# 1 MONTH OF
# FREE
## READING

at

## www.ForgottenBooks.com

By purchasing this book you are eligible for one month membership to ForgottenBooks.com, giving you unlimited access to our entire collection of over 1,000,000 titles via our web site and mobile apps.

To claim your free month visit:

www.forgottenbooks.com/free1099697

ISBN 978-0-331-30180-9
PIBN 11099697

No. 61.—JULY, 1898, to JULY, 1899.

# GEER'S
# HARTFORD CITY DIRECTORY;
## JULY, 1898:

*COMPRISING THE*

*Names of Residents; where Living; where in Business; where Employed; Copartnerships; Corporations; Signs; Societies; Migrations; Marriages; Births; Necrology; Divorces; Streets and Avenues;*

# HARTFORD ILLUSTRATED;
## GEER'S CONNECTICUT GEOGRAPHICAL DIRECTORY

### OF 6,172 PLACES, WITH TOWN AND COUNTY LOCATIONS; OF

CITIES, TOWNS, BOROUGHS, POST OFFICES, SCHOOL DISTRICTS, VILLAGES, HAMLETS, PRECINCTS; RAILROAD, EXPRESS, TELEGRAPH AND TELEPHONE STATIONS; MOUNTAINS, ISLANDS, LAKES, PONDS, Etc.

## POST OFFICE AND BUSINESS DIRECTORIES,

Also, ELIHU GEER'S SONS' NEW MAP OF HARTFORD,

And all Desirable Information, about the CITY OF HARTFORD, for Citizens and Strangers.

ALSO, A DIRECTORY OF THE

# TOWN OF EAST HARTFORD,

*COMPRISING THE*

*Names of Residents, Location and Occupations; Town Offices; Courts; Corporations; Churches; Public Schools; Societies; Marriages; Births; Deaths; Classified Business Directory, Street and Avenue Directory.*

HARTFORD, CONN., U. S. A.;
THE HARTFORD PRINTING COMPANY, PRINTERS AND PUBLISHERS;
ELIHU GEER'S SONS', CANVASSERS AND COMPILERS.
1898.

# PREFACE.

——◆——

N this, the 61st volume of GEER'S HARTFORD CITY DIRECTORY, we have incorporated, following page 32, an index to the RE-NUMBERING of Main street, giving both the old and the new numbers, and the names of the firms or persons occupying the same on the first of May. We feel confident it will be found an exceedingly useful and valuable table for reference by our citizens and business men, and of special value to the insurance interests, and those tracing deeds, etc.

The total number of names enumerated is 35,949, a gain of 1,051 over last year, making the population of the city at the present time 78,253.

The First Regiment, C. N. G. (Hartford Companies), as they were organized at the time they left to join the United States Volunteers, will be found on page 680, and a list of those that passed examination and entered the U. S. service will be found on page 393.

Divorces, numbering 74, are on page 392.

Commencing with page 395 will be found a list of 1,304 persons who left the city during the past year and the places to which they have gone.

Deaths numbering 1,182 commence with page 401.

Marriages to the number of 680 will be found on page 406.

Births numbering 1,799 commence with page 409.

The War Revenue Taxes will be found on page 759.

From last year's Directory have been erased 7,180 names; added 8,231 new names, and altered the residence and business location of 9,387; making 24,798 changes from last year's book.

For the number of names in each issue of this work for the past sixty-one years, with the changes and new names added, see the following table and next page.

| VOL. | YEAR. | NAMES. | GAIN. | VOL. | YEAR. | NAMES. | GAIN. |
|---|---|---|---|---|---|---|---|
| 1 | 1838, | 1,625, | | 18 | 1855, | 6,175, | 48 |
| 2 | 1839, | 1,631, | 6 | 19 | 1856, | 6,326, | 151 |
| 3 | 1840, | 1,797, | 166 | 20 | 1857, | 6,377, | 51 |
| 4 | 1841, | 1,818, | 21 | 21 | 1858, | 7,030, | 653 |
| 5 | 1842, | 2,300, | 482 | 22 | 1859, | 7,196, | 166 |
| 6 | 1843, | 2,890, | 590 | 23 | 1860, | 8,428, | 222 |
| 7 | 1844, | 3,110, | 220 | 24 | 1861, | 8,471, | 43 |
| 8 | 1845, | 3,140, | 30 | 25 | 1862, | 8,683, | 212 |
| 9 | 1846, | 3,166, | 26 | 26 | 1863, | 9,115, | 422 |
| 10 | 1847, | 3,175, | 9 | 27 | 1864, | 9,354, | 239 |
| 11 | 1848, | 3,810, | 635 | 28 | 1865, | 9,382, | 28 |
| 12 | 1849, | 4,170, | 360 | 29 | 1866, | 10,089, | 707 |
| 13 | 1850, | 4,963, | 793 | 30 | 1867, | 10,127, | 38 |
| 14 | 1851, | 5,361, | 398 | 31 | 1868, | 10,276, | 149 |
| 15 | 1852, | 5,877, | 516 | 32 | 1869, | 11,291, | 1015 |
| 16 | 1853, | 6,093, | 216 | 33 | 1870, | 12,345, | 1054 |
| 17 | 1854, | 6,127, | 84 | *Erasures, etc. were not kept previous to* 1871. | | | |

# PREFACE.

| VOL. | YEAR. | NAMES. | GAIN. | NAMES ERASED. | NAMES ALTERED. | NEW NAMES. |
|---|---|---|---|---|---|---|
| 34 | 1871 | 13,576 | 1,231 | 2,218 | 4,076 | 3,449 |
| 35 | 1872 | 14,351 | 775 | 2,189 | 2,761 | 3,231 |
| 36 | 1873 | 14,672 | 321 | 2,302 | 4,424 | 2,891 |
| 37 | 1874 | 15,409 | 737 | 2,925 | 5,617 | 3,981 |
| 38 | 1875 | 15,871 | 462 | 3,540 | 4,737 | 4,002 |
| 39 | 1876 | 16,312 | 441 | 3,641 | 5,246 | 4,404 |
| 40 | 1877 | 16,444 | 132 | 3,530 | 5,383 | 3,662 |
| 41 | 1878 | 16,526 | 82 | 3,241 | 4,122 | 3,423 |
| 42 | 1879 | 16,584 | 58 | 3,482 | 4,394 | 3,540 |
| 43 | 1880 | 16,658 | 74 | 3,387 | 4,253 | 3,461 |
| 44 | 1881 | 16,929 | 271 | 3,706 | 4,919 | 3,977 |
| 45 | 1882 | 18,314 | 1,385 | 3,484 | 8,108 | 4,869 |
| 46 | 1883 | 19,341 | 1,027 | 3,319 | 7,012 | 5,075 |
| 47 | 1884 | 20,015 | 674 | 3,630 | 5,472 | 4,304 |
| 48 | 1885 | 20,253 | 238 | 4,129 | 7,280 | 4,387 |
| 49 | 1886 | 20,665 | 412 | 3,810 | 6,310 | 4,222 |
| 50 | 1887 | 21,514 | 849 | 3,660 | 6,635 | 4,509 |
| 51 | 1888 | 22,504 | 990 | 4,175 | 8,753 | 5,165 |
| 52 | 1889 | 23,492 | 988 | 3,722 | 8,185 | 4,710 |
| 53 | 1890 | 24,452 | 960 | 4,128 | 7,629 | 5,088 |
| 54 | 1891 | 26,427 | 1,975 | 3,999 | 8,377 | 5,974 |
| 55 | 1892 | 26,913 | 486 | 4,767 | 8,064 | 5,253 |
| 56 | 1893 | 29,175 | 2,262 | 4,748 | 9,630 | 7,010 |
| 57 | 1894 | 29,880 | 705 | 5,151 | 9,752 | 5,856 |
| 58 | 1895 | 31,105 | 1,225 | 5,296 | 8,089 | 6,521 |
| 59 | 1896 | 33,396 | 2,291 | 5,805 | 7,051 | 8,096 |
| 60 | 1897 | 34,898 | 1,502 | 6,079 | 9,055 | 7,581 |
| 61 | 1898 | 35,949 | 1,051 | 7,180 | 9,387 | 8,231 |

## RECAPITULATION.

NAMES of Residents, etc., in this City, July, 1898, pages 35 to 389, .................................................. 35,949
REMOVALS or MIGRATIONS out of the City, whose names were in the 1897 DIRECTORY, pages 395 to 400, 1,304
NECROLOGY, from June 1, 1897, to June 1, 1898, pages 401 to 406, ........................................ 1,182

    TOTAL number of NAMES in Hartford City Directory ............................................ 38,435

From the Names in last year's Directory we have ERASED ....................................... 7,180
To Names in last year's Directory we have made CHANGES in residence and business locations ............... 9,387
NEW NAMES added this year, ............................................................... 8,231

    TOTAL NUMBER OF CHANGES in names from the last year's Directory ...................... 24,798

Population of Hartford, July, 1898, estimated on the ratio of 2.1768 ............................... 78,253

Total Number of Names enumerated in Hartford ................................................. 38,435
Number of Names of Residents, etc., in East Hartford (pages 761 to 785) ...................... 2,364
Necrology in East Hartford (page 786) ................................................. 103    2,467

    Grand Total number of Names in this year's Directory ................................. 40,902

The Hartford Directory shows a gain of 1,051.

The East Hartford Directory shows a gain of 103.

Yours very truly,

ELIHU GEER'S SONS.

HARTFORD, CONN., July 19, 1898.

# ADVERTISERS' INDEX. .

# East Hartford Advertisers' Index.

# Contents of East Hartford Directory.

# INDEX TO CONTENTS.

| | PAGE. |
|---|---|
| A. D. VORCE Co. | 718 |
| Abatement of taxes — Officers | 674 |
| Abbreviations and Explanations | 33 |
| Acme Machine Screw Co. | 736 |
| Additions, etc., too late for regular insertion | 34 |
| Admission of each State to the U. S. | 645 |
| Advertisers Index | 9–12 |
| Ætna Indemnity Company | 736 |
| Ætna Insurance Co. | 442, 443 |
| Ætna Life Insurance Co. | 449 |
| Ætna Machine Co. | 736 |
| Ætna National Bank | 481 |
| African Methodist Episcopal Zion Church | 691 |
| Agents Sundry Benevolent Societies | 718 |
| Aldermen | 673 |
| Allen Drum Band | 718 |
| Allotment of Judges and Terms, July 1, '98 | 649 |
| Allyn Memorial Chapel | 692 |
| Alms House, | 674 |
| Alumni Association of Hfd. Public High School | 718 |
| American Board of Com. for Foreign Missions | 718 |
| Amateur Bowling League of Connecticut | 718 |
| American Emigrant Company | 718 |
| American National Bank | 481 |
| American Publishing Co. | 473 |
| American School at Hfd. for Deaf and Dumb | 718 |
| American Specialty Mfg. Company | 736 |
| American Type Founders Co. | 471 |
| Ancient Burying Ground Association | 735 |
| Ancient Order of Foresters of America | 738 |
| Ancient Order of Hibernians | 718 |
| Ancient Order of United Workmen | 738 |
| Andrus & Naedele Co. | 485 |
| Apothecaries | 594 |
| Appointed Officers (city) | 674 |
| Ararat Lodge, I. O. B. B. No. 18 | 718 |
| Arba Lankton Total Abstinence Society | 734 |
| Archæological Society, see Hartford | 722 |
| Architects | 594 |
| Area, Capitals and Population of each State | 563 |
| Area, Capitals, Population, Countries of the World | 643 |
| Armories | 594 |
| Army and Navy Club | 22 |
| Army and Navy Volunteers | 398 |
| Arsenal School | 716 |
| Art Society of Hartford, 624 Main | 718 |
| Artists | 595 |
| Ashes Removed, | 891 |
| Assessors | 668 |
| Assistant Town Clerk | 668 |
| Association Adas Israel | 694 |
| Association Brothers, Children of Israel | 696 |
| Asylum Avenue Baptist Church | 688 |
| Asylum Hill Congregational Church | 685 |
| Attorneys at Law | 595 |
| Auditors City of Hartford | 674 |
| Auditors Public Accounts (State) | 652 |
| B. H. Webb Council, No. 702, R. A | 718 |
| Bachelors | 718 |
| Bakers | 596 |
| Balf Edward Co. | 426 |
| Bands of Music | 596 |
| Bank Commissioners | 658 |
| Bankers | 596 |
| Banks | 596 |
| Baptist Social Union of Connecticut | 658 |
| Baptist Young People's Union | 718 |
| Barbers | 596 |

| | PAGE. |
|---|---|
| Bathing House | 888 |
| Beach Manufacturing Co. | 736 |
| Beacon Falls Mill & Power Co. | 736 |
| Beethoven Lodge, No. 98, I. O. O. F. | 731 |
| Benevolent and Protective Order of Elks, Hartford Lodge, No. 19 | 728 |
| Benevolent Societies agents of | 718 |
| Billings C. E. Manufacturing Co. | 736 |
| Billings Sidewalk and Masons Supply Co. | 736 |
| Billings & Spencer Co. of Hartford, Conn. | 736 |
| Birkery Manufacturing Company | 736 |
| Births one year previous to January, 1898 | 409 |
| Blacksmiths | 598 |
| Blind Educational Board | 658 |
| Blodgett & Clapp Co | 736 |
| Board of Aldermen and Councilmen | 674 |
| Board of Charities of Connecticut | 661 |
| Board of Education (State) | 663 |
| Board of Education of the Blind | 658 |
| Board of Pardons | 658 |
| Board of Relief | 674 |
| Board of School Visitors | 715 |
| Board of Trade | 719 |
| Board Trustees Firemen's Ben. Society | 721 |
| Board Trustees Young Men's Christian Association | 718 |
| Boarding Houses | 598 |
| Boardman Wm. & Sons Co. | 736 |
| Boiler Inspectors | 663 |
| Bonner-Preston Company | 737 |
| Bonsilate Box Co. | 737 |
| Book Publishers | 599 |
| Boot and Shoemakers | 599 |
| Boroughs in Connecticut | 556 |
| Boundaries of City of Hartford | 670 |
| Boundaries City Wards | 670 |
| Boundaries School Districts | 671 |
| Box Makers | 600 |
| Branch No. 86, National Asso. of Letter Carriers | 719 |
| Bricklayers' and Plasterers' Union | 719 |
| Bridge Commissioners, City, see Street Com'rs | 677 |
| Bridge Commissioners (State) | 658 |
| Bridges History of | 567 |
| British Empire, Colonies of | 644 |
| Broad Brook Co. | 737 |
| Brokers | 600 |
| Brokers Board | 719 |
| Brotherhood of Andrew and Philip, 4th Church | 696 |
| Brown School | 715 |
| Brown, Thomson & Co's Emp. Mut. Aid Asso. | 719 |
| Buckingham Assembly No. 213 | 719 |
| Buckingham Council No. 4, Jr. Order, O.U.A.M. | 732 |
| Builders and Carpenters | 600 |
| Building Inspector | 674 |
| Buildings, Halls, etc. | 681 |
| Bureau of Labor Statistics | 651 |
| Burr Index Co. | 737 |
| Burying Grounds and Cemeteries | 735 |
| Bushnell Council. No. 213. O. U. F. | 719 |
| Business Directory, July, 1898 | 593 |
| Business Failures in Connecticut | 392 |
| Business Failures in the United States | 392 |
| Business of Hartford Clearing House | 642 |
| Business Panics and Depressions | 462 |
| Calendar for year, July 1898 to July 1899 | 22 |
| Calhoun Printing Co. | 737 |
| Canoe, Hartford Canoe Club | 722 |
| Capewell Horse Nail Co. | 737 |
| Capitol City Bowling Club | 719 |

SIXTY-ONE YEARS AGO, in the year 1838, there were 1,625 Names in the first Hartford City Directory; to-day the following are the only ones living.

Barnard Henry Dr.
Beach George.
Bolter James.
Butler J. V. B.
Chamberlin Nelson H.
Church Abner.
Gill Alfred, San Francisco.
Granger Erastus, Boston.
Judson Curtis.
Marcy E. E., Orange. N. J.

Nicholson Ruel, East Hartford.
Parsons E. W.
Pettibone Franklin E.
Phelps R. R., Otis, Mass.
Russell Gurdon W. Dr.
Starkweather Nathan.

CORPORATIONS.
Ætna Insurance Co.
Am. Asylum for Deaf & Dumb.
City Hotel.
Collins Co.
Connecticut River Banking Co.
Courant Office.
Exchange Bank.
Farmers and Mechanics Bank.
Firemen's Benevolent Society.

Hartford Bank.
Hfd. Co. Mutual Fire Ins. Co.
Hartford Fire Insurance Co.
Hartford Orphan Asylum.
Phoenix Bank.
Retreat for the Insane.
Society for Savings.
Times Office.
Trinity (Washington) College.
United States Hotel.

Curtis Judson is the oldest hotel keeper in the United States. Of the 17 Institutions, with their 800 odd Directors, Trustees and Officers, there remain only 6 Banks, 3 Fire Insurance Companies, and 7 corporations.

Only 1 Business Firm is in active operation to-day, the same as 61 years ago, viz.:—N. H. Chamberlin, truckman. Only 16 of all the firms in Hartford to-day are direct successors to the business houses of 60 years ago. Of the City Government only Abner Church and James Bolter are still with us. This list 11 years ago had 70 more names in it.

There has died the past year: S. S. Chamberlin, William Isham.

## Calendar, July, 1898, to July, 1899.

### JULY.—1898.

| Sund. | Mon. | Tues. | Wed. | Thur. | Frid. | Sat. |
|---|---|---|---|---|---|---|
| ... | ... | ... | ... | ... | 1 | 2 |
| 3 | 4 | 5 | 6 | 7 | 8 | 9 |
| 10 | 11 | 12 | 13 | 14 | 15 | 16 |
| 17 | 18 | 19 | 20 | 21 | 22 | 23 |
| 24 | 25 | 26 | 27 | 28 | 29 | 30 |
| 31 | ... | ... | ... | ... | ... | ... |

### AUGUST.

| Sund. | Mon. | Tues. | Wed. | Thur. | Frid. | Sat. |
|---|---|---|---|---|---|---|
| ... | 1 | 2 | 3 | 4 | 5 | 6 |
| 7 | 8 | 9 | 10 | 11 | 12 | 13 |
| 14 | 15 | 16 | 17 | 18 | 19 | 20 |
| 21 | 22 | 23 | 24 | 25 | 26 | 27 |
| 28 | 29 | 30 | 31 | ... | ... | ... |

### SEPTEMBER.

| Sund. | Mon. | Tues. | Wed. | Thur. | Frid. | Sat. |
|---|---|---|---|---|---|---|
| ... | ... | ... | ... | 1 | 2 | 3 |
| 4 | 5 | 6 | 7 | 8 | 9 | 10 |
| 11 | 12 | 13 | 14 | 15 | 16 | 17 |
| 18 | 19 | 20 | 21 | 22 | 23 | 24 |
| 25 | 26 | 27 | 28 | 29 | 30 | ... |

### OCTOBER.

| Sund. | Mon. | Tues. | Wed. | Thur. | Frid. | Sat. |
|---|---|---|---|---|---|---|
| ... | ... | ... | ... | ... | ... | 1 |
| 2 | 3 | 4 | 5 | 6 | 7 | 8 |
| 9 | 10 | 11 | 12 | 13 | 14 | 15 |
| 16 | 17 | 18 | 19 | 20 | 21 | 22 |
| 23 | 24 | 25 | 26 | 27 | 28 | 29 |
| 30 | 31 | ... | ... | ... | ... | ... |

### NOVEMBER.—1898.

| Sund. | Mon. | Tues. | Wed. | Thur. | Frid. | Sat. |
|---|---|---|---|---|---|---|
| ... | ... | 1 | 2 | 3 | 4 | 5 |
| 6 | 7 | 8 | 9 | 10 | 11 | 12 |
| 13 | 14 | 15 | 16 | 17 | 18 | 19 |
| 20 | 21 | 22 | 23 | 24 | 25 | 26 |
| 27 | 28 | 29 | 30 | ... | ... | ... |

### DECEMBER.

| Sund. | Mon. | Tues. | Wed. | Thur. | Frid. | Sat. |
|---|---|---|---|---|---|---|
| ... | ... | ... | ... | 1 | 2 | 3 |
| 4 | 5 | 6 | 7 | 8 | 9 | 10 |
| 11 | 12 | 13 | 14 | 15 | 16 | 17 |
| 18 | 19 | 20 | 21 | 22 | 23 | 24 |
| 25 | 26 | 27 | 28 | 29 | 30 | 31 |

### JANUARY.—1899.

| Sund. | Mon. | Tues. | Wed. | Thur. | Frid. | Sat. |
|---|---|---|---|---|---|---|
| 1 | 2 | 3 | 4 | 5 | 6 | 7 |
| 8 | 9 | 10 | 11 | 12 | 13 | 14 |
| 15 | 16 | 17 | 18 | 19 | 20 | 21 |
| 22 | 23 | 24 | 25 | 26 | 27 | 28 |
| 29 | 30 | 31 | ... | ... | ... | ... |

### FEBRUARY.

| Sund. | Mon. | Tues. | Wed. | Thur. | Frid. | Sat. |
|---|---|---|---|---|---|---|
| ... | ... | ... | 1 | 2 | 3 | 4 |
| 5 | 6 | 7 | 8 | 9 | 10 | 11 |
| 12 | 13 | 14 | 15 | 16 | 17 | 18 |
| 19 | 20 | 21 | 22 | 23 | 24 | 25 |
| 26 | 27 | 28 | ... | ... | ... | ... |

### MARCH.—1899.

| Sund. | Mon. | Tues. | Wed. | Thur. | Frid. | Sat. |
|---|---|---|---|---|---|---|
| ... | ... | ... | 1 | 2 | 3 | 4 |
| 5 | 6 | 7 | 8 | 9 | 10 | 11 |
| 12 | 13 | 14 | 15 | 16 | 17 | 18 |
| 19 | 20 | 21 | 22 | 23 | 24 | 25 |
| 26 | 27 | 28 | 29 | 30 | 31 | ... |

### APRIL.

| Sund. | Mon. | Tues. | Wed. | Thur. | Frid. | Sat. |
|---|---|---|---|---|---|---|
| ... | ... | ... | ... | ... | ... | 1 |
| 2 | 3 | 4 | 5 | 6 | 7 | 8 |
| 9 | 10 | 11 | 12 | 13 | 14 | 15 |
| 16 | 17 | 18 | 19 | 20 | 21 | 22 |
| 23 | 24 | 25 | 26 | 27 | 28 | 29 |
| 30 | ... | ... | ... | ... | ... | ... |

### MAY.

| Sund. | Mon. | Tues. | Wed. | Thur. | Frid. | Sat. |
|---|---|---|---|---|---|---|
| ... | 1 | 2 | 3 | 4 | 5 | 6 |
| 7 | 8 | 9 | 10 | 11 | 12 | 13 |
| 14 | 15 | 16 | 17 | 18 | 19 | 20 |
| 21 | 22 | 23 | 24 | 25 | 26 | 27 |
| 28 | 29 | 30 | 31 | ... | ... | ... |

### JUNE.

| Sund. | Mon. | Tues. | Wed. | Thur. | Frid. | Sat. |
|---|---|---|---|---|---|---|
| ... | ... | ... | ... | 1 | 2 | 3 |
| 4 | 5 | 6 | 7 | 8 | 9 | 10 |
| 11 | 12 | 13 | 14 | 15 | 16 | 17 |
| 18 | 19 | 20 | 21 | 22 | 23 | 24 |
| 25 | 26 | 27 | 28 | 29 | 30 | ... |

### NATIONAL HOME FOR DISABLED VOLUNTEER SOLDIERS.

BRANCHES.—*Central*, Dayton, Ohio; *Marion*, Marion, Indiana; *Eastern*, Togus, Maine; *Northwestern*, Milwaukee, Wisconsin; *Southern*, Elizabeth City, Virginia; *Western*, Leavenworth, Kansas; *Pacific*, Los Angeles, California.

*Managers.*—The President of the U. S., the Chief Justice, the Secretary of War, *ex-officio;* Gen. William B. Franklin, Hartford, Conn., *President;* Gen. Wm. J. Sewell, Camden, N. J.; Gen. Thomas J. Henderson, Princeton, Ill.; Col. J. L. Mitchell, Milwaukee, Wis.; Col. Sidney G. Cooke, Herington, Kan.; Gen. John Marshall Brown, Portland, Me.; Col. George W. Steele, Marion, Indiana; Gen. Alfred L. Pearson, Pittsburgh, Pa.; Gen. Charles M. Anderson, Greenville, Ohio; Maj. A. W. Barrett, Los Angeles, Cal., *Vice Pres'ts;* Gen. Martin T. McMahon, *Secretary*, Times Building, New York City.

### ARMY AND NAVY CLUB OF CONNECTICUT.

Simeon J. Fox, New Haven, Pres't; William B. Wooster, Derby, Alfred B. Beers, Bridgeport, Francis B. Allen, Hartford, John T. Crary, Norwich, Vice Pres't's; Julius Knowlton, Bridgeport, Sec'y; Sidney M. Gladwin, Hartford, Treas. Leonard A. Dickinson, 1901, Frank A. Monson, 1899, George A. Hammond, 1900, Executive Committee.

### SOCIETY OF THE WAR OF 1812 IN CONN.

Morgan G. Bulkeley, Hartford, *Pres't;* John E. Heaton, New Haven, William W. Skiddy, Stamford; Henry W. Wessells, Litchfield, A. Floyd Delafield, Noroton, Jesup Wakeman, Southport, *V. Pres'ts;* O. Storrs Seymour, 80 Broad street, New York city, *Sec'y and Treas.* Instituted April 5, 1894. Incorporated April 6, 1894.

### ST. FRANCIS HOSPITAL.

Rt. Rev. Michael Tierney, Pres't; Rev. Walter Shanley, Sec'y; Rev. John A. Mulcahy, Treas. Board of Incorporators.—John O'Flaherty, Pres't; D. F. Sullivan, Secretary; Rev. Thomas Broderick, Thomas McManus, John W. Coogan, Patrick Garvan, Matthew Hogan, Cornelius Ryan, D. F. Sullivan, Geo. C. Bailey, John O'Flaherty. Corner Woodland and Collins sts. Incorporated, February, 1897.

### SOCIETY OF CONNECTICUT ARTISTS.

Frederick E. Church, Hudson, N. Y., *Hon. Pres't;* Walter Sanford, Hartford, *Pres't;* E. S. Woods, Hartford, *V. Pres't;* Charles Noel Flagg, Hartford, *Rec. Sec'y;* D. F. Wentworth, Hartford, *Cor. Sec'y;* the above officers and R. M. Shurtleff, N. Y. City, *Council.* Organized 1892. Annual election third Saturday in Oct.

### SOCIETY OF THE SONS OF REVOLUTION IN CONNECTICUT.

Morgan G. Bulkeley, Hartford, Pres't; Daniel N. Morgan, Bridgeport, Vice Pres't; Henry N. Wayne, New Britain, Sec'y; Henry W. Wessels, Litchfield, Treas.

### EXCELSIOR LODGE No. 3, F. & A. M.

James S. Taylor, W. M.; Benjamin F. Johnson, Sr. W.; Joseph C. Lee, Jr. W.; Frederick O. Cross, Treas.; Watkins W. Christian, Sec'y., 29 Wolcott st. Meets 2d and 4th Mondays at 302 Asylum st.

### CHURCH OF SACRED HEART.—ITALIAN CATHOLIC, 125 MARKET ST.

This church was recently purchased from the German Lutherans, and was dedicated on Sunday morning, June 5, 1898.

### YOUNG MEN'S TOTAL ABSTINENCE SOCIETY.

J. J. Gaffey, Pres't; W. H. Hutchinson, Vice Pres't; J. J. Derby, Fin. Sec'y; M. J. Hines, Rec. Sec'y. J. J. Gaffey, P. J. Hutchinson, J. L. Guilfoil, Trustees.

### HARTEORD REAL ESTATE EXCHANGE.

George H. Woods, Pres't; Francis Chambers, Vice Pres't; Howard G. Bestor, Treas.; Fred. M. Lincoln, Sec'y; E. Dillingham, Chairman; E. B. Dillingham, Francis Chambers, H. W. Woodward, Geo. H. Woods, H. G. Bestor, S. C. Doty, F. M. Lincoln, H. B. Donovan, Directors. Organized March 10, 1896. Meets Tuesday at 92 Pearl street. Annual election first Tuesday in September.

### OUR SAVIOUR'S DANISH EVG.-LUTH. CHURCH, 284 PEARL ST.

B. Gregersen, Pastor; L. Petersen, Pres't; Chr. Nielsen, Vice Pres't; A. C. Brown, Sec'y; Thomas Wind, Treas; Chr. G. Potholm, John Bossen, Martin Petersen, Peter Nielsen, Jens K. Kristensen, Trustees.

### COURT ABRAHAM LINCOLN, No. 121, F. OF A.

G. B. Schwartz, Chief Ranger; I. Kempner, Rec. sec'y; D. E. Krauss, Fin. Sec'y; L. Levitow, Treas.; S. Tuck, A. Kesler, E. Elowitz, Trustees.

### MORGAN STREET MISSION SCHOOL.

CHAPEL, 52 MORGAN ST. *Organized March 21, 1852.* Allen H. Newton, Sup't; Hattie Gillette, Ass't; Miss Mary E. Coyle, Sup't Infant Department; Lizzie R. Bill, Ass't; Henry Ney, Sec'y; Howard Hayden, Ass't Sec'y; Russell C. Northam, Treas. Teachers 22; Scholars 90; School, 2.30 P. M.; in summer, 6 P. M. Annual meeting in January.

### INDUSTRIAL FREE SCHOOLS.

COOKING AND TRAINING SCHOOL; Saturday morning. Mrs. Elizabeth Ayres, *Manager*, 239 Market st.

DAY NURSERY; 239 Market st.

DIET KITCHEN; Union for Home Work, 239 Market st. Supplies for the sick, as ordered by physicians.

GIRLS SEWING SCHOOL; Saturday mornings, during the winter only, at 239 Market st. Organized, 1872.

KITCHEN GARDEN; on Saturdays in the afternoon, at 239 Market street, during the winter only.

READING ROOMS AND PARLORS, for Young Women; from 6.30 to 9.30 P. M. daily. United Workers' 49 Pearl st.

### TAXES ON PROPERTY IN HARTFORD.

| Year.. | '87 | '88 | '89 | '90 | '91 | '92 | '93 | '94 | '95 | '96 | '97 |
|---|---|---|---|---|---|---|---|---|---|---|---|
| | Mills. | Mills. | Mills. | Mills. | Mills. | Mills. | Mills. | Mills. | Mills. | Mills. | Mills. |
| City ...... | 9½ | 9½ | 9 | 9 | 9½ | 10¼ | 10 | 11½ | 16 | 16 | 16½ |
| " Sinking. | ... | ... | ... | ... | ... | ... | ... | ½ | ½ | 1 | 1 |
| Town...... | 6½ | 7 | 7 | 5 | 4 | 3½ | 4 | 3½ | ... | ... | ... |
| " Sinking. | 1 | 1 | 1 | 1 | 1 | ½ | ½ | ½ | ½ | ... | ... |
| T. F'd. Debt | ... | ... | ... | ... | ... | ... | ... | ... | ... | ... | ... |
| Asy. st. br.. | ... | ... | ½ | ½ | ... | ... | ... | ... | ... | ... | ... |
| Total....... | 17 | 17½ | 17½ | 15½ | 14½ | 14¼ | 14½ | 16 | 17 | 17 | 17½ |

### STATE SCHOOL FUND

At the end of fiscal year, Sept. 30, 1897, amounted to $2,007,088.97; nine-tenths of which is invested in real estate mortgages, and the balance in bank stocks and cash on hand. In the year 1795 this fund amounted to $1,200,000.00. From the income of this fund there has been distributed to the common schools of this state between the years 1796 and 1897 inclusive $8,818,946.51. The Oct. 1897 census of children in the State between four and sixteen years of age, was 184,264, being an increase of 5,001 children over the previous year's enumeration. There are 1,840 school districts in the 167 towns of Conn. The school population in the agricultural towns has decreased the past decade. HERBERT E. BENTON, Commissioner.

# ELIHU GEER'S SONS
# GUIDE TO STREETS, AVENUES, ETC.

*The figures 1. 2. 3. 4. 5. 6. 7. 8. 9. 10 on the right of the names of each street indicate the wards in which the same are located,—the ward boundaries generally run in the center of streets.—See Table of Contents.*

*This Guide indicates at a glance the proximate locality of any required number on any street; for example, if you desire to know about where No. 800 Asylum street is located, this guide shows you that, being an even number, it will be found on the north side, and about mid-way between Sumner and Huntington streets.*

*The streets running north and south are numbered from the south excepting Wethersfield, Maple and Franklin avenues, Hopkins, Babcock, and Columbia sts. and Park Terrace, those running east and west are numbered from Main st., or from end of street pointing thereto, excepting North st.   Odd numbers on SOUTH and WEST sides, uniformly.*

*The names of all streets running north and south ( except Main, Broad and Laurel ), change at Park river, and all east and west at crossing Main street.*

---

**Affleck.** 8
146 Ward, N. to 341 Park.

**Albany Avenue.** 3,4
1419 Main, N. W. to City line.
No.   1, at Tunnel, 1419 Main.
" 15, Lumber, S.
" 77, Chestnut, S.
" 90, Belden, N. E.
" 90, East, N.
" 97, Edwards, S.
" 106, Center, N.
" 124, Green, N.
" 131, Williams, S.
" 164, Brook, crosses.
" 204, Garden, crosses.
" 276, Vine, N.
          Sigourney, S.
" 284, Lenox place, N.
          Woodland, S.
          Harrison, S.
          Blue Hills av. N.
          Scarborough, S.
          Bloomfield, N.
          Prospect av. S.

**Alden.** 7
71 Wethersfield, W. to 52 Dean.

**Allen Place.** 8
65 Washington, W. to Summit.
No.   1, Washington.
" 54, Broad, crosses.
" 140, Summit, end.

**Allyn.** 5
89 Trumbull, W. to 42 Union place.
No. 122, Trumbull, 89.
" 250, Ann, crosses.
" 372, High, crosses.
" 432, Union place, 42, end.

**American Row.** 1
101 State, S. to 64 Prospect.

**Amity.** 10
878 Park, N. to Davenport.

**Ann.** 5
258 Asylum, N. to 1367 Main.
No. 26, Asylum, 258.
" 55, Allyn, crosses.
" 70, Church, crosses.
" 92, Chapel, E.
" 99, Oriental alley, W.
" 123, High, W.
" 128, Main, 1367, end.

**Annawan.** 7
97 Wethersfield, W. to 74 Franklin.
          Nos. 1 to 73.

**Arch.** 1
524 Main, E. to 7 Front.
No.   1, Main, 524.
" 38, Prospect, N.
" 99, Front, 7, end.

**Asylum.** 4,5,9,10
819 Main, W. to 950 Prospect av.
No.   1, Main, 819.
" 126, Trumbull, crosses.
" 213, Haynes, S.
" 258, Ann, N.
" 379, Ford, S.
" 380, High, N.
" 464, Union place, N.
" 470, Railroad, crosses.
" 504, Spruce, N.
" 511, Hurlburt, S.
" 572, Spring, N.
" 594, Garden, N.
" 597, Hopkins, S.
" 629, Farmington, S. W.
" 711, Asylum place, S.
" 778, Sumner, N.
" 822, Huntington, N.
" 872, Sigourney, crosses.
" 920, Willard, N.
" 978, Atwood, N.
" 1023, Gillett, S.
" 1076, Woodland, crosses.
          Girard, S.—Kenyon, S.
          Scarborough, N.
          Prospect avenue, 950, end.

**Asylum Place.** 2
711 Asylum st. to 70 Farmington av.

**Arthur Place.** 2
26 Russell, S.

**Ashley.** 4
209 Garden, W. to 132 Woodland.
No. 80, Huntington, crosses.
" 118, Sigourney, crosses.
          Atwood, S.
" 150, May, N.
" 268, Woodland, end.

**Ashton.** 10
Heath street, W.

**Atheneum.** 1
642 Main, E. to 35 Prospect.

**Atlantic.** 4
231 High, W. to railroad.

**Atwood.** 4,10
978 Asylum, N. to Ashley.
No.   4, Townley, E.
          Collins, crosses.
          Ashley, end.

**Avon.** 2
64 Windsor av. E. to 339 Front.
No.   1, Windsor av. 64.
" 28, Railroad, crosses.
" 45, Portland, S.
" 54, Windsor, crosses.
" 82, Front, 339,—branch railr'd.

**Babcock.** 9
405 Capitol, S. to 342 Park.
No.   1, Capitol.
" 80, Russ, crosses.
" 152, Grand, E.
" 342, Park, end.

**Back Lane.** 7
Maple, S. to Preston.

**Barbour.**    3
124 Capen, N. to Windsor line.
No. 1, Capen, 124.
"   88, Nelson, crosses.
"   132, Judson, crosses.
"   184, Westland, crosses.
     Charlotte, W.
     Frankfort, crosses.
     Tower, crosses.

**Barnard.**    7
Maple av. W. to Washington.

**Bartholomew Avenue.**    8
Park, southerly, W. of Park river.
     Hamilton, crosses.
     Belmont, E.
     Rose, E.
     Olive, E.

**Beach.**    9
89 Farmington, S. to R. R. track
     and E. to 41 Flower.

**Beacon.**    10
Warrenton, N. crossing 641 Farm-
     ington to Cone.

**Belden.**    3,4
47 Windsor av. W. to 90 Albany.

**Bellevue.**    3
32 Canton, N. to 31 Sanford.
No. 2, Canton, 32.
"   88, Pavilion, W.
"   147, Suffield, crosses.
"   192, Warren, E.
"   221, Cranes court, W.
"   226, Loomis, E.
"   248, Sanford, end.

**Belmont.**    8
Wellington, W. to Bartholomew av.

**Benton.**    7
145 Wethersfield, W. to Webster.
No. 1, Wethersfield, 145.
"   72, Franklin av. crosses.
"   140, Maple, end.

**Berkeley Place.**    1
19 Front, W.

**Bloomfield Avenue.**    4
West end Albany av., N.

**Blue Hills Avenue.**    4
Tavern on Albany av., N.
     Westland, E.
     Tower, crosses.

**Blumenthal Place.**    5
1263 Main, W.

**Bodwell.**    7
299 Wethersfield, W. to Franklin.

**Bond.**    7
197 Wethersfield, W. to Maple.
     Mannz, N.
     Franklin crosses.

**Benner.**    8
99 Zion, W.

**Boulanger.**
Prospect av. W.

**Brady Place.**    8
1140 Broad, E. to 85 Wolcott.

**Brisley Place.**    5
230 Asylum, N.

**Broad.**    8,9
Maple, N. to 15 Farmington.
No.   1, Maple.
"   65, White, laid out.
"   524, New Britain, crosses.
"   610, School, E.
"   700, Brownell, E.
"   808, Vernon, crosses.
"   852, Allen, crosses.
"   900, Lincoln, E.
"   948, Madison, E.
"   998, Jefferson, E.
"   1022, Ward, crosses.
"   1110, Park, crosses.
"   1150, Brady place, E.
"   1178, Grand, crosses.
"   1268, Russ, crosses.
"   1370, Capitol, crosses.
"   1386, Park river.
"   1438, Howard, W.
"   1455, Railroad, crosses.
"   1471, Queen, W.
"   1478, Hopkins, E.
"   1566, Farmington, 15, end.

**Brook.**    3,4
16 Liberty, N. to 145 Mather.
No. 1, Liberty, 16.
"   64, Albany, crosses.
"   84, Fairmount, E.
"   120, Winter, E.
"   138, Mather, 145, end.

**Brown.**    7
331 Wethersfield, W. to George.
No. 1, Wethersfield, 331.
     Franklin, crosses.
     Winship, crosses.

**Brownell Avenue.**    8
23 Washington, W. to 525 Broad.
     Nos. 1 to 40.

**Buckingham.**    8
311 Main, W. to 148 Washington.
No. 1, Main, 91.
"   11, John, S.
"   18, Whitman, N.
"   31, Hudson, S.
"   53, Wadsworth, S.
"   56, West, N.
"   69, Cedar, S.
"   94, Washington, 148, end.

**Bushnell.**    7
Franklin W. to Back Lane.

**Canton.**    2,3
156 Windsor av. E. to 187 Windsor.
No. 1, Windsor av. 156.
"   16, Wooster, N.
"   32, Bellevue, N.
"   46, Windsor, junction R. R. end.

**Capen.**    3
375 Windsor av. W. to Vine.
No.   1, Windsor av. 375.
"   78, Clark, N.
"   124, Barbour, N.
"   170, Martin, N.
"   216, Garden, crosses.
"   350, Vine, end.

**Carpenter.**    10
Madison av. W.

**Capitol Avenue.**    6,9,10
393 Main, W. to Willow.
No. 1, Main, 393.
"   27, Whitman, S.
"   91, West, crosses.
"   142, Clinton, N.
"   174, Trinity, N.
"   191, Washington, S.
"   261, Oak, S.
"   293, Hungerford, S.
"   333, Broad, crosses.
"   371, Lawrence, crosses.
"   405, Babcock, S.
"   437, Putnam, S.
"   479, Columbia, S.
"   491, Park Terrace, S.
"   511, Park river.
"   532, Sigourney, N.
"   585, Woodbine, crosses.
"   620, Laurel, crosses.
"   659, Willow, S., end.

**Caya.**
Prospect av. W.

**Cedar.**    6
130 Park, N. to 69 Buckingham.

**Cemetery.**    5
84 Mather, N. to Catholic Cemetery.
     Pliney st. W.
     Mahl av. E.

**Center.**    3
106 Albany, N. to 73 Mather.
No. 2, Albany, 106.
"   12, Fairmount, crosses.
"   30, Seyms, E.
"   42, Mather, 73, end.

**Central Row.**    1
766 Main, E. to 65 Prospect.
No. 15 Woods place, S.

**Chadwick Avenue.**    10
332 Park, N.

**Chapel.**    5
141 Trumbull, W. to 92 Ann.

**Charles.**    1,2
24 Kilbourn, N. crossing Morgan.
No. 1, Kilbourn, 24.
"   32, Talcott, crosses.
"   70, Morgan, 81, crosses.

**Charlotte.**    3
Barbour, W. to Waverly.

**Charter Oak Avenue.**    1,7
310 Main, E. to Vandyke.
No. 1, Main, 310.
"   25, Charter Oak place, S.
"   28, South Prospect, N.
"   56, Governor, crosses.
"   72, Woodbridge, N.
"   94, Union, crosses.
"   105, Vanblock, S. E.
"   106, Taylor, N.
"   115, Wyllys, S. W.
"   117, Huyshope, S. E.
"   128, Vredandale, crosses.
"   141, Vandyke, end.

**Charter Oak Place.**    7
24 Wyllys, N. to 25 Charter Oak av.
     Nos. 1 to 40.

**Church.**　　4,5
971 Main, W. to 60 Spring.
No. 1, Main, 971.
" 44, Trumbull, crosses.
" 80, Ann, crosses.
" 108, High, crosses.
" 122, Foot Guard place.
" 125, Union place, S.
" 130, Huntley av. N
" 136, Spruce, crosses.
" 140, Spring, 60, end.

**Chestnut.**　　4
34 Walnut, N. to 77 Albany.

**City Hall Place.**　　1
Between City Hall and Post Office,
from 51 State st. to 12 Central row.

**Clark.**　　3
78 Capen, N. to Westland.
No. 1, Capen, 78.
" 44, Elmer, E.
" 99, Nelson, W.
" 185, Judson, W.
" 188, Westland, end.

**Claremont.**　　8
Maple, W.

**Clifford.**　　8
Maple, W.

**Clinton.**　　6
142 Capitol, N. to 93 Elm.

**Collins.**　　4,9,10
4 Myrtle, N. W. to 106 Woodland.
No. 1, Myrtle, 4.
" 110, Garden, crosses.
" 155, Sumner, S.
" 189, Huntington, crosses.
" 227, Sigourney, crosses.
" 265, Willard, S.
" 309, Atwood, crosses.
" 379, Woodland, 106, end.

**Columbia.**　　9
479 Capitol avenue, S.

**Commerce.**　　1
348 Sheldon, N. to 94 Morgan.
No. 1, Swing bridge.
" 30, Potter, crosses.
" 40, Keeney, E.
" 98, Grove, crosses.
" 122, State, crosses.
" 149, Ferry, crosses.
" 178, Kilbourn, W.
" 191, Talcott, W.
" 241, Morgan, 94, end.

**Concord.**
N. from Farmington avenue, town
of West Hartford.

**Cone.**　　10
Whitney st. W. to 684 Prospect av.
Tremont, S.
Oxford, S.
Beacon, S.
Prospect avenue, end.

**Congress.**　　7
12 Morris, N. to South Park.

**Cottage Grove Avenue.**　　4
W. end Tower av. N. to Bloomfield.

**Cottage Place.**　　7
263 Wethersfield, W. to Franklin.

**Cranes Court.**　　3
450 Windsor av. to 221 Bellevue.

**Crown.**　　8
Webster, W. to Julius.

**Curcombe.**　　7
Hendricxsen W. and S. to Wawarme.

**Cushman.**　　10
9 Sigourney, W. to Woodbine.

**Dartmouth.**　　8
Maple, W.

**Davenport Avenue.**　　10
W. from Smith to Rowe.
Smith, crosses.
Amity, S.
Heath, S.
James, S.
Rowe, S.

**Dean.**　　7
From below Alden, N. to 23 Morris.
No. 18, S. of Alden.
" 52, Alden, E.
" 68, Morris, 23, end.

**Donald.**　　2
Kennedy, N. to Russell.

**Douglas.**　　7
Franklin, W. to George.
Winship, crosses.

**Dutch Point.**　　1
Junction of Conn. and Park rivers.

**East.**　　3
90 Albany, N. to 45 Mather.
No. 1, Albany, 90.
" 11, Fairmount, W.
" 12, Florence, E.
" 27, Seyms, crosses.
" 39, Mather, 45, end.

**Easton.**　　8
Fairfield, W. to New Britain, laid out.

**Eaton.**　　7
458 Wethersfield, W. to Franklin.

**Edwards.**　　4
118 Spring, N. to 97 Albany.
No. 2, Spring, 118.
" 58, Walnut, crosses.
" 112, Albany, 97, end.

**Ellery.**　　1
Park river, N. to 78 Potter.

**Elliott.**　　8
169 Wethersfield W.to 170 Franklin.
No. 21, Elliott place, S.

**Elliott Place.**　　7
Elliott, S.

**Ellsworth.**　　8
19 New Britain, S. to Crown.
King, E.

**Ellsworth Place.**　　2
9 Morgan, southerly.

**Elm.**　　6
488 Main, W. to 48 Trinity.
No. 1, Main, 488.
" 35, Linden, S.
" 69, West, S.
" 98, Clinton, S.
" 115, Trinity, 48, end.

**Elm Place.**　　6
47 Elm, S.

**Elmer.**　　3
421 Windsor av. W. to 44 Clark.

**Ely.**　　2
1382 Main, N. E. to 17 Winthrop.

**Evergreen.**　　10
Warrenton N. to 585 Farmington.
Gray, E.
Fales, E.

**Faience.**
Hamilton, S.

**Fairfield Avenue.**　　8
Maple, N. to New Britain.
No. 1, Maple avenue.
Freeman, E.
White, W.
Easton, W., laid out.
" 80, Freeman, E.
New Britain avenue, end.

**Fairmount.**　　3
11 East, W. to 84 Brook.
No. 1, East, 11.
" 36, Center, crosses.
" 62, Green, crosses.
" 112, Brook, 84, end.

**Fales.**　　10
Sisson W. to Evergreen.

**Farmington Avenue.**　　9,10
629 Asylum, W. to City line.
No. 1, Asylum, 629, N.
" 15, Broad, S.
" 70, Asylum place, N.
" 71, Flower, S.
" 89, Beach, S.
" 185, Sigourney, crosses.
" 221, Imlay, S.
" 259, Laurel, crosses.
" 296, Marshall, N.
" 337, Forest, S.
" 346, Gillett, N.
" 374, Woodland, N.
" 394, North branch Park river.
" 428, Owen, S.
" 454, Lorraine, N.
" 470, Sherman, N.
" 477, Sisson av., S.
" 506, Girard av., N.
" 535, Evergreen, S.
" 538, Kenyon, N.
" 565, Smith,
" 568, Whiting, N.
" 588, Tremont, crosses.
" 612, Oxford, crosses.
" 642, Beacon, crosses.
" 670, Prospect av.; town line.
Hamilton, N.
Concord, N.
Highland, N.
Vanderbilt hill, N.
Whiting av.
Quaker lane.

**Fern.**
Prospect av. to and in W. Hartford.

**Ferry.**                                    I
106 Front to Connecticut river.
No.  1, Front, 106.
"    65, Commerce, S.
"    66, Valley, N.
"    74, Commerce, N.
"    78, ends at Connecticut river.

**Fishfry.**                              2,3
912 Windsor av. E.

**Flatbush Avenue.**                       8
53 Zion, W. crossing Town line.
South Laurel, S.

**Florence.**                              3
85 Windsor av. W. to 12 East.

**Flower.**                                9
Park river, N. to 71 Farmington.
No. 14, Howard, E.
"    21, Railroad crossing.
"    41, Beach, W.
"    44, Queen, E.
"    89, Farmington, 71, end.

**Foot Guard Place.**                      4
149 High, W. and 122 Church, N.

**Ford.**                                  5
346 Pearl, N. to 379 Asylum.
No. 2, Pearl, 346.
"    6, Riverside place, E.
"   20, Asylum, 379.

**Forest.**                               10
Railroad, N. to 337 Farmington.
No.  1, Railroad tracks.
"    38, Hawthorn, crosses.
"    73, Farmington, end.

**Francis Avenue.**                       10
713 Park, S. crossing Hamilton, and
     W. of Railroad track.

**Frankfort.**                             3
807 Windsor av. W.

**Franklin Avenue.**                       7
150 Maple, S. to City line.
No.  1, Maple, 150.
"    2, Morris, E.
"    74, Annawan, E.
"    93, Pawtucket, W.
     Schultas place, E.
"   152, Benton, crosses
"   165, Warner, W.
"   170, Elliott, E.
"   209, Whitmore, W.
'   234, Bond, crosses.
     Cottage place.
     Bushnell, W.
     Preston, crosses.
     Franklin place, W.
"   430 Bodwell, E.
     Douglas, W.
     Gilman, W.
     Brown, crosses, laid out.
     Standish, E.
     South, crosses.

**Freeman.**                               8
Maple, W. to Fairfield.

**Front.**                               1,2
224 Sheldon, N. to N. Y. & N. E. R.
No.  1, Sheldon, 224, at bridge.
"    7, Arch, W
"    19, Berkley place, W.
"    24, Potter, E.
"    70, Grove, crosses.
"    98, State, crosses.
"   106, Ferry, E.
"   186, Kilbourn, E.
"   187, Kilbourn court, W.
"   155, Temple, W.
"   180, Talcott, crosses.
"   218, Morgan, crosses.
"   290, Water, N. E.
"   291, Pleasant, W.
"   309, North, W.
"   389, Avon, W.
"   374, N. Y. & N. E. R. end.

**Garden.**                            3,4,9
594 Asylum, N. to Westland.
No.  1, Asylum, 594.
"   100, Myrtle, E.
"   174, Collins, crosses.
"   209, Ashley, W.
"   229, Sargeant, W.
"   240, Hfd. & Conn. Western R.
"   246, Walnut, E.
"   264, Liberty, E.
"   338, Albany, crosses.
"   404, Mather, crosses.
"   450 Pliney, E.
"   524, Capen, crosses.
     Nelson, E., laid out.
     Woodruff, W.
     Judson, E., laid out.
     Westland, end.

**George.**                                7
Preston, S. to South.
Olive, E.
Gilman, E.
Brown, E.

**Gillett.**                              10
346 Farmington, N. to 1023 Asylum.
No.  1, Farmington, 346.
"    74, Niles, crosses.
"   118, Asylum, 1023, end.

**Gilman.**                                7
Franklin, W. to George.
Winship, crosses.

**Girard Avenue.**                        10
506 Farmington, N. to Asylum.

**Glendale Avenue.**                       8
141 Zion, W.

**Gold.**                                  5
655 Main, W. to 100 Wells.

**Goodman Place.**                         2
1182 Main, easterly and northerly.

**Goodwin.**                               2
34 Windsor av. E. to railroad track.
     Nos. 2 to 28.

**Governor.**                            1,7
34 Wyllys, N. to 169 Sheldon.
No.  1, Wyllys, 34.
"    44, Charter Oak, crosses.
"    85, Sheldon, 169, end.

**Grace.**                                10
New Park av. W. to Greenwood.

**Grand.**                               6,9
13 Lafayette, W. to Putnam.
No.  1, Lafayette, 13.
"    11, Oak, crosses.
"    28, Hungerford, crosses.
"    50, Broad, crosses.
"    56, Lawrence, crosses.
     Babcock, crosses.
     Putnam, end, laid out.

**Grand Avenue.**                          8
Laid out, 7 Zion, W. to New Park av.
No.  1, Zion.
     S. Laurel, N.
     S. branch Park river.
     Newfield av. crosses.
     Oakwood av. crosses.

**Gray.**                                 10
Sisson, W. to Evergreen.

**Green.**                                 8
124 Albany, N. to 97 Mather.
No.  2. Albany, 124.
"    26, Fairmount, crosses.
"    77, Winter, W.
"    95, Mather, 97, end.

**Greenwood.**                            10
375 Park, S.

**Grove.**                                 1
710 Main, E. to Connecticut river.
No.  1, Main, 710.
"    81, Prospect, crosses.
"    96, Front, crosses.
"   117, Mechanic, S.
"   146, Commerce, crosses.
"   154, ends at Connecticut river.

**Hamilton.**                           8,10
177 Zion, W. to New Park.
No.  1, Zion.
     South branch of Park river.
     Wellington, crosses.
     Bartholomew, crosses.
     Faience, S.
     Francis, crosses.
     New Park, end.

**Hamilton Heights.**
Farmington avenue, N. in town of
     West Hartford.

**Harbison Avenue.**                       8
155 Zion, W.

**Harper.**                                3
Love Lane, N. to Keney Park.

**Harrison.**                              4
Albany, S. and E. to Woodland.

**Hawthorn.**                             10
41 Sigourney, W., crossing Forest.
No.  1, Sigourney.
"    32, Imlay, N.
"    88, Laurel, crosses.
"   153, Forest.
     Extended to North Branch
     of Park river.

**Haynes.**                                5
218 Asylum, S. to 200 Pearl.

**Hazel.**                                10
720 Park, N.

**Heath.** 10
914 Park, N.
No. 1, Park.
  Ashton, W.
  Pike, W.
  Davenport, crosses.

**Hendricxsen Avenue.** 7
Wawarme, N. W. to Wyllys.
No. 1, Wawarme.
  Curcombe, W.
  Masseek, E.
  Weehassat, E., laid out.
  Sequassen, E., laid out.
  Wyllys, crosses.

**Hicks.** 5
17 Trumbull, W. to 8 South Ann.
  Nos. 2 to 68.

**High.** 4,5
380 Asylum, N. to 1389 Main.
No. 1, Asylum, 380.
 " 62, Allyn, crosses.
 " 127, Church, crosses.
 " 149, Foot Guard pl., westerly.
 " 203, Walnut, W.
 " 206, Oriental alley, E.
 " 231, Atlantic, W.
 " 268, Ann.
 " 269, Worcester place, W
 " 281, Main, 1389, end; junc. Ann.

**Highland.**
Farmington av., N. to Fern, in the
  town of West Hartford.

**Holcomb.** 4
End of Vine st. W. to Bluehills av.

**Hopkins.** 9
597 Asylum, S. & W. to 1478 Broad.
  Nos. 2 to 116.

**Howard.** 9
1438 Broad, W. to 14 Flower.

**Hudson.** 6,7
64 Jefferson, N. to 31 Buckingham.
No. 25, Jefferson, 34.
 " 51, Park, crosses.
 " 106, Buckingham, 31, end.

**Hungerford.** 6,9
260 Park, N. to 293 Capitol.
No. 1, Park, 256.
 " 29, Grand, crosses.
 " 83, Russ, crosses.
 " 141, Capitol, 293, end.

**Huntington.** 4,9
822 Asylum, to 80 Sargeant.
No. 1, Asylum
  Collins,
  Ashley,
  Sargeant.

**Huntley Avenue.** 4
27 Walnut, S. to 130 Church.

**Huntley Place.**
9 Huntley av. E. 400 feet.

**Huyshope Avenue.** 7
Wawarme, N. to 117 Charter Oak.
No. 1, Wawarme.
 " 39, Masseek, crosses.
 " 57, Weehassat, crosses.
 " 77, Sequassen, crosses.
  Wyllys, W.
 " 109, Charter Oak av. 117, end.

**Hurlburt.** 10
511 Asylum, S.

**Imlay.** 10
22 Hawthorn, N. to 221 Farmington.
  Nos. 1 to 80.

**James.** 10
Laid out from Park, N.
  Ashton, E.
  Pike, crosses.
  Davenport, crosses.

**Jefferson.** 7,8
1 Main, W. to 998 Broad.
No. 2, Main, 1.
 " 64, Hudson, N.
 " 77, South Hudson, S.
 " 112, Seymour, crosses.
 " 164, Washington, crosses.
 " 288, Broad, 988, end.

**Jewell.** 5
13 Trumbull, W. to 2 Ford.

**John.** 6
38 Park, N. to 11 Buckingham.

**Johnson's Lane.** 8
Near Stone Pits, on New Britain av.

**Jordan Lane.**
In the town of Wethersfield.

**Judson.** 3
185 Clark, W. to 184 Martin, end.
No. 25, Barbour, crosses.

**Julius.** 8
27 New Britain, S. to Crown.
  King, E.
  Crown, E.

**Keeney.** 1
40 Commerce, E. to river.

**Kennedy.** 2
82 Windsor av. E.

**Kenneth.** 8
Maple, W.

**Kenyon.** 10
Laid out from 586 Farmington, N. to
  Asylum.

**Kibbe.** 10
New Park, W., crossing Madison av.

**Kilbourn.** 1
136 Front, E. to 173 Commerce.
No. 1, Front, 136.
 " 24, Charles, N.
 " 39, Valley, S.
 " 47, H. & C. V. R. R. crosses.
 " 58, Commerce, 173, end.

**Kilbourn Court.** 1
137 Front, W.

**King.** 8
Webster, W. to Julius.

**Kinsley.** 1
374 Main, E. to 69 Market.

**Lafayette.** 6
194 Park, N. to 147 Washington.
No. 1, Park, 194.
 " 13, Grand, W.
 " 53, Russ, W.
 " 67, Washington, 147, junction.

**Laurel.** 10
Park N. to Niles, also laid out from
  New Britain av. N. to Park.
No. 1, Park, N.
  Park river.
 " 20, Riverside, E.
 " 25, Willow, W.
 " 122, Capitol, crosses.
 " 174, Hawthorn, crosses.
 " 308, Farmington, crosses.
 " 390, Niles, 65, end.

**Lawrence.** 8,9
118 Ward, N. to Park river and
  Flower street bridge.
No. 1, Ward, 54.
 " 68, Park, crosses.
 " 124, Grand, crosses.
 " 194, Russ, crosses.
 " 280, Capitol, crosses.
 " 303, Park river, end.

**Lenox Place.** 4
284 Albany, N.

**Lewis.**
100 Wells, N. to 81 Pearl.

**Lexington.** 7
Laid out from Franklin av., W.

**Liberty.** 4
31 Williams, W. to 264 Garden.
  Nos. 1 to 61.

**Lifkey Place.** 10
660 Park, N.

**Lincoln.** 8
71 Washington, W. to 900 Broad.
  Nos. 1 to 68.

**Linden Place.** 6
439 Main, W. and N. to 35 Elm.

**Loomis.** 3
226 Bellevue, E. to Windsor.

**Lorraine.** 10
454 Farmington, N. and W.
  to Sherman.

**Love Lane.** 3
Westland, N. W. to Vine.

**Lubeck.**
Prospect av. W.

**Lumber.**
15 Albany, S.

**Madison.** 8
75 Washington, W. to 948 Broad.

**Madison Avenue.** 10
911 Park, S., crossing Kibbe.
  Carpenter, W.

**Mahl Avenue.** 3
267 Windsor av. W. to 247 Cemetery.

**Main,** 1,2,3,4,5,6,7
Jefferson and Wyllys, N. to 1 Windsor av.
No.   1, Jefferson, W.
"      2, Wyllys, E.
"    117, Park, W.
"    310, Charter Oak, E.
"    311, Buckingham, W.
"    398, Capitol, W.
"    439, Linden, W.
"    480, Sheldon, E.
"    488, Elm, W.
"    500, Main st. single arch bridge.
☛ 524, Arch, E.
"    527, Wells, W.
"    615, Mulberry, W.
"    642, Atheneum, E.
"    655, Gold, W.
"    710, Grove, E.
"    763, Pearl, W.
"    766, Central, E.
"    819, Asylum, W.
"    850, State, E.
"    874, Kinsley, E.
"    891, Pratt, W.
"    910, Temple, E.
"    971, Church, W.
"  1008, Talcott, E.
"  1048, Morgan, E.
"  1062, Village, N. E.
"  1068, Windsor, N.
"  1126, Phelps, N.
"  1131, Trumbull, N.
"  1146, Sigourney place, N.
"  1182, Goodman, N. E.
"  1252, Pleasant, N. E.
"  1263, Blumenthal, N.
"  1367, Ann, S.
"  1382, Ely, N. E.
"  1389, High, S.
"  1410, Railroad tunnel.
"  1419, Albany, W.

**Maple Avenue.**   7,8
South Park, S. W. to City line.
No.   2, South end of South Park.
"     47, Retreat av. W.
"    150, Morris, E.
"    156, Franklin, S. E.
        Barnard, W.
        Pawtucket, E.
        Benton, E.
        Warner, E., laid out.
        Whitmore, E.
        Bond, E.
        Webster, N.
        Back lane, E.
        Claremont, W.
        Kenneth, W.
        Clifford, W.
        Dartmouth, W.
        Freeman, W.
        South, E.
        Fairfield, N.

**Mannz.**   7
201 Wethersfield, W. to Elliott pl.

**Market.**   1,2
104 State, N. to 75 Pleasant.
No.   1, State, 10½.
"     69, Kinsley, W.
"     96, Temple, crosses.
"    154, Talcott, crosses.
"    202, Morgan, crosses.
"    269, Marsh, W.
"    326, Pleasant, 75, end.

**Marsh.**   2
26 Village E. to 266 Market.

**Marshall.**   10
296 Farmington av. N. to 69 Niles.

**Martin.**   3
170 Capen, N. to Westland.
No.   1, Capen, 170.
"     84, Nelson, E.
"    184, Judson, E.
"    188, Westland, end.

**Martin Avenue.**   8
New Britain, N.

**Masseek.**   7
From Vandyke, W. to Hendricxsen.
    Huyshope, crosses.

**Mather.**   3
157 Windsor av. W. to Vine.
No.   1, Windsor av. W.
"     45, East, S.
"     78, Center, S.
"     84, Cemetery, N.
"     97, Green, S.
"    145, Brook, S.
"    187, Garden, crosses.
"    265, Vine, end.

**May.**   4
150 Ashley, N. to Sargeant.

**Mays Court.**   1
28 Temple, N.

**Meadow.**   7
220 Wethersfield, E.

**Mechanic.**   1
18 Potter, N. to 117 Grove.

**Moseleys Court.**   6
Rear 28 Linden.

**Morgan.**   2
1048 Main, E. to Conn. river bridge.
No.   1, Main, 1048.
"      9, Ellsworth place, S.
"     32, Market, crosses.
"     64, Front, crosses.
"     81, Charles, crosses.
"     90, Railroad, crosses.
"     94, Commerce, 241, at bridge.

**Morris.**   7
51 Wethersfield, W. to 150 Maple.
No.   1, Wethersfield, 51.
"     12, Congress, N.
"     23, Dean, S.
"     29, Maple, 150, end.

**Mulberry.**   5,6
615 Main, W. to 84 Wells.

**Myrtle.**   4
118 Spring, W. to 100 Garden.

**Nelson.**   3
99 Clark, W. to 84 Martin.
    Barbour, crosses.

**Newfield Avenue.**   8
Laid out from New Britain N. to
Flatbush bridge over south branch
Park river, crossing Grand av.

**Newington Avenue.**   8
New Britain, S.W., under Cedar hill.

**New Britain Avenue.**   8
1 Washington, S. W. to town line.
No.   2, Washington, 1.
"     19, Ellsworth, S.
"     37, Julius, S.
"     51, Broad, crosses.
"     78. Martin.
"     98, Johnsons Lane, N.
"    125, Summit, N.
"    150, Fairfield, S.
        Zion, N.
        White, E.
        Newington, S.
        Newfield, N.
        City line crosses.

**New Park Avenue.**   10
775 Park, S. W. to City line.
No.   1, Park.
        Hamilton, E.
        Grace, W.
        Kibbe, W.
        Prospect av. N.
        Flatbush av. crosses.
        Grand av. crosses.

**Niles.**   10
125 Sigourney, W. to Woodland.
No.   1, Sigourney, 125.
"      4, Plinys court, N.
"     55, Laurel, S.
"     69, Marshall, S.
"     90, Gillett, crosses.
"    124, Woodland, end.

**Norman.**   7
Laid out from Franklin av., W.

**North.**   2
309 Front, W. to 76 Windsor.

**Oak.**   6
228 Park, N. to 261 Capitol.
No.   1, Park, 228.
"     18, Grand, crosses.
        Russ, crosses.
        Capitol, 261, end.

**Oakwood Avenue.**   8
New Britain av., N. to Grand av.

**Olive.**   8
Wellington, W. to Bartholomew.

**Orchard.**   2
37 Windsor, W.

**Oriental Alley.**   5
99 Ann, W. to 206 High, op. Walnut

**Owen.**   10
423 Farmington, S.

**Oxford.**   10
Warrenton N., crossing 613 Farmington to Cone.

**Park.**   6,7,8,9,10
117 Main, W. to 884 Prospect av.
No.   1, Main, 117.
"     38, John, N.
"     70, Hudson, crosses.
"    100, Wadsworth, N.
"    119, Seymour, S.
"    130, Cedar, N.
"    168, Washington, crosses
"    194, Lafayette, N.
"    207, Squire, S.
"    228, Oak, N.

No. 225, Wolcott, S.
" 260, Hungerford, N.
" 288, Broad, crosses.
" 310, Lawrence, crosses.
" 341, Affeck, S.
" 342, Babcock, N.
" 371, Putnam, crosses.
" 405, Zion, S.
" 535, Laurel, N. and laid out S.
" 646, Park river.
" 660, Zifkey Place, N.
" 690, Bartholomew av. S. W.
　　Railroad crosses.
" 713, Francis av. S. W.
" 720, Hazel, N.
" 775, New Park av. S. W.
" 770, Sisson, N.
" 822, Chadwick.
" 856, Smith, N.
" 876, Greenwood, S.
" 878, Amity, N.
" 914, Heath, N.
" 911, Madison av. S.
　　James, N.
" 974, Rowe, N.
" 1010, Prospect av. end.

**Park Terrace.** 10
491 Capitol av. south.

**Pavilion.** 3
268 Windsor av. E. to 88 Bellevue.
No. 2, Wooster, E. crosses.

**Pawtucket.** 7
90 Franklin, West to 151 Maple.
Nos. 1 to 48.

**Pearl.** 5
763 Main, W. to 2 Ford.
No. 1, Main, 763.
" 81, Lewis, S.
" 141, Trumbull, crosses.
" 200, Haynes, N.
" 254, South Ann, crosses.
" 346, Ford, 2, at Park river, end.

**Phelps.** 2
1126 Main, N. and E. to 15 Windsor.

**Pike.** 10
Heath, W. crossing James.

**Pleasant.** 2
1252 Main, E. to 291 Front.
No. 1, Main, 1252.
" 22, Winthrop, N.
" 36, Portland, N.
" 44, Windsor, crosses.
" 50, Village, crosses.
" 61, Pleasant court, S.
" 75, Market, S.
" 90, Railroad, crosses.
" 104, Front, 291, end.

**Pleasant Court.** 2
From 61 Pleasant st. southerly.

**Pliney.** 3
Cemetery, W. to 450 Garden.

**Pliny's Court.** 10
4 Niles, N.

**Portland.** 2
36 Pleasant, N. to 45 Avon.
No. 1, Pleasant, 36.
" 139, Avon, 45, end.

**Potter.** 1
24 Front, E. and S. to Dutch point.
No. 1, Front, 24.
" 18, Mechanic, N.
" 56, Commerce, crosses.
" 73, Ellery, S.

**Pratt.** 5
891 Main, W. to 84 Trumbull.

**Preston.** 7
287 Wethersfield av. W. to Back lane.
　　Winship, S.
　　George, S.

**Prospect.** 1
88 Arch, N. to 25 Central row.
No. 1, Arch, 88.
" 35, Atheneum, W.
" 54, Grove, crosses.
" 65, Central row, 25, end.

**Prospect Avenue.** 4,10
New Park av. N. to Albany av.
No. 1, New Park.
　　Lubeck, W.
" 884, Park, crosses.
" 446, Davenport, laid out.
" 510, Warrenton, E.
" 600, Farmington, crosses.
　　Fern, W.
" 684, Cone, E.
" 950, Asylum, crosses.

**Putnam.** 8,9
174 Ward, N. to 487 Capitol.
No. 1, Ward.
" 89, Park, crosses.
" 99, Grand, E., laid out.
" 199, Russ, E.
" 256, Capitol, end.

**Quaker Lane.**
From Farmington av. southerly,
　and W. of Prospect av.

**Queen.** 9
1471 Broad, W. to 44 Flower.

**Retreat Avenue.** 7
47 Maple av. S. W. to 44 Washington.
No. 1, Maple, 47.
" 96, South Hudson, N.
" 164, Seymour, N.
" 286, Washington, 44, end.

**Rice Court.** 4
Rear 1419 Main.

**Riverside.** 10
20 Laurel, E. to 2 Woodbine.

**Riverside Place.** 5
6 Ford, eastward.

**Rose.** 8
Wellington, W. to Bartholomew.

**Rowe.** 1
974 Park, N. to Davenport.

**Russ.** 6,9
53 Lafayette, W. to 199 Putnam.
No. 1, Lafayette, 53.
" 43, Oak, crosses.
" 77, Hungerford, crosses.
" 113, Broad, crosses.
　　Lawrence, crosses.
　　Babcock, crosses.
　　Putnam, end.

**Russell.** 2
108 Windsor av. E. to 175 Windsor.
26, Arthur place, S.

**Sanford.** 3
466 Windsor av. E. to Railroad track.
No. 2, Windsor av. 466.
" 31, Bellevue, S.
" 81, Windsor, S.
" 103, Railroad track, end.

**Sargeant.** 4
229 Garden, W. to 146 Woodland.
No. 80, Huntington, S.
" 118, Sigourney, crosses.
" 150, May, S.
" 272, Woodland, end.

**Scarborough.** 4
Laid out from 148 feet W. of Park
river bridge on Albany av., southerly
to Farmington av.

**School.** 8
9 Washington, W. to 610 Broad.

**Schultze Place.** 7
119 Wethersfield, W. to Franklin.

**Sequassen.** 7
Vandyke, W. to 78 Vanblock.
Vredendale, N.
Huyshope, crosses.

**Seymour.** 7
164 Retreat, N. to 119 Park.
No. 1, Retreat, 165.
" 120, Jefferson, crosses.
" 201, Park, 119, end.

**Seyms.** 3
123 Windsor av. W. to 30 Center.
No. 1, Windsor av. 123.
" 31, East, crosses.
" 47, Center, 30, end.

**Sherman.** 10
470 Farmington av., N. to Lorraine.

**Sheldon.** 1
480 Main, E. to Commerce st. bridge.
No. 1, Main, 480.
" 71, South Prospect, S.
" 169, Governor, S.
" 223, Woodbridge, S.
" 224, Front street bridge, N.
" 273, Union, S.
" 343, Taylor, S.
" 343, Commerce st. bridge, end.

**Sigourney.** 4,9,10
532 Capitol, N. to Sargeant.
No. 1, Capitol, 532.
" 9, Cushman, W.
" 25, Railroad crosses.
" 41, Hawthorn, W.
" 85, Farmington, crosses.
" 125, Niles, W
" 151, Asylum, crosses.
" 213, Collins, crosses.
　　Ashley, crosses.
　　Sargeant, end.

**Sigourney Place.** 2
1146 Main, N. rear Sigourney house.

**Sisson Avenue.** 10
770 Park, N. to 477 Farmington.
　　Gray, W.
　　Fales, W.

**Smith.**          10
856 Park, N. to 557 Farmington.
   Davenport, crosses.
   Warrenton, crosses.
   Farmington, end.

**South.**          7
361 Wethersfield, W. to Maple.
No.  1, Wethersfield.
   Franklin, crosses.
   George, N.
   Maple, end.

**South Ann.**          5
70 Jewell, N. crossing at 253 Pearl.
No.  1, at Jewell.
 "  8, Hicks, E.
 "  20, Pearl, crosses.
 "  31, end, rear 271 Asylum.

**South Hudson.**          7
96 Retreat av., N. to 77 Jefferson.

**South Park Place.**          7
From Wyllys to Jefferson, crossing
  south end of Main.

**South Prospect.**          1
28 Charter Oak, N. to 71 Sheldon.

**Spring.**          4
572 Asylum, N. to 2 Edwards.
No.  1, Asylum 572.
 "  60, Church, E.
 "  113, Myrtle, W.
 "  118, Edwards, end,

**Spruce.**          4
504 Asylum, N. to railroad shops.
No.  1, Asylum, 504.
 "  61, Church, crosses.
 "  83, Railroad tracks, end.

**Squire.**          8
28 Ward, N. to 207 Park.

**Standish.**          7
345 Wethersfield, W. to Franklin av.

**State.**          1
850 Main, E. to Conn. river.
No.  1, Main, 850.
 "  51, City hall place S.
 "  101, American row, S.
 "  104, Market, N.
 "  203, Front, crosses.
 "  258, Commerce, crosses.
 "  287, Connecticut river, end.

**Suffield.**          3
850 Windsor av. E. to Windsor.
No.  1, Windsor av. 350.
 "  11, Wooster, S.
 "  35, Bellevue, crosses.
 "  59, Windsor, end.

**Summit.**          8
New Britain av. N. to Zion.
No.  1, New Britain.
   Vernon, E.
   Allen place, E.
   Zion, unites.

**Sumner.**          9
778 Asylum, N. to 155 Collins.

**Talcott.**          1,2
1008 Main, E. to 191 Commerce.
No.  1, Main, 1008.
 "  8, Webb court, N.
 "  30, Market, crosses.
 "  66, Front, crosses.
 "  80, Charles, crosses.
 "  90, Railroad crosses.
 "  96, Commerce, 191, end.

**Taylor.**          1
106 Charter Oak, N. to 843 Sheldon.

**Temple Place.**          1
86½ Temple street, N.

**Temple.**          1
910 Main, E. to 153 Front.
No.  1, Main, 910.
 "  28, May's court, N.
 "  86½, Temple place, N.
 "  46, Market, crosses.
 "  84, Front, 153, end.

**Tower Avenue.**          3,4
Laid out from 948 Windsor av. W.
to Cottage Grove av., crossing Barbour and Blue Hills av.

**Townley.**          10
37 Willard, W. to 4 Atwood.

**Tremont.**          10
Warrenton, N. crossing 585 Farmington to Cone.

**Trinity.**          6
174 Capitol, N. to 1 Ford.
No.  1, Capitol, 174.
 "  48, Elm, E.

**Trumbull.**          5
101 Wells, N. to 1131 Main.
No.  2, Wells, 101.
 "  13, Jewell, W.
 "  17, Hicks, W.
 "  49, Pearl, crosses.
 "  66, Asylum, crosses.
 "  84, Pratt, E.
 "  89, Allyn, W.
 "  106, Church, crosses.
 "  141, Chapel, W.
 "  147, Main, 1131, end.

**Union.**          1
Charter Oak, N. to 273 Sheldon.

**Union Place.**          4,5
464 Asylum, N. to 125 Church.
No.  1, Asylum, 464.
 "  42, Allyn, E.

**Valley.**          1
66 Ferry, N. to 89 Kilbourn.

**Vanbleck Avenue.**          7
S. of Masseek, N. to 105 Charter Oak.
No. 40, Masseek, crosses.
 "  58, Weehassat, E.
 "  78, Sequassen, E.
 "  108, Wyllys, crosses.
 "  119, Charter Oak, 105, end.

**Vanderbilt Avenue.**          8
So. Farmington, N. to Grand av.

**Vandyke Avenue.**          7
Wawarme, N. to 141 Charter Oak.
   Weehassat, W.
   Sequassen, W.

**Vernon.**          8
45 Washington, W. to Summit.
No.  1, Washington, 45.
 "  54, Broad, crosses.
 "  186, Summit, end.

**Village.**          2
1062 Main, N. to 54 Avon.
No.  1, Main, 1062.
 "  26, Marsh, E.
 "  60, Pleasant, crosses.
 "  70, North, crosses.
   Avon, 54, end.

**Vine.**          3,4
276 Albany av. N. to Holcomb
No.  1, Albany av. 276.
   Mather, E.
   Capen, E.
   Woodruff, E.
   Westland, E.
   Love lane, E.
   Holcomb st., end.

**Vredendale Avenue.**          1
Sequassen, N. to Commerce st. br.,
  crossing Charter Oak av.

**Walker.**          7
Laid out from Franklin av., W.

**Wadsworth.**          6
100 Park, N. to 53 Buckingham.

**Walnut.**          4
203 High, W. to 246 Garden.
No. 27, Huntley avenue, S.
 "  29, Railroad crossing.
 "  84, Chestnut, N.
 "  59, Edwards, crosses.
 "  70, Williams, N.
 "  108, Garden, 246, end.

**Ward Place.**          8
125 Zion, W.

**Ward.**          8
101 Washington, W. to 224 Zion.
No. 28, Squires, N.
 "  25, Wolcott, N.
 "  96, Broad, crosses.
 "  118, Lawrence, N.
 "  146, Affleck, N.
 "  174, Putnam, N.
 "  204, Zion, end.

**Warner.**          
165 Franklin, W. to Maple.

**Warren.**          3
192 Bellevue, E. to Windsor.

**Warrenton Avenue.**          10
Sisson av. W. to 510 Prospect av.
   Evergreen, N.
   Smith, crosses.
   Tremont, N.
   Oxford, N.
   Beacon, N.
   Prospect av.

**Water.**          2
290 Front, N. E. through meadow.

**Waverly.**          3
Love lane N. to Keney Park.

**Way Place.**          2,3
Windsor st. extension, E. to meadow.

**Washington.** 6,7,8
Webster st. junction New Britain
av. N. to 191 Capitol.
No. 1, New Britain.
" 9, School st. W.
" 23, Brownell av. W.
" 44, Retreat, E.
" 45, Vernon, W.
" 65, Allen place, W.
" 71, Lincoln, W.
" 77, Madison, W.
" 90, Jefferson, crosses.
" 101, Ward, W.
" 118, Park, crosses.
" 147, Lafayette, W.
" 148, Buckingham, E.
" 156, Capitol, 191, end.

**Wawarme Avenue.** 7
116 Wethersfield, E. to Vandyke.
Curcombe, N.
Hendricxsen, N
Vanblock, N., laid out.
Huyshope, N.
Vandyke, end.

**Webb Court.** 2
8 Talcott, N.

**Webster.** 7,8
From Maple N. to 1 Washington.
No. 1, Maple.
" 14, Bond, E.
" 96, Benton.
" 119, New Britain.
" 120, Washington, end.

**Weehansat.** 7
Vandyke, W. to 58 Vanblock, crossing Huyshope.

**Wellington.** 8
West of south branch Park river.
Hamilton, crosses.
Belmont, W.
Rose, W.
Olive, W.

**Wells.** 5,6
527 Main, W. and N. to 1 Lewis.
No. 1, Main, 527.
" 84, Mulberry, E.
" 100, Lewis, 1, end

**West.** 6
56 Buckingham, N. to 69 Elm.
No. 1, Buckingham, 56.
" 14, Capitol, crosses.
" 38, Elm, 69, end.

**West Hartford Avenue.**
City line 3 miles to reservoirs.

**Westland.** 3
565 Windsor av. W. to Blue hills av.
Clark, S.
Barbour, crosses.
Martin, S.
Garden, S.
Love lane, N.
Vine, crosses.

**White.** 8
Fairfield, W. to New Britain.

**Whitman Court.** 6
18 Buckingham, N. to 27 Capitol.

**Whitmore.** 7
209 Franklin av., W. to Maple av.

**Whitney.** 10
568 Farmington, N. to Cone.

**Wethersfield Avenue.** 7
2 Main, S. to Wethersfield town.
No. 2, Main, 2.
" 51, Morris, W.
" 71, Alden, W.
" 97, Annawan, W.
" 116, Wawarme, E.
" 119, Schultas, W.
" 145, Benton, W.
" 169, Elliott, W.
" 197, Bond, W.
" 201, Bodwell, W.
" 201, Mannz, W. to Elliott place.
" 220, Meadow, E.
" 268, Cottage place, westerly.
" 287, Preston, W.
" 299, Bodwell, W.
" 331, Brown, W., laid out.
" 345, Standish, W.
" 361, South, W.
" 491, Eaton, W.
" 506, City line, end.

**Willard.** 10
920 Asylum, N. to 265 Collins.
No. 1, Asylum, 920.
" 37, Townley, N.
" 69, Collins, 265, end.

**Williams.** 4
70 Walnut, N. to 131 Albany.
No. 1, Walnut, 70.
" 81, Liberty, W.
" 112, Albany, 131, end.

**Willow.** 10
25 Laurel, W. and N. to 659 Capitol.
Nos. 1 to 100.

**Windsor Avenue.** 3
Previous to May, 1898, this was 710
to 1074 Main st.
1410 Main to City line.
No. 2, Railroad tunnel.
" 34, Goodwin, E.
" 47, Belden, W.
" 64, Avon, E.
" 82, Kennedy, E.
" 88, Florence, W.
" 108, Russell, E.
" 123, Seyms, W.
" 156, Canton, E.
" 157, Mather, W.
" 264, State Arsenal.
" 267, Mahl, W.
" 268, Pavilion, E.
" 350, Suffield, E.
" 375, Capen, W.
" 421, Elmer, W.
" 450, Cranes court, E.
" 565, Westland. W.
" 588, Sanford, E.
" 807, Frankfort, W.
" 943, Tower, W.
" 912, Fishfry, E.
" 1187, City line, end.

**Windsor.** 2,3
1068 Main, N. to Sanford.
No. 15, Phelps, W.
" 37, Orchard, W.
" 53, Pleasant, crosses.
" 76, North, E.
" 134, Avon, crosses.
" 161, N. Y. & N. E. R.
" 175, Russell, W.
" 181, N. Y., N. H. & H. R. crosses.
" 187, Canton, W.
Suffield, W. Warren, W.
Loomis, W. Sanford, crosses.

**Wilson.**
113 Zion, W.

**Winship.**
South, N. to Preston.
Brown, crosses.
Gilman, crosses.
Douglas, crosses.

**Winter.** 3
77 Green, W. to 120 Brook.

**Winthrop.** 2
22 Pleasant, N. W. to railroad.
No. 17, Ely, S.

**Wolcott.** 5
52 Ward, N. to 235 Park.

**Woodbine.** 10
33 Riverside, N. to 50 Cushman.
No. 2, Riverside, 33.
" 112, Capitol, crosses.
Cushman, end.

**Woodbridge.** 1
72 Charter Oak, N. to 223 Sheldon.

**Woodland.** 4,10
374 Farmington, N. to Albany.
No. 50, Niles, E.
" 74, Asylum, crosses.
" 106, Collins, E.
" 132, Ashley, E.
" 146, Sargeant, E. laid out.
" 166, Conn. Western R. R. bridge.
" 192, Harrison av., W. and N.
" 223, Albany, end.

**Woodruff.** 3
Laid out from Garden, W. to Vine.

**Woods Place.** 1
15 Central row, southerly to alley.

**Wooster.** 3
16 Canton, N. to 11 Suffield.
No. 2, Canton, 16.
" 68, Pavilion, crosses.
" 120, Suffield, 11, end.

**Worcester Place.** 4
269 High, W.

**Wyllys.** 7
2 Main, N. E. to 115 Charter Oak av.
No. 2, Main, 2.
" 24, Charter Oak place, N.
" 34, Governor, N.
Hendricxsen, S.
Union, N.
Vanblock, crosses.
Huyshope, S.
Charter Oak av. 115, end.

**Zion.** 8
New Britain av. N. to 405 Park.
No. 7, Grand av. W., laid out.
" 53, Flatbush av. W.
" 99, Bonner, W.
" 113, Wilson, W.
" 125, Ward place, W.
" 141, Glendale av., W.
" 155, Harbison, W.
" 177, Hamilton, W.
" 200, Summit, S. E.
" 224, Ward, E.
" 252, Park, 405, end.

## Obsolete Street Names with Present Names.

A VALUABLE TABLE for tracing old land titles.

| OBSOLETE NAMES. | ALTERED TO |
|---|---|
| Adams st. | Pleasant st. |
| Allen's road, | Flatbush av. |
| Asylum av. | Asylum st. No. 629 westw'd. |
| Back st. | Trumbull st. |
| Baker's lane, | Ward st. |
| Bliss st. | East from Park tool house. |
| Bridge st. | Morgan st. |
| Brinley court, | South Ann st. |
| Buckingham lane, | Whitman st. |
| Burr st. | 490 Main, to and in Alb.av. |
| Cemetery lane, | Pine st. |
| Coles st. | Governor st. |
| College place, | Trinity st. |
| College st. | Capitol av. |
| Cooper lane, | Lafayette st. |
| Creek st., | Morgan st. |
| Dee lane, | Tower av. |
| Dorrs st. | Market st. Nos. 1 to 202. |
| Division st. | Temple st. |
| Factory lane, | Mulberry st. |
| Franklin st. | Allyn st. |
| Griswold st. | Broad st. Nos. 481 to 711. |
| Grove lane, | Mechanic st. |
| Highways by Little river, | Arch, Wells, Sheldon & Elm. |
| Hubbard st. | Sisson av. |
| Jones lane, | Ferry st. |
| Kingsley st. | Kinsley st. |
| Knox court, | Hungerford st. |
| Lee st. | Kinsley st. |
| Leet st. | Webster st. |
| Linwood st. | Lawrence st. Nos. 1 to 69. |
| Little river to No. Meadow | Front st. |
| Lower Ferry road, | Charter Oak av. |
| Maiden lane, | Wells st. to Trumbull. |
| Malt lane, | Park st. No. 168 westward. |
| Market bridge, | Main st. stone bridge. |
| McKegg road, | Prospect av. |
| Meadow lane, | Front st. Nos. 180 to 291. |
| Meadow lane, | Village st. and Water st. |
| Meeting house to Mill, | Pearl and Wells st. |
| Middle road, | Farmington av. |
| Mill st. | Wells st. |
| Myrtle av. | Collins st. |
| New Haven turnpike, | Maple av. |
| Nichols lane, | Gold st. |
| North av. | Windsor st. |
| North end of Wells st. | Lewis st. |
| North Meadow lane, | Water st. |
| North Prospect, | Winthrop. |
| North Sheldon st. | Kennedy st. |
| Oil Mill lane, | Capitol av. No. 191 westw'd. |
| Orient st. | Grove st. |
| Prison st. | Pearl st. Nos. 1 to 129. |
| Railroad place, | Union place. |
| Railroad row, | Spruce st. |
| Rifle av. | Capitol av. |
| School st. | Arch st. |
| Sentinel hill to Palisado, | Main st., 4th Church, south. |
| Sentinel hill to Seth Grants, | Trumbull st. |
| Shaving lane, | South Prospect st. |
| Sheldon av. | Kennedy st. |
| Soldiers Field lane, | Front st. No. 291 north. |
| South Winthrop st. | Goodman pl. |
| Talcott Mountain turnpike, | Albany av. |
| Tanner's lane, | Elm st. |
| The Neck, | Main st. above No. 718. |
| Theatre st. | Temple st. |
| Thrall st. | Girard av. |
| Town Hill st. | Asylum st. |
| Upper Mill st. | Trinity st. |
| Wadsworth lane, | Atheneum st. |
| Water st. | Sheldon st. Nos. 1 to 169. |
| Welles place, | Linden st. |
| West st. | Washington st. |
| Workhouse lane, | Pearl st. Nos. 129 to 346. |
| Zachary lane. | Vernon st. |

# ΛAIN STREET AS RENUMBERED,
## MAY, 1898.

| Old | New | |
|---|---|---|
| 1 | 5 | Chaffer Julia A. wid. John H. |
| | | Smith Elector P. wid. J. Milton. |
| | | Featherbridge Emeline, Mrs. |
| | | Cheney Minnie P. nurse. |
| | | Comerford Elizabeth. |
| 3 | 9 | Eberle Frederick. |
| | | " Edward. |
| 5 | 21 | Costello James V. |
| | | " Elizabeth M. |
| | | Comerford Elizabeth. |
| 7 | 29 | Newton Elizabeth A. wid. Philo S. |
| | | Hawley Anna C. Mrs. |
| 9 | 37 | White Cornelia A. wid. Francis A. |
| | | " Harry W. |
| 11 | 47 | Hills John R. |
| | | Willis Caroline M. wid. Charles. |
| 13 | 53 | Gillette Hattie. |
| | | " Norman. |
| | | " Henry C. |
| 15 | 67 | Farrell James. |
| | | " James E. teamster. |
| | | Wall James E. |
| | | Roach Edward B. |
| | 75 | South Park M. E. Church. |
| 19 | 89 | Comp Nelson. |
| | | Whalen Michael J. |
| | | McFarlan Bert, dressmaker. |
| | | Sweet C. H. Mrs. dressmaker. |
| | | Beebe Ira. |
| | | " Fred S. |
| 19½ | 91 | Sheehan Edward J. |
| | | O'Brien John. |
| | | Egan John. |
| | | McManus Edward K. |
| | | " John F. |
| | | " Harry F. |
| | | " Thomas E. L. |
| 21 | 95 | Tracy Henry C. grocer. |
| 21½ | 97 | Birmingham Michael. |
| | | Buckley James W. |
| | | Harris Eugene C. |
| | | McAuley George A. |
| | | McCann Mary, wid. John. |
| | | Dettenborn William F. |
| | | Collins Edward T. |
| | | " Elizabeth Mrs. |
| | | Dower John J. |
| 23 | 99 | Lee Charlie, laundry. |
| 23½ | 101 | Buckley Bridget, wid. John. |
| | | Long Jeremiah. |
| | | " John. |
| | | " Patrick. |

| Old | New | |
|---|---|---|
| 23½ | 101 | Waller Robert. |
| | | McMahon Annie, wid. Bernard. |
| | | Godman Mary. |
| | | Daniels Charles E. |
| | 103 | Natine John, barbershop. |
| 25½ | 105 | Cella Joseph. |
| 27 | 107 | Coleman Cornelius F. saloon. |
| 27½ | 109 | Hale Martha, wid. John. |
| | | Hogaboom Homer A. |
| | | Hartleben Hermann. |
| | | Spieler Frederick T. |
| 29 | 111 | Hawksworth Harry, saloon. |
| 29½ | 113 | Hooper Charles E. |
| | | " George. |
| | | Brett John J. |
| 31 | 115 | Graves Frank E. drugstore. |
| | | *Park Street, W.* |
| 33 | 131 | Strong Charles H. market. |
| 33½ | 133 | Williams John H. furniture repairer. |
| | | McManus Brothers, cigar factory. |
| 35 | 141 | Attleton James P. Mrs. |
| | | Mellen C. B. |
| | | Mayer R. A. Mrs. |
| 37 | 143 | Graham James R. |
| | | Hollister Fidelia, wid. Charles W. |
| | | Preston Albert B. |
| 39 | 151 | Hollister Ida M. Mrs. |
| | | " Lillian, wid. Martin. |
| | | " Robert. |
| | | Pierce William N. |
| 41 | 153 | Field Monroe F. |
| | | Naylor James H. physician. |
| 43½ | 169 | Balfe Dennis. |
| | | Coughlin James A. |
| | | Downey Andrew. |
| | | Landaugh Emil. |
| | | Ward Patrick. |
| 45 | 171 | Saled David, tailor. |
| 45½ | 173 | Sardella Leberato, fruits. |
| 47 | 181 | Claffey Kate, wid. Charles B. |
| | | Dunn George F. |
| 51 | 189 | **LOTKER KARL,** furrier. |
| | | Wheeler Sophia A. wid. Charles W. |
| 51½ | 197 | Enginehouse No. 1. |
| 53 | 207 | Bolles Cora, wid. S. P. |
| | | Crane Harry. |
| | | " Sarah, Mrs. |
| 55 | 209 | Duffy Katharine. |
| | | " Rose. |
| | | Helion Mary B. |
| | | " Margaret. |
| | | " John J. |

| | | |
|---|---|---|
| 55 | 209 | Helion Daniel J. |
| 57 | 215 | **WITTE ROBERT C.** cutlery and hardware. |
| | 219 | Witte Julia, wid. Charles. |
| | 217 | Murphy William J. cigar manufacturer. |
| 59 | 221 | Claffey ohn R. |
| | | " Harry J. |
| | | Tucker Henry. |
| | | McGhee John C. |
| | | Morrissey Thomas. |
| | 223 | Claffey John R. saloon. |
| 61 | 231 | Reardon Timothy F. |
| 63 | 233 | Languish Thomas J. |
| | | " Frank J. |
| | | Stone John F. |
| | | Boudreau Frank. |
| | | " Alfred. |
| | | " Frederick. |
| | | Kelleher Alice J. wid. Timothy C. |
| 65 | 241 | Riley William A. |
| | | Kendall Fred. |
| | | Fowler Alice N. |
| 67 | 253 | Cooley James E. |
| | | Hawkins David S. |
| | | Mix Eliza. |
| | | Cooley Cora Vineta. |
| | | Kelley Michael. |
| | | Smith F. Bruce. |
| | | Doran Patrick. |
| 69 | 255 | Carpenter J. A. Mrs. |
| | | Loomis William F. |
| | | Gaylord Louis A. |
| | | Roulston Robert H. |
| | | " Martha L. Mrs. |
| | | Scofield Charles E. |
| | | " Viola M. Mrs. |
| | | McLouth Benjamin F. |
| 71 | 261 | Bertty George, fruit. |
| | | Kilty John. |
| | | Murphy Mary A. |
| | | " Bridget, wid. Bartholomew. |
| | | " Daniel. |
| | | Buntin William G. |
| | | Johnson August. |
| | | Istmand Otto. |
| | | Maddin Thomas. |
| | | Lundberg Ernest. |
| | | Boulanger Joseph. |
| | | " Arthur. |
| | | Goncas Ernest. |
| | | Lefeve Frederick. |
| 73 | 265 | Corrigan Rose J. boardinghouse. |
| | | " Katherine, wid. Bernard. |
| | | " Timothy. |
| | | " Catharine E. |
| | | Egan Keron. |
| | | Sullivan Patrick J. |
| | | Grogan Thomas. |
| | | Thomas William. |
| | | Probst Frederick F. |
| | | Kane Peter. |
| | | Fahy Mary, wid. Edward. |
| | | " John F. |
| | | " Timothy B. |
| | | " Thomas J. |

| | | |
|---|---|---|
| 73 | 265 | Coulter Peter. |
| | | McCafferty Janette Mrs. |
| | 267 | Citizens Grocery and Provision Co. |
| 75 | 269 | Hackett Thomas J. saloon. |
| | 271 | McNeill Marion, wid. William. |
| | | Emerson Samuel. |
| | | Neilson Neils. |
| | | Hansen Peter. |
| | | " Henry A. |
| | | Banks William. |
| | | McDermid Thomas. |
| 77 | 275 | Moore & Holbrook, market. |
| | 277 | Wheeler Henry E. |
| | | " George L. |
| | | Hayden Ellen. |
| | | Brace E. Mrs. dressmaker. |
| | | Fagerhorn Carl. |
| | | Lucas Mary. |
| | | Cahill William F. |
| | | Ellis John. |
| | | Taylor James A. |
| | | Dolquist Gotfried C. |
| | | McKeilson Evert. |
| | | Gordon James M. |
| | | Bain William. |
| | | Forbes Alexander. |
| | | Greenland George W. |
| | | Broomhall Mary Ann. |
| | | Deluhery John M. |
| | | Anderson Christina, wid. Andrew. |
| | | Evans Blanche M. wid. Evan E. |
| | | Crawford Flora, wid. Frank. |
| | | Michaelson Edward. |
| 79 | 279 | Hirth Joseph, saloon. |
| 81 | 281 | Goldstein Max, barber shop. |
| | 283 | Watson James. |
| | | Williams Frank J. |
| | | Flynn Roger. |
| | | Patterson Robert. |
| | | Kennedy Robert. |
| | | Brown Jane, wid. John. |
| | | " Alexander. |
| 83 | 285 | Schuman's bakery. |
| 85 | 287 | Markowitz Heyman, shoemaker. |
| | 293 | Booth James Webb, physician. |
| | | " James W. Jr. |
| | | Rudge William H. |
| 87 | 295 | South Charles F. |
| | 307 | South Congregational Church. |
| | | *Buckingham Street, W.* |
| 91 | 341 | Tillinghast Alvah H. groceries. |
| | 343 | Miner John F. boardhouse. |
| | | Bryan John E. |
| | | Slocum Charles. |
| 93 | 345 | Fischer Fannie, wid Gustav, boardingh |
| | | " Gustav. |
| | | Winship Henry C. |
| | | Ludwig Arthur |
| | | Miller John L. |
| | | Orkonsky Edward. |
| | | Jenney Harry L. |
| | 347 | Griswold John H. drygoods. |
| | 349 | Straus Herman. |
| | | Porteous Robert. |
| 95 | 351 | Hong Fred W. laundry. |

| | | |
|---|---|---|
| 95 | 353 | Yores Paul, fruit. |
| | 355 | Green Joseph, cigars. |
| 97 | 357 | Franzen F. W. |
| | | Dunn Thomas J. |
| | | Miner John. |
| | 359 | Franzen Francis William, saloon. |
| 99 | 361 | Vogel Solomon, German delicacies. |
| | 363 | Warren Jessie C. Mrs. dressmaker. |
| | | Bartlett Samuel P. |
| | | Farrell Joseph E. |
| | | Hunt John. |
| | | " Owen. |
| | | Foster Arthur. |
| | | Samblin William. |
| | | Brandt E. |
| 101 | 365 | Reid William D. |
| | | MacGowan James P. |
| | | Gibbons John. |
| | | Mink Moses. |
| | | " Rose. |
| | | " Victor. |
| | 367 | Japan Product Co. |
| | 371 | Miller James Plinery. |
| | | Hertel Albert G. veterinary. |
| 103 | 373 | Montgomery Hugh G. market. |
| | 375 | Van Houten Arthur A. |
| | | Bogue Harriet M. Mrs. dressmaker. |
| | | Abbey Edward M. |
| | | Harris William J. |
| | | Storrs Ella E. Mrs. |
| | | Goodwin Alice H. |
| | | Tinkham Emily A. |
| | | Sweet S. A. Mrs. |
| 105 | 377 | Lyons Bridget, wid. Edmund. |
| | | Stein Henry. |
| | | Bloomingdale James. |
| | | Brick Jeremiah. |
| | | Lyons Mary J. |
| 105½ | 379 | Dean's Steam Laundry. |
| 107 | 385 | Sickles Charles H. bakery. |
| 109 | 387 | Morgan & Pratt, undertakers. |
| | | McDougall Alexander. |
| 111 | 389 | Hotel Capitol, D. W. C. Pond. |
| | | Bancroft M. Mrs. |
| | | Clark H. W. |
| | | Connors Thomas. |
| | | Doolittle Marie P. |
| | | Farris John. |
| | | Frederick H. O. Mrs. |
| | | Judson Curtis. |
| | | Knowlton James E. |
| | | Madden W. J. |
| | | Rourke John. |
| | | Sisson Charles E. |
| | | Simonds John B. |
| | | Steele Charles A. |
| 111½ | 389½ | Trant Thomas, plumber. |
| 113 | 391 | O'Flaherty Maurice, drugstore. |
| | | Main Louis, ice. |
| | | *Capitol Avenue, W.* |
| 115 | 407 | Hubbard Charles L. drugstore. |
| 115a | 409 | Dow Peter, shoemaker. |
| 115b | 413 | Blazier J. F. & Co. |
| 115c | 415 | Marenhaltz Otto, barbershop. |
| 117 | 419 | Burke John E. gent's furnishings. |

| | | |
|---|---|---|
| 119 | 423 | Fleming Thomas G. groceries. |
| 119½ | 425 | Marchant George, harness. |
| | | Murray Charles, plumber. |
| 121 | 427 | The Linden Building. |
| | | Ackley Elton E. rm. 2. |
| | | Emmersly Henry P. rm. 3. |
| | | Farwell Fannie C. rm. 4. |
| | | Dennison Jessie K. nurse, rm. 5. |
| | | Nuttell Mattie F. nurse, rm. 5. |
| | | Martin W. J. rm. 6. |
| | | Hanson C. B. wid. Daniel D. rm. 8. |
| | | Grogan Anna M. wid. Frank G. rm. 9. |
| | | Doyle Edward R. rm. 9. |
| | | Way Charles L. rm. 10. |
| | | Bonar Samuel, rm. 11. |
| | | North Albert W. rm. 12. |
| | | Clapp John B. rm. 13. |
| | | Whiting Elsie B. wid. R.E.K. rm. 15. |
| | | Whiting William H. C. rm. 15. |
| | | Brown George M. rm. 16. |
| | | Smith Robert T. rm. 18. |
| | | Bartholomew Dana W. rm. 20. |
| | | Burroughs William S. rm. 21. |
| | | Hotchkiss May B. wid. Levi H. rm. 22. |
| | | Hotchkiss Philip Lee, rm. 22. |
| | | Marshall Marg't, wid. Thos. rm. 22. |
| | | John M. C. nurse, rm. 23. |
| | | Knapp Jesse, nurse, rm. 23. |
| | | Thacher John H. rm. 24. |
| | | Clark Harriet A. rm. 25. |
| | | " Mary E. wid. Henry H. rm. 25. |
| | | Beebe Robert L. rm. 27. |
| | | Watson Herbert W. rm. 28. |
| | | Dickinson G. L. rm. 29. |
| | | Leinhard H. A. rm. 32. |
| | | Holt Henry T. rm. 33. |
| | | Ayres William A. rm. 34. |
| | | Stibbs George R. rm. 35. |
| | | Shipman Agnes, rm. 36. |
| | | Sugden Frank W. rm. 36. |
| | | Rines James A. rm. 38. |
| | | Faucon James P. Rev. rm. 40. |
| | | Thayer George B. rm. 45. |
| | | Geer E. J. E. wid. Elihu, rm. 47. |
| | | Simonds William E. attorney, rm. 48. |
| | | Donovan John P. rm. 51. |
| | | Pitkin N. T. rm. 52. |
| | | Pease Lena K. wid. Augusta L. rm. 53. |
| | | Maxim Hiram P. rm. 54. |
| | | Cheney Ward, rm. 55. |
| | | Sheldon Lewis P. rm. 55. |
| | | Swords Joseph F. coal, rm. 61. |
| | | Whittelsey Edgar G. rm. 62. |
| | | Henney Charles M. rm. 63. |
| | | Saunders Herbert H. rm. 64. |
| | | " P. H. B. Mrs. rm. 64. |
| | | Vail M. G. wid. Thomas. J. rm. 65. |
| | | " Thomas G. rm. 65. |
| | | **TRYON E. S.** builder, rm. 71. |
| | | Center Addison P. rm. 71. |
| | | Hubbell Emeline, wid. LeP. rm. 72½. |
| | | Smith Cath. M. wid. Elisha T. rm. 72½. |
| | | Newton Philo W. rm. 73. |
| | | Freeborne James L. rm. 74. |
| | | Lawson Robert C. rm. 75. |

| | | |
|---|---|---|
| 121 | 427 | Lyman Richard P. rm. 81. |
| | | Billings Harry E. rm. 82. |
| | | Dodd Charles, rm. 83. |
| | | Ryder Elisha, rm. 84. |
| | | " George H. rm. 84. |
| | | Allen W. G. rm. 85. |
| | | Lewis George S. rm. 86. |
| | | Brainard Sarah W. |
| | | Harrington H. E. |
| 121½ | 431 | Beam Alfred C. bicycle repairs. |
| 123 | 433 | Duffy James F. plumber. |
| 125 | 437 | Premier Mfg. Co. carriages. |
| | | *Linden Place, W.* |
| | 455 | South Baptist Church. |
| | | *Elm Street, W.* |
| 127 | 485 | Noll Brothers, shoes. |
| | 487 | Wing Yee, laundry. |
| 129 | 489 | Lewis Mary, Mrs. dressmaker. |
| | | Perkins Alice. |
| | | White Nettie, Mrs. |
| | | Campbell Joseph. |
| | | Hector Ellen, wid. Harmon. |
| | | Peck Stephen B. |
| | | Jackson James. |
| 131 | 491 | Debato Carmine, fruit. |
| 133 | 493 | **FLYNN JOHN,** market. |
| 139 | 515 | Tracy D. Wallace, drug store. |
| 141 | 517 | Kane Thomas F. physician. |
| | | Carlon Philip P. physician. |
| | | Conway Mary A. dressmaker. |
| | | Nichols Henry F. |
| | | Glynn Ellen. |
| | | Sewell Albert C. |
| 143 | 519 | Campagna John, fruit. |
| 145 | 521 | Lawrence James, shoes. |
| 147 | 523 | Muller Ernest, barber shop. |
| | | Smith Alex, harness shop. |
| | | Clark Joseph D. |
| | | Harrigan Mary, wid. Jeremiah. |
| | | Sawan Thomas J. |
| | | Scanlan Maurice M. |
| | | Scanlan Alice, wid. Dayton. |
| | | Sarvan Frank H. |
| 149 | 525 | Curtin John D. saloon. |
| | | *Wells Street, W.* |
| 151 | 539 | Lacy Thomas, saloon. |
| 153 | 543 | Brucker Charles F. |
| 161 | 553 | Reinert Emil G. physician. |
| 155 | 545 | Ahern John B. |
| | | Beccu William. |
| | | Blythe Eliza, Mrs. |
| | | Broomhall Louise, Mrs. |
| | | " William. |
| | | Callahan Patrick M. |
| | | Carson Alice, wid. Anderson. |
| | | " Joseph F. |
| | | " William G. |
| | | Coleman John J. real estate. |
| | | Coles Clifford M. |
| | | Curtin John D. |
| | | Dewey George M. |
| | | " Howard R. E. |
| | | Estes Martha S. wid. Lucius J. |
| | | Foisey Joseph A. |
| | | Fowler Emerson B. |

| | | |
|---|---|---|
| 155 | 545 | Fowler Lucy M. wid. Francis. |
| | | Gagnon Felix. |
| | | Healey Annie, wid. Thomas. |
| | | " Thomas. |
| | | Kurtcher Margaret, Mrs. |
| | | Larkin Mary, wid. D. M. |
| | | Moyer William N. shirt mfgr. |
| | | Santhouse Susan, wid. Robert. |
| | | Sheperdson Daniel F. |
| | | Skinner Sarah E. wid. John T. |
| | | Stagg Jennie M. Mrs. |
| | | Thibault Lucy, wid. Samuel. |
| | | Walsh Daniel. |
| 157 | 547 | Griswold Hosmer, groceries. |
| 159 | 551 | Mittau Adolph, watchmaker. |
| | | Dix & Co. gent's furnishings. |
| | | Lamb Lorenzo, real estate. |
| 165 | 557 | Kenney & Dillon, undertakers. |
| | | Buckley & Reardon. |
| 175 | 571 | Kingsley & Smith, butter and eggs. |
| | 573 | Edwards Herbert C. |
| | | Keller Edward F. |
| | | " Dennis F. |
| | | Beecher Edward. |
| | | Jones James H. |
| | | Stewart John. |
| | | Torry Harlan W. |
| | | " Harry W. |
| | | Laughman John. |
| 177 | 575 | Centennial American Tea Co. |
| 179 | 579 | Keller Brothers. |
| 179½ | 581 | Cummings Cyrus D. |
| | | Perkins Nelson S. |
| | | Davis Daniel. |
| | | Oliver William. |
| | | Barrett Robert. |
| | | Cummings Cyrus D. Mrs. |
| 181 | 583 | Long John C. café-saloon. |
| | 585 | Meyer Henry, furniture. |
| | 587 | Shea William. |
| | 589 | Standard Boot and Shoe Co. |
| 185 | 591 | Rosenthal Chas. tobacco and cigars. |
| 187 | 598 | Lux Peter & Son, furniture. |
| | 587 | Staer Kate, wid. Christopher. |
| 187½ | 597 | **ENTRESS ALBERT,** sculptor. |
| | | Sinnott P. carpenter. |
| | | Malone John J. cigar shop. |
| 189 | 599 | **BULL N. B. & SON,** stoves and tinware. |
| 195 | 605 | Heublein Edmund, saloon. |
| 197 | 607 | Werder Fritz, confectionery. |
| 199 | 609 | **JONES GEORGE E.** Turkish baths. |
| | | Jones Harry. |
| | | McNally John. |
| | | Audolf Carl. |
| | | Gaffey John F. |
| | | Trobeck Enoch O. |
| | | McElhinney John M. |
| 205 | 613 | **FENN LINUS T.** furniture. |
| | | *Mulberry Street, W.* |
| 207 | 627 | Gloscio & Romont, bootblacks. |
| | 629 | Kennelly & Co. drug store. |
| 209 | 633 | Robbins Brothers, furniture. |

| | | |
|---|---|---|
| 211 | 635 | Axtelle John F. physician. |
| | | Moore Emma N. dressmaker. |
| | | " John C. |
| | | Edgerton Charles H. |
| 211½ | 637 | Lawler John J. saloon. |
| 213 | 637½ | Dalessio Tony, poolroom. |
| | 639 | Bell Charles H. drugstore. |
| 215 | 643 | Churchill Geo. G. second-hand store. |
| 215½ | 645 | Hartford Bowling Alleys. |
| 217 | 647 | McAuley George A. barber shop. |
| | 651 | City Hotel. |
| | | Brennan James. |
| | | Herth Frank. |
| | | Lewis Henry B. |
| | | Waterman Joseph R. |
| | 653 | Public Market. |

*Gold Street, W.*

| | | |
|---|---|---|
| 219 | 657 | Sheehan Edward J. saloon. |
| 221 | 659 | Branch Maria, wid. David. |
| | | " George D. |
| | | Wood Sarah L. |
| 223 | 675 | Center Church. |
| 235 | 687 to 695 | **ECKHART J. H. & CO.** art store. |
| 237½ | 697 | Tilton Abner F. merchant tailor. |
| | | Quinn P. H., American Tea Co. |
| 239 | 701 | **BESSE P. & J.** caterers. |
| 241 | 703 | West End Land Co. real estate. |
| | | Fletcher & Rosenthal, barber shop. |
| | | Roeske & Fernald, printers, rm. 3. |
| | | Waldron William F. physician, rm. 6. |
| | | Gerety & Sullivan, builders, rm. 7. |
| | | Albu Max, physician, rm. 8. |
| | | Bailey William, Jr. rm. 9. |
| | | Pease James R. rm. 10. |
| | | Kent Frank D. |
| | | Zimmerman Charles H. |
| | | Crowley William L. rm. 11. |
| | | Caldwell Albert M. rm. 12. |
| | | Hills Corinthea E. wid. Myron, rm. 12. |
| | | Yates Wells, rm. 13. |
| | | Jones John, rm. 13. |
| | | " Edwin A. rm. 14. |
| | | Watkinson David, rm. 14. |
| 243 | 705 | Loeffler George J. drug store. |
| 245 | 709 | **DILLINGHAM E. B.** real estate, rm. 1. |
| | | Munger Everett P. rm. 4. |
| | | Parks Harrison W. |
| | | Thorman James W. rm. 5. |
| | | Morgan M. E. Mrs. rm. 6. |
| 247 | 711 | Russell Charles H. groceries. |
| 249 | 715 | Grand Union Tea Co. |
| 251 | 719 | Foster & Morrill. |
| 253 | 721 | Waverly Building. |
| | | Charter Oak Park Office, rm. 1. |
| | | Webster & Baker, insurance, rm. 1. |
| | | Pomeroy W. H. dentist, room 2. |
| | | Griswold F. A. insurance, rm. 3. |
| | | Knox Robert C. insurance, rm. 3. |
| | | Seelye Ezra N. insurance, rm. 3. |
| | | Pierson Fred'k A. real estate, rm. 3. |
| | | Morris Charles E. physician, rm. 5. |
| | | **GREENE JACOB H.** real estate and insurance, rm. 8. |

| | | |
|---|---|---|
| 253 | 721 | Haub & Son, merchant tailors, rm. 7. |
| | | Emory & Co. merc. agency rm. 9. |
| | | Hamlin John, attorney, rm. 9. |
| | | Peiler Ernst, music teacher, rm. 10. |
| | | Johnston Edwin P. broker, rm. 12. |
| | | Bachimont Stephane, rm. 14. |
| | | Ware M. F. Mrs. nurse, rm. 14. |
| | | Fagan P. H. rm. 15. |
| | | King Mary, wid. Harry, dressm. rm. 16. |
| | | Greene Jacob H. broker, rm. 17. |
| | | Saunders, Kate C. Mrs. millinery. |
| | | Wood, Harmon & Co. rm. 19. |
| | | Benedict C. M. H. electro therapeutics, rm. 20. |
| | | " Everett R. rm. 20. |
| | | " Elmer C. rm. 20. |
| | | Keenan D. F. contractor, rm. 21. |
| | | Pratt Elmore L. rm. 23. |
| | | **HOFFMAN JOHN R.** civil engineer, rm. 24. |
| | | Flynn Martin, contractor, rm. 24. |
| | | Morgan Ely, physician, rm. 28. |
| | | Hooker Edward B. physician. rm. 29. |
| | | **HARTFORD DREDGING CO.** contractors, rm. 30. |
| | | Heubler Alfred, rm. 31. |
| | | Dubes Mary, dressmaker, rm. 32. |
| | | Cobey John W. rm. 33. |
| | | Downer William V. rm. 33. |
| | | Brigham Charles S. rm. 34. |
| | | Ramsey Martha L. rm. 35. |
| | | Miskill Minnie, dressm. rms. 38, 40. |
| | | Thomson James M. rm. 39. |
| | | McNerny Marg't E. dressm. rm. 41. |
| | | " Anna L. rm. 41. |
| | | Metropolitan Life Ins. Co. rm. 42. |
| | | Cowles Louise M. rm. 45. |
| | | Miner Louise M. wid. Seth, rm. 45. |
| | | Boulanger Francois, rm. 46. |
| | | Kennedy Julia A. Mrs. dressm. rm. 50. |
| | | Brown George, rm. 51. |
| | | Halligan Jennie, rm. 52. |
| | | Cook C' P. H. Co. rm. 53. |
| | | Dowling Jennie J. millinery, rm. 54. |
| | | Hanqt'l Rose L. dressmaker, rm. 55. |
| | | Loomis Carrie M. Mrs. dressm. rm. 56. |
| | | Powers Mary J. hairdressing, rm. 57. |
| | | Forsythe Jane, rm. 58. |
| | | Dyes Pauline, rm. 61. |
| | | " Susanna, rm. 61. |
| | | Boardman James W. rm. 62. |
| | | " Fred B. rm. 62. |
| | | Main Edward T. rm. 62. |
| | | Green Frederick M. rm. 65. |
| | | " Carolyn N. music teacher, rm. 65. |
| | | Tuttle Constant L. rm. 67. |
| | | Watkinson J. Russell, rm. 69. |
| | | Alling Alma L. Mrs. dressmaker, rm. 71. |
| | | Coudry Anna, wid. J. W. |
| | | Frye Margaret A. Mrs. |
| 255 | 725 | Mellen & Hewes Co. crockery. |
| 259 | 729 | **SISSON T. & CO.** wholesale druggists. |
| 265 | 739 | Robbins Edward D. attorney. rm. 1. |

265 739 Broughel Jr. Andrew J. att'y, rm. 1
Kellogg George A. attorney, rm. 1.
Sumner George G. attorney, rm. 1.
Loomis Dwight, attorney, rm. 1.
Hamersley William, attorney, rm. 1.
McKeon Mary L. dressm. rm. 8.
Stebbins Charles W. rm. 8.
Kellogg E. P. photographer, rm. 11.
Tracher Michael L. massage.
267 741 Krug & Powers, cigars and tobacco.
271 747 Stuart-Charles T. photographer.
273 751 Boston Branch, W. W. Walker.
275 753 Goodwin N. J. dentist, rm. 1.
Barrett Charles E. dentist, rm. 1.
Miller Geo. M. dancing acad. rm. 7.
Chase A. Elenora, photog. rm. 5.
277 755 Goodwin, C. L. & G. R. shoes.
279 757 Doty Sam'l C. real est. and inv. rm. 1.
Chesebro James L. architect, rm. 1.
New Eng. Loan and Trust Co. rm. 1.
Middlesex Banking Co. rm. 1.
Whitney Harry.
Sinnott Robert.
Richardson Frank.
Hall Ira D.
Bill Rollin H.
Schneider Nicholas.
Pierce Mary F. laundry.
281 759 **MOORE GEO. W. & CO.**
investment securities.
Boston Dental Association.
Harney William J. photographer.
Goldstein Benj. J. dancing.
283 761 **CONN. RIVER BANK-ING CO.**
285 785 **CONN. TRUST & SAFE DEPOSIT CO.** securities.
287 783 **CONN. MUTUAL LIFE INSURANCE CO.**
**CITY BANK OF HART-FORD.**
National Home for Disabled Volunteer Soldiers.
Goodwin J. J. & F. rm. 7.
Richards Alfred T. insurance.
Jarman James H. insurance.
785 **COLLINS CO.** office.
789 Grosch Edward, barber shop.
295 791 **DIME SAVINGS BANK.**
297 793 **HARTFORD COUNTY MUT. FIRE INS. CO.**
Welles J. N. dentist.
Case Uriah, attorney.
Curtis John F. real estate.
McCarthy John J. architect.
O'Flaherty Hugh, attorney.
Mildeberger Henry D. attorney.
Kennedy Henry, real estate.
299 795 **STATE BANK.**
301 801 **HATCH & NORTH COAL CO.**
Smith & McDonough, stationers.
Brooks Emma Elmore, stenographer.
303 803 **PHOENIX NATIONAL BANK.**

303 803 **AMERICAN NATION-AL BANK.**
**RICHARDS FRANCIS H.**
patent solicitor
Brokers Board.
Howe & Collins.
Skinner Henry H. broker.
305 805 **ADAMS EXPRESS CO.**
McClunie George G. florist.
309 811 Starr Pierre S. physician.
Eberle Frederick, attorney.
" Frederck G. attorney.
Prudential Insurance Co.
Rancor Charles R.
Perkins Albert G.
Hempstead Lorenzo.
Laws Martha L. wid. Edward E.
311 815 **MECHANICS SAVINGS BANK.**
Ward W. Jacobs & Co., R.R. tickets.
313 817 Werder Fritz, confectionery.
*Asylum Street, W.*
325 835 Sawyer George O. store.
327 841 Becher Frank, saloon.
329 843 **BONNER, PRESTON & CO.** decorators.
331 845 Geary T. J. & Co. cloaks.
333 847 McConville Wm. J. city attorney, rm. 2.
Quinn James J. attorney, rm. 2.
Grant Ralph M. attorney, rm. 2.
**BILL & TUTTLE,** attorneys. rm. 4.
Dickenson Robert C. attorney, rm. 4.
Ross Herbert A. attorney, rm. 4.
Prentice Charles H. real estate, rm. 6.
Hills J. Coolidge, rm. 6.
**WILLIAMS FRANK B.** attorney, rm. 8.
Fielding Wm. C. deputy sheriff, rm. 8.
Forrest George C. agent, rm. 8.
**STAPLES GEO. W.** general agent N. Y. Life Ins. Co. rm. 10.
Graham James R. constable, rm. 10.
Foote John M. Jr. rm. 10.
Rist Owen D. rm. 1.
**BOND ALBERT H.** manager Mass. Mutual Life Insurance Co. of Springfield, rm. 3.
**ROGERS F. WILLSON,** insurance, rm. 3.
Welles Roger, attorney, rm. 5.
**McMANUS THOMAS,** attorney, rm. 5.
Tuller George W. real estate, rm. 5.
**NEW ENGLAND TYPE-WRITER EXCH.** rm. 7.
Williams Rosamond M. rm. 7.
**MILLS HIRAM R.** attorney, rm. 9.
Smith Herbert Knox, attorney, rm. 9.
Stoeckel Robbins B. attorney, rm. 9.
Lyman Theodore, attorney, rm. 9.
Schirmaier Frederick, rm. 13.
Martin David T. rm. 15.
Callery William C. rm. 17.

| | | |
|---|---|---|
| 333 | 847 | Neal Charles W. rm. 17. |
| | | Warner Nellie L. dressm. rm. 19. |
| | | **BENNETT & BROTT,** attorneys, rm. 23. |
| | | Taintor Henry E. attorney, rm. 23. |
| | | Roberts Walter W. rm. 24. |
| | | Hampshire Parker, engraver, rm. 24. |
| | | Austin Leverett N. attorney, rm. 23. |
| | | Day Edward M. attorney, rm. 22. |
| | | Bligh Edward, rm. 26. |
| | | Booth A. F. rm. 27. |
| | | Dickinson H. Wallace, artist, rm. 29. |
| | | Doerr Adolph, tailor, rm. 35. |
| | | Jackson Edward, architect, rm. 37. |
| 335 | 851 | **CASE C. H. & CO.** jewelers. |
| 337 | 853 | **RAPELYE CHARLES A.** drug store. |
| 341 | 857 | Fowler & Miller Co. printers. |
| 343 | 859 | **FRANCIS & CO.** hardware. |
| 345 | 863 | **PARKER FRANCIS H.** attorney, rm. 3. |
| | | Steele & Steele, attorneys, rm. 3. |
| | | Stoughton John A. attorney, rm. 2. |
| | | Sill George G. attorney, rm. 1. |
| | | Vail Thomas G. attorney, rm. 1. |
| | | **WARD WM.** real estate, rm. 5. |
| | | Hartford Street Sprinkling and Supply Co. rm. 5. |
| | | Griffin Chat A. shirt mfgr. rm. 6. |
| | | **PERKINS JAMES A. & CO.** plate printers, rm. 8. |
| | | Petit Joseph, tailor, rm. 11. |
| | | Smith George M. |
| | | Hurd Charles H. |
| 347 | 865 | Chapin Lyman A. newsdealer. |
| | | Smith Charles F. watchmaker. |
| | | Harvey & Lewis, opticians. |
| 349 | 867 | Soby Charles, cigars. |
| 351 | 869 | Moran John F. men's furnishings. |
| | 871 | Weildon Thomas C. hair store. |
| | | Clark Alfred C. engraver. |
| | | Staudinger August D. |
| 355 | 875 | Jacobs, Avery & Northam Co. |
| 357 | 877 | Calhoun David S. attorney, rm. 1. |
| | | Calhoun J. Gilbert, attorney, rm. 1. |
| | | Garvan Edward J. attorney, rm. 1. |
| | | Goslee Henry S. attorney, rm. 3. |
| | | Ellsworth Ernest B. attorney, rm. 3. |
| | | Parsons Francis, attorney, rm. 3. |
| | | Markham Daniel A. attorney, rm. 1. |
| | | Coogan John W. attorney, rm. 2. |
| | | " James T. 2d. attorney, rm. 2. |
| | | Newberry Leslie W. attorney, rm. 6. |
| | | Jackson Sarah J. wid. Silas, rm. 7. |
| | | Welton Jennie E. rm. 9. |
| | | Johnston Margaret, rm. 10. |
| | | Gemmill Agnes, rm. 10. |
| | | Jordan Kittie L. rm. 11. |
| | | " Mary A. rm. 11. |
| | | " Lizzie A. rm. 11. |
| | | Andrews Margaret, wid. Hugh, rm.12. |
| | | Beach Sarah, rm. 14. |
| | | Chidsey Almira, rm. 15. |
| | | Sperry S. M. Mrs. rm. 16. |
| 361 | 881 | Hempstead Adelaide R. hairstore. |

| | | |
|---|---|---|
| 361 | 881 | Samuels Charles, tailor. |
| 365 | 885 | Hills Charles S. & Co. store. |
| | | *Pratt Street, W.* |
| 369 | 901 | Simmons W. G. & Co. shoes. |
| 371 | 903 | Columbia Building. |
| | | Doebler John F. dentist, rm. 1. |
| | | Maginn William F. tailor, rm. 2. |
| | | O'Keefe Michael, advertisement writer, rm. 2. |
| | | Pillion Henry J. dentist, rm. 3. |
| | | **GREENSTEIN R. A.** ladies' tailoring, rm. 4. |
| | | Mill Misses, hairdressers, rm. 9. |
| | | Taylor Thomas B. rm. 8. |
| | | " Hurlburt R. rm. 8. |
| | | " George B. rm. 8. |
| | | Holmes Electric Protective Agency. |
| | | Olin Frederick, rm. 13. |
| | | Bennett William, rm. 13. |
| | | Brennan Lizzie M. dressm. rm. 15. |
| | | Ferrell Frances, millinery, rm. 18. |
| | | Brewer Fred. R. photog'r, rm. 19. |
| | | Hedican Misses, dressmakers, rm. 20. |
| 373 | 907 | **BRAINERD H. B.** wall paper, etc. |
| 375 | 909 | Russell Charles H. groceries. |
| 377 | 911 | Wright & Dunham, dentist, rm. 1. |
| | | **LINCOLN FREDERICK M.** real estate, rm. 2. |
| | | Hartford Calcium Light Co. rm. 2. |
| | | Blair & Coxeter, jewelers, rm. 4. |
| | | Brooks A. E. rm. 5. |
| | | Chamberlin Edgar, rm. 7. |
| | | Risley Edward F. rm. 8. |
| | | Goodman Lena Mrs. |
| 379 | 913 | Aishberg Edwin, shoes. |
| 385 | 921 | Wise, Smith & Co. store. |
| 391 | 929 | Charleton E. P. & Co. store. |
| 393 | 931 | Heublein G. F. & Bros. saloon. |
| 395 | 933 | Hartford Opera House. |
| | | Manns Geo. W. barbershop, rm. 1. |
| | | People's Credit Clothing Co. rm. 2. |
| | | Roberts W. Henry, rm. 5. |
| | | Lathrop A. E. Mrs. |
| | | Jennings H. H. Jr. rm. 15. |
| | | Converse Isaac A. rm. 16. |
| | | Charleton J. D. rm. 29. |
| | | Byer Lavina L. rm. 19. |
| | | Grou George W. rm. 24. |
| | | Wilson Cora, rm. 25. |
| | | Maloney John F. rm. 21. |
| | | Clark William M. rm. 43. |
| | | Case A. David, rms. 39 and 40. |
| | | Pratt C. W. cloaks. |
| 397 | 937 | **SCHROEDER,** confectionery. |
| 403 | 941 | **ASSOCIATE DENTISTS,** rm. 3. |
| 405 | 943 | |
| | | Schroeder Charles, rm. 6. |
| | | Crane Charles L. rm. 19. |
| | | Damon Harriet, wid. Urias, rm. 20. |
| | | Buck Mary J. Mrs. rm. 20. |
| | | Dillon Lewis T. rm. 14. |
| | | Luther Mrs. rm. 15. |
| | | Strong Idella L. Mrs. |
| | | Adkins John B. rm. 17. |

| | | |
|---|---|---|
| 405 | 943 | Doyle Nora E. rm.-22. |
| | | Kenyon M. E. wid. Albert, rm. 24. |
| | | Davis William S. rm. 25. |
| | | Durand Fannie B. rm. 26. |
| | | Rogers Ellen M. wid. Henry C. rm. 27. |
| | | Avery Frank L. rm. 29. |
| | | Pfund Katharine, wid. T. G. rm. 32. |
| | | " Annie K. rm. 32. |
| | | Brown Charlotte A. wid. W. O. rm. 34. |
| | | " Clara A. rm. 34. |
| | | Eberle Jacob, rm. 35. |
| | | Calhoun Mrs. rm. 36. |
| | | Wallace Etta Mrs. rm. 38. |
| | | Shaw Thomas A. rm. 39. |
| | | Fish Arthur W. janitor. |
| | | Strong Mrs. rm. 15. |
| 407 | 945 | Larned & Hatch, shoes. |
| | 955 | Christ Church. |

*Church Street, W.*

| | | |
|---|---|---|
| 423 | 973 | Williams John K. drugstore. |
| 425 | 975 | Bennett & Rathget, restaurant. |
| 427 | 979 | Great Atlantic & Pacific Tea Co. |
| 439 | 981 | Mallery J. Hammond, dentist. |
| | | Colonial, Ayer George S. |
| | | Hammer Joseph C. |
| | | Broderick James N. |
| | | Reed L. M. Mrs. nurse. |
| | | Kelly Matthew. |
| | | " Michael. |
| | | Miller Emma M. |
| | | Pratt A. D. |
| | | Roy H. V. Mrs. |
| | | Saunders O. E. |
| | | Mugler Harry. |
| | | Parsons H. E. Mrs. |
| | | Belcher Edith. |
| | | Shannon E. V. |
| | | Martin William. |
| | | Severn Frank W. |
| | | Rourke T. E. |
| | | Alvord Ida J. |
| | | Burr Sidney E. |
| | | Williams Elizabeth, nurse. |
| | | Chase A. L. |
| 433 | 983 | Case H. J. & Co. groceries. |
| 435 | 985 | Dowling Thomas F. |
| | | Fairchild Daniel. |
| | | Mahon William J. physician. |
| | | Mullaly Daniel. |
| | | Kennedy Michael. |
| | | Munsill Edward. |
| | | Kennedy Daniel. |
| | | Fitzgerald Patrick. |
| | | Lynch Patrick. |
| | | " Dennis. |
| | | Schroeder Christian. |
| | | Knudsen Louis. |
| | | " Charles. |
| | | Nison Hans W. |
| | | Maher James. |
| | | Missal Abraham. |
| | | Bradley George F. |
| 437 | 987 | Sherlock Mattie, dressmaker. |
| | | Clarkin Michael. |
| | | Ehlers Hans. |

| | | |
|---|---|---|
| 437 | 987 | Winter Neils. |
| | | Chapman George A. |
| | | Sturtzel Mary C. Mrs. |
| 439 | 989 | Smith P. B. & Co. saloon. |
| | 995 | Clark & Phelps, livery. |
| | | Lyman Richard P. veterinary surg. |
| | | Webster William S. harnessmaker. |
| 443 | 997 | Berry & Cosgrove, saloon. |
| 445 | 999 | Arlington Hotel, Sidney H. Allen. |
| | | Blinn Hattie. |
| | | Carr O. S. |
| | | Dwesteg August. |
| | | Gray Fred. H. |
| | | Flynn James L. |
| | | Maguire Lettie. |
| | | Marsh Joseph. |
| | | Merritt Mable. |
| | | Penn Julian M. |
| | | Peardon A. |
| | | Penders Bernard. |
| | | Segur F. P. |
| | | Stone Claud W. |
| | | Warburton George B. |
| | | White Daniel. |
| | | Whalan John. |
| | | Wheeler J. E. |
| | | Yost John. |
| 449 | 1005 | Schmeltz & Hammer, shoes. |
| 451 | 1007 | Atro James D. fruit. |
| 453 | 1013 | Willes Jabez H. art store. |
| 455 | 1015 | Weeks George H. cigars. |
| | 1031 | Goodell George M. shoes. |
| 469 | 1037 | Leschke & Pletcher, cigars. |
| 471 | 1039 | Johnson Frank M. photographer. |
| | | Elwood Thomas F. |
| | | Tudor Charles C. |
| | | Herrick M. F. Mrs. |
| | | Fisk Henry A. |
| | | Grennan Lawrence J. |
| 473 | 1043 | Bonnee Joseph, fruit. |
| 475 | 1045 | Needham M. C. Mrs. |
| | | " John A. |
| | | " George A. |
| | | Conners James N. |
| | | Cullen Andrew. |
| | | Danehy John. |
| | | " Cornelius. |
| | | Denehy John, |
| | | Drew E. |
| | | Ford John P. |
| | | Harrison Samuel S. |
| | | John Napoleon. |
| | | Kashman Morris. |
| | | Keefe Michael. |
| | | Maloy John. |
| | | Montag Henry. |
| | | Shea Dennis J. |
| | | Stetzner Louis. |
| | | Turner William. |
| | | Wadsworth Henrietta Mrs. |
| | | Wall James. |
| | 1047 | Donaghue William & Co. |
| 477 | 1049 | Avery Frank L. restaurant. |
| 479 | 1055 | Lauria Donato, fruit. |
| 483 | 1059 | Sheehan Nellie, wid. William. |

| | | |
|---|---|---|
| 483 | 1059 | Burns Mary, wid. Richard. |
| | | Prass Frederick. |
| | | Talcott W. L. Mrs. |
| | | Courtney Thomas. |
| 485 | 1061 | Hartnett & Bartley, saloon. |
| | 1063 | Pibbles John, livery. |
| | | Lee Thomas J. veterinary. |
| | | Kowalsky Godfrey, blacksmith. |
| | | Elkin Brothers, upholsterers. |
| 487 | 1065 | City Market. |
| 489 | 1067 | Ball Charles G. |
| | | Gilbert |
| | | Bush Philip. |
| | | Eggleston Mary A. |
| | | O'Connell John Mrs. |
| | | Keefe John R. |
| | | Mohr Edward E. |
| | | O'Brien James J. |
| | | Curran James. |
| | | " William. |
| 491 | 1069 | Ball Julius, barbershop. |
| 493 | 1071 | Rooney Peter F. |
| | | " Thomas F. |
| | | Rooney Kate. |
| | | Rosenthal Albert C. |
| | | Leighton Frank. |
| 495 | 1073 | King Horace H. shoes. |
| 499 | 1079 | Smith Bros. furniture. |
| 501 | 1081 | O'Callaghan Julia. |
| | | " Nana. |
| | | Murphy Anna. |
| | | " Mary. |
| | 1091 | Fourth Church. |
| 515 | 1101 | Saunders William O. |
| | | Allen William H. |
| | | Fargo Sarah E. |
| | | " Nellie R. |
| 517 | 1105 | Lawrence William J. shoes. |
| 521 | 1107 | Willis William. |
| | | Atwell John. |
| 523 | 1109 | Manock Edmunt, shoemaker. |
| 525 | 1111 | Barrows & Thalheimer, market. |
| 527 | 1113 | Brewer Julia, wid. Eliab. |
| | | Peirce A. E. Mrs. |
| | | Delner Edwin. |
| | | Howe Nathan C. |
| | | Clark Thomas J. |
| | | Adams Roswell. |
| | | Moran Michael. |
| | | Brooks Almond. |
| | | Heslow Thomas. |
| | | Nelson Lewis. |
| | | Guilfoil William. |
| | | Brown Michael. |
| | | Price James. |
| 529 | 1115 | Wadsworth Alfred J. cigars. |
| 531 | 1117 | Scott Julia, wid. Patrick. |
| | | " Mary M. |
| | | Smith Columbus A. |
| | | " Desire, wid. Maynard S. |
| | | Krahenbuhl Fred. |
| | | Johnson Charles. |
| | | Oliver Seth. |
| 533 | 1119 | Kiely Michael J. saloon. |
| 535 | 1123 | **PEASE C. A. & CO.** flour. |

| | | |
|---|---|---|
| 537 | 1125 | Higgins M. Thomas. |
| | | Haynes Frank T. |
| | | Crocker Jeremiah. |
| 539 | 1127 | Hoxie Royal S. |
| 541 | 1129 | Griswold Charles R. drugstore. |
| | | *Trumbull Street, S.* |
| 547 | 1143 | Hills H. E. & Son. groceries. |
| 549 | 1145 | Griswold Julia E. Mrs. |
| | | Stickney Charles L. |
| | | Brown Owen M. |
| | | Parkman James. |
| 551 | 1147 | Brace Olin N. |
| | | " Jennie. |
| | | Moore William. |
| | | " M. J. Mrs. |
| 553 | 1149 | McGurk Bernard, market. |
| 555 | 1151 | Saraceno Battista, barbershop. |
| 557 | 1153 | Abel Orpha E. wid. S. P. boardingh. |
| | | Dunham Adeline M. wid. Washbun. |
| | | McKinley Mattie. |
| | | Copeland Edward B. |
| | | Layden Thomas. |
| | | Odeman Oscar. |
| | | Pierson Walter. |
| 559 | 1155 | Summerhill John M. |
| | | Boardman Belle C. wid. William. |
| 561 | 1157 | Litchfield County Market. |
| 563 | 1159 | Rollo Louis M. barbershop. |
| 565 | 1163 | Moriarty Thomas. |
| | | " James. |
| | | " Dennis. |
| | | Farley Patrick. |
| | | Danehy James. |
| | | " Mary, boardinghouse. |
| | | Battey William H. |
| 567 | 1165 | Harding & Holbrook, market. |
| 567½ | 1165½ | Zimmerman Samuel, shoemaker. |
| 569 | 1167 | Clancy Timothy M. saloon. |
| 571 | 1171 | Curley John. |
| | | Seeley May. |
| 573 | 1173 | Collins C. Irving. |
| | | " Alice Mrs. boardinghouse. |
| | | Strong Daniel. |
| | | Hayes John W. |
| 575 | 1175 | D'Esopo Domonic, fruit. |
| 577 | 1175½ | Niles D. B. livery. |
| | | Lettievi John. |
| | | Montani Carl. |
| | | Pinto Carl. |
| | | Meehan Patrick J. |
| 579 | 1179 | D'Esopo Pasquale M. |
| | | " Joseph. |
| | | " Rocco A. |
| | | " Salvator |
| | | " Donato. |
| 581 | 1181 | Barry Albert, saloon. |
| 583 | 1183 | Cunningham Maria J. boardingh. |
| | | " Thomas. |
| | | Barry Albert. |
| | | Carroll Charles A. |
| | | Gorman Patrick. |
| | | Gallagher Patrick. |
| | | Bastrom Oscar. |
| | | Mullen James. |
| | | Lee William. |

583 1183 Dwyer Michael.
     Fox Martin.
     Murley Daniel.
     Dunn Thomas.
585 1185 Furrey Ervin L.
     Furrey Leonard M.
587 1187 Sill L. B. stationery.
589 1189 McCorkle George A. drugstore.
591 1191 Case William C.
     Hotchkiss Sophia Mrs.
     Hughes Melvin C.
     Montague Marg't A. wid. Welles W.
593 1193 Knox John M.
     " Charles N.
     " Virginia M. wid. Daniel G.
     Gaines Margaret, wid. Nelson.
     " Dudley A.
595 1195 Frost Henry D. groceries.
599 1197 George Adonio, fruit.
601 1199 Pratt George W.
     " George W. Jr.
     Wilson Patrick.
     " Martin F.
     " Mary L.
603 1201 Loveland Rose.
     Dickenson Ferdinand.
     Filley Margaret, wid. Thomas.
605 1203 **GOODRICH S. & CO.**
     drugstore.
607 1205 Sweet Henry T. physician.
611 1209 Smith Alice W. boardinghouse.
     Dupre John.
     Lips Albert.
     Johnson Henry.
     Sullivan James.
     Waterhouse Harry E.
613 1211 Pattison Joseph, saloon.
615 1213 Deming Charles A. bakery.
     1215 Barnard Carlos A.
     Dannehy William.
     Manion John.
619 1219 Stickney Charles L. saloon.
615 1213 Minzie William P. store.
621 1221 Tillotson Florence.
     Baker Charles.
625 1223 Southergill Margaret Mrs.
     " Francis.
     Tatro George.
     Fleming Patrick.
     Gladding Wilbur M.
627 1225 Sing Frank, laundry.
     Danneh John P.
     Wickham Rosa J. wid. Wm. H.
     " Edwin H.
629 1231 Garrity Michael, livery.
     Ford J. M. builder.
     Kibbe & Penfield, painters.
629 1233 Quincy House, T. E. Foley.
     Normand Alfred L.
     Adams Emma J.
633 1235 Taft Joel C. coal.
     Bassevitch & Glotzer, furs.
635 1237 Cirigliano Joseph.
641 1243 Harris Elizabeth.
     Ellsworth Henry S.

641 1243 Ellsworth Benjamin G.
     Hills Howard E.
     " Alonzo K.
     Blake Albert E.
     Gammerdinger Wm.
637 1239 Gallon Joseph.
     " Charles J.
     Clay Edwin.
     Gamerdinger Christian.
     " William.
     " George H.
     " Charles F.
643 1245 Baldwin Charles A.
     Jorey James A.
     Phelps Arthur.
     Robinson John E.
     Miller Margaret E. Mrs.
645 1255 Meafoy Ellen Mrs. boardinghouse.
     Brainard Eliza S.
     Smith Mary A.
     Phelps John.
     Parshley Sadie.
     Walsh Elizabeth, nurse.
     Wilcox Fred M.
647 1259 Laschever Nathan, tailor.
649 1261 Britton Kate, wid. John.
     " Thomas A.
     Brewer Charles M.
     Buckley William F.
     Buckley James.
     Martin Louis.
     Preston George P.
     Preston Louisa E. wid. Benjamin F.
     Rourke Michael J.
     Wilson George E. nurse.
651 1263 Cross Frederick O. shoemaker.
     Bliss Edward, tinner.
     Maddock Hopkin, tinner.
     Williams E. D. cigar manufacturer.
     Winslow Nelson, tile.
     *Blumenthal Place, S.*
655 1271 Baxter H. Ella.
     Fielding William C.
     " John A.
     Dalton Marshall H.
     " Albert W.
     Bradley William E.
     Thompson James W.
657 1273 Clark M. E. Mrs. clairvoyant.
     English David.
     Westphal William.
     Hurd Gilbert P.
     Russell Dora.
     Gordon Walter N.
     Thomas John U.
659 1279 Herrick Louis B.
     Bowman Charles M.
     Bassett Ernest E. C.
661 1281 Ames Charles L.
     Waterman James.
     Baldwin Ada L.
     Moore Jennie Mrs.
     Babcock E. Dorance C.
     Goff Leroy M.
     Derby Don H.

| | | |
|---|---|---|
| 663 | 1293 | Farrell Eliza, wid. Thomas. |
| | | Fitch Emily E. wid. William H. |
| | | Cole R. Brooks. |
| | | Murdock George H. |
| | | Finn David. |
| | | Porter Eugene A. |
| | | Thalheimer Robert. |
| | | Goldenblum Emma. |
| | | Fannon Thomas F. |
| | | Costello Sadie E. dressmaker. |
| 665 | 1295 | Cowan Arthur B. |
| | | Welch Margaret A. |
| | | " Mary, wid. John. |
| | | Thrall Flavia A. Mrs. |
| | | Wilcox Fred. B. |
| | | Lester Newell. |
| | | Shea William E. |
| 667 | 1303 | Bartlett Alonzo. |
| | | Chapman Albert. |
| | | Whitney Leon D. |
| | | Bartlett Burton A. |
| | | Pierson Wilbur E. |
| | | " Wilbur B. |
| 669 | 1305 | Pattison Joseph. |
| | | " Alice. |
| | | Needham William F. |
| | | Schmeltz Henry H. |
| | | " Louis. |
| | | Woods James J. |
| | | Healy William. |
| | | Meyers Frederick. |
| | | Kelly Catherine, wid Thomas. |
| 671 | 1313 | Bundy Horace L. |
| | | " Harriet M. |
| 673 | 1315 | Dowling John F. physician. |
| | | Dowling Elizabeth M. |
| 675 | 1325 | Smith Frank B. |
| | | Kellogg Elizabeth S. Mrs. |
| 677 | 1329 | Goodrich Arthur L. |
| 679 | 1333 | Newton Theodore. |
| | | " Frank E. |
| 681 | 1337 | Kellogg George F. |
| | | " Rich W. |
| 685 | 1341 | Woodworth Frances A. wid. Arthur. |
| | | " Walter G. |
| | | Kimberly Thomas A. |
| | | Abels George F. |
| | | Shaw George L. |
| 687 | 1343 | Sawyer Flora L. wid. William E. |
| | | " Harry W. |
| | | Lynch Ada. |
| | | Wood William. |
| | | Beckwith James B. |
| | | Murray Chas. F. |
| 689 | 1355 | Leroy Peter. |
| 693 | 1357 | Marsharsky Meyer, shoemaker. |
| | 1359 | Leroy Brothers, store. |
| 693 | 1361 | Arnold Frank M. |
| | | Langdon Burton H. |
| | | " Mary E. wid. Merrick C. |
| | | Whiting Loren A. |
| | | " Walter F. |
| | | Dahme Hubert Rev. |
| | | Deming Charles A. |
| | 1363 | Leroy Brothers, store. |

| | | |
|---|---|---|
| | | *Ann Street, S.* |
| | | *High Street, S.* |
| 699 | 1391 | Coleman William H. drugstore. |
| 701 | 1393 | Botsford Charles P. physician. |
| | | Brown Abial. |
| | | " George W. |
| | | Simmons Lizzie F. wid. Oramel. |
| | | " Edward H. |
| | | " Myra B. |
| 703 | 1395 | Sleeper George E. |
| | | Hickey James D. |
| | | " Edward C. |
| | | " John H. |
| | | " Hattie. |
| | | " Kate, wid. Christopher. |
| | | Green Alvin W. |
| | | " Eva, wid. William. |
| 705 | 1397 | Patterson George, market. |
| 705½ | 1399 | Anderson William J. store. |
| 707 | 1407 | Bridge Lewis N. |
| | | Winott May. |
| | | Stannard John S. |
| | | Wilbraham George. |
| 709 | 1409 | Post Charles A. groceries. |
| 711 | 1411 | Yates E. P. & Co. grain. |
| 713 | 1413 | Wolfe Charles. |
| | | Smith Fannie M. wid. Joseph. |
| | | Lewis William G. |
| | | Dart Theodore S. |
| 715 | 1415 | Couch George C. |
| | | Phillips William E. |
| | | Drake Timothy. |
| | | Fay Edward E. |
| | | " Frederick N. |
| 717 | 1417 | Thomas Albert L. market. |
| 719 | 1419 | **BROWN EDMUND,** carpenter and builder. |
| | | Phipps Edward D. |
| | | *Rice Court, S.* |
| 8 | 54 | Beach George Watson. |
| | | Jarvis John S. Mrs. |
| 10 | 60 | Botelle Ellear. |
| | | " Edmund R. |
| | | " Andrew E. |
| | | Doolan Mary, wid. Michael. |
| 12 | 66 | Egan John. |
| | | " Peter. |
| 16 | 80 | Farmer Roderick W. |
| | | Havens Frances B. Mrs. |
| | | " Ellen S. |
| 22 | 96 | Higgs William H. |
| | | Delaney John O. |
| 24 | 104 | Goodrich Elizur S. |
| 28 | 118 | Barnard Henry. |
| | | " Josephine E. |
| | | " Emily V. |
| | | Patrick Julia S. |
| 32 | 134 | Reilly P. Harvard, |
| | | Bond Joseph H. |
| | | Strong Charles H. |
| 34 | 136 | Sawtelle Alfred W. |
| | | " Albert G. |
| 36 | 140 | Lazzaro Albert E. |

| | | |
|---|---|---|
| 38 | 158 | Broderick Thomas W. Rev. |
| | | " Edward J. Rev. |
| | | Lally Francis J. Rev. |
| | | Laden Thomas J. Rev. |
| | | Broderick Catharine A. |
| 46 | 188 | Antonia, sister, mother super. |
| 44 | 170 | St. Peters Church, |
| 60 | 214 | Peck Cornelia C. Miss. |
| | | Weeks Victoria. |
| 64 | 232 | Redfield Henry A. |
| | | Kelly Michael, gardener. |
| 68 | 244 | Clark Mary, daugh. late David Clark. |
| | | Clark Mary E. wid. Andrew D. |
| | | Fitts Thomas K. |
| 72 | 256 | Smith Patrick B. |
| 76 | 270 | Varney Jennie S. Mrs. dressmaker. |
| | | " Fred. H. cutter. |
| | | " William S. |
| | | Lavin James J. |
| | | Mitchell Ernest Brownell. |
| | | Kenneally Joseph F. |
| 76a | 278 | Pierce William J. |
| | | Brigham Oliver H. |
| | | " Herbert E. |
| | | Dooley Michael F. |
| | | Wise Michael J. |
| 76b | 280 | Talcott Caleb M. |
| | | " H. Louise. |
| | | Bill Austin R. |
| | | Robinson R. Maud. |
| | | Linke Emil F. |
| 78 | 288 | McCarty Timothy M. plumber. |
| 80 | 290 | Leek Amanda M. Mrs. |
| | | " Philanda. |
| | | Watrous John H. |
| 84 | 294 | Sing War, laundry. |
| | 296 | Bartlett John. |
| | | Roser Max. |
| 86 | 298 | Regan Bridget, wid. Dennis. |
| | | Duffy Maria. |
| | | Regan Dennis F. |
| 88 | 302 | Harrington Daniel J. |
| 90 | 304 | Emmons Joseph B. |
| | | " Elwyn N. |
| | | Hoffman Mitchell. |
| 92 | 306 | Ford Jarvis O. |
| | | " Willie K. |
| | | Mellen Frank C. |
| | | Scott Ripley A. |
| | | " Leland D. |
| | | " Frank R. |
| | | Boucher John B. physician. |
| | | McCormick James J. |
| 94 | 308 | Sawtelle Alfred W. drug store. |
| | | *Charter Oak Street, E.* |
| 96 | 330 | Melrose & Keane, liquors. |
| 96½ | 334 | Dunn Mary, wid. Andrew. |
| | | Doty Margaret. wid. George. |
| | | " John. |
| 98 | 336 | Day Fred E. |
| 100 | 338 | Dodge & Brewer, market. |
| 102 | 346 | McManus, John C. stoves, etc. |
| 102½ | 350 | Benton Charles F. |
| | | Barnard Edward R. |
| | | Greenleaf M. A. wid. Henry. |

| | | |
|---|---|---|
| 102½ | 350 | Greenleaf Sarah E. |
| | | Hubbard Carrie W. wid. Charles. |
| | | Welch Clara C. |
| 104 | 356 | Boardman Chauncey B. livery stable. |
| | | Stroud Thompson C. vet. surgeon. |
| 106 | 360 | Daly Lawrence, stoves, etc. |
| 106½ | 364 | Winn Mary. |
| 108 | 366 | Woolley Fred. P. livery stable. |
| 114 | 390 | McCook John B. physician. |
| | 396 | " John J. Rev. |
| | | " Philip J. |
| | | " George Sheldon. |
| | | " Eliza L. |
| 116 | 406 | O'Flaherty John, physician. |
| 118 | 420 | Robinson Henry C. |
| | | " Henry S. |
| | | " John T. |
| | | " Mary S. |
| 120 | 434 | Moran Louisa. |
| | | " Theresa. |
| 122 | 448 | Schall Ernst. |
| | | Gilbert William J. |
| | | " Augustus H. |
| 124 | 450 | **MURRAY WILLIAM A.** plumber. |
| | 452 | Barrett Elizabeth J. Mrs. boardingh. |
| | | Coleman Cornelius F. |
| | | Conehoven James G. |
| | | " Theodore H. |
| | | Dudley Joseph L. |
| | | " William G. |
| | | Hilon Thomas. |
| | | Mack John. |
| | | Manion Joseph. |
| | | Tuttle William H. |
| 126 | 454 | Wah Charlie A. laundry. |
| 128 | 456 | Arcari Brothers, barber shop. |
| | 458 | McCann Arthur. |
| | | Smith Louis. |
| | | Penfield William H. |
| | | Cahill Evelyn, wid. William J. |
| | | Wenk Fred W. |
| 130 | 460 | Horse Guard Armory. |
| | | Cunliffe Janette, wid. John. |
| | | " Frederick R. |
| | | " Richard W. |
| 130 | 462 | **PEASE C. A. & CO.** flour, grain and feed. |
| 132 | 466 | Allen Brothers, grocers. |
| | | *Sheldon Street, E.* |
| 134 | 484 | Forst Charles, bakery. |
| 136 | 486 | Greenwald William, gents furnishings. |
| 138 | 488 | Wellington Building. |
| | | Forst Charles. |
| | | Chadwick Mary, rm. 3. |
| | | Bernard Emery. |
| | | Marshall A. D. Mrs. |
| | | Leveillie Napoleon P. |
| | | Kelley John. |
| | | Porter Lettie, wid. Charles. |
| | | Frazier Wm. B. engineer. |
| | | Commier Lizzie E. wid. William. |
| | | Schlattery Mrs. nurse. |
| | | Sanford Homer D. |
| | | Morse Edward N. |

| | | |
|---|---|---|
| 138 | 488 | Conlin Philip F. |
| | | Olynn Bernard. |
| | | Sickles Charles H. |
| | | VanSyckel William H. |
| | | Carter Horace L. |
| | | Seeley Edward M. |
| | | Wilcox Margaret, wid. Henry L. |
| | | Smith E. Shipman. |
| | | " Ellen H. wid. Henry J. |
| 140 | 490 | Bacon Franklin N. market. |
| 142 | 516 | Franklin Market, E. H. Harris. |
| | 518 | Allen Emily J. boardinghouse. |
| | | " Moses D. |
| | | Smith C. Edward. |
| | | Arthur John. |
| | | Welch William. |
| | | Kuhn Henry. |
| | | Leitch Louisa, wid. Constantine. |
| 142½ | 520 | Langley John L. |
| | | Smith Wm. B. |
| | | Thayer Wm. W. |
| | | Martin Michael. |
| | | Weldon Frank. |
| | | " Louis. |
| | | Murphy John. |
| | | Meaney Daniel. |
| | | Costigan Mary, wid. John. |
| 142 | 522 | Farrell John H. saloon. |
| | | *Arch Street, E.* |
| 144 | 532 | McKernan Edward F. saloon. |
| 146 | 534 | Tillotson Margaret J. wid. Chas. L. |
| | | " Edward P. |
| | | Modoc Geo. A. toolkeeper. |
| | | Furey Peter M. driver. |
| | | Frankenfield John. |
| | | Dalton Lewis. |
| | | Lee James. |
| 148 | 536 | Prisk Alfred J. |
| 150 | 538 | Nussbaum Kaufman, market. |
| 152 | 540 | American Cycle Repair Co. |
| 154 | 542 | Estlow Elizabeth, wid. Alfred. |
| | | Bullock Joseph. |
| | | Clark Martin. |
| | | Conlin Daniel. |
| | | Hughes John. |
| | | Thurber Edward. |
| 156 | 544 | Miller Max. tailor. |
| 158 | 546 | Rogers Laura, wid. Fred'k D. dressm. |
| | 548 | Conroy John, book store. |
| 160 | 550 | Lawler Edward, plumber. |
| | 552 | Manion James J. |
| | | Potter Annie, wid. Fred J. |
| | | Slaboszewski Hilery A. |
| 162 | 554 | **FRENCH HARRY A.** doors, sash and blinds. |
| 164 | 556 | Woolley Geo. W. & Son, undertakers. |
| | 558 | Marvin John. |
| | | Bernard Napoleon P. |
| | | Eitel E. music teacher. |
| 166 | 560 | Black M. J. vet. surg. livery stable. |
| | | Dudley J. L. veterinary dentist. |
| 168 | 564 | Drew Fannie L. wall papers, etc. |
| 170 | 566 | Mathies John H. |
| | | Evans Archie. |
| | | " George. |

| | | |
|---|---|---|
| 170 | 566 | Mathies Nettie Mrs. dressmaker. |
| | | Connor Lizzie. |
| | | Fitzgerald Annie Mrs. |
| | | Sullivan Eugene. |
| | | " William. |
| | | Hagerty Edward. |
| | | Sullivan Margaret Mrs. |
| | | Burke Alice, wid. Patrick. |
| | | " James J. |
| | | " Dennis F. hackman. |
| | | " John. |
| | | " William J. |
| 172 | 568 | Martel Louis J. laundry. |
| | 570 | Frost Nellie. |
| | | McGinn James. |
| | | Vining Almon C. |
| | | Quinn Mary. |
| | | Carroll Margaret E. wid. Patrick. |
| | | " John F. |
| | | McDonald William. |
| 178 | 580 | St. Johns Church. |
| 184 | 590 | Nichols Delbert L. |
| | | Dawe Emma L. |
| | | Jordan David. |
| | | Ritchie Jordan W. |
| | | Brainard Hartwell H. |
| | | Wyatt William. |
| | | Juster W. J. |
| | | Brackley W. |
| | | Perkins Eugene P. |
| 186 | 592 | Hubbard Jane, wid. Wm. Franklin. |
| | | " William F. |
| | | " George S. |
| 188 | 596 | Martel L. J. Mrs. employment. |
| | | Carroll Samuel J. electrician. |
| 206 | 624 | Art Galeries. |
| | | Connecticut Historical Society. |
| | | Hartford Free Public Library. |
| | | Wadsworth Atheneum. |
| | | *Atheneum Street, E.* |
| 214 | 644 | **AETNA NAT'L BANK.** |
| 216 | 648 | **SMYTH MFG. CO.** |
| 218 | 650 | **AETNA LIFE INS. CO. HARTFORD STEAM BOILER INSPECTION AND INSURANCE CO.** |
| | | Ætna Indemnity Co. |
| | | **SPERRY, McLEAN & BRAINARD,** attorneys. |
| | | Hascall H. E. music teacher, rm. 15. |
| | | Branes H. T. H. broker, rm. 17. |
| | | Williams Charles H. Rev. 18. |
| | | Isham Mary T. rm. 20. |
| | | Williams Mary E. Mrs. rm. 33. |
| | | French Almo E. rm. 39. |
| | | Stanton Louis E. rm. 40. |
| | | Hitchcock Carrie M. Mrs. rm. 41. |
| | | Brocklesby Wm. C. rm. 42. |
| | | Browning Maranda A. Mrs. rm. 43. |
| | | Sykes V. A. rm. 44. |
| | | Pember E. M. Mrs. rm. 45. |
| | | " Hubert. |
| | | National Trotting Association, rm. 47. |
| | | Clark Olin H. rm. 52. |
| | | Smith Elizabeth G. private school. |

218 650  Gates L. C. Mrs. rm. 54.
         Hubbard Louisa D. Mrs. rm. 56.
         Garves & Robinson, civil engineers,
            rm. 57.
         Hubbell Elizabeth, nurse, rm. 58.
         Gardner Elizabeth D. dressm. rm.59.
         Schott James S. rm. 60.
         Berry Annie F. Mrs. rm. 61.
         Moldenhour Frieda, rm. 62.
         " Dora Mrs. rm. 62.
         Conn. River Bridge & Highway
            District Commission, rm. 64.
         Hawkins C. H. Mrs. rm. 65.
220 654  Shepard Charles E. insurance.
222 658  **KIMBALL & McCRAY.**
224 664  **DICKINSON L. A. & CO.**
226 666  **AETNA INS. CO.**
230 676  Republican Club.
232 678  McNamara Thomas, livery stable.
234 686  Church of The Redeemer.
236 700  Hartford City Gas Light Co.
         **SCOVILLE ALBERT W.**
            contractor and builder.
         Adams Sherman W. attorney.
         Baker W. E. & Son, insurance.
         Bayley & Goodrich, architects.
         Egan Maria J. millinery school.
         Hardy Herbert C.
         Hannum T. W. Jr.
         Mix Gertrude L. stenog, rm. 11.
         Morgan William D. physician.
         Root Edward K. physician.
         Stewart John D.
         United Workers Club.
         Whitmore Franklin G. real estate.
238 702  Coombs John, florist.
240 704  Hartford Wheel Club.
         Traute A. H. real estate.
         **CONN. CATHOLIC PUB-
            LISHING CO.**
         Barnes George H. plate printing.
         Dawson Joseph, city marshal.
242 706  Seide David, barbershop.
246 716  **BURR BROS. "TIMES"**
248 720  **WAKEFIELD WALTER
            L.** fire insurance and real estate.
         **WAKEFIELD AGENCY,**
            real estate and loans.
         **SCOVILLE WM. H.** archi-
            and builder.
         New England Construction Co.
         Eckhardt Christian H. rm. 3.
         Theis Frank W. rm. 6.
         Alexander Samuel, rm. 7.
         Whitaker F. P. rm. 10.
         Kelleher J. J. rm. 11.
         Deegan James, rm. 12.
         Lutz Reinhold, tailor, rm. 17.
250 722  **NEW ENG. COAL CO.**
         Price Robert C. real estate.
         Maxfield Brothers, brokers.
254 724  Johnson George F. printer.
         Smith Robert, rm. 5.
         Atchison Joseph, rm. 9.
         Andross G. physician rm. 11.

254 724  Slattery Mary Mrs. rm. 17.
         de Granval Walter, rm. 18.
         Keys K. Mrs. rm. 21.
         Neff Bernard, tailor, rm. 25.
         Weed Sue Mrs. rm. 26.
256 726  Herbert Art Co.
258 730  Saunders P. H. B. & Son, tailors.
         Wentworth George B.
         Kissler Abraham B. tailor.
         Germania Cycle Club.
         Salvation Army.
260 732  **CO-OPERATIVE SAV-
            INGS SOCIETY OF
            CONN.**
262 734  Hewins Matt H.
         **TOPPING JAMES R.**
            pattern maker.
         Goodacre Brothers, cigar factory.
264 738  Goodacre W. H. saloon.
266 740  Cusick Frederick H. tailor.
         Brown Charles M.
         Williams David J.
268 742  Mayer Nathan, physician.
         Cairns John.
         " John Jr.
         " Joseph M.
270 744  Alexander & Elmer, bicycles.
272 746  **MASON W. C. & CO.** coal.
274 750  **STATE MUTUAL FIRE
            INSURANCE CO.**
         **CROSS & MORLEY,** fire
            insurance.
         Safford Charles A. attorney, rm. 1.
         **CROSS, HYDE & SHIP-
            MAN.** attorneys at law, rm. 8.
         Gillett A. B. real estate.
         Chapman Thos. B. constable, rm. 14.
         Greene Charles B. constable, rm. 14.
         Freeman J. H. B. attorney, rm. 16.
         Scott Frederick A. attorney.
         Wolcott Frank, rm. 20.
         Eddy Willard, attorney, rm. 24.
         **DENISON CHAS.** broker,
            rm. 25.
         White John H. attorney, rm. 26.
         Yeomans Edw. M. attorney, rm. 26.
         Brocklesby John H. attorney, rm. 27.
         **WILLIAMS HARRY R.**
            patent solicitor, rm. 28.
         Tyler Heman A. insurance, rm. 29.
         Todd Milo A. insurance, rm. 29.
         Smith G. Fred, rm. 29.
         Tyler Manufacturing Co. rm. 29.
         Pierce Willis A. constable, rm. 30.
         Barbour Sylvester, attorney, rm. 30.
         Burke Harry M. attorney.
         Sherman Ernest A. engraver, rm. 32.
         Stewart Charles, rm. 33.
         Healy Frank E. attorney, rm. 34.
         " Thomas L. real estate, rm. 34.
         Humphry Henry, builder, rm. 37.
         Gerstl Max, architect, rm. 38.
         **OLMSTEAD'S COM-
            MERCIAL COLLEGE,**
            rm. 40.

| | | |
|---|---|---|
| 274 | 750 | Keller George, architect, rm. 43. |

274  750  Keller George, architect, rm. 43.
Brocklesby Wm. C. architect, rm. 45.
Butler & Helion, real estate, rm. 46.
Becker Willis E. architect, rm. 47.
John Hancock Mutual Life Insurance
Co. rm. 49.
Leonard Agustus T. rm. 51.
276  752  **VORCE A. D. CO.** art store.
278  754  **HARTFORD COAL CO.**
Hills John R. contractor and builder.
Woods George H. real estate.
Garvie John B. contractor.
760  Hogan M. plumber.
284  764  **HARTFORD TRUST CO.**
*Central Row, E.*
300  800  Preston Miles B. mayor.
Strong Charles C. city treasurer.
Robins Charles H. auditor.
Water Commissioners.
Board of Health.
Roberts E. D. sealer of weights, etc.
Board of Aldermen Chamber.
"    Common Council Chamber.
Street Commissioners Office.
Bunce Charles H. city engineer.
Building Inspector.
Dawson Joseph, city marshal.
Counor Peter, janitor.
*State Street, E.*
334  852  **GOODWIN LESTER H.**
drug store.
338  856  Alexander Edward W. merch. tailor.
**TALCOTT WILLIAM H.**
bookbinder.
340  858  Ballerstein Benjamin, store.
342  862  Levy Heyman P. jewelry.
344  866  Way Hardware Co.
346  868  Bullock Henry C. dentist.
Fox Horace P.
"  H. P. Mrs. dressmaker.
Hartford Paving & Construction Co.
Olmsted Charles E. physician.
348  872  **UNITED STATES BANK**
*Kinsley Street, E.*
354  882  J. Samuels & Co. shoes.
356  884  Clarke Sidney E. attorney.
White Watson L. real estate.
Wiley Louis N. dentist.
Peterson Kathrine.
Robinson Winter D.
Scott George D.
"  William G.
Buckley Patrick T.
Dunn Michael J.
Goff Angie D. wid. Hatsell S.
"  Harry H.
O'Neill Margaret Mrs.
McInnis Catharine, wid. Donald.
Galpin Robert J.
McManus Robert.
Hurley James.
Turry Frank.
358  886  **HANSEL, SLOAN & CO.**
jewelers.

360  890  **KOHN HENRY & SONS,**
jewelers.
362  892  Gilman Jacob, tailor.
364  896  **SAGE, ALLEN & CO.**
dry goods.
**HART CHAS. R. CO.**
carpets, etc.
902  Case Erastus E. physician.
DeLamater R. S. & Son, photographers.
372  904  Ballerstein Building.
Ballerstein Raphael.
Cooper J. furs. rm. 2.
Collis Alison V. rm. 12.
King C. B. rm. 15.
Seide Henry W. insurance, rm. 16.
Angell A. physician, rms. 22, 25.
Pike L. E. & Co. brokers, rms. 27, 28.
**BOYNTON EDWARD B.**
investments, rms. 30, 31.
Well & Devine, opticians, rm. 34.
**CLAUSSEN EDWARD
E.** mech. engineer, rms. 38, 39.
Turner Annie F. milliner, rm. 40.
Bairstow Thomas, rm. 46.
Griswold G. M. dentist, rm. 53.
Little Samual A. dentist.
Clark, S. W. com. mcht. rm. 75.
Barrington Alfred, music, rm. 78.
Bunce N. Gedney, astist, rm. 78.
Oneill Mary E. dressm. rm. 79.
Southwaite F. M. millinery, rm. 81.
Carroll J. R. insurance, rms. 83, 84.
Graham W. C. stenographer, rm. 85.
**ALLEN ISAAC A. Jr.**
architect, rms. 87, 92.
Willson Vesta H. copyist, rm. 88.
Mix Fred'k E. dentist, rm. 93.
**MARQUARDT H. C.** real
estate and insurance, rms 95, 96.
Steele T. Sedgwick, artist, rms. 97, 98.
**DES JARDINS B. M.** mechanical engineer, rms. 99, 100.
**HONEY FREDERICK R.**
mechanical engineer, rms. 99, 100.
Wentworth D. F. artist, rm. 102.
Vorce C. B. civil engineer. rm. 103.
Fenety Andrew C. artist, rm. 105.
Carney William C. rm. 108.
Bundy H. L. photogr. rm. 109.
Bunce W. Gedney, artist, rm. 112.
Flagg Charles Noel. artist, rms. 113.
378  908  **BALLERSTEIN R. & CO.**
milliners.
*Temple Street, E.*
380  920  **BROWN, THOMSON &
CO.** dry goods, etc.
382  926  Brown, Thomson & Co's Building.
Buck John H. attorney, rm. 3.
Keefe Misses, milliners, rm. 8.
Hathaway Chas. H. chiropodist, rm. 9.
Gentlemen's Driving Club, rm. 10.
Pierce & Roulston, milliners, rm. 11.
**BUCK & EGGLESTON,**
attorneys.

382 926 Grannis S. H. wid. Eri, dressm. 12.
   " Cora L. milliner, rm. 12.
   Martin Thomas J. rm. 15.
   Heath C. J. wid. Benj. F. dressm. 16.
   Murray May Mrs. nurse, rm. 16.
   Kelly Catherine, rm. 17.
   Egan Annie, rm. 17.
   Morrell M. A. wid. A. W. nurse, rm.18.
   Andrews James P. attorney, rm. 19.
   Fowler George B. attorney, rm. 19.
   Morrison L. W. stenographer, rm. 19.
   Leete William H. attorney, rm. 19.
   **BRISCOE CHARLES H.**
    attorney, rm. 20.
   St. Hilarre Emma J. rm. 24.
   Peck G. Herbert, rm. 27.
   Wasserbach Eliza, wid. John C.
   Kimball John C. Rev.
   Robert O. Tyler Post, No. 50, G.A.R.
   Bryant Charles K. dentist, rm. 32.
   Bacon Fred J. music teacher, rm.33.
   " Albert C. rm. 35.
   Martin Thomas H. Mrs. rm. 36.
   Cornish James P. electrician, rm. 37.
   Rouse C. O. physician.
   Givans John Jr. rm. 41.
   Scott Alex. rm. 42.
   Peltier Pierre D. physician, rm. 43.
   Starr Thomas K. dentist, rm. 44.
   Barrett George F. dentist, rm. 45.
   Buckland G. W. Mrs. architect, 47.
   Buckland Arthur J. rm. 47.
   Seybold Mind. teacher, rm. 48.
   Bradley Ruth A. pianist, rm. 49.
   **MERRIAM A. E. COLT**
    **MRS,** electric physician, rm. 51.
   Sparrow Fannie L. rm. 54.
   Newton Clinton H. teacher, rm. 55.
   " Clinton H. Mrs. teacher, rm.55.
   Wiggin George, rm. 59.
   " M. E. Mrs. inventor, rm. 59.
   Howe Joseph F. rm. 64.
   " J. F. Mrs. dressmaker, rm. 64.
   Wenk Henry C. rm. 65.
   Semple Lilla B. Mrs. rm. 66.
   Turmey Sarah, rm. 67.
   Converse H. Mrs. rm. 68.
   Linsley M. M. rm. 70.
   Camp Fannie Grimes, rm. 72.
   Loomis M. C. Mrs. rm. 73.
   **LAW & PRENTISS,** dentists, rm. 76.
   Curtis & Johnson, architects, rm. 77.
   Cole H. P. physician, rms. 81,82,83.
   " Hills, physician, rms. 81, 82,83.
   Dillingham A. F. rm. 84.
   Potts & Brabazon, artists, rm. 86.
   Allen N. H. music teacher, rm. 87.
   Brown Frederick E. Jr. rm. 94.
   Kelly J. W. rm. 98.
   Lattimer George, janitor, rm. 99.
384 928 Strong David E. shoes.
400 942 **BROWN, THOMSON &**
   **CO.** dry goods, etc.
406 956 Fox G. & Co.

428 980 **NEAL, COFF & INGLIS**
   **CO.** carpets, etc.
432 986 The Windsor, Mrs. C. H. Latham.
   Latham Charles H.
   Case Charles Z.
   Doolittle Maria P.
   Hubbard Chas. E.
   Stueck J. William Jr.
   Whittelsey Wm. F. Jr.
   Williams Harry F.
  988 Nolan J. F. carpenter.
   Missell William, upholsterer.
  990 Robertson Lafayett J. fruit.
436 992 Fromberg Thomas, jeweler.
436½ 994 Priore Joseph, shoemaker.
   Romano George, bootblack.
438 996 Garfinkle Morris, jeweler.
   *Talcott Street, E.*
450 1014 First Baptist Church.
456 1026 Sisson Elizabeth Mrs.
458 1028 Manufacturers Cash Shoe Store.
460 1030 Union Grocery Co.
462 1032 Tillotson Katherine E. Mrs.
   Scribner H. A.
   Williams E.
   Schlaefer Charles.
464 1034 **MARSH HENRY T.**
   dancing school.
   Marsh Elizabeth R. wid. Truman.
   " Ellen Mrs. dressmaker.
   Cotton William.
   Dillon Charles.
   Gladding Albert.
466 1086 **STUECK JACOB W. Jr.**
   bakery.
  1042 The Cadden.
   Beckwith A. F.
   Dunham A. I. Miss.
474 1046 New York Tea Store.
   Kennedy Philip S.
   *Morgan Street, E.*
476 1050 Union Market, J. S. Pilgard.
478 1052 Spieske Henry, furniture.
480 1056 Janson Henry, saloon.
   Germania Hall.
486 1070 **BREEN PATRICK J.**
   marble works.
488 1072 Couch George M. plumber.
   Tuttle Samuel.
   Starr John C.
   Fox Clarinda, wid. Dudley.
490 1074 Crary David Jr. physician.
492 1076 Marsh Thomas & Co. painters.
   Jackson James L. watchmaker.
   Snow Char es L. plumber.
   Chesky H. & Co. fruit.
494 1078 Johnson Andrew B.
   " Christian.
   Lyon Joseph.
496 1080 Adams Elizabeth, wid. Mecena C.
   " Lizzie May.
   " Able S.
   Young Frank.
   Robinson Almon.
   Walker William.

| | | |
|---|---|---|
| 496 | 1080 | Morrell Edward M. |
| | | Savoy Anlor. |
| | | Rowland Harvey. |
| | | Devine Matthew. |
| 500 | 1084 | Cadwell & Jones, hardware. |
| 502 | 1086 | Martin Mary V. wid. Chester. |
| | | Bradley Burton. |
| | | Butler Albert. |
| | | Flint Fred. |
| | | Levee Nathan F. |
| | | " Bessie M. |
| 504 | 1088 | Whaples Anna Mrs. |
| | | Goodman Arthur P. |
| | | Shavalear Josephine, wid. Edwin. |
| 506 | 1090 | Goodman D. A. estate, furniture. |
| 508 | 1092 | Hopper & Sweeney, plumber. |
| | | French C. S. painter. |
| 510 | 1094 | Nelson Frank. |
| | | " Frank Mrs. boardinghouse. |
| 512 | 1096 | Smith Matilda, wid. Elliott, hotel. |
| | | " Margaret M. |
| | | Bauer John L. |
| | | Johnson Kittie. |
| | | Patron Josie. |
| | | Cotter Mabel Mrs. |
| | | Murphy Agnes. |
| 514 | 1098 | Roesner August, restaurant. |
| 516 | 1100 | Sing Tan, laundry. |
| | | Kibbe William E. bicycles. |
| | | Gardner Samuel A. oil. |
| 518 | 1102 | Belden Oscar C. |
| | | Lux Ellis. |
| | | " J. George. |
| 520 | 1104 | Nason Cora B. wid. William S. |
| | | Davis Fred. |
| | | Behan John F. |
| | | Counehan Daniel D |
| | | Martin James. |
| | | Roberts Fred. |
| | | Ingalls Harriet Mrs. |
| 522 | 1106 | Bradley Henry E. paints. |
| 524 | 1108 | Lee Wing, laundry. |
| 526 | 1110 | Backus Jason. |
| | | " Sarah A. |
| | | Kenefick John J. |
| | | Champlin Jennie A. Mrs. |
| 528 | 1112 | Stowe Henry. |
| | | Wilbur Elizabeth E. wid. Gilderoy. |
| | | Stowe Josephine F. Mrs. dressm. |
| | | Hall Noadiah K. |
| | | Welden Hattie, wid. Horace N. |
| 530 | 1116 | Behner F. Edward, tinner. |
| 532 | 1118 | Horenstein Bros. cigars. . |
| 534 | 1120 | Camp Charles W. |
| | | Bradley May. |
| 536 | 1122 | Cooley Samuel A. |
| | | " Mary A. |
| | | Wall Josephine Mrs. |
| | | " Edward. |
| | | Decker Samuel. |
| | | Daley John. |
| | | Alderman Elbert T. |
| | | Waters James. |
| | | Doyle Thomas. |
| 538 | 1124 | **WHITE F. W.** stoves, etc. |

| | | |
|---|---|---|
| 540 | 1128 | Nott Charles D. livery. |
| | | Munsell Mary F. wid. Chester W. |
| | | " Robert C. |
| | | Epsar Frank. |
| | | Walters Aretus. |
| | | " Harry. |
| | | Losty John F. |
| | | Hammond William H. |
| | | " William T. |
| | | Collins William. |
| 542 | 1130 | Pierce's Steam Laundry. |
| 546 | 1136 | Cody Charles. |
| | | Nolan Morris J. |
| | | Tracy John W. |
| | | Freeman Edwin L. |
| | | " Mary E. |
| | | McCoy George S. |
| 548 | 1140 | Gould Elizabeth, wid. Thomas. S. |
| | | " Charles E. |
| | | " Kate A. |
| | | Denslow Ferdinand D. |
| | | Flagg Frank. |
| | | Judd P. S. W. |
| | | *Sigourney Place, N.* |
| 552 | 1146 | Pietsch & Hinkley, painters. |
| | 1148 | Brown William, harness store. |
| 554 | 1150 | **SIGOURNEY HOUSE.** |
| | | Coyle N. J. Mrs. |
| | | " Mary E. |
| | | Adams Charles Hemingway. |
| | | " Mary S. Mrs. |
| | | Baker Alice M. |
| | | Bill Elizabeth R. |
| | | Daniels Timothy A. |
| | | Drake Helen A. wid. Nathaniel. |
| | | Graham William A. |
| | | Hartstall Max. |
| | | " Sarah E. |
| | | " Isabel. |
| | | Heubler Dora, wid. Julius. |
| | | Judd Cornelius M. |
| | | Martin Osgood C. |
| | | McNierny Thomas. |
| | | O'Brien John J. |
| | | Perkins Daniel C. |
| | | Perry M. M. |
| | | Reese Isaac J. |
| | | Senk George H. |
| | | Upson Frederick P. |
| | | Wilcox Florence M. |
| 556 | 1152 | Mahl George & Son, plumbers. |
| | | " Benjamin F. builder. |
| | 1154 | French & Hurlock, painters. |
| 558 | 1156 | Schneider N. groceries. |
| 560 | 1158 | Cadwell Hattie J. wid. Starr D. |
| 562 | 1160 | Mulligan Edward. |
| | | Fitzgerald Thomas. |
| | | Lynch John. |
| | | Lane Albert E. |
| | | " Edgar A. |
| | | Puffer Jennie E. wid. Charles E. |
| | | Shea William J. |
| 564 | 1162 | Henry James J. tinner. |
| 566 | 1164 | Warner Mary A. wid. Charles S. |
| | | Griswold Gertrude E. |

| | | |
|---|---|---|
| 566 | 1164 | Hamlin Fred. |
| | | Leek William S. |
| | | " Carrie, wid. John D. |
| | | " Grace D. |
| | | Potter Wm. L. |
| 568 | 1166 | **FOSTER & FURREY,** |
| | | undertakers. |
| 572 | 1170 | **NIMS, WHITNEY & CO.** |
| | | doors sash and blinds. |
| 574 | 1172 | Moran Mary, boardinghouse. |
| | | " Catharine, wid. John. |
| | | Brown William. |
| | | Fleming Andrew. |
| | | Kilgannon John. |
| | | Rollo Victor A. |
| | | Sullivan Patrick. |
| | | Sullivan Michael. |
| | | Wadsworth William S. |
| | | Worton Elizabeth, wid. Samuel. |
| | | Neff Fred W. |
| 576 | 1174 | Cohn Brothers, signpainters. |
| | | Silver Brothers. |
| 578 | 1176 | Wheelwood Ambrose. |
| | | Adams James. |
| | | Donahue John. |
| | | Roach Patrick. |
| | | Whittemore Edmund J. |
| 580 | 1178 | Hunter Jane, wid. Joseph. |
| | | Abbie Lulu. |
| | | Bleo Minnie Mrs. |
| | | Daily Kate. |
| | | Rollo Louis M. |
| 582 | 1180 | Abels George F. furniture. |
| 594 | 1192 | Goldenthal Moses, tinner. |
| | | Levy Louis, shoemaker. |
| 596 | 1194 | Boucher Mary, wid. Thomas F. |
| | | Ashwell Charles E. |
| | | Broderick T. A. Mrs. |
| | | Bryton Edwin. |
| | | Byron Thomas. |
| | | Handy Silas. |
| | | Peeples Eldridge F. |
| 598 | 1196 | Day P. R. & Sons, fence builders. |
| | | Barnett Simon, tailor. |
| 600 | 1198 | Deutsch Morris. |
| 602 | 1200 | Capitol Tea & Coffee Co. |
| 604 | 1202 | Clark Thomas J. Mrs. boardingh. |
| | | Avery Arnold P. |
| | | Burns Peter. |
| | | Cummings Thomas. |
| | | Dahill Margaret. |
| | | Edwards Thomas. |
| | | Featherstone Benjamin F. |
| | | Landry Albert. |
| | | " Peter. |
| | | O'Brien Honora, wid. John. |
| | | " Dennis R. |
| | | Rourke John. |
| | | Sheehan John J. |
| | | Welch David F. |
| | | White John F. |
| 606 | 1204 | Mahl Edward, plumber. |
| 610 | 1208 | Potter Wilson. |
| | | " Wilson Mrs. dressmaker. |
| | | Mallison Henry S. |

| | | |
|---|---|---|
| 610 | 1208 | Blythe George A. |
| | | Pass Fred. |
| | | Clark E. H. Mrs. dressmaker. |
| | | Columbe Joseph. |
| 612 | 1210 | Puffer Emma J. Mrs. |
| | | " Julia, wid. Charles. |
| | | Neal Charles H. Mrs. |
| | | Baldwin John. |
| | | Drew John. |
| | | Curley John. |
| | | Willard Abbie M. wid. Charles E. |
| 614 | 1212 | Harding Thomas H. painter. |
| | | Reid James W. tailor. |
| | | Leonard Augustus T. jeweler. |
| 616 | 1214 | Otis J. Henry, livery. |
| | | Mills Patrick H. |
| | | Jackson Cornelius. |
| | | Jacklin Lottie, wid. William. |
| | | Hawley Mary E. Mrs. |
| | | Freeman Edward W. |
| | | Reynolds Forest. |
| | | Mahoney John. |
| 618 | 1216 | Bethel Mission Church. |
| 620 | 1218 | Hayes John. |
| | | " Mary Mrs. |
| | | " Joseph. |
| | | Stoll Lisetta Mrs. boardinghouse. |
| | | Finan Patrick. |
| | | " Michael. |
| | | Cady Thomas. |
| | | Munsell William F. |
| | | Kanza John. |
| | | Hartenstein Ivan. |
| | | Voiral Julius. |
| 620½ | 1220 | Hayden William T. |
| | | " Henry A. |
| | | Brooks James. |
| | | Guest Fred. |
| 622 | 1222 | Ryan Patrick J. harness. |
| 624 | 1224 | Gillette Horace S. |
| | | Keleher William F. |
| | | Wheeler Floren A. |
| | | Meyn Henry. |
| | | Daley Mathew A. |
| | | O'Donnell Edward. |
| | | Reid William. |
| | | Wilbur J. Nelson. |
| | | Wilson Robert. |
| 630 | 1230 | Langdon & Daley, plumbers. |
| 632 | 1232 | Chickering John W. |
| | | Hosford George. |
| | | Lucas Caroline, wid. Thomas. |
| | | Sheedy Catharine, dressmaker. |
| | | Duggan Mary Mrs. |
| | | Allen Mary Mrs. |
| | | Pike Dora. |
| | | Johnson Thomas. |
| 634 | 1234 | Cohn R. & Co. leather. |
| 636 | 1236 | Leonard Chester A. |
| | | Eastman Charles A. |
| | | Taylor Alice. |
| | | " Fannie. |
| 640 | 1242 | Arnold & Phelan, saloon. |
| 642 | 1244 | Collins Wm. M. |
| | | Daniels Eugene. |

| 642 | 1244 | Lyons Howard. |
| | | Murtress Thomas. |
| | | Renard George. |
| | | Riley James. |
| | | Smith Jennie Mrs. dressmaker. |
| 644 | 1246 | Merrill Ira. |
| | | McCoy George. |
| | | Clark Thomas A. |
| | | Russell John S. antiques. |
| | | Robbinson Fannie, rooms to rent. |
| | | Hatheway Harris D. |
| 646 | 1248 | Crawford & Co. groceries. |
| | | *Pleasant Street, E.* |
| 650 | 1260 | **NEW ENG. GRANITE WORKS,** monuments. |
| 652 | 1274 | Crane Charles L. painter. |
| | | Taylor Geo. H. Carpenter. |
| 668 | 1304 | Ely Charlotte. |

| 668 | 1304 | Morgan Annie. |
| | | Beach Helen, wid. John. |
| | | " Charles. |
| 682 | 1336 | Baker Hattie, wid. Fred'k D. |
| | | Harding Anna. |
| | | Maligan Charles Mrs. |
| | | Hoskins William H. |
| | | Turner Lavinia Mrs. |
| | | Smith Horace M. |
| 684 | 1338 | " Mary J. wid. Frank H. |
| | | Sharples Samuel. |
| | | " James. |
| | | Hamlet Edward. |
| | | Fuller Frank S. |
| 696 | 1388 | Wright George E. |
| | | *Ely Street, E.* |
| 702 | 1400 | Goodwin Fannie B. wid. J. N. |
| | | Whitmore Harriette B. wid. O. H. |

+++++++++++++++++++++++++++++++++++++++++++++++++++++++++++++++++++

## STATE SENATORS;

*From District No. 1, since this State was Districted.*

Samuel Hart, 1830.
Romeo Lowrey, '31, '44, '48.
Samuel B. Woodward, '32.
James Dodd, 1833.
Joseph B. Gilbert, 1834.
Levi Barnes, 1835.
Wm. W. Ellsworth, 1836.
Martin Kellogg, 1837.
Charles A. Goodrich, 1838.
Julius S. Barnes, 1839.
Job Allyn, 1840.
William Robbins, 1841.
Alfred Smith, 1842.
Horace Gridley, 1848.
Isaac W. Stuart, 1845, '46.
Thomas C. Perkins, 1847.
James Dixon, 1849, 1854.
Isaac Toucey, 1850.
Henry C. Deming, 1851.
James T. Pratt, 1852.
Geo. M. Landers, '53, '69, '78.
Sam'l G. Merriman, 1855.
James B. Crosby, 1856.

Charles R. Chapman, 1857.
Dwight W. Pardee, '58, '59.
Elisha Johnson, 1860, '61, '70, '71.
Henry K. W. Welch, 1862.
Henry R. Bradley, 1868.
Amzi P. Plant, 1864.
Samuel Rockwell, 1865.
George Beach, 1866, '67.
Nathaniel B. Stevens, '68.
Charles M. Pond, 1872, '74, '75, '76. '77.
John R. Hills, 1878, '79, '81, '82, '83.
John R. Buck, '80; '81, J.R. B.resigned part this term.
Francis B. Cooley, '84. '85.
Edward S. Cleveland, 1886.
George G. Sumner, 1887.
Edward S. Cleveland, 1889, 1891, 1893.
John M. Hall, 1895.
Linus B. Plimpton, 1897.

## HISTORY OF EXPRESSES.

About 1840 a tri-weekly EXPRESS between this city and New York was commenced, which was sold to Harnden & Co. in 1842, but not proving remunerative, in a few months they sold out to Daniel Phillips, who carried on this business until he consolidated with other Expresses, July 1st, 1854, as the Adams Express Company. Adolphus Harnden was the pioneer expressman between Boston and New York, and was lost with 150 other passengers, on the burning steamer Lexington, on Long Island sound, Jan. 1840. Alvin Adams did errands and carried packages from Boston to New York via Norwich in 1840; and from the numerous post riders, who prior to 1849, used to visit cities, weekly, before the era of daily papers began, and distribute the weekly papers in all directions, as well as carrying light produce to cities and making purchases for persons on their routes; these post riders were the expressmen of former generations, announcing to customers their arrival, by blowing tin horns, instead of steam whistles. Previous to 1846 the redemption of the bills by the Hartford Banks was made weekly at the Suffolk Bank, Boston, by paying expenses of some Hartford business man, who might be going thither, to take on their carpet bag filled with bank bills and notes, and bring back their bills that had been redeemed by the Suffolk bank.

## REPRESENTATIVES FROM HARTFORD

*To the General Assembly of the State of Connecticut,*
SINCE ADOPTION OF THE 1818 CONSTITUTION.

Thomas S. Williams, 1819, '25, '27, '28, 29.
Michael Olcott, 1819.
Nathan Johnson, 1820, '21, '22. '23.
Henry Seymour, 1820.
Luther Savage, 1821.
Jeremy Hoadley, 1822, '23, '26, '28.
John Russ, 1824, '29.
Joseph Pratt, 1824, '33.
Henry Kilbourn, '25, '27, '35.
John M. Niles, 1826.
Henry L. Ellsworth, 1830.
Cyprian Nichols, 1830.
Thos. K. Brace, 1831, '32.
Eli Todd, 1831.
Jos. Trumbull, '32, '48, '51.
William Hayden, 1833.
Wm. Hungerford, 1834, '36.
Truman Hanks, 1834.
Wm. W. Ellsworth, 1835.
Jonathan Goodwin, 1836.
Henry Barnard, '37, '38, '39.
Roderick Terry, 1837.
Francis Parsons, 1838.
Melvin Copeland, 1839.
Thomas C. Perkins, 1840, '42, '43, '45, '46.
Charles Chapman, 1840, '47, '48, '62, '64.
Alfred Smith, 1841, '49.
Samuel Whitman, 1841.
Allyn S. Stillman, 1842.
Timothy M. Allyn, 1843.
James Dixon, 1844.
Isaac W. Stuart, 1844.
Ezra S. Hamilton, 1845.
David F. Robinson, '46, '54.
Chauncey Howard, 1847.
Henry C. Deming, 1849, '50, '59, '60 '61.
W.J.Hamersley, '50, '67, '70.
Edmund G. Howe, 1851.
Isaac Toucey, 1852.
James B. Crosby, 1852.
Wm. W. Eaton, 1853, '63, '68, '70, '71, '73, '74.
Alfred E. Burr, 1858, '66.

Daniel Phillips, 1854.
Rich'd D. Hubbard, '55, '58.
Edwin D. Tiffany, 1855, '59.
Alonzo W. Birge, 1856.
Charles R. Chapman, 1856.
Eliphalet A. Bulkeley, 1857.
Nathaniel Shipman, 1857.
Chas. H. Northam, '58, '60.
Thomas H. Seymour, 1861.
Abner Church, 1862.
Chas. M. Pond, 1863, '68.
Henry K.W. Welch, '64, '65.
Franklin Chamberlain, '65.
Nath'l B. Stevens, 1866, '67, '75, '76, '77.
Elisha Johnson, '69, '75, '76.
Norman Smith, 1869.
Monroe E. Merrill, 1871.
Charles R. Chapman, 1872.
Charles E. Perkins, 1872.
Sam'l F. Jones, 1873, '74.
Mahlon R. West, 1877, '81.
Stiles D. Sperry, 1878.
Thomas McManus, 1878.
Henry C. Robinson, 1879.
Lucius A. Barbour, 1879.
Lewis E. Stanton, 1880.
Gustavus F. Davis, 1880.
Joseph H. Sprague, 1881.
George G. Sill, 1882.
Charles H. Cooley, 1882.
Edward S. Cleveland, 1883.
Wilbert W. Perry, 1883.
Stephen A. Hubbard, 1884.
Leverett Brainard, 1884.
Charles M. Joslyn, 1885.
George O. Kinne, 1885.
William Hamersley, 1886.
John E.Scanlan, '86, '87, '88.
Frank E. Hyde, '87, '88, '89.
Andrew Smith, 1889.
Albert H. Walker, 1891.
Philip H. Fagan, 1891.
William Hamersley,*1893.
Patrick D. Ryan, 1893.
Wm. H. Watrous, 1895.
Rob't W. Barrett, 1895.
Joseph L. Barbour, 1897.
Robert A. Griffing, 1897.

*Resigned to accept appointment as Judge of the Superior Court.

# ABBREVIATIONS AND EXPLANATIONS.

The business location of individuals engaged in business for themselves, is first mentioned in connection with their names, and then their place of residence; *persons not thus engaged, but employed by others, are mentioned first as* AT THE *No. and street or* AT THE *company where employed, and then their place of residence.*

\* Signifies that only one partner of the firm name could be ascertained.

Where female names are mentioned without a prefix of Mrs. such are understood to be a Miss.

When two numbers are given in connection with one name, and only one street mentioned, the number first given is the place of business, and the second the residence, and both in the same street.

The letter h. signifies house; b. boards; l. lodges or rooms at; at. street; av. avenue; r. rear; u. upper tenement; pl. place; c. corner; ct. court; rd. road; ter. terrace; t. town; v. village; n. near; rm. room; etc.

We have omitted at the end of each line, av. pl. and ct. except in cases where streets and avenues have the same name. Therefore where the residences of individuals are put down as at New Britain, Farmington, Maple, etc., the word avenue is understood to follow. Abbreviations of names of streets, etc., are made as follows:—

| | | | | | | | |
|---|---|---|---|---|---|---|---|
| Alb. | Albany. | E.H.t. | East Hartford town. | Mar. | Market. | S.Ann. | South Ann. |
| Aly. | Allyn. | | | Mec. | Mechanic. | S.Hud. | South Hudson. |
| Am. | American. | Ev. | Evergreen. | Mor. | Morgan. | S.M.v. | South Manchester village. |
| Ash. | Ashley. | Fmt. | Fairmount. | Mul. | Mulberry. | | |
| Asy. | Asylum. | Far. | Farmington. | N.B. | New Britain av. | S.Pro. | South Prospect. |
| Bab. | Babcock. | Flow. | Flower. | N.B.t | New Britain town | St.Ry. | Street Railway. |
| Barb. | Barbour. | Fkn. | Franklin. | N.P. | New Park av. | T.v. | Thompsonville village. |
| Bart. | Bartholomew. | G t. | Glastonbury town. | N.t. | Newington town. | | |
| Blo. | Bloomfield. | | | N.E.R. | New York & New England R. R. | Tru. | Trumbull |
| B.t. | Bloomfield town. | Good. | Goodman. | | | Un.pl. | Union pl. |
| Blu. | Bluehills. | Gov. | Governor. | N.Y.R. | New York, New Haven & Hartford R. R. | Wads. | Wadsworth. |
| Bkm. | Buckingham. | Haw. | Hawthorn. | | | W.P.v. | Warehouse Point village. |
| B.v. | Burnside village. | Hdx. | Hendricxsen. | | | | |
| | | H.v. | Hockanum village. | Pk.ter. | Park terrace. | Wash. | Washington. |
| Cap. | Capitol. | | | Pav. | Pavilion. | Waw. | Wawarme. |
| Chas. | Charles. | Hung. | Hungerford. | P.&R. | Philadelphia and Reading R. R. | W.H.t. | West Hartford town. |
| Ch.O. | Charter Oak av. | Hun. | Huntley. | | | | |
| C.O.pl. | Charter Oak pl. | Huy. | Huyshope. | Ple. | Pleasant. | Weth. | Wethersfield av. |
| Chst. | Chestnut. | Jef. | Jefferson. | Por. | Portland. | Weth.t. | Wethersfield town. |
| Com. | Commerce. | Kil. | Kilbourn. | Pro. | Prospect. | | |
| Cong. | Congress. | Laf. | Lafayette. | Riv. | Riverside. | W.t. | Windsor town. |
| Cur. | Curcombe. | Law. | Lawrence. | Sey. | Seymour. | W.L.t. | Windsor Locks town. |
| Cush. | Cushman. | Mn. | Main. | Shel. | Sheldon. | | |
| Dvpt. | Davenport. | M.t. | Manchester town | Sig. | Sigourney. | Wdbg. | Woodbridge. |

# ADDITIONS, JULY, 1898.

Barker W. E. pianoteacher, h. 119 Albany.
**BEAULAC T. F.** manager for F. R. Slocum Marble Works, 1 Ford, h.u. 38 Wooster.
*See outside back cover.*
Bentley J. W. insurance agent, h. 189 Bellevue.
Bissell Catherine E. Mrs. removed to E.H.t.
Blake Charles S. at Harford Steam Boiler Insp. & Ins. Co. 650 Main, b. 215 Sigourney.
Bromley Daniel T. physician, 121, b. 121 Pearl.
Calef Edward B. grocer, h. 108 Capen.
Carlson Charles J. carpenter, h. 27 John.
Carpenter R. H. Mrs. h. 124 Church.
Carroll Henry T. mach. at Colts, h. 152 Brown.
Clark F. D. dentist, b. 189 Bellevue.
" Marion D. stenog. 197 Asy. b. 189 Bellevue.
Cole R. Brooks, with Potter & Payne, 405 Allyn, b. 1293 Main.
Colla Paul A. clerk at 1248 Main, b. 42 Village.
Collins L. J. attorney, 847 Main, b. 109 Wooster.
Cunningham Peter, bartender, b. 114 State.
Delorme Fred, h. 1081 Main.
Erley K. H. h. 231 Franklin.
Foly Dennis, mason, h.r. 259 Front.
Foster George H. engineer, 51 Ann, h. 32 Beach.
Gaffey J. J. weigher 70 Huy. h. 231 Franklin.
Harvey C. E. physician, 68 Pratt, rm. 44.
Hazard Nelson T. toolm. at Colts, h. 254 Weth.
Luther George H. h. 19 Center.
McLean Edward, janitor 666 Mn. h. 98 Walnut.
Murray Richard J. asst.supt. 756Mn. h. 67Julius.
Smith William C. grocer, 1248 Main, h. G.t.
Smith Gershom, auditor at Popes, h. 19 Girard.

## CYCLONES OR BLIZZARDS.

August 14, 1787, in Rockyhill, Glastonbury, Bolton and Coventry.
Over Litchfield, Hartford, Windham and New London counties, July 15, 1799.
In the last century near Meriden and Wethersfield; at Wallingford in 1878; at Winsted, July 2, 1883; at Burnside, Sept. 12, 1886.
March 11–13, 1888, occurred the heaviest snow and ice storm ever known, which shut off all communication from the city for nearly a week except by the long distance telephone.
July 18, 1893, a heavy thunder shower accompanied with cyclonic wind and hail visited Hartford, unroofing buildings and uprooting trees, doing great damage also to growing crops and tobacco in the towns of East Hartford and Glastonbury.
April 12, 1894, snow and high gale; drifts 8 feet deep in some parts of the state.
January 27–28, 1897, heaviest snow storm since the blizzard of 1888.
July 12–13, 1897, heavy wind and rain, causing a 19 foot freshet.

**JOB PRINTING** AT 16 STATE ST.

## FRESHETS IN THE CONN. RIVER.

All the highest freshets were caused by southeast rain storms of three to four days duration.

| | |
|---|---|
| 1639, great flood Mar. 10. | 1882, May 31, 14¾ feet. |
| 1642, great flood May, June | 1883, April 14, 20½ feet. |
| 1683, flood July, Aug. 26 ft. | 1883, April 25, 17⅞ feet. |
| 1692, water rose 26 ft. 2 in. | 1884, March 29, 21½ feet. |
| 1801, March 1, 27 feet 8 in. | 1884, April 21, 19¾ feet. |
| 1839, Jan. 29, 24 feet 2 in. | 1885, Jan. 5, 15 ft. 2 in. |
| 1841, 26 feet 4 inches. | 1885, April, 18 feet. |
| 1843, 27 feet 2 inches. | 1885, Nov. 8, 16 feet 9 in. |
| 1850, May, 21 feet 8 in. | 1886, Jan. 7, 18 feet 5 in. |
| 1852, April, 28 feet. | 1886, May 4, 21 feet 9 in. |
| 1854, May 1, 29 feet 10 in. | 1887, April 13, 23 feet 6 in. |
| 1856, Aug. 5, 18 feet. | 1888, April 8, 19 feet 5 in. |
| 1857, Feb. 22 feet 5 in. | 1889, April 21, 11 feet 9 in. |
| 1859, March, 26 feet 5 in. | 1889, Nov. 30, 15 feet 7 in. |
| 1861, April, 21 feet 6 in. | 1890, May 9, 15 feet. |
| 1862, April, 28 feet 8 in. | 1890, Oct. 26, 16 feet. |
| 1865, March, 24 feet 9 in. | 1891, Jan. 24, 17 feet 6 in. |
| 1867, April 19, 21 feet. | 1891, April 17, 19 feet 9 in. |
| 1868, Feb. 19, 21 feet 6 in. | 1893, May 6, 24 feet. |
| 1868, May 23d, 20 feet. | 1894, April 25, 13 8.10 feet. |
| 1869, April 23, 26 feet 8 in. | 1895, April 16, 25 feet 8 in. |
| 1869, Oct. 6, 26 feet 3 in. | 1896, March 3, 26 ft. 4 in. |
| 1870, Jan. 4, 19 feet 2 in. | 1897, March 25, 14 feet. |
| 1870, April 21, 25 feet 4 in. | 1897, April 10, 16 ft. 2 in. |
| 1872, April 13, 21 feet. | 1897, April 19, 16 ft. 3 in. |
| 1874, Jan. 9, 23½ feet. | 1897, May 16, 14 ft. 8 in. |
| 1876, April 16, 22 feet. | 1897, June 12, 19 feet 7 in. |
| 1877, April 30, 18½ feet. | 1897, July 16, 19 feet 9 in. |
| 1878, Dec. 13, 24½ feet. | 1898, March 16, 20 feet. |
| 1879, May 1, 21¼ feet. | 1898, March 22, 20 ft. 3 in. |
| 1881, April 26, 16 feet. | |

## POSTAGE STAMP AGENTS.

*Appointed by the Post Office Department, where the public can procure Stamps same as at the Post Office.*

90 Albany avenue, M. Greenbaum.
376 Asylum street, C. A. Rapelye.
5 Congress street, J. J. Seinsoth.
55 Farmington avenue, F. B. Edwards.
308 Main street, A. W. Sawtelle.
515     "     D. W. Tracy.
629     "     Kennelly & Co.
639     "     C. H. Bell.
852     "     L. H. Goodwin.
973     "     J. K. Williams.
1399     "     W. J. Anderson.
155 Windsor av. N. K. Morgan.
879     "     A. D. Pierce.
12 New Britain, H. Townsend.
205 Park street, Edwin Crary.
143 Trumbull street, T. R. Shannon.

## RAIN FALL.

Previous to 1872 the average rain fall in this city was about 50 inches. Since then the annual average has been 41.53 inches. In 1819 it was only 34 inches. Since 1872 there has been an averaged decrease. In 1888 35.46 inches; 1884, 41.24 inches; 1885, 48.71 inches; 1886, 55.07 inches; 1887, 45.07 inches; 1888, 58.91 inches; 1889, 43.97 inches; 1890, 50.01 inches; 1891, 52.39 inches; 1892, 39.10 inches; 1893, 49.00 inches; 1894, 43.05 inches; 1895, 48.36 inches.

## No. 61:

# GEER'S HARTFORD CITY DIRECTORY;
## JULY, 1898.

**A. D. VORCE CO.** art pictures, frames, etc. 752 Mn. Trust Co's bldg. *See p. 418.*
Aab Edith M. stenographer, b.2u. 15 Imlay.
" Emma E. clerk, b.2u. 15 Imlay.
" Kate, wid. Charles E. h.2u. 15 Imlay.
Abair Edward, wirew. at 618 Cap. b. 36 Laurel.
Abato Michael, bootblack, b.u. 64 Morgan.
Abbe Charles R. engineer, h. 223 Jefferson.
" E. H. painter at 20 Central, h. E.H.t.
" Elizabeth M. nurse, h. 48 Church.
" Ferren Wm. fi'e n. at 1189 Bd. b.u. 39 Grand.
" Harry A. G. theological student, 1507 Broad.
" Herbert C. electrician, h. 22 Spring.
" Lester G. wholesale fish,183 State,h. 24 East.
" Robert L. clerk at 658 Main, b. 24 East.
" Thomas, banker, 80 Pearl, rm. 4, h. Fkr.t
" William L. h. 110 High.
Abbey Edward M. builder, b. 375 Main.
" Eugene E. painter, b.u. 5 Atlantic.
" Geo. Myron, forem. 581 Cap. h.u. 18 Imlay.
" George W. carpenter, b.u. 5 Atlantic.
Abbie Lulu, b.2u. 1178 Main.
Abbot Edward H. b. 138 Jefferson.

**ABBOT JOHN C.** banker, bonds and investments, 49 Pearl, h. 138 Jefferson.
*See page 430.*

Abbott Chas. B. machinist at 388, b. 371 Capitol.
" Chas. W. helper at 1 Laurel, b. 371 Capitol.
" Lincoln H. h.u. 413 Garden.
" Louisa, wid. Merrill, h. 58 Buckingham.
Abel Alfred, stonecutter, b. 15 Martin.
" Chas. D. toolm. Popes, h. 83 Buckingham.
" Joseph, h 15 Martin.
" Solon H. repairer at 40 Gov. b. 19 Capitol.
Abell Earle F. clerk at 154 Pearl, b. 96 Ann.
" Orphie,wid. S P. h. 1153 Main.
" Sarah E. h. 96 Ann.
Abells Edward J. clerk at 98 Kil. h. 142 Mather.
Abels George F. furniture, 1180,h.u. 1341 Main.
Abelsohn John, agent, h. 231 Franklin.
Abernethy Edw'd T.toolm.at Colts,b.42 Seymour.
" William Henry, machinist at Thorne Type Setting Machine Co. 581 Cap. h. 42 Sey.
Abernovitch B. peddler, h.3u. 62 Avon.
Abery Harry, tinner at 164 State, b. E.H.t.
Abild Lydik C. painter, b. 93 Whitmore.
Abodie Frank, engineer, b. 141 Market.
Abrahamson A. deckhand, 285 State.
" Hans, blindmaker, 8 Sigourney, h.u. 43 Glendale.
Abram Patrick G. pressman at Popes, b. 53 Maple.

# Allyn House Drug Store,
## PHILO W. NEWTON,
# Druggist.
## SURGICAL INSTRUMENTS.
### No. 142 ASYLUM STREET,
**Corner of Trumbull st.**

Abramowitz Morris, tailor, h. 305 Market.
A. E. **ABRAMS**, Physician and Surgeon. Office 78 High street, house, 350 Laurel.
Hours—9 to 10 A. M.,
2 to 4 P. M.
Sunday no office hours.
Mondays, Wednesdays and Saturdays,
7 to 8 P. M.
Telephone 601-2.

Abrams Alva E. physician, 78 High, h.350 Laurel.
" Henry, cigarmkr. 867 Main, b. 74 Temple.
Abronza Alphonzo, barber, 20, h. 20 Kilbourn.
Abroza Charles, restaurant, 189, h.u. 189 Front.
Academy Immaculate Conception, 89 Church.
" Mount St. Joseph, 150 Farmington.
" of Sacred Heart, 158 Main.
Ackerly Theo. B. city physician, 2 Holcomb, h. 166 Franklin.
Ackerman Muna C. boilermaker at H. B. Beach & Son, 135 Grove, h.u. 31 Wolcott.
" Nels, filer at Popes, b. 31 Wolcott.
" Samuel, tailor at 149, h. 149 Front.
" Sidney W. clk. Adams Ex. Co. b. 117 Ann.
Ackley Elton E. agent at 427, h. 427 Main.
" Frank E. clerk at Popes, b. 41 Hungerford.
" Louise, clerk at 867 Main, b. 58 Church.
Acme Machine Screw Co. Vredendale.
Adair Arthur S. rubberwkr. at 690, h. 865 Park.
" Fred D. clerk at 818 Park.
" George A. rubberworker at 690 Park, h. 7 Washington.
" Jas. H. rubberwkr. 690 Park, h. 17 Sisson.
" Moses, rubberwkr. at 690, h. 865 Park.
Adam A. storage batterym. 266 Pearl, b. 18 Bkm.
Adams Abel S. clerk at 159 Asy. b. 1080 Main.
" Addison L. painter at 41 Albany, h. Suffield.
" Albert R. clerk at 852 Main, b. 77 Elm.
" Alex C. ass't secretary Ætna Insurance Co. 666 Main, b. 111 Elm.

Adams Alfred M. carpenter, h. 397 Capitol.
" Arthur, carpenter, h. 54 Prospect av.
" & Atkins, wagon manufacturers, 10 Charles.
  Edward Adams.          George A. Atkins, Jr.
" Burt M. clerk at 319 Cap. h. 249 Lawrence.
" C. F. Co. household goods, Ernest C. Shepard, manager, 261 Asylum.
" C. George, waiter 33, b. 33 Prospect.
" Charles F. printer, h. 302 Asylum.
" Charles F. (C. F. A. Co.) h. Erie, Penn.
" Charles H. advertising solicitor, 7 Central, h. 28 Hopkins.
" Charles H. constable, h. 28 Madison.
" Charles Hemmenway, associate editor Hartford Courant, 66 State, b. Sigourney House, 1150 Main.
" Chauncey H. bkkpr. at 690 Park, b. 53 Cap.
" Clifford G. at 369 Capitol, b. 249 Lawrence.
" Edward (A. & Atkins) h. W.H.t.
" Edward T. tailor, 25 Asy. b. 26 Sanford.
" Effie M. at 133 Sheldon, b. 302 Asylum.
" Elizabeth, wid. M. Clark, boardinghouse, 1080 Main.
" Elizabeth V. teacher Arsenal school, b. Cromwell t.
" Emma C. wid. George, h. 300 Wethersfield.
" Emma J. housekeeper, 1233 Main.
**ADAMS EXPRESS CO.** office 805 Main, branch office Union R. R. depot, 466 Asylum.        *See page 553.*
" Ezra S. h. 77 Elm.
" F. Amelia, wid. J. M. h. 320 Windsor av.
" Frank D. carpenter, h.u. 140 Maple.
" Frank P. at 77 Pearl, b. 140 Maple.
" Frank S. grinder, 388 Capitol, b. W.H.t.
" Fred. A. engir. 650 Mn. h.u. 41 Buckingham.
" Fred. L. machinist at Sigourney Tool Co. 9 Sigourney, b. 397 Capitol.
" Geo. H. night train despatcher, Union depot, l. 44 High.
" George L. clerk, 164 State, h. So. Weth.
" Harry M. clerk at 193, b. 32 Asylum.
" Henry, waiter steamer Hartford, 285 State.
" Henry J. plumber at 450 Mn. b. 31 Village.
" Hotel, M. Colburn, Albany c. Blue Hills.
" J. D. bkkpr. 145 State, h. Wethersfield.
" James, b. 1176 Main.
" Jas. M. printer at Hartford Times, 716 Main. h.u. 10 Canton.
" Jane A. wid. John, laundress, h. 51 Mather.
" Jane J. wid. Franklin D. h. 140 Maple.
" Jennie M. clerk, b. 140 Maple.
" Jessie A. wid. W. J. h. 167 Clark.
" John Q. clerk, h. 140 Maple.

Adams Lizzie M. b. 1080 Main.
" Margaret T. wid. John W. h. 9 Harrison.
" Mary H. b. 91 Ann.
" Mary S. Mrs. b. 1150 Main.
" Mary S. clerk at 1189 Broad, h. 48 Grand.
" Roswell, b. 1113 Main.
" Samuel G. plumber, h. 149 Maple
" Sarah, wid. Chester, h. 22 Winthrop.
" Sarah, wid. Henry, h. 15 Huntley pl.
" Seth B. insp'r at Hartford Steam Boiler Insp. & Ins. Co. 650 Mn. h.u. 17 Ashley.
" Sherman W. attorney, 700 Main, room 7, *sec'y park commissioners,* b. 125 Park.
" Susan A. clerk National Life Association, 53 Trumbull, b. 77 Elm.
" W. J. motorman St.Ry. h. 49 Dean.
" William, hackdriver at 15½ Babcock.
" Wm. C. janitor, Trinity Col. h.u. 26 Sanford.
" Wm. H. goldbeater 41 Tru. b. 15 Huntley pl.
" William J. conductor St.Ry. h. 8½ Park.
Adamson Alex. foreman at 133 Shel. h. 50 Mahl.
" Geo. coremaker at 1 Flower, b.u. 179 Law.
" Henry P. assemb. at 556 Cap. b.u. 179 Law.
" Mary, wid. Henry, b. 5 Curcombe.
" Mary, wid. John, h. 179 Lawrence.
" Robert F. coremaker, b.u. 179 Lawrence.
Adcock Herbert, insp'r, 1 Flow. h. 36 Hopkins.
" John W. mach. at 1 Flow. h. 54 Barbour.
Addis Fred W. printer at 141 Pl. b. 19 Capitol.
" Martin O. toolmaker at 476 Capitol, h. 21 Woodbine.
" T. Emmett, student at Trinity College, b. 21 Woodbine.
Adelsohn Israel, peddler, h.u. 243 Market.
" Samuel, grocer, 70, h. 70 Windsor.
Adiano Joseph, masontender, h. 33 North.
Adianolfi Antonio, grocery, 176, h. 192 Front.
Adkins Frank H. mach. at 1 Flow. h. 145 Collins.
" Frederick A. brushmaker, h. 200 Evergreen.
" John B. printer at 252 Pearl, l. 943 Main.
" ☞ see also Atkins.
Adler Abraham Moriss, b.u. 264 Front.
" H. S. floorwalker at 921 Main, b. 66 Capitol.
Adlund Peter, at 142 Russ, h. 164 Babcock.
Adriance Francis H. h. 81 Vernon.
Aemuro Giovanni, barber, 83 Windsor, h 119 Front.
Ætna Indemnity Co. 650 Main.
**AETNA INSURANCE CO.** (*Fire*), office 666 Main.  *See pages 442 and 443.*
**AETNA LIFE INSURANCE CO.** office 650 Main.         *See page 449.*
**AETNA MACHINE CO.** special machinery, 77 Commerce.  *See page 532.*
**AETNA NATIONAL BANK,** 644 Main, cor. Atheneum.   *See page 481.*
" Pyrotechnic Co. Albert Marwick, jr. 377 Asylum.
**AETNA STAMP WORKS,** F. E. Smith, 25 Asylum.  *See page 429.*
Agard Charles, mach. at Popes, h. 49 Wdbg.
" Charles F. carpenter, 53 Vernon, h. 70 Bond.
Aghamalian Malcom G. mach. 26 High, h.u. 15 Church.

Agillo Paul, laborer, b. 7 Charles.
Agnew Seymour P. const. 29 Pearl, h. 68 Hung.
Agney Fred'k W. postal clerk, h.u. 27 Ward.
Ahern Anna J. teacher South School, 36 Wadsworth, b. 55 Sigourney.
" Bert, plumber at 11 Haynes, h.u. 2 May ct.
" Catharine, wid. Nicholas, h. 259 Front.
" Catherine, wid. William, h. 90 Ward.
" Cornelius, laborer, b.u. 82 Front.
" Daniel, mason, 38, h. 38 Crown.
" Daniel, carpenter at 141 Tru. b. New Park.
" Daniel B. carpenter, b. 207 Sheldon.
" Daniel W. blacksm. at 54 Arch, h. 207 Shel.
" David, brickmason, b. 38 Crown.
" David, deckhand str. Hartford, 285 State.
" David J. assembler at Colts, h. 47 Huyshope.
" Edward, mason, b. 38 Crown.
" Edward J. b. 348 Front.
" Ellen, wid. Patrick, h.u. 107 Windsor.
" Eugene, brakeman, N.Y.R. h.3u.r. 28 Wal.
" Eugene F. brakeman, b.u. 107 Windsor.
" Francis, mason, b. 190 Pearl.
" Hannah N. b. 55 Sigourney.
" Henry M. yardman, 25 Front, h. 3 Center.
" J. deckhand, steamer Hartford, 285 State.
**AHERN JAMES,** plumber, gas fixtures, 280 Asy. h. 55 Sigourney. *See page 505.*
" John, h. 77 Elm.
" John, casehardener at Popes, h. 23 Sargeant.
" John, electrician at St.Ry. h.u. 338 Park.
" John, farmer, h. New Park av.
" John, laborer, h. 40 Ward.
" John, laborer, 556 Capitol, h. 90 Ward.
" John, student, b. 3 Center.
" John A. h. 76 Hudson.
" John B. carptr. at 133 Sheldon, h. 545 Main.
" John J. clerk, 29 Morris, b. 144 Capitol.
" John J. steamfitter, h. 107 Windsor.
" John J. (*McCarthy & A.*) b. 194 Pearl.
" John W. asst. supt. 721 Main, h.u. 91 Jef.
" Kate N. dressmaker, 144, h. 144 Capitol.
" Margaret, dressmaker, b. 23 Sargeant.
" Margaret, wid. Edward, h. 348 Front.
" Margaret, wid. Thomas, b. 34 Flower.
" Margaret M. b. 55 Sigourney.
" Matthew J. stonecutter at New England Granite Works, 1260 Main, h. 3 Center.
" Maurice, ast. foreman, 556 Cap. h.u. 142 Bab.
" Maurice, shoemaker, 176 Windsor av. h.u. 142 Windsor.
" Michael, molder at 54 Arch, h. 43 Huyshope.
" Michael F. molder at 54 Arch, h. 43 Huy.
" Nicholas, ostler, b. 259 Front.
" Patrick F. molder 556 Cap. b. 107 Windsor.
" Patrick J. storekeeper, State Prison, h.2u. 133 Maple.
" Peter D. b. 91 Jefferson.
" Thos. P. shoemaker, at 91 Windsor av. h. 16 Russell.
" William, corem. 556 Capitol, h.u. 13 Front.
" William J. switchman, h.u. 62 Loomis.
" William T. saloon, 49, h.u. 49 Sheldon.
Ahlbrecht Wm. F. trav. salesm. h. 187 Bellevue.
Ahler John G. machinist at 1 Flower, b. 22 Bab.
Ahlgreen Herman, bakery, 12 Queen, b.u. 61 Haw.

Ahlstrom Alma, laundress at 20 South Hudson.
Aishberg Edwin, boots, shoes, 913 Mn. h. 30 Bkm.
" Lena M. wid. Henry, h. 30 Buckingham.
Aitken James C. machinist at 1 Flower, h. S.M.t.
Akerberg Charles, milkman, h. Fishfry.
**AKERLIND JOHN A.** tailor, 205 Park, h.u. 40 Grand. *See page 424.*
Albert John, clerk, 858 Main, b. 44 Sumner.
" Louis, soda water, 211, h.u. 232 Front.
Albin Fred. W. brakeman N.Y.R. h. 78 Chestnut.
" James J. painter at 352 Albany, 70 Union pl.
Albiston James A. carpenter, 53 Vernon, h.S.M.t.
Albrecht Fritz, baker at 238, b. 238 New Park.
Albro J. H. motorman, St.Ry. b. 80 State.
" Jas. W. shoemaker, 18 N.B. h.u. 189 Maple.
" Mary A. nurse, 33, b.u. 33 Wooster.
**MAX ALBU,** physician, office 703 Main, room 8. Hours—2 to 3.30 P.M. 6 to 7.30 P.M.
Albu Max F. physician, 703 Main, h. 32 Capitol.
Albun Abraham, peddler, h. 40 North.
Alcock [☞ *see Elcock.*
**ALCORN HUGH M.** attorney at law, 57 Pratt, b. Suffield t. *See page 485.*
" Robert T. carpenter, h.2u. 93 Chestnut.
Alden Charles A. agent, 756 Main, b. 197 Jef.
" Frank H. painter, b. 197 Jefferson.
" Herbert W. foreman, 1 Laurel, h. 464 Far.
" Mary Mrs. h. 197 Jefferson.
" Moses, harnessmaker, h. 518 Main.
Alderman A. C. Mrs. dressm. 14, h. 14 Church.
" A. Paul, clerk at 852 Main, b. M.t.
" Alice H. wid. Alfonso, b. 33 Allen pl.
" Elbert T. butcher at 493, l.u. 1122 Main.
" Horace F. butcher, 123 Ann, b.u. 54 Wooster.
" James S. grocer, 472, h. 474 Windsor av.
Aldrich Bertel V. carpenter, h. 222 Maple.
" Charles E. electrician, h. 45 Park.
" D. E. cashier, 375 Asylum, b. 96 Church.
" Frank H. h.u. 11 Canton.
" Louis M. carpenter, h. 224 Maple.
" Pertia W. taxidermist, h. Franklin pl. 3d h.
" S. P. seamstress, h.3u. 40 Asylum.
Aldridge Geo. T. printer 141 Pl. h. 823 Broad.
Aldro Pratzel, laborer, b. 29 Commerce.
Alesantra Joseph, bootblack, h.u. 83 Windsor.
" Pepino, laborer, h. 319 Front.
Aleshiusky Casper, saloon, 92 Front.

Alexander Andrew, tailor at 544 Main, h. E.H.t.
" Benjamin, tailor, 168 Front, h. 68 Pleasant.
" Edward W. tailor, 856, l. 856 Main.
" Ellen Frances Mrs. h.u. 10 Lewis.
" & Elmer, bicycles and sundries, 744 Main.
        Robert M. Alexander.     Lucius N. Elmer.
" Emma G. wid. John C. dressm. b.51 Windsor.
" Geo. W. jeweler, 125, h. 125 Maple.
" Joel S. blacksmith at 54 Com. h. 41 Laurel.
" John, bricklayer, b. 51 Lafayette.
" John, electroplater, 39 Tru. h.u. 31 Bellevue.
" Louis, shoemaker, 251, b. 279 Park.
" Moses, clothing, 144, h. 144 Front.
" Robert M. ( A. & Elmer) b. 4 Huyshope.
" Rose, music teacher, b. 68 Pleasant.
" Samuel, agent, l.u. 720 Main, rm. 7.
" Sarah, wid. Charles, b. 75 Clark.
" William L. operator, 388 Capitol, b. E.H.t.
Alfarno Tony, fruit store, 31, h. 31 Laurel.
Alfier Vittorio, grocer, 174, h. 174 Front.
Alfred Merritt A. salesman, 201 Asylum, h. 116
    Huntington.
" Rachel E. wid. Augustus B. h. 116 Hunt-
    ington.
Alger John, mach. A. S. Cook Co. h. 79 Seymour.
" Lucien, firem. str. Middletown, h.u. 230 Aly.
" Lucien J. machinist 80 Huy. h.2u. 92 Park.
" ☞ See also Allger.
Allarde Amelia M. b.u. 220 Sheldon.
" Camille, dropforger, h.u. 220 Sheldon.
" Josie, clerk, 921 Main, b.u. 220 Sheldon.
Allardyce Charles B. boilermaker, h.u. 37 Center.
" M. M. Miss, at Travelers Insurance Co. 56
    Prospect, b.u. 37 Center.
Allen Adelaide A. h. 37 Huntington.
" Albert, operator, 388 Cap. b. 96 Chestnut.
" Albert B. frescopainter, h.2u. 29 Kennedy.
" Albert L. ( Allen Bros.) h.u. 183 Seymour.
" Albert O. stocker at Colts, b. 31 Woodbridge.
" Alden J. machinist, h. 31 Woodbridge.
" Alex. secy. Spring Brook Ice Co. 4 Central,
    h. 280½ Laurel.
" Alfred H. mach. at Colts, b. 31 Woodbridge.
" Aline M. musicteacher, b. 234 Sigourney.
" Alonzo A. molder at 1 Flower, b. 365 Main.
" Ann, h.u. 72 Governor.
" Annie P. wid. B. Rowland, h. 84 Vernon.
" Aven L. foreman stocking department at
    Colts, h.u. 69 Seymour.
" Bert A. boxm. 274 Pearl, b.2u. 129 Albany.
" Brothers, grocers, etc., 466 Main.
        Albert L. Allen.     Irving W. Allen.
" Caroline S. teacher Arsenal sch. b. 38 Brook.
" Charles, b. 51 Imlay.
" Charles, b.3u. 279 Asylum.
" Charles, mason, h.3u. 49 New Britain.
" Charles, motorman, St.Ry. h. 48 Windsor.
" Charles A. machinist at Pratt & Whitney
    Co. 1 Flower, h. 80 Hopkins.
" Charles Dexter, bookkeeper at 31 Pratt,
    literary editor Hartford Post, h.78 Vernon.
" Charles Dwight, clerk, 8 Hurlburt, b. 133
    Sargeant.
" Charles Mrs. clerk, Brown, Thomson & Co.
    942 Main, h. 48 Windsor.

Allen Charles M. Mrs. (Ida F.) b. 59 Capitol.
" Charles W. bkkpr. 2 S. Ann, h. 105 Hung.
" Dwight, shade holders 284 Asy.h.Springfield.
" E. Henry, clerk at Popes, h.u. 33 Julius.
" Edgar, insp. at Popes, h. 258 Jefferson.
" Edward, laborer, h. 4 Putnam.
" Edward C. bookkeeper at Hartford Tele-
    gram, 12 Central, h. 70 Congress.
" Edward H. bkkpr. at Popes, h. 531 Broad.
" Edwin S. at Ætna Ins. Co. 666 Main, b. 61
    Williams.
" Elizabeth, at 1 S. Ann, b. 7 Hungerford.
" Elmer A. toolmaker at Popes, h. Ellsworth.
" Emily Mrs. prop. Franklin house, 518 Main.
" Emily S. wid. Albert N. b. 31 Woodbridge.
" Emma G. h. 41 Webster.
" Eustace L. b. 859 Prospect av.
" Francis B., 2d v.pres't Hartford Steam Boiler
    Insp. & Ins. Co. 650 Main, h. 61 Willard.
" Francis N. at Ætna Life Ins. Co. 650 Main,
    h. 234 Sigourney.
" Frank S. chief inspector Hfd. Steam Boiler
    Insp. and Ins. Co. 650 Mn. h.u. 42 Seymour.
" Frederick, h. 40 Babcock.
" Frederick I. clerk, 466 Main, b.u. 183 Sey.
" Frederick V. pressman at 690 Park b. 47
    Woodbine.
" Geo. E. machinist at 581 Cap. h. 46 Grand.
" Geo. E. salesm. 1 Flower, b. 41 Hungerford.
" Geo. F. driver, h.u. 96 Chestnut.
" George H. h. 112 Maple.
" George I. clerk at State Capitol, Highway
    Commission, rm. 27, h. Middletown t.
" George M. h. 48 Allen pl.
" Grace M. nurse, b.2u. 96 Chestnut.
" Grosvenor N. correspondent at Popes, b. 18
    Garden.
" Harry, farmer, b. 990 Windsor av.
" Henry C. rubberw. 690 Park, h. 19 Sisson.
" Henry S. mach. 1 Flower, b. 236 Jefferson.
" Howard, clerk, Pratt & Whitney Co. 1
    Flower, b. 96 Chestnut.
" Irving W. ( Allen Bros.) h.u. 171 Seymour.
**ALLEN ISAAC A. Jr.** architect, 904
    Main, Ballerstein building, rm. 87, h. 34
    Mahl.                  See page 519.
" James, teamster at 153, b. 153 Zion.
" Jas. B. storehouse, Popes, h.u. 5 Hungerford.
" James H. laborer, h.u. 81 Green.
" Jas. P. secy. and treas. Hartford Carriage
    Co. h. 370 Asylum, rm. 34.
" James W. bridgebuilder, b.u. 289 Asylum.
ALLEN JEREMIAH M. president Hartford Steam
    Boiler Insp. and Ins. Co. 650 Main, h. 138
    Collins.              See page 446.
" John, brickmaker, b. Windsor av.
" John, machinist at N.Y.R. h.r. 28 Walnut.
" John, treasurer Hartford Theological sem-
    inary, 1507 Broad, h. 65 Washington c.
    Allen pl.
" John C. clerk at 197 Asy. b. 280½ Laurel.
" John S. iceman, 4 Central, l.u. 58 Grove.
" Joseph, tailor, l. 10 Goodman.
" Julian S. civil engineer, b. 859 Prospect av.

Allen L. F. Mrs. h.u. 39 Wooster.
" Leonard M. credit clerk, Popes, 436 Capitol, b. 258 Jefferson.
" Lewis W. physical instructor at High school, h. 67 Ashley.
" Libbie M. nurse, 96, b. 96 Church.
" Lizzie G. wid William, h. 51 Liberty.
" Lizzie M. at 690 Park, b. 28 Walnut.
" Louis G. conductor St.Ry. b. 80 State.
" Lucy F. wid. Davenport, h. 54 Babcock.
" Mary Mrs. h.u. 1232 Main.
" Mary, wid. Bernard, h. 7 Hungerford.
" Mary, teacher at 690, b. 690 Asylum.
" Mary Catherine, dressmaker, b. 4 Putnam.
" Mary W. student, b. 520 Farmington.
" Moses D. harnessmaker at 8 Sig. h. 142 Main.
" Nathan H. music teach. 926, h. 926 Mn. rm. 87.
ALLEN NORMAND F. (Sage, Allen & Co.) dry goods, etc., 894-902 Main, h. 520 Farmington.
" Patrick, enameler, 581 Cap. b. 101 Sheldon.
" Rachel, wid. Alonzo, b. 283 Collins.
" Ripley D. furnaces, 3 Grove, h. 133 Sargeant.
" Russell J. mach. at 1 Flower, h. 853 Park.
" Sadie R. stenographer, 267 Asy. b. W.P.v.
" Samuel, bookkeeper, b.u. 75 Chestnut.
" Samuel, molder at 1 Flower, b. 401 Capitol.
" Samuel H. pastor Catholic Apostolic church, h. 859 Prospect av.
" Samuel W. h. 103 Webster.
" Sidney H. prop. Arlington house, 999 Main.
" Simeon J. pinm. Jewell Pin Co. h.u. 289 Asy.
" Theophilus, pinm. at Brown, Thomson & Co. 942 Main, h. Windsor t.
" Thomas, teamster, b. 18 Dean.
" Thomas T. enameler, 581 Cap. b.u. 5 Affleck.
" Thomas W. driver, b. 15 Mather.
" W. Bradford, secy. and treas. Premier Mfg. Co. 437 Main, h. 371 Laurel.
" Walter B. student at Yale, b. 61 Willard.
" William, laborer, b.u. 11 John.
" William, laborer, h2u. 180 Walnut.
" William A. laborer, h.u. 16 Arch.
" William G. supt. 135 Sheldon, h. 427 Main.
" Wm. H. driver 1177, Main, h. 45 Windsor.
" William J. mach. at P.&R. h.u. 72 Walnut.
" William J. policeman, b2u. 289 Asylum.
" Wm. R. clerk at 149 State, b. 280 Laurel.
" ☞ see also Allyn; Alling.
Allender James H. mechanic, b. 4 Village.
Allge Geo. J. patternmkr. Colts, h. 34 Annawan.
Allger Manley H. motorm. St.Ry. b.2u. 126 Mar.
" William, driver at 356 Main, b. 39 John.
Alling Alma A. Mrs. dressmaker, 721, h. 721 Main, rm. 71.
ALLING BUEL B. mgr. Walnut Lodge Hospital Co. 56 Fairfield, h. 29 Allen pl. See page 712.
" Charles R. clerk, b. 70 Spring.
" Eliza, wid. Marcus B. b. 29 Allen pl.
" Frank N. car repairer, 53 Vernon, h.u. c. Maple and King.
" Jane, wid. Chas. J. h. 70 Spring.
Allis Ferdinand W. printer at Times, 716 Main, h. 405 Wethersfield.

Allis Frances M. b. 90 Edwards.
Allison David, blksm. at 366 Allyn, b. 42 Church.
" Margaret J. wid. Fred. A. h. 169 Ashley.
" Jane, wid. Hugh, h. 63 Spring.
" Whittaker, driver at 71 Asy. h. 63 Spring.
" William, carpenter, P.& R. h. 71 Williams.
Allston John, porter, h.u. 45 Liberty.
Allyn Robert Mrs. (Belle M.) h. 44 Garden.
" Ella C. Mrs. b. 12 Whitney.
ALLYN HOUSE DRUG STORE, 142 Asylum. See page 35.
" House, 152 Asylum, John J. Dahill, mgr.
" John W. clerk, b. 6 Buckingham.
" Robert J. h. 44 Garden.
" Wm. W. carpenter at 252 Pearl, h. Bloomfield.
" ☞ see also Allen; Alling.
Alms House, 2 Holcomb.
Alpress Sarah M. Miss, h.u. 4 Marsh.
Alquist Clara, bkpr. 13 Haynes, b. 58 Church.
Alston Theodore M. laborer, h. Brady.
Altemus Edw. S. clerk at 97 Asy. h. 103 Ann.
" W. F. & Co. Mfg. Diamond Compound, 9 Asylum.
" Wm. F. (W. F. A. & Co.) h. 526 Pro. av.
Alter Fred. E. machinist at Pratt & Whitney Co. 1 Flower, b.u. 44 Hopkins.
" M. H. Mrs.: h.u. 44 Hopkins.
" Wm. Hale, mach. 1 Flow. b.u. 44 Hopkins.
Altman Philip, barber at 187 Front, h. 8 North.
Alton Chas. inspector at 476 Capitol, h. E.H.t.
" Charles D. physician, 86, h. 86 Farmington.
Alvord Alfred B. contractor at James L. Howard & Co. 438 Asylum, h.u. 105 Windsor av.
" Carrie L. wid. J. C. h.u. 8 Ashley.
" Edwin D. (C. H. Strant & Co.) h. Vernon t.
" Ida J. insurance, b. 981 Main.
" Wm. E. pres't and mgr. Merchants National Trading Association, 66 State, h. M.t.
Ambro Michael, barber, 144 h. 180 Front.
Ambruso Frank, laborer, b.u. 64 Morgan.
Ameluxen John P. screwmkr. 476 Cap. h. E.H.t.
Amentello Mark M. laborer, h.u. 210 Front.
American Cycle Repair Co. 540 Main.
    E. L. Wheeler.    Robert Painter.
" Dist. Telegraph & Messenger Co. 6 Central.
" Emigrant Co. 25 Forest.
" Gang Syphon Well Co. 220 State.
" Hotel, Geo. T. Arthur, manager, 103 State.
AMERICAN NATIONAL BANK OF HARTFORD, 803 Main. See page 431.
AMERICAN PUBLISHING CO. 424 Asylum. See page 473.
" Real Estate Co. 904 Main, rm. 30.
" School for Deaf, 690 Asylum.
" Specialty Co. 135 Sheldon.
" Steam Laundry, W. H. Clements, 788 Park.
Amerman Charles A. boilermaker, 109 Commerce, h. 16 Pawtucket.
" Chas. B. machinist, h. 16 Atwood.
" Edward R. inspector Popes, h.2u. 38 Park.
" James P. (P. A. & Son,) h. 16 Atwood.
" Katherine A. wid. Chas. D. h.2u. 7 Goodwin.
" Mariam, at 59½ Trumbull, b. 365 Weth.

Amerman Peter (*P. A. & Son,*) h. 204 Weth.
" Peter & Son, boilerworks, 109 Commerce.
    P. Amerman.          J. P. Amerman.
" Rhoda, at 59½ Trumbull, b. 365 Weth.
" Wm. foreman, 109 Com. h. 365 Wethersfield.
Ames Bert T. florist, b. Quaker lane, W.H.t.
" Charles H. farmer, b. Quaker lane, W.H.t.
" Charles L. principal Brown school, 160 Market, h. 1281 Main.
" Eugene D. farmer, h. Quaker lane, W.H.t.
" Frederick P. carpenter at 155 Charter Oak, h.u. 876 Broad.
" Louis M. billing clerk, P.&R.R. h. 131Tru.
" May D. Mrs. music teacher, h.131 Trumbull.
" Samuel, b. 9 Preston.
" ☞ *see also Eames.*
Amick Chas. L. brakeman, N.Y.R. h.u. 36 Pratt
AMIDON FREDERICK S. wire screens, etc., r. 60 Temple, h. 50 Westland.  *See page 40.*
" Henry, h.u. 18 Russell.
" Willie Henry, carpenter, h. Park st. W.H.t.
Ammann Henry, baker, h.u. 45 Morgan.
Ammon John, b. 2 Holcomb.
Amorose Michael, lab. Pope Tube Co. h.u. 67 Mor.
Anders ☞ *See also Enders.*
Andersen Andrew J. polisher at 476 Capitol, h.u. 21 Hamilton.
" Hans, brazier at Popes, b. 12 Woodbine.
" Thomas, asst. supt. Prudential Ins. Co. h. Whiting lane, W.H.t.
Anderson Adelphia, wid. George, b.2u. 8 State.
" Adolph, carpenter, b.u. 147 Babcock.
" Albin, pressman at 690 Park, h. 27 Francis.
" Alexander, cabinetm. 69 Front, b.191 Capen.
" Alfred, carpenter, h. 31 Hungerford.
" Alfred, shoem. 59 Farmington, b.31 Putnam.
" Amandus P. filer at Popes, b. 151 Babcock.
" Andrew, at Hartford Electric Light Co. b. 234 Pearl.
" Andrew, laborer at 618 Capitol, b. 4 Elm.
" Andrew, motorm. St.Ry. b.u. 80 State.
" Andrew, watchman 476 Cap. h. 1157 Broad.
" Andrew G. mach. 581 Cap. b. 167 Babcock.
" Andrew G. mach. at 30 Cush. h. 110 Ward.
" Andrew J. buffer at Popes, h. Burnside v.
" Andrew M. cutter, 15 Tru. b. 23 Hamilton.
" Andrew S. beltm. at 15 Tru. h. 50 Willow.
" Annie Mrs. h. 18 Gold.
" Anthon S. b. 16 Squire.
" August, at 59½ Tru. b.r. 16½ Affleck.

Anderson August, mach. at 1 Flow. b. 301 Law.
" August W. blacksmith, 201 Smith, h. Fairview.
" Augusta, restaurant, 301, h. 301 Lawrence.
" Augustus A. mason, b. 301 Lawrence.
" Carl, coachman at 466, b. 466 Farmington.
" Carl J. mach. at Popes, h.2u. 164 Putnam.
" Carl J. rubberwrkr. 690 Park, b.u. 147 Bab.
" Carrie L. dressmaker, h. 17 South Ann.
" Charles, builder, h.r.u. 48 Cedar.
" Charles, butcher at Newton & Burnett, b. 13 Hungerford.
" Charles, cook at 149 High, h. 45 Chestnut.
" Charles, laborer Pope Tube Co. b. 291 Park.
" Charles A. at 618 Capitol, b.2u. 74 Putnam.
" Charles A. steamfitter at Popes, h. 291 Park.
" Charles C. porter at 273 Asylum, h. E.H.t.
" Charles G. footman at 30, b. 30 Wethersfield.
" Charles H. rubberwrkr. 690 Pk.h.99 Hamilton.
" Charles J. bank watchman, h. 22 Morris.
" Charles J. cook, b.u. 49 Green.
" Charles J. laborer, h. 153 Washington.
" Charles J. restaurant 613, h. 611 Capitol.
" Charles O. carpenter, b. 17 Walcott.
" Charles O. cutter at 59½ Tru. h.u. 8 Brady pl.
" Christena, wid. Andrew, h.3u. 277 Main.
" Christian J. milkman, 1, h. 1 Flatbush.
" Christian T. laborer, b. Whitinglane, W.H.t.
" David, boilermaker at H. B. Beach & Son, 135 Grove, b. 21 Wadsworth.
" Edward, helper 133 Sheldon, b. 80 Front.
" Edward, teamster, b.u. 17 Affleck.
" Edw. P. washer at r. 1214 Mn. h. 12 Village.
" Elbert, printer, b.2u.r. 1048 Broad.
" Elbridge P. clerk, 20 Sargeant, b. 66 Williams.
" Emil, carpenter, b. 31 Hungerford.
" Emma, wid. David, h.2u. 38 John.
" Emma L. stenogr. 62 Market, b.2u. 38 John.
" Eric, roofer, h.u.r. 23 West.
" Eric J. patternmaker, b. 167 Babcock.
" Ernest, baker at 385 Main, h.r. 16 Squire.
" Frank, carpenter, b. 98 Babcock.
" Gustav, b. 167 Babcock.
" Gustavus, gardener at 687, b. 687 Asylum.
" Hannah, wid. David, h. 136 State.
" Hans, deckhand str. Middletown, 285 State.
" J. B. quarterm. str. Hartford, h. Brockways.
" James, at 1 Flower, b.u. 1204 Broad.
" John, (*Anderson L. & Co.*) h. 44 Putnam.
" John, carder at 59½ Tru. h. 4 Brady pl.
" John, laborer, h. Fairview.
" John, ostler at 143, b. 143 Capitol.
" John A. stairbldr. Taft Co. h.2u. 74 Putnam.
" John A. buffer at Popes, b.u. 291 Park.
" John D. mach. at 388 Capitol, b. 136 State.
" John E. at 734 Main, h. 167 Babcock.
" John G. h.u. 110 Ward.
" Joseph, sawyer, 335 Sheldon, b. 37 Liberty.
" Joseph A. laborer, b. 37 Liberty.
" Justus D. secretary Hartford Rubber Works, h. 63 Kenyon.
" Knut, filer, b.r. 9 Hungerford.
" Knut H. stonecutter, h. 613 Capitol.
" Larson & Co. books, stationery, etc. 322 Asy.
    John Anderson.          Oscar Anderson.
" Louis G. operator at 40 Gov. b. 46 Putnam.

Anderson Louis J. carpenter, b.2u. 74 Putnam.
" Mads Peder, carpenter, h. 26 Elmer.
" M. Albin, bartender at 282 Park, h.2u. 4½ Hungerford pl.
" Margaret, wid. Peter, h.2u. 74 Lawrence.
" Matthias, cabinetm. at 225 Shel.h. 16½ Alden.
·" Montague, janitor South school, h. 6 Squire.
" Neils E. laborer, h.u. 55 Grand.
" Nels, mech. at Popes, b. 53 Woodbridge.
" Ollie, laborer, b.u. 278 Pearl.
" Orlorf, gardener at 83, h.r. 83 Woodland.
" Oscar, carpenter, b.u. 12 Putnam.
" Oscar, clerk, b.u. 20 Park.
" Oscar, inspctr. 581 Cap. h. 137 Babcock.
" Oscar, painter, h. 6 Brady pl.
" Paul, carpenter, h. 131 Ward.
" Peter, h.u. 8 Elliot pl.
" Peter, beltmaker at 15 Tru. b. 23 Hamilton.
" Peter, carpenter, h. 40 Rowe.
" Peter, gardener at 41 Weth. h.u. 15 Park.
" Peter, laborer, h.2u. 62 Sheldon.
" Peter, melter at 54 Arch, h. 8 Elliot pl.
" Peter, steamfitter at Popes, h. 8 Olive.
" Peter G. mach. at 1 Flower, b. 376 Park.
" Pliny S. bookkeeper at Gemmill, Burnham & Co. h. 66 William.
" Rebecca, h. 53 Allen pl.
" Robert, draughtsman, 1 Flow. b. 275 Asy.
" Robert J. printer at 141 Pearl, h. 10 Woos.
" Sarah J. wid. Andrew J. b.u. 14 Goodwin.
" Timothy W. mach. at 1 Flow. b. 31 Spring.
" Victor, carder at 59½ Tru. b. 37 Putnam.
" W. deckhand scow Newton, 285 State.
" Walter R. clerk at Colts, h. 55 Franklin.
" Wm. H. mech. engir. at Popes, h. 63 Forest.
" Wm. J. variety store, 1399 Main, h. 18 Chapel.
Andorff Gustaf, mach. b. 699 Main.

G. A. ANDRE, Physician, office and house 303 Park street.
· Hours—8 to 10 A. M.
1 to 3 and 7 to 9 P. M.
Telephone 429-3.

Andre G. A. physician, 303, h. 303 Park.
" Louis, tinner at 1072 Main, b. 32 Church.
Andren Andrew, shipjoiner, h. 159 Babcock.
Andretta Antonio, civil engineer, h. 16 Village.
Andrew Clair L. clerk at 1 Flower, b. 9 Avon.
" William E. salesman, h. 9 Avon.
Andrews Alex. G. clerk at Brown, Thomson & Co. 942 Main, h. 74 Martin.
" Alledo S. (G. C. A. & Co.) h.u. 20½ N.B.
" Alvin E. machinist at 26 High, h.u. 32 Cedar.
" Anna H. teacher High school, b. 164 Seymour.
" Anne, matron, h. 1 Pavilion.
" Benjamin, helper at St. Ry, 115 State.
ANDREWS CHARLES, (A. & Creedon) 446 Asylum, h. East Hartford t.
" Clarence A. driver at 71 Asy. h. 121 Oak.
**ANDREWS & CREEDON**, steamfitters, 446 Asylum. See page 542.
Charles Andrews. John Creedon.
" Dwight H. at 20 N.B. b. 101 Webster.
" Edward L. mach. at 1 Flower, b. 121 Oak.
" Elbert J. secretary of Thorne Typesetting Machine Co. 581 Capitol, h. New York.

Andrews Elizabeth, wid. Lyman, h.u. 11 May.
" Ellen, wid. Woodbridge, h. 72 Governor.
" Erwin, clerk, 745 Main, b. 43 Linden.
" Frank D. h.2u. 15 Seymour.
" Frederick B. at 336 Asy. h.2u. 26 Hopkins.
" George, decorator at Baxter the Decorator, 231 Asylum, h. 34 Hopkins.
" Geo. C. (Geo. C. A. & Co.) h. 101 Webster.
" Geo. C. & Co. groceries, etc. 20 New Britain.
Geo. C. Andrews. Alledo S. Andrews.
" George H. W. carpenter, b. 124 New Britain.
" Gustavus J. carpenter, b. 124 New Britain.
" Harriet, h. 4 Marsh.
" Harriet, wid. Hudson, h.u. 13 Seyms.
" Helen B. teacher, b. 164 Seymour.
ANDREWS HORACE M. alderman 4th ward, (A. & Peck,) h. 80 Williams.
" James, carpenter, h. 124 New Britain
ANDREWS JAMES P. supreme court reporter, attorney, 926 Main, h. 37 Willard.
" Jane C. wid. William O. h. 9 Oak.
" Lillian A. teacher Lawrence st. school, h. 164 Seymour.
" Margaret, wid. Hugh, seamstress, h.u. 877 Main, rm. 12.
" Mary Mrs. b. 2 Holcomb.
" Myron A. cashier Charter Oak National Bank, 124 Asylum, h. West Hartford t.
" Nathan H. h. 167 Sigourney.
" Oregon F. Mrs. nurse, 124, b. 124 N.B.
**ANDREWS & PECK**, doors, windows, and blinds, 88 Market, factory 155 Charter Oak. See page 509.
Horace M. Andrews. Austin L. Peck.
" Rudolph, butcher, 203 State, b. 41 Mulberry.
" Samuel J. pastor Catholic Apostolic church, h. 956 Asylum.
" Samuel W. machinist at Colts, h. N.B.t.
" Sidney W., U. S. storekeeper, (H. W. Palmer & Co.) b. 13 Lafayette.
" Walter C. clerk at 20, h. 20½ New Britain.
" William A. mason, h. 164 Seymour.
" William Stanton, ass't cashier Hartford National Bank, 58 State, h. 108 Washington.
Andreykovits Julia, dressmaker at 270 Main, b.u. 24 Grand.
" Vincent, cutter, 8 Sigourney, h.u. 24 Grand.
Andross George, physician, 724 Main, rm. 11, h. Manchester t.
" J. Burt, clerk at 49 Pearl, h. E.H.t.
Andrus Charles B. carpenter, h.2u. 32 Kinsley.
" Charles B. mason builder, 11, h. 11 Seyms.
" Frank H. clerk, b. 11 Seyms.
" Harry C. blacksmith, 48 Ann, b. W.H.t.
ANDRUS HENRY (Andrus & Hermann,) 300 Asylum, h. 53 Buckingham.
**ANDRUS & HERMANN**, bicycles & sporting goods, 300 Asylum. See p. 484.
Henry Andrus. Fred N. Hermann.
" Joseph, b. 135 Front.
" Mary, wid. Luman J. h.2u. 24 Seyms.
**ANDRUS & NAEDELE CO.** bicycles and sporting goods, 272 Asy. See page 485.
Frank Jewett, Manager.
Andruss Mary P. h.u. 46 John.
Anender Oscar, clerk at 983 Main.

Angali Joseph, at.30 Cushman, h. Lifkey pl.
Angel John, cook at 152 Asylum.

AUGUSTUS ANGELL, Physician, specialist in
Eye and Ear Diseases, Ballerstein build-
ing, 904 Main, room 22.
Hours—9 A.M. to 1 P.M.
2 to 5 P.M.
Tuesday and Saturday—7 to 8 P. M.

Angell Augustus, physician, 904 Main, rm. 22,
h. 30 Vernon.
" William E. bkkpr. 754 Main, h. 62 Williams.
Angelo Dan, fruits, etc. 365 Cap. h. 80 Madison.
" Dell, tailor at 66 Asylum, b. 6 Goodman.
" Peter, laborer, h. 56 Portland.
Angier Silas, blacksm. 366 Allyn, b. 20 Linden.
Angilillo Domenico, laborer, h.u. 64 Morgan.
Angstrom Albin, assembler at 556 Capitol, h. 10
South Forest.
Angus Alex. (*Angus & Chesebro*) h. 27 Warner.
**ANGUS & CHESEBRO,** building con-
tractors, 27 Warner, office 757 Main.
.                              *See page 519.*
Alex. Angus.          E. L. Chesebro.
" James, b. 110 Oak.
" William, builder, h. 110 Oak.
" William, Jr. b. 110 Oak.
Aninger Benj. helper at James L. Howard & Co.
438 Asylum, b. 44 John.
Annese Michael, barber at 9, b. 21 Morgan.
Annex House, 204 Asylum.
Anninger Frank, at 29 Wells, b. 33 Wooster.
Annis Burleigh S. teacher at High school, h.
244 Collins.
" Nellie W. stenographer at Popes, b. M.t.
" William J. driver Hook and Ladder truck,
275 Pearl, h.u. 64 Hicks.
" ☞ *see also Ennis.*
Anthony Leonard H. foreman 1 Laurel, b. 49
Sigourney.
Antonia Mother Superior, 188 Main.
Antrim Eli, farmer, b. 1016 Windsor av.
" Elmer, milkman, 1016, b. 1016 Windsor av.
" Oliver, farmer, h. 1016 Windsor av.
Antupitzky Barney,butcher at 186,b.u. 184 Front.
" Samuel, market, 186, h. 184 Front.
Antz Henry, barber, 27 Pearl, h.u. 124 Hung.
Apgar Maud,dressmaker, 45, b. 45 Main.
Apple Louis, carpenter, b. 1143 Broad
Applebaum Max, laborer, b. 2u. 55 Pleasant.
Applebee William, gearcutter at 1 Flower, h.u.
38½ New Britain.
Appleman Max, screwmr. at 476 Cap. b. 55 Ple.
Appleton Fred. L. clerk at Popes, b. 147 Wash.

Appley Lyman H. mach. 110 Com. b. 214 Hi
Appoon Emil H. cigarmaker, h. 273 Asylum.
Apter Joseph A. cattle dealer, h. 122 Windsor.
" Max, peddler, h.u. 263 Market
Arand Ada, at 690 Park, b. 155 Lawrence.
Aranofski Albert, peddler, h.u. 89 Morgan.
" Barney, peddler, h.u. 55 Morgan.
Arcari Antonio, barber, 456 Main, h. 176 Front.
" Donanta, laborer, b.u. 64 Morgan.
" Joseph A. laborer, b.u. 64 Morgan.
" Louis, barber at 456 Main, b. 13 Morgan.
" Michael, laborer, b.u. 64 Morgan.
" Nicolo, laborer, h. 64 Charles.
Arcelli Pepino, laborer, h. 78 Charles.
Archer John, coachman, 47 Garden, h. 80 Spring.
" John, laborer, h.u. 22 Lawrence.
" John, Jr. clerk at 325 Asylum, b. 80 Spring.
" Joseph, at Travelers Ins. Co. 56 Prospect,
b. 227 Sigourney.
Arens Henry O. tailor at 41 Asylum, h.r. 110
Bluehills.
Arenson Morris, photographer, b. 84 Windsor.
Arenzanno August, laborer, b. 2 Charles.
" Philoberto, laborer, b.u. 4 Charles,
Arian Bernard, collector, 261 Asy. h. 88 Madison.
Arikoski Joseph, stonecutter, b. 21 Arch.
Arlington Danford P. slater, b.2u. 34 Laurel.
" House, Sidney H. Allen, prop. 999 Main.
Armeluxen.☞ *see also Amaluxen.*
Armes Mary E. housekeeper, b. 39 Willard.
Armitage Charles A. machinist at 476 Capitol,
h. Wilson station.
" Clarence J. at Veeder Mfg. Co. h. 32 Chapel.
Armor George M. stenographer at Capewell
Horse Nail Co. b. 157 Capitol.
**ARMOUR & CO.,** dressed beef & provis-
ions, F. W. Hale, mgr. 501 to 507 Asy.
Arms Alvah C. polisher at Colts, h. Burnside v.
" Carleton S. clerk, 336 Asy.b. 27 Townley.
" Edith L. teacher, b. 27 Townley.
" James C., Arms Pocket Book Co. 336 Asy-
lum. h. 27 Townley.
" James D., Arms Pocket Book Co. 336 Asy-
lum, b. 27 Townley.

P. H. C. ARMS, Physician and Surgeon.   Office
94 Walnut street.
Hours—8 to 10 A. M.
1 to 3 and 6 to 8 P. M.
Telephone—412-12.

Arms P. H. C., physician and surgeon, 94, h. 94
Walnut.
**ARMS POCKET BOOK CO.** manu-
facturers, 336 Asylum.  *See page 504.*
James C. Arms.        James D. Arms.
" Publishing Co. 336 Asylum.
" Sarah A. b. 14 Walnut.
Armstrong Bridget Ann Mrs. b. 53 Madison.
" Christopher, b. 112 Laurel.
" John, b. 241 Forest.
" John, filer at Colts, b. E.H.t.
" John Mrs. h. 18 Gold.
" William, pressman, 690 Park, b. 37 Haw.
Arnd August H. helper at 30 Cush. h. 92 Francis.
" Edith M. at 690 Park, b. 155 Lawrence.
Arnofski ☞ *see Aranofski.*

Arnold Charles E. ins. agent and bookkeeper at 97 Asylum, h. 86 Hudson.
" Charlotte L. wid. Albert, h.u. 41 Congress.
" Diana M. Mrs. h. 86 Hudson.
" E. H. & Son, prop. Trout Brook Ice and Feed Co. 48 Ann.
Edwin H. Arnold.    Frederick W. Arnold.
" Edwin H. (E. H. A. & Son,) h. W.H.t.
" Ephraim, ship. clerk Popes, b. 14 Grand.
" Everett E. bkkpr. at Pratt & Whitney Co. 1 Flower, b. E.H.t.
" Frank M. barber at 706, h. 1361 Main.
" Frederick W. (E. H. A. & Son,) b. W.H.t.
" George F. pilot steamer Middletown, 285 State, h. Tylerville v.
" George H. operator 40 Gov. h.2u. 49 Elliott.
" H. George, patternmaker at 556 Capitol, h. 249 Putnam.
" John B. carpenter, b. 531 Garden.
" John George, h. 25 West.
" Perry M. student, b. 34 Vine.
" & Phelan, saloon, 1242 Main.
Smith C. Arnold.    Alfred B. Phelan.
" Sarah, wid. Walter T. b.u. 5 Morris.
" Smith C. (A. & Phelan) h. 34 Vine.

**ARNOLD WALTER T.** architect, builder, 80 Pearl, h. 47 South Hudson.
" Wm. E. inspector 388 Cap. h. Hockanum v.
" Wm. F. bookkeeper at 225 State, h.u. 150 Allyn.
" William R. rubberw. at 690 Pk. b. 17 Bkm.
Arnott Alexander, student at Trinity college, b. South Manchester t.
" Daniel, brakeman P.&R.R. b.u. 73 Albany.
" George E. rubberw. 690 Park, h. 43 Bkm.
Arons Samuel, tailor, 1362 Broad, dyeing, 296, h. 296 Pearl.
Aronson Charlie, blacksmith, 207 Front, h.2u. 52 Pleasant.
" Herman, peddler, h. 78 Talcott.
Arsenal, 1¼ miles no. City Hall, 264 Windsor av.
Art Gallery, Alice W. Gay, custodian, 624 Main.
Art Society of Hartford, 624 Main.
Arthur Chas. P. brakem. N.Y.R. b.u. 82 Walnut.
" George T. manager American hotel, 103 State, h. 29 Sherman.
" Jas. W. butcher at 308 Asy. b.u. 82 Walnut.
" John, stonemason, b. 518 Main.
" Patrick, stonemason, h.u. 82 Walnut.
Arundel Walter B. student Trinity college, 7 Jarvis hall, Summit.
Ash Margaret, concert dept. 336, b. 336 Weth.
Ashberg Harry, grocery, 34, h. 34 North.
Ashby Wm. clerk 119 Pearl, h. 71 Charter Oak.
Ashcroft Amos B. at 198 Pearl, h.r. 12 Village.
Asheim Herbert, floorw. 921 Main. h. Meriden t.
Asher Edwin, h. 51 Lafayette.
" Joseph E. laborer, b. 30 Wolcott.
" Maria, wid. Eldridge E. h. 30 Wolcott.
Ashforth Charles, solderer at 62 Market, h.u. 240 Martin.
Ashjian Mardiers, helper at 141 Pearl.
Ashley Elizabeth J. wid. Henry, h. 216 Windsor av.
" George D. h.u. 35 Annawan.

Ashley Henry, b. 143 Collins.
" Lora A. wid. James, b. 24 Hopkins.
Ashmead J. H. & Son, goldbeaters, safes, 41 Tru.
Robert H. Ashmead.
" Marie A. widow Austin T. h. 14 Spring.
" Robert H. (J. H. A. & Son,) h. Windsor t.
Ashmore Andrew, carpet layer at Chas. R. Hart. Co. 898 Main, h. 20 Huntley pl.
" William, mechanic at Popes, h. 32 Loomis.
Ashwell Chas. confectioner, h. 198 Capen.
" Chas. E. foreman Billings & Spencer Mf'g Co. 142 Russ, h. 2 u. 1194 Main.
" Frank B. clerk at 142 Russ, h. 32 Albany.
" George H. clerk at 103 Asy. h. 65 Hung.
" Robert R. cabinetmaker, b. 77 Williams.
Ashworth Annie, at 690 Park, b. 15 Francis.
" Thos. R. carpr. at 54 Arch, h.u. 15 Francis.
Aspenwall Mary, wid. George, h. 188 High.
" Mary P. b. 188 High.
Aspromonte Leonard, brickl. h.u. 81 Windsor.
**ASSOCIATE DENTISTS,** 943 Main.
See page 423.
Associated Press, 7 Central, rm. 5.
Aston Geo. D. driller at Colts, h.u. 7 Curcombe.
Atcheson Albert C. signpainter, h.u. 12 Smith..
" James A. machinist, b. 14 Smith.
" Margaret Mrs. h. 14 Smith.
" Rob't H. molder 690 Park, h. 89 Madison av.
" William A. rubberw. 690 Park, h. 14 Smith.
Atchison Everett B. clerk, b. 56 Hudson,
" Frank S. printer, b. 56 Hudson.
" Fred. H. clerk at 30 State, b. 56 Hudson.
" John, engineer, h. 56 Hudson.
" John L. printer, b. 56 Hudson.
" Joseph, supt. Commercial Cable Co. 3 Central, b. 724 Main, rm. 9.
" Nellie, wid. Walter T. h.u. 19 Foot Guard.
Atheneum Library, 624 Main.
Atherton E. Newton, h. 160 Commerce.
" Fred E. conductor St.Ry. h. King c. Julius.
Atkins Chas. A. Jr. lumber dealer, h. 51 Sumner.
" Fred, teamster, h. 53 Sanford.
" George A. Jr. (Adams & Atkins) h. E.H.t.
" Jacob P. A. salesman 54 Ann, b. 128 Maple.
" Nathan, h. 53 Sanford.
" Sam'l, dry goods, real est. and h. 128 Maple.
" Simon A. salesman, 54 Ann, b. 128 Maple.
" ☞ see also Adkins.
Atkinson Edward, physician at Insane Retreat, 30 Washington.
Atlantic & Pacific Tea Co. 974 Main.
" Screw Works, David Tilton, proprietor, 70 Huyshope.
Atro James D. fruits, 1007 Main, h.r. 29 Albany.
Attleton James P. Mrs. (Salome L.) h. 141 Main.
Atwater Richard, h.u. 217 Ashley.
Atwell Chas. W. conduc. St.Ry. b.u. 230 Allyn.
" George C. editor Conn. Quarterly, (Hartford Engraving Co.) 66 State, h. New Britain t.
" Hattie B. at 44 Pratt, b.u. 230 Allyn.
" Hattie C. wid. Chas. W. h.u. 230 Allyn.
" John C. butcher at 344 Windsor av. b. 64 Capen,
Atwood Eleanor, wid. Julius C. h.u. 8 Wooster.
" Eleanor D. clerk, 739 Main, b.u. 8 Wooster.

**ATWOOD EUGENE F.** Rev. gen'l agent Co-Operative Building Bank of N. Y. 212 Asylum, rm. 5, h. 590 Garden.
" Evelyn E. teacher Brown school, b. N.B.t.
" Faience Co., Faience cor. Hamilton.
" Henry S. farmer, h. 419 New Britain.
" Mary L. Mrs. h. 26 Whitney.
" William C.purchaser at Popes,h. 496 Pro.av.
Auagnostopralos J. machinist, 13 Central.
Aubanel Emma, French and German teacher, b. 56 Willard.
Aubrey John, polisher at Colts, h. 71 Franklin.
Aubry John, polisher at Colts, b. 35 Front.
Auernig Peter, laborer, b. 95 Harper.
Aufmkolf George, cigarm. at 104 Asy. b.41 Mul.
Auger Joseph, brickmaker, b. 775 Windsor av.
Augur George E. C. machinist at 133 Sheldon, h. 46 Governor.
" Herbert B. student, b. 68 Charter Oak.
" William C. with Security Co. 62 Pearl, h. 68 Charter Oak.
Augustus Emeline, wid. Ezekiel, h.u.r. 213 Pearl.
Auld Frances, head nurse at 20 South Hudson.
Aupry Alex. clerk at 956 Main, h. 121 Ann.
Austin Abe B. clerk at 97 Asy. b. 106½ Trumbull.
" Alden B. butcher at 516 Main, l. 70 Capitol.
" Alfred, messman stm. Hartford, 285 State.
" Elbert B. mach. at 135 Shel. b. 28 Spring.
" Elwyn L. clerk 4 Church, h. 250 Jefferson.
" Emily M. wid. J. H. b. 251 Farmington.
" Eugene G. letter carrier at Station A, h. 250 Putnam.
" Frank,clerk at 55 Maple.b.177 Wethersfield.
" George engineer at P.&R. h.u. 40 Liberty.
" George C. carpenter, b. 462 Farmington.
" Horace B. at Travelers Insurance Co. 56 Prospect, h.u. 64 Russ.
" James L. inspector at Popes, b. 49 Governor.
" Leverett N. attorney, 847 Main, rm. 23, h. Suffield t.
" Minnie B. bookkeeper, h. 22 Winthrop.
" Omer, teamster, h. 129 Barbour.
Automatic Electric Musical & Novelty Co. 118 Asylum, rm. 6.
Avedision Aaron (Hartford Wood Yard Co.) b. 25 Charter Oak.
Averberg Israel, painter, h. 13 North.
" Sam, h.3u. 22 North.
Averill Cyrus B. mach. at 80Huy. h. 225 Park.
Avery Antoinette A. cashier, Brown, Thomson & Co. 942 Main, b. 244 High.
" Arnold P. plumber at 1204, b. 1202 Main.
" Charles, boots and shoes, 160 Asylum, h. 97 Edwards.
" Elizabeth P. wid. George W. h. 76 Garden.
" Frank J. foreman at 476 Cap. h.Windsor t.
" Frank L. manager at 1049, h. 943 Main.
" F. Herbert, clerk at 160 Asylum b. 97 Edwards.
" Frederick H. treas. Jacobs, A. & N. Co. 875 Main, h. E.H.t.
" George, grocer, 614, h. 610 Capitol.
" Henry, foreman at Billings & Spencer Co. 142 Russ, h.2u. 44 Cedar.
" Henry C. forem. at 291 Aly., h. 60 Williams.

Avery Julia M. Mrs. nurse, 14, b. 14 Church, rm.
" Marshall A. mach. at 1 Flower, h. S.M.v.
" Samuel C. at Hartford Fire Ins Co. 53 Trumbull, b. 97 Edwards.
" Thos. E. diesinker at 142 Russ, h. 35 B
Avizn Louis, hodcarrier, h.u. 143 Commerce
Axtelle Ella M. Mrs. h. 40 Pliny.
" J. Frank, physician, 635, h. 635 Main.
Ayer D. O. wid. Robert, h. 55 Capitol.
" George S. proprietor the Colonial, 981 M
Ayers Albert R. toolmaker, h. 23 Heath.
" Bessie M. dressmaker, b. 23 Heath.
" Charles J. bottler, 25 Union, h. 26 Gov
" Edson F. mach. at Popes, b.2u. 1350 B
" Frank J. bootmaker at 454 Asylum, b. Sumner.
" Frank J. manager, b.u. 4 Squire.
" John, bookkeeper, b. 26 Governor.
" Wm. F. clerk at Brown, Thomson & Co. d goods, 942 Main, h. 100 Retreat.
" ☞ see also Ayres.
Aylardo Andrea, laborer, b.3u. 56 Portland.
Ayotte John, laborer, h.2u. 6 Talcott.
Ayres Elizabeth Sluyter Mrs. assistant superi tendent Union for Home Work, 239 M ket, h. 427 Main, rm. 34.
" Frederick H. telegraph editor at Hartf Post, 23 Asylum, h. Whiting.
" Henry W. civil engineer, 66 State, b. 57 Fs
" William, painter, b.u. 40 Village.
" William A. journalist, editorial writer Hartford Times, 716, h. 427 Main.
" ☞ see also Ayers.
BABASINIAN Vahan S. theo. student, 1507 Broa
**BABCOCK A. H. MRS.** practi optician, supporters and trusses for ladies and children, 265 Asylum.
" Ben. roller at 62 Market, h. Windsor t.
" Charles M. enameler at 581 Cap. h. E.H.t.
" E. Dorance, driller at Colts, b. 1281 Main.
" Edward F. machinist at 690, h. 819 Park.
" Albert D. clerk at Brown, Thomson & Co. 942 Main, b. 206 Asylum.
" Fannie A. attendant at 30 Washington.
" Frank S. stationery engineer, h. 44 Hicks.
" George, fireman tug Ward, 285 State.
" Geo. J. (Waterville Cut. Co.) h. 199 Laurel.
" Harvey S. mach. at 9 Sig. h. 50 Fairmount
" Henry E. assistant postmaster, 65 State, h.2u. 7 Canton.
" Henry M. carpenter at 141 Tru. h. Weth.t.
" I. M. Mrs. h. 206 Asylum, flat 2.
" James L. waiter at 107, l. 112 State.
" John P. buffer, h.u. 257 High.
" P. A. Mrs. h. 123 Trumbull.
" Robert, at 8 Sigourney, b.2u. 36 Flower.
" Traverse C. jobber, h. 171 Windsor.
" William, carpenter, b. 819 Park.
" Wm. H. manager, 247 Pearl, h.u. 19 Beach.
Bach Abraham, market, 206 Front, h. 28 Mor.
" Isaac, butcher at 206, h. 192 Front.
Bacharach Henry, meats, 13, h. 211 Park.
" Milton, student, b. 9 Canton.
" Samuel, clerk at 13, h. 211 Park.

PIANOS RE-BUILT AS GOOD AS NEW BY LEO. H. BATTALIA, Warerooms, 943 MAIN ST.

Bacall Charles H. secretary Hartford Life Ins.
Co. 252 Asylum. h. South Highland st.

Bacharach Sidney L. *councilman 2d ward,* buyer at 921 Main, b. 9 Canton.
" Wm. com. traveler, h. 9 Canton.
Bacher Nicholas, jeweler, b.u. 83 Pleasant.
Bachimont Stephane, French teacher, 721 Main.
Bachmeyer Annie Mrs. nurse, 175, b. 175 Maple.
Backe Peter H. screwmaker at 476 Capitol, b. 32 Laurel.
Backer Jacob, butcher, h.2u. 190 Front.
BACKES FRED. W. bakery, 169, h. 167 Asylum. *See page* 45.
Backman Charles, mach. 44 Arch, b.21 Mulberry.
" Emil, carpenter, b.2u. 54 Flower.
" Victor, printing dept. 336, b. 336 Weth.
Backstrom Andrew G. saddler at 8, b. 45 Sig.
Backus Jason, magnetic healer, 1110, h. 1110 Mn.
" Mary, wid. Thomas, h. 216 Windsor av.
" Sanford H. helper, 165, h.u. 153 Windsor.
" Sarah A. teacher 2d North school, 249 High, b. 1110 Main.
Bacon Albert C. bookkeeper at 155 Charter Oak, h.u. 926 Main, rm. 35.
" Alice C. stenographer, b. 106 Capen.
". Alta M. clerk, 885 Main, b. 120 Maple.
" Andrew J. h. 86 Maple.
" Bellamy A. bottler, 13 Morris, h. 120 Maple.
" Chas. L. trimmer, 266 Pearl, h. 21 Talcott.
" Cornelia, wid. Hiram, h.u. 216 Windsor av.
" Elizabeth, dressmaker, 106, h. 106 Capen.
" Franklin N. market, 490 Main, h. Berlin t.
" Fred J. banjo teacher, h. 223 Asy. rm. 115.
" Fred T. steamfitter, h. 4 Atlantic.
" Frederick H. butcher at 490 Main, h. E.H.t.
" Frederick J. stenographer at Ætna Life Ins. Co. 650 Main, h. 1146½ Broad.
" Frederick S. student at Trinity College, 27 Jarvis Hall, Summit.
" G. Frank, varnish agent, h. 147 Albany.
" Geo. L. repairer at 266 Pearl, h. 84 Maple.
" Harriet E. matron, Insane Ret. 30 Wash.
" Harry C. clerk at 123 Ann, h. 1 Avon.
" Harry W. clerk, Pope Tube Co. h. Weth. t.
" Horace W. Jr. decorator at Baxter the Decorator, 231 Asylum, h. 106 Wooster.
" James G. printer at 141 Pearl, h. 106 Capen.
" John, carriagemaker at 597 Mn. h.r. 61 Tru.
" Josephine S. teacher, b. 102 Ann.
" Marcus M. bottler, r. 13 Morris, h. 105 Weth.
" May W. stenographer at 650 Mn. b. 61 Tru.
" Merton H. pressm. 668 Mn. b. 40 Atlantic.
" Mortimer C. actor, b. 80 Hicks.
" Ora A. clerk at Phœnix Mutual Life Ins. Co. 49 Pearl, b. 120 Maple.
BACON SAMUEL A. sec'y Chas. R. Hart Co. 896 Main, h. 249 Collins. *See Advtrs. Index.*
" Sarah A. b. 249 Collins.
" Stiles S. burnisher at Wm. Rogers Mfg. Co. 66 Market, h. 2 Orchard.
" William, carpenter, b.r. 44 Pleasant.
" William E. clerk at 921 Main, b. 18 Clark.
" William H. printer Hartford Life Ins. Co. Co. 252 Asylum, b. 4 Atlantic.
" William T. physician, 11 Pratt, h.195 Collins.
Badger George E. *(A. G. King & Co.)* h.u. 23 Benton.

Badke William, b. 215 Bellevue.
Baeder Fritz, laborer, b.2u. 98 Albany.
Baedor Anthony C. engineer at I. B. Davis & Son, 40 Cushman, h. 1148 Broad.
" Anthony Louis, clerk at 882 Mn. h.u.10 Fmt.
" George H. clerk at 945 Main, h. E.H.t.
" William A.*( W.A.B.& Co.)* h.u. 31 Windsor.
" Wm. A. & Co., Union Printing Co. 90 Asy.*
Bagdigian Charles, laborer at 116, b. 125 Ch.O.
" Zeron, *(Hfd. Wood Yard Co.)* b. 125 Ch.O.
" Martin, *(Hfd. Wood Yard Co.)* b.125 Ch.O.
Bagg Mary, h.u. 2½ Grand.
Baggett J. H. foreman Hartford Telegram, 12 Central, b. 126 Trumbull.
Bagley Charles, at 830 Main, b. 57 Church.
" William I. printer at Case, Lockwood & Brainard Co. 141 Pearl, h. 53 Oak.
Baglin C. clerk at 885 Main, b. 150 Allyn.
Bagnolo Domenics, laborer, h.u. 82 Morgan.
Bagot John R. rest'nt, 107 State, b.u. 28 Morgan.
Bagshaw Herbert, mach. at 133 Shel. b. 98 Huy.
" Leonard, operator, b. 151 Martin.
" William, repairer at Capewell Horse Nail Co. 40 Governor, h.u. 151 Martin.
" William Jr. solderer at Wm. Rogers Mfg. Co. 66 Market, b.u. 151 Martin.
Bahnson Rudolph F. painter at 581 Cap. h. Blu.
Bahre Robert, conductor St.Ry. h.u. 382 Park.
Bailey Benjamin D. hosedriver No. 3, h. 19 Seyms.
" Bessie M. nurse, 13, b. 13 Avon.
" Catherine F. h.u. 22 Seyms.
" Charles L. daughtsman at 581 Capitol, b.u. 226 Sargeant.
" Charles W. clerk at 95 Ple. h. Plainville t.
" Chas. W. woodworker, b. 65 Elm.
" Dwight E. polisher, Popes, h.u. 102 Hopkins.
" Edwin T. h.u. 108 Barbour.
" Ellen, wid. of Michael, h. 22 Seyms.
" Florence M. at Hartford Life Ins. Co. 252 Asylum, h. East Berlin v.
" Fred, teamster, b. 27 Morgan.
" George C. physician, 65, h. 65 Church.
" · George S. at Brown, Thomson & Co. manager advertising dept. 942 Mn. h. 13 Avon.
" Georgietta A. at 867 Main, b. 78 Chestnut.
" Hannah C. wid. Charles, h. 817 Windsor av.
" Hannah F. teacher at Brown school, 160 Market, b. 65 Church.
" Harrie E. clerk at Pratt & Whitney Co. 1 Flower, b. Cromwell t.

Bailey Herbert G. clerk, superintendent Charities Commission. h. 13 Avon.
" James C. upholsterer at Seidler & May. 306 Pearl. b. 65 Elm.
" Jane B. teacher South school, 36 Wadsworth, b. 5 Linden.
" Jennie E. bookkeeper at H. Brainerd, b. 10 Townley.
" Joseph. ostler. 82 Hudson.
" L. D. b. 104 Church.
" Margaret A. milliner at Brown, Thomson & Co. 942 Main. b. 22 Seyms.
" Marion E. upholsterer, b. 65 Elm.
" Martha M. wid. Horace, h. 150 Albany.
" Mary Mrs. b. 35 Oxford.
" Mary Ann, wid. Simeon, h. 65 Elm.
" Michael A. physician, 65, b. 65 Church.
" Minnie A. teacher Brown sch. b. 65 Church.
" Nellie E. b. 65 Church.
" Orra B. cook, b.u. 108 Babcock.
" Roy W. salesman at 66 Asy. b.u. 39 Wooster.
BAILEY WILLIAM Jr. alderman 5th ward, sec'y Warner & Willard Co. 110 Asylum, h. 703 Main, rm. 9.
" William E. carpenter, 78, h. 78 Chestnut.
" Vincent I. mach. at 1 Flow. b. 114 Hopkins.
" ☞ see also Bayley.
Bain Margaret A. h.2u. 387 Capitol.
" Mark, clerk 745 Main, b.2u. 387 Capitol.
" William, b.2u. 387 Capitol.
" ☞ see also Bane, Bayne.
Baird M. E. electrician, h. 339 Laurel.
" ☞ see also Beard.
Bairman John R. with Columbia Brewing Co. h. 58 Bellevue.
Bairstow Ink Co. mfrs. chemists, 281 Allyn.
" M. A. dressmaker, 904, h. 904 Main, rm. 46
" Thos. B. (B. Ink Co.) h. 904 Main, rm. 46.
Baisden James S. carpenter at Taft Co. h. 230 Windsor av.
" R. captain barge 3, 285 State.
Baker Albert R. journalist, b. 70 Capitol.
" Alice M. teacher Arsenal sch. b. 1150 Main.
" Annie, b. 62 Pleasant.
" Arthur F. helper at 164 State, b. 897 Windsor av.
" Benj. B. painter, h.u. 43 Seyms.
" Charles, I. 1221 Main.
" Charles, brakeman, N.Y.R. b.r. 26 Walnut.
" Charles E. machinist at 1 Flower, b. 54 Bkm.
" Charles W. ticket agt. N.Y.R. h. 1221 Main.
" Christian, mach. at 1 Flow. b.u. 82 Hudson.
" Daniel, carpenter, h.2u. 6 Green.
" David, laborer, b.2u. 33 Mechanic.
" E. L. b. 62 Grove.
" Edward F. clerk at 323, h. 317 Asylum.
" Edward P. repairer at Popes, b. 1262 Broad.
" Frank A. hackman 16, h.u.r. 16 Squire.
" Frank P. patternm. 216 Law. h. 37 Barbour.
" Frank P. Mrs. dressm. 37, h. 37 Barbour.
" Fred'k N. clerk at 1079 Main, h. 112 State.
" Geo. L. (Marcy Bros. & Co.) h. 276 Weth.
" George W. (W. E. B. & Son,) b. W.H.t.
" Hattie, wid. Fred'k, dressm. h. 1336 Main.
" Henry C. clerk b. 11 Greenwood.

Baker Henry S. operator at 95 Pleasant, h. 11 Greenwood.
" Herbert C. mechanical eng. h. 50 Linden.
" Herman L. mach. at Popes, h. 293 Weth.
" Herman W. mach. at 80 Huy. b. 54 Capitol.
" Isabella A. at 1 So. Ann, b. 43 Bellevue.
" Isaiah Jr. (Webster & B.) fire insurance, 721 Main, h. 37 Kenyon.
" Johanna, wid. James, h. 43 Bellevue.
" John F. clerk at Brown, Thomson & Co. 942 Main, b. 57 Church.
" John J. caster, 110 Com. b. 47 Talcott.
" John J. laborer, b.2u. 33 Mechanic.
" Josephine R. wid. Henry E. h. 70 Capitol.
‡ Josiah Q. at Ætna Life Insurance Company, 650 Main, h. 280 Wethersfield.
" Julia A. at 1 So. Ann, b. 43 Bellevue.
" Kittie. at So. Ann, b. 43 Bellevue.
" Lottie May, h. 276 Maple.
" Louis E. mech. at Colts, h. 70 Charter Oak.
" Louise, wid. Edward A. h. 11 Myrtle.
" Max. tailor at 730 Main, b. 41 North.
" Minnie B. W. stenographer, rm. 42 State Capitol. b. Plainville t.
" Nathan, peddler, h.u. 271 Market.
" Nettie A. bkkpr. 323 Asy. b. 254 Jefferson.
" Penrose H. engr. Pope Tube Co. h. u. 9 Amity.
" Richard, laborer, h. 14 North.
" Richard, ostler, 12 Wells, h.r. 1 Orchard.
" Richard H. journalist, b. 70 Capitol.
" Ruth H. Mrs. b. 112 High.
" Samuel M. printer at 141 Pearl, h.u. 15 Bkm.
" Thomas, laborer, b.2u. 33 Mechanic.
" Timothy, teamster, h. Talcott c. Market.
" Victor H. mach. at 13 Central.
" W. E. & Son, insurance agents, 700 Main.

Wm. E. Baker.        Geo. W. Baker.

" Walter J. ruler at 254 Pearl, h. 52 Madison.
" William, laborer, b. 120 Mather.
" Wm. E. (W. E. B. & Son) h. 17 Highland.
" William E. at 126 Church, b. 22 Hopkins.
" William F. finisher at 581 Capitol, b. 129 Bellevue.
" ☞ see also Becker; Becher; Bekker; Besker.
Bald May B. teacher High sch. b. 25 Sherman.
Baldasaria Carlo, laborer, b. 247 Front.
" Gabriel G. barber, 18 Kilbourn, b. 247 Front.

**BALDWIN BROS.** general express forwarders to all foreign ports via fastest mail steamers. Wilbur F. Dodge, agent in connection with Adams Express Co.
" Ada L. Mrs. dressm. 1281, h.u. 1281 Main.
" Charles A. clerk at Popes, b. 63 Oak.
" Chas. A. express, 1245, h. 1245 Main.
" Charles O. stamps, stencils, etc. 8 State, h. 41 Huntington.
" Courtland R. clerk at National Fire Ins. Co. 95 Pearl, h. 230 Jefferson.
" Dwight D. clerk at 98 Kil. b. 19 Williams.
BALDWIN EDWARD M. (Rice & B.) 214 Pearl, b. 22 Niles.        See page 494.
" Fred L. b.u. 234 Wethersfield.
" Grove B. b. 405 Windsor av.
" Harry S. draughtsman, 1 Lau. b. 181 Capitol.
" James, gatetender N.Y.R. h.u. 25 Sigourney.

Baldwin John, clerk at Brown, Thomson & Co. 942. l 1210 Main.
  " John F. carriagemaker, h. 250 Lawrence.
  " John J. cutter at 8 Sigourney, h. 43 Grand.
  " Lyman H. upholsterer at Neal. Goff & Inglis Co. 980 Main, h.u. 17 Seymour.
  " Minnie F. at 247 Pearl. b. 43 Grand.
  " Nicholas D. mach. at 1 Flow. b. 1316 Broad.
  " Rollin D. sec'y E. S. Kibbe Co. 149 State, h. 405 Windsor av.
  " William F. carpenter foreman for W. H. Relyea, h.u. 234 Wethersfield.
Balf Dennis, teamster, h.u. 169 Main.
  " Edward, laborer, h.r. 68 Temple.
  " Edward, pres. Edward Balf Co. h. 174 Sey.
  " Edward P. laborer, b.u. 38 Temple.
  " Mich. J. mach. 30 Cush. h.u. 16 Huntley pl.
  " Michael J. Jr. machinist, b.u. 16 Huntley pl.
**BALF EDWARD CO. (THE)**, general contractors, office 2 Chapel, coal yard, 276 Market. *See page 426.*
  " John, laborer, h.4u. 55 Spruce.
  " Sadie, domestic at 20 South Hudson.
  " Thomas, driver, b. 61 Judson.
  " William, teamster, b.u. 147 Market.
  " William H. mech. at Popes, b.2u.r.23 Spruce.
  " ☞*see also Balf: Bolf.*
Balfe Patrick, teamster at 8 Front.
Balfour Jas. mach. at 1 Flow. h.u. 44 Glendale.
  " James, Jr. steamf. at N.Y.R. b. 44 Glendale.
Balgley Alexander, b.u. 41 Windsor.
  " Benjamin, clerk at Lincoln, Seyms & Co. 34 Market, b. 41 Windsor.
  " Jacob, b.u. 41 Windsor.
  " Paul, h. 41 Windsor.
Balinsky Ignace, laborer, h.2u. 95 Sheldon.
Balkin Barnard, painter, h.2u. 64 Village.
Ball Annie, b. 66 Niles.
  " Bessie B. h. 66 Niles.
  " Charles G. laborer at Capitol, h. 1067 Main.
  " Emma Mrs. h. 16 Trinity.
  " Frederick W. bookkeeper National Life Association, 53 Trumbull, h. 16 Trinity.
  " Geo. W. watchmaker, 25 Asylum, h. 66 Niles.
  " Harry, restaurant, 8, l. 7 Central.
  " John E. weigher at 172 Commerce, h. 66 Charter Oak.
  " Julius, barber, 1069 Main, h. 17 East.
  " Martha S. nurse at 20 So. Hudson.
  " Mary E. teacher West Middle school, 927 Asylum, b. 66 Niles.
  " Samuel, watchman, h.u. 37 Pleasant.
  " Samuel L. barber, 46 Church, b. 37 Chapel.
  " Stephen, president National Life Association, 53 Trumbull, h. 106 Park,
Ballance James, draughtsman, h. 32 Wooster.
Ballantine Geo. A. pattern clerk, 1 Flower, b.2u. 234 Putnam.
  " Henry J. mach. 581 Cap. h.2u. 234 Putnam
  " James, gardener, 103, b. 135 Woodland.
  " Jane, wid. Robert, h.2u. 234 Putnam.
  " Sarah D. wid. Ebenezer, b. 128 Oxford.
Ballard Emma M. clerk at Brown, Thomson & Co. 942 Main, b. 512 Windsor av.
  " Harriet K. wid. Porter, h. 23 Wadsworth.

Ballerstein Benjamin, gent's furnishing, 858 Main, h. 44 Sumner.
**BALLERSTEIN R. & CO.** milliners, wholesale and retail, 908 Main.
  R. Ballerstein.    C. Dillon.
*See page 421.*
  " Raphael (*R. Ballerstein & Co.*) h. 904 Main.
Ballis Dominie, laborer at 335 Shel. b. 19 Mec.
Ballou Chas. printer at Case, Lockwood & Brainard Co. 49 Pearl, b. 98 Trumbull.
  " Ella, b.u. 19 Foot Guard.
  " Geo. W. filer, 581 Cap. b.u. 19 Foot Guard.
  " Hosea E. pressman at 141 Pearl, b.u. 19 Foot Guard pl.
  " Julia A. Mrs. h.u. 19 Foot Guard pl.
  " Lydia W. at Hartford Life Insurance Co. 252 Asylum, h. 78 Barbour.
  " William J. theological student, 1507 Broad.
Balmer Daniel, h. 98 Ashley.
Bamman Henry F. engineer at 65 Suffield.
Bancroft Arthur C. mach. at 1 Flow. b. 67 Russ.
  " H. Wallace, clerk at 142, b. 67 Russ.
  " Harry S. clerk, b.u. 69 Babcock.
  " M. E. Mrs. b. 389 Main.
  " Mary C. wid. Samuel, h.u. 69 Babcock.
  " Samuel M. rubberworker at 690 Park, h. Glastonbury t.
Bane Carey, laborer at 276 Market, h. 60 Albany.
  " Thomas, at 216 Lawrence, h. 133 Ward.
  " Thos. J. machinist at 1 Flow. h.u. 72 Law.
  " William, carpenter, b.2u. 277 Main.
  " ☞*see also Bain, Bayne.*
Baney John, b. 56 Buckingham.
Banfield Charles E. helper at Trinity College, h. 1 South Laurel.
  " Edward clerk at 705 Main, b. 1 Flatbush.
  " Edward, at 715 Main, b. 1 So. Laurel.
Bank Charles A. conductor St.Ry. b. 68 Lincoln.
Banker Annie, dressmaker, b. 34 Charter Oak pl.
Banks Arthur, boxm. at r. 133 Shel. b. 22 Hicks.
  " Edward A. mason, h. 22 Hicks.
  " George B. rubberw. 690 Park, h. 40 Heath.
  " J. H. Mrs. lodgings, 245 State.
  " Jefferson H. restaurant, 244, h. 245 State.
  " John, ostler at 212 Park, h.u. 3 Wolcott.
  " Raymond, ostler, 173 State, b. 10½ Gold.
  " Sarah R. Mrs. teacher, h. 1 Webster.
  " Walter F. mach. at 30 Cush. b. 22 Hicks.
  " William, helper at 366, l.2u. 271 Main.
Bannan Ellen J. wid. James, h.2u. 50 Wells.
  " James J. at 581 Capitol, b.2u. 50 Wells.
  " John H. foreman at 556 Cap. h.u. 20 Grace.
  " Matthew J. mach. at 556 Cap. b. 35 Hawthorn.
  " Michael F. mach. at 556 Capitol, h. N.B.t.
  " Michael S. b.u. 20 Grace.
Banning John, conductor St.Ry. b. 151 Weth.
  " John, saloon, 17 Mulberry, b. 23 Benton.
  " Kate, wid. Michael, h.u. 16 Albany.
  " Robert J. teamster, 268 Shel. b.u. 16 Albany.
  " Rufus C. janitor Northeast school, h. 223 Barbour.
  " William A. teamster, 138, h. 138 Barbour.
  " William A. Jr. printer, b. 138 Barbour.
Bannon Edward J. h. 56 Smith.
  " Katie F. at 690 Park, b. 56 Smith.

Bansemer Charles, barten.at 26 Un.pl. b. 428 Asy.
"   Gottlieb, market, 34, h. u. 83 Front.
"   Gustaf, baker, h.2u. 83 Front.
"   Louise wid. August, dressmaker, h.u.r. 65 Temple.
Banson Alfred, laborer, b. 296 Park.
"   Edward, asst. janitor at Parkville school, b. 833 Park.
Barachani Frank, baker at 178, h. 178 Front.
Baratochi Nicola, laborer, h. 265 Front.
Barbeau Benj. J. h. 57 Bellevue.
"   Benjamin J. Jr. buffer at Wm. Rogers Mfg. Co. 66 Market, h.u.r. 68 Vanblock.
"   Leodo clerk at 921 Main, h. 57 Bellevue.
"   Leon H. buffer at 66 Market, h.u.72 Bellevue.
"   Wilfred, buffer, b. 57 Bellevue.
"   ☞see also Barber, Barbour.
Barbeaulte Edward, mach. at Colts, h.u. 3 Hdx.
Barbello Cona, laborer, h. 78 Charles.
Barber Andrew, saddler at 8 Sig. h. 25 Putnam.
"   Benjamin, yardman, 17 Alb. h. 57 Bellevue.
"   Charles A. clerk, h.u. 127 Barbour.
"   Cornelia G. wid. Alfred A. b.2u.1206 Broad.
"   Daisy, stenographer at 851 Main, b. 241 Windsor av.
"   Edw. S. h. 113 Oak.
"   Francis A. conductor St. Ry. h. 44 Brook.
"   Frank O. at 902 Main, b. 157 Capitol.
"   Fred. J. toolm. at 581 Cap. h. 11 Harbison.
"   Geo. H. foreman 1 Flower, h. 62 Allen pl.
"   George R. carpenter, h. 265 Jefferson.
"   George W. real estate, b.r. 843 Park.
"   Hamlet P. cutter, 59½ Tru. h. 232 Garden.
"   Harriet, domestic, b. 187 High.
"   Harry A. warmer at 690, b. 551 Park.
"   Henry G. milkman,375,h.u. 375 New Britain.
"   Horace I. Mrs. h. 241 Windsor av.
"   James, farmer, h. 475 New Britain.
"   Jane, seamstress, b.u. 42 Village.
"   Jessie M. teacher, b. 460 New Britain.
"   Joel A. mechanic at Popes, h.u. 24 Squire.
"   Joseph E. assistant delivery clerk N.Y.R. 98 Kilbourn, h. 7 Lewis.
"   Louis E. clerk, 252 Pearl, b. 232 Garden.
"   Mark, farmer, h. 460 New Britain.
"   Mary, wid. Ezra, h. 128 Babcock.
"   Mary E. teacher at South school, 36 Wadsworth, b. 34 West.
"   Nellie M. wid. Melvin, clk. h. 370 Asy. rm. 68.
"   Rebecca H. wid. H. K. b. 16 Girard.
"   Sarah, wid. Orrin, b.u. 51 Williams.
**BARBER WILLIAM P.** manufacturer Barber's ink extracts, clerk at Orient Ins. Co. 5 Haynes, h. 16 Girard.   *See page 188.*
"   ☞see also Barbour; Barbeau.
Barbour Amy L. teacher High school, b. 58 Beacon.
"   Arthur E. painter, 185 Asylum, h. E.H.t.
"   Charles S. plater at 62 Mar. h. 10 Bellevue.
"   Collin H. clerk at Neal, Goff & Inglis Co. 980 Main, b. 58 Beacon.
"   David H. bkkpr. at 85 Pratt, b. 30 West.
"   Frank O. porter at Chas. R. Hart Co. 898, l. 898 Main.
"   Harry, electrician, b. 2 Church.

**BARBOUR JOS. L.** attorney at law, 50 State, First Nat. B'k Bldg. h. 81 Gillett.
BARBOUR LUCIUS A. pres. and treas. Williman-tic Linen Co. 391 Allyn, h. 130 Washington.   *See page 544.*
"   Lucius B. b. 130 Washington.
"   Lucy A. private school, 44, b. 44 Beacon.
"   Marion E. clerk at Brown, Thomson & Co. 942 Main, b. 58 Beacon.
"   Mary C. wid. Ansel S. b. 49 Governor.
"   Pamela J. wid. Henry S. h. 44 Beacon.
"   Robert W. student, b. 81 Gillett.
"   Samuel L. secretary Barbour Silver Co. 62 Market, h. 114 Woodland.
"   Silver Co. silversmiths, 62 Market.
"   Sylvester, attorney, 756 Main, h. 58 Beacon.
"   ☞see also Barber; Barbeau.
Barby Fritz J. manager, 931 Main, h.2u. 6 Church.
Barchel Joseph, screwmaker, h.u. 7½ Oak.
Barchfeld Amelia, artist, b. 12 Bond.
"   Bernard, bootmaker, 4 Kinsley, h. 12 Bond.
"   Helen M. teacher Wethersfield av. school, b. 12 Bond.
"   Jacob, cigarm. at 867 Mn. h.2u. 39 Brown.
"   John G. machinist, b.2u. 39 Brown.
"   Josephine, teacher Parkville sch. b.12 Bond.
"   Matilda, art. at Elmwood pottery, b. 12 Bond.
Barden Andrew, clerk, b. 347 Front.
"   Lillie, domestic, b. 485 Capitol.
"   ☞see also Borden.
Bardin Jas. N. forem. at Popes, h.u. 49 Williams.
Bardol Edward A. *(E. P. Charlton & Co.)* h. 37 Girard.
Bardons Charles A. bookkeeper at A. Hollander's Sons, 82 Asylum, h. 26 Talcott.
"   Philip H. machinist at Pratt & Whitney Co. 1 Flower, h.u. 233 Jefferson.
"   ☞see also Barton.
Bardwell Arthur F. supt. Popes Motor Carriage department, 1 Laurel, b. 49 Sigourney.
"   William S. laundryman at 438 Asylum.
Bares Nathan, irondealer, 80, h.3u. 78 Front.
Barker Alfred, dentist at 943 Main, b. 70 Law.
"   Charles S. W. bookkeeper at Hartford Trust Co. 764 Main, h. 354 Garden.
"   E. nurse, 14 Church, rm. 4.
"   Edward B. b. 49 Girard.
"   Egbert L. diesinker at Colts, h. 51 Huyshope.
"   Harry, student, b. 58 Asylum.
**BARKER F. W. & CO.** doors, sash and blinds, 86 Morgan.*   *See page 519.*
                    Frank W. Barker.
"   James E. b. 3 Whitman.
"   John C. com. merchant, h. 205 Wethersfield.
"   J. & Co. pianofortes, music, 153-155 Asy.*
"   Ludlow *(L. Barker & Co.)* h. 659 Farmington.
"   Mary G. wid. Daniel, b. 122 Clark.
"   Russell F. draughtsman, 2 Central, b. 354 Garden.
"   Samuel L. toolmaker at Popes, h.u. 45 Smith.
"   Wm. E. pianotuner, teacher, h.u. 58 Asylum.
"   Wm. H. draughtsman, h. 223 Asy. rm. 129.
"   William H. salesman, b. 27 Arch.
"   Wm. L. B. with L. Barker & Co. h. 49 Girard.
"   Willis P. engir. engine No. 8, h.u. 70 Law.

Barlow Arthur J. carpenter at r. 22, b. 15 Grand.
" Charles H. carpenter at r. 22, h. 15½ Grand.
" Howard C. at Ætna Life Insurance Co. 650 Main, b. 53 Capitol.
" Jas. W. carptr. builder, r. 22, h.u. 15 Grand.
" John A. machinist at Pratt & Whitney Co. 1 Flower, b. 283 Park.
" John H. grand secretary masonic orders, 51 Ann, h. Shelton t.
" Joseph K. mach. at 31 Hicks, h. 18 Trinity.
" Joseph R. books, stationery, 366 Asylum, b. 18 Trinity.
" Timothy F. washer at 366 Main, b. 63 Dean.
" Walter E. at 366 Asylum, b. 18 Trinity.
" William, h. 63 Dean.
" Wm. J. mach. at 1 Laurel, h.u. 228 Garden.
" Winifred, wid. Joseph, h.u. 283 Park.
Barnard Carlos A. h.r. 1219 Main.
" Charles, plumber, b. 255 Asylum.
" Dorus C. bookkeeper at Hiram Bissells, b. 43 Wadsworth.
" Dwight E. foreman at 154 Pl. h. 98 Maple.
" Edward E. cabinetmaker at 103 Asylum, b.u. 32 Hopkins.
" Edward R. city express, 64 State, stables 35 Woodbridge, h. 350 Main.
" Ellen S. b. 417 Windsor av.
" Emily V. b. 118 Main.
" Frank W. clerk, b. 315 Pearl, rm. 403.
" George H. milkman, h. Bloomfield av.
" Grace M. stenog. at Popes, b. 58 Church.
" Harry S. baker, b. 53 Liberty.
" Henry, book publisher, 118, b. 118 Main.
" John G. driver chemical engine, h. 64 Hicks.
" Josephine E. b. 118 Main.
" Lucretia W. wid. John, b.u. 289 Allyn.
" Mark, carpenter at N.Y.R. h.u. 51 Fairmount.
" Newrie W. steamfitter at 164 Sta. b.98 Maple.
" Samuel W. at 53 Ann, b. 52 Babcock.
" W. E. car inspec. N.Y.R. h.u. 51 Bellevue.
" W. Lincoln, clerk at Pratt & Whitney Co. 1 Flower, h. 37 Brown.
" Willard C. Jr. painter, b.u. 6 Huntley pl.
" William C. agent, h.u. 6 Huntley pl.
" William H. superintendent of printing at 154 Pearl, h. 223 Asylum, rm. 74.
" William M. carpenter N.Y.R. h. W.t.
" ☞ see also Bernard.
Barnards Clara A. wid. William, restaurant, 12, h.u. 10½ Ford.
Barneckey Chas. E. tailor at 66 Asy. h.u. 14½ N.B.
" Eli, tailor at 66 Asylum, b. 14 New Britain.
Barnedy Tony, lab. at 618 Capitol, b. 41 North.
Barnell Dan'l A. rubberw. 690 Park, b. Meriden t.
Barnes Ada F. assistant matron, 1 Pavilion.
" Arthur G. oiler at 70 Commerce, b. W.t.
" Carrie, winder at 34 Morgan, b. 36 Pratt.
" Chester E. teamster, h. 20 Morgan.
" Elizabeth, wid. James T. b. 58 Madison.
" Ella L. h. 158 Sargeant.
" Fannie C. dressmaker, h. 67 Willard.
" Frank, laborer, h. 17 Windsor.
" Frank M. rubberw. 690 Pk. b. 95 Hamilton.
" George C. clerk at James L. Howard & Co. mfg. car goods, 438 Asylum, h. 29 Spring.

Barnes Geo. H. plateptr. 704 Mn. b.u. 165 State.
" Harry L. with Security Co. 62 Pearl, b. 143 Collins.
" Irving R. electrician, 214 Pearl, h. 22 Jefferson.
" James, collarmaker at 8 Sig. b. 95 Hamilton.
" James, janitor, 36 Jefferson.
" James A. G. mach. at 133 Sheldon, b. E.H.t.
" John J. plater 581 Capitol, b. 13 North.
" L. Algernon, carpenter at 50, b. 50 Oxford.
" Loren W. builder, 50, h. 50 Oxford.
" Louis H. mach. at Colts, b. 36 Charter Oak.
" Maria L. Mrs. b. 36 Jefferson.
" Mary A. b. 36 Jefferson.
" Michael, car inspector, b. 24 Howard.
" Miranda R. wid. Jonas, h. Park, W.H.t.
**BARNES PHILLIP S.** builder, 416, h. 416 Franklin.          *See page* 481.
" R.T.H. broker, 650 Main, rm. 17, b.98 Wells.
" Robert, clerk at 729 Main. b. W.t.
" W. F. clerk at 206 State, b. Wethersfield t.
" William C. mach. at 581 Cap. h. 2 James.
Barnett James L. bkkpr. at 322 Pearl, b. 87 High.
**BARNETT JOHN F.** bicycle repairing, mfr. sulky wheels, 322 Pearl, h. 87 High.
" Simon, tailor, 1196 Main, l. 145 Front.
" & Tucker, sulky and carriage wheels, 302 Asylum.

| J. F. Barnett. | W. W. Tucker. |

" William, salesman at 304 Asy. b. Buckland t.
Barney John, h.u. 144 Madison av.
Barnofski Ferdinand, tailor, h.u. 77 Temple.
Barnsley Arthur, mach. at 198 Pearl, b. 87 High.
Barnum Belle M. dressmaker, 25½, b.25½ Florence.
" Charles H. with the Sunday Journal, 284, b.u. 223 Asylum, rm. 118.
" James G. h. 284 Franklin.
**BARNUM JOSEPH H.** publisher Hartford Journal, Foster block, 284; h. 223 Asylum, rm. 118.          *See page* 466.
" Mary Mrs. b.r. 230 Asylum.
Barone George A. lithographer at 42 Union pl. h.u. 1 Worcester pl.
" ☞ see also Barron.
Barr Rosa J. bookkeeper at R. S. Peck & Co. printers, 26 High, b. 71 Tremont.
Barrell Wm. E. wirew. at 618 Cap. h. 89 Arch.
Barrett Allen M. driver at Bill Bros. 46 Ann,
" Bros. builders, 10 Trumbull.

| Thomas Barrett. | Robert W. Barrett. |

" Charles E. carpenter, h. 63 Harrison.
" Charles E. dentist at 753 Mn. h. 200 Ashley.
" Elizabeth J. Mrs. boardinghouse, h.452 Main.
" Frank J. salesman at 898 Main, h. 43 Pliny.
" Frederic W. bkkpr. 10 Tru. b. 81 Bluehills.
" George F. dentist, 926 Mn. rm. 45, h. 63 Sig.
" Grace L. nurse, b.u.r. 230 Asylum, rm. 13.
" Herbert T. conductor St.Ry. h. 78 Benton.
" Herbert T. nightlunch, h.u. 65 Hudson.
" James F. driver at 33, b. 43 Market.
" James S. b.u. 15 Heath.
" John, blacksmith, h. 43 Market.
" John Jr. (A. Squires & Son,) b.u. 43 Market.
" Mary, wid. James, h.u. 15 Heath.
" Michael J. shipping clerk at 142 Russ, b.u. 60 Woodbine.

Barrett Patrick, machinist, h. 60 Woodbine.
" Patrick J. engineer 618 Cap. h.u. 354 Park.
" Robert, mason, b. 581 Main.
" Robert W. (B. Bros.) h. 81 Blaehills.
" Robert W. joiner, b. 3 Harrison.
" Syrell H. steamfitter, 164 State, h. 496 Broad.
" Thomas, (B. Bros.) h. 3 Harrison.
" Thomas F. rubber w. 690 Park, h. 44 Heath.
" Wm. E. baker, b. 43 Market.
" William F. at 7 Haynes, b. 98 Babcock.
" William H. b. 37 Heath.
" Wm. R. carpenter, b. 3 Harrison.
Barrila Domenico, laborer, b.u.r. 10 Charles.
" Francesco, laborer, b. 17 Morgan.
" John, laborer, b.3u. 89 Morgan.
" Rocco, shoemaker, 3, h. 3 Charles.
Barrington Alfred, vocal teacher, 904 Main, rm. 78, h. 85 Jefferson.
Barron Charles L. b.u. 24 Wolcott.
" Lewis, at 59½ Trumbull, b.u. 24 Wolcott.
" Wm. H. carptr. at 20 Potter, h. 214 Garden.
" ☞ see also Baron.
Barrows A. Herbert, patternmaker, b. 322 Weth.
" Andrew O. l. 189 High.
" Andrew R. (B. & Thalheimer,) h. 9 Belden.
" Andrew S. clerk at 40 Ple. h.u. 53 Windsor.
" Arthur C. brakeman, b. 45 Sigourney.
" Benj. S. physician, 78, h.u. 228 High.
" Chas. A. market, 61 Village, b. 46 Windsor.
" Chas. A. Jr. market, 40 Ple. b. 46 Windsor.
" Charles L. grocer, Sisson av. and Park, h.u. 239 Park.
" Charlotte E. wid. Albert, h. 25 Madison.
" Clarence E. teamster at 1411 Main, h.r. 417 Garden.
" Edgar E. buffer, h. 45 Sigourney.
" Edwin K. at Travelers Ins. Co. 56 Prospect, b. 21 Townley.
" Edwin L. builder, b. 25 Madison.
" Elizabeth, wid. Andrew, h. 9 Belden.
" Ellen A. wid. Edwin G. h. 21 Townley.
" Frank R. machinist at 83 Woodbine, b. 240 Asylum.
" Frank W. clerk at 2 So. Ann, h. W.H.t.
" Franklin P. livery stable, 291 Allyn, h. 29 Florence.
" Fred'k M. bookkr. at 88 Market, h. 8 Mahl.
BARROWS FREEMAN W. councilman 3d ward, manager at Talcott, Frisbie & Co. druggists, 273 Asylum, h. 123 Bellevue.
" Harriet F. teacher at Brown school, 160 Market, b. 8 Mahl.
" Harriet H. wid. Frederick F. h. 8 Mahl.

Barrows Harry H. proofreader at Case, L. & Brainard Co. 141 Pearl, b. 157 Franklin.
" Irving M. draughtsm. 252 Asy. b.127 Bellevue.
" John, mach. at 62 Market, h.u. 157 Franklin.
" Julia R. wid. George J. metaphysician, h.u. 127 Trumbull.
" Kate Mrs. h. 24 Howard.
" Nellie M. at Travelers Ins. Co. 56 Prospect, b. 25 Madison.
" Samuel W. h. 12 Sumner.
" & Thalheimer, grocers and meat, 1111 Main.
    Andrew R. Barrows.    Robert Thalheimer.
" Thos. W. engraver, 62 Market, h. Cromwell t.
" Walter C. filer at 556 Capitol, b. E.H.t.
" Walter D. diesinker at 62 Market, b.u. 157 Franklin.
Barry Albert, saloon, 1181, b. 1183 Main.
" Edward, waiter, 80 State.
" Frank L. packer, h.u. 39 Windsor.
" J. deckhand str. Hartford, 285 State.
" Johanna Mrs. h.2u.r. 23 Spruce.
" John, blacksmith at N.Y.R. h.r. 25 Spruce.
" John, carpenter, b. 96 Jefferson.
" John, painter at N.Y.R. h. 7 Oak.
" John, shipcarpenter, b. 53 Governor.
" John J. bricklayer, b. 12 Center.
" John J. butcher, 128, h. 128 New Britain.
" Martha, wid. Robert, h. 612 Garden.
" Mary, domestic, h. 57 Church.
" Patrick, teamster, h.u. 36 Woodbridge.
" Patrick H. shipcarpter. h. 53 Governor.
" Thomas, laborer, h. 38 Wells.
" Thomas, ostler, b. 61 Ann.
" Thomas, saloon, 217 Front, h. 231 Market.
" Thomas J. b. 198 High.
" William, bartender, 80 State.
" Wm. J. coachman at 30, b. 30 Woodland.
" ☞ see also Berry.
Barstow Byron P. bookkeeper at Potter & Payne, 405 Allyn, l. 61 Spring.
Barta Frank J. confect'ry, etc. 150, h. 150 Russ.
Bartels Lucas F. machinist at 388 Capitol, h. 42 Madison.
Barth Joseph J. carriagemr. h. 26 So. Prospect.
Bartholomew Dana W. (Mayer & B.) h. 427 Mn.
" Fred C. clerk at 314 Asylum, h.u. 40 Church.
" George, clerk at 941 Main, b. 18 Central.
" George H. draughtsman, Hfd. Steam Boiler Insp. & Ins. Co. 650 Main, h. G.t.
" George M. h. 13 Prospect.
BARTHOLOMEW W.W. pres't & treas. Hfd. Provision Co., Valley, h. 77 Sigourney. See p. 586.
" William C. secretary Hartford Provision Co., Valley, b. 77 Sigourney.
" William F. b. 13 Prospect.
" Wilson T. salesman at Hfd. Provision Co., Valley, h. 53 Bellevue.
Bartholomy Frank, clerk, 590 Park, b.u. 12 Hung.
" Jennie, at 254 Pearl, b. 12 Hungerford.
" Jennie, wid. John, h. 12 Hungerford.
" John N. machinist at Pratt & Whitney Co. 1 Flower, b. 12 Hungerford.
Bartlett Anna E. stenographer, b. 33 Russ.
" Arthur L. clerk at W. C. Mason & Co. 746 Main, b. 33 Russ.

Bartlett Arthur M. salesm. 45 Asy. b. 31 Ashley.
" Burton A. clerk, 206 State, b.u. 1303 Main.
" Charles A. mach. at 476 Capitol, l. 119 Oak.
" Charles B. bookb. at 141 Pearl, b. 145 High.
" Edna J. b.u. 47 Wooster.
" Edwin S. office 212 Asylum, h. 14 Belden.

**BARTLETT F. W. & F. E.** real
estate and storage, 212 Asylum. *See p.* 420.
Fred. W. Bartlett.    Frank E. Bartlett.
" Fanny P. wid. D. E. h. 31 Farmington.
" Frank E. *(F. W. & F. E. Bartlett)* real es-
tate, 212 Asylum, b. 14 Belden.
" Fred. W. h. 212 Asylum, rm. 4.
" G. M. architect, 35 Wall st. N.Y., b. 14 Belden.
Geo. D. mer. tailor, 25 Asylum, h. Naubuc v.
" Geo. W. carpenter, h.u. 47 Wooster.
" Harry B. clerk at 755 Main, b. 8 Barnard.
" Harry C. at Ætna Life Ins. Co. 650 Main,
b. Tariffville v.
" Hugh J. operator at 40 Governor, b. E.H.t.
" James B. at Phœnix Insurance Co. 64 Pearl,
h. 162 Sargeant.
" John, market, 552 Asylum, h. 30 Hopkins.
" John, operator at 40 Governor, h. 296 Main.
" John B. b. 80 Bond.
" John L. mach. at 1 Flow. b. 48 Hungerford.
" John O. christian scientist, 53 Trumbull, h.
26 Ashley.
" Lucius W. bookkeeper, h. 33 Russ.
" Margaret W. private school, h. 31 Farmington.
" Mary I. assistant at Hartford Library, 5
Athenæum, b. Tariffville v.
" Mary L. musicteacher, h. 31 Farmington.
" Otis G. at Ætna Life Ins. Co. b. 90 Ashley.
" Patrick, fireman at 476 Cap. h. 47 Lawrence.
" Samuel O. toolm. 20 Sargeant, h. 80 Bond.
" Samuel P. inspector at Popes, b.u. 363 Main.
" Sherman N. printer at 16 State, h. 38 Church.
" Wallace E. drugclerk, b. 57 Pratt.
" Warren T. asst. bookkeeper at Hartford
Trust Co. 764 Main, b. 33 Russ.
" Wm. C. bkkpr. at 341 Main, h.u. 12 Alden.
" William M. student, b. 162 Sargeant.
Bartley James, *(Hartnett & B.)* h. Holyoke.
" Wm. J. mach. at 1 Flower, b. 1413 Broad.
Barton Albert L. machinist, h. 136 Martin.
" Alex. H. mach. at 1 Flow. b. 52 Edwards.
" Charles E. driver St.Ry. h.2u. 80 Madison.
" Dwight J. machinist, b. 52 Edwards.
" Edward T. foreman, 690 Park, b. 115 Oak.
" F. B. machinist, b. 52 Edwards.
" Fannie E. b. 690 Farmington.
" Frank H. mach. at 1 Flower, h. 248 Putnam.
" Frank L. toolmaker 9 Sigourney, h. 199 Russ.
" Fred. mechanic at 26 High, b. 39 Frankfort.
" G. E. finisher, 69 Front, h. E.H.t.
" George H. at National Fire Insurance Co.
95 Pearl, h. 690 Farmington.
" Henry P. Mrs. b. 690 Farmington.
" John C. mach. at 1 Flower, h. 22 Ashley.
" Mary E. clerk at Sage, Allen & Co. 898, b.
277 Main.
" Matthew H. salesman, b.u. 56 Wooster
" Minnie A. clerk at Brown, Thomson & Co.
942 Main, b. 136 Martin.

Barton Ray, at James Ahern, 280 Asy. b. Sisson.
" Seymour, boxm. 1 Flower, b.2u. 80 Madison.
" William, inspector at 700 Main, h. E.H.t.
" William, painter at 5 Mechanic, h. E.H.t.
" Wm. E. mach. at 142 Russ, b. 40 Frankfort.
" ☞ *see also Bardon.*
Barts William, dentist, 759 Main, b. 88 Church.
Bartschmid Alois, music teach. organist, h. 55 Russ.
Bascom Caroline L. wid. Christopher R. business
medium, 68, h. 68 Pratt.
" Mary M. manicure, 68, h. 68 Pratt, rm. 21.
" Richard S. janitor Unity Church, h. 68 Pratt.
Bascombe M. Mrs. dressmaker, 2, h. 2 Wadsworth.
" Cyrus H. machine hand 225 Shel h. 2 Wada.
Basey Mary, domestic at 27, b. 27 Wethersfield.
" Mattie E. b. 239 Bellevue.
" Sidney S. Mrs. h. 239 Bellevue.
" Sidney S. Jr. b. 239 Bellevue.
Bashner Louis, grocer, h. 40 Commerce.
Basiar Isaac, rollermaker, b. 236 Front.
" Nathan, peddler, b.u. 236 Front.
" Simon, peddler, b.u. 261 Market.
Baskerville John J. clerk at 690 Park, b.u. 34
Madison.
" Wm. F. toolmaker, Popes, h.u. 34 Madison.
Basney Deming S. modelmaker at Popes, h. 191
Jefferson.
" Herbert F. mechanic, b. 249 Jefferson.
" Lloyd, elevatorer, 921 Main, b. 141 Bellevue.
" Marshal J. clerk, 1391 Mn. b. 191 Jefferson.
" Nicholas, mach. 476 Cap. b. 53 Buckingham.
Bason Henry, helper, h.u.r. 28 Morgan.
Bassett Alice W. wid. O. B. Jr. h. 51 Oxford.
" Austin B. professor at Hartford Theological
Seminary, 1507 Broad.
" Eldorus A. carpenter, b. 90 Ann.
" Elizabeth C. wid. William T. h. 123 Clark.
" Ernest E. C. asst.clerk at P.O. h.2u. 1279 Mn.
" Etta, wid. George, h.u. 73 Albany.
" Mary E. Mrs. nurse, b.u. 56 Albany.
" Mary G. wid. E. J. h. 1 Charter Oak pl.
" Merton W. watchmak. 20 State, b.u. 16 Mahl.
" Nelson B. clerk at 197 Asylum, b. 51 Oxford.
" William B. notice clerk at Phœnix National
Bank, 803 Main, b. 51 Oxford.
Bassevitch & Glotzer, furs, 1235 Main.
Julius Bassevitch.    Samuel J. Glotzer.
" Julius, *(B. & Glotzer,)* h. 81 Pleasant.
Bassinger Jacob, b.u. 126 Albany.
" Paul A. florist, h.u. 126 Albany.
Bastrom Oscar, helper, b. 1183 Main.
Batchelder Joseph Warren, at National Fire Ins.
Co. 95 Pearl, h. 15 Clinton.
" ☞ *see also Bachelder.*
Batcheller Frank W. clerk, 342 Asy. h. 165 Ash.
Bates Adaline A. wid. J. D. h. 29 Gillett.
" Agnes Mrs. attendant, 30 Washington.
" Albert C. librarian, Historical society, 624
Main, b. 202 High.
" Albert H. machinist at Cheney Brothers, 34
Morgan, h. E.H.t.
" Edward J. toolmaker at 581 Cap. b. 376 Park.
" Ezra F. bookkeeper at Brown, Thomson &
Co. drygoods, 942 Main, h. 240 Laurel.
" Geo. D. lunch room, 196, h. 223 Asy. rm. 51.

# BAXTER,

## The DECORATOR.

| Wall Papers, | INTERIOR |
|---|---|
| Room Mouldings, | AND EXTERIOR |
| Metal and Canvas | WORK |
| Ceilings, | PROMPTLY ATTENDED |
| Parquet Floorings. | TO. |

## 231 ASYLUM STREET.

Bates Helen A. Mrs. nurse, 82, h. 82 Franklin.
" Henry C. printer at 175 Pl. h. 73 Governor.
" Herbert S. clerk at 81 Pratt, b. E.H.t.
" R. M. collector at 61 Asylum, b. 57 Church.
" Walter L. clerk at 928 Mn. b. 98 Trumbull.
" William, printer at 175 Pearl, b. 73 Gov.
Batson Emily S. wid. Henry, h. 722 Asylum.
" William P. clerk at Hartford Fire Ins. Co.
  53 Trumbull, h. 722 Asylum.
**BATTALIA LEO. H.** dealer in pianos,
  rebuilding a specialty, 943 Main.
Battalin Maurice, screwmaker at 476 Capitol, b.
  20 Cedar.
Batte Geo. H. creammaker at 701 Mn. b. 33 John.
Batteline Ralph, setter at Jewell Belting Co. 15
  Trumbull, h.2u. 19 Ellery.
Batterbury Richard B. laborer at Colts, h. 70
  Vanblock.
Batterson Emily L. at Travelers Insurance Co.
  56 Prospect, b. 1 Vine.
" George S. real estate agent, 370 Asylum,
  b. Highland, s. of Farmington.
" George T. Mrs. b. Highland, s. of Far.
BATTERSON JAMES G. president Travelers Ins.
  Co. 56 Prospect, president N. E. Granite
  Works, 1260 Main, h. 1 Vine.
                          See page 456.
" James G. Jr. vice president N. E. Granite
  Works, 1260 Main, b. New York city.
Battey Wm. H. agent, h. 1163 Main.
Battisla Donato, laborer, b.u. 83 Windsor.
Batty Geo. H. diesinker at Popes, h. 97 Laurel.
Batups Albert, laborer, h. 112 Heath.
Bauder Edward S. chief conduct. St.Ry.h. E.H.t.
Bauer John, chef, h.u. 150 Mather.
" John L. (Green & B.) h. 1096 Main.
Baum Wendel, b. 14 Pawtucket.
Baumann Francis, h. 36 Hudson.
" ☞ see also Bowman.
Baumgarten Albert, screwmaker at 476 Capitol,
  h. 269 Park.
Baumgartle Paul A. filer, 388 Cap. h.u. 80 Kibbe.
Baumgartner Albert L. toolmaker, l.2u. 29 Elm.
Baumstein Israel, butcher, h.2u. 203 Front.
Baun William, tailor at 720 Main, h. 25 Brook.
Baxter Geo. S. at Ætna Insurance Co. 666 Main,
  b. 34 Charter Oak pl.
" H. Ella, bookkeeper, b. 70 Edwards.
" Martin, screwm. 476 Capitol, h. 8 Forest.

Baxter Mary A. at 690 Park, b. 22 Francis.
" Michael, screwmaker, h.r. 2 Forest.
BAXTER WILLIAM G. decorator, wall paper,
  231 Asylum, h. 70 Edwards.
                          See page 52.
" William Henry, teamster at Potter & Payne,
  405 Allyn, h. 45 New Britain.
**BAYLEY & GOODRICH,** architects,
  700 Main, rooms 10 and 11.
  L. D. Bayley.      D. Parsons Goodrich.
" Lewis D. (B. & Goodrich) b. 104 Church.
" ☞ see also Bailey.
Bayless M. Bertha, buyer, 835 Mn. b. 169 Ashley.
Bayliss Grace L. stenographer, 926 Main, rm.
  77, b. 129 Trumbull.
" Isadora E. wid. James E. h. 129 Trumbull.
" James E. Mrs. h. 129 Trumbull.
Bayne John, laborer, h.3u. 57 Spruce.
" ☞ see also Bane; Bain.
Baytopp Annie L. weaver, b. 87 Maple.
" Mary, wid. Wm. dressm. 87, h. 87 Maple.

CHARLES C. BEACH, Physician. Office Hartford
  Fire Insurance Company building, 53
  Trumbull, h. 54 Woodland.
Hours—2 to 5 P. M.
     Sundays 4 to 5 P. M.
          Telephone 549.

Beach Chas. C. physician, 53 Trumbull, h. 54
  Woodland.
" Chas. M. (Beach & Co.) treasurer Broad
  Brook Co. 209 State, h. W.H.t.
" Charles T. student, h. 1304 Main.
" Clarence C. bookkeeper, 54 Ann, b. N.B.t.
**BEACH & CO.** importers, aniline dyes,
  chemicals, 209 & 211 State. See page 591.
" Edward D. h. 739 Asylum.
" Frederick E. salesman E. S. Kibbe Co. h.
  64 Oxford.
" George, (Beach & Co.) importers, chemi-
  cals; 209 State, h. 131 Farmington.
" George S. foreman, b. 5 Vandyke.
" George Watson (Beach & Co.) chemicals,
  209 State, h. 54 Main. See page 591.
**BEACH H. B. & SON,** waterfront
  boilerworks, 135 Grove. See page 538.
  H. B. Beach.      Harry L. Beach.
" Harriet Mrs. h.u. 20 Brown.
" Harry L. (H. B. Beach & Son,) boilerworks,
  135 Grove, h. 14 Buckingham.
" Helen, wid. John, h. 1304 Main.
" Henry B. (H. B. Beach & Son) boilerworks,
  135 Grove, h. 43 Winthrop.
" Jacob, machinist, b. 24 Chestnut.
" Jacob M. porter, b.r. 116 Albany.
" James C. borer at Colts, h.u. 33 Union.
" Josephine E. wid. J. W. b. 78 Wethersfield.
" Mfg. Co. underclothes, etc. 209 State.
" Mary R. teacher at High school, 39 Hop-
  kins, b. 71 Buckingham.
" Sarah, seamstress, h.2u. 877 Main, rm. 14.
" Selden, b. 73 Oxford.
" T. Belknap, (Beach & Co.) importers, chem-
  icals, 209 State, h. 99 Elm.
Beacon Falls Mills & Power Co. 209 State.

Beadle Elizabeth E. nurse, 205, h. 205 Ashley.
" H. Leonard, assistant bookkeeper at Society for Savings, 31 Pratt, h. 209 Ashley.
Beakey Michael, waiter, l. 96 State.
Beakley Fred. W. foreman at Jewell Belting Co. 15 Trumbull, b. 107 Pratt, rm. 2.
Beal George W. waiter, 29, h. 29 Windsor av.
" Mary Mrs. domestic, 29, b. 29 Windsor av.
Beale Hannah, at 336, b.u. 426 Asylum.
" Phœbe M. b.u. 426 Asylum.
Beals Edwin M. mach. 1 Flow. b. 146 Windsor av.
Beam Alfred C. bicycle repairs, 431 Main, h. 70 Maple.
Bean Henry S. clerk, 372 Asylum, b. 27 Lewis.
" James. laborer at N.Y.R. b.u.r. 23 Spruce.
" Joseph, buffer, b. 237 Lawrence.
" Walter F. engineer, b. 113 Albany.
Beard Amanda F. Mrs. music teacher, h.u. 61 Elm.
" Elisha S. clerk, 30 State, h.u. 40 Retreat.
" ☞ see also Baird.
Beardoe G. traveling salesman, b. 48 Asylum.
Beardslee B. Mrs. h. 73 Edwards.
" Clark S. Rev. prof. Theological Seminary, 1507 Broad, h. W.t.
Beardsley Benj. F. physician, 90, h. 90 Edwards.
BEARDSLEY CLARENCE I. (L. A. Dickinson & Co.) fire insurance agency, 664 Main, h. 1 Bellevue. See page 444.
" Edward R. sec'y and tr. P.&R. h. 52 Imlay.
BEARDSLEY EDWARD W. local agent Phœnix Fire Insurance Co. 64 Pearl, h. 20 Girard av. See page 460.
" Guy E. at Ætna Ins. Co. 666 Main, b. 90 Edwards.
" Harold J. bkkpr. 126 Church, b. 1 Bellevue.
" Mary J. assistant at 171 Putnam.
Beaton M. Mrs. b. 41 Woodbridge.
" Neil, stonecutter, b.r. 36 Temple pl.
Beattie Robert (Davies & B.) h. 37½ Church.
" Robert Mrs. millinery, 37½, h. 37½ Church.
Beatty Michael, teamster, b.u. 51 Front.
Beauchamp Geo. screwm. 476 Cap. l. 284 Asylum.
" Joseph, bicycle repairer at Andrus & Herrmann, 300, l. 284 Asylum, rm. 88.
" Joseph, teamster, 283 Shel. b. 1470½ Broad.
" Wm. messenger, Adams Ex. b.u. 144 Albany.
Beauchemin Emory, carpenter, h.2u.r. 348 Windsor av.
" Herman, cigarmaker, 867 Main b. 97 Russ.
Beaudet David, oiler, 142 Russ, h. 283 Capitol.
Beaudion Peter, laborer, 690 Park, b. Prospect av.
Beaudoin Alexander, carpenter, h. Pro. nr. N.P.
" Alfred, carpenter, b. 148 Albany.
" Filias, carpenter, h. 306 Wethersfield.
" Frank, carpenter, h. 148 Albany.
Beaumeir Jos. rubberw. 690 Park, h. 24½ Grace.
Beaune Edwin P. barber, 255, b.u. 37 Lawrence.
" Henry W. fitter, 556 Capitol, h.2u. 6 Talcott.
" Leon, joiner, h.u. 37 Lawrence.
" William J. mach. Popes, h. 37 Lawrence.
Beaupre Exies, dropforger, b.u. 28 Laurel.
" Frederic, dropforger, b. 50 Amity.
" Henry, carpenter, h. 33 Pleasant.
" Joseph, plasterer, b. 50 Amity.
" Mark, dropforger at Popes, b. 50 Amity.

Beaupre Middie W. clerk, 690 Park, b. 28 Law.
" ☞ see also Baupre.
Beauregard Ellen, h. 3 Riverside pl.
" Frank, waiter, 98 Wells, b. 150 Allyn.
" James, harnessm. at 8 Sig. b. 613 Capitol.
Beccu William, bartender, b.2u. 545 Main.
Beccuchi Antonio, laborer, b.3u. 31 North.
Becher August, printer, 252 Pearl, b.2u. 4 Talcott.
" Chas. W. bartender, 42 Asy. h.u. 50 Temple.
" Frank, saloon, 841 Main, h. 111 Trumbull.
" Fred. Otto, bookbinder at 856 Main, b.2u. 4 Talcott.
" Julius, porter, 841 Main, h. 36 Grand.
" ☞ see also Baker; Becker; Bekker.
Bechstedt Chas. O. barber, 258 Law. h. 198 High.
Beck Abram, meats, 206 Front, h.r. 28 Morgan.
" Addie M. justifyer, Evening Post, 23 Asylum, l. 75 Allen pl.
" Alice, clerk, 921 Main, b. E.H.t.
" Annie C. clerk, Brown, Thomson & Co. 942 Main, b. E.H.t.
BECK CURT. E. furniture upholsterer, 262 Allyn, h. 146 Capitol. See p. 505.
" Franz H. packer, 867 Main, .h.u. 204 Fkn.
" George, butcher at 493 Main, b. 75 Allen pl.
" Hans H. screwm. 476 Cap. h.2u. 144 Mather.
" Henry, bartender, 841 Main, h. E.H.t.
" Henry, butcher, h. 13 Portland.
" Isaac, h.2u. 60 Morgan.
" Isaac, butcher, 206, h.2u. 190 Front.
" Jacob, peddlor, h. 222 Front.
" John E. burnisher, 62 Market, b. 75 Allen pl.
" John L. bookb. 252 Pearl, h. 75 Allen pl.
" Joseph, h.u. 60 Morgan.
" Julius, at 273 Asylum, b. 192 Front.
" Lizzie, at 59½ Trumbull, b. 75 Allen pl.
" Lottie E. nurse, 75, b. 75 Allen pl.
" Lydia, b. 146 Capitol.
" Meyer, laborer, 1 Flower, h 134 Front.
" Paul G.M. mach. at 388 Cap. h. 6 Hungerford.
" Peter H. screwm. at 476 Cap. h.u. 32 Laurel.
" William L. clerk, 295 Asy. b. 79 Allen pl.
Becker Benjamin, peddler, h.3u. 19 North.
" Catherine Mrs. b. 73 Laurel.
" Emma, nurse, b. 14 Church, room 3.
" Fannie, b. 19 North.
" Ferdinand E. bartr. 651 Main, h. 73 Laurel.
" Fred, rubberw. 690 Park, b.2u. 82 Francis.
" George, molder, h.2u. 84 Francis.
" H. peddler, b. 75 Pleasant.
" Hyman, tailor at 730 Main, b. 41 North.
" Jacob, h. 75 Pleasant.
" Jacob, butcher, h.u. 190 Front.
" Louis J. toolm. at 803 Main, h.u. 65 Madison.
" Morris, clerk, b. 58 Pleasant.
" Oscar, tinner, b.2u. 82 Francis.
" Samuel, harnessm. at 8 Sig. h. 58 Pleasant.
" Tobias, h. 58 Pleasant.
" Willis E. architect, 756 Main, rm. 47.
" ☞ see also Baker; Beecher; Becher; Bekker.
Beckett Lucas A. roller, h. 160 Sisson.
Beckley Edward L. machinist, 142 Russ, h. 72 Hopkins.
" Elizabeth, wid. Edgar, h. 399 Wethersfield.
" Ernest I. clerk, 295 Asylum, b. Rocky Hill t.

Beckley Harry C. helper, C. C. Fuller & Co. 14
    Ford, b. 399 Wethersfield.
  " Hattie E. b. 399 Wethersfield.
Beckman Charles O. mach. at 54 Arch, b. 21 Mul.
Beckwith Eugenia, wid. Alpheus, h. 26 Russ.
  " Albert F. painter, 39 Ann, b.2u. 1042 Main.
  " Allen B. clerk, 40 Ann, h. 152 Wethersfield.
  " Charles, conductor P.&R. h. 93 Chestnut.
  " Daniel P. toolm. at Popes, h. Windsor t.
  " Frank T. conductor at V. Div. N.Y.R. 450
    Asylum, h. Middletown t.
  " Isbon T. Rev. professor Trinity College, 14
    Seabury hall, Summit.
  " J. E. capt. barge E. S. Tyler, 285 State, h
    Saybrook t.
  " J.L. barge Nauticus, 285 State, h.Saybrook t.
  " James B. h. 1343 Main.
  " Merrill F. student, b. 233 Sargeant.
  " Richard L. b. 90 Gillett.
  " Thomas F. conductor Valley division N.Y.R.
    h. 273 Windsor av.
Bedard Wm. F. at 336 Asylum, h.2u. 14 Talcott.
Bedford George T. screwmaker, h.2u. 5 Sisson.
  " John, screwmaker at 476 Cap. h. 179 Law.
  " William, laborer, h.r. 213 Pearl.
  " Wm. R. livery, 15½ Babcock, h.u. 5 Sisson.
Bedigan Donald, laborer, 690 Park, h. 2 Putnam.
Bednar Lawrence, laborer, h.2u. 216 Sheldon.
Bedworth Francis T. clerk, Brown, Thomson &
    Co. 942 Main, b.2u. 25 Alden.
  " Wm. E. assembler at Colts, h.2u. 25 Alden.
Bee Cigar Co. 220 State.
  " Hive office, Wm. H. Bulkeley, 650 Main.
  " Wm.G. electrician at 1 Laurel, b. Burnside t.
Beebe Arba B. engineer at N.Y.R. h.u. 6 Foot
    Guard pl.
  " Charles E. salesman, Case, Lockwood &
    Brainard Co. 141 Pearl, b. 9 Clinton.
  " Emily C. b.u. 58 Russ.
  " Emma E. housekeeper at 20 South Hudson.
  " Everett M. salesman, 34 Mar. h. 15 Crown.
  " Fred.S. mach. hand at 135 Shel. b.3u. 89 Mn.
  " Frederick H. captain steamer Hartford, 285
    State, h. Essex t.
  " Henry E. letter carrier, h. 44 Madison.
  " Hobart A. driver, h.2u. 246 Wethersfield.
  " Ira, repairer at 40 Governor, h.3u. 89 Main.
  " J. Rosco, conductor St.Ry. b. 28 Alden.
  " Robert L., U. S. Army, b. 427 Main.
  " S. wid. J. R. b.u. 58 Russ.
Beecher Edward, policeman, h.3u. 573 Main.
  " George W. agent, 811 Main, b. 227 High.
Beehan Hattie A. clerk at 921 Mn. b. 10 Walnut.
  " Mark J. gardener, h.u. 10 Walnut.
**BEEMAN & HATCH ORCHES-**
**TRA,** Charles P. Hatch, manager, 18
    Windsor av.
Beeman Mary L. violinist, 18, h.u. 18 Windsor av.
  " Wm. M. jeweler, 272 Asy. h.u. 18 Windsor av.
Beers Arthur B. conductor St.Ry. h. Burnside v.
  " Edith D. teacher of dancing, b. 64 Allen pl.
  " Eliza, nurse, b. 11 Elmer.
  " George M. clerk at Pratt & Whitney
    Co. 1 Flower, h. 64 Allen pl.
  " Geo. M. Mrs. dressmaker, 64, h. 64 Allen pl.

Beers Robert, clerk at Hartford St.Ry. Co. 11
    State, b. 44 Cedar.
  " Samuel, laborer at 30 Weth. h. 83 Huysbope.
  " William D. mach. at Colts, b. 63 Annawan.
  " ☞ see also Behre; Beyer.
Beerwort Wilbert E. milkman, b. 286 N.B.
Beesch Frank E. painter, N.Y.R. b. 79 Clark.
  " Jacob M. helper N.Y.R. b. 116½ Albany.
Begenski Bill, laborer, b.u. 40 North.
Begg William, b. 1339 Broad.
Beggs Edith, bkkpr. at 721 Main, b.u. 15 John.
  " Nathaniel, mach. at 80 Huy. h.u. 15 John.
Begler Frank, teamster, h. 192 State.
Begley Annie, b. 70 Church.
  " Charles, teamster, 165, b. 115 Windsor.
  " Mary Mrs. clerk at 835 Main, h. 11 S. Pro.
  " Michael, laborer, h. 113 Windsor.
  " Thomas, laborer at N.Y.R. b. 104 Portland.
Begoney Bertha, at 835 Main, b.u. 19 Church.
Behan Fenton P. machinist at 30 Cushman, h.u.
    52 Chestnut.
  " John, helper, h.2u. 57 Windsor.
  " John F. clerk, at 95 Pleasant, b. 1104 Main.
Behner F. Edward, tinner, 1116 Mn. h. 3 Alden.
  " Louis, fire insurance, 51 Tru. h. 79 Pearl.
Behre Henry, machinist at Colts, b. 77 Huyshope.
  " William, mach. at Colts, h. 77 Huyshope.
  " ☞ see also Beyer; Beers.
Beiderman Gotfried, at Popes, h.u. 28 Sanford.
Beissner Henry, butcher, h.u. 74 Martin.
Beiswanger Barbara, wid. Michael, h.133 Market.
Beizer Jacob, rollercaster at 141 Pearl.
  " Nathan, peddler, h. 236 Front.
Bekker John H. mach. 30 Cush. h.2u. 47 Wdbn.
  " ☞ see also Baker; Becher; Becker; Beker.
Beladean John, carpenter, b.2u. 147 State.
Belanger Joseph B. trimmer, 266 Pl. b. 2 Mannz.
  " Philip, carptr. at 158 Woodland, h.2u. 33 Asy.
Belcher Clarence, stenographer at W. C. Mason
    & Co. 746 Main, b. E.H.t.
  " Dean E. draughtsman at 1 Flower, h. S.M.v.
  " Edith, clerk at 835, l. 981 Main.
  " John, machinist, h. 90 Chestnut.
  " John N. toolm. at 1 Flow. h. 238 Jefferson.
  " Leroy H. clerk at 1143 Main, b.u. 90 Chst.
  " Roosevelt, coachman at 44, l. 44 High.
  " Thomas N. conductor St.Ry. h.3u. 90 State.
  " Warren J. draughtsman at 142 Russ, h.u.
    30 Hopkins.
Belcourt Henry, burnisher 62 Mar. h. 126 State.
  " Oscar, gardener, 26, h. 26 Whitney.
Belden Caroline B. wid. Emerson W. h. 98 Hudson.
  " Channing S. at Hartford Steam Boiler
    Insp. & Ins. Co. 650 Mn. b. 57 Farmington.
  " Charles, painter, r. 96 N.B. h. 74 Bond.
**BELDEN CHARLES R.** pres. and treas. Hartford
    Coal Co. 754 Main, h. 905 Asylum.
    See page 492.
  " Clifford H. b. 217 Laurel.
  " Edgar A. woodw. at 69 Front, h. 166 Ashley.
  " Edward W. salesman 47 Ann, h. 71 Tremont.
  " Eugene S. contractor, h. 217 Laurel.
  " Frank E. secretary Colt's Pat. Fire Arms
    Mfg. Co. h. 329 Laurel.

Belden Frederick S. asst. secy. Hartford Coal Co. h. 8 Park ter.
" Herbert E. at Hartford Fire Ins. Co. 53 Trumbull, b. 217 Laurel.
" Jas. S. (S. B. & Son) h. 44 Buckingham.
" Oscar C. insurance agt. 721, h. 1102 Main.
" Russell B. at Travelers Insurance Co. 56 Prospect, b. 98 Hudson.
" Seabury, shipbuilder, h. 3 Girard.
**BELDEN SETH & SON,** flagstone, 69 Commerce. See page 508.
James S. Belden.
Beleski Isaac, harnessm. at 8 Sig. b. 12 North.
Belfi Ernest J. machinist at 28 High, b. 61 Ann.
Belfield Homer B. shipping clerk at 142 Russ, h. 14 Linden.
" Stiles, messenger Adams Ex. h.u. 14 Linden.
Belisie Tancrede, carpenter, b. 48 Temple.
Belknap Charles H. at National Fire Insurance Co. 95 Pearl, b. 5 Vine.
" Edward L. at Phœnix Ins. Co. 64 Pearl, b. 5 Vine.
" Leverett (B. & Warfield,) h. 5 Vine.
" Sarah M. Mrs. h. 5 Vine.
**BELKNAP & WARFIELD,** booksellers, publishers, 77 Asylum. See p. 421.
Leverett Belknap.    George F. Warfield.
Bell Alex. McC. carpenter, h. 9 Girard.
" Azilda, dressmaker, b. 46 Canton.
" Chas. H. druggist, 639 Main, h. 118 Weth.
" Clarence E. mach. at 13 Cen. h.u. 27 Albany.
" Edward C. clerk at Popes, b. 68 Lawrence.
" Etelrite D. wid. James, h. 46 Canton.
" Eugene R. machinist at 2 So. Ann, b. E.H.t.
" Frank, painter, h. 206 Asylum, flat 6.
" George H. S. Rev. b. 183 Capen.
" George L. toolmaker at 20 Sargeant, h.u. 72 Hopkins.
" George N. physician, 44 High, h. 211 Garden.
" Harriet. clerk 835 Main, h. 231 Lawrence.
" James A. boxm. 254 Pearl, b.2u. 129 Albany.
" John, conductor at St. Ry. b. E.H.t.
" John A. M. upholsterer, b. 9 Girard.
" John B. at 1 Spruce, b. 20 Charles.
" Lillian G. stenogr. at 273 Asy. b. 96 Ann.
" Martha, at 336 Asylum, b. 58 Church.
" Mary, wid. Lewis, h.r. 6 Squire.
" Patrick F. repairer at Popes. h.u. 242 Pearl.
" Richard, cabman, l.u. 126 Windsor.
" Samuel H. janitor at Ætna Insurance Co. 666 Main, h. 185 Capen.
" Sarah, clerk at Brown, Thomson & Co. 942 Main, b.u. 129 Albany.
" Wilfred F. carpenter, h.u. 49 Governor.
Bellado Charles, bellman at 152 Asylum.
Bellamy Robert B. student Trinity college, b. 69 Vernon.
" Walter, finisher at 62 Market, h.26 Congress.
Bellanger Joseph, carpenter, b.u. 112 Windsor.
" Theophile, joiner at 158 Woodland.
Bellardini Lucca A. laborer, h.3u. 2 Charles.
**BELLER BERNHARD,** cabinetmaker, 43, b. 43 Linden. See page 511.
Bellenski Isaac, peddler, h.3u. 24 North.
Bellerin Francis, carpenter, h. 18 Douglas.

Bellew Peter, repairer 532 Asy. b. 25 Walnut.
Belli Antonio, laborer, b. 2 Charles.
Bellows Frank R. baggagemaster at V. Div. N. Y.R. h. Saybrook t.
Bellsborrow ☞ see Billsborrow.
Belmont Joseph A. barber at 415 Main.
Belter Herman, cabinetm.155 Ch.O. h.300 Maple.
Belyea Annie A. wid. Joshua, nurse, l. 61 Spring.
Bemis Mary C. Mrs. h. 111 Ann.
" Thomas B. with Hartford Life Ins. Co. 252 Asylum, h. 21 Lincoln.
Bender Emery E. teacher at Huntsingers, 30 Asylum, h.u. 502 Windsor av.
" ☞ see also Binder.
C. M. H. BENEDICT, Professional Massage and Electro Therapeutics, Manicure and Chiropody, Facial and Hand Treatments a speciality; also Scalp Treatments and Shampooing. Room 20, Waverly building, 721 Main.
Benedict Caroline M. H. wid. Chauncey, massage and electrican, 721, h. 721 Mn. rm. 20.
" Elmer C. clerk, 1 Flow. b. 721 Main, rm. 20.
" Everett R. nightclerk P.O. b. 721 Mn. rm. 20.
" Frank C. at Conn. Building & Loan Asso. 252 Asylum, h. 44 Westland.
" George H. engineer, h. 9 Hendricxsen.
" Harry, baggagem. Union Station, b. W.H.t.
" Louis H. tester, 556 Cap. h.u. 10 Glendale.
" Samuel N. assessor, 114 Pearl, h. 54 Bkm.
Benerman William A. lab. b. 10 New Britain.
" Edith, bookkeeper, b. 73 Park.
Bengston Henning, pressman at 69C, h. 853 Park.
" Jacob, tailor, h. 67 Governor.
" John, mech. at Popes, b.2u. 177 Lawrence.
" Nils, machinist at 581 Cap. b.177 Lawrence.
Bengtson Alfred, b. 296 Park.
" Olof, tailor, h.2u. 2 Elm pl.
Benham Hattie J. wid. Nathan, b. 5 Winthrop.
" Mary E. wid. James L. h. 72 Chestnut.
" Wm. Perkins, mach. at Popes, b. 72 Chestnut.
" William Pitkin, h. 317 Wethersfield.
Benjamin Daniel, bkkpr. 555 Capitol, b. W.t.
" Edson M. carptr. at 141 Tru. h. 104 Wooster.
" Frank L. clerk 139 Asylum, b. 104 Wooster.
" George, carpenter, h. 104 Wooster.
" Howard W. clerk at Phœnix Mut. Life Ins. Co. 49 Pearl, h. Windsor t.
" John W., Hfd. Charcoal Co. h. 108 Wooster.
" Lizzie, at 59½ Trumbull, b. 104 Wooster.
" Mabel Mrs. boardinghouse, 38 Temple.
" Nellie M. wid. Wm. H. h. 21 Evergreen.
" Prosper, bricklayer, h. 36 Temple.
" Roland H. ship'g clk. 54 Arch,b.108 Wooster.
" Scott R. gen. agt. at Hartford Steam Boiler Insp.& Ins.Co.650 Main, b.57 Farmington.
" William M. architect 756 Mn.l. 104 Wooster.
Benkert Agnes, wid. Charles, b. Maple c. King.
Bennedetto Geo. fruit, 261 Mn. h.2u. 64 Morgan.
" Leonard, tailor, b.u. 27 Kilbourn.
Benner Adoniram J. builder, 99, h. 99 Babcock.
Bennett James, carpenter, h. 43 New Britain.
" Albert, laborer, b. 113 Front.
" Alice N. b. 300 Farmington.

Bennett Alvin, mech. at Popes, b. Burnside v.
" Amos, foreman, h. 67 Laurel.
" Amos T. Jr. toolm. at Popes, h. 67 Laurel.
" Arthur P. with National Fire Insurance Co. 95 Pearl, b. 206 Sisson.
**BENNETT & BROTT,** attorneys at law, 847 Main, room 23.   *See page* 483.
Edward B. Bennett.   George Olney Brott.
" C. Frederick, telegraph operator, 12 Central, h. 222 Garden.
" Edward B. attorney at law, (*B. & Brott,*) 847 Main, rm. 23, b. 67 Collins.
" Edward F. finisher at 62 Market, h. E.H.t.
" Edward W. carpenter, b. 2 Church.
" Elizabeth A. clerk Sage, Allen & Co. 898 Main, b. 5 Grand.
" Ella S. bookkpr. at 176 Allyn, b. 307 Weth.
" Elmer P. shipper at 15 Tru. h. 11 Warner.
" George S. silvers. 62 Market, b. 36 Pleasant.
" J. watertender str. Middlet'n, h. Hamburg t.
" James, casehardener at Popes, h. 67 Laurel.
" James, machinist at Pratt & Whitney Co. 1 Flower, b. East Hartford t.
" James H. drug clerk at 853 Main, b. 194 High.
" Jane S. wid. William A. h. 8 Trinity.
" John S. clerk at 114 Asylum, b. 67 Laurel.
" Joseph A. foreman, 1 Flower, h. 42 Lincoln.
" Joseph J. clerk at 95 Main, b. 80 Allen pl.
" M. Toscan, b. 300 Farmington.
" Margaret, wid. P. H. h. 5 Grand.
" Margaret D. cashier Brown, Thomson & Co. 942 Main, b. 5 Grand.
" Martin, manager Lion Fire, Scottish Union and National Ins. Co. 197 Asylum, h. 300 Farmington.
" Mary J. clerk at Brown, Thomson & Co. 942 Main, b. 5 Grand.
" Mary M. teacher Wilson St. school, b. 67 Lau.
" Michael, laborer, h.r. 28 South Prospect.
" Nancy Mrs. h. 118 Albany.
" Norman B. h. 56 Willard.
" Philo P. sup't Bradstreets Com. Agency, 49 Pearl, rm. 18, h. 206 Sisson.
" & Rathgeb, restaurant, 975 Main.
Edward W. Bennett.   Henry Rathgeb.
" Tasker, student, h. 300 Farmington.
" Wm. machinist at Colts, h.u. 78 Vanblock.
" William H. lineman at 247 Pearl, h. 27 N.B.
" William J. toolmaker at Popes, h. 67 Laurel.
" Wm. R. hardener at 388 Capitol, b. N.B. t.
" William W. bookkeeper at Popes, l. 903 Main, rm. 13.
Bennie John, iceman, b. 22 Elm.
Benning Annie M. b. 77 Bellevue.
" Barbara, wid. Frederick, h. 77 Bellevue.
Bennis Abraham, groceries, 19, h. 23 Hawthorn.
" James F. machinist at Pratt & Whitney Co. 1 Flower, h.u. 168 Windsor.
" William J. repairer at Popes, h. 3u. 514 Broad.
Bennison Richard Harry, guide at Pope Tube Co. b. W.H.t.
Bensemer August, h.u. 83 Front.
" ☞ *see also Bansemer.*
Benson Alfred, carpenter at 158 Woodland, b. 34 Putnam.

Benson Andrew, engineer, 93 Ch.O. h. Weth.
" Charles E. gardener, h.u. 28 Rowe.
" Eliza M. h.u. 10 Village.
" Fred W. teamster, b. 107 Hungerford.
" Jennie C. dressmaker, 10, h.u. 10 Village.
" Isaac, barber 296 Asylum, h.u. 304 Market.
" Levi B. clerk, 2 So. Ann, h. 70 Windsor av.
" Lloyd R. student at Trinity college, 6 Northam Tower, Summit.
" Nils, rubberworker, b.u. 55 Grand.
" Reuel A. student at Trinity College, 2 Northam Tower, Summit.
" Rudolph, painter, h. Bluehills.
Bent Thomas B. salesman, h. 44½ Wooster.
Bentley J. W. insurance agent, h. 40 Wooster.
" Joseph, steamfitter at 53 Vernon.
" Mary, h. 2 Orchard.
" Mary E. teacher at Arsenal school, b. 149 Windsor av.
" Wm. F. builder, architect, 219, h. 219 Ashley.
" Wm. S. rubberworker at 690, b. 816 Park.
Benton Charles F. b. 2 Holcomb.
" Collins W. with Hartford Life Ins. Co. 252 Asylum, b. So. Manchester v.
" Frederick H. teamster, h.u. 18 Sanford.
" George, laborer, h.u. 211 Pearl.
" Henry A. screwm. at 476 Cap. h. 232 Weth.
" Herbert E. school fund commissioner, State Capitol, room 5, h. New Haven c.
" John R. instructor at Trinity college, 1 Jarvis hall, Summit.
" Rebecca, wid. William, h.u. 12 West.
Bentz Arthur O. machinist at 223 State, h. 30½ Harbison.
Bentzen Carl J. P. helper at 15 Tru. b. 17 Elmer.
Benzamere Charles, bartender at 26 Union pl. b. 428 Asylum.
Bercovitz Jacob, tailor, h.u. 299 Market.
Berdansky Samuel, driver at 10 Ple. h. 304 Mar.
Berdrick Thomas A. clerk at 909 Mn. h. 14 Gov.
Berenson Benj. filer at Popes, b. 41 Windsor.
" Bros. barbers, 296 Asylum.
Ike Berenson.   Max Berenson.
" Ike (*B. Bros.*) h. 304 Market.
" Max (*B. Bros.*) h.u. c. Market and Pleasant.
Berg Abraham, cutter at 8 Sig. b. 56 Pleasant.
" Andrew, carpenter, h.u. 111 Lawrence.
" August, mechanic at 216 Law. h.r. 48 Cedar.
" Charles, G. h. 21 Hamilton.
" Emil J. polisher at Popes, h.u. 151 Babcock.
" Ida T. b. 82 Gillett.
Bergen James, painter, h. 109 Windsor.
" Katherine, wid. Thomas B. h. 109 Windsor.
" Keron, saloon, 84 Walnut, h. 46 Liberty.
" Maria L. wid. Jeremiah P. h. 84 Hudson.
" Mary, b. 109 Windsor.
Bergenholst John A. rubberw. at 690, h. 525 Park.
Berger Hyman, peddler, h. 2u. 232 Front.
" Karl, oiler at 581 Capitol, h. 82 Madison av.
" Max H. mach. at 30 Cush. h. 56 Hawthorn.
Bergerstrom John H. mechanical engineer, 252 Asylum, h. 64 Madison.
Berggren Alfred L. machinist at 1 Flower, h. 97 Hamilton.
" Carl F. peddler, b. 55 Harrison.

Bergman Annie wid. Maurice, h.u. 49 Chestnut.
" Fred E. nickleplater at Popes, b. Shannon pl.
" Henry A. barber, 77 Trumbull, b.u. 49 Chst.
" John, mechanic at Popes, h. Shanahan pl.
" Samuel, barber at 22 State, b. 49 Chestnut.
Bergquist David, h.u. 3 Brady pl.
" John, rubberw. at 690 Park, h. 10 Putnam.
" Joseph, watchman, h.u. 3 Brady pl.
" Otto, operator at 40 Gov. b.r. 56 Albany.
Bergron John B. rubberworker, h. 10 Amity.
Beringer Max, tailor at 2 State, b.u. 36 Temple.
Berkey Michael, waiter, 80 State.
Berkley Anderson, laborer, b.r. 118 Albany.
Berkman Harris, dry goods, h.u. 192 Front.
Berkovitch Abraham, 2d hand furniture, 64 Morgan, h. 270 Front.
" Moses, tailor, h.2u. 203 Front.
" Sam, peddler, h.u. 91 Front.
Berlin Victor, printer at 11, b. 110 Pratt.
Berman A. D. peddler, h.u. 207 Front.
" Bernard, carpenter, h. 60 Avon.
" Isaac, h. 28 Pleasant.
" Louis, h. 207 Front.
" Max D. peddler, h. 11 Morgan.
" Rachael, clerk, b. 207 Front.
" Samuel, helper at 135 Sheldon, b. 60 Avon.
" ☞ see also Behrman.
Bermingham J. M. general treasurer National Home for Disabled Volunteer Soldiers, office 783 Main, b. 27 Spring.
" ☞ see also Birmingham.
Bernard Carlos A. mech. at Popes, b. 1219 Main.
" David, buyer at 921 Mn. h.u. 36 Bellevue.
" Emery, assembler at Colts, h. 488 Main.
" Frank, carver at 20 Potter, h. 66 Bond.
" Isadore, clerk, b 550 Asylum.
" Luke, groceries, 121, h. 119 Windsor av.
" Napoleon P. toolmr. at Popes, b.u. 556 Mn.
" Oscar, Jr. carpenter, b. Gilman c. George.
" Petre, carpenter, h.u. 89 Windsor.
" Philomene, wid. Oscar, h. Gilman c. George.
" W. H. driver at 37 Wells, b.u. 6 Bond.
Bernhardt Fred A. gardener at Retreat farm, 262, h. 262 New Britain.
" Winona, b. 262 New Britain.
Bernier Arthur, clerk at 653 Mn. h. 33½ Russell.
" Bosile, laborer, h.2u. 105½ Windsor.
" Frank, teamster, h.u.r. 105½ Windsor.
" Louis, carpenter, h.2u. 369 Park.
" Theophile, carpenter, b.u. 40 John.
Bernstein Harris, peddler, h.u. 164 Front.
" Joseph Abram, tailor, 46 Asy. b. 84 Windsor.
Beront Charles, laborer at 335 Sheldon, h. 21 South Prospect.
Berquist Gustave, potter at Faience, h. 8 Olive.
" Solomon, inspector at Popes, h. 1 Wolcott.
Berrigan Daniel, printer at 284, b. 279 Asylum.
Berrington Geo. H. patternm. at Colts, h. E.H.t.
Berry Anna F. wid. Benj. h. 650 Main, rm. 61.
" Carl J. polisher at Popes, h. 21 Hamilton.
" Charles, baker, h. 22 North.
" & Cosgrove, saloon, 997 Main.
    Thomas F. Berry.        Bernard H. Cosgrove.
" Dennis J. (P. B. & Sons,) h.2u. 6 Walnut.
- " Edwin W. waiter, h.u. 273 Jefferson.

Berry Ellen, wid. Patrick, b. 76 Franklin.
" Florence A. b. 234 High.
" Frances E. wid. William, h. 234 High.
" Fred. D. bookkeeper at Water Commissioners, City hall, 800 Mn. h. 31 Ward.
" George G. mach. at 388 Cap. h. 273 Jefferson.
" Howard, optician at 865 Main, b. 28 Spring.
" James, laborer at 95, b. 69 Pleasant,
" Jas. P. (P. Berry & Sons) b. 17 Windsor av.
" John F. (P. Berry & Sons,) h.2u. 52 Flower.
" John H. coremaker at 556 Cap. b. 289 Asy.
" Joseph E. clerk 223 Asylum, h.u. 111 Oak.
" Julia H. b. 76 Franklin.
" Lucinda, wid. Edwin B. b.u. 273 Jefferson.
" Margaret, h.u. 22 South Prospect.
" Mary, wid. Peter, h. 17 Windsor av.
" Michael, h.2u. 71 Avon.
" Nelson, driver, b. 342 Wethersfield.
" P. & Sons, wholesale fruits, 4 American.
    Dennis J. Berry.        James P. Berry.
    Peter M. Berry.         Thomas A. Berry.
              John F. Berry.
" Patrick E. grocery, 74, h. 74 Franklin.
" Peter M. (P. Berry & Sons,) b. 17 Windsor av.
" Rose, wid. Michael, h.2u. 10 Charter Oak.
" Samuel H. clerk at Phœnix Mutual Life Ins. Co. 49 Pearl, h. 60 Oak.
" Thomas, helper at 54 Arch, h. 22 S. Pro.
" Thomas A. (P. Berry & Sons,) h.u. 23 Elmer.
" Thos. F. (B. & Cosgrove,) h. 65 Windsor av.
" Thomas R. toolmaker, h.u. 107 Hungerford.
" W. M. moterman St.Ry. h. E.H.t.
" Wm. driver at 15 Albany, h.u. 105 Windsor.
" Wm. R. at Ætna Life Ins. Co. 650 Main, b. 234 High.
" ☞ see also Barry.
**BERRYMAN  MANUFACTUR-ING CO.** 40 Cushman. *See p. 546.*
Bersen Max, barber, h.u. 81 Pleasant.
Berslav Isaac, cleaner street dept. h.u. 176 Front.
Bertelsen Christesen, beltmaker at 15 Trumbull, h.r. 23 Morgan.
" Hans, shoemaker, 15, b. 12 Morgan.
Berthold H. Mrs. housekeeper, 13 Seyms.
" Mary, forewoman at 20 Sargeant, b. 113 Babcock.
Bertram William, mach. at N.Y.R. h. 23 Walnut.
Bertrand Henry J. blacksmith, 5 Mechanic, h. 37 Lawrence.
" Ubeld, carpenter, h. 37 Lawrence.

Bertty George, fruits, &c. 261 Mn. h. 64 Morgan.
Bertuccio Antonio, beltmaker at 15 Trumbull, b.2u. 36 Windsor.
" Vincent, (Muzio & B.) h.u 12 Kilbourn.
Berube Edward, carpenter N.E.R.R. h.u.r. 105½ Windsor.
" Joseph, carpenter, h.u.r. 89 Windsor.
Besse Joseph L. (P. & J. B.) h. 187 Sisson.
" Peter (P. & J.B.) 701 Main, h. Boston, Mass.
BESSE P. & J. ice cream, pastry, and confectionery, 701 Main.              See page 57.
     Peter Besse.          Joseph L. Besse.
Best Calvin L. carpenter, h. 30 New Britain.
" Charles R. discount clk. at Conn. Trust & Safe Deposit Co. 785 Main, b. 57 Buckingham.
" George, h. 57 Buckingham.
" Helen E. clk. at 871 Main, b. 24 New Britain.
" Herman J. joiner, b. 24 New Britain.
" James J. builder, 24, h. 24 New Britain.
Bestor Clarissa, wid. Geo. R. b.u. 236 Jefferson.
" Cyrus S. salesman, Ingraham, Swift & Co. 126 Church, h.u. 236 Jefferson.
" Howard G. real estate, and auctioneer, etc. 82 Pearl, h.15 Lincoln.
" Robert L. clerk at 82 Pearl, b. 15 Morris.
" S. J. Mrs. h.u. 15 Morris.
Betancourt Roberto A. insurance, 92 Pearl, h. Brookfield t.
Beterman Gottfried J. enameller at 581 Capitol, h. 28 Sanford.
Betts Edward H. salt & fish, 216 State, h. 121 Huntington.
" Frederick A. insurance commissioner, rm. 18, State Capitol, h. New Haven t.
" George B. clerk at 544 Asylum, b. 56 Put.
" James, laborer, b. 124 Potter.
Betzer Charles, carpenter, h.u. 22 Morgan.
Beulich Hermann, lab. at 490, b. 490 Windsor av.
Bevins Vernah L. at National Fire Ins. Co. 95 Pearl, b. 575 Farmington.
Beyer Frank, burnisher at 62 Mar. h.2u. 77 Gov.
" ☞ see also Beers, Behre.
Biangamano John, ragpicker, l.3u. 20 Charles.
" Michael, ragpicker, h.2u. 20 Charles.
Bibbins Frances, seamstress, h.2u. 28 Julius.
" Julia, wid. William W. h.2u. 28 Julius.
Biche Zee, polisher at Hartford Typewriter Co. 476 Capitol, h. Prospect av.
Bickel August H. patternmaker at 1 Flower, b. 86 Hamilton.
" Charles M. machinist at Hartford Cycle Co. 581 Capitol, h. 86 Hamilton.
" Richard W. patternmaker at 1 Flower, b. 86 Hamilton.

HENRY BICKFORD, Physician.    Office, 98 Ann street.
Hours—8 to 9 A.M.
          1 to 2 and 7 to 8 P.M.
               Telephone 849-2.

Bickford Henry, physician, 98, h. 98 Ann.
" John B. carpenter at 158 Woodland, h.2u. 346 Windsor av.
Bickmore William, carpenter, h.u. 42 Pleasant.
Biddle Edward G. clerk at Popes, b. 15 Sherman.
" George, b. 15 Sherman.
" George J. compositor at Case, Lockwood & Brainard Co. 141 Pearl, b. 15 Sherman.
Bidelik Michael, helper at 1 Flower, h. 75½ Ple.
Biderman Jos. screwm. at 476 Cap. b. 54 Ple.
Bidgood Edward H. clerk at 372 Asy. h. E.H.t.
" Frederick, clerk at 26, b. 26 State.
" Laura, clerk, b. 19 Benton.
" Marcus L. Mrs. h.u. 19 Benton.
Bidwell Ada C. proofreader, 154 Pearl, b. 828 Broad.
" Albert W. painter, h. 12 Union.
" Daniel D. reporter Hartford Times, 716 Main, h. East Hartford t.
" Delia A. teacher at South school, 36 Wadsworth, b. Bloomfield t.
" Elizabeth W. Miss h. 89 Buckingham.
" Ella A. cloakfitter at Stillman & Co. furriers, 59 Pratt, b. 58 Church.
" Eunice, wid. Alfred, h. 12 Avon.
" Frank, painter at 1106 Main, h. E.H.t.
" Frank W. at Ætna Life Ins. Co. 650 Main, h. 5 Brownell.
" Frederick, b. 2 Holcomb.
" Frederick C. clerk at 78 Asy. h. Bloomfield t.
" Grace C. stenographer Phœnix Mutual Life Ins. Co. 49 Pearl, b. 197 Park.
" Harry, manager, 77 Pratt, l. 14 Church.
" Herbert, collector, h. 10½ Ford.
" Howard E. clerk at Beach & Co. 209 State, b. East Hartford t.
" Jas. H. (H. C. Judd & Root,) 389 Allyn, h. 89 Buckingham.
" Jane E. b. 27 Atwood.
" Jennie E. wid. Lorenzo, b.u. 5 Brownell.
" John C. (John C. Bidwell & Co.) h. 5 Clinton.
" John C. & Co. Goodyear Rub. Store, 237 Asy.*
" John W. boardinghouse, 37 Winthrop.
" Kate L. bookkeeper at Sage, Allen & Co. 898 Main, b. 197 Park.
BIDWELL, MARTIN A. trees, etc. h. 24 Vine.
                                      See page 59.
" Percy W. clerk, 154 Pearl, b. 20 Lewis.
" Phœbe, h.u. 9 Kinsley.
" Samuel J. mechanic at Popes, h. 197 Park.
" Samuel W. coal and lumber, h. 72 Bkm.
" William H. clerk, b. 126 Trumbull.
Bieckel Chas. mach. at 581 Cap. h. 86 Hamilton.
Biederman Gottfried J. at Popes, h.u. 28 Sanford.
Bigelow Eugene C. foreman, 59½ Tru. h. 24 Mahl.
" Harry W. bookkeeper at 865 Main, rm. 6, h. 18 Scyms.
" Henry, toolmaker, h. 8 Canton.
" Henry W. chemist, test department at Popes, b. 18 Garden.

Biggs Henry B. lab. at 276 Mar. h.2u. 40 Hicks.
Bigley Martha E. h.u. 198 Allyn.
Bigot Augustus, hodcarrier, b. 197 State.
Bilek Joseph F. tailor at 81 Asy. b. 27 Mulberry.
Bill Albert C. (Bill & Tuttle) 487 Main, rm. 4. judge police court, h. 27 Annawan.
" Albert C. b. 98 Vine.
" Alice M. stenogr. at 750 Main, b. S.M.v.
" Austin R. supt. at Adams Express Co. 805 Main, h.u. 280 Main.

**BILL BROTHERS,** carmen and city express, 46 Ann. *See page 550.*
Francis P. Bill, est. of.    Fred R. Bill.
Dwight H. Bill.
" Clarence A. at Hartford Fire Ins. Co. 53 Trumbull, b. South Manchester v.
" Dwight H. (Bill Bros.) h.u. 128 Trumbull.
" Edward S. eng. N.Y.R. h. 378 Windsor av.
" Edwin S. b. 230 Asylum.
" Emery E. clerk at 164 State, b. 27 Vine.
" Francis W. H. at Ætna Life Insurance Co. 650 Main, b. 113 Albany.
" Fred R. (Bill Bros.) 46 Ann,h. 128 Trumbull.
" George F. chief of police, 38 Kinsley, b. 98 Vine.
" George S. engineer N.Y.R. h. 87 Brook.
" Harry C. clerk at Pope Tube Co. b. 27 Vine.
" Harry L. musician, b. 334 Wethersfield.
" Homer C. Mrs. h. 113 Albany.
" Julia A. wid. C. C. b. 27 Annawan.
" Lizzie R. b. 1150 Main.
" M. fireman tug Coulston, 285 State.
" Mary E. wid. George W. h. 27 Vine.
" Robert P. clerk at 1 Flower, b. 27 Vine.
" Rollin H. clerk at 372 Asy. b. 757 Main.
" Sarah A.N. wid.Francis P.h.u. 128 Trumbull.
" Tony, sidewalk layer at 154 Charter Oak, h. 20 Kilbourn.

**BILL & TUTTLE,** attorneys at law, 847 Main. *See page 482.*
Albert C. Bill.    Joseph P. Tuttle.
BILLINGS C. E. MFG. Co. mach. 142 Russ.
*See page 531.*
BILLINGS CHAS. E. prest. & gen. mgr. The Billings & Spencer Co. 142 Russ, *fire commissioner,* h. 86 Buckingham.
*See page 531.*
" Eugene G. bkkpr. at 80 State, h. 45 Walnut.
" Fred H. at Popes, h. 45 Walnut.
" Frederick C. superintendent at The Billings & Spencer Co. 142 Russ, h. 171 Capitol.
" Harry E. asst. supt. The Billings & Spencer Co. 142 Russ, h. 427 Main, rm. 28.
" Henry E. president Billings Sidewalks and Masons Supply Co. h. 17 Allen pl.
" Henry F., clerk railroad commissioner, rm. 43, State Capitol, h. 35 Ward.
" May Mrs. h.2u. 24 Mulberry.
" P. H. merchant tailor, 11 Asy. h.173 Collins.
" Sarah F. seamstress, b. 79 Willow.
" Sidewalk & Masons Supply Co. 154 Ch. O.

**BILLINGS & SPENCER CO** The dropforgings, etc. 142 Russ, c. Lawrence.
*See page 531.*

Billsborrow Frank H. stenographer at Ætna Ins. Co. 666 Main, h. 52 Lincoln.
" Hannah, wid. James, b. 52 Lincoln.
Billups Albert Mrs. h. 523 Park.
Bilodeau Joseph H. A. tailor at 71 Asylum, h.u. 119 Windsor av.
Bingham Clinton, clerk at 745 Mn. b. 66 Hopkins.
" Edwin H. clerk at Jewell Belting Co. 15 Trumbull, h. 11 Alden.
" Frances A. nurse, b. 14 Spring.
" Geo. A. supervisor of bridges at N.Y.R. h. 251 Lawrence.
" George C. motorman St.Ry. b. 4 Elliott ct.
" Grace J. stenographer at Popes, b. 251 Law.
" Herbert C., Prospect Stock Farm and h. 856 Prospect av.
" Hezekiah C. iceman at 4 Central, h. E.H.t.
" J. Rev. clergyman, h. 484 Farmington.
" Julia C. wid. Orsemus, b. 15 Foot Guard pl.
" Nancy L. wid. Henry A. h. 11 Alden.
" Wallace R. at Travelers Insurance Co. 56 Prospect, b. 53 Capitol.
" Warren A. tillerman str. No. 4, h. 18 S.Ann.
Biondi Frank, laborer, b.u. 73 Morgan.
Birch Albert T. at 68 Mar. b.2u. 50 Chestnut.
" Eva E. at 252 Pearl, b.2u. 50 Chestnut.
" Ellen, wid. Thomas, h. 209 Garden.
" Herbert R. bkkpr. at 20 Church, h. E.H.t.
" John. h. 61 Whitmore.
" Louis H. toolm. at 142 Russ b. 178 Ashley.
" Mary A. at 68 Market, b.2u. 50 Chestnut.
" Nellie, wid. of Thomas, h.2u. 50 Chestnut.
" Richard, plumber, 20 Church, h. E.H.t.
" Thomas S. foreman at Billings & Spencer Co. 142 Russ, h. 178 Ashley.
Birckmayer William, carpenter, h. 49 Heath.
Bird Fred W. h. 185 Smith.
Birden Charles H. carpenter, h.2u. 264 Capen.
" J.S. & Co.,Capitol City Pickle House,84 Vine.
" John S. student, b. 84 Vine.
" Jas. S. (J. S. Birden & Co.) h. 84 Vine.
Birge Esther, wid. Edwin, h. 40 Allen pl.
" William H. bookkeeper, h.u. 51 Pleasant.
Birkenmayer Helen J. stenographer at Hartford Fire Ins. Co. 53 Trumbull, b. 84 Capitol.
Birkery Cornelius J. prest. Birkery Mfg Co. h. 111 Bellevue.
" Edward L. student, b. 111 Bellevue.
" Mfg. Co. plumbers' supplies, 65 Suffield.
" Michael E. brassfinisher, b. 163 Front.

# E. C. BISHOP & CO.,

MANUFACTURERS OF

## Ladders & Step-Ladders of all kinds.

The New Improved Hartford Extension Ladder.

Painters' Stage Ladders.    Ladder Hooks, etc.    Cyprus
Wood Eave Trough and Conductors of all kinds.

## 34 CAPEN STREET.

Birkholtz John, helper at 1 Flow. b.u. 248 Law.
Birmingham Ann, wid. Thomas, h.u.r. 78 Ward.
" Bernard, mach. at 581 Cap. h. 1421 Broad.
" Hannah J. clerk at 885 Main, b. E.H.t.
" John B. b.u.r. 78 Ward.
BIRMINGHAM JOSEPH M. alderman 9th ward,
     asst. supt. at Popes, h. 256 Putnam.
" Lizzie, b.u. 57 Dean.
" Mary, proofrdr. at 704 Mn. b. 1421 Broad.
" Mary, store 74, h. 74 Ward.
" Mary, vestmaker, h. 271 Jefferson.
" Mary, wid. Thomas, h.u. 57 Dean.
" Michael, teamster at 2 Chapel, h. 97 Main.
" Michael T. at Neal, Goff & Inglis Co, 980
     Main, b. 86 Madison.
" Nellie, laundress, St. Marys Home, W.H.t.
" Patrick, mason, h.u. 84 Ward.
" Patrick H. toolm. at Popes, h.2u. 308 Park.
" Patrick J. plumber, b. 373 Broad.
" Solomon F. fireman, h. 298 Park.
" Thomas F. peddler, h. 15 Benton.
" Thomas P. h. 133 Babcock.
" ☞ see also Bermingham.

## BIRNEY REGINALD, special agent
Mutual Benefit Life Ins. Co. Newark, N.
J. 29 Pearl, h. 43 Huntington.
Birth Joseph, wagonm. at 10 Ferry, h. 26 Pro.
Bishop Alonzo W. electrician, b.2u. 84 Grove.
" Carlos E. h. 27 Bluehills.
" Carrie O. bkkpr. at 319 Asy. b. 152 Wash.
BISHOP E. C. & Co. ladder manufacturers, 34
     Capen.                    See page 60.
                 Edwin C. Bishop.
" Edna L. b. 27 Bluehills.
" Edward, operator at 135 Shel. b. 26 Church.
" Edward R. mechanic, b. 34 Capen.
BISHOP EDWIN C. (E. C. B. & Co.) h. 34 Capen.
" Elizabeth F. Mrs. b. 59 Capitol.
" Elsie Mrs. b.u. 37 Liberty.
" Esther, wid. Roscoe E. h.2u. 84 Grove.
" Frank F. clerk at Connecticut General Life
     Ins. Co. 49 Pearl, b. 94 Huntington.
" Frederick L. h. 76 Farmington.
" Karl, printer at 141 Pearl, h.u. 34 Capen.
" Nellie V. cashier at Brown, Thomson &
     Co. 942 Main, b. 84 Grove.
" Nelson, carpenter, h. 15 Davenport.
" Nelson Jr. rubberw. 690 Park, b. 15 Dvpt.
" Rens, benchman, b. 15 Davenport.
" Reuben J. clerk 254 Pearl, h. 14 Warner.
" Richard K. native lumber, h. 603 Garden.
" Sylvester S. skiver at 15 Tru. h. 152 Wash.

Bissell Arthur T. b. 95 Ann.
" Birge A. janitor, 315, h. 315 Pearl.
" Caroline D., Miss, h. 93 Spring.
" Catharine B. b. 462 Farmington.
" Catharine E. wid. Sylvester, h. 462 Far.
" Frances Louisa Mrs. h. 44 Spring.
" H. Edgar, clerk, N.Y.R. h. West Haven t.
" Henry, bookkeeper and cashier at F. H.
     Richards, 803 Main, h.u. 38 Huntington.
" Herbert G. clerk at Phœnix Mutual Life
     Ins. Co. 49 Pearl, b. 44 Spring.
BISSELL HIRAM, mason, builder, 43,
     h. 43 Wadsworth.        See page 516.
" Howard C. draughtsman, b. 38 Huntington.
" J. Walton, b. 34 Chapel.
" James M. tobacco, 220 State, h. 34 Chapel.
" Julia S. D. wid. Geo. P. h. 93 Spring.
" Lilian L. musicteacher, 44, b. 44 Spring.
" Luzurne E. apprentice 1 Laurel, b. 173 Ash.
" M. Elleanor, b. 95 Ann.
" Mary, teacher at kindergarten Brown school,
     b. 38 Huntington.
" Roger W. clerk at 95 Ple. b. 38 Huntington.
" Samuel T. musicteacher and pianotuner, 851
     Main, h. 38 Kenyon.
" T. Clarence, chief clerk comptrollers office,
     rm. 2, State capitol, h. Willimantic t.
" Thomas H. real estate and loans, h. 95 Ann.
" William P. milkman, 10, b. 10 Holcomb.
Bisshoff Morris, painter, h. 262 Front.
Bitgood Edward H. clerk 372 Asylum, h. E.H.t
Bixbee ☞ see Byxbee.
Bizari Nicolo, laborer, b.u. 64 Morgan.
" Peligreni, laborer, b.u. 64 Morgan.
" Raphael, laborer, b.u. 64 Morgan.
Bjork Matilda J. wid. of Chas. J. h.2u. 18 Tru.
Bjorkgreen John, laborer, b.u. 80 Front.
Bjorklund Chas. clerk at Smith, Bourn & Co.
     8 Sigourney, b. 320 Capen.
" Earnest W. carpenter, b.u. 67 Governor.
" Ellen, massage, b. 1332 Broad.
" John E. carpenter at 69 Front, b. 320 Capen.
" Knut, mach. at 133 Sheldon, h.r. 14 Affleck.
" Louisa, dressmaker, b. 320 Capen.
" Victor, clerk at Baxter the Decorator, 231
     Asylum b. 320 Capen.
Bjorkman L. W. A. pastor Swedish Zion Con-
     gregational Church, h. 87 Russ.
" ☞ see also Byorkman.
Bjorn Carl, driver at 48 Ann, b. W.H.t.
Bjurling John, machinist, h. 34 Wooster.
Blachansky A. b.u. 85 Morgan.
" Esar, peddler, h.u. 85 Morgan.
" Lena, operator, 172 Front, b.u. 85 Morgan.
Black Agnes, stenographer, 424 Asylum, b.
     Glastonbury t.
" Burton A. fitter at 164 State, h. 461 Broad.
" Gertie H. at 1 South Ann, b.u. 189 Maple.
" Lucy H. Mrs. prop. Madison house, 110 Pratt.
" Madison J. prop. Empire Stables, veterinary
     surgeon, 560 Main, h. 111 Pratt.
" Martha J. forelady at 83, b. 55 Woodbine.
" Robert, stonemason, h. 264 Capen.
" Samuel, machinist at 83, h. 55 Woodbine.

Blackburn Wm. blacksmith, b.u. 224 Park.
Blackman Charles C. h.u. 257 Windsor av.
" Cyrus M. hardener at 1 Flow. b. 28 Spring.
" J. machinist, 13 Central.
Blackmer Walter R. theo. student, 1507 Broad.
Blade Charles, waiter at 389 Main.
" Frances M. Mrs. h. 4 Elm.
" Robert H. clerk at 547 Main, b. 4 Elm.
Bladon Geo. L. goldbeater, 41 Trumbull, h. 112 Wooster.
Blair & Coxeter, manufacturing jewelers, 911 Mn.
Robert C. Blair.        Wm. G. Coxeter.
" Edgar S. bookkeeper at 25 Front.
" Edward, carpenter, h. 404 Franklin.
" Frank, carpenter, h. 106 Mather.
" James, clerk at 745 Main, h. 107 Albany.
" Joseph, carpenter, h. 58 Bond.
" Robert C. (B. & Coxeter,) h. 66 Capen.
Blais Joseph, blacksmith, b. 61 Albany.
Blake Albert E. clerk at Charles R. Hart Co. carpets, 898, l. 1243 Main.
" Alvin, boilermaker at H. B. Beach & Son, 135 Grove, h. 5 Blumenthal.
" Alvin F. teamster, h.u. 10 Blumenthal.
" Bridget, wid. John, h.u. 1432 Broad.
" Chas. E. turner at 62 Mar. h. Cromwell t.
" Charles L. carpenter, 1 Flower, h. New Park.
" Edward G. traveling salesman, h. 30 Imlay.
" Edwin A. pastor First M. E. church, h. 98 Edwards.
BLAKE EDWIN J. (T. J. Blake & Son,) 143 Commerce, b. 23 Vine.
" Francis, waiter, h.u. 37 Mather.
" Frank, mechanic at Popes, b.r. 143 Zion.
" Fred W. teamster, Pope T. Co. h. 25 Grand.
" Harry, h. 140 Barbour.
" James, blacksmith at Pope Tube Co. h.2u. 137 Lawrence.
" Jas. Edward, machinist at 1 Flow. h. 8 Fales.
" John, fireman P.&R. b. 152 Mather.
" John F. clerk at 15 Albany, h. New Park.
" John F. salesman at 263 Asylum, h. C.O.pl.
" Lillie G. clerk at Brown, Thomson & Co. 942 Main, b. 225 High.
" Mabel A. b. 23 Vine.
" Mary J. teacher, h. 1432 Broad.
" Peter, machinist at Lincoln & Co., 54 Arch, h.u. 39 Spring.
" Sylvester J. clerk at 117 Asy. b.u. 39 Spring.
BLAKE T. J. & SON, brass and coppersmiths, 141 and 143 Commerce.
See page 489.
Thomas J. Blake.        Edwin J. Blake.
" Thos. P. pressfeeder 12 Central, b. 80 State.
" Thomas J. charity commissioner, (T. J. Blake & Son,) h. 23 Vine.
" Thomas J. Jr. drug clerk 385 Cap. b.23 Vine.
BLAKE WALTER P. painter, 219 to 221 Pearl, h. 234 Zion.
" Wilbur H. bookkeeper, special U. S. custom house storekeeper, 141 Com. b. 23 Vine.
Blakely Bertram L. salesm. 43 Asy. b. 110 High.
" Frank W. at 37 New Britain, b. 60 Seymour.
Blakeman George H. patternmaker 33 Wells, b. 9 Lafayette.

## G. G. BLANCHARD,

# Butter and Eggs.

### SPECIALTY,

# FRESH EGGS.

## 40 VINE STREET.

Blakeslee A. D. photoengraver at A. Mugford, 177 Asylum, b. 119 Capitol.
" Fred. G. at Ætna Ins. Co. 666 Main, b. 192 Sargeant.
" Havilah A. h. 791 Park.
" Helen E. wid. Capt. Harry, h.u. 192 Sargeant.
" Henry J. b. 791 Park.
" Jessie B. accountant at 476 Cap. b. 791 Park.
" Leila H. kindergarten teacher Arsenal school, b. 192 Sargeant.
" Wilber H. forem. Burr Index Co. h. 120 Park.
Blakesley George D. clerk at Insurance Dept. State Capitol, rm. 16, h. 30 Lewis.
" Harley M. insurance clerk, rm. 14, State Capitol, b. 30 Lewis.
Blanc H. waiter steamer Hartford, 285 State.
Blanchard Archibald W. clerk at Factory Ins. Association, 95 Pearl, b. 110 Babcock.
" Frank O. salesman at 304 Asy. b. 168 Sig.
BLANCHARD GEORGE G. groceries and meats, 170 Capen, creamery butter and eggs, 40, h. 40 Vine.        See page 61.
" Henry C. clerk, b. 22 Hopkins.
" Homer, h. 73 Buckingham.
" Joseph L. b. 73 Buckingham.
" Oland H. manager N. E. Div. of agents National Life Association, h. 168 Sigourney.
" Paul, lather, h. 52 Lawrence.
" Paul P. carpenter, h. 13½ John.
" Samuel N. clerk, b. 168 Sigourney.
Blanchette Charles S. carptr. b. 5 Davenport.
" Louis, carptr. at 10 Tru. h.u. 5 Davenport.
" Valmore, steamfitter at 1 Flow. b. 40 Amity.
Blanchfield James, farmer, h. 566 Windsor av.
" James E. rubberw. at 690 Pk. b. 49 Sanford.
" John, contracting grading, 49, h. 49 Sanford.
Bland Albert, pressman at Case, Lockwood & Brainard Co. 141 Pearl.
" Fred. C. bkkpr. at Billings & Spencer Co. 142 Russ, h. 40 Lincoln.
" John R. blacksm. N.Y.R. h.u. 104 Walnut.
" Robert W. machinist, l. 284 Asylum, rm. 84.
" Wm. W. printer at 29 Union pl. h. 22 Village.
Blanejr Julius, carptr. 53 Vernon, b. 127 Ward.
Blase John, fruit, h. 23 Windsor.
Blatchford Francis M. h. 41 Willard.
Blazer & Co. confectionery, 413 Main.
Frank Blazer.        John Blazer.
" Frank (F. Blazer & Co.) h. 58 Pleasant.
" John (F. Blazer & Co.) h. 23 Windsor.
Blease Alfred H. shipping clerk at Wm. Rogers Mfg. Co. 66 Market, h. 14 Pliny ct.

Bleehdorn Charles, b. 222 Sargeant.
" Victoria, wid. William, b. 222 Sargeant.
" William, upholsterer, 2 Tru. h. 194 Russ.
" ☞ see also Bluehdorn.
Bleik Isaac, grocery, 75½, h. 75½ Pleasant.
Blenkhorne Sadie, nurse, 20 South Hudson.
Blesso Rocco, porter at 637 Main, b. 58 Pleasant.
Bletcher Frank O. stenographer at 783 Main, b. 18 Buckingham.
Blevins David, slater, 383, h. 383 Park.
" Wm. engineer, h.u. 385 Park.
" William B. butcher, h. 246 Park.
Blicq Edgar T. clerk at Sage, Allen & Co. 898 Main, b.3u. 80 Pearl.
Bligh Edward J. mgr. cafe 26 State, l. 847 Main.
Blinn D. H. & Co. watchmakers, 175 Asylum.
    Daniel H. Blinn.    Edward R. Blinn.
" Daniel H. (D. H. B. & Co.) h.u. 366 Maple.
" Edward R. (D. H. B. & Co.) h. Cromwell t.
" Hattie, b. 999 Main.
" Ira, electrician, l. 16 Village.
" Philip, electrician, l. 16 Village.
" Rex E. salesman at 725 Main, b. 25 Alden.
" Wm. W. engineer at 555 Cap. h. 14 Imlay.
Blise ☞ see also Blazer.
Bliss Abby G. wid. Benjamin, h. 73 Farmington.
" Alfred L. clerk at Orient Insurance Co. 5 Haynes, b. 54 Willard.
" Amelia F. wid. Elisha, h. 166 Sigourney.
" Arthur W. (W.H.B.& Sons) h. 190 Sargeant.
" Charles L. clerk at Popes, b. Cromwell t.
" Chas. W. foreman, 1 Flow. h. Springfield,
**BLISS EDWARD,** furnaces and ranges, repairing a specialty, 1263 Main, h. 231 Sigourney, See page 494.
" Edw. A. clerk at 372 Asylum, h. 167 Albany.
" Edward B. at Ætna Insurance Company, 666 Main, b. 231 Sigourney.
" Edward M. shipping clerk at Pratt & Whitney Co. 1 Flower, b. 54 Willard.
" Elisha F. b. 169 Sigourney.
" Emily H. wid. Edward A. h. 54 Willard.
" Francis E. president American Publishing Company, 424 Asylum, h. 169 Sigourney.
" Francis E. Jr. bookkeeper, b. 169 Sigourney.
" Fred J. (W. H. Bliss & Sons,) h. 47 Weth.
" Frederick S. h. 73 Farmington.
" Harry E. timekeeper, b. 49 Wethersfield.
" Hayden W. b. 36 Jefferson.
" Mary T. wid. Ralph, h. 25 Wadsworth.
" Thomas, blacksm. at 476 Cap. b. 216 Shel.
" Walter, secretary American Publishing Co. 424 Asylum, h. 166 Sigourney.
" Watson H. (W. H. Bliss & Sons,) h.49 Weth.
**BLISS WATSON H. & SONS,** builders, 158 Woodland. Office 17 Lewis.
    W. H. Bliss.    Fred. J. Bliss.    Arthur W. Bliss.
Bloch Simon, peddler, h. 211 Front.
Block John, carpenter, b. 276 Lawrence.
" Himan, groceries, 72, h. 72 Temple.
" Simon, setter at 15 Trumbull, b. 81 Pleasant.
Blodgett Agnes E. wid. Wm. H. b. 147 Sigourney.
" Alden M. teamster at 71 Asy. h. 15 Windsor.
**BLODGETT & CLAPP CO.** iron, steel, etc. 47–55 Market. See page 541.

Blodgett Frank A. overseer 42 Seyms, h. 32 Vine
" Geo. A. machinist at 1 Flower, b. 1204 Broad.
" Roswell F. secretary Pratt & Whitney Co. 1 Flower, h. 3 Farmington.
" William H. patent attorney at F. H. Richards, 803 Main, h. 147 Sigourney.
Bloise Vincent, tailor, 31½ Alb. b. 47½ Morgan.
Blomberg ☞ see Blamburg.
Blomeke Elizabeth, wid. H. G. h. 1 Worcester pl.
Blomgren John L. polisher at Popes, b. 13 Hung.
Blomquist Martin, toolmaker at Popes, h.u. 15 Harbison.
Blondin Alphoso, contractor, h. 61 Park.
Blonin Louis, joiner, b.u. 59 Windsor.
Blood Louis H. designer of machinery, 49 Pearl, h.u. 217 Ashley.
" William, at 1189 Broad, b. 231 Lawrence.
Bloom Alfred M. trav. salesman, h.u. 77 Franklin.
" Joseph B. peddler, h.u. 73 Charles.
" Samuel, tailor at 66-Asylum, b.u. 195 Front.
" ☞ see also Blume.
Bloomingdale James, pat. medicine, l. 377 Main.
" Martha, musician, h. 719 Asylum.
Bloomquist Carl O. clerk at 197 Asy. b. Bristol t.
Bluehdorn Ernest C. machinist, 1 Flower, h. 71 Woodbine.
" ☞ see also Bleedorn.
Blum Martha J. wid. Henry, h.u. 9 Howard.
Bluman Michael, wirew. at 618 Cap. b. 22 North.
" Samuel, wirew. at 618 Capitol, b. 206 Front.
Blume Fred. W. screwm. 476 Cap. h. Newington j.
" Theo. W. toolm. at 1 Flower, l. 46 Babcock.
" ☞ see also Bloome.
Blumenthal Abe, screwm. at 476 Cap. b. 80 Mor.
" Abraham, tinner at 1192 Main, h. 54 Ple.
" Albert J. clerk at 82 Asylum, h. Weth. t.
" Benj., German delicacies, 229, h. 225 Market.
" Etta, wid. Aaron, h. 72 Hungerford.
" Harry roofer, h. 66 Village.
" Isaac R., Excelsior Sale and Exchange Stables, 20 Morgan, b. 106 Ann.
" Mollie, dressmaker, h. 72 Hungerford.
" Moses, salesm. 908 Main, b. 72 Hungerford.
" Samuel, driver at 20, b. 20 Morgan.
" Sarah, wid. Meyer, groceries, 80, h. 80 Mor.
Blush Clark D. assembler, h. 235 Asylum.
Blydenburgh Ralph G. shipcaulker, h.u. 2 Union.
Blythe Chas. A. machinist, h. 49 Huyshope.
" Elizabeth Mrs. h.u. 1155 Main.
" Elizabeth C. h. 799 Asylum.
" Eva Mrs. housekeeper, 98, b. 98 Wells.
" George A. printer 252 Pearl, b.u. 1208 Main.
" Mabel M. clerk, b. 30½ Cedar.
" Margaret, h. 799 Asylum.
Board of Trade, P. H. Woodward, sec. 49 Pearl.
Boarding Home for Young Women, 58 Church. See Woman Christian Association of Hfd.
Boardman Alfred, carpenter, b. 148 Albany.
" Belle C. wid. William, h.u. 1155 Main.
" Benjamin, bartender, 36 Park, b.2u.163 Bab.
" Charles, h. 42 Webster.
" Chauncey B. livery, 356 Main, h. 23 Wash.
" Elizabeth, wid. William H. h.u.163 Babcock.
" Elizabeth H. teacher at Woodside Seminary, 1204, b. 1204 Asylum.

Boardman Elmina, wid. Henry, h.u. 240 Weth.
" Florence, b.u. 163 Babcock.
" Frances M. b. 42 Webster.
" Frank, carpenter, h. 148 Albany.
" Frank R.engraver at 29 Union pl.h.u.99 Oak.
" Fred B. clerk, b. 721 Main, rm. 62.
" Geo. W. machinist at 24 Mec. b. 330 Weth.
" Harry R. bookkeeper at Capewell Horse Nail Co. 40 Governor, b. 119 Capitol.
" Howard F. treasurer Wm. Boardman & Sons Co. h. 193 Evergreen.
" James W. blksm. 133 Shel.l. 721 Main,rm.62.
" John S. h. 330 Wethersfield.
" Margaret A.wid.Charles H.h.25 Washington.
" Robert A. clerk, First National Bank, 50 State, b. 25 Washington.
" T. Jefferson, president Wm. Boardman & Sons Co. h. 77 Buckingham.
" Thomas J. inspector Factory Ins. Ass'n, 95 Pearl, h. Warehouse Point v.
" William, laborer, h. 7 Oak.
" Wm. E. clerk, 304 Asy. b. 77 Buckingham.
" Wm. F. driver, 15 Alb. h. 103 Windsor av.
" William F. J. h. 74 Farmington.
" William G. h. 10 Marshal.
" Wm. H. mach. 83 Wdbn. h.2u. 163 Babcock.
" Wm. & Sons Co. tea,coffee, etc.,304 Asylum.
Bochner Solomon, agent, 756 Mn. h.231 Franklin.
Bock August, baker at 169 Asylum.
" Henry, b. 119 High.
" Sadie, at 690 Park, b. 104 Windsor.
Bockins Harry N. rubberw. 690 Park, h.9 Hung.
Bockus Ernest W. nightwatchm. h. 26 Cottage pl.
" Silas, helper, St.Ry. b. E.H.t.
" William, foreman St.Ry. h. E.H.t.
Bocorselski Raymond F. draughtsman at 141 Trumbull. b. 153 Ward.
Bode Ivan M. foreman for W. S. Williams, 285 State, b. 38 Woodbridge.
Bodenstein Chas.F.mach.at 1So. Ann,h. 25Brook.
" Herman, cigarmaker, 29, h. 29 Brook.
" Mary, wid. Herman, b. 25 Brook.
Bodge Geo. R. agent, 81, h.3u. 81 Asylum, rm. 10.
" Margaret, clerk at 349 Main, b. 2 Chestnut.
" Margaret, wid. Dwight C. h. 2 Chestnut.
" Nellie, at 83 Woodbine, b. 2 Chestnut.
" Wm. C. machinist at 581 Cap. b.2 Chestnut.
Bodwell Chas. S. mach. at 142 Russ,h.11 Clinton.
" E. A. wid. Thos. L. nurse, b. 127 Oak.
" Emma Louise, wid. J. H. b. 18 Ch. O.
" Geo. A. electrotyper at 177 Asy. b.11 Clinton.
Boel William H. painter at N.Y.R. h. W.t.
Boettger J. Gustav, rubberworker at 690 Park, h.2u. 20 Kibbe.
Bogardus Adelbert U. dropforger at Colts, h.r. 74 Vanblock.
Bogert Dorcas wid. David B. A. h. Alb. c. Brook.
Bogle Henry, motorman, St.Ry. h.4u. 18 S.Ann.
Bogue Arthur T. supt. money order dep't at P. O. h. 42 Bond.
" David R. salesman, 61 Asylum, b. Weth.t.
" Harriet M. Mrs. dressm. 375, h. 375 Main.
" John C. police, b. 103 Capitol.
Bohan James J. h.u. 147 Sheldon.
" ☞ see also Bowen.

Bohman Alfred, filer, 556 Cap. h.u.r. 17 Wolcott.
" William E. helper, h.2u. 47 Lawrence.
Bohner Theodore, teamster, l. 556 Main.
Boice Frances, wid. Isaac W. h. 101 Hungerford.
" Harriet C. cashier, 45 Asy.b. 101 Hung.
" Webb C. salesm. 956 Main, b. 101 Hung.
Bois Catherine E. nurse at 20 South Hudson.
Boisseau Henry A. mach. 476 Cap. b. 84 Pro. av.
" John B. A. carpenter, h. 92 Prospect av.
" Jos. B. machinist, 476 Cap. h.84 Prospect av.
Boissier Agnes, wid. Charles, b. 260 Laurel.
Boisvert Felix, blacksmith N.Y.R. h. 25½ Flower.
Bolan Anthony F. hose driver at No. 8 Engine house, h.u. 129 Babcock.
" Ella, wid. Patrick, h. 72 Seymour.
" James, laborer at stone pits, b. Zion.
" James H. screwmaker, 476 Cap. h.u. 39 Har.
" John, laborer at stone pits, h.u. 15 Ellery.
" Joseph, helper, 1 Flower, h.u. 39 Harbison.
" Mary J. b.u. 39 Harbison.
Boland Alice, at 690 Park, b.u. 2 Harbison.
" Bridget, wid. Michael, h.u. 2 Harbison.
" Frederick A. mechanical engir. h.64 Vernon.
" John, b. 2 Holcomb.
" John E. buffer at Wm. Rogers Mfg. Co. 66 Market, b. 29 Mechanic.
" Michael, b. 2 Holcomb.
" William, laborer, h.u. 29 Mechanic.
" William, park officer, b.u. 35 Park.
" ☞ see also Bolan, Bowlan.
Bolanger Joseph, carpenter, b.u. 112 Windsor.
Bolar Edward, tinner at 360 Main, h.u. 60 Bond.
Bolard John J. machinist at N.Y.R. b.1326 Broad.
Bolden Geo. L. coachm. 130, l.r. 130 Washington.
Bolder Patrick W. laborer, Popes, b. 57 Spruce.
Boldizar Joseph, harnessm. 8 Sig. b. 28 Lawrence.
Bolf Wm. M. truckman, 51, h. 51 Martin.
" ☞ see also Balf.
Bolger Belle R. b.u. 99 Maple.
" John F. actor, b.u. 99 Maple.
Bolles Addie R. wid. George A. h. 852 Asylum.
" Carrie A. b. 9 Clinton.
" Charles H. h. 471 Farmington.
" Charles R. student, b. 471 Farmington.
" Cora B. wid. Samuel P. b. 207 Main.
" Edward M. strapm. 15 Tru.b. 17 Goodman.
" Ernest F. shipclk. 1 S.Ann,h. Manchester t.
" George J. cutter, 1 S. Ann,h. 201 Capen.
" Harry K.clerk, 709 Main, b.471 Farmington.
" Herman L. clerk at 155 Asy. h.u. 22 Williams.
" Jane Mrs. h. 17 Goodman.
" John C. bookkeeper, h. 121 Hungerford.
" Minnie, wid. John F. h. Farmington.
" O. Elmer, pressman, h. 261 Park.
" William C. h. 27 Girard.
" ☞ see also Bowles.
Bolt Cora T. Mrs. steno. Popes, b. 94 Hawthorn.
" William W. student, b. 94 Hawthorn.
Bolter James, president Hartford National Bank, 58 State, h. 1067 Asylum.
Bolton J. Hyde, Jr. h. 457 Wethersfield.
" James A. physician, 30 Washington.
" John, blacksmith at 8 Front,h. 15 Harbison.
" L. A. Mrs. nurse, h. 13 So. Hudson, rm. 10.
" Peter, carpenter, 155 Ch.O. b. 72 Seymour.

## A. H. BOND,

### Manager

## MASSACHUSETTS

## Mutual Life Insurance Company,

### SPRINGFIELD, MASS.

Office, 847 MAIN St., Hills' Block, Room 3.

*Old Number, 333.*

**F. WILLSON ROGERS, General Agent.**

*The Massachusetts Law Guarantees Cash and Paid-up Values after two annual premiums. It also compels an annual distribution of Surplus, thereby giving a clear, definite and fair contract.*

Bolton Thomas, stonemason, h.u. 11 S. Pro.
Bomstar Michael, enameler, Popes, h.135 Law.
Bonaparte Joseph H. butler, 888, b. 888 Asylum.
Bonar Samuel, floorwalker at R. Ballerstein & Co. b. 427 Main, rm. 11.
BOND ALBERT H. insurance agent, 847 Main, rm. 3, h. 24 Townley. (8) *See page 64.*
" Alfaretta, wid. William, h. 45 Woodbridge.
" Austin M. salesman, 851 Main, h. Windsor t.
" Charles E. h. 518 Prospect av.
" Charles W. b. 45 Woodbridge.
" Ferdinand, clerk, 1056 Main, h. 20 Pleasant.
" George M. mechanical engineer at Pratt & Whitney Co. 1 Flow. b. 141 Washington.
" Joseph, attendant, 134, b.u. 134 Main.
" Marion W. stenographer at 843 Main, rm. 3, b. 24 Townley.
" Owen W. toolm. at 20 Sargeant, b. 240 Laurel.
" R. E. Mrs. b. 68 Wooster.
" Robert, b. 45 Woodbridge.
" W. G. grocer, h.u. 68 Bellevue.
Bonded Warehouse, r. 74 Trumbull.
Bondison A. deckhand, 285 State.
Bondy Sigmund, saloon, 42 Asylum, h. 14 Morris.
Bone John, h. 48 Bond.
" John, annealer at 40, h. 28 Governor.
" Robert D. *assessor and city ratemaker*, 114 Pearl, b. 48 Bond.
" William, builder, 48, b. 48 Bond.
Bonee Frank, clerk at 488 Asylum, h. 33 Albany.
" Jos. fruit, 1043 Main, groceries 81, h. 81 Mor.
" Michael, fruit, etc. 2 Ford, h.2u.r. 33 Albany.
" Nicholas, fruit, etc. 116, h.u. 116 Lawrence.
" Nicholas, laborer, Pope Tube Co. h. 88 Mor.
" Peter, fruits, etc. 488 Asylum, h.r. 33 Albany.
Bonfoey B. Clayton (*Bonfoey Bros.*) b. 25 Spring.
**BONFOEY BROS.** carpenters and builders, 109 Windsor av. *See page 518.*
    B. Clayton Bonfoey.    Frederick L. Bonfoey.
" Frederick L. (*Bonfoey Bros.*) h. 17 Avon.
Boniface James, fruits, h. 31 Albany.
" John D. clerk at 197 Asylum, b. 20 Mahl.
Bonimasso Vito, bootblack, b. 49 Morgan.
Bonn Mary, wid. Herman, h.u. 77 Temple.
" ☞ *see also Bonney.*
Bonneau Louis O. carpenter, h. 54 Winship.
Bonnecuora Antonio, baker at 59 Village.

Bonneilo Domenico, laborer, h.u. 82 Morgan.
Bonnel Charles F. mach. at Popes, h.u. 50 Amity.
" Diana, wid. Wm. D. b.u. 50 Amity.
" Martin, laborer, 335 Sheldon, h.u. 34 S. Pro.
" William P. caterer, h. 29 Heath.
" Wm. D. rubberw. at 690 Park, b.u. 51 John.
" ☞ *see also Bunnell.*
Bonner Charles F. plumber, b. 255 Asylum.
" John D. *fire commissioner*, pres. Bonner, Preston Co. 843 Main, h. 42 Huntington.
**BONNER, PRESTON CO.** painters supplies, paper hangings, photographic supplies, 843 Main. *See page 425.*
" William steamfitter at Popes, b. 134 Martin.
" Wm. J. foreman at Popes, h.u. 134 Babcock.
" ☞ *see also Bonar.*
Bonney John F. filer at 1 Laurel, h.2u. 6 Heath.
" Wm S. elevatorer, 75 Pratt, h.u. 25 Hun. pl.
" ☞ *see also Bonee.*
Bonsilate Box Co. mfrs. corkaline handles, 24 Mechanic.
Bontelle John S. rubberw. 690 Park, b. 236 N.P.
Bontempo Angelo A. laborer, b. 263 Front.
" Vincenzo, laborer, h. 263 Front.
Booker Charles D. barber, h. 30 Ferry.
Bools Oliver E. pressman at Popes, h. 261 Park.
Boorstein Harry M. clerk, 921 Main, b. 91 Front.
Bootay David N. driver, 256 Main, h.2u. 19 Good.
Booth Albert F. merchant tailor, 55 Pratt, L. 847 Main, room 27.
" Alfred J. filer at Popes, h. 46 Wells.
" Charles W. inspector, 581 Cap. b. 18 Imlay.
" & Condos, confectionery, 224 Asylum.
    Peter Booth.    A. Condos.
" Edwin R. baker at 185, h. 138 Albany.
" Edwin S. repairer, 40 Gov. h.u.r. 8 Ch. O.
" Fred. N. at Travelers Ins. Co. 56 Prospect, b.u. 14 Linden.
" James Webb, physician, 293, h. 293 Main.
" James W. Jr. clerk, 74 Tru. b. 293 Main.
" John A. helper, Popes, h. 46 Grove.
" Minnie Day, teacher at 44, b. 44 Beacon.
" Peter (*Booth & Condos*) h. 20 Trumbull.
" Samuel F. lineman, 284 Asylum, b. 936 Main.
" Thos. ostler, Adams Ex. Co. b. 522 Garden.
" Thomas B. draughtsman, 1 Laurel, b. 25 Huntington.
" Wallace M. blacksmith, h.u. 69 Fairmount.
" Walter, mach. at 1 Flower, b. 51 Sigourney.
" Walter C. mach. at 1 Flower, b. 51 Sigourney.
" Wm. F. clerk 1195 Main, h.u. 232 Windsor av.
" William G. painter, h.2u. 275 Asylum.
Bora Henry J. lather, h.u. 46 Seymour.
Borce Harriet C. cashier, 45 Asy. h. 101 Hung
Borcorselski Frank E. draughtsman at 1 Flower, h. 228 Zion.
Borden Elias W. carpenter at 158 Woodland, h. 81 Seymour.
Borcham Robert, gardener, 210 Far. h. 4 Niles.
Borg Carl, traveling salesman, b. 169 Babcock.
Borgeson Martin, laborer, h.u.r. 44½ John.
Borgiman Max, laborer, h.u. 92 Front.
Borjeson John E. gardener at 135 Washington, h.u. 125 Ward.
" Linus, mach. at Popes, b.u. 74 Lawrence.

Born Rudolph, buffer at Popes, h.2u. 51 Babcock.
" Samuel, h. 42 Grand.
" ☞ see also Bourn.
Borst George F. b. 223 Asylum, rm. 11.
Borup Elenora, dressmaker, b.u. 222 Park.
Bosanko S. Arthur Mrs. nurse, 20 So. Hudson.
Boshur T. F. helper 581 Cap. b. 37 Albany.
Bosquet August H. skiver at Jewell Belting Co. 15, b. 97 Trumbull.
Boss Austin D. mgr. Willimantic Linen Co. 34 Morgan, h.u. 22 Suffield.
" Chauncy M. mach. at 111 Sheldon, b. W.t.
Bossen Christian, watchman, h. 381 Park.
" Christian, Sr. hostler, r. 50 State, h.381Park.
" Jens, clerk at 78 High, b. 350 Laurel.
" John J. reporter Bradstreet Co. b. 381 Park.
" Oscar, bookkeeper, b. 381 Park.
" Peter, laborer, b. 381 Park.
Bosson Frank H. manager bookkeeper at Popes, 436 Capitol, h. Cone.
Boston Branch, W. W. Walker, 745-751 Main.
" Dental Association, 759 Main.
" Furniture house, Julius A. Kellogg, 147 Asy.
Bostwick M. Annie, b. 74 Arch.
Boswell Charles E. foreman at 24 Mechanic, h.u. 38 Temple.
Bosworth D.A. electrician, 214 Pearl, b.119 High.
" Edith M. wid. N. h. 57 Garden.
" Edwin H. porter at 152 State, h. 3 Sherman.
" Eugene, carpenter, h.u. 35 Hudson.
" Fred E. clerk at Connecticut Fire Ins. Co. 51 Prospect, b. 3 Sherman.
" Louis, mach. at 581 Cap. h. Wethersfield t.
" Mary J. wid. James, b. 209 Garden.
" Nellie I. clerk at 109 State, b. E.H.t.
" Stanley B. pottery, 38 Front, h. 1506 Broad.
" William, painter, b.r. 321 Windsor av.
Botelle Andrew E. b. 60 Main.
" Charles W. solderer at 62 Market, h.u. 61 Hudson.
" Edmund R. electrician, b. 60 Main.
" Ellelar, foreman on city St.Wks. h. 60 Main.
Botsford Arthur T. brassfinisher, b.u. 147 State.
" Charles P. physician, 1393, h. 1393 Main.
" Hannah, wid. H. A. h. 121 Sigourney.
" Ingraham & Swift, now Ingraham, Swift & Co.          See page 585.
" Isaac B. foreman at Colts, h. 85 Huyshope.
" Mary B. h. 121 Sigourney.
" Winton E. clerk 745 Main, b.u. 147 State.
Bottger Fred E. printer at 91 Asy. b. 2 Church.
Bouchard Arthur, h.u. 31 Lawrence.
" Henry A. clerk at 122 Capen.
" James W. mach. at 133 Sheldon, h.r. 31 Law.

JOHN B. BOUCHER, physician. Office 306 Main street.
Hours—8 to 9 A. M.
1 to 3.30 and 7 to 9 P. M.
Telephone 1014-12.

Boucher John B. physician, 306 Mn. b. 12 Bkm.
" John B. painter, b. 17 Kilbourn.
" Mary J. wid. Thomas F. h. 1194 Main.
Boudereau Henry, carpenter, h. 44 Windsor.
Bouderoe Joseph J. foreman St.Ry. l. 80 State.

Boudreau Alfred, lather, b. 233 Main.
" Frank, lather, b. 233 Main.
" Frederick, lather, b. 233 Main.
Boughton Belle L. clerk at National Life Association, 53 Trumbull, b. 119 High.
" Edward G. clerk Sage, Allen & Co. 898 Main, b. 119 High.
Bouin Joseph, elevatorer Conn. Mutual Life Ins. Co. 783 Main, b. 37½ Church.
Boulanger Arthur, brazier, h.3u. 261 Main.
" Frank, blacksm. at Popes, l. 721 Main, rm. 46.
" Joseph, brazier at Popes, h.3u. 263 Main.
Boulet Louis, operator, 7 Central, h.u. 8 Clinton.
Bourgard Frank, clerk 369, b. 281 Capitol.
Bourn Eldon A. cutter at 8, h. 123 Sigourney.
" William S. clerk at Smith, Bourn & Co. 8 Sigourney, h. 15 Eaton.
" ☞ see also Born; Borne.
Bourque Fred, mech. at Popes, h.u. 252 Law.
Boutelle Gertrude L. at 424 Asylum, b. 45 Park.
" John A. helper, 690 Park, h.u.236NewPark.
" William, cabinetmaker at Strickland & Shea, 20 Potter, h.u. 45 Park.
Bouvier Gilbert, harnessmaker at 8 Sigourney.
Bowden Charles, attendant, 30 Washington.
Bowdoin Edward W.( W.H.B.& Son,) h.42 Clark.
" W. H. & Son, grocers, meat market, 48 Clark.
Walter H. Bowdoin.     E. W. Bowdoin.
" Walter H. ( W. H.B.& Son,) h. 75 Clark.
Bowe Albert H. painter, h.2u. 1 Elm pl.
" Anna E. clerk Brown, Thomson & Co. 942 Main, b. 36 Franklin.
" August, captain barge 14, h.3u. 5 Kilbourn.
" Daisey, clerk, 53 Tru. b. 25 Washington.
" Frank E. clerk at 356 Main, b. 25 Wash.
" Fred, painter, h. 27 Canton.
" Fred E. clerk at 581 Cap. b. 25 Washington.
" Harry, b. 25 Washington.
" Katherine M. clerk 745 Main, h. 36 Franklin.
" Michael, laborer, h.u. 40 Sheldon.
" Thomas, molder at 556 Cap. h. 36 Franklin.
Bowen Charles T. clerk 175 Asylum, b. Far. t.
" Edward, blacksmith, h. 284 Asylum, rm. 68.
" Edwin C. at Ætna Life Ins. Co. 650 Main, h. Meriden t.
" Emma F. at 1189 Broad, h. 48 Grand.
" Jerome, mach. at 9 Sig. h.u. 101 Hungerford.
" John R. mach. at 1 Flower, h. 129 Lawrence.
" Joseph, b. 37¼ Church.

Bowen Marcellus, prof. at Theological Seminary, 1507 Broad.
" Richard S. waiter, h.u. 56 Grand.
" ☞ see also Bohen.
Bower John, electrician, b. 1096 Main.
" William H. repairer, 201 Asylum, h. W.t.
Bowers Carrie E. at 59½ Tru. b. 58 Church.
" Chas. E. mach. at 9 Sig. h.u. 41 Buckingham.
" E. W. clerk, 599 Main, b. No. Cromwell v.
" Ellsworth T. clerk, 98 Wells, h.u. 98 Church.
" Frank A. clerk, 69 Albany, h. 107 Brook.
" George H. rubberw. at 690 Park, b. 81 Sey.
" Henry, b. 109 Elm.
" John H. at Ætna Life Ins. Co. 650 Main, b. 18 Buckingham.
" Kate A. secretary Christian Scientist, 252 Asylum, b. 109 Elm.
" Mary A. wid. Edward H. h. 50 Pleasant.
" William, painter, b. 3 Pleasant.
" ☞ see also Bauer.
Bowker Fertilizer Co.218 Sta. E. F. Jennison, agt.
Bowler Charles, carpenter, b.u. 8 Hawthorn.
Bowles Chas. A. butcher, h.u. 60 Walnut.
" Helen A. b. 370 Asylum.
" ☞ see also Bolles.
Bowman Alfred G. assemb. 556 Cap.h.17½ Wolcott.
" Charles M. division freight agent N.E.R. Union Depot, h.u. 1279 Main.
" Frank R. clerk at 61 Asylum, h. 241 Pearl.
" James H. laborer, b.2u. 173 Windsor.
Bowne Garrett D. foreman at 8 Sig. h.u. 113 Hung.
" ☞ see also Bone; Beone.
Bows J. fireman str. Middletown, 285 State.
Bowser Georgiana, wid. B. h.u. 100 Walnut.
Boyagian John, screwm. 476 Cap. b. 1442 Broad.
Boyar A. machinist at 13 Central, h. 86 Pleasant.
Boyce Alfred T. cigarmaker, b. 38 Woodbridge.
" Alice A. dressmaker, b. 38 Woodbridge.
" Edward, mach. at 142 Russ, b. 38 Wdbg.
" Eliza, wid. Ed. h. 38 Woodbridge.
" George J. foreman at Popes, h. 175 Babcock.
" Jas. E. foreman at 581 Cap. h.17 So.Laurel.
" John, boilermaker, h.2u. 138 Mather.
" John W.draughtsm.556Cap.h2.u.1427Broad.
" John Y. machinist, h.2u. 962 Broad.
" Robert H.foreman at 476 Cap. h. 12 Amity.
Boyd Charles T. decorator at Brown, Thomson & Co. 942 Main, h. 132 Jefferson.
" Edward E. b. 6 Girard.
" Fred. R. student, b. 40 Annawan.
" George W. E. carman, b.u. 5 Wolcott.
" James, weigher at Hartford Coal Co. 100 Commerce, h.u. 5 South Hudson.

Boyd Laura A. wid. Chas. O. b. 85 Wethersfield.
" Marguerite A. clerk at 75 Pearl, b. 92 Hudson.
" Sarah D. wid. John, h. 92 Hudson.
" Thomas, chief clerk collector's office, 114 Pearl, h. 40 Annawan.
Boyden Charles S. b. 2 Holcomb.
" ☞ see also Bryden.
Boyes Thomas H. mach. at 54 Arch, h. E.H.t.
Boykett Charles H. gardener, b. 126 Westland.
Boyle Bridget A. at 1 So. Ann, b. 90 Willow.
" Catherine F. wid. Wm. h. 125 Babcock.
" Daniel J. clerk, b. 2 Worcester pl.
" Dennis F. plumber at 302 Pl. b. 43 Babcock.
" Frank, laborer, b. 1416 Broad.
" Jas. M. machinist, h.u. 118 Asylum.
" John F. mason, b. 125 Babcock.
" John J. asst. dentist 86 Pratt, b. 55 Fairfield.
" John W. mason, h. 2 Worcester pl.
" Josephine E. at 254 Pearl, b. 125 Babcock.
" Julia A. wid. Christopher, h. 90 Willow.
" Kittie A. at 254 Pearl, b. 125 Babcock.
" Mary, dressmaker, 21, b. 21 Sumner.
" Mary T. dressmaker, b. 125 Babcock.
" Michael R. polisher, 581Cap.h. 77 Woodbine.
" Richard, h. 43 Babcock.
" Sarah J. clerk, b. 90 Willow.
" William, clerk, 835 Main, h. E.H.t.
" William, janitor Law. st. sch. h.u. 61 Grand.
" William B. crater at 581 Cap. h. 391 Allyn.
BOYNTON EDW. B. councilman 4th ward, gen'l ag't American Real Estate Co. 904 Main, h.u. 26 Williams.
" Henry M. carpenter, h. 38 Williams.
" Susan E. dressmaker at 265, h. 265 Asylum.
Boysen Peter, carpenter, h. 15 Winter.
Boysseau John B. A. carptr. 476 Cap. h. 92Pro.av.
Boyter John, clerk at Brown, Thomson & Co. 942 Main, b. 225 High.

## BRABAZON ANDREW, stonecutter,
cor. Garden and Liberty, h. 21 Pavilion.
See page 511.

Samuel Brabazon.
" Frank L. printer at 141 Pearl, b. 21 Pavilion.
" Jane, wid. Robert, h. 16 Waverly.
" John, carpenter, b. 21 Pavilion.
" John, farmer, b. 945 Park.
" Lizzie, dressm. at 270 Main, b. 945 Park.
" Robert, b. 945 Park.
" Samuel, stonecutter, b. 175 Barbour.
" Samuel D. clerk at 110 Asy. h. Carpenter.

Brabazon Thos. printer at 141 Pearl, b. 21 Pav.
" Thomas F. artist, 926 Main, b. 16 Waverly.
" William J. stonemason, h. 945 Park.
" William Jr. stonemason, b. 945 Park.
Brace Emily M. b. 144 Washington.
" Eveline, wid. Frederick, dressmaker, 277,
  h. 277 Main.
" Gertie A. carpet sewer at C. R. Hart Co.
  carpets, etc. 898 Main, b. 33 Church.
" Jennie, clerk, b.u. 1147 Main.
" John M. G. seed leaf tobacco, 214 State, h.
  West Hartford t.
" Olin N. enameler at Popes, h.u. 1147 Main.
" S. C. wid. Orrin. h. 33 Church.
" Sarah J. wid. Edwin J. b. 127 Oak.
Bracken Caroline L. stenographer at 904 Main,
  rm. 30, b. Wethersfield t.
" Francis H. hackman, h.u. 76 Potter.
" Frank, driver, h.2u. 32 Kinsley.
" James, gatetender N.Y.R. h. 21 Howard.
" James Jr. polisher, b. 21 Howard.
" Michael J. molder at 556 Capitol, h. Weth-
  ersfield t.
Brackett Edward S. teacher, b. 92 Barbour.
" F. A. principal Northeast school, h. 92 Barb.
Brackley M. W. mach. 13 Central, b. 64 Capitol.
" W. machinist, b. 590 Main.
Bradbury Mary E. wid. C. W. boardingh. 343 Mn.
Braddock Annie, b. 13 Capitol.
Bradford Geo. B.tinner,599Main, h.231Bellevue.
" Irving, trimmer, 835 Main, b. 25 Spring.
Bradin Isabel J. b.2u. 5 Linden.
" James W. Rev. rector St. Johns church,
  h. 6 Park ter.
" James W. Jr. student Trinity college, b. 6
  Park ter.
" Selina F., Japanese lunchroom, 389 Capitol,
  b. 6 Park ter.
Bradley Arthur A. mgr. shoe dept. at 45 Asy-
  lum, h. 131 Ashley.
" Arthur H. at Phœnix Insurance Co. 64
  Pearl, b. 847 Asylum.
" Arthur J. agent, 756 Main, b. 12 Village.
" Arthur L. clk. at 614 Cap. h.2u. 29 Babcock.
" Burton, carpenter, l. 1086 Main.
" Dominick, driver 40 Elm, h.u. 752 Windsor.
" Elizabeth Mrs. b. 21 Elliott.
" Ella L. at Hartford Life Ins. Co. 252 Asylum,
  b. 40 Tremont.
" Francis A. Jr. clerk, 145 Asy.h. 15½ Martin.
" Frank A. peddler, h. 15½ Martin.
" Frank P. bkkpr. at 1106 Main,b. 30 Capen.
" George Fred. trimmer at 266 Pearl, l.2u.
  985 Main.
" Grace E. teacher Northeast school, b. 30
  Capen.
" Henry, engineer N.Y.R. h. 60 Ashley.
" Henry E.paints & oils,1106 Main,h.30 Capen.
" James, blacksm. at Colts, h. 3 Hendricxsen.
" Joseph H. laborer, b. 11 Elmer.
" Kate, wid. Michael, b. 7 Kilbourn.
" Lewis H. mach. at Popes, h.u. 1500 Broad.
" Marshall J. rubberworker at 690 Park, b.
  Bloomfield t.
" May, h.u. 1120 Main.

Bradley Patrick, station engineer, N.Y.R. h. 20
  Huntley pl.
" Ruth A. music teacher, 926 Main. rm. 49
" Thomas, laborer at 15 Tru. b. 7 Kilbourn.
" William, dropforger at Popes, h. 3 Queen.
" Wm. E. bookkpr. 193 Asy. b.2u. 1271 Main.
" William F. framer, 15½, b. 15½ Martin.
" Willis G. signist, 8 Kinsley, h. 1 Pleasant.
Bradowich Michael, lab. at 581 Cap. b. 19 Com.
Bradstreet Co.,P.P.Bennett, supt.49 Pearl, rm.18.
Brady Bros. bottlers, 1 Brady place.
    Thomas A. Brady.        Stephen A. Brady.
" Catharine, wid. Thomas, b. 38 Putnam.
" Christopher, b. 72 Ward.
" Edward, carpenter, 72, b. 72 Ward.
" Edward J. cordmaker at 15 Trumbull, b. B.v.
" Florence J. cook, b.u. 21 Arch.
" James H. printer at Phœnix Insurance Co.
  64 Pearl, b. 63 Sheldon.
" John, horseshoer, h. 40 Glendale.
" John F. bookbinder at 141 Pearl. h.44 Wells.
" John J. at 1 Brady pl. h. 72 Ward.
" John T. porter, Lincoln, Seyms & Co. 34
  Market, h.Wethersfield t.
" Margaret, wid. Thomas, h.u. 16 Commerce.
" Mary, wid. Christopher, h. 72 Ward.
" Owen, painter at 20 Central, b. 63 Prospect
" Owen E. mech. engir. at Popes, h. 63 Flower.
" Patrick, b. Home for the Aged, W.H. t.
" Philip, h.u. 49 Hawthorn.
" Stephen A. (Brady Bros.) h. 326 Park.
" Thomas, moulder at 556 Cap. h. 175 Law.
" Thomas A. (Brady Bros.) b. 72 Ward.
" Thomas H. shippingclerk at 13 Central,
  h.u.r. 34 South Prospect.
" Thos. J. machinist, b. 44 Wells.
Bragaw E. M. Mrs. h. 14 Suffield.
" Isaac, manager Way Hardware Co. 866
  Main, h. 343 Windsor av.
Bragg Frank, woodworker, h.u. 18 Atlantic.
" Fred. S. painter at 188 Asy.h.u.92 Wooster.
" George S. carpenter, h.u. 22 Canton.
" Geo. S. clerk, 372 Asy. h. South Windsor t.
" Harry G. machinist at Colts, b. 18 Atlantic.
Brahich Janco, laborer, b. 15 Mechanic.
Brainard Albert E. laborer, h. 141 Capen.
**BRAINARD AUSTIN,** (Sperry, Mc-
  Lean & B.) attorney at law, 650 Main,
  h. 29 Kenyon. (15)      See page 494.
" Charles E. h. 265 Wethersfield.
" Daniel E. clerk at 10 Market, b. 147 Collins.
" Eliza S. b. 1255 Main.
" Everett C. sten'er P.&R. h. 147 Collins.
" George L. b. 36 Jefferson.
" Harriet E. b.u. 156 Washington.
" Harrison, at Evening Post, 25 Asylum, b.u.
  98 Hopkins.
" Harry, teacher, b. 162 Washington.
" Hartwell H. traveling salesman Brown,
  Thomson & Co. 942 Main, b. 64 Capitol.
" Herman B. felspar, b.2u. 128 Albany.
" Homer W. teacher, High sch.h. 88 Kenyon.
Brainard Leverett, pres. of The Case, Lock-
  wood & Brainard Co. 141 Pearl, h. 185
  Washington.      See page 475.

Brainard Louisa E. wid. Olive, h. 73 Hungerford.
" Lydia M. wid. Lewis H. h. 162 Washington.
" Lyman B. asst. treas. Hfd. Steam Boiler Insp. & Ins. Co. 650 Main, b. 149 High.
" Margaret F. bkkpr. 7 Haynes, b. 88 Kenyon.
" Rebecca M. h. 94 Ann.
" Sarah W. b. 427 Main, rm. 40.
" Walter A. compositor, 252 Pearl, h. 26 East.
" William H. trunkmaker at 182 Asy. h. E.H.t.
" William R. bookkeeper, h. 88 Kenyon.
Brainerd Addison G. clerk at Hartford National Bank, 58 State, b. 45 Wethersfield.
" Amaziah, sec. and treas. Hartford Paper Co. 49 Trumbull, h. 48 Huntington.
" David E. clerk at 40 Gov. b. 45 Wethersfield.
" Fred J. gen. agt. for D. Appleton & Co. 248 Main, h. 20 Lincoln.
**BRAINERD HARVEY B.** wall papers, draperies, window shades, 84 Pratt, h. 30 Townley. (10)  *See p. 503.*
" Henry F. b. 45 Wethersfield.
" Henry L. h. 45 Wethersfield.
" Thomas, painter, b. 70 Front.
Brake Joseph, h. 145 Flatbush.
" Manuel, b. 145 Flatbush.
Braman Dennis, b. 2 Holcomb.
" Edward S. conductor St.Ry. b. 39 Julius.
" Henry T. insurance, h. 72 Niles.
Bramhall Richard, polisher at Popes, b. 118 Shel.
Bramley William, decorator at Baxter the Decorator, 231 Asylum, h.u. 108 Wooster.
Branagan Edward C. salesm. at 45, b. 289 Asy.
" Thomas J. molder at 54 Arch, h. 40 Temple.
Branch Ellen, domestic, b.u. 33 Ferry.
" George, fireman, b.u. 659 Main.
" Maria, wid. David, h.u. 659 Main.
" Mary A. wid. Elisha P. h.u. 26 Beach.
" Sarah Mrs. h.u. 32 Wells.
Branchier Rocco, laborer, b.3u. 67 Morgan.
**BRAND ROBERT,** cabinetmaker, 5½ Morris, b.2u. 66 Putnam.  *See page 507.*
" Smart, clerk 921 Mn. b. 11 Foot Guard pl.
" Wm. carpenter at 141 Tru. h. 68 Putnam.
Branden William, laborer, b. Pleasant.
Brandenberger J. Robert, laborer, b. Elizabeth Park.
Brandon Ellen, wid. William, h.u. 85 Governor.
" John, b.u. 85 Governor.
" May, bkkpr. at 921 Main, b. 85 Governor.
" Peter, carman, h. 29 Front.
Brandow Charles F. machinist at 110 Commerce, h. 82 Grand.
Brandriss Marcus M. grocer, 34, h. 34 Front.
Brandt E. h.u. 363 Main.
" Elizabeth M. teach. language, b. 25 Sherman.
" Edw. H. mach. at N.Y.R. h. 320 Maple.
" Hans B. trav. salesm. 690 Park, h. 25 Sherman.
" John, baker at 484 Main.
" Oscar C. h.u. 85 Harbison.
" *see also Brant.*
Brannigan Frank, mechanic, b. 138 Trumbull.
" Joseph R. polisher at Popes, h.u. 7 Zion.
" William F. at 581, b. 381 Capitol.
Bransfield John E. laborer P.&R. h.r. 21 Chst.
Bransgrove A. G. wigmaker, 25, b. 25 Central.

Brant Nellie M. Mrs. dressm. 37, h. 37 Amity.
" *see also Brandt.*
Brassill Annie, b. 43 Hungerford.
" Bridget, wid. John, h.u. 85 Windsor.
" Edward A. laborer at Pope Tube Co. h. 11 Sisson.
" Eva K. clerk at Brown, Thomson & Co. 942 Main, b. South Manchester v.
" Frank A. mach. at 133 Shel. b. 38 Russell.
" Frank A. messenger at P.O. b. 38 Russell.
" James, h.u. 80 Walnut.
" John, b. 35 Windsor.
" Mary E. at 252 Pearl, b. 43 Hungerford.
" Michael M. tinsmith, h. 38 Russell.
" Frank, h. 43 Hungerford.
" William Mrs. h. 43 Hungerford.
" William, pressfdr. at L. Wileys, b. 43 Hung.
" *see also Brazel.*
Bratt Patrick, enameler at Popes, b. 284 Asylum.
Brauer Jacob, toolm. at Colts, h.u. 33 Hamilton.
Braun August F. machinist, h. 25 Brook.
" Robert C. cutter, b.2u. 25 Brook.
" William, tailor, b.2u. 25 Brook.
Braxton Fairfax, laborer, h.u. 76 Albany.
" Moses, coachman, 91 Ann, h. 45 Liberty.
" William, janitor, h. 37 Liberty.
Bray Edward, h.3u. 106½ Trumbull.
" Daniel W. assembler at Colts, b.u.r. 76 Vanblock.
" James C. b. 24 Woodbridge.
" Mary, wid. William, h.u.r. 76 Vanblock.
" Michael, machinist, Colts, h. 45 Woodbridge.
**BRAY WILLIAM J.** contractor and builder, 35, h. 35 Imlay, storehouse r. 550 Park.  *See page 512.*
Brayman Edward S. conduc. St.Ry. b. 39 Julius
Brazel Charles H. clerk 979 Main, b. 220 Ashley.
" Eliza, wid. Peter, h. 1 Imlay.
" Elizabeth, wid. Matthew, h. 220 Ashley.
" Frank F. fireman at 30 Washington.
" James, helper, h.u. 80 Walnut.
" Margaret, wid. Terrance, h.u.r. 23 West.
" Matthew T. build. remover 220, h. 220 Ashley.
" Patrick F. papercut. at 141 Pearl, h.u. 15 Laf.
" Terrance W. policeman, b. 16 Cedar.
" Wm. F. building mover, 10, h. 10 Center.
" *see also Brassill.*
Brazers Elmer C. cutter at 188 Asylum, b.2u. 32 Hopkins.
Brazina Ignaz C. fitter at Colts, h.r. 60 Wells.
Brazos Annie E. nurse at 54, h. 54 Church.
Brechtel Robert, helper 1 Flow. h.2u. 4 Kil. ct.
" Robert, Jr. b.2u. 4 Kilbourn ct.
Breck Carl H. waiter at 276, b. 276 Lawrence.
Breckenridge W. W. Rev. pastor Presbyterian church, h. 61 Oak.
Breed Charles A. clerk at 973 Mn. b. 61 Gillett.
" George, vice president Blodgett & Clapp Co. 51 Market, h. 61 Gillett.
Breen Charles, at N.E.R. b.u. 52 Edwards.
" Daniel W. clerk, 75 Windsor, b. 29 Pleasant.
" John, carpenter, h.u. 39 Lawrence.
" John A. foreman at 276 Cap. h. 1413 Broad.
" John H. mechanic, h.u. 1413 Broad.
" Patrick F. teamster, h.2u. 62 Sheldon.

**BREENPATRICK J.** monuments,1070 Main, market, 75 Windsor, h.u. 29 Pleasant. *See outside front cover.*
Breer Charles, chef at 701 Main, b. 33 John.
Brehm Anthony, helper at 217 Windsor, b. 4 Bellevue.
" Jas. S. inspector at Popes, h.u. 11 Oak.
Breining Anton, rubberw. 690 Park, h. Lifkey.
" Joseph, rubberworker, b.u. Lifkey.
Bremser C. Frederick, upholsterer at 898 Main, h. 28 Vernon.
Breneiser Frank S. cigarmaker at 104 Asylum, h.2u.r. 58 Temple.
Brennan Alice. dressmaker, 326½, b. 326½ Park.
" Anna, wid. Michael, h.2u. 13 North.
" Cornelius J. machinist, h. 326½ Park.
" Edward A. saddler at 8 Sig. b. 401 Capitol.
" Ellen, wid. William Sr. h. 28 Avon.
" Eugene, bartender at 18, l.u. 16 Market.
" Frank, salesman at 501 Asy. b. 51 Chestnut.
" James, h.u. 20 Commerce.
" James, carpenter, h. 89 Fairmount.
" James, chef at 651, b. 651 Main.
" James, salesman, b. 16 Avon.
" James C. mach. at 142 Russ, h. 326½ Park.
" John, coachman at Far. c. Highland.
" John, driver, 126 Church.
" John, slater, b.u. 270 Front.
" John F. teamster, 232 Shel. b.2u. 8½ Ellery.
" John J.carpenter, b. 28 Avon.
" John T. plumber at 280 Asylum, b. W.L.t.
" Joseph, gate tender N.Y.R. b. 28 Avon.
" Joseph P. (Gately & B.) h.u. 3 Seyms.
" Julia, dressm. 903 Main, rm. 15, h. 16 Avon.
" Kate, wid. Keron, b. 103 Commerce.
" Lizzie, dressm. 903 Main, rm.15, h.16 Avon.
" Lizzie A. bookkeeper,1050 Main, b.16 Avon.
" Margaret, wid. Michael, h. 42 Green.
" Margaret, wid. Thos. h. 51 Chestnut.
" Margaret A. milliner,908 Main, b. 15 Avon.
" Margaret L. clerk, Brown, Thomson & Co. 942 Main, b. 89 Fairmount.
" Mary, b.2u. 8½ Ellery.
" Mary E. operator at 8 Sig. b. 326½ Park.
" Michael, hodcarrier, b. 52 Linden.
" Michael, laborer, stone pits,h.109 Hamilton.
" Michael, machinist, b.2u. 8½ Ellery.
" Michael A. brakeman, b. 28 Avon.
" Minnie R. stenographer, 690 Park,h. E.H.t.
" Nora, dressmaker, b. 51 Chestnut.
" P. F. marketman, b. 51 Chestnut.
" Rose, wid. James, h. 326½ Park.
" Thomas, butcher, b. 51 Chestnut.
" Thomas, laborer, b. 103 Commerce.
" Thomas,marketman, 319 Asy. b.35 Chestnut.
" Thomas, polisher, 66 Market,b.u. 64 Village.
" Thomas A. polisher, b. 16 Avon.
" Timothy F. printer at 857 Main, b. 28 Avon.
" William, rubberw. 690 Park,b.109 Hamilton.
" William J. at Pope Tube Co. b. 28 Avon.
Brenton Cranston, student at Trinity College, 8 Jarvis hall.
Breslar Ike, tailor, 46 Portland.
Bresnahan Michael J. brazer, 581 Cap. b.275 Asy.
Bress Bennett, peddler, h.u. 244 Front.

# C. S. Brewer & Co.,

Wholesale——

## FRUIT DEALERS AND COMMISSION MERCHANTS.

Agents for——

CELEBRATED EXCELSIOR FIREWORKS.

## 238 and 240 ASYLUM ST.

Brestlin John J. h.u. 25 Wyllys.
Bretman David, (Teisler & Co.) 54 Pleasant.
Brett John H. watchman at 28 Laurel, h.u. 52 Woodbine.
" John J. tinner at 346, h. 113 Main.
" M. A. mfg. agent, 190 Pearl, b. 14 Spring.
" ☞see also Britt.
Brewer Alfred R. foreman, 15 Albany, h. E.H.t.
" Arthur L. bookkeeper, 51 Market, b. E.H.t.
" Ashbel H. captain barge No. 5, 285 State, h. E.H.t.
" Bryon Z. manager Peoples Credit Clothing Co. 933 Main, room 2, h. 55 Brook.
" C. E. Miss, b. 120 Trumbull.
BREWER C. S. & Co. wholesale fruit, 238 and 240 Asylum. *See page 69.* Charles S. Brewer. Russell M. Burdick.
" Charles H. (Dodge & B.) h. 97 Washington.
" Charles M. with A. D. Vorce Co. art store, 752, h. 1261 Main.
" Charles S. (C. S. B. & Co.) h. 240 Collins.
" Clarissa A. Mrs. physician, 120, h. 120 Tru.
" Ernest J. bookkeeper, 164 State, b. E.H.t.

Mrs. C. A. BREWER, Physician. Office, 120 Trumbull street.
Hours—8 to 10 A.M. 2 to 4 and 7 to 8 P.M.

Brewer Everett E. pilot steamer Hartford, 285 State, h. E.H.t.
" Everett P. clerk at 164 State, h. E.H.t.
" Frank C. at L. A. Dickinson & Co. insurance agency, 664 Main, h. E.H.t.
" Fred R. commercial photographer, 903 Main, rm. 19, h. 120 Trumbull.
" Geo. A. bookkeeper Hartford Courant Co. 66 State, h. 105 Park.
" Gertrude, b. 29 Center.
" Howard E. with Conn. Mutual Life Ins. Co. 783 Main, b. E.H.t.
" Jacob, mach. at Popes, h. 19 Julius.
" James, brazier, 581 Capitol, b. 47 Sigourney.
" Joshua B. b. 419 New Britain.
" Julia, wid. Eliab, h. 1113 Main.
" Leslie L. clerk, 124 Asylum, b. E.H.t.
" Linwood R. bookkeeper, 164 State, b. E.H.t.
" Maggie C. wid. Frank J. h.u. 19 Church.
" Mary J. wid. Frederick O. h. 6 Wooster.
" Murray D. clerk, 342 Asylum, h. 38 Brook.
" O. P. h. 13 Buckingham.
" Ralph C.collarmaker, 8 Sigourney, h. E.H.t.

Brewer Rich'd E.clerk, 933 Mn. rm.2, h.55 Brook.
" Risdon A. mach. at N.Y.R. h. 8 Belden.
" Sidney R. bluer at Colts, h. E.H.t.
" Waldo B. mechanic, Colts, h. 61 Dean.
" William, finisher, 141 Commerce, h. E.H.t.
" William E. framemaker at 752 Mn. h. E.H.t.
Brewster Alfred L. leather findings, 186 Pearl,
    h. 26 Goodwin.
" Chauncey B. Rt. Rev. h. 98 Woodland.
" George H. brakeman, h.u. 17 Village.
" James H. assistant manager Lion Fire, &
    Scottish Union & National Ins. Co. at 197
    Asylum, h. 36 Gillett.
" Lizzie L. wid. Henry T. h.u. 10 Village.
" Merrick, laborer, h.r. 229 Pearl.
" Robert M. dis. clerk at Farmers & Mechanics
    Nat. Bank, 106 State, h. 554 Prospect av.
" Samuel, moulder at James L. Howard & Cos.
    438 Asylum, h.u. 20 Goodman.
Brezina Ignaz, mach. at Colts, h.r. 60¼ Wells.
Brick Jeremiah, plumber, b. 377 Main.
Bride Thos. H. foreman, 690 Park, h. 58 Putnam.
Bridge Lewis N. driver, 484, h. 1407 Main.
Bridgman Delia L. nurse, b. 171 Collins.
" Federal B. mason, 45, h. 45 Sumner.
" Geo. J. baker at 27, h. 27 Sherman.
" Luella, dressmaker, 171, b. 171 Collins.
" Myron H. teller, Hartford National Bank,
    58 State, h. 45 Huntington.
" William S. cashier, Hartford National Bank,
    58 State, b.149 High.
Bridgwater Frank L. pressman at 252 Pearl,
    h. 221 Capen.
" Herbert E. machinist, 1 Flower, h. N.t.
" Thomas F. pressm. 254 Pearl, h.u. 221 Capen.
Brien Mary A. bkkpr at 725 Main, b. 66 Hudson.
Brierton Kittie C. clerk, b.2u. 103 Mather.
" Margaret, dressmaker, b.2u. 103 Mather.
" Mary, dressmaker, b.2u. 103 Mather.
" Philip, laborer, 389 Allyn, h.2u. 103 Mather.
Briganty Domenico, bricklayer, h.3u.14 Kilbourn.
" Gaspero, carpenter, h.3u. 14 Kilbourn.
Briggaman George Mrs. h. 281 Capitol.
" ☞ see Bruigaman.
Briggs Alfred L. clerk, 843 Main, b.u.57 Barbour.
" Charles O. clerk, P.&R. b. 228 High.
" George D.salesm.45 Asylum, b.56 Winthrop.
" H. laborer, b. 126 Westland.
" Helen R. b. 638 Asylum.
" J. Frank, salesm. 227 Asy. h. 125 Trumbull.
" Marie A. at Travelers Ins. Co. 56 Prospect,
    b. 25 Wethersfield.
Brigham Charles S. conductor, N.E.R. h. 721
    Main, room 34.
" Clement H. clerk, b. 114 Wooster.
" E. M. at Bushnell Park Cafe, b. 270 Main.
" Ernest A. E. printer at 174 Pearl, b. 33 Tru.
" Ernest W. clerk, 389 Allyn, h. 206 Sisson.
" George S. (Bushnell Park Cafe,) h.14½ Pav.
" Harriet M. wid. Don F. h. 114 Wooster.
" Herbert E. clerk, 98 Wells, h.u. 278 Main.
" L. Louise, physician, 52, h. 52 Church.
" Lincoln L. laborer, h. 33 Trumbull.
" Oliver H. manager, 98 Wells, h.u. 278 Main.
" Samuel H. beltm. at 15 Tru. b. 15 Sanford

**L. LOUISE BRIGHAM, Physician.    Office, 52
    Church street.
    Hours—9 to 10 A.M.
        2 to 4 and 6.30 to 7.30 P.M.
        Sundays 12 to 2 P. M.
        Telephone 908.**

Brigham Wm. M. mach. at 1 Flow. h. 83 Bkm.
Brill Michael, laborer, b. 68 Potter.
Brimble Charles H. crater, 581 Cap. b. 150 Allyn.
" Ernest William, mason, b.u. 130 Ward.
" George, inspector, b.u. 130 Ward.
" Joseph, painter, h.u. 130 Ward.
" Joseph Jr. painter, b.u. 130 Ward.
Brines Moses J. student at Trinity College, 2
    Jarvis Hall, Summit.
Brink Alfred, machinist at 1 Flower, b. S.M.t.
" Fritz, mach. at 1 Flower, h.r. 1074 Broad.
" Jessie H. forewoman, 133 Shel. b.10 Liberty.
" Margaret, wid. William F. h. 10 Liberty.
" Otto, barber, 92, h. 70 Flower.
" Rudolph A. machinist at 1 Flow. h.53 Maple.
" Wm. Frank, mach. at 1 Flow. h. 10 Liberty.
" William Fred. machinist at 1 S. Ann, h. 321
    Windsor av.
Brinkley Levi, waiter, steam. Hartford, 285 State.
Brinkman Dorus, gardener, 45, h. 45 Woodbine.
" Edward P. gardener, 300 Far. h.55 Harrison.
Brinley George at Hartford Fire Insurance Co.
    53 Trumbull, b. Newington t.
" Godfrey, student, Trinity college, 30 Jarvis
    Hall, Summit.
" John H. W. mail clerk, Popes, h. Newington t.
Brinton Joseph P. plumber at 11 Haynes, b.E.H.t.

**BRISCOE CHAS. H.** attorney, 926
    Main, h. Thompsonville v.    *See page* 484.
Briscoe George W. driver, h. 36 Chapel.
Brisebois Peter, laborer r. 25 Front, h. 117 Mar.
Brislin Thomas J. h.u. 10 Charter Oak.
Brissenden Thos. waiter, 1049 Mn. l. 168 Front.
Brisson Joseph, carpenter, h. 358 Park.
Bristlin Thomas J. electrician at 581 Capitol,
    h. 10 Charter Oak.
Bristol Alfred S. mach. at 1 Flow. h.u.35 Lincoln.
" Cornelius G. Rev. rector Church of the
    Good Shepherd, h. 92 Wethersfield.
" Edwin S. mach. at 1 Flower, b. 147 Babcock.
" Frank B. painter at 20 Central, b. 30 Char-
    lotte.
" Mary M. teacher, South school, b. W.H.t.
" Mortimer L. draughtsman at Colts, h. W.H.t.
Britt Edward F. printer at 252 Pearl, b.287 Cap.
" John, groceries, 102, h. 100 Mather.
" John M. barber at 84, h.r. 30 Temple.
" Lena L. dressmaker, b.u. 9 Asylum.
" Minnie, wid. John, h.u. 9 Asylum.
" Samuel, forem. Pope Tube Co. h. 1236 Main.
" Simeon, forem. Pope Tube Co. h. 33 Putnam.
" Stephen, driver, b. 61 Judson.
" ☞ see also Brett.
Britten Thomas H. patternmaker, h. 59 Flower.
Britton Ernest J. b. 54 Governor.
" Harry, filer at Popes, h. 80 Madison.
" James C. special agent United States Depart-
    ment of Labor, h. 54 Governor.
" James J. artist, b. 54 Governor.

Britton Kate, wid. John, h. 1261 Main.
" Ralph D. traveling salesman, b.102 Kenyon.
" Susan, wid. James, h. 54 Governor.
" Thomas, boxmaker, b. 1261 Main.
" Thomas H. patternmaker at 1, h. 59 Flower.
" ☞ see also Breton.
Broad Brook Co. 211 State.
" John, machinist, h.u. 91 Windsor.
Broadhurst Leon P. assistant bookkeeper Phœnix
National Bank, 803 Mn. h.u. 41a Allen pl.
" Thomas, mach. at 1 Laurel, h. 214 Jefferson.
Broad View Dairy & Stock Farm, J. Dart & Son,
286 New Britain.
Broadman Hyman, shoem. 187 State, h. 76 Talcott.
Brock Otto, flyman Parsons theatre, b.u. 9 Grand.
Brockett Chas. W. painter, N.Y.R. b.u. 1333 Broad.
" George H. painter at N.Y.R. b.r.1333 Broad.
Brocklesby Arthur K. at Ætna Life Insurance Co.
650 Main, h. 126 Washington.
" John H. collector of customs, attorney, 750
Main, room 27, h. 3 Preston.
" William C. architect, 756, h. 650 Main.
Brockley Mary, h.u. 10 Chapel.

# U. H. BROCKWAY & CO.,
## Merchant Tailors,
**DEALERS IN FIRST QUALITY**

### READY-MADE CLOTHING and
### GENT'S FURNISHING GOODS.

*Particular Attention to Custom Work.*

### 132 STATE STREET.

BROCKWAY U. H. & Co. merchant tailors,
132 State. *See page 71.*
" Ulysses H. *water commissioner, (U. H.
Brockway & Co.)* h. 16 Chapel.
" George A. clerk, l. 556 Main.
" Wm J. harnessm. at 1222 Main, h. M.t.
**BROCKWAY & TUTTLE,** carriage
repository, 19 Mather. *See page 550.*
Brodaur ☞ *see Brodeur.*
Broder Stephen, coachm. at 12 Myrtle, 21½ Chst.
Broderick Bonaventure Rev. h. 352 Collins.
" Catherine, wid. John, h. 41 Hamilton.
" Catherine, wid. Thomas, b. 64 Williams.
" Catherine A. h. 158 Main.
" Clement M., Ideal Machine Works, h. 64
Hopkins.
" David F. mach. at 1 Flower, b.u. 200 Laurel.
" Dennis F. electrician h.u. 33 Front.
" Edward J. Rev. assistant pastor St. Peters
Roman Catholic church, b. 158 Main.
" James, printer at 141 Pearl, b. 981 Main.
" Margaret, wid. John H. h. 200 Laurel.
" Sarah A. wid. John, h. 14 Governor.
" Thomas A. Mrs. h.u. 1194 Main.
" Thomas W. Rev. pastor St. Peters Roman
Catholic church, h. 158 Main.

Broderick William, blacksmith at 1 Laurel, b.
176 Putnam.
Brodersen Nissine, dressm. 222, h.u. 222 Park.
Broderson Christine, laundress 30 Washington.
Brodeur Adolph, tailor, h.2u. 45 Kinsley.
" Henry, harnessmaker, 15, h. 15 Portland.
" Norbert, harnessm. at 8 Sig. h.' 79 Kibbe.
" Peter, harnessmaker at 784 Park, b. Pros-
pect av. so. of Park.
Brodeure Arthur J. rubberworker at 690 Park,
h. 45 Amity.
Brodie Alice L. stenographer at 721 Main, rm.
3, b. 70 Hudson.
" Frank W. clerk at 9 Central, b. 70 Hudson.
" J. F. h.u. 44 Hicks.
" John, mach. at 83 Woodbine, h. 70 Hudson.
Brodrib John, mach. at 9 Sig. h. 6 Meadow.
Brodrick David H. sexton St. Patricks ceme-
tery, b.u. 31 Center.
" John, bricklayer, b.u. 31 Center.
Brody Israel, clerk at 198 State, h. 64 Pleasant.
Brogdon E. motorman St.Ry. 115 State.
Brokaw Wm. P. engineer, h. 16 Benton.
Brokers' Board, 803 Main.
Brolin Alvin E. nickel plater at Popes, b. 13 Hung.
" Joseph, polisher at Popes, h. 13 Hungerford.
Broman Frank Emil, Rev. pastor First Swedish
Methodist church, 402 Asy. h. 1152 Broad.
Bronkie Fred A. machinist at 1 Flower, h. S.M.v.
Bronley William, driver at r. 87 High.
Bronsdon Lillian L. clerk at T. Sisson & Co. 729
Main, b. 45 Farmington.
Bronson Arthur H., U. S. Army, h. 18 Niles.
" Cooley J. motorman St.Ry. h. 94 Chestnut.
" Elizur D. clerk at 564 Main, b. 16 Village.
" & Fitzgerald, succeeded by R. N. Fitzgerald.
" Nettie L. Mrs. musicteach.b.u.18 Windsor av.
" Robert T. h. 56 Sumner.
BRONSON SAMUEL M. sec'y & treas. National
Machine Co. 133 Shel. h. 28 Charter Oak.
" Sanford F. general agent Hartford Life Ins.
Co. 252 Asylum h. 75 Edwards.
" W. S. Mrs. h. 54 Sumner.
" William, painter, b. 49 Franklin.
" Wm. W. Jr. mach. at 9 Sig. b. 18 Windsor av.
Bronsord John, machinist at 83 Woodbine, b. 55
Madison.
" Louis, burnisher at Wm. Rogers Mfg. Co.
66 Market, h.u. 55 Madison.
" Louis, machinist at 142 Russ, b. 55 Madison.
Brookbanks George H. painter at Baxter the
Decorator, 231 Asylum, b. 463 Broad.
" Henry, (H. B. & Son,) b. 463 Broad.
" Henry & Son, painters, 463 Broad.
Henry Brookbanks.    James H. Brookbanks.
" James H. (H. B. & Son,) b. 463 Broad.
Brookman James, boilerm. 109 Com. b. 90 Grove.
" Thos. boilermaker, h. 90 Grove.
Brooks Abel E. antiques, 911 Mn. rm.5, h.54 Mahl.
" Addie B. at 53 Ann, h. 140 Trumbull.
" Albert H. (W. H. Dodd & Co.) h. 210 Weth.
" Albert H. Jr. clerk at 42 Union pl. b. 210
Wethersfield.
" Adolph G. laborer, b. 100 Commerce.
" Almond, engineer, l. 1113 Main.

Brooks Arthur T. carpenter, h. 3 Harrison pl.
" Bert, painter at 175 Pearl, h. 67 Albany.
" C. J. wid. L. M. b.u. 125 Park.
" Calvin M. attorney, 71 Asy. h. Bloomfield t.
" Charles E. 2d engineer steamer Middletown, 285 State, h. Hadlyme t.
" Charles F. conductor St.Ry. h. 39 Julius.
" Chas. H. motorm. St.Ry. h. 45 Hungerford.
" David W. florist, 53 Farmington, and 5 also, h. 3 Fairfield.
" Edith D. b. 3 Fairfield.
" Edward, h.u. 125 Park.
" Emma Elmore, stenographer and type-writer, 801 Main, b. 32 Atwood.
" Ernest, cashier, 75 Pratt, h. 460 Maple.
" Frank, carpenter, h. 53 Wadsworth.
" Frank, operator at 40 Gov. b.3u. 90 Sheldon.
" Frank M. agent, h. 411 Garden.
" Fred A. engineer, h. 100 Commerce.
" George, coachman at 800, h.r. 800 Asylum.
" H. A. at ·Travelers Insurance Co. 56 Pros-pect, h. Windsor Locks t.
" Henrietta, wid. Henry P. b.326 Windsor av.
" Henry, glazier at 23 Wells, b.2u. 90 Sheldon.
" Henry A. toolmaker at Popes, b. 57 Church.
" Herbert, florist, h. 388 Franklin.
" James E. bridgebuilder, l. 10 Garden.
" James S. l. 1220 Main.
" Jennie E. clerk at 247 Pearl, b. 3 Fairfield.
" Joseph, clerk, 490 Main, h.3u. 101 Sheldon.
" Louise M. wid. Orson, dressm. 42, h.42 Village.
" Lucy D. wid. Augustus O. b. 13 Florence.
" Lydia, b. 149 High.
" M. S. Mrs. nurse, 71 Asylum, rm. 23.
" Mary W. Mrs. 53 Farmington, b. Fairfield.
" Newton S. operator, b. 145 High.
" Philip A. builder, 496, h. 496 Broad.
" Rostine A. inspec'r 476 Cap. h.u.100 Hudson.
" Roswell B. farmer, h. 25 Scarborough.
" Susan F. clerk at Brown, Thomson & Co. 942 Main, b. 96 Ann.
" William, machinist, h.3u. 90 Sheldon.
" William D. h. 1163 Main.
Broomhall Louisa wid. Wm. laundress, h.2u. 545 Main.
⁙ Mary A. wid. Richard, burnisher at Colts, h.3u. 277 Main.
" Richard, assembler at Colts, h.u. 180 Sheldon.
" Richard Jr. polisher at Popes, b.u. 180 Shel.
" Sarah, wid. Richard, h.2u. 180 Sheldon.
" William, assemb. at 476 Cap. b.2u. 545 Main.
Brophy Andrew, teams. Colts, h.40 Woodbridge.
" John T. stonemason, h. 42 Harbison.
" Thomas A. plumber at 280 Asylum, b. 40 Woodbridge.
Brordman Henry, shoes, 187 State, b. Talcott.
Brosmith William, at Travelers Ins. Co. 56 Pros-pect, h. 3 May.
Brosnan William, helper, 165 Windsor, b. 18 Kennedy.
BROTT GEO. O. alderman 8th ward, (Bennett & Brott,) attorneys at law, h. 117 Wash-ington.        See page 483.
" James O. brakeman, N.Y.R. h. 220 Bellevue.
" Oliver, b. 220 Bellevue.

Broucek Joseph T. filer at Colts, h. 50 Harbison.
Broughal Jane wid. Peter, h.u. 13 Portland.
" John J. driver engine No. 7, h. 9 Sanford.
" Katie, b.u. 13 Portland.
" Lizzie, winder at 34 Mor. b.u. 13 Portland.
Broughel Andrew J. master mech. h. 40 Spring.
**BROUGHEL ANDREW J. JR.** attorney at law, 739 Main, telephone in office, h. 40 Spring.
" David A. soliciting ag't P.&R. b. 40 Spring.
Broughton Lyman B. apprentice, 690 Park, b.u. 64 Whitmore.
" Mary, wid. James, h.u. 64 Whitmore.
Brousso Frank, tinner at 291 Asylum.
Brouthers ☞ see Brodeur.
Browe Ernest, foreman, Pope Tube Co. h. 65 Madison.
Brower Edwin, at Phœnix Ins. Co. 64 Pearl, h. h. 41 Kenyon. (23)
" House, Sherman & Crowley, 25 Central.
" Walter, laborer, h.2u. 40 Sheldon.
Brown Abial, h. 1393 Main.
" Abner E. clerk at 700 Mn. h.u. 201 Jefferson.
" Abram P. h. 270 Farmington. ↘
" Agnes A. wid. Henry, h. 112 Albany.
" Albert E. shipping clerk at 581 Capitol, h.2u. 80 Putnam.
" Albert F. clerk at 197 Asylum, b. 227 High.
" Albert S. mach. at 1 Flow. h.So.Manchester v.
" Alex. carpenter at 141 Tru. b.3u. 283 Main.
" Alexander L. toolm. Popes, h. Wilson station.
" Alice, b. 131 Hamilton.
" Allen W. salesman, 40 High, h. 9 S. Hudson.
" Alma, helper at 133 Sheldon, b. 64 Hicks.
" Almira J. wid. Eli, h.u. 49 Clark.
" Alpha, wid. William, h.u. 128 Albany.
" Amariah L. coachman, b. 38½ Beach.
" Andrew C. foreman at 581 Capitol, h. 24 Bushnell.
" Angeline R. Mrs. h. 36 Cedar.
" Annie B. stenographer at Insurance Journal, 53 Trumbull, b. 26 Williams.
" Arthur L. clerk at Lincoln, Seyms & Co. b. 189 Sigourney.
" Arthur M. mach. at 581 Cap. h. 56 Judson.
" Augustus F. mach. at 1 Flower, h. 25 Brook.
" Benjamin, wood and coal, 34 Avon, h.u. 72 Bellevue.
" Bessie A. teacher West Middle school, 927 Asylum, b. 48 Huntington.
" C. E. Mrs. h. 1470 Broad.
" Carrie Mrs. b.u. 88 Fairmount.
" Catherine L. wid. Fred. h.u. 284 Asy. rm.100.
" Chas. M. watchman, h.u. 740 Main.
" Chas. W. tinner at r. 464, b. 464 Windsor av.
" Charlotte A. wid. W. O. h. 943 Main, rm. 34.
" Christine W. stenogr'r, 389 Allyn, b. 704 Mn.
" Clara, miliner, h.3u. 943 Main, rm. 34.
" David H. clerk, b. 58 Oxford.
" David J. baggagemaster N.E.R. h.u.33 Avon.
" David J. motorman St.Ry. b. 231 Market.
" E. F. ins. gen. 783 Main, b. 29 Buckingham.
**BROWN EDWARD J.** watchmaking and repairing, 162, h. 727 Asylum.

Brown E. Vincent, draughtsman at Pope Tube Co. h.2u. 244 Putnam.
" E. W. conductor St.Ry. h. 50 Linden.
" Edward E. scourer at 15 Tru. h. 2 Rice ct.
" Edwin W. foreman printing dept. at Popes, h. 71 Russ.
" Elisha P. foreman, r. 17 Alb. h. Bloomfield t.
" Elmer E. reporter Bradstreet, h. 35 Allen pl.
" Elmer R. clerk, 365 Allyn.
" Emily W. wid. Arba H. b. 73 Church.
" Emory L. insp. at 700 Main, b.u. 64 Madison.
" Esther, wid. Lucius, h.u. 46 Seymour.
" Eunice M. wid. George W. b. 66 Williams.
" F. C. O. janitor at Ætna Life Insurance Co. 650 Main, b. 14 Center.
" Fannie F. b. 270 Farmington.
" Frances A. seamstress, h.u. 21 Albany.
" Francis J. at 20 Central, l. 29½ Lewis.
" Frank, b. 574 Windsor av.
" Frank, bookkeeper, h. 18 Ashley.
" Frank H. teamster, 46 Ann, h. 153 Weth.
" Frank J. machinist at 1 Flow. b. 918 Park.
" Fred E. clerk, 1149 Main, b. Weth.t.
" Fred. E. printer at Times office, h. 574 Windsor av.
" Fred. E. Jr. pressman at 141 Pearl, h. 926 Main, rm. 94.
" Fred. J. clerk at Smith, Bourn & Co. 8 Sigourney, h. East Hartford t.
" Frederick S. Mrs. (Almera Olive,) h. 17 Cap.
" Freeman M. salesman, h. 189 Sigourney.
" George, h. 721 Main, rm. 51.
" George Mrs. h. 223 Asylum, rm. 130.
" George C. farmer, h. 16 Brown.
" George H. bkkpr. at 14 Ford, b. 62 Walnut.
" George H. carpenter at Strickland & Shea, 20 Potter, h. 227 Jefferson.
" Geo. M. office, 427, h. 427 Main, rms. 14, 16.
" Geo. P. molder at 24 Potter, b.u. 83 Grove.
" Geo. W. boxm. at 223 State, b. 1393 Main.
" George W. (Easton & B.) h. 18 Elmer.
" George W. waiter, h.u.r. 227 Pearl.
" Gerald H. clerk, 700 Main, h. 58 Oxford.
" & Gross, now Belknap & Warfield, 77 Asy.
" Harry, helper, 48 Ann, b. Walnut.
" Harry F. washer, 690 Park, b. 131 Hamilton.
" Henry H. beltmaker at Jewell Belting Co. 15 Trumbull, h.r.3.u. 64 Hicks.
" Harvey, laborer, h.u. 128 Windsor.
" Hattie E. at 690 Park, b. 30 Pleasant.
" Hattie E. wid. G. W. b. 40 Green.
" Helen, Miss, h. 140 Washington.
" Henry. mason contractor, 51, h.u. 51 N.B.
" Henry P. mach. at 28 Laurel, h. Newington t.
" Henry S. bookkeeper, h.3u. 106 Hopkins.
" Herbert E. iceman, 4 Central, b.u. 37 Canton.
" J. H. at 15 Trumbull, l 14 Spring.
" J. Jay, clerk at 338 Mn. b. 242 Wethersfield.
" James, helper, 556 Cap. h.u. 175 Lawrence.
" James, h. 18 Affleck.
" James, mach. at 142 Russ, b. 21 Arch.
" James A. barber, h.2u. 348 Windsor av.
" James B. comp. at Popes, b.u. 175 Lawrence.
" James H. T. golftrainer, h. 22 Highland.
" James M. engir. N.Y.E. h.u.u. 12 Wooster.

Brown Jane, wid. John, h.3u. 283 Main.
" Jennie D. 690 Park, b. 105 Babcock.
" John, joiner, b.u. 117 Zion.
" Joseph, coachman, 614 Asy. h. 112 Albany.
" Joseph B. collarm. 8 Sig. b. 21 Riverside.
" Joseph E. mach. at 1 Flower, h. 22 Pearl.
" Joseph Henry, mason, 1079, h. 1079 Broad.
" Josie M. nurse, h. 230 Asylum, rm. 8.
" Julia Mrs. b. W.H. Home for Aged, Albany.
" J. William, carpenter, b. 45 Lincoln.
" Leon P. with Ætna Life Insurance Co. 650 Main, b. 223 Asylum.
" Lena, clerk at 97 Asylum, b. Windsor t.
" Leroy D. correspondt. Popes, h. 68 Allen pl.
" Lewis H. clerk, Popes, b. Unionville t.
" Lewis L. helper, 126 Church, h. 56 Bkm.
" Lillian, b.2u. 128 Albany.
" Lillie, b. 49 Clark.
" M. Grace, kindergarten teacher Arsenal School, b. 107 Wooster.
" Margaret, wid. James T. h. 36 Pratt, rm. 4.
" Margaret, wid. John J.nurse, h.u. 290 Market.
" Margaret, wid. John, laundress, h. 125 Ch.O.
" Margaret W. Mrs. (B. & St.John) h.u.704 Mn.
" Mary, wid. Horace, h.u. 210 Windsor av.
" Mary, wid. James W. h. 29 Bellevue.
" Mary, wid. Michael, h. 210 Barbour.
" Mary, wid. Patrick, b. Home for the Aged.
" Mary A. wid. George T. h. 574 Windsor av.
" Mary B. Mrs. matron, 334, b. 336 Weth.
" Mary E. b. 120 Trumbull.
" Mary E. nurse at 30, b. 30 Wethersfield.
" Mary M. nurse, b. 73 Buckingham.
" Matthew J. cigarm. 104 Asy. b.140 Mather.
" Michael, painter, l. 1113 Main.
" Minnie B. bkkpr. 75 Pearl, b. 45 Farmington.
" Nellie A. dressm. 574, h. 574 Windsor av.
" Oliver, laborer, b. 286 Market.
" Orlando L. carptr. at 141 Pl. h. 177 Retreat.
" Orrin M. machinist, b. 1145 Main.
" Oscar D. lettercarrier, h.2u. 2 Belden.
" Oscar L. mach. at 690 Park, b. 225 High.
" Owen M. b. 1145 Main.
" Patrick, salesman, 219 Asy. h.3u. 12 Affleck.
" Patrick J. machinist, b. 18 Affleck.
" Peter, peddler, b.3u. 89 Morgan.
" Richard, laborer, h. 1 Forest.
" Roancie M. wid. Thomas, h.u. 64 Madison.
" Robert D. student at Yale, b. 1470 Broad.
" Robert E. coachman, b. 19 Foot Guard pl.
" Rosella, wid. James, b. 36 Pratt, room 4.
" Roswell W. Mrs. b. 140 Washington.
" Rowland C. bkkpr. 66 State, h. 64 Wooster.
" & St. John, millinery, 65 Pratt.
   Mrs. M. W. Brown.        C. L. St. John.
" Sarah Mrs. h. 7 Pleasant.
" School, 160—170 Market.
" Thomas, h. 76 Putnam.
" Thomas, belper, Pope Tube Co. b. 24 Putnam.
" Thomas, moulder, 618 Capitol, b. 82 Laurel.
" Thomas, helper P.R.R. b. 53 Liberty.
" Thomas P. molder at 556 Cap. b. 112 Laurel.
" Thomas P. Jr. student, Trinity college, 25 Jarvis hall, Summit.
" Walter H. conductor St.Ry. h. E.H.t.

Brown Walter S. bookkeeper, 1 South Ann, b. b. 270 Farmington.

**BROWN, THOMSON & CO.** drygoods, millinery, children's clothing, books, boots and shoes, etc. ♭20–942 Main.
        *See page 499.*
Geo. A. Gay,      Harry E. Strong.
" Walter, carriagepainter, 17 Elm, b. 32 North.
" William, motorman, b.r.u. 25 Morgan.
" William, dog doctor, 114, h. 114 Albany.
" William, painter, b. 6 Lewis.
" William, gardener, b. 1172 Main.
" Wm. harness, etc. 1148 Main, l. 239 Pearl.
" William, screwm. 476 Capitol, b. 76 Putnam.
" William A. ins. clerk, 197 Asy. b. 15 Beach.
" William B. b. 36 Jefferson.

**BROWN WILLIAM B.** tinner, r. 464 h. 464 Windsor av.
" William G. policeman, h. 6 Preston.
" William H., U. S. Army, h. 140 Retreat.
" William J. iceman, 4 Central, b.u. 37 Canton.
" William P. student at Trinity college, 33 Jarvis hall, Summit.
" Wm. S. salesman at 91 Morgan, b. 94 Church.
" Willis H. b.u. 64 Madison.
" ☞ *see also Braun.*
Browne A. M. wid. Dr. G. S. h. 19 Capitol.
" Albert G. welldriver, 370, h. 370 Asy. rm. 75.

**BROWNE EDMUND,** builder, r. 1419 Main, h. 13 Florence.  *See page 518.*
" Etta, clerk, b. 271 Jefferson.
" Frederick T. mach. at Popes, h. Windsor t.
" John D. president of Connecticut Fire Ins. Co. 51 Prospect, h. 19 Kenyon. (9)
" Marion B. stenographer at Hungerford, Hyde, Joslyn & Gilman, 49 Pearl, b. 13 Florence.
" Pauline, b. 271 Jefferson.
" Sarah E. Mrs. metaphysician, 370, h.u. 370 Asylum, rm. 17.
" Virginia F. b. 19 Kenyon.
Brownell Charles D. mach. at Popes. b. 401 Cap.
" Stephen C. bookkeeper, Ætna National Bank, 644 Main, b.u. 260 Laurel.
Browning Miranda A. wid. Gilman, h. 650 Main, room 43.
" Rosa, h. 284 Asylum, room 2.
Brownlee Thomas, gardener, h. 41 Forest.
" Thomas J. dropf. at Popes, h. 35 Harbison.
" William, ostler, 1128 Main. b. 14 Huntley pl.
Bruce, Filley & Co. furniture, 103 Asylum.
John E. Bruce,  W. J. Filley,  L. J. Filley.
" Fred W. woodworker, 5 Mec. h. E.H.t.

Bruce Geo. P. inspector at r. 59½ Tru. b. E.F².t.
" Gibson, whitewasher, h.r. 213 Pearl.
" John E. (B., Filley & Co.) h.u. 163 Ashley.
" Willard H. notary, 197 Asylum, h. 13 Seyms.
Brucker Charles F. bakery, 543, h.2u. 545 Main.
Bruckner Carl Rev. pastor Our Saviour's Danish Evangelical Lutheran Ch. h. 64 Babcock.
Brucksech Frederick, coachman, 242, b. 242 Windsor av.
Bruehl G. Charles, cabinetmaker at 1170 Main, h.2u. 9 Green.
Bruggestrat Henry, baker, h. 77 Temple.
Bruiggaman Frederick J. machinist at 142 Russ, b. 38 Cedar.
" George H. mach. at 1 Flower, h. 387 Capitol.
" John F. machinist at 40 Gov. h. 38 Cedar.
" Wm. A. mach. at Colts, h. 92 Charter Oak.
Brunader Emil, painter, b.u. 12 Putnam.
Brunell Eli, cigarmaker, 867 Main, h. 180 High.
" Joseph, polisher, b. 61 Ann.
Brunet Elmira, wid. Jos. washer, h.u. 48 Temple.
Brunett William, helper, 54 Arch, h.u. 24 Dean.
Brunette August, bunker No. 3 enginehouse.
Brunette Francis, dropforger, h.u. 18 Ashley.
" Frank Jr. b.u. 18 Ashley.
Brunner & Co. bicycles, 198 Pearl.•
" Louise, at 88 Woodbine, b. 112 Laurel.
" Melnote M. (Brunner & Co.) h. 41 Spring.
Bruno Anthony, h.u. 14 Putnam.
" Antonio, laborer, h.2u. 7 Charles.
" Ed. machinist at 1 Flower, b. 14 Putnam.
Brunotte August, machinist, b. 58 Front.
" William, barber, 58, h. 58 Front.
" William, Jr. barber at 58, b. 58 Front.
Brure Ernest, bootblack, h.u. 40 Village.
" Ernest U. bootblack, 27 Pearl, b. 40 Village.
Brusie Lillian A. Mrs. dressm. 61, h. 61 Hudson.
Brusoe Frank, turner, h.2u. 131 Ward.
Brust Frank G. h. 153 Wethersfield.
Bruyn Abram, carpenter, h.r. 9 South Prospect.
Bryan Agnes C. music teacher public schools, b. 389 Main.
" John, laborer, b. 20 Spring.
" John E. painter at 20 Central, b. 343 Main.
" Thomas R. trav. salesman, h. 5 Lafayette.
" William J. harnessm. at 8 Sig. b. Capitol.
Bryans Wm. J. clerk, 983 Main, b. Hockanum v.
Bryant Caroline F. wid. W. A. h. 61 Huntington.
" Charles K. dentist, 926 Main, rm. 32, h. 61 Huntington.
" & Co. pasteurized cream, 5 Lenox pl.
W. M. Bryant.    Bert W. Chapman.
" Clarence at Ætna Insurance Co. 666 Main, h. Windsor t.
" Edward B. at Ætna Insurance Co. 666 Main, h. 12 Atwood.
" Frances A. wid. Chas. dressm. 4, b. 4 Marsh.
" Fannie, bkkpr. 83 Woodbine, h. 462 Far.
" Frederick G. toolmr. at Popes, h.u. 89 Jef.
" Geo. A. finisher, 581 Cap. b.2u. 56 Asylum.
" George Albert, 13 Central, h. 19 Elliott.
" Hannah W. stenographer, 801 Mn. b. E.H.t.
" Harry E., U. S. Army, b. 61 Huntington.
" Henry, designer at New England Granite Works, 1260 Main, h. 81 Edwards.

Bryant Harry E. clerk, Hartford Life Ins. Co. 252 Asylum, b. 462 Farmington.
" Henry G. artist, clerk Conn. Trust and Safe Deposit Co. 785 Main, b. 81 Edwards.
" James E. Mrs. h. 291 Park.
" James P. shipping clerk, 83 Woodbine, h. 462 Farmington.
" James S. cashier at Colts Pat. Fire Arms Mfg. Co. b. 81 Edwards.
" Percy L. student at Trinity College, b. E.H.t.
**BRYANT PERCY S.** attorney at law, 57 Pratt, h. E.H.t. *See page 485.*
" Willard M. (*Bryant & Co.*) h. 5 Lenox pl.
" William H. at Ætna Life Ins. Co. 650 Main. h. Windsor t.
Brydon Frank R. carpenter at 10 Trumbull, h. 82 Whitman.
Bryson Jane A. nurse, 14, b. 14 Church, rm. 4.
Bryton Edwin, L2u. 1194 Main.
Buanchetto Secondo, fireman, 835 Mn. h. 13 Mor.
Bubbell Frank, laborer at 8 Front.
Bublitz John, carpenter, h.2u. 4 Lawrence.
Bubser Annie A. teacher at Normal school, b. 172 Putnam.
" Augusta A. wid. Reinhold, h. 172 Putnam.
" Fidel, supt. at Pope Tube Co. b. 186 Laurel.
Buch George, tailor, 10, h. 98 Charter Oak.
" John, woodcarver, 69 Front, h. Forestville t.
Buchanan Chas. O. plumber, 228 Pearl, h.u. 14 Bond.
" Wm. A. salesman, 97 Asylum, b. 6 Church.
Bucher Albert, at Colts, b. 139 Front.
" Emil C. mach. at 1 Flower, b. 7 Putnam.
" Julius, laborer, b. 139 Front.
" Mary, wid. John, h. 139 Front.
Buck Chas. A. conductor St.Ry. h. 68 Linccoln.
" Chas. L. motorman St.Ry. h.u. 80 Madison.
" Charles T. floorwr. 956 Main, h. 6 Avon.
" Edward L. attendant, 30 Washington.
" Edward W. at Travelers Insurance Co. 56 Prospect, h. Wethersfield t.
**BUCK & ECCLESTON,** attorneys at law, 926 Main, room 3. *See page 481.*
John R. Buck.      Arthur F. Eggleston.
" Elizabeth Mrs. laundress, h.r. 14 Martin.
" Frances, wid. B. E. h. 197 High.
" Fred'k F.E. printer at 174 Pearl, h. Whiting lane, south of Farmington av.
" Henry R. draughtsman. 800 Main, h. Weth. t.
" Howard C. at Phœnix Ins. Co. 64 Pearl, b. 197 High.
" John H. attorney, 926 Main, rm. 3, exc. secy to Gov., State Capitol, rm.35, b. 37 Forest.
" John R. (*B. & Eggleston*) attorney at law, 926 Main, h. 37 Forest.
" Leon C. ins. agent, 756 Mn. h. 16 Jefferson.
" Mamie, operator, b. 68 Lincoln.
" Mary J. Mrs. b. 943 Main, rm. 20.
" Percy, clerk, h.2u. 271 Jefferson.
" Lemuel A. seacaptain, h. 5 Ellsworth.
" Thomas, waiter at 29 Central, b. 80 State.
" Winthrop E. brakeman, N.Y.R. h.u. 4 Ellsworth pl.
Buckerselski Raymond, sexton Jewish cemetery, h. 153 Ward.

Buckerselski Raymond F. draughtsman, 141 Trumbull, b. 153 Ward.
Buckingham William F. clerk, city auditor, 800 Main, h. 54 Brook.
Buckland Arthur J. clerk, 956 Main, h. Rocky Hill t.
" C. Edward, ins. agent, 721 Main, rm. 3, h. Glastonbury t.
**BUCKLAND C. W. MRS.** resident architect, 926, h. 926 Main, rm. 47.
" Henry H. painter, h.r. 44½ John.
" Henry H. Jr. painter, h.r. 44½ John.
" William, b. 182 Collins.
Buckley Andrew J. finisher, 65 Suffield, b. 10 Chst.
" Anna L. b.u. 12 Liberty.
" Annie, domestic, 20 South Hudson.
" B.A. employment agency, 112 Tru. h.166 Aly.
" Bridget, wid. John, h. 101 Main.
" Bridget, wid. Patrick, h.u. 25 Seyms.
" Bros. & Co. painters, 10 Ford.
Wm. O. Buckley.   Chas. H. Buckley.
George Buckley.   Wm. O. Buckley, Jr.
" Catharine, wid. Dennis, h.u. 24 Flower.
" Carrie S. Mrs. b. 5 South Prospect.
" Catherine G. milliner, 956 Mn. b. 12 Liberty.
" Charles H. (*B. Bros. & Co.*) h. 50 Grand.
" Chas. J. at 62 Market, b. 196 New Park.
" Delia A. at 29 Union pl. b. 17 East.
" Dennis P. butcher, 1046 Mn. h. 194 Capen.
" Edward L. h.u. 18 Winthrop.
" Elizabeth, b.u. 254 Putnam.
" Elizabeth C. clerk, 956 Main, b. 12 Liberty
" Ellen, wid. Michael, h. 18 So. Prospect.
" Eugene J. ship.clerk, Colts, h.2u. 200 Shel.
" Fannie, wid. Amos, washer, h. 100 Walnut.
" George, (*Buckley Bros.*) h.u. 3 Squire.
" George H. carpenter, Pratt & Whitney Co. 1 Flower.
" J. deckhand steamer Hartford, 285 State.
" James, b.u. 1261 Main.
" James, operator, Evening Post, 23 Asylum, b.r. 40 Vanblock.
" James E. machinist at 9, h. 23 Sigourney.
" James G. paymaster, 556 Cap. b. 24 Flow.
" James W. h.u. 97 Main.
" Jeremiah, hodcarrier, h. 17 East.
" Jeremiah F. (*B. & Reardon,*) h. 122 Hung.
" Jeremiah J. b. 196 New Park.
" John, b. W.H. home for aged, Albany.
" John, engineer, N.Y.R. h. 12 Liberty.
" John, gardener, h.u. Hawthorn extension.
" John F. diesinker at Colts, b. 40 Vanblock.
" John F. Jr. fireman, N.Y.R. b. 12 Liberty.
" John P. dock foreman, 285 State, h.196 N.P.
" Joseph M. cutter, 154 Windsor, b. 53 Ple.
" Keron, gardener, 30 Weth. b. 76 Vanblock.
" Lawrence, foreman, 65 Suffield, h. 560 Windsor.
" Lewis E. millwright, Colts, h.r. 44 Vanblock
" Louis M. mach. at Colts, h.u. 47 Huyshope.
" Mary A. clerk, Brown, Thomson & Co. 942 Main, b. 17 East.
" Mary G. dressmaker, b.u. 25 Seyms.
" Mary J. h.r. 13 Belden.
" Michael, carpenter, h. 14 Ward pl.

*Established, 1854.*

# N. B. BULL & SON,

## PARLOR STOVES AND RANGES,

## HOT AIR. FURNACES. HOT WATER.

**Housekeeping Goods.**
**Sanitary Plumbing and Roofing.**
**Refrigerators.**

Telephone 1028-5.   **599 AND 601 MAIN ST.**
**Old Nos. 189 and 191.**

Buckley Mich. R. engir. h. Quaker lane, W.H t.
" Miles J. upholsterer at r. 258 Main.
" Nellie, b. 12 Liberty.
" & O'Loughlin, saloon, 22 Central.
    Patrick T. Buckley.        John J. O'Loughlin.
" Patrick T. (*B. & O'Loughlin*) h.u. 884 Mn.
" & Reardon, teas and coffees, 28 Wells.
    Jeremiah F. Buckley.        Chas. J. Reardon.
" Thomas J. laborer, b. 362 Front.
" W. S. h. 63 Hungerford.
" Wickliffe S. clerk, Mechanics Savings
    Bank, 815 Main, h. 63 Hungerford.
" Wm. F. cigarstripper, 104 Asy. b. 1261 Mn.
" William J. painter, h.u. 224 Allyn.
" William J. toolmaker, Colts, h. 18 John.
" Wm. O. 3d, clerk, 146 State, b. 47 Wooster
" Wm. O. (*B. Bros. & Co.*) h.u. 14 Squire.
" Wm. O. Jr. (*B. Bros. & Co.*) h. 47 Wooster.
" ☞ *see also Bulkeley; Bulkley.*
Buckman William E. foreman printer at the
    Sunday Globe, 25 Asylum, h.u. 96 Park.
Buckner Sherman, waiter 25 Central, b. 43 Liberty
" William L. ostler at 51 Farmington.
Budd Michael, asst. janitor, Popes, b. 188 Ward.
Budde Augustus W. *1st selectman*, mason and
    builder, 107, h. 107 Hungerford.
" Charles, mason, b. 39 Putnam.
" Eliza, wid. William, h. 39 Putnam.
" Henry A. mach. at 1 Flower, h. 39 Putnam.
" Henry A. mason, h.u. 103 Hungerford.
" Minnie E. D. stenographer at 921 Main,
    b. 39 Putnam.
" Minnie L. stenogr. 141 Asy. b. 107 Hung.
Budge Benjamin, at Travelers Ins. Co. 50 Pros-
    pect, b. 1 Union.
" Edward C. asst. bookkeeper, Jewell Belt-
    ing Co. 15 Trumbull, b. Wethersfield t.
" Jessie C. wid. James, h.2 u. 1 Union.
" Matthew, watchman, 556 Cap. h. 109 Bab.
" William C. machinist at Popes, b.2u.1.Union.
Budreau Joseph J. roadmaster St.Ry. b. 80 State.
Budro Frank A. lather, h.u. 12 Trumbull.
Buell Caroline M. wid. James N. h.u. 68 Chst.
" Lillian Mrs. b. 29 Center.
" Robert Catlin, clerk at Hartford Nat. Bank,
    58 State, h. 21 Columbia.

**BUELLESBACH WILLIAM,** or-
    namental & plain iron work for builders,
    columns, beams, etc. 75 Commerce, h.u.
    19 Avon.          *See page 478.*

Buffin William, at Case, Lockwood & Brainard
    Co. b.2u. 19 Church.
Bugbee H. J. Miss, Travelers Insurance Co. 56
    Prospect, b. 1 Amity.
" John B. driver, h. 11 Washington.
" Julia, wid. Franklin, h.2u. 216 Windsor av.
Bugby Harriet, wid. Charles E. h. 6 Amity.
Buger Albert, helper, b. 139 Front.
" George, laborer, b. 139 Front.
" Julius, helper, b. 139 Front.
" Mary Mrs. washing, h. 139 Front.
" William, laborer, b. 139 Front.
Buggie Catharine, wid. of James, h.u. 24 Avon.
" Edward L. clerk, 93 Kil. b.u. 24 Avon.
" James, varnisher, 556 Main, b.u. 24 Avon.
" Michael J. helper at 1 Flower, h. 108 Ward.
Buggle James J. driver, 544 Asy.b.r. 25½ Flower.
" Michael, filer, h.r. 25½ Flower.
Buglisi Chris. barber, 791 Main, h. 36 Windsor.
Buion Michael, b.u. 13 Mechanic.
Bukovitch ☞ *see Berkovitch.*
Bulkeley Emma J. Mrs. h. 8 Belden.
" John C. Ætna Life Ins. Co. 650 Main,
    h. 9 Park ter.
BULKELEY MORGAN G. president Ætna Life
    Ins. Co. 650 Main, h. 136 Washington.
                        *See page 449.*
" William E. A. cashier Ætna Life Ins. Co.
    650 Main, b. 134 Washington.
" William H. auditor Ætna Life Ins. Co. 650
    Main, h. 134 Washington.
Bulkley Clarendon C. clerk at Colts armory, h.
    47 Sumner.
" George E. clerk at Conn. General Life Ins.
    Co. 49 Pearl, b. 924 Asylum.
" George G. clerk at Orient Ins. Co. 5 Haynes,
    h. Rocky Hill t.
" Helen E. inspector at 110 Commerce, b.
    Rocky Hill t.
" Henry S. b. 924 Asylum.
" Mae E. Miss, Travelers Ins. Co. 56 Prospect,
    b. Wethersfield t.
" Mary S. wid. George L. h. 924 Asylum.
Bull Benjamin N. bookkeeper at 599 Main, h.
    118 Park.
" Edward W. bicycles, 328 Asylum, h. 280
    Laurel.
" Edward W. cabinetmaker, State Capitol,
    h. 103 Wooster.
" George, ostler, 370, b. 370 Albany.
" Geo. S. (*N. B. Bull & Son,*) h. 260 Franklin.
BULL N. B. & SON, stoves, tinware, plumbers,
    etc. 599 and 601 Main.   *See page 76.*
    Norris B. Bull.        Geo. S. Bull.
" Norris B. (*N.B.Bull & Son*) h. 118 Park.
" Wellington E. clerk at Mechanics Savings
    Bank, 815 Main, b. 39 Spring.
Bullard Anna W. teacher at West Middle school,
    927 Asylum, b. 20 Niles.
" Clarissa Mrs. b. 234 Barbour.
" Herbert S. atty. at law, 2 Central, b. 20 Niles.
" John E. (*B., Johnson & S.*) h. Middletown t.
" Johnson & Shipman, ins. etc. 175 Asylum.
    John E. Bullard.   Myron H. Johnson.   Jas. Shipman.
Bullock Edmund L. b. 60 Vernon.

Bullock Henry C. dentist, 868, h.u. 868 Main.
" Joseph B. gunsmith, Colts, b.u. 542 Main.
" Joseph W. toolmaker at 581 Capitol, h.u. 271 Jefferson.
" N. Florence, teacher at Washington Street school, b. 60 Vernon.
" William Joseph, foreman at 24 Mechanic, h. 97 Franklin.
Bulman Edward, bartender at 134, b. 80 State.
Bumgartner Albert L. toolm. Popes, h. 29 Elm.
Bumstein Israel, butcher, h.u. 203 Front.
Bumster John J. filer at Popes, h.u. 22 Putnam.
" Michael, mach. at 40 Gov. h. 135 Lawrence.
" William J. harnessmaker, h. 192 Jefferson.
Bunce Alexander, student at Yale, b. 61 Edwards.
" Alice, b. 104 Niles.
" Arthur M. clerk, Brown, Thomson & Co. 942 Main, b. 175 Capitol.
" B. F. (Bunce & Pelton,) l. 61 Prospect.
" Charles H. city surveyor, City Hall, 800 Main, h. 175 Capitol.
" Edward M. secretary Conn. Mutual Life Ins. Co. 783 Main, h. 78 Elm.
" Emma, b. 149 High.
" Fred. W. machinist at Colts, b.r. 20 Grand.
" Frederic L. cashier Phœnix National Bank, 803 Main, h. 104 Niles.
" Henry L. president United States Bank, 872 Main, h. 114 Capitol.
" Hezekiah, h.r. 20 Grand.
" John L. b. 78 Elm.
" Jonathan B. president Phœnix Mutual Life Insurance Co. 49 Pearl, b. 61 Edwards.
" M. E. Miss, at Travelers Insurance Co. 56 Prospect, b. 637 Farmington.
" & Pelton, brokers, 7 Central.
B. F. Bunce.                    L. C. Pelton.

PHILLIP D. BUNCE, Physician.  Office, 50 Pratt.
Hours—9 to 10 A. M.
          2 to 4 and 7 to 8 P. M.
          Sundays—3 to 4 P. M.
          Telephone connection.

Bunce Philip D. physician, 50, h. 50 Pratt.
" Walton C. clerk, Popes, b. 114 Capitol.
" William Gidney, artist, 904 Main, rm. 112, b. 21 Woodland.
" William N. salesman, b. 36 Imlay.
Bundy Harriet M. artist, b. 1313 Main.
" Horace L. photographer, 904, rm. 109, h.u. 1313 Main.
Bunke William, baker, h.2u. 101 Sheldon.
Bunn John B. student at Trinity College, 42 Jarvis hall, Summit.
Bunnell Catherine, wid. George, h.u.r. 25 Spruce.
" Charles A. gardner, b. Vanderbilt hill.
" Edith L. teacher, Brown school, b.u. 127 Alb.
" Ernest P. machinist, b.u. 127 Albany.
" Harry, helper at 57, b. 51 Albany.
" James A. inspect. Popes, h.2u. 242 Putnam.
" Seymour, toolmaker, 70 Huy. h. 127 Albany.
" ☞ see also Bonnel, Bonnell.
Bunner Joseph, carpenter, h.u. 5 Davenport.
Buntin John A. rubberworker at 690 Park, b. 23 Sherman.
" Wm. G. molder at 1 Flower, h.u. 263 Main.

Burbank George G. student Trinity college, 4 Jarvis hall, Summit.
" James B. major U.S.A. h. 714 Asylum.
" Julia B. private school, 714, h. 714 Asylum.
" Katherine, teacher, High school, b. 714 Asy.
Burbidge Charles H. foreman. patternmaker, 1 Flower, h. 429 Capitol.
Burch Ellen, wid. Thomas, b. 209 Garden.
**BURCH GEO. W.** rubber stamps, 91 Asylum, (B. & Tarbox,) h. 209 Garden.
                                  See page 497.
Burch & Tarbox, printers, 91 Asylum.
George W. Burch.      Charles H. Tarbox.
Burchmore Stephen W. printer at 668 Main, l. 53 Trumbull.
Burckard George, mach. at 690 Park, b. 19 Sisson.
Burden John, mach. at 1 Flower, b. 39 Putnam.
Burdett Charles L. attorney at law, solicitor of patents, 68 Pratt, h. 188 Sigourney.
" Ralph, student, h. 188 Sigourney.
" Thomas, b. 188 Sigourney.
Burdette Enos J. builder, h.u. 50 Heath.
Burdick Asa I. salesman, Charles R. Hart Co. 898 Main, h.u. 40 Wooster.
" Eliza, wid. George H. h. 205 Sigourney.
" Frances A. Mrs. h. 756 Park.
" Francis L. clerk at 690, h. 756 Park.
" Frank E. 690 Park, h. 52 Capitol.
" Gertrude A. at Phœnix Ins. Co. 64 Pearl, b. 12 Canton.
" Howard H. mach. at 1 Flow. b. 205 Sig.
" Orlo D. machinist at 40 Gov. h. 71 Madison
" Rollin D. salesman  t C. S. Hills & Co. 885 Main, h. 12 Canton.
" Russell M. (C. S. Brewer & Co.) h. 166 Sig.
" William L. Mrs. b. 48 Asylum.
Burdon John, mach. at 1 Flower, b.u. 39 Putnam
Bureau Alphonse T. barber at 933 Main, h.u. 4 Russell.
Burg George, blacksmith at Popes, h.u. 43 N.B.
Burgenson John, gardener at 135 Washington.
Burgess Cornelia E. b. 72 Buckingham.
**BURGESS HENRY C.** coal, 15 Albany, b. 72 Buckingham.      See page 493.
" Mary, wid. Henry W. h.u. 52 Russell.
" Robert, helper, 1 Flow. h. Thompsonville v
" Sarah G. b. 72 Buckingham.
Burgey Fred. meat peddler, h. 67 Hudson.
Burghardt Harold D. mach. 1 Laurel, h.113 Park.
Burk Ann, wid. Nicholas, b. 74 Pleasant.
" Annie, clerk, 956 Main, b. 87 Fairmount.
" George W. operator at 40 Gov. h. E.H.t
" James F. salesman at Chas. R. Hart Co. 898 Main, b. Meriden t
" John, farmer, St. Marys Home, W.H.t
" Joseph F. coachman, 366 Garden.
" Joseph J. Jr. undertakers assistant at 387 Main, h.u. 86 Grove.
" Michael, helper St. Ry. 115 State.
Burke Alice, wid. Patrick, h.u. 566 Main.
" Augustus H. motorman St. Ry. h.u. 7 Sig. pl.
" Bartholomew J. collector Hartford Telegram, b.u. 68 Sheldon.
" Burton H. clerk, 690 Park, h. 10½ Sisson.
" Daniel, rubberw. at 690 Pk. h. 134 Madison.

Burke Daniel F. teamster at 25, b.u. 247 Front.
" Daniel L. repairer at Popes, b. 90 Capitol.
" Dennis F. driver at 356, b.u. 566 Main.
" Edward B. helper at Pratt & Whitney Co. 1 Flower, h. 82 Francis.
" Frank H. engraver at R. S. Peck & Co. 26 High, b. 29 Bellevue.
" Fred. E. foreman at Downing & Perkins, 128 Commerce, h.u. 31 Pleasant.
" Harry M. attorney, 756 Main, h. S.M.v.
" James, clerk at 571, b.u. 566 Main.
" James, helper at Popes, b. 90 Capitol.
" James, laborer, h. 21 Canton.
" James A. plater at Wm. Rogers Mfg. Co. 66 Market, b. 35 Pleasant.
" James J. steamfitter, 1 Flower, b. 109 Russ.
" James L. polisher at 581 Cap. h. 6 Putnam.
" John, laborer, h.u. 68 Sheldon.
" John E. (Mrs. Hannah M.) gents' furnishings, 419 Main, h. 47 Annawan.
" John F. teamster, b. 566 Main.
" John M. tailor at 76 Asylum, h. 16 Wooster.
" John W. clerk at 419 Main, b. 47 Annawan.
" Joseph, bottler at r. 7 Brady, b. 373 Broad.
" Joseph F. clerk, 82 Asylum, b. 47 Annawan.
" Joseph F. coachman at 366 Garden.
" Julia, wid. Patrick, h.u. 29 Bellevue.
" Julia E. stenog. 197 Asy. b. Talcottville v.
" Julia M. clerk at Brown, Thomson & Co. 942 Main, b. 29 Bellevue.
" Lottie, wid. Patrick A. h. 878 Broad.
" Margaret, dressmaker, b. 85 Governor.
" Margaret Mrs. h. 85 Governor.
" Martin, brazier at Popes, b.2u. 22 Lawrence.
" Mary, wid. Patrick, h. 5 Hendricxsen.
" Mary E. dressmaker, b. 29 Bellevue.
" Michael, laborer, h.u.r. 23 Spruce.
" Michael, teamster, h. 87 Fairmount.
" Morris, b.2u. 26 Flower.
" Patrick, hartder. 194 State, b.u. 150 Market.
" Patrick, helper, b. 39 So. Prospect.
" Patrick J. mach. at Colts, b. 5 Hendricxsen.
" Patrick J. night forem. St.Ry. h.u. 230 Weth.
" Patrick N. coachman, 23 C.O.pl. b. 261 Main.
" Paul J. enameler at Popes, b. 85 Governor.
" Richard, carpenter, b. 338 Franklin.
" Thomas, buffer at 62 Mar. b. Wethersfield t.
" Thomas, brakem. at N.Y.R. h.2u. 26 Flower.
" Thomas, clerk Brown, Thomson & Co. 942 Main, b.u. 153 Market.
" Thomas, coachm. 10 Myrtle, h.2u. 56 Flower.
" Thomas, painter, b.3u. 40 Sheldon.
" Thos. E. elevatorer, 14 Church, b.u. 68 Shel.
" Timothy J. sec'y at 25 Front, h. 28 Imlay.
" William, lab. Pope Tube Co. b. 80 Madison.
" William, laborer, b. 39 South Prospect.
" William E. bookkeeper, New England Brewing Co. b. 33 Canton.
" William J. clerk at 571, b.u. 566 Main.
" William J. clerk, 28 Union pl. h. 38 Spring.
" ☞ see also Burk.
Burkholder John D. shipping clerk, 556 Capitol, h. 6 So. Forest.
Burkle Edwin C. mach. at Colts, h.u. 8 Union.
" Henry W. mach. b.u. 92 Charter Oak.

Burkle Paulina, wid. John G. h.u. 92 Ch.O.
Burkman Harris, peddler, h.u. 190 Front.
Burleigh Chester, farmer, 81, b. 81 Bluehills.
Burlingham Charles H. shipping clerk at Seidler & May, 306 Pearl, h.2u. 42 Madison.
" John F. mach. at 30 Cush. b. 21 Wolcott.
Burnell Calvin J. treasurer Beach Manufacturing Co. 209 State, h. 35 Willard.
" Francis C. clerk at Popes, b. 35 Willard.
" Joseph, inspector at Popes, b. 61 Ann.
BURNET JAMES G. (Newton & B.) meats, 319 Asy. h.u. 27 Huntington. See page 487.
Burnett Albert D. ostler at and b. 20 Tremont.
" Arthur E. traveling salesman at Popes, h. New York city.
" Edward Joseph, painter at 29, b. 29 Vine.
" Elizabeth, wid. Robert, h.u. 10 John.
" Frank R. motorman St.Ry. h. 15 John.
" Jennie, assistant at 171 Putnam.
Burnham Albert M. clerk 50 Asy. b. 13 Sherman.
" Annie, clerk, 956 Main, b. E.H.t.
" Annie M. dressm. 107, b.u. 107 Jefferson.
" B. E. oiler steamer Hartford, 285 State.
" C. D. & H. D. marble works, 54 Windsor av. Chester D. Burnham.    Herbert D. Burnham.
" Charles E. agent, b. 79 Allen pl.
" Charles L. b. 49 Oak.
" Chester D. (C. D. & H. D. B.) h. 337 Windsor av.
" D. S. b. 119 Capitol.
" Dwight L. at Ætna Life Insurance Co. 650 Main, b. E.H.t.
" Dwight T. manager Hartford Grocery Co. 369 Capitol, h.u. 24 Madison.
" Edgar A. at Ætna Life Insurance Co. 650 Main, b. E.H.t.
" Edgar F. (Gemmill, Burnham & Co.) 66 Asylum, h. 621 Farmington.
" Edmund A. theological student, 1507 Broad, h. 753 Asylum.
" Edward A. machinist, h. 51 John.
" Ellen A. b. 13 Sherman.
BURNHAM ELLERY D. councilman 7th ward, (Marcy Bros. & Co.) h. 269 Wethersfield.
" Etta M. bkkpr. at 342 Asy. b.u. 24 Madison.
" F. A. president Mutual Reserve Fund Life Association, 904 Main.
" Frank G. life ins. agt. 29 Pearl, b. 52 Wooster.
" Frederick C. at Ætna Insurance Co. 666 Main, h. 170 Sargeant.
" Fred. C. at Phœnix Ins. Co. 64 Pearl, b. 52 Wooster.
" George H. (Miller & B.) b. 48 Asylum.
" George L. with Ætna Ins. Co. 666 Main, b. 39 Russ.
" Herbert D. (C. D. & H. D. B.) h. 52 Wooster.
" Herbert E. cutter at 66 Asy. b. 52 Wooster.
" Howard D. clerk at 197 Asy. b.u. 24 Madison.
" Ida J. music teach. 337, b. 337 Windsor av.
" J. Edward, clerk, 353 Mn. b. 4 Buckingham.
" J. William, diesinker, b. 13 Sherman.
" Julia, h. 786 Asylum.
" L. Katherine, wid. Joseph D. h. 79 Pearl.
" Lottie E. at Hartford Life Ins. Co. 252 Asylum, b. 170 Sargeant.

Burnham Martha wid. Edwin, h. 79 Allen pl.
" Martha C. wid. P. H. h. 170 Sargeant.
" Mary, wid. John T. h. 13 Sherman.
" Mary B. wid. Alfred A. h. 786 Asylum.
" Olen H. blacksmith, 366 Allyn, h. 25 Vine.
" Percy O. B.(*Crawford & Co.*) b.u.6Church.
" Philip, clerk, b.u. 88 Hudson.
" Philip D. discount clerk at Phœnix National Bank, 803 Main, b. 79 Pearl.
BURNHAM RALPH, *alderman 6th ward*, foreman Jewell Belting Co. 15 Tru. h.u. 49 Oak.
" Sarah F. dressmaker, 15, b. 15 Sherman.
" Thomas G. machinist at Pratt & Whitney Co. , 1 Flower, h. 24 Beach.
" Wm.W. tobacco packer, h.u. 9 Riverside pl.
Burns Agnes, b. 19 Wadsworth.
" Agnes L. dressmaker, b.2u. 74 Walnut.
" Bernard, foreman at Popes,h.u,66 Lawrence.
" C. J. G. clerk at Pope Motor Carriage dep't, 1 Laurel, b. 54 Sumner.
" Daniel J. laborer at 65 State, b. 25 Spruce.
" David F. steamfitter, h. 90 Franklin.
" Dominick F. grocer, 304, meat, 310 Park, h. 64 Lawrence.
" Ellen, wid. Dennis, h.u. 36 Hicks.
" Edward, fireman, b. 18½ Howard.
" Edward, screwmaker at 70 Huy. h. 40 Park.
" Edward A. crater 581 Cap. b. 19 Foot Guard.
" Edward A. toolm. at Popes, b.u. 64 Russ.
" Edward F. boilermaker, b. 1318 Broad.
" Edward F. ironworker, h.u. 51 Pleasant.
" Edw'd J. boilerm. at 40 Cush. b.2u. 135 Law.
" Elizabeth, wid. William, h. 308 Park.
" Ellen, wid. Michael, h.2u. 53 Front.
" George, mechanic at 26 High, b. 78 Brook.
" George H. saloon, 136, b. 134 Windsor.
" Henry, cook, h.u. 51 Sanford.
" James, at 100 Commerce, h. 61 Ann.
" James, cook at 80 State.
" James, grocer, 134, h. 134 Windsor.
" James, laborer, b. 79 Chestnut.
" James, machinist, b. 16 Chestnut.
" James, screwmaker at Popes, b. 308 Park.
" James Mrs. boarding house, 61 Elm.
" James F. bookkeeper Brown, Thomson & Co. 942 Main, h.u. 95 Park.
" James F. harnessmaker, b. 36 Laurel.
" James F. jobber, b. 134 Windsor.
" James J. boxm. at 581 Cap. b. 16 Chestnut.
" James V. barber, b. 200 Asylum.
" John, captain, h. 48 Front.
" John, farmer, 146, h. 146 Bluehills.
" John, helper, b.2u. 13 North.
" John, laborer, h. 16 Chestnut.
" John, laborer, 306 Park.
" John, laborer, 95 Pleasant, h. 78 Brook.
" John, oiler, 556 Capitol, h.u. 47 Hawthorn.
" John, paper ruler, b. 111 Pearl.
" John J. saloon, 238 Zion, b. 41 Glendale.
" John J. b. 2 Holcomb.
" John J. screwm. at Popes, b.u. 36 Laurel.
" John J. policeman, h. 31 Pleasant.
**BURNS JOHN J.** plumber and gasfitter, 14 Trumbull, b. 152 Bluehills.
" Kittie C. clerk at 942 Main, b.2u 53 Front.

Burns Kittie J. bookkeeper at 304, b. 308 Park.
" Lawrence J. repairer, Popes, h. 135 Barbour.
" Mamie A. bookkeeper at 544 Asy.b.: 08 Park.
" Margaret, wid. James, h.u. 36 Laurel.
" Martin H. buyer at 956 Main, h. 44 Mahl.
" Mary, wid. Richard, h. 1059 Main.
" Mary M. b. 19 Wadsworth.
" Max, stonemason, b.u. 69 Pleasant.
" Michael, mason, b.2u. 40 Sheldon.
" Michael, setter at Jewell Belting Co. 15 Trumbull, h.2u. 59 Pleasant.
" Patrick, laborer, b. 1139 Broad.
" Patrick, laborer at State Capitol, h. E.H.t.
" Patrick F. forger at Popes, h.2u. 4 Affleck.
" Patrick F. molder 556 Cap. b. 16 Chestnut.
" Peter, plumber, b. 1202 Main.
" Philip, gardener at 345 Collins, b. 146 Blu.
" Phœbe, wid. Joseph G. dressm. h. 54 Sumner.
" Rose, b.u. 142 Grove.
" Rose, wid. Jeremiah, h. 270 Front.
" Stephen, mach. at 556 Capitol, h. 78 Brook.
" Thomas, helper h.r. 25 West.
" Thomas, h.2u. 92 Walnut.
" Thomas, brakeman, h.2u. 17 Windsor.
" Thomas, shoemaker, 1357, h. 1357 Main.
" Thomas A. clerk at 134, b. 134 Windsor.
" Thos. F. bartender at 17 Central, h. 220 Park.
" Thomas J. lineman, h. 13 Curcombe.
" Walter F. plater, h.2u. 53 Front.
" William, enameler at Popes, h.u. 34 Park.
" William F. wringer, 15 Tru. b.2u.59 Pleasant.
" Wm. H. assembler, 556 Cap. h. 52 Liberty.
" Wm. H. carpetlayer, h. 355 Asylum.
" William H.mach. at 1 Flower, b. 62 Sheldon.
" William J. clerk, b. 61 Ann.
" Wm. J. meat and vegetable market, 544 Asylum, h.u. 12 Center.
" ☞ *see also Byrne ; Byrnes ; O'Byrne.*
Burpee Alice J. teacher, b. 38 Huntington.
" Caroline L. wid. William H. nurse, h.u. 230 Windsor av.
" Chas. W. state editor Hartford Courant, 66 State, b. 49 Forest.
" J. Frederick, merchant, h. 33 Huntington.
" Robert L. clerk, 198 Pearl, b. 69 Church.
" Susan J. wid. Henry L. h. 33 Huntington.
" ☞ *see also Baupre.*
Burr Alfred E. (*B. Brothers.*) editor Hartford Times, 716 Main, h. 102 Windsor av.
" Alice, b. 155 Franklin.
" Alice E. b. 243 Sargeant.
" Andrew W. h.u. 7 King.
**BURR BROTHERS,** publishers of Hartford Daily Times, 716 Main.
A. E. Burr.   Franklin L. Burr.   W. O. Burr.
" Carl E. bookkeeper, 118 Asylum, l.112 Oak.
" Clara Mrs. dressmaker, 155, b. 155 Franklin.
" Clara J. at Travelers Insurance Co. 56 Prospect, b. Rocky Hill t.
" Clarence H. at Travelers Insurance Co. 56 Prospect, b. 12 Church.
" Colin C. draughtsman 177 Asy.b. Rocky Hill t.
" Edgar B. at Phœnix Insurance Co. 64 Pearl, h. 243 Sargeant.
" Frances Ellen, b. 102 Windsor av.

Burr Franklin L. *(B. Brothers,)* editor Hartford Times, 716 Main, h. 136 Windsor av.
" Fred. W. miller at 24 Mec. h.u. 79 Hudson.
" Frederick E. *( Otis & Burr,)* h. Bristol t.
" George S. saddler, 8 Sig. h. 200 Windsor av.
" Harris L. bookkeeper, Popes, h. 24 Imlay.
" Harry L. at Ætna Insurance Co. 666 Main, h. 7 Windsor av.
" Howard C. clerk, 66 Asylum, h.u. 26 East.
" Index Co. 336 Asylum.
" Jason F. carpenter h.2u. 13 Goodman.
" John B. & Co. publishers, 336 Asylum.*
" Nellie, at 20 Sargeant, b. 12 Hungerford.
" Robert, baker at 20 South Hudson.
" Sidney, floorwalker, 921, b. 981 Main.
" Wallace H. blacksm. at 1 Flow. h.u. 192 Russ.
" William B. cashier, 7 Am. h.u. 10½ Ford.
" Wm. J. harnessm. at 8 Sig. b.2u.13 Goodman.
" Willie O. *(Burr Bros.)* editor Hartford Times, 716 Main, b. 102 Windsor av.
" Willoughby F. mech. 581 Cap. h. Plainville t.
Burrell Henry J. barber, h. 89 Arch.
" William E. h. 89 Arch.
" William H. inspector, 690 Park, b. 89 Arch.
Burrill Henry W. vice president at 875 Main, h.u. 18 Belden.
Burritt Harry E. finisher, 24 Mechanic, h.2u. 19 Williams.
Burroughs William A. clerk, 97 Asylum, b. 427 Main, rm. 21.
" Grace, theological student, 1507 Broad, b. 62 Hawthorn.
Burrows George, tinsmith at 599 Main, b.45 Park.
" Frank O. ostler, b. 40 Tremont.
" John, saloon, 1 Morgan, h. 2 Church.
" Percy, laborer, 940, b. 940 Windsor av.
Burt Ada E. b. 28 Charter Oak.
" Charles R. secretary Connecticut Fire Ins. Company, 51 Prospect, h. 181 Capitol.
" George H. cashier State Bank, 795 Main, h. 15 Marshal.
" Harold L. at 39 Pearl, b. 42 West.
" Howard S. clerk, b. 61 Ashley.
" Lilla M. h. 236 Wethersfield.
" Lucius, sidewalk inspector, h. 61 Ashley.
" Luther H. student, Trinity college, b.42 West.
**BURT LUTHER W.** civil engineer, 39 Pearl, h. 42 West.          *See page 421.*
" Seaborn, coachm. U. S. Hotel, h. Benton.
" William E. brakeman, P.&R. h. E.H.t.
Burton Henry C. timekeeper, Hartford Cycle Co. h. 248 Franklin.
" James S. veterinary surgeon, 2 American, h. 281 Windsor av.
" John, h. 189 Zion.
" Jonas W. clerk, Orient Insurance Company, 5 Haynes, h. Rocky Hill t.
" Julia L. wid. Augustus W. h. 127 Bellevue.
" Rachel C. wid. Rev. N. J. h. 2 Sumner.
" Robert H. clerk, 755 Main, h. 127 Bellevue.
" Robert H. Jr. clerk, Popes, b. 127 Bellevue.
" Sperry Mrs. furrier, h. 68 Pratt.
" Sterling, clerk, Orient Insurance Company, 5 Haynes, h. 208 Wethersfield.

Burwell John S. at Ætna Life Insurance Co. 650 Main, h. 49 Sumner.
" W. C. clerk, 921 Mn. h. 223 Asylum, rm. 54.
Buschman Herman, cigarm. at 867 Mn. b.97 Russ.
Bush Benjamin F. mach. at 1, h.u. 70 Flower.
" Edward, bartender, 60 Front, b.47 Morgan.
" Elizabeth, wid. William, h. 17 Church.
" Elizabeth A. Mrs. b. 211 Garden.
" Henry, carpenter at 155 Sheldon, h. W.H.t.
" James R. filer at Colts, h. 62 Maple.
" Joseph H. cigarmaker at 867 Main, h. W.H.t.
" Lewis, b. 2 Holcomb.
" Peter H. carpenter, b. Quaker lane, W.H.t.
" Philip, carpenter, l. 1067 Main.
" Simon J. upholsterer at 613 Main, h. Quaker lane, W.H.t.
" William P. brickmason, h. 56 Maple.
" William S. machinist at 1 Flower, b. E.H.t.
Bushie P. carpenter, l. 1067 Main.
Bushnell Charles H. repairer at Popes, h.u. 28 Huntley pl.
" Dwight, marketman, 319 Asy. h. Windsor t.
" Giles R. machinist at 133 Sheldon, h. E.H.t.
" Hattie A. at Hoadleys, b.u. 28 Huntley pl.
" Henry S. pianotuner, 201 Asy. b. 63 Church.
" Horace Mrs. h. 30 Winthrop.
" Lewis B. machinist at Colts, h.u. 5 Morris.
" Louisa, b. 30 Winthrop.
" Park Cafe, 323 Pearl, George S. Brigham.
" Russell H. carriagemaker, r. 792, h.u. 792 Windsor av.
Buskirk John, b. 14 Spring.
Buss John S. mach. at 133 Sheldon, b.12 Church.
Busse Frank A. overseer, Hartford Cycle Co. b. 21 Sumner.
BUTHS JOSEPH, collector State Savings Bank, 39 Pearl, *street commissioner,* h. 34 Allen pl.
" Karl A. plumber, b. 36 Temple.
Butler Adelaide W. wid. Charles F. h.821 Asylum.
" Albert B. motorman, St.Ry. h. 16 Elm.
" Albert J. tinner, b. 1086 Main.
" Alfred C. engraver, l. 27 Seyms.
" Alice, dressmaker, b.u. 125 Charter Oak.
" Andrew, laborer, Popes, h.2u. 38 Wells.
" Arthur G. carpenter, h.u. 433 Windsor av.
" Charles H. supt. State Capitol, h. Oxford t.
" Charles W. at State Library, Capitol building, h. 204 Collins.
" Charlotte A. teacher at South school, 36 Wadsworth, b. 821 Asylum.
" Clara M. clerk, National Life Insurance Co. 53 Trumbull, b. 1461 Broad.
" Frances, wid. Nicholas, h.u. 125 Charter Oak.
" Frank E. manager claim depart. National Life Association, 53 Tru. h.u. 22 Atwood.
" Frank H. clerk, 1451, h. 1461 Broad.
" Frank T. mason, h.u.r. 44 Village.
" George, driver, 379 Main, h.r. 27 John.
" George E. engineer, 1 Laurel, b. E.H.t.
" George E. mach. at 1 Flower, b. 66 Hopkins.
" George O. at 981 Main, h. Simsbury t.
" George W. brickmason, h.u. 41 Park.
" Harriet E. wid. Henry, h. 192 Sargeant.

Butler & Helion, real estate, 756 Main, rm. 46.
   Patrick F. Butler.       John J. Helion.
" Herbert P. bookb. 336 Asy. h.u. 72 Retreat.
" J. Hartwell, U.S. Army, h. 276 Laurel.
" J. V. B. h. 10 Garden.
" James A. machinist, b.u. 44 Grand.
" James E. saloon, 35, h. 35 Mulberry.
" Jane, dressmaker, b.u. 147 Maple.
" Jeannette E. artist, 29, h. 29 John.
" John, janitor, Trinity college, h. 736 Broad.
" John, laborer, b. 81 Governor.
" John A. Jr. at Pope Tube Co.h. 92 Church.
" John F. fireman, h. 159 Lawrence.
" John F. sergeant police, b.u. 44 Grand.
" John J. pressman, 141 Pearl, b.u. 91 Asylum.
" John S. plumber, b. 333 Park.
" Joseph P. A. clerk, 304 Park, b.u. 44 Grand.
" Levi, b. 58 Niles.
" Louis F. at Travelers Insurance Co. 56 Prospect, b. 276 Laurel.
" Lydia A. Mrs. h.r. 64 Dean.
" Mary, b. 54 Grand.
" Michael, laborer, city works, h.2u.157 Zion.
" Nicholas, mason, h.u. 44 Grand.
" Oscar M. machinist at Colts, h. 150 Capen.
" Patrick F. b. 81 Governor.
" Patrick F. (B. & Helion,) b.u. 147 Maple.
" Patrick J. bartender, b. 115½ Ann.
" Thomas, barrel mfr. 30 Ferry, h.u. 9 Kil.
" Thomas, engineer, h.2u. 89 Arch.
" ,Thomas, molder at 54 Arch, b. 159 Law.
" Thomas J. clerk, 197 Asylum, b.44 Harbison.
" William, burnisher, 62 Market, h. 27 Seyms.
" William G. bookkeeper, Barbour Silver Co. 62 Market, h. 35 Lincoln.
" William K. clerk, E. S. Kibbe Co. wholesale grocers, 149 State, h. 58 Niles.
" William L. clerk, b.r.44 Village.
" William M. toolmaker at 70 Huyshope, h. 38 Annawan.
Butnario Geo. barber at 3 Asy. h.3u. 181 Market.
Butter Michael, laborer, stone pits, h. Dean.
Butters Willard S. stock clerk, Capewell Horse Nail Co. 40 Governor, h. 81 Hudson.
Buttles Wallace L. mech. 581 Cap. b. 236 N.P.
Buttner Gustave H. mach. N.Y.R. h.116 Babcock.
" Shepstein, tailor, h. 30 North.
Butto Cyprian, chef at restaurant, N.Y.R. h.u. 11 Goodman.
Button Louis W. clerk at Orient Insurance Co. 5 Haynes, b.u. 1206 Broad.
" William A. foreman, Pratt & Whitney Co. 388 Capitol, h.u. 224 Putnam.

**BUTTS & CROSBY,** architects and engineers, 49 Pearl.    *See page 427.*
   Edward P. Butts.      Francis W. Crosby.
" Edward P. (*Butts & C.*) b. 119 Capitol.
" Fred. H. toolmaker, Popes, h.2u. 296 Park.
" George C. signpainter, b. 245 Park.
" J. Harry, bookb. at 141 Pearl, b. 83 Arch
" James M. painter, h. 245 Park.
" James M. Jr. painter, b. 245 Park.
Buzzell Fannie E. wid. George H. b.u. 11 Good.
Byers Samuel C. b.2u. 62 Village.
" William, mach. 1 Flower, h.2u. 62 Village.

Byington Frank P. clerk, 901 Main, h. 8 Canton.
Byles Frederick K. mixer, 690 Park, h. Flatbush.
Byorkman Wm. M. foreman, Popes, b. 56 Park.
" ☞ *see also Bjorkman.*
Byrd Enos H. porter, 593 Main.
Byrne Chas. E. lineman, 266 Pearl, h. 60 Retreat.
" George J. clerk, b. 28 Park.
" James, ostler, 1046 Main, b. 79 Chestnut.
" James J. clerk, 921 Main, b. 28 Park.
" John, tailor, 8 State, h.u. 28 Park.
" John B. plumber at 433 Mn. b.50 Governor.
" John J. paper ruler, 856 Main, b. 111 Pearl.
" Michael, steamfitter at 556 Cap. h.265 Park.
" ☞ *see also Burns; Burnes; O'Byrnes.*
Byrnes M. Edward, farmer, 9 Harrison.
Byron Thomas, steamfitter, b.2u. 1194 Main.
Bysen Christian P. carptr. 88 Mar. h.15 Winter.
" ☞ *see Baysen.*
Byswinger L. Mrs. 133 Market, rm. 4.
Byxbee Theodore M., United States deputy collector, 65 State, h. Meriden t.
" ☞ *see also Bixby.*

CABACK Frank, h.2u. 34 Flower.
Cachman John, helper, 556 Cap. b. 25 Sigourney.
Cadden Abraham, office 100 Asy. h. 36 Sumner.
" Simon B. (*Union Clothing Co.*) h. 7 Canton.
Cadieu Phillippe, motorman, St.Ry. h. 148 Alb.
Cadigan Catharine, wid. Morris, h. 60 Governor.
" Frank J. plumber at 433 Mn. b.60 Governor.
" Maurice B. plumber at 389½ Mn, b. 60 Gov.
Cadisky Philip, peddler, h. 196 Front.
Cadwell Albert, foreman, r. 1128, h. 703 Main.
" Cassius E. clerk, 1082 Main, b. 4 Belden.
" Charles S. janitor, 448 Mn. h.u. 78 Barbour.
" Ernest W. farmer, 581 Cap. b. 234 Putnam.
" Eugene E. cutter, 1 S.Ann, h. 37 Julius.
" Frank J. salesman, 744 Main, b. Elmwood.
" George M. toolm. 556 Cap. b.u. 78 Barbour.
" George T. mach. at 302 Asy. b. 63 Bluehills.
" Gordon, driver, 48 Ann, h. Williams.
" Harry B. plumber at 584 Asylum, b. 80 Hopkins.
" Hattie J. wid. Starr D. dressm. h.1158 Main.
" Herbert, salesman, 34 Capen, b. 234 Putnam.
" Jennie, wid. Charles, b. 234 Putnam.
" John B. 2d engineer steamer Hartford, 285 State, h. New Britain t.
" John P. repairer at Popes, h. Elmwood.
" & Jones, seeds, hardware, etc. 1082-1084 Mn.
   Samuel F. Cadwell.   W. Frank Jones.
" Louis E. assembler at Popes, b. 234 Putnam.
" Samuel F. (*C. & Jones,*) b. 4 Belden.
" Sarah T. h. 61 Church.
" ☞ *see also Caldwell.*
Cady Arthur M. (*C. & Lombard,*) h. 19 Florence.
" Clayton F. machinist at 581 Cap. b. 266 N.P.
" Cornelius C. machinist at 9 Sig. h. 35 Bkm.
" Ernest, *water commiss'r*, h. 249 Farmington.
" Ernest H. clerk at Pratt & Cady Co. 556 Capitol, b. 249 Farmington.
" F. Dwight, operator, 40 Gov. b. 24 Wdbg.
" George E. at 556 Capitol, h.2u. 23 Babcock.
" Geo. F. at Conn. Mutual Life Ins. Co. 783 Main, b. 98 Hudson.

Cady & Lombard, meats, groceries, 69&75 Albany.
 Arthur M. Cady.  Martin E. Lombard.
" M. B. wid. Ferris W. h. 32 Buckingham.
" Mary A. dressmaker, 15, h.2u. 15 Goodwin.
" Mary L. saleswoman at 45 Asylum, h. E.H.t.
" Thomas, plater, b.u. 1218 Main.
" William, bartender at 1181, h. 1178 Main.
Cafero Joseph, mason, h.4u. 36 North.
Cafferty Richard, b. 2 Holcomb.
Caffrey Maria, widow Thomas, h. 2 Grand.
Cahill Benj. M. polisher, b.u. 8 Elm.
" Catherine, wid. John M. h.u. 8 Elm.
" Daniel, laborer at N.Y.R. h.u. 21½ Chestnut.
" Edward P. merchant tailor, 105 Pratt, h. 197 Russ.
" Evelyn, wid. William, J. b. 458 Main.
" Frank J. pressman at Popes, b.u. 8 Elm.
" H. C. hostler at 173 State, b. 38 Barbour.
" James, h. 49 Linden.
" James, foreman, 115 State, h. 140 Weth.
" John A. machinist at Colts, h. 30 Congress.
" John L. framem. at 251 Pearl, h. 30 Temple.
" Joseph H. physician, 51, h. 51 Church.
" Mary Mrs. h.u. 117 Benton.
" Morris, blacksm. at N.Y.R. h.u.r. 30 Chst.
" Patrick, blacksmith at 142 Russ, h.u. 1062 Broad.
" Philip, helper, 1 Flower, b.u. 18 Trumbull.
**CAHILL WILLIAM H.** dentist, D.D.S. 75 Pratt, b. 51 Church.
 See page 423.
Cairnes Jane S. wid. James, h. 76 Retreat.
Cairns Annie M. teacher at Northeast school, b. 80 Clark.
" Bessie, bkkpr. 281 Asylum, b. 41 Seyms.
" Edward T. inspector at Factory Ins. Association, 95 Pearl, h.u. 106 Capen.
" Elizabeth J. principal Washington Street school, b. 80 Clark.
" Ella L. attendant at 30 Washington.
" Gilbert J. carpenter, b. 80 Clark.
" James R. carpenter, h.u. 41 Seyms.
" John, machinist, h.u. 742 Main.
" John Jr. clerk, b.u. 742 Main.
" Joseph M. artist, b.u. 742 Main.
" Margaret R. b.u. 742 Main.
" Robert, carpenter, 80, h. 80 Clark.
" ☞ see also Cairnes; Carnes; Kearns.
Calabrese Ricco, b.2u. 40 Windsor.
Calado Leon, (T. Rates & Co.) b. 33 Albany.
Calaher Thomas, b. 22 Pliney.
Calano Inncenzia, fruit, 615, h. 615 Capitol.
" James, clerk at 20 Central, b. 68 Front.

Calano Joseph, fruit, 15 Central, h. 68 Front.
" Joseph, 25 Flower, b. 615 Capitol.
" Tony, clerk at 15 Central, b. 68 Front.
Calanos J. fruit and confectionery, 216 Allyn, h. 235 Front.
Calantrillo Moritz, h. 31 Mechanic.
" Rossana, h.u. 31 Mechanic.
Calback Joseph A. printer at Courant, 66 State, b.u. 224 Maple.
" Robert, carriagetrimmer, 5 Mechanic, h.u. 222 Maple.
Calberg Walfred, filer at 581 Cap. b.u. 56 Haw.
" ☞ see also Carlburg.
Calder Geo. builder, 288 Sig. h. 140 Sargeant.
" Helen B. b. 140 Sargeant.
" John, carpenter, h.u. 294 Maple..
" Matilda S. teacher, b. 140 Sargeant.
" Wm. P. draughtsman at Hfd. Steam Boiler Insp. & Ins. Co. 650 Mn. b. 140 Sargeant.
Caldwell Albert M. h.2u. 703 Main, rm. 12.
" Geo. E. engir. at 217 Windsor, h. 19 Canton.
" Gordon, iceman, h. 71 Williams.
" Harriet, wid. Frank W. h. 25 Capitol.
" Harry H. fireman, N.Y.R. h. 60 Walnut.
" James, machinist, b. 23 John.
" Jane, wid. Archie, h.2u. 54 Chestnut.
" Julia Mrs. h.2u. 42 Windsor.
" ☞ see also Cadwell; Coldwell.
Calef Ed. B. conductor St.Ry. b. E.H.t.
Calhoun Charles, at 62 Market, b. 17 Church.
" David, clerk at Conn. Fire Insurance' Co. 51 Prospect, b. 274 Farmington.
" David S. attorney, 877 Main, rm. 1, h. 274 Farmington.
" Geo. H. nightwatchm. Capitol, h. 62 Russ.
" Hubbard W. clerk, Pope Mfg. Co. b. 290 Sigourney.
" Isabella, wid. John C. h. 59 Church.
" J. Gilbert, prosecuting attorney, 877 Main, rm. 1, h. 360 Laurel.
" John J. blacksmith, 843 Park, h. 236 N.P.
" Myrtie C. teacher at kindergarten Warburton chapel, b. 62 Russ.
" Printing Co. 29 Union pl.
" Rebecca K. wid. Alexander, h. 290 Sig.
Calkins Chas. H. draughtsm. at 476, b. 381 Cap.
" Frank W. polisher, 476 Cap. b. 62 Hung.
" Frederic H. sec'y National Life Association, 53 Trumbull. h. 63 Gillett.
" William, carptr. 224 Sargeant, h. 36 Imlay.
" William, mach. at 1 Flower, h. 18 Oak.
" ☞ see also Caulkins; Corkins.
CALLAGHAN CORNELIUS J. boxmaker, etc. 42 Union place, h. 96 Albany. See p. 83.
" Daniel D. porter at 165, h.u. 108 Windsor.
" ☞ see also Callahan; O'Callaghan.
Callahan Ann Mrs. b. 2 Holcomb.
" Bridget, wid. John, h. 23 Sigourney.
" Catharine Mrs. b. 2 Holcomb.
" Catharine and Mary, h. 86 Ann.
" Charles, clerk 372 Asylum, b. 111 Maple.
" Cornelius, laborer at 165, h. 102 Windsor.
" Cornelius J. laborer at 12 Pratt, b. 2 Portland.
" Daniel, carpenter, h.u. 23 Congress.

Callahan Daniel, laborer, h. 2 Portland.
" Daniel, laborer, h.2u. 36 Sheldon.
" Daniel P. lab. at 98 Kilbourn, h. 58 Village.
" Ellen, wid. Thomas, h. 153 Washington.
" Hannah, shirtm. at 93 Asy. b. 51 Walnut.
" James, b.2u. 200 Sheldon.
" James, carpenter, h. Boulanger.
" James W. fireman at N.YR. b.u. 111 Maple.
" Jeremiah H. carptr. N.Y.R. h.u. 111 Maple.
" John, at 129 State, h. 37 Lafayette.
" John, driver at 37 Wells, b. 55 Liberty.
" John, laborer, b.u. 88 Wells.
" John F. bkkpr. 133 State, b.u. 111 Maple.
" John F. at 242 State, b. 5 Charles.
" John H.wireworker at 618 Cap. b. 36 North.
" John P.coremak. at 556 Cap. h. 156 Bellevue.
" John W. printer at 154, l. 315 Pearl, rm. 404.
" Joseph A. policeman, h.u. 10 Warren.
" Katharine A. teacher at Parkville school, b. 86 Ann.
" Mary, wid. Patrick, groceries, 36, h. 36 North.
" Mary C. clerk at Brown, Thomson & Co. 942 Main, b.u. 111 Maple.
" Michael laborer, b. 24 Chestnut.
" Michael, laborer 65 Suffield, b.u. 12 S.Pro.
" Michael, tinner, h. 51 Walnut.
" Michael J. driver, h.u. 156 Bellevue.
" Michael O. h. 156 Bellevue.
" Nicholas, laborer at 1, h. 28 Flower.
" Patrick, fireman at 266 Charles, h.u. 5 Charles.
" Patrick J. carpenter, h.u. 33 Canton.
" Richard M. mach. at 388 Cap. b. 23 Sig.
" Robert A. at 17 Elm, h. 13 Crown n. Webster.
" Thomas, porter, 149 State, b. 43 Franklin.
" Thomas, stonelayer, h.u. 391 Park.
" Thomas J. blacksm. N.Y.R. h.177 Lawrence.
" Thos. W. stonelayer, 154 Ch.O. b. 29 North.
" Thos. W. teamster, h.2u. 13 Front.
" Wm. L. clerk, 1046 Main, b. 53 Walnut.
" ☞ see also Callaghan; O'Callaghan.
Callan Francis, tailor, 2 Ford, h. 40 Hungerford.
Callandrillo Frank, h. 75 Charles.
" Joseph, clerk, h.u. 13 Charles.
Callandrilloo John, barber, h. 15 Charles.
Callen James A. at 581 Capitol, h. 759 Park.
Callender Charles, driller at Colts, h. E.H.t.
" Charles E. Jr. machinist at Colts, h. E.H.t.

**CALLENDER BROS.** restaurant, 296 Asylum.
Wm. S. Callender.    Eugene H. Callender.
" Eugene H. (Callender Bros.) h. 27 Imlay.
" Frederic E. diesinker at 142 Russ, h. 54 Putnam.
" Louisa C. wid. Warren, h. 5 So. Prospect.
" Ralph, teamster at 8 Front.
" Wm. S. (Callender Bros.) h. Waterbury t.
Callere Joseph, grocery, 264, h. 264 Front.
Callery Frank J. forem. 556 Cap. b. 1337 Broad.
" James, teamster, 1, h.u. 13 So. Ann.
" James J. foreman at R. S. Peck & Co. 26 High, h.2u. 2 Queen.
" John, at 556 Capitol, h. 1335 Broad.
" William, cutter at R. S. Peck & Co. 26 High, h. 6 Whitmore.
" Wm. C. jeweler, 847 Main, h. 6 Whitmore.

**C. J. CALLAGHAN,**

MANUFACTURER OF

**PAPER ✹ BOXES**
*of every description.*

PAPER, LEATHERETTE, CHAMOIS CASES
FOR JEWELRY AND SILVERWARE.    **44 Union Place.**

Telephone Connection.    Established 1883.

Calnen Dennis P. druggist, h. 1329 Broad.
Calsey Fred, motorman St.Ry. h. 703 Main.
Caverly Arthur, h. 272 Maple.
" Frank C. at Jewell Belting, Co. 15 Trumbull, b. 18½ Church.
" Thomas J. mason at 164 State, b.18½ Church.
Cambridge Annis B. dressmaker, 67, b. 67 Green.
" Carrie S. b. 67 Green.
" Charles, b. 2 Holcomb.
" Ebenezer S. Mrs. musicteacher, h. 67 Green.
" Eva L. dressmaker, 67, b. 67 Green.
" Ichabod L. landscape gardener, h. 67 Green.
" Walter J. ostler, h.u. 14½ Martin.
Cameran Michael, peddler, h.u. 75 Charles.
Cameron Alexander, stereotyper at Daily Times, 716 Main, h. 164 Ashley.
" Catherine, dressmaker, h. 76 Albany.
" George F. blacksmith, b. 27 Kennedy.
" Hattie, wid. Malcolm, h. 870 Broad.
" Kate, dressmaker, h.u. 215 Windsor.
" Robert, horseshoer, h.2u. 27 Kennedy.
Camp Albert, driver at 46 Ann, h. 132 Grove.
" Albert B. engineer No. 6, h. 50 Wdbg.
" Chas. H. bookbinder, 336 Asy. b. 28 Village.
" Charles W. painter, h. 147 Market.
" Cornelia E. h. 117 Woodland.
" Fannie G. Mrs. l.4u. 926 Main, rm. 72.
" Geo W. saloon, 161 State, b. 117 Albany.
" H. E. Mrs. h. 90 Church.
" Henry P.mach. at 1 Flow. b.2u. 11 Goodman.
" Howard A. (S. S. Scranton & Co.) h. 28 Wooster.
" J. C. salesman, h. 570 Prospect av.
" John S. v. prest. and treas. Pratt & Cady Co. 556 Capitol, organist Park church, office 391 Allyn, h. 1021 Asylum.
" Kate F. b. 141 Bellevue.
" Katherine C. b. 117 Woodland.
" Laura, wid. David C. h. 141 Bellevue.
" Lewis M. manager, 218 Asy. b. 30 Spring.
" Mabel, b. 90 Church.
" Samuel J. builder, h. 110 Capitol.
" Walter G. at National Fire Ins. Co. 95 Pearl, h. 817 Windsor av.
" William D. clerk at Connecticut Fire Ins. Co. 51 Prospect, h. 141 Bellevue.
" ☞ see also Kampf.
Campagna John, fruit and confectionery, 519 Main, h. 81 So. Prospect.
Campbell Alice G. bkkpr. at 651 Mn. b. 35 Mahl.
" Charles F. engir. at 42 Seyms, h. 54 Chestnut.
" Charles H. draughtsman at Pope Tube Co. h. 20 Fairview.

Campbell Cynthia S. wid. Herbert B. b. 900 Asy.
" Emma E. h. 165 Collins.
" Fred, plumber at 389½ Main, b. Flatbush.
" George, at 29, h.u. 70 Albany.
" George A. carpenter, l. 1 Linden.
" George C. b. 34 Village.
" George C. butcher, 65, h. 171 Ashley.
" Georgia, bookkeeper, 65 Asylum, b. 35 Mahl.
" H. B. wid. A. C. h. 97 Trumbull.
" Henry A. janitor, Phœnix Mutual Life Ins. Co. 49 Pearl, l. 8 Gold.
" J. W. clerk at 921, b. 1088 Main.
" James, gardener, Pope Tube Co. h. Lubeck.
" James, *health commissioner,* physician, 2, h. 2 Congress.
" James A. mechanic at 26 High, b. 16 Village.
" James J. h. 35 Mahl.
" James J. Jr. manager, 651 Main. b. 35 Mahl.
" Janet A. nurse, 20 South Hudson.
" John, laborer, h. 23 Huntley pl.
" John, screwm. 70 Huyshope, h.u. 6 Union.
" John, weigher, b. 35 Liberty.
" John W. carpenter at Colts, h.u. 128 Jefferson.
" Joseph, ostler, h. 489 Main.
" Margaret J. nurse, b. 37 Allen pl.
" Mary, wid. John, h. 36 Temple pl.
" Mary T. clerk, 70 Huy. b. 72 Vanblock.
" Nancy J. b. 36 Jefferson.
" Neil C. tailor at 66 Asylum, h.2u. 2 Elm pl.
" Polly A. wid. Charles C. b. 165 Collins.
" Terence J. electrician, h.2u. 20 Park.
" Thomas F. buffer, h.r. 72 Vanblock.
" Thomas W. operator at N.E.R. h. E.H.t.
" William, b. Hotel Hartford.
" William, bricklayer, h.u. 25 Pawtucket.
" William, operator at Popes, l. 16 Village.
" William Mrs. h. 115 Elm.
" Wm. W. waiter at 98 Wells, b. 32 Capitol.
Campion Agnes, b. 192 Jefferson.
" William, coachm. at 24 Cap. h.2u. 55 Wdbg.
Campon Peter T. waiter, 33, b. 33 Prospect.
" ☞ *see Kampmann.*
Camsell William H. mach. at 476 Cap. h. 36 Brook.
Camyre Joseph, ostler at 51, b. 51 Farmington.
Canales George F. at St. Ry. b. 54 Eaton.
" Lillian, b. 54 Eaton.
Canary Kate, wid. Dennis, b. 51 Wadsworth.
Candee C. M. wid. Stephen M. coaldealer, 21, h. 21 Allen pl.
" John D. treas. 154 Ch.O. h.u. 17 Allen pl.
Canedy Clarence T. b.u. 65 Williams.
" Cora A. clerk, b.u. 65 Williams.
" I. S. h.u. 65 Williams.
" Lilla F. b.u. 65 Williams.
Canfield Merrill N. polisher, Colts, b. Newington j.
" Robert H. h. 79 Windsor.
" Walter J. polisher at Colts, h. Newington t.
Cannavan James, driver at 54 Huntley pl. b.2u. 18 Trumbull.
Canning Eliza, wid. Thomas, h. 175 Barbour.
" James, carpenter, h. 208 Capen.
" Robert, carpenter, b. 175 Barbour.
Cannon Archie L. clerk, 336 Asy. b. 198 Jefferson.
" Catherine C. milliner at 75 Pratt.
" Ed. J. assembler at Popes, h.2u. 32 Wells.

Cannon Frank, forger at Popes, h. 26 Flower.
" & Flanagan, grocers, 230, meats, 236 Park.
    Thomas F. Cannon.    Thomas F. Flanagan.
" John, h. 56 Oak.
" John, b. 148 Albany.
" Julia L. Miss, at Travelers Insurance Co. 56 Prospect, b. 10 Village.
" Katherine, cashier, b. 56 Oak.
" Michael J. butcher at 230 Park, h. 5 Oak.
" Patrick, laborer, h.u. 148 Albany.
" Peter, pickler at Popes, h. 44 Wells.
" Thomas F. *( C. & Flanagan,)* h.u. 3 Oak.
" Thomas P. molder at 556 Cap. h. 1423 Broad.
Cant William S. porter, Brown, Thomson & Co. 942 Main, h.u. 121 Pearl.
Canterbury George B. h.u. 107 Edwards.
Cantervitch Harris, shoemaker, 51 Albany, h.u. 276 Front.
Cantro Joseph, clerk, 90 Albany, b. Chestnut.
Cantner Nathan, tailor, h.2u.r. 67 Pleasant.
Cantwell John, machinist at 388 Capitol, b.u. 147 Lawrence.
" Margaret, wid. Patrick, h. 45 So. Hudson.
Canty John, deckhand str. Middletown, 285 State.
Capen Ada, folder at 26 High, b.u. 75 Gov.
" Harry R. mach. at 1 Flower, b. 24 Elmer.
" James R. cattle dealer, h. 24 Elmer.
" Jane, wid. Geo. T. h.u. 75 Governor.
" Julia R. b. 24 Elmer.
Capewell George J. vice prest. and sup't C. Horse Nail Co. 40 Governor, h. 903 Asylum.
" George J. Jr. b. 903 Asylum.

**CAPEWELL HORSE NAIL CO.**
factory and office, 40 Governor. *See p. 524.*
Capitol Avenue House, Eli Daigneau, 276 Law.
" Brick Co. 268 Prospect av.
" City Carriage Co. 291-303 Allyn.
" City Furniture House, 78 Sheldon.
" City Lumber Co. 25 Front.

**CAPITOL CITY OIL CO.** 195
State.    *See page 541.*
" City Pickling house, 84 Vine.
" City Roofing Co. 110 Pratt, H. B. Kingsley.
" Loan Office, 32 Asylum.
" or State House on Bushnell Park.
" Tea and Coffee Co. 1200 Main.
    S. D. Tulin.    L. Toft.    S. S. Tulin.
Caplan B. peddler, h.u. 16 North.
" Max, screwmr. 476 Capitol, h.u. 195 Front.
" Samuel, peddler, h.2u. 61 Pleasant.
Caples Edward C. steward, h. 6 Waverly.
Caporale Peter, stonemason, b.3u. 82 Morgan.
" Rocco, bootblack, 18 State, h.u. 21 Windsor.
Cappel Peter, laborer, b. 2 Huntley.
Cappello Angelo M. laborer, b. 12 North.
" Joseph, laborer, b.u. 64 Morgan.
" Ricco, laborer, h.3u. 12 North.
Cappelluzzi Rock, laborer, b. 82 Potter.
Cappelo Frank, laborer, b.u. 319 Front.
" Vito, laborer, b.u. 319 Front.
Capron Eunice M. wid. S. M. h. 41 Willard.
Capucci Antonio, laborer, h.r. 99 Windsor.
Carberry Jas. J. tobacco pkr. 231 State, b. E.H.t.
" Mary, at W. H. Home for Aged, Albany.
" Mary A. dressmaker, b.u. 53 Wadsworth.

**CARBON PHOTO STUDIO,** Wm. M. Kellogg operator, 92 Pearl. *See outside front cover.*
Carbone Carlo, laborer, b.3u. 2 Charles.
" Joseph, helper at 40 Ann, h.3u. 82 Morgan.
Carcavallo Luigi, laborer, h.u.r. 268 Front.
Cardenje Domenico, laborer, h.3u. 158 Front.
Cardomon Frank, laborer, b. 7 Charles.
" Peter, grocery, 5, h. 7 Charles.
Care Benjamin, 690 Park, h.u. 11 Kibbe.
Carey Bernard, h. 258 Front.
" Daniel J. polisher at James L. Howard & Co. 438 Asylum, h. 39 Chestnut.
" David S. blacksm. at 142 Russ, h. 36 Flower.
CAREY FRANK S. secy. Hartford Courant Co. 66 State, h.u. 45 Wadsworth. *See page 463.*
" Fred'k A. foreman at 335 Shel. h. 21 Morris.
" Frederick R. toolm. 581 Cap. h. 92 Franklin.
" George A. clerk, Popes, b. 464 Windsor av.
" George B. mach. at 1 Flow. h.u. 1469 Broad.
" Geo. S. hairdr. 903 Main, h. 464 Windsor av.
" John, at 556 Capitol, b. 1443 Broad.
" John E. driver Hook & Lad.Co.h.u. 242 Pearl.
" John E. plumber at 12 Mul. h. 37 Franklin.
" John F. brakeman, b.3u. 21 Spruce.
" John H. horseshoer, 29 Wells, h.2u.r. 22 S.Pro.
" John J. polisher at Popes, h. 84 Albany.
" Lillian, dressmaker, b.u. 9 Blumenthal.
" Mamie J. at 690 Park, b. 10 Wellington.
" Mary Mrs. h.u. 9 Blumenthal.
" Michael, h. 23 Howard.
" Michael, laborer, b.3u. 38 Flower.
" Michael, laborer, h. 10 Wellington.
" Michael, teamster at Downing & Perkins, 128 Commerce, h.u. 117 Market.
" Patrick, repairer, P.&R. b. 55 Liberty.
" Patrick M. motorman St.Ry. h.3u. 38 Flower.
" Patrick T. foreman, P.&R. h.u. 137 Mather.
" Robert E. (Eastern Brass Works,) h. N. Y.
" Sarah E. at 690 Park, b. 10 Wellington.
" Stephen, bartender at 1047 Main, h. 29 Ple.
" Thomas, brakeman, h.u. 1427 Broad.
" Thomas, laborer, h.2u. 19 Howard.
" Wm. car inspector, P.&R. h. 55 Liberty.
" William, teamster at 100 Com. b. 1443 Broad.
" Wm. S. steam fitter, h.2u. 39 Chestnut.
" ☞ *see also Cary.*
CARHART C. E. editor Hartford Globe, 25 Asylum, b. 109 Trumbull. *See page 465.*
Carl Jonathan, h.u. 192 Vernon.
" John, teamster, h.u. 20 Julius.
Carleton Amos L. foreman 1 Flow. h. 1485 Broad.
" Bernard S. at Ætna Life Insurance Co. 650 Main, h. 1485 Broad.
" Denny, secretary and treasurer Williams & Carleton Co. h. 620 Farmington.
" Guy M. b. 620 Farmington.
" John W. at Ætna Insurance Co. 666 Main, h. 200 Sargeant.
" L. Clinton, moulder at 1 Flow. h.u. 199 Russ.
" Winfred G. salesm. 206 State, b. 41 Willard.
" ☞ *see also Carlton.*
Carley Frank S. rubberw. 690 Pk. h.u. 47 Amity.
" John, deckhand str. Middletown, 285 State.
Carliell Arthur J. laborer, 581 Cap. b. 284 Asylum.

Carlin Catherine, wid. Charles, h.u. 25 West.
" Henry E. assistant, 387 Main, l. 119 Capitol.
" J. A. machinist at 13 Central.
" John, engineer, b.u. 83 Governor.
" John J. expressman, b. 42 Hudson.
" Joseph, expresser, 42, h. 42 Hudson.
" Joseph, Jr. expressman, b. 42 Hudson.
" Peter, teamster at 335, b.2u. 172 Sheldon.
Carlisle Alex'r M. asst. mgr. at 581 Cap. b. 57 Far.
" Arthur, l. 284 Asylum, rm. 78.
Carlo Giovanni, ragpicker, h.u. 76 Charles.
Carlon Ann, wid. Hugh, h. 284 Allyn.
" John, machinist, h. 284 Allyn.
" Philip, physician, b. 284 Allyn.
Carlson Axel, helper, 133 State, b. 64 Flower.
" Albert, clerk at 149, h.2u. 129 Babcock.
" Albert J. bricklayer, h. Pros. av. south Park.
" Albertina Mrs. h.u. 99 Hamilton.
" Alfred S. cabinetm. at 147 Shel. h. 96 Albany.
" Amandus, helper at 556 Cap. h.u. 35 Wolcott.
" Andrew, enameler, 581 Cap. h.u. 47 N.B.
" Andrew, motorman St.Ry. h.2u. 289 Asy.
" August, laborer, b.u. 28 Putnam.
" August, teamster, h.r. 226 Garden.
" C. deckhand, 285 State.
" Carl J. helper, 142 Russ, b. 162 Putnam.
" Charles A. assembler at 581 Capitol, h.u. 39 Glendale.
" Charles A. filer, h.3u. 10½ Ford.
" Charles J. buffer at Popes, h.u. 150 Ward.
" Charles John, carpenter, h.u. 49 Green.
" Claus, carpenter, h.r. 37 Washington.
" David, mechanic at Popes, b. 123 Babcock.
" E. Samuel, mach. at 142 Russ, b. 147 Bab.
" Edward, farmer at 30 Washington.
" Emil, teamster, h. 822 Park.
" Frank, helper, 581 Capitol, b. 282 Laurel.
" Frank, lab. Pope Tube Co. b. 24 Wolcott.
" Fred. clerk, Hfd. Grocery Co. h.u.r. 27 John.
" Fred. fireman at 70 Com. h.r. 22½ Alden.
" Gustav O. diesinker at 142 Russ, h.u. 25 Putnam.
" John, teamster, 4, b. 4 Huyshope.
" John, teamster at 283 Sheldon, b. 45 Laf.
" John A. coachm. at 764 Asy. b. 162 Sisson.
" John A. ostler at 319 Asylum.
" John J. laborer, h.u. 80 Commerce.
" Lina M. clerk at Phœnix Mutual Life Ins. Co. 49 Pearl, b. 69 Webster.
" Nils A. mechanic at 40 Cush. h.u. 23 Hamilton.
" Oscar, clerk at 1090 Main, h.2u. 4 Village.
" Oscar, waiter at 98 Wells, l. 27 Linden.
" Oscar E. mach. at 1 Flower, h.u. 9 Putnam.
" Otto, piano tuner at 227 Asy. b. 31 Putnam.
" Samuel, at 142 Russ, b. 147 Babcock.
" William, mech. at Popes, b. 29 Hamilton.
Carlton Isabel, wid. William T. h. 60 Lincoln.
" William N. asst. librarian at Watkinson Library, 5 Atheneum, b. 60 Lincoln.
" ☞ *see also Carleton.*
Carlucci Frank, laborer, b.u. 86 Morgan.
" Jerome, laborer, h. 75 Charles.
" Nunzio F. laborer, b.u. 86 Morgan.
Carman Florence E. nurse, b. 14 Church, rm. 4.
" Nancyiette, wid. Geo. G. h.u. 38 Church.

Carmenski Frank, laborer at 690 Park.
Carmer Isaac H. floorwalker at Brown, Thomson
   & Co. 942 Main, b. E.H.t.
Carmine Delia, fruit, 83, h. 83 Windsor.
Carmody Bessie A. school teacher, b. 86 Fkn.
" James L. electrician at 1152 Main, b. 86 Fkn.
" John P. painter, h. 10 Smith.
" John T. plumber at 280 Asy. b. 86 Franklin.
" Thos. foreman Water Works, h. 86 Franklin.
Carnes James, porter, 209 State, h. 24 Potter.
" ☞ *see also Cairnes; Cairns; Kearns.*
Carney Catherine, wid. Timothy, h.u. 9 Curcombe.
" Chas. J. rubberw. at 690 Park, b. 41 John.
" Daniel, laborer, h. 41 Glendale.
" Daniel P. benchm. Pope Tube Co. b.u. 9 Cur.
" Frank, teamster, b.u. 117 Mather.
" John, plumber at 1092 Main, h. E.H.t.
" John J. millman at 690 Park, h. 111 Hamilton.
" John W. dentist at 868 Main, b.u. 24 Canton.
" Joseph, cigarm. at 287 Allyn, h.u. 24 Canton.
" Jos. B. mech. 83 Woodbine, b. 111 Hamilton.
" Julia, at Perkins Switch Co. b. 111 Hamilton.
" Margaret A. dressmaker, b.u. 24 Canton.
" Mary, wid. John, h.u. 24 Canton.
" Michael, machinist, b. 16 Hawthorn.
" Michael, millwright at Popes, b. 1416 Broad.
" Rose E. clerk at 956 Main, b. 7 Green.
" Timothy J. driller at Colts, h. 78 Vanblock.
" William C. artist, 904 Main, rm. 106.
" ☞ *see also Kearney.*
Carolan Catherine, wid. Charles, h. 25 West.
" Margaret, dressmaker, b. 25 West.
Caron Omsine, carpenter, h2.u. 13 Hendricxsen.
" ☞ *see also Carron.*
Carootgen Morris, peddler, h.r. 207 Front.
Carpen James, laborer, h. 29 Arch.
Carpenter A. Raleigh, trav. salesman, 146 State,
   b. 12 Belden.
" Charles R. draughtsm. 1 Flow. b. 9 Hamilton.
" Clarence E. bkkpr. 1152 Main, b. 36 Mahl.
" Guthrie, porter at 30 Washington.
" James, laborer, h.u.r. 552 Park.
" James B. Mrs. h. 22 Buckingham.
" Jared W. janitor, h. 111½ Ann.
" Josephine A. wid. D. B. h. 255 Main.
" Louis A. machinist, h. 88 Hudson.
" Lucy A. Mrs. b. 95 Bellevue.
" R. H. Mrs. h. 20 Linden.
" Sophia T. wid. Elisha, h. 122 Garden.
" Victor I. clerk at 197 Asylum, h.u. 117 Hung.
" W. H. rubberw. at 690 Park, h. 75 Laurel.
" Wm. G. decorator at Baxter the Decorator,
   231 Asylum, b. 622 Main.
" William O. h. 12 Belden.
" Wm. R. printer, 356 Asy. b. 153 Windsor av.

**CARPENTER & WILLIAMS,** now
   Frank B. Williams. *See page* 496.
" Winfred H. clerk, 690 Park, b. 75 Laurel.
Carr Annie R. wid. Thomas, h. 56 Benton.
" Arthur, clerk, b. 33 Mather.
" Bernard, teamster, b. 64 Vanblock.
" Bertha E. stenographer, National Life Asso-
   tion, 53 Trumbull, h. 56 Benton.

**CARR ELLEN R.** dentist, 68 Pratt, rm.
   19-20, h. Collinsville t.

Carr George H. Mrs. h. 33 Mather.
" Hawley, janitor. b. 33 Mather.
" Marshall L. drugclerk at 155 Windsor av.
   b. 33 Mather.
" Mary L. musicteacher, 33, b. 33 Mather.
" Oscar L. carpenter, b. 999 Main.
" Patrick H. paperruler, 141 Pearl, b. 94 Alb.
" Peter, teamster, 42, h. 42 New Britain.
" William M. Rev. pastor Parkville M.E.
   church, h. 25 Sisson.
Carrick Margaret M. dressmaker at 75 Pratt.
Carrier Carrie M. b. 1534 Broad.
" Edmund D. painter at 10 Ford, h.2u. 245 Jef.
" John H. at 154 Pearl, l.u. 11 Goodwin.
" Margaret, dressmaker, h. 96 Hudson.
" Mary, wid. Thomas H. h.2u. 15 Chestnut.
Carrigan Annie, wid. William, b. 25 Bellevue.
" Annie C. cashier, 372 Asy. b.u. 52 Flower.
" Chas. S. clerk, b.u. 52 Flower.
" Edward J. clerk, b.u. 52 Flower.
" James, moulder, 556 Cap. b. 147 Babcock.
" Joseph, beltmaker at 15 Tru. h.u. 5 Francis.
" William, h.u. 52 Flower.
" ☞ *see also Kerrigan; Corrigan.*
Carroll Agnes A. dressmaker, 199, h. 199 Sheldon.
" Bridget, wid. John, h.u. 68 Washington.
" Chas. A., U. S. Army, b. 6 Pavilion.
" Charles E. machinist, b. 1183 Main.
" Cornelius A. machinist, b. 903 Park.
" Cornelius C. stonemason, h. 903 Park.
" Deglan, teamster at 476 Cap. h.u. 18 Putnam.
" Dennis, h. 32 Grace.
" Dennis A. traveling salesman, b. 903 Park.
" Edward C. mach. at 556 Cap. h. 12 Putnam.
" Edward J. at Popes, b. 25 Sigourney.
" Edward J. paper, 867 Main, h. E.H.t.
" Eli, messenger Adams express, h.u. 44 Alb.
" Emma M. stenogr. 690 Park, b.u. 68 Wash.
" Frank, shippingclk. 835 Mn. b. 18 Putnam.
" Fred W. captain tug Coulston, 285 State.
" George, b. 227 High.
" George F. b. 373 Asylum.
" Henry T. mechanic at Colts, h. 3 Curcombe.
" James, mach. at 30 Cushman, h.u. 11 Queen.
" John, coachman at 47 Main, h.u. 60 Retreat.
" John A. clerk at town clerk's office, 114
   Pearl, h.u. 68 Washington.
" John E. screwm. 476 Cap. b. 53 Fairfield.
" John F. b.r. 570 Main.
" John H. machinist, h.u. 153 Capen.
" John J. b. 6 Pavilion.
" John L. hackdriver at 19 Mather, h. 97 Vine.
" Joseph R. ins. agent, 904 Main, h. E.H.t.
" Katherine B. stenographer, b. 903 Park.
" Keron, packer at 40 Gov. h.u. 46 Benton.
" Lottie, buyer, 835 Main, b.u. 153 Capen.
" Margaret Mrs. h.r. 570 Main.
" Maria, wid. John. h.u. 113 Windsor.
" Martin, mechanic at Popes, b. W.L.t.
" Mary A. dressmaker, b. 6 Pavilion.
" Michael, h.3u. 55 Spruce.
" Michael J. plumber, 690 Park, h. 31 Spring.
" Owen P. mechanic at Popes, b. 1326 Broad.
" Patrick, b. W.H. Home for the Aged, Albany.
" Patrick, bootm. 7 Huntley av. h. 6 Pavilion.

Carroll Patrick, coachm. at 50, h.r. 50 Fairfield.
" Patrick, helper at 1 Flower, h. 8 Hawthorn.
" Patrick F. porter at Brown, Thomson & Co. 942 Main, b. 52 Chestnut.
" Patrick Henry, b. 6 Pavilion.
" Richard F. law student, dep. clerk U.S. dist. and circuit courts, 65 State, b. 6 Pavilion.
" Robert, mech. 581 Cap. h. 2 Hungerford.
" Samuel J. electrician at 596 Main, h. W.H.t.
" Sarah, wid. Bartholomew, h. 214 High.
" Stephen A. barber at 46 Asylum, h. 32 Park.
" Thomas, l. 88 Church.
" Thomas, oiler at 476 Cap. h.u. 10 Putnam.
" Thomas, ostler, rear 173, b.r. 173 State.
" Thomas E. salesman at Charles R. Hart Co. 898 Main, h.u. 13 Canton.
" Thomas J. mechanic at Popes, h. Windsor t.
" Wilfred B. at Ætna Life Ins Co. b. E.H.t.
" William J. clerk at 197 Asylum, b. 240 Sig.
" William J. sectionhand St.Ry. b. 903 Park.
Carron David F. butcher, b. 19 Morris.
" Edward A. tinner at 599 Main, b. 19 Morris.
" Joseph C. h. 197 State.
" Kate, milliner at 908 Main, b. 19 Morris.
" Salome Mrs. boardinghouse, 197 State.
" Thomas, h. 19 Morris.
" Thos. F. carpenter, b. 19 Morris.
Carson Alice, wid. Anderson, h.2u. 545 Main.
" Henry S. bookkeeper, h.u. 51 John.
" Joseph F. cleaner at 37 Wells, b.2u. 545 Main.
" Oscar, h. 9 Putnam.
" William G. h.2u. 545 Main.
Carstensen H. Peter, screwmaker, b 46 Laurel.
" Jurgen, screwm. at 476 Cap. h. 32 Laurel.
" Marius C. screwm. at 476 Cap. h. 32 Laurel.
" Mary, laundress, h. 32 Laurel.
" Nicolia F. screwm. at 476 Cap. b. 38 Smith.
Cartellano Cona, laborer, h.2u. 6 Charles.
Carter Alfred R. marblecutter, h. 317 Asylum.
" Ambrose B. peddler, b. 16 Warren.
" Bessie M. b. 440 Windsor av.
" Charles P. at Conn. Mutual Life Ins. Co. 783 Main, b. Glastonbury t.
" David, market, 8 Church, h. 37 Capen.
" Edwin J. traveling salesman, h.u. 1 East.
" Eliza L. wid. Everell, dressm. h. 188 Laurel.
" Elizabeth S. bookkeeper at 898 Main, b. 440 Windsor av.
" Eva A. b.3u. 40 Sheldon.
" Flora H. wid Eliza B. b. 27 Wethersfield.
" Franklin P. board of relief, contr. at Pratt & Whitney Co. 1 Flower, h. 124 Collins.
" Fred W. cook at 18 Central, l. 175 Windsor.
" Hezekiah, laborer, h.u. 287 Albany.
" Horace L. blacksm. at 29 Wells, h.2u. 488 Mn.
" Ivy Grace, b. 317 Asylum.
" J. Weston, harnessm. 59½ Tru. h. 21 Mahl.
" James, borer at Colts, h. 71 Franklin.
" James, rubberw. at 690 Park, h. 5 Kibbe.
" James, teamster, b. Albany.
" Jas. P. sergeant police, h.u. 173 Seymour.
" James S. drug clerk, 308 Mn. b. 173 Seymour.
" John, mechanic at Popes, h. 21 Mahl.
" John D. pressman at Colts, b. 71 Franklin.
" John H. blacksm. at 110 Com. b.u. 32 Wells.

Carter John W. engineer, b. 125 Brook.
" John W. mechanic at Popes, b. 31 Hamilton.
" Julia, wid. Abraham, h. 16 Warren.
" Lincoln, printer at 26 High, h. Manchester t.
" Lyman R. mach. at 1 Flower, h. 55 Mahl.
" Mattie A. bookkeeper, b. 440 Windsor av.
" Maud A. nurse at 20 So. Hudson.
" Philip, laborer, b.u. 287 Albany.
" Samuel W. b. 36 Jefferson.
" Sarah, wid. John, h.2u. 210 Windsor av.
" Stephen, driller, Colts, h. 440 Windsor av.
" Wm. H. foreman at 1 Flower, h. 79 Franklin.
" William L. assistant at Hartford Public Library, 5 Athenæum, b. 188 Laurel.
Cartlidge William, chef at 26 State, h. 21 Central.
" William Mrs. boardinghouse, 21 Central.
Carty Charles E. teamster, 283 Sheldon, h.2u. 33½ Lafayette.
Carukin Michael, mechanic at Popes, b. 26 Park.
" Patrick, mechanic at Popes, b. 26 Park.
" Peter, mechanic at Popes, b.2u. 26 Park.
Carver Selden S. inspector at Popes, h. Bristol t.
Cary John L. fireman N.E.R. b.2u. 73 Albany.
" John W. clerk, 745 Mn. b. 91 Buckingham.
" William R. draughtsman at Tube Co. b. 91 Buckingham.
" ☞ see also Carey.

Casale Carmine, laborer, h.2u. 78 Charles.
Case Albert M. policeman, h. 346 Albany.
" Alvin C. at Jewell Belt. Co. h. 11 Warner.
" Archibald L. clerk at Popes, b. 25 Capitol.
" Charles, clerk at 342 Asylum, b. 28 Spring.
" Chas. G. with O. D. Case & Co. b. 741 Asy.
" Charles H. carpenter, h.u. 27 Mahl.
" Charles P. (Bartlett & Case,) h. Simsbury t.
" Charles Z. b. 986 Main.
" Charlotte G. teacher South school, 36 Wadsworth, b. Wethersfield t.
" Clara B. nurse at 20 South Hudson.

**CASE C. H. & CO.** watches, jewelry, diamonds, etc. 851 Main. See outside front cover.

Clayton H. Case.          Mortimer H. Miller.

" Clarence N. clerk, 201 Asylum, b. 109 Ann.
" Clayton H. (C. H. C. & Co.) jewelers, 851 Main, h. 493 Prospect av.
" Clifford M. mach. at Popes, h. 54 Babcock.
" Cornish E. mach. 1 Flower, b. 28 Spring.
" David, engineer at 933, h. 933 Main, rm. 40.
" David N. at Travelers Insurance Co. 56 Prospect, b.u. 27 Mahl.
" Edward B. farmer, h. 63 Bluehills.
" Elizabeth T. clerk at Internal Revenue office, 65 State, b. 66 Willard.
" Ellen M. h. 305 Farmington.

ERASTUS E. CASE, Physician, after Aug. 1st, 1898, at Sage-Allen building, 902 Main, rms. 68 and 69.

Hours—10.30 to 12 A.M.          Evenings, 7 to 8,
          2 to 4 P.M.              excepting Thursday
Thursday, 10.30 to 12 A.M. only.   and Sunday, at resi-
Sunday, 12 to 1 P.M. only.         dence, 109 Ann st.
     Telephone at office and residence.

Case Erastus E. physician, 902 Main, h. 109 Ann.
" Ernest L. clerk, 908 Main, h.u. 42 Beach.

Case G.Burton, pianotuner 241 Asy. b. 147 Wash.
" George D. assembler at Popes, h.u. 9 John.
" George R. deputy collector Internal Revenue, 65 State, h. 66 Willard
" H. J. & Co. grocers, 983 Main.
Horace J. Case.        Edward B. Phillips.
" Harry, at 59½ Trumbull, b. 64 Capitol.
" Harry, at N.E.R. b. 80 Church.
" Helene E. b. 109 Ann.
" Herbert M. student, b. 109 Ann.
" Herbert M. b. 247 Sigourney.
" Hobart W. carpenter, h. 19 Williams.
" Horace J. (H.J. C. & Co.) h. 180 High.
" Horace N. clerk at Pratt & Whitney Co. 1 Flower, b. South Manchester v.
" Horace O. g. sec'y K. of P. 89 Pearl, h. E.H.t.

**CASE, LOCKWOOD & BRAINARD CO.** printers, bookbinders, etc. 141 Pearl.        *See page 475.*
" Mabel D. stenographer National Exchange Bank, 76 State, b. E.H.t.
" Marion, wid. Mason N. h.u. 196 Windsor av.
" Miron J. bookkeeper, Pope Mfg. Co. 436 Capitol, h. W.H.t.
" Myra W. b.u. 196 Windsor av.
" Nellie E. at 62 Market, b.u. 346 Windsor av.
" O. D. & Co. publ'rs. school furn. 302 Asylum.*
" Oliver C. round cordm. 15 Tru. b. 11 Warner.
" Orlando D. (O. D. C. & Co.) h. 741 Asylum.
" Raymond W. stenog. 25, b. 25 Atwood.
" Ruth E. b. 36 Jefferson.
" Sarah E. L. wid. Dr. Chas. R. b. 218 Collins.
" Theo. G. student Trinity college, 17 Jarvis hall, Summit.
" Uriah, attorney, 793 Main, h. 247 Sigourney.
" Wilbert S. bkkpr. 84 Pratt, b. 51 Oxford.

**CASE WILLIAM C.** attorney at law, 57 Pratt, h. Granby t.        *See p. 485.*
" William C. clerk at 745, h. 1191 Main.
" William O. at Hfd. Steam Boiler Insp. & Ins. Co. 650 Main, b. 25 Capitol.

**CASE WILLIAM S.** judge court of common pleas; attorney at law, 57 Pratt, h. 4 Park ter.        *See page 485.*
" Willis B. at Phœnix Ins. Co. 64 Pearl, h. 142 Collins.
" ☞ *see also Kase.*
Casey Agnes, at 83 Woodbine, b.u. 9 Ellery.
" Edward, cook, h.u. 21 Windsor.
" Elizabeth, wid. Thomas, h.u. 59 Market.
" Eugene R. musician, b. 25 Beach.
" J. O. (Sedgwick & C.) b. 57 Farmington.
" James E. polisher, b.u. 9 Ellery.
" John, cigarm. at 40 Mul. b.2u. 15 Talcott.
" John, laborer, h.2u. 120 Portland.
" John J. molder at 556 Cap. h. 7 Curcombe.
" John P. helper at 152 State, b.2u. 146 Grove.
" Marcus A. vice president Case, Lockwood & Brainard Co. 141 Pearl, h. 25 Beach.
" Mary, b.r. 56 Albany.
" Michael J. mech. at Popes, b. 146 Grove.
" Patrick, turner at 62, b. 59 Market.
" Patrick J. screwm. 476 Cap. b. 36 Trumbull.
" Richard D. b. 24 Elmer.

Casey Richard J. patternm. 556 Cap. h. 42 Hung.
" Sarah, h. 206 Asylum.
" Thomas, laborer, h.r. 11 Bellevue.
" Thomas F. helper, h.u. 9 Ellery.
" Wm. driver at 169 Front, b.u. 9 Ellery.
" William, driver at 356 Main.
" William, laborer, stone pits, h. New Britain.
Cashen John W. dropforger 142 Russ, h.u. 26 N.B.
" Mary, dressm. 14 Church, b. 98 New Britain.
" William, dropforger 142 Russ, h. 98 N.B.
" William Jr. b. 98 New Britain.
Cashin Michael, blacksmith, N.Y.R. h. 6 Chapel.
Cashman Dennis F. lab. 40 Gov. h.u. 57 Wdbg.
" Eliza, wid. Daniel, h.u. 65 Temple.
" John, helper, b. 25 Sigourney.
" John, laborer, b. 34 So. Prospect.
" Maurice W. butcher at 1050, b. 1043 Main.
" ☞ *see also Kashmann.*
Casiero Joseph, tailor at 293 Park, b. 15 North.
Caskey Mary O. theological student at 1507 Broad, b. 62 Hawthorn.
Casol Thomas, lab. 24 Mechanic, b. 72 Potter.
Casperson Charles, cook at 30 Washington.
" John, 2d cook, b. 31 Putnam.
Cassannova Joseph, baker at 26, b. 26 State.
Cassell Alfred, coachman, 7, b. 7 Vine.
Cassells Frank J. motorman St.Ry. h. 94 Jefferson.
" John J. enameler at Popes, b. 4 Lawrence.
Casserly Kate F. wid. John, h.u. 8 Queen.
" Nellie, trimmer at Pope Mfg. Co. b. 8 Queen.
Cassiday James L. clerk, 96 Tru. b. 63 Bkm.
" James W. horseman, 15, b. 15 Sumner.
" John, laborer, 690 Park, b.2u.r. 23 Spruce.
" Margaret, wid. John, h. 5 Curcombe.
" Michael, laborer at N.Y.R. b.3u.r. 49 Spruce.
" Patrick, blacksmith at 29 Wells, h. 143 Law.
" Peter, helper at P.&R. l. 1427 Broad.
" Peter, laborer, b.2u.r. 23 Spruce.
" Thomas J. burnisher, h. 206 Asylum, flat 5.
" William H. operator, 135 Shel. b.5 Curcombe.
Cassien Edward, helper at 48 Ann.
Castle Grove E. mach. at 1 Flow. h. 21 Putnam.
" Harry A. bkkpr. at Popes, h. Plainville t.
" Patrick, h.u. 71 Governor.
" Wm. G. repairer at Popes, b. 109 Lawrence.
Castles John, b. 4 Lawrence.
Castonguary David, carpenter at 158 Woodland, h. 249 Jefferson.
Caswell Charles H. at Ætna Life Ins. Co. 650 Main, b. 42 Imlay.
" Charles S. market, 295 Asy. h. 42 Imlay.
" Frank B. inspector at Popes, b. N.B.t.
" Frederick K. mech. engir. h.u. 238 Laurel.
" Henry K. Mrs. h. 238 Laurel.
" John W. butcher, b. 27 Wooster.
" Lizzie F. Mrs. milliner, 75 Pratt, b.1293 Main.
" Louis S. with Daniels Mill Co. b. 81 Wash.
" Thomas M. secy. Hatch & North Coal Co. 801 Main, h. Cone.
Catauldo Joseph, laborer, h.u. 37 Albany.
Caternovitch Abram, tailor, h.u. 64 Morgan.
Cathedral Lyceum, 227 Lawrence.
Cathie Richard, draughtsm. 177 Asy. b. 99 Tru.
Catholic Apostolic Church, 1520 Broad, Rev. John A. R. Rogers, rector.

Catholic Club, 11 Grove.
**CATHOLIC TRANSCRIPT,** weekly, office 704 Main. *See page* 467.
Catlin A. K. Mrs. b. 36 Jefferson.
" Abijah, cotton, 210 Pearl, h. 966 Asylum.
" Clarence F. toolm. 9 Sig. b. 72Buckingham.
" George S. Mrs. b. 583 Farmington.
" Jane, b. 36 Jefferson.
Catran M. Emma, cashier, 97 Asy. b. 58 Church.
Catzen Louis, porter Neal, Goff & Inglis Co. 980 Main, h. 83 Pleasant.
Caulfield E. V. organist, h. 30 Webster.
" Henry R. trav. salesman, b. 47 Farmington.
" John, laborer at 95, b. 69 Pleasant.
Caulkins Alice, wid. Edgar, b. 68 Beacon.
" C. at Hfd. Mach. Screw Co. b. 381 Capitol.
" Fred A. electrician at 690 Park, b. 18 Oak.
CAULKINS WILLIS E. *(Stoddard & C.)* 155 Charter Oak, h. 14 Florence. *See p.* 518.
" ☞ *see also Calkins; Corkins.*
Caum Frank, supt. 115 State, h. 263Windsor av.
Causby Benj. F. farmer 2d house w. Asylum av. on Prospect av.
Cavanaugh Edward, b. Franklin.
" Frank, driver at Brown, Thomson & Co 942 Main, b. 174 Barbour.
" Hannah Mrs. h.2u. 202 Sheldon.
" John, laborer, b.u. 84 Arch.
" John, laborer, 690 Park, b. 4 Francis.
" John J. filer at Colts, h. Burnside t.
" John J. teamster, 174, h. 174 Barbour.
" John J. Jr. teamster at 174, b. 174 Barbour.
" Kate, domestic, 20 South Hudson.
" Thomas, teamster at 174, b. 174 Barbour.
" William, plumber, b.2u. 202 Sheldon.
Cavenaugh Kate, wid. James, h.u.r. 27 John.
" Morris H. lineman 266 Pearl, h. 107 Wooster.
" Rose, wid. Martin, h. 3 Sigourney pl.
" ☞ *see also Cavanagh; Kavanagh; Caveno.*
Cavens Geo. orderly at 2 Holcomb, h.u. 24 Alden.
Caverley Frank C. helper 15 Tru. b. 18½ Church.
Cawley Patrick, helper at 9 Sig. h. 21 Lawrence.
" Thos. J. helper at 1 Flower, b. 10 Putnam.
Caya Bernard, contractor and builder, Prospect av. c. Caya, h. Prospect av.
" Wilfred, carpenter, b. Prospect av. c. Caya.
Cedar Hill Cemetery, Maple, c. Fairfield, office 785 Main.
Cederwall Oscar, ship. clerk 581 Cap. b. 139 Bab.
Cella Joseph, creammaker at 701, h.u. 105 Main.
" Louie, asst. cook at 701 Main, b. 33 John.
Celli Carmine, laborer, h.r. 262 Front.
Centennial Amer. Tea Co.,Wm. Stuart, 575 Main.
Center Addison P. assistant cashier at Popes, b. 427 Main, rm. 71.
Central Labor Union Hall, 11 Central.
" New England Brick Exchange Co., Hartford Division, 704 Main.
" Row Restaurant, Harry Ball, 8 Central.
Cersosimo A. Raphael, laborer, h.3u. 67 Morgan.
" Antonio, foundryman, b.3u. 51 Morgan.
" Carmine, wood peddler, h.u. 220 Bellevue.
" Francesco, laborer, b.3u. 79 Morgan.
" Joseph & Co. fruit and groceries, 558 Asy. Jos. Cersosimo. Salvatore Satriano. Tony Perone.

Cersosimo Jos. *(Jos. Cersosimo & Co.)* h. 49 Mor.
" Joseph, driver, h.u. 210 Front.
" Joseph, laborer, h.3u. 67 Morgan.
" Louis, tailor, h.u. 79 Morgan.
Chace Raymond A. machinist at 476 Capitol, b. 57 Sigourney.
Chadbourne Wm. H. hostler, 126 Church, h.u. 4 Charter Oak.
Chadwick Earl L. at Colts, b. 24 Woodbridge.
" Fannie Mrs. h. 842 Park.
" Mary, h. 488 Main, rm. 3.
" Patrick J. h. 842 Park.
" Thomas, clerk, 160 Windsor av.
Chaese Nora, photo artist, 753 Main.
" ☞ *see also Chase.*
Chaffee Abner C. helper at 61 Asylum, h.2u. 37 Chestnut.
" Charles, marketm. at 369 Cap. h. 90 Laurel.
" Charles W. Adams Ex. messeng. h. 55 Julius.
" Cornelius V. h. 459 Broad.
" Julia A. wid. John H. h. 5 Main.
" Nellie L. h. 20 Suffield.
" Nellie M. dressmaker, b. 58 Church.
" Norman P. steamfitter at 152 State, b. 3 Sherman.
" Orrin W. Jr. electrician, h.u. 7 John.
" Theodore D. shipping clerk at 100 Trumbull, h. Manchester t.
" William R. clerk at 377 Asylum.
Chalker Caroline, wid. Sylvester C. h. 236 Windsor av.
" Margaret, wid. Allen S. h.u. 67 Russ.
Challiss Raymond E. mach. 1 Flower, b. 3 Far.
Chamansky Adolph B. clk. 882 Mn. b.4u. 80 Pearl.
Chamberlain Arthur M. trav. salesm. at Potter & Payne, 405 Allyn, h. 169 Albany.
" Edgar H. mach. at 1 Flower, b. 911 Main.
" Mary J. attendant at 30 Washington.
" Minnie B. teacher Wadsworth Street school, b. 52 Capitol.
CHAMBERLIN ALBERT S. *councilman 1st ward,* *(S. D. C. & Sons,)* provisions, 179 State, b. 16 Prospect.
" Alvin W. bookbinder at Case, Lockwood & Brainard Co. 141 Pearl, h. 28 Benton.
" Charles E. expresser, h.2u. 80 Grove.
" Clayton P. clerk at Hartford Daily Times, 716 Main, b. 28 Benton.
" Frank D. *(S. D. Chamberlin & Sons,)* provisions, 179 State, h. 17 Seyms.

Chamberlin G. Burton, clerk at 107 Grove, b.
    16 Prospect.
" George W. clerk at Jewell Belting Co. 15
    Trumbull, h. W.H.t.
" Henry A. machinist at 15, h.u. 6 Trumbull.
" Henry H. timekeeper at Taft Co. b. 16 Pro.
" John H. carman, b. 27 Hudson.
" Mary, wid. Franklin, h. 341 Farmington.
Chamberlin Nelson H. carman, 27, h. 27 Hudson.
" Reuben, h. 17 Lafayette.
" Samuel D. (S. D. C. & Sons,) provisions,
    179 State, h. 16 Prospect.
CHAMBERLIN SAMUEL D. & SONS, provisions,
    179 State.          See page 89.
      Samuel D. Chamberlin.  Frank D. Chamberlin.
           Albert S. Chamberlin.
" Harriet E. wid. Samuel S. h. 120 Capitol.
" Samuel S. (C. & Shaughnessy,) b. 2A Belden.
" & Shaughnessy, gents furnishings, 65 Asy.
      Samuel S. Chamberlin.    D. J. Shaughnessy.
CHAMBERLIN, WHITE & MILLS, now Hiram R.
    Mills.              See page 491.
Chambers Francis, attorney at law, 68 Pratt,
    rm. 1, h. 58 Imlay.
Champ Peter, bartender, 146 Front, h. 31 S.Pro.
Champaign Philip, barber, b. 45 Park.
Champion Bathsheba J. wid. H. A. h 37 Mather.
" Charles P. laborer, h.u. 114 Albany.
" Charles S. patent attorney at F. H. Rich-
    ards, 803 Main, h.2u. 17 Belden.
" Edgar R. clerk, 377 Asy. h. 148 Seymour.
Champlin Charles C. foreman, 46 Ann, h.u.51 Sey.
" Charles J. compositor, 252 Pearl, b. Weth.t.
" Charles W. assistant shipping clerk, William
    Rogers Mfg. Co. 66 Mar. h.u. 100 Capen.
" Elizabeth H. wid. Henry B. h. 64 Gillett.
" Frank D. boilermaker, b. 154 Windsor av.
" Jennie Mrs. b.u. 1110 Main.
" W. Craig, entry clerk, 273 Asy.b.1110 Main.
" Wm. A. foreman, 152 State, h. 154 Windsor av.
" William H. bookkeeper, State Savings Bank,
    39 Pearl, h. 29 Gillett.
Chandler Arthur W. market, 58 Sheldon, b.
    1271 Main.
" Charles V. clerk, 164 State, b. So.Windsor t.
" Ed. R. pressman, 16 State, b. 1271 Main.
" Frederick L. bookkeeper, 164 State, b. So.
    Windsor t.
" George A. clerk, T. Sisson & Co. 729 Main,
    b. 715 Asylum.
" George F. clerk, b. 1271 Main.
" Geo. P. (T. Sisson & Co.) wholesale drug-
    gists, h. 715 Asylum.      See page 560.

## CHANDLER SHORTHAND
SCHOOL, 252 Asy.    See page 710.
" William, bookb. 141 Pearl, h. 1271 Main.
Chaney Albert L. b. 38 Sumner.
" Etta M. Mrs., Domestic Bakery, 44 Pratt,
    h. 38 Sumner.
Chapaitz ☞ see Chapote.
Chapel Alice M. clerk, 725 Main, b. 58 Church.
" Ernest, brickmaker, b. Windsor av.
Chapin Albert D. clerk, Hartford Coal Co. 754
    Main, h. 193 Wethersfield.
" Annie C. wid. Henry, h.u. 47 Sumner.
" Arthur, b. Harrison.
" Arthur D. mason, 74, h. 74 Seymour.
" Atlas, machinist at 9 Sigourney, b.41Asylum.
" Elmer, mach. at 388 Cap. b.u. 224 Putnam.
" Francis A. cabinetm.180 Aly.h.215 Jefferson.
" Fred E. b. Harrison.
" Frederick H. (T. Sisson & Co.) wholesale
    druggists, h. W.H.t.      See page 560.
" Frederick P. clerk, Orient Ins. Co.5 Haynes,
    b. 47 Sumner.
" Gilbert W. actuary at Society for Savings,
    31 Pratt, h. 900 Asylum.
" Lyman A. newsdealer and bookseller, 865
    Main, h.u. 30 Huntington.
" M. A. Miss, nurse, 122, l. 122 High.
" Mary L. clerk, 908 Main, b. 215 Jefferson.
" Merrick W. bookkeeper, American National
    Bank, 803 Main, b. 193 Wethersfield.
" Robert D. clerk, United States Bank, 872
    Main, b. 193 Wethersfield.
Chapmadi Tony, fruit, 225, h. 225 Park.
Chapman Adelbert, mach.388 Cap.b.u.1303 Main.
" Albert M. cigarm. at 876 Main, h.u. 91 Asy.
" Alice M. b. Windsor av.
" Annie E. Mrs. b. 63 Spring.
" Bert W. (Bryant & Co.) h. 7 Lenox.
" Birge, blacksmith, b. Windsor av.
" Charles H. printer at Hartford Times, 716
    Main, h. 17 Goodwin.
" Charles M. laborer at 690, b. 983 Park.
" Charlotte F. Mrs. h.2u. 44 Hopkins.
CHAPMAN DWIGHT, councilman 4th ward; with
    Ætna Ins. Co. 666 Main, b.131 Sargeant.
" Edgar W. clerk, 188 Asylum, h. 26 Russell.
" Edward, mach. Pope Tube Co.b.17 Goodwin.
" Edward N. laborer, 690, h. 983 Park.
" Eleazer P. (C. B. Goodwin & Co.) h. 49
    Sargeant.
" Emma, wid. Edwin, b. 28 Huntington.
" Emma A. wid. Fred. T. h. 280 Sigourney.
" Frank L. mgr. at 24 Mec. h. 128 Oxford.
" Frederick B. driver at 175, l. 173 Ashley.
CHAPMAN FREDERICK P. councilman 6th ward,
    traveling salesman, h.u. 58 Russ.
" Frederick S. draughtsman at 1 Laurel,
    b. 113 Edwards.
" George, woodw. 352 Albany, b.24 Chestnut.
" George A. diesinker, 142 Russ, h.u.987 Main.
" Harriet B. wid. Charles R. h. 337 Laurel.
" Henry E. clerk, Hartford Life Insurance
    Co. 252 Asylum, b. 29 Girard.
" Henry E. student, b. 114 Huntington.
" Henry E. clerk, 700 Main, h. 114 Huntington.

Chapman Henry E. checker, Colts, h.u. 31 Benton.
" Henry H. buyer at Brown, Thomson & Co. 942 Main, h.107 Bellevue.
" Hubert W. at Hartford Fire Insurance Co. 53 Trumbull, h. 11 Columbia.
" I. E. bookkeeper at 54 Huntley, h. Capen.
" James O. carpenter at 556 Cap. h. 15 Seyms.
" John C. machinist at 1 Flower, b. 50 Cedar.
" John W. draughtsman at 1 Laurel, b. Garden cor. Asylum.
" John W. salesman, Popes, b. 57 Farmington.
" Joseph L. foreman at 388 Cap. h.1266 Broad.
" L. B. carpenter, b. 27 Spring.

**CHAPMAN LESLIE G.** dentist, 86 Pratt, h.55 Fairfield. *See front page cover.*
" Louis B. at Phœnix Insurance Co. 64 Pearl, b. 128 Oxford.
" Louisa B. Mrs. h. 29 Girard.
" Lucius, bootcutter, h.u. 27 Wooster.
" Mabel, nurse at 20 South Hudson.
" Marion G. principal Charter Oak school, b. 68 Church.
" Maro S. superintendent U.S. envelope works 1 South Ann, h. South Manchester v.
" Mary J. Mrs. nurse, 12, h. 12 Squire.
" May E. organist and music teacher, b. 29 Girard.
" Millie W. bookkeeper at J. H. Eckhardt Co. 695 Main, b. Rocky Hill t.

**CHAPMAN & MUCKLOW,** real estate, insurance and loans, 370 Asylum.
Rush P. Chapman. William B. Mucklow.
" Orin P. carpenter, h. 7 Lenox.
" Oscar A. farmer, h. 281 Albany.
" Robert H. b. 337 Laurel.
" Rush P. *(C. & Mucklow,)* h. 113 Edwards.
" Samuel A. steamfitter, h. 36 Sheldon.
" Sarah, wid. Lucius, b. 628 Windsor av.

**CHAPMAN SILAS Jr.** fire insurance agency, 51 Trumbull, h. 335 Windsor av.
" Susie M. tel. op. 42 Union pl. b. 63 Spring.
" Thomas B. deputy sheriff, constable, 750 Main, rm. 14, h. 13 Canton.
" Thomas B. manufacturer, h. 10 Park ter.
" Whitfield S. clerk at 10 Central, b. 63 Spring.
" Wilfred M. carpenter, h. 628 Windsor av.
" William, clerk, 1 South Ann, h. 89 Brook.
" William R. clerk at Connecticut Fire Ins. Co. 51 Prospect, h. E.H.t.
" William R. presshand, 581 Cap. h.89 Brook.
Chappell Albert E. toolmaker at Popes, h.6 Haw.
" Burton L. clerk 745 Main, h. Ingleside.
" George C. mach. at Popes, b. 36 Charter Oak.
" William H. diesinker, 142 Russ, b 80 State.
Chaput Jos. laborer, Pope Tube Co. h. 8 Water.
" Joseph, swager, h. 1 North.
" Joseph Jr. harnessmaker, b. 1 North.
Charbonneau Octave, painter, h.2u. 7½ Oak.
Charest Alfred, carpenter, h.u. 129 Ward.
" George, waiter at 358 Asylum, b.10½ Village.
Charity Organization Society, 57 Trumbull.
Charlie Bros. laundry, 14 New Britain.
Charlton Augustus H. pres. Hartford Dredging Co. 4 Central, b. 244 High.

Charlton E. P. & Co. notions, etc. 929 Main.
Earl P. Chariton. Edward A. Bardol.
Charleston J. D. l. 933 Main, rm. 29.
Charney Fannie, wid. Jacob, h. 64 Pleasant.
" Simon, operator at Popes, b. 64 Pleasant.
Charter George H. superintendent at 4 Central.
" Oak Hall, 125 Charter Oak.

**CHARTER OAK NATIONAL BANK,** 124 Asylum. *See page 432.*
" Oak Park, office 721 Main.
" Oak school, 105 Charter Oak.
" Wesley I. with Hartford Life Insurance Co. 252 Asylum, b. 234 High.
Chase A. R. Mrs. at 223 Asylum, rm. 10.
" Abbie Mrs. h.2u. 6 Ford.
" Abraham L. floorw. at 956, b. 981 Main.
" Charles E. assistant secretary Hartford Fire Ins. Co. 53 Trumbull, h. 914 Asylum.
" Cornelia S. wid. J. G. h. 76 Church.
" Fessenden N. stenographer at F. H. Richards, 803 Main, h. 40 Brook.
" George L. pres't Hartford Fire Insurance Company, 53 Trumbull, h. 888 Asylum. *See page 458.*
" Hiram H. mach. at 476 Cap. h.198 Evergreen.
" J. Seymour, sec'y board of water commissioners, City hall building, h. 12 Whitney.
" Joseph Stannard, clerk, P.&R. b. 792 Asy.
" Lucy A. wid. Joseph D. h. 12 Whitney.
" Nelson, laborer at 690 Park, b.u.73 Albany.
" Oak A. grocery, 88, h. 88 Walnut.
" Stanley A. theological student, 1507 Broad.
" ☞ *see also Chase.*
Chatel Joseph, painter, b.u. 21 Central.
Chatfield Thomas L. watchman at State Prison, h. 4 Buckingham.
Chatterley Harry Y. general agent at 197 Asylum, h. 352 Laurel.
Chaves Antonio C. machinist at 1 Flower, b. 220 New Britain.
Cheesick Michael, helper, 1 Flower, h. 19 Mahl.
" Michael Mrs. groceries, 19, h. 19 Mahl.
Cheetham William L. filer at Colts, h.u. 63 Hudson.

**CHENEY BROTHERS,** Silk Manufacturers, 34 Morgan and South Manchester. *See inside front cover, and page 545.*
" C. L. Mrs. b. 1 Ward.
" Emily L. wid. Thomas B. h. 733 Asylum.
" Frances E. teacher, h. 733 Asylum.
" Frank Jr. vice president Cheney Brothers, 34 Morgan, h. South Manchester v.
" Frank W. Col. treasurer, secretary Cheney Brothers, 34 Morgan, h. So. Manchester v.
" Fred. H. machinist at 9 Sig. h.u. 44 Beach.
" Horace F. W. mach. at 135 Sheldon, h.2u. 16 Alden.
" Howell, supt. at Cheney Bros. silk mill, 34 Morgan, h. So. Manchester v.
" Knight D. president Cheney Brothers, 34 Morgan, h. South Manchester v.
" Laura M. Mrs. h.2u. 16 Alden.
Cheney Louis R. councilman 10th ward, h. 40 Woodland.

Cheney Minnie P. nurse, b. 5 Main.
" Walter A. molder at 556 Cap. b. 248 Law.
" Ward, exchange editor, Courant, 66 State, b. 427 Main, rm. 55.
Cherniavsky Samuel, groceries, 42, h. 42 North.
Chesba B.ladies tailor,29 Church,h.122 Windsor.
CHESEBRO EUGENE L. (Angus & Chesebro,) builders, h. 39 Seymour.   See page 519.
**CHESEBRO JAMES L.** architect, 757 Main, rms. 1 and 2, h. 51 Seymour.
Chesebrough L. Anna, teacher, b. 751 Asylum.
Chesky Harris, (H. C. & Co.) h. 84 Barbour.
" H. & Co. wholesale fruits, 1076 Main.
        Harris Chesky.        Max Rivkin.
Chesler Benjamin, tailor, h.u. 28 North.

WESTON CHESTER, Physician.   Office, 110 High street.
        Hours—8 to 9 A.M.
        2 to 4 and 7 to 8 P.M.
        Sundays, 12 to 1 P.M.

Chester Weston, physician, 110, h. 110 High.
Chiaputto Bennedetto, laborer, h.3u. 86 Morgan.
" Michael, laborer, b. 16 Kilbourn.
" Nicholas, helper, h.u. 82 Morgan.
Chiarizia John M. at C. S. Brewer & Co. 238 Asylum, h. 66 Chestnut.
Chiarizio Giovannio, laborer, h.2u. 67 Morgan.
Chiasciono Michael, watchman, h. 21 Morgan.
" Richard, barber, at 222 Asy. b. 21 Morgan.
Chickering John, shoemaker, b.u. 1232 Main.
Chickey Nicholas, laborer, h.u.r. 57 Front.
Chiclau Antony, laborer, b. 29 Commerce.
" Thomas, laborer, h. 29 Commerce.
Chidley Jennie E. clk. 82 Tru. b. Newington t.
Chidsey Almira, dressmaker, 877, h. 877 Main, rm. 15.
" Robert C. mach. at 476 Cap. h. Windsor t.
Child Albert Kennedy, b. 36 Charter Oak.
" Edgar A. pianotuner at 201 Asylum, h. 44 Williams.
" Frederick D. supt. Conn. Institute for Blind, h. 12 Wadsworth.
" Josephine M. Mrs. h. 13 So. Hudson, rm 5.
Children's Aid Society, 223 Asylum, room 10.
Childs Arthur R. draughtsman, b. 9 Holcomb.
" Charles R. at Hartford Fire Insurance Co. 53 Trumbull, h. 27 Marshall.
" Frances R. nurse at 20 So. Hudson.
" Francis R h. 186 Collins.
" Grace, asst. lib. 5 Atheneum, b. 26 C.O.pl.
" John R. nightclerk, 852 Mn. h.u. 95 Bellevue.
Chimp Peter, laborer, h. 31 So. Prospect.
Chinkis Benjamin, peddler, h. 8 North.
" David, peddler, h. 8 North.
Chinn Herbert, foreman, 581 Cap. h. 238 N.B.
Chipman Horace E. h. 36 Wooster.
" Martha J. h. 115 Wooster.
Chipps Fred J. cabinetm. h. Pros. av. n. N.P.
Chisholm John, lineman, 247 Pearl, b. 298 Park.
Chisich Michael, mach. at 388 Cap. h. 19 Wells.
Chlopkowiak L. cigarmaker, h. 58 Temple.
Chofnos Abram, tailor, h. 73 Charles.
Chokellian Michael, screwm. at 476, l. 381 Cap.
Chong Fang, laundry, 100½ Trumbull.
" Flang, laundry, 208 Sheldon.

Chong Quong, laundry, 116 Market.
" Sung, laundry, 229 Park.
Choquette Clifford C. carpenter, h.u. 303 Park.
Christ Margarethe, attendant at 30 Washington.
" Wilhelm, screwm. at 476 Cap. b. 276 Law.
Chrisley George, driver, b. 61 Ann.
Christensen Andreas, polisher, b. 1155 Broad.
" Andrew, gardener, h.r. 1168 Windsor av.
" Annie, wid. Niel, h. 49 Elliott.
" Carl, polisher at 581 Capitol, b. 234 Park.
" Carl, laborer, b. 29 Elliott.
" Carl J. farmer, h. Bloomfield av.
" Christian, tailor, 41, b.2u.r. 41 Asylum.
" Christian L. mach. at 30 Cush. h. W.H.t.
" Eleanor Mrs. h. 42 Lawrence.
" Frederick, clerk Jewell Pin Co. 31 Hicks, h. Wethersfield t.
" Iver, pressman, 690 Park, h.u. 1 Brady pl.
" Iver M. laborer at 335 Shel. h. 25 Sargeant.
" John, helper at Jewells, h.u. 29 Elliott.
" John P. roller at 15 Tru. b. 29 Elliott.
" Kruse, rubberw. at 690 Park, b.u. 40 Hung.
" Martha, wid. Dennis, b. 21 King.
" Neils, gardener, h.r. 1168 Windsor av.
" Neils, tailor at 97 Asylum, h.u. 1061 Main.
" Niels K. beltmaker at Jewells, h. 533 Broad.
" Nicoles, rubberw. 690 Pk. h.u. 31 Putnam.
" Peter, stretcher at 15 Tru. b. 1078 Main.
" Peter, sweeper at Popes, h. 1155 Broad.
" Peter, toolmaker, h. 109 Laurel.
" Peter, waiter, h. 24 Talcott.
" Peter C. shipper at 8 Sig. b. 1204 Broad.
" Peter C casehardener Popes, h. 1148 Broad.
Christenson Peter, diesinker at 142, b. 40 Russ.
" Wilhelm M. gardener at 83 Woodland, h. 234 Park.
Christian Frank, decorator, b. 255 Asylum.
" Remington P. conduc. P.&R. h. 72 Walnut.

CHRISTIAN SCIENCE READING ROOMS, the first established in Hartford, 252 Asylum c. Ann, K. A Bowers secretary.      

" Watkins W. lettercarrier, h. 29 Wolcott.
Christiansen John, mechanical engineer at 1 Flower, h. 236 Laurel.
" John, clerk at 1030 Main, h.u. 28 Church.
" John, operator at 388 Cap. b. 16 Wooster.
" S. P. A. cabinetmaker at 80½ Ann, h. E.H.t.
Christianson Chris, coachman, 69, b. 69 Gillett.
" John, carpenter, h. 114 Heath.
Christie Chris J. brazier, 581 Cap. b. 55 Putnam.
" David, janitor at 783 Main, h. 298 Maple.
" Fred D. brazier at 942 Main, h. 65 Dean.
" James, conductor, St.Ry. h.u. 64 Hicks.
" James, Jr. janitor, 36 Jefferson, h.u. 7 Park.
Christino Gustano, shoemaker, h. 7 Charles.
Christoffersen Erasmus, upholsterer at 103 Asylum, b. E.H.t.
" James J. beltmaker, 15 Tru. b. 39 Asylum.
Christoph George W. manager B. F. Sturtevent Co., Vredendale, h. 8 Westland.
Christopher David, teamster, b. 548 Park.
" James, enameler at Popes, b.u. 123 Babcock.
" John, fireman, 690 Asy. h.2u. 123 Babcock.

Christy Albert, helper, b. 16 Affleck.
" Charles M. polisher at Popes, h. 16 Affleck.
" Florence M. clerk at Brown, Thomson & Co. 942 Main, b. 16 Affleck.
Chritchley George, forem. 22 Trinity, b. 61 Ann.
Chudoba Frank F. draughtsmam at Popes, b. 148 Brown.
" Mary, wid. Ferdinand, laundr. h. 148 Brown.
Chump Pietro, laborer, h.2u. 64 Morgan.
Chung Charles, laundry, 114, h. 114 Laurel.
" Charles, laundryman, b. 96 Flower.
" George, laundry, 96, h. 96 Flower.
" W. laundry, 954, h. 954 Broad.
" Wah, laundry, 229, h. 229 Park.
Church Abner, b. 779 Asylum.
" Albert, landscape gardener, h. 108 Pro. av.
" Alonzo C. inspector motor carriage department at Popes, h. 68½ Laurel.
" Earl Douglas, at Travelers Insurance Co. 56 Prospect, b. 122 Garden.
" Edgar E. foreman, 581 Cap. b. 188 Putnam.
" Edwin J. laborer at 690 Park, h. Prospect av. s. of Park.
" Edwin T. gardener, b. Prospect av. s. of Park.
" Elizabeth, wid. Edward, h. 241 Windsor av.
" Eugene A. mach. at 476 Cap. l. 51 Babcock.
" George O. inspec. 581 Cap. h.u. 91 Chestnut.
" Grace M. clerk at Brown, Thomson & Co. 942 Main, b. 91 Chestnut.
" Home, Episcopal, 76 Bellevue.
" Julia E. wid. Samuel, b. 17 Annawan.
" Lewis Mrs. boardinghouse, 19 Central.
" M. Gertrude, Lu. 123 Hungerford.
" Street House, 80 Church.
" William, dancing master, 104, h. 104 Clark.
" William F. machinist, b. 47 Hawthorn.
" William G. apprentice at 1, b. 68½ Laurel.
" William G. foreman 70 Huy. h.u. 104 Clark.
" William T. J. machinist at 30 Cushman, b. 108 Prospect av.
Churchill Alvord S. clerk at Gemmill, Burnham & Co. 66 Asylum, h. 112 Washington.
" Charles D. painter, h.2u.r. 60 Temple.
" Charles N. painter, b. 16 Wellington.
" George G. 2d hand furniture, 643 Main, h.u. 44 Cedar.
" Cora B. Mrs. laundress, h.u.r. 60 Temple.
" Henry P. carpenter at 54 Arch, h. 11 Olive.
" William T. h. 7 Seyms.
" Wm. T. musicteacher, b.u. 16 Wellington.
Ciarizio John, laborer, h.u. 30 Kilbourn.
" Maryangello, laborer, b.u.r. 10 Charles.
Cidilli Joseph, laborer, b. 17 Morgan.
Cigal M. shoem. at 38 Windsor, h.2u. 32 Portland.
Cigarmakers Union, No. 42, 11 Central.
Cinqmars Leon, cleaner at N.Y.R. b. 238½ Zion.
" Prospect J. carptr. at N.Y.R. h. 237½ Zion.
Cion Isaac, cigarmaker, 51, h. 51 Morgan.
" Joseph, b. 241 Market.
" Michael, h. 241 Market.
Cirelli Antonio, grocery, 26, h. 26 Kilbourn.
Cirigliano Felice, wid. Frank, h. 83 Windsor.
" Joseph, barber, 1237 Main, h. 49 Morgan.
" Vito, groceries, 40, h.u. 40 Village.
Citizens Grocery and Provision Co. 267 Main.

**CITIZENS' MEAT AND FISH MARKET,** JOHN FLYNN, 493 Main.
*See page 587.*
**CITY BANK OF HARTFORD,** 783 Main. *See page 432.*
" Court Room, in Aldermens room, 800 Main.
**CITY DIRECTORY,** Elihu Geer's Sons, compilers, book and job printers, 16 State, up stairs. *See page 474.*
" Dispensary, store, 182 Pearl.
" Hall, 800 Main, the old State House.
" Hotel, 651 Main, James Campbell, prop.
" Market, John J. Foley, 1065 Main.
" Mission Society, building, 234 Pearl.
Civitillo Michael, laborer, b. 67 Morgan.
Clabby Jas. T. cutter at 28 High, h. 10 Chestnut.
Claffey Alice, wid. Michael J. h.u. 22 Dean.
" Catharine, wid. John, h. 68 Retreat.
" Ellen, wid. Patrick, h. 12 Huntley pl.
" Frank, at 1 So. Ann, b.u. 22 Dean.
" Frank, mach. at 388 Capitol, b.u. 22 Hicks.
" Frank E. patternm. at 40 Cush. h. 41 Laurel.
" George F. h. 26 Hicks.
" Harry J. clerk at 223, b. 221 Main.
" Kittie, at 476 Capitol, b.u. 1214 Broad.
" John H. carpenter, h.3u. 174 Sheldon.
" John H. engineer, h.u. 22 Hicks.
" John R. saloon, 223, h. 221 Main.
" Kate, wid. Chas. B. h. 181 Main.
" Keron, carpenter, h. 111 Maple.
" Keron, helper at 54 Arch, b.u. 12 Huntley pl
" Maria, wid. John, h.u. 853 Park.
" Michael J. driller at Colts, h.u. 11 Curcombe.
" Patrick E. helper, Popes, b.u. 12 Huntley pl.
Claffin George H. carpenter, h. 34 New Britain.
Claffy Ed. J. patterntender, 1 Flow. b. 275 Pearl.
" James, fireman at Popes, b. 1316 Broad.
" Thomas H. finisher at 62 Mar. b. 275 Pearl.
Clancy Daniel Mrs. h.r. 343 Collins.
" John, porter at 165, h. 151 Windsor.
" Joseph, laborer at State Capitol, b. 2u. 40 Park.
" Mary A. dressmaker, b. 22 Grand.
" Michael, teamster, h. Newfield.
" Peter D. carpenter, h. 351 Albany.
" Timothy A. bartend. 61 Elm, b. 132 Tru.
" Timothy A. saloon, 1167 Mn. h. 11 Goodwin.
" Thos. molder at 54 Arch, h.u. 54 Lawrence.
" William F. h. 47 Hawthorn.
Clano James, laborer, b. 68 Front.
Clapp Allen C. salesman at E. S. Kibbe Co. 149 State, h.u. 24 Lewis.
" Arthur C. agent at Parsons Theater, b. 24 Lewis.
" Chloe E. wid. Samuel F. b. 48 Ashley.
" Ella J. wid. Willis M. h. 24 Lewis.
" Ellen L. wid. C. C. h.u. 24 Church.
" Fred. C. plumber, 24, b.u. 24 Church.
" George I. (C. & Treat,) h. 115 Bellevue.
" Howard, hostler at 231, b. 231 Lawrence.
" Inez J. stenog. at Popes, b. East Windsor t.
" John B. (John B. Clapp & Son,) b. 427 Main, rm. 13.
**CLAPP JOHN B. & SON,** iron and steel, 61 Market. *See page 529.*
John B. Clapp.      Roswell J. Clapp.

Clapp Jos. B. tinner, 26 Kinsley, h. 13 Morris.
" Leslie T. clerk at 342 Asy. b. 147 Wash.
" Margaret Mrs. b. 2 Holcomb.
" Martha A. wid. J. Hooker, h.u. 112 Hopkins.
" Roswell J. (John B. Clapp & Son,) 61 Market, h. 48 Willard.
" Sarah M. wid. Caleb, h. 24 Lewis.
" Susan P. teacher 2d North school, 249 High, b. 11 Winthrop.
" & Treat, hardware, 64 State.
     George I. Clapp.    Irving C. Treat.
Clare Frank D. asst. proof reader at Hartford Courant, 66 State, h. 21 Barnard.
" Mary A. F. cashier, 590 Park, b. 32 Grace.
Clark A. oiler str. Middletown, 285 State.
" Abel S. teacher, 690 Asylum, h. 20 Atwood.
" Alexander W. bkkpr. at Belknap & Warfield, 77 Asylum, b. 247 Sigourney.
" Alfred, b.r. 60 Bluehills.
" Alfred C. engraver 871 Mn. h. 223 Asy. rm. 22.
" Alice, b. 268 Farmington.
" Alice A. Mrs. h. 50 Pleasant.
" Alida R. teacher Brown school, 160 Market, b.2.u. 16 Florence.
" Allan S. at National Fire Ins. Co. 95 Pearl, b. Wethersfield t.
" Ann, wid. Patrick, h. 18 Russell.
" Anna A. wid. Patrick F. h.u. 34 Wilson.
" Anna S. h.2.u. 16 Florence.
" Anna W. stenographer at Hartford Fire Ins. Co. 53 Trumbull, b. Wethersfield t.
" Benj. sawyer at 335 Sheldon, h. 37 Liberty.
" Charles, clerk at 690 Park, b. 1¼ East.
" Charles, tel. operator, Popes, b. 1½ East.
" Charles A. at 302 Asylum, h. 62 Maple.
" Charles A. accountant, b. 32 Capitol.
" Charles E. teamster, 250 State, b. 57 Elliott.
" Charles E. toolmaker at Colts, h. N.B.t.
" Charles H. b.u. 148 Seymour.
" Charles H. carpenter, N.Y.R. h.u. 4 Rice ct.
CLARK CHARLES HOPKINS, vice pres. Hartford Courant Co. asso. editor Hartford Courant, 66 State, h. 14 Prospect. *See page 463.*
" Charles W. b. 125 Washington.
" Charles W. clerk, U. S. Envelope Agency, 1 South Ann, h.u. 13 Washington.
" Charlotte, b. 268 Farmington.
" Chester J. motorman St. Ry. h.u. 57 Elliott.
" Clarence B. clerk at 273 Asylum, b. M.t.
" Clemence L. wid. Kirk M. h. 129 Hamilton.
" Clinton C. apprentice at 1 Laurel, b. 129 Hamilton.
CLARK & CO. See L. L. Ensworth & Son, page 592.
" Clyde A. clerk, 409 Allyn, b. Windsor t.
" & Crane, fish, 323 Asylum.
     Edward E. Clark.    Charles E. Crane.
" Daniel Milton, butcher at 165, h. 165 Clark.
" David H. clerk, 109, b. 109 Trumbull.
" Diamond & Clark, leaf tobacco, 225 State.
     Eugene S. Clark.   Levi Diamond.   John S. Clark.
" E. fireman, tug Ward, 285 State.
" E. H. Mrs. dressmaker, b.u. 1208 Main.
" Ed. W. diesinker at Popes, h.u. 1183 Broad.
" Edgar D. clerk at 388 Cap. h. Windsor t.

**CLARK EDRED W.** machinist, etc. 31 Wells, h. 56 Bond.    *See page 526.*
" Edward E. (Clark & Crane,) h. 172 Clark.
" Edward F. roofer, h.2u. 114 Mather.
" Edward H. secretary Willimantic Linen Co. 391 Allyn, h. 906 Asylum.
" Edward J. driver at 250 State, b. 5 Kilbourn.
" Edward A. attend. 30 Wash. h. 118 Webster.
" Edward S. mach. at 31 Wells, b. 56 Bond.
" Edwin E. engineer, 34 Pratt, h. 80 Grove.
" Edwin E. Jr. repairer, 198 Pearl, b. 80 Grove.
" Elizabeth, b. 36 Collins.
" Elizabeth B. at Hartford Fire Ins. Co. 53 Trumbull, b. Wethersfield t.
" Elizabeth M. Mrs. h. 130 Retreat.
" Ellen, h.r. 39 Forest.
" Emma Mrs. dressmaker, 1208, b. 1208 Main.
" Emma J. Mrs. h.u. 53 Pleasant.
" Ernest W. toolmkr. at 9 Sig. h. 1185 Broad.
" Erwin B. b. 10 Wyllys.
" Ethel M. stenographer at Popes, b. 38 West.
" Eugene A. jewelry, 208 Asy. b. 113 Trumbull.
" Eugene R. clerk, 859 Main, h. 24 Belden.
" Eugene S. (Clark, Diamond & C.) h. Poquonock v.
" F. Dewey, dentist, b. 40 Wooster.
" Frank, driver, 1130 Main, h. 22 Windsor.
" Frank, motorman St. Ry. 115 State.
" Frank A. b. 2 Holcomb.
" Frank E. clerk at 95 Pleasant, b. 172 Clark.
" Franklin, office with U. H. Brockway & Co. merchant tailors, 132 State, b. U. S. hotel.
" Frederick B. clerk, 1084 Mn. b. 165 Clark.
" Frederick H. clerk, 115 Pearl, b. 439 Capitol.
" Fred. P. packer, 254 Pearl, b. Manchester t.
" Frederick W. trav. salesman at Lincoln, Seyms & Co. 34 Market, h. Waterbury t.
" George B. builder, 199, h. 199 Barbour.
" Geo. D. discount clerk at United States Bank, 872 Main, b. West Hartford t.
" George E. butcher, 160 Windsor av b. 136 High.
" George H. Rev. h. 125 Washington.
" George J. patternm. 33 Wells, b. 52 Capitol.
" George L. (C. & Phelps,) h. 189 High.
" George N. clerk at Belknap & Warfield, bookstore, 77 Asylum, b. 13 Capitol.
" Grace, h.u. 10½ Ford.
" Harmony E. wid. Seth H. h. 14 Wyllys.
" Harriet A. b. 427 Main, rm. 25.
" Harriet E. wid. Albert, matron at Union Depot, h. 33 Walnut.
" Harry A. carpenter, h. 78 Madison av.
" Harry W. adv. manager at Evening Post, 23 Asylum, l. 389 Main.
" Henry S. mach. at 31 Wells, b. 6 Buckingham.
" Henry W. b., 389 Main.
" Herbert G. civil eng. h. Windsor av. station 4.
" Horace, student at Yale, b. 14 Prospect.
" Howell G. clerk at 61 Far. b. 24 Babcock.
" James, h. 5 Kilbourn.
" James J. clerk, 721 Main, b.2u. 152 Allyn.
" Jas. H. coachman at 268, b. 268 Farmington.
" James M. steamfitter, 440, b. 739 Asylum.
" John, h.u. 34 Wilson.

Clark John, (*Hunter & Clark,*) h. 15 Windsor.
" John, laborer, Colts, b. Charter Oak hall.
" John, nightwatchm. 142 Russ, h. 106 Ward.
" John C. foreman, 581 Capitol, h.u. 10 Imlay.
" John J. assembler, 581 Capitol, b. 34 Wilson.
" John J. saloon, 245 State, h. 226 Jefferson.
" John L. bkkpr. 87 Asylum, h. 67 Windsor av.
" John S. (*C., Diamond & C.*) h. 64 Bluehills.
" Joseph C. driver, b.2u. 1½ East.
" Joseph D. machinist, h. 523 Main.
" Joseph M. bkkpr. at 48 Ann, h. 163 Clark.
" Josiah C. manager at 721 Main, rm. 19, h. 153 Allyn.
" Julia Mrs. b. 46 Seymour.
" Julius G. mechanic, 1 Laurel, b.u. 11 Imlay.
" Kittie Spencer Mrs. b. 90 Ann.
" Levi G. painter at 20 Central, b. 16½ Pratt.
" Lewis G. clerk, Brown, Thomson & Co. 942 Main, b. 13 Avon.
" Lucy M. teacher, 690 Asy. b. 20 Atwood.
" Luella T. wid. Addison, h.u. 17 Belden.

MME. M. E. CLARK, the gifted business and test medium, at 1273 Main st. Hartford, who has an established reputation for mediumist work by correspondence. Persons sending articles of their own with $1 and stamp, will receive prompt attention.

Clark M E. Mme. medium, 1273 Main.
" M. Isabel, stenographer at Conn. General Life Ins. Co. 49 Pearl, b. 67 Windsor av.
" Mahlon N. at Phœnix Insurance Co. 64 Pearl, h. 38 Willard.
" Marcellus N. salesman, h. 223 Asy. rm. 112.
" Margaret, wid. John, h. 199 Barbour.
" Margaret, wid. Joseph C. h.2u. 1½ East.
" Marion D. stenogr. 197 Asy. b. 40 Wooster.
" Martin T. cigarmaker at 867, b. 542 Main.
" Mary,daughter late David Clark,h.244 Main.
" Mary, wid. Andrew D. b. 244 Main.
" Mary, wid. James, h.u. 47 Linden.
" Mary A. wid. Lemuel, b.u. 265 Wethersfield.
" Mary E. wid. Henry H. h. 427 Mn. rm. 25.
" Mary M. b. 10 Foot Guard pl.
" Maud,stenographer,Popes, b. 129 Hamilton.
" May E. dressmaker at 199, b. 199 Barbour.
" Merlin F. roofer, 19, h. 19 Center.
" Miles, farmer, h.r. 60 Bluehills.
" Olin H. at Ætna Life Insurance Co. 650, h. 650 Main.
" Osmyn P. toolm. at 476 Cap. h. 253 Putnam.
" Peter, brickmaker, b. Windsor av.
" & Phelps, livery stables, r. 995 Main.
George L. Clark. George M. Phelps.
" Ray, clerk at 323 Asylum, b. 172 Clark.
" Richard J. teamster, 250 State,h. 33½ Front.
" Robert G. draughtsm. 1 Laurel, h.u. 40 N.B.
" Rose, b. 181 State.
" Sophia A. wid. Russell, h. 24 Belden.
" Samuel, (*C. & Smith,*) b. Wethersfield t.
" Samuel, laborer, h. 49 Francis.
" Samuel, laborer, b.r. 24 South Prospect.
" Samuel A. mach. at 9 Sig. h.2u. 397 Capitol.
" Samuel P. roofer, h. 114 Mather.

Clark Seymour,forem.124 Front,h.2u. 13 Talcott.
" Sidney Williams, commission agent, 904 Main, rms. 75, 76, h. 40 Willard.
**CLARK & SMITH,** job and book printers, 49 Pearl.          *See page 95.*
Samuel Clark.     Est. Andrew Smith.
" Stella, musician,336 Weth. h. 53 Pleasant.
" Stephen E. musician, b. 1120 Main.
" Susan B. Mrs. h.u. 16 Florence.
" Susan T. h. 799 Asylum.
" Susie, h. 8 Gold.
" Susie B. cook, b. 3 Farmington.
" Thomas, tallyman, 95 Ple. b. 227 Market.
" Thomas A. optician, l. 1246 Main.
" Thomas J. painter, h. 1113 Main.
" Thomas J. Mrs. boardinghouse, 1202 Main.
" W. F. rubberworker, h. 49 Francis.
" Walter, molder at Alfred Ricker's, 26 Potter, h. 25 Barnard.
" Walter B. asst. supt. fire alarm, 43 Pearl, h. 51 Capitol.
" Walter S. inspector, 581 Cap. h.u. 195 Park.
" Walter waiter str. Hartford, 285 State.
" Wayne D. clerk, 155 Asylum, b. 150 Allyn.
" William, waiter str. Middletown, 285 State.
CLARK WM. B. president, Ætna Insurance Company, 666 Main, h. 268 Farmington.
                              *See pages 442, 443.*
**CLARK WILLIAM M.** bellhanger, locksmith and electrician, 22 Church, h. 933 Main, rm. 43.
" William M. Jr. U.S.A. b. 933 Main.
" Wm. P. collector, 118 Asy. h. 230 Weth.
" Winnibell M. teacher Brown school, kindergarten, 160 Market, b.2u. 16 Florence.
**CLARKE CHAS. H.** attorney at law, 3 Asylum, h. 18 Garden.
" & Duffy, merchant tailors, 73 Asylum.
James Clarke.          Robert J. Duffy.
" E. W. & Son, asphalt pavers, r. 32 Village.
Rienzi A. Clarke.
" Elias R. clerk at 57 Albany, h.u. 271 High.
" Ellis E. machinist at Popes, h. 12 Babcock.
" Elma A.wid. Horace P. nurse, b. 28 Hopkins.
" George H. machinist at 1 Flow. b. 157 Cap.
" Gertrude F. stenographer at Pope Mfg. Co. b. 38 West.
" James, (*C. & Duffy,*) h. 23 Evergreen.
" L. Walter, asst. secretary Connecticut Fire Ins. Co. 51 Prospect, h. 191 Farmington.

Clarke Maud, stenographer at Pope Mfg. Co. b. 129 Hamilton.
" Rienzi A.(E.W.C.&Son,)h.521 Prospect av.
" Sarah P.wid. Elbridge W. h.521 Prospect av
" Sidney E. attorney, 884 Main, h. 15 Spring.
" Walter Irving, h. 227 High.
" William F. laborer,690 Park, b.49 Francis.
" Wm. F. night dep. 42 Seyms, h. Windsor av.
Clarkin Agnes M. clerk at Brown, Thomson & Co. 942 Main, b. 81 Maple.
" Catherine M. wid. Peter, nurse, b.u. 147 Shel.
" Ella B. stenographer, 142 Russ, b. T.v.
" Eugene, clerk, 745 Main, h. 112 Huyshope.
" Michael M. (McIntire & C.) h. 987 Main.
" Peter A. b.u. 81 Maple.
" William, steamfitter at 164 State, h.2u. 73 Williams.
Clarkson James H. ornamenter at 438 Asylum, h. E.H.t.
Clary Annie A. wid. R. John, b. 102 Hungerford.
" Frank, driver at 156, b. 156 Front.
" Michael, machinist, h. 73 Temple.
" William, engineer, h.u. 50 Westland.
" ☞ see also Clarey; Cleary.
Claudecrant Claude E. helper at 15 Trumbull, b. Burnside v.
Claussen Ed. E. mechanical engineer, 904 Main, rm. 38, h. 255 Putnam.
Clausson Matthew, laborer, h.2u. 81 Sheldon.
Clawson Ellen, wid. James, h. 238 Park.
Clay Charles E. managing editor Telegram, 12 Central, b. 26 State.
" Edwin, machinist at Popes, h.u.r. 1239 Main.
" William, h. 68 Clark.
Clayton Frederick, supt. 721 Main, h. 3 Wash.
Clearing house, 803 Main.
Clearkin John, laborer, h. 112 Huyshope.
Cleary Frank M. driver, h. 72 Wooster.
" Henry, driver, 48 Ann, b.2u. 63 Flower.
" James M. laborer, 690, b. 902 Park.
" John, printer, h. 35 Avon.
" John J. screwmaker at 476 Capitol, h. 13 Lawrence.
" John S. teamster for city, h. 427 Broad.
" John W. driver at 48 Ann. h.2u. 63 Flower.
" Jos. N. bookkeeper at 902, b. 902 Park.
" Kate, wid. Charles, laundress, 34 Pratt, h. 206 Asylum.
" Michael, receiving clerk at 581 Capitol, b. 258 New Park.
" Michael T. brazier, Popes, b. 258 New Park.
" Patrick, ostler, 29 Wells, b. 33 Wooster.
" Patrick, laborer, b.u. 71 Windsor.
" Patrick H. caterer, b. 29 Heath.
" Thomas, laborer, b. 125 Barbour.
" ☞ see also Clary.
Cleasby Harold L. student at Trinity college, b. 6 Mahl.
" William H. salesman, h. 6 Mahl.
Cleaveland Frank E. lawyer and legal blanks, 66 State, h. 4 Florence.
" ☞ see also Cleveland.
Clemens Elizabeth, at 965 Main, b.u. 84 Ward.
" Everett O. mach. at N.Y.R. h.u.62 Bkm.
" James, b.u. 84 Ward.

Clemens Jennie, clerk at 956 Main, b. 84 Ward.
" John, filer at 581 Capitol, h.u. 173 Zion.
" John, laborer, stone pits, h. 173 Zion.
" Samuel L. author, (Mark Twain) b. 351 Far.
" Wilbur, at Popes, b.u. 84 Ward.
Clement D. V. conductor St.Ry. 115 State.
" John K. student at Trinity College, 9 Jarvis hall, Summit.
" Martin W. student Trinity College, 26 Jarvis hall, Summit.
Clements Clifford E. at 788 Park, h. 24 Amity.
" W. H. Mrs. dressmaker, 68, h. 68 Heath.
" Wm. H. laundry, 788 Park, h. 68 Heath.
Clemons Henry D. forem. at 476 Cap. h. 97 Allen pl.
" Lizzie, wid. Edward, b. 83 Allen pl.
Clemson Andrew, woodworker at 5 Mechanic, h. Manchester t.
Clen Charles, laborer, h.2u. 82 Sheldon.
Cleveland Annie I. wid. John, h. 134 Sigourney.
" Celia T. clerk at Brown, Thomson & Co. 942, b. 884 Main.
" Edmund J. h. 59 Beacon.
" Edmund J. Jr. b. 59 Beacon.
" Edward S. water commissioner, h. 134 Sig.
" Frank, mach. at 1 Flow. h. 41 Hungerford.
" Orange, com. dep. 42 Seyms, h. 142 Mather.
" Vernet E. clerk, 702 Main, b. 19 Capitol.
" William, farmhand, 55, b. 55 Bluehills.
" ☞ see also Cleaveland.
Clifford Alfred P. engineer at 5 Athenæum, h. 217 Sargeant.
" Ellen, wid. Patrick, h. 293 Market.
" Frank, paperhanger 88 Mar. h. 13½ John.
" Henry A. evangelist, Religious Census, 1091 Main, b. 78 High.
" James, hodcarrier, b.2u. 12 So. Prospect.
" John, b.2u. 1442 Broad.
" John, farmer, b. 2 Orchard.
" John J. Jr. h.u. 263 High.
" Mary, h.2u. 95 Shelden.
" Mary, wid. Cornelius, h.r. 98 New Britain.
" Mary, wid. William, h. 2 Orchard.
" Michael P. saloon, 117, h. 113 Windsor.
" Patrick, laborer at 1 Flow. h. 1442 Broad.
" William, laborer at 8 Front, b. 2 Orchard.
Climan I. tailor, 108 Pratt, h. 265 Market.
Climouski Charles, laborer, b. 95 Sheldon.
" ☞ see Klaman.
Cline Edward N. molder 1 Flow. h. 1444 Broad.
" Frank, polisher, b.u. 66 Potter.
" Fred. conductor St.Ry. b. 3 Chapel.
" Lillian A. musician, b. 1432 Broad.
" Marie J. musician, b. 1432 Broad.
" Michael, molder at 1 Flower, h. 1432 Broad.
" Paul, laborer, h.u. 66 Potter.
" Wm. J. employed 273 Asy. b.u. 66 Potter.
" ☞ see also Kline; Clyne.
Clintsman Fred W. clerk, 732 Main, h. 152 Weth.
" Grace E. b. 152 Wethersfield.
" Susan R. Mrs. h. 152 Wethersfield.
" William D. clerk, b. 152 Wethersfield.
Clodge Jennie Mrs. boardinghouse, h.u.234 Allyn.
Clonnan James H. foreman at Pope Tube Co. h. 47 Francis.
" Joseph W. clerk at 450 Main, b. 47 Francis.

Clonnan Mary, wid. Andrew, h. 47 Francis.
" Walter P. steamfitter, b. 47 Francis.
Cloonan Catherine, h. 56 Talcott.
" John, helper at 1 Flower, h. 1430 Broad.
Close Alfred A. oper. 6 Central, b.2u. 21 North.
" James H. h.2u. 21 North.
" William H. helper at Popes, b2.u. 21 North.
Clossey Charles, foreman, b. 5 Vandyke.
Closson Chas. J. baggagem. N.Y.R. b. 30 Spring.
Clough Bros. express, h. 11 Morris.
   Clarence D. Clough.   Nathaniel Clough.
" Clarence D. (Clough Bros.) b. 11 Morris.
" Emma J. clerk 223 Asylum, b. 58 Church.
" Fred W. compositor at Popes, h. 28 West.
" George H. screwm. 476 Cap. h. 23 Wolcott.
" Horace W. rubberworker, h. 17 James.
" John R. screwm. at 476 Cap. b. 11 Morris.
" Lucy, wid. Robert, b. 70 Sheldon.
" Nathaniel, (Clough Bros.) b. 11 Morris.
" Thomas, b. 11 Morris.
" William, h. 11 Morris.
" William Jr. expressman, h.2u. 279 Park.
Cloy Charles E. captain, h. 223 Asylum, rm. 121.
Cloyes Charlotte B. h. 11 Julius.
Cluff William H. filer at Colts, h.2u. 874 Broad.
Clune Patrick, helper at N.Y.R. b. 27 Spruce.
Clutis Carlton E. correpondent Popes, l. 25 Cap.
Clyde Frank S. clerk at 338 Mn. h. 210 Franklin.
" Samuel T. foreman at Colts, h. 3 S. Hudson.
Clyne Thomas, signalman N.Y.R. h.35 Hawthorn.
Coakley Patrick, helper at 54 Arch, b. 159 Law.
" Thomas, helper at 54 Arch, b. 102 Center.
Coate Ernest, carpenter, h.u. 20 Howard.
Coates Ida Mrs. asst. matron, 71 Putnam.
" Thomas, ostler, b.r. 26 Front.
Coatman Thomas, molder at 54 Arch, h. 4 Ellery.
Cobb Elisha L. bkkpr. 149 State, h. Windsor t.
" F. P. (Geo. N. Merrill & Co.) 75 Pratt.
" Frank H. b. 77 Grove.
Cobett Samuel F. mason, h.2u. 26 East.
Cobey John, collector at 721 Main, rm. 33.
" Lucy E. teacher Northwest sch. b. 30 Imlay.
" Minnie, artist at 747 Mn. h. New Britain t.
Coburn Charles, lime, cement, etc. 154 State, h.
   105 Edwards.
" Chas. H. Jr. salesm. 154 State, h. 97 Williams.
" Frank E. clerk at 154 State, h. E.H.t.
" Frank L. machinist, h.u. 21 Kennedy.
" G. Louis (Hartford Undertaking Co.) b.
   106½ Trumbull.
" George B. bkkpr. at 154 State, h. 38 Mahl.
" George L. Rev. b.u. 49 Webster.
" George L. (Hartford Undertaking Co.) b.
   106½ Trumbull.
" Herbert E. teamster, 154 State, h. E.H.t.
" Jonathan, mach. at 1 Flower, h. 51 Grand.
" Julia, nurse, 122, l. 122 High.
" ☞ see also Colburn.
Cochran L. B. physician U.S. Army, b. 43 Far.
" Robert W. pressman at Popes, h. N.B. t.
Cochrane Hattie E. stenographer at State Cap-
   itol, b. Newington t.
" Robert, cabinetmaker at L. T. Fenn, 613
   Main, h. New Britain t.
" ☞ see also Corcoran.

Coclough Kate, wid. Jos. boardingh. 198 Allyn.
Code James, painter at 17 Elm, h. 15 South Laurel.
Codet George W. b. 202 Barbour.
Cody Charles, bartender, l. 1136 Main.
" Ellen E. wid. John, h. 16 Jefferson.
" Geo. W. painter, h. 52 Retreat.
" Helen, milliner, 16, b. 16 Jefferson.
" John, laborer at 556 Capitol, h. 5 Riverside.
" John, helper at 8, h.2u.r. 13 Front.
" John H. Mrs. h.u. 95 Seymour.
" Lillian M. teacher Wethersfield av. school,
   b. 95 Seymour.
" M. Isabel, b. 16 Jefferson.
" Nellie T. teacher, b.u. 95 Seymour.
" William V. plumber, b. 16 Jefferson.
Coe Carleton W. forem. at 476 Cap. h. Windsor t.
" Clara M. elocutionist, b. 8 Spring.
" Clinton S. mach. at 476 Cap. h. 50 Judson.
" Charles C. Mrs. (E. M.) h. 320 Farmington.
" Ernest W. mach. at 142 Russ, h. 85 Allen pl.
" Felix, h. 17 Morgan.
" Isaac H. at Ætna Insurance Co. 666 Main,
   h. 42 Sumner.
" O. W. freight clerk str. Hartford, b. Por. t.
" Theodore I. draughtsman at 904 Main, rm.
   87, b. 42 Sumner.
Coffee Frank J. mach. at N.Y.R. h.2u. 74 Sanford.
Coffey James E. at 370 Front, h. 61 Elliott.
" James J. helper 142 Russ, b. 1143 Broad.
" Jere. H. blacksmith at 1 Flow. h.37 Harbison.
" John, firem. at Pope Tube Co. h. 24 Grace.
" John H. Jr. blacks. 1 Flow. b. 37 Harbison.
" John J. laborer, h.2u. 20 Trumbull.
" Nellie A. at 690 Park, b. 37 Harbison.
" Peter G. mach. at 30 Cushman, h. 27 John.
" Richard, b. 2 Holcomb.
" Timothy, foreman blacksmith department,
   Billings & Spencer Mfg. Co. 142 Russ,
   h.u. 74 Ward pl.
Coffin Marietta O. wid. Geo. B. b. 46 Bellevue.
Coffrin Erma P. stenographer at 68 Pratt, b.u.
   70 Washington.
" Merrill L. carpenter at Strickland & Shea,
   20 Potter, h.u. 70 Washington.
Coggeshall Evelyn C. stenog. at Popes, b. 217 Ash.
Coggles Thos. conductor, P.&R. h.u. 70 Walnut.
Coggshall Albert O. buffer at Wm. Rogers Mfg.
   Co. 66 Market, h. 130 Clark.
" D. Frank, clerk, 370 Albany, h.u. 130 Clark.
" Frank B. driver at Brown, Thomson & Co.
   942 Main, b.u. 130 Clark.
Coggswell John B. carpenter, h. 161 Capitol.
Coghlan Wm. harnessm. at 1222 Mn. h. 80 Pearl.
Cogswell Frank L. Jr. at 84 Tru. b.u. 4 Chapel.
" Henry J. jeweler, 84 Trumbull, h.u. 4 Chapel.
Cohen Araham, tailor at 19, b. 19 Church.
" Gustav, clothing, 115, h.u. 143 Front.
" Harry F. bkkpr. 131 Main, h. 124 Jefferson.
" Jacob, buffer at Wm. Rogers Mfg. Co. 66
   Market, b. 25 Kilbourn.
" Joseph, (C. & Silberman,) h. 57 Front.
" Joseph, teacher, h. 194 Front.
" Moses, h. 72 Windsor.
" & Silberman, tailors, 64 Trumbull.
   Joseph Cohen.   Charles Silberman.

Cohen Sidney, buyer at 956 Main, h. 173 High.
Cohn A.&Co.leaftobacco,H.Palmer,agt.231 State
" Abram, mach. at 1 Flower, b. 46 Portland.
" Abram, ragpicker, h.2u. 258 Front.
" Bros. sign painters, 1174 Main.
    Simon Cohn.          Morris Cohn.
" Elias, watchmaker, 104 Tru. h. 11 Morgan.
" Frank, barber, 206, h. 201 Front.
" Henry, grocer, 29, h.2u. 29 Mulberry.
" Isaac, clothing, 110 State, h.u. 78 Morgan.
" Isadore, butcher, h.r. 87 Windsor.
" Jacob, peddler, h. 64 Pleasant.
" Jacob, shoemaker, h. 80 Morgan.
" Meyer Rev. hardware, 180, h. 180 Front.
" Meyer, tailor, 35, h. 35 Sheldon.
" Michael, peddler, h.r. 87 Windsor.
" Morris, (C. Bros.) h. 180 Front.
" Morris, shoemaker, 115, h. 115 Front.
" Phillip, peddler, h.u. 79 Avon.
" R. & Co. leather and findings. 1234 Main.
    Robert Cohn.         Eff. Congreso.
" Robert, (R. C. & Co.) b. 44 North.
" Rosie, confec. and groc. 55, h. 55 Morgan.
" Samuel, helper at 1 Flower, h. 279 Market.
" Simon, (C. Bros.) h. 180 Front.
" Thersie, grocer, 29, h.2u. 29 Mulberry.
" ☞see also Cohen; Cowan; Cowen; Kohn.
Coho Emily R. teacher at E. M. Huntsinger, 30
    Asylum, h. 22 Linden.
Colberg Walfred, mech. at 581 Cap. b.r. 9 Hung.
Colbert Bertha, wid. Frank, h.r. 44 Wells.
" Daniel, saloon, 130Front, b. 7 Kilbourn.
" Ellen, wid. Michael, h.2u.r. 157 Maple.
" James Francis, b.2u.r. 157 Maple.
" Mary, h. 1492 Broad.
Colburn Chas. M., Adams hotel, 370 Albany.
" ☞see also Coburn.
Colby Cynthia L. wid. Alonzo, h. 62 Francis.
" Fred W. molder at A. T. Ricker, 26 Potter,
    h. 42 Franklin.
" George, clerk 231 State, b. 849 Windsor av.
" James H. molder at Alfred T. Ricker, 26
    Potter, h. 23 Lincoln.
" Mary Mrs. nurse, 100, b. 100 Madison av.
Coldwell Harriet, wid. Richard, h. 109 Mather.
" Julia, wid. Edward, h. 42 Windsor.
Cole Albert E. laborer, 242, b. 242 Wethersfield.
" Alice L. teacher High school, b. 213 Garden.
" Chas. J. compositor, 2 State, b. 15 Kennedy.
" Charles W. constable,2 State, h. 15 Kennedy.
" Elisabeth H. wid. Chas. J. h. 106 Woodland.
" Frank E. mechanic, h. 89 Williams.
" Frank J. glasscutter, h. 76 Bellevue.
" George, laborer, h. 86 John.

DRS. H. P. & HILLS COLE, Physicians. Office,
    Cheney building, 926 Main, room 82.
H. P. COLE M.D.          HILLS COLE, M.D.
    Surgeon.             Medical Electricity.
Hours—11 to 12 A.M.     Hours—9 to 12 A.M.
    3 to 4 P.M.             1 to 5 P.M.
House, 133 Sigourney.   Telephone 1012-6.

Cole Harlan P. physician and surgeon, 926
    Main, rm. 82, h. 133 Sigourney.
" Henry, grocer, 2, h. 2 Talcott.
" Henry C. rubberw. 690 Park, b. 240 Laurel.
" Henry J. clerk. b. 2 Talcott.
" Hills, physician and medical electricity, 926
    Main, rm. 82, h. 133 Sigourney.
" James, teamster, b. 128 Albany.
" John C. mach. at 690 Park, h. 55 Putnam.
" Morris, peddler, h.u. 152 Front.
" R. Brooks, conductor, St.Ry. l.u. 1293 Main.
" Richard H. student, b. 106 Woodland.
" Warren W. carptr. at N.E.R. h.231 Barbour.
" William F. clerk at 2 State, b. 15 Kennedy.
Coledezky Abraham, dyer, b.u. 68 Morgan.
" Ozias, grocer, 68, h.u. 68 Morgan.
Coleman Albert E.mach.at 1 Flow.b.u.33Babcock.
" Albert H. collector, h. 167 Clark.
" Annie E. dressmaker, b. 15 Belden.
" Cornelius F. saloon, 107, l. 452 Main.
" Emma B. clerk, Popes, b.u. 167 Bellevue.
" Emma J. at 336 Asylum, b. 88 Retreat.
" Francis H. b. 221 Garden.
" George C. at 745 Main, b.u. 11 Liberty.
" James A. conductor St.Ry. b. 48 Prospect.
" James J. at Ætna Life Ins. Co. h. 7 Goodwin.
" Joanna, wid. John, h. 15 Belden.
" John, clerk at 108, b. 98 Trumbull.
" John, porter at 1047 Main, l. 1436 Broad.
" John, woodyard, James st. h. 938 Park.
" John D. clerk at 193 Asylum, b. 15 Belden.
" John F. clerk, b. 1436 Broad.
" John J. real estate, 545 Main, h. 37 John.
" John P. solderer at 62 Mar. h.u. 65Governor.
" John W. clerk at 745 Main, h. 60 Wooster.
" Kidney, laborer, h.2u. 194 Sheldon.
" Lizzie M. clerk at 942 Main, b. 15 Belden.
" Lucy, wid. Levi, h.u. 167 Bellevue.
" Mary, at 235 State, b. 15 Belden.
" Mary, wid. Daniel, h.u. 11 Liberty.
" Mary A. clerk at 372 Asylum, b. 11 Liberty.
" Mary E.teacher N.E.school,b.u.167 Bellevue.
" Mary R. wid. James, h. 33 Hungerford.
" Michael A. dropforger Popes, h.u. 69 Laurel.
" Nellie, clerk at 956 Main, b. 15 Belden.
" Thomas, enameler at Popes, h. 46 Hicks.
" Thomas J. teamster, h.r. 44 Village.
" Thomas P. at N.E.R. h.u. 20 Hicks.
" William H.druggist,1391 Main,h.55 Church.
" ☞see also Collman.
Coles Albert E. fireman on steamer Hartford,
    h.2u. 5 Whitman.
" Burnice, clerk at 835 Main, b. 89 Williams.
" Charles, bartender, l. 367 Asylum.
" Chas. H. mach. at Colts, b. 183 Seymour.
" Clifford M. lineman, 266 Pearl,b.u. 545 Main.
" Edgar R. printer at Phœnix Insurance Co.
    64 Pearl, b. 14 Charlotte.
" Edna L. clerk at 884 Main, b. 89 Edwards.

COLES FRANCIS, *abatement of taxes,* printer at Phœnix Ins. Co. 64 Pearl, h. 14 Charlotte.
" Jennie, b.u. 345 Wethersfield.
" Mary, h.u. 9 Kinsley.
" Mary, wid. William, b. 183 Seymour.
" Rosa Mrs. b. 3 Huntley.
" Samuel, laborer, h. 49 Mather.
" William. apprentice at Colts, b. 97 Capitol.
" William H.foreman at Colts, h.183 Seymour.
" ☞ *see also Cowles.*
Coley Patrick, helper, b. 21 Lawrence.
Colishaw ☞ *see Cowlishaw.*
Colla Felix, clerk at C. S. Brewer & Co. 238 Asylum, h.2u. 42 Village.
" J. Peter, clerk, 174 Asylum, b.2u.42 Village.
" Joseph, carpenter, b. 75 Hudson.
" Paul, clerk at 119 Pearl, b. 42 Village.
Collard John A. clerk, 835 Main, h.133 Trumbull.
" John P. clerk at 25 Central, h. 133 Trumbull.
" Lester W. draughtsm. 1 Flow. h. 104 Laurel.

# MONEY TO LOAN
## On Watches and Diamonds,
### No. 71 ASYLUM STREET.

COLLATERAL LOAN CO., F. N. Sharpe, 71 Asylum, rm. 10.
Collazo Lila S. dressmaker, h. 67 Green.
Collier Arthur, janitor, b. 2 Church.
" Arthur J. conductor, P.&R. h. Winsted t.
Collin Alphonse, carptr. Colts, h.u. 3 Seymour.
Collins Abbott C. (fish and game commissioner,) at Conn. Mutual Life Ins. Co. 783 Main, h. 18 Preston.
" Adella E. dressm. at 71, h. 71 Asylum, rm. 11.
" Alfred B. foreman, b.u. 138 Mather.
" Alice Mrs. boardinghouse, 1173 Main.
" Ann E. housekeeper, 63 Church.
" Arthur,·at and b. Hospital farm.
" Atwood, president Security Co. 62 Pearl, h. 1010 Asylum.
" Catherine, wid. James, h. 17 Howard.
" Charles B. engineer N.Y.R. h. 20 Atlantic.
" Charles I. bookkeeper, h. 1173 Main.
" Clarence Lyman, b. 1054 Asylum.
**COLLINS COMPANY,** works at Collinsville, Conn.; office 785 Main.
*See page 521.*
" Cornelius J. machinist, h. 68 Avon.
" Cornelius S. switchman, h. 108 Windsor.
" Cornelius W. foreman at 115 State, h.u. 4½ Hungerford pl.
" Daniel, hackdriver, h. 20 Trinity.
" Dennis, switchman, N.Y.R. h.u. 21 Loomis.
" Dryden P. carpenter, h.u. 66 Wooster.
" E. Miss, h. 1054 Asylum.
" Edward, machinist at 40 Governor, h.3u. 97 Main.
" Edward J. operator, b. 4 Union.
" Emily P. wid. Zimri, b. 187 High.
" Eugene A. clerk at 97 Asy. b.u. 30 Hudson.
" Faith W. b. 149 High.
" Francis L. manager 711 Main, b. 4 Union.

Collins Frank, machinist, h. 17 Howard.
" Frank, teamster, b. 108 Windsor.
" Frank E. nightclerk at postoffice, b.18 Avon.
" Geo. B. conductor St.Ry. h.u. 2 Winthrop.
" Geo. H. ins. clerk, 197 Asy. b. 75 Madison.
" George L. machinist, b. 30 Hudson.
" Helen R. Mrs. h. 99 Farmington.
" Henrietta A. Mrs. l. 56 Trumbull.
" Howard S. h. 99 Farmington.
" Ira, barber, 985 Main, h. 24 Church.
" Irving, bookkeeper, b. 1173 Main.
" James M. machinist, N.Y.R. b. 66 Hopkins.
" Jeremiah, laborer 107 Grove, h.u. 87 Front.
" Jeremiah, ostler, h.u. 110 Windsor.
" Jerry, carpenter, b.2u. 1053 Broad.
" John, fireman at 70 Com. h. 3 Elliott ct.
" John, deckhand, str. Middletown, 285 State.
" John H. teamster at 46 Ann, h.u. 7 Mays ct.
" John J. carptr. at r. 116 Mar. b. 1053 Broad.
" John J. manager at 80, l. 80 State.
" John P. *board of relief,* butcher at 1046 Main, h. 31½ Russell.
" John T. inventor at 26 Laurel, h. 96 Haw.
" Joseph, helper, b. 4 Forest.
" Joseph A. carpenter, b. 10 Arch.
" Joseph F. clerk, b. 30 Hudson.
" Joseph P. clerk at 711 Main, b. 4 Union.
" Leonard J. law student 847 Mn.b.109 Wooster.
" Lucius D. clerk 100 Asy. b.u. 66 Wooster.
" Margaret T. wid. William, h. 4 Union.
" Mark, engineer at 100 Com. h. 140 Albany.
" Mary, h.u. 133 Market, rm. 5.
" Mary E. wid. William, h. 28 Village.
" Mary F. h. 94 Woodland.
" Maurice, lineman at 247 Pearl, b. 168 Allyn.
" May F. stenog. at Popes, b. 12 Walnut.
" Michael, hackman, b. 20 Trinity.
" Morris, driver at 366 Main, h. 30 Hudson.
" Samuel, (S. Collins & Co.) b. 58 Oak.
" Samuel & Co. flagging,stone,etc.283 Sheldon.
   Samuel Collins.   Charles Courtice.
" Thomas, stitcher at 15 Tru. h.2u. 35 S.Pro.
" Timothy, teamster, r. 211 Bellevue.
" William, b.u.r. 1128 Main.
" William A. farmer, b. 71 Asylum, room 20.
" Wm. Erastus Mrs.(Era Lee,) h. 990 Asylum.
" William G. h.u. 71 Asylum, rm. 20.
" Wm.H.stationmaster Un.Depot,h. 232 High.
" Wm. J. driver at 47 Ann, b.u. 168 Allyn.
" Wm. J. rubberworker at 690, h. 771 Park.
" Wm. J. tilesetter at 164 State, b.u. 33 Elm.
" Wm. M. clerk at 1028, h. 1244 Main.
" Wm. V. accountant P.&R. h. 12 Walnut.
" ☞ *see also Kollenz.*
Collis Alison V. agt. 904 Mn. rm. 12, h. 58 Allen pl.
Collman Augusta, wid. Francis H. b.221 Garden.
" Francis H. mail clerk, b. 221 Garden.
Collorton Patrick, enameler, Popes,h.90 Sheldon.
Colloque Orrok P. student, 7 Northam, Summit.
Collum Annie Mrs. boardinghouse, 31 Spring.
" George S. president Collum Manufacturing Co. 9 Asylum, h. 68 Pratt, rm. 27.
" Manufacturing Co. 9 Asylum.
" Mary F. electric needle specialist, h. 68 Pratt, rm. 33.

# COMMERCIAL HOUSE,

**Opposite Allyn House,**

## 165 Asylum Street.

### G. F. JOHNSON, PROPRIETOR.

## Good Home for Commercial Men.

**TWO MINUTES WALK FROM DEPOT.**

Colonial The, G. S. Ayer, proprietor, 981 Main.
" Club, 47 Prospect.
Colony May E. printer at 141 Pearl, b.166 Russ.
Colpitts Arthur B. employee 59½ Tru. h.50 Grand.
" Manfred, clerk at 369 Capitol, h.u. 91 Russ.
" Samuel C. cutter at 59½ Tru. b. 91 Russ.
" Wm. W. harnessm. at 8 Sig. h.u. 91 Russ.
Colson Frank, fireman at 152 Asylum.
Colston Theo. machinehand at Colts, h. 131 Jef.
Colt David H. clerk at Popes, b. Elmwood v.
" Jane A. wid. Samuel H. b. 310 Collins.
" Samuel Mrs. (Elizabeth H.) h. "Armsmear,"
    30 Wethersfield.
" Samuel T. inspector at Colts, h. Farmington t.
Colton Charles A. at 555 Capitol, h. 106 Bluehills.
" Charles. b. 90 Church.
" Daniel P. secretary Hfd. Electric Light Co.
    266 Pearl, b. 31 Allen pl.
" Edward M. packer, 30 Cush. h. 127 Bluehills.
" Frank B. market gardner, 90, h. 90 Bluehills.
" Lester H. Mrs. h. 31 Allen pl.
" Maria A. wid. Fred P. h.u. 210 Windsor av.
COLTON OLCOTT B. (Smith, Bourn & Co.) h.
    255 Laurel. See page 547.
" Sidney B. market gardener, h.u. 90 Bluehills.
" Walter S. beltm. at 15 Tru. h.u. 64 Wooster.

## COLTS PATENT FIRE ARMS MANUFACTURING CO.
17 Vandyke. See page 543.

Columbe Joseph, barber, h.u. 1208 Main.

## COLUMBIA BICYCLES, See p 796.
" & Hartford Bicycle Agency. See p. 485.

## COLUMBIA BREWING CO. lager
beer and ale, 245 Windsor. See p. 417.
" Hotel, T. F. Meagher, prop. 28 Market.
Columbus Joseph L. carpenter, h. 27 Judson.
Colver Sarah B. h.u. 18 Congress.
" ☞see also Culver.
Combs Edward F. lab. 20 Vredendale, h. 26 Gov.
" Foster W. b. 995 Windsor av.
Comeford Elizabeth, milliner, b. 21 Main.
Comer John, helper, h. 1035 Broad.
" Joseph J. timekeeper at Popes, b.1035 Broad.
" Thomas E. mechanic at Popes, b.1035 Broad.
Comfort Powder Co. 61 Albany.
Comiske Charles, carpenter at 1 Flower, h.S.M.t.
Commander Miles, insurance, b. 140 Trumbull.
Commeraw Augusta, laundress, h.u. 8 Gold.
Commercial Cable Co. 3 Central.

COMMERCIAL HOUSE, Geo. F. Johnson. prop.
    165 Asylum. See page 100.
" Record, M. A. Brett, mgr. 190 Pearl.

Commerford Zelotus W. student, Theological
    Seminary, 1507 Broad.
Commerman Simon, tailor at 221 Pearl, h.4 KiLct.
Commier Lizzie, wid. William, h. 488 Main.
Commins Edward, helper at 581, b. 381 Capitol.
Common Council rooms, in City Hall, 800 Main.
Comp Chas. E. operator, 40 Governor, b.89 Main.
" Harry E. repairer at 40 Governor, b.89 Main.
" Nelson, clerk at Brown, Thomson & Co.
    942, h. 89 Main.
" William O. clerk at Brown, Thomson & Co.
    942, b. 89 Main.
Comry Edmonia, wid. Philip, h. 85 Mather.
Comstock Alvin W. stenographer at Pope Mfg.
    Co. b.u. 43 Lincoln.
" Charles S. machinist at Colts, h. 316 Maple.
" Charles W., U. S. district attorney, 65 State,
    h. Montville t.
" Frederic R. architect, 252 Asylum, h.69 Sig.
" Gilbert, h.u. 123 Hungerford.
" Hannah S. wid. Albert H. b. 285 Capitol.
" Harry F. clerk at 1 Flower, h. E.H.t.
" John D. at Hartford Fire Ins. Co. l. 53 Tru.
" John P. at 25 Asylum, h. Newington t.
" Mary, wid. Edward E. h. 206 Asylum, flat 15.
" Royal D. at 252 Asylum, rm. 36, h. 69 Sig.
" Tracy S. clerk at Potter & Payne, 409
    Allyn, b. E.H.t.
Cona Barbello, laborer, h. 78 Charles.
Conant Albert A. b. 375 Laurel.
" Earl B. clerk, Y.M.C.A. b. 315 Pearl.
" George A. clerk superior court, 85 Trum-
    bull, h. 375 Laurel.
" Lillian R. teacher West Middle school,
    927 Asylum, b. 167 Sigourney.
Condolora John, laborer, h. 76 Charles.
Condon George, laborer, b.2u. 15 Mechanic.
" Jerry, roofer, b.r. 20 Commerce.
" John C. helper at 1 Flower, b. 12 Putnam.
" Michael W. coachman at 22 Woodland, h.
    22 Liberty.
" William, plumber, b. 22 Liberty.
Condos A. (Booth & C.) b. 20 Trumbull.
" Harry, clerk at 224 Asy. h. 20 Trumbull.
Condren Annie, h.3u. 6 Ellery.
" Annie, dressmaker at 270 Mn. b.u. 56 Dean.
" Elizabeth A. teacher, b.u. 56 Dean.
" Margaret, dressm. at 270 Main, b.u. 56 Dean.
" Mary, wid. James, b.u. 56 Dean.
" Minnie, clerk at Brown, Thomson & Co. 942
    Main, b.u. 56 Dean.
Condron Catherine, wid. Thos. h.u. 133 Market.
" Hattie, milliner, b. 63 Ward.
" Hetty, wid. John, h. 63 Ward.
" Jas. belt repairer at Colts, h. 50 Vanblock.
" James F. filer at Colts, b. 50 Vanblock.
" James F. laborer, b.u. 54 Front.
" John, coachm. 128 Woodland, h. 255 Ashley.
" John, painter, b. 63 Ward.
" John A. polisher at Colts, b. 50 Vanblock.
" Joseph A. clerk at 48, b.u. 54 Front.
" Margaret, checker at Colts, b. 50 Vanblock.
" Mary L. tailoress, h.2u. 133 Market.
" Patrick, driver at 29, h. 74 Albany.
" Patrick, laborer, h.u. 28 So. Prospect.

Condron Patrick J. painter, 63, b. 63 Ward.
" Thomas, teamster, h.u. 54 Front.
" Thomas F. machinist at 54 Arch, b. 54 Front.
" ☞ see also Conran.
Cone Charles, filer at Colts, b. 3 Squire.
" Charlotte R. clerk at 700 Mn. b. 53 Allen pl.
" Harry F. clerk at 581 Cap. b. 784 Asylum.
" Herbert, fireman str. Hartford, 285 State,
   h.2u. 3 Whitman.
" J. H. & W. E. hardware, etc. 87 & 89 Asy.
   William E. Cone.
" James B. h. 640 Farmington.
" John B. bookkeeper at Ætna National
   Bank, 644 Main, h. 132 Collins.
" John W. b. 55 Bacon.
" Joseph W. at Ætna Insurance Co. 666 Main,
   h. 182 Collins.
" Martha I. wid. Jos. H. h. 784 Asylum.
" Mary C. teacher at West Middle school, 927
   Asylum, h. 55 Beacon.
" Ogden F. machinist at 40 Cushman. h.
   Warehouse Point v.
" Orson T. machinist at I. B. Davis & Son, 40
   Cushman, h. Warehouse Point v.
" W. deckhand tug Ward, 285 State.
" Wm. E. (J. H. & W. E. Cone,) b. Allyn house.
" ☞ see also Cohen; Cohn; Kohn.
Conehoven James G. h.u. 452 Main.
" Theo. H. mach. at 135 Shel. b.u. 452 Main.
Confitto Antonio, laborer, b. 17 Morgan.
" Frank, laborer, b.u. 264 Front.
" Vencenzo, laborer, b.u. 264 Front.
Conforto Bastiano, laborer, b.u. 78 Charles.
Congdon Chas. S. driver at C. S. Brewer & Co.
   240, h. 251 Asylum.
" Herbert B. paperhanger 843 Mn. h 49 John.
" M. fireman str. Middletown, 285 State.
Congreso Eff, (R. Cohn & Co.) b. 44 North.
Conkey Benj. F. carpenter, h. 38 Windsor av.
" D. Frank, traveling salesman at 149 State,
   b. 38 Windsor av.
Conklin Annie, wid. Merrill, h.u. 2 A. Wadsworth.
" C. W. b. 983 Asylum.
" Emory A. brewer at Ropkins & Co. 232
   Sheldon, b. 157 Capitol.
Conklin H. W. & Co. insurance and real estate.
                See page 101.
  H. W. Conklin.   H. S. Conklin.   M. O. Wells.
Conklin H. W. (H. W. C. & Co.) insurance
   and real estate, 9 Central, h. 983 Asylum.
" Harry S. (H. W. C. & Co.) b. 983 Asylum.
" Henry W. inspector at Popes, h.u. 1 Wolcott.
" Jas. H. clerk at 55 Maple, b. 234 Jefferson.
" Jefferson, supt. h. 270 Prospect av. s. Park.
" John, plumber at 11 Haynes, b. 74 Grove.
" John, plumber, 128, b. 126 State.
" John A. agent Citizens' Grocery and Pro-
   vision Co. 267 Main, h. 86 Cedar.
" John P. b.2u. 212 Sheldon.
" John R. bartender at 161 State, b. 586 Park.
" Patrick, laborer, h.2.u. 212 Sheldon.
" Patrick D. laborer at 1 Flower, h. 77 Arch.
" Wm. at Colts, b.2A. Wadsworth.
" William, plumber at 128, b. 126 State.

---

## H. W. CONKLIN & CO.,

## Insurance &

## Real Estate

## Agency,

## 9 CENTRAL ROW.

Conklin Wm. M. machinist at Pratt & Whitney
   Co. 1 Flower, h. 874 Park.
" William P. bookkeeper at First National
   Bank, 50 State, b. 983 Asylum.
Conlan Celia, dressmaker, b. 90 Capitol.
" William H. A. sup. police, h. 127 Maple.
" William J. h. 90 Capitol.
Conley Patrick, laborer, h.u. 88 Sheldon.
" ☞ see also Connelly.
Conlin Daniel, switchm. N.Y.R. h.2u. 46 Portland.
" James, motorman St.Ry. h.2.u. 37 Wdbg.
" James, teamster, h.r. 53 Front.
" Philip F. dropforg. 142 Russ, h.u. 488 Main.
" William J. carptr. at N.Y.R. h. 19 Wolcott.
Connahan Daniel, lab. at 95 Ple. b. 1104 Main.
Conn. Bible Society, 323 Pearl, Y.M.C.A. bldg.
" River Bridge & Highway District Com-
   mission, 650 Main, rm. 64.
**CONNECTICUT BUILDING &**
   **LOAN ASSOCIATION,** 252
   Asylum.       See page 430.
" Car Service Asso'n, Union depot, 466 Asy.
" Children's Aid Society, 223 Asylum, rm. 10.
" Congregational Club, Memorial Hall, 426 Asy.
**CONN. COURANT.**   See page 463.
**CONN. FARMER,** Noah Cressy, M.D,
   editor, 284 Asylum.   See page. 466.
**CONNECTICUT FIRE INSUR-**
   **ANCE CO.** 51 Pros. See page 457.
**CONNECTICUT GENERAL**
   **LIFE INS. CO.** 49 Pearl. See
   page 448.
" Historical Society, 624 Main.
" Home Missionary Society, 426 Asylum.
" Humane Society, 51 Prospect.
" Institute and Industrial School for the
   Blind, 336 Wethersfield.
" League of Art Students Association, 370
   Asylum, rm. 80.
**CONNECTICUT MUTUAL LIFE**
   **INSURANCE CO.** 783 Main.
             See pages 450, 451.
**CONN. POST.** 23 Asylum.
" Prison Association, room 45, in Capitol.
**CONNECTICUT QUARTERLY,**
   66 State.       See page 477.
   George C. Atwell, Editor.
**CONNECTICUT RIVER BANK-**
   **ING CO.** 761 Main.   See page 433.

**CONN. RIVER LUMBER CO.** of Holyoke, G. Fred Smith, 756 Main, rm. 29.

**CONN. RIVER STEAMBOAT CO.**          *See page 555.*

**CONNECTICUT TRUST AND SAFE DEPOSIT CO.** 777, 785 Main.          *See page 437.*

Connell Arthur, clerk, b. 71 Asylum, rm. 18.
" George W. clerk, 843 Main, b. 39 Sisson.
" James Balfour Rev. Olivet Baptist church, h. 39 Sisson.
" James J. clerk at 45 Asylum, b. 29 Hudson.
" Mich. porter at 165 Windsor, h.u. Kennedy.
" Morris, laborer, h.3u.r. 32 Wells.
" Morris F. laborer, b.u.r. 34 So. Prospect.
" Paul, at Popes, b.3u. 32 Wells.
" Thomas, helper at 54 Arch, b. 2 Union.
" Thomas, waiter at station, b. 7 Atlantic.
" Thomas H. ( *O'Brien & C.* ) b. 160 Allyn.
" Timothy, helper at N.Y.R. h.u. 118 Portland.
" William, helper at 356 Main, b.2u. 57½ Gov.
" ☞ *see also McConnell; O'Connell.*
Connelly Ann, wid. Francis, b. 29 Sherman.
" Charlotte, housekeeper at 146, b. 146 Weth.
" Dennis F. driver, b.u.r. 95 Sheldon.
" Francis A. clerk, h. 23 Williams.
" Jerry, night clerk, 651 Mn. h.2u.15 Windsor.
" Thomas F. assembler, h.u. 89 Franklin.
" William, at 266, b. 111 Pearl.
" Wm. L. brassmolder, 556 Cap. h. 37 Flower.
" ☞ *see also Conley, Connolly.*
Conner Henry, bookbinder, h.2u. 306 Market.
" James H. draughtsman, 26 High, b.3 Marsh.
" John, laborer, b.2u.r. 34 So. Prospect.
" John F. driver at 46 Ann, h. 3 Marsh.
" Mamie F. Mrs. b. 849 Windsor av.
" Peter, janitor city hall, 800 Mn. h.3 Marsh.
" Peter, Jr. plumber at 1230 Mn. b. 3 Marsh.
" ☞ *see also Connor; O'Conner; O'Connor.*
Conners Andrew, laborer, b.u.r. 12 S. Pro.
" Bridget, wid. Patrick, h.3u. 20 Park.
" Bridget, wid. Thomas, h. 19 Hawthorn.
" Catherine, wid. Timothy, h. 333 Front.
" Daniel, lab. Valley div. N.Y.R. h.u. 51 Por.
" David, driver at 145 State, h.u. 14 Charles.
" David D. at 288 Asylum.
" Garry, h. 38 Walnut.
" Honora, wid. John, b. 17 Kennedy.
" James, blacksmith, b.u. 12 Clinton.
" James, laborer, b. 22 Commerce.
" James N. l. 1045 Main.
" Jas. R. machinist at Colts, h. 1158 Main.
" James S. painter, h.u. 16 Commerce.
" Jeremiah L. polisher, 581 Cap. b. 147 Law.
" John, laborer, h.u. 36 Sheldon.
" John, laborer, h.u.r. 12 So. Prospect.
" John, news agent, h. 239 Martin.
" John, ostler at 1061, l. 1061 Main.
" John J. rubberworker at 690, b.3u. 20 Park.
" Martin, laborer, h. 199 Windsor.
" Mary, h2u.r. 34 So. Prospect.
" Michael, brakeman P.&R. b. 10 Queen.
" Michael, helper, h.r. 56 Albany.
" Michael, laborer, b.u. 258 Front.

Conners Michael D. assistant deputy jailor, 42 Seyms, h. Russell.
" Patrick, blacksmith at 22 Wells, b.u. Clinton.
" Patrick, laborer, b. 114 Windsor.
" Sylvester, teamster, h.u. 111 Potter.
" Thomas J. supt. carriers, 66 Sta.h.u.37 Park.
" Timothy, painter, h.u. 333 Front.
" William, clerk at 193 Asylum, b. 11 Hung.
" William, fireman at N.Y.R. h. 10 Queen.
" William, saloon, 14, h. 14 Albany.
Connerton James, corem. 54 Arch, h. 134 Martin.
" John P. bartender, b. 86 Fairmount.
" Owen, helper, h. 86 Fairmount.
" Patrick, laborer, h.u. 90 Sheldon.
" Patrick, teamster, h. 74 Avon.
" Thomas M. hackdriver, b. 86 Fairmount.
Conniff James, clerk, b.2u. 24 Lawrence.
" John, laborer, b.2u. 24 Lawrence.
CONNIFF JOHN F. *alderman 1st ward*, mason, b. 63 Ward.
" Mary, wid. Michael, notions, 64, h. 64 Front.
" Peter, laborer, h.u. 24 Lawrence.
Connihan Frank, assembler at Colts, b. 40 Park.
Connolly Frank A. box clerk P.O. h. 23 Williams.
" Frederick F. mason, b.2u. 3 Goodman.
" Henrietta, b.2u. 3 Goodman.
" Jas. M. tailor at 76 Asy. h.2u. 3 Goodman.
" Jas. M. Jr. b.2u. 3 Goodman.
" Nell, goldleafer, b.2u. 3 Goodman.
" Thomas F. mech. at Popes, h. 89 Franklin.
" Thomas J. mach. Colts, h. 370 Asylum, rm.39.
" William, deckh. str. Middletown, 285 State.
" ☞ *see also Connelly.*
Connor Alice V. clerk at Brown, Thomson & Co. 942 Main, b. 11 Hungerford.
" Elizabeth, nurse at 20 South Hudson.
" Francis F. helper at Popes, h.u. 45 Hawthorn.
" George A. carpenter, h.u. 147 Collins.
" James F. laborer, h.u. 10 Winter.
" James J. mach. at 1 Flower, b. 61 Front.
" Jeremiah F. machinehand at 83 Woodbine, b. 35 Russell.
" Jeremiah J. clerk, 236 State, b.u. 79 Windsor.
" John, dipper at 83 Woodbine, h. 35 Russell.
" John F. clerk at 206 State, b.u. 79 Windsor.
" John J. patternmaker, b. 61 Front.
" Joseph, mach. at 581 Cap. b. 46 Wilson.
" Josephine, b. 58 Church.
" Julia A. stenogr. at 66 State, b. 46 Wilson.
" Keron, switchman, h.u. 45 Hawthorn.
" Lizzie, h.u. 566 Main.
" Mary K. stenographer at Brown, Thomson & Co. 942 Main, b. Windsor Locks t.
" Margaret, h. 155 Babcock.
" Michael, b. 66 Sigourney.
" Michael, dropf. at Popes, b 1333 Broad.
" Michael, gardener, 140 Wash. h. 11 Hung.
" Michael, laborer, h.u. 10 Winter.
" Patrick, blacksm. at 29 Wells, h.2u. 67 Gov.
" Patrick, laborer at 1 Flower, h. 46 Wilson.
" Patrick F. porter, 236 State, b.u. 79 Windsor.
" Patrick F.mach. Pope Tube Co. b. 46 Wilson.
" Robert, mach. at N.Y.R. l.2u. 1158 Main.
" Thomas, helper at 1 Flower, h.u. 1079 Broad.
" Thomas Jr. teamster, b.r. 61 Front.

Connor William J. machinist at 388 Capitol, b. 373 Asylum.
" William O. mach. at 556 Cap. h. 61 Haw.
" ☞ see also Conner; O'Conner; O'Connor.
Connors Annie, laundress at 30 Washington.
" Hugh, teamster, h.r. 61 Front.
" James, b. 2 Holcomb.
" James, horseshoer at 22 Wells, h.u. 47 Fkn.
" Jerry J. mechanic at Popes, b. 74 Putnam.
" Jos. A. assembler at Popes, b.49 Walnut.
" Martin, flagman, P.&R. b. 400 Albany.
" Michael, coremaker at 54 Arch, h. 19 Squire.
" Michael, elevatorer at 141 Pearl.
" Minnie, ward maid at 20 South Hudson.
" Patrick, laborer, bu. 1 Union.
" Patrick, mach. at 388 Cap. h.Wilson station.
" Thomas, h.r. 61 Front.
" Thomas, night clerk at 389, b. 389 Main.
" Thos. laborer, 556 Capitol, b. 177 Lawrence.
" Thomas E. laborer, Keney Park, h. Tower.
" W. J.steamfitter at 164 State, b. 10½ Village.
Connover Herbert J. ostler r. 87 High, h. 88 Fmt.
" William H. waiter, h.2u.r. 88 Fairmount.
Conrad Philip, saloon and restaurant, 50-52 Market, h. 95 Park.
Conrads Carl H. sculptor at N.E.Granite Works, 1260 Main, h. 142 Windsor av.
CONRAN FRANK E. plumber, 237 Asylum, h. 69 Allen pl.　　See page 103.
" James, belter, h. 50 Vanblock.
" James F. filer, b. 50 Vanblock.
" ☞ see also Condron.
Conrick Michael P. bartender at 98, l. 90 State.
Conrey John E. milkman, b. Bloomfield av.
" Wm. H.farmer and milkm. h. Bloomfield av.
Conroy C. deckhand stmr. Hartford, 285 State.
" David F. woodturner, b.u. 28 Woodbridge.
" Jas. B. stenog. 44 Market, b. 60 Windsor av.
" John F.ticket agt.etc. 548 Mn.h.u. 12 Arch.
" Peter, laborer, 9 Sigourney.b.u. 35 Liberty.
" Thos. at Woven Wire Mat. Co. h. 962 Broad.
" William, helper at 54 Arch, h. 962 Broad.
" William H. salesman at Neal, Goff & Inglis Co. 980 Main, b. Windsor Locks t.
" William J. linem. at 266 Pearl, h. 12 Village.
Considien Ann, h. 13 Charter Oak.
Considine John B. train despatcher at N.E.R. b. 809 Asylum.
" Thomas, b.u. 25 Flower.
Console Francesco, barber, 253 State, b. 16 Kil.
Consumers Ice Co. 80 State.
　　George H. Dunlap.　　Roswell M. Deming.
Conti Angelo & Co. grocery 161 Front, h. 78 Temple.
" Frank, h.u. 15 Charles.
Contoro Nicholas, plater, h.u. 19 Ellery.
Converse Ella F. wid. James, h.u. 43 Lincoln.
" Helen E. wid. Jos. H. h.u. 926 Main, rm. 7.
" I. Austin,butcher at 116 Albany,b. 933 Main.
" Julia I. wid. Wm. W. h. 270 Farmington.
" Lawrence A. clerk, 54 Mor. b. 186 Barbour.
" Lorenzo D. clerk at Adjutant Gen'l office, rm. 19, State Capitol, h. Windsor t.
" Sarah E. wid. Stillman A. b. 24 Preston.
Convey Michael, laborer, b.2u. 40 Sheldon.

**FRANK E. CONRAN,**
ﾟ ﾟ　**SANITARY PLUMBER**
and **GAS FITTER. ∴ ∴ ∴**
Special Attention Given to Ventilation.
House Drainage Tested Free of Charge.
**No. 237 ASYLUM STREET.**

Conway Charles, grocer, 293, h.u. 293 Lawrence.
" Charles A. Jr. b.2u. 293 Lawrence.
" Chas. J. molder at 556 Cap. b. 72½Seymour.
**CONWAY CO-OPERATIVE CREAMERY,** 53 High.　See p. 586.
" Dennis J. helper at 1 Flower, h.u. 32 Girard.
" Francis J. b.u. 293 Lawrence.
" Honora, wid. Martin, h.2u. 49 Front.
" James, fireman steamer Hartford, 285 State.
" James, inspector at 690 Park, b.2u. 49 Front.
" Jas. J. mechanic at Popes, b. 293 Lawrence.
" John.lab. at W.C.Mason & Co.b.u.250 Front.
" John, enameler at 581 Capitol, b.42 Amity.
" John, helper at 556 Capitol, b.u. 293 Law.
" John B. corem. at 556 Cap. b. 72 Seymour.
" John F. filer at Popes, h. 15 Kibbe.
" John J. laborer, 5, b. 7 Lenox.
" John James, teamster. b. 8 Winter.
" John M. engineer at Hartford Daily Times, 716 Main, h. 17 Seyms.
" John W. filer at 556 Capitol, h. 6 Union.
" John W. Jr. foreman at 556 Cap.h.45 Crown.
" Katherine R. music teacher. 2, h. 2 Orchard.
" Maria, laundress, h.u. 49 Mather.
" Martin, Jr. stonecutter, h.2u. 149 Maple.
" Mary, wid.John, h. 51 Wilson.
" Mary A. dressm. 517 Main, h. 149 Maple.
" Michael F. brassturner, h. 25 Francis.
" Patrick, b.2u. 49 Front.
" Stephen, bellman at 152 Asylum.
" Terence, bricklayer at 556 Cap. h.u. 77 Gov.
" Thomas, apprentice, 5 Mec. b. Burnside v.
" Thomas F. clerk, b. 2 Orchard.
" Thomas K. plumber, 34 Shel. b. 72 Seymour.
" Wilbur H. pressfeeder at Case, Lockwood & Brainard Co. 141 Pearl, b. 17 Seyms.
" William A. polisher at 581 Cap.b.u.293 Law.
" William G. fireman, 70 Com. b. 2 John.
Coogan James T. 2d, attorney, 877 Main, rm. 2, h. Windsor Locks t.
" Jane, h. 33 Elm.
" John W. atty. 877 Main, rm. 2, b. 26 State.
" Rose Mrs. h. 44 Trumbull.
Coogle Charles, driver, 4, b. 4 Huyshope.
Cook A. Dudley, letter carrier, P.O. h. 416 Windsor av.
" Albert S. attorney, with Asa S. Cook Co. 80 Huyshope, h. 90 Gillette.
" Ansel G. physician, 164, h. 164 High.
" Asa S. president and treasurer Asa S. Cook Co. 80 Huyshope, h. 20 Charter Oak pl.
**COOK ASA S. CO.** machinery manufacturers, 80 Huyshope, Colts west armory.
　　　　　　　　See page 525.
" Bessie, seamstress, b. 58 Church.

Cook C. P. H. Co. novelties, 721 Main, rm. 53.
" Carlyle C. bookkeeper at Hartford Electric Light Co. b. 46 Mahl.
" Caroline A. wid. Andrew T. dressmaker, 406, b. 406 Wethersfield.
**COOK CHARLES C.** contractor and builder, 141 Tru. h. 4 Highland. *See p.419.*
" Charles P. H. mgr. 721 Main, h.u.23 Pleasant.
" Curtis C. bookkeeper at Hartford Electric Light Co. h. 46 Mahl.
" D. P., Yankee notions, newspapers, music, instruments, etc. 92 State, h. 173 High.
" Daniel P. Jr. ins. agent, h.u. 171 State.
" Edith L. music teacher, 173, b. 173 High.
" Edward, clerk at 197 Asy. h.u. 533 Garden.
" Edward, laborer. h.2u.r. 12 S. Prospect.
" Edward B. at Phœnix Insurance Co. 64 Pearl, h. 11 Foot Guard pl.
" Edwin T. painter,185 Asylum, l.u. 234 Pearl.
" Edw. W. Jr. clerk, b. 40 Pliny.
" Elihu S. secretary and assistant treasurer J. N. Shedd Co. 109 Asy. h. 21 Williams.
" Elizur, proofreader at Case, Lockwood & Brainard Co. 141 Pearl, h. 117 Ann.
" Emily, wid. Albert, h. 400 Windsor av.
" Ephraim, janitor, h.u. 76 Edwards.
" Etta A. wid. John R. b. 75 Hudson.
" Frank A. foreman at 581 Capitol, h. E.H.t.
" Frank W. toolmaker at Popes, h. Windsor t.
" George, h. 432 Windsor av.
" George E. farmer, b. 432 Windsor av.
" Hans, driver, b.u. 16 Trumbull.
" Harriet A. Mrs. h. 164 High.
" Harris J. toolmaker at 476 Cap. h. 20 Russ.
" Henrietta F. wid. Moses, h. 312 Windsor av.
" Henry E. fireman, N.Y.R. b. 117 Ann.
" Horace T. b. 173 High.
" Horace W. driver, h.2u. 34 John.
" Howard W. asst. secretary, Orient Insurance Co. 5 Haynes, h. 236 Ashley.
" James, yardman, 17 Albany, h. E.H.t.
" James S. farmer, h. 429 Windsor av.
" John F. secretary A. S. Cook Co. 80 Huy-shope, h. 28 Warner.
" John M. mach. at 111 Sheldon, b. W.L.t.
" John W. clerk, h. 67 Franklin.
" Joseph L. clerk, Pope Tube Co. h.u.38 Lewis.
" Kate, wid. William, h. 1 Pleasant ct.
" Lewis P. orderly at 20 South Hudson.
" Lizzie P. bookkeeper, b. 173 High.
**COOK LOUISE H.** wid. Wm. T. type-writers copyist and supplies, 80 State, rm. 113, b. 115 Trumbull. *See page 710.*
" Lucinda A. h.2u. 346 Windsor av.
" Lucy A. wid. John, b. 46 Mahl.
" Maria E. Mrs. b. 36 Jefferson.
" Mary A. at 690 Park, b. 40 Amity.
" Mary E. Mrs. manager Hartford Viavi As-sociation, h. 117 Ann.
" Millard F. asst. treas. Asa S. Cook Co. 80 Huyshope, b. 20 Charter Oak pl.
" Nancy, wid. John, h.u. 16 Gold.
" Orrin H. fish peddler, h. 458 Broad.
" Patrick J. steamfitter at Popes, h. Lifkey.

Cook Richard G. foreman at Colts, b. 54 Capitol.
" Thomas A. painter, h.2u. 293 Wethersfield.
" Thomas H. storekeeper, Colts, h. 136 Sey.
" Wallace A. mach. at 476 Capitol, b. 58 Russ.
" Willard B. forem. at 111 Sheldon, h. W.P.v.
" William F. forem. at 1 Flower, b. 373 Asylum.
" Wm. G. mach. at 1 Flow. b. 57 Farmington.
" William K. prof. at E. H. Morse's Business College, 370 Asylum, teacher of writing in public schools, b. 9 Preston.
Cooke Annie E. b. 149 High.
" Augustus D. h. 9 Fairfield.
" Ella, wid. E. Ludlow, h. 821 Asylum.
" Fred. M. clerk at 66 Asy. b. 278 Windsor av.
" John B. collector, h.2u. 198 Allyn.
" John H. prest. and treas. Sigourney Tool Co. 9 Sigourney, h. 340 Farmington.
" John W. at Connecticut Mutual Life Insur-ance Co. 783 Main, b. 149 High.
" Lorrin A. governor State of Connecticut, room 39, State Capitol, h. Winsted t.
" Samuel W. student Trinity college, b. 24 Jarvis hall, Summit.
" Wm. P. clerk at 74 Trumbull, h. 8 Lewis.
" ☞ *see also Cook: Koch.*
Cooking and Housework School, 239 Market.
Cooksley Chas. E. bkkpr. at 71 Asy. h. 47 Julius.
" Chas. W. Jr. at 71 Asylum, b. 47 Julius.
" Percy O. clerk, b. 47 Julius.
Cooley Arthur H. clerk at American National Bank, 803 Main, b. 192 Sargeant.
" Caroline L. wid. Anson, h. 19 Suffield.
" Chas. H. appraiser, 882 Mn. h. 18 Annawan.
" Charles H. Jr. agent, 904 Main, rm. 30, b. 18 Annawan.
" Charles P. treasurer Fidelity Co. 49 Pearl, b. 119 Farmington.
" Chester, b. 43 Sumner.
" Cora Vinetta, b. 253 Main.
" Edward S. teamster, b. 152 Seymour.
" Francis B. office 904 Main, h. 119 Far.
**COOLEY FRANCIS R.** banker, 49 Pearl, h. 12 Marshall. *See page 428.*
" Frederick H. assem. at Popes, h.u. 246 Jef.
" George A. Jr. clerk at 31, b.u. 31 Church.
" George E. state inspect. steam boilers, first cong. district, h.u. 429 Windsor av.
" George L. farmer at 106, b. 106 Bluehills.
" Geo. W. assembler, Popes, h.u. 31 Church.
" Henry B. mach. at 254 Pearl, b. 103 Capitol.
" Herbert C. cigarm. 104 Asylum, h. 56 Mahl.
" Horace E. mechanic at Popes, h. Windsor t.
" James E. mach. at 80 Huy. h. 92 Retreat.
" James E. toolmaker at 254 Pearl, h. 253 Main.
" Joseph W. h.u. 59 Sigourney.
" Mary A. h. 1122 Main.
" Samuel A. chemist, h. 1122 Main.
" Sarah, wid. Almon, nurse, h. 216 Windsor av.
" William, assembler at Popes, b. 19 John.
" William H. cigarmaker, b. 56 Mahl.
" William J. motorman St.Ry. l.u. 740 Main.
Coolidge Edmund B. finisher at C. C. Fuller Co. 14 Ford, h. East Hartford t.
Coombs J. F. manager, 409 Allyn, b. 228 High.

Coombs John, florist, 702 Main, greenhouses, 114, h. 118 Benton.
" Joseph F. florist at 702 Main, b. 118 Benton.
" Thomas J. clerk, 575 Main, h.u. 874 Broad.
" ☞ see also Cumbs.
Coomer ☞ see Kummer.
Coomes Claud S. clerk, 865 Main, b. 28 Spring.
" Gilbert H. machinist, h. 967 Asylum.
" L. C. wid. William W. b. 255 Laurel.
" Wm. M. floorm. Adams Ex.h. 370 Asy. rm.20.
Coon Adelbert J. screwmaker at 476 Capitol, h.2u. 490 Windsor av.         •
Cooney Dennis F. driller at Colts, h. 25 Wyllys.
" James, conductor, N.Y.R. h.u. 59 Bellevue.
" John W. helper, 1230 Main, b. 59 Belden.
" Lillie J. bookkeeper, b.u. 59 Bellevue.
" Margaret M. clerk Brown, Thomson & Co. 942 Main, b. 15 Portland.
" William, fireman at 266 Pearl, h. E.H.t.
Coons Samuel W. student at Trinity college, 26 Jarvis hall, Summit.
" Ambrosine, h. 133 Market.
Cooper Bernard, peddler, h. 222 Front.
" Charles J. machinehand at Colts, h. E.H.t.
" Chas. W. plumber at 690 Park, h. 107 Heath.
" Frank P. electrician at 1 Laurel, b. E.H.t.
" George, at 299, b.u. 299 Windsor av.
" George A. watchm. 141 Pearl, h.u. 61 Mahl.
" George B. draughtsman at 904 Main, rms. 87-92, b. 42 Sumner.
" Harriet L. stenographer, insurance dept. rm. 16, State Capitol, b. 31 Russ.
" Honora, wid. John C. h.u. 219 Pearl.
" J. Sulla Rev. pastor African M. E. Zion church, h. 17 So. Ann.
" Jessica E. saleslady at 904 Mn. b. 1339 Broad.
" John A. clerk, h. 56 Grove.
" John C. clerk at Popes, b. 219 Pearl.
**COOPER JOSEPH,** cloaks, suits, furs, wraps, etc. Ballerstein building, 904 Main, rm. 2, h. 208 Collins.
" L. M. Mrs. modiste, 58, h. 58 Grove.
" Leroy W. driver at 213 State, b. 39 Madison.
" Mary A. wid. Judah, h.2u. 490 Windsor av.
" R. S. at 40 Governor, b. 231 Lawrence.
" Sam, cigarmaker, b. 34 Avon.
**COOPER SAMUEL C.** *(Hebard &* C.) h. 39 Madison.    See page 552.
" Samuel C. Jr. clerk, 87 Asy. b.u. 39 Madison.
" William, laborer at 93 Ch. O. b. 36 Hicks.
Co-operative Building Bank of New York, Rev. E. F. Atwood, manager, 212 Asylum.
" Provision Co. 149 Bab., H. Medeen, mgr.
" Savings Society of Connecticut, 782 Main.
Cooperman Louis, peddler, h. 34 Avon.
Cope Brothers, plumbers and gasfitters, 94 State.
George Cope.        John Cope.
" George, (*Cope Bros.*) h. 252 New Park.
" George, laborer, N.Y.R. h. 2 Francis,
" John, (*Cope Bros.*) h. Oakwood av. W.H.t.
Copeland Chas. H. mach. at 1 Flow. h. 71 Capitol.
" Edward, builder, b. 1153 Main.
" Frank D. mach. at 223 State, h. 373 Asy.
" Grace M. at 336, b. 336 Wethersfield.
" Ike, h. 9 Kennedy.

Copeland James S. designer at Popes, 436 Cap. h. 176 Sargeant.
" James S. mechanical engineer at Popes, h. 176 Sargeant.
" Joseph, l. 14 Spring.
" Minnie S. Mrs. h. 45 John.
" Samuel, peddler, b. 61 Pleasant.
Copp Laura M. clerk at Brown, Thomson & Co. 942 Main, b. 355 Park.
Coppelli Michael, saloon, 146 Front, h. 31 S. Pro.
Copperberg Gus. bartender at 287 Asylum, h. 6 Foot Guard pl.
" Julius, Jr. saloon, 107, h. 71 Asylum, rm. 7.
" ☞ see also Kopperburg.
Copperstein Louis, h.u. 70 Avon.
Coppicke Antonio, laborer, b.r. 99 Windsor.
" Tony, laborer, h.r. 99 Windsor.
Coppinger Thomas, dropforger at 133 Sheldon, h. 9 Willow.
Cora John, at 97 Asylum, b.u. 18 Trumbull.
Corbally W. H. drop forger 142 Russ, b.9 Grand.
Corberg August, painter, b.u. 12 Putnam
Corbet Margaret, h. 43 Windsor.
Corbett Ann, wid. William. h.u. 275 Asylum.
" Anna E. stenographer at 690 Pk. h. N.B.t.
" E. deckhand steamer Hartford, 285 State.
" John, janitor at 106 State, h.u. 232 Park.
" Margaret, wid. Michael, h. 188 Ward.
Corbin A. mason, b. 276 Lawrence.
" Annie E. wid. Lewis D. h. 171 Seymour.
" Harvey W. clerk at Conn. Trust & Safe Deposit Co. 785 Main, b.u. 57 Willard.
" Josephine W. wid. Wm. M. h.u. 57 Willard.
" L. mason, b. 276 Lawrence.
" Lula T. clerk at Brown, Thomson & Co. 942 Main, b. 171 Seymour.
" Mary S. wid. David P. h.u. 57 Willard.
" Milford, waiter str. Middletown, 285 State.
Corcoran Daniel, h.u. 133 Mather.
" Daniel, clerk, b. 76 Heath.
" Frank, carpenter, 155 Ch.O. h.24 Commerce.
" Frank J. driver, b. 24 Commerce.
" Jeremiah, laborer at 690 Park, b. 76 Heath.
" Jeremiah, operator, 40 Gov. h.r. 18 Babcock.
" John, at 859 Main, b. 76 Heath.
" John J. mach. at N.Y.R. h. 133 Mather.
" Margaret, wid. Humphrey, h. 76 Heath.
" Michael, h. 1 Queen.
" Michael, carcleaner, St.Ry. h. 5 Queen.
" Michael, woodworker, h.u. 2 Wawarme.
" Michael J. clerk, b. 76 Heath.
" Patrick, laborer, h.u. 112 Grove.
" Timothy, laborer, b.u. 133 Mather.
" ☞ see also Cochrane.
Cordier George B. boxmaker, b. 22 Chestnut.
" Henry, porter at 209 State, h.u. 20 Winter.
" Jacob Mrs. h. 22 Chestnut.
" Kate, dressmaker, 22, b. 22 Chestnut.
" Lewis, harnessm. 195 State, b. 22 Chestnut.
Corette Joseph, carpenter at N.Y.R. h. W.H.t.
Corey Sarah M. wid. William A. h. 207 Barbour.
" Wm. W. asst. forem. 1 Flow. h.u. 207 Barb.
" ☞ see also Cory.
Corletto Nicolo, laborer, b. 73 Morgan.
Corliss A. W. photographer at 902 Main.

Corkins Fred A. rubberw. 690 Park, b.u. 18 Oak.
" Wellington M. bkkpr. 11 Haynes, b. 18 Oak.
" William M. machinist, h.u. 18 Oak.
" ☞ *see also Caulkins.*
Cormack David N. carpenter, h. 5 Squire.
Cormier Homer, clerk, 745 Main, b. 1139 Broad.
" Joseph A. molder at 1 Flower, h. 771 Park.
Cornelius Allie L. nurse, 98½, h. 98½ Ann.
Cornell George A. state armorer, 264, h. 264 Windsor av.
Cornfield Frank, peddler, h. 20 North.
" Harry, clerk at 188 State, b.u. 8 North.
" Harry, clerk, h. 104 Windsor.
" Morris, peddler, h.u. 296 Market.
" Samuel, peddler, h.u. 8 North.
**CORNING H. F. & CO.** horse goods, etc. 83 Asylum.
    Harry F. Corning.    Henry Corning.
" Harriet E. h.4u. 80 Pearl.
" Harry F. *(H. F. C. & Co.)* h. W.H.t.
" Henry, *(H. F. C. & Co.)* h. 52 Spring.
" James B. at Ætna Life Ins. Co. 650 Main, b. 75 Hudson.
" John J. l. 102 Pearl.
" Louisa, wid. John B. h. 102 Pearl.
Cornish De Witt C. builder, 3, h. 3 Seyms.
" Electa C. wid. Horton, b. 285 Albany.
" Eliza E. wid. Edward, h.3u. 279 Asylum.
Cornwall Charles H. clk. at Lincoln, Seyms & Co. teas, coffees, etc. 34 Market, h. Windsor t.
" Horace, attorney, 68 Pratt, h. Broad c. Far.
" Seth A. fireman, N.Y.R. h. 57½ Governor.
Cornwell Albert E. expressman at 335 Sheldon, h.u. 995 Main.
" Bridget, h. 39 Chapel.
" Clara W. Mrs. h. 34 Kenyon.
" Emna J. b. 36 Jefferson.
" George L. b. 152 Seymour.
" Harriet, wid. Reuben, b. 43 Wooster.
" Irving W. watchman at 9 Sigourney, h. 370 Asylum, rm. 59.
" L. A. Mrs. matron, 2 Holcomb.
" Leroy A. machinist at Colts, h. 152 Sey.
" Margaret, h. 39 Chapel.
" Richard D. b. 36 Jefferson.
" Silas H. cashier at Phœnix Mutual Life Ins. Co. 49 Pearl, h. 34 Kenyon.
Corone Joseph, laborer, b. 75 Charles.
Coroso Rosco, laborer, b.3u. 67 Morgan.
Corpe Laura A. wid. Wm. corsets, 31, b. 31 Church.
Corr Eliza, wid. Austin B. h.3u. 38 Spring.
" John, porter, 97 Asylum, b. 18 Trumbull.
" Sarah, b. 38 Spring.

Corrett Ceasar, brickmr. b. Caya av. near Pro.
" Frank, laborer, h. Caya av. near Pro. av.
Corrigan Ann, wid. Peter, h.2u. 88 Walnut.
" Annie M. cashier at Brown, Thomson & Co. 942 Main, b. 88 Walnut.
" Catharine E. at Plimptons, b. 265 Main.
" Bernard F. repairer at Popes, h. 964 Broad.
" Ellen, wid. Patrick, h. 54 Flower.
" Frank, painter, b. 54 Flower.
" James, coachm. at 31 Gillette, b.2u. 60 Flow.
" John M. carpenter, h.u. 92 Hudson.
" Kate, wid. Bernard, h. 265 Main.
" Maggie M. at 42 High, b.2u. 88 Walnut.
" Mary A. clerk at 956 Main, b2u. 88 Walnut.
" Rose J. b. 265 Main.
" Timothy, coachman, b. 54 Flower.
" Timothy, painter, b. 265 Main.
" William H. driver, b. 92 Hudson.
" ☞ *see also Carrigan; Kerrigan.*
Corser Fred E. foreman Pope Tube Co. b.u 12 Affleck.
Corson Donald S. student at Trinity college, 18 Seabury hall, Summit.
" Wm. R. C. with Eddy Electric Mfg. Co. h. 127 Oxford.
Corvaglia Suigi, laborer, b. 68 Front.
Corwin Edith P. and Marie R. Misses, b. 145 Ash.
" Harriet L. Mrs. (Wm. A.) h. 145 Ashley.
Corry John M. calenderer, 690 Park, b. 21 Sisson.
Cory Charles E. architect with Wm. H. Scoville, 720 Main, h. 4 Goodman.
Cosanello Briani, laborer, h.u. 86 Morgan.
Cosderfer David, watchman, h.u. 10 Goodman.
Cosette Victor, mach. at 388 Cap. b. 1470½ Broad.
Cosgrove Bernard H. *(Berry & C.)* h. b. 20 Morgan.
" Bridget, wid. John, h. 33 Chestnut.
" Edward, laborer at 1 Flower, b.2u. 138 Law.
" James, teamster at 2 Chapel.
" James E. butcher, b. 33 Chestnut.
" John, bartender at 365 Asylum.
" John, laborer at 1 Flower, b. 24 Lawrence.
" John B. carpenter, h. 109 Russ.
" John F. buyer at 956 Main, b. 189 Russ.
" Jos. T. screwmaker, 476 Cap. b. 33 Chestnut.
" Mary, h. 42 Village.
" Michael, helper at N.Y.R. h.2u. 49 Hawthorn.
" Michael, machinist at 556 Cap. h.u. 189 Russ.
" Michael J. mach. at 556 Cap. b.u. 189 Russ.
" P. A. clerk at 197 Asylum, b. 49 Hawthorn.
" Patrick J. assembler at 556 Cap. b.u. 189 Russ.
" Patrick J. bricklayer, b. 20 Morgan.
" Peter J. mach. at 1 Flower, h. 38 Lawrence.
" Thomas, coachm. 19 Pro. h.r. 22 So. Prospect.
" Thomas, laborer, 1 Flow. b.2u. 138 Lawrence.
" Thomas V. bricklayer, h. 20 Morgan.
" William H. silverplater, b. 33 Chestnut.
" William J. plumber at 433 Mn. h. 389 Capitol.
Coshinsky Peter, tailor at 881 Main, h. 93 Sheldon.
Cosker Christopher H. painter, h. Hawthorn ex.
" James J. engr. at 30 Cush. h. 167 Hawthorn.
" William D. gardener, 103, b.r. 135 Woodland.
Coss Mary Mrs. b. St. Marys Home, Albany.
Costain Catherine E. clerk at P.O. b.u. 103 Tru.
Costello Dominick D. elevatorer at Popes, h.u. 56 Hicks.

Costello Edward H. policeman, h.2u. 18 Affleck.
" Eliza M. wid. William, b.u. 44 Lawrence.
" Elizabeth M. bookkeeper, b. 21 Main.
" Frank J.storekeeper at Popes,b.u. 56 Hicks.
" James V. shoemaker, 21, h. 21 Main.
" James W. toolm. 556 Capitol, h. 30 Babcock.
" John, deckhand, str. Middletown, 285 State.
" John, b. 2 Holcomb.
" John, laborer, h.u.r. 12 South Prospect.
" Margaret, h.3u. 33½ Spruce.
" Martin, engineer at 26 State, h. 92 Grove.
" Mary,wid.James,housekeeper,h.119Mather.
" Mathew, laborer at Hfd. Prov.Co. b.86 State.
" Minnie Mrs. b. 2 Holcomb.
" Nathaniel, meatcutter, b. 80 State.
" Nicholas J. mechanic at Popes,h.u. 44 Law.
" Patrick, b. 40 John.
" Patrick, bartender, 16 Sheldon,h u.20 Dean.
" Patrick, laborer, b.u.r. 12 South Prospect.
" Patrick, teamster, h. 202 Sheldon.
" Richard,molder, 54 Arch,b. 24 Woodbridge.
" Sarah, wid. Richard, h.u. 88 Fairmount.
" Sarah E. dressmaker, b.2u. 1293 Main.
" William, saloon, 86 Albany, h. 23 Belden.
Costen James, waiter at 296 Asylum, b.90 Pearl.
" Walter, cook at 296 Asylum, l. 90 Pearl.
Costigan James F.polhr.at Colts,b.16 Pawtucket.
" John A. mach. at N.Y.R. b. 111 Lawrence.
" Mary, wid. John, b. 520 Main.
Cote Alphonse, brickmaker, h. 173 Barbour.
" Alphonse Jr. brickmaker, b. 173 Barbour.
" Chas. carpenter, N.Y.R.h.r. 1470½ Broad.
" Charles A. Jr. bartender, 167 State, b.r. 1470¼ Broad.
" Eugene, h.u. 371 Capitol.
" Oliver, brickmaker, b. 173 Barbour.
" Urban, brickmaker, b. 173 Barbour.
Cotter Agnes B. at 690 Park, b. 30 Amity.
" E. J. motorman, St.Ry. h. 47 Flower.
" Edward, h.u. 47 Flower.
" Daniel, foreman at 19, b. 19 Buckingham.
" Jeremiah F.clerk at 1 So. Ann,h.19 Bellevue.
" John, buffer at 581 Capitol, b.246 Lawrence.
" John J. h. 7 Wolcott.
" Mabel Mrs. b. 1096 Main.
" Michael, fireman at 1 Flower, b. 170 Ward.
" Thomas W. mach. at Colts,b.19 Buckingham.
" Timothy, mason, b. 19 Bellevue.
" William, livery stable, 19, h. 19 Buckingham.
" William, registrar of electors, 114 Pearl, h. 42 Windsor av.
Cotton Charles H. farmer, h. Albany, W.H.t.
" Charles L. ostler at 1177, l. 1177 Main.
" Edward A. ostler at 1177 Main,l. 17 Church.
" Edwin A. silversmith at Wm. Rogers Mfg. Co. 66, b. 150 Market.
" Julius H. floorwalker at Brown, Thomson & Co. 942 Main, h. E.H.t.
" Sumner H. mach. at 388 Cap. b. 242 Putnam.
" William G. collarmaker at 8 Sig. l.1034Main.
Cottrell Harry L. asst. clerk Board of Health, City Hall, 800 Main, h. 69 Webster.
Couch Arthur R. student, b. 43 Farmington.
" Edward N. tinner at 1072 Mn. h.u. 9 Morgan.
" Elbert L. musician, b. 43 Farmington.

Couch Elbert M. draughtsman 1 Flow. b. 43 Far.
" George C. laborer, h. 1415 Main.
" George M. plumber, 1072 Mn. h. 60 Bellevue.
" James G. clerk at 28 Laurel, b. S.M.t.
" Julia Mrs. h.u. 1 Riverside pl.
" Nicholas, slater, b. 12 Center.
" Samuel, operator, b. 145 High.
" Sarah C. wid. William G. b. 60 Bellevue.
" Thomas E. mach. at 1 Flow. b.43 Farmington.
Coudemarche Mr. carpenter, h. 1 Kibbe.
Coudray Robert D. jeweler at Hansel, Sloan & Co. 886 Main, h. Wethersfield t.
Coudry Anna, wid. J. W. h. 721 Main.
Coughlan D. J. & Co. 180 Asylum, rm. 3.
    Daniel J. Coughlan.    Eugene Coughlan.
" Daniel J. (D. J. & Co.) b. 26 West.
" Eugene, (D. J. & Co.) b. 26 West.
" Matthew A. gardener, h. 26 West.
Coughlin Bridget,wid.James,at 87, h.2u.23 Wells.
" Bridget S. wid. John F. h. 16 Walnut.
" Edward E. freight agt.N.Y.R.h.14 Pavilion.
" Fannie, wid. John, b.u. 15 Belden.
" Frank, motorm. St.Ry. b. 66 Madison.
" James, laborer, h. 6 Cedar.
" James A. laborer, 13 Central, h.u. 169 Main.
" James P. pressfeeder, 141 Pl. h. 52 Vanblock.
" Jeremiah, boilerm. at N.E.R. h. 106 Walnut.
" John, b.u.r. 34 South Prospect.
" John, laborer at 80 Huy. b. 34 So.Prospect.
" John, teamster at 556 Capitol, h. 1 Harrison.
" John F. clerk at 690 Park, b. 136 Babcock.
" John F. Jr. mach. at Colts, b. 52 Vanblock.
" John J. driver at 232 Shel. b. 63 Governor.
" John J. paperruler at 141 Pearl, h. 13 Oak.
" John J. with St.Ry. h.u. 11 Arch.
" John N. printer, b. 5 Russell.
" Joseph, plumber, b.u. 15 Belden.
" Kittie E. inspector, 70 Huy. b. 52 Vanblock.
" Martin, roofer, h. 283 Allyn.
" Matthew E.trav.salesman at 54 Ann,b.14 Pav.
" Matthew J. foreman at 556 Cap.b.1 Harrison.
" Michael, mason, b.3u. 23 Wells.
" Michael, b. 2 Holcomb.
" Michael, barnman, Adams Ex.Co.h.1 Queen.
" Michael, laborer, h. 11 Arch.
" Michael, Jr. laborer, b. 11 Arch.
" Patrick, h. 11 So. Prospect.
" Patrick, laborer at H. B. Beach & Son, 135, h. 112 Grove.
" Patrick, laborer, h.u. 77 Arch.
" Patrick F. helper at 1 Flow.h.u.18 Glendale.
" Patrick H. plumber at 142 Russ, h. 136 Bab.
" Peter, helper at 556 Capitol, b.35 Hawthorn.
" Sarah Mrs. h. 50 Russell.
" Thomas, enameler, h.2u. 34 South Prospect.
" William, molder, h. 74 Tru. h. 52 Chestnut.
" William H. molder, h. 52 Chestnut.
" ☞see also Caughlin, Coghlan.
Coulter Peter, lather, b.2u. 265 Main.
Coulthard Abe, porter at 161, b. 161 State.
Counahan Cornelius, boxmaker.h.28 Woodbridge.
" Dennis F. porter at 8 Hurlburt, b. 28 Wdbg.
" Frank, at Colts, b. 40 Park.
" John J. engineer, b. 28 Woodbridge.
" Patrick, baker, h. 28 Woodbridge.

## E. S. COWLES,

**General Manager for Connecticut,**

## FIDELITY & DEPOSIT CO. OF MARYLAND.

**Manager of Branch Office,**

## GERMAN-AMERICAN INSURANCE CO. of New York.

**Agent,**

## THE MUTUAL LIFE INSURANCE CO. of New York.
## THE TRAVELERS INSURANCE CO. of Hartford.

Fire, Life, Accident, Employers Liability, and other
Insurance and Surety Bonds, placed only in best
Companies and at the Lowest Rates.

### Office, 25 PEARL ST., 3 Doors from Main St.

Counehan Daniel D. b. 1104 Main.
COUNTRYMAN WILLIAM A. *councilman* 10*th*
    *ward*, editor The Post,23Asy.h.204 Sisson.
County Commissioners Office, 85 Trumbull.
    " House, 85 Trumbull and 127 Allyn.
    " Jail, E. J. Smith, jailor, 42 Seyms.
**COURANT** Hartford Daily. *See page 463.*
Court of Common Pleas. 85 Trumbull.
    " John, waiter, b. 74 High.
Courtemanche H. cutter at 8 Sig. b. 13 Putnam.
Courtice Chas. (*S. Collins & Co.*) 283 Sheldon,
    h. 58 Oak.
Courtney James, coachman, b. 8 Concord.
    " Samuel, screwmaker at 476 Capitol, h. N.t.
    " Thomas, expressman, b.u. 1059 Main.
Courtright E. E. nurse, 14 Church, rm. 3.
Covel Charlotte E. b. 13 Belden.
    " F. T. Mrs. h. 13 Belden.
    " Frank B. foreman at Popes, h. 55 Allen pl.
Covell F. D. Mrs. h.u. 86 Pratt.
    " Irving S. Syndicate Prem. Co. h. 86 Pratt.
Covello James, laborer, h.u. 49 Morgan.
Covey Amasa D. mach. at 24 Mechanic, h. E.H.t.
    " George, mach. at 24 Mechanic, h. E.H.t.
Covil Wm.B.Jr. conductor St.Ry. h.63 Madison.
Cowan Andrew L. compositor at Popes, h. 108
    Hopkins.
    " Arthur B. salesman, h. 1295 Main.
    " Dennis, laborer, b. 14 Huntley pl.
    " Frank L. machinist, b. 8 Woodbine.
    " George W. clerk at 423 Main, b. 8 Woodbine.
    " Jos. W. carpenter,N.Y.R. h. Hayden station.
    " Nellie, h.u. 55 Hawthorne.
    " ☞*see also Cohen.*
Cowles Albert W. mech. at Popes, b. Weth. t.
    " Alfred, elevator man at Popes, h. 70 Capitol.
    " Almira H. wid. Lester, h.u. 15 Goodwin.
    " Arthur H. motorman, St.Ry. h.E.H.t.
    " Charles H. bartender at 178, b. 367 Asylum.
    " Cornelia B. wid. Horace B. h. 23 Girard.
    " Edgar C. physician, b. 15 Clinton.
    " Edward A. foreman at 1 Laurel, b.63 Church.
COWLES EDWIN S. surety bonds, life and acci-
    dent ins. agent, 25 Pearl, h. 373 Laurel.
        *See page 108.*
    " Elizabeth, b. 21 Preston.
    " Eunice, wid. Edgar P. h. 15 Clinton.

Cowles Fannie M. h. 106 Park.
    " Frank, salesman, 224 State, h.u. 51 Spring.
    " Frank, washer, 1128, l. 703 Main.
    " H. Leslie, at Travelers Insurance Co. 56
        Prospect, b. 225 High
    " Harry, machinist at 690 Park, h. 240 Laurel.
    " Hubert L. clerk, b. 51 Barbour.
    " James B. steamfitter, h. 29 Elm.
    " Louis, carpenter at N.Y.R. h. E.H.t.
    " Louise M. h. 721 Main, rm. 45.
    " Matilda Mrs. h.r. 26 Trumbull.
    " S. W. real estate, 295, h. 295 Windsor av.
    " Sarah J. wid. Oliver, h. 21 Preston.
    " Thomas M. treasurer Anchor Mills, h. 147
        Washington.
    " Truman, farmer, h. 21 South.
    " Walter A. h. 65 Forest.
    " Walter G. at Travelers Ins. Co. 56 Pros-
        pect, h. 287 Windsor av.
    " Wm. J. pressfeeder at 141 Pearl, h. E.H.t.
    " ☞*see also Coles.*
Cowley Annie, folder at 26 High, b. 35 Linden.
    " Edward F. bkkpr. at 54 Ann, b. 35 Linden.
    " Eugene J. foreman at 581 Cap. b. 35 Linden.
    " Francis, h. 35 Linden.
    " Francis T. Jr. sup. police, b. 35 Linden.
    " Joseph P. pressman at 141 Pearl,b.35 Linden.
**COWLISHAW HENRY,** cutler, etc.
    162 Pearl, h. 51 Congress. *See page 535.*
Cox Chas. H. salesm. at 54 Ann, b. 50 Williams.
    " Charles B. manager sales department at
        Popes, h. 1 Cone.
    " Fannie S. h. 50 Williams.
    " Geo. E. salesman, 248 Asy. h.2u. 95 Chestnut.
    " George H. clerk at Popes, b. 3 Farmington.
    " J. Fred. correspondent at Popes, h.u. 67 Sig.
    " James, blacksmith, 142 Russ, b. 237 Law.
    " James, farmer, h. 64 Bluehills.
    " James E. carpenter, N.Y.R. h. 50 Williams.
    " John E. sec. Fowler & Miller Co. h.862 Broad.
    " John T. carptr. at N.Y.R. h.u. 14 Squire.
    " May E. b. 862 Broad.
    " Michael, helper at 1 Flow. b. 185 Lawrence.
    " Wm. F. manager at 42 Asylum, h. 49 Ward.
Coxeter Wm. G. (*Blair & C.*) h.51 Congress.
Coxon John, laborer, b. 93 Madison av.
Coyle Barney, laborer, b. 60 Front.
    " Dennis J. barkpr. 80 State, h. 121 Albany.
    " Frank P. mach. at 70 Huy. b. 65 Flower.
    " Gertrude W. dressmaker, b. 19 Alden.
    " Hannah, wid. Thomas, h. 95 Sheldon.
    " James J. clerk at Adams Ex. h. 128 Avon.
    " James J. nickle plater at Popes, b. 65 Flow.
    " John A. clerk at N.Y.R. b.u. 65 Flower.
    " Mary, wid. James J. h. 65 Flower.
    " Mary E. b. Sigourney house, 1150 Main.
**COYLE N. J.** Mrs. proprietor Sigourney
    house, 1150 Main.        *See page 561.*
    " Thos. J. driller at 581 Cap. b. 95 Sheldon.
Coyne James E. laborer at 40 Gov. h. 91 Arch.
    " James J. b. 8 Francis.
    " Martin, machinehand at 581 Cap.b.8 Francis.
    " Thomas, laborer on city works, h. 8 Francis.
Crafts Otto, helper Popes Tube Co. h.u. 34 John.

Craig Albert F. clerk, b. 16 Oak.
" Herbert E. at 10, b. 10 Fairfield.
" J. E. & Co. wholesale liquors, 239 State.*
" James E. (*J. E. C. & Co.*) h. 16 Oak.
" John F. h. 16 Oak.
" John M. brassmolder, h. 41 Franklin.
CRAIG JOHN S. plumber, 59 Farmington, h.2u. 64 Ashley.  *See page 109.*
" Lottie Mrs. b. 124 Market.
" Saline, crater, b.r. 49 Spring.
" William, carpenter, h.r. 59 Dean.
" William G. physician,11 Pratt, l. 122 Garden.
Craiger Andrew, laborer at 8, b. 19 Front.
Cramer Henry, tinner at Colts, h. E.H.t.
" Jacob, bottler, 27, b. 27 Mulberry.
" William H. attendant 30 Washington.
Crampton Ruth S. teacher West Middle school, b. 167 Sigourney.
Crandall Georgie L. wid. Joseph A. b. 24 Babcock.
" Mary A. wid. Cranston C. b. 18 Annawan.
Crane Chas. E. butcher, r. 175, h. 177 Ashley.
" Chas. L. signpainter,1274,h. 943 Main,rm.19.
" Charles W. mach. at 1 Flower, h. 29 Benton.
" Daniel, laborer, b.r. 14 Arch.
" E. B. clerk, b. 175 Ashley.
" Edward E. motorman, St.Ry. h. 20 Julius.
" Emma, at 247 Pearl, b. 30 Hopkins.
" Eugene, laborer, h.r. 14 Arch.
" Francis B. dentist, 8 State, b. 751 Asylum.
" Fred.A.foreman painterN.Y.R.h.u.277High.
" Harry C. laborer at 690 Park, b. 207 Main.
" Iphigenia E. Mrs. dressm. 7, h. 7 Belden.
" Irving H. clerk at 83 Woodbine, b. E.H.t.
" John E. teacher at 690 Asylum, h.189 Sisson.
" John W. treas. WhitlockC.P.Co.h.45Grand.
" Orson W. conductor St.Ry. h.u. 53 Cong.
" Patrick W. carptr. 52 John, h.3u. 111 Maple.
" S. L. G. dentist, 8 State, h. 751 Asylum.
" Sarah Mrs. b. 207 Main.
" Sarah, wid. Peter, laundress,h.2u.36 Flower.
" Stephen D. cigars, 213, h. 213 Pearl.
" William A. attendant 30 Washington.
Cranick Charles, driver, b. 20 Talcott.
Cranigan John M.night watchman at 98Kilbourn, h.u. 73 Temple.
Cranitch Patrick, laborer, b. 74 Albany.
Cranney Luke G. collarm. at 8, b. 43 Sigourney.
Cropulli Raphael, barber, 9 Market, h.21 Morgan.

DAVID CRARY, JR., Physician.  Office and house, 1074 Main street.
Hours—8 to 9 A.M. 1.30 to 4 and 7 to 9 P. M.

Crary David Jr. physician, 1074,h. 1074 Main.
" Edwin, druggist, 206, h.u. 208 Park.
" Frank, b. 27 Lewis.
" Hattie L. Mrs. b. 80 Maple.
Crase Richard H. patmkr. at 33 Wells,h.u. 239 Jef.
Craven Lawrence, molder,141 Com. b.u. 42 Wdbg.
" Martin V. bartender, h.u. 42 Woodbridge.
" Wm. upholsterer at 633 Main, h. 223 Asy.
Cravengard Christie, at 9 Sig. h. 109 Laurel.
Crawford Chas. grocer, 75 Ch.O. h. 93 Huyshope
" Charles M. sec'y Hfd. Paving & Construction Co. 868 Main, h. 94 Asylum.

## JOHN S. CRAIG,

*PRACTICAL—*

## PLUMBER AND GASFITTER,

*Dealer in FIRST CLASS PLUMBING and GAS-FITTING MATERIALS.*

Sanitary Plumbing a Specialty.

Agent for The Archer & Pancoast Co. Gas Fixtures, etc.

## 59 FARMINGTON AVENUE,

*Farmington Avenue Hotel Building.*

Crawford & Co. groceries, 1248 Main.
Malcolm Crawford.    Percy O. Burnham.
" Eliza, wid. Alexander, h.u. 43 Windsor.
" Flora, wid. Frank, h.3u. 277 Main.
" Harry, bartender, h. 14 So. Ann.
" J. B. l. 315 Pearl, rm. 402.
" James, laborer, h. 290 Pearl.
" Malcolm (*Crawford & Co.*) b. 1220 Main.
" Norman McD. general manager St.Ry. 115 State, h. 946 Asylum.
Creanick Chas. A. clerk at 1079 Mn. b. 20 Talcott.
Credenza Archangello, laborer, h.u. 210 Front.
Creech William P. salesman at 45 Asylum. b. 56 Winthrop.
Creed Daniel L. bartender at 522, b. 739 Main.
Creedon Elizabeth, wid. Patrick, h.2u. 159 Front.
" John, (*Andrews & C.*) h. 71 Seymour.
" John, policeman, h. cor. Russ and Hung.
" Thos. F. assembler, b.2u. 159 Front.
Crehan Eugene, helper N.Y.R. h. 14 Arch.
Creighead Lucy, wid. Glasgon C. h. 352½ Front.
Creighton Bernard, bricklayer, b.r. 181 Bellevue.
" Thos. J. compositor 254 Pearl,h. 29 Barbour.
Creller Leigh F. conductor St.Ry. b.u. 206 Fkn.
Cremin J. lab. Pope Tube Co. h.u. 110 Laurel.
Cresel Carmine, barber at 1237 Main.
Cressy Louis A. sec'y and treas. Conn. Farmer, 284 Asylum, b. 104 Huntington.
" Morton S. student at Yale, b.104 Huntington.
" Noah, M.D. editor Conn. Farmer, 284 Asylum. h. 104 Huntington.
Creston Peter, at 142, b. 156 Russ.
Crilly John A. adjuster St.Ry. 115 State, h. 146 Wethersfield.
" Thomas, hodcarrier, b. 16 Market.
Crimmin Patrick, laborer, h.u. 35 Avon.
Crimmins Daniel J. pistolm. at Colts, b. 53 Fkn.
" James, bartender, b. 7 Atlantic.
" John, wiredrawer at 40 Gov. h. 110 Laurel.
" Mary, wid. James, h.r. 44 Village.
" Mary, wid. John, h. 53 Franklin.
" P. Henry, assembler, Popes,h.2u. 108 Ward.
" William, helper, b. 79 Chestnut.
Critchie Arthur W. B. at 54 Ann, b. E.H.t.
Critchley Agnes, dressmaker, b. 16 Spring.
" Burt H. mach. at Popes, b.2u. 550 Asylum.
Crittenden Charles E. printer at 141 Pearl, h.u. 67 Hungerford.
" Elmer F. machinist at 476 Cap. l.192 Russ.
" George A. mach. at 476 Cap. h. 192 Russ.

Crittenden Leroy S. toolm. 476 Cap. b. 192 Russ.
" Ralph, mach. at 133 Sheldon, b. 47 Sumner.
" ☞ see also Cruttenden.
Crocker Albert N. clerk at Pratt & Whitney Co. 1 Flower, b. 63 Glendale.
" Alice M. asst. librarian at Hartford Public Library, 5 Athenæum, b. 20 Pavilion.
" Benjamin B. draughtsman at 756 Main, rm. 32, b. 20 Pavilion.
" Chas. E. painter at 843 Main, h. 63 Glendale.
" Chas D. bkkpr. at 1204 Main, h. 36 Mahl.
" Cynthia M. wid. Jeremiah, h. 20 Pavilion.
" E. A. lunchroom, 18 Central, h. 62 Edwards.
" Frank, painter, h.u. 230 Asylum.
" Fred'k W. clerk at Orient Ins. Co. 5 Haynes, b. 20 Pavilion.
" Hattie C. nurse, 95, h. 95 Jefferson.
" Howard, nightclerk, P.O. b. Wethersfield.
" Jeremiah R. laundrym. 1130, h. 1125 Main.
" John M. painter, h. 18 Sanford.
Crockett Matilda C. at 690 Park, b. 73 Francis.
Crockford Edmund M. Jr. farmer 301, b. 301 N.B.
Crofton Edward, motorm. St.Ry. b.2u. 387 Cap.
" Walter, coachman at 1067, b. 1067 Asylum.
Crofut James K. sec'y Blodgett & Clapp Co. 51 Market, h. Simsbury t.
" Sidney W. bank commissioner at State Capitol, rm 35, h. Killingly t.
Croke Wm. R. machinist, h. 287 Capitol.
Croll Benjamin, pressman, 690 Park, h. 11 Kibbe.
" Jacob, peddler, h. 210 Front.
Crolle Michael, laborer, b.u. 190 Front.
Crombie Albert H. butcher at 201 State, l. 90 Cap.
Cronan Corn, laborer at 8 Front.
Crondahl Cornelius, b.2u. 101 Sheldon.
" Hannah, wid. Daniel, h. 76 Vernon.
Cronin Catherine, wid. Daniel, h.2u. 36 Sheldon.
" Dennis, mach. r. 223 State, b.u. 48 Bellevue.
" James, l.u. 234 Pearl.
" Jeremiah F. clerk, 26 Front, b.u. 49 Wdbg.
" John, laborer, b.u. 49 Woodbridge.
" John B. molder at 54 Arch, h. 51 Potter.
" John F. helper, h. 93 Sheldon.
" John J. laborer, b. 33 Liberty.
" John J. mach. at 1 Flower, h. 224 Pearl.
" Mary, wid. Patrick, h.u. 30 Huntley pl.
" Mary Mrs. b. 828 Park.
" Maurice, quarrym. stone pits, h.r. 93 Sheldon.
" Michael, helper at 556 Cap. b. 33 Liberty.
" Patrick, ostler at 12, b. 52 Wells.
" Robert, coachman, h. 61 Elm.
" Thomas, coachman, h.u. 12 Clinton.
" Thomas, helper at Capitol, h.u. 89 Front.
" Thomas, mach. at 1 Flower, b. 10 Hawthorn.
" Timothy, laborer, b.2u. 101 Sheldon.
" Timothy, livery stable, 12, h.u. 52 Wells.
" William, dropforger at Popes, h.u. 43 Haw.
" William, helper, b. 9 Hawthorn.
" William F. screwmaker, b.u. 89 Front.
Cronnin Cornelius, laborer, h.u. 33 Liberty.
" Daniel F. clk. Pope Tube Co. b.u. 49 Windsor.
" Jeremiah, laborer, h.u. 49 Windsor.
" Joseph, barber at 55 High, b.u. 49 Windsor.
" Patrick H. helper, b.u. 49 Windsor.
" Robert E. mach. 1 Flower, b. 42 Hopkins.

Crosby A. O. treas. 868 Mn. h. E. Glastonbury v.
" Albert H. at Conn. Mut. Life Ins. Co. 783 Main, manager The Church Review, h. 39 Williams.
" Benjamin F. h. 98 Jefferson.
" Edward H. foreman at 20 Sargeant, h.u. 44 Atwood.
" Elizabeth B. wid. William S. h. 117 Wdld.
" Erastus H. clerk at 885 Main, h. 10 Florence.
CROSBY FRANCIS W. (Butts & C.) architects, 49 Pearl, b. 119 Capitol.
" Fred R. barber at 291 Park, h. 40 Ward.
" George B. at 9 New Britain, b. 27 Linden.
" Geo. E. laundry, Hawthorn, h.u. 15 Beach.
" George E. Jr. at Ætna Ins. Co. 666 Main, b. 15 Beach.
" George W. blacksm. at N.Y.R. b. 173 High.
" Gertrude, h. 117 Woodland.
" Howard L. clerk at 853 Main, b. 15 Beach.
" Isabella, wid. Erastus H. h. 785 Asylum.
" Leslie J. carpenter, h.r. 655 Farmington.
" Lester D. laundry, h. 21 Crown.
" Mary E. h. 98 Jefferson.
" Richard N. clerk at 197 Asy. b. 10 Florence.
" Thomas, compositor at Evening Post, 23 Asylum, h. New Britain t.
" William L. bkkpr. 69 Albany, b. 51 Oxford.
Cross B. Frank, bookbinder at 49 Trumbull, b. 115 Edwards.
" Edward, gardener, h. Hawthorn extension.
" Frederick O. shoem. 1263 Mn. h. 181 Capen.
" George, shoemaker, 328 Pearl.
" Harriet B. wid. Philemon, h. 115 Edwards.
CROSS ISAAC Jr. (C. & Morley,) prest. & treas. State Mutual Fire Ins. Co. 750 Main, h. 151 Capitol.          See page 445.
" L. D. doorplates, 103, b. 103 Ann.
" Maria D. Mrs. dressmaker, 10, h.2u. 10 Martin.
" Marian A. clerk at 70 Huy. b.u. 20 Union.
" Mary G. wid. James C. b. 19 Florence.

**CROSS & MORLEY,** insurance agents, 750 Main.          See page 445.
          Isaac Cross, Jr.          Franklin A. Morley.
" Rachael, wid. Henry, h.u. 20 Union.
" Thomas, operator at Popes, b.u. 20 Union.
" Wm. F. mach. at 30 Cush. b.u. 20 Union.
" William D. porter at P. O. h. 43 Wolcott.
" Wm. P. H. restaurant, 257 State, h.u. 10 Martin.
Crosscup & Gaudett, fresco painters, 75 Pratt.
          William A. Crosscup.          Amos Gaudett.
" Wm. A. (C. & Gaudett,) h. 345 Wethersfield.
Crossen Timothy, deckhand, str. Middletown, 285 State.

FREDERIC S. CROSSFIELD, Physician. Office, 75 Pratt street, Stearns building.
Hours—9 A.M. to 4 P.M.

Crossfield Frederic S. physician, 75 Pratt, b. 149 High.
" Lucy I. Mrs. b. 136 Trumbull.
" Rowland, cigarmaker, h. 48 Retreat.
Crost Andrew, photo engraver at 177 Asylum, b. 48 Retreat.

**CROSTHWAITE F. H.** Hartford Wire Works, 247 Asylum, h. 205 Laurel.
See page 488.
Crotean Daniel J. machinist at Pope Tube Co. h. 206 Asylum.
" David J. mach. 30 Cushman, h. 2 Putnam.
" Louis A. salesm. at 956 Mn. b. 110 Trumbull.
**CROTHERS T. D.** physician, Walnut Lodge, for inebriates, 56 Fairfield.
See page 712.
Crow James, teamster at 128 Commerce, b.u c. Temple and Front.
" John, porter at 207 Allyn, h. 14 Charles.
" John, stevedore, h.u. c. Temple and Front.
" John. Jr. teamster, 128 Commerce, b.u. c. Temple and Front.
Crowell Albert B. h. 79 Buckingham.
" Edward H. correspondt. at Popes, b. 79 Bkm.
" Frank B. steward, tug L.C.Ward, 285 State.
" John W. meat peddler, 455, h. 455 Garden.
" Wesley V. machinist 1 Flow. b. 66 Hopkins.
Crowley Alex. stonemason, h.2u. 33 Mechanic.
" Alice Mrs. b. 2 Holcomb.
" Andrew, laborer, h.u. 95 Sheldon.
" Cornelius, fireman at 20 Sargeant, h. 38 Hudson.
" Cornelius J. polisher, b. 38 Hudson.
" Daniel, bricklayer, b. 84 Albany.
" Daniel, teamster at 25, b.u. 247 Front.
" Daniel J. monumental carver, 34, h. 34 Williams.
" Edward, laborer, h.u. 84 Albany.
" Edward J. ins. agent, 721 Main, h. 7 Green.
" Ellen, wid. Cornelius, h.2u.r. 105 Windsor.
" Fred, driver at 25, b. 26 State.
" James, blacksmith at 48 Ann, b. W.H.t.
" James, motorman St.Ry. b. 64 Grove.
" Jas. C. polisher at Popes, h. New Britain t.
" James J. laborer, 690 Park, b. 14 Albany.
" Jeremiah M. plumber at 164 State, b. 38 Hudson.
" John, clerk at 130 Albany. b. 7 Green.
" John, laborer, 95 Pleasant, h. 16 Goodwin.
" John F. hodcarrier, h. 6 Douglas.
" John R. driver, 147, l. 550 Asylum.
" Joseph J. laborer, 335 Shel. b. 14 Union.
" Margaret, wid. Thomas, h.u. 14 Albany.
" Nellie T. boxtrimr. at 133 Shel. b. 7 Center.
" Patrick, laborer, h. 7 Center.
" Rose. wid. John, h. 7 Green.
" Sam. painter at 158 Woodland, b. 17 Center.
" Thomas J. helper at Popes, b. 38 Hudson.
" Wm. H. lineman at 266 Pearl, b. 87 High.
" William, cook, l. 87 High.
" William, laborer, b.u. 247 Front.
" William L. (Sherman & C.) h.2u. 703 Main.
Crowshaw Joseph, carpenter, h.r. 204 Asylum.
Crowther Frank H. mach. at 581, b. 317 Capitol.
" Harry, polisher at Popes, b.u. 44 Hopkins.
Crozier DeGrey F. salesman, h. 366 Garden.
Crum Francis A. mgr. at 732 Main, h. 22 Kenyon.
" Susan M. wid. F. W. b. 189 Ashley.
Crummey David H. mach. at 1 Flow. h.u. 295 Law.
" James A. tool clerk at 1 Flow. b. 295 Law.
" Sadie A. clerk, b.u. 295 Lawrence.

Crusberg Gabriel A. painter, h. 56 Judson.
Cruse Thomas, gardener, h.u. 22 Howard.
Crusius Robert, clerk, P.&R. h. Tariffville v.
Cruttenden Robert S. bookkeeper at National Fire Ins. Co. 95 Pearl, h. 65 Ashley.
" ☞ see also Crittenden.
CRYGIER FRANK H. cigars and tobacco, 248 Asylum, h. 70 Buckingham.
See page 111.
Cucuel Arthur L. mach. at 133 Shel. h. Bristol t.
Cuddigan Dennis, mach. at 556 Cap. b. 153 Bab.
" John J. brazier at Popes, b. 153 Babcock.
" Margaret, wid. Maurice, h. 153 Babcock.
" Michael, molder at 556 Cap. b. 153 Babcock.
" William, molder at 556 Capitol, h.r.552 Park.
Cudiski Abram, photographer, b.4u. 190 Front.
Cudney Christopher W. lineman at 247 Pearl, l. 166 Allyn.
Cudworth Henry J. toolm. at Popes, h.u.51 Grand.
Cuff Edward Charles, b. 23 Kilbourn.
" Patrick J. harnessmaker, h. 23 Kilbourn.
" Thos. G. bartender, b. 27 Morgan.
Culd Fred D. gen. supt. 336 Weth. h. 12 Wads.
Cull Bridget, h.2u. 20 Church.
" Daniel, pressm. at Popes, b.2u. 20 Church.
" John, engineer, 306 Pearl, h.2u. 20 Church.
" John, b. W. H. Home for the Aged, Alb.
" Katie, b.2u. 20 Church.
" Patrick J. polisher, b.2u. 20 Church.
Cullen Andrew S. clerk, 33 Asy. b. 1045 Main.
**CULLEN CHAS. A.** galvanized iron cornice and skylight manf. 44 Ann, h. 26 Center.
See page 489.
" Charles H. draughtsman, 904 Main, rm. 87, b. 198 Jefferson.
" Chas. W. plumber at 20 Church, h. N.B.t.
" Elizabeth A. clerk at Popes, b.u. 198 Jef.
" Gertrude M. bkkpr. Popes, b. 198 Jefferson.
" Margaret, pressfeeder at Case, Lockwood & Brainard Co. b.u. 29 Spruce.
" Margaret Mrs. b. 13 Putnam.
**CULLEN MICHAEL,** manager Peerless Oven Co. 44 Ann, h.u. 198 Jefferson.
See page 506.
" Michael, painter at r. 16 N.B. h. N.B.t.
" Michael J. packer at 1 So. Ann, h. 29 Spruce.
" Peter E. repairer at Popes, b. 144 Capitol.
Cullorton Charles, laborer, b.u. 101 Sheldon.
Culley Jacob H. mach. at 388 Cap. h. 27 Elm.
" Eliza G. Mrs. h.u. 37 Liberty.

## F. B. CUMMINGS,

## Livery & Boarding Stable,

Rear of Brown Stone Church, Asylum Street,
Corner of Huntington.

**820 Asylum Street.          14 Huntington Street.**

Telephone Connection.

Cullinane Bartholomew, driver, b.u. 64 Front.
Culliton Thomas H. secretary Calhoun Printing Co. 29 Union pl. b. 53 Capitol.
Culver A. J. Rev. pastor Christian Union Church, Wethersfield, h. 433 Windsor av.
" Walter B. chief cashier freight department N.Y.,N.H.&H. and N.E.R. 98 Kibourn, h. 62 Edwards.
" ☞ see also Colver.
Cumbs Clarence, laborer, b.2u. 278 Pearl.
" George, waiter, b.2u. 278 Pearl.
" ☞ see also Coombs.
Cummings Alice T. cataloguer, Hartford Public Library, 5 Atheneum, b. 180 Sargeant.
" C. D. Mrs. boardinghouse, 581 Main.
" Cyrus D. ironw'r at 618 Cap. b. 162 Sisson.
" Dennis B. engineer, h.u.r. 28 Walnut.
" Francis A. (C. & Garvin,) h. 180 Sargeant.
CUMMINGS FRANK B. livery, 14 Huntington, h. 5 Sumner.          See page 112.
" & Garvin, flour & grain, 37 Spruce.
Francis A. Cummings.          Charles H. Garvin.
" Hattie L. music teacher, 66, b. 66 Allen pl.
" James, laborer, b. 61 Potter.
" Jane, wid. James, h. 21 Sumner.
" John, clerk at 866 Main, b.u. 22 Franklin.
" Joseph F. P. engineer, h. 21 Sumner.
" Lawrence, profiler at Colts, h.u. 22 Franklin.
" Leonard G. real estate, h. 100 Edwards.
" Lizzie, dressmaker, b. 113 Maple.
" Margaret E. dressmaker, 128, h. 128 Ann.
" Margaret S. b. 60 Allen pl.
" Mary, tailoress, b.u. 22 Franklin.
" Mary, wid. George, boardinghouse, 16 Tru.
" Matthew J. conductor St.Ry. b. 32 Benton.
" Michael, porter, 207 Allyn, h.u. 147 Market.
" Patrick, gardener, b. 21 Sumner.
" Peter A. foreman St.Ry. b. 31 Benton.
" Sarah Mrs. h. 16 Lewis.
" Thomas B. carpenter, h.u. 144 Babcock.
" Thomas F. driver, 132 Market, b. 192 State.
" Thomas J. painter, b. 1202 Main.
" William, at Ætna Life Insurance Co. 650 Main, h. 66 Allen pl.
" ☞ see also Comings.
Cunliffe Frederick R. driver at Adams Ex. Co. b. 460 Main.
" Janet, wid. John S. h.u. 460 Main.
" Richard, signpainter at 104 Asylum, b. 460 Main.
Cunneen Martin, motorman, St.Ry. 115 State.
" Patrick, foundryman, 618 Cap. h. 48 Bonner.

Cunningham Alexander H. inspector, Hartford Steam Boiler Insp. & Ins. Co. 650 Main, l. 66 Capitol.
" Bridget, wid. Morris, h. 91 Windsor.
" Charlotte, b. 51 Sigourney.
" George G. h. 51 Sigourney.
" Harriet P. nurse at 20 South Hudson.
" Harvey M. mach. at 1 Flower, b. 51 Sig.
" James, b. 74 Retreat.
" James, b. 2 Holcomb.
" James, laborer, 556 Capitol, b. 7 Hawthorn.
" James, baggage master steamer Hartford, 285 State, b. 29 Bellevue.
" John C. laborer, h. 9 Hendricxsen.
" John E. mach. at P.&R. h.3u. 1422 Broad.
" John F. helper, 225 Sheldon, h. 13 Hdx.
" John G. mach. at P.&R. h. 1422 Broad.
" John J. butcher at 203 State, h. 52 Hicks.
" John W. molder, h.u. 82 Front.
" Lucy, milliner at 904 Main, b. 51 Sigourney.
" Margaret Mrs. b. 29 Bellevue.
" Margaret, wid. John, b.u. 63 Madison.
" Margaret, wid. John F. h.u. 118 Front.
" Margaret, wid. Matthias, h. 99 Windsor.
" Maria J. Mrs. boardinghouse, 1183 Main.
" Mary, wid. John, h.2u. 34 South Prospect.
" Mary E. bkkpr. 875 Main, b.2u. 11 Goodwin.
" Matthew, laborer, 556 Capitol, b. 7 Haw.
" Matthias, Jr. clerk, 273 Asy. b. 99 Windsor.
" Michael, chipper at 556 Capitol, b. 7 Haw.
" Michael, helper, 228 Pearl, b. Newington t.
" Michael, laborer, b.2u. 114 Windsor.
" Michael J., Florence House, 114 State.
" P. deckhand steamer Hartford, 285 State.
" Patrick, coremaker, b.u. 34 So. Prospect.
" Peter, bartender, 1001 Main, h.u. 74 Gov.
" Rose, b. W. H. Home for the Aged, Alb.
" Thomas, brazier, h. 1183 Main.
" Thomas, driver, h.u. 65 Pleasant.
" Thomas H. machinist at Pratt & Whitney Co. 1 Flower, b.u. 20 Babcock.
" Timothy, laborer, h.2u. 114 Windsor.
" Wilbur F. farmer, Blo. opp. school farm.
" Wm. captain, h.2u.r. 61 Front.
" William, engineer, 27 Potter, b. 19 Central.
" William H. molder 1 Flow. h.u 20 Babcock.
" Wm. J. salesman, 206 State, h. 11 Westland.
Cuntz Hermann F., M. E. patent clerk Pope Mfg. Co. b. 2 Columbia.
Curcio Gilardo, laborer, h. 190 Front.
Curley David, teamster, h.3u. 4 John.
" David, wringer at 15 Trumbull, b. 4 John.
" Ellen, h.u. 47 Spruce.
" John, bartender, b. 1171 Main.
" John, clerk at 990, b. 1210 Main.
" Patrick J. clerk at Charles R. Hart Co. 898 Main, h.u. 27 Talcott.
Curran Edward, silverplater, b. 80 State.
" James, printer at Sunday Journal, 284 Asylum, l.2u. 1067 Main.
" John, fireman N.Y.R. b. 45 Albany.
" Patrick, laborer, b.u. 106 Windsor.
" William, tinner, b.u. 1067 Main.
Currie Ann Mrs. h. 138 Madison av.
Currier Herman D. mach. 1 Laurel, b. 419 Maple.

Curry Emma F. wid. John A. b. 110 Retreat.
" Eugene H. manager at 169 Front, h. 2u. 249 Jefferson.
" F. C. at Travelers Ins. Co. 56 Prospect, b. 34 Vine.
" Fannie J. Mrs. b. 36 Jefferson.
" Howard W. clerk, 690 Park, b. 110 Retreat.
" Isabella, wid. Alexander, h. 110 Retreat.
" James A. farmer and milkman, b. 39 Vine.
" James S. mech. at Popes, b. 138 Madison.
" John, collarmaker at 8 Sig. h. 39 Vine.
" John M. rubberworker, b. 21 Sisson.
" Kate L. at 690 Park, b. 138 Madison av.
" Martin, cigarmaker, h. 235 Park.
" Thomas, h.u. 19 Alden.
" Thomas, laborer at 1 Flower, h. 21 Smith.
" Thomas F. mech. at Popes, b. 138 Madison.
Curtain John, coachman, h. 99 Arch.
Curtin Annie, operator at 97 Asy. b. 1422 Broad.
" Cornelius, driver, r. 13 Wells, h.2u.53Wads.
" D. F. clerk at 197 Asylum, b.2u. 53 Wads.
" David, coachman at Mrs. Colts, 30 Wethersfield, h. 28 Park.
" David W. mach. at 1 Flow. h. 1206 Broad.
" Dennis, helper at 1 So. Ann, b. 66 Hopkins.
" Edward, painter at 29, b. 29 Vine.
" Frank H. clerk at 42 High, h.u. 75 Ward.
" James, motorman St.Ry. h. 23 Liberty.
" James H.clerk 197Asy. b.2u.53Wadsworth.
" John, driver at 1123 Main, b. 10 Ellery.
" John, helper at 1 Flower, h. 303 Lawrence.
" John, pressman, b. 97 Windsor.
" John, tinner at N.Y.R h. 44 John.
" John D. saloon, 525, h.u. 545 Main.
" Mary, wid. David, h.u. 1422 Broad.
" Mary, wid. Mich. groceries, 10, h. 10 Ellery.
" Michael, filer at Popes, b. 27 Affleck.
" Michael, helper at P.&R. h. 84 Walnut.
" Michael, mach.hand Colts, b. 42Woodbridge.
" Patrick, teamster at 40 Elm, b. 15½ Wads.
" Thomas P. mach. at Popes, h. 1 Orchard.
" Walter, clerk, b. 44 John.
" William H. tinner at N.Y.R. h.u. 111 Law.
Curtis Alfred C. market, 16 Queen, h.3u. 82 Sargeant.
" Curtis C.wattdr.str.Middletown,h.Hamburg.
u Charles W. elevatorer 650 Mn. h. 51 Center.

**CURTIS D. J. & SON,** brickmakers, 737 Windsor av.    *See page 517.*
Daniel J. Curtis.        Daniel J. Curtis, Jr.
Curtis Daniel J. *(D. J. Curtis & Son,)* builder, brickm. 737 Windsor av. h. Springfield c.
u Daniel J. Jr. *(D.J.C. & Son,)* b. 651 Main.
" Edward, assistant supt. at N.Y.R. 450 Asylum, h. 62 Gillett.
" Fred C. magician, h.u. 37½ Church.
" George D. state editor at Hartford Times, 716 Main, h. 96 Windsor av.
" George H. machinist, b. 135 Capen.
u Gerard, clerk, 650 Mn. rm. 17, b. 84 Garden.
Curtis Grosvenor W. vice president Charles R. Hart Co. 898 Main, h. station 19, W.t.
    *See page 179.*
" Harry, mason, h. 17 Kibbe.
u Hattie E. h. 42 Elliott.

Curtis Henry, gardener, h. 185 Capen.
" Henry J.sec.Curtis Hull Mfg.Co.h.61 Imlay
" Henry T. clerk, 72 Front, h.2u. 52 Judson.
" Herman W. motorman, St.Ry. h. 24 Vernon.
" Hull Mfg. Co. 42 Union pl.
" James A. jobber, h. 54 Grand.
" John A. h.u. 15 Eaton.
" John F. real estate, 793 Main, h. 30 Imlay.
" & Johnson, architects, 926 Main, rm. 77.
T. Alden Curtis.        Wm. D. Johnson.
" Josiah, b. 2 Holcomb.
" Lucius Q. Rev. b. 52 Imlay.
" Robert W. student, b. 4 Girard.
" Sarah A. Mrs.: h. 61 Imlay.
" Sidney B. cashier, Western Union Telegraph Co. 6 Central, h. 4 Girard.
" T. Alden, *(C. & Johnson,)* h. Windsor t.
" Thomas, clerk at P.O. h.u. 37½ Church.
" Wm. E. clerk at 4, b.u. 37½ Church.
" Wallace E. carptr. 224 Sargeant, h.36 Imlay.
" Wm. H. screenm. 247 Asylum. h. 2 Morris.
" Wm. J. helper, N.Y.R. b.r. 26 Walnut.
Curtiss Everett P. sec'y & treas. Hitchcock & Curtiss Knitting Co. h. 624 Asylum.
" John, h. 303 Lawrence.
" Payson L. student Theol.sem. 1507 Broad.
" Samuel H. secy. and treas. of Western Automatic Machine Screw Co. h. 125 Oak.
Curvo Cristofer, stonecutter, b.4u. 190 Front.
Cusanelli Marieangello, laborer, h. 73 Morgan.
Cushing Thomas, 2d mate str. Middletown, 285 State, h. New York.
Cushman Austin F. pres't Cushman Chuck Co. h. 141 Sigourney.
" Chuck Co. manufacturers, 30 Cushman.
" Dwight, waterwheels, h.r. 29 Church.
" Elvie M. clerk at Brown, Thomson & Co. 942 Main, b. East Hartford t.
" Eugene L. sec'y and treas. Cushman Chuck Co. h. 32 Atwood.
" Frances V. wid. Elisha, h. 69 Chestnut.
" Frank S. conductor, St.Ry. h. 626 Broad.
" Harry M. b.2u. 54 Chestnut.
" Lucius E. painter, h. 7 Sigourney pl.
" Merritt S. carpenter, b.2u. 54 Chestnut.
" Solomon M. carpenter at 334 Asylum, b.u. 866 Broad.
Cushner Benjamin, ragpeddler, h.u. 20 North.
Cusick Charles T. cutter at 740, l. 740 Main.
" Fred'k H. merchant tailor, 740, l. 740 Main.
" George, molder, b.2u. 18 Gold.
" John, machinist at Colts, h. 2 Wawarme.
" John J. clerk, 319 Asylum, b. 53 Flower.
" Michael T. machinist at 1, h. 53 Flower.
" Patrick, driver, h.u. 22 Commerce.
" Thos. J. polisher at Popes, b. 2 Wawarme.
" Walter, laborer, b. 22 Commerce.
" Wm. E. machinist at Colts, b. 2 Wawarme.
Custalow Chas. W. waiter, 941 Mn. h. 160 Barb.
Custerbater Fred, harnessmaker, b.u. 25 Brook.
Custis Chas. W. elevatorer,650 Mn.h. 154Mather.
Custus Henrietta, wid. Charles, b. 20 Wads.
Cuterpacer Barned, peddler, h. 244 Front.
Cutler Benj. laborer, 128 State, h. 27 Kilbourn.
" Bradford J. agent, 715 Mn. b.110 Babcock.

Cutler Geo. S. screwm.476 Cap. l. 16 Columbia.
" James M. mach. at 1 Flower, b. 40 Allen pl.
CUTLER RALPH W. president Hartford Trust
    Co. 764 Main, *fire commissioner*, h. 101
    Washington.
" Samuel A. clerk, 6 Central, b. 29 Kilbourn.
Cutting Arthur, helper at 3 Far. l. 1500 Broad.
" Ezra M. cashier at Popes, b. 217 Ashley.
Cuttz George, screwm. at 476 Cap. b. 151 Weth.
Cuykendall D. M. clerk at 69 Albany, b. E.H.t.
" F. H. h.u. 68½ Wooster.
Cycle Supply Company, 20 Sargeant.
Cyclopedia of Insurance, H. R. Hayden, 53 Tru.
Cygolf Shoe, The, 218 Asylum.

DABATO Carmine, fruits, 491 Main, h. 12 Elm.
Dabeau Napoleon, forger at Popes, h. 54 Market.
Daberkow Carl E. janitor, h.u. 5 Pleasant.
" Max R. printer at Hartford Times, 716
    Main, h. 25 Pleasant.
Dabrama Nicolo, laborer, h.3u. 27 North.
Daccy James B. printer, b. 45 Windsor.
" James F. packer, b.2u. 52 Avon.
" John, laborer, b.2u. 40 Sheldon.
" Maggie, winder at 34 Morgan, b. 49 Wooster.
" Margaret, wid. Patrick, h. 49 Wooster.
" Michael J. helper, b. 52 Avon.
" Michael M. compositor 23 Asy.b.45 Windsor.
" Thomas, driver, h. 45 Windsor.
" Thomas, pressfdr. 141 Pearl, b.2u. 52 Avon.
" ☞ *see also Darcy.*
Daggett W. H. H. awnings, 71 Asy. h. 70 Martin.
Dagle Henry J. toolm. at 476 Capitol, h. E.H.t.
Dahill Cornelius, ship fastener, h. 7 Front.
" Cornelius,teamster,128Com. b Front c.Arch.
" Daniel F. ship carpenter, h. 111 Potter.
" Daniel J. carptr. Popes, h.2u. 35 Harbison.
" John, teamster, b.2u. 89 Front.
" John J. manager Allyn House, 152 Asylum.
" Margaret, clerk at 921 Main, b. 168 Allyn.
" Margaret, wid. Thomas, h. 77 Temple.
" Mary, cook at 20 South Hudson.
" Nellie C. cashier, b. 77 Temple.
" Thomas, helper, h. 76 Pleasant.
" W. T. machinist, b. 76 Pleasant.
" William, helper at 54 Arch, b. 258 Front.
" William F. expressman, h. 47 Green.
Dahl Andrew, clerk, 1038 Main, b.2u. 28 Church.
" C. F. helper at Colts, b. 133½ Barbour.
" George T. mach. at Colts, b. 133½ Barbour.
Dahlberg Nils, filer at 581, b. 317 Capitol.
Dahlen Alex D. janitor1507 Broad, h.u.53Wdbg.
Dahlin Aaron A. screwm. 476 Cap. h.u. 240 Zion.

Dahlman Sevren, saddler at 8, b. 143 Sigourney.
Dahm Emma M. clerk, Brown, Thomson & Co.
    942 Main, b. 23 Wolcott.
" Herman, polisher, h.u. 23 Wolcott.
" Herman, Jr. mach. 555 Cap. b.u. 23 Wolcott.
" Rudolph, harnessmaker, h.u. 2 Putnam.
Dahme Hubert Rev. h. 1361 Main.
Daigneau Eli, Capitol Ave. House, 276 Lawrence.
" Harmidas, carpr. at N.Y.R.h.u.37 Lawrence.
Dailey Bridget, wid. Keron, h.r. 35 Front.
" Dennis, boilermaker at N.E.R. h. 22 Center.
" Horace E. painter at 1 Flow. b. 1469 Broad.
" James, plater at Wm. Rogers Mfg. Co. 66
    Market, b.r. 35 Front.
" Jas. P. harnessm. 1148 Main, h.u. 9 Sig. pl.
" John, switchman, St.Ry. h.3u.r. 25 Spruce.
" John W. operator at 40 Gov. b. 1122 Main.
" Keron, helper at 128 State, b.r. 35 Front.
" Mary Mrs. h. 68 Albany.
" Patrick, teamster, 250 State, h. E.H.t.
" Timothy J. helper at Baxter the Decorator,
    231, b. 284 Asy. rm. 79.
" Warren Clair, music teacher, b. 153 Capen.
" William E. lab. Pope Tube Co. b. 139 Zion.
" William J. assistant superintendent, 731
    Main, h. 4 Foot Guard pl.
" William P. horsedealer, h. Windsor av.
" ☞ *see also Daily, Daley, Daly.*
Daily Kate, b.2u. 1178 Main.
" Patrick, b. 2 Holcomb.
Daina Lawrence, chef,152 Asy.h.2u. 42½Windsor.
Dairy restaurant, H. N. Strong, 189 Asylum.
Daisnarois Oscar, lather, b. 192 State.
Dakin Edward, decorator at Baxter the Deco-
    rator, 231 Asylum, h. 4 John.
Daleno Giovanni A. fruits, 262, h. 262 New Park.
Dalessio Antonio, laborer, b.r. 33 North.
" Tony, poolroom, 637½ Main, h. 49 Morgan.
" Tony, shoem. 355 Park, h.2u. 33 Albany.
Daley Ann, wid. John, h.u. 37 Lafayette.
" Bridget, laundress at 30 Washington.
" Charles, teamster, h. 73 Pleasant.
" Charles F. mach. at 1 Flower, h. 108 Ward.
" Crohen, laborer, h.u. 106 Windsor.
" Dennis, laborer at 1 Flower, h. 108 Ward.
" Edward, clerk at L. L. Ensworth & Son,
    iron merchants, 104, h. 252 Front.
" Edward W. clerk at 341 Main, h. 3 East.
" Francis, engineer, h. 3 Lewis.
" Francis Mrs., Parkview house, 3 Lewis.
" Francis J. drug clerk, b. 3 Lewis.
" George W. clerk L. L. Ensworth & Son, iron
    store, 104 Front, h. 30 Windsor av.
" Hugh J. laborer, 1 Flow. b. 303 Lawrence.
" Jas. woodworker, 352 Alb. b. 39 Harrison.
" Jas. A. salesm. 66 Asy. b.u. 37 Lafayette.
" John, l.u. 1122 Main.
" John, porter at 306 Pearl, h. 6 Hungerford.
" John F. machinist, h.u. 67 Bellevue.
" John J. mechanic at 581 Capitol, b. 10 Arch.
" John P. toolmaker at 1 Flow. b. 1331 Broad.
" John W. druggist at 1189 Main, b. 3 Lewis.
" Joseph F. plumber, 1230 Main, b. 15 Belden.
" Joseph T. druggist, 200 Fkn. h. 65 Elliott.
" Mae J. cashier at 909 Main, b. 45 N.B.t.

Daley Margaret A. b.u. 37 Lafayette.
" Matthew, clerk at 372 Asylum, b. 31 Park.
" Matthew A. bkkpr. at 1230, b. 1224 Main.
" Michael, laborer, h. 29 Arch.
" Michael, mach. at 1 Flower, h. 1331 Broad.
" Michael, piper, P.&R. b.2u. 53 Liberty.
" Miles F. drug clerk, 407 Mn. h.u. 7 Morris.
" Nellie, dressmaker at 48, h.2u. 48 Windsor.
" Patrick, laborer, b.3u. 36 Sheldon.
" Patrick, laborer, b.u. 259 Front.
" Patrick, laborer at Popes, b. 159 Lawrence.
DALEY PATRICK H. councilman 2d ward, (Langdon & Daley,) h. 11 Pleasant.
" Patrick J. conductor, St.Ry. b.2u. 40 Park.
" Stephen H. mach. at 70 Huyshope, h.45 N.B.
" Thomas, at 20 Sargeant, b. 6 Hungerford.
" William, helper, 133 Shel. b. 52 Linden.
" William, ostler, 366 Main, h. 136 Albany.
" William, rubberworker, b. 8 Amity.
" William C. clerk at 909 Main, b. 86 Pratt.
" Wm. H. mach. at 1 Flower, h.2u. 226 Zion.
" ☞ see also Dailey· Daily; Daly.
Dalgleish John L. treas. Barbour Silver Co. 62 Market, h. 69 Washington.
Dalleas Jennie Mrs. b. 187 Sisson.
" Peter, collector, b. 187 Sisson.
Dalton Ada, nurse, h. 14 Church, rm. 10.
" Albert W. clerk, b.u. 1271 Main.
" John, filer at Popes, b.u. 9 Hawthorn.
" John, mason, h. 2 Orchard.
" John J. grocery, 77 Sheldon, h. 138 Maple.
" John J. blacks. 556 Cap. h. 49 Wadsworth.
" John P. teamster, b. 74 Windsor.
" John S. mach. at 13 Central, h.u. 100 Bab.
" Joseph, h. 9 Hawthorn.
" Kittie, at 70 Huyshope, b. 138 Maple.
" Lewis, lineman, l. 534 Main.
" Marshall H. tinsmith at 446 Asylum, h.2u. 1271 Main.
" Michael, laborer, Colts, b.u. 45 Woodbridge.
" Nora T. inspec. at 70 Huy. b. 49 Wadsworth.
" Richard J. toolmkr. at 556 Cap. h.u. 100 Bab.
" William J. at 70 Huyshope, b. 138 Maple.
" William J. motorman St.Ry. b. 86 Flower.
Daly Catherine, wid. John, h. 56 Liberty.
" Charles, polisher, h.u. 61 Potter.
" & Eardley, painters, r. 1331 Broad.
Patrick Daly.     John Eardley.
" Elizabeth Mrs. h. 13 Charter Oak.
" Ellen, wid. Thomas, b.3u. 338 Park.
" Fergus, fireman at 70 Com. b.2u. 35 Elliott.
" James, carpenter at 141 Trumbull, b. Liberty.
" James A. conductor, N.Y.R. h.u. 3 Hamilton.
" James F. molder, h.2u. 68 Sheldon.
" Jas. R., U.S. gauger, 65 State, h. 66 Hudson.
" John, casehardener, 581 Cap. h. 133 Law.
" John F. machinist, h. 67 Bellevue.
" John J. bkkpr. 360 Main, b. 13 Lawrence.
" John J. screwmaker, 476 Cap. b. 180 Front.
" John J. machinist, b. 17 Curcombe.
" Joseph, laborer, h.u. 20 Commerce.
" Katherine I. clerk, 956 Main, b. 126 Maple.
" Lawrence, gardener, 118 Benton, b. 338 Park.
" Lawrence, stoves, etc. 360 Main, h. 13 Law.
" Marg. Mrs. seamstress Watkinson schl. farm.

Daly Margaret, wid. Keron, b.u. 1447 Broad.
" Margaret J. clerk at Brown, Thomson & Co. 942 Main, b. Warehouse Point v.
" Mary, wid. Patrick, h.2u. 52 Green.
" Mary, wid. Charles, h. 17 Curcombe.
" Mary, wid. Patrick, h.2u. 102 Windsor.
" Mary E. wid. James F. h.2u. 9 Hendricxsen.
" Michael, helper, b. 23 Chestnut.
" Michael W. printer at Hartford Times, 716 Main, b.u. 66 Hudson.
" Patrick, (D. & Eardley.) h.u. 1331 Broad.
" Patrick, helper, h. 23 Chestnut.
" Patrick, helper, h. 18 So. Prospect.
" Peter A. clerk at 908 Main, h.u. 130 Babcock.
" Thomas, coachman, h.u. 36 Woodbridge.
" Thomas, helper at 556 Cap. h.u. 13 Front.
" Thos. F. letter carrier station A. h.51 Hudson.
" Timothy, casehardenner, 581 Capitol, h. 104 Windsor.
" Timothy, coachman at 2, b. 2 Congress.
" Timothy, mach. at Popes, h.u. 104 Windsor.
" Wm. molder at 54 Arch, h.u. 61½ Governor.
" ☞ see also Dailey; Daily; Daley.
Dalzell Adello, laborer, N.Y.R. h.2u. 369 Park.
" J. P. electrician, b. 66 Hopkins.
D'Amato John, tailor at 299 Mar. b. 20 Charles.
Damato Biasi, laborer, h.3u. 76 Charles.
" Carlo, laborer, b.3u. 76 Charles.
" Domenico, ragpicker h. 78 Charles.
" Francisco, laborer, b. 78 Charles.
" John, laborer, b.3u. 76 Charles.
" Joseph, laborer, b. 78 Charles.
" Vencenzio, bootblack, h. 78 Charles.
Damcke Emma Mrs. h. 186 Laurel.
Damery Eliza, wid. John, b.u. 80 Hudson.
" Geo. D. conductor St.Ry. h.u. 80 Hudson.
" Wm. H. clerk, 436 Asylum, h.u. 80 Hudson.
Damiano Rocco, bootblack, 706 Mn. h. 190 Front.
Damico Domenico, laborer, b. 78 Morgan.
Damon Christine, wid. David, h. 133 Mar. rm. 6.
" Fannie E. dressmaker, 54, h. 54 Maple.
" Harriett G. wid. Uriah E. h. 54 Maple.
" William A. dentist, 103, l. 103 Pratt.
Damroy William, laborer, h.2u. 15 Mechanic.
Damstrom John E. roller at Pope Tube Co. b. 70 Lawrence.
Danahy Cornelius, baker, l. 1045 Main.
" Edmund W. at Ætna Life Ins. Co. 650 Main, b. 38 Collins.
" James, h. 38 Collins.
" Jas. L. proofreader, 252 Pearl, b. 38 Collins.
" John, blacksmith, 92 Albany, l. 1045 Main.
" ☞ see also Danehy; Denehy.
Danaker Ambrose, motorm. St.Ry. b. 2 Goodman.
" Joseph H. motorm. St.Ry. h. 2 Goodman.
Dananey John J. laborer at N.Y.R. h. 44 Avon.
Danbury Hat Co. 214 Asy. J. E. Raynor, mgr.
Dandurand Adolph, carpenter, h. 42½ Windsor.
Danehy James, laborer, b.u. 1163 Main.
" ☞ see also Danahy; Denehy.
Danforth Joseph W. waiter at 931, b. 933 Main.
" Kate C. h. 22 Francis.
" Mary G. wid. John W. h. 67 Buckingham.
D'Angillo Donato, laborer, b.r.3u. 20 Charles.
" Francesco, laborer, b.4u. 2 Charles.

Dangona Nincenzo, laborer, h.r.n. 10 Charles.
Daniel Chas. Z. ad. writer, 76 Tru. b. Highland.
" David, (*H. & D. Daniel,*) h. Highland.
" H. & D. clothers, 76 Trumbull.
    Harry Daniel, Springfield.    David Daniel.
Daniels Aaron M. varnishes, b. 12 Walnut.
" Albert N. bookkeeper, 726 Main, h. 392 Wethersfield.
" Angelo C. filer at 388 Capitol, b. 2 Atlantic.
" C. D. conductor St.Ry. h. 212 Allyn.
" C. S. Mrs. h.u. 2 Belden.
" Charles E. h.u. 101 Main.
" Charles F. bartender at 330 Main.
" Clarence E. elevatorer, 835 Mn. b. 2 Martin.
" Edward, b. 50 Village.
" Eugene H. painter, b. 1244 Main.
" Eva A. clerk at Hartford Life Ins. Co. 252 Asylum, b. 17 Haynes.
" Frank K. steogr. 654 Main, b. Middletown t.
" Frank L. mach. at 1 Flower, b. 20 Linden.
" Fred, b. 50 Village.
" Fred. A. mach. at 1 Flower, h. 180 Putnam.
" Fred. E. cabinetm. at 147 Asy. h.u. 19 Chapel.
" Fred H. bunker engine No. 5, b. 129 Sig.
" Geo. C. asst. janitor, 223 Asy. h.u. 2 Martin.
" Harry W. mach. at 1 Flower, h.u. 26 Imlay.
" Henry C. printer, 284 Asylum, h. 12 Walnut.
" James A. at Hartford Fire Ins. Co. 53 Trumbull, h. Glastonbury t.
" James T. mach. at 581 Capitol, h.2u. 26 Imlay.
" Julia A. wid. James A. h. 120 Trumbull.
" Leonard C. (*Daniels Mill Co.*) 40 Elm, h. 64 Farmington.
" Lorenzo D. janitor at 676, h. 676 Main.
" Louis, laborer, b. 72 Pleasant.
" Louise M. wid. Fred. M. b. 278 Windsor av.
" Matilda, wid. Morgan, b. 60 Benton.
" Mill Co. flour, feed, grain, 40 Elm, 353 Albany, and Bloomfield.
" Newell P. printer, 25 Asylum, h. E.H.t.
" Rhoda, wid. John M. h. 50 Village.
" Timothy A. b. 1150 Main.
" William, driver, 250 State, b. Riverside pl.
" William R. ship. clerk, 175 Pearl, b. Weth. t
Danielson Albin, lab. 690 Park, b. 99 Hamilton.
" Charles G. mech. at Popes, h.u. 74 Lawrence.
" Fred, machinist, b. 23 So. Hudson.
" George E. foreman at Popes, h.u. 11 Imlay.
" Gustav, baker, 1213 Main, h. 23 So. Hudson.
" Herman, carpenter, h. 51 South Hudson.
Danks Frank W. dispatcher, P.&R. h. Tariffville t.
Danley Anna M. attendant at 30 Washington.
Dannehy John J. teamster, h. 1225 Main.
" William, h. 1219 Main.
Dantrich Fred L. artist, 57, b. 57 Park.
Darby Burt A. clerk, 1079 Main, h. 20 Talcott.
" James, bartender, 539 Main, h. 66 Hicks.
" John, driver at 1036 Main, b. 80 Hopkins.
DARBY JOHN (*Wolcott & D.*) mechanical engineer, h. 6 Columbia.    *See page 493*
**DARBY THEODORE T.** fresco painter, 37, h. 37 Martin.    *See page 529.*
Darcey William. inspector P&R. b. 92 Walnut.
D'Arche Carl A. clerk, b.u. 46 Canton.
" Carl F. machinist, h. Park.

D'Arche David J. operator at N.Y.R. h.u. 46 Canton.
" Emil, bricklayer, b.u. 46 Canton.
" Meclea A. mach. at 28 Laurel, h.u. 9 Smith.
Darcy Albert F. actor, b. 7 Barbour.
" Mary, wid. John, h. 7 Barbour.
" Michael, b. 2 Holcomb.
" Patrick J. inspector health board, City Hall, 800 Main, h. 144 Retreat.
" ☞ *see also Dorsey.*
Dare Emily C. dressmaker, 71, h. 71 Asy. rm. 22.
Darling Charles A. carpenter, h. 11 John.
" Edgar C. rubberw. 690 Park. h. 60 Heath.
" George A. mach. at Popes, h. 68 Madison.
" George W. coachman at 20 Highland, h. 11 Fales.
" Jennie L. stenographer at rm. 27, State Capitol, b. West Hartford t.
" John D. salesman, 25 Asy. h. 43 Buckingham.
" William E. dentist at 53 Tru. b. 68 Madison.
" Martin, b. 61 Ann.
Darnstaedt C. R. die sinker, l. 67 Pearl.
" Frederick W. electric. at Popes, h. 964 Broad.
" Herman J. toolm. at Popes, h. 964 Broad.
Darrell Albert, farmer, b. Bloomfield av. opposite school farm.
Darrow Elizabeth, h.r. 8 Seyms.
" George H. h.r. 8 Seyms.
" Sarah A. wid. Christopher M. h. 28 Mahl.
Darsey John, molder at 54 Arch, h. 101 Sheldon.
Dart Benj. machinist at 388 Capitol, h. E.H.t.
" Charles T. molder, 1 Flower, h. Newington t.
**DART EDMUND,** builder, 14 Hicks, h. 577 Farmington.    *See page 552.*
" Fred W. (*West End Land Co.*) h. 374 N.B.
" Harry E. elevatorer at N.Y.R. h. 6 Atlantic.
" J. & Son, milkmen & stock farm, 286 N.B.
    Joseph Dart.    Fred W. Dart.
" Joseph, (*J. D. & Son,*) h. 286 New Britain.
" M. John, inspector at 388 Capitol, b. E.H.t.
" Marking Machine Co. 235 State.
" Mary J. wid. Fred. L. h.u. 2 Chestnut.
" Matilda, wid. Theodore G. h. 6 Atlantic.
" Theodore S. blacksm. at 9 Kil. h. 1413 Main.
" Walter C. mach. at 388 Capitol, h. E.H.t.
" Warren T. coachman, h. 28½ Beach.
Darziel Alderd, repairer, P.&R. h. Burnside v.
Daugherty Abbie L. b. 9 Walnut.
Daughn Eugene, bookkeeper, b. 61 Ann.
Davenport Charles A. at Hartford Life Insurance Co. 252 Asylum, b. 64 Capen.
" & Co. bottlers, 39 Front.
    Joseph C. Davenport.
" Elizabeth E. wid. Charles, b. 64 Capen.
" Jane C. Mrs. nurse, 449, b. 449 Broad.
" John S. Rev. h. 1057 Asylum.
" Joseph C. restaurant, 7, h.u. 5 American.
David John, stonecutter, b. 20 Morgan.
" Martin J. painter at 1 Flower, h.u. 20 Law.
Davidson Chas. S. div. supt. N.Y., N.H. & H.R. 450, h. 915 Asylum.
" David, h.2u. 48 Sheldon.
" Hugh, bricklayer, h. 352 Park.
" John F. porter at Conn. Trust and Safe Deposit Co. 785 Main, b. 6 Elm.

Davidson Wm B. teller United States Bank, 872 Main, *fire commissioner*, b. 915 Asylum.
" ☞ *see also Davison.*
Davie Archibald R. shipping clerk at National Machine Co. 133 Shel. h.u. 426 Asylum.
" John, clerk, 310 Park, b. 149 Babcock.
Davies James R. (*D. & Sawyer*,) b.u. 49 Wooster.
" & Sawyer, plumbers, 53 Farmington.
James R. Davies.      DeForest A. Sawyer.
Davin Peter B. mechanic at Popes, b. 749 Broad.
Davis A. G. at Travelers Ins. Co. 56 Prospect, h. 169 Seymour.
" A. P. nurse, 14, b. 14 Church, rm. 1.
" Arthur P. toolm. 1 Flower, b. 169 Seymour.
" Adella Mrs.: h. 31 Walnut.
" Albert B. C. clerk, 372 Asy. b. 5 Harrison.
" Arthur, at Colts, b.u. 23 Wells.
" & Beattie, barbers, 36¼ Church.
" Belle C. teach. Arsenal school, b. 192 High.
" Bertha, nurse, 20 South Hudson.
" Beulah Mrs. b. 145 Collins.
" Bros. market and grocers, 1451 Broad.
Charles F. Davis.      Silas H. Davis.
" C. E. wid. Rev. Samuel A. h. 192 High.
" C. M. wid. W. B. h. 5 Wadsworth.
" Carl W. at Travelers Insurance Co. 56 Prospect, b. 79 Vernon.
" Charles E. h. 53 Westland.
" Charles F. (*D. Bros.*) h. 257 Lawrence.
" Chas. L. rubberw. at 690 Park, h. 604 Main.
" Charles M. sawyer at 69 Front, h. E.H.t.
" Clarence C. ostler at 43 Mar. h. 11 Elliott pl.
" Courtland P. conductor V. Div. N.Y.R. 450 Asylum, h. 34 Ashley.
" Daniel R. bookbinder at Case, Lockwood & Brainard Co. 141 Pearl b. 581 Main.
" Edward L. repairer at 40 Gov. h. 37 Elm.
" Eliza Mrs. laundress, h. 5 Huntley av.
" Ernest, barber at 299, h.u. 299 Windsor av.
" Fannie R. clerk at Brown, Thomson & Co. 942 Main, b. 56 Church.
" Ferdinand J. boardinghouse, 32 Church.
" Frances L. wid. Joseph S. h.u. 46 Wooster.
" Francis W. blacksm. 1 Flow. h.2u. 167 Cap.
" Fred, carpenter, b. 1104 Main.
" Fred, porter at 851 Main, h. Cottage Grove.
" Frederick C. clerk at 27 Asy. h. 61 Lincoln.
" Frederick W. barber at 3 Asy. h. 34 Smith.
" Frederick W. with J. J. & F. Goodwin, 783 Main, h. 79 Vernon.
" G. Pierrepont, physician, medical examiner Travelers Ins. Co. 56 Pro. h. 30 Woodland.
" George, clerk, 55 Maple, h. 17 Buckingham.
" George, painter, b. 41 Asylum.
" George C. toolmaker at Popes, b. 56 Bkm.
" George D. helper at 353 Albany, h. N.t.
" George F. (*D. & Beattie*,) h.48 Park.
" George M. mach. at 40 Cush. h.37 Woodbine.
" George S. student at Yale, b.u. 46 Wooster.
" Georgine A. dressmaker, 192, b. 192 High.
" Grace, stenogr. at 745 Main, b. 37 Elm.
" Gustavus F. h. 1493 Broad.
" Harris, tailor, 94½ Trumbull, h. 220 Front.
" Harrison W. goldbr. at 265 Asy.l.97 Wash.
" Hugh, laborer, b.u. 62 Front.

**DAVIS I. B. & SON,** mfrs. Berryman heaters & pumps, 40 Cush. *See page 546.*
John O. Davis.
" J. C. conductor, St.Ry. h.2u. 15 Center.
" J. R. (*D.& Sawyer*,) h.u. 49 Wooster.
" James, clerk at 40 Elm, b. Bloomfield.
" John, painter at 1106 Main.
" John, b.u. 41 Vernon.
" John E. traveling salesman h. 271 Jefferson.
" John H. K. student at Trinity college, 32 Jarvis hall, Summit.
Davis JOHN O. (*I. B. Davis & Son,*) 40 Cushman, h. 183 High.      *See page 546.*
" John R. engineer at 124, b. 124 Front.
" John W. market, 38, h.u. 40 Grand.
" Joseph, carpenter, b. 79 Chestnut.
" Joseph, car contractor, h.2u. 15 Center.
" Joseph M. upholsterer, h. 99 Trumbull.
" Josephine H. wid. Isaac B. h. 333 Laurel.
" Lizzie, h.u. 52 Edward.
" Llewellyn L. butler, 320, b. 320 Farmington.
" Lucius B. salesman at Charles R. Hart Co. 898 Main, h. 35 Sumner.
" Marion L. stenogr. at 205 State, b.192 High.
" Marshall, bookkeeper at 13 Central, b. Terryville v.
" Martin, painter at 1 Flower, h. 20 Lawrence.
" Mary T. wid. Isaac P. h.u. 435 Capitol.
" Maud E. teacher, Arsenal school, b.169 Sey.
" Minnie S. metaphysician, b. 192 High.
" Rose, h. 79 Chestnut.
" Samuel, merchant tailor, 66, h. 53 Morgan.
" Sarah E. b. 771 Asylum.
" Silas H. (*D. Bros.*) h. 1493 Broad.
" Solon E. at Travelers Ins. Co. 56 Prospect, b. 169 Seymour.
" Solon P. teacher of drawing in public schools, h. 86 Edwards.
" Thomas C. with St.Ry. h 36 Vernon.
" Thomas P. clerk, 438 Asylum, b.5 Harrison.
" Truman, carpenter, b.u. 66 Wooster.
" Vincent E. coachman at 300, h.r. 300 Far.
" W. R. satinfinisher at 62 Market, h. E.H.t.
" Walter W. supt. at 75 Pratt, b. 28 Bkm.
" William, carpenter, h. 5 Harrison.
" William, cook, h.u. 126 Windsor.
" Wm. R. draughtsman at Factory Ins. Association, 95 Pearl, b. 2 Garden.
" William S. insurance agt. l.943 Main,rm.25.
" William W. mason, h. 53 Westland.
" ☞ *see also Davies.*
Davison Luther A. physician, 11, l. 11 Pratt.
" Suvia, wid. C. D. b. 66 Forest.
" Walter W. operator at 111 Sheldon, b. W.t.
" ☞ *see also Davidson.*
Davitt Donald J. salesman at 501 Asy. b. 80 Church.
Davoll Frank A. salesm. at 57 Alb. h. 532 Garden.
Davoud Vahram, b. 51 Marshall.
Dawe Emma L. b. 590 Main.
Dawes William H. machinehand, Colts, h. E.H.t.
Dawley Thomas A. laborer, 690 Park, h.2 Ashton.
Dawsey Albert L. h. 152 Russ.
Dawson Catherine, wid. John, h.u. 10 S. Pro.
" Charles, b.u. 10 South Prospect.
" Fred M. bkkpr. at 266 Pearl, b. 105 Clark.

Dawson James, forem. 235 State h.u. 36 Pratt.
" Joseph, city marshal, h.u. 704 Main.
" P. H. bricklayer, h.u. 12 Church.
" Thomas, teamster at 335 Sheldon, b.10 S.Pro.
" Willard, mach. at 1 Flow. h.u. 152 Babcock.
Day Abraham, helper at r. 64 Asy. b.2u. 9 Park.
" Albert P. general supt. Pope Mfg. Co. 436
   Capitol, h. 364 Laurel.
" Anna C. teach. Weth. av. school, b.32 Bkm.
DAY ARTHUR P. treas. The L. E. Rhodes Co.
   28 High, h. 2 Farmington. *See page 548.*
**DAY C. W.** creamery butter, 53 High,
   h. Windsor t.          *See page 586.*
" Caroline E. b. 152 Asylum.
" Charles E. meat dealer, 158, h. 158 Capen.
" Chas. W. bookbinder at Case, Lockwood &
   Brainard Co. 141 Pearl, h. Newington t.
" Clive, teacher, b. 2 Farmington.
" Edward M. attorney, 847 Main, b. 109 Elm.
" Elizabeth wid. Abraham,dressm.h.2u.9 Park.
" Ernest C. clerk at Capewell Horse Nail Co.
   40 Governor, b. 24 Allen pl.
" Frank H. Mrs. b. 24 Allen pl.
" Frank W. bag.master, N.Y.R. h.37 Chestnut.
" Frederick E. saloon, 336 Main, h. 29 West.
DAY GEORGE H. vice pres. manager, Pope Mfg.
   Co. 436 Capitol, *park commissioner,* h. 78
   Wethersfield.
" Gordon B. bricklayer, h. 388 Wethersfield.
" Helen L.stenog. at Popes, b.78 Wethersfield.
" Henry A. B. (*P.R. Day & Sons,*) h. W.H.t.
" John B. painter,h.u. 83 Governor.
" Kittie E. Mrs. at 11 Pratt, b. 143 Trumbull.
" Nellis E. (*P. R. Day & Sons,*) h. W.H.t.
" Noah D. collarm. 8 Sig. h.2u.r. 151 Babcock.
" Nursery, Union for Home Work, 239 Mar.
" P. R. & Sons, fence builders, 1196 Main.
Philemon R. Day.  Henry A. B. Day.  Nellis E. Day.
" Philemon R. (*P. R. Day & Sons,*) h.W.H.t.
" Samuel, cigarm. at 104 Asy. h.u. 17 Walnut.
" Sara C. h. 2 Farmington.
" Thos. H. electrician, 280 Asylum, h. 4 Pliny.
" Thomas M. h. 2 Farmington.
" Thomas M. agent, 83, b.u. 83 Governor.
" Welthea T. wid. Robert E. h. 29 Bkm.
" William H. clerk, b. 37 Chestnut.
" William J. printer at 1 Flower, b. 91 Russ.
Dayo [☞ *see Deyo.*
Dayton Fred E. assist. treas. 66 Pro. b. 202 High.
" Julia E. wid. Henry H. b. 202 High.
" Lydia, b. 36 Jefferson.
Daze Peter, molder, h. 91 Russ.
Deacon George W. engir. N.Y.R. h. 289 Asylum.
Deady Delia, at 252 Pearl, & 41 Lafayette.
" Jeremiah T.cutter, 252 Pearl,b.41 Lafayette.
" John, woodfinisher, h.u. 219 Bellevue.
" Maggie, dressmaker, b.u. 219 Bellevue.
" Mary, wid. David, h. 41 Lafayette.
" Stephen D. painter at 254 Pearl, b. 41 Laf.
" [☞ *see also Deedy.*
Deagan George H.assembler at Popes,b.17 Ward.
Dealing B. H. b. 23 Chapel.
Dean Andrew, assembler at 556 Cap. h. 47 Haw.
" Carlista A. teacher at Brown school, 160
   Market, b. 223 Asylum, rm. 76.

Dean Charles, carpenter, h.u. 8 Hendricxsen.
" Charles M. laundry, 379 Mn.b.2 Wadsworth.
" Edward, mach. at 556 Cap.b.u.47 Hawthorn.
" Fred. H. clerk at 30 Cush. h. 189 Ashley.
" H. S. stamper at Postoffice, b. E.W.t.
" Henry, machinist at 1 Flow. b. 147 Babcock.
" Joseph, polisher at 581 Cap.b.237 Lawrence.
" Susan M. housekeeper, 19 Suffield.
" William F. toolm. at 1 Flower, b. 10 Garden.
Deane Mary, b. St. Marys Home for Aged, W.H.t.
" Mary, b. 37 Park.
DeAngelis Ella, b. 52 Front.
DeArche [☞ *see Darche.*
Deasy James, driver at 133 State, b.Alb.W.H.t.
DeBar [☞ *see Delbar.*
**DE BARTHE ALBERT W.** manager
   New Method Laundry Co. 438 Asylum.
DeBerio John M. teamster, b. 73 Morgan.
" Pasquale, laborer, h.2u. 11 Charles.
Debler F. Jos. shoem. at 755 Mn. h.22 Madison av.
" William, conductor St.Ry. h. 8 Mannz.
DeBlois Edward A. traveling salesman at Popes,
   b. Wethersfield t.
DeBone Gaetane, store, 38, h. 38 Canton.
" Prospero, b.u. 220 Bellevue.
DeBonis Dominick, physician, Italian consul,
   office for changing Italian money, 24, h.24
   Morgan.
DeCarlo Julia, boardinghouse, u. 17 Ellery.
Decatur Edward C. packer, h. 52 Sanford.
Dechan Charles, harnessmaker at 334 Asylum,
   h.r. 15 Park.
Dechene Peter, carpenter, b. 36 John.
Decker Alpheus J.mach. at 40 Gov. b. 189 Smith.
" Harvey B. at 883 Main, h. 2B Wadsworth.
" Horace E. toolmaker at Popes, h. 56 Maple.
**DECKER JOHN A.** blacksmith & horse-
   shoer, 201, h. 205 Smith. *See page 548.*
" John A. Jr. student, b. 205 Smith.
" Louis, cigarmaker at 867 Main, b. 163 Front.
" Samuel W. M. b.u. 1122 Main.
" Theo. foreman at 40, h. 28 Governor.
DeColigny W. Gaspard, salesman at Popes, h.
   West Roxbury, Mass.
DeCraney George W. mech. at Popes, b.237 Law.
Deedy William, helper, 54 Arch, b. 41 Lafayette.
" [☞ *see also Deady.*
Deegan James M.telegrapher, h.720Main,rm.12.
" James T. painter, b. 42 Francis.
" George S. enameler at Popes, h.80 Putnam.
" Michael, enameler at Popes, b.Forestville t.
" Patrick, h.r. 13 Lawrence.
" Sarah A. wid. Edward, h.u. 2 State.
" T. S. h. 103 Capitol.
" William F. inspector at 581 Cap.b.u.2 State.
Deehan Patrick, at Jewells,h.r.u. 9 So. Prospect.
Deeschanck Franz, baker at 368 Asy. b. 23 West.
D'Elia Carmine, grocer, 83, h. 83 Windsor.
DeFelice Alfonzo, restaurant, 52, h. 52 Front.
DeFoe Joseph, laborer, b.u. 319 Front.
" Raffaele, restaurant, 262, h. 262 Front.
DeForest Charles H. dropf. 142Russ,h. 54 Hung.
" Cornelia L. wid. Wm. B. h. 360 Laurel.
" George H. inspect.at 142Russ,h.2u. 47 Bab.

Degnan Annie L. tailoress, b.u. 50 Retreat.
" Bernard H. clerk at 913 Main, b. 43 Walnut.
" George M. shipper at 725 Main, b. 43 Walnut.
" John, feeder at 175 Pearl, b. 43 Walnut.
" Margaret, clerk at 956 Main, h.u. 50 Retreat.
" William, Jr. carpenter, b.u. 43 Walnut.
" William W. carpenter, h.u. 43 Walnut.
DeGranvall Walter, fireman 70 Com. b. 724 Main.
DeGray Alton, screwmaker, h. 35 Russell.
Degredior Rocco, laborer, h.2u. 265 Front.
DeGrey James, teamster, b.u. 11 John.
DeGroat Wm. E. mach. at 26 High, h.u. 23 Wells.
Delafera Frank, tailor at 532, b. 24 Albany.
" Luciano, shoem. at 532, b. 24 Albany.
" Michael, shoemaker, 25, h. 33 Albany.
Delahanty Frederick A. painter, h.2u. 45 Kinsley.
" Helena A. wid. John J. h. 118 Mather.
" John J. Jr. painter, 12, h. 12 Warner.
" Lottie E. dressmaker, b. 118 Mather.
" Wm. E. clerk, b. 118 Mather.
DeLamater Richard S. ( De L. & Son,) h. 84 Bkm.
" Richard W. (DeLamater & Son,) b. 84 Bkm.
" & Son, photographers, 902 Main.
   Richard S. DeLamater.   Richard W. DeLamater.
Delaney Benjamin, machinist, b. 80 Hopkins.
" Catherine, wid. Thomas, nurse, h. 56 Hicks.
" James E. mach. at 9 Sigourney, b. 80 Hopkins.
" John, blacksmith at Popes, h.u. 46 Smith.
" John, coachman at 96, l.r. 96 Main.
" John, sidewalk layer, 154 Ch. O. h. 74 Windsor.
" John J. repairer 744 Mn. b. 33½ Russell.
" Lizzie, clerk at 956 Main, b.u. 20 Avon.
" Maria, wid. William, h.u.r. 27 John.
" Martin, laborer, h.r. 33 Russell.
" Martin Mrs. h.u. 286 Maple.
" Mary, clerk at 956 Main, b. 108 Albany.
" Mary, wid. Patrick, h.u. 20 Avon.
" Michael, clerk, b.r. 33 Russell.
" Michael, solderer at 62 Mar. h. Weth.t.
" Patrick, b. 2 Holcomb.
" Patrick W. helper at N.Y.R. h.u. 299 Law.
" Thomas, emp. at 59½ Tru. b.r. 33½ Russell.
" Thomas J. mech. at Popes, b.u. 46 Smith.
" Wm. Joseph, b.u. 286 Maple.
" Wm. L. foreman 581 Cap. h. 50 Putnam.
" Wm. P. messenger, 3 Central, b.u. 20 Avon.
" Wm. T. enameler at Popes, b. 51 Albany.
DeLaNiepce Marie, tchr. High sch. l. 18 Garden.
Delano Nicolo, barber, 377 Cap. b.u. 27 Kilbourn.
Delap Catherine, wid. Nathan, b. 532 Garden.
" Edward, grocer, 30, h.2u. 18 Trumbull.
" Geo. N. inspector Hartford Steam Boiler Inspection & Ins. Co. 650 Mn. h.u. 32 Mahl.
Delasantra Frank, laborer, h.u. 22 Charles.
" Michael, laborer, b. 365 Front.
Delasio Angelo, laborer, h.u. 22 Charles.
" Frank, mason, h.3u. 32 Morgan.
" Vincenzo, laborer, h.2u. 22 Charles.
Delbar Stephen, gardener for M. G. Bulkeley, 136 Washington.
Delee Frank, laborer, h. 33 Mechanic.
DeLeeuw Hyman, clerk at 7 Asy. b. 88 Edwards.
" Leopold, (Salomon & DeL.) tobacco and cigars, 7 Asylum, b. 88 Edwards.
" Rose Mrs. ( Salomon & De L.) h. 88 Edwards.

DeLeo Dominco A. laborer, h.2u. 73 Morgan.
Delesky John, laborer, b. 215 Bellevue.
DelGandio Frank, shoemaker, b.u. 47½ Morgan.
" John, helper, b.u. 47½ Morgan.
DelGudicio Domenico, laborer, h.u. 83 Windsor.
Dellert Frank J. foreman, 48 Ann, b. W.H.t.
Delliber Charles H. real estate, h. 218 Park.
Delman Fred, driver at 543 Main.
Delmastra Rasino, laborer, h. 3 North.
Delner Edwin, agent, l. 1113 Main.
DeLorenza Joseph, barber at 281 Main.
Delorme Fred, h.u. 44 Woodbridge.
Deloughery John J. carptr. N.Y.R. h.u. 62 Flow.
Deloury Demas, lather, b. 197 State.
" Dennis, foreman N.Y.R. h. 115 Babcock.
" ☞ see also Dillourey.
DeLuca Angelo M. laborer, b. 47½ Morgan.
" John, laborer, h.3u. 20 Charles.
Delucca Joseph, baker at 68 Talcott, h. 30 Kil.
DeLucre John, laborer, b. 57 Pleasant.
" Joseph, pressman, b. 57 Pleasant.
" Margaret, wid. Martin, h. 57 Pleasant.
" Michael D. printer, b. 57 Pleasant.
" Thomas H. b. 57 Pleasant.
Deluhery John M. carpenter, h.3u. 277 Main.
Demar David, lineman fire department, 43 Pearl, h. 66 Hicks.
Demars Peter, corem. at 556 Cap. h. Weth.t.
Demarto Angelo, laborer, h.2u. 29 Mechanic.
deMauriac Octave, at Ætna Ins. Co. 666 Main, b. Middletown t.
Dember Isaac, peddler, h.u. 41 North.
Deming Albert C. salesm. 126 Church, h. 22 Seyms.
" Alice M. teacher N.E. school, b. 145 Babcock.
" Charles A. baker, 1213, h.2u. 1361 Main.
" Charles O. b.u. 16 Arch.
" Clarice E. clerk at Brown, Thomson & Co. 942 Main, b. 39 Seyms.
" D. W. watchman 1 Flow. h. 23 Hungerford.
" Edward, secy. The L. T. Frisbie Co. 79 Talcott, h. 14 Avon.
" Edwin N. mason, h. 39 Seyms.
" Elizabeth, wid. Ernest, b. 131 Sigourney.
" Elsie F. clerk, b. 39 Seyms.
" Eva E. h. 39 Seyms.
" Fanny C. clerk, b. 83 Buckingham.
" Fred A. express, 20, h.3u. 20 Morgan.
" George L. farmer, h. Windsor road.
Deming Geo. M. councilman 3d ward (Deming Printing Co.) h. 145 Barbour.
" George W. watchm. at 1 Flow. h. 223 Fkn.
" Henry A. jewelry and watches, 87 Pratt, h. 30 Charter Oak.
" Hobert W. watchman, l. 53 Trumbull.
" Horace C. traveling salesman, 15 Trumbull, h. Pleasant Valley v.
" Leslie F. salesman at Neal, Goff & Inglis Co. 980 Main, b. Bloomfield t.
" May R. b. 1361 Main.
" Printing Company, 2 State.
" Roswell M. ( Consumers Ice Co.) carman, h.u. 478 Wethersfield.
" Roxy B. wid. Stillman N. h. 83 Buckingham.
" Wesley E. farmer, h. Windsor road.
" Wm. B. carpenter, Taft Co. h. 79 Madison.

Deming Wm. H. asst secy. Connecticut Mutual
    Life Ins. Co. 783 Main, h. 16 Highland.
" William L. at Phœnix Ins. Co. 64 Pearl, b.
    43 Washington.
Demo Joseph, laborer, b.u. 56 Portland.
Demont Wilbur, helper, 133 Shel. b. 94 Windsor.
Dempsey Annie, wid. Benjamin, h.u. 59 Market.
" James, b. 2 Holcomb.
" James J. helper at 581 Cap. b. 14 Glendale.
" John, teamster city works, h.u. 9 Wilson.
" John J. conductor St.Ry. h.2u. 36 John.
" Lawrence, teamster, b. 14 Glendale.
" Mary, wid John, h. 14 Glendale.
Demuro Giovanni, barber at 83 Windsor, h. 219
    Front.
Demyer Louis, laborer, b. 1 North.
Denby Joseph H. trav. salesman, b. 26 Chapel.
Denches Joseph, helper at 1 Flow. b. 66 Windsor.
Deneen James, finisher at 147 Asy. h. 133 Mather.
" James E. brazier at Popes, b. 133 Mather.
" Jeremiah J. polisher at Popes, b. 133 Mather.
Denehy Cornelius, helper at 57 Alb. b. 78 State.
DeNezzo Felix, laborer, h.u. 86 Morgan.
" Frank, fruit, 82, h. 82 Morgan.
" ☞ see also Nezzo.
Dengstrom Frank G. brazier Popes, b. 232 Putnam.
**DENISON CHARLES,** stockbroker,
    756 Main, h. 48 Imlay.      *See page 426.*
" Chas. capt. barge 4, 285 State, h. Saybrook t.
" Clara M. bookkeeper, b. 207 Laurel.
" Frank R. bkkpr. at 190 Pearl, b. 207 Laurel.
**DENISON GEO. E.** contractor and
    builder, 190 Pearl, h. 207 Laurel. *See p.518.*
" Learned B. nurse, b. 26 Huntington.
" Marion B. acct. 1082 Mn. h. 97 Huntington.
" ☞ see also Dennison.      •
Dennehey William, laborer at 466 Asylum.
" ☞ see also Danahy; Danehy.
Denney Pearl A. stenographer at Johns-Pratt Co.
    555 Capitol, b. E.H.t.
Dennis & Co. brickyard, Prospect av. s. of Park.
    James Dennis.    Thomas Dennis.    Wm. H. Dennis.
" Geo. F. lineman, 3 Central, h. 32 Cedar.
" James W. clerk at Ætna Indemnity Co. 650
    Main, h. 83 Franklin.
" Jared, mach. at 152 State, h.u. 259 Capen.
" Rodney, president Conn. Humane Society,
    office, 51 Prospect, h. 98 Washington.
" Thomas (D. & Co.) h. Pros. av. s. of Park.
" William H. (D. & Co.) h. New Britain t.
Dennison James, mate tug Smith, 285 State.
" Jessie K. nurse, 427 Main, rm. 5.
" John L. at Travelers Insurance Co. 56
    Prospect, h. 26 Huntington.
Denniston Chas. E. train desp. P.&R. b. High.
Dennit Peter, cabin watchman str. Middletown.
Denoyers S. Charles, laborer 1 Flow. h. 5 Francis.
Denslow Eddie U. milkman, h.u. 915 Windsor av.
" Edward D. h. 915 Windsor av.
" Ferdinand D. horsedealer, b. 1140 Main.
" Helen P. Mrs. h.u. 15 Imlay.
" Mary E. stenographer at 847 Main, rm. 4, b.
    1040 Windsor av.
" Phil'r W. (P. & W. D.) h. 1130 Windsor av.

Denslow P. & W. milkmen, 1130 Windsor av.
    Philander W. Denslow.    Welton U. Denslow.
" Welton U. (P. & W. D.) h. Windsor t.
Depalma Nicola, laborer, h.u. 56 Portland.
" William, cook, b. 280 Front.
" Vingen, h. 280 Front.
Depatic Luger, tilesetter, 164 State, h.u. 9 Law.
DePaulo Alphonso, laborer, b.u. 20 Charles.
Deperro Rocco, bootblk, 18 State, h. 73 Windsor.
DePhilip Michael, ragpicker, h. 78 Charles.
" Vincenzo, laborer, b. 78 Charles.
Depuy Augustus, helper, N.E.R. b. 12 Center.
deQuetteville Clifford N. clerk 98 Wells, b. 167 Cap
Derby Arthur H. polisher, h. 93 Madison av.
" Aubrey H. student Trinity college, 7 Nor-
    tham tower, Summit.
" Don H. l.2u. 1281 Main.
" John J. watchmaker, 992 Mn. b. 45 Walnut.
" Joseph F. deliv. clk. 98 Kil. b.u. 45 Walnut.
" Joseph H. laborer at 98 Kil. h.u. 45 Walnut.
" Mary J. wid. Charles H. b. 165 Bellevue.
Derdinger Mechoir, b. 2 Holcomb.
DeRick William W. clerk, 97 Asy. b. Meriden t.
Dermont Leon J. mach. at 9 Sig. h.u. 270 Park.
" William, engraver, b.u. 270 Park.
DeRoehn Henry E. carptr. h.u. 45 New Britain.
Derosa Jacob, barber, 9, h.r. 9 Spruce.
" Nicolo, laborer, b.u. 78 Charles.
Derrick Harry, elevatorer 581 Cap. h.57 Madison.
" John A. forem. at 581 Cap. h. 73 Congress.
" John A. Mrs. dressmaker, 73, h. 73 Congress.
Derrin Abbey G. h. 811 Asylum.
" Carrie E. h. 811 Asylum.
" Nettie, h. 811 Asylum.
DeSalvio Alphonse, student Trinity college, 5
    Jarvis hall, Summit.
Deschamps Alphonse, carpenter, b. 46 Canton.
" Napoleon, h. 46 Canton.
Desgardins Joseph, carpenter, b.2u. 7½ Oak.
**DESJARDINS BENJAMIN M.**
    mechanical engineer, 904 Main, rms. 99-
    110, h. Buena Vista, W.H.t.
                    *See page 490.*
Deslongchamps Eugene, carpenter, b.u. 17 Chst.
Desmond Ann, h. 354 Park.
" Catharine, wid. Jeremiah, h.u. 20 Cedar.
" Cornelius, laborer, b.u. 82 Front.
" Dennis, gardener at 73 Wash. b.u. 20 Cedar.
" Dennis F. ironworker, 618 Cap. b. 354 Park.
" John, deckh. str. Middletown, 285 State.
" John, laborer at 48 Kilbourn, b. 28 Front.
" Nora J. dressmaker, 354, h. 354 Park.
" Patrick H. assemb. at Popes, b.u. 354 Park.
" Timothy J. brazier at Popes, b. 354 Park.
Desmore M. Louise, bkkpr. 901 Main, b.166 Allyn.
" Sarah J. wid. John D. h.u. 166 Allyn.
Desmorier Hubert, carpenter, b.u. 17 Chestnut.
**D'ESOPO BROTHERS,** carpenters
    and builders, r. 1179 Main.
    Joseph D'Esopo.          P. M. D'Esopo.
" Bros. Orchestra, 1179 Main.
    Dominic D'Esopo.    Pasquale M. D'Esopo.
           Rocco A. D'Esopo.
" D. & M. fruits, 269 Asylum.
    Daniel D'Esopo.          Michael D'Esopo.
" Daniel, (D. & M. D'E.) b. 21 Windsor.

D'Esopo Dominic, (D'E. Bros. Orchestra,) musi-
   cian, fruits, etc. 1175 Main, h. 190 Front.
" Donato, h. 1179 Main.
" James, peanuts, h. 64 Morgan.
" Joseph, (D'E. Bros.) h. 1179 Main.
" Michael, (D. & M. D'E.) fruits, 269 Asylum,
   h. 64 Morgan.
" Oscar, (R. A. & O. D'E.) b. 21 Windsor.
" Pasquale, milk peddler, h.u. 64 Morgan.
" Pasquale M. (D'E. Bros.) (D'E. Bros. Or-
   chestra,) h. 1179 Main.
" R. A. & O. cigars and tobacco, 88 State.
   Rocco A. D'Esopo.   Oscar D'Esopo.
" Rocco, (R. A. & O. D'E.) h. 1179 Main.
" Salvator, student, b. 1179 Main.
Despard Geo. P. filer, 30 Cush. h.u. 43 Hawthorn.
" Michael, helper at 476 Cap. h. 25 Sigourney.
Desrosiers Adolph L. mach. at 581, b. 381 Cap.
Dessell Joseph O. molder 1 Flow. h. 50 Glendale.
Dettenborn Louis F. foreman, 69 Front, h.u. 57
   Seymour.
" Wm. F. cabinetm. at 133 Shel. h.2u. 97Main.
Dettling Martin J. mech. at Popes, b. 9 Queen.
Deukess Fred. laborer, b. 60 Front.
Deascher Arthur, engir. 245 Windsor, b. 4 Nelson.
Deuse Simeon, mach. at 54 Arch, h. Hockanum v.
Deutsch Dora Mrs. dressmaker, 54 Village.
" Morris, portraits, 1198 Main, h. 54 Village.
Deuty Harrison M. driver, h. 14 Huntley.
D'Evanney Edward, helper, b.u. 22 Huntley pl.
" John, steamfitter at 267 Asylum, h. 39 S. Pro.
" Margaret, wid. Patrick, h.2u. 22 Huntley pl.
Devanney Edward, engineer, b.2u. 68 Sheldon.
" Michael, b.2u. 68 Sheldon.
" Thomas, engineer at 232, h. 204 Sheldon.
Deveau Claudius A. filer at Popes, h.u. 435 Broad.
" Napoleon, dropforger, Popes, h.u. 54 Market.
Devery James, helper at 232 Shel. b. 14½ Gov.
Devine Edward, lab. Pope Tube Co. b.u. 1053 Broad.
" James, steward, 2 Holcomb.
" John, at Popes, h. 35 Francis.
" John, lab. at Pope Tube Co. b.u. 1053 Broad.
" Martin, rubberw. at 690 Park, b. 35 Francis.
" Martin J. expressman, h. 12 Village.
" Matthew M. clerk at 921 Mn. b. 39 Chapel.
" Minnie J. clerk at 921 Main, b. 12 Village.
" Patrick, barrel striker, Colts, h.u. 1053 Broad.
" Patrick, gatetender, P.&R. h.2u. 69 Avon.
" Walter W. (Wells & D.) b. 484 Weth.
" ☞ see also Divine.
Devito Joseph, shoem. 42 Pratt, b. 33 Albany.
" Peter, shoemaker at 42 Pratt, b. 37 Albany.
Devlin Edward, mason, b.2u. 3 Park.
" Frances, b.u. 63 Sigourney.
" John T. motorman, St.Ry. b.u. 56 Benton.
" Mary R. h.u. 63 Sigourney.
Devoe George A. boilerm. at N.Y.R. b. 145 High.
Dewey C. L. Mrs. h.2u. 124 Windsor.
" Chas. T. bkkpr. 981 Main, b. 14 Church.
   Dwight M. E. bookkeeper at 273 Asylum,
   h.2u. 273 Jefferson.
" Edward W. county commissioner, 85 Trum-
   bull, h. Granby t.
" George N. printer at Hartford Times, 716,
   h.2u. 545 Main.

Dewey Howard R. E. clerk, b.2u. 545 Main.
" Patrick, laborer, b. 14 Huntley pl.
" Welthia, at 201 Asy. l. 17 Haynes, rm. 25.
Dewing Fred. M. mach. 1 Flow. h. 51 Hungerford.
" Leonard H. b. 80 Buckingham.
" Susan, wid. Leonard C. h. 80 Buckingham.
DeWitt George W. b. 119 Capitol.
" Naomi, wid. John E. h. 370 Laurel.
DeWolf Ephraim, groceries, 350 Windsor av. h.
   59 Clark.
Dexter Edward M. bkkpr. 140 State, h. 209 Jef.
" John, b. 626 Broad.
" Joseph C. printer at 753 Mn. h. 204 Capen.
Deyo Elting T. clerk at 885 Main, b. 30 West.
Diamond Cora Belle, b. 161 Franklin.
" Edward P. filer at Popes, b. 57 Babcock.
" Levi, (Clark, D. & Clark,) h. 161 Franklin.
Diano Leonordo, barber, 253 State, h. 16 Kil.
Dibble Emma E. Mrs. employment, 54 Pratt, h.
   160 Allyn.
" Emma E. wid. George, h. 24 Babcock.
" Henry C. conductor St.Ry. h. 160 Allyn.
" Hinman A. tobacco, 35 Capen, h. 336
   Windsor av.
" Howard A. clerk at Popes, b. 160 Allyn.
" Susan E. compositor, 141 Pearl, b. 48 Russ.
" William, h. 38 Ashley.
Dicken Bertie, sorter at 34 Pratt, b. 58 Church.
Dickenson Edwin C. b. 6 Bond.
" Ferdinand, h.u. 1201 Main.
" Gertrude E. teacher Arsenal school, b.6 Bond.
" Harriet H. wid. Nathaniel, b. 58 Imlay.
" Henry W. b. 2 Holcomb.
" Linus, h. 6 Bond.
" Robert C. attorney at law, 847 Main, clerk
   Police Court, h. 223 Wethersfield.
Dickerman Charles W. cutter at 154 Pearl, h.
   91 Chestnut.
" S. J. wid. Charles, h.2u. 91 Chestnut.

WILTON E. DICKERMAN, Physician, 51 Pratt.
   Hours—8 to 10 A. M.
      2 to 4 and 7 to 8 P. M.
      Telephone 967.

Dickerman Wilton E. physician, 51, b. 51 Pratt.
Dickerson Anna E. wid. George H. b.u. 62 Capen.
" Chas. quartermaster, str. Hfd. h. Haddam t.
" Frank R. strapper, 15 Trumbull, h. 100 Vine.
" Geo. N. brickyard, h. 37 Washington.
" Josephine L. wid. Leander, news, 56, h. 58 Tru.
" Mary A. wid. Alfred, h. 172 Sigourney.
" Theodore B. clerk at National Home for
   Disabled Volunteer Soldiers, 783 Main,
   b. 37 Washington.
Dickinson Albert A. baggageman N.Y.R. h. 62
   Wooster.
" Andrew Mrs. h.u. 116 Retreat.
" Calvin P. express, 46, h. 46 Pratt.
" Chas. F. diesinker at Billings & Spencer
   Co. 142 Russ, h. 30 Freeman.
" Daniel E. expressman, h. 171 Windsor.
" E. M. (Dickinson & Miller,) h. 199 Collins.
" Edith L. Mrs. b.u. 18 Windsor av.
" Emery, mach. at 1 Flower, h.u. 39 Putnam.
" Frederick C. chief clerk, N.Y., N.H. & H. and
   N.E.Rys. h. 144 Capitol.

Dickinson Frederick L. machine hand at Colts, b. 116 Retreat.
" George A. mach. at Colts, b. 116 Retreat.
" George K. alterative medicine, 25 h. 25 Ev.
" George L. advertising dept. Courant, 66 State, h. 427 Main, rm. 29.
" H. F. driver at 46, b. 46 Ann.
" H. Wallace, artist at 847, l. 847 Main, rm. 29.
" Harry L. machinist, b. 144 Capitol.
DICKINSON HENRY H. (Newton, Robertson & Co.) h. 43 Ward.          See page 486.
" John, mach. at N.Y.R. h. Wethersfield t.
" John R. patternmaker, h. 52 Capitol.

**DICKINSON L. A. & CO.** local agents
Ætna Ins. Co. 664 Main.     See page 444.
Leonard A. Dickinson.  Clarence I. Beardsley.
" Leonard A. (L. A. D. & Co.) h. 1 Bellevue
" Mary A. b. 26 Congress.
" & Miller, leaf tobacco, 215 State.
E. M. Dickinson.          M. C. Miller.
" Orland N. molder at 1 Flower, h. 128 Bab.
" Sidney O. chief box clerk P.O. h. 856 Broad.
" Truman H. mason, l. 593 Main.

**DICKINSON TYPE FOUNDRY.**
Boston, Mass.          See page 471.
" William A. driller, Colts, h.u. 17 S.Hud.
" Wm. E. at motor carriage works, h. 261 Weth.
" William E. mach. at 1 Flow. b. 261 Weth.
" Wolcott A. ostler at 1214 Main, h. E.H.t.
Dicks Geo. B. salesman at 33 Asy. b. 985 Park.
" Thomas, rubberworker at 690, h. 985 Park.
" ☞ see also Dix.
Dickson Alex. machinist at 1, b. 86 Flower.
" John F. tinner, b. 86 Flower.
" L. L. fireman str. Hartford, 285 State.
Didrikson Anna Mrs. bookkeeper at 149 Babcock, h. 72 Putnam.
" John, clerk, h. 72 Putnam.
Diederick Edward, painter, 352 Albany, b. 1178 Main.
Diehl Louis, diemaker at Popes, h. Unionville t.
Diesick Chas. bartender, 110 Asy. h. Pliny's ct.
Diostell Joseph F. washer, 232 Shel. h. 71 Gov.
Dietel John, brewer, 315 Park, b. 182 Ward.
Dietrich Carl J. architect, 904 Main, h. 34 Webster.
" Chas. G. h. 22 Pliney.
" Charles J. C. driver at 279 Mn. h. 37 Talcott.
" Emma K. stenogr. 51 Market, b. 58 Temple.
" Ludwig M. mechanical engineer at Popes, b. 2u. 289 Capitol.
" Margaret, wid. Theodore, h. 58 Temple.
" Millard Mary Mrs. musician, b. 3 Asylum.
" Theodore, policeman, h.u. 2 Talcott.

Dietz Clifton J. clerk 881 Main, b. 19 Walnut.
Diggs Joseph, porter at 45 Asy. h. 3 Huntley av.
" Oscar, capmaker at 76 Asy. b. Bloomfield.
" Wm. H. clerk at 91 Pratt, b. 43 Liberty.
Dignam Annie A. comp. 336 Asy. b. 32 Hudson.
" Arthur M. polisher, h. 26 Cedar.
" John H. mach. at 40 Governor, b. 32 Hudson.
" Mary Mrs. h. 32 Hudson.
" Thomas F. printer, Hartford Times, 716 Main, h. 8 Whitmore.
Dilea Dominick, laborer, h. 2u. 73 Morgan.
" Louis, laborer, b. 2u. 73 Morgan.
Dilena Nicolo, barber, b. 2 Kilbourn.
Dill Bertha M. clerk at 956, h. 373 Main.
" Walter E. clerk at 285 State, h. New York.
Dilliber Nelson C. toolm. Popes, h. 51 Woodbine.
" ☞ see also Delliber.
Dillingham A. F. Miss, h. 926 Main, rm. 84.
DILLINGHAM E. B. advertising agency, 709 Main, h. 491 Farmington.     See page 122.
" Julia H. wid. Albert, b. 24 Walnut.
Dillon Annie, cook at 466 Asy. l. 111½ Hung.
" Annie, wid. James, h. 8 Bonner.
" Carlos, carpenter, h.u. 226 Zion.
" Catherine, b. 66 Church.
DILLON CHARLES, (R. Ballerstein & Co.) b. 66 Church.          See page 421.
" Chas. J. (Kenney & D.) h. 573 Main.
" Charles L. mechanic at Popes, h. 1034 Main.
" Christopher J. clk: 1 So. Ann, h.r. 232 Zion.
" Edward, driller, stone pits, b. 8 Bonner.
" Edward, dropforg. at 142 Russ, h. 15 Putnam.
" Edward F. policeman, h. 39 Babcock.
" James, harnessmaker, h. 2u. 44 Village.
" James, laborer at 8, b. 19 Front.
" James, machinist, b. 72 Vanblock.
" James D. groceries, 244, h.u. 242 Pearl.
" James J. printer at 175 Pearl, h. 12 Cedar.
" John, carptr. at 155 Ch.O. h. 31 Pawtucket.
" John, mason, h. 284 Allyn.
" John B. tinner at 346 Main, b. 6 Cedar.
" Jos. machinist at Colts, b. 72 Vanblock.
" Louis T. operator at Plimpton Manufacturing Co. 252 Pearl, h. 943 Main, rm. 14.
" Margaret, h. 72 Vanblock.
" Mary, at 1 So. Ann, b. 8 Bonner.
" Nicholas, boilermaker at H. B. Beach & Son, 135 Grove, b. 261 Front.

Dillon Richard J. foreman at L. B. Davis & Son, 40 Cushman, b. 261 Front.
" Richard J. restaurant Union station, 466, Asylum, h. 100 Church.
" Thomas, b. 2 Holcomb.
" Thomas, laborer at Colts, h.u. 74 Vanblock.
" Timothy, mason, h.u. 39 Hudson.
" William, laborer at stone pits, b. Flatbush.
Dilloucre Matthew, laborer at 690 Park.
Dilloucrey Joseph, pressman at 141 Pearl, h. 57 Pleasant.
Dillourey Patrick, laborer, h. 34 Laurel.
" Wm. J. helper at 618 Cap. b. 34 Laurel.
" ☞ see also Deloury.
DiLorenzo Andrew, barber,175 State, b. 57 Front.
" Minervino, barber at 120 Front, h. 21 Mor.
**DIME SAVINGS BANK** of Hartford, 791 Main. See page 439.
Dimene Albert, laborer, b.2u. 88 Front.
" Nicola, laborer, h.2u. 88 Front.
Dimick Morrison, helper at 1152 Mn. b. 9 Good.
Dimock Edith L. b. Vanderbilt hill, Farmington.
" Ira, president Nonotuck Silk Co. 133 Sheldon, h. Vanderbilt hill, Farmington.
" Irving, student, b. Vanderbilt hill, Far.
" Oliver W. inspector, Colts, h. 177 Asy. rm. 2.
" Stanley K., U.S.A. b. Vanderbilt hill, Far.
Dimon Arthur L. clerk at Popes, b. E.H.t.
" Earle E. b. 147 Woodland.
" George B. supt. at 147, h.r. 147 Woodland.
" John J. farmer, h.r. 147 Woodland.
Dimond Clara S. wid. Joseph L. b.u. 3 Lafayette.
Dineen Dennis, moulder, 556 Cap. b. 191 Law.
" ☞ see also Deneen.
Dingwell A. E. insp. at 266 Pearl, h. 5 Kilbourn.
" Arthur E. laborer, h. 5 Kilbourn.
" Charles H. beltmaker at Jewell Belting Co. 15 Trumbull, h.r. 269 Wethersfield.
" Wm. B. jobber, b. 5 Kilbourn.
DiNicola Domenico A. laborer, b.u. 83 Windsor.
" Nicolo, shoemaker, h.u. 190 Front.
" Vincenzo, laborer, b.u. 82 Morgan.
" ☞ see Del Gudicio.
Dion Albertine M. clerk at 921 Main. b. 88 Amity.
" Alfred, carpenter, h.u. 2 Church.
" Celestine H. mach.at 1 Flow. b. 38 Amity.
" Frank, brickmaker, b. Windsor av.
" Louis, carpenter, h. 44 Canton.
" Louis, carpenter at N.Y.R. h. 45 Amity.
Diono Frank, restaurant, 74, h. 74 Talcott.
DiPaulo Pietro, laborer, b.u. 73 Main.
**DIRECTORY,** office, 16 State.
Disanza Teresa, groceries, 92 Francis.
Distell Joseph, ostler, b.2u. 220 Sheldon.
DiTono John, laborer, b. 73 Morgan.
Dittenborn ☞ see Dettenborn.
Divine Arthur H. farmer, b. 484 Wethersfield.
" John H. engineer, h. 484 Wethersfield.
" Lewis H. mechanic, b. 484 Wethersfield.
" ☞ see also Devine.
Divinsky Josie, grocer, 192, h. 198 Front.
" Sarah, lunch room, 198, h. 198 Front.
Dix & Co. hatter & gents furnishings, 551 Main.
" Edward B. (D. & Co.) h.u. 154 Seymour.

Dix Frank R. clerk at 33 Mar. h. Wethersfield t.
" Jennie L. clerk at 937 Mn. b. 32 Buckingham.
" Leonard R. clerk, Hartford Coal Co. 754 Main, b. Wethersfield t.
" ☞ see also Dicks.
Dixon Alex, laborer, Pope Tube Co. b. 9 Francis.
" Burton, b. 40 So. Prospect.
" Charles H. mach. at 1 Flower, b. 16 Elm.
" Elizabeth, h. 159 Farmington.
" Frank Rev. pastor So. Baptist Church, h. 28 Capitol.
" Frank E. cutter at 254 Pearl, h. 87 Williams.
" George, laborer at Pope Tube Co. b. 91 Madison av.
" James F. polisher at 581 Cap. b. 110 Laurel.
" John, porter at 205 State.
" John, tinner at 4 Ford, b. 86 Flower.
" John Wm. papermaker, b. 8 Winter.
" Julius, teamster, 28 Francis, b.u. 6 Huntley.
" Marcia, wid. Nelson C. h.u. 16 Elm.
" Robert, laborer, Pope Tube Co. b. 9 Francis.
" Thomas P. b. 22 Ward.
" William H. jobber, h.3u. 37 Liberty.
" William J. teller at American National Bank, 803 Main, h. 4 Ward.
Djorio Frank, boardinghouse, h. 74 Talcott.
D'Muro John, barber at 83 Windsor.
Doane Charles S. salesman at Charles R. Hart Co. 898 Main, b. Rockville t.
" Ernest, clerk at 81, b.u. 24 Church.
" Samuel E. clerk, 476 Capitol, h. 98 Laurel.
" Sumner A. clerk,374 Asy.h. So.Manchester t.
" Sumner L. prop. Hotel Brainard, 119 Cap.
Dobbs Frank P. rubbercutter, b. 38 Babcock.
Dobbin Edward S. student, Trinity college, 8 Jarvis hall, Summit.
Dobmeier Michael, baker, h.3u. 70 Morgan.
Dobson Henry F. brazier at Popes, b. 25 West.
" Maria S. wid. William, b. 36 Jefferson.
" Richard W. teamster at 46 Ann, b. 85 Gov.
" William, mach. at 1 Flower, h. 25 West.
" William A. modelm. at Popes, b. 144 Bab.
Dockrell Thos. H. 164 State, h. 100 Madison av.
Dodd Charles A. cashier at Orient Insurance Co. 5 Haynes, h. 427 Main, rm. 83.
" Charles A. h. 116 Hopkins.
" W. H. & Co. lithographers, 42 Union place.
  W. H. Dodd.        Albert H. Brooks.
" W. H. (W. H. D. & Co.) h. 9 Russell.
Dodez Wm. engr. at N.Y.R. h. 1202 Broad.
Dodge & Brewer, market, grocers, 340 Main.
  Charles N. Dodge.        Charles H. Brewer.
" Chas. N. (D. & Brewer) h. 242 Wethersfield.
" Edwin H. foreman at Hartford Type-Writer Co. h. 57 Sigourney.
" Elmer L. blacksmith at 352, b. 299 Albany.
" Employment agency,98½ Trumbull.
" Gilbert P. foreman, r. 64 Asy. h.u. 86 Pratt.
" Grover W. b. 173 High.
" Harry, fireman at P.&R. b. 73 Albany.
" Merriam E. foreman, Jewell Belting Co. 15 Trumbull, h. 27 Alden.
" Minnie, waiter, b.u. 168 Allyn.
" Wilbur F. chief clerk Adams Express Co. h. 44 Hopkins.

**THE POST DELIVERED AT YOUR HOME DAILY, PER MONTH, FIFTY CENTS.**

Doe Alton C. attendant at 30 Washington.
Doebler Charles F. h. 220 Collins.
" John F. dentist, 903 Main, h. 27 Florence.
" ☞see also Deobler.
Doehler Fred A. blacks. N.Y.R. h.u. 50 Temple.
" Max, clerk, 882 Main, b. 50 Temple.
Doem Rose R. clerk, Brown, Thomson & Co. 942 Main, b. 37 North.
Doerfler Theo. cigarmaker at 104 Asylum.
Doerr Adolph, tailor at 847, h. 847 Main, rm. 35.
" John, cutter & mgr. at 263 Asy. h. 71 Hudson.
Doherty Charles, painter, b. 23 Grand.
" Charles, carriagem. at 17 Elm, h. 23 Grand.
" Charles A. h. 149 Lawrence.
" Edmund, clerk at 581 Cap. b. 35 Glendale.
" Edward, machinehand at Colts, b. 10 Arch.
" Edward J. inspector, Popes, h. 31 Law.
" Elizabeth Mrs. h. 172 Ward.
" George, apprentice at 581 Cap. b. 23 Grand.
" James, at 365 Allyn, b.u. 12 Church.
" Margaret, housekeeper, h.u. 38 Spring.
" Margaret, wid. Charles E. h. 35 Glendale.
" Mary, wid. Patrick, h. 33 Chapel.
" Patrick, molder at 54 Arch, h. 51 Front.
" Richard W. finisher at 556 Cap. b. 172 Ward.
" Robert T. finisher at 556 Cap. h. 91 Front.
" W. A. helper at 48 Ann, h. W.H.t.
" ☞see also Doeherty; Dauherty; Dougherty.
Dohlberg Frank, harnessmaker at 8 Sigourney, b. 58 Woodbine.
Dolan Bridget, h. 28 Babcock.
" Charles, b. 28 Babcock.
" Dennis, helper, N.Y.R. h.u. 19 Spruce.
" Dennis W. electroplater, h. 265 Park.
" Edward, teamster at 5, b. 3 Fairfield.
" Edward P. b. 7 Chapel.
" Francis, painter, h. 111 Hungerford.
" Frank, liquors, wholesale, 39 Kinsley, h. 63 Buckingham.
" James A. laborer, b.u. 26 Union.
" James H. screwm. at 476 Cap. b. 39 Harbison.
" John P. mach. at 1 Flower, b.u. 60 Hicks.
" John, 27 Mechanic, died June 19, aged 23.
" John, laborer, 100 Com. h. 138 Grove.
" John, solderer, b.u. 19 Spruce.
" John J. painter, b. 23 Spruce.
" John Jr. laborer, 100 Com. b. 138 Grove.
" John P. b. 28 Babcock.
" John P. assem. at 581 Cap. h.u. 149 Law.
" Lawrence Mrs. h. 60 Hicks.
" Lawrence J. clerk, 108 Asy. h. 60 Hicks.
" Margaret, at 28 High, b.2u. 1316 Broad.
" Martin, melter at 1 Flower, h. 236 Zion.
" Mary, wid. James, h. 65 Governor.
" Michael, corem. at 1 Flow. h.2u. 1316 Broad.
" Michael, laborer, h.r. 9 So. Prospect.
" Michael, laborer, b. 25 Sigourney.
" Mary J. clerk, Brown, Thomson & Co. 942 Main, b.2u. 1316 Broad.
" Patrick, driver, h. 27 Mechanic.
" Patrick E. gardener, h. 43 Evergreen.
" Stephen, carpenter, b. 80 State.
" Thos. F. 1st mate str. Middletown, 285 State.
" Thos. J. clerk, 1046 Main, b.2u. 306 Market.
" Wm. J. cigarmaker, h.u. 98 Retreat.

Dolan William J. steelhardener at 388 Capitol, b.2u. 1316 Broad.
" Winifred, wid. John, h.u. 28 Albany.
" ☞see also Doolan.
Dolbeare William B. teamster, b. 79 Franklin.
Dole Augustus O. machinist, h.u. 15 Seymour.
" Fred. J. supt. at F. H. Richards, 803 Main, b. 112 Edwards.
" Frederick E. repairer at Popes, b.u. 15 Sey.
Dolin James F. h. 7 Windsor av.
" ☞see also Dooling.
Doll Helen T. bkkpr. 437 Main, b. 38 Capen.
Dolquist Gotfried C. salva. army, h.2u. 277 Main.
Domarus Otto T. l. 284 Asylum, rm. 61.
Domestic Sewing Machine Co. John H. Post, 726 Ma.
Domico Domenico, peanuts, b. 24 Morgan.
" Tony, laborer, r. 29 Albany.
Don David, blacksmith at 5 Mec. h. Bluehills.
Dona Anton P. harnessm. 8 Sig. h.u. 2 Law.
Donaghue Chas. deckh. str. Middletown, 285 State.
" Edw'd, saloon, 352 Asylum, h. 20 Florence.
" John, deckhand str. Middletown, 285 State.
" Patrick, wholesale liquors, 133 State, h. 135 Capitol.
" William, wholesale liquors and wines, 28 and 30 Union pl. h. 195 High.
" William & Co. liquors, wines, etc. 1047 Main.
William Donaghue. P. S. Kennedy.
Donahue Anthony F. mach. at N.Y.R. h.u. 62 Wilson.
" C. deckhand str. Hartford, 285 State.
" Daniel, laborer Pope Tube Co. h.u. 226 N.P.

**DONAHUE DANIEL J.** brickyards, 685 Windsor av. h.u. 171 Barb. See p. 520.
" E. T. nurse, 14, b. 14 Church, rm. 1.
" Hubert J. stonemason, h. 72 Avon.
" James, clerk at 234 Park, b. 5 Oak.
" James, machinist, b. 28 Buckingham.
" James P. mach. at 30 Cush. b. 93 Hawthorn.
" James W. clerk, b. 376 Park.
" Jeremiah, laborer, b. 47 Hamilton.
" Jeremiah C. polisher, b. 350 Front.
" Jeremiah J. operator at 40 Gov. h. 24 Fkn.
" John, clerk, 230 Park, b. 5 Oak.
" John, clerk at 309, b. 307 Park.
" John, clerk, 690 Park, b. 55 Bartholomew.
" John, laborer, b.u. 104 Trumbull.
" John F. teamster, b. 44 Green.
" John J. assembler at Popes, b. 376 Park.
" John J. clerk at 921, b. 1176 Main.
" John J. machinist at N.Y.R. b. 5 Oak.
" Mary, wid. John J. b.u. 367 Asylum.
" Katherine, h. 55 Bartholomew.
" Lawrence, b. 2 Holcomb.
" Margaret, bkkpr. 424 Asy. b. 6 Goodman.
" Margaret, wid. Peter, h.u. 88 Windsor.
" Mary Mrs. b. St. Mary's Home, Albany.
" May, clerk at Brown, Thomson & Co. 942 Main, b. 376 Park.
" Michael, h. 40 Village.
" Michael, blacks. at 1 Flower, h. 62 Wilson.
" Michael, coachman and b. 655 Farmington.
" Michael, laborer at Popes, h.u. 6 Queen.
" Michael, mason tender, h.u. 41 Wilson.
" Murthay, bag'em. Union depot, h. 17 Howard.

AN ▲ NEWSPAPER, THE POST LEADS.

Donahoe Patrick, laborer at 690 Park, b. 5 Oak.
" Patrick, stonemason, h.u. 16 Arch.
" Peter, grocer, 309, h. 307 Park.
" Sylvester, bricklayer, b. 50 Church.
" Terrence. mason, h. 23 Brook.
" Thos. coachman, h. 66 Sigourney.
" Thomas, clerk, 236 Park, b. 5 Oak.
" Thomas, laborer. h. 44 Green.
" Thomas, at N.Y.R. h. 25 Flower.
" Thomas, saloon, 263 Park, h. Poquonock v.
" Thomas J. b. 44 Green.
" ☞ see also Donaghue; Donahoe; Donohue; O'Donohue.
Donaldson Andrew, carpenter, h.u. 62 Lawrence.
" Edward, blacksmith, h. 33 Mulberry.
" Jennie E. folder 26 High, b.u. 62 Lawrence.
" Margaret, folder at 154 Pearl, b.u. 62 Law.
" Peter, bartdr, 178 Asylum, h.u. 143 Collins.
Donchian S.B. oriental rugs,75 Pearl,h.85 Gillette
Dondero Andrew, h.2u. 117 Albany.
Donegan ☞ see also Dungan.
Doner Israel, peddler, h. 5 North.
Donlan Martin, cook, h. 54 Windsor.
Donley Arthur F. toolm. at Colts,h. 83 Madison.
" James R. engineer, P.&R. h. 31 Brook.
" Josephine P. wid E. P. h. 83 Madison.
" Lillian C. stenog. at Perkins Electric Switch Mfg. Co. 83 Madison, b. 83 Madison.
" William, helper, b. 139 Lawrence.
" ☞ see also Danley.
Donlon Thos. laborer, h. 33 Avon.
Donnelly Edward, laborer, b. 179 Albany.
" Francis, mason, h. 66 Green.
" James, engineer at N.Y.R. h. 50 Linden.
" James, helper, 1152 Main, b.u. 15 Goodwin.
" James, plumber, b. 61 Ann.
" James J. painter at N.Y.R. b. 50 Linden.
" John, laborer, h. 25 Kilbourn.
" John J. goldbeater at 41 Tru. b. 47 Franklin.
" Joseph, b. 116 Whitmore.
" Matthew L. carpenter, b. 66 Green.
" Mary, wid. Michael, h. 6 Alden.
" Patrick, assembler, h.u. 47 Franklin.
" Patrick H. b. 7 Highland.
Donofreo Archangello, lab. b.3u. 81 Morgan.
" Michael, laborer, b.3u. 81 Morgan.
Donolo Carlo, helper, 267 Asylum, b.u. 12 North.
Donoghue Michael S. boilermaker at 40 Cushman, h. 13 Squire.
Donohue Frank, laborer, b. 33 Front.
" Herbert, laborer, b. 26 Union.
" Jas. papercut. at 141 Pearl, b. 29 Bellevue.
" Jeremiah, operator, h. 24 Franklin.
" John, blacksm. at 142 Russ, b. 38 Lawrence.
" John, draughtsman, b. 93 Hawthorn.
" Walter, carpenter, h.2u. 84 Albany.
" ☞ see also Donaghue; Donahoe; Donahue, O'Donohue.
Donovan Anthony, carpenter, r. 116 Market, h.u. 9 Hungerford.
" Arthur C. cigarm. at 104 Asy. b. 55 Ferry.
" Catherine, wid. Patrick, h.2u.r. 27 John.
" D. J. salesman, 501 Asy. b. 109 Trumbull.
" Daniel, helper, Hfd. Prov. Co. b. 55 Ferry.
" Daniel, hodcarrier, b.r.u. 25 Morgan.

Donovan Dominick. electrician, h.2u. 83 Gov.
" Elizabeth, wid. John, h.2u. 297 Lawrence.
" Ellen, wid. Patrick, h.u. 52 Hicks.
" Fredk. B. brassmoulder at 38, b.u. 55 Ferry.
" James, blacksmith at N.Y.R. h. 1445 Broad.
" James, carpenter, r. 116 Market, b. 9 Hung.
" James F. clerk, E. Tucker's Sons, 100 Trumbull, h.u. 169 Windsor.
" Jas. G. brass foundry, 38–40, b. 55 Ferry.
" James P. Rev. h. 140 Farmington.
" Jeremiah, h. 55 Ferry.
" Jeremiah, Jr. brassmolder, 38, b. 55 Ferry.
" John, crater, 581 Capitol, b. 102 Albany.
" John, painter at P.&R. h.u. 107 Retreat.
" John, traveling salesman, b. 55 Ferry.
" John P. travel. salesm. b. 427 Main, rm.51.
" Harry, cigarmaker, b. 56 Albany.
" Kate H. Mrs. h.u. 104 Trumbull.
" Lillie G. cashier, 921 Main, b. 66 Capitol.
" Margaret, clerk at 921 Main, b. 66 Capitol.
" Mary, wid. Daniel D. h.u. 44 North.
" Mary, wid. Thomas, h. 32 North.
" Mary A. tailoress, b.2u.r. 27 John.
" Michael, laborer, b. 4 Donald.
" Michael, salesman at H. B. Brainerds, b. B.v.
" Nellie, domestic at 36 Jefferson.
" Patrick, carpenter, b. 320 Asylum.
" Patrick,deckhand str. Middletown,2×5 State.
" Patrick B. real estate, 92 Pearl, h. 191 Russ.
" Theodore F. florist, b.u. 44 North.
" Thomas, bartender, h. 26 Trumbull.
" Thomas, teamster, b. 32 North.
" Timothy, helper at 54 Arch, h. 28 Union.
" Timothy, teamster, h. 4 Donald.
" Walter M. brassmolder, 38, h. 55 Ferry.
" ☞ see also Dunivan.
Donzo Michael, laborer, h.3u. 20 Charles.
Doocey Fannie H. wid. Daniel, h. 61 Judson.
" ☞ see Ducey.
Doocy Patrick, stonecutter, 42 Alb. h. 149 Martin.
Doody Catherine, wid. James, h. 447 Capitol.
" Joseph F. clerk, b.u. 57 Hudson.
" Thomas, expresser, h.u. 57 Hudson.
" ☞ see also Duddy.
Doolan Frank, painter, N.Y.R. b.u. 111 Hung.
" Mary, wid. Michael, h.u. 60 Main.
" Thomas, bellman, 26, b. 26 State.
" Thomas, mason, h. 29 Pleasant.
" ☞ see also Dolan.
Dooley Alice J. clerk at 700 Main.
" Annie G. clerk, P. O. b.u. 55 Charter Oak.
" Daniel, carpenter, h.u. 47 Portland.
" James, b. 41 Asylum.
" John, carpenter, b.u. 25 Flower.
" Joseph H. mixer at 690 Park, b. Boulanger.
" Maria, wid. Michael, h.2u. 36 Hicks.
" Mary, wid. John, b. 23 Williams.
" Mary A. teacher Brown school, 160 Market, b. 55 Charter Oak.
" Michael F. national bank examiner, h.2u. 278 Main.
" Michael J. helper at N.Y.R. b. 66 Hopkins.
" Nicholas, molder, 556 Cap. h. 9 Hawthorn.
" Phillip, janitor, 81 Ann, h. 121 Mather.
" Philip J. engineer, h. 121 Mather.

Dooley Timothy, fireman, P.&R. h.2u. 51 Walnut.
" William, bottler, 84, b. 84 Vine.
" William J. foreman N.Y.R. h. 1214 Broad.
" ☞ see also Duley.
Dooling John, painter at 17 Elm, b. Union.
" John, watchman at 783 Main, h.u. 137 Zion.
" ☞ see also Doling.
Doolittle Charles J. machinist at 111 Shel. h.W.t.
" Ernest J. mach. at 302 Asylum, h.92 Wooster.
" Frances E. b. 36 Jefferson.
" Fred E. operator at 111 Sheldon, b. W.t.
" Frederick, agent State board of education, rm. 42, State Capitol, h. Cheshire t.
" Gilbert C. horse dealer, b.u. 16 Elmer.
" Lewis J. draughtsm. at 1 Laurel, b. 36 Ch.O.
" Marie P. clerk at 937, b. 986 Main.
Door Henry C. captain Barge 1, 285 State, h. Black Hall v.
Doorley Edward, laborer, h. 117 Mather.
" James E. printer at 66 State, h.u. 35 Canton.
Doran Annie J. b. 34 Russell.
" Charles H. clerk, b. 18 Fairmount.
" Edward J. salesman, 273 Asy. b.20 Wooster.
" Ephraim, barber, b. 5 Wolcott.
" James P. driver, b. 34 Russell.
" James R. car acct. P.&R.h.u. 53 Hungerford.
" John J. plumber at St.Ry. h.u.r. 56 Grove.
" Joseph, engineer at 20, b. 20 South Hudson.
" Margaret P. b. 34 Russell.
" Patrick, policeman, l. 253 Main.
" Peter, laborer, h. 34 Russell.
" R. helper at 217 Windsor.
" Rosanna, wid. James, h.u. 20 Wooster.
Dorsey Dennis L. printer at Hartford Life Ins. Co. 252 Asylum, b.u. 130 Front.
" John, stonecutter at 93 Ch.O. h.u. 130 Front.
" John, Jr. stonecutter, b.u. 130 Front.
Dorenbaum Morris, machinist at 388 Capitol, h. 55 Pleasant.
Dorey John, b. 343 Main.
Dorgan Charles P. tallyman, 98 Kil. h.302 Market.
" Mamie, at 19 Foot Guard pl. b. 302 Market.
Dorman Esther O. wid. Julius, b.u.210 Windsor av.
" Hiram, blacksm. at 618 Cap. b. 16 North.
" Samuel A. wireworker, 618 Cap. b.16 North.
Dorr Cephas, brickmaker, N.P. av. h. 13 Amity.
" Walter, asst. engir. at 427 Main, b.u. 2 Elm pl.
" William, laborer at 690 Park, b. 13 Amity.
Dorrity A. deckhand, steamer Hartford, 285State.
Dorsey Annie Mrs. h. 33 Ferry.
" Bridget, wid. Patrick, h.u. 157 Zion.
" Dollie, bookkeeper, 843 Main, b. Ch.O.pk.
" Edward J. carpenter, h.u. 7 Lawrence.
" Henry, clerk at 995 Main, b. 33 Ferry.
" Henry Mrs. h. 33 Ferry.
" James, quarryman at stone pits, b. 94 N.B.
" James T. hacks, 10, h. 10 Commerce.
" John, h. 104 Walnut.
" Katherine A. stenog. at 690 Park, h.Oakwood.
" Lizzie F. bkkpr. at 454 Asylum, b. Ch.O. pk.
" Martin, laborer at 8 Front, h. 23 North.
" Thomas A. clerk at 8 Church, b. 37 Capen.
" William F. J. bookkeeper, b. 23 North.
" ☞ see also Darcy.
Dottoro James, fruits, etc. 1007 Mn.h.2u.29 Albany

Doty Alex. H. brickmaker, h. 78 Barbour.
" Alfred E. harnessm. 8 Sig. h. 216 New Park.
" Cyrus B. mach. at 388 Cap. b. 11 Goodman.
" Harrison E. laborer at 690 Park, h. 20 N.P.
" John, laborer, b. 334 Main.
" Margaret, wid. George, h. 334 Main.

**DOTY SAMUEL C.** real estate and management of property, 757 Main, h. 78 Barbour.

Dougherty Bernard, lab. N.Y.R. h.2u. 32 Flower.
" Bros. groceries, 55 Spruce.
    Joseph A. Dougherty.    Philip J. Dougherty.
" Charles b. 47 Spruce.
" Charles, b.2u. 91 Front.
" Charles W. polisher at 142 Russ, h. 237 Law.
" John J. carpenter, h. 32 Hopkins.
" Joseph A. (D. Bros.) b. 72 Spring.
" Joseph F. corem. 556 Cap. h.2u. 91 Front.
" Mary wid. Patrick, h. 33 Chapel.
" Michael, cigarm. 867 Main, h. Windsor t.
" Philip, saloon, 44, h.u. 44 Spruce.
" Philip J. (D. Bros.) h. 606 Farmington.
" Robert F. machinist, b.2u. 91 Front.
" Wm. plumber at 164 State, b.u. 53 Dean.
" William J. b. 72 Spring.
Doughty James, motorman, St.Ry. b. 1044 Main.
Douglas Edward, civil engir. b.u. 24 Windsor av.
" Henry Lee, clerk at 122, h. 180 Capen.
Douglass Chauncey, coachman, h.r. 35 Willard.
" Daniel, jobber, b.u. 51 Sanford.
" E. E. physician, 36½, h.u. 42 Church.
" E.O. captain, 285 State, h. Thompsonville v.
" Edward O. clerk at Hartford Transportation Co. 285 State, h. Windsor Locks t.
" Mary A. bookkeeper at 142 Asy. b. N.B.t.
" Maurice D. woodw. 69 Front, l. 63 Prospect.
" W. L. Shoe Co. Herbert A. Ensign, 192 Asy.
Douthwaite Fannie M. milliner, 904 Main, rm. 81, b. 96 Ann.
" Geo. F. printer at 252 Pearl, h. 7 Mahl.
" George S. b. 7 Mahl.
" Harry W. printer at Hartford Times, 716 Main, b. 7 Mahl.
" Ina L. stenogr. at 2 South Ann, b. 7 Mahl.
" Sarah A. wid. Robert H. b. 96 Ann.
Dow Alice J. wid. Irville, dressmaker, 399, b. 399 Wethersfield.
" Anna G vocal teacher, b. 39 Willard.
" Arthur M. printer, h.u. 58 Clark.
" Carlos E. salesm. 206 State, h. Wethersfield t.
" Charles F. at Hartford Steam Boiler Inspection and Insurance Co. 650 Main, h. 2 Belden.
" Cortez N. mach. at 80 Huy. h.u.106 Seymour.
" Etta M. teach. at Arsenal school, b.9 Florence.
" Everett E. h. 188 Sargeant.
" Frederick D. (Dow & Hatch,) h. 2 Belden.
" & Hatch, grocers, 2 Church.
   F. D. Dow.     Charles E. Hatch.
" Henry F. mach. at 1 Flower, b. 66 Hopkins.
" James M. building inspector, h. 9 Florence.
" John Henry, waiter, h.r.u. 2 Center.
" Peter, shoemaker, 409 Main, h. 97 Hudson.

**DOW PETER JR.** leather and findings, 278 Asylum, b. 97 Hudson. *See p. 551.*

**If You Want all the News, Read THE POST.**

Dow Richard F. designer, h. 199 Jefferson.
" Riou L. salesman at 278 Asy. h.u. 36 Ward.
" Sarah A. wid. Riou D. h.u. 106 Seymour.
Dowd Gaylord, b. 116 Franklin.
" Hugh P. teamster, h. 35 Woodbridge.
" James, b. 2 Holcomb.
" James, farmer, h. 28 Lenox.
" James, laborer, b.u. 44 Hicks.
" James W. farmer, b. 1169 Windsor av.
" John, shoemaker at 89, h. 89 Clark.
" John J. painter, b. 28 Lenox.
" John L. clerk at 206 State, h. 37 Bellevue.
" Kittie J. clerk at 835 Main, b. 35 Woodbridge.
" Nora J. Mrs. clairvoyant, h. 89 Clark.
" Patrick, pressm. at 25 Asy. b. 35 Woodbridge.
" William, plumber at 280 Asy. b. 13 Russell.
Dowdall Edward K. helper at 266 Pearl, h. 1326 Broad.
Dowden John W. janitor U. depot, h. 39 Walnut.
Dower James P. milkman, 50, h. 50 New Park.
" John J. plumber at 20 Church, h.u. 295 Windsor av.
" John L. manager, 33 Asylum, l. 54 Prospect.
" William M. policeman, h. 170 Putnam.
Dowling Annie M. clerk, 885 Main, b. 40 Francis.
" Elizabeth M. dressmaker, b. 1315 Main.
" James, helper, h. 52 Woodbine.
" James C. mach. at 581 Cap. h. 52 Woodbine.
" James F. h. 19 Huntley pl.
" Jennie J. millinery parlors, 721 Main, rm. 54.
" John, mach. at 581 Capitol, b.r. 60 Wells.

JOHN F. DOWLING, Physician and surgeon. Office, 1315 Main.
Hours—Until 9 A. M.
2 to 4 P. M. 7 to 9 P. M.
Telephone 716.

Dowling John F. physician, 1315, h. 1315 Main.
" Martin T. hydraulic pressman, 141 Pearl, b. 61 Ann.
" Mary, h. 3u. 1449 Broad.
" Mary, stenographer, b. 40 Francis.
" Thomas, carpenter, N.Y.R. h. 40 Francis.
" Thomas F. compositor at 141 Pearl, b. 19 Huntley pl.
" Thomas F. motorman St.Ry. h. 985 Main.
" Thomas L. plumber, 446 Asy. h. 38 Francis.
" William, plumber at 446 Asy. b. 40 Francis.
" William J. engir. 30 Cush. b. 52 Woodbine.
Down Edwin A. physician, 2 State, h. 703 Asylum.

**DOWN EUGENE C.** typewriter supplies, 847 Main, rm. 7, h. 17 Lincoln. See p. 422.
" ☞ see also Downs.
Downer Burdette W. clerk at 342 Asylum, b. 30 Chapel.
" Harry E. laborer at 690 Park, h. 11 Rowe.
" William V. manager at 721 Main, rm. 33.
Downes Mich. W. clerk at Popes, b.u. 594 Garden.
" Wm H. J. messenger at Capitol, b. 60 Grand.
Downey Andrew, h. 2u. 169 Main.
" Edward, laborer h. 2u. 11 Seymour.
" James, clerk, b.u. 17 Putnam.
" James, grocery, 38, h. 38 New Britain.
" John, coachman, h.u. 17 Putnam.
" John, laborer, b.u. 20 Green.

**DOWNING & PERKINS, CARMEN.**

Teams constantly in readiness for transportation of all kinds of merchandise to or from ... cars or boat, and about town. ...

**GOODS FORWARDED WITH DESPATCH.**

128 Commerce St. Telephone, 1009-3.

Downey John J. Rev. assistant at St. Patrick's church, h. 82 Church.
" John P. mach. at 1 Flower, b.u. 17 Putnam.
" Joseph C. driver at 366 Main, b. 17 Putnam.
" Katie M. clerk at Brown, Thomson & Co. 942 Main, b.u. 17 Putnam.
" Patrick, helper, h. 2u. 10 Queen.
" Sarah G. b. 17 Putnam.
" Terence, b. 38 New Britain.
" William, teamster at 93 Ch.O. b. 38 N.B.
Downie Alex. clerk, h. 2u. 169 Main.
Downing Freda, b. 131 Trumbull.

**DOWNING & PERKINS, carmen,**
128 Commerce. See page 552.
Daniel C. Perkins. Mrs. Henrietta Downing.
" Henrietta, wid. Emery (D. & Perkins,) h. 500 Farmington.
" Martha W. Mrs. b. 131 Trumbull.
" Michael, laborer, b.u. 70 Vanblock.
Downley Charles, painter at 618 Capitol, h. 42½ Windsor.
Downs Albert C. carpenter, 257, h. 257 Capen.
" Byron, carpenter, 53 Vernon, h. E.H.t.
" Catherine, wid. John, h. 51 Albany.
" Charles A. student, Thelogical Seminary, 1507 Broad.
" Edward, laborer, b. 327 Front.
" Edward, machinist N.Y.R. h. 12 Wooster.
" Elizabeth, musicteacher, 12, b. 12 Wooster.
" Frank B. machinist at 83 Woodbine, b. E.H.t.
" Frank C. stereotyper at Hartford Times, 716 Main, b. Springfield, Mass.
" James, enameler, 581 Cap. b.u. 36 Sheldon.
" James, teamster, b. 327 Front.
" James C. clerk, b. 7 Avon.
" James, Jr. laborer, h. 327 Front.
" John J. blacksm. at 690 Park, b. 248 Law.
" Mary, wid. Patrick, h.u. 36 Sheldon.
" Nellie, wid. Thomas H. h.u. 60 Grand.
" Patrick, mason, b.u. 594 Garden.
" Thomas, laborer, h. 2u. 81 Sheldon.
" Thomas F. machinist, b. 142 Windsor.
" William J. cigarm. at 104, b. 255 Asylum.
" ☞ see also Down, Downes.
Doyle Albert, carpenter, h.u. 39 South Prospect.
" Bridget, wid. Lawrence, h.u. 194 Sheldon.
" Catherine, operator, 97 Asy. b. 62 Green.
" Daniel, enameler at Popes, b. 177 Lawrence.
" Daniel P. at Popes, h. Chadwick.
" Dennis N. bartender, 109, b. 113 Front.
" Edmund P. inspec. at Popes, b.u. 52 Wdbg.
" Edward, enameler at Popes, b. 159 Law.
" Edward Mrs. h. 2u. 2 Portland.

**THE POST is a 20th-Century Newspaper.**

Doyle Edward R. *health commissioner*, pres. Hfd. Telegram Co. 12 Central, h. 427 Main.
" Elizabeth A. wid. Alexander, h.u. 7 S. Pro.
" Henry F. machinist at 1 Flow. b. 84 Laurel.
" Henry S. gardener, h. 1478 Broad.
" James, laborer, h.u. 9 Kinsley.
" James F. bartdr. at 161 State, b. 52 Wdbg.
" James M. carpenter at 155 Ch.O. h.81 Gov.
" James M. woodworker, b.2u. 81 Governor.
" John, helper at Popes, h.u. 70 Putnam.
" John, laborer, stone pits, b. Flatbush.
" John D. coachman at 112, b. 112 Edwards.
" John E. cigarm. at 867 Main, h. 41 Green.
" John Henry, b.u. 194 Sheldon.
" John J. cigarmaker, 104 Asy. h. 121 Mather.
" John J. mechanic at Popes, h.2u. 72 Retreat.
" John T. coremaker, 556 Cap. h. 15 Kilbourn.
" Joseph, waiter at 33, b. 33 Prospect.
" Joseph M. lithogr. 42 Union pl. b. 190 Ward.
" Kate Mrs. h.u. 18½ Church.
" Kate, wid. Patrick, h. 85 Governor.
" L. D. electrotyper at 177 Asy. b. 21 Spruce.
" Lawrence, l. 192 State.
" Lawrence P. driver, b. 194 Sheldon.
" Margaret, b.u. 194 Sheldon.
" Margaret, operator, 97 Asy, b.u. 62 Green.
" Margaret, wid. John, h.u. 52 Woodbridge.
" Margaret, wid. John, h. 190 Ward.
" Margaret A. nurse b. 14 Spring.
" Maria J. tailoress, b.u. 7 South Prospect.
" Martin, boilermaker, b. 320 Asylum.
" Mary Mrs. b. W.H.Home for the Aged, Alb.
" Mary, wid. Maurice, b. 49 Spruce.
" Matthew C. helper, N.Y.R. h.2u.r. 44½ John.
" Matthew C. Jr. b.2u.r. 44½ John.
" Michael, laborer, h.u.r. 56 Albany.
" Michael, laborer, h.2u. 16 Potter.
" Nancy, h.2u. 72 Hopkins.
" Nora E. dressmaker, 943 Main, rm. 22,
" Patrick, hodcarrier, b.u. 44 Hicks.
" Patrick, saloon, 23, h.4u. 21 Spruce.
" Patrick J. engineer, r. 867 Main, h. E.H.t.
" Patrick J. gardener, 1 Vine, h.u. 281 Albany.
" Patrick J. laborer, h.u. 138 Windsor.
" Patrick J. Jr. burnisher at 62 Market, b.u. 138 Windsor.
" Peter, blacksmith, h.u. 21 Spruce.
" Richard, clerk 372 Asylum, b. 1478 Broad.
" Robert J. clerk, 96 Albany, b. 19 Mather.
" Thomas, l.u. 1122 Main.
" Thomas, laborer, b. 340 Front.
" Thomas J. actor, b.u. 52 Woodbridge.
" Thos. J. operator at 135 Shel. h. 340 Front.
" Thomas P. polisher, b. 21 Spruce.
" William, enameler at Popes. b. 159 Law.
" William, porter at 24, b. 24 Market.
" William H. b. 1478 Broad.
" William J. polisher at 476 Capitol, b.u. 194 Sheldon.
" Wm. J. printer at 174 Pearl, b. 190 Ward.
Drago Frank J. b. 80 Temple.
" John, tailor, h.u. 80 Temple.
Drahaus John, laborer, b.u. 4 Ellery.
Drake Anna B. wid. Francis S. h. 44 Imlay.
" Arthur, pressman, b.u. 21 Hawthorn.

Drake Cornelius, molder 690 Park, h. 35 Heath.
" Eugene S. mach. 9 Sig. h. West Hartford t.
" Frank J. bartdr. 25 Central, b.u. 12 Union.
" Helen, wid. Nathan, b. 1150 Main.
" Henry, molder at 690 Park. h. 35 Heath.
" John, head gardener, 30, h.r. 30 Wethersfield.
" John, machinist at 30 Cush. h. 23 Hawthorn.
" John M. marblecutter, 1070 Mn. h. 82 State.
" Lucy T. h.r. 39 Forest.
" Timothy, civil engineer, 1415 Main, h. 6 Sumner.
" W. Henry, recording clerk, 690 Park, h. 64 Putnam.
Draxler Max, blacksm. at Popes, h. 23 Portland.
Drechsler Louise Mrs. b. 61 Prospect.
" Max, blacksmith, h.r. 23 Portland.
Drescher Albert R. barkpr. 98 Wells, b. 33 Mul.
Dresner Peter, cigarmaker, b.u. 181 Market.
Dresser Charles H. woodturner, 225 Sheldon, h. 15 Clark,
" Franklin J. machine hand, 225 Sheldon, b. 15 Clark.
" George C. clerk, Valley div. N.Y.R. 450 Asylum, h.2u. 65 Babcock.
" Jennie M. justifier at Hartford Post, 23 Asylum, b. East Hartford t.
" John A. timekeeper at N.Y.R. h. E.H.t.
" Susie E. asst. matron Watkinson sch. farm.
" Wilfred H. mach. hand 255 Shel. b. 15 Clark.
Drew Alfred, laborer, l. 16 Village.
" Allen, mangr. 564 Main, b. 16 Buckingham.
" Allen, waiter, l. 16 Village.
" Bridget Mrs. b. W. H. Home for Aged, Alb.
" E. l. 1045 Main.
" Fannie L. at 564 Main, h. 16 Buckingham.
" John S. clerk at 921, b. 1210 Main.
" John W. foreman, 690 Park, h. 99 Heath.
" Joseph N. civil engineer, 800 Main, b. 129 Huntington.
" Mary S. wid. Aaron, h. 99 Heath.
" Milton A. mach. r. 223 State, b. 12 Sisson.
Drieu Louis, helper, 70 Com. b. Poquonock v.
Driggs Frank S. screwmaker at 476 Capitol, b. Burnside v.
Driscoll Clarence J. trav. salesman, b. 42 High.
" Cornelius W. bkkpr. 74 Tru. h. 94 Capitol.
" David C. saloon, 18, h. 22 Albany.
" David S. harnessmaker at 59½ Trumbull, b. 48 Asylum.
" Ella A. seamstress, b. 58 Church.
" J. F. conductor St.Ry. b. 57 Congress.
" James C. manager at 42, h. 42 High.
" John, laborer, b.u. 71 Windsor.
" John M. b.u. 265 Market.
" Mary, wid. Daniel, h.u. 265 Market.
" Michael T. rubberw. 690 Park, b. Colchester t.
" Thomas, carpenter, b. 6 Charter Oak.
" Timothy A. operator, N.Y.R. b. 265 Mar.
Drisnack Albert M. mach. 1 Flow. b. 86 Hopkins.
Drivers' Ice Co., John N. Risley, 490 Main.
Driving Club Park, opp. Adams hotel, Albany.
Drobegg Charles, German pharmacy, 60, h.u. 60 Village.
Droitcour Michael A. at R. S. Peck & Co. 26 High, b. 119 Capitol.

Drohan Margaret, wid. Richard, h.u. 1088 Broad.
" Michael, laborer, h. 4½ Hungerford pl.
" Richard H.screwm. 476 Cap.b.u.1088 Broad.
" Thomas P. mach. at 9 Sig. b.u. 1088 Broad.
Drolet George, Jr. carpenter, b. 883 Westland.
" Henry, carpenter, h.2u. 34½ Church.
Drollet Joseph, carpenter, h.u. Windsor av.
Dron Celestine, machinist at 1 Flow. h. 39 Amity.
Dropper Samuel, painter, h.u. 193 Front.
Drown Alvin R. train dispatr. N.Y.R. h. E.H.t.
Drummond Alice G. nurse, b.2u. 9 Park.
Dryden Thos. J.coachman 103, h. 135 Woodland.
Drysdale Richard,mach. fixer, 34 Mor.h.36 Pratt.
Duane Bridget, wid. Patrick, h.u. 86 Franklin.
" James. polisher at 41 Trumbull.
" Patrick, clerk at 1 So. Ann, h.u. 86 Franklin.
Dubar Dominic, laborer, h.u. 14 Ellery.
Dube Frank, carpenter, h.u. 112 Windsor.
Dubeil Joseph, laborer, h. 32 Portland.
Dubes Mary, dressmaker, 721, h.u. 721 Main.
Dubreuil Arthur T. burnisher at 62 Market.
" Edward, finisher, 62 Mar. b. 317 Asylum.
" John F. burnisher at 62 Mar. b. 2 Church.
Dubrow Abraham, furrier, h.u. 4 Pleasant ct.
Dubuth Joseph, lather, b. 21 Central.
Ducey Edward J. machinist, Popes, b. 565 Main.
" James J. millwright at Popes, b. 173 Zion.
" John J. machinist, 1 Flower, h.u. 2 Suffield.
" Wm. H. mechanic at Popes, b. 149 Martin.
" William J. mechanic at Popes,b.u. 242 Zion.
" ☞see also Doocey.
Ducharme John I. painter, h.u. 7 Goodman.
" Kate Mrs. h.u.r. 36 Temple.
" Patrick, carpenter, h. 38 Prospect.
Duchesne F. shoemaker, 27½, h.u.r. 27½ Lewis.
" John J. painter, b.u.r. 27½ Lewis.
Dudrowicz John, tailor at 23, h. 23 Sheldon.
Dudley Edward E. cigarm. at 867 Main,h. N.B.t.
" Jennie N. bookkeeper at 721 Main, rm. 19,
    b. 58 Church.
" Jos. L. veterinary surg. 560, h.u. 452 Main.
" Nettie S. wid. James F. b.u. 60 Niles.
" Wm. A. foreman at Popes, h.u. 15 Oak.
" William G. b.u. 452 Main.
Due Niels, coachman at and h. 645 Prospect av.
Duerr Charles A. laborer, h.u. 65 Elm.
Duese ☞see Deuce.
Dufault Odelia, screwmaker, h.2u. 21 Wolcott.
Duff Alice, b.u. 80 Hopkins.
Duff Daniel, helper, b. 41 Huyshope.
" Maggie M. nurse, b. 703 Asylum.
" Mary J. dressmaker, b. 53 Church.
" Rosanna, wid. Patrick, h. 53 Church.
Duffey Frank J. physician, b. 27 Buckingham.
" Mary, wid. Thomas F. h. 27 Buckingham.
" Thomas A. clerk, b. 27 Buckingham.
" ☞see also Duffy.
Duffie Lawrence, mach. 1 Laurel, b.Manchester t.
Duffy Bridget, tailoress at 2 State, b.u. 19 John.
" Catherine, b. 107 Park.
" Catherine E. artist at 747 Main,b. 10 Mahl.
" Catherine T. milliner, 19 Pratt,h. 209 Main.
" Edward F.mach. at 556 Cap. h. 126 Babcock.
" Edward T. clerk at 82 Asylum, b. 30 Cedar.
" Frank, clerk at P.&R. b. 47 Washington.

Duffy James, coachman, h.u. 30 Cedar.
" James A. helper 433 Main, b. 50 Governor.
" James B. manager, 174 Asylum,b. 30 Cedar.
" James F. plumber, 433 Main, h.50 Governor.
" James F. sweeper at Colts, h. 43 Huyshope.
" John, building mover, b. 10 Center.
" John, farmer, 30 Washington, b. 99 N.B.
" John F. storekeeper, Popes, b.4u. 312 Asy.
" John P. at 501 Asylum, h. 4 Dean.
" John W.inspector 690 Park,b.19 Wellington.
" Joseph, clerk at 466, b.u. 312 Asylum.
" Joseph, clerk at 637 Main, b. 59 Maple.
" M. deckhand steamer Hartford, 285 State.
" Margaret T. at 690 Park, b. 19 Wellington.
" Maria, b. 298 Main.
" Mary, wid. Stephen, dressm. h. 30 Temple.
" Mathew J. firem. 556 Cap. h.u. 29 Hawthorn.
" Michael, laborer, h. 32 Portland.
" Michael, U. S. army, b. 59 Maple.
" Michael J. clerk at 97 Asy. h.u. 17 Kennedy.
" Patrick, deckhand str. Middletn. 285 State.
" Patrick, finisher, 556 Cap. h.u. 1422 Broad.
" Peter, h.4u. 312 Asylum.
" Robert J. (Clarke & D.) h. 10 Mahl.
" Rose, h. 106 Ann.
" Sarah I. asst. bkkpr. 372 Asy. b. 30 Cedar.
" Stephen J. b. 30 Cedar.
" Thomas, h. 47 Washington.
" Thomas, rubberworker, h. 19 Wellington.
" Thomas A. insurance clerk at 197 Asylum,
    b. 27 Buckingham.
" Thomas F. stonemason, h. 59 Maple.
" Thos. F. Jr. teamster 701 Mn. b. 59 Maple.
" Timothy, helper at Popes, h. 4½ Hungerford.
" William H. marblecutter at 1070 Main, h.
    40 Chestnut.
" Wm.J.fireman at Trinity college, h.159 Zion.
" William L. clerk at 97 Asylum, b. E.H.t.
" ☞see also Duffey.
Dugan J.William, motorman,St.Ry.b.74 Sanford.
" John, h.u.r. 173 State.
" John P. electrician, b. 26 Alden.
Duggan Alice G. at 59½ Tru. b. 98 Jefferson.
" Ann, wid. Michael, h. 1337 Broad.
" Cornelius, molder at 54 Arch, h. 70 Sanford.
" E. photographic engraver, b. 98 Jefferson.
" Fannie, at 59½ Trumbull, b. 98 Jefferson.
" George, driver at 7 Brady, h. 78 Ward.
" J. deckhand str. Hartford, 285 State.
" Jennie, clerk at Brown, Thomson & Co.
    942 Main, b. 1337 Broad.
" Martin, contractor, b. 11 Goodman.
" Martin H. barber, h.u. 51 Wadsworth.
" Mary, wid. John, h.u. 1232 Main.
" Patrick, bottler, b. 10 Whitmore.
" Richard F. mach. 388 Cap. b. 8 Hawthorn.
" Sarah, wid. Patrick C. h.u. 98 Jefferson.
" Thomas S. Rev. editor Catholic Transcript,
    704 Main, h. 140 Farmington.
" William C. clerk 59½ Tru. h.u. 98 Jefferson.
Duhr Pauline, nurse, 217, b. 217 Ashley.
" Rose, nurse, 217, h. 217 Ashley.
Duiguan Patrick, laborer, h.u. 44 Hicks.
" Peter, laborer, b.u. 44 Hicks.
Dhlasko Thomas, operator at 8 Sig. b. 95 Sheldon.

**DULEY JULIA E. MRS.** prop. Hotel
    Prospect, 119 High.    See page 561.
" ☞ see also Dooley.
Dully Jos. F. clerk, 1150 Broad, h.u 27 Affleck.
" Patrick, dropf. at 142 Russ, b. 4½ Hung.pl.
Dumas Henry, clerk, 121, b. 119 Windsor av.
" Wm. H. rubberw. at 690 Park, h.u. 11 Sisson.
Dumont Agapit, carpenter, b.u. 17 Chestnut.
" Alfonse, at Ætna Life Ins. Co. 650 Main, b.
    46 Buckingham.
" Napoleon, carpenter, b.u. 17 Chestnut.
" Normandine A. h. 46 Buckingham.
Dun R. G. & Co. mercantile agcy. 223 Asy. rm.8.
Dunbar George, polisher at James L. Howard
    & Co. 438 Asylum, b. New Britain t.
" James, b. 186 Sigourney.
" Joseph, ostler at 128 Commerce, h. E.H.t.
" Lorenzo D. carriagemaker at 37 New
    Britain, h. Bloomfield t.
" William J. foreman at Popes, h.u. 159 Russ.
" William J. tallyman at 98 Kil. h. E.H.t.
Dunberry H. R. trimmer at 266 Pearl, h.u. 17
    Talcott.
Duncan Agnes A. clerk at Brown, Thomson &
    Co. 942 Main, b. 1056 Broad.
" Edgar, b. 35 Woodbridge.
" Jas. A. butcher at 99 Albany, b.u. 16 Center.
" John, carpenter, r. 334 Asy. h.u. 121 Pearl.
" Kearns, h. 167 Capitol.
" Ralph H. nickleplater at Popes, h. Windsor t.
" Roger, clerk at 650 Main, h. Windsor t.
" William S. salesman at 241 Asylum.
Dundon John, mail clk. Un. depot, h.u. 35 Hung.
" John P. (Major & D.) h.2u. 44 Beach.
Dungan Agnes M. clerk at Brown, Thomson &
    Co. 942 Main, b. 26 Morris.
" Francis P. corem. 54 Arch. h.u. 88 Ward.
" James H. mach. at 1 Flow. b. 1056 Broad.
" John F. h. 98 Huyshope.
" John Francis, hoseman, chemical engine,
    h. 1139 Broad.
" Joseph H. mach. at 1 Flower, h. 1056 Broad.
" Kitty, dressm. at 270 Main, b. 26 Morris.
" Louis E machinist at 70 Huy. b. 26 Morris.
" Margaret J. b. 1056 Broad.
" William, machinist at Colts, h. 26 Morris.
" William E. corem. at 54 Arch, b. 26 Morris.
" William, Jr. mach. at 1 Flow. b. 1040 Broad.
" ☞ see also Donegan.
Dunham A. I. Miss, h.2u. 1042 Main.
" Adeline M. wid. Washbun, b. 1158 Main.
" Alice G. schoolteacher, b.u. 43 Hudson.
" Austin & Sons, wool, 66 State.
    Austin C. Dunham.    Samuel G. Dunham.

Dunham Austin C. (A. D. & Sons,) h. 19 Pro.
" Caroline, wid. Lucien, at 867 Main, h.u. 43
    Hudson.
" Carrie, at 66 Market, b.u. 43 Hudson.
" Donald A. student, b. 17 Marshall.
**DUNHAM FRANK W.** (Wright & D.) dentist,
    901 Main, rm. 1, h. 212 High.
**DUNHAM HOSIERY CO.** camel
    hair underwear, 66 State.  See page 547.
" Isabelle B. teach. china paintg. h. 8 Spring.
" Lydia, wid. E. H. h.2u. 28 Pleasant.
" Marcus G. farmer, h. 386 Wethersfield.
" Mary E. h. 19 Prospect.
" Nettie, h.2u. 28 Pleasant.
" Olive P. at 265 Asylum, b.u. 43 Hudson.
" Samuel G. (A. D. & Sons,) health commis-
    sioner, vice pres't St.Ry. h. 1030 Asylum.
" Sarah R. h. 19 Prospect.
" Sylvester C. attorney; at Travelers Ins.
    Co. 56 Prospect, h. 17 Marshall.
Dunian John, at Hartford Woven Wire Mat-
    tress Co. h. 162 Sisson.
Dunivan ☞ see Donovan.
Dunlap Charles Mrs. h.u. 16 Warren.
" Charles V. b. 372 Windsor av.
" Edward W. sewingmachine agent, 9 Haynes,
    b. 1113 Main.
" George G. roofer, 4 American.
" George H., Consumers Ice Co. h.u. 2 Good.
" Harvey H. salesman, 145 Asylum, b. 372
    Windsor av.
" James V. h. 372 Windsor av.
" Judson, iceman at 4 Central, h. 74 Walnut.
" Lucy W. teacher, b. 1506 Broad.
" Nannie W. wid. Henry, b. 1506 Broad.
" Robert, iceman at 4 Central, h. E.H.t.
Dunlay J. deckhand str. Hartford, 285 State.
Dunn Albert, bartender, h.2u. 304 Market.
" Anna J. padm. at 8 Sig. b.u. 18 Howard.
" Annie, b. 283 Park.
" Bridget, dressmaker, 136, h. 136 Maple.
" Catherine, wid. John J. b.u. 219 Sheldon.
" Chas. H. forem. at 15½ Babcock, h. 60 Smith.
" Daniel, helper at 228 Pearl, b. 81 Front.
" David, waiter str. Middletown, 285 State.
" Dennis, stonemason, h. 132 Babcock.
" Edward, ironworker, b.r. 26 Walnut.
" Edward S. mach. at 1 Flower, h. 18 Union.
" Elizabeth, dressmaker, b. 132 Babcock.
" Elizabeth, wid. John, h. 305 Park.
" Frank, helper at 9 Sigourney, h. 136 Maple.
" Frank C. screwm. 476 Cap. h. 226 N.P.
" Frank W. h.u. 226 New Park.
" George E. repairer, 9 Haynes, h. 83 Sargeant.
" Geo. F. clerk at Brown, Thomson & Co.
    942 Main, b. 88 Park.
" George F. polisher at Colts, b. 181 Main.
" George H. carpenter, b. 60 Smith.
" Grace, wid. Jeremiah, h.u. 74 Putnam.
" Harry, screwmaker at 476 Cap. b. 60 Smith.
" James, clerk, b.u. 305 Park.
" James, laborer, b.u. 219 Sheldon.
" James, inspector at 690 Park, h. 57 Spruce.
" James A. stonemason, N.Y.R. b. 132 Bab.

Dunn Jas. D. blacksmith at 1 Flow. h. 60 Wilson.
" James D. policeman, h.2u. 27 Alden.
" James F. painter, h.u. 4 Chestnut.
" James J. b.u. 18 Howard.
" James J. nickleplater at Popes,h.1427 Broad.
" John, laborer, h. 40 Bluehills.
" John, plumber at 94 State, b. 132 Babcock.
" John E. mach. at 1 Flower, b. 223 Park.
" John F. receiving clk. Popes, h.u. 68 Laurel.
" John J. clerk, b.2u. 14 Arch.
Dunn John J. alderman 1st ward, clerk at 801 Main, b.u. 219 Sheldon.
" John Joseph, plumber at 550 Main, h.u. 12 Affleck.
" John M. mason, h.u. 21 Windsor.
" John P. helper, b. 198 Allyn.
" John T. conductor St.Ry. h.u. 74 Walnut.
" Joseph, apprentice, b.2u. 14 Arch.
" Joseph, sash and blind maker at 554 Main, h. 32 Woodbridge.
" Joseph, at Ætna Life Ins Co. 650 Main, h. 88 Park.
" Joseph E. painter at h. 4 Chestnut.
" Joseph H. plumber at 476 Capitol,h.60 Smith.
" Joseph P. laborer at 690 Park, b. 82 Laurel.
" Lawrence A. h.u. 285 Park.
" Louis, peddler, h.u. 20 North.
" Maggie, wid. Joseph, h.2u.r. 14 Arch.
" Margaret, wid. Michael, h. 283 Park.
" Margaret, wid. Patrick, h.u. 22 Franklin
" Mark F. molder at 54 Arch, h. 74 Madison.
" Mary, wid. James, h. 4 Chestnut.
Mary, wid. John, h. 1421 Broad.
Mary A. wid. Andrew, h. 334 Main.
Mary E. cashier at 929 Mn. b. 132 Babcock.
Mary F. wid. Peter J. h. 18 Union.
Mary J. b. 283 Park.
" Michael, h.u. 18 Howard.
" Michael, engineer at Lincoln, Seyms & Co. whl. grocers, 34 Market, h. 81 Front.
" Michael E. b. 40 Bluehills.
" Michael H. h. 9 Huyshope.
" Michael J. mach.hand at Colts, h. 69 Huy.
" Michael J. driver No-pariel Laundry, h.2u. 884 Main.
" Michael J. toolmaker at Popes, h. 11 Oak.
" Patrick, laborer, h.2u. 2 John.
" Patrick, molder at 556 Capitol, h. 77 Arch.
" Patrick H. mantels, 218 Pearl, h. 76 Capitol.
" Patrick J. polisher at Colts,b.2u.22 Franklin.
" Patrick P. car inspec. b. 312 Asylum, rm. 10.
" Thomas, h.u. 80 Windsor.
" Thomas, mason, b. 1183 Main.
" Thos. F.mach. at 1 Flower, h.u. 171 Babcock.
" Thomas J. h.u. 357 Main.
" William F. b.2u. 27 Alden.
" William H. salesman at H. B. Brainerd, b. 88 Park.
" Wm. H. machinist at 1 Flow. h.2u. 223 Park.
" William H. polisher at Colts, h.22 Kennedy.
" William J. foreman at Hartford Telegram, 12 Central, h.u. 50 Governor.
" Wolf, peddler, h. 37 North.
Dunnell Geo. H. trimmer 266 Pearl, b. 296 Maple.
" Herbert H. b.u. 40 Trumbull.

Dunnell Louis G. assembler at 581 Capitol, h. 32 Temple.
" Sarah, wid. Elbridge G. h.2u. 32 Temple.
" William H. helper, h. 1136 Main.
Dunnells Sylvester, driver at 71 Asylum, h. 26 Flower.
Dunner Isa, peddler, h. 5 North.
Dunning Emily A. wid. Wm. B. h.u. 43 Niles.
" Margaret, dressmaker, b.u. 54 Potter.
" Mary, wid. Thomas, h.u. 54 Potter.
" Morton D. theological student, 1507 Broad.
" Stewart N. at Ætna Ins. Co. 666 Main, b.u. 43 Niles.
Dupar Edw. B. salesman at 304 Asylum, h. So. Glastonbury t.
" Frederick M. clerk at 115 Main, h. 58 Maple.
" Oliver A. clerk, b. 58 Maple.
Duplessis Arthur J. stenographer at 750 Main, b. Meriden t.
Dupont Marie, h.2u. 245 State.
Dupre Alfred N. laborer, 252 Pearl, b. E.H.t.
" John, carpenter, b. 1209 Main.
" Joseph, carpenter, 252 Pearl, b. E.H.t.
" Wm. M. painter, h. 148 Albany.
" Wm. T. painter, b. 148 Albany.
Duprey Harry F. machinist at Colts, h.u. 66 Vanblock.
Duquett Andrew, laborer, h.u. 16 Bonner.
Durand Fannie B. artist, b. 943 Main, rm. 26.
Durant John, driver at 46 Ann, h. E.H.t.
" Sadie, boxmaker, 223 State, b.u. 146 Albany.
Durfinsky Joseph, tailor, h. 41 Village.
Durie Alex. carpenter, h. 41 Harbison.
" Alex. Jr. lineman, b. 41 Harbison.
" David, printer at 29 Union pl. h. 54 Glen.
" Thomas, blacksmith at 17 Elm, b. 126 Front.
Durkin John, helper at Pratt & Whitney Co. 1 Flower, b. 248 Lawrence.
" Michael, teamster at 91 Morgan.
Duryee William E. trav. salesman, b. 49 Girard.
Duschane John, finisher at Neal, Goff & Inglis Co. b. 27½ Lewis.
Dussette Frank, (D. & Wrisley,) h. 233 Barbour.
" Frederick, brickmaker, b. 233 Barbour.
" & Wrisley, brickyard, Frankfort.
Frank Dussette.          W. G. Wrisley.
Dustin Charles E. electrical office, 11 Central, h. 519 Farmington.
" Geo. Rev. supt. Orphan Asylum, 171 Putnam.
" George Mrs. matron 171 Putnam.
" Guy K. student at Yale, b. 519 Farmington.
Dutton Daniel F. meat, etc. 1150, h. 1150 Broad.
" John F. plumber, b. 350 Park.
" Robert L. jobber, h. Whiting.
Duty Henry, brakeman N.Y.R. h.u. 27 Albany.
Duval Arthur E. dentist, 9 Asylum, h. 26 Russell.
" Caroline, wid. Theodore, b. 26 Russell.
" Ellsworth E. burnisher at Wm. Rogers Mfg. Co. 66 Market, h. 26 Russell.
" Joseph A. burnisher at Wm. Rogers Mfg. Co. 66 Market, b. 26 Russell.
" Theodore, laborer at 496, b. 496 Broad.
Duveney H. waiter, str. Hartford, 285 State.
Duzak Henry, laborer at 20, b. 22 Morgan.
Dwesteg, Augustus, laborer, b. 999 Main.

**The Up to Date Merchant ADVERTISES in The Post.**

# JOHN W. DWYER,
## Contractor
## and Builder.

*STORE AND OFFICE FITTING a Specialty.*
*Special Attention Given to*
*JOBBING AND REPAIRING.*

## Residence and Shop, No. 386 PARK STREET.

TELEPHONE.

Dwight Chas. A. clerk, 207 Allyn, b. 23 C.O.p.
" Edward F. machinist at Pratt & Whitney
  Co. 1 Flower, h. E.H.t.
DWIGHT HENRY C. *(D., Skinner & Co.)* 207
  Allyn, h. 23 Charter Oak pl. *See p. 483.*
" Henry Cecil Jr. h. 5 Linden.
" M. Grace, teacher, b. 30 Lincoln.
**DWIGHT, SKINNER & CO.** wool-
  dealers, 207 Allyn. *See page 483.*
  Drayton Hillyer. Henry C. Dwight. Wm. C. Skinner.
**DWIGHT SLATE MACHINE**
  **CO.** machinists, 13 Central. *See p. 526.*
" Wm. B. at 207 Allyn, b. 636 Prospect av.
Dwils John, laborer, h.2r. 34 So. Prospect.
Dworski Henry, feed, 373, h. 373 Park.
" Louis, variety store, 375, h. 373 Park.
" Wm. salesman, 9 Haynes, h.2u. 46 Portland.
Dwyer Albert E. clerk, 82 Asy. h.2u. 31½ Russell.
" Alice, wid. Richard, h.u. 16 Cedar.
" Annie, clerk at 956 Main, b. 23 Pleasant.
" Bartholomew, forem.watermains, h. 33 Imlay.
" Benjamin R. bookkeeper, L. L. Ensworth
  & Son, iron merchants, 104 Front, b.
  145 High.
" Elizabeth, cook at 36 Jefferson.
" Ella, wid. J. Robert, h. 103 Hudson.
" Eunice C. wid. Robert, b.u. 59 Market.
" George H. polisher at Wm. Rogers Mfg. Co.
  66 Market, b. 1048 Main.
" George K. at Ætna Life Ins. Co. 650 Main,
  b. 19 Florence.
" James F. b. 33 Imlay.
" John, carpenter, h. 36 Russell.
" John E. asst. treas. Duncan Co. b. 33 Imlay.
" John E. groceries, 146 Ward, h. 2 Affleck.
" John J. architect, 78 Trumbull, b. 36 Russell.
" John J. attorney, 68 Pratt, rm. 7, h. 181 Mar.
" John J. saloon, 30, h.2u. 32 Albany.
DWYER JOHN W. contractor and builder, r. 386,
  h. 386 Park. *See page 132.*
" Julia A. waitress, b.u. 19 Foot Guard.
" Katherine C. stenographer at 78 Trumbull,
  b. 36 Russell.
" Mabelle E. stenographer, National Life As-
  sociation, 53 Trumbull, b. 103 Hudson.
" Martin, mach. at N.Y.R. h.u. 27 Spruce.
" Mary A. clerk, Brown, Thomson & Co. 942
  Main, b. 8 Foot Guard.
" Mary A. wid. Thomas, h. 181 Market.
" Mary C. dressm. 270 Main, b. 181 Market.

Dwyer Mary M. clerk, Brown, Thomson & Co.
  942 Main, b. 16 Cedar.
" Michael J. bartender, 1167, b. 1183 Main.
" Nellie K. clerk, 956 Main, b. 277 High.
" Patrick T. filer at Colts, h.u. 20 Morris.
" Richard J. clerk at Popes, b. 16 Cedar.
" Richard J. clerk, secretary of state office,
  rm. 38, State Capitol, b. 36 Russell.
" Robert W. teller at Hartford Dime Sav-
  ings Bank, 791 Main, b. 33 Imlay.
" Thos. screwm. at 476 Cap. h. 185 Lawrence.
" Thomas H. printer at 336 Asy. b. 33 Imlay.
" William S. teller at First National Bank,
  50 State, h.u. 19 Florence.
" ☞ *see also Dyer.*
Dyer Bridget, b. W. H. Home for Aged, Albany.
" Charles E. h. 8 Imlay.
" Louis M. salesman at H. J. Knox, plumber
  supplies, 2 So. Ann, b. 66 Capitol.
Dyes Pauline, teacher of modern languages, 721,
  h. 721 Main, rm. 61.
" Susanne, teacher of languages, b. 721 Main,
  rm. 61.
Dysky Joseph, tailor at 892 Main, b. 41 Village.

EADIE JAMES, *councilman 6th ward,* toolmaker
  at 1 Flower, h. 158 Washington.
Eagan Alice, wid. James P. h. 2 Rice.
" Ann, wid. Michael, h.3u. 34 Park
" Edward, laborer, h.u. 106 Windsor.
" Frank, carpenter, h. 47 Linden.
" James, mason, b.2u. 36 Flower.
" James J. mach. at 54 Arch, h.u. 10 Union.
" John, painter, b. 47 Linden.
" Joseph F. mech. at 581 Cap. b. 8 Huntley pl.
" Julia, wid. Peter, h. 8 Huntley pl.
" Kate J. clerk, Brown, Thomson & Co. 942
  Main, b.3u. 34 Park.
" Luke, laborer, h.u. 36 Hicks.
" M. B. stenographer, 197 Asy. b. 36 Hicks.
" Owen, blacksmith, h. 49 Hawthorn.
" Patrick, driver, b. 36 John.
" Patrick, laborer, h.u. 93 Sheldon.
" Patrick, mach. at Colts, h.90 Charter Oak.
" Patrick J. screwm. 476 Cap. h. 61 Haw.
" Peter A. brakem. N.Y.R. b. 8 Huntley pl.
" Thomas F. mach. at 1 Flower, b. 28 Spring.
" Wm. helper, Pope Tube Co. h. 236 N.P.
" ☞ *see also Egan.*
Eagle Dye House, 11 Wells.
" Eyelet Co. 24 Mechanic.
Eakins James,shoemaker,r.1086, h.r.1086 Broad.
" John, express, 15, h. 15 Hawthorn.
" John J. mechanic, b. 15 Hawthorn.
" Thomas, h.u.r. 53 Front.
" Thomas J. b. 15 Hawthorn.
Eames Harold H. secretary & manager at Pope
  Tube Co. h. 1 Park ter.
" Helen, b. 58 Church.
" Helen M. clerk, 881 Main, b. 19 Walnut.
" Fannie Mrs. housekpr. at 30, b. 30 Weth.
Eardley John, *(Daly & E.)* h.u. 107 Park.
Earl Fanny M. sec. and treas. Insurance Journal
  Co. 53 Trumbull, h. 34 Charter Oak.
" Katherine N. stenog. Popes, b. 21 Girard.

Earl Lewis M. engraver at 62 Market, b. 5 West.
" Lizzie C. b. 21 Mather.
" Allan W. electrotyper at A. Mugford, 177 Asylum, b. 5 West.
" William L. silversmith at 62 Mar. h.u. 5 West.
Earle Ann, wid. Cornelius, 2u. 141 Mather.
" House, Thomas J. Winter, prop. 74 High.
" John M. h. 196 Collins.
Earley John, carpenter, b.u. 119 Pearl.
Earling J. W. conductor, St.Ry. b. 56 Maple.
" Joseph, mach. at 1 Laurel, h. 56 Maple.
Earls Michael, mason, h. 75 Hamilton.
" Michael Jr. mason, b. 75 Hamilton.
" William, mason, b. 75 Hamilton.
Earnright J. deckh. str. Hartford, 285 State.
Easland Fred. A. machinist at 20 Sargeant, h.u. 245 Jefferson.

**EAST HARTFORD MFG. CO.** mfrs. of high grade writing and ledger papers. *See page* 480.
East Hartford Express. *See page* 559.
" Wm. coachm. at L. Barker, h. Whiting.
**EAST SIDE PAPER STORE,** 53 Morgan. *See page* 472.
Easterby Alfred, grocer, 26, h. 28 Commerce.
" Alfred J. mach. at 30 Cush. h. 148 Albany.
" Charles, cigarm. at 867 Mn. b.u. 148 Albany.
" Chas. Jr. cigarm. at 867 Main, h. 23 Center.
" Henry E. printer at R. S. Peck & Co. 26 High, h.u. 30 Woodbridge.
Easterman Wm. F. at 581 Cap. b. 232 Putnam.
Eastern Brass Works, 221 State, Robt. E. Carey.
Eastman Chas. A. coachm. 116 Ann,b. 1236 Main.
" DeWitt H. clerk, Popes, b. 3 Farmington.
" Florence S. h.u. 171 Seymour.
" Harlow O. rubberw. 690 Park, b. 50 Smith.
" Herbert, supt. lamp dept. 83 Woodbine, h. 11 Sherman.
" Herbert O. mech. at Popes, b. 49 Governor.
" Joseph S. h.u. 54 Wooster.
" M. Jennie, wid. Ervin S. h. 49 Governor.
" Otto, cabinetm. at 69 Front, b.3u. 261 Main.
Easton Alonzo, carpenter, b.2u. 93 Chestnut.
" Apollos, cigarm. at 867 Main, b. 277 High.
" Arthur B. carpenter, b.2u. 93 Chestnut.
" & Brown, plumbers, 20 Kinsley.
George Easton.            George W. Brown.
" Frank, alligner at 476, b.u. 433 Capitol.
" George (E. & Brown,) h. Springfield t.
" Mary J. wid. Francis, b. 18½ Church.
" Wm. A. yardmstr. at N.Y.R. h. 48 Hopkins.
Eaton Ada B. Mrs. b. 54 Westland.
EATON EDWARD B. life insurance and advertising, 50 State, b.u. 439 Windsor av.
                          *See page* 505.
" Frank H. bartender, 1219 Mn. h. 59 Market.
" Fred. J. humorous writer, b. 439 Windsor av.
" Harriet I. music teacher, 25, b. 25 Weth.
" Henry J. chief engineer Hartford Fire Department, rear 43, h.u. 92 Pearl.
" Henry J. Mrs. real laces cleaned, h.u. 92 Pearl.
" Howard C. musician, b. 251 Putnam.
" John W. machinist, h. 27 Spruce.
" Newbury J. salesman, h.u. 439 Windsor av.

Eaton Norman, draughtsman at 388 Capitol, h. 31 Wooster.
" Robert O. deputy dairy com. at State Capitol, rm. 54, h. No. Haven t.
" W. Bradford, physician, 2, h. 2 Garden. Telephone 1106.
" William Hamner, student at Trinity college, 11 Jarvis hall, Summit.
" William L. attorney, b. 86 Church.
" William W. attorney, 86, h. 86 Church.
Eaves Elam, machinist at Pratt & Whitney Co. 1 Flower, h.u. 57 Barbour.
" Minnie F. teacher, N.E. school, b.u. 57 Barb.
Ebbets Avery, trimmer, 835 Main, h. 33 Sumner.
" Mary C. wid. Joseph P. h. 33 Sumner.
Ebbitts Robert E. foreman, Pope Tube Co. b. b. 357 Capitol.

EBERLE EDWARD, D.D.S. dentist, Unity building, 68 Pratt, rm. 31.
   Hours—9 to 11.30 A. M.
          1.30 to 5 P. M.

Eberle Alex. D. decorator, h. 150 Wethersfield.
" Edward, D.D.S. dentist, 68 Pratt, h. 9 Main.
" Fred. G. attorney at law, 811, h. 427 Main.
" Frederick, attorney, 811, h. 9 Main.
" Geo. electrician, St.Ry. b. 150 Weth.
" Helen M. dressm. at 150, b. 150 Wethersfield.
" Jacob C. condtr. St.Ry. b. 150 Wethersfield.
" Sophia, dressm. at 150, b. 150 Wethersfield.
Ebert Ann, wid. Fred, h.u. 48 Prospect.
" George F. lettercarrier, h. 90 Grove.
" Maggie F. b. 48 Prospect.
Eberwein Caroline, wid. Fred. b. 206 Windsor av.
Eccler Etta, stenog. at 336, b. 335 Wethersfield.
Echols Francis G. manager at Pratt & Whitney Co. 388 Capitol, h. 137 Sigourney.
Ecihelman Isor, dressmaker, h.u. 214 Front.
Eckersen David T. clerk at Wm. Rogers Mfg. Co. 66 Market, h. 38 Capen.
Eckhardt Christian H. clerk at J. H. Eckhardt Co. 693, b. 720 Main, rm. 3.
**ECKHARDT J. H. CO.** art store, artists' materials, picture frames, etc. 687 to 695 Main. *See page* 418.
" Malcom M. student at Yale, b. 5 May.
" Salome, wid. J. H. h. 5 May.
Eckman Hulda, domestic at 20 South Hudson.
" Ida, ward maid at 20 South Hudson.
Eckmeter George L. meat peddler, h. 70 Walnut.
Eckstein Louis, boots & shoes, 199, h. 199 Front.
Eckstrom Gustaf, polisher at Popes. h. 147 State.
Eddy Arthur H. president Eddy Electric Mfg. Co. secretary Spencer Automatic Machine Screw Co. 111 Sheldon, h. 318 Collins.
**EDDY ELECTRIC MFG. CO.** Windsor, Conn. *See page* 536.
" Willard, atty. 756 Main, rm. 24, h. Haddam t.
Ede Edgar, b. 23 New Britain.
**EDE EDGAR F.** carpenter and builder, 3, h. 3 Morris. *See page* 429.
" Thomas E. b. 63 Hawthorn.
Edel LouisM. burnish. 62 Mar. h.u. 318 Windsor av.
Edelmann William, P. assembler at Colts, h. B.v.

Edgar Alexander F. physician, 219, h. 219 Park.
" Matthew, lineman, b. 18 Trumbull.
Edgerly John H. salesm. 139 Asy. b.u. 106½ Tru.
" Susan Mrs. h.u. 104 Albany.
Edgerton Albert C. mach.at 1 Flow.h. 54 Amity.
" Charles H. machinist, b.u. 635 Main.
" Clinton D. Mrs. b. 45 Smith.
" Ferre C. mach. at 30 Cushman, h. 51 Amity.
" James C. mach. at 1 Flower, b. 1163 Broad.
" Lloyd P. inspector at Popes, h. 1163 Broad.
Edgeworth Bartley, molder at 556 Cap. h. N.B.
Edlin Jacob, mach. at 388 Capitol, h. 82 Windsor.
Edlott Marchese, laborer, 613 Cap. b. Parkville.
Edlund Peter A. dropforger at Billings & Spencer
    Co. 142 Russ, h.u. 23 Babcock.
Edman Ernest, painter, h.u. 346 Windsor av.
Edmond Charles A. steamfitter at 276 Asylum,
    h.u. 32 Chapel.
Edstrom Alfred, driver, 4, b. 4 Huyshope.
" Charles A. grinder at Popes, h. 154 Ward.
" Christine, nurse, 82, h.u. 82 Madison.
" Gustav A. carpenter, b. 154 Ward.
Edwards Alexander Bruce, theatrical manager,
    h. 43 Vine.
" Alonzo, carman, 75, b. 75 Hudson.
" Arthur J. clerk, b. 2 Walnut.
" Benjamin W. printer at Case, Lockwood &
    Brainard Co. 141 Pearl, h. 9 Goodwin.
" Charles W. B. real estate, h.u. 63 Albany.
" Eva J. nurse at 20 South Hudson.
" Frederick B. druggist, 55 Farmington, h.
    218 Laurel.
" George R. printer, h. 2 Walnut.
" Herbert C. hose driver at 197, h. 573 Main.
" Hiram, carptr. 264 Windsor, h. 11 FootGuard.
" J. Arthur, clerk at Phœnix Mutual Life Ins.
    Co. 49 Pearl, b. 8 Walnut.
" John, laborer, h.r. 21½ Chestnut.
" John L. Jr. draughtsman at F. H. Richards,
    803 Main, b. New Britain t.
" John M. motorman St.Ry. b. 35 Elliott.
" Linus W. foreman, 62 Market, h. 43 Lincoln.
" Mary, wid. James, h.2u. 15 Mechanic.
" Nelson, mason, h.2u. 1 Ellsworth pl.
" Samuel, car inspector, N.Y.R.b.u.73 Albany.
" Sprague W. policeman. b. 80 State.
" Thomas, baker at 57 Judson, l. 1202 Main.
" Thomas O. physician, 540 Prospect av.
" William B. janitor, 154 Pearl, h. 24 Wads.
" William W. mechanic, b. 25 Morris.
Eff Louis, groceries, 203, h. 205 Front.
" Max, shoemaker, 205, h. 205 Front.
Effemia George, bootblack, b.4u. 190 Front.
Egan Abbie, wid. Patrick, h. 122 Heath.
" Alice, dressmaker, b. 122 Heath.
" Annie, compositor, h. 49 Walnut.
" Annie T. clerk at Brown, Thomson & Co.
    942, b. 926 Main.
" Catherine Mrs. h.u. 25 Green.
" Catherine Mrs. h. 122 Heath.
" Daniel D. polisher at Popes, h.r. 44 Wells.
" Daniel F. clerk at 697 Main, b. 38 Franklin.
" Edward A. fireman, Colts, h.86 Charter Oak.
" Edward J. delivery clerk, 98 Kil.h. 24 Center.
" Edward J. laborer, h. 86 Charter Oak.

Egan Ellen, wid. William, h. 103 Potter.
" Frank, iceman, b.u. 31 Chapel.
" James F. builder, h. 34 Bellevue.
" James F. laborer at 98 Kil. b. 24 Center.
" James T. expressman, 48, b. 48 Wilson.
" John, conductor St.Ry. b.u. 91 Main.
" John, molder at 556 Cap. b.u.90 Charter Oak.
" John, teamster, 25, b.u. 25 Greenwood.
" John J. operator at 40 Governor, h. 66 Main.
" John J. teamster, b. 122 Heath.
" Joseph M. laborer at Popes, b. 48 Wilson.
" Keron, laborer at 40 Governor, b. 265 Main.
" Keron, laborer at stone pits, h. 48 Wilson.
" Keron Jr. tinner, 48, b. 48 Wilson.
" Lawrence, laborer at N.Y.R. h. 1436 Broad.
" Margaret, wid. John, h.u. 31 Chapel.
" Margaret, wid. Keron, h. 38 Franklin.
" Margaret, wid. Thomas, h.u.90 Charter Oak.
" Margaret L. at 1 So. Ann, b.2u. 38 Franklin.
" Margarite, teacher, b. 23 Greenwood.
" Maria J. dressmaker, 700, h. 700 Main.
" Mary T. at 34 Morgan, b. 38 Franklin.
" Michael, farmer, h. 2 Francis.
" Michael, laborer at stone pits, h. 7 Flatbush.
" Patrick, laborer, b.u. 32 Portland.
" Peter, helper at 70 Huyshope, b. 66 Main.
" Rose, h. 138 Windsor.
" Thomas, operator, 70 Huy. b.u.90 Charter Oak.
" Thomas M. butcher, h. 7 Hawthorn.
" William, h. 232 New Park.
" William J. brazier at 581 Capitol, b. 18
    Trumbull.
" ☞ see also Eagan.
Eggirs William, waiter, 25 Mar. h.u. 25 Windsor.

**ECCLESTON ARTHUR F.** state
    attorney, (Buck & E.) attorney at law, 926
    Main, h. 29 Windsor av. See page 481.
" Charles E. conductor St.Ry. h. 211 Park.
" Isabelle, teacher at Washington st. school,
    b. 4 Barnard.
" Mary A. carpetsewer, 219 Asy. h.u. 1067 Mn.
Egley Roxey, wirew. at 618 Cap. b. 56 Portland.
Egney Patrick, lab. Colts, b. 68 South Prospect.
Egrew ☞ see also Edgrew.
Ehbets Carl J. mechanical engineer at Colts, h.
    14 Vernon.
Ehlers Hans, h. 987 Main.
" John, machinist at 1 Flower, b.22 Babcock.
" Julius, cook at 33 Prospect, h. 165 Babcock.
" Wilhelm, machine hand, Colts, b. 435 Main.
Ehret Abbie Mrs. h. 46 Wooster.
" Frank E. b. 46 Wooster.
" Jennie L. milliner, b. 46 Wooster.
Eicenberg Carl M. mach.at 690 Park, h. Shannon.
Eichel Adolph, at N.Y.R. h. 43 Francis.
" Annie Mrs. h. 17 Morgan.
" Louisa, b. 17 Morgan.
" Mamie, b. 17 Morgan.
Eichelman Isaac, tailor, 214, h. 214 Front.
Eichhorst Paul Richard, h. 272 Maple.
Eichler John F. mach. at 1 Flower, h. 40 Hung.
Eichenger Joseph, cellarman, 245 Windsor, b.
    48 Bellevue.
Eignor Frank, fireman P.& R. b. 140 Mather.

Eininholdt John, baker, 195 Albany, l. 84 Front.
Eisele Louis F. cigarm. at 867 Mn. h. 2u. 18 Seyms.
Eisenberg Henry A. barber, 356 Park, b. 7 Sumner.
Eisenman Harry, capmaker at 76 Asylum, h. E.H.t.
Eiswirth John. tailor, h.u. 100 Seymour.
Eitel Emil, bookbinder at 141 Pearl, zither teacher 558, h. 2u. 558 Main.
Ek Nils Rev. pastor Swedish Baptist Church, h. W.H.t.
Ekstrom Gustave, polisher, Popes, h. 2u. r. 147 State.
Ekwall John Eric, shoem. 10 Ch.O. b. 248 Jef.
Elardl Carlo, h. 35 North.
Elborn Abram, fruit peddler, h. 40 North.
Elcha Clayton E. coachman at 943, b. 320 Asylum.
" Clifton H. laborer, h.u.r. 213 Pearl.
" William J. waiter, 25 Central, h.r. 41 Mather.
Elcock Charles A. painter, h.u. 4 Rice.
" Frederick, barber, b.u.r. 60 Temple.
" Henry G. janitor, 159 High, h.u. 30 Huntley pl.
" Rena, at 867 Main, b. 4 Rice ct.
Elder Elizabeth H. nurse, h. 14 Church, room 3.
" Harry, clerk at postoffice, b. 21 Central.
" Maria D. wid. Nathan, h. 49 South Hudson.
Eldredge Company, 110 Commerce.
" Geo.L.R. manager Eldredge Co. h.u. 39 Pearl.
Eldridge & Co. insurance agents, 2 State.
" George K. clerk, 956 Main, b. 99 Trumbull.
" George P. at Brown, Thomson & Co. 942 b. 821 Main.
" Hannah M. wid. Chas. W. h. 24 Buckingham.
" James W. real estate, 2 State, storage warehouse, 1 Meadow, h. 31 Wethersfield.
" Richard S. optician at Brown, Thomson & Co. 942 Main, h. 821 Broad.
" Samuel Ervine, at 690 Park, b. 821 Broad.
Electric Carpet Beating Co., Charles L. Hatch, proprietor, 226 Putnam.
Elfstrom John G. painter, h.u. 12 Putnam.
Elin Meyer, clerk at 48 Pratt, b. 25 Morgan.
Elite Lodging House, 249 Asylum.
Elkey Lucinda, wid. Austin, h. 128 Windsor.
Elkin Bros. upholsterers, 1061 Main.

Samuel Elkin.    Louis Elkin.

" Louis, (E. Bros.) b. 39 Portland.
" Meyer Rev. Rabbi of Congregation Beth Israel, h.u. 14 Florence.
" Samuel, (E. Bros.) 1061 Main.
Ellegard Robert, blacksmith at 476 Capitol, h. 39 Glendale.
Ellern Joseph, tailor at 104 Asylum, b. 3 Chapel.
Ellery Arthur S. lather, 581 Capitol, h. 52 Green.
Elliott Charles, at N.Y.R. h.u. 53 Walnut.
" Charles W. operator at 111 Sheldon, b. W.t.
" Floyd H. photographer at Pratt & Whitney Co. 1 Flower, h. 29 Ward.
" George T. janitor, h. 2u.r. 41 Mather.
" H. L. clerk at 901 Main, b. 4u. 80 Pearl.
" Matilda, wid. William, h. 1096 Main.
" Robert, janitor Trinity church, h. 86 Spring.
Ellis Alfred L. at Travelers Insurance Co. 56 Prospect, b. 27 Wethersfield.
" Amy A. wid. Gregory, b. 6 Wadsworth.
" Augustine L. b. 550 Farmington.
" Benjamin F. b. 27 Wethersfield.
" George, farmhand, 105, b. 105 Bluehills.

## ELM POULTRY YARDS,

**F. O. GROESBECK, Proprietor,**

*Breeder of Exhibition and General Utility Birds.*

### Office, 30 SUMNER STREET,

*Yards, W. HARTFORD and MANCHESTER.*

State Agent for

**CYPHERS INCUBATORS AND BROODERS.**

**PEEP 'O DAY INCUBATORS AND BROODERS.**

Machines in operation cheerfully shown.

**EGGS HATCHED AT REASONABLE RATES.**

Ellis George, 27 Wethersfield, died June 25, aged 55.
" George M. foreman at Thos. Oakes & Son, steamfitters, 11 Haynes, h. 51 Brown.
" George W. at Travelers Ins. Co. 56 Prospect, h. 73 Beacon.
" Gertrude M. clerk at Brown, Thomson & Co. 942 Main, b. 111 Edward.
" Ida M. teacher at Brown school, b. Weth.t.
" John, molder at Lincoln & Co. 54 Arch, h.u. 277 Main.
" Kate F. stenog. 11 Central, b. 6 Wadsworth.
" Leonard A. b. 550 Farmington.
" Rachel, wid. Eli, h. 43 Liberty.
" Sarah J. wid. Fred. A. h. 2u. 235 Asylum.
Ellison Elizabeth, wid. William, h. 46 Smith.
" Frank D. plumber at 690 Park, h. 46 Smith.
" George F. at r. 13 Forest, h.u. 53 Francis.
" Herbert E. carpenter, b. 46 Smith.
" James, plumber, h. 46 Smith.
" Thomas, compounder at 690, h. 551 Park.
" ☞ see also Allison.
Ellovitch Charles, dyer at 37 Wells, b. 2u. 304 Mar.
" Elias, dyer at 37 Wells, h. 2u. 304 Market.
Ellsworth Arthur E. painter, h. 227 Bellevue.
" Benjamin G. clerk at Bradstreets, 49 Pearl, rm. 18, b. 2u. 1243 Main.
" Burt, brazier at Popes, b. 118 Bellevue.
" Chas. H. bookkeeper at 48 Ann, b. W.H.t.
" Christiana, wid. John H. b. 75 Flower.
" Edith C. stenographer at National Fire Ins. Co. 95 Pearl, b. East Windsor t.
" Elizabeth, stenographer, 801 Main, b. W.H.t.
" Ernest B. attorney at law, 877 Main, rm. 3, b. 68 Collins.
" Frederick, fertilizers, 44 Market, h. 7 Vine.
" H. Mrs. musician, b. 227 Bellevue.
" Henry S. signpainter, h. 2u. 1243 Main.
" Julia Dow Mrs. h. 68 Collins.
" May, b. 75 Flower.
" Robert H. clerk at Conn. Fire Ins. Co. 51 Prospect, b. West Hartford t.
" Watson J. h. 19 Spring.
" William H. musician, b. 227 Bellevue.
ELM POULTRY YARDS, 30 Sumner.
Elmer Alfred G. foreman, 690 Park, h. 54 Smith.
" Clinton B. tallyman at 95 Ple. h.u. 8 Grand.
" Edward O. physician, 813, h. 813 Park.
" Elisha S. carpenter, h. 66 Wooster.

**To Rent Advertisements Bring Results in The Post.**

Elmer Emma, wid. Oliver, h. 3 Whitman.
" Emma B. b. 61 Francis.
" Emma F. b. 3 Whitman.
" Harry W. (*E. & McClellan,*) b. 3 Whitman.
" Hattie G. bkkpr. at 552 Asylum, b. E.H.t.
" Herbert T. clerk at 95 Ple. h.u. 46 Beach.
" Hiram W. rubberw. 690 Park, h. 61 Francis.
" Jennie B. teach. Parkville sch. b. 61 Francis.
" Lizzie M. bookkeeper, b. 66 Wooster.
" Lucius H. (*Alexander & E.*) b. Hockanum v.
" & McClellan, market, 108 Trumbull.
　　Harry W. Elmer.　　Charles R. McClellan.
" Walter F. clerk at 197 Asy. b. 61 Francis.
Elmore Bertha, stenogr. at 801 Main, b. N.B.t.
" Charles B. treasurer Dwight Slate Machine
　　Co. h.u. 43 Oxford.
" Charles M. musicteacher, l.u. 5 Center.
" Frank H. salesman, b. 98 Farmington.
" Henry D. clerk at Hartford Dime Savings
　　Bank, 791 Main, b. 98 Farmington.
" Samuel D. lawyer, b. 98 Farmington.
" Samuel E. president Connecticut River
　　Banking Co. 761 Main, h. 98 Farmington.
" William, joiner, 69 Front, b. 12 Buckingham.
Elmwood House, John Mills, 145 High.
Elovich Louis, Wayside Print, 66 State, h. 125
　　Maple.
Elsner Gustav, b. 11 Kilbourn.
" Louis, clerk, b. 11 Kilbourn.
" Minnie, cashier at 956 Main, b. 99 Bellevue.
" Morritz, confect. 129 Front, h. 11 Kilbourn.
" Rosa, wid. Moses E. h. 99 Bellevue.
Eltz Elizabeth, 10 Kilbourn, died June 8, aged 81.
" Henry J. sup. police, h. 10 Kilbourn.
Elwin Chas. cigarmaker at 847 Mn. h. 44 Amity.
" Wm. C. lettercarrier, P.O. h. 18 Elmer.
Elwood Charles, at 180 Ann, l.u. 241 Pearl.
" John J. cutter at 1 South Ann, h. 59 Ward.
" Joseph J. boxmaker at Popes, b.u. 36 Flower.
" Lawrence, switchm. N.Y.R. b.u. 36 Flower.
" Thomas F. policeman, h. 1039 Main.
" Thomas J. cutter at 1 So. Ann, h.u. 88 Grove.
Ely Annie A. clerk at National Life Association,
　　53 Trumbull, b. 44 Ashley.
" Charlotte M. h. 1304 Main.
" Henry, h. 45 Capen.
" Mary, b. 44 Ashley.
Embury Geo. A. clerk at National Fire Ins. Co.
　　95 Pearl, h. 37 Allen pl.
Emerick Arni, teamster, 2 So. Ann, h. 37 Francis.
" George E. at Hfd. Cycle Co. h. 59 Julius.
" Melvin L. mach. hand, 581 Cap. b. 37 Francis.
Emerson Chas. W. clerk Hartford Life Insur-
　　rance Co. 252 Asylum, h. 32 West.
" Edward, machinist at 1 So. Ann, b. 31 N.B.
" Irving, musicteacher, h. 63 Girard.
" John, machinist at 1 Flow. b. 1 Wawarme.
" Mary E. teach. West Mid. sch. b. 63 Girard.
" Samuel, machinist, 30 Cush. h. 1 Wawarme.
" Sophia Mrs. b. 36 Jefferson.
Emery & Co. 721 Mn. rm. 9, R. P. Griswold, mgr.
" E. machinist at 13 Central.
Emmel Peter, cabinetmaker, h. 6 Kilbourn ct.
Emmersly Henry, h. 427 Main, rm. 3.
Emmet Minnie Mrs. h. 6 Village.

Emmett Catherine, wid. Robert, h.u. 3 7 Congress.
" Sarah, dressmaker at 59, h. 59 N.B.
Emmonds Joseph, saloon, 88 Front, h. 24 Martin.
Emmons Alice, stenogr. 803 Main, b. S.M.v.
" Elwyn N. at Connecticut Mutual Life Ins.
　　Co. 783, b. 304 Main.
" Frank B. Mrs. h.u. 168 Allyn.
" Hattie I. wid. Franklin B. h. 20 Canton.
" Joseph B. h. 304 Main.
" Mary Mrs. housekeeper, 80 Ann.
" Whitmore, clerk at 51 Tru. h. 22 Congress.
Empire Coal Co., Henry S. McClory, 146 Tru.
" Stables, Madison J. Black, prop. 560 Main.
**EMPIRE STEAM LAUNDRY,** W.
　　E. Fanning, prop. 34 Pratt. Quick work.
Enander Emil, helper, 26 Potter, b.u. 54 Flower.
" Oscar, clerk, h.u. 54 Flower.
Enders Fred. August driver at 305, h.u. 305 Law.
" Harriet A. wid. Thos. O. h. 6 Highland.
" John O. office 872 Main, h. 15 Highland.
" Richard E. assembler, Popes, h.11½ Hamilton.
" Thomas B. Dr. b. 7 Highland.
" ☞ *see also Anders.*
Endress Geo. P. cig. mfr. 23 Kennedy, h.5 Seyms.
Engart Henry, filer at Popes, h.2u. 86 Hamilton.
Engel Fannie, wid. David, b. 16 Elmer.
" Frederick, tailor, l.u. 3 Goodman.
" Louis E. clerk at 180 Allyn, b.u. 4 Orchard.
" William, bootmaker, 10 State, h.u. 4 Orchard.
Engelhardt F. Wm. ironworker at 618 Capitol,
　　h.2u. 9 Kinsley.
" Henry, assembler at Colts, b. Hockanum v.
" William, billposter, h.u. 130 Ann.
Engelke Marion, with Hartford Life Insurance
　　Co. 252 Asylum, h. West Hartford t.
Engessor John, driver, 163 Front, h.u. 72 Temple.
Engine house No. 1, 197 Main.
Engleman Nathan, h. 14 Wooster.
Engler Vincent, bartdr. 315 Park, h.u.1035 Broad.
English Celia, wid. Eli, h. 124 Windsor.
" David, b. 1273 Main.
" Edward, policeman, h. 40 Hungerford.
" James, laborer, b. 114 Windsor.
" James, waiter at 12, l. 10½ Ford.
" Joel L. secretary Ætna Life Insurance
　　Company, 650 Main, h. 12 Fern.
" Michael, helper at 1 Flower. h. 1048 Broad.
Engstrand Chas. cutter 59½ Tru. b.u. 37 Wolcott.
" Christine, wid. Jonas, h.u. 37 Wolcott.
" Edward, carptr. at N.Y.R. h. 18 Squire.
" Gustav, filer at Popes, b.u. 37 Wolcott.
Engstrom Albin V. assembler at 556 Capitol, h.u.
　　12 South Forest.
" Arthur A. mach. at 1 Flower, b. 171 Babcock.
" Aug. employed at 59½ Tru. b. 312 Asylum.
" August, b.r. 16 Affleck.
" Axel R. mach. at 30 Cush. b.u. 16½ Affleck.
" Frank G. brazier, Popes, b.2u. 232 Putnam.
" Mary E. Mrs. b. 18 Squire.
Ennis Bessie, proofreader, b.u. 76 Governor.
" Jennie, cashier at 2C1 State, b. 76 Governor.
" Elizabeth, wid. William, b.r. 60 Portland.
" Frank, policeman, h.u. 76 Governor.
" John C. mach. hand, Colts, h.u. 24 Franklin.

**You'll Get ALL THE NEWS, if you READ THE POST.**

Ennis John P. painter at 185 Asy. h. 25 Canton.
" Mary B. at 1 South Ann, b.r. 60 Portland.
" Patrick J. mach. at 1 Flow. h. 22 Glendale.
" Thomas S. bluer at Colts, b. 76 Governor.
" ☞ *see also Annis.*
Ennison Walter J. mechanical engineer at 581
     Capitol, h. 944 Windsor.
Eno Arthur M. disp. St.Ry. h. 16 Elmwood.
" Edw. E. mach. at 1 Flow. h.u. 1462½ Broad
" Frank H. traveling salesman at E. Tucker's
     Sons, 100 Trumbull, h. 240 Jefferson.
" Henry C. laborer, 1 Flower, h.u. 23 Howard.
Enright Mary, Mrs. h. 74 Ann.
Ensign Edwin L. machinist 30 Cush. b. E.H.t.
" Henry, h. 165 Sigourney.
" Herbert A. manager 192 Asy. h.81 Madison.
" Mary A. teacher 2d North school, 249, b.
     234 High.
" Thomas W. clerk 192 Asylum, l. 81 Madison.
Ensling Philip Jr. machinist at 70 Huyshope, b.
     36 Charter Oak.
Ensworth Antionette L. b. 310 Farmington.
" George, b. 510 Farmington.
" Henry L (*E. & Parsons,*) h. 5 Whitman.
" Horace H. (*L. L. Ensworth & Son,*) 104
     Front, b. 510 Farmington.
" Jerusha A. wid. Horace, b. 510 Farmington.

**ENSWORTH L. L. & SON,** iron,
     steel, 104 Front,        *See page 592.*
     Lester L. Ensworth.        Horace H. Ensworth.
" Lester L. (*L. L. Ensworth & Son,*) 104
     Front, h. 510 Farmington.
" & Parsons, meatmarket, 77 Front.
     Henry I. Ensworth.        Wm. S. Parsons.
" ☞ *see also Ainsworth.*

**ENTRESS ALBERT,** sculptor, r. 597
     Main, h. 51 Allen pl.        *See page 511.*
Epps John H. jobber, h.u. 38 Village.
Epsar Frank, tailor, r. 1128, h.u. 1128 Main.
Epstein Abram, blacksmith, 201, h. 213 Front.
" David N. salesman, h.u. 192 Front.
" Jacob, teamster, 315 Park, h.u. 255 Market.
" Max, cabinetm. 155 Ch. O. h. 86 Pleasant.
" Otto, plumber at 94 State.
" Samuel, tailor 114 Tru. h.2u. 130 Windsor.
Erdin Charles R. machinist at Pratt & Whitney
     Co. 1 Flower, b. So. Manchester v.
Erely James, teamster, h. 74 Walnut.
Erichson August, cabinetmaker at Seidler & May,
     furniture store, 306 Pearl, h. 30 Cedar.
" Chas. B. (*E. & McLean,*) h. Berlin t.
" & McLean, dentists, 3 Asylum.
     Emil B. Erichson.        Geo. O. McLean.
" ☞ *see also Ericson.*
Erickson Albert, carpenter, b.u. 150 Ward.
" Andrew, h. 12 Smith.
" Andrew, mechanic, h. 296 Park.
" Arthur, machinist, h.u. 28 Elm.
" Carl, helper at 476 Capitol, b. 296 Park.
" Carl W. carpenter, b.u. 29 Hamilton.
" Edward, mach. 70 Huyshope, h.u. 40 N.B.
" Emil, stonecutter, 275 Park, l. 157 Lawrence.
" Gustav F. painter, l. 109 Lawrence.
" Hans G. boilermaker at 109 Com. h. 21 King.
" Herman, sawyer at Taft Co. h. 72 Putnam.

Erickson John, coachman at 568, h.r. 568 Far.
" John, harnessm. at 8 Sig. h.u. 20 Wolcott.
" Karl, cabinetm. at 69 Front, b. 34 Wooster.
" Martin H. carpenter, h. 77 Ward.
Ericsen Andrew, filer, 581 Capitol, h. 12 Smith.
" & Harman, 133 Sheldon.
     Emil Ericsen.        Harry Harman.
" Emil, (*E. & Harman,*) h. 16 Douglas.
Ericson Knut, screwm. 476 Cap. b.u. 66¼ Laurel.
Ernst Henry, saloon, 27, b. 27 Mulberry.
Erving Henry W. cashier Connecticut River
     Banking Co. 761 Main, h. Prospect av.
" Rollin K. treas. Burr Index Co. h. 50 Willard.
" Stine, clerk, 365 Allyn.
" William A. sec'y Hartford County Mutual
     Fire Ins. Co. 793 Main, h. Pro. av. W.H.t.
" William G. student, b. Prospect av.
" ☞ *see also Irving.*
Erwin Robert G. h. 687 Asylum.
Esbensen Hans, at 30 Cushman, b. 1153 Broad.
" Holga, mach. at 30 Cushman, b. 1153 Broad.
" Lawritz M. mach. at 30 Cush. h. 1153 Broad.
Esbo Samuel P. coachman at 83 Woodland, h.
     1142 Asylum.
Escherich Annistan, h. 38½ Woodbine.
" Eugene, yeast agent, b. 38½ Woodbine.
Eschholz Hermann, bakery and h.238 N.P.c.Ham.
Estadrooks Albert J. at 581 Capitol, b. 8 Smith.
Estes Martha S. wid. Lucius J. h.2u. 545 Main.
Estlow Alfred J. clerk at 690 Park, b. 25 Russ.
" Charles W. machinist, b. 69 Congress.
" Elizabeth, wid. Alfred, boardh. 542 Main.
" George, printer, 336 Asy. h.u. 38 Congress.
" Martin, cigarm. at 217 Main, b.u.69 Congress.
" Niles S. mechanic at Popes, h. 33 Lewis.
" Sarah S. wid. Martin, h.u. 69 Congress.
Etheridge James L. carpenter, 165, h. 165 Russ.
Etherington C. Arthur Jr. clerk at Popes, b. 228
     Putnam.
" Charles A. b. 228 Putnam.
" Charles A. Mrs. h.u. 86 Pratt.
" Henry C. foreman 9 Sig. h.u. 228 Putnam.
" James F. mach. at 9 Sig. h.u. 17 Williams.
" Mahala, wid. James, h.u. 17 Williams.
Ethier Joseph, carpenter, h. 3 Lawrence.
Eustace Wm. F. grocer, 119 Pearl, h.u. 110 Hung.
Evangelist Mary, Sister Superior, 89 Church.
Evanosich John, laborer, h. 99 Potter.
Evans Adella, wid. Edgar, h.3u. 40 Sheldon.
" Albert F. rubberw. 690 Park, b. 47 Laurel.
" Archibald, mach. at 135 Shel. b. 566 Main.
" Blanche Mrs. wid. Evan E. h.3u. 277 Main.
" Charles, conductor, St.Ry. b. 52 Retreat.
" Charles S. motorman, St.Ry. b.u. 74 Seymour.
" Edward S. machinist, 9 Sigourney, h. E.H.t.
" Emma M. stenog. 2 State, b. 43 Buckingham.
" George A. b. 500 Farmington.
" George H. mach. at 135 Shel. b. 566 Main.
" George L. brakeman, h. 25 Loomis.
" Herbert, gardener, h. 28 Chestnut.
" & Hanmer, millinery, 75 Pratt.
     K. E. Evans.        Mrs. F. C. Hanmer.
" Isaiah F. clerk at 55 Far. h. 88 Fairmount.
" John D. student Trinity col. b. 114 Vernon.
" K. E. (*E. & Hanmer,*) h. 721 Main.

**THE NEWS PRINTED IN THE POST IS RELIABLE.**

Evans Lester S. engineer, h. 13 Huntley pl.
"   Owen, cabinetm. at 24 Potter, b. 24 Wdbg.
"   Thomas, sec'y Hartford City Gas Light Co.
     700 Main, h. 114 Vernon.
"   William O. operator, b. 55 Babcock.
"   Wm. W. traveling salesman, h. 17 Belden.
Evarts Frank L. blacksm. 16 Hicks, b.23 Liberty.
"   Howard A. patternmaker at 556 Capitol, b.
     23 Liberty.
"   Reuben L. blacksmith, h.u. 23 Liberty.
Eveleth James A. clerk at 1 Flower, b. E.H.t.
Even Charles W. bkkpr.at 261 Asy. b. 58 Hung.
"   Charles F. blacksm. 476 Cap. h.58 Hung.
**EVENING POST ASSOCIATION,**
daily and weekly, 23 Asylum.
Everett Archie C. clerk at Wm. Rogers Mfg.
     Co. 66 Market, h.u. 7 Atlantic.
"   Irving, watchman stone pits, h. Albany.
"   Irving S. rubberw. 690 Park, h. 348 Windsor.
"   Martin R. supt. Prudential Ins. Co. 811
     Main, h. 47 Allen pl.
Evers Mary E. wid. Michael, h. 28 Spring.
Eversberg Chas. baker at 132 Tru. h. Temple.
Everts Arthur S. operator, 40 Gov. b. 39 Dean.
Ewart Mary A. clerk at 690 Park, b. 17 Smith.
"   Samuel, dropforger, 142 Russ, h. 17 Smith.
Ewell Chas. F. clerk, 97, l. 223 Asylum.
"   Daniel J. b. 80 Church.
"   Daniel L.clerk at 115 Asylum, h. 15 Liberty.
Ewens David, sidewalklayer 154 Ch.O. h.161 Bab.
Ewing Chas. H. chief eng. P.&R. h. 25 Imlay.
"   Christine, b. 185 Wethersfield.
"   J. Hunter, clerk at P.&R. b. 25 Imlay.
"   John, conductor St.Ry. h.u. 48 Prospect.
"   Rachel W.wid. Henry C.h.185 Wethersfield.
Ewins Adam, waiter, b. 161 Babcock.
"   Harry R. b. 77 Governor.
"   Henry W. silversman at William Rogers
     Mfg. Co. 66 Market, h. 77 Governor.
**EXAMINER,** 45 Brown. *See page 468.*
Excelsior Sale and Exchange Stables, I. R. Blu-
menthal, prop. 20 Morgan.
Eyesenger Charles, teamster at 2 Central, l.u.
     85 South Prospect.

FACETTE Joseph, harnessmaker at 8 Sigourney,
     b.2u. 37 Lawrence.
"   Uldege, blacksmith, b.2u. 37 Lawrence.
Factory Insurance Association, 95 Pearl, Charles
     G. Smith, manager.
Faden Nathan, peddler, b.u. 182 Front.
Fagan Bartholomew, b.W.H. home for aged, Alb.
"   Bridget, wid. Peter, b. 290 Flatbush.
"   Catherine, wid. Robert, h. 64 Hungerford.
"   Katharine F. stenogr. 11 Central, b. 221 Jef.
"   John T. policeman, h. 82 Laurel.
"   Joseph A. farmer, h. 14 Squire.
"   Lawrence F. quarryman at stonepits, h. 290
     Flatbush.
"   Martin, saloon, 1076, h. 1076 Broad.
"   Mary, b. 256 Flatbush.
"   Mary E. musicteacher, b. 64 Hungerford.
"   Matthew E. policeman, h. 221 Jefferson.
"   Michael A. screwmaker at 476 Capitol, b.
     30 Harbison.
"   Minnie A. bkkpr. at 719 Mn. b. 221 Jefferson.
"   P. H. h. 721 Main, rm. 15.
"   Patrick, screwm. at 476 Cap. h.u. 16 Putnam.
"   Philip J. carpenter, h. 12 Cedar.
"   Robert J. Jr. student, b. 64 Hungerford.
"   Thomas F. toolm. at 476 Cap. l. 14 Squire.
Fagerhorn Carl, painter, b. 271 Main.
Faherty John E. porter at 152, b. 152 Asylum.
Fahey Dennis, screwmaker at 476 Cap. h. Mt.
"   Frank, at N.Y.R. b. 1478 Broad
"   Hannah, wid. Michael J. h.2u. 49 Hawthorn.
"   John, at N.Y.R. b. 1478 Broad.
"   John F. lather, b.2u. 265 Main.
"   John J. laborer at 476 Cap. h.2u. 84 Ward.
"   Kate, at 37 Wells, b.3u.r. 25 Spruce.
"   Mary, wid. Edward, h.2u. 265 Main.
"   Patrick J. clerk, h. 46 Benton.
"   Thomas, b. 2 Holcomb.
"   Thomas J. lather, b.2u. 265 Main.
"   Timothy B. lather, b.2u. 265 Main.
Fahy Edward H. trav. salesm. Popes, b. 68 Ward.
"   James, teamster at 2 Chapel, h. 45 N.B.
"   Patrick, engineer, h. 68 Ward.
"   Thomas, h.2u. 67 Avon.
"   Thomas W. instructor at Popes, b. 68 Ward.
"   ☞ *see also Fay; Fahey.*
Fairbairn Susan D. wid. Walter, h. 14 Myrtle.
Fairbanks Amos, plumber, b. 43 Linden.
"   Francis P. painter, b.u. 11 Goodman.
"   George, at 59½, b. 135 Trumbull.
"   George H. joiner, h.u. 60 Hawthorn.
"   Sophronia, 16 White, died June 14, aged 90.
Fairbrother Arthur L. clerk 141 Tru. b. 1 C.O.pl.
"   Howard, traveling salesman at 15 Trumbull,
     h. Providence, R. I.
Fairchild Daniel W. agent, 985, l. 985 Main.
"   Margaret S. wid. Stephen B. h.u. 177 Retreat.
Fairfield Edgar G. diesinker at 142 Russ, h.u. 251
     Putnam.
"   Edmund J. sec'y Hartford Typewriter Co.
     476 Capitol, h. 906 Asylum.
"   Geo. A. pres't & treas. Hfd. Machine Screw
     Co. *park commissioner,* h. 50 Fairfield.
"   George E. b. 50 Fairfield.

Fairfield John M. pres. and treas. Hfd. Type-writer Co. *water commissioner*, h. 207 Sig.
" Lizzie J. wid. Henry H. b. 40 Clark.
" Minnie D. wid. Edmund D. h. 5 Wadsworth.
" Philip E. clerk at Pope Tube Co. b. 207 Sig.
" Samuel E. clerk Hartford Typewriter Co. b. 5 Wadsworth.
Fairman Henry M. cutter at 59½ Tru. h.u. 8 Avon.
" John, h. 8 Avon.
Fairview House, A. Leavitt, 87 High.
Fairweather Myles W. rubberworker, 690 Park, h. Wethersfield t.
Falck Charles M. H. mach. Popes, h.u. 228 Zion.
" Hans, bartender, 302 Park, h. 964 Broad.
" Peter, milkman, h. 110 Bluehills.
" ☞ *see also Falk; Folk.*
Fales Anna G. wid. Thomas J. h. 21 Evergreen.
Falk Benjamin, peddler, h. 180 Sheldon.
" Levie, bookbinder, b. 180 Sheldon.
" Max, rubberw. 690 Park, b. 176 Sheldon.
" Tillie Mrs. groceries, 176, h. 180 Sheldon.
" ☞ *see also Falck; Folk.*
Falkenbury Emma F. teacher, b.u. 123 Hung.
Fall Charles V. painter, h.u. 111 Lawrence.
Fallon Bridget, wid. John, h.u. 24 Affleck.
" Catharine, wid. William, h.2u.r. 151 Maple.
" Frank H. b.u. 24 Affleck.
" Frederick, blacksmith, 352 Albany, b. 39 Harbison.
" Joe, laborer at N.Y.R. h. 16 Arch.
" Thomas P. laborer, b.u. 24 Affleck.
Fallow Gavin S. toolmaker at Pratt & Whitney Co. 1 Flower, h. 53 Julius.
" George J. mach. 70 Huy. b. 157 Capitol.
Falls Alice, wid. Michael, h. 3 Chapel.
" Margaret A. bkkpr. at 94 Tru. b. 3 Chapel.
Falotico Rocco, bootblack, h.3u. 16 Kilbourn.
Falvey Jerry L. mach. 1 Laurel, b. 615 Capitol.
" Jeremiah M. helper at 476, b. 615 Capitol.
" Thomas, teamster, h. 57 Hawthorn.
Fanelle Louis, clerk, 1177 Main, h. 79 Windsor.
Fanjoy Howard J. mech. 54 Arch, h. 31 Bart.
Fanning Fannie E. bkkpr. 34 Pratt, b.u. 30 Blu.
" Timothy A. clerk at Brown, Thomson & Co. 942 Main, b. New Britain t.
" William E. proprietor Empire Steam Laundry Co. 34 Pratt, h. 30 Bluehills.
" Wm. W. trav. salesman, h. 139 Ashley.
Fannon Thomas F. cigarm. 867, h. 1293 Main.
Fantoney Charles E. at 490, b. 615 Capitol.
Fantoni John, setter at 15 Tru. b. 13 Kilbourn.
Farand Napoleon, carptr. N.Y.R. h. 10 Warren.
Farber Louis, peddler, h. 22 North.
" Morris, peddler, h.u.r. 26 North.

**FARBER MORRIS,** manufacturer fine bedding, mattresses, cot beds, etc. 8 Walnut, h. 62 Pleasant.

Fargo Nellie R. inspector, h.u. 1101 Main.
" Sarah E. wid. Samuel S. h. 1101 Main.
" Theodore C. painter, b. 713 Main.
Farina Louis, collarm. 8 Sig. b. 262 New Park.
Farley Ann, wid. James, h.2u. 91 Windsor.
" Benjamin L. 6 Talcott.
" Charles F. bartender, 989 Mn. b. 6 Talcott.

Farley Edward J. clerk, 690 Park, b. 13 James.
" Edward M. h. 58 Governor.
" Ernest A. clerk, 37 Church, b. 217 Jefferson.
" James H. carbonm. 33 Wells, b. 72 Grove.
" John, b. 2 Holcomb.
" May Mrs. h.u. 48 Wells.
" Michael P. ins. agt. 721 Mn. h.2u. 1432 Broad.
" Patrick, corem. at 556 Cap. b. 14 Pratt.
" Patrick, laborer, b.u. 1163 Main.
" Patrick J. driver, b. 6 Talcott.
" Thomas, bartender, b. 6 Talcott.
Farmer John J. foreman, b. 20 Albany.

**FARMER PUBLISHING & PRINTING CO.** 284 Asylum. *See page 466.*
" Roderick W. treasurer Hartford Heating Co. h. 80 Main.

**FARMERS & MECHANICS NAT. BANK,** 106 State. *See page 433.*
Farmilo George H. ins. clerk, 197 Asy. b. 91 Bkm.
" Henry, mason, h. 91 Buckingham.
" Howard, mach. at 388 Capitol, b. 91 Bkm.
Farmington Av. Grocery, A. C. Rose, prop. 61 Farmington.
" Av. Hotel, 57 Farmington.
" River Power Co. Pearl.

**FARMINGTON VALLEY HERALD & JOURNAL.** See p. 470.
Farnam Charles N. Mrs. 223 Asylum, rms. 33, 34.
Farnham Adeline Mrs. 867 Mn. b. 120 Trumbull.
" Alice M. teacher Weth. av. sch. b. S.W. t.
" Elias B. salesman at W. C. Mason & Co. 746 Main, h. 32 Bellevue.
" Ellen, wid. John M. b. 144 Retreat.
" Mabel, wid. William A. h. 117 Albany.
" Type Setter Mfg. Co. office 53 Trumbull.
Farnsworth Harry A. gen. agent Conn. General Life Ins. Co. 49 Pearl, h. 36 Ashley.
" Mary A. nurse, 54, b. 54 Church.
" William E. clerk at T. Sisson & Co. 729 Main, h.u. 102 Hudson.
Farr Burt J. machinist, N.Y.R. b. 76 Hopkins.
" Frank, restaurant, 148, h. 148 Front.
" Fred. H. painter, b. 206 Asylum, flat 7.
" George P. canvasser, b. 206 Asylum, flat 7.
" Warner M. clerk at 643 Main, b. 44 Cedar.
Farraday John J. mach. at r. 64 Asy. h. 9 Mor.

DR. I. FARRAR, at Allyn House every 3d Friday and Saturday in each month:
Hours—Fridays, 1 to 10 P. M.
Saturdays, 8 to 11 A. M.
Specialty: Chronic diseases, also Rupture, Hydrocele and Varicocele.
Send 10c. to lock box 2315 for his sealed book on Rupture, Hydrocele, etc., 28 King Street, Dorchester District, Boston, Mass.

Farrar I. physician, 152 Asy. h. Boston, Mass.
Farrell Andrew, fireman, N.E.R. h.u. 1444 Broad.
" Ann, wid. Thomas, h.u. 92 Retreat.
" Ann, wid. William, h.3u. 45 Spruce.
" Annie T. clerk advertising department at Popes, b. 170 Seymour.
" Bernard, upholsterer, 219 Asy. h.u. 20 Avon.
" & Co. saloon, 203 State.
Thomas P. Farrell.

**The Post, 12 Cents a Week, Delivered at Your Home.**

Farrell Cornelius F. driver for city, h. 28 N.B.
" Daniel, plumber at 3 Grove, b.u. 22 Ford.
" Edward J. policeman, b. 26 Alden.
" Edward W. tinner at 128 State, h. 170 Sey.
" Eliza, wid. Thomas, h.u. 1293 Main.
" Francis H. painter, b. 53 Church.
" Garrett J. police, h.u. 27 Talcott.
" Gerritt, helper at 450 Main.
" James, carman, h. 67 Main.
" James, clerk at 715 Main, b. 3 Seymour.
" James, clerk at 65 Asylum, b. 170 Seymour.
" James E. blacksmith at Colts, h. 94 Jefferson.
" James E. Jr. teamster at 335 Shel. h. 67 Main.
" James T. deputy U. S. marshal, *assessor*, h. 137 Park.
" James V. clerk at Brown, Thomson & Co. 942 Main, b. New Britain.
" James W. porter, 54 Ann, b. 168 Allyn.
" John, coachman, 341, h.r. 341 Farmington.
" John, machinist at 133 Shel. h. 92 Chestnut.
" John, skiver at 15 Trumbull, b. 3 Lewis.
" John A. saloon, 340 Park, h. 129 Babcock.
" John E. tilesetter, 218 Pearl, b.u. 33 Elm.
" John H. saloon, 522 Main, h. 98 Maple.
" Joseph E. screwm. 476 Cap. b.2u. 363 Main.
" Kate, wid. Patrick, h.3u. 34 Park.
" Kate A. clerk at Brown, Thomson & Co. 942 Main, b.3u. 34 Park.
" Lizzie, clerk at 70 Huyshope, b. 37 Cong.
" Margaret, wid. James, h.u. 37 Arch.
" Margaret, wid. James, h.3u. 4 Ellery.
" Mary, b.u. 92 Retreat.
" Mary, dressmaker at 73, h.u. 73 Huyshope.
" Mary, wid. Garrett, h.u. 3 Center.
" Mary, wid. James, h.2u.r. 57 Spruce.
" Mary E. clerk at Popes, b. 170 Seymour.
" Mary E. dressmaker, 1295, b. 67 Main.
" Michael, b.u. 22 Ford.
" Michael J. laborer at 54 Arch, h.r. 15 Park.
" Michael P. mason, b. 29 Lawrence.
" Morris, saloon, 20, h. 22 Ford.
" Nellie, clerk at 956 Main, b. 3 Center.
" Patrick A. carpenter at 10 Tru. b. 3 Lewis.
" Patrick F. coachm. 99 Ann, h.2u. 41 Chst.
" Patrick R. mason, h. 3 Seymour.
" Richard, gardener, h. Fairview.
" Robert J. telegraph operator, b. 53 Church.
" Rose, wid. Thomas R. h. 53 Church.
" Rosella, b. 53 Church.
" Thomas, coachman, b.r. 341 Farmington.
" Thomas, helper at Capitol, h. 7 Queen.
" Thomas, ostler at 51, b. 51 Farmington.
" Thomas, teamster, h.u. 47 New Britain.
" Thomas J. brickmason, h. 29 Lawrence.
" Thos. P. (*Farrell & Co.*) h. 39 Woodbridge.
" Thomas P. salesman at 66 Asy. b.3u. 34 Park.
" Thomas R. painter at 9 Sig. b. 53 Church.
" Timothy F. engineer, P.&R. b. 101 Ann.
" Walter, b. 170 Seymour.
" William, gardener at 49, h.r. 49 Woodland.
" William, decorator at Baxter the Decorator, 231 Asylum, b. 2 Wadsworth.
" William, molder, 54 Arch, h.2u. 1035 Broad.
" William, rubberw. at 690 Park, h. 45 Spruce.
" Wm. C. Jr. bkkpr. 61 Mar. b.r. 49 Woodland.

Farrell Wm. H. painter, 185 Asy. b. 36 Temple pl.
" Wm. J. bartender, 245 State, b. 32 Albany.
" William J. teamster, 280 Asy. h.u. 23 Lav.
" ☞ *see also Ferrall.*
Farrelly John, motorman St.Ry. h.2u. 153 Weth.
Farrington James F. machinist at 388 Capitol, h. 6 Kibbe.
Farris Hannah C. Mrs.: h.u. 25 Allen pl.
" John, music, banjo, 173 Asylum, b. 389 Main.
Farvey John, hodcarrier, b. 13 Goodman.
Farwell Fannie C. b. 427 Main, rm. 4.
Fassett Charles, plumber, 3 Grove, h. 41 John.
" Geo. T. ins. agent, 811 Main, h. 32 John.
Fat Sung, laundry, 365, h. 365 Park.
Fathers of Our Lady of LaSalette, New Park.
Faucon James P. Rev. assistant rector Christ church. h. 427 Main, rm. 40.
Faulds Robert, h.u. 516 Broad.
Faulton Michael, machinist, b. 38 Temple.
Faust Charles, painter St.Ry. h.u. 3 Rice.
Faxon Alfred H. painter, h. 108 Hungerford.
" Edward R. contrac. 1 Flow. h. 50 Huntington
" Edward R. Jr. mach. 1 Flow. h.u. 8 Haw.
" Ellen A. wid. George A. h. 88 Buckingham.
" Walter C. asst. secy. Ætna Life Insurance Co. accident dept. 650 Main, h. 29 Huntington.
Fay Catharine, wid. Patrick, h. 61 Heath.
" David P. molder at 54 Arch, b. 27 Grand.
" Edward E. coremaker at Lincoln & Co. 54 Arch, h. 27 Grand.
" Edward E. laundry, 21, h. 21 Albany.
" Elizabeth, teacher at 690 Asy. b. 6 Atwood.
" Etta H. milliner at 25 Pratt, b. 49 Sigourney.
" Frank, blacksmith at N.Y.R. b. 1418 Broad.
" Frank T. receiving clerk motor carriage department, Popes, h. 48 Sigourney.
" Frederick D. clerk at 1 Laurel, b. 49 Sig.
" Frederick N. laundryman, 21, b. 21 Albany.
" George H. motorman St.Ry. h. 259 High.
" Gilbert O. teacher at 690 Asy. h. 6 Atwood.
" James, plasterer at 30 Cush. h.u. 173 Barbour.
" James J. molder at 54 Arch, b. 27 Grand.
" John, helper N.E.R. b.r. 49 Spring.
" John, motorman St.Ry. h. 36 Benton.
" John, plater at Wm. Rogers Manufacturing Co. 66 Market, h.u. 15 Buckingham.
" John J. molder, 555 Capitol, b. 48 Asylum.
" Lawrence, woodw. at 618 Cap. h. 61 Heath.
" Michael, plumber at 94 State, h. W.L.t.
" Milton B. foreman at Jewell Belting Co. 15 Trumbull, b.u. 79 Clark.
" Nellie F. dressmaker, 49, h. 49 Sigourney.
" Noney J. at 1189 Broad, b. 27 Grand.
" Patrick, h. 70 Ward.
" Wm. nightwatchman, h.u. 128 Martin.
" ☞ *see also Fahey; Fahy.*
Faye Jules Lee, hostler, 173, l. 173 State.
Feagener Sedonei, wid. Belthazar, seamstress, 10 Charter Oak, h.2u. 37 Mulberry.
Fearsall Henry, filer at 581 Cap. b. Hamilton.
Featherbridge Emeline Mrs. stenog. b. 5 Main.
Featherstone Benj. F. clerk at Brown, Thomson & Co. 942, b. 1202 Main.
" James J. brakeman, h. 35 Pleasant.
" Thos. F. laborer, b. 35 Pleasant.

**For Sale Advertisements Bring Results in the Post.**

Febvre Daniel, builder, 56 Tru. b. Windsor t.
Fechner Adolph, filer at Popes, h.u. 172 Ward.
" Adolph, mech. at 54 Arch, h. 172 Ward.
Feeck Charles, Jr. clerk, 885 Main, b. 19 Walnut.
Feeley George, deckh. str. Middletown, 285 State.
" Joseph O. bartender 24 Front, b.2u. 17 Good.
" Matthew J. saloon, 24, groceries, 26, b.u.
26 Front.
" Thomas W. bluer at Colts, b.2u. 17 Goodman.
" W. M. coachman at 77, h.r. 30 Wethersfield.
" William J. laborer at 70 Huy. b.r. 30 Weth.
Feeney Bernard, peddler, h.u.r. 65 Temple.
" Frank J. driver at 39 Front, b.r. 17 Albany.
" John, laborer at r. 17, h.r. 17 Albany.
" Mary E. dressmaker, 76, b.u. 76 Walnut.
" Matthew E. potter, h.u. 93 Madison av.
" Richard J. cigarm. 40 Mul. b. 17 Albany.
" Thomas, helper at P.& R. b.u. 76 Walnut.
" William, laborer, 389 Allyn, h.u. 76 Walnut.
Feery Michael J. mach. N.Y.R. h. 13 So. Laurel.
Fehan George, mason, b. 84 Grove.
Fehmer Albert, architect, 1260 Main, h. 68 Capen.
Fehr Albert, polisher, 581 Cap. b.2u. 296 Park.
Feiane John, laborer, b.u. 82 Morgan.
Feigener B. A. Mrs. tailoress h.3u. 37 Mulberry.
Feighn John N. carpenter, h.2u. 146 Mather.
Feil Louis, bakery, 115, h. 115 Windsor.
Fein Simon, peddler, h.u. 78 Talcott.
Feinberg Bernard, operator, h. 76 Talcott.
Feingold George, umbrella mfr. 13, h. 13 Morgan.
Felblum Simon, peddler, h.u.r. 8 North.
Felch W. Farrand, at Travelers Insurance Co. 56
Prospect, h. 286 Sigourney.
Feldburg William, setter at 15 Tru. b. 13 North.
Felder Charles, at 436 Capitol, h.3u. 4½ Hunger-
ford pl.
" John, mechanic, Popes, h. 4½ Hungerford pl.
Felhage Charles, b. 2 Holcomb.
" Edward, painter, h.u. 4 South Forest.
Felhusen John, tailor, h.u. 47 Talcott.
Fellerman Fred, tailor, 2 State, h. 23 Morgan.
Fellerter Ann, wid. Patrick, laundress, h.2u. 80
Windsor.
" Ellen, h.u. 31 Hudson.
" Helen T. saleslady at H. B. Brainerd, b. 4
Bartholomew.
" James, mason, h.u. 4 Bartholomew.
" James P. driver at 896 Main, b. 77 Francis.
" Jane, wid. John, h. 147 Zion.
" Patrick J. polisher at Popes, b. 147 Zion.
Felley George, deckh. str. Middletown, 285 State.
Fellipse Nicola, laborer, h.u. 41 North.
Fellowes Charles E. attorney, clerk Court of Com-
mon Pleas, 85 Trumbull, h. 44 Forest.
" Mary E. Miss, b. 44 Forest.
Fellows George, mach. 80 Huy. b. 157 Capitol.
Felt Levi L. cashier at Travelers Insurance Co.
56 Prospect, h. 142 Jefferson.
" William, at Travelers Ins. Co. 56 Prospect,
b. 142 Jefferson.
Felth John, gardener, 72, l.r. 72 Washington.
Felty J. Wellington, physician, 340, h. 340
Windsor av.
Feminello Michael, farmhand, b. 81 Morgan.
Fenan Thomas, mason, l.u. 24 Church.

Fendow Charles, at 476, h.2u. 615 Capitol.
Fenety Andrew C. artist 904, h. 904 Mn. rm. 105.
Fenn A. I. Mrs. b. 983 Asylum.
" Andrew W. painter, h. 438 Windsor av.
FENN CHARLES W. councilman 5th ward, sales-
man at 175 Pearl.
" Clarence A. polisher at 65 Suffield, b. 438
Windsor av.
" David, l.u. 1293 Main.
" E. Hart, city editor of Hartford Post, 23
Asylum, b. U. S. hotel.
" Francis S. b. 152 Asylum.
" Frederick P. accountant at 175 Pearl, h.
Wethersfield t.
" J. Lincoln, attorney at law, 85 Trumbull,
asst. clerk superior court, h.u. 45 Sumner.
" John Roberts, manager L. T. Fenn, furniture
store, 613 Main, b. 655 Farmington.
" Keron, b.u. 7 Putnam.
FENN LINUS T. furniture, etc. 613 Main.
h. 655 Farmington.		*See page 501.*
" Mary R. b. 655 Farmington.
" W. S. salesm. 84 Market, h. Westminster, Vt.
" Wallace T. sec'y & treas. of Kellogg & Bulkeley
Co. 175 Pearl, h. Wethersfield t.
" Wilson L. foreman at 135 Sheldon, h. 5 Mahl.
" ☞ *see also Finn.*
Fennell Michael L. carpenter, h.u. 45 Chestnut.
" Timothy H. supt. N.Y. & N.E.R.R. b. 152
Asylum.
Fenner Alex. E. conductor St. Ry. h.u. 20 Benton.
" Wm. O. electrician at St. Ry. 115 State, h.u.
86 New Britain.
Fennessey Daniel, teamster at 50, b.u. 50 Wdbg.
Fennessy Frank, machinist, h.u. 1328 Broad.
" Frank J. machinist at Pope Tube Co. h. 1328
Broad.
" John, lookout str. Middletown, h. Brooklyn t.
" John J. boilermaker, at H. B. Beach & Son,
135 Grove, h. 9 Wells.
" Thos. J. mach. at Popes, b. 276 Lawrence
" William J. laborer, h.u. 10 Winter.
" ☞ *see also Finnessey.*
Fenning Edward S. engineer, 40, h. 30 Gov.
Fenoglio Alexander A. lithographer at 42 Union
pl. h. 62 Madison.
Fenton Dennis, steamfitter, h. 697 Windsor av.
" Dennis A. printer at 141 Pearl, b. 12 Haw.
" Edward, helper at 165 Windsor, b. 18
Kennedy.

Fenton Ellen, wid. Jeremiah, b.u. 46 Wells.
" Isaac M. woodworker, 352 Albany, h.u. 183 Woodland.
" James, h.2u. 15 Wells.
" James, electrotyper at A. Mugford, 177 Asylum, b. 12 Hawthorn.
" John, laborer, b.u. 30 Flower.
" Michael, carpenter, h.2u.r 12 So. Prospect.
" Patrick, plumber at 280 Asy. b. 12 Haw.
" Robert C. clerk at 98 Kilbourn, l. 98 Capitol.
" Roger, h. 12 Hawthorn.
Fenwick David, restaurant, 111, h. 90 Pearl.
Feree Wm. E. mach. at 1 Flow. b. 34 Hopkins.
Ferenz Joseph, laborer, 25 Front, b. 56 Sheldon.
Fergerburg Charles, silversmith, b. 88 Church.
Fergstrom August B. teamster, h.u. 199 Shel.
Ferguson Albin S. cigarmanufacturer, fruits, etc. 53 Albany, h.u. 56 Liberty.
" Andrew, stenographer at Capewell Horse Nail Co. 40 Gov. h. Talcottville v.
" Augustus, teamster, h.u. 199 Sheldon.
" Clarence W. wirew. 618 Cap. b. 257 N.P.
" Henry Rev. professor at Trinity College, h. 123 Vernon.
" Herbert D. foreman at 581 Cap. b. 257 N.P.
" Herbert F. rubberw. 690 Park, b.u. 14 Heath.
" Hugh, fireman St.Ry. h. 21 Squire.
" James D. rubberw. 690 Park, b. 257 N.P.
" John, blacksmith, h. 257 New Park.
" John, plumber, b. 21 Squire.
" Julia E. trained nurse, b. 257 New Park.
" Owen J. barber at 291 Park, b. 21 Squire.
" Robert W. boilermaker, h. 40 Williams.
" Robert W. Jr. machinist at 40 Cushman, b. 40 Williams.
" Samuel, draughtsman at 266 Pearl, b. 123 Vernon.
" Walter W. clerk at 69 Alb. b. 40 Williams.
" William J. mach. at 1 Flow. h. Manchester t.
Fernald Robert P. h.u. 212 Asylum.
Fernquist Hilma C. teacher at Parkville school, b. 62 Webster.
Ferrall Frances, milliner, 903 Main, rm. 18, b. 225 Barbour.
" John J. gardener, b. 225 Barbour.
" Matthew gardener, b. 225 Barbour.
" ☞ see also Farrell.
Ferranto Aricangello, laborer, b.2u. 82 Morgan.
" Daniel, laborer, b.u. 168 Front.
" Joseph, grocery, 17, h. 17 Charles.
" Joseph M. excavating contr. h. 17 Charles.
Ferrier James W. carpenter, h. 10 Wadsworth.
Ferris Sarah B. wid. Chas. R. b.u. 183 Seymour.
Ferriter Maurice, machinist, b.2u. 126 Albany.
Ferro Frank, laborer, b.r. 20 Charles.
" John, laborer, b.r. 20 Charles.
" Luigi, laborer, b.r. 20 Charles.
Ferry Charles, driver at r. 32, b. 32 Church.
" William H. collarm. at 8 Sig. h. E.H.t.
Festa Joseph, laborer, b.u. 168 Front.
Fester John, laborer, h.u. 262 Front.
" Peter, laborer, h.u. 262 Front.
Festermaker Jackson D. brakeman at N.Y.R. b. 180 Capen.
Fetherstone ☞ see Featherstone.

Fetzer Frederick, laborer at 335 Sheldon, h.r. 32 South Prospect.
Feulner John, brewer, 315 Park, h.u. 2 Brady pl.
Fialkoweski Victor, draughtsman at Pope Tube Co. b. 238 Laurel.
Fiance Joseph, laborer, b.4u. 190 Front.
Fichman Max, peddler, h. 262 Front.
Fichtner Frederick P. b. 230 High.
" Pauline A. wid. C. h. 230 High.
Ficocelli Joseph, laborer, b.4u. 190 Front.
" Munzio, laborer, b.u. 83 Windsor.
Fidelberg Joseph, screwm. at 476 Cap. b.32 North.
Fidelity & Casualty Co. The, 49 Pearl.
**FIDELITY COMPANY,** 49 Pearl.
*See page 438.*
" & Deposit Co. of Maryland, 25 Pearl.
Fiege Augustus F. h. 27 Congress.
Field Alice B. nurse, l. 97 Trumbull.
" Benjamin D. foreman at 164 State, h. 225 Franklin.
" Charles H. special agent U.S. stamped envelope works, 1 S. Ann, h. 33 Niles.
" Edgar A. com. trav. at Tucker & Goodwin, 8 Hurlburt, h.u. 13 Mahl.
" Edward B. salesman at Popes, b. 33 Niles.
" Eugene D. at Travelers Ins. Co. 56 Prospect, b. 68 Beacon.
" Francis E. apprent. at 1 Laurel, b. 33 Niles.
" Jennie R. nurse, b. 108 Ann.
" Joseph F. at Ætna Insurance Co. 666 Main, h. 68 Beacon.
" Monroe S. driver, h. 153 Main.
" Nancy M. Mrs. h. 38 Sumner.
" William E. experimenter, 690, h. 757 Park.
" Wm. H. elevator at 15 Tru. b. 8 Goodman.
Fielder George L. publisher Hartford Evening Post, 23 Asylum, h. 164 Sargeant.
Fielding Chas. R. carpenter at N.Y.R. h. 179 Barb.
" John A. foreman at 62 Market, h. 1271 Mn.
" William C. electric burglar protection, deputy sheriff, 847, rm. 8, h. 1271 Main.
Fields Calvin S. asst. pressman at Courant, 66 State, b. E.H.t.
" John H. ostler at 401, b. 401 Albany.
" Lottie, housekeeper, b. 30 Ferry.
Filand James, b. 2 Holcomb.
" ☞ see also Filon.
Filbue Simon, peddler, h.3u.r. 8 North.
Filer ☞ see also Fyler.
Filiau Joseph T. blacksmith, r. 580 Windsor av. h. 4 Charlotte.
Filipowaki John, b.u. 5 Front.
" Kazimer, h.u. 92 Front.
Filley Charles T. h.u. 32 Canton.
" George L. conductor St.Ry. h. 32 Center.
" Louis J. (Bruce, Filley & Co.) h. Bloomfield t.
" Margaret, wid. Thomas, b.u. 1201 Main.
" Sophia Mrs. dressmaker, b.u. 32 Canton.
" Wilbur J. (Bruce, Filley & Co.) h. 202 Sargeant.
Fillian Mary C. Mrs. b.St.M.Home for Aged, Alb.
Fillinger Joseph, candymaker, b. 14 Morgan.
Fillmore John, asst. cook at 323 Pearl, h. 566 Mn.
Filon Frank J. at 59½ Tru. b. 22 Liberty.
" Mae T. stenogr. at 811 Main, b. 22 Liberty.

Filon Margaret H. wid. David J. h. 22 Liberty.
" Mary, wid. Hugh, h.u. 67 Avon.
" Sarah, at 37, b.u. 48 Wells.
" Thomas, h.u. 63 Avon.
" Thomas, laborer, h.r. 35½ Linden.
" ☞ see also Filand.
Finan Michael, mason, l.u. 1218 Main.
" Patrick, mason, l.u. 1218 Main.
Finch Merritt, laborer, h. 69 Bluehills.
Findon Ada B. b. 32 Pliney.
" Alice, clerk, b. 32 Pliney.
" Fred, machinist, b. 28 Buckingham.
" John, mach. at 135 Shel. h. 28 Buckingham.
" Lenora, b. 28 Buckingham.
" Sadie, dressmaker, b. 32 Pliney.
" William F. machinist, h. 32 Pliney.
Fine Art Glass Co. 72 Niles.
" Charles A. mech. at 26 High, b.2u. 276 Mar.
" Esther, wid. Sam, h.2u. 276 Market.
" Lewis, peddler, h.u. 73 Charles.
" Morris, fruit peddler, h.u. 8 North.
" Morris, tinner, 4 Ford, b. 276 Market.
" Philip, peddler, h. 176 Front.
" Shem, ragpeddler, h.u. 78 Talcott.
Fineberg Louis, crock.& tin w. 20½, h. 119 Front.
Finebloom Mayer, tailor at 73 Pratt, h.2u. 226 Front.
Finer Max, peddler, h. 216 Front.
Finesilver Nathan, portrait artist, h.u. 277 Mar.
Fing Ferdinando, grocery, 180, h. 180 Front.
Fingel James, barber at 144, b 180 Front.
Finigan Joseph J. clerk at 45 Asylum, b. 56 Winthrop.
Fink Ignatz, helper at 142 Russ, h.u. 5 Kil. ct.
" Jacob, at 194 Pearl, b. 177 Asylum.
Finklestein Mike, setter at 15 Tru. h. 13 North.
Finklestern, Max, laborer, h.u. 15 North.
Finlay Bros. printers, 25 Asylum.
  James Finlay.   William F. Finlay.
" James, (F. Bros.) h. 30 Ashley.
" William F. (F. Bros.) h. 94 Ashley.
Finley Anna, wid. George, h.2u. 24 Babcock.
" Ellen, h.2u. 63 Madison.
" Elmer J. bkkpr. at 145 Asylum, b.13 Avon.
" Fred'k D. toolm. at 476 Capitol, b. 9 John.
" H. A. instructor at Hfd. Business College, 370 Asylum.
" John A. carptr. jan. at 234 Pearl, h. 71 Asy.
" Mary Ann, h.2u. 63 Madison.
" Michael, policeman, h.u. 148 Albany.
" Patrick J. policeman, h. 84 Chestnut.
" Robert P. secy. Workingmen's Ex.Y.M.C.A.
Finn Annie, b.r. 59 Zion.
" David, spicegrinder at 146 State, l. 1297 Mn.
" George, motorman St.Ry. 115 State.
" James, farmer at 30 Wash. b. 99 N.B.
" James, laborer, b. 6 Lewis.
" James A. mach. at 1 Flow. b. 1316 Broad.
" John, stonemason, h.r. 19½ Buckingham.
" John, teamster at 462 Main, h. 14 S. Pro.
" John P. mach. at 388 Capitol, h. 367 Park.
" Michael, gardener at 83 Woodland, h. 1190 Asylum.
" Michael, laborer, b. 12 South Prospect.
" Patrick S. polisher at Popes, h.u. 51 Alb.

Finn Wm. express driver, 15½ Babcock, h.u. 242 Zio'i.
Finnegan Edward W. mechanic, 581 Cap. b. N.t.
" Frank, bartdr. at 287 Park, b. 1145 Broad.
" Hubert, clerk at Sisson c. Park, h. 874 Park.
" J. J. clerk at 45 Asylum, b. 56 Winthrop.
" John A. apprentice, b. 20 Brook.
" John M. enameler at 581 Capitol, b.2u. 81 Governor.
" Margaret P. wid. Peter, h. 1335 Broad.
" May, bkkpr. at 835 Main, b. 20 Brook.
" Patrick, stairbuilder at 133 Shel. b. 101 Ann.
" Patrick T. baggagem. P.&R. h. 20 Brook.
" ☞ see also Finigan.
Finneran Sarah, h.4u. 47 Spruce.
Finnerty Edward, enam. at Popes, h. 373 Broad.
" John, screwm. at 476 Capitol, b. 373 Broad.
" Peter, b.u. 51 Albany.
" Peter, expressman at 373, b. 373 Broad.
Finnessey John, engir. at 110, h.u. 10 Commerce.
" ☞ see also Fennessey.
Finney Charles H. machinist, b. 19 Atlantic.
" Joseph, laborer, b. 1 North.
Finucane John, steamfit'r at 110 Com. h. 96 State.

**FIRST NATIONAL BANK OF HARTFORD,** 50 State. See p. 484.
Fischenick Gaspard, cook, 427 Mn. h.u. 83 Grove.
Fischer A. C. cigarmaker at 867 Main, h. E.H.t.
" Albert C. laborer, h.u. 15½ Martin.
" Camillo L. vice president & treasurer The H. Fischer Brewery, h. 52 Oak.
" Fannie, wid. Gustave, boardingh. 345 Main.
" George B. diemaker at Popes, h. 26 Grand.
" Gustav, printer at 91 Asy. b. 345 Main.
Fischer Gustave, newsdealer, 259 Asylum, b. 68 Pleasant. See page 14.
" Harry Z. woodworker at Strickland & Shea, 20 Potter, h.u. 18½ Church.
" Henry A. upholsterer at Neal, Goff & Inglis Co. 980 Main, b. 45 Talcott.

**FISCHER HUBERT, BREWERY,** 315 Park. See page 492.
" Hubert, president Hubert Fischer Brewery, saloon, 158 Front, h.u. 315 Park.
" John, salesman at Popes, b. 114 Hung.
" John P. teamster at 273 Asy. h.r. 10 Russell.
" Julius, cabinetmaker, h.2u. 295 Park.
" Jennie, domestic, b.u. 68 Pleasant.
" Joseph, teams. at Taft Co. 15, b.u. 116½ Alb
" Laura, saleslady at 908, b. 345 Main.
" Maggie, at 34 Morgan, b. 222 Franklin.

**Established 1872.**

# Ransom N. FitzGerald,

Wholesale Dealer in

*Salt, Salt Fish, Canned Goods, and Grocers' Sundries, Pickles, Jellies, Preserves, Beans, Peas, etc.*

Proprietor of Mascot and Phœnix Brands of Canned Vegetables and Fish.

**Office and Store,**

## 44 and 46 MARKET STREET.

Fischer Olga, b. 345 Main.
  " Simon, h.u. 13 Wethersfield.
  " W. Frederick, con. St.Ry. b.u. 200 Allyn.
  " Wm. T. conductor St.Ry. b. 36 Vernon.
  " ☞ see also Fisher.
Fish Alfred B. clerk at Beach & Co. chemicals, 209 State, h. 116 Capen.
  " Arthur W. janitor at 943 Mn. h. 43 Liberty.
  " Edgar W. mech. at Popes, h. Wethersfield t.
  " Ella E. dressmaker, 13, b.u. 13 East.
  " Frederick S. engir. N.Y.R. h. 43 Bellevue.
  " Geo. H. clerk, h. 27 Pavilion.
  " Hamlin W. dropf. at 142 Russ,h. 68 Wooster.
  " H. Maria, h. 64 Buckingham.
  " Harris, peddler, h. 277 Market.
  " Helen M. wid. Samuel A. nurse, h.u. 13 East.
  " Hyman, tailors trimmings, 48 Pratt, h.u. 25 Morgan.
  " Sarah C. wid. A. M. h. 64 Buckingham.
  " W. J. clerk at 304 Asylum, b. Newington t.
**FISHEL & LEVY,** wholesale liquor dealers, 189 State.
Joseph M. Fishel.    Morris Levy.    Adolph Levy.
  " Joseph M. *(F. & Levy,)* h. New York.
Fisher Abe, clerk at 188 State, h. 2 Ellsworth pl.
  " Andrew, salesman, h. 52 Clark.
  " Annie, asst. at Pub. Library, b. 68 Pleasant.
  " Arthur W. linem. N.E.R. h.u. 50 Chestnut.
  " Bessie, proofreader, 141 Pearl, b. 62 Capen.
  " Charles A. foreman at Case, Lockwood & Brainard, 141 Pearl, b. 197 Collins.
  " Charles E. mach. at 476 Cap. b. 45 Talcott.
  " Charles F. carpenter, b. 73 Webster.
  " Chas. F. carpetlayer at 22, h. 22 Preston.
  " Charles G. freight agent, N.Y.,N.H.&H.R. and N.E.R. Cos. h. 100 Huntington.
  " Chas.R.salesm.at 462 Mn.b.100 Huntington.
  " Charles R.Mrs.(Susan B.G.)h.101 Trumbull.
  " Florence L.-student, h. 197 Collins.
  " Francis, Mrs. h.u. 43 Woodbridge.
  " Frederick F. assistant bookkeeper at Conn. River Banking Co. 761 Main, b. 15 Beach.
  " Frederick H. h.u. 62 Morgan.
  " Frederick H.Jr.clerk at 885 Mn. b.u. 62 Mor.
  " George A. woodw. at 133 Shel. h. 411 Maple.
  " Geo. B.local ins. agent 197 Asy. h. 166 Collins
  " George W. h. 231 Market.
  " Gilbert, barber at 83 Front, h.3u. 80 Shel.
  " Jacob, newsdlr. at 259 Asy. b. 68 Pleasant.

Fisher John F. agent, b. 19 Spring.
  " John T. upholsterer, b. 45 Talcott.
  " Joseph W. h. 26 Vernon.
  " Michael, capmaker, h.2u. 68 Pleasant.
  " Nellie, stenog. at Popes, b. 43 Woodbridge.
  " Louis, mach. at 1 Flower, b. 68 Pleasant.
  " Robert E. clerk at 74 Tru. b. 26 Vernon.
  " Warren H.inspector at 690 Park,h.266 N.P.
  " ☞ see also Fischer.
Fishman Max, peddler, h.u. 262 Front.
Fisk Amelia, b.r. 44 Village.
  " Grace A. clerk at 224 Asy. b. 44 Village.
  " Henry A. b.u. 1039 Main.
**FISK HENRY J., D. D. S.** dentist, 53 Trumbull, rm. 306, h. Windsor t.
  " Leonard D. *(Daniels Mill Co.)* 40 Elm, h. Farmington cor. Prospect.
**FISK LOUIS H., D. D. S.** dentist, 53 Trumbull, rm. 306.
  " Mary E. teacher Washington street school, b. 33 Allen pl.
Fiske Carrie Mrs. dressm. 284 h.u. 284 Asy. rm 89.
  " Charles C. h. 10 Ellsworth.
  " DeLancey W. student at Trinity, 24 Jarvis Hall, Summit.
  " John D. *(J. D. Fiske & Co.)*h. 50 Niles.
**FISKE JOHN D. & CO.** succeeded by Peter Dow Jr., 278 Asy. *See p. 551.*
  " Reginald, student, Trinity college, 6 Jarvis hall, Summit.
  " Samuel A. student Theological seminary, 1507 Broad.
Fistler Frank, paperhanger, h. 23 Sigourney.
Fitch A. P. Mrs. forelady at 908 Main. h. 96 Ann.
  " Asa P. at Hartford Fire Ins. Co. 53 Trumbull, h. 96 Ann.
  " B. T. driver at 368 Asylum.
  " C. Raymond, supt. at Hartford Cycle Co. h. 5 Girard.
  " Charles G. agent, 756 Main, b. 44 Hudson.
  " Charles G. conductor St.Ry. h. 44 Hudson.
  " Emily E. wid. W. H. h.u. 1293 Main.
  " Florence M. bkkpr.121 Windsor av.b.8 East.
  " Frank M. clerk at Hartford Life Ins. Co. 252 Asylum, h.u. 110 Wooster.
  " Fred. L. molder at 556 Capitol, h. E.H.t.
  " Horace S. h. 297 Windsor av.
  " Irving D. screwm. at 476 Cap. h.2u. 6 John.
  " J. Patten, b. 103 Trumbull.
  " Mattie M. stenog. at 556 Capitol, b.E.H.t.
  " Nathan D. nightwatchman at Brown, Thomson & Co. 942 Main, h. 8 East.
Fitts Frank M. sales. Chas. R. Hart Co. rugs and carpets, 898 Main, h.u. 222 Jefferson.
  " H. Mrs. l. 32 West.
  " Henry E. cashier at Travelers Insurance Co. 56 Prospect, h. 20 Marshall.
  " Maria, wid. Joseph P. b. 20 Marshall.
  " Thomas K. gardener at 244, b. 244 Main.
Fitzger Thomas, buffer, 182 Allyn, h. 261 State.
FitzGerald Ransom N. *city tax collector,* 114 Pearl, commission merchant, 44-46 Market; *fire commissioner,* h. 110 Edwards.
            *See page 144.*

Fitzgerald Andrew, driver at 366 Main, b. 1335 Broad.
" Ann Mrs. b. 2 Holcomb.
" Annie Mrs. h.u. 566 Main.
" Catherine A. b. 12 Center.
" Edward, mach. at Colts, b. 42 Woodbridge.
" Eugene, plumber, b. 488 Main.
" F. engineer at 388 Capitol, h. 10 Putnam.
" J. H. b. 315 Pearl, rm. 406.
" James, h.u. 23 North.
" James, laborer, b.2u. 81 Sheldon.
" James, laborer, 8 Front, l.72 Charter Oak.
" James H. at Popes, b. 20 Linden.
" Jeremiah, h. 42 Woodbridge.
" Johanna, wid. Michael, h. 12 Center.
" John, bricklayer, b. 24 Union.
" John, helper at N.E.R. b. 4 Donald.
" John, laborer at Colts, h. 42 Woodbridge.
" John, ostler at 87 High, b. 61 Ann.
" John E. helper at 54 Arch, b.u. 45 Wdbg.
" John J. assemb. at 556 Cap. b. 9 Hawthorn.
" John J. conductor at St.Ry. h. 41 Chestnut.
" Kate, ward maid at 20 So. Hudson.
" Louis, waiter at 33 Prospect.
" Margaret T. clerk at Brown, Thomson & Co. 942 Main, b.u. 52 Green.
" Mary, wid. Michael, h. 866 Broad.
" Mary E. Mrs. b. 2 Holcomb.
" Mary E. clerk at Brown, Thomson & Co. 942 Main, b.u. 52 Green.
" Maurice J. clerk at 12 State, b.u. 52 Green.
" Michael, laborer, b.r.u. 25 Morgan.
" Michael, laborer at and b. 776 Windsor av.
" Michael, helper at 54 Arch, b. 28 Potter.
" Michael J. b. 42 Woodbridge.
" Michael J. office mgr.206 State, b.866 Broad.
" Patrick, engineer, 1 Flower, b.u.10 Putnam.
" Patrick, hodcarrier, h. 24 Putnam.
" Patrick E. buffer at Wm. Rogers Mfg. Co. 66 Market, b. 20 Avon.
" Patrick F. clerk, b. 12 Center.
" Patrick J. teamster at 1 Flower, b.985 Main.
" Peter, stairbuilder, b.u. 572 Windsor.
" Peter J., United States army, b. 26 Market.
" Robert, helper, h.2u. 39 Woodbridge.
" Robert E. clerk at 885 Main, b. Rockville t.
" Robert F. Rev. vice president St. Thomas seminary, h. 352 Collins.
" Thomas, b. 2 Holcomb.
" Thomas, helper at Colts, h.u. 52 Green.
" Thomas, helper at 54 Arch, b. 28 Potter.
" Thomas, teamster, b. 1160 Main.
" Thomas, tester, 556 Cap.b.4½Hungerford pl.
" Thomas Jr.lab.556 Cap. b.4½ Hungerford pl.
" Thomas M. buffer, h.3u. 261 State.
" Timothy E. brittaniaworker at 62 Market, h. 28 Albany.
" William, b.2u. 39 Woodbridge.
" William H. bartender, h. 371 Capitol.
" William J. clerk at 125 Albany, b. 12 Center.
Fitzgibbon Henry,molder,54 Arch,h.78 Franklin.
" James D. assembler at Popes, b. 78 Franklin.
" John J. carpenter, h. 4 North.
" Josephine, clerk, 942 Main, b. 78 Franklin.

Fitzgibbon Mary A. clerk at Brown, Thomson & Co. 942 Main, b. 78 Franklin.
" Stephen, laborer, h. 94 Harper.
Fitzpatrick Anna Mrs. h.2u. 18 Lawrence.
" Bridget, wid. Matthew, b. 70 Walnut.
" Daniel A.printer at 141 Pearl,h.u. 5 Atlantic.
" F. deckhand, str. Middletown, 285 State.
" Frank, helper at 54 Arch, h. 20 John.
" J. H. trav. salesm. 15 Tru. h. Salem, Mass.
" James, driver at 245, h. 99 Windsor.
" James, enameler, b.u. 4 Putnam.
" James, machinist, b.2u. 18 Lawrence.
" James, painter, b. 111 Pearl.
" John, bartender, b.u. 33 Spruce.
" John, coachman at 54, b. 54 Woodland.
" John, mach. at 1 Flower, b. 45 Sigourney.
" John J.plumber at 164 State,b.103 Windsor.
" Joseph, helper at Popes, h. 45 Spruce.
" Margaret, wid. William, h. 33 Spruce.
" Mary, wid. John, h.u. 16 Westland.
" Michael J.asst.forem. 48 Ann,h. 18 Walnut.
" Mr. molder at Colts, l. 381 Capitol.
" Patrick, farmer, b.3u.r. 60 Temple.
" Peter, laborer, Pope Tube Co.b. 55 Laurel.
" Thomas J. machinist at 1 Flower, b. 5 Queen.
" William, bartender, b.2u. 18 Lawrence.
" William, bartender, 17 Central, b.25 Chapel.
" William, laborer, h.2u.r. 93 Sheldon.
" William, porter at 583 Mn. b.u. 18 Lowrence.
Fitzsimmons Bernard, plumber at 1152 Main, b. 145 High.
" Charles, teamster, h.2u. 184 Sheldon.
" James, butcher, 552 Asy. b. 2 Worcester pl.
" James, groceries, 126, h. 126 Martin.
" John, clerk at 756 Main, b. 2 Worcester pl.
" John, shoemaker, h. 3 Rice.
" Patrick, mason, h. 7 Avon.
" Thomas F. carriagem. Alb. b. 126 Martin.
" William J. clerk at 921 Main, b. 7 Avon.
Fivenson Julius, peddler, h.u. 28 North.
" Nathan, b.2u. 28 North.
Flad Amelia, wid. Charles F. h. 1330 Broad.
" ☞ see also Flood.
Flagg Augusta S. wid. Lorenzo G., Quaker lane.
" Charles E. chief clerk at Evening Post, 23 Asylum, b. 48 Church.
" Charles H. farmer, h. Park, W.H.t.
" Charles N. artist, 904 Mn. h. 90 Washington.
" E. Gurdon, salesman, b. 11 Winthrop.
" Edward, painter, h.u. 550 Park.
" Elizabeth A. h. 118 Trumbull.
" Ellen E. h. 90 Washington.
" Eugenia E. stenographer at Factory Ins. Co. 95 Pearl, b. 58 Church.
" Eva L. clerk at 725 Main, l. 60 Walnut.
" Frank S. discount clerk at Charter Oak National Bank, 124 Asylum, b. 1140 Main.
" George E. salesman 206 State, h. W.H.t.
" Grace E. b. 11 Winthrop.
" Howard A. clerk at Conn. Fire Ins. Co. 51 Prospect, b. W.H.t.
" Mary E. wid. Edward A. h. 11 Winthrop.
" Stuart R. teamster at 843 Main, b.60 Walnut.
" Wilbur F. b. 96 Laurel.
" Wm. B. forem. shoe shop 690 Asy.h. 96 Laurel

Flahavan Delia, clerk, b. 4 Whitman.
" James, woodworker, 556 Main, b.4 Whitman.
" Margaret, wid. Morris, h. 4 Whitman.
" Michael, helper, 556 Main, b. 4 Whitman.
Flaherty Daniel M.saloon,17Central,h.198Laurel.
" John, porter at 152 Asylum.
" Morris, helper at 556 Capitol,h.u.134Martin.
" ☞see O'Flaherty; Faherty.
Flaishman Adolph,tailor at 19Church,h.42Village.
Flanagan E. deckhand str. Hartford, 285 State.
" John F. porter at 389 Allyn,h.2u.r. 61 Front.
" John J. grocer, 97, h. 97 Windsor.
" John J. laborer, b.2u. 275 Asylum.
" Michael, corem. 556 Capitol, b.147 Babcock.
" Owen, laborer at stone pit, b. Zion.
" Thomas, h.2u.r. 61 Front.
" Thomas, laborer at 1, b. 36 Flower.
" Thomas F. foreman mattress department at
    334 Wethersfield, h. 26 Franklin.
" Thomas F. (Cannon & Flanagan,) b. 3 Oak.
" William J. asst. bkkpr. 372 Asy.b. 227 High.
" ☞see also Flannigan.
Flanegan Annie, dressmaker, b.r. 15 Belden.
" James F. car rep. P.&R. h. 78 Walnut.
" Julia, wid. James, h.r. 15 Belden.
Flanigan Edward, deckhand str. Middletown,
    285 State.
" J. laborer at Pope Tube Co. b. 65 Laurel.
" James E. printer at 857 Main, h. E.H.t.
" John F. swager, b. 94 Madison av.
" Patrick, helper, 556 Capitol, h.u. 166 Ward.
" Thomas F. clerk at Connecticut General
    Life Ins. Co. 49 Pearl, h. 115 Albany.
" Thomas F. at 336 Weth. h. 26 Franklin.
" William H. printer at 29 Union pl. h. E.H.t.
Flannery Ann,wid.Keron,grocer, 139,h.139 Zion.
" James, iceman, 4 Central, h. 40 S.Prospect.
" James, stonemason, h.u. 62 Governor.
" John, policeman, h.u. 37 Woodbridge.
" Keron S. helper, b. 62 Governor.
" Margaret, wid. Patrick, h.u. 24 Commerce.
" Patrick, laborer, h.r. 44 Pleasant.
" Thomas (O'Brien & F.) h.2u. 119 Maple.
" William, brakeman, N.Y.R. h.r. 90 Ward.
Flansburg Chas. conduct. St.Ry. h.u. 47 Elliot.
Flato Michael C.barber at 703Mn.h.214Franklin.
Flattery Ann, wid. John, h.2u. 113 Hungerford.
" Elizabeth A. at Case, Lockwood & Brainard
    Co. b.2u. 113 Hungerford.
" John J. engir. N.Y.R. b.2u. 113 Hungerford.
" Keron, painter, 48 Ann, b. W.H.t.
Fleig Fred, at 217 Windsor, b. 4 Bellevue.
Fleischmann & Co. yeast, 42 High.

Fleming Andrew, b. 1172 Main.
" Christina, wid. Charles, h.u. 56 Seymour.
" Edward, telegraph operator, b. 14 Kilbourn.
" Grace, bkkpr. at 423 Main, b. 56 Seymour.
" Mary, wid. Thomas, h.2u. 275 Asylum.
" Mary J. seamstress, b. 16 Howard.
" Michael, laborer, h. 16 Howard.
" Michael, laborer, h. 111 Maple.
" Patrick, mason, b. 1223 Main.
" Thomas, teamster, h. 228 Maple.
" Thomas G. grocery, 423 Mn. h. 56 Seymour.
Flentye Fred H. barber, 34 Temple, h. 17 Belden.
Fletcher Clarence V.clerk at Pope Tube Co. b.
    277 Windsor av.
" Elizabeth Mrs. h.u. 60 Trumbull.
" Emerson C. bkkpr. 2 S.Ann, b. 37 Congress.
" Harry A.forem. 581 Capitol,h.u.52 Kenyon.
" John P. waiter at 26 State, b. 246 Bellevue.
" Joseph G. toolmaker at Colts, h. 37 Congress.
FLETCHER N. P. & Co. book publishers, ink ex-
    tract mfrs. 31 Niles. (Nathan F. Peck.)
" Oscar S. (F. & Rosenthal,) b. 647 Main.
" William V. brassfinisher, b. 37 Congress.
" & Rosenthal, barbers, 703 Main.
Fleury Frank, b. 48 Temple.
Flibbart George, mach. 1 Flower, b. 52 Avon.
" Melvina, wid. Medie, h.u. 52 Avon.
Flint Addie Mrs. l. 1113 Main.
" Benj. F. domestic bakery, 150, h. 150 Capen.
" Byron W. b. 2 Holcomb.
" Daniel A. repairer, Capewell Horse Nail Co.
    40 Governor, h. 9 Front.
" Daniel W. at 53 Vernon, b.2u.31 Hungerford.
" Edward L. peddler, l.u. 1155 Main.
" Frederick, at 53 Vernon, h.u. 31 Hungerford.
" Frederick, painter, b. 1086 Main.
" George N. h. 31 Chapel.
" Geo. W. (Geo. W. F. & Co.) h. 310 Collins.
FLINT GEO. W. & Co. furniture, etc. 61 Asylum.*
    *See page 147.*
" Harold F. C. real estate, etc. 252 Asylum,
    rm. 15-16, b. 10 Westland.
" Lottie M. housekpr. h.2u. 31 Hungerford.
" Rupture Cure Co. 252 Asylum.
" William E. mech. 26 High, b. 31 Chapel.
" Wm. E. salesman at 185 Asylum, h. 49 Green.
" William S. coachm. 30 Cush. h. 98 Walnut.
" ☞see also Flynt.
Flood William, engineer, P.&R. h. 40 Liberty.
" ☞see also Flad.
Florence Arthur W.clerk,852 Mn.b.2u. 27 Russell.
" Delia, dressm. 24 Morgan, h. New Britain t.

Florence House, M. J. Cunningham, 114 State.
" William, policeman, h.u. 27 Russell.
Floss Reuben, teamster, 2 American, h. 89 Front.
Flower Edward D. bootcutter, 59½ Trumbull, h. 48 Windsor av.
" Ellen M. h. 432 Windsor av.
" Spencer L. h. 10 Fern.
Flynn Agnes M. clerk, 921 Main, b. 29 Lafayette.
" Alfred A. clerk at 745 Main, b. 70 Brook.
" Alfred W. papercutter at 141 Pearl, b. 10 Franklin.
" Ann Mrs. h. 1262 Broad.
" Ann, wid. Francis, h. 29 Lafayette.
" Annie E. at 86 Woodbine, b. 1262 Broad.
" Catherine, wid. Patrick, b. W. H. Home for the Aged, Albany.
" Charles P. carpenter, h. 413 Garden.
" Daniel, at 1 South Ann, b. 70 Brook.
" Daniel, clerk, 653 Main, b. 96 Hudson.
" Daniel, insp. Popes, b. Warehouse Point v.
" Dennis, bricklayer, b. 261 Lawrence.
" Dennis, helper at 581 Capitol, b. 2 Chestnut.
" Edward J. bkkpr. at 942 Main, b. 18 Center.
" Elizabeth L. clerk, 835 Main, b. 62 Lincoln.
" Francis T. mason, b. 1262 Broad.
" George W. clerk, 9 Central, b. 59 Allen pl.
" James, molder, 54 Arch, b. 261 Lawrence.
" James D. policeman, h u. 32 Albany.
" Jas. E. molder, Pratt & Cady, b.u. 1421 Broad
" James F. mason, h.2u. 24 So. Prospect.
" James K. engir. at 427 Main, h. Lif'key.
" James L. cigarmaker at 867, b. 999 Main.
" Jane C. teacher Wilson st. sch. b. 148 Wash.
" Jeremiah, helper, 266 Pearl, h. 299 Market.
" Jerry, ostler, b. 74 Potter.
" John, fireman stmr. Hartford, 285 State.
" John, helper, h.2u. 22 Kennedy.
" John, laborer, b. 459 Broad.
" John, laborer at 70 Com. h.u. 163 Barbour.
" John, laborer at 179 State, h. 94 Windsor.
" John, mason, l. 3 Grand.
" John, mason, b. 261 Lawrence.
" John, teamster, b.u. 94 Windsor.
**FLYNN JOHN,** meat, fish, vegetables, 493 Main, h. 59 Allen pl.   *See page* 587.
" John F. engineer at N.Y.R. b. 18 Center.
" John L. bartender at 583 Main, b. 18 Buckingham.
" John M. contr. and builder, 858, h. 858 Broad.
" John P. policeman, h.2u. 10 Charter Oak.
" Joseph C. clerk, 690 Park, b. 75 Laurel.
" Joseph D. tutor, b. 96 Hudson.
" Julia, milliner, 921 Main, b.u. 85 Elliott.
" Katherine, dressmaker, b. 29 Lafayette.
" Lawrence, switchm. at N.Y.R. h. 85 Loomis.
" Margaret, dressmaker, h.u. 891 Allyn.
" Margaret F. musicteach. b. 119 Hungerford.
" Martin, bricklayer & builder, 721 Main, rm. 24, h. 62 Lincoln.
" Martin J. mason, b. 1262 Broad.
" Mary, burnisher, b. 1329 Broad.
" Mary Ann, b.u. 459 Broad.
" Mary E. musicteacher, 119, b. 119 Hung.
" Mary G. dressm. 148, b. 148 Washington.
" Mary Mrs. b. W.H. Home for aged, Albany.

Flynn Matilda, h. 279 Park.
" Michael, blacksm. at 29 Wells, h. 74 Potter.
" Michael, driller at stone pits, h. 3 Flatbush.
" Michael, gardener, h. 38 John.
" Michael, helper at 1204 Main, b. 12 Loomis.
" Michael 2d, b. 2 Holcomb.
" Michael A. blacksmith, 92 Alb. h. 70 Brook.
" Michael H.draughtsm. 49 Pearl, h. 119 Hung.
" Michael J. blacksm. 92 Alb. h. 24 Franklin.
" Michael J. brazier, b. 1262 Broad.
" Mich. W. plumber at 280 Asy. b. 10 Loomis.
" Nellie, wid. James F. h.2u. 17 Goodwin.
" Patrick, canvasser, b. 1316 Broad.
" Patrick, laborer, b. Pleasant c. Windsor.
" Patrick J. conductor St.Ry. h. 41 Putnam.
" Patrick J. gardener, h.2u. 8 Queen.
" Patrick J. laborer, b.u. 76 Potter.
" Peter, cutter at 97 Asy. h.2u. 110 Trumbull.
" Roger, laborer, b.u. 283 Main.
" Rosella F. milliner, 921 Main, b.29Lafayette.
" Thomas, laborer, h. 34 Front.
" Thomas, mason, h.u. 98 New Britain.
" Thomas, mason, b. 261 Lawrence.
" Thos. mason and builder, 148, h. 148 Wash.
" Thomas E. repairer, Popes, b. 45 Chestnut.
" Thos. H. bkkpr. at 493 Main, b. 59 Allen pl.
" Thomas J. at 556 Main, b. 88 Pleasant.
" Valentine J. mason, b. 62 Lincoln.
" William, cashard. at Popes, h. 25 Glendale.
" William, watchm. 624 Main, h. 299 Market.
" William F. clerk, 206 State, b. 74 Potter.
" William J. elevatorer at Phœnix National Bank, 805 Main, b. 88 John.
" ☞*see also Flinn.*
Fogarty John P. salesm. Popes, h. Springfield, Ill.
" Joseph, helper at 438 Asy. b. 119 Maple.
" William H. mason, h.u. 119 Maple.
Fogelburg Chas. J. silversm. 62Mar. b.88 Church.
Fogg Chas. S. mach. at 581 Cap. b.u. 46 Seymour.
" Elmer H. at Ætna Life Insurance Co. 650 Main, h. 347 Windsor av.
" Joseph H. b. 172 Collins.
Foisey Anthony, carpenter, h. 47 New Britain.
" George, engineer at 24 Mechanic, h. 5 Park.
" Joseph A. engineer at 335 Shel. h. 245 Main.
" ☞*see also Farsey.*
Folco Thomas, barber at 75, b. 75 Morgan.
Foley Abina, wid.Jeremiah, washer, h.u.62 Avon.
" Allan J. carpenter, h.u. 19 Church.
" Anna, clerk, b. 195 Russ.

# FORBES DECORATING CO.,

### 3 ASYLUM STREET, Cor. Main.

## FLAGS

### AND DECORATIONS

*For Grand Festivals, Fairs, Public*
*... Halls and Buildings, ...*
*Celebrations, etc.*

Foley Bart, engineer, h. 29 Chestnut.
" Bridget, wid. Andrew, h.3u. 25 Spruce.
" Cornelius J. laborer, b.u. 3 Cranes.
" Daniel, saloon, 6 Franklin, h. 171 Maple.
" Daniel W. apprentice at Popes, b. 195 Russ.
" Daniel W. bluer at Colts, h. E.H.t.
" Dennis, h.u. 1048 Broad.
" Dennis, laborer, P.&R. b. 103 Mather.
" Dennis, mason, h.r.u. 25 Morgan.
" Dennis G. boilermak. N.Y.R. h. 1048 Broad.
" Edward, teamster, at 335 Shel. b. 97 Main.
" Edward F. waiter at 651 Main, b.u. 15 Good.
" Elizabeth, dressmaker, b.u. 15 Goodman.
" Ellen, wid. Michael, h. 39 So.Prospect.
" Frank I. agt. N.Y. News Co. h. 91 Chestnut.
" Hannah, seamstress, b. 68 Church.
" Hannah, wid. Dennis, b. 4 Franklin.
" Helen C. teacher at Second North school,
    249 High, b. 11 Lafayette.
" Herbert, janitor at 11 Pratt, h. 52 Brook.
" Hugh H. b.u. 171 Babcock.
" James, at Plimptons, b.u. 62 Avon.
" James F. machinist, b. 15 Goodman.
" John, bluer at Colts, h. E.H.t.
" John, engir. 147 Shel. h.3u.34 So. Prospect.
" John, salesman at Neal, Goff & Inglis Co.
    980 Main, h. E.H.t.
" John, steamfitter, b. 29 Spruce.
" John B. brakeman, h.u. 30 Canton.
" John B. b.u. 22 Affleck.
" John J. inspector at Popes, b.u. 195 Russ.
" John J. market, 1065 Main, h. 110 Ann.
" John L. draughtsm. at 252 Asy. b. 28 Bkm.
" John T. inspector, 690 Park, b. 2 Winthrop.
" Joseph, clerk at 193 Asylum, b. 16 Center.
" Julia A. b.u. 195 Russ.
" Kitty, dressmaker, 22, b.u. 22 Affleck.
" Michael, deckh. str. Middletown, 285 State.
" Michael, laborer, h.3u.r. 28 South Prospect.
" Mich. nightwatchm. Popes, h.2u. 1074Broad.
" Michael A. mason, h.u. 7 Hamilton.
" Michael J. butcher, 1065 Mn. h. 20 Morgan.
" Michael J. laborer, h.2u. 34 South Prospect.
" Michael J. mach. at 690 Park, b. 22 Affleck.
" Morris, laborer, h.u. 15 Goodman.
" Morris C. pressm. 141 Pearl, b.u. 15 Good.
" Patrick, b. 2 Holcomb.
" Patrick, foreman at Popes, h. 230½ Zion.
" Patrick, laborer, h. 81 Avon.
" Patrick, laborer, h. 16 Center.

Foley Patrick, mach. at 581 Cap. h. 1329 Broad.
" Patrick J. helper at Popes, h. 195 Russ.
" Patrick J. machinist, h. 14 Huntley.
" Richard, laborer, N.Y.R. h.3u. 33½ Spruce.
" Richard C. joiner, h. 44 Lawrence.
" Terence, plumber, b. 39 South Prospect.
" Thomas, butcher, 369 Cap. h. 1333 Broad.
" Thomas, gardener at Francis Goodwin,
    h.2u. 55 Spruce.
" Thos. F. bookkeeper at 5 Mechanic, b. E.H.t.
" Thomas F. polisher at 476 Cap. b.u. 195 Russ.
" Thomas J. expressman, b. 195 Capen.
" Thomas W., U.S. army, b. 11 Lafayette.
" Timothy E. prop. Quincy House, 1233 Mn.
" William, bartender, 1047 Mn. b.u. 63 Flower.
" William A. saloon, 98 State. h. E.H.t.
" Wm. B. hack driver, h.u. 22 Center.
" Wm. Hebert, janitor, 31 Pratt, l 52 Brook.
" Wm. J. mach. at 83 Woodbine, b. 15 Good.
" William J. machinist at 20 Vredendale, b.
    100 Village.
" Wm. M. laborer, N.Y.R. h.3u. 55 Spruce.
" William R. carpenter at Cheney Bros. silk
    mill, 34 Morgan, h. 11 Lafayette.
Follett George, druggist at 143 Tru. h.u. 26 Beach.
Follis Margaret, wid. Cornelius, h.2u. 10 Ellery.
Folts Geo. H. manager R. G. Dun & Co. mer-
    cantile agency, 223 Asy.h. 243 Farmington.
" George W. b. 243 Farmington.
Foo Wong, laundry, 17 Church.
Foorde William, meatcutter, 131 Main, h. 1 John.

**FOOT GUARD HALL,** Edson Ses-
    sions, manager, 159 High.   *See page 496.*

Foote Catharine F. wid. Richard, h.u. 15 Portland.
" Charles, wirew. at 618 Cap. b. Madison.
" John M. jr. deputy sheriff, 847 Main, rm. 10,
    h. W.H.t.
" Myron M. splicer, 690 Park, h. 131 Hamilton.
" Samuel, bootblack at 281 Mn. h. 47½ Morgan.
Foran Frank L. inspector, 690, h. 548 Park.
" James M. coachman, h. Quaker lane.
Forand Napoleon, at N.Y.R. h. 10 Warren.
Forastiere Antonio, shoemaker, 57 Woodbridge,
    h.2u. 219 Sheldon.
" Frank, b.2u. 219 Sheldon.
" Michael, barber, h.2u. 219 Sheldon.
" Richard, harnessm. 8 Sig. b. 219 Sheldon.
Forbes Alex, carpenter, b.2u. 277 Main.
" Cornelia B. Mrs. pres. S.W.C.T.U. h. 206
    Wethersfield.
" Decorating Co. flags, bunting, etc. 3 Asylum.
**FORBES EDWARD P.** manager Forbes Decorat-
    ing Co. sign painter and decorator, 3
    Asylum, b. 110 Pratt.    *See page 148.*
" Frank S. at Conn. Mutual Life Ins. Co.
    783 Main, h. East Hartford t.
" Fredric H. clerk at Connecticut General
    Life Insurance Co. 49 Pearl, b. 35 Niles.
" George G. asst. bookkeeper First National
    Bank, 50 State, b. 35 Niles.
" Henry S. clerk at Orient Ins. Co. 5 Haynes,
    b. 206 Wethersfield.
" Ira E. telegraph editor at Hartford Times,
    716 Main, h. 75 Windsor av.

Forbes Jennie P. teacher Wethersfield av. school, b. 35 Niles.
" Miner O. chief engineer str. Hartford, 285 State, h. Higganum v.
" Samuel B. pastor Wethersfield avenue Congregational ch. h. 206 Wethersfield.
FORBES WARREN L. agent New Home Sewing Machine, at Brown, Thomson & Co. 942 Main, h. 35 Niles. *See advt.*
Forby Mary R. wid. Wm. F. h. 85 Buckingham.
Ford Edmund H. printer, b. 33 Townley.
" Edwin R. painter, h. 2 Oak.
" Elizabeth Mrs. h. 46 Cedar.
" Evelyn B. foreman Perkins Electric S. Mfg. Co. 83 Woodbine, h. 387 Capitol.
" Fred. L. boss carpenter at Pratt & Whitney Co. 1 Flower, h. Windsor t.
" Frederick L. asst. city surveyors office, 800 Main, h.u. 53 Oak.
" Hattie A. stenogr. 210 Pearl, b.155 Franklin.
" Henry, coachman at 1008 Asylum, h. 33 Townley.
" Ira W. auctioneer, b. 117 Trumbull.
" J. Harry, at Ætna Life Ins. Co. 650 Main, b. 33 Townley.
" J. M. painter, r. 1231 Main.
" James J. tinner, b. 32 Church.
" J. P. roofer, 373 Asy. rm. 6, l. 1045 Main.
" Jarvis O. machinist, h.u. 306 Main.
" John H. h. 155 Franklin.
" John J. lab. at 556 Capitol, h.2u. 36 Hicks.
" John P. plumber, 297 Park, b. 27 Putnam.
" Joseph H. driver, h.r. 227 Pearl.
" Joseph M. painter, h. 57 Pratt.
" Mary E. b. 78 Clark.
" Mary L. clerk at Brown, Thomson & Co. 942 Main, b. 155 Franklin.
" Michael, laborer, h.u. 21 Wolcott.
" Michael, ostler at 12, b. 52 Wells.
" Michael F. polisher, 476 Cap. h.u. 21 Wolcott.
" Nelson G. clerk at Phœnix Mutual Life Insurance Co. 49 Pearl, b. 59 Capitol.
" Patrick, machinist at 142 Russ, b. 23 West.
" Philo H. farmer, b. 302 Albany.
" Romulus W. h. 59 Capitol.
" Sarah A. folder at Popes. b. 78 Clark.
" Thomas, coachman at 127 Wash. h. 27 Putnam.
" Thos. J. Jr. carpenter, b. 27 Putnam.
" William, bootmaker, 78, h. 78 Clark.
" Wm. K. mach. at 40 Gov. h.u. 306 Main.
Foreman Abraham, laborer, h. 40 North.
Forest Isaiah, carpenter, h.u. 962 Broad.
" John, laborer, b.u. 962 Broad.
Forlen John, tailor, h.u. 35 Asylum.
Forni Albert, cook at 931 Main, h. 37 Mulberry.
Forred Benjamin, steamfitter, 70 Com. h. 36 John.
Forrest Charles R. h. 1045 Asylum.
" George C. broker and mfr. agent, 847 Main, rm. 8, b. 1045 Asylum.
" Mary Mrs. h.u. 25 Wyllys.
" Patrick, conductor at St.Ry. h. E.H. t.
" Wm. J. mach. at 30 Cush. b. 2u. 29 Hawthorn.
" ☞ *see also Forest.*
Forrestiere Michael, barber at 103 Main, h. 219 Sheldon.

Forristall Agnes, at 1 So. Ann, b. 90 New Britain.
" Alice, at 1 So. Ann, b. 90 New Britain.
" Mary, at 1 So. Ann, b. 90 New Britain.
" William, blacksmith at N.Y.R., h. 90 N.B.
" William N. clerk Adams Ex. h.u. 10 Sisson.
Fors Fred. G. polisher, Popes. h.u.r. 14 Maysct.
Forsberg Joseph, coachman at 7 Alden.
Forsell Alfred, mechanic, Colts, b. 29 Hamilton.
" Gustav S. mechanic, Popes, h. 29 Hamilton.
Foisey George N. engineer at 24 Mechanic, h. 3u. 5 Park.
Forsey U. harnessm. 8 Sigourney, b. 13 Putnam.
Forshaw Harry, carpenter, h. 140 New Park.
" Harry Mrs. dressmr. 140, h. 140 New Park.
Forss Charles F. roller, Pope Tube Co. h. 10 Rose.
Forst Charles, baker, 484, h.u. 488 Main.
Forster Jacob, cornicem. at 93 Fkn. h. 270 Maple
" John R. blacksmith at Popes, h. 181½ Law.
" Ludwig, market gardener, 375, h. 375 N.B.
Forsyth Clara J. Mrs. dressm. 14, h. 14 Church·
" John S. machinist, h. 14 Church, rm. 9.
Forsythe James, mach. at 142 Russ, h. 9 Brady.
" Jane, dressmr. 721 Main, rm. 58, h. 71 Cong.
Fortett Joseph, at 690 Park, b. 24 Heath.
Fortin Frank, brickmaker, b. Windsor av.
" Joseph A. motorman St.Ry. h. 36 Church.
Forto Sam, bootblack, h.3u. 47½ Morgan.
Fortune Trifley J. ostler, b. 24 Chestnut.
Fosler Arthur, at 1 Flower, b.2u. 305 Lawrence.
" George C. cigarmaker, h.2u. 305 Lawrence.
" John, molder at 556 Cap. h. 305 Lawrence.
" Matilda, b. 305 Lawrence.
Foss Frank H. student at Trinity college, 5 Jarvis hall, Summit.
Fossard Henrietta A. wid. Frank R. b. 7 Belden.
Fossum Nelson H. contractor at Johns-Pratt Co. b. Bloomfield t.
Foster A. L. & Co. clothiers, 45 Asylum.*
" Armand D. mach. at 388 Cap. h. 363 Main.
" Arthur, at 1 Flower, b.2u. 363 Main.
" Arthur L. (*A. L. F. & Co.*) h. 945 Asylum.
" Bessie C. attendant at 30 Washington.
" Caroline Miss, b. 29 Kenyon.
" Caroline B Mrs. h. 36 West.
" Charles A. engineer, h. 242 Pearl.
" Charles F. laborer, 335 Shel. h. Wethersfield.
" & Co. wholesale grocers, 72 Front.
    Fred'k R. Foster,    Geo B. Foster.
" E. E. granite cut'r 1 Ford, b. 19 Foot Guard.
" E. M. Mrs. clerk at 928 Main, b. E.H.t.
" Effie W. clerk National Life Association, 53 Trumbull, b. 111 Whitmore.
" Elliott C. paper agent, h. 17 Girard.
" Frank G. at Ætna Insurance Co. 666 Main, h. 36 West.

# FOSTER & FURREY,

57 Church St.　　　1187 Main St.

## Funeral Directors

### AND

## Embalmers,

Lady Assistant.
Attendance Day or
Night.　::: 　　1166 MAIN STREET.

Old Number, 568.

Telephone 142-5.　Connected with house.

Foster Frederick R. (Foster & Co.) h. 77 Weth.
FOSTER & FURREY, undertakers, 1166 Main.
　　Ralph Foster.　　　Erwin L. Furrey.
　　　　　　　　　See page 150.
" George B. (Foster & Co.) h. Prospect av.
" George H. engir. at 51 Ann, h. 32 Asylum.
" Harry J. at Travelers Ins. Co. 56 Prospect,
　　b. 90 Hudson.
" Harry O. brakem. N.E.R. b.u. 46 Hopkins.
" Hattie M. stenographer at National Fire Ins.
　　Co. 95 Pearl, b. 337 Windsor av.
" Herbert B. apprentice 1 Laurel, b. 51 Oak.
" J.Frank, mach at 388 Capitol,h.u. 873 Broad.
" Jacob, cornicemr. 93 Franklin, h. 270 Maple.
" Jas. M. office 284 Asylum, rm. 4, h. 172 Sig.
" James P. Mrs. (Sarah D.) h. 68 Governor.
" Mabel E. stenographer at Popes, b. E.H.t.
" Mary E. wid. Joseph H. b. 249 Capen.
" Mary G. Mrs. teacher South school, 36 Wads-
　　worth, b. 90 Hudson.
" & Morrill, merchant tailors, 719 Main.
　　Wilbur B. Foster.　　　Charles W. Morrill.
FOSTER RALPH, (F. & Furrey,) h. 337 Wind-
　　sor av.
" Ralph H.drug clerk at 142 Asylum, b.u. 238
　　Windsor av.
" Reuben R. 308 Asy. h. 17 Haynes, rm. 114.
" Walter A. clerk at 803 Main,h. Springfield t.
" Walter C. salesman, b. 8 Walnut.
" Wilbur B. (F. & Morrill,) h. Rockville t.
" William E. h. 17 Haynes, rm. 114.

## FOSTER WM. H. (Frayer & F.) coal,446

Asylum, h. 275 Collins.　See page 490.
Fothergill Ed W. draughtsman at 756 Main, rm.
　　28, h. 9 Hamilton.
Foundation Patrick J. mach. 1 Flow. b. 45 Sig.
Fountanelli John, city sweeper, b. 12 North.
Fountin Alexander A. glazier, 86 Mor. h. E.H.t.
Fowler Alice N. teacher at South school, 36
　　Wadsworth, b. 78 Allen pl.
" Arthur C. commercial trav. b u. 48 Wooster.
" Benjamin E. h. 76 Allen pl.
" Braziller H. ins. agt. b.u. 3 Whitman.
" Charles A. salesman at Lincoln, Seyms &
　　Co. 34 Market, h. Rocky Hill t.
" Clarkson N. charity commissioner, cashier at
　　197 Asylum, h. 24 Allen pl.
" Edgar C.insurance agent, b.u. 48 Wooster.
" Edward C. clerk at 856 Main, h. Bloomfield t.
" Emerson D. plumber, b.u. 545 Main.
" Emma G. stenographer at F. H. Richards,
　　803 Main, b. 24 Allen pl.

Fowler Evelyn J. G. salesman at 216 State, b.
　　2 Charlotte.
" Frances Mrs. h. 53 Wooster.
" Frank D. toolm. at 388 Cap. h. 181 Maple.
FOWLER GEO. B. attorney at law, 926
　　Main, b. Thompsonville v.
" Geo. T. engir. at 83 Woodbine, h. 2 Walnut.
" Georgiana A. wid. M. Newton, b. 113
　　Windsor av.
" Harry P. modelmakr. Popes, h. 830 Broad.
" Harry R. mach. at Colts, b.2u. 3 Whitman.
" & Huntting, wholesale fruits, etc. 47 Ann.
　　　　　Charles H. Huntting.
" Jas. B. electrician at 284 Asy. l. 173 High.
" Jeremiah, h. 181 Maple.
" Jeremiah C. h.u. 48 Wooster.
" Lucy M. wid. Francis, h.u. 545 Main, rm. 13
" M. Louise, bkkpr. 369 Cap. b. 101 Babcock
" Margaret T. wid. Joseph S. h.u. 96 Ch.O.
" Mary E. b. 146 Wethersfield.
" & Miller Co. printers, 857 Main.
" Richard W. insur. special, b.u. 48 Wooster.
" Walter B. delivery clerk at 745 Main, b.2u.
　　3 Whitman.
" William, clerk at 852 Main, b. 53 Wooster.
Fox A. I. Mrs. b. 84 Edwards.
" Albert A. inspector water works, 800 Main,
　　City hall, h. 119 Trumbull.
" Albert E. burnisher at Wm. Rogers Mfg. Co.
　　66 Market, b.2u. 23 Seyms.
" Albert H. burnisher at the William Rogers
　　Mfg. Co. 66 Market, b.2u. 23 Seyms.
" Alice S. employment office, 119, b. 119 Tru.
" Ann, wid. Thomas, h. 35 South Prospect.
" Anna M. wid. Clinton, b. 36 Jefferson.
" Annie, wid. Thomas, h.u. 241 Pearl.
" Annie M. inspector at 70 Huy. b. 55 Hudson.
" Bridget wid. James, at 37 Wells, b. 13 S.Pro.
" Carrie M. assistant matron, 36 Jefferson.
" Clarinda, wid. Dudley, h.u. 1072 Main.
" Daniel J. molder, 556 Cap. h.u. 35 Babcock.
" David, compositor at Hartford Times, 716
　　Main, b. 81 Chestnut.
" David C. driver, h.u. 53 Congress.
" Edgar H. driver at Adams Express Co. h.u.
　　32 Temple.
" Edgar H. Jr. crater at 581 Cap. b. 81 Asy.
" Edward W. sexton cathedral, h.r. 140 Far.
" Edwin, student, b. 18 Governor.
" Edwin W. filer at Colts, b. 36 Charter Oak.
" Elizabeth J. Mrs. matron at 36 Jefferson.
" Eugene D. driver at L. L. Ensworth & Son,
　　iron merchants, 104, h.u. 33½ Front.
" Ezra, plater at 556 Capitol, h. 82 Madison.
" G. & Co. dry goods, 956 Main.
　　Moses Fox,　Jacob L. Fox,　Morris F. Marks.
" George, mach. at P.&R. b.u. 140 Mather.
" Geo. H. burnisher, b.2u. 23 Seyms.
" Geo. H. shoemaker at 3 Spruce, h. 84 Spring.
" Geo. J. builder, 64, h. 64 New Britain.
" Harrison W. burnisher at William Rogers
　　Mfg. Co. 66 Market, h. 709 Main.
" Harvey, engineer, h.u. 8 Atlantic.
" Henry A. foreman, Popes, h.2u. 250 Putnam.
" Henry J. awningm. at 71 Asy. b. 70 Martin.

Fox Horace P. (*Simons & F.*) h.u. 868 Main.
" Horace P. Mrs. dressm. 868, h.u. 868 Main.
" Horace W. pres. C. C. L. Co. h. Warrenton.
" Isaac, l. 230 High.
" J. Rose, stenog. at 721 Main, h. E.H.t.
" Jacob, (*Schmidt & F.*) h. 54 Oak.
" Jacob L. (*G. Fox & Co*)956 Mn. b.23 Morgan.
" James J. inspector at Johns-Pratt Co. b.u. 35 Babcock.
" James P. teamster, h. 81 Chestnut.
" John, enameler, b. 81 Chestnut.
" John, Rev. b. 35 South Prospect.
" John, sexton at St. Joseph's cathedral, h. 61 Hawthorn.
" John A. teamster, b. 81 Chestnut.
" John S. bartender, b. 18 Governor.
" Joseph, engineer, b.u. 84 Arch.
" Joseph, tailor, 373 Park, h.3u. 20 North.
" Josephine A. clerk, b. 84 Spring.
" Louise, b. 36 Jefferson.
" M. C. clerk at 700 Main, h. 35 So. Prospect.
" Martin, carpenter, h. 1183 Main.
" Martin, saloon, 214 Sheldon, h. 18 Governor.
" Mary, wid. Keron, h. 29 Hawthorn.
" Mary A. clerk at 715 Main, b. 46 Windsor.
" Michael J. saloon, 57 Market, h. 142 Weth.
" Moses, (*G. Fox & Co.*) h. 534 Prospect av.
" Patrick F. bartender at 57, h.u. 59 Market.
" Pat'k J. engir. 556 Main, h.u. 29 Portland.
" Phœbe J. wid. Walter, b. 564 Windsor av.
" Robert H. architect and bookkeeper at 22 John, h. 58 Annawan.
" Roderick H. student at Trinity college, 36 Jarvis hall, Summit.
" Sam'l P. crater at 581 Cap. h. 68 Chestnut.
" Thomas E. clerk at Popes, b. 58 Annawan.
" Thomas J. laborer at Popes, b. 35 Babcock.
Fox THOMAS R. (*Hills & Fox*) mason builders, h. 58 Annawan. *See page 515.*
" William, at 476 Capitol, b. 61 Hawthorn.
Foye Mary, h.r.u. 45 Spruce.
" Thomas E. foreman 581 Cap. b. 47 Laurel.
Frad N. grocery, 194, h. 190 Front.
Framberg August, enameler at Popes, h. 8 Hung.
Francis Albert A. bookkeeper at Pope Mfg. Co. 436 Capitol, b. 5 New Britain.
" Albert N. clerk at 1 So. Ann, h. 208 Capen.
" Albert N. Jr. designer, b. 208 Capen.
" Anna B. wid. Frederick A. b. 3 Farmington.
" Arthur D. piano tuner, 5, b.u. 5 N.Britain.
" Austin N. driver at 47 Ann, b. 297 Asylum.
" Chas. D. inspector Hfd. Steam Boiler Inspection & Ins. Co. 650 Main, h.u. 5 N.Britain.
" Charles R. clerk, 690 Park, b.150 Madison av.

**FRANCIS & CO.** hardware, grindstones, twine, etc. 859 Main. *See page 546.*
William Francis.  Edward M. Francis.
William F. Girard Jr.
" Daniel W. tinner at 843 Park, h. 8 Woodbine.
" Edmund H. clerk at 2 So. Ann, b. 208 Capen.
" Edward M. (*Francis & Co.*) 859 Main, b. 154 Washington.
" Edward M. h. 95 Wethersfield.
" Edward S. supt. electrical dept. Thos. Oakes & Son, 11 Haynes, h. 63 Lincoln.

Francis Evelina H. Mrs. h.u. 147 Capen.
" Everett M. paymaster Hartford Street Railway Co. 115 State, b. 95 Wethersfield.
**FRANCIS FREDERICK W.** prop. U. S. Photo-Chemical Mfg. Co. photoengraving, developing, printing, etc. 29 Pearl, b. 101 Elm. *See page 419.*
" Jas. H. machinist, b. 106 Hungerford.
" James P. headwaiter at 53 Ann, h.r. 24 S. Pro.
" Mary E. b.u. 147 Capen.
" Mary H. b. 54 Wadsworth.
" Robert, contr. at 1 Flower, h. Newington t.
" Sarah Miss, b. 50 Williams.
" Thomas E. enameler at Pope Manfg. Co. h.u. 351 Albany.
" William, (*Francis & Co.*) h. 101 Elm.
" William C. mason, h. 147 Capen.
" William M. inspector Hartford Steam Boiler Insp. & Ins. Co. 650 Main, h. Atlanta, Ga.
Francolina Domenico, teacher of Italian at 17, h.u. 17 Morgan.
" Franklin, student, b.u. 17 Morgan.
" Nito A. laborer, b. 67 Pleasant.
" Prospero, student, b.u. 17 Morgan.
Franey Edward F. enameler at Popes, b.53 Potter.
" Thomas, b. 2 Holcomb.
" Thomas C. gatetender, N.Y.R. h.u. 5 Queen.
Franjesc Louis, laborer, h. 16 Ellery.
Frank Abraham, painter, b.r. 26 North.
" F. August, tailor, h. 36 Trumbull.
" Fritz, mach. at N.Y.R. h.2u. 46 Grand.
" Joseph, patterncutter, h.2u. 42 Beach.
" Julius, helper at 1 So. Ann, b. 43 Avon.
" Julius E. buffer at 581 Cap. h.u. 36 Grand.
" Michael, laborer, b.u. 86 Morgan.
" Nezzo, b. 13 Charles.
" Nunzio, laborer, b.u. 86 Morgan.
" Paule, laborer, b. 11 Charles.
" Wm. H. printer at 141 Pearl, b.34 Trumbull.
Franke Paul, ostler r. 50 State, b. 165 Front.
Frankel Morritz H. at 20 Sargeant, h. 121 Mather.
Frankenfield John, lineman, l. 534 Main.
Franklin Albert, laborer, l.u. 10½ Gold.
" Clarence N. driver at 48 Ann, b. W.H.t.
" George A. motorman, St.Ry. h.u. 952 Broad.
" House, Mrs. Emily Allen, prop. 518 Main.
" Lysander W. toolmaker at 83 Woodbine, b. 57 Pratt.
" Market, 516 Main.
Ed. H. Harris.      Howard G. Newton.
" William, cook, h. 38 Village.
" William B. Gen., pres. board of mgrs. of Nat. Soldiers Home, 783 Main, h. 144 Wash.
Franks Adella, milliner, 36 Pratt, b. 42 Beach.
Frankum Wm. H. clerk at 197 Asy. b. 244 High.
Fransmic Nicholas, h. 82 Potter.
Franz Annie, b. 58 Church.
" Reinherz, packer at 867 Mn. h.u. 15 Chestnut
Franzen Andrew, machinist, h.u. 156 Russ.
" Frank, mech. at 54 Arch, h. 10 Winship.
" Frederick W. saloon, 359, h. 357 Main.
" Peter, dropforger at James L. Howard & Co. 438 Asylum, h.u. 1143 Broad.
" S. C. Rev. pastor Swedish E. Lutheran Emanuel church, h. 187 Russ.

Fraser Alexander, elevatorer, 738, b. 138 Main.
Frasier ☞ see Frazier.
Fraternal News office, 2 State, rm. 9.
Frawley John, laborer, b.2u. 81 Sheldon.
Fray Louis C. piano tuner, 301 Main, h. 204 Sargeant.
Frayer Clarence B. clerk, 1 Laurel, b. 249 Capen.
**FRAYER & FOSTER,** coal, 446 Asylum.        *See page 490.*
" Mary E. wid. Seymour A. h. 249 Capen.
" William W. clerk at 446 Asy. b. 249 Capen.
Frary John, bricklayer, h.2u. 117 Albany.
Frazier Albert, cigarmaker at 1015 Main, h. 284 Asylum, rm. 82.
" Andrew, laborer at 285 State.
" Charles U. publisher, 7 Central, h. 24 Cong.
" Elizabeth, wid. Edward H. h. 15 Meadow.
" George W. harnessmaker, h. 11 Madison av.
" Homer, blacksmith, P.&R. h.u. 116 Mather.
" Homer E. clerk at 139 Asy. b. 116 Mather.
" Robt. hallwatch str. Middletown, 285 State.
" S. M. Mrs. h. 809 Asylum.
" William S. harnessmaker at Smith, Bourn & Co. h.u. 49 Spruce.
" William B. engineer at 651, h. 488 Main.
" William G. assem. at Popes, h. 51 Laurel.
" ☞ see also Frasier.
Freberg Edward, mach. at Popes, h. N.Britain.
" Louis, carpenter at 53, b.u. 53 Webster.
Freden Carl, mech. at Popes, b. 98 Babcock.
Frederick H. O. Mrs. b. 389 Main.
Frederickson Carl N. machinist at 30 Cushman, b.u. 296 Park.
" Nicholas, boxmaker at Popes, b. 296 Park.
Fredrick Joseph, driller at Colts, b. 35 Front.
" Louis, filer at 142 Russ, b. 60½ Wells.
Fredine August, machineh. at Colts, h. 157 Law.
Freeborne James L. manager Standard Oil Co. 370 Front, b. 427 Main, rm. 74.
Freeburg Emil. pressm. at 690 Park, h.u. 42 Smith.
Freed John H. toolmaker at Popes, h. 20 Crown.
" Wolf, peddler, h.r. 74 Temple.
" ☞ see also Fried.
Freeman Albert, driver at 373 Main, h.u. 26 Fkn.
" Alexander, h.u. 26 Franklin.
" Charles, toolmaker, h. 17 So. Hudson.
" Charlotte M. wid. Geo. A. h. 54 Sanford.
" Edmund B. commission, b.u. 24 Market.
" Edward, machinist at 1 Flow. b. 1136 Main.
" Everett W. porter at 835, h.r. 1214 Main.
" Fayette F. salesm. at 45 Asy. b.54 Winthrop.
" Geo. Fred. elevatorer, h. 54 Sanford.
" Harrison B. attorney, judge probate, 114 Pearl, h. 780 Prospect av. north of Cone.
" Harrison Barber Jr. attorney, 750 Main, rm. 16, b. 780 Prospect av. north of Cone.
" Henry, machinist, h. 227 Wethersfield.
" Jacob, peddler, h. 159 Front.
" Josephine, h. 133 Market.
" Julia, wid. Thomas, h.u.r. 41 Mather.
" Mary E. h.u. 11½ Clinton.
" Mary E. rooms to rent, h. 1136 Main.
" Philip, peddler, h. 32 Benton.
" Simon G. treasurer Freeman-Tibbals Co. 34 Asylum, b. 80 Edwards.

Freeman Sol. I. president Freeman-Tibbals Co. 34 Asylum, h. 80 Edwards.
" Tibbals Co. clothiers, 34 Asylum,
Freer William D. city reporter at Hartford Courant, 66 State, h. W.H.t.
Freeze Munroe A. at 218 State, h. 9 Walnut.
Fregogliatte Philip, bottler, h.2u. 268 Front.
French Almo E. superintendent at 554, L 650 Main, room 39.
" Arthur W. at Ætna Life Ins. Co. 650 Main, b. 103 Ashley.
" Chas. C. compositor, 141 Pearl, h. 60 Judson.
" Chas. Sheldon, tcamster at 25 Front, h.u. 44 Woodbridge.
" Chauncey B. clk. at 325 Asy. b. 74 Hudson.
" Dwight S. mechanic, b. 74 Hudson.
" Elden L. draughtsman at 20 Sargeant, b. 3 Grand.
" Erwin R. machinist at 1 Laurel, h. E.H.t.
" Ethelbert, toolmkr. at Colts, h. 103 Ashley.
" Everett J. at Case, Lockwood & Brainard Co, b. 74 Hudson,
" Frank S. sup't at 24 Mechanic, h. 68 Hudson.
" George H. Jr. (*F.&Hurlock*) h.u. 26 Liberty.
" Greville W. grocer, Franklin, c. Annawan, h. 56 Annawan.
**FRENCH H. A.** mfrs. doors, sash and blinds, 554 Main, h. Wethersfield t.        *See page 512.*
" Henry E. clerk at 338 Main, h.u. 168 Putnam.
" Henry L. b. 63 Gillett.
" Henry L. tcamster, 1 Flow. h.u. 52 Babcock.
" & Hurlock, painters, 1152 Main.
George H. French.        Walter Hurlock.
" Mabel P. bu. 54 Sanford.
" Martha L. wid. Edward S. h. 74 Hudson.
" Mary Mrs. bkkpr. 928 Main, h. 3 Grand.
" John L. joiner, h.u. 54 Sanford.
" William, at Elmwood pottery, h. 81 Wilson.
" William, helper at 54 Arch, b. 81 Wilson.
" William A. machinist, h. 29 Morgan.
" William C. clerk at 690 Pk. b. 195 Sigourney.
" William H. mach. at 13 Central, h. E.H.t.
Freney James, bartender, 47, h.u. 47 Spruce.
Frese Albert, brewer, 315 Park, b.2u. 52 Law.
" Louis, brewer at 315 Pk. h.2u. 164 Babcock.
Fresher Sam. H. brakeman N.Y.R. h.r. 23 Spruce.
Freshmann Andrew, carwiper at N.E.R. b. 78 Walnut.
Frey Wm. J. asst. bookkeeper at C. S. Brewer & Co. 238 Asylum, h. 63 Church.
Friar Alonzo E. painter, N.Y.R. h. 277 High.
" John, h.u. 4 Hungerford.
" John C. b. 4 Hungerford.
" Winfield S. h. 4 Hungerford.
Friars Mary, wid. David A. b. 42 Windsor av.
Frick William W. h. 19 Pavilion.
Frida Ernest, barber at 362 Asy. b. 74 Edwards.
Fridine August, driller at Colts, h.u. 157 Law.
Fridman Himan, tailor, h. 77 Windsor.
Friebe William S. at Ætna Life Ins. Co. 650 Main, b. 23 King.
Fried Rose, clerk at 955 Main, h. 82 Pleasant.
" Simon, tailor at 94½ Tru. h.r. 65 Temple.
" ☞ see also Freed.

Friedman Davis, peddler, h.u. 55 Morgan.
" Edward, buffer at 110 Com. b. 229 Francis.
" Elias, tinware, 210½ Front, h. 21 Morgan.
" Jacob, peddler, h.u. 159 Front.
" Hariss, clerk at 192 Front, h. 56 Pleasant.
" Harry, tailor at 881 Main, b. 28 North.
" Henry, capmaker at 76 Asy. b. 213 Front.
" Herman, buffer at 110 Com. b. 229 Francis.
" Jacob L. repairer, b. 24 Morgan.
" & Kaplan, boots and shoes, 65 Morgan.
  Elias Friedman,           David Kaplan.
" Louis, peddler, h.2u. 56 Pleasant.
" Max, shoemaker at 139, h. 135 Trumbull.
" Morris, cloakmaker, h.u. 8 Marsh.
" Morris, farmhand, 30, b. 30 Bluehills.
Friedricks Frederick E. clerk at 98 Kilbourn,
  b. 126 Ann.
" H. O. Mrs. b. 389 Main.
Friend Elizabeth M. matron at 20 So. Hudson.
" ☞ see also Damico.
Friendly Visitors Club, Union for Home Work,
  239 Market.
Fries Adam A. fireman, h. 2 Bartholomew.
" Benjamin J. machinist at 476 Capitol, b.
  243 Lawrence.
Frieze Rudolph, screwm. at 476 Cap. b. 243 Law.
Frink Charles D. ( Goodale & F. ) h. 251 Asy.
" Edward P. tinner at 881 Main, b. 52 Mahl.
" Emilie A. Mrs. h. 228 High.
" George H. horsedealer, b. 140 Trumbull,
" Nausic, packer at 618 Capitol, b. 42 State.
Frisbie Belle Welles, wid. Chas. G. h. 10 Sumner.
" Caroline E. wid. Lemuel T. h. 800 Asylum.
" Edw. C. ( Talcott, F. & Co. ) h. 136 Collins.
" Edward J. tinner at 599 Main, b. 10½ Ford.
" Eva E. housekeeper, b. 221 Garden.
**FRISBIE L. T. CO.** hides, skins, tal-
  low, salt, 79 Talcott.    See page 585.
" Thomas S. com. agent, h. 221 Garden.
Frish Gertrude E. Mrs. b.u 132 Market.
Frith Reginald M. clerk at 1082 Main, b. Albany
  c. Bloomfield.
Fritsche Chas. J. foreman, Billings & Spencer
  Mfg. Co. 142 Russ, h. 301 Park.
Fritz August, laborer, b. 60 Front.
Fritze John L. toolmaker at Colts, h. 1076 Broad.
Fritzsom Chas. W. screwm. 476 Cap. b. 243 Law.
Frobel Albert D. bartdr. at 430 Asy. h 6 Queen.
Froelich Charles E. physician, 108, h. 103 Pratt.
Frohock A. H. capt. barge No. 10, 285 State,
  h. Lincolnville, Me.
Fromberg Thos. jeweler, 992, h. 992 Main.
Fromkueckt Gabriel, baker at 238, b. 238 N.P.
Frosch Bernhardt, toolm. 581 Cap. h. 35 Hudson.
Fross Fred, laborer, h. 14 Mays ct.
Frost Annie, wid. George E. b. 21 Wethersfield.
" Carl F. coppersm. at 141 Com. b. 80 Front.
" Chas. Z. chaser at 62 Mar. h. New Britain t.
" Henry D. grocer, 1195 Main, h. 90 Wooster.
" John A. dealer in tea and coffee, h.u. 42 Beach.
" Nellie, b. 570 Main.
" Otto E. h.2u. 37 Canton.
" Sam'l E. painter at 843 Mn. b.2u. Portland.
" William B. paperh. at 843 Main, h.2u. 2 Por.
Frostle ☞ see Trostle.

Frumansky Abe, drygoods, 142 Front, h. 293 Mar.
" Joseph, laborer, b.u. 293 Market.
" Louis, clerk at 142 Front, b.u. 293 Market.
" Wm. at 1 Laurel, b.u. 293 Market.
Fruvente Antonio, laborer, h. 168 Front.
Fry Louis, machinist at 54 Arch, h. Burnside v.
" Margaret A. Mrs. chiropodist at Brown,
  Thompson & Co. 942, b. 721 Main.
" Thomas, clerk at 98 Kilbourn, b. W.P.v.
Frye Mr. at 238 Asylum, b. 63 Church.
" Chas. H. clerk at 547 Main, b. 108½ Wash.
" Ellen, wid. Charles W. h. 108½ Washington.
" Melvin, clerk, State Prison, b. 62 Edwards.
Fryer George, coachman, 210 Far. b. 6 Niles.
Fuldner Adolph, mach. 338 Cap. h.3 Kilbourn ct.
Fuller Adell E. bookkeeper, 5 Asy. b. 36 Russ.
" Albert B. salesman, h. 170 Sargeant.
" Alice M. teacher, b. 11 Girard.
" Alice S. stenographer at State Capitol, rm.
  5, b. 105 Oak.
" Arminia B. teacher, b. 96 Webster.
" Bertha M. bookkeeper at 304 Asylum, b.
  105 Wooster.
**FULLER C. C. & CO.** furniture, 14 and
  16 Ford.              See page 500.
  Chauncey C. Fuller.      Alva W. Spaulding.
" Charles, painter, b. 556 Main.
" Charles J. salesman, 725 Main, h. 29 West.
" Chauncey C. ( C. C. F. & Co. ) h. 14 Seyms.
" Cornelia M. wid. A. H. b. 206 Sisson.
" Cynthia M. Mrs. mental and magnetic
  healer, 96, h. 96 Webster.
" Dexter M. machinist at 1, b. 68½ Laurel.
" E. A. & W. F. leaf tobacco, 236 State.
  Edward A. Fuller.      Wm. F. Fuller.
" Edgar W. bookkeeper at Lincoln, Seyms &
  Co. whl. teas, etc. 34 Market, h. E.H.t.
" Edw'd A. ( E. A. & W. F. Fuller ) h. Suffield t.
" Edwin C. mach. 476 Cap. b. 373 Asylum.
" Elizabeth L. Mrs. b. 95 Jefferson.
" Ella A. teacher Brown school, 160 Market,
  b. 34 West.
" Ernest S. machinist at Popes, b. 45 Smith.
" Eugene S. mech. at 225 Shel. h.u. 23 Wads.
" Frank A. driver, 48 Ann, b. W.H.t.
" Frank R. salesman, b. 170 Sargeant.
" Frank S. teamster, 164 State, h.u. 1338 Main.
" Fred. E. stenographer at Gross, Hyde &
  Shipman, 2 Central, h. E.H.t.
" Fred'k R. clerk at 110 Tru. h.u. 50 Village.
" Geo. advertising agent, 933 Main.
" George, toolm. at 581 Cap. h.2u. 13 Sanford.
" Geo. A. harnessm. Weth. t. b.u. 29 Benton.
" Geo. D. nightwatchman, h.u. 29 Benton.
" Geo. P. chief engir. 690 Park, h. 21 Sisson.
" Geo. W. trunks, etc. 182 Asy. h. 96 Webster.
" Henry C. teamster, b. 61 Judson.
" Henry W. apothec'y at hosp'l, h. 95 Jefferson.
" Henry W. mach. at 133 Shel. l.r. 41 Asylum.
" Horace S. physician, and medical examiner
  for the city, 95, b. 95 Trumbull.
" Hurbert M. helper P.&R. l. 19 Goodman.
" J. Weston, clerk, 487 Main, h.u. 10 Morris.
" John H. waiter, h.u. 105 Front.
" Josephine I. dressmaker, 36, h. 36 Russ.

Fuller Leon L. draughtsman at 1 Flow. b. E.H.t.
" Louis A. janitor Char.Oak bank, h. 48 Heath.
" Marshall H. salesman at Smith, 'Northam
   & Co. 129 State, h. East Douglas, Mass.
" Mary E. Mrs. h. 29 West.
" Mary P. b.u. 105 Wooster.
" Minerva A. wid. Amasa B. h.u. 105 Wooster.
" Robert, at 254 Pearl, b. 70 Charter Oak.
" William A. gardener, h. 51 Lafayette.
" Wm.F.( *E.A.& W. F.Fuller,*) b. 152 Asylum.
" William L. B. toolm. at Popes, b. 36 Russ.
" Willis J. asst. supt. 581 Cap. h.u. 45 Lincoln.
Fullerton Jennie, dressmaker, h. 5 Sigourney.
Fulner Adolph, machinist, b. 3 Kilbourn ct.
" ☞ *see also Feulner.*
Fulton Albert C. theological student, 1507 Broad.
  " Goodrich H. beltmaker, 15 Trumbull, b. 88
    Retreat.
  " Ross, gardener, h.u. 4 Cedar.
Funck Carlton H. printer, 258 Law. l. 198 High.
Fungaroli Gelsomino, shoemaker, 114 Laurel,
   b. 615 Capitol.
Funnie Joseph, porter str. Middletown, 285 State.
Furberg Andrew, sidewalk layer at 154 Charter
   Oak, h. 34 Cedar.
Furen Wm. E. teamster, h.u. 215 Bellevue.
Fureno Rocco, laborer, h.2u. 20 Kilbourn.
Furey Andrew T. switchm. N.Y.R. h. 8 Warren.
" James F. laborer, h.u. 8 Blumenthal.
" Peter M. teamster at 46 Ann, h. 534 Main.
" ☞ *see also Furrey, Fury.*
Furlong Edward, laborer, b.2u. 33 Union.
" Ellen, wid. John, h.u. 25 Waverly.
" Frank P. postmaster, 65 State, (*F. & How-
   ard,*) h. 273 Collins.
" & Howard, grocers, 160, meats, 164 Wind-
   sor av.
    Frank P. Furlong.    Daniel C. Howard.
" John F. teamster, h. 1 Cemetery.
" Lawrence F. electrical engineer, 237 Asy-
   lum, h. 169 Barbour.
" Mark, laborer, h.u. 1 Cemetery.
" Michael J. sawyer, 169 Front, h.2u. 33 Union.
" Thomas, driver, b.2u. 33 Union.
" William, hackdriver, h. 415 Garden.
Furman Ezra, brakem. at P. & R. b.u. 73 Albany.
" W. D. screwmaker at 1 Lau. b. 81 Pleasant.
Furness Addison G. polish. 581 Cap. b. 366 Maple.
Furniss William T. agent, h. 149 Sigourney.
Furrey Ervin L. (*Foster & F.*) undertakers,
   1166, h. 1185 Main.    *See page* 150.
" Leonard M. carpenter, b. 1185 Main.
" Michael C. foreman, b. 29 Mahl.
" ☞ *see also Furey; Fury.*

Furshpan Wolf, mach. at 388 Cap. h. 238 Front.
Furst Lewis, h. 206 Asylum, flat 14.
Furtinato Luigi, laborer, b. 79 Morgan.
" Vincenzo, laborer, b. 79 Morgan.
Fury Francis X. sexton, St. Patrick's church,
   h. 288 Allyn.
" ☞ *see also Furey; Furrey.*
Fusari Leo, ornamental plaster. 418 Asy. h. N.B.t.
Fusler Wm. H. cont'r 618 Cap. b. 1330 Broad.
Fussell Horace S. at 581 Capitol, h. 74 Allen pl.
Futter Leon, b. 153 Maple.
" Simon, clerk at 261 Asylum, h. Maple.
Fyler Anson P. order clerk at 141 Pearl, b.
   Warehouse Point v.
" Orsemus R. railroad commissioner at State
   Capitol, rms. 41–43, h. Torrington t.
" ☞ *see also Filer.*

Gabb Mary, wid. Thomas, b. 93 Hudson.
Gable Bert C. bookkeeper at Hills & Co. 372,
   374 Asylum, h. 4 Whitmore.
Gabriel John, h. 202 Barbour.
Gabrielle Antonio, laborer, b. 19 Mechanic.
" Burton Lynde, clerk at 197 Asy. b. 60 Dean.
" Ernest S. b. 60 Dean.
Gabrielle Sanford A. *councilman 7th ward,*
   machinist at 40 Governor, h. 60 Dean.
Gadbois George, plumber, b. 2 Church.
Gadd George, assembler at Colts, b. E.H.t.
Gade Fred, janitor, h.2u. 32 Wells.
Gadsby William, painter, h. 935 Park.
Gaffey Agnes, clerk at 956 Main b. 52 Wdbg.
" Daniel, laborer, h.u. 12 Union.
" Elizabeth, wid. Thomas, h. 27 John.
" John, laborer, h.u. 53½ Governor.
" John, b. St. Mary's Home, W.H.t.
" John, machinist, h.2u. 19 Babcock.
" John, oiler at Cheney Bros. silk mill, 34
   Morgan, b. 27 John.
" John F. saloon, 116 State, h.u. 609 Main.
" John J. laborer, b. 27 John.
" John J. weigher at 70 Huy. h.u. 19 Babcock.
" John S. machinist, b.3u. 121 Maple.
" Joseph E. tinner at 360 Main, b. 29 Linden.
" Kate, wid. Patrick, h.u. 104 Trumbull.
" Kate R. wid. Peter, h. 52 Woodbridge.
" Kittie, clerk at 956 Main, b. 52 Woodbridge.
" Lena M. E. clerk at Brown, Thomson & Co.
   942 Main, b. 180 Seymour.
" Mary A. seamstress, b.3u. 121 Maple.
" Mary E. clerk at Brown, Thomson & Co.
   942 Main, b. 180 Seymour.
" Michael, laborer, h.u. 27 John.
" Michael, policeman, h. 99 Maple.
" Patrick F. fireman at Popes, h. 34 Park.
" Peter J. baggage ex. Un. depot, h. 27 Chapel
" Rose, wid. Keron, h. 180 Seymour.
" Rose M. b. 180 Seymour.
" Tenia, b. 52 Woodbridge.
" William J. assembler, b.u. 12 Union.
Gaffney James, clerk, 653 Main, h.2u. 57 Pleasant.
" James, plumber, b. 76 Bellevue.
" James A. filer at Popes, h.u. 42 Avon.
" Sadie A. clerk at Brown, Thomson & Co.
   942 Main, b. 225 High.

Gage Caroline A. wid. Rev. W. L. h. 747 Asylum.
" Edward L. porter at 30 Wash. h. 8 Ellsworth.
" Hannah W. wid. Joseph, h. 277 High.
" Henry E. clerk at Conn. Fire Insurance Co. 51 Prospect, b. 8 Ellsworth.
Gager Charles E. L 75 Pratt, rm. 15.
" Chauncey F. cond. St.Ry. h. 10 Elliott pl.
" Frederick, helper, L 29 Washington.
" John S. at 180 Allyn, b. Glastonbury t.
Gaghan Ann, wid. Thomas, h.2u. 8 Lawrence.
" Bridget, wid. Thomas, h. 12 Lawrence.
" John A. polisher, 581 Cap. h.u. 35 Franklin.
" Joseph F. polisher at 581 Cap. b.2u. 8 Law.
" Michael F. laborer, b. 12 Lawrence.
" Thomas J. bartender, b. 12 Lawrence.
" Thomas P. laborer, h.u. 7 Squire.
" ☞ see also Geoghagan; Ghagan.
Gagnon Felix, carpenter, b.2u. 545 Main.
" Onesiphore, brickmaker, b. 186 Barbour.
Gahan Samuel, mach. at 1 Flow. h.u. 49 Spring.
Gaherty William J. conductor St.Ry. h. 10 Owen.
Gahn Carl, at 690 Park, h.2u. 40 New Britain.
Gahne Emil, brushmaker, h.u. 13½ John.

**CAINES CHAS. M.** printer, 66 State, h. 427 Main. *See page 478.*

" David L. city express, 6, h.u. 6 Alden.
" Dudley A. drug clerk at 639, b. 1193 Main.
" Edward H. clerk at 267 Main, h. 55 Ward.
" Fred. S. horse dealer, b. 522 Windsor av.
" Jared, captain tug L. C. Ward, 285 State.
" John C. toolmaker at 9 Sigourney, h. W.H.t.
" Margaret, wid. Nelson, h.u. 1193 Main.
" Raymond S. clerk at 885 Main, b. E.H.t.
" Robert A. at Conn. Mutual Life Ins. Co. 783 Main, b. W.H.t.
Gaioski Louis, laborer, h.u. 19 Front.
Galbraith Christina, teacher, Lawrence street school, b. 214 New Britain.
Galdreau Fred, lather, b. 197 State.
Gale Arthur S. veterinary surgeon, r. 20 Morgan, h.2u. 110 Trumbull.
" George, supt. shipyd. 285 State,b.5 Vandyke.
" Henry A. supt.at 155 Ch.O. h.u. 26 Madison.
" Thomas, deckhand, 285, b. 197 State.
Galer Ralph, conductor St.Ry. b. 12 Bond.
Galivan Thomas F. polisher at Colts, b. 3 Dean.
Gallage Nicola, laborer, h.u. 39 North.
Gallagher Bernard, at Cedar Hill Cem.h.Weth.t.
" Catherine, wid. Thomas O.h. Albany.
" Charles F. machinist at 556 Cap. b. 246 Park.
" Charles J. helper at 154 State, h. 16 Winter.
" Clara A. clerk, 956 Main, b. Albany, W.H.t.
" George E. farmer, b. Albany, W.H.t.
" Henry, mason, h.r. 259 Front.
" Henry J. mach. 9 Sigourney, h. 43 Babcock.
" James, b. 68 Flower.
" John, gardener, 159 Farmington, h. 68 Flow.
" John, mason, h.r. 259 Front.
" John F. brakeman, b.r. 259 Front.
" John J. clerk at Sage, Allen & Co. 898 Main, h. 70 Windsor av.
" John J. farmer, b. Albany, W.H.t.
" Maria, wid. John, b. 14 Winter.
" Mary C. h.3u. 47 Spring.

Gallagher Michael, gardener, b. 62 Flower.
" Michael W. painter, b.r. 259 Front.
" Patrick, h.r. 39 Forest.
" Patrick, bartender at 75, b. 75 Windsor.
" Patrick, mason, b. 1183 Main.
" Thomas F. saloon, 75, h.u. 75 Windsor.
" William, filer at 1 Laurel, h. Farmington t.
Gallehawk Francis Mrs. h. 111 Heath.
" Olive E. b. 111 Heath.
Gallery of Paintings and Statuary, 624 Main.
Gallevsky Harry, jeweler, 2 State, h.27 Kennedy.
Gallichio Nicholas J. mechanic at 581 Capitol, h.3u. 39 North.
Gallivan Jeremiah J. salesm. 725 Mn. h. 1 Seyms.
Gallon Charles J. printer, b.r. 1239 Main.
" Joseph, h.r. 1239 Main.
Galloway Nesbit B. mach. at 9 Sig. h. 29 Affleck.
Gallup Bessie M. teacher, b. 37 Bluehills.
" Christopher M. draughtsman at 800 Main, b. 300 Wethersfield.
" Emma H. stenogr. at Popes, b. Manchester t.
" Erastus, marketman, h. 37 Bluehills.
" John M. (G. & Metzger,) h. 39 Forest.
GALLUP & METZGER, music store, 201 Asylum.
    John M. Gallup.    Simon C. Metzger.
" William M. clerk, b. 37 Bluehills.
Galleotti Nicola A. helper at 15 Trumbull, notary, b. 34 Windsor.
" Rocco, h. 34 Windsor.
Galpin Robert J. clerk, h.3u. 884 Main.
Galt John R. correspondent, Popes, h.331 Laurel.
Galtner Adolph, driver at 315 Park.
Galvin Catherine, wid. Thomas F. h.u.127 Maple.
" James B. printer at 66 State, b. 28 Russell.
" James J. diesinker at Popes, h.u. 1338 Broad.
" John, b.u. 1338 Broad.
" John, laborer, b.2u. 4 Portland.
" John C. bartender at 222 Front,h. 60 Talcott.
" John F. mach. at 1 Flower, h.u. 156 Russ.
" May F. stenog. at Ingraham & Swift, 126 Church, b. 127 Maple.
" Michael, h.4u.r. 23 Spruce.
" Nellie, bookkeeper, 845 Main, b. 127 Maple.
" Patrick, switchman at N.Y.R. h. 28 Russell.
" William, teamster, b. 180 Seymour.
" ☞ see also Gallivan.
Gamerdinger Charles, packer, b.r. 1239 Main.
" Christian, mach. at 556 Cap. h.r. 1239 Main.
" George H. stairbuilder, b.r. 1239 Main.
" William, b.r. 1239 Main.
" William, boxmaker, b.r. 1239 Main.
Gammach George W. at 53 Vernon, b. W.H.t.
Gammack Frederick S. at 209 State, b. W.H.t.
Gammons Mildred B. bookkeeper at 45 Pratt.
" W. E. bkkpr. 188 Asylum, b. Manchester t.

Gandett Matthew, b. 59 Market.
Gandy Charles, conductor St.Ry. 115 State.
Ganey William A. operator at 721 Main, rm. 12.
Gangloff Henry P. mechanic at 581 Cap. h. N.B.t.
Ganion Hugh, laborer, b. 350 Front.
" James, engineer N.Y.R. h.u. 1418 Broad.
" Joseph, b. 1418 Broad.
" Thomas, tinner at 346 Main.
" ☞ see also Ganyon.
Ganley Edmund E. mach. at Colts, b. 9 S. Pro.
" John, butcher, h.3u. 70 Walnut.
" Margaret A. dressmaker, b. 9 So. Prospect.
" Mary I. folder at R. S. Peck & Co. 26 High,
    b. 9 So. Prospect.
" Michael J. bunker, engine 2, b. 70 Windsor av.
" Thomas J. telegrapher, b. 70 Windsor.
" William J. machinist at 328 Asy. b. 9 S. Pro.
Gannon Cora, nurse, h.u. 20 John.
" James, screwm. at 476 Capitol, b. 13 Russell.
" Thomas F. mech. at Popes, b.u. 59 Maple.
Gans Barbara, wid. William, b. 63 Clark.
" Frank A. barber at 22 State, h. 67 Clark.
" John B. b. 63 Clark.
" Lizzie, h.r. 72 Temple.
" Louis R. bunker, engine 7, b. 63 Clark.
" Mayer, tailor, h.u. 61 Pleasant.
" Nathan (Rome & G.) h. 200 Front.
" Samuel, laborer, b.r. 72 Temple.
Ganthrie Michael, helper, 1 Flow. h. 47 Spruce.
Ganyon John, polisher, h.u. 25 Hamilton.
" ☞ see also Ganion; Guinan.
Ganz Israel, helper at 7 North, h. 200 Front.
" Louis H. roofer 199, h. 195 Front.
" Myers, tailor at 720 Main, h. 61 Pleasant.
Garber Israel, peddler, h. 60 Avon.
Gardell Charles J. janitor, 732 Main, h.3u. 177
    Asylum.
Gardiner George, steamfitter, h.r. 22 Jefferson.
" William G. clerk, 78 Asy. b.147 Washington.
Gardner A. driver, 315 Park.
" Benjamin, clerk, 711 Mn. b. 16 Buckingham.
" Charles E. brakem. P.&R. h.u. 214 Asylum.
" Charlotte C. wid.C.H. dressm. h.u.17 Chapel.
" Christopher, diesinker at 142 Russ, h.7Good.
" Edith, b.u. 28 Alden.
" Edward S. h. 78 High.
" Elizabeth B. dressm. 650, h. 650 Main, rm.59.
" Ellen E. wid. William H. h.u. 28 Alden.
" Frank B. mach. at 30 Cush. h. 65 Willow.
" Henry, mach. at 1 Flower, h. 55 Ashley.
" Henry B. clerk at 197 Asylum, b. 55 Ashley.
" James A. waiter at 26 State, b.3u.290 Pearl.
" Julian E. veterinary surg. h. 118 Trumbull.
" Marcia Mrs. b. 2 Holcomb.
" Mary A. wid. Moses F. grocer,15,h.15 Ellery.
" Moses, h. 2 Holcomb.
" Robert N. clerk at Orient Ins. Co. 5 Haynes,
    b. 55 Ashley.
" Samuel A. lamp oils, 1100 Mn. h.Burnside v.
" W. H. candy, l. 284 Asylum, rm. 59.
" William J. clerk at 78 Asylum, b.335 Pearl.
Gardula Mary Mrs. striper, 1037 Mn. h.44½ John.
Garfield Benjamin F. baggagemaster, Union
    depot, h. 19 Crown.
" Ellen H. wid. Edwin, b. 19 Crown.

Garfinkel Morris, watchmaker, 996 Main, h. 229
    Franklin.
" William, jeweler, 154, h. 160 Front.
Garlan Patrick, driver at 560, l. 560 Main.
Garland Adelaide, h. 22 Grand.
" Edward W. inspector, 690 Park, b. 25 Smith.
" Ellen, wid. William, h. 5 Green.
" Frank, teamster, b. 74 Windsor.
" James N. ostler at Linus T. Fenn, 613
    Main, h. 116½ Albany.
" John T. lacquerer at James L. Howard &
    Co. 438 Asylum, h. 25 Smith.
" Robert, porter, 195 State,l. 52 Buckingham.
Garlock Charles, helper, 84, b. 84 Vine.
Garman Louis, filer at 581 Capitol, b. 26 Flower.
Garneau Xavier, painter at 25 Church, h. 144
    Brown.
Garner Thomas W. repairer, Popes, h.u.86 N.B.
Garney John, helper, P.&R. h. 23 Chestnut.
" Peter, laborer. P.&R. b. 23 Chestnut.
Garrache Fred, laborer, b.u. 30 Kilbourn.
Garrett Arthur T. iceman, 4 Cen. b. 7 Goodwin.
" Effie M. b. 7 Goodwin.
" John, insurance, h. 645 Farmington.
Garrette Edward D. b. 112 Whitmore.
" J. Frank, trav. salesman, h. 26 Florence.
" Joseph W. bookkeeper at Bill Bros. h.u.
    112 Whitmore.
Garrison Charles A. painter, h.r. 60 Portland.
" Fred S. clerk at P.&R. b. 28 Spring.
" Wesley, painter, h. 49 John.
" Weyant, b.2u. 31 Mechanic.
Garrity Daniel J. clerk at Popes, h.u. 9 Ward pl.
" Edward J. machinist at Pope Tube Co.
    h. 26 Village.
" Emily, b.u. 326½ Park.
" Helen, dressm. at 270 Main, b.u. 121 Maple.
" Jane, wid. Patrick, h.u. 28 Madison.
" John, gardener, 30 Weth. h.u. 326½ Park.
" John, laborer at stone pits, h.r. 50 Wilson.
" John F. clerk, b.u. 121 Maple.
" John F. piper, h. 34 John.
" John F. repairer at Popes, b. E.H.t.
" Keron F. at stone pits, b.r. 50 Wilson.
" Margarette, nurse, 28, b.u. 28 Madison.
" Michael, livery, r. 1231 Main, h. 1 Goodman.
" Patrick, driver, b.u. 28 Madison.
" Peter F. laborer for city, h.u. 121 Maple.
" Sarah D. nurse, 20 South Hudson.
" Thomas, repairer, P.&R. b. 20 Affleck.
" William, clerk, b. 1 Goodman.
" William, laborer, 83 Woodland, h.26 Village.
" ☞ see also Gerety.
Garsden John H. forem. at Popes, h. 71 Hung.
Gartland Ed. J. buffer, b. 29 Morgan.
Garvan Agnes W. teacher at High school, b. 236
    Farmington.
" Edward J. attorney 877 Main, rm. 1, clerk
    city court, b. 236 Farmington.
" Frank P. student, b. 236 Farmington.
**GARVAN PATRICK,** paper dealer,
    207 State, *park commissioner,* h. 236
    Farmington.        *See page 472.*
" John, student, b. 236 Farmington.
" Thomas F. at 205 State, b. 236 Farmington.

Garvey John, mach. at P.&R. h.u. 23 Chestnut.
" John J. teamster, h.u. 25 Front.
" Joseph, lineman at 80 State, b. 23 Florence.
" Patrick, helper at 165 Windsor, b. 37 Avon.
" William M. salesm. 45 Asy. b. 80 Hopkins.
Garvie Annie L. nurse, 20 South Hudson.
" George S. polisher at Popes, h. E.H.t.
" Harry G. polisher, b. 88 Ann.
" John, machinist, h. 23 Chestnut.
" John B. builder, 754 Main, h. 240 Park.
" John S. clerk at Brown, Thomson & Co. 942 Main, b. 16 Russ.
" Peter, laborer, b. 23 Chestnut.
" Robert, plumber, 12 Mulberry, h. 40 Russ.
" William S. polisher, Popes, h. 44 Vanblock.
Garvin Chas. H. (Cummings & G.) h. 181 Sisson.
" Cornelius F. mach. at N.Y.R.b.r.63 Albany.
Garwood Samuel, machinist, h.r. 30 Temple.
Gaspare Brighenti, carpenter, h. 12 North.
" Domenico, hodcarrier, b. 12 North.
" Peter, hodcarrier, b. 12 North.
Gass Thomas B. manager restaurant, N.Y.R. 466 Asylum, l. 30 Spring.
Gast Fred, plumber at 1230, b. 1220 Main.
Gastner August, ostler, b. 3 Ellsworth.
Gastonguay Godemier, machinist at 1 Flower, b. 25 Greenwood.
" Jos. B. mach. 1 Flower, b. 25 Greenwood.
" Wilfred J. mach. 1 Flow. b. 25 Greenwood.
Gately & Brennan, house furnishers, goods installment, 118 Asylum, room 1.
    E. Gately.        J. P. Brennan.
" Thomas, b. W.H. Home for Aged, Albany.
Gates Andrew F. attorney at law, 11 Central, rm. 6, h. 42 Willard.
" Benjamin, mach. at 388 Cap. b. 213 Law.
" Carrie L. h. 102 Hudson.
" Chas. S. foreman, Popes, h.u. 1206 Broad.
" Edith S. school teacher, b. 48 Asylum.
" F. E. Mrs. h. 48 Asylum.
" Frank A. clerk at 24 State, b. 48 Asylum.
" Herbert D. motorman St.Ry. h. 11 Sey.
" Julian H. stamp clerk, P.O. h.u. 19 Canton.
" L. C. Mrs. humane agent, 650 Main.
" Maria Miss, h.u. 133 Market. rm. 7.
" Mary E. wid. Justin J. h.u. 53 Dean.
" Thomas, farmer, 868, h. 868 Windsor av.
" W. D. engineer tug Smith, 285 State.
" Wilbur S. salesman at 476 Cap. h. 46 Wads.
" William E. with The E. S. Kibbe Co. grocers, 149 State, h. Glastonbury t.

**GATLING GUN CO.** firearms, office, 17 Vandyke av. Colts Armory.
                    See page 565.
Gaudet Matthew, carpenter, b.u. 59 Market.
" Oliver, helper, b. 6 Oak.
" Patrick S. carpenter, h. 409 Franklin.
" Patrick S. Mrs. Hartford laundry, 403, h. 403 Franklin.
" Timothy, carpenter, h.u. 4 Oak.
" Valentine, laborer, b.u. 4 Oak.
Gaudett Amos P. (Crosscup & G.) h 224 Franklin.
" Simon F. carpenter, h. 22 Bushnell.
Gauggel Hubert, h.u. 232 New Park.

Gaughan Frank, teamster, h.2u. 14 Lawrence.
Gauthier Arthur, machinist at 1 Flower, h.2u. 25 Greenwood.
" Fred, barber at 27 Pearl, b. 109 Trumbull.
" Sarah A. Mrs. h. 59 Albany.
Gavel Michael, helper at 476 Cap. b. 260 Shel.
Gavin Bryan N. dropfogr. Popes, h. 1149 Broad.
" Jas. J. boots & shoes, 83 Tru. h.u. 38 Spring.
" James W. bartendr. at 98 Wells, h. 87 Fmt.
" James W. Mrs. clerk, 956 Main, h. 65 Cap.
" Lillie, dressmaker, 19, b. 19 Alden.
" Mary A. dressmaker, h.u. 38 Spring.
" Michael, policeman, h. 19 Alden.
" Michael J. dropfgr. Popes, b. 1149 Broad.
" Nellie, dressmaker, 19, b. 19 Alden.
" Peter B. operator at Popes, b. 1149 Broad.
Gavitt Arthur P. supt. 29 Union pl., h. 99 Oak.
Gay Alice M. b. 61 Huntington.
" Alice W. wid. Wm. P. custodian at 624 Main, h.u. 61 Huntington.
" Frank B.librarian Watkinson Library, supt. Wadsw. athenæum, 624 Main, h. 658 Far.
GAY GEORGE A. (Brown, Thomson & Co.) dry goods, etc. 920-942 Main, h. W.H.t.
                    See page 499.
" Mary Y. b. 62 Chestnut.
Gaylor Charles, pinmaker, h. 77 Windsor.
" Max, laborer, h. 77 Windsor.
Gaylord C. Walter, organist, h. 20 Imlay.
" Edward B. clerk, 197 Asylum, b. 15 Girard.
" Emily N. b. 15 Girard.
" Hezekiah, h. 15 Girard.
" Joseph H. theological student, 1507 Broad.
" Luther L. clerk at Capewell Horse Nail Co. 40 Governor, b. 255 Main.
Gaynor Frank J. operator at 40 Gov. b. 25 John.
" Thomas, helper at 556 Capitol, h. 25 John.
Geadbois George, tinner at 291 Asylum.
Gear Rus. E. foreman r. 133 Shel. b. 18 Wooster.
" William A. mechanic, b. 18 Wooster.
" ☞ see also Geer.
Gearin James J. blacksmith, 20 Morgan, b.u. 41 Windsor.
" Michael J. blacksmith, h.u. 41 Windsor.
" Michael, Jr. b.u. 41 Windsor.
Geary David C. machinist, 1 Flower, b. 285 Park.
" Frank P. policeman, h. 119 Brook.
" James T. (Keho & Geary,) h. 233 Market.
" John J. inspector at Popes, b. 285 Park.
" Margaret J. clerk at Brown, Thomson & Co. 942 Main, b. 285 Park.
" Maria Mrs. wid. Terrance, h. 615 Capitol.
" Mary, wid. Michael, h. 285 Park.
" Patrick, laborer, b.u. 22 Albany.

**GEARY THOMAS J. & CO.** cloaks and furs, 845 Main.*
" Thos. J. (Thos. J. G. & Co.) h. 40 Hopkins.
" ☞ see also Garey.
Gebhardi Gustav, music teacher, 46, h. 46 N.B.
Geckley George G. pressman at Popes, h.u. 9½ Hamilton.
Geddes Annie, dressmaker, b. 227 Sigourney.
" Chas. E. toolm. 26 Lau. h.u. 84 Whitmore.
Geddie David, carpt. at r. 334 Asy. b.2u 265 Mn.

**THE NEWS PRINTED IN THE POST IS RELIABLE.**

Gee George N. rubberwkr. at 690 Park, h. B.v.
" Ying, laundry, 130, h. 130 Windsor.
Geeley Henry, The Clothier, 27 Asylum, h. 631 Farmington.
Geer Anna B. teacher So. school, 36 Wadsworth, b. Highland, south of Farmington.
" E. Howard, sec'y and sup't Hartford Printing Co. 16 State, h.u. 111 Trumbull.
" E. Jennie E. wid. Elihu, h. The Linden, 427 Main.

**GEER ELIHU SONS,** See Hartford Printing Co. 16 State. *See page 474.*
" Eliza S. teacher Lawrence St. school, b. 57 Farmington.
" Erastus C. treasurer Hartford Printing Co. 16 State, h. 12 Garvan, E.H.t.
" Erskine Hart, director Hartford Printing Co. h. Hadlyme v.
" Ethel Ellsworth, and Elene E. Misses, b. The Linden, 427 Main.
" Everett S. printer at Ætna Fire Ins. Co. 668 Main, h. 64 Niles.
" Geo. L. molder at 556 Cap. h. New Britain t.
" Hattie E. wid. Charles G. h. Highland, south of Farmington.
" Mary L. teacher, 690, l. 714 Asylum.
" ☞ *see also Gear; Geary.*
Geertz Frank, cabinetm. at r. 16 Forest, h. W.H.t.
Geetersloh Fred. H. mach. at 556 Cap. h. 23 Haw.
" James T. machinist, 556 Cap. h. 35 Laurel.
" John, gardener, b. 43 Hawthorn.
" Wm. J. mach. 556 Cap. h.u. 213 Hamilton.
Gehring Emilie L. vocalist, b. 379 Wethersfield.
Geib Wm. chaser at 62 Market, h. 49 Lincoln.
Geibelhansen Ludwich, cabinetmaker at 225 Sheldon, h. Wethersfield t.
Geidel Paul, bartdr. 163 Front, h. 2u. 25 Francis.
Geiger Bartholomew, shoemaker at 10 State, b. 80 Temple.
" John L. painter, h.u. 6 Marsh.
Geipel Frederick, twister at Cheney Bros. silk mill, 34 Morgan, h. 1 Orchard.
Geisel Adam, screwmkr. 476 Capitol, h. 7 Kibbe.
" Adam Jr. b. 7 Kibbe.
" William, machinist at 1 Flower, b. 7 Kibbe.
Geiselhart Frederick. laborer, h.u. 123 Front.
Gelbart Hallie F. public reader, b. 427 Main.
" Theo. F. engraver, h. 427 Main.
Geldman Davis, grocer, 82, h. 82 Avon.
Gelinas Joseph, patternmaker, b. 22 Morgan.
" Josie, actress, b. 201 Lawrence.
" Maria Mrs. h. 201 Lawrence.
Gellert Anna, wid. U. Hansen, b.u. 207 Capen.
" Anton, carpenter at Andrews & Peck, 88 Market, h. East Hartford t.
" Hans L. carpenter, h.u. 207 Capen.
" John C. carpenter, b.u. 207 Capen.
Gelman Michael, tailor, 160, h. 160 Front.
Gelsh David, peddler, h.r. 198 Front.
Gelston Hollister, carpenter, b. 26 Chapel.
" Jennie S. Mrs. b. 26 Chapel.
" M. Olive, manicure, b. 26 Chapel.
Gemmill Agnes, stitcher at 15 Trumbull, b. 877 Main, rm. 10.

Gemmill, Burnham & Co. merchant tailors, etc. 66 Asylum.
    John Gemmill.    Edgar F. Burnham.
" John, ( G., Burnham & Co. ) h. 66 Farmington.
" Margaretta, b. 66 Farmington.
Gendreau Luc, carpenter, h. Lubeck.
Gendron C. H. laundryman, b.u. 17 Wells.
" Flora Mrs. b.u. 51 New Britain.
" Fred, painter, 37 N.B. h. Windsor Locks t.
" Hermine Mrs. laundress, h.u. 17 Wells.
" Hector, burnisher, h.u. 17 Wells.
Gent John J. butcher, b. 33 Mechanic.
Gentlemens Driving Club, 926 Main. .
Geoggin ☞ *see Goggins.*
Geoghagan Patrick, laborer, h.u. 72 Sanford.
" Peter J. coachman at 356 Main, h. 143 Law.
" ☞ *see also Gaghan; Ghagan.*
George Abraham, sidewalk layer at 154 Charter Oak, h. West Hartford t.
" Adonis, fruit, 1197 Main, h. 33 Albany.
" Christebel, wid. Charles, h. 336 Franklin.
" Domenico, laborer, h.u.r. 7 Charles.
" Ed. F. expressman at 4 Central, b. 46 Village.
" Elizabeth C. b. 249 Collins.
" Henry, express, 4 Central, h. 46 Village.
" Isabelle L. stenographer, b. 29 Pearl.
" Jerome, laborer, b.u. 33 North.
" John L. driver at 4 Central, b. 46 Village.
" Joseph, harnessmaker at 8 Sigourney.
" Napoleon, h. 54 Bond.
" Nicola, laborer, h. 47½ Morgan.
" Prospero, clerk at 1197, b. 1197 Main.
" Rocco, laborer, h.u. 33 North.
" William, at 1 Flower, b. 73 Park.
" William H. expressman, h. 20 Chapel.
Geotz August, laborer, 53 Vernon, h. 5 S. Hud.
" John B. mach. at 1 Flower, b.u. 280 Park.
Ger Louis, tailor, b.u. 3 North.
Gerald Catherine, wid. Guy, h.u. 40 Wooster.
Gerard Henry, painter. b.u. 306 Park.
Gerety George J. ( G. & Sullivan, ) h. 247 Weth.
" & Sullivan, builders, 703 Main, rm. 7.
    George J. Gerety.     Timothy J. Sullivan.
Gerhardt Karl, mechanical engineer at Popes, h. 53 Webster.
Germaine Remi, carpenter, b. 197 State.
German American Insurance Co. of New York, E. S. Cowles, manager, 25 Pearl.
Germania hall, 1056 Main.
Gernhardt Harry F. artist, h. 20 Crown.
Gernreich Oscar, polisher at Wm. Rogers Mfg. Co. 66 Market, h. 80 Temple.
Gerrity Patrick, driver, b. 274 Front.
Gerrish Edwin J. attendant, 30 Washington.
" Thomas, laborer, N.Y.K. b.u. 20 Affleck.
" Thomas F. bricklayer, b. 274 Front.
Gerry Charles O. carpenter, h. 2u. 1 Orchard.
" Cathleen, teacher at 1205, b. 1205 Asylum.
" Nellie G. clerk at Wm. h. 9 Pleasant.
Gershel L. & Bro. tobacco, Ellery Darlin, agent, 232 State.
Gerson Albert, clerk at 76 Tru. h. Springfield t.
Gerstein Isaac, foreman at 172, h.r. 174 Front.
Gerstl Max, architect, 756 Main, rm. 38.
Gerwin Anthony, filer h. 69 Potter.

**The Post, 12 Cents a Week, Delivered at Your Home.**

Getchel Fred H. molder 690 Park, h.u. 48 Heath.
" John, molder at 690 Park, h. 48 Heath.
" Wm. H. tirecollector at 690 Park,h.48 Heath.
Gett George, teamster at 2 Chapel, b. 11 John.
Getter Frank, painter, b. 21 Mulberry.
Gettier William M. painter at 88 Mar. h.126 Ann.
Gettner Aldolph, brewer, 315 Park, b. 50 Law.
Getty George A. clerk at 928 Main, b. 66 Bkm.
" Henry, mechanic at Popes, b, 20 Morgan.
Getz Aaron, cigarsalesman, b. 23 Morgan.
" Carrie Mrs. h. 54 Village.
" Gilbert, clerk at Sage, Allen & Co. 898 Main, h.2u. 65 Elliott.
" Jacob, new and secondhand clothing, 122 State, h. 23 Morgan.
" Louis, clerk at 122 State, b. 23 Morgan.
" Mary, wid. Moritz, h.u. 117 Front.
" Sarah, wid. Michael, h.2u. 65 Elliott.
" Solomon, clerk at 122 State, b. 23 Morgan.
" ☞ see also Katz.
Giacinnio Angello, laborer, h.u. 82 Morgan.
Giannettino Brothers, barbers, 2 State.
Louis Giannettino.  Philip Giannettino.
" John, printer at R. S. Peck & Co. 26 High, b. 2 Dean.
" Louis (G. Bros.) h. 2 Dean.
" Louis Z. machinehand, 40 Gov. b. 2 Dean.
" Philip (G. Bros.) h.2 u. 55 Windsor.
Gibb Hattie Mrs. h.u. 64 Hicks.
" William N. mach. at 476 Capitol, l. 60 Ann.
Gibben John, harnessmkr. 59½ Tru· b. 87 High.
Gibbins Frank, helper at 1204 Main.
Gibbons Annie, wid. James, h. 92 Grove.
" Bridget, wid. John, h.u. 86 Charter Oak.
" Frank H. b.u. 86 Charter Oak.
" James M. dentist at 868 Main, b. 92 Grove.
" John A. toolmaker, 581 Cap. h.u. 365 Main.
" Lizzie P. Mrs. h.u. 289 Asylum.
" Maurice F. mach. at Colts, b. 92 Grove.
" P. Joseph, clerk Conn. Trust & Safe Deposit Co. 785 Main, b. 80 Capitol.
" Thomas J. printer at Catholic Transcript, 704 Main, b. 92 Grove.
" William A. teamster, b. 92 Grove.
" Wm. F. mach. at 135 Shel. b.u. 86 Ch. O.
Gibbs Edward, b. 71 Sigourney.
" Electric Mfg. Co., Jacob S. Gibbs, 302 Asy.
" George S. agent, 715 Main, h. E.H.t.
" Jacob S. (G. E. Mfg. Co.) b. 119 Sherman.
" James W. chief clerk at Conn. Car Service Asso. 466 Asylum, h.u. 26 Atwood.
" John H. clerk at 466 Asylum, b. 55 Capitol.
" Matthew J. clerk, 4 Central, b. 8 Wadsworth
" Matthew P. foreman, N.Y.R.h.71 Sigourney.
" Richard J. mgr. 583 Main, b. 8 Wadsworth.
" Samuel L.mach. at 1 Flower, h.u.1147 Broad
" William, b. 60 Ann.
Giblin James, laborer at Popes, b.u. 22 Union.
Gibney John, vulcanizer, 555 Cap. b.2u. 79 Gov.
Gibson Andruss J. jobber, b. 4 Elm.
" Carrie Mrs. h. 14 Goodwin.
" Frank J. burnisher, b. 35 Front.
" George P. attorney at 2, b. 80 State.
" John, carptr. at N.Y.R. b. 1329 Broad.
" Katie, domestic, 50 John.

Gibson Mary, wid. Edward, h.u. 85 Front.
" Michael, helper, N.Y.R. b. 1329 Broad.
" Patrick, fireman 142 Russ, b. 1329 Broad.
" Peter, blacksmith, h.u. 50 Willow.
" William, l.2u. 175 Windsor.
" William, tailor, 956 Main, b. 1329 Broad.
" ☞ see also Gipson.
Gidart August W. helper, 556 Cap. b. 154 Ward.
Giddings Chas. E. clerk Board of Assessors and Bd. of Relief, 114 Pearl, h. 239 Sigourney.
" Daniel W. clerk at 556 Capitol, b. 41 Asylum.
" Edith M. teacher Lawrence street school, b. 341 New Britain.
" Emery B. reporter Hartford Telegram, b. 28 Huntington.
" Eugene A. at Conn. Mutual Life Ins. Co. 783 Main, b. 341 New Britain.
" Harrison K. b. 341 New Britain.
" Howard A., U.S.A. h. 13 Alden.
" Hulda S. wid. H. A, b. 97 Webster.
" Joseph R. secretary Holly Steam Engineering Co. 28 High, b. 170 Sigourney.
" Susan M. wid. Edwin, h. 341 New Britain.
Gierginsky Albert H.filer at Colts, h.u.88Madison.
Giersch John, at 74 Tru. h. 230 Asylum, rm. 2.
Gies Wilhemina, wid. Chas. h. 18 S.Hud. rm. 3.
Giese Charles H. grocery, 51, h. 51 Ferry.
Giesler Martin, tailor, h. 52 Temple.
" Mary Mrs. midwife, h. 52 Temple.
Giestein J. peddler, h. 88 Windsor.
Gifford Alenza T. toolm. 388 Cap. b. 72 Hopkins.
" Charles R. painter at 1148 Main, h. 4 Walnut.
" James R. carpenter, h. 26 Chestnut.
" Richard T. mach. 388 Cap. b.2u. 72 Hopkins.
" Theron M. rubberw. 690 Park, h.u. 30 Smith.
Giggey Chas. E. photo eng. 177 Asy. b. 119 Cap.
Gilbert Alfred T. wtchm.N.Y.R. h.122Wellington.
" Augustus H. cigarmaker, 741, h. 448 Main.
" Benjamin S. supt. Hartford Hospital, 20 So. Hudson, h. 1 Barnard.
" Charles, fireman, N.Y.R. h. 9 Grand.
" Charles A. clerk at Alfred T. Ricker, moldings, 26 Potter, h. 89 Webster.
" Charles E. assistant secretary Ætna Life Insurance Company, 650 Main, h. 60 Gillett.
" Charles O. b. 80 State.
" Cornelius B. toolm. at 476, b. 381 Capitol.
" Elizabeth S. wid. Erastus, h.18 Charter Oak.
" F. E. travel. salesman, Popes, h. N. Y. city.
" Fred, liner at Popes, b. 86 Trumbull.
" George A. mach. at 1 Flower, b. 51 Oak.
" George A. salesman at 47 Ann, b. 67 Willard.
" George H. architect, 67, h. 67 Willard.
" Grace, at r. 59½ Tru. b. 247 Lawrence.
" Harriet P. wid. Charles B. b. 19 Vernon.
" Helen A. nurse, 20 South Hudson.
" Ida M. b. 2 Winthrop.
" John W. builder, 15, h. 15 Capitol.
" Julia E. h. 145 Sigourney.
" Julie K. stenographer at Popes, b. E.H.t.
" Lewis S. inspector at 581 Cap. b. Burnside v.
" Minnie J. teach.Northwest sch.b.99 Webster.
" Normand B. discount clerk at Hartford National Bank, 58 State, b. 145 Sigourney.
" Seth L. clerk, 2 So. Ann, h. 99 Webster.

**For Sale Advertisements Bring Results in the Post.**

Gilbert William H. Rev. b. 714 Asylum.
" William H. bookkeeper at Hartford National Bank, 58 State, h. 145 Sigourney.
" William H. bookkeeper at Frank J. Knox & Son, plumbers, h. 80 Webster.
" William J. cigarmfr. 159 Asy. h.u. 448 Main.
Gilchrest Edward, carpenter, 109 Windsor av.
Gildard E. J. cigarm. at 867 Main, b. 170 High.
Gilday John H.engir. Almshouse,h.r. 91 Bluehills.
Gilde Adeline C. wid. Fred. W. h. 14 Cottage.
" Albert H.cigarmaker at 847 Main, h. E.H.t.
" Augustus E. engineer at 158 Woodland, b.14 Cottage.
" Frank C. helper, 135 Sheldon, b. 59½ Gov.
Gilderdale Catherine, clerk in ins. dept. rm. 14 State Capitol, b. 5 Lenox.
Gile Loren D. conductor St.Ry. h. E.H.t.
Giler Lillian, at 336, b. 336 Wethersfield.
Giles Edgar W. musician, b. 334 Wethersfield.
" John F. electrician, N.Y.R. h.u. 69 Willow.
" John F. laborer, h. 293 Market.
Gilfoil ☞see Guilfoil.
Gilks Chas. E. bartdr. 17 Mulberry, l. 1171 Main.
Gilkyson John, motorman. St.Ry. h.u. 11 Talcott.
Gill Albert, rubberworker, b. 551 Park.
" Alice V. wid. Thomas J. h. 44 Imlay.
" Delia, wid. John, h.u. 116 Hungerford.
" Frank C. assistant bookkeeper at U. S. Bank, 872 Main, b. 44 Imlay.
" James, laborer, b.u. 84 Arch.
" John, laborer, 40 Governor, b. 349 Main.
" Joseph B. printer at Telegram, 12 Central, b.u. 116 Hungerford.
" Louie, helper at 690, b. 551 Park.
" M. H. physician, 151, h. 151 Windsor av.
" Mark B. toolmaker at Popes, b.u. 116 Hung.
Gillen William, clerk at 261 Asy. h. 36 Hicks.
Gilleood John, waiter, 26 State.
Gillespie & Co. roofing, paints, etc. 219 State.
                Horace E. Gillespie.
" Frank B. janitor, b. 80 State.
" George W. h.2u. 49 Governor.
" Horace E. (G. & Co.) b. 275 Asylum.
" Lucia C. dressmaker, 49, b.2u. 49 Governor.
Gillett Albert B. general agent Girard Fire Ins. Co. 744 Main, h. 943 Asylum.
" Albert M. clerk, 37 Church, h. 14 Trinity.
" Arthur L. Rev. instructor, associate prof. at Hfd. Theol. Seminary, b. 1 Wethersfield.
" Cornelia H. wid. Albert J. b.320 Farmington.
" Horace S. h. 1224 Main.
" Lucius L. repairer at Popes, b. 3 Whitman.
" Walter C. molder at A.T. Rickers, 26 Potter, b. 18 Elm.
" William, actor, playwright, h. 49 Forest.
Gillette Chas. H. correspondent at Popes, h. Cone.
" Charles O. manufac. baskets, h. 28 Linden.
" Ellery C. clerk, 350 Windsor av. h. 22 Pratt
" Frank W. mach. 135 Sheldon, b. 17 Suffield.
" Hattie, h. 53 Main.
" Henry C. clerk at 581 Cap. b. 53 Main.
" Henry J. missionary City Missionary Society, 234 Pearl, h. 17 Suffield.
" Mary P. teacher at 2d North school, 249 High, b. 17 Suffield.

Gillette Norman, clerk at Conn. Trust and Safe Deposit Co. 785, b. 53 Main.
" Sarah J. wid. Harrison A. h. 257 High.
Gillick Catherine Mrs. b. 2 Holcomb.
Gilligan Austin, helper at Capitol, h. 36 Flower.
" James, helper at 142 Russ, h. 16 Putnam.
" James M. enameler at Popes, b. 421 Broad.
" John, foreman 302 Asylum, b. 87 High.
" Robert, elevatorer, Popes, b. 421 Broad.
" Robert, Jr. assmbler at Popes, b. 421 Broad.
" Thomas, car inspector, h. 90 Pleasant.
" Thomas, fireman, h. 1060 Broad.
Gilliland Caroline A.attendant at 30 Washington.
" Edward J. carpenter, h. 44 Liberty.
" John T. deliv.clerk at 745 Main, h.u. 13 John.
" Robert T. sawyer at 26 Potter, h. 27 John.
" William M. dropforg. 142 Russ, h. 203 Maple.
Gillis Jas. ship carptr. 285 State, b.u. 61 Potter.
" John, laborer at 20 South Hudson.
Gillum Elizabeth H. h. 6 Charter Oak pl.
" Ellen H. wid. George S. h. 63 Lafayette.
" Frederick G. bookpublisher, b. 6 C.O.pl.
" William, b. 36 Jefferson.
GILMAN GEO. H. (Hungerford, Hyde, Joslyn & G.) attorney at law, 49 Pearl, h. 63 Lafayette.        See page 488.
" Jacob, tailor at 392 Main, h. 40 Windsor.
" Julius S. h. 5 Morris.
" Michael, clothing, 160, h. 160 Front.
" Rebecca Mrs. b. 2 Holcomb.
Gilmartin Daniel J. steamfitter, 164 State, h. 65 Glendale.
" James, laborer, b. 12 Center.
" John, harnessm. 1148 Mn. h. 110 Windsor.
" Joseph V. machinist, h.3u. 212 Sheldon.
" Thomas, helper at N.Y.R. b.u. 118 Portland.
Gilmore Alex, patternm. 1 Flow. b. Rocky Hill t.
" David A. clerk at Brown, Thomson & Co. 942 Main, b. New Britain t.
" Frank J. mach. hand. 40 Gov. b. 239 Martin.
" John, hodcarrier, h.r. 60 Woodbine.
" John J. h. 25 Talcott.
" M. J. broommaker, 336, b. 336 Wethersfield.
" Nellie, writer, b. 284 Asylum, rm. 33.
" William H. trav. salesm. Smith, Northam & Co. 129 State, h. Springfield, Mass.
Gilmour John, (Kinberg & G.) h. 46 Harrison.
Gilnack Martin, mach. at N.Y.R. h. 242 Martin.
Gilpin John E. machinist, h.u. 130 Ann.
" Joseph H. clerk at 223, b. 815 Asylum.
Gilson James W. salesm. 690 Park, b. 25 Girard.
Gilstein Isaac, watchm. 956 Main, h. 11 North.
" Jacob, soda water, 215 Front, h. 53 Pleasant.
Gimbert Bessie, nurse, 171 Putnam.
Ginger Aram, peddler, h.3u. 213 Front.
Gingras Alfred, carpenter at N.Y.R. h. 4 Amity.
" Joseph A. rubberw. 690 Park, b. 4 Amity.
Ginsberg Louis, mach. at 388 Cap. b. 276 Market.
" Samuel, peddler, b.u. 130 Windsor.
" Solomon, machinist at 1, h. 26 Flower.
Ginsburg Samuel, screwm. h.u 57 Hawthorn.
Gipson Andrew J. janitor, 80 Pearl, l. 104 Church.
Gipstein Harry G. barber, 615 Cap. h.86 Pleasant.
" Peter, bottler at 198 Front, b. 42 North.
" Sam, barber, h. 86 Pleasant.

Girard David, agent at 721 Main, b. 41 Asylum.
" Delia, wid. William F. h. 229 Pearl.
" Dennis, ostler at 19, b. 19 Buckingham.
" Edmund, painter, 227, b. 229 Pearl.
" Frank J. rubberw. 690 Park, h. New Britain.
" Louis, carpenter, h.u. 48 Sheldon.
" William F. Jr. (*Francis & Co.*) 859 Main, b. 230 High.
Girdwood Florence A. matron at Watkinson Farm School, Bloomfield.
Giszewsky Annie, wid. George, prop. German Republic house, 163 Front.
" George, b. 163 Front.
Gitelson Morris, clerk at 76 Tru. b. 37 Chapel.
Gito Tony, cigarmaker, 88 State, h. 198 Front.
Given Catharine, wid. James, h. 22 Talcott.
" Frank P. printer at 49 Pearl, h.u. 20 Talcott.
" James E. hackdriv. r. 87 High, b. 22 Talcott.
" James J. clerk at 179 State, h. 127 Front.
" John, b. 127 Front.
" John F. Jr. engir. at 926, l.3u. 926 Main, rm.14.
" Thomas J. printer at 252 Pearl, b. 22 Talcott.
" Robert J. blacks. at 5 Mech. h. 20 Talcott.
Givens Bridget Mrs. b. 16 Atlantic.
Gladden Chas. W. floorwalker at Brown, Thomson & Co. 942 Main, h.u. 27 Mather.
Gladding Albert, painter, b. 1034 Main.
" Alice E. teacher, N.W. school, b.u. 9 Belden.
" Arthur, asst. engineer, 98 Wells, h. E.H.t.
GLADDING CHARLES F. *councilman 9th ward;* with Phœnix Mutual Life Ins. Co. 49 Pearl, h. 36 Huntington.
GLADDING CURTIS P. (*S. Goodrich & Co.*) apothecaries, 1203 Main, h.u. 2 Belden.
           *See page 164.*
" Fred. W. mech. at Popes, h.u. 82 Franklin.
" Helen M. teacher, b. 36 Huntington.
" Lewis, driver at 4 Central, h.u. 17 Wells.
" Timothy, market gardener, h. 23 Harrison.
" Wilbur M. mach. at 1 Flower, b. 1223 Main.

ELLEN HAMMOND GLADWIN, Physician. Office, 705 Asylum avenue.
Hours—8.30 to 9.30 A.M.,
2 to 4 P.M.
Telephone 303.

Gladwin Ellen Ham'nd, physician, 705, h.705 Asy.
" Frank, painter, b. 246 Jefferson.
" H. P. machinist at 13 Central.
" L. A. Mrs. State instructor Rebecca Lodges, h. 868 Broad.
" Randolph P. bottler, 7 Brady, h. 868 Broad.
" Russell Selden, investments, 49 Pearl, h. 1566 Broad.
" Sidney M. at Dwight, Skinner & Co. 207 Allyn, h. 705 Asylum.
Glaeser George, upholsterer at 262 Allyn, b. 36 Church.
Glanville Richard H. filer at Popes, b.u. 34 Hicks.
Glanz Benjamin, peddler, h. 35 North.
" Harry, screwm. at 476 Capitol, b. 35 North.
" Joseph, assembler, b.u. 35 North.
" Morris, screwm. at 476 Capitol, h. 44 North.
Glaser Robert, cashier, Columbia Brewing Co. 245 Windsor, h. 107 Bellevue.

Glass Sarah Mrs. h.3u. 46 North.
Glasser Benjamin M. cigarm. l. 115 Trumbull.
Glasson Mary F. clerk, b. 2 Franklin pl.
Glasteter Emil, cook, h.2u. 6 Mays.
" Louis, chef, 365 Allyn, h. 29 Chestnut.
Glater Morris, blacksm. r. 46, h.u. 46 North.
Glazebrook Haslett McK. student at Trinity, 34 Jarvis hall, Summit.
Glazier A. Judson, real estate, 8 State, h.3 Sumner.
" Charles H. salesman, 304 Asy. h. 26 Chapel.
" Charles M. ins. clerk, 197 Asy. b.67 Edwards.
" Clara M. wid. Isaac, h. 67 Edwards.
" Daniel F. h. 3 Sumner.
" Daniel J. at Hartford Fire Ins. Co. 53 Trumbull, b. 57 Farmington.
" Edward L. salesm. 1115 Main, b.u.26 Belden.
" Elisha J. traveling salesman, l. 739 Asylum.
" Fred. D. salesm. at 47 Market, b. 67 Edwards.
" G. wid. Harrison A. h. 61 Prospect.
" H. Viola, kindergarten teacher at Arsenal school, b. E.H.t.
" Ida, at 26 High, b. 58 Church.
" Luther C. 42 Union pl. h. 212 Collins.
" Mary C. l. 4 Atwood.
" Myron L. clerk, 1 So. Ann, h.u. 26 Belden.
" Nellie E. wid. Harry, h.2u. 33 Bellevue.
" Phœbe, wid. Carlos, b. 212 Collins.
" Robert C. teller Charter Oak National Bank, 124 Asylum, b. 67 Edwards.
Gleason Alonzo A. teamster, 335 Sheldon, h. 25 Morris.
" Ann L. Mrs. h.u. 236 Windsor av.
" Dennis Rev. pastor Italian Catholic church, b. 82 Church.
" Edward, at 24 Mechanic, b. 125 Barbour.
" Edward H. at St.Ry. b. 201 Front.
" Edward N.cigarst.222 Asy.b.r. 180 Barbour.
" Isaac C. inspect. at Popes, h.u. 69 Allen pl.
" Joseph, porter at 225 State, h. 267 Front.
" Kate, wid. Thomas, h. 226 Jefferson.
" Lena, wid. John, h. 14 Chapel.
" Martha W. wid. F. L. b. 12 Willard.
" Michael, laborer, l. 148 Market.
" Lillian E. wid. Chauncey W. h. 50 Albany
" Newton W.manag. at 222Asy.h.125 Barbour.
" Patrick, coachman, 43 Pro. h. 20 Atheneum.
" Patrick, helper at 135 Shel. b.3u. 113 Maple.
" Thomas, lineman, 266 Pearl, h. 64 Windsor.
" Thomas, tinner at 16 Mulberry, h. 201 Front.
" Timothy, coachman, 570, b. 521 Windsor av.
" Timothy, farmer, b. 11 Westland.
Glegl Frank, driver 490 Windsor av. h. 8 Warren.
Glen Christine F. teacher Ch. O.sch.b.56 Seymour.
" Samuel, painter at 1062 Mn. h. 200 Allyn.
Glennon James, laborer, b.u. 69 Pleasant.
Glessman John J. C. mach. at Colts, l. 54 Capitol.
Gleszer Samuel, (*G. & Seltzer,*) h. 489 Windsor av.
" & Seltzer, real estate, 2 State.
    Samuel Gleszer.        Bernard Seltzer.
Gleisman Geo. A. mach. at 1 Flow. b. 1330 Broad.
Globe John, painter, h.2u. 165 Front.
**GLOBE PUBLISHING CO.** Sunday Globe, 25 Asylum.     *See page 465.*
Glodell Leroy M. electrician at St.Ry. 70 Commerce, b.u. 15 South Prospect.

**If you have anything to Sell, Advertise it in The Post.**

Gloe John, painter at 34 Temple, h. Front.
Gloscio Mike, bootblack, 627 Main, h. 190 Front.
" & Romont, bootblack, 627 Main.
 Mike Gloscio.   James Romont.
Gloster Margaret, wid. Patrick, h.2u. 51 Portland.
" Margaret, b.2u. 51 Portland.
" Mary, dressmaker, b.2u. 51 Portland.
" Mathew, laborer, b.2u. 81 Sheldon.
Glotzer Samuel J.(*Bassevitch & G.*)h.81 Pleasant.
Glover Leonard M. traveling salesman, 38 Ann, h. 14 Westland.
" Thomas, toolm. at 142 Russ, h. 65 Hudson.
Glueck Bernard, carpenter, h.2u. 294 Park.
Gluick Adolph, bkkpr. 189 State, h. 14 Morris.
Glynn Elizabeth, boardinghouse, 10 Arch.
" Ellen, h. 517 Main, rm. 11.
" James, engineer, 690 Asylum, h. 82 Walnut.
" James, laborer, h.u. 10 Ellery.
" James F. laborer at 70, b. 98 Huyshope.
" Jennie A. dressmaker, b. 82 Walnut.
" John, driver at 356 Main, b.r. 27 John.
" John, enginedriver, No. 6, h. 98 Huyshope.
" John, teamster at 232, h.u. 16½ Governor.
" John F. grocery, 144, h.u. 99 Maple.
" John F. teamster, b. 78 Martin.
" Michael, laborer, h.u. 32 Flower.
" Nellie S. laundress, 351 Asy. b. 82 Walnut.
" P. deckhand str. Hartford, 285 State.
" Patrick, laborer, h.u. 138 Lawrence.
" Richard A. machinist at 1 Flower, b. 185 Lawrence.
" Thomas, painter at N.Y.R. 450 Asylum.
" Thomas, roofer, l. 24 Gold.
" William, laborer, h. 26 Howard.
" William, plumber, b.u. 27 John.
" Zitam, inspector at 70, b. 98 Huyshope.
" ☞ *see also* Glenn.
Gobellman Iman, bottler, h. 488 Main, rm. 3.
Gober Gus A. machinist, h.2u. 20 Sheldon.
" Gus F. clerk at Brown, Thomson & Co. 942 Main, h. 27 Sheldon.
Gobernman Ise, bottler, r. 198 Front.
Gocher W. H. sec'y National Trotting Association, 650 Main, h. 209 Woodland.
Godbee Jas. Edgar, sec'y Hfd. Woven Wire Mattress Co. 618 Cap. h. 223 Asylum, rm. 12.
Godbout Arthur W. celluloid worker at Popes, b. 303 Park.
" Francis, carpenter, h. 51 Windsor.
" Fred. Jos. tinner at 291 Asy. b. 51 Windsor.
" Louis J. saddler at 8 Sig. b. 51 Windsor.
" Louise M. clerk at 921 Main, b. 51 Windsor.
" Prosper J. burnisher, l. 51 Windsor.
" Ulric B. bartdr. at 997 Main, h. 20 Goodwin.

Goddard Arthur P. printer at 175 Pl.b. 122 **Heath.**
" Chas. P. asst. forem. 1 Flower, l. 10 **Garden.**
" Frank E. at Travelers Ins. Co. 56 **Prospect,** h. 144 Woodland.
Godfrey Annie L. h.u. 9 Kinsley.
" Margaret, wid. Michael, h.u. 30 **Flower.**
" Patrick, laborer, h. 1443 Broad.
" Thomas, laborer, h. 19 Howard.
Godkin James H. compositor at Hartford **Post,** 23 Asylum, h.u. 6 Goodman.
Godman Mary, dressmaker, l.u. 101 **Main.**
Godreau Bertha M. organist, b. 364 Park.
Godwin Martin, laborer, h.u.r. 23 Spruce.
Goebel Charles, at 63 Woodbine, h. 42 **Laurel.**
" Fred. Jr. & Co. cafe, 358 Asylum.
 Fred Goebel, Jr.  Charles L. Herrmann.
" Fred. Jr.(*F.G., Jr. & Co.*)h. 195 **Evergreen.**
" Frederick, h. 195 Evergreen.
" J. Chas. mach. at 83 Woodbine, h. 42 **Laurel.**
" William B. temperer at Colts, b. 35 **Front.**
Goepel Louis, at 7 American, b. 206 **Windsor.**
Goetz August F. machinist at 53 Vernon, h.u. 5 South Hudson.
" Caroline Mrs. b. 4 Francis.
" Frederick, baker, h.u. 6 Elliott.
" Fritz, baker at 53 Ann, b. 187 **Wethersfield.**
" John E. h.u. 92 Hudson.
" Sigmund, filer at Colts, h. Hockanum v.
Goff Angeline D. wid. Hatsell S. dressmaker, h.2u. 384 Main.
" Cordelia Mrs. b. 36 Jefferson.
" Harry H. b.2u. 884 Main.
" Maria, wid. Daniel, h. 191 Park.
Goff EDWARD F. vice pres. & sec'y Neal, Goff & Inglis Co. 980–984 Main, b. 191 **Park.**
       *See page 498.*
" Leroy M. forem. at Pope Tube Co.b. 1281 **Mn.**
" Max, tailor at 881 Main, b. 296 **Pearl.**
Gogarty John F. clerk for L. E. **Stanton,** 16 State, b. Windsor Locks t.
Goggins David, laborer, b.u. 71 Windsor.
" J. S. & Co. saloon, 71 Windsor.*
" Jas. J. assistant eng. at 98 Wells, b. 74 Green.
" James S. (*J. S. G. & Co.*) h.u. 71 Windsor.
" John, laborer, h. 44 Pleasant.
" Michael, porter at 26 State, b. 74 Green.
" Patrick, laborer, h.u. 104 Windsor.
Gohan Michael, laborer at Popes, b. 4½ Hung.
Gohring Irvin, assembler, 556 Cap. b.2u. 24 Bab.
Gold Hyman, peddler, h.2u. 19 North.
Goldberg David, clerk at 67 Morgan, b. 11 North.
" David, at 28 Market, h. 28 North.
" Harris, h. 881 Park.
" Ike E. bookkeeper, b. 11 North.
" Jacob, peddler, h.u. 160 Front.
" Kolman, grain, etc. 67 Morgan, **feed,** 22, grocery, 24, h. 11 North.
" Lewis, shoemaker, h. 30 Kilbourn.
" Max, clerk at 26, b. 11 North.
" Michael, clerk at 69 Morgan, b. 11 North.
" Michael Mrs. 25 North.
" Minnie, notions, 881, h. 881 Park.
" Nathan, machinist at 1 Flower, confectionery, 22, h. 22 Howard.
" William, clerk at 1118, b. 1118 Main.

Golden Catherine L. wid. Jas. b. 18 Francis.
" Catherine P. b. 37 Canton.
" Edward, carpenter, 352, b. 354 Albany.
" Edward T. operator at Catholic Transcript, 704 Main.
" Elizabeth F. bookkeeper, b. 37 Canton.
" Frank A. repairer at Popes, b. 37 Canton.
" Frank H. h. 99 Maple.
" Henry, painter, 352, b. 354 Albany.
" James, apprentice, 857 Main, b. 34 Madison.
" John, blacksmith, 352, h. 354 Albany.
" John, h.u. 80 Grove.
" John, teamster, h. u. 21 Kilbourn.
" John J. policeman, h. 34 Madison.
" Lewis, peddler, h.2u. 30 Kilbourn.
" Mary, wid. James, h.2u. 40 So. Prospect.
" Mary, wid. Patrick, h.2u. 33½ Front.
" Michael, watchman at Phœnix Mutual Life Ins. Co. 49 Pearl, h. 37 Canton.
" Michael J. polisher, b.2u. 40 South Prospect.
" Patrick, coachman, h. 20 Ely.
" Peter J. druggist in Bristol, b. 34 Madison.
" Stanley, carpenter, b.u. 110 Hopkins.
" Thomas F. mech. at 581 Cap. b. 33½ Front.
" Wolf, tailor, h.u. 46 North.
" Thomas, filer at 581 Capitol, h. 5 Fairfield.
Goldenberg Israel,carptr.builder,h.u.24 Kennedy.
" Joseph, h. 38 Congress.
" Joseph, drygoods, 30, h.u. 30 Pleasant.
Goldenblum Emma, cashier at 58 Trumbull, b.2u. 1193 Main.
" Herman R. traveling salesman at 908 Main, h. 76 Edwards.
Goldenthal David, h. 11 Morgan.
" Julius, at 956 Main, b. 15 Affleck.
" Moses, tinner, 1192 Main, h. 15 Affleck.
Goldfarce Morris F. peddler, b. 30 Kilbourn.
Goldfer Harris, shoemaker, 244, h. 244 Front.
Goldfine Davis, harnessmaker, h.u. 79 Avon.
" Jacob, clerk, 137, b. 147 Front.
" Jacob, tailor at 104 Asy. h.3u. 15 Morgan.
Golding Felix D. helper, 266 Pearl, b.55 Hudson.
" Katherine R. clerk at Brown, Thomson & Co. 942 Main, b. 80 Grove.
Goldman Lewis, shoemaker, 145, h. 145 Front.
Goldschmidt Herman (H. G. & Son.) h. 18 Ple.
" H.& Son, dry and fancy goods, 52–54 Ann.
Herman Goldschmidt. Louis S. Goldschmidt.
" Louis S. (H. G. & Son.) b. 18 Pleasant.
Goldsmith Bertha, clerk at 921 Main, b. 48 Bkm.
" Etta, designer, 908 Mn. b. 48 Buckingham.
" Henry J. trav. salesman, b. 48 Buckingham.
" Isaac, b. 48 Buckingham.
" Lizur, h. 48 Buckingham.
" Pauline P. clerk, 908 Mn. b. 48 Buckingham.
Goldson James, mach. at N.Y.R. h. New Park.
Goldstein Benj. J. dancing teacher, 759 Main, h. 209 Front.
" Fanny Mrs. bakery 216, h.u. 209 Front.
" Gus. grocer, 237 Park, h. 47 Hungerford.
GOLDSTEIN HENRY, councilman 1st ward, market, 218 Sheldon, h.u. 29 Woodbridge.
" Ike, tailor, b. c. Morgan & Front.
" Max, barber, 281 Main, h. 85 Seymour.
" Moriss, peddler, h.u. 37 North.

Goldstein Morris, (Simon, Ragovin & Co.) h.2u. 255 Market.
" Samuel, baker at 46 North, h. 86 Pleasant.
" Simon, shoem. 359 Asylum, h. 306 Market.
" Solomon, baker, h. 209 Front.
Goligian Sarkis, (Hartford Woodyard Co.) b. 125 Charter Oak.
Gona Stephen, helper, 26 Potter, b. 34 S.Pro.
Goncas Ernest, carpenter, b.3u. 263 Main.
Gonnella George, time clerk at N.E.R. b. E.H.t.
Gonyon William, driver at 1214, b. 1210 Main.
Gomond J. W. photographer, h. 14 Church, rm. 11.
Gompf Effie S. copyist, b. 19 Beach.
" Emma J. wid. W. S. proofreader at Hfd. Courant, 66 State, b. 17 Haynes, rm. 104.
" Willard C. stenographer at Connecticut Fire Ins. Co. 51 Prospect, h. 19 Beach.
Good James H. mach. at 1 Flower, b. 64 Russ.
" John, nickelplater at Popes, h. 95 Sheldon.
Goodacre Arthur S. (G.Bros.) h.u. 72 Seymour.
" Bros. cigar manufacturers, 738 Main.
Arthur S. Goodacre. Charles E. Goodacre
" Charles E. (G. Bros.) b. 72 Seymour.
" E. P. cigarmaker, b.u. 72 Seymour.
" Francis, bartender, 738 Main, h. 67 Elm.
" James, cigarmaker, h.u. 72 Seymour.
" William H. cigarm. at 104 Asy. h. W.H.t.
" Wm. H. saloon, 738 Main, h. 67 Elm.
Goodale Burton, clerk at 372 Asy. l. 30 Spring.
" Carolyn L. stenog. at Popes, b. 38 West.
" Edward W. box clerk, P.O. h.u. 329 Capitol.
" Elizur H. real estate, 124, h. 124 Market.
" & Frink, restaurant, 253 Asylum.
William N. Goodale. Charles D. Frink.
" H. A. b. 329 Capitol.
" Hubert D. student at Trinity col. b. Suffield t.
" Mary F. wid. Charles N. h. 41 Winthrop.
" Toote, h. 46 Temple.
" William N. (G.& Frink,) h.u. 51 Asylum.
Goodbery John,dropf.at 142 Russ,h.70 Lawrence.
Goodchilds Oliver A. bartender at 314 Asylum, h.3u. 28 Church.
Goodell Frances C.wid.Dwight G. h. 109 Wooster.
" Geo.M.boots & shoes,1029 Mn.h.85 Chestnut.
" James R. clerk at 1029 Mn. b. 85 Chestnut.
" Louis A. clerk at Factory Ins. Asso. 95 Pearl, b. 25 Congress,
" Martha Mrs. h. 25 Congress.
" Mary A. artist, b. 25 Congress.
" Mary E. wid. Edmund B. h.u. 17 Goodman.
" Mary F. wid. Alfred, b.u. 8 South Forest.
" Olive L. cook at 171 Putnam.
" Reuben S. draughtsman at 141 Trumbull, b. 25 Congress.
" Silas, h. 25 Congress.
" Wm. H.mach. at Pope Tube Co.h.8 S.Forest.
Goodenough Francilla J. teacher Second North school, b. 58 Church.
Goodnoh Edwin H. mach. 1 Flow. h.u. 20 Francis.
Goodfellow William H. millwright at Pope Tube Co. b. 373 Asylum, rm. 13.
Goodhart Michael, peddler, h.u. 71 Avon.
Goodman Aaron C. h. 834 Asylum.
" Abraham, ladies' tailor, 19, h. 19 Church.
" Adolph, roller at 690 Park, h. 94 Francis.

**As A NEWSPAPER, THE POST LEADS.**

# S. GOODRICH & CO.,

## 1203 and 1205 MAIN ST.
Old Numbers, 605 and 607.

### DRUGGISTS.
*Surgical Instruments and Physicians'*
*Supplies, Trusses, Elastic Stock-*
*ings, Shoulder Braces,*
*and Crutches.*

PRESCRIPTIONS A SPECIALTY.
Best Goods.          Lowest Prices.

Goodman Arthur P. bkker. Farmers & Mechanics
    National Bank, 106 State, h. 1088 Main.
" Don Alonzo, estate of, furniture, 1090 Main.
" Dora, groceries, 85, h. 85 Front.
" Edna M. b. 911 Main, rm. 7.
" Frank, foreman at 1 Flower, h. 45 Oak.
" G. Ray, at Hartford Fire Insurance Co. 53
    Trumbull, b. 45 Oak.
" George, at 17 Albany, b.2u. 1 Goodman.
" Joseph, secretary Bicycle World, 66 State,
    rm. 21, h. 74 Congress.
" Lena Mrs. clerk at 372 Asy. b. 911 Main.
" Max, tailor at 892 Main, b. 122 Windsor.
" Richard J. student at Yale, b. 834 Asylum.
" Samuel, h. 85 Front.
" Wolf, tailor at 892 Main, b. 122 Windsor.
Goodness Edmund, filer at Popes, b. 23 Spring.
Goodrich Alice, nurse at 20 South Hudson.
" Alice G. wid. Stephen, *(S. G. & Co.)* h.
    636 Prospect av.
" Arabella M. Mrs. b. 84 Flower.
GOODRICH ARTHUR L. treas. Hartford Courant
    Co. 66 State, h. 1329 Main. *See page 463.*
GOODRICH CHARLES C. gen. manager The Hart-
    ford & N. Y. Transportation Co. h. 168
    Washington.          *See pages 554, 555.*
" Charles C. merchant, N.Y. h.55 Wethersfield.
" Chas. E. machinist, h. 373 Asylum, rm. 12.
" Chas. N. toolm. at Colts, h. 70 Buckingham.
" Clarence L. draughtsm. 1 Flow. h.u. 197 Jef.
" D. Charles, fitter at 62 Mar. h. 44 Park.
" D. Parsons *(Bayley & G.)* architects, 700
    Main, b. 145 Capitol.
" Dexter T. groceries, h. 43 Windsor.
" Elizur S. pres't Hartford Street Railway
    Co. 115 State, h. 104 Main.
" Frank, burnisher at 62 Mar. h. Meriden t.
" Frank C. compositor at Case, Lockwood &
    Brainard Co. 141 Pearl, h. 126 Retreat.
" Frank H. clerk at Phoenix Mutual Life Ins.
    Co. 49 Pearl, b. 89 Buckingham.
" Geo. H. printer at Hartford Courant, 66 State.
" Georgia, b. 54 Church.
" Harry R. buffer at Wm. Rogers Mfg. Co.
    66 Market, h. Glastonbury t.
" Herbert V. forem. 1 Flower, h. 72 Hopkins.
" Isaac F. carpenter at Pratt & Whitney Co.
    1 Flower, b 373 Asylum.
" J. B. Mrs. nurse, h.u. 16 Belden.
" J. Harry, clerk at Lincoln & Co. 54 Arch,
    b.u. 16 Belden.

Goodrich James B. h.u. 16 Belden.
" James H. supt's clerk at Popes, b. N.B.t.
" James R. general inspector, 53, h. 46 Vernon.
" Jane E. Mrs. b. 36 Jefferson.
" Lucy F. b.u. 16 Belden.
" Luther G. salesm. at Popes, h. Dryden, N.Y.
" Mary A. wid. W. W. h. 98½ Ann.
" Riley F. local freight agent at Hartford &
    N. Y. Trans. Co. 285 State, h. Weth.t.
" Samuel G. b. 57 Farmington.
" Samuel R. piano tuner, 153 Asy. h. Bristol t.
GOODRICH STEPHEN & Co. druggists, 1203
    Main.          *See page 164.*
    Curtis P. Gladding.     Mrs. Alice G. Goodrich.
" Theodore H. chief operator at 6 Central,
    h. 73 Washington.
" W. Wells, artist, novelties, 36 Pratt, h.98½ Ann.
" William S. mail. clerk at P.O. h.u. 63 Market.
Goodridge T. Welles, clerk at Motor Carriage.
    dept. 1 Laurel, b. 149 High.
Goodsell Wm. T. foreman, 8 Sig. h. 39 Lincoln.
Goodwill Chas. A. watchm. 1 Flow. b. 121½ Alb.
" Club, 98 Pratt.
" Henry J. watchman at 1 Flow.h.121½ Albany.
" Justin, policeman, h.2u. 249 Putnam.
Goodwin Alice H. h.u. 375 Main.
" C. B. & Co. boots and shoes, 163 Asylum.
    Clarence B. Goodwin.    Eleasur P. Chapman.
" C. L. & G. R. boots and shoes, 755 Main.
    Charles L. Goodwin.     George R. Goodwin.
" Carolyn A. h. 190 Sigourney.
" Charles A. student at Yale, b.103 Woodland.
" Chas. L. *(C. L. & G.R.)* b. 29 Wethersfield.
" Chas. R. contractor, 555 Cap. h. 45 Green.
" Clarence B. *(C.B.G.&Co.)* h. 49 Sargeant.
" Claude E. foreman at 690, h. 1600 Park.
" Croswell H. horsedealer, h. 15 Bloomfield.
" Effie M. compositor at R. S. Peck & Co. 26
    High, b. Bloomfield t.
" Elizabeth W. b. 56 Winthrop.
" Francis Rev. *(J. J. & F. G.)* 783 Main, room
    5, h. 103 Woodland.
" Francis S. student at Yale, b. 103 Woodland.
" George, at Ætna Life Ins. Co. 650 Main, b.
    Burnside v.
" George A. florist, h. Whiting.
" Geo. E. at Strickland & Shea, 20 Potter,
    h. 15 Seymour.
" George O. packer at Jewell Belting Co.
    15, b. 16 Trumbull.
" George R. *(C.L.&G.R.)* b. 29 Wethersfield.
" Grace A. seamstress, b.u. 23 Canton.
" Harriet B. wid. Edwin O. h. 79 Spring.
" Harriet F. b. 73 Sigourney.
" Harry F. clerk, 310 Park, h.u. 29 Babcock.
" Harry F. contrac. 555 Cap. b. 106 Bluehills.
GOODWIN HENRY H. *(Tucker & G.)* wholesale
    grocers at 8, 10 & 12 Hurlburt, h. 576
    Farmington.          *See page 585.*
" J. J. & F. office, 783 Main, room 5.
    James J. Goodwin.      Rev. Francis Goodwin.
" James J. *(J. J. & F. G.)* 783 Main, room 5,
    *park commissioner,* b. 103 Woodland.
" James L. student, b. 880 Asylum.
" James N. Mrs. *(Fannie)* h. 1400 Main.
" Jeannette, b.u. 281 New Britain.

**Advertise Your Real Estate in THE POST.**

Goodwin John G. coachman, h. 14 Warren.
" Joseph O. secretary, 732 Main, h. E.H.t.
GOODWIN LESTER H. druggist, 852 Main, h. 880 Asylum.  *See page 165.*
" Martin, laborer, h.r. 23 Spruce.
" Mary A. b. 36 Jefferson.
" Mary J. Mrs. h.u. 23 Canton.
" Minnie A. operator, b. 30 Spring.
" Moses A. h. 792 Windsor av.
" Nellie, operator, 247 Pearl, b.41 Hungerford.
" Nelson J. dentist, 753 Main, rm. 1, h. 335 Laurel.
" Richard E. b. 36 Jefferson.
" Wilbur E. (*West End Land Co.*) h. Elm-wood v.
Goothold Isaac, driver, b. 15 Avon.
Gordon A. M. Mrs. h.u. 16 Alden.
" Allan H. at Colts, b.u. 16 Alden.
" Arthur W. optician at 865 Mn. b.u.16 Alden.
" Chas. F. clerk at 446 Asy. h. 99 Huntington.
" E. A. mgr. Conn. Car Service Asso. office Union station, 466 Asylum, h. Boston.
" E. William, carpenter, b.u. 93 Hudson.
" Effie Grace, teacher, b. 30 Lincoln.
" Herbert A. painter, b. 231 Laurel.
" James, carptr. at 155 Ch.O. h. 41 Walnut.
" James Jr. laborer, h. Whiting lane, W.H.t.
" James M. carpenter, h.2u. 277 Main.
" Jennie E. Mrs. b.3u. 36 Church.
" Joseph, engineer at 37, h.u. 32 Wells.
" Mary Mrs. b. 2 Holcomb.
" Michael J. manager at 52, h. 230 Asylum.
" Morris, store, 73 Windsor, h.r. 34 North.
" Peter G. trav. salesman, b. 30 Lincoln.
" Walter N. clerk, 98 Kilbourn, b. 1273 Main.
" William, carpenter, b.u. 93 Hudson.
" William, clerk, b.u. 16 Alden.
" William, forem. at 868 Mn.rm.8,b.u.44 Hicks.
Gordy Wilbur Fisk, principal Second North school, 249 High, h. 104 Gillett.
Gore Joseph, porter at 152 Asylum.
Gorfine David, saddler at 8 Sig. h. 79 Avon.
" Wolf, tailor at 118 Asylum, b. 46 North.
Gorfinkel. ☞ *see Garfinkel.*
Gorham Daniel J. clerk at Lincoln, Seyms & Co. 34 Market, b. 8 Union.
" George A. florist at 5, b. 3 Fairfield.
" John J. currer at 15 Trumbull, h. 8 Union.
Gorie W. G. litho. at 42 Union pl. b. 170 High.
Gorman Annie J. at 1 S.Ann, b.u. 9½ Hamilton.
" Arthur J. b. 38 Park.
" Bridget, wid. Terence, h. 151 Windsor.
" Chas. F. drug clerk at 142 Asy. h. 87 Capitol.
" Clifton W. at Ætna Ins. Co. 666 Main, b. 148 Seymour.
" Eleanor, h.u. 40 Ward.
" James O. saloon, 287 Allyn, h. 255 Asylum.
" James W. sweeper at Colts, h. 74 Vanblock.
" John, laborer, b.u. 151 Windsor.
" John, sexton St. Peter's Church,h.2u. 28 Park.
" Joseph, machinist, h.3u. 38 Park.
" Kate Mrs. b. 2 Holcomb.
" Lizzie, at 252 Pearl, h.2u. 14 Queen.
" Louise, b.2u. 14 Queen.
" Mary E. at 252 Pearl, h.2u. 14 Queen.

**Goodwin's Drug Store.**

OPEN ALL NIGHT.

*The Best Goods and Low Prices.*   L. H. GOODWIN, APOTHECARY.

Cor. MAIN and STATE STS.

Gorman Patrick, b. 2 Holcomb.
" Patrick, laborer, h. 4 Green.
" Patrick O. scourer at Jewell Belting Co. 15 Trumbull, b. 1183 Main.
" Thomas, laborer at 214, b. 214 Woodland.
" William D. mach. 252 Pearl, h. 103 Capitol.
Gorton Alice May, b. 450 Farmington.
" Charles, painter, b.2u. 82 Francis.
" John, painter, b.2u. 82 Francis.
" Joseph O. clerk at Connecticut Gen'l Life Ins. Co. 49 Pearl, h. 450 Farmington.
" L. Bell, b. 785 Asylum.
" Lydia V. wid. Stephen, h. 785 Asylum.
" Maria A. wid. Thomas, h.2u. 82 Francis.
" Mary G. wid. Horace S. h. 450 Farmington.
" Philip G. deputy collector U. S. custom house, 65 State; special agent Ætna Life Ins. Co. 654 Main, b. 450 Farmington.
Goselin Alphonse, carpenter, h.u. 17 Chestnut.
Goslee Earl S. toolmaker at 476 Capitol, b. W.t.
" Henry S. attorney, 877 Main, rm. 3, b. G.t.
" Howard L. toolm. at Popes, b. Windsor t.
Goss Bernard F. clerk, 16 Church, h.2u. 15 Seyms.
" Charles A. waiter, l. 175 Windsor.
" John R. painter, h.u. 138 Madison.
" Jennie L. Mrs. seamstress, h 175 Windsor.
" Julia, wid. Thomas, h. 4 Cedar.
" Margaret, wid. Thomas, h. 175 Lawrence.
Gossel Louis, coppersm. N.Y.R.h.u.32Lawrence.
Gossman John B. lettercarrier, P.O.h. 177 Capen.
" Joseph B. h. 250 Lawrence.
Gothers Delia, b. 17 Eaton.
" James, at 175 Pearl, b.u. 129 Albany.
" John J. saloon, 65, h.u. 65 Sheldon.
" Joseph D. bartender at 65, b.u. 63 Sheldon.
Gotihell Louis, laborer, b. 54 Pleasant.
Gothold Louis, screwm. at 476 Cap. b. 74 Temple.
Gotthold Louis, tobaccoshipper, b. 54 Pleasant.
Gott Henrietta M. wid.Daniel, h.u. 263 Windsor av.
Gotthold Louis, tobaccoshipper, b. 54 Pleasant.
Gouch Hector, brickmaker, b. Windsor av.
Gouge George Louis, clerk, 54 Ann, b. 30 Beach.
" George S. bookbind. 141 Pearl, h. 30 Beach.
Gough Arthur C. letter carrier, h. Franklin, c. Annawan.
" Benjamin R. agent, 811 Main, b. 87 High.
Gould Alice J. Mrs. h. 64 Oxford.
" Arthur F. toolmaker at Popes, b. 101 Ann.
" B. F. b. 113 Windsor av.
" Charles E. clerk, b. 1140 Main.
" Elizabeth E. wid. Thomas S. h. 1140 Main.
" Geo. F. carpenter at 33 Wells, h. 101 Ann.
" Kate, b. 1140 Main.
" Roy S. clerk at Popes, b. 64 Oxford.

**If You Want all the News, Read THE POST.**

Goulet A. barber at 34 Mul. b.u. 167 Asylum.
" Alex. carptr. at N.Y.R. b. 1470½ Broad.
" Edmund, barber, 34 Mul. h.u. 29 West.
" Frank, b. 70 Charter Oak.
" Georgina M. dressm. 721, h. 721 Main, rm. 51.
" Louis Jr. engir. 268 Pro. av. h. 52 Francis.
" Wm. barber at 34 Mulberry, b.u. 167 Asylum.
Goulette Marcel J. F. mach. Colts, b. 70 Ch.O.
Gourlay Jessie R. Mrs. nurse, h.3u. 32 Park.
Gourley Henry, freight clerk, stm. Middletown, 285 State, h. New York.
Gousett John, machinist, h.u. 47 John.
Govan James, saloon, 119, h. 119 Front.
" Thomas, bkkpr. 232 Shel. b. 46 Annawan.
" William G. brazier at 581 Cap. b. 119 Front.
Governor of State of Conn., Lorenzo Cooke, rooms 35–39 State Capitol. h. Winsted t.
**GOVERNOR'S FOOT GUARD HALL,** 159 High. *See page 496.*
" Horse Guard Armory, 460 Main.
Gow George A. salesm. 304 Asy. b. 14 Evergreen.
GOWEN JOSEPH H., Hartford Apron and Towel Supply Co. 49 Market, h. 428 Maple.
Gowdy Charles A. electrician, h. 3 Clark.
" Francis B. operator, Popes, h.u. 32 Sumner.
" H. R. electrical engineer, b.u. 32 Sumner.
" Lorin B. grocery, 1 Whitmore, h. 211 Franklin.
Goyt Emma R. b. 46 John.
" George, h. 46 John.
Grace James J. *(G. Jewelry Co.)* b. 40 Asylum.
" Jewelry Co. 40 Asylum.
" Philip A. motorman, St. Ry. h. 148 Albany.
" R. E. Pomroy Mrs. h. 45 Washington.
Gracy Abraham, dropforger at 142 Russ, h.2u. 46 New Britain.
Gradisky Louis, carpenter, b. 225 Capen.
**GRADISKY L. W. H.** carpenter, builder and jobber; orders promptly attended to; shop 80½ Ann, h. 225 Capen.
Grady Bridget, wid. Wm. h.2u. 32 Front.
" Cornelius, driver, 1411 Mn. h. 133 Mather.
" Cornelius N. printer at Hartford Courant, 66 State, b. 44 Russell.
" David, porter, 77 Charles, h.u. 28 Albany.
" David O. laborer at Popes, b.r. 2 Putnam.
" Dennis, janitor at 95 Pearl, h.u. 63 Front.
" Francis, cigarmaker, h. 47 Annawan.
" James C. porter, 165 Windsor, h. 50 Avon.
" Jas. J. drugclerk at 377 Asy. b. 44 Russell.
" James P. mach. at 110 Com. b. 44 Russell.
" John C. saloon, 147, h. 149 Windsor.
" John J. lab. at State Capitol, h.u. 28 Cedar.
" John J. machinist at 70 Huy. b.2u. 32 Front.
" John J. porter, h. Winter.
" John T. porter, b. Green c. Fairmount.
" Margaret, wid. Cornelius, h.u. 50 Russell.
" Mark, policeman, h. 92 Fairmount.
" Martin, mech. at 581 Capitol, b. 247 Front.
" Mary, b. 47 Annawan.
" Michael, helper, b.u. 50 Russell.
" Michael, teamster, b.r. 61 Front.
" Michael J. bartender, 61, b.2u. 89 Front.
" Michael S. porter, 1123 Main, h. 28 Albauy.
" Patrick, foreman at 165 Win. h. 44 Russell.
" Patrick, helper, 1 Flow. b.u. 29 Commerce.

Graeney Edward, at 581 Capitol, b. 10 Arch.
Graf Adolph, saloon, 36, h. 36 Temple.
" Charles, bartender at 36, b. 36 Temple.
" Charles, watchman at Wm. Rogers Mfg. Co. 66, b. 65 Market.
" Elizabeth, b. 57 Heath.
" Frank, cigarmaker, b. 36 Temple.
" John, filer at 30 Cushman, h. 57 Heath.
Graff Charles, saddler at 8 Sig. b.u. 18 Babcock.
" John, saddler, 8 Sigourney, h.u. 18 Babcock.
" John P. clerk at 358 Asy. h.3u. 18 Babcock.
" Joseph, bakery, 255, h. 255 Park.
" Joseph Jr. policeman, b. 255 Park.
" Joseph P. butcher, b.u. 18 Babcock.
" S. H. M. wid. William, h. 46 Putnam.
" Richard F. h. 118 Madison av.
" William H. clerk at Hartford Life Ins. Co. 252 Asylum, b. 46 Putnam.
Grager Adolph, laborer, P.&R. b. 140 Mather.
Graham Albert H. mach. at 111 Sheldon, h. W.t.
" Alfred S. mach. at 1 Flower, h.u. 220 Park.
" Charles J. assembler, Popes, h.u. 19 Spruce.
" Cyrus R. carpenter at Colts, h. 37 Wadsworth.
" Ellen, wid. Emanuel, b. 18 Fairmount.
" George M. salesman at 40 Elm, h. 164 Wash.
" George R. printer, 45 Pratt, b. 37 Wads.
" George T. clerk at Hansel, Sloan & Co. 886 Main, h. 11 Florence.
" James R. constable, 847, rm. 10, h. 143 Main.
" James T. toolm. Popes, h. 194 Windsor av.
" Jason, grocer, 125 Albany, h. 90 Williams
" John J. h. 14½ Morris.
" Jos. floorwalker, 956 Main, b. 109 Trumbull.
" Julietta, dressmaker, b. 14½ Morris.
" Laura Carrie, h. 17 Haynes. rm. 119.
" Mabel A. nurse, 29, b. 29 Allen pl.
" Malachi, b. 50 John.
" Mary, clerk at 1036 Main, b. 61 Ann.
" Mary, dressmaker, h. 14½ Morris.
" Matthew, clerk at 73, b. 81 Asylum.
" Rebecca N. wid. Donald, b. 220 Park.
" Rosalia I. b. 29 Allen pl.
" Thomas A. engineer, h. 9 Atlantic.
" Thomas B. scourer, 15 Tru. b. 11 Warner.
" W. H. undertaker's asst. 387 Mn. b. 119 Cap.
" William A. city editor Courant, 66 State, b. Sigourney house, 1150 Main.
" Winfield C. stenog. 904, b.u. 904 Mn. rm. 36.
Graml Annie, wid. Henry, dressm. h. 143 Front.
" Thomas, helper, 747 Main, b.u. 143 Front.
Gramophone Mr. the talking machine, 118 Asylum.
Grana Giovanni Dr. h. 70 Morgan.
Grand Army Hall, Cheney building, 926 Mn. rm. 22.
" Union Tea Co., 715 Main, H. L. Metcalfe, manager.
Grandahl John A. shoem. 10 Ch. O. h. 248 Jef.
Graney James, laborer, h. 62 Avon.
" Thomas, clipper, 556 Cap. b. 92 Francis.
Granfield M. J. painter, b. 1153 Main.
Granger Alice L. stenogr. at Conn. Building & Loan Association, b. Bloomfield t.
" Charles W. toolmaker at Popes.
" Edward, farmer, 1016, b. 1016 Windsor av.
" George, carriage painter, 580 Windsor av. b. Fishfry.

**THE POST is a 20th-Century Newspaper.**

Granger W. F. at Travelers Ins. Co. 56 Prospect, b. Bloomfield t.
" William, painter, 580 Windsor av.
Grannigan Frank, helper N.Y.R. h. 8 Huntley pl.
Grannis D. A. baggagem. N.Y.R. h.u. 23 Walnut.
Granniss Cora, milliner, 926, h.2u. 926 Mn. rm.12.
" Susan H. wid. Eri, dressm. 926, b.2u. 926 Main, rm. 12.
Grant Ann Mrs. b. 2 Holcomb.
" Cephas, coachman at 266 Far. h. Asylum.
" Cephas C. farmer, Whiting, W.H.t.
" Charles C. driver, h.u. 96 Wooster.
**GRANT CHARLES L.** wellborer, 22, h. 22 Belden.    *See page 535.*
" David, saddler at 8, b. 45 Sigourney.
" Edwin M. at 46 Ann, l. 284 Asylum, rm. 73.
" Ernest W. clerk, 197 Asylum, b. Rockville t.
" Fred. S. carpenter, h. 256 New Park.
" Fred. Wm. asst. bookkeeper at Popes, b. East Windsor Hill.
" Henry T. salesman, h. 223 Asylum, rm. 28.
" Horace R. clerk, 476 Cap. b. 256 New Park.
" James, helper at St.Ry. 115 State.
" James M. farmer, h. 51 Vine.
" James M. Jr. h. 53 Vine.
" Jenifer, teamster, b. Park n. Prospect.
" John B. laborer, h.r. 34 Sumner.
" Jonas, cabin str. Hartford, 285 State.
" Kate L. wid. Arthur E. h.2u. 24 Hopkins.
" Nellie A., Jewell Pin Co. b.u. 24 Hopkins.
" Nellie J. attendant at 30 Washington.
" Ralph M. lawyer, 847 Main, h. So.Windsor t.
" Richard A. skiver at 15 Tru. h. 29 Linden pl.
" Robert, clerk, 57, b. 57 Farmington.
" Robert J. Jr. clerk, 76 Trumbull, b. S.G.t.
" Thomas, polisher at Popes, b. 54 Eaton.
" Thos. teamster at, b.c.Park, and Prospect av.
" William J. clerk at 579 Main, l. 298 Park.
Grasser Fred W. b.2u. 3 Kilbourn ct.
" Jacob, wirewkr. 618Cap. h.2u. 3 Kilbourn ct.
" Rosa, dressmaker, h.2u. 3 Kilbourn ct.
Grassier Eugene T. mach. 54 Arch, h. 168 Fkn.
" Helen M. b. 168 Franklin.
Grater Fred'k. mach. at Colts, b.u. 5 Vandyke.
Grattan Maria, wid. Thomas, h. 51 Liberty.
" Sarah, wid. John, h.2u. 516 Broad.
Graudy Charles, conductor, St.Ry. b. 80 State.
Grauer Albert, cigarm. at 867 Mn. h.u. 26 Talcott.
" Lena, wid. William, h.u. 26 Talcott.
" Walberg, wid. Albert, h. 53 Madison.
Graul August E. baker, 292, h. 294 Park.
Gravel Esther, wid. Prosper, h. 236 Barbour.
" Felix, brickmaker, b. 236 Barbour.
Gravengaard Christien, helper at 9 Sigourney, h. 109 Laurel.
Graves Ada E. wid. Seth D. b. 638 Asylum.
GRAVES CHAS. E. treasurer Trinity college, 89 Pearl, h. New Haven t.   *See pages* 706, 707.
" DeWitt C. lettercarrier P.O. b. 118 Asylum.
" Edw. G. bkkpr. 160 Windsor, b.118 Collins.
" Edward M. investments, 933 Main, h. 273 Collins.
" Edwin D. (*G.&Robinson,*) 650 Main, rm. 64, State Bridge Commission, b. 101 Kenyon.

Graves Elmer C. butcher, 11, h. 11 Elmer.
" Francis C. supt. envelope department, 252 Pearl, h.u. 52 Wooster.
**GRAVES FRANK E.** druggist, 115 Main, b. 109 Pearl.
" G. A. Mrs. yeast, 22, h. 22 Barbour.
" George A. h. 22 Barbour.
" Joseph A. principal South school, 36 Wadsworth, h. 28 Charter Oak pl.
" Julia A. b. 638 Asylum.
" Lewis E. roller at 690, h. 819 Park.
" Mary J., Christian Scientist, 93, h. 93 Russ.
" Miles W. treasurer State Savings Bank, 39 Pearl, h. 638 Asylum.
" & Robinson, civil engirs. 650 Main, rm. 57.
   Edwin D. Graves.     Halbert G. Robinson.
" Wm. H. toolmaker, 70 Huy. h. 95 Franklin.
Gray Albert M. architect, 756 Mn. b. 815 Asylum.
" Charles A. engineer, 57, b.r. 59 Albany.
" Charles R. mach. 1 Flow. b. 123 Hungerford.
" Clara B. wid. John W. h. 22 Niles.
" Ellen W. Miss, h. 198 Farmington.
" Fred H. clerk at 999 Main.
" George, helper at 48 Ann, b. W.H.t.
" Henry J. enameler at Popes, b. 70 Ward.
" Janet E. teacher Parkville school, b. South Manchester v.
" Jessie L. wid. Robert, h.u. 52 Seymour.
" John, clerk at 885 Main, h.u. 71 Williams.
" John, clerk at 1 Flower, h. 70 Ward.
" John, steamfitter, h. 4 Wadsworth.
" John S. h. 198 Farmington.
" Leonard B. janitor, Popes, h. 96 Madison av.
" Margaret A. wid. Isaac A. h. 292 Sigourney.
" Mary, wid. Neil, h.u. 193 Sisson.
" Philip B. operator at 12 Central, b. 12 Bkm.
" Robert W. h. 22 Niles.
" Telephone Pay Station Co. r. 64 Asylum.
" William, supt. r. 64 Asylum, h. 193 Sisson.
" William D. mach. at 476 Cap. h. 18 Smith.
" William M. carpenter, h. 260 Jefferson.
Grayson Marion C. stenographer at Conn. Fire Ins. Co. 51 Prospect, b. 219 High.
Greaney Michael, laborer, 51 Avon.
" Patrick, laborer, h.u. 99 Windsor.
" Thomas, chipper, h.u. 83 Huyshope.
Great Atlantic and Pacific Tea Co. James T. Morris, manager, 979 Main.
Grebel Gertrude T. clerk, Popes, b. 447 Capitol.
" Paul A. clerk at Popes, h. 447 Capitol.
Greeley Kate S. clerk, 842 Asy. b.u. 23 Affleck.
" William, at 34 Pratt, b. 14 Gold.
" Valentine, laborer, h. 14 Gold.
Green A. M. custodian station A, Capitol av. h. 164 Russ.
" Albert W. janitor at State Capitol, h.u. 45 Wolcott.
" Alfred W. pension and ins. agt. 82 Pearl, city reporter at Courant, h. 161 Seymour.
" Alvin W. mach. at 1 Flower, h. 1395 Main.
" Austin, driver at 46 Ann, b.r. 40 Temple pl.
" & Bauer, manufacturers, 31 Wells
   Henry Green.     John L. Bauer.
" Bert L. dropforger, 142 Russ, b. 243 Law.
" Carl A. tailor, 53 Pratt, h.u. 87 Maple.

**Merchants say it PAYS to Advertise in The Post.**

Green Carolyn N. music teacher, 721, h. 721. Main, rm. 65.
" Charles, janitor Asylum av. Congregational church, h. 146 Capen.
" Charles J. clerk, 215 State, h. S.Windsor t.
" Charles R. mailing clerk at Hartford Courant, 66 State, b. 161 Seymour.
" David I. supt. Charity Organization Society, 57 Trumbull, h. 86 Edwards.
" Dwight, clerk at Hartford Grocery Co. h. 90 Laurel.
" Eliza, assistant matron at 690, b. 690 Asylum.
" Emily, b.2u. 1206 Broad.
" Eva, wid. William, h.2u. 1395 Main.
" Frank I. janitor at Phœnix Mutual Life Ins. Co. 49 Pearl, b. 8 Gold.
" Fred T. clerk, 136, h.3u. 126 Albany.
" Frederick M. bookkeeper at 129 State h. 721 Main, rm. 65.
" Frederick W. foreman at Colts, h. Fairfield.
" George C. foreman at Colts, h. 19 Bkm.
" Geo. H. dropfgr. 142 Russ, b.u. 25 Wolcott.
" Hannah M. Mrs. b. 37 Mather.
" Harry D. student at Trinity college, 32 Jarvis hall, Summit.
" Henry, gardener, 11, l. 11 Charter Oak pl.
" Henry, (Green & B.) h. 50 Ashley.
" Henry R. wireworker at 247 Asy. h. 50 Smith.
" Isaac W. waiter, h. 33½ Harbison.
" James, bartender at 109, b. 109 Trumbull.
" James, cigarmaker, 867 Main, b. 74 Pleasant.
" James, waiter at 80 State, b. 19 Central.
" James E. clerk at Baxter the Decorator, 231 Asylum.
" James W. bookkeeper at Pratt & Whitney Co. 1 Flower, b. 57 Farmington.
" John, fireman N.E.R. b.r. 26 Walnut.
" John, machinist at N.Y.R. b. 27 Spruce.
" John, watchman, b. 209 Hamilton.
" Joseph, cigar store, 355 Main, h. 107 Laurel.
" Laura, b. 13 Walnut.
" Lucinda, wid. Richard, h.u. 100 Walnut.
" Maria, wid. Reuben, b.2u. 1206 Broad.
" Michael, mason, h.u. 180 Front.
" M. Estelle, b. 164 Russ.
" Michael, asst. foreman 1, h.3u. 40 Flower.
" Milton E. helper at N.Y.R. h.3u. 126 Albany.
" Nancy, wid. Joel B. b. 10 Florence.
" Patrick, motorman St.Ry. b.3u. 188 Market.
" Patrick M. mach. at 1 Flower, h. 2 Queen.
" Ralph, janitor at 391 Allyn, b. 45 Wolcott.
" Samuel W. helper, 1204 Main.
" Sarah F. laundress, b. 100 Walnut.
" Thomas S. laborer, h.u.r. 2 Center.
" William, solderer at 66 State, h. 147 Martin.
" William H. janitor at 197 Asylum, h.r. 36 South Prospect.
" William P. at Conn. Mutual Life Ins. Co. 783 Main, b. South Windsor t.
" ☞ see also Greene.
Greenback Jacob, mach. at 1 Flow. h. 34 North.
Greenbaum Amelia, wid. Leopold, h.u. 94 Edwards.
" Fannie, milliner, b.u. 94 Edwards.
" Moses, Corner Pharmacy, 90 Albany, h. 96 Edwards.

Greenberg Abram, gents furnishings, 178 State, h. 33 Windsor.
" Benjamin, screwmkr. 476 Cap. h. 13 Mor.
" David, screwm. at 476 Cap. h.u. 13 Morgan.
" Harry, h. 8 Marsh.
" Jacob, machinist, h.u. 34 North.
" Kune, dry goods, 84, h.2u. 84 Morgan.
" Leon, saloon, 72 Trumbull, h. 13 Weth.
" Louis, h. 82 Windsor.
" M. (A. C. Loveland & Co.) h. 58 Pleasant.
" Meyer (G. & Sigal,) b. 33 Windsor.
" Michael, screwm. 476 Cap. h.u.r. 164 Front.
" & Sigal, barbers, 175 State.
    Mayer Greenberg.    Samuel Sigal.
Greene Arthur H. mach. at 1 Flow. h. 12 Squire.
" Charles B. constable, 750 Main, rm. 14, h. 14 Linden.
" Daniel E. tinner, 4 Ford, h. 112 Hopkins.
" Edmund B. cigarmkr. 597 Mn. h. 28 Martin.
" Edward, at 1 Flower, b. 26 Imlay.
" Eugene H. salesman, b. 278 Windsor av.

**GREENE JACOB H.** real estate and fire insurance, 721 Main, rm. 8, h. 184 Sigourney.    *See page 425.*
" Jacob L. pres't Connecticut Mutual Life Insurance Co. 783 Main. h. 113 Woodland.
" Mary W. musicteacher, 1204, b. 1204 Asy.
" Patrick E. tinner at 4 Ford, b. 112 Hopkins.
" ☞ see also Green.
Greenland Ann Mrs. b. 13 So. Hudson.
" George W. toolmaker, Popes, h.r. 286 Park.
" John, F. b.u. 33 Chapel.
Greenlaw Margaret C. matron, 690, b. 690 Asy.
Greenleaf Mary A. wid. William, clairvoyant, 350, h. 350 Main.
" Sarah, h. 350 Main.
Greeno Margaret, nurse, h. Barnard.
" William, carpenter, b. Barnard.
Greenstein Abraham, ladies tailor, 903, room 4, h. 183 Market.
" Adeline, at 903 Main, rm. 4, h. 183 Market.
" Israel, peddler, h.u.r. 204 Front.

**GREENSTEIN R. A.** ladies tailor, 903, rm. 4, h.u. 183 Market.    *See page 562.*
Greenwald William, gents furnishings, 486 Main, h. 38 South Prospect.
Greenway Robert J. Jr. machinist at 1 Flower, b.u. 104 Hungerford.
Greenwood Felix, blacksm. N.Y.R. h. 25¼ Flow.
" Peter, mechanic at Popes, b. 25¼ Flower.
Greer R. C. mechanl. engir. at Popes, h 155 Ash.
" William, laborer Pope Tube Co. h. 9 Francis.
Gregg Alice L. Mrs.: dressmaker, 165, h. 165 Capen.
" George W. (G. W. G. & Co.) h. 165 Capen.
" George W. Jr. clerk at 2 Un.pl. b. 165 Capen.
" George W. & Co. carriages, 2 Union pl.*
Gregory Chas. patternm. at 54 Arch, b. 54 Brown.
" George H. Sr. joiner, h. 117 Babcock.
" George M. Jr. carpenter, h. 117 Babcock.
" Louis, carpenter, b.u. 34 Wooster.
" Martha, wid. S. W. h.u. 13 Walnut.
" Napoleon, carpenter, h.u. 34 Wooster.
" Wm. T. patternm. at 33 Wells, h. 54 Brown.
Greiner Edward, bricklayer, h.u. 36 Canton.

**GREINER GEORGE F.** painter and decorator, 19, h. 19 East. *See page 520.*
" Napoleon, drop forger at 142 Russ, h.u. 3 Goodman.
Grelish Michael, laborer, h. 45 Albany.
Grennan Ellen, wid. Hugh, h.2u.r. 44 Village.
" James A. printer at Calhoun Printing Co. 29 Union pl. b.u. 74 Avon.
" John J. typesetter, b. 74 Ann.
" Lawrence J. machinist, h. 1089 Main.
" William, carpenter r. 334 Asylum.
Gressor J. woodworker, h. 3 Kilbourn ct.
Greyer Lida, wid. William, b. 62 Willard.
Gribben John, harnessmaker at 8, b.45 Sigourney.
Gribbons Frank H. machinist at 40 Governor, b.u. 95 Hudson.
Grice John H. laborer, b.2u. 14 Gold.
Gridley Ann A. wid. Henry R. h. 21 Annawan.
" Carrie L. teacher South school, 36 Wadsworth, b. 55 Capitol.
" Henry R. real estate and ticket agent, 18 State, b. 21 Annawan.
" John P. night superintendent Adams Express, h. 61 Ward.
" John S. carriageshop, r. 35 Front, h. 50 Barbour.
**GRIEBEL WILLIAM H.** merchant tailor, 56 Pearl, b. 152 Asylum.
Grierson James A. machinist at Pope Tube Co. b. 33 Woodbine.
" Janet S. aligner at 476 Cap. b. 33 Woodbine.
" Margaret, b. 33 Woodbine.
" Peter C. painter, h. 41 Laurel.
" ☞ *see also Grearson.*
Griffeth Charles W. driver engine No. 2, h.2u. r. 35 Pleasant.
Griffin Adolphus, laborer, h. 34 Village.
" Alice Mrs: h. 1 Orchard.
" Bridget Mrs. b. 2 Holcomb.
" Charles E. machinist at 9 Sigourney, b.u. 33 Babcock.
" Chat A. shirts, 863, h.u. 863 Main, rm. 6.
" Dan, helper at 1 Flower. b.u. 101 Sheldon.
" Daniel, laborer, h. 101 Zion.
" Dennis, headwaiter at 98, h.u. 52 Wells.
" Dennis, hodcarrier, h.u. 25 John.
" Duane N. Rev. pastor North M. E. church, h. 411 Windsor av.
" Ellen, at 42 High, h.u. 52 Wells.
" Emanuel, helper, 1 Flower h. 17 Ellsworth.
" George, brazier at Popes, b. 520 Garden.
" George, foreman at 8 Front.
" George F. canvasser, b. 69 Governor.
" J. E. Mrs. h. 22 Hopkins.
" James, laborer at Pope Tube Co. b. 297 Law.
" John, benchman, h.u. 3 Lawrence.
" John, clerk at 629 Main, b. Burnside v.
" John, saloon at 32, h. 12 So. Prospect.
" John, ostler, 20 South Hudson.
" John F. clerk at 376 Asylum, b. Burnside v.
" John H. car inspector, h.u. 19 Goodman pl.
" Julia E. wid. E. L. h. 22 Hopkins.
" Kate, h.2u. 34 South Prospect.
" L. Christine, clerk at Phœnix Mutual Life Ins. Co. 49 Pearl, b. Farmington t.

Griffin M. J. blacksmith, b. 80 State.
" Mary, dressmkr. 86 Pratt, b.u. 52 Wells.
" Michael, b. 2 Holcomb.
" Michael, hodcarrier, h.u. 52 Linden.
" Michael, laborer at P.&R. h.u. 75 Avon.
" Michael, laborer, b.u.r. 11 Bellevue.
" P. H. clerk at 1 Laurel, b. Burnside v.
" Patrick J. clerk at 80, b. 80 State.
" Ralph U. student, b. 625 Asylum.
" Thomas, helper at 54 Arch, h. 27 Walnut.
" Wm. J. clerk at 25 Wells, b. 101 Zion.
" William L. carpenter, h. 9 Winship.
Griffing Robert A. president Ætna Indemnity Co. 650 Main, h. 112 Ann.
Griffith Chas. pool & bilds. 235 Asy. h.u. 6 Queen.
" Job C. h.u. 15 Benton.
" John E. manager at 249 Pearl, h. 40 Ashley
" M. A. clerk at 249 Pearl, b. Bristol t.
" William, harnessmkr. 217 State, b. 52 Bkm.
**GRIFFITH WILLIAM RICHARD** real estate and insurance agent, notary public, 66 State, h. 544 Prospect av.
*See page 427.*
Grigersen Chris, helper at Daniels Mills Co. Bloomfield av., b. Bloomfield av.
Griggs Edward H. orderly at 20 S. Hudson.
" Ellen E. Mrs. cashier, 117 Asy. b. 2 Florence.
" George, driver at 4, b. 4 Huyshope.
" John B. physician, h. 1067 Asylum.
" Sabine E. clerk at Popes, b. 28 Spring.
Grimes John, laborer at 98 Kil. h.3u. 26 Hun.pl.
" Joseph, engineer N.Y.R. h.2u. 62 Flower.
Grimley Ann, wid. John, b.2u. 166 Washington.
" Caroline B. teacher physical culture, 166, h.2u. 166 Washington.
Grimm Henry A. at Dwight Slate Machine Co. b. 1336 Broad.
Grippo Frank A. helper at 15 Trumbull.
Grische Richard, cook at 1098 Mn. h.u.r. 20 Tru.
Griswold Adelaide M. Mrs. stenographer at Popes, h. 223 Asylum.
" Austin F. laborer at Pope Tube Co. b. 91 Madison av.
" Bertha H. teacher at South school, b. South Wethersfield t.
" Charles, at 2 Union pl. h. 95 Huntington.
" Charles, b. 95 Huntington.
" Chas. E. rubberw. at 690 Park, b. 98 Bab.
" Chas. R. drugs, 1129 Mn. h. 197 Collins.
" Clara B. wid. Dennis K. h. 9 Walnut.
" Delos, motorman St.Ry. h. 120 Wooster.
" Edith G. at Travelers Insurance Co. 56 Prospect, b. So. Wethersfield t.
" Edwin B. painter, h. 13 Fairmount.
" Eliza, wid. Caleb, h. 346 Windsor av.
" Elizabeth C. b. 6 Belden.
" Elizabeth F. b. 36 Jefferson.
" Ella A. clerk, b. 58 Church.
" Ellen M. b.2u. 36 Capen.
" Everett C. at Conn. Mutual Life Ins. Co. 783 Main, b. Rocky Hill t.
" Frank C. sup't agencies Conn. General Life Ins. Co. 49 Pearl, h. 95 Huntington.
" Frank W. molder at James L. Howard & Co. 438 Asylum, b. W.H.t.

**THINKING PEOPLE Read The Post Daily.**

**GRISWOLD FREDERICK A.**
manager Northwestern Mutual Life Ins.
Co. 721 Main, rm. 3, h. Wethersfield t.
" Fred'k B. engraver, 29 Un.pl. h. 43 Beacon.
" George G. clerk at 223 Asylum, h. Berlin t.
" George T. stenographer at 149 State, h. 223 Asylum, rm. 117.
" Georgia Miss, b. 88 Retreat.
" Gertrude, b.u. 1164 Main.
**GRISWOLD GILBERT M.,**
D.D.S. dental rooms, 904 Main, rm. 53, h. 241 Laurel.
" Hattie S. Mrs. h.u. 185 Smith.
" Henry S. electrician, b.2u. 48 Prospect.
" Hosmer, grocer, 547 Main, h. 53 Ch.O.
" Howard R. at Phœnix Ins. Co. 64 Pearl, b. 53 Charter Oak.
" Isabella L. b. 6 Belden.
" James B. mach. at 581 Cap. b. Newington t.
" James L. foreman at 581 Cap. h. 38 Putnam.
" Jesse H. mach. at 40 Gov. h.u. 38½ Hudson.
" Jessie D. teacher Parkville school, b. Rocky Hill t.
" John B. carptr. at 556 Capitol, h. W.H.t.
" John B. molder at James L. Howard & Co. 438 Asylum, h. E.H.t.
" John D. clerk at 152 Asylum.
" John H. dry goods, notions and toys, 347 Main, h. 2 Whitman.
" Joseph F. painter at 1106 Main.
" Josephine M. agent at Children's Aid Society, 223 Asylum, room 10, h. W.H.t.
" Julia E. wid. Edwin, h.u. 1145 Main.
" Katherine, at 59½ Trumbull, h. 9 Walnut.
" Lestina, at 247 Pearl, h. 9 Walnut.
" Malcom R. Mrs. h. 185 Smith.
" Mary, wid. Josiah, h. 9 Belden.
" Monroe, dentist, 51, h. 51 Pratt.
" Nettie, b. 43 Vine.
" Oswald, at Pope Tube Co. b. 91 Madison av.

R. S. GRISWOLD, Physician and Surgeon. Office, 44 Church street.
Hours—Until 10 A. M.
1.30 to 3.30 and 7 to 8 P. M.
Sundays 2 to 4 P. M.
Telephone.

Griswold R. S. surgeon U.S.A. h. 44 Church.
" Robert S. at 547 Main, h. 13 Alden.
" Roland E. salesman, b. 6 Belden.
" Samuel A. farmer, h. Fern.
" Sanford A. janitor, h.2u. 48 Prospect.
" Truman, clerk at 56 Pearl, b. 16 Prescott.
" Walter B. bkkr. at 547 Main, b. 53 Ch.O.

Griswold William, at 12 Pratt, h. 206 Asylum.
" William B. toolm. at 581 Cap. b.u. 53 Hung.
" William D. cond. St.Ry. h. 22 Jefferson.
" Wm. S. at Ætna Life Ins. Co. 650 Main, b. Fern, West Hartford t.
" Wolcott L. mach. r. 223 State, h. 16 Preston.
Groeninger Chris, cigarmaker at 867 Main.
Groenke Chas. L. mach. at N.Y.R. h. 203 Fkn.
GROESBECK FREDERICK O. bookkeeper at Neal, Goff & Inglis Co. 980 Main, prop. of Elm Poultry Yards, office, 30, h. 30 Sumner.
" John K. at Hartford Fire Insurance Co. 53 Trumbull, b. 10 Garden.
Grogan Anna M. wid. Frank G. treas. Hartford Telegram Pub. Co. 12 Central, h. The Linden, 427 Main, room 9.
" Bridget, wid. Owen, h.u. 28 Trumbull.
" Gerald, helper at N.Y.R. b. 1350 Broad.
" James J. mech. at Popes, b. 27 Forest.
" John, clerk at 581 Cap. b.u. 28 Trumbull.
" John, farmer, h. 222 Albany.
" John J. mach. at 476 Capitol, b. 27 Forest.
" Owen J. assem. at 581 Cap. b. 28 Trumbull.
" Patrick, laborer, h. 27 Forest.
" Thomas F. machinist, h.u. 265 Main.
" Walter, clerk at 302 Main.
Grohman Bernhard F. watchman at 175 Asylum, b. 30 Alden.
" Carl L. chief draughtsman at Pratt & Whitney Co. 1 Flower, h. 5 May.
Grooll Alois, coppersmith, N.Y.R. h. 32 Lawrence.
Groom James H. salesm. 57 Alb. h. 17 Williams.
Gropp Emilia B. wid. Frederick, b.u. 1 Lawrence.
" Frank, cigarm. at 867 Main, b.u. 1 Lawrence.
" Fred A. h. 38 Grand.
" Richard, driver, b.u. 1 Lawrence.
Grosch Edward H. barber, 789 Main, h. 36 Wdbg.
Gross Adolph, peddler, h. 59 Bellevue.
" Alfred B. clerk at 933 Main, rm. 2, b.u. 5 Goodman.
GROSS CHARLES E. (*Gross, Hyde & Shipman,*) 2 Central, *park commissioner,* h. 840 Asylum. See page 486.
" Charles H. pressm. 252 Pearl, h. 232 Capen.
" Charles W. student at Yale, b. 840 Asylum.
" Edward, bottles and metals, 63–65 Ferry, h.u. 306 Market.
" Ellen Mrs. b. 105 Capitol.

Gross Emory, at and b. hospital farm.
" Flora C. cashier at 921 Main, b. 5 Goodman.
" Henrietta, wid. Frank B. h. 5 Goodman.
GROSS HERMAN, bottles, 198–200 Front, h. 262
   Market. *See page 486.*

**GROSS, HYDE & SHIPMAN,** attorneys at law, 2 Central, room 8.
   *See page 486.*
Charles E. Gross. Wm. Waldo Hyde. Arthur L. Shipman.
Gross Isador, groceries, 209, h. 209 Front.
" Jacob, peddler, h. 71 Avon.
" Jacob, laborer, h. 276 Front.
" Morris, assembler at 556 Cap. h.3u. 79 Avon.
" Morris, peddler, h. 262 Front.
" Otto W. b.u. 5 Goodman.
" Pauline, wid. Charles J. h.u. 19 Church.
" Sam, peddler, b. 71 Avon.
" Selma H. clerk at 941 Main, b. 5 Goodman.
" Simon, clerk at 14 State, b. 264 Front.
" Zahweira, polisher at 556 Cap. h.r. 132 Mar.
Grosvenor Charles W. state treasurer, at State
   Capitol, b. 152 Asylum.
Grou Ellen, wid. John, h. 115 Sigourney.
" George W. h.u. 933 Main, room 24.
" William D. h. 237 Farmington.
" ☞ *see also Grau.*
GROVER LEWIS C. supt. Colts Pat. Fire Arms
   Mfg. Co. h. 23 Wethersfield. *See p. 548.*
" O. F. at Hartford Fire Insurance Co. 53
   Trumbull, b. Middletown t.
" S. Wesley, foreman at 13 Central, b. E.H. t.
Groves Elizabeth, wid. Albert, h.r. 36 So.Prospect.

**GROZIER & MOORE,** contractors and
   builders, Vredendale c. Taylor. *See p. 510.*
James H. Grozier. Robert Moore.
GROZIER JAMES H. (*G. & Moore*) h. 50 Warrenton.
Gruber Jacob, tailor, 293, h. 293 Park.
" Louis, b. 293 Park.
Gruentler Catherine Mrs. h. 25 Morris.
" Edward K. appren. 28 Laurel, b. 25 Morris.
" Henry N. operator at 40 Gov. b. 25 Morris.
Gruet Ellen M. Mrs. h.u. 7 Canton.
" Walter D. at Phœnix Insurance Co. 64
   Pearl, h.u. 7 Canton.
Grumman Wm. E. attendant at 30 Washington.
Grundshaw Ed. J. cigarm. 52 Pratt, h. 157 Capen.
" James, cigarm. 52 Pratt, h.2u. 180 Capen.
Grundt Chas. F. assistant engineer steamer No.
   4, h. 19 Talcott.
Gruninger Fred. tailor, 14, h.u. 14 Goodman.
Guarcio Joseph, laborer, b.u. 33 North.
Gubaty Jacob, screwm. at 476 Cap. b. 20 North.
Gubitz August C. filer at Colts, h. 101 Huyshope.
" Charles, machinist at Colts, b. 57 Dean.
" Fred, mach. at Pope Tube Co. h. 236 Zion.
" Henry J. machinist, b. 101 Huyshope.
" Minnie M. b. 101 Huyshope.
" Otto, filer at Colts, h.2u. 101 Huyshope.
" Richard, filer at Colts, h. 314 Maple.
Gueno William S. carpenter, b. 22 Barnard.
Guerico Luigi D. shoem. at 524 Asy. b. 33 Alb.
Guerra George, h. 49 Morgan.
" Pietro, laborer, h.u. 73 Morgan.
" Sulvon, tailor, 65, h. 65 Pleasant.

Guerriero Luca, barber, 75, h. 75 Morgan.
Guerro Antonio, bartender at 80 Windsor, b.u.
   81 Morgan.
" Bros. saloon, 80 Windsor.
Joseph Guerro. Peter Guerro.
" Joseph (*G. Bros.*) h u. 81 Morgan.
" Peter (*G. Bros.*) h. 12 North.
Guertin Alvis V. mach. at Colts, b. 45 Huyshope.
" Napoleon, carpenter, b. 34 Prospect av.
Guethlein Anton, bartdr. at 605 Mn. h. 47 Shel.
" George, bartender, h.2u. 47 Sheldon.
" Leo F. saloon and restaurant, 33, b. 29 Pearl.
Guett Monroe, supt. at 26 High, b. 55 Walnut.
Guidott C. J. h. 230 Asylum, rm. 8.
Guild Fred. A. carpenter, 690 Park, h.u. 8 James.
" Harry G. rubberw. 690 Park, h. 64 Smith.
" Louis L. clerk, 103 Asy. h.3u. 32 Hopkins.
" Robert, h. 64 Smith.
" Wilbur A. polisher at 40 High, h. 64 Smith.
Guilfoil Annie L. teach. Brown school, b. 33 Elm.
" Frank, machinist at 13 Central, b. 33 Elm.
" Grocery Co. grocers, 193 Asylum.
" James, clerk at 115 Pearl, b. 269 Park.
" John, teamster, 335 Sheldon, b.u. 64 Village.
" John L. printer, b.u. 269 Park.
" John W. bookkeeper at 17, b. 33 Elm.
" Joseph P. secretary and manager, Guilfoil
   Grocery Co. h. 181 Laurel.
" Kate E. teacher at Parkville school, b. 33 Elm.
" Margret, wid. Michael, h. 33 Elm.
" Margaret A. envelopemaker, b. 87 Mather.
" Sarah, clerk at 956 Main, b. 87 Mather.
" Stephen, b. 87 Mather.
" Thomas, expressman, b. 198 High.
" Thomas J. cook at 107 State, l. 204 Asylum.
" William, waiter, l. 1113 Main.
" William E. b. 33 Elm.
" ☞ *see also Gilfoil.*
Guilmartin James, laborer 30 Weth. h.u. 15 Cur.
" John, harnessmaker, h.2u. 110 Windsor.
" Joseph B. mach. at 388 Cap. h. 212 Shel.
" ☞ *see Gilmartin ; Kilmartin.*
Guinan Alice, at 1 So. Ann, b. 16 Wilson.
" Anna C. dressmaker, 22, h.u. 22 Beach.
" Charles F. polisher at Popes, h. 28 Grace.
" Chas. H. blacksmith, b. 16 Wilson.
" Christopher, helper, N.Y.R. h. 1322 Broad.
" Elizabeth, dressmaker, 22, h.u. 22 Beach.
" Elizabeth R. Mrs. h.u. 22 Beach.
" Gerald J. carpenter, h. 28 Seymour.

Guinan Hubert, cooper, h. 350 Front.
" James W. engir. at 581 Cap. h. 82 Ward.
" John, helper at 618 Capitol, h. 162 Sisson.
" John, blacksmith at N.Y.R. h. 16 Wilson.
" John, polisher at Popes, h.u. 25 Hamilton.
" John F. machinist, N.Y.R. b. 16 Wilson.
" John J. wirew. at 618 Cap. b. So. Forest.
" Joseph, carpenter, b. 1322 Broad.
" Joseph E. braizer, 581 Cap. b. 1418 Broad.
" Keron, polisher at Colts, b. 5 Vandyke.
" Lily, at 1 South Ann, b. 16 Wilson.
" Mary, at 690 Park, b.u. 25 Hamilton.
" Mary, at 1 South Ann, b. 16 Wilson.
" Mary E. teacher at 2d North school, 249 High, b.u. 22 Beach.
" Michael J. wirew. at 618 Cap. h. 42 Amity.
" Michael, Sr. lab. at 618 Capitol, h. So. Forest.
" Rose, wid. Patrick, h. 298 Park.
" Thomas, foreman, 618 Capitol, b.1 So. Forest.
" Thomas, tinner, 102 Main, h. 81 Governor.
" Thomas, watchman, Colts, b. 53 Huyshope.
" Thomas, wireworker, 618 Cap. h. So. Forest.
" Wm. F. wireworker, 618 Cap. b. So. Forest.
" ☞ see also Ganyon, Guinion, Guynan.
Guinee Wm. C. assembler at 556 Cap. b. 53 Potter.
Guinen James, engineer N.Y.R. h. 1418 Broad.
Guiney James J. clerk, h. 5 East.
" Kathryn L. stenog. 756 Main, b. 5 East.
" Mary, wid. James, h. 5 East.
Guinion Maggie T. inspector at 70, b.53 Huyshope.
" Mary B. inspector at 70, b. 53 Huyshope.
" Thomas, watchman, Colts, h. 53 Huyshope.
" Wm. E. machinist, b. 53 Huyshope.
Guiwits Fred W. cigarmaker at 867 Main, h.u. 23 Belden.
" Katherine, wid. Uriah, h.u. 23 Belden.
Gullberg Otto, dropf. at 142 Russ, h. 358½ Park.
Gun Chung, laundry, 769, h. 769 Park.
Gundlach E. & Co. jewelers, 20 State.
Mrs. Louis Gundlach.    Emma Gundlach.
" Emma, (E. G. & Co.) b. 212 Laurel.
" Louis, clerk at Hansel, Sloan & Co. 886 Main, b. 212 Laurel.
" Louis Mrs. (E. G. & Co.) h. 212 Laurel.
Gundry Chas. E. bkkpr. 1 Laurel, h. 10 Imlay.
Gunkel John C. h. 240 New Britain.
" Louis, screwm. 476 Cap. b. 240 New Britain.
Gunn Charles A. foreman at Pratt & Whitney Co. 388 Capitol, h.u. 54 Retreat.
" James H. bookkeeper at R. Ballerstein & Co. 908 Main, h. E.H.t.
" Thomas F. clerk at 742 Main, b. 23 Bellevue.
" Thomas H. mach. at 388 Cap. b. 54 Retreat.
" William F. lieutenant police, 38 Kinsley, h. 83 Maple.
Gunning Chas. J. plumber, b. 103 Babcock.
" Daniel, mechanic at 599 Main, h. 164 Ward.
" Daniel, plumber, b. 103 Babcock.
" Ellen Mrs. b. 2 Holcomb.
" James W. medical student in N.Y. b. 9 Zion.
" John, mechanic, h.2u. 1062 Broad.
" John, superintendent stone pits, h. 9 Zion.
" Michael, porter at Brown, Thomson & Co. 942 Main, h.u. 1060 Broad.
" Michael L. barber at 415 Main, h. 15 Park.

Gunning Sarah A. dressmaker, 9, b. 9 Zion.
" Thomas, nightwatchman at Mrs. Colts, 30 Wethersfield, h. 103 Babcock.
" Thomas J. police, h. 5 Zion.
" Thomas J. Jr. plumber, b. 103 Babcock.
" William J. b. 2 Holcomb.
Gunshanan James, city express, 19, h. 19 Affleck.
" James P. printer at 857 Main, b. 19 Affleck.
" John, clerk Catholic Transcript, b.17 Affleck.
" John F. baseballist, h. 17 Affleck.
" Joseph A. expressman, b. 19 Affleck.
" Maggie M. b. 19 Affleck.
" Mich. H. investigator, 182 Pearl, b.19 Affleck.
" Terrence M. marketman, 319 Asylum, h. 164 Pearl.
" Thos. W. deputy collector, U. S. inspector, 65 State, h. 85 Madison.
Gurley Stacey, cook at 296 Asy. h.u. 290 Pearl.
Gurney E. T. driver at 126, l. 124 Church.
Gurra ☞ see also Guerra.
Guset John P. helper at 185 Sheldon, h. 47 John.
Gustafsen Christina Mrs. h.u. 53 Webster.
" Elon W. carpenter, h. 49 Webster.
" Frank Hilgo, joiner, b.u. 53 Webster.
Gustafson Charles, gardener, h. 938 Park.
" Chas. machinist at 1 Flower, h. 34 Cedar.
" Chas. ostler, 51, b. 51 Farmington.
" Chas. W. mach. 1 Flower, h. 37 Hungerford.
Gustayson Gustav, screwmaker at 476 Capitol, h.u. 23 Glendale.
Gutfleish Sam, peddler, b.u. 292 Market.
Gutharz Philip, agent, h.u. 34 Avon.
Guthrie Michael, helper, h. 47 Spruce.
Guttman Rose, teacher of drawing in public schools, b. 106 Ann.
Guy Albert Rev. b. 90 Edwards.
Gydesen Carl F. salesm. at 1 Flow. b. 25 Belmont.
" Hans C. mach. at 1 Flower, b. 25 Belmont.
" Hans Christian, woodyard, 25, h. 25 Belmont.
" Morris A. mach. at 476 Cap. b. 25 Belmont.
" Peter, toolmaker at 476 Cap. b. 25 Belmont.
HAAS Barney, bricklayer, h.u. 164 Front.
" Benjamin L. salesm. 150 State, b. 5 Florence.
" Felix S. salesman, 150 State, h. 18 Whitney.
" John, saddler at 8 Sig. b. 401 Capitol.
" Louis B. charity commissioner, leaf tobacco, 150 State, h. 5 Florence.
" Wm. F.(Standard R.& C.R.Co.) h.u.12 Arch.
" Wm. P. salesm. at 150 State, b. 5 Florence.
" ☞ see also Hass.
Haaser Joseph, tailor, 19, h. 19 Goodwin.
Habel Anton, machinist, h. 73 Hamilton.
" Paul, driver, h. 54 Bond.
Habenstein Edw'd, caterer, 53 Ann, h. 187 Weth.
" Edward Jr. bkkpr. at 53 Ann, b. 187 Weth.
Hack Fred'k H. packer, 252 Pearl, h. 13 Warner.
Hackett John J. assembler, Popes, b. E.H.t.
" Mary, wid. Peter, b. 22 Avon.
" Michael, stonecutter at 283 Shel. h. E.H.t.
" Minnie A. dressmaker, 88, h. 88 Ch. Oak.
" Morris, laborer, h. 88 Charter Oak.
" Thos. J. saloon, 269, h. 271 Main.
Hadden David, assembler at Popes, b. 80 Heath.
" Winifred F. helper at 690 Park, b. 80 Heath.

Hadley Charles L. mechanical engineer at Popes, h. 462 Farmington.
" E. M. at 501 Asylum, b. 149 High.
" O. C. assistant matron, 76, h. 76 Temple.
Hadlock George W. toolmaker at 142 Russ, h. 56 Lincoln.
Hadron R. motorman St.Ry. h. 40 Retreat.
Haenagen Julius, pressman, 252 Pl. b. 59 Madison.
Hafey Michael J. foreman at Lincoln & Co. Phœnix Iron Works,54 Arch, h. Wethersfield t.
Haff Isaac, boots & shoes, 146 State, h. 136 Grove.
" Joel P. toolmaker at 70 Huy. h. 215 Franklin.
Haffey Bridget, h.u. 27 John.
Haffke Emil G. woodturner at 20 Potter, h. 53 Woodbridge.
" Jennie, wid. Frederick, h. 53 Woodbridge.
Hagan Edward, h. Gilbert, c. Bluehills.
" Mary, h.u. 10 Chapel.
Hagarty Frank A. clerk, 70 Huy. b. 57 Franklin.
" James P. mach. at 83 Woodbine, h. 57 Fkn.
" Joseph, grocer, 75 Front, h.u. 57 Franklin.
" Patrick, switchman, h. 57 Franklin.
" Thomas, clerk at 75 Front, b. 57 Franklin.
" ☞ see also Haggerty.
Hagedorn Fred. J. spinner at James L. Howard & Co., 438 Asylum, b. Wapping v.
Hagelin Andrus, rubberw. h.2u. 177 Lawrence.
" John F. inspector, 581 Cap. b. 169 Babcock.
" Oscar, tailor, b. 21 Mulberry.
Hagenow James S. mach. at 1 Flow. h. S.M.v.
Hagerman Charles laborer at 335, b. 33 Sheldon.
Haggerty D. F. motorman St.Ry. h. E.H.t.
" Edward H. painter, b.u. 566 Main.
" Maggie, assistant at 171 Putnam.
" Michael, laborer at N.Y.R. b. 6 Donald.
" Michael, teamster at 46 Ann, b. 5 Kilbourn.
" ☞ see also Hagarty.
Hagner Gus A. clerk at 921 Main, b. 28 Hopkins.
Hagopian George (Hartford Woodyard Co.) b. 125 Charter Oak.
Hahn George, driver at 315, h.u. 324 Park.
" John, b. 78 Jefferson.
" Lillian, wid. William H. h.u. 62 Wooster.
" Mary, wid. John, h. 78 Jefferson.
" Morris, peddler, h.u. 4 Portland.
Haight Monroe G. student at Trinity college, 11 Jarvis hall, Summit.
Haines ☞ see also Haynes.
Haist Albert R. stenographer at William Rogers Mfg. Co. 66 Market, h. E.H.t.
Hakanson August, lab. N.Y.R. b.2u. 108 Ward.
" Charles, laborer N.Y.R. h.2u. 108 Ward.
Hakes Curtis, mach. at 1 Flow. b.2u. 86 Hopkins.
Hakewessell Augusta, wid. Reinholt, Sr. h. 222 Sargeant.
" Reinholt. asst. treas. Acme Machine Screw Co. h. 222 Sargeant.
Hale Annie M. h.u. 35 John.
" Charles H. engineer at 956 Main, h. 67 Park.
" Charles R. mach. at 9 Sig. h. 1264 Broad.
" Charles W. clerk at Popes, b. 109 Elm.
" Charlotte, wid. John B. b. Harrison.
" Clarence F. clerk, Popes, b. 59 Capitol.
" David, h.r. 61 Trumbull.
" Edwin C. saloon, 30, h. 30 Church.

Hale Edwin J. messenger court of common pleas, b. 12 Linden.
" Frank H. conductor St.Ry. b. 6 Chapel.
" Francis M. toolmaker at 9 Sig.h. 1264 Broad.
" Frank, h.u. 399 Windsor av.
" Frank E. student at Yale, b. 1264 Broad.
" Frank R. porter at Adams Ex. h.u. 1 Elm.
" Fred W. mgr. Armour & Co. 501 Asylum, b. 109 Trumbull.
" Fred'k W. at 149 State, b.u. 440 Windsor av.
" George A. motorman St.Ry. h.u. 6 Avon.
" George F. b.2u. 82 Madison.
" George L. com. agent, h. 109 Elm.
" Gordon B. patternmaker, b. 12 Linden.
" Homer R. manufacturer, h. 77 Allen pl.
" J. Wilber, salesman at 1013 Main, h. E.H.t.
" James W. salesman at Charles R. Hart Co. 898 Main, h.u. 9 Belden.
" John, telescope manufac'tr,18, b.2u.18 Clark.
" John D. carptr. at 53 Vernon, h. Burnside v.
" L. W. (Jennie A.) Mrs. h. 27 Benton.
" Leonard W.asst. foreman,1 Flow.b.u.16 Elm.
" Louis W. Jr. b. 27 Benton.
" Lucretia M. wid. Junius, h. 12 Linden.
" Martha R. wid. John H. h.u. 109 Main.
" Mary A. wid. George T. h.2u. 82 Madison.
" Mollie J. boardinghouse, h.u.r. 26 Walnut.
" Owen G. cashier at Hfd. & N. Y. Transportation Co. 285 State, h.u. 9 Wadsworth.
" William, trav. salesman, h.u. 25 Hudson.
Halem Morris, tailor at 881 Main, b. 279 Front.
Haley Jeremiah, blacksmith, 34 Elm, h. 62 Bkm.
" John, carptr. at 1 Flower, h.u. 32 Harbison.
" John, driver at 544 Asylum, b. 1447 Broad.
" Thomas W. screwm. 581 Cap. h. Ch.O. park.
" ☞ see also Healey; Healy.
Halfin Rosa, milliner at 908, b. 389 Main.
Haling Louis H. rubberw. b. 128 Madison av.
" Randall H. carpenter at 83 Woodbine, h.u. 32 Kinsley.
Hall Adeline E. h. 103 Wooster.
" Amasa C. student, Trinity college, b. W.H.t.
" Andrew, laborer, h.r. 37 Front.
" Carl, porter, h.2u. 68 Temple.
" Caroline B. wid. Lucius J. h. 14 Fairmount.
" Carrie L. clerk at money order dept. P.O. b. Hockanum v.
" Chas. E. mach. at 9 Sig. h.2u. 1266 Broad.
" Chas. H. artist,45 Pratt, h. 244 Wethersfield.
" Charles W. (H. B. Little & Co.) h.u. 44 Annawan.
" Clarence L. clerk at Colts, b. 61 Weth.
" Daniel, rubberw. 690 Park, h. 40 Evergreen.
" David P. carpenter, h.2u. 52 Linden.
" David S. b. 98 Pratt.
" Emeline F. wid. Lambert C. h. 34 Ch.O.
" Emma M. wid. Charles, b.u. 68 Chestnut.
" Emmet R. dentist at 721 Main, rm. 26, b. 40 Evergreen.
" Ernest A. asst. engir. 690 Pk. b. 1148 Broad.
" Frances E. foreman 690 Park, h. 17½ Sisson.
" Frank A. toolmaker at Popes, h. Quaker lane, W.H.t.
" Fred J. clerk, 206 State, b. 68 Chestnut.
" George H. porter, Adams Ex. h. 21 Kennedy.

**A Good Investment-Your Advertisement in The Post.**

Hall George R. clerk at 20 Sargeant.
" Harry M. mach. at 1 Flower, b.u. 11 Clinton.
" Henry H. student, b. 27 Niles.
" Henry J. cashier at Postoffice, h. 31 Canton.
" Henry J. mach. at Colts, h. 138 Maple.
" Ira, machinist at 1 Flower, h. 373 Park.
" Ira D. fireman at 650, h. 757 Main.
" James E. mach. at 110 Com. h. 50 Liberty.

**HALL JAMES P.** State Agent of the Mutual Benefit Life Ins. Co. of Newark, N. J. 29 Pearl, b. 27 Niles.

" James W. carpenter, h. 28 Chestnut.
" Joel E. meatdealer, h. 2u. 38 Capen.
" John, laborer, b.3u. 68 Sheldon.
HALL JOHN H. vice president and treasurer, Colts Patent Fire Arms Manufacturing Co. h. 61 Wethersfield. *See page 543.*

JOSEPH B. HALL, Physician and Surgeon. Office 57 Pratt street.
Hours—9 to 10 A. M.
2 to 4 and 7 to 8 P. M.
Telephone connection.

Hall Joseph B. physician, *clerk Board of Health,* 57 Pratt, h. 827 Asylum.
" L. A. 284 Asylum, rm. 88.
" Lewis, mechanic, b.u. 188 Market.
" Lewis H. mechanic at Popes, h.u. 109 Law.
" Lydia B. h. 103 Wooster.
" Mary, attorney, 98, l. 98 Pratt.
" Mary J. clerk at Popes, b. 58 Church.
" Mellisa E. wid. John S. b. 43 Park.
" Noadiah K. laundrym. 542, h.u. 1112 Main.
" Orilla B. wid. Joseph, h. 827 Asylum.
" Ransom B. instructor at 1507 Broad.
" Robert R. musician, b. 244 Wethersfield.
" Rufus W. grainer, h. 79 Bellevue.
" Samuel B. cutter at 108 Asy. l. 32 Hopkins.
" Sidney, h. 127 Trumbull.
" Thomas, driver at C. S. Brewer & Co. 238, h. 329 Asylum.
" William, gunmaker, h.u. 138 Maple.
" William A. clerk, b. 80 State.
" William E. engineer at 690, h. 821 Park.
" William T. mach. hand, Colts, h.u. 285 Park.
Hallahan Gertrude, clerk, 881 Mn, b.94 Retreat.
" Kitty, clerk at 908 Main, b. 94 Retreat.
" Louise, dressm. at 270 Main, b. 94 Retreat.
" Maria, wid. Thomas, h.u. 8 Lawrence.
" Mary, wid. John, b. 59 Allen pl.
" Michael, laborer, h.u. 128 Albany.
" Wm. J. enameler at Popes, h. 94 Retreat.
Hallauer Frank, h.u. 78 Jefferson.
" Frank Jr. screwmkr.at Popes, h.u. 30 Alden.
" Henry C. assembler at Colts, h. 3 Dean.
Hallbauer Agnes, b. 78 Jefferson.
" Otto, brewer, h. 182 Ward.
Hallberg Bernhard, at A. W. Scoville, h.2u. 22 Dean.
" Ernest W. bartender at 80, b. 163 Front.
Hallet Charles, porter at Brown, Thomson & Co. 942 Main, h. 68 Temple.
Hallenbeck Harry, engineer at 26 Potter, h. 202 Maple.
Hallett Emma V. b. 2 Sumner.

Hallgren Axel, florist, h. Whiting lane, W.H.t.
Halliday Arthur S. student, b. 41 Vine.
" Charles H. lettercarrier, h. 41 Vine.
" Ernest C. at 131 Front, b. 68 Williams.
" George W. rubberworker, 690, h. 828 Park.
" Hiram C. b. 828 Park.
" Hiram S. pressman at 690, h. 828 Park.
" James W. mach. at 30 Cushman, b. 19 Smith.
" Louis, cook at 370 Albany, h. Windsor.
" Robert, machinist at N.Y.R. h. 19 Smith.

**HALLIDAY WILBUR H.** locksmith, bellhanger, electrician, etc. 131 Front, h. 68 Williams. *See page 506.*

" Wilbur T. assistant town clerk, 114 Pearl, h. 68 Williams.
" William S. mach. at 1 Flow. b.u. 828 Park.
" ☞ *see also Halladay; Holaday; Holiday.*
Hallin Fritz, b. 301 Lawrence.
Hallinan Chas. J. screwmkr. 476 Cap. b.29 Beach.
" David, laborer at 1230 Mn. h.u. 120 Albany.
" Frank C. mach. at 30 Cushman, b. 29 Beach.
" Katherine, dressmaker, 29, h. 29 Beach.
Halligan Eleanor, tailoress at 856, b. 721 Main.
" Jennie, b. 721 Main, rm. 52.
Hallisey John, laborer, h. 136 Grove.
" Charles J. operator, b. 136 Grove.
" Patrick, laborer, h.u. 65 Avon.
Hallison John, watr. str. Middletown, 285 State.
Halloran Richard, coachm. 140, h.u.r. 140 Wash.
Halls of Record, 114 Pearl.
Halperin David, laborer, b. 71 Avon.
Halpin John, farmer, St. Marys Home, W.H.t.
" Mary Mrs. dressmaker, 17, b.u. 17 S. Pro.
Halstad Fred, blacksm. at 25 Wells, h. 101 Ann.
Halstead M. J. Miss, matron Shelter for Women, 76, h. 76 Temple.
Ham Oliver H. modelm. at Popes, l. 124 Hung.
Hamel George, nightlunch, h. 19 Goodman.
Hamersley Elizabeth, h. 65 Vernon.
" Sophia, h. 65 Vernon.
" William, *judge supreme court,* attorney, 709 Main, h. 65 Vernon.
Hamilton Alex. clerk at C. S. Brewer & Co. 238, h.u. 835 Asylum.
" Annie L. stenogr. 800 Mn. b. 23 Windsor av.
" Carrie F. teacher, b. 29 Ashley.
" Elizabeth S. asst. librarian at Theological Seminary, 1507 Broad, h. W.H.t.
" Emma E. b. 7 Vine.
" Ernest E. builder, 180 Asy. h. 45 Webster.
" G. Willis, superintendent firealarm, r. 43 Pearl, h. 29 Ashley.
" George A. carpenter at 1 Flow. h. New Park.
" George E. at Hartford Fire Insurance Co. 53 Trumbull, h. 29 Ashley.
" Harvey, mason at 164 State, h.u. 9 S.Pro.
" Hattie H. Mrs. h. 11 Winthrop.
" James E. law student, 650 Mn. b. 15 Capitol.
" Joseph D. real estate at 2 State, h. E.H.t.
" Mary W. operator at 6 Central b. Weth.t.
" Morrison C. roadmaster N.Y.R. h. 139 Sig.
" Sarah H. musicteacher, b. 74 Niles.
" Thomas, machinist at N.Y.R. h. 67 Hung.

Hamilton Thomas M. builder, h. Warrenton.
" William, b. 4 Elm.
Hamlen Charles G. attendant at 30 Washington.
Hamlett Edward, paperhanger, b. 1338 Main.
Hamlin Fred, conductor St.Ry. b. 1164 Main.
" George W. foreman at Popes, h. Bristol t.
" John, attorney, 721 Mn.h. Thompsonville v.
" Kate L. G. h.2u. 1 Wooster.
Hamm George, sawyer, 169 Front, h. 20 Walnut.
" Katie N. housekeeper, b. 69 Walnut.
Hammann Jacob, tailor, 2 State, h.2u. 52 Temple.
Hammar Carl, mach. at 78 Com. h.u. 7 Wells.
Hammer Frederick, barber at 1069 Main, b.r. 60 Temple.
" Joseph C. (Schmeltz & H.) b. 981 Main.
Hammerstrom Charles (Jacobs & H.) h.u. 111 Lawrence.
Hammond Aaron L. carpenter, b.u. 98 Walnut.
" Clarence L. restaurant, 326, h. 320 Asylum.
" E. Payson Rev. h. 25 Atwood.
" Frank, clerk at 310, b. 279 Asylum.
" Fred. H. L. asst. secy. Y.M.C.A. 315 Pearl, h. 16 Atwood.
" Joseph, beltmaker, h.3u. 279 Asylum.
" Joseph M. Jr. enameler at Popes, h. 279 Asy.
" William H. h.r. 1128 Main.
" Wm. T. conductor St.Ry. b.r. 1128 Main.
Hammonstrom Martin, assembler at 556 Capitol, h. 133 Mather.
Hampe Max A. clerk, 653 Main, h.2u.13 Portland.
Hampke William, baker, b. 55 Judson.
Hampshire Parker, engraver, 847 Main, rm. 24, b. 106 Retreat.
Hamston James, laborer, h.u. 8 Winter.
Hamstrom Charles, painter, b. Lawrence.
Hanahan James, contractor & jobber, h. Grand.
Hancock Harvey, driver, h. Bluehills.
" Herman, farmer, r. 147 Woodland.
" Marah E. wid. Jesse M. h.2u. 23 Howard.
" Walter J. beltman at 1 Flower, h.2u. 8 Ch.O.
" Samuel, painter, h.u. 180 Barbour.
" William, filer at 1 Laurel, h. 12 John.
Handel Bertha, b. 76 Jefferson.
" Rose L. dressm. 721, h.u. 721 Main, rm. 55.
Handford John H. machinist at 133 Sheldon, h. 18 Westland.
Handley Catherine H. wid.Thos. K. h.u. 251 Park.
" Ellen, at 252 Pearl, b.u. 251 Park.
" John T. b.u. 251 Park.
Hands William, machinist, h. 12 John.
HANDY H. L. wholesale provisions, 31 Church. *See page 175.*
" Silas, harnessmaker at 523, h. 1194 Main.
Hane Fred. filer, b.u. 355 Park.
Haneber Margaret T. tailoress at 881 Main, b. 76 Putnam.
Hanford [☞ *see* Handford.
Hanger William J. mach. at 9 Sig. h. 74 Law.
Hankenberg Albert, carpenter, h.r. 105 Windsor.
Hanlay Ann, b. 26 Sanford.
Hanley Harry, signwr. 185 Pearl, b. 20 Church.
" Johannah Miss, h.2u. 36 Trumbull.
" Nora A. dressmaker, 53, b. 53 Grove.
" Thomas, tailor at 76 Asylum, b. 110 Pratt.

Hanlon Edward J. .b. 48 Vanblock.
" Jeremiah, shoem. 79 Front, h. 107 Babcock.
" Mark J. bookkeeper at James Ahern, 280 Asylum, b. 107 Babcock.
" Nora, b. 107 Babcock.
" Thomas fireman at Colts, h.r. 48 Vanblock.
" Thomas J. molder, 54 Arch, b. 48 Vanblock.
Hanmer A. Elizabeth, stenographer, 115 State, b. Wethersfield t.
" Caroline E. wid. William, b. 149 High.
" F. C. Mrs. (Evans & H.) h. Newington.
" Fay B. clerk at Phœnix Mutual Life Ins. Co. 49 Pearl, b. Wethersfield t.
" John, laborer at Hartford & N.Y. Transportation Co. 285 State, h. Wethersfield t.
" Walter, at Hartford Life Insurance Co. 252 Asylum, h.u. 53 Oak.
" William, clerk 206 State, b. Wethersfield t.
Hanna Annie R. attendant 30 Washington.
" George W. molder at 690 Park, h. 35 Amity.
" Walter W. attendant at 30 Washington.
Hannah John, screwmkr. 476 Capitol, b. 3 Grand.
Hannahan [☞ *see* Heneghan.
Hannan Cornelius, laborer, h. 43 Lafayette.
" Hugh, carpenter, h.u. 55 Putnam.
" Hugh S. foreman at 155 Ch.O. h. 19 Putnam.
Hanniford Robert M. draughtsman at 1 Flower, b. 223 Asylum, rm. 16.
Hannis Louis, bic. repairer, 10 Mul. b. Windsor.
Hannon Chas. P. druggist, 110 Trumbull, h.u. 85 Edwards.
" Edward W. clerk at 110 Tru. b. 85 Edwards.
" Frank, laborer, h. 26 Flower.
" Michael D. molder at 1 Flow. h.u. 18 Law.
" Michael D. mach. at 54 Arch, b. 147 Law.
" Patrick, b.u. 18 Lawrence.
" Patrick, clerk 310 Park, b2u. 50 Lawrence.
Hannum Fred. N. auctioneer, 208, b. 253 Asylum.
" Geo. A. bkkpr. 24 Mechanic, b. 68 Church.
" Theodore W. school, 302 Asylum, h. Weth.t.

Hanophy Michael at 13 Morris, h.2u. 18 Dean.
Hanover Morris, casehardner 476 Cap. h. 76 Put.
Hansel Amelia L. b. 34 West.
" Bertha, wid. Chas. (C. H. & Son) h. 34 West.
" Charles & Son, merch. tailors, 69 Pearl.
Mrs. Charles Hansel.      Edward H. Hansel.
HANSEL CHARLES R. (H., Sloan & Co.) jewelers, 886 Main, b. 71 Elm.
" Edward H. (C. H. & Son,) b. 58 Niles.

## HANSEL, SLOAN & CO., Jewelers.

**New Location, 886 MAIN ST.,**

*Old Number, 358,*

**Nearly Opposite Old Stand.**

*Telephone, 833-4.*

**HANSEL, SLOAN & CO.** jewelers, etc. 886 Main.     *See page 176.*
Charles R. Hansel.     Frederick R. Sloan.

Hansell Caroline, h. 73 Forest.
Hansen A. Marie, asst. principal Parkville school, b. 71 Ward.
" Anna E. milliner, b. 71 Ward.
" B. M. W. foreman at 388 Cap. h. 65 Sig.
" C. deckhand str. Hartford, 285 State.
" Carl K. mach. 142 Russ, b. 138 Brown.
" Charles J. coachm. 20, l. 20 Charter Oak pl.
" Chris. cook, 358 Asylum, h.2u. 150 Mather.
" Chris. A. screwm. 476 Cap. h.u. 177 Law.
" Christian, b. 36 Jefferson.
" Christian, tailor, 215, b. 373 Park.
" Christopher, janitor 933 Main, h. 31 Union.
" Detlef M. P. stretcher, 15 Tru. b. 21 Wads.
" Ernest, finisher, h.u. 2 Fairfield.
" Ernst, gardener Popes park, h.u. 638 Maple.
" H. C. carpenter, b. 231 Pearl.
" Hans C.C. jan. Hfd.Opera House, h.31 Union.
" Henry A. carpenter, b.2u. 271 Main.
" John, at 690 Park, b. 4 Sisson.
" John, diesinker at 142, h. 160 Russ.
" John, finisher, b. 45 Green.
" John, helper at L. T. Fenn, 613 Main, h.2u. 34 Lawrence.
" John N. molder at 690 Park, h. 44 Francis.
" Lauritz, mach. at 9 Sig. h. 12 Woodbine.
" Lauritz, shoemaker 928 Main, h. 20 Church.
" Lena, h.u.r. 23 Morgan.
" Louis, pressman, h. 9 Winship.
" Martin, molder at 690 Park, h.u. 27 Heath.
" Neils, mach. 30 Cush. h.2u. 179 Lawrence.
" Nicholas, screwmaker, 476 Cap.b.u.177 Law.
" Peter, baker at 484, b.2u. 271 Main.
" Peter, carpenter, h. 105 Mather.
" Peter, engir. at N.Y.R. h.u. 33½ Lafayette.
" Peter, tailor at 1362 Broad, h. 156 Russ.
" Peter O.laborer 335 Shel. h. 5 Kilbourn ct.
" Peter O. lab. at 335 Sheldon, h. 131 Ward.
" Robert, mach. at 9 Sig. h.u. 46 Laurel.
" Samuel H. molder, h. 5 Kilbourn ct.
" Soren, laborer at 335 Sheldon, h. 71 Ward.
Hansheltz Rudolph, clerk, 1143 Main, b. 49 Mahl.
Hansling Charles E. meat dealer, b.u. 73 Williams.
" Philip, h.u. 73 Williams.
HANSLING PHILIP JR. *alderman 8th ward,* asst. supt. at Pope Mfg. Co. h. 385 Park.
Hanson August, mech. at Popes, h. 162 Putnam.
" Benjamin P. rubberworker at 690 Park, h.u.r. 23 Morgan.
" Charles, ironw. at 555, h.u. 625 Capitol.

Hanson Charles A. laborer 98 Kilbourn, h.E.H.t.
" Cornelia B. wid. Daniel D. h. 427 Main, rm.8.
" Edward K. mach. at 1 Flower, b. 31 Union.
" Fred S. mach. at 1 Flower, b. 31 Union.
" George, cashier, 3 American, b.u. 46 Temple.
" Gustaf, tender str. Hartford, 285 State.
" Hans N. polisher at 581 Cap. h. 4 Sisson.
" Harry J. clerk at 1 Flower, b. 1204 Broad.
" Mary, wid. Iver V. Lu. 1204 Broad.
" John, bricklayer, h.u. 84 Albany.
" Neils P. blacksmith, h.2u. 106 Windsor.
" Wm. B. forem. 1 Flower, h.u. 65 Sigourney.
" William J. mach. at 1 Flower, h. 77 Park.
Hansult Louis, bartdr. at 31 Temple, h. 56 Talcott.
Hanvey Dennis J. foreman at N.Y.R. h. 61 Glendale.
" John L. J. b. 61 Glendale.
Hapgood, Edward T. (*Hapgood & Hapgood,*) h. 83 Gillett.
" & Hapgood, architects, 141 Trumbull.
Melvin H. Hapgood.     Edward T. Hapgood.
" Melvin H. (*Hapgood & Hapgood,*) h. 142 Woodland.
Hara Fred, at 475, b. 475 New Britain.
Haran Annie C. at N.Y. laundry, b. 15 Howard.
" Hannah J. b. 15 Howard.
" Mary A. b. 15 Howard.
" Michael D. h. 15 Howard.
Harbison Alexander, gen. agent N. Y. Life Ins. Co. 2 Central, h. 104 Washington.
" Hugh, h. 104 Washington.
" Isaac, b. 36 Jefferson.
" Jane Miss, b. 102 Vernon.
" John P. treasurer Hfd. City Gas Light Co. 700 Main, h. 102 Vernon.
" Robert, at Travelers Ins. Co. 56 Prospect, l. 53 Trumbull.
Hardeman William H. elevatorer at State Capitol, h.u.r. 25½ Flower.
Harden Charles J. machinist, b. 30 Hopkins.
" Leon D. mech. at Popes, h. 233 Sigourney.
Hardendorff Horatio,builder,102, h.102 Hudson.
Harder Eugene H. asst. janitor at Y.M.C.A. u.r. 88 Fairmount.
" Levi D. coachman, h.u. 25 Wolcott.
" P. T. clerk at C. C. Fuller & Co., 14 Ford, b. Windsor t.
" Richard, laborer at and h.r. 78 Edwards.
" William T. b. 2 Holcomb.
Hardie Thos. C. saloon, 287 Park, h. 1145 Broad.
" Thos. C.Jr. bartdr. 287 Park,b. 1145 Broad.
" William J. helper at 299 Pk. b. 1145 Broad.
Hardigan Luke, lab. N.E.R. b.3u. 33½ Spruce.
Hardiman W. B. Miss, nurse, 36, b. 36 Church.
Harding Albert W. mach. 9 Sig. h. 48 Francis.
" Anna, l. 1336 Main.
" Caleb E. mach. at 1 Flower, h. 56 Francis.
" Chas. H. printer, 284 Asy. b.2u. 73 Gov.
" Clarence, clerk 183 State, b.u. 28 Wooster.
" Geo. engineer 109 Commerce, h. 54 Francis.
" Herbert A. carpenter, b. 1153 Main.
" & Holbrook, fish, 1165 Main.
Samuel E. Harding.     William J. Holbrook.
" Jennie, wid. Joseph, h. 15 Smith.
" Job, carpenter, h. 58 Francis.

Harding John, printer, b.2u. 73 Governor.
" John L. blacksm. 352 Albany, h. 84 Mather.
" Joseph, carpenter at N.Y.R. h. 58 Francis.
" Lillian I. stenogr. at 476 Cap. b. 58 Francis.
" Mabel E. acct. at 476 Capitol, b. 58 Francis.
" Sam'l E. (H. & Holbrook,) h. 28 Wooster.
" Thomas, carpenter, h.r. 22 Trumbull.
" Thomas H. painter 1212 Main, h.u. 149 Clark.
" William, carptr. 581 Cap. h. Prospect av.
" William, clerk, 75 Windsor, h.2u. 306 Market.
" William A. inspector, 690 Park, b. 15 Smith.
" William P. painter, h.2u. 73 Governor.
" ☞ see also Herding.
Hardy Harriet N. wid. Benj. D. h. Park n. Prospect av. W.H.t.
" Herbert C. instructor, 700 Main, h. N.Y. c.
" R. D. carpenter, b. 36 Imlay.
" Thomas, painter, b.u. 245 Jefferson.
Hare Chas. R. toolm. at 581 Cap. h. 11 Sanford.
Harevick Moses, woodworker, h. 32 Portland.
Harford Margaret, wid. Edward, h.u. 74 Albany.
Harger Burton F. carpenter, b.u. 173 Ashley.
" Fannie M. b.u. 173 Ashley.
" Isabel N. bkkpr. 34 Pratt, b.u. 173 Ashley.
Hargey John M. painter, 24, h. 24 Charlotte.
Hargood Priscilla, seamstress, b. 171 Putnam.
Hargrave John G. student Trinity-college, 18 Northam tower, Summit.
Hari Henry, slater, b. 55 Green.
Harkins Bessie, cook at 375 Asy. b.r. 64 Hicks.
" F. B. plumber at 237 Asylum, b. 64 Hicks.
Harlem Lena, wid. Julius, h.u. 9 Hungerford.
Harlow Fred. M. (J. H. Silsby & Co.) h.288 Weth.
" Herman W. h. 62 Niles.
James, steamfitter, 11 Haynes, b. 1094 Main.
" Milan P. (Pitkin & H.) b. 62 Niles.
Harman Frank G. carpenter, h. 58 Clark.
" Harry (Ericsen & H.) h. Winship c. Douglass.
" Nicholas F. carpenter, N.Y.R. b. 44 Hopkins.
Harmon Frederick, mach. 1 Flow. h.u. 17 Talcott.
" Harry L. plumber at 440 Asy. b. 30 Chapel.
Harney Bridget, wid. John, h. 266 Maple.
" Delia F. clerk at Brown, Thomson & Co. 942 Main, b. 266 Maple.
" George, waiter at 427 Main, b. 64 Hicks.
" James D. barber 1159 Main, h. 144 Trumbull.
" Julia, dressmaker, b. 266 Maple.
" Mary C. artist at 759 Main, b. 266 Maple.
" Michael, blacksmith, N.Y.R. h.r. 17 Wolcott.
" Wm.J. photographer at 759 Mn.h.266 Maple.
Harold Joseph, peddler, h.3u. 66 Avon.
Harowitz Harris, painter, h.u. 40 North.
" Morris, laborer, h.u. 32 Portland.
Harper Alexander, messenger Farmer & Mech. Nat. Bank, 106 State, l. N.B.t.
" Allan, stonemason, h. 14 Ellsworth.
" Cecil, professor Hartford Theological Seminary, 1507 Broad.
" J. W. dentist, 50 State, l. 813 Asylum.
" John, plasterer, h. 949 Park.
" John M. florist, 10 Windsor av. h. 14 Goodwin.
" Joseph P. pressman at Popes, b. 88 Church.
" Lewis E. asst. supt. 1 Flow. h.u. 41 Vernon.
" Lincoln A. mach. at 1 Flower, b. 73 Park

Harper Ruth A. teacher, 690 Asylum.
" Thomas A. rubberworker at 690 Park.
Harrigan David, helper at 152 State, b. 33½ Front.
" John, fireman P.&R. b. 20 Chestnut.
" John, painter at 185 Asylum.
" John F. boilermaker, b. 33½ Front.
" John H. plumber, 1152 Main, h.u. 16 Elm.
" Joseph, laborer, h. 103 Commerce.
" Mary, wid. Jeremiah, h. 523 Main.
" ☞ see also Horrigan.
Harrington Andrew F. moulder at 556 Capitol, h.2u. 191 Lawrence.
" Arthur, janitor at Popes, h. 91 Willow.
" Clayton G. stenographer at Phœnix Ins. Co. 64 Pearl, b. 35 Wadsworth.
" Colton R. asst.deliv.clerk at P.O.b. 35 Wads.
" Daniel J. market, 302 Main, h. 20 Alden.
" Edith M. musicteacher, 24, b.u. 24 Hopkins.
" Edward, painter, b.u. 117 Mather.
" Emerson F. discount clerk at First National Bank, 50 State, h. 287 Sigourney.
" Florence W. cigarmaker, 88 State, b. E.H.t.
" Frank, draughtsm. at 1 Flow. h. 35 Girard.
" Frank H. stenog. at 581 Capitol, b. W.P.v.
" Frank W. clerk at 903 Main, b. 35 Wads.
" Fred, driver at 552 Asylum, b. 76 Spring.
**HARRINGTON HENRY E.** mgr. Mutual Life Ins. Co. of N.Y. 50 State, rm. 69, h. 5 Linden.
" James B. porter at 66 Asylum, h. 51 Center.
" John, mason, h.r. 81 Avon.
" John F. horseshoer, 10 Charles, b. E.H.t.
" Joseph A. clerk at 690 Park, h. 35 Chapel.
" Lewis Mrs. h. 35 Wadsworth.
" M. W. cashier Hfd. Op. house, b. 27 Linden.
" P. deckhand str. Hartford, 285 State.
" Thomas F. motorman St.Ry. b.u. 27 Pleasant.
" Timothy, butcher at 302 Main, b. 20 Alden.
" William A. h. 28 Beach.
" Wm. H. printer at Case, Lockwood & Brainard Co. 141 Pearl, h.u. 24 Hopkins.
" ☞ see also Herrington.
Harris Abraham, barber, 22 Shel. b. 142 Maple.
" Asa, h.u. 51 Hudson.
" Carrie F. dressmaker, b. 17 South Ann.
" Charles, b. 142 Maple.
" Charles, tailor at 526 Asylum, h. 1069 Broad.
" Charles A. painter, 580 Windsor av. h..W.t.
" Chas. B. conductor St.Ry. b. 99 Trumbull.
" Charles J. clerk at L. L. Ensworth & Son, iron merchants, 104 Front, h.2u. 298 Park.
" Edward, laborer, h. 70 Temple.
" Edward H. (Franklin Market,) h.u. 51 Hudson.
" Elizabeth, h. 1243 Main.
" Ella R. clerk at Sage, Allen & Co. 898 Main, b. 129 Trumbull.
" Elsie, milliner at 908 Main, b. 70 Fairmount.
" Eugene, horse trainer, b. 234 Barbour.
" Eugene C. motorman St.Ry. l.u. 97 Main.
" F. E. l. 284 Asylum, rm. 57.
" Frank, solicitor at 393 Allyn.
" George F. salesman at 501 Asy. b. 6 Church.
" Geo. J. porter at 77, b. 118 Asylum.

**It Pays Big Interest-Your Advertisement in The Post.**

Harris Harriet E. milliner, 908 Mn. b. 86 Laurel.
" Harry A. rubberw. at 690 Park, h. Weth. t.
" Henry Mrs. h. 202 Ashley.
" Henry, cigarm. 867 Mn. h. 431 Windsor av.
" Henry, watches, etc. 34 Asy. h. 202 Ashley.
" Herman, painter, h. 266 Market.
" Jacob A. barber, 22, b. 142 Sheldon.
" James A. porter 239 State, h.2u. 1281 Main.
**HARRIS JAMES,** sanitary plumbing, 302 Pearl, h. 70 Fairmount.
" Jennie Mrs. h. 213 Pearl.
" John J. plumber, 302 Pearl. h. 70 Fmt.
" Jonas, waiter. h.u. 60 Pleasant.
" Joseph, bartender, 103 State, h. Pleasant.
" Leonard S. mgr. Side Weight Horse Shoe Co. 26 Mechanic, h. 32 Charter Oak.
" Luther, marketman at 121 Windsor av. h. 20 Suffield.
" Luther R. machinist at 1 Flower, h. Weth. t.
" Mary A. dressmaker, b. 70 Fairmount.
" Mary M. teacher at South school 36 Wadsworth, b. 41 Capitol.
" Mary N. Mrs. b. 50 Cedar.
" Max, grocer, 30 Morris, h. 142 Maple.
" Moses, h. 304 Wethersfield.
" Moses, merchant, h. 1044 Main.
" N. O. horsetrainer. h. 161 Barbour.
" Philip H. expressman, h. 72 Pleasant.
" Rose, clerk at Brown, Thomson & Co. 942 Main, b. 266 Market.
" Samuel, barber, b. 142 Maple.
" Samuel, machinist at Colts, h. 9 Williams.
" Thos. A. plumber, 302 Pearl, b. 70 Fmt.
" Thomas L. bookbinder at 856 Main, h. W.t.
" Walter G. at 273 Asylum, h. 186 Sargeant.
" William, roofer. h.u. 545 Main, rm. 6.
" William B. waiter at 53 Ann, h.r. 1 Marsh.
" William E. inspector at Colts, h. Weth. t.
" William H. h. 8 Lawrence.
" William H. policeman, h.2u. 39 Spring.
" Wm. J. machinehand, b. 375 Main.
" ☞ *see also Abramovitz.*
Harrison Alexander S. h. 196 Sigourney.
" Annie, wid. William H. h.u. 85 Fairmount.
" Arthur E. assistant foreman at Pope Tube Co. h. 237 Lawrence.
" Benj. blacksmith at N.Y.R. h. E.H.t.
" Carrie L. b. 24 Madison.
" Edward F. clerk at Hartford County Mutual Fire Ins. Co. 793 Main, h. 196 Sigourney.
" Ellen M. b. 196 Sigourney.
" George B. machinist at N.Y.R. h. E.H.t.
" James, h.3u. 208 Sheldon.

Harrison Jay D. traveling salesman, **149 State,** h. Springfield, Mass.
" John, helper at 1, h. 30 Flower.
" John, mason builder, 156, h. 156 **Franklin.**
" Joseph P. brassfinisher at 65 **Suffield.**
" Mary, wid. Herman, h. 24 **Madison.**
" Mary A. wid. Henry, h.u. 35 Spruce.
" May M. bkkpr. at 310 Park, b. 64 **Lawrence.**
" Nelson A. jobber, b. 37 Mather.
" P. H. & Son, contractors, 343 Main.
   P. H. Harrison.   H. L. Harrison.   L. B. **Harrison.**
" Robert, screwm. at 476 Cap. b. **Burnside v.**
" Samuel S. fitter at 62 Mar. b. 1045 **Main.**
" Sanford B. janitor St. John's church, h.u. 54 Grand.
" Sarah, matron, 20 South Hudson.
" Strabo, teamster, h.u. 13 Mechanic.
" Wm. F. announcer at N.Y.R. h.u. 3 **Asylum.**
" Wm. F. engir. at 556 Cap. b. 57 **Farmington.**
" William P. cleaner at 37 Wells, b. 29 **Linden.**
Harrman Caroline, wid. John A. h. 6 **Lewis.**
Harss Hans P. ostler at r. 50 State, b.r. 36 **Temple.**
Hart A. Elijah, treasurer Society for Savings, 31 Pratt, h. 846 Asylum.
" Albert B. lettercarrier, b. 104 Capen.
" Alfred D. mach. at 1 Flower, h. Whiting.
" Anna E. wid. A. E. h. 36 Buckingham.
" Augustus J. Mrs. h.u. 40 Hungerford.
" Charles H. mach. at Wm. Rogers Mfg. Co. 66 Market, h.3u. 90 State, rm. 6.
" Chas. R. president The Chas. R. Hart Co. h. station 19, Windsor t.
**HART CHARLES R. CO. (THE)** carpets, rugs, etc. 898 Main. *See page 179.*
" Clarence W. foreman at 581 Capitol, h.u. 100 Francis.
" Edward G. realestate, 18 State, h. 69 Willard.
" Edwin, ins. agent, 721 Main, b. 166 Russ.
" Edwin R. h.u. 51½ Wooster.
" Ferdinand A. agent Ætna Life Insurance Co. for Massachusetts, h. 417 Windsor av.
" Ferdinand, Jr. b. 417 Windsor av.
" Frances E. Mrs. h. 90 Mather.
HART GERALD W. pres. Hart & Hegeman Mfg. Co. 28 High, h. 5 Highland.
" Harrie E. patent dept. at Popes, b. N.B.t.
" Harry C. Jr. printer at 284, b.u. 289 Asylum.
**HART & HEGEMAN MFG. CO.** electric light supplies, 26 High.
   *See page 539.*
" Henry C. painter, h.u. 56 Hudson.
HART HENRY F. alderman 3d ward, machinist, Wm. Rogers Mfg. Co. 66 Mar. h. 104 Capen.
" Henry H. carriagem. 41 Alb. h. 197 Sisson.
" Henry L. machinist at Wm. Rogers Mfg. Co. 66 Market b. 30 Barbour.
" James E. blacksmith at 14 Huntington, b. 98 Sargeant.
" John, insurance agent, b.2u. 36 Lawrence.
" Joseph C. h. 368 Laurel.
" L. C. groceries, etc. 63, h. 202 Albany.
" Lewis O. at 879 Windsor av. b. 104 Capen.
" Lizzie I. Mrs. dressm. 51½, h.u. 51½ Wooster.
" Lucius R. asst.supt. at 751 Mn. h. 27 Russell.

# The CHAS. R. HART CO.

*Sell more goods in their line than any name mentioned in these pages.*

*REMEMBER THAT WE SELL*

**Wall Papers,
Ceiling Decorations,
Draperies, Shades,
and Ornamental
Outfittings, at
Close Cut Prices.**

# ‖ Carpets, Rugs, Oil Cloths,
# ‖ Linoleums, Mattings.

*Buying in immense quantities for the Jobbing Trade, enables us to sell to the Retail Trade*
*AT LESS THAN REGULAR PRICES.*

## The CHARLES R. HART CO.,

### 894, 896, 898, and 900 MAIN STREET, Hartford, Conn.

Hart Mary Mrs. music teacher, 166, b. 166 Russ.
" Otis J. clerk at 114 Pearl, b.u. 15 Center.
" Patrick, polisher at Popes, h. N.B.t.
" Patrick H. horseshoer at 14 Huntington, h. 98 Sargeant.
" Samuel, D.D. Rev. professor of literature, Trinity college, 22 Jarvis hall, Summit.
" Simeon T. inspec. 690 Park, b.129 Hamilton.
" Thomas, laborer, b. 100 Francis.
" William, waiter at 1049 Mn. l. 33 Windsor.
" Wm. H. painter at 20 Central, b. 56 Hudson.
Hartenstein Frank, cabinetmaker at C. C. Fuller & Co. 16 Ford, h.2u. 1443 Broad.
" Harry, barber at 24 Mul. b.4u. 80 Pearl.
" Ivan, machinist at Billings & Spencer Co. 142 Russ, b.u. 1218 Main.
Hartford Advertising Co. Albert E. Lazzaro, manager, 7 Central, rm. 4.
**HARTFORD APRON & TOWEL SUPPLY CO.** J. H. Gowen, 49 Market.
" Beef Co. wholesale meats, 54 Huntley av.
" Bill Posting Co. Foot Guard hall, 159 High.
" Board Fire Underwriters, 53 Trumbull.
" Board of Trade, 49 Pearl.
" Bologna factory, 480 Windsor av.
Theodore Maurer, proprietor.
" Boltless and Noiseless Thrill Coupling Co, 173 Asylum. John Farris, manager.
" Bowling Co. 645 Main.
**HARTFORD BOX CO.** E. W. Smith, proprietor, 223 State. *See page 532.*
**HARTFORD BREWING CO.** 232 Sheldon. *See page 491.*

**HARTFORD BUILDING AND LOAN ASSO.** 370 Asy. rms. 4–5. *See page 424.*
**HARTFORD BUSINESS COLLEGE,** 370 Asylum. *See page 711.*
E. H. Morse.
" Calcium Light Co. room 2, 911 Main.
" Carpet Co. office 10 Market.
**HARTFORD CARRIAGE CO.** 300 Allyn. *See page 549.*
" Chair Co. 42 Seyms.
J. Henry Martin.          Frank Blodgett.
" Chemical Co. soap mfrs. 235 State.
" Cigar Co. cigar manufacturers, 54 Pratt, C. H. Glazier, manager.
**HARTFORD CITY DIRECTORY,** Elihu Geer's Sons, canvassers, compilers, printers, publishers, 16 State. *See p. 474.*
" City Gas Light Co. 700 Main.
" Club, 33 Prospect.
**HARTFORD COAL CO.** office 754 Main, yard 100 Commerce. *See page 492.*
Hartford & Conn. Western R. office Philadelphia & Reading Railroad, 59 Spruce.
" County Jail, 42 Seyms. *See index.*
" County Medical Society. *See index.*
**HARTFORD COUNTY MUTUAL FIRE INS. CO.** 793 Main. *See page 445.*
**HARTFORD COURANT CO.** publishers daily, semi-weekly and weekly Courant, 66 State. *See page 463.*
**HARTFORD CYCLE COMP'Y,** bicycles, 581 Capitol. *See page 796.*

**THINKING PEOPLE Read The Post Daily.**

THE

# HARTFORD HEATING CO.

Steam, Hot Water, and Hot Air Heating,
Ventilation, General Steam
Fitting, Mill Work.

Wrought Iron }
Cast Iron }**BOILERS.**

### 267 ASYLUM STREET.

*Telephone, 1043-5.*

HARTFORD DECORATING Co. J. Alex. McClunie,
177 Asylum.    *See Advertisers' Index.*
"  Dental Co. 96 Trumbull, W. C. Messinger.
"  Diamond Polish Co. 118 Asylum.

**HARTFORD, DIME SAVINGS
BANK OF,** 791 Main.    *See p. 439.*
"  Dispensary, 2 Talcott.
"  Dredging Co. 721 Main.
"  Drug Co. 852 Main.
"  Electric Laundry, L. J. Martel, 568 Main.

**HARTFORD ELECTRIC LICHT
CO. WORKS,** office, 266 Pearl,
works 70 State.    *See page 542.*
"  Employment Office, 596 Main.

**HARTFORD ENGINE WORKS,**
r. 223 State.    *See page 539.*

**HARTFORD ENGRAVINC CO.**
Geo. C. Atwell, Fred C. Wessel, 66 State.
*See page 477.*

**HARTFORD FIRE INSURANCE
CO.** 53 Trumbull.    *See page 458.*
"  Graphophone Co. (The) C. A. Q. Norton,
manager, 80 Trumbull.
"  Grocery Co. 369 and 375 Capitol.
HARTFORD HEATING Co. THE, 267 Asylum.
*See page 180.*

**HARTFORDER HEROLD,** 31 Mulberry.    *See page 470.*
"  Hollow Ware Co. 17 Florence.

**HARTFORD HOSPITAL,** 20 South
Hudson.    *See page 701.*
"  Hotel, Alfred A. Pocock, prop. 365 Allyn.
"  Ice Co. 4 Central.
"  Laundry, 403 Franklin.
Mrs. P. S. Gaudet.

**HARTFORD LIFE INSURANCE
CO.** 252 Asylum.    *See page 454.*
"  Light & Power Co. office, 266 Pearl.

**HARTFORD LUMBER CO.** r. 17
Albany.    *See page 515.*
"  Machine Screw Co. 476 Capitol.

**HARTFORD MANILLA CO.** office,
1 South Ann.    *See page 479.*
"  Messenger Co. 3 Central.

**HARTFORD MOULDINC W'KS,**
Alfred.T. Ricker, 26 Potter. *See page 517.*

**HARTFORD NATIONAL BANK,**
58 State.    *See page 434.*

**HARTFORD AND NEW YORK
STEAMBOATS,** 285 State.
*See page 555.*

**HARTFORD AND NEW YORK
TRANSPORTATION CO.**
285 State.    *See page 554.*

**HARTFORD NURSERY,** C. O. Pur-
inton, 75 New Britain.
"  One Price Clothing Co. 114 & 116 Asylum.
"  Orphan Asylum, 171 Putnam.

**HARTFORD PAPER CO.** mfrs. white
and colored paper, 141 Pearl. *See p. 480.*
"  Paving & Construction Co. 868 Main, rm. 2.
"  Plating Co. 249 Pearl.

**HARTFORD POCKET CUIDE,**
252 Asylum.    *See page 505.*
"  Portrait Co. 1198 Main.

**HARTFORD POST,** daily and weekly,
23 Asylum.

**HARTFORD PRINTINC CO.**
Elihu Geer's Sons, City Directory, 6
State, 2d, 3d & 4th stories.  *See page 474.*
Hartford Prohibition Club, 91 Asylum.

**HARTFORD PROVISION CO.**
Valley street.    *See page 586.*
"  Public Library, 5 Athenæum.  *See Index.*
"  Publishing Co. now A. D. Worthington & Co.
"  Real Estate Exchange, 911 Main.
"  Real Estate Improvement Co. 436 Capitol.
"  Real Est. & Investm. Agency, 118 Asy. rm.6.

**HARTFORD RUBBER WORKS
CO.** mfrs. factory 690 Park. *See p. 796.*
"  Seminary Press, publishers, etc. 1507 Broad.
"  Sewing Machine Co.—See Pope Mfg. Co.
"  Silverware Co. John E. Griffith, 249 Pearl.
"  Social Settlement, h. 6 North.
"  Society of Natural Sciences, 65 Pratt.
"  and Spring Brook Ice Co. 4 Central.

**HARTFORD STEAM BOILER
INSPECTION AND IN-
SURANCE CO.** 650 Main, 2d
story, room 8.    *See pages 446, 447.*
"  Street S rin ling and Supply Co. 863 Main,
rm. 5. p  k

**HARTFORD** *(Sunday)* **GLOBE,** 25
Asylum.    *See page 465.*

**HARTFORD SUNDAY JOUR-
NAL,** 284 Asylum.   Jos. H. Barnum, 284
Asylum, room 36.    *See page 466.*

**HARTFORD TELECRAM CO.** 12
Central row.    *See page 464.*

**HARTFORD THEOLOCICAL
SEMINARY,** Congregational, 1507
Broad.    *See pages 708, 709.*

**HARTFORD TIMES,** daily and weekly,
Burr Bros. 716 Main.

**HARTFORD TRUST CO.** 764 Main
and 1 Central row.    *See page 437.*
"  Typewriter Co. 476 Capitol.
"  Street Railway Co. office,115 State, barns,
157 Wethersfield, 53 Vernon.

**HARTFORD UNDERTAKING CO.** funeral directors and embalmers, 106 Trumbull.

G. Louis Coburn.                George L. Coburn.
"  Water Works office 800 Main, City hall.
"  Weekly Guide, E. B. Eaton, editor, 252 Asy.
"  Wheel Club, 704 Main.
"  Woodyard Co. 116 Charter Oak.

Aaron Avedision.        Kirikor Kazariom.
Sarkis Goligian.        Zeron Bogdigian.
Martin Bogdigian.       George Hagopian.

**HARTFORD WIRE WORKS,** 247 Asylum, F. H. Crosthwaite, proprietor.
*See page 488.*

**HARTFORD WOVEN WIRE MATTRESS CO.** 618 Capitol.
*See page 522.*

Hartigan Martin, machinist, b. 249 Asylum.
"  Nellie J. housekeeper at 249 Asylum.
Hartleben F. E. bartdr. 637 Main, h. 2A Wads.
"  Hermann, gardener, b. 109 Main.
Hartley Tom. W. h. 5 Mays ct.
"  William, marblecutter, h. 25 Florence.
"  Wm. N. plumber at 1230 Main, h. E.H.t.
Hartman Adam, bootmaker, 27, h. 27 Lafayette.
Hartnett Anna J. clerk at Brown, Thomson & Co. 942 Main, b. 10 Chapel.
"  & Bartley, saloon, 1061 Main.

John T. Hartnett.        James Bartley.
"  Edward E. steamfitter, h. 209 Hamilton.
"  Edward J. clerk at 1129 Main, b. 46 Elliott.
"  James, carpenter, h. 46 Elliott.
"  James G. carpenter, h.u. 2 Ellery.
"  John, screwmaker, 476 Capitol, h.u. 7 Oak.
"  John F. molder, b. 10 Chapel.
"  John T. (*H. & Bartley,*) h. Holyoke, Mass.
"  Mary, wid. William, h. 10 Chapel.
"  Mary A. compositor, R. S. Peck & Co. 26 High, b. 46 Elliott.
"  Michael, screwm. at 476 Cap. b. 15 Howard.
"  Nellie E. clerk at Brown, Thomson & Co. 942 Main, b. 46 Elliott.
"  Rich. T. clerk at 6 Central, b. 46 Elliott.
"  Wm. F. trimmer, 180 Allyn, h. 520 Garden.
Hartranft Chester D., D.D. pres't Hartford Theological Seminary, 1507 Broad, h. 82 Gillett.
*See pages 708, 709.*
Hartstall Isaac, clerk at 273 Asy. b. 26 Chapel.
"  Isabell, clerk at 908, b. 1150 Main.
"  Max clerk at 97 Asylum, b. 1150 Main.
"  Moses A. h. 170 Seymour.
"  Sarah E. clerk at 904, b. 1150 Main.
Hartung Annie, wid. Jacob, h.u. 74 Temple.
Hartz Hermann T. ins.agt. 721 Mn. h.u. 49 Amity.
Hartzmark Abraham, clerk, 881 Mn. b. 24 Brook.
Harvey Daniel, carpenter, 5 Ellery.
"  Foster E. (*H. & Lewis*) h. 14 Florence.
"  George, b. 13 Warner.
"  George P. policeman. h. 260 Capen.
"  James R. saloon, 26 Market, h.u. 50 Green.
"  L. W. music teacher, 171, h. 171 High.
"  & Lewis, opticians, 865 Main.

Foster E. Harvey.        Robert H. Lewis.
"  Peter L. cigarmaker, b. 1149 Broad.
"  Wm. E. engraver at 177 Asy. h. 133 Barbour.

Harvich Morris B. wireworker at 618 Capitol, h.u. 82 Portland.
Harwood Frederick A. clerk at Hfd. Life Ins. Co. 252 Asylum, h. East Hartford t.
"  Nancy C. wid. F. W. b. 114 Huntington.
"  Wm. laborer, b.u. 26 Union.
Harworth Joseph, helper, 142 Russ, h. 51 Ferry.
Hascall Arthur I. b. 54 Capitol.
"  H. E. Miss, music teacher, 650 Main, rm. 15.
"  Mary J. Mrs. h. 54 Capitol.
"  S. Howard, clerk 51 Market, b. 54 Capitol.
Haskell Chas. B. produce, 145 State, h. 98 Weth·
"  George S. bookk. at 224 State, h. 200 Smith.
"  Ruth M. b. 15 Marshall.
Haskins Elizabeth A. h. 80 Maple.
Haslam James, motorman St.Ry.h. 122 Trumbull.
Haspey William, plumber, h. 297 Park.
Hass Abraham, plasterer, h.2u. 64 Pleasant.
"  Bernard H. screwmaker at 476 Capitol, b. 160 Front.
"  ☞ *see also Haas.*
Hasselbrock Warne S. polisher at 111 Sheldon, b. Windsor t.
Hassett Arthur W. operator at 6 Central, h.3u. 35 Pleasant.
"  James, laborer, b.u. 148 Mather.
"  John, janitor So. Cong. church, h. 45 Ward.
"  John A. repairer at Popes, b. 45 Ward.
"  John D. baggagemaster N.Y.R. h. 10 S.Pro.
"  Margaret, wid. Arthur, h.u. 35 Pleasant.
"  Patrick J. laborer at Pope Tube Co. h.u. 1316 Broad.
"  Richard J.pressm.at 141 Pl.b.3u. 35 Pleasant.
"  Thos. H. printer at 141 Pearl, b. 45 Ward.
"  William, helper at 1152 Main. b.3.u. 35 Ple.
Hastie Estelle J. wid. Alex. clerk at Brown, Thomson & Co. 942 Main, b. 18 Bellevue.
"  Jennie E. ass't librarian at 5 Atheneum, b. 18 Bellevue.
"  Ralph A. joiner, b. 18 Belden.
Hastings Anna C. Mrs. h. 69 Elm.
"  Arthur B. groceries, 30, h.u. 17 Grand.
"  Ellen A. wid. Frederick, b. 17 So. Prospect.
"  Emma B. music teach. 1185, b.u. 1185 Broad.
"  Francis H. chemist 42 Union, h. 49 Willard.
"  Herbert E. mason,b. 15 Canton.
"  Herbert E. patternmaker at 1 Flower, h. Hockanum v.
"  Inez A. b.u. 26 Smith.
"  James F. gen. agent National Fire Ins. Co. 95 Pearl, h. 174 Sigourney.
"  Joel, splicer at 690 Park, h.u. 26 Smith.
"  Lewis W. mason. h. 15 Canton.
"  Lizzie J. h. 39 Wadsworth.
"  Louis M. cashier at Ætna Life Ins. Co. 650 Main, b.u. 1185 Broad.
"  Mary A. teacher of art, h. 35 Spring.
"  Mary A. wid. Eldridge G. h. 190 Sigourney.
"  Mary L. teacher at High School, 39 Hopkins, b. 69 Elm.
"  Peter P. coachm. 1010 Asy. h.r. 343 Collins.
"  Samuel S. mason, h.u. 1185 Broad.
"  Wallace S. roller 690 Park, b.u. 26 Smith.
"  Walter S. mach. 476 Capitol, b. 11 Atlantic.

HASTINGS WILLARD D. councilman 4th ward, beltmaker, Jewell Belting Co. 15 Trumbull, h. 11 Atlantic.

Hatch Augustus Capt. clerk Popes, h. 230 Putnam.
" Burton, clerk at 2 Church, b. W.H.t.
" Carrie L. dressmaker, 11, h. 11 Goodwin.
" Charles E. (Dow & H.) h. W.H.t.
" Chas. E. (Larned & H.) h. 211 Ashley.
" Charles L., Electric Carpet Beating Co. 226 Putnam, h. 66 Westland.
" Charles P. cornet teacher, h. 18 Windsor av.
" Charles P. watchm. 1 Flow. h. 226 Putnam.
" E. J. Mrs. business medium, h. 230 Putnam.

HATCH EDWARD B. president Johns-Pratt Co. 555 Cap. h. 208 Sig.    See page 540.
" Eliza, dressmaker, 11, h. 11 Goodwin.
" Ernest G. supt. John Hancock Life Ins. Co. 756 Main, h. 155 Ashley.
" Frank D. mach. at Johns-Pratt Co. h. W.H.t.
" Frederick A. machinist, h.u. 90 Retreat.
" Geo. E. prest. The Hatch & North Coal Co. 801 Main, h. 203 Sigourney.
" Herbert L. machinist at 20 Vredendale, h. 23 Seymour.
" John C. beltmaker at 15 Tru. h.u. 88 Retreat.
" Julia A. h. 238 Wethersfield.
" Lillis dressmaker, 11, h. 11 Goodwin.
" Lloyd W. clerk at 556 Capitol, h. 23 Sisson.

**HATCH MILITARY BAND,** Charles P. Hatch, director, 18 Windsor av.

**HATCH & NORTH COAL CO.** office, 801 Main, yard 56 Com. See p. 491.
" Phoebe A. wid. Edwin B. b. 83 Franklin.
" Susan M. wid. Charles, h.u. 10 Lewis.
" Winifred, wid. William A. h. 230 Franklin.

Hatfield Daniel W. iceman at 48 Ann, b. W.H.t.
" Martha P. wid. John, b.u. 10 West.

Hathaway Chas. H. chiropodist, 926, l. 926 Main.
" E. O. (Geo. N. Merrill & Co.) 75 Pratt.
" Louis C. chiropodist, 926, b. 926 Main.

**HATHEWAY EARLE,** architect & builder, h. 29 Imlay.    See page 495.
" Edward F. salesman, h.u. 50 Barbour.
" Emory G. machinist at 13 Central.
" Harris D. bartender at 1242, l. 1242 Main.
" Ida L. b. 29 Imlay.
" Lyman E. b. 29 Imlay.
" Sarah, dressmaker, 29, b. 29 Imlay.

Hatstat John W. forem. at 8 Front, l. 105 Capitol.

Hatton Charles Mrs. h.u. 76 Sanford.
" Fred, b. 76 Sanford.

Haub Agnes, laundress at 20 South Hudson.
" George, (H. & Sons) h. 299 Market.
" George, Jr. (H. & Sons) b. 299 Market.
" & Sons, merchant tailors, 721 Main, rm. 7.
    George Haub.    George Haub, Jr.
" Otto, tailor, b. 721 Main.

Haughton ☞ see also Horton.

Haupt Frederick, bartdr. at 330 Main. h. 17 John.
" Wm. driver at 245 Windsor, h. 48 Bellevue.

Hauser Fred. uphols. at 306 Pearl, h. 57 Seymour.
" John, gardener, h.u. 123 Front.

Hausken Julius, bookb. 252 Pearl, b.u. 59 Madison.

Hauson ☞ see also Haaser, Houser.

Hausmann Henry, foreman at Popes, h.u. 11 Hamilton.
" William F. buffer at Popes, h.u. 18 Affleck.

Hausser Gustav F. Rev. pastor German Methodist Episcopal Church, h. 99 Jefferson.

Haussler Otto J. machinist at 9 Sig. h. 19 Oak.

Hauver Philip E. cond. St.Ry. h.u. 74 Seymour.

Havel Anton, mach. in Springfield, h. 73 Hamilton.

Havemeyer Chas. W. Mrs. h. 131 Washington.

Haven Charles B. clerk, b. 194 Windsor av.
" Emma, wid. S. C. h. 194 Windsor av.
" George, adjutant general, State capitol, h. New London t.

Havens Dudley W. asst. inspector Hfd. water works, 800 Main, City hall, h. 23 Mahl.
" Edwd. F. screwm. 476 Cap. h2u. 1331 Broad.
" Ellen S. b. 80 Main.
" Frances B. wid. Walter, b. 80 Main.
" Frank C. mach. at 1 S. Ann, b. Burnside v.
" Frank S. stu. at Yale, b. 603 Farmington.
" Frank W. editor "Safety Fund Advocate" with Hartford Life Ins. Co. 252 Asylum, h. 603 Farmington.
" Irving W. h.u. 58 Oak.
" James, h.2u. 4 Affleck.
" James F. policeman, h. 21 Ward.
" John L. helper at 266 Pearl, b. 80 Church.
" Olive H. wid. Sylvester, b. 862 Windsor av.
" Peter, laborer at 476 Cap. b. 303 Lawrence.
" Ralph G. farmer, b. 862 Windsor av.
" Samuel H. bookkeeper at Henry Kohn & Sons, 890 Main, b. 23 Mahl.
" Susan B. wid. William H. h. 30 Wooster.
" William W. carpenter, h. 31 Wadsworth.

Hawes Albert H. painter at 88 Mar. h. 17 Grand.

Hawkins Alice S. kindergarten teacher Northwest school, b. 46 Madison.
" C. H. Mrs. h. 650 Main, rm. 65.
" Clara P. b. 15 Clinton.
" David, bartender at 46 Union pl. h. E.H.t.
" David S. draughtsm. at 1 Laurel, h. 253 Main.
" Emma W. proofreader at Hartford Times, 716 Main, b. 46 Madison.
" Frank M. collector at 700 Main.
" Fred W. rubberw. at 690 Park, b. 426 Asy.
" George A. patternmaker at Pratt & Whitney Co. 1 Flower, b. 102 Hopkins.
" Harry, ostler, h.r. 173 State.
" Harry P. clerk at 131 Main, b. 46 Madison.
" James H. jobber, h.2u. 213 Windsor.
" James W. motorman St.Ry. h. 22 Jefferson.
" John F. carpenter, h.u. 71 Albany.
" Merritt V. clerk, 39 Church, h.u. 71 Albany.
" Mortimer C. carpenter at 101½ Hudson, h.u. 40 Fairmount.
" Sadie L. kindergarten teacher Northeast school, b. 46 Madison.
" Sarah, boxm. at 254 Pl. b.u. 35 Lafayette.
" Walter E. music teacher, h. 27 Pliny.
" Westel, clerk at 215 Main, b. 426 Asylum.
" William, mach. at Popes, h. 46 Madison.
" William G. carpenter, h. 238 Park.

Hawks Clarence A. at and h. hospital farm.
" Fred W., Retreat farm, 99, b. 99 New Britain.
" William C. asst. librarian, 1507 Broad.

**THE POST is a 20th-Century Newspaper.**

Hawksworth Henry, saloon, 111 Mn. h. 70 Sey.
" William, bartdr. at 111 Main, h. 34 Park.
Hawley Anna C. Mrs. h. 29 Main.
" Cynthia M. b. 36 Jefferson.
" Frank W. bkkpr. at 273 Asy. h. 190 Ashley.
" Fredk. R. salesm. at 190 Pearl, h. 149 Alb.
" George, expressdriver, b.u. 284 Pearl.
" Hattie C. b. 355 Windsor av.
" James J. artist sculptor, b. 2 Columbia.
" John G. headclerk at Capewell Horse Nail Co. 40 Governor, h. 98 Capitol.
" Joseph R., United States Senator, h. Washington, D.C.
" Jotham B. h. 355 Windsor av.
" Louis F. clerk, b. 149 Albany.
" Mary A. wid. E. E. h. 145 Washington.
" Mary E. Mrs. h.r. 1214 Main.
" Robert R. clerk at Popes, b.u. 20 Ellsworth.
" Timothy E. forem. Popes, h.u. 20 Ellsworth.
" Udora, h. 145 Washington.
" V. E. Co. 254 Asylum.
" Victoria E. Mrs. secretary and treasurer V. E. Hawley Co, b. 223 Asylum, rm. 15.
" William P. correspondent at Popes, 436 Capitol.
Hay John, boilermaker, h. 20 Spring.
" Samuel, bkkpr. at 1 Flow. b. 143 Woodland.
Hayden Ellen A. Mrs. h. 277 Main.
" George A. clerk at city collector's office, h. 335 Wethersfield.
" Harry L. clerk at 132 State, l. 36 Collins.
" Hascall A. clerk, 859 Mn. h. Hayden station.
" Henry R. editor Weekly Underwriter, 53 Trumbull, h. East Hartford t.
" Howard C. bkkpr. at 299 Allyn, b. 63 Imlay.
" James, waiter at 80 State, l. 19 Central.
" John D. cutter at 252 Pearl, h. 47 Lafayette.
" John M. laundry, 351 Asylum, b. 219 Collins.
" Lawrence S. shoemaker, h. 168 Front.
" Myron L. inspector at 581, b. 445 Capitol.
" Warren, editor Insurance Journal at 53 Trumbull, b. E.H.t.
" Warren E. clerk at 745 Main, b. 36 Collins.
" William A. ornamentor at 438 Asylum, b. 1220 Main.
" William T. carpenter, h. 1220 Main.
Haydenberg Andrew, pressman at 690 Park. b. 17½ Wolcott.
Hayes Agnes M. clerk at Brown, Thomson & Co. 942 Main, b. 51 Ward.
" Annie Mrs. W.H. Home for the Aged, Alb.
" Anthony, cooper, b. 1335 Broad.
" Arthur D. physician, 18 Spring.
" Edward, driver patrol wagon, b. 80 State.
" Edward W. driver at 356 Main, h. 74 Gov.
" George C. clerk at 742, b. 474 Windsor av.
" James, laborer, b. 10 Cone.
" James E. inspector, h.u. 51 Ward.
" John, polisher at 556, b. 1218 Main.
" John, laborer, h. 1 Lawrence.
" John F. clerk, at P.&R. h. 20 Green.
" John J. mach. at Popes, b. 115 Hungerford.
" John W. lineman, h.u. 1173 Main.
" Joseph, steamfitter at 164 State, h. S.M.t.
" Joseph B. clerk, b. 1218 Main.

Hayes Joseph M. packer 1 S. Ann, h. 2u. 242 Pearl.
" Mary, wid. Patrick, h.u. 94 Park.
" Mary Mrs. h. 1218 Main.
" Michael, laborer, b.r. 25 West.
" Minnie A. dressmaker, b.u. 94 Park.
" Patrick, b. 69 Governor.
" Patrick, laborer at N.E.R. h.3u. 49 Spruce.
" Patrick D. foreman, Pope Tube Co. h.E.11.t.
" Patrick F. lineman, h. 50 Retreat.
" Thomas F. lettercarrier, h.u.39 Woodbridge.
" Thomas J. bookb. at 252 Pearl, b. 123 Tru.
" Thomas J. molder, b.u. 94 Park.
" Thomas P. engir. at 427 Mn. h. 28 Linden.
" William, painter, b. 147 Babcock.
" William E. toolm. at Popes, b. 28 Linden.
" ☞ see also Hays.
Haynes Alfred W. assembler Popes, b. 26 Union.
" Charles D. mach. at 40 Gov.b. 18 Pawtucket.
" Charles W. Mrs. h. 74 Windsor av.
" Chauncey E. forem. at Jewells, h. 18 Lewis.
" Elizabeth, wid. John J. h. 35 Waverly.
" Frank T. laundrym. at 1130, b.u. 1125 Main.
" George A. boilermaker, h.2u. 4 Squire.
" Helen, wid. Benjamin F. h. 201 Retreat.
" Henry M. goldbeater at 41 Trumbull.
" Henry R. printer at 668 Mn. h. 46 Allen pl.
" Howard, lithog. at r. 34 Pratt, b. 26 Union.
" John H. machinist at 142 Russ, b. 26 Union.
**HAYNES J. W.**      See page   557.
" ☞ see also Haines.
Hays George, patternmaker at 1 Flower, h. 143 Woodland.
" Richard, tailor, h.u. 93 Windsor.
" Robert L. machinist, b.u. 9 Kilbourn.
" Wm. R. machinist at 1 Flower, l. 197 Main.
" ☞ see also Hay, Hayes.
Haythorn Winifred, wid. Daniel, h.u. 224 Putnam.
Hayward Andrew J. bookkeeper at Hatch & North, 56 Commerce, h. 24 Alden.
" Harold J. with Travelers Ins. Co. 56 Prospect, b. 24 Alden.
" Jennie L. stenographer at Eddy Electric Manufacturing Co. b. 24 Alden.
" Mamie, wid. E.W. clerk at 928 Main, h. 223 Asylum, rm. 15.
Hazard Frank, carpenter at 1 Flow. h.435 Capitol.
" Lucy and Lucia, Misses, h. 33 Lafayette.
" Nelson T. toolm. at Colts, h.u. 7 Congress.
Hazel Charles F. plumber, b.u. 46 Portland.
" George, molder, b. 34 Village.
" John F. hodcarrier, b. 548 Park.
" R. cook at 80 State.
" Robert J. clerk, h.u. 46 Portland.
" William, laborer, h. 548 Park.
" Wm.H.cutter at Pope Tube Co. h. 19 Kibbe.
Hazelwood Stephen S. machinist at 70 Huyshope, b. 24 Woodbridge.
Hazell George A. clerk 556 Cap. b. 34 Pleasant.
" Madge, clerk at 99 Pratt, b. 34 Pleasant.
" Robert W. tinner at F. W. White's stove store, 1124 Main, h. 34 Pleasant.
Hazen Charles E. foreman at 252 Pearl, h.Blo.t.
" Edward W. circulating mgr. at Hartford Post, 23 Asylum, h. 205 Sargeant.

**If You Want all the News, Read THE POST.**

Heacox Charles, asst. foreman at Pratt & Whitney Co. 1 Flower, b 249 Lawrence.
" Charles E. mach. at 1 Flow. b. Unionville t.
" Fred A. machinist at 1 Flow. h. Unionville t.
Heald Charles L. laborer. b. 20 Talcott.
Healey Annie, wid. Thomas, h.u. 545 Main.
" Annie K. clerk at Brown, Thomson & Co. 942 Main, h 17 Canton.
" Bertrand N. profiler at Colts,h. 417 Garden.
" Daniel, boilerman, h. 16 Atlantic.
" Daniel, laborer at 98 Kilbourn, b. 4 North.
" Daniel, teamster, b. 3 Ellery.
" Ellen, h.2u. 105 Windsor.
" Ellen, wid. Richard, h.u. 4 North.
" James, machinist at 556 Cap. b. 95 Sheldon.
" James F. baggagem. N.Y.R. depot, h.E.H.t.
" John, h. 17 Canton.
" John, framemaker, h.2u. 79 Avon.
" John E. engraver, b. 17 Canton.
" John J. assembler at Popes, b. 10 Potter.
" John J. framer at 581 Capitol, b. 79 Avon.
" Joseph D.mach.at 30 Cush. b. 138 Lawrence.
" & Ledoux, barbers, 46 Asylum.
 William A. Healey. Joseph Ledoux.
" Mabel T. asst. bkkpr. at 97 Asy.b.31 Spring.
" Michael, clerk, b. 40 John.
" Michael, laborer, h.2u. 79 Avon.
" Michael Jr. laborer, h.2u. 79 Avon.
" Robert E. mach. at 30 Cush. b. 138 Lawrence.
" Thomas W. toolm. at Popes, b. 545 Main.
" William A. (H. & Ledoux,) l.2u. 1305 Main.
" William F. machinist, Popes, b. 10 Potter.
" ☞ see also Haley; Healy.
Health Commissioners office in City hall, 800 Mn.
" Underwear Co. 66 State.
Healy Andrew, teamster at 1, h. 15 South Ann.
" Ann, h. 265 Jefferson.
" Annie, b. W.H. Home for the Aged, Albany.
" Daniel G. carptr. at 141 Tru. h.u. 68 Park.
" Declan, tinner, h.u. 138 Lawrence.
" Declan F.machinist, 388 Cap. b. 33 Wdbg.
" Dennis, driver at 71 Asy. h. 184 Ward.
" Edward, mason, b. 76 Bellevue.
" Elizabeth A. h. 7 Chapel.
" Frank E. attorney at 750 Main, h. W.L.t.
" James, lumberman, 335 Shel. h. 33 Wdbg.
" James J. Jr.clerk,27 Asy. b. 33 Woodbridge.
" Jeremiah, bartdr. at 130 Front, b. 220 Shel.
" John, barber at 347 Allyn, b. 97 Trumbull.
" John, laborer, b.2u. 258 Front.
" John E. machinist at 9 Sig. h. E.H. t.
" Jos. J. horseshoer at 276 Allyn, b. 5 Chapel.
" Patrick, hodcarrier, h.u.r. 228 Maple.
" Patrick H. clerk at 47 Ann, h.2u. 36 Ward.
" Peter F. janitor at Wethersfield av. school, h.u. 406 Franklin.
" Phillip, at National Life Association, 53 Trumbull, b. 545 Main.
" Timothy, b. 98 Chestnut.
" Thomas, shoemaker, 8, h. 10 Potter.
" Thomas, surveyor, b.u. 1333 Broad.
" Thomas, Jr.molder,114 Grove, b. 10 Potter.
" Thomas L real estate, 756 Main, h. W.L.t.
" Thomas M. carpenter, h. 49 Pawtucket.
" ☞ see also Haley; Healey; Heley.

Hearn Albert P. H. motorman St.Ry. h. 14½ N.B.
" Timothy J. screwm. 476 Cap. h. 58 Seymour.
Hearns William, screw. at 476 Cap. b. 4 Brady.
Heath Ada E. at Hartford Steam Boiler Inspection and Ins. Co. b. 112 Windsor av.
" B. nurseryman, b. 161 Capitol.
" Calvin, laborer, b. 45 Wolcott.
" Cornelia J. wid. Benjamin F. dressmaker 926, h. 926 Main, rm. 16.
" George, carpenter, b. 336 Franklin.
" Otis E. florist, h. 16 Fern.
" Samuel, carpenter, b. 5 Charlotte.
" William, laborer at 305 Far. h. 18 Owen.
" William, papermaker, h.u. 6 Huntley.
Heaton Charlotte G. wid. Edward, h. 811 Asylum.

**HEBARD & CO.** carmen and heavy teaming, 213 State. *See page 552.*
 George H. Hebard. Samuel C. Cooper.
" Geo. H. (H. & Co.) h. 144 Wethersfield.
" ☞ see also Hibbard.
Hebb Maurice, diemaker at Popes, b. 252 Law.
Hebbe Rudolf, laborer at 335 Sheldon, h. Weth. t.
Hebeler Christ, driver at 245 Windsor, b. 56 Bellevue.
Heber George, baker, b. 139 Front.
" William, mach. at 1 Flower, b. 139 Front.
Hebert Luke, carpenter, h.2u. 112 Windsor.
Heckaman Elizabeth, wid. Edw. b.249 Putnam.
" Frank E. mach. 388 Capital, h. 249 Putnam.
Heckenback Matthew J. baker, h. 19 Kibbe.
Hecker Edward, tinner at 1116 Main, h.r. 44 Village.
Hector Ellen, wid. Harmon, h.u. 489 Main.
Hedden John F. trainmaster P.&R.l. 63 Church.
" Margaret T. teacher High school, b. 3 Far.
Heddenberg Andrew, at .690 Park, b.u.r. 17 Wolcott.
Heddle James, carpenter, b. 373 Capitol.
" Malgal, carpenter, b. 373 Capitol.
Heddrick, Barbara, wid. Alex. h. 40 Fairmount.
" William, painter, b. 40 Fairmount.
Hedges Thomas, bookkeeper at Brown, Thomson & Co. dry goods, 942 Main, h. 18 Grand.
Hedican Kate, dressmaker, 903, h. 903 Main.
" Lizzie, dressmaker, 903, h. 903 Main.
Hedlund John, coachm. 78 Weth. h. 9 Elliott pl.
" John Emil, at 98 High, h. 1151 Broad.
" Levin, tailor, h.2u. 31 Putnam.
Hedrick, Albert P. mach. 1 Flower, b. Enfield t.
" Chas. B. student at Trinity, b. 122 Vernon.
Hedstrom Anna, wid. Gustave, h. 162 Russ.
" Arvid G. receivingclerk, Popes, h. 162 Russ.
" Ellen A. clerk at 366 Asylum, b. 162 Russ.
Heeber William, mach. at 1 Flow. b. 139 Front.
Heeney John F. polisher,Popes,h.2u. 12 Affleck.
" Wm. L. engir. 365 Allyn, h. 20½ Goodwin.
Heffernan Chas. C. opera. 40 Gov. b. 1 Orchard.
" James, blacksmith, h. 1 Orchard.
" Michael, teamster, h.u. 111 Potter.
" Patrick, moulder at 618 Cap. h. 362 Front.
" Patrick Mrs. (Bridget) groc. 66, h. 66 Front.
" Patrick J. clerk at 197 Asylum, b. 66 Front.
Hefferon Edwin F. machinist, b. 47 Sigourney.
" James, printer, 25 Asy. b.u. 74 Lawrence.
" Thomas, firem. N.E.R. b.2u. 50 Russell.

**Advertise Your Real Estate in THE POST.**

Heffon Alice M. attendant at 30 Washington.
Heffron Thos. boilerm. N.Y.R.h.u. 47 Sigourney.
  " Thomas Jr. at 1 Laurel, b.u. 47 Sigourney.
Hegarty Timothy A. driver at Lincoln, Seyms & Co. 34 Market, h.u. 18 Goodwin.
Hegeman George S. vice prest. Hart & Hegeman Mfg Co. h. New York. *See page 539.*
Hegman Gustavus A. tailor at 720 Main, h. 21 Mulberry.
  " Oscar, tailor at 720 Main, h. 21 Mulberry.
Heider Max, machinist, b. 8 Belden.
  " Nellie B. Mrs. stenographer at Case, Lockwood & Brainard Co. 141 Pearl, b. 8 Belden.
Heiding Frank H. packer at 252 Pearl, h. 5 Hungerford.
Heidroth Henry, laborer at 335, b. 80 Sheldon.
Heim J. W. rubberworker at 690, h. 819 Park.
Heil Joseph, musician, h. 10 Lawrence.
  " Louisa, wid. Frank, b. 28 Vernon.
Heilpern James, inspector 690 Park, b. 71 Avon.
Heimer Bruno, machinist at 1 Flower, b. E.H.t.
Heimgartner Louis, (*H. & Sutter,*) h. 153 Weth.
  " & Sutter, saloon and h. 39 Mulberry.
    Louis Heimgartner.    Jacob Sutter.
Hein Chas. harnessman at 8 Sig. h. 14 Kibbe.
  " Frank, h. 31 Grace.
  " Louisa, wid. Frederick, h.u. 26 Talcott.
Heindle Theodore, filer at Colts, h. 1088 Broad.
Heine Jacob, cook at Allyn house, 152 Asylum.
Heins Brothers saloon, 26 Union pl. 430, hotel, 428 Asylum.
    Frank W. Heins.    Wm. F. Heins.
  " Frank W. (*Heins Bros.*) h. 430 Asylum.
  " John W. rubberworker at 690 Park, h. Hazardville v.
  " William F. (*Heins Bros.*) h. 430 Asylum.
  ☞ *see also Hines; Hynes.*
Heints Geo. H. pressman, 668 Main, b. 68 Church.
  " Philip, h. 68 Church.
Heinz Anton, filer at Colts, h. 50 Harbison.
  " Thomas, filer at Colts, h. 65 Dean.
Heinze Meta, dressmaker, 1148, b. 1148 Broad.
Heise Frank A. policeman, h. 26 Church.
  " George C. policeman, h. 49 Grand.
  " Henry A. storekpr. Popes, h.u. 20 Babcock.
Helbig Christian, cabinetmaker, b.2u. 80 Grove.
Helender Markum, plumber, h.3u. 18 Trumbull.
Helene Charles, cutter at 91, h. 91 Front.
  " Madame, hairdressing, etc. 223 Asy. rm. 56.
  " Manuel, clothier and tailor, 91, h. 91 Front.
Helfricht Charles J. contractor, h. 175 Maple.
  " Cuno A. engraver at Colts, h. 83 Webster.
Helgerson Andrew J. b. 72 Charter Oak.
Helin Andrew W. repairer at Popes, h. 109 Law.
Helion Daniel J. collection clerk at National Exchange Bank, 76 State, b. 209 Main.
  " John J. (*Butler & Helion,*) b. 209 Main.
  " Margaret, teacher Charter Oak school, 91 Charter Oak, b. 209 Main.
  " Mary B. h. 209 Main.
Heller Asher, buyer at 921 Main, b. 25 Windsor.
Hellgren Per A. shoemaker at 92 Tru. h. E.H.t.
Hellman Anton, clerk at 143 Trumbull, b. 502 Windsor av.

Hellman Emmy, milliner, 908 Main, b. 502 Windsor av.
  " Ludwig, h. 502 Windsor av.
  " Minna, teacher at Brown school, 160 Market, b. 502 Windsor av.
Hellyar Charles, bricklayer, b. 142 Windsor.
  " Frank C. mason, h. 577 Park.
  " Frederick, mason, h. 240 New Park.
  " Joseph, mason, h. 577 Park.
  " Margaret, wid. Thomas E. b. 142 Windsor.
Helm Christopher L. h.r. 10 Russell.
  " George J. bartender, h.u. 192 Jefferson.
Hellstrom Oscar, gardener at Mrs. Colts, 30, b.r. 30 Wethersfield.
Helstrom Gustave, watchm. 581 Cap. h. 139 Bab.
Heminway Edwin H. cashier at W. C. Mason & Co. 746 Main, b. 5 Wadsworth.
  " Minnie E. b. 5 Wadsworth.
Hemmerle August, pressman at 690 Park, h.2u. 38 Temple.
  " Henry J. pressman at 25 Asy. b.u. 38 Temple.
Hempstead Adelaide R. hair store, 881, h.4u. 926 Main, room 74.
  " Lorenzo, telegrapher at 6 Central, h.811 Main.
Hendee Sarah J. Miss h. 74 Buckingham.
Henderson Chas., Pros. Casino, h. 10 Highland.
  " Charles, wine clerk at 200, b. 204 Asylum.
  " Charles H. laborer, b. 94 Walnut.
  " Charles L. molder at 1 Flow. b. 1212 Broad.
  " Ella, dressmaker, 37, b. 37 Madison.
  " George A. motorman St. Ry. h. 14 Benton.
  " J. D. clerk at Popes, b. Manchester t.
  " James, at Popes, b.2u. 306 Market,
  " James, golf trainer, b. Park, W.H.t.
  " James D. printer, 336 Asylum, b.2u. 109 Windsor.
  " John, clerk at Brown, Thomson & Co. 942 Main, b. 97 Trumbull.
  " John F. paperruler, b.2u. 109 Windsor.
  " Mary, wid. James, h.2u. 109 Windsor.
  " Oscar, filer at James L. Howard & Co. 438 Asylum, h. E.H.t.
  " Wm. G. gard. at H. C. Judd, h. 10 Highland.
Hendley Arthur, J. mach. 476 Cap. h. 100 Laurel.
Hendrick George, teamster, b.r. 14 Martin.
  " Harriet, nurse, b. 14 Church, rm. 3.
  " James, laborer, b.r. 14 Martin.
Hendrickson John, helper, b. 42 Lawrence.
  " Neils, b. 42 Lawrence.
  " Peter H. carpenter, h. 1 Kilbourn ct.
Hendron George, teamster at Seidler & May, 306 Pearl, h.u. 88 Mather.
  " John, expressman, h.u. 3 Cranes ct.
  " Maggie, laundress at 20 South Hudson.
Heneber Jas. E. mach. 1 Flow. b.2u. 86 Madison.
  " Morris, casehardener at 476 Capitol, h.2u. 76 Putnam.
Heneford Maurice, machinist, b.2u. 35 Mechanic.
Heneghan Michael, helper at 1 Flower, h.2u. 10 Lawrence.
  " Michael 2d, laborer, b.2u. 10 Lawrence.
  " Owen, masonstender, h.2u. 19 Howard.
  " William, saloon, 141 Windsor, h. 52 Avon.
Heniher John, b. 48 Bonner.
Henion Charles Irving, carpenter, h. 76 N.B.

**As A NEWSPAPER, THE POST LEADS.**

Henke Adolph, tailor, h. 48 Seymour.
" Amalie M. teacher at South school, 36 Wadsworth, h. 48 Seymour.
" Charles, baker at 238 N.P. h. 41 Francis.
" Francesca A. teacher at Brown school, 160 Market, b. 48 Seymour.
Henken Diedrich H. tailor, h. 10½ Village.
" Geo. P. plumber at 280 Asy. b. 10½ Village.
Henkin William H. musician, h. 28 Pleasant.
Henley A. B. trav. salesm. at Popes,h. Jersey City.
" Johanna, h. 36 Trumbull.
Henn Albert W. secretary and treasurer Acme Machine Screw Co. h. 44 Allen pl.
" Barbara, wid. Frank A. b. 6 Russell.
" Christina, wid. Wm. washer, h.3u. 9 Kinsley.
" Edwin C. president Acme Machine Screw Co. h. Bloomfield t.
Hennessey Alice Mrs. h.3u. 36 Sheldon.
" Edward J. ostler 356 Main, h.2u.39 S.Pro.
" Frank A. conductor St.Ry. b. 36 Hicks.
" James F. policeman, h.u. 25 Talcott.
" John, at 1, b. 32 Flower.
" John, machinist, b. 46 Grand.
" John, teamster at 100 Commerce, h. 64 Front.
" Kate, wid. John, h. 36 Hicks.
" Lawrence, teamster, b.u. 103 Commerce.
" Michael, teamster, h.u. 103 Commerce.
" Patrick, blacksmith, b.u. 49 Lawrence.
" Patrick, farmer, h.r 13 New Park.
" Thomas, molder at 556 Cap. h.2u. 16 Elm.
" Timothy, machinist at Colts, h.2u. 165 Front.
" William, teamster at 571 Main, b. 16 Winter.
" William N. bricklayer,b.2u. 117 Hungerford.
Henney Charles M. freight agent, Penn. R.R. 18 State, h. 427 Main, rm. 63.
" David, president, treas. Hartford Light and Power Co. 266 Pearl, h. Unionville t.
" James B. gen. manager Hartford Light and Power Co. h. 90 Vernon.
**HENNEY WM. F.** attorney at law, 11 Central, b. 32 Vernon.
Hennig Anton, polisher at Wm. Rogers Mfg. Co. 66 Market, h. Addison v.
Henning Otto, saloon, 31, h. 33 Temple.
" William L. barber, 77 Trumbull, h. 17 Pratt.
Henrechon Geo.N. mach. at 1 Flow.b. 874 Broad.
" John B. machinist at Pratt & Whitney Co. 1 Flower, h. 1214 Broad.
Henrichson Peter, tailor, 45, h.u. 45 Ann.
Henry Abbie E. teacher, b. 17 Haynes, rm. 116.
" Albert W. mangr. at 1028 Main, h. 284 Sig.
" Blanch S. b. 284 Sigourney.
" Carter, teamster, b.r. 88 Fairmount.

Henry Chas. E. packer,725 Mn. h.r.88 Fairmount.
" Charles W. student at Trinity college, 6 Northam tower, Summit.
" Della, b. 116 Ann.
" Esther, h. 17 Haynes, room 116.
" George B. electrician, b. 284 Sigourney.
**HENRY GEORGE H.** manager Associate Dentists, 943, h. 943 Main.
*See page 423.*
" Harriet W. bookkeeper at Hartford Post, 23 Asylum, b. 55 Ashley.
" Isaac W. machinist, h. 891 Windsor av.
" Jas. G. tinner at 1162 Main, h. 15 Russell.
" John, mason, b.u. 34 Lawrence.
" John E. waiter, l.r. 88 Fairmount.
" John M. supt. police, h. 49 Green.
" Nellie M. stenographer at Pope Tube Co. b. 55 Ashley.
" Rob't A. forem. 135 She. h. 50½ Annawan.
" Robert G. clerk at 1162 Main, b. 15 Russell.
" Thomas, mason, h.u. 18 Gold.
" William, ostler at 11, b. 11 Winthrop.
Hensley Willam C. mechanic at Popes, h.60 Bond.
Henson Annie M. wid. Johanson, b. 36 Harrison.
" Hubert, teamster, h.u. 63 Pleasant.
" James, laborer at 8 Front, h. 18 Dean.
" James H. operator at 40 Governor, b. E.H.t.
" Keron, laborer at 8 Front, h. 41 Glendale.
" Mary Mrs. b. 2 Holcomb.
" Peter, blacksmith at 5 Mec. h. 106 Windsor.
" ☞see also Hansen; Hanson.
Hepburn Alex. porter at 745 Main, h. Ingleside.
" George H. h. 225 High.
" John, shipping clerk at Potter & Payne, 405 Allyn, h. 48 New Britain.
Hepp Peter, machinist at 476 Cap. h. 324 Park.
Heppe A. Elizabeth, teacher at Washington street school, b. 223 Asylum.
Herbert Art Co. fancy goods, 726 Main.
" Elias, peddler, h.2u. 78 Talcott.
" Maurice J. toolm. Popes, h.2u. 1212 Broad.
" Nathan, harnessmaker, 186 Front.
" Thomas F. lineman, 3 Central, b. 80 State.
Herbst W. Edward, bootmaker, 71, h. 71 Asylum.
Herding Frank H. packer, 252 Pearl, h. 10 Hung.
Herdllin Louise J. clerk at 913 Main, b. 200 Wethersfield.
Hergan Mary, operator, 97 Asy. b. 1418 Board.
Herlihy Florence, clerk at 372 Asy. b. 27 Spruce.
Herlitschek Isaac, bkkpr. 221 State, h. 35 Brook.
" Marcus, h. 82 Pleasant.
" Samuel, clerk, b. 82 Pleasant.
Herman Caroline, wid. John A. h. 6 Lewis.
" Christoph, buffer at Popes, h. N.B.t.
" John, coachman at 510, h. 510 Farmington.
Hermann Anthony, screwmaker, b.u. 23 Sheldon.
" Frederick B. mechanic at 581 Capitol, h. New Britain.
**HERMANN FRED. N.** (*Andrus & Hermann*,) 300 Asylum, b. 44 Hopkins.   *See page 484.*
" Joseph, helper at 142 Russ, h.r. 11 Ellery.
" Leonard, bartender at 72 Tru. h.u. 96 Maple.
" Maurice, assembler at Popes, h.u. 193 Front.
" Nicholas F. carpenter, N.Y.R. b.1212 Broad.
" ☞see Herrmann.

Hernes Charles B. at 690 Park, h.2u. 10 Rose.
Herold Charles Mrs. (Emilie,) h. 71 Church.
Herr John M. steamfitter, b.2u. 198 Allyn.
Herrick Albert A. ostler, h. 51 Talcott.
" Lewis B. h. 1279 Main.
" Louis A. shipping clerk at 221 State, h.u. 2 Kilbourn ct.
" Mary F. wid. Benjamin, h.2u. 1039 Main.
Herridge Richard, filer, 476 Cap. h. 83 Allen pl.
Herrington Alfred G. machinist at 1 Flower, h. 76 Spring.
" Ernest W. telegraph operator, b. 76 Spring.
" Frederick E. clerk, 552 Asy. b. 76 Spring.
" Herbert S. clerk, 44 Asylum, b. 76 Spring.
" Louisa, wid. Alfred, b.u. 19 Buckingham.
" ☞ see also Harrington.
Herriott Emma F. Mrs. h. 24 Vernon.
" Randolph R. clerk at Kimball & McCray, 558 Main, b. Windsor t.
" William Howard, b. 24 Vernon.
Herrmann Chas. L. artist, 111, h. 111 Trumbull.
" Frederika J. wid. Carl, h. 111 Trumbull.
" Kathariner M. b. 111 Trumbull.
" Katherine Mrs. h.2u. 1075 Broad.
" Lizzie M. b. 111 Trumbull.
" W. D. & Co. cafe, 106 Asylum,*
" Wenzel, market, 162, h. 164 Front.
" William, polisher, 581 Capitol, b.u.17 Affleck.
" Wm. D. (W. D. H. & Co.) b. 111 Trumbull.
" ☞ see also Herman.
Herron John, pickler at Popes, h. 58 Flower.
" Robert, machinist, b. 1447 Broad.
" William, assembler at 556 Cap. b.1447 Broad.
Herrup Eli, h.u. 199 Front.
" Louis, salesman, b. 199 Front.
" & Raphael, barbers, 278 Asylum.
    Solomon Herrup.        Harry Raphael.
" Sam. barber, 1 Spruce, h. 304 Market.
" Solomon (H. & Raphael,) b. 201 Front.
Hersey George M. general secretary Y.M.C.A. 315 Pearl, h. Farmington av. W.H.t.
            See pages 704, 705.
Hershinor B. rags, 102, h. 102 Windsor.
Hertel Albert G. veterinary surgeon, r. 371 Main, h.u. 16 Trumbull.
Herter Louis A. engrav. at 30 Asy. b.5 Pleasant.
" Wm. C. horse bootm. 8 Sig. h.u. 42 Laurel.
Herth Frank, cook at 651, b. 651 Main.
Herting Edward W. b. 61 Prospect.
" Theo. M. cigar mfr. r. 173 State.
Hertsch Bernhardt, teamster at Hartford Provision Co. h. Glastonbury t.
Hertzler George C. groceries, 193, h. 78 Park.
Herzer Charles, map colorer, 40, b.u. 40 Wolcott.
" Theodore, printer at Case, Lockwood & Brainard Co. 141 Pearl, h. 39 Ashley.
Herzfeld Harry, clerk, b. 23 Pavilion.
" Julius, lettercarrier, P.O. h.u. 23 Pavilion.
" Leo, clerk at 956 Main, b.u. 23 Pavilion.
Herzog John, brushm. 176 Allyn, h. 17 Sanford.
Heslow Thomas, b. 1113 Main.
Hess Benedict, farmer, b. Park, W.H.t.
" Bernard, plasterer, h.u. 164 Front.
" Chas. T. clerk at 47 Ann, h. 20 Brown.
" Conrad, laborer, h.u. 64 Vanblock.

Hess Conrad, stocker at Colts, b. 64 Vanblock.
" Frederick J. at Nims, Whitney & Co. h.u. 153 Market.
Hessert Wm. F. cigarmaker 597 Mn. h. 146 Alb.
Hessian Thomas, helper at 30 Cush. h.r. 21 Haw.
Hester Lewis E. engineer, P.&R. b. 110 Brook.
Hetherton Richard B. deputy sheriff, constable, 85 Trumbull, h. 37½ Church.
Hetschel Albert A. rubberw. b.2u. 81 Front.
" Emil, clerk at 705 Main, b.2u. 81 Front.
" Sophia, wid. Emil, clerk at 701 Main, h.2u. 81 Front.
Hettrich Louis, bottler at 480, b. 428 Asylum.
Hetzel George J. buffer at Wm. Rogers Mfg. Co. 66, h. 149 Market.
" Geo. J.Mrs. confectionery,149,h.149Market.
" George M. cutter, 1260 Mn. b. 210 Barbour.
Heublein Albert F. bartender at 480 Asylum, h.u. 63 Chestnut.
" Andrew, bottler at 605, b. 603 Main.
" August, h.u. 86 Wells.
" Edmund, saloon, 605, h.u. 603 Main.
" Frederick W. h. 9 Fairfield.
" G. F.& Bro. wholesale liquors, 74 Trumbull, saloon, 931 Main.
    Gilbert F. Heublein.    Louis F. Heublein.
" Gilbert F. (G.F.H.& Bro.) h. Prospect av.
" Hotel, 98 Wells, c. Gold.
" Hugo, bartender at 931, b.u. 603 Main.
" Louis F. (G. F. H. & Bro.) b. 98 Wells.
" W. E. at 74 Trumbull, b.u. 86 Wells.
Heubner ☞ see Huebner.
Heussler Frank F. mailing clerk, daily Times, 716 Main, b. 1336 Broad.
Hevenor Anna E. wid. John F. h.u. 194 Laurel.
" Chas. L. mach. at 1 Flower, b.u. 194 Laurel.
Hewes Dwight N. sec'y M. & H. Co. h.u. 158 Sargeant.
" Nathaniel, b.u. 158 Sargeant.
" ☞ see also Hughes.
Hewins Caroline M. librarian Hartford Public Library, 5 Athenæum, b. 705 Asylum.
" Matt H. billiard saloon, 734 Main, h. 281 Collins.
Hewitt Andrew, pressman, 690 Park, h. 8 Amity.
" Arthur R. stereotyper at Hartford Times, 716 Main, b. 256 New Park.
" Edward E. patternm. 556 Cap. h. 91 Russ.
" Frank, driver at r. 87, b.r. 87 High.
" George F.rubberw.690 Park, h.5 Davenport.
" Henry H market, 1157 Main, l. 118 Asylum.
" John B. engir. 24 Mechanic, h. 236 N.P.
Hewson David, h.u. 152 Mather.
" Henry W. laborer, r.u. 65 Elm.
" John, carpenter, b.u. 152 Mather.
Heyer Charles E. clerk at 581 Cap. b. 816 Park.
" Frank E. mach. at 1 Flower, h. Elmwood v.
" Jas. K. Sr. mach. at 1 Flow. h. 449 Capitol.
" James Kort, Jr. machinist, b. 76 Hopkins.
" John Worth, contractor, 1 Flow. h. Elmwood.
" Paul, tinner, h. 272 Maple.
Heyne Chas. H. clerk 273 Asy. b.2u. 50 Temple.
Hibbard Ralph G. teacher of elocution High school, 39 Hopkins, h. New Britain t.
" ☞ see also Hebard.

Hick Edwin H. machinist at Colts, b. 59 Huy.
" John H. machinist at Colts, h. 59 Huyshope.
Hickey Bartholomew, at 843 Main, b.r. 155 Washington.
" Catharine, wid. Christopher, h.u. 1395 Main.
" Catharine, wid. Daniel, h.u. 40 So. Prospect.
" Edmund, engir. 24 Mec. b. 216 Sheldon.
" Edmund B. brusher, 62 Market, b.216 Shel.
" Edward, helper, 1 Flow. h.4½ Hungerford pl.
" Edward C. clerk, b.u. 1395 Main.
" Hattie, clerk at 956, b.u. 1395 Main.
" James, clerk, b.u. 1395 Main.
" James, deckh. str. Middletown, 285 State.
" John H. pressfeeder at Case, Lockwood & Brainard Co. 141 Pearl, b.u. 1395 Main.
" John J. painter, h.u. 47 Albany.
" Margaret, wid. Thomas, h.u. 8 Cedar.
" Margaret, wid. Thomas, h.u. 216 Sheldon.
" Maria Mrs. h.2u. 55 Hawthorn.
" Michael, h. 67 Harrison.
" Michael, machinist at 1 Flower, h.3u. 135 Lawrence.
" Patrick, deckh. str. Middletown, 285 State.
" Thomas, helper, b. 1442 Broad.
Hickman William J. driver at 30 State, h. 242 Bellevue.
Hickmott Edward P. at Ætna Life Insurance Co. 650 Main, b. 161 Maple.
" Lincoln S. at Conn. Mutual Life Insurance Co. 783 Main, b. 161 Maple.
" Martha E. teacher, b. 161 Maple.
" William J. at Conn. Mutual Life Ins. Co. 783 Main, h. 268 Wethersfield.
Hickox Charles A. janitor at 234, h. 234 Pearl.
Hicks Bros. stables, r. 173 State.
        William Hicks.        Job Hicks.
" Charles V. B. painter, h. 11 Talcott.
" Cornelius, ostler, b. 38 Barbour.
" Edward E. carpenter, h.u. 14 Glendale.
" Frank, b. 255 Asylum.
" Job, (Hicks Bros.) h. 38 Barbour.
" Julia, wid. Charles, b. 43 Beacon.
" Lewis W. Rev. h. 1 Farmington.
" Mary A. umbrella repairer at Brown, Thomson & Co. 942 Main, h. 11 Talcott.
" Minnie, nurse, b. 97 Webster.
" Nooman, fireman, P.&R. b. Winsted t.
" Parker J. machinist at 1 Flower, b. 101 Hungerford.
" Thomas, insurance agent, h.2u. 38 Canton.
" William, (Hicks Bros.) h. Waterbury t.
" ☞ see also Hick.
Hickson☞ see Hixon.
Hidroth Henry, laborer, l. 80 Sheldon.
Hiemer Bruno, machinist at 1 Flower, b. E.H.t.
Higbie William W. clerk at 116 Albany, b. B.v.
Higgins Barnard, bartender, 278, b. 255 Asylum.
" Cuhim M. conductor, St.Ry. h. 31 Vernon.
" Drusilla, wid. Stephen, b. 220 High.
" Ed. W. brazier at 581 Cap. b. 14 Chestnut.
" Edward W. insp. at Popes, b.u. 357 Asylum.
" Fred W. engraver at Wm. Rogers Mfg Co. 66 Market, h.u. 176 Clark.
" George W. commercial traveler, b.7 Chapel.
" Grace A. b. 81 Beacon.

Higgins John, driver at 2 Am. b.u. 46 Temple.
" John E. h. 29 Sumner.
" Joseph F. h.u. 61 Elm.
" M. Thomas, asst. pressman at Courant, 66 State, h.u. 1125 Main.
" Margaret, clerk at 956 Main, b.u.26 Putnam.
" Mary A. Mrs. h. 81 Beacon.
" Mary E. attendant at 30 Washington.
" Mary E. feeder at 154 Pearl, b. 111 Hung.
" Mary J. wid. Martin, h.u. 26 Putnam.
" Michael, laborer at 8, h. 19 Front.
" Michael J. clerk at Brown, Thomson & Co. 942 Main, h.u. 4 Putnam.
" Pat. teamster at 128 Com. b.u. 46 Temple.
" Sylvester B. b.u. 357 Asylum.
" Thomas, dropforger, Popes, h.2u.r. 61 Front.
" Thos. B. machinist, h. 111 Hungerford.
" Thomas M. helper, b. 40 Liberty.
" W. Dudley, clerk at Ætna Insurance Co. 666 Main, b.u. 26 Hopkins.
Higginson Frederick H. machinist at 476 Capitol, b.u. 41 Hudson.
Higgs William H. president Calhoun Printing Co. 29 Union pl. h. 96 Main.
Highland☞ see also Hiland; Hyland.
Highway Mission, 1216 Main.
Higley Franklin P. teamster, h.u. 38 Grand.
" M. Phinett, wid. Oliver C. h. 24 Vine.
" Sarah A. wid. Lyman O. b. 149 High.
" Warren H. carpenter, h. 62 Harrison.
" Wm. J. painter, h.u. 4½ Hungerford pl.
Hiland ☞ see also Highland; Hyland.
Hilbert James, blacksm. 276 Allyn, h.u.86 Walnut.
Hildebrand Charles, ass't actuary, Conn. Mutual Life Ins. Co. 783 Main, h. 30 Allen pl.
Hildoshoim Max, driver, h. 29 Huntley pl.
Hile Alice, wid. E. J. nurse, h. 22 Columbia.
Hilfiker Fred O. mach. at 1 Flower, b. 23 John.
Hilgen Peter, h.u. 4 New Park.
Hilinski John, ostler at 1061, b. 1061 Main.
Hill Allison S. mach. hand 40 Gov. b.15 Goodwin.
" Arthur, carpenter, b. 320 Asylum.
" Benjamin, b.u. 60 Judson.
" Benjamin E. printer, h. 26 Clark.
" Bernall F. porter at 407 Main, b. 52Sanford.
" Braxton E. porter at 852 Mn. h. 52 Sanford.
" Charles H. machinist, h.u. 26 Goodwin.
" Chas. P. assistant foreman, Hartford Times, 716 Main, h. 14 Russell.
" Eben B. (Hill & Robinson,) h. 136 Tru.
" Elizabeth Mrs. b. 30 Niles.
" Florence C. b. 11 Clinton.
" Frank J. bricklayer, b. 74 Grove.
" Frank M. driver, h.2u. 103 Commerce.
" Fred A. mach. at 1 Flower, b. Middletown t.
" Frederick A. clerk 901 Main, h.u. 14 Russell.
" Frederick J. bricklayer, b. 74 Grove.
" George, teamster, h. 51 Sanford.
" Geo. E. meat cutter, 329 Asy. b. 14 Russell.
" George F. laborer at Popes, h. 59 Windsor.
" George H. laborer at 40 Gov. h. 60 Judson.
" George S. clerk, b.u. 9 Canton.
HILL GEORGE W. mgr. Hartford Lumber Co. r. 17 Albany, h. 19 Ashley. See page 515.

Hill Helen I. wid. Jonathan T. h. 216 Windsor av.
" Henry J. foreman motor carriage department, 1 Laurel, h. 18 Sherman.
" Ichabod, machinist, h.u. 191 Lawrence.
" James A. polisher at 476 Cap. h. 59 Zion.
" John J. baggage agent N.Y.R. h. 122 Ann.
" John J. salesman, h. 18 Cottage.
" Marshall L. bkkpr. 57 Albany, h. 26 Clark.
" Mary E. b. 51 Barbour.
" & Robinson, cigarbox makers, r. 133 Shel.
    Eben B. Hill.    Arthur D. Robinson.
" Sarah E. h. 64 Clark.
" Thomas F. salesman, h. 16 Westland.
" Thomas W. harness m. at 8, b. 43 Sigourney.
" Warren Mfg. Co. cond. punches, 174 Pearl.
    John B. Holaday.
" Wm. A. printer at Courant, h.u. 57 Benton.
" Wm. A. printer at 141 Pearl, h. 115 Trumbull.
" William Cameron, student at Trinity college, 9 Jarvis hall, Summit.
" William S. lab. at 40 Gov. b.u. 60 Judson.
" ☞ see also Hills.
Hillard George A. b. 62 Bluehills.
" John, mason, h.r. 59 Zion.
" Joseph, at N.Y.R. h. 4 Lawrence.
" Thomas, laborer at stone pits, b.r. 59 Zion.
" Timothy J. steamfitter 555 Cap. h. 62 Blu.
Hille Charles, jeweler, 34 So. Prospect.
" Oscar, filer at Popes, h.2u. 8 Marsh.
Hillee Michael. clerk at 391 Main, b. 40 John.
Hillender Malcolm, tinner at 599 Mn. h. 16 Tru.
Hilliard Dennis, carpenter, b.u. 68 Park.
" Elisha C. vice president Hfd. Life Ins. Co. h. 19 Charter Oak pl.
" Maria, wid. John, bakery, 44, h. 44 Park.
Hillman Louis G. clerk at 2 S. Ann, h. 57 Village.
Hills A. Starkey, bookb. at 141 Pl. h.u. 34 Elmer.
" Addie, b. 46 Temple.
" Albert, h. 226 Garden.
" Albert M. at Conn. Mutual Life Ins. Co. 783 Main, b. 280 Garden.
Hills ALFRED L. (Hills & Fox,) builders, 22 John, h. 216 Jefferson. See page 515.
" Alonzo (H. E. H. & Son,) b. 1243 Main.
" Amelia B. wid. Oscar K. h. 75 Seymour.
" Anna B. wid. Charles E. h. 29 Center.
" Anna M. nurse, b. 370 Asylum, room 28.
" Burton, bookbinder at Case, Lockwood & Brainard Co. 141 Pearl, b.464 Windsor av.
" Burton L. with Atwood F. Co. h. 56 Park.
" Caroline, wid. Wells, b. 163 Ashley.
HILLS C. S. & CO. dry goods, etc. 883–885 Main.
    Charles S. Hills.    E. V. Vedder.
" Charles E. agent, 715 Main, b. Wethersfield t.
" Chas. E. peddler horseradish, h.u. 9 Kinsley.
" Charles H. mason, h. 70 Franklin.
" Charles S. (C. S. Hills & Co.) h. 215 Laurel.
" Chas. S. undertaker, 1166 Main, b.226 Garden.
Hills CHARLES W. (Hills & Marchant,) h. 200 Collins. See page 189.
" Clarence I. b. 226 Garden.
" Clothes Dryer, M. A. Brett, agt. 190 Asylum.
" Corinthea E. wid. Myron E. b.2u. 703 Main, rm. 12.

**HILLS & MARCHANT,**
∴ PRACTICAL ∴

**Undertakers & Embalmers,**
58 ANN STREET, corner ALLYN STREET.
*Burial Lots for Sale.*
CHARLES W. HILLS.    W. T. MARCHANT,
Residence, 200 Collins Street.    Residence, 7 Belden Street.

**HILLS & CO.** grocers, staple and fancy, fruits, etc. 372, 374 Asylum. See p. 485.
    E. Hamilton Hills.    Lee H. Hills.
" Dexter W. mason, h. 4 Village.
" E. Hamilton, (Hills & Co.) h. 64 Imlay.
" Edson, machinist, l. 90 Pearl.
" Ellen E. wid. Charles Isaac, h. 354 Laurel.
" Ellen M. wid. William, h.3u. 152 Allyn.
" Emma J. Mrs. b. 16 Buckingham.
" Ernest S. clerk, 58 Ann, b. 200 Collins.
" F. R. Mrs. boardinghouse, 98 Trumbull.
" Florence M. wid. Frank R. b. 54 Hung.

**HILLS & FOX,** masons and builders, 22 John. See page 515.
    Alfred L. Hills.    Thomas R. Fox.
" Francis H. at Connecticut Mutual Life Ins. Co. 783 Main, h. 202 Windsor av.
" Frank, machine hand at Colts, b. 14 Clark.
" Frank, teamster, h.2u. 103 Commerce.
" Frank F. clerk at 372 Asylum, h. 57 Imlay.
" Frank R. chef at 1049 Mn. h. 98 Trumbull.
" Fred. K. machinist, b. 70 Franklin.
" Frederick Arthur, printer, b. 20 East.
" Frederick K. mach. at 388 Capitol.
" Frederick W. boilersetter, h. 20 East.
" George, clerk at L. L. Ensworth & Son, iron merchants, 104 Front.
" George F. president State Bank, 795 Main, h. 50 Gillett.
" Geo. R. cashier Adams Ex. Co. h. 95 Capitol.
" Gilbert H. painter, 352 Alb. h.u. 73 Hudson.
" H. E. & Son, groceries, 1143 Main.
    Howard E. Hills.    Alonzo K. Hills.
" Henry, watchmaker, 19 Pearl, h.67 Hudson.
" Herbert C. ass't sup't Hartford and N. Y. Transportation Co. 285 State, h. E.H.t.
" Horace K. clerk, 700 Main, b.200 Windsor av.
" Howard E. (H. E. H. & Son,) b. 1243 Main.
" I. & Sons, (estate,) 847 Main.
" Ichabod, mach. 142 Russ, h. 191 Lawrence.
" J. Coolidge, office 847 Mn. rm.6, h. 19 Atwood.
" John, jobber, b.u. 253 Market.
" John P. plumber, b. 70 Franklin
" John R. builder, 754 Main, sec. Hfd. Coal Co. street commissioner, h. 47 Main.
" Jos. E. machinist at 28 Laurel, b. 90 Pearl.
" Julia G. wid. A. C. h. 243 Laurel.
" Katherine L. teacher, b. 200 Windsor av.
" Laura K. teacher, b. 200 Windsor av.
HILLS LEE H. (Hills & Co.) grocers, 372, 374 Asylum, h. 143 Ashley. See page 485.
" Leonie May, stenographer at National Life Association, 53 Trumbull, b. 79 Williams.
" Lottie, laundress, 30 Washington.
" Louis C. salesman, h. 367 Laurel.
" Lucy B. wid. Frederick, h. 7 John.

HILLS & MARCHANT, undertakers, 58 Ann.
     See page 189.
  Charles W. Hills. William T. Marchant.
" Maria D. wid. C. H. b. 15 Clinton.
" Maria L. wid. Francis H. h. 202 Windsor av.
" Mark H. decorator at Baxter the Decorator, 231 Asylum, h. Rocky Hill t.
" Matilda Mrs. b.2u. 95 Chestnut.
" Maurice, gardener, b.3u. 37 Liberty.
" May J. operator at 19½ Trumbull.
" Myra G. teach. Washington st. school, b. 202 Windsor av.
" Nelson P. mason, 64, h. 64 Clark.
" Porter, assembler at Popes, b. Main.
" R. Judson, b. 7 John.
" Raleigh Hill, teamster, l. 175 Windsor.
" Raymond, clerk, 164 State, b. 79 Williams.
" Roland B. h. 79 Williams.
" Roland B. Jr. clerk at 95 Pearl, b. 79 Williams.
" Ruez B. mach. hand at Colts, b. 14 Clark.
" Ruez H. capt. str. Middletown, h. E.H.t.
" Sarah E. b. 64 Clark.
" Stuart F. clerk at Jewell Belting Co. 15 Trumbull, b. 243 Laurel.
" W. R. clerk, 197 Asylum, b. Burnside v.
" William, clerk at 4 State, b. 115 Trumbull.
" William H. quartermaster, str. Middletown, h. Perth Amboy, N J.
" Wm. H. toolmaker at Popes, h.u. 55 Babcock.
" ☞ see also Hill.
Hillyer Appleton R. office at Ætna National Bank, 644 Main, h. 288 Windsor av.
" Clara E. Miss, h. 521 Windsor av.
HILLYER DRAYTON, (Dwight, Skinner & Co.) 207 Allyn, h. 96 Woodland.   See page 483.
" Joseph, h.u. 4 Lawrence.
Hilon Thomas, lineman, b. 452 Main.
Hilton Burton E. assem. 556 Cap. h.u. 21 South.
" Daniel D. waiter, 701 Main, h. 181 Capen.
" Eugene S. painter, h.2u. 90 Grove.
" Harry L. asst. accountant, Conn. Building & Loan Asso. 252 Asylum, b. 93 Seymour.
" John, rubber w. at 690 Park, h. 92 Laurel.
" Robert W. draughtsm. at Popes, b. 56 Park.
" Seymour E. assemb. 556 Cap. h. 58 Brown.
" Wm. F. clerk at Phœnix Mutual Life Insurance Co. 49 Pearl, h. 93 Seymour.
" Wm. H. carpenter, 690 Park, h. 23 Sherman
Hiltz Susan G. wid. John, b. 356 Windsor av.
Hiltzen Peter, lab. at 690 Park, b. 4 New Park.
Himan ☞ see Hyman.
Himberg Herman, machinist, b. 14 Pavilion.
Himelblum Hyman, mach. at Colts, h. 70 Vanblock.
Hinchey Annie, at 1 So. Ann, b. 41 Wilson.
" Bernard, b. 41 Wilson.
" John F. mach. Pope Tube Co. h. 41 Wilson.
" Patrick, laborer at stone pits, b. 41 Wilson.
" Sarah, at 1 So. Ann, b. 41 Wilson.
Hinckley Henry D. model maker at Dwight Slate Mach. Co. 13 Central, h. 111 Whitmore.
" Homer R. painter, b.u. 150 Allyn.
" Howard A. repairer 744 Mn. b. 111 Whitmore.
HINCKLEY HOWARD N. sec'y and gen. manager Dwight Slate Machine Co. 13 Central, h. 187 Sigourney.   See page 525.

Hinckley Nelson G. h. 829 Asylum.
" Watson W. newspaper agent, l.u. 236 Allyn.
" William G. foreman, Hartford Cycle Co. 581 Capitol, h. 38 Woodbine.
" ☞ see also Hinkley.
Hinds Wm. A. splicer, 690 Park, h. 18 Carpenter.
Hine Charles D. secretary State Board Education, room 42, State capitol, h. New Britain t.
" Chester, at 59½ Trumbull, h. W.H.t.
" George H. mach. at 1 Flower, b.u. 139 Zion.
" Sylvester Rev. h. 25 Huntington.
Hines Christopher, laborer, b.2u. 35 Mechanic.
" Daniel B. lab. at 476 Capitol, b. 1062 Broad.
" Eliza, wid. Michael, h.2u.r. 35 Mechanic.
" Ellen, wid. John, h.u. 55 Governor.
" George J. cond. St. Ry. b. 884 Main, rm. 36.
" James B. profiler at Colts, h.2u. 111 Maple.
" John B. machinist at Popes, b.u. 133 Ward.
" John P. machinist, h.u. 26 Cedar.
" Margaret, wid. Daniel, h.3u. 1 Front.
" Margaret, wid. John, at Phœnix Ins. Co. 64 Pearl, h. 40 Lewis.
" Mary, h.u. 27 Spruce.
" Mary, wid. Patrick, h.u. 192 Sheldon.
" Matthew, clerk at Brown, Thomson & Co. 942 Main, b.3u. 1 Front.
" Michael, porter at 26, b. 26 State.
" Samuel F. refiner at 265 Asy. l. 97 Wash.
" Thos. E. plumber, 94 State, b. 41 Amity.
" Thomas J. machineh. Colts, b. 55 Governor.
" William A. h.u. 18 Carpenter.
" Wm. A. corem. at 1 Flower, b.u. 55 Gov.
" ☞ see also Hynes, Heine.
Hing Charles W. laundry, 258, h. 258 Allyn.
" Simon, helper P.&R. b. 65 Fairmount.
Hingley Frank Edgar, machinist at 70 Huyshope, b. 25 Pawtucket.
Hinkley A. Guy, at Ætna Life Ins. Co. 650 Main, b. 150 Allyn.
" Albert H. (Pietsch & H.) h. 150 Allyn.
" Homer R. painter at 1146 Main, b. 150 Allyn.
" ☞ see also Hinckley.
Hinman Arthur, clerk at 40 Gov. b. 21 Walnut.
" Charles, conductor P.&R. h. 21 Walnut.
" Charlotte M. clerk, 334 Weth. b. 58 Church.
" Ellen, cook, 20 South Hudson.
" Harry R. mgr. at 45 Asy. h.2u. 156 Wash.
" Henry, steward tug Coulston, 285 State.
" Orrin M. carptr. 690 Park, h. 32 Heath.
" Robinson S. chief clerk in secretary of state office, State capitol, rm. 36, b. 152 Asylum.
Hinton Harry, painter at 25 Wells, b. E.H.t.
" John, filer at Colts, h. East Hartford t.
Hinsdale F. B. wid. E. P. b. 439 Capitol.
Hinz Herman, b. 39 Mulberry.
Hipp Peter, screwmaker, h. 324 Park.
Hipple William H. at Phœnix Insurance Co. 64 Pearl, h. 9 May.
Hirsch Arthur, clerk at 1 S. Ann, h. 63 Congress.
" Jacob, h.u. 28 Sanford.
" Louis, mason, h.u. 100 Jefferson.
Hirschfield Annie Mrs. groceries, 56, h. 56 Mar.
" David, porter at 956 Main, h. 56 Market.
" Otto G. engraver at R. S. Peck & Co. 26 High, h. Meriden t.

Hirst Arthur J. ass't cook, 53 Ann, b.u. 14 Fmt.
"   George, mach. 1 Flower, b.r. 30 Wethersfield.
"   ☞ *see also Hurst.*
Hirth Angustus C. student, b. 76 Jefferson.
"   Joseph, saloon, 279 Main, h. 76 Jefferson.
"   Joseph E. student, b. 76 Jefferson.
Hislop Thomas, helper, b. 1113 Main.
Historical Rooms, 624 Main.     *See Index.*
Hitchcock Alfred M. teacher at High School, 39 Hopkins, b. 41 Willard.
"   Burritt C. bkkpr. at 372 Asy. h. 112 Wooster.
"   Carrie M. Mrs. dressmaker, 650, h. 650 Main, rm. 41.
"   & Curtiss Knitting Co. 1189 Broad.
"   Emily E. wid. Henry, h.u. 216 Windsor av.
"   Ernest, painter, h.u. 766 Park.
"   Henry P. merchant tailor, 10 State, h. 59 Garden.
"   Hiram, painter, h.u. 12 Sisson.
"   K. E. Mrs. b. 116 Wooster.
"   Marcena, president Hitchcock & Curtiss Knitting Co. h. 1183 Broad.
"   Wm. mailing dep't Hfd Post, 23, b. 289 Asy.
Hixon George O. ship. clk. 690 Pk. b. 64 Putnam.
"   Lula M. stenographer at 49 Pearl, rm. 19, b.u. 64 Putnam.
HJERPE EMIL, councilman *9th ward*, messenger at Popes, h. 1151 Broad.
"   Oscar W. cutter, 59½ Tru. h. 212 Asylum.
Hoadley Edward J. confectioner, 19 Foot Guard pl. h. 16 Garden.
"   Francis A. teller Hartford Trust Company, 764 Main, h. 78 Ann.
"   George E. h. 78 Ann.
"   Manufacturing Co. mfgrs. of confectionery, 19 Foot Guard.
Hoadly Chas. J. state librarian in Capitol,h. 78 Ann.
Hoagland Oscar F. toolm. 1 Flower, b. 74 Putnam.
Hoar Ann, wid. Michael, h.2u. 41 Mechanic.
Hoban Edward A. filer at Popes, h. 23 Spring.
"   John J. machinist at 9 Sig. b. 81 Asylum.
"   Michael J. chipper, 556 Cap. h. 29 Chestnut.
Hobb Alexander, jobber, b.u. 253 Market.
Hobbey James N. & Co. brokers, 75 Pratt.
Hobbs Chappell, watchm. r. 87 High, l. 34 Village.
Hoben James, tinner, h. 45 Green.
"   John, mach. N.Y.R. shop, h. 18 Glendale.
"   Michael, h. 21 Chestnut.
"   Thomas F. painter Colts, h.u.r. 72 Vanblock.
Hobine Henry, polisher at Popes, l. 118 Asylum.
HOBSON ARTHUR E. *councilman 7th ward*, supt. 62 Market, h. 21 Wethersfield.
"   George W. h. 732 Park.
"   Harry C. mach. 1 Flower, b.u. 56 Francis.
"   Mary C. nurse, 221, b. 221 Capen.
Hodge A. B. & Co. infants' and children's wear, 64 Pratt.*
"   Annie B. *(A. B. H. & Co.)* b. 86 Ann.
"   Arthur, h.2u.r. 60 Temple.
"   Edward B. machinist at 54 Arch,h. Naubuc v.
"   Edgar, motorman, St.Ry. h.u.r. 60 Temple.
"   Eugene L. elevator. 68 Pratt, b. 111 Pearl.
"   Frank C. mech. 26 High, h. 50 Albany.
"   Franklin A. printer, Hartford Courant, 66 State, h. 105 Jefferson.

HODGE GEO. W. special agent American Real Estate Co. 904 Main, rms. 30–31, h. Rainbow v.
"   Harriet F. b. 19 Capitol.
"   Homer L. patternm. Popes, h.u. 196 Russ.
"   Lulu, waitress, 255 Asylum, b. 36 Liberty.
"   Minnie A. b.u. 11 Bellevue.
Hodnett Thomas, painter, b. 6 Chapel.
Hodus Lewis, theological student, 1507 Broad.
Hoelst Jean, cook, 98 Wells, b. 33 Mulberry.
Hoey Jas. machinist at 1 Flower, b. 49 Walnut.
"   Robert, b. 2 Holcomb.
"   ☞ *see also Hoye.*
Hofer John, assembler at Colts, h. 2 Kilbourn ct.
"   Victor, machinist, h. 2 Kilbourn ct.
Hoff Aron, h.u. 190 Front.
"   George, screwm. at 476 Cap. b. 190 Front.
"   Isaac, shoemaker, 146 State, h.u. 138 Grove.
"   Julius, shoem. at 1192 Main, h.u.r. 174 Front.
"   Louis, barber, 71 Potter, h.u. 90 Front.
Hoffberg George, mach. 1 Flow. h. 46 Portland.
Hoffman Belle, wid. Bardy, h. 285 Market.
"   C. F. Paul, court stenog. b. 26 Huntington.
"   David, tailor, 104 Trumbull, h. 262 Front.
"   George A. stenographer at F. H. Richards, 803 Main, b. 234 High.

HOFFMAN JOHN R. civil engineer, 721 Main, rm. 24.     *See page 441.*
"   Joseph, driver, h. 26 North.
"   Louis, tailor, 296, h. 296 Market.
"   Samuel, peddler, h. 26 North.
"   William J. inspector, Popes, h. 88 Whitmore.
"   William J. Mrs. dressm. 88, h. 88 Whitmore.
Hoffmer Anton, mason, h.u. 12 Woodbine.
Hoffmokel Theodore, brewer at 315 Park, h.2u. 52 Lawrence.
Hogaboom Homer A. policeman, h. 109 Main.
Hogan Anna Mrs. h.2u. 44½ John.
"   Charles L. bkkpr. 280 Asy. b. 41 Woodbine.
"   Delia, wid. John H. h.u. 15 Talcott.
"   Dennis F. manager at Robert Walker's, paints, &c., 12 Church, b. 17 Morris.
"   Edward, deckh. str. Middletown, 285 State.
"   Edward D. saddler at 8 Sig. b. 41 Woodbine.
"   Ellen, wid. Thomas, h. 17 Morris.
"   Honora, wid. James, h.u. 8 Potter.
"   James, laborer, b.2u. 101 Sheldon.
"   John, enameler at Popes, h.u. 227 Bellevue.
"   John F. bookkeeper at 74, b. 53 Grove.
"   John H. switchman, N.Y.R. h.u. 197 Windsor.
"   John P. clerk at 521 Main, h.u. 209 Sheldon.
"   Josephine H. clerk, b. 41 Woodbine.
"   Julia A. clerk at 1213, b. 1213 Main.
"   Keron, foreman at Popes, h. 33 Center.
"   Lenore S. bookkeeper, b. 41 Woodbine.
"   Lewis F. brakeman, b.u. 15 Talcott.
"   Malachi, plumber, 760 Main, b. 41 Wdbg.
"   Mfg. Co. plumbers' supplies, 74 Grove.
"   Margaret A. dressmaker, 17, b. 17 Morris.
"   Mary T. clerk at Brown, Thomson & Co. 942 Main, b. 227 Bellevue.
"   Mathew M. b. 53 Grove.
"   Matthew, (Hogan Mfg. Co.) 74, b. 53 Grove.
"   Michael, laborer at 1 Flower, h. 133 Law.

## W. B. HOGAN & BRO.,

### Plumbers, Steam and Gas Fitters,

81 Trumbull St., Allyn House Block,

Dealers in all kinds of Brass and Plated Goods, Plumbing and Gas Fitting Materials. Gas Fixtures furnished at short notice.

Hogan Michael, shoemaker, 41,. h. 41 Woodbine.
" Nellie M. teacher Law. st. sch. b. 17 Morris.
" Patrick, laborer, b.u. 250 Front.
" Pat'k, porter, depot restaurant, b. 23 Spring.
" Thomas F. carpenter, b.u. 44½ John.
" Thos. F. gen. forem. N.Y.R. h.u. 1302 Broad.
" Thomas F. moulder at 556 Cap. b. 7 Haw.
" Thomas H. mech. at 476 Cap. h. 80 Madison.
" Thos. M. (W. B. H. & Bro.) h. 17 Morris.
" Thomas N. clerk at 739 Main, b. 53 Grove.
" William B. (W. B. H. & Bro.) h.u. 17 Morris.
HOGAN WM. B. & BRO. plumbers, 81 Trumbull.          See page 192.
        Wm. B. Hogan.          Thos. M. Hogan.
" Wm. E. Jr. carptr. 147 Shel. h.u. 44½ John.
" William J. h. 140 Trumbull.
" William J. clerk at 74, b. 53 Grove.
" William J. gardener, h.u. 44½ John.
" ☞ see also Hargan.
Hogerty William T. machinist at 54 Arch, b. Unionville v.
Hogle Henry J. cutter, Pope Tube Co. b.u. 150 Fkn.
" Herman H. rubberw. 690 Park, h. 4 Ashton.
Hohnquist William, moulder at 54 Arch, h. 22½ Alden.
Hokanson August, helper, N.Y.R. b. 108 Ward.
" Charles A. painter at N.Y.R. h. 108 Ward.
Holaday John B. (W. Hill Mfg. Co.) h. 50 Niles.
" Mary L. wid. Thomas H. h. 101 Hudson.
" ☞ see also Holiday; Halliday.
Holbrook David W. (Moore & H.) h. 33 Elmer.
" F. S. wid. David B. b. 33 Elmer.
" Lucy, wid. Newton, h. 3 Park ter.
" Newton D. salesman at Popes, b. 3 Park ter.
" William J. (Harding & H.) h. 1158 Main.
Holcomb Amy I. b. 109 Ann.
" Annie L. sec'y High School, b. 154 Capitol.
" Annie M. wid. Joel R. h. 154 Capitol.
" Armand E. hotel manager, h. 194 High.
" Arthur, at 46 Ann, b. 16 Trumbull.
" Bessie G. clerk at Sage, Allen & Co. 898 Main, b. 50 Lincoln.
" Burton B. driver at 54 Ann, l.u. 29 Benton.
" Clara F. wid. Amherst L. h. 10 Holcomb.
" Clarence S. cook, b.u. 216 Sheldon.
" Clinton, at 618 Capitol, b. 34 Hopkins.
" Edward V. b. 36 Jefferson.
" Edwin L. toolm. at Popes, h. 317 Capitol.
" Ellen E. wid. Alfred, h. 50 Lincoln.
" George N. police commissioner; with Ætna Life Insurance Co. 650 Main, b. 154 Cap.
" Ida G. teacher Washington st. school, b. 148 Seymour.
" Inez C. bookkpr. 386 Asy. b. 27 Congress.
" Johanna, wid. Rockwell, h. 69 Pleasant.

Holcomb John E. engineer, P.&R. h. Winsted t.
" Lewis H. mechanic at Popes, b. 55 Babcock.
" Lizzie J. b. 109 Ann.
HOLCOMB MARCUS H. (H. & Pierce,) county treasurer, 85 Trumbull, attorneys at law, 68 Pratt, h. Southington t.
                                        See page 487.
" Mary A. wid. Schuyler, b. 21 Arch.
" Mortimer, lab. 252 Pearl, h. 17 Lafayette.
**HOLCOMB & PIERCE,** attorneys, at law, 68 Pratt.          See page 487.
    Marcus H. Holcomb.          N. E. Pierce.
" William R. clerk, h. 20 Ely.
Holcombe George A., U. S. N. b.u. 98 Hopkins.
" Gilbert H. h.u. 98 Hopkins.
" Harold G. clerk at Fidelity Co. 49 Pearl, b. 79 Spring.
" Henry W. drugclk. 367 Cap. b.u.98 Hopkins.
" John M. health commissioner, vice president Phœnix Mutual Life Insurance Co. 49 Pearl, h. 79 Spring.
Holden Alexander, waiter, b. 33 Ferry.
" Benedict M. attorney, 11 Central, L 22 Spring.
" Constance A. nurse, 20 South Hudson.
" Fred. cook, b.2u. 10½ Gold.
" John F. mechanic at Popes, b. 27 John.
" Kate Mrs. b. 2 Holcomb.
" Mary, dressmaker, 56, h. 56 Albany.
" Mary, wid. James, h.u.r. 27 John.
" Walter S. electrician at 1, b. 110 Laurel.
Holehouse Abram, mach. at 28 Laurel, b. 69 Heath.
" Frank, foreman painter, 1 Flow. h.350 Park.
" John R. machinist at 1 Flow. b. 69 Heath.
" Mary, wid. John, h. 69 Heath.
Holgerson John H. bartender, 263, b. 291 Park.
Holliday Louis J. chef, h. 23 Sanford.
" Susan Mrs. h. 23 Sanford.
" ☞ see Halladay; Halliday; Holaday.
Holland Alice, b.u. 53 Oak.
" Annie, at 59½ Trumbull, b. 58 Church.
" Edmund J. engrav.at 175 Pearl,h.4 Orchard.
" Gustave A. filer at Colts, h. 22 Glendale.
" Harry A. filer at Colts, h. East Hartford t.
" James P. porter at 342, h. 297 Asylum.
" Johanna, wid. John, h. 4 Orchard.
" Michael, b. 4½ Hungerford pl.
" Thomas, hostler, r. 50, l.r. 50 State.
" ☞ see also Hulland; Hollond.
Hollander A. Sons, clothiers, 82 to 88 Asylum.
        Aaron Hollander.          Simon Hollander.
" Aaron (A. Hollander's Sons) b. 107 Ann.
" Abraham, h. 107 Ann.
" Samuel, manager at 177 Asy. l.u. 150 Allyn.
" Simon, (A. Hollander's Sons,) b. 107 Ann.
Holle Elizabeth, wid. Gottlieb, b. 34 Franklin.
" H. Eaton, plumber at 81 Tru. b. 152 Allyn.
" Hattie M. Mrs. dressm. 152, h. 152 Allyn.
" ☞ see also Holly.
Holleran John T. polisher at Wm. Rogers Mfg. Co. 66 State, h.2u. 31½ Russell.
Hollings Harriet E. Mrs. b.u. 192 Vernon.
" Henry H. grainer, 556 Main, l. 118 Asylum.
" John F. pianopolisher, u. 28 Mulberry, h. 34 Julius.

**For Sale Advertisements Bring Results in the Post.**

Hollingshead Albert M. clerk at Phœnix Mutual Life Ins. Co. 49 Pearl, h. 49 Annawan.
Hollingworth Effie M. teacher South school, 86 Wadsworth, b.u. 56 Seymour.
Hollis Daniel W.(*D. W. H. & Son,*) h. 62 Laurel.
**HOLLIS DANIEL W & SON,** builders. Office 212 Asylum. *See page 514.*
Daniel W. Hollis.     Eben Hollis.
" Eben, (*D. W. H. & Son,*) b. 62 Laurel.
" Frank G. machinist, h. 41 Hudson.
" Frank L. clerk, b. 62 Laurel.
" Hattie G. b. 62 Laurel.
Hollister Albert G. h. 370 Asylum, rm. 36.
" Carrie E. teacher West Middle school, b. 234 Wethersfield.
" Charles E. farmer, h.u. 4 John.
" Emily L. forewoman 59½ Tru. b.u. 47 Green.
" Fidelia, wid. Charles W. b. 143 Main.
" George, carpenter, 234, h. 234 Wethersfield.
" George Edgar, clerk 866 Main, b. 234 Weth.
" Herbert H. bkkpr. 15 Tru. h. 30 Highland.
" Ida M. Mrs. toilet preparations, h. 151 Main.
" John R. clerk at 124 Asylum, b. 30 Highland.
" Josephine, wid. Thomas A. h. 76 Wells.
" Lillian, wid. Martin, h. 151 Main.
" Robert Jr. engineer, Lincoln & Co. 54 Arch, h. 151 Main.
" Roswell, engineer at Popes, h. 27 Woodbine.
" Tracy, carpenter, b. 128 Maple.
" William, engineer at 62 Market, h. E.H.t.
" William H. b. 47 Green.
Hollond James P. porter at 342, h. 297 Asylum.
" ☞ *see also Holland.*
Holloran Dennis J. polisher at Wm. Rogers Mfg. Co. 66 Market, h. New Britain t.
" John, mason, b.u. 62 Front.
" Michael, helper at 1 Flower, b. 4½ Hung. pl.
Holloway Geo. A. pressman, 690 Park, b. 212 Jef.
" Henry W. bkkpr. 690 Park, b. 25 Evergreen.
" James F. deliverym. 145 State, b.u. 39 John.
" John H. painter, b.u. 39 John.
" Mary, wid. Michael, h.u. 39 John.
" Rose, dressmaker, b.u. 39 John.
Holly Steam Engineering Co. 28 High.
" ☞ *see also Holley.*
Holman Benzoin (*Holman & M.*) b.u. 78 Front.
" Justin B. conductor valley division N.Y. R. h. Saybrook point.
" & Meister, cloth hat and cap mfgrs. 76 Asy.
Benzoin Holman.     Rubi Meister.
Holmes Alfred, h.u. 9 Kinsley.
" Alice M. theo. student at 1507 Broad, b. 62 Hawthorn.
" & Co. brokers, 10 Central.
" Charles E. polisher at Popes, b. 149 Asylum.
" Elbridge R. mach. at 1 Flower, b. Weth.t.
" Electric Protective Co. 903 Main, rm. 13.
" Elmer, driver at 69 Albany, b. E.H.t.
" Ernest C. polisher at Popes, h. 81 Asy. rm. 9.
" Ethan J. painter at 10 Ford, h.u. 37 Park.
" Frank, motorman St.Ry. h. 8 Bond.
" Fred. G. bkkpr. at 197 Asylum, b. E.H.t.
" George E. painter, h.r. 56 Albany.
" Howard M. receiving clerk at 98 Kilbourn, h. 20 Morris.

Holmes James, laborer, h.r. 56 Albany.
" James, ostler, 17 Albany, h.2u. 82 Avon.
" James V. machinist at Colts, b. 20 Seyms.
" Joseph T. gardener, h.u. 30 Wolcott.
" Richard J. bkkpr. at Popes, b. 98 Capitol.
" W. Clark, traveling salesman for Popes, h. Brooklyn, N. Y.
" William R. painter, h. 40 Village.
" William R. teamster, h. 56 Portland.
" William R. Jr. bricklayer, b. 56 Portland.
" William S. mechanic at Popes, h. 58 Fmt.
Holmquist August Wm. molder, h.u.r. 22½ Alden.
" Charles N. mach. at Colts, h.u. 49 Elliott.
" Frank L. engir. at 266 Pearl, h.u. 58 Broad.
" Matilda, wid. Edward, h. 252 Franklin.
Holmstrom Emanuel, cutter at Popes, 690 Park, h. 47 Belmont.
Holmwood A. helper at 346 Main.
Holst Geo. M. teamster at 335 Shel. h. 73 Ward.
" Lauritz B. filer at 30 Cushman, h. 1159 Bd.
Holstein EdwardJ. clerk at 26 Asy. b.2u. 28 Mor.
" Isaac, diamond setter, 890 Main, h.2u. 28Mor.
" John H. cutter, 252 Pearl, b. E.H.t.
" Joseph, barber, b.2u. 28 Morgan.
" Leonard, fireman at Pope Tube Co. h.u. 96 Madison av.
Holston Lee, porter at 257, b. 297 Asylum.
Holt Anna M. wid. William K. h. 8 Atwood.
" Charles H. dentist, h. 100 Wooster.
" Charles W. at Connecticut Mutual Life Insurance Co. 783 Main, b. 8 Atwood.
" Fred P. supt. safe deposit vaults, Hfd. Trust Co. 764 Main, h. 130 Capitol.
" Geo. C. ornamental painter, h.u. 84 Jefferson.
" Hannah W. wid. Henry S. h. 40 Bond.
" Henry T. asst. bookkeeper at Ætna National Bank, 644, h. 427 Main, rm. 33.
" John, dentist, b. 171 Capen.
" Lester A. supervisor at 690 Asylum, h.u. 23 Sargeant.
HOLT Lucius H. treasurer The Billings & Spencer Co. 142 Russ, h. 66 Buckingham. *See page 531.*
" Rhine, baker at 69, b. 69 Morgan.
Holtman John, assembr. 556 Cap. b.188 Putnam.
Holton John J. clerk, 197 Asylum, b.2u. 1 East.
" Thomas F. printer, b.2u. 1 East.
Holtz Abraham, artist, b. 61 Pleasant.
" Hyman, junk dealer, h.u. 57 Pleasant.
" William, bottler, 232 Sheldon, b. 133 Front.
Holtzerhiemer Henry, driver, h.u.r. 58 Temple.
Holzapfel Edward, mach. at 1 Flow. b. Suffield t.
Homan Etta, h. 7 Wadsworth.
" Eveline, wid. Henry, h. 7 Wadsworth.
" Ida. clerk at 82 Trumbull, b. Meriden t.
" Nellie L. stamping, 82 Trumbull.
Homberg Herman A. machinist at 245 Windsor, b. 4 Pavilion.
Home of Woman's Aid Society, 1 Pavilion.
Honce Alfred, livery, 82 Hudson h. 21 John.
Hondlow David L. foreman at 336, h. 336 Weth.
Honer August W. operator, 8 Sig. h. 82 Sargeant.
" Gustave, harnessm. 8 Sig. h. 94 Babcock.
" Martin J. carpenter, b. 94 Babcock.

**The Post, 12 Cents a Week, Delivered at Your Home.**

**HONEY FREDERIC R.** instructor
mechanical drawing, 904 Main, rm. 99.
professor Trinity college, h. N. Haven t.
See page 422.
Honeyman William, coachm. 1045, h.r. 1045 Asy.
Hong Fred W. laundry, 351 Main.
**HONISS THOS. A.** oysters, wholesale
and retail, and the best oyster restaurant
in the state, 30 State, h. 1 Mahl.
See page 589.
" Wm. H. mech. engir. 370 Asy. h. 51 Oak.
Hood Charles, blacksmith, 36 Alb. b.2u. 251 Asy.
" James, clerk at Brown, Thomson & Co.
942 Main, h.u. 94 Wooster.
" John J. laborer, 555 Cap. h. 19½ Putnam.
" Nellie Mrs. h.3u. 18 South Ann.
" Patrick F. mixer at 555 Cap. h.u. 20 Affleck.
" Percy W. clerk at Hartford Rubber Co.
690 Park, b. 211 Garden.
Hooker Alfred M. engir. at James L. Howard &
Co. 438 Asylum, h.u. 135 Capen.

EDWARD B. HOOKER, Physician. Office 721
Main street, Waverly Building, room 29.
Hours—10.30 to 12 A.M. } Except Saturday.
     2 to 3.30 P.M. }
Saturdays 10 A. M. to 1 P. M.
Sunday, 12 to 1 P.M.
Evenings at Residence, 70 Farmington av.
Telephone Residence 723.

Hooker Edward B. physician, 721 Main, rm. 29,
h. 70 Farmington.
HOOKER EDWARD W. treasurer Perkins Electric
Switch Mfg. Co. h. 10 Myrtle. *See p. 536.*
" John, lawyer, h. 16 Marshall.
" Martha, wid. B. E. b. 149 High.
" Thomas W. clerk, b. 149 High.
Hooper Charles E. sawyer at 335 Shel. b. 113 Main.
" George, shipcarp. 285 State, h. 113 Main.
" Henry, blacksmith at N.Y.R. b. 28 High.
" Wm. clerk at 956 Main, h.2u. 27 Russell.
Hop Gwong, laundry, 76½ Temple.
Hope George, painter, b.u. 338 Park.
" Norman L. salesman Cheney Bros. silks,
h. 106 Wethersfield.
Hopewell Carl, helper at 1152 Main, b. E.H.t.
" James W. mach. at 556 Capitol, h. E.H.t.
Hopkins Alex. S. bitters, r. 138, h. 138 Windsor av.
" Arthur B. machinist, b.u. 204 Laurel.
" Benj. G. foreman at 618 Cap. h.u. 204 Laurel.
" George F. h.2u. 329 Capitol.
" John G. real estate, 49 Pearl, h. 55 Capitol.
" Leroy, builder, h. 26 Mahl.
" Roselle A. teacher N. E. sch. h.u. 204 Laurel.

Hopper Jas. H. farm. 1130, b. 1130 **Windsor av.**
" John W. (*H. & Sweeney,*) h.u. 11 Belden.
" Joseph, at Popes, b. 58 Asylum.
" & Sweeney, plumbers, 1092 Main.
   John W. Hopper.    Thomas A. Sweeney.
Horahan John, stage manager at Parsons thea-
ter, b.u. 9 Grand.
Horan Annie M. B. clerk at Brown, Thomson
& Co. 942 Main, b. 174 Seymour.
" Catherine, h. 41 Sheldon.
" Edward, laborer, h. 9 Lawrence.
" Edward, teamster, 268 Pros. av. h. 19 Grace.
" Frances M. repairer, b. 7 Concord.
" Francis P. mach. at 1 Flow. b. 52 Lawrence.
" James, brazier at 581 Cap. b.r. 27½ Lewis.
" James, engineer at stonepits, b. 129 Zion.
" James, laborer at 70 Com. b.3u. 38 Park.
" James, painter, 4, h. 4 Waverly.
" John, forem. at Hfd Cycle Co. b.r. 27½ Lewis.
" John, gardener at 30 Weth. b. Sherman.
" John, laborer at 70 Com. h. 32 Portland.
" John, teamster at 8 Front, b. 16 Arch.
" John, teamster at 190 Com. b. 129 Zion.
" John, molder at 54 Arch, h.2u. 2 Union.
" John Mrs. b.W. H. Home for the Aged, Alb.
" John B. helper at 1 Flower, h.u. 52 Lawrence.
" Joseph, b. Concord, West Hartford t.
" Joseph, molder, b.u. 6 Union.
" Joseph H. motorman St.Ry. b. 12 Church.
" Katie, wid. Edward, h. 1316 Broad.
" Keron, conductor St.Ry. b.u. 94 Retreat.
" Keron, gardener, Whiting lane, b. Concord.
" Keron, laborer at 70 Commerce, h. B.v.
" Keron, screwm. at 476 Capitol, h. 7 Putnam.
" Martin, moulder at 556 Cap. b.u. 6 Union.
" Mary, h. 41 Sheldon.
" Michael, actor, b. 129 Zion.
" Michael, laborer, b. 32 Elm.
" Michael, plumber, b. 31 Chapel.
" Michael, engineer, h. 60 Wells.
" Michael, coremaker 1 Flow. h.u. 7 Putnam.
" Neal, at 15½ Babcock.
" Patrick, enameler, b.u. 58 Dean.
" Patrick, laborer, h.129 Zion.
" Patrick, laborer, 70 Huy, h.u. 236 Maple.
" Patrick J. mach. at 1 Flower, h.u. 18 Center.
" Thomas, bartender, 186 Shel. b. 92 Retreat.
" Thomas, laborer, St.Ry. h. 115 State.
" Thomas F. polisher 581 Cap. b. 1316 Broad.
" William, helper, h.2u. 17 Howard.
" William A. b. 52 Lawrence.
" Wm. J. gardener, b. Concord, W.H.t.
Horenson C. H. blacksmith, 207 Front.
Horenstein Abraham (*H. Bros.*) b. 1118 **Main.**
" Bernard (*H. Bros.*) h. 1118 Main.
" Bros. tobacco and cigars, 1118 Main.
   Abraham Horenstein.   Bernard Horenstein.
Horey Joseph, janitor Ch. O. school h.u.67 Fkn.
" Margaret, dressmaker, 67, b.u. 67 Franklin.
Horgan John, fireman N.Y.R. b. 20 Chestnut.
" John C. polisher at Popes, h. 8¼ Queen.
" ☞ *see also Hogan.*
Horman John E. plumber at 11 Haynes, h.
5 Chapel.
Horn P. deckhand str. Hartford, 285 State.

Horse Samuel B. com. bureau labor statistics, rm. 48, State capitol, h. Winsted t.
" Thomas, tinner, h. 155 Windsor.
Horner Fave, driver, 37 Wells.
" Harry A. student at Trinity college, 41 Jarvis hall, Summit.
" Robert J. coachman, h. 16 Owen.
Horowitz Harris, builder, h.u. 40 North.
" Samuel, shoemaker, 40 State, h. 238 Front.
Horpoltds Herman, cigarmaker, h. 210 Front.
Horr Ann, wid. Michael, h.2u. 41 Mechanic.
" Chas. F. woodturner at Strickland & Shea, 20 Potter, h. 285 New Britain.
Horrigan D. deckh. str. Hartford, 285 State.
" David, helper at 152 State, b. 33½ Front.
" Henry B. painter at 185 Asylum, b.21 John.
" John, boilerm. at 152 State b. 33½ Front.
" John J. annealer at Popes, h. 47 Hawthorn.
" ☞ see also Harrigan.
Horse Guard Armory, 460 Main.
Horsfall Luke( H. & Rothschild,)h.52 Huntington.
" Martha, wid. Edward, b. 52 Huntington.
" & Rothschild, hatters, etc. 97 Asylum.
    Luke Horsfall.    Wm. B. Rothschild.
Horsman Joseph R. assembler at Popes, b. 56 Jefferson.
Horstman August, cigarmaker at 104 Asylum, b. 33 Temple.
Horton Amenus, car inspector, h. 20 Russell.
" Charles, electrician at 1 Laurel, b. 744 Park.
" Charles H. rubberw. at 690, b. 902 Park.
" Edwin K. h. 952 Park.
" George A. machinist at 1 Flower, b. W.P.v.
" Harry Irving, clerk at 197 Asy.b.u.43 Canton.
" Harvey, h.u. 31 Grand.
" Henry W. solicitor, h.u. 43 Canton.
" James W. clerk at P.&R. l. 22 Spring.
" Lucien S. clerk at Brown, Thomson & Co. 942 Main, b. Wethersfield t.
" Manfred E. machinist at Popes, h.76 Putnam.
" Thomas L. waiter, b. 90 Pearl.
" Walter, clerk at P.&R. b. 28 Spring.
" ☞ see also Haughton.
Horvitch Harry, laborer, b. 238 Front.
Horwitz Charles, dry goods, 174½, h. 174½ Front.
" Isaac, rabbi, h.r.u. 176 Front.
Hosby John, coachman, Prospect av. b. Sig.
Hosch William, cigarmaker, b.u. 150 Market.
Hosford George, roofer, l.u. 1232 Main.
" Mary, wid. George, h. 43 Ann.
Hoskins Alfred J. musician, b. 334 Wethersfield.
" Ernest J. clerk at 886 Main, b. 33 Allen pl.
" Francis D. Rev. sec. and treas. Society for Increase of the Ministry, b. 34 C.O.pl.
" Henry, teamster at 745, b. 1336 Main.
" Preserved B.printer at 703 Mn. h.33 Allen pl.
" William, carpenter, l. 1336 Main.
Hosley Edward M. mech. 26 High, b.100 Mather.
" Eugene J. at N.E.R. h. 100 Mather.
" Irma G. stenographer, b. 100 Mather.
Hosmer Arthur, carpenter, h.u. 54 Wadsworth.
" Hall, 1507 Broad.    See pages 708, 709.
" Henry F. electrician at 53 Vernon, h.u. 35 Benton.
" James R. carpenter, 224 Sargeant, h. W.t.

Hosmer Mattie R. clerk at Popes, b. E.H.t.
" Thomas, h. 235 Wethersfield.
" Walter, h. 235 Wethersfield.
" William H. purchasing agent, 53 Vernon, h.u. 35 Benton.
Hosty Patrick, carpenter at 53 Vernon, h.u. 40 Retreat.
Hotchkiss Clayton E. b.u. 18 Windsor av.

**HOTCHKISS E. EUGENE,** plater, 182 Allyn, h.u. 18 Windsor av.
" Frances A. wid. L. M. h. 765 Asylum.
" Lizzie, dressmaker, b. 46 John.
" Mary B. wid. Levi H. b. 427 Main, rm. 22.
" Mary F. h. 765 Asylum.
" Philip L. at Ætna Life Insurance Co. 650, b. 427 Main, rm. 22.
" Samuel M. notary public, b. 119 Capitol.
" Sophia, Mrs. b. 1191 Main.
" William C. h. Quaker lane.
Hotel Brainard, S. L. Doane, 119 Capitol.
" Capitol, 389 Main.

**HOTEL HARTFORD,** A. A. Pocock, proprietor, 365 Allyn.
" Heublein The, 98 Wells, corner Gold.

**HOTEL PROSPECT,** Mrs. Julia E. Duley, proprietor, 119 High. See p. 561.
Hotine George, carpenter, h. 248 New Britain.
Hotoph Charles H. foreman at 30 Cushman, h. 84 Prospect av.
Hough Charles W. teamster, h. 256 Capen.
" Chester E. peddler, b. 256 Capen.
" Collis S. pressman at Popes, h. Plainville t.
" F. Marie, nurse, b. 49 Governor.
" Fannie, b. 36 Jefferson.
" Harriet L. wid. Samuel, h.u. 112 Hopkins.
" Niles E. manager at 10 Central, h. W.H.t.
" Prescot W. woodworker, b. 41 Seyms.
" Warren H.glazier, 88 Market, b. 41 Seyms.
" Warren P. h. 41 Seyms.
" ☞ see also Huff.
Houghmaster Albert, coachman, 288 Windsor av. h. u. 89 Wooster.
" Theron E. clerk at 342 Asy. b. 89 Wooster.
Houghton Albert, laborer, N.Y.R. h. Hayden sta.
" Arthur H. polo player, b.2u. 3 Park.
Houle Alma F. carpenter, h. 47 Wilson.
" Usebe, plumber at 6 Church.
Houlihan Patrick, molder, 556 Cap. h.18 Howard.
House Anna, dressmaker, b. 58 Church.
" C. A. Mrs. massage, 258, b.258 Wethersfield.
" Elizabeth, wid. William W. h. 133 Wash.
" Eugene, machinist, 13 Central, b. E.H. t
" Fred. H. foreman, Taft Co. h. 49 Harrison.
" Henry E. instructor, 42 Seyms,h.u.37 Center.
" Henry S. manager sub. dept. Connecticut Quarterly, h. 133 Washington.
" Herbert B. driver at N.Y.& B.D. Ex. Co. h. East Hartford t.
" Hezekiah K. h. 112 Wooster.
" Mary Mrs. seamstress, h.3u. 289 Asylum.
" Mary A. Mrs. h. 28 Buckingham.
" Mary E. b. 289 Asylum.
Houser ☞ see also Hauser.

**You'll Get ALL THE NEWS, if you READ THE POST.**

Houston Agnes N. h.2u. 61 Whitmore.
" Alex. machinist at Colts, b.2u. 3 Whitman.
" George H. watchmaker, b. 21 Bellevue.
" James G. b. 36 Russ.
" Jennie C. Mrs. h. 36 Russ.
" Robert G. mach. at 1 Flow. b. 108 Hopkins.
" Robert N. canvasser, b.2u. 61 Whitmore.
" William, canvasser and bill distributor, b.2u. 61 Whitmore.
Hovey Frederick E. h. 23 Seyms.
" Henry R. accountant, h. 57 Oxford.
" Mary E. wid. Henry R. h. 23 Seyms.
Howard Arthur E. deputy collector customs, 65 State, h. 218 Wethersfield.
" Catherine P. wid. Chas. F. h. 116 Farmington.
" Charles P. secretary J. L. Howard & Co. 438 Asylum, b. 116 Farmington.
" Daniel C. (Furlong & H.) h.u. 378 Windsor av.
" Edward, janitor, h. 42 Chestnut.
" Frank E. clerk at James L. Howard & Co. 438 Asylum, b. 150 Collins.
" Frank L. treasurer, J. L. Howard & Co. 438 Asylum, h. 150 Collins.
" Frank W. b. 149 High.
" Frederick, painter, l. 118 Asylum.
" George, operator at 388 Cap. h.284 Asylum.
" Hale S. salesman at 42 High, b.2u. 200 Allyn.
" Herbert S. agent, 715 Main, h.u. 45 Wooster.
" Jas. storekeeper, 98 Wells, h. 60 Seymour.
" James L. president J. L. Howard & Co. railroad car goods, 438 Asylum, h. 67 Collins.
**HOWARD JAMES L. & CO.** mfrs. car furnishing goods, 438 Asy. *See p. 527.*
" John, clerk, 160 Windsor av. b. 42 Chestnut.
" John, physician, 119, h. 119 Trumbull.
" John J. foreman at 581 Cap. h. 38 Putnam.
" Margaret, wid. Joseph, h. 91 Madison av.
" Matilda F. wid. Woodbury, h. 25 Evergreen.
" Nellie G. dressm. 721 Main, b. 42 Chestnut.
" Sarah, dressmaker, b. 91 Madison av.
" William, mach. at 142 Russ, b. 20 Sheldon.
" William, stonec. at 93 Ch.O. h. 585 Garden.
Howarth Joseph, helper, h. 51 Ferry.
" Mazzini G. mach. 1 Laurel, h.u. 49 Francis.
Howd Charles, at St.Ry. b.u. 29 Wooster.
Howe Albert S. clerk, 319 Asylum, h. 14 Trinity.
" Albert S. secy. Hartford Building & Loan Asso. 370 Asylum, h. Windsor t.
" Annie I. teacher, Second North school, b. 24 Windsor av.
" Chas. B. instructor High school, h. 153 Ash.
" & Collins, 803 Main, Phœnix bank building.
    Daniel R. Howe.        Atwood Collins.
" Daniel R. treas. Hartford Street Railway, (H. & Collins,) office 803 Mn. h. 1008 Asy.
" Emma B. Mrs. h. 6 Wadsworth.
" George, clerk, 2 Wash. h.u.14½ New Britain.
" Hannah, wid. Soloman, h. 244 High.

HARMON G. HOWE, Physician. Office and h. 137 High, c. Church.
Hours—8 to 9 A.M.
    3 to 4 and 7 to 8 P.M.
    Sundays, 3 to 4 P.M.
        Telephone 529.

Howe Harmon G. physician, 137, h. 137 High.

Howe Horace S. student, b. 137 High.
" Joseph F. framer, at J. H. Eckhardt Co. 693 h. 926 Main, rm. 64.
" Joseph F. Mrs. dressm. 926, b.926 Main, rm.64.
" Nathan C. bartender, b. 1113 Main.
" Thomas B. profiler at Colts, h. 10 Wyllys.
" W. T. b. 152 Asylum.
" Will S. cashier at 690, h. 901 Park.
" William W. machinist at N.Y.R. b. E.H.t.
Howell Charles, stairbuilder, b.u. 21 Preston.
" H. A. trav. salesm. 908 Main, b.13 Winthrop.
Howes A. C. painter, h.3u. 10½ Ford.
" Frank C. laborer at 1, b. 41 Laurel.
Howich Harry, mach. at 388 Cap. h. 238 Front.
Howitz W. A. l. 19 Spring.
Howland Edward D. printer, h. 52 Glendale.
Howlett Chas. A. ornamentor, 438 Asy. h.E.H.t.
Howley Edward T. clerk at Pope Tube Co. b.u. 120 Hungerford.
" John, printer at 1 Flow. b.u.120 Hungerford.
" Mary, wid. Michael, h.u. 120 Hungerford.
" William, laborer, 335 Sheldon, b.2u.13 Front.
Hoxie Geo. B. mach 1 Flower, b. 8 Foot Guard.
" Geo. C. contractor, 1 Flow. h. 8 Foot Guard.
" Royal S. machinist at Pratt & Whitney, 1 Flower, h. 1127 Main.
Hoye James E. carpenter, h.u. 109 Hungerford.
" Paul, baker at 1036 Main, h. 1 Worcester.
" Peter, b.2u. 34 Laurel.
" Thomas, plumber at 599 Mn. b.2u. 34 Laurel.
" ☞ see also Hoey.
Hoylan Edward, laborer, stone pits, b. Flatbush.
Hoyle May, b. 193 State.
Hoyt Frank N. civil engineer at Highway com. office, State capitol, rm. 27, h. 70 Wash.
" J. M. Miss b. 61 Spring.
" R. M. Mrs. h. 61 Spring.
" Thomas, guide, State capitol, h. 147 Wash.
Hub Loan Company, 180 Asylum.
Huband Albert, car inspector, h. 94 Windsor.
Hubbarback Samuel, peddler, h. 24 North.
Hubbard Adeline M. wid. Fred.M. h.u.32 Kinsley.
" Albert, driver at 82 Francis, b.u. 551 Park.
" Albert H. silversm. 62 Market, b.88 Church.
" Ann E. h. 483 Farmington.
" Arthur E. bkkpr. at 20 N.B. h.u. 449 Broad.
" Carrie W. wid. C. F. b. 350 Main.
" Charles E. bkkpr. at Taft Co. h. 986 Main.
" Charles E. lumber dealer, 69, h. 69 Bluehills.
" Charles L. druggist, 407 Main, h. 166 Wash.
" Christian, motorman, St.Ry. h. E.H.t.
" Dudley W. b. 14 Highland.
" Edwin F. diesinker at 62 Mar. h.u.57 Lincoln.
" Elizabeth A. wid. Stephen A. h. 791 Asy.
" Elizabeth S. wid. Norman, h. 54 Prospect.
" Ellen Mrs. h.u. 449 Broad.
HUBBARD FRANK E. electrical expert, (H. & Mortson,) h. 26 Ward. *See page 428.*
" Frederick H. at Ætna Insurance Co. 666 Main, b. 904 Asylum.
" George B. helper, 15 Tru. b. 32 Kinsley.
" George S. toolmaker at Popes, b. 592 Main.
" Gideon M. b. 56 Bond.
" Harriett Mrs. h. 9 Seyms.
" Hiram H. carpenter at 142 Russ, l.34 Cedar.

Hubbard James E. b. 45 Capen.
" James H. toolmaker at Popes, h.u. 21 Imlay.
" James L. (*H. & Monson*,) h. Newington t.
" Jane Mrs. wid. W. F. h. 592 Main.
" Jennette, h. 483 Farmington.
" Joseph T. milkman, 116, h. 116 Bluehills.
" Lester, mason, b. 88 Church.
" Lincoln D. strapper, 15 Tru. b. 84 Retreat.
" Louisa D. police matron, 38 Kinsley, h.u. 650 Main, rm. 56.
" Mary C. at 856 Main, h. 48 Wadsworth.
" Mary S. wid. Lester S. h. 166 Washington.
" & Monson, incandescent lamps, 358 Asylum.
James L. Hubbard.　　William R. Monson.

**HUBBARD & MORTSON,** automatic time switch clocks, 42 Union pl.
Frank R. Hubbard.　　George Mortson.
*See page 428.*

" Richard D. Mrs. h. 126 Washington.
" Roland, at 1 Flower, b. 551 Park.
" Susan V. h. 483 Farmington.
" William, motorman, St.Ry. h. 168 Allyn.
" William D. pres. & treas. Side Weight Horse Shoe Co. 9 Central, h. 14 Highland.
" William F. Jr. jeweler, b. 592 Main.
" William H. machinist, b. 50 Judson.
Hubbell Elizabeth, nurse, b. 650 Main, rm. 58.
" Emeline C. wid. LePorte h. 427 Mn. rm. 72½.
" Frank, at 1 Flower, b. 66 Hopkins.
" Gershom W. B. clerk, 207 Allyn, l. 23 Spring.
" Lindley D. draughtsman at 581 Capitol, h. 1500 Broad.
Hubbs Wm. D. driver, h.u. 35 Bellevue.
Hube Henry C. baker at 484 Main, h. 24 Suffield.
Hubel Fred, mach. at 1 Flower, b. 66 Hopkins.
Huber Jacob, upholst. 147 Asy. h.2u. 140 Mather.
" Jacob G. saddler at 8 Sig. b. 65 Laurel.
Huberman Joseph, mineral water mfgr. 1098 Main, h.2u. 22 North.
" Moriss, soda fountain, 198 Front, h. 22 North.
Hubert Leopold, fruit peddler, h. 19½ Elmer.
" Herman, confectioner at 607, b. 609 Main.
Hubnar Charles, filer at Colts, h.2u. 44 Wells.
Huchstedt Henry, harnessmaker at 8 Sigourney, h. 70 Temple.
Hudner William F. saloon, 61, h.u. 61 Front.
" ☞ *see also Heubner.*
Hudson Abraham, machinist at 40 Governor, h. 91 Jefferson.
" Ann, wid. Henry, b. 4 Marsh.
" Charles S. driver, h. 119 Ann.
" Delia P. wid. Henry, h.u. 202 Windsor av.
" Edmund, editorial writer at Hartford Times, 716 Main, b. 10 Garden.
" Frank G. mach. at Colts, b. 91 Jefferson.
" Fred. V. secretary Connecticut General Life Insurance Co. 49 Pearl, b. Allyn house.
" George, pantryman str. Hartford, 285 State.
" Grenville M. clerk at Phœnix Mutual Life Ins. Co. 29 Pearl, b. 185 Ashley.
" Hattie B. Mrs. art work, b. 119 Ann.
" Henry at 62 Market, h. 18½ Church.
" John S. shippingclerk at 2 So. Ann, h. 200 Windsor av.
" Julia E. b. 185 Ashley.

Hudson William, solderer at Barbour Silver Co. 62 Market, h. 18 Church.
" William M. physician, h. 105 Elm.
Huebler Alfred, saloon, 287 Asylum, h. 721 Main, rm. 31.
" Charles R. b. 36 Grand.
" Dora, wid. Julius, 1150 Main.
" Frank R. machinist at Pratt & Whitney Co. 1 Flower, b. 226 New Park.
Huff Abram, shoemaker, 335 Asy. h.r. 174 Front.
" ☞ *see also Hough.*
Huffman William A. rubberworker at 690 Park, b. 266 New Park.
Hugentobler Elizabeth S. wid. George J. h. 122 Huntington.
" Georgia L. stenographer, at 904 Main, rm. 12, b. 122 Huntington.
Hugett Josie A. Mrs. h.u. 38 Lewis.
Huggard Robert, collector, 261 Asy. b. 71 Williams.
Hughes Amos C. carpenter, b. 242 Wethersfield.
" Arthur L. at Travelers Ins. Co. 56 Prospect, b. Wethersfield t.
" Cecilia, clerk at 956 Main, b.u. 200 Russ.
" D. P. woodturner at 308 Allyn.
" Ellen, wid. James, h.u. 200 Russ.
" James C. attendant at 30 Washington.
" John, laborer, b. 542 Main.
" John F. attendant at 140, h.2u. 158 Wash.
" John J. clerk, l. 62 Grove.
" John P. stonecutter, b. 346 Front.
" John W. carpenter, b. 242 Wethersfield.
" Jos. C. watchm. at 1 S. Ann, h.2u. 79 Chestnut.
" Lorie Mrs. h.2u. 210 Windsor av.
" Lucy, wid. John, h. 346 Front.
" Mary A. b.u. 200 Russ.
" Meloin C. conductor St.Ry. h.u. 1191 Main.
" Nellie, at 1 So. Ann, b. 44 Beach.
" Patrick T. brickmason, h.u. 159 Babcock.
" Peter, blacksmith, 59, h. 59 New Britain.
" Philip, engineer at stone pits, b. 25 Zion.
" Rose Mrs. dressm. 110, h. 110 Trumbull.
" Samuel, journeyman, l. 30 Spring.
" Samuel, mach. 581, b. 371 Capitol,
" Sarah, wid. John M. h.r. 14 Chapel.
" Thomas, farmer, h. 25 Zion.
" Thomas Jr. engineer at Brown school, h. 3 So. Laurel.
" Thos. F. boxcutter at 1 S. Ann, h. 22 Avon.
" Thos. H. painter, b. 200 Allyn.
" W. deckhand str. Hartford, 285 State.
" William T. laborer, b.u. 200 Russ.
" ☞ *see also Hewes.*
Hulbert Ellard O. painter, h. 154 Capen.
Hull Aaron E. prest. Curtiss Hull Mfg. Co. h. 62 Imlay.
" Burton W. entry clerk, 273 Asy. b. 4 Canton.
" Charlotte S. stenographer at Hfd. St. Ry. Co. 115 State, b. 2B Belden.
" Clara K. Mrs. h.u. 39 Pearl.
" Elizabeth, wid. Wm. b. 532 Garden.
" Frank, manager, 75 Pratt, b. 28 Buckingham.
" George O. at Ætna Life Insurance Company, 650 Main, b. 48 Church.
" Harriet H. wid. Reuben, h. 20 Lewis.
" Harry, b. 15 Village.

Hull Harry A. plumber, h.u. 49 Grand.
" Herman T. foreman city park, h. 77 Windsor av.
" Joseph C. coachman at r. 49 Forest.
" M. Jenny, wid. Andrew R. h. 48 Ashley.
" Philander, upholsterer at 15, h. 9 Sig. pl.
" Philetta H. tailoress, 20, h. 20 Lewis.
" Reuben S. b. 20 Lewis.
" Selden B. ins. agt. at 721 Main, b. 168 Allyn.
Hullpitch William, driver at 250 State, b.u. 46 Temple.
Hultgerent John, mach.hand, Colts, b. 80 Front.
Hultman Chas. W. roller at 690 Pk.h. 77 Francis.
" John, assemb. 556 Capitol, l.u. 188 Putnam.
" Segrid, wardmaid at 20 So. Hudson.
Humason J. Irving, iceman at 4 Central, h.2u. 24 Kennedy.
" John P. b. 36 Jefferson.
" Meritt J. watchman, St.Ry. h. 58 Dean.
Humes Emily, wid. William, h. 16 Spring.
" William Y. C. manager advertising department at Popes, h. 6 Columbia.
Hummel Becker E. carpenter, h. 54 Wooster.
Hummell A. C. captain barge No. 6, 285 State.
" Madison, driver 175 Ashley, h. 19 Sargeant.
Humpage A. clerk at 28, b.u. 40 Grand.
Humphrey A. H. engineer at 75, h. 75 Pratt.
" Alfred H. mach. at 1 Flower, b. 58 Bkm.
" Harold D. stenographer at Kimball & McCray, 658 Main, b. Unionville v.
" Henrietta S. wid. H.B. h. 301 New Britain,
" Henry, contractor and builder, 750 Main, rm. 37, h. Rocky Hill t.
" Walter B. mach. at 490 Cap. h. 48 Putnam.
Hunciker Jacob H. screwm. 476 Cap.h.23 Smith.
" Kittie, clerk at 369 Capitol, b. 23 Smith.
Hungerford Caroline C.wid.Anson,h.45 Prospect.
" Clarence C. b. 45 Prospect.
HUNGERFORD FRANK L. (H., Hyde, Joslyn & Gilman,)attorney at law,49 Pearl,h.N.B.t.

**HUNGERFORD, HYDE, JOSLYN & GILMAN,** attorneys at law, 49 Pearl. See page 488.
Frank L. Hungerford. E. Henry Hyde,
Chas. M. Joslyn.
Geo. H. Gillman. Wm. C. Hungerford.
" Newman, salesman at Blodgett & Clapp Co. 51 Market, b. 45 Prospect.
" William C. (H., Hyde, Joslyn & Gilman) attorney, 49 Pearl, h. New Britain t.
Hunn George A. gardener at 31, b. 31 Annawan.
" L. J. Fitta, wid. George A. h. 11 Clinton.
" Paul R. physician, 47, h. 47 John.
" Valentine L. helper, P.&R. b. 43 Seyms.
" Wm. Wells, bkkpr. 247 Asylum, b. 47 John.
Hunt Albert L. at Travelers Insurance Co. 56 Prospect, h. 124 Trumbull.
" Alvin A. dentist at 8 State, b. 79 Seymour.
" Barney, helper, b. 1447 Broad.
" Burritt A. bookkeeper at Ingraham, Swift & Co. 126 Church, b. 18 Prospect.
" Charles W. teamster,88 Mar. h.u. 26 Center.
" Cornelia M. dressmaker,137,b.137 Trumbull.
" Eunice S. h. 137 Trumbull.
" Frederick C. at 236 Asylum, b.u. 26 Center.

Hunt James, foreman 690 Park, h. 94 Francis.
" James, pressman at 141 Pearl, h. 89 Pratt.
" James H. warmer at 690 Park, b. 266 N.P.
" James J. helper at 690 Park, h. 168 Ward.
" James Mrs. stamping, 89, h. 89 Pratt.
" Jennie J. wid. James H. h. 16 Trinity.
" John, blacksmith at 476 Cap. b.2u. 363 Main.
" Milo, h. 190 Laurel.
" Milo S. at Ætna Life Ins. Co. 650 Main, h. 190 Laurel.
" Minnie E. dressmaker, b.u. 26 Center.
" Owen, waiter, b.2u. 363 Main.
" Unice S. milliner, 137, h. 137 Trumbull.
" Thos. gardener, h. 33 Bellevue.
" Thomas, bartender and b. 1076 Broad.
" W. W. & Co. nurserymen, 24 State.*
" William B. printer, 133 Shel. b. 68 Spring.
" William Chapin, clerk, h.u. 223. Asy. rm. 62.
" William F. engineer, 9 Sig.b.u.r. 33 Bellevue.
" Wm. W. ( W. W. H. & Co.) h. 236 Allyn.
Hunter A. Belle, clerk at 701 Mn. b. 96 Wooster.
" Agnes, wid. Robert, h.u. 121 Pearl.
" Alexander, roofer at 32 Village.
" Andrew, milkman, h. 10 Holcomb.
" Bertha E. wid. Wm. W. h. 9 Riverside pl.
" Charles, cook at 8, b. 8 Central.
" Chas. A. clerk at Hartford Trust Co. 764 Main, b. 15 Washington.
" & Clark, saloon, 123 Pearl.
Robert Hunter. John Clark.
" Edward J. carptr. at 155 Shel. h. 192 Jef.
" Harness Co. N. W. Hunter, 162 Asylum.
" Howard W. clerk at 162 Asy. b. 41 Vernon.
" Hugh, mach. 476 Capitol, h. 37 Laurel.
" Hugh Jr. mach. at 476 Cap. b. 37 Laurel.
" James, at 59½ Trumbull, b. 26 Flower.
" James, machinist at 476 Cap. h. 244 Putnam.
" James L. teamster at 71 Asy. h.2u. 26 Flower.
" Jane, wid. Joseph, h. 1178 Main.
" Jane, wid. William, b. 169 Ashley.
" John, teamster at 154 Ch.O. b. Woodbridge.
" John S. pres't water commissioners, supt. water works, 800 Main, h. 15 Washington.
" Margaret D. nurse, 48, b. 48 Church.
" Nathaniel W. (Hunter Harness Co.) h. 41 Vernon.
" Rich. H. engineer, 155 Ch.O. h.u. 21 Arch.
" Robert (Hunter & Clark,) h.u. 121 Pearl.
" Thomas G. farmer, b. 7 Washington.
" William, clerk at Brown, Thomson & Co. 942 Main, h. 217 Capen.
" Wm. B. patternm. 33 Wells, h.u. 56 Wooster.
Huntington Alonzo, blacksm. 9 Sig. h.Poquonock.
" Benj. F. mach. at 30 Cush. b. 234 Franklin.
" Bert D. bakery, 185, h. 195 Albany.
" C. W. 223 Asylum, rm. 19.
" Caroline T. b. 18 Prospect.
" Chas. A. mach. at 581 Cap. h. 43 Babcock.
" Chas. G. advertising department, Popes, real estate, h. 23 Wethersfield.
" Clark, foreman 250 State, b. 26 C.O.pl.
" Edward F. foreman at 690 Park, b.9 Amity.
" Ernest H. toolmaker at Colts, b. 30 West.
" Eunice E. clerk, b. 200 Russ.
" Francis H. driver, 128 Com. h.u. 128 Albany.

Huntington Henry A. attorney, 2 Central, h. Windsor t.
" Henry G. clerk Connecticut Fire Insurance Co. 51 Prospect, h. 96 Kenyon.
" Henry L. machinist at Pratt & Whitneys, 1 Flower, b. 96 Kenyon.
" John T. Rev. rec. St. James ch. h. 17 Clinton.
" Lillie L. teacher N.E.school, b. 113 Edwards.
" Lottie, clerk, b. 200 Russ.
" Mary G. ass't librarian, 5 Atheneum, b. 26 Charter Oak pl.
" Misses, h. 336 Collins.
" Rich. T. toolmaker at 388 Cap. h. 200 Russ.
" Richard T. Jr. clerk Y.M.C.A. b. 200 Russ.
" Robert W. Jr. actuary at Conn. Gen. Life Ins. Co. 49 Pearl, h. 336 Collins.
" Samuel G. clerk at Conn. General Life Insurance Co. 49 Pearl, b. 96 Kenyon.
" Sarah W. b. 17 Clinton.
" William, (H. W. Palmer & Co.) h. 26 Charter Oak pl.
" Wm. W. h. Prospect av. 1st h.n. of Asylum.
Huntley Seth, carpenter, b. 66 Capitol.
Huntoon Edward W. toolmaker at Popes, h. Windsor t.
Huntsinger Camilla A. teacher at E. M. Huntsingers, 30 Asylum, h. 7 Linden.
**HUNTSINGER EMANUEL M.** business college, 30 Asylum, h. 2u. 7 Linden.
*See outside back cover.*
Huntting Chas H. (Fowler & H.) h. 19 Townley.
" Wm. L. & Co. leaf tobacco, 214 State.
Wm. L. Huntting. Wm. S. Huntting.
" Wm. L. (Wm. L. H. & Co.) h. E.H.t.
" Wm. S. (Wm. L. H. & Co.) h. E.H.t.
Hunziker John, mach. at 1 Flower, b. 2u. 213 Law.
" Hans, toolmaker, 1 Flow. b. 213 Lawrence.
Hurbut Francis V. cabinetmaker, h.u. 9 N.B.
Hurd Charles F. real estate, 80 Pearl, rm. 2, h. 211 Collins.
" Chas. H. inspector at Popes, h.u. 863 Main.
" George E. shipper at 725 Mn. b. Bloomfield t.
" Gilbert S. machinist at 13 Central, h.2u. 1273 Main.
" Hiram, carpenter at N.Y.R. h. 23 Ward.
" Hubert L. brassfinisher, 65 Suffield.
" Ida M. wid. Charles H. h. 47 Green.
" Phœbe, wid. William D. h. 211 Collins.
" Wm. A. inspec. 245 Pearl, h.u. 5 Ellsworth.
" Wm. F. packer 725 Main, h. Bloomfield t.
" William M. toolm. at 581 Cap. b. N.B.
Hurlburt Anna L. b. 576 Farmington.
" Cornelia, wid. Benjamin F. b. 146 Weth.
" Cornelia M. b. 305 Farmington.
HURLBURT E. E. provisions, Valley st. h. 34 Sumner. *See page 199.*
" Edwin M. machinist, 1 Flower, h.u. 6 Grand.
" Henry W. Mrs. (Mary L.) h. 576 Far.
" Nellie May, b. 576 Farmington.
" Thomas, electrician, b. 25 Central.
Hurlbut Block, 373 Asylum.
" George S. b. 754 Asylum.
" Harry, screwm. at 476 Cap. b. 82 Windsor.
" Howard C. b. 754 Asylum.
" Sarah C. wid. Amanda M. h. 754 Asylum.

Hurley Brothers, machinists, r. 223 State.
James H. Hurley. John J. Hurley.
" Cornelius, helper at 232, b. 36 Sheldon.
" Daniel, driver at 172 Com. h.3u. 192 Shel.
" Daniel, molder at 556 Cap. b. 1335 Broad.
" Ellen, wid. Cornelius, h.u. 34 Hudson.
" Ellen, wid. Michael, h.u. 68 Vanblock.
" Florence, clerk, 885 Main, b.3u. 25 Spruce.
" George, lineman, b.2u. 36 Sheldon.
" James, bartender at 77, b.2u. 36 Sheldon.
" James, helper at N.Y.R. h.u. 22 Huntley pl.
" Jas. F. (Woods&Hurley,)b.114 Hungerford.
" James H. (H. Bros.) h.u. 884 Main.
" John, teamster, h.u.r. 54 Potter.
" John, watchman at Cheney Bros. Silk Mill, 34 Morgan, h. 114 Hungerford.
" John A. at Travelers Insurance Co. 56 Prospect, h. 61 Hudson.
" John H. teamster at 74 Mor. b. 20 Village.
" John J. (Hurley Bros.) mach. at 1 Flower, b. 34 Hudson.
" John J. mach. hand, Colts, b.u. 68 Vanblock.
" Margaret, wid. John F. h.u.r. 44 Village.
" Martin P. blacksmith, h. 9 Morgan.
" Michael, lineman, b.2u. 36 Sheldon.
" Michael, mach. 135 Sheldon, b. 34 Hudson.
" Patrick, blacksmith, b. 9 Morgan.
" & Staudinger, electricians&mach. 223 State.
Jas. H. Hurley. August D. Staudinger.
" Thomas, plumber, b. 114 Hungerford.
" William, laborer, b.2u. 36 Sheldon.
" William G. b. 24 Wadsworth.
Hurlock Walter (French & H.) h.2u. 13 Liberty.
Hurst Frank S. clerk at 852 Main, b. 21 N.B.
" George, cigarm. at 867 Main, h. 68 Spring.
" Stephen, tailor, 21, h. 21 New Britain.
" Thomas E. tinner,3Grove, h. 891 Windsor av.
" William B. printer r. 133 Shel. b. 68 Spring.
" ☞see also Hirst.
Hurter Rudolph, manager at 84, h.u. 84 Front.
Huse F. clerk at 835 Main, b. 75 Seymour.
Husinsky M. J. physician, 1042, h. 1042 Main.
Hussey Alice, and Maggie, b. 72 Maple.
" Edward, ostler, 171, h.u. 258 Front.
" James, polisher, b. 300 Allyn.
" John, laborer, b. 3 Ellery.
" Katherine L. (S.J.H.& Co.) h.u. 164 Wash.
" Joseph H. woodworker, 20 Potter, h.W.H.t.
" Samuel J. (S. J. H. & Co.) h. 99 Edwards.
" Samuel J. & Co. paints, etc. 20 Central.
Samuel J. Hussey. Katherine Hussey.

Hussey Stephen J. mach. at 1 Flow. h. 70 Putnam.
" Stephen L. Jr. assemb. Popes, b. 70 Putnam.
" William F. mech. at Popes, b. 70 Putnam.
Husted James H. buffer, b.u. 33½ Lafayette.
" Nels, lettercarrier, h.u. 33½ Lafayette.
Hutchings Claud J. clerk, 929 Mn. h.49S.Hudson.
Hutchins C. E. teamster, b. 74 High.
" Edward, clerk, h. 2 Webb.
" Frank, painter, b. 2 Webb.
" George A. foreman at Popes, h. 236 N.P.
" George A. helper, h.u. 41 Canton.
" Harriet, wid. Lyman D. h. 2 Webb.
" H. Gordon, b. 699 Asylum.
" J. Herbert, life ins. 721 Main, rm. 3, h. G.t.
" Llewellyn A. painter, h. 2 Webb.
" M. Evangeline, compositor at 25 Asylum,
   b.u. 41 Canton.
" Mary O. wid. of Nelson O. b.u. 41 Canton.
" Nelson, trimmer, b.u. 41 Canton.
" Robert H. b. 699 Asylum.
" Sophia A. wid. Llewellyn, b. 35 Lafayette.
Hutchinson Benjamin P. cutter 8 Sig. h. 65 Laurel.
" Clair S. clerk at Smith, Northam & Co. 129
   State, h. 366 Windsor av.
" Eliza A. wid. H. W. h. 109 Wooster.
" George W. clerk at Brown, Thomson & Co.
   942 Main, b. 17 Talcott.
" Ida B. wid. E. W. h.r. 193 Park.
" James A. mach. 1 Flower, h. 104 Albany.
" John, toolm. at 581 Cap. b. 276 Lawrence.
" John I. agent Ætna Life Ins. Co. 650 Main,
   h. Essex t.
" John J. engraver, 62 Market, h. 92 Park.
" Kate W. principal kindergarten, Brown
   school, b. 11 Winthrop.
" Louis H. accountant. b. 109 Trumbull.
" Louisa D. wid. Jewett E. Sr. b. 366 Windsor av.
" Nellie, b.r. 193 Park.
" Nellie M. Cannon Mrs. h. 104 Albany.
" Patrick J. clerk at 419 Main, h. 92 Park.
" Sarah, wid. William, h.u. 92 Park.
" William, compositor at Case, L. & Brainard
   Co. 141 Pearl, b. 92 Park.
Hutchison Robert, lab. 556 Cap. h.2u. 36 Laurel.
" Robert J. molder at 556 Cap. h. 25 Putnam.
Hutner Max, rubberw. at 690 Park, b. 9 Kibbe.
Hutt Albert W. butcher at E. E. Hurlburts, Valley,
   h.2u. 108 Mather.
" ☞ see also Huot.
Hutter Abraham, buyer, 956 Main, b. 225 Market.
" Eva, clerk at 956 Main, b. 225 Market.
Huttner Frederick, driller at Colts, h.u. 9 Kibbe.
Hutton Arthur, laborer, h. 1068 Broad.
" David, stonecutter, h.2u. 3 Oak.
" James (Smith & H.) h. 202 Jefferson.
" Jean A. clerk at Brown, Thomson & Co.
   942 Main, b. 202 Jefferson.
Hutzler Edward, cooper 315 Park, h. 52 Grand.
Huxstep Seth, clerk 216 Sta. h.u.r.348 Windsor av.
Hyatt Edgar H. ship. clerk at Brown, Thomson
   & Co. 942 Main, h. 9 Lafayette.
" Theo. cabinetfinisher, h. 63 Willow.
Hyde Almon, foreman, h.u. 6 Avon.
" Arthur S. sec. and treas. Whitlock Coil Pipe
   Co. h. 63 Niles.

Hyde Chas. blacksm. at 17 Elm, b. 18 Trumbull.
" Chas. O. teamster, 154 State, l. 171 Windsor.
" Clarissa T. wid. Charles, b. 61 Barbour.
" Clement C. teacher High sch. h. 1470 Broad.
HYDE E. HENRY, JR. (Hungerford, Hyde,
   Joslyn & Gilman) attorney, 49 Pearl,
   charity commissioner, h. 597 Farmington.
                              See page 488.
" Emma J. stenog. 756 Main, b.u. 445 Capitol.
" Emma R. b. 406 Wethersfield.
" Empson B. at Phœnix Ins. Co. 64 Pearl, b.
   109 Elm.
" Eugene A. h. New Park.
" F. Elizabeth, wid. Alvan P. h. 37 C.O.pl.
" Frank E. attorney at law, Paris, France,
   h. 37 Charter Oak pl.
" Fred E. horsetrainer, b. New Park.
" George, employee at 59½ Tru. h.u. 6 Walnut.
" Harold A. b. 206 Asylum, rm. 9.
" Harry J. mach. 133 Shel. b.u. 445 Capitol.
" Harry T. clerk at 719 Main, h. 9 Canton.
" James A. engir. at 581, h.u. 445 Capitol.
" Jesse A. operator at 388 Capitol, b. W.t.
" John, gardener at 56, b. 56 Fairfield.
" John S. inspector at Colts, b. E.H. t.
**HYDE, JOSLYN & GILMAN,** now
   Hungerford, Hyde, Joslyn & Gilman.
                              See page 488.
" Richard W. sexton Christ ch. h.u.15 Church-
" Salisbury, h. 12 Myrtle.
" Thomas M. asst.supt. 811 Main, h.u.6 Walnut.
HYDE WM. WALDO, (Gross, H. & Shipman,)
   attorneys, 756 Main, street commissioner,
   h. 37 Charter Oak pl.      See page 486.
Hydel Fred'k C. clerk, 690 Park, h. 260 Laurel.
Hyer Charles, at Popes, h.u. 22 Grand.
Hyland Dan'l, janitor¹ St. Jos. sch. h.142 Babcock.
" Edward, laborer, h. 22 Commerce.
" Helen, clerk at 835 Main, b. 142 Babcock.
" John, b. 30 Temple.
" John, lab. at Zion Hill cemetery, h. 5 Affleck.
" John, screwm. at 476 Capitol, h. 151 Law.
" Joseph, painter at P.&R. h. 293 Lawrence.
" Kate, nurse, b. 703 Asylum.
" Mary A. dressmaker, h.2u. 54 Pratt.
" Michael, teamster at 9, b. 9 Zion.
" Minnie, dressmaker, b. 142 Babcock.
" Thomas, watchman at 476 Cap.h.u.15 Squire.
" ☞ see also Hiland; Highland.
Hyman Herman, grocer, 246, h. 246 Front.
" Morris, harnessmaker, b. 246 Front.
Hynds Bernard, clerk 310 Park, b.u. 133 Ward.
" John, gardener at Popes, h.u. 133 Ward.
" John Jr. plumber at 280 Asy. b.u. 133 Ward.
Hynes David, iceman, b. 141 Commerce.
" David N. conductor St.Ry. h. 55 Wdbg.
" Delia, inspector at 476 Cap. b. 30 Fairfield.
" James, polisher at 581 Cap. b. 41 Amity.
" James M. bartender, 134, h.u. 136 State.
" Kittie M. clerk, b. 30 Fairfield.
" Malachi, b. 30 Fairfield.
" Martin, farmer and milkm. 30, h. 30 Fairfield.
" Martin J. asst. clerk 476 Cap. l. 86 Hopkins.
" Matthew, liquors, 134 State, h. 72 Capitol.

Hynes Patrick, tobaccosorter, h.u. 5 American.
" Thomas, blacksmith, h. 41 Amity.
" Thomas, porter at 26, b. 26 State.
" Thomas D. teamster, h.u. 133 Ward.
" Thomas J. h.2u. 1048 Broad.
" Thomas W. packer at 40 Gov. h.u. 53 Wdbg.
" William, blacksmith, b. 18 Central.
" William, milkman, 40, h. 45 Fairfield.
" William J. elevatorer at Phœnix Mutual Life
    Ins. Co. 49 Pearl, b. 40 Lewis.
" ☞ see also Hines.

IACOVONO Masinino, laborer, b. 22 Kilbourn.
" ☞ see also Yackavon.
Ibbott Charles, shipper at Popes, h.u. 421 Broad.
Ideal Mach. Works, models, punches, dies, 328 Asy.
Iffland Alexander, brushm. 176 Allyn, h. 51 Ferry.
Ignatius Sullivan A. salesm. 139 Asy. h. 126 Capen.
Igo Lawrence, coachm. 356 Mn.h. 2 C Wadsworth.
" Thomas A. shoemaker, h. 270 Park.
Igoe Nellie M. stenogr at 1 Laurel, b. 93 Park.
" Thomas, plumber, b. 80 State.
" Wm J. cigarm. 104 Asy. h. 2u. 153 Windsor av.
Ils Christine J. nurse, b. 448 Main.
Imlin John, cabinetm. 69 Front, h. 12 Kilbourn ct.
Immeln Leo, joiner, h.2u. 102 Ward.
" Peter, stairbuilder, h.2u. 6 Kilbourn ct.
Imparatrice Prospro, bootblack, b. 21 Windsor.
Impey Stephen T. mason at 8 Front, h. Ingleside
    pl. Bluehills.
Indian Bulletin, (quarterly by Conn. Indian
    Association,) 714 Asylum.
Industrial Home for the Blind, 335, store 334 Weth.
Ingalls Edward H. conductor St. Ry. b. 14 Bond.
" Frederick C. student at Trinity college, 17
    Seabury hall, Summit.
" Harriet Mrs. h.u. 104 Main.

P. H. INGALLS, Physician.    Office, 112 High
    street.
    Hours—11.30 A.M. to 3 P.M.
                Telephone 342.

Ingalls P. H. physician, 112, h. 112 High.
Ingerson Louise, clerk at 53 Ann, h. Cottage.
Ingle Huldah S. Mrs. h.u. 289 Capitol.
Inglehart William, helper at 618 Cap.h.9 Kinsley.
INGLIS WM. SLOANE, pres. Neal, Goff & Inglis
    Co. h. 44 Willard.          See page 498.
Ingraham Chas. E. mach. 133 Shel. b.u. 7 Clinton.
INGRAHAM CLARENCE B. (I., Swift & Co.)
    126 Church, h. 171 Sigourney.
                See page 585.
" Delia O. b. 36 Jefferson.
" Edward R. student, b. 171 Sigourney.
" Fred C. celluloidw. at Popes, b. 19 Church.
" Lewis W. farmer, b. 235 Barbour.
" Melissa, wid John B. b.2u. Winter.

INGRAHAM, SWIFT & CO.
    dressed beef, sheep, provisions, poultry,
    butter, eggs and cheese, 126 Church.
                See page 585.
Clarence B. Ingraham.
    Gustavus F. Swift, Chicago, Ill.
            Edwin C. Swift, Boston, Mass.

Ingraham Walter, electrician at 70 Commerce,
    h.u. 189 Retreat.
" Warren, blacksmith at 201 Smith, h. 26
    Whitney.
" William F. undertakers assistant, 58 Ann,
    h. 4 Kennedy.
" William Thomas, painter, 34 h.34 Lawrence.
Ingram Frank A. veterinary surgeon, 367 Allyn,
    h.3u. 14 Church, rm. 6.
Inns John, painter, h.u. 2 Ellery.

**INSANE RETREAT,** 30 Wash-
    ington.          See pages 698, 699.
Inskip Fred, machinist at Popes, b. Burnside v.
Insurance Journal Co. 53 Trumbull.
International Loan Office, H. Runbaken, 2 State.
" Sunday School Index Co. 336 Asylum.
Iorgensen Martin, saddler at 8 Sig. h. 25 Putnam.
Iowa Mortgage Co. 40 Asylum.
Ipsar ☞ see Epsar.
Iribas Juan L. Spanish interpreter, at Travelers
    Ins. Co. 56 Prospect, h. 169 Seymour.
Irving Charles, h.u. 26 Elmer.
" Henry J. bookfinisher at 141 Pearl, h. 2
    Whitman.
" William H. painter, h.2u. 18 Elmer.
" ☞ see also Erving.
Irwin Thomas A. rubberw. at 690, h. 771 Park.
" Wm. J. inspector at Popes, h.2u. 15 Oak.
Isenberg H. A. barber, h. 7 Sumner.
Isham Henry G. h. 211 High.
" Mary T. b. 650 Main, rm. 20.
" Oliver K. physician, 211, h. 211 High.

OLIVER K. ISHAM, Physician.    Office, 211 High,
    corner Walnut.
    Hours—11.45 A.M. to 3 P.M. and 7 to 8 P.M.
                Telephone 1110.

Isleib Charles A. plumber at 1204 Main.
" Frederick, buffer at Popes, h. 189 Zion.
Isler John, cabinetm. 69 Front, h. 16 Franklin.
Islieb George H. electrician at 1 Laurel, b.S.M.t.
Israeli Elimelech, dry goods, 232, h. 232 Front.
" Esaias, student, b. 232 Front.
" Simon, b. 232 Front.
Istrand Otto, carpenter, l.2u. 263 Main.
Itzak Warrenton, market, 80, h.u. 80 Potter.
Itzkovitz Leon, screwm. at 476 Cap. h. 4 Kil. ct.
" Rosa, wid. Harry, b. 4 Kilbourn ct.
Ives Annie C. wid. John S. h. 70 Niles.
" Annie L. teacher at Second North school,
    b. 70 Niles.
" Annie M. Mrs. 223 Asylum, room 106.
" Edward K. bkkpr. at 335 Shel.h.59 Lincoln.
" Frederick C. at Hartford Fire Insurance
    Co. 53 Trumbull, h. 18 Girard.
" Ralph B. manager at 164 State, b. 70 Niles.
" Sarah E. wid. Silliman B. h.u. 11 May.
" Susan B. stenog. at Popes, b. 26 C.O. pl.
" William W. clerk in labor statistics office,
    rm. 48, State capitol, h. Norwich v.
Izzard Thos. 2d cook, str. Middletown, 285 State.

JACK Wm. A. cabinetm. 69 Front, h. 232 Capen.
Jacklin Lottie, wid. William, h.u.r. 1214 Main.
Jacklyn William H. porter at T. Sisson & Co.
   729 Main, h. 14 Warren.
Jackman Elmer A. supt. at Andrews & Peck,
   155 Charter Oak, h. 104 Franklin.
Jackson Albert, waiter at 389, b. 389 Main.
" Alex.M. painter at 185 Asylum, h.85 Benton.
" Allen, butler at 131 Far. h. 96 Walnut.
" Andrew J. waiter at 53, b. 53 Ann.
" Arthur A. bookkeeper at 154 Charter Oak,
   b. 19 Congress.
" Charles, carpenter, h.2u. 76 Madison.
" Charles, inspector at Hfd. Steam Boiler In-
   spection & Ins. Co. b. 87 Madison.
" Charles, lettercarrier, P.O. h. 19 Congress.
" Charles L. mach. at 80 Huy. b. 19 Congress.
" Charles S. cook at 323 Pearl, b.r. 70 Temple.
" Cornelius, at 599 Main, h.r. 34 Village.
" Cornelius, clerk, h.u.r. 1214 Main.
" Daniel, janitor, 650 Main, h. 14 Center.
" Dawson, hodcarrier, b. 45 Wolcott.
" Edward, at 847 Main, rm. 37, b. S.M.t.
" Edward Q. at Ætna Insurance Co. 666 Main,
   h. Middletown t.
" Elizabeth, wid. George J. h. 62 Vernon.
" Elizabeth, wid. William, h.3u. 59 Ferry.
" Frances E. clerk at insurance department,
   rm. 20, State capitol, b. New Haven t.
" Fred. C. supt. city delivery, P.O. 65 State,
   dentist, h.u. 110 Capen.
" George A. waiter, b. 1 Marsh.
" Jack, laborer at 335 Sheldon, h. 6 Oak.
" James J. waiter at 26 State, h.u. 489 Main.
" James L. watches and jewelry, 1076 Main,
   h. 176 Clark.
" Joanna Mrs. h.u. 33 Sumner.
" John W. bartender, 65 Shel. h.2u. 41 S.Pro.
" Leonidas S. clerk at N.Y.R. 450 Asylum,
   h. 35 Washington.
" Lizzie, wid. Jesse H. h. 789 Windsor av.
" Louisa J. wid. Lewis W. b. 181 High.
" Niles, carpenter, h. 38 Rowe.
" Orion, clerk at Popes, b. 35 Washington.
" Peter, polisher at 476 Capitol, h. 232 Park.
" Rufus R. business manager, Hartford Daily
   Times, 716 Main, b.u. 33 Sumner.
" Sarah J.wid.Silas,seamstress,h.877 Mn.rm.7.
" Susan, wid. Charles, h. 53 Lincoln.
" Wm. H. inspector at Popes, h. 67 Madison.
Jacobs Alfred W. discount clerk at City Bank,
   783 Main, b. 4 Barnard.
" Arthur I. inventor, 9 Sig. h. 253 Collins.

Jacobs, Avery & Northam Co. crockery, 875 M
" Belle, clerk at 835 Main, b. 4 Walnut.
" Caroline A. teacher at High school, b. 815
   Asylum.
" Delia A. wid. Jeremiah, h. Davenport.
" Henry, clerk, b. 44 Village.
" Henry M. pres. 875 Main, h. 19 Vernon.
" Jacob, h. 45 Morgan.
" Jacob Mrs. midwife, 45, h. 45 Morgan.
" Jeremiah Sr. h. Prospect av.
" John A. l. 74 High.
" Joseph, capm. at 76 Asylum, b. 213 Front.
" Julia Mrs. milliner, 908 Main, h. Walnut.
" Louise, wid. Henry, b.r. 44 Village.
" Matthew M. porter at Charles R. Hart Co.
   898 Main, h. 23 West.
" Nellie, bookkeeper, b. 7 Kennedy.
" Nicholas V. dropfor. 142 Russ, h. 241 Park.
" Raymond K. machinist, b. 97 Russ.
" Robert M. laborer, b. 7 Kennedy.
" Ward S. mach. at 1 Flow. b. 530 Farmington.
" Ward W. (W. W. J. & Co.) treasurer
   Mechanics Savings Bank, etc. 815 Main,
   h. 530 Farmington.
" Ward W. & Co. ticket agents, 815 Main.
" William, jobber, h. 7 Davenport.
" Wm. C. filer at Colts, h. 4 Barnard.
" Wm. R. mach. at 9 Sigourney, b.u. 97 Russ.
Jacobson Alex. H. assembler at 556 Capitol,
   h.u.r. 355 Park.
" Andrew, (J. & Hammerstrom,) h. 109 Law.
" Charles, mach. at 1 Flow. h.u. 82 Madison.
" Charles, mechanic at Popes, b. 121 Babcock.
" Emil, painter, b.u.r. 355 Park.
" Frank, at Newton & Burnett, 319 Asylum,
   b.u. 64 Flower.
" George, carpenter, b.u. 64 Flower.
" Gustavus, harnessmaker at 83 Asylum,
   h.2u.r. 355 Park.
" & Hammerstrom, painters, 14 Hungerford.
   Andrew Jacobson.        Charles Hammerstrom.
" John (Olsen & J.) b. 80 Front.
" John, cabinetm. 147 Shel. h.u.r. 126 Ward.
" John, laborer, h.u. 64 Flower.
" Peter, blacks. 697 Windsor av. b. 182 Clark.
Jacobus Melancthon W. Rev. prof. Hfd. Theo.
   Seminary, 1507 Broad, h. 14 Marshall.
Jacques Arthur L. clerk, Popes, b. 1148 Broad.
" Ernest, bartender, b. 534 Main.
" Maria, wid. Thomas, h. 1148 Broad.
Jaeger Johann Heinrich Wilhelm, pastor Ger-
   man Lutheran church, h. 28 Julius.
Jaffar Abraham, plater at Popes, h.u.r. 132 Mar.
Jager Andrew, bricklayer, l. 30 Church.
" Arthur, at 690 Park, b. 37 Francis.
Jaggerman Mary Mrs. b. 2 Holcomb.
Jainsen Carl, painter, h. 152 Babcock.
James Alfred, gardener, 67 Weth. h. 194 Maple.
" Celia, wid. Silas J. h.u. 9 Avon.
" Charles H. porter at 143 Tru. h. 83 Mather.
" Flora, dressmaker, b.u. 9 Avon.
" H. B. machinist at 13 Central, b. 1 Linden.
" Martin, rubberworker at 690, b. 15 Park.
" Michael T. mach. at 142 Russ, h.72 Hopkins.
" Philip, painter, 352 Albany, b. 70 Trumbull.

James W. Samuel, janitor Second North school, 249 High, h.u. 6 Winter.
"   William E. mechanic at Popes, h. 9 Avon.
Jameson Henry, cabinetm. at 556 Main, h.233 Jef.
"   William J. carpenter, h. 908 Park.
Jamieson Carey A. carpenter, r. 334 Asylum, b. 228 Franklin.
"   George D. mach.at 133 Shel.b.228 Franklin.
"   Harley W. boxm. at Popes, b. 228 Franklin.
"   Robert W. cigarm. at 88 State, h.1179 Main.
"   Thomas, iceman at 48 Ann, h. W.H.t.
"   Victoria B. teacher at South school, 36 Wadsworth, b. Middletown t.
Janes William R. roller, 690 Park, h.u.13 Francis.
Janke Julius, filer at 142 Russ, b. 81 Front.
Janner John, laborer, 245 Windsor,h.56Bellevue.
Janoski Alexander, laborer, b.r. 11 Ellery.
Jansen Alfred C. pocketbookmaker at 336 Asylum, b. 60 Church.
"   Carl C. conductor, St.Ry. h. 16 Jefferson.
"   Charles J. mach. at N.Y.R. h. Elmwood.
Janson Henry, saloon, 1056 Main, h.117 Albany.
"   ☞see also Johnson.
Japsen Nils, laborer at 476 Capitol, h. 240 Zion.
Jaqua Frank, painter, b. 21 Walnut.
"   Sophia, at 49 Trumbull, b.u. 69 Babcock.
Jaquith Arthur G. motorman, h. 30 Woodbridge.
"   F. Arthur, mach. at 54 Arch, h. 40 Putnam.
"   Horace D. carpenter, h.2u.r. 36 Sanford.
Jardine Robert, toolm.at 388 Cap.h.u.66 Congress.
"   Robert S. mach. at 581 Cap. b.u.66 Congress.
Jarman Emma M. teacher Northwest school, b. Burnside v.
**JARMAN JAMES H.** agent Conn. Mutual Life Ins. Co. 783 Main, h. 274 Wethersfield.            *See page 451.*
"   William S. at Conn. Mutual Life Ins. Co. 783 Main, b. Burnside v.
Jarvis Edward W. dentist at 53 Tru. b. Portland t.

GEO. CYPRIAN JARVIS, Physician. Office, 98 High street.
Hours—2 to 5 P. M.
Telephone 338.

Jarvis Geo. Cyprian, physician, surgeon, 98, h. 98 High.
"   John S. Mrs. (Elizabeth) h. 54 Main.
"   Joseph, brickmaker, h. New Park.
"   Richard W. H. president Colt's Patent Fire Arms Mfg. Co. b. 30 Wethersfield.
Jasper Fannie M. b. 16 Winthrop.
Jasperson Andrew, clerk, 369 Cap. b.1461 Broad.
Jassay Boldi, cutter at 8 Sig. h.u.r. 28 Lawrence.
Jaycox Elizabeth, wid. Leander H. b. 27 Pliny.
Jaynes Chauncey, b. 103 Ann.
Jedikin Joseph, watchmaker at 862 Main, h. 56 Pleasant.
Jeffers Cornelius, cigarm. 867 Main, h.Windsor t.
"   Patrick, hodcarrier, b. 6 Cedar.
"   Robert J. clerk at 1082 Main, h. 60 Wells.
Jefferson Arthur, barber 99 State,h.u.55 Madison.
"   Emma Mrs. h.u. 55 Madison.
"   Jeff P. apprentice at 1092 Main, b. M.t.
"   Morris S. rubberw. 690 Park, b. 91 Willow.
"   Peter, driver, 46 Ann, h.2u.r. 33½ Lafayette.

Jenison Eunice C. Miss, stenographer at Tucker & Goodwin, 8 Hurlburt, b. 9 Chapel.
"   Mary E. nurse, 9, b. 9 Chapel.
Jenkins Arthur B. stenographer, notary public, at 68 Pratt, h. 35 Oxford.
"   Charles H. clerk at Factory Ins. Asso. 95 Pearl, b. 53 Sigourney.
"   H. M. wid. Joseph F. h. 35 Oxford.
"   Henry, 2d pantryman steamer Middletown.
"   Wm. G. Mrs. (Lillie H.) h. 53 Sigourney.
Jenks Bertha, at 59½ Trumbull, b. 48 Hudson.
"   Frank M. compositor at Popes,h.u.104 Hung.
"   Frederick R. timeclk. 1 Flow. h.48 Hudson.
"   Julia, teacher, b. 48 Hudson.
"   Rebecca, at 59½ Trumbull, b. 48 Hudson.
Jenne A. E. motorman St.Ry. h. Pearl.
Jenney Harry L. mach. at Colts, b. 345 Main.
Jennings Charles L. clerk 885 Main, b. 97 Tru.
"   Edgar H. burnisher at 62 Market, b. Hawthorn ex.
"   Elijah, laborer Pope Tube Co.h. 588 Garden.
"   Elijah Jr. laborer at Pope Tube Co. b. 588 Garden.
"   Elizabeth A. Mrs.: b.r. 110 Barbour.
"   Frank B. mach. at 9 Sig. b. 52 Babcock.
"   George G. mach. 1 Flower, b. 3 Farmington.
"   & Graves, prop. Opera House, 933 Main.
    Henry H. Jennings.          E. M. Graves.
"   Henry H. (*J. & Graves,*) h. Bridgeport t.
"   Henry H. Jr. adv. agent, l. 933 Main, rm. 15.
"   John F. pressm. at Popes, b. 588 Garden.
"   Lewis, at 883 Main, b. 6 Avon.
"   Mary E. stitcher at 8 Sig. b. 588 Garden.
"   Theodore, cigarmaker, b. 23 Church.
"   Tillie, seamstress, 171 Putnam, b. 118 Hung.
Jennison Edward F. fertilizers, 218 State, h. Wethersfield t.
Jensen Bagnar, b. 56 Putnam.
"   Carl, h. 6 Oak.
"   Carl, laundryman at 30 Washington.
"   Hans, driver, h. 57 Judson.
"   James P. carpenter, h. 74 Putnam.
"   John P. machinist at 54 Arch, b. 4 Elliott pl.
"   Neil, screwm. at 476 Capitol, h.r. 322Capen.
"   Niels, porter at 273 Asylum, b. 1155 Broad.
"   Peter, laborer, h.r.2u. 44½ John.
"   R. Randloe, woodwkr.u.16 N.B.b.533 Broad.
"   Sophie, attendant at 30 Washington.
"   Soren, laborer at 15 Tru. b. 15 Morgan.
Jentile Pasquale, laborer, h.u. 168 Front.
Jepson Christian, stuffer at 15 Tru. h. Burnside v.
"   Jeppe, painter, b. 50 Willow.
"   Neils, mechanic, b. 240 Zion.
"   Peter M. blacksm. at 476 Cap. h.u.50 Willow.
Jerin Jacob, filer at Colts, h. 7 King.
Jester William S. driver, 547 Main, b. 64 Capitol
Jeter William, teamsr. 82 Francis, h.r. 21 Squire.
Jett William, fireman N.E.R. h.2u. 10 Martin.
Jette Joseph, bicyclerepairer, b. 87 High.

**JEWELL BELT HOOK CO.**
15 Trumbull.            *See page 548.*

**JEWELL BELTING COMPANY,**
hides, leather, leather belting, etc. 15 Trumbull.            *See page 530.*

**Advertise Your Real Estate in THE POST.**

Jewell Charles A. treasurer Jewell Belting Co. 15 Trumbull, h. 140 Washington.
" Charlotte A. h. 140 Washington.
" Lyman B. vice pres't Jewell Belting Co. 15 Trumbull, h. 113 Elm.
" P. & Sons, 15 Trumbull.
   P. Jewell,   L. B. Jewell,   Chas. A. Jewell.

**JEWELL PAD COMPANY,** 49 Hicks.	*See page 534.*

**JEWELL PIN COMPANY,** 31 Hicks.	*See page 534.*
" Pliny, pres. Jewell Belting Co. 15 Trumbull, pres. Jewell Pin Co. h. 210 Farmington.
Jewett Almena, wid. Josiah, b. 380 Windsor av.
" Benjamin, motorman St. Ry. h. 2u. 2 Talcott.
" David B. student at Trinity college, 17 Jarvis hall, Summit.
" Edward A. pressman at 141 Pearl.
" Frank (*Andrus & Naedele Co.*) 272 Asylum, h. 330 Windsor av.
" Fred. D. (magician) trick-rooms r. 240, h. 238 Windsor av.
" George D. machinist, h.u. 10 West.
Jillson Camella, b. 67 Wethersfield.
" Emily, wid. William, b. 59 Sargeant.
" Frank, lunch wagon, h. 59 Sargeant.
" Hannah E. wid. Asa W. h. 67 Wethersfield.
Joblintz Otto, laborer, b. 39 Mulberry.
Jobson A. fireman tug Ward, 285 State.
Jockisch Charles, cabinetmaker at 225 Sheldon, h.u.r. 165 Front.
Joddick Elizabeth, h. 37 Arch.
Johansen Johanna, wid. L. Peter, h. 11 Holcomb.
" Mads, machinist at 335 Shel. h.u. 6 Oak.
Johanson Carl J. filer, 581, b. 279 Capitol.
" William B. mach. at 1 Flower, b. 154 Ward.
John Hancock Mutual Life Ins. Co. of Boston, 756 Main, Ernest G. Hatch, supt.
" Mary C. nurse, h. 14 Church.
" Napoleon, carpenter, l. 1045 Main.
Johnantonio Julian, laborer, b. 73 Morgan.
Johnesky Alex, laborer at 8 Front.

**JOHNS-PRATT CO.** mfr. vulcanized Asbestos packing and electric goods, 555 Capitol.	*See page 540.*
Johnson Aaron, trimmer 180 Allyn, b. 28 Temple.
" Adolph F. carpenter, b.3u. 102 Albany.
" Albert, driver at 53 Ann, b. 4½ Bond.
" Albert J. driver at 53 Ann, b. 187 Weth.
" Albert L. packer at 40 Gov. b. 81 Seymour.
" Albert W. dieskr. 142 Russ, h. 182 Putnam.
" Alex. cabinetmaker at 69 Front, b. 29 Park.
" Alfred, coachman at 126 Far. h.r. 35 Forest.
" Alfred, machinist, b.u. 80 Front.
" Alice H. wid. James D. h. 41 Niles.
" Allen H. clerk at Popes, b. 49 Allen pl.
" Alma, nurse, b. 193 Russ.
" Amanda, dressmaker, 43, h. 43 N.B.
" Andrew, blacksm. 352 Alb. b. 39 Harrison.
" Andrew, carpenter, b.2u. 179 Lawrence.
" Andrew, carpenter, b. 234 Park.
" Andrew, saloon, 282, h. 280 Park.
" Andrew, screwm. at 476 Cap. 66½ Laurel.
" Andrew B. saloon, 44 Temple, h.u. 1078 Mn.

Johnson Annie, wid. Julius, h.u.r. 173 **Windsor.**
" Antony C. machinist at 1 Flow. b. 181 **Law.**
" Arthur C. draughtsm. 1 Flow. b. 315 **Pearl.**
" Arvid G. rubberw. at 690 Park, b. 301 **Law.**
" August, cabinetmaker, b.2u. 54 **Flower.**
" August, at 59½ Trumbull, b. 27 **Wolcott.**
" August, coachman, b.2u. 263 **Main.**
" August, machinist at 142 Russ. h. 40 N.B.
" August M. stonema. h. Quaker lane, W.H.t.
" Barnett, laborer, h. 19 Sanford.
" Benj. sexton 1st Meth. church, h.u. 112 Alb.
" Berger, machinist at 1 Flower. b. 154 Ward.
" Bernard, laborer, h.2u. 18 Kilbourn.
" Bort, coachman at 104 Wash. h.u. 8 Hung.
" C. J. machinst at 1 Laurel, b. 150 Ward.
" Carl J. mach. at 476 Capitol, h. 12 Smith.
" Carlos M. salesman at 367 Mn. l. 17 Walnut.
" Case, ostler at 372 Asylum, l. 257 High.
" Catherine, wid. Henry J. h. 106 Gillett.
" Catherine, wid. William, dressm. h. 69 Willow.
" Charles, at 1 So. Ann, b. 67 Albany.
" Charles, deckh. str. Middletown, 285 State.
" Charles, gardener, b. 1117 Main.
" Charles, plumber, h.u. 206 Allyn.
" Charles, steamfitter, h. 4 Walnut.
" Charles, teamster, h. 6 Oak.
" Charles A. molder at 618 Cap. b. 74 Putnam.
" Charles A. carpenter, h.u. 13 Affleck.
" Charles C. screwm. 476 Cap. h. 273 Capen.
" Charles E. helper at 142 Russ. b. 43 N.B.
" Charles E. saloon, 163 Front, h. 52 Oak.
" Charles E. toolmaker at Colts, h. 118 Asy.
" Charles F. brazier at Popes, b. 291 Park.
" Charles F. prof. Trinity college, h. 69 Vernon.
" Charles G. baker wagon, b.u. 14 Fairmount.
" Charles G. filer at Popes, b. 62 Lawrence.
" Charles G. polisher at Colts, h. N.B.t.
" Charles H. marketman, 319 Asy. b. 13 Hung.
" Charles J. mech. at Popes, b. 60 Jefferson.
" Charles J. printer at Hartford Times, 716 Main, h.u. 288 Park.
" Charles J. stonecutter, 283 Shel. b. 613 Cap.
" Charles M. printer at 141 Pearl, b. 69 Park.
" Charles O. stonec. at 283 Shel. b. 301 Law.
" Charles P. sawyer at 93 Ch.O. h.r. 98 N.B.
" Charles R. at 59½ Trumbull, h. 7 Wolcott.
" Charles S. shoem. 59 Far. h.u. 46 Grand.
" Charles W. h. 79 Elm.
" Charles W. h. 231 Lawrence.
" Charlotte D. wid. Henry, b. 133½ Barbour.
" Charlotte H. wid. Edwin E. b. 119 Bellevue.
" Chauncey R. b. 132 Jefferson.
" Chauncy R. Jr. machinist at 1 Flower, b. 50 Cedar.
" Christian, helper at 30 Cush. b. Mulberry.
" Christian Mrs. b. 43 New Britain.
" Christian, laborer, h.2u. 1 Pleasant ct.
" Christian, operator at 8 Sig. h. 13½ Hamilton.
" Christian A. screwmaker at 476 Capitol, h. 275 Capen.
" Christian C. screwmaker at 476 Capitol, h. 273 Capen.
" Christian Clemsen, b. 11 Kibbe.
" Christian S. linem. 266 Pearl, h. 1078 Main.
" Christie P. machinist, b.2u. 613 Capitol.

**As A NEWSPAPER, THE POST LEADS.**

Johnson Christine A. mail clerk at Popes, b. 125 Charter Oak.
" Christopher, carpenter, h. 10 Bond.
" D. Waldo Mrs. h. 103 Trumbull.
" Daniel E. engineer at Billings & Spencer Co. 142 Russ, h. 431 Capitol.
" Daniel S. polisher at 142 Russ, l. 52 Oak.
" David, laborer, 285 State, b. Elizabeth park.
" Edward, laborer, l. 1078 Main.
" Edward A. musician, mach. at 1 Flower, h. 365 Laurel.
" Edward A. salesman at 219 Asy.b. N.B.t.
" Edwin, policeman, h. 66 Spring.
" Edwin B. at Ætna Life Ins. Co. 650 Main, h. 119 Bellevue.
" Elijah C. cashier at National Exchange Bank, 76 State, h. Windsor t.
" Eliza S. Mrs. h. 35 Pliny.
" Ella, at 20 Sargeant, b.u. 20 Cedar.
" Ellery A. watchmaker at H. Kohn & Sons, 890 Main, h.u. 21 Elmer.
" Emil, at 142 Russ, b.u. 43 New Britain.
" Emil, tailor at Patten Dye Works, 37 Wells, h. 37 Woodbridge.
" Emily P. dressmaker, b. 171 Seymour.
" Eric, laborer, b.r. 30 Wethersfield.
" Ernst, laborer, h. 11 Kibbe.
" Esther, wid. Thos. h. Whiting lane, W.H.t.
" Ethel E. clerk 140 State, h.u. 133½ Barbour.
" Fannie, b. 106 Gillett.
" Francis August, mach. 1 Flow. b. 59 Madison.
" Francis G. bricklayer, h.u. 24 Goodwin.
" Francis M. clerk at Popes, b. 809 Asylum.
" Frances Mrs. h.u. 42 Windsor.
" Frank A. driver at 44 Mar. h. 39 Chestnut.
" Frank E. driver, 56 Niles, h.u. 61 Hawthorn.
" Frank E., U. S. A. pres. Loan and Guarantee Co. 49 Pearl, h. 142 Collins.
" Frank E. motorman, St.Ry. h.r 42 Bkm.
" Frank H. b. 32 Madison.
" Frank H. coachman 640 Far. h. 43 Amity.
" Frank J. superintendent Hartford Heating Co. 267 Asylum, h. Hayden station.
" Frank M. photogr. 1039 Main, b. 35 Pliny.
" Fred. E. clerk at 1046 Main, h. E.H.t.
" Frederick W. printer at Case, Lockwood & Brainard Co. h.u. 41 Hungerford.
" George, screwmkr. 476 Cap. h. 18 Babcock.
" George D. lineman at 247 Pearl.
" Geo. F. job printer, 724 Main, h. 138 Weth.
JOHNSON GEORGE F. prop. Commercial House, 165 Asy. opp. Allyn house. See p. 100.
" George L. helper, 15 Tru. b. 15 Sanford.
" George M. foreman bindery, Case, Lockwood & Brainard Co. 141 Pearl, h.69 Park.
" Geo. W. at 13 Central, h. 59 Julius.
" Gertrude E. stenographer National Life Asso. 53 Trumbull, b. Manchester t.
" Gertrude J. bookkeeper, b. 55 Woodbridge.
" Gilbert, teamster, b.u. 61 Potter.
" Godfrey, driver 130 Church, h.u. 358 Park.
" Grace J. clerk at 96 Tru. h. Wethersfield t.
" Gus, caster at 62 Market, b.u. 151 Babcock.
" Gustav, asst. shipping clerk at 556 Capitol, h.u. 24 Wolcott.

Johnson Gustav A. operator, 8 Sigourney, h.u. 58 Woodbine.
" Gustavus, tailor, 93 Pratt, h. 49 Allen pl.
" H. B. Mrs. h. 47 Grand.
" H. W. l. 30 Spring.
" Hans, at 78, b. 78 Avon.
" Hans P. motorman St.Ry. h.2u. 20 Lawrence.
" Hans P. screwm. at 476 Cap. h. 275 Capen.
" Hans W. screwm. 476 Cap. h. 181 Lawrence.
" Harriet, b. 53 Oak.
" Harriet, h. 87 Elm.
" Harriet Howe, teacher vocal culture, 23, h. 23 Wadsworth.
" Harry, waiter, h.2u.r. 213 Pearl.
" Harry E. at Nat. Life Asso. 53, h. 103 Tru.
" Harry F. laborer, h. 8 Smith.
" Helen, nurse, b. 193 Russ.
" Henry, butler at 195, b. 195 Collins.
" Henry, laborer at 75, b. 75 Bluehills.
" Henry, undertaker at 1166, h.u. 1209 Main.
" Herbert W. toolm. at Popes, b. 47 Grand.
" Herman, coachman, b. 510 Farmington.
" Herman, laborer, b.r. 12 Fern.
" Horace, auctioneer, etc. storage, r. 170 Commerce, h. Middle Haddam t.
" Hilma, dressmaker, 193, b. 193 Russ.
" Horace L. foreman at Billings&Spencer Mfg. Co. 142 Russ, h. 62 Hungerford.
" Hugh M. rubberw. at 690 Park, h. 166 Allyn.
" Hulda, laundress at 20 S. Hudson.
" J. C. head waiter at 152 Asylum.
" J. Edmund, carriage painter, 580 Windsor av. h. 45 Barbour.
" J. Peter, h.u. 7 Willow.
" Jacob, woodyard, 30 Union, h. 36 Village.
" Jacob O. carptr. at 15 Tru. b. 98 Babcock.
" James, at 169 Front, b. 330 Pearl.
" James, deckhand str. Middletown,285State.
" Jennie, b. 62 Chestnut.
" Joel, machinist, b. 59 Madison.
" John, at 690 Capitol, h. 18 Putnam.
" John, at 690 Park, b. 147 Babcock.
" John, filer, b.2u. 54 Flower.
" John, harnessmaker at 83 Asy. b. 291 Park.
" John, helper, b. 330 Pearl.
" John, helper at stone pits, b. 52 Village.
" John, laborer, h. 3 Brady.
" John, laborer at 556 Capitol, h. 56 Harrison.
" John, laborer at Popes, b.r. 30 Wethersfield.
" John, laborer at 142 Russ, h. 880 Broad.
" John, laborer at 581 Capitol, h.u. 35 Wolcott.
" John, mason, h.u. 47 Woodbine.
" John, printer, b. 234 Pearl.
" John Jr. machinist, h. 33 Laurel.
" John A. at Popes, h.r. 239 Jefferson.
" John A. lab. at 295 Sheldon, b. 21 Mulberry.
" John A. mach. at 581 Cap. h. 181 Babcock.
" John A. mason, h. 55 Grand.
" John A. polisher at Popes, h. 99½ Jefferson.
" John A. stonecutter, 54 Windsor av. b. 301 Lawrence.
" John C. mach. at 1 Flower, b. 91 Willow.
" John E. coachman, 66 Washington.
" John F. state deputy K.O.T.M. h.u. 9 Squire.
" John G. driver at 501 Asylum.

Johnson John J. bricklayer, b.u. 47 Woodbine.
" John M. polisher, 476 Cap. h. 2u. 29 Hamilton.
" John P. coachm. Prospect av. h. Fairview.
" John R. at 141 Pearl, l. 118 Asylum.
" John W. Mrs. (Phoebe A.) h. 74 Windsor av.
" John W. solderer at 62 Mar. h. 64 Francis.
" Joseph A. printer at 141 Pearl, h. 111½ Hung.
" Justus, diesinker, 142 Russ, h. 34 Putnam.
" Katie, housekeeper, h.u. 30 Ferry.
" Kittie, laundress, b. 1096 Main.
" Lars, miller, 48 Ann, b. W.H.t.
" Lars A. at Ætna Life Ins. Co. 650 Main, h. West Hartford t.
" Laura, h. 87 Elm.
" Leroy F. packer, 1 S. Ann, h.u. 248 Putnam.
" Lewis, porter at 10 State, b. Wolcott.
" Lewis, rubberw. at 690 Park, b. 11 Kibbe.
" Louis S. collector at Evening Post, 23 Asylum, b. 13 Florence.
" Louise, laundress, 171 Putnam.
" Lucius M. clerk at 885 Main, b. 50 Sumner.
" Lucretia, b. 45 Capen.
" Lydia M. h. 55 Grove.
" M. Carlyle, president V. E. Hawley Co. h.u. 19 Congress.

M. M. JOHNSON, Physician. Office, 92 Pearl street.
Hours—9 to 10 A.M.
2 to 3.30 and 7 to 8 P.M.
Telephone 573.
Sanitarium 220-6.

Johnson Marcus M. physician, 92 Pearl, h. 122 Woodland.
" Marshall B. mach. at 1 Flow. h. 34 Vernon.
" Mary Mrs laundress, h. 108 Huyshope.
" Mary E. wid. Lyman B. h. 182 Putnam.
" Mary F. bookkeeper, b.u. 120 Jefferson.
" Matilda, h. 206 Asylum, room 19.
" Merritt F. cutter at 1 S. Ann, h. 67 Albany.
" Mollie, cook at 76, h.r. 60 Wells.
" Morgan, foreman at Dwight Slate Machine Co. 13 Central, h. 9 Morgan.
" Myron H. (Bullard, J. & Shipman) h. Middletown t.
" Nancy, laundress, h.u.r. 37 Albany.
" Neil, laborer, 54 Arch, h. King.
" Neils, helper at 1 Flower, b. 157 Babcock.
" Neils P. bricklayer, b.2u. 20 Lawrence.
" Nicholas, repairer at 40 Gov. b. 118 Asylum.
" Nicoline, wid. Samuel, h.u. 20 Cedar.
" Nils, at 273 Asylum, b. 1155 Broad.
" Olaf, coachman at 62 Woodland, h.u. 60 Harrison.
" Oscar, b. 37 Woodbridge.
" Oscar, coachman at 207, b. 282 Laurel.
" Oscar, teamster at 82 Francis, b. 646 Park.
" Oscar C. mach. 476 Cap. b.u. 167 Babcock.
" Oscar Julius, mach. 1 Flow. b. 59 Madison.
" Osmond C. patternmaker Pratt & Whitney Co. 1 Flower, h. 43 Congress.
" Patrick, b. 37 Woodbridge.
" Pende A. polisher at 581 Cap. b. 50 Willow.
" Percy, gardener, 76, b.r. 76 Wells.
" Perrie A. carpenter, h. 17 Wolcott.
" Peter, baker at 169 Asy. h.2u. 82 Windsor.

Johnson Peter, miller, b. Bloomfield.
" Peter, laborer at 252 Pearl, b.2u. 28 Church
" Peter, molder at 54 Arch, h. 28 Putnam.
" Peter, porter at 462 Main, h. 7 Willow.
" Peter C. mach. at 28 Laurel, b. 386 Park.
" Peter E. bricklayer, h. 40 Evergreen.
" Peter H. screwm. at 476 Cap. h. 275 Capen.
" Ransom, cook, b.r. 140 Albany.
" Reynold A. diemr. at 26 High, h. 42 Windsor.
" Rhienhart, mach. at 1 Flow. b. 181 Lawrence.
" Richard, contractor, b. 39 Chapel.
" Richard, laborer, h.u. 35 Spruce.
" Robert H. cigarmaker at 88 State, and musician, h.u. 201 Park.
" Rose. b. 106 Gillett.
" Rose A. wid. Edward A. h. 55 Woodbridge.
" Rufus, driver, Adams Ex. Co. h. 68¼ Wooster.
" Sally C. wid. John, b. 568 Farmington.
" Samuel, cooper at Valley, h.u. 40 Temple.
" Samuel E. h. 206 Asylum.
" Sarah Mrs. h. 60 Albany.
" Sarah B. h. 87 Elm.
" Selden L. salesman, 149 State, h. 66 Lincoln.
" S. Georgina, wid. Wm. G. h.23 Wadsworth.
" Stewart P. switchm. N.Y.R. b.u.106 Walnut.
" Swan, polisher at Popes, b.2u. 29 Hamilton.
" Thomas, blacksm. 295 Shel. h. 204 Franklin.
" Thomas, machinist, b.u. 1232 Main.
" Thomas B. molder at 618, b. 371 Capitol.
" Thomas M. at 71 Asylum, b.r. 4 Martin.
" Thos. P. collector, 4 Central, b. 106 Gillett.
" Thomas P. gardener, h.3u. 62 Sheldon.
" Victor, laborer, h. 43 Ann.
" W. E. civil engir. at and h. Farmington, City Water works reservoir.
" Walter, b. 49 Windsor.
" Walter, driver at and b. Fishfry.
" Walter B. motorman, St.Ry. h. 32 Madison.
" Walter L. clerk, b. 35 Pliny.
" Wilbur A. painter, h.2u. 230 Windsor av.
" Wilbur C. clerk at 581 Capitol, b. 813 Asylum.
" William, carpenter, b.u. 54 Flower.
" Wm. clerk at Brown, Thomson & Co. 942 Main, h.u. 54 Barbour.
" William, driver, 4, b. 4 Huyshope.
" William C. clerk, h. 809 Asylum.
" Wm. D. (Curtis & J.) h. 64 Bond.
" Wm. F. cutter 1 So. Ann, h. 31 New Britain.
" William J. helper, b. 31 Lawrence.
" William R. clerk at 3 Central, b. 35 Pliny.
" William S. laborer. b.u. 112 Albany.
" Willis H. brakeman, P.&R. h.u. 73 Albany.
" Yoel W. mach. at 1 Flower, b. 59 Madison.
" ☞ see also Johnston; Johnstone; Janson.

Johnston Annie, teacher. b. 216 Wethersfield.
" Edwin P. broker, 721 Main, rm. 12.
" George, clerk, b. 36 Bond.
" Hector, buyer at Brown, Thomson & Co. 942 Main, h. 30 Westland.
" James, mach. at 1 Flower, b. 10 Affleck.
" Joseph, instructor, h. 36 Bond.
" Margaret, clerk, h.u. 877 Main, rm. 10.
" Thos. L. profiler at Colts, h. 254 Jefferson.
" Warren G. borer, Colts, h. 216 Wethersfield.
" ☞ see also Janson; Johnson; Johnstone.

**If you have anything to Sell, Advertise it in The Post.**

Johnstone Charles, real estate, 9 Asylum, b.3u. 36 Church.
" Christopher A. photographer, 45 Pratt, h. 161 Sisson.
" Christopher S. foreman at Lincoln & Co. 54 Arch, h. 201 New Park.
" George, laborer at stonepits, 7 Flatbush.
" John J. clerk at 54 Arch, b. 201 New Park.
" John R. printer at 141 Pearl, h. 118 Asylum.
" Robert A. at 45 Pratt, h. 201 New Park.
" Walter, mason, h. 101 Glendale.
" ☞ see also Janson; Johnson; Johnston.
Jolidon Charles J. toolm. at Colts, h.u. 57 Pratt.
Jonas Henry, grocer, 50, h. 50 Temple.
Joncas Jos. E. carptr. at 53 Vernon, b. 263 Main.
Jondreau Fred, plasterer, b. 197 State.
Jones Albert F. b. 116 Ann.
" Alice W. at 336, b. 336 Wethersfield.
" Alma, bkkpr. at 1031 Main, b. 555 Garden.
" Almeron H. Mrs. h.r. 555 Garden.
" Anna L. milliner at Brown, Thomson & Co. 942 Main, b. 7 Clinton.
" Booker, coachman at 29, b. 29 Windsor av.
" Charles A. insurance agent, h. 37 Lewis.

CHARLES E. JONES, Physician. Office and Residence 116 Ann street.
Hours—9 to 10 A.M., 3 to 4 and 7 to 8 P. M.
Wednesdays—9 to 10 A. M. only.
Sundays—3 to 4 P.M. only.
Telephone 965.

Jones Chas. E. physician, office and h. 116 Ann.
" Charles T. assembler at Colts, h. 84 Webster.
" Charles T. Jr. clerk, 581 Cap. b.84 Webster.
" Charles W. machinist, Popes, b. 119 Oak.
" Chas. W. solderer 62 Mar. h. 25 Sargeant.
" Daniel T. saddler at 8 Sig. b. 47 Laurel.
" Delia R. Mrs. cook at 30 Washington.
" Edward A. mach.at Colts, h.u. 151 Retreat.
" Edward J. clerk at Popes, b. 37 Lewis.
" Edward R. teamster, h. 81 Green.
" Edward W. brazier, h. 106 Windsor.
" Edwin A. bookkeeper at 276 Market, h. 703 Main, rm. 14.
" Elizabeth, wid. Wm. b. 137 Hamilton.
" Elizabeth, stenogr. at 843 Main, b. E.H.t.
" Everett P. clerk at 1082 Main, b. 55 Kenyon.
" Frank H. teamster, b. 61 Judson.
" Frank M., U. S. A. b.r. 555 Garden.
" Fred. plumber at 164 State, b. Windsor t.
" Fred. A. lather, b. 107 Mather.
" Frederick C. at Phœnix Life Ins. Co. h. 128 Woodland.
" George, painter at 1 Flower, h. 7 Clinton.
" George A. mach. at 1 Flow. b. 7 Clinton.
" George C. gardener, 21, b. 21 Vine.

JONES GEORGE E. magnetic physician, 609, h. 609 Main.    See page 421.
" George H. steward steamer Middletown, 285 State, h. Goodspeed.
" George S. ship. clerk 921 Mn. h.2u. 17 Chst.
" Harriet L. Mrs. h. 46 Seymour.
" Harry, b. 609 Main.
" Henry O. motorman St.Ry. h.u.r. 98 N.B.
" Henry W. h.u. 59 Ferry.

Jones Horace K. h. 35 Spring.
" James, blacksmith P.&R. h. E.H.t.
" Jas. printer at 252 Pearl, b.152 Washington.
" James H.draughtsm. at Pope Tube Co. h.137 Hamilton.
" James H. floorwalker at 835, h. 573 Main.
" James S. blacks. P.&R. h. 137 Madison av.
" Jane, wid. John, h.u. 5 Huntley.
" Joel, b. 785 Windsor av.
" John, b.3u. 703 Main.
" John F. coachman at 85, l. 85 Ann.
" John H.elevatorer at 835 Mn. b. 35 Spruce.
" John H. waiter at 53, b. 53 Ann.
" Joseph, distributor, Hartford Post, 23 Asylum, b. 137 Madison av.
" Joseph, tinner, 26 Hicks, b.u. 118 Asylum.
" Laura B. clerk at Lincoln, Seyms & Co. 34 Market, b. 119 Oak.
" Levis O. chief clerk 247 Pearl, h.6 Westland.
" Lucy M. wid. Samuel F. h. 192 Farmington.
" Margaret H. clerk at National Life Association, 53 Trumbull, b. 77 Elm.
" Maria, wid. Robert, notions, 70, h. 70 Sheldon.
" Marion E. nurse, b. 87 Laurel.
" Mary Mrs. h.u. 35 Spruce.
" Mary G. Mrs. h. 198 Bellevue.
" Mary V. b. 7 Clinton.
" Moses J. gardner, b. 2 George.
" Owen H. plumbers specialties, r. 279 High, b. 1 May.
" Robert, teamster, 26 Potter, h. 4½ Squire.
" Robert, waiter, b.r. 1 Marsh.
" Robert W. coachman, h. 63 Lafayette.
" Rosa, wid. Lewis, h.u. 35 Spruce.
" Russell Lee, clerk at Phœnix Mutual Life Ins. Co. 49 Pearl, b. 128 Woodland.
" Sarah H. wid. Henry N. b. 93 Huyshope.
" Thomas A. motorman, h.u. 2 Mannz.
" Truman B. mach. at 133 Shel. b. 91 Asylum.
" W. Frank (Cadwell & J.) h. 55 Kenyon.
" W. W. painter, 185 Asylum, b. 197 State.
" Wayland H. fishdealer, h.u. 419 Garden.
" Wm. A. saddler at 8 Sig. h.2u. 200 Russ.
" William E. lather, b. 81 Green.
" William F. foreman at 158 Wdld. h.25 Eaton.
" William H. lather, h. 107 Mather.
" Willis P. finisher, h.u. 95 Huyshope.
Jons Mary F. nurse, 14, b. 14 Church, rm. 4.
Jordan Charles, helper at Old North Cemetery, h. 2 Center.
" David J. inspector at Colts, b. 590 Main.
" Edward, tailor at 11 Wells, h. 358 Weth.
" James, carpenter, h.u. 20 Canton.
" James, mach. at 142 Russ, b. 118 Babcock.
" James J. filer at 30 Cushman, h.u. 579 Park.
" John J. machinist, 30 Cush. b.2u. 34 Laurel.
" Kate A. dressmaker, 20, h.u. 20 Canton.
" Katherine, nurse at 20 South Hudson.
" Kittie, clerk, h.u. 875 Main, rm. 11.
" Lizzie, h.u. 877 Main, rm. 11.
" Margaret, wid. Michael, h. 145 Zion.
" Mary A. h.u. 877 Main, rm. 11.
" Michael, carpenter, h.u. 145 Zion.
" Moses, dropforger at Colts, h.u. 1 Curcombe
" Nancy B. wid. Elisha S. h.u. 81 Albany.

**THE POST is a 20th-Century Newspaper**

Jordan Patrick, b. 2 Holcomb.
" Stephen J. woodw. 155 Ch.O. b. 358 Weth.
" William J. artist, b.u. 20 Canton.
Jorey James A. janitor, h.u. 1243 Main,
Jorgenson Hans, screwm. 476 Cap. h.3u. 26 Park.
" John A. elevatorer at 427 Main, b. 26 Park.
" Ulrich, at 15 Trumbull, h.u. 28 New Britain.
Joseph Aaron, tailor at 104 Asy. h. 126 Market.
" Louis A. janitor police station, h.u. 27 Loomis.
" Morris, drugclerk at 254 Asy. b. 126 Market.
" Samuel, cigarm. 104 Asy. h.2u. 15 Portland.
Josephs John J. at 581 Capitol, h. E.H.t.
Josephson Oscar A. painter at 186, h. 186 Ward.
Joslin Josiah, machinist, 1 Flower, b. 26 Imlay.
Joslyn Bessie L. operator, b. 719 Asylum.
JOSLYN CHARLES M. (*Hungerford, Hyde, J. & Gilman*) attorneys at law, 49 Pearl, h. 245 Farmington.      *See page 488.*
" Clarence R. doors, sash and blinds, 23 Wells, h. 11 Ellsworth.
" James N. peddler, l. 24 Church.
" Josiah, machinist at 1 Flower, h. 26 Imlay.
" Richard L. asst. bookkeeper at State Bank, 795 Main, b. 11 Ellsworth.
" Vern V. clerk at 983 Main, b. 56 Winthrop.
" Wm. Bell, engir. at 165 Windsor, h. 54 Avon.
Joubert Moses, carptr. 750 Main, rm. 37, h.u. 86 Madison.
Jourgeson Ulrich, miller at 15 Tru. b. 28 N.B.
Journal of Inebriety, 56 Fairfield.
Journeymens International bakery, 78 Morgan.
Jovina Rossi, laborer, h.u. 57 Front.
Joy Patrick, laborer, h.2u. 12 So. Prospect.
" William L. rubberw. at 690 Park, h. N.B.t.
Joyce Annie E. b.u. 55 Bellevue.
" Elizabeth, wid. Mich. seamstress, h. 7 Front.
" James, Jr. traveling salesman at Popes, b. South Manchester v.
" John, laborer, h.4u.r. 23 Spruce.
" John C. brakeman P.&R. h. Canaan t.
" John F. mason, b.u. 55 Bellevue.
" Kate, l. 75 Hungerford.
" Mamie E. saleslady at Wm. Rogers Mfg. Co. 66 Market, h. 55 Bellevue.
" Michael, stonecutter, h.u. 55 Bellevue.
" Patrick, helper at 4 Central, b. 1 Elm pl.
" Thomas H. hardener at Popes, h. Bloomfield t.
" William, teamster at 2 Chapel, h.u. 4 Affleck.
Joyner Alfred S. carptr. 69 Front, h.u. 25 Albany.
" E. P. Mrs. dressmaker, 864, h. 864 Broad.
" Edward P. marketman, 319 Asy. h. 864 Broad.
" Herbert, trimmer, 16 Mul. h. Manchester t.
Judatz Oswald, cabinetmaker at 69 Front, h. King, n. Julius.
Judd Allen B. druggist, b. 28 Hopkins.
" Anna M. wid. George D. h. 155 Washington.
" Araunah, h. 46 Park.
" Cornelius M. traveling salesman at 8 Hurlburt, b. 1150 Main.
" David E. clerk, h. 141 Ashley.
" Edward H. *selectman*, machinist, 24 Mechanic, h. 28 Hopkins.
" Edwin D., U. S. Army, h. 58 Garden.
" Edwin Y. (*H.C.J.& Root,*) b. 10 Highland.
" Eugene K. clerk at 335 Shel. b. 86 Hudson.

Judd Etta M. physician, 141, h. 141 **Ashley.**
" George F. cellarman at 232 **Sheldon,** b. 155 Washington.
" H. C. & Root, wooldealers, 389 **Allyn.**
    H. C. Judd.      J. H. Root.      E. D. **Judd.**
        J. H. Bidwell.         E. Y. **Judd.**
" Henry C. (*H. C. J. & Root,*) h. 10 **Highland.**
" Mary R. wid. Willis W. h. 102 **Babcock.**
" Melissa D. wid. John F. h. 58 **Garden.**
" Philip S. W. salesman, b. 1140 **Main.**
Judge Dominick, molder at 54 Arch, h. 32 **Hudson.**
" Matthew J. student, b. 32 Hudson.
" William J. student, b. 32 Hudson.
Judson Albert A. inspector at Popes, h. **E.H.t.**
" Albert H. glazier at 88 Market, h. **E.H.t.**
" Albert S. b. 127 Brook.
" Curtis, b. 389 Main.
" Dwight R. clerk at 729 Main, b. E.H.t.
" Helen L. stenographer at Orient **Ins. Co.** 5 Haynes, b. East Hartford t.
" John C. cutter, 8 Sig. h.u. 31 Barbour.
" Truman H. dynamo man, 266 Pearl, b. 8 Foot Guard.
Juliani Vito, laborer, b.3u. 51 Morgan.
Julio Nicolas, grocery, 268, h. 268 Front.
Jurezak Michael, laborer, h. 68 Potter.
Juster W. J. b. 590 Main.

KADISKI Abram, peddler, h.u. 211 Front.
" Lewis, tailor, h. 196 Front.
Kaeser Albert, upholsterer, 61 Asy. h. **Whiting.**
" Frederick H. farmer, h. Whiting.
Kahn Henry, groceries, 105, h. 136 **Mather.**
" Isador, butcher, b.r. 87 Windsor.
" Mitchell, peddler, b.r. 87 Windsor.
Kaiser William, steamfitter at 1 Flow. h. E.H.t.
Kaizer Rudolph, gardener, 138, b. 138 **Wash.**
Kaitz Joseph, woodcarver, 69 Front, b. 74 Grove.
Kalagian Charles, screwmaker at 476 Capitol, b. 1443 Broad.
Kalausch John J. molder, 690 Park, b. 32 Francis.
" Wenzel A. machinist at Colts, h. 32 Francis.
Kalber Chas. J. gardener at Cedar Hill cemetery, b. New Park.
" Conrad, mach. Pope Tube Co. b. 181 N.P.
" Henry, filer, h. 15 New Park.
Kalberg ☞ *see Calberg.*
Kalher ☞ *see Kelleher; Keleher.*
Kalish David F. b. 9 Charter Oak.
" Emily B. bkkpr. 921 Main, b. 9 Charter Oak.
" Pauline, wid. Hermann, h. 9 Charter Oak.
" Theo. M. toolm. at Popes, b. 9 Charter Oak.
Kalkhof John, tailor, 2, h.2u. 2 Kilbourn ct.
" Louis, tailor at 2, h.2u. 2 Kilbourn ct.
Kallajian Kircher, screwmaker at 476 Capitol, h. 24 Howard.
" Misak, screwm. at 476 Cap. b. 1443 Broad.
Kallenbach John M. expressm. 42, h. 42 Madison.
" Lena, clerk at 956 Main, b. 42 Madison.
Kalowski Tony, laborer, h.u.r. 18 Sheldon.
Kalver John, h. 17 New Park.
Kamerer Charles, driver, 633 Mn. h.u. 48 Retreat.
" Frank, clerk at 538 Main, b. 249 Front.
" Fred, butcher, h. 249 Front.
" ☞ *see also Kemerer.*

Kamienski Frank, laborer, rub.wks. b. 31 S.Pro.
Kamleiter John, gardener at 107, b. 107 Ann.
Kammerman Isadore, tinner at 1192 Main, h. 4 Kilbourn ct.
Kammritz August, painter, h. 36 Belmont.
Kampfmann Adam,bottler,60Front,h.47 Morgan.
" Joseph, h. 23 Bellevue.
Kanary ☞ see also Canary.
Kandrick Joseph, laborer, b.2u. 2 Ellery.
Kane B. clerk at Brown, Thomson & Co. dry goods, 942 Main, b. 33 Morris.
" Barbara Mrs. laundress, h.r. 139 Martin.
" Bridget, wid. Patrick, h. 147 Maple.
" Honora, wid. Dennis, b.u. 61 Judson.
" J. Robert, clerk, 31 Pratt, b.r. 119 Far.
" James, clerk, b. 33 Morris.
" James, groceries, 258, h. 258 Front.
" James H. b. 170 New Park.
" Jeremiah, laborer, h.3u. 68 Sheldon.
" Jeremiah J. b. 33 Morris.
" John, clerk at 989 Main, h. 20 Center.
" John, coachman at 119,h.r.119 Farmington.
" John, deckhand str. Middletown,285 State.
" John, engineer at P.&R. h. 22 Brook.
" John, porter at Brown, Thomson & Co. 942 Main, h. 33 Morris.
" John, teamster, h.u. 140 Grove.
" John J. laborer, h.u. 248 Front.
" John Jr. teamster, 74 Mor. b. 76 Pleasant.
" John Jr. b. 31 Morris.
" Jos. L. barber, 66 Sheldon, h. 52 Linden.
" M. Matilda, teacher at Brown school 160 Market, b. 147 Maple.
" Margaret, b. 33 Morris.
" Mary E. milliner at Brown, Thomson & Co. 942 Main, b. 33 Morris.
" Mary J. teacher at South school, 36 Wadsworth, b.147 Maple.
" Matthew, molder, 54 Arch, h.2u. 2 Putnam.
" Michael, brickyard, 170, h. 170 New Park.
" Patrick F. carpenter, b. 28 Grace.
" Peter A.at 581 Capitol, b.u. 265 Main.
" Robert,elevatorer, Colts, h.u.r. 74 Vanblock.
" Sarah, b. W. H. Home for Aged, Albany.
" Thomas, ostler at P.&R. h. 24 Pliny ct.
" Thomas, teamster, r. 50 State, h. 140 Grove.
" Thomas F. health commissioner, physician, 517 Main, b. 147 Maple.
" Thomas F. h. 776 Park.
" Thomas F. printer, b. 214 High.
" Thomas W. conductor, h.3u. 73 Avon.
" William E. teamster at 476 Cap. h. 108 Ward.
" William F. bkkpr. 170, b. 170 New Park.
" William M. mach.at 133 Shel. h. 5 Elliott.
" ☞ see also Keane; Kean; Keene; Keine.
Kannair Frank E.cashier,78 Asy.h.101 Whitmore.
Kannuski August, laborer, h.3u.r. 44½ John.
Kanza John, electrician, b.u. 1218 Main.
Kapcheske Herman A.woodworker, 155 Charter Oak, b. 15 Windsor.
" William, woodworker, b. 15 Windsor.
Kapitke Otto, clerk at 5 Asylum, b. 126 Ann.
Kaplan Bessie, b. 9 Kennedy.
" David (Friedman & K.) b. 65 Morgan.
" Isaac, commercial traveler, h.u. 9 Kennedy.

Kaplan Max, screwmaker, h.u. 195 Front.
" Rubie, peddler, h.2u. 159 Front.
" Samuel, peddler, h.2u. 159 Front.
Kapp Martin, cigarm. 104 Asy. h.2u. 58 Temple.
" Peter, laborer at 141 Com. b. 2 Ellery.
Kaptuller Emil, carpenter, b. 133 Front.
Karbaum Annie E.clerk, 956 Main, b. 17 Alden.
Karotke Jacob, tinner, 1192 Main, h. 205 Front.
Karotkin Isaac,barber, 91 Windsor, b. 205 Front.
" Morris, peddler, h. 205 Front.
Karr Arthur V. elevatorer, 835 Mn. b.33 Mather.
" Lucasta N. wid. Wm. S. h. 2 Atwood.
" Mary L. musicteacher, 2, b. 2 Atwood.
Kasanof Reuben, tailor, 822, h. 822 Park.
Kaschefski Henry, laborer, b. 98 Albany.
Kase Helwig, bartender at 357 Asylum.
" ☞ see also Case.
Kasfreski Charles, laborer, b. 21 Arch.
Kashman Benjamin, at 26 Mul. b. 143 Capitol.
" Morris, butcher, l. 1045 Main.
" Seymour, clerk at 26 Mul. b. 143 Capitol.
Kashmann Isaac. gents furnishings, 12 State, h. 11 Canton.
" Isaac H.clerk at 26 Mulberry,b. 143 Capitol.
" Jacob at 162, b. 162 Clark.
" Joseph,meats.etc.26 Mulberry,h.143 Capitol.
" Simon, wholesale butcher, 46, h. 46 Sumner.
" ☞ see also Cashman.
Kasnicky Abram, laborer, h.u. 224 Front.
" Frank, laborer, b.u. 224 Front.
" Jacob, peddler, b.u. 224 Front.
Kassenbrook Theo.fresco painter,office 262 Allyn, h. 22 Goodwin.
Kassnick Michael, laborer, h. 15 Mechanic.
Kastberg Eric F. mech. at Popes, h. 169 Babcock.
Katten Abraham, Hartford One Price Clothing Co. 114 & 116 Asylum, h. 31 Summer.
" ☞ see also Cadden.
Katz Abe A. b. 192 Front.
" Esau, milkman, h. 82 Pleasant.
" Harris, bottler, h. 190 Front.
" Isaac, peddler, h.2u. 11 North.
" Jacob, h. 194 Front.
**KATZ JACOB,** scrap iron, copper, brass, etc. 9, h. 7 North.    See page 502.
" Jacob, laborer, h. 54 Pleasant.
" Jacob, screwm. at 476 Cap. h. 74 Temple.
" Joseph, clerk at 215 Front, b. 61 Morgan.
" Joseph R. barber, 9, b.u. 19 Morgan.
" Louis, market, 205 Front, h.u. 40 Avon.
" Louis, milkman, h. 82 Pleasant.
" Louis, screwmaker, h.2u. 180 Windsor.
" Max, cigar store,1074 Broad,h. 64 Windsor.
" Max, cigars & tobacco, h. 259 State.
" Max, laborer at 40 Gov. h.u. 57 Morgan.
" Max, tailor at 94½ Trumbull, b. 78 Morgan.
" Michael, peddler, h.u. 130 Windsor.
" Michael, tailor, h.u. 78 Morgan.
" Morris H. market,51 Morgan, h. 248 Front.
" Nathan, driver, h. 80 Pleasant.
" Nathan, grocer, 215 Front, b. 61 Morgan.
" Samuel, clerk, h.3u. 55 Morgan.
" Samuel, mach. at 388 Cap. h. 60 Pleasant.
" Samuel, painter, h. 165 Front.

**If you have anything to Sell, Advertise it in The Post.**

Katz Samuel, peddler, h.u. 101 Windsor.
" Simon, peddler, h.u. 190 Front.
" ☞ *see also Getz, Kaitz.*
Katzenstein Benj. B. (*K. Bros.*) h.u. 17 Bellevue.
" Bros. meats, 132 Windsor and 201 Front.
Benjamin Katzenstein.   Moses Katzenstein.
Solomon Katzenstein.
" Minnie, wid. Wm. h. 67 Bellevue.
" Moses, (*Katzenstein Bros.*) b. 15 Weth.
" Solomon, (*Katzenstein Bros.*) b. 67 Bellevue
Katzman Bennie, barber at 178 State, b. 198 Front.
" David, carriagem. at 36 Ferry, b. 198 Front.
" Lewis, peddler, h.r. 198 Front.
" Solomon, barber, 178 State, h. 78 Madison.
Katzung Berthold, pressm. 252 Pearl, h. 15 Belmont.
" John F. pressm. 252 Pearl, h. Newington t.
" William, mach. at 133 Shel. b. Newington t.
Kaufman Howard E. engineer, b. 80 State.
Kaufmann Jacob, molder at 114 Grove, h. 111 Madison.
Kaughmann Leo, b. 119 Ann.
Kavanagh Rose, at 34 Morgan, b.2u. 121 Maple.
Kavanaugh Edward A. sawyer at 225 Sheldon, h. 220 Franklin.
" John T. enameler at 581 Cap. b.u. 65 Avon.
" ☞ *see also Cavanaugh; Cavanagh.*
Kay John D. coachman, b.u. 73 Windsor.
" William W. shoemaker, 73, h. 73 Windsor.
" Wilson, filer at 28 Laurel, h. 35 Linden.
Kazariom Kirikor, Hfd.Woodyd. Co.b.125 CH.O.
Keach Frank, teams. at 213 State, h. 52 Retreat.
" George B. pressman at 690, h. 548 Park.
Kean Joe M. Mrs. h.2u. 16 Goodman.
" L. J. Darnstædt Mrs. physn. 67, h. 67 Pearl.
" ☞ *see also Kane; Keane; Keen; Keine.*
Keane Chas. M. floorwkr. at 956 Mn. b. 109 Tru.
" Eugene, laborer, h. 9 Green.
" Hannah, wid. Matthew F. h.u. 84 Walnut.
" Henry P. h. 22 Alden.
" James H. (*Melrose & K.*) h.u. 46 Annawan.
" John, laborer, h. 9 Green.
" Mary A. clerk at 921 Main, b. 72 Walnut.
" Matthew P. at Station A, b. 22 Alden.
" Peter, buyer at 956 Main, b. 22 Alden.
" ☞ *see also Keen; Kane; Kean; Keine.*
Keanchan Jas. lab. Pope Tube Co. b. 111 Zion.
Kearney Dennis, Pope Tube Co. h.u. 41 Glendale.
" Harry C. rubberworker at 690, b. 765 Park.
" Henry, b.u. 21 Ward.
" James A. patternm. at 1 Flow. b.u. 21 Ward.
" James J. rubberworker at 690, h. 765 Park.
" Patrick, enameler at 581 Cap. h.u. 21 Ward.
" Patrick J. assembler at 581 Cap. b. 3 Ward.
" Peter J. enameler at Popes, h. 47 Hudson.

Kearns Bridget, wid. Timothy, b. 2 Holcomb.
" Dennis, inspector at Colts, h. 63 Huyshope.
" James, b. 2 Holcomb.
" James, at 211 State, b. 24 Babcock.
" James F. mach. at 388 Cap. h. Burnside v.
" John, laborer, h. 16 Francis.
" John, laborer, b.2u. 24 Babcock.
" John F. printer at 141 Pearl, b. E.H.t.
" John Jr. helper at 581 Cap. b. 16 Francis.
" Matthew, machinist, h. 37 Congress.
" Michael A. enam. at Popes, b. 80 Putnam.
" Michael H. (*McKee & K.*) h. E.H.t.
" Patrick, labr. at 581 Cap. b.2u. 24 Babcock.
" Thomas, laborer, city works, b. 8 Bonner.
" Thomas, pressm. at 690 Park, h. 24 Belmont.
" Thomas P. mach. at 30 Cush. b. 16 Francis.
" William, screwmaker, b. 1 Brady pl.
" William J. pressman, b.u. 32 Trumbull.
" ☞ *see also Carnes; Cairns; Cairnes; Kerns; Currans.*
Keas ☞ *see Keyes.*
Keasick John, b. 2 Holcomb.
Keasley Emma A. wid. George R. h.u. 83 Jef.
" George Jr. bartender, b.u. 266 Maple.
Keating Catherine Mrs. b. 2 Holcomb.
" Daniel J. plumber, 30 Washington.
" Daniel J. rubberworker, h. 22 Howard.
" Edward, teamster at 462 Main, b. 7 Willow.
" Francis J. polisher, b. 21 Loomis.
" James, teamster, b. 58 Judson.
" John, laborer, h. 60 Portland.
" John W. brazier, b.r. 52 Linden.
" Margaret, clerk at 956 Main, b. 1 Orchard.
" Mary, at 8 Central, b. 520 Main.
" Maurice B. laborer at 15 Alb. h. 66 Chestnut.
" P. Joseph, porter, b. 21 Loomis.
" Patrick, machinist, h. 21 Loomis.
" Philip, laborer at 98 Kil. h. 55 Albany.
" Thomas F. mach.bd.at Colts, h. 68 Vanblock.
" •William R. mech. at 581 Cap. b. 52 Linden.
" William T. barber, h.u. 52 Linden.
Keaton Wm. H. labr. at 385. Shel. h. 85 Green.
Kee Sing, laundry, 297 Lawrence.
Keech Jessie Mrs. h.2u. 46 Asylum.
Keefe Anastasia, wid. John, b.u. 29 Portland.
" Christopher, driver, h.u. 44 Village.  .
" Cornelius, laborer, h.r. 105 Windsor.
" Daniel, laborer, b. 24 Chestnut.
" Jas. horseshoer at 7 Spruce,h.19 Foot Guard.
" John, blacksmith, h.u. 350 Park.
" John, feeder at 141 Pearl, b.u. 350 Park.
" John, laborer, h. 19 Foot Guard.
" John J.electrotyper at 177 Asy.h.56 Albany.
" John R. painter at 1106, b.u. 1067 Main.
" Margaret M. dressmaker at 926 Main, rm. 8.
" Mark, coachman at 22, b. 22 Niles.
" Mary, wid. John, h. 96 Windsor.
" Michael, b. 1045 Main.
" Michael, plumber at 164 State, b. 1045 Main.
" Michael, laborer, h. 26 Center.
" Michael W. brassw. at 223 State, b. 202 Jef.
" Misses The, milliners, 926 Main, rm. 8.
" N. Frances, dressmaker, 926 Main, rm. 8.
" Nellie, wid. David, h.2u. 146 Grove.
" Patrick J. janitor, h.u. 29 Portland.

Keefe Robert J. bkkpr. 1092 Mn. b. 52 Bellevue.
" Thomas J. plumber, 12 Mul. h.u. 72 Bellevue.
" Timothy M. clerk at Conn. Fire Insurance
    Co. 51 Prospect, h. 19 Ashley.
" William, foreman at 223 State, b.u. 202 Jef.
" ☞ *see also O'Keefe.*
Keefer ☞ *see Keifer.*
Keegan Margaret, wid. Thomas, h.2u. 1418 Broad.
" Mary, operator at 97 Asy. b.2u. 1418 Broad.
" Michael A. market, 283 Park, b. 59 Ward.
" Rose, b. W.H. Home for the Aged, Albany.
" Sarah, oper. at 203 Asy. b.2u. 1418 Broad.
" Thomas, salesm. at 76 Tru. b.2u. 1418 Broad.
Keehn Henry, baker at 69 Mor. h. 13 Kilbourn.
Keehner Christina, wid. Geo. F. h.r. 44 Village.
" Frederic E. repairer St.Ry. h.u. 5 Park.
" George A. trimr. at 164 State,h.r. 44 Village.
" William H. mach. at 556 Cap. h.u. 5 Ple. ct.
Keeler Orville, electrician, h.u. 71 Albany.
" Ralph H. asst. dentist at 903 Main, rm. 1,
    h. 18 Prospect.
" Ralph W. supervisor at 690, b. 690 Asylum.
Keeley Emma, wid. Michael, h. 193 State.
Keelly John, laborer, b. 488 Main.
Keen Chas. B. carptr. at P.&R. h.u. 115 Lawrence.
" Frank A. carpenter, b. 54 Williams.
" George, carpenter, h.3u. 23 Wells.
" Sarah Mrs. b. 100 Retreat.
" ☞ *see also Keane; Kean; Kane; Keine.*
Keena Ellen, wid. Andrew, h. 75 Governor.
" James T. mach. at 476 Capitol, b. 8 Squire.
" John, screwmaker at 476 Cap. b. 15 Francis.
" Michael T. driller at 581 Cap. b. 147 Law.
" Patrick, blacksm. at Popes, h. 8 Squire.
" Thomas, screwm. at 476 Cap. b. 15 Francis.
" Thomas J. Rev. rector St. Lawrence
    church, 18 South Laurel.
Keenan Ann, wid. John, h.u. 19 John.
" D. F. railroad contractor, 721 Main, rm. 21.
" James, laborer, b. u. 18 Commerce.
" James, pianist, b. 24 Market.
" James F. skiver at 15 Trumbull, b. 80 State.
" John, laborer, h. 75 Avon.
" John, mechanic at 26 High, b. 31 Chapel.
" John. C. plumber at 164 State, b. 1045 Main.
" Mary Mrs. b. 2 Holcomb.
" Mary C. dressmaker, 80, h. 80 Trumbull.
" Matthew, laborer, h.u. 10 Chapel.
" Matthew J. coremaker, b. 9 Riverside.
" Nellie C. b. 80 Trumbull.
" Patrick J. rubber, 581 Capitol, b.u. 9 Ellery.
" Richard. at 556 Capitol, b. 9 Riverside.
" Thomas, hodcarrier, h.u. 18 Commerce.
" Thomas, Jr. laborer, b.u. 18 Commerce.
" Thomas P. gardener, h.r. 48 New Britain.
" William, annealer at 556 Cap. h. 9 Riverside.
" William H. machinist at Colts, h. 96 Ch.O.
Keene George H. at Travelers Insurance Co. 56
    Prospect, b. 54 Williams.
" George M. carpenter at 80½ Tru. h.12 Seyms.
" Patrick F. propr. Cycle pool rm.19,h. 19 Park.
" Wm. C. machinist at 54 Arch, b. 54 Williams.
" Wm. H. forem. carptr. N.E.R. h.54 Williams.
Keeney Chas. R. carriages,123 Church,b.27 Julius.
" Ernest A. ins. clerk, 197 Asy. b. 227 High.

**KEENEY GEORGE E.** prest. Conn.
    Building & Loan Association, 252 Asylum,
    h. Somerville t.      *See page 430.*
" Lee L. b. 36 Jefferson.
" Reid A. carriagesmith at 123 Ch.h. 27 Julius.
" Reid H. gardener at 22, b. 22 Bluehills.
" William, bricklayer, h.u. 47 Lawrence.
" William, mechanic at 556 Capitol, h. E.H.t.
" Winfield G. driver, h.u.r. 22 Trumbull.
" ☞ *see also Keney.*
Keep Charles D. clerk at Phœnix Mutual Life
    Ins, Co. 49 Pearl, h. 246 Laurel.
KEEP HOWARD H. *alderman 9th ward;* clerk at
    Phœnix Mutual Life Ins. Co. h. 202 Sig.
" William E. builder, 97, h. 97 Webster.
Keesler Ambrose E. carpenter at 20 Vredendale,
    h. Bloomfield t.
Keevers Matthew J. mach. 133 Shel. h. 13 Grand.
Kehner ☞ *see Keehner.*
Keho Charles J. *(K. & Geary,)* h.u. 233 Market.
" & Geary, saloon, 167 State.
    Chas. J. Keho.          Jas. T. Geary.
" Mary, wid. Garrett, b.u. 233 Market.
" Michael H. dropfor. at Popes,h. 38 Liberty.
" Patrick, at gaswks. 8 Front, b. 69 Governor.
" Patrick J. laborer, b. 8 Marsh.
Kehoe Charles, laborer at Keney park, b.u. 666
    Windsor av.
" James, laborer at Colts, b. 69 Governor.
" James, teamster, h.u. 666 Windsor av.
" John, laborer, h. Tower av. c. Barbour.
" Michael, scourer at 15 Tru. b. 33 Spruce.
" Michael C. fireman at 1 Laurel, b. 86 Tower.
" Patrick, laborer, b. 80 State.
" Patrick K. laborer, h. 114 Windsor.
" Susie, Mrs. h. r. 213 Pearl.
" ☞ *see also Keough; McKeough.*
Keidel John G. mach. at 556 Cap. h.u. 918 Park.
Keifer George, butcher at 516 Main, h. 33 Elliott.
Keiler John, at 15 Albany, h.2u. 51 Liberty.
Keily Alice T. h.2u. 53 Chestnut.
" Daniel W. conductor, St.Ry. b.2u. 53 Chst.
" John, laborer, b. 14 Huntley pl.
" John A. conductor St. Ry. b.2u. 53 Chestnut.
" Minnie A. clerk at Lincoln, Seyms & Co. 34
    Market, b.2u. 53 Chestnut.
Keirnan John, carpenter, h.u. 299 Lawrence.
Keisch Edward C. operator, 135 Shel. b. 52 Jef.
" Frederick A. mach. at Colts, b. 96 Jefferson.
" Wilhelm, molder, 54 Arch, h.u. 96 Jefferson.
" William, driver, b.u. 96 Jefferson.
" William, at 229 Market, b. 32 Wells.
" William F. molder at 54 Arch, h. 32 Wells.
Keith C. H. h. 234 High.
" John, machinist at Colts, b. 45 Huyshope.
" William B. mach. at Colts, h.u. 17 Curcombe.
Keithly John, helper at Colts, b. 116½ Albany.
Kelhassa Frank, baker at 115 Windsor, h.W.H.t.
Keleher Bridget, h.r. 60 Temple.
" Daniel, salesm. 54 Huntley, h. 18 Goodwin.
" Michael, plumber at 14 Mul. b. 265 Front.
" Wm. A. mach. Colts, h. Wethersfield t.
" Wm. F. *(Ripley Bros. Co.)* l. 1224 Main.
Kelleher Alice J. wid. Timothy C. h. 233 Main.
" Andrew, laborer, h.2u. 105 Commerce.

Kelleher Andrew, packer, h.u. 146 Grove.
" Daniel, buyer at Jewells, 15 Tru. h. 8 Elm.
" Dennis, sawyer, h. 7 Ellery.
" Dennis J. woodw. at 618 Cap. b. 7 Ellery.
" Edward C.plumber at 164 State,b.1045Main.
" J. J. l. 720 Main, rm. 11.
" James, painter, h.u.r. 25 Spruce.
" James, teamster at 100 Com. b.u. 25 Front.
" James F. driver, b. 265 Front.
" Jeremiah, helper at St.Ry. 115 State.
" Johanna, b.W.H. Home for the Aged, Alb.
" John, bartender, l. 651 Main.
" John, laborer, b.2u. 107 Windsor.
" John, teamster at 997 Main, b. 265 Front.
" John,watchman at 172 Com. h. 29 Windsor.
" John J. driver, h. 23 North.
" John J. mach. at 54 Arch, b.u. 90 Willow.
" John J. mach.at 135 Sheldon, h.u. 90 Willow.
" Mary, h.u. 1421 Broad.
" Mary, wid. Patrick, h. 265 Front.
" Patrick, corem. at 1 Flow. b. 147 Babcock.
" Patrick J. news, 534 Asy. b.2u. 1421 Broad.
" Thomas, driver chem. engine, h. 265 Front.
" Thomas F. helper, b.2u. 1421 Broad.
" Timothy, milkman, h. 10 So. Prospect.
" William, enameler at Popes, b. 1329 Broad.
" William, expressman, h. 49 Linden.
" William, laborer at 335 Shel. h. 26 Union.
" William, machinist at 1 Flower, b. 86 Elm.
KELLEHER WILLIAM J. councilman 1st ward,
  teamster, 79 Talcott, h. 29 Windsor.
" ☞see also Kallaher; Keleher.
Kelleman Henry F. draughtsman at 1 Flower,
  h. 36 Hudson.
Keller Bros. dry goods, 579 Main.
  D. F. Keller.        E. F. Keller.
" Dennis F. (Keller Bros.) b.u. 573 Main.
" Edward F. (Keller Bros.) b.u. 573 Main.
" George, architect, 756 Main, h. 11 Park ter.
" Henry J. mach. at 556 Cap.h.u.17 Harbison.
" J. deckhand, steamer Hartford, 285 State.
Kelley Annie, clerk at Popes, b. 35 Harbison.
" Annie, wid. Patrick, h. 94 New Britain.
" Bernard J. carpenter, h.u. 83 Front.
" Catherine, h. 926 Main, rm. 17.
" Cecelia A. clerk at Popes, b. 175 Babcock.
" Daniel, laborer, h. 59 Potter.
" Daniel, tinner at 360 Main, b. 32 Church.
" Daniel J. polisher, h.u. 59 Potter.
" Edward, carpenter at N.Y.R. h. 46 Avon.
" Edward, helper at 1 S.Ann, b. 18 Trumbull.
" Edward, laborer at 476 Capitol, h.u. 36 Ward.
" Edward H. laborer at 95 Pleasant, h. N.B.t.
" Edward H. machinist at Colts, b. 18 Ely.
" Edward J. machinist, h. 46 Avon.
" Eugene, laborer, b.u. 59 Arch.
" Eugene, laborer, b. 57 Potter.
" Francis J. mach. at 30 Cushman, b. E.H.t.
" George R. h. 43 Canton.
" Henry J. mason, b. 46 Liberty.
" James, helper at N.Y.R. h.u. 36 Hicks.
" James, laborer, b.u. 25 Sigourney.
" James E. clerk at Brown, Thomson & Co.
  942 Main, b.u. 10 Center.
" James J. assembler, Popes, b.u. 19 Howard.

Kelley James M. saloon, 15, h. 13 Spruce.
" James T. carpenter, h. 45 Francis.
" Jeremiah J. tailor, b. 14 Ellery.
" Joe F. clerk at Baxter the Decorator, 231
  Asylum, b. Rocky Hill t.
" John, fireman, State capitol, b. 133 Babcock.
" John, laborer, h.u. 10 Center.
" John, mach. at 30 Cush. h. 2½ Hungerford.
" John, mason, h.u. 46 Liberty.
" John Mrs. dressmaker, b.u. 133 Babcock.
" John F. bartender, 246 State, h.u. 10 Center.
" John F. bricklayer, h.u.r. 147 State.
" John J. engir. at 232 Shel. h.r. 28 Morgan.
" John J. helper, h.r. 14 Arch.
" John J. inspector at Popes, b. 43 Sigourney.
" John T. clerk, b. 43 Canton.
" Katherine C. clerk at Brown, Thomson &
  Co. 942 Main, b. 300 Albany.
" Lizzie S. clerk at Brown, Thomson & Co.
  942 Main, b. 13 Russell.
" Margaret R. bookeeper at Potter & Payne,
  405 Allyn, b. 13 Russell.
" Marion L. stenog. at Conn. General Life
  Ins. Co. 49 Pearl, b. 133 Sargeant.
" Mary, seamstress, b.u. 10 Center.
" Mary O. wid. Daniel, h.2u. 101 Sheldon.
" Matthew F. mech. at Popes, b. 90 Ward.
" Matthew J.paperruler at Case, Lockwood &
  Brainard Co. 141 Pearl.
" Michael, gardener at 232, l. 253 Main.
" Michael, laborer, b.u. 59 Arch.
" Michael, mason, b. 16 Commerce.
" Michael J. polisher at Popes, h. W.L.t.
" Nora, wid. Owen, h. 3 Ellery.
" Pat, helper at 1 Flower, b.u. 1442 Broad.
" Patrick, clerk, 956 Main, b.2u. 36 Lawrence.
" Patrick, laborer, b. 2 Winthrop.
" Patrick J. b. 20 Chestnut.
" Patrick J.mason at Colts, h. 2 Hendricxsen.
" Peter, b.u. 10 Center.
" Peter, laborer, h.u. 27 Mechanic.
" Peter, laborer, 133 Sheldon, b. 69 Governor.
" Robert, at 37, b.2u. 32 Wells.
" Samuel J. waiter, 3 Am. h.r. 5 Pleasant ct.
" Solon C. investm'ts, h. c. Pros.&Warrenton.
" Stephen, polisher at Popes, h. 4A Hung.
" Stephen F. b. 4A Hungerford.
" Thomas F.cashardener at Popes,b.269Main.
" Thomas J. city editor at Hartford Post,
  23 Asylum, b. 130 Babcock.
" Thomas J. polisher at Popes, b. 19 Howard.
" Thomas W. screwm at 476 Capitol, h.W.P.t.
" William, h. 4A Hungerford.
" William, filer at Popes, b. 2½ Hungerford.
" William J. b. 28 Morgan.
" ☞see also Kelly.
Kellogg Arthur B. physician, 53 Trumbull,
  rm. 213, b. 748 Asylum.
" & Bulkeley Co. lithographers. 175 Pearl.
" Charles E. machinist at Johns-Pratt Co. 555
  Capitol, h. 71 Governor.
" Charles C. b. 77 Washington.
" Chester B. clerk at C. C. Fuller & Co. 14
  Ford, b. Elmwood.
" Ebenezer N. office, 373 Asy.h. 20 Prospect.

EDWARD W. KELLOGG, Physician. Office, 53 Trumbull, rm. 209, Hfd. Fire Ins. Co. Bdg.
Hours—9 to 10 A.M., 2.30 to 4 P.M.
At office daily except Thursday and Sunday P.M.
Telephone—Office, 137-2; Residence, 359.

Kellogg Edward W. physician, 53 Trumbull, rm. 209, h. 748 Asylum.
" Edwin P. photographer, 739 Main, rm. 11, h. 8 Wooster.
" Elizabeth S. Mrs. b. 1325 Main.
" Emily Mrs. b. 73 Sigourney.
" Florence H. assistant at Hartford Public Library, 5 Atheneum, b. 1337 Main.
" Frank H.clerk,147 Asylum, b.94 Windsor av.
" Frank S. charity commissioner; at 207 Allyn, h. 70 Church.
" George A. attorney, 739 Main, h. 5 Whitney.
" George B. salesman at 389 Allyn, b. Weth. t.
KELLOGG GEORGE F. councilman 5th ward, market, 123–125 Ann, h. 1337 Main.
" Harry G. salesman, h. 22 East.
" Henry H. insurance, b. 61 Oxford.
" Henry Mrs. h. 24 Capitol.
" Jane B. teacher, 690, b. 690 Asylum.
" John H. b. 61 Oxford.
" Julius A., Boston Furniture House, 147 Asylum, h. 94 Windsor av.
" L. A. S. Mrs. h. 5 Whitney.
" M. Bertha, h. 62 Chestnut.
" Nathaniel O. wool, 373 Asy. b. 20 Prospect.
" Richard W. clerk at Orient Ins. Co. 5 Haynes, b. 1337 Main.
" Robert W. deputy jailor, 42, h.u. 16 Seyms.
" Rodney, manager Washington Life Ins. Co. h. 61 Oxford.
" Samuel N. h. 77 Washington.
" Sarah C. wid. George, b. 57 Farmington.
" Wm. H.at Ætna Life Ins.Co.650 Mn.h.8 Fern.
**KELLOGG WILLIAM M.** photographer, 92, h. 92 Pratt. See outside front cover.
Kelly Alice, wid. Bernard, h. 74 Retreat.
" Andrew, painter at 352, h. 299 Albany.
" Bros. stoneyard, 93 Charter Oak.
  John Kelly.          Michael Kelly.
" Catherine, b. 36 Jefferson.
" Catherine, wid. Andrew, h. 300 Albany.
" Catherine, wid. Thomas, b.2u. 1305 Main.
" Charles, clerk at 48, b.u. 83 Front.
" Daniel, helper, 1 Flower, h.2u. 88 Walnut.
" Daniel, printer, 25 Asylum, h.u. 24 Russell.
" Dennis, bricklayer, b. 94 New Britain.
" Dennis, jobber, h.2u. 72 Pleasant.
" Dennis, laborer, b. New Park.
" Edward, laborer, b. 300 Albany.
" Ellen, wid. Edmund, h. 47 Woodbridge.
" Francis M. cond. St.Ry. h.u. 139 Lawrence.
" George, painter at 352, b. 300 Albany.
" Hugh B.electrician at 85 Pratt, b.6 Chestnut.
" James, h.u. 41 Williams.
" James, carpenter, h. 60 Woodbine.
" James, stonec. at 93 Ch.O. b. 24 Union.
" James B. laborer, h.2u. 9 Sigourney.
" James C. clerk, b. 74 Retreat.
" James H. machinist, 1 Flow. h. 1463 Broad.

Kelly James W. electrician, h. 295 Lawrence.
" John, elevatorer, Un. Depot, h.u. 19 Howard.
" John, (Martin & K.) b.3u. 265 Asylum.
" John, laborer, b. 14 Huntley pl.
" John, laborer, h. 13 Russell.
" John, laborer at Colts, b. 61 Vanblock.
" John, (Kelly Bros.) h. 94 New Britain.
" John, laborer at 694 Park, b. 300 Albany.
" John, laborer, 556 Capitol, h. 14 Lawrence.
" John, laborer, b. 53 Potter.
" John, laborer, Pope Tube Co. h.u. 139 Zion.
" John, motorman, St.Ry. h. 300 Albany.
" John A. h. 490 Farmington.
" John B. bartender at 738 Main, b. 74 Retreat.
" John D. stonecutter at 93 Ch.O. b. 24 Union.
" John L. molder at 556 Cap. b. 4 A Hung.
" John Mrs. b.W.H.Home for Aged, Albany.
" John W. b.u. 41 Williams.
" Julia Anna, at 40 Governor, b.u.41 Williams.
" Keron, helper, h.u. 90 Ward.
" Margaret, wid. Thomas, h.2u. 18 Alden.
" Martin, clerk at 745 Main, h. 64 Hicks.
" Mary, wid. Keron, h. 40 John.
" Mary, wid. William, h. 22 Hicks.
" Matthew, gardener, 386, b. 386 Park.
" Michael, b. 981 Main.
" Michael, laborer. b. 101 Sheldon.
" Michael, buffer, h.u. 12 Elm.
" Michael, (Kelly Bros.) h. 96 New Britain.
" Michael, b.2u. 185 Lawrence.
" Michael, helper, 1 Flower, h.2u.26 Lawrence.
" Michael J. molder at 618 Cap. b. 27 Grand.
" Patrick, b.u. 1423 Broad.
" Patrick, deckhand str. Hartford, 285 State.
" Patrick, fireman at Colts, h. 61 Huyshope.
" Patrick, helper, 9 Sigourney, b. 19 Howard.
" Patrick, laborer, h.2u. 26 Flower.
" Patrick, laborer, b.u. 16 Ely.
" Patrick J. paperstock, Dutch Pt. h.243 Weth.
" Patrick J. oiler at Colts, h.2u. 18 Alden.
" Paul W. driver at 356 Main, h.u. 33 Sheldon.
" Peter, mach. at 1 Flower, b.u. 26 Lawrence.
" Peter J. bookbdr. at 141 Pearl, b. 10 Center.
" Robert, laborer, b.2u. 50 Russell.
" Thomas, mechanic, b.u. 185 Lawrence.
" William, helper at 152 State, b.27 Mechanic.
" William, janitor, Northw. sch. b. 300 Albany.
" William, painter at N.Y.R. b. 1333 Broad.
" William J. carpenter, b. 255 Asylum.
" ☞ see also Kelley.
Kels Charles, baker at 238 N.Park, h. 71 Temple.
Kelsey Charles B. clerk at 241 Asy. b. 147 Wash.
" E. A. trav. salesman, 15 Tru. h. Meriden t.
" Emily A. wid. Wm. H. h. 886 Asylum.
" Geo. W. toolm. at 476 Cap. h. 100 Laurel.
" Henry H. Rev. pastor Fourth Congregational church, h. 108 Ann.
" James T. elevatorer at 581 Capitol, h.2u. 47 South Hudson.
" Julia M. h. 31 Lafayette.
" Maria, h.u. 122 Trumbull.
" Richard F. h.u. 103 Webster.
" Sarah I. seamstress, b.16 Spring.
" William, joiner, b.u. 29 Church.
Kelting Kate, laundress, h.3u. 4 Lewis.

Kelton Robert H. C.clerk, 690 Park,h.2 Columbia.
Kelty James H. molder at 54 Arch, h. 341 Main.
Kemerer☞see also Kamerer.
Kemler Jacob, h. 5 Pleasant ct.
" Louis, clerk at 110 State, b. 5 Pleasant ct.
**KEMLER MICHAEL,** paper, etc. 53, h.2u. 53 Morgan. *See page 472*
Kemmerer Herman, painter, b. 43 Martin.
" John R. pressm. 668 Main, h. 57 Westland.
" ☞see also Kamerer.
Kempner David, student at Yale, b. 7 Sumner.
" Isadore, (*N.Kempner & Son,*) b. 7 Sumner.
" Joseph, h. 222 Putnam.
" Nathan,(*N.Kempner & Son,*) h. 7 Sumner.
" Nathan, grocer, 117 Law. b. 222 Putnam.
" Nathan & Son, real estate, 57 Morgan.
    Nathan Kempner.    Isadore Kempner.
Kempton Arthur W. clerk, Popes, b. 3 Far.
Kendall Charles E. conductor, St.Ry. b.u. 48 Pro.
" Fred S. motorman St.Ry. l. 241 Main.
" George H. cutter at 8 Sigourney.
" George T. student at Trinity college, 18 Seabury hall, Summit.
" John F. conductor at N.Y.R. b. 1462½ Broad.
" Susan, b. 36 Jefferson.
" Wm. R. ins. agent, 721 Main, h. 51 Spring.
Kendrick Ella B. Mrs. at 336 Weth. h. 370 Asy.
" Henry H. auctioneer, l. 370 Asy. rm. 27.
Kendziora Paul, laborer, b. 68 Potter.
Kenefick Ann E. h.u. 6 Ellery.
" James F. laborer at 40 Gov. b. 6 Ellery.
" John, b.u. 6 Ellery.
" John J.cigarmaker,104 Asy. b.u.1110 Main.
" Joseph, laborer, h.u. 6 Ellery.
" Kitty E clerk at Brown, Thomson & Co. 942 Main, b. 35 Canton.
" Margaret G. clerk at Brown, Thomson & Co. 942 Main, b. 35 Canton.
" Michael, expressman, h. 6 Ellery.
" Thomas J. porter at Brown, Thomson & Co. 942 Main, h. 35 Canton.
Kenehan Hugh, laborer. h.u. 28 Front.
Kenehan John F.benchm. Tube Co. b. 111 Zion.
" Lillie, b. 111 Zion.
" Michael, laborer at stonepits, b. Zion.
" Patrick J. helper at 142 Russ, b. 4½ Hung.
Kenelly Eugene, ship. clerk at 177, b. 56 Asy.
Keney Hall, 98 Pratt.
" Roberts & Co. now Tucker & Goodwin.
" Walter, clerk at Phœnix Mutual Life Ins. Co. 49 Pearl, h. 143 Washington.
" ☞see also Keeney.
Kenig Aron, real estate, h. 147 Front.
Kenna Michael, U. S. Army, b.u. 147 Laurel.
Kennard Mary J. wid. William B. h. 9 Squire.
Kenneally Joseph F. l. 270 Main.
Kennedy Ann J. F. teacher at South school, 36 Wadsworth, b. 10 Wyllys.
" Bridget, wid. Thomas, h. 64 Ward.
" Charles, night watchman at Brown, Thomson & Co. 942 Main, h. 34 Canton.
" Clara, clerk at 835 Main, h. 106 Spring.
" D. J. laborer at 8 Front.
" Daisy, candymaker, b.u. 104 Albany.
" Daniel, engineer, l.u. 985 Main.

Kennedy Edmond B. painter at 5 Mechanic, b. 34 Canton.
" Edward J.clerk at 1046 Main, b. Windsor t.
" Edward J. clerk Board of Street Commissioners, b. 10 Wyllys.
" Eliza M. wid. John J. h.u. 78 Green.
" Grace, stenographer, b. 56 Asylum.
" Henry, office, 793 Main, h. 614 Asylum.
" Henry M. clerk at Sigourney Tool Co. 9 Sigourney, h.2u. 46 Beach.
" James, receiving clerk at 98 Kil.h. 254 Front.
" James J. buffer at Popes, h.u. 338 Park.
" Jean, carpetsewer at Brown, Thomson & Co. 942 Main, b. 34 Canton.
" John, gardener, h.4u. 61 Spruce.
" John, laborer, h. 52 Kennedy.
" John, plasterer, b. 214 High.
" John, signpainter at 104 Asy. b. 78 Green.
" John A. bricklayer, b.u.59 New Britain.
" John C. celluloidwkr. Popes, b. 61 Hudson.
" John J. polisher at 581 Cap. h.2u. 44 Benton.
" John J. waiter,l. 1 Avon.
" John W. bkkpr. 72 Front, h.2u. 30 Franklin.
" John W. enameler at Popes, b. 69 Hudson
" Joseph, clerk at 304 Park, b. 64 Ward.
" Joseph, clerk at 92 Pearl, b. 106 Spring.
" Joseph A. clerk, b. 10 Wyllys.
" Joseph L. clerk at 125 Albany, b. 78 Green.
" Joseph T. shipper at Popes, b. 114 Hopkins.
" Julia A. wid. Ralph, dressmaker, 721, h. 721 Main, rm. 50.
" Kate, clerk, b. 69 Hudson.
" Kate E. Mrs. b. 25 East.
" Maggie, dressmaker, l. 106 Spring.
" Margaret, wid. Philip, h.2u. 29 Pleasant.
" Mary, b. W. H. Home for the Aged, Alb.
" Michael, lab. at stone pits, h.u. 59 N.Britain.
" Michael C. clerk, 95 Pleasant, b. 985 Main.
" Michael Jr. bricklayer, b. 59 New Britain.
" Nellie B. wid. Jas. A. dressm. 56 h.u. 56 Asy.
" Nora A. clerk, 1046 Main, b. 29 Pleasant.
" Patrick, coachman, h. 106 Spring.
" Patrick, laborer at 8 Front, b.3u. 192 Shel.
" Patrick, laborer, b.u. 84 Albany.
" Patrick J. bartender, 269 Main, b. 5 John.
" Philip S.grocer,1046 Main,h. 83 Edwards.
" Richard, laborer, 1 Flower, b. 9 Hawthorn.
" Richard, laborer, h. 39 Amity.
" Robert, woodwkr. 5 Mechanic, h.u.283 Main.
" Robert H. instructor at Popes, b. 64 Ward.
" Thomas, bartender at 49, b.u. 49 Sheldon.
" Thomas, fireman, P.&R. b. 73 Albany.
" Thomas, laborer at stonepits. h. 59 N.B.
" Thomas, stonecutter at 93 Charter Oak, h. 47 Hawthorn.
" Thomas, watchman at Colts, h. 10 Wyllys.
" Thomas C. actor, b. 31 Lewis.
" Thomas J. h.u. 64 Ward.
" Thos. J. foreman at Popes, h. 78 Putnam.
" Thos. K. attorney, b. 10 Wyllys.
" William Rev. assistant at St. Patricks church, b. 82 Church.
" William, Jr. laborer, b.u. 4 Green.
" ☞see also Cannedy.
Kennehan Patrick, b. 4½ Hungerford pl.

**The Up to Date Merchant ADVERTISES in The Post.**

Kennelly & Co. druggists, 629 Main.
    James A. Kennelly.      C. L. Kennelly.
" James, h. 36 Charter Oak pl.
" James A. (Kennelly & Co.) b. 36 C.O.pl.
" John, h.2u. 138 Windsor.
" John A. hardener, b.u. 138 Windsor.
" John F. clerk at 956, b. 270 Main.
" John M. glazier at Andrews & Peck, 88 Market, h.2u. 20 Babcock.
Kenneth Annette, dressmaker, h. 75 Niles
Kenney Ann, wid. Patrick, h.2u. 142 Grove.
" Anna I. at 904 Main, b. 43 Evergreen.
" Bridget, wid. Arthur, h. 46 Wells.
" Daniel, driver, h.r. 56 Albany.
" & Dillon, undertakers, 557 Main.
    Estate of Martin Kenney.    Charles J. Dillon.
" Edward J. mech. at Popes, b. 44 Vanblock.
" Eldridge L. motorman St.Ry. b.u. 6 Avon.
" Frank J. machinist, b.r. 56 Albany.
" George, laborer, 231 State, b.2u. 142 Grove.
" James F. traveling salesman, h.u. 22 Imlay.
" James J. b. 34 Sumner.
" Jane M. wid. Martin, h. 59 Buckingham.
" John, laborer, h. 20 Elm.
" John H. machinist, h. 56 Albany.
" John J. (Warren & K.) machinist at 70 Huyshope, b. 44 Vanblock.
" John W. laborer, b.2u. 142 Grove.
" Jos. clerk at 571 Main, b. 59 Buckingham.
" Joseph, ostler at 371 Main, h. 19 Sheldon.
" Joseph F. helper at 70 Huy. h. 20 Elm.
" Julia A. insp. at 70 Huy. b. 44 Vanblock.
" Katherine, dressmaker, h.u. 387 Capitol.
" Margaret J. clerk, b. 59 Buckingham.
" Michael, hackdriver, 15½ Babcock, l.74 High.
" Michael, woodwkr. 352 Alb. h.35 Sumner.
" Patrick E. lettercarrier, P.O. b. 20 Elm.
" Peter, laborer, b. 255 Ashley.
" Peter, millwright at Colts, h. 44 Vanblock.
" Peter J. Jr. polisher, Popes, b.u.44 Vanblock.
" Robert, brakeman, b. 5 Chapel.
" Sabina, wid. Thomas, b. 15 Liberty.
" Thomas H. operator, b.2u. 142 Grove.
" Thomas T. billposter, h.r. 69 Windsor.
" William C. & Dillon, b. 59 Bkm.
" Wm. E. enameler at 581 Cap. l. 33 Church.
" Winifred K. teacher at Second North School, 249 High, b. 35 Sumner.
" ☞ see also Kinney.
Kensler Bernhard, mach.at 133 Shel. h.u.26 West.
" Myer, tailor at 97 Asylum, h. 17 Windsor.
Kent Albert, at Pratt & Whitney Co. 1 Flower, h.u. 19½ Putnam.
" Angeline E. wid. Albert M. h.u.433 Capitol.
" Bros. builders, 8 Barnard.
    Irving S. Kent.    Frank D. Kent.
" Frank D. (Kent Bros.) b. 708 Main, rm. 10.
" Irving S. (Kent Bros.) b. 8 Barnard.
" Mark, painter at N.Y.R. b.u. 1478 Broad.
" Maurice, molder at 54 Arch, h.u. 256 Park.
" Michael, street cleaner, b.u. 76 Avon.
" William P. field manager Conn. Building & Loan Association, h. 104 Ashley.
Kenton Harry R. filer at Colts, h.r. 48 Vanblock.
Kenworthy Mary, wid. John, h. 15 Grand.
" Thomas, h.u. 13 Oak.

Kenyon Benj. L. signw. 185 Pearl, b. 28 Church.
" Benj. W. (Preston & K.) h.u. 37¼ Church.
" E. L. Mrs. h. 297 Albany.
" Edgar M. telegrapher, h.2u. 150 Allyn.
" Edward F. sales stable, 287, h. 285 Albany.
" Elijah A. farm. and milkm. h. 105 Bluehills.
" Eliza, wid. John, b. 24 Florence.
" Francis, nurse and masseur, h.u. 19 Wads.
" Frederic H. at Phœnix Insurance Co. 64 Pearl, b. 24 Florence.
" H. L. clerk at 173 Asylum, b. 25 Allen pl.
" Irving R. clerk, 91 Pratt, b. 50 Prospect av.
" Jennie, wid. Edwin W. h. 24 Florence.
" John, laborer, b. 6 Martin.
" Lorenzo W. clerk at 91 Pratt, b. 50 Pro. av.
" M. E. wid. Albert, h. 943 Main, rm. 24.
" Milford, driver at 219 Asylum, h. Franklin
" R. P. Co. hats, caps, furs, 91 Pratt.*
" Rinaldo P. (R. P. K. Co.) h. 50 Prospect av.
" William E. h. 13 Walnut.
" ☞ see also Kinyon.
Kenzie ☞ see Kinzie.
Keohine Dennis, laborer, Pope Tube Co. b. 14 Huntley pl.
Keonig ☞ see also Koenig.
Keough Thomas W. bartdr. 738 Mn. h.u. 81 Gov.
Kepler Ernest, messenger at P. O. h. 37 Center.
" Joseph E. del. clerk at 98 Kil. h.2u. 9 East.
" Mabel, stenographer, b.2u. 9 East.
Kerchmarsic Powell, laborer, h.2u. 6⅛ Ellery.
Kern Otto, baker, b. 165 Front.
" ☞ see Kearns, Kerns.
Kernan Frank E. lineman, 266 Pearl, b.41 Mul.
" Frank P. polisher, 581 Cap. b.2u. 884 Main.
Kerns Samuel P. rubberwkr. 690, h. 960 Park.
Kerr Edward J. mach. at 581 Cap. b. 297 Law.
" John H. machinist at Colts, b. 152 Allyn.
" John R. H. clerk at 273 Asy. b. 162 Collins.
" Peter, boilerm. at 40 Cush. b.2u.54 Chestnut.
" William, sidewalklayer, 154 Charter Oak, h. 77 Hudson.
Kerrigan ☞ see also Carrigan; Corrigan.
Kersey Patrick, boilermaker, h. 250 Front.
" Patrick, Jr. stonecutter at 1070 Main, h.u. 250 Front.
" William J. burnisher, b. 250 Front.
Kershaw John, laborer, h.2u. 93 Windsor.
" Richard J. laborer, h.2u.r. 23 Spruce.
" Thomas, shoemaker, 42, h. 42 Bonner.
" Wm. W. rubberw.at 690 Park, b.41Bonner.
Kerwin Edward, nightlunch, h.u. 71 Hudson.
" Garret, blacksmith, b. 44 Rose.
" Garrett, laborer, h.3u. 6⅛ Ellery.
" George S. B. dispatcher N.Y.R. 450 Asylum, h.u. 65 Babcock.
" John J. steamfitter at 253 Asylum, h. 43 Zion.
" Joseph, employed at 273 Asy. b. 47 Albany.
" Kate, dressmaker, 161, b. 161 Zion.
" Lawrence, h. 44 Rose.
" Lawrence E. carpenter, b. 161 Zion.
" Michael, farmer, h. 161 Zion.
" Michael J.mach. at N.Y.R.h. 39 Harbison.
" Nicholas C. conductor St.Ry. b. 183 Market.
" Thomas, steamfitter at 253 Asy. b. 161 Zion.
" ☞ see also Kirwin, Kurwin.

`**THINKING PEOPLE Read The Post Daily.**

Kessler Abraham B. tailor, 730 Main, h.42 North.
" Annie, wid. Abraham, h.u. 176 Front.
" Ida, dressmaker, 42, h. 42 North.
" John, bakery, 305, h. 305 Lawrence.
Ketchum John E. fireman, 252 Pearl, b. 48 Oak.
Ketter Christ Henry,printer,175Pearl, h.27Arch.
" Edwin H. mach. at 1 Flower, b. 27 Arch.
Kettin William, laborer, h.u. 85 Green.
Ketz Louis, screwm. at 476 Cap. h. 130 Windsor.
Keuhnhold☞see Kuehnold.
Keyes Annie M. music teacher, b. 2 Avon.
" Frank R. machinist at 1 Flow. b. 117 Oak.
" Kittie Mrs. b.u. 724 Main, rm. 21.
" Mary Mrs. b. 36 Winthrop.
" Samuel B. h. 2 Avon.
Keyser John H. b. 1204 Asylum.
Kibbe Angeline M. Mrs. h.3u. 200 Allyn.

**KIBBE E. S. CO. THE,** wholesale grocers, spices, etc. 149 to 155 State.
See page 587.
" Edward W. repairer, 1100Main, b.200Allyn.
" H. A. (K. & Penfield,) h. 1231 Main.
" Harriet, wid. Henry A. h.u. 839 Asylum.
" & Penfield, painters, r. 1231 Main.
  H. A. Kibbe.        W. T. Penfield.
" Prosper D. clerk, 547 Main, h. Manchester t.
" Prosper D.Mrs. stenog.Hartford Courant Co.
  66 State, b. Manchester t.
" Wm. E. bicycles,1100 Main, b.3u. 200 Allyn.
" William H. machinist, h.u. 839 Asylum.
Kidd John, diesinker at 1 Flow. h. 38 Hopkins.
" Louise J. clerk at The E. S. Kibbe Co. 149
  State, b. 38 Hopkins.
Kidney Annie, dressmaker b.2u. 194 Sheldon.
" Coleman, h.2u. 194 Sheldon.
" John, laborer, h. 144 Mather.
" Michael, gardener, b.2u. 32 Park.
" Michael Mrs. dressmaker, b.2u. 32 Park.
" Nellie M. bkkpr. at 835 Main, b. 32 Park.
Kiefer Andrew J.salesman,281 Allyn,h.r. 33 Asy.
" Louis J. butcher at 8 Church, b.u. 264 Capen.
Kiely James, at William Rogers Mfg. Co. 66
  Market, b. 26 Huntley pl.
" James, helper Pope Tube Co. h.241Williams.
" James, pressman Pope Tube Co. h. 579Park.
" James, teamster, b. 192 State.
" John W. benchman at Pope Tube Co. b.
  241 Williams.
" Michael J. saloon, 1119, h. 1117 Main.
Kiem Allois, mach. at 1 Flower, h. 50 Lawrence.
" John, draughtsm. 177 Asy. b.u. 50Lawrence.
" Louis, machinist at Pratt & Whitney Co. 1
  Flower, h.u. 50 Lawrence.
Kiernan Bernard, bricklayer, h.2u. 352 Park.
" John, carpenter, b.u. 299 Lawrence.
" John, filer at Popes, b. 205 High.
Kierstead Grace A. stenographer at 98 Wells,
  b. 127 Babcock.
" Grant U. clerk at Hatch & North Coal Co.
  801 Main, h. 127 Babcock.
" William, salesman 34 Capen, b.127Babcock.
Kies Richard, lab. at brickyard, b. Windsor av.
Kiesul Thomas, laborer, h.u. 72 Potter.
Kilbourn Alonzo J. h. 169 Russ.
" Charles R. toolmaker, h. 76 Retreat.

Kilbourn Ella C. wid. W. F. musicteacher 34,
  b. 34 Annawan.
" Emma C. b. 34 Windsor.
" Fanny A.Mrs.dressm.2u.33,h.2u.33 Windsor.
" Grace L. saleswoman at Brown, Thomson
  & Co. 942 Main, b. 84 Retreat.
" John F. salesman National Cash Register Co.
  118, h. 223 Asylum, rm. 32.
" Jos. A. physician, 771 Park, h. 139 Collins.
" Wm. A. bookbinder at 336Asy. h. 84 Retreat.
" William R. engir. at Prospect av. h. 8 Smith.
Kilbourne Frank E. undertaker, h.r. 1 Orchard.
Kilby Arthur E. confectioner, 39, h. 39 Sargeant
" Eva F. supervisor at 30 Washington.
" Fred A. barber at 22 State, h.2u. 18 Spring.
Kilfoil Robert J. molder, h.2u. 92 Willow.
" Thomas H. molder at 54 Arch, h. 24 Affleck.
Kilgannon John, laborer, b. 1172 Main.
Killard Benard, laborer, b. 60 Hungerford.
" Patrick, lab. at 1 Flower, h.2u. 267 Park.
" Timothy, coachman, 1 Vine, h. 27 Brooks.
Killcoyne Thomas, laborer, b.2u. 81 Sheldon.
Killeen Peter J.mach. at 1 Flower, h. 13 Atlantic.
Killian Annie, b. W.H. Home for aged, Albany.
" Ellen, wid. James, h.u. 62 Governor.
" Frank J. clerk at Brown, Thomson & Co.
  942 Main, b. 2 A Wadsworth.
" James, blacksmith, b. 2 A Wadsworth.
" Terence, saloon, 83, h. 81 Sheldon.
" Thomas, mechanic, b.u.r. 65 Temple.
" Thomas F. enameler 581 Cap. b.2u. 47 Com.
" Thomas J. b.u. 2 A Wadsworth.
Killin James & Sons, wholes. liquors, 74 Morgan.
  William H. Killin.        James F. Killin.
" James F. (James Killin & Sons,) h. 100 Ann.
" Kate, wid. Thomas J. h.u. 4 Portland.
KILLIN WILLIAM H. alderman 2d ward, (James
  K. & Sons,) h. 72 Morgan.
Killmer John S. car insp. h.u. 10 Foot Guard.
Killmurray Cornelius J. 581 Cap. b. 94 Cushman.
" Jane, wid. Cornelius, h.u. 295 Lawrence.
" John B. mach. at 1 Flow. b. 295 Lawrence.
" Joseph A. operator at 8 Sig. b. 295 Lawrence.
Killoran Michael, bottler h.r. 7, h. 2 Brady.
Killy John A. genl. agent, 197Asy. h. 490 Far.
Kilmartin Edw'd J. painter at 133 Shel.b.20Dean.
" James, gardener, h. 13 Curcombe.
" James, laborer, b. 12 Center.
" John, mach. at 54 Arch, h.3u. 192 Sheldon.
" Michael, cellarman, 232 Sheldon, b. 63 Gov.
" & O'Brien, saloon, 38 Sheldon.
  Patrick Kilmartin.        James J. O'Brien.
" Patrick (K. & O'Brien,) h. 14½ Governor.
" Patrick, helper at Popes, b. 4 Chestnut.
" ☞see also Guilmartin.
Kilmurray John, laborer, h. 49 Cushman.
" Michael J. trucker, 690Park, b. 94 Cushman.
" William, watchman at Colts, h.2u. 20 Dean.
Kilpatrick Catherine M.wid.Jos. h. 3 Ellsworth pl.
" Robert E. mech. at Popes, h. Park, W.H.t.
Kilray Edward F.mach. at Popes, h. 1424 Broad.
" John E. rubberw. 690 Park, b. 23 Spruce.
" Joseph, grinder, 556 Cap. b.2u.r. 23 Spruce.
" Mary, wid. John, h.2u.r. 23 Spruce.
Kilroy John, mach. at 1 Flower, h. Ch.O. Park.

Kiltner Mary, at 252 Pearl, b. 58 Church.
Kilty John, at 54 Arch, b. 263 Main.
Kimball Carlos C. (*K. & McCray*,) ins. agents, 658 Main, h. 266 Farmington.
**KIMBALL & M'CRAY,** insurance agents, 658 Main, Ætna Life building.
          *See page 444.*
  Carlos C. Kimball.     William B. McCray.
" Frederick S. clerk at Kimball & McCray, 658 Main, b. 266 Farmington.
" George C. sec'y and treas. Smyth Mfg. Co. 648 Main, b. 266 Farmington.
" George E. patternm. 54 Arch, l. 315 Pearl.
" John C. Rev. h.3u. 926 Main, rm. 20.
" Richard H. drug clerk, 206 Park, h. 25 Ward.
Kimberly Carrie A. dressm. 38, b. 38 Ashley.
**KIMBERLY THOMAS A.** dentist with Dr. L. G. Chapman, 86 Pratt, h. 1341 Main.    *See outside front cover.*
Kimmall Rosie, at 15 Tru. b. 102 Windsor.
Kimmell Barbara, wid. Frank, b. 150 Babcock.
" Jacob, laborer, h.u. 102 Windsor.
" John J. machinist, h. 150 Babcock.
Kinberg Andrew, (*K. & Gilmour*,) b. 49 Green.
" & Gilmour, carprts. and builders, 23 Squire.
  Andrew Kinberg.     John Gilmour.
Kincaid Fredrick M. screwm. h. 351 Wethersfield.
" J. Harvey, clerk at 18 State, b. Middletown.
" Sarah, wid. Joseph, b. 351 Wethersfield.
Kind Albert, filer at Colts, h. 19½ Putnam.
Kindser Morris, bartdr. 197 Front, b. 51 Morgan.
Kindsler David, barber, h.2u. 44 Pleasant.
Kinerney Thomas, b. 60 Vernon.
King Adelaide S. wid. Herbert, h. 57 Park.
" Adeline C. wid. Jas. h. 57 Farmington.

**KING A. C. & CO.** engineers and contractors, steam and hot water heating and ventilating, 440 Asylum.
  Alfred G. King.    George E. Badger.
" Alfred G. (*A.G.K.&Co.*) h. 924 Windsor av.
" Allen, fireman at N.Y.R. b. 67 Madison.
" Angeline E. wid. Dan. W. h. 370 Asy. rm. 77.
" C. B. at Colts, b. 904 Main, rm. 15.
" Carrie G. operator at Hartford Post, 23 Asylum, b. 38 Williams.
" Charles, h. 371 Windsor av.
" Charles H. bookkeeper at 150 State. h. E.H.t.
" Donald E. asst. ticket agent N.Y.R. b.2u. 30 Hopkins.
" Edward L. crater at 581 Capitol, b. E.H.t.

EMMETT C. KING, Physician. Office, 21 Capitol avenue.
    Hours—8 to 10 A.M.
       2 to 4 and 7 to 8 P.M.
       Sundays 2 to 3 P. M.
       Telephone 548.

King Emmett C. physician, 21, h. 21 Capitol.
" Ernest T. livery, 19, b. 26 Gold.
" Eugene J. toolmaker at Popes, h. E.H.t.
" Everett E. mach. at 30 Cushman, b. E.H.t.
" Frank, assembler, 302 Asy. b. 131 Hamilton.
" Frank A. rubberw. at 690 Park, b. 19 Sisson.
" Fred. E. with Ætna Ins. Co. 666 Main, b. 31 Girard.
" George A. h. 135 Bellevue.

King George B. mach. at 80 Huy. h. 904 Main.
" George F. assem. at Colts, h. 102 Seymour.
" George P. barber at 206 Asy. b. 26 Church.
" George S. foreman at 690, h. 875 Park.
" Gertrude M. clerk, 62 Market, h. 26 Cong.
" Harvey A. clerk, b.2u. 17 Goodman.

**KING HARVEY B.** artesian well driller, 38, h.u. 38 Williams.    *See page 484.*

" Henry A. car builder, 19 Florence.
" Herbert E. photographer, 57, h. 57 Park.
" Herbert S. bkkpr. 336 Asy. h. 198 Jefferson.
" Herbert S. clerk, h. 68 Russ.
" Horace H. boots, etc. 1073 Main, h. 200 Windsor av.
" Howard A. clerk at 342 Asy. b. 30 Chapel.
" J. E. Mrs. h.u. 26 Congress.
" James, carinspector, b.u. 33 Chapel.
" James, laborer, h.u. 103 Windsor.
" John, b.r. 12½ So. Prospect.
" John, carpenter, b.2u. 30 Hopkins.
" John, repairer, P.&R. b.u. 33 Chapel.
" John R. treas. N. E. Brew. Co. 217 Windsor.
" John T. cigarmaker, 867 Mn. h. 76 Governor.
" Joseph, laborer, b. 77 Madison.
" Joseph, mach. at 1 Flow. h.u. 220 New Park.
" Joseph B. carpenter, h. 49 Liberty.
" Joseph H. cashier American National Bank, 803 Main, h. Arnolddale road, W.H.t.
" L. Elizabeth, teacher vocal music, h.20 Beach.
" Lewis H. nickelplater at Popes, b. E.H.t.
" Louis, cigarmaker, h.2u. 172 Sheldon.
" Lydia A. wid. Adolphus, h. 20 Beach.
" Maria, wid. John, h. 32 Elm.
" Mary, h. 36 Jefferson.
" Mary, h.2u.r. 34 So. Prospect.
" Mary, wid. Thomas, h. 261 New Britain.
" Mary A. wid. Harry, dressm. 721 Main, rm. 16
" Mason, mach. at 1 Flower, b. 220 New Park.
" Michael, b.2u.r. 34 So. Prospect.
" Michael, laborer 189 State, b.u. 74 Windsor.
" Michael H. saloon, 2, h.u. 2 Lawrence.
" Minnie Mrs. cook 1049 Main, h. 17 Windsor.
" Nathan, 2d pantrym. str. Hartford, 285 State.
" Nelson E. lineman 266 Pearl, b. 935 Main.
" Olcott F. messenger at Ætna National Bank, 644 Main, b. So. Windsor t.
" P. Arthur, (*K.& Starkey*,) h.2u. 30 Hopkins.
" Patrick, laborer, N.Y.R. h. 103 Windsor.
" Robert H. driver, Adams Ex. b. 38 Williams.
" Simon, machinist, b.u. 65 Fairfield.
" & Starkey, builders, 30 Hopkins.
  Arthur King.    Samuel R. Starkey.
" Tessie R. clerk at Brown, Thomson & Co. 942 Main, b. 66 Sequassen.
" Thomas, b. 70 Governor.
" Thomas, at Pope Tube Co. h. 230 Maple.
" Thomas, stove polisher, b.u. 32 Wells.
" Timothy, laborer, h. 65 Fairmount.
" William, laborer, stone pits, h.u. 1063 Broad.
" William H. secretary Ætna Ins. Company, 666 Main, h. 509 Farmington. *See p. 442.*
" William H. laborer at 40 Gov. b.1 Kilbourn.
" William J. b. 66 Sequassen.
" William S. painter, b. 200 Allyn.

**THE POST is a 20th-Century Newspaper.**

Kinghorn Geo. diesinker, 142 Russ, b.84 Franklin.
" George, forem. 141 Tru. h.84 Franklin.
" H.Henry, horseshoer at 10 Charles, h. E.H.t.
" Henry, carptr. at 158 Woodland, h.83 Allen pl.
" Jennie G. clerk at 956 Main, b.84 Franklin.
" John, mach. at 83 Woodbine, b. 4 Morris.
" Joseph, carpenter at 141 Tru. b. 84 Franklin.
" William, b. 64 Grove.
" William, machinist at Colts, h. E.H.t.
" William, teamster at 39 Front, b.7 American.
" William B. diesinker at 142 Russ, b.4 Morris.
Kingsbury Albert N. turner, h.2u. 2 Wooster.
" Frank P. machinist at Pope Tube Co. h. 117 Madison av.
" George, mach. at 59½ Trumbull, b. Enfield t.
" Laura A. h. 73 Sigourney.
" Lewis K. polisher at Popes, h. 19 Park.
Kingsley Albert, ostler at 38, b. 38 Vernon.
" Alice Mrs. h.u. 44 Liberty.
" Caralyn, clerk at 725 Main, b. 67 Park.
" Charles A. bookkeeper at H. B. Beach & Son, 135 Grove, b. 196 Sargeant.
" Charles F. clerk at Lincoln, Seyms & Co. 34 Market, b. 81 Williams.
" & Co. grocers, 436 Asylum.
          Kendrick C. Kingsley.
" Dumont, bkkpr. at Lincoln, Seyms & Co. 34 Market, h. 81 Williams.
" Edward J. rubberw. at 690 Park, b.113 Heath.
" Edwin W. butcher at 331 Cap. h.60 Jefferson.
" Ferdinand C. collector, 247 Pearl, b.64 Capen.
" George W. engineer fire steamer No. 2, h.u. 23 Pleasant.
" Harry H. clerk at 956 Main, b. 67 Park.
" Henry B., Cap. City Roofing Co. h. 110 Pratt.
" Jennie B. wid. Frederick A. h. 64 Capen.
" John A. toolmkr. at 13 Central, h.2u.61 Russ.
" Joseph L. butcher at 544 Asy. h. 25 Westland.
" Kendrick C. (K. & Co.) h.u. 22 Ashley.
" Lucy J. h.u. 26 Grand.
" Michael W. b. 51 Heath.
" Robert C. clerk at 254 Pearl, b. 32 Bellevue.
" Sadie, h. 67 Park.
" & Smith, butter store, 571 Main.
 Richard J. (Kingsley) Kinsella.     Thomas A. Smith.
" Thomas, clerk at P.O. b. 21 Sheldon.
" Wm. baggage master at N.Y.R. h. 115 Heath.
" William J. b. 343 Main.
Kiniry James J. laborer at 98, b. 9 Kilbourn.
" John J. boilermaker at 40 Cushman, h.2u. 61 Hawthorn.
Kinlan Catharine, wid. Martin, h.u. 49 Walnut.
" Julia, b.u. 49 Walnut.
Kinlock William, farmer, b. 205 Woodland.

Kinnarney Bridget, wid. Thomas, h. 60 **Vanb.**
" James, teamster at Colts, h. 62 **Vanblock.**
" James P. Jr. oiler at Colts, b. 62 **Vanblock.**
" John, machine hand at Colts, b.62 **Vanblock.**
" Lizzie, clerk, 956 Main, b.84 **Vanblock.**
" Michael J. oiler at Colts, b. 60 **Vanblock.**
Kinne Andrew L. roller, 690 Park, b. 357 **Capitol**
" E. motorman, St.Ry. b. 740 Main.
" Eugene F. mach. at 1 Laurel, h. 49 **Hung.**
" Kate E. b. 305 Farmington.
Kinney Alfred W. draughtsm. at 556 **Capitol, h.** 99 Hungerford.
" Delia C. wid. Huntington, h.u.216 Windsor av.
" Walter A. printer at R. S. Peck & Co. 26 High, b. 99 Hungerford.
" William H. clerk, b. 99 Hungerford.
" ☞ see also Kenney; Keaney.
Kinnure John F. laborer, b.u. 257 Front.
Kinsella James, b.2u. 1 East.
" Michael, carpenter, h.2u. 1 East.
" Richard J. (Kingsley & Smith,) h. 26 Linden. h. 26 Linden.
" T. W. clerk at 921 Main, b. 86 Ann.
" William J. elevatorer, 65 State, h.26 Linden.
" William J. gardener at 33, b. 33 Prospect.
Kinsler Anna, wid. George, h. 12 Hungerford.
" David, barber, 42, h. 42 Pleasant.
" George B. J. mach. at 1 Flow. b.u. 12 Hung.
" Moriss, bartender, h.2u. 51 Morgan.
" Rebecca, h.2u. 104 Windsor.
Kinsley Arthur, patternmkr. 33 Wells, b.323 Pearl.
Kinsman Charles L. mach. 30 Cush. b.18 Woodbine.
" Edward C. at Ætna Life Insurance Co. 650 Main, b. Rocky Hill t.
" Henry E. machinist, h. 18 Woodbine.
" Louise H. teacher, b. 18 Woodbine.
" Myer, tailor, h.u. 17 Windsor.
" William M. machinist at 30 Cushman, b. 18 Woodbine.
Kinyon Frank S. horse dealer, h. 111 **Edwards.**
" Seth, farmer, h. 302 Albany.
" ☞ see also Kenyon.
Kinzie William D. supervisor of clerks, N.E.R. h. 173 High.
Kip A. R. Mrs. bkkpr. 853 Main, b. 56 Allen pl.
" Arthur R. instructor at Morse's Hartford Business College, 370 Asy. h. 56 Allen pl.
Kipp Edgar W. fresco painter. b. 164 **Russ.**
" Fred. W. clerk at 6 Cen. b.2u. 82 Sheldon.
" George W. assemb. at 581 Cap. b.2u. 82 Shel.
" Joseph F. mach. at Popes, b.u. 82 Sheldon.
" Mary, wid. Michael, h.2u. 82 Sheldon.
" Matthew J. browner, b.2u. 82 Sheldon.
Kippen Elizabeth F. b. 36 Jefferson.
" Henry A. b. 36 Jefferson.
Kirbell Benj. J. harnessm. at 8 Sig. b.u. 133 Tru.
Kirby Cornelius J. h. 259 Front.
" Phil. laborer, h. 168 Front.
" William, blacksmith at 25 Wells. h. N.B.t.
Kirch Jacob, bootmaker, b.2u. 31 Flower.
Kirchner Chas. C. foreman, 535 Shel. h. 419 Fkn.
Kirk Chas. H. insp. at Colts, h.u. 32 Woodbridge.
" Edmund, rubberw. at 690, b. 587 Park.
" Hugh, laborer at 154 Ch.O. b. 76 Madison.
" James N. ins. agent, 721 Main, b. 225 High.

Kirk Samuel J. machinist at Pratt & Whitney Co. 1 Flower, h.u. 105 Hungerford.
Kirkbride C. W. motorman, St.Ry. h. Windsor t.
" George B. mechanic at Popes, b. 152 Allyn.
Kirke Alexander W. clerk at Brown, Thomson & Co. 942 Main, b. 90 Church.
Kirkegaard Mads, porter at 207 State, b. 59 Mar.
Kirkley Robert, plumber at 425 Main.
Kirkorian Charles, screwm. at 476, l. 381 Capitol.
" M. screwmaker at 476, l. 381 Capitol.
Kirkpatrick Elizab'h, wid. Jas. nurse, h. 33 Julius.
" John, carpenter, h. 33 Julius.
" Letitia E. wid. James. h.u. 133 Market.
" Robert J. machinist, Colts, h.u. 13 Warner.
Kirsche Richard, bartender 279 Mn.h. 47 Hudson.
Kirwan Cornelius A. mech. Popes, b. 24 Commerce.
Kirwin Cornelius T. plater at 62 Mar. b. 66 Chst.
" Patrick J. molder at 1 Flower, h.u. 185 Law.
" ☞ see also Kerwin.
Kitchen Frank H. engineer at 70 Com. b. W.t.
" Ira G. engineer, h.u.r. 1 Orchard.
" John, at 252 Pearl, l.u. 48 Oak.
" Lizzie E. teacher, b.u. 166 Windsor av.
" Sarah J. wid James, h.u. 166 Windsor av.
Kith Sallie, wid. King, h. 3u. 290 Pearl.
Kitson Agnes J. clerk at 956 Main, b. 33 Wilson.
" Martin J. molder, 54 Arch, b. 70 Potter.
" Michael, laborer, h. 70 Potter.
" Rosa, clerk at Brown, Thomson & Co. 942 Main. b. 33 Wilson.
" S. J. helper at 48 Ann, b. Walnut.
" Samuel, b. 2 Holcomb.
" Simon J. molder at 54 Arch, h. 33 Wilson.
Kittal Adolph, helper. h.u. 12 Trumbull.
Kittredge Warren G.clerk,130 Alb.h.69 Babcock.
Kittridge C. V. N. b. 57 Farmington.
Kivney John, switchm. N.Y.R. h. 60 Flower.
" Thomas, helper at N.Y.R. h.u.183 Lawrence.
Kjelleren C. J. painter, 10½ Ford, h. W.H.t.
Klaman Israel, tailor, 42 Pratt, h. 265 Market.
Klanberg Josephine, at 835 Main, b.15 Woodbine.
Klebau Edward, painter, h.3u. 4½ Hungerford pl.
Klein Adolph, barber at 27 Pearl, h. 283 Allyn.
" Henry, barber at 5 Central, b. 5 Kilbourn.
" Jacob, groceries, 270, h.u. 284 Market.
" Max, h. 263 Market.
" Nathan, peddler, h.u. 292 Market.
Klett Christina, wid. Peter, h. 282 Market.
" Fred. at 99 Pratt, b. 282 Market.
" John, painter at 41 Albany, b. 92 Chestnut.
" Louis, clerk, Stillman & Co. furs, etc. 59 Pratt, h. E.H.t.
" Oscar, filer at Colts, b. 282 Market.
" Otto, h. 282 Market.
" Valentine, machinist, h.u. 49 New Britain.
Kley Louis, pressman Hartford Times, 716 Main.
Klimonski Anthony, laborer, h.2u. 93 Sheldon.
Klincuk Peter, laborer at 15 Albany, h. Morgan.
Kline Delia B. wid. Harlan P. h. 112 Woodland.
" Mary, wid. Columbus, b. 4 Huyshope.
" Milo, laborer at Spring Grove Cemetery, h. 297 Windsor av.
" Robert H. bookkeeper at Orient Insurance Co. 5 Haynes, h. 206 Sargeant.
" ☞ see also Cline.

Klinger Adeline P. asst. 690 Asy. b. 133 Ashley.
" Bertha H. teacher West Middle School, b. 133 Ashley.
" Clara M. teacher at West Middle School, b. 133 Ashley.
" Katherine, wid. Henry F. h. 133 Ashley.
Klingler Charles, supt. Jas. L. Howard & Co 438 Asylum, h. 4 Preston.
" ☞ see also Gloekler.
Klodgk John, butcher at 162, h. 190 Front.
Klominski John, laborer, h.u. 84 Potter.
Klosinski Piot, laborer, h. 93 Sheldon.
Knapp Alfred M. asst. supt. at 721 Main, h. 27 Florence.
" Charles A. conductor St.Ry. b. 152 Allyn.
" Frank, bartender at 605 Main, h. 20 Benton.
" Frederic, expert acc't, h. 14 Columbia.
" Harry S., U. S. Navy. b. 14 Columbia.
" Irving, flagman at N.Y.R. h. 47 Walnut.
" Jessie E. nurse, b. 427 Main, rm. 23.
" Margaret L. b. 14 Columbia.
" Mary Clissold, kindergarten teacher Second North school, 249 High, b. 14 Columbia.
Kneeland William, bkkpr. at 80 State, b.21 East.
Kneen James, machinist at 690, b. 821 Park.
Knevett Frederic, gardener, b. 47 Laurel.
" Thos. M. molder at 618 Cap. h. 2 Forest.
" William, gardener, h. 47 Laurel.
Knickerbocker C. A. Miss, teacher, h. 870 Asylum, rm. 23.
" Engine Works, 490 Capitol.
" R. W. mechanic, l.u. 18½ Church.
" Webster, clerk, 885 Main, b. 86 Hudson.
Knight Clarence P. master cabinet shop, 690 Asylum, b. 315 Pearl, rm. 407.
" Elias, helper at C. C. Fuller & Co. 14 Ford, b. 2 Huntley.
" Franklin H. atty. 11 Central, rm.7,h.W.H.t.
" James, inspector at Popes, h. 72 Madison av.
" James H. coachman, h. 334 Pearl.
" James H. president First National Bank, 50 State, h. 6 Charter Oak pl.
" Willard, Jr. modelm. at Popes, h.54 Vernon.
" William, porter at 140 State, b. 2 Huntley.
" William W. physician, office 96, l. 96 Tru.
Knightly Thomas E. driver at 13 Morris, h.u. 4 Whitmore.
Knoek Hattie, wid. Gilbert J. h. 35 Windsor.
" Leviat S. pawnbroker, hardware, etc 188, h. 190 State.
Knotts David, car inspector, N.Y.R.h.3 Warren.
Knous Caroline, wid. Jacob, h. 633 Prospect av.
" John, h. 95 Washington.
Knowlden James G. b. 2 Walnut.
Knowles G. William, at 58 Ann, b.2u. 152 Allyn.
" Walter, driver at 484 Main.
Knowlton Archer, toolmaker at 581 Capitol, h. 70 Madison av.
" Blanche H. dressmaker, 48, b. 48 Hopkins.
" Clarence A. toolm. at 476 Cap. b. 35 Wash.
" Eliza W. C. h. 51 Russ.
" Harlan P. clerk, 633 Main, b.35 Washington.
" James E. b. 389 Main.
" Nancy J. Mrs. h. 51 Russ.
Knox Almira, wid. William, b. 28 Marshall

# FRANK J. KNOX,

### JOBBER IN
## Steam Fitters, Gas Fitters and Plumbers' Supplies,

*Engineers' and Mill Supplies,*

*Steam and Gas Fitters' Tools,*

*Pipe Cut and Threaded to Sketch.*

Show-room with Plumbing Fixtures erected and in operation, to which Inspection is invited.

### No. 2 SOUTH ANN STREET.

*Long Distance Telephone.*

Knox Chas. N. electrician, 210 Pearl, h. 701 Asy.
" Chas. Norton, comp. at 49 Pearl, b.1193 Mn.
" Dwight W. salesm. 2 So. Ann, b. 28 Marshall.
" Frank H. train desp. N.Y.R. h. 45 Wooster.
KNOX FRANK J. wholesale dealer in steam, plumbers supplies, 2 So. Ann, h. 28 Marshall.
*See page 220.*
" Harry R. bookkeeper at Geo. W. Moore & Co. 759 Main, h. 281 Wethersfield.
" John A. machinist, b.u. 30 Canton.
" John B. assist. secretary Phœnix Ins. Co. 64 Pearl, h. 222 Collins.
" John B. Jr. at Phœnix Ins. Co. 64 Pearl, b. 222 Collins.
" John Malcolm, agent, h. 1193 Main.
" Joseph W. laborer, h.u. 2 Portland.
" Robert, machinist at Popes, h.u. 25 Russell.
" Rob't C. agent Northwestern Mutual Life Insurance Co. 721 Main, h. 26 Marshall.
" Sarah L. wid. Chester, h. 26 Marshall.
" Virginia M. wid. Daniel G. h.u. 1193 Main.
" Wm. R. machinist, N.Y.R. b. 30 Canton.
Knudson Charles, laborer, l.2u. 985 Main.
" Katrina, wid. Hans, h.u.r. 36 Temple.
" Louis, l.2u. 985 Main.
Kober Edw. G. messenger at P. O. b.2u. 104 Alb.
" George, baker, h.2u. 104 Albany.
Koch Anton, helper at 142 Russ, h. 7½ Oak.
" August, cafe, 29 Central, h. 39 Buckingham.
" Charles, manager, h. 55 Prospect.
" George, grinder at Popes, b.u. 10 Squire.
" Gustave, baker at 548 Main, h. 51¼ Wooster.
" Michael slater, h.2u. 116 Mather.
" Samuel P. operator at N.E.R. b. 145 High.
" ☞ *see also Cook; Cooke.*
Kochler Josephine, b. 36 Jefferson.
Koeber Augusta J. win.trim. 956 Mn. b. 28 Bkm.
Koech Edward R. laborer at 335, h. 80 Sheldon.
Koedski William, laborer, b. 4 Elm.
Koehler Louis H. steamfitter at 50 Church.
Koenig August, filer at Colts, h. 17 Harbison.
" C. A. A. grocer, 42, h. 44 Temple.
" Charles F. clerk at 42, b. 44 Temple.
" Emil L. mach. at 1 Flower, h. 72 Madison.
" Oscar, teacher violin, 71, h. 71 Church.
" William J. mach. at 70 Huy. b. 118 Babcock.
" William T. mach. at 1 Flow. b. 92 Madison.
Koerber Anthony, b. 119 Ann.

Koffinke Paul, assembler at Colts, h. Burnside v.
Koffman A. peddler, h.r. 67 Pleasant.
" Mitchel, clothing, 324 Asy. h.u. 304 Main.
Kofsky Bernhard, dry goods, etc. 300, h.u. 300 Park.
Kohler Charles, laborer, h.u. 12 Francis.
" John B. h. 12 Francis.
Kohlus Henry, wood engraver at 177 Asylum, b. 179 Babcock.
" Nicholas, mach. at N.Y.R. h. 179 Babcock.
Kohn Albert M (*Henry Kohn & Sons,*) jewelers, 890 Main, h. 19 Niles.
" Edmund P.(*H.Kohn & Sons,*)b.48 Winthrop.
" Geo. E. clerk at Henry Kohn & Sons, 890 Main, b. 48 Winthrop.
" Henry, (*H. Kohn & Sons,*) h. 48 Winthrop.
**KOHN HENRY & SONS,** wholesale jewelry, diamonds, 890 Mn. *See page 797.*
Henry Kohn. Albert M. Kohn. Oscar W. Kohn.
Edmund P. Kohn.
" John, mechanic at 26 High, b. 1218 Main.
" Oscar W.(*H.Kohn & Sons,*) b. 48 Winthrop.
Kolkoski Joseph, laborer, h.u. 5 Ellery.
" Simon, foundrym. 618 Capitol, h. 5 Ellery.
Kollenz Christian, cigarm. 867 Mn. h.u. 24 Talcott.
Koller John, filer at Colts, h. 56 Whitmore.
Kolur Samuel, clerk at 956 Main, b. 221 Front.
Koluskie Michael, porter, 98 Wells, h. 23 Sheldon.
Komoko Social Club, 709 Main, rm. 7.
Koplan Reuben, peddler. b. 159 Front.
" Sam, clothing, 159, h. 159 Front.
Koppelman Henry C. machinist, Colts, h. 23 Pawtucket.
" Herman P. agent, 283 Asy. b. 29 Pawtucket.
Kopplemann Becky G. clerk at 368 Asylum, b. 23 Pawtucket.
" Herman, b. 23 Pawtucket.
Korn Lena S. b. 77 Elm.
Kornell Charles, laborer, h.u. 9 Hendricxson.
Korngiebel Arthur, carpenter, h. 27 Spring.
Korrose Roxey, wirew. 618 Cap. h. 66 Morgan.
Koruski John, laborer, b.u. 4 Ellery.
Koryatta Karmel, laborer, h.u. 57 Front.
Kosenski Ignance, laborer at 335, b. 80 Sheldon.
Kosetzke Albert, engineer at Pope Tube Co. b. 1432 Broad.
" August, mach. Pope Tube Co. h.3u. 338 Park.
" Hennetta, wid. Charles, h.u. 16 Howard.
Koshefsky George, machinist, h.2u. 98 Albany.
" Henry, machinist, b.2u. 98 Albany.
" Max, laborer, b.2u. 98 Albany.
Kosillian Kirchoff, laborer, b. 14 Putnam.
" Martin, laborer, b. 14 Putnam.
Kossick Simon, cigarm. 104 Asylum, h. E.H.t.
Kostenbader Mary, wid. Frederick, h. 43 Martin.
Koster John L. porter at Brown, Thomson & Co. 942 Main, b. 242 Putnam.
" Mary H. wid. David, h. 242 Putnam.
Kotchmarte Joseph, laborer, h.2u. 6½ Ellery.
Kotoski Michael, laborer, h. 2 Ellery.
Koufman Alfred, peddler, h.r. 76 Pleasant.
" Philip, manufacturer, b. 104 Windsor.
Kowalske J. Fred. motorm.St.Ry.h.u.74 Sanford.
Kowalsky Frank, wireworker at 247 Asylum.
" Godfrey, blacksmith at 1061 Main, h. E.H.t.
" Rudolph, screwm. 476 Cap. b. 1088 Broad.

**THINKING PEOPLE Read The Post Daily.**

Kowelski Antonio, laborer, h.2u. 17 Ellery.
Kowisky Alec. chipper at 556 Cap. b. 23 Shel.
Koztonski James, laborer, h. 21 Arch.
Krah Thomas, machinist at 1 Flower, b. N.B.t.
Krahenbuhl Fred, baker at 1117 Main.
Krahl George, uphols. at 1079 Main, h. 28 Mays.
" Reynold, mech. at Popes, h. 35 Hamilton. •
Krajeroski Victor,laborer at 142 Russ,b.21 Arch.
Kramer August, teamster, h.u. 12 Elm.
" Benj. barber at 1069 Main, h. 34 Avon.
" George, tinner, h. 9 Whitmore.
" Michael, peddler, h. 34 Avon.
" Philip, salesman, 261 Asylum, h. 6 Kibbe.
" Samuel, peddler, h. 6 Kibbe.
" Sarah, groceries, 6, h. 6 Kibbe.
" ☞ see also Cramer.
Kramm Joseph, rabbi Association Brothers
    Children of Israel, h. 53 Morgan.
" Lewis, teacher, b. 53 Morgan.
Krapsch W. Frank, cabinetmaker at Seidler &
    May, 306 Pearl, h. Burnside t.
Krause Leo. H. machinist at P.&R. b. 415 Garden.
" Otto H. foreman at P.&R. h. 415 Garden.
Krauss Benj. carpenter, h.3u. 53 Morgan.
" David E. clerk at Brown, Thomson & Co.
    942 Main, b.u. 28 Morgan.
" Isidore, clerk at 188 State, h. 6 Pleasant ct.
" Louis, clerk at 114 Asy. h.u. 19 Morgan.
" Philip, shoemaker, 14 Mulberry, h. 32 Cap.
" Solomon, tailor, h.u. 28 Morgan.
" ☞ see Krause.
Kranthoff Charles, cigarm. 151, h. 149 Market.
Krazewski Paul, candymaker, b.u. 74 Sanford.
Kregie Andrew, laborer, h.u. 19 Front.
Kreimendahl Fred.W. lettercar. h.u. 13 Sanford.
" George R. tinner at 16 Mul. b.u. 10½ Village.
" Julius, baker, 94, b. 94 Hudson.
" Julius R. machinist, h.r. 36 Grand.
Krenoski Peter, rubberwkr. at 690, b. 15 Park.
Kress Charles R. harness.at 8 Sig.b.386 Weth.
Kreuter Louis, assembler at Colts, h.u. 143 Zion.
Kreuzer Edmund L. cutter, 252 Pearl, b. 76 Ann.
" Mary, wid. Casper, h. 76 Ann.
Krist William, screwm. at 476 Cap. b. 276 Law.
Krocher John S. agent,236 Asy.h.106½ Trumbull.
" Hans P. lodginghouse, 24 Gold.
Krogig Frank, at 176 Flatbush, h. 75 Hamilton.
Kroher John A. saloon, 66, h. 66 Temple.
" Otto, manager Commercial Cable, 3 Central,
    h. 17 Bond.
Krohn Charles, watchm. 157 Weth. h. 6 Mannz.
" Theodore, watchm. at 157 Weth. h. 6 Mannz.
Kronsberg August, stonecutter, h. 110 Hung.
Kropp Chas. F. b. 3 Kilbourn ct.
" G. Adolph, at Ætna Life Insurance Co. 650
    Main, h.u. 53 Sigourney.
" Minnie F. wid. Charles, h.3.u. 3 Kilbourn ct.
Krotoshiner Joseph,(J.Samuels&Co.)b.1 Spring.
" Yetta Mrs. h. 1 Spring.
Krough James P. bkkpr. at 690, b. 756 Park.
Krug Chas. B. pressman, 1 So. Ann, h.u. 15 Fmt.
" Eliza, b. 74 Williams.
" Fred. C. cigarm. 741 Main, h. 62 Williams.
" George P. bkkpr. at 126 Church, b. 15 Fmt.
" Jno.G.mach.Pope Tube Co.h.u.86 Hamilton.

Krug Louis, (K., Powers & Co.) h. 46 Huntington.
" Powers & Co. tobacconists, 741 Main.
    Louis Krug,      Michael Powers.
Krull August, b. 2 Holcomb.
" Otellie Mrs. b. 2 Holcomb.
Krum Alice J.inspector at 40 Gov. b.63 Franklin.
" Clifford E. printer at Hartford Life Ins. Co.
    252 Asylum, b. 63 Franklin.
" Elizabeth A. b. 63 Franklin.
" Rosalia J. wid. Henry, h. 63 Franklin.
Krumgold Henry, saloon, 60 Ple. h. 37 Chestnut.
Krupp Rudoff, rubberworker at 690 Park, h. 42
    Madison av.
Kudelli Andrew, repr. at Popes, h.u. 35 Hamilton.
Kuebler George F. clerk at 885 Main, h.7 Grand.
" Robert B. printer at 252 Pearl, h. E.H. t.
" William, cigarm. at 104 Asylum, h. E.H.t.
Kuehn Henry, (Steinbrueck & K.) h. 72 Temple.
Kuehnold Chas. cigarm. 46 Market, h. 22 Talcott.
" Fred W. cigarmaker, 46 Mar. h. 22 Talcott.
Kuen Alois, at Colts, h. 1 Curcombe.
Kuenzli Aug. mach. at 13 Central, h.u. 1 Russ.
" Charles K. b. 196 Sargeant.
" Josephine K. stenographer, b. 196 Sargeant.
" Sophia, wid. August, h. 196 Sargeant.
Kuffs William, cigarmaker at 104 Asylum.
Kugler Christian G. baker, h.3u. 11 Whitmore.
Kuhn Emil, teamster, h. 68 Temple.
" Henry, teamster, 385 Sheldon, b.u.518 Main.
" Jacob, laborer, h. 76 Sanford.
" Rosie, wid. Louis, groceries, 25 North.
Kuhne Edward J. h. 24 Belden.
Kuhrt Otto, filer, 388 Capitol; musician,h.65 Elm.
Kulig John, laborer, b.2u. 56 Sheldon.
Kulle Karl C. bkkpr. at 100 Tru. b. W.L.t.
Kullgren Fred. K. h.r. 37 Washington.
Kuhn Albert, lithogr. at 42 Union pl. b.170 High.
Kumm Lewis A. machinist at 690 Park, h. N.B.t.
Kummel Augustus F. foreman at Pratt & Whit-
    ney Co. 1 Flower, h. 183 Retreat.
" Charles F. contr. at 1 Flow. h. 41½ Russ.
" Henry J. clerk at 865 Main, b. 130 Retreat.
Kummer Charles Jr. painter, b.r. 228 Maple.
" Charles H. clerk, h.r. 228 Maple.
" Lucy, b. 228 Maple.
Kumpitsch Jacob, bottler, 279 Main, b. 38 Wells.
" John, screwmaker at 431 Main, b. 38 Wells.
" Magdalene, wid. Jacob, h.3u. 6 Kilbourn ct.
" Mary, dressmaker, 6, b.3u. 6 Kilbourn ct.
" Ollis, baker, b.u. 38 Wells.

**KUMPITSCH P. F.** dentist, 75 Pratt,
    h.2u. 42 Grand.  *See outside back cover.*

" Ursula, h.u. 38 Wells.
Kundsen John, shoem. at 945 Main, l. 33 Asy.
Kunkel Emily R. wid. Edward, h. 69 Congress.
" Frederick W. b. 69 Congress.
" Harris, tailor, h.u. 52 Windsor.
" Minnie E. stenographer at Sage, Allen &
    Co. 898 Main, b. 69 Congress.
" Susan, wid. Valentine, h. 78 Hudson.
Kunz Albert, varnisher at 633 Main, b. 8 Fkn.
" Peter J.corem. at r. 223 State, b.3u. 88 Shel.
Kurjill Joseph, laborer, b.u. 4 Ellery.
Kurtcher Margaret Mrs. h.2u. 545 Main.

Kurth Karl F. F. student at Trinity college, 11 Northam tower, Summit.
Kurth Wilfred, clerk at 197 Asylum, b. N.B.t.
Kurz Frederick, baker at 368 Asy. b. 28 Prospect.
Kussie Frank, laborer, h.u. 84 Potter.
Kutscher Ferdinand, grocer, 77, h. 75 Temple.
Kutshleach Frank, baker at 368 Asy. b. 41 Mul.
Kuznitzki Abe. pinma. at 31 Hicks, b. 224 Front.
" Jacob, peddler, h.u. 224 Front.
" Louis, wheelturner, 581 Cap. b. 224 Front·
Kzerian Kirkor, screwm. at 476, l. 381 Capitol·
" Martin, screwmaker at 476, l. 381 Capitol·

LABADIE Aurall, molder, h.u. 8 Warren.
" Omer, carpenter at N.Y.R. h.2u. 4½ Hung.
" Joseph, mason. b.u. 42 Canton.
" Louis, carpenter, h.u. 42 Canton.
" Wilfred, tailor, b.u. 42 Canton.
Labere Joseph, hodcarrier, b. 197 State.
LaBoeuf Felix, mason, h.u. 16 Heath.
LaBoiteaux E.M.toolm. 20 Sargeant, b. 55 Garden·
LaBonta Alvie, clerk at Popes, b. 51 Putnam.
Labreck, Frederick P. engineer, h. 30 Canton.
" Joseph E. b. 30 Canton.
" Melvina, wid. Joseph, h.r. 87 Windsor.
LaCart William, bottler at 430, b. 428 Asylum.
Lacass John, cigarm. 867 Mn. h.u. 18 Douglas.
Lacava Domenico, barber, 16 Mor. h.18 Kilbourn.
" Margaret, wid. Peter, h.3u. 79 Morgan.
" Rocco, old iron, copper, etc. h. 18 Kilbourn.
Lacey Charles, filer at Popes, l. 289 Asylum.
" George, mason, h. 79 Park.
" James G. h.u. 866 Broad.
Lachepelle Louis, driver 568 Main, b. 54 Market.
Laclure Joseph, painter, b. 144 Brown.
Lackard Joseph W. bookeeper, h.u. 13 Amity.
Lackey Otis C. foreman engine house at N.Y.R. h. 100 Hopkins.
Lackie Lawrence, firem. str. Hartford, 285 State.
Lackmann Frank, cooper at 232 Shel. h. E.H.t.
Lacy Edward J. collector at 245 Windsor, b. 53 Chestnut.
" Joseph, b. 58 Hawthorn.
" Lawrence, machinist at Pope Tube Co. b. 58 Hawthorn.
" Patrick, blacksmith, h.u. 58 Hawthorn.
" Thomas, saloon 539 Main, h. 53 Chestnut.
Ladd Wallace G. polisher at 23 Mulberry, h. 125 Barbour.
Laden Thomas J. Rev. b. 158 Main.
Ladue Lovina, wid. John S. h.u. 173 State.
Laduke Fred. carpenter at Colts, b. 39 Wolcott.
" John H. machinehand, Colts, h. 39 Wolcott.
" Mary, h. 13 Talcott.
Lady of Sorrow, Roman Catholic Church, Grace c. Greenwood, Parkville.
LaFargue John S. mach. at P.&R. b. E.II.t.
Lafayette John J. carpenter, b. 1153 Main.
Laflin George W. carpenter, b.u.r. 3 East.
LaFogg Benjamin, waiter at 12, b.u. 10½ Ford.
" Lewis A. coachman, h. Quaker lane.
LaFortune Victor E. conductor St.Ry. h. E.H.t.
Lagan Edward, clerk, 210 Asylum, b. 32 Village.
" Frank, teamster, Daniels Mill Co. Blo. av.
" Frank W. clerk Pope Tube Co. b.32 Village.

Lagan Jas. teamster Daniels Mill Co. b. Bl...
" James H. clerk at Brown, Thomson &... 942 Main, b. 32 Village.
" Margaret, wid. Bernard, h. 57 Annawa...
" Margaret C. clerk Brown, Thomson &... dry goods, 942 Main, b. 57 Annawa...
" Mary W. dressmaker, b. 57 Annawan.
" Michael, clerk, b. 57 Annawan.
" Terence, blacksmith, b. 32 Village.
Lahaie Arthur, burnisher at 62 Mar. b. 126 St...
Laharpe Joseph, shoemaker, h. 40 So. Prosp...
Lahey James, laborer, b.2.u. 81 Sheldon.
" Jeremiah, engineer, h. 88 Grove.
" Jeremiah, plumber at 14 Mul. b. 88 Gro...
" John, h.u. 20 Sheldon.
" Patrick H. driver, 560 Main, b. 6 Trumb...
" William, boilermaker, b. 88 Grove.
" ☞ see also Lahy; Leahy.
Laidlow Hannah, wid. Charles, nurse, h. 2 Ma...
Laiman Mary A. wid. John, b.u. 117 Albany...
" Theodore W. engineer at Cheney Bros. ... mill, 34 Morgan, h. 7 Goodwin.
Laing Hugh, carpenter, h. 96 Windsor.
" John, carpenter, h.2u. 2 Squire.
Laird Thomas, foreman at 158 Woodland, h. ... Harrison.
Laity Matthew H. mach. 1 Flow. b.u.86 Hopki...
Lajauness Louis, filer at Popes, b. 23 Spring.
LAKE EVERETT J. sec'y and treasurer Har... ford Lumber Co. r. 17 Albany, h. 55... Farmington.            See page 513.
" Thomas A. internal revenue collector, pres... Hartford Lumber Co. r. 17 Albany, ... Rockville c.
Laksar Alexander, harnessmaker at 8 Sigourney... h. 171 New Park.
LaLibirte Theodore, carpenter, h. Boulanger.
Lalley James F. policeman, h. 202 Laurel.
Lally Francis J. Rev. b. 158 Main.
" James F. Jr. mach. at 30 Cush. h. 43 Haw.
" John, inspector at 700 Main, b. 51 Capen.
" Mary, wid. Thomas, b.2u. 29 Hawthorn.
" Mary J. stenographer, b. 51 Capen.
" Michael, laborer, h.2u. 55 Hawthorn.
" Michael K. diemaker, 476 Cap. h. 55 Haw.
" Michael L. filer at 30 Cushman, h. 43 Haw.
" Patrick, coachman at 911 Main, h. 51 Capen·
" Thomas, filer, h.2u. 8 John.
" Timothy W. operator, b.u.r. 74 Vanblock.
" William F. at 30 Cush. b.2u. 29 Hawthorn·
LaMarche Felix J. b.u. 146 Mather.
Lamb Albert L. clerk at Hartford Life Ins. Co. 252 Asylum, h. Elmwood.
" Chauncey B. salesman, b. 132 Trumbull.
" Edwin E. mach. at 581 Cap. h. 18 Belmont·
" Edwin J. bakery, 132, h. 132 Trumbull.
" James, blacksmith, 10 Ferry, h. 16½ Morris·
" John, blacksmith at 10 Ferry, h. 16½ Morris·

LAMB JOHN W. general agent Phœnix Mutual Life Ins. Co. 49 Pearl, h. 219 Jefferson.
" Joseph, blacksm. 12 Ferry, b.2u. 16½ Morris·
" Lorenzo, real estate, 551 Main, h. 154 Sey·
" Mary wid. William b.u. 22 Huntley pl.

Lamb Mary E. wid. Albert, b. 117 Oak.
" O. Frank, clerk at 323 Asy. b.u. 32 Chapel.
" Wm. A. engineer at 1 Flower, h. 117 Oak.
Lambe Emma G. attendant at 30 Washington.
" John J.fire depart.supplies, h.6 Buckingham.
" Mary F. b. 6 Buckingham.
Lambert Aleck, asst. cook at 109, b. 109 Tru.
" John, cond. N.E.R. h.u.r. 49 Spring.
" John, driver, h.u. 50 Avon.
" Joseph, bootmkr. 454 Asylum, b. 87 High.
" Martin T. driver at 91, b. 28 Morgan.
Lamenza Tony, fruits, 48, b. 70 Union pl.
Laminger Adolph, cornicemaker at 93 Franklin, h. 33 Pawtucket.
Lamkins Fred W. clerk at Sage Allen & Co. 898 Main, h.u. 2 Wooster.
Lamoureaux Charles, carptr. b. 246 Lawrence.
" Henry, carpenter, b. 246 Lawrence.
Lamoureux F. G. Mrs. b. 219 High.
Lamoy J. Byron. pressman, b. 433 Madison.
Lamphear Erwin A. machinist, h.41 Ward.
" Mason G. wheelturner, b.127 Front.
" Oliver C. teamster at 149 State, h.127 Front.
" William O. brazier, b. 127 Front.
Lamphere Jennie W. wid. Albert W. h.u. 29½ Lewis.
" ☞See also Lanphere.
Lampone Frank, barber, h. 156 Front.
Lampson Amanda, wid. Julius, h. 80 Farmington.
" Frank W. carpenter at 14 Hicks, h. 15 King.
Lamroux Ame, cabinetm. at 133 Shel. b. 312 Asy.
Lamson Chas. M. Rev. pastor First (Center) Church of Christ, h. 142 Washington.
" Elsie J. wid. Frank A. h.u. 28 Martin.
Lancaster Edw. h.u. 75 Flower.
" Edward J. helper at Baxter the Decorator, 231 Asylum, b.u. 75 Flower.
Lanctan William A. barber, 275, h. 275 High.
Landell Charles, brazier at Popes, b. 291 Park.
Lander Abram, peddler, h. 53 Pleasant.
Landerman Oses, screwmaker at 476 Capitol, groceries, 18, h. 20 Cedar.
Landers Florence, Mrs. h. 1 Mays ct.
" Florence A. clerk at Brown, Thomson & Co. 942 Main, b. 28 Temple.
" Garrettee, blacksm.at 352 Alb. b. 88 Mather.
" Maurice W. mach. at 581 Cap. h. 194 Haw.
" Robert H. painter at Baxter the Decorator, 231 Asylum, h. 41 Bellevue.
" Thomas, plasterer, b. 197 State.
" William E. F. asst. adjutantgeneral, State Capitol, rm. 19, h. New London ct.
Landfear Louise B. musict. 102, b.u. 102 Wooster.
" N. Maria, h.u. 102 Wooster.
Landin August P. blacks. N.Y.R. b. 31 Wolcott.
Landon Carl, teamster, b.u. 251 Park.
" Caroline M. wid. Daniel, h.2u. 12 Goodman.
" Frank H. livery, 212, h. 214 Park.
" Frank H. Jr. at Travelers Ins. Co. 56 Prospect, b. 214 Park.
" Herbert E. h. 114 Capen.
" Raymond H. driver, h.2u. 12 Goodman.
Landough Emil, gunsmith, h. 169 Main.
Landrigan Daniel, laborer at stone pits, h. Zion.
" Daniel J. machinist at Popes, b. 41 Hamilton.

Landrigan John F. cutter 8 Sig. b. 41 Hamilton.
" Joseph, carptr. at Tube Co. h.2u. 22 Cedar.
" Kate, at 1 South Ann, b. 41 Hamilton.
" Kate M. wid. John, dressm. h.u. 72 Lawrence.
" Mary, at 690 Park, b. 41 Hamilton.
" William, laborer, b.u. 63 Flower.
" ☞see also Lundrigan.
Landry Albert, carpenter, b 1202 Main.
" Clifton E. clerk, 314 Asy. h.u. 50 Pleasant.
" Joseph M. brakem. P.&R. b. 110 Mather.
" Joseph P. mach. at 388 Cap. h. 1139 Broad.
" Peter, carpenter, b. 1202 Main.
Landurand Joseph, groceries, Prospect av. near New Park.
Lane Alice S. wid.Fred. J. h. Whiting lane, W.H.t.
" Arthur E., U. S. Army, h. 1160 Main.
" Arthur M. bookkeeper Wm. Rogers Mfg. Co. 66 Market, h. Windsor t.
" Charles M. milkman at 40, h. 40 Clark.
" Charles S. contractor, h. 25 Ashley.
" Con M. mixer at 690, h. 548 Park.
" Daniel, laborer St.Ry. h.u. 3 Park.
" Daniel D. machinist at Lincoln & Co. iron works, 54, b. 21 Arch.
" David, motorman at St.Ry. h.u. 17 Benton.
" Davis E. dentist, 17 Pratt, h. E.H.t.
" Edgar A. engineer at 1130, h. 1160 Main.
" Edward, driver, b. 20 Chapel.
" Enos H. bookkeeper at Pratt & Cady Co. 556 Capitol, h.u. 122 Huntington.
" Enos J.driver at 54, b.u. 21 Arch.
" Ezra M. cabdriver, b.u. 8 State.
" Frank, farmer, b. 776 Windsor av.
" Frank, machinist, h.u. 104 Jefferson.
" Frank A. Jr. clerk at 700 Main, b. 776 Windsor av.
" Frank Arthur, cabman, b. 316 Wethersfield.
" George, driver at 1231 Main.
" Hannah, wid. Edward, h.u. 75 Avon.
" James, blacksmith at 5 Mech. b. 18 Walnut.
" John, agent, h. 24 Chestnut.
" John, steward at Popes, l. 436 Capitol.
**LANE JOSEPH G.** wholesale grocer, liquors, 224 State, h. 20 Highland.
*See page 589.*
" Kathryn J. clerk at Brown, Thomson & Co. 942 Main, b. 3 Park.
" Margaret, wid. Thos. grocery, 33½ Morris, h. 4 Franklin.
" Margaret N. Mrs. h. 246 Lawrence.
" Nicholas N. moulder at 556 Cap. b. N.B.c.
" Oliver W. clerk at Popes, b. 64 Russ.
" Patrick, teamster at 40 Elm, h.u. 35 S. Pro.
" Peter C. drug clerk, 853 Main, h. 6 Winter.
" Robert E. carpenter, h.2u. 8 State.
" Rollin D. supt. Old North Ceme. h. 3 Mahl.
" Sarah Mrs. store, 776, h. 776 Windsor av.
" Theodore A. porter at T. Sisson & Co. 729 Main, h. 316 Wethersfield.
" Timothy, helper at Lincoln & Co. iron works, 54, h.u. 21 Arch.
" W. A. & Co. groceries, 37 Church.*
" Walter A. ship'gclk, 389 Allyn, h. 118 Hung.
" Walter H.public carriage driver,b.316 Weth.
" Washington Mrs. agent, h.2u. 8 State.

**RIDER ERICSSON**

# Hot Air Pumping Engines.

## T. H. LANGDON,

**PLUMBER, Steam and Gas Fitter,**

### No. 228 PEARL STREET.

*Telephone, 140.*

Lane Washington H. jobber, h.u. 8 State.
" William C. ostler at 995, h. 173 Main.
" Willis A. (*W. A. L. & Co.*) h. 217 Jefferson.
Landfersweiler Edward, clerk at 342 Asylum, h. 47 Bellevue.
Lang Archer W. Mrs. h.u. 167 Asylum.
" William C. clerk at Popes, b. Manchester t.
Langan William, carpenter, b. 112 Laurel.
Langdon Burton H. clerk at 956, b.u.1361 Main.
" Charles S. special agent National Fire Ins. Co. 95 Pearl, h. 108 Gillette.
" & Daley, plumbers, 1230 Main.
    John F. Langdon.        Patrick H. Daley.
" Edward K.machinist at 1 S. Ann.b. 255 Asy.
" Edward W. at 1 Laurel, b. 61 Spring.
" Ellen J. wid. Wm. W. b. 57 Farmington.
" Eveline, b. 213 Retreat.
" Frank I. b. 197 Sigourney.
" George, Mrs. b. 197 Sigourney.
" George H. machinist at 142 Russ, h. 12 Tru.
" George M. at 228 Pearl, b. 38 Madison.
" Hervert B. clerk at Conn. Fire Ins. Co. 51 Prospect, h. 197 Sigourney.
" James P. mason, h.u. 7 Center.
LANGDON JOHN F. (*Langdon & Daley,*) h.u. 38 Bellevue.
" Mary, wid. John, h.u. 155 Windsor.
" Mary E. wid. Merrick C. h.u. 1361 Main.
" Ralph, laborer, b. 111 Maple.
LANGDON THOMAS H. plumber, steam and gas-fitting, 228 Pearl, h. 38 Madison.
                                *See page 224.*
" Wm. E. drug clerk, h. 41 Laurel.
Langdow Amil, mach. at Popes, h. 20 Cottage.
Lange Antonio, laborer, b.4u. 190 Front.
" Arthur, baker at 1036 Main.
" F. C. painter, 212 Asy. rm. 5, h. 73 Laurel.
**LANGE & FLAD,** fresco painters, 13 Central.          *See page 512.*
                Henri Lange.
LANGE HENRI, (*L. & Flad,*) painters, 13 Central, h.u. 272 Park.
" William F. printer at R. S. Peck & Co. 26 High, b.u. 9 South Hudson.
Langenban Christian P. mach. h.u. 17 Atlantic.
" Louis, mach. at 30 Cush. h. 157 Lawrence.
Langhans Carl, tailor 69 Pearl, h. 284 Franklin.
Langley John L. h u. 520 Main.
Langlois Fortuna, painter, h. 130 Brown.
Langrish Edward J. at Neal, Goff & Inglis Co. 970 Main, b. 29 Woodbridge.

Langrish Edward J. policeman, h. 29 Wdbr
" Frank J. woolpacker, b. 233 Main.
" Thomas, painter, b. 233 Main.
Languth George, stereotyper, b.2u. 22 Hopk
Langzettel Robert C. A. barber at 27 Pea 55 Governor.
Lanigan Charles J. helper, b.u. 11 Liberty.
" Edward, watchman, h.u. 11 Liberty.
**LANKTON ARBA,** gospel temper evangelist, mfr. salve, etc. 2, h. 2 Ma
                                *See page 56*
" George H. lettercarrier at P.O. b. 113 T
" Henry L. stocker at Colts, h. Wethersf
" T. Wilbur, foreman, 252 Pearl, h. 6½ I
" ☞ *see also Langton.*
Lanman David T. Mrs. h. 10 Clinton.
" Joseph K. asst. treasurer Hartford Mach Screw Co. 476 Capitol, h. 10 Clinton.
Lannon James, blacksmith, b. 121 Madison
Lantange Lange, joiner, b.3u. 220 Sheldon.
Lanyon Eliza, wid. Wm. H.h.u. 17 So. Prosp
Lanze Antonio, laborer, b.3u. 51 Morgan.
Lapalme Tancrede, carpenter, b.u. 121 Ann.
LAPAUGH JOHN D. councilman 6th ward, buil r. 46 John, h. 68 Park.
Lapen Joseph, laborer, b. 71 Potter.
" Rocco, laborer, b. 71 Potter.
Lapenta Louis, helper, h. 12 North.
" Rocco, laborer, h. 67 Pleasant.
LaPlace Bertha L. b. 15 Mahl.
Laplant Louie, carpenter, b. 18 New Park.
" Theodore, carpenter, h. 18 New Park.
Laplante Louis J. typeworker at 476 Capit b. 276 Lawrence.
Lapoint Albert W. clerk, 581 Cap. b.2u. 11 Que
" Peter, carpenter, h. 126 Heath.
Lapointe Claranda G. clerk, 701 Mn. b. 887 Par
" J. N. Mrs. h.u. 918 Park.
" Joseph N. foreman at 1 Flow. h.u. 918 Par
" Louis, b. 12 North.
" Rocco, laborer, h. 12 North.
" Stanislas S. machinist at 1 Flower, watch maker at 883, h. 887 Park.
Laporte Eugene F. driver, 1 Flow. h. 80 Madison.
" Joseph, carpenter, h.u. 11 Davenport.
" Mitchell, boxmaker at Pratt & Whitney Co. 1 Flower, h. 171 Zion.
" Philip, mach. 9 Sigourney, b. 80 Madison.
Lappie William M. forem. 690 Park, h. 42 Heath.
Lappen D. stoves, etc. 166, h.u. 166 Front.
" Israel, mgr. stove store, 166, h.u. 166 Front.
Laprise C. M. Mrs. h. 67 Windsor.
Laragy Edward, lab. at 223 State, b.u. 80 Sheldon.
" Francis A. molder, 114 Grove, b. 51 Ch.O.
" James, helper at 54, h.u. 77 Arch.
" James J. coremaker, 114 Grove, b. 51 Ch.O.
" John, molder, b.u. 80 Sheldon.
" Patrick, foundry, 114 Grove, h. 51 Ch.O.
" William, molder, h.u. 80 Sheldon.
" Wm. T. molder, h.u.51 Charter Oak.
Laramee Alfred, machinist, h. 853 Park.
Laraway Wm. P. mechanical draughtsman at 581 Capitol, h. 196 Laurel.
Lardick Elizabeth, h. 37 Arch.

**If You Want all the News, Read THE POST.**

Lardner Patrick J. enameler at Popes, h. W.L.t.
Larendeau Mederick, carptr. b. 255 Asylum.
Larenson John, stuffer at 15 Trumbull, b. E.H.t.
Largary William Jr. cigarmaker at 173 State,
   b.2u. 80 Sheldon.
Larkin Keron, electrician, 26 High, b. 87 Maple.
  " James, laborer at stonepits, h. 33 Hamilton.
  " Jos. stonecutter, b. 33 Hamilton.
  " Keron J. blacksm. at 9 Sig. h.2u. 7 Putnam.
  " Keron J. mech. at 26 High, b. 87 Maple.
  " Mary, wid. Dennis M. h. 545 Main, rm. 15.
  " Michael, laborer, h. 87 Maple.
  " Thomas, b.2u. 7 Putnam.
Larkum Georgie, wid. Horace H. h. 37 Imlay.
  " Harry H. teller at National Exchange
    bank, 76 State, h. 37 Imlay.
  " Newton W. b. 37 Imlay.
  " Wilbur N. clerk at 388 Capitol, h. 46 Beach.
Larned Amos, (L.&Hatch,) h. 2 Townley.
  " & Hatch, boots, etc. 945 Main.
      Amos Larned.    Charles E. Hatch.
  " ☞see also Learned.
Larochelle Seraphin, brickmaker, h. 775 Wind-
   sor av.
LaRock Frances, wid. Jos. h. 154 Washington.
  " John, helper at 1 Flower, h. 971 Park.
LaRocque Edmund J. barber at 275 High, l.
   97 Williams.
  " Henry W. carpenter, b. 13 Kennedy.
  " Mary,wid. Napoleon, dressm. h. 13 Kennedy.
LaRose Joseph, woodworker, b. 36 John.
LaRoza E. buffer at 62 Market, b. 36 Canton.
  " Leonard, silversmith, 62 Mar. h. 36 Canton.
Larraway William P. draughtsman at 581 Cap-
   itol, h. 196 Laurel.
Larsen August, laborer at Popes, h. Burnside t.
  " Emil,screwm. at 476 Cap. b. 109 Lawrence.
  " George, at 476 Capitol, h.u. 25 Glendale.
  " John, b. 354 Park.
  " Louis, baker at 368 Asylum, h. Douglass.
  " Marinus, screwm. at 476 Capitol, b. E.H.t.
  " Michael, clerk at 1030 Main, h. 45 Talcott.
  " ☞see Lawson.
Larson Adolph, rubberworker, b. 64 Flower.
  " Alfred, screwm. at 476 Cap. b. 54 Flower.
  " Andrew G. carptr, 224 Sargeant, b. 5 Amity.
  " August, stonecutter, h.r. 56 Albany.
  " August, teamster at 252 Pearl, h.2u. 115
    Lawrence.
  " Augusta, laundress at 20 South Hudson.
  " Carl, blacksm. at 581 Cap. h. 138 Albany.
  " Charles, bartender, 306 Park, h.u. 195 Russ.
  " Chas. L. mach. 1 Flower, h. 177 Lawrence.
  " Chas. W. mach. at 1 Flower, h. 28 Francis.
  " Chas. W. mach. 476 Cap. b. 164 Putnam.
  " Christian, screwm. 476 Cap. b.u. 25 Glendale.
  " Clara, wid. Erick J. h.2u. 177 Lawrence.
  " David, b.u. 55 Grand.
  " Emil, coachm. 98 Washington, b. 2 Squire.
  " Frank, butcher, 84 Madison, b. 2 Squire.
  " Frank, carptr. 158 Woodland, h. 61 Grand.
  " Hjelmar, farmer, b. 47 Bluehills.
  " Ida, dressmaker at 173, b. 173 Babcock.
  " John, driver at 543 Main, h.u. 16 Elm.
  " John, iceman at 48 Ann, b. W.H.t.

Larson John, screwm. 476 Cap. b.u. 25 Clinton.
  " John, screwmaker, b. 33½ Lafayette.
  " John L. at 556 Capitol, h.2u. 232 Putnam.
  " Jonas W. helper, 1 Flower, h. 59 Madison.
  " Louis, clerk at 149, h.u. 171 Babcock.
  " Nels. clerk at 140 State, h. East Hartford t.
  " Oscar, h. 1 Queen.
  " Peter, ostler at 19 Gold, h. 58 Temple.
  " Peter C. screwm.at 476 Cap.h.33½ Lafayette.
  " Peter N. mach. at 581 Cap. h. 56 Hawthorn.
LaSalette College, New Park.
Lasbury Edwd. G. (H.Lewis&Co.) h.17 Pleasant.
  " Frank S. at National Fire Insurance Co.
    95 Pearl, b. 17 Pleasant.
  " Fred. T. clerk at Connecticut Fire Insur-
    ance Co. 51 Prospect, b. 17 Pleasant.
L'Aschevar Abram, clerk at 908 Main, h.2u.
   272 Market.
Laschever L. tailor, 29 Church, h.2u. 272 Market.
  " Nathan, tailor at 1259 Main, h. 78 Talcott.
Laselle Merton, bartender, b. 47 Prospect.
Lashaway Jos. carptr. at 155 Ch.O. h.u.63 Avon.
Lasher Frank H. clerk at 886 Main, b. 236 High.
  " Louis H. engir. 476 Cap. h. 891 Park.
  " Morgan, b. 8 Center.
  " Perry, farmer Watkinson Farm School,
    Bloomfield av.
  " Zacharius G. clerk at 4 Central, h. 8 Center.
Lashorn Geo. L. machinist. h.u. 47 Sheldon.
Laslitt Harry, mason, h. 310 Capen.
Lasquenza Frank, laborer, h.u. 78 Charles.
Lassen Andrew, at 218 State, h.u. 55 Front.
Laster Raymond, at 330, b. 330 Pearl.
LATE JAMES C. (North & L.) 336 Asylum, h.
   W.H.t.          See page 470.
Laten Charles, waiter, b.u. 30 Ferry.
Later Max, 2d hand clothing, h. 80 Temple.
  " Morris, market, 196, h. 196 Front.
Lates Frederick W. engraver at Calhoun Print-
   ing Co. 29 Union pl. h. 45 Oxford.
Latham Charles H. supt. Hfd. Dredging Co. b.
   986 Main.
  " Charles H. Mrs. boardinghouse, 986 Main.
  " George, b. 3 Davenport.
  " Maurice C. agent at 715 Mn. b. Manchester t.
  " Robert, helper St.Ry. b. 3 Davenport.
Lathrop A. E. Mrs. housekeeper, h.u. 933 Main.
  " Arthur E.druggist at 55 Far. l. 63 Church.
  " Edwin F. machinist at Colts, b. 20 Union.
  " Elisha E. clerk at 314 Asylum, b. 38 Imlay.
  " Ella S. dressmaker, 20, b. 20 Union.
  " George T. at 20 Central, b. 20 Union.
  " Hayden R. bookkeeper at Tucker & Good-
    win, 8 Hurlburt, b. 67 Sigourney.
  " Jennie T. b. 236 High.
  " Maria L. wid. Samuel B. h. 20 Union.
  " Oliver S. machinehand at Colts, b. 56 Oak.
  " Walter H. liquors, 314 Asylum, h. 38 Imlay.
  " Walter H. Jr. clerk at 314 Asy. b. 38 Imlay.
Latimer Bell, at 34 Pratt, b. 58 Church.
  " Edward H. inspector, b. 71 Buckingham.
  " Franceita, wid. James A. h.u. 15 Imlay.
  " George A. janitor, 926 Main, h. 90 Mather.
  " Richard R. com. salesm. h. 71 Buckingham.
Latin Samuel D. carpenter, b.u. 49 Francis.

**For Sale Advertisements Bring Results in the Post.**

Latter Nettie S. wid. Walter, h. 25 Mahl.
" Moriss, blacksmith, h.u. 46 North.
" Wilbert S. cashier at 95 Ple. b. 25 Mahl.
Lau Charles, b. 2 Wooster pl.
" G. Frank, inspector, b.u. 2 Wooster pl.
" George F. toolmaker at Popes, b. 263 High.
" John, shoem. at 39 Ann, h.u. 2 Wooster pl.
" ☞see also Law; Laws.
Laufersweiler Edward, clerk, h.u. 47 Bellevue.
Laughland John, slater at Colts, h.u.227 Jefferson.
Langblin Edward, blacksmith, b. 3 Hungerford.
" James, carpenter, h. 3 Hungerford.
" John E. screwm. at 476 Cap. h. 28 Wolcott.
" Michael, operator at 135 Shel. h.37 Madison.
" Robert, bottler r. 85 Wolcott, b. 3 Hung.
" William, foundrym. 618 Cap. h.u.21 Howard.
" ☞see McLaughlin, O'Laughlin, O'Loughlin
Langhton Nellie E. wid. Thos. R. h. 1 Pleasant.
" ☞see also Lawton.
**LAUREL PARK,** See page 557.
Lauria Donato, fruits, 1055 Main, h. 56 Portland.
Lauridsen Albert C. toolm. at Popes, h. 358 Park.
" Julius A. diesinker, h. 12 Affleck.
Laurie Nettie, insurance dept. State capitol, b.
155 Washington.
Lauriedsen Claus A. mach. Popes, h.2u. 358 Park.
Laurio Domenico, h.u. 64 Morgan.
" Joseph, bootblack, 352 Asy.h.3u. 82 Morgan.
Lauritsen Hans, buffer, 581 Cap. b.u. 1204 Broad.
Lauritzen Lauritz, baker, 368 Asy. h. 11 Douglas.
Lavago Joseph, helper at 110 Alb. h. 64 Morgan.
Lavaie Rocco, laborer, b. 73 Morgan.
Lavelli George J. with Security Co. 62 Pearl, b.
22 Florence.
" ☞see also Le Valley.
Laven Henry, laborer, b. 64 Vaublock.
Laverty Wm. motorman St.Ry. h.u. 63 Dean.
Lavery Frank, driver, 4, b. 4 Huyshope.
" James, driver, 4, b. 4 Huyshope.
" John H. driver, h.u. 149 Windsor.
" John P. mach. at 581 Cap. h.2u. 952 Broad.
" Robert, coachman, 92, b. 92 Farmington.
Lavett Mattie, b. 40 Bellevue.
Laviere Frank, laborer, h.u. 1 North.
" George, grocery, 10, h. 10 North.
" J. P. carpenter, b.u. 10½ Ford.
" John, laborer, h.u. 1 North.
Lavin Hyman, at 1 Flower, b. 1 Forest.
" Hyman, grocery, 160, h. 164 Front.
" Jacob, tailor, h.u. 164 Front.
" James J. dentist at 926, b. 270 Main.
" John, laborer, b. 54 Avon.
" Joseph, tobacco & confectionery, h. 9 Queen.

Lavin Julius, helper at 618 Capitol, b. 1 Forest.
" Moriss, peddler, h.u. 190 Front.
" Thomas F., Engine No. 1, h.u. 64 Vanblock.
Laviolet H. Alex. cigarmaker, 104 Asylum, h.
17 Windsor av.
Lavoie August, millwr. 133 Shelden, h. 9 Law.
" Elie, carpenter, h.u. 28 Lawrence.
" Elie, mason, h. 50 Amity.
" Eugene J. operator, b.u. 28 Lawrence.
" Israel, carpenter, h. Lubeck.
" Louis, carpenter, b. 9 Lawrence.
Lavorni Biaso, ragpicker, h. 13 Charles.
**LAW & PRENTISS,** dentists, 926 Main,
rm. 76.          See page 427.
William H. Law, D.D.S.    Chas. C. Prentiss, M.D.
" Fred. A. toolm. at 1 Laurel, h. 419 Maple.
" George F. machinist, b. 265 High.
" Homer L. Dr. h. 100 Washington.
**LAW WILLIAM H.** D.D.S. (Law &
Prentiss,) dentists, 926 Main, rm. 76, h.
16 Trinity.
" ☞see also Lau; Laws.
Lawler Andrew A. machinist at 80 Huyshope,
h.u. 23 Morris.
" Bridget, wid. Francis, h.u. 140 Windsor.
" Edward, b. 2 Holcomb.
" Edward, plumber, 550Mn.h.138Wethersfield.
" Frank, bookkeeper, Popes, b. 202 Maple.
" James F. saloon, 202 State, b. 30 Front.
" John A. butcher, 271, h. 271 N.B.
" John F. bkkpr. at 550 Main, b. 138 Weth.
" John J. plumber, 548 Asy. b.u 72 Maple.
" John J. saloon, 637 Main, h. 60 Madison.
" John W. h.r. 202 Maple.
" Mary, wid. Thomas, h. 30 Front.
" Mary A. bkkpr. 745 Main, b. 43 Hudson.
" Mary A. wid. James, h.u. 72 Maple.
" Mary J. h. 51 Wadsworth.
" Michael J. brassturner, 556 Cap. h. 43 Haw.
" Thomas, h. 44 Village.
" Thomas, h.u. 100 Retreat.
" Thomas A. blacksm. 142 Russ, h. 56Madison.
" Thos. J. enameler, Popes, h. 15 Curcombe.
" William F. bricklayer, b.u. 72 Maple.
" William J. mach. at 581 Cap. h. 153 Law.
" Wm. T. painter, h.u. 40 John
Lawlor B. S. Miss, manager 375, b. 370 Asy. rm.57.
" David M. restaurant, 375 Asy. h. Prov., R.I.
" Raymond W. steamfitter at 164 State, h.u.
25 Center.
" William P. mach. 142 Russ, b.2u. 9 S.Pro.
Lawrence Alexander, carpenter, b. 48 Linden.
**LAWRENCE CHARLES H.** sec'y Phoenix Mutual
Life Insurance Co. 49 Pearl, police com-
missioner, h. 199 Sigourney.
See pages 452, 453.
" Dominic, laborer, h.u. 19 Ellery.
" Edwin H. foreman at Popes, b. 357Capitol.
" Frank, molder, 618 Capitol, h. 104 Ward.
" Frank V. draughtsm. Popes, h. 22 Highland.
" Gertrude M. stenographer at 223 Asylum,
b. 82 Grove.
" Herbert E. mach. at Colts, h. 82 Grove.

Lawrence Herman Arthur, machinist at 1 Laurel, b. 179 Hawthorn ex.
" James, boots & shoes,521 Main, h. 110 Weth.
" James W. clerk, 521 Main, b. 110 Weth.
" Jennie E. stenogr. at Popes, b. Middletown t.
" Michael, horseshoer, 7 Spruce, h. Kinsley.
" Ned, foreman, h. 357 Capitol.
" Oscar, filer at Popes, b.u. 23 Spring.
" Richard B. special agent Ætna Indemnity Co. 650 Main, h. 22 Highland.
" Thomas, operator at 388 Cap. b. 4 Gilbert.
" Thomas F. student at Yale, b. 199 Sig.
" William, h.u. 23 Sheldon.
" Wm. plumber at 164 State, b. 21 Central.
" William J. boots, etc. 1105 Main, h.108 Weth.
Lawrensen Charles, coachman, h. 282 Laurel.
Lawrenson Ludwig, gardener at h.r. 12 Fern.
" ☞ see also Laurensen.
Laws Luther S. del. clerk, 745 Main, b. 103 Tru.
" Martha S. wid. Edward E. h.3u. 811 Main.
" Peter S. mach. 388 Capitol, b. 459 Broad.
" ☞ see also Lau; Law.
Lawson Chas. bartender, 302 Park, h.u. 195 Russ.
" Charles, helper, 142 Russ, h. 47 Lawrence.
" Charles E. at 476 Capitol, b. 164 Putnam.
" Christina, h.u. 16 Trumbull.
" Daniel H. shoem. at 546 Asylum,b.New Park.
" Fulton Q. traveling salesman, h. 876 Broad.
" John, cabinetm. at 225 Sheldon, h.u. King, n. Julius.
" Peter H. filer at 581 Capitol, h.56 Hawthorn.
LAWSON ROBERT, councilman 6th ward; with Pope Mfg. Co. h. 72 Hungerford.
" ☞ see also Laughson.
Lawton Edward F. foreman at 266 Pearl, b.u. 35 Lincoln.
" Franklin L. physician, 18, h. 18 Congress.
" Henry A. gardener at 112, b. 112 Edwards.
" ☞ see also Laughton.
Lay Charles H. ship. clerk at Popes, h.u. 232 Jef.
" Eliza M. wid. J. W. h.u. 29 Lincoln.
" Horace E. photogr. 212 Asy. h. 113 Wooster.
" ☞ see also Leigh.
Layden Thos. harnessmaker, 8 Sig. b.1153 Main.
Layland Chas. mach. at 1 Flow. h. 53 Grand.
" Edmund W. machinist at 9 Sigourney, h. 69 Hungerford.
" William L. toolm. at 9 Sigourney, h. E.H.t.
Laylor George R. lacecutter at 15 Trumbull, b.2u. 120 Wooster.
" Mary E. wid. John, dressmaker, 120, h.2u. 120 Wooster.
Layton Emma H. laundress, h. 8 Gold.
" Olive J. Mrs. nurse, h. 144 Capen.
" William C. mach. at N.Y.R. b. 66 Hopkins.
" ☞ see also Leighton.
Lazarus Benj. cigarmaker at 867 Mn. b. 115 Tru.
Lazzaro A. D. wid. Andrew, h.u. 140 Main.
" Albert E. publisher, 7Central,rm.4, h.140Mn.
Leach Charles D. lab. 15 Alb. h.u. 74 Windsor.
" James J. stonecutter, h.u. 3 John.
" ☞ see also Leitch.
Leadbitter F. G. cigarm. at 867 Main, h. E.H.t.
Leader Rebecca, wid. Rev. S. b. 12 Lenox.
Leag August, lab. at Bushnell Park, h. 38 Wells.

Leahy David J. painter, h. 3 Orchard.
" Ellen, wid. William, h.u. 8 Putnam.
" John, coachman at 131, b. 131 Washington.
" John J. carpenter, b. 112 Windsor.
" John J. mach. at 581 Cap. b. 276 Lawrence.
" Mary, b.u. 8 Putnam.
" Patrick, laborer, b.3u. 55 Spruce.
" Patrick, shoemaker, 26, h. 26 Howard.
" Patrick J. assembler, 476 Cap. h. 8 Putnam.
" Thomas J. letter carrier, h.2u. 82 Walnut.
" Thomas J. molder, 1 Flower, h. 13 Putnam.
" William, peddler, h. 112 Windsor.
" William H. laborer, b. 112 Windsor.
" ☞ see also Lahey; Lahy.
Leamy Martin, waiter at 80 State.
Leaney Thomas P. clerk at P.&R. b.u. 3 Ellery.
Learned Letty H. teacher Brown School, (kindergarten,) b. New Britain t.
" Newton M. Rev. ins. 252 Asy. h. 176 Sig.
" ☞ see also Larnerd; Leonard.
Leary Daniel J. helper, 26, b. 26 State.
" George, plumber at 128 State, b. 38 S.Pro.
" Edward, laborer, b. 192 State.
" Jerry, molder at 555 Capitol, h. 90 Ward.
" John C. bartender at 352 Asy. b. 18 Kennedy.
" Lawrence, switchman, N.Y.R. h.u.7 Warren.
" Michael C. laborer, b. 1327 Broad.
" Timothy, at N.E.R. h.2u. 35 Canton.
" William, steamfitter, l. 17 Church.
" ☞ see also O'Leary.
Leas John H. temperer at 40 Gov. h. Weth. t.
Leasche ☞ see Leische.
Leatherwood Jesse H. mach.at690Park,b.49Russ.
Leavenworth Addie J. Mrs. musicteacher, 56, h. 56 Winthrop.
" George W. stonemason, h. 226 Barbour.
" Willard M. h. 56 Winthrop.
Leavey John, carptr. at 155 Ch.O. h.u. 3 Ellery.
" ☞ see also Levy.
Leavitt Abraham, clerk, h. 87 High.
" Clarence A. clerk at Brown, Thomson & Co. 942 Main, b. 87 High.
" Edith W. theological student, 1507 Broad, b. 62 Hawthorn.
" Floyd, engraver at Wm. Rogers Mfg. Co. 66 Market, b. E.H.t.
" Harry W. conductor, h.u. 40 Bellevue.
Lechner Fritz, brewer, b. 55 Laurel.
" Matthew, electrician at 1, b. 51 Laurel.
" Nicholas, shoemaker, 55, h. 55 Laurel.
Leclerc Joseph L. at 185 Asylum, b. 144 Brown.
Lecor Olga E. clerk at 715 Main, b. 32Babcock.
Lecreiner Harry G. tinsmith at Popes, h. 150 Madison av.
Leddy Michael, b. 2 Holcomb.
" Peter, machinist at Colts, h. E.H.t.
Ledgard Samuel P.mach.133Shel.h.u.53Wooster.
Ledger William L. buyer at Brown, Thomson & Co. 942 Main, h. 119 Oxford.
Ledoux Joseph, (Healy & L.) b.u. 3 Goodman.
Ledoyt Frank, mech. at Popes, b. 59 Flower.
Leduc John, barber, h.u. 38 Russell.
" Methiemias,barber,91Windsor,h.38 Russell.
" Otto, helper at·133 Sheldon, b. 105 Windsor.
" Peter, machinehd. at Colts, b. 105 Windsor

**THE NEWS PRINTED IN THE POST IS RELIABLE.**

Ledwith Bridget, wid. James, h. 121 Hamilton.
" Edward, machinist, h.2u.r. 28 Walnut.
" Edward F. Jr.mach. N.Y.R. b. 12 Wilson.
" Ellen, wid. Edward. h. 12 Wilson.
" James, at 141 Zion, b. 12 Wilson.
" John, bartender at 255 State, l.u. 33 Front.
" Mary, b. 12 Wilson.
" Philip, machinist at N.Y.R. b. 12 Wilson.
" Sadie E. clerk at 875 Main, h. 39 Spring.
" Thomas, farmer, h.r. 98 New Britain.
" Thomas, screwmaker, h.2u.4 Putnam.
" Thomas J. laborer at N.Y.R. h.r. 82 Ward.
Lee Albert, mason, b. 2 Church.
" Alice, nurse at 20 S. Hudson.
" Ann, wid. Patrick, h.u. 35 Spruce.
" Branch, butler at 1054, b. 1054 Asylum.
" C. A. Mrs. wid. George, b. 13 Sisson.
" Cecelia Mrs. h.2u. 211 Pearl.
" Charlie, laundry, 99 Main.
" Chung, laundry, 98 Park.
" Edward H. motorman St.Ry. b. 26 Alden.
" Frank H. machinist, b. 62 Francis.
" George, at 146 State, h. 128 Bellevue.
" George, mason, h. 11 Affleck.
" George M. electrical engineer, b. 20 Vernon.
**LEE H. K.** mechanical engineer 223 State, h. 223 Asylum, rm. 67. *See page 539.*
" Harry, mason, b. 11 Affleck.
" Harry A. carpenter, h.u. 35 Chestnut.
" Harvey S. watchman, 30 Weth. h. 26 Alden.
" Homer, motorman St.Ry. b. 26 Alden.
" Hop, laundry, 222 Windsor av.
" James, bartdr. at 340 Park, b.u. 4 Grand.
" James, dropforger at Colts, b.u. 37Mulberry.
" James, motorman St.Ry. b. 48 Asylum.
" James P. inventor, h. 20 Vernon.
" John, teamster, b. Donald.
" John, watchman at N.Y.R. h.3u. Spruce.
" Joseph C. janitor N.Y.R. h. 43 Liberty.
" Julius, porter at 76 Tru. b. 5 Huntley.
" Louise M. b. 138 Washington.
" Margaret A. h. 60 Fairmount.
" Margaret B. teacher, Brown school, b. 20 Belden.
" Mary, wid. Patrick, h. 42 Liberty.
" Mary C. housekeeper, 21 Vine.
" Peter J. bartender, h.2u. 50 Avon.
" Quong, laundry, 132 Front.
" Rob't E. clerk at 193 Asylum, h. 14Wooster.
" Robert H. mach. at 1 Flow.h. 157 Babcock.
" Sam, laundry, 59 Maple.
" Sing, laundry, basement 175 State.
" Sing, laundry, 92, h. 92 Sheldon.
" Thomas, teamster at 100 Com. h. 19 Ellery.
" Thomas E. waiter at 53 Ann, h. 14 Gold.
" Thomas C. fireman at Capitol, b. 255 Asy.
" Thomas J. veterinary surgeon, 1061 Main, b. 10 Chapel.
" Thomas V. machinist, b. 389 Capitol.
" William, helper, b. 1183 Main.
" Wm. C. rubberw. at 690 Park, h. 13 Sisson.
" William H. Mrs.h. 138 Washington.
" Wing, laundry, 1108, h. 1108 Main.
" ☞*see also Leigh.*

Leek Amanda M. Mrs.: corsetfitter, h.u. 290 Main.
" Carrie E. wid. John D. h.2u. 1164 Main.
" Grace D. b.2u. 1164 Main.
" Philander, carriagetr. 17 Elm, h.u. 290 Main.
" William S. undertkr. 1166, b.2u. 1164 Main.
Leep Francis, laborer, b. 147 Sheldon.
" Peter, lab. at 335 Shel. h.2u.r. 34 S. Prospect.
Leese John, laborer, h.2u. 2 Ellery.
Leete Joseph, h.u. 83 Bellevue.
" William H. attorney at law, 926 Main, rm. 19, b. Thompsonville t.
Lefebre Everest E. brazier, h.u. 23 Kennedy.
" Homer, milkman, Windsor av. c. Tower.
" Zoella, wid. Solime, h.2u.r. 15 Wells.
Lefebvre Joseph, polisher, h.u. 48 Sheldon.
Lefeve Frederick, clerk, b.3u. 263 Main.
Leffingwell Adella E. h. 5 Arch.
" George E. manager, h. 7 Linden.
" ☞*see also Lleffyngwell.*
Lefkovitz Arnol, cigarm. 1115 Mn.h.u. 14Wooster.
Legaee Louis A. mech. at Popes, l. 71 Russ.
Legal Frank, bolognamaker, h.2u. 8 Warren.
Legasey William A. clerk at Brown, Thomson & Co. 942 Main, h. 153 Martin.
Legate William H. plater, Wm. Rogers Mfg Co. 66 Market, h.u. 38 Capen.
Legendre William, clerk, b. 8 Center.
LeGeyt Geo. H. teamster, b. George c. Preston.
" James P. carman, h. George c. Preston.
" James W. teamster, b. George c. Preston.
Legg Cornelius E. butcher, 203State, h. 11 Cong.
" Nicholas H. at 8 Front, h. 86 Arch.
Leggett Estola, wid. William H. h. 24 Cottage.
LeGrange Grant, agt. 756 Main, b. 12 Village.
Lehan James, hodcarrier, h. 18 Walnut.
" James F. laborer, b. 18 Walnut.
" James F. mach. N.Y.R. h.2u. 139 Law.
" Jerry, wiper, h. 139 Lawrence.
" Lizzie, clerk at 835 Main, b. 18 Walnut.
" Thomas J. enameler at Popes, h. 93 Sheldon.
" Timothy, blacksmith, h.2u. 93 Sheldon.
Lehann Alina, wid. Carl, b.u. 28 Harbison.
Lehmann Otto, mach. at 1 Flower, h. 28 Harbison.
" Pauline, wid. Frederick W. midwife, h.u. 139 Front.
Lehnemann Dora, wid. August, b. 28 Florence.
" H.August cigarm.at 104 Asy.h.u.37 Bellevue.
" John W.printer at 1089 Main,b.37 Bellevue.
Lehner August G. machinist, b. 36 Capitol.
" Joseph J. salesman at 97 Asy. b. 64 Church.
Lehr John J. mach.at Colts, b.72 Charter Oak av.
" Mary, wid. Jacob, h. 72 Charter Oak av.
Lehwald M.J.manager at 77 Pratt, l. 14 Church.
Leibert Charles F. at 28 High, b.u. 371 Capitol.
" Edward T. clerk at Kimball & McCray, 658 Main, b. 478 Wethersfield.
" George, finisher, 17 Elm, b. 347 Wethersfield.
" Joseph, tinner at 16, b. 41 Mulberry.
" ☞*see also Liebert.*
Leibler Frank, molder at 54 Arch, h. Weth. t.
Leibman Lewis, dry goods, 208, h. 208 Front.
Leichner Bernard, grocer, 80, h. 80 Talcott.
" Pinkus, tailor, h. 187½ Front.
Leidich B.W. porter, Adams Ex. b.u. 31½ Russell.
" ☞*see Liedrich.*

Leigh Enoch, engraver, 32, h. 32 Ward.
" Lewis L. machinist 1 Flower, b. 739 Asylum.
" ☞ see also Lay; Lee.
Leighton Frank H. clerk, 556 Cap. l.u.1071 Main.
" William H. laborer, b.u. 16 Gold.
" ☞ see also Layton.
Leineweber Charles F. machinist at 556 Capitol, h.u. 57 Park.
Leinhard Henry A. special correspondent Popes Mfg. Co. 436 Capitol, h. 427 Main rm. 32.
Leink Sam, tailor at 118 Asylum, b. 22 North.
Leipziger Jacob, collector, 261 Asy. b. 37 Chapel.
Leische Amelia, wid. Godfried, h. 217 Franklin.
" Frank, carptr. & build. 217, b. 217 Franklin.
" Sophia, b. 217 Franklin.
Leitch Bertha E. bkkpr. 291 Asy. b.29 Williams.
" Henry, stoves, plumbing, 291 Asylum, h. 29 Williams.
" Louisa, wid. Constantine, h. 518 Main.
" William, gardener, h.u. 14 Affleck.
" William, laborer, b. 28 Babcock.
" William R. mach. at 1 Laurel, h.u. 297 Park.
" ☞ see also Leach.
Leitz John E. repairer locks, etc. 328 Asylum, h. 153 Windsor av.
Leland Agnes O. Mrs. b.u. 63 Albany.
" Lewis Mrs. b. 40 Buckingham.
Leman Charles I. salesman, b. 52 Windsor.
Lemance James, clerk, 371 Park, b. 55 Lawrence.
Lemire Eddie, mach. at 1 Flower, b. 14 Putnam.
" Joseph, machinist at Pratt & Whitney Co. 1 Flower, b. 14 Putnam.
Lemke Paul Rev. h. 62 Babcock.
Lemonte Patrick, laborer at N.Y.R. r. 465 Asy.
Lemmon David, peddler, h.u. 52 Windsor.
Lenan Michael, b. 15 Huntley pl.
Lendrick Charles, butcher, b. 5 Vandyke.
Lenehan John T. bartend .125 Pearl, h.2u. 46 Tru.
" Julia C. bkkpr. 25 Asylum, b. 41 Williams.
" Kate Mrs. h. 46 Trumbull.
" Margaret T. b. 41 Williams.
" Michael G. saloon,125 Pearl, h.u.46 Trumbull.
" Michael J. coachman, h. 41 Williams.
" ☞ see also Linehan; Lennehan; Linnihan; Linnehan; Lynehan.
Lenhoff Chas. butcher at 26 Mulberry, h.4 Talcott.
Lenihan Catherine, dressm. 50, b.u. 50 Francis.
" John J. apprentice, 389½ Main, h. 42 Chst.
" Mary J. clerk at Brown, Thomson & Co. 942 Main, b.u. 42 Chestnut.
" Owen, watchman, 476 Cap. h.u. 50 Francis.
" Thomas, laborer, P.&R. h. 42 Chestnut.
Lennhoff Helen, cashier, 1030 Main, b. 4 Talcott.
Lennihan Jerry G. brakeman, b. 58 Spring.
" ☞ see also Lenahan; Lennehan; Linehan; Linnehan; Lynehan.
Lennon James F. grinder at 388, h. 625 Capitol.
" John, nickel plater, h.2u. 19 Talcott.
" Michael W. helper, h.2u. 38 South Prospect.
" Patrick, b. 16 Talcott.
" ☞ see also Linnon.
Lennox Alb. E. mail. clerk, P.O. h.u. 61 Madison.
" Arthur, clerk, h.u. 264 Jefferson.
" Charles W. cabinetmaker, b. 28 Woodbine.
" Eli, cabinetm. at 556 Main, h. 28 Woodbine.

Lennox Jennett Mrs. h.u. 52 Seymour.
" John, carpenter, h. 864 Broad.
" William J. plumber, 11 Haynes, b. 370 Asylum.
Lent George D. molder, b. 9 Kennedy.
" Ida A. b. 9 Kennedy.
" John L. molder, h. 9 Kennedy.
Lentz Edwin H. cigarmaker, h.u. 7 Blumenthal.
" John, cigarmanufacturer, h. 43 Sigourney.
Lenz Fred, pastry cook, b. 14 Morgan.
Leon Jerry, helper at N.Y.R. h. 183 Lawrence.
Leonard August W. mach. 30 Cush. b.46 Grand.
" Augustus T. jewelry, 1212, l.756 Main, rm.51.
" Benj. F. electrician, h.u.r. 28 Lawrence.
" Charles B. painter, h.u. 21 Huntley pl.
" Charles B. Jr. clerk at 711 Main, b. 21 Huntley pl.
" Charles S.J.O. mach. at 476 Cap. l. 109 Law.
" Chester A. letter carrier to Cap. h.u.1236 Mn.
" Cornelius, clerk at 3 Central, b. 66 Village.
" Cornelius M. salesman at Linus T. Fenn, 613 Main, h.u. 55 Hudson.
" Edward J. driller at Colts, h.u. 2 Oak.
" Estelle Mrs. dressmaker, 53, b.u. 53 Maple.
" Fred. T. painter, b.u. 21 Huntley pl.
" Hannah, wid. Thomas, h.2u. 66 Village.
" John, machinist at 581 Capitol, h. 22 Cedar.
" Joseph, clerk, h.r. 64 Ward.
" Kathryn H. clerk, b. 53 Madison.
" Louis H. clerk at 131 Main, h.r. 60 Church.
" Margaret, wid. Michael, h.u. 22 Cedar.
" Mary A. wid. Michael, b. 108 Hungerford.
" Matthew, laborer, b.u. 17 Kilbourn.
" O. W. clerk at 61 Albany, h. 12 Avon.
" Patrick, laborer, h.u. 10 Lawrence.
" Ralph Y. operator at N.E.R. b. 173 High.
" Sara G. dressmaker, 53, b.u. 53 Maple.
" Thomas, fireman, str. Hartford, 285 State.
" Thomas F. operator, b. 3 Talcott ct.
" William, mechanic, b.u. 46 Grand.
" William F. mach. at 130 Cush. b. 66 Willow.
" ☞ see also Larned, Learned.
Leopold Alfred, machinist, b. 45 Kinsley.
" Charles, helper at 1 Flower, h. 45 Kinsley.
LePard Frank H. floorwalker at Brown, Thomson & Co. 942 Main, h. 878 Asylum.
" Frederick P. selectman, h. 878 Asylum.
Lepper Adam D. mach. at 1 Flow. h.2u. 109 Law.
" Alfred, mach. at 1 Flow. h. 109 Lawrence.
" Bernard, mach. at 1 Flow. h.6 Bartholomew.
Lequoi John H. L. h.2u. 117 Benton.
Leresque Ernest, carptr. N.Y.R. h.252 Lawrence.
LeRoy Bros. h. 67 Morgan.
" Bros. fruit dealers, etc. 1859-1863 Main.
   J. B. LeRoy.   Jos. M. LeRoy.   Dominic A. LeRoy.
" D. & N. N. saloon, 212 Front.
   Donato LeRoy.   N. N. LeRoy.
" Donato, (D. & N.N. LeR.) h.u. 82 Morgan.
" Dominic A. (LeRoy Bros.) h. 180 Ann.
" J. Baptiste, (LeRoy Bros.) h.r. 3 East.
" John, laborer, h.3u. 67 Morgan.
" Joseph M. (LeRoy Bros.) h.2u. 1361 Main.
" Nicholas N. (D.&N.N.LeR.) h.u. 67 Morgan.
" Peter A. real estate, h. 1355 Main.
" Rocco, helper, b.u. 67 Morgan.
" Sarah J. wid. Augustus N. b. 80 Kenyon.

**For Sale Advertisements Bring Results in the Post.**

LeSantry Daniel, laborer, h.2u. 158 Front.
" Rock, motorman St.Ry. h.2u. 158 Front.
" Salvatori, cigarmaker, b.2u. 158 Front.
Leschke Emil, (*L. & Pletcher*,) h. 28 Chapel.
" & Pletcher, tobacconists, 1037 Main.
  Emil Leschke.  Jacob Pletcher.
Leshane William,driver at 1128 Main, h. Albany.
Leslie Wm.H.printer at 2 State, b.5 Ellsworth pl.
Lesnia Albert, helper, 1 Flower, h. 1035 Broad.
Lessard William,clerk, 114 Asy.b.24 Greenwood.
Lessel Lucy, h. 13 South Hudson.
" S. M. Mrs. h. 13 South Hudson.
Lessizza Antone, laborer, 285 State, h. Dutch pt.
" Paul, laborer, 285 State, h. Dutch pt.
Lester Arvilla Mrs. h.4u. 18 Trumbull.
" Charles E. W. cutter at 59¼ Tru. h. E.H.t.
" F. Josephine, wid. G. W. b. 37 Niles.
" Frank B. cutter at 60 Asylum, h.u. 57 Russ.
" George, at 367 Capitol, b. 57 Russ.
" George R. clerk at Conn. Fire Insurance
  Co. 51 Prospect, b. 37 Niles.
" George W. Mrs. h. 17 Russ.
" Harry B. at 476 Capitol, h. 211 Ashley.
" Henry E. clerk at 95 Pleasant, b. 57 Russ.
" Henry H. plater at William Rogers Mfg.
  Co. 66 Market, h. E.H.t.
" Howard W. sec. Veeder Mfg. Co. b. E.H.t.
" Irene S. clerk at 843 Main, h. 100 Hopkins.
" James, conductor St.Ry. h. 35 Capen.
" James G.inspector at Pope Mfg. Co. h.E.H.t.
" Jennie M. clerk at 115 State, b. 35 Capen.
" Leon E. machinist at 1 Flower, b.u.173 Russ.
" Mabel E. teacher at Arsenal school, b.E.H.t.
" Mabel P. accountant at T. Sission & Co.
  729 Main, b. 35 Capen.
" Mary, wid. Charles E. h.u. 25 Allen pl.
" Michael J. blacksmith, h.u. 47 Hawthorn.
" Newell, cutter, b.u. 1295 Main.
" William W. druggist, 367, h. 329 Capitol.
Lettiere John, carpenter, h.r. 1177 Main.
" Joseph, clerk, b. 81 Morgan.
" Pasquale, carpenter, h. 2 North.
" Roxy, clerk at 745 Main, b. 27 Kilbourn.
" Theresa, wid. Carlo, h.u. 27 Kilbourn.
Leutzenkirchen☞ *see Luetzenkirchen.*
LeValley Benj. W. l. 373 Asylum, room 10.
" George S. b. 36 Jefferson.
" James, marblepolisher. 40 High, b.u. 35 Law.
LeValli Joseph A. barber,26 State, h. 22 Florence.
" ☞ *see also Lavelli.*
Levee Anna, at 99 Pratt, h. 3 Asylum.
" Bessie M. stenographer, b.u. 1086 Main.
" Nathan F. carpenter, h.u. 1086 Main.
Leveillie Napoleon P.assem. at Popes,b.u.488 Mn.
Leven Jacob, dressmaker, 164, h. 164 Front.
Levenson David, tailor, b.u. 174 Front.
" Hyman, harnessm. at 8 Sig. h. 13 Affleck.
" Levi, tailor, h.u. 174 Front.
" Louis, tailor. b.u 174 Front.
" Morris, harnessm. at 8 Sig. b. 13 Affleck.
" ☞ *see also Levinson.*
Leventhal Frank, jewelry, 15, h. 15 Florence.
" Louis, peddler, h.u. 80 Morgan.
" Simon, enameler at Popes, h. 56 Chestnut.
" Solomon, peddler, h.u. 21 North.

Lever John, mach. at 1 Flow. b. 303 Lawrence.
Levesque Ernest,carptr. at N.Y.R. h.u. 252 Law.
" Hector I. painter at St.Ry. h.u. 43 Amity.
" Joseph F. carpenter, h. 154 Brown.
" Joseph R. mach. at 1 Flower, b. 43 Amity.
" Nelson, h. 7 Davenport.
" Oscar P.machinist at 1 Flower, h. 41 Grand.
" Philip A. mach. at 1 Flow. h.u. 43 Amity.
" Rebecca, b.u. 43 Amity.
Levin Bernhard, barber at 85 Front, b.3u. 80 Shel.
" George, shoemaker, 147, h. 147 Front.
" Holman, peddler, h.u. 15 North.
" Joseph, inspector at Popes, h. 9 Queen.
" Max, agent at 108 Trumbull, h. 11 Pleasant.
" Max, paper, twine, etc. 41, h. 41 North.
" Max, shoemaker, 11, h. 11 Park.
" Meyer, peddler, h. 22 North.
" Morris, pressman at 618 Cap. h. 190 Front.
" Samuel, tailor, b. 22 North.
" Samuel, tailor at 556 Asylum, h.2u. 22 Ford.
Levine Julius, h. 8 Forest.
Levinson Abraham J. bottler at 70, h. 68 Temple.
" P. peddler, h.u. 57 Morgan.
" ☞ *see also Levenson.*
Levintow Louis, clerk at 956 Main, b. 21 North.
" Samuel, barber at 51 Windsor, h. 21 North.
Levierge A. W. cigarmaker at 104 Asylum,
  h.2u. 17 Williams.
" Emma L. milliner,756 Mn. b.2u.17 Williams.
Levitt Joseph L.clerk at Brown, Thomson & Co.
  942 Main, b. 176 Front.
" Louis, hardware, 174½, h. 176 Front.
" Stephen, carptr. at 155 Ch.O. h. 176 Front.
Levoie ☞ *see Lavoie.*
Levy Adolph (*Fishel & L.*) h. New York c.
" Heyman P. jeweler, 862 Main, h.u. 190 State.
" Isaac, butcher, h.u. 84 Barbour.
" Josiah W. attorney, 9 Asy. h. 198 High.
" Louis, salesman, 501 Asylum, h. 162 Clark.
" Louis, shoem. at 1192 Main, h.u.101 Windsor.
" Morris, (*Fishel & L.*) 189 State, h. N. Y.
" Morris, fruit, h. 33 Windsor.
" Morris, operator, h. 52 Governor.
" Morris L. tailor at 46 Asy. h. 52 Governor.
" Samuel, ladies wrappers, 228, h. 228 Front.
" Thomas, laborer, h.u. 3 Ellery.
" William,laborer at 2 Union pl. h. 70 Martin.
" ☞ *see also Leavy.*
Lewellyn Henry, machinehand at Colts, h.u.r. 62
  Vanblock.
Lewis Albert A. mach. 13 Central, h. 245 Putnam.
" Arthur, rubberworker at 690, b. 565 Park.
" Brayton S. draughtsman at 581 Capitol, b.
  50 Lincoln.
" Caroline L.wid. Norman V. h.2u.42 Hopkins.
" Chas. H.engineer at 24 Mec. h. 221 Sheldon.
" Charles T. inspec. at 690 Park, b. 12 Heath.
" Daisy, nurse, 48, h.u. 48 Church.
" David A. blacksm. at 352 Alb.h.u. 218 Allyn.
" David W. machinist, b. 218 Allyn.
" Dennis, lather, b. 33 Mechanic.
" E. W. at 98 Asylum, b. 68 Woodbine.
" Edwin P. machinist, 1 Flow. b. 315 Pearl.
" Ella M. at Hartford Life Ins. Co. 252 Asy-
  lum, b. 21 Greenwood.

Lewis Elizabeth, b. 1469 Broad.
" Fred C. signpainter, b. Eaton.
" Fred Hawley, at 185 Pearl, b. 21 Greenwood.
" Fred. T. Jr. clerk at 197 Asy. b. 13 Niles.
" Frederick E. bookkeeper, b. 1469 Broad.
" Geo. A. engineer, h. 60½ Walnut.
" George B. butcher, h. 93 Hudson.
" Geo. C. helper at 232 Shel. b.u. 218 Allyn.
" George S. millinery, 145 Asy. l. 427 Main.
" Harriet, wid. Geo. W. h. 9 Avon.
" Harriet M. wid. James, b. 14 Seyms.
" Henry, (H. L. & Co.) h. 32 Clark.
" Henry & Co. merchant tailors, 174 State.
　　Henry Lewis.　　　　　　E. G. Lasbury.

**LEWIS HENRY B.** hacks, livery and boarding stable, 22 Trinity, b. 651 Main. Telephone 819-2.
" Isaac, tailor, 80 State, rm. 8, h. 9 Chapel.
" Jackson A. laborer, h. 60½ Walnut.
" James C. painter, h. Eaton.
" John, laborer, h. 16 Ellery.
" John B. medical director at Travelers Insurance Co. 56 Prospect, h. 312 Farmington.
" John H. driver at 554, b. 86 Flower.
" John R. plumber at 20 Church, h. E.H.t.
" Justus P. superintendent Pratt & Cady Co. 556 Capitol, h. 175 Sigourney.
" Leroy S. h. 115 Ann.
" Mary, wid. Jesse, dressm. 489, h. 489 Main.
" Mary B. b. 312 Farmington.
" Mary P. teacher at 44, b. 44 Beacon.
" Mehitable, wid. Wm. H. h. 21 Greenwood.
" Richard D. inspec. at Popes, b. 116 Franklin.
" Robert E. buffer at Wm. Rogers Mfg. Co. 66 Market, b.u. 218 Allyn.
" Robert H. (Harvey & L.) h. 16 Florence.
" T. Jarvis, at Phœnix Ins. Co. 64 Pearl, h. E.H.t.
" Thomas, repairer at Popes, h. 230 Franklin.
" Timothy, painter, h. 33 Mechanic.
" Timothy Jr. lather, b. 33 Mechanic.
" Walter E. diesinker at Popes, h.u. 18 Imlay.
" William B. clerk at 97 Asylum, b. E.H.t.
" William G. painter, b.2u. 1413 Main.
" William W. b. 2 Holcomb.
" ☞ see also Luis.
Lexell Victor, gardener, b. 37 Park.
Leycett Fred W. patterm. at 40 Cush. h. 179 Haw.
Leyden John T. enam. at Popes, b.2u. 57 Spruce.
Libby Lawrence R. engir. 164 State, h. 96 Maple.
" Locke A. trav. salesman at Tucker & Goodwin, 12 Hurlburt, h.u. 438 Windsor av.
Libutzke Fred, clerk at 818 Park, b. 24 Smith.
" John G. mach. at 388 Capitol, b. 24 Smith.
Lichtblau Morris (Model Tailoring Co.) 222 Pearl, h. 18 South Ann.
Liebert Arthur C. at Connecticut Mutual Life Ins. Co. 783 Main, h. East Hartford t.
" Mitchel O. policeman, h.u. 25 Pleasant.
" ☞ see also Leibert.
Liebler Mary, clerk at Brown, Thomson & Co. 942 Main, b.2u. 20 Alden.
Lietschuh Gustaf, screwm. at 476 Cap. b. 622 Mn.
Lifschitz D. carpenter, h. 5 North.
" Samuel, peddler, h. 190 Front.

Lilja Julius B. machinist at Pratt & Whitney Co. 1 Flower, h. 9 Putnam.
Lillis Bridget, wid. Frank, b. 235 Park.
Lilly Howard J. driver at 185 Asy. b.u. 31 Chapel.
" O. K. barber at 347 Allyn, l. 22 Hopkins.
Lims Wm. W. saddler, 8 Sig. h.u. 29 Lawrence.
Limyanski Myer. peddler, h.u. 201 Front.
Linane Michael, b. 15 Huntley pl.
Lincks George, teamster at 165 Win. b. 20 Hicks.
" John F. baker, 156, h. 156 Front.
Lincoln Lillian, wid. Brooks M. h.2u. 264 Jef.
LINCOLN CHARLES G. (L., Seyms & Co.) 34 Market, h. 68 Niles. See page 522.
" Charles L. president The Lincoln Co. 54 Arch, h. 73 Wethersfield.
" Charles P. with The Lincoln Co. 54 Arch, h. 82 Wethersfield.

**LINCOLN CO. THE,** proprietors Phœnix Iron Works, 54-70 Arch. See p. 522.
" Dwight F. h. 56 Park.
" Elizabeth B. wid. George S. h. 129 Capitol.
" Ella E. b. 56 Park.
" Eunice M. wid. Ivers, h. 210 Windsor av.
" Eveline, wid. S. W. h. 189 Sigourney.

**LINCOLN FREDERICK M.** real estate, appraiser, notary, auctioneer; sec'y Hartford Real Estate Exchange, 911 Main, h. 129 Capitol. See page 427.
" Gilbert, salesman at Lincoln, Seyms & Co. 34 Market, b. 68 Niles.
" Kate Mrs. laundress, h.u. 4 Huntley.
" Mary J. wid. Theo. M. senior, h. 104 Capitol.
" Robt. M. clerk at 1417 Main, h. Windsor av.
" Theodore M. secy. and treas. The Lincoln Co. 54 Arch, h. 86 Wethersfield.

**LINCOLN, SEYMS & CO.** wholesale teas, coffee and spices, tobacco, etc. 34 Market. See page 588.
　　Charles G. Lincoln.　　　Robert N. Seyms.
Lind George, at Adams Exp. Co. b. 39 Chapel.
" Geo. carptr. &c. Bushnell park, h.u. 6 Lewis.
" Jesse N. clerk at 278 Asylum, h. 43 Dean.
" Nicholas A. teamster, h. 146 Mather.
" Peter L. laborer, b. 26 Trumbull.
" ☞ see also Lynde.
Lindberg Anders G. dropforger at 142 Russ, b. 1316 Broad.
Lindblad Alfred, coachm. at 2, l. 2 Wethersfield.
Lindbloom Herman, printer, h. 54 Lawrence.
Linde Annie, nurse, 14 Church, rm. 2.
" Ulrich E. polisher at Popes, h. 1143 Broad.
Linden Albert, washer at 690 Park, h. 69 Francis.
" Building, 427 Main.
" Louise, b. 69 Francis.
" William, millm. at 690 Park, b. 69 Francis.
Lindell Frank, gardener, 58, b 58 Prospect av.
Linder Jacob J. chef at 835 Main, b.r. 206 Asy.
Linderoth Victor, diesinkr. at Popes, b. 230 Zion.
Lindgren Arynid E. machinist at 556 Capitol, b. 137 Babcock.
" Oscar, dropfor. 142 Russ, b.2u. 1322 Broad.
" Oscar, screwm. at 476 Cap. b. 41 Mulberry.
" Per O. dropfgr. at 142 Russ, h. 54 Flower.

**THE POST DELIVERED AT YOUR HOME DAILY, PER MONTH, FIFTY CENTS.**

*H. B. LITTLE.*          *C. W. HALL.*

# H. B. LITTLE & CO.,
## Pattern Makers
### AND MANUFACTURERS OF
## Cutting Blocks,
### 33 WELLS STREET.

Lindner Alvin, engraver at 177 Asy. h. 23 Morris.
" Anne E. wid. August, h. 8 Fales.
" Fred. machinist at 476 Capitol, b. 8 Fales.
" Henry, forem. at Pope Tube Co. h. 8 Fales.
Lindsay Mary H. b. 301 New Britain.
" Samuel, clerk at Pope Tube Co. b. 58 Dean.
Lindsey Joseph, laborer, h. 34 Hudson.
" Joseph Jr. apprent. 556 Mn. b. 34 Hudson.
Lindsley Benjamin, clerk at 852 Main, h. Fkn.
" Carl V. clerk at 921 Mn. b. 24 Windsor av.
" Edgar C. pressfeeder at Case, Lockwood & Brainard Co. 141 Pearl, b. 157 Franklin.
" Herbert E. machinist, h. 157 Franklin.
" ☞ see also Linsley.
Lindholm August, carpenter, b. 14 Rose.
Lindstrom Agnes, domestic, 20 South Hudson.
" John A. mach. at 77 Com. h.u. 23 Wells.
Linehan Mary L. teacher South sch. b. 58 Bkm.
" ☞ see also Lenahan; Lennehan; Lennihan; Linnehan; Lynehan.
Lines Ellen, wid. Timothy, h.u. 27 Mechanic.
" Howard E. clerk at 921, b. 642 Main.
" William S. b. 12 Highland.
Ling Andrew, tailor 37 Wells, b. 108 Hopkins.
Lingard Frank, clerk at 1079, h. 580 Main.
Lingleton Daniel, ostler at 4 Central.
Lingren John J. molder at 54 Arch, h.u. 39 Chst.
Link Charles, machinist at 388 Cap. h. 70 Ward.
" John, filer at Colts, b. 133 Front.
" Pauline, wid. Paul, h. 99 Hudson.
Linke Emil F. treas. The Unitype Co., Manchester t. h.u. 280 Main.
" Sophia, wid. William, b. 19 Wethersfield.
" Wm. L. cashier at George W. Moore & Co. farm loans, 759 Main, h. 19 Wethersfield.
**LINN EDGAR G.** sec'y Conn. Building & Loan Association, 252 Asylum, h. 356 Laurel.          *See page 430.*
" Iosette, nurse, 20 South Hudson.
Linnon James W. at 175 Pearl, b. 23 West.
" John M. machinist at 1 Flower, b. 4 Queen.
" John J. bricklayer, h. 23 West.
" John J. Jr. drugclerk, 391 Main, b. 23 West.
" Michael W. janitor at Brown school, 160 Market, h. 4 Queen.
" ☞ see also Lennon.
Linsley John, mech. at 54 Arch, b. 7 Wadsworth.
" Marcus M. trav'g salesman at E. Tucker's Sons, 100 Trumbull, h.u. 926 Main, rm. 69.
" William H. driller at Colts, h. 7 Wadsworth.
" ☞ see also Lindsley.

Linton Earl L. mach. at 1 Flow. b. Burnside v.
" Mary, wid. Alexander, h. 10 Franklin.
" Nettie Mrs.: b.3u. 6 Trumbull.
Lints George, helper at 61 Asylum.
Lion Fire Ins. Co. agency, 197 Asylum, Martin Bennett manager, J. H. Brewster, asst. manager.
Lippert Charles C. rubberworker at 690 Park, h.2u. 21 Wadsworth.
Lippmann Bernard, rabbi, h.u. 47 Morgan.
" Solomon, clerk at 172 Front, b.u. 47 Morgan.
Lippold Alfred B. machinist, h.r.u. 45 Kinsley.
" Charles, helper, h.u.r. 45 Kinsley.
" Lewis, machinist. h.2u.r. 7½ Oak.
Lips Albert, music teacher, b. 1209 Main.
Lipsey Robert G. bkkpr. Willimantic Linen Co. 391 Allyn, b. 23 Ward.
Litchfield County market, 1157 Main.
" George, laborer, h. 48 Madison av.
Litnow Joseph B. mach. 142 Russ, b. 198 Capen.
Littell Elton G. student, Trinity, b. 122 Vernon.
Little Arthur H. driver at Adams Express Co. h. 87 Brook.
" Augustus S. engineer at 225 Sheldon, h. 100 Jefferson.
" George H. salesman at Smith, Northam & Co. 129 State, h. 87 Buckingham.
**LITTLE H. B. & Co.** pattern and model makers, 33 Wells.          *See page 232.*
H. B. Little.          C. W. Hall
" Harry R. carpenter at N.Y.R. b. 101 Ann.
" Horace B. (*L.H.B.& Co.*) h. 44 Annawan.
" James Oliver, carpenter, b. 118 Webster.
" Robert S. carpenter, h. 1 Worcester pl.
**LITTLE SAMUEL A.**, D.D.S. dentist, rm. 53, Ballerstein building, 904 Main, b. 32 Buckingham.
" ☞ see also Littell.
Littlefield Ambrose B. framer at 251 Pearl, h.u. 108 Albany.
" Jesse L. mach. 142 Russ, h.u. 26 Hopkins.
Littlejohn Robert, b.u. 33 Chapel.
Livingston James, landscape gardener, h. Quaker lane
" Mich. J. carptr. 116 Mar. h.2u. 1053 Broad.
" Thos. gardener, h. 99 Whitmore.
" William, gardener, h.u. 74 Flower.
" Wm. F. carpenter, h. 41 Woodbridge.
" Wm. F. Mrs. boardinghouse, 41 Woodbridge,
Lizzerani Charles, painter, h.4u. 190 Front.
Ljungquist John W. driver, h.u. 140 Martin.
Lleffingwell ☞ see Leffingwell.
Llewellyn ☞ see Lewellyn.
Lloyd A. P. Miss, b. 200 Evergreen.
" Addie J. nurse, 200, b.3u. 200 Allyn.
" Annie L. steno. at 66 State, b. 22 Morris.
" Charles H. policeman, h.u. 22 Morris.
" Charles R. watchmaker, l. 118 Asylum.
" David, h.2u. 10 Goodman.
" Edward J. mason at 56, h. 56 Buckingham.
" Hugh, painter at 158 Woodland.
" Lottie, b.u. 22 Morris.
" William B. Mrs. photographer, 11 Pratt, h. 143 Trumbull.

**As A NEWSPAPER, THE POST LEADS.**

**LOAN AND GUARANTEE CO. OF CONN.,** 49 Pearl. *See page 441.*
Lobdell Bell, wid. Edwin S. h.u. 23 Affleck.
" Bessie, teacher, b.u. 23 Affleck.
" Eugene S. mach. at 1 Laurel, h. 300 Park.
Lobermeyer Alex. R. mach. 133 Shel. h. 23 John.
Locke Ira J. beltmaker at Jewell Belting Co. 15 Trumbull, h.u. 17 Sanford.
" Thomas F.horsesh'r, 29 Wells, h.33 Wooster.
Lockhart John, watch. str.Middletown, 285 State.
Lockwood Albert, laborer N.Y.R. h. 284 Allyn.
" Charles, coachman, b. 10 Highland.
" Chas.M.sash & blindmkr.554Mn.h. 32 Wdbg.
" Frank P. foreman, 41 Trumbull, h. Newington junction.
" Fred T. carpenter, 155 Ch.O. h. 28 Wdbg.
" James J. helper, N.Y.R. b.u. 284 Allyn.
" James L. electrotyper at 41 Tru. b. 68 Far.
" James M. driver at 71 Asy. b.u. 98 Hopkins.
" Millard F. polisher at 476 Cap. b. 252 Law.
" William H. electrotyper, 41 Tru. h. 68 Far.
" Wm. W. teamster, 2 Chapel, b. 58 Governor.
Locomotive,quarterly, Steam Boiler Co. 650 Main.
Lodge Walter B. shadehanger at Brown, Thomson & Co. 942 Main, b. 44 Wooster.
Lodovowski Henry, laborer, b.2u. 56 Sheldon.
" John, laborer, b.2u. 56 Sheldon.
Loeb Helena, wid. Charles, groceries, 54½, h. 54 Wooster.
Loeffler George J.druggist, 705 Mn. h. 99 Hudson.
Loescher Anton F. mach. 9 Haynes, h.u. 69 Ward.
" Christina, wid. August, h.2u. 69 Ward.
" Frank L. pinmaker, Jewells, h.2u.110 Ward.
" Gustav H. pinm. at 31 Hicks, h. 55 Elliott.
" Herman C. wireworker at 618 Capitol, b.2u. 69 Ward.
" Mary Mrs. h.u. 23 Wolcott.
" Wilhelm, h. 232 Windsor av.
Loeser Alfred W. *(F. C.& A.W.L.)* h. 295 Park.
" Fred C. *(F.C. & A. W. L.)* b.u. 289 Park.
" Frederick C. & Alfred W. saloon, 289 Park.
Frederick C. Loeser. Alfred W. Loeser.
" George, bottler at 291, b. 289 Park.
" Lena, wid. Peter, h.u. 289 Park.
" Peter, b. 289 Park.
Lofferty Michael, laborer, h.u. 319 Front.
Loffmin Alexander, driver at 501 Asylum.
Loft Lazarus, (Capitol Tea and Coffee Co.) h. 33 Bellevue.
Loftus J.J. Rev. asst. at St.Patrick's, b.82 Church.
Logan Jesse G. laborer, h. 68 Albany.
" Matilda, dressmaker, 229, h.u. 229 Pearl.
" Theresa, dressmaker, 229, b.u. 229 Pearl.
Lohnes Hardy T. foreman 247 Pearl, h. 166 Allyn.
Lohs Frederic A. tailor, 88 Pearl, h. 48 Windsor.
Lomax Robert, harnessmaker at 454 Asylum, h. Wilson station.
Lombard Arthur D. mechanic at 83 Woodbine, h.u. 89 Hawthorn.
" Frank, foreman at Billings & Spencer Co. 142 Russ, b. 127 Oak.
" Frank A. theological student, 1507 Broad.
" Martin E. *(Cady & L.)* h. 15 East.
" Nicholas, laborer, b. 105 Commerce.
" S. Anna, wid. F. B. h. 53 Capitol.

**The Post, 12 Cents a Week, Delivered at Your Home.**

## LONG'S HOTEL AND PALACE DINING ROOMS,

### 78, 80, AND 82 STATE STREET.

*Open Day and Night.*
*Private Tables for Ladies.*

**Board by the Week, 21 Meals, $3.50.**
**Rates, $1.00 per Day and upward.**

*900 Furnished Rooms.*
*Steam Heat and Electric Light in Every Room.*
*Fine Wines and Lager Delivered for family use.*

### ROOF GARDEN

**LONG BROTHERS,** *Connected with the Hotel.*
*Proprietors.*

Lombardi Rocco, laborer, h. 319 Front.
London Benjamin, operator. h. 101 Windsor.
Londonski Thos. lab. Pope Tube Co. b. 4 Elm.
Londrigan William, teamster, b.r. 105 Windsor.
Londry Ashil E. saloon, 290 Park, h. 1137 Broad.
Lonergan Augustine, law clerk at 14 State, b. Rockville c.
Long Arthur E. buyer at Brown, Thomson & Co. 942 Main, h. Springfield, Mass.
LONG BROS. proprietors Mirror Palace Dining Rooms, 78–82 State. *See page 233.*
John C. Long. Timothy J. Long. J. M. Long.
" Carl Herman, clerk at 78 Asy. b.2u. 33 Bab.
" Clarence E. clerk, 700 Main, b. 12 Belden.
" Fred W. mach. at 1 Flow. b. 15 Williams.
" G. Clarke, porter, b. 47 Prospect.
" Geo. A.patternm. at 1 Flow.h. 244 Putnam.
" Geo. H. iceman, 48 Ann, l. 373 Asy. rm. 14.
" James, mechanic, b.2u. 55 Liberty.
" James T. polisher at Popes, h. N.B.t.
" Jeremiah, laborer, b. 101 Main.
" Jeremiah M. *(Long Bros.)* h. 28 Congress.
" John, motorman St.Ry. h.2u. 33 Babcock.
" John, repairer, b. 101 Main.
" John, rubberw. at 581 Capitol, h. 102 Ward.
" John C. *(Long Bros.)* saloon, 583 Main, h. 73 Grove.
" Margaret, wid. Michael, b. 73 Grove.
" Mary A. teacher Arsenal school, b. 73 Grove.
" Mary E. Mrs. h. 15 Williams.
" Michael C. shipper at Popes, b. 39 Russ.
" Patrick, waiter at 835, b. 101 Main.
" Patrick J. laborer at 98 Kil. h.u. 55 Liberty.
" Timothy J. *(Long Bros.)* b. 73 Grove.
" Wah, laundry, 287, h. 287 Asylum.
Longdon Arthur C. boxmaker, h. 80 Madison.
" Emma A. wid. Thomas, h.u. 231 Capen.
" John W. carpenter at 30 Washington, h. 78 Webster.
Longfield Doc. painter, b. 25 Central.
Longworth John C. butcher at 250, h. 250 N.B.
" Joseph, saloon, 27, h.u. 29 North.
" Joseph F. h.2u. 29 North.
" Mary, dressmaker, 29, b.u. 29 North.
Look Frank B. physician, 104, b. 104 Church.
Loomis A. Clayton, bookkeeper at 133 Sheldon, h. 141 Washington.

Loomis A. L. Miss, stenographer at 1 Laurel, b. 141 Washington.
" Archibald G. president Ætna National Bank, 644 Main, h. 142A Washington.
" Archie H. ass't teller Society for Savings, 31 Pratt, b. 142A Washington.
" Augustus, engineer, engine No. 7, 480 Windsor av. h. 130 Clark.
" Bessie R. stenog. 154 Pearl, b. 251 Lawrence.
" Burdett, manufacturer, h. Prospect av.
" Burdett Jr. h. Far. c. South Highland av.
" Carrie M. Mrs. dressmkr. 721 Main, rm. 56.
" Charles, carpenter, 128, h. 128 Jefferson.
" Chas. Russell, artist, h. 15 Vernon.
" Charles W. clerk at Brown, Thomson & Co. 942 Main, h. 40 Russell.
" Clara, instructor at Morse's Hartford Business college, b. 58 Church.
" Clarissa, b. 36 Jefferson.
" Clinton F. commer. traveler at 44 Market, h.u. 53 Sargeant.
" Dwight, ex-state referee and attorney, 739 Main, h. 278 Farmington.
" Edwin R. roadmastr. N.Y.R. h.u. 32 Hopkins.
" Eliza A. b. 36 Jefferson.
" Elizabeth, b. 36 Jefferson.
" Florence M. stenographer, b. 78 Chestnut.
" Florence Mrs. treasurer, 933 Main, h. Rockville t.
" Frances A. wid. W. G. h. 20 Buckingham.
" Frank W. surveyor, 114 Pearl, h.u. 67 Sigourney.
" Geo. A. contractor at Popes, h. 12 Columbia.
" Harry S. clerk at 83 Asy. b. Windsor t.
" Helen, Mrs. nurse, h. 39 Wadsworth.
" Helen A. cashier at Sage, Allen & Co. 898 Main, b. 39 Wadsworth.
" Helen F. at Hartford Life Ins. Co. 252 Asylum, b. 27 Spring.
" Hiram G. surveyor, 114 Pearl, h. 193 Sigourney.
" Howard, teamster, h.u. 68 Sheldon.
" James M. condu. N.Y.R. h.u. 73 Windsor av.
" John W. at Ætna Life Insurance Co. 650 Main, h. 149 High.
" Mary, b. 36 Jefferson.
" Melvena C. Mrs. h. 926 Main, rm. 73.
" Neland, salesman at Lincoln, Seyms & Co. 34 Market, h. 104 Hungerford.
" Susie H. stenographer at Silas Chapman, Jr. 51 Trumbull, b. 335 Windsor av.
" Thos. R. clerk, Phœnix Mutual Life Ins. Co. 49 Pearl, h. 320 Farmington.

Loomis Wm. F. asst. sec'y at National Machine Co. 111 to 133 Sheldon, b. 255 Main.
" ☞ *see also Lokmis ; Lumis.*
Looney Catherine, wid. Jeremiah, h. 35 Church.
" Daniel E. asst. form. 128 Com. b.u. 11 Morris.
" James, waiter at 244, b. 245 State.
" Jeremiah T. teamster, h.u. 220 Sheldon.
" Mary & Kate, laundry, 35, h.u. 35 Church.
Loong Sun, laundry, 284 Park.
Lopachine ☞ *see Lupachira.*
Loper Edward T. painter at 17 Elm, b.2u. 168 Windsor av.
" Mary Mrs. dressm. 168, h.2u. 168 Windsor av.
Lopianski Benjamin, grocer, h. 20 Russell.
" Morris, grocer, 19, h. 19 Morgan.
Loprete Domencio, laborer, h. 190 Front.
" Pasguale, barber, 47, h. 47 Albany.
" Rodolph, barber, 9½ Wells, h. 105 Front.
" Savirio, laborer, h.u. 78 Charles.
Lorber Harriet A. nurse, 14 Church, rm. 10.
Lord Anna M. wid. Frank J. h. 34 Ch.O. pl.
" Chas. H. yeast, office, 281 Allyn, h. 15 Center.
" Clifford A. operator at 40 Governor, l. 24 Windsor av.
" Frank J. billiards, 32 Asylum, h.u.55 Garden.
" Fred. C. mach. at 1 Flower, h. 34 C.O.pl.
" Frederick E. mach. at 1 Flower, h. W.P.v.
" George F. h. 5 Lafayette.
" Harlow A. miller at 40 Elm, h.u. 16 Beach.
" Hezekiah B. machinist, N.Y.R. b. 110 Pratt.
" Horace G. foreman drop shop at Colts, h.u 254 Jefferson.
" J. M. machinist at 28 High, b. W.L.t.
" James J. rubberw. 690 Park, b. 28 Walnut.
" James W. barber, 299, b.u. 299 Windsor av.
" John R. insp. 142 Russ, b. 24 Windsor av.
" Jos. E. gearcutter, 1 Flower, h. W.P.v.
" Leon H. machinist at 1 Flower, b. W.P.v.
" Malcolm Eugene, carpenter at 155 Charter Oak, h. 24 Belden.
" S. Clarke, organist of Asylum Hill church, h. 111 Elm.
" Sylvester S. bookkeeper, h.u. 30 Wooster.
Lorentson John, mechanic at 581 Cap. h. 56 Haw.
Lorenz Richard R. bottler, h. 55 Kibbe.
" Wm. A. mechanical engineer, 370 Asylum, h. 96 Garden.
Lorenzen Edmund J. draughtsman at 1 Laurel, b. 41 Madison.
" Immanuel, mach. 142 Russ, h.u. 41 Madison.
Loshnock Albert, mach. at 388 Cap. h. 83 Temple.
" Albert Jr. operator, 388 Cap. b. 83 Temple.
" John A. operator at 388 Cap. b. 83 Temple.
Losty Agnes, wid. Edward, h.2u. 137 Zion.
" Ann, wid. Patrick, h. 49 Chestnut.
" Ed. T. policeman, h. 39 Hamilton.
" James A. blacksmith, h.u. 57 Village.
" John F. h.u.r. 1128 Main.
" Joseph L. mach. at 30 Cush. b. 50 John.
" Mary, grocer, 115, h. 115 Zion.
" Patrick, teamster, 115, h. 115 Zion.
" William, teamster, b. 115 Zion.

**LOTKER KARL,** furrier, 189, h. 189 Main.                    *See page 420.*

Lotze Alfred, h. 29 Mulberry.
"   Charles A. h. 77 Hungerford.
"   Fred, b.u. 29 Mulberry.
"   Otto H. grocer, 3 Clark, h. 72 Grove.
"   Reinholt, tailor, 720 Mn.rm.17, h.29 Mulberry.
"   Reinholt Jr. tailor at 720 Main, h. 26 Tru.
"   ☞ see also Lutz.
Louden Frank, b. 2 Holcomb.
Loughlin Ann, wid. John, h.u. 25 Flower.
"   John, painter, h.u. 4 Donald.
"   John, slater at Colts, h.2u. 95 Jefferson.
"   Patrick, hackdriver, h. 18½ Howard.
"   Peter, mach. at 1 Flow. b. 1478 Broad.
"   William, molder at 616 Cap. h.u. 15 Howard.
"   ☞ see Laughlin; McLaughlin;  O'Laugh-
        lin; O'Loughlin.
Loughman John, h.u. 573 Main.
"   Patrick F. marblepolisher at 54 Windsor av.
        h.2u. 40 Flower.
"   Patrick F. Mrs. groceries, 40, h.2u. 40 Flow.
Louis Antonio, lab. Pope Tube Co.h. 206 Asylum.
"   Charles, agt. at 576 Main, h. 16½ Morris.
Lounsbury Cooke, attorney, 75 Pratt, h. 19 High-
        land.
Love Wm. DeL. Jr. Rev. pastor Pearl St. Cong.
        Church, park commissioner, h. 354 Laurel.
Lovejoy Mr. machinist, b. 97 Trumbull.
Loveland A. C. & Co. junk shop, 65 Pleasant
        A. C. Loveland.         M. Greenberg.
"   A. C. (A. C. L. & Co.) h. 18 Avon.
"   A. L. motorman St.Ry. 115 State.
"   Annie Mrs. at 265 Asylum, h. E.H.t.
"   Benjamin W. at Conn. Mutual Life Ins. Co.
        983 Main, h. 5 Preston.
"   Celestia, h. 283 Windsor av.
"   Charles E. b.2u. 41 Wooster.
"   Elizabeth R. wid. F. Harvey, h.2u. 216 Wind-
        sor av.
"   Ella W. at 34 Asylum, b. 163 Ashley.
"   Frederick, polisher at Popes, h. 54 Eaton.
"   George C. h. 18 Ford.
"   Henry E. salesman 9 Haynes, h. 41 Bellevue.
"   Lillian E. Mrs. prop. Park Hotel, 18 Ford.
"   Mason J. bookkeeper, b. 1153 Main.
"   Wilbur F. mach. 1 Flower, h. 1214 Broad.
Loveless William E. machinist, b. 41 Flower.
Lovell Charles D. grocer, 50, h. 50 Front.
"   & Tracy Co. oils, grease, 218 State.
Lovenbein Adolph, printer, 174 Pearl, b. 63 Pro.
Loveridge Wm. J. filer at Colts, h.u. 50 Bond.
Lovett Henry, teamster, h.r. 105 Windsor.
Low David, mer. tailor, 60 Asylum, h. 355 Park.
LOW DO YAN, oriental restaurant, 182
        State.                           See page 512.
"   Elizabeth B. wid. Frederick A. h. 8 Wyllys.
"   Emerson G. clerk, 98 Kilbourn. h. 8 Wyllys.
"   James G. draughtsman at 476 Capitol, b.
        37 Hamilton.
"   James J. screwm. 476 Cap. b. 12 Hungerford.
"   Jessie G. b. 37 Hamilton.
"   John, plumber at 24 Church, b. 37 Hamilton.
"   Margaret G. h. 37 Hamilton.
"   Robert G. carpenter, h. 14 Francis.
"   William B. carpenter, 37, h. 37 Hamilton.
"   Wm. B. Jr. carptr. at 37, b. 37 Hamilton.

Lowe Amelia, wid. William, b. 12 Ellsworth.
"   Charles, teamster at 50, b.u. 50 Woodbridge.
"   Edward A. printer, 284 Asy. b. 7 Goodman.
"   Frank P. mach. at 20 Sargeant, b. 127 Brook.
"   Fred. helper at 15 Trumbull, b. 14 Spring.
"   George W. mach. at 9 Sig. b.u. 39 Babcock.
"   James, motorman, St.Ry. b. 22 Spring.
"   John E. carpenter, 141 Tru. h. 7 Goodman.
"   Lawrence, foreman pump wks. b. 14 Spring.
"   Lawrence F. mechanic at Jewell Belting
        Co. b. 14 Spring.
"   Lawrence J. clerk at 295 Asy. b. 2 Water.
"   Mattie, concert dept. 336, b. 336 Weth.
"   Oswold, mason, h.u. 2 Martin.
"   Robert, molder at 1 Flower, h.u. 39 Babcock.
"   William N. mgr. at 2 Wash. h.u. 6 Ellsworth.
"   William T. joiner, h. 6 Martin.
Lowenhaupt John P. electrician, 85 Pratt, h.
        Burnside v.
Lowery Harry, clerk 342 Asy. b.2u. 72 Hopkins.
"   Henry, laborer at 54 Arch, b.u. 15 Park.
"   James, helper at 54 Arch, b. 16 Union.
"   Thomas, helper at 1 Flower, h.u. 29 Arch.
Lowrie Alfred W. clerk at 983 Main, b. 43 Mahl.
"   Arthur J. clerk at 552 Asylum, b. 43 Mahl.
"   Fred W. clerk at 983 Main, b. 43 Main.
"   Nettie D. Mrs. clerk Insurance Dept. State
        capitol, h. 155 Washington.
Lowry Daniel, barber, 37, h.r. 37 Albany.
"   James, engineer at Colts, h.u. 75 Huyshope.
"   Joseph J. butcher, b.u. 75 Huyshope.
"   Michael J. mach. at Colts, h. 75 Huyshope.
Lowski Joseph, laborer at 335, b. 56 Sheldon.
Loy Edward J. machinist at Colts, b. 30 Spring.
Loyd Elmer B. laborer at Popes, b. 267 Park.
Loydon Ada J. b.u. 13 East.
"   Albert H. bookkeeper at 40 Elm, h. 370
        Asylum, rm. 61.
"   Alice J. b.u. 13 East.
"   Fred. R. state agent Travelers Ins. Co. 56
        Prospect, h. 15 Niles.
"   Mary M. wid. Marshall, b. 370 Asy. rm. 16.
Lozell Walter J. at Travelers Insurance Co. 56
        Prospect, b. 113 Park.
Lozier Harry L. asst. bookkeeper at 501 Asylum,
        b.u. 7 Atlantic.
Lubblein Benjamin, peddler, h.2u. 26 North.
Lucas Amelia Mrs. boardinghouse, 401 Capitol.
"   C. C. compositor at 141 Pearl.
"   Caroline, wid. Thomas, h. 1232 Main.
"   E. J. capt. barge Frank Jones, 285 State, h.
        Middletown t.
"   Elmer E. engr. at 70 Com. h.4 Wadsworth.
"   Francis M. b. 401 Capitol.
"   Frank T. capt. Gracie Williams, 285 State,
        h. Cromwell t.
"   Geo. E. machinist, h. 52 Seymour.
"   James H. clerk at Pratt & Whitney Co. 1
        Flower, b. 52 Seymour.           •
"   John, mach. hand at Colts, h. 52 Seymour.
"   Mary, h.u. 277 Main.
"   Winfield, steamfitter, b. 4 Wadsworth.
Lucca John, laborer, h.r.u. 20 Charles.
Luce Jennie, wid. Leander L. h.2u. 132 Market.
"   ☞ see also Luse.

**You'll Get ALL THE NEWS, if you READ THE POST.**

Lucey Dennis, prop. Crystal House, 249, b. 249 Asylum.
" James, mach. at 1 Flower, h. 1445 Broad.
" James A. diesinker, 142 Russ, h. 623 Capitol.
" John W. mach. at 1 Flow. b. 49 Hungerford.
Luchenta Andrea, laborer, h.2u. 12 North.
Luckingham Bridget, wid. Jos. h.u.r. 38 Temple.
" Charles, hackman at 356 Main, h. 78 Spring.
" Frank, machinist, b.r. 38 Temple.
" Hannah, wid. Adam, h.r. 25 Morgan.
" John A. mach. at 62 Market, h. 36 Temple.
" William, brakeman, b. 27 Seyms.
Ludwig Alice M. saleslady, 45 Asy.h. 1212 Broad.
" Arthur, carpenter, b. 345 Main.
" Fred. grinder, 388 Capitol, h. 1212 Broad.
" Herman, machinist at Pratt & Whitney Co. 1 Flower, h. 13 Francis.
" Lizzie, hairdresser, b. 1212 Broad.
" Louisa, wid. John, h.u. 20 John.
" Otto, machinist at 133, b. 199 Sheldon.
" Solomon, tailor, 97 Asy. h.u. 270 Market.
Lueth Louis C. barber at 791 Mn. h.2u. 117 Hung.
Luftig Henry M. clerk at 110 State, b. 32 North.
" Louis, jewelry, 29 Church, h.3u. 32 North.
Luis Antonio, benchman at Pope Tube Co. h.u. 12 Affleck.
Luke John A. mason, h. 206 Asylum, flat 1.
Lull Fred H. engineer, h. 155 Windsor.
" Lysander, h. 35 Annawan.
Lumholdt Fred, gardener, b. 126 Westland.
Lumis George H. clerk at 921 Main, h. E.H.t.
" Thomas J. machinist, 581 Cap. h. 52 Laurel.
" ☞ see also Lohmis: Loomis.
Lumpone Frank, barber at 2 State, h. 156 Front.
Lund Carl, b. 279 Capitol.
" Henry T. pattternm. 33 Wells, b. 101 Ann.
" John K. polisher at Popes, h. Burnside v.
Lundberg Ernest, operator at 133 Sheldon, b.2u. 263 Main.
Lundeberg Carl F. mach. at 1 Laurel, h. 14 Affleck.
Lundeen Chas. W. tailor 2 State, b.u. 48 Hopkins.
Lundgren Gustavus A. porter, h. 72 Windsor.
Lundh Martin, toolm. Colts, b. 32 Buckingham.
Lundin Solomon, foreman, Popes, h. 121 Babcock.
Lundrigan Annie, b. 17 Kilbourn.
" John, teamster at 128 Com. b. 15 Kilbourn.
" Morris E. lab. 252 Pearl, b. 15 Kilbourn.
" Thos. teamster, 79 Talcott, h. 17 Kilbourn.
Lundy Edw. M. saloon, h.2u. 46 Windsor.
" George A. assemb. at 476 Cap. b. 7 Kilbourn.
" Joseph F. aligner at 476 Cap. b. 80 Flower.
Luney Catherine Mrs. b. 2 Holcomb.
Lung Ching, laundry, 108 State.
" Lee Yee, laundry, 90 Albany.
" Sam, laundry, 361 Asylum.
" Wung, laundry, 11 Morgan.
Lungholm Martin, tailor, h. 75 Ward.
Lungo Jenaro, laborer, b.3u. 27 North.
Lunny Robert, bookkeeper at State Bank, 795 Main, h. 29 Wooster.
" Robert J. collarmaker, 8 Sig. h. 151 Babcock.
Lupschino Angelo M. laborer, b.u. 83 Windsor.
" Frank, laborer, b.u. 80 Kilbourn.
" Ralph, laborer, b.u. 83 Windsor.
" Sarafino, laborer, b.u. 83 Windsor.

Lurea Aaron, tinner, h.u. 66 Village.
Luscomb Henry H. sec'y & supt. at Johns-Pratt Co. 555 Capitol, h. 277 Collins.
Luse ☞ see also Luce.
Lussier Louis, assembler at 581, b. 613 Capitol.
Luth Henry J. h. 74 Fairmount.
Luther Alice A. h. 943 Main, rm. 15.
" Emma A. wid. Fred. A. h.r. 21 Hawthorn.
" Flavel S. Rev. professor at Trinity college, Summit, h. 1 Columbia.
" George H. h.u. 27 Judson.
" Hurvey M. clerk at 304 Asy. h. 53 Dean.
" L. M. deck watchman str. Hartford, 285 State, h. Hadlyme v.
" Louis H. machinist, h.r. 21 Hawthorn.
" Peter S. manager at Beach & Co. 27 Potter, l. 58 Grove.
Lutton Joseph, motorman, St.Ry. h.2u. 40 Park.
" William J. motorman St.Ry. h. 48 Avon.
" ☞ see Sutton.
Lutwack Wm. cigarmaker, 191, h. 191 Front.
Lutz Charles, helper, the Times, b.u. 139 Market.
" Daisy M. bkkpr. 160 Windsor av. b. 32 Russell.
" Frederick, shoemaker, 187, h.u. 139 Market.
" Frederick, Jr. buffer at William Rogers Mfg. Co. 66, h. 139 Market.
" Henry E. painter, 175 Pearl, h.r. 299 Market.
" John, woodworker, 41 Albany, h. 32 Russell.
" John G. plater at 62 Market, b. 32 Russell.
" Joseph, laborer, h.2u. 22 Charles.
" Joseph H. polisher at 581 Cap. b. 4 Sisson.
" ☞ see also Lotze.
Lutzenkirchen Henry, machinist at 476 Capitol, h.u. 21 Affleck.
" William H. at 476 Capitol, h.u. 964 Broad.
Lux Carl E. clerk at 1082 Main, h. 114 Weth.
" Ellis, upholsterer at C. C. Fuller & Co. 14 Ford, h. 1102 Main.
" George L. clerk at 1105 Main, h. 114 Weth.
" George S. clerk at 115 Asy. b. 1102 Main.
" Harry E. clerk at 1105 Main, b. 103 Weth.
" J. George, clerk, b. 1102 Main.
" Peter, (P. L. & Son,) h. 103 Wethersfield.
" Peter & Son, furniture, 593 Main.
    Peter Lux.        William K. Lux.
" Wm. K. (P. L. & Son,) h. Wethersfield t.
Luzmoor John E. burnisher, 62 Mar. b. 209 Capen.
" John T. inspector at Popes, h. 209 Capen.
" William, plumber, b. 209 Capen.
" William H. plater at Wm. Rogers Mfg. Co 66 Market, h. 209 Capen.
Lybeck J. R. asst. engir. tug Ward, 285 State.
Lycett Fred. W. patternmaker at 40 Cushman, h. 179 Hawthorn ex.
" George H. foreman at Pratt & Whitney Co. 1 Flower, h.u. 48 Hopkins.
Lykke John P. carpenter, h.u. 36 Rowe.
Lyman Albert B. mach. at 1 Flow. h.u. 27 Benton.
" Albert E. machinist, h.u. 179 Barbour.
" Chas. R. jeweler at 20 State, b.u. 62 Capen.
" Dayton W. painter, h. 14 Ellery.
" Dwight E. supt. at 80 Huy. h. 30 Annawan.
" Edward O. clerk, 554 Asylum, h. 65 Flower.
" Eleazer H. slater at 18, h.u. 18 Elmer.

Lyman Elias L. asst. forem. Popes, h. 4 Wooster.
" Everett M. mech. 476 Cap. b.u. 35 Annawan.
" Frank P. printer at 29 Un.pl. h. 125 Mather.
" Frank Pitkin, mach. 80 Huy. b. 30 Annawan.
" Frank W. at 118, b. 15 Benton.
" Frank W. b. 14 Trinity.
" Frederick B. theolog. student, 1507 Broad.
" G. E. machinist at 13 Central.
" G. W. Mrs. housekeeper, b. 15 Morris.
" George J. general agent for the Christian at
    Work, h.u. 6 Canton.
" George W. b.u. 27 Benton.
" Hattie C. wid. Chas. K. proofreader at Case,
    L.& Brainard Co. 141 Pearl, h.u. 62 Capen.
" Helen M. b. 34 Sumner.
" Henry M. motorman, St.Ry. h. 6 Canton.
" Howard L.repairer, 328 Asy. b. 18 Elmer.
" Irving L. machinist, b. 18 Elmer.
" Joseph T. janitor 4th church, b.u. 6 Canton.
" Julian G. pressm. 154 Pearl, h.2u. 76 Hopkins.
" Luke W. clerk, Conn. Trust & Safe Deposit
    Co. 785 Main, b. 341 Laurel.
" Mary J. wid. Dan. P. dressm. 214, b. 214 Jef.
" Nathan G. h. 303 Capitol.
" Ralph W. restaurant, 977 Main, b. 62 Capen.

**LYMAN RICHARD P.** veterinary surgeon, office, St. Johns stables, 997, h. 427
Main, rm. 81. Telephone, 123 and 1165.

" Richard P. mach. 80 Huyshope, h. 108 Fkn.
" Sarah J. wid. Luke, h. 341 Laurel.
" Theodore, attorney, 847 Main, rm. 9, h. 22
    Woodland.
Lynberry D. forwd. cabin, str. Hartford, 285 State.
Lynch Abbie S. h.2u. 26 Elm.
" Ada, dressmaker, 75 Pratt, b.u. 1343 Main.
" Allen E. b. 7 Washington.
" Annie Mrs. h.u. 255 Park.
" Annie C. clerk at Brown, Thomson & Co.
    942 Main, b. 37 Park.
" Bernard, helper, h.2u. 220 Sheldon.
" Charles H. engineer at Case, Lockwood &
    Brainard Co. 141 Pearl, h. Wilson station.
" David, painter at Baxter the Decorator,
    231 Asylum, h. 13 Church.
" Declan J. rubberworker at 690 Park, h.
    105 Madison av.
" Dennis, l.u. 985 Main.
" Dennis J. repairer at Popes, h. 33 Riverside.
" Dora, cook at 20 South Hudson.
" Eugene S. roller at 690 Park, h. 28 Elm.
" Frank, b.u. 9 Putnam.
" Frank, cigarm. r. 173 State, h. Wethersfield.
" Frank P. bartender at 103, b. 103 State.
" George W. clerk at 68 Hicks, h.u. 62 Webster.
" J. deckhand, steamer Hartford, 285 State.
" James. toolm. at 476 Capitol, h. 128 Ward.
" James D. machinist, P.&R. h.u. 120 Albany.
" James F. machinist at N.Y.R. h. 119 Zion.
" Jeremiah J. forem. 556 Cap. b.2u. 9 Putnam.
" John, helper, 556 Capitol, h.u. 10 Hawthorn.
" John, laborer, h.u. 27 Mechanic.
" John, laborer, b. 1160 Main.
" John, yard forem. 1 Flower, h. 9 Hawthorn.
" John F. cigarmanufacturer, r. 192 Asylum.

Lynch John F. steamfitter at 152 State, h.u
    125 Mather.
" John H. appren. at 1 Laurel, b.10 Hawthorn.
" John H. mechanic at Popes, b. 9 Affleck.
" John J. machinist at 556 Cap. h. 25½ Flower.
" Joseph A. screwm. 476 Cap. b. 25½ Flower.
" Maggie, cook at 430, b. 428 Asylum.
" Maggie, wid. John, h.2u. 115 Windsor.
" Mary A. wid. John, h. 37 Park.
" Matthew, laborer, b. 9 Affleck.
" Michael, motorman St.Ry. h. 1438 Broad.
" Michael J. bartdr. at 734 Main, b. 25 Central.
" Michael W. h. 15 Chestnut.
" Michael W. brazier, h. 23 Kennedy.
" Nellie, b. 174 Farmington.
" Patrick, b.u. 985 Main.
" Patrick F. porter, 207 Allyn, b. 1202 Main.
" Peter, hodcarrier, h. 11 Douglass.
" Richard D. signpainter at 111, b. 83 Front.
" Rosa, wid. Patrick, b. 9 Squire.
" Susan, h.u. 53 Front.
" Thomas, pressfeed. 141 Pearl, b.u. 255 Park.
" Thomas C. rubberw. 690 Park, b. 75 Laurel.
" Thomas J. clerk, Park c. N.P. b. 9 Affleck.
" Viola, assistant matron, b. 1205 Asylum.
" William, mach. at 1 Laurel, h. 1449 Broad.
" William, tinner, b. 15 Hawthorn.

WILLIAM J. LYNCH, Physician. Office, 272
    Park street.
    Hours—Until 9 A. M.
        1 to 2.30 and 7 to 8.30 P. M.
            Telephone 429-6.

Lynch William J. physician, 272, b. 272 Park.
Lynde May B. b. 81 Asylum.
" Weltha A. wid. Duane W. h. 81 Asylum.
" ☞ see also Lind.
Lynehan Cornelius, engir. P.&R. h. 36 Liberty.
" ☞ see also Lenahan; Lennehan; Linnehan;
    Linnihan; Linehan.
Lyon Benjamin, (Jacob Lyon & Sons,) b. 15 Weth.
" Bridget, wid. Edmund, h. 377 Main.
" Charles Woolsey, student, b. 26 Buckingham.
" Cigar Co. 40 Mulberry.
" Clark, gardner, b. 152 Seymour.
" Edith, student, b. 58 Church.
" Felix, (Jacob Lyon & Sons,) b. 15 Weth.
" Harry G. clerk at 1 Flower, b. 10 East.
" Horace G. cabinetm. 158 Woodland, h. 10 East.
" Irving P. physician, b. 26 Buckingham.
" Irving W. Mrs. h. 26 Buckingham.
" Jacob, (Jacob Lyon & Sons,) b. 15 Weth.
" Jacob & Sons, stoves, tinners, 128 State.
        Jacob Lyon.     Felix Lyon.     Benj. Lyon.
" John, plumber at 11 Haynes, h. 250 Zion.
" Joseph, plumber, l. 1078 Main.
Lyons Alice, h.2u. 44 Village.
" Augustus P. engineer No. 5, h. 129 Sigourney.
" Bessie, wid. Dennis, h.r. 56 Albany.
" Dennis, cigarm. 40 Mulberry, b. 30 John.
" Edward F. mach. 556 Cap. b. 35 Putnam.
" Edward F. plumber, b. 22 Dean.
" Edward T. (Lyon Cigar Co.) h. 46 Windsor.
" Emma A. stenographer at Security Co. 62
    Pearl, b. South Manchester t.

**Merchants say it PAYS to Advertise in The Post.**

Lyons Frank, bootm. 22 Un. pl. h. 47 Morgan.
" Frank, laborer, b. 24 Vine.
" Fred H. clerk, 45 Asy. b. 156 Washington.
" Howard G. clerk, b. 1244 Main.
" James, carpenter at Popes, h. 30 John.
" James J. helper, 490 Cap. b. 305 Farmington.
" John, brass molder at 38 Ferry, b.u. 87 Front.
" John J. mach. at 1 Flower, h. 46 Babcock.
" Joseph, (F. Rates & Co.) b.u. Cap. c. Laurel.
" Joseph P. boxm. at Popes, b. 11 Hamilton.
" Keron, coachman, h.r. 305 Farmington.
" Margaret, at 83 Woodbine, b. 159 Babcock.
" Mary E. wid. T. J. h.2u. 27 Mechanic.
" Mary J. stripper, 40 Mulberry, b. 377 Main.
" Michael, carpenter, h. 22 Dean.
" Michael P. salesman, Popes, h. 11 Hamilton.
" Patrick J. waiter, l. 20½ Goodwin.
" Timothy J. varnisher at Seidler & May. furniture store, 306 Pearl, h.u.r. 259 Front.
" Wm. machinist at 556 Cap. h. 35 Putnam.
" William O. at Travelers Insurance Co. 56 Prospect, h. 10 Preston.
Lytle Eugene S. clerk at 80 State, b. 54 Capitol.
" James A. theological student, 1507 Broad.
" William F. asst. bkkpr. 48 Ann, b. 54 Capitol.

MAASEN Henry, mech. at Popes, h. 40 Wolcott.
Mabraski Minnie, boardinghouse, h. 7 Ellery.
Macalaugh Joseph, tinner, b. 59 Pleasant.
MacCullum ☞ see McCollum, Collum.
MacDonald Duncan B. Rev. prof. Theological Seminary, 1507 Broad, h. 815 Asylum.
" James H. highway commissioner, State Capitol, rm. 27, h. New Haven.
" ☞ see also McDonald.
Macer Mandel, peddler, h.u. 204 Front.
Macey Peter, bricksetter, h. Windsor av.
Macfarlane Eugene, clerk at Hills & Co. 372 Asylum, h. 12 Hungerford.
" Henry B. at 371 Asylum, h.2u. 16 Goodman.
MacGarry M. C. Miss, nurse, b. 48 Church.
MacGowan James P. artist, h.u. 365 Main.
MacGranor Robert J. salesm. 956 Mn. h. 30 Pliny.
Macholowitz Wolf, tailor, h. 144 Front.
Macia Rocco, laborer, b.u. 10 North.
Mack Alfred M. paperhanger, h. 64 Whitmore.
" Crohen, laborer, u. 106 Windsor.
" Elizabeth M. bkkpr. 711 Main, h. 12 Pratt.
" George S. porter, 725 Main, h. 55 Fairmount.
" Harold K. painter, b. 64 Benton.
" Harry A. dentist at 926 Main, rm. 32, b. 4 East.
" Herbert D. plumber at Thos. Oakes & Son, b. 64 Whitmore.
" James, slater, h.u. 514 Broad.
" John, driver at 452 Main.
" John, mason tender, h.u. 76 Avon.
" John F. clerk at 852 Main, b. 63 Church.
" John J. buyer at 956 Main, b. 48 Mahl.
" Myron J. printer at 252 Pearl, h. 4 East.
" Patrick, laborer, b.u. 69 Pleasant.
" Sarah, wid. John, laundress, h.u. 36 Pratt.
" Thomas, painter, b. 140 Trumbull.
" Wesley O. rubberw. 690 Park, b. 626 Broad.
" ☞ see also Mark.

Mackay Alexander, carpenter at r. 334 Asylum, h.u. 57 Wooster.
" ☞ see also McKay.
MacKenzie Fred. A. clerk, Atlantic Screw Works, 70 Huyshope, b. 70 Capitol.
Mackessy William H. b. 227 High.
Mackie David, b. 2 Holcomb.
" Hugh, patternm. at 734 Main, h. 29 Pawtucket.
Mackin Robert D. cigarm. 867 Main, h. Windsor t.
" Timothy, asst. farmer, St. Marys Home, W.H.t.
Mackinnon Alex. D. bookkeeper at National Exchange Bank, 76 State, h. 134 Barbour.
Mackleria Antonio, porter, 145 State, b. 86 Morgan.
MacLeod Angus, stonecutter, b.u. 36 Canton.
MacNabb J. Albert, plumber, 228 Pearl, b.u. 1322 Broad.
" Katherine, wid. Joseph F. h.u. 1322 Broad.
MacNaught Geo. K. Rev. pastor Grace chapel, Parkville, b.u. 7 Sisson.
MacNutt Lulu R. clerk at Brown, Thomson & Co. 942 Main, b. 58 Church.
Macomber Delmar L. machinist at 1 Flower, b. 34 Charter Oak pl.
Macreedy ☞ see also McCray.
Madara Samuel, carpenter, l. 98 Trumbull.
Maddaleeni Pasquale, barber, 16, b. 3u. 67 Morgan.
Madden Ellen, h. 279 Park.
" Francis F. teamster at stone pits, h. 35 Zion.
" Francis J. laborer at stone pits, b. 35 Zion.
" Frank J. molder at 54 Arch, h. 50 Annawan.
" John, h. 220 Jefferson.
" John, motorman, St. Ry. b.2u. 34 Park.
" John, stonemason, h. 18 Cedar.
" Joseph A. foreman at Hartford Post, 23 Asylum, b. 389 Main.
" Martin A. enameler at Popes, b. 220 Jefferson.
" Michael, saloon, 36, h. 92 Park.
" Thomas, b.2u. 263 Main.
" Thomas, enameler at Popes, b. 80 Putnam.
" W. J. b. 389 Main.
Maddoch Harry, tinner at 267 Asy. b. 1 Blumenthal.
Maddock George, clerk, b. 38 Wolcott.
Maddox Frank H. plumber at 11 Haynes, h.u. 160 Clark.
Mader John, helper at Pope Tube Co. b. 165 Front.
Madigan James B. electrician, b.u. 88 Williams.
" John, machinist, h. 14 Chestnut.
" John, teamster, 128 Com. b.u. 31 Pleasant.
" John F. hackdriver, 87 High, h.2u. 31 Pleasant.
" Martin, laborer, h.r. 44 Village.
" Martin W. Jr. driver r. 87 High, b.r. 44 Village.
" Michael, coachman, h.u. 88 Williams.
" Morris, teamster at 250 State, h.2u. 90 Shel.
" Thomas, carptr. at 155 Ch. O. h. Wethersfield t.
" Walter J. clerk, 133 Sheldon, b. 88 Williams.
" William, laborer at 1 Laurel, h. 42 Amity.
" William, laborer at 20 Church, b. Weth.t.
Madison C. H. messman, str. Hartford, 285 State.
" Charles, carpenter, h. Bartholomew.
" House, 110 Pratt, Mrs. Lucy H. Black.
" Samuel M. carpenter, h. 48 Church.
Madnick Joseph, blacksmith, h.u. 40 North.
Madran Elodie, wid. Godfrey, h. 8½ Ellery.
Madsen Christina, wid. Iver, h.u. 105 Mather.
" Christine M. clerk at 745 Main, b. 28 Center.

Madsen Edward C. machinist at 142 Russ, b. 105 Mather.
" John, laborer at 335 Sheldon, h.u. 131 Ward.
" John, musician, b. 334 Wethersfield.
" Larens J. drug clerk, 1129 Mn. b. 28 Center.
" Lewis C. laborer, h. 766 Park.
" Margaret, laundress at 30 Washington.
" Matthias, bootmaker, 39 Ann, h.u. 28Center.
" Neils C. screwm. at 476 Capitol, h. E.H.t.
" Nicholas, laborer, h.u. 234 Park.
" Peter, mason, h.u. 318 Capen.
Madurin Albert, cook at 931 Main, l. 2 Church.

**MAERCKLEIN HERMAN,** manufacturer of sofa beds, 104 Asylum, h. 22 Woodbine. *See page 562.*
" Herman J. assistant cashier Conn. River Banking Co. 761 Main, h. 213 Laurel.
" Hubert L. at Phœnix Ins. Co. 64 Pearl, h. 3 Linden.
Maffes Matteo, laborer, b. 148 Front.
Magaro Louis, joiner r. 60 Temple, h. 29 Albany.
Magazina Joseph, baker, 46, h. 44 North.
Magee Herbert J. printer at Phœnix Ins. Co. 64 Pearl, b. 31 Francis.
" John T. canvasser, b.u. 147 State.
" Mary, h. 133 Market, rm. 2.
" Minnie, at Jewell Pin Co. b. 58 Church.
" Robert, laborer at 1 Flower, h. 31 Francis.
" ☞ *see also McGee.*
Magill ☞ *see McGill.*
Maginn James J. painter, h.u. 570 Main.
" John H. b. 61 Sigourney.
" Wm. F. mer.tailor, 903 Main, rm.2, h. 61 Sig.
" ☞ *see also McGinn.*
Maginnis Edward, laborer, b. 60 Front.
Magnell Carl E. buffer at 1 Laurel, b. 1332 Broad.
" Charles J. drug clerk at 55 Farmington, l. 28 Spring.
Magnus Patrick, laborer at 285 State, h. E.H.t.
Magnuson Adolph, buffer Popes, b. 1332 Broad.
" Albin, pressman, 141 Pearl, b. 1332 Broad.
" Alfred J. helper, h. 125 Ward.
" Charles, helper, b.u. 1332 Broad.
" John F. patternm. at 784 Mn. b. 1332 Broad.
" Mary, wid. Jansen, h. 1332 Broad.
Magonigal James, tillerman No. 3, 124 Front, h. 20 Village.
" Robert, driver engine No. 8, l. 385 Park.
Maguire Edward F. buffer at 581 Cap. b. 98 Bab.
" John F. mach. at 888 Capitol, b. 223 Park.
" Kate, wid. John B. h.u. 223 Park.
" Kittie J. clerk, 921 Main, b. 223 Park.
" Letta B. clerk at 898, b. 995 Main.
" Richard, at Pope Tube Co. b. 20 Linden.
" Thomas, machinist, h.u. 6 Huntley.
" Thomas, real estate, h.u. 67 Pleasant.
" Thomas, toolmaker, h. 116 Hungerford.
" WilliamT. clerk station A, P.O. b. 223 Park.
" ☞ *see also McGuire.*
Maguy Louis, finisher at 110 Com. b. 255 Asy.
" ☞ *see also Mahon; Mehan.*
Mahanowich Andrew, laborer, b. 15 Mechanic.
Maher Ann, wid. Patrick, h.u. 42 Beach.
" Bridget, wid. James, h.r. 60 Wells.

Maher Bridget, wid. Michael, h.u. 33½ Front.
" Catherine, wid. Patrick, h. 231 Pearl.
" Edward A. enameler, h.u. 49 Hudson.
" Ellen, h.u. 15 Portland.
" George, blacksm. 352 Alb. b. 12 Windsor.
" James, teamster, l.2u. 985 Main.
**MAHER JERRY.** *See page 559.*
" John, blacksmith, ʋ Mech. b.u. 33½ Front.
" John, ostler at 250 State. h. 168 Front.
" John E. driver at 250 State, b. 168 Front.
" John J. b. 27 John.
" Margaret, at 37 Wells, h. 15½ Wadsworth.
" Maria J. h. 15½ Wadsworth.
" Martin, helper at 54 Arch, h.u. 27 John.
" Mary, wid. William, h.u. 91 Arch.
" Mary M. clerk at 956 Main, b. 32 Wells.
" Michael, coachman, b. 74 High.
" Michael, laborer, b.u. 33½ Front.
" Michael M. painter, b. 60 Loomis.
" Nellie, b. 231 Pearl.
" Patrick, molder at 556 Cap. h. 1 Worcester.
" Patrick, molder at 1 Flower, h. 73 Governor.
" Patrick F. driver at 250 State, b. 168 Front.
" Patrick H. bartender, h. 18 Westland.
" Patrick J. tailor, 219 Pearl. h. 20 Hicks.
" Thomas, laborer, b. 1 Vine.
" William, laborer at Colts, b. 60 Vanblock.
" William J. clerk at Brown, Thomson & Co. 942 Main, b. 7 Front.
" William M. teamster, b. 168 Front.
" ☞ *see also Mayer; Meyer, Meagher.*
Mahl Arabella, wid. Fred. h. 277 Windsor av.
" *Chas. printer at 141 Pearl, h.u. 37 Barbour.
**MAHL EDWARD,** *alderman 7th ward,* plumber, 1204 Main, h. 24 Annawan.
" Edward M. builder, b. 277 Windsor av.
" Elizabeth, wid. Benjamin, h.u. 61 Mahl.
" Fred. Benj. builder, 1152 Main, b. 277 Windsor av.
" George *(G. M. & Son,)* h. 329 Windsor av.
" George Jr. *(G.M.&Son,)* b. 329 Windsor av.
" Geo. & Son, plumbers, 1152 Main.
    George Mahl.        George Mahl, Jr.
" Herman, builder, 12, h. 12 Pavilion.
" Stephen J. architect, b. 277 Windsor av.
" William, printer, b.u. 61 Mahl.
Mahler Gustave E. glassworker, 83 Woodbine.
Mahon Austin, h.u. 23 Huntley pl.
" Bridget M. music teacher, b. 105 Windsor.
" Edward, student, b.u. 105 Windsor.
" Egbert G. clerk at P.&R. l. 117 Ann.
" James, clerk at 47, b. 47 Sheldon.
" James, laborer b. 88 Grove.
" John, gardener, h. 22 Grace.
" John F. clerk at Brown, Thomson & Co. 942 Main, b.u. 72 Hopkins.
" John J. driller at Colts, b. 45 Hudson.
" John T. trav. salesman, h. 15 Goodman.
" Joseph F. motorman St.Ry. h. 88 Grove.
" Kate, housekeeper, h. 88 Grove.
" Maria, wid. Peter, grocery, 47, h. 47 Sheldon.
" Martin, h.u. 60 Wells.
" Martin W. diem. at 476 Cap. h. 1462½ Broad.
" Mary, wid. Martin, h. 1 Brady.

Mahon Michael, mason, h. 37 Pleasant.
" Patrick, shoemaker, 13, h. 22 Grace.
" Patrick J. clerk 105 Windsor, b. 37 Pleasant.
" Thomas F. conductor St.Ry. h. 150 Market.
" William J. physician, 985 Mn. h.105 Windsor.
" William J. A. meats, 105, h.u. 105 Windsor.
" ☞ see also Mahan.
Mahoney Alex. J. signalman, N.Y.R. b. 6 Tru.
" Annie, dressmaker, 10, h. 10 Atlantic.
" Annie, wid. Stephen, h.u. 33 Mechanic.
" Catherine, clerk at 921 Mn. b. 8 Atlantic.
" Daniel D. enameler at Popes, b. 29 Arch.
" Daniel J. engineer, l. 4 Winthrop.
" Dennis, rubberw. 690 Pk.h.10 Bartholomew.
" Dennis P. porter at Brown, Thomson & Co.
      942 Main, h.u. 9 Goodman.
" Edward, laborer, b.u. 95 Windsor.
" Edward F. polisher, h.r. 95 Windsor.
" Edward J. upholsterer, b.u. 312 Asylum.
" Edward James, operator, b. 22 Affleck.
" Elizabeth, wid. Dennis, h. 9 Goodman.
" Ellen J. dressmaker, 10, b. 10 Atlantic.
" Henry L. clerk 288 Asylum, b. 80 Trumbull.
" Henry P. plumber, b. 8 Atlantic.
" Jeremiah J. driv. 28 Union pl. h. 55 Pleasant.
" Jeremiah M. lab. 98 Kil. h.2u. 32 Pleasant.
" John, ostler at 1214, l.r. 1214 Main.
" John, storekeeper, N.Y.R. h.u. 312 Asylum.
" John B. clerk, b. 16 John
" John F. b. 312 Asylum.
" John F. at Pope Tube Co. b. 13 Westland.
" John J. miller at 40 Elm, h.3u. 202 Sheldon.
" John J. plumber at 1204 Main, h. 43 Wbdg.
" John O. lab. at 40 Governor, h. 111 Potter.
" John P. mach. at 1 Flower, b. 9 Goodman.
" John P. mach. 20 Sargeant, h. 10 Atlantic.
" Joseph T. clerk at 858 Main, b. 8 Atlantic.
" Lawrence J. teamster, b. 111 Potter.
" Margaret, wid. John, h.2u. 7 Green.
" Mary, wid. William O. h. 6 Trumbull.
" Michael, laborer at 95 Pleasant, h. 2 North.
" Michael, printer at 252 Pearl, h. Windsor t.
" Michael F. mach. at Colts, b.2u. 1053 Broad.
" Mich'l J. enameler, 581 Cap.h.2u. 95 Windsor.
" Michael J. helper 1 Flow. b.r. 15 Woodbine.
" Patrick, policeman, h. 8 Atlantic.
" Peter, blacksmith, h. 16 John.
" Thomas, watchman at 1 Laurel, h. 22 Affleck.
" Thomas F. pressf. 141 Pearl, b. 22 Affleck.
" William, clerk at P.&R. b. 95 Windsor.
" William, machinist at Popes, h. Burnside v.
" William, teamster, b.2u. 7 Green.
" William E. boss steamf. 1 Flow. h. 5 Atlantic.
" Wm. H. mach. at 1 Laurel, h. 22 Affleck.
Maialli Pompero, laborer, b. 365 Front.
Main Edward T. toolm. Colts, b. 721 Main, rm.62.
" Emily S. wid. Martin V. h.4 Huyshope.
" Frank, b. 40 Trumbull.
" Julian H. salesman 263 Asylum, h. 73 Hung.
" Louis S. ice, office, 391 Main, h. 4 Huyshope.
" William D. motorman St.Ry. h. 344 Weth.
Mainello Felix, saloon, 222 Front, h. 60 Talcott.
Mairson David, janitor at 241 Asy. b. Kennedy.
" Joseph, dep. collector U.S. internal revenue,
      65 State, h. 10 Goodman.

Maislen David, clerk at 65 Mor. b. 278 Market.
" Isaac, peddler, h. 278 Market.
" Max, peddler, h. 243 Market.
Maisvk John, lab. at 335 Sheldon, h. 66 Potter.
Majestic Portrait Studio, 721 Main, rm. 33.
      Wm. V. Downer, Manager.
Major & Dundon, signpainters, 104 Asylum.
      Oliver Major.          John P. Dundon.
" Oliver J. (M. & Dundon,) b. 118 Asylum.
Makinson Hattie, b. 69 Seymour.
" Peter L. painter, h. 69 Seymour.
Malberg Benj. yardman, 17 Alb. b.u. 80 Front.
MALCOLM THOMAS, (Purves & Malcolm,) r. 334
      Asylum, h. Warrington.   See page 422.
Maligan Charles Mrs. b. 1336 Main.
Maligian John G. screwmaker at 476 Capitol,h.u.
      38 Lawrence.
Malins A. W. at Trav. Ins. Co. b. 13 Prospect.
Mallender John G. painter 185 Asy. h. 207 Capen.
Mallery J. Hammond, dentist, 981, h. 981 Main.
Mallett S. Benedict, roadmaster's clerk, N.Y.R.
      450 Asylum, h. 223 Garden.
Malley Abram, dry goods, 87½, h. 87½ Windsor.
" Bernard, molder at 54 Arch, h. 19 Howard.
" J. deckhand str. Hartford, 285 State.
" James, polisher at 581 Cap. b. 1430 Broad.
" Joel, grocer. 137, h. 147 Front.
" John, bricklayer, b. 1335 Broad.
" Simon, dry goods, h. 142 Front.
" Thomas P. toolmaker, b. 1430 Broad.
" ☞ see also Melley.
Malling Chas. J. filer at 30 Cush. h. Bloomfield t.
Mallinger Michael, waiter at 80 State.
Mallison Henry S. printer, h.u. 1208 Main.
Mallner Hans, draughtsman at 370 Asylum, b.
      22 Hopkins.
Mallon Edward, fireman str. Hartford, 285 State.
" Edward A. carman at 1 S. Ann,h.103 Mather.
" Edward C. porter, b. 47 Prospect.
" Jennie, dressmaker, 10, b. 10 Chapel.
" Michael F. attendant, 30 Washington.
Mallory Frederick, teamster, 1, h. 81 Flower.
" William H. mach. 110 Com. h. 146 Albany.
" Willis M. mach. at 77 Com. b. 146 Albany.
Malloy Alice, b. 6 Carpenter.
" Barney T. rubberw. 690 Park, b.14 Francis.
" D. T. policeman, h. 47 Walnut.
" John, laborer, city works, h. 6 Carpenter.
" John F. molder at 1 Flower, h. 16 Bonner.
" Mark F. helper 164 State, b.u. 14 Francis.
" Marshall A. clerk, P.&R. b. 47 Walnut.
" Mary, wid. Bernard, h.u. 14 Francis.
" Wm. H. molder at 690 Park, h. 18 Heath.
" ☞ see also Maloy; Molloy.
Malm O. William, salesman, 52 Ann, l.u. 68 Russ.
Malone Bessie, wid. Peter, h. 112 Babcock.
" Charles, city driver, b.u. 58 Flower.
" Edward, laborer at 8 Front.
" Emma J. at Travelers Insurance Co. 56
      Prospect, b. 249 Franklin.
" George H. carptr. 147 Sheldon, h.12 Church.
" James G. laborer, h.2u. 36 Sheldon.
" James J. carpenter, b. 1335 Broad.
" James T. buildingm. 12 Center, h. 2 Winter.
" John, bottler at 109, b. 113 Front.

Malone John J. cigarmaker, u. 597 Main.
" John J. collarm. at 8 Sig. h. 162 Ward.
" Michael F. machanic N.Y.R. h.u. 111 Hung.
" Philip,laborer,95 Pleasant,h.2u.18 Windsor.
" Thomas, foreman at 737, b. 697 Windsor av.
" Thomas E. h. 249 Franklin.
Maloney Ann, wid. Michael, h. 208 Maple.
" Bridget, wid. Thomas, h. 1340 Broad.
" Charles D. (*Snow & M.*) b. 28 Spring.
" Henry, machinist, l. 155 Washington.
" James, mason, b. 208 State.
" James, plumber at 389½ Main, h.u. 105 Jef.
" James, policeman, h. 72 Bellevue.
" John, h.u. 9 East.
" John, at Popes, h. 412 Broad.
" John, cook at 3 Central, b. 124 Market
" John J. bartender, b. 933 Main.
" John J. enameler at Popes, h. 412 Broad.
" Josephine, bkkpr. 2 Church, b. 1340 Broad.
" Kate, operator at 34 Morgan, b. 259 Front.
" Michael, helper, N.Y.R. b.u. 139 Lawrence.
" Michael, helper at 16 Hicks, h. 272 Front.
" Michael, ostler at Hills & Co. h.r. 29 Albany.
" P. deckhand str. Hartford, 285 State.
" Philip J. engineer, l. 236 High.
" Richard J. clerk,1046 Main,h.u. 27 Pleasant.
" Theresa A. stenographer, b. 272 Front.
" Thos. steamfitter at 203 Asy. h. 190 Sisson.
" Timothy, watchman, b. 141 Trumbull.
" Wm. J. bkkpr. at P.&R. b. 1340 Broad.
" William James, enam. 581 Cap.b. 412 Broad.
" ☞ *see also Meloney, Moloney.*
Maloy Bernard, quarryman, h. 41 Mechanic.
" Charles,laborer at 54 Arch,h.3u. 74 Sheldon.
" Daniel, teamster at 51, b. 78 Martin.
" Edward, helper at 266 Pearl, b. 68 Retreat.
    Edward J. assembler, 581 Cap. b. 20 Bonner.
‖ J. Edward, printer, 141 Pearl, h. 464 Maple.
" James, benchm. Pope Tube Co. b. 10 Bonner.
" John, carptr. at 158 Woodland,l. 1045 Main.
" John H. inspector plumbing for city, h. 36
    Annawan.
" John J. helper, h.u. 3 Curcombe.
" Joseph P. enameler at Popes, h. 117 Zion.
" Keron, car inspector, h.2u. 96 Windsor.
" Keron, policeman, h. 422 Maple.
" Keron F. plumber at James Ahern, 280
    Asylum, h. 1 Imlay.
" Lawrence, laborer at stonepits, b. Mechanic.
" Margaret A. at 921 Main, b.u. 14 Francis.
" Mary A. teacher So. school, b. 36 Annawan.
" Rose A. teacher Brown sch. b. 36 Annawan.
" Thos. F. shoem. 270½ Park, h. 66 Hudson.
" William, machinist, b. 14 Francis.
" Wm. B. meterman, 266 Pearl, b. 68 Retreat.
" Wm. J. appren. 34 Shel. b. 36 Annawan.
" William J. polisher, 1 Flow. b. 317 Capitol.
" Winnifred J. h. 422 Maple.
" ☞ *see also Molloy; Malloy.*
Maltbie Abbie H. b. 15 Church.

**MALTBIE THEODORE M.** attorney at law, 3 Asylum, corner Main, h. Granby t.                    *See page 489.*
Malumphy ☞ *see Molumphy.*

Malyere Gennaro, mason, h.u. 89 Morgan.
" M. Angelo, laborer, b.u. 73 Morgan.
Mancini Domencio, (*M. & Silvestri*) h.3u. 45 Por.
" & Silvestri, grocery, 33 North.
    Domencio Mancini.        Frank Silvestri.
Manco Oscar, laborer, b.3u. 7 Charles.
Mancy Frank, carpenter, h.u. 38 Amity.
" John A. printer at 336 Weth. b. 32 Bkm.
" Julia A. Mrs. h. 25 Harper.
Mandeville Bert M. plater at Wm. Rogers Mfg.
    Co. 66 Market, b. 27 Martin.
" Carlton, plater at Wm. Rogers Mfg. Co. 66
    Market, h.u. 27 Martin.
" Carrie, clerk at 901 Main, b. 27 Martin.
" Fred. G. trimmer at 62 Mar. b. 27 Martin.
" Giles, b. 218 Laurel.
" Mary E. wid. Fred. G. h. 27 Martin.
" P. L. clerk, b. 41 Grand.
" Robert, plater at 66 Market, b. 27 Martin.
Mandigo Charles R. dynamoman at 266 Pearl,
    h. 119 Albany.
" William J. mach. 1 Flower, h. 58 Spring.
Mandlebaum Emanuel, h. 37 Chapel.
Mandorian Albert, chef, b. 2 Church.
Mandrus Delia, dressm. r. 132, h.r. 132 Market.
Manecy Frank, fruits, 335 Asylum, 336 Pearl, h.
    27 Flower.
Manee James T. cigarm. 104 Asy. h.u. 60 Seyms.
Manell William, carpenter, h.2u.153 Windsor av.
Manelli Dominick, fruit, 36 State, h. 40 Hung.
" Joseph, clerk at 36 State, b. 40 Hungerford.
Mangan Ellen, wid. Daniel, h. 102 Hungerford.
" John, hackdriver, b.u. 47 Green.
" Mary, dressmaker, h. 102 Hungerford.
Mangarell Carlo, laborer, h.u. 102 Windsor.
" Frank, laborer, b.u. 1 North.
" John, laborer, h.3u. 119 Front.
" Joseph, laborer, b.u. 1 North.
Mangerson Albert, laborer at 285 State.
Manginess Joseph, grocer, h. 19 Mechanic.
Mangoson John, coachm. at and b. Prospect av.
Manierre Arthur, plumber, h.u. 51 Wooster.
" Leon, printer, b. 51 Wooster.
" William P. painter, h. 51 Wooster.
Manion Ann, wid. Lawrence, h.u. 53 Potter.
" Edward, building mover, b. 10 Union.
" Edward J. teamster, b. 10 Union.
" Eliza, wid. William, h. 33½ Chestnut.
" Frank, blacksmith, b. 10 Union.
" Henry, switchman P.&R. h. 33½ Chestnut.
" James, mach. at 1 Flower, h. 13 Smith.
" James J. wiper N.Y.R. h.2u. 34 Flower.
" James J. agent, h. 552 Main.
" John, h. 30 So. Prospect.
" John, baggagem. at N.Y.R.h.u.r.1219 Main.
" John, driver, 98 Wells.
" John A. molder, 54 Arch, b.u. 25 Pawtucket.
" John T. mach. at 9 Sigourney, b. 13 Smith.
" Joseph, painter at 452 Main.
" Joseph H. helper at 164 State, b.u. 10 Union.
" Keron, blacksmith, h.u. 55 Front.
" Michael, laborer, b. 369 Park.
" Michael, laborer, b. Lifkey.
" Michael J. blacksm.352 Alb. b.u.35 Franklin.
" Patrick, laborer, h.u. 35 Liberty.

**If you have anything to Sell, Advertise it in The Post.**

Manion Patrick, laborer at Colts, b.u. 38 S. Pro.
"   Patrick, woodwkr. at 352 Alb. h. 72 Capitol.
"   Peter, bartender, h.u. 85 So. Prospect.
"   Peter A. clerk, b. 25 Pawtucket.
"   Richard, stonemason, h. 137 Mather.
"   Thomas W. brazier, Popes, b.u. 10 Union.
"   William F. saloon, 55, h.u. 53 Potter.
Mankis Anthony, packer, 618 Cap. h. 49 Front.
"   John, packer at 618 Capitol, b. 49 Front.
Manley Henry W. polisher, 1 Flow. b. 83 Church.
"   John, motorman St.Ry. h.2u.r. 126 Market.
"   Joseph P. mach. at Colts, h. 76 Vanblock.
"   William L. h. 10 New Britain.
Mann Adelbert W. h. 13 Kennedy.
"   Arthur, cigarmaker at 4 Mulberry, h. South
       Glastonbury v.
"   Arthur, teamster at 128 Com. h. 227 Market.
"   Arthur W. clerk at Popes, b. 25 Capitol.
"   Frank D. sec'y Ernst Schall Co. h.u.303 Park.
"   Gottlieb G. cigarm. 867 Mn. b. 212 Franklin.
"   Henry, sign painter, b. 2 Church.
"   Mandy Mrs. h.2u. 213 Pearl.
"   Mary A. teacher at 690, b. 690 Asylum.
Mannel August, gardener, h. 123 Retreat.
"   August Jr. mech. at Popes, b. 123 Retreat.
"   Charles, h. 67 Hudson.
"   Lizzie R. clerk at 150, b. 150 Russ.
Manner Joseph P. helper, 142 Russ, h. 6 Kil ct.
Manning Augusta M. h. 49 Willard.
"   Dennis, leverman, N.Y.R. h. 33 Russell.
"   Geo. W. mach. at 556 Cap. h.u. 42 Grand.
"   John, helper at 1 Flower, h. 24 Albany.
"   John J. teamster, h. Lifky.
"   Keron, enameler at Popes, b. 55 Front.
"   Patrick F. laborer, h. 11 Hendricxsen.
"   William H. shipping clerk, Colts, h. 41 Cong.
Mannisevitz Fannie, wid. Isaac, confectionery,
       204, b. 174½ Front.
Mannix Henry, laborer, h.u. 13 Front.
"   James, horseshoer, 22 Wells, h. 7 Morris.
"   James M. mach. 1 Flower, b.u. 168 Ward.
"   John P. pattrnm. at 1 Flow. b.u. 168 Ward.
"   John J. b.u. 1427 Broad.
"   Katie, clerk at 928 Main, b. 7 Morris.
"   Michael, (M. & Ritchie,) h. 103 Oak.
"   Patrick, polisher at James L. Howard &
       Co. 438 Asylum, h. 22 Brook.
"   Patrick, porter at 152 Asylum.
"   & Ritchie, carpenters and builders, r. 133
       Sheldon.
       Michael Mannix.            David Ritchie.
"   Rose, b. 7 Morris.
"   Thomas, boxmaker at Pratt & Whitney Co.
       1 Flower, h.u. 168 Ward.

Manns George W. barber, 933 Main, h. E.H.t.
"   Gottfried, carpenter at 690 Park, h. 143
       Madison av.
Mannz Gottfried, h. 179 Wethersfield.
Manock Edmund, shoemaker, 1109 Mn. h. E.H.t.
Manogue Kate, dressm. 108, b.2u. 108 Windsor.
Manscault Adolphus, carptr. b. Pro. av. c. N.P.
"   Stephen, carpenter, h. Prospect av.
Manook Mr. screwmaker, b. 381 Capitol.
Mansfield Enos O. h. 30 Lewis.
"   John, helper at 1, h.u. 32 Flower.
"   Matt. blacksm. at 22 Wells, h. 5 Curcombe.
Manson George M. painter at 352 Alb. b. 140 Tru.
"   James, coachman, h. 58 Vernon.
"   Jessie, milliner at 904 Main, b. 58 Vernon.
"   Samuel, stonecutter at 40 High, b.58 Vernon.
Mansuy Clara Mrs. boardinghouse, 48 Prospect.
"   Louis J.(M.& Smith,) h. Oakwood av. W.H.t.

**MANSUY & SMITH,** carriage manfg.
   and horseshoeing, 17, 18, 20 and 21 Elm.
   Louis J. Mansuy.        T. Hammond Smith.

"   William N. finisher at 17, b. 15 Elm.
Mansworth Elizabeth, wid. Matt. h. 136 Maple.
Manternach Geo. lab. Pope Tube Co. b. 88 Shel.
"   Harry, lab. at Pope Tube Co. b. 88 Sheldon.
"   John C. clerk at Pope Tube Co. b. 55 Green.
"   Kate Mrs. h.3u. 88 Sheldon.
Mantie Charles, policeman, h.u. 28 Church.
"   Frank, clerk, b.2u. 1204 Broad.
"   Herrman, lab. city park, h.2u. 1204 Broad.
"   Otto, upholsterer, h.u. 1204 Broad.
Mantille Vito, laborer, b.u. 27 Kilbourn.
Manton James L. cigarm. 867 Main, b. 255 Asy.
Manufacturers Governor Co. 223 Asy. rm. 11,
Manuppello Michael, laborer, h.u. 88 Front.
"   Sconio, laborer, b.u. 88 Front.
Manville Covering Co. 249 Pearl.
Manwaring Chas. W. genealogist, h. 25 Mather.
"   Fannie J. indexstamper, b. 25 Mather.
"   Mary E. h. 25 Mather.
Manwell Augustine P. theo. student, 1507 Broad.
Mapes Formula & Peruvian Guano Co. H. H
       Stafford, manager, 242 State.
Maples James G. carpenter, h. 49 Dean.
Mara Daniel, machinist at N.Y R. b. 111 Weth
"   John, laborer, b. 39 So. Prospect.
"   Patrick, helper at N.Y.R.
Marble Ellen E. Mrs. h. 123 Clark.
"   Eugene S. toolm. 476 Capitol, h. 66 Allen pl.
Marceau Corine, dressmaker, b. 767 Park.
"   Raymond, machinist, h.u. 767 Park.
"   Robert, lab. at Pope Tube Co. b.u. 767 Park.
March Christian R. clerk, 835 Mn. h. 47 Williams.
"   John G. barber, 9 Asylum, l. 9 Canton.
"   William, teamster, h.u. 339 Front.
"   ☞ see also Marsh.
Marchand Clodion S. nicklep. at Popes, l. 58 Asy.
Marchant Caroline, wid. Wm. nurse, b. 189 Ash.
"   Geo. harnessm'r, 425 Main, h. 57 Congress.
"   George Jr. bkkpr. E. E. Hurlbut, h. 57 Cong.
"   Mary, teacher Ch.O. school, b. 11 Congress.
"   Robert, florist, r. 13, h. 13 Huntington.
"   William T. draughtsman, 141 Trumbull, h.
       b. 57 Congress.

MARCHANT WM. T. (*Hills & M.*) undertakers, h.u. 7 Belden. *See page 189.*
" ☞*see also Merchant.*
Marchello Joseph, barber at 103, l. 105 Main.
Marches Fred'k, barber at 222 Asy. b. 181 Mar.
Marcovitz Hyman, shoemaker, h. 204 Front.
" Sam. M. shoemkr. at 59 Maple, h. 135 Grove.
" Solomon, restaurant, 201, b. 201 Front.
Marcus Rollie, clerk at 908 Main, l. 74 Park.
" Solomon, grocer and market, 72, h. 74 Park.
Marcy Andrew W. clerk, 287 Asy. h. 2u. 80 Hopkins.
" Bros. & Co. shoe manufacturers, 14 Ford.

| W. P. Marcy. | E. D. Burnham. |
| G. L. Baker. | A. E. Rankin. |

" Chas. H. supt. at 155 Ch.O. h. 61 Madison.
" E. Edgerton, travelingsalesm. b. 60 Capitol.
" Frederick A. *selectman*, h. 60 Capitol.
" Merrick A. h.u. 269 Wethersfield.
" Wm. D. clerk at 78 Asy. b.u. 80 Hopkins.
" Wm. P. (*M. Bros. & Co.*) h. 24 Huntington.
Marene Isal, bkkpr. at 54 Morgan.
Marenboltz Fred. apprent. at Colts, b. 42 John.
" Otto, barber; 415 Main, h. 42 John
Marguliers Charles, cabinetmaker at Linus T. Fenn, 613 Main, h.u. 220 Front.
" Jacob, cabinetmaker, b. 220 Front.
" Simon, cabinetmaker, h. 120 Portland.
Mariangello Angello M. mason, h.u.r. 268 Front.
Marion Edwin T. salesman at 334 Asy. h. E.H.t.
Mark Fred, laborer St.Ry. h.u.r. 29 Albany.
Markel Emerick, engineer, h. 10 Walnut.
Markham Daniel A. attorney at law, 877 Main, rm. 3, h. 22 Sumner.
" Henry C. carriagemaker, h.2u. 21 Vernon.
Markman Christopher, deckhand str. Middle-town, 285 State.
Marks Abraham H. clerk at 97 Asy. b. 52 Bkm.
" Arthur J. clerk at 226 Asylum.
" Bella, clerk, b. 52 Buckingham.
" Brothers, fruit, 39 Church.●
" Caroline, wid. Marks, h.u. 77 Windsor av.
" David, removed to Springfield, Mass.
" Eugene R. grainer, house 26 Crown.
" James, peddler, h. 59 Windsor.
" Leopold, (*M. Bros.*) h. 39 Sumner.
" Mark, clerk at 108 Asy. b. 52 Buckingham.
" Matthew, shoemaker, 1 Martin, h. 7 Winter.
" Matthew Jr. boxmkr. at Popes, h. 7 Winter.
" Melina, wid. Henry J. b. 39 Sumner.
" Morris F. (*G. Fox & Co.*) b.u.77 Windsor av.
" Morris J. painter, 312 Alb. h.u. 13 Liberty.
" Richard J. foreman at Popes, b. 7 Winter.
" Rosie, clerk, 956 Main, b. 52 Buckingham.
" Samuel, peddler, h. 52 Buckingham.
" ☞ *see also Marx.*
Marlow Agnes, dressmkr. 19, h. 19 Wadsworth.
" John F. toolmaker, Popes, h. 19 Wadsworth.
" Mary M. dressmaker, 19, h. 19 Wadsworth.
" Patrick J. trav. salesman, b. 19 Wadsworth.
" Peter, machinist, b. 19 Wadsworth.
Marone Rocco, bootblack, h.3u. 30 Kilbourn.
" Vito, laborer, h.u. 190 Front.
Maroney Daniel, b. 398 Broad.
" Hannah, at 40 Governor, b. 398 Broad.
" John, laborer at stonepits, h. 398 Broad.

Maroney John Jr. mach. at Colts, b. 398 Broad.
" Lizzie I. dressmaker, 6, b. 6 Village.
" Mary, at 40 Governor, b. 398 Broad.
" Mary, dressmaker, h.u. 6 Village.
" Thomas, helper at 1 Flower, b. 398 Broad.
" ☞ *see also Meroney.*
Maros M. laborer, Popes Tube Co. h.67 Morgan.
Marose Dominic, harnessmaker at 8 Sigourney, b. 67 Walnut.
" ☞ *see Amorose.*
Marquardt Frederick G. pressman at Hartford Courant, h. 12 Village.
MARQUARDT HERMAN C. ins. and real estate, 904 Main, rm. 95, h. 53 Brown.
Marquette Joseph L. bartender at 29 Central, h.u. 35 Park.
Marr Anna M. Mrs. attendant 30 Washington.
" Atwood B. attendant 30 Washington.
" Frank, (*Vickery & M.*) b. 651 Main.
Marrett Thomas A. real estate, h. 58 Trumbull.
Marron Thomas, helper 433 Main, b. 1445 Broad.
Marroto George, printer, h. 20 Charles.
" Mary, wid. Frank, h. 20 Charles.
Marry John, at 1 Flower, b.u. 248 Lawrence.
Mars Eugene V. mach. 133 Shel. h. 59 Francis.
Marsden John S. buyer at Brown, Thomson & Co. 942 Main, b. 126 Collins.
" Nehemiah L. blacksmith, h.u. 23 Martin.
Marsh Arthur M. at 25 Front, b. Windsor t.
" B. Frank, chief clerk Treas. office at State capitol, b. 59 Capitol.
" Chauncey S. hackman, h. 260 Franklin.
" Clara Mrs. matron, 171 Putnam.
" Clara B. b. 260 Franklin.
" Digby Mrs. h. 239 Farmington.
" Edward W. gasfitter at James Ahern, 280 Asylum, h.u. 105 Clark.
" Elizabeth, wid. Truman, b. 1034 Main.
" Ellen Mrs. dressmaker, h. 1034 Main.
" Frank T. civil engineer, b.u. 105 Clark.
" George L. clerk at Hartford Life Ins. Co. 252 Asylum, b. Vernon t.

**MARSH HENRY T.** teacher of dancing, office and private academy, 1034, h. 1034 Main. *See page 496.*

" John, millman, at 690 Park, h. Boulanger.
" John, janitor Chapter house, Trinity college, Summit, h.u. 159 Zion.
" John E. farmer, h. 1168 Windsor av.

## J. HENRY MARTIN,

MANUFACTURER OF

# Cane Chair Settings

Also, RE-SEATING OF CANE SEAT CHAIRS,
AND WOVEN CHAIRS—Piazza
and Veranda.

### Address, 42 SEYMS STREET.

Marsh John H. salesman at Smith, Northam & Co. 129 State, h. 131 Sigourney.
" Martha, milliner, 926 Main, b. 58 Church.
" Mary A. wid. Hazard, h. 164 Babcock.
" Mary A. wid. Seth E. h. 658 Farmington.
" Mary E. wid. Frank, b. 42 Clark.
" Mary I. musicteacher, 105, b.u. 105 Clark.
" Mary L. nurse, h. 14 Church, rm. 3.
" Myron G. bkkpr. at 987 Main, h. Windsor t.
" O. Vincent, h. 43 Sargeant.
" Priscilla A. bookkeeper, 835 Mn. b. 18 Avon.
" Thomas, (T. M. & Co.) h. 54 Fairmount.
" Thomas & Co. painters, 1076 Main.*
" Warren R. clerk at Bonner-Preston Co. 843 Main, h.2u. 144 Albany.
" William B. clerk, 142 Russ, b. 164 Babcock.
" William H. clerk, 51 Tru. b. 54 Fairmount.
" ☞ see also March.
Marshall A. D. Mrs. h. 488 Main.
" Annie, h.u.r. 68 Albany.
" Annie J. wid. James, clerk, Lincoln, Seyms & Co. 34 Market, h. 17 Haynes, rm. 69.
" Daisy, at 20 Sargeant, b.2u. 149 Lawrence.
" Eliza A. wid. William C. b. 26 Wolcott.
" Ellen F. wid. Thomas, h. 210 Windsor av.
" Eugene, driver at 180 Allyn, h.u. 9 Sig. pl.
" Eva L. teacher Lawrence st. school, b. 17 Haynes, rm. 69.
" Ezra J. compositor, h.u. 50 Williams.
" Geo. musicteacher at 1205 Asy. h. 2 Avon.
" Joseph B. machinist, 1 Flow. h. 65 Madison.
" Julia, dressmaker, 37, h. 37 Brook.
" Margaret, wid. Thomas, h. 427 Main.
" Philena C. b. 50 Williams.
" Robert, foreman, h.u. 37 Brook.
" Robert, machinist, h.u. 50 Cedar.
" Sarah A. dressmaker, b.u. 50 Cedar.
" Warren W. asst. foreman, 1 Flow. h. N.B.t.
" William, patternmaker, b.u. 50 Cedar.
" Wm. E. checker, stone pits, h.u. 131 Zion.
" William H. clerk at U. S. Photo. Chemical Co. 29 Pearl.
" William H. policeman, h. 20 Morgan.
" Wilson C. painter, h.u. 61 Dean.
Marsharsky Meyer, shoemaker, 1357 Main.
Marsicano Frank, laborer, b. 319 Front.
Marston A. driver at 74 Trumbull, b. E.H.t.
" David D. filer at Colts, h. E.H.t.
" Herbert C. filer Colts, b. East Hartford t.
" Mary P. wid. Charles. b. 134 Farmington.
Marte Otto, barber at 362 Asy. b. 74 Edwards.
" Paul H. barber, 362 Asylum, h. 74 Edwards.
Martel Ann Mrs. employment, 596 Main, h. 43 Annawan.
" Daniel, cutter at 336 Asy. b. 51 Morgan.

Martel Harry J. mgr. 568 Mn. h. 106 Whitmore.
" Louis J. laundry, 568 Main, h. 43 Annawan.
" Rocci, laborer, h.2u. 51 Morgan.
Martell Jane, tailoress, h.3u. 172 Sheldon.
Martello Antonio, printer, 336, b. 336 Weth.
Martenson John, carpenter, h.u. 29 Hamilton.
" John, operator at 40 Gov. h. 2½ Elliott pl.
Martin Alfred W. clerk at 1 Flower, h. 27 Beach.
" Alice, b.u. 86 Jefferson.
" Andrew, mason, b. 86 Jefferson.
" Archie, clerk at Silas Chapman, Jr. 51 Trumbull, h. 39 Mahl.
" Arthur E. foreman at 556 Cap. b. 83 Sig.
" Bertha C. clerk at 908 Main, b. 26 Belden.
" Chas. A. conductor at St.Ry. h. 78 Benton.
" Charles C. engraver at 62 Mar. h. 53 Lincoln.
" Charles E. bkkpr. at 78 Asy. b. 42 Williams.
" Charles H. mangr. at 50 Asy. b. 26 Belden.
" Charles J. bartdr. 583 Main, h. 69¼ Madison.
" Charles T. at Ætna Life Ins. Co. 650 Main, h. 2 Girard.
" David, expressman, h. 20 Affleck.
" David T. writing teach. h. 847 Main, rm. 15.
" Edward F. bkkpr. at 54 Ann, h. 1352 Broad.
" Edward G. at Travelers Insurance Co. 56 Prospect, h.u. 39 Capen.
" Edward J. clerk, 237 Park, b. 20 Affleck.
" Edward J. enameler, 302 Asyum, h. Weth.t.
" Edwina B. teacher Lawrence st. school, b.u. 97 Washington.
" Elizabeth Mrs. h. 400 Windsor av.
" Etta, b.u. 18 Congress.
" Eva Mrs. wid. Melmoth, h.u. 61 Albany.
" Francis, laborer, h.u. 86 Jefferson.
" Frank G. plater at James L. Howard & Co. 438 Asylum, h. 40 Temple.
" Frank J. conductor, St.Ry. b. 81 Bellevue.
" Fred. M. machinist, b. 42 Williams.
" George E. h. 83 Sigourney.
" George E. brakem. P.&R. h.u. 55 Spruce.
" George E. iceman, 4 Central.
" Geo. P. toolmkr. at Colts, h. 48 Franklin.
" George R. draughtsman, 556 Cap. b. 83 Sig.
" Harry C. teamster, b. 8 Walnut.
" Henrietta L. wid. J. D. h. 7 Buckingham.
" Henry A. mach. at 1 Flower, h.u. 31 Mather.
" Henry F. printer at Sunday Journal, 284 Asylum, b. East Hartford t.
" Herbert, at 8 Sigourney, h.r. 143 Zion.
" Horatio A. agent at 721 Main, h. 26 Belden.
" Hugh J. pressfeeder at 12 Central, h.E.H.t.
" Iola E. wid. Philip, h. 126 Trumbull.
MARTIN J. HENRY, contractor, 42 Seyms, h. 159 Capen.            See page 244.
" James, baker, h.u. 80 Temple.
" James, hack driver, b. 1104 Main.
" James, hackman, b. 38 Church.
" Jas. F. casehardener at 581 Cap. h. 32 Hicks.
" James J. molder at 54 Arch, h.u. 108 Huy.
" James P. clerk, b. 14 John.
" James P. laborer, h. 33¼ Russell.
" Jane, wid. William, h. 42 Williams.
" John, expressman, h. 29 Putnam.
" John, foreman at 15 Tru. h. 5 Whitman.
" John, laborer, b. 14 Huntley pl.

## A Good Investment—Your Advertisement in The Post.

Martin John, laborer, h.2u. 95 Sheldon.
" John, laborer, b.2u. 265 Asylum.
" John A. penmanship, public sch. h. 39 Capen.
" John F. bookkeeper at Capewell Horse Nail Co. 40 Governor, h. 71 Capitol.
" John G. motorman St. Ry. h.u. 4 Elliott.
" John H. helper at 356 Main, h. 5 John.
" John H. porter at Charles R. Hart Co. 898 Main, b. Windsor Locks t.
" John J. express. 690 Park, h. 29 Putnam.
" John K. carpenter, h. 39 Annawan.
" Joseph A. clerk at Brown, Thomson & Co. 942 Main, b. 33½ Russell.
" Joseph J. clerk at 12 Maple, b. 58 Lincoln.
" & Kelly, painters and decorators, 265 Asy. Thomas Martin. John Kelly.
" Leon E. teamstr. 335 Shel. h.995 Windsor av.
" Louis, cigarmaker, l.u. 1261 Main.
" Louis N. driller at Colts, b. 36 Charter Oak.
" Margaret, wid. James, h. 14 John.
" Maria, wid. James, cook at 389 Main.
" Mary Mrs. clerk at 835 Main, h. E.H.t.
" Mary, wid. Patrick, b. 111½ Hungerford.
**MARTIN MARY V.** wid. Chester, furnished rooms, h. 130 Ann.
" Michael, hackman, l. 520 Main.
" Osgood C. clerk, 901, b. Sigourney house, 1150 Main.
" Owen, h. 95 Whitmore.
" Patrick, fireman, h.2u. 183 Lawrence.
" Patrick, hodcarrier, h. 78 New Park.
" Patrick E. carpenter, b. 114 State.
" Peter R. blacksmith at 37 N.B. b. 69 Sey.
" Rebecca D. wid. George E. h. 113 Ann.
" Richard P. manager Postal Telegraph Cable Co. 3 Central, h. 16 Whitney.
" Robert J. carpenter St.Ry. h. 281 Albany.
" Robert M. clerk, b. 8 Walnut.
" Rufus N. conductor St.Ry. b. 64 Grove.
" Sarah C. clerk at 921 Main, b. 82 Brook.
" Thomas, h. 120 Windsor.
" Thos. bartender, 57, h.u. 59 Potter.
" Thomas, laborer, h. 8 James.
" Thomas, laborer, h. 4 Donald.
" Thomas, (M. & Kelley,) h.3u. 265 Asylum.
" Thomas J. clerk 139 Asylum, b. 926 Main.
" Thos. J. printer, 29 Union pl. b.2u.15 S.Pro.
" Thomas S. clerk 26 Mul. b. 33½ Russell.
" Tillie, wid. John, h. 8 Walnut.
" Walter C. bricklayer, b. 8 Walnut.
" William E. clerk, b. 83 Sigourney.
" Wm. H. carptr. at Popes, h. 26 Wellington.
" William J. supt. P.&R. h. 427 Main, rm. 6.
" William P. operator at 12 Central, b. 981 Main.
" Winfred Robert, prof. Trinity college, b. 21 Jarvis hall, Summit.
Martindale William W. envelope cutter, 252 Pearl, h. 59 Hungerford.
Martine Tobia, laborer, h.u. 73 Morgan.
Martinsen Andrew, buffer, h. 110 Ward.
Martinson Joshua, granitecutter, b.u.550 Asylum.
Martocci Joseph, laborer, b.u. 64 Morgan.
" Salvator, laborer, b.u. 64 Morgan.
Marturello Alphoso, florist, h. 39 North.

Martyn Herbert W. harnessm. 8 Sig.h.r. 143 Zion.
" Sidney, electrotyper at 41 Tru. b. 72 Ward.
Marvel Arthur C. clerk, b. 6 Fales.
" Earle H. trav. salesman at C.S.Brewer & Co. 238 Asylum, b. 6 Fales.
" Eugene, at 302 Asylum, b. 12 Atlantic.
" Harry E. traveling salesman Hartford Rubber Co. 690 Park, b. 64 Russ.
" Joseph E. contractor at Pratt & Whitney Co. 1 Flower, h. 6 Fales.
" Louis M.engr.PopeTubeCo.h.u.184 Putnam.
" Marion E. clerk at Billings & Spencer Co. 142 Russ, b.12 Atlantic.
" Sylvester, salesman, h. 12 Atlantic.
" Walter S. asst.forem. 1 Flow. h.u.53 Lincoln.
" ☞ see also Marble.
Marvin Charles H. cigarmaker at 847 Main, b. 230 Asylum.
" Edwin E. attorney, clerk U. S. District and Circuit Courts, United States commissioner, 65 State, h. 51 Gillett.
" Frank W. at 20 Central, h. E.H.t.
" George K. delivery clerk at Case, Lockwood & Brainard Co. 141 Pearl, h. 250 Franklin.
" John, h.u. 558 Main.
" L. P. Waldo, attorney at law, 2 Central, h. 36 Woodland.
Marwedel Wm. H. mach. 1 Flow, b.237 Lawrence.
Marwick Albert Jr. druggist, 877 Asylum, h. 97 Farmington.
" Virginia P. Mrs.: teacher vocal music, h. 97 Farmington.
Mascara Thomas, fruit, 18 Church, h. 37 Albany.
Masconitz David, b. 272 Market.
Masele Antonio, laborer, b.u. 265 Front.
Maskers Harry, goldbeater, 100 Love lane, b.36 Liberty.
" Samuel C. carpenter at N.Y.R. h. 36 Liberty.
Maslen Charles C. clerk at 40 High, b. 83 Wash.
" Joseph B. asst.forem.at 40 High, h.u. 222 Jef.
" Lewis, peddler, h. 37 Pleasant.
**MASLEN STEPHEN,** monumental works, granite, marble, etc. 40 High, h. station 20, W.t. *See outside back cover.*
Mason Adella, wid. Charles, h.u. 1 Huntley.
" Anna, wid. Abel, h. 210 Windsor av.
" Anna A. wid. Samuel, h.u. 2 Elm pl.
" Edward C. at 722 Main, b. 61 Prospect.
" Edward J. K. student Trinity college.
" Ella A. wid. George H. chiropodist and massage, 240, h.u. 240 Sigourney.
" Ellen A. wid. Edward P. h. 101 Trumbull.
" Frank A. E. mach. N.Y.R. h.1469 Broad.
" Frank E. bindery forem. at Case, Lockwood & Brainard Co. 141 Pearl, h.u. 67 Russ.
" Frederick F. bkkpr. 66 State, b. 522 Garden.
" Frederick M. teamster, b. 53 Mather.
" Frederick T. clerk at Hartford Courant, 66 State, b. 522 Garden.
" George C. gearcutter at 1 Flow. b. 83 Arch.
" George L. draughtsman at 469 Cap.h.W.P.v.
" George William, shoemaker, h. 83 Arch.
" James, coachman, 77 Washington.

**It Pays Big Interest-Your Advertisement in The Post.**

Mason James A. machinist at 1 Flow. h. W.P.v.
" John, at 284 Asylum, b. 61 Prospect av.
" Mary J. Mrs. b. 40 Bond.
" Matthew, helper at 9, h. 45 Sigourney.
**MASON W. C. & CO.** coal and wood, 746 Main. 172 Commerce, 169 Front. *See page* 417.
" Walter H. pressm. at 24 Mec. h.73 Hudson.
MASON WILLIAM C. ( *W. C. Mason & Co.* ) h. 282 Farmington.
Masonic Hall Association, 53 Ann.
" Temple, 51, 53, 55 Ann, c. Allyn.
MASSACHUSETTS MUTUAL Life Ins. Co. A. H. Bond, agent, 847 Main. *See page* 64.
Massara Leonardo, fruit peddler, b. 35 North.
Masschatzsky Samuel, tailor at 139 Asylum, h. 224 Front.
Masterton Elizabeth, wid. Robert, nurse, 52, b.u. 52 Seymour.
Masur Harry, clerk at 956 Main, b. 112 State.
" Louis, barber, b. 112 State.
" Maurice, clerk at 88 Asylum, h. 112 State.
Matello ☞ *see Martello.*
Materazio Joseph, laborer, h. 7 Charles.
Materson Charles, helper, b.3u. 59 Ferry.
Mather Albert E. engineer, h. 564 Windsor av.
" Alice C. b. 762 Windsor av.
" Allen C. farmer, h. 536 Windsor av.
" Arthur, milkman, h. 958 Windsor av.
" Charles, farmer, h. 762 Windsor av.
" Charles E. printer at Hartford Courant, b. 356 Windsor av.
" Clara S. wid. Henry, h.u. 24 New Britain.
" Dexter P. b. 990 Windsor av.
" Elizabeth Mrs. h. 64 Grove.
" Frank H. h. 926 Windsor av.
" Frank J. carpenter, h. 15 Goodwin.
" Frank M. attorney, clerk Probate court, 114 Pearl, b. 821 Asylum.
" George D. night mail clerk, P.O. h. 512 Windsor av.
" Horace E. geneaologist, h. 747 Asylum.
" John C. printer at Courant office, 64 State, h. 356 Windsor av.
" L. L. Mrs. nurse, h. 13 So. Hudson, rm. 11.
" Laura M. b. 762 Windsor av.
" Lizzie D. Mrs. christian scientist, h. 1040 Windsor av.
" Lucy O. teacher High school, 39 Hopkins, b. 747 Asylum.
" Mary A. teacher West Hartford, b.u. 24 N.B.
" Mary B. teacher High school, b. 747 Asy.
" Mary H. wid. Charles, b. 67 Edwards.
" Mary S. b. 1169 Windsor av.
" Oliver T. milkman, h. 1040 Windsor av.
" Raymond T. head shipping clerk at Popes, 436 Capitol, h. 51 Putnam.
" Richard H. electrician, b. 1169 Windsor av.
" Robert A. machinist, b. 536 Windsor av.
" S. Alpheus, clerk at 472, b. 522 Windsor av.
" Susan M. wid. George. b. 16 Suffield.
" Thomas S. ( *Tuttle & M.* ) h.522 Windsor av.
" Walter P. janitor Phœnix Ins. Co. 64 Pearl, h. 38 Lewis.

Mather Walter S. farmer, h. 990 Windsor av.
" William A. theological student, 1507 Broad.
Mathers Thomas W.cigarm.at 867 Mn. h.42 Avon.
Matheson Duncan, mason, h.u. 2 Webb.
Mathias Louis, cigarm. at 104 Asylum, b. E.H.t.
Mathies John H. laborer, 70 Huy. h. 566 Main.
" Nettie Mrs. dressmaker, h. 566 Main.
Mathieu Albert, nickelplater b.u. 244 Park.
" Edward, barber at 281, b.u. 244 Park.
Mathieuson ☞ *Matthieuson.*
Mathison, Morris, painter, b. 23 John.
Mathson Baden, belper, 142 Russ, b. 880 Broad.
" William, helper, 142 Russ, b. 880 Broad.
Matkow Elias, filer at Colts, h. 4 John.
Matson James, clerk at 8 Ford, b. 3 Riverside pl.
" William L. broker, 55 Tru. h. 47 Garden.
" William R. at Travelers Ins. Co. 56 Prospect, b. 47 Garden.
Matte Albert J. machinist, h.u. 55 Hawthorn.
Mattebbe Chas. tailor at 730 Main, b.58 Temple.
" John, streetsweeper, h. 58 Temple.
Matteo Carmine, laborer, b.u. 83 Windsor.
" Ja Francisco, laborer, b.u. 83 Windsor.
Mattesen Arthur C. engineer str. Middletown, b.3u.r. 60 Temple.
" Lillian E. Mrs. h.u.r. 60 Temple.
Matteson Christian, laborer at State capitol, h.u.r. 60 Temple.
Matthews Albert, b. 58 Seymour.
" Albert, deckhand str. Middletown,285 State.
" Clayton, machinist, b.u. 119 Albany.
" Edward A. carpenter, h.u. 119 Albany.
" Edward E. painter at 10 Ferry, b.26 Church.
" George H. driller at Colts, h. 107 Jefferson.
" Henry, farmer at 16, b. 16 White.
" J. Frank, conductor St.Ry. h. 79 Willow.
" James W. painter at 1106 Main, h.79 Willow.
" Susan T. wid. James R. h. 141 Maple.
Matthewson Oluf, fireman at 315, h.u. 296 Park.
" Robert H. clerk, state treasurer's office, State capitol, rm. 1, b. 3 Farmington.
" ☞ *see also Mathewson.*
Matthieu Archibald, shoem. 784 Park, h.W.H.t.
" Edward F. assembler, b. 58 Seymour.
" John Jr. boxmaker, h.u. 244 Park.
" Louis, carpenter, b.u. 244 Park.
Mattia G. shoemaker 24, h.r. 31 Albany.
Mattieson Olaf, gardener, 86 Weth. h. 29 Elliott.
Mattoon Fred. J. con. N.E.R. h. 75 Hungerford.
Maurer Dominick, h. 120 Babcock.
" Madeline J.stenog. 690 Park, b.120 Babcock.
" Theo.( *Hartford Bologna Factory* ) r. 490, h. 490 Windsor av.
Maurice George, machinist at 1 Flower, b. 50 Hungerford.
" George B. attendant at 30 Washington.
" J. H. clerk at 759 Main, b. 50 Hungerford.
" Joseph, machinist at 1 Flower, h. 50 Hung.
Maurmann Peter, h. 54 Temple.
Maxfield Brothers, brokers, 722 Main.
    Charles F. Maxfield.   George C. Maxfield.
" Chas. F. ( *Maxfield Bros.* ) h. New Hartford t.
" Geo. C. ( *Maxfield Bros.* ) h. New Hartford t.
Maxim Hiram P. mechanical expert at 1 Laurel, h. 427 Main, rm. 54.

Maxwell Emma C. supt. Industrial Department Womens Home, 54, b. 58 Church.
" Eugene A. agent, b. 119 Capitol.
" Frank, fireman, b. 7 Goodwin.
May A. L. Mrs. b. 223 Asylum, rm. 20.
MAY CHARLES, (*Seidler & M.*) 306 Pearl, b. 82 Kenyon. *See page* 500.
" Charles, assembler, b. 6 Kilbourn ct.
" Charles, harnessm. at 8 Sig. h. 262 N.P.
**MAY D. W.** *See page* 559.
" Gustave, b. 6 Kilbourn ct.
" James H. molder at 1 Flower, h. 39½ Sisson.
" John, barber, h. 6 Kilbourn ct.
" John, photographer at 177 Asy. b. 29 West.
" John Jr. b. 6 Kilbourn.
" John M. conductor N.Y.R. h. 60 Pliney.
" Lynde E. conductor N.Y.R. h. 105 Whitmore.
" Max, cook at 931 Main, h. 72 Temple.
" Peter, at 8 Sigourney, b. 234 New Park.
" William B. gardnr. at 83, h.r. 83 Woodland.
" Wyman J. agent, Phœnix Mutual Life, h.u. 94 Huntington.
Mayer & Bartholomew, real estate, 7 Central.
    Jerome Mayer.    Dana W. Bartholomew.
" Henry C. asst. principal Brown school, h. 223 Asylum, rm. 17.
" Jerome (*M. & Bartholomew*), b. 107 Ann.
" Louis, traveling agent, h. 107 Ann.
" Nathan, physician, 742 Main, h.u. 29 Pearl.
" R. A. Mrs. b.u. 141 Main.
" William, peddler, h.r. 17 Portland.
" ☞ *see also Maher ; Myer ; Meyer.*
Mayhew George P. foreman Hartford Times composing room, 716 Main, h. 50 Madison.
Maylew Michael, h. 55 Hudson.
Maynard C. B. Mrs. h. 206 Asylum, flat 13.
" Charles E. mach. at 142 Russ, b. 80 State.
" Daniel H. coachman, 748, h. 748 Asylum.
" Edward W. traveling salesman at 690 Park, h. Springfield, Mass.
" Mary S. wid. Lester J. b. 827 Broad.
" Napoleon, carpenter, h.u. 13 Putnam.
" Wm. L. electrician, 142 Russ, h. 827 Broad.
Mayne William E. signpainter, 1274 Main, h. 167 Clark.
Mayo Charles H. rubberw. at 690, h. 848 Park.
" James J. machinist at 690, h. 902 Park.
" Joseph Mrs. h. 13 Vernon.
" March C. Rev. b. 13 Vernon.
" Samuel, boxm. at 690 Park, h. 144 Madison av.
Mays John E. groceries, 122, h. 122 Capen.
Maytum Daniel, mason, h. 4 Village.
Maziatti Leonard, carpenter, h. 339 Front.
Mazza Philip, laborer, b.u. 78 Charles.
Mazzuchi Luigi, baker at 178, b. 178 Front.
McAdam Charles F. operator, 135 Shel. b. 26 Gov.
" Francis A. machinist, 252 Pearl, h. 18 John.
" Joseph F. machinist, b. 26 Governor.
" Lucius, clerk at Hartford Life Insurance Co. 252 Asylum, b. 57 Farmington.
" Patrick, hackman, h.u. 56 Sheldon.
" Thos. J. mach. at 77 Com. b. 26 Governor.
McAdams Bridget, b.u. 1421 Broad.
" Richards, teamster, h. 79 Sheldon.
McAdoo James L. laborer, h.u. 180 Putnam.

McAffe Wm. clerk at Frank J. Knox, plumbers' supplies, 2 South Ann. b. 24 Windsor av.
McAleer Alice, dressm. 18 Beach, b. 80 Flower.
" Edward, plumber, 12 Mulberry, b. 80 Flower.
" James P. bookkeeper, b. 80 Flower.
" Patrick, janitor, h. 80 Flower.
" Samuel F. clerk at 133 State, b. 80 Flower.
" William B. at 476 Capitol, h. 80 Flower.
McAll Edward S. draughtsm. at Popes, b. W.t.
McAloon Rosie, clerk at 956 Main, b. E.H.t.
McAlvon James, teamster at 32, Lu. 24 Church.
McArthur A. H. motorm. St. Ry. b.u. 289 Asylum.
" John, carptr. r. 334 Asylum, h. 33 Julius.
" Joseph, beltmaker at Jewell Belting Co. 15 Trumbull, b. 152 Mather.
" William, setter 15 Trumbull, b. 152 Mather.
McAuley George A. barber, 647 Mn. h.u. 77 Park.
" John, b. 2 Holcomb.
McAuliffe Daniel, porter 77 Chas. b. 18 Kennedy.
" Eugene D. fireman, h.u. 16 Russell.
" James, clerk at 614 Capitol, b. 30 Willow.
" James, foreman 165 Windsor, b. 18 Kennedy.
" James, laborer, h. 19 Ellery.
" John, clerk at 310 Asylum, b.u. 49 Front.
" John M. corem. at 556 Cap. b. 30 Willow.
" Lizzie, stitcher at 8 Sigourney, b. 30 Willow.
" Michael, trucker P.&R. b. 66 Hopkins.
" Nellie, clerk at 835 Main, b. 16 Russell.
" Thomas, laborer, h.u. 19 Ellery.
" Timothy J. helper at P.&R. b. 66 Hopkins.
" William, laborer, h. 30 Willow.
" William F. clerk at 614 Cap. b. 30 Willow.
McAvoy ☞ *see McEvoy.*
McBride James H. bkkpr. 110 Asy. b. 58 Gov.
" John, farmer, b. Albany, W.H.t.
" John, fireman N.Y.R. h.u. 36 Flower.
" Josephine, at 745 Main, b. 264 New Park.
" Margaret, wid. John, h.u. 58 Governor.
" Samuel, asst. foreman, b. 264 New Park.
" Thomas J. enameler at 581 Cap. b.u. 58 Gov.
McCabe Alice E. bkkpr. 866 Main, b. 6 Putnam.
" Bernard, helper, b. 44 Sanford.
" Edward, fireman, N.Y.R. h. 44 Sanford.
" Edward, helper at 388 Capitol, b. 6 North.
" Elizabeth, wid. James, h. 2u. 29 Hungerford.
" Ellen F. h. 227 High.
" Emma, pressfeeder at 668 Mn. b. 131 Law.
" Frank, solicitor, b. 191. Lawrence.
" Helen B. clerk at 908 Mn. b. 131 Lawrence.
" Howard A. helper, N.Y.R. b. 162 Ward.
" James, b. 2 Holcomb.
" Jas. B. mach. 30 Cush. h.2u. 43 Hawthorn.
" Jas. J. mach. at Johns-Pratt Co. b. 615 Cap.
" John, tinsmith, b. 5 Center.
" Kate, b. 131 Lawrence.
" Lizzie A. clerk at Brown, Thomson & Co. 942 Main, b. 5 Center.
" Martin, switchtender N.Y.R. b. 5 Center.
" Owen F. clerk at 197 Asy. b.u. 6 Putnam.
" Peter J. clerk, 252 Pearl, b.u. 112 Hung.
" Thomas, helper at N.Y.R. h.u. 6 Putnam.
" Thomas J. mach. hand at Colts, b. B.v.
" William, foundryman at 618, b. 615 Capitol.
" William H. signalman N.Y.R. h. 131 Law.
" William T. brakeman N.Y.R. b. 5 Center.

**THINKING PEOPLE Read The Post Daily.**

J. M. McCARTHY.                J. J. AHERN.

## McCARTHY & AHERN,
# Funeral Directors
### AND
## Embalmers,

LADY
EMBALMER.          **149 PEARL STREET.**

**Telephone Call, 1049-2.**

McCafferty Jeannette,wid.Edw'd A.h.u.265Main.
"   Mary, printing dept.336,b.336Wethersfield.
McCaffery Edward J. bricklayer, h.2u. 11 Queen.
"   Sarah A.wid. Bernard J. h. 94 Albany.
McCall Pat, dropforger, at Colts, h. 49 Hudson.
McCallan ☞ see also MacCallan.
McCallum John, clerk at Brown, Thomson & Co.
    942 Main, h. 10 Russell.
McCandless Catherine,wid.Jas.h.2u. 64 Hopkins.
"   Charlotte, nurse, b. 111 Ann.
"   Margaret C. b.2u. 64 Hopkins.
"   Ralph C. rubber 581 Cap. b.2u. 64 Hopkins.
McCann Arthur, janitor, h. 458 Main.
"   James, b.2u.r. 22 So. Prospect.
"   James, roofer at 32 Village.
"   James A. mech. at Popes, b.u. 84 Hudson.
"   John, laborer at Pope Tube Co. h. 25 Pearl.
"   John D. h.2u.r. 22 So. Prospect.
"   John H. bkkpr. at 91 Morgan, h.u. 221 Shel.
"   Joseph, b.2u.r. 22 South Prospect.
"   Julia Mrs. at W.H. Home for Aged, Albany.
"   Mary, wardmaid at 20 So. Hudson.
"   Mary, wid. John, h. 97 Main.
"   Mary A. clerk at 227 Asy. b. 221 Sheldon.
"   Michael J. clerk 227 Asy. b.u. 221 Sheldon.
"   Patrick A. builder, h. 23 Vernon.
McCarter Al. engineer at 80 State.
"   Harry E. mach. St.Ry. h. 35 Woodbridge.
"   Joseph, b. 152 Mather.
"   William, b. 152 Mather.
McCarthy Alfred, electrotyper at 41 Trumbull,
    h. 27 Harrison.
McCARTHY & AHERN, undertakers, 194 Pearl.
    John M. McCarthy.      John J. Ahern.
                            See page 248.
"   Andrew J. clerk at Brown, Thomson & Co.
    942 Main, b. 1333 Broad.
"   Anna, clerk at 835 Main, b. 14 Talcott.
"   Annie L. stenog. at 64 State, h. 21 Ashley.
"   Catherine B. clerk at Brown, Thomson &
    Co. 942 Main, b. Burnside v.
"   Charles J. assemb. at Colts, h. 32 Franklin.
"   Chas. M. clerk, 288 Main, h. 214 Bellevue.
"   Cornelius,helper at 581 Cap.h.2u.r. 44½John.
"   Daniel, porter at 149 State, h. 45 Portland.
"   Dennis, h. 61 Hamilton.
"   Dennis,lab. at PopeTubeCo.h.u.44 Francis.
"   Dennis, laborer, b. 190 Ward.
"   Dennis C. carpetlayer at Charles R. Hart
    Co. 898 Main, h. 102 Whitmore.

McCarthy Elizabeth, h. 21 Sheldon.
"   Ellen Mrs. h. 5 Queen.
"   Hannah, cook at 103, b. 103 State.
"   Hannah, wid. James, h.u. 15 So. Prospect.
"   James, b. 2 Holcomb.
"   Jeremiah,coachman at 121,b.121Sigourney.
"   Jeremiah, teamster, b.2u. 28 Cedar.
"   Jeremiah, teamster at 335 Shel. h. 62 Front.
"   Jeremiah J. at 20 South Hudson.
"   Jeremiah J.cutter,154 Pearl,b. Rocky Hill t.
"   John, teamster at 158, b.r. 160 Woodland.
"   John, benchman at Pope Tube Co.b.5 Queen.
"   John, machine hand at Colts, h. 52 Hudson.
"   John, mason tender, h. 51 Hamilton.
"   John J. barber, 347 Allyn, h. 25 Hawthorn.
"   John J. b. 104 Jefferson.
**McCARTHY JOHN J.** architect, 793
    Main, rm. 7.   The most modern designs
    rendered in the different styles of archi-
    tecture at lowest terms; h. New Britain t.
"   John J. machinist, b. 104 Jefferson.
"   John M. (McC. & Ahern,) h.u. 40 Spring.
"   Josie, dressmaker, b. 21 Ashley.
"   Katie F. stenog. 700 Main, b. Rocky Hill t.
"   Lizzie, at 690 Park, b. 82 Hamilton.
"   Mamie T. clerk at 374 Asylum, b. N.B t.
"   Margaret, dressmaker, b. 104 Jefferson.
"   Margaret Mrs. b. 2 Holcomb.
"   Mary E. clerk at Popes, b. 21 Ashley.
"   Michael, carptr. 52 John, h.3u. 111 Maple.
"   Michael, laborer, b. 156 Woodland.
"   P. deckhand str. Hartford, 285 State.
"   Patrick, janitor High school, h. 21 Ashley.
"   Thomas A. laborer 556 Cap. b.r. 124 Main.
"   Thomas J. screwm. Popes, b. 104 Jefferson.
"   Thomas W. filer at 581 Cap. b. 51 Hamilton.
"   Timothy, laborer, h.u. 45 Portland.
"   Timothy,laborer, h.u. 104 Jefferson.
"   Timothy F. engineer N.Y.R. h. 12 Winter.
"   Timothy J. b. 82 Hamilton.
"   Timothy L. bartdr. 238 Zion, b. 51 Hamilton.
"   Timothy M. plumber, 288 Mn. h. 94 Retreat.
"   William, at 554 Main, b. 14 Arch.
"   William, laborer at N.Y.R. h.u. 14 Arch.
"   ☞ see also McCarty.
McCartney Samuel, laborer, b.r. 64 Ward.
McCarty Annie, wid. John, b. 82 Hamilton.
"   Anthony,woodw. at 155 Ch.O. b. 80 State.
"   Charles, laborer, h. 2 North.
"   Cornelius, truckman, h.u. 33 Hudson.
"   Daniel, b. 2 Holcomb.
"   Daniel, teamster at 8 Front, h. 90 Windsor.
"   Daniel B. coachman, b. 106 Albany.
"   Dennis F. mach. at 1 Flow. b.104 Jefferson.
"   Elizabeth A. dressm. 214, h. 214 Bellevue.
"   Florence, dropforger, b.u. 33 Avon.
"   Fred D. electrotyper, h. 59 Harrison.
"   Harry E. engineer at 70 Com. h. 35 Wdbg.
"   James, laborer, h.r. 44 Village.
"   James D. bartender, 53½, b. 55 Windsor.
"   John, deckhand str. Middletown, 285 State.
"   Jeremiah, laborer, b.2u. 12 So. Prospect.
"   Jeremiah G. printer, l. 17 Church.
"   John, laborer, h. 1449 Broad.

McCarty John, saloon, 53 Windsor, h.2u. 29 Mor.
" Mary, boarding house, 18 Central.
" Mary E. bookkeeper, b. 214 Bellevue.
" Michael, laborer, b.u.r. 12 So. Prospect.
" Michael, laborer, b.u. 82 Front.
" Nora, h.u.r. 61 Front.
" Nora, b.3u. 32 Wells.
" Patrick, driver at 126 Church, h. 76 Walnut.
" Simon G. molder 690 Park, b. 214 Bellevue.
" Timothy, helper, h. 82 Hamilton.
" Timothy M. plumber, 288 Mn.h.u.94 Retreat.
" William, teamster, b.u. 104 Trumbull.
" William F. h 48 Clark.
" William J. helper, b. 36 Imlay.
" ☞see also McCarthy.
McCaulley Edwin H. patternm. 1 Flow. b.28West.
McCauliff Dennis, mach. 388 Cap. b. 145 Wash.
" James, b. 41 Sheldon.
" John, mach. at 388 Cap. b. 145 Washington.
McCausland Clarence Elmer, foreman at Popes,
    h.u. 39 Allen pl.
" Ralph E. modelm. at Popes, b. 39 Allen pl.
McChesney George R. supt. agencies Hartford
    Life Ins. Co. 252 Asylum, b. 149 High.
" William, trav. salesman, h.u. 56 Sumner.
McClary John, mfg. office fixtures, etc. 69 Front,
    h.2u. 7 Linden.
McClay Lizzie P. wid. James S. h. 162 Collins.
McClean Joseph, rest't, 10 Gold, h.3u. 82 Sheldon.
" Joseph A. clerk, 203 State, b.3u. 82 Sheldon.
" Thomas, clerk, 283 Park, b.3u. 82 Sheldon.
McClellan Albert M. rubberwkr. at 690 Park, h.
    Burnside v.
" Ann Mrs. seamstress, h.u. 133 Market, rm. 8.
" Charles R. (Elmer & McC.) b. 3 Whitman.
" Joseph W. asst. engineer No. 7, 480 Windsor
    av. h.u. 22 Kennedy.
" Mae B. cashier at 711 Main, h. E.H.t.
McClelland Milton H. teamster at 46 Ann, h. E.H.t.
McClerman Ann Mrs. b. St. Marv's Home for
    Aged, Albany.
McClory Henry S. coal, 146 Tru. h. 39 Kinsley.
McCloskey John, ostler at r. 173, b.r. 173 State.
" Patrick, driver at 15 Albany, h.46 Liberty.
McClunie Annie, dressmaker, 464, b. 464 Far.
" G. Wm. florist at 805 Main, h. 31 Annawan.
" Geo. G. florist at 805 Main, b.u. 25 Alden.
" Helen, teacher, Charter Oak school, 91
    Charter Oak, b. 464 Farmington.

**McCLUNIE J. ALEXANDER,**
    landscape architect, Hartford Decorating
    Co. 177, h.u. 823 Asylum. *See page 249.*
" Thomas, landscape gardener, h. 464 Far.
" Thomas R. truant officer, h. 42 Cedar.
McClure Carrie, b. 13 East.
" Chas. E. salesman 175 Pearl, h.u. 23 Seyms.
" David L. carpenter, h. 13 East.
" Jos. C. carpenter at 88 Mar. h. 153 Franklin.
" Peter E. clerk at 653 Main, h. 22 Village.
McCollum John, h. 206 Asylum, flat 15.
" John, b. 2 Holcomb.
" Olin S. machinist at 20 Vredendale, b.u.
    104 Hungerford.
" ☞see also McCallum.

McConkey James A. assembler, Popes, h.N.B.t.
McConn J. benchman at Pope Tube Co. h. 109
    Hamilton.
McConnell James, clerk at Smith, Bourn & Co.
    8 Sigourney, b. 8 Hawthorn.
" John, b.u.r. 41 Front.
McConville Peter, screwmaker, 476 Cap. b. M.t.
" William J. city attorney, attorney at law,
    847 Main, rm. 1, h. 25 Ashley.
McCook Eliza L. b. 396 Main.
" George Sheldon, U. S. army, b. 396 Main.
" John B. physician, U. S. army, b. 396 Main.
" John J. Rev. prof. Trinity college, h. 396 Mn.
" Philip J. b. 396 Main.
McCoombs James, fireman N.Y.R. b. 60 Walnut.
" Robert, porter at 734 Main, h. 6 Meadow.
McCorkell, Alex. K. accountant at C. S. Hills &
    Co. 885 Main, h. 16 Imlay.
" James, cutter at 8 Sigourney, h. 28 Hudson.
McCorkle George A. druggist, 1189 Main, h.
    10 Belden.
" Sarah, wid. William, h. 10 Belden.
McCormick Andrew, h.2u. 15 Howard.
" Bridget, h. 31 Cedar.
" Christopher, h. 60 Wells.
" Ellen, b. St. Mary's Home for Aged, Albany.
" Frank, engir. High school, b. 114 Hopkins.
" Grace, wid. Matthew, h.u. 37 Avon.
" James H. clerk 197 Asylum, b. Bloomfield t.
" James H. farmer, b. 2 Fairfield.
" James J. clerk at 306 Main, b. 1442 Broad.
" John, h.2u. 1447 Broad.
" John, clerk at 371, b. 1445 Broad.
" John F. enameler at 581 Cap. b. 60 Wells.
" John F. laborer at stonepits, b. 2 Fairfield.
" John H. cutter at 15 Trumbull, b. E.H.t.
" Leontine J. wid. William, h.r. 59½ Albany.
" May, clerk at 368 Asylum, b. 116 Hopkins.
" Michael, blaster stonepits, h. 2 Fairfield.
" Michael Jr. helper at stonepits, b. 2 Fairfield.
" Patrick W. mach. hand at Colts, b. 60 Wells.
" Robert J. salesman at The E. S. Kibbe Co.
    149 State, b. Windsor t.
" William, b. 2 Fairfield.
" William, decorator, b. 19 Central.
" William, molder, h.3u. 74 Walnut
" William H. molder at Pratt & Whitney Co.
    1 Flower, h.u. 74 Walnut.
" William J. blacksmith, h. 18 Alden.
McCourt Jas. fireman at Popes, h.u. 15 Park.
" Patrick, tailor, h. 1 Orchard.

McCoy Christopher, machinist at N.Y.R. h.r.
  26 Walnut.
" Geo. D. salesman, b. 42 Wooster.
" George S. salesman at Neal, Goff & Inglis
  Co. 980, b. 1246 Main.
" James, mach. at 1 Flower, b. 86 Hopkins.
" Jane, wid. John, h. 42 Wooster.
" John, laborer at 18, b. 18 Barbour.
" John J. ins. agt. at 756 Main, b. Windsor av.
" Thomas, musician, b. 336 Wethersfield.
" William, builder, 55, b. 55 Lincoln.
" William H. asst. bookkeeper at Farmers and
  Mech. Nat. Bk. 106 State, h. 55 Lincoln.
" William J. clerk at 66 State, b. 42 Wooster.
McCray Calvin C. bookkeeper at C. S. Brewer &
  Co. 238 Asylum, h. 450 Wethersfield.
" Chas. C. landscape gardener, b.u. 112 Laurel.
" Katharine, wid. Samuel, h. 450 Wethersfield.
" S. Warren, at Ætna Life Insurance Co. 650
  Main, b. 141 Washington.
" Theodore H. conductor St.Ry. b. 450 Weth.
McCRAY WILLIAM B. (*Kimball & McCray,*) 658
  Main, h. 44 Gillett.  See page 444.
" ☞ *see also Macrae.*
McCreary Howard S. stenographer Ætna Life
  Ins. Co 650 Main, b. 54 Ashley.
" Ralph W. stenographer at Ætna Life Ins.
  Co. 650 Main, b. 54 Ashley.
McCrenor James, machinist at 83 Woodbine, b.
  Buckland v.
McCrimmon Belle M. J. nurse, 20 So. Hudson.
McCrone James, b. 2 Holcomb.
" Jeannette, wid William, h. 84 Williams.
" Richard, blacksmith, h. 171 Zion.
" Richard F. clerk at 419 Mn. b. 16 Franklin.
" Wm. M. salesman, 690 Park, h. 84 Williams.
McCrossen Dennis, enameler at Popes, h.87 Com.
" Mary, wid. James, h.u. 250 Front.
McCrosson William H. vulcanizer at 555 Capitol,
  h. Bloomfield t.
McCrum George R. machinist at 388 Capitol, h.
  252 Putnam.
McCue Bernard, bricklayer, b. 24 Union.
" Charles T. manager tire department at 690
  Park, h. 17 Russ.
" Edward J. painter, b.3u. 200 Sheldon.
" James F. mach. at Colts, b.3u. 200 Sheldon.
" John, mason, h. 147 Lawrence.
" John A. driller at Colts, h. 26 Park.
" Julia A. wid. Michael, h. 98 Albany.
" Kate, at mattress department, 334 Wethers-
  field, b. 26 Franklin.
" Martin, laborer, h.u. 33 Russell.

McCue Michael J. telegraph operator, 3 Central,
  b. 98 Albany.
" Owen, at mattress department, 334 Weth-
  ersfield, b. 26 Franklin.
" Patrick, moulder, 556 Cap. h. 48 Windsor.
" Thomas, laborer, b.u. 5 Affleck.
" Thomas, laborer, h.3u. 200 Sheldon.
" Thomas, policeman, h. 26 Park.
" Thos. J. Jr. machineh. Colts, b.u. 128 Ward.
" ☞ *see also McHough; McKeough.*
McCullough Felix, carptr. at 53 Vernon, h. E.H.t.
" John, plumber at 1152 Main, b. 14 Chapel.
" Margaret A. clerk at Brown, Thomson &
  Co. 942 Main, b. 14 Chapel.
" P. deckhand steamer Hartford, 285 State.
" Thomas F. machinehand at Colts, b. E.H.t.
" Wm. H. operator at 40 Governor, b. E.H.t.
McCune Bernard, molder, h. 24 Flower.
" Catherine, b. 24 Flower.
" ☞ *see also McKeown; McKone; McKeon.*
McCunn James M. bookkeeper at 74 Trumbull,
  b. 34 Charter Oak.
McCusker Daniel J. steamfitter at 33 Vernon,
  b. 58 Benton.
" John Lawrence, carptr. P.&R. h. 76 Green.
" Michael, blacksmith, b. 46 Liberty.
" Patrick, laborer at 15 Albany, h. 46 Liberty.
McDermid Thomas, carpenter at r. 334 Asylum,
  h.3u. 271 Main.
McDermott Catharine, wid. James, h.u. 5 Amity.
" Christopher J. laborer, b. 13 Front.
" Eddie, gardener, l. 84 Arch.
" James, caterer at and b. Trinity college.
" James J. saloon 25, h. 30 Temple.
" James J. cook at 375 Asy. h.u.r. 299 Mar.
" John, blacksmith, h. 13 Front.
" John F. painter, b.u. 52 Woodbridge.
" John F. policeman, h.2u. 184 Putnam.
" Maurice E. rec. clerk at 98 Kil. b. 13 Front.
" Thomas, hackman at 13, b. 13 Front.
McDiarmid Joseph, bookkeeper at Brown, Thom-
  son & Co. 942 Main, b. Manchester t.
McDonald Catharine, wid. James, h.r. 9 Queen.
" Charles H. clerk at Popes, b. 51 Elm.
" Daniel, finisher, h. 15 Wadsworth.
" Daniel F. carpenter, h. 23 Lawrence.
" Edward, laborer at Capitol, h. 82 Jefferson.
" Edward F. clerk at 78 Asy. b. 82 Jefferson.
" Edward P. machinist N.Y.R. h.u. 22 Amity.
" Ellen, wid. Patrick, h.u. 11 Affleck.
" George E. carpenter, h.u. 26 Elm.
" Geo. F. blacksm. at 581 Cap. h. 188 Capen.
" James, cigarmaker 104 Asy, b. 42 Canton.
" James, lab. State capitol, h.2u. 65 Flower.
" James, molder at 556 Cap. h. 7 Hawthorn.
" James, screwmaker, 476 Cap. b.u. 11 Affleck.
" Jasmes A. plumber at 94 State, b. 22 Amity.
" Jennie, at 254 Pearl, b.2u. 110 Hungerford.
" Jeremiah M. clerk 885 Mn. h. 97 Seymour.
" John, laborer, h.2u. 140 Windsor.
" John, laborer at Spring Grove Cemetery,
  h. 43 Mather.
" John, carpenter at 155 Ch.O. b. 5 Vandyke.
" John C. currier at Jewell Belting Co. 15,
  b. 30 Trumbull.

McDonald John F. Mrs. h. 18 Russell.
" John J. clerk at 254 Pearl, h.2u. 110 Hung.
" John P. polisher at Popes, b. 1262 Broad.
" Margaret, wid. John, h.2u. 110 Hungerford.
" Margaret L. aligner at Hartford Typewriter Co. b. 9 Girard.
" Nellie J. b. 82 Jefferson.
" Patrick H. laborer, b.u. 11 Affleck.
" Peter, molder, h.2u. 57 Spruce.
" Peter, plumber at 291 Asy. h.u. 29 Hudson.
" Peter, screwmaker, 476 Cap. b. 84 Ward.
" Thomas F. agent, 721 Mn. b. 158 Babcock.
" Thomas J. painter, b.2u. 275 Asylum.
" William, conductor St.Ry. h.u. 216 Fkn.
" William, laborer, h.r.u. 570 Main.
" William B. painter, h.u. 114 Mather.
" Wm. B. janitor 1st Reg't Arm'y, h.u.51 Elm.
" William J. buffer at William Rogers Mfg. Co. 66 Market, b. 348 Front.
" Winifred, foreman drapery dept. Neal, Goff & Inglis Co. 980 Main, b. E.H.t.
" ☞ see also MacDonald.
McDonnell Annie R. teacher N.E. school, b.u. 378 Windsor av.
" Bridget, wid. John, h.u. 20 Albany.
" Charles C. pressman at Case, L. & B. Co. 141 Pearl, b.2u. 378 Windsor av.
" Cornelius, teamster, b. 259 Front.
" Elizabeth, dressmaker, h. 65 Flower.
" James, porter at 219 Asy. h.u. 1335 Broad.
" John B. clerk at Halls of Record, 114 Pearl, h.2u. 378 Windsor av.
" Maggie, clerk at 270 Main, b.u. 20 Albany.
" Mary E. stenogr. at 690 Park, b. 65 Flower.
McDonough Bernard, coachman, b. 28 Babcock.
" Edward J. rubberw. 690 Park, h. 623 Cap.
" Eugene, tinner at 4 Ford, h. 29 Hudson.
" Frank P. brakeman P.&R b. 51 Brook.
" Geo. F. electrician, 690 Park, b. 60 Willow.
" Henry J. mach. at 30 Cush. b. 60 Willow.
" James, laborer, Pope Tube Co. b. Riverside.
" John, helper, h.u. 20 Russell.
" John E. conductor P.&R. h. 51 Brook.
" John, Jr. b.u. 20 Russell.
" Maria, h.u. 16 Flower.
" Michael, b.u. 20 Russell.
" Michael, laborer, h. 60 Willow.
" Patrick, helper at Pratt & Whitney Co. 1 Flower, h.2u. 22 Babcock.
" Peter, laborer, h.2u. 57 Spruce.
" Robert H. pat.mkr. 556 Cap. b. 56 Willard.
" Thomas, painter, 352 Alb. h. Manchester t.
" William J. (Smith & McD.) 801 Main, h.u. 344 Wethersfield.
McDougall Alexander, clerk at Brown, Thomson & Co. 942, b. 387 Main.
" John, jan. Phœnix Nat. Bank, h.u. 803 Main.
McElhinney John M. cabinetm. 556. b.609 Main.
McElhone John M. mech. Popes, b. 55 Babcock.
McElliott Stephen J. assist. supt. John Hancock Mutual Life Ins. Co. 756 Mn. b. 105·Ann.
McElroy George C. electrotyper at A. Mugford, 177 Asylum, h. 48 Lincoln.
" Grace, at Wileys, b. 15 Atlantic.
" Margaret, wid. George, h. 15 Atlantic.

McElwain Alfred H. contractor, h. 59 Chestnut.
" Frank A. student at Trinity college, 5 Northam tower, Summit.
McEnroe Michael, mason, h. 47 Congress.
McEntee Elizabeth, b. 245 Wethersfield.
" John. foreman at Colts, h. 245 Wethersfield.
" John Jr. molder at 54 Arch, b. 979 Park.
" Patrick H. machinist, b. 245 Wethersfield.
McEvoy Joseph F. bartdr. 36 Wells, h. 72 Retreat.
" Joseph L. bartender at 25, b. 25 Central.
" Nora E. teach. at Parkville sch.b.u.147Maple.
" Patrick, rubberw. 690 Park, h. 40 Glendale.
" William, general foreman street department, 800 Main, h.u. 147 Maple.
" ☞ see also McAvoy.
McFadyen James, carpenter at William Rogers Mfg. Co. 66·Market, h. 172 Barbour.
" John, supt. at William Rogers Mfg. Co. 66 Market, h. 28 Mahl.
" Joseph, baker at 94 Hudson, h. 29 Morgan.
" Samuel, bookkeeper at William Rogers Mfg. Co. 66 Market, h.u. 20 Mahl.
McFall James, joiner, b. 565 Park.
McFarlan Armour J. blacksmith at 82 Francis, h. 550 Park.
" Bert, dressmaker, h.u. 89 Main.
McFarland Armour N. roller 690, h. 865 Park.
" Elizabeth, fancy goods, superintendent P.O. in Parkville, 761, h. 761 Park.
" Jas. N. rubbw. 690 Park, b. 7 Washington.
" John J. teamster. h. 73 Francis.
" ☞ see also Macfarlane.
McFarlane Alex. toolm. at Colts, b. 34 Ch. Oak.
" John H. beltmaker, 15 Trumbull, h. Weth. t
" William T. beltmaker at 15 Trumbull, h.u. 170 Windsor av.
McFetridge Joseph, machinist at Pratt & Whitney Co. 1 Flower, h. 23 Affleck.
" Robert, janitor Trinity college, h. 72 N.B.
" Thomas, salesman 335 Sheldon, h.u. 72 N.B.
McGann Edward, mach. at N.Y.R. h.u. 117 Zion.
" John P. operator at 6 Central, h. 71 Laurel.
" Patrick, machinist, h.u. 62 Governor.
" Thomas, engir. 476 Cap. h. 138 Lawrence.
McGary Alexander, stonecutter at 93 Charter Oak, h. 33 Hudson.
McGauley Frank P. driver, h.r. 58 Grove.
" Owen, mason, b.u. 105 Jefferson.
" Wm. F. butcher 2 Church, h.u. 76 Windsor.
McGavock John, laborer on city works, h. 119 Madison av.
McGeachie James C. steamfitter at 446 Asylum, h.u. 93 Hudson.
McGeary Mary, nurse, l.2u. 36 Church.
McGee Cornelius T. (McGee Mfg. Co.) h.78 Park.
" Howard H. clerk, b. 78 Park.
" John, barber, 3 Asylum, b. 19 Goodwin.
" John, mason tender, h. 140 Lawrence.
" Kate, wid. Michael, h.u. 180 Front.
" Levy S. carptr. at 60 Temple, h.u. 23Ward.
" Mfg. Co., druggist rubber sundries, 78 Park. Cornelius T. McGee.
" Robert S. buffer at Popes, b.u. 23 Ward.
" Wm. L. salesm. 45 Asy. b.u. 106½ Trumbull.
" ☞ see also Magee.

McGehon Marcus J. clerk, 319 Asylum, b. E.H.t.
McGhee John C. agent, l. 221 Main.
McGibbon Lewis C. attendant at 30 Washington.
"   Peter S. attendant at 30 Washington.
McGill Annie, b. W.H.Home for the Aged, Alb.
"   Ellen P. Miss, matron 239, b.u. 307 Market.
"   James, fireman, h.u. 45 Spruce.
"   Jas. F. life ins. agt. at 721 Mn. h.u. 426 Asy.
"   John, blacksmith at H. B. Beach & Son, 135 Grove, h.u. 307 Market.
"   John, driver, b. 24 Chestnut.
"   Joseph W. laborer, b. 307 Market.
"   Margaret, wid. Michael, b.u. 45 Spruce.
"   Patrick, laborer, h.u. 75 Windsor.
"   Robert, deckhand,str. Middletown,285State.
"   ☞see also Magill.
McGilton James, machinist at Pope Tube Co. h. 7 Prospect av near New Park.
McGinley Hugh F. watchman, h.r. 91 Bluehills.
McGinn Charles, mason, h. 29 Liberty.
"   Charles Mrs. groceries, 29, h. 29 Liberty.
"   Hugh, blacksm. 41 Annawan, h. 80 Franklin.
"   John, laborer, h.u. 25 West.
"   ☞see also Maginn.
McGinnis E. fireman, str. Middletown, 285 State.
McGoe Ann, h.u. 72 Governor.
McGoldrick Jas. J. pressm. Popes, h. 381 Park.
McGonnell Joseph, machinist at Pratt & Whitney Co. 1, h.3u. 30 Flower.
McGovern James, enameler at 1, b. 63 Flower.
"   Mary C. clerk at Brown, Thomson & Co. 942 Main, b. 3½ Elliott pl.
"   Nora Mrs. h. 3½ Elliott pl.
"   Owen, at Popes, b.u. 71 Governor.
"   Patrick, at Ætna Life Ins. Co. 650 Main, h. 46 Buckingham.
"   Patrick, carpenter, b.u. 18 Central.
"   Thomas J. tailor, 76 Asylum, l. 61 Prospect.
McGowan Andrew, ostler at 995, l. 995 Main.
"   David, tinner, 346 Main, h.u. 40 Hicks.
"   John, helper at 98 Wells, b. 33 Mulberry.
"   Margaretta J. teacher Law. st. sch. b. 27 Bkm.
"   Michael, porter at 224, b. 80 State.
"   Michael C. boilerm. N.Y.R, h.2u. 4 Queen.
"   Michael H. manager at 589 Main.
"   Patrick N. laborer, 556 Cap. b. 43 Sigourney.
McGrady Patrick, at 1 Flower, b. 43 Linden.
McGrain Thomas G. operator, 40 Gov. b. 15 S. Pro.
McGrane Julia, wid. James, h.r. 45 Sheldon.
McGranor Robert J. floorwalker at 956 Main, b. 56 Winthrop.
McGrath Alice, h. 29 Trumbull.
"   Andrew, stonecutter, h.u. 11 Ellery.
"   Catharine T. wid. James J. h.u. 53 Potter.
"   Daniel, carpenter, b.u. 121 Ann.
"   Daniel J. assembler at Popes,b. 28 Grace.
"   Daniel S. lettercarrier, P.O. h.u 87 Chestnut.
"   Edward A. plumber, 824 Park, h. 22 Greenwood.
"   Frank Mrs. h.u. 142 Grove.
"   Fred. W. clerk, 3 American, b. 4 Ellsworth.
"   James J. bartender at 55, b.u. 53 Potter.
"   John H. helper, h.u. 41 South Prospect.
"   John J. machinist at Popes. b. 43 Madison av.
"   John J. operator at 8 Sigourney, b. 80 State.

McGrath John P. carpenter at 1 Flower, h.u. 50 Glendale.
"   John W. mach. at 388 Cap. l.u. 1328 Broad.
"   Lawrence, bottler, b.u. 53 Potter.
"   Mary S. wid. Stephen, h. 43 Madison av.
"   Michael, laborer, N.Y.R. h.u. 25 Flower.
"   Nellie, b. 62 Grove.
"   Nellie, clerk at 956 Main, b. 28 West.
"   Nora A. dressmaker, 43, b. 43 Madison av.
"   Patrick, laborer, 1 Flower, l.u. 1328 Broad.
"   Patrick V. bartender, 269 Main, h. 44½ John.
"   Rose, wid. Stephen, h.u. 312 Asylum, rm. 10.
"   Rose E. boardinghouse, 5 Chapel.
"   Sarah, h. 29 Trumbull.
"   Thomas, b. W.H.Home for the Aged, Albany.
"   Thomas, mach.at Pope Tube Co.h.34 Amity.
"   Thos. S. pressm. Pope Tube Co. b.470 Broad.
"   Thos. W. screwmaker at Popes, b. N.B.t.
"   Timothy, laborer on St.Ry. b.u. 22 Albany.
"   Timothy F.( T. F.McG.& Co.) h.u.820 Park.

**McGRATH T. F. & CO.** contractors and builders, 820 Park.   See page 520.
"   Timothy J. packer, l. 3 Marsh.
"   William, saloon at 29, h.u. 31 Sheldon.
"   William F.mach. at 1 Flow.h.2u.118 Market.
McGregor E. Peter, screwmaker at 476 Capitol, b. 67 Hamilton.
"   James, carpenter, N.Y.R. h. 67 Hamilton.
"   John, United States army, h. 49 Amity.
McGrevy Martin, laborer, h. 24 Union.
"   Richard, bicycle repairer at 328 Asylum, b. 24 Union pl.
McGuckin Michael, carptr.P.&R.h.u.1328 Broad.
McGuiniss Thomas, helper at 98 Kil. h. E.H.t.
McGuinness John L. Rev. asso. editor Catholic Transcript, 704 Main, h. 140 Farmington.
McGuira Norton, shipr. 581 Cap. h.21 Lawrence.
McGuire Arthur G.mach.at 1 Flow. h.u.238 Park.
"   B. b. 63 Market.
"   Charles, clerk at 243, b. 223 Park.
"   Charles M. mach. at 1 Flower, b.u. 238 Park.
"   Christopher, roofer r. 32 Village.
"   Edward, finisher at 17 Elm, h. N.H.t.
"   Elizabeth, b. W.H. Home for the Aged, Alb.
"   John, laborer, h.3u. 1447 Broad.
"   John, teamster at 100 Commerce, h. 28 Front.
"   John H. teas, etc. 16, h. 36 Church.
"   Margaret Mrs. b. W. H. Home for Aged, Alb.
"   Margaret A. wid. Cornelius, h. 18 Francis.
"   Martin, conductor, P.&R. h.2u. 31 Liberty.
"   Martin, helper at 581 Cap. h. 21 Lawrence.
"   Mary H. Mrs. h.u. 6 Trumbull.
"   Patrick, laborer, b. 147 Sheldon.
"   Patrick, laborer at stone pits, h. Park.
"   Patrick F. laborer, h. 19 Putnam.
"   ☞see also Maguire.
McGullers Simon, carpenter, h. 120 Portland.
McGuone John, stonectr. at 93 Ch.O. b. 94 N.B.
McGurk Annie, bkkpr. at 352 Alb. b. 39 Harrison.
"   Barney, deckhand, str. Hartford, 285 State.
"   Bernard, market, 1149 Main, h.u. 7 Avon.

**McCURK BERNARD L.** carriagemaker, 352 Albany and Woodland, h. 39 Harrison.

McGurk Catherine, housekeeper, h. 7 Avon.
" Minnie F.stenographer,N.E.R.b.200 Ashley.
" Nellie, wid Phillip, at 11 Pratt, b.1094 Main.
" Nellie A. wid. William, h. 200 Ashley.
" Patrick, deckhand; str. Hartford, 285 State.
McHugh Charles, mach. at 1 Flow.b.66 Hopkins.
" Thomas, helper at 9 Sigourney, h. 128 Ward.
McIlvaine John G. student at Trinity college, 24 Jarvis hall, Summit.
McIndue George, h. 57 Elliott.
" Margaret A. clerk at Brown, Thomson & Co. 942 Main, b. 57 Elliott.
McIneary Joseph F. engineer, b. 54 Potter.
" Mamie A. b. 54 Potter.
" Marks, laborer, b. 54 Potter.
" Thomas, h. 54 Potter.
McInnis Catherine, wid. Donald, b. 884 Main.
" Henry J. teamster at 46 Ann, h. 109 Windsor.
" Norman A. painter, h.u.r. 66 Vanblock.
" Richard, errandboy at Colts, b. 66 Vanblock.
McIntee John, molder at 54 Arch, h. 751 Park.
McIntosh David B. machinist at Pope Tube Co. h. 89 Madison.
" George F. diesinker at Popes, h.246 Putnam.
" Howard E. machinist, b. 37 Amity.
" Hugh, gilder at 693, b. 343 Main.
" John, dyer at 37 Wells, b. Wethersfield t.
" Underhill H. gilder, b. 35 Buckingham.
" William C. diesinker at Popes, h. 37 Amity.
McIntyre Archibald, carpenter at 141 Trumbull, h. Arnsdale, W.H.t.
" Bridget, wid. Joseph, h.u. 19 Mechanic.
" Clara. h.u. 316 Windsor av.
" & Clarkin, undertakers, 12½ Church.
   James McIntyre.   Michael M. Clarkin.
" Ed. T. mach. at 70 Huy. b.u. 11 Seymour.
" Edward E. F. saloon, 109 State, h.u. 1 Webb.
" Fannie, h.u. 216 Windsor av.
" Fred. G. porter at 207 Allyn, b. 23 Spring.
" Henry E. bartend. 109 State, b.u. 6 Talcott.
" Henry J. helper at James L. Howard & Co. 438 Asylum, b. 19 Mechanic.
" Hugh A. h. 10 Hungerford.
" James, (McI. & Clarkin,) h.u. 6 Talcott.
" John, watchman at Colts, h.r. 56 Vanblock.
" John D. bookbinder, h.u. 219 Pearl.
" John H. clerk, 1165 Main, b.u. 19 Mechanic.
" John J. Jr. assistant engineer at 124 Front, b.r. 56 Vanblock.
" Kittie, wid. Hugh, h.u. 219 Pearl.
" Kittie F. stenog. secretary of state, rm. 36, State capitol, b.u. 219 Pearl.
" Leonard, carpenter, b. 23 Spring.
" Marv, wid. John, h.u. 1 Webb.
" Oscar E. driver, 14 Huntington.
" Peter, engineer, b. 36 Temple pl.
" Peter, horse trainer, b. 428 Asylum.
" Thos. assembler at 556 Capitol, b. 60 Flow.
" William, carpenter, h.u. 4 Morris.
" William J. appren. at Colts, b. 56 Vanblock.
McIsaac Allen, lineman, b.u. 59 Market.
" Angus A. beltmaker at Jewell Belting Co. 15 Trumbull, b. 21 Central.
McJunkins Robert, clerk, 164 State, b.117 High.
McKaig Dolphin L. painter at N.Y.R. h. W.t.

McKay Donald, collector, steamer Middletown, h. Portland t.
" Frances, wid. John, h.u. 162 Ward.
" Howard, caller at N.Y.R. b.u. 162 Ward.
" James, baker at 745 Main, h.u. 31 Putnam.
" William, helper at 135, b. 88 Sheldon.
" ☞ see also Mackay.
McKean Annie S. b. 28 Franklin.
" James, painter, 5 Mechanic, b. 28 Franklin.
McKee George C., U. S. gauger, b. 111½ Ann.
" John B. printer at 141 Pearl, b. 41 Dean.
" Joseph E. b. 23 Elliott.
" & Kearns, saloon, 220 Front.
   William J. McKee.   Michael H. Kearns.
" Nancy, wid. Robert, h. 41 Dean.
" Patrick F. clerk at 693 Mn. b. 245 Jefferson.
" Sophia, wid. James, h. 245 Jefferson.
" William J. (McK. & Kearns,) h. E.H.t.
McKeen Bedford, salesman at 335 Sheldon, b. 86 Hudson.
McKegg Elizabeth, wid. James, h. 10 Affleck.
McKeilson Evert, h.2u. 277 Main.
McKenna Francis T. joiner, h. 1053 Broad.
" James, tinner at 50 Church.
" John, b. W. H. Home for the Aged, Albany.
" John, builder at 11, h. 11 Bellevue.
" John J. marketm. at 33 Market,b.2u.96 State.
" Lewis, fireman P.&R. h. 86 Fairmount.
" Patrick F. marketm. 33 Mar. l.2u. 96 State.
" Patrick H. tailor at 66 Asy. h. 1416 Broad.
" ☞ see also McKinney; Kinney; McKenney.
McKenney Robert H. rubberworker at 690 Park, b. 46 Smith.
McKenzie Carl, carpenter, b.u. 68 Flower.
" Elma, b. 70 Capitol.
" Emeline, wid. Thomas J. h.u. 68 Flower.
" Frank T. cigarm. at 867 Main,b.u.68 Flower.
" Fred, b. 70 Capitol.
" G. E. clerk at 304 Asylum, b. 70 Capitol.
" Jessie, dressmaker, 294, b. 294 Franklin.
" John A. carpenter, b. 1430 Broad.
" Theodore H. civil engineer, 75 Pratt, h. Southington t.
McKeon Agnes J. clerk at Brown, Thomson & Co. 942 Main, b. 7 Kennedy.
" James, painter, b. 548 Park.
" Mary E. clerk at Brown, Thomson & Co. 942 Main, b. 7 Kennedy.
" Mary L. dressmaker, 739, h. 739 Main, rm. 8.
" Matthew R. brass finisher at 65 Suffield, b.u. 7 Kennedy.
" Nora E. bkkpr. at 1046 Main, b. 83 Edwards.
" Philip, coremaker, h.u. 7 Kennedy.
" ☞ see also McCune; McKone; McKeown.
McKeough Annie, dressmaker, b. 282 Bellevue.
" John, apprentice, 5 Mechanic, b. 155 Maple.
" Martin, saloon, 110, h. 110 Albany.
" Patrick J. laborer, h. 232 Bellevue.
" William, blacksmith at 5 Mec. h. 155 Maple.
" ☞ see also Kehoe; Keough.
McKeown James A. marketman, 319 Asylum, b. 21 So. Hudson.
" James E. driver at 149 State, h. 24 Walnut.
" William, h. 205 Woodland.
" ☞ see also McKeon; McKone; McCune.

**If You Want all the News, Read THE POST.**

McKernan Edward F.saloon,532 Mn.h.63 Capitol.
" Francis, janitor, h. 94 Albany.
" John, h. 24 Avon.
" John H. bartender at 532 Main, h.u. 8 John.
" Mary Mrs. h.3u. 312 Asylum.
McKichney Bert, steamfitter, b. 80 State.
McKinley Frank, b. 2 Holcomb.
" Mattie, b. 1153 Main.
McKinney Albert R. at Ætna Life Insurance
    Co. 650 Main, b. 17 Seymour.
" Essie, butler, b. 149 Sigourney.
" Henry S. foreman st. dept. h. 17 Seymour.
" John H. with Graves & Robinson, b. 17
    Seymour.
" John M. clerk, h.u. 15 Liberty.
" Maggie, wid. John, h.r. 23 West.
" Mary B. wid. H. b. 177 Retreat.
" Monroe, b.u. 15 Liberty.
" Robert H. rubberworker, b. 46 Smith.
" Scott D. butcher at 373 Main. h.12 West.
" ☞ see also McKenna; McKenney; Kinney.
McKinnon James, tinner at 1116 Main, h. 50 Alb.
" James Mrs. h. 50 Albany.
McKinstry John, clerk at 197 Asy. b. Ellington t.
McKirdy Andrew, carpenter, h.u. 32 Grand.

EVERETT J. McKNIGHT, Physician and Sur-
    geon. Office 110 High street.
    Hours—8 to 9 A.M., 2 to 4 and 7 to 8 P.M.
    Sundays—2 to 3 P.M.
    Telephone—503-2.

McKnight Everett J. physician, 110, h. 149 High.
" James B. engineer, h.u. 1074 Broad.
" Patrick, laborer, h.u. 93 Sheldon.
McKone Brothers, builders, etc. 147 Sheldon.
    Christopher J. McKone.    William McKone.
" Christopher J. (McK. Bros.) h. 109 Weth.
" James N. student, h. 174 Farmington.
" John J. clerk, b. 131 Oak.
" Mary, h.r. 44 Village.
" Patrick, builder, r. 131, h. 131 Oak.
" Peter, teamster, 153, h. 153 Zion.
" Robert A. builder at 131, b. 131 Oak.
" William, (McK. Bros.) b. 174 Farmington.
McKune ☞ see also McCune; McKeon; Mc-
    Keown.
McLachlan David, patternm. at 556, b. 287 Cap.
" John C. clerk at P.&R. h. 110 Hopkins.
McLaren Matthew J. plasterer, h.u. 53 Liberty.
McLaughlan William, b. 22 Squire.
McLaughlin Alida, at 141 Pearl, b.926 Mn. rm.67.
" Arthur, salesman at Neal, Goff & Inglis Co.
    980 Main, h. 1148 Broad.
" Catherine, wid. Owen, b. 16 Center.
" Charles C. painter, b. 14 Potter.
" Daniel F. b. 15 Zion.
" Eugene, driver at 356 b. 362 Main.
" Frank, mason, b.2u. 131 Lawrence.
" George J. helper, 135 Shel. b. 46 Vanblock.
" Hugh H. b. 14 Potter.
" James, h. 48 Vanblock.
" James A. helper at 1 Laurel, b. 1035 Broad.
" James F. salesman at 232 Shel. h. 21 Vernon.
" James H. sta. engine at P.&R. b. 15 Williams.
" John, coachman, 137, l. 137 High.
" John, sidewalklayer, h. 22 Squire.

McLaughlin John F. bart. 33 Pearl, b. 14 Potter.
" John F. mach. at 40 Gov. h. 14 Jefferson.
" John F. mason, h. 15 James.
" John J. enameler at Popes, b. 12 Arch.
" John J. grocery and meats,141, h. 141 Zion.
" Kate. dressm. 1232 Main, h.2u. 15 Williams.
" Martin J. mach. at 581 Cap. b. 1421 Broad.
" Mary, laundress at 30 Washington.
" Mary, wid. Terrance, h. 14 Potter.
" Michael, farmer, r. 147 Woodland, h.u. 15
    Williams.
" Michael, mason, h.u. 131 Lawrence.
" Patrick J. molder at 556 Cap. h. 94 Windsor.
" Peter, watchman at Colts, h. 46 Vanblock.
" Peter H. Jr. machineh. Colts, b. 46 Vanblock.
" Peter J. plumber at 128 State, h. 15 Zion.
" Terrance, dropforger at Colts, b. 39½ Laf.
" Vesta, nurse, 20 South Hudson.
" ☞ see also Laughlin.
McLean Annie Mrs. dressm. h. 117 Jefferson.
" Benjamin, b.u. 23 Russell.
" Chas. O. inspector at Popes, h. 117 Jefferson.
" Duncan, carpenter, b. 112 Laurel.
" Dwight, express, h.u. 136 Albany.
" Edward, janitor at Ætna Insurance Co. 666
    Main, h.u. 23 Russell.
" Ethel A. clerk at 197 Asylum, b. 38 Pliny.
" Frank, carpenter, h. 82 Franklin.
" Frank, teamster, h. 457 Windsor av.
" George C. grocer, meats,16 Maple, h. 120 Jef.
" George L. factory inspector, State capitol,
    rm. 26, h. Ellington t.
" George O. (Erichson & McL.) h. 3 Asylum.
McLean GEORGE P. (Sperry, McL. & Brain-
    ard,) attorney, 650 Main, h. Simsbury t.
        See page 494.
" Lewis D. clerk, b.u. 117 Jefferson.
" Lillian F. b. 117 Jefferson.
" Mary, teacher Lawrence st. school, b. E.H.t.
" Nicholas W. engineer str. Middletown, h.u.
    19 Congress.
" P. H. Rev. h. 140 Farmington.
" William H. h. 38 Pliney.
McLear Wm. B. carptr. 476 Cap. h. 1425 Broad.
McLeod Arthur, policeman, h.u. 59 Market.
" Arthur A. electrician, b.u. 67 Pleasant.
" Donald, stereotyper at the Courant, 66
    State, h. 459 Maple.
" Samuel F. boxmaker at Popes, b.u. 59 Mar.
McLoughlin Francis J. machinist at 1 Flower,
    b. 1035 Broad.
" Peter, elevatorer at Pratt & Whitney Co. 1
    Flower, h. 1035 Broad.
McLouth Benjamin F. at Conn. Mutual Life
    Ins. Co. 783, b. 255 Main.
McMahon Annie, dressmaker, b.u. 51 Front.
" Annie C. wid Bernard, h.u. 286 Park.
" Anthony J. bartender, b. 15 Spruce.
" Daniel, laborer at 95 Pleasant, b. 54 Avon.
" Henry P. polisher at 581 Cap. b. 25 Putnam.
" John, helper at 1 Flower, b. 15 Huntley pl.
" John, helper at 556 Cap. b. 246 Lawrence.
" John, laborer at 79 Talcott, h. 14 Wads.
" John, laborer at N.Y.R. b.2u. 38 Lawrence.

**As A NEWSPAPER, THE POST LEADS.**

McMahon John J. draughtsman at 252 Asylum,
 b. 14 Wadsworth.
" John J. engineer, P.&R. h.u. 144 Mather.
" Margaret, wid. Michael, h.2u. 38 Lawrence.
" Joseph M. clerk at 581 Cap. b.u. 286 Park.
" Mary, h. 126 Babcock.
" Mary, laundress, b.2u. 38 Lawrence.
" Matthew, chipper at 556 Cap. b. 7 Hawthorn.
" Michael F. enameler at Popes, b. 14 Wads.
" Oscar, brickmaker, b. Windsor av.
" Patrick, b.r. 60 Woodbine.
" Patrick, laborer at r. 147 Woodland, h.
 Scarborough.
" Timothy, filer at 581 Cap. b. 246 Lawrence.
" William A. driver, h. 6 Goodman.
McMann Annie Mrs. h.u. 4 Chapel.
" Harry A. apprentice, b.u. 4 Chapel.
McManus Anna and Rose Misses, b. 80 Pratt.
" Arthur J. at 346 Main, b. 255 Jefferson.
" Bessie M. teacher at Second North school,
 249 High, b. 255 Jefferson.
" Bros. cigar factory, 133 Main.
  John F. McManus. Harry F. McManus.
" Charles, (Jas. McM. & Sons,) dentists, 80
 Pratt, h. 109 Washington.
" Edward, driver Adams Exp. b. 41 Asylum.
" Edward F. baggageman N.Y.R. b. 80 State.
" Edward K. driver at 13 Morris, h.2u. 91 Mn.
" Frank C. at 346 Main, b. 255 Jefferson.
" Fred'k G. clerk, b. 60 Edwards.
" Harry F. (McManus Bros.) b. 91 Main.
" Harry John, b.u. 232 Wethersfield.
" Henry, (Jas. McM. & Sons,) dentists, 80
 Pratt, h. 550 Prospect av.
" J. Henry, clerk at Hartford Trust Co. 764
 Main, b. 255 Jefferson.
" J. Ward, at Ætna Life Ins. Co. 650 Main, b.
 60 Edwards.
" James, (Jas. McM. & Sons,) h. 80 Pratt.

**McMANUS JAMES & SONS,**
dentists, 80 Pratt.  See page 423.
 Jas. McManus, Chas. McManus, Henry McManus.
" James, cigar m. at 867 Main, h. 7 Chapel.
" John, carpenter, h.u. 41 Asylum.
" John C. stoves, etc., 346 Main, h. 255 Jef.
" John F. (McManus Bros.) b.2u. 91 Main.
" John H. h. 20 Center.
" John J. helper at Colts, b.2u. 184 Sheldon.
" John J. moulder at 618, b. 371 Capitol.
" John Mrs. boardinghouse, 41 Asylum.
" Joseph, clerk at 242, b. 41 Asylum.
" Mary, stitcher, b. 31 Arch.
" Mary W. wid. John T. h. 60 Edwards.
" Michael, helper at St.Ry. 115 State.
" Michael J. laborer at 153, h.u. 232 Weth.
" Patrick, hodcarrier, b.2u. 10 Lawrence.
" Robert D. janitor, h.2u. 884 Main.
" Rosanna, wid. John, h.u. 6 Marsh.
" Thomas, clerk at 242 Asylum, b.2u. 91 Main.
" Thos. polisher at 581 Capitol, b. 6 Marsh.

**McMANUS THOMAS,** attorney at
law, 847 Main, rm. 5, h. 125 Park.
      See page 490.
" Ward, at Ætna Life Insurance Co. 650
 Main, b. 60 Edwards.

McManus William J. florist at 702 Main, b. 232
 Wethersfield.
McMaster Mahlon K. coachman, at 30 Wash.
McMenemy John, at National Fire Ins. Co. 95
 Pearl, b. Manchester t.
McMillen Alexander, at 24 Potter, b. 43 Linden.
" Margaret, wid. Carson, h. 13 Babcock.
McMonegle Daniel, ostler, b. 5 John.
McMonogal Edw.wiper at N.Y.R. h.u. 57 Spruce.
McMullen Alexander, laborer, h. 44 Hicks.
McMullin Enos B. hackdriver, r. 50, b.r. 50 State.
McMurray Charlotte L. Mrs. teacher Wadsworth
 street school, h. 68 Church.
" Fred. S. quartermaster U.S.N. b. 68 Church.
" James, at Pattens dye wks, 37, b.2u, 32 Wells.
" James, porter at 942 Main, b. 248 Asylum.
" Michael, laborer at Colts, b. 5 Vandyke.
McNally Bernard, carptr. N.Y.R. h. Rocky Hill t.
" James, molder, h.u. 29 Commerce.
" John, l. 609 Main.
" John, laborer, b. 88 Ward.
" John J. at 476 Capitol, h. 88 Ward.
" Thomas, coachman, h. 8 Highland.
McNamar Erwin N. clerk, b. 25 Pliney.
" George A.drug clerk at 142 Asy.b.25 Pliney.
" James B. h. 25 Pliney.
McNamara Anna, wid. Daniel, h.2u. 89 Windsor.
" Bridget, wid. Thomas, h. 232 Zion.
" Brothers, butchers, 113 Hungerford.
  John B. McNamara. Timothy McNamara,
    Joseph M. McNamara,
" Daniel J. clerk at 1111 Main, b. 89 Windsor.
" Francis P. clerk at 581 Capitol b. 315 Pearl.
" James, laborer, b.u. 38 Wells.
" James, laborer at 556 Capitol, b. 30 Flower.
" John, bartender, h. 21 Huntley.
" John, expressman, b.2u. 89 Windsor.
" John, pressman at 141 Pearl, h. 12 Lawrence.
" John B. (McN. Bros.) h. 113 Hungerford.
" Joseph M. (McN.Bros.) b. 106 Hungerford.
" Nellie A. bkkpr. at 25 Front, b. 106 Hung.
" Patrick, b.u. 30 Huntley pl.
" Thomas, coachman and b. Prospect av.
" Thomas, polisher, b.u. 51 Albany.
" Thomas, livery stable, 678 Main.
" Thomas, mason, h.r. 234 Zion.
" Timothy W. (McN.Bros.) h. 214 Woodland.
McNary Catherine, wid. Richard, h.u. 57 Dean.
" Geo. F. mach. at 1 Flower, h. 155 Babcock.
" John, coachman, b. 110 Edwards.
" Lizzie F. inspector at 70 Huy. b.u. 57 Dean.
" Mary J. housekeeper, h.u. 57 Dean.
McNaught Wm. J. blacks. at P.&R. 116 Mather.
McNaughton Mabel, nurse at 20 So. Hudson.
McNear Louis D. furniture repairer, b. 69 Fmt.
McNearny John E. lathe hand, b. 54 Potter.
" Joseph, salesman, h. 54 Potter.
" ☞ see McIneary.
McNeil Anthony, carptr. at 285 State, h. 2 Union.
" Arthur, rubber w. at 690 Park, h. 20 Kibbe.
" Joseph, ship carpenter, h.u. 53½ Governor
" Joseph, stonecutter at 93 Ch.O. b. 2 Union.
" Matthew F. machinist, b. 2 Union.
" William J. student Trinity college, 18 Jarvis
 hall, Summit.

**THE POST is a 20th-Century Newspaper.**

McNeill Marion, wid. William, h.u. 271 Main.
McNerny Anna L. l. 721 Main, rm. 41.
" Margaret, dressm. h. 721 Main, rm. 41.
McNevin Michael, laborer at Pope Tube Co. h. 45 Hicks.
McNickle James, gilder at J. H. Eckhardt Co. art store, 693 Main, h. 13 Oak.
**McNIE MALCOLM,** paperruler, 336 Asylum, h. 227 Ashley. *See page 504.*
" Mary C. wid. Robert, b. 1145 Broad.
" William H. painter N.Y.R. b. 285 Asylum.
McNierney Thomas, sec'y New England Brewing Co. 217 Windsor, h. 46 Bellevue.
McNierny Thomas, b. 1150 Main.
McNulty John J. laborer, h. 34 Flower.
" Joseph, gardener, h. 234 Jefferson.
" Joseph M. mach. at 1 Flow. b. 234 Jefferson.
" Michael, mason, h. 6 Cedar.
" Nettie D. bkkpr. at 436 Asy. b. 234 Jefferson.
" Patrick, laborer, h.u. 1416 Broad.
" Sarah, dressmaker, b.u. 1416 Broad.
" Thomas, groom, 103, b. 103 Woodland.
McPhee Alex. mach. at 388 Cap. h. W.H.t.
" James, mach. at 388 Capitol, h.u. 19 Park.
McPherson A. L. teamster, b. 1153 Main.
" Charles, brassmolder at 38 Ferry.
" Frank B. bookkeeper at Case, Lockwood & Brainard Co. 141 Pearl, h. 46 Lincoln.
McPhillips Wm. profiler at Colts, 14 Vanblock.
McQuade Andrew P. printer at Clark & Smith, 49 Pearl, h. 6 Goodman.
McQueen Annie, h.u. 12 Potter.
" Kate, h.u. 12 Potter.
McQueeny Dennis, helper N.Y.R. h. 27 Harbison.
" John, laborer at 133 Sheldon, b. 76 Walnut.
McQuillan Alice T. hair store, 17, h. 17 Pratt.
" John, bricklayer, h.2u. 110 Ward.
" Samuel, bricklayer, h.u. 31 Center.
McRoe Bridget, b. W.H.Home for aged, Albany.
McRonald Thos. florist, Cemetery st. h. 50 Albany.
**McRONALD T. J.** florist, 66 Mahl, h. 2 Pliny.
McRossie ☞ *see MacRossie.*
McRoy Elizabeth, bookkeeper at Newton, Robertson & Co. 342 Asy. b.u. 82 New Britain.
McShane Hugh A. foreman at 15 Trumbull, h.u. 29 Kennedy.
" John E. skiver at 15 Tru. b. 29 Kennedy.
McSweegan David F. dri. hose, 2, h. 49 Wooster.
" John, h.2u. 19 Goodwin.
" Rose, housekeeper, h. 19 Goodwin.
" Thos. blacksmith, 41 Alb. h.2u. 19 Goodwin,
McTernan Patrick, b. 2 Holcomb.
McTigue Cath. wid. Jas. notions, 69, h. 69 Potter.
" James, laborer, b. 69 Potter.
" John P. laborer, h. 103 Potter.
McVein Alex. at 556 Capitol, h. 26 Elm.
" William, machinist, b. 26 Elm.
McViney John, waiter at 80 State.
" L. E. h. 24 Wadsworth.
McWilliams John A. clerk, 909 Main, h. 46 Pratt.
Meacham Maurice R. vulcanizer 555 Capitol, b. Bloomfield t.
Meachem Alice, b.2u. 346 Windsor av.

Meachem C. E. Mrs. h.2u. 346 Windsor av.
" Ella, b.2u. 346 Windsor av.
Mead Benjamin P., State comptroller, State capitol, rm. 2, h. New Canaan t.
" Charles M. b. Allyn House, 152 Asylum.
" James A. eclectic physician, 80 Pearl, rm. 9, b. 230 Putnam.
" Michael J. scrpwm at 476 Capitol, b. 9 Haw.
Meafoy Ellen F. Mrs. boardinghouse, 1255 Main.
" Florence, nurse, 1255, h. 1255 Main.
Meagher Edward A polisher Colts, h. 49 Hudson.
" Jeremiah, b. 24 Market.
" Joseph, mach. at 142 Russ, b. 86 Walnut.
" Michael W. bartender 24 Mar. h. 150 Brown.
" Thomas F. polisher, Colts, h. 458 Maple.
" Timothy F. proprietor Columbia House, 24 Market, h. 86 Grove.
" William E. b. 1150 Main.
" Wm. F. drug clerk, b. 86 Ann.
Meaney Daniel, lineman, l. 520 Main.
" Edward J. mach. at 9 Sig. h. 8 Hawthorn.
" J. J. conductor St.Ry. 115 State.
" William T. foreman at 581, b. 381 Capitol.
Meara Sarah, wid. John, 867 Mn. b.u. 84 Grove.
Meceale Jacino, fruit peddler, h. 12 North.
**MECHANICS SAVINGS BANK,** 815 Main.    *See page 439.*
Me'cune ☞ *see also McCune.*
Medbury Daniel H. clerk at 64 State, h. Bloomfield.
Medeen Hjalmar, mgr. 149 Bab. b. 164 Putnam.
Meech Huntington Phelps, at Nat'l Fire Ins. Co. 95 Pearl, h. 53 Annawan.
Meegan Patrick, shoem. at 172, b. 58 Asylum.
Mechan Austin W. laborer, h. 23 Huntley pl.
" Daniel, lineman 266 Pearl, b. 520 Main.
" John, laborer at 8, h. 21 Front.
" John J. bartdr. 1177 Mn. h. 17 Huntley pl.
" Margaret, wid. John, b.u. 31 Hungerford.
" Patrick J. saloon, 1177 Mn. h.u. 31 Pleasant.
" ☞ *see also Mahan; Mahon.*
Meek Walter L. superintendent, h.u. 9 Francis.
Mehegan Bartholomey, at 1 Flow. b.u. 52 Hicks.
" Dennis Timothy, joiner, b.u. 52 Hicks.
Meheran Francis, helper at 45, b. 45 Lafayette.
" James, grocer, 45, h.u. 45 Lafayette.
Meier Christian, mach. at 1 Flower, h. Wilson sta.
Meincus Tony, laborer, h. 49 Front.
Meisselman Solomon, peddler, h.u. 70 Windsor.
Meissner Emma, b. 103 Ann.
" Fred. h. 103 Ann.
" Louis, waiter at 98 Wells, b. 150 Allyn.
" Rudolph, waiter at 98 Wells, b. 150 Allyn.
Meister R. *(Holman & M.)* h.3u. 78 Front.
Meisterling Charles, tinner, 60, h. 60 Temple.
" Jacob, laborer at 1 Flower, h. 170 Ward.
Mekel George, laborer, h. 130 Ward.
Melaven Wm. W. cond. St.Ry. b. 3¼ Elliott pl.
Melberger L. G. conductor St.Ry. b. 61 Madison.
" Louis G. barber at 484 Asy. b. 61 Madison.
Melbourne Emma, stenog. 252 Asy. b. Meriden t.
Melby Alfred, bookkpr. at 52 Asy. b. 54 Capitol.
Melcher John, tailor at 56 Pearl, h.u. 26 Cedar.
Melekoske Andrew, saloon, 125, h. 123 Front.
Melicorsky J. plumber, b. 207 Front.

**Merchants say it PAYS to Advertise in The Post.**

Melins Cyrus, teamster, 2 Chapel, h.u. 37 Hudson.
Mell Augustus, painter, h. 17 Talcott.
Mellein George F. mach. at 1 Flower, h. 17 Squire.
Mellen Chas. B. forem.mach.shopColts,h.141Main.
"  Frank C. machinist at Colts, b.u. 306 Main.
"  Frank G. treas. M.& Hewes Co.b.215 Collins.
"  & Hewes Co. crockery, etc. 725 Main.
"  Moses, president Mellen & Hewes Co. h.
    215 Collins.
Meller Richard, U. S. army, h. 60 Hicks.
Mellgren Chas. E. stockkpr. 476 Cap. h. 25 Hudson.
"  Matilda, wid. Frederick, b. 25 Hudson.
Melly William, laborer, h. 179 Albany.
Melody Charles, blacksm. Hartford Woven Wire
    Mattress Co. 618 Capitol, b.u. 354 Park.
"  Joseph H. engineer, Hartford Woven Wire
    Mattress Co. 618 Capitol, b.u. 354 Park.
**MELONEY WILLIAM H.** manager
    Capitol City Oil Co. 195 State, h. 52
    Buckingham.          *See page 541.*
"  William H. Jr. bicycles, 217 State, b.52 Bkm.
"  ☞ *see also Maloney; Moloney.*
Melrose James *(M. & Keane,)* h. 120 Jefferson.
"  John, h. 24 Village.
"  & Keane, saloon, 332 Main.
        *James Melrose.        James H. Keane.*
"  William, clerk at 843 Main, b. 257 High.
"  William, copyholder at Evening Post, 23
    Asylum, b. 24 Village.
Memorial Hall, (Eldredge) 426 Asylum.
Mendelsohn Castle, barber at 46, h. 55 Church.
Meniere Peter, plumber at 1204 Mn. h. Wooster.
Menihan William, corem.556 Cap. h.2u. 9 Putnam.
Mentze William, tailor at 66 Asylum, h. 1 Webb
Meranski David, tailor, h. 15 Morgan.
Mercadande Francisco P. barber, 88½ Trumbull,
    b.u. 27 Kilbourn.
"  Michael, ragpicker, h.u. 27 Kilbourn.
"  Vito, waiter, b.u. 27 Kilbourn.
Mercantile Agencies, 223 Asylum; 49 Pearl.
"  National Bank, 53 Trumbull.
Mercer Charles B. carptr. 57 Elliott, l. 63 Spring.
"  Edward, mach. at 1 Flow. b. 109 Babcock.
"  Frank B. driver at 48 Ann, h.u. 66 Chestnut.
**MERCHANTS' NATIONAL
    TRADING ASSOCIATION,**
    66 State.          *See outside back cover.*
Merchenz Richard, engineer, h. 4 Bellevue.
Mercier Arsene, helper 1 Flow. h. Caya, W.H.t.
"  Edward, painter, h.u. 7 Huntley.
Merk ☞ *See Murk.*
Merkle L. sewingmachine agent, b. 80 State.
Meroney ☞ *see also Maroney.*
Merriam Alex. R. Rev. prof. Theological Semi-
    nary, 1507 Broad, h. 314 Collins.
MERRIAM A. E. COLT Mrs. eclectic physician
    and cabinet baths, 926 Main, rm. 51, h.
    38 Church.          *See page 257.*
"  Amy, bkkpr. at 201 Asylum, h. Rocky Hill t.
"  Charlotte Mrs. clerk, 30 Washington.
"  Ezekiel R. h. 38 Church.
"  Frederick F. steamfitr. 266 Pl.h.2u. 66 Hicks.
**MERRIAM C. C. & CO.** *See p. 497.*
"  L. B. Mrs. h. 36 Lincoln.

---

# Dr. A. E. Colt Merriam,

## ECLECTIC AND
## CLAIRVOYANT
## PHYSICIAN.

### Static Electric & Massage Treatments,
### Cabinet Baths.

#### CONSULTATION FREE.

**Office, CHENEY BLOCK, SUITE 51.**

Hours, 8 to 9.30 A.M.    1.30 to 6.30 P.M.

**Residence, 38 CHURCH STREET.**

---

Merrick George, tinner at 4 Ford, b. 54 Trumbull.
"  J. T. Mrs. boardinghouse, 27 Spring.
"  William A. engir. at 154 Pearl, h. 42 Church.
Merrifield Alfred S. clerk at Popes, h. 860 Broad.
Merrill Arthur H. real estate, 378 Asylum, h.
    6 Tremont.
"  Charles E. clerk at Adams Ex. l. 119 High.
"  Chas. J. foreman Case, Lockwood & Brain-
    ard Co. 141 Pearl, h.u. 52 Kenyon.
"  Dwight H. clerk at 87 Asy. b. Newington t.
"  G. N. *(G. N. M. & Co.)* 75 Pratt.
**MERRILL GEORGE N. & CO.**
    civil and consulting engineers, 75 Pratt.
                                *See page 428.*
    G. N. Merrill.    E. O. Hatheway.    F. F. Cobb.
"  I. M. conductor St.Ry. h. 34 Franklin.
"  Ira M. mech. at 42 Union pl. h. 1246 Main.
"  John F. h.r. 50 State.
"  Lena J. wid. Merton C. b. 28 Marshall.
"  Lorenzo D. hotel, 54, h. 54 Prospect.
"  Roswell E.rubberw. 690 Park,h.u.96 Madison.
"  Wm. A. conductor St.Ry. b. 155 Windsor av.
Merrills George S. farmer, h. 30 Charlotte.
Merriman Franklin, mason, h.u. 84 Arch.
"  G. A. Mrs. boardinghouse, 25 Spring.
"  Gaius A. salesm. 126 Church, h. 25 Spring.
"  J. Jetson, b. 25 Spring.
"  Robert G. conductor, N.Y.R. h. 225 Garden.
Merriter Morris, helper P.&R. b. 127 Albany.
Merritt Chas. B. mach. 30 Cush. h.u. 23 Elliott.
"  Fred'k M. cond. St.Ry. b.u. 117 Kenyon.
"  George P. expert acct. b. 117 Kenyon.
"  George S. at Ætna Life Ins. Co. 650 Main,
    h. 117 Kenyon.
"  Harry C. bookkeeper, b. 117 Kenyon.
"  Jos. mech. engineer 581 Cap. b. 119 High.
"  Mabel, waitress, 999 Main.
"  Maria S. wid. Edwin, h. 69 Webster.
Merrow George W. sec'y and treas. Merrow
    Machine Co. h. 34 Forest.
"  Joseph M. president Merrow Machine Co.
    h. 54 Niles.
**MERROW MACHINE CO.** machine
    mfgrs. 26-28 Laurel.    *See page 535.*
"  Wilmont M. cutter at 68 State, h. 96 Chst.
Merry Arthur M. forem. 581 Cap. h. 69 Madison.
"  Benjamin C. mach. at 581 Cap. h. 89 Haw.
Mertens Eugene R. mach. at 9 Sig. b. 1258 Broad.
"  John B. machinist N.Y.R. h. 1258 Broad.
"  Paul W. buffer at Popes, h.2u. 3 Rice ct.

**People who have Money to Spend, Read The Post.**

Mertz Frank J. steamfitter at Popes, b. Elmwood.
Mertzking Manuel, milkman, 145, h. 145 Flatbush.
Merwin Edward, gardener at 51, b. 51 Vine.
" George J. clerk at Phœnix Mutual Life Ins. Co. 49 Pearl, b. Windsor t.
" Harry I. draughtsman, R. S. Peck & Co. 26 High, b. 431 Capitol.
" Sadie M. stenographer at Q. M. General's office, State capitol, rm. 56, b. Windsor t.
Merz Anthony H. h.u. 103 Hudson.
" Frederick, tailor, h. 35 Park.
" George, blacksmith, h. 12 Warren.
" Grace M. tailoress, 35, h. 35 Park.
" Gustav, butcher, h.u. 151 Wethersfield.
" Gustav C. at Jewel Pin Co. b. 35 Park.
" Mamie C. music teacher, 35, b. 35 Park.
" Mathew, barber, 615, b. 615 Capitol.
Mesker Theodore, oiler at Colts, b. 66 Vanblock.
Messenger Jarvis T. messenger U.S. court, b. 103 Pratt.
Messier Medric, carpenter at 53 Vernon, h. West Rocky Hill v.
Messinger Charles F. mach. at Colts, b. 12 Bkm.
" Wⁿ· C. dental supplies, 96 Tru. h. 66 Imlay.
Messler Louis S. foreman, h.u. 140 Barbour.
Metcalf Geo. A. operator at 8, b. 45 Sigourney.
" George, papermaker, h. 58 Edwards.
" Grace E. stenog. at 68 Pratt, b. 815 Asylum.
Metcalfe Harry L. mgr. 715 Main, h. 173 Albany.
" William S. draughtsm. 254 Pearl, h. 26 Crown.
Metkoff Emil, laborer, h. 4 John.
Metropolitan Hotel, J. O. Gorman, 255 Asylum.
" Life Ins. Co. of N. Y. 721 Main, rm. 42.
Mettler Adolph, machinist, b. 63 Crown.
" Annie wid. Casper, h. 63 Crown.
" Casper W. inventor, h. King, n. Julius.
" Jacob, inventor, b. 63 Crown.

METZGER SIMON C. (*Gallup & M.*) h. 28 Kenyon.
Metzner Joseph, cook, h.u. 101 Windsor.
Meudona Katie, groceries, 15, h. 15 Mechanic.
Meyer Albert, clerk at 1056 Main, b. 63 Congress.
" August, blacksmith, 352 Alb. h.r. 53 Front.
" August J. upholst'r at r. 585 Mn. b. 44 Park.

Meyer Emma C. Mrs. h. 13 John.
" Frederick, clerk at r. 585 Mn. b.u. 44 Park.
" George J. foreman, h.u. 57 Bellevue.
" Harry F. special delivery, P.O.
" George P. laborer, h. 1063 Main.
" Grace C. at 1 So. Ann, b.u. 20 Goodwin.
" Henry, furniture, r. 585 Main, h. 44 Park.
" Henry B. painter, b. 44 Park.
" Herman, mach. at 1 Flow. b. Manchester t.
" Herman W. teamster, 245 Windsor, b. 180 Ward.
" Joseph, mach. at N.Y.R. h. 28 Harbison.
" & Noll, printers, 302 Asylum.
　William L. Meyer.　　　William Noll.
" Otto, ostler at 315 Park, h. 180 Ward.
" Sophia, wid. Bernhardt, b. 28 Harbison.
" William H. clerk at 639 Main, h. 13 John.
" Wm. L. (*M. & Noll,*) b.u. 44 Park.
" ☞ *see also Maher ; Myer ; Mayer ; Myers.*
Meyerhoff Aaron, peddler, h.u. 96 Windsor.
Meyers Charles, peddler, b. 105 Commerce.
" Fred, rubberw. at 690 Park, h. 4 Francis.
" Frederick, cigarm. at 867, l.2u. 1305 Main.
" George, blacksmith, h. 12 Warren.
" Robert, teamster at 46 Ann, h. 75 Governor.
Meylew Michael, pistolmaker, h. 55 Hudson.
Meyn C. Henry, modeler at Sanford Co. 438 Asylum, b. 1224 Main.
Micchelson V. M. printer, b.u. 234 Pearl.
Michael Emanuel M. mechanic, h. 124 State.
" Isaac E. barber at 34 Mul. h. 75 Williams.
" Laura C. wid. John, h. 94 Hudson.
" Solomon, fish market, 205, saloon, 182 Front, h. 233 Market.
Michaels Flora, clerk at 956 Mn. b. 233 Market.
" Minnie, clerk at 956 Main, b. 233 Market.
Michaelson Edward, blacksmith, h.u. 277 Main.
" Harris, shoemaker at 52, h. 52 Sheldon.
" Howard W. clerk at 98 Kil. h. 126 Ann.
" Hyman, tailor at 80 State, h. 1 Mays ct.
" Valdemar, harnessmaker at 8 Sigourney, b. 141 Market.
" Walter, harnessmaker, b. 141 Market.
" William, b.u. 141 Market.
Michaud Benjamin L. engir. Popes, h. 9 Smith.
Michelsen Edward, wireworker, b.2u. 275 Main.
" Hans, bookbinder at 141 Pl. b.21 Wadsworth.
Michelson Peter, teamster, h. 48 Harrison.
" William, laborer, b.2u.r. 56 Temple.
Michener Edwin A. rubberworker at 690 Park, b. 13 Suffield.
Middlebrook Louis F. ass't sec'y Htfd. Steam Boiler Insp. & Ins. Co. h. 147 Ashley.
**MIDDLESEX BANKING CO. OF MIDDLETOWN, CONN.** S. P. Townsend, agent, 49 Pearl, rm. 28.
Middleton James E. mgr. 759 Mn. h. Springfield.
" John R. clerk at Brown, Thomson & Co. 942 Main, b. 227 High.
Middledorf William, b.2u. 26 Church.
Midura Ignace, screwm. 476 Cap. b. 34 S.Pro.
Midler Meyer, tailor at 956 Mn. h.2u. 34 Avon.
Micke Ernst, waiter, h.u. 40 Chestnut.
Miel Ernest deF. Rev. rector Trinity church, h. 120 Sigourney.

Mielke Julius C. mach. at Colts, h.2u. 104 Jef.
Mielnyk Mike, wiredrawer at 40 Governor, b. 29 Commerce.
Mikkelson Peter, ostler at 995 Main, h. E.H.t.
Milaney James, ostler at 372 Asy. l. 257 High.
" Michael, ostler at 372 Asylum, l. 257 High.
Milano Antonio, laborer, h. 190 Front.
" Michael, teamster, h. 29 Albany.
Milcke Otto, solderer at 62 Mar. h. 14 Westland.
Mildeberger Henry D. attorney at law, 793 Main, h. 17 Benton.
Mildner Adolph, baker at 69, b.u. 69 Morgan.
Mildrum Hattie, b. 34 Allen pl.
Miler H. R.W. musician, 336, b. 336 Wethersfield.
Miles Adolphus F. printer at Hartford Times, 716 Main, h. 73 Park.
" Bernard J. helper at 9 Sig. h.u. 99 Windsor.
" Fred T. operator at 20 Sargeant, b. 73 Park.
" Harry R. Rev. pastor Windsor ave. Cong. church, h. 294 Windsor av.
" Katie, domestic, h.3u. 99 Windsor.
" Lewis W. foreman, 70 Huy. h.u. 74 Retreat.
" Margaret Mrs. h.u.r. 61 Front.
" Oscar A. printer at Hartford Times, 716 Main h. 1 Dean.
" Rose, wid. John, h. 63 Francis.
" Thomas, printer, h.2u. 75 Seymour.
Milesi Battisto, laborer, b. 148 Front.
Milgard Peter, blacksm. at 476 Cap. h. 50 Willow.
Milikowski Carl, pressman, 690 Park, h. 13 N.P.
" Michael, engineer at 245 Windsor, h.u. 232 Bellevue.
Milk Patrick H. janitor at 650, h. 616 Main.
Milkey Otto, buffer, 62 Market, h.u. 14 Westland.
Mill Charlotte J. (*The Misses Mill,*) b. 27 Allen pl.
" Isabel L. (*The Misses Mill,*) b. 27 Allen pl.
" John, rubberworker, h. South Forest.
" Kittie B. b. 27 Allen pl.
" The Misses, hairstore and manic. 903 Main.
    Charlotte J. Mill.     Isabel L. Mill.
" ☞ *see also Mills.*
Millard Cornwall T. teller, 31 Pratt, b. 36 Lewis.
" Maria wid. Charles, h. 3 Asylum.
" Samuel T. h. 36 Lewis.
Miller Adam C. carpenter, h. 58 Benton.
" Addie, wid. Charles, h.2u. 2 Orchard.
" Albert H. mach. at 111 Shel. b.u. 141 Market.
" Andrew, at Billings & Spencer Co. 142 Russ, h. 4 Oak.
" Anna, b.u. 165 Front.
" Anna B. bookkeeper, b.u. 1339 Broad.
" Annie E. bookkeeper, b. 43 Bellevue.
" Archibald, overseer at Cheney Bros. silk mill 34 Morgan, b. 23 Huntington.
" Archibald Jr. student, b. 23 Huntington.
" Arthur H. mach. at 581 Cap. b. 47 Laurel.
" August, printer, h.u. 5 Pleasant.
" Belle M. b. 223 Asylum, room 34.
" Benj. N. B. supt. Open Hearth Mission, 135 Front, h. 15 Church.
" Beulah, b. 58 Benton.
" & Burnham, undertakers, 180 Allyn.
    G. O. Harrison Miller.     George N. Burnham.
" Christ H. sweeper at 62 Mar. h. 88 Mather.
" Carl N. operator at 388 Cap. b. Newington t.

Miller Carrie E. stenographer at 57 Trumbull, b.u. 234 Pearl.
" Catherine, at 476 Capitol, b.2u. 188 Putnam.
" Catherine A. wid. Wiley B. h. 719 Asylum.
" Chandler E. sec'y Humane Society, 51 Prospect, h. 11 Belden.
" Charles, borer at Colts, h. 81 Front.
" Charles, machinist at 142 Russ, h. 9 Hung.
" Chas. B. at National Fire Insurance Co. 95 Pearl, h.u. 24 Elmer.
" Chas. F. bookbinder at 141 Pearl, h. 47 Law.
" Chauncey F. carpenter, N.Y.R. h.u. 31 Grand.
" Christian, silverplater at 66 Market, h.2u. 88 Mather.
" Christie, helper, b. 68 Temple.
" Christopher, b.u. 33 Chapel.
" Edward R. finisher, 69 Front, h.u. 27 North.
" Edwin P. printer at 857 Mn. h.u. 37½ Church.
" Elizabeth G. wid. Aug. C. h. 325 N.B.
" Ellen Mrs. h. 943 Main.
" Emma M. dressmaker, b. 981 Main.
" Emory H. motorm. at St.Ry. h. 13 Benton.
" Emory H. Mrs. dressm. 13, b.' 13 Benton.
" Ernest J. bookkeeper, Case, Lockwood & Brainard Co. 141 Pearl, b. W.P.v.
" Florence C. clerk, 18 Pratt, b. 238 Windsor av.
" Florence I. clerk, b. 57 Laurel.
" Eugene D. printer at 703, h. 1153 Main.
" Frank, screwm. at 476 Capitol, b.u. 17 John.
" Frank B. Jr. mach. 28 High, b. Bloomfield t.
" Fred. C. printer at 703 Main.
" Fred S. b. 67 Webster.
" Frederick W. asst. superintendent St.Ry. 115 State, h.u. 31 Benton.
" George, clerk, b. 52 Park.
" George, helper at 69 Front, b. Burnside v.
" George, painter, b.u. 20 Trumbull.
" George F. mach. at 388 Cap. h.u. 14 Kibbe.
" George J. engir. at 315 Park, h. 68 Law.
" George M. pressman Popes, h.2u. 329 Capitol.
" George R. physician, 182, h. 182 High.
" George S. Dr. supt. agencies Phœnix Mutual Life Ins. Co. 49 Pearl, h. 68 Imlay.
" George W. horseman, h. 39 Barbour.
" Guy P. correspondent at Popes, l. 18 Garden.
" Harold, student, b. 128 High.
" Harrison G. O. (*M. & Burnham,*) h. 52 Mahl.
" Harry G. clerk at Lincoln, Seyms & Co. 34 Market, b. South Glastonbury v.
" Harry L. printer at 66 State, b. E.H.t.
" Harvey, b.u. 31 Grand.
" Hattie A. teacher Northeast school, b. Bloomfield t.
" Hattie E. nurse, b. 49 Oak.
" Helen, wid. Harvey, b. 48 Prospect.
" Helen E. wid. James C. h. 57 Laurel.
" Henry, bookkeeper, b. 75 Flower.
" Henry, tailor at 2 State, h. 8 Loomis.
" Henry E. machinist at 1 Flow. h. 16 Kibbe.
" Henry P. repairer at Popes, h. New Britain t.
" Herbert P. inspector at 40 Gov. h. 57 Hudson.
" Homer, at 300 Asylum, b. 48 Babcock.
" Hugh I. correspondent, Popes, l. 18 Garden.
" Jackson A. mach. at 133 Shel. b. 999 Main.
" James H. brazier, Popes, h. 48 Babcock.

**Advertise Your Real Estate in THE POST.**

Miller Jas. P. livery stable, r. 371 Main, h. G.t.
" James P. motorman, St.Ry. h.u. 13 Benton.
" Jeffrey D. carpenter, h. 1339 Broad.
" John, b. 2 Holcomb.
" John, cellarman, 245 Windsor, b. Bellevue.
" John, pressman at 690 Park, h. 585 Garden.
" John L. painter at Baxter the Decorator, 231 Asylum, b. 345 Main.
" John W. conductor, St.Ry. b. 13 Benton.
" Jonas, leaf tobacco, 210 State, h. 43 Wooste
" Kate, wid. John, h.u. 81 Front.
" Katherine A. theo. student, 1507 Broad.
" Lawrence J. mach. 9 Sig. h.u. 224 Putnam.
" Letitia, wid. Henry, h. 14 Benton.
" Lewis C. machinist at 54 Arch, b. 68 Law.
" Louis, bartender at 41 Mulberry, h. 2 Oak.
" Louis, clerk at 921 Main, b. 16 Elmer.
" Louis, tailor, h. 8 North.
" Louise, at 252 Pearl, b.u. 141 Market.
" Lucia E. wid. James H. h. 238 Windsor av.
" Margaret, b.2u. 188 Putnam.
" Margaret, wid. Charles G. h.2u. 12 Village.
" Margaret, wid. Elijah T. b.2u. 1245 Main.
" Martin, cabinetmaker, h.u. 152 Mather.
" Mary A. b. 4 Florence.
" Mary A. wid. Benjamin W. clerk at 1036 Main, b. 56 Liberty.
" Mason C. (Dickinson & Miller,) b. 325 N.B.
" Matilda Mrs. b.r. 24 Trumbull.
" Max, clerk at 921 Main, b. 16 Elmer.
" Max, tailor at 544 Main, h. 82 Front.
" Morris, shoemaker, h. 64 Village.
MILLER MORTIMER H. (C. H. Case & Co.) diamonds and jewelry, 851 Main, h. 40 Kenyon.     See front cover outside.
" Nathan, agent, h. 97 Whitmore.
" Nathan, wirew. at 618 Cap. h. 21 Hawthorn.
" Nathan F. clerk Hartford County Mutual Fire Ins. Co. 793 Main, h. Bloomfield t.
" Nellie C. clerk at Brown, Thomson & Co. 942 Main, b. 81 Pleasant.
" Phila, b. 97 Trumbull.
" Philip, at 62 Market, b. 81 Front.
" Richard, filer at 581 Capitol, h. 60 Hicks.
" Robert, electrotyper at 177 Asy. b. Com.
" Robert, sidewalk layer at 154 Charter Oak, h. 284 Asylum, rm. 39.
" Rufus L. roller at 690 Park, h. 38 Heath.
" Russell, trav. salesm. 210 State, h. 43 Wooster.
" Samuel, harnessm. at 8 Sig. h. 278 Market.
" Samuel, sidewalk layer at 154 Charter Oak, b. 284 Asylum, rm. 39.
" Sarah, clerk at Brown, Thomson & Co. 942 Main, b. 64 Village.
" Thomas, rubberw. at 690 Park, b. S.Forest.
" W. J. barber, 55 High, h. 20 Spring.
" Warren T. driver at 4 Central, h. 1 Elm pl.
" William E. mach. 1 Flower, h. 7 Francis.
" William F. toolkeeper at 28, b. 57 Laurel.
" William F. tailor at 8 State, b. 5 Pleasant.
" William H. bkkpr. at 1411 Main, h. N.H.t.
" William H. draughtsman at Pratt & Whitney Co. 1 Flower, h.u. 57 Babcock.
" Wm. H. H. salesman, Lincoln, Seyms & Co. whl. spices, 34 Mar. h. So. Glastonbury v.

Miller William P. mach. at 70 Huy. h. 40 Ward.
" Willis E. saloon, 200 Asy. h. Springfield.
" ☞ see also Meller; Muller.
Millett Edward W. molder, 690 Pk. h.u. 234 N.P.
" Eugene, teamster, h. 551 Park.
" Eugene Jr. mach. 1 Flow. h. 67 Hamilton.
" Joseph F. teamster, b. 551 Park.
" Thomas, elevatorer, b. 66 Hopkins.
Millette Josephine, wid. Louis, b.u. 149 Maple.
Milli Abbe D. adv. agt. 386 Weth. b. 6 Florence.
Milligan Edward, secy. Phœnix Insurance Co. 64 Pearl, b. 111 Elm.
Milliken Arthur J. b. 86 Hopkins.
" Jerome B. machinist, h. 86 Hopkins.
" John B. accountant at Conn. Building and Loan Asso. 252 Asy. h. 63 Ashley.
" John B. mach. at 1 Flow. b. 86 Hopkins.
Millott Patrick, expressman, b.2u. 78 Walnut.
Mills Abbie D. b. 10 Florence.
" Charlotte A. b.u. 209 Jefferson.
" Edward T. machinist, Pratt & Whitney Co. 1 Flower, b. Thompsonville v.
" Elijah, (M. & Son,) h.u. 16 Elmer.
" Elijah & Son, brickmakers, Tower.
   Elijah Mills.          Eugene D. Mills.
" Elizabeth, wid. James, h. 71 Hamilton.
" Eugene D. (M. & Son,) h. 230 Barbour.
" Hattie V. dressm. 370, b. 370 Asy. rm. 65.
" Henry, tailor, b. 36 Temple.
**MILLS HIRAM R.** attorney at law, 847 Main, rm. 9, h. Bloomfield t. Successor to Chamberlin, White & Mills. See p. 491.
" Jennie Miss, nurse, h. 34 Chapel.
" John, blacksmith, b. 145 High.
" John H. porter, b.u. 130 Windsor.
" Julius G. barber at 9 Asy. h.u. 264 Market.
" Mary, b.u. 130 Windsor.
" Minnie, boxmaker, b. 15 Bellevue.
" O. William, driver, 57 Alb. b. 90 Chestnut.
" Patrick H. janitor Ætna building, 650, h. 1212 Main.
" S. W. wid. Timothy, b. 234 Ashley.
" Susan E. wid. George K. h. 106 Hung.
" Vernica, wid. Gustave, h.u. 130 Windsor.
" Winn C. teamster, h. 232 Barbour.
" ☞ see also Mill; Milz.
Milofski John, laborer, b.3u. 55 Morgan.
Milrot M. helper at 1 Flower, h. 13 North.
" Peter, laborer, b.3u. 13 North.
Miltimore Rufus C. h.2u.r. 153 Wethersfield.
Miltner Adolph, baker at 69, b. 69 Morgan.
Milton Alfred, carriageptr. 352 Alb. h. 211 Barb.
" Benjamin F. painter, h.u. 44 Wooster.
" Branch D. carpenter at 69, h. 63 Front.
" Carrie A. dressmaker, 211, b. 211 Barbour.
" Charles, machinist, h.u. 25 Westland.
" James S. molder at 690 Park, h. 14 Smith.
" John, painter, h.u. 45 Barbour.
" Mary, wid. William, h. 23 Westland.
" Wm. H. Jr. decorator at Baxter the Decorator, 231 Asylum, h.u. 63 Madison.
Milvæ John, carptr. at r. 334 Asy. h.u. 17 Martin.
Milyer Meyer, tailor, h.3u. 34 Avon.
Milz Henry T. tailor, 847 Main, h. 36 Temple.
" ☞ see also Mills.

Minberg George, filer at 581, b. 613 Capitol.
Minckler Barney, cook at 1219 Mn. l. 7 Pleasant.
Mineham Patrick, laborer, h.u.r. 61 Front.
Mineiky J. W. Mrs. h. 721 Main, rm. 31.
Miner Caroline A. wid. Wm. h. 104 Church.
" Charles A. shipping clerk, 70 Huyshope.
" Charles H. clerk at Popes, b. 127 Jefferson.
" Edward H. conductor, St.Ry. h. 55 Hung.
" George H. clerk at 581, h. 437 Capitol.
" Grace, waitress at 30 Washington.
" Jacob, laborer, h. 6 Kilbourn ct.
" Jacob, lab. Pope Tube Co. h.u. 71 Hamilton.
" Jacob, shoemaker, h. 71 Hamilton.
" John, helper, h. 6 Kilbourn ct.
" John, watchman, l.u. 357 Main.
" John F. boardinghouse, 343 Main.
" John O. marketman, h. 149 Clark.
" Josiah L. conductor St.Ry. h. 56 Maple.
" Louise M. wid. Seth, h. 721 Main, rm. 45.
" Morton F. bookkeeper at Atlantic Screw
    Works, 70 Huyshope, h. 127 Jefferson.
" O. Herbert, private hotel, 149 High.
" Samuel A.bkkpr.389 Allyn,b.77 Windsor av.
" Wm. H. Mrs. prop. Am. hotel, 103 State.
Minett Eugene A. overseer at Cheney Bros. 34
    Morgan, h. 28 Pleasant.
Minge Gustav, gardener, b. 6 Wellington.
Minke Moses, floorwa. at 956, b.2u. 365 Main.
" Rose, clerk at 956, b.2u. 365 Main.
" Victor, butcher at 538, l.2u. 365 Main.
Minnerly Ferris A. clerk at Popes, h. 107
    Whitmore.
Minse Louis, stairb. 20 Potter, h.u, 6 Blumenthal.
Minssen Alfred, asst. inspector Hfd. Steam
    Boiler Inspection & Ins. Co. b. 54 Bkm.
Mintha Mary, typewriter, 336, b. 336 Weth.
Minza Veronica, wid. Jacob, h.u. 31 Trumbull.
Minzie William P. at 1213, l. 1213 Main.
Mirande Cosmo, collarm. at 8 Sig. h. 262 N.P.
Mirkesis Oliver, laborer, b.u. 17 Mechanic.
Mirrow, Franz W. tailor, h.u. 93 Chestnut.
Mischou Fred, laborer, h.u. 62 Sheldon.
Misheau Frank A. bartdr. at 931 Mn. h. 129 Alb.
Misker John, filer at Colts, b. 64 Vanblock.
" Theodore, laborer, h.u.r. 64 Vanblock.
Miskill Edward, carptr. at 10 Tru. b. 3 Harrison.
" Geo. E. carpenter, h. 74 Flower.
" Minnie, dressm. 721, h. 721 Main, rm. 38.
Missal Abram, barber at 985 Mn. b. 24 Morgan.
" Isaac S. tailor at 2 State, b. 24 Morgan.
" Joseph, tailor at 2 State, b. 42 North.
Missel Joseph W. barber at 1151 Main, h. 107
    Wooster.
" Wm. E. uphol. 988 Main, h.u. 44½ Wooster.
Missell Chas. tailor, 30½ Tem. h. 29 Windsor.
" Michael, tailor, h. 29 Windsor.
" William J. buffer, h. 29 Windsor.
Missett James, trav. salesman, h.u. 61 Ward.
Missionaries of LaSalette, N.P. south of Grace.
Mitchell Alfred L. cond. N.Y.R. h. 72 Vernon.
" Andrew D. com. trav. 110 Asy. h. 31 Church.
" Angeline C. Mrs. housekpr. h.u. 181 Capen.
" Arthur, clerk, b. 31 Church.
" Arthur B. barber at 209 Pearl, b.u. 251 Asy.
" Charles C. helper, b. 181 Capen.

Mitchell Charles E. coal, h. 1534 Broad.
" Charles T. correspt. Popes, b. 1534 Broad.
" Dennis, laborer, b. 33 Avon.
" E. oiler, steamer Middletown, 285 State, h.
    Saybrook t.
MITCHELL E. V. (Smith, Northam & Co.) 129
    State, h. 14 Charter Oak pl. See page 590.
" Edwd. mechanic, Popes, h. 32 New Britain.
" Edward B. meatcutr.552 Asy.h. 56 Putnam.
" Edwin Knox prof. Theological Seminary,
    1507 Broad, h. 57 Gillett.
" Ellen J. wid. James H. h.u. 9 Green.
" Ernest B. clerk at 197 Asy. b. 270 Main.
" Filmore S. waiter, 314 Asy. h. 34 Village.
" Frederick A. clerk at 1 So. Ann. h. W.H.t.
" Frederick A. machinist at 1 Flow. h. E.H.t.
" Frederick L. assistant foreman at Popes,
    b.u. 166 Allyn.
" George C. at Hfd. Fire Ins. Co. 53 Trum-
    bull, b. 11 James.
" Hattie P. h. 152 Washington.
" Henry C. clerk at 242 Asy. b. 31 Church.
" Herbert W. conductor St.Ry. h. 1 Orchard.
" J. Alfred, h.u. 40 Cedar.
" James E. clerk at Popes, h. 119 Oak.
" James E. oiler, str. Middletown, 285 State,
    b. 32 New Britain.
" James H. mach. 1 Flow. h. 85 Whitmore.
" John H. mach. at 1 Flower, b. Plainville t.
" John H. vice president Phœnix Insurance
    Co. (Fire) 64 Pearl, h. 56 Niles.
" Joseph, mach. at 13 Central, b.u. 20 Albany.
" Marietta Mrs. h. 197 Franklin.
" Marion, at Hartford Life Insurance Co.
    252 Asylum, b. 167 High.
" Morris, porter at T. Sisson & Co. 729 Main,
    h. 29 Wolcott.
" Nellie Mrs. laundress, 1130 Mn. h. 9 Green.
" Patrick, laborer, b. 33 Avon.
" Patrick J. plumber, b. 23 Spring.
" Ralph, gardener, h. 40 Cedar.
" Robert, laborer, h.u.r. 101 Windsor.
" Ruby, wid. Andrw A. h.u. 40 Cedar.
" T. fireman str. Middletown, h. Saybrook t.
" Thomas E. stonemason, h. Lifkey.
" Tony, laborer, b.u. 82 Sheldon.
" Victor E. draughtsman at 54 Arch, h.2u.
    35 Hungerford.
" Walter A. student Trinity col. b. 73 Vernon.
" Walter H. janitor at State Bank,h.10 Martin.
" Walter H. Jr. porter, b. 10 Martin.
" William A. janitor at Ætna Insurance Co.
    666 Main, h. 5 Wolcott.
" William H. musician, h. 31 Church.
" Wm. S. printer at 175 Pearl, h. 83 Governor.
Mittag Clara, b. 144 Albany.
" Frances,wid. Henry A. nurse, h. 144 Albany.
" Lena M. b. 144 Albany.
" Lulu, b. 144 Albany.
" Marjorie, b. 144 Albany.
Mittau Adolph, watchmkr. 551 Main, h. 28 West.
" Frederick, shoem. at 172 Pearl, h. 128 West.
Mitteldorf Wm. electro. at 177 Asy. b. 26 Church.
Mitton Alex. R. mach. 1 Flower, h.u. 227Park.
Mix Clifford C. student at Yale b. 9 Lenox.

**THINKING PEOPLE Read The Post Daily.**

Mix Eliza F. h. 253 Main.
" Frederick E. dentist,904 Main, h.172 Collins.
" Gertrude, stenogr. at 700 Main, b. 9 Lenox.
" Royal C. clerk, Hartford Life Insurance Co. 252 Asylum, h. 9 Lenox.
Miyanaga S., Japanese goods, h. 367 Main.
Mochan Morris, carpenter, h. 20 Bloomfield.
Modeen Joseph, clerk at 149, b. 167 Babcock.
Model Tailoring Co. 222, 224 Pearl.
    Benjamin Schoer.        Morris Liothblau.
Modern Pharmacy, G. M. Allen, mgr. 299 Park.
Moeller August, piano dealer at 92, h. 92 Pearl.
" Emil, machinist at 1 Flow. h.2u. 110 Ward.
" Louis, bartender at 74 Park.
Moers Catherine, h.u. 16 Charles.
Moffatt James, machine hand at Colts, b. B.v.
" Phil, bartender at 127, h.u. 116½ Albany.
Mohan Peter F. (P. B. Smith & Co.) b. 6 Tru.
" Thomas, saloon, 61 Elm, b. 6 Trumbull.
Mobegan Bartholomew, helper at 1 Flower, b. 52 Hicks.
Mohr Edward E. transferer at 175 Pearl, h.2u. 1067 Main.
Moisner Elmer, carpenter, h. 30 Elm.
Moisson Theodore, carpenter at N.Y.R. h. R.H.t.
" ☞ see also Moyson.
Mold Charles, laborer, h. 121 Front.
Moldenhouer Dora, wid. Wm.J.F. h. 650 Main.
" Frieda, teacher of languages, b. 650 Main.
Molin Carl P. Rev. bookstore, 205 Park, h. 312 Asylum, rm. 3.
Molitor Fred. F. finisher at James L. Howard & Co. 438 Asylum, h.2u. 92 Windsor.
" William F. Mrs. h. 63 Pleasant.
Moll Max E. farmer, b. 235 Barbour.
" Ulrich J. h. 235 Barbour.
Moller Laurentz B. contractor, James L. Howard & Co. 438 Asylum, h. 84 New Britain.
Molloy Patrick C. coachm.847 Asy.h.r.226Garden.
" ☞ see also Maloy; Molloy.
Molnar Louis, tailor, h.2u.r. 34 South Prospect.
Moloney ☞ see also Maloney; Meloney.
Molton ☞ see Moulton.
Molumphy Catherine, clerk at 921 Main, b. 2B Wadsworth.
" David, engraver at A. Mugfords, 177 Asylum, b. 2B Wadsworth.
" Edward J. painter, h. 28 Mulberry.
" Ellen, wid. David, h. 2B Wadsworth.
" Mamie, at 252 Pearl, b.u. 2B Wadsworth.
" Maurice W. printer, b. 2B Wadsworth.
" ☞ see also Malumphy.
Monacella Angelling Mrs. h.u. 79 Windsor.
" Pasquate, h.u. 79 Windsor.
Monagan Kittie I. stenographer at Lincoln, Seyms & Co. 34 Market, b. 7 Avon.
Monahan Francis, b. 111 Wethersfield.
" Maurice, laborer, h. 209 Sheldon.
" Michael, b. 2 Holcomb.
" Michael, laborer, b. 111 Maple.
" Michael, laborer, h.3u.r. 34 South Prospect.
" Patrick J. expressman, b. 88 Mather.
" Patrick J. mechanic, 54 Arch, b. 14 Chapel.
" Thomas, saloon, 70 Front, h. 111 Weth.
Mongan Thomas, laborer, h.2u.r. 25½ Flower.

Mongrain Frank, carptr. N.Y.R. h.2u. 52 Ple.
Monihan M. deckhand, str. Middletown,285 State.
Monitz Herman, mason, b. 70 Front.
Monk Edwin E. metalworker, 44 Ann, b. 73 Park.
" George D. publisher, l. 7 Central.
" Rose, at 252 Pearl, b. 15 Belmont.
" Sam. boilerm. at 109 Com. h. 15 Belmont.
Monks Herbert, mach. 70 Huy. b. 11 Eaton.
" James, mach. at 70 Huy. b. Park n. Pro.av.
" Rubert, b. 11 Eaton.
" Samuel, clerk at Colts, b. 88 Jefferson.
" William, machinist at 70 Huy. h. 11 Eaton.
Monnier William D. teacher Northwest school, h. Springfield t.
Monogue Kate, dressm. 108, b.2u. 108 Windsor.
Monroe Austin G. mach. at 9, h. 57 Sigourney.
" Ernest, assembler at 83 Woodbine, b. 281 Capitol.
" John W. clerk at Kimball & McCray, insurance, 658 Main, b. 57 Sigourney.
" ☞ see also Munroe.
Monson William R. (Hubbard & M.) h. N.t.
Montag Henry J. engraver at 62 Mar.b.64 Capitol.
" John J. engraver at 62 Mar. h.u. 108 Wooster.
Montague A. deckhand, str. Middlet'n, 285 State.
" Frederick C. salesman, h.u. 70 Maple.
" Margaret, wid. Welles W. b.u. 1191 Main.
Montaino Antonio, mason, b.3u. 18 Kilbourn.
" Dominic, laborer at 46 Un.pl. h. 154 Front.
" Lucca, mason, b.3u. 18 Kilbourn.
" Nardo, laborer, h.3u. 56 Portland.
" Peter, harpist, h.2u. 81 Windsor.
" Prospero, lab. street dept. h.2u. 81 Windsor.
Montani Carl, bootblack, h.u.r. 1177 Main.
Montano Dominic, laborer, h. 33 Windsor.
" Joseph, mason, b. 21 Windsor.
Montany Tony, tailor, l.u. 81 Windsor.
Montgomery Hugh G. market,373 Mn. h.142 Sey.
" James, polisher, b.2u. 1427 Broad.
" Lawrence R. machinist, h.u. 20 Chapel.
" Matthew, toolm. at 476 Cap. h. 32 Putnam.
" Philip, at Ætna Ins. Co. 666 Main, b. 142 Sey.
Montie Frank, clerk at 956 Main, b. 1204 Broad.
Montle Homer, at Colts, h.u. 74 Seymour.
Montry John, laborer, 300, b. 300 Wethersfield.
" John Jr. at 9 Morgan, b. 300 Wethersfield.
Moodie William, carpenter, h. 152 Mather.
Moody Adelbert J. at Ætna Life Ins. Co. 650 Main, b. 16 Smith.
" Brazilla E. clerk at 742 Park, h.u. 16 Smith.
" Edward H. clerk at 98 Asylum, h.u. 50 Niles.
" Effie B. china painting, b. Allen pl.
" Francis O. mach. at 1 Flow. h. 97 Babcock.
" George B. steward at 26 State.
" George F. bookkeeper, h. Allen pl.
" Henry, watchman 30 Cush. h.u. 16 Beach.
" John, groceries, etc. 120 Alb. h. 23 Center.
" Osborn W. woodw. at 155 Ch.O. b. B.v.
" Rachel, wid. Joseph, h.u. 16 Smith.
" Ralph, oiler steamer Hartford, 285 State, h. Thompsonville v.
" William A. carriagemaker, 37, h. 41 N.B.
" William C. patternmaker, b. 6 Canton.
" Wilfred L. mach. at 40 Cush. b. 6 Canton.

Mooers Henry A. h. 49 Park.
" M. E. Mrs. dressmaker, 49, h. 49 Park.
Moon Frank D. builder, 78, h. 78 Bond.
Mooney Daniel, laborer, h.r. 3 Pleasant ct.
" Daniel J. h. 39 Hudson.
" James P. shipper at 581 Cap. b. 51 Albany.
" John, b. 2 Holcomb.
" John, bellboy at 98 Wells, b. New Park.
" John, carpenter, h. New Park.
" John Mrs. boardinghouse, u. 1421 Broad.
" Joseph G. blacksmith, 249 Pearl.
" Margaret, wid. Charles, h.u. 1049 Broad.
" Matthew, laborer, b. 57 Albany.
" Michael, laborer, b. 38 South Prospect.
" Nicholas, helper at N.Y.R. h.2u. 38 Wells.
" Patrick, carpenter, h. 111 Zion.
" Thomas, laborer, h.2u.r. 57 Spruce.
" Thomas J. teamster, 25 Front, h.u.28 Church.
Moore Alice L. teacher, Washington st. school,
    b. 25 Allen pl.
" Anne W. b. 15 Columbia.
" Augustus P. mason, h. 289 Allyn.
" C. Howard, ship. clerk at 252 Pearl, h. Weth.
" Catherine, h.r. 16 Charles.
" Charles D. engineer, N.Y.R. h.u. 40 Green.
" Charles H. stereotyper at Hartford Courant,
    66 State, h. 228 Jefferson.
" Charlotte, b. 202 Maple.
Moore Clifford O. (Sage, Allen & Co.) dry
    goods, etc. 902 Main, b. 119 High.
" Edward F. machinist at 1 Flower. E.H.t.
" Emma N. Mrs. dressm. 635, h.u. 635 Main.
" Frank E. mach. at 142 Russ, h. 94 Church.
" Frank E. Mrs. stenographer, Smith, North-
    am & Co. 129 State, h. 94 Church.
" Franklin J. clerk at 33 Market, h.2u. 232
    Windsor av.
" Frederick C. inspector at Factory Ins.
    Association, 95 Pearl, h. 62 Kenyon.
" George C. b. 85 Wethersfield.

**MOORE GEO. W. & CO.** western farm
    loans, 7 & 8 per cent. 759 Main. *See p.429.*
    James H. Tallman.    Jas. B. Moore.
" Grace M. piano dept. Brown, Thomson &
    Co. 942 Main, b. 98 Trumbull.
" H. A. motorman, St.Ry. h. 49 Park.
" Harry, planer at 175 Pearl, b.r. 298 Market.
" Harvey F. at 158 Woodland, h. E.H.t.
" Hattie M. Mrs. h. 126 Ann.
" Henry, laborer, h.u. 254 Front.
" Henry H. painter at Pratt & Whitney Co.
    1 Flower, b. Manchester t.
" & Holbrook, meat and fish, 275 Main.
    Reuben T. Moore.    David W. Holbrook.
" James, fireman, P.&R. h. 73 Albany.
" James, tinner, b. 21 Eaton.
" James B. (G.W.M.& Co.) h.88 Wethersfield.
" James M. inspector, Hartford Steam Boiler
    Insp. and Ins. Co. 650 Main, h. 25 Allen pl.
" James P. baggageman. N.Y.R. b. 33½ Spruce.
" James R. R. gen. manager Hartford Hol-
    low Ware Co. h.u. 17 Florence.
" Jennie Mrs. boardinghouse 2u. 1281 Main,
" Jesse, solicitor for Hartford Courant Co. 66
    State, h. Farmington t.

Moore John, laborer, h. 5 Green.
" John C. conductor St.Ry. h.u. 635 Main.
" John K. b. 15 Columbia.
" Joseph, waiter, str. Middletown, 285 State.
" Laura C. wid. George W. h. 85 Wethersfield.
" Louisa M. wid. Jonathan, b. 631 Farmington.
" M. J. Mrs. physician, h. 1147 Main.
" Marjorie, teacher at 8, b. 8 Spring.
" Martin J. blacksm. 276 Allyn, h. 52 Grand.
" Mary, wid. Edward, h. 1442 Broad.
" Mary, wid. Michael, h. 254 Front.
" Michael J. labor. Pope T. Co. h.u.r.15 Belden.
" Peter F. bartender, 989 Main, h. 6 Trumbull.
" Reuben T. (M. & Holbrook,) h.54 Park.
" Richard, laborer, b.u. 14 Arch.
Moore Robert (Grozier & M.) 339 Sheldon,
    h. 203 Franklin.        *See page 510.*
" Robert (W. C. Smith & Co.) h. 19 Russ.
" Thomas, h. 21 Eaton.
" Thomas, farmer, h.r. 147 Woodland.
" Thomas F. brakem. N.Y.R. h.u. 198 Front.
" William, h. 1147 Main.
" William A. assistant secretary Phœnix Mu-
    tual Life Ins. Co. 49 Pearl, h. 23 Madison.
" William D. signalman, N.Y.R. h. 40 Green.
" William F. painter at 12Church, h.88 Mather.
" Wm. H. harnessm. at 8 Sig. b. 94 Babcock.
" William H. laborer, h.r. 103 Vine.
" William H. Rev. sec'y of Missionary Society
    of Conn. 426 Asylum, h. 15 Columbia.
" William J. clerk at 372 Asylum, b. 12 Pratt.
" Winthrop B. student, b. 15 Columbia.
" ☞ *see also Mohr; Mooers.*
Moors Edward N. screwm. at 476 Cap. b. Weth t.
" William M. coremaker at 556 Cap. h. Weth.
Moran Agnes, b. 60 Madison.
" Annie, b. 64 Hopkins.
" Anthony, sweeper at Popes, h.u. 3 Lawrence.
" Bridget, wid. James, h. 39 Lafayette.
" Catherine, wid. John, h. 1172 Main.
" Daniel, laborer, h.r. 23 Spruce.
" David S. musician, h. 16 Ely.
" Dennis, helper, h. 76 Windsor.
" Edward, embosser at 141 Pearl, b.76 Windsor.
" Frank, carpenter, h. 33 Elliott.
" Frank J. brazier at Popes, b.u. 98 Babcock.
" James, b. 2 Holcomb.
" James, helper, h.u. 34 South Prospect.
" James, teamster at 165, b. 169 Windsor.
" James A. steward at 365 Allyn, h. 49 Spring.
" James F. cabinetm. at 69 Front, h. E.H.t.
" James F. mason, h. 124 Babcock.
" James F. painter, b. 52 Hudson.
" James J. foreman on N.Y.R. h. 121 Mather.
" James P. mach. at Colts, h.u. 63 Governor.
" John, baggagem. at N.Y.R. h. 35 Liberty.
" John, laborer, h.u. 55 Liberty.
" John, painter, l. 70 Front.
" John C. engineer fire department, b. 63 Gov.
" John F. men's furnishings, 869 Main, b. 48
    Church.
" John J. harness stitcher, h. 39 Lafayette.
" John P. printer at 175 Pearl, h. 76 Windsor.
" Kate, at 254 Pearl, b. 60 Madison.
" Louise A. h. 434 Main.

**As A NEWSPAPER, THE POST LEADS.**

Moran Margaret, b. W. H. Home for Aged, Alb.
" Margaret, clerk at 956 Main, b. 76 Windsor.
" Martin, steamfitter, h.2u. 48 Windsor.
" Mary, at 254 Pearl, b. 60 Madison.
" Mary, boardinghouse, 1172 Main.
" Mary, wid. Michael, h. 263 Front.
" Mary, wid. Patrick T. h.2u. 1088 Broad.
" Mary, wid. Thomas J. h. 58 Village.
" Michael, groceries 46, h.2u. 81 Sheldon.
" Michael, laborer, h.u. 16 Huntley pl.
" Michael C. l.u. 1113 Main.
" Michael F. assembler at Colts, h. 58 Village.
" Michael F. steamfitter, Colts, h. 8 Wawarme.
" Patrick, clerk, 174 Asylum, b.2u. 81 Shel.
" Patrick F. motorman St Ry. h.u. 281 Market.
" Rose, wid. James, h. 65 Windsor.
" Theresa, h. 434 Main.
" Thomas, brakeman, b.u. 16 Huntley pl.
" Thomas, polisher at Colts, b.u. 58 Village.
" Thomas, plumber, h. 1049 Broad.
" Thomas, teamster at 385 Shel. h. 50 Gov.
" Thomas J. boilermaker at I. B. Davis & Son,
      40 Cushman, h.u. 263 Front.
" Thomas J. painter and decorator, h. 14 Ch.O.
" William Mrs. h.2u. 33 Mechanic.
" William, plumber at 1092 Mn. h. 60 Madison.
" William H. clerk at 869 Main, b. E.H.t.
" William J. b. 1335 Broad.
" ☞ see also Morin.
Morarty James, laborer, b.2u.r. 12 So. Prospect.
Morba Bertha, wid. Hans, h. 32 Capitol.
" Karl P. assistant at Hartford Library, 5
      Atheneum, b. 32 Capitol.
Morcom Frederick C. at Ætna Life Insurance
      Co. 650 Main, b. 27 Sumner.
" James J. at Travelers Insurance Co. 56
      Prospect, h. 27 Sumner.
" Will J. at Travelers Ins. Co. 56 Prospect,
      b. 27 Sumner.
Moreau Mary, wid. Pierre, h.2u. 26 Church.
Morehouse E. K. Mrs. nurse, 14 Church.
" Frank S. student Trinity college, 8 Nor-
      tham tower, Summit.
Moren Alfred E. mach. at 1 Flow. b. 371 Capitol.
" Alfred E. mach. at 581 Cap. b. 1202 Broad.
" Edward A. mach. 1 Flow. b.u. 1202 Broad.
" John, molder, h.2u. 1202 Broad.
Moretzki Ignatz, city street cleaner, h. 180 Ward.
Morey Polly Ann, wid. Nelson, b. 52 Kenyon.
Morg John, baker, b.2u. 76 Sanford.
Morgan Albert, at Hartford Fire Ins. Co. 53
      Trumbull, b. 92 Pearl.
" Alfred E. clerk at 247 Asylum, h.u. 18 Avon.
" Annie, nurse, b. 1304 Main.
" Bridget, wid. Michael, h.2u. 71 Governor.
" Catherine, h.r. 219 Pearl.
" Edward, marketman, 319 Asy. b. 26 Chst.
" Eliza J. wid. Wallace, h. 1463 Broad.
" Elizabeth Mrs. h. 2 Columbia.
" Ely, physician, 721 Main, rm. 28.
" Emily M. b. 108 Farmington.
" Emma E. Mrs. h.u. 153 Windsor av.
" Forrest. h. 227 Sigourney.
" Frank T. steamfitter, Popes, h. 65 Glendale.
" Fred. H. foreman at 690, h. 819 Park.

Morgan Harriet E. wid. Nath'l H. h. 55 Grove.
" Henry C., Asst. Q. M. General, State Cap-
      itol, room 56, h. Colchester.
" Henry K. h. 108 Farmington.
" Hugh T. vice-prest. New England Brewing
      Co. 217 Windsor.
" James, commer. traveler, h.u. 125 Jefferson.
" James, policeman, h. 84 Arch.
" James H. clerk, 335 Shel. b.u. 125 Jefferson.
" James P. driver at 120 Albany, b. 48 Brooks.
" Jeremiah, watchman, b. 40 John.
" John, driver at 430, b. 428 Asylum.
" John, laborer, h.2u. 45 Spruce.
" John F. cigars, b. 48 Brooks.
" John J. laborer, h. 34 Chestnut.
" Joseph, pickler at Popes, b. 40 John.
" Joseph Mrs. h. 44 Church.
" Lena, wid. Otto, h.2u. 56 Sheldon.
" M. E. Mrs. nurse, h. 709 Main, rm. 6.
" Mary A. h.u. 48 Wadsworth.
" Mary E. clerk at 871 Main, b. 48 Brooks.
" Michael, laborer, h. 45 Spruce.
" Nathaniel K. drug. 155, h. 320 Windsor av.
" Patrick, teamster, h. 76 Fairmount.
" Patrick F. at 238 Zion, h. 25 Hamilton.
" Patrick J. shoemaker, 25 Alb. h.u. 48 Brook.
" & Pratt, undertakers, 387 Main.
      Wm. R. Morgan.        James T. Pratt.
" Robert A. clerk at 241, h. 223 Asy. rm. 68.
" Street Mission, 52 Morgan.
" Thomas, laborer at 8 Front, h. 84 Arch.
MORGAN THOMAS W. *councilman 5th ward;* with
      Phœnix Insurance Co. 64, b. 92 Pearl.
" Victor F. student at Trinity college, b.
      227 Sigourney.
" Watkin Ede, painter, h. 230 Maple.
" William, cashier at Wm. Rogers Mfg. Co.
      66 Market, h. 18 Prospect.
" William, coachman. 420 Main, h. 20 Grace.
" William, driver at 901 Main, b. 48 Brook.
" William, helper, h.u. 36 North.
" William, molder at 618 Capitol, h 36 North.
" William A. chief night clerk at P.O. h.u. 40
      Williams.
" William D. & Co. manufacturers of check
      books, 9 Columbia.
      William D. Morgan.        William G. Morgan.
" Wm. Denison, *(W. D. Morgan & Co.)* dis-
      count clerk Ætna National Bank, 644
      Main, b. 9 Columbia.
🖝 Wm. D. physician, 700 Main, h. 108 Far.
" William G. *(W. D. Morgan & Co.)* editor of
      The Ætna, at Ætna Life Insurance Co.
      650 Main, h. 9 Columbia.
" William R. *(Morgan & Pratt,)* b. 28 Capitol.
Morginson Mary, laundress, h.u. 7 Affleck.
Morhardt Chas. ins. clerk at 197 Asy. b. 26 Grace.
" Frederick, h. 26 Grace.
Moriarty Bartholomew, coachman 198, h. 198 Gray
" Dennis J. laborer, b.u. 1163 Main.
" James, porter at 47, b. 47 Prospect.
" James, laborer, b.u. 1163 Main.
" James, laborer, b.2u. 81 Sheldon.
" James, masontender, h.u. 18 Dean.
" James J. barber at 77 Tru. h.u. 279 Asylum.

PIANOS RE-BUILT AS GOOD AS NEW BY LEO. H. BATTALIA, Warerooms, 943 MAIN ST.

Moriarty Jeffrey, screwmaker at 476 Capitol, b. 28 Grand.
" John, laborer, b. 34 So. Prospect.
" John,laborer at 70 Commerce,b.u.1163 Main.
" Julia, h.r. 103 Windsor.
" Mary Mrs. boardinghouse, 1163 Main.
" Mary, wid. James, h.2u. 103 Windsor.
" Michael, laborer, h.2u. 8 Winter.
" Patrick, laborer, h.u. 118 Windsor.
" Patrick J. bricklayer, b. 1327 Broad.
" Thomas, hodcarrier, h.u. 1163 Main.
" Thomas B. mach. at P.&R. h. 53 Liberty.
" Thomas F. clerk at 928 Main, b. 9 Gray.
Morin J. E. baker at 751 Main, b. 103 Trumbull.
Morkan Bridget, wid. John, h.3u. 38 So. Prospect.
" Michael J. conductor St.Ry. b.3u. 38 S.Pro.
" Michael W. watchm. Colts, h.r. 68 Vanblock.
" William, driver at 1123 Main, b. 61 Judson.
MORLEY FRANKLIN A. councilman 5th ward, (Cross & Morley,) h. 223 Asylum, rm. 70.
See page 445.
" William, mechanic, b. 34 Smith.
Moroney Mary, wid. Lawrence, h.3u. 19 Spruce.
" Michael, joiner, b.u. 22 Dean.
" Patrick J. joiner, b.u. 22 Dean.
" Thomas, carbuilder, N.Y.R. h.3u. 19 Spruce.
" ☞ see also Maroney, Meroney.
Morran Thad. D. clerk, h.u. 14½ Morris.
" William J. toolmkr. Colts, h. 65 Huyshope.
Morrell Daniel, sec'y Hartford Machine Screw Co. 476 Capitol, h. 14 Myrtle.
" Edward M. cigarmaker, b. 1080 Main.
" Daniel S. clerk at 476 Capitol, b. 14 Myrtle.
" John W. ass't sec'y, 476 Cap. b. 14 Myrtle.
" M. A. wid. A. W. nurse, h. 926 Main.
Morrill Chas. W. mangr. 719 Mn. h. 131 Bellevue.
" Joseph E. molder at 1 Flower, h. 213 Law.
" Sarah J. wid. Orin, b. 131 Bellevue.
Morris Alfred J. carpenter, h. 52 Washington.
" Augusta, wid. Isadore, b.2u. 11 Belden.
" Bessie, 521 Windsor av.
" Bridget, 521 Windsor av.
" C. Sheras, clerk at Popes, b. 77 Elm.
" Charles E. physician, 721 Main, rm. 5, b.2u. 3 Seyms.
" Chas. W. printer at 141 Pearl,h.u. 88 Hudson.
" Clara, student, b.u. 100 Hudson.
" Cornelia A. teacher at Brown school, b. 52 Washington.
" Edward B. b. 2 Ward.
" Edward E. rubberworker at 690 Park, h. 144 Madison av.
" Elijah, machinist at Popes, h. 31 Hamilton.
" Ellen, wid. Patrick, b. 159 Babcock.
" Fannie A. wid. Henry A. h. 298 Pearl.
" Felix C. tester at 556 Cap. b. 159 Babcock.
" Frank, salesman, h.u. 9 Pleasant.
" Fred, helper at 44, b. 44 Woodbridge.
" George H. salesman at 20 Central, h.u. 21 Seymour.
" George R. mach. at 54 Arch, h.u. 150 N.P.
" Grace M. cashier at 908 Main, b. 32 Canton.
" Henry A. waiter, b.u. 289 Pearl.
" Henry G. porter at 41 Tru. h. 224 Park.

Morris James A. at Hartford Fire Ins. Co. 53 Trumbull, b. 298 Pearl.
" James J. at 79 Talcott, h. 18 So. Prospect.
" James T. manager Great Atlantic & Pacific Tea Co. 979 Main, h. 3 Seyms.
" John, gatetender at N.Y.R. h. 20 Chestnut.
" John E. assistant secretary Travelers Insurance Co. 56 Prospect, h. 2 Ward.
" John F. b. 2 Ward.
" Jonathan F. office at Charter Oak National Bank, 124 Asylum, h. 80 Farmington.
" Joseph, assembler at Popes, h. 31 Hamilton.
" Joseph T. steward at 80, h.r. 173 State.
" Mary, wid. Martin, b. 202 Laurel.
" Mary E. teacher, b. 52 Washington.
" Michael, carcleaner, h.u. 6 Green.
" Nathan, clerk at 324 Asy. h.2u. 11 Belden.
" Phillip J. conductor St.Ry. b. 48 Prospect.
" Rachel, clerk at 908 Main, b.u. 11 Belden.
" Richard C., U. S. marshal, 65 State, h. New London t.
" Robert, inspector at 690 Park, b. 150 N.P.
" Sarah, wid. Thomas, h. 31 Hamilton.
" Sarah, wid. Thomas, h.u. 10 Rose.
" William, manager at 80, b. 80 State.
" William, mechanic at Popes. b.u. 248 Law.
" William S. salesm. at 49 Pratt, h. 624 Broad.
Morrison Agnes C. h. 50 Albany.
" Daniel D. stereotyper at Hartford Times, 716 Main, h. 49 Sigourney.
" Dennis, carptr. at 165 Windsor,h. 38 Canton.
" Edward J. clerk at Popes, b. 27 Hawthorn.
" Frank P. foreman at Popes, b. 71 Russ.
" Frederick S. teacher High school,39 Hopkins, h. 209 Laurel.
" John, b.3u. 194 Sheldon.
" John, plumber at 164 State, b. 21 Central.
" John H. janitor at West Middle school, h. 27 Hawthorn.
" Joseph, h.u. 10 Rose.
" Joseph F. packer, h.2u. 29 Hawthorn.
" Joseph T. modelmkr. at Popes, b. 401 Cap.
" Lincoln W. stenographer, 926 Main, rm. 19, h. Thompsonville v.
" Mary Mrs. b. 2 Holcomb.
" Michael B. engineer at 556 Capitol, h.2u. 149 Lawrence.
" Rose wid. James, h.3u. 192 Sheldon.
" Theodore, carptr. N.Y.R. h. Rocky Hill t.
" Thomas, harnessmkr. 8 Sig. l. 5 Hawthorn.
" Thomas J. assembler, b.2u. 192 Sheldon.
" W. A. conductor St.Ry. b. 80 State.
Morrisey John E. clerk at 372 Asy. b.50 Liberty.
Morriss Fred E. clerk, 84 Albany, b. 30 Lewis.
Morrissey Catherine,wid.Thomas,h. 127 Albany.
" James F. groceries, 84 Alb. h. 84 Chestnut.
" John, laborer at Jewell Belting Co. 15 Trumbull, h.u. 47 Walnut.
" John J. saloon, 122, b. 127 Albany.
" John J. trimmer at 266 Pearl, b. 127 Albany.
" Maurice, brakeman, h.u. 50 Liberty.
" Michael, b. 2 Holcomb.
" Michael, driver, b.u. 69 Pleasant.
" Michael, molder at 54 Arch, b. 345 Main.
" Thomas, coachman, l. 221 Main.

Morse Albert B. agent, 200, b. 200 Allyn.
"  Apollos C. carpenter, h. 13 Talcott.
"  Bryan K. student at Trinity college, 38
    Jarvis hall, Summit.
"  Charles R. b. 529 Broad.
"  Charles S. extracts, perfumes, h. 529 Broad.
"  E. H. Mrs. instructor at Hartford Business
    college, 370 Asylum, h. 7 Brownell.
**MORSE EDWARD H.** proprietor of
    the Hartford Business college, 370 Asy-
    lum, h. 7 Brownell.    *See page 711.*
"  Edward L. clerk, h. 35 Bellevue.
"  Edwin N. engineer at 379, h.u. 488 Main.
"  Emma M. b.r. 257 Windsor av.
"  Ernest H. carpenter, b. 115 Oak.
"  Everett H. at Travelers Insurance Co. 56
    Prospect, b. 7 Walnut.
"  Florence Hovey, wid. E. L. h. 7 Walnut.
"  Frederick G. painter, 32, h. 32 Lawrence.
"  Fred J. physician, 55 b. 55 Church.
"  Harriet L. wid. John H. b.r. 257 Windsor av.
"  Hattie G. clerk at Phœnix Mutual Life Ins.
    Co. 49 Pearl, b. 257 Windsor av.
"  Huldah, wid. Luke, b. 127 Bellevue.
"  J. Howard, h. 20 Fairfield.
"  John H. machinist at 581, b. 381 Capitol.
**MORSE LEONARD,** attorney at law,
    recorder city court, 2 Central, room 3, b.
    14 Spring.    *See page 492.*
"  M. Irving, salesm. 111 Shel. h. Wilsons sta.
"  Matthew O. market, 179 Asy. h.u. 49 S.Hud.
"  Ralph, teamster at 88 Market, h. E.H.t.
Mortensen Hans, carptr. N.Y.R. h. 46 Laurel.
"  John, carpenter, 69 Front, h. Parkville.
"  Joshua, stonecutter at 40 High, b. 513 Capitol.
Morton Douglas, teamster, h.u. 28 Huntley pl.
"  Edward S. painter, b. 140 Trumbull.
"  Frank, polisher, h. 116 Retreat.
"  Frank K. iceman, 4 Central, h. 39 Linden.
"  Fred. A. clerk at 237 Asylum, h. 57 Lincoln.
"  George B. motorman St.Ry. b.u. 34 Pratt.
"  Geo. E. iceman at 4 Central, h. 2 Elm pl.
"  George W. rubberworker at 690 Park, h.
    80 Madison av.
"  Grace Mrs. h. 138 Market.
"  John, bookbdr. 141 Pearl, h. Wethersfield t.
"  Jos. bookbinder at 141 Pearl, h. 10 Grand.
"  William S. carpenter, h. 20 Smith.
MORTSON GEORGE, *(Hubbard & M.)* time
    clocks, etc. b. 110 High.    *See page 428.*
Morway Edward N. annealer at 1 Flower.
"  Lewis J. annealer, 1 Flow,.h. Southington t.

Moscarri Thos. fruit, etc. 18 Church, h.r.35 Alb.
Mosco Salvator, poolroom, 180 Front, h. 30 Kil.
**MOSELEY DAVID S.** publisher and
    printer, 336 Asylum, h. W.H.t.
                        *See page 477.*
"  Edward E. bkkpr. at 399 Allyn, b. 63 Imlay
"  G. W. & Son, wholesale grocers, 399 Allyn.
    George W. Moseley.     Herbert C. Moseley.
"  George W. *(G. W. M. & Son,)* h. 63 Imlay.
"  Georgia M. teacher N. E. school, b. W.H.t.
"  Herbert C. *(G. W. M. & Son)* h.Thomps'ville.
"  Mary W. wid. David B. h. 339 Asylum.
"  S. Belle, b. 63 Imlay.
Moses Geo. E. bookkeeper at Woven Wire Mat-
    tress Co. h. 37 Ward.
"  Linwood K. ledger clerk Popes, b. 37 Ward.
"  Louisa M. wid. Luther J. h.u. 51 Spring.
"  Luther M. clerk at 97 Asy. b. 236 Ashley.
"  Sophia, wid. Andrew A. h. 9 Fern, W.H.t.
"  Victor, waiter steamer Hartford, 285 State.
Mosesson Samuel, dye works, 143, h. 143 Front.
Mosher Anna, wid. Edgar A. b. 160 Franklin.
"  Edward H.civil eng. 70Com.h.u.150Franklin.
"  Fannie, b. 16 Belden.
"  John H. motorman St.Ry. b.u. 150 Franklin.
"  Lewis W. rubberw. at 690 Park, b.12 Sisson.
Moshier John, b. 56 Wethersfield.
Mosinsky Abram, peddler, h. 54 Avon.
"  Nathan, grocer, 54, h. 54 Avon.
Moskovitz Daniel, tailor, b. 31 North.
"  Sam. salesman 261 Asylum, h. 282 Front.
Mossel Meyer E. clerk at 862 Main, b.190 State.
Most Martin H. waiter 358 Asylum, b. 70 Front.
Mothes Herman E. rubberworker at 690 Park,
    h. 27 Madison av.
Mott John, teamster at 38 Front, h. 22 Hicks.
"  John T. molder at 1 Flower, h. 35 Wolcott.
Motta Giovanni, saloon 79, h. 79 Windsor.
Motto Nicola, fruits and confect. 8, h. 10 Maple.
Mottram Albert, foreman 62 Mar. h. 240 Martin.
"  Albert, Jr. solderer, 62 Mar. b. 240 Martin.
"  Alfred, solderer at 62 Market, b. 15 Harper.
"  Charles, solderer 62 Market, h. 26 Loomis.
"  Simon, buffer at 62 Market, h. 15 Harper.
Moules Lillian B. wid. Charles R. b. 75 Hudson.
Moulthrop R. J. Mrs. h. 67 Pearl.
Moulton Alfred S. framer at 581, b. 381 Capitol.
"  Frank P. teacher High school, h. 247 Collins.
Mount St. Joseph Convent, 152 Farmington.
Mourman Peter, woodworker at 133 Sheldon.
Mousette Echton, fish peddler, h. 105 Commerce.
"  Joseph, bartender, h.u.r. 143 Commerce.
Moussette Toune, bartender, h. 9 Kilbourn.
Mow Charlie, laundry, 113, h. 113 Lawrence.
"  Quong, laundry, 54 Sheldon.
Moyer Annie, wid. William W. h. 57 Putnam.
"  Burness, at 83 Woodbine, b. 57 Putnam.
"  Curtis H. secy. and treas. J. H. Eckhardt
    Co. art store, 693 Main, h. 22 Girard.
"  Edward A. draughtsman at 690 Park, b.
    57 Putnam.
"  Gilbert L. electrician at 83 Woodbine, h.
    57 Putnam.
"  Henry C. b. 223 Asylum, rm. 17.

Moyer Mahlon H. stenographer Court Common Pleas, h. 73 Madison.
" Olivia J. wid. Wm. boardinghouse, 64 Cap.
" Wm. N. shirtmaker, 545, h. 545 Main.
Moylan Bridget, wid. Cornelius, h. 75 Wilson.
" Cornelius, lab. Pope Tube Co. b. 75 Wilson.
" Dennis, laborer, h. 44 Glendale.
" John J. b. 75 Wilson.
" Thomas, carptr. 335 Shel. h. 34 Chestnut.
Moynahan Maurice, teamster at 189 State, h. 209 Sheldon.
" Patrick, driver, h. 57 Wooster.
" Thomas, driver, b.u. 51 Albany.
Mt. St. Joseph's Convent Corporation, 152 Far.
Mucci Joseph, laborer, h. 1 North.
" Sullivan, laborer, h.u. 19 Ellery.
" William, b. 1 North.
Muchman Alder, peddler, h.u. 214 Front.
Mucklow Alfred W. agent Building and Loan Association, h. 51 Clark.
" William B. (Chapman & M.) 370 Asylum, h. 51 Clark.
Mudry George, at Hartford Machine Screw Co. b. 251 Park.

**MUGFORD ALBERT,** wood engraver and electrotyper, 177 Asylum, h. 129 Kenyon.             *See page 476.*
" Edwin S. salesman at A. Mugford, 177 Asylum, b. 129 Kenyon.
Muggleton John E. mach. at Popes, b.2u. 75 Flow.
Mugler Harry, printer, b. 981 Main.
Muhleib Sophia Mrs. b.u. 143 Zion.
" William H. at Popes, b.u. 143 Zion.
Muir William S. clerk at 98 Kil. b. 63 Spring.
Mulcahy Annie, b. 1413 Broad.
" Arthur W. painter, h.u. 110 Barbour.
" Bridget T. teacher, W.H.t. b. 56 Vanblock.
" David M. cutter at 76 Asylum, b. 115 Hung.
" Edward J. *street commissioner,* gents furnishings, 33 to 41 Asylum, h. 5 Chestnut.
" James, laborer, h.u. 40 John.
" James, laborer at 98 Kil. h.2u.r. 61 Front.
" Johanna, dressmaker, b. 114 Hungerford.
" John A., Very Rev. vicar general, pastor St. Patrick's church, h. 82 Church.
" John J. carptr. & builder, 11 h. 11 Kennedy
" John J. clerk at 33 Asylum, b. 115 Hung.
" Joseph P. assembler, b. 17 Green.
" Julia, proofreader at 1 So. Ann, b. 116 Hung.
" Michael M. screwm. 476 Cap. h. Newington t.
" Michael J. helper 1 Flower, h.u. 21 Law.
" Thos. engineer at Capitol, h. 115 Hungerford.
" Thomas F. mach. at 1 Flow. b. 1413 Broad.
" Thomas L. laborer at N.Y.R. h. 1413 Broad.
" Timothy, blacksmith at Colts, h. 56 Vanblock.
" Wm. H. Jr. painter, b. 17 Green.
" William J. Mrs. b. 1333 Broad.
Muldoon Bridget, wid. Roger, h. 23 Seymour.
" James J. operator, 35 Sheldon, b. 86 Arch.
" John F. mason, b.u. 86 Arch.
" Margaret, at 34 Morgan, b. 86 Arch.
" Martin, laborer, h.u. 86 Arch.
" Mary, dressmaker, b. 23 Seymour.
" Mary A. dressmaker, b.u. 86 Arch.

Muldoon Michael F. mech. at Popes, b. E.H.t.
" Patrick J. toolm. at 388 Cap. h.u. 4 Grand.
Muldowney Jas. fireman 165 Windsor, h. 48 Avon.
" James F. bartendr. 30 Union pl. h. 152 Russ.
" Michael, mach. at N.Y.R. h.u. 59 Spruce.
Mulhall Catherine, housekeeper, h. 67 Elm.
MULHALL JAMES, real estate, etc. 29 Pearl, h. 7 Florence.           *See page 267.*
" Jeremiah J. screwm. 476 Cap. h. 42 Francis.
" Jeremiah Jr. machinist, b. 42 Francis.
" John, clerk at 928 Main, b. 7 Florence.
" Mary A. h.u. 17 Wolcott.
" Mary E. h. 67 Elm.
" Matthew F. blacksmith at 17, b. 67 Elm.
" Nellie T. teach. Wilson st. sch. b.u. 17 Wolcott
" William H. mach. at 581 Cap. b. 42 Francis.
Mullady Patrick, assemb. at Colts, h.r. 9 S. Prospect.
Mullally Bridget, wid. Thomas, h.2u. 47 Green.
" Daniel J. foreman at 95 Ple. h.u. 985 Main.
" Edward F. b.2u. 47 Green.
" John, tinner N.Y.R. h. Windsor t.
" Thos. J. bricklayer, b.2u. 47 Green.
" William H. bricklayer, h. 29 Hungerford.
Mullander ☞ *See also Mallender.*
Mullane Daniel J. head clerk N.Y.N.H.&H. freight station, 98 Kilbourn, h.u. 8 Russell.
" Catherine E. clerk at Brown, Thomson & Co. 942 Main, b.u. 78 Franklin.
" Ellen, wid. William, h.u. 78 Franklin.
" William F. painter, h.u. 3 Warren.
Mullaney John, bartdr. 365 Allyn, h. 7 Atlantic.
" John, helper at 1, b.u. 30 Flower.
Mullarky Chas. woodyard, 135 Ch.O. h.u. 1 Front.
" Henry, teamster at 213 State, b.u. 1 Front.
" Louisa, laundress at 4 Lewis, b.u. 1 Front.
Mullberd Benjamin, laborer, b.u. 80 Front.
Mullen Elizabeth, wid. Thomas, h. 21 Grace.
" James, mason, b. 1183 Main.
" James F. mach. 83 Woodbine, b. 248 Law.
" James W. clerk at 224 State, h. 65 Oxford.
" John, laborer, b. Cone.
" John E. clerk at L. L. Ensworth & Son, iron merchants, 104 Front, b. 83 Oxford.
" John S. molder at 556 Cap. b. 21 Grace.
" Nellie, dressm. 68 Pratt, rm. 26, b. 83 Oxford.
" Mamie, clerk at 956 Main, b. 15 Flower.
" Mary E. dressmaker, 21, b. 21 Grace.
" Matthew, helper, b. Cone.
" Michael, mech. 581 Cap. b.u. 47 Commerce.
" Rose Mrs. b. 2 Holcomb.

Mullen Thomas, farmer, h. Cone.
" Thomas F. landscape gardener, b. Cone.
" Thos. F. salesman at 47 Mar. b. 83 Oxford.
" Thomas Francis, forem. at 66 Sta.b.21 Grace.
" William, h. 83 Oxford.
" ☞ see also Mullane; Mullin; O'Mullane.
Muller August, lithographer at 42 Union pl. h.
   5 Pleasant.
" Ernest, barber, 523 Main, h. Newfield.
" Leonard, stocker at Colts, b.2u. 9 S.Pro.
" Martin, cabinetmaker, b.u. 152 Mather.
" Peter, laborer, b.2r. 34 So. Prospect.
" ☞ see also Miller.
Mulligan Ambrose, lettercarrier Station A. b.
   27 Windsor.
" Annie Mrs. b.u. 21 Huntley pl.
" Blanche, clerk 169 Asylum, h. 56 Oak.
" Cyprian J. letter carrier, P.O. h. 5 Warren.
" Edward, molder 54 Arch, h.2u. 1160 Main.
" Fred. J. engineer at 835 Mn. h. 58 Madison.
" Isabella M. teacher Washington st. school, b.
   22 Linden.
" James M. clerk at 581 Cap. b. 27 Windsor.
" John, laborer, b. 39 South Prospect.
" John G. bartender h.u. 32 Kilbourn.
" Theresa A. wid. John F. h.u. 56 Oak.
" Thomas, b. 2 Holcomb.
" Walter A. operative at 388 Cap. b. 56 Oak.
Mullin Joseph, reporter at Hartford Daily Times,
   716 Main, b. 90 Church.
" Matthew, clerk, b. 80 State.
" ☞ see also Mullen.
Mullings John, steamfitter at 548 Asylum, b.
   38 Hudson.
Mullins Thomas, clerk at Brown, Thomson &
   Co. 942 Main, b. 90 Church.
Mulqueen Annie and Kate, h.2u. 12 Potter.
Mulraine James, laborer, h.2u. 32 Elm.
" John, bottler at 539 Main, b. 32 Elm.
Mulrane Edward J. h.u. 94 Grove.
" James, laborer at Colts, b. 28 South Prospect.
" Joseph M. enameler at Popes, b.u. 54 Law.
" Patrick, h. 55 Front.
" Patrick, enameler at Popes, b.u.54 Lawrence.
" Thomas, enameler at Popes, h. 19 Commerce.
Mulverhill Edward, laborer, b.2u. 41 Mechanic.
Mulvey James, clerk at 108 Asy. b. Meriden t.
" Michael A. toolm. 1 Flow. b. 34 Hopkins.
Mulville Francis X. Rev. teacher, b. 352 Collins.
Mumford James P. bookb. at 141 Pearl, h. E.H.t.
Muncey Henry, asst. janitor, 66, b. 66 Prospect.
" Wm. A. janitor Parsons theater, h. 66 Pro.
Munger Alonzo N. engineer at E. S. Kibbe Co.
   149 State, h.u. 37 Hungerford.
" Everett P. captain, h.u. 709 Main.
" Frank D. supt. reg. dept. P.O. h. 24 Lincoln.
Munn Annie A. stenographer at Jewell Belting
   Co. 15 Trumbull, b.u. 222 Garden.
" Edwin J. bookkeeper at W. L. Wakefield,
   insurance, 720 Main, b. 222 Garden.
" Emma B. wid. John B. h.u. 222 Garden.
Munoz Charlotta, nurse, 20 South Hudson.
Munro John, coachman at 2 Wethersfield, b.
   2 Franklin pl.
" Kenneth M. b.u. 2 Franklin pl.

Munroe Geo. I. carptr. 14 Hicks, h. 88 Wooster.
" James, machinist, b. 28 Buckingham.
" ☞ see also Monroe.
Munsell Charles C. florist, 87 Tru.l.3u. 36 Church.
" Chester W. carpetlayer at 1130 Main, h.2u.
   5 Orchard.
" Edward B. clerk at 95 Ple. l.u. 985 Main.
" Francis R. carpenter, h. 65 Williams.
" Fred'k H. operator, h.u. 65 Williams.
" Geo. H. painter at 133 Sheldon, h. 43 Ann.
" Mary F. wid. Chester W. h.r. 1128 Main.
" Robert C. driver, b.r. 1128 Main.
" Wm. F. clerk, b.u. 1218 Main.
Munsill Gail B. h. 4 Wethersfield.
" Eva M. wid. Marcus, h. 113 Collins.
" F. E. motorman St.Ry. h. E.H.t.
" Mary J. wid. Mills S. h. 2 Wethersfield.
Munson Alice G. nurse, l.3u. 14 Church, room 10.
" Harry B. agent, b. 80 Hopkins.
" Thomas H. cigarm. at 867 Main, h. W.H.t
" Wallace A. clerk at 921 Main, h. 874 Broad.
Munyan Chester G. inspector of loans, at Trav-
   elers Ins. Co. 56 Prospect, h. 37 Gillett.
Murdock Archibald G. clerk at Brown, Thom-
   son & Co. 942 Main, b. 3 Bellevue.
" Geo. A. toolkeeper at 133 Shel. b. 534 Main.
" George H. conductor St.Ry. l.u. 1293 Main.
" John, b. 2 Holcomb.
" John, foreman at r. 1061 Main, h. 288 Allyn.
" John, toolm. at 388 Capitol, h. 22 Barnard.
" Wm. machinist at 581 Cap. h.u. 3 Bellevue.
" William N. Jr. clerk, b.u. 3 Belden.
Murk Gustav, b.u. 1 Kilbourn ct.
" Herman G. brushm. 176 Allyn, h.2u. 55 Bab.
" Jacob, laborer, h.u. 1 Kilbourn ct.
Murley Daniel, laborer, b. 1183 Main.
Murnane Richard J. apprentice at 1092 Main,
   b.u. 11 Belden.
Murphy Agnes, b. 1096 Main.
" Andrew C. casehardener at Popes, h.8 Queen.
" Ann Mrs. h. 60 Grand.
" Ann, wid. Talbot, grocery, 143, h. 143 Zion.
" Anna, h.u. 1081 Main.
" Annie, dressmaker, 19, b.u. 19 Wolcott.
" Arthur P. blacksmith, h. 29 Elliott.
" Bernard, clerk, 75 Windsor, b.u. 306 Market.
" Bessie, wid. James, h. 19 Russell.
" Bridget, wid. Bartholomew J. h. 263 Main.
" Catherine, wid. Patrick, h. 256 Flatbush.
" Catherine A. J. dressm. 33, b.2u. 33 Avon.
" Charles H. prompter, b.u. 19 Wolcott.
" Cornelius A. Mrs. h. 49 Hawthorn.
" D. H. real estate, l. 23 Chapel.
" Daniel, student, b.u. 261 Main.
" Daniel, tailor, 59, h.u. 59 Pleasant.
" Daniel F. driver at 212 State, b. 703 Main.
" Della T. clerk at Brown, Thomson & Co.
   942 Main, b. 19 Russell.
" Dennis, laborer h.2u. 33 Avon.
" Dennis, laborer at 172 Com. b. 192 State.
" Dennis F. porter, 207 Allyn, b. 1202 Main.
" Dennis J. abstracter of titles, b. 3 Linden.
" Dennis J. laborer, h. 41 Loomis.
" Dennis J. special ins. Board of Health, City
   hall, 800 Main, h.u. 54 Morgan.

**For Sale Advertisements Bring Results in the Post.**

Murphy Dominic, plumber, b. 64 Hungerford.
" Edward, machinist, b. 343 Main.
" Edward J. bkkpr. at 98 Wells,h.24 Goodwin.
" Edward J. driver, b. 108 Windsor.
" Edward J. mach. at P.&R. b. 12 Hung. pl.
" Edward J. mec. engineer at Hartford Steam
    Boiler L & Ins. Co. 650 Mn. h. 15 Capitol.
" Edward M. salesman, h.u. 27 Florence.
" Edward T. machinist, b. 60 Ann.
" Elizabeth T. Mrs. hairdresser at 881 Main,
    b. 90 Retreat.
" Ellen, wid. Thomas, b.u. 33 Martin.
" Ellen M. bookkeeper, b. 3 Linden.
" Frank T. bartender, h.u. 47 Windsor.
" Fred'k J. salesman, b.u. 1333 Broad.
" Frederick W. clerk at Popes, b. 19 Russell.
" Hannah, wid. Jere. washer, h.2u.r. 105 Win.
" Henry, mechanic at Popes, b. 342 Front.
" Henry J. forger at 142 Russ, h.u. 33 Laurel.
" James, b. 2 Holcomb.
" James, bartender at 212 State, b. 24 S.Pro.
" James, coachman, b.u. 12 Clinton.
" James, coachman 67 Collins, h.u. 90 Walnut.
" James, enameler at 581 Cap. b.u. 5 Affleck.
" James, laborer, h. 21 Arch.
" James, laborer, h. 35 Russell.
" James E. engineer tug Coulston, 285 State,
    h.u. 111 Laurel.
" James J. bricklayer, b. 114 State.
" James J. plumber at James Ahern, 280 Asy-
    lum, h. 88 Windsor.
" James L. clerk at Brown, Thomson & Co.
    942 Main, b. 91 Mather.
" James W. apprentice at 20 Vredendale, b.
    115 Windsor.
" Jennie, clerk at Brown, Thomson & Co.
    942 Main, b. Wethersfield t.
" Jeremiah J. h.u. 50 Hicks.
" Johannah, wid. Richard, washer, h. 9 Sig.pl.
" John, l. 520 Main.
" John, boilermaker at H. B. Beach & Son,
    135 Grove, h. 91 Mather.
" John, plumber, h.2u. 8 Goodman.
" John, laborer, b.u. 71 Windsor.
" John, hodcarrier, h.2u. 34 South Prospect.
" John, laborer, h.u. 232 Zion.
" John, laborer, h.2u. 50 Russell,
" John, laborer, h. 352 Front.
" John, musician, h.u. 20 Walnut.
" John E. clerk, b. 301 Park.
" John F. clerk at 956 Main, b. 59 Pleasant.
" John F. groceries, 29, h. 5 Hawthorn.
" John F. l. 12 Huntley pl.
" John H. teamster, b. 256 Flatbush.
" John J. bricklayer, h.u. 149 Martin.
" John J. helper at N.Y.R. b. 198 Allyn.
" John J. helper N.E.R. b.u. 4 Donald.
" John Mrs. dressmaker, 20, h. 20 Walnut.
" John P. assistant to City Surveyor, at city
    hall 800 Main, h.u. 19 Wolcott.
" John W. waiter at 80 State.
" Joseph, carptr. at 155 Ch.O. h. 176 Putnam.
" Joseph H. foreman at Jewell Belting Co. 15
    Trumbull, h.u. 19 Greenwood.
" Kate, housekeeper, h.u. 110 Laurel.

Murphy Kate S. teacher at Brown school, 160
    Market, b. 3 Linden.
" Kittie, waiter at 8 Central.
" Lawrence F. assembler at 581 Capitol, b.
    256 Flatbush.
" Maggie J. clerk at 908 Main, b. 19 Russell.
" Malvina E. vocal teacher, b. 19 Russell.
" Margaret Mrs. b. 2 Holcomb.
" Margaret Mrs. h.u. 168 Front.
" Margaret, wid. Richard, h.u. 27 Affleck.
" Margaret, wid. Edward, h. 44 Benton.
" Margaret J. saleslady, b. 19 Russell.
" Martha C. bkkpr. at 83 Asy. b.u. 261 Main.
" Mary, h.u. 108 Main.
" Mary, h. 73 Avon.
" Mary A. clerk at Brown, Thomson & Co.
    942, b. 263 Main.
" Mary Mrs. h. 118 Windsor.
" Mary, wid. Daniel, h. 23 Benton.
" Mary E. ribbon weaver, b. 19 Russell.
" Michael, deckh. str. Middletown, 285 State.
" Michael, laborer, b. 352 Front.
" Michael, laborer, b. 101 Sheldon.
" Michael, rubberw. 690 Park, h. 50 Francis.
" Michael F. helper, b.u. 110 Laurel.
" Michael E. boxmaker, b. 118 Windsor.
" Michael J. mechanic at Popes, b. 106 Hung.
" Mich. M. painter at 618 Cap. b. 2u. 202 Shel.
" Patrick, carrepairer, h. 40 Avon.
" Patrick, engineer at Allyn House, 152 Asy.
" Patrick, mechanic at Popes, h.r. 2 Putnam.
" Patrick, screwmkr. at 476 Cap.h.2u. 133 Law.
" Patrick, teamster at 40 Elm, h. King.
" Patrick M. brazier, b. 118 Windsor.
" Patrick J. plumber at 581 Capitol, b. 256
    Flatbush.
" Patrick P. mechanic, h. 3 Cranes.
" Patrick P. toolm. at Popes, b. 387 Capitol.
" Patrick, Sr. b.u. 49 Spruce.
" Pasqual, driver, h.u. 137 Commerce.
" Peter, mechanic at 335 Shel. h. 17 Affleck.
" Peter R. janitor at 1, b. 110 Laurel.
" Philip P. chief clerk at N.E.R. Union sta-
    tion, b. 60 Grand.
" Richard, casehardener at 476 Capitol, h.u.r.
    232 Zion.
" Robert. wholesale liquors, 212 State, l.
    708 Main.
" Stephen, laborer, b.u. 4 Ellery.
" Stephen A. repairer at Popes, h. 24 Russell.
" Susie M. clerk at Brown, Thomson & Co.
    942 Main, b. 126 Trumbull.
" Thomas, h. 12 Chestnut.
" Thomas, clerk, b. 15 So. Ann.
" Thomas, machinist, b.u. 24 South Prospect.
" Thomas D. filer at Popes, b. 27 Affleck.
" Thomas F. mason, h. 140 Windsor.
" Thomas J. machinist, h.u. 24 South Prospect
" Thos. J. polisher at 476 Capitol, h. 2 John.
" Jeremiah J. upholsterer, h. 212 Center.
" Timothy, laborer, h. 13 Goodman.
" Timothy, machinist, h.u. 110 Laurel.
" Timothy J. brazier, b. 118 Windsor.
" Timothy J. porter at Brown, Thomson &
    Co. 942 Main, b. 13 Goodman.

**The Post, 12 Cents a Week, Delivered at Your Home.**

# WILLIAM A. MURRAY,

## Plumber and
## Gas Fitter,

### Dealer in Plumbers' Materials.

Special attention
given to Sani-
tary Matters.

**450** MAIN
STREET,
Old Number, 124.

Murphy William, b. 88 Ann.
" William, helper at 1 Flower, h.u. 5 Affleck.
" William, helper at 388 Cap. h.u. 54 Wdbg.
" William, laborer N.E.R. h.u. 4 Donald.
" William, teamster, h. 257 Front.
" William F. brakeman, h. 73 Avon.
" William J. cigar mfr. 217, l. 219 Main.
Murray Annie L. clerk, 956 Main, b. 25 Wyllys.
" B. C. lineman at 266 Pearl, b. 124 Church.
" Bartholomew, laborer at Pratt & Whitney
    Co. 1 Flower, h.u. 4 Lawrence.
" Bernard W. painter, b. 107 Park.
" Bros. carriage build. and repair. 25 Wells.
        John J. Murray.      Christopher Murray.
" Charles, h.u. 111 Hungerford.
" Charles, carriagemaker, h.2u. 28 Cedar.
" Charles, plumber, 425 Main, h. 35 Franklin.
" Charles F. circulation mgr. at Hartford
    Telegram, b. 1343 Main.
" Christopher, (M. Bros ) h. Wethersfield t.
" David, at 312, b. 312 Farmington.
" Elizabeth, wid. Charles, h. 25 Wyllys.
" Ellen, wid. Edward, h.u. 11 Hendricxsen.
" Frank, carpenter, h. 88 Ann.
" Frank A. bookkeeper, at 75 Pratt, b. S.M.v.
" Hugh, painter, 267, b.2u. 267 Park.
" J. machinist at 13 Central.
" James, butcher, h.2u. 38 Flower.
" James, blacksmith, at N.Y.R. h.1035 Broad.
" James, carptr. 44 Market, h. 56 Hawthorn.
" James, joiner, h. 105 Windsor.
" James B. butcher, h.2u. 28 Cedar.
" James E. mech. at Popes, b.u. 179 Babcock.
" James F. clerk at 44 Asylum, b. 107 Park.
" James J. mach. at 142 Russ, b. 185 Lawrence.
" James T. enameler at Popes, h.u. 50 Wells.
" James T. steamfitter, 253 Asy. h. 190 Sisson.
" John, groceries, 3, h. 3 Wawarme.
" John, painter at 9 Sigourney, h. 12 Church.
" John F. plumber, 136, h. 136 Maple.
" John F. mechanic, 581 Cap. b. 1445 Broad.
" John J. laborer, 14 Capen.
" John Joseph, (M. Bros.) h. 24 So. Prospect.
" John W. engineer, N.Y.R. h.u. 99 Hung.
" Joseph, mechanic, h. 118 Babcock.
" Joseph E. helper, 450 Mn. b. 11 Hendricxsen.
" Joseph H. mech. at 54 Arch, b. 88 Ann.
" Josephine, b.r. 116 Albany.
" Kate, wid. Dennis, h.u. 61 Potter.
" Kate, wid. William, h.2u. 116 Albany.

Murray Leon, paperhanger, b.u. 76 Governor.
" Maggie T. laundress at 30 Washington.
" Margaret, machine operator at 8 Sigourney,
    b.u. 38 Spring.
" Margaret, wid. Daniel, h. 38 So. Prospect.
" Margaret, wid. Martin, h. 185 Lawrence.
" Martin F. helper at 9 Sig. b. 185 Lawrence.
" Mary, clerk at 956 Main, b. 25 Wyllys.
" Mary Mrs. 46 Retreat.
" Mary, wid. Robert, h.u. 28 Franklin.
" Mary A. wid. William, h. 2 Trumbull.
" May Mrs. nurse, h. 926 Main, rm. 16.
" Michael, b. 37 Grand.
" Michael, beltman at 1 Flow. h. 23 Lawrence.
" Michael, 2d mate str. Hartford, 285 State.
" Michael, shoem. at 30 Park, h. 134 Martin.
" Nellie, clerk, b. 35 Franklin.
" Owen, gardener, h.u. 179 Babcock.
" Patrick F. switchman, h. 37 Grand.
" Patrick J. park policeman, h. 103 Vine.
" Patrick T. mech. at Popes, h. 183 Lawrence.
" Peter, butcher, b. 107 Park.
" Peter, helper, h.u. 50 Wells.
" Peter, laborer, h. 35 Front.
" Peter J. machinist, h.u. 194 Maple.
" Richard J. asst.supt. 756 Mn.h.u.118 Mather.
" Robert, painter, b.u. 28 Franklin.
" Robert, painter at 17 Elm, b. 44 Jefferson.
" Robert, salesman b. 5 Squire.
" Rose, h.2u. 46 Benton.
" Rose, wid. Patrick, h. 107 Park.
" Thomas, laborer, h. 25 Elm.
" Thomas F. plumber, b. 35 Front.
" Thomas J. molder, 556 Cap. b. 1445 Broad.
" William, brickburner, b. 915 Windsor av.
" William, clerk, 344 Windsor av. b.2 Suffield.
MURRAY WILLIAM A. plumber, 450 Main, h.
    11 Smith.              See page 270.
" William F. enameler at Popes, h. 2 Trumbull.
" William J. forem. Popes, h.2u. 245 Putnam.
Murtagh James, coachman at 68 Collins, h.u.
    49 Liberty.
Murtha Anna, wid. James, h. 53 Pleasant.
" James, conductor, N.Y.R. h.u. 28 Loomis.
" John J. clerk at 210 Pearl, b. 53 Pleasant.
" Matthew, teamster, b. 18 Dean.
Murtress Thomas, painter, b. 1244 Main.
Muscatelli Michael, laborer, b.u. 82 Morgan.
Mushatyky Samuel, tailor, 139 Asy. h.224 Front.
Mussgnug Martin, newsdealer 90 Asy. h. 30 Tru.
Muth John, repairer at Popes, b.u. 58 Edwards.
MUTUAL BENEFIT LIFE INS. Co. of Newark,
    N. J., James P. Hall, state agent, 29 Pearl.
MUTUAL LIFE INS. Co. of New York, 25 Pearl.
    E. S. Cowles, special agent. See page 108.
" Reserve Fund Life Asso. 904 Main, rm. 83.
Muzio & Bertucci, barbers, 222 Asylum.
        Joseph M. Muzio.      Vincent Bertucci.
" Joseph M. (M. & Bertucci.) b. 64 Morgan.
" Serafino, harnessm. at 8 Sig. b. 262 N.P.
**MUZZEY MARY R. MRS.** restau-
    rant, 14½ Church.         See page 561.
Myer Andrew, carpenter, b. 10 Squire.
" ☞ see also Maher · Mayer ; Meyer.

**Want Advertisements Bring Results in THE POST.**

Myers Charles E. clerk, 732 Main, h.2u. 29 West.
" Charles W. beltm. at 15 Tru. h. 183 Market.
" Charles W. laborer, h. 240 Zion.
" Edward, b. 2 Holcomb.
" George W. carpenter, h.2u. 239 Park.
" Hattie W. wid. Jas. dressm. h.2u. 312 Asylum.
" Henry A. laborer, h.2u. 93 Madison av.
" Henry W. inspector Hfd. Steam Boiler Insp. & Ins. Co. 650 Main, h. 3 Congress.
" Isaac, jeweler, h. 15 Avon.
" Jane Mrs. h. 30 Chestnut.
" Robert L. driver, 46 Ann, h.2u. 75 Governor.
" William, h. 13 John.
" William F. printer at 336 Asylum, b.2u. 93 Madison av.
" William G. blacksm. 10 Ferry, h. 110 Brooks.
" William W. inspec. at Popes, h. 73 Webster.
" 𝄪 see also Meyer.
Myerson Louis, blacksmith, 201 Front, h.3u. 17 North.
Myrick George, tinner, l.u. 56 Trumbull.

NABE Catherine, wid. Louis, b. 1254 Broad.
Nædele Anna, wid. Theo. C. h. 330 Windsor av.
" John G. A. supt. 252 Pearl, h. 49 Mahl.
Naghn Jacob, screwmaker, l. 381 Capitol.
Nagle Benjamin, clerk at 474 Main, b. 14 Talcott.
" Frank, clerk at 82 Asylum, b. 24 Village.
" John, porter at 150 State, h. 14 Talcott.
" John E. teamster, b. 134 Albany.
" John J. at Travelers Ins. Co. 56 Prospect, b. 14 Talcott.
" John J. messenger, b. 24 Village.
" Patrick, helper at 98 Kil. h.u. 24 Village.
" Philip, bartender, 202 State, b. 14 Talcott.
" Thomas, bricklayer, h. 84 Grove.
" Thomas, laborer, 128 Com. h. 134 Albany.
" Thomas F. laborer at 98 Kil. b. 24 Village.
" William F. clerk at 493 Main, b. 50 John.
" William R. helper, 15 Tru. b. 134 Albany.
Nagy Andrew, harnessm. 8 Sig. b.u. 2 Lawrence.
Nahigion Matthew N. helper at 618 Capitol, b. 24 Howard.
" Peter, at 40 Governor, b.2u. 1427 Broad.
Nairn John J. accountant at T. Sisson & Co. 729 Main, h. 30 Atwood.
Nairns Patrick, b. 28 Lawrence.
Najarian Peter, carpenter, h.u. 1443 Broad.
Nalen Frank, sidewalk layer at 154 Charter Oak, h. 74 Windsor.
Nally Bridget, h. 20 Putnam.
" Edmund P. machinist, b. 137 Lawrence.
" Edward P. blacksmith at N.Y.R. h. 137 Law.
" James A. molder at 54 Arch, h. 29 Com.
" James H. mach. at 581 Cap. b. 137 Lawrence.
" John J. toolkeeper at 476 Capitol, h. 88 Ward.
" Margaret, b. 137 Lawrence.
" Margaret, h. 20 Putnam.
" Patrick, screwm. 476 Cap. h. 17 Wolcott.
" Patrick E. screwm. at 476 Cap. h.r. 17 Wolcott.
" Thomas A. appren. 476 Cap. b.u. 20 Putnam.
Nangle Lily L. teacher Parkville sch. b. 791 Park.
Napolatano Domenico, laborer, b.u. 64 Morgan.
Narragansett Brewing Co. 132 Market.

Nash Dora, h. 152 Allyn.
" Frank, painter, h. W.H.t.
" George, painter, b. Quaker lane, W.H.t.
" Harry G. salesm. 904 Mn. rm.12, b.194 High.
" John, machinist at P.&R. h.u. 13 Liberty.
" Louis, teamster at 2 Chapel, b.u. 11 John.
" Thomas, carptr. at 155 Charter Oak, h. T.v.
" Willard F. mach. at 581 Cap. b. 152 Allyn.
Nason Charles R. at Ætna Life Ins. Co. 650 Main, b. 20 Madison.
" Cora B. wid. Wm. S. boardingh. 1104 Main.
Nass David, peddler, h. 3 North.
Nast Herman, laborer, h.3u. 9 Kinsley.
Nathan Hale cigar manufactory, 88 State.

**NATIONAL BISCUIT CO.** cracker bakery, 59 Albany.

**NATIONAL CASH REGISTRY CO.** 118 Asylum, rm. 2, Charter Oak Bank building, J. F. Kilbourn, salesman.

**NATIONAL EXCHANGE BANK,** 76 State. See page 435.

**NATIONAL FIRE INSURANCE CO.** 95 Pearl. See page 459.
" Home for Disabled Volunteer Soldiers, office 783 Main, rm. 16.

**NATIONAL LIFE ASSOCIA- TION,** 53 Trumbull. See page 455.

**NATIONAL MACHINE CO.** 111 to 133 Sheldon. See page 540.
" Trotting Association, 650 Main, rm. 47.
Nauman Richard G. screwmaker at 476 Capitol, h.2u. 188 Putnam.
Naval John, b. 255 Asylum.
Navat John, laundryman, h.u. 118 Wooster.
Navins Peter, foreman P.&R. h. 28 Lawrence.
Nax Carl P. cutter at 160 Pearl, h. 2 Trumbull.
Naylor Edw. C. molder at 1 Flower, b. T.v.
" James H. physician, 153, h. 153 Main.
" William, mach. 1 Flow. h. Thompsonville v.
" William A. toolm. at 581 Capitol, h.M.t.
Nazlian Jacob, screwm. at 476, l. 381 Capitol.
Neal Alfred, molder at 556 Cap. b. 7 Hawthorn.
" Amelia, wid. Andrew, h. 459 Broad.
" Andrew, clerk at 388 Cap. b. 459 Broad.
" Charles W. watch repairer, 847, rm. 17, l. 1210 Main.
Neal Christopher R. treas. of Neal, Goff & Inglis Co. 976-984 Main, h. 7 Fales.
See page 498.
" Daisy, b. 459 Broad.

**NEAL, GOFF & INGLIS CO.** car- pets, draperies & wallpaper, furniture, 976-984 Main. See page 498.
" Mary A. teacher at 1205 Asylum.
Nealon Matthew J. machine hand at 581 Capitol, h.u.r. 234 Zion.
Nearing Albert H. ins. agent, h. 24 Hopkins.
" Fred. A. rubberw. 690 Park, b. 25 Greenwood.
" L. L., Bristol express, office, 46 Ann.
" Sarah, wid. Henry T. h.u.r. 29 Church.
Neary Annie E. boardinghouse, 38 Charter Oak.
" John, laborer at 142 Russ, l. 16 Putnam.
" Thomas, driver, h. 51 Albany.

**THE NEWS PRINTED IN THE POST IS RELIABLE.**

Neary Thomas F. expressman, h.r. 51 Albany.
" Thos. F. mach. at 70 Huy. h. 16½ Governor.
Neddo Joseph R. mach. 1 Flow. b. 373 Asy. rm. 25.
Needham Arthur, polisher, 26 Laurel, h.54 Smith.
" Barbara, wid. Cornelius, h. 88 Grove.
" Bridget, wid. Michael, h.r. 25 Spruce.
" Ellen, wid. Michael C. h. 1045 Main.
" George A. b. 1045 Main.
" John A. b. 1045 Main.
" Margaret, b.r. 25 Spruce.
" The, restaurant, F. L. Avery, mgr. 1049 Mn.
" William F. musician, h.u. 1305 Main.
" William W. l. 46 Temple.
Neelan Anthony, painter, h. 50 Russell.
" Frank, sidewalk layer, b. 74 Windsor.
" Mary A. h. 50 Russell.
Neff Bernard, tailor, 724 Mn. h.2u. 50 Retreat.
" Calla, at 336, b. 336 Wethersfield.
" Fred W. signpainter, b.2u. 1172 Main.
Negro Michael, bootblack, h. 158 Front.
Neill Henry W. restaurant, 3 Am. h. 4 Ellsworth.
Neillson Andrew, helper, 618 Cap.h. 1416 Broad.
Neilson A. cabinetm. at 69 Front, h. 26 Barbour.
" Carl, coachman at 79, l. 79 Church.
" Carl, inspector at 581 Capitol, b. 65 Laurel.
" Carl J. mach. at 30 Cush. b. 171 Babcock.
" Charles, driver at 7 Haynes, h. Walnut.
" Charles, waiter at 14½, b.r. 1½ Church.
" Hilbreth, toolmaker at 476, b. 279 Capitol.
" James, toolmaker at 581 Cap. h. 318 Capen.
" Jeff. J. shipper at 8 Sig. h. 13 Riverside.
" John, laborer at stonepits, h. 45 Zion.
" John A. toolmaker at 1 Laurel, h. 286 Park.
" Lars C. lettercarrier P.O. b. 234 Pearl.
" Neil, painter, h.2u. 271 Main.
" Neils N. gluer at 15, b. 18 Trumbull.
" Otto, washer at 366 Main, h.2u. 32 Kinsley.
" Theodore, clerk, b. 46 Grand.
" William A. carptr. at r. 334 Asy. h. 17 King.
" ☞ see also Nelson; Nilsen.
Neiveot Benjamin, peddler, h.u. 30 Pleasant.
Nellegan Anna H. milliner at Brown, Thomson &
      Co. 942 Main, b. Kensington v.
Nellgan Mary T. h. 115 Ann.
" William H. h. 117½ Ann.
Nellis Jennie O. stenog. at 370 Asy. b. 167 High.
Nelsen Anton, rubberw. 690 Park, h. 109 Laurel.
Nelson Alexander W. machinist at 476 Capitol,
      h. 109 Lawrence.
" Alfred, coachman, b. 856 Prospect av.
" Alfred G. waiter, 26 State, h. 241 Bellevue.
" Andrew P. carpenter at N.Y.R. h. 50 Ward.
" August S. laborer, 581 Cap. b. 119 Babcock.
" Balthasar, mach. at 581 Cap. b. 31 Union.
" Benjamin, porter at 752 Main.
" Charles, carpenter, b.u. 54 Flower.
" Charles, clerk at 1457 Broad, h. 4 Brady.
" Chas. teamster at 335 Shel. b.u. 94 Walnut.
" Chas. A. pressman, Popes, h.u. 15 Hamilton
" Christian, mach. 1 Flow. b. So.Manchester t.
" Christian, watchman at Jewell Belting Co.
      15 Trumbull, h. 2 Elliott pl.
" Cora A. Mrs. dressm. 241, h. 241 Bellevue.
" Edwd. deckhand str. Middletown, 285 State.
" Edward A. mach. at 1 Flower, h. 7 Putnam.

Nelson Emil, filer at Popes, h.2u. 271 Jefferson.
" Frank, stonecutter, h. 1094 Main.
" Frank Mrs. boardinghouse, 1094 Main.
" Fred, laborer at 690 Park, b. 26 New Park.
" George, polisher at 581 Cap. h. 26 New Park.
" Gustaf, baker, 106, h. 106 Jefferson.
" Hans, painter, h.u. 373 Park.
" Harry, polisher at 581 Cap. b. 24 N. Park.
" Henrik, mason, b. 85 Heath.
" Henry, porter, 973 Main.
" Herbert, polisher at 581 Cap. b. 26 N. Park.
" James, h. 318 Capen.
" John, at Popes, b.2u. 29 Hamilton.
" John, baker, 12 Queen, h. 33 Liberty.
" John, dropfor. at 142 Russ, b. 109 Lawrence.
" John, laborer at 283 Shel. b. 301 Lawrence.
" John, laborer at P.&R. b. 58 Bond.
" John, shipper at 8 Sigourney, h. 9½ Kibbe.
" John P. rubberw. at 690 Park, h. 85 Heath.
" John J. coachman, h.r. 205 Laurel.
" John J. machinist at 1 Flow. h. 37 Putnam.
" John N. blacksmith, 697 Windsor av. h.
      182 Clark.
" Joseph V. mixer at 690 Park, h. 3 Davenport.
" Leland E. mach. at 388 Capitol. h. E.H.t.
" Lewis, l. 1113 Main.
" Ludwig, carptr. at r. 334 Asy. h. Burnside v.
" Maria, wid. John, laund. h.u.r. 124 Market.
" Morris, carpenter at N.Y.R. h. 40 Church.
" N. deckhand scow Newton, 285 State.
" Neils, laborer, h.u. 14 Lawrence.
" Neir, florist at 30 Washington, h. 316 Maple.
" Nels, carpenter, b.u. 234 Park.
" Nels P. laborer, h. 68 Harrison.
" Nils, screwm. at 476 Cap. h. 43 Glendale.
" Olin B. mach. at 476 Capitol, l. 17 Church.
" Oscar, rubberw. at 690 Park, b.u. 17 Affleck.
" Paul, farmer, b. 990 Windsor av.
" Peter, beltmaker at 15 Tru. h. 68 Harrison.
" Peter, driver, b. 18 Gold.
" Peter J. polisher at Popes, h. E. Hartford t.
" Theodore, shoem. at 10 Ch.O. b.u. 46 Grand.
" Wilbur F. roller at 690 Park, h. 19½ Sisson.
" William, machinist, l. 17 Church.
" William, machinist, 1 Flow. b. Prospect av.
" ☞ see also Neilson; Nilson.
Nemiah J. W. 783 Main, rm. 5, h. Windsor t.
Nemser Louis, filer at 581 Capitol, h. 32 Flower.
Nero Antonio, laborer, h. 31 Mechanic.
Nerstein Moses, packer at 172 Front.
Nesbit William, carpenter, h. 18 Clark.
Nesi Joseph, cook at 701 Main, b. 33 John.
Nesson Andrew, teamster at 15 Tru. h. Blo.
" N. laborer at 15 Trumbull, b. W.H.t.
Nestasia Frank, laborer, h.u. 180 Front.
Nestor Austin, helper at 1 Flow. h.u. 962 Broad.
" Michael, helper at N.Y.R. b. 25 Spruce.
" Michael J. helper, 1 Flow. h.u.47 Hawthorn.
" Thure, mach. at 1 Flower, b.2u. 358 Park.
Neth Geo. electrician, 85 Pratt, b.u. 59 Seymour.
Nettleton Chas. E. cashier at 732 Main, h. N.t.
" Geo. E. carptr. at 690 Park, h. 20 Sherman.
" Joseph at 66 Temple, l.u. 118 Asylum.
" Wilbur E. foreman at Popes, h. 102 Kenyon.
Netzold Henry C. carpenter N.Y.R. h. Elmwood.

Neubert Caroline, wid. August, h.3u. 61 Morgan.
" Lizzie, b.3u. 61 Morgan.
Neuischeler Fred. driver, 315, h.u. 322 Park.
Neumann Louis N. fresco painter at Baxter the decorator, 231 Asylum, h.u. 57 Rose.
" Otto A. W. toolmaker at 328 Asy. h. 57 Rose.
" Robert, painter, h. 57 Rose.
" ☞ see also Newman.
Neuschulten William F. bartdr. h.u.r. 165 Front.
Nevels Andrew, carpenter, b. 10 Arch.
" Michael J. carpenter, b. 10 Arch.
" Thomas J. carpenter, b.u. 10 Arch.
Nevers Frank W. rubberw. 690 Park, b. 15 Smith.
" George, clerk board of street commissioners, 800 Main, City hall, h. 8 Buckingham.
" Roderick E. patternm. at 734 Mn. h. 32 Sey.
Neville Bartholomew, tinner at 1116 Main, b. 48 Hicks.
" John, b. 48 Hicks.
" Joseph, tinner at 1116 Main, b. 48 Hicks.
" Margaret, wid. of William, h. 48 Hicks.
Nevin Matthias W. bookbinder at William H. Talcott, 856 Main, l. 46 Temple.
Nevins Michael, boilerm. at H. B. Beach & Son, 135 Grove, h. 194 Sheldon.
" Peter, h. 28 Lawrence.
Newarfo Louis, laborer, b. 335 Front.
Newberth Annie, h.u. 26 Trumbull.
Newberry Edith, teacher at Chandler Short-hand school, 522 Asy. b. So. Windsor t.
" Leslie W. attorney at law, 877 Main, room 6, h. S. Windsor t.
" Wm. A. clerk, 921 Mn, b. 315 Pearl, rm. 415.
Newbury Alice C. wid. Charles C. h. 30 Spring.
Newcity Louis, buyer at 956 Main, b. 38 Bkm.
New Dom Hotel, 109 Tru. J. F. Weeden, prop.
Newell Alfred, mason, b. 1079 Broad.
" Charles M. patternmaker at 556 Capitol, b. 17 Townley.
" Clifton T. gardener at 276, b. 276 Weth.
" Fred. D. mach. at 1 Flower, h. 1254 Broad.
" George E. painter, 42, h.u. 42 John.
" Jessie N. teacher of drawing, South school, b. 57 Farmington.
" Joseph, h.u. 26 Commerce.
" W. H. at Ætna Life Ins. Co. 650 Main, h. 315 Capitol.
" England Bakery, Schuman Bros. 69 Morgan.

**NEW ENGLAND BREWING CO.**
217-231 Windsor.          *See page 504.*
New England Coal Co. office 722 Main.
                           *See page 273.*

**NEW ENGLAND CONSTRUC-TION CO.** contractors and builders,
720 Main.          *See page 424.*
" England Despatch Company, general for-warders. *See Bill Brothers, page 550.*
" England Fancy Dye Works, 94 Trumbull.

**NEW ENGLAND GRANITE WORKS,** J. G. Batterson, president,
1260 Main.          *See page 533.*
" England Loan and Trust Co. 757 Main.
" England Steam Laundry, Geo. E. Crosby, r. West Hawthorn.

New England Trading Coupon Co. 77 Pratt, Harry Bidwell, manager.

**NEW ENGLAND TYPE-WRITER EXCHANGE,** 847
Main, room 7.          *See page 422.*
          E. C. Down, agent.
" Home Sewing Machine. See W. L. Forbes.

**NEW METHOD LAUNDRY CO,**
438 Asylum, Albert W. DeBarthe, mgr.
Newhall Clifford E. mach. at 388 Cap. b. 9 Laf.
" Frank E. motorman St. Ry. h. 56 Benton.
Newhouse Ewd. waiter at 1049 Mn. l. 33 Chapel.
Newman Arthur, mach. at 40 Gov. b. 63 Bkm.
" Charles A. laborer at 35, h.u. 174 Sheldon.
" Claus N. biddler at 2 Sig. h. 32 Grand.
" David, tailor at 118 Asylum, h. 11 Morgan.
" Edwad, tinner' b. 40 Trumbull.
" Fred. mechanic at Popes, b. East Hartford t.
" George H. mechanic at Popes, b. E.H.t.
" Gus, fireman, tug Smith, 285 State.
" Gustaf R. mach. at Popes, b.u. 174 Sheldon.
" Jas. F. mach. hand at 40 Gov. b. 71 Ch.Oak.
" John Arthur, repairer at 40 Gov. h. 63 Bkm.
" L. E. Mrs. h.2u. 18 South Ann.
" Solomon, h. 40 North.
" Solomon, gatetender at Capewell Horse Nail Co. 40 Gov. h. 71 Charter Oak.
" ☞ see also Neumann.
Newschafer Chas. A. clerk, Popes, b. 170 High.
" Frederick W. reporter Sunday Globe, 25 Asylum, b. 170 High.
" George, cigarmaker, 867 Main, h. 170 High.
Newsham William, painter, h.u. 19 Park.
Newton Abby D. wid. Charles C. h. 4 Wadsworth.
" Allen H. bookkeeper at Conn. Trust & Safe Deposit Co. 785 Main, h. 218 Collins.
Newton Andrew L. councilman 8th ward, ma-chinist at 1 Flower, h. 15 Hamilton.
Newton Arthur D. sec'y and treas. Eddy Elec-tric Mfg. Co. Windsor t. h. 17 Niles.
                           *See page 536.*

**NEWTON & BURNET,** meats,
poultry, fish, oysters, vegetables, etc,
319 Asylum.          *See page 487.*
Edwin A. Newton.          James G. Burnet.
" Burt L. (*Theo. Newton & Co.*) h. 16 Vernon.
" Charles E. secretary Jewell Belting Co. 15 Trumbull, h. 19 Marshall.
" Charles W. (*G. W. N. & Son*) h. 120 Ann.
" Clinton H. vocal teacher, h. 926 Mn. rm. 55.

Newton C. H. Mrs. vocal teacher, 926 Mn. rm. 55.
" Duane E. traveling salesman, 15 Trumbull,
b. 17 Townley.
" Edith, b. 17 Townley.
" Edward, student, b. 72 Farmington.
" Edward H. painter, h. 20 Canton.
" Edward N. clerk at Smith, Northam & Co.
129 State, h. Springfield t.
" Edward W. farmer, h. 23 A Sisson.
" Edwin A. (N. & Burnet,) h.u. 216 Garden.
" Elizabeth A. wid. Philo S. h. 29 Main.
" Elizabeth P. Mrs. h. 56 Vernon.
" Ernest E. decorator at Baxter the Deco-
rator, 321 Asylum, b. 106 Wooster.
" Frank E. (T. Newton & Co.) b. 1333 Main.
" Frank E. market garden, 810, b. 810 Park.
" Frank G. bartender at 187, h. 126 State.
" Frank W. polisher at Colts, h. 106 Franklin.
" G. W. & Son, coal, 107 Grove, office, 15 Pearl.
George W. Newton.    Charles W. Newton.
" George B. secretary Hartford Carpet Co.
10 Market, h. 20 Huntington.
" Geo. H. painter, h. 18 Carpenter.
" Geo. W. (G. W. N. & Son,) h. 11 Windsor av.
" Harriet A. wid. Horace, b. 20 Canton.
" Herbert H. b. 810 Park.
" Howard G. (Franklin Market,) b.u.47 Cong.
" J. G. D. florist, 810, b. 810 Park.
NEWTON JOEL P. (N., Robertson & Co.) h. Say-
brook t.                  See page 486.
" Joseph K. farmer, b. 91 Bluehills.
" Katherine L. teacher at South school, 36
Wadsworth, b.u. 17 Congress.
" Lewis R. mason, h. 28 Martin.
" Loomis A. secretary at Fidelity Company,
49 Pearl, b. 491 Farmington.
" Mattie A. Mrs. b. 106 Retreat.
" Mary G. wid. John, h.u. 47 Congress.
" Murray A. conductor St. Ry. b. E.H.t.
NEWTON PHILO W., Allyn house drug store, 142
Asy. h. 427 Main, rm. 78.  See page 35.
NEWTON, ROBERTSON & CO.
grocers, fruit, creamery butter, teas, 338
and 342 Asylum.          See page 486.
J. P. Newton.  W. P. Robertson.  H. H. Dickenson.
" Theodore, (T. Newton & Co.) h. 1333 Main.
" Theodore & Co. builders, 77 Pearl.
Theodore Newton.      Burt L. Newton.
" Ralph, clerk at 983 Main, b. E.H.t.
" Rosilla R. teacher West Middle school, 927
Asylum, b.u. 47 Congress.
" Roswell W. builder, office 29 Pearl, room 5,
h. 72 Farmington.
" Thomas S. mason, h. 116 Clark.

New York & Boston Despatch Express Co. 236
Asylum, John S. Krocher, agent.
" York & Eastern News Co. Union depot.
" York Forced Sale Co. 175 Asylum. D. H.
Blinn, manager.
" York Laundry, Looney Sisters, 35 Church.
L. Mary Looney.        Kate Looney.
" York Leather Co. H. J. Weingartner, man-
ager, 21½ Mulberry.
" York Life Insurance Company, 847 Main,
George W. Staples, general agent.
" York & New England R. R. Co. station,
Union depot, 466 Asylum; offices, repair
shops, and round houses, East Hartford;
freight depot, 95 Pleasant.
" York, New Haven & Hartford R.R. Co.
station 466 Asylum; freight depot, 98
Kilbourn.
**NEW YORK STEAMBOATS,**
285 State.              See page 554.
" York Tea Store, P. S. Kennedy, 1046 Main.
Ney Dora, wid. Frank, b.2u. 38 Lewis.
" Edward M. at 265, b. 1015 Asylum.
" H. Clinton, at 265, b. 1015 Asylum.
" Henry F. machinist at 80 Huy. h.u. 37 John.
" John F. clerk, 265 Asy. h.u. 96 Windsor av.
" John M. (J. M. N. & Co.) h. 1015 Asylum.
" John M. & Co. goldrefiners, etc. 265 Asy.*
" Paul S. student, b. 1015 Asylum.
" ☞ see also Nye.
Nezzo Antonio D. scissorgrinder, h.u. 83 Windsor.
" ☞ see DeNezzo.
Nice ☞ see Nies.
Nicholl Peter, laborer, b. 21 Arch.
Nichols Alrima, wid. William, h. 33 Brown.
" Arthur C. machinist at 24 Mechanic, h. 12
Pawtucket.
" Carolyn, teacher at West Middle school,
927 Asylum, b. 54 Church.
" Charles F. policeman, h. 55 Park.
" Charles L. b.2u. 90 State. rm. 6.
" Clifford D. manager at 356 Asy. h.u. 15 Canton.
" Clinton G. clerk at 223 Asylum, b. S.M.v.
" Delbert L. carpr. at r. 334 Asy. h. 590 Main.
" Elmer A. teacher High sch. b. 28 Hopkins.
" George, clerk at Phœnix Mutual Life Ins.
Co. 49 Pearl, h. Highland, s. Farmington.
" George F. salesman at Lincoln, Seyms &
Co. wholesale spices, 34 Mar. h. Windsor t.
" George L. janitor Courant building, h.2u.
90 State, rm. 6.
" Grace M. clerk at Brown, Thomson & Co.
942, b. 573 Main,
" Harry, waiter at 931 Main, b. 2 Church.
" Harry L. clerk at Popes, b.2u. 28 Hopkins.
" Henry F. turner at Colts, h.u. 517 Main.
" Howard E. cutter, 356 Asy. h.u. 3 Goodman.
" Ida F. (Nichols Paper Box Co.) h. 230
Windsor av.
" James, president National Fire Insurance Co.
95 Pearl, h. 948 Asylum.
" James, bookkeeper at Conn. Mutual Life
Ins. Co. 783 Main, h. Warrenton, n. side.
" John W. student at Trinity college, 31
Jarvis hall, Summit.

Nichols Julia K. clerk Brown, Thomson & Co. 492 Main, b.u. 90 State.
" Louise S. b. 54 Church.
" Lucinda M. Mrs. h. 230 Windsor av.
" Lucius H. mach. at 1 Laurel, h.2u.28 Hopkins.
" Paper Box Co. 356 Asy. Ida F. Nichols.
" Patrick, waiter at 296 Asy. h.18 Trumbull.
" Pluma E. wid. George B. h. 44 John.
" Richard E. toolm. at Colts, h.u. 83 Jefferson.
" Theo. M. repairer, at Popes, h. 35 Babcock.
" Walter C: pressm. at 141 Pearl, b.u. 20 South.
" Walter J. porter at 139 Asy. b. 244 Putnam.
" William, laborer, b.u. 8 Gold.
" William M. student at Trinity college, 31 Jarvis hall, Summit.
" Wm. H. Jr. toolmkr. 1 Flower, b. 62 Russ.
" Winfred U. mach. at 1 Flow. b. 33 Brown.
" ☞ see also Nicoll.
Nicholson Frank, machinist at 20 Sargeant, b. East Hartford t.
" James, blacksmith, b.u. 2 Ashton.
" Walter, harnessm. at 8 Sig. b.u. 141 Market.
Nickerson Harriet I. b. 10 Atwood.
Nicolini Dominic, helper at 135 Sheldon, b.3u. 7 Charles.
" John B. barber at 80 State, b. 7 Charles.
" Nicola, laborer, h. 7 Charles.
Nicoll the tailor, 52 Asylum, h. New York city.
" Annie W. clerk at 885 Main, b. E.H.t.
" David H. jeweler, 911 Main, b. 73 Park.
" Frederick, bartender, h. 100 Albany.
" ☞ see also Nichols.
Nieberg Charles J. inspector at 581 Capitol, b. 12 South Forest.
Niehofen Peter, plumber, 550 Mn. b. 78 Benton.
Nichofer William, watchman at 62 Market.
Nielson Anton, rubberw. 690 Park, b. 19 Willow.
" Carl C. inspector at 581 Cap. b. 65 Laurel.
" ☞ see also Neilson; Nelson.
Nieretz August, tailor, h. 77 Temple.
Nies Emma, b.u. 218 State.
" Joseph, helper, b. 218 State.
" Sarah, wid. George, h.u. 218 State.
" William, driller at Popes, b.u. 218 State.
" ☞ see also Nice.
Niesig John, laborer, b.u. 208 Sheldon.
Nighigian Robt. mech. at 26 High, h. 24 Howard.
Nihan Joseph, telegraphr.49 Pearl, b.2u. 26 Park.
" Michael, mason, h.2u. 26 Park.
Nihill Mary, wid. Matthew, boardg.house 69 Gov.
" Nora, boarding house, 147 Sheldon.
Nihon William, laborer, 40 Gov. b. 24 Union.
Nilan Charles, driver at 4 American.
" Patrick, b. 2 Holcomb.
Niles Daniel B. livery stable, r.1177 Mn.h.9 Chapel.
" Frances Z. h. 73 Forest.
" Henrietta W. wid. Lucas H. b. 457 Weth.
" Nellie L. Mrs. h. 232 High.
" Stillman, h. 203 Maple.
Nils E. K. pastor Swedish Baptist Church, h.u. 389 Capitol.
Nilson Hans, painter, b.2u. 985 Main.
" Nils, at 476 Capitol, h. 74 Ward pl.
" Nils, carpenter, 155 Ch.O. h. 119 Babcock.
" Peter, at 1, b. 1 Flatbush.

**NIMS, WHITNEY & COMPANY,** doors, sashes and blinds, 1170 Main, Ned C. Wardwell, manager. *See p. 511.*
Nirenstein E. groceries, 76, h.u. 76 Sheldon.
Nirolek John, laborer, b.u. 208 Sheldon.
Nisinsky Frank, filer at 388 Cap. h. 27 Francis.
Nissen Christ, farmer, h. Prospect av.
" Niels, pressman at 690 Park. b. 40 Prospect.
" Nis, farmer, h. Prospect av. W.H.t.
Nitsche Frederick, mach. 490 Cap. b. 4½ Hung. pl.
" John A. pressfdr.141 Pearl, h.2u.87 Windsor.
" Mary, h.2u. 87 Windsor.
" Reynold, upholsterer, h.2u. 87 Windsor.
Nixon Ellen, at 53 Ann, b. 214 Pearl.
" Elmer E. mach.at 30 Cushman, h.u. 17 Bkm.
" Walter G. machinist, 30 Cush. b. 17 Bkm.
Nizinski Mary Mrs. b. 2 Holcomb.
Nizlian Bogus, mechanic, 26 High, h.14 Putnam.
Noacco Louis, helper at 1 Flower.
Noad Lillian, clerk at 835 Main, b. 48 Hopkins.
Nobert D. N. burnisher, 62 Mar. b. Meriden t.
Noble Averitt, b. 123 Clark.
" Charles H. bank commissioner at State Capitol, room 55, h. New Milford t.
" Charles S. produce, 9 Morgan, h. 300 Weth.
" Charles S. (*Noble Drug Co.*) b. E.H.t.
" Drug Co. druggists, 153 Wethersfield. William B. Noble, E.H.t.  Charles S. Noble.
" Edward J. b. 300 Wethersfield.
" Henry D. mach. 142 Russ, b.u. 39 Wolcott.
" Isabelle, wid. Leroy, h.u. 39 Wolcott.
" James H. farmer, h. 10 Brown.
" John B. dairy commissioner at State Capitol, room 54, h. East Windsor t.
" John M. machinist at 13 Central h. 50 Fkn.
" Richard H. clerk 71 Asylum, b. 18 Brown.
" Samuel, waiter at 244, b. 245 State.
" Wilfred H. screwmkr. 476 Cap. h.50 Hudson.
Nobles Elon B. salesman at Popes, b. G.t.
Nocetu John, hodcarrier, b. 335 Front.
Nocher John, sidewalklayer, b. 77 Hudson.
Nodine Angie, compositor at 336 Wethersfield, h. 12 Squire.
" David W. mach. at 142 Russ, h. 12 Squire.
" Wm. H. messenger at P.O. b. E.H.t.
Noel Clifford N. mach. at 1 Flow. h. 19 Julius.
" Napoleon, carpenter, h.2u. 32 Wooster.
Nohert Francis X. burnisher at 62 Market, h. Meriden t.
" F. X. Jr. burnisher, 62 Market, h. Meriden t.
Nolan Anna M. b. 238 Zion.
" Carroline L. bkkpr. 46 Ann, b.u.51 Windsor.
" Daniel, stonemason, h. 25 Walnut.
" Elizabeth, wid. James, h. 1327 Broad.
" Frank J. clerk at 909 Main, h. E.H.t.
" Frank M. toolmkr. at 185 Shel. b. 64 Grove.
" James, builder, b. 59 Franklin.
" James, plumber, 3 Grove, b. 25 Walnut.
" James F. laborer, b. 1327 Broad.
" James P. mgr. at 6 Central, b.u. 51 Windsor.
" Jennie C. dressmaker, b.u. 27 Beach.
" John, assembler at Popes, b. Meriden t.
" John, bartender, b. 119 High.
" John, gateman at N.Y.R. h.u. 1423 Broad.
" John, ostler at 356 Main, h.2u. 113 Maple.

Nolan John F. managr. at 365, b.3u. 312 Asy.
" John J. carptr. r. 988 Mn. h. 59 Franklin.
" John W. printer, 876 Main, h. 186 Capen.
" Joseph N. plumber at James Ahern, 280 Asylum, h.u. 48 Ward.
" Joseph J. waiter, b. 1327 Broad.
" Katherine, at 956 Main, b.2u. 113 Maple.
" M. Gerald, clerk, 30 Union pl. b. 119 High.
" Mary, wid. James J. h.u. 81 Seymour.
" Mary A. tailoress, b. 1423 Broad.
" Mary E. dressmaker, b. 113 Maple.
" Maurice J. jeweler at 851, b. 1136 Main.
" Nellie, clerk at Brown, Thomson & Co. 942 Main, b. 51 Windsor.
" Nicholas, clerk, b. 15 Fairmount.
" Patrick, h. 62 Grand.
" Patrick, carpenter, b. 6 Chestnut.
" Patrick, laborer, b. 93 Madison av.
" Patrick J. bkkpr. at 956 Mn. b. 113 Maple.
" Patrick J. finisher, 556 Cap. b. 1335 Broad.
" Patrick P. carpenter. h. 6 Chestnut.
" Terence F. driver, 46 Ann, h.2u. 17 Affleck.
" William A. at 62 Market, b. 1327 Broad.
" William F. porter 219 Asy. b.u. 1335 Broad.
" William H. carpenter, b.u. 59 Franklin.
Noland Eliz. C. stenographer at Popes, b. N.t.
Nolet Frank, barber, b. 15 Portland.
Noll Brothers, boots and shoes, 485 Main.
    Jacob Noll.        Harris Noll.
" Harris, (Noll Bros.) h. 74 Temple.
" Ike, clerk at 485 Main, b. 74 Temple.
" Isaac, shoem. at 173 State, b. 190 Front.
" Jacob, (Noll Bros.) h. 190 Front.
" Louis W. printer at Courant, b. 98 Retreat.
" Rosa, wid. Anthony, h. 98 Retreat.
" William, (Meyer & N.) b. 98 Retreat.
Nolquist ☞ see also Nordquist.
Nonotuck Silk Co. 133 Sheldon.
Noonan Alice F. dressmaker, b. 18 Beach.
" Andrew, painter, b.2u. 79 Governor.
" Dennis, at Pope Mfg. Co. b. 58 Flower.
" Edward C. clerk, 1203 Main, b. 188 Albany.
" James, miller, 40 Elm, h.u. 49 Linden.
" James F. foreman at Popes, h. 29 Babcock.
" James F. policeman, b. 33 Lawrence.
" John, coachman, 183 High, h. 19 Spruce.
" John P. b. 33 Lawrence.
" Josephine, and Margaret, b. 188 Albany.
" Margaret, wid. Patrick, h. 33 Lawrence.
" Mary, dressmaker, h. 18 Beach.
" Mary, seamstress, h.2u. 24 Huntley pl.
" Mary F. teach. Parkville sch. b.u. 49 Linden.
" Morris J. mach. at 42 Russ, b.u. 49 Linden.
" Nellie, b. 188 Albany.
" Patrick, b. 1427 Broad.
" Thomas, elevatorer Popes, h.u. 24 Huntley pl.
" W. A. cashier P.&R. h. Manchester t.
" William, h. 188 Albany.
" William, helper at Popes, b. 58 Flower.
" William J. engineer, h. 76 Brook.
Noone John, bkkpr. at 70 Huyshope, b. 48 John.
Noord Olaf, mach. at 1 Laurel, h. 285 Capitol.
Noot ☞ see also Nott.
No-Pareil Laundry Co. r. 366 Windsor av. F. O. Stewart, manager.

Nordberg August, waiter, 98 Wells, h. 27 Linden.
Nordburg Edward, laborer, b. Elizabeth park.
Nordfors Charles Peter, assembler at 556 Capitol, h. 301 Lawrence.
Nordlund Enoch, coachman, h.u. 56 Hawthorn.
Nordquist Gustaf A. assem. 581 Cap. b. 23 Hamilton.
Nordstrom Chas. A. mach. 1 Flower, h. W.H.t.
" Charles W. shipfastener, h. 57 Maple.
Noren Frederick, h.r. 9 Hungerford.
Noridge Edward, bartender, 84, h.u. 82 Sheldon.
Norman Alfred, clerk, 219 Asy. h.2u. 37½ Church.
" Nathan, laborer at 690 Park, b.u. 42 Smith.
Normandin Alphonse, bartdr. at 1233 Main, b.u. 61 Albany.
Normoyle Daniel J. stenogr. at Pratt & Whitney Co. 1 Flower, b.u. 46 Hopkins.
Norrgard A. Arnold, tailor, 312, h.4u. 312 Asy.
Norrman Charles F. mach. 1 Flow. h. 42 Putnam.
Norris Carrie S. seamstress at 20 So. Hudson.
" Delia, wid. Michael, h.r. 36 Hicks.
" George, helper, b. 13 Talcott.
" Kingsley F. Rev. associate pastor Fourth church, 1091 Main, h. 16 Belden.
" Mary Louise, h.2u. 243 Jefferson.
" Michael H. clerk, h. 64 Edwards.
" Michael J. brassmolder, b.u. 62 Front.
" Richard D. insurance, h. 32 Canton.
" Richard J. bricklayer, h. 74 Windsor.
" T. May, stenographer at Sanford Co. 438 Asylum, b. 64 Edwards.
" William G. operator at 247 Pearl, b.2u. 243 Jefferson.
Norse M. b. 227 High.
Norstrom Chas. J. mach. at 388 Cap. h. W.H.t.
NORTH ALBERT W. treas. Hatch & North Coal Co. 301, h. 427 Main, rm. 12.
                  See page 491.
North Alice B. clerk Factory Insurance Association, 95 Pearl, b. East Hartford t.
" Dwight, clerk at Belknap & Warfield, 77 Asylum, b.u. 19 Pleasant.
" Charles R. toolm. at Colts, h. 41 Seymour.
" Gertrude N. stenog. at Popes, b. 63 Oak.
" Henry A. carptr. at N.Y.R. h. 59 Flower.
" John A. (N. & Late,) h. Collinsville t.
" Lydia G. wid. Benjamin W. b. 26 Vernon.
**NORTH & LATE,** publishers Farmington Valley Herald and Journal, 336 Asylum.    See page 470.
    John A. North.      James C. Late.
" Robert, clerk, b. 63 Oak.
" Robert B. clerk at Popes, b. 63 Oak.
" Sarah H. wid. Dwight, h.u. 19 Pleasant.
NORTHAM CHAS. H. (Smith, Northam & Co.) 129 State, street commissioner. h. 12 Charter Oak pl.    See page 590.
" Edwin T. clerk at Smith, Northam & Co. 129 State, b. 12 Charter Oak pl.
" Estelle F. wid. Robt. C. h. 95 Hungerford.
" Robert C. sec'y 875 Main, h. 95 Hungerford.
" Russell C. clerk at Smith, Northam & Co. 129 State, b. 12 Charter Oak pl.
NORTH END CARRIAGE CO. r. 34 Capen.
                  See page 277.

Northend C. A. Mrs. h. 56 Willard.
" Henry H. at Hartford Fire Insurance Co. 53 Trumbull, h. 317 New Britain.
Northrop Edwin, musician, b. 334 Wethersfield.
Northrup Frank J. conductor, St.Ry. h. 150 Fkn.
" George Mrs. dressmaker, 150, h. 150 Fkn.
" George S. motorman St.Ry. h. 150 Fkn.
" Jesse, carpenter, l.u. 110 Hopkins.
Northway Alfred C. market 319 Asy. h.17 Canton.
North West school, 304 Albany.

**NORTHWESTERN MUTUAL LIFE INSURANCE CO.** F. A. Griswold, manager, 721 Main, rm. 3.

Northwood Edward C. helper at 11 Haynes, b. 36 Walnut.
" George, *(Geo. N. & Son,)* h. 1 Chestnut.
" George & Son, grocers, 36 Walnut.
    George Northwood.    George H. Northwood.
" Geo. H. *(Geo. N. & Son,)* b. 1 Chestnut.
" W. H. spinner, b. 1 Chestnut.
Norton Arthur W. toolm. at James L. Howard Co. 438 Asylum, h. Manchester t.
" C.A.Q.,Hfd. Graphophone Co. h. 48 Church.
" Claressa L. b. 1407 Main.
" Clara A. at 80 Trumbull, b. 48 Church.
" Edwin N. filer at Popes, b. 389 Capitol.
" Elizabeth E. wid. Seth P. h. 16 Chapel.
" Emma, wid. Francis B. b. 100 Ann.
" Frank C. ins. agt. at 721 Main, b.35 Linden.
" George N. tinner, h. Windsor av. c. Suffield.
" Henry H. laborer, 335 Shel. b.42 Webster.
" James, carman 283 Shel. h.u. 50 Wdbg.
" John, helper at 54 Arch, h.u. 46 Wells.
" Lucius B. manager National Mercantile Co. 66 State, h. New Britain t.
" Malcolm A. builder, h. 32 Highland.
" Margaret, at 921 Main, b. 58 Church.
" Maria, wid. Thomas, h. 13 Chapel.
" Mary, h. 19 Suffield.
" Nellie L. b. 13 Chapel.
" Winifred S. clerk at Brown, Thomson & Co. 942 Main, b. 42 Webster.
Norwich house, 1094 Main.
Norwick Max, cabinetm. 69 Front, h. E.H.t.
Noslia Jacob, laborer, b. 14 Putnam.
" Paul, laborer, h. 14 Putnam.
Notine Anthony L. sup. policeman, l. 430 Asy.
" John, barber, 103, h. 105 Main.
" Joseph, barber, 454, h.u. 428 Asylum.
Nott Charles D. livery, r. 1128 Main, h.3 Avon.
" Samuel, office 709 Main, b. 6 Belden.
" Selah W. mach. 388 Cap. h.u. 18 Grand.
" ☞ *see also Noot.*
Nourse Edward E. professor at Hartford Theological Seminary, 1507 Broad, h. Berlin t.
" M. W. draughtsm. at 177 Asy. b. 227 High.
Novelle John, ragpicker, h. 2½ Charles.
Noxon Louis C. draughtsman at 78 Trumbull, h.u. 26 South Prospect.
Noyce William, assembler at Popes, b. 218 State.
Noyes Flora L. supervisor, 690, b. 690 Asylum.
" George N. h.u. 19 Seyms.
" James W. driver, h. 8 John.
" Joseph F. supt. at 133 Shel. h.u. 14 Grand.

Noyes Mary J. teacher at 690, b. 690 Asylum.
" Wm. H. mach. at 1 Flower, h. 167 Sigourney.
·Nugent Edward J. mach. at 581 Cap. b. 7 Green.
" James, plumber, 228 Pearl, h.u. 59 Chestnut.
" James, teamster, b. 74 Windsor.
" John F. slater, h.2u. 17 Kennedy.
" Michael, carman, 31, h. 31 Mather.
" Thomas, driver, b. 31 Mather.
" Wm. H. engraver, 177 Asy. h.94 Huntington.
Nuhu Dora H. milliner, l. 222 Sargeant.
Nuilen Exel, laborer at 556 Cap. b. 2 Green.
Nunan Dennis J. blacksm. at Popes, b. 52 Flower.
Nursery Day, Union for Home Work, 239 Mar.
Nuss William, brakeman N.E.R. b.2u. 73 Albany.
Nussbaum Kaufman, meats, 538Mn.h.80Hudson
Nussman Joe, clothing, 157, h. 157 Front.
Nuthmann Conrad, filer Colts, h. Burnside v.
Nutile Gabrielle, groceries, 136, h. 136 Front.
Nuttell Mattie F. nurse, h. 427 Main, rm. 5.
Nutter Harrie Yates, correspdt.Popes, b. 809 Asy.
Nutting Charles D. h. 34 New Britain.
" Mary Howard, nurse, 14, b. 14 Spring.
" Walter G. draughtsm. at 1 Flow. b. 175 Russ.
Nyberg Charles J. filer, h. 12 So. Forest.
Nye Aline S. student, b. 24 Bluebills.
" Chas. H. screwm. at 476 Cap. h.u. 26 Elm.
" Robert P. purser str. Middletown, h. Falmouth, Mass.
" Watson, mach. 1 Flower, h.u. 27 Williams.
" ☞ *see also Ney.*
Nylen Claus O. mech. at Popes, b.u. 98 Babcock.
Nyman Charles J. machinist at 1 Flower, b. Russ.
" P. N. harnessm. 8 Sig. h.2u. 115 Lawrence.
Nyquoit Alfred, rubberworker, b. 42 Smith.
Nyser John C. F. photog'r, 2 Ford, h. 36 Smith.

*THOMAS OAKES.*          *T. EDWARD OAKES.*

## THOS. OAKES & SON,

*Contractors for*

## Plumbing, Heating, Gas Fitting and Electric Wiring.

*We carry the largest stock of Plumbing Goods in the city. Also Electrical Supplies in great variety.*

*Telephone Connection.*          **11 HAYNES STREET,**

OAKES Ernest A. blacksm. 690 Park, b. 426 Maple.
" Frank B. clerk, b. 114 Franklin.
" J. Albert, plumber at 11 Haynes, b. 124 Huntington.
" Rebecca, wid. Frederick, b. 77 Elm.
" Thomas, *( T. O. & Son,)* h. 124 Huntington.
**OAKES THOMAS & SON,** plumbers, gasfitters, etc. 11 Haynes. *See p. 278.*
Thomas Oakes.          T. Edward Oakes.
" T. Edward, *( T. O. & Son,)* h.u. 29 Elmer.
Oakey P. Davis, state agent J. M. Hobby & Co. 75 Pratt, b. 136 Trumbull.
Oakley Ernest F. h. 90 Webster.
" Fred. A. foreman 1 Flower, b. 76 Hopkins.
" Marcelina J. Mrs. midwife, h. 255 Putnam.
Oates James F. mach. 1 Laurel, h. 45 Hawthorn.
" John C. clerk, h.2u. 46 Hopkins.
Oatman Alva Mrs. h. 217 Farmington.
Obbat O. assistant cook at 152 Asylum.
Obert & Puglisi, barbers, 124 Asylum.
Joseph Obart.          Philip Puglisi.
" Joseph, *( O. & Puglisi,)* h. 36 Windsor.
O'Beirne Alloysius, b.u. 240 Maple.
" Mamie L. operator, b. 240 Maple.
" Margaret, wid. Michael, h.u. 240 Maple.
Ober Philip H. pressman at Popes, h. 286 Fkn.
Oberer Albert Frank, mach. 388 Cap. b. 16 Kibbe.
Oberman John M. helper N.Y.R. h. 78 Potter.
O'Bery Wm. waiter str. Hartford, 285 State.
O'Brien Alice G. clerk, b. 81 Arch.
" Andrew, lab. 165 Windsor, h. 40 Chestnut.
" Andrew J. finisher 556 Cap. h. 43 Hawthorn.
" Ann, wid. Patrick, h.u. 245 Park.
" Annie wid. Daniel J. h. 30 Center.
" Bridget, groceries, 106, h. 106 Huyshope.
" Bridget, wid. Patrick, h. 33 Front.
" Catherine, wid. Michael, h. 339 Front.
" & Connell, saloon, 194 State.
Michael O'Brien.          Thomas H. Connell.
" Cornelius, stonemason, h.r. 52 Bond.
" Daniel, b. 2 Holcomb.
" Daniel, helper 165 Windsor, h.u. 34 Russell.
" Daniel, laborer, P.&R. h. 42 Village.
" Daniel, mach.hand. at Popes, b. 32 Flower.
" Daniel, mason, b.r. 121 Maple.
" Daniel B. laborer, h.u. 33 Front.
" Daniel F. feeder 141 Pearl, b.u. 19 FootGuard.
" Daniel J. mach. at 556 Cap. h.u. 43 Hawthorn.
" Daniel S. rec. clerk at 98 Kil. b. 263 Front.
" Dennis, expressman, 141, h. 141 Barbour.

O'Brien Dennis, laborer, h.u. 87 Maple.
" Dennis R. blacksm. at 20 Mor. b. 1202 Main.
" Edward, blacksmith at Pratt & Whitney Co. 1, h.u. 76 Flower.
" Edward, grinder, 388 Cap. h. 35 Lawrence.
" Edward D. agent at 721 Main, b. 30 Center.
" Edward L. painter, b.r. 181 Bellevue.
" Ellen, wid. James, b.3u. 38 So. Prospect.
" & Flannery, stoneyard, r. 6½ Ellery.
George O'Brien.          Thomas Flannery.
" Francis D. b. 10 Cedar.
" Francis P. meatcutter. 329 Asy. b. 12 Cedar.
" Frank, pressman at 581 Cap. h. 594 Garden.
" George, *( O'B. & Flannery,)* b. 94 Hudson.
" Hannah, wid. Thomas, b. 32 Russ.
" Henry J. polisher at Colts, b. 81 Arch.
" Honora, wid. John, b. 1202 Main.
" James, b. 2 Holcomb.
" Jas. *(Kilmurtin & O'B.)* h. 14½ Governor.
" James, brassm. at 141 Com. h.u. 22 Albany.
" James, deckhand str. Middletown, 285 State.
" James, laborer, h.u. 72 Charter Oak.
" James, machinist at 1 Flow. h. 49 Hawthorn.
" James, polisher at Colts, h. 81 Arch.
" James H. stonecutter, h.2u. 32 Chestnut.
" James I. carinspector, b.u. 19 Goodman.
" James J. b. 88 Charter Oak.
" James J. bartender, 202 State, b.u. 29 Front.
" James J. engraver at A. Mugford, 177 Asylum, h.u 51 Dean.
" James J. molder at 54 Arch, b. 10 Cedar.
" James J. plumber, l.2u. 1067 Main.
" James P. clerk at 30 Wells, b.u. 147 Sheldon.
" James P. conductor St.Ry. b. 271 Jefferson.
" Jeremiah, foundryman at 65 Suffield.
" Jerry, helper, b. 263 Front.
" Jerry, screwmaker at Popes, b. 55 Babcock.
" John, b. 2 Holcomb.
" John, bottler at 13 Morris, h.u. 91 Main.
" John, carcleaner, h.2u. 57 Spruce.
" John, deckhand str. Middletown, 285 State.
" John, gardener at 34 Pro. h. 594 Garden.
" John, laborer, b. 4 Green.
" John, laborer, h. 263 Front.
" John, laborer, h.2u. 14 Kilbourn.
" John, laborer at 79 Talcott, b. 214 Allyn.
" John E. policeman, h.2u. 142 Babcock.
" John F. bkkpr. at 556 Cap. h. 106 Laurel.
" John F. inspector, 690 Park, b. 55 Putnam.
" John F. porter at 908 Main, h. 281 Allyn.
" John J. clerk at 1150, b. 1150 Main.
" John J. engineer at 42 Union pl. h.u. 312 Asylum, rm. 5.
" John J. teamster at 1411 Main, b.r. 75 Fmt.
" John M. hatter at 36, l. 36 Pratt.
" Joseph, b. 32 Russ.
" Kathryn, at 270 Main, b. 151 Retreat.
" Lawrence J. plumber at 81 Tru. b. W. L. t.
" Luke T. printer at Hartford Printing Co. 16 State, h.u. 1068 Broad.
" Margaret, b. W.H. Home for the Aged, Alb.
" Martin, laborer, b.3u. 36 Sheldon.
" Martin F. polisher, b.u. 72 Charter Oak.
" Martin H. assem. at 556 Cap. h. Bloomfield t.
" Mary, laundress 30 Washington.

O'Brien Mary, wid. Cornelius, h.r. 181 Bellevue.
" Michael, (*O'B. & Connell,*) h. 160 Allyn.
" Michael, at 365 Allyn.
" Michael, helper, h.u 35 Hawthorn.
" Michael, laborer, h.u. 147 Sheldon.
" Michael, laborer, h. 6 John.
" Michael, mason, h.u. 101 Sheldon.
" Michael J. waiter at 33, b. 33 Prospect.
" Michael J. mach. at 581 Cap. h. 2 Douglas.
" Michael J. teams. at 206 State, h.u. 84 Fmt.
" Michael P. trimmer, 352 Albany, h. 20 Blo.
" Morris, driver, h.r. 56 Albany.
" Nora, at 8 Central, b. 60 Wells.
" Patrick, h. 121 Maple.
" Patrick, at Cedar Hill cem. h.u.r. 5 Fairfield.
" Patrick, bartender at 359 Main.
" Patrick, bartender at 20 Ford, b. 41 Asylum.
" Patrick, carpenter, h.u. 6 Chestnut.
" Patrick, driver, b.2u. 4 Portland.
" Patrick, laborer, b.u. 259 Front.
" Patrick, laborer, b. 79 Chestnut.
" Patrick, laborer at 40 Governor, h. 37 John.
" Patrick B. coremaker at 54 Arch, h. 10 Cedar.
" Patrick M. laborer at 581 Cap. h. 66 Fmt.
" Patrick J. gardener, b. 594 Garden.
" Patrick J. law student, 11 Central, b. N.B.t.
" Patrick J. machinist, b. 339 Front.
" Patrick J. sweeper at Colts, b. 63 Governor.
" Patrick William, agent, b. 58 Fairmount.
" Peter, driver, h.u. 9 Sigourney pl.
" Peter F. driver at 273, h.2u. 242 Pearl.
" Robert E. packer at 40 Gov. b. Bloomfield t.
" Richard, deckh. str. Middletown, 285 State.
" Thomas, bartender, l. 31 Trumbull.
" Thomas, carpenter, h.u, 12 Trumbull.
" Thomas, driver for city, h. Wawarme.
" Thomas, express, h. 66 Windsor.
" Thos. head porter, 26 State, h. 23 Congress.
" Thomas Sr. farmer, h.u. 147 Sheldon.
" Thomas Jr. mason, b.u. 147 Sheldon.
" Thomas A. driver engine No. 1, h.u. 63 Park.
" Thomas J. antique furniture warehouse, 12 Elm, b. 32 John.
" Thomas J. cashier at 98 Wells, h.2u. 51 Wads.
" Thomas L. carptr. at 12 Elm, h. 32 John.
" Thomas, L. carpenter at 12 Elm, h. 32 John.
" Timothy, machinist, b. 339 Front.
" Timothy W. laborer at 98 Kil. b. 26 Elmer.
" William, h. 26 Elmer.
" William, carptr. & bldr.136, h. 136 Retreat.
" William, deckh. str. Middletown, 285 State.
" William, polisher, 65 Suffield,b.2u.24 Cedar.
" William J. teamster Hartford Provision Co., Valley, h.3u. 11 Queen.
" William P. inspector, h.3u. 88 So.Prospect.
" William S. plumber, b.u. 6 Chestnut.
" Wm. W. saloon, 178 Asylum, h.u. 108 Hung.
O'Byrne James, lab. stone pits, h. 10 Glendale.
" Michael, steamfitter, b. Park.
O'Callaghan Catherine, wid. James. h.u. 13 Good.
" Dennis, clerk, h.u. 13 Goodman.
" Ellen Mrs. b. 321 Windsor av.
" Hannah, weaver, b. 13 Goodman.
" Jeremiah, h. 321 Windsor av.
" John, porter at 129 State, h. 39 Lafayette.

O'Callaghan John J. barten'r 184,h.u. 182 State.
" Julia, dressmaker, h. 1081 Main.
" Nano, dressmaker, h. 1081 Main.
" Patrick M. bartender at 425, h. 545 Main.
" ☞*see also Callaghan; Callahan.*
Ochaby O. filer at 556 Capitol, h. 84 Potter.
O'Connell Bartholomew, b. 2 Holcomb.
" Daniel, bartender at 107 Main, b. 32 Park.
" Daniel, laborer, h. 17 Green.
" Daniel, polisher at Popes, h.u. 32 Park.
" Daniel, waiter at 80 State.
" Henrietta P. Mrs. dressmaker, 75 Pratt.
" John, brassmolder at 65 Suffield.
" John F. shipper at C. C. Fuller & Co. 16 Ford, h.2u. 174 Sheldon.
" John J. bartender, h.r. 27 Morgan.
" John J. enameler at Popes, b. 34 S.Pro.
" John J. splicer at 690, l. 771 Park.
" Kate, wid. Peter, b.2u. 66 Village.
" Mary, wid. John, h.u. 1067 Main.
" Michael, contractor and builder, h. Lubeck.
" Maurice, expressman, h. 76 Bellevue.
" Maurice Mrs. boardinghouse, 76 Bellevue.
" Michael, fireman, P.&R. b. 36 Liberty.
" Patrick, laborer, h.u. 57 Spruce.
" Peter, clerk at 51 Market, b.u. 1210 Main.
" Thos. helper 54 Arch, b.2u. 2 Union.
" Thos.laborer at city water works,h.u.140Law.
" William M. saloon, 69, h. 69 Pleasant.
" ☞*see also Connell.*
O'Conner David F. shipping clerk, 1 Hurlburt, h.u. 23 Portland.
" Geo. T. molder, 556 Capitol, h. 22 Dean.
" Mary, clerk at 835 Main, b. 24 West.
" Michael, coachm. at 29 Collins, h. 78 Flower.
" Michael, waiter, h.2u. 1 Elm pl.
" ☞*see also Conner; Connor.*
O'Connor A. night clerk at Adams express, b.u. 4 Foot Guard.
" Andrew J. h. 22 Linden.
" Bell F. bookkeeper, b. 22 Linden.
" Daniel, packer 70 Huy. h.r. 76 Vanblock.
" Daniel F. bartender, h. 11 Russell.
" Don, clerk, h. 66 Lawrence.
" Edward P. switchtender, h.u. 75 Fairmount.
" Eliza, wid. Michael, h. 24 West.
" Geo. E. with M. J. O'Connor, b.u. 1542 Broad.
" Jeremiah, engineer, 20 South Hudson.
" Jeremiah, stonemason, h.2u. 28 Grand.
" John, b. W. H. Home for the Aged, Albany.
" John,flagman at 95 Pleasant,h. 90 Windsor.
" John, laborer, b. 209 Sheldon.
" John J. machinist, b.r. 61 Front.
" Mary, inspector at 70 Huy. b. 6 Hendricxsen.
" Mary, wid. Matthew, h. 124 Potter.
" Michael, coremaker, 54 Arch, h. 19 Squire.
" Michael H. real estate, h.2u. 40 Hungerford-

**O'CONNOR MICHAEL J.** con.
tractor and builder, president Windsor Red Stone Co. h. 1542 Broad. *See p. 508.*

" Patrick, laborer at 70 Huyshope, h. 1 Union.
" Susan, wid. Henry, h.u. 33 Francis.
" Thomas, clerk at 115 Pearl, b.u. 33 Francis.
" Thomas, driver, h.u. 28 Grand.

O'Connor Thomas F. brazier, h.r. 61 Front.
" Thomas F. clerk, b. 17 Kennedy.
" Thomas F. printer 23 Asylum, h. 13 Spruce.
" William, assistant pressman at Times office, 716 Main, b. 24 West.
" ☞ see also Conner; Connor.
O'Connors James, steamf. 164 State, b. 475 Main.
" William, mach. at 556 Cap. h. 61 Hawthorn.
Octigan James J. bartender at 868 Allyn, b. 66 New Britain.
O'Day James T. clerk, b. 48 John.
" Martin, ragpicker, h.u. 53 Avon.
" Mary, wid. James, h. 48 John.
" Minnie, dressmaker, 48, b. 48 John.
Odell Adam, b. 2 Holcomb.
" Charles H. teamster at Smith, Northam & Co. h.u. 28 Russell.
" Frank H. h.u. 177 Asylum.
" William, teamster, 268, b. 270 Prospect av.
Oderman Oscar Y. painter, b. 1153 Main.
Odlum James B. bartend. 359 Mn. h. 49 Franklin.
O'Donaghue Michael, helper at 1 Flower, h. 62 Wilson.
O'Donnell Ann, wid. Anthony, h. 66 Retreat.
" Annie, clerk at 956 Main, b. 23 Spruce.
" Edward, clerk at 90 Albany, l. 1224 Main.
" Francis, machinist, l.u. 53 Front.
" Garrett, mach. at 556 Cap. h.2u. 1438 Broad.
" Jerry, machinist at 556 Cap. h. 1448 Broad.
" John, mach. at 1 Flower, h. 1444 Broad.
" John, porter at 52 Ann, h.2u. 265 Asylum.
" John H. harnessmaker at 8 Sig. h. N.B. t.
" Louis, engineer at 304 Asylum, b. 26 Chapel.
" Owen, florist at 118 Benton, h. 45 Elliott.
" Patrick, laborer, 276 Mar. h.4u.r. 23 Spruce.
" Patrick E. engir. 1 So. Ann, h. 74 Green.
" Richard, machinist, b.u. 53 Front.
" Thomas F. toolmaker, h. 1214 Broad.
" William, b. 66 Retreat.
" William J. clerk at 95 Ple. b.u. 14 Pratt.

**O'DONOHUE MICHAEL,** church architect, 93, h.u. 93 Hawthorn.

O'Donovan Dominick, electrician at Popes, h.2u. 83 Governor.
" Eugene, carpenter, h. 66 Capitol.
O'Dosha Emma O. bookkeeper at 77 Commerce, b. 35 Buckingham.
Oehlhof Christian, cigar mfr. 30 Park, h.45 Hudson
O'Farrell James Mrs. h. 331 Front.
" John, lettercarrier, h. 13 Wells.
Officer John W. foreman, St. Ry. h.u. 149 Weth.
" John W. Mrs. dressm. 149, h.u. 149 Weth.
Offman David, tailor, h.u. 262 Front.
" Hyman, laborer, h.4u. 34 North.
O'Flaherty Bridget, wid. John, h.u. 87½ Windsor.
" Daniel E. mech. at 581 Cap. h. 35 Sigourney.
" Daniel J. mech. at 581 Capitol, b. 31 Flower.
" Grace, typewriter, b. 40 Buckingham.
" Hugh, attorney, 793 Main, b. 40 Bkm.
" Hugh, laborer at 335 Shel. h.2u. 15 S.Pro.
" Jeremiah, at 247 Pearl, b. 14 Huntley pl.
" John, laborer, b.r. 53 Front.
" John, physician, 406, h. 406 Main.
" John J. at 581 Capitol, b.u. 31 Flower.

O'Flaherty Mary Mrs. h.r. 53 Front.
" Maurice, druggist, 391 Main, h. 12 Morris.
" Patrick, mason, h.3u. 216 Sheldon.
" ☞ see also Flaherty.
Ogden Charles W. B. b. 26 Congress.
" Franklin S. molder at 1 Flow. h. 23 Howard.
" James A. mach. at 581 Cap. h. 318 Maple.
" Susan, wid. Clarence, h. 26 Congress.
Ogg Alexander, forem. 54 Arch, h. 22 New Park.
" John S. mach. at 54 Arch, b. 22 New Park.
Ogilvie George, stonecutter, h. 585 Garden.
Ogilvy Harry, plumber, b. 36 Prospect.
" James A. supt. of Phœnix Mutual Life Ins. Co. building, 49 Pearl, h.u. 51 Mahl.
" William, blacksmith, h. 36 Prospect.
O'Hallorhan Michael, helper at 1 Flower, b. 4½ Hungerford.
O'Hara Ann M. wid. Francis, h.u. 53 Flower.
" Catherine, wid. Edward, h.2u. 25 Flower.
" Geo. M. clerk, 575 Main, b. 53 Flower.
" Jas. tinner at 16 Mul. grocer, 71, h.u. 71 Potter.
" Julia, clerk at 956 Main, b. 42 Madison.
" Nellie, clerk at 956 Main, b. 42 Madison.
" Patrick, laborer, 1 Flower, h.u. 1442 Broad.
" Thos. J. clerk at 1046 Main, b. 79 Chestnut.
" Thomas J. mach. at 581 Cap. h.147 Lawrence.
Ohliger August, carptr. r. 321, h. 321 Windsor av.
" Charles, carpenter, h. 72 Sanford.
" Ernest A. sawyer, h. 182 Clark.
Ohlsen John, carpenter, h. 62 Lawrence.
Oiley George, confectionery, 174 Windsor av h. 46 Bellevue.
O'Keefe Arthur, operator, 388 Cap. b.28 Center.
" Catherine, dressmaker, b. 105 Zion.
" Charles P. engraver at R. S. Peck & Co. 26 High, b. 65 Flower.
" Cornelius, teamster at stone pits, b. 105 Zion
" Daniel, barber, 55 High, h.u. 42 Hopkins.
" James, helper at 1, b. 28 Flower.
" James, nightwatchm. Cap. h. 1462 Broad.
" James Jr. messenger at Cap. b. 1462 Broad.
" John, molder at 1 Flower, b. 16 Russell.
" John J. helper at 1 Flower, b. 1 Queen.
" Joseph Rev., St. Marys Home, W.H.t.
" Katherine, stenographer, b. 65 Flower.
" Marga. wid. Cornelius, grocer, 105, h. 105 Zion
" Mary, wid. Owen, b.2u. 29 Hungerford.
" Michael, advertisement writer, 903 Main, h. 28 Russell.
" Patrick, helper at 1 Flower, h. 1 Queen.
" Thomas, clerk at 114 Asylum, h. 12 Wells.
" Timothy, barber at 387 Allyn, h. 51 Chestnut.
" ☞ see also Keefe.
O'Koomian Jasper, screwm. 476 Cap. b. 15 Bab.
O'Laughlin Bridget, wid. Patrick, h.u. 87 Com.
" Daniel, b. 2 Holcomb.
" Dennis, helper, b. 50 Green.
" Edward, laborer, h.u. 87 Commerce.
" James, ostler at 560 Main, b.2u. 20 Cedar.
" John, molder at 556 Cap. b. 43 Evergreen.
" John J. ship'ngclerk at 62 Mar. h.u. 44 Green.
" Joseph J. clerk at Brown, Thomson & Co. 942 Main, h. 79 Hudson.
" Mary Mrs. laundress at 34 Pratt, h. 87 Com.
" Michael, ostler, r. 371 Main, h.2u. 20 Cedar.

O'Laughlin Michael J. carpenter, h.u. 46 Green.
" Patrick, helper, 48 Ann, b. W.H.t.
" Pat'k, laborer Sp'g Grove Cem'y,h. 50 Green.
" Patrick J. driver, h.u. 18½ Howard.
" Peter, driver at 25, h.u. 18 Union.
" Peter J. printer at 29 Union pl. h. 17 East.
" Thomas, tobacco pack.231 State, b.23 Front.
" Thomas F. plater at 62 Market, b. 50 Green.
" ☞ see also O'Loughlin.
Olcott George C. buffer at Popes, h. 82 Benton.
" Harry E. mach. at 1 Flow. b. 46 Hopkins.
" James H. clerk, 95 Pleasant, h. 290 Market.
Olcuder Frank, laborer, h.2u. 95 Sheldon.
Olcutt George B. b. 47 Farmington.
" Harry H. stenog. 388 Cap. b.47 Farmington.
**OLD PEOPLE'S HOME,** 36 Jefferson.　　　See pages 702, 703.
Oldbelt Ike, roller at 62 Market, h. 60 Morgan.
Older Abraham, poolroom, 211 Front, h.u. 304 Market.
" Barnard, peddler, h.r. 25 Kilbourn.
" Morris, city reporter at Hartford Courant; 66 State, b. 89 Morgan.
Oldfield Luke H. h. 106 Seymour.
Oldroyd Charles G. machinist at Pratt & Whitney Co. 1 Flower, h. 47 Babcock.
" Joseph A. machinist 1 Flower, h. Windsor t.
Olds Alfred A. ( O. & Whipple, ) h. 252 Laurel.
" Charles R. theological student, 1507 Broad.
" Sophronia, b. 36 Jefferson.
" & Whipple, agricultural impl.164 to 168 State.
Alfred A. Olds.　　　Frank H. Whipple.
" William, supt. at 225 Sheldon, h. 1 Squire.
Olea Frederick, at 252 Pearl, h. 108 Mather.
O'Leary Daniel, laborer, h.2u.r. 101 Windsor.
" German, molder at 555 Cap. h.2u. 90 Ward.
O'Leary James F. physician, 4, l. 4 Village.
" James F. waiter, 375 Asy. h.u. 28 Pleasant.
" Jeremiah, bricklayer, b. 197 Windsor.
" Joshua F. architect at 756 Main.
" Patrick, melter 66 Suffield, h. 197 Windsor.
" ☞ see also Leary.
Olekuck Edward, plater at Wm. Rogers Mfg. Co. 66 Market, h. East Hartford t.
Olin Andrew F. oper. 252 Pearl, h. 108 Mather.
" Frederick, ins.broker, 903,rm.13,l.903 Main.
" Joel W. cutter at 252 Pearl, b. 106 Mather.
" Otto B. operator at 252 Pearl, h. Wilson sta.
Oliver Catherine, laund. 34 Pratt, h.u. 11 Ellery.
" Catherine T. B. b. 88 Chestnut.
" Frank C. brazier at Popes, b. East Hartford t·
" Harry W. repairer,911 Mn.h.153 Windsor av.
" John William, machinist, h. 98 Chestnut.
" Rose, clerk at 921 Main, b. 58 Church.
" Sidney, painter, b.r. 1117 Main.
" William, mach. at 1 Flower, b. 581 Main.
" William E. clerk, 135 Shel. h. 124 Church.
" Wm. F. boxmaker at 133 Shel. b. 11 Ellery.
Olkuck Rose E. stenog. at E. M. Huntsinger, 30 Asylum, h.u. 38 Capen.
Olmsbee John, clerk at 319 Asylum, b. 198 High.
Olmsker Harris, at 314 Asylum, h. 263 Market.
Olmstead A. W. glassworker at 20 Sargeant, b. 55 Garden.
" Clarence F. toolm. at Popes, b. 289 Capitol.

**OLMSTEAD COMMERCIAL COLLEGE,** 756 Main. See p. 710.
" Ella M., Commercial College, 756 Main, rm. 40, b. 25 Spring.
" Henry W. mach. at 1 Flower, b. 55 Gillett.
" Osmond W. h. c. Sargeant and Garden.
Olmsted Ashbel W. machinist at 20 Sargeant, b. 55 Garden.
" Charles E. ins. agent, h.u. 26 Church.
" Charles E. physician, 868, h. 868 Main.
" Clara J. h. 29 Spring.
" Elihu, machinist at 388 Capitol, h. E.H.t.
" Ellen G. bookbdr. at 141 Pearl, b. 58 Church.
" Fannie M. h. 29 Spring.
" Frank, clerk at 217 Albany, b. E.H.t.

**OLMSTED C. N.** Waltham Comet agency; Lovell Diamond, Hunter and Waverly bicycles; trading and repairing, 186 Pearl, h. 55 Garden.
OLMSTED GEORGE H. prest. Hartford Carriage Co. 300 Allyn, h. E.H.t. See page 549.
" George K. student, b. 177 Bellevue.
" Hannah L. wid. Lucius D. h. 74 Niles.
" Harriet M. teach. Second no. sch. h. 68 Pratt.
" Harry, salesman at Hartford Carriage Co. 300 Allyn, b. E.H.t.
" Harry D. at Conn. Mutual Life Ins. Co. 783 Main, h. E.H.t.
" Jessie S. b. 74 Niles.
" John L. b. 26 State.
" Joseph N. h. 177 Bellevue.
" Margaret P. wid. Woodbridge S.h. 55 Gillett.
" Ormond, foreman, 9 Sargeant, h. 77 Clark.
" Walter B. cashier Conn. Mutual Life Ins. Co. 783 Main, h. 55 Gillett.
" Walter B. Jr. b. 55 Gillett.
Olney Jeremiah, h. 117 Washington.
Oloslegesi Joseph, blacksm. h.u.r. 3 Pleasant ct.
O'Loughlin Elizabeth, wid. Patrick,h.79 Hudson.
" James, contr. and builder, 25, b. 25 Central.
" John, laborer, b. 23 Front.
" John J. (Buckley & O'L.) h.2u. 233 Market.
" Margaret, wid. John, h.2u. 389 Capitol.
" Michael, filer at 70 Huy. h. 37 Madison.
" Thomas, b. 23 Front.
" ☞ see also O'Laughlin; McLaughlin; Loughlin.
Olschefskie Chas. harnessm. at 8 Sig. b. 28 Grand.
" Frederick, harnessm. at 8 Sig. h. 24 Grand.
" Gotfried, Jr. ( Wise, Smith & Co. ) h. 19 Mahl.
Olsen Ada, wid. Charles, boardingh. u. 80 Front.
" Andrew, chipper, 556 Cap. h.2u. 47 Sheldon.
" Charles, scourer, 15 Tru. b. 54 Lawrence.
" Christian, laborer at Capitol, b. 24 Gold.
" Fred, baker, 1036 Main, b. 279 Capitol.
" George, awning maker at 124, b. 124 State.
" Gustaf, ( O. & Jacobson,) b.u. 80 Front.
" Jacob, carpenter, b. 98 Babcock.
" & Jacobson, saloon, 80 Front.
Gustaf Olsen.　　　John Jacobson.

**OLSEN JOHANN,** photographer, 89 Pratt, h. 76 Ann.
" John, helper, 15 Trumbull, b. 54 Lawrence.
" Martin, cook, h. 24 Gold.

**You'll Get ALL THE NEWS, if you READ THE POST.**

Olsen Nelson, cutter at 690 Park, b. 28 Putnam.
" Nils, rubberw. at 690 Park, b. 28 Putnam.
Olson Henry A. laborer, b. 28 Buckingham.
Olsson Holger, ship. clk. 424, h. 284 Asy. rm. 55
Olstrom Teder, laborer, h. 3 Brady.
Olynn Bernard, painter, h.2u. 488 Main.
O'Malley A. E. machinist at 13 Central.
" Edward J. machinist, b. 24 Canton.
" Irene M. stenographer, b. 24 Canton.
" John, deckhand str. Hartford, 285 State.
" John, policeman, h. 24 Canton.
" John M. tinner, b. 24 Canton.
O'Mara Dennis, at N.Y.R. b. 47 Sigourney.
" Frank, foreman at 62 Market, h. 200 N.P.
" James, helper, b.3u. 86 Walnut.
" James, repairer at Popes, h. 72 Potter.
" P. 2d engineer, tug Coulston, 285 State.
" Rodger, laborer at 169, b.u. 250 Front.
Omassee Stephen, janitor at 50, b. 52 Market.
O'Meara Edward J. lab. P.& R. h.2u. 86 Walnut.
" James, helper, b.2u. 86 Walnut.
" John, tillerman, 275 Pearl, h.u. 44 Lawrence.
" Maurice, teamster at 100 Com. b.3u. 184 Shel.
" Patrick, laborer at P.&R. b. 78 Walnut.
" Patrick, watchman, N.Y.R.h.u.47 Sigourney.
O'Mullane Lillie, clerk 921 Main, b.u. 70 Flow.
Onderdonk Adrian H. student at Trinity college, b. 122 Vernon.
O'Neil Andrew F. chief clerk at P.&R. l. 15 Williams.
" Annie, at 476 Capitol, b.u. 412 Broad.
" Bartholomew, policeman, h. 112 Hungerford
" Bridget, wid. William, h.2u. 65 Pleasant.
" Cornelius J. lab. at 95 Ple. b.3u. 12 S. Pro
" Dennis Jr. joiner, 68 Hudson, b.u. 373 Broad
" Dennis C. gardener, h. Hawthorn ex.
**O'NEIL EDWARD,** contractor and builder, 68, h.u. 68 Hudson. *See p. 520.*
" Edward, fireman. Trinity college, b. Grand.
" Elizabeth M. cashier at R. Ballerstein & Co. b. 62 Church.
" Eugene, h.u. 23 Spring.
" Francis, h.u. 232 Zion.
" Frank B. mason, b. 24 Pawtucket.
" George C. clerk at 97 Asylum, b. 62 Church.
" Geo. E. bkkpr. at 236 Park, b. 24 Pawtucket.
" Gerald, conductor St.Ry. h. 39 Hungerford.
" J. bookkeeper at Popes, h.u. 102 Hopkins.
" James, laborer, Pope Tube Co. b. 412 Broad.
" James, molder, 54 Arch, b. 24 Pawtucket.
" James, teamster, h.u. 7 Park.
" Jas. A. bookkeeper, 234 State, b. 62 Church.
" Jeremiah, plumber, 1230 Mn. b. 88 Church.

O'Neil John, expressman, b.u. 47 Green.
" John, gardener, h. 351 Farmington.
" John, laborer at 581 Capitol, b. 12 Putnam.
" John C. drug clerk, 204 State, b. 112 Hung.
" John F. brakeman, b. 220 Allyn.
" John F. benchman at Pope Tube Co. b. 102 Hopkins.
" John J. engineer at P.O. h. 22 Pawtucket.
" John M. musician, h.2u. 12 Church.
" Joseph E. at Ætna Life Ins. Co. 650 Main, b. 62 Church.
" K. Wm. pressman at 62 Mar. h.2u. 211 Fkn.
" Margaret Mrs. h.3u. 884 Main.
" Margaret, wid. Timothy, h.2u. 7 Park.
" Margaret E. h. 62 Church.
" Marguerite, milliner, 908 Mn.b.24 Pawtucket
" Martin, tinsmith, h.u.r. 44 Village.
" Mary, wid. Dennis, h.u. 373 Broad.
" Mary, wid. Peter, h.u. 150 New Park.
" Michael, laborer, h.u. 95 Windsor.
" Michael, mason & contrctr. h. 24 Pawtucket.
" Michael J. clerk at Popes, b. 102 Hopkin.
" Patrick, laborer, b. 12 South Prospect.
" Patrick, laborer, 98 Kilbourn, h.3u.r.12 S.Pro.
" Patrick J. teamster, 4 Am.b. 17 Windsor av.
" Thomas, conductor, N.E.R. h.2u. 2 Elm pl.
" Thomas, laborer, b. 23 Brook.
" Thomas, laborer, h. 30 Hicks.
" Thomas A. engineer N.Y.R. h. 7 East.
" Thomas E. clerk at 30 State, b. 62 Church.
" Timothy J. screwm. at Popes, h.u. 22 Hicks.
" William, mason, b. 12 Village.
" William F. mason and builder, 172, h. 172 Farmington.
O'Neill Anna, dressmaker, b. 64 Ashley.
" Charles P. machinist at 9 Sig. h. 50 Oak.
" Margaret Mrs. h.2u. 884 Main, rm. 56.
Oneill Mary E. dressm. 904 Main, rm. 80, h.W.t.
Ongley George B. actor, b. 112 Vernon.
" M. J. Mrs. matron, h. 112 Vernon.
Opdyke Harry H. clerk 160 Asy. h. 22 Hopkins.
Open Hearth Mission, 135 Front, Benj. N. B. Miller, superintendent.
Oppelt Adam, spinner at 62 Market, h. 25 Francis.
" Andrew, at Popes, h. 71 Hamilton.
" Barthel, grocery, 234, h. 284 New Park.
" Fred, b. 224 New Park.
" Fred, at 690 Park, b. 4 New Park.
" George, b. 4 New Park.
" Herman, pressman at 690 Park, b. 4 N.P.
" John, clerk at 234, b. 284 New Park.
" John, pressman at 690 Park, b. 4 New Park.
" Michael, shoem. & notions, 224, h. 224 N.P.
" William, mach. at 581 Capitol, h. Lubeck.
Opper Fred. C. manager, 189 State, h. 40 West.
Oppermann Frederick, h.u. 130 Martin.
" Henry, grocer, h. Crown, c. Julius.
" Herman, printer, b.u. 130 Martin.
Oppoon Emil H. cigarmaker, h.u. 4 Village.
O'Reilly Daniel J. toolsharpener at 93 Charter Oak, b. 49 Woodbridge.
" Eugene A. mech. at 335 Shel. b. 11 Ellery.
" Eugene P. rubberworker at 690 Park, b. 266 New Park.
" James, blacksmith, b. 11 Ellery.

O'Reilly John G. miller at 165 Windsor, h.2u. 53 Walnut.
" Patrick, b. 2 Holcomb.
" Patrick, blacksmith, b. 11 Ellery.
" Patrick H. b. 11 Ellery.
" Phillip, lithographer at 66 Prospect, b.N.B.t.
" Thomas F. plater at 62 Mar. b.2u. 116 Alb.
" Wm. J. laborer at 70 Com. h. 11 Ellery.
" ☞see also Reilly; Riley.
Orens Jacob, ins. agent, h.3u. 282 Front.
Orensten Henry, screwm. at 476 Cap. h. 306 Mar.
" Mendel, peddler, h.u. 303 Market.
ORGILL ADOLPHUS J. councilman 8th ward, machinist at 1 Flow. h. 33 New Britain.
" Ernest, b. 257 Windsor av.
" John, photog. 753 Main, h. 257 Windsor av.
**ORIENT INSURANCE CO.** 5 Haynes, c. Pearl. See page 461.
Orlander Charles A. foreman, 556 Capitol, h. 48 Windsor av.
Orns John L. agent at 721 Main, h. 282 Front.
Ornsteen Henry, screwm. at 476 Cap. h. 306 Mar.
O'Rourke Edward S. machinist at Popes, b.u. 72 Governor.
" Frank, helper at Popes, h.2u. 254 Front.
" Frank, painter, h.r. 60 Temple.
" James T. blacksm. at Colts, h.u. 72 Governor.
" Michael, janitor, h. 55 Spruce.
" Michael J. laborer, b. 60 Front.
" ☞see also Rourke.
Orphan Asylum, boys and girls, 171 Putnam.
Orr Caroline Mrs. h.u. 462 Windsor av.
" Frank, proofreader at 141, h.u. 71 Pearl.
" Harry E. salesm. at 45 Asy. b. 56 Winthrop.
" John Henry, carpenter at 1 Laurel, h.u. 462 Windsor av.
" Louis G. C. printer at 252 Pearl, b. 462 Windsor av.
" Robert, buyer at 921 Main, h. 18 Clark.
Orton Alice H. wid. Alfred, h. 23 Sanford.
Osbaldiston William H. propr. Household Oil Co. h.u. 66 Westland.
Osborn Burtis J. clerk at 1130 Mn.h.u.31 Canton.
" Charles F. teamster, h.u. 40 Village.
" George, oil peddler, h.u. 278 Market.
" George S. greenhouse, c. Sargeant and Atwood, h. 248 Sargeant.
OSBORN HENRY, police commissioner, secretary Dunham Hosiery Co. 66 State, h. 23 Capitol. See page 547.
" John W. mgr. at 9 Haynes, h. New Haven t.
" Orvil C. coachman at 903 Asylum.
" Thomas, clerk, 4 American. h. 73 Pleasant.
" William E. typewriter, h.u. 38 Brook.
Osborne Adelaide D. masseuse, 167, b. 167 High.
" Fred F. photo-engraver, at A. Mugford, 177 Asylum, b. 80 State.
Osgood Charles, painter, h. 167 Zion.
O'Shaughnessy Peter H. h.3u. 21 Spruce.
O'Shea Gerald, screwm. at 476 Cap. h. 55 Haw.
Osiks Michael, coachman at 948, l. 943 Asylum.
Osmond Isabelle, wid. William, h. 5 New Britain.
" Joseph H. engineer at N.Y.R. h. 6 Atlantic.
Osterblom John, coachm. 74 Far. h. 108 Hopkins.

Osterling Alfred, coachman, h. Highland.
Osterlund Oscar, carpenter, b. 66½ Laurel.
Ostland Charles, coachman, b. 30 Townley.
Ostlund Axel R. polisher at Popes, h. 58 Haw.
Ostrander F. M. collector at 9 Haynes, h. 336 Windsor av.
" John P. mach. 9 Haynes, b. 336 Windsor av.
" Samuel W. clerk at Wm. Rogers Mfg. Co. 66 Market, b. 29 Mulberry.
Ostroski Frank, laborer, b.r. 11 Ellery.
O'Sullivan John, policeman, h. 28 Cedar.
" Michael, laborer, h.r. 11 Bellevue.
" ☞ see also Sullivan.
Otis Alma E. Mrs. b. 36 Jefferson.
" & Burr, planing mill, 169 Front.
" J. Henry, livery stable, r. 1214 Mn. h.3 Avon.
" John, (O. & Burr,) h. 41 Wadsworth.
" Ralph S. toolm. at 581 Cap. h. 67 Madison.
O'Toole Catherine wid. Patrick, h. 54 Vanblock.
" James J. assemb. at Popes, b.u. 49 Lawrence.
" Mary, wid. Lawrence, h.u. 49 Lawrence.
". Wm. P. nickel plater at Popes, b.u. 49 Law.
Ott Andrew, h.2u. 55 Babcock.
" Andrew A. stairbuilder at Taft Co. b.u.r. 125 Hungerford.
" Emil, bartender, h.u.r. 125 Hungerford.
" Frederick M. mach. at Water Wks. h. 63 Elliott.
" George, b.r. 125 Hungerford.
" George, bartdr. at 5 American, h.2u. 24 Mor.
" George, bartdr. 315 Park, h. 53 Wadsworth.
" Jacob A. salesm. at 55 Alb. h.u. 82 Sergeant.
" John, b.r. 125 Hungerford.
" Joseph, at Pope Tube Co. b.r. 125 Hung.
" Nellie, wid. Anton, h. 1352 Broad.
Ottman F. Jr. Rev. b. 25 Elmer.
Otto Hugo F. mach. at 142 Russ, h. 753 Main.
" Paul, painter, 352 Albany, h. 1618 Broad.
" William, tailor at 66 Asylum, h. 56 Village.
" William C. collector, b. 56 Village.
Ottowitz Peter, filer at Popes, h. 19 Lawrence.
Ough John, carpenter, h.u. 415 Garden.
Overand Annie, milliner at 908 Mn. b. 60 Allen pl.
Overman Wheel Co. 847 Main.
Overton Grace M. stenog. at 690 Park, h. E.H.t.
Ovulock Obed S. attendant, 30 Washington.
Owen Albert, helper at 1152 Main, b. 145 High.
" Alfred G. conductor St.Ry. h.u. 26 N.B.
" Elijah, asst. civil engineer at 39 Pearl, b. Buckland v.
" Herbert A. laborer, h.u. 53 Chestnut.
" Hugh T. gardener at 305 Far. b.u. 41 Flow.
" Jennie M. clerk at Brown, Thomson & Co. 942 Main, b. 26 New Britain.
" John, carpenter, h. 44 Wolcott.
**OWEN JOSEPHINE M.** wid. Eber E. boardinghouse, 57 Church, until Oct. 1; on and after Oct. 1, 164 High.
" Katherine B. teacher Second North school, b. Buckland v.
" Mary, wid. Thos. Jr. nurse, h.u. 82 Madison.
" Maud, milliner at 904 Main, b. 53 Chestnut.
" Thomas, stonecutter & sidewalk contractor, r. 38, h.u.r. 38 Annawan.
" Thomas S. J. inspec. at 690 Park, b. 91 Haw.

**A Good Investment-Your Advertisement in The Post.**

Owens Albert, plumber, b. 145 High.
" Edward, b. 231 Pearl.
" George, plumber at 1152 Main, b. 145 High.
" John R. elect. at Pope Tube Co. b.u. 91 Haw.
" Margaret, wid. Edward, h. 231 Pearl.
" Martin A. machinist at Pope Tube Co. h. 91 Hawthorn.
" Michael F. electrician at Pope Tube Co. b. 91 Hawthorn.
" Patrick, helper at Colts, b.2u. 81 Sheldon.
" Patrick, screwmaker, h.u. 63 Hawthorn.
Ozon Wallace, oil peddler, h. 52 Smith.

PAASKE Johann St. draughtsman at 1 Flower, b. 57 Farmington.
Packard Anna Marshall, b. 50 Gillett.
" Bessie K. stenog. at Popes, b. New Britain t.
" C. F. (Packards Pharmacy,) 12 N.B.
" Caleb L. h. 15 Suffield.
" Elmer C. (Packards Phar.) 12, h. 12 N.B.
" Pharmacy, 12 New Britain.
C. F. Packard.          Elmer C. Packard.
" Philomela, b. 36 Jefferson.
Packer Emily J. nurse, b. 22 Winthrop.
Paddock Geo. rubberw. at 690 Park, b. 30 Grace.
" Nellie M. stenog. at Conn. Building and Loan Association, 252 Asy. b. Meriden t.
Paddoli Joseph, carpenter, b.u. 21 Morgan.
Paganelle Vito, laborer, b. 7 Charles.
Page Bertrand A. clerk at Travelers Insurance Co. 56 Prospect. b. 219 High.
" Charles, laborer, h.u. 57 Mather.
" Frank M. driver at 2 American.
" Irving W. telegraph operator, h. 171 Capen.
" James, driver, b. 4 Huntley.
" Jeanette A. nurse, b. 223 Garden.
" Joseph, laborer, h. 4 Huntley.
" Mary, h. 6 Village.
" Mary E. wid. Jonathan B. b. 343 Main.
Page Mary Jane, wid. Geo. matron, 1205 Asylum
" Ralph E. clerk at 859 Main, b. 25 Evergreen.
" Wenona, stenographer at State capitol, rm. 54, b. 241 Main.
" Wm. W. painter, h. 15 Windsor.
" ☞ see also Paige.
Pagram Anna and Fidelia, Misses, h. 62 Webster.
" John, saloon, 68 Hicks, b. 62 Webster.
" Louisa, h. 62 Webster.
Paige Mary I. teacher at South school, 36 Wadsworth, b. 21 Capitol.
Paine ☞ see also Payne.
Painter Charles S. enam. at Popes, h. 285 Capitol.
" Robert F., Amr. Cycle Repair Co. h. E.H.t.
Pairman John R. foreman at 245 Windsor, h. Bellevue.
Paistick Peter, laborer, b.2u. 95 Sheldon.
Palace Laundry, 4 Lewis, Mrs. M. Reinhardt, pr.
Palerma Nicolo, fruit peddler, h.2u. 81 North.
Palette Robert N. clerk, 554 Asy. b. 78 Spring.
Pallatza Domenico, laborer, b. 17 Morgan.
Pallette Augusta, wid. William, b. 22 Hopkins.
Pallotte Rocco, watchm. Taft Co. h.u. 35 Albany.
Palm Charles, inspector at 581 Cap. h. 43 N.B.
Palmberg, Justice, shoem. 18 Howard, h. 18 Law.

Palmer Carrie E. Mrs. h. 28 Chestnut.
" Clarence L. market, etc. 115, h. 113 Pearl.
" Edgar M. meats, etc. 130 Alb. h.u. 411 Garden.
" Edith M. bkkpr. 130 Albany, b. 411 Garden.
" Edmond G. janitor at 17 Haynes, rm. 122.
" Edward, pressman at 690 Park, h. 10 Rose.
" Edward C. clerk at 115, b. 113 Pearl.
" Edward O. clerk at 130 Alb. b. 411 Garden.
" Emily, nurse, 70, h. 70 Wooster.
" F. L. at Travelers Ins. Co. 56 Prospect, b. Rocky Hill t.
" Frances C. wid. W. H. h. 1054 Asylum.
" Frank L. clerk at 853 Main. b. 96 Ann.
" H. W. & Co. carmen, 250 State.
Sidney W. Andrews.       William Huntington.
" Harry H. telegraph editor at Hartford Post, 23 Asylum, h. 24 Bluehills.
" Harry W. dynamo man at 266 Pearl, b. 849 Windsor av.
" Henry, agt. at 231 State, h. 849 Windsor av.
" John C. discount clerk at State Bank, 795 Main, h. 59 Church.
" John Erving, policeman, h.u. 25 Bellevue.
" Josiah C. at Travelers Ins. Co. 56 Prospect, h. Rocky Hill t.
" Laura, at 247 Pearl, b.u. 80 Seymour.
" Mary A. b. 1130 Windsor av.
" Nellie, clerk at 956 Main, b. 58 Church.
" Nicholas L. potter. h. 98 Madison av.
" Rae C. clerk at 782 Main, b.2u. 29 West.
" S. B. Mrs. b. 389 Main.
" William J. ship. clerk at Popes, h. 78 High.
Palmes Mary E. h. 46 Park.
Palmisano Frank, fruitpeddler, h. 93 Windsor.
Palotta Matia, laborer, b. 73 Morgan.
" Peter, laborer, b.3u. 5 Charles.
" Peter, laborer, b.r. 73 Morgan.
" Rocco, laborer, h. 158 Front.
" Tony, bootblack, h.2u. 68 Pleasant.
Paltilowitz Isa, laborer, b. 144 Front.
" Moriss Rev. h. 144 Front.
Palutze John, bootblack, b.4u. 190 Front.
Pannone Antonio, bartdr. 190 Front, b.u. 86 Mor.
" Pietro, saloon, 190 Front, h.u. 86 Morgan.
Pansullo Alfonso, shoemaker at 139 Trumbull, h. 33 Albany.
Panter George, tinner at 1072, h. 456 Main.
Pantolfe Domenico, laborer, b.2u. 79 Morgan.
Pape Frank, laborer, b.u. 64 Morgan.
Papillion Elzear, mach at 1 Flow. h.2u. 32 Law.
" Frank, teamster at 25 Front, h. Madison.
" George, painter, b.2u. 32 Lawrence.
Papp Andrew, cabinetm. b.2u.r. 34 So. Prospect.
Paquett Alfred, carpenter, h. 137 Babcock.
Paquette Melvina, wid. Frank, boardgh. 192 State.
Parchall Joseph F. screwmaker at 476 Capitol, h. 35 South Prospect.
Pardee Martha, b. 95 Bellevue.
" Sarah N. & Cora W. Misses, h. 62 Capitol.
" William, at Popes, b. 145 High.
Pardi Francisco, laborer, h.3u. 2 Charles.
Parent Emily, operator at 247 Pearl, b.u. 47 Laf.
Parenti John, laborer, b.u. 11 Charles.
" Michael, laborer, h.u. 73 Morgan.
Parigo Joseph, barber, 1019 Mn. h. 30 Kilbourn.

Parish Ella A. teacher South sch. b. 123 Hung.
" George T. artist, h. 47 Laurel.
" Roswell, Jr. clerk at 389 Allyn, l.53 Tru.
" Wm. lineman, 266 Pearl, h. 488 Main.
" ☞ see also Parrish.
Park Bros. & Co. steel and copper, 13 Central,
George E. Leffingwell, manager.
" Central Stables, W. Tewksbury, r. 87 High.
" Commissioners' office, 800 Main.
" Knitting Works, C. C. Plaisted & Co. 336
Asylum.
" View Hotel, Heins Brothers, 430 Asylum.
" View House, 3 Lewis.
" ☞ see also Parkes; Parks.
Parker Almon G. messenger P.O. b.116 Franklin.
" Anna, wid. Stephen, b. 36 Jefferson.
" Annie A. clerk at Brown, Thomson & Co.
942 Main, b. 45 Farmington.
" Arthur V. foreman Keney park, b. 12 Blu.
" Benjamin, bookkeeper, 302 Asylum.
" Benton N. stenographer, b. 279 Capitol.
" Charles, driver for city, h. 2 George.
" Charles A. mach. at 1 Flow. h. 88 Franklin.
" Charles E. with Kimball & McCray, insur-
ance agency, 658 Main, h. 14 Whitney.
" Charles F. toolmaker, h. 40 Hudson.
" Cyrus C. joiner at 690, h. 952 Park.
" Edward D. mech. at 437 Mn. h. 40 Hudson.
" Edwin A. steamfitter, h.r. 8 Village.
" Edwin D. upholsterer at 921, b.1244 Main.
" Edwin P. Rev. pastor South Congregational
church, h. 47 Buckingham.
" Emerson M. barber at 706 Mn. h.u. 116 Fkn.
" Enoch, carpenter, h. 88 Franklin.
" Ernest L. drugclk. 1203 Main, h.111 Albany.
" Felton, patent clerk, Popes, b. 2 Columbia.

**PARKER FRANCIS H.** attorney at
law, 863 Main, rm. 3, h. 122 Wethersfield.
See page 493.
" Frank E. messenger at P.O. b.u.116 Franklin.
" Frank J. clerk at Conn. General Life Ins.
Co. 49 Pearl, b. 22 Pavilion.
" Frederick, foreman at Hartford Cycle Co.
h. 71 Laurel.
" Frederick D. h. 40 Hudson..
" Frederic J. polisher, 581 Cap, h.u. 4 Sisson.
" Genio S. carptr. 188 Asy. h.u. 22 Pavilion.
" George A. supt. Keney park, h. 12 Bluehills.
" George C. rubberwkr. 690 Park, h. 30 Grace.
" Geo. P. Jr. trav. salesman, b. 88 Church.
" Geo. W. mach. at 388 Capitol, b.38 Babcock.
" Harry S. clerk, 149 State, b. 98 Trumbull.
" Harry V. stamper at P.O. h.u. 12 Canton.
" Henry D. clerk, 66 Asy. h.2u. 36 Wooster.
" Howard W. electrician, b. 49 Spring.
" John D. 2d vice president Hartford Life
Insurance Co. 252 Asylum, h. 77 Seymour.
" John Dwight, asst. secretary Conn. Mutual
Life Ins. Co. 783 Main, h. 183 Sigourney.
" John M. collector, b. 8 Preston.
" John M. Jr. at Ætna Life Ins. Co. 650 Main,
h. 8 Preston.
" Kate, wid. James H. h. 141 Maple.
" Leon M. mach. 388 Capitol, h. 38 Babcock.

Parker Leon W. bookkeeper at Pratt & Whit-
ney Co. 1 Flower, h. 12 Imlay.
" Lewis D. treasurer & manager Hartford
Rubber Works, 690 Park, h. 633 Pro. av.
" Lillie L. stenographer, E. B. Dillingham, b.
238 New Park.
" Lucius R. clerk Hartford Life Ins. Co. 252
Asylum, b. 314 Farmington.
" Lucy M. b. 88 Church.
" Lucy M. teacher at Brown school, b. 122
Wethersfield.
" Mary A. wid. James E. h. 315 Capitol.
" Matilda, wid. George, h. 88 Church.
" Merrill R. toolmaker, h.u. 40 Hudson.
" Percy, at 581 Capitol, h. 90 Heath.
" Philip, waiter at 296 Asylum.
" Richard L. mach. at Colts, h. 40 Hudson.
PARKER RIENZA B. president Hartford Life
Ins. Co. 252 Asy. h. 314 Farmington.
See page 454.
" Robert P. traveling salesman, 690 Park,
b. 47 Buckingham.
" Samuel K. foreman 581 Cap. h.238 N.Park.
" Sarah, wid. John H. h. 50 John.

**PARKER THOMAS M.** stencils, etc.
71 Asylum, rm. 27, h. 51 Dean.
See page 534.
" Tillie, wid. George, h. 88 Church.
" Wm. C. inspector at Popes, h.u. 45 Hung.
" Wm. D. special agent Conn. Bureau of
Labor Statistics, rm. 48, h. Meriden t.
" William H. h.u. 49 Spring.
" Wm. H. bkkpr. 206 State, h.12 Buckingham.
" Wm. H. toolmaker at 556, h. 279 Capitol.
" William J. foreman, Case, Lockwood &
Brainard Co. 141 Pearl, h. 44 Ward.
" William K. collector, h. 49 Spring.
Parkes Alfred, painter, 185 Asy. h. 19 Bond.
" Alfred, Jr. mach. at 1 Flower, b. 19 Bond.
" Eliza A. H. dressmaker, b. 19 Bond.
" ☞ see also Park; Parks.
Parkhurst A. Mabel, teacher at Arsenal school,
b. 109 Oak.
" Albert, painter, 10 Ford, h. 109 Oak.
" Charles G. insurance clerk, b.u. 60 Wooster.
" Edward G. mechanical engir. h. 50 Sumner.
" Eva E. operator at Popes, b. 109 Oak.
" Guilford F. watchman, h. 60 Wooster.
" Harry E. clerk 154 Pearl, b. 128 Park.
" J. Etta, clerk, b.u. 60 Wooster.
" Louis E. city editor Hartford Daily Times,
716 Main, h. 128 Park.
" Lucy A. clerk, b.u. 60 Wooster.
Parkman Jas. A. barber at 77 Tru. b.u.1145 Main.
Parks Harrison W. b. 709 Main, rm. b.
" Robert C. com. traveler, h. 44 Retreat.
" Wm. T. manager 57 Albany, h.u. 189 High.
Parkville Post Office, E. McFarland, postmaster,
761 Park.
Parlee Hoyt, carpenter, u. 22 Goodwin.
" Lizzie, at 956 Main, b. 58 Church.
" Murray, builder, h. 57 Elliott.
" Payson, iceman at 4 Central.
" William J. M. foreman, Popes, b. 145 High.

**You'll Get ALL THE NEWS, if you READ THE POST.**

Parmele George L. dentist, 65, h. 65 Pratt.
Parmelee Burton M. clerk, 97 Asy. h. 48 Hopkins.
" Charles C. mach. at Colts, h. 55 Franklin.
" Emily, wid. William, b. 68 Hungerford.
" Frederick W. salesman L. L. Ensworth & Son, iron and steel store, 104 Front, h. 59 Oak.
" Julia A. Mrs. at Hartford Life Ins. Co. 252 Asylum, b. 29 Elmer.
" Paul E. bkkpr. trust dept. Conn. Trust & Safe Deposit Co. 785 Mn. h. 218 Jefferson.
Parmlee Dwight B. bible reader, h.u. 67 Tremont.
Parnell Nora, dressmaker, b.u. 1328 Broad.
" ☞ see also Parquette.
Parrish Elisha E. b. 2 Holcomb.
" Herbert L. bookkeeper at 26 High, h. 17 Haynes, rm. 22.
" ☞ see also Parish.
Parry John, mach. hand at Colts, b. 54 Vanblock.
" Kate G. Mrs. b. 13 So. Hudson.
" Thomas, browner at Colts, h.r. 54 Vanblock.
Parshley Sadie, b. 1255 Main.
Parsons A. H. electrotyper at 177 Asy. h. 49 Vine.
" Advertising Agency, 71 Asylum, rm. 26.
" Albert R. clerk at Sec'y of State, rm. 36 State Capitol, h. 242 Sigourney.
" Arthur D. bkkpr. r. 334 Asy. b. 10 Wooster.
" Arthur T. woodworker at 158 Woodland, h.u. 18 Seyms.
" B. M. wid. John G. h. 146 Windsor av.
" Charlotte R. wid. William, b. 70 Clark.
" David N. Mrs. h. 10 Wooster.
" Edward W. office, 9 Central, h. 145 Capitol.
" Emery S. machinist at 1 Laurel, h. 109 Oak.
" Fitzroy B. cashier, 8 Central, l. 244 High.
" Francis, attorney at law, 877 Main, rm. 3, h. 960 Prospect av.
" George K. tinner at 164 State, b. 392 Fkn.
" Harriet E. stenographer at National Life Association, b. 981 Main.
" Herbert C. mgr. Parsons Theatre, 66 Pros.
" Hiram W. printer, 668 Main, b. 21 Florence.
" J. K. b. 244 High.
" John, gardener, b. Quaker lane, c. Far.
" John H. bottler at 84, b. 84 Vine.
" John W. mach. at Colts, h. 25 Pawtucket.
" Lyman J. postal clerk V.R.R. h. Saybrook t.
" Mary J. at Case, Lockwood & Brainard Co. 141 Pearl, b. 18 Trinity.
" May E. wid. Charles H. b. 370 Asy. rm. 28.
" Philip A. painter at 10 Ford, b. 17 Church.
" Rob't E. mach. at 1 Flower, h. 1204 Broad.
" Sam. T. molder, 690 Park, h.u. 11 Francis.
" Sarah L. wid. Lines, b.2u. 108 Albany.
" Theater, 66 Prospect.
" Tirzah M. h. 5 Avon.
" W. D. at Popes, b. 25 Capitol.
" Will S. (Ensworth & Parsons,) h. 177 Capen.
" William N. painter, b. 10 Wooster.
Paschuci Luigi, laborer, h.u. 210 Front.
Pasco F. L. at Travelers Ins. Co. 56 Prospect, b. 65 Annawan.
" Jane, wid. Henry A. h.2u. 12 Charter Oak.
" W. E. draughtsm. at 252, b. 223 Asy. rm. 30.
Pascoe Isabell, nurse at 20 So. Hudson.

Pasmateia Julia Mrs. h.2u. 12 North.
Pass Fred. clerk at Brown, Thomson & Co. 942, b.u. 1208 Main.
Patchet Edward W. electr. h. 223 Asylum, rm. 127.
" Robert, gardener, 103, h.r. 135 Woodland.
Paternost Antinio, h.r. 25 Windsor.
" Dominic, bootblack, h.r. 25 Windsor.
" Dominico, laborer, b. 11 Charles.
Pathe Dennis Mrs. h.u. 40 Commerce.
" Joseph, stonecutter, b.u. 40 Commerce.
Paton John, mason, h.u.r. 4 Pleasant ct.
" Lewis B. professor, Hartford Theological Seminary, 1507 Broad, h. 50 Forest.
" ☞ see also Patten, Patton.
Patrick Geo. at r. 98 Wells, h2u.r. 54 Temple.
" Geo. B. clerk at Nat. Home for Disabled Volunteer Soldiers, 783 Main, b. 55 Capitol.
" Julia S. b. 118 Main.
" William, carpenter, h.u. 159 Front.
Patricks Joseph, laborer, h.u. 6 Charles.
" Michael, ragpicker, b.3u. 6 Charles.
Patrizy Frank, laborer, b.u. 64 Morgan.
Patron Josie, b. 1096 Main.
Patronsky Dominic, porter at 74 Trumbull.
" Isaac, shoemaker, 34, b. 34 North.
Patten Ann Mrs. b. 2 Holcomb.
" Bessie, dressmaker, 206 Asylum, rm. 16.
" Harry R. head clerk order dept. at Popes, b.u. 36 Westland.

**PATTEN HENRY E.** dyer, carpet beating by superheated steam, 37 Wells, h. 39 Russ c. Oak.        *See page* 591.
" M. Celinda, at H. E. Patten's dyeworks, 37 Wells, h. 39 Russ.
" Solon L. h.u. 36 Westland.
" ☞ see also Paton; Patton.
Pattenden George, gardener, h. 967 Asylum.
Patterson Caldwell, h. 33 Washington.
" Charles, at Popes, b. 98 Babcock.
" Chas. blacksmith, h. 133 Commerce.
" Charles H. lab. at 98 Kil. b. 33 Washington.
" Edward R. sewer contract. h.2u. 11 Belden.
" Emma E. musician, b. 336 Wethersfield.
" Fannie, wid. Joseph, b. 133 Wethersfield.
" George, market, 1397 Mn. h.u. 90 Chestnut.
" Harry, laborer, b. 24 Vine.
" Lucy, wid. James C. b. 144 Capen.
" Martha A. teacher Arsenal sch. b. 33 Wash.
" Mary E. teacher at Wash. st. sch. b. 33 Wash.
" Mary I. teacher at South school, 36 Wadsworth, b. 55 Capitol.
" Olivia, wid. Daniel S. h. 90 Fairmount.
" Robert, b. 2 Holcomb.
" Robert, engir. at 5 Mechanic, h.2u. 283 Main.
" William J. bookkeeper, h. 50 Fairmount.
Pattie Veronica, wid. Joseph, h. 58 Front.
Pattison Alice V. stenog. at Factory Ins. Association, 95 Pearl, b. 1305 Main.
" E. C. Mrs. b. 3 Park ter.
" Emma, b. 334 Wethersfield.
" Harold Rev. pastor First Baptist church, h. 31 Winthrop.
" Jennie L. steno. at Popes, b. 3 Park ter.
" John C. printer, b. 61 Spring.

**To Rent Advertisements Bring Results in The Post.**

Pattison John C. head clerk bicycle department at Popes, h. 3 Park ter.
" Joseph, saloon, 1211, h. 1305 Main.
Patty Ira, painter, b.u. 8 Hawthorn.
Patulo Pasquale, laborer, b. 2 Charles.
Patz Bertha, clerk, b. 16 East.
" Bertha, wid. Ferd. h. 16 East.
" Hugo E. clerk at Henry Kohn & Sons, 890 Main, h.u. 18 Belden.
" Theodore G. clerk at 98 Kilbourn, b. 16 East.
Paubel Robert H. bkkpr. at 867 Mn. h. Meriden t.
Paul Desdemona, laundress, h.2u.r. 25 Wolcott.
Pauli Frederick, screwm. 476 Cap. h. 13 Hamilton.
Paulinni Pasquale, laborer, h.u. 190 Front.
**PAULISCH FRANK G.** bandmaster Popes Band, h. 391 Allyn, rm. 11.
Paulsen Adolph, saddler at 8 Sig. b. Elmwood v.
Pausch Albert, bookkeeper at Connecticut Fire Insurance Co. 51 Prospect, h. 51 Ashley.
" Annetta, wid. Henry, h.u. 69 Sargeant.
" Clara A. teacher at 249 High, b. 69 Sargeant.
" Emily F. teach. Arsenal sch. b. 69 Sargeant.
Payeure Joseph, lineman, h. 18 Trumbull.
Paynadge Frank, lab. 53 Vernon, b.u. 82 Potter.
Payne Abbie E. wid. William, b. 33 Sargeant.
" Dudley J. conductor P.&R. h. Winsted t.
PAYNE EDWARD S. (*Potter & Payne,*) provisions, etc. 405 Allyn, h. Windsor t. *See p. 586.*
" Frank B. asst. paymaster U.S. navy, b. 27 Girard.
" Frank W. stenogr. at Ætna Life Ins. Co. 650 Main, h. 9 Sargeant.
" Fred F. *messenger board of councilmen,* toolmaker at 476 Capitol, h. 36 Seymour.
" Fred. W. at Travelers Ins. Co. 56 Prospect, h. 40 Huntington.
" Henry G. clerk at 1124 Main, b. 15 Good.
" Stella M. at Hartford Life Ins. Co. 252 Asylum, b.u. 52 Wadsworth.
" ☞*see also Paine.*
Payson H. N. ins. agent, h. 30 Hopkins.
" W. H. capt. barge Josie Williams, 285 State, h. Middletown t.
Payton F. P. restaur. 330 Pearl. h.u. 198 Bellevue.
Payung Charles, mach. N.Y.R. h. 16 Hawthorn.
Peabody Eva R. attendant, 30 Washington.
Peak Daniel, painter, 192, h. 192 Vernon.
" ☞*see also Peek.*
Pearce Isaiah, rubberworker, h. 9 Olive.
" Walter, clerk Adjutant General's office, rm. 19, State capitol, h. 14 Trinity.
" ☞*see also Pierce.*
Peard James J. asst. superintendent at Colts Pat. Fire Arms Mfg. Co. h. 23 Allen pl.
" Richard L. inv. clerk at Colts, b. 23 Allen pl.
Peardon A. salesman at 835, b. 999 Main.
Pearl Arthur, teacher of writing, 24, b. 24 Julius.
" Charles E. clerk at 653 Main, h. 57 Brook.
" Harris, shoemaker, 30 Mul. h.u. 40 North.
" Morris, at Popes, h.u. 28 Flower.
" Samuel, blacksmith, h.u. 431 Windsor av.
" Samuel, laborer, 252 Pearl, h. 431 Main.
" Samuel T. minister at Catholic Apostolic church, b. 41 Sumner.

All Nerve and Chronic Diseases are treated, with wonderful results.

OFFICE HOURS 12 to 1, and after 6 P. M. **H. A. PEASE,** Consultation Free

*MAGNETIC PRACTITIONER.*
Dealer in the Great Liver and Kidney Cure.
Best of References furnished if desired. **58 Wooster St.**

Pearl Simon, at 273 Asylum, b. 28 Flower.
" William M. minister at Catholic Apostolic Church, h. 41 Sumner.
" ☞*see also Purl.*
Pearman John, brewer, h. 47 Bellevue.
Pearsall Henry, filer at 581 Cap. h. 45 Hamilton.
Pearson August, baker, 34, h. 34 Spring.
" Austin, mechanic at Popes, h. 64 Putnam.
" Burdette, inspector, 581 Cap. b. 64 Putnam.
" Charles, dropforger at 142 Russ, h. 14 N.B.
" Chas. A. salesman 302 Asy. h u. 30 Madison.
" Charles F. gardener and coachm. 1205 Asy.
" Edward J. b. 81 Buckingham.
" Edward J. bkkpr. at 15 Tru. h. 81 Bkm.
" George H. bookkeeper, b.u. 172 Sheldon.
" Geo. W. violinist, 25, h.u. 25 Bellevue.
" Henry, saloon, 170, h.u. 172 Sheldon.
" Jeannette wid. Lucien T. h. 81 Buckingham.
" Louis, coachman at 700 Farmington.
" Olof J. gardener, b. Whiting lane.
" Thomas E. mechanic at Popes, h. 382 Park.
" William T. artist at Hartford Times, 716 Main, b. 119 Capitol.
" ☞*see also Pierson.*
Pease Albert A. mechanic at 164 State, h.u. 877 Windsor av.
" Alex, helper St.Ry. h. E.H.t.
PEASE ALFRED H. treas. Hart & Hegeman Mfg. Co. h. 17 Charter Oak pl. *See page 539.*
" Allison L. diamonds, 756 Main, h. 43 Wash.
" Amelia A. h.u. 4 Canton.
" Ansel, painter, h. 14 Governor.
" Augusta, wid. Zeno K. h. 427 Main, rm. 53.
" Austin H. clerk at 1 Flower, b. 4 Canton.
" Charles A. assistant bookkeeper at 31 Pratt, b. 4 Canton.
**PEASE CHARLES A. & CO.** flour, grain, etc. 462 and 1123 Main, 77 Charles.
Charles A. Pease. William O. Pease.
*See page 589.*
PEASE CHARLES A. (*C. A. Pease & Co.*) flour, grain, and feed, 462 Main, h. 369 Laurel.
" Chas. E. clerk, 1 So. Ann, h. 47 Oak.
" Charles H. conductor St.Ry. h. 2 Winthrop.
" Chas. L. agt. 904 Mn. rm. 30 b. 27 Spring.
" Clara A. teacher at High sch. b. 1492 Broad.
" Clifford A. clerk, 391 Aly. b. Windsor Locks t.
" Edward T. clerk at T. Sisson & Co. 729 Main, b. No. Bloomfield t.
" Edward S. machinist 30 Cushman, h.E.H.t.
" Frank J. salesman at 242 State. h. Enfield t.
" Fred E. clerk at 369 Cap. h.2u. 1461 Broad.
Pease Fred L. clerk at 885 Main, b.u. 21 Walnut.
" Harriet E. teacher Brown school, 160 Market, b. 33 Wooster.

**The Up to Date Merchant ADVERTISES in The Post.**

PEASE HENRY A. magnetic practitioner, 33, h. 33 Wooster.        See page 287.
" Henry H. discount clerk, Hartford Trust Co. 764 Main, b. 4 Canton.
" Ida L. clerk at Brown, Thomson & Co. 942 Main, b. 24 Hopkins.
" J. Austin, h. 4 Canton.
" James R. engineer, h.u. 703 Main, rm. 10.
" John W. clerk at 711 Main, b. E.H.t.
" L. & Co. stationers and printers, 13 Haynes.*
" Lewis, (L. Pease & Co) h.u. 13 Hungerford.
" Mary C. wid. Chas. W. h. Brook, c. Alb.
" Mary J. Mrs. h.u. 373 Asylum, rm. 34.
" Myron A. janitor Arsenal sch. b. 33 Wooster.
" Orrin L. clerk at 1203 Main, h. 153 Albany.
" Robert R. supt. Hfd. Woven Wire Mattress Co. 618 Capitol, h. 183 Hawthorn.
" Sewall L. rubberw. 690 Park, b. 10 Grand.
PEASE WILLIAM C. (C. A. P. & Co.) flour, grain, and feed, 462, 1123 Main, h. 38 Charter Oak pl.
" Wm. H. (Warner Photo Co.) b. 19 Canton.
" Wm. H. woodw. 618 Cap. b. 183 Hawthorn.
" Willis L. clerk Conn. General Life Ins. Co. 49 Pearl, b. Windsor Locks t.
Pebbles Elizabeth, wid. Franklin, h. 8 Wash.
" Harriet A. wid. Aden, h. 8 Russell.
" Mary Mrs. h. 7 Goodwin.
" ☞ see also Pibbles.
Pecan Henry, clerk at 342 Asylum, l. 28 Spring.
Peck Alfred H. at National Fire Ins. Co. 95 Pearl, b. 45 Farmington.
" Alice C. wid. Charles H. h. 20 Barbour.
" Arthur B. stenog. at Popes, b. 80 Hopkins.
PECK AUSTIN L. (Andrews & P.) sash, doors, etc. 88 Market, h. 99 Ann.    See p. 509.
" Austin L., Lumber Co. 88 Market.
" Carlos C. student Trinity college, 28 Jarvis hall, Summit.
" Charles C. teamster 67 Front, h.u. 4 Ch.O.
" Charles E. with R. S. Peck & Co. 28 High, b. 43 Ashley.
" Charles R. carpenter, h. 273 Jefferson.
" Cornelia C. h. 214 Main.
" Edward A. importer of glass, 88 Market, h. Saybrook t.
" Edward B. ass't sec'y Conn. General Life Insurance Co. 49 Pearl, h. 100 Capitol.
" Ellen H. wid. George K. h. 52 Wadsworth.
" Frank, clerk, b. 80 State.
" Frederick M. sec. and treas. Heublein Hotel Co. h. 100 Capitol.
" G. Herbert, policeman, h.2u. 926 Mn. rm. 27.
PECK HARRY H. lumber dealer, r. 32 Church, h. 264 Franklin.    See page 509.
" Ira C. clerk at Smith, Northam & Co. flour and feed, 129 State, h.u. 21 Evergreen.
" Lois S. nurse, b. 94 Church.
" Mary A. wid. Adw. dressm. h.u. 1 Goodman.
" N. Alice, bookkeeper, b. 283 Capitol.
" Nathan F. h. 31 Niles.
PECK R. S. & CO. job printers & wood engravers, 26–28 High.    See page 473.
" Rial S. (R. S. Peck & Co.) h. 43 Ashley.

Peck Richard E. student Trinity college, 28 Jarvis hall, Summit.
" Robert L. draughtsm. 1 Flow. h. 34 Hopkins.
" Samuel W. carpenter at W. H. Scoville, h.u. 2 Squire.
" Stephen B. driver, Lu. 489 Main.
" Theodore, glazier at 88 Market, b. 99 Ann.
" Walter K. commer. trav. h. 32 Huntington.
" Wilbur N. machinist, h. 124 Hungerford.
" Wm. W. diesinker, 142 Russ, h. 124 Hung.
Peckham A. B. Mrs. h. 28 Huntington.
" Bros. meats, 8 Ford and 331 Capitol.
        Frank B. Peckham.        George H. Peckham.
" Charles H. agent at 715 Main, h. 27 N.B.
" Frank B. (P. Bros.) h. 64 Williams.
" George H. (P. Bros.) h. 249 Lawrence.
" Joseph R. stenographer, b. 200 Allyn.
" Mary J. Mrs. dressmaker, h. 64 Williams.
" Mattie E. wid. Henry W. h. 200 Allyn.
Pedlow Mary, operator at Hartford Post, 23 Asylum, b. 392 Wethersfield.
Peebles Mary, wid. John, h. 18 Ely.
" Wm. J. clerk at 109 Asylum, h. 18 Ely.
" ☞ see also Peoples.
Peek DeWitt J. ins. broker, h.u. 280 Sigourney.
Peel Frank, toolsharpener, l. 157 Lawrence.
Peeples Eldredge, driver 15 Tru. h.2u. 1194 Main.
" James D. tinsmith, h.3u. 753 Main.
" ☞ see also Peoples.
Peer Bernard P. mach. 388 Cap. h. 2 Atlantic.
" Frank B. mach. at 388 Cap. b. 2 Atlantic.
" Howard J. caster, b. 2 Atlantic.
" L. B. mach. at 388 Cap. h.2u. 88 Madison.
**PEERLESS OVEN CO.** 44 Ann, Michael Cullen, mgr.    See page 506.
Peet Charles G. ins. agt. 811 Main, h.4u. 426 Asy.
Peglau Rudolph, brazier at Popes, b. Weth.t.
Pegram Edward S. secretary Ætna Indemnity Co. 650 Main.
Pehl Edmond, foreman at 315 Park, h. 52 Law.
" Herman, tailor, h.u. 42½ Windsor.
Pehrson Louis, coachman 700, b. 700 Farmington.
Peiler Ernst, musicteacher, 721 Mn. h. 14 Suffield.
" Max H. at Ætna Life Insurance Co. 650 Main, h. 36 Allen pl.
Pelatt Dominic, laborer 618 Cap. h. 67 Morgan.
Pell Maurice, mechanic at Popes, h. 28 Flower.
Pellett Alonzo D. builder, 190, h. 190 Smith.
" Henry G. clerk, b. 190 Smith.
" Louis E. clerk, b. 190 Smith.
" Milton F. carpenter, 190, b. 190 Smith.
Pelloso Joseph, laborer, b.3u. 51 Morgan.
Pelnso Vengenzo, bootblack, h. 11 Charles.
Pelos Frank, laborer, h. 29 Mechanic.
Pelrin Louis, burnisher at 62 Market, b. Meriden t.
" Romeo, burnisher at 62 Market, b. Meriden t.
Peltier Andrew, carpenter, h.2u. 49 Green.
" Andrew, Jr. carpenter, b.2u. 49 Green.

FRANK H. PELTIER, Physician.    Office, 926 Main street, room 15, Cheney building.
        Hours—11 A.M. to 1 P.M.
                7 to 8 P.M.
                Telephone 507-2.

Peltier Frank H. physician, 926 Mn. h. 187 High.

**THINKING PEOPLE Read The Post Daily.**

Peltier Mrs. b. 981 Main.
" Omer, carpenter, b.u. 17 Chestnut.

PIERRE D. PELTIER, Physician, Office, 926 Main,
    street, Cheney building.
    Hours.—8.30 to 10 A. M.
        3 to 5 and 7 to 8 P. M.
    Thursdays—8.30 to 10 A. M. only.
    Sundays—5 to 7 P. M. only.
    Office Telephone, 507-2. Residence Telephone, 535.

Peltier Pierre D. physician, 3u. 926 Mn. h. 187 High.
" Richard F. carpenter, b.2u. 49 Green.
Pelton Charles H. molder, h. 56 New Park.
" Charles H. rubberw. 690 Park, h. N.P.
" Charles M. machinist, 1 Flower, h. E.H.t.
" Charles N. baker, 41, h. 41 Laurel.
" George, teamster at Frank J. Knox, 2
    South Ann, b. 884 Main.
" L. C. (Bunce & P.) b. Windsor t.
" Rena, at 252 Pearl, b. 100 Seymour
" William H. at Hartford Fire I.'s  Insurance Co.
    53 Trumbull, b. 792 Asylum.
" William N. h. 792 Asylum.
Pember A. Mrs. clerk at 908, b. 1210 Main.
" Chauncey H. (M. W. P. Sons,) b. 163 Sisson.
" E. M. wid. Joseph S. h. 650 Main, rm. 45.
" Edward E. (M. W. P. Sons,) h. 221 Collins.
" Elisha H. trav. salesman, 78 Asy. b. 8 Bkm.
" Herbert, b. 650 Main.
" M. W. Sons, woolens, 292 Asylum.
    C. H. Pember.          E. E. Pember.
" Milo W. salesman, 292 Asylum, h. 163 Sisson.
" Nathaniel B. clerk at 197 Asy. b. 650 Main.
Pendergast Barney, mason, b. 999 Main.
" Dennis, expressman, 20, h. 20 Cedar.
" Mary C. at 904 Main, b. 108 Walnut.
" Matthew J. machinist, b. 108 Walnut.
" Michael, laborer, h. 108 Walnut.
" Thomas, carptr. at 141 Tru. b. 108 Walnut.
" Thomas J. toolmaker, 581, b.u. 371 Capitol.
" William J. machinist, h. 6 Walnut.
" ☞ see also Prendergast.
Penders Agnes A. clerk at Brown, Thomson &
    Co. 942 Main, b. 84 Francis.
" Bernard, mason, b. 999 Main.
" Charles J. b.u. 82 Francis.
" Edw. F. iceman, 4 Central, h.2u. 31 Mechanic.
" James, mason, b.u. 82 Francis.
" Lawrence, driller at Colts, b. 70 Walnut.
" Mary A. at 270 Main, b.u. 82 Francis.
Penderville Michael, h. 8 Chestnut
" Timothy C. mach. at Colts, h.2u. 5 Squire.
Pendleton Henry, laborer h. 19 South Prospect.
" Sophronia, wid. Rodney, h. 31 Wooster.
Penet George H. broommaker, 336, b. 336 Weth.
Penfield Chas. M. clerk at 142 Russ, b. 127 Oak.
" Elmore, traveling salesman, h. 107 Ashley.
" Emma, wid. Chas. b. 30 Sumner.
" George R. clerk at Popes, b. 103 Huntington.
" George S. at Travelers Insurance Co. 56
    Prospect, h.u. 103 Huntington.
" Harry, machinist, b. 189 Zion.
" Harry, Jr. mach. at 1 Flower, b. 263 High.
" Henry E. Sr. mach. at 1 Flower, b. 263 High.
" Henry N. motorman St.Ry. h. 127 Oak.
" Mae, wid. Frank A. b. 189 Zion.

## JOHN PEPION & CO.,

## House and Sign Painters,

## and Decorators.   ∴   ∴

Wholesale and Retail Dealers in

**Paints, Oil, Glass, Varnishes, Brushes,
Wall Papers, etc.**

A Full Line of Painters' Materials.

## 25 CHURCH ST.

Penfield Raymond W. stairbuilder, 24 Potter, h.
    124 Huntington.
" Schuyler, tinner at P.&R. h.u. 11 Sargeant.
" Wm. A. boilerm. at N.Y.R. h.u. 11 Sargeant.
" William H. mach. at 133 Shel. b. 458 Main.
" William T. (Kibbe & P.) h.r. 36 Temple.
Penn Julian M. cigarm. at 104 Asy. b. 999 Main·
" Newton L. b. 29 Allen pl.
Penn. railr'd fr'ght office, C. M. Henney, 18 State.
Pennock James S. watchman at 252 Pearl, b.
    228 Garden.
Pearce Morris, with Hartford Rubber Works Co.
    690 Park, b. 31 Girard.
" William, special agent at Ætna Life Ins.
    Co. 654 Main, h. 14 Girard.
" William R. clerk at 700 Main, b. 14 Girard.
Penskie Louis, beltm. at 15 Tru. b. 80 Pleasant.
Peoples Alex. F. (Peoples Ex. Co.) b. 11 Queen.
" Credit Clothing Co., B. Z. Brewer, 933 Main.
" Eldridge F. teamster at 15 Trumbull, h.2u.
    h.2u. 1194 Main.
**PEOPLES EXPRESS CO.** 42 Union
    pl.                    See page 559.
    Alex. F. Peoples. John J. Peoples. Thos. Peoples.
" James D. tinsmith, h.3u. 275 Main.
" John J. (Peoples Express Co.) b. 11 Queen.
" Thomas, (Peoples Express Co.) b. 11 Queen.
" William F. blacksmith, h. 11 Queen.
" ☞ see also Peeples.
Pepion Andrew M. painter at John Pepion &
    Co. 25 Church, l. 284 Asylum, rm. 8.
" Andrew S. helper, b. 123 Bellevue.
" Chas. plumber, 120 Market, b. 123 Bellevue.
" Frank, painter, h. 123 Bellevue.
" John, (J. P. & Co.) h.u. 25 Church.
" John Jr. bookkeeper, b.u. 25 Church.
PEPION JOHN & Co. painters and decorators,
    25 Church.*              See page 289.
" Nettie, bookkeeper at John Pepion & Co.
    25, b.u. 25 Church.
Pepper Bennett H. messenger police court, b.
    51 Woodbridge.
" Harriet A. wid. G. C. b. 97 Babcock.
" Patrick, blacksm. at N.Y.R. b.177 Lawrence.
Pera Lewis, barber, b.3u. 21 Morgan.
Percy Charles D. coachman, h.u. 53 Lafayette.
" Clarence L. janitor at 704 Main, h. 53 Laf.

**THE POST is a 20th-Century Newspaper**

Pere Joseph, tailor at 892 Main, h. 41 Village.
Perelman Jos. S. machinist, 1 Flow. b. 9 Putnam.
Perham Melvin A. shoemaker, 65, h. 65 Albany.
Perine Frederic G. journalist, h. 118 Huntington.
" ☞see also Perrin.
Perkins Albert G. barber, 22 State, h. 288 Franklin.
" Alice, laundry, 489, h. 489 Main.
PERKINS ARTHUR, (Perkins & Perkins,) attorney at law, 14 State, h. 95 Niles.
" Bessie J. wid. Eleazer J. h.u 33 Babcock.
PERKINS CHARLES E. (Perkins & Perkins,) attorney at law, 14 State, h. 49 Woodland.
" Chas. G. president Perkins Electric Switch Mfg. Co. 83 Woodbine, h. 12 Girard.
" Charles N. saddler at 8 Sig. h. 22 Sanford.
" Clara J. stenographer at Popes, b. 31 Ashley.
PERKINS DANIEL C. (Downing & P.) carmen, 128 Commerce, b. 1150 Main. See p. 552.
" Edward Carter, student, b. 55 Forest.

## PERKINS ELECTRIC SWITCH MFG. CO. 83 Woodbine. See p. 536.

" Eli H. blacksmith at N.Y.R. l. 31 Trumbull.
" Elisha L. blacksmith, h.r. 23 Mather.
" Elliot J. clerk at 66 State, h. 14 Mahl.
" Eugene, engineer at 133 Shel. b. 590 Main.
" Frederic W. Rev. pastor Church of the Redeemer, h. 34 Collins.
" George S. carpenter at shipyard, h. Weth.t.
" Gertrude S. wid. Rev. Fred'k J. b. 91 Ann.
" Gustavus S. engineer at Conn. Mutual Life Ins. Co. 783 Main, h. 19 Lewis.
" Henry A. student, b. 55 Forest.
" James A. (J. A. Perkins & Co.) 863 Main, h. Wethersfield t.
PERKINS JAMES A. & Co. plate printing & engraving, 863 Main. See page 290.
James A. Perkins. Jared B. Standish.
" James H. coachm. at 73 Wash. h. 81 Allen pl.
" Lillian, stenog. at Popes, b. 109 Elm.
" Lyman B. gen. agt. Hfd. Steam Boiler Insp. & Ins. Co. 650 Main, h. 13 Girard.
" Mabel H. h. 43 Prospect.
" Martin, architect & builder, 887, h.u.887 Park.
" Mary, wid. Thomas, b. 49 Woodland.
" Mary D. wid. Edward H. h. 55 Forest.
" Mary R. wid. George, h. 43 Prospect.
" Myron W. printer at Hfd. Daily Times, 716 Main, h. 62 Edwards.
" Nelson S. trimmer, b. 581 Main.
PERKINS & PERKINS, attorneys, 14 State.
Charles E. Perkins. Arthur Perkins.
" Thomas C. b. 49 Woodland.

Perkins Timothy A. conductor, h. 31 Trumbull.
" Wm. H. inspec. at Hfd. Steam Boiler Insp. & Ins. Co. 650 Main, h. 18 Mahl.
Perl Morris, machinist, h. 30 Pleasant.
Perline Mary, boardinghouse, 68 Front.
Perlitz Henry, musician, h.u. 150 Front.
" Madalene, midwife, h.u. 150 Front.
" William H. musician, h.u. 18½ Church.
Perlmutter Jacob, woodturner, h. 271 Market.
Peronne Anthony (J. Cersosino & Co. ) h. 210 Front.
Perrault Louis N. dyeworks, 36, h.u. 36 Pratt.
Perricolo Ralph, barber, h.3u. 30 Kilbourn.
Perrin Holbrook Foote, organist and pianist, h.u. 125 Huntington.
" Morris L. conductor N.E.R. b.u. 46 Hopkins.
" Philena Foote, wid. H. M. music teacher, h.u. 125 Huntington.
" ☞see also Perine.
Perrine Harvey L. conductor St.Ry. h. 258 Weth.
Perrozzo Michael Angelo, laborer, h.3u. 25 North.
Perry Abbie J. wid. M. L. h. 27 Lewis.
" Alfred T. Rev. librarian, 1507 Broad, h. 731 Asylum.
" Charles D. b. 90 Chestnut.
" Charles D. molder at 1 Flow. b. 77 Woodbine.
" Charles O. plater at 66 Market, h. E.H.t.
" Chas. W. ship. clerk 62 Mar. b. Elmwood v.
" Cora E. clerk at Conn. Building & Loan Association, 252 Asylum, b. Manchester t.
" DeWitt C. h. 61 Russ.
" Edwin L. salesman, 1411 Main. b. Wilson sta.
" Ellen M. Mrs. clerk, b. 1029 Main.
" Ernest A. salesman, 921 Mn. h. 11 Florence.
" Esther C. principal West Middle school, 927 Asylum, h. 55 Beacon.
" Gilbert, saddler at 8 Sig. h. 31 Putnam.
" Jane E. wid. Emile, b. 615 Capitol.
" Jennie M. bkkpr. at 57 Alb. b. 69 Sargeant.
" John, b.u. 6½ Charter Oak.
" John H. inspector 142 Russ, h. 69 Sargeant.
" Julian E. moulder, h. 91 Laurel.
" Kate C. wid. Wilbert W. b. 122 Garden.
" Louis A. at 956 Main, b. 31 Putnam.
" M. M. b. 1150 Main.
" Mary A. music teacher, 61, h. 61 Russ.
" Mary E. wid. Vellette D. h. 34 Sumner.
" Milledge E. driver 71 Asy. h.u. 114 Hopkins.
" Peter A. carptr. & contcr. 159, h. 159 Russ.
" Rodolph Del. inspector at 476 Capitol, h. 118 Asylum.

Perry Wilbert L. at Ætna Insurance Co. 666 Main, b. 315 Pearl, rm. 408.
Person John, at 581 Capitol, h.u. 31 Wolcott.
Persons C. E. clerk 843 Main, l. 61 Spring.
Persse Theophilus B. h. 41 Capitol.
Perwo Geo. rubberw. 690 Park, h. 105 Babcock.
Peters A. M. Mrs. h. 284 Market.
" Charles H. ostler at 995 Main, h. 16 Gold.
" Courtney C. salesm. 334 Asy. b. 287 Collins.
" James, laborer at 581 Capitol, h. 16 Ellery.
" John, laborer at 618 Capitol, h. 9 Forest.
" Mary E. wid. John T. h. 287 Collins.
" Meinert C. janitor, h. 4 Morgan.
" Walter, laborer, b. 284 Market.
Petersen Andrew, driver at 315, h. 326 Park.
" Christian B. plum. at 128 State, h. Ingleside.
" Christopher, b.u.r. 386 Park.
" Frank L. carpenter at 158 Woodland.
" Gertrude, clerk at 16 Church, h. Ingleside.
" John, laborer, h.u.r. 386 Park.
" Katherine, nurse, b. 884 Main.
" Nels, laborer, 287, b. 285 Albany.
" Nicholas C. farmer & milkm. h. 125 Bluehills.
" Otto, apprentice at 690 Park, b. 147 Market.
" Peter, carpenter, b.u. 1204 Broad.
" Peter, laborer, 335 Sheldon, h. Bloomfield t.
" Peter C. at Popes, h. 441½ Temple.
" Peter L. carpenter, h.u. 49 Amity.
Peterson A. P. joiner, h.u. 176 Putnam.
" Albert, milkman, h.u. 36 Village.
" Albert, painter, b. 26 Wolcott.
" Alex. A. filer at Popes, h. 153 Lawrence.
" Alfred, mach. at 476 Cap. b. 181 Babcock.
" Alfred J. polisher at Popes, h. 121 Babcock.
" Alma, wid. Alfred, h.u. 147 Babcock.
" Alof, gardener, l. 34 Spring.
" Amanda, dressmaker, h. 37 Hungerford.
" Andrew, mach. at 24 Mech. h. 62 Sheldon.
" Andrew, mechanic, h.u. 533 Broad.
" August, polisher at Popes, h. Wethersfield t.
" Axel, packer at 40 Gov. b.u. 115 Lawrence.
" Benjamin, paperhanger, h. 153 Clark.
" Carl C. gardener, b. 55 Harrison.
" Carl P. mechanic at Popes, h. 44½ Temple.
" Carson, farmer at Watkinson farm school.
" Charles, florist, h. Whiting.
" Charles, farmer, 47, b. 47 Bluehills.
" Charles, helper at 69 Front, b. E.H.t.
" Charles, shipper at Popes, b. 98 Babcock.
" Chas. V. watchman at 690 Park, h. 7 Olive.
" Christie, laborer, h.u.r. 60 Temple.
" Clarence, U.S. Army, b.u. 34 Village.
" Elof, assembler at 556, h. 625 Capitol.
" Fritz T. driver at 868 Asy. b.u. 18 Trumbull.
" Gustavus, coachman, Pro. av. h. 36 Rowe.
" John, at 618 Capitol, h. 1 Forest.
" John, helper at N.Y.R. h. 615 Capitol.
" John, laborer, h.2u.r. 60 Temple.
" John, laborer at Popes, h. 16 Trumbull.
" John B. carptr. at N.Y.R. h. 20 Trumbull.
" John E. screwm. at 476 Cap. h.r. 66½ Laurel.
" John F. laborer at 26 Laurel, h. 93 Bluehills.
" John Mrs. h.2u. 613 Capitol.
" Joseph, shipg. clerk 149 State, b. 14 Warner.
" Martin, beltm. at 15 Tru. h.2u. 152 Mather.

Peterson Martin, coachm. 109, b. 109 Edwards
" Neils R. mach. at 1 Flower, h. 43 Ann.
" Paul C. gardener at 83 Woodland, h. 52 Harrison.
" Peter, gardnr. 83 Woodland, h.u. 56 Harrison.
" Peter, laborer, h.3u.r. 60 Temple.
" Philip, b.u.r. 41 Mather.
" Robert, coachman at, b. 576 Farmington.
" Rose, wid. John, h. 238 Zion.
" Samuel, blacksmith at N.Y.R. h. 46 Laurel.
" Swan, at 643 Main, h.u. 26 Wolcott.
" Thomas, helper at 54 Arch, h. 2 Kilbourn ct.
" Walter, driver at 21, b. 21 Capitol.
" Wilson, gardener, h. 224 Bellevue.
Petherbridge Emelyn, stenogr. at 650, b. 5 Main.
Petit Charles, stonemason, b.r. 44 Wells.
" Joseph, tailor, 863 Main, h. 56 Wooster.
Petrizo Antonio, laborer, h. 76 Charles.
" Tom, laborer, h. 22 Charles.
Petrizzo Giuseppo, laborer, h.2u. 6 Charles.
" Michael, ragpicker, h.u. 6 Charles.
Petroraeio Basello, laborer, b. 86 Morgan.
" Raphael, laborer, b.u. 86 Morgan.
Petrossi Louis, foreman, h.2u. 88 Front.
Petroy John, laborer, b.u. 67 Morgan.
" Raphael, laborer, b.u. 86 Morgan.
Petrozilo Fedello, laborer, h. 1 North.
Petschke Charles, at 30 Cush. b.u. 56 Hawthorn.
Pettee Charles L. W. chem. at Popes, h. 3 Far.
Pettibone Frank E. h. 220 High.
" William F. at Conn. Mutual Life Insurance Co. 783 Main, h. 492 Farmington.
Pettingill Fred A. Mrs. laundress, 34 Pratt.
Pettit John S. adjuster National Life Association, 53 Trumbull, b. 119 Capitol.
" Rosie, laundress at 34 Pratt, b. 9 Green.
Pettys George, engir. P.&R. h. 106 Hopkins.
" George Jr. clerk, 87 Asy. b. 106 Hopkins.
Peyton Agnes J. dressmaker, b. 51 Walnut.
" James, at Trav.Ins.Co. 50 Pro. b. 51 Walnut.
" Thomas, h.u. 51 Walnut.
Pfaff Moritz, h.u. 58 Temple.
Pfeiffer Andrew O. gilder, 752 Mn. h.u. 231 Capen.
" Bertha J. cashier at 909 Main, h. 231 Capen.
" George, German books, 31, h.u. 31 Mulberry.
" Jacob, b. 163 Front.
**PFEIFFER PAUL F.** editor Hartforder Herold, 31, b. 31 Mulberry.
See page 470.'
Pfeil John, tailor, 81 Asylum, h. 9 Center.
Pfund Annie K. music teacher, b. 943 Mn. rm. 32.
" Katherine, wid. T. G. h. 943 Main, rm. 32.
" Samuel T. assistant foreman at Hartford Post, 23 Asylum, h. 203 Ashley.
" Wm. A. printer, 60, tobacconist, 62, h. 62 Mor.
Pfunder Emil, mach. at 133 Shel. b. 45 Wooster.
Phair Philip D. instructor at Trinity college, 1 Jarvis hall, Summit.
Phalen Jennie, seamstress, b.2u. 84 Albany.
" Mary, dressmaker, h.2u. 84 Albany.
" Patrick, h.u. 36 Lawrence.
Phelan Alfred B. (Arnold & P.) h. 75 Chestnut.
" Lewis L. teamster, b. 11 John.
" William P. h. 95 Hudson.
Pheland Harry A. carpenter, h.u. 33 Chapel.

Phelon Annette, wid. Charles, h. 46 Hopkins.
Phelps A. C. Mrs. h.4u. 289 Asylum.
" Albert P. inspector at Pratt & Whitney Co. 1 Flower, h.u. 36 Hopkins.
" Antoinette R. h. 72 Washington.
" Arthur, b.u. 1245 Main.
" Charles, b. 2 Holcomb.
" Charles, secretary of State at State capitol, rm. 40, h. Rockville t.
" Chas. H. foreman, 155 Ch.O. h.u.168 Allyn.
" Charles H. miller at 40 Elm, b. 62 Walnut.
" Chas. R.dynamoman,266 Pearl,b.u.22 Hicks.

**PHELPS, DALTON & CO.** prop's Dickinson Type Foundry, Boston, Mass. *See page* 471.
" David L. h. 62 Walnut.
" Delia, bookkr. at 956 Main, b. 68 Wooster.
" Dexter S. salesman at Charles R. Hart Co. 898 Main, h. 552 Windsor av.
" Dwight H. measurer at Chas. R. Hart Co. 898 Main, h. 150 Allyn.
" Edward M. at 14 Hicks, h.u. 36 King.
" Edwin D. machinist, b.u. 26 Huntley pl.
" Emily R. wid. George B. h.u. 26 Huntley.
" Florence G. Mrs. h.u. 15 Imlay.
" Frank B. collector at C. C. Fuller & Co. 14 Ford, h. 62 Walnut.
" Fred A. dentist,911 Main,rm.1,h.21 Canton.
" Fred H.fgt. agent, P.&R. h. 223 Asy. rm. 77.
" Geo. H. toolm. 476 Cap. h. 810 Windsor av.
" George M. (*Clark & P.*) h. Bloomfield t.
" Grace H. wid. Walter G. teacher Arsenal school, h. 109 Wooster.
" Guy R. family of, 72 Washington.
" Henry E. clerk, h. 67 Williams.
" Henry M. mason, b. 48 Asylum.
PHELPS J. O. JR. *water commissioner*, treasurer Blodgett & Clapp Co. office 51 Market, h. 242 Windsor av.        *See page* 541.
" J. Wesson, clerk, b.u. 13 Belden.
" Jeffery O. president Blodgett & Clapp Co. 51 Market, h. Simsbury t.
" John W. at Travelers Ins. Co. 56 Prospect, h. 153 Windsor av.
" Lawrence, motorm. St.Ry. b. 48 Asylum.
" Mary J. wid. Elihu H. dressm.h.u.289 Allyn.
" Nancy M. wid. Erastus, h. 9 Walnut.
" Orville, b. 2 Holcomb.
" Oscar A.supt.Warburton chapel,h.u.232 Sig.
" Richard O. musicteacher, h. 18 Suffield.
" S. F. deckhand tug L. C. Ward, 285 State.
" Samuel, clerk at 149 State, b.u. 33 Brook.
" Samuel O. clerk at 1 So. Ann, h. 33 Brook.
" Walter G. bkkpr. at 462 Main, h. 105 Park.
" William C. clerk, h.u. 124 Capen.
Phenix Joseph N. bkkpr.at 47 Ann,h. 22 Brown.
Philadelphia, Reading & New England R. R. Co. station, 59 Spruce.

**PHILBRICK HALSEY B.** *select-man*, builder, 111, h. 111 Edwards. *See page* 519.
" Harry W. clerk at Sage, Allen & Co. 898 Main, b. 111 Edwards.

Philip James, helper at 135 Shel. h. 51 Front.
" Rocco, laborer, b. 67 Pleasant.
" Simon, laborer, h.3r. 34 South Prospect.
Philipo Lorenzo, laborer, b.3u. 41 North.
" Nicolo, laborer, b.3u. 41 North.
Phillips Albert C. clerk at 983 Mn. h. 32 Brook.
" Chas G. asst.ticket agt. N.Y.R.h.u. 2 Walnut.
" Daniel, h. 1 Farmington.
" E. May, b. 23 Columbia.
" Edward B. (*H.J. Case Co.*)h. 38 Windsor av.
" Elizabeth, wid. Charles, h.u. 8 Green.
" Ellen M. b. 128 Bellevue.
" Harry C. mach. at Colts, b. 43 Woodbridge.
" Henry J. porter at 1203 Main, b. 8 Green.
" Henry L. clerk at Factory Insurance Association, 95 Pearl, b. 57 Farmington.
" J. C. l. 315 Pearl, rm. 402.
" J. Henry, at Ætna Insurance Co. 666 Main, h. 27 Congress.
" James C. plumber at 11 Haynes, b. 251 Asy.
" James F. laborer, city works, h. 15 Squire.
" Jas. H. teamster at 78 Asy.h.u. 11 Goodman.
" James S. overseer at Hartford Cycle Co. 581 Capitol, h. 281 Ann.
" John M. inspector at 466 Asy. b. 42 Hopkins.
" Lizzie, wid. Charles, h. 8 Green.
" Patrick, b. 2 Holcomb.
" Patrick, laborer, b.2u. 47 Sheldon.
" Richard J. blacksm. at 1 Flow, h.u. 43 Grand.
" Samuel C. sawyer at 335 Shel. b. 9 East.
" Sidney, conductor, St.Ry. 115 State.
" Thos. H. asst. forem. at 69 Front, h. 17 Zion.
" Wm. messman str. Middletown, 285 State.
" William E. laundryman, h.2u. 1415 Main.
" Wm. H. pistolm. at Colts, h.r. 42 Vanblock.
" William J. clerk at 690 Park, h.Kensington v.
" Wm. S. saddler at 8 Sig. b. 284 Asylum.
Philomina Nisa, laborer, h. 31 Mechanic.
Phinney Glennie F. stenographer at 732 Main, b. 181 Maple.
" Lucinda R. wid. Emerson E. b. 181 Maple.
" Robert H. mach. at 1 Flow. b. 1163 Broad.
Phippeney Chas. W. gardnr. h.r. 321 Windsor av.
" Daniel, butcher, b.r. 321 Windsor av.
" Daniel, driver 1128 Mn. h.r. 321 Windsor av.
Phipps A. A. Mrs. h. 4 Brown.
" Bessie, b. 4 Brown.
" Edward D. general repairer, r. 1419 Main, h.u. 13 Fairmount.
" Henry E. at Travelers Insurance Co. 56 Prospect, h. 211 High.
" Solon P. bookkeeper at Pope Mfg. Co. h. 179 Hawthorn ex.
Phœnix Brass Foundry company, James Terry, manager, 223 State.
" Fred, inspector at Popes, h.u. 246 Putnam.

**PHOENIX INSURANCE COMPANY,** 64 Pearl. *See page* 460.
**PHOENIX IRON WORKS,** Lincoln Co. props. 54 to 70 Arch. *See page* 522.
" James W. machinist at Popes,b. 177 Bab.
**PHOENIX MUTUAL LIFE INSURANCE COMPANY,** 49 Pearl. *See pages* 452, 453.

**PHOENIX NATIONAL BANK,**
803 Main. *See page 435.*
" Walter, mechanic at Popes, music teacher, h. 177 Babcock.
Phyfe R. Eston, teacher High school, b. 625 Asy.
Pibbles John, prop. Union livery stables, 1061 Main, b. 99 Windsor av.
" ☞*see also Pebbles.*
Picard Charles L. machinist, b.u. 40 Canton.
" Chas. N. saddler at 8 Sig. h.u. 40 Canton.
" George H. pressman at 254 Pearl, h.2u. 51 Bellevue.
" Henry, mach. at 1 Flow. b.u. 50 Lawrence.
Piche Zenophite, at 476 Cap. h. 86 Prospect av.
Pickering James E. tilesetter at 164 State, b. Warrenton.

**PICKERING W. H. & CO.** machin- ists, 110 Commerce. *See page 537.*
" Wm. H. (*W. H. P.& Co.*) h. 83 Grove.
Pickett Robert M. screwm. at Popes, b.163 Front.
Piddock Charles A. Rev. supt. Baptist State Missions, h. 185 Sigourney.
" John E. W. b. 185 Sigourney.
Pidge Frank L. blacksmith at 40 Governor, h. 15 Woodbine.
Pidgeon Delia Mrs. housekeeper, h. 851 Park.
" Joseph, laundry, b. 851 Park.
Pierce A. E. Mrs. clairvnt. phys.1113,h. 1113 Mn.
" Albert H. forger at 142, h. 68 Russ.
" Austin D. druggist, 379, h. 387 Windsor av.
" Charles, stairbuilder h. 42 Ward.
" Clayton E. clerk at 51 Mar. h. 63 Franklin.
" E. T. Mrs. (*P. & Roulston.*) h. Burnside t.
" Edward H. clerk at Brown, Thomson & Co. 942 Main, b. 119 High.
" Edwin T. forger at 142 Russ, h. 71 Sergeant.
" Frank A. clerk, 142 Asylum, b.u. 68 Russ.
" Fred A. clerk at 372 Asylum, b.u. 869 Main.
" Gilbert E. machinist at 581 Capitol, h.u. 244 Wethersfield.
" Harry N. mech. at Popes, b. 63 Prospect.
" Herbert W. stenog. at Ætna Insurance Co. 666 Main, h. 51 Annawan.
" Isaiah, rubberwkr. at 690 Park, h. 9 Olive.
" Isabella Mrs. h. 92 Mather.
" Joseph B. sec'y and treas. Hartford Steam Boiler Insp. & Ins. Co. 650 Main, h. 23 Windsor av.
" Leslie D. plater, 476 Cap. h. 126 Huntington.
" Lucy B. teacher at Weth. b. 75 Sargeant
Pierce Mary F. Mrs. proprietor Pierce's steam laundry, 1130, h.u. 757 Main.
" Morris D. inspector at Factory Insurance Association, 95 Pearl, b. 4 Willard.
" Nancy M. wid. Albert T. b. 387 Windsor av.
" Nathan W. h. 63 Prospect.

**PIERCE NOBLE E.** (*Holcomb & P.*) attorneys at law, 68 Pratt, h. Bristol t.
*See page 487.*
Pierce & Roulston, milliners, 926 Main, rm. 11.
E. T. Pierce. M. K. Roulston.
" Roxanna, wid. Sam. washer, h. 18 Fairmount.

**PIERCE'S STEAM LAUNDRY,**
Mary F. Pierce, 1130 Main.

---

**PIERCE & ROULSTON,**
**MILLINERY,**
**Room 11, Cheney Building, 926 MAIN ST.**

Pierce Wm. H. wastepa.33 Ferry,h.18 Fairmount.
" William J. cashier at Hartford Steam Boiler Inspection & Ins. Co. 650, h. 278 Main.
" William J. clerk, h. Fairview.
" Wm. M. barber at 334 Pearl, h. 175 Windsor.
" William N. electrician, h. 151 Main.
" Willis A. constable, 756 Main, h. 9 Morgan.
" ☞*see also Pearce.*
Pierson Adolph, mason, b. 1153 Main.
" C. Wesley, agent, b. 3 Pleasant.
" Caleb W. collarmaker at 8 Sig. h. 795 Asy.
" Charles, at 216 Law. h.u. 40 New Britain.
" Charles W. bkkpr. at 28 Pratt, b.795 Asylum.
" D. Baldwin,clerk at 1 South Ann,h. 84 Brook.

**PIERSON FREDERICK A.** real estate and .business agent, 721 Main, Waverly building, room 3, h. 38 Lincoln.
" George W. violinist, 230, h. 230 Garden.
" Mary S. milliner, 70 Pratt, b. 795 Asylum.
" May B. clerk at 851 Main, b. 42 Wooster.
" P. A. wid. D. B. b. 25 Ashley.
" Swan M. at 118 Benton, b.u. 147 Babcock.
" Walter, mason, b. 1153 Main.
" Wilbur B. clerk at 273 Asy. b.2u. 1303 Main.
" Wilbur E. tinner at 1162, h.2u. 1303 Main.
" William W. clerk at Ætna Indemnity Co. 650 Main, b. 38 Lincoln.
" ☞*see also Pearson.*
Pietsch Chas. H. (*P. & Hinkley,*) h.u. 44 Wolcott.

**PIETSCH & HINKLEY,** fresco paint- ers, 1146 Main.
Charles H. Pietsch. Albert H. Hinkley.
Pigott Michael J. (*Sherman & Pigott,*) b. 48 Prospect.
Pihl Frank O. toolsharpr. 40 High, b. 153 Law.
Pihlgren Axtel, laborer, 302 Asy. b. 42 Putnam.
Pikard Henry, machinist at Pratt & Whitney Co. 1 Flower, b. 52 Lawrence.
Pike Clarence A.fireman N.Y.R.b.4u.289 Asylum.
" Dora, waitress, h.u. 1232 Main.
" George W. at 154 Asylum, b. 80 Church.

**PIKE L. E. & CO.** general agents New York Life Insurance Co. dealers in stocks, bonds and investment securities, 904 Main, rms. 27 and 28.
" Lafayette E. (*L.E.P.& Co.*) h. 62 Willard.
" Sherman, watchman at 30 Washington, h.u. 47 So. Hudson.
" Walter L. attendant at 30 Washington.
Pilgard John A., Union Grocery Co. h. 82 Ann.
" Katherine D. nurse, b. 14 Church, rm. 4.
Pilgrim Anna E. h. 362 Windsor av.
" Ella F. teacher, h. 362 Windsor av.
Pillar Paul, blacksmith at 75 Com. b.3u. 40 Park.
Pillion Elizabeth, wid. James, h.u. 5 Amity.
" George, helper at 388 Capitol, b. 1107 Main.
" George F. at 25 Front, h. 57 Madison.
" Henry J. dentist, 903 Mn. rm. 3,b.126 Weth.

**As A NEWSPAPER, THE POST LEADS.**

Pillion Jane Mrs. h.u. 84 Grove.
" John H. barber, h. 76 Pleasant.
" Joseph T. student at 721 Main, rm. 2, b. 126 Wethersfield.
" Kieran, mach. at Colts, h. 126 Wethersfield.
" Mary, b. 3 Brownell.
" Michael, laborer at 169, b. 168 Front.
" Thomas J. police, h. 165 Zion.
Pillon Frank, laborer, h. 41 Madison.
Pimm Alfred B. stenographer at 5 Central, b. Newington t.
Pindar Alfred, engraver, at A. Mugford, 177 Asylum, h. 55 Westland.
Pinkney Henry, pantryman str. Middletown, 285 State.
Pinnelo Gaetano, carpenter, h. 120 Windsor.
Pinney Bertha E. stenographer at Hartford Post, 23 Asylum, b. 58 Church.
" Charlotta, b.u. 30 Madison.
" David Williston, clerk at 690 Park, b. W.L.t.
" Florence, b. 137 Windsor av.
" Gerald W. teamster, 44 Mar. b.52 Woodbridge.
" Gertrude M. clerk at Phœnix Mutual Life Insurance Co. 49 Pearl, b. 13 Squire.
" Harry H. mach. at 1 Flower, h. 57 Babcock.
" Joseph, clerk, b. 58 Governor.
" Joseph C. waiter at 26 Un.pl. b. 428 Asylum.
" Joseph H. mach. at 1 Flower, h. 13 Squire.
" Marshall N. b. 2 Holcomb.
" Mather E. traveling salesman at 54 Ann, h. 137 Windsor av.
" Nellie, wid. George H. h. 27 Bellevue.
" S. B. machinist at 1 Flower, b. 238 Park.
" William R. mach. at 388 Cap. b. 37 Imlay.
Pinto Angelo M. h. 56 Portland.
" Carlo, fruits and confec. h.u.r. 1177 Main.
" Jeannaro, handorgan, h. 22 Charles.
" Joseph, laborer, b.3u. 64 Morgan.
" Nicoli, carpenter, h.u. 10 Front.
" Salvatore, laborer, h. 210 Front.
" Vite Michael, laborer, b.u. 64 Morgan.
Pintus Sarah, wid. Harris, dry goods, 64, h. 64 Morgan.
Pisano Peter, creammkr. 701 Main, b. 33 John.
Pisicttano Frank, mason, h.3u. 27 Kilbourn.
Pistor William, packer at 104 Asylum, h.113 Park.
Pitblado Colin B. artist, solicitor at 658 Main, h. 156 Sargeant.
" Harriet C. Mrs. music teacher, 156, h. 156 Sargeant.
Pitcher George, clerk at 20 Vredendale, b. B.t.
" Sam C. foreman, Pope Tube Co. b. 115½ Ann.
Pitkin Albert H. with Conn. Mut. Life Ins. Co. 783 Main, rm. 16, h. 106 Niles.

**PITKIN BROS. & CO.** steam boilers, &c. 152 State.
Norman T. Pitkin.
" Chester M. clerk at 721 Mn. h.2u. 70 Wooster.
" Eliza A. wid. Leonard, h. 115 Bellevue.
" Emeline R. wid. William L. h.u. 60 Capen.

**PITKIN & HARLOW,** rubber goods, 26 and 28 Asylum.
J. A. Pitkin.        M. P. Harlow.
" Horace E. silversmith, h.u. 36 Capen.

Pitkin Howard S. reporter at Evening Post, 23 Asylum, h. East Hartford t.
" J. Louise G. wid. Albert P. h. 190 Sigourney.
" James A. (P. & Harlow,) h. 290 Weth.
" Maria G. b. 212 Laurel.
" Mary F. wid. Wm. S. boardingh. 175 Capitol.
" Norman T. (Pitkin Bros. & Co.) h. 427 Main, rm. 52.
" Ralph, agent real estates, 575, h. 575 Far.
" Susie H. stenog. at National Fire Insurance Co. 95 Pearl, b.u. 60 Capen.
" William T. asst. bookkeeper, 152 State, h. 42 Winthrop.
Pitney Sarah Mrs. h. 20 Grand.
Pittman Edward H. life ins. h.u. 239 Jefferson.
" Helen, wid. Edward, h.u. 59 Madison.
Pitzanto Angelo M. laborer, h.4u. 190 Front.
" Nicola A. laborer, b.4u. 190 Front.
Place Carrie E. h. 48 Church.
" William, clerk at 48 Clark, h.r. 139 Martin.
Plaisted C. C. & Co. Park knitting works, 336 Asy.
" Chas. C. (C.C.P.& Co.) h. 848 Park c. Smith.
Plant Harry, machinist at Pratt & Whitney Co. 1 Flower, b. 36 Pleasant.
Plasikowski August, furrier, 47 Pratt, b. 124 Martin.
Plato Alfred I. at Travelers Insurance Co. 56 Prospect, h.u 14 Martin.
" Benager H. real estate, 71 Asy. b. 20 Wads.
" Gertrude, seamstress, b. 20 Wadsworth.
" Harry A. at Ætna Ins. Co. 666 Main, b.2u. 14 Martin.
Platt Ada L. stenographer at Hartford Fire Insurance Co. 53 Trumbull, b. 56 Willard.
" Charles T. instructor at Hartford Business College, 370 Asylum, h. 9 Brownell.
" Edith J. stenographer at Orient Ins. Co. 5 Haynes, b. 56 Willard.
" Harriett A. Mrs. matron young women's boardinghouse, 58, h. 58 Church.
Plaut Harry, machinist, 1 Flower, b.36 Pleasant.
" Henry, carpenter, h.u.r. 95 Sheldon.
" Julius R. jeweler, h.u. 101 Whitmore.
" Solomon. barber. 5 Central, h. 36 Pleasant.
Playford Ella M. Mrs. h.2u. 36 Capen.
" Lizzie E. bookkeeper, b.3u. 36 Capen.
" Myrtle, stenog. r. 60 Temple, b. 36 Capen.
Plefing John, cutter at 881 Main.
Pletcher Jacob, (Leschke & P.) h. 28 Florence.
Plikunas Jastin, saloon, 92, b. 51 Front.
Plimpton Frederick, treasurer, Plimpton Mfg.Co. 252 Pearl, h. 21 Marshall.
" Harry J. trav.salesm.252 Pearl, h.43 Willard.
" Howard D. bkkpr. 252 Pearl, b. 21 Marshall.
" James M. secretary, Plimpton Mfg. Co. 252 Pearl, h. 192 Farmington.
" Jennie L.T. wid. Fred. W.h.134 Farmington.
" Jessie E. clerk at 937 Main, b. 258 Weth.
" Linus B. president Plimpton Mfg. Co. 252 Pearl, h. 847 Asylum.
" Mfg. Co. printers, 254 Pearl.
" William T. bookkeeper at 252 Pearl, h. 134 Farmington.
Plohn Emil, clerk at 921 Main, b. 52 Capitol.
Plow Henry, clerk at 690 Park, h. 25 Girard.

**If You Want all the News, Read THE POST.**

Plum Frank H. coachman at 27 Charter Oak pl.
Plumb Andrew, helper, Tube Co. h. 133 Weth.
" Arthur W. rubberw. 690 Park, b. 19 Sisson.
" Nathaniel S. butcher at 373 Main, h. 133 Wethersfield.
Plummer Chas. B. mfr. potato chips, h.u. 388 Weth.
" Frank L. machinist at 30 Cush. h.u. 10 Bond.
" Geo. L. at National Fire Insurance Co. 95 Pearl, b. 22 Marshall.
" Oliver A. b.u. 10 Bond.
Plunkett Thos. E. cond. St.Ry. h.118 Asy. rm.12.
Pocock Alfred A. prop. Hotel Hartford, 365 Allyn.
" William A. mach. 1 Flower, b. 365 Allyn.
Poder Ernest, tailor at 2 State, h. 126 Hung.
" Francisca, wid. Joseph, b. 126 Hungerford.
Poindexter Charles E. at Ætna Ins. Co. 666 Main, h. 10 Lenox.
Poland Joseph, laborer at Colts, h.r. 78 Vanblock.
" Mary A. b.r. 78 Vanblock.
Polaski Joseph, bootblack, h. 64 Morgan.
Polder William, painter, 352 Albany, b.188 Capen.
Polenetz Blosh, laborer, h.u. 86 Morgan.
Police Commissioners office, City hall, 800 Main.
" Station, 38 Kinsley.
Polino Michael, laborer at stone pits, h. Ellery.
Pollard Alice E. clerk, b. 33 Babcock.
" Della A. wid. John, matron State capitol, rm. 53, h.u. 57 Garden.
" Frederick, assistant foreman at 1 Flower, b. 71 Woodbine.
" J. S. Mrs. h. 33 Babcock.
" M. Luther, wheelwright, b. 66 Spring.
Pollette Philip, b.u. 54 Market.
Pollock Benj. R. trainmaster at N.E.R. Union depot, h. 370 Asylum, rm. 30.
" Ivar, dropforger at 142 Russ, h. 230 Zion.
Pollotti Domenico, laborer, h.3u. 67 Morgan.
" Nicholas, h. 16 Village.
" Rocco, laborer, h.u. 35 Albany.
Pomerons Morris, peddler, b.u. 270 Market.

**POMEROY A. H.** bicycles and athletic goods, 98 Asylum, h. 13 Spring.

" Everett C. mach. at 1 Flow. h. 57 Sigourney.
" Frank, callman at N.Y.R.b. 45 Hungerford.
" Geo. E. dentist at 721, rm. 2, h. 721 Main.
" Mary J. wid. Noah, h. 646 Asylum.
" Theodore Wat, clerk at Conn. Building and Loan Asso. 252 Asylum, h. Meriden t.
" Wm. H. dentist, 721 Mn. rm.2, h.91 Bellevue.
Pomroy George W. safety check book, 279 High, h. 1 May.
Pond Charles G. h. 34 Hopkins.
" DeWitt C. h. 719 Asylum.
" DeWitt C. prop. Hotel Capitol, 389 Main.*
" Elizabeth J. wid. David H. h.u.58 Wooster.
" Frank A. tiresetter, b.u. 58 Wooster.
" William H. clerk, School Fund office, rm. 5 in State capitol, h. Old Saybrook t.
Ponds John D. repairer at 40 Gov. b.u. 243 Jef
Ponsaing John, massage, 1524, h. 1524 Broad.
" Matilda Mrs. massage, h. 1524 Broad.
Pontillo Domenico, laborer, b.u. 86 Morgan.
" John, driver, h.3u. 79 Morgan.
" Michael, laborer, b.3u. 89 Morgan.

Pontillo Peter, laborer, b.3u. 79 Morgan.
" Peter, laborer, b.r.u. 10 Charles.
Pontino Carmen, laborer, b. 79 Morgan.
Pontoppidan Reinholt, screwmaker at 476 Capitol, b. 98 Laurel.
Pooler Jane Mrs. h. 133 Market, rm. 3.
Pooley William, mach. at 142 Russ, b. 112 Hung.
Pope Albert A. president The Pope Mfg. Co. 436 Capitol, h. Boston, Mass.
" Albert L. sec'y Pope Mfg. Co. 436 Capitol, h. Prospect av. c. Fern.
" Edward, l. 284 Asylum, rm. 64.
" Edward, machinist at 1 So. Ann, b. 4 East.
" George, l. 284 Asylum, rm. 64.
" George, treas. Pope Mfg. Co. sec'y and treas. Hartford Cycle Co. street commissioner, h. 648 Asylum.
" Harry M. mech expert at 1 Laurel, h.59 Ash.

**POPE MANUFACTURING CO.** manufacturers of Columbia bicycles, 436 Capitol. See page 796.

" Manufacturing Co. Motor Carriage department, 1 Laurel.

**POPE TUBE CO.** Hamilton street.
See page 796.

" Military Band, office 104 Asylum.
" Rebecca E. Mrs. b. 18 Trinity.
Popp Fred, Jr. clerk 581 Cap. b. 70 Windsor.
" Frederick, tailor, h.u. 80 Windsor.
Porass Reuben, 2d hand furn. 298, h. 298 Front.
Porch Kate, wid. Samuel H. h. 51 Fairmount.
" Seymour, woodworker, b. 45 Dean.
Porter A. Leonard, expressman, h.u. 115 Barbour.
" Addie J. dressm. 284, h. 284 Asylum, rm. 33.
" Katheryne I. wid. Clifford W. b. 4 Florence.
" Charles E. clerk at 95 Pearl, h. 41 Pliny.
" Charles Mrs. h.3u. 16 Trumbull.
" Edwin T. clerk at 49 Ann, h. N. Britain t.
" Eleanor E. teacher, Hartford Business College, 370 Asylum, b. South Windsor t.
" Ella C. Mrs. boardinghouse, 8 Village.
" Eugene A. trav. salesman, l.u. 1293 Main.
" F. M. wid. Harry B. h.u. 20 Goodwin.
" Fanny E. Mrs. h. 51 Governor.
" Fidelin, b. 36 Jefferson.
" Frederick L. supt. Hfd. Street Sprinkling & Supply Co. 863 Main, h. So. Windsor t.
" Gertrude L. dressmaker, 13, b. 13 Ellsworth.
" Howard F. toolmkr. at Popes, b. 67 Webster.
" Ida S. Mrs. b.u. 20 Goodwin.
" Ira W. plumber, 20 Church, b. 20 Linden.
" J. S. wid. John A. h. 320 Collins.
" James T. h. 80 Ann.
" Jennie Mrs. b. 80 State.
Porter John A. secretary to the president, Washington, D. C. president Evening Post Association, 23 Asylum.
" John J. at National Fire Insurance Co. 95 Pearl, b. 80 Ann.
" Lettie, wid. Charles, h. 488 Main.
" Levi H. ostler at 57 Albany, h.u. 78 Chst.
" Marietta, wid. Nelson O. h. 51 Barbour.
" Samuel W. laborer, h. 97 Hawthorn.
" Slidell N. compos. 141 Pearl, b.u. 39 Barbour.

Porter Wm. ins. agent, 721 Main, h. 379 Weth.
" William F. agent, h. 8 Village.
" Wm. H. carptr. at hospital, h. 13 Ellsworth.
" William H. Jr. painter, b. 67 Webster.
" Wm. Jr. physician, 391 Allyn, h. 69 Forest.
" Wm. L. patternm. 1 Flower, b. 98 Hopkins.
Porterfield Geo. mach. 1 Flow. h.2u. 29 Affleck.
Porteus Angelina, bkkpr. at 120 Alb. b. 3 Forest.
" James, farmer, h. 3 Forest.
" John, h. 5 Forest.

**PORTEUS ROBERT,** contractor and
builder, r. 13, h. 13 Forest.  *See p. 495.*
" Robert, carpenter, h. 349 Main.
Porto John, laborer, b.4u. 190 Front.
Posner Isaac, tailor, h.u. 3 North.

**POST,** daily, 23 Asylum.
" Chas. A. grocer, 1409 Main, h. 156 Capitol.
" Charles W. elevatorer, b. 32 John.
" David J. treas. Veeder Mfg. Co. h. 23 Wash.
" Elmer E. helper, 1162 Mn. b.2u. 45 Albany.
" George W. at Ætna Life Ins. Co. 650 Main,
h. 41 Mahl.
" Harriet, wid. Spencer A. h.u. 45 Albany.
" Herbert A. clerk at Lincoln, Seyms & Co.
spices, etc. 34 Market, b. 33 Chapel.
" Jessie, h. 7 Chapel.
" John H. prest. Herbert Art Co. 730 Main,
h. 71 Pearl.
" Office, Frank P. Furlong, P. M. 65 State.
" William, electrician, b.u. 5 Lewis.
" William C. clerk at 45 Asylum, b. 32 John.

**POST WM. H. CARPET CO.**
curtains, carpets, rugs, 219 Asylum and
15 Haynes.
" Wm. H. president Wm. H. Post Carpet Co.
h. 706 Prospect av. north of Cone.
" William Strong, v.pres't & sec'y Wm. H.
Post Carpet Co. b. 706 Prospect av.
Postal Telegr. Cable Co. 3 Cent. and 42 Union pl.
Potenza James, fruit store, 35, h. 35 Albany.
" Michael, laborer, h. 190 Front.
" Tony, laborer, b. 190 Front.
Potholm Christian, cabinetmaker at 133 Sheldon,
h. 405 Franklin.
Potter A. V. conductor N.E.R. h.u. 426 Asylum.
" Bradford W. mach. at 1 Flower, h. 7 Clinton.
" Charles H. driver at 547, b. 552 Main.
" Chas. S. foreman stairbuilder at Taft Co. h.
Warehouse Point v.
" Daniel, l. 758 Main, rm. 52.
" Franc E. principal Parkville school, h.u.
791 Park.
" Fred J. Jr. clerk at 1397, b. 552 Main.
" Fred. J. Mrs. h.u. 552 Main.
" George, h.r. 14 Chapel.
" George B. mailclerk at Potter & Payne, 405.
Allyn, b. 37 Garden.
" Giles, agent state board education, State
capitol, rm. 42, h. New Haven t.
" Hosea A. carpenter at Hartford Cycle Co.
h. 17 Wadsworth.
" Joseph H. laborer, 15 Tru. b.17 Wadsworth.
" L. T. Mrs. dressmaker, 1208, h. 1208 Main.

Potter LeRoy, druggist at 367, b. 283 Capitol.
**POTTER LESTER L.** (*Potter & Payne,*) 405–407
Allyn, h. 37 Garden.  *See page 586.*
" Martha J. wid. George A. b. 19 Seyms.
" Maurice H. cab. mkr. 133 Shel. h.u.5 Atlantic.
**POTTER & PAYNE,** wholesale gro-
cers and flour dealers, 405 Allyn.
*See page 586.*
Lester L. Potter.    Edward S. Payne.
" Robert A. *county commissioner,* 85 Trum-
bull, h. Bristol t.
" William, carriagemaker, b. 188 Capen.
" Wilson L. salesman, 393 Allyn, h. 1164 Main.
Potts S. Warren, draughtsman, F. H. Richards,
803 Main, b. Bloomfield t.
" Wm. S. clerk at Popes, b. 926 Main, rm. 86.
Potwin Thos. Fred. clerk, 342 Asy. b. 72 Hopkins.
Poulin Thos. H. trimmer, 266 Pearl, b. 20 Village.
Pousner Michael M. molder at 618 Capitol, b.
41 Windsor.
Powel Edward F. student Trinity college, 23
Jarvis hall, Summit.
" James B. president Mercantile National
Bank, 53 Trumbull, h. 127 Washington.
" Joseph S. cigarm. at 104 Asy. h.u. 56 Smith.
" Sarah E. Mrs. h.r. 76 Albany.
" Ward C. accountant, b. 127 Washington.
" William T. floorwalker at Brown, Thomson
& Co. 942 Main, b. 4 Pliny.
Power Declan, at Pope Tube Co. h.u. 27 Harbison.
" John, b.u. 27 Harbison.
" Patrick, b. W. H. Home for Aged, Albany.
" Walter A. com. traveler, h. 7 Sherman.
Powers Adelia, wid. Law. laundress, h. 74 Sanford.
" Anastasia Mrs. h.2u. 57 Spruce.
" Arthur W. laborer, u. 10½ Gold.
" Chas K. engineer N.Y.R. h. 11 Sargeant.
" Daniel, laborer, Pope Tube Co. h. 10 Putnam.
" Edmund, b. 2 Holcomb.
" Edward H. clerk at 201 Asy. b. 53 Windsor.
" Edward L. mach. 54 Arch, b.u. 32 Front.
" Frank H. bottler at 142 State, h. 32 Front.
" Frank T. clerk at 1409 Main, b. 21 Albany.
" George F. carman, b. 53 Windsor.
" James, helper at 54 Arch, h. 35 Mechanic.
" James F. printer at 66 State, b. E.H.t.
" James J. laborer, b.u. 74 Pleasant.
" James J. police, h.u. 35 Pleasant.
" Jane, wid. John, h. 74 Vernon.
" John, carpenter at r. 334 Asy. h. 52 Hicks.
" John, laborer at stonepits, h. Hamilton.
" John, teamster at 46 Ann, h.u. 74 Pleasant.
" John, watchman, b.u. 35 Pleasant.
" John F. rubberw. at 581 Cap. b. 56 Flower.
" John J. bunker engine No. 7, b. 21 Albany.
" Mary, wid. Patrick, h. 21 Albany.
" Mary J. hairdressing, h. 721 Mn. rm. 57.
" Michael, laborer at stonepits, h. 53 Wilson.
" Michael, helper at 1 Flow. b. 1442 Broad.
" Michael, (*Krug, P. & Co.*) h. 53 Windsor.
" Michael J. grinder at Popes, b.3u. 57 Spruce.
" Patrick, helper at 1 Flower, h. 45 Wilson.
" Patrick, machinist at 54 Arch, h.u. 32 Front.
" Patrick F. printer at Case, Lockwood &
Brainard Co. 141 Pearl, b. 21 Albany.

**Merchants say it PAYS to Advertise in The Post.**

Powers Richard J. polisher, 476 Cap. b. 35 Mec.
" Thos. H. teamster at 46 Ann, h.u.r. 52 Gov.
" Thomas M. machinist at Colts, b.u. 45 Wdbg.
" Walter, machinist at Pratt & Whitney Co.
1 Flower, b. 1442 Broad.
" Wilbur J. clerk at 197 Asy. b. 74 Vernon.
" William, at N.Y.R. b.u. 52 Hicks.
" William, at 4 Lewis, b.u. 33 Martin.
Powlick Frank, laborer, b.u. 82 Sheldon.
Pownall Casper W. h. Bartholomew c. Belmont.
" Maud, 77 Pratt, b. Bartholomew c. Belmont.
" Thomas, shoemaker, 68 Albany, h. Chapel.
Pozloski James, laborer, 142 Russ, h. 21 Arch.
Pradella Joseph, restaurant, 90, h. 90 Front.
Prain James, machinist at 388 Capitol, h. W.H.t.
Pranasky Parlo, tailor at 892 Main, b. 10 North.
Prarie Chas. A. mach. at 690 Park, h. 262 N.P.
Prass Frederick, bartendr. 1061, h.u. 1059 Main.
Pratt A. D. baker at 745 Main, h. 21 Belden.
" A. W. carpenter at 155 Capitol, h. Williams.
" Abram W. contractor, 125, h. 125 Huntington.
" Ambrose E. tuner at 241 Asy. h.u. 59 Weth.
" Ambrose L. cabinm. 633 Main, h. 59 Weth.

**PRATT & CADY CO.** manufacturers, valves, 556 Capitol, c. Sig. *See page 527.*
" Cassius P. patternmaker at Pratt & Whitney Co. 1 Flower, b. 117 Oak.
" Charles F. b. 466 Farmington.
" Charles W. cloaks and ladies furnishings, 937 Main, h. 466 Farmington.
" Clarence, teamster, h. 88 Fairmount.
" Clarence B. patternmaker at Pratt & Whitney Co. 1 Flower, b. 55 Ward.
" Edward, blacks. 697 Windsor av. b. Kinsley.
" Dwight, sawyer, 225, h.r. 93 Sheldon.
" Edward A. millwright, 1 Laurel, h. 79 Pearl.
" Edward B. salesman, h. 11 Winthrop.
" Edwina M. teacher Arsenal school b. 137 Windsor av.
" Elmore L. pianos at 241 Asylum, h. 721 Main, rm. 23.
" F. Ernest, clerk at Popes, b. 59 Wethersfield.
" Fannie W. h. 896 Asylum.
Pratt FRANCIS A. consulting engineer Pratt & Whitney Co. 1 Flower, h. 29 Collins.
" Francis C. mechanical engineer Pratt & Whitney Co. 1 Flower, b. 29 Collins.
" Frank W. screwm. 476 Capitol, h. 34 Brook.
" Frederick L. discount clerk at American Nat. Bank, 803 Main, b. So. Glastonbury v.
" G. L. Mrs. at 336, b. 336 Wethersfield.
" George W. bookkeeper at 110 Commerce, h. 1199 Main.
" George W. Jr. clerk, b. 1199 Main.
" George W. Mrs. dressm. 1199, h. 1199 Main.
" George W. salesman, h. 206 Asylum, flat 20.
" Grace L. stenogr. at Popes, b. E.H.t.
" Harry L. inspector at Popes, b. E.H.t.
" Henry S. h. 833 Asylum.
" Howard J. clerk at Brown, Thomson & Co. 942 Main, h. 50 Brown.
" Ida L. b. 69 Church.
" James C. h. 700 Farmington.
" James T. *(Morgan & P.)* h. 84 Capitol.

Pratt Jennie A. teacher High school, b. South Glastonbury v.
" John C. carpenter, h. 69 Church.
" Joseph H. student at Yale, b. 700 Far.
" Lawrence M. teamster for Hartford Lumber Co. h. 88½ Fairmount.
" Mary D. bookkeeper at Hartford Printing Co. 16 State, b. 239 Sigourney.
" Mary H. b. 36 Jefferson.
" N. B. b. 721 Main, rm. 23.
" Rufus N. treasurer of Johns-Pratt Co. 555 Capitol, h. 170 Sigourney.
" Seymour A. asst. ticket agent, N.Y.R. h.u. 19 Williams.
" Waldo S. professor Hfd. Theological Sem.; instructor Trinity college, h. 86 Gillett.
" Walter W. at Travelers Insurance Co. 56 Prospect, l. 821 Asylum.

**PRATT & WHITNEY CO. (THE)** machinists, iron founders, 1 Flower.
*See page 523.*
Pray William N. salesman at Potter & Payne, 405 Allyn, h. 111½ Ann.
Precort Adelard, carpenter, h. 6 Church.
Preissner Arnold, baker, 59, b. 101 Sheldon.
" August *(P. Bros.)* h.u. 59 Sheldon.
" Bros. bakery, 59 Sheldon.
August Preissner. John Preissner.
" Emanuel, builder, 206, h. 206 Franklin.
" John, *(P. Bros.)* h.u. 59 Sheldon.
" Julius, baker at 59, h.u. 59 Sheldon.
Premier Manufacturing Co. 437 Main.
Premo David E. repairer at 40 Gov. h. 3 Queen.
Prendergast Agnes, at 83 Woodbine, b. 286 Maple.
" Charles H. mach. at Popes, h.u. 137 Lawrence.
" James, laborer at 15 Tru. b. 151 Windsor.
" Margaret, wid. Joseph, h. 286 Maple.
" Mary, at 12 Pratt, b. 286 Maple.
" Michael, bricklayer, b. 70 Capitol.
" Nellie L. clerk at 942 Main, b. 286 Maple.
" Robert E. clerk at 901 Main, b. 286 Maple.
" William, laborer at Jewell Belting Co. 15 Trumbull, b. 151 Windsor.
" William J. printer, b. 286 Maple.
" Wm. T. machinist, b.u. 38 Congress.
" ☞ *see also Pendergast.*
Prenevost Hubert, helper at 690 Park, b. 552 South Forest.
Prentice Charles H. real estate, 847 Main, rm. 6, h. 366 Laurel.
" Frank I. asst. teller, 31 Pratt, h. 109 Elm.
" Harriet, wid. George W. b. 74 Bond.
" Kate B. wid. Charles Hills, h. 366 Laurel.
" Samuel O. judge of Superior Court, 85 Trumbull, h. 111 Elm.

**PRENTISS CHAS. C.,** M. D. *(Law & P.)* dentists, 926 Main, h. 16 Benton.
*See page 427.*
" Edwin S. toolmaker, h. 30 Vine.
Prescott Albert N. clerk at Ingraham & Swift, b. 229 Sigourney.
" Daniel K. Mrs. b. 229 Sigourney.
" Fred G. mason, h. 21 Seymour.

**THE POST DELIVERED AT YOUR HOME DAILY, PER MONTH, FIFTY CENTS.**

Prescott Ward G. clerk at Popes, b. 29 Bkm.
" William C. teller Mechanics Savings Bank,
815 Main, h. 229 Sigourney.
Preskowitz W. tailor at 29 Pearl, rm. 6, b.
186 Putnam.
Press Benjamin, peddler, h.u. 244 Front.
Presto Antonio, laborer, b.2u. 7 Charles.
Preston Albert B. bank watchman, h.u. 18 Lewis.
" Edward, b. 135 Front.
" Edward V. sup't agencies Travelers Insur-
ance Co. 56 Prospect, h. 31 Gillett.
" Ellen E. wid. Truman W. h. 200 Allyn.
" Frank J. instructor High school, h. 16 Cone.
" Frederick J. machinist, h.u. 13 Russell.
" George B. h.u. 1208 Broad.
" George B. stock broker, b. 275 Wethersfield.
" George F. printer, b. 1261 Main.
" George O. b. 4 Preston.
" Hugh F. pinm. at 31 Hicks, b.u. 2 Tru.
" James, bottler, r. 141, h. 141 Front.
" James A. lithographer, b. 61 Park.
" James G. filer at Colts, h. 50 John.
" James J. letter carrier, h. 7 Lewis.
" John B. b. 2 Trumbull.
" Joseph, machinist at Colts, b.u. 6 Alden.
" Joseph A. driver at r. 141, b.141 Front.
" Jos. S. boxmaker at Popes, b. 61 Park.
" Joshua, h. 17 Haynes, rm. 63.
" & Kenyon, signpainters, 185 Pearl.
   Miles B. Preston.  Benjamin W. Kenyon.
" Leroy S. ship. clerk 26 High, b. 34 Hopkins.
" Louisa E. wid. Ben. h. 1261 Main.
" Margaret, wid. Andrew, h.u. 61 Park.
" Martha C. b. 36 Jefferson.
PRESTON MILES B. *mayor of Hartford*, secy. &
treas. Bonner-Preston Co.(*P. &Kenyon,*)
h. 214 Collins.   *See page 425.*
" Sarah, wid. Thomas, h. 2 Trumbull.

**PRESTON THOMAS P. M.** meat
market, 308 Asylum and 48 Front, h. 77
Harrison.  Successor to Davis & Foster.
" Wm. C. lettercarrier station A, h.4 Winthrop.
" William J. farmer, h. 275 Wethersfield.
Preu Annie, wid. Paul J. h. 32 Harbison.
" Paul J. bkkpr. at 273 Asy. b. 32 Harbison.
Price Arthur D. clerk at 205 State, h.u.79 Allen pl.
" Clara M. at Travelers Ins. Co. 56 Prospect,
b. 68 Church.
" Dora, dressmaker, h.u. 868 Park.
" Esau J. coachman at 91 Wethersfield, h.
47 Pawtucket.
" Geo. T. (*R. P. & Son,*) h. 41 Sisson.
" Harvey E. laborer, h.u. 171 Windsor.

---

Price J. Isabella, principal at Northwest school,
b. 78 Allen pl.
" James, carpenter, b. 1113 Main.
" James, rubberworker at 690, h. 864 Park.
" John M. h. 44½ John.
" Joseph, bookkeeper, b. 36 Pleasant.
" L. Eudora, teacher at Northwest School, h.
73 Allen pl.
" L. F. salesman at 140 State, h.W.P.v.
" Louis, real estate, h. 225 Market.
" Margaret J. housekeeper, h.u. 12 Church.
" Percy F. instructor at Popes, b. 30 Church.
" Robert, (*R. P. & Son*) h. W.H.t.
" Robert & Son, coal, feed, blacks. 82 Francis.
   Robert Price.  George T. Price.
" Rob't C. real estate, 722 Main, h. 59 Seymour.
" Robert W. carpenter, b. 16 Smith.
" Thomas, silverworker at 62 Market, b. 226
Franklin.
PRICE W. T. & Co. insurance agents, 95 Pearl.*
               *See page 298.*
" Walter H. papercut. at 141 Pearl, h. 5 Cranes.
PRICE WM. T. (*W.T.Price & Co.*) h. 363 Laurel.
Prickett Frank L. foreman at L. A. Wiley &
Son, 251 Pearl, h. 217 Capen.
Primus Hettie, wid. Holdridge, h. 20 Wadsworth.
" Thronieve B. seamstr's, 20, b. 20 Wadsworth.
Prince F. Welles, student Trinity college, b.
66 Vernon.
PRINCE FREDERICK W. *councilman 8th ward,*
secretary Gatling Gun Co. h. 66 Vernon.
Prindle Frank B. machinist, h. 21 Williams.
" Geo. E. pressman 252 Pearl, h.u. 33 Elm.
" Geo. E. Mrs. variety store, 31, h.u 33 Elm.
" Leda G. clerk at 82 Tru. b. 21 Williams.
Prior Andrew, laborer, b. 36 Imlay.
" Chas. E. toolmaker 1 Flow. h.u. 30 Hopkins.
" Chas. Edw. treasurer and secretary Security
Co. 62 Pearl, h. 165 Collins.
" Chas. Edw. Jr. with Security Co. 62 Pearl,
b. 165 Collins.
" Domingo N. motorm. St. Ry. h.118 Asy. rm. 16.
" Frank N. conductor St. Ry. h. East Wind-
sor Hill.
" Fred W. clerk at Popes, h.u. 62 Hung.
" Fredk. H. com. traveler, b. 38 Wooster.
" Geo. A. mach. at 581 Cap. h. 232 Putnam.
" Grace M. stenographer, b.u. 232 Putnam.
" Jane, wid Abbott G. h.u. 232 Putnam.
" Julia R. wid. Edward, h. 202 Sargeant.
" Mary, wid. Patrick, b.u. 51 Chestnut.
" Mary B. wid. George F. h. 222 Jefferson.
" Wilbur F. inspector at Popes, h. 38 Wooster

Priore Jos. shoemaker, 994 Main, h.u 214 Front.
Prisk J. Alfred, clerk at 556, h.u. 536 Main.
Probst Fred. F. operator 135 Shel. b. 265 Main.
Proctor Harry C. toomaker at 9 Sig. h. 52 Putnam.
Proffitt Emily, wid. John G. h. 36 Benton.
" Frederick H. barber, b.u. 36 Benton.
" Mary Mrs. nurse, 36, b.u. 36 Benton.
Proller Morris, clothing, 111, h. 134 Front.
" Morris, peddler, b. 8 North.
Prossett Caira, dressmaker, b. 39½ Sisson.
Prothero John, mech. at 581 Cap. h.2u. 233 Jef.
Prouty Clarence, farmer, b. 30 Washington.
" Judson I. printer at Hartford Daily Times, 716 Main, h. 30 Wooster.
" Robert, printer at 284 Asy. b. 30 Wooster.
" Walter S. teamster, h. 36 Imlay.
Provinchi Eugene, baker at 238, b. 238 New Park.
Provo Lawrence, barber at 281 Park, b. 43 Hung.
Provost Frank D. carpenter, h. 134 Brown.
" Oliver, carpenter, b. 142 Brown.
" Napoleon L. carpenter, h. 142 Brown.
Pruden Albert J. clerk at Sage, Allen & Co. 898 Main, h. Middletown t.
Prudential Ins. Co. of America, 811 Main.
Prue Annie M. laundress, 171 Putnam, b. 38 Harbison.
" Charles, at Hartford Lumber Co. h. E.H. t.
Prumbaum Nicholas W. mach. 388 Cap. h. E.H.t.
" Peter, tinner at 164 State, h. E.H.t.
Prutting Arthur J. machinist at Pratt & Whitney Co. 1 Flower, b. 231 Pearl.
" George, musician, h. 241 Pearl.
PRUTTING GEORGE, Jr. teacher of dancing, 53 Trumbull, h.u. 54 Annawan. *See p.* 299.
" Harry, machinist at 1 Flower, h. 52 Hung.
" John W. clerk, b. 241 Pearl.
" Robert, b. 54 Annawan.
" William, machinist at 1 Flow. h. 17 Walnut.
Psytulski Michael, harnessm. 8 Sig. h. 82 Potter.
Public Free Library and Art Gallery, Wadsworth Athenæum, 624 Main and 5 Athenæum street.
" Market Co., W. C. Wade, 653 Main.
Pucella Peter, laborer, b. 110 Grove.
Pucci Charles, clerk at 63, b. 106 Albany.
" R. Emmett, mach. at P.&R. h.2u. 106 Albany.
" Robert F. helper P.&R. b.2u. 106 Albany.
Puffer Emma J. Mrs.: boardinghouse, 1210 Main.
" Jennie E. wid. Chas. E. h.2u. 1160 Main.
" Julia T. wid. Charles E. Jr. b. 1210 Main.
Puglisi N. Christ. barber, h.3u. 36 Windsor.
" Peter, shoem. 40 Church, b. 36½ Windsor.
" Philip, barber, b.2u. 36 Windsor.
" Tony, laborer, b.3u. 36 Windsor.
Pullar Andrew, (*J. P. & Co* ) h. 10 Pawtucket.
" Charles, (*J. P. & Co.*) h. 52 Annawan.
" James, (*J. P. & Co.*) h. 33 Front.
" James & Co. carriage makers, 5-13 Mechanic. James Pullar. Andrew Pullar. Charles Pullar.
Pullman Joseph, apprentice at 1 Flower, b.u. 9 Putnam.
Pulver Elmer, timek. at 690 Park, h.u. 189 Smith.
" John J. farmer, h. 189 Smith.
" Marvin, notions, 820, foreman at 690 Park, h. 8 Sisson.

Puntillo John, teamster at 154 Charter Oak, h.u. 79 Morgan.
Purcell Catherine, wid. Patrick, h.r. 236 Maple.
" Edward, plumber at 52 Allyn, b. 170 Front.
" George, laborer, b.r. 236 Maple.
" John, teamster, b.u. 261 Front.
" John C. operator, 40 Gov. b.r. 236 Maple.
" John J. mechanic at Popes, b. 146 Grove.
" John L. plumber, 550 Main, b. 261 Front.
" Kate, wid. Martin, h. 146 Grove.
" Martin L. teamster at 225 Shel. h. 146 Grove.
Purcelli Antonio, laborer, h.r.u. 14 Charles.
Purdue Albert J. trav. salesman, h. 25 Marshall.
Purdy Frank, jobber, b.u. 1 Riverside pl.
" Hugh, molder at 1 Flower, h. 72 Madison.
" Hugh Jr. draughtsm. at 1 Flow. b. 72 Madison.
" James M. mach. at 1 Flow. b. 72 Madison.
Purinton A. Estella, bkkpr. 139 Asy. b. 75 N.B.
" Chas. O. pottery and nursery, r. 77, h. 75 N.B.
" Frank L. clerk at 197 Asylum, b. 75 N.B.
" John L. h. 32 Seymour.
" Oscar B. toolmaker at 9 Sig. h. 32 Seymour.
" Samuel C. potter at 75, b. 75 New Britain.
Purl Maurice, clerk at 342 Asy. h. 30 Pleasant.
" ☞ *see also Pearl.*
Purlee George, helper at 48 Ann, b. Walnut.
Purple Caroline A. wid. Edward, b. 439 Capitol.
" William R. clerk at P.O. station A, b. 439 Cap.
Purtell Thomas M. cigarm. 867 Main, h.u. 7 Green.
PURVES ADAM (*P. & Malcolm,* ) h. 27 Pawtucket.
PURVES & MALCOLM, contractors and builders, r. 334 Asylum. *See p.* 422.
Adam Purves.　　Thomas Malcolm.
" Robert W. laborer at Pope Tube Co. h. 43 New Britain.
Puscher Martin, machinist at 142 Russ, h.u. 299 Lawrence.
Putnam Abe P. insp. at 690 Park, b. Wilson sta.
" Charles F. carpenter, N.Y.R. h. 18 S. Ann.
" Edwin W. patternmaker at Popes, h.u. 20 Ellsworth.
" Frank L. diemaker at Popes, h. Wilson sta.
" George K. patternmaker, 33 Wells, b. E.H.t
" Giles H. inspector at Colts. h. E.H.t.
" Phalanx Armory, 6 Haynes.
" William H. newspaper artist at The Courant. State, h. 47 Harrison.
Pye Charles D. at Orient Ins. Co. 5 Haynes, b. 101 Wethersfield.
" Rebecca M. b. 142 Wethersfield.
" Thomas F. h. 101 Wethersfield.
" Thomas F. Jr. at Travelers Insurance Co 56 Prospect, b. 101 Wethersfield.
Pynchon Lauriston F. L. at Ætna Insurance Co. 666 Main, b. 34 Charter Oak pl.

Pynchon Thomas R. Rev. professor Trinity college, 15 Seabury hall, Summit.
" William H. C. instructor at Trinity college, h. 13 Columbia.
Pyne James W. foreman at Sunday Journal, 284 Asylum, h. 113 Park.
**PYNE ROBERT,** editor Weekly Examiner, 45, h. 41 Brown.   *See page 468.*
" Robert E. printer, h.u. 39 Brown.
" Thomas M. conductor St.Ry. b. 149 Weth.
Pyott George D. mach. Popes, h. 172 Putnam.

QUAILE Michael J. janitor at 109 State, h.u. 44½ John.
Quain Daniel J. ostler, l. 90 Front.
Quebec Fred, clerk, b. 5 Grand.
Queeny Delia, h. 13 South Hudson.
Quellar James, at 47 Ann, h. 49 Morgan.
QUIGGLE ELMER C. president The E. S. Kibbe Co. 149 State, h. Farmington av. W.H.t.
                              *See page 587.*
Quigley Edward, machinist, b. 125 Charter Oak.
" Ernest M. hosedriver Co. No. 4, h. 168 Allyn.
" James, mach. at Colts, b. 125 Charter Oak.
" John, gardener at 1008 Asy. h.r. 21 Atwood.
" John, laborer, h.2u. 6 Union.
" John K. at National Fire Insurance Co. 95 Pearl, h. 99 Brook.
" Michael, polisher at Colts, b. 125 Ch.O.
" Michael F. b. 125 Charter Oak.
" Thomas, expressman at Colts, h.1 Wehasset.
Quill Annie, clerk at Brown, Thomson & Co. 942 Main, b. 24 Center.
" Daniel, laborer, h. 24 Center.
" Nellie, clerk at Brown, Thomson & Co. 942 Main, b. 24 Center.
" Nora, stitcher at 19½ Tru. b. 24 Center.
" Patrick, laborer, b. 24 Center.
Quillar James H. laborer, h. 116 Albany.
Quimby Annie Mrs. bookkeeper at 759 Main.
" Charles J. motorman St.Ry. h. 5 Charlotte.
Quin DeWitt C. P. printer, b. 30 Chapel.
" J. Scrugham, ticket agt. N.Y.R. h. 30 Chapel.
" Louis C. printer at Hartford Life Ins. Co. 252 Asylum, b. 30 Chapel.
Quincher John, wiredrawer at 40 Gov. b. 6½ Elm.
Quincy House, Timothy E. Foley, prop. 1233 Main.
Quinlan James, laborer, b. 274 Front.
" Mary Mrs. h.u. 117 Zion.
" Patrick H. confectionery, 263, h. 263 High.
" Thomas R. screwm. 476 Cap. b.u. 52 Woodbine.
" William J. mach. 30 Cush. b. 52 Woodbine.
Quinn Andrew G. clerk, b. 97 Windsor.
" Bridget, wid. Martin, h.u. 119 Zion.
" Bridget, wid. William, h.2u 72 Hopkins.
" Charles H. printer at 29 Union pl. h. 60 Windsor av.
" Daniel J. mechanic at Popes, b. 25 Putnam.
" Edward, laborer, h.u. 29 Hawthorn.
" Edward, laborer, 1 Flow. b.u. 1438 Broad.
" Edward, rubberw. at 690 Park, b. N.t.
" Edward J. agent at 756 Main, h. Rockville t.
" Edward W. machinist, b. 119 Zion.
" Elizabeth, b. W.H. Home for Aged, Albany.

Quinn Felix J. policeman, h.2u. 15 Chestnut.
" George E. toolmaker at Popes, b. 36 Ch.O.
" Hanora, wid. Patrick, b. 39 Franklin.
" Hugh, mechanic at Popes, h.2u. 22 Francis.
" Hugh H. screwmaker, b. 68 Laurel.
" James, brickmaker, h. 13 James.
" James, butcher at 1065 Main, h.u. 20 Morgan.
" James A. plumber at 280 Asylum, b. Weth.t.
QUINN JAMES J. clerk city court, attorney, 847 Main, rm. 2, b.u. 5 East.
" John, gardnr. 147 Woodland, h.u. 15 Chestnut.
" John, gardener, h. 10 Cone.
" John F. wirew. at 618 Capitol, b. N.B.t.
" John H. rubberw. 690 Park, h.u. 20 Kibbe.
" John H. Jr. at Pope Tube Co. b.r. 25 Putnam.
" John J. bartender at 997 Main, h. 8 Huntley.
" John J. clerk 342 Asylum, b.2u. 72 Hopkins.
" John J. enameler, b.u. 59 Market.
" John L. printer at 336 Asy. b. 60 Windsor av.
" Joseph T. mach. at Popes, b.r. 25 Putnam.
" Kate M. wid. John L. h. 60 Windsor av.
" Laura, wid. Albert, seamst. h.u.r. 65 Temple.
" Mary, b.2u. Hopkins.
" Mary, bitters, h.u.r. 570 Main.
" Mary, wid. John, h.u. 8 Huntley pl.
" Maurice, nightwatchman 95, h. 88 Pleasant.
" Michael, assembler, 556 Cap. h. 8 Winter.
" Michael J. assembler at Colts, h. 52 Vanblock.
" Patrick F. mach. at Colts, h. 52 Vanblock.
" Patrick H. wholesale tea dealer, 697 Main, h. 150 Capitol.
" Patrick J. clerk at 977 Main, b.u. 8 Huntley.
" Patrick M. laborer, 1 Flow. b.u. 1438 Broad.
" William J. clerk at 1065 Main, h.u. 5 East.
" William M. profiler at Colts, h.u. 30 Hudson.
" ☞ *see also Quin.*
Quinnott Alex. mach. at Colts, h.u. 78 Vanblock.
Quint Alanson D. manufacturer turret drills, 80 Huvshope, h. 8 Clinton.
Quintard H. Harrison, h. 80 Capitol.
" Helen R. forelady at R. Ballerstein & Co. 908 Main, b. 16 Prospect.
" Herbert A. h.u. 23 Windsor.
Quirk Andrew, wid. William J. h.u. 104 Clark.
" Dennis, laborer, h. 1 Imlay.
" John, fireman, h. 230 Maple.
" John, lineman, 266 Pearl, h.u. 150 Market.
" Kate, dressmaker, 1, h. 1 Imlay.
" Mary T. clerk at 921 Main, b. 88 Pleasant.
" Maurice, nightwatchman, 95, h. 88 Pleasant.
" Michael, driver, 701 Main, b.r. 87½ Windsor.
" Morris, Jr. clerk, 65 Asylum, b. 88 Pleasant.
" Patrick, helper at Popes, h. 24 Amity.
" Patrick H. laborer, Pope Tube Co. b.1 Imlay.
" Terence P. coachman, 12 C.O. pl. h.u. 32 Elm.
" Timothy J. mach. at 1 Flow. b.2u. 159 Law.
Quish Michael J. mach. at 13 Central, b. 29 Smith.
" William J. contractor at Johns-Pratt Co. 555 Capitol, h. 29 Smith.
Quist Alfred, cutter at 690 Park, h. 8 Putnam.
Quong Wong (*Yuen Sing & Co.*) 108 State.

**JOB PRINTING** AT 16 STATE ST.

RABBIT Bernard, laborer, h.r. 236 Maple.
" Julia A. at Capewell Horse Nail Co. 40 Governor, b. 236 Maple.
" Mary, at 1 So. Ann, b.r. 230 Maple.
Rabbitt John, laborer on city water works, b.u. 120 Albany.
Rabe Fred W. at 34 Pratt, b. 19 Central.
Rabinovitz E. groceries, 39, h. 39 Portland.
Rabitsch Nicholas, assembler at Colts, h. 98 N.B.
Racaniello Michael, handorgan, h.3u. 5 Charles.
Rackett Mary J. wid. J. Conklin, b. 27 Sherman.
" Samuel, pressm. 690 Park, h.2u.47 Belmont.
Raco Franzesco, fruits, etc. Un. pl. h. 33 Albany.
Racynsky Frank, laborer, b.2u. 95 Sheldon.
Radcliffe William G. machinist at 1 Flower, h. 54 Barbour.
Rader Psisuch, barber, b. 5 North.
Radey John, h.u. 130 Front.
" Nellie, clerk, b.u. 3 Goodman.
Radican Patrick, driver at 342, b. 342 Weth.
" Peter, blacksmith at stonepits, h.75Glendale.
" Peter F. machinist at Pratt & Whitney Co. 1 Flower, h.u. 75 Glendale.
" ☞ see also Radigan.
Radigan Edward M. enameler, 581 Cap. b.88 Shel.
" James W. laborer at Sigourney Tool Co. 9 Sigourney, b. 46 Beach.
" John, laborer, N.E.R. b.3u.r. 23 Spruce.
" Michael, stonemason, h.u. 78 Walnut.
" Patrick, sub. fireman, h. 1418 Broad.
" William, helper at r. 13 Wells, b. E.H.t.
" ☞ see also Redican.
Radin Harris, peddler, h.2u. 257 Market.
Radle Philip, laborer, b. 938 Park.
Radomskoff Ignatz, cabinetmaker at 633 Main, h. Collinsville v.
Radowich Frank, laborer at 581 Cap. b. 99 Potter.
" Tony, laborer at 581 Cap. b. 99 Potter.
Rady Eugene, butcher at 516, b. 518 Main.
Rafferty Celia, wid. John, h.u. 55 Liberty.
" Margaret, wid. Francis, h. 29 Lawrence.
" Mary, wid. Farrell, h.u. 27 Harbison.
" Patrick, driver at 15 Alb. h.2u. 22 Lawrence.
Rafter Joseph J. sup't R. S. Peck & Co. printers, 26 High, b. 53 Capitol.
" Manfg. Co. printers sundries, 26 High.
Ragan Annie M. stenog. at Popes, b. 88 Ch.O.
" Patrick, forem.560 Mn. h.u. 88 Charter Oak.
" Peter, saloon, 48 Temple, h.u. 22 Talcott.
" Peter, steamfitter, b. 209 Hamilton.
" Timothy F. blacksm. at Popes, b. 8 Queen.
" Wm. P. nickelpr. at Popes, b.u. 88 Ch.O.
" ☞ see also Reagan; Regan.
Ragataky Benj. bottler, h.u. 198 Front.
Ragna Salvatore, tailor at 41, b.u. 41 Asylum.
RagoFrank,candy and fruit,22Un.pl.h.23Albany.
Ragovin Morris (Simon, R. & Co.) h. 35 Benton.
Rahba Mary, h. 22 Morgan.
" Sophia, wid. John. boardingh. 22 Morgan.
Rahnenfubrer Adolph, trimr. 41 Alb. h.30½ Cedar.
Raible Frank H.engineer N.Y.R. h.u.1260 Broad.
" Frank W. b. 1260 Broad.
Raichel Michael, laborer, b. 5 North.
Raicis Leon, filer at Colts, h. 55 Pleasant.
Rainey Thomas, helper, 54 Arch, b.r. 61 Front.

CHAS. A. RAPELYE,

APOTHECARY.

Prescriptions a Specialty.

HOMEOPATHIC MEDICINES.
TRUSSES AND ELASTIC STOCKINGS.

376 Asylum Street 🖅

853 Main Street.

Raites Henry J. inspector at Popes, h. W.P.v.
Ramilloid Frank, machinist, h.2u. 40 John.
Ramsdell Amos W. porter at Adams Express, 805 Main, h. 615 Capitol.
" Chas. A. forem. at Pope Tube Co. h. 121 Oak.
" Mary M. draperysewer, 219 Asy. b.u. 15 Ple.
" P. O. Rev. pastor Bethel Mission church, h.u. 11 Bellevue.
" Roswell C. h.u. 15 Pleasant.
" William F. carptr. at 155 Ch.O. b.u. 15 Ple.
Ramsden Charles L. policeman, b.u. 29 Beach.
" Irene M. J. clerk at Popes, b. 29 Babcock.
" Robert H. clerk at 115, b. 92 Pearl.
Ramsey Alfred F. trimmer at 17 Elm, h. 271 High.
" Charles M. machinist, h.u. 44 John.
" Martha L. h. 721 Main, rm. 35.
" William H. painter, h. 271 High.
Rancor Charles, clerk at 745, b. 811 Main.
" Chas. R.press forem. 141 Pearl,h.3u. 811 Mn.
" Herbert C. polisher at Popes, b. 31 Center.
Rand E.H.carptr.at 158Woodland,h.Windsor av.
" Frank H. mach. at 476 Capitol, h.u. 9 Park.
" Frederick K. machinist at 20 Vredendale, h. 244 Jefferson.
" Harry E. machinist at 1 Flower, h. E.H.t.
" Mary H. wid. C. C. h.u. 9 Park.
Randall Ann, wid. John, h. Whiting lane.
" Ann, wid. Robinson, h.u. 88 Chestnut.
" Arthur M. painter, b. 60 Temple.
" Burt W. clerk at 2 South Ann, b. 64 Hicks.
" Estella M. wid. William R. b.u. 88 Chestnut.
" Franklin C. traveling salesm. h. 17 Ashley.
" George, clerk, b.u. 51 Sanford.
" Harriet, laundress, 139, h. 139 Capen.
" James F. waiter at 26 State, h.u. 43 Wolcott.
" Martha A. wid. Jesse A. b. 32 Hicks.
" Susan Mrs. laundress, h.2u. 51 Sanford.
" William, laborer, h.u. 2 Center.
" William F. jobber, b.2u. 51 Sanford.
Randles G. Earl, mach. 1 Flow. b.45 Farmington.
Randolph Albert, hackdriver, h.u. 52 Village.
" Ira, jobber, b. u. 52 Village.
" John F. Jr. clerk,466 Asy. b. 11 Foot Guard.
Rankin Adolphus Erwin (Marcy Bros. & Co.) h. 377 Laurel.
" William, helper at P.&R. h. 10 Huntley pl.
" William J. wireworker at 60 Temple, b. 10 Huntley pl.
Ranney Benj. W. cigarmaker, b. 226 Ashley.
" Charles K. groceries, 96 Alb. h. 50 Brook.

**THINKING PEOPLE Read The Post Daily.**

# F. D. RATHBUN,

## Insurance
## Broker.

**Office with F. F. STREET,**

### 118 ASYLUM STREET.

—————P. O. BOX, 902.

Telephone, 126-5.————

Ranney Frank D. florist at 805 Main, h. E.H.t.
" Louise J. Mrs. nurse, b. 23 Windsor av.
" Salvador O. cigars, h. 226 Ashley.
" William W. Rev. pastor of Park church, b. 811 Asylum.
Ransom E. N. b. 21 Capitol.
" Henry C. Mrs. b. 104 Ann.
RAPELYE CHARLES A. druggist, 376 Asylum, and 853 Main, h. 107 Washington.
See page 301.
Raphael Aaron, confectionery, 183, h. 184 Front.
" Abbie Mrs. h. 101 Hudson.
" Charles, asst. forem. Popes, h.u. 92 Francis.
" Harry, tailor at 730 Main, h. 299 Market.
" Henry (Herrup & R.) h. 184 Front.
" Isaac, barber, 32 Shel. h.u. 40 Woodbridge.
" Louis, barber, b. 184 Front.
" Rudolph, farmer, h. Lifkey.
" William, clerk at 956 Main, h. 184 Front.
Raphey John, laborer, b. 1447 Broad.
" Maggie, h. 1447 Broad.
" Thomas, laborer, b. 1447 Broad.
Rapport George, grocer, 86, h. 86 Retreat.
" George Jr. drugclerk at 703 Mn.h. 86 Retreat.
" Louis A. clerk, b. 86 Retreat.
Rarett James A. mechanic at Popes, b. 32 Elm.
Rarity John, teamster, b.2u. 32 Front.
" Thomas J. teamster, b.2u. 32 Front.
Rasmunson James, carpenter, h. 47 Amity.
Rasmusen Peter, driver, 366 Mn. b.r. 58 Temple.
" Peter, pressman at 690 Park, h. 33 Laurel.
Rasmussen Hanson. carpenter at 158 Woodland, b.u. 80 Front.
" Robert, packer at 273 Asy. h. E.H.t.
" Nils, rubberw. at 690 Park, b. 65 Hawthorn.
Ratcliffe William G. h. 54 Barbour.
Ratell Josephine, housekeeper, h.u. 263 Front.
Rates Frank F. (R. & Co.) h. 55 Grand.
" Frank & Co. groceries, 348 Park.
Frank Rates.          Joseph Lyons.
" Michael, fruit store, 31, h.u.r. 29 Albany.
" Peter, h.3u. 18 Kilbourn.
" Thomas (T. R. & Co.) h. 33 Albany.
" Thomas & Co. fruit, cigars, etc. 90 Albany.
Thomas Rates.          Leon Calador.
" Rath G. pressman,252 Pearl, b. 27 Williams.
RATHBUN FRED. D. insurance, 118 Asylum, h. 160 Sargeant.          See page 302.
" Helen B. teacher West Middle school, b. 17 Columbia.

**RATHBUN JULIUS C.** district agent National Life Ins. Co. Montpelier, Vermont, also accident insurance 80 Pearl, h. 17 Columbia.
Rathgeb Henry, cigarmaker at 867 Main, b. E.H.t.
Ratner A. watchmaker at 30, h.u. 30 Kilbourn.
Ratigan Thomas, screwm. Popes, b.u. 72 Hopkins.
Rattigen Patrick, laborer, b.2u. 55 Liberty.
Rattray Celia A. nurse, 64, b. 64 Russ.
Rau Conrad, mach. at 30 Cushman, h. 53 Heath.
" Edward F. express, 7 Central, h. 39 Brook.
" Frank B. clerk at 1 Flower, b. 14 Atlantic.
" George Jr. bottler, 132 Market, b. Burnside.
" Wilson D. engir. at 921 Main, h. 14 Atlantic.
Rauchel Jacob, cook, 26 State.
Rauscher William, bottler, 7, b. 7 Affleck.
Ray Benj. C. journalist, b. 346 Capen, c. Vine.
" Charles R. mach. at 1 Flow. b.2u. 382 Park.
" Edward, clerk, b. 14 Grace.
" Frank E. bookkeeper at H. C. Burgess, 15 Albany, h. 348 Capen, c. Vine.
" Frank F. cigarm. at 867 Main, h.u. 94 Retreat.
" George, h. 21 Smith.
" Grace M. clerk at Brown, Thomson & Co. 942 Main, b. 55 Annawan.
" James H. millwright, h. 220 New Park.
" Robert, at 1 Flower, h. 21 Smith.
" Robert K. shipclk. at 388 Cap. h. 21 Smith.
" Robert Jr. clerk at 690 Park, b. 21 Smith.
" William, harnessm. at 8 Sig. b. 168 Allyn.
" Wm. H. carpenter at 556 Cap. h. 14 Grace.
" William J. b. 14 Grace.
" Wm. J. h. 284 Pearl.
" Wm. P. porter, 72 Front, b. 60 Portland.
" 🖙see also Wray.
Raymond Asa L. farmer, h. 22 Cottage.
" Charles, driver, h.u. 152 Front.
" Clarice, musicteacher, 82, b.u. 82 N.B.
" Daniel W. agent, h. 55 Annawan.
" Donato, laborer, h.u. 64 Morgan.
" Domenico, laborer, h.u. 64 Morgan.
" Francisco, laborer, h.2u. 64 Morgan.
" John W. pianotuner, 82, h.u. 82 New Britain.
" Mary F. M. teacher at 1204, b. 1204 Asylum.
" Oliver A. (R. & Sloan,)h. 15 Mahl.
" Samuel N. l. 223 Asylum, rm. 110.
" Samuel W. evangelist, h.u. 15 Goodwin.

**RAYMOND & SLOAN,** sales stables, horses, etc. 19 Mather.          See page 549.
Oliver A. Raymond.          Jerome H. Sloan.
Raynor J. E. manager at 214 Asy. b. Trumbull.
Read Alex. M. clerk at 690 Park, b. 373 Capitol.
" Frank H. machinist, h. 9 Kinsley.
" George H. bookkeeper at 32 Church, b. 115 Trumbull.
" Wallace F. conduc. St.Ry. h. King, c. Julius.
" 🖙see also Reed; Reid.
Readel Frances A. wid. Henry O. b. 217 Sargeant.
" George H. operator, b.u. 26 Elm.
" 🖙see also Redell, Reidel.
Reader Geo. H. toolm. at 581 Cap. b. 94 Babcock.
" Mary J. Mrs. h. 18 Elm.
" Thomas, woodt. 69 Front, h. 127 Hamilton.
" Wm. G. diesinker, 142 Russ, h.u. 94 Babcock.

Readett Daniel, night dispatcher, N.Y.R. depot, fire commissioner, h. 91 Wooster.
Reagan John, machinist, b.u. 32 Pleasant.
" John, plumber at 280 Asy. b. 69 Huyshope.
" Peter, steamfit. at 581 Cap. b. 209 Hamilton.
" Thomas F. mach. at. Colts, h. 69 Huyshope.
" William J. mach. at Colts, b. 41 Woodbridge.
" ☞see also Regan; Ragan.
Reaphy Thomas, laborer, b.2u. 23 Spruce.
Rearden John, sec'y Case, Lockwood & Brainard Co. 141 Pearl. h. 246 Collins.
                    See page 475.
Reardon Abbie J. dressmaker, b. 115 Collins.
" Charles, at Colts, b.u. 36 Woodbridge.
" Charles J. (Buckley & R.) h.u. 115 Collins.
" Daniel, laborer at 29 Alb. h.2u. 33 Liberty.
" David F. lab. at 581 Cap. h.2u. 113 Windsor.
" David Jr. machinist, h.2u. 113 Windsor.
" Edward T. hardener, 388 Cap. h.u. 338 Park.
" Eliza, wid. Dennis, b. 115 Collins.
" John, laborer, h.u. 47 Windsor.
" John, printer at Hartford Times, 716 Main, h. 19 Pleasant.
" John F. porter at 216, b.u. 192 State.
" John J. carpenter, b. 70 Albany.
" John J. porter, h. 73 Williams.
" Julia, wid. William, h.u. 102 Albany.
" Mamie, milliner, 835 Main, b. 11 Winthrop.
" Mary Mrs. b. W.H. Home for Aged, Albany.
" Mary, wid. Andrew, h. 337 Front.
" Michael, laborer, b.u. 102 Windsor.
" Michael F. laborer, b.u. 338 Park.
" Patrick, bartender, h.u. 35 Mechanic.
" Patrick, boilerm. P.& R. h.2u. 88 Walnut.
" Patrick, carinspector, N.E.R. h. Albany.
" Patrick E. gardener, h. 10 Owen.
" Patrick J. pressm. 141 Pearl, h.153 Windsor.
" Thomas, cigarm. at 867 Main, b. 255 Asylum.
" Thomas, coachm. at 98 Wells, b. 26 Morgan.
" Thomas, florist at 14 Huntington.
" Thomas, laborer at Colts, b. 89 Front.
" Thomas F. mason, b. 70 Albany.
" Timothy F. engraver, b. 231 Main.
" Timothy J. helper at 54 Arch, h. 49 Wdbg.
" Timothy S. b.u. 47 Windsor.
" Wm. J. buffer, Pope Tube Co. b. 44 Sanford.
" ☞see also Rearden; Riordon.
Rearty Charles, teamster, b. 9 Front.
" John, teamster, h. 9 Front.
" Michael, machinist, b. 9 Front.
" Thos. J. teamster, h. 9 Front.
Reccarda Diuradi, laborer at 1152 Main, h. 74 Pleasant.
" Raphael, laborer, b.u. 67 Morgan.
Recor Albert H. polisher at 388 Capitol, h. E.H t.
Record J. Richard, annealer at 1 Flower, h. 47 Hamilton.
Reckard Helen D. b.u. 84 Webster.
" Jerusha K. wid. Abner W. h.u. 84 Webster.
Reckel Julius, confectioner, h.u. 73 Windsor.
Redden John, teamster, 170, b. 170 New Park.
Redding Amos P. toolm. at Colts, h. 32 Webster.
" Dennis, laborer 1 Flower, h. So. Windsor t.
" John, car inspector, h.u. 49 Liberty.
" Lawrence, painter, h. 45 Chestnut.

Reddy John, mech. at Popes, b. 60 Hungerford.
Redell ☞see also Readel, Reidel.
Redfield Alfred B. office, 239 State, h. 764 Asylum.
" Edward D. cashier City Bank of Hartford, 783 Main, h. 4 Columbia.
" Henry A. president Phœnix National Bank, 803, h. 232 Main.
" Henry S. (Stedman & R.) h. 124 Washington
" Hosmer P. asst. treas. & teller Conn. Trust & Safe Deposit Co. 785 Main, h. 45 Niles.
" John R. president National Exchange Bank, 76 State, h. Farmington c. Prospect av.
" William T. at 239 State, h. 160 Collins.
Redican Patrick, driver, b. 342 Wethersfield.
Redicau Peter, laborer, stonepits, h. So. Laurel.
Reddigan Patrick F. helper P.&R. h. 61 Spruce.
Redhead Ernest E. clk. 369 Cap. b. 112 Whitmore.
" James O. b. 112 Whitmore.
Redigan Patrick, h. 2 Wawarme.
" William, laborer, l.u. 12 Arch.
Redington John, clerk, h.u. 100 Jefferson.
" Judson T. salesman, b. 152 Allyn.
Redlund Emil, assemb. at 556 Cap. h. 110 Laurel.
" William, driver, h. 56 Woodbine.
Redmond Jas. teamster at 230 State, b. 47 Talcott.
" James, teamster, h. 58 Talcott.
" John F. porter, 207 Allyn, h.u.r. 130 Front.
" John W. teamster, 128 Com. b.u. 58 Talcott.
" William F. policeman, h. 34 Russell.
Redway Mary E. b. 36 Jefferson.
Reed A. Douglass, clerk, 131 Mn. b. 95 Franklin.
" Alex. D. h.u. 100 Wooster.
" Agnes D. b. 100 Wooster.
" Andrew, helper, N.Y.R. h.2u. 151 Lawrence.
" Andrew H. butcher at 65, h.2u. 173 Ashley.
" Charles, h.u. 11 Foot Guard.
" Chas. O. bkkpr. 19 Ft. Guard b. Scotland v.
" Clarence J. drug clk. 973 Mn. b. 52 Allen pl.
" Edward Y. machinist at Colts, h. E.H.t.
" Fred. M. clerk at 928 Main, b. 56 Bkm.
" George R. bkkpr. at 66 State, b. 52 Allen pl.
" George W. M. second vice president and gen. manager Pratt & Whitney Co. 1 Flower, h. Tunxis house, Tariffville.
" Herbert Warren, h.u. 27 Alden.
" James, h.u. 288 Park.
" James R. collector, 15 Albany, h. 220 Capen.
" John, baker at 78 Morgan, h. 81 Front.
" John, cook str. Middletown, 285 State.
" John U. foreman at 1 Laurel, h. 52 Allen pl.
" Leonard J. machinist at 328 Asylum, b. 97 Whitmore.
" Lucia M. Mrs. nurse, l. 981 Main.
" Martin Mrs. b. 373 Capitol.
" Michael W. mach. at Colts, h. 97 Whitmore.
" Myron W. mechanic at Popes, h.u. 203 Park.
" Patrick, laborer for city, h.u. 288 Park.
" William H. bkkpr. at 103 Asy. h. 75 Laurel.
" ☞see also Reid; Read.
Reepenhousen Wm. M. steamfr. at 690, h. 867 Park.
Rees Henry E. assistant secretary Ætna Insurance Co. 666 Main, h. 60 Niles.
Reese Isaac J. steamfitter at 70 Com. b. 1150 Main.
" Joseph, laborer, b.2u. 208 Sheldon.
" Milton P. mach. at 135 Sheldon, b. 28 Dean.

Reeve Alice I. bookkeeper, b.u. 104 Whitmore.
" Wm. M. machinist 9 Sig. h.u. 104 Whitmore.
" Wm. R. machinist at Colts, h. 104 Whitmore.
Reeves Mark, clerk advertising dept. at Popes, h. 2 Columbia.
Regan B. Mrs., Catholic books, h. 298 Main.
" Charles, carpenter, b. 68 Carpenter.
" Dennis F. lineman, h. 298 Main.
" Eugene F. at 581 Capitol, b. 47 Flower.
" Michael A. mach. at 54 Arch, h. 47 Flower.
" Patrick, teamster, 435, h.u. 435 Broad
" Peter J. steamfitter, 581 Cap. b. 209 Hamilton.
" ☞ see also Reagan; Ragan.
Regneuf Victor, orderly at 20 So. Hudson.
Regtsky Ben, helper, 198, h. 198 Front.
Reheiser Florence, cook, h.u. 58 Temple.
" Simon, cook at 53 Ann, b.u. 24 Mulberry.
Rehse Augustus, tailor, h.u. 22 Jefferson.
" Edward A. b.u. 22 Jefferson.
Reinbert E. T. at 254 Pearl, b. 119 Capitol.
Reiche Charles E. manufacturer of billiard tables, r. 599 Main, h. 16 Walnut.
" Hermann C. saloon, 357 Asy. h.2u. 29 West.
" Hermann C. Jr. printer at 154 Pearl, h. 55 Madison.
" Robert, waiter at 358 Asylum, h. E.H.t.
Reid Ann, wid. Patrick, h.4u. 49 Spruce.
" Bridget, h.u. 286 Park.
" Francis, b.u. 286 Park.
" Fred M. painter, h. 60 Loomis.
" Fred. T. forem. Pope Tube Co.h.u. 41 Spring.
" Jas. W. merchant tailor,1212 Mn. h. 10 Avon.
" John J. carpenter, b. 548 Park.
" John P. crater at 581 Capitol, b. 214 Allyn.
" Lewis F. Dr. instructor Trinity college, h. 117 Woodland.
" Mary, h.2u. 286 Park.
" Mary, wid. Edward, h.u. 214 Allyn.
" Robert, compositor at Sunday Globe, 25 Asylum, b. 19 Goodwin.
" Robert J. machinist at 26 Potter, h. E.H.t.
" Thomas D. machinehand at Colts, h. E.H.t.
" William C. cabinetmaker, h. 15 Buckingham.
" William D. h. 365 Main.
" Wm. G. mach. at 30 Cush. h.u. 36 Belmont.
" William L. mach. at Colts, h.u. 45 Hudson.
" William M. floorwalker at Brown, Thomson & Co. 942, l. 1224 Main.
" Wm. R. carpenter, h. 48 Oak.
" ☞ see also Read; Reed.
Reidel Arthur E. clerk, b. 130 State.
" Ernest, beltmaker at 15 Tru. h. 31 Grace.
" Louise, tailoress at 130 State, b. 1078 Main.
" W. Moritz, tailor, 130, h.u. 130 State.
" ☞ see also Readel, Redell.
Reidy Bridget, wid. John, h. 130 Front.
Reiff Chas. F. cigarmaker at 867 Main, h. E.H.t.
Reighenzi Alexander, cook at 30 Washington.
Reiley Alan C. correspondent at Popes, b. 156 Sargeant.
" Michael H. enameler at Popes, b.u. 16 Avon.
" William J. enameler at Popes, b. 16 Avon.
Reilly Annie, h. 57 Walnut.
" Cathrine, wid. Edw. dressm. h.u. 12 Cedar.
" Charles J. telegrapher, 756 Main, h. 37 Dean.

Reilly Edward, hodcarrier, h.u. 52 Hicks.
" Elizabeth, wid. Christopher, h. 57 Walnut.
" Frederick J. clerk, 6 Central, b. 37 Dean.
" James, b. 2 Holcomb.
" Jas. H. liv. stable, r. 173 State, h.u. 60 Gov.
" John, toolmaker at 436 Cap. h. 1423 Broad.
" John F. electrician, b. 57 Walnut.
" Joseph F. b. 67 Congress.
" Julie Smith, teacher of dancing, City Mission hall, 234 Pearl, h. 65 Imlay.
" Margaret, wid. John, h. 75 Avon.
" Margaret, wid. Thomas, h. 67 Congress.
" Mary Mrs. h.u. 2 Rice ct.
" Mary E. clerk at Brown, Thomson & Co. 942 Main, b. 72 Chestnut.
" Mary J. assist. at 5 Athenæum, b. 12 Cedar.
" P. Harvard, teacher of dancing, 6 Haynes, h.u. 134 Main.
" Philip, livery stable, 19, h. 26 Gold.
" Philip B. bartender at 22, b. 21 Central.
" Philip H. molder at 690 Park, h.u. 134 Madison av.
" Richard J. tinner at 346 Main, b. 67 Congress.
" Sara C. Mrs.: h. 65 Imlay.
" William J. operator, 756 Main, b. 37 Dean.
" ☞ see also Riley; O'Reilly, Reiley.
Reimann Annie R. burnisher, b.u. 1 Wooster.
" William, cigarm. at 741 Main, h.u. 1 Wooster.
Reine James, operator at 135 Sheldon, b. 4 Elm.
Reinert Emil G. physician, 553, h. 553 Main.
Reinhardt John, cigarmaker, h.u. 33 Martin.
" N. Mrs., Palace laundry, h. 33 Martin.
Reinhart Jacob, laborer, 490, b. 490 Windsor av.
Reinholtz Robert, tinner, h.2u. 72 Sanford.
" William H. machinist, N.Y.R. h.u. 16 Chst.
Reinkendoff Albert, laborer, h. 13 New Park.
Reipenhouse Wm.M. steamfitter,690, h.867 Park.
Reis Lillian M. teach. West Mid. sch. b. 22 Girard.
" Philip J. cutter 132 State, h. 112 Windsor av.
" ☞ see also Rice; Ryce.
Reise Milton P. helper, 135 Shel. b. 22½ Alden.
" William, operator, 135 Shel. b. 22½ Alden.
Reisel Edward, salesman at Neal, Goff & Inglis Co. 980 Main, h.u. 29 Florence.
Reisman E. tailor, h.u. 88 Sheldon.
Reitz Frank, fruit store, 31, h.r. 29 Albany.

**RELIGIOUS HERALD,** R. H. Smith, editor and proprietor, 336 Asylum.
           See page 469.
Relihan Edward, stonemason, b. 41 Hamilton.
" Edward Jr. policeman, h.2u. 32 Franklin.
" Francis J. at 956 Main, b. 223 Park.
" James J. machinist at 1 Flow. h. 223 Park.
" John F. machinist 556 Cap. h. 39 Hamilton.
" Michael J. gardn'r 1054 Asy. h. 345 Collins.
" Michael J. pressm. 555 Cap. b. 117 Woodland.
Relles Joseph A. laborer at 9 Sig. h.r. 12½ S. Pro.
Relyea Charles A. bookkeeper at 2 Chapel b. 260 Wethersfield.
" Rena, b. 260 Wethersfield.

**RELYEA WILLIAM H.** architect and builder, 260, h. 260 Wethersfield.
Remillard Frank H. mach. 133 Shel. h. 40 John.

Remington Charles H. clerk at Orient Ins. Co. 5 Haynes, b. 147 Washington.
" Edgar A. salesman 249 Pearl, b. 19 Capitol.
" Henry S. butcher at 125 Alb. h. 147 Wash.
" Mary C. Mrs. b. 147 Washington.

**REMINGTON STANDARD TYPEWRITER,** Frederick S. Squier, mangr. Phœnix Life Building, 49 Pearl, rm. 19.

Remsen J. J. conductor St.Ry. b. 17 Chapel.
Remson Charles F. teacher at E. M. Huntsingers, 30 Asylum, h.2u. 22 Seyms.
Renals Edmund, clerk at 581 Capitol.
Renard Charles F. janitor at 764 Mn. h. 66 Hung.
" George, elevatorer, b. 1244 Main.
" Lena, dressmaker, b. 19 Trumbull.
" Wm. T. bartender at 26 State.
Rengstrom Israel, helper, N.Y.R. h. 19¼ Putnam.
Rennacker Charles A. (*Rennacker & Co.*) h. 159 Ashley.

**RENNACKER & CO.** clothiers141 Asy*
Renney Charles A. clerk, h. 336 Maple.
Renshaw Annie, dressmaker, 202, b. 202 High.
" Joseph B. mach. at 1 Flower, h. 202 High.
Renwick Wm. R. shipper at 956 Mn. b. 76 Flower.
Renz Frank, harnessmaker, b.u. 82 Potter.
" William, harnessmaker, 8 Sig. b. 82 Potter.
Resnik Philip, tailor, 38, h. 38 .Windsor.
" Sam. tailor, b.u. 30 Kilbourn.
Respess John, at 149 State, b. 98 Trumbull.

**RETREAT FOR THE INSANE,** 30 Washington.        *See pages* 698, 699.
Rettig Paul, tailor, h. 27 Russell.
Reuber Henry, tailor, 8 State, h. 27 Williams.
Reuschel Ernst, cabinetm. at 633 Main, h. 17 King.

**REUSS HUGO,** designer and engraver, 30 Asylum, h. 27 Morris.
Reuthe Adolph C. lettercarrier, h. Hockanum v.

**REVIEW PUBLISHING CO.** 8 State.        *See page* 472.
Rexford ElizabethR.wid.Steuben,h.81Sigourney.
Reyneke Charles, chef 98 Wells, h. 33 Mulberry.
Reynolds Alden H. blacksmith at 5 Mechanic. h. 102 Capen.
" Amos, carpenter, h. 183 Woodland.
" Benjamin, b. 65 Albany.

**REYNOLDS & CO.** electrical engineers, 85 Pratt.        *See page* 507.
" Charles R. (*Reynolds & Co.*) h. 17 Alden.
" Eliza J. h. c. Davenport and Smith.
" Forest, ostler at 1214, l. 1214 Main.
" Frank D. operator 11 l Sheldon, b. 16½ Pratt.
" Frank P. asst. treas. Sigourney Tool Co. 9, h. 232 Sigourney.
" Fred W. horsetrainer, h. New Park.
" George A. cashier at Pratt & Whitney Co. 1 Flower, clerk *fire commissioners,* h. 15½ Vernon.
" Geo. E. bartender, 1119 Mn. h. 96 Windsor.
" Geo. E. teamster, h. 37 So. Hudson.
" Granville, teamster, b. 37 So. Hudson.
" Harry M. musician, b. 27 Atwood.

Reynolds Henry H. agent 811 Mn. b. 27 Spring.
" James, carpenter, h. 46 Francis.
" James E. teamster at 232 Shel. h. 86 Ward.
" James H. lacquerer at 62 Mar. h.r.1 Orchard.
" John R. supt. Smyth Mfg. Co. h. 27 Atwood
" John V. (*Reynolds & Co.*) h. 17 Alden.
" Lafayette L. forem. 24 Potter, h. 63 Madison.
" Michael, harnessmaker, h. 82 Potter.
" Oms W. teacher at E. M. Huntsinger, 30 Asylum, b. 232 High.
" Steve, fireman steamer Hartford, 285 State.
" Wm. blacksmith at 22 Wells, h. Bloomfield t.
Rheaume Edward, carpenter at 158 Woodland, b. 32 Windsor.
Rheddick Alice A. b. 241 Bellevue.
" Enoch H. clerk, 1 So. Ann, h. 14 Elmer.
Rhein Isaac, h. 198 Front.
" Rubien, clothier, 68 Talcott, h. 72 Village.
" Samuel, h. 198 Front.
Rhetigan Michael, clerk, b. 86 Hopkins.
Rhoades Chas. A. clerk 84 Pratt, h. 56 Capitol.
" Galen M. carpenter, h. 56 Capitol.
Rhoads May E. milliner, h.u. 106½ Trumbull.
" S. E. Mrs. h.u. 106½ Trumbull.
Rhodes Chas. B. toolmkr. Colts, h. Wethersfield t.
" Chauncey, h. 51 Buckingham.
" Chauncey E. collector, 82 Pearl, b. 51 Bkm.
" Eddie J. teamster r. 334 Asy. b. 31 Chapel.

**RHODES L. E. CO.** machine manufacturers, 26 High.        *See page* 548.
" Leverett E. president L. E. Rhodes Co. 26 High, h. 51 Oak.
" Wm. H. real estate, 49 Pearl, h. 111 Retreat.
Ribeck A. helper at 1 Flower, h. 39 Putnam.
Riando Blase, waiter 90, b. 90 Front.
Ribella Andeia, ragpicker, h. 20 Charles.
" Domenico, ragpicker, h. 20 Charles.
" John, bootblack, b.u. 20 Charles.
Ricard Geo. H. pressm. 252 Pearl, b. 40 Canton.
Ricco Tony, bakery, 178, b. 178 Front.
Rice Bros. saloon, 257 Asylum.
William C. Rice.        Francis W. Rice.
" Abraham, cigar store, 92,h. 92 New Britain.
" Albert L. carpenter at 1, b. 1 Rice ct.
" Ann, wid. Luke, h. 10 Village.

**RICE & BALDWIN,** electrical engineers, 214 Pearl.        *See page* 494.
Willard A. Rice.        Edward M. Baldwin.
" Charles D. mechanical engineer at Popes, h. 78 Seymour.
" Edward J. ostler at 342 Asy. b. 5 Chapel.
" Francis W. (*Rice Bros.*) h. 1425 Broad.
" David, twister at Cheney Bros. silk mill, 34 Morgan, h.u. 4 Winthrop.
" Frank, laborer, h.3u. 1 North.
" George H. machinist, b.u. 4 Winthrop.
" George S. blacksmith at Colts, h. 46 Willard
" Harry, clerk at 956 Main, b. 50 Governor.
" Harry L. student Trinity college, 17 Northam tower, Summit.
" Henry W. carpenter, 1, h. 1 Rice ct.
" Henry W. clerk, 257 Asylum, b. 75 Flower.
" Jos. helper at Pratt & Cady Co. b. 75 Gov.
" Joseph P. electrician at 556 Cap. b. 75 Gov.
" Mary, wld. Christian, h. 75 Flower.

Rice Mary L. clerk Hartford Seminary Press, b. 175 Sigourney.
" Michael J. clerk, b.u. 50 Governor.
" Oliver, ostler at 149 State, h. 1 Elliott pl.
" Richard J. inspector Hartford Steam Boiler Insp. & Ins. Co. 650 Main, h. 65 Governor.
" Richard W. salesman, h.u. 215 Garden.
" Salvator, laborer, h. 70 Avon.
" Thos. R. machinist at 80 Huy. h. E.H.t.
" Walter C. mach. at 1 Flower, h. 248 Law.
" Willard A. (R. & Baldwin,) 214 Pearl, h. 42 Hopkins.
" William C. (Rice Bros.) b. 75 Flower.
" Wm. F. general agt. at 197 Asy.h. 1 Sumner.
" Wm. H. head clerk at N.Y.R. 95 Pleasant, b. 46 Willard.
" ☞ see also Reis; Ryce.
Rich Alfred T. letter carrier, P.O. b. 58 Maple.
" Edna E. Miss, h. 896 Asylum.
" Ernest A. student Trinity college, 9 Northam tower, Summit.
" Joseph, clerk at 76 Trumbull, b. 37 Chapel.
" Samuel S. b. 8 Flatbush.
Richard Alfred, teamster, b. 128 Albany.
" Don C. clerk at 338 Main, b. 242 Weth.
" Elmer I. machinist at 1 Flow. b. 231 Law.
" Jacob, saddler at 8 Sigourney, h. 118 Asylum.
" William A. Rev. pastor South Park M. E. church, h. 137 Jefferson.
Richards Alfred, mach. at 13 Central, b. E.H.t.
" Alfred E. student at Yale, b. 15 Townley.
" Alfred H. machinist at P.&R. h. E.H.t.
**RICHARDS ALFRED T.** general ag't Conn. Mutual Life Ins. Co. 783 Main, rm. 16, h. 15 Townley. See pages 450, 451.
" Amanda Mrs. laundress, b. 242 Belevue.
" Byron O. paint. 53 Vernon, h. 126 Hamilton.
" Charles S. b. 41 Wooster.
" Edith K. teacher W. M. Sch. b. 15 Townley.
" Ellis G. vice pres't and secretary National Fire Ins. Co. 95 Pearl, h. 897 Asylum.
**RICHARDS FRANCIS H.** mechanical engineer, patent attorney, 803 Main, h. 112 Edwards. See outside front cover.
" Frederick, carpenter, h. 113 Trumbull.
" Henry W. clerk at Brown, Thomson & Co. 942 Main, h.u. 41 Wooster.
" Hubert P. supt. at F. H. Richards patent office, 803 Main, h. New Britain t.
" Joseph H. blacksmith, b.u. 12 Mays ct.
" Louis A. electrician, h. Park, W.H.t.
" Louis W. clerk at 238 Park, b.u. 8 Oak.

Richards Mattie, milliner, b. 25 Spring.
" Thomas H. h. 41 Wooster.
" Wm. buffer at 62 Market, h. 56 Westland.
" William E. helper at 133 Sheldon, b. E.H.t.
" Zephir, clerk at 149 Babcock, h. 45 Amity.
Richardson C. H. cook str. Hartford, 285 State.
" Ellen L. h. 164 High.
" Frank, l. 757 Main.
" George, driver at 2 American.
" George, photo eng. 177 Asy. b. 119 Capitol.
" Geo. F. electrician at Popes, b. 18 Ellsworth.
" George H. office 721 Main, rm. 1, h. 55 Oak.
" Israel, ostler, h. 3 Wolcott.
" James A. porter 45 Pratt, b.u. 15 Mechanic.
" Joseph S. enameler at Popes, b. 84 Putnam.
" Leonard E. physician, 99, h. 99 Park.
" M. Arthur, clerk, b. 96 Wooster.
" Susan A. wid. W. E. h. 96 Wooster.
" Walter A. clerk 197 Asylum, b. Rockville t.
Richelieu John, hodcarrier, b. 16 Market.
Richie Jordan W. cabinetm. Taft Co. b. 64 Cap.
" Robert M. laborer, h. 29 Judson.
" ☞ see also Ritchie.
Richman Jacob M. wrapper mfg. 172, h. 174 Front.
Richmann Saml. barber, 291 Park, b. 104 Windsor.
Richmond Augusta R. wid. Robt. W. h. 7 Preston.
" Charles E. helper at Colts, h.u. 45 Huyshope.
" Chester B. photographer, b.u. 84 Jefferson.
" Denison, student Trinity college, 14 Northam tower, Summit.
" Eugene H. at Travelers Insurance Co. 56 Prospect, b. 25 Florence.
" Frank B. treas. 135 Shel. b. 32 Buckingham.
" Frank L. painter, 28 Temple, h. 18 Barbour.
" George W. mach.hand Colts, h. Burnside v.
" Henry U. h. 7 Preston.
" James, painter at 10 Ford, h. E.H.t.
" James G. foreman at 581 Capitol, h. 65 Woodbine.
" John L. engir. 370 Asylum, b. 167 Albany.
" Susan J. wid. Henry A. h. 5 So. Prospect.
Richter Albert E. architect 700 Mn. b. 25 Capitol.
RICHTER FERDINAND, councilman 1st ward, manager 803 Main, b. 75 Temple.
Rickaby Georgia H. stenographer at Popes, b.2u. 166 Washington.
**RICKER ALFRED T.** proprietor Hartford Molding Works, 26 Potter. h. 89 Webster.          See page 517.

Ricker Catherine Mrs. b. 335 Wethersfield.
" Nellie T. attendant, 30 Washington.
" Rufus W. h.u. 61 Whitmore.
Riddell Andrew J. mach. at Popes, h. 14 Ellsworth.
" George, stonecutter, h. 78 Maple.
" George B. engir. Orph. Asy. h. 38 Harbison.
" Thomas, laborer at Popes, b. 14 Ellsworth.
Rider ☞ see also Ryder.
Ridett Alexander, machinist at 1 Flower, h. South Manchester v.
Rieckel Albert, blacksmith, h. 23 Putnam.
" William, foreman at Popes, h.u. 254 Putnam.
Riedel Alwyne C. clerk, 700 Main, b. 130 State.
Riedlinger Joseph, b.u. 67 Hudson.
Riedmann Matthias, tailor, h.u. 5 Orchard.
Rielley Patrick, b. 2 Holcomb.
Rieu Oliver, laborer, h. 129 Ward.
Rigby May E. teach. Lawrence st. sch. b. 67 Russ.
**RIGGS CHARLES H.** dentist, 68 Pratt, rm. 34, h.u. 25 Marshall.
" Robert B. prof. in chemistry, Trinity college, h. 35 Forest.
Righenzi Alexander, chef at 30 Washington, h. h.u. 28 Julius.
Rigney Edward J. polisher at James L. Howard Co. 438 Asylum, b.2u. 39 South Prospect.
" Ellen, wid. James, h.u. 39 So. Prospect.
" James P. enameler at Popes, b.u. 39 S.Pro.
" Joseph, carpenter, b. 28 South Prospect.
" Thomas, blacksm. at 12 Ferry, h. 28 S.Pro.
Riley Agnes, forewoman Neal, Goff & Inglis Co. 980 Main, b. 27 Windsor.
" Annie E. stenographer at Popes, b. E.H.t.
" Austin J. bartender at 25, b. 30 Temple.
" Charles D. cashier First National Bank, 50 State, h. 1 Ward.
" Charles F. bricklayer, b. 68 Bond.
" Chas. F. quarrym. at stonepits, h. 5 Flatbush.
" Charles S. machinist at 1 Flow. b. 90 Ann.
" Edmund D. sup't at Matt. Hewins, billiards, 734 Main, h. 16 Morris.
" Edward, mason, h.3u.r. 95 Sheldon.
" Edward T. clerk at 904 Main, b. 15 Belden.
" Ellen, wid. Luke, h.u. 13 Kilbourn.
" Eugene, at 690 Park, b. 266 New Park.
" Frances D. clerk at Popes, h. E.H.t.
" Frank P. pressman 252 Pearl, b. 21 Talcott.
" George P. farmer, b. 67 Francis.
" George W. machinist, h.3u. 40 So.Prospect.
" James, h.u. 16 Avon.
" James, at Cathedral Lyceum, h. 67 Francis.
" James, blacksmith, h. 11 Ellery.
" James, cook at 80 State, l.u. 160 Allyn.
" James, laborer, b. 1300 Asylum.
" James J. carpenter, b. 5 South Laurel.
" John, cigarm. at 88 State, b. 58 Talcott.
" John, cigarm. at 104 Asy. b. 56 Chestnut.
" John, gardener at 158, h. 158 High.
" John, lab. 147 Woodland, h.2u. 45 Green.
" John, printer, b.2u. 5 Goodman.
" John, quarrym. at stone pits, b. 5 Flatbush.
" John C. miller at 165, h.u. 169 Windsor.
" John G. laborer 165 Windsor, h. 53 Walnut.
" John J. toolmaker, h.2u. 1423 Broad.

Riley John Mrs. tailoress, h.u. 1443 Broad.
" John P. hackdriver at 571 Main, h. 40 S.Pro.
" John P. machinist, h. 14 Hawthorn.
" Mary A. teacher Charter Oak sch. b. 60 Gov.
" Mary A. h. 6 Talcott.
" Mary E. nurse, 205, h. 205 Ashley.
" Mary J. designer at 908 Main, b. 16 Avon.
" Michael, inspector at Popes, b. 98 Babcock.
" Michael, peddler, h.r. 64 Vanblock.
" Patrick, h.2u. 5 Goodman.
" Patrick, b. 70 Front.
" Patrick, laborer, h. 58 Talcott.
" Peter, roadmaker, h. 5 So. Laurel.
" Philip, helper at Case, Lockwood & Brainard Co. 141 Pearl, h. 21 Talcott.
" Philip, teamster, h.r. 15 Belden.
" Richard gardener, h.2u. 116 Albany.
" Richard Jr. plater at 62 Mar. h.2u. 116 Alb.
" Stanley J. policeman, h.u. 61 Russ.
" Stephen, engineer P.&R. h. 18 Liberty.
" Thomas, h. 220 Allyn.
" Walter A. h. 241 Main.
" William, enameler at Popes, b.u. 16 Avon.
" Wm. A. bkkpr. at 205 State, h. Burnside v.
" Wm. J. barber, 248, h.u. 250 Park.
" William J. driver at 701 Main, h.r. 15 Belden.
" ☞ see also Reiley; Reilly; O'Reilly.
Rinck Augustus, lab. at 70 Com. h.2u. 86 Retreat.
Rines James A. merchant tailor, 30 Asylum, b. 427 Main, rm. 38.
Ring Julia, wid. John, h.u.r. 33½ Front.
" Patrick J. comp. 141 Pearl, b.u.r. 33½ Front.
Ringrose John T. coachman, h.u. 56 Maple.
Ringstrom Annie, wid. Peter Jr. h. 22 Putnam.
" Israel, helper, h.u.r. 19½ Putnam.
Ringwood Daniel, carpenter, 191 Lawrence, h. 44 Canton.
Rinnie Richard, carpenter, b. 41 Asylum.
Riordan Carroll, bartender at 30, b. 70 Albany.
" David B. lab. at Popes, b. 70 Albany.
" Ellen, wid. Martin, b. 30 Florence.
" James I. polisher at Popes, b.u. 102 Albany.
" John, polisher, h. 102 Albany.
" John J. assembler at Popes, h.u. 102 Albany.
" John J. brazier at Popes, h.2u. 36 Lawrence.
" Wm. J. brazier at Popes, b.u. 295 Lawrence.
" Mary E. dressmaker, h. 71 Sigourney.
" ☞ see also Rearden; Reardon.
Rioux Eugene, carpenter, h.u. Lubeck.
" Fred, carpenter, b. 52 Russell.
" H. L. carpenter, h. Prospect av. n. Park.
" Oliver, carpenter, h. 137 Ward.
" Wilfred, carpenter, h.u. 54 Prospect av.
Ripkin Mark, h. 84 Barbour.
Ripley Bros. Co. carpets, wall paper, 84-88 Pratt.
" Charles E. at Hartford Steam Boiler Insp. & Ins. Co. 650 Main, b. 550 Farmington.
" Charles H. joiner, b. 241 Pearl.
" E. Elton, inspector, 690 Park, b. 218 N.P.
" George W. (R. Bros. Co.) h. E.H.t.
" John C. with The J. H. Eckhardt Co. art and picture frame store, 695 Main, b. 215 Jef.
" Laura M. h. 200 Sigourney.
" Lewis W. president Ripley Bros. Co. h. Glastonbury t.

Ripley W. G. Mrs. bkkpr. at 295 Asy. h. E.H.t.
" William S. clerk at Lincoln, Seyms & Co. 34 Market, b. 241 Pearl.
Rippilo Frank, laborer, b. 56 Portland.
Rippolone James, barber, b.u. 73 Morgan.
" Joseph, peddler, h.u. 73 Morgan.
Risby James, laborer, h.2u. 2 Center.
Rising Addie, wid. Charles A. h.u. 68½ Laurel.
" Charles A. mach. at 1 Flower, b. 68½ Laurel.
Risley A. L. h.2u. 39 Kingsley.
" Adelaide E. Mrs. h. 281 Allyn.
" Albert E. teller at Ætna National Bank, 644 Main, h. 399 Capitol.
" Arthur L. sawyer at 335 Shel. b. 6 John.
" Cassius E. helper 164 State, b. Hockanum v.
" Charles, foreman, 285 State.
" Chas. S. motorman at St. Ry. h. E.H.t.
" Clara I. clerk at 881 Main, b.u. 128 Maple.
" Edith L. b. 399 Windsor av.
" Edward F. helper at 164 State, h.2u. 911 Main, rm. 8.
" Elisha, supt. agencies Conn. Mutual Life Insurance Co. 783 Main, h. 70 Gillett.
" Geo. L. clerk, 881 Main, h. 385 Windsor av.
" Henry A. mech. at Popes, b. 90 Capitol.
" Isadore, wid. Henry E. h.u. 128 Maple.
" James, painter, b. 1244 Main.
" Jane A. wid. Caleb, h.u. 10 Lewis.
" John A. assembler at Colts, h. E.H.t.
" John N. (Drivers' Ice Co.) h. 346 Weth.
**RISLEY LEON S.,** Ph. G., druggist, 385 Capitol, h. 8 Columbia.
" Levi D. conductor St.Ry. b. 80 State.
" Lorenzo, farmer, h. 99 Windsor av.
" Ralph M. patternm. 133 Sheldon, h. E.H.t.
" Rollin, clerk at 87 Asylum, b.u. 128 Maple.
" William, boilermaker at 152 State, b. E.H.t.
" Wm. D. potter, h.2u. 86 Grove.
" ☞ see also Wrisley.
Rist Owen D. jeweler, 847 Main, rm. 1, h. E.H.t.
Risteen Allan D. asso. editor Locomotive at Hfd. Steam Boiler Insp. & Ins. Co. 650 Main.
Rita Vito, laborer, b.3u. 51 Morgan.
Ritchie Annie, bookkeeper, b. 66 Dean.
" Herman, printer, h.u. 55 Madison.
" David (Mannix & Ritchie,) h. 66 Dean.
" David Jr. apprent. 133 Shel. b. 66 Dean.
" Harry, cook at 80 State.
" James R. mach. at Colts, h. 117 Trumbull.
" Joseph, waiter, h.2u. 2 Affleck.
" Robert, gardener, 102 Windsor av. h. Judson.
" Robert, waiter at 358 Asy. l. East Hartford t.
" W. C. purser str. Hartford, 285 State.
" ☞ see also Richie.
Ritter Joseph, b. 24 Elmer.
Rival Peter, assem. at Colts, h. Hockanum v.
River House, Edward N. Atherton, 76 Ferry.
Rivers Fannie M. wid. John H. h. 210 Windsor av.
" Nelson, h. 47 New Britain.
Rivkin Isaac, assembler at Colts, b. 34 Avon.
" Max, (Chesky H. Co.) h. 84 Barbour.
" Morris, h. 34 Avon.
" Nathan, assembler at Popes, b.u. 34 Avon.
Rixinger Matilda, wid. Otto, h. 47 Park.

Riz Ina, b. 103 Webster.
Rizy Joseph A. rubberw. 690 Park, h. 41 Laurel.
Rizzo James, fruits and groceries, 100 Park, h. c. Park and Broad.
" Leon, fruits, 59, h. 59 Spruce.
Roach Andrew, waiter at 931 Mn. b. 2 Church.
" Edward, expressman, b. 141 Barbour.
" Edward, stonecutter, b.u. 48 Avon.
" Frank, fireman, h. 6 Huntley.
" Garrett, lettercarrier, h.u. 74 Pleasant.
" George, iceman at 4 Central, h. 96 Chst.
" John F. mach. at N.Y.R. b.2u. 82 Front.
" Lawrence, blacksmith N.Y.R. h. 29 Chestnut.
" Mary J. b. 51 Spring.
" Michael, mason, b. 88 Church.
" Michael, stonecutter, h.2u. 48 Avon.
" Morris, mech. 83 Woodbine, b. 134 Martin.
" Nicholas, carptr. at N.Y.R. h. 163 Babcock.
" Nicholas Jr. polisher at 142 Russ, b. 163 Bab.
" Thomas, laborer, h. 6 Green.
" Thomas, teamster, 189 State, h.2u. 82 Front.
" Thos. F. helper at 135 Shel. b.2u. 82 Front.
" William, b. 2 Holcomb.
" ☞ see also Roch; Roche.
Roache Patrick, bridgebuilder, h.u. 1176 Main.
Roahen John, laborer, h.2u. 72 Walnut.
Roane Abraham, laborer, h.u.r. 41 Mather.
" ☞ see also Rhone.
Roarty ☞ See Rorty.
Roatch William, plumber, 3 Grove.
Robarge Benj. lab. at 685, b. 685 Windsor av.
Robatz Anthony, laborer, h.2u. 12 Ellery.
Robb Alexander, conduc. St.Ry. l.u. 10 Church.
" David, laborer h.2u. 128 Windsor.
" James, laborer, b. 9 Holcomb.
" James W. salesman at 145 Asylum, h.u. 375 Windsor av.
" Louis, woodpeddler for W. C. Mason & Co. b. 330 Pearl.
" Robert L. driver, b. 330 Pearl.
" William Lispenard, professor of physics, Trinity college, h. 118 Vernon.
Robbins Brothers, cabinet furniture, 633 Main. Frederick A. Robbins. Philemon W. Robbins.
" Charles S. at Travelers Insurance Co. 56 Prospect, b. 85 Buckingham.
" Edward D. attorney at law, 739 Main, rm. 1, h. Wethersfield t.
" Edward H. foreman at H. B. Beach & Son, 135 Grove, h. 47 Clark.
**ROBBINS ELIPHALET D.** repairing in wood and metal, general jobbing, 54 Pratt, h. Wethersfield t.
" Frederick A. (Robbins Bros.) h. 181 High.
" George, lather, b. 191 Lawrence.
" James P. clerk at 690 Park, b. 44 High.
" John, brakeman at N.E.R. h. 8 Warren.
" Jos. B. chief clerk, P.&R. b. 57 Farmington.
" May E. teacher at Brown sch. b. Rocky Hill t.
" Mary W. b. 379 Wethersfield.
" Philemon W. (R. Bros.) h. 16 C.O.pl.
" Richard H. at Conn. Mutual Life Ins. Co. 783 Main, b. Rocky Hill t.
" Robert W. clerk Phœnix Mutual Life Ins. Co. 49 Pearl, h. Wethersfield t.

**THINKING PEOPLE Read The Post Daily.**

**ROBBINS SILAS W.** The A. D.
Vorce Co. h. Wethersfield t. *See p.* 418.
" Silas W. Rev. b. 5 Preston.
" Susan, b. 36 Jefferson.
" ☞ *see also Robins.*
Roberts Abby W. wid. Walker W. b. 12 Willard.
" Abraham, apprent. at 690 Park, b. 42 Smith.
" Albert, pressm. at 690 Park, h.u. 42 Smith.
" Albert O. salesman, b. 23 Girard.
" Arthur D. filer at Colts, b. East Hartford t.
" Caroline F. b. 655 Farmington.
" Charles F. machinist at 30 Cushman, h. 18½ Church.
" Chas. F. real estate, 190 Pearl, h.18 Marshall.
" Charles H. builder, h. 45 Webster.
" Charles S. carpenter, b. 45 Webster.
" E. Cornwall, clerk at Tucker & Goodwin, 8 Hurlburt, h. 22 Columbia.
" Edmund D. sealer weights and city inspector, City hall, 800 Main, h. 21 Imlay.
" Edwd. E. at Eddy Electric Co. b. 113 Ann.
" Edwin M. h. 577 Farmington.
" Edwin Mrs. h.r.u. 1 Orchard.
" Eliza J. Mrs. seamstress, b. 18½ Church.
" Fred C. engir. at 98 Wells, h. 20 Lawrence.
" Fred H. lineman at 266 Pearl, b. 87 High.
" Frederick, painter, 1106, b. 1104 Main.
" George, engineer, b. 36 Woodbridge.
" George, prest. and treas. Hartford Carpet Co. 10 Market, h. 63 Washington.
" George Mrs. (Elvira) h. 59 Lafayette.
" Geo. D. manager, 54 Huntley, h. 9 Walnut.
" George F. polisher, b. 75 Governor.
" George Jr. b. 63 Washington.
" Grace L. h.u. 55 Willard.
" Hamlet F. clerk at P.O. h. 30 West.

ROBERTS HENRY, *alderman 6th ward*, president Hartford Woven Wire Mattress Co. 618 Capitol, h. 59 Lafayette.
" Henry C. h. 32 Village.
" Herbert S. foreman of framing at Colts, h.u. 39 Congress.
" Homer C. at Conn. Mutual Life Ins. Co. 783 Main, h. East Hartford t.
" Hugh, gardener at 118, b. 15 Benton.
" James B. gardener, h.r. 18 Congress.
" Jane E. wid. of Wm. J. h. 31 Townley.
" John, engineer, b. 197 State.
" John J. W. express, 236 Asy. h. 930 Park.
" Julia, wid. William S. h. 7 Lafayette.
" Mary E. b. 36 Jefferson.
" Mary J. b. 18½ Church.
" Martha A. wid. Ozim, bkkpr. at 1148 Main, h. 55 Green.
" Pearl, student, b. 58 Church.
" R. Henry, mach. at 252 Pearl, h. 42 Brook.

**ROBERTS S. F.** awning and tent maker, 124, h. 124 State. *See page* 502.
" Sarah R. b. 113 Ann.
" W. Henry, b.u. 933 Main.
" Walter W. jewelry, 847 Main, rm. 24, h. N.B.
" Wm. R. foreman at 476 Cap. h. Windsor t.
" Wm. A. driver at 169 Asy. h.2u.r. 36 Temple.

Robertson Andrew S. baker, 57 Alb. h. 48 Vine.
" Charles H. teamster, h. 21 Wolcott.
" Christopher, joiner, b. Hawthorn ex.
" Frank, teamster, 56 Com. h.u. 124 Windsor.
" Harry, washer at 690 Park, b. 69 Francis.
" Henry G. clerk, 653 Main, b. E.H.t.
" James A. carptr. at 141 Tru. h.u. 66 Putnam.
" James A. Jr. mach. at 1 Flow. b.u. 234 Zion.
" John, foreman, 57 Albany, h. 103 Bellevue.
" John, rubberworker at 690 Park, b. W.P.v.
" John T. baker, 57 Albany, h. 50 Barbour.
" Lafayette J. fruits and confectionery, 990 Main, h. 73 Church.
" Mamie Mrs. h.u. 18 Trumbull.
" Robert, carpenter at 13, h. 3 Forest.
" St. Clair, carpenter, h.u. 111 Lawrence.
" Sybil R. wid. Gurdon Y. b.101 Huntington.
" Wm. F. mach. 1 Flow. h. Warehouse Point v.
" William B. clerk at 204 State, b. 66 Putnam.
" Wm. J. wiredrawer at 40 Gov. h. 12 Ch.O.
ROBERTSON WILLIAM P. *(Newton, R. & Co.)* grocers, h. 101 Huntington. *See p.* 486.
" William T. mach. at 1 Flow. b. 1478 Broad.
" William W. inspect. at Popes, h.u. 16 Haw.
" ☞ *see also Roberson.*
Robin Charles, carpenter, h.2u. 96 State.
" Louie C. plumber at 120 Mar. b. 96 State.
ROBINS CHARLES H. *city auditor* at City hall, 800 Main, h. 26 Lincoln.
" ☞ *see also Robbins.*
Robinson A. Maud, stenog. at Phœnix Mutual Life Ins. Co. 49 Pearl, b. 197 Park.
" Algernon S. mach. at 556 Cap. h.u.1163 Broad.
" Almen, cigarmaker at 867, b. 1080 Main.
" Arthur D. *(Hill & R.)* h.u. 22 Belden.
" Arthur J. h. 98 Walnut.
" Beverly, driver, b. 60½ Walnut.
" Catharine, wid. Wm. H. h. 200 Wethersfield.
" Charles A. Mrs. b. 152 Asylum.
" Chas. F. switchm. N.Y.R. h.2u. 34 Wooster.
" Charles H. driver, h. 335 Asylum.
" Charles S. mason, h.u. 154 Windsor av.
" Charles W. b. 335 Asylum.
" Edith H. wid. Charles A. h. 152 Asylum.
" Edward C. inspector, Popes, h. 55 Babcock.
" Edwin S. carptr. at 581 Cap. h. 30½ Grace.
" Emily P. wid. Alfred S. h. 35 Lewis.
" F. C. Mrs. h.4u. 20 Trumbull.
" F. E. Miss, boardinghouse, 1246 Main.
" Frederick H. engineer, P.&R. h. 24 Pliny.
" Fredk. P. rubberw. at 690 Park, b. 14 Bart.
" George, h. 20 Allen pl.
" George, hostler at 164 State, l. 30 Ferry.
" Grace Mrs. b. 9 Belden.
" Grace C. teacher, 690, b. 725 Asylum.
" Halbert G. *(Graves & R.)* b. 152 Asylum.
" Henry C. *(Robinson & Robinson,)* h.420 Main.
" Henry N. *(Tracy & R.)* h. 49 Kenyon.
" Henry S. sec'y Conn. Trust & Safe Deposit Co. 785, b. 420 Main.
" Hezekiah, waiter, b. 2 Huntley.
" Honoria M. J. wid. Henry W. dressmaker, h.3u. 312 Asylum, room 2.
" Howard B. toolm. 1 Flow. h.u. 142 Seymour.

**The Up to Date Merchant ADVERTISES in The Post.**

Robinson Isaac H. carpenter h. 40 Smith.
" J. Cæsar, jobber, h.2u. 173 Windsor.
" James B. h. 307 Wethersfield.
" Jas. C. conductor St.Ry. h. S. Glastonbury v.
" James F. mach. at 690 Park, h. 63 Flower.
" John E. salesm. at 272 Asy. h.3u. 1245 Main.
" John T. (R. & Robinson,) b. 420 Main.
" John T. blacksm. Pope Tube Co. h.u. 12 N.B.
" Joseph S. butler 646 Asylum, h.u. 6 Squire.
" Julius, laborer at 70 Huy. b. 30 Pleasant.
" Loren H. mach. at Colts, h. 810 Windsor av.
" Lucius F. (Robinson & Robinson,) 11 Central, park commissioner, h. 45 Forest.
" Mary S. b. 420 Main.
" Nells P. h.2u. 33 Laurel.
" & Robinson, attorneys at law, 11 Central.
    John T. Robinson.    Henry C. Robinson.    Lucius F. Robinson.
" R. Maud, h.u. 280 Main.
" Sarah D. h. 307 Wethersfield.
" Theron I. clerk at 15 Tru. b. 5 Pliny's ct.
" W. B. special examiner bureau pensions, 65 State.
" William H. butler at 210 Far. h. 5 Pliny's ct.
" Winter D. motorman St.Ry. h.u. 884 Main.
Robotham Clara, stenog. at 197 Asy. b. 38 Pliney.
Roch Geo. B. patternmaker, h. 13 Center.
" Geo. B. Jr. mach. at 1 Flower, b. 13 Center.
" William B. plumber, b. 13 Center.
Roche Bridget, nurse, h.3u. 20 Sheldon.
" Edward B. conductor St.Ry. b. 99 Main.
" John J. painter, 17 Elm, h. 103 Whitmore.
" Matthew J. J. boilermkr. b.3u. 20 Sheldon.
" Michael, granitecutter, h.2u. 48 Avon.
" Patrick, blacksmith, h.2u. 51 Front.
" Thomas, blacksmith, h. 15 Elm.
" Thomas, profiler at Colts, h.u. 76 Hudson.
" ☞ see also Roch; Roach.
Rochette Joseph V. mach. N.Y.R. h. 301 Park.
Rock Corinth S. machinist at 1 Flower, b. 118 Asylum, rm. 12.
" Edward Jr. laborer at 133 Shel. b. 51 Wdbg.
" Edward W. engineer, h. 51 Woodbridge.
" Frederic C. stampingclerk at Wm. Rogers Mfg. Co. 66 Market, h.u. 51 Woodbridge.
" H. L. at N.Y.R. b. 78 High.
" John L. helper at 1 Flow. h. 118 Asylum.
" ☞ see also Roch.
Rockenfeller Kittie A. clerk at Brown, Thomson & Co. 942 Main, b. 600 Garden.
" Max W. foreman 581 Capitol, h. 101 Mather.
" Rudolph A. driver, 1204 Main, h. 198 Capen
Rockett Patrick W. mech. at 581 Cap. h. 137 Zion.
Rockwell Alanson L. machinehand at Colts, h. South Windsor t.
" Ann M. wid. Frank, h.u. 216 Windsor av.
" Arthur A. machinehand at Colts, b. S.W.t.
" C. Perry, ass't cashier at Popes, b. 145 Collins.
" Charles, carman at Wm. Rogers Mfg. Co. 66 Market, h. 18 Florence.
" E. H. Mrs. dressmaker, h.2u. 44 Hopkins.
" Frank D. salesman at 126, h. 94 Church.
" Fred A. clerk at 690 Park, b. 30 Grace.
" Fred. C. Bonsilate Box Co. 24 Mechanic, h. 461 Prospect av.

Rockwell Gilbert, b.u.r. 93 Sheldon.
" J. W. mfr. pack. boxes, 67 Front, h.u. 80 Sey.
" Owen L. machinehand at Colts, b. S.Wt.
" Samuel W. engir. at 2 So. Ann, h. Weth. t.
" Walter, machinehand at Colts, h. S.W.t.
Rockwood Harry J. draughtsman at 556 Capitol, b. 83 Sigourney.
Rocky Hill Foundry Co. 9 Asylum.
" Hill stone pits, Zion, opposite Vernon.
Rodblatt Goodman, b. 2 Holcomb.
Rodda Awilda, b. Franklin, c. Annawan.
" James, h. Franklin, c. Annawan.
" Richard, machinist at 30 Cushman, h. Franklin, c. Annawan.
Rodgers Anthony, carpenter, b. 41 Asylum.
" Clarence M. draughtsman at Hfd. Steam Boiler Insp. & Ins. Co. h. 35 Beacon.
" Delia, housekeeper, h. 30 Ferry.
" John, special agent Hartford Steam Boiler Insp. and Ins. Co. 650 Mn. h. 292 Sigourney.
" John A. cook, h. 30 Ferry.
" ☞ see also Rogers.
Rodgerson Andrew, rubberworker at 690 Park, b. 203 Sheldon.
Rodias William, boxm. at 1 Flow. h. 17 S.Pro.
Rodonski Thomas, laborer, b.u. 82 Sheldon.
Rodowski Jacob, laborer, h.u.r. 81 Front.
" Maurice, tailor, 86, h. 86 Front.
Roe Edward L. decorator at Baxter the Decorator, 231 Asylum, h. Rocky Hill t.
Roeben Bernard, cabinetmaker at 225 Sheldon, h. 54 Judson.
Roedel Ernest B. filer at Popes, h.2u. 29 Grace.
Roeder Frederick, tailor at 136, h.3u. 136 State.
Roedlinger Conrad N. foreman gardener on Popes Park, h. 638 Maple.
Roehm Dorothea, clerk at 229, b. 225 Market.
" Emil W. mechanic at Popes, b. 73 Heath.
" Gustav, tinner at 222 State, h. 78 Heath.
Roemer George A., U.S.A. b. 45 Webster.
" Otto, carpenter, h. 112 Brook.
" Roesner August, restau. 1098, h. 1098 Main.
Roennert Alfred, driver, b. 133 Front.
Roeske & Fernald, printers, 703 Main.
    Henry H. Roeske.    R. P. Fernald.
" Henry H. (R. & Fernald,) h.u. 1 Elm pl.
Roessler Henry, screwm. at 476 Capitol, h. H.v.
" Marie, dressmaker, 127, h. 127 Albany.
Rofkess David, b. 31 North.
" Moses S. h. 31 North.
" ☞ see Ruffkess.
Roffler Anton, cook at 30 Washington.
" Ida S. cook at 30 Washington.
Rogers Barnett, saloon 165 Front, h. 104 High.
" Charles, laborer, b. 4 Elm.
" Charles, laborer. h.u. 13 Mechanic.
" Charles A. bookkeeper at Smith, Bourn & Co. 8 Sigourney, h. 41 Niles.
" Chas. C. mach. at Popes, h.u. 48 Bonner.
" Chas. O. painter at 12 Church, b.u. 11 Good.
" Christian, coachman at 98, l. 98 High.
**ROGERS (THE) CUTLERY CO.**
    mfrs. of cutlery and plated goods, 66-68 Market.        *See page 471.*
" Daniel S. clerk, 303 Allyn, h. 195 Jefferson.

Rogers Edward E. clerk at 110, b. 110 Pratt.
" Ellen M. wid. Henry, milliner and dress-
maker at 943 Main, rm. 27, h. 31 Mahl.
ROGERS FRANK WILLSON, insurance agent, 847
Main, rm. 3, h. 32 Florence. *See p. 311.*
" Fred, clerk at 1 So. Ann, b. 22 Morgan.
" Fred W. b. c. Bluehills and Holcomb.
**ROGERS GEORGE B.** architect, 49
Pearl, rm. 39, b. 815 Asylum.
" Harriet H. wid. Thomas F. h. 240 Sigourney.
" Henrietta, wid. D. M. h. 108 Church.
" Henry B. laborer, h. 13 Mechanic.
" Henry E. rubberw. at 690 Park, h. 58 Heath.
" James H. aligner at 476 Cap. h. 47 Amity.
" James H. carpenter 141 Tru. h.u. 20 East.
" Jane B. wid. William T. h. 43 Linden.
" John A. expressman, h.u. 278 Pearl.
" John A. R. Rev. pastor Catholic Apostolic
church, h. Windsor t.
" Joseph W. screwm. at 476 Cap. b. 237 Law.
" Laura A. wid. F. D. dressm. 546 h. 546 Main.
" Louis, tailor, h.u. 190 Front.
" Margaret H. wid. Simeon S. h. 41 Niles.
" Sarah A. wid. William T. h. 43 Linden.
" William, architect, b.u. 11 Goodman.
" Lucy J. wid. Wm. h. 9 Holcomb c. Bluehills.
" William H. steampipe & boiler covering, etc..
ins. agent, 259 Asylum, h. 47 Wadsworth,
" William H. lab. at 252 Pearl, h. 121 Albany.
**ROGERS (THE) WILLIAM
MANUFACTURING CO.**
electro plated goods, 66, 68 Market.
*See back cover outside.*
" Wm. M. clerk at 618 Cap. h. 1352 Broad.
ROGERS WILLIAM W. (*Woodward & R.*) ma-
chinists, h. Concord, W.H. t. *See page 526.*
Roginsky Vincent, at Smith, Bourn&Co. h. Caya.
Rohan John, engineer at Colts, h.u. 49 Franklin.
" John F. plumber at 280 Asy. b.u, 49 Franklin.
" Jos. electrician at 214 Pearl, h.u. 49 Franklin.
" Thomas, teamster at 100 Com. b.2u. 184 Shel.
" ☞ *see also Rowen.*
Rohne Chas. W. treas. 732 Main, h. 7 Girard.
Rohofsky Jacob, mach. at 1 Flower, h. 81 Front.
Rohowsky Maurice, clothing, 86, h. 85 Front.
Rohrer John, laborer at Cap. h.2u. 24 Mulberry.
Rohrmayer George, dyeing and clothes cleaning,
88 Trumbull, and 11, h. 11 Wells.
" George M. helper at 11, b. 11 Wells.
" John W. clerk at 11, b. 11 Wells.
Rohwer John, h. 58 Judson.
Roland Edward P. collarm. at 8 Sig. h. 38 Webster.
Rolletschek Max, baker at 94 Hud. h.u. 139 Front.
**ROLLINS ROBERT W.** sup't Hart-
ford Electric Light Co. 80 State, h. 25
Wethersfield. *See page 542.*
Rollo Louis M. barber, 1159, h.u. 1178 Main.
" Victor A. pressman at Elihu Geer's Sons,
16 State h.2u. 1172 Main.
Roloff John F. B. harnessm. at 8 Sig. h. 18 Smith.
Rolston Ella, b. 16 Winter.
" Elmer F. pressm. at 618 Cap. b. 16 Winter.
" Sophia, wid. John, h.u. 16 Winter.

Romano Frank, bootblack, h.u. 190 Front.
" George, bootblack, 994, h.r. 988 Main.
Romanski Alex, laborer at Pope Tube Co. h.2u.
34 South Prospect.
Romanus Mary, superior at St. Mary's Home
for the Aged, Albany.
Rome & Gans, jobbers of dry goods, 206 Front.
Samuel Rome. N. Gans.
" Jacob, shoemaker at 209 Law. b. 200 Front.
" Jacob, peddler, b. 4 Portland.
" Lipman, peddler, h. 78 Talcott.
" Louis, h. 23 Pleasant.
" Rive, peddler, h.u. 193 Front.
" Samuel, (*R. & Gans,*) h. 193 Front.
" Simon, peddler, h. 4 Portland.
" ☞ *see also Raum.*
Romeo Joseph, laborer, b.u. 78 Charles.
Rommel Fred C. polisher at Popes, h. 1232 Main.
" J. Wesley, clerk at 197 Asy. l.u. 13 Chapel.
Romont James, (*Gloscia & R.*) h. 78 Charles.
Ronald Charlotte K. stenographer at 88 Market,
b. 23 Beach.
" James T. machinist at N.Y.R. h.u. 23 Beach.
" Jessie M. stenograp'r at 13 Cen. b. 23 Beach.
Ronan Hannah E. wid. Wm. H. h. 15 Mather.
" Owen, at Pope Tube Co. b.2u. 89 Chestnut.
" Thomas, helper at P.&R. h. 78 Walnut.
" Thomas J. clerk at 34 Asy. h.2u. 89 Chestnut.
Rone Abram, jobber, h.u.r. 41 Mather.
" Louis, peddler, b. 23 Pleasant.
Ronne Anthony B. mach. 70 Huy. h.2u: 94 Park.
Ronzino Domencio, laborer, b.u. 6 Charles.
Rood Alfred H. mach. at 1 Flower, h.2u. 147 Law.
" Arthur W. manager U. S. hotel, 26 State.
" Augusta M. saleslady, 835 Main, b. 811 Asy.
" David A. proprietor U. S. hotel, 26 State.
" Elsie A. teacher Northeast school, b. 811 Asy.
" Frank D. executive clerk, room 35, State
capitol, h. 18 Columbia.
" Emma T. Mrs. h. 811 Asylum.
" Fred L. mechanic, b. 123 Trumbull.
" H. T. Mrs. boardinghouse, 147 Babcock.
" Harry A. lab. at Pope Tube Co. h. 401 Cap.
" Myles H. at 265, b. 811 Asylum.
Roome Charles L. joiner, b. Lubeck.
Roomy James, laborer, l. 4 Elm.

Rooney Benjamin R. assembler, b. 3 Wawarme.
" Bernard, steamfitter at Colts, h. 41 Huyshope.
" Catharine, h. 75 Governor.
" Catharine, wid. James, b. 271 New Britain.
" Edward, machinist, b. 41 Huyshope.
" Eliza, wid. Francis, h. 152 Front.
" Francis, manager 7, h.u. 71 American.
" Francis F. clerk, h.r. 4 Pleasant ct.
" Hugh F. hackdriver r. 50 State, b. 152 Front.
" Hugh L. electrician at Reynolds & Co. 85 Pratt, h.u. 21 Kilbourn.
" John F. bartender, b. 152 Front.
" John J. painter at 1106 Mn. b. 128 Martin.
" Kate, b. 1071 Main.
" Lawrence P. driver 7 Brady, b.2u. 50 Wells.
" Michael, laborer at Popes, b. 30 Flower.
" Michael, laborer at 8 Front, b. 84 Arch.
" Peter F. farmer, h. 1071 Main.
" Peter F. machinist, b. 128 Martin.
" Thomas F. clerk, b. 1071 Main.
" William, ostler, r. 173 State, b. 38 Barbour.
Root A. J. b. 185 Wethersfield.
" Abigail W. wid. Horatio, h. 185 Weth.
" Albert J. carptr. at 921 Main, h.u. 6 Russell.
" Amelia M. Mrs. h. 12 Lewis.
" Arthur G. clerk at 389 Allyn, h. W.H.t.
" Clarence R. foreman at Sanford Co. 438 Asylum, h. New Britain t.
" Cynthia C. h. 144 Trumbull.
" E. Buell, h. 124 Ann.
" E. Buell Mrs. dressmaker, 124, h. 124 Ann.
" Edward K. medical inspector health board, physician, 700 Main, h. 160 Garden.
" Erastus S. h. 41 Allen pl.
" Esther A. wid. Franklin, eclectic physician, 1201, h. 1201 Main.
" Frank C. painter, b. 39 Elm.
" Fred. H. carpenter, 166, h. 166 Clark.
" Harriet, Mrs. h. 39 Elm.
" Hattie, clerk at 162 Pearl, b. 39 Elm.
" Herbert, farmer, 30 Washington, b. 99 N.B.
" John G. president Farmers & Mechanics National Bank, 106 State, h. 197 High.
" John H. salesman at 54 Ann, h. 12 Preston.
" John R. h. 23 Florence.

JOSEPH E. ROOT, Physician.  Office, 67 Pearl street.
Hours—10.30A.M. to 12 M.
3.30 to 5.30 and 7.30 to 9 P.M.
Sundays, 12 to 2 P.M.
House 71 Pearl.       Telephone 723.

Root Joseph E. physician, 67, h.u. 71 Pearl.
" Judson H. (H. C. Judd & Root,) 389 Allyn, h. 66 Washington.
" Julia C. Miss, h. 794 Asylum.
" Louis S. clerk at 898 Main, h. 26 Brook.
" Louise, wid. George E. dressmaker, 166, b.2u. 166 Windsor av.
" Lyman, U.S.N. b. 202 Sigourney.
" Martha C. wid. Jas. N. seamstrs. h. 111½ Ann.
" Matilda C. wid. Elisha K. h. 160 Garden.
" Mary P. b. 39 Elm.
" Samuel Elbert, mach. at 133 Shel. b. 39 Elm.
" Samuel M. h. 39 Elm.
" Smith A. painter, 1106 Main, h. Rockville t.

Root Susan, wid. G. W. b. 48 Madison.
" William, carpenter, b. 121 Pearl.
" Winifred, dressmaker, b. 39 Elm.
Roper Hubert, machinist, h.u. 520 Garden.
" Hugh F. polisher at Popes, h. 8½ Queen.
" James L. mech. at Popes, h.2u. 79 Governor.
" John, l.u. 71 Asylum.
" Timothy M. butcher, b.u. 234 Allyn.

**ROPKINS & CO.** brewers Canada malt ales and porter, 232–242 Shel. See p. 491.
Edgar L. Hopkins.

Ropkins Edgar L. (R. & Co.) h. 155 Washington.
Rops John, laborer, b. 4 Elm.
Rorabeck Ezra T. engineer, 8 Sig. h. 65 Francis.
Rorty Charles J. carpenter, h. 7 Martin av.
" Hugh, bricklayer, b. 74 Putnam.
" Katie, at 476 Capitol, b. 7 Martin av.
" Mary L. at 476 Capitol, b. 7 Martin av.
" Nellie J. inspectress at 476 Cap.b.7 Martin av.
Rosario Francesco, ragpicker, h. 22 Charles.
Rosasco Charles D. laborer, h. 335 Front.
Rosberg Charles, b.r. 14 Affleck.
Rosbrook Fred. L. buffer at Wm. Rogers Mfg. Co. 66 Market, h. East Hartford t.
" William R. buffer at Wm. Rogers Mfg. Co. silver plated ware, 66 Market, h. E.H.t.
Rose Alexander C. (Farmington avenue grocery,) h. 247 Lawrence.
" Daniel, carpenter, b. 148 Front.
" Frank, shoemaker, h.u. 31 North.
" Fred, l. 373 Asylum, rm. 24.
" J. Howard, draughtsman, b. 29 West.
" John Henry, physician,11 Pratt, h. 12 Garden.
" Louis, conductor St.Ry. b. 94 Park.
" Mary Mrs. b. 646 Asylum.
" Michael, hostler 745 Main, b. 93 Sheldon.
" Reginald K. bkkpr. 335 Shel. b. 39 Spring.
" Thomas, coachman, h.r. 656 Farmington.
Rosell Harry, b. 24 Woodbridge.
Rosen Bros. carpenters and joiners, 279 Market.
Joseph Rosen.            Louis Rosen.
" Charles, milkman, b. 29 Market.
" Gustavus, carptr. at 155 Ch.O. b.u. 80 Com.
" Joseph, (R. Bros.) h.2u. 279 Market.
" John W. lab. at 111 Sheldon, h. Windsor t.
" Louis, (R. Bros.) h.u. 89 Madison av.
" Marx, paperhanger, h.u. 132 Market.
Rosenbaum Carrie, clerk at 908 Mn.b. 35 Windsor.
" Jake, fruit, etc. 55 Windsor, h.u. 73 Avon.
" Samuel, clerk at 76 Trumbull, b. 37 Chapel.
" Samuel, peddler, h.2u. 73 Avon.
" William, barber at 281 Main, h. 17 Wells.
Rosenbeck Bert, filer at 581, h.u. 615 Capitol.
" Frank, filer at 581 b.u. 615 Capitol,
" John S. H. agent at 715 Main, h. 157 Zion.
Rosenberg Benj. barber shop, 187, h.u.187½ Front.

**ROSENBERG DAVID,** tailor, 17 Albany, b. 41 North.
" Ruben, screwmaker at 476, l. 381 Capitol.
" Samuel, laborer, h.u. 137 Commerce.
Rosenblatt Barney (Rosenfeld & R.) h.u. 17 North.
" Benjamin, h. 37 Windsor.
" Benjamin, (R. & Shevitz,) b. 292 Market.
" Israel, tailor at 45 Asy. h.u.r. 1 Mays ct.

Rosenblatt Moses, grocer, 44 Village, b. 37 Windsor.
" & Shevitz, barbers, 327 Capitol.
Benjamin Rosenblatt. Louis Shevitz.
Rosenfeld Libbie, groceries, 196, h. 170 Front.
" Isaac, (Rosenfeld & R.) h.u. 15 Morgan.
" Max, grocer, h. 174 Front.
" & Rosenblatt, real estate, 15 Morgan.
Isaac Rosenfeld. Barney Rosenblatt.
Rosenfield Mr. screwmaker, b. 57 Hawthorn.
Rosenthal Albert (Fletcher&R.)h.u. 1071 Main.
" Charles, cigars, 591 Main, h. 49 Annawan.
" Frederick, clerk 591 Main, b. 59 Hudson.
" Lena, domestic, h.3u. 61 Morgan.
Rosenwall Wm. F. laborer, b. 173 Babcock.
Roser Matthias, coachman, h.u. 296 Main.
Rosita Salvador,grocer,295Park,h.118Lawrence.
Ross Albert E. grocery, 55, h. 55 Vernon.
" Charles B. ins. clerk at 197 Asy. b. 227 High.
" Donato, laborer, b.3u. 81 Morgan.
" Frederick H. cook at 375, l. 373 Asylum.
" George G. screwm.at 476 Cap. b. 63 Francis.
" Herbert A. attorney,847 Mn.rm.4, b.27Vine.
" Jackson, jobber, h.u. 96 Walnut.
" James, helper, St.Ry. 115 State.
" James H. laborer 56 Com. h. 13 Mechanic.
" John,helper at Barbour Silver Co.62 Market, b. 58 Asylum.
" John A. clerk at 581 Capitol, h. 27 Smith.
" John D. machinist at 9 Sig. h. 6 Grand.
" Joseph R. musician, h.u.r. 227 Pearl.
" Julia, wid. Perry, b.u.r. 227 Pearl.
" Simon, laborer, h. 139 Martin.
" Peter, laborer, b.u. 44 Hicks.
" William S. mach. at Colts,h.u. 126 Retreat.
Rossa Francesco; laborer, b. 22 Charles.
Rossberg Karl, mech. at 581 Cap. b.r. 14½ Affleck.
Rosseter Charles W. clerk at 956 Main, h.u. 230 Asylum, rm. 3.
" L. G. h. 241 Windsor av.
Rossiter Helena R. wid. Dan'l W. registrarCharity Org. Society, 57 Tru. h. 105 Clark.
Rossmeisl Anton, machinist at 388 Capitol, h.u. 1 Kilbourn ct.
" Joseph, mach. at 26 High, b.u. 165 Front.
Rossner Charles H. carpenter, h. 163 Barbour.
" Lewis P. b. 163 Barbour.
Rosso Domenico, laborer, b.u. 27 Kilbourn.
" Girado, laborer, b. 27 Kilbourn.
" James, laborer, b. 27 Kilbourn.
" Joseph, laborer, b.u. 27 Kilbourn.
" Michael, laborer, h. 158 Front.
Roszelle Edward M. foreman, 867 Main,h.89 Chst.
Rotberg Morse, laborer, h.u.r. 176 Front.
Roth Anthony, stonemason, h. Prospect av.
" Charles J. laborer, h. Elizabeth pk.
" David M. tailor at 76 Tru. b. 345 Main.
" Edith A. nurse at 20 South Hudson.
" Gust W. mach. at 1 Flower, h. Elizabeth pk.
" Katherine C. stenographer at Pope Tube Co. b. New Britain t.
Rothe Gustave B. printer, b. 27 Williams.
Rothschild David,salesm.221State,h.118Webster.
" Mary Mrs. b. 2 Holcomb.
" William B. (Horsfall & R.) h. 117 Collins.

**ROTHWELL PERCY** (Whitney&R.)
patent attorney, 49 Pearl, b. 240 Sigourney.
See page 502.
Rotman Samuel, peddler, h.r. 20 North.
Rotundo William, bartdr. 190 Front, b.u. 86Mor.
Roudett Duncan,watch str.Middletown,285State.
Roulston Archibald J. electr. b. 216Wethersfield.
" Archibald W. mach. at 1 Flower, b. 5 Affleck.
" John, laborer at State capitol, h. 244 Park.
" Martha L. Mrs. voice culture, b. 255 Main.
" Mary, wid. Archibald, h.u. 216 Wethersfield.
" Mary K. (Pierce & R.) b. 216 Wethersfield.
" Rob't G. mach. at 388 Cap. h.2u. 48 Ward.
" Robert H. mailing clerk at P.O. b. 255 Main.
" William J. driller on bicycles, b. 244 Park.
" ☞ see also Rolston.
Rounds Arthur C. clerk at 835 Main.
Rounsavelle Joseph H. horsetrainer,b. 935 Park.
" Annie M. wid. Wm. H. h. 935 Park.
Rourke David J. motorman St.Ry. b. 64 Grove.
" Edward J. printer at 29 Union pl. b.u. 164 Babcock.
" Frank P. assemb. at Popes, h.u. 254 Front.
" John, agent, b. 389 Main.
" John, janitor Lawrence street school, h.u. 164 Babcock.
" John F. salesm.126Church, b.u. 164Babcock.
" John M. clerk at Brown, Thomson & Co. 942, b. 1202 Main.
" John M. driver at Blodgett & Clapp Co. 51 Market, b. 45 Albany.
" Julia C. clerk 347 Main, b.u. 164 Babcock.
" Mary, at 37, h.2u. 32 Wells.
" Michael, fireman at 476 Cap. h. 1062 Broad.
" Michael, janitor, b. 55 Spruce.
" Michael J. expressman, b. 1261 Main.
" Minnie, clerk at 956, h. 981 Main.
" Sarah, wid. Peter, h.u. 42 Green.
" Thomas E. buyer at 956, h. 981 Main.
" Timothy, clerk at P.&R. b. 55 Spruce.
" William, blacksm.at Popes, b.2u. 80 Walnut.
" William A. printer, h.u. 164 Babcock.
" ☞ see also O'Rourke.
Rouse Ann J. wid. Asa W. h. 52 Laurel.
" Arthur D. rubberw. at 690 Park, h. 9 Amity.
Rousselle Joseph, carpenter, h.u. 42 Madison av.
Roussos Geo. J. mach. 13Central, b.2u. 47 Elliott.
Routier Oscar, driver, b. 342 Wethersfield.
Rouviere Charles C. clerk, h.u. 75 Chestnut.
" Ellen, wid. John R. h.u. 23 Westland.
" George R.baggagemasterValley Div.N.Y.R. b.u. 23 Westland.
" Louis H. goldbeater, 100 Love lane, b.u. 23 Westland.
" Nellie, stenogr. 42 Union pl. b. 23 Westland.
Rovick Benjamin, shoemaker, h.3u. 147 Front.
Rowbothan John, polisher at 581 Capitol, h.u. 21A Sisson.
" Joseph J. rubberw. at 690 Pk. b. 21 A Sisson.
**ROWE ALLEN H. & CO.** manufacturers of Rowe's improved shoulder shoe calk, 5 Rowe av. See page 529.
" Allen H. (A. H. Rowe & Co.) h. 5 Rowe av.
" B. fireman tug Smith, 285 State.

Rowe Benjamin, grinder 388 Cap. h. 449 Broad.
" C. O. physician, 926 Main, rm.37, h. 109 Tru.
" George W. clerk at Popes, b. 283 Capitol.
" James E. mach. at 1 Flow. b. Wethersfield t.
" Mary, wid. Lawrence, h.u. 40 Chestnut.
" Mary F. clerk, b.u. 40 Chestnut.
" Nicholas J. driver at U. S. Express Co. b.u.
    40 Chestnut.
" William, lab. at Pope Tube Co. h. 449 Broad.
Rowell Harriet, h. 25 Lewis.
" Warren L. clerk at Brown, Thomson & Co.
    942 Main, b. 56 Winthrop.
Rowen Jane, wid. Robert, b. 24 Congress.
Rowitt Peter, coachman, h. 32 Elm.
Rowland Albert B. tinner at 342 Pearl, h. 25 Judson.
" Guy F. mach. at 30 Cushman, b. 25 Judson.
" Harvey, mach. at 34 Morgan, b. 1080 Main.
" Thomas, rodman with city surveyor, 800
    Main, b. 41 Madison.
Rowley Arthur M. clerk at Popes, b. Bloomfield t.
" Carrie, wid. Wm. R. b. 813 Park.
" Clayton W. clerk at Hartford Times, 716
    Main, b. Bloomfield t.
" Edward W. b. 41 Windsor av.
**ROWLEY FRANK H.** builder, 190
    Asylum, h. 30 Brook. *See page 441.*
" John H. (*R. & Wilcox*,) h.u. 188 Capen.
" Juliana A. b. 36 Jefferson.
" L. A. Mrs. asst. matron, 2 Holcomb.
" Warren, h. 41 Windsor av.
**ROWLEY & WILCOX,** builders, 188
    and 253 Capen. *See page.562.*
    John H. Rowley.      Wilber A. Wilcox.
" William H. bookkeeper at United States
    Bank, 872 Main, h. 198 Sigourney.
Roy James P. B. polisher Popes, h.2u. 183 Mar.
" Harriet V. wid. John, milliner, 908 Main, b.
    153 Washington.
" P. E. Rev. pastor St. Ann's Roman Catho-
    lic church, h. 364 Park.
**ROYAL INSURANCE CO.** general
    agency, 720 Main. *See page 445.*
Royce George W. at Neal, Goff & Inglis Co. 980
    Main, b. Wethersfield t.
" Herman B. experimntr. 690 Park, h.189 Russ.
" Herman S. machinist at Popes, h. 189 Russ.
ROYCE PHILANDER C. secretary Hartford Fire
    Ins. Co. 53 Trumbull, h. 301 Asylum.
Roys Louis C. salesman at 304 Asy. h.u. 17 Avon.
Rube Charles, ostler at 995, l. 995 Main.
Ruben Abram, peddler, b.u. 3 North.
" Himan, peddler, h.u. 3 North.

Rubena James A. at 15 Tru. h.2u. 137 Commerce.
Rubenbauer Charles, clerk 882 Main, h.136 Front.
" George, mach. at Popes, b. 139 Front.
" George J. mach. at Colts, h. 139 Front.
" John, machinist at Colts, h. 139 Front.
" Martin, bottler at 7, b. 7 Affleck.
Rubie James, setter at 15 Tru. b. 37 Collins.
Rubinson M. J. jeweler, h. 16 Huntley pl.
Rubright Benj. A. captain barge No. 2, 285 State.
" George W. captain barge No. 7, 285 State.
" M. V. captain barge Marston, 285 State.
Ruby Ellen, wid. Daniel, h.3u. 2 John.
" John, operator at Popes, b.3u. 2 John.
" Michael, coremaker at 65 Suffield, b. 2 John.
Rucci Donato, laborer, b.u. 86 Morgan.
" Giuseppe, laborer, b. 73 Morgan.
" Nicolo, mason, b.3u. 89 Morgan.
Rucienski Vincent, harnessm. at 8 Sig. h.W.H.t.
Rudd A. Holley, foreman electric signal, N.Y.R.
    450 Asylum, h. 282 Sigourney.
" Harold H. student Trinity college, 6 Jarvis
    hall, Summit.
Ruderman Jacob, market, 56, h. 56 Pleasant.
Rudge Wm. A. machinist at Colts, l. 293 Main.
Rudolf Philip, filer at Popes, h.u. 35 Francis.
Rudolph Andrew C. mach. 1 Flow. b.2 Wadsworth.
" August, patternm. 556 Cap. h. 34 Trumbull.
" Frederick, tailor, h.u. 2 Wadsworth.
" Fred. A. clerk, 243 State, h. 29 Church.
" George, musician, h. 20 Village.
" Geo. A. inspector at Popes, h.u. 449 Capitol.
" James O. machinist, 13 Central, b. 2 Wads.
" Philip, repairer at Popes, h. 35 Francis.
" William B. mach. 13 Central, h.u. 60 Maple.
Rudy Isaac, tailor, at 544 Main, h. 82 Front.
Rue Henry, at 17 Albany, h. 53 Mather.
" William Henry, lather, b.u. 53 Mather.
Rueger Emil, painter at 30 Wash. h. 221 Maple.
Ruez Joseph, laborer, h.u. 92 Front.
Ruffemach Clements, gardener, b. 118 Bellevue.
Ruffkes Benjamin, mechanic at 581 Capitol, h.
    59 Hawthorn.
" David, teamster, 67 Morgan, b. 30 North.
" Israel, laborer, b. 31 North.
" Joseph, inspector at 690 Park, h. 31 North.
" Morris, h.u. 31 North.
" William I. machinist, 133 Shel. b. 31 North.
Rulon Edwin, clerk at 973 Main, b. 4 Chapel.
Rumark Antonio, laborer, h.u. 72 Avon.
Rummell Edw. G. polisher, 142 Russ, h. 118 Asy.
" J. Henry, bookkeeper at W. H. Bliss & Son,
    b. 98 Capitol.
" John W. clerk, b.u. 13 Chapel.
Runatelli Domenico, laborer, b. 365 Front.
Rundbaken Henry, jewelry, 8, h. 8 Goodman.
" John, real estate, 2 State, h. 19 Chestnut.
Rungee Augustus H. clerk, 705 Main, h.49 Hung.
" William C. inspector 40 Gov. b. 157 Capitol.
Runyan B. pressman at 690 Park, h. 5 Squire.
Runzelli John, laborer, h.3u. 319 Front.
Runzina Joseph, laborer, h. 12 North.
Ruppert Leopold, bartender, 315 Park, h.2u.
    38 Temple.
Rusden Ethelbert A. h. 15 Fern.
Rushton Sidney, clerk at Popes, h. 69 Ward.

Russ Andrew J. cigar manufr. 28, h.u. 24 Church.
" Charles J. Mrs. (Mary) b. 149 High.
" Elizab. C. wid. Chas. T. h. 117 Woodland.
" Fred, at 59½, b. 135 Trumbull.

H. ELMORE RUSSEGUE, Physician. Office, 95
Farmington ave.
Hours—8 to 9 A. M.
2 to 3.30 and 7 to 7.45 P. M.
Sundays—3 to 4 P. M. only.
Telephone, 1000.

Russegue H. Elmore, physician, 95, h. 95 Far.
Russell Albert T. b.r. 173 State.
" Annie, b. W. H. Home for Aged, Albany.
" Annie, h.u. 163 State.
" Annie J. wid. Frederick W. h. 103 Elm.
" Arthur S. clerk at 78 Asylum, b. 14 Beach.
" Bridget Mrs. b. W. H. Home for Aged, Alb.
" Charles, Mrs. boardinghouse, 76 Hopkins.
" Charles E. policeman, h. 150 Mather.
" Charles H. wholesale and retail grocer, 711
and 909 Main, h. Boston, Mass.
" Chas. S. clerk at 690 Park, b. Farmington t.
" David, laborer, h.3u. 68 Sheldon.
" Diodate B. janitor at Washington street
school, h. 83 Benton.
" Dora, b.2u. 1273 Main.
" Edith D. stenographer at Popes, b. 109 Elm.
" Ellen, wid. John, h. 4 Ellery.
" F. Grenville, trav. salesm. at Popes, b. 103 Elm.
" Fannie B. wid. Harry T. h. 3 Grand.
" Frank H. saloon. 107 Front, h. 11 Kilbourn.
" Fred, carpenter, b.u.r. 5 Hungerford.
" Gurdon W. park commissioner, physician,
207, h. 207 Farmington.
" Henry, assembler at Popes, b. 54 Market.
" Henry B. h. 236 Collins.
" James W. plater, b. 236 Barbour.
" John C. mate steamer Hartford, 285 State,
h. Haddam t.
" John E. mate tug L. C. Ward, 285 State.
" John S. antiques, 1140, h. 1246 Main.
" Joseph D. saloon, 246, h.u. 248 State.
" Joseph I. inspector at Popes, h. 26 Avon.
" Joseph W. at Ætna Ins. Co. 666 Main, b.
112 Wethersfield.
" Julia A. wid. Westell, h. 4 Pavilion.
" Lillian M. teacher at 1205 Asylum.
" Maria Mrs. h. 236 Barbour.
" May W. h. 103 Elm.
" Nicholas, bartender at 84 h.u. 72 Walnut.
" Paul L. b.u. 83 Benton.
" R. La Motte, bookkeeper at Conn. River
Banking Co. 701 Main, b. 3 Vine.
" Raymond, clerk at 342 Asylum, h. 84 Park.
" Robert L. h. 3 Vine.
" Sarah E. Mrs. h. 76 Hopkins.
" Sarah A. wid. Wm. b. 101 Oak.
" Thomas J. carpenter, h. 564 Windsor.
" Thomas W. president Connecticut General
Life Ins. Co. 49 Pearl, h. 774 Asylum.
" William, bookkeeper at Water Commission-
ers, city hall, 800 Main, h. 112 Weth.
" Wm. A. operator at 252 Pearl, h. 61 Barbour.
" William C. h. 645 Prospect av.
Rust Eliza T. nurse, h. 13 South Hudson, rm 8.

Rustemeyer Charles F. h. 825 Broad.
" Charles P. engineer, h. 43 Julius.
" Joseph, framer at J. H. Eckhardt Co. art
store, 693 Main, b. 35 Buckingham.
Ruth Wm. T. draughtsman, Popes, h. 53 Ward.
Rutherford Kate, dressmaker, h.u. 10 Wyllys.
Rutt Joseph, laborer, h.u. 10 Squire.
" Morris, tailor, h. 50 Sheldon.
Rutter John A. electrician N.Y.R. b.u. 3 Grand.
Ryan A. B. laborer, h. 126 Ward.
" Alice, wid. Thomas, h.u. 3 Brady pl.
" Ann H. h.2u. 40 Spring.
" Annie, dressmaker, 1, h. 1 Chestnut.
" Bridget, b. W. H. Home for Aged, Albany.
" Catherine, dressmaker, 285, b. 285 Park.
" Charles F. operator at N.Y.R. l. 145 High.
" Cornelius, captain of police, 38 Kinsley, h.
131 Park.
" Dennis F. bookkeeper, b. 131 Park.
" Edward, expressman, 413, h. 413 Broad.
" Edward, fireman N.Y.R. b. 80 State.
" Edward, laborer, b.u. 44 Hicks.
" Edward J. foreman Conn. Farmer, 284
Asylum, h. 55 Dean.
" Edward L. U. S. Army, b. 55 Dean.
" Edward T. farmer, h. 400 Albany.
" Edward W. weigher at Hartford Coal Co.
100, b.u. 100 Commerce.
" Ellen, dressmaker, 1, h. 1 Chestnut.
" Ellen S. b. 131 Park.
" George M. laborer at 8 Front, h. 99 Arch.
" Harry, clerk at Popes, b. 60 Church.
" J. Howard, printer, b. 55 Dean.
" James, beltmaker, h. 25½ Flower.
" James, mechanic at Popes, b.u. 387 Capitol.
" James F. bricklayer, b. 108 Babcock.
" James P. laborer at 581 Cap. h. 25½ Flower.
" Jas. J. switchman N.Y.R. b.2u. 118 Mather.
" Jerry, bricklayer, b.2u. 36 Lawrence.
" Johanna, wid. Daniel, b.u. 27 Windsor.
" John, coachman at 152, b. 152 Farmington.
" John, coachman at and b. 30 Washington.
" John, foreman at Hartford Coal Co. 100,
h.u. 100 Commerce.
" John, teamster, h.u. 65 Temple.
" John, Jr. clerk, b.u. 100 Commerce.
" John D. casket trim'r at 556, h. 558 Main.
" John F. foreman, r. 50 State, h.r. 38 Temple.
" John F. Rev. assistant at St. Patrick's
Church, b. 82 Church.
" John L. painter, l.u. 15 Chestnut.
" John T. motorman St.Ry. h. 19 Talcott.
" Joseph, sweeper at Colts, b. 1 Wehasset.
" Joseph C. postal clerk, h.u. 27 Windsor.
" Julia, wid. Henry, h.u. 36 Babcock.
" Kittie, clerk at 965 Main, b. 65 Temple.
" Julia A. tel. operator at Popes, b. 55 Dean.
" Katie T. stenograpr. at Capitol, h.u. 6 Atlantic.
" Lena, wid. Owen, h.r. 230 Market.
" Margaret Mrs. b.2u. 72 Retreat.
" Margaret, wid. James, b.2u. 118 Mather.
" Margaret A. milliner at Brown, Thomson &
Co. 942 Main, b. 285 Park.
" Martin, laborer at 556 Cap. b. 36 Lawrence.
" Mary, bookkeeper, b. 172 Farmington.

Ryan Mary, clerk at 956 Main, b. 65 Temple.
" Mary, wid. Peter, h.2u. 47 Commerce.
" Mary A. wid. William M. h. 35 Ashley.
" Mary C. bkkpr. at 76 Asylum, b. 60 Church.
" Mary C. clerk at Brown, Thomson & Co
.942 Main, b. 285 Park.
" Mary C. teacher Brown sch. b.u. 66 Hudson.
" Mary J. wid. John, dressm. h.u. 66 Hudson.
" Mary L. bkkpr. at 308 Asy. b. 88 Church.
" Matt, helper at 1 Flower, b. 194 Sheldon.
" Matthew, laborer at Pratt & Whitney, 1
Flower, b.u. 4 Lawrence.
" Michael, clerk at Brown, Thomson & Co.
942 Main, b.u. 84 Hudson.
" Mich. deckhand str. Middletown, 285 State.
" Michael, tailor at 76 Asylum, h. 58 Village.
" Michael, teamster, b.u. 258 Front.
" Mich. B. molder at 54 Arch, h.u. 224 Maple.
" Michael J. blacksmith, h. 76 Green.
" Michael W.porter,906 Main,h.2u.153 Maple.
" Nellie, dressmaker, b. 108 Babcock.
" Nona, clerk at Brown, Thomson & Co.
942 Main, b. 36 Babcock.
" Patrick, b. 2 Holcomb.
" Patrick, assistant foreman, Jewell Belting
Co. 15 Trumbull, h.u. 7 Kilbourn.
" Patrick, deckhand str. Hartford, 285 State.
" Patrick, farmer, b. 400 Albany.
" Patrick, laborer at 1 Flower, b.u. 4 Law.
" Patrick, laborer at 1 Flower, h.2u. 303 Law.
" Patrick, packer at Popes, b. 38 Flower.
" Patrick D. mer. tailor, 76 Asy. h. 60 Church.
" Patrick J. harnessm. 1222 Mn.h.30 Florence.
" Patrick J. mach. 30 Cush. b. 41 Woodbine.
" Patrick Jr. b. 2 Holcomb.
" Philip F. mechanic a Popes, h. Unionville v.
" Philip S. machinist at 1 Flow. b. 250 Zion.
" The tailor, 76 Asylum.
" Thomas, plumber at 548 Asylum.
" Thomas, president New England Brewing
Co. 217 Windsor.
" Thomas E. mechanic at Popes, h. Bristol t.
" Thos. J. trimmer at 556 Main, h.2u. 82 Grove.
" Thomas K. clerk, 956 Mn. b. 108 Babcock.
" Timothy, silverplater, b. 145 High.
" Timothy W. driver at r. 7, b.u. 3 Brady pl.
" William, laborer, h. 101 Sheldon.
" William, motorman St.Ry. h. 43 Vernon.
" Wm.F.painter at 20 Central,h.2u.54 Temple.
" William F. weigher, b.u. 100 Commerce.
" Wm. H. mach. 1 Laurel, h.u. 36 Babcock.
" Wm. H. teamster, St.Ry. h. 108 Babcock.
" William J. bartender at 86 Alb. h.u.3 East.
" Wm. J. machinist at Popes, h. 26 Putnam.
" William S. lumberman, b. 99 Arch.
" William T. teamster, b. 61 Judson.
" Winifred A. teacher at Brown school, b.
131 Park.
Ryberg Charles H. coachman, b. 301 Lawrence.
" Frank, laborer, h.r. 12 Fern.
Ryder Anna, wid. Daniel S. h. 62 Green.
" Elisha, manager Western Union Telegraph
Co. 6 Central, h. 427 Main, rm. 84.
" Geo. H. helper at 34 Morgan, b. 62 Green.
" George H. student, b. 427 Main.

Ryder Geo. W. mach. P.&R. h.99 Windsor av.
" Geo. W. Jr. salesman, b. 99 Windsor av.
" Ira M. ship. clerk 690 Park,h.114 Babcock.
" Patrick, stonecutter, b. 9 Arch.
" Thomas F. mason and builder, h. 9 Arch.
" Wm. E. cigarmaker at 867 Main, b. 99
Windsor av.
Rydquist Augustus, mechanic at 581 Capitol, h.
193 Russ.
" Martin A. filer at 581, b. 613 Capitol.
Rytel Stanislaw, laborer 8 Front, h. 31 Mechanic.

St. Anne's Convent, sister Mary Bonaventure,
246 Farmington.
St. Augustine School for Boys, West Hartford
Sisters of Mercy, 152 Farmington.
St. Catherine Girls' Orphan Asylum, 93 Church,
sister Evangelist, superior.
St. Clair Joseph, mason, h.u. 58 Spring.
St. Clare Hector B. agent, h. 1½ East.

**ST. FRANCIS' HOSPITAL,** 110
Woodland.

St. George Eva A. clerk at 937 Main, b. 56
Sumner.
" Matilda A. clerk at Brown, Thomson & Co.
942 Main, b. 56 Sumner.
St. Germain Remi, saloon, 85 Front, h. 197 State.
St. Hilaire Emma J. h. 926 Main, rm. 24,
St. James Orphan Boys' Asylum, 93 Church.
St. John Adele, laundress, h.2u. 42½ Windsor.
" Caroline, wid. Charles R. h. 31 Elmer.
" Carrie Louise, teach. vocal music, b. 835 Asy.
" Catherine L. *(Brown & St. John,)* h. E. H.t.
" Charles H. clerk at 61 Market, b. 31 Elmer.
" Daness, dressmaker, h.u. 42½ Windsor.
" Daniel B. farmer, h. 217 Barbour.
" Edward C. compositor at Hartford Times,
716 Main, h. 195 Capen.
" Edward D. farmer, b. 611 Garden.
" Eliza C. b. 114 Washington.
" Frederick M. laborer, b. 611 Garden.
" George H. plumber at 608 Main, h.u. 120
Wooster.
" Harry M. brakeman N.E.R. b. 31 Elmer.
" Henry, h. 835 Asylum.
" Howell W. actuary Ætna Life Insurance Co.
650 Main, h. 194 Farmington.
" John J. motorman St.Ry. h. 43 Village.
" Jennie, wid. William R. h. 20 Hicks.
" Joseph, motorman, h.u. 42½ Windsor.
" Josephine F. teacher Brown school, b. E.H.t.
" Louis S. bricklayer, h.u. 149 Maple.
" Marie D. clerk at Brown, Thomson & Co.
942 Main, b. 15 Pleasant.
" Marshall, stoker at Colts, h. E.H.t.
" Nancy E. wid. Charles G. h. 611 Garden.
" Samuel B. physician, 68 Pratt, h. 114 Wash.
" Samuel M. clerk, b. 31 Elmer.
" William E. janitor at 85 Tru. b. 31 Elmer.
" William H. treas. Spencer Automatic Ma-
chine Screw Co. b. 194 Farmington.
St. Joseph's Cathedral, 150 Farmington.
" Convent, 160 Farmington, mother superior,
sister M. J. Fabian.

# SAGE, ALLEN & CO.

### OFFER THE

## Largest Variety at Lowest Prices

#### IN THE FOLLOWING DEPARTMENTS:

| | | |
|---|---|---|
| Cloaks,  Silks, | Kid Gloves, | Laces, |
| Linens and | Silk Waists, | Trimmings, |
| Housekeeping Goods, | Colored Dress Goods, | Wool and Cotton |
| Ladies' Suits, | Hosiery, | Underwear, |
| Black Goods, | Cotton Shirt Waists, | Ribbons. |

# EVERY UP TO DATE NOVELTY

### AS THEY APPEAR.

# SAGE, ALLEN & CO.

St. Lawrence Charles, brickmaker, b. Windsor av.
St. Mary Wolfert, joiner, b. 197 State.
St. Mary's Home for the Aged, Albany, W.H.t.
St. Peters Convent, 188 Main.
St. Thomas Seminary, 352 Collins.
Sabo Paul, harnessm. at 8 Sig. h.u. 116 Zion.
Sachaklian Aaron, clerk at Brown, Thomson & Co. 942 Main, b. 52 Capitol.
" Stephen, clerk, 24 Pratt, b. 52 Capitol.
Sachodoski John, laborer at Pope Tube Co. h. 64 Sheldon.
Sachtman☞ see Sechtman.
Sacini Joseph N. laborer, b. 56 Portland.
Sacino Domenico, laborer, b.3u. 51 Morgan.
Sack Harris, drygoods, 70, h. 70 Morgan.
" John, clerk at 70 Morgan, h. 200 Park.
Sackett Charles C. b. 19 Russ.
" Emerson, carpenter, h. 14 Lawrence.
" F. Adelaide, clerk at St.Ry. b. 2B Belden.
Sadd Arthur, baker at 69, b. 69 Morgan.
" Fred T. piano tuner, b. 80 Trumbull.
Saddela Joseph,' fruit peddler, h. 10 North.
Sadler Cora E. clerk, b. 54 Brown.
" Jean A. at T. Sisson & Co. 729 Main, h. Windsor Locks t.
" Joseph F. forem. at 53 Vernon, h. 7 Webster.
Sadoian Kanriel, laborer at 40 Gov. h. 33 S.Pro.
" Michael, screwmaker at 486, b. 381 Capitol.
Saegart George W. helper at 133 Sheldon, b. Poquonock v.
Saengerbund Hall, 11 Central.
Safety Fund Advocate, monthly, 252 Asylum.
**SAFFORD CHARLES A.** attorney at law, 750 Mn. rms. 1 and 2, b. 268 Weth.

Safford Kate P. teacher Parkville school kindergarten, l. 101 Trumbull.
" William C. clerk at 197 Asy. b. 171 Albany.
Sagarino Dominick, groceries, h. 15 Mechanic.
" Felix, laborer, h. 34 Windsor.
" Frank, beltmaker at 15 Tru. h. 32 Windsor.
" Oscar, helper at 15 Tru. b. 34 Windsor.
" Rocco, beltmaker at 15 Tru. b. 34 Windsor.
Sage Albert P. horse undertaker, h.u. 1 Chapel.
**SAGE, ALLEN & CO.** dry goods, silks, gloves, etc. 894-902 Main.
Jerome E. Sage. Normand F. Allen. Clifford O. Moore.
*See page 317.*
" E. W. & Co. hides & wool, 64 Albany.
Edwin W. Sage.  Harry D. Sage.
" Edwin A. farmer, h. 1087 Windsor av.
" Edwin W. (E. W.S. & Co.) h. 23 Columbia.
" Eugene R. clerk at Wm. Rogers Mfg. Co. 66 Market, h. 34 Babcock.
" Eugenia Mrs. h. 34 Babcock.
" Frank H. Jr. b.u. 34 Babcock.
" Fred L. farmer, h. 1087 Windsor av.
" George W. farmer, h. 995 Windsor av.
" Harold, clerk at 940 Park, b. 34 Heath.
" Harry D. (E. W. S. & Co.) b. 149 High.
SAGE JEROME E. (S., Allen & Co.) dry goods, etc. 894-902 Main, h. 109 Edwards.
*See page 317.*
" Lucy M. at 690 Park, b. 34 Heath.
" Walter F. machinist, h. 34 Heath.
" William A. junior department secretary, 315 Pearl, h. 113 Park.
" William P. Rev. b. 23 Columbia.
" Willis R. salesman, 140 State, h.u. 876 Windsor av.

## For Sale Advertisements Bring Results in the Post.

## SALOMON & DeLEEUW,

*Cigars and*

*Smokers' Articles,*

*Wholesale and Retail.*

### PIPE REPAIRING A SPECIALTY.

#### NEW LOCATION, ·

## 7 ASYLUM STREET, Near Main St.

Sagebiel Herman, baker, h. 124 Portland.
Sailor Wm. M. cigarm. at 867 Mn. h. 12 Douglass.
Salad Witte, wid. Julius, gents furnishings, 325 Capital, h.u. 1350 Broad.
" Simon, tailor at 11 Asylum, b.u. 24 Morgan.
Salamovitz Leon, peddler, h. 66 Avon.
Salberg Edward P. clerk at 197 Asylum, b. 10 Winthrop.
Salce Antonio, laborer, h.2u. 12 North.
" John, laborer, b.2u. 12 North.
Salcer Emil, baker at 69 Morgan, h.u.r. 28 S.Pro.
Saled Abey, b.u. 70 Temple.
" David, tailor, 171 Main, h.r. 70 Temple.
" Levi, b.r. 70 Temple.
Salesberg Henry M. canvasser, h. 255 Market.
Salicki Frank, lab. at Pope Tube Co. b. 15 Wells.
Sall John A. h.u. 1144 Broad.
" William E. diesinker, Colts, h.u. 26 Alden.
" ☞ *see also Saul.*
Salmon Charles R. mach. 1 Flower, h. 207 Collins.
" Thomas E. timekeeper at 1 Flower.
SALOMON & DeLEEUW, tobacconists, 7 Asylum.
          *See page 318.*
    Leopold DeLeeuw.          Mrs. Rose DeLeeuw.
Salomone Mariano, barber at 458 Asy. b. 158 Front.
" ☞ *see also Solomon.*
Salsberg Henry M. clerk at 261 Asylum.
Salsburg A. H. mason, b.u. 11 Bellevue.
Salter Abram, clerk at 234, b. 238 Front.
Saltonstall Lindall W. Rev. rector Christ church.
    Office hours daily 12 to 1 p. m. in the chapel, h. 16 Winthrop.
Salvation Army, local headquarters, 730 Main.
Salvator Michael, laborer, h. 135 Commerce.
" Sarfine, laborer, b.u. 82 Morgan.
Salvatore Louis, bootblack, h. 47 Portland.
Salzer John W. electrician N.Y.R. h.u. 3 Grand.
Samblin William, gardner, b.2u. 363 Main.
Sames Elias, coachman, h. 202 Maple.
" Harry C. electrotyper at 41 Tru.b. 202 Maple.
Samilson Louis (*S. & Shulman,*) h. 296 Pearl.
" & Shulman, trimmings, 108½ Trumbull.
    Louis Samilson.          Samuel Shulman.
Sammartino John, laborer, b. 148 Front.
Sammis Elwood F. helper at 690 Park, b. 22 Howard.
" Hortense F. at 690 Park, b. New Park.
" Lydia N. wid. Foster M. dressmaker, h. N.P.
Sampson Arthur A. (*Wade & S.*) h. Benton, n. Webster.
" Arthur L. clerk at 869 Mn. b.2u. 24 Hopkins.
" Chas. P. band sawyer, 225 Shel. h. 44 N.B.

Sampson Charles W. woodturner, b.2u. 44 N.B.
" George W. supt's clerk at Popes, b. 283 Cap.
Samson Frederick, general agent Hartford Fire Ins. Co. 53 Trumbull, h. 641 Farmington.
" George, blacksmith at r. 580 Windsor av. b. Windsor t.
Samuels Isaac F. meats, 42, h. 42 Wooster.
" J. Charles, tailor, 881 Main, h. 24 Brook.
" J. & Co. New Eng. Boot & Shoe H. 882 Main.
    Joel Samuels.          Mrs. Minnie Samuels.
                      Jos. Krotoshiner.
" Joel, (*J. Samuels & Co.*) h. 128 Collins.
" Minnie, wid. Louis (*J.S.& Co.*) b. 128 Collins.
" Samuel E. clerk at 882 Main, b. 128 Collins.
Samuelson Carl E. printer at 141 Pearl, h.u. 48 Clark.
" John, driver, b. 55 Judson.
" Martin, driver, b. 55 Judson.
Sana Frank, peddler, h. 43 Windsor.
Sanborn Charles H. driver, b. 3 Pleasant.
" S. Sidney, cutter at 56 Pearl, h. 22 Imlay.
" William A. h. Farmington c. Highland.
Sanborne Annie E. Mrs. h. 51 Russ.
" George E. Rev. h. 51 Russ.
Sand Chris N. stonecutter, h.u. 38 Rowe.
" Lan, laundry, 486 Asylum.
" Wil H. assistant at Huntsinger Business College, 30 Asylum.
Sandberg Albert, coachman, 117, h. 117 Wash.
" Andrew F. carpenter, b. 56 Woodbine.
" Ingrid Mrs. b.u. 77 Franklin.
" John A. carpenter, h.u. 154 Ward.
Sandbough Frank, operator, b. 145 High.
Sanders Annie, wid. Clarence, h. 34 Church.
" Augustus, machinist, h.u. 71 Jefferson.
" C. C. lookout str. Hartford, 285 State.

## J. C. SANDERS,

## BAKERY.

**The Best Home-Made Goods at Lowest Prices.**

#### 94 HUDSON STREET.

SANDERS JOSEPH C. baker, 94, h. 94 Hudson.
" ☞ *see also Saunders.*
Sanderson Edward F. theological student at 1507 Broad.
" Herbert A. foreman at 34 Morgan, h.2u. 263 Windsor av.
" Isaac B. carpenter, b. 40 Hudson.
Sands Henry W. driver, h. 215 Windsor.
Sanford Charles B. clerk 61 Asylum, h. E.H.t.
**SANFORD CO. THE** manfrs. of architectural and decorative relief ornament. Office and factory, 438 Asylum.
          *See page 448.*
" Geo. W. at Conn. Mutual Life Ins. Co. 783 Main, b. 189 Retreat.
" Harrison, clerk at Popes, b. 63 Oak.
" Homer D. porter 44 Market, h.u. 488 Main.
" Louis A. teamster, h. So. Forest.
" Mabel, b.u. 112 Laurel.
" Mary A. Mrs. h.u. 112 Laurel.
" S. A. wid. Dwight E. h. 189 Retreat.

**The Post, 12 Cents a Week, Delivered at Your Home.**

SANFORD WALTER, artist, sec'y and treasurer Sanford Co. 438 Asylum, h. 28 Gillett.
      *See page* 448.
" Wilbur G. machinist at Pratt & Whitney Co. 1 Flower, h. 33 Union.
" William E. express, b. 19 Church.
Sankbel Fred, carpenter, h. 28 John.
Sano A. M. buyer, b. 15 Seyms.
 " Vincent F. buyer, h. 10 Pavilion.
Sansabrino Giovanni, laborer, h.u. 14 Kilbourn.
" Rosie, dressmaker, 12, h. 12 Kilbourn.
Sansoe Frank, h. 25 Kilbourn.
Sansone Salvatore, candy manfr. 849,h.851 Park.
Santa Moraco, laborer, b. 73 Morgan.
Santamo William H. hostler, 73, b. 73 Grove.
Santerson John W. tailor at 730 Main, h. 23 Por.
Santhouse Susan wid Rob't, h. 545 Main.
Santorra Frank, policeman, b.2u. 1208 Broad.
 " Margaret F. clerk at Brown, Thomson & Co. 942 Main, b. 1208 Broad.
" P. Hugh, pressfeeder at 141 Pearl, l. 5½ Ple.
Santocopito Raphael, laborer, b. 247 Front.
Santry William, filer at Popes, l. 278 Asylum.
Sanzo Lawrence, laborer, h.3u. 190 Front.
 " Nicolo M. laborer, b. 73 Morgan.
Sapolskey Samuel, screwm. at 476, l. 381 Capitol.
Saraceno Battista, barber, 1151, h. 1098 Main.
" Michael, barber at 1151, b. 1098 Main.
" Nicodemo, harnessmaker at 8 Sigourney, h. 68 Pleasant.
Saracino Angelo, barber at 9 Mar. b. 21 Morgan.
Sarafino Salvator, laborer, b.2u. 82 Morgan.
Sardella Leberato, fruits, 173 Main.
Sardello Joseph, fruit peddler, h. 10 North.
Sargeant Edward J. painter at 53 Vernon, b. 1255 Main.
Sargent Asa, car inspector, N.E.R. h. 43 Walnut.
" Chester A. conductor, St.Ry. h.u. 80 N.B.
" Edward S. machinist at 1, h. 84 Flower.
" George, mason, h. 46 Cedar.
" Geo. K. painter at 185 Asy. h. 35½ Chestnut.
" Mary E. wid. Geo. H. boardingh. 84 Flower.
" Peter, waiter, 100, b. 100 Sheldon.
" William, teamster, 46 Ann, b.u. 212 Sheldon.
Sarvan Frank H. messenger, P.O. b.u. 523 Main.
 " Thos. J. porter at Sage, Allen & Co. 898, h.u. 523 Main.
Sarvent Sylvia Mrs. h. 103 Bellevue.
Sassano Biagio, barber, 37 Albany, b. 33 Morgan.
Satelin Jacob, clerk, h.r. 176 Front.
Satriano Salvatore (*J. Cersosimo & Co.*) h.3u. 49 Morgan.
Satter Jacob, groceries, 234, h. 234 Front.
Sauberlie Gottfried, rubberw. at 690, h. 767 Park.
Saudalo Angelo, laborer, b. 64 Front.
 " Cesira, laborer, b. 64 Front.
Saudner Joseph, helper at 142 Russ, h. 40 Park.
Sauer Edward J. barber at 94 Asy. b. 22 Hopkins.
" Elizabeth, clerk at 484, b. 484 Main.
" ☞ *see also Souer.*
Saum E. E. toolmaker, h.u. 45 Jefferson.
Saunders Alex. F. mach. at Pratt & Whitney Co. 1 Flower, h. 1208 Broad.
 " Alfred E. mach. at 1 Flower, h. Harbison.
 " Alfred H. clerk at Popes, b. 218 Franklin.

Saunders Archibald F. machinist at Pratt & Whitney Co. 1 Flower, h.u. 59 Zion.
" Charles C. clerk, 78 Asy. b. 391 Wethersfield.
" Chas. D. supt. 821 Main, h. 48 Mahl.
" Chas. W. supt's clerk at Popes, b. 218 Fkn.
" Edwin F. porter, Adams Express Co. h. 100 Albany.
" Elizabeth, h. 167 High.
" Frank J. saloon at 302, h. 302 Park.
" Frank M. toolm. at 581 Capitol, h. S.M. v.
" Fred. woodworker, h. 218 Franklin.
" Fred J. b. 218 Franklin.
" George S. clerk at 78 Asylum, b. 391 Weth.
" George W. compositor at 141 Pearl, h. 31 Lewis.
" Gustavus A. toolm. at 135 Shel. h. 271 Jef.
" Henry, clerk at Popes, b. 218 Franklin.
" Henry H. (*P.H.B.S. & Son*)427 Main,rm.64.
" J. Frank, framemaker at J. H. Eckhardt Co. 695 Main, b. 15 Ward pl.
" James H. carriagemaker, r. 16, h. 16 N. B.
" Jennie, b. 391 Wethersfield.
" Jennie L. clerk at 903 Main, b. 16 N.B.
" Jessie E. b. 167 High.
" John, laborer at Popes, b. 11 Harbison.
" John B. painter, h. 391 Wethersfield.
" Joseph, buffer at 182 Allyn, b.u. 32 Wells.
" K. C. milliner, 721 Main, rm. 18, h. 3 Seyms.
" Lucinda W. wid. Prince H. B. (*P. H. B. S & Son*) h. 427 Main, rm. 64.
" Oscar E. clerk at Lincoln, Seyms & Co. 34 Market, b. 981 Main.
**SAUNDERS P. H. B. & SON,** merchant tailors, 730 Main.
  Lucinda W. Saunders.  Henry H. Saunders
" Thos. W.cutter at 730 Main, h. 3 Seyms.
" Walter M. mach. 1 Flow. b.So.Manchester v.
" William,asst.foreman at Popes, h.15 Ward pl.
" William M. toolm. 302 Asy. h. 246 Weth.
" Wm. O. carptr. 9 Sig. h.3u. 1101 Mn. rm. 5.
" ☞ *see also Sanders.*
Sauren Wm. chipper at 556 Cap. h. 32 Sheldon.
Sauter Edward, machinist 1 Flow. h.u. 53 Grand.
Savacool George, helper, P & R. b. 11 Liberty.
Savage Goff R. at Ætna Life Ins. Co. 650 Main, l. 18 Buckingham.
" Harry F. clerk, 145 Asy. h.u. 44 New Britain.
" John, engineer, P.&R. h. 148 Mather.
" Laura M. wid. E. C. h. 14 Walnut.
" Mary, wid. William, h. 8 Cedar.
" Olive M. wid. Dwight, h. 12 Suffield.
" Thomas W. b. 8 Cedar.
" Wilfred W. treas. at 235 State, b. Weth. t.
" Willis M., Comfort Powder Co. 61 Albany, h. Wethersfield t.
Savard Arthur M. mach. 1 Flow. h. 34 Windsor.
Savochsky Michael, laborer, h.3u. 15 Park.
Savoni Angello A. laborer, b.3u. 51 Morgan.
Savoy Anlor, lather, b. 1080 Main.
Sawtelle Albert G. clerk, b. 136 Main.
" Alfred W. druggist, 308, h. 136 Main.
" Caroline, wid. Albert G. b. 530 Farmington.
Sawyer DeForest A. (*Davies & S.*) h. 15 Pleasant.
" E. M. wid. C. B. h. 439 Capitol.
" Edith Pingree, b. 4 Townley.

**The Post, 12 Cents a Week, Delivered at Your Home.**

Sawyer Elizabeth E. wid. Elmer, b. 7 So. Pro.
" Ernest M. carpenter at Baxter the Decorator, 231 Asylum, h. 11 King.
" Flora L. wid. William E. h.u. 1343 Main.
" George, painter at 20 Central, b. E.H.t.
" George O. drygoods, 835 Main, h.4 Townley.
" Guy A. b. 230 Putnam.
" Harry W. bkkpr. 266 Pearl, b.u. 1343 Main.
" R. W. rubberw. at 690 Park, b. 230 Putnam.
" Willis E. mach. at 133 Sheldon, h.u. 5 S. Pro.
Sayer John M. tailor, at 76 Asy. h. 51 Liberty.
" Margaret, clerk at Brown, Thomson & Co. 942 Main, b. 28 Pleasant.
" Sarah, wid. Edward, h. 35 Pleasant.
Sayers Garrett, Jr. helper at 266 Pearl, b.u.r. 61 Front.
" Garrett Mrs. h.u.r. 61 Front.
" Thomas, baggagem. N.Y.R. h.u. 51 Liberty.
" William, mason, b. 180 Seymour.
Sayles Mina R. stenographer at 197 Asy. b. 94 Cap.
Scailes Frances H. Mrs. h.u. 25½ Florence.
" Geo. W. salesm. 54 Ann, h. 25½ Florence.
" John, helper at 169 Front, h. 124 Potter.
Scalizi Lorenzo, laborer, h. 41 Mechanic.
Scalley Edwd. brakesm. P.&R. h.u. 28 Russell.
Scanlan Alice, wid. Dayton, h.u. 523 Main.
" B. boxmaker, l. 38 Church.
" Hanora, wid. Michael, b. 60 Church.
" John E. laborer, h. 14 Chestnut
" Maurice M. painter h.u. 523 Main.
" Michael F. journalist, h. 60 Church.
" Patrick H. b. 60 Church.
" Peter J. coachman, 207, b. 207 Farmington.
" Thomas, laborer, 556 Cap. b. 33 Riverside.
" ☞ see also Scanlon.
Scanlon Bartho. mech. at Popes, h. 17 Putnam.
" Bridget, wid. John, h.2u. 21 Lawrence.
" Ellen E. wid. Timothy, h. 25 Alden.
" Henry E. carpenter at 703 Main, h. Morris.
" John, carpenter, h. 338 Franklin.
" John, laborer at Spring Grove Cemetery, h.2u. 119 Maple.
" John, laborer, b. 4 Huntley pl.
" John, painter, b.u. 54 Hudson.
" John, painter, b. 75 Hudson.
" Mary E. stenographer Dime Savings Bank, 791 Main, b. 25 Alden.
" Michael J. laborer, h.u. 8 Winter.
" Patrick, laborer, h.2u. 151 Windsor.
" Peter, helper at 9 Sig. b.2u. 151 Windsor.
" Richard, laborer at 1 Flow. h. 31 Lawrence.
" Thomas, laborer, b.u. 26 Union.
" Thomas, laborer, b.2u. 151 Windsor.
" Thomas, stonecut. at 93 Ch.O. b. 2 Edwards.
" Thomas, teamster, b. 53 Windsor.
" Thos. M. molder, 690 Park, h. Newington t.
" Timothy A. b. 25 Alden.
" William, helper at Baxter the Decorator, 231 Asylum, b. 16 Trumbull.
" ☞ see also Scanlan.
Scannell John, teamster, b. 2 Brady.
Scanno Fernenello, laborer, b. 81 Morgan.
Scarborough Edwin, clerk at Popes, h. E.H.t.
" George F. at Hartford Fire Insurance Co. 53 Trumbull, h. West Hartford t.

Scarono Angelo M. laborer, h.u. 210 Front.
Scarritt Jennie, wid. Wm. seamstress, b. 120 Jef.
Sceery Elizabeth, wid. Bernard, h. 52 Wells.
" Ellen N. dressm. 60, h.u. 60 Fairmount.
" James, brakeman, b. 1½ Avon.
" James J. porter at 97 Asy. b. 18 Trumbull.
" John, clerk at 10 Church, h.u. 33 Pawtucket.
" John B. b. 52 Wells.
" Kate, at 1 So. Ann, b. 58 Vanblock.
" Louisa, at 1 So. Ann, b. 58 Vanblock.
" Margaret, at 1 So. Ann, b. 58 Vanblock.
" Mary, wid. James, h.u. 38 So. Prospect.
" Mary E. dressm. 60, h.u. 60 Fairmount.
" Michael, laborer at Colts, h. 58 Vanblock.
" Michael S. clerk at 76 Asy. b. 58 Vanblock.
" Thomas, furniture, 10 Church, h.u. 37 Arch.
" Thomas H. painter, at 1 Flow. b. 52 Wells.
" William, at 904 Main, b. 6 Trumbull.
" William, enameler at Popes, b. 39 Arch.
" ☞ see also Seery.
Schaal John, filer at 142 Russ, h. 108 Ward.
Schacher Casimir, clerk, 730 Mn. b.u. 56 Village.
" Etienne, forem. at 730 Main, h.u. 56 Village.
Schadel Joseph, baker, h.u. 32 Grand.
Schadow Julius R. machinist at 1 Flower, b. 238 New Britain.
Schaefer Conrad, barber at 1159 Main, h. 54 Wooster.
" Geo. W. cigarm. at 159 Asy. h.u. 38 Barbour.
" John H. brazier at Popes, b. 46 Hopkins.
Schaeffer Mark A. pianotuner, 153, b. 63 Asylum.
" Richard C. H. clerk at 881 Mn. b. 19 Walnut.
" Rosie Mrs. h.u. 46 Hopkins.
Schaerer Eliza, b. 52 Temple.
Schafer Hugo, master mechanic at P.&R. b. 223 Asylum, room 56.
Schaffer Paulina, dressm. 277, h. 277 Market.
" Peter, filer at 581 Capitol, h. 277 Market.
Schaffman Bennett, tailor, h. 206 Front.
" Joseph, peddler, b.u. 64 Pleasant.
Schaffner Martin, filer at Popes, h. 140 Mather.
Schall Ernst, (Ernst Schall Co.) h. 448 Main.
" Ernst Co. jewelers, 5 Asylum.
" John, filer, 142 Russ, h.u. 108 Ward.
Schapirow Harry, needlem. 28 Laurel, b. 30 Kil.
" Samuel H. filer at Colts, h.r. 60 Vanblock.
Scharf George, cellarman at 245 Windsor, h.u. 72 Wooster.
Scharoff Mr. mattressm. r. 8 Walnut, b. 72 Ple.
Scharole John, laborer, b. 319 Front.
Schattgen J. watchm. at 32 Asylum, h. N.B.t.
Schaubel Geo. D. foreman N.Y.R. h. 23 Lincoln.
Scheck Rosa Mrs. h. 27 South Hudson.
**SCHECK THEO. C.** fresco painter and designer, 113, h.u. 113 Main.
Schectman ☞ see also Sechman.
Schedvin Chas. lab. at Popes, h.u.r. 1048 Broad.
Scheer Antoine, tailor, 35 Church, l.u. 147 State.
" Eugene, tailor, 35 Church, l.u. 147 State.
Scheidler Tony, molder at 114 Grove, b. 284 Fkn.
Scheld Theodore, florist, h. Cays. W.H.t.
Schenkel Aug. W. brazier, h.u. 242 New Britain.
Schierbolz Emil C. agt. 132 Market, h. 11 Congress.
Schiessl Peter, driver, h u. 10 Squire.
Schiffranschi Ferd. mason helper, h. 7 Wells.

Schildge Geo. K. mach. at 1 Flower, b. S.M.v.
" Katherine E. stenog. at 721 Main, b. South Manchester v.
Schiller Arthur, driver at 607, b. 609 Main.
" Charles A. policeman, h. 10½ Village.
" Emanuel, clerk, b. 4 Winthrop.
" Joseph F. carpenter, b.u. 10½ Village.
Schimonsky M. brewer, 315 Park.
Schindler Jonas, cigarm. at 867 Mn. h. 153 Martin.
Schiolovitch Max, peddler, h.u. 81 Pleasant.
Schirm Ernst, blacksm. 28 Shel. b. Maple c. King.
" Frank, Jr. blacksm. 28 Shel. b. Maple c. King

**SCHIRM FRANK F.** blacksmithshop, 28 and 30 Sheldon, h. Maple c. King.
*See page 551.*
" Rose, music teacher, b. Maple c. King.
Schirmaier Fred, pressf. at Popes, b.u. 293 Law.
" Frederick, jeweler, 847 Main, rm. 13, h. 293 Lawrence.
" John, at 890 Main, b.2u. 293 Lawrence.
Schisler John, h.u. 16 Affleck.
Schlaefer Charles, waiter at 931, b. 1032 Main.
Schlag Frederick A. printer with Hartford Life Ins. Co. 252 Asylum, h. 89 Jefferson.
" Harry A. clerk, b. 89 Jefferson.
" William F. manager, 169 Zion, h. 89 Jef.
" Wilmar A. bkbdr. 141 Pearl, h. 89 Jefferson.
Schlatter Lottie Mrs. nurse, 488 Main, rm. 16.
" William, goldbeater, 265 Asy. h. 31 Center.
Schleicher Ernest, woodw. at Taft Co. h. E.H.t.
" John W. polisher at Popes, h.2u. 58 Flower.
" William F. machinist, h.2u. 5 Affleck.
Schleifenbaum Jacob, h. 113 Park.
Schlemmer Oscar P. confectr. 44 Ann, h. 9 Oak.
Schlutter Otto B. teach. of language High school, 39 Hopkins, h. 14 Morgan.
Schmavonian Arsene B. theological student, 1507 Broad.
Schmedegard Peter, gardener, h. 60 Morgan.
Schmelz Chas. F. mechanical engineer at F. H. Richards, 803 Main, h. 194 Laurel.
" Louis, gardener, b.u. 1305 Main.
" & Hammer, boots and shoes, 1005 Main.
" Henry H. (*S. & Hammer,*) h. 1305 Main.
Schmelzkopf Emanuel F. beltm. h. 62 Babcock.
" Fred. W. E. clerk at 15 Tru. h. 60 Babcock.
Schmidt Aleck, carpenter at N.Y.R. h. E.H.t.
" Andrew, painter, b. 22 Morgan.
" Anthony, laborer, h. 72 Avon.
" August H. (*S. & Fox,*) h.u. 54 Oak.
" Emil, horse food, r. 8, h. 8 Bond.
" Ernest, screwm. at 476 Cap. b. 159 Front.
" F. Louis C. pianotuner, h. 35 Chapel.
" Henry J. waiter, 50, b. 52 Market.
" & Fox, jewelers, 19 Pearl.
<small>August H. Schmidt. Jacob Fox.</small>
" Joseph, mach. at 80 Huyshope, h.2u.84 Arch.
" Martin, tailor, h. 79 Hungerford.
" Michael, h.u. 68 Potter.
" Michael, shoemaker at 139, b. 135 Trumbull.
" Paul, baker, h.u. 82 Hudson.
" Peter, tailor at 719 Main, h. 60 Portland.
" Regina, dressmaker, h.2u. 84 Arch.
" Robert H. mech. at Popes, b. 54 Annawan.
" Roger, laborer, b. 159 Front.

Schmidt Theo. teamster, 132 Mar. b. 2 Holcomb.
" William, bartender, 107 Asy. h. 48 Windsor.
" *see also Smith.*
Schneeloch Walter E. machinist, l. 14 Spring.
Schneider Bernard, baker at 484 Main, h.2u. 76 Sanford.
" Charles, butcher at 8 Ford, h.u. 37 Grand.
" Charles H. at 54 Arch, h. 160 Franklin.
" Christian C. student, h. 156 Front.
" Frank, barber at 272 Park, b. 24 Avon.
" Herbert, baker, h.2u. 76 Sanford.
" Julian, laborer, b. 276 Front.
" Mary, clerk at Brown, Thomson & Co. 942 Main, b. Windsor Locks t.
" Mary, wid. Simon, b.u.r. 132 Market.
" Michael, laborer, h.u. 28 Talcott.
" Michael, machinist at 1 Flower, h.u. 7¼ Oak.
" Nicholas, (*Hills & S.*) l. 757 Main.
" Otto, brewer at 315 Park, h.u. 25 Putnam.
" Samuel, screwm. at 476 Cap. b. 276 Front.
" *see also Snyder.*
Schnester Fred. H. mach. at 1 Flow. h. 38 Wolcott.
Schoel George H. bricklayer, b. 132 Market.
Schoen Benjamin, (Model T. Co.) b.u. 33 Chapel.
Schoenberger John J. insp. at Popes, b.2u. 29 Bab.
Schoenborn Gustav C. mach. 1 Flow. b. 158 Ward.
" Julius, cigarm. at 867 Main, b. 158 Ward.
" Louis M. harnessmaker, 334 Asy. h.u. 100 Sey.
" Paul, cigarmaker at 867 Main, b. 158 Ward.
" William T. watchman at Werder park, h. 158 Ward.
Schoenfeld Jacob, clerk, 956 Main, b. 37 Windsor.
" Moses, h. 29 Morris.
Schoepflin George F. cigarm. 741 Mn. h. 66 Julius.
Schoewald Robert, cornicemaker, h. 59 Franklin.
" Theodore, cabinetm. 69 Front, h. 53 Elliott.
Schofield David, plumber at 12 Mul. h. 57 Oak.
" John J. steward Colonial club, 47 Prospect.
" William, at Popes, b. 439 Capitol.
" William F. painter at 20 Central, h. Eaton.
" *see also Scofield.*
Scholnik M. laborer, h.2u. 82 Avon.
Scholz Albert A. cigarm. at 867 Main, h.2u. 98 Retreat.
Schonburn Ernst, driver at 238, b. 238 N.P.
Schonhaar Frederica, wid. Casper, h.u. 25 Brook.
" Robert W. machinist, b.u. 25 Brook.
Schott Carl, clerk, 6 State, l. 53 Trumbull, rm. 5.
" James S. tobacconist, 6 State, l. 650 Mn. rm. 60.
Schottmuller Theodore, baker, b. 57 Judson.
Schrauth Joseph, butcher, 835 Main, h. 84 Front.
Schreiber Charles J. brazier, b. 70 Front.
" Henry C. W. machinist, h.2u. 12 Church.

**SCHREPFER MICHAEL,** bakery, 368, h. 370 Asylum, rm. 22.
Schremmer William, mach. at 1 Flower, h.83 Fmt.
" Frank, mach. at 1 Flow. h. 83 Fairmount.
Schrieber Bruno, contractor, h. 185 Sisson.
" Charles, boardinghouse, 70 Front.
Schriftgiesser Emil S. bookkeeper at Columbia Brewing Co. h.u. 14 Pavilion.
Schroeder Aug. harnessmaker, b. 401 Capitol.
" Charles H. confectioner, caterer at 941, h. 943 Main, rm. 6.
" Christian J. lineman, h.2u. 985 Main.

SCHROEDER FRED. G. confectioner, 941 Main, b. 14 Morgan.          *See page 322.*
" Kittie E. b. 14 Morgan.
" Otto, baker at 292, b. 294 Park.
Schubert Harry, ragicker, h.u. 78 Talcott.
Schudlesch Eva, wid. William, h. 28 Grand.
Schufeldt ☞ *see Shufelt.*
Schuler Isaac, tailor, h. 46 North.
¢ Louis A.clerk,372 Asylum,b.32 New Britain.
Schulten ☞*see Neuschulten.*
Schultz Albert A. mech. Popes, b.145 Lawrence.
" Carl H. clerk at 793 Main, b. 31 Elliott.
" Charles, helper at Pratt & Whitney Co. 1 Flower, h. 156 Babcock.
" Charlotte F. Mrs. nurse, h. 33 Elliott.
" Christina, wid. Jacob, h. 145 Lawrence.
" Frank, pinmaker 31 Hicks, b. 156 Babcock.
" Henry, wireworker 618 Cap.b. 156 Babcock.
" John, carpenter, h.u. 35 Wolcott.
" John, wirewkr. at 618 Cap. b. 156 Babcock.
" Julia, at 476 Capitol, b. 145 Lawrence.
" Leo, screwm.at476 Capitol, b.145 Lawrence.
" Margaret, clerk at 956 Main, h. 146 Weth.
" Rose A. at 476 Capitol, b. 145 Lawrence.
" William, chipper,556 Capitol, b. 27 Sheldon.
" ☞*see also Schulze; Schulz.*
Schulz Carl, laborer at 335 Sheldon, h. 57 Julius.
" Carl, music teacher, 202, h. 202 Capen.
" Carl F. Jr. waiter, 835 Main, b. 202 Capen.
" Charles, laborer at 335 Sheldon, h. 57 Julius.
" Charles, machinist at Colts, b. 7 Park.
" Herman C. clerk, 745 Main, b.2u. 50 Temple.
" Herman R.cigarm. at 867 Main, b. 57 Julius.
" William, h. 231 Bellevue.
" William G. driver, h.r. 1061 Main.
Schulze Bernard G. policeman, b. 110 Trumbull.
SCHULZE EDWARD, *councilman 9th ward,* cabinetmaker at Capitol, h. 1256 Broad.
" Gertrude A. stenographer at Factory Ins. Asso. 95 Pearl, b. 1256 Broad.
" Henry B. h.u. 146 Wethersfield.
" William E. clerk at Popes, b. 1256 Broad.
" ☞*see also Shultz.*
Schumacher Augustus H. gen'l bkkpr. at Ch. O. National Bank, 124 Asy. b. 136 Seymour.
" Charles, cigarm. 867 Main, h. 136 Seymour.
" Charles F. patternmaker, h. 62 Putnam.
" Charles Jr. printer at 716 Mn.b.136 Seymour.
" John N. patternmaker, h.u. 66 Putnam.
" Leonard, foreman at r. 32 Church, h.3u. 69 Williams.
Schumaker Frank, lumberman, h.u. 27 Pleasant.
" Frank Jr. at 17 Albany, h. 27 Pleasant.

Schuman Bros. New England bakery, 69 Morgan and 285 Main.
     J. Fred. Schuman.    Paul F. Schuman.
          Edw. Schuman.
" Edward *(S.Bros.)* h. 446 Windsor.
SCHUMAN JOHN F. *(Schuman Bros.)* councilman 2d ward, h. 283 Main.
" Max, baker at 69, b.u. 69 Morgan.
" Oswald, baker at 69, b.u. 69 Morgan.
" Paul F. *(S. Bros.)* h. 462 Windsor av.
Schumann Paul T.mach.at P.&R. h. Foot Guard.
Schumansky Valentine, brewer, h.2u. 49 Law.
Schumer Max, peddler, b.2u. 24 North.
Schumonsky John, expressman, h.2u. 187 Front.
Schuster Fred H.mach. at 1 Flow. h. 38 Wolcott.
" William, machinist, b. 47 Morgan.
Schutz Elizabeth P. wid. Aug. h. 699 Asylum.
" Robert H. asst. secy. Smyth Thread Book Sew. Mach. Co. 648 Mn. b. 699 Asylum.
" Walter Stanley, student, b. 699 Asylum.
" William, cellarman at 245 Windsor, h.u. 28 Sanford.
Schwab Joseph, insurance, 51 Tru. h. 24 C.O.pl.
" Josephine H. teacher at Brown school, b. 24 Charter Oak pl.
" Martha, b. 24 Charter Oak pl.
Schwalb Max, tailor at 118, h. 118 Asylum.
Schwarting Henry, ornamental plasterer, 438 Asylum, h.u. 20 Squire.
Schwartz Aaron, bottler, h. 81 Pleasant.
" Abraham, clerk at 52 Am. b.u. 283 Market.
" David L. student at Trinity college, 35 Jarvis hall, Summit.
" George B. real estate, 83, h. 83 Pleasant.
" Joseph, laborer, b. 119 Front.
" Joseph, notions, h. 20 Talcott.
" Louis, butcher at 56, b. 56 Pleasant.
" Morris. carpenter, 20 Potter, h. 62 Pleasant.
" Ozias, bartender, 182 Front. h. 283 Market.
" Samuel, nightwatch, h. 80 Pleasant.
Schwartzman Michael, machinist, h. 60 Avon.
Schwarz Carl, machinist, b.u.r. 165 Front.
" Moxie, machinist, 26 High, b. 165 Front.
Schwarzer Albert,cabinetm.u. 33 Wells, h.18 Bab.
Schwazt Abe, salesman, 54 Ann, b. 283 Market.
Schwegler Andrew, screwm. 476 Cap.b.2 Ellery.
" Peter, screwm. at 476 Capitol, b. 2 Ellery.
Schweighart Caspar M.helper, 30 Cush.h. Lifky.
" Joseph M. mach. at 30 Cushman, h. Lifky.

Schwenzfeire Charles W. machinist at 1 Laurel, b. 27 Williams.
Schwikowski Mary, wid. John, h.u. 141 Market.
Schwingler Fred S., Hfd. Hat Mfg. & Repairing Co. 71 Asylum, rm. 9, h. 202 Barbour.
Schwirz Carl, machinist, h.u.r. 165 Front.
Schworer Anna Mrs. milliner at 904 Main, b. 133 Market, rm. 9.
Scoble William J. patternm.at 54 Arch,h. 31 Bart.
Scofield Charles E. salesman, b. 255 Main.
  " Viola M. Mrs. chiropodist, b. 255 Main.
  " William F. painter, h. 17 Eaton.
  " ☞see also Schofield.
Scollon Mary, dressmaker, 110,b.110 Windsor.
Scotland Thomas H. at Hfd. Fire Ins. Co. 53 Trumbull, h. 42 Allen pl.
Scott Alex. clerk at Brown, Thomson & Co. 942, b. 926 Main.
  " Alonzo B. nightwatchman, 154 Pearl, h. 65 Williams.
  " Anna, wid. James, h.u. 19 Front.
  " Austin W. ostler, h. 139 Martin.
  " Bell, cook, b.r. 213 Pearl.
  " Bridget, wid. James, h. 41 Green.
  " Charles Dr. h.u. 57 Garden.
  " Dennis, manager, 72, h.u. 72 Pleasant.
  " Edgar, dyer at H. E. Patten, dye works, 37 Wells, h. 17 Russell.
  " Edgar L. clerk at Brown, Thomson & Co. 942 Main, h.2u. 21 Williams.
  " Elizabeth, wid. Andrew, h. 261 Lawrence.
  " Everett R. box clerk at P.O. h.u.s 329 Capitol.
  " F. A. at Travelers Ins. Co. 56 Prospect, b. East Windsor Hill.
  " Frank R. driller at Colts, b. 306 Main.
  " Fred. A. attorney, 750 Main, h. Terryville v.
  " George D. janitor, h.u. 884 Main.
  " George H. at 26 Church, b. 29 Chapel.
  " George P. polisher at 476 Cap. h. 44 Grand.
  " Geo. T. harnessm. at 8 Sig. b. 51 Fairmount.
  " George W. polisher, 142 Russ, h. 33 Grand.
  " H. Walter, at Hartford Fire Insurance Co. 53 Trumbull. l. 17 Haynes, room 60.
  " Harlow B. b. 65 Williams.
  " Harriet C. wid. John, b. 107 Jefferson.
  " Harris E. mach. at N.Y.R. b. 145 High.
  " Hobart C. clerk at 653 Main, h. 125 Brook.
  " Isaac A. b. 139 Martin.
  " Isaac A. 42 Seyms.
  " J. Stanley, at Travelers Insurance Co. 56 Prospect, h. 85 Buckingham.
  " James, agent, h.2u. 9 Goodman.
  " James, carpenter, h.u. 35 Front.
  " James, helper, b. 19 Front.
  " James W.foreman, Keney park, b. 182 Clark.
  " John, h.u. 22 Wells.
  " John, carpenter, h. 13 King.
  " John, carpenter at r. 334 Asy. h. 1 Spruce.
  " John,laborer at Pope Tube Co. h.r. 15 Park.
  " John, waiter at 26 State, b. 43 Wolcott.
  " John B. physician, 71, h. 71 Asylum, rm. 2.
  " John G. carpenter, h.r. 23 Spruce.
  " John J. at Connecticut Mutual Life Insurance Co. 783 Main, b. 17 Russell.
  " John W.painter,104 Asy.b.u.2B Wadsworth.

Scott Julia, wid. Patrick, h.u. 1117 Main.
  " Julia A. bookkeeper at 27 Asy. b. 41 Green.
  " Laurence, lather, r. 14 Elmer.
  " Leland D. machinist at Colts, b.·306 Main.
  " M. Bradford, cashier Hartford Fire Ins. Co. 53 Trumbull, h. 78 Edwards.
  " Maggie, wid. William, h. 40 Hicks.
  " Marion, wid. Andrew D. h.u. 329 Capitol.
  " Mary E.clerk at Brown, Thomson & Co. 942 Main, b. 2B Wadsworth.
  " Mary M. clerk, b.u. 1117 Main.
  " Nathaniel J. cond. St.Ry. b.u. 56 Benton.
  " Nellie A. clerk at Brown, Thomson & Co. 942 Main, b. 17 Russell.
  " Peter, clerk, h. 2B Wadsworth.
  " Ripley A. foreman at Colts, h. 306 Main.
  " Seymour L. clerk at 335 Sheldon, b.33 Grand.
  " & Smith, undertakers, 26 Church.
    Thomas Scott.    William J. Smith.
  " Thomas, helper at 54 Arch, h.u. 28 Wells.
  " Thomas, (Scott & Smith,) h. 29 Chapel.
  " Walter G. forem. at 476 Cap. h.154 Babcock.
  " Wm.carriagem.at r.1128 Main,h.55 Wooster.
  " William, porter, h. 884 Main.
  " William G. asst.clerk, 59½ Tru. h. 884 Main.
  " Wm. T. inspector at 700 Mn. b.u. 19 Front.
Scottish Union & National Ins. Co. 197 Asylum.

**SCOVILLE A. W. WOODWORK-ING CO.** Vredendale, c. Taylor.
                              *See page 516.*

**SCOVILLE ALBERT W.** contractor, builder, office 700 Mn. factory 286 to 292 Sheldon, h. 15 Sumner. *See page 513.*
  " Clifford E. bkkpr. at 581 Cap. b. 18 Imlay.
  " Lester, clerk, b. 15 Sumner.
  " Roscoe, helper at 450 Main.
  " Royal L. traveling salesman at 690 Park, b. 211 Garden.

**SCOVILLE WILLIAM H.** alderman *7th ward,* architect and builder, office 720 Main, h. 7 Alden. *See page 515.*

Scow Christopher, helper at 54 Arch.
Scranton Florence C. bkkpr. 745 Mn.b. 12 Lenox.
  " Louis H. traveling salesman, h. 12 Lenox.
  " S. S. & Co. bookpublishers, 281 Asylum.
    Wm. L. Matson.    Howard A. Camp.
  " Wilber L. traveling salesman, b. 12 Lenox.
Screver Peter, mech. at 581 Capitol, b. 23 John.
Scribner Harry M. clerk at Frank J. Knox, plumber supplies, 2 So. Ann, b. 1032 Main.
Scriko Pasquale, laborer, h.u. 4 Charles.
Scrimgeour Andrew D. machinist at 490 Capitol, h.u. 61 Hungerford.
Scrivener Robt. supt. Cedar Hill cem. h.1 Fairfield.
  " William H. clerk at Mechanics Savings Bank, 815 Main, b. 1 Fairfield.
Scriver John A. driver at 236 Asy. h.u. 90 State.
Scronick Joseph, laborer, 24 Mec. h.2u. 2 Ellery.
Sculley John, laborer, h.u. 267 Front.
  " Thomas, teamster at 100, h. 103 Commerce.
Scully Jos. F. butler, 83 Woodland, h.1140 Asy.
  " Michael, mach. at Colts, b.u. 43 Woodbridge.
  " Vincent J. clerk at 304, b.u. 308 Park.
  " William, casehardener at Popes, b. 8 Queen

## JOHN J. SEINSOTH,

### Licensed ∴ Pharmacist,

A FULL LINE OF

Drugs, Chemicals and Fancy Articles,

Sponges, Chamois, etc.

Proprietor of Jake's Spruce Gum Cough Syrup, Jake's
Sarsaparilla, Jake's Liver Pills, etc.

Paints, Oils, Glass, Varnish, Putty, etc.

## 12 MAPLE AVE. AND 5 CONGRESS STREET.

Seabury Hall, Trinity College, Summit.
Seaholm Charles E. harnessmaker at 1222 Main,
 h. 91 Hamilton.
" Walfred, carpenter, N.Y.R. h. 125 Ward.
Seal Michael, boilerm. stonepits, h.2u. 514 Broad.
Seale Arthur M. at Hartford Life Ins. Co. 252
 Asylum, h. 92 Willow.
Seamans Eli J. machinist at 1 Flower, h. Ware-
 house Point v.
" Harrison, machinist at Case, Lockwood &
 Brainard Co. 141 Pearl, h. 83 Jefferson.
" Otis H. clerk at Wm. Rogers Mfg. Co. 66
 Market, h. 83 Jefferson.
Seaptmas Michael, helper, 1 Flow. b. 289 Market.
Seargeson Edward, laborer, h.2u. 33 Pleasant.
Searle Alfred L. with Connecticut Mutual Life
 Ins. Co. 783 Main, b. 24 Windsor av.
" Ellen, wid. Henry L. h. 24 Windsor av.
" Franklin H. at Connecticut Mutual Life
 Insurance Co. 783 Main, h.u. 26 Ashley.
" Frederick A. asst. bookkeeper at Hartford
 Nat'l Bank, 58 State, h. 112 Huntington.
Sears David L. student at Yale, b. 964 Asylum.
SEARS EDWARD H. pres. The Collins Company,
 Collinsville, h. 964 Asylum.    See p. 521.
" William H. teamster at L. L. Ensworth & Son,
 iron & steel, 104 Front, h.u. 51 Talcott.
Seary James B. brakeman N.Y.R. h. 1½ Avon.
Seattledi Guisippi, laborer, h.u. 37 Albany.
Seaver Cora J. teach. Parkville sch. b. 206 Laurel.
" Frederick A. machinist, h. 206 Laurel.
" Julia A. wid. Heber, h. 206 Laurel.
" William A. machinist, b. 206 Laurel.
" ☞ see also Seifert.
Sebalsky Peter, ragpicker, h.3u. 6 North.
" Sam, ragpicker, h.2u. 6 North.
Sechtman B. peddler, h. 42 Market.
" . Charles, clerk at 908 Main, b. 220 Front.
" David, screwm. 476 Capitol, h.u. 220 Front.
" Harry, screwm. at 476 Cap. h.2u. 220 Front.
" Louis, fruit store, h. 81 Windsor.
" Max. foreman at 476 Cap. h.u. 280 Front.
" William, barber at 356 Park, b. Windsor.
" ☞ see also Schechtman.
Secoll Frank, machinist at Colts, b. 53 Francis.
" Joseph, filer at Colts, h. 53 Francis.
Secor James H. fireman at P.&R. h. 148 Mather.
" Jas. S. foreman at Popes, messenger board
 aldermen, h. 32 Babcock.
" Theodore C. mach. 252 Pearl, h. 32 Babcock.

SECURITY COMPANY, bankers,
 62 Pearl.        See page 438.
Sedelsky Barnett, clothing, 86 Shel. h. 209 Front.
Sedgwick Benjamin, clerk at Brown, Thomson
 & Co. 942 Main, b. 2 Church.
" & Casey, music store, 227 Asylum.
 Frank A. Sedgwick.        J. O. Casey.
" Charles F. asst. cashier Farmers & Mech.
 Nat. Bank, 106 State, h. 42 Buckingham.
" Ellen J. wid. Levi, b. 76 Farmington.
" Frank A. (S. & Casey,) h. 119 Ann.
Seefeldt Frederick, gateman, b. 572 Windsor.
Seegermeyer Henry G. machine hand at Colts,
 h. 69 Laurel.
Seegers Herman, clerk 1030 Main, b. 36 Temple.
Seeley Edward M. machinist, b.2u. 488 Main.
" May, h.u. 1171 Main.
" Wm. H. chief clerk P.&R. h.370 Asy. rm. 33.
Seelye Ezra N. ins'. agent 721 Main, h. 213 Garden.
Seery James, janitor at 93 Asy. b. 18 Trumbull.
" Mary, dressm. 60, h.u. 60 Fairmount.
" William M. clerk at 908 Mn. h. 6 Trumbull.
" ☞ see also Sceery.
Segal Israel, peddler, h.r. 65 Temple.
" Jake, photographer, 124, h.r. 124 Market.
" Joseph, peddler, h.r. 124 Market.
Segalla Aaron, at 591 Main, h. 9 Mahl.
Segar Edward E. correspondent at Popes, h. M.t.
Segarson Michael, laborer, b.u. 102 Windsor.
Segel Louis, painter, h. 51 Morgan.
" ☞ see also Siegal.
Segerson Edward, laborer, h. 40 Canton.
" James F. mechanic at Popes, b. 33 Pleasant.
Segur Frank P. insurance, b. 999 Main.
" Gideon C. physician, 67, h. 67 Farmington.
Seibart Nicholas, janitor, 703, l. 697 Main.
Seibert Harry C. cafe at Popes, l. 312 Asy. rm. 7.
Seide Barnett, h. 67 Williams.
" David, barber, 706 Main, h.2u. 185 Seymour.
" Henry W. insurance agent, real estate, 904
 Main, rm. 16, h. 95 Russ.
" Morris M. barber, 57 Maple, h. 67 Williams.
Seidler Arthur L. upholsterer at Seidler & May,
 306 Pearl, b. 118 Bellevue.
" Clarence P. at Seidler & May, 306 Pearl,
 b. 118 Bellevue.
" Frederick A. upholsterer at Seidler & May,
 306 Pearl, b. 118 Bellevue.
" George M. bookkeeper at Seidler & May,
 306 Pearl, b. 876 Windsor av.

SEIDLER & MAY, furniture, 306 to
 318 Pearl.        See page 500.
 George N. Seidler.    Charles May.
" George N. (S. & May,) h. 118 Bellevue.
Seidman Nathan, barber at 51 Windsor, b. 81 Ple.
Seifert John O. stenographer at F. H. Richards,
 803 Main, b. 50 Temple.
Seigel Morris, tailor, h.u. 92 Windsor.
" ☞ see Segel: Siegel.
Seinsoth Franklin A. motorm. h.u. 19 Buckingham.
SEINSOTH JOHN J. druggist, 5 Congress, and
 12 Maple, h. 58 Lincoln.    See page 324.
" Lindolin W. tailor at 132 State, h. 7 Wells.
Seipel Louis, buffer at Popes, b. 1350 Broad.
Seitz E. A. b. 389 Main.

**THE NEWS PRINTED IN THE POST IS RELIABLE.**

Sekoll Mary, l.u. 29 Pearl.
Selbie Frank, cabinetmaker, h. 158 Franklin.
Selby Arthur, b.u. 14 Bond.
" Frank, driver 4, b. 4 Huyshope.
" J. Edith, bkkpr. at 554 Asy. b. 30 Hopkins.
Selden C. Waite, mach. at 1 Flow. b. 161 Capitol.
" Edward M. milkman, h. 54 Eaton.
" Ella J. Mrs. h.u. 130 Babcock.
Seliger Wendel, chiropodist, 15, h. 15 Waverly.
" Wilbelmina Mrs. author Garden Notes, h. 15 Waverly.
Seligman Ida Mrs. h.u. 70 Village.
Sellers Amanda, stenog. at 884 Mn. b. 97 Hamilton.
" Charles John, forem. Popes, h.u. 97 Hamilton.
" Hulda, b.u. 97 Hamilton.
Sellew Ernest B. draughtsman at 1 Flower, b.u. 22 Hopkins.
" George O. mach. at 40 Governor, h. E.H.t.
" Harry H. mach. at 1 Laurel, h. 24 Morris.
Selling David H. clerk at 100 Asy. h. 96 Ashley.
Selta Joseph, lodginghouse. 37 Albany.
Seltzer Barnett, (Gleszer & Seltzer,) h.u.40 Park.
" Max, assembler at Popes, b. 24 Lawrence.
" Nathan, groceries, 24, h. 24 Lawrence.
Semple Lilla B. clerk at Brown, Thomson & Co. 942, b. 926 Main.
" William A. b. 926 Main.
Senato Samuel, fruit and candy, 35 Sigourney.
Senatro Clement, confect. h.3u. 56 Portland.
Senger George C. mach. at 1 Flow. b. 272 Park
" Harry, clerk N.Y. News Co. h.u. 8 Chestnut
" Martha K. stenographer, b. 272 Park.
" Martin, barber, 272, h. 272 Park.
Senior Bridget, nurse, 1445, l. 1445 Broad.
" Susan A. Mrs. dressmaker, 51, h. 51 Pratt.
Senk George H. deputy sheriff, 85 Trumbull, b. 1150 Main.
" John, cabinetmaker, h.u. 161 Barbour.
" John R. gunstocker at Colts, h.u. 9 Morris.
" Wm. grocer, 8 Capen, 448, h.446 Windsor av.
Sensenbaugh John W. clerk at 95 Ple. b. 145 High.
Sentener Arabella B. Mrs. attendant at 30 Washington.
" Ella M. attendant at 30 Washington.
" Olive A. attendant at 30 Washington.
Sequeira Augustus, contractor at Pratt & Whitney Co. 1 Flower, b.u. 152 Allyn.
Seraphin Peter, clerk at 106 Asy. h. 36 Windsor.
" Samuel, harnessm. at 8 Sig. h. 36 Pleasant.
Seregensi Constanci, laborer, h.u. 12 North.
" Domenico, laborer, h.u. 12 North.
Serene Mae, clerk, b. 148 Mather.
" Nathaniel, h. 148 Mather.
Sergason John, at city water wks. h.2u. 201 Park.
Sergerson Edward, plasterer, h. 23 Pleasant.
" Richard, laborer, b. 23 Pleasant.
Service Helen, wid. William, h. 54 Allen pl.
" James H. baggagemaster at Union depot, b. 54 Allen pl.
" John W. druggist, 299 & 243 Park, h. 42 Allen pl.
Servie Frank, brewer, h. 223 Bellevue.
Servitch Louis, barber, h. 64 Pleasant.
Sessarsky Lewis, peddler, h.2u.r. 190 Front.
" Nathan, grocer, 30, h. 30 North.

**SESSIONS EDSON,** mangr. Foot Guard hall, 159 High, h.u. 20 Belden.
*See page 496.*
" Lillian, student, 30 Asylum, b.u. 10 Chestnut.
" Margaret Mrs. h.u. 10 Chestnut.
Setterberg Edward, coachm. at 108 Farmington, h. 115 Lawrence.
Severn Edmund, music teacher at 45, h. 45 Far.
" Frank W. insurance agent, l. 981 Main.
Sevwana Minnie, printing dept. 336, b. 336 Weth.
Seward DeWitt K. machinist, h. 58 Seymour.
" Ernest R. mach. at 133 Shel. b. 58 Seymour.
" Frank R. student, b. 58 Seymour.
Sewell Albert C. upholsterer at Neal, Goff & Inglis Co. 980, h. 517 Main.
Sexton Carrie L. h.2u. 42 Hopkins.
" Charles H. helper, b.u. 104 Wooster.
" Edward, mach. at 1 Flower, b. 177 Asylum.
" Fred. G. cashier United States Bank, 872 Main, h. 496 Farmington.
" George K. h. 278 Windsor av.
" James J. saloon, 116 Front, b. 20 Center.
" Joel B. superintendent at I. B. Davis & Son. 40 Cushman, h. 17 Forest.
" John M. clerk at 62 Market, b. 88 Ann.
" Lawrence B. stairbuilder at 133 Sheldon, h. 10 Foot Guard.
" Louis M. clerk at Phoenix Mut. Life Ins. Co. 49 Pearl, b. Highland, so. of Far.
" Mary, wid. H. L. h.u. 104 Wooster.
" Mary, wid. Patrick, h. 20 Center.
" Michael, motorman St.Ry. b. E.H.t
" Minnie Hyde, wid. George, h. 12 Myrtle.
" Thomas R. printer at 175 Pearl, h. 20 Center.
" Walter H. clerk 206 State, b.u. 104 Wooster.
" ☞ *see also Saxton.*
Seybold Mme. French teacher, 926 Main, rm. 48.
Seymour Albert H. clerk, b.u. 38 Woodbridge.
" Albert H. clerk at 64 State, h.u. 21 East.
" Alonzo M. waiter, h.u. 316 Wethersfield.
" Arden A. l.u. 19 Atlantic.
" Ashbel, Favorite Oil Co. 163 Asy.h. 281 N.B.
" Bela C. clerk at 32 Walnut, h. 19 Atlantic.
" C. M. Mrs. nurse, h.u. 38 Woodbridge.
" Carrie L. teacher, b. 229 New Britain.
" Charles, waiter, h.u. 213 Windsor.
" Charles M. mach. at 24 Mechanic, h. W.H.t.
" Clarence H. painter, b. 17 Church.
" Dudley S. contractor at Pratt & Whitney Co. 1 Flower, h. 102 Huntington.
" Edgar H. farmer, h. Park, W.H.t.
" Edith C. hairdresser, 68 Pratt, h.u. 38 Wdbg.
" Edward S. machinist at 26 Laurel, b.W.H.t.
" Eliza C. wid. Wooster B. h.u. 281 New Britain.
" Ellen M. Miss, h. 167 Main.
" Emily, h. 88 Collins.
" family of Horace, 167 Main.
" Frank H. engr. at 15 Tru. h.u. 19 Atlantic.
" Frank W. mach. at 1 Flow. b. 15 Fairfield.
" Fred B. cashier National Fire Insurance Co. 95 Pearl, b. 358 Laurel.
" Frederick A. farmer, h. Park, W.H.t.
" Frederick W. lettercarrier, b. 5 Cranes.
" Freeman P. foreman at Popes, b. 10 Fairfield.
" Harriet L. teacher Parkv. sch. b. 26 Madison.

Seymour Herbert P. forem. at Popes, h.u. 247 Jef.
" Horace S. clerk at Popes, h. 8 Girard.
" Howard A. clerk at 15 Tru. b. 15 Fairfield.
" Howard C. clerk at 49 Ann, b. 47 Ward.
" Isabella O. wid. H. P. h.u. 247 Jefferson.
" J. Howard, clerk at L. L. Ensworth & Son, iron and steel store, 104 Front, b.u. 247 Jef.
" John, cider & vinegar, 16 Park, h. 47 Ward.
" John L. farmer, h. 15 Fairfield.
" Julia Mrs. h. 167 Main.
" Julius L. laborer, h. 88 New Britain.
" L. Eugene, lettercarrier, h. 10 Martin.
" Laura, wid. Walter, h. 106 Retreat.
" Laura H. wid. Henry T. h. 102 Huntington.
" Lemuel W. milkman, h. 247 New Britain.
" Leverett K. (Wakefield Agency,) h. Park, West Hartford t.
" Lillie dressmaker at 30 Wash. b. 229 N. B.
" Lillie E. wid. Henry, 867 Mn. h.u. 52 Hudson.
" Linville B. clerk at Brown, Thompson & Co. 942 Main, b. 281 New Britain.
" Lloyd G. janitor, h. 1 Atlantic.
" Louis C. clerk, h.u. 38 Woodbridge.
" Luthera P. wid. Albert h. 303 Capitol.
" M. Louise, wid. Michael L. h. 229 N.B.
" Mary O. wid. Freeman, h. 10 Fairfield.
" Mira A. dressmaker, 31, h.u. 31 Wadsworth.
" Nathan W. builder, h. Park, W.H.t.
" Norman B. farmer, h. 460 Broad.
" Ralph Russell, clerk at American National Bank, 803 Main, b. 15 Fairfield.
" Richard, h. 31 Park.
" Richard W. clerk, h.u. 31 Wadsworth.
" Robert T. bookkeeper at W. C. Mason & Co. 746 Main, h. 179 Ashley.
" S. Francis, farmer, h. 420 New Britain.
" Sophia Miss, h. 167 Main.
" Spencer H. clk. 216 State, h. 26 Madison.
" Susan T. Miss h. 167 Main.
" William, milkman, h. Oakwood av. W.H.t.
" William L. printer at Hartford Life Insurance Co. 252 Asylum, b. 10 Martin.
" William O. railroad commissioner, rm. 41 State capitol building, h. Ridgefield t.
Seyms George H. h. 181 Collins.
SEYMS ROBERT N. (Lincoln, S. & Co.) 84 Market, h. 85 Ann.        See page 588.
"  ☞ see also Sims.
Shack Anton, laborer, h.u. 4 Ellery.
Shackley Frank W. coal, h. c. Park, n. Prospect.
" Mabel, student, Theolog. sem. 1507 Broad.
Shadow Julius R. mach. at 1 Flow. h. 238 N.B.
Shaffer Charles O. accountant, h. 57 Woodbine.
" Mary C. Mrs. clerk at Brown, Thomson & Co. 942 Main, b. 297 Lawrence.
" Samuel Mrs. h. 297 Lawrence.
" William H. lettercarrier at station A, P.O. h.u. 41 Grand.
"  ☞ see also Schaffer.
Shaffner Martin, engin. P.&R. h. 140 Mather.
Shahbaz Baba N. theolog. student, 1507 Broad.
Shailer C. A. Mrs. h. 98 Capen.
" Clifford B. photographer at A. Mugford, 177 Asylum, b. 224 Sargeant.
" Collard A. bartender 152 Asy. h. 98 Capen.

Shailer Eliza F. wid. Joseph N. h. 98 Capen.
" Emory C. bookkeeper, b. 2 Avon.
" Robert E. clerk at 252 Pearl, b.224 Sargeant.
" Rollo L. contractor & bldr. h. 224 Sargeant.
" Wells R. stonetrim. 283 Shel. h. 224 Sargeant.
" William P. bartdr. at 109, h. 125 Trumbull.
Shamgochin George, at 476 Cap. h. 18 Babcock.
Shanks Abraham, operator, 388 Cap. b.33 Windsor.
Shanley Catherine, h.u. 101 Mather.
" Patrick, helper, b. 306 Park.
" Thomas, laborer, h.2u. 101 Mather.
" Walter J. Rev. h. 140 Farmington.
Shannahan John, carpenter N.Y.R. b.19½ Putnam.
" John J. railm. at 618 Cap. b. 19½ Putnam.
" Patrick, molder at 618 Cap. h.u. 26 Flower.
Shannon Ann, wid. Owen, h. 85 Putnam.
" E. V. b. 981 Main.
" Fred J. foreman, b.u. 171 Barbour.
" George, conductor St.Ry. b. 19 Central.
" H. G. cigarm. at 867 Main, h. Windsor t.
" Hugh E. helper at 2 So. Ann, b.u. 270 Front.
" Isabel F. nurse, 20 South Hudson.
" James B. physician, 119, b. 119 Capitol.
" James J. driver at Adams Express Co. b. 68 Chestnut.
" James W. h. 35 Putnam.
" John, at N.Y.R. shops, h. South Forest.
" John E. assem. at 581 Cap. b. 68 Chestnut.
" Jos. S. pressman, 252 Pearl, h.u. 207 Sheldon.
" Lucy M. Mrs. b. 147 Trumbull.
" Owen, U. S. Army, b. 16 Walnut.
" Patrick, laborer at 98 Kil. b. 270 Front.
" Patrick, laborer, h. 26 Flower.
" Philip, laborer at 98 Kil. h. 60 Pleasant.
" Robert H. student, l. 147 Trumbull.
" T. R. & Co. druggists, 143 Trumbull.*
" Thomas A., clerk at the Fidelity Co. 49 Pearl, h.u. 255 Jefferson.
" Thomas A. clerk, h. 255 Jefferson.
" Thomas R. (T. R. S. & Co.) h. 147 Trumbull.
" William H. blacks. at 34 Elm, h. 10 Lewis.
Shapirio Abraham, painter, h. 86 Pleasant.
" Joseph, grinder at 388 Cap. h.2u. 32 North.
Shapiro Benjamin, operator, h. 32 North.
" Joseph, shoemaker at 40 State, b. Front.
" Morris, teacher, h. 261 Market.
Sharff Louis, barber at 46 Temple.
Sharfman Barned, peddler, h.u. 206 Front.
" Joseph, peddler, b.u. 60 Pleasant.
Sharkey James F. screwm. at Popes, b.u. 54 Law.
Sharp Edward, at 209 State, h. E.H.t.
" Harry E. contractor, h.u. 153 Clark.
" Ormond V. clerk at 98 Kil. b. 13 Belden.
" Thomas, helper at 40 Elm, h. E.H.t.
Sharpe Charles H. teamster, h.2u. 96 Walnut.
" Frank N., Collateral Loan Co. 71 Asylum, b. 1544 Broad.
" George W. toolm. at 20 Sargeant, h.39 Seyms.
" Howard J. nurse, h. 1220 Asylum.
Sharper Ernest, clerk at 310 Park, b. 152 Bab.
Sharples James, stonecutter, b. 1338 Main.
" Samuel, painter, b. 1338 Main.
Sharrott David, cook, l. 10½ Village.
" George, waiter, l. 10½ Village.
Shasholfski Meyer, laborer, b. 72 Pleasant.

Shattuck D.W. salesm. at Popes, h. Salem, Mass.
" Etta S. wid. G. M. h. 69 Fairmount.
Shaughnessy Ann, wid. Peter, h. 24 Dean.
" Daniel J. (*Chamberlin & S.*) b. 55 Hung.
" James, polisher at 142 Russ, h. 36 Lawrence.
" John, h. 55 Hungerford.
" John J. b. 24 Dean.
" John J. mach. 388 Cap. b. 55 Hungerford.
" Mary, dressmaker, b. 24 Dean.
" N. H. clerk, b.u. 21 Bellevue.
" Walter R. clerk, b.u. 21 Bellevue.
Shavalar Josephine, wid. Edwin, h. 1088 Main.
Shavers Maria, h.3u. 284 Pearl.
Shaw Albert A. builder, h.2u. 46 Temple.
" Alexander L. foreman at Pope Tube Co. b.u. 1147 Broad.
" Charles, ostler, l.r. 87 High.
" Charles L. etcher at Wm. Rogers Mfg. Co. 66 Market, h. 810 Windsor av.
" David, ostler at 87 High, l.r. 34 Village.
" Dawson, coachman, l.r. 131 Farmington.
" Elwin A. beltmaker at 15 Tru. b. 11 Russell.
" George, agent at 721, b. 1221 Main.
" George L. clerk at 1180, b.u. 1341 Main.
" John L. mason, b.u. 1147 Broad.
" Joseph, at 59½ Trumbull, b. E.H.t.
" Margaret, wid. Alexander, b.u. 1147 Broad.
" May E. stenog. at 15 Tru. b. Manchester t.
" Nellie D. wid. Fred. dressm. h.2u. 177 Asy.
" Robert, bookkeeper, l. 24 Windsor av.
" Robert, laborer at 690 Park, b. 8 Sisson.
" Samuel, plumber, 1204 Mn. b.u. 1147 Broad.
" Thomas, polisher at 581 Capitol, h. N.B.t.
" Thomas A. b.u. 943 Main, rm. 39.
" William, machinist at 83 Woodbine, b. 45 Hamilton.
" William R. mach. at 83 Woodbine, h. M.t.
" William S. janitor at 370 Asy. h. Windsor t.
" William Y. at Travelers Ins. Co. 56 Prospect, h. Quaker lane, W.H.t.
Shay Daniel J. h. 70 Hungerford.
" Margaret J. dressmaker, h. 70 Hungerford.
" Timothy J. carpenter, b. 70 Hungerford.
" ☞ *see also Shea.*
Shea Ann, wid. Michael, h.u. 263 High.
" Annie, dressmaker, b.u. 263 High.
" Bridget, wid. John J. b.u. 331 Front.
" Catherine, b. 1350 Broad.
" Catherine, wid. Patrick F. h.u. 57 Ward.
Shea Chas. W. (*Strickland & S.*) wood mantels, etc. h. 13 Lafayette. *See page 516.*
" Cornelius, b. 266 New Park.
" Cornelius, lab. Pope Tube Co. b. 76 Heath.
" Cornelius, laborer at 690 Park, h. 12 Grace.
" Cornelius, laborer at 556 Cap. h. Weth.
" Cornelius, masontender, h. 34 So. Prospect.
" Cornelius J. rubberworker at 690 Park, b. 74 Putnam.
" Daniel, bartdr. at 32 S.Pro. h. 5 Goodman.
" Daniel, laborer, h.u. 26 Village.
" Daniel J. driver, 205 State, h. 36 Temple.
" Dennis, peddler, h. 344 Front.
" Dennis, teamster, h.u. 2 Ashton.
" Dennis B. conductor, h. 335 Front.
" Dennis J. floorwalker, 835, b. 1045 Main.

Shea Edward, waiter 107 State, b. 28 Morgan.
" Edward F. foreman, N.Y.R. h. 174 Putnam.
" Edward F. helper at N.Y.R. h. 40 Flower.
" Edward F. watch. at 158, h.r. 160 Woodland.
" Edwd. F. Jr. benchm. Popes, b. 174 Putnam.
" Frank E. polisher at Popes, h.2u. 350 Park.
" Gerald, screwm. 476 Cap. b. 55 Hawthorn.
" Hannah, b.u. 14 Queen.
" Ida M. b.u. 3 Lafayette.
" James, inspector at N.Y.R. h. 25 Flower.
" James C. clerk at 407 Main, b. 70 Hung.
" James F. laborer, b. 119 Windsor.
" James J. baseballist, b. 174 Putnam.
" James J. operator at Popes, b.u. 147 Law.
" James L. conductor St.Ry. h. 1 Ellsworth pl.
" John, coachman, h. 37 Park.
" John, feeder, 42 Union pl. b. 174 Putnam.
" John, laborer, b. 63 Flower.
" John, switchtender at 98 Kil. b.u. 35 Russell.
" John A. laborer at 476 Cap. h. 30 Flower.
" John A. laborer, b. 69 Avon.
" John B. painter, h.2u. 40 Green.
" John D. barber, 2, l. 14 State.
" John F. polisher at Popes, h.2u. 144 Babcock.
" John J. bartender, b. 55 Windsor.
" John J. engineer, b. 12 Grace.
" Lizzie, bkkpr. at 956 Main, b.u. 57 Ward.
" Mary, wid. James, h.2u. 118 Portland.
" Matthew O. mechanic, h.u. 87 Windsor.
" Michael, at N.Y.R. h.u.r. 23 West.
" Michael, expressman, h. 41 South Prospect.
" Michael, laborer, h. 118 Portland.
" Michael, mason, h. 6 John.
" Michael J. saloon, 53½, h.u. 55 Windsor.
" Morris A. printer at 2 State, b.u. 33 Russell.
" Mortimer, carpenter, h. 388 Park.
" Nicholas, teamster at 46 Ann, h.2u. 140 Grove.
" Patrick, laborer, b.u. 12 South Prospect.
" Patrick, laborer, b. 101 Sheldon.
" Patrick, motorman St.Ry. h.u. 34 Park.
" Patrick J. cigarms. at 867 Main, b. 180 High.
" Robert S. at 466 Asylum, b. 174 Putnam.
" Thomas, laborer, h. 24 Church.
" Thomas, motorman St.Ry. b. 40 John.
" Thomas, plumber's asst. h.u. 119 Windsor av.
" Timothy, b. 266 New Park.
" Timothy, blacksm. 22 Wells, b. 12 S.Prospect.
" Timothy, carpenter, h. 40 Park.
" Timothy, carptr. N.Y.R. b. 70 Hungerford.
" Tim. F. molder at 690 Park, b. 74 Putnam.
" Timothy H. barber, b. 135 Maple.
" William, machinist, b. 46 Grand.
" William A. plater at Popes, b. 40 Flower.
" William E. printer at Hartford Times, 716, h.u. 1295 Main.
" William H. mach. at 1 Flow. b.u. 57 Ward.
" William J. driver at 48 Ann, h. 1160 Main.
" William L. harnessmaker at 59½ Trumbull, h. 587 Main.
" William L. mech. at Popes, b. 34 Lawrence.
" ☞ *see also O'Shea, Shay.*
Sheard Ellen, wid. Peter L. h. 148 Market.
" Frances, milliner, 908 Main, b.u. 57 Barbour.
" William, assistant pressband at Hartford Times, 716 Main, b. 148 Market.

**If you have anything to Sell, Advertise it in The Post.**

Shearer Mary M. stenographer at 177 Asylum, h. Manchester t.
Shechtman Louis, fruit, h.u. 81 Windsor.
Sheckman Harry, screwmaker, h.3u. 33 Pleasant.
Shedd J. N. Co. hatters, etc. 109 Asylum.
" James N. president and treas. J. N. Shedd Co. h. 193 Farmington.
Sheedy Catharine, dressm. 1232, h. 1232 Main.
" James, bricklayer, b. 75 Franklin.
" John J. boilermaker, h. 42 Canton.
" Matthew F. blacksm. N.E.R. h. 80 Walnut.
" Michael, contractor at 75, h. 75 Franklin.
" Thomas, brickmason, b. 75 Franklin.
" William J. brickmason, h. 462 Maple.
Sheehan Andrew, laborer, h. 433 Broad.
" Andrew F. driller at Colts, h. 49 N.B.
" Catherine F. b. 433 Broad.
" Daniel, cashier at 80, l. 80 State.
" Dennis, laborer, b.3u.r. 12 South Prospect.
" Edward, b. 2 Holcomb.
" Edward J. saloon, 657, h. 91 Main.
" F. J. lineman at 3 Central, b. 84 Grove.
" Frank, hodcarrier, b.r. 2 South Forest.
" James, agent, h. 101 Mather.
" James, laborer at Capitol, b. 18 Kennedy.
" James F. mach. at 581 Cap. b. 103 Commerce.
" Jere. helper at 165 Windsor, b. 18 Kennedy.
" John, b. 137 Zion.
" John, helper, b. 18 Kennedy.
" John, laborer at 95 Ple. b. 18 Kennedy.
" John, policeman, h.2u. 28 Front.
" John, stretcher at 15 Tru. h. 120 Mather.
" John, teamster, b. 433 Broad.
" John A. clerk at 95 Pleasant, b. 145 High.
" John H. molder, h.2u. 94 Grove.
" John J. laborer, b. 1202 Main.
" Kittie D. clerk at 956 Main, b. 53 Chestnut.
" Michael, laborer, b. 102 Windsor.
" Michael, laborer at 15 Tru. h.2u. 1½ Avon.
" Michael, laborer, h.u. 11 John.
" Michael T. b. 2 Holcomb.
" Nellie, wid. William, h. 1059 Main.
" Norine G. at 14 Pratt, b. 433 Broad.
" Patrick, teamster 100 Com. h.2u. 23 Spruce.
" Patrick E. lettercarrier at station A, h.u. 3 Queen.
" Patrick J. sup. policeman, h.u. 108 Mather.
" Richard, engir. 266 Pearl, h.u. 120 Hung.
" Robert, h.u. 8 Lawrence.
" Samuel, operater, b. 145 High.
" Timothy, tender, 34 Morgan, b. 119 Tru.
" William, porter at 8 Hurlburt, h. 54 Village.
" William P. machinist at N.Y.R. h. 46 Green.
Sheeley Norman, fireman P.&R. b. 73 Albany.
Sheeran Margaret, boardinghouse, 18 Trumbull.
Sheffield Henry C. bookkeeper at C. R. Hart Co. 898 Main, h. 88 Ashley.
Sheiber Theo. L. wireworker at 618 Capitol, h. 15 Greenwood.
Sheidler Tony, molder, b. 284 Franklin.
Sheldon Anna O. h. 105 Windsor av.
" E. E. electrotyper at 177 Asylum, h. E.H.t.
" Edward A. real estate, h. Whiting lane.
" Elizabeth B. b. 88 Collins.
" George R. Mrs. b. 109 Elm.

Sheldon Grace B. b. 230 High.
" Jane L. h. 124 Trumbull.
" Louis P. clerk at Popes, b. 427 Main.
" Louise M. b. 149 Windsor av.
" Sarah M. nurse, 14, h. 14 Church, rm. 4.
" W. Carrie, h.u. 57 Willard.
" see also Shelton.
Sheldrick Fenner E. clerk at 372 Asy. b. Blo.
Shelley Bern, motorman St.Ry. 115 State.
" George P. electrician at 581 Cap, h.W.H.t.
" James, painter, 352 Albany, b. 39 Harrison.
" Wm. O. chief clerk at Factory Ins. Association, 95 Pearl, h. 22 Lincoln.
Shellington William J. clerk at 921 Main, b. 17 Chestnut.
Shelly John J. boxm. at 67 Front. b.u. 53 Potter.
" John Philip, helper at Strickland & Shea, 20, h.u. 53 Potter.
" Philip A. agent, h.u. 53 Potter.
Shelter for Women, 76 Temple.
SHELTON CHARLES E. alderman 3d ward, with Adams Express Co. b. 310 Windsor av.
**SHELTON EDWARD**, real estate, insurance, etc. 66 State, h. 310 Windsor av.
                                        See page 426.
" Eva S. stenographer at 904 Main, rm. 100, b. Rockville t.
" see also Sheldon.
Shepard Addie M. h.u. 48 Wadsworth.
" Almyr J. clerk at 885 Main, h. Burnside v.
" Chas. E. general agt. Ætna Life Ins. Co. 654 Main, h. Highland, south of Farmington.
" Ernest C. manager at 261 Asy. h. 205 Garden.
" Fred, driver at 82 Francis, b.u. 551 Park.
" Frederick C. bookkeeper at Popes, 436 Capitol, h. 217 Ashley.
" Frederick O. lather, b.u. 48 Wadsworth.
" Jason J. at Ætna Life Insurance Co. 650 Main, h. 225 Wethersfield.
" Jennie E. Mrs. b.u 15 Morris.
" John G. toolmaker at 9 Sig. h. 166 Putnam.
" Kate B. clerk, b.u. 80 Cedar.
" L. C. clerk at 109, b. 109 Trumbull.
" Lucia M. wid. D. A. b. 95 Jefferson.
" Lucy A. Mrs. embroiderer at 762 Main.
" Minnie A. D. at 59½ Tru. b. 166 Putnam
" Nellie F. clerk at 141 Pearl, b. 166 Putnam.
" Theron, painter, h. 35½ Chestnut.
" W. fireman str. Middletown, 285 State.
" Walter W. h. 15 Mechanic.
" William, head waiter str. Hartford, h. N.Y.
" William J. plater at 581 Cap. l. 90 Pearl.
" Willis S. motorman St.Ry. b. 111 Pearl.
" see also Shepherd; Sheppard; Chaput.
Shepardson Daniel F. plumber, h. 545 Main.
" Francis G. b. 42 Mahl.
" Hattie, wid. Harold, h. 68 Wooster.
SHEPHERD FORREST, councilman 9th ward, law student, b. 667 Asylum.
" Fred, laborer, h. 15 Mechanic.
" George, filer at 581 Capitol, h. E.H.t.
" George, laborer at 690 Park, h. 26 Lawrence.
" George R. physician, 32 Far. h. 667 Asy.
" see also Shepard; Sheppard; Chaput.

Shepp Frances, wid. John, h.u. 83 Front.
Sheppard Harry N. clerk, h.u. 44 Chestnut.
" John J. machinist at 1 Flower, b. 169 Russ.
" Thomas M. driver at 55 Mar. h.u.44 Chestnut.
" William F. contractor at Pratt & Whitney
Co. 1 Flower, h. 169 Russ.
" William G. mach. at 1 Flow. h.u. 173 Russ.
" Wilson, carpenter, h.u. 22 Smith.
" ☞ see also Shepard; Shepherd; Chaput.
Sherer John, laborer, b. 1st h. w. of Asy. on Pro.
Shereshevsky Moses, clerk, 110 State. h. 270 Mar.
Sheridan Andrew J. mach. at 556 Cap. h.256 Park.
" Annie F. dressmaker, 8, b. 8 Wellington.
" Ellen Mrs. washer, h.2u. 31 Mechanic.
" James, helper N.Y.R. h. 8 Wellington.
" James, laborer, b.2u. 31 Mechanic.
" John, laborer at 100 Com. h. 61 Potter.
" Patrick, laborer, h.2u. 38 Wells.
" Patrick, tailor, 41, h.2u. 41 Mechanic.
" Philip, barber at 98 Francis, b. 23 Sisson.
Sheriden Fred W. student, b. 242 Putnam.
Sheriff Hartford County, E. J. Smith, 85 Tru.
Sherlock Mattie L. dressmaker, 987, h. 987 Main.
Sherman Alice, with the Hartford Globe, 25
Asylum, h. East Haddam t.
" Charles, mach. at 388 Cap. h. 224 Putnam.
" Charles A. marketman 319 Asy. h. 198 High.
" Clark A. rubber w. at 690 Park, h.u. 28 Rowe.
" Clifton L. managing editor Courant,66 State.
b. 54 Buckingham.
" Drucilla, b. 32 Clark.
" Ernest A. designer and engraver, 756 Main,
room 32, h. Wethersfield t.
" Ernest A. salesm. at 45 Asy.b.106½ Trumbull.
" Eugene M. bkkpr. at Popes, 436 Capitol.
" Frank, broommaker at 336, b. 336 Weth.
" George W. foreman at 388 Capitol, h.
Springfield t.
" Israel, fruit peddler, h.3u. 15 North.
" M. Alice, teacher Brown school, b. 35 Center.
**SHERMAN M. W. & SON,** general
trucking, Donald street. *See page 551.*
Mason W. Sherman.      Roger W. Sherman.
" Maria, laundress at 20 So. Hudson.
" Mason W. (*M. W. S. & Son,*) h. 35 Center.
" Morgan J. prop. Brower house, 23 Central.
**SHERMAN & PIGOTT,** carmen, 234
State.
Roger W. Sherman.      Michael J. Pigott.
" Roger W. (*S. & Pigott,*) h. 6 East.
" Seth E. slater & painter, h. 238 Martin.
" William H. machinist at 581 Capitol, h.u.
46 Laurel.
Sherris Jacob, iceman at 4 Central.
Sherry James, machinist, b. 9 Wadsworth.
" John, machinist, h. 9 Wadsworth.
" Michael, machinist at 1 Flower, b. 9 Wads.
" William, mach. at 30 Cush. h.u. 305 Law.
Shertman B. peddler, h. 42 North.
" Louis, helper, b. 42 Windsor.
Sherwood Clarence B. h. 183 Bellevue.
" Daniel, b. 23 Sumner.
" Frank G. clerk, 154 Pearl, h. Rocky Hill t.
" Granville H. student at Trinity college, 3
Northam tower, Summit.

Sherwood Levi H. printer at 252 Pearl,h. R.H.t.
" Luther H. printer at 154 Pearl, h. 167 Ash.
Shew John W. farmer, h. 251 Wethersfield.
" Wm. A. bookkeeper at Conn. Fire Ins. Co.
51 Prospect, b. 251 Wethersfield.
Shevitz Louis (*Rosenblatt & S.*) b. 64 Pleasant.
Shghian Peter, laborer at Capewell Horse Nail
Co. 40 Governor, b. 1443 Broad.
Shield Bros. barbers, 334 Pearl.
William H. Shield.      Richard M. Shield.
" Richard M. (*Shield Bros.*) 27 Huntley
" Wm. H. janitor at 49 Pearl,h. 85 Fairmount.
Shields Archie, mach. at 388 Cap. b. 119 Albany.
" David P. lineman, h. 19 John.
" Howard L. butcher at 1111, b. 1113 Main.
" Morris H. brickmaker, h.u.r. 31 Albany.
" Nellie L. b. 348 Capen.
" James, h.u. 61 Hawthorn.
" William G. engineer P.&R. h. 24 Pliny.
Shiloh Ada A. Mrs. b. 44 Elliott.
" Josephine C. wid. John, b. 44 Elliott.
" William B. butler at 30 Weth. h. 44 Elliott.
Shindler Jonas, cigarmaker, h.u. 153 Martin.
Shine Mr. motorman St.Ry. b. 19 Central.
" Philip, laborer, b. 41 South Prospect.
Shipman Agnes G. teacher Brown school, 160
Market, l. 427 Main, room 36.
" Louis J. mason, h. 123 Clark.
**SHIPMAN ARTHUR L.** (*Gross, Hyde & Ship-
man*) b.u. 33 C.O.pl.      *See page 486.*
" Jas. (*Bullard, Johnson & S.*) h. 163 Ashley.
" James H. laundryman at 30 Washington.
" Nathaniel, judge U. S. Circuit Court of
Appeals, P. O. building, 65 State, h. 33
Charter Oak pl.
" Morris H. mach. at 476 Cap. h. 84 Windsor.
" Simon, tailor, h.u. 84 Windsor.
" Walter S. machinist, b. 163 Ashley.
" William, tailor at 730 Main, b.u. 84 Windsor.
Shippee Charles N. market, 116 Alb. h. 259 Law.
Shippey Elmer W. machinist at 335 Sheldon, b.
78 State.
Shirley Charles H. silversmith at 62 Market,
h. 254 Franklin.
" Herbert, harnessm. 83 Asy. h.u. 106 Mather.
" Thomas, silversm. at 62 Mar. b. 226 Franklin.
" Wm. T. silversm. at 62 Mar. h. 226 Franklin.
Shirrell Abbie I. wid. William, b. 7 Belden.
" Ida V. teacher of music, 7, b. 7 Belden.
Shocher Solomon L. teacher, h. 272 Market.
Schoenle Theodore, cabinetmaker, h. 33 Elliott.
Shoemaker Percy E. machinist at 690 Park, b.u.
17½ Sisson.
Sbold Charles O. painter, l. 109 Lawrence.
Shontell Augustus, beltmaker at 15 Trumbull,
h.u. 45 Barbour.
Shooks Theodore, conductor, P.&R. h. E.H.t.
Shorey Ernest, brickmaker, b. Windsor av.
" William, brickmaker, b. Windsor av.
Shortell Fred J. mach.hand at Colts,b. 113 Park.
" Frederick J. machine hand at Colts, b. 42
Vanblock.
" James F. profiler at Colts, h. 42 Vanblock.
" Thomas, helper at 142 Russ, b. 135 Lawrence.
Shortensick Michael, stonemason,b.u. 69 Pleasant.

Shosho Lorenzo, laborer, b.u. 47½ Morgan.
Show Isaac, tailor, h.u. 46 North.
Shroder Henry E. mach. 70 Huy. h. 19 Benton.
ShuckerowJas.J.yardm.N.Y.R.h.2u.118Mather.
" William, conductor, N.E.R. h. 20 Goodman.
" ☞see also Shugrue; Sughrue; Sugrue.
Shufelt Albert E. city editor Hartford Telegram,
    12 Central, b. 26 State.
Shugrue John, carpenter, b.u. 26 Village.
" ☞see also Shuckerow; Sugrue; Sughrue.
Shulansky Henry, paperhanger, h.r. 17 Portland.
Shulman Samuel, (Samilson & S.) h. 296 Pearl.
Shulthiess Augusta, clerk 203 State, b. 4 Kil. ct.
" John, mach. at 388 Cap. h.u. 4 Kilbourn ct.
" John F. barber at 9 Asylum, h. 21 Mather.
" Rosie, b.u. 4 Kilbourn ct.
Shultz William, laborer, b. 4 Elm.
" ☞see also Schultz.
Shumaker John, engir. 70 Com. b. 27 Pleasant.
Shumm Adolph, motorm. St. Ry. b. 289 Asylum.
Shumway Arthur C. at National Fire Insurance
    Co. 95 Pearl, b. 335 Windsor av.
" Clarence S.draftsm. at Hartford Steam Boiler
    Insp. & Ins. Co. 650 Main, h. 3 Alden.
Shurter Elijah T. telegraph editor Courant, 66
    State, h.u. 25 Imlay.
Shuster Andrew, blacksmith, h. 5 Kilbourn ct.
Sibalsky Penier, butcher, h. 22 North.
Sibley Preston B. special agt. factory inspector,
    State capitol, rm. 26, h. Danielson t.
Sibon Nathan, clerk at 65 Asy. b. 21 Bellevue.
" Thomas H.ins. agt. 721 Mn. h. 21 Bellevue.
Siboolski Jake, helper at 1 Flower, h. 8 North.
Sichler Chas. engir. 217 Windsor, h. 58 Loomis.
" Geo. saloon, 44 Union b.2u. 312 Asylum.
" Geo. Jr. bartdr. at 44 Un.pl. b.u. 312Asylum.
Sickels George II. telegrapher at Courant, 66
    State, h. East Hartford t.
Sickler Tony, laborer at stone pits, h. Ellery.
" Valentine, laborer at stone pits, h. Ellery.
Sickles Chas. II. baker, 385, h.2u. 488 Main.
Sickmann Otto, cigarmaker, h. 1 Pleasant ct.
Siddons John, porter at 24, b. 24 Market.
Side Weight Horse Shoe Co. 9 Central.
Sidelow John, waiter, 7 American, b. 21 Central.
Sidney Frederick, porter at 110, b. 110 Pratt.
Siegel Annie, wid. William, h.u. 257 Market.
" Benny, laborer, b.u. 257 Market.
" Henry, tailor at 66 Asylum, h. 101Windsor.
" Morris, tailor, h. 92 Windsor.
Siegle Morris, shoemaker, h. 32 Portland.
Siehert Annie, wid. Joseph, h.3u.r. 60 Temple.
Siehm August, fireman 315 Park, h. 4½ Hung. pl.

Sientz Araham, tailor, 19, b. 19 Church.
Siewert Herman, musician, b. 35 Chapel.
Sigal Samuel, (Greenberg & S.) h.r. 299 Market.
Sigmund Michael, laborer, h.u. 6½ Ellery.
Sigourney A. M. traveling salesman, 126 Church,
    h. Bristol t.
**SIGOURNEY HOUSE,** Mrs. N. J.
    Coyle, prop. 1150 Main.    See page 561.
**SIGOURNEY TOOL COMPANY,**
    manufacturers of contract machinery, 9
    Sigourney.                 See page 537.
Sihoert John, blacksmith, h.2u. 38 So. Prospect.
Sikes Orson B. machinist at 1 Flower, b. T.v.
Sila Joseph, laborer, b.3u.r. 54 Temple.
Silberman Aaron, mach. at James L. Howard &
    Co. 438 Asylum, h. 20 Trumbull.
" Charles, (Cohen & S.) h. 133 Maple.
" Harry, shoemaker, b. 70 Temple.
" Jacob, tailor at 730 Main, h. 42 Market.
" ☞see Silverman.
Silivitski Max, laborer, b.u. 82 Pleasant.
Silk Albert E. trav. salesm.15Tru.h.Detroit,Mich.
" Edward A. draughtsm. 1 Flow. b. 25 Spruce.
" Michael J. helper at 556 Main, h. 150 N.P.
" Patrick J. saloon, 25, h. 25 Spruce.
Sill Emilie M. metaphysical books, periodicals,
    89 Trumbull, h. 223 Asylum. rm. 24.
" Geo. G. attorney, 863 Main, h. 124 Garden.
" Hattie C. stenographer, b. 11 Goodwin.
" Howard A. clerk,1187 Main, l. 223 Asylum.
" John, toolmaker at Popes, b. 86 Hopkins.
" Louis B. notions, 1187 Main, h. 223 Asylum.
" Samuel J. mach. at 70 Huy. h. 59 Elliott.
Sillence Herbert, driver, h.u. 249 Jefferson.
" Stephen, butcher, h.2u. 4 Goodman.
Silliman Robert N. clerk at 581 Capitol, l. 315
    Pearl, rm. 409.
Silloway Wm. F. engineer, h. 80 Capitol.
Silman Ike, tailor, 532 Asylum, h. 62 Village.
Silsby J. H. & Co. lumber, 148 Allyn.
    Jonas H. Silsby,      F. M. Harlow.
    W. C. Morse, Springfield, Mass.
" Jonas H. (J. H. Silsby & Co.) h. 150 Allyn.
Silver Bros. confectionery, 1174 Main.
    Israel Silver,        Joseph Silver.
    Jacob Silver,         Wolf Silver.
" Israel, (Silver Bros.) h. 56 Pleasant.
" Jacob, (Silver Bros.) h. 29 Kennedy.
" Joseph, (Silver Bros.) h. 27 Kennedy.
" Novelty Co. 180 Allyn.
" Wolf, (Silver Bros.) b. 77 Bellevue.
Silverman Harry, harnessmaker at 8 Sigourney,
    h. 79 Avon.
" Israel, laborer, h. 22 North.
" Joseph, machinist at 388 Cap. h. 22 North.
" Joseph, peddler, h. 104 Windsor.
" Kibbe, shoemaker, 169 State, h. 70 Temple.
" Morris, tailor, 66 Asylum, h. 249 Front.
" Nathan, peddler, h.u. 262 Front.
Silvernail Louis, clerk, 252 Pearl, b. 192 Far.
Silversmith Hascal, peddler, h. 67 Pleasant.
" Nathan, peddler, h.u. 193 Front.
" Oscar, peddler, h. 67 Pleasant.
Silverstein Bernard, tailor 19 Church, b.66 Avon.
" Solomon, clothier, 198, h.u. 196 State.

Silvestri Antonio, mason, h.2u. 47 Portland.
" Frank, (*M. & Silvestri,*) h.3u. 45 Portland.
" Gastano, mason, h. 45 Portland.
" Marco, mason, h.3u. 47 Portland.
Simendinger Alexander L. machinist at 1 Flower,
    b. 3 Francis.
" Florence, mechanic at James L. Howard &
    Co. 438 Asylum. b. 3 Francis.
" George W. machinist, b. 3 Francis.
" Theodore, contractor, h. 3 Francis.
" Theodore D. spinner 62 Market, h. 196 N.P.
Simes Frank J. molder 1 Flow. b. 272 Lawrence.
" Robert P. b.2u. 75 Governor.
Simkin Frank R. machinist at 1 Flower, h. 116
    Hopkins.
Simmons Byron A. h. 895 Asylum.
" George A. printer at 336 Asy. h. 95 Hamilton.
" James H. operator at 24 Mec. h. Bloomfield t.
" John, at 581 Capitol, b. 179 Lawrence.
" Minnie, wid. Ralph, h.3u. 10½ Ford.
" R. Mrs. h. 57 Pratt.
" W. Clayton, U. S. Army, h. 109 Jefferson.
" W. G. & Co. boots and shoes, 901 Main.
    W. G. Simmons.    Anthony H. Speath.
" Wm. G. (*W. G. S. & Co.*) h. 112 Park.
" Wm. S. agent State Board Education, rm.
    42, State capitol, h. Central Village v.
" ☞ *see also Simonds; Simons.*
Simms Henry A. bkbdr. 252 Pearl, h.u. 129 Alb.
" Robert H. clerk at Brown, Thomson & Co.
    942 Main, b. 1 Wooster.

**SIMMS WILLIAM J.** contractor and
•   builder, 54 Pratt, h. 1 Wooster.
         *See page 517.*

" ☞ *see also Sims; Seyms.*
Simon Gustavus, clerk 908 Main, h. 69 Williams.
" Herman, peddler, h. 64 Avon.
" Minnie, wid. Edward F. boardgh. 133 Front.
" Ragovin & Co. wholesale cloak mfrs. 73 Pratt.
    Joseph Simon.   Morris Ragovin.   Morris Goldstein.
Simonds Casper J. student at 2 Central, b. 427
    Main, rm. 48.
" Ellen T. wid. Thomas, h. 27 Affleck.
" Ernest L. student at Trinity, b. 33 Ward.
" Fred. R. contractor at Pratt & Whitney Co.
    1 Flower, h. 33 Ward.
" Geo. H. butcher, 818 Park, h. 211 Hamilton.
" John B. machinist, 1 Flower, b. 27 Affleck.
" Julia G. teacher at West Middle school, 927
    Asylum, b. 47 Ashley.
" Stillman A. traveling salesman, h. 47 Ashley.
" Thomas B. printer, b. 27 Affleck.

**SIMONDS WILLIAM E.** patent law-
    yer, 2 Central, h. 427 Main, summer resi-
    dence, Collinsville v. *See outside back cover.*

" ☞ *see also Simmons; Simons; Symonds.*
Simons Charles H. teamster, 7, h.r. 7 Washington.
" Charles H. Jr. teamster, b.r. 7 Washington.
" Edward H. machinist, b.2u. 1393 Main.
" Edwin F. clerk, b. 146 Capitol.
" & Fox, awnings, tents, 7 Haynes.
    Geo. O. Simons.    Horace P. Fox.
" George O. (*S. & Fox,*) h. u. 86 Pratt.
" James, carpenter, b. 6 Cedar.
" John B. b. 389 Main.

Simons Laura Mrs. b. 10 Ellsworth.
" Lizzie F. wid. Oamel, h.2u. 1393 Main.
" Moses, clerk at 921 Main, b. 7 Sumner.
" Myra B. printer, b.2u. 1393 Main.
" Robert, assembler at Colts, h. E.H.t.
" Thomas C. Mrs. h. 60 Vernon.
" William Mrs. h. 23 New Britain.
" ☞ *See also Simmons; Simonds; Symonds.*
Simpkins Oliver H. mach. 133 Shel. b. 7 Webster.
" William, b. 7 Webster.
" Wm. F. bookkeeper, 214 Pearl, h. 32 Russ.
Simpson Charles, driver at 15 Albany, h. E.H.t.
" Chas. W. mason, h.u. 68 Wooster.
" Edgar P. clerk, 745 Main, h. 50 Windsor av.
" Edith L. stenographer, b. 58 Church.
" Eliza J. nurse, b.3u. 279 Asylum.
" Frank P. clerk at Brown, Thomson & Co.
    942 Main, b. 76 Hopkins.
" Fred'k T. physician, 122, h. 122 High.
" . George, helper at 20 Sargeant, h. E.H.t.
" George A. blacksmith, h.u. 38 Harbison.
" H. Warren, traveling salesman, h. 53 Capitol.
" Hattie M. stenographer, 744 Main, h. S.W.t.
" Irwin A. toolm. at 1 Flower, h. 185 Hamilton.
" James, carpenter at N.Y.R. h.3u. 279 Asylum.
" James F. mach. 1 Flower, h. 143 Madison.
" John M. clerk at 956 Main, h. 33 Lewis.
" Martha B. b. 63 Ashley.
" Robert, foreman N.Y.R. b.u. 1383 Broad.
" Selden S. millw. at Popes, h. 14 Queen.
Sims ☞ *see also Seyms; Simms.*
Sinclair J. K. painter, 185 Asylum, b. E.H.t.
Sing Charlie, laundry, 24 Mulberry.
" Charlie, laundry, 1360 Broad.
" Charlie Wong, laundry, 118 Albany.
" Frank, laundry and tea store, 1225 Main.
" Hong, laundry, 780 Park.
" Lung, laundry, 57 Windsor.
" Quong, laundry, 1156 Main.
" Quong, laundry, 1174 Main.
" Quong, laundry, 20 Morgan.
" Tam, laundry, 1100 Main.
" Wah, laundry, 294 Main.
" Wing, laundry, 117 Windsor av.
" Wong T. laundry, 62 Trumbull.
" Yee, laundry, 273 Lawrence.
SING YUEN & Co. teas, silk and chinaware, 118
    State. *See Yuen, Sing & Co.*
Singer Sewing Machine agency, 9 Haynes.
Single Arthur E. carriage shop, 295 Sheldon
    h. 426 Maple.
Singleman Louis, engineer, b.u. 84 Arch.
Singleton Annie, b. 56 Flower.
" Daniel, ostler at 756 Main, b. 66 Front.
" Eliza, wid. Daniel, h. 56 Flower.
" Julia, wid. Michael, h. 79 Arch.
" Margaret, at 254 Pearl, b. 56 Flower.
" Michael, enameler at Popes, h. 56 Flower.
" Richard V. attendant at 56 Fairfield, h.u.
    10 New Britain.
" Timothy J. helper at 15 Tru. h. 50 Hicks.
Sinington George J. laborer at James L. Howard
    & Co. 438 Asylum, h. 44 John.
Sinnott Bros. carpenters, 26 Harbison.
    William J. Sinnott.    Robert E. Sinnott.

**Advertise Your Real Estate in THE POST.**

Sinnott Edward, expressman, h.r. 81 Front.
" Elizabeth E. teacher at Wilson st. school, b. 26 Harbison.
" James, mechanic at Popes, h. 447 Capitol.
" John J. celluloidw. at Popes, b. 447 Capitol.
" John J. prop. Trinity Phar. b. 26 Harbison.
" Julia, wid. William, h. 26 Harbison.
" Mary, b.u. 447 Capitol.
" Peter W. assemb. at Popes, b. 447 Capitol.
" Patrick C. builder 597 Main, h.u. 42 Wells.
" Robert, stonecutter at 93 Ch.O. l. 757 Main.
" Robert E. (Sinnott Bros.) b. 26 Harbison.
" Therese, wid. of John, h.u. 1048 Broad.
" Thos. B. rubberw. 690 Park, b. 447 Capitol.
" Thomas J. plum. at 248 Park, h. 33 Harbison.
" William J. (Sinnott Bros.) b. 26 Harbison.
Sinsigalli Frank, shoemaker, 73, h. 73 Morgan.
Sion Inman, tailor, h. 61 Morgan.
Sippe Oscar W. storekpr. P.&R. b. 71 Williams.
Siple Charles W. tailor, b.r. 33 Russell.   .
" Louis, at Popes, b.u. 1350 Broad.
Sipple Chas. S. polisher at 111 Sheldon, b. W.t.
" Christopher, teamster, b. 180 Seymour.
" J. H. cigarm. at 867 Main, h. Poquonock v.
Sirine Wm. mach. at 13 Central, b. 47 Walnut.
Sirrocco Nathan, jewelry peddler, h.u. 84 Alb.
Siska William, tailor, h.2u. 196 Russ.
Sissa Angelo P. physician, 82 Mor. b. 1150 Main.
" Bros. druggists, 82 Morgan.
      Angelo P. Sissa.          Silvio Sissa.
" Silvio, (S. Bros.) 82 Morgan.
Sisson Alvin E. clerk at Pope Tube Co. h. W.t.
" Antoinette, operator, b. 189 Maple.
" Charles E. engineer at 389, b. 389 Main.
" Charles L. h. 170 Sisson.
" ' Dwight E. gearcutter at 1 Flower, b. 60 Ann.
" Elizabeth Mrs. h. 1026 Main.
" Eugene D. machinist, l. 60 Ann.
" Everett S. fireman P.&R. b. 24 Pliney.
" Frederick W. machinist at 9 Sigourney, h. Wethersfield t.
" J. A. watchman at Pope Tube Co. h. Windsor t.

**SISSON T. & CO.** wholesale druggists, 729 Main.          *See page 560.*
      Thos. Sisson, Geo. P. Chandler, Fred. H. Chapin.
" Thos. (T. Sisson & Co.) h. 126 Farmington.
" Willard H. at N.E.R. h. 63 Chestnut.
Sista Joseph, laborer, b. 17 Morgan.
Sisters of Mercy, 89 Church & 246 Farmington.
" of St. Joseph, 110 Woodland.
Sitzer Andrew, laborer, 15 Albany, h.147 Martin.
" Franklin B. operator, Popes, h.u.520 Garden.
Size Barney, b. 2 Holcomb.
Sizer Andrew J. supervisor at 30 Washington, h. 221 Maple.
" Ralph W. E. clerk at Hartford Cycle Works, b. 218 Franklin.
" Viola A. wid. Oliver B. h. 218 Franklin.
Sizkind Barney, tailor, 79, h. 79 Governor.
" Barney Mrs. candy, etc., 79, h. 79 Governor.
" Louis, clerk at 300 Park, b. 79 Governor.
Sjogren Amanda, dressm. r. 14, b.r. 14 Affleck.
Skaber John, screwm. at 476 Cap. b. 56 Sheldon.
Skahill Stephen, porter 252 Pearl, h. 45 Kinsley.

Skau Andrew H. Mrs. h. 40 Willow.
" Hans L. screwm. at 476 Cap. h. 40 Willow.
" Martin B. screwm. at 476 Cap. b. 40 Willow.
" Peter L. screwm. 476 Cap.h.u.48 New Britain.
Skeahan John A. bartender at 26, b. 28 Market.
Skehill Thomas, expresser, 1063, h.r. 1063 Broad.
Skelly Isaac, laborer, b. 80 State.
" Patrick, laborer at Popes, h.2u. 4 John.
" Thomas J. mechanic at Popes. b.2u. 4 John.
Skidgell Oscar T. mach. at 1 Laurel, b. 49 Sig.
Skiff Harry R. at Travelers Ins. Co. 56 Prospect, b. 833 Asylum.
" Frank B. painter, 5 Mec. h. 36 Webster.
" Frederick W. clerk at insurance department, State capitol, h. West Haven v.
" Kate L. wid. Royal G. b. 833 Asylum.
SKILTON DeWITT C. president Phoenix Ins. Co. 64 Pearl, h. 958 Asylum.   *See page 460.*
" Nellie C. teacher West Middle school, b. 177 Sigourney.
Skinner Arthur, at 334 Weth. b. 16 Preston.
" Arthur, driver at 12 Pratt, b. Weth. t.
" Bessie M. stenog. at 109 State, b. 43 Elm.
" Chas. R. traveler, h. 25 Huntington.
" Charles W. h. 2 Mahl.
" Fannie T. at ins. dept. State capitol,h. 4 Bond.
" George L. mach. at 1 Flower, h. 55 Garden.
" Harriet, wid. Horace, b. 16 Preston.
" Harriet L. wid. James, nurse, h. 41 Vine.
" Henry H. broker, 803 Main, h. Sp'gfield, Mass.
" James, waiter at 25 Central, h.r. 488 Main.
" Jennie S. metaphysician. b.u. 127 Trumbull.
" John E. driver, h. 17 Gold.
" John H. salesman at Neal, Goff & Inglis Co. 980 Main, h. 45 Bellevue.
" Lewis B. collector, h. 43 Elm.
" S. C. mate tug Coulston, 285 State.
" Sarah E. wid. John T. h.2u. 545 Main.
" Timothy P. at 1 Ford, h.u. 76 Capitol.
" Wealtha G. wid. Alfred R. b. 112 Park.
SKINNER WM. C. (Dwight, S. & Co.) wool, 207 Allyn, h. 61 Woodland.   *See page 483.*
Skirrow Benjamin R. mach. at Colts, b.68 Brown.
" Robert W. at 209 State, h. 421 Franklin.
" Susan A. stenog. at 133 Shel. b.421 Franklin.
Skow Christie, gardener, b.u. 1204 Broad.
Slaboszewski Hilari A. tailor, h.2u. 552 Main.
Slade Charlotte, wid. Marion, h. 10 Foot Guard.
" George, pianomover, h. 23 Kennedy.
Slamons Jas. J. buffer, 182 Allyn, h. 12 Kennedy.
" Patrick, buffer at 182 Allyn, b. 12 Kennedy.
Slamovitch Barned, peddler, h. 282 Front.
Slate Charles D. mach. at 13 Central, h.u. 26 Russ.
" D. N. & Co. commis'n merchants, 42 Ann.
" Daniel N. (D.N.S. & Co.) h. 186 Sigourney.
" Dwight, president Dwight Slate Mac. Co. 13 Central, h. 187 Sigourney.
**SLATE (DWIGHT) MACHINE CO.** special machinery, mfrs. and dealers, office, 13 Central.   *See page 52.*
Slater Alice, operator, b. 42 Ward.
" Charles B. carpenter, h.u. 48 Ward.
" Frank A. filer, h. 64 Vanblock.
" Isaac, h. 42 Ward.

Slater Maurice P. mach. at Colts, h.u. 10 Oak.
" William T. screwmaker at 476 Capitol, b. 42 Ward.
Slattery Austin P. carpenter, h. 25 Harbison.
" Edward, lineman, b. 18 Trumbull.
" James P. collarm. at 8 Sig. b. 66 Hopkins.
" John, at 8 Sigourney, b. 66 Hopkins.
" John, laborer, stonepits, h. Ellery.
" John A. carpenter, h.u. 9½ Hamilton.
" Joseph, carpenter, b. 25 Harbison.
" Joseph M. polisher at 581 Capitol, h. N.B.t.
" Martin J. manager Conn. Catholic Publishing Co. 704 Main, h. 2 Winthrop.
" Mary wid. Patrick, b. 724 Main, rm. 17.
" Mary A. b. 29 Elm.
" Patrick J. b. 66 Hopkins.
" Thomas, carpenter at 26, b. 25 Harbison.
" Wm. J. machinist at P.&R. h. 78 Green.
Slavenski Charles, tailor, b. 70 Morgan.
Slavin Anna Mrs. h.u. 62 Village.
" Sarah, b.u. 62 Village.
Sleeper Fred. A. toolm. at 581 Cap. b.80 Madison.
" George E. physician, h. 1395 Main.
Sleeth John C. at 843 Main, h. 21 Affleck.
" Wm. J. storekeeper at Popes, h. 21 Affleck.
Slemholtz Henry M. electrician, 85 Pratt, h. 110 Whitmore.
Slesinger Henry, assembler at Popes, h. 57 Oak.
" Lotta L. musicteacher, 57, b. 57 Oak.
Slimbaum Samuel, tailor at 780 Mn. b. 262 Front.
Sliney Annie M. inspector at 70 Huy. b. 57 Gov.
" Edward J. machinist at Colts,b. 57 Governor.
" James, U. S. Navy, b. 57 Governor.
" John J. enameler at Popes, b. New Britain t.
" Mary, wid. Thomas, h. 57 Governor.
Slingland Frank, plumber, h.2u. 183 Babcock.
Sloan Adrian P. superintendent at 30 Cushman, h. 61 Woodbine.
" Aurelia T. wid. J. R. h. 15 Alden.
" Edgar J. special agent-Home Insurance Co. of New York, h.u. 227 Ashley.
SLOAN FREDERICK H. (Hansel, S.& Co.) jewelers, 886 Main, h. 15 Alden.
" James A. with C. E. Bishop & Co. 34 Capen.
SLOAN JEROME H. (Raymond & S.) sale stables, 19 Mather, b. 15 Mahl.  See page 549.
" John,laborer at Pope Tube Co.b.1326 Broad.
" John, machinist, l. 284 Asylum.
" Mary E. b. 61 Woodbine.
" Michael, b. 202 Sheldon.
" Michael, groceries, 44, h. 44 Benton.
" Neil, barber, 80 State, h.u. 81 Maple.
" Richard F. brassworker, h. 1449 Broad.
Sloane Anna, h. 39 Windsor.
" Burdett H. teamster, 2 Chapel, b. 3 John.
" Clarence H. clerk at Brown, Thomson & Co. 942 Main, b. 833 Asylum.
" Edward, laborer at 581 Capitol, h. 18 Grace.
" Henry A. meats, 32 Walnut, h. 26 Williams.
" John, h. 22 Williams.
" John Jr. h. 201 Capen.
" John R. bkkpr. r. 64 Asylum, h. 296 Maple.
" Louisa R. b. 296 Maple.
" Robert, carpenter, h.2u.r. 9 So. Prospect.

Sloane Ruby G. b. 296 Maple.
" William, lather, b. 147 Sheldon.
" Wm. H. clerk at 32 Walnut, b. 26 Williams.
Slocum Amy M. wid. Charles, h.u. 9 Kinsley.
" Charles H. manager, 343, b. 343 Main.
" Charles H. clerk city treasurer office, City hall, 800 Main, h. 3 Fales.
" Franklin R. coal, and monumental works, 1 Ford and 40 Albany, h. 24 Walnut.
" Lucius F. engineer, N.Y.R. h. 101 Laurel.
" Raymond L. clerk at Popes, b. 3 Fales.
" Wellington R. secy. and treasurer Edward Balf Co. b. 24 Walnut.
Slonim Bernard, coal agent, h.u. 238 Front.
" Nathan, peddler, h. 15 Morgan.
Slosson Annie T. Mrs. h. 722 Asylum.
" Hans, deckhand, str. Middletown, 285 State.
" ☞ see also Schlossen.
Slowey Bernardi, janitor Colt Memorial house, b. 24 Woodbridge.
Sluyter Elizabeth L. wid. Stephen G. supt. Union for Home Work, h. 239 Market.
" Laura H. assistant at 239, h. 239 Market.
Slynay Mary Mrs. domestic, h. 236 Front.
Small Charles G. asst. supt. at 135 Sheldon, h. 20 Pawtucket.
" Frederick F. ass't cashier Phœnix Mutual Life Ins. Co.49 Pearl, h. 520 Prospect av.
" Henry, carpenter, h. 41 Spring.
" Henry T. special agent Hartford Life Insurance Co. 252 Asy. h. 520 Prospect av.
" John, gardener at 34, h.r. 34 Forest.
" Lewis H. clerk at Kimball & McCray, insurance, 658 Main, h. 250 New Park.
" William C. foreman at Pratt & Whitney Co. 1 Flower, h. 250 New Park.
Smallyon Edward J. helper, 266 Pearl, h. 51 Woodbine.
Smart Charles T. student Trinity col. b. 8 Sisson.
" Emma, b. 416 Windsor av.
" Ezra, machinist at 31 Hicks, h. 7 Sisson.
" Ezra E. Jr. machinist at 40 Gov. b. 35 Bkm.
" Frank C. toolmaker at Popes, b. 8 Sisson.
SMART GEORGE E. councilman 10th ward, supt. Ætna Mach Co. 77 Com. h. 192 Laurel.
" John, asst. supt. 77 Commerce, b. 7 Sisson.
" Leila M. musicteacher at Northeast school, b. 8 Sisson.
" Martha B. nurse, 20 South Hudson.
SMART THOMAS, alderman 10th ward, foreman at Popes, h. 8 Sisson.
" William, at 15 Trumbull, h.u. 124 Heath.
" Wm. E. machinist at 31 Hicks, h. Parkville.

Smead Edwin B. principal Watkinson Farm school, h. Albany, c. Bloomfield.
" H. Preston, b. Albany, c. Bloomfield.
Smedkear Peter, gardener, h.2u. 60 Morgan.
Smike Harry, sweeper at 1 Flow. b. 280 Front.
Smiley Edward H. principal Public High School, 39 Hopkins, h. 244 Collins.
Smith A. H. Mrs. (Capitol City Furniture Co.) h. 24 Julius.
" Abram, patternm. at 77 Com. h.u. 59 Sey.
" Adelaide L. at Hartford Life Ins. Co. 252 Asylum, b.u. 12 West.
" Albert E. jobber, h. 213 Windsor.
" Albert G. at 218 State, h. Wethersfield t.
" Alexander, bicycle dealer and repairer, 10 Mulberry, h. 66 Laurel.
" Alexander, harnessm. 523 Main, h. E.H.t.
" Alexander L. mach. at 70 Huy.h.962 Broad.
" Alice, wid. Walter, b. 33 Ferry.
" Alice A. h. 19 Walnut.
" Alice M. nurse, b. 14 Church, rm. 10.
" Alice W. boardinghouse, 1209 Main.
" Alvina M. Mrs. dressmaker, b. 3 Pleasant.
" Andrew, lab. street dept. h.u.r. 17 Wolcott.
" Andrew, laborer, h. 69 Avon.
" Andrew L. driver, b.u. 23 Martin.
" Andrew T. ins. agt. 10 Central,h. 637 Pro.av.
" Ann Mrs. h. 29 Linden.
" Ann, wid. James, b. 13 Squire.
" Annie, b. 181 State.
" Anton, machinist, h.r. 17 Wolcott.
" Ariadne K. wid. Henry G. h. 72 Vine.
" Arthur A. mach. at 555 Cap. b. 43 Sigourney.
" Arthur B. clerk at Hartford Box Co. 223 State, b. 841 Asylum.
" August E. mach. at P.&R. h. 106 Mather.
" August H. (Schmidt) watchmaker and jeweler, 19 Pearl, h. 54 Oak.
" Augustus, laborer, b.u.r. South Prospect.
" Austin, farmer, h.u. 265 Wethersfield.
" Bernard, bartender, b. 96 State.
" Bessie M. clerk at Brown, Thomson & Co. 942 Main, b. 587 Park.
**SMITH, BOURN & CO.** saddlers, 334 Asy. factory 8 Sig.    See page 547.
Chas. B. Smith.        Olcott B. Colton.
" Bridget, wid. Bernard, b. 16 Walnut.
" Bridget, wid. Owen, h.u. 29 Commerce.
" Bros. furniture, 1079 Main.
Minot M. Smith.        Columbus A. Smith.
" Bruce F. foreman at 266 Pearl, b. 253 Main.
" Burdett F. profiler, h. 55 Park.
" C. Edward, mach. at 30 Cush. b. 518 Main.
" Caroline T. Mrs. b. 77 Wethersfield.
" Carrie T. at 336 Asylum, b.2u. 4 Martin.
" Carrie, clerk at 832 Main, b. 42 Hopkins.
" Catherine M. wid. Elisha T. h. 427 Main.
" Charles, h. 4 Donald.
" Charles, captain barge No. 11, 285 State, h. Rocky Hill t.
" Charles, mach. at 142 Russ, b. 21 Arch.
Smith Charles B. (S., Bourn & Co.) h. 66 Forest.    See page 547.
" Charles D. clerk at 83 Asylum, b. E.H.t.
" Charles E. b. 39 Talcott.

Smith Charles E. manager, b. 278 Laurel.
" Charles F. watchm. 865 Mn. h. 57 Willard.
" Charles G. manager Factory Ins. Association 95 Pearl, h. 111 Elm.
" Chas. H. office 49 Pearl, h.593 Farmington.
" Charles H. teamster, h. 4 James.
" Chas. H. Jr. Mrs. (Katherine) h. 593 Far.
" Charles J. mach. at 556 Cap. b. 1338 Broad.
" Charles L. foreman at Sigourney Tool Co. 9 Sigourney, h. 27 Niles.
" Charles M. foreman at Popes, h. 71 Laurel.
" Charles W. machinist at 133 Sheldon, b. Windsor Locks t.
" Christian, carriagemaker, h. 31 Village.
" Chauncey L. engir.' 30 Wash. h. 355 Maple.
" Clarence H. at Travelers Insurance Co. 56 Prospect, b.u. 18 Oak.
" Clarissa wid. William T. h.u. 4 Martin.
" Chester P. b. 25 Fairfield.
" Clarence A. student at Trinity college. 43 Jarvis hall, Summit.
" Clyde P. at Hartford Fire Insurance Co. 53 Trumbull, b. 201 Evergreen.
" Clyde R. clerk at 64 State, b. 72 Vine.
" Coleman, motorman St.Ry. 115 State.
" Columbus A. (Smith Bros.) h.u. 1117 Main.
" Curtis, blacksmith, N.Y.R. h.u. 51 Williams.
" Curtis, student at Trinity college, 39 Jarvis hall, Summit.
" Daisy, teacher, b. 215 Garden.
" Dennis D. waiter, b. 6½ Ellery.
" Desire, wid. Maynard S. b.u. 1117 Main.
" De Witt, engineer, h.u. 71 Williams.
" Dudley C. foreman at Popes, 436 Capitol, h.u. 41 Congress.
" E. B. conductor St.Ry. b. East Hartford t.
" E. Barrie, bkkpr. at 20 Sergeant, l. 62 Russ.
" E. Florence, stenog. at 424, b. 32 Asylum.
" E. J. Mrs. nurse, 71, h.2u. 71 Asylum, rm.21.
" E. Shipman, reporter Hartford Telegram, 12 Central, h. 488 Main.
Smith Eben E. treas. National Life Association, 53 Tru. h. 11 Marshall.   See page 455.
" Edgar, capt. barge No. 9, 285 State, h.E.H.t.
" Edgar L. sec'y and ass't treas. Hartford and N. Y. Tran. Co. 285 State, h. 10 Columbia.
" Edgar W. salesman at 219 Asy. b. Talcottville v.
" Edmund S., U. S. Army, b. 19 Russ.
" Edward, machinist at Pratt & Whitney Co. 1 Flower, h. Wethersfield t.
" Edward A. Mrs. h. 107 Elm.
" Edward L. cigarm. at 867 Mn. h. 7 Chapel.
" Edward A. cutter at 8 Sig. b.2u. 106 Mather.
" Edward C. machinist at 31 Wells, b.518 Main.
" Edward L. student at Yale, b.u. 18 Oak.
**SMITH EDWARD W.** proprietor Hartford Box Co. 223 State. h. 841 Asylum.    See page 532.
" Edward W. sexton Pearl street M. E. Zion church, h. 80 Fairmount.
" Edwin C. h.u. 304 Wethersfield.
" Edwin J. sheriff, 85 Trumbull, jailor 42. h. 42 Seyms.
" Edwin J. Jr. b. 42 Seyms.

**PIANOS RE-BUILT AS GOOD AS NEW BY LEO. H. BATTALIA, Warerooms, 943 MAIN ST.**

Smith Electa P. wid. Milton, b. 5 Main.
" Eliza W. wid. James, h.u. 238 Wethersfield.
" Elizabeth G. priv. school, h.650 Main,rm.53.
" Ellen, wid. Frederick, h.u. 63 Capitol.
" Ellen H. J. Mrs. h.2u. 488 Main.
" Ellen T. wid. Mather H. h. 17 Huntington.
" Elmer L. captain scow No. 12, 285 State, h. 90 Walnut.
" Elmer E. toolma. 1 Flower, h. 47 Babcock.
" Elvira, wid. John, b. 120 Windsor av.
" Elwood J. at F. J. Knox, plumber supplies, 2 South Ann, h.u. 40 Babcock.
" Emeline T. wid. H. M. h. 11 Girard.
" Emma A. wid. F. Webb, h. 31 Ashley.
" Emma F. clerk at 956 Main, b. 34 Lawrence.
" Emor A. chief op. at 247 Pearl, h. 160 Wash.
" Ernest A. b. 80 Bluehills.
" Ernest W. student, b. 107 Elm.
" Erwin J. expressman, h.u. 13 Center.
" Erwin R. student, b. 72 Vine.
" Esther L. ass't principal, b. 1204 Asylum.
" Ethel C. stenographer at Smith, Bourn & Co. 8 Sigourney, b. 57 Benton.
" Eugene E. driver at 288 Asy. b. 78 State.
" Eugene R. rubberw. at 690 Park,h. 75 Laurel.
" Eugene W. h. 286 New Britain.
" F. E. wool, h. 7 Columbia.
" F. Haskell, chemist at 690 Park, b. 73 Bab.
" Fannie M. wid. Joseph, h.2u. 1413 Main.
" Fannie M. Mrs. 223 Asylum, rm. 78.
" Felix, hackdriver, l.2u. 24 Mulberry.
" Ferdinand, (S. & Hutton,) h. 85 Sigourney.
" Ferdinand W. b. 85 Sigourney.
" Francis, h. 115 Edwards.
" Francis A. Mrs. h.2u. 166 Washington.
" Francis A. salesm. at 300 Asy. b. 119 High.
" Francis H. papercut.223 State,h.48 Madison.
" Frank, baker at 57 Albany, b. 218 State.
" Frank, meat peddler, l. 22 Walnut.
" Frank A. clerk at C. S. Brewer & Co. 240 Asylum, h. 76 Williams.
" Frank B. bookkeeper at City Bank of Hartford, 783, h. 1325 Main.
" Frank B. clerk at Hartford Daily Times, 716 Main, l. 192 Sargeant.
" Frank B. engraver at 177 Asy. b. 54 Capen.
" Frank Boardman, polisher, h. 47 Belmont.
" Frank E. screwm. at 60 Temple, b. E.H.t.
" Frank E. stereotyper at 25 Asylum, h. E.H.t.
" Frank G. machinist at 1 Flow. b. 31 Spring.
" Frank G. at Dwight, Skinner & Co. 207 Allyn. h. 7 Columbia.
" Frank H. b. 33 Pliney.
" Frank M. drug clerk, 273 Asy. h.u. 16 East.
" Frank P. at 26 Church, b. 29 Wadsworth.
" Frank P. assem. at Popes,b.u.248 Lawrence.
" Frank Peter, saloon, 62 Front.
" Frank W. brakeman at P.&R. h. 13 Liberty.
" Frank Waldo, machinist at 581 Capitol, h. 10½ Ford, rm. 10.
" Frank Webb, clerk at 1 S. Ann, b. 31 Ashley.
" Franklin, carptr. shop r.8 Ash.h.215 Garden.
" Fred A. genl. deliv. at P.O.h.u.79 Governor.
" Fred G. trav. salesman, h.2u. 86 Hopkins.
" Fred S. (J. E.S. & Son,) 49 Pearl, b.W.H.t.

Smith Frederick, engineer, b. 66 Prospect.
" Frederick, teamster, b. 35 East.
" Frederick C. clerk at P.&R. b. 27 Niles.
" Frederick H.cutter at 76 Asy.h.u. 14 Warren.
" Frederick J. barber, 42 Union pl. h. 58 Ash.
" Frederick M. agent Hartford & New York Transportation Co. 285 State, h. 25 Niles.
" G. Brainard, accountant. h. 24 Preston.
" G. Chester, inspector at Popes, h. 201 Park.
SMITH G. FRED, secretary Conn. River Mfg. Co. of Holyoke, office 756 Main, room 29, Trust Co's block, h. 30 Niles.
" George, buffer at 62 Mar. h. Glastonbury t.
" George, helper, h. 140 Trumbull.
" George, laborer, h. 12 Arch.
" George A. forem. at 476 Cap. h. 254 Putnam.
" George F. inspector Factory Ins. Association, 95 Pearl, grocery and market, 2 Washington, h. 6 Ellsworth.
" George G. caterer, h.u.r. 24 South Prospect.
" Geo. M. beltmaker at Popes, h.u. 863 Main.
" George M. b. 31 Ashley.
" George N. helper at 346 Main, h.2u. 3 Park.
" George N. traveling salesman, b. 149 High.
" George T. b.u. 1208 Broad.
" George W. b.3u. 80 Pearl.
" George W. at Connecticut Mutual Life Ins. Co. 783 Main, h. Wethersfield t.
SMITH GEORGE WILLIAMSON Rev. president Trinity College, office 13, Seabury hall, Summit, h. 115 Vernon. See pp. 706, 707.
" Gershon, auditor at Popes, h. 19 Girard.
" Gertrude C. matron at 42, b. 42 Seyms.
" Grace, milliner, b. 103 Wooster.
" Grace, stenog. at 75 Pratt, b. 254 Putnam.
" H. Hilliard, draughtsman at 756 Main, b. 320 Farmington.
" H. Louise, wid. James A. h. 15 C.O.pl.
" Harriet E. Mrs. h.3u. 80 Pearl.
" Harry, porter at 20, b. 20 South Hudson.
" Harry F. fireman N.Y.R. b. 60 Walnut.
" Harry R. driver at 979 Main, h. 41 Brook.
" Harry S. at 20 Sargeant, b. 31 Ashley.
" Helena M. wid. Daniel G. h.u. 54 Capen.
" Henry, b. 2 Holcomb.
" Henry, clerk at 197 Asylum, b. 53 Grand.
" Henry A. mach. at 1 Flow. h. 39 Putnam.
" Henry A. stonecutter, h.u. 29 Commerce.
" Henry C. salesm. 1123 Main, h. Wilson sta.
SMITH HENRY F. town and city clerk, 114 Pearl, h. 46 Annawan.
" Henry H.molder at 54 Arch,h.18 Wadsworth.
**SMITH H. M. & CO.** manufacturers H. O. Polish, 179 High. See page 419.
" Henry P. engir. at 252 Pearl, h.u. 48 Oak.
" Henry T. driver at C. S. Brewer & Co. 238 Asylum, h. 126 Windsor.
" Henry V. toolmaker, h. 51 Sigourney.
" Henry W., Merchants package express, 44 Asylum, h. 40 Tremont.
" Herbert Knox, attorney at law, 847 Main, rm. 9, h. 107 Elm.
" Herbert W. brakem. P.&R. b.u. 73 Albany.

**If You Want all the News, Read THE POST.**

*JAMES E. SMITH.*        *FRED S. SMITH.*

# JAMES E. SMITH & SON,

### General Agents

## *Phœnix Mutual Life Insurance Co.,*

### *No. 49 PEARL STREET, Room 13,*

*Phœnix Mutual Building.*

SMITH HORACE M. (*H. M. S. & Co.*) l. 1336 Main.
" Horace W. coachman, 199, b. 199 Collins.

HOWARD FRANKLIN SMITH, Physician and
Surgeon.  Office, 609 Main street.
Hours—9 to 10 A.M.
2 to 4 and 7 to 8 P.M.
Sundays, 3 to 4 P.M.
Telephone at office and residence.

Smith Howard Franklin, physician and surgeon,
609 Main, h. 215 Garden.
" Howard W. draughtsman at Pope Tube Co.
h. Quaker lane.
" & Hutton, mantels, tiles, etc. 1446 Broad.
Ferdinand Smith.        James Hutton.
" Hyman F. president and treasurer Guilfoil
Grocery Co. h. W.H.t.
" Inez J. teacher, b. 72 Vine.
" Isabelle M. b. 278 Laurel.
" J. Aborn, clerk, 376 Asy. h. 65 Sargeant.
" J. C. conductor St.Ry. b. 52 Retreat.
" J. M. Mrs. artist, h.u. 370 Asylum, rm. 12.
" J. Charles, storehouse r. 36, h. 36 Bkm.
" J. Fred'k, mach. at 388 Cap. h. 85 Sigourney.
" James, driver, b. 192 State.
" James, gardener, h. 261 Laurel.
" James, machinist 1 Flower, b.u. 31 Benton.
" Jas. merch. tailor, 33, b. 223 Asylum, rm. 72.
" James, teamster, b. 35 Mulberry.
" James A. at Connecticut Mutual Life Insur-
ance Co. 783 Main. h. 214 Garden.
" James C. h. Sisson.
" James E. (*J. E. Smith & Son,*) h. W.H.t.
SMITH JAMES E. & SON, general agents Phœnix
Mutual Life Ins Co. 49 Pearl. *See p. 336.*
James E. Smith.        Fred. S. Smith.
" James E. bookkeeper Hartford Fire Ins.
Co. 53 Trumbull, h. 201 Evergreen.
" James H. mach. at Colts, b.r. 58 Vanblock.
" James H. milkman, h. 25 Fairfield.
" James H. waiter at 142 Asy. h.u. 30 Wolcott.
" James M. clerk 745 Main, h.2u. 24 Dean.
" James R. at Yale, b. 15 Charter Oak pl.
" Jeanette A. b. 10 Fairfield.
" Jennie Mrs. dressmaker, h.u. 1244 Main.
" Jesse G. (*S. & McDonough,*) 801 Main, h.
150 Albany.
" John, dropforger, h. 118 Babcock.
" John, plumber, 18, h. 389 Allyn.
" John, signalman, 95 Pleasant, b. 270 Front.
" John A. bartdr. at 1211 Main, l. 164 Allyn.

Smith John C. carpenter, b. 98 Trumbull.
" John C. teach. dancing, 40 Pratt, l. 33 Lewis.
" John E. at 61 Asylum, b. E.H.t.
" John F. helper 66 Prospect, b. 218 State.
" John F. letter carrier, h.u. 49 Wadsworth.
" John H. painter, b.r. 14 Chapel.
" John J. mach. at Colts, b.r. 58 Vanblock.
" John M. city express, h.u. 1044 Main.
" John W. molder at 690 Park, h.u. 32 North.
" John W. of Hartford Steamboat Co. h.u.
114 Wooster.
" Jonathan C. conductor St.Ry. 115 State,
h. 52 Retreat.
" Joseph, hackman, b. 29 Commerce.
" Joseph, janitor, h. 35 Lafayette.
" Joseph, ostler at 356 Main.
" Joseph, porter at 867 Main, b. 47 Sheldon.
" Joseph E. motorman, St Ry. b. 19 Central.
" Joseph F. carpenter, b. 94 Madison av.
" Joseph F. laborer, h.2u. 27 Mechanic.
" Joseph M. salesman Ransom N. FitzGerald,
44 Market, h.u. 370 Asylum, rm. 49.
" Joseph P. barber, 86 Tru. h. 90 Retreat.
" Josephine S. wid. Robert H. h.u. 54 Sanford.
" Julia A. wid. Andrew J. h.u. 18 Oak.
" Kate Mrs. b. 2 Holcomb.
" Kate F. wid. Samuel P. h. 124 Potter.
" Katherine stenogr. at Popes, b. Weth. t.
" Katherine F. teacher of gymnastics, South
school, b. 54 Capitol.
" Katharine L. wid. Isaac D. teacher West
Middle school, h. 27 Marshall.
" Knighton, with Security Co. 62 Pearl, h. 27
Marshall.
" Lawrence, machinist at 13 Central.
" Lee W. motorman third rail, h.2u. 146 Alb.
" Lewis W. lettercar, sta. A, h.2u. 228 Putnam.
" Lizzie M. wid. Stebbins, b. 66 Wooster.
" Lotta Korn, professional singer, h. 25 Niles.
" Lottie A. laundress, h.u. 10 Green.
" Louis, b. 458 Main.
" Louis, plumber, b.u. 60 Portland.
" Louis, plumber, 72, h. 72 Morgan.
" Louis E. clerk, b. 75 Laurel.
" Louis F. at 40 Elm, b. 637 Prospect av.
" Lucy A. b. 21 Allen pl.
" Lyman, police sergeant, h. 42 Russell.
" Lyman D. writing teacher public schools, h.
33 Madison.
" Mabel R. b. 278 Laurel.
" Maitland B. saloon, 288 Asy. h. 278 Laurel.
" Marcie, wid. John N. h.u. 131 Jefferson.
" Margaret C. clerk, 921 Main, b. 90 Retreat.
" Margaret M. bookkeeper, b. 1096 Main.
" Maria H. wid. Edmond, b. 124 Collins.
" Marion G. teacher Lawrence street school,
b. 33 Madison.
" Martha, wid. Michael J. h. 74 Albany.
" Martha E. wid. Charles F. h.u. 34 Cedar.
" Martha M. h. 90 Charter Oak.
" Martin, electrician at 70 Com. h. 15 Warner.
" Mary, wid. James T. h.u. 248 Lawrence.
" Mary, wid. William J. h. 759 Park.
" Mary A. wid. Pat'k H. h. 29 Wadsworth.
" Mary Ann, b. 1255 Main.

**Merchants say it PAYS to Advertise in The Post.**

Smith Mary E. Mrs. h. 32 Temple.
"    Mary E. dressmaker, b. 39 Congress.
"    Mary J. wid. Frank H.boardingh.1338 Main.
"    Mary J. wid. John, nurse, 48, b.u. 48 Grand.

**SMITH MARY L. MRS.** stenographer, 2 Central, rm. 6, h. 24 Preston.

"    Mary M. Mrs. attendant 30 Washington.
"    Mary M. inspector at 70 Huyshope, b.r. 58 Vanblock.
"    Mary R. h.2u. 278 Pearl.
"    Matilda, h. 74 Ann.
"    Matilda, wid. Elliott, boardingh. 1096 Main.
"    Mattie, clerk at 7 Haynes, b. 51 Spring.
"    Mattie A. attendant at 30 Washington.
"    Maynard S. manager, h. 194 Capen.
"    & McDonough, books & stationery, 801 Mn. Jesse G. Smith.        Wm. J. McDonough.
"    Merth, h.u. 238 Wethersfield.
"    Michael, h.u. 218 State.
"    Michael, bricklayer, h. 96 Harper.
"    Millie L. bkkpr. at 45 Asy. b. 42 Russell.
"    Minnie Mrs. h. 14 Warren.
"    Minnie J. stenographer, at Adams Express Co. b. 120 Hungerford.
"    Minot M. (S. Bros.) h. 184 Barbour.
"    Myrton T. printer at 328 Asy. b. 72 Vine.
"    Nancy M. wid. George, h. 17 Girard.
"    Nehemiah, expressman, b. 34 Village.
"    Nelson P. floorwkr. 956 Main, h. 32 Brook.
"    Newton M. carpenter, h. 57 Benton.
"    Philura L. wid. Noah A. h. 14 Spring.

**SMITH, NORTHAM & CO.** flour, feed, grain,meal, etc. 129 State; warehouse & steammills, 165 Windsor. *See page 590.*
Chas. H. Northam.        E. V. Mitchell.

OLIVER C. SMITH, Physician and Surgeon. Office, 44 High street.
Hours—9 to 10 A.M.
2 to 3.30 and 7 to 8 P.M.
Office telephone 238-2.    House telephone 1016-4.

Smith Oliver C. physician, 44 High, h. 39 Imlay.
"    Oliver T. machinist, b. 134 Farmington.
"    Oscar H. machinist, 20 Vrendale, b. 34 Fkn.
"    P. B. & Co. liquors and cigars, 989 Main. P. B. Smith.        Peter Mohan.
"    Patrick, laborer at Colts, h.r. 58 Vanblock.
"    Patrick, lather, h.u. 22 Union.
"    Patrick, teamster, h. 29 Commerce.
"    Patrick B. (P. B. & Co.) h. 256 Main.
"    Patrick S. h. 94 Madison av.
"    Pauline E. stenogr. 25 Pearl, b. 11 Girard.
"    Perry Mrs. h. 74 Arch.
"    Peter, bartender, 32 Front, h. 3 Orchard.
"    Peter, tailor, h.u. 60 Portland.
"    Philip, machinist, 388 Cap. h.34 Pleasant.
"    Philip J. shoemaker, 532, b. 532 Asylum.
"    R. Wilson, Jr. clerk 497 Asy. b. 149 High.
"    Ransley D. b. 72 Vine.

**SMITH REUBEN H.** editor Religious Herald, 336 Asylum, h. 80 Bluehills.
*See page 469.*

"    Richard, h. 90 Charter Oak.
"    Richard, rubberw. at 581 Cap. b.2u. 81 Gov.
"    Robert, Lu. 724 Main, room 5.

Smith Robert, polisher, h. 53 Brook.
"    Robert D. assembler at 26 Laurel, h. N.B.t.
"    Robert E. polisher at Colts, h. 61 Elliott.
"    Robert T. salesman, h. 427 Main, rm. 18.
"    Rose, wid. Joseph, h.u. 71 New Britain.
"    S. C. Mrs. dressmaker, 69, h. 69 Laurel.
"    Samuel, cook at 8, b. 8 Central.
"    Samuel J. machinist at 581 Cap. h. N.B.t.
"    Samuel S. at 1077 Main.

**SMITH SARA J.** young ladies seminary, h. 1204 Asylum.        *See page 710.*

"    Sarah J. Mrs. b. 8 Girard.
"    Sarah O. wid. William E. h. 28 Atwood.
"    Seymour C. engineer, 69 Front, h. E.H.t.
"    Seymour E. foreman at Billings & Spencer Co. 142 Russ, h.u. 48 Grand.
"    Seldon S. auctioneer, h. 24 Julius.
"    Sherman C. patternm. 555 Cap. h.u. 69 Laurel.
"    Silas N. engineer P.&R. h. 152 Mather.
"    Stephen R. at Conn. Mutual Life Ins. Co. 783 Main, h. 34 Seymour.
"    Thomas, driver, Adams Ex. Co. b. 44 Beach.
"    Thomas, fireman at 70 Com. h.2u. 43 N.B.
"    Thomas, laborer at stonepits, h. Parkville.
"    Thomas, laborer, b. 16 Putnam.
"    Thomas A. *police commissioner*, (Kingsley & S.) h. 61 Green.
"    Thos. Hammond, (Mansuy & S.) h.39 Imlay.
"    Thomas M. treasurer Dime Savings Bank, 791 Main, h. 711 Prospect av.
"    Thomas W. engineer St. Mary's Home, Albany av. W.H.t.
"    Virginia T. wid. Wm. B. office 223 Asylum, rm. 10, h. 39 Imlay.
"    Walter, clerk at 61 Farmington, b. Capen.
"    Walter F. b. 90 Retreat.
"    Walter F. at Ætna Life Insurance Co. 650 Main, h. 18 Garden.
"    Walter H. mach. at 9 Sig. h. 48 Ashley.
"    Walter W. police sergeant, h. 39 Talcott.
"    Warren, painter, b. 33½ Chestnut.
"    Wayne E. at Hartford Fire Insurance Co. 53 Trumbull, b. 201 Evergreen.
"    Wenna, teacher, b. 254 Putnam.
"    Welsey H. b. 19 Foot Guard.

**SMITH & WHITNEY,** agents for the Clipper Bicycles, also a full line of sundries, 13 Haynes.
Myron T. Smith.        Clifton W. Whitney.

"    Wilder Mrs. (Charlotte M.) b. 111 Wash.
"    William, bartdr. at 107 Asy. h. 48 Windsor.
"    William, mach. at 388 Capitol, b. 242 Zion.
"    William, teamster, b. 35 Mulberry.
"    William A. clerk at 197 Asy. b. 15 Capitol.
"    William B. mason, b. 520 Main.
"    Wm. Bro. at Travelers Ins. Co. 56 Prospect, h. 3 May.
"    Wm. C. (W. C. S. & Co.) h. Glastonbury t.
"    William C. & Co. grocers, 119 Pearl. Wm. C. Smith.        Robert Moore.
"    William E. h. 146 Wethersfield.
"    William E. machinist, h.u. 21 John.
"    William F. collarmaker, h.u. 59 Hudson.
"    William F. conductor St.Ry. h. 59 Hudson.

**The Up to Date Merchant ADVERTISES in The Post.**

Smith Wm. F. hospital steward, jail, h. 23 Canton.
" Wm. F. solderer at 62 Mar. h.u. 24 Martin.
" William G. mach at 476 Cap. b. 59 Hudson.
" Wm. G. molder at 581 Cap. b.u. 100 Francis.
" Wm. H. fireman at N.Y.R. h. 28 Babcock.
" William H. polisher at 70 Huy. h. 213 Law.
" William H. printer at 49 Pearl, b.u. 18 Oak.
" Wm. H. stereotyper at 66, b. 218 State.
" William I. cigarmaker at 104 Asylum.
" Wm. J. engir. steamer No. 1, h. 31 Hudson.
" William J. (Scott & S.) h. 29 Wadsworth.
" Wm. S. bunker at engine No. 8, 124 Front.
" Wm. T. foreman at 581 Capitol, h. 49 Oak.
" Wm. W. cashier, Farmers and Mechanics
    Nat'l Bank, 106 State, h. 664 Farmington.
" Willis E. real estate, Allyn House, room 11,
    h. 28 Atwood.
" Winfield D. clerk at 8 State, b. 58 Sigourney.
" ☞ see also Smyth.
Smitton Charles H. foreman at 147 Sheldon, h.
    227 Jefferson.
Smyly Mary R. Mrs. b. 86 Gillett.
Smyth David G. teacher at High Sch. h. 46 Willard.

**SMYTH MANUFACTURING
CO.** bookbinders' machinery, 648 Main.
                        See page 528.
" Philip, ass't cashier 197 Asy. h. 39 Oxford.
" Sarah J. wid. James, h. 39 Oxford.
" ☞ see also Smith.
Smytheman T. George, boots, shoes, 92 Trumbull,
    h. 22 Pavilion.
Snatch Henry R. b.u. 1 Goodman.
Snell Aleck R. painter at 185 Asylum, b.2u. 37
    Hungerford.
" Carl, carpenter, h.2u. 37 Hungerford.
" Charles W. operator, 40 Governor, b. W.P.v.
" Cullen B. report clerk at Popes, h. W.H.t.
" Harry B. civil engineer at 70 Commerce
    b. 25 Capitol.
" Howard, helper at H. B. Beach & Son, 135
    Grove, b.3u. 8½ Ellery.
" Oscar W. carptr. h. Arnoldale road, W.H.t.
" Thomas C. B. civil engineer at 70 Com-
    merce, b. 25 Capitol.
Snider ☞ see Schneider; Snyder.
Snook Wm. B. screwm. at 476 Cap. h.u. 146 Mather.
Snow Alfred E. scrmkr. 476 Cap. h. 243 Lawrence.
" Annie G. nurse, b. 58 Church.
" Bertha M. Miss, teacher at 1205 Asylum.
" Charles L. plumber, 1076 Main, h. 6 Russell.
" Edwin T. farmer, b. 234 Barbour.
" Edgar W. electrician, 284 Asy. b. Burnside v.
" Ellen, artist, b. 99 Washington.

Snow F. S. physician, medical director Hartford
    Life Insurance Co. 252, b. 152 Asylum.
" G. Winfield, (S. & Maloney,) b. 27 Spring.
" Geo. A. plumber at 1152 Main, b. Burnside v.
" Geo. E. painter N.Y.R. h. 243 Lawrence.
" Greenleaf, machinist, at 20 Sargeant, h.
    10 Fairmount.
" Linus A. mach. at 476 Cap. b.2u. 51 Babcock.
" & Maloney, builders, 27 Spring.
    G. Winfield Snow.     Charles D. Maloney.
Snowman Benjamin W. salesman at 690 Park.
Snyder Charles H. foreman patternmaker at 54
    Arch, h. 160 Franklin.
" Herman, tailor at 921 Main, b. 271 Market.
" Rob't E. driver at 1130 Main, b. 56 Grand.
" Sophia, Mrs. h. 56 Grand.
" ☞ see also Schneider.
Sobolevsky Samuel, groceries, 106, h. 106 Windsor.
Soby Charles, cigarmfr. store, 867 Mn. l. 284 Asy.
" George H. clerk, 867 Main, b.2u. 14½ Morris.
" Geo. W. clerk, 867 Main, b.2u. 14½ Morris.
" James, fruit stand, 195 State, b. 64 Morgan.
" John A. b. 259 Lawrence.
Society for Savings, 31 Pratt.
Sodafsky Harris, peddler, h.3u. 80 Morgan.
Sodasky Joseph, baths, 77, h.u. 79 Morgan.
Soden John C. joiner, h.u. 176 Front.
Soderberg Hans, operator at 388 Capitol, h.
    26 Wolcott.
" Linus, mach. at 388 Capitol, b. 26 Wolcott.
Soderberg Reynolds, blacksmith, 133 Sheldon,
    h.u. 84 Park.
Soderquist Ernest F. machinist at 252 Pearl, h.
    106 Mather.
Soderstrom Erik, mach. 476 Cap. h. 71 Hung.
" Godfrey L. mach. at 476 Cap. b. 71 Hung.
Sokutie A. tailor at 108 Pratt, b. Front.
Solar Peter, tailor, 2u. 117, h.2u. 117 Market.
Solodofsky Louis, peddler, h.u. 205 Front.
Soloman Alexander, h.2u. 236 Front.
" Sigmond, tailor, h.2u. 78 Front.
Solomon Emma, Mrs. h.u. 1075 Broad.
" Israel, peddler, h.r.u. 67 Pleasant.
" Joseph H. harnessm. at 8 Sig. h. 21 Morgan.
" Louis, tailor at 730 Main, h. 42 Windsor.
" M. Mrs. h.r. 22 Trumbull.
" Richard, b.u. 1075 Broad.
" William, peddler, h.u. 369 Park.
" Zrezman, clerk at 956 Main, h. 82 Front.
" ☞ see also Salomon.
Somers Abraham L. inspector, 266 Pearl, b. 7 Am.
" Cora E. wid. Clarence E. b. hospital farm,
    New Britain.
" John T. mechanic at Popes, b. 17 John.
" Joseph F. clerk at Brown, Thomson & Co.
    942 Main, b. 17 John.
" Lawrence E. mach. at 80 Huy. b. 17 John.
" Margaret H. clerk at Brown, Thomson &
    Co. 942 Main, b. 17 John.
" Mary, h. 17 John.
" ☞ see also Summers.
Somerset Chas. H. mach. at 1 Flow. l. 48 Babcock.
" James, mach. at 690 Park, h. 13 Warner.
Somerville Jennie, at 254 Pearl, b. 273 Jefferson.
Sommer Chas. O. barber at 22 Sta. h. 99 Williams.

Sommerman Mr. cigarm. 867 Main, h. 212 Fkn.
" Albert E. machinist, 142 Russ, b. 72 Hudson.
" August A. upholsterer, 219 Pearl, h.u. 72 Hudson.
" August A. Jr. machinist at 142 Russ, b. 72 Hudson.
" Edward, engineer str. No. 4, h. 178 Putnam.
" Edward Jr. clerk, b. 178 Putnam.
Sonblaski Fred, laborer at Popes, h. Newington t.
Song Charles, laundry, 102 Trumbull.
" John, laundryman, 954, b. 954 Broad.
Sontheimer Thos. cabinetmaker, h. 11 Francis.
Sooter Henrietta, h. 22 Winthrop.
Sope☞ see D'Esopo.
Soper Eunice B. wid. Charles C. b. 36 Jefferson.
" H. P. painter, b. 1153 Main.
" Helen G. nurse, b. 14 Church, rm. 3.
" Mary Mrs. trim.at 180 Allyn,h.2u.1158 Main.
Soppian Joseph, mach. at 476 Cap. b. 113 Hung.
Sorbo Michael, laborer, b. 17 Morgan.
Sorensen Niles, driver at Bill Bros. h. 204 Fkn.
" Henry H. porter at 973 Mn.b.123 Trumbull.
Sorg George Mrs. h. 215 Bellevue.
Soritzki Solomon, cutter, h. 12 Mays ct.
Sormani Louis, driver at 701 Main.
Sossasky Lewis, peddler. h.u. 190 Front.
Souer John, filer at 556 Capitol, h. Burnside v.
" ☞ see also Sauer.
Soule Georgiana Mrs. h.u. 26 Woodbridge.
" William F. clerk, Hartford Telegram, 12 Central, b. 232 Franklin.
" Willis L. carpenter, h. 262 New Britain.
South Charles F. tailor, b. 295 Main.
" Sidney F.merchant tailor,77Pearl,b.26 State. 26 State.
" William R. cook, h.r. 65 Sheldon.
Southeimer Sebastian, mach. 1 Flow. h. 35 Grand.
Souther Henry, mech. engineer at Popes, h. Cone.
Southergill Francis, gardener, h. 1223 Main.
" George L. milkman,1017,h.1017 Windsor av.
" Louis, milkman, 1017, h. 1017 Windsor av.
" Margaret Mrs. boardinghouse, 1223 Main.
" Robert H. bookbinder at 141 Pearl, h.u. 82 Jefferson.
" Robert H. Jr. machine hand, 40 Governor, b.u. 82 Jefferson.
" ☞ see Suthergill.
Southern New Eng'd Paving Co. 141 Trumbull.
" New England Telephone Co. 247 Pearl.
Southmayd Jane, wid. J. K. b. 868 Windsor av.
Southner Joseph, locksmith, h.3u. 40 Park.
Southwick Fred L. bookkeeper at 149 State, h.u. 196 Trumbull.
" Henry, teamster at 46 Ann, h.u. 78 Front.
Southworth Charles F. electrician at 228 Pearl, h. Manchester t.
" Georgia A. operator,3 Central, b.215Garden.
Sozo Donato, laborer, b.2u. 81 Morgan.
Spafard Harry P. clerk 803 Mn. b. Glastonbury t.
Spafford Charles L. machinist at 20 Vredendale, b. 5 Vandyke.
Spain James W. mach. at 133 Shel. b. 111 Pearl.
Spainer Hugo, clerk at Nat'l Home for Disabled Volunteer Soldiers, 783 Main, h. 78 Allen pl.

Spalding Frank B. salesm. at Popes, h. 64 Oxford.
" John A. b. 833 Asylum.
" Carrie P. wid. John Edward, h. 29 Collins.
" Samuel Mrs. h. 92 Ann.
" ☞ see also Spaulding.
Spalter James J. rubberworker at 690 Park, b. 263 Market.
Spaniollo Pasquale, laborer, b. 73 Morgan.
Spanza James, h.u. 2 Charles.
Sparks Charles, driver at 53 Vernon, b. 15 John.
" Dwight W. toolm. at 476 Cap.h.2u.101 Bab.
" Ella,wid.John,dressm.16,h. 16 Buckingham.
" Fred, mach. at 53 Vernon, h. Wetherfield t.
" Frederic, optician, 82 Pearl, h. 16 Bkm.
" George E. machinist at 1, h. 68 Laurel.
" John, driver at 53, b. 53 Vernon.
" Leslie W. clerk at 76 Tru. b. 79 Madison.
" Lyman, helper at 53 Vernon, h. Weth.t.
" Thomas H. J. mach. at 70 Huy. h. 10 Rose.
" Wm. A. filer at Colts, h. 50 Chestnut.
Sparrow Amos L. engineer at Y.M.C.A. building 315 Pearl, h. 242 Sargeant.
Sparvento Raphael,setter at 15 Tru. b.19 Ellery.
Spatcher James, Jr. b.u. 18 Sheldon.
" John, gardener, at City park, h.u. 18 Sheldon.
" Walter R. driver at 103 Asy. h.u. 21 Grand.
Spatra Max, laborer, Pope Tube Co.b. 33 North.
SPAULDING ALVA W. ( C. C. Fuller & Co.) h. 21 Vine.     See page 500.
" Clinton E. b. 21 Vine.
" ☞ see also Spalding; Spollen; Sporlan.
Spear David A.florist, 242 Asy.h. 91 Wethersfield.
" Howard W. b. 14 Benton.
" John M. conductor St.Ry. h. 14 Benton.
" John M. Mrs. dressm. 14, h. 14 Benton.
" Minnie L. cashier at 45 Asy. b. 14 Benton.
Speath Anthony H. ( W. G. Simmons & Co.) l. 31 Elmer.
" George E. upholst. at 219 Asy. b. 20 South.
" Pauline, wid. George M. h. 20 South.
Speck Wm. G. contractor 618 Cap. b. 18 Smith.
Specter Max, laborer at N.Y.R. h.2u. 78 Front.
" Samuel, rubberw. at 690 Park, b. 78 Front.
Speers Elizabeth wid. John, h. 28 Smith.
" Isaac, rubberworker, b. 28 Smith.
" John, elevatorer at 690 Park, h. 28 Smith.
" Robert, rubberworker, h. 28 Smith.
Speirs Charles A. operator, 8 Sig. h. 33 Capitol.
" E. H. clerk at 908, b. 389 Main.
" Robert G. plumber at 20 Church, h.2u. 25 Center.
" Thomas C. draughtsman at H. B. Beach & Son, 135 Grove, h. 14 Beach.
Spellacy Frank P. contractor, b. 115 Weth.
" James E. drug clerk, b. 57 Front.
" John F. mason, b. 115 Wethersfield.
" Julia C. teacher at Brown school, 160 Market, b. 115 Wethersfield.
" Katharine, wid. James, h. 115 Wethersfield.
" Martin M. mason, b. 115 Wethersfield.
Spellman B. J. steward tug Smith, 285 State.
" Frank, sawyer at 93 Ch.O. h. 48 Green.
" Frank N. engineer, b.2u. 48 Green.
" Fred W. needlemaker at 26 Laurel, h.2u. 48 Green.

**THINKING PEOPLE Read The Post Daily.**

Spellman Henry A. machinist, h.u. 2 Goodman.
" Henry I. machinist, b.u. 2 Goodman.
" J. fireman str. Middletown, 285 State.
" Laura, wid. John, h. 69 Fairmount.
" Leslie A. dentist, b.2u. 2 Goodman.
" Nelson, mechanic at Popes, h.2u. 48 Green.
" Theresa, b. 2 Holcomb.
" William, butcher, h.3u. 8 Ellsworth pl.
" William, teamster at Bill Bros. 46 Ann,
    h.u. 212 Sheldon.
" William N. butcher, h. 8 Ellsworth pl.
Spencer Abiatha H. carpenter at 1 Flower, h.
    15 Babcock.
" Alfred Jr. cashier Ætna National Bank, 644
    Main, h. 16 Niles.
" Ambrose, asst. tr. 31 Pratt, h. 855 Asylum.
" Arthur E. painter, b.u. 14 Winter.
" Automatic Machine Screw Co. 111 Sheldon.
" Brainard, elevator er at 926 Mn.h.u.40 Lewis.
" Carnot O. chief clerk School Fund office,
    room 5, State capitol, h.u. 105 Oak.
" Charles E. with W. C. Mason & Co. 172
    Commerce, h. 47 Niles.
" Charles T. foreman at Hartford Electric
    Light Co. h.u. 21 Talcott.
" Christopher M. prest. Spencer Automatic
    Machine Screw Co. h. Windsor t.
" Clarissa M. wid. Calvin, h. 181 Sigourney.
" Clinton, special agt. 654 Main, h. Suffield t.
" Edgar E. carpenter, h. 23 Center.
" Florence M. teach. Brown school,160 Market,
    b. 18 Chapel.
" Frances E. wid. H. E. at Travelers Ins.
    Co. 56 Prospect, h. 7 Buckingham.
" Francis H. ( G. F. S. & Co.) h. 65 Sargeant.
" Frederick S. tinner at 291 Asylum, h u.
    39 Sargeant.
" Geo. A. iceman 4 Central, h.u. 37 Canton.
" George F. ( G. F. S. & Co.) h. 1534 Broad.
**SPENCER GEORGE F. & CO.**
    carmen, 71 Asy. rm. 25.    See page 550.
    George F. Spencer.        Francis H. Spencer.
" Grace C. kindergarten teacher at North
    East school, b. 98 Church.
" Harriet A. wid. Uriel, h.u. 52 Judson.
" Henry C. lockmaker at James L. Howard &
    Co. 438 Asylum, h. 35 Chapel.
" Herbert D. engineer, b.u. 52 Judson.
" Howard F. repairer, Popes, h.u. 14 Winter.
" Ira H. supt. 28 High, h.u. 52 Judson.
" James A. foreman, N.Y.R. b. 1202 Broad.
" Jane, h. 34 Buckingham.
" Joseph, cigarm. at 867 Main, h.3u. 177 Asy.
" Jos. B' mach. at r. 223 State, h. Windsor t.
" Juliette H. wid. Joseph N. h. 10 Suffield.
" Martha E. wid. L. A. h. 98 Church.
" Mary, h. 855 Asylum.
" Mary Catlin, h. 135 Oxford.
" Mary E. Mrs. b. 104 Albany.
" Mary L. b. 98 Church.
" Norman C. student at Yale, b. 779 Asylum.
" Norman H. salesman, h. 779 Asylum.
" R. Donald, real estate, 373 Asylum, h.u. 11
    Ellsworth.
" Richard M. carpenter, h. 24 Martin.

Spencer Samuel E. engir. at N.Y.R. h. 101 Bab.
" Sarah, wid. Andrew M. h.u. 14 Winter.
" Truman J. printer, b. 10 Suffield.
" William Mrs. h. 90 Ann.
Sperber Geo. H. tinner, 16 Mul. b.2u. 152 Allyn.
Sperl Julius, baker at 78 Morgan, h. 204 Barbour.
Sperry Clara M. h. 109 Washington.
" E. W. b. 27 Pavilion.
" Edward, machinist at 1 Flower, h. W.P.v.
" Elicia E. wid. George. b. 7 Belden.
" Elisha P. bart. at 336 Mn. h. 116 Whitmore.
" Emily J. h. 115 Ann.
" Francis B. clerk at Popes, b. 31 Winthrop.
" Franklin M. h. 4 Chapel.
" Henry M. discount clerk National Exchange
    bank, 76 State, b. 31 Winthrop.
" Henry T. h. 31 Winthrop.
**SPERRY LEWIS,** (S. McLean &
    Brainard ) attorney at law, 650 Main, h.
    East Windsor Hill.        See page 494.
" Louis A. Mrs. h. 284 Asylum, rm. 60.
" Mary B. Miss, private kindergarten school,
    323 Pearl, 3d floor, b. 31 Winthrop.
**SPERRY, McLEAN & BRAIN-
ARD,** attorneys at law, 650 Main. See
    page 494.
    Lewis Sperry.        George P. McLean.
            Austin Brainard.
" Nathan A. inspector at Popes, h. 75 Webster.
" Susan M. Mrs. dressm. 877, h.u. 877 Mn. rm. 16.
Spicer Edwin A. mech. at Popes, h. Rocky Hill t.
" J. W. at 34 Pratt, b. 30 Bluehills.
Spidell Geo. M. compositor, 252 Pearl, h. 29 Hung.
Spiegel David, toolm. at Popes, h. 57 Seymour.
" Herman, cutter at 30 Asylum, b.u. 66 Windsor.
" Nathan, clerk at Brown, Thomson & Co.
    942 Main, b. 66 Windsor.
" Raphael, tailor at 2 Kinsley, h.u. 66 Windsor.
Spiegelman Max, grocer, 106, h. 106 Ward.
Spiehsl Joseph, filer at Popes, h. 10 Squire.
Spielvogel John, carpenter at 133 Sheldon, h.u.r.
    71 Temple.
Spieske Bertha, music teacher, 77, b. 77 Edwards.
" Emma, music teacher, 77, b. 77 Edwards.
" Henry, furniture, etc. 1052 Mn.h.77 Edwards.
" Louise, music teacher, 77, b. 77 Edwards.
Spillane Michael J. machinist at Pratt & Whit-
    ney Co. 1 Flower, b. 45 Lafayette.
Spiller Fred. T. drug clerk at 515, b. 109 Main.
Spielly Philip, helper at 20 Potter, h. 25 Avon.
Spitylie M. nurse, b. 14 Church, rm. 4.
Splaun Michael, driver at 725 Main, h. 24 Cedar.
Spollen Annie, cashier, 745 Main, b.3½ Elliott pl.
" Dennis A. b. 3½ Elliott pl.
" Mary, wid. Matthew, h. 3½ Elliott pl.
" Patrick, saloon, 186, h.u. 184 Sheldon.
Sponsel Chas. W. ass't supt. at Capewell Horse
    Nail Co. 40 Gov. h 22 Huntington.
" John A. machinist, h. 27 South Hudson.
" John A. Jr. machinist at Pope Tube Co. h.
    27 South Hudson.
Spooner Celia B. stenographer at 197 Asylum,
    b. 259 High.
" Isabell, wid. Eugene T. h.u. 259 High.
Sporer Matthias, foreman, 476 Cap. h.u. 295 Park.

**As A NEWSPAPER, THE POST LEADS.**

Sporlan Charles H. salesman, h. 21 Seymour.
" Edward M. cond. St.Ry. b. 21 Seymour.
Sposito Laueiza, laborer, h.u. 78 Charles.
Spragg Chas.R.rubberw. 690 Park, b.1478 Broad.
" Harding, driver, 71 Asy.rm. 25, b. 63 Spring.
Sprague Charles E. insurance agent, b. 46 Bond.
" Charles H. messenger Adams Express Co.
    b.2u. 44 Hopkins.
" Charles W. superintendent streets, 800
    Main, City hall, h. 111½ Ann.
" Cyrus, farmer, b. 7 Washington.
" Effie, at ins. dept. State cap. h. 21 Winthrop.
" Elwin L. watchman at 70 Com. h. 46 Bond.
" Eva, at 336, b. 336 Wethersfield.
" Harriet B. teacher at Lawrence street
    school, h. 111½ Ann.
" Joseph H. at Ætna Life Ins. Co. 650 Main,
    h. 21 Winthrop.
" Sarah, wid. Benjamin, b. 37 Sumner.
" Sarah F. teacher, 690 Asylum.
" T. Dwight, clerk at 98 Kil. b. 223 Asylum.
" William, cattle commissioner at State capi-
    tol, rm. 54, h. Andover t.
Spring Brook Ice Co. 4 Central.
" Duffy, bartdr. 187 State, b. 106½ Trumbull.
" Grove Cemetery, N. C. Wilder, sup't, 196
    Windsor av.
" Henry, saloon, 187 State, h. 8 Marsh.
" P. Charles, foreman, b. 58 Wooster.
" Rudolph, screwm. 476 Cap. h. 139 Market.
" Theo. L. watchm. 20 Sargeant, b.115 Barb.
" William F. barber at 42 Un.pl. h. 115 Barb.
Springer Enos O. shirts, overalls, etc. 28 High,
    h. 1 Atlantic.
Spugnardo Liborio, fruit, 10½, h. 12 Village.
Spurr George W. mechanic at 20, h. 82 Sargeant.
Squier Frederick S. agt. Remington Typewriter
    Co. 49 Pearl, rm. 19, h. 130 Main.
" James V. dep. collector, 65 State, h. W.L.t.
Squires A. & Son, meats, oysters, 33-43 Market.
    Elisha B. Squires.        J. Barrett, Jr.
" Alvin, h. 16 Linden.
" Alvin E. clerk at 33 Mar. b. 167 Seymour.
" Charles A. b. 14 Fairmount.
" Charles B. plater at 62 Market. h. E.H.t.
" Charles B. railway postal clerk, h.u. 512
    Windsor av.
" Charles W. bkkpr. at 33 Mar. b. 52 Park.
" Elisha B. (A. Squires & Son,) h. 167 Sey.
" George W. salesman, 33 Market, h. 52 Park.
" Henry N. polisher at 111 Sheldon, h. W.t.
" John, brakeman, P.&R. h. 58 Spring.
" Walter L. builder, 149, h.u. 149 Clark.
St. ☞ see Saint, beginning of letter "S" page 316.
Stacey Everett E. student, Trinity college, 8
    Northam tower, Summit.
Stach Howard J. foreman at National Machine
    Co. 111-133 Sheldon, h.u. 101 Babcock.
Stack Patrick, laborer at Popes, b. 27 Affleck.
" Thomas, laborer, h.r. 117 Woodland.
" Timothy, driver, 15 Albany, b. 24 Chestnut.
" William, cabinetm. at 633 Mn. b. 18 Central.
Stacker John, shoemaker, 546 Asy. h.r.58 Temple.
Stackpole Charles O. molder at 1 Flower, b.
    120 Hungerford.

Stacy Almira, wid. Henry, h.2u. 210 Windsor av.
" Ina B. cor. fittings, waists, 58, b. 58 Church.
" Oliver H. draughtsman at 1 Flower, b. 48
    Hopkins.
Staderman Richard C. screwmaker at 476 Capi-
    tol, h.u. 1075 Broad.
Stafford Charles J. toolm. at Popes, b.Rockville t.
" Dudley J. bkkpr.650 Mn. rm.47, h.14 Union.
" Emma A. 71 Capitol.
" H. H. fertilizers, 242 State, b. 59 Capitol.
" John, iceman at 4 Central, h. 14 Union.
" John, teamster, 71, h. 71 New Britain.
" Joseph, harnessm. at 195 State, h. 33 Martin.
" Joseph A. b. 33 Martin.
" Mary, h.u. 270 Maple.
" Nathan E. agent Denamore Typewriter, 7
    Central, h. 44 Lincoln.
" Thomas, grading contractor 65, h. 65 N.B.
Stager Cornelius C. clerk, 342 Asylum, b. B.v.
" Frank, porter, h.3u. 23 Wells.
" Michael, blacksmith, b.3u. 23 Wells.
Stagg Jennie M. Mrs. b.2u. 545 Main.
Staib Emma C. b. 67 Huyshope.
" George W. patternm. at Colts, h. 71 Huy.
" John A. machinist at 70, h. 67 Huyshope.
Stain Aaron, peddler, b.u. 190 Front.
" ☞ see also Stein.
Stalker E. E. secy. & treas. Stalker Mfg. Co. h.
    New Park.
" Mfg. Co. horse goods, 452 Asylum.
" Neil, mgr. Stalker Mfg. Co. h. New Park.
Stall Arthur W. train dispatcher, N.E.R. h.E.H.t.
" Joseph S. cigarmaker, b. 3 Chapel.
Stamm Rosena, wid. John, h. 34 Allen pl.
Stancheski Elizabeth, wid.Charles,h.561Garden.
" Eva H. music teacher, h. 561 Garden.
Stancliff Amelia, wid. J. W. b. 254 Jefferson.
" Henry J. b. 54 Capitol.
Standard Boot and Shoe Co. 589 Main.
    M. H. McGowan, Mgr.
" Oil Co. James L. Freeborne, mgr. 370 Front.
" Rug and Carpet Renovating Co., William F.
    Haas, prop. r. 13 and 15 Wells.
" Tea House, 16 Church, J. H. McGuire, prop.
Standinger Charles, b. 25 Mulberry.
Standish Harry, clerk at 89 Trumbull, b.Weth.t.
" Howard A. clerk at 372, h.u. 212 Asylum.
" J. Herbert, physician,378, h.378Windsor av.
" Jared B. (J. A. Perkins & Co.) engraver at
    177 Asylum, h. Wethersfield t.
" Miles, trav.salesm. 65 Suffield, h.Griswold t.
" Thomas, secretary and treasurer Birkery
    Mfg. Co. 65 Suffield, h. Wethersfield t.
Stanfinbil Rudolph, collector at 118 Asylum,
    h.2u. 110 Barbour.
Stanley Alice L. stenog. at Popes, b. 58 Church.
" Charles O. clerk at Brown, Thomson & Co.
    942 Main, b. 231 Market.
" Frank G. mfgr. bicycle stands,11,b.11 Good.
" Grant, student, b. 11 Goodman.
" James, buffer at Wm. Rogers Mfg. Co. 66
    Market, h.u. 9 Hendricxsen.
" Joseph E. sewing machine agt. h. 11 Good.
" Joseph T. polisher, b. 81 Governor.
" L. J. Mrs. h. 191 State.

# GEORGE W. STAPLES,

### GENERAL AGENT,

# New York Life Insurance Co.,

## 847 MAIN STREET,

**Old Number 333.          ROOM 4, HILLS' BLOCK.**

Stanley Louis H. principal East school, Whiting
    lane, b. 462 Farmington.
" Peter, nurseryman, b. 7 Lenox.
Stannard Ellen L. nurse, h. 5 Ellsworth pl.
" Frank L. asst. foreman at Pratt & Whit-
    ney Co. 1 Flower, h.u. 45 Sigourney.
" John S. clerk at T. A. Honiss, 30 State,
    h.u. 1407 Main.
" Mason, machinist at 9 Sig. h.u. 10 Talcott.
" Monroe, foreman Pratt & Whitney Co. 1
    Flower, h. 48 Imlay.
" Walter M. bookkeeper at Brown, Thomson
    & Co. 942 Main, b. South Manchester v.
Stanners Thomas J. at 183 State, b. 3 Wawarme.
Stansbury Edward, at, b. Hospital farm.
Stanton Charles A. clerk, 52 Temple, h. 34 Wdbg.
" George F. traveling salesman at Popes, b.
    North Adams, Mass.
" George H. paperhanger at Baxter the Deco-
    rator, 231 Asylum, h. 58 Grove.
" John C. polisher at Popes, h.2u. 1445 Broad.
**STANTON LEWIS E.** attorney, 16
    State, h. 650 Main, room 40. *See p. 495.*
" Sarah, wid. Samuel, b. 185 Smith.
Staples Chas. S. mach. at 555 Cap. h. 231 Lawrence.
STAPLES GEORGE W. general agent New York
    Life Insurance Co. 847 Main, rm. 10, h.
    West Hartford t.          *See page 342.*
" M. S. Miss, b. 223 Asylum.
Stapleton Fred, clerk, 1031 Main, h. 85 Chestnut.
" James, engineer, h.u. 82 Avon.
" Richard P. engineer, h. 51 Potter.
" Thomas, helper at Telegram, 12 Central.
Starbuck Bessie G. music teacher, b. 43 Niles.
" Mary E. music teacher, b. 43 Niles.
**STARBUCK R. M. & SON,**
    plumbers and electricians, 249 Pearl.
                    *See page 425.*
    R. M. Starbuck.    R. M. Starbuck, Jr.
" R. M. *(R.M.S.& Son,)* h. 57 Barbour.
" R. M. Jr. *(R.M.S.& Son,)* b. 57 Barbour.
Starenstein Ellis, shoem. at 254 Law. b. 30 Kil.
Stark Sam Petersen, bricklayer, h. 38 Rowe.
Starkel Ernest J. clerk, 466 Asy. h.u. 15 Kibbe.
" Henry, baggagem.at Un.depot,h.u.15 Kibbe.
Starkey Ada, b.3u. 198 Allyn.
" Dennis J. shippingclerk, Case, Lockwood &
    Brainard Co. 141 Pearl, h.2u. 41 Green.
" Harry, engineer at Pope Tube Co. b. 153
    Windsor av.
" John, ropemaker, h.u. 34 Canton.

Starkey John J. Jr. clerk, 66 Asy. h. 15 Florence.
" Mary, wid. Thomas, h. 216 Windsor av.
" Samuel R. *(King & S.)* b.u. 1478 Broad.
" Thomas J. assembler, 556 Cap. b.u. 34 Canton.
" Walter, lineman, 266 Pearl, h.u. 48 State.
Starkie William A. engineer, h. 15 Bellevue.
Starkweather Charles M. correspondent at Pope
    Mfg. Co. 436 Capitol, h. 36 Forest.
" Nathan, surveyor, 948, h. 948 Asylum.
Starr Benjamin M. b. 27 Charter Oak pl.
" Charlotte M. wid. Burgis P. h. 30 Townley.
" Edmund, salesm. 273 Asy. h. Newington t.
" Francis E. mason at 164 State, h. 461 Maple.
" Fred, driver Pierces laundry, b.19 Central.
" Fred'k W. head clerk repair department at
    Popes, h. Newington t.
" George H. circular distribr. 312 Asy. rm. 6.
" J. Edward, painter, r. 16 N.B. h. 57 Hudson.
" John C. steamfitter, 15 Kinsley, h.u. 120
    Mather, after Sept. 1, h. 133 Albany.
" Kate, wid. Christopher, h. 587 Main.
" Lottie E. Mrs. h. 44 Wooster.

PIERRE S. STARR, Physician, 811 Main, h. 179
    Sigourney street.
    Hours—8 to 9.30 A.M.
        2 to 3.30 and 7.30 to 8.30 P.M.
        Telephone—House 1027-3.

Starr Pierre S. physician, 811 Main, h. 179 Sig.
" Robert S. b. 179 Sigourney.
" Thomas K. dentist, 926 Main, Cheney
    building, h. 36 Beacon. (2)
" Wilbur H. mason, h. 16 Elm.
" ☞ *see also Staer.*
Start Edwin H. clerk 843 Main, h. 47 Lafayette.
Starum John, laborer, b. 29 Commerce.
Stasne Frank C. tailor, 730 Main, h. 84 Park.
State Arsenal, 264 Windsor av.
**STATE BANK,** 795 Main. *See page 436.*
" House or State Capitol, on Bushnell Park.
" Library, C. J. Hoadly, librarian, in Capitol.
**STATE MUTUAL FIRE INSUR-
    ANCE CO.** 750 Main.    *See p. 445.*
" Prison Association, room 45, in Capitol.
**STATE SAVINGS BANK,** 39 Pearl.
    Miles W. Graves, treas.    *See page 440.*
Station House and Police, 38 Kinsley.
Staudinger August D. *( Hurley& S.)* h.u. 871 Main.
" Rudolph E. toolmaker, h.2u. 48 Retreat.
Staugler Edward F. assembler at 690 Park, b.
    4 Foot Guard.
" Wm. F. tailor, h.u. 4 Foot Guard.
Staunton Mary Gray, h. 645 Farmington.
Stavalo Dominic, laborer, b.u. 76 Charles.
" Joseph, laborer, h.3u. 4 Charles.
" Vencenzo, laborer, h.u. 76 Charles.
Stavo Nunzianto, ragpicker, h. 20 Charles.
Stead Daniel, helper 1 Flow. b.u. 12 New Britain.
Steaklum Robert, laborer, h. 32 Grand.
Steamboat storehouses, 112 Com. and 285 State.
" wharves at the foot of State street.
Steane Abram, peddler, h. 190 Front.
" Isaac James, pres't Barbour Silver Co.
    62 Market.

**THE POST DELIVERED AT YOUR HOME DAILY, PER MONTH, FIFTY CENTS.**

Stearns Alice M. b. 76 Flower.
" Bert. N. clerk at 31 Church, h.2u. 4 Chapel.
" Charles. C. private school for boys, 126, h. 126 Garden.
" Charles S. real estate, 75 Pratt, h. 83 Elm.
" Frank Monroe, h. 7 Elliott pl.
" Frederic S. clerk at 34 Asylum, h.r. 57 Gov.
" Henry, mach. at 388 Capitol, b. 4 Chapel.
STEARNS HENRY P.superintendent and physician Retreat for the Insane, 30 Washington, h. 190 Retreat. *See pages* 698, 699.
" Isaac, traveling salesman, b. 57 Pratt.
" Persis M. wid. Experience, h. 76 Flower.
" Thomson, student, b. 126 Garden.
" ☞see also Sterns.
Stebbins Alonzo, mach. at 80 Huy. h.u. 46 Bond.
" Charles W. driller at Colts, l. 739 Main.
" Daniel H. repairer, 115 State, h. Rainbow v.
" George D. foreman at 476, h. 381 Capitol.
" Henry M. toolm. at 476 Cap. b. 228 High.
" James K. screwm. 476 Cap. h.2u. 1352 Broad.
" Joseph B. machinist, h. 17 Squire.
" Mary J. Mrs. clerk at 882 Main, b. 12 Bkm.
Stecher Nicholas, filer at Popes, b. Burnside v.
Stedman Chas. E. clerk at 690 Park, h. 123 Oak.
" Edmund A. h. 79 Elm.
" Elizabeth Mrs. h. 145 Collins.
" Elizabeth S. Miss, h. 79 Elm.
" Harry B. *(S. & Redfield,)* h. 533 Far.
" Herbert P. clerk Hfd. Lib'y, b. 145 Collins.
" Jeannette, b. 36 Jefferson.
" John A. butcher, 25, b. 25 Greenwood.
" John E., U. S. Army, b. 145 Collins.
" Lewis H. clerk at Belknap & Warfield, 77 Asylum, h.u. 82 Sargeant.
" & Redfield, commercial paper, 5 Central.
 Harry B. Stedman. H. S. Redfield.
" William H. superintendent Merrow Machine Co. 26–28 Laurel, h. 173 Seymour.
Steele Adelbert, machinist, h. Oakwood.
" Albert S. helper at 353 Albany, h. W.H.t.
" Albion B. bkkpr. at 209 State, b. 846 Park.
" Andrew G. b. 846 Park.
" Arthur G. salesman, 149 State, h. 53 Mahl.
" Charles A. b. 389 Main.
" Charles J. box clerk at P. O. b. 21 Florence.
" Chauncey A. machinist, h. 57 Dean.
" Clinton G. carptr. at 155 Ch.O. b. E.H.t.
" Edward, machinist, b.u. 16 Ely.
STEELE EDWARD L. councilman 3d ward *(Steele & S.)* attorney, 863 Main, b. 27 Clark.
" Edward P. mach. at 388 Capitol, h. W.H.t.
" Geo. Whipple music teach. 8, h. 8 Spring.
" Geo. W. Mrs. day school for girls, 8 Spring.
" Goodwin, patternm. at Popes, h. 846 Park.
" Harriet, b. 36 Jefferson.
" Henry W., U. S. Army, h.2u. 28 Pleasant.
" Hugh A. butcher at 1050 Main, h.u. 16 Ely.
" Jennie, wid. John W. h. 1339 Broad.
" Les. P. L. coachman, b.2u. 28 Pleasant.
" Samuel A. gatetender at 1 Flow. b. 378 Asy.
" & Steele, attorneys at law, 863 Main, rm. 3.
 Timothy E. Steele. Edward L. Steele.
" Thos. Sedgwick, artist, 904 Main, rm. 98, h. 71 Woodland.

## William P. Steinmetz,

Formerly with J. C. Wasserbach,

### REAL ESTATE BROKER,

APPRAISER AND NOTARY PUBLIC,

80 PEARL STREET, Kenmore Bldg.

*PROPERTY: For Sale or Exchange in all parts of the city. Farms and Business Opportunities.*

*REAL ESTATE: Special attention paid to the Care of Property, Renting and Collection of Rents, and General Management, also Sales of Real Estate.*

Steele Timothy E. *(Steele & S.)* attorney, 863 Main, h. 27 Clark.
" W. R. clerk at Tucker & Goodwin, 8 Hurlburt, b. 27 Clark.
" Wilbur S. bkkpr. 1072 Main, h. 17 Chestnut.
" William C. policeman, h. 21 Florence.
Steen Alexander, saddler at 8 Sig. b. 98 Hopkins.
Steer Trayton, expresser, h. 84 Fairmount.
Steeves Wm. H. toolm. at Popes, h. 39 Grand.
Stehli Jacob, at 476 Capitol, h. 72 Russ.
Steidel Henry, tailor at 2 State, h. 238 Bellevue.
Stein Adolph, filer at 142 Russ, h. 28 Front.
" Carl L. mach. at 28 High, b. Glastonbury t.
" Henry, driver at 366, l. 377 Main.
" Israel, harnessm. at 8 Sig. h. 228 Front.
" Joseph, laborer street dept. h. 49 Morgan.
" Moriss, dry goods, 140, h. 140 Front.
" Morris, peddler, h.2u. 196 Front.
" Moses, peddler, h. 21 Wadsworth.
" ☞see also Steane.
Steinbrueck Charles, helper at 70, b. 70 Temple
" Christian, *(S. & Kuehn,)* h. 70 Temple.
" & Kuehn, saloon, 70 Temple.
 Christian Steinbrueck. Henry Kuehn.
Steinkamp Geo. barber at 706 Mn.b. 224 Franklin.
Steiner & Co. saloon, 29 Temple.
 Sigmund Steiner. Carl Stern.
" Emma J. h. 12 Suffield.
" Sigmund, *(Steiner & Co.)* 29 Temple.
" Solomon, jewelry peddler, h. 4 Goodman.
Steinhoff John A. trav. salesman, h. 12 Lenox.
Steinholtz Henry, electrician, h. 110 Whitmore.
Steinmetz August G. clerk 835 Main, b. 49 Sig.
" Jacob F. clerk, b. 5 Hawthorn.
" Robert C. real estate, 80 Pearl, h. 49 Sig.
STEINMETZ WILLIAM P. real estate broker, 80 Pearl, h. 266 Jefferson. *See page* 343.

### STELLING FRED W. sheet metal work, 93 Franklin, h. 14 Pawtucket.
 *See page* 487.

Stemchuck Michael, bottler 182 Front, h. 17 Mec.
Stengelin Andrew, bkkpr. 315 Park, h.u. 206 Jef.
" Fred. C. cutler, 5 Grove, h.u. 78 Jefferson.
Stengle Frederick W. carpenter, b.u. 76 Ward.
" Harry S. treas. Parson's Theatre, h. 66 Pro.
" William, laborer, b.u. 8 Village.
Stenner Charles, mach. 476 Cap. h. 1336 Broad.
Stenson Oliver E. carpenter, h. 16 Cone.
" ☞see also Stinson.

**It Pays Big Interest-Your Advertisement in The Post.**

# W. T. STEVEN,

*Manufacturing
Optician,*
*Jeweler and
Watchmaker,*

## No. 4 STATE STREET.

Stenstrom Theo. rubberworker, b. 109 Laurel.
Stentafore Chas. pressman 690 Park, b. 42 Smith.
Stepan Wm. E. mach. at 1 Flow. h. 55 Francis.
" William J. mach. at 1 Flow. b. 55 Francis.
Stephan Charles E. saloon, 197 Front, foreman
   Columbia Brewing Co. h. 143 Bellevue.
" Maurice, U. S. Army, b. 143 Bellevue.
Stephens Harry H. carptr. 155 Ch.O. h. 51 Bab.
" George, helper at Pratt & Whitney Co. 1
   Flower, h. 124 Heath.
" George H. at 164 State, b. 124 Heath.
" James F. mach. at 1 Flower, b. 124 Heath.
" John, mach. at 30 Cushman, b. 124 Heath.
" Walter T. baker at 30 Washington.
Stephenson [☞ *see also Stevenson.*
Steppe Mark E. salesm. Popes, b. Brooklyn, N.Y.
Sterbenz Geo. brewer at 315 Park, h. 50 Law.
Sterling [☞ *see Stirling.*
Stermer John, machinist N.Y.R. h. 15 Oak.
Stern Aaron, h. 13 Congress.
" Carl (*Steiner & Co.*) h. Bellevue c. Suffield.

CHARLES S. STERN, Physician.    Office, 75
   Pratt street.
     Hours—10 A. M. to 3 P. M.
       6.30 to 7.30 P. M.
     Sunday—9 to 10 A. M.
       Telephone 121-13.

Stern Charles S. physician, 75 Pratt, h. 29 Pearl.
" E. Belle, bkkpr. at 956 Main, b. 13 Congress.
" Isaac, buyer at 956 Main, b. 13 Congress.
" Jos. S. (*Stern & Weidl,*) h.u. 61½ Governor.
" Minnie, teacher Northw. sch. b. 13 Congress.
" Moses A. buyer at 956 Mn. h. 12 Goodman.
" Samuel L. clerk at Brown, Thomson & Co.
   942 Main, b. 13 Congress.
" & Weidl, barbers, 6 Charter Oak.
     Joseph S. Stern.        Edward Weidl.
" [☞ *see also Stearns.*
Sternberg John C. clerk at Popes, b. W.H.t.
Sternchitz Joseph, peddler, h.u. 262 Front.
Sterrman August, at 690 Park, h.u. 84 Francis.
Sterzing Augustus, contractor at James L. How-
   ard & Co. 438 Asy. h.3u. 16 Trumbull.
" Emil J. toolm. at 581 Cap. h. 19 Greenwood.
" George, filer at 142 Russ, h. 203 Lawrence.
" George H. contractor at James L. Howard &
   Co. 438 Asylum, h. 860 Park.
" [☞ *see also Stetson.*
Stetson Charles R. engineer, b. 1067 Main.
" George, laborer, h.u. 303 Lawrence.
" Jane V. wid. Horace W. h. 60 Buckingham.
" William E. mach. 1 Flow. b. 52 Hungerford.
Stetzner Louis, carpenter, l. 1045 Main.

STEVEN WILLIAM T. optician, 4 State, h. 99
   Trumbull.        *See page 344.*
Stevens Abbott A. painter, 843 Mn. b. 640 Weth.
" Albert H. furniture, b. 81 Benton.
" Albert H. painter at 843 Main, h. 460 Weth.
" Albert J. mach. at 1 Flow. b.u. 88 Franklin.
" Albert T. motorm. St.Ry. b. 48 Prospect.
" Alfred A. clerk at 342 Asylum, h. 63 Oak.
" Alfred M. clerk at 272 Asy. b. 96 Chestnut.
" Anthony, agt. Time Lock Co. b. 33 Brown.
" Bridget, wid. Michael, h.2u.r. 60 Temple.
" Charles B. rubberw. 690 Park, h. 90 Hudson.
" Charles E. photoeng. at 177 Asy. b. 80 State.
" Charles G. conductor St.Ry. b. 150 Franklin.
" Charles M. bkkpr. at 108 Asy. b. 11 Whitney.
" Clara A. principal Lawrence street school,
   b. 107 Washington.
" Clarissa F. wid. Lyman, b. 33 Oak.
" Daniel H. gen. repairer, h. 81 Benton.
" David, h. 11 Whitney.
" David J. clerk at 1 Flow· b. 11 Whitney.
" Edward, cigarm. at 867 Main h. E.H.t.
" Edwin W. assemb. at Colts, h. 88 Franklin.
" Edwin W. woodmolder, h. 1 Preston.
" Fannie B. nurse, 20 South Hudson.
" Emma W. stenog. at Popes, b. 63 Oak.
" Enos, brickmaker, h. 389 Wethersfield.
" George W. assembler at 476, b. 161 Capitol.
" Halsey, at Hartford Steam Boiler Inspection
   and Ins. Co. 650 Main, b. Newington t.
" Herbert E. b. 460 Wethersfield.
" Horace, awningmaker, h.r. 22½ Alden.
" Horace, helper at 135 Shel. b. 460 Weth.
" Howard E. finisher at 17 Elm. h. 389 Weth.
" James R. clerk at 5, h. 727 Asylum.
" Jane, wid. J. N. B. h. 9 Fales.
" John, hallman str. Hartford, 285 State.
" John, laborer at 15 Tru. b. 1423 Broad.
" John B., U. S. Army, b. 41 Hungerford.
" John H. P. at Hfd. Steam Boiler Insp. &
   Ins. Co. 650 Main, b. Newington t.
" John S. clerk at 329 Asylum, b. 9 Fales.
" Joseph R. painter, h.2u.r. 68 Temple.
" Julia A. teacher, South school, 36 Wads-
   worth, b. 1 Preston.
" Martin Van, condtr. St.Ry.h.u. 12 Babcock.
" Mary B. wid. Edwin, h. 1 Preston.
" Mary K. stenographer at Orient Ins. Co. 5
   Haynes, b. Newington t.
" Maud, attendant at 30 Washington.
" Michael, helper at 556 Cap. b. 1427 Broad.
" Michael F. setter at 15 Tru. b. 1425 Broad.
" Nellie H. b. 9 Fales.
STEVENS NEWELL H. proprietor National Meat
   Market, 329 Asylum, h. 9 Fales.
        *See page 345.*
" Patrick, cabinetm. at 633 Mn. h. 22 Cedar.
" Paul E. clerk at 654 Main. b. 727 Asylum.
" Rachel, musicteacher, b. 40 Mahl.
" Robert D. deputy collector and inspector
   Custom House, h.u. 40 Mahl.
" Sarah, h. 36 Jefferson.
" Sarah A. Mrs.: teacher South school, 36
   Wadsworth, h. 1 Preston.

Stevens Thomas, carpenter, h.2u. 28 Babcock.
" Thomas, painter, b.2u.r. 68 Temple.
" W. Fisk, clerk at Popes, b. Newington t.
" William, brewer at 217 Windsor, h. 219 Bellevue.
" William, plumber at 94 State, b. 125 Heath.
" William, teamster at 40 Elm. b. 29½ Lewis.
" Wm. E. mach. at 1 Flow. b. 88 Franklin.
" William H. vice president Ripley Bros. Co. h. 17 Huntington.
Stevenson Chas. H. mach. 1 Flow. h. 79 Francis.
" Henry C. mach. at 1 Flower, h. 122 Madison.
" Henry C. molder at 556 Cap. h. 196 Russ.
" John H. mach. at 1 Flower, h. 79 Francis.
" John Henry, melter, h.u. 196 Russ.
" Marie D. bkkpr. at 350 Windsor av. b. 79 Francis.
" Sophia, wid. John, b. 79 Francis.
" ☞ see also Stephenson.
Stewart Abigail Mrs. laundress, 10, h. 10 Green.
" Archibald, diem. at Popes, h.u. 245 Putnam.
" Charles, coachman, h.r. 36 South Prospect.
" Charles W. l. 756 Main, rm. 33.
" Frank O. manager Nopareil laundry, r. 366 Windsor av. h. 140 Martin.

STEWART GORDON W. expert accountant and bookkpr. Address, Portland, Conn.

" Henry B. laborer, b. 10 Green.
" J. Ernest, clerk First National Bank, 50 State, b. Windsor t.
" James A. mech. at 581 Capitol, b. 64 Flower.
" Jennie L. dressm. 200, b. 200 Wethersfield.
" John C. manager cafe, 835, b.3u. 573 Main.
" John D. janitor at 700, b. 700 Main.
" Thomas, helper at 690 Park, b.91 Madison av.
" Timothy B. h.u. 61 Whitmore.
" Walter A. W. bookkeeper and stenographer at 26, h. 102 Laurel.
" ☞ see also Stuart; Steward.
Stibbs George H. steam heating, etc. 50 Church, l. 427 Main, rm. 35.
Sticklor Max, teacher, h.2u. 64 Morgan.
Stickney Chas. L. saloon, 1219, h. 1145 Main.
" Geo. G. patternm. at Colts, b. 39 Governor.
Stiehl William, h. 134 Mather.
Stiles Austin, carsealer at 95 Pleasant, h. E.H.t.
" Charles W. scientist, b. 141 Washington.
" E. W. h. 141 Washington.
" Edgar C. teacher, b.u. 20 Imlay.
" Frances B. Mrs. h.u. 20 Imlay.
" Frank B. h.u. 273 Jefferson.
" George L. hose driver, Co. No. 5, l. 129 Sig.
" Josephine, b. 141 Washington.
" Samuel M. Rev. stenographer at Ætna Life Ins. Co. 650 Main, h. 141 Washington.
" Walter F. clerk 732 Main, b. 149 Windsor av.
" William J. motorman St.Ry. h. 49 Dean.
Still George A. boilerm. at N.Y.R. b. 3 Lafayette.
" Sarah, wid. Frank, h.2u. 3 Lafayette.
" Wm. C. mach. 1 Flow. h.2u. 33 Hungerford.
Stillman Augustus M. foreman at 476 Capitol, h. 16 Columbia.
" Benjamin R. asst. secretary National Fire Ins. Co. 95 Pearl, h. 39 Woodland.

STILLMAN & CO. furs, etc. 59 Pratt street.          See outside front cover.
William H. Stillman.
" Edw. B. h. 255 Farmington.
" Henry A. h. 100 Woodland.
" Henry A. clerk at Popes, b. Rocky Hill t.
" William E. proofreader at Evening Post, 23 Asylum, b. Meriden t.
STILLMAN WILLIAM H. (Stillman & Co.) furs, etc. 59 Pratt, h. 22 Charter Oak. pl.
" William W. supt. board of charity commissioners, 222 Pearl, h. 2 Holcomb.
Stillwell John, h.u. 203 Maple.
Stinson Roger W. tailor, 71 Asy. h.2u. 1 Goodman.
" S. C. conductor, St.Ry. h. 289 Asylum.
" Thomas J. at 37 Wells, h.u. 455 Garden.
" ☞ see also Stenson.
Stirckler Charles N. clerk at Brown, Thomson & Co. 942 Main, h. 51 Capitol.
Stirling Clarence C. electri. 66 State, b. 11 Girard,
" J. Carolus, treasurer Pratt & Whitney Co. 1 Flower, h. 145 Woodland.
" Robert, laborer, b.u. 47 Green.
" ☞ see also Sterling.
Stitch Eva A. wid. Martin, b. 49 Mahl.
Stitt James H. clerk at 589 Main, h. 27 Lewis.
Stivers William C. brakeman, h.u. 26 Liberty.
Stockall Daniel H. harnessmaker at 8 Sigourney, h.2u. 112 Laurel.
" William, harnessm. at 8 Sig. b. 112 Laurel.
Stockbridge John, carptr. at 39, h.2u. 39 Kinsley.
" Sophia, h. 39 Windsor.
STOCKER EBEN H. secretary Billings & Spencer Co. 142 Russ, h. 40 Allen pl. See page 531.

FRANK H. STOCKER, Physician.  Office, 40 Allen pl.
Hours—8.30 to 9.30 A.M.
         2 to 3 and 7 to 8 P.M.
With Dr. C. E. Jones, 116 Ann—10 to 11 A.M.
Sundays—2 to 3 P.M.
         Telephone connection.

Stocker Frank H. physician, 40, b. 40 Allen pl.
" Jane B. h. 521 Windsor av.
" John, shoemaker, h.3u. 54 Temple.
Stockham Alfred S. laborer 40 Gov. h. 145 Shel.
" Edward, labr. at 40 Gov. h. 12 S. Prospect.
" Harry, oper. at 40 Gov. h. 34 S. Prospect.
Stocking Frank, screwm. 476 Cap. b. 250 Law.
" Louis, clerk at 956 Main, b.u. 51 Babcock.
" Mahler, wid. B. H. h.u. 51 Babcock.

Stocking Mammie Mrs. clerk 956 Mn. h. 236 High
" Sarah M. housekeeper at 171 Putnam.
Stockton Frank, rubberw. 690 Park, b. 106 Sey.
" Frank M. roller at 690 Park, h. 106 Seymour.
Stockvis Frank, salesman, h. 149 Wethersfield.
Stockwell Joseph C. h. 120 Preston.

**STODDARD & CAULKINS,** contractors, 155 Charter Oak. *See page 518.*
Stephen D. Stoddard,     Willis E. Caulkins.
" Frederick H. engineer, h. 29½ Lewis.
" John E. clerk at Popes, b. Newington t.
" Jonathan H. Jr. h.r. 13 Washington.
" Stephen D. (*S. & Caulkins,*) h. 219 Laurel.
" William B. clerk at 1129 Main, b. 225 High.
Stodel Charles J. cigarmaker at 34 Temple, h. 181 Market.
Stoeckel Robbins B. attorney, 847 Main, rm. 9, b. 109 Elm.
Stoehr Fred G. bartdr. at 50 Mar. h. 71 Bluehills.
" Henry W. cigar mfr. r. 75, h.r. 75 Bluehills.
Stokes Fred'k, meat market, 371 Asylum, h. 107 Wethersfield.
" John, clerk at 115 State, b. Glastonbury t.
" Martin C. clerk at 690 Park, b. 156 Collins.
" Samuel, farmer, h. Davenport c. Heath.
Stoll Emil J. cigarmaker at 104 Asy. b. 3 Chapel.
" Ferdinand A. harnessm. 8 Sig. h.u. 65 Francis.
" George, joiner, h. 20 Commerce.
" Lizzetta Mrs. boardinghouse, 1218 Main.
Stone Albert E. roller at 690 Park, h.u. 11 Squire.
" Anna M. dressmaker, h. 11 Squire.
" Arthur J. enginr. r. 60 Temple, b. 100 Pratt.
" Claude W. cigarmaker, b. 999 Main.
" Charles, at 13 Morris, h.u. 14 Warner.
" Charles, bookbdr. at 141 Pearl, b. Windsor t.
" Charles E. b. 64 Hopkins.
" Charles G. at 13 Morris, b.u. 14 Warner.
STONE CHARLES G. *councilman 4th ward,* at Travelers Insurance Co. 56 Prospect, h. 240 Ashley.
" Charles H. pressm. 66 State, h.u. 4 Walnut.
" Charles S. machinist at Colts, h. E.H.t.
" Edward C. patternmaker at Billings & Spencer Co. 142 Russ, h. 60 Putnam.
" Edwd. Collins, student at Yale, b. 26 Allen pl.
" Edwin M. civil engineer at 39 Pearl, b. 76 Hopkins.
" Elbert L. coachman at 23, b. 23 Capitol.
" Elizabeth W. teacher at High School, b. 26 Allen pl.
" Frank E. buffer at Wm. Rogers Mfg. Co. 66 Market, h.r. 62 Vanblock.

Stone Frank E. special agent National Fire Insurance Co. 95 Pearl, h. 171 Collins.
" Frederick T. clerk, h. 46 Lincoln.
" George, b. 2 Holcomb.
" George F. teacher, 690, h. 991 Asylum.
" Geo. M. Rev. pastor Asylum avenue Baptist church, h. 22 Townley.
" Grace, at r. 59½ Trumbull, b. 58 Church.
" Henrietta E. b. 26 Allen pl.
" Henry W. teamster, 46 Ann, h.u. 105 Com.
" Herman C. mach. at 1 Flow. h. 36 Hopkins.
" Howard M. machinist, b.u. 86 Ward.
" James B. h. 23 Marshall.
" James H. painter, h. 6 Cottage.
" Jesse E. wool & cotton rags, r. 44, h. 44 Wdbg.
" John A. mach. at 1 Flow. b. 72 Charter Oak.
" John F. cashier at 247 Pearl, b. 233 Main.
" John P. mach. at 83 Woodbine, b. 234 Pearl.
" Lucy M. h. 813 Asylum.
" Mabel E. teacher West Middle school, h. 167 Sigourney.
" Mary C. wid. Edward C. h. 26 Allen pl.
" Melville, salesman, h. 39 Ward.
" Robert E. checker at Colts, h. 14 Clark.
" Sarah E. teacher, b. 11 Squire.
" Theodore H. clerk at 97 Asy. b. 101 Ann.
" Thomas, painter at 1 Flow. h. 226 Putnam.
" Wilbur A. teamster at 46 Ann, h.u. 31 Tru.
" Willard, helper, h. 11 Squire.
Stoneburner Charles E. lab. at 40 Gov. h.r. 98 N.B.
" Edgar E. b. 98 New Britain.
Stoner George J. law student, b.u. 118 Wooster.
" Louis E. clerk at City Bank of Hartford, 783 Main, b. 118 Wooster.
" Merrick A. supt. 34 Pratt, h.u. 118 Wooster.
Stopfer John L. filer at Popes, h.r. 58 Temple.
" Leopold, laborer, h.r. 58 Temple.
Storer Mary F. attendant at 30 Washington.
Storey George A. clerk at Brown, Thomson & Co. 942 Main, h. 32 Chapel.
" May G. proofr. 254 Pearl, b. 122 Huntington.
Stork Alfred, at 902 Main, b.u. 51 Chestnut.
" Jacob, carptr. at 155 Ch.O. h. 32 S. Prospect.
" Julia S. clerk at 956 Main, b. 57 Chestnut.
" Meyer, cigarm. at 104 Asy. h.u. 51 Chestnut.
Storms Albert F. diem. Popes, h.2u. 52 Putnam.
Storrs Ella Mrs. dressmaker, b. 375 Main.
" F. H. & Co. mfrs. agents, 42 Church.*
" Frank H. (*F. H. S. & Co.*) b. 91 Ann.
" Harry, clerk, b.u. 101 Oak.
" Henry C. h.u. 122 Clark.
" Henry C. electrician at 1 Flower, h. 101 Oak.
" Henry W. architect, 50 State, b. 122 Clark.
" Herbert H. clerk at 6 State, h. 33 Congress.
" Herbert E. assistant bookkeeper at Neal, Goff & Inglis Co. 980 Main, b. 33 Cong.
" J. F. Dillingham Mrs. physician, h. 122 Clark.
" Joseph W. h. 122 Clark.
" Mabel N. teacher, b.u. 33 Congress.
" Melancthon, physician, 91, h. 91 Ann.
" Rose W. stenographer at Popes, b. 122 Clark.
" William M. h. 24 Columbia.
Story Otis J. student at Trinity college, 35 Jarvis hall, Summit.
" Pearl A. clerk, b. 122 Huntington.

Stotz Mary J. wid. Jacob. h.2u. 164 Babcock.
Stoughton D. G. & Co. druggists, 204 State, and Park c. New Park, Parkville.*
" Dwight G. (D. G. S. & Co.) candy manufacturer, 219 State, h. 752 Park.
" George H. investment broker, 7 Central, rm. 1, h. 66 Oxford.
" John A. attorney, 868 Main, rm. 2, h. E.Ht.
" John F. clerk at 98 Kilbourn, b. 80 Church.
" Norman F. (S. & Taylor,) h. So.Windsor t.
" & Taylor, grates, etc. 38 Avon.
   Norman F. Stoughton.   John C. Taylor.
Stowe Elmert C. porter, 1411 Main, b. 30 Vine.
" Etta W. Mrs. nurse b. 14 Church, rm. 4.
" Henry, painter, h.u. 1112 Main.
" Josephine F. Mrs. dressm. h.u. 1112 Main.
Stowell Ernest C. clerk 254 Pearl, b.u. 63 Julius.
" George, carpenter, h. 20 Commerce.
" Joseph C. b.u. 58 Benton.
Strachan Adam, blacksmith, h. 25 Warner.
Strahan John W. h. 85 Williams.
Strant C. H. & Co. U. S. Club and hotel stables. r. 50 State.
   Charles H. Strant.   Edwin D. Alvord.
" Charles H. (C. H. S. & Co.) h.'82 Williams.
Stratton Albert, machinist at Popes, h. 28 N.B.
" Charles R. mach. 1 Flower, b. 72 Hopkins.
" Daniel F. rub.wkr. 690 Park, b. 7 Hamilton.
" Daniel J. engir. at stone pits, h. 7 Hamilton
" Frank W. filer at Capewell Horse Nail Co. 40 Governor, h. 168 Franklin.
" Fred S. wirestraightener at 31 Hicks, h. Wethersfield t.
" James D. barkeeper at 203 State, b. 5 Zion.
" Jared O. mach.at 40 Gov. h.406 Wethersfield.
" Sanford E. bookbinder at Case, Lockwood & Brainard Co. 141 Pearl, h. 243 Jefferson.
" William A. mach. at 40 Gov. b. 157 Cap.
" William H. assist't manager Factory Ins. Association, 95 Pearl, h. 4 Willard.
Strauss Amos, cigarm. 867 Main, h.u. 35 Park.
" Augusta Mrs. h.2u. 27 Asylum.
" Ernest, laborer, h. 685 Windsor av.
" Fred. assemb. at 556 Cap. h. 2 Pleasant ct.
" Henry, laborer at 40 Gov. h.u. 349 Main.
" Herman, h.r. 349 Main.
" Nathan, clerk at 921 Main, h. 20 Squire.
Straw Henrietta, nurse, b. 97 Webster.
Street Commissioners office, City hall, 800 Main.
" Edwin R. musical novelties, 225 Sheldon, h. 28 Brook.
" Frederick F. sec'y Pratt & Cady Co. fire ins. agent, 118 Asylum, prop. Grove's Herb Extract, h. 270 Laurel.
" John E. tillerman, 275, h.u. 275 Pearl.
" Joseph, stairbuilder at 20 Potter, h. 43 Brook.
" Jos. Jr. cabinetm, 20 Potter, h.2u. 92 Grove.
Streeter A. T. electrician at 66 Pro. h. Holyoke.
" Augusta A. wid. Asa C. b. 91 Wooster.
" F. V. clerk at 155 Asylum, h. NewBritain t.
" Willis C. mach. P.&R. h.2u. 120 Mather.
Strehlan Chas. F. apprentice N.Y.R. b. 35 Laurel.
Strehlau George, jeweler at 5 Asy. b. 35 Laurel.
" Otto, brazier, h.u. 35 Laurel.
Strempfer John, boardingh. & saloon, 60 Front.

Strickland A. Elizabeth, wid. Stephen, h. 17 Annawan.
STRICKLAND ABEL (S. & Shea,) scroll sawyers, etc. h. 32 Russ.    See page 516.
" Allen M. carpenter at 155 Ch.O. h. E.H.t.
" Eugene, brickmaker, h.u. 19 Seyms.
" Frank C. salesman at 78, b. 78 Park.
" Fred H. conductor St.Ry. b. 8 Wooster.
" George E. policeman, h. 8 Grand.
" George H. motorm. St. Ry. b.2u. 36 Capen.
" Harry J. paperruler 141 Pearl, b. 8 Grand.
" Helen A. wid. Jacob A. b. 911 Asylum.
" Herbert W. clerk at Popes, b. Windsor t.
" Irvin E. bkkpr. at 9 Haynes, h.2u. 21 Seyms.
" Merton H. clerk at Hartford Daily Times,   716 Main, b. South Manchester v.

**STRICKLAND & SHEA,** scrollsawing, mantels, 20 Potter.   See page 516.
   Abel Strickland.   Charles W. Shea.
" Sidney E. h. 8 Wooster.
" Viola, wid. William, b. 43 Ann.
Striker Frank, saddler, 8 Sigourney, b. 401 Cap.
Strobel Caroline, wid. Bernard, b.u. 80 Kibbe.
" Harry, clerk 745 Main, b.u. 110 Hopkins.
" Howard, machinist at 20 Sargeant, b.u. 110 Hopkins.
" Lottie, clerk at 385 Main, b.u. 110 Hopkins.
" Mary Jane, wid. Joseph, h.u. 110 Hopkins.
" Seward P. clerk, 374 Asy. b.u. 110 Hopkins.
Stroh George, foreman at 98 Kil. h. 32 Asylum.
Strom Louis, stonemason, h. 28 Putnam.
Stromberg Chas. J. at 1 So. Ann, b. 123 Babcock.
" David, machinist at Popes, h. 123 Babcock.
Stronach George, carpenter at Jewell Belting Co. 15 Trumbull, h. 221 Capen.
" Mabel, stenogr. 252 Asylum, b. 221 Capen.
" Raymond E. asst. bookkeeper at City Bank of Hartford, 783 Main, b. 221 Capen.
STRONG CHARLES C. city treasurer, 800 Main, City hall, h. 853 Asylum.
" Charles H. grocer, 134 Mn. h. 187 Seymour.
" Charles O. mach. at 476 Cap. b. 232 Putnam.
" Charles R. teamster, h. 212 Capen.
" Daniel, tailor, h.u. 1173 Main.
" David E. boots & shoes,928 Mn. h. 103 Wash.
" Edwin, h. 79 Church.
" Edwin A. b. 79 Church.
" Ethel A. stenographer, b. Quaker lane.
" Frank C. coachman at 417 Windsor av. h. 27 Loomis.
" George, laborer, h. 213 Pearl.
" Geo. M. officer st. prison, h.2u. 2 Winthrop.
STRONG HARRY B. (Brown, Thomson & Co.) 920 942 Main, h. 361 Laurel.   See page 499.
" Henry L. telegraph editor Hartford Daily Times, 716 Main, h. 19 Vernon.
" Henry N. restaurant, 189, l.u. 284 Asylum.
" Henry S. mach. at 1 So. Ann, h.2u. 25 Elm.
" Herbert E. at National Fire Insurance Co. 95 Pearl, b. 218 Sargeant.
" Idella L. Mrs. dressm. 943, h. 943 Mn. rm.15.
**STRONG IRA J.** new and second-hand machinery, 267 Asylum, h. 42 Wooster.   See page 524.

**People who have Money to Spend, Read The Post.**

# J. W. STUECK, Jr.,

**HIGHEST GRADE**

## 🌾 BAKERY,

**German Tarts and Pastry to Order.**

### ICE CREAM PARLORS AND

### LIGHT LUNCH.

### 1036 MAIN ST., near Morgan St.

Old No. 466.          *Telephone, 128-3.*

Strong Jennie D. teacher Arsenal sch. b. 8 Avon.
" Joseph, trainer, h. Quaker lane.
" Julius L. Mrs. h. 266 Farmington.
" Louie P. b. 79 Church.
" Maria E. C. wid. Rev. Caleb, h. 94 Woodland.
" Rebecca, wid. Mathew, h. 336 Pearl.
" Wm. H. machinist at 1 So. Ann, b. 29 Morgan.
Stropel ☞ *see Strobel.*
Stroud Thompson C. veterinary surgeon, 356 Main, h.u. 39 John.
Strucks Louis, foreman, 8 Sig. h. 19 Babcock.
Strunk John T. brakem. N.E.R. b.u. 25 Hun. pl.
Struthers Graham, condtr. St. Ry. h.u. 86 Retreat.
" Jas. carpenter at Taft Co. h.u. 112 Mather.
Strycharski Albert, laborer, h. 6 Ellery.
Stuart Chas. T. photogr. 747 Mn. h. 201 Laurel.
" George W. artist, b. 201 Laurel.
" Joel C. engir. at 13 Central, b. 4 Winthrop.
" Willard H. mach. 13 Central, h. 4 Winthrop.
" Wm. prop. Centennial American Tea Co. 575 Main, h. 18 Lincoln.
" ☞ *see also Stewart.*
Stubbs M. R. b. 81 Sigourney.
Stubenranch Joseph, clerk at 118 Asylum, rm. 2,
Stubenrauch Frank, painter, b. 17 Morgan.
b.3u. 152 Allyn.
Studley Charles J. b. 83 Park.
" Theodore, inspector at Colts, h. 83 Park.
STUECK J. WILLIAM, Jr. bakery, 1036, b. 986 Main.          *See page 348.*
Stumm Ferdinand, baker, h.u. 1 Worcester pl.
Stumpf William E. screwmkr. 476 Cap. h. B.v.
Stupel Frank, salesman, h. 84 Windsor.
Sturgeon Joseph C. teamster, 128 Commerce, b. 14 Chapel.
Sturm I. shoemaker, 154, dry goods, 150, h. 154 Front.
" John C. mach. at 30 Cush. b. 13 Riverside.
" Louis, stonemason, h. 28 Putnam.
" Olaf, machinist at 30 Cush. h. 13 Riverside.
" Simon, shoemaker, 157 Maple, b. 154 Front.
Sturman August, cutter, 690 Park, b. 82 Francis.
Sturmdorf Leonice C. M. music'n b. 98 Sargeant.
Sturtevant Albert M. b. 105 Washington.
" Ernest W. trav. salesm. at Popes, h.u. 109 Oak.
" F. Raymond, student Trinity college, b. 105 Washington.
" Francis C. egg food, 216 State, h. 105 Wash.
" George P. foreman 216 State, b. 105 Wash.
" Harold E. mach. at 133 Shel. b. 24 Warner.

Sturtevant Robert B. machinist at 80 Huyshope, h. 24 Warner.
" Samuel F. trav. salesman, h. 20 Seyms.
Sturtzel Agnes L. seamstr. 937 Mn. b. 41 Canton.
" Mary C. wid. Frank P. b. 987 Main.
" Sarah, wid. H. P. laundress, h. 41 Canton.
Stuttaford John W. harnessmkr. 8, b.u. 43 Sig.

## STUTZ EUGENE, German massage and magnetic treatment, 9, h. 9 Asylum.

*See page 422.*

" Frederic J. pressman, h. Quaker lane.
St. ☞ *see Saint, beginning at letter "S," page 316.*
Suartfiguer Samuel, painter, 295 Sheldon. h. E.H.t.
Suchadolski John, grocer, 64 Shel. h. 27 Hamilton.
Suchawolsky Louie Rev. h.2u. 265 Market.
Sucker Frank, filer at 556 Capitol, h. 80 Talcott.
Suda Francis, Jr. clerk at T. Sisson & Co. 729 Main, b.2u. 33 Capitol.
Sudarsky Jos. peddler, baths, 77, h.u. 79 Morgan.
Sudder John, teamster, h.u. 12 Woodbine.
Suessbrick William F. bookkeeper at 78 Asylum, b. 106 Hungerford.
Sugden A. W. at National Fire Ins. Co. 95 Pearl, b. Rocky Hill t.
" Emily R. b. 20 Niles.
" Frank W. salesman at Charles R. Hart Co. 898, h. 427 Main, rm. 36.

SUGDEN WILLIAM E. treasurer Charles R. Hart Co. 898 Main, h. 58 Capitol.

*See page 179.*

Sugermeyer Dominick, mach. 1 Flow. b. 69 Laurel.
" Henry G. machine hand, h.u. 69 Laurel.
" Joseph, oiler at 70 Commerce, b. 34 Wdbg.
Sughrue Michael, mach. 388 Cap. b. 8 Whitmore.
Sugrue John, joiner, b. 26 Village.
" John F. b. 44 Avon.
" Kate H. clerk, b. 44 Avon.
" Mary, laundress at 34 Pratt, b. 23 Wolcott.
" Mary J. clerk at Brown, Thomson & Co. 942 Main, b. 44 Avon.
" Michael, blacksm. and h. Bloomfield c. Alb.
" Patrick, carpenter, h. 44 Avon.
" Patrick, clerk, b. 44 Avon.
" Timothy A. plumber, b. 44 Avon.
" ☞ *see also Sughrue; Shuckerow; Shugrue.*
Suhanek James D. wid. Joseph, h.u. 4 Barnard.
Suisman Max, tobacco, 206, h. 206 Front.
" Samuel N. clerk at 206, b. 206 Front.
Suldo Antonio, laborer, b.u. 88 Front.
Sullivan Andrew F. h.2u. 232 New Park.
" Anna, h. 4 Cedar.
" Annie, clerk, b. 219 Bellevue.
" Annie M. clerk at Brown, Thomson & Co. 942 Main, b. 52 Green.
" Barry, plumber at 237 Asy. h. Franklin.
" Bartholomew J. h. 94 Park.
" Bridget, domestic at 36 Jefferson.
" Bridget, wid. Daniel J. h.2u. 81 Chestnut.
" Bridget, wid. Timothy, grocer, 78, h. 78 Avon.
" Catherine, seamstress, h. 20 Spring.
" Catherine, wid. Jeremiah, h. 117 Mather.
" Christopher, laborer, h. 118 Windsor.
" Cornelius, deckh. str. Middletown, 285 State.
" Cornelius, engir. N.Y.R. h.u. 30 Albany.

**If You Want all the News, Read THE POST.**

Sullivan Cornelius B. manufacturer of bakers' peels, 60 Loomis.
" Cornelius J. clerk at 98 Kil. b. 50 Liberty.
" Cornelius J. machinist at 581 Capitol, h.u. 5 Hawthorn.
" Daniel, b. 56 Front.
" Daniel, inspector, h.u.r. 74 Sheldon.
" Daniel, laborer, b. 101 Sheldon.
" Daniel, laborer, b. 199 Windsor.
" Daniel, mason, b. 80 State.
" Daniel, molder at 556 Cap. b. 23 Hawthorn.
" Daniel, teamster at 153, b. 153 Zion.
" Daniel, teamster at 373, h. 354 Broad.
" Daniel D.enam.at 581Cap.b.2u.107 Windsor.
" Daniel D. machinist at Popes, h. Lifkey.
" Daniel F. corem.556 Cap.b.2u.120 Windsor.
" Daniel F. physician, 64, h. 64 Church.
" Daniel F.plumber at 228 Pearl,b.23 Babcock.
" Daniel J. clerk, 365 Allyn, l. 20¼ Goodwin.
" Daniel J. inspector at 581 Cap. h. E.H.t.
" Daniel J. mach. at 30 Cush. b. 28 Cedar.
" Daniel J. steward at Allyn house, 152 Asy.
" Daniel Jr. machinist, b.2u. 107 Windsor.
" Daniel R. rubberw. 690 Park, h. 81 Heath.
" Daniel S. mason, h.r. 23 Spruce.
" Daniel T. rubberworker, h.u. 107 Windsor.
" David, engineer at South sch. h.u. 20 Park.
" Dennis, laborer, h.2u. 96 Windsor.
" Dennis, mason, b. 11 Bellevue.
" Dennis, plumber, h. 23 Babcock.
" Dennis, polisher at Popes, h.u. 41 Chestnut.
" Dennis F. forem. at N.Y.R. h.2u.126 Albany.
" Dennis J. hoseman chemical engine company, b.3u. 96 Windsor.
" Dennis J.pressman 252 Pl. h.u. 39 Congress.
" Dennis J. carman, h. 354 Broad.
" Dennis M. gardener at 13 Prospect, h. 4 Squire.
" Dennis W. screwm. at 70 Huy. h.2u. 8 Union.
" Edward F. clerk at 581 Cap. b. 39 Congress.
" Ellen Mrs. boardinghouse, 14 Huntley pl.
" Eugene J., U. S. Army, b.u. 566 Main.
" Florence, laborer, h.u. 34 Flower.
" Francis A. mach. at 1 Flow. b. 1424 Broad.
" Humphrey, laborer, h.u. 34 Avon.
" Ignatius A. salesm. 141 Asy. h.u. 126 Capen.
" J. deckhand, steamer Hartford, 285 State.
" James, apprentice at 5 Mechanic, b. E.H t.
" James, buffer at 62 Market. h.u.163 Barbour.
" James, fireman, h. 117 Mather.
" James, mason, h.2u. 1424 Broad.
" James, mason, l.u. 1209 Main.
" James F. brazier, b. 49 Lawrence.
" James H. mach. at Colts, b. 70 Francis.
" James J. cigarm. at 104 Asy. b. 57 Windsor.
" James J. hodcarrier, h. 67 Avon.
" James J. mach. at 47.6 Cap. b. 23 Babcock.
" James J. packer, h. 76 Avon.
" Jeremiah, clerk at 45, b. 45 Lafayette.
" Jeremiah, conduc. at N.Y.R. b.u.117 Mather.
" Jeremiah, laborer, b. 101 Sheldon.
" Jeremiah, teamster, 470, h. 470 Broad.
" Jeremiah J. clerk at 372 Asy. b. 39 Congress.
" Jeremiah J. painter, h.2u. 88 Ward.
" Jerry, helper at 54 Arch, b. 2¼ Belden.

Sullivan Johanna, h.u. 122 Windsor.
" Johanna, wid. Patrick, tailoress at 2 State, h. 61 Front.
" John, b. 57 Windsor.
" John, boardinghouse, 4 Huntley pl.
" John, carpenter, b. 16 Market.
" John, coachman at 321, h. 321 Windsor av.
" John, gardener at and b. Prospect av.
" John, helper, b. 250 Front.
" John, laborer at 98 Kilbourn, b. 60 Pleasant.
" John, laborer, h.u. 12 Ellery.
" John, laborer, h. 199 Windsor.
" John, laborer, h.2u. 65 Avon.
" John, laborer, h.u. 120 Portland.
" John, laborer, h.2u. 96 Windsor.
" John, laborer, h. 81 Pleasant.
" John, laborer, h.2u. 74 Sheldon.
" John, plasterer, h.u. 32 Wooster.
" John C. clerk at 230 Park, b. 4 Squire.
" John F. policeman, h. 25 Pavilion.
" John J. bookkeeper, 818 Park, b. 81 Heath.
" John J. chipper at 556 Capitol, b. 23 Haw.
" John J. laborer at 98 Kil. b. 35 Avon.
" John J. mach. 1 Flower, b. 1424 Broad.
" John J. plumber, h.2u. 121 Maple.
" John J. pressman, b. 57 Windsor.
" John J. salesman at 126 Church.
" John K. carpenter, h. 18½ Grace.
" John L. laborer at N.Y.R. b. 120 Portland.
" John M. laborer, h. 81 Heath.
" John P. laborer at 8 Front.
" Joseph F. packer, b. 22 Franklin.
" Joseph P. helper at 54 Arch, h.u.r. 27 John.
" Julia, wid. Benjamin, h.u. 18 Kennedy.
" Julia, wid. Daniel, h.u. 7 Kilbourn.
" Julia, wid. James, h.u. 1427 Broad.
" Julia A. Mrs. boardinghouse, 88 Sheldon.
" Julia B. bkkpr. at 201 State, b. 1337 Broad.
" Katherine, clerk at 61 Albany, b. 70 Francis.
" Kittie T. cashier at Brown, Thomson & Co. 942 Main, b. 49 Walnut.
" Margaret, wid. Michael R. h.u. 566 Main.
" Margaret Mrs. h.u. 15 Putnam.
" Margaret D. clerk at Brown, Thomas & Co. 942 Main, b. 49 Walnut.
" Mary, h. 62 Green.
" Mary, b.u. 7 Kilbourn.
" Mary, wid. Charles, b. 139 Zion.
" Mary, wid. Michael, h.3u. 84 Albany.
" Mary, wid. Michael, h.2u. 120 Windsor.
" Mary, wid. Michael, h.3u.r. 12 So. Prospect.
" Mary, wid. Patrick, b. 70 Francis.
" Matthew N. molder at 1 Flower, h. 267 Park.
" Maurice, repairer at Popes, h. 23 Babcock.
" Michael, b. 14 Huntley pl.
" Michael, helper, 26, b. 26 State.
" Michael, lab. at P.&R. b.u. 120 Albany.
" Michael, laborer, b. 102 Windsor.
" Michael, laborer, h.r. 11 Bellevue.
" Michael, laborer, h.2u. 122 Windsor.
" Michael, laborer, h. 114 Windsor.
" Michael, laborer, h. 105 Windsor.
" Michael, laborer, b. 49 Walnut.
" Michael, lab. Pope Tube Co. h. 1172 Main.
" Mich. mason contractor, 373, h.u. 373 Broad.

Sullivan Michael, laborer, b.2u. 101 Sheldon.
" Michael E. carpenter, b. 18½ Grace.
" Michael J. polisher at 556 Capitol b.u. 84 Flower.
" Michael J. bartend. 931 Main,b. 3 Orchard.
" Michael J. pressman at Popes,h. 19 Howard.
" Michael R. painter, b. 21 Sargeant.
" Morris P. electrician, 556 Cap. b. 22 Village.
" Mortimer, teamster, 157, h.2u. 157 Zion.
" Nora, h. 23 West.
" Patrick, fireman at 70 Com. h. 40 Windsor.
" Patrick, hackdriver, h.3u. 55 Spruce.
" Patrick, laborer, b. 1172 Main.
" Patrick, laborer, 40 Gov. b.2u. 88 Sheldon.
" Patrick, laborer, b.u. 106 Windsor.
" Patrick, laborer, h.u.r. 38 Temple.
" Patrick, laborer, h.u. 42 Pleasant.
" Patrick, laborer, h.u. 143 Commerce.
" Patrick. motorman, St.Ry. h.2u. 17 Wells.
" Patrick, section forem. N.Y.R. h.u. 85 Avon.
" Patrick E. brakeman N.Y.R.h.2u. 8 Winter.
" Patrick J. butcher, 138 Front, h. 210 Fkn.
" Patrick J. laborer at 40 Gov. b. 265 Main.
" Peter A. policeman, h. 56 Dean.
" Richard P. driver at 54 Huntley, h. 10 Huntley pl.
" Robert, boilerm. 109 Com. h. 39 Kinsley.
" Sylvester, laborer, h.u. 25 Canton.
" Thomas, at Popes, b. 81 Heath.
" Thomas, b.u. 5 Hawthorn.
" Thos. J. mach. at 1 Flower, b. 5 Hawthorn.
" Timothy, coachman, 834, h. 834 Asylum.
" Timothy, helper, b. 35 North.
" Timothy, laborer, b. 190 Ward.
" Timothy, laborer, b. 85 Governor.
" Timothy, laborer, b.r. 14 Arch.
" Timothy, saloon, 18, h.u. 16 Market.
" Timothy F. clerk, 690 Park, b2u.23 Williams.
" Timothy J. (Gerety & S.) h. 226 Zion.
" Timothy J. mason, h. 113 Maple.
" William, helper at N.Y.R. b. 59 Spuce.
SULLIVAN WM. A. councilman 2d ward, buffer at Wm. Rogers Mfg.Co.h.2u.120 Windsor.
" William F. butcher at 1065, b.u. 566 Main.
" Wm.J.supernumary police,b.3u. 84 Albany.
" William J. salesman for E. E. Hurlbut, Valley st. h. 86 Williams.
" William J. pressh. at 581 Cap.b. 23 Babcock.
" ☞ see also O'Sullivan.
Sulze Isaac, driver at 14 Morgan.
Summer Frances A. clerk at Brown, Thomson & Co. 942 Main, b. 136 Trumbull.
" Minnie E. clerk at 956, b. 1222 Main.
Summerhill John M. shipping clerk, 690 Park, h. 1155 Main.
Summerman ☞ see Sommerman.
Sumner Charles F. Jr. clerk State Treasurer, office State Capitol, room 1, h. Bolton t.
" E. F. wid. William H. h. 12 Alden.
SUMNER FRANK C. sec'y and treas. Hartford Trust Co. 764 Main, health commissioner, h. 609 Farmington      See page 437.
" Geo. A. draughtsman at 926 Main, room 77, b. 133 Washington.

Sumner George G. attorney, 739 Main, b. 583 Farmington.
" Henry M. inspector at 709 Mn.h.60 Tremont.
" Juliette C. wid. William, h. 11 Myrtle.
" Sarah E. wid. George A. b. 133 Washington.
**SUNDAY JOURNAL,**  See page 466.
Sunderland Hannah, wid. Samuel, b. 107 Weth.
" Peter, clerk at 371 Asylum, h. 141 Mather.
Sundstrom Fred, mach. at Popes. b.u. 46 Grand.
Sunny Side house, T. E. Templeton, 80 Church.
Superior Court Room, 91 Trumbull.
Surabian Kayajan, screwmaker at 476 Capitol, b. 252 Lawrence.
Surmaliam Kahajan, laborer at 116, b. 125 Ch.O.
Surine W. machinist at 13 Central.
Surridge Frederick J. engineer. h.u. 180 Capen.
" John, laborer at 1 Flower, h. 1424 Broad.
Sutcliffe Jos. finisher, 69 Front, h. 13 Francis.
" Joseph, painter at 1106 Main, b. 1 John.
" Matthew H. machine hand at 40 Governor, h.u. 60 Seymour.
Suthergill ☞ see also Southergill.
Sutherland Alexander G. clerk at Brown, Thomson & Co. 942 Main, h. 86 Hopkins.
" F. W. conductor St.Ry. h. 183 Market.
" Heath, patent attorney at F. H. Richards, 803 Main, h. 26 Hopkins.
" J. A. Jr. draughtsm.at 388 Cap.b.26 Hopkins.
" J. H. publisher, h. 177 Asylum.
" John M. foreman at Popes, h. 209 Jefferson.
" Margaret Mrs. dressmaker, h. 22 Elm.
" Robert T. screwmaker at Popes, b. 22 Elm.
Sutter Jacob (Heimgartner & S.) h. 39 Mulberry.
" W. A. cigarmaker at 867 Main.
Svanson Augusta, assistant, 171 Putnam.
Svenson August, carpenter at 158 Woodland.
" Carl F. cabinetm. 20 Potter, h.u. 67 Gov.
**SVENSON CHARLES,** general contractor, 54, h. 54 Woodbine. See p. 482.
" Charles, mach. 30 Cushman, b. 175 Russ.
" Lorentz, gardener, b.u. 74 Flower.
" Neils P. farmer, 958, b. 958 Windsor av.
Swain Daisy M. stenog. 30 Cush. b. 106 Wooster.
" George, laborer, h. 106 Wooster.
" John W. printer, b. 95 Chestnut.
" William M. parcel delivery, h. Capen c. Vine.
Swallow Joseph, driver, h. 4 Rice.
Swan Arthur R. clerk, 197, h. 81 Asylum, rm. 6.
" Charlotte E. stenog.739 Mn.l.223 Asy.rm.21.
" Edward C. clerk at Pope Tube Co.b. 48 Park.
" Emma D. stenog. 868 Main, b. 141 Capen.
" Harriet C. wid. Egbert P. b. 223 Asy. rm. 21.
" Isaac S. printer at Hartford Daily Times,716 Main, h. 141 Capen.
" Theron C. clerk, adjutant general office, room 19 in State Capitol, h. 52 Russ.
" William H. collector, b. 81 Asylum.
Swansen John, cutter, 15 Tru.b. 153 Lawrence.
Swanson Adolph, carpenter, b.u. 28 Woodbridge.
" Albert, screwm. at Popes, h.u. 188 Putnam.
" Albert, screwm. 476 Capitol, h. 2 Harbison.
" Andrew M. operator at 40 Gov. h.36 Putnam.
" Anshelm, carpenter, h.u. 273 Jefferson.
" John, clerk at 1248 Main, b. 25 Vine.

Swanson John, farmer, 958, h. 958 Windsor av.
" Malcolm, gardener, at & b. 856 Prospect av.
" Nils, carpenter, h.u. 28 Woodbridge.
" Oscar, joiner, b. 28 Woodbridge.
" Solomon, at 690 Park, b. 553 Broad.
" Swan, filer at 581 Capitol, b. 54 Flower.
" ☞ see also Svenson.
Swartenberger Joseph, peddler, h. 30 Pleasant.
Swartfiguer Herbert M. watchmaker, 81 Pratt, h. 117 Hungerford.
Swartz ☞ see Schwartz.
Swathel William Henry, miller at Lincoln, Seyms & Co. 34 Market, h.u. 3 Avon.
Sweeney Annie J. clerk at Brown, Thomson & Co. 942 Main, b. 120 Albany.
" C. A. Mrs. nurse, h.2u. 1350 Broad.
" Della Mrs. nurse, b. 20 Marshall.
" Edward, coachman at 188, b. 138 Weth.
" Edward, laborer, b. 111 Maple.
" Edward J. machinist, b.u 53 Liberty.
" Eugene, firem. at 476 Capitol, h. 103 Heath.
" Eugene, laborer, h. 2½ Commerce.
" Frank C. engineer, N.Y.R. b. 1350 Broad.
" Henry W. buyer at Brown, Thomson & Co. 942 Main, h. 8 Winthrop.
" John, b. 102 Hungerford.
" John, bartender, b. 204 Asylum.
" John, electrician at 1 Laurel, b. 13 Russell.
" John F. molder at 1 Flow. h. 85 Hungerford.
" Lillian J. b.2u. 1350 Broad.
" Maggie A. clerk, b. 85 Hungerford.
" Mary, h.u. 48 Wadsworth.
" Michael F. helper, b.u. 28 Commerce.
" Michael J. h.u. 96 State.
" Thomas A. (Hopper & S.) h. 7 Kennedy.
" William, laborer, h.u. 49 Front.
" William E. mgr. at 745 Main, b. 8 Brownell.
Sweet C. H. Mrs. h.u. 89 Main.
" Caroline C. teacher at 690, b. 690 Asylum.
" Charles F. oils and greases, 174 Pearl, h. 637 Farmington.
" Edward W. buffer at Wm. Rogers Mfg Co. 66 Market, b. 57 Bellevue.
" Elizabeth, wid. William, h.u. 4 Oak.
" George B. b. 39 Buckingham.
" Henry T. bonesetter, 1205 Mn. h. 22 Bluehills.
" James H. engineer, b. 194 High.
" Lester H. at Travelers Insurance Co. 56 Prospect, h. 58 Buckingham.
" Louisa A. Mrs. music teacher, h. 58 Bkm.
" S. A. Mrs. clairvoyant, h. 373 Main.
" William B. mach. at 1 Flow, h.u.102 Seymour.
Sweetser Edward E. h. 29 Washington.
Swell Thomas, laborer at 8 Front, b. 99 Arch.
Swendsen Sol. molder, 690 Park, b. 533 Broad.
Swenson August, at 618 Capitol, b.u. 46 Grand.
" Charles, carpenter. b.2u 177 Lawrence.
**SWENSON CHARLES K.** florist, 210 Asylum, h. Elmwood v. See page 565.
" John, at Jewell Belting Co. 15 Trumbull, b. 153 Lawrence.
" Louis G. carpenter at N.Y.R. h. 2 Queen.
" Magnus, at 40 Governor, b. 36 Putnam.
Swers Edmund, butler at 722, b. 722 Asylum.

Swett Ralph K. salesman at Popes, b. Winchester, Mass.
Swettenham Edwin A. forem. Popes, h. 603 Garden.
Swickler Andrew, laborer, h.u. 2 Ellery.
Swift Charles F. orderly at 20 So. Hudson.
" Ernest H. (M.H.S.& Sons,) b. 100 Love lane.
" Evelyn, h. 30 Gillett.
" Frank T. carpenter, h. 531 Garden.
" Helen T. wid. Orlando, h. 30 Gillett.
" Joseph A. clerk at 556 Cap. h.u. 151 Law.
" M. H. & Sons, goldbtrs. etc. 100 Love lane.
    Matthew Swift.   M. Henry Swift.
        Ernest H. Swift.
" Matthew, (M.H.S.& Sons,) h.100 Love lane.
" Matthew Henry, (M. H. S. & Sons,) b. 100 Love lane.
" Raymond, rubberw. at 690 Park, b. 4 Avon.
" Rosa C. cutter at 100, b. 100 Love lane.
" Rowland, president American National Bank, 803 Main, h. 1 Wethersfield.
" Tallmadge, h. 30 Gillett.
Swin John W. pressman at Evening Post, 23 Asylum, b. 115 Trumbull.
" William E. pressman at Evening Post, 23 Asylum, h.2u. 22 Hopkins.
Swindell Walter S. electrician at 266 Pearl, h.2u. 44 Church.
Swing Annie, at 254 Pearl, b. 74 Madison.
**SWORDS JOS. F.** treas. New England Coal Co. 722, h. 427 Main.
                *See page 273.*
" Lewis H. b.u. 136 Seymour.
Sydenham Frederick, clerk, b.u. 279 Asylum.
" Thomas G. carpenter, b.u. 279 Asylum.
" Walter L. h.2u. 39 South Prospect.
" William E. barber at 80 State, b.u.279 Asylum.
Sykes Edward S. druggist, secretary Comfort Powder Co. h. 158 High.
" Francis A. h. 18 Belden.
" Nathan P. clerk at 547 Main, h. 67 Russ.
" V. Alfred, baker at 543, l.u. 650 Mn. rm.44.
Sylvester James, mason, h. 180 Front.
Symonds Charles, at Ætna Life Ins. Co. 650 Main, b. 48 Church.
" ☞ see also Simons; Simmons; Simonds.
Syndicate Premium Co., I. S. Covell, 78 Pearl.
Synott John Rev. pres. & sec. St. Thomas Seminary, h. 352 Collins.
" William, mach. at 1 Flow. b. 58 Jefferson.
Syo Charles, at 476 Capitol, b.2u. 109 Lawrence.

**A Good Investment-Your Advertisement in The Post.**

**TABOR MALLERY,** carpenter, r. 281
   Allyn, h. Higganum v.   *See page* 513.
" Mallery W., U. S. Army, b. 284 Asylum.
Tadusch Keshinski, packer, 618 Cap. b. 42 State.
Taft Albert J. bkkpr. at 29 Albany, h. E.H.t.
" Charles E. physician, 98, b. 98 High.
" Co. The, woodworkers. Lumber st. r. 15 Alb.
" E. H. butcher, b. 181½ Lawrence.
" Edwin R. photog. at 11 Pratt, h. 1 East.
" Ellen C. wid. Cincinnatus A. h. 97 Elm.
" Fred A. traveling agent, h. 59 Sigourney.
" Joel C. coal dealer, 29 Albany, h. E. H.t.
" Laura W. h. 97 Elm.
" Wm. E. weigher, 240 Garden, b. E.H.t.
" ☞ *see also Tifft; Tefft.*
Tagerty John, carptr. N.Y.R. h.3u.r. 12 S.Pro.
Taidell John, laborer, h.r. 1048 Broad.
Taillefair Edward, laborer, b. 52 Russell.
" Leon, carpenter, h. 52 Russell.
Taintor Alice, h. 28 Garden.
" George E. real estate agent, rep. J. J. & F.
   Goodwin, 223 Asy. rm. 6, h. 129 Wash.
" Henry E. vice president Security Co. at-
   torney, 847 Mn. rm. 23, h. 112 Woodland.
" James S. student at Yale, b. 862 Asylum.
" James U. secretary Orient Insurance Co. 5
   Haynes, h. 862 Asylum.
" Wm. W. sec'y Hartford and Spring Brook
   Ice Co. 4 Central, h. 18 Vernon.
Taksar Alexander, at 8 Sig. h. 171 New Park.
" Thomas, at stonepits, h.u. 171 New Park.
Talcott Caleb M. h. 280 Main.
" Carrie C. wid. Frank H. h. 43 Sumner.
" Charles H. (*T. Frisbie & Co.*) h. 863 Asylum.
" Edward C. trav. salesman, Jewell Belting Co.
   15 Trumbull, b. 863 Asylum.
" Frisbie & Co. wholesale drugs. 273 Asylum.
   Edward C. Frisbie.   Charles H. Talcott.
" George J. conductor St.Ry. 115 State.
" H. Louisa, b. 280 Main.
" Harry E. laborer at 95 Ple. h.u. 44 Village.
" Hart, *selectman* ; at Travelers Insurance Co.
   56 Prospect, h. 139 Bellevue.
" Mary K. b. 815 Asylum.
" Morton C. draughtsman at Pope Tube Co.
   h. 139 Bellevue.
" Seth Mrs. (Sarah A.) h. 863 Asylum.
" W. L. Mrs. dressmaker, b. 1059 Main.

**TALCOTT WM. H.** bookbinder, 856
   Main, h. 52 Sumner.   *See page* 478.
" Wm. Hart, bkkpr. 197 Asy. h.u. 24 Seyms.
Talemadge Clayton J. carpenter, b. 428 Asylum.
Tallman Alice P. b. 25 Niles.
" Grace, b. 25 Niles.
TALLMAN JAMES H. (*G. W. Moore & Co.*) farm
   loans, 759 Main, h. 25 Niles. *See page* 429.
Talmadge Bert W. helper, 142 Russ, b. 12 Bkm.
" Elliott F. theological student, 1507 Broad,
   h. 3 Webster.
" Mae H. bkkpr. at 103 Asy. b. 65 Hungerford.
Tangney Daniel, helper at 54 Arch, h. 50 Hicks.
" Patrick, laborer, b. 50 Hicks.
Tannebaum Israel M. barber at 178 State.
Tansey May B. stenographer at Potter & Payne,
   405 Allyn, b. 1328 Broad.

Tansey Roger, h. 1328 Broad.
" Roger, Jr. clerk at 921 Main, b. Windsor t.
" William, at Schroeders, b. 1328 Broad.
Tansley Geo. H. foreman at Colts, h. 54 Madison.
" M. A. dressmaker, 75 Pratt, suite 16.
Tappert Otto F. mach. at 1 Flow. b. 62 Babcock.
Tapley Grace, clerk at 956 Main, b. 27 Spring.
Tarbell Edward N. correspondent at Popes, h.
   221 Franklin.
" Horace D. h. 96 Washington.
Tarbox Charles, polisher at Colts, h.2u. 4 Union.
" Chas. H. (*Burch & T.*) h.u. 263 Jefferson.
" George E. clerk, b.2u. 4 Union.
" Henry E. polisher at Colts, h.u. 47 Wdbg.
" William F. assembler 581 Cap. b.2u.4 Union.
Tarpy Edward M. bartdr. 17 Central, h.u. 27 Beach.
Tasey Louis, driver at Hartford Lumber Co.
   r. 17 Albany, b.u. 20 Trumbull.
Tashjian George, screwm. at 476, l. 381 Capitol.
" Harry, screwmaker at 476, l. 381 Capitol.
Tate M. Elizabeth, teacher Wadsworth street
   school, b. Windsor Locks t.
Tatem Frank, pattermaker at r. 64 Asylum, b.u.
   10 Bellevue.
" Joseph, turnkey, 42 Seyms, h.u. 10 Bellevue.
Tatro Alexander, motorman St.Ry. b. 72 Grove.
" Charles T. machinist, b. 15 Windsor.
" George, stairbuilder, b. 1223 Main.
" Mary E. b. 36 Jefferson.
" Sarah, wid. Peter, h. 15 Windsor.
Tattam Emma, at 254 Pearl, h. 457 Windsor av.
" Louisa, wid. Geo. nurse, b.u. 457 Windsor av.
Taub Johanna, groceries, 52, h. 52 Pleasant.
Taussig Chas. constable, 2 State, h. 10 Winthrop.
" Harry, clerk at 862 Main, b. 10 Winthrop.
" Jennie H. b. 10 Winthrop.
" Sophie, asst.bkkpr. 908 Mn. b. 10 Winthrop.
Taylor Adelia, b. 36 Jefferson.
" Alexander, painter at 1152 Mn.h.r.36 Chapel.
" Alice, h.u. 1236 Main.
" Alice M. h. 97 Washington.
" Allen W. teamster, h. 116 Mather.
" Ann, wid. Michael, h.2u. 28 Flower.
" Antoinette A. wid. F. A. h. 244 High.
" Austin B. machinist at 9 Sig. b. 21 Imlay.
" B. H. (*Taylor Bros.*) h. 3 Huntley.
" Bertha, b. 13 Capitol.
" C. waiter, steamer Middletown, 285 State.
" Charles C. carptr. 1 Flow. h.u. 1470 Broad.
" Charles E. poolroom, 6 Ford, b.156 Mather.
" Charles F. mfr. at Burnside, h. 772 Asylum.
" Charles L. engineer at 54 Arch, b. 41 Weth.
" Charlotte, wid. John, b. 187 Wethersfield.
" Charlotte, wid. O. S. h. 13 Capitol.
" Cornelia S. canvasser, h.u. 12 Alden.
" Daniel, porter at 25, b. 25 Central.

**TAYLOR E. & SONS,** steam planing
   mill, 335 Sheldon.   *See page* 510.
   Samuel Taylor.   Edwin F. Taylor.
" Edward, bookkeeper at 128 Commerce, h.
   Warehouse Point v.
" Edward H. mach. at 20 Vredendale, h.B.t.
" Edward P. machinist at Popes, b. 100 Sey.
" Edwin P. (*E. T. & Sons*) h. 41 Wethersfield.
" Edwin P. Jr. student at Trinity, b. 41 Weth.

# GEORGE M. TAYLOR,
# Carpenter and Builder
### AND BREEDER OF
### White Plymouth Rocks and S. C. White Leghorns,
### 1274 MAIN STREET,

Old No. 652.   Residence, Station 18, Windsor, Conn.

Taylor Elizabeth R. b.u. 12 Alden.
" Emerson G. student at Yale, b. 64 Garden.
" Fannie, h.u. 1236 Main.
" Frank, cook, h.u. 113 Front.
" Frank H. bricklayer, h.2u. 57 Village.
" Frank S. bkkpr. at Colts, h. 66 Webster.
" Frank T. carpenter, l. 118 Asylum.
" Franklin H. teacher at High school, h. 86 Allen pl.
" Fred H. cook, h.r. 37 Front.
TAYLOR FREDERICK D. secretary Sigourney Tool Co. 9 Sig. h. 29 Niles.    See p. 537.
" Frederick E. mach. at 9 Sig. h. 30 Putnam.
" Fred. M. machinist at Colts, h. 206 Jefferson.
" Fred M. pressman at 15 Tru. b. 64 Russ.
" Fred. N. optician, 162 Asy. h. Windsor t.
" Fred R. blacksmith N.Y.R. h. 5 Temple.
" George, enameler at Popes, b. 69 Governor.
" George, lather at 24 Mec. b. 116 Mather.
" George B. elevator 921, b.903 Main, rm. 8.
" George F. b.2u. 28 Flower.
TAYLOR GEORGE M. carpenter and builder, 1274 Main, h. Station 18, Windsor t.
" George W. driver, h. 2 Center.
" George W. insp. at 555 Cap. b. Bloomfield t.
" Georgia A. wid. George B. h. 48 Cedar.
" Gertrude R. wid. Howard, b. 11 FootGuard.
" Henry S. enameler Popes, h.u. 72 Governor.
" Hettie, peddler, h.3u. 78 Morgan.
" Howard J. machinist at 9 Sig. b. 21 Imlay.
" Hurlburt R. night clk. P.O. b. 903 Main, rm.8.
" Hyman, tailor, h.3u. 190 Front.
" Irving, mach. at 1 Flower, b.u. 4 Winthrop.
" J. E. Mrs. h. 82 Sargeant.
" James, driver, h.2u. 90 Walnut.
" James A. mach. at 13 Central, h.u. 277 Main.
" James G. mach. at Colts, h.u. 32 Madison.
" James H. printer, b. 90 Hudson.
TAYLOR JAMES P. pres't Charter Oak National Bank, 124 Asylum, h. 84 Garden.
                                    See page 432.
" Jas. S. porter Adams Ex. Co. b.u. 40 Cedar.
" Jennie H. b. 100 Seymour.
" John A. engineer N.Y.R. h.u. 30 Babcock.
" John C. (Stoughton & T.) secretary Conn. Prison Ass'n, room 45 in State Capitol, h. 137 Kenyon.
" John E. carpenter, 347, h. 347 Weth.
" John E. contractor at 476 Cap. h. 41 Putnam.
" John E. toolmaker at 476 Capitol.

# Mrs. Nellie L. Taylor,
### PROFESSIONAL MASSAGE
### —AND—
### ELECTRO THERAPEUTICS,
Middle Bell.   *24 Hopkins St.*

Taylor John E. Jr. bookkeeper, b. 347 Weth.
" John H. packer at James L. Howard & Co. 438 Asylum, h. 17 Congress.
" John M. vice president Conn. Mutual Life Insurance Co. 783 Main, h. 64 Garden.
" John O. porter at 875 Main, h. 4 Martin.
" John S. cigarm. at 867 Main, h. 64 Spring.
" John S. engir. at Pope Tube Co. h. 56 Hung.
" John S. jobber, h. 156 Mather.
" Joseph, mach. at 581 Cap. b.2u. 28 Flower.
" Levi C. dentist, 68 Pratt, h. 107 Edwards.
" Lillian M. clerk at 875 Main, b. 64 Spring.
" Martha L. wid. Francis, h. 21 Imlay.
" Mary F. wid Stephen, h. 98 Jefferson.
" May F. bookkeeper at Sigourney Tool Co. 9 Sigourney, b. 21 Imlay.
TAYLOR NELLIE L. Mrs. prof. massage, 24, b.u. 24 Hopkins.    See page 353.
" Oscar, carpenter at 252 Pearl, h. B.v.
TAYLOR PETER, councilman 8th ward, builder, h. Bartholomew.
" Philip, tailor at 20 Church, h.2u. 138 Grove.
" Ralph B. painter, b. 3 Pleasant.
" Samuel, (E.T. & Sons) h. 30 Charter Oak pl.
" Samuel, bookbinder, b. 51 Ashley.
" Samuel, carpenter, h. 54 Wadsworth.
" Samuel W. h.u. 59 Hawthorn.
" Solon, janitor at 82 Asylum, h. 14 Martin.
" Stephen, filer at Popes, h. 106 Seymour.
" Theo. D. machinist at 1 Flow. b. 1194 Main.
" Thomas, b. 2 Holcomb.
" Thomas B. janitor, 835, h.u. 903 Mn. rm. 8.
" Thomas F. bricklayer, b. 116 Mather.
" Thomas J. mach. at 1 Flower, b. 50 Cedar.
" Thomas S. b.2u. 28 Flower.
" Thomas W. painter, h. 77 Heath.
" Warren S. broker, h. 55 Walnut.
" William, clerk, b. Whiting lane.
" William, driver, 399 Allen, b. 24 Chestnut.
" William F. clerk at Wm. Rogers Mfg. Co, 66 Market, b. 172 Barbour.
" William H. b. 156 Mather.
" William H. helper at 164, h.r. 173 State.
" Wm. J. mach. at 20 Vredendale, b. M.t.
" William O. teller at State Bank, 795 Main. b. 13 Capitol.
Tebai John, at Pope Tube Co. h. 35 Francis.
Tefft Fred'k H. trimmer at 266 Pearl, h.r. 92 N.B.
" Frederick M. clk. at 389 Allyn, b. 26 Atwood.
" M. Josephine, b. 26 Atwood.
" Sarah L. wid. Daniel R. h. 26 Atwood.
" Stephen A. at Phœnix Ins. Co. 64, b. 2u. 71 Pearl.
" Virginia A. wid. Stephen A. b.2u. 71 Pearl.
" Waldo D. motorman at St. Ry. h. 38½ N.B.

### Want Advertisements Bring Results in THE POST.

Tefft Walter R. collector 48 Ann, b. 26 Atwood.
" William L. at National Fire Ins. Co. 95 Pearl, b. 26 Atwood.
" ☞ see also Tifft; Taft.
Tegarty John, painter, h.4u.r. 12 So. Prospect.
Teisler H. A. (T. & Co.) h. 54 Pleasant.
" H. A. & Co. dry goods, 54 Pleasant.
  H. A. Teisler.  David Bretman.

**TELEGRAM,** 12 Central. *See page 464.*

Telle Chas. A. trav. salesm. 42 High,b.u.200 Allyn.
Telleen Oscar, laborer, b.u. 80 Front.
Tembroeck Cora J. clerk at Brown, Thomson & Co. 942 Main, b. 58 Church. •
Temperance Reading Rooms, 102 Sheldon.
Temple James,helper at 556 Cap.h.u. 24 Putnam.
" Joseph, chipper at 556 Cap. b. 20 Putnam.
" Keron T. laborer stonepits, h. 34 Wilson.
Templeman Lucius E. machinist, b. 80 Church.
" Thomas E., Sunny Side House, 80 Church.
Templeton Isabella, clerk 865 Main, b.58 Church.
" William D. beltmaker at Jewell Belting Co. 15 Trumbull, h. 66 Hopkins.
Tencellent J. C. conductor St.Ry. h.u. 70 Ch.O.
Tengeon Fred'k, barber 1151 Mn. b. 59 Windsor.
Tennert Charles E. clerk Hartford Life Ins. Co. 252 Asylum.
Tenney Charles H. trav. salesm. h. 578 Pro. av
" Dewitt C. electricn. 1 Laurel, b. 272 Asylum.
Tennyson James E. polisher at Popes, h. R.H.t.
Tererice Fred A. rubberworker at 690 Park, b. 128 Madison.
Terhune William, b. 2 Holcomb.
Terragna Salvatore, mer. tailor, 33, h. 41 Asy.
Terrell Charles E. foreman Popes, h. 48 Hung.
" Emma L. nurse, b. 14 Church, rm. 10.
Terrett John, stables, r. 106, h. 106 Hopkins.
Terrill Oscar J. salesm. 45 Asy. b. 56 Winthrop.
Terry Adeline, wid. Joseph A. b. 1300 Asylum.
" Charles A. farmer, h. 1300 Asylum.
" Edward C. mfr. 50 State, h. 175 Collins.
" James, secretary and treas. Phœnix Brass Foundry Co. b. 175 Collins.
" John J. mach. at Pope Tube Co. b. 226 N.P.
" Lucretia, wid. Stephen, h. 771 Asylum.
" Mabel F. teacher at West Middle school, 927 Asylum, b. 17 Columbia.
" Mary A. h. 97 Ann.
" Solon M. b. 771 Asylum.
" Wm. E. laborer Pope Tube Co. b. 226 N.P.
Teske Alcliffe T. Mrs. h. 81 Bellevue.
" Charles, jeweler and watch repairing, 214 Asylum, h. 81 Bellevue.

Tetzner Michael G. painter at Pope Tube Co h.u. 12 South Forest.
Teuscher Arthur, clerk Columbia Brewing Co. h. 5 Nelson.
Tevin Stephen, laborer at 8 Front.
Tewksbury Wilbur, livery stable, 87 High, h. 8 Pavilion.
Thacher John H. cashier Conn. Fire Insurance Co. 51 Prospect, h. 427 Main, rm. 24.
Thalheimer A. L. mech. engir. 2 Central, rm. 21.
" Robert, (Barrows & T.) h. 1293 Main.
Thanlow Valdemar, pressman at 690, h. 757 Park.
Thatcher Herb't E. clerk, 476 Cap. h.u. 39 Wads.
Thayer Andrew L. cabinetm. 556 Main, h. E.H.t
" Arthur E. mach. at 1 Flower, l. 34 Collins.
" Calista M. wid. William A. b. 22 Barbour.
" Edward, at Travelers Insurance Co. 56 Prospect, l. 721 Main.
" Elizabeth F. wid. Nathan, h.u. 68 Madison.
" Francis J. mason, 39, h. 39 Linden.
" Frank H. clerk at 843 Main, b. 61 Spring.
" George B., U. S. Army, b. 427 Main, rm. 45.
" George F. clerk at Popes, b. Manchester t.
" Grace D. clerk at Popes, b.u. 68 Madison.
" Hudson D. clerk at Brown, Thomson & Co. 942 Main, b. 51 Church.
" Joseph S. bkkpr. at 339 Sheldon, h. 56 Bkm.
" L. Mrs. agent, 373 Asylum, rm. 2.
" Laura R. wid. Marshall, h. 21 Greenwood.
" Wilbur J. buyer 956 Main, b. 10 Fairmount.
" William, carpenter, l. 520 Main.
" Willis M. clerk at 266 Pearl, b. Enfield t.

**THE FIDELITY CO.** 49 Pearl street.
*See page 438.*

Theis Frank W. supply clerk at Travelers Insurance Co. 56 Prospect, l. 720 Mn. rm. 6.
Theological Ins. of Conn. 1507 Bd. Now The Hfd.
 Theological Seminary. *See pages 708, 709.*
Theriau Hilarion C. carpenter at 142 Russ, b.2u. 44 Hungerford.
" John, carptr. at 142 Russ, b. 44 Hungerford.
Thibeault Lucy, wid. Sam'l, dressm. h.2u.545 Mn.
Thielen August, carpenter, h.u. 157 Zion.
Thierfelder Richard, mach. 1 Flow. h. 20 Green.
Thirlkel Samuel, cigarm. 40 Mul. b.18 Pawtucket.
" Thos. H. cigarm. 867 Mn. h. 18 Pawtucket.
Thoer William T. inspec. at Popes, h. 97 Madison.
Thomas Abbie S. wid. Archibald, h. 52 Laurel.
" Albert L. meat market, 1417 Mn. h. 109 Alb.
" Alexander, b. 23 Sanford.
" Alexander, gardener, b. 53 Sanford.
" August D. waiter at 26 State, h.u. 83 Green.
" Carrie J. clerk at 937 Main, b. 149 High.
" Charles, head waiter str. Middletown, 285 State, h. New York.
" Charles C. janitor 83 Woodbine,h.2 Huntley.
" Charles R. at 83 Woodbine, b. 2 Huntley.
" D. Webster, marketman, 1417 Main, h. E.H.t.
" Daniel, laborer, h. 41 Mather.
" David A. waiter at 107 State, h. 27 Elm.
" Emily J. wid. Emerson B. h.u. 28 Martin.
" Frank, coachman, b. 2 Huntley.
" Frank H. painter, b. 20 Talcott.
" Frederick, h.u. 224 Bellevue.

**For Sale Advertisements Bring Results in the Post.**

Thomas Frederick E. h.2u. 125 Charter Oak.
" George B. foreman at 88 Woodbine, h. 53 Putnam.
" James B. civil engineer, b. 126 Woodland.
" John B. at r. 64 Asylum, h. 2A Belden.
" John U. B., U. S. Army, b.2u. 1273 Main.
" Lovina, wid. George H. b.2u. 106 Hopkins.
" Mary, wid. David, b. 130 Ann.
" Milton H. foreman, 56 Com. b. 290 Pearl.
" Nicholas F. engineer, h.u. 220 Bellevue.
" Peter J. farmer, h. 58 Bluehills.
" Rebecca P. wid. Charles, b. 20 Wadsworth.
" Robert W. laundryman at 379 Main.
" Roscoe C. night clerk at P.O. b.103 Bellevue.
" Sarah A. Mrs. wid. William E. h.u. 253 Mar.
" William, helper at 135 Shel. b.u. 265 Main.
" William A. laborer, b. 53 Sanford.
" William H. carpenter, h. 16 Franklin.
" William J. jobber, h.u. 253 Market.
Thompson A. machinist at 1, b. 34 Laurel.
" Alex. helper, b. 44½ John.
" Alfred C. clerk at Brown, Thomson & Co. 942 Main, b. 68 Clark.
" Alice J. wid. Henry, h.u. 35 East.
" Ann C. wid. Gilbert W. b. 68 Clark.
" Arthur R. b. 51 Imlay.
" Augustus C. professor at Hartford Theological Seminary, 1507 Broad.

**THOMPSON BROS.** mason and contractors, 19 Rowe. See page 513.
Niels Christian Thompson. George Thompson.
" Charles, painter at 175 Pearl, h. 1 Union.
" Charles C. painter, h.u. 256 Capen.
" Charles E. at Conn. Mutual Life Insurance Co. 783 Main, h. 51 Imlay.
" Charles W. laborer, 56 Com. h. 171 Windsor.
" Edward M. watchm.at 851 Main, h. 32 West.

THOMPSON FRANK A. insurance agent for Phœnix Mutual Life Insurance Co. 49 Pearl, h. West Hartford t.
" Frank E. farmer at 90, h. 90 Bluehills.
" Fred, porter at 160 Windsor av. h. Pearl.
" George, salesm. at 9 Haynes, h. 130 Capen.
" George (Thompson Bros.) h. Manchester t.
" Gilbert W. clerk at Brown, Thomson & Co. 942 Main, b. 68 Clark.
" H. A. motorman at St.Ry. h. 10 Ellsworth.
" H. M. Rev. pastor Memorial Baptist Church, h. 17 Vernon.
" Hattie Mrs. h. 75 Edwards.
" Henry John, steward at Retreat for Insane, 30, b. 30 Washington.
" Herbert W. bkkpr. at 49 Pearl, h.u. 16 Mahl.
" Isabelle, b. 8 Alden.
" James, painter, b.2u. 15 Goodman.
" James A. clerk, h.u. 88 Wooster.
" James R. coachm. 195 High, h.u. 83 Mather.
" James R. machinist at Pratt & Whitney Co. 1 Flower, h. 32 Ashley.
" Jennie, wid. Charles F. h. 114 Whitmore.
" John, blacksmith at N.Y.R. h. 1338 Broad.
" John E. electrician, h. 114 Hopkins.
" Judson A. foreman at 48 Ann, b. Walnut.
" Katherine, wid. Jesse, h. 59 Sargeant.

Thompson Laura, attendant at 30 Washington.
" Lewis W. mach. at Courant, h. 88 Allen pl.
" Lizzie, dressmaker, b. 58 Church.
" Louis H. coachman, 320, b. 320 Collins.
" Maria. D. wid. William, h. 29 Atwood.
" Mary M. wid. Charles, h. 32 Ashley.
" Mary N. asst. at Orphan Asylum, 171 Putnam.
" May Belle, stenog. 164 State, b.u.88 Wooster.
" Minnie, wid. Charles W. h. 32 Ashley.
" N. Christian (T. Bros.) h.u. 19 Rowe.
" Niels, woodturner at 147 Shel. h. 19 Rowe.
" Oscar R. captain scow Newton, h. 8 Brady.
" Peter, carpenter, h.2u. 229 Franklin.
" Robert, tailor at 18 Park, h. 80 Benton.
" Robert M. clerk at 247 Asy. b. 88 Wooster.
" Sadie E. saleswoman at 45 Asy. h. 32 Ashley.
" Susan A. Mrs. dressmaker, b. 18 Suffield.
" Suzanne C. kindergarten teacher Charter Oak school, b. 8 Alden.
" Thomas, molder at 54 Arch, h. 54 Hudson.
" Thomas H. h. 8 Alden.
" Wallace, forem.at H.B.Brainerd, h.17 Elmer.
" Walter A. elevatorer, 650 Mn. b. 35 Spruce.
" Willard H. profiler, h.r. 50 Vanblock.
" William, at Travelers Insurance Co. 56 Prospect, b. Windsor t.
" William J. h. 278 Farmington.
" Wm. J. engineer, tug L. C. Ward, 285 State, h. East Haddam t.
" ☞ see also Thomson.
Thomson Chas. watertender str. Hfd. 285 State.
" Christian, at 20 Potter, h. 8 Elliott pl.
" Hilda, bookkeeper at 66 State, b. 58 Church.
" James L. student at Yale, b. 944 Asylum.
" James M. h. 944 Asylum.
" James W. clerk at 983, h. 1271 Main.
" Margaret Mrs. b. 2 Holcomb.
" Ole, b.2u. 229 Franklin.
" ☞ see also Thompson.
Thoren Claus, mech. at Popes, b. 110 Laurel.
Thorman James, clerk at 37, b. 37 Bluehills.
" James W. operator at 8 Sigourney, h.u. 709 Main, rm. 5.
Thorn Edgar E. coachman at 65 Washington, h.u. 81 Allen pl.
Thorne Edwin M. h. 245 Wethersfield.
" Everett M. conductor at St.Ry. b.u. 136 Sey.
" William, at Popes, b. 48 Hopkins.
Thornton John W. washer at 690 Park, h. 33 Francis.
Thorpe Lena B. bkkpr. 921 Mn. b. 279 Asylum.
" Thomas E. splicer, 690 Park, h. Park,W.H.t.
Thorstenson Fred, driver at 12 Queen, l. 61 Haw.
" John, bakery, 12 Queen, l. 58 Hawthorn.
Thrall Charles W. condr. at St.Ry. h. 873 Broad.
" Dwight A. b. 219 High.
" Dwight W. gen. agent Conn. Humane Society, 51 Prospect, h. 219 High.
" Dwight W. Mrs. h. 219 High.
" Edward B. plow parts, stove repairs, etc. 63, h. 63 Church.
" Elmer G. clerk at Perkins Electric Switch Co. b. 610 Capitol.
" Flavia A. Mrs. medical clairvoyant, 1295 Main, h. Poquonock v.

**The Post, 12 Cents a Week, Delivered at Your Home.**

Thrall Frank C. clerk 45 Asylum, h. 110 High.
" Franklin W. carpenter at·86 Morgan, h.3u.
   18 South Ann.
" Ida R. kindergarten, 63, b. 63 Church.
" Louise B. wid. Samuel, b. 215 Garden.
" Oliver H. at Travelers Insurance Co. 56
   Prospect, b. 219 High.
" Pliny E. driver at C. C. Fuller Co. 14 Ford,
   h. 172 Windsor av.
**THRASHER E. E. MISS,** teacher
   Chandler Shorthand school, 252 Asylum,
   h. 202 High.　　　　*See page 710.*
" William, tinner at 346 Main.
Thresher Arthur, fishery, h. 494 Wethersfield.
" Delia M. wid. William, h. 478 Wethersfield.
" Julia C. wid. Wm. B. h. 484 Wethersfield.
Thuer Alex. F. filer at 30 Cush. h.u. 58 Flower.
" Charles E. night clerk at 103, b. 103 State.
" John H. assembler at Colts, h. Hockanum v.
" Wm. T. filer at Popes, h. 97 Madison av.
Thulin Otto C. at 581 Cap. b.u. 46 New Britain.
" Otto E. fresco painter, 84 Pratt, h.u. 46 N.B.
" Sylvia S. b.u. 46 New Britain.
Thurber Edward, joiner, b. 542 Main.
Thurston Geo. B. engir. at P.&R. h. 36 Collins.
" Louise, b. 888 Asylum.
Thwing C. H. traveling salesman at Popes, h.
   Boston, Mass.
Thydell John P. wiredr. at 40 Gov. b. 1048 Broad.
Tiagwad Christen, filer, 30 Cush. h. 1048 Broad.
Tibbals Edwin C. b. 1393 Main.
" Irvin N.secy.Freeman-Tibbals Co.l.29 Pearl.
" Marshall V. mechanic at Lincoln & Co. 54
   Arch, h.u. 31 Woodbridge.
" Sarah D. wid. William, h. 31 Bellevue.
" Wm. A. signs, 68½ Temple, b. 31 Bellevue.
Tibbitts Ralph G. machinist at Pratt & Whitney
   Co. 1 Flower, h. 31 Trumbull.
Tidlund Edwin, draughtsman at 1 Laurel, b.
   119 Capitol.
Tiernay Michael, Right Rev. Bishop of Hartford,
   h. 140 Farmington.
" Michael, laborer, b. 36 Temple pl.
Tierney David, mech. at Popes, b. 27 Harbison.
" John, joiner, b. 80 State.
" Martin E. helper at 54 Arch, b.u. 22 Law.
" Mamie, at 149 State, b. 370 Asylum.
" Thomas B. mech. at Popes, b. Burnside v.
Tiffany Ellen F. b. 757 Asylum.
" F. B. painter, b. 1153 Main.
" Lucien, h. 757 Asylum.
" M. Adelene, artist, 757, b. 757 Asylum.
Tifft Ada L. Mrs. manf. cake tins, 115, h. 115 Oak.
" ☞*see also Tefft; Taft.*
Tighe Michael J. clerk at 711, b. 184 Main.
" Thomas A. laborer at 98 Kil. b. 65 Pleasant.
Tilden Bert O. sanitary engineer at 164 State, h.
   103 Webster.
" Walter L. agent at 715 Main, h. Windsor t.
Tiley James T. machinist, b.u. 83 Governor.
" Michael, bartender at 637 Main.
Tilley Henry C. clerk at Brown, Thompson &
   Co. 942 Main, h. 22 Jefferson.
" John S. helper at 48 Ann, b. W.H.t.

Tillinghast Alva H. grocer, 341 Main, h. 65 Bkm.
Tillman Charles A. pressm. at Popes, h. 36 Wolcott.
" Louis, peddler, b.u. 210 Front.
Tillotson Albert S. coachman 30, h.r. 30 Weth.
" Edward P. h. 534 Main.
" Florence M. furnished rooms, 1221 Main.
" Fred A. chef at 583 Main, l.u. 36 Temple.
" H. H. clerk at 197 Asylum, h. W.H.t.
" Katherine E. Mrs. fur. rooms, 1032 Main.
" Margaret J. Mrs. h. 534 Main.
" Sherman H. telegraph opera. b. 57 Church.
Tilton Abner F. mer. tailor, 697 Mn. h. 58 Asylum.
" David, proprietor Atlantic Screw works,
   70, h. 81 Huyshope.
" Fred. N. bookkeeper at 70, h. 79 Huyshope.
" Geo. E. lawyer, 9 Asylum, b.3u. 36 Church.
**TIMES OFFICE,** 716 Main.
Timmons Jas. F. operator, 247 Pearl, b. 194 High.
Tims Howard, mach. at 388 Cap. b. 23 Lawrence.
" Jane A. b.u. 23 Lawrence.
" William H. machinist, b. 23 Lawrence.
" William W. saddlemaker, h.u. 28 Lawrence.
Tiney John, at 8 Sigourney, b.2u. 36 Flower.
Tinguad Christian, laborer, h.u.r. 1048 Broad.
Tinker Herbert E. policeman, h.2u. 40 Hopkins.
" Leroy D. machinist at 1 Flower, L 109 Oak.
Tinkham Andrew J. b. 2 Holcomb.
" Emily A. clairvoyant, h.r. 373 Main.
" Ernest W. mach. at 9 Sig. b. 33 Babcock.
" George H. mach. at 9 Sig. b. 33 Babcock.
" Joseph, b. 36 Jefferson.
Tippett John, h. 1476 Broad.
" John Jr. clerk at 493 Main, b. 114 State.
Tipton Isaac, mach. at 1 Flower, b. 317 Capitol.
" John F. patternm. at 1 Flow. b. 371 Capitol.
Tirrell A. R. b. 25 Spring.
" Louis R. ostler at 126 Church.
Tisca Martin, laborer, h. 93 Sheldon.
Tischenbach Nicholas, operator at Capewell
   Horse Nail Co. 40 Gov. h. 89 Arch.
Tisdale Edw. mach. 1 Flower, h.u. 551 Park.
Tishcoff Toffey, laborer, b.u. 6½ Ellery.
Titcomb John W. writing teacher public schools,
   instructor Hartford Business college, h.
   24 Charter Oak.
Titus Allen S. student at Trinity college, 34
   Jarvis hall, Summit.
" Lona S. clerk, b. 11 Preston.
Tivey Frank, tailor, 2u. 9, h.2u. 9 Goodman.
Tobey Caroline M. head nurse at 20 S. Hudson.
" Edwin S. clerk at 581 Cap. b. 196 Laurel.
" James W. S. clerk at 20, b. 20 So. Hudson.
" Mary J. wid. William, h. 39 Imlay.
Tobias Hermann, brakeman N.Y.R. h.u. 399 Fkn.
" Theodore, jeweler, h. 399 Franklin.
Tobie Wilbur O. machinist at 20 Vredendale.
Tobin James P. bkkpr. at 4 American, b. E.H.t.
" Michael, laborer, b. 25½ Flower.
" Patrick, b.u. 20 Affleck.
" William F. policeman, h. 107 Windsor.
Toccio John, laborer, b.3u. 16 Kilbourn.
" Joseph, harnessmaker, h.3u. 16 Kilbourn.
" Nicholas, harpist, h.u. 16 Kilbourn.
" Nicholas, laborer, h. 82 Potter.

Todd James H. agent at 811 Main, h. 81 Maple.
" Milo A. ins. agt. 756 Main, h. 16 Huntington.
" Samuel D. crater at 581 Cap. h. 33 Asylum.
Tolhurst Edwin, at T. A. Honiss, oyster depot, 30 State, h.u. 41 Seymour. *See page 589.*
" Frank E. clerk at 55, b. 94 Maple.
" Norman J. clerk, 55 Maple, h. 63 Hudson.
" William C. clerk at 55, b. 94 Maple.
" Wm. J. groceries, meats, etc. 55, h. 94 Maple.
Tolles Charles L. clerk at Jewell Belting Co. 15 Trumbull, b. 18 Marshall.
" Edwin, woolens, etc. 49 Ann, h. 251 Far.
" George F. forem. at Colts, h. 213 Retreat.
Tolx Eugene F. mechanic, 581 Cap. h. 50 Linden.
Tomkins Harry, carpenter, l.u. 6 Church.
Tomlins Wm. J. bartdr. 116 Front, h. 20 Village.
Tomlinson Charles C. superintendent, 335 Sheldon, h. 50 Buckingham.
" Frederick C. at Ætna Life Ins. Co. 650 Main, b. 50 Buckingham.
" George R. at Travelers Ins. Co. 56 Prospect, b. Plainville t.
" S. Lewis, student at Trinity col. b. 50 Bkm.
Toner Daniel, b. 2 Holcomb.
" John, butcher, b. 65 Avon.
" John F. motorman St.Ry. h. 27 Talcott.
" Kate, wid. Hugh A. h.u. 24 Commerce.
" Patrick, stonepolisher, 1260 Mn. h. 65 Avon.
Tong Sing, laundry, 294, h. 294 Asylum.
Tonguay Peter, carpenter, h. 196 Mather.
Tonkinson John, filer at Colts, h.r. 70 Vanblock.
Tonlinson Wm. R. mach. at 1 Flow. b. 5 Squire.
Toohey James, polisher at Popes, b. 25 Flower.
· " Jane Mrs. b.u. 20 Ely.

**TOOHEY JOHN A.** attorney at law, 49 Pearl, b. 119 Capitol.
" Thomas, laborer, h. 228 Maple.
" Thos. J. Mrs. dressmaker, 45, h. 45 John.
Toohill Mamie, clerk at 956 Mn. b. 51 Pleasant.
Toohy Cornelius, goldbeater at 14 Mulberry, b. 25 Waverly.
" Dennis, teamster, h. 25 Waverly.
" John, clerk, b. 25 Waverly.
" Wm. laborer, h.u. 17 Squire.
" ☞ *see also Twohey.*
Tooker A. B. captain tpg Smith, 285 State, h. Hamburg v.
" Fred, driver at 34 Pratt, b. 1341 Main.
" Morris S. at Ætna Life Ins. Co. 650 Main, b. 10 Alden.
" William R. rubberw. 690 Park, h. 11 Francis.
Toole Charles, waiter at 80 State.
" James, assembler, 302 Asy. b.u. 49 Lawrence.
" Mary, wid. Lawrence, h.u. 49 Lawrence.
" William P. plater, b.u. 49 Lawrence.
Tooley Chas. M. painter, h. 1320 Broad.
Toomey Annie T. b. 11 Kilbourn.
" Barbara, b. 11 Kilbourn.
" Daniel, deckhand str. Hartford, 285 State.
" John J. coachman at 244 Mn. h.u. 96 Maple.
" Kate Mrs. b. 2 Holcomb.
" Mary, tailoress, b. 343 Main.
" Morris E. at 107 Front, b. 11 Kilbourn.
" Patrick, laborer, h. 11 Kilbourn.

Toomey Thomas F. teamster, b. 11 Kilbourn.
" Thomas H. engineer P.&R.R. h. 104 Walnut.
" Wm. J. foreman at 46 Ann, b. 11 Kilbourn.
Toorney ☞ *see Turney.*
Tooth Stephen, helper, 142 Russ, b.u.r. 28 Law.
Toothaker Henry G. cutter at 66 Asy. h. 12 Mahl.
" Horace W. cutter at 719 Main, b. 12 Mahl.
Tophan Lawrence, at 436, h.u. 283 Capitol.

**TOPPING JAMES R.** pattern and model maker, 734 Main, h. 1 Woodbridge av. East Hartford t. *See page 541.*
" Wm. W. patternm. at 734 Mn. b. 58 Grove.
Torgerson Edward, mason, b. Highland.
Torp Christian, mach. 581 Cap. h. 97 Madison av.
Torpy ☞ *see also Tarpy.*
Torrey Arthur H. woodw. 556 Mn. h.2u. 76 Park.
" Frank B. clerk, b.2u. 884 Main.
" Frank W. compositor, b. 35 Lafayette.
" Harlan W. woodworker, 556, h.2u. 573 Main.
" Harry W. drugclerk, b.2u. 573 Main.
" Wm. W. toolmkr. at Popes, h. 35 Lafayette.
Torrington Joseph, janitor at Union station, h.2u. 6 Ford.
Tossa Nicholas, mechanic at 83 Woodbine, b. 82 Potter.
Tougas Odianna, b. 54 Market.
Tourtellott James E. asst. sup't at Hartford Rubber Works, 690 Park, h.u. 64 Kenyon.
Tourtellotte William F. plumber at 81 Trumbull, h. E.H.t.
Toutant Eugene J. burnisher at 62 Market, h.u. 55 Wooster.
Tower Thomas, helper, h. 13 Morgan.
" Wesley B. asst. foreman at 690 Park, b. 26 Smith.
" Wesley W. painter at 554 Main, h. Windsor t.
Towler John, laborer, 1 Flower, b. 10 Hawthorn.
" William, b. 25½ Howard.
Town House, 2 Holcomb av. end of Vine.
" Mary E. wid. Luther, b. 100 Hopkins.
" Store, now city store, 182 Pearl.
Towne Arthur P. bookkeeper at Dime Savings Bank, 791 Main, h. 610 Farmington.
" Clinton D. carriagepainter, h. 43 Seyms.
" Elizabeth Mrs. dressmaker, 4, h. 4 Village.
" Hattie A. dressmaker, b. 43 Seyms.
" Isabella, wid. Jos. H. Jr. h. 610 Farmington.
" Leroy M. pressman, b.u. 242 Putnam.
" Lewis E. machinist, h.u. 31 Putnam.
" Nellie E. clerk, b. 43 Seyms.
" Sarah, wid. Rev. E. S. h.u. 242 Putnam.
" Susan E. teacher at 2d North school, b. 219 High.
Towner John H. clerk 375 Capitol, b. 129 Sargeant.
Townsend Alice, wid. Wm. B. h.u. 125 Park.
" Drusilla M. wid. Joseph R. h.u. 105 Front.
" Eliza, wid. Henry, b. 58 Hungerford.
" Heber, druggist, 9, h. 9 New Britain.
" Henry W. clerk at Smith, Bourn & Co. 8 Sigourney, b. 5 Atlantic.
" Jacob, laborer, b.2u. 15 Mechanic.
" James H. barber, h.u. 34 Village.
" S. P. investments and broker, 49 Pearl, rm. 28, b. 109 Elm.

Townsend Stephen H. beltmaker at Jewell Belting Co. 15 Trumbull, h. 58 Hungerford.
" William, h.u. 34 Village.
Townson Lewis P. machinist at 1 Flower, b. T.v.
Toy John, screwmkr. at 476 Cap. b. 18 Francis.
" Patrick, screwm. at 476 Cap. b. 18 Francis.
Tozzo Angello M. laborer, b.u. 268 Front.
" Antonio, laborer, b.2u. 64 Morgan.
" Joseph, laborer, h. 1 North.
" Luigi, laborer, h.u. 268 Front.
" Peter, laborer, b.u. 268 Front.
" Tony, laborer. h. 1 North.
" Vito, laborer, b.2u. 64 Morgan.
Tracey Coral E. teacher Washington St. school, b. 31 Vernon.
" James. coachman, h. 66 Woodland.
" John, b.2u. 76 Walnut.
" Wm. J. plumber at 548 Asy. b.u. 39 Portland.
" Sadie, silverplater, b.u. 39 Portland.
" 〰see also Tracy.
Tracher Michael L. massage, h.2u. 739 Main.
Tracy Albert J. fireman N.Y.R. b.u. 7 East.
" Angeline, b. 36 Jefferson.
" Annie, wid. John F. h.2.u. 181 Market.
" Annie Mrs. at 37, h.u.r. 60½ Wells.
" Annie H. teacher, b. 80 Kenyon.
" Charles H. at 334 Weth. h. 106½ Trumbull.
" Charlotte G. teacher, b. 80 Kenyon.
" Clarence H. shipping clerk, Ransom N. FitzGerald, 44 Market, b. 78 High.
" D. Wallace, druggist, 515 Main, h. 100 Weth.
" Edward, clerk at 1195 Main.
" Edward F. temperer at 40 Gov. b. 14 S.Pro.
" Elizabeth, wid. Patrick, h.u. 39 Portland.
" Elizabeth, wid. Thomas, h.u. 266 Maple.
" Ellen, wid. Peter, h. 14 So. Prospect.
" Ellsworth M. student at Trinity college, 11 Northam tower, Summit.
" Florence G. at Hartford Steam Boiler Insp. & Ins. Co. 650 Main, b. 112 Windsor av.
" Frank E. repairer at 40 Gov. h. 19 Chapel.
" Frederick, teamster, 283 Shel. h. 2 Elm pl.
" Frederick P. clerk at Connecticut Fire Insurance Co. 51 Prospect, h. 511 Farmington.
" Garret S. clerk, 95 Main, h. 816 Park.
" George H. electrician, b.u. 98 Maple.
" Gertie N. Mrs. clairvoyant, b. 19 Chapel.
" H. M. Mrs. b. 69 Congress.
" Harriet, wid. Robert F. b. 23 Sherman.
" Henry C. groceries, 814 Park and 95 Main, butter, etc. 940, h. 816 Park.
" Henry J. linem. 6 Central, h.u. 44½ Temple.
" Hubert D. at Ætna Life Insurance Co. 650 Main, h. 8 Buckingham.
" James, boilermaker N.Y.R. h.u. 7 East.
" James A. filer at 40 Gov. b. 14 So. Prospect.
" John, iceman at 48 Ann, b.2u. 63 Flower.
" John, laborer at 8, h.2u. 19 Front.
" John F. (T. & Robinson,) h. 95 Kenyon.
" John J. lineman, 6 Central, h.3u. 58 Temple.
" John W. carpenter, l. 1136 Main.
" Joseph, electrician, b. 45 Farmington.
" Joseph H. b.u. 7 East.
" Joseph H. clerk at 266 Pearl, b. 1150 Main.
" Kate J. inspector at 70, b. 57 Huyshope.

Tracy L. Howard, clerk 515 Main, h. 124 Jef.
" Louis A. clerk at 690 Park, h. 4 Avon.
" Maria C. b. 36 Jefferson.
" Mary, h.u.r. 34 South Prospect.
" Mary, wid. John, b. 76 Capitol.
" Michael, h.u. 98 Maple.
" Michael, porter at Colts, h. 57 Huyshope.
" Michael J. clerk Adams Ex. h.u. 53 Wads.
" Miles P. inspector at Colts, h. 48 Hudson.
" & Robinson, hardware, 78 Asylum.
  John F. Tracy.    Henry N. Robinson.
" Samuel G. sec'y L. & T. Oil Co. h.u. 1 Kibbe.
" Sophia D. teacher at High sch. b. 80 Kenyon.
" Thomas, helper at 37 Spruce, h. 76 Walnut.
" Thos. C. laborer at 40 Gov. h.2u. 91 Arch.
" Willis S. h. 816 Park.
Tragansa Clarence, artisan at 22 Belden, b. 56 Winthrop.
Train Addison W. carpenter at 1, b. 1 Rice ct.
Trainer E. A. tinner at 164 State, h.2u. 172 Windsor av.
Trant Bartholomew, molder at 556 Capitol, h.2u. 20 Alden.
" E. M. Mrs. teacher German and French, b. 20 Niles.
" John C. painter, 20 Central, h. 40 Franklin.
" Josephine R. h. 9 Seyms.
" Mamie A. clerk at Brown, Thomson & Co. 942 Main, b.u. 64 Congress.
" Maurice, helper at 133 Shel. h. 10 Congress.
" Morris B. clerk 374 Asy. b.u. 64 Congress.
" Thomas, plumber 389½ Mn. h.u. 64 Congress.
" Timothy, machinehand, Colts, b.u. 64 Cong.
Trante Vito, laborer, b. 75 Morgan.
Trask Arthur, b. 2 Holcomb.
" Frank H. policeman, b. 1463 Broad.
" Minnie A. wid. of Wm. A. clerk at Brown, Thomson & Co. 942 Mn. h.2u. 3 Whitman.
Traub David, teacher, h. 279 Market.
Traute Alfred, h. 181 Wethersfield.
" Alfred H. real estate, 704 Mn. h. 16 Alden.
" Hulda, b. 181 Wethersfield.
" Selma, b. 181 Wethersfield.
Trauz Frank, h. 178 Putnam.

**TRAVELERS INSURANCE CO.**
life and accident, 56 Prospect, corner of Grove. *See page 456.*

" Record, pub. monthly 56 Prospect.
Travere Fred C. helper St.Ry. 115 State.
Travis Elwood B. salesman, b. 47 Farmington.
Treadwell Harry A. (E. M. Young & Co.) b. 14 Russell.
" James O. painter r. 60 Temple, b. 50 Barb.
" Wm. B. machinist, b. 73 Babcock.
Treall Cloffie Miss, at 690 Park, b. 8 Bonner.
" Delia, dressmaker, b. 8 Bonner.
" Joseph, brickmaker, h. 8 Bonner.
" Lewis E. helper at 581 Capitol, b. 8 Bonner.
Treat Adelaide, wid. Trall, h. 8 Smith.
" Ann E. wid. Charles, h.u. 83 Seymour.
" D. Louise, bookfolder, Case, Lockwood & Brainard Co. 49 Trumbull, b. 58 Church.
" Edwin A. at 118 Asylum, h. Naubuc v.
" Emeline, wid. John W. dressm. h. 110 High.

Treat Emerson D. clerk, 1082 Mn. h. 24 Seyms.
" Frank, butcher, h.2u. 152 Mather.
" Frank S.steamfitr.Pope Tube Co. b. 8 Smith.
" Ira B. helper St.Ry. b. 80 State.
" Irving C. (Clapp & T.) b. 103 Wethersfield.
" Jerome, brakeman, h. 110 High
" Susan A. b. 69 Church.
Trebbe Chas. F. butcher at 33 Mar. h. 71 Temple.
" Herman, teamster, b. 130 Martin.
Trebert Frank, machinist at 1 Flower, h. Ch.O.
" John J. machinist 30 Cushman, h. W.H.t.
Tredeau T. Charles, coachman, 134 Washington, h. 392 Franklin.
Tredo Henry, motorman at St. Ry. b. 57 Pratt.
" William J. motorman St.Ry. b. E.H t.
Tree Fred J. waiter, 98 Wells, h. 29 West.
TreFethren Eugene B. theo. student, 1507 Broad.
Tregoning John, supt. Perkins Electric Switch Mfg. Co. 83 Woodbine, h. 89 Hawthorn.
" Rosa, housekeeper, 89 Hawthorn.
" Wm. electrician, 83 Woodbine, b. 89 Haw.
Trehy Dennis J. mach. at 555 Cap. h. 305 Park.
" Edward M. clerk, b. 8 Elm.
" John J. enameler, h.u. 8 Elm.
" John, Jr. inspector at Popes, b.u. 8 Elm.
" Mary, wid. James, h.u. 269 Park.
" Michael F. machinist at 1 Flow. b.u. 8 Elm.
" William J. at N.Y.&B. Despatch Co. 236 Asylum, b.u. 8 Elm.
Treisbach Harry F. carptr. at 70 Huy. b. 36 C.O.
Treloar James, filer, h.u. 30 South Prospect.
" John H. barber, 92 Flower, b. 349 Main.
" William J. musician, b. 6½ Charter Oak.
Tremont Antonio, fruits, 31 Pearl, b.u. 214 Front.
" Louis, clerk, 31 Pearl, b.u. 214 Front.
Tremonte Brothers, grocers, 53 New Britain.
  Peter Tremonte.          Joseph Tremonte.
" Joseph, (Tremonte Bros.) h. 51 N.B.
" Peter, (Tremonte Bros.) b. 51 New Britain.
Trerice Annie, wid. Robt. F. h. 128 Madison av.
" Charles, h. 128 Madison av.
" Fred A. rubberworker, h. 128 Madison av.
" James E. rubberworker at 690 Park, b. 128 Madison av.
" John, driver, h.u. 80 Sheldon.
Tresch Abraham, cigarm. 867 Main, h.u. 222 Fkn.
" Frank, cigarm. at 867 Mn. h.u. 208 Franklin.
" John, stonecutter, 69 Com. b.r. 71 Temple.
Treslin Gustaf, laborer, h.2u. 10 Winter.
Tressy Alexander, laborer, h. 7 Squire.
" Michael, rubberw. at 690 Park. b. 7 Squire.
" Patrick J. mech. at 581 Cap. b. 7 Squire.
" Timothy J. rubberworker at 690 Park, b. 7 Squire.
Trevor James E. machinist, h. 81 Franklin.
Triebert Delia, wid. William, h. 45 Hamilton.
" Fred. J. molder at 438 Asy. h.u. 61 Spruce.
" Henry, toolmaker at 556 Cap. h.u. 230 Zion.
" James, machinist at 40 Cush. h.u. 615 Cap.
Trieschmann Luther H. barber at 706 Main, h. 870 Asylum, rm. 40.
Trimble Alexander B. driver, h. 31 Smith.
" Joseph F. mach. at 1 Flower, b. 31 Smith.
Trinity Church, 120-130 Sigourney, Rev. Ernest DeF. Miel, rector.

**TRINITY COLLEGE,** Summit st. 1 mile south of Capitol.   See pages 706, 707.
Trinity College Societies.        See page 726.
" Pharmacy, J. J. Sinnott, prop. 169 Zion.
" Tablet, monthly, 7 Jarvis hall, Trinity college.
Trio Tool & Machine Co. 356 Asylum.
  J. U. Reed.     H. A. Lawrence.     G. A. Prior.
Tripp Alfred H. tinner at 164, b. 80 State.
" Harold W., U. S. Army, b. 143 Collins.
" Margaret J. wid. Henry G. h. 5 Oak.
" Richard E. clerk at Wm. Rogers Mfg. Co. 66 Market, h. 30 Barbour.
Trishman George W. foreman at r. 87, l.r. 87 High.
Trobeck Enoch O. mach. at Popes, h.u. 609 Main.
Troedson August, helper, 556 Cap. l. 37 Wolcott.
Trolan Robert L. inspector at Hfd. Steam Boiler Insp. & Ins. Co. 650 Main, h.u. 97 Hung.
Trolin Carl L. mach. at 1 Flower, h.2u. 358 Park.
Trombley Adolphus, h. 198 Capen.
" Frank, plumber at 1204 Main, b. 198 Capen.
" Fred'k helper at 1204 Main, b. 198 Capen.
" Wm. L. laborer at 581 Cap. h. 151 Martin.
Tropp Gustaf, carpenter, b. 18 Lawrence.
Trostel Frank A. bartender, b. 17 Lawrence.
" Fred, driver, h. 17 Lawrence.
Trotter Henry, b. 214 Woodland.
" William, toomaker at Colts, h. 34 Ch.O.
Trotzowaki Fritz, helper at 308 Allyn, b. 29 Vine.
Trout Brook Ice & Feed Co. 48 Ann.
" Frank, saloon, 21, h.u. 21 Kilbourn ct.
" John M. student Theo. seminary, 1507 Broad.
Trowbridge, Edward C. advertising solicitor, Evening Post, 23 Asylum, b. 56 Willard.
Troy Frank K. domestic, and b. 32 Congress.
Trudeau Charles J. benchman, b. Prospect av. n. New Park.
" John, carpenter, h. Prospect av. c. N.P.
Truding Erwin, machinist, h. 14 Affleck.
Trumbull Alexander, electrician at 190 Pearl, b. 14 Church.
" Anna M teacher Wadsworth st. school, b. 54 Buckingham.
" Annie Eliot, literary editor, Courant, 66 State, b. 734 Asylum.

**TRUMBULL BROS.** electrical engineers, 190 Pearl.        See page 420.
  John H. Trumbull.          Frank S. Trumbull.
TRUMBULL CHARLES P. general agent Adams Express Co. h. 118 Ann.   See page 553.
" Frank S. (Trumbull Bros.) b. 14 Church.
" Gurdon, h. 970 Asylum.
" Henry, electrician at 190 Pearl, b. 14 Church.
" Hugh, bookbinder at 141 Pearl, h. 84 Park.
" Sarah A. wid. J. Hammond, h. 734 Asylum.
" James V. A. superintendent Valley Division, N.Y.R. 450 Asylum, h. 226 Farmington.
" John H. (Trumbull Bros.) b. 14 Church.
" Joseph, janitor Parkville sch. h. 833 Park.
" Joseph H. livery, b. 833 Park.
" Joseph P. bookkeeper at Beach & Co. 209 State, b.u. 84 Jefferson.
Trumpeno Pasquale, laborer, h.u. 30 Kilbourn.
Truscott Mary, b. 23 Affleck.
Trutting Urban, helper at 1 Flower, h. 14 Affleck.

**THE POST is a 20th-Century Newspaper**

# EDWARD S. TRYON,

## Carpenter,
## Contractor,
## and Builder,

**427 MAIN St., The Linden, Room 71.**

Old No. 121.

### Shop, 28 TEMPLE ST.

Trux Melville E. manager building department
 Conn. Building and Loan Association,
 252 Asylum, h. 27 Huntington.
Tryon Charles F. gardener, h.u. 279 Park.
" Charles E. clerk at 653 Main, h. 82 Hudson.
TRYON EDWARD S. builder, 28 Temple, b. 427
 Main, room 71. *See page 360.*
" George B. Jr. machinist at 80 Huyshope, b.
 Manchester t.
" George F. carpenter at 109 Windsor av. b.
 1 Chapel.
" John A. toolmaker at Popes, h. 36 Ch. O.
" Samuel, janitor at 65 State, h. Bloomfield t.
Tubbs George E. engineer, h. 39 Francis.
" William H. ass't auditor Ætna Life Ins.
 Co. 650 Main, h. 107 Oak.
Tuchandler Aaron P. mach.at 581 Cap.b.13 North
Tuck David, painter, 618 Cap. b.u. 306 Market
" Louis, peddler, h. 298 Market.
" Michael, molder, h. 49 Morgan.
" Samuel, peddler, h.u. 306 Market.
" Simon, peddler, h. 49 Morgan.
Tucker Abbie A. wid. Frederick O. b.u. 94 Haw.
" Amelia M. wid. Talcott M. h. 160 Barbour.
" Charles W. groceries, h. N.P. n. city line.
" Curtis A. draughtsman at Popes, b. 23 Russ.

**TUCKER'S E. SONS**, straw boards,
 papers, twine, 100 Trumbull. *See p. 481.*
" Edwin H. teller at City Bank of Hartford
 783 Main, h. 122 Garden.
" Frank L. mach. 1 Flower, b. 94 Hawthorn.
" Frederick N. salesm. 399 Allyn, b. 285 N.B.

**TUCKER & GOODWIN**, wholesale
 groceries, flour, 10 Hurlburt. *See p. 585.*
William Tucker. Henry H. Goodwin.
" Henry, cutter, l. 221 Main.
" Henry E. repairer at Popes, b. 28 Elm.
" Howard J.butcher at 1050 Mn. h.34 Windsor.
" James E. with E. Tucker's Sons, paper deal-
 lers, 100 Trumbull, h. 6 Myrtle.
" John D. *(E. Tucker's Sons,)* paper, twine,
 etc. 100 Trumbull, h. 84 Edwards.
" Louis E. mach. 1 Flower, b. 94 Hawthorn.
" Perley E. machinist at 1 Flow. h. W.H.t.
" Phil, solderer at 62 Market, b. Hawthorn ex.
" Richard, b. Prospect av.
TUCKER WM. *(Tucker & Goodwin,)* wholesale
 grocers, h. 84 Edwards. *See page 585.*

# GEO. W. TULLER,
# Real Estate Broker,

*Special Agent for*

# Fire Insurance,

## No. 847 MAIN STREET,

Old Number, 333,

*Room 5, Second Floor, Hills' Block.*

Tucker William E. policeman, h. 233 Capen.
" Wm. E. mach. at 1 Flow. h.2u. 1152 Broad.
" Wm. W. contrac. 1 Flow. h. 105 Huntington.
Tudor Charles C. h.u. 1039 Main.
Tuft Peter C. polisher at 30 Cush. 18 Wolcott.
Tufts Charles H. painter, h. Caya.
Tuill Chas. P. stenographer P.&R. b. 28 Spring.
Tuite Mary A. wid. Patrick, h. 60 Hungerford.
" Mary E. teacher at Lawrence street school,
 b. 60 Hungerford.
" Nellie, bookkeeper, 956 Main, b. 114 Hung.
Tulin Isaac, shirt manuf. 285, h. 231 Market.
" Loft & Tulin, tea, etc. 1200 Main.
 S. D. Tulin. L. Loft. S. S. Tulin.
" S. D. *(T. Loft & T.)* h.u. 231 Market.
" S. S. *(T. Loft & T.)* b. 77 Bellevue.
Tullar Cerelia, wid. E. B. h. 9 James.
" Allen H. machinist at Popes, h. 9 James.
Tuller Charles D. h. 43 Park.
TULLER GEORGE W. real estate, 847 Main, rm. 5,
 h. 177 Sigourney. *See page 360.*
" Hubert M. engineer, b.u. 16 Goodman.
" Marshall J. clerk, 165 Windsor, b. 43 Park.
" Mary E. wid. William J. b. 170 Sisson.
" Ralph D. machinist, h. 43 Park.
" Robert A. laborer at 252 Pearl, b. 62 Grove.
Tully Geo. J. mach. 26 Mechanic, h.2u. 6 Lewis.
" Mary M. b. 19 Wadsworth.
" Owen, blacksmith at P.&R. h.u. 20 Howard.
" Patrick, blacksmith at 1 Laurel, h.2u. 232
 New Park.
Tuloski August, teamster, h.u. 92 Sheldon.
Tumillo Nito M. laborer, h. 31 North.
Tumin Samuel, cashier at N.E. Brewing Co.
Tummillo Joseph, bootblack at 10 State, b. 31
 South Prospect.
Tunstell Isaac C. laborer, h. Whiting.
Tunxis Worsted Co. 66 State.
Tuohey Michael F. reporter Hartford Courant,
 66 State, h. Manchester t.
" ☞ *see also Toohey Twohey.*
Tupp Alfred H. tinner at 164, b. 80 State.
Tupper Mary E. b. 36 Jefferson.
Turgeon Fred S. barber, b. 59 Windsor.
Turin Clos, at Popes, b. 110 Laurel.
Turley Catharine, wid John, h.2u.r. 259 Front.
" John, loomfixer, h.r. 250 Front.
" Patrick, laborer, 70 Huyshope. h.u. 1 Union.
" Patrick J. brakeman, h.u. 54 Loomis.
Turmey Sarah, carpet sewer at Brown, Thomson
 & Co. 942 Main, b. 926 Main.
" Thomas, janitor, h.u. 23 Pleasant.

Turnberg John F. filer at Popes,l.u. 153 Lawrence.
Turnbull Bertha J. stenographer, 254 Pearl, b. 109 Hungerford.
" Charles D. clerk at 252 Pearl, 109 Hung.
" James, mach. at 581 Capitol, h. 109 Hung.
" James A. clerk at Phœnix Mutual Life Ins. Co. 49 Pearl, h. 584 Prospect av.
" Mary, stenographer at Ætna Indemnity Co. b. 109 Hungerford.
" Thomas, assistant secretary Hartford Fire Ins. Co. 53 Trumbull, h. 201 Sigourney.
Turnee Jennie P. sewing machine agent at Brown, Thomson & Co. 942 Main, b. 17 Florence.
Turner Alice B. at Hartford Life Ins. Co. 252 Asylum, h. East Berlin v.
" Alice B. stenog. 197 Asylum, h. 39 Ashley.
" Annie F. milliner, 904 Main, b. 54 Bkm.
" Arthur O. bookkeeper at Capewell Horse Nail Co. 40 Governor, b.u. 69 Babcock.
" Bently S. rubberw. 690 Park, h. 30 Grace.
" Bertram H. printer at Hartford Courant, 66 State, b. 888 Windsor av.
" Charles R. painter, h.2u. 3 Squire.
" Charles W. clerk at 650 Main, h. W.H.t.
" David M. screwm. at 476 Cap. b. 33 Hung.
" E. B. Mrs. h. 132 Washington.
" Elizabeth Mrs. h. 33 Hungerford.
" Frank H. superintendent, 690, h. 580 Park.
" Fred. H. agent, b.u. 106½ Trumbull.
" Fred. M. carpenter at 247 Asylum.
" Fred. W. assistant foreman, Hartford Courant, 66 State, b. 888 Windsor av.
" George, saloon, 44 Union pl. h. 100 Francis.
" George D. screwmaker, b. 33 Hungerford.
" Guy B. foreman, 690 Park, h. 14 Heath.
" J. Henry, treas. Case, Lockwood & Brainard Co. 141 Pearl, h. 20 Belden.
" J. Ross, clerk at 1 Flower, h. 28 Hopkins.
" Jacob A. foreman at Hartford Courant, 66 State, h. 888 Windsor av.
" James, mach. at 581 Capitol h. 476 Broad.
" Jennie J. clerk at Brown, Thomson & Co. 942 Main, h. 17 Florence.
" John, hard wood finisher, h. 20 Wolcott.
" John, machinist, b. 110 Trumbull.
**TURNER JOHN,** stairbuilder, 24 Potter, b. New Britain t.
" John J. coremaker, b. 61 Governor.
" John J. deliv.clk.98 Kil.h.u.125 Charter Oak.
" Joseph,blacksm. at 123 Church,h.474 Broad.
" Joseph F. machinist at Colts, b. 61 Governor.
" Kate A. inspector at 70 Huy. b. 61 Governor.
" Lavinia Mrs. h. 1336 Main.
" Mark C. carpenter, h. 12 Chapel.
" Mary, wid. William, h. 61 Governor.
" Mary E. inspector at 70 Huy. b.61 Governor.
" Nathan B. canvasser, h.u. 9 Kinsley.
" Rachel, wid. Thomas, b. 298 Pearl.
" Robert E. printer, 3 Spruce, h. E.H.t.
" Robert H. rubberw. 690 Park, h.13½ Francis.
" Thomas F. polisher, h.u. 125 Charter Oak.
" Walter I. clerk at 193 Asy. h.u. 39 Ashley.
" William, coachman at 100, b. 100 Church.

Turner Wm.A. coremaker, 556 Cap. b.61 Gov.
" William J. polisher at Colts, h.u. 125 Ch.O.
" William J. saloon, 44 Un. pl. l. 1045 Main.
Turo Thomas, beltm. 15 Trumbull, b. 13 Morgan.
Turpen Jacob B. waiter, b.u. 109 Mather.
Turretski Charles, ragpeddler, h.3u. 20 North.
Turton Benj. b.u. 21 A Sisson.
" Edwin, polisher at Popes, h.u. 10 Smith.
" John, polisher at Popes, b. 10 Smith.
Tusell Alfred, mach. hand, Colts, b. 29 Hamilton.
Tuttle Albert G. special freight agent, N.Y.R. h. 37 Sumner.
" Alice G. b. 105 Trumbull.
" Charles L. farmer & milkm. 47,h.47 Bluehills.
" Constant L. (T. & Mather,) b. 721 Main.
" Frances A. Mrs. b. 597 Farmington.
" Frank D. clerk at 750 Main, h.u. 24 Belden.
" Fred L. salesman, h.u. 24 Belden.
" Harry U. at National Fire Insurance Co. 95 Pearl, b. 47 Bluehills.
" Horace H. mach. at 1 Flow. b. 45 Sigourney.
" Jane Miss, h. 36 Winthrop.
" Jewett, engineer at 80 State, h.u. 6 Putnam.
" John, blacksmith at 142 Russ, h. 3 East.
" John F. laborer, h.u.r. 3 East.
" JOSEPH P. (Bill & Tuttle,) attorney at law, 847 Main, rm. 4, h. 133 Windsor av.
                                See page 482.
" Josiah G. trav.salesm. 725 Main, h.u. 31 Mahl.
" Mary A. housekeeper 30 Washington.
" & Mather, carmen, 2 American.
   Constant L. Tuttle.       Thos. S. Mather.
" Merwin, electrician, l. 30 Lewis.
" Michael, laborer at P.&R. b. 70 Union pl.
**TUTTLE N. J.** carriages and wagons, 19 Mather, h.u. 133 Windsor av.
                                See page 550.
" Plating Co. 41 Trumbull.
" Robert C. farmer, b. 47 Bluehills.
" Samuel I. (Tuttle & Sons,) h. 105 Trumbull.
" & Sons, grindstones, 1072 Main, S. I. Tuttle.
" William H. plater, h.u. 452 Main.
Tuzzillo Nicola, laborer, h.u. 210 Front.
Twaddell Jas. A. motorm. St.Ry. h.2u. 952 Broad.
Twaddle William B. cond. St.Ry. h.u. 973 Park.
Twain Mark, Samuel L. Clemens, author "Innocents Abroad," etc. h. 351 Farmington.
Twardoks Gustave F. foreman at 581 Capitol. h. 112 Hungerford.
" John F. insp. 581 Cap. b. 112 Hungerford.
Twartz Lulu, milliner at 956 Mn. b. 58 Church.
Twarz Arthur, grinder at 388 Cap. b.1212 Broad.
" Max, filer at 142 Russ, b. 1212 Broad.
Twichell Burton P. student at Yale, b. 125 Woodland.
" David C., U. S. Army, b. 125 Woodland.
" Edward C. b. 125 Woodland.
" Harmony, b. 125 Woodland.
" Joseph H. pastor Asylum Hill Congregational church, h. 125 Woodland.
" Susan L. b. 125 Woodland.
" ☞ see also Twitchell.
Twilley Benj. F. laborer, 95 Ple. b. 7 Atlantic.
Twiss Clayton W. clerk, 852 Mn. b. 110 Wooster.
" Ernest B. clerk at Colts, b. 110 Wooster.

**THE NEWS PRINTED IN THE POST IS RELIABLE.**

Twiss Herbert M. trav. salesm. Brown, Thomson & Co. 942 Main, h. 110 Wooster.
" John H. mechanic, 26 High, b.u. 7 Clinton.
" Marshall C. insp. at Colts, h. 30 Franklin.
Twitchell Willis l. *park commissioner,* principal Arsenal school, h. 31 Atwood.
" ☞*see also Twichell.*
Twohey Alice W. wid. James, h.u. 63 Woodbine.
" Dennis, mason, b. 63 Woodbine.
" James E. b.u. 63 Woodbine.
" ☞*see also Toohey, Toohy.*
Twohill John J. clerk at 26, b. 26 State.
Tygwent Michael, helper at Colts, h. 6½ Ellery.
Tyler Adrian H. patrnm. 556 Cap. h.u. 1447 Broad.
" Allys E. b. 179 Seymour.
" Charles C. supt. at Pratt & Whitney Co. 1 Flower, h. 7 May.
" Clarence M. at 154 Pearl, b. 179 Seymour.
" Clayton H. b. 179 Seymour.
" Edwin S. coal, office 746 Main, h.22 Marshall.
" Frederick A. clerk at 618 Cap. b. 5 Meadow.
" Geo. W. Rev. pastor Shiloh Baptist Church, h. 14 Martin.
" Harold R. at Phœnix Ins. Co. 64 Pearl, b. 43 Washington.
" Heman A. insurance, 756 Main, rm. 29, h.u. 179 Seymour.
" Heman A. Jr. at Yale, b. 179 Seymour.
" James T. mach. at 13 Central, b.u. 83 Gov.
" Manufacturing Co. 756 Main, rm. 29.
" Melvin, engineer at 177 Asy. h.u. 48 Park.
" Michael, waiter, b.r. 64 Hicks.
Tyler Ogden S. b. 368 Broad.
" Robert S. clerk at 388 Capitol, b. 7 May.
" Samuel, builder, r. 55 Park, h. 36 Ward.
" Selden W. agt. for Carter Ink Co. b.54 Capitol.
" Wm. F. patternm. at 618 Cap. h. 5 Meadow.
Tynan Thomas, washer at 560, l. 560 Main.
Tyroll Amy, milliner, b. 110 Babcock.
" Henry A. mach. 581 Cap. h.u. 110 Babcock.
" John W. clerk at 690 Park, b. 110 Babcock.
Tyrrell Harry A. paperhanger, h.u. 55 Green.

UDAPSKY Lewis, peddler, h.3u. 190 Front.
Udervitch David, ragpeddler, h.3u. 73 Charles.
Ufford Harry, bricklayer, h.r. 29 Albany.
Uhler J. Knight, clerk, Popes, b. 29 Buckingham.
Ulbert Bruno, buffer at Wm. Rogers Mfg. Co. 66 Market, b. 17 Sanford.
Ullrich Ferdinan, taxidermist, saloon, 5 Vandyke.
" Karl, cigarmaker at 104 Asy. h.2u. 33 Temple.
" Louis, barbershop, 5, b. 5 Vandyke.
" Wilhelmina, prop. Armory house, 5 Vandyke.
Ulrich Anna, wid. Conrad, h. 14 Alden.
" Arthur L. stenog. at Colts, h.u. 33 Congress.
" Augustus F. toolm. at Colts, h.u. 18 Morris.
" Frank, electrician at 53 Vernon, b. 116 Bab.
" Frederick H. messenger at State Bank, 795 Main, b.u. 18 Morris.
" George, teller State Savings Bank, 39 Pearl, *fire commissioner,* b. 14 Alden.
" Herman, engraver at Colts, b. 14 Alden.
Umberfield Burton L. police sergeant, h.u.617 Cap.
" Burton L. Jr. drugstore, 619, h. 617 Capitol.
" Kate, wid. George, b. 240 Collins.
Underwood Blanche Mrs. boardingh. 20 Talcott.
" G. M. painter, h.2u. 20 Church.
Unger Jacob, decorator, h.2u. 20 North.
Union Clothing Co. 100 Asylum.
S. B~r~ Cadden & Co.
" for Home Work, 239 Market.
" Grocery Co. John Pilgard, prop. 1030 Main.
" Pacific Tea Co., J. B. Duffy, magr. 174 Asy.
" Printing Co., W. A. Baedor & Co. 90 Asylum.
" Railroad Station, 466–478 Asylum.
" Stables, John Pibbles, prop. r. 1061 Main.
United Lines Telegraph Co. 3 Central.
" States Baking Co. 409 Aly. J.F.Coombs, mgr.

**UNITED STATES BANK,** 872 Main, cor. Kinsley. *See page 436.*
" States Bonded Warehouse, r. 74 Trumbull, office at 65 State.
" States Circuit and District Courts, 65 State.
" States Circuit Judge, Nathaniel Shipman, 65 State.
" States Collector of Customs, John H. Brocklesby, 65 State.
" States Commissioner's office, 65 State.
" States Court House and Post Office, 65 State.
" States courts' clerk, Circuit court, and District court, Edwin E. Marvin, 65 State.
" States Deputy Collector of Customs, Arthur E. Howard, 65 State.
" States District Attorney, Charles W. Comstock, 65 State.
" States Express, 236 Asy. John S. Krocher, agt.
" States Hotel, David A. Rood, prop. 26 State.
" States Hotel and Club Stables, r. 50 State.
" States Internal Revenue Office, 65 State.
" States Marshal, Richard C. Morris, 65 State.

**UNITED STATES PHOTO. CHEMICAL MFG. CO.** photo engraving, etc. Fred W. Francis, 29 Pearl. *See page 419.*
" States Stamped Envelope Agency, 1 So. Ann.
" States Stamped Envelope Works, H. J. & C. H. Wickham, 1 South Ann.

United Workers Club, 700 Main.
Upham Gilbert S. foreman at N.Y.R. h. 356 Park.
Upshur Susan, wid. Grant U. h.r. Edwards.
Upson Edwin L. foreman at 556 Capitol, h.u. 23 Huntington.
  " Fred. P. superintendent at Hartford Electric Light Co. 266 Pearl, b. 1150 Main.
  " Theron, chief clerk Insurance Department at Capitol, h.u. 51 Russ.
Upton Chas. H. clerk at Brown, Thomson & Co. 942 Main, h. 21 East.
  " Ernest C. agent, b. 67 Franklin.
  " Isaac J. elevator at 756 Main, h. 8 Ashley.
  " William T. electrician at 1 Laurel, b. E.H.t.
Ure James G. mach. 1 Flow. b. 104 Hungerford.
  " Walter B. clerk, h. 127 Brook.
Urgo Joseph, bootblk. 162 Asy. h.u. 11 Charles.
Uricchio Frank, laborer. b.u. 56 Portland.
  " Gaetano, barber at 454 Asylum, h. 158 Front.
  " Joseph, barber, 219, h. 219 Sheldon.
  " Joseph, shoemaker, h. 33 North.
  " Pasquale, carpenter, h.2u. 27 Kilbourn.
Urraro Joseph, laborer, h.u. 210 Front.
Ursino Luca, laborer, h. 11 Charles.
Ursone Donato, fruits, 139½ Tru. h. 23 Albany.
  " Donato, teamster, h.2u. 73 Morgan.
  " Tresa, b.3u. 82 Morgan.
Uschmann May, milliner at 75 Pratt, b. 125 Tru.
Usher Geo. latheman, 24 Mec. b. 41 Woodbridge.
Utley Charles H. farmer, h. 71 Bluehills.
  " Herbert S. milkman, b. 55 Bluehills.
  " Lucius H. farmer, h. 55 Bluehills.
  " Martin T. farmer, b. 55 Bluehills.
  " Mary L. b. 55 Bluehills.
Uttore Fred E. at 995 Main, h. 19 Foot Guard.
Utzig Henry, baker at 56, h. 56 Front.
  " Jacob, driver at 132 Market, h. 28 Talcott.
Uvino Carmine, ragpicker, b. 13 Charles.
  " Michael, laborer, h. 13 Charles.
Uzelmeier William, machinist at 1 Flower, h. T.v.

Vail Annie E. clerk, 956 Main, b. 44 Liberty.
  " George, physician, b. 87 Windsor.
  " James, grocer & saloon, 87, h.u. 87 Windsor.
  " James H. beltmaker at Jewell Belting Co. 15 Trumbull, h.u. 17 Goodwin.
  " John J. mach. at 1 Flow. h.2u. 50 Lawrence.
  " Joseph, clerk at 87, b.u. 87 Windsor.
  " Margaret, wid. Louis, h.u. 12 Warren.
  " Morris, laborer at St.Ry. h.u.r. 25 Spruce.
  " T. J. Mrs. b. 427 Main, rm. 65.
  " Thos. mach. at 1 Flower, h.2u. 50 Lawrence.
  " Thos. G. attorney, 863, b. 427 Main, rm. 65.
  " Wm. D. trav. salesm. Popes, b. 275 Collins.
Vaillant Henry L. saloon, 36 Wells, h.u. 3 Whitman.
Valario Joseph, laborer, h.u. 234 Front.
Valdivia Jos. H. buyer, 210 State, h.u. 16 Florence.
Valencia Sister, mother sup. St. Francis Hospital.
Valentine August L. machinist at 1 Flower, b. 40 Hungerford.
  " Charles M. driver at Brown, Thomson & Co. 942 Main, h. 115 Barbour.
  " George L. clerk 44 Asy. h.2u. 49 S.Hudson.
  " George W. clerk at Brown, Thomson & Co. 942 Main, b. 11 Florence.

Valentine H. E. Mrs. h. 68 Washington.
  " Nathaniel G., U.S.A. h. 68 Washington.
  " Robert, b. 255 Asylum.
Valiquette Alfred, cigarmfr. r. 90, h. 90 Heath.
  " Cyrille, barber, 837, h. 837 Park.
  " Frank, peddler, h. 837 Park.
Vallan Joan, laborer, h. 105 Commerce.
Vallente Gabriel, laborer, b. 247 Front.
  " Joseph, barber, 46 Temple, h. 86 Morgan.
Vallett Leander J. brakem. P.&R. h. 25 Walnut.
Vallette Edward A. filer at Popes, h.u.r. 64 Ward
Valley Division N.Y.N.H.&H.R.R. 450 Asylum.
VanAllen Chester L. section foreman P.&R. b. 1443 Broad.
VanAusdall Charles C. clerk at Lincoln, Seyms & Co. 34 Market, b. 20 Westland.
  " Conklin, trav. salesman, h. 20 Westland.
VanBuren Henry S., U. S. Army, b. 32 Bkm.
VanBuskirk John, l. 14 Spring.
  " John H. gateman N.E.R. b. 2 Walnut.
Vandenburg Charles B. painter, h.r. 61 Front.
Vanderbeck Willard H. printer at Popes, b.u. 175 Babcock.
Vanderbeek Abraham, Vanderbeek Tool Works, 490 Capitol, h. 902 Asylum.
  " Herbert, drughtsm. 1 Laurel, b. 902 Asylum.
VanDerburg Henry, dynamo man at 266 Pearl, h. E.H.t.
Vanderman Augustus, helper Colts, b. 112 State.
Vandewag John, decorator at Baxter the Decorator, 231 Asylum, h. 106 Jefferson.
VanDeWater Arthur R. student Trinity college, 19 Seabury hall, Summit.
Vanditto Christian, beltmaker at 15 Trumbull, h. 56 Portland.
VanDusen James R. finisher 133 Shel. h. E.H.t.
VanDyne Giles, attendant at 56, b. 56 Fairfield.
VanEpps E. J. Mrs. h. 7 South Hudson.
VanGasbeck LauraJ.wid.Wm.h.u.200Windsorav
VanHoudt Louis, fresco painter, h.u. 9 John.
VanHouten Arthur A. contractor, b. 375 Main.
Vankeirsbilck Fred. machinist, b. 19 Belmont.
  " Jean, machinist, h. 19 Belmont.
VanKeuren Louis N. quartermaster general at State Capitol, rm. 56, h. Bridgeport t.
VanLoon Bella J. h. 12 Trumbull.
VanMelsen J. H. cook at 921 Main, b. 28 Temple.
VanMeter Allen R. student Trinity college, 5 Northam tower, Summit.
VANNAIS GEORGE L. councilman 3d ward, bookkeeper at 956 Main, h. 42 Mahl.
VanName George E. Jr. machinist at Hartford Times, 716 Main, h. 32 Asylum.
  " Joseph M. (VanN.&Co.) lime, 35 Walnut, 45 Vine.
Vanni Joseph F. carptr. at Colts, h. 66 Vanblock.
  " Peter, browner at Colts, b. 66 Vanblock.
VanOrmer Frank, oiler, 70 Com. b. 45 Park.
  " Herman, ch. engir. at 70 Com. h. 201 Ashley.
VanOstrem Geo. brakeman, b.u. 22 Avon.
  " John, blacksmith 252 Pearl, h.u. 22 Avon.
VanOverstraeten John, clerk at Brown, Thomson & Co. 942 Main, b. 35 John.
  " Joseph S. h. 35 John.
  " Martin, cabinetm. at 225 Shel. h. 35 John.

VanPatten Wyman, machinist at 581 Capitol, h. 1469 Broad.
VanSchaack David, telegraph editor Hartford Telegram, 12 Central, h. 5 Park ter.
VanSchuyver Charles G. b. 8 Trinity.
VanSteenberg Ellen Mrs. b. 21 South Hudson.
Van Syckel Wm. H. baker at 385, b.2u. 488Main.
Van Vliet Marion, teacher Washington street school. b. 33 Allen.
VanWort Bert, at 17, b. 73 Albany.
VanZile Edward S. author, h. 19 Columbia.
Varley Henry, foreman at 283 Shel. h.Newfield.
Varney Edward H. cutter, 10 State, b. 33 Cap.
"   Fred H. cutter, b. 270 Main.
"   Mme. (Jennie S.) modiste, h. 270 Main.
"   William S. chiropodist, h. 270 Main.
Varrole John B. laborer, h. 12 North.
Vasco Michael, harnessmaker, h.u. 91 Windsor.
Vashjain Charles, screwm. at 476, b. 381 Capitol.
Vasilo Nicolo, laborer, b. 2 Charles.
Vasquenza Frank, laborer, b. 22 Charles.
"   Gaetano, laborer, b. 22 Charles.
"   Michael, laborer, h. 6 Charles.
Vater William, cigarm. 104 Asy. h. 69 Windsor.
Vaughan Richard J. b. 56 Buckingham.
Vaughn James, porter, 98 Wells, b. 28 Cedar.
Veasey Samuel R. agt. 721 Main, b. 25 Spring.
Vedder Edwn. V. ( C. S. Hills & Co.) b. 152 Asy.
Veeder Mfg. Co. cycle cyclometers, 20 Sargeant.
"   Curtis H. pres't V. Mfg. Co. b. 40 Willard.
Veite Max, at 17 Albany, h. 1 Goodman.
Veitz Clarence A. lab. at 335 Shel. h. 238 Martin.
Velhage Frank R. machinist, h. Lubeck.
Vellette Lee, brakeman, h. 25 Walnut.
Velte Charles J. engraver 30 Asy. b. 4 Francis.
"   George B. instructor at Trinity college, b. 4 Francis.
"   Henrietta, wid. John, h. 4 Francis.
Vendetto Christian, laborer, h.u. 56 Portland.
Vendicta James, laborer, b. 105 Commerce.
Vennart William, clerk at 12, h.2u. 40 Church.
Vensel C. A. machinist at 1 Flower, h. N.B.t.
Ventere Luigi, laborer, b.3u. 27 North.
Venton Fred'k, coal peddler, h.r. 321Windsor av.
Ventres Fred B. toolm.at 476 Cap. h.u. 64Francis.
"   Hubbard N. shipping clerk at Capewell Horse Nail Co. 40, h.u. 28 Governor.
Verchor Stephen, cigarm. at 40 Mul. h. Weth.t.
Verliegger Juliess, cabinetmaker, h. 35 South.
Vermilyea Geo.W. helper at 142 Russ, b.283 Cap.
VerValin Gideon, caser. h.u. 18 Pawtucket.
Very William, bookkeeper Phœnix National Bank, 803 Main, h. 23 Sumner.
Vesey Edward J. polisher atPopes, h.u.78 Flower.
"   Winnie, wid. Hugh, h.u. 78 Flower.
"   ☞ see also Veazey.
Vessels Silas, jobber, h. 4 Martin.
Vester Thomas N. mason, h.u. 11 Rowe.
Veteran Volunteer Fireman's Association of Hartford, Conn., 27 Arch.
Vetor Frederick, teamster, h.2u. 17 So.Prospect.
Vetter Louis, plumber, h.u.r. 36 Trumbull.
"   Mary wid. Alfred B. h.u. 36 Trumbull.
Vettmock Neil, helper at 54 Arch, h. 29 Elliott.

Vew Shin, laundry, 157, h. 157 Maple.
Vibber Abel, screwm. at 476 Cap. b. 55Pleasant
Vibbert Aubrey D. student at Trinity college, 10 Jarvis hall, Summit.
"   Caroline Mrs. h. 40 Trumbull.
"   L. M. Mrs. dressmaker, 71 Asylum, rm. 24.
Vibberts Ida L. attendant at 30 Washington.
"   Russell, b. 2 Holcomb.
Vibert J. S. conductor St.Ry. h. Wethersfield t.
"   James M. baggagemaster V. Div. N.Y.R. 450 Asylum, h. Wethersfield t.
"   Mary E. wid. Benjamin, h. 13 Washington.
Vicini Luigi, laborer, b. 67 Morgan.
"   Rocco, laborer, b. 75 Morgan.
Vickery & Marr, bowling alley, 645 Main.
          Thos. G. Vickery.      Charles Marr.
"   Thomas G. ( V. & Marr,) h. 81 Hudson.
Vidbourne Jos. gardener, b. Elizabeth park.
Videon Albert H. toolm. at 111 Shel. b. W.L.t.
"   Charles H. mach. at 1 Flow. b. 248 Lawrence.
Vieberg Victor, laborer, b. 301 Lawrence.
VIENNA BAKERY, 167–169 Asylum. See p. 45.
"   Pressed Yeast Co. Chas. H Lord, 281 Allyn.
Viering Paul, farmer, h. 236 Maple.
Viets Clarence, laborer, h.u. 238 Martin.
Viggiano Antonio, barber, 377 Cap. b.u. 27 Kil.
Vigiano James, barber, 14½ New Britain.
Vigle Samuel A. machinist at 83 Woodbine, b. 77 Windsor.
Vignone Nicholas A. laborer, h. 4 Charles.
"   Pasquale, laborer, b.2u. 82 Morgan.
Vile William, grocery, 280, h. 280 Front.
Vilentski Moriss, tailor, h.u. 182 Front.
Villiancourt Mr. hodcarrier, b. 197 State.
Vinal Frederick, lawyer, h. 149 Collins.
Vincensa Mainello, harnessm. 8 Sig. b.Frankfort
Vindetto Cresenzio, laborer, h. 56 Portland.
Vingenzo Galgotto, laborer, h.4u. 64 Morgan.
Vining Almanzor C. candies, 570, h. 570 Main.
"   Clarence J. plumber at 690 Park, b. 234 Jef.
"   Ernest W. mach. at 30 Cush. h. 952 Broad.
Vinton Charles S. machinist, 1 Laurel, h. 8 Oak.
"   Cora C. bkkpr. at 61 Asy. b. 45 Hungerford.
"   Della M. clerk at 711 Main, b. 8 Oak.
Vintschger Gus C. Jr. clerk Popes, b. 113 Park.
Viola Frank, shoemaker, 260, h. 260 New Park.
"   Tony, fruits, 950, h. 950 Broad.
Virtue William W. b. 26 Ashley.
Vissell George, operator at 476 Cap. b. 8 Forest.
Vitari Joseph, laborer, h.u. 210 Front.
Vitt Max, bakery & grocery, 151, h.u.r.151 Maple.
Vizner Marcell F. carpenter, h.u.r. 239 Jefferson.
"   Marcell F. Jr. carpenter, h. 239 Jefferson.
"   William, tinsmith, h.u.r. 239 Jefferson.
Vlanzo John Mrs. h.u. 12 Elm.
Voelter Robert, butcher, h.2u. 70 Sanford.
Vogel Anna E. teacher, 719, h. 719 Asylum.
"   Charles R. clerk, b. 175 Zion.
"   Christian, contractor at 1 Flow. h. 175 Zion.
"   Solomon, groceries, 361, h. 363 Main.
"   William, watchmaker, 191 Front, h. N.B.t.
"   Wm. C. machinist at 1 Flower, b. 175 Zion.
Vogelberg Charles, silversmith, b. 88 Church.
Vogt Jessie, wid. Joseph, h.u. 113 Albany.
"   Warren A. engir. N.Y.R. b.u. 113 Albany.

Voigt Richard, driver at 93 Fkn.b.14 Pawtucket,
Voirol Julius, cigarmaker, b.u. 1218 Main.
Voleman Max, laborer, h. 79 Avon.
Volenzano Victor, barber, h. 21 Morgan.
Vondra Joseph, tailor, h.2u. 54 Temple.
Vonna Peter, molder at 690 Park, h.u. 224 N.P.
VonWettberg Anna Mrs. h. 223 Asy. rms. 79-80.
" Edward, at Conn. Mutual Life Ins. Co. 783 Main, b. 223 Asylum.

**VORCE THE A. D. CO.** art store, mirrors,agts.art unions, 752 Mn. *See p.*418.
" C. B. civil engineer, 904 Main, b. 149 High.
" William S. gilder at A. D. Vorce Co. 752 Main, h. 15 Warner.
Vorrey Minnie J. at 273 Asylum, b. 16 Morris.
VosBurgh H. K. stove repairer, h.2u. 111 Tru.
" Leonard L., U.S. Army, b.2u. 111 Trumbull.
Vosko Michael, harnessm. 8 Sig. h. 91 Windsor.
Voss Fred. A. machinist 30 Cush. h. 19 James.
Vossler Adella E. dressm. 160, h. 160 Allyn.
" Max, upholsterer at Neal, Goff & Inglis Co. 980 Main, h. 160 Allyn.
Vurgenski A. Mrs. h.r. 60 Temple.
" Frederick, b.u.r. 60 Temple.

WACHNIANSKEY S. machinist at 1 Flower, h.u. 279 Market.
Wachtner Frank, watchmaker at Hansel, Sloan & Co. 886 Main, b. 25 Capitol.
Waddel John, laborer, b.3u. 40 Park.
" Michael, laborer, b.3u. 40 Park.
Wade Arthur C. clerk at 653 Main, h.u. 38 John.
" Benjamin C. butcher, h. 82 Hudson.
" John F. mach. at 388 Cap. h. 427 Broad.
" Louis W. filer at 851 Cap. h.2u. 42 John.
" O. A. capt. barge Hatch, h. Poors Mills, Me.
" & Sampson, market, 203 State.
    Walter C. Wade.        Arthur A. Sampson.
" Walter C.(*PublicMarketCo.*) h.71 Edwards.
" William, helper 11 Haynes, h.r. 57 Spruce.
Wadhams John H. assistant clerk Comptroller's office State capitol, h. Goshen t.
" John M. agent State Board of Education, rm. 42, State capitol, h. Goshen t.
" Louis W. carpenter, h. 26 New Britain.
Wadleigh Nancy M. wid. Lorenzo M. h.14 Walnut.
Wadstrom Justus, at Popes, b. 21 Wadsworth.
" Lewis, fireman at 581 Cap. b. 153 Lawrence.
" Titus A. janitor at Popes, l.u. 110 Hopkins.
Wadsworth Alfred J. cigarmaker at 1115 Main, h. 105 Wooster.
" Athenæum, 624 Main.
" Charles B. clerk at 556 Main, b. 124 Capitol.

**WADSWORTH DANIEL S.** "Wadsworth Inn," h. 104 Albany.
" FrederickE.blacks.r.44½John, h.40 Glendale.
" Gallery of Paintings, 624 Main.
" George N. joiner, b. 40 Glendale.
" Henrietta Mrs. b. 1045 Main.
" Herbert C. at Hartford Fire Insurance Co. 53 Trumbull, h. 60 Willard.
" Lucy, b. 401 Albany.
" Martha, wid. Edward, h. 124 Capitol.
" Martha Louisa, h. 124 Capitol.

Wadsworth Mary R. wid. Josiah, b.u. 15 Fmt.
" Robert A. at Connecticut Mutual Life Ins. Co. 783 Main, b. 124 Capitol.
" William S. butcher, h.u. 1172 Main.
Waegelein Herman, baker at 169 Asy. b. 26 West.
" Louis P. baker at 169 Asylum, b. 26 West.
Waenstaen Max, helper at 1 Flow. b. 81 Front.
Waghorn Albert H. clerk 197 Asy. b. Elmwood v.
" Daisy L. clerk at National Life Association, 53 Trumbull, b. Elmwood v.
" Elijah S. carpenter at N.Y.R. h. Elmwood v.
Waglum Howard, helper at Popes, l. 109 Bab.
Wagner Charles, upholst. 638 Main, h. 9 Morris.
" Clara M. clerk at 745 Main, b. 9 Morris.
" George, barber at 272, b. 272 Park.
" John P. engineer, h. 16 Pliney.
" Maria C. b.u. 177 Capen.
" Wm. F. mach. at 252 Pearl, h. Wilson station.
Wagstaff Wm. rubberw. 690 Park, b. 32 Francis.
Wah Charlie A. laundry, 454 Main.
" Sam, laundry, 328 Pearl.
" Sing, laundry, h. 1075 Broad.
" Yet, laundry, 211 Lawrence.
Wahl John, filer at Popes, h. 88 Hamilton.
" ☞ *see Wall.*
Wahlquist Alfred, molder at 556 Cap. h. 167 Bab.
" August P. machinist at 28 Laurel, h.u.r. 16 Affleck.
" John, mason, b. 47 Woodbine.
Wainwright Jonathan M., U.S.A. b. 58 Wash.
" Helena B. wid. Wm. A. M. h.58 Washington.
Waite Albert J. foreman at Popes, h.u. 107 Oak.
" Elbridge G. foreman at 111 Edwards, h. 302 Maple.
" Ernest N. foreman at Popes, h. 47 Atwood.
" Frank Louis, physician,68 Pratt, h.259 Weth.
" Frederick, toolm. at 476 Cap. h. 20 Grand.
" George E. clerk at 372 Asylum, h. E.H.t.
" James N. h. 50 Wadsworth.
" Joseph Rev. pastor Unity church, h. 109 Kenyon.
" Luzerne C. millwright at 581 Cap. b. B.v.
" Mary A. Mrs. asst. matron, 690, b. 690 Asy.
" William M. agent at 756 Main, b. 2 Whitman.
Waitman Isaac, fruits, h.u.r. 26 North.

**WAKEFIELD AGENCY,** real estate, loans, etc. 720 Main. *See page 424.*
    W. L. Wakefield.        F. W. Wakefield.
" Anna, wid. J. Percival, b. 28 Hudson.
" Atwood, agent cigars and tobacco, 259 Asylum, h. 421 Maple.
" Eugene H. salesman, Valley, h. 207 Ashley.
" Fred W.(*Wakefield Agency,*) b. 421 Maple.

**WAKEFIELD WALTER L.** fire ins. agent, 720 Main, rm. 1, h. 64 Webster. *See page 445.*
Wakeman Mark W. gardener at 119, l.r. 119 Far.
Wahlberg Herman, coachm. 550 Far. h. 11 Fales.
Walbridge Charles H. teamster at L. T. Fenn, furniture store, 613 Main, h.u. 214 Park.
" Robert, bkkpr. at 16 Mul. b.u. 214 Park.
Walch James, laborer, h. 54 Hungerford.
" Thomas, bartender, b. 82 Francis.
" William J. machinist 1 Flow. b. 1413 Broad.

# ROBERT WALKER,

## House Painter & Decorator,

### 12 AND 14 CHURCH STREET.

**Storehouse and Paintshop, 187 PEARL STREET.**

**New Store After October 1st, at**

### 1017 MAIN STREET.

**All kinds of Painters' Supplies, Wall Papers, Artists' Materials, etc.**

Walchensteimer Peter, at 8 Sig. b. 55 Laurel.
Walden Timothy, helper, 232 Shel. h. 9 Curcombe.
Walder Aaron, real estate broker. 10, h. 10 Morris.
" Bros. gents' furnishings, 120 State.
   I. J. Walder.       H. W. Walder.
" Herman W. (*Walder Bros.*) b. 10 Morris.
" Isaac J. (*Walder Bros.*) b. 10 Morris.
Walding W. C. clerk at 88 Market, h. E.H.t.
Waldo W. F. tel. operator, N.Y.R. b. 45 Wooster.
Waldron Arthur M. operator Western Union
   Telegraph Co. 6 Central, h. 64 Lincoln.
" Frank, buffer at 62 Market, h. E.H.t.
" H. G. brazier at 62 Market, b. E.H.t.
" James H. bookkeeper, h. 10 Buckingham.
" Patrick, helper at 1 Flow. b. 138 Lawrence.
" Thomas, lab. at 1 Flow. h.2u. 140 Lawrence.

WILLIAM F. WALDRON, Physician. Office, 703
   Main street, room 6.
     Hours—7 to 9 A. M.
          2 to 4 P. M.
            7 to 9 P. M.
               Telephone 410—5.

Waldron William F. physician, 703 Main, b.
   39 Woodbridge.
Wales James A. student at Trinity college, 4
   Jarvis hall, Summit.
Walgren Robert, gardener, h.r. 655 Farmington.
Walker Albert H. attorney, h. 133 Hawthorn.
" Andrew, driver at 399 Allyn, l.u. 6 Squire.
" Barbara, b. 1 Farmington.
" Charles E. assistant manager sale depart-
   ment at Popes, h. 488 Prospect av.
" Eugene, clerk at 745 Main, b. W.H.t.
" Frank, plumber at 164 State, b. 8 Flower.
" Frank S. conductor, P.&R. b. 255 Asylum.
" Fred W. at 20 Sargeant, l. 22 Hopkins.
" George, at 302 Asylum, b. So. Windsor t.
" George Leon Rev. pastor Emeritus First
   ' Church of Christ (Center), h. 46 Prospect.
" James M. student at Trinity college, 34
   Jarvis hall, Summit.
" John, h. 83 Bellevue.
" John, helper at 48 Ann. b. W.H.t.
" John H. conductor St.Ry. l. 703 Main.
" John L. at 956 Main, b. 83 Bellevue.
" John W. slater, h.3u. 180 Sheldon.
" Matthew, b. 41 Mather.
WALKER ROBERT, painter and decorator, 12 and
   14 Church, shop 187 Pearl, h. 70 Williams.
               *See page 366.*

Walker Weston W., Boston Branch, groceries,
   745 Main, h. Arnoldale road, W.H.t.
" Wilbur C. credit clerk at Popes, h. 496
   Prospect av.
" William R. stairbuilder, b. 1080 Main.
" Williston, professor Theological Seminary,
   1507 Broad, b. 46 Prospect.
Walkey Samuel, carpenter, h.u. 7 Sigourney pl.
Walkley A. W. bricklayer, h. 44 Brook.
" Caroline E. stenographer at L. L. Ensworth
   & Son, 104 Front, b. Wethersfield t.
" Chandler H. porter, 304 Asy. h.2u. 6 John.
" Frank H. mach. at 30 Cush. b. 42 Spring.
" Harry H. clerk at Conn. River Banking Co.
   761 Main, b. Wethersfield t.
" Richard W. b.u. 43 Vernon.
" Warren, h.u. 43 Vernon.
Wall Alice, wid. Michael, h. 9 Ward pl.
" Anna B. at 690 Park, b. 40 Evergreen.
" Charles H. mach. 28 High, h. 55 Warrington.
" Charles J. elevatorer, h.u. 72 Vanblock.
" Dennis, teamster, b. 9 Ward pl.
" Edward, clerk at 376 Asy. h.u. 1122 Main.
" Edward, helper, h.r. 25 Spruce.
" Francis, polisher at 476 Cap. b. 125 Mather.
" Garrett, saloon, 184 State, h. 88 Jefferson.
" James, machinist at 54 Arch, b. 125 Mather.
" James, steamfitter, 164 State, b. 1045 Main.
" James C. rubberworker at 690 Park, b. 40
   Evergreen.
" James E. h. 25 Wolcott.
" James E. conductor, St.Ry. b. 67 Main.
" John, laborer, h.u. 45 Green.
" John F. machinist at Popes, b. 9 Ward pl.
" Josephine Mrs. rooms to rent, h.u. 1122 Main.
" Martin, mach. Pope Tube Co. b. 9 Ward pl.
" Mary, wid. James, h.2u. 40 Evergreen.
" Michael, b. 2 Holcomb.
" Michael, mach. Pope Tube Co. b. 9 Ward pl.
" Patrick, tinsmith, h. 125 Mather.
" Patrick F. steamfitter, b. 80 State.
" Peter (Mary) Mrs. h. Warrenton.
" Peter J. driver at Brown, Thomson & Co.
   942 Main, b. 45 Green.
" Pierce C. carpenter, b. 125 Mather.
" Robert, motorman, b. 101 Main.
" William B. jobber, h.r. 21 Squire.
" ☞see also Wahl.
Wallace Alex. manager at 226, b. 230 Asylum.
" Alfred M. bookkr. 152 State, h. 190 High.
" Daniel T. coachman at 136 Washington, h.
   38 Cedar.
" David F. molder 556 Capitol, h.u. 32 Elm.
" Edward J. laborer at 54 Arch, h.u. 9 Front.
" Frank, coachman at 135, b. 135 Washington.
" Frank S. bkkpr. 118 Asy. b. Windsor Locks t.
" Henrietta, wid. Frederick, at Brown, Thom-
   son & Co. 942, h. 943 Main, rm. 38.
" Howard, clerk at 705 Main, b. 445 Capitol.
" Jane R. boardinghouse, 79 Front.
" John, laborer at 618 Capitol, h. 52 Hicks.
" John B. gateman N.Y.R. h. 49 Brook.
" John W. M. carptr. at Popes, h. 445 Cap.
" Mary, wid. David, b. 35 Laurel.
" Michael, molder, 618 Capitol, h. 35 Laurel.

# W. E. WALLACE,

*Importer, Dealer, and Grower of*

**Hardy Roses, Azalias, Rhododendrons, Shrubs, Fruit and Ornamental Trees, Clematis, etc.**

NURSERIES, **FARMINGTON AVENUE**, BETWEEN

WHITING STREET AND QUAKER LANE.

### P. O. BOX 370, HARTFORD.

*Electric car passes the grounds every ten minutes.*

WALLACE WM. E. nurseryman, office 57, h. 57 Farmington. *See page 367.*
" Wm. J. conductor N.Y.R. h. 47 Brook.
Wallbeoff James E. con. St.Ry. h. 158 Franklin.
Walledman Max, peddler, h.u. 24 North.
Waller Fred J. printer, b. 189 Maple.
" Robert A. agent, b. 189 Maple.
" Robert E. motorman St.Ry. h. 189 Maple.
Walley William, rubberworker, b. 38 Smith.
Wallin John, cabinetm. at 133 Shel. h. 43 Amity.
Wallwork Maggie L. at 5 Sigourney pl.
Walmsley Daniel P. machinist, h.r. 44 Village.
" John, printer at 141 Pearl, b. 62 Capen.
" William, plumber, b. 62 Capen.

## WALNUT LODGE HOSPITAL

CO. hospital, 56 Fairfield av.
*See page 712.*
Walquist ☞ *see Wahlquist.*
Walrath W. Harry Mrs. b. 1150 Main.
Walsh Benedict C. night manager at Western Union Telegraph, 6 Cen. h. 52 Wadsworth.
" Bernard F. crater, 581 Cap. b. 2u. 1445 Broad.
" Cornelius J. conduc. St.Ry. h.u. 80 Franklin.
" Daniel, rubber at 581 Cap. b. 2u. 545 Main.
" Daniel F. clerk at 218 Asy. b. 15 So. Ann.
" Edward, bartender, b. 21 Central.
" Elizabeth, nurse, b. 1255 Main.
" James, carpenter at N.Y.R. h. 167 Zion.
" James, deckh. str. Middletown, 285 State.
" John J. farmer at 105, b. 105 Bluchills.
" John J. laborer at Popes, h. 11 Wilson.
" Joseph J. shipg. clk. 690 Park, b.u. 105 Bab.
" Joseph P. driver, b.2u. 1445 Broad.
" Martin, ostler at 12 Wells, b. 355 Asylum.
" Mary R. b. 1445 Broad.
" Michael, laborer, 14 Huntington.
" Michael, ship carpenter, h.u. 31 Sheldon.
" Morris, machinist at 110 Com. b. 31 Chapel.
" Peter A. printer, 29 Un.pl. b.2u. 1445 Broad.
" Redmond, at 690 Park, h.u. 40 Smith.
" Richard, deckh. str. Middletown, 285 State.
" Richard, driver, b. 20 Affleck.
" Robert, clerk at 120 Alb. h. 66 Fairmount.
" Sarah, wid. Michael, h.2u. 1445 Broad.
" Thomas, at r. 32 Church.
" Thomas, forem. at Pope Tube Co. h. 105 Bab.
" Thomas, hodcarrier, h.u. 8½ Ellery.
" Thomas J. h.u. 105 Babcock.
" Thomas J. mach. 20 Vredendale, h. 32 Por.
" W. helper at 164 State, h. 46 Avon.

Walsh William, foreman, h.u. 31 Elliott.
" William H. carpenter, h. 119 Maple.
" Wm. H. contr. state prison, h. 14 Preston.
" ☞ *see also Welch; Welsh.*
Walter Anna C. teacher at High School.
" Fred, driver at 863 Main, h. 16 Westland.
" Gustav, shoemaker, 883, h. 853 Park.
" Herman, laborer, b. 853 Park.
" Louis, tailor at 76 Asylum, b. 5 North.
" William, market, 19, h. 19 Elmer.
Walters Aretus, driver, h.r. 1128 Main.
" Catharine, wid. Fred A. h. 41 Huntington.
" Harry, b.r. 1128 Main.
" Joseph, with New England Brewing Co. h. 20 Maple.
Walton Charles, clerk at 115 Pearl, b. 22 Hicks.
Walz Fred C. carpenter, h.u. 1332 Broad.
" Jacob, grocer, 54, b. 54 Temple.
" Jacob, music teacher, 103, h.u. 103 Pratt.
" John M. engineer at 1507, h. 1337 Broad.
" John Jr. carpenter, b. 1337 Broad.
" Lola H. stenog. at 690 Park, b. 1337 Broad.
" Mary, wid. Christian, b. 54 Temple.
Wander Emil C. (*W. W. & Sons,*) h.u. 61 Kenyon.
" Eugene A. (*W. W. & Sons,*) h. 175 Maple.
" William (*W. W. & Sons,*) h. 48 Forest.
" William & Sons, pianos, 241 Asylum.
Wm. Wander. Emil C. Wander. Eugene A. Wander.
" ☞ *see also Wunder.*
War Charlie, laundry, h. 47 Morgan.

## WARBURTON C. B. decorator, painter, agent for Reliance Oil & Grease Co. warerooms, 1092, office, 999, h. 999 Main.

Ward C. Clayton, clerk at C. H. Case & Co. jewelers, 851 Main, b. 493 Prospect av.
" Catherine Mrs. clerk at 37 Wells.
" Chas. H. motorman St.Ry. b.u. 16 Goodman.
" David, filer at 581 Capitol, h. 86 Pleasant.
" Edward, laborer, h.r. 25 Spruce.
" Edward M., U. S. Army, b. 166 Russ.
" George, b.2u. 2 Elm pl.
" George E. operator at 8 Sig. h. 166 Russ.
" Herbert W. steamfitter, h. 32 Chapel.
" James, tinner at 360 Main, b. 23 Spruce.
" James A. h. 1 Sumner.
" James J. coachman at 356 Main, h. 4 Weth.
" James W. clerk at 872, b. 32 Asylum.
" James W. physician, 437, h. 437 Capitol.
" John, b. 2 Holcomb.
" John, h. Quaker lane.
" John J. laborer, h.u. 53½ Governor.
" John J. traveling salesman at 690 Park, h. 10 Canton.
" Joseph H. plumber, b. 35 Amity.
" Kate, wid. Patrick F. h. 35 Amity.
" M. Josephine, stenographer, b. 35 Amity.
" Mamie, at 1 South Ann, b. 15 Goodman.
" Margaret Mrs. cook at 30, h.u.r. 30 Weth.
" Mary, wid. James, h. 12 Buckingham.
" Mary A. stenog. at 690 Park, b. 10 Canton.
" Mary W. wid. Nathaniel C. h. 889 Asylum.
" Michael T. Jr. joiner, h.u. 261 Park.
" Patrick, laborer, h.u. 169 Main.
" Thomas J. compositor at Evening Post, 23 Asylum, h. 9 Center.

**Merchants say it PAYS to Advertise in The Post.**

# WILLIAM WARD,

(Successor to JOHN McGOODIN.)

Care of
Real
Estate a
Specialty.

## Real Estate

### AND

## House Agent,

Twenty Years' Experience.

## No. 863 Main Street.

Old Number 345.

WARD WILLIAM, real estate agent, 863 Main,
    rm. 5, b. 119 High.     See page 368.
Wardell Caroline, wid. William, clerk at 745
    Main, b.2u. 153 Windsor av.
" Minnie, h.u. 126 Market.
Wardenski August, brewer 315 Park, h. 29 Affleck.
Wardstrom Linus, at 581 Cap. l.u. 153 Lawrence.
Wardwell J. Frank, at 335 Sheldon, b. 25 Morris.
WARDWELL NED C. manager Nims, Whitney
    & Co. doors, sash and blinds, 1170 Main,
    h.u. 109 Albany.     See page 511.
Ware Clarence W. polisher at 111 Sheldon, b.
    Windsor t.
" Edw. T. b. 125 Woodland.
" Harry E. h. 104 Trumbull.
" Jennie M. wid. Alfred C. h.2u. 19 Church.
" M. F. Mrs. nurse, 721 Main, room 14.
" ☞see also Wear.
Warfield Abijah B. bookkeeper at H. E. Patten,
    dye works, 37 Wells, h. 454 Windsor av.
WARFIELD GEORGE F. (Belknap & Warfield,)
    77 Asylum, b. 25 Spring.    See page 421.
Waring John, electrician at 83 Woodbine, b.
    141 Washington.
Wark John, conductor St.Ry. b. 80 State.
Warnecke Henry, filer at Colts, h. King, n. Julius.
Warner Alfred O. bkkpr. at 77 Chas. b. 19 Avon.
" Alonzo W. mach. at 1 Flow. h. 48 Cedar.
" Arthur N. asst. forem. at Popes, b. 56 Capitol.
" Bruce D. molder, h. 100 Willow.
" Carrie M. Mrs. attendant at 30 Washington.
" Charles Dudley, pres't Hartford Courant
    Co. editor Hartford Courant, 66 State,
    park commissioner, h. 37 Forest.
" Clarissa B. b. 2 Brown.
" Edward T. plumber at 1072 Mn. h. 82 Spring.
" Edward T. Jr. plumber, b. 82 Spring.
" Eugene W. foreman at 581 Cap. h. 28 Martin.
" Everett E. optician at 865 Main, b. 28 Spring.
" Frank A. filer at Colts, b. 48 Cedar.
" Frank G. (W. Photograph Co.) b. 49 Forest.
" Fred A. mach. at 26 High, b. 82 Spring.
" Fred. W. treas. W. & Willard Co. h. Weth. t.
" Geo. B. electrician at 190 Pearl, h. Elliott pl.
" George H. h. 49 Forest.
" Geo. R. Rev. rector St. Thomas Episcopal
    church, h. 60 Capen.
" George W. machinist, 1 Flower, h. 46 Cedar.
" Gilbert F. mach. at 388 Cap. h.u.249 Putnam.

Warner Grace M. pianist, b.u. 30 Sumner.
" Harriet, seamstress, h. 312 Windsor av.
" Henry R. clerk at 27 Asylum, h. 58 Edwards.
" Herbert O. at Conn. Mutual Life Insur-
    ance Co. 783 Main, h. 7 Park ter.
" Illine, waitress at 30 Washington.
" James L. clerk at 110 Asy. b. 28 Spring.
" Lucius P. boss polisher at 1 Flow. h. 2 Brown.
" Luman, janitor, 1½, h. 13 So. Hudson.
" Maria H. wid. Allan W. h.u. 30 Sumner.
" Mary, wid. Chas. S. h.u. 1164 Main.
" Minnie C. music teacher, b. 60 Capen.
" Photograph Co. 75 Pratt.
    William H. Pease.     Frank G. Warner.
" Robert, machinist at 40 Cush. h. 151 Collins.
" Robert G. plumber, h. 82 Spring.
" Robert J. bookkeeper, h. 143 Collins.
" Sarah M. S. wid. Dr. Eli, h. 3 Farmington.
" Timothy P. pilot str. Middletown, 285 State.
    h. Goodspeed v.
" Webb S. clerk Adams Ex. Co. b.u. 56 Asylum.
" & Willard Co. merchant tailors, 108-110 Asy.
" Wm. A. student Trinity college, b. 60 Capen.
" William H. clerk at 197 Asy. h. Weth. t.
Warren Annie J. justifyer at Hartford Post, 23
    Asylum, b. 40 Vanblock.
" Charles N. peddler, h.u. 14 Goodwin.
" Francis M. carriages, horse goods, etc. 393
    Allyn, h. 32 Woodbine.
" Fred H. millwright at 40 Gov. h. 100 Retreat.
" Fred'k F. janitor 389 Allyn, b. 32 Woodbine.
" George E. bridge superintendent N.Y.R.
    h.u. 37 Williams.
" George W. h. 25 Seyms.
" Herbert C. contractor at Pratt & Whitney
    Co. 1 Flower, h. 283 Collins.
" J. C. dressmaker, h.u. 363 Main.
" John, helper at Colts, h. 40 Vanblock.
" John F. clerk 222 Sheldon, b. 40 Vanblock.
" & Kenney, saloon, 3 Front.
    M. J. Warren.     John J. Kenney.
" Mabel B. stenogr. b. 66 Charter Oak.
" Mary G. Mrs. b. 108 Farmington.
" Michael J. (W. & Kenney,) grocers, 222
    Sheldon, h. 40 Vanblock.
" Mortimer A. agent State Board Education,
    rm. 42, State capitol, h. Collinsville t.
" Robert H. clerk at 729 Main, h. 83 Green.
" Sidney A. barber at 84 Albany, h.u. 96 Chst.
" William, h. 41 Mather.
" William Dana, h. 7 Riverside st.
Warrillow James H. mach. at 1 Flow. h.u. 19 Julius.
Warring Robert, porter at T. Sisson & Co. 729
    Main, h. 14 Warren.
Warrington Frank J. polisher at 111 Sheldon,
    b. Windsor t.
" Sarah J. at 867 Main, b. 58 Church.
" Wm. cigarmaker at 867 Main, h. Windsor t.
" William C. operator at 111 Sheldon, b.W.t.
Wart Wellington H. stenographer Phœnix Ins.
    Co. 64 Pearl, h. 82 Putnam.
Washburn Albert L. asst. engineer at 800 Main,
    h.3u. 80 Pearl.
" Alvin, printer, h.u. 32 Wells.
" Anna, wid. Thomas, h.u. 35 Mechanic.

Washburn Christiana, wid. Jas. b. 753 Asylum.
" Ella A. teacher N.E. school, b. 35 Clark.
" Frank R. bricklayer, h. 34 Elmer.
" George C. h. 13 Wadsworth.
" Henrietta Mrs. h. 96 Church.
" Herbert E. printer at 133 Shel. h. 76 Fmt.
" Lucius F. bricklayer, h. 35 Clark.
" Lucy A. wid. Ed. M. h.u. 20 Grand.
" Mary A. wid. A. H. h. 22 Prospect.
" Nellie H. teacher Ch.O. sch. b. 80 Pearl.
" S. P. Mrs. h. 199 Russ.
" S. Alice, at 39 Pearl, b.3u. 80 Pearl.
" William, mason, h. 85 Clark.
Washington Charles, jobbing, l. 33 Ferry.
" George, b. 41 Mather.
" James F. coachman at 98, l.r. 98 Ann.
" Life Ins. Co., R. Kellogg, mgr. 61 Oxford.
" Nancy, wid. Harrison, b. 14½ Martin.
Wasserbach Eliza, wid. John C. h.926 Main, rm 28.
Water Commissioners' office in city hall, 800 Main.
Waterhouse Burton S. toolmaker at Popes, h.u.
    70 Wooster.
" Elijah F. machinist, h. 70 Wooster.
" F. H. electrician, b.u. 100 Wooster.
" Harry E. mach. at Popes, h.u. 1209 Main.
" J. E. printer at 1 Flower, b. 100 Wooster.
" Lillian, clerk, b. 70 Wooster.
" W. machinist, 13 Central.
Waterman Arthur B.motorm. St.Ry.h.52 Retreat.
" Edgar F. b. 61 Lafayette.
" Edward H. b. 96 Sargeant.
" Francis E. student Trinity college, b. 61 Laf.
" Eugene F. laborer, 56 Com. h.u. 14 Gold.
" George N. hostler 50 State, h. 11 Talcott ct.
" Gertrude, assistant, 171 Putnam.
" Harlan P. carpenter, h.2u. 82 Madison.
" Harry, cook, b. 16 Gold.
" Ira, helper, h.2u. 53 Sanford.
" James H. piano mover, h.u. 1281 Main.
" James N. conductor St.Ry. h.r. 26 Walnut.
" James N. plumber, b.r. 26 Walnut.
" John L. helper, h. 1 Huntley.
" Joseph R. engineer at 8 Front, b. 651 Main.
" Lucy S. wid. Edgar, h. 61 Lafayette.
" Mary S. teacher Brown school, h.96 Sargeant.
" Robert H. clerk at Brown, Thomson & Co.
    942 Main, b. Naubuc v.
" S. G. Miss, h. 41 Congress.
" William H. clerk at 98 Kil. b. 96 Sargeant.
" William P. teamster, b. 230 Barbour.
" Wyllys B. clerk at Brown, Thomson & Co
    942 Main, b. Naubuc v.
Waterous Annie R. Mrs. h. 775 Asylum.
" Richard G. real estate, 3 Asylum, h. E.H.t.
" Richard G. Jr. b. 775 Asylum.
" Thos. C. attorney at law, 49 Pearl, b. 775 Asy.
" ☞see also Watrous.
Waters Charles, farmer, b. 16 White.
" David, gardener, h. 99 Allen pl.
" Edward, brakeman, b.r. 23 Portland.
" Emma Mrs. nurse, b. 14 Grand.
" Henry, farmer, h. 16 White.
" Henry B. carpenter, 252 Pearl, h. 222 Park.
" James, machinist, l.u. 1122 Main.
" James Jr. mach. at 1 Flower, h. 17 Squire.

JOHN B. WATERS, Physician.    Office, 103
    Trumbull street.    -
    Hours—8 to 10 A. M.
    1 to 3, and 7 to 9 P. M.
        Telephone 950.

Waters John B. physician, 103, h. 103 Trumbull.
" Lucy J. nurse, h. 32 Hopkins.
" Samuel E. lettercarrier, h. 43 Walnut.
" William A. inspector, h.u. 12 Goodman.
Watkins Clara S. cashier at 711 Main, b. 90 State.
" Chas. F. carpenter, 1170 Main, h.3u. 90 State.
" Charles W. druggist, 839, h. 891 Park.
" Whitney W. mach. at 581 Cap. h.u. 10 Haw.
" Willard W. mach. at 581 Cap. h. 10 Haw.
" William R. gardener, h.2u.r. 132 Market.
Watkinson Alfred H. at Hfd. Steam Boiler Insp.
    & Ins. Co. 650 Main, b. 57 Grove.
" Caroline, wid James, b. 9 Grand.
" David, mach. at 133 Sheldon, b. 91 Asylum.
" David, machinist, b. 703 Main, room 14.
" J. Russell, printer at 668, h. 721 Main, rm. 69,
" Jane H. wid. Alfred, h. 57 Grove.
" Juvenile Asylum and Farm School, Albany
    c. Bloomfield avs.
" Library, 5 Athenæum.
" Louise S. wid. E. B. h. 725 Asylum.
Watrous Charles D. carpet layer, 43, h. 43 John.
" Charles F. watchman, h. 8 Washington.
" Cornelia A. teacher 2d North school, 249
    High, h. 8 Washington.
" Edgar R. plater at Wm. Rogers Mfg. Co.
    66 Market, h. 165 Bellevue.
" Frank C. clerk at William Rogers Mfg. Co.
    66 Market, h.u. 16 Avon.
" George W. secretary Wm. Rogers Mfg. Co.
    66 Market, h. 16 Suffield.
" Hattie L. b. 32 Buckingham.
" Henry, engineer, h.2u. 77 Temple.
" Ida, clerk at 835 Main, b. 58 Church.
" J. Hubbard, medicine, 71, l. 71 Asy. rm. 17.
" John H. leaf tobacco, 230 State, L 290 Main.
" Mary A. Mrs. b. 55 Annawan.
" Ralph, teamster, Daniels Mill Co. b. Blo.
" Robert N. foreman mailing, P.O. h. W.L.t.
" Sarah A. wid. S. DeLoss, b. 6 Wooster.
" William H. lithographer, h. 59 Kilbourn.
WATROUS WILLIAM H. president and treasurer
    Wm. Rogers Mfg. Co. & Rogers Cutlery
    Co. 66 Market, h. 548 Windsor av.
        See outside back cover.
" ☞see also Waterous.
Watson Alex. A. foreman at 154 Charter Oak,
    h. 32 Lincoln.
" Alexander, at Adams Express Co. h. 3 Rice.
" Arthur B. pressf. at 724 Main, b. 59 Willow.
" C. H. motorman, 115 State, h. E.H.t.
" Daniel, laborer, b. 28 Elm.
" Eliza W. wid. George W. h. 203 Sigourney.
" Elizabeth J. wid. of Wm. B. h. 59 Willow.
" Frank J. salesman at Potter & Paynes, 405
    Allyn, l. 38 Church.
" Frank P. bricklayer, h. 59 Market.
" George E. mech. at Popes, b.u. 42 Lawrence.
" George M. mason, b. 47 Park.
" Harry, at 581 Capitol, b.u. 3 Rice.

**To Rent Advertisements Bring Results in The Post.**

Watson Harry S. carpenter, b. 47 Park.
" Hobert W. auditor at P.&R. h. 427 Main.
" Idelle B. teacher French, High school,
b. 719 Asylum.
" James, clerk at Tucker & Goodwin, 10-12
Hurlburt, h. 49 Amity.
" James, woodw. at 5 Mechanic, b.u. 283 Main.
" John, collarmaker at 8 Sig. h.u. 44 Putnam.
" John H. hackdriver, supernumerary police-
man, h.u. 5 North.
" Joseph R. asst. bkkpr. 44 Mar. b. 59 Capitol.
" Margaret, wid. William, h.u. 42 Lawrence.
" Mary J. dressmaker, h. 28 Elm.
" Minnie E. wid. G. L. clerk at 956 Main,
h.3u. 36 Church.
" N. G. clerk at 745 Main, b. 4 Ashton.
" Peter J. repairer at Popes, b.u. 5 North.
" Robert, b. 56 Fairfield.
" Sarah, wid. Alexander, nurse, b. 13 King.
" William G. clerk, h. 4 Ashton.
" William J. lacer at Popes, b.u. 42 Lawrence.
" William L. turner, b.u. 3 Rice.
" William T. machinist at 9 Sig. b. 47 Park.
Waugh James, farmer, b.u. 21 Squire.
" James, laborer, h. 25 Wolcott.
" James E. ostler, b. 5 Wolcott.
" William B. ostler, 87 High, h.r. 21 Squire.
Waverly building, 721 Main.
Way A. Sidney, b. 86 Windsor av.
" Chas. L. sec.& treas. 866, b. 427 Main, rm. 10.
" Clarence H. agent, b. 5 Sherman.
" Ernest N. clerk, b. 5 Sherman.
" George L. h. 86 Windsor av.
" George L. Jr. mgr. 933 Mn. b. 86 Windsor av.
" Hardware Co. 866 Main.
" Helen C. teacher dancing and deportment,
6 Haynes, b. 86 Windsor av.
" Henry P. instruct. Popes, b. 86 Windsor av.
" Henry R. (H.R.W.& Co.) h. 5 Sherman.
" Henry R. & Co. leaf tobacco, 219 State.*
" Howard D. b. 86 Windsor av.
" Leonard D. b. 86 Windsor av.
" Newton F. mechanic, b. 5 Sherman.
" Samuel L. prest. 866 Main, h. 142 Bellevue.
Wayner A. C. architect, New England Brewing
Co. 217 Windsor.
Wayside Print Shop, L. Elovich, mgr. 66 State.
Weatherby William, clerk at 329 Asy. b. 9 Fales.
Weatherhead Frank W. formn. at Colts, h.u. 76 Park.
Weaver Edward W. lineman at 6 Cen. h. 9 Park.
" Elbert L. bookkeeper at Charter Oak Nat'l
Bank, 124 Asylum, b. 115 Wooster.
" Frederick J. mach. at 1 Flow. b. 85 Laurel.

Weaver Laura A. b. 115 Wooster.
" John N. dropforger, h. 115 Wooster.
" Thomas S. city reporter at Hartford Courant,
66 State, h. 115 Wooster.
Webb C. Eastman, clerk at Tucker & Goodwin,
8 Hurlburt, h. 5 Columbia.
" Charles, ship carpenter, 285 State.
" Charles O. expressman, b. New Park.
**WEBB ELDORUS M.** boots & shoes,
546 Asylum, h. 16 New Park. *See p. 795.*
WEBB GEORGE M.              *See page 559.*
" Harry P. salesman, h. 32 Clark.
" Herbert A. driver, h. 5 Goodman.
" Louis J. bkkpr. at 283 Shel. b. 61 New Park.
" Myron, h. 193 Farmington.
" R. L. h. 57 Farmington.
" Walter G. at 42 Union pl. h. Windsor t.
" Watson Mrs. b. 149 High.
" William A. attend. 30 Wash. h. 75 Seymour.
Webber Frank W. clerk, 152 Asylum.
Weber Amos M. finisher at 613 Mn. h.u. 64 Hicks.
" Daniel J. pressman, 252 Pearl, h.u. 119 Hung.
" Gustavus A. turner, h.3u. 26 Trumbull.
" Henry, blacksmith at 48 Ann, h. W.H.t.
" John, laborer, h.2u. 26 Flower.
Weberg Victor, stonecutter, b. 301 Lawrence.
Webster Alvier D. carriage manufacturer, 303
Allyn, h.u. 29 Vine.
" Annie R. h. 60 Williams.
" Antoinette H. wid. Wm. E. h.34 Charter Oak.
" Arthur A. supt. r. 221 State, b. 18 Morris.
**WEBSTER & BAKER,** fire insur-
ance agents, 721 Main.
Charles M. Webster.          Isaiah Baker, Jr.
" Benjamin F. machinist, h.u. 150 Allyn.
" Benjamin F. Jr. employment, 154 Allyn,
h. 30 Chestnut.
" Caroline A. Mrs. h.u. 181 State.
" Charles C. toolm. at Colts, h.u. 70 Hudson.
" Chas. E. blacksm. 34 Elm, h. 212 Jefferson.
" Chas. M. (W.& Baker) 721 Mn. h. 159 Sey.
" Chas. R. salesman, 98 Asy. b. 92 Barbour.
" Chas. S. tinner at 530 Asy. h. 146 Brook.
" Cora M. music teacher, 29, b. 29 Vine.
" Dana, assist. foreman, 690, h. 985 Park.
" Dwight A. painter at 29, b.u. 29 Vine.
" Edward, furnaces, 530 Asy. h. 60 Williams.
" Edward R. traveling salesman, b. 16 Seyms.
" Elizabeth S. wid. Henry, teacher oil paint-
ing. h. 210 Windsor av.
" Elmer E. roller at 690 Park, h. 52 Heath.
" Emeline, b. 475 New Britain.
" Emily, wid. Dr. A. J. b. 77 Allen pl.
" Fred. clerk at 25 Front, l. 97 Washington.
" Harry, plumber, h.3u. 128 Albany.
" Irva C. at Brown, Thomson & Co. 942
Main, b. 64 Bond.
" James, helper at 20 Church, h. Albany.
" Jennie, attendant at 30 Washington.
" John C. tinner at 530 Asylum, h. 117 Brook.
" John C. vice president Ætna Life Insurance
Company, 650 Main, h. 686 Farmington.
" Louis M. motorman St.Ry. h. 109 Whitmore.
" Roy C. clerk at 1 Flower, b. 739 Asylum.

Webster Wm. H. boardinghouse, 98 Babcock.
" William S. harnessm. 995 Main, h. 16 Seyms.
Wechsler Sam, wholesale fruits, h. 51 Morgan.
Wedburg Frank E. mach. 1 Flow. h. 66½ Laurel.
Wedge Joseph, linem. 266 Pearl, h.u. 2 Winthrop.
Wedley William J. painter, h. 36 Capen.
Weed Edward S. mach. at 98 Asy. h. 44 Park.
" Francis P. h. 83 Elm.
" George C. clerk, b.u. 112 Wooster.
" Julius, postal clerk, h. 98 Wooster.
" Sue Mrs. h. 724 Main, room 26.
" William T. conductor St.Ry. b. E.H.t.
Weeden J. F., New Dom Hotel, 109 Trumbull.
**WEEKLY EXAMINER,** 45 Brown.
*See page 468.*
" Underwriter, H. R. Hayden, 53 Trumbull.
Weeks Albert P. salesman at Sage, Allen & Co.
898 Main, h. 18 Sherman.
" Annie Gordon, wid. Harry A. h. 22 Atwood.
" Champion A. linem. 247 Pearl, h. Ingleside.
" Edgar, carpenter, b. 36 Imlay.
" Edgar S. carptr. 224 Sargeant, h. 36 Imlay.
WEEKS EGBERT O. *councilman 10th ward,* vice
president Ætna Ins. Co. 666 Main, h. 580
Farmington.
" Frank M. cooper, 57, h.u. 61 Albany.
" Geo. H. tobacconist, 1015 Mn. h. 18 Florence.
" Herbert S. clerk 1015 Main, b. 18 Florence.
" James L. clerk at 885 Main, h.u. 9 Morgan.
" Jane E. wid. John C. h. 58 Wooster.
" Lewis A. trim. 266 Pearl, h. Oakwood, W.H.t.
" M.J. Mrs. employmt. 98½ Tru. h. 102 Wooster.
" Mabel, kindergarten teacher at Lawrence
street school, b. 18 Sherman.
" Mary A. h. 6 Wyllys.
" Melvin J. trav. salesman, b. 102 Wooster.
" Olive, wid. George, cook, h.u. 1 Huntley.
" Robert, painter, h.u. 22 Grand.
" Victoria, b. 214 Main.
" William H. teacher at 690 Asy.h.22 Atwood.
Weelenski Joseph, clothier, h.u. 84 Morgan.
Wegner Charles, upholstr. 663 Mn. h. 9 Morris.
" Charles Jr. clerk at 581 Cap. b. 9 Morris.
" Frederick, mail clerk at Popes, b. 9 Morris.
Wehe William, b. 2 Holcomb.
Wehner August, confectioner at 607 Main.
" George, shoemaker, 28, h. 28 Trumbull.
Wehrly Herman, market, 52, h. 60 Temple.
Weiczorek Anthony J. machine hand at Colts,
h. 3 Wawarme.
" George A. mach. hand, Colts, b. 3 Waw.
Weidell Frank G. blacksm. N.Y.R. b. 16 Squire.
Weidermann Charles F. draughtsman at 1 Flow.
b. 119 High.
Weidl Edward, (*Stern & Weidl,*) h.r. 35 Wolcott.
Weidlich August, musicteacher, h. 40 Lewis.
" Herman, saloon, 5 Am. h. 206 Windsor av.
" Herman J. at 5 Am. b. 206 Windsor av.
" Julius, cigarm. at 104 Asy.b.206 Windsor av.
" Oscar L. electrician at 53 Vernon, h. 105
Madison av.
Weigel Samuel, laborer, b. 77 Windsor.
Weigelt Bernhart, h. 1334 Broad.
" Wm. P. tinware, 16 Mulberry, h. 1334 Broad.

Weil Jacob, screwm. 476 Capitol, h.u. 7 Oak.
Weiland Fred F. baker, 20 South Hudson.
Weildon Fred. W. hairstore, 871 Mn. h.u. 254 Jef.
" Thos. C. hairdresser at 871 Mn. h. 17 Elmer.
" ☞see Weldon.
Weills Andrew, laborer, b.3u. 6 Ellery.
Weinberg Michael, pressm. 555 Cap. b.u.r. 67 Ple.
" Minnie, pastry cook, 98 Wells.
Weinburgh Harry B. pinm. 31 Hicks, b. 137 Com.
Weindrof Louis, tailor at 835 Mn. h. 124 Martin.
Weiner Abe, (*W. Bros.*) h. 47½ Morgan.
" Bros. produce dealers, 54 Morgan.
Max Weiner.  Abe Weiner.
" Max, (*W. Bros.*) b.2u. 47½ Morgan.
Weinerman Benjamin, peddler, h.3u.78 Morgan.
Weingarten Herman G. leather, 21½, h.2u.21 Mul.
Weingrow Samuel, tailor, 79, h. 79 Windsor.
Weinmann Philip, saloon, 132, h. 132 Market.
Weins Thomas, shoem. 62 Trumbull. b. 69 Potter.
Weinstein Hyman, shoem. at 206, h. 206 Front.
" Israel, tailor at 94½ Trumbull, h. 3 North.
" Louis, tailor, b. 4 Portland.
" Max, grocer at 80, h. 80 Talcott.
" Max, laborer, h.r. 81 Front.
" Michael, filer at Colts, h. 30 Kilbourn.
" Moriss, tailor, h.3u. 34 Avon.
" Sam, shoemaker at 86 State, h. 14 Kilbourn.
" Sophie, wid. Solomon, h. 7 South Prospect.
Weintrout Louis, tailor, h.r. 124 Market.
Weir Charles D. driller at Colts, h. 54 Hudson.
" David, h.u. 16 Beach.
" Della Mrs. h. 39 Linden.
" Emma, wid. James, h. 43 Sigourney.
" Grace L. stenog. 197 Asylum, b.u. 16 Beach.
" Janet M. physician, 38, h. 38 West
" Lottie, b. 43 Sigourney.
" Mary, wid. Harvey, h. 210 Windsor av.
" William, laborer, 300, b. 300 Wethersfield.
" William E. clerk at Hartford Steam Boiler
Ins. & Insp. Co. 650 Main, b.u. 16 Beach.
" Winifred D. bkkrp. 851 Mn. b. 139 Bellevue.
" ☞see also Wier.
Weis Emil, tailor, h.2u. 58 Temple.
Weise Emma, housekeeper at 705 Asylum.
" ☞see Wise.
Weisiet Henry L. driver at 484 Main, h.u. 86 Jef.
Weisman John, manager at 197, h. 78 Front.
Weisner Amos, molder 54 Arch. h. 162½ Franklin.
" August, molder at 54 Arch, h. 160½ Franklin.
Weiss Conrad, butcher, 98 Wells, b. 83 Mulberry.
" Harry, clerk at 261 Asylum, h. Huntley pl.
" Hugo, baker, b. 57 Judson.
" Joseph, confectioner, 59, h. 59 Morgan.
" Wm. J. carptr. 158 Woodland, b.u. 76 Gov.
Weitze Philip, tailor at 105 Pratt, h. 214 Front.
Weitzel Conrad, cabinetmaker at 633 Main, h.u.
212 Capen.
Welch Archibald A. actuary Phœnix Mutual Life
Ins. Co. 49 Pearl, h. 21 Woodland.
" Bridget, wid. Daniel, h. 82 Francis.
" Catharine, wid. William H. h. 13 Crown.
" Clara C. tailoress, b. 350 Main.
" Daniel, b. 82 Francis.
" Daniel, bricklayer, b. 15 Lafayette.
" David S. polisher at 9 Sig. h. 1202 Main.

**THINKING PEOPLE Read The Post Daily.**

Welch Delcan, helper, 1 Flower, h. 21 Howard.
" Edward, carriagep. 352 Alb. b. 39 Harbison.
" Edward, foreman at 8 Front, h. 97 Arch.
" Eliza, wid. George M. b. 149 High.
" Elizabeth Mrs. b. Home for Aged, Albany.
" Elizabeth J. b. 144 Garden.
" Fannie, attendant at 30 Washington.
" & Farrell, dressmakers, 1295 Main.
       Margaret A. Welch.       Mary E. Farrell.
" Fernando C. h. 72 Westland.
" Frank, b. 2 Holcomb.
" George H. h. 116 Trumbull.
" Geo. K. physician, 103 Pratt, h. 144 Garden.
" Helen, b.2u. 27 Spruce.
" Henrietta, wid. George A. h. 30 Madison.
" Jacob, helper at 388 Cap. h. 145 Lawrence.
" James, filer at Popes, h.u. 77 Hamilton.
" James, helper at Popes, h. 177 Zion.
" James, laborer, h.u. 75 Seymour.
" James, lab. at stonepits, h.u. 77 Hamilton.
" James E. laborer, h.u. 39 Lawrence.
" James F. polisher 476 Cap. b. 19 Mechanic.
" James F. Jr. screwm. at Popes, b.u.177Zion.
" Jerry, helper at 54 Arch, h. 5 Park.
" John, laborer, l.2u. 26 Church.
" John, laborer, h.2u. 39 Lawrence.
" John, laborer, h. 29 Mechanic.
" John, rubberworker at 690, h. 908 Park.
" John H. conductor St. Ry. h. 20 Dean.
" John J. screwm. at 476 Cap. h. 386 Park.
" John W. sec'y Hartford Dime Savings Bank,
       791 Main, h. 624 Asylum.     See page 439.
" Joseph, bricklayer, b. 15 Lafayette.
" Joseph J. motorman, St.Ry. h. 1350 Broad.
" Joseph M. conductor St.Ry. b. 32 Madison.
" M. C. Mrs. h. 234 Ashley.
" Margaret, dressmaker, b.r. 13 Belden.
" Margaret A. dressmaker, h. 1295 Main.
" Martin, ostler at 12 Wells, b. 355 Asylum.
" Mary, h. 234 Ashley.
" Mary, wid. Andrew, h. 23 Front.
" Mary, wid. John, h.2u. 1295 Main.
" Michael, b. 2 Holcomb.
" Michael, laborer, h.u. 26 Union.
" Michael J. toolm. at Popes, h.Wilson station.
" Morris, engineer at N.Y.R. h. Loomis.
" Patrick, b. 2 Holcomb.
" Patrick, bartender at 659 Main, b. 33 Elm.
" Patrick, mason, h. 82 Francis.
" Pierce T. polisher at 9 Sig. h. 125 Mather.
" Richard, ostler, b. 20 Affleck.
" Samuel, mason, b. 82 Francis.
" Sarah A. clerk at Capewell Horse Nail Co.
       40 Governor, b. 103 Capitol.
" Sebina, wid. Edward F. h. 53 Madison.
" Stephen, screwm. at 476 Cap. b.u. 7 Haw.
" Susan L. G. wid. H. K. h. 65 Edwards.
" Thomas, casehardener at Popes, h. 60 Wells.
" Thomas, helper at 476 Capitol, b. 4 Affleck.
" Thomas, mason, h. 15 Lafayette.
" Thos. J. repairer at 40 Gov. h.u. 208 Maple.
" Timothy J. helper, N.Y.R. b. 198 Allyn.
" William, lineman at 6, b. 19 Central.
" William, screwm. h.2u. 35 Lawrence.
" William, stonecutter, b. 518 Main.

Welch William A. screwm. 476 Cap. h. 42 Law.
" William B. clerk at 653 Main, h. 10½ Ford.
" William F. screwm.476Cap. b. 29 Mechanic.
" William H. cutter 175 Pearl, h.u. 25 Talcott.
" William J. engineer, h. 86 Madison.
" William J. pressman at141 Pearl, b. 20 Dean.
" William J. repairer at 40 Gov. b. 157 Capitol.
" William L. screwm. 476 Cap. b. 177 Zion.
" William P. h. 46 Avon.
" William P. assembler at Popes, b. 68 Hudson.
" William R. mach. at 1 Flow. b. 43 Lafayette.
" ☞see also Welsh; Walsh.
Weldon Annie, wid. Joseph, h.2u. 58 Temple.
" Charles H. at National Fire Insurance Co. 95
       Pearl, h. 133 Kenyon.
" Edward G. clerk at Brown, Thomson & Co.
       942 Main, h. Hockanum v.
" Frank W. machinist, b. 520 Main.
" Hattie, wid. Horace N. b.u. 1112 Main.
" Lewis, carpetweaver, 31 Wells, b. 520 Main.
" ☞see also Weildon; Whelden; Welton.
Welke Jacob, at 1 Flower, h.u. 145 Lawrence.
" William A. at 490 Cap. b.u. 145 Lawrence.
Welker Henry, musician, mechanic at Popes, h.
       53 Putnam.
" Jacob, at Popes, b. 53 Putnam.
Weller C. S. painter at 1106 Main, h. Liberty.
" Jacob, peddler, b. 241 Front.
" John, bottler, 84, h. 84 Vine.
" Robert, h. 18 Buckingham.
" Robert Jr. designer, 180 Asy. h. 147 Weth.
" William J. carptr. at 180Allyn, b.13 Belden.
Welles Albert A.rubberw. 690 Park, b.u.54 Heath.
" Charles T. president City Bank of Hartford,
       783 Main, h. 111 Washington.
" Florence A. wid. L. V. h.u. 54 Heath.
" Hoadley C. clerk at Conn. Trust and Safe
       Deposit Co. 785 Main, h. 766 Asylum.
" Ida E. b. 66 Charter Oak.
" James G. driver at 46 Ann, b. 16 Westland.
" John N. dentist, 793 Main, h.Wethersfield t.
" Louisa, wid. A. D. h. 88 Retreat.
" Maria H. wid. John S. h. 104 Ann.
" Maude, wid.Thomas G.h. 11 Charter Oak pl.
" Ralph C. mechanic at Popes, b. 54 Heath.
" Roger, attorney, 847 Main, h. Newington t.
" S. Maria, h.u. 24 Atwood.
" ☞see also Wells.
Welling J. C. Mrs. h. 159 Farmington.
Wellington The, 488 Main.
Wellman Max, molder at 555 Capitol, h. Avon.
Wells Anna, wid. James, washer, h.u. 14 Warren.
" Anna R. Mrs. attendant at 30 Washington.
" Arthur, teamster at 46 Ann, h. 257 Market.
" Arthur B. forem. at 62 Mar. h. 54 Westland.
" Arthur C. mach. at 30 Cush. b. 42 Spring.
" Arthur J. carptr. 703 Mn. h.2u. 23 Seymour.
" Charles, helper at 87 Wells.
" Charles Arthur, h. 21 Elliott.
" Charles G. h. 21 Elliott.
" Charles T. h. 17 Spring.
" Christopher A.mach.388Cap.h.2u.36Church.
" Daniel H. actuary Connecticut Mutual Life
       Ins. Co. 783 Main, h. 38 Allen pl.

**As A NEWSPAPER, THE POST LEADS.**

Wells & Devine, refractionists and opticians, 904 Main, rm. 34.
Walter E. Wells.      Walter W. Devine.
" Edward V. mach. at 1 Flow. b. 21 Elliott.
" Ernest Alden, student at Yale, b. 38 Allen.
" F. E. conductor St.Ry. 115 State.
" Frank G. mach. at 1 Flower, h. 171 Albany.
" Georgiana, b. 21 Elliott.
" Harry C. clerk at 197 Asy. b. 171 Albany.
" Henry E. clerk at Brown, Thomson & Co. 942 Main, b. 809 Asylum.
" James D. clerk at Hartford Trust Co. 764 Main, b. Wethersfield t.
" Jane L. Mrs. h. Albany, W.H.t.
" John S. trav. salesman, h. 73 Sigourney.
WELLS JORDAN C. councilman 7th ward, painter and decorator, 60, h. 60 Benton.
" Katie T. attendant at 30 Washington.
" Marshall O. (H. W. Conklin & Co.) real estate and ins. 9 Central, h. 156 Collins.
" N. G. Mrs. dressmaker, 86, h. 86 Pratt.
" Nancy, wid. Oscar, b.u. 54 Wadsworth.
" Richard B. clerk at 142 Russ, b. 809 Asylum.
" S. Maria, h.u. 24 Atwood.
" Stephen, painter, h.u. 60 Benton.
" Thomas, laborer, h. 884 Main.
" Thomas S. clerk at Brown, Thomson & Co. 942 Main, b. Wethersfield t.
" Virginia T. b. 52 Church.
" Walter E. (W. & Devine,) h. 16½ Morris.
" William B. clerk, h.u. 76 Ann.
" William H. machinist at 490 Capitol, b. 21 Elliott.
" William L. b. 60 Benton.
" William Tate, at Ætna Insurance Co. 666 Main, h. Wethersfield t.
" ☞see also Welles.
Wellwood Ambrose, 1176 Main, died June 5, aged 52.
Welsh Catharine Mrs. h.2u.r. 124 Market.
" Charles, at 37 Wells, b. 24 Gold.
" Daniel, b. 545 Main.
" Eleanor Mrs. seamstress, 937 Mn. h. 36 Bond.
" J. deckhand str. Hartford, 285 State.
" J. M. conductor St.Ry. h. 32 Madison.
" James, saloon, 16 Sheldon, h.2u. 32 Asylum.
" James Mrs. h. 28 Talcott.
" John, blacksmith, h: 4 Winter.
" John, laborer, b.u. 39 Lawrence.
" John H. teamster at 100 Com. h.r. 61 Front.
" Margaret, clerk at 956 Main, b. 31 Sheldon.
" Mary A. dressmaker, 80, h. 80 Walnut.
" Mary E. b. 36 Bond.
" Michael, shipcarpenter, h.u. 31 Sheldon.
" Stephen, machinist, b.u. 9 Hawthorn.
" Thomas, helper at 54 Arch, h. 5 Park.
" Thomas P. printer at Hartford Times, 716 Main, b. 4 Winter.
" William, blacksmith, b. 4 Winter.
" William, laborer, h.2u.r. 124 Market.
" ☞see also Welch ; Walsh.
Weltin Anna, wid. Joseph, h.2u. 58 Temple.
" Josephine, at Hartford Life Ins. Co. 252 Asylum, b. 58 Temple.
Weltner Adam, baker, 68, h. 68 Windsor.

Weltner Adam, Jr. baker, 68, b. 68 Windsor.
" Conrad, clerk Johns-Pratt Co. b. 68 Windsor.
" George, baker at 68, b. 68 Windsor.
" Herman, helper at 164 State, b. 68 Windsor.
" William, policeman, b. 68 Windsor.
" William, porter at 956 Main, h. 48 Village.
Welton Henry A. h. 1514 Broad.
" Jennie E. b. 877 Main, rm. 9.
" Lucy B. b. 36 Jefferson.
" Nellie Goyt, wid. Louis C. h. 46 John.
" ☞see also Weldon; Whelden; Weildon.
Wengler Marks H. laborer, b.u. 20 Park.
Wenis Thomas, saloon, 84, h.u. 84 Sheldon.
Wenk Fisher A. B. cashier at 756 Mn. b.u. 60 Bab.
" Fred. W. rubberw. at 690 Park, h.u. 458Mn.
" H. Charles, at National Fire Ins. Co. 95 Pearl, b. 926 Main.
" Margaret, wid. J. H. W. h.u. 60 Babcock.
" Wm. C. modelmaker Popes, h.u. 60 Babcock.
Wenn Peter, walklayer at 283 Sheldon.
Wennerstrom John, ostler 51, b. 51 Farmington.
Wentworth Daniel F. artist, 904 Mn. h. 43 Sumner.
" George B. framem. 730 Main, h. 43 Sumner.
" John D. bkkpr. at 288 Asy. h.u. 12 Avon.
" Lucius M. at Travelers Ins. Co. 56 Prospect, h.u. 40 Annawan.
" W. S. captain barge No. 8, 285 State, h. Poors Mills, Me.
Wenwick William R. clerk, b. 76 Flower.
Wenzel Frank A. clerk 33 Asy. b.4u. 80 Pearl.
Wenzloff Adolph, carpenter, b. 53 Brown.
" Arthur, mech. at 335 Sheldon, h. 55 Brown.
" Gustaf R.mechanic at 335 Shel. h. 157Maple.
" Paul, baker at 167 Asylum, h. 55 Brown.
Werder Fritz, confectioner, 607, 817, h. 609 Main.
" Helen, at 607, b. 609 Main.
" Paul, confectioner at 607, b. 609 Main.
Werner Nellie L. dressm. 847 Main, rm. 19, b. Elmwood v.
" Wilhelm F. tailor, 29 Pearl, h. 186 Putnam.
Werup Konrad, mech. at Popes, b.u. 55 Green.
" Siewert, baker at 368 Asylum, b.u. 55 Green.
Wescott Adelaide M. teacher West Middle school, b. 794 Asylum.
" Alex. T. clerk at Popes, b. 111 Laurel.
" Alex. T. fireman, b. 10 Heath.
" Christina Mrs. h. 111 Laurel.
" William A. machinist, b. 111 Laurel.
" ☞ see also Westcott.
Wesley C H. janitor at 49 Pearl, h.u. 16 Gold.
" Hattie, wid. Frank, nurse, h. 128 Windsor.
Wessel Fred, (Hartford Engine Co.) 223 State, h. New Britain t.
" Julius A. molder 555 Cap. h. Prince, W.H.t.
West A. M. (A.B.West&Co.) h. Boston, Mass.
" Abbie A. wid. Philo, b. 238 Sigourney.
" Andrew B. (A.B.West&Co.) h. 31 Lincoln.
" Sarah J. wid. Berzilla R. h.2u. 4 Chapel.
" End Land Co. 703 Main.
F. C. Rockwell.    F. W. Dart.    W. E.Goodwin.
" Erastus C. carpenter, h.u. 7 Pleasant.
" Frank, yardmaster, h. 67 Williams.
WEST FRED. A. alderman 4th ward, contractor at 1 Flower, h. 238 Sigourney.
" Harriet Mrs. dressmaker, 7, h.u. 7 Pleasant.

**PIANOS RE-BUILT AS GOOD AS NEW BY LEO. H. BATTALIA, Warerooms, 943 MAIN ST.**

West Harry J. ship.clerk 581 Cap.h.u.52 Francis.
" Irving H. milkman, h.2u. 100 Hudson.
" James R. timekeeper, l. 236 High.
" Joseph M. bookkeeper, b. 148 Mather.
" Jos. G. butcher at 1065 Main, h. 148 Mather.
" Marcia A. wid. Mahlon R. h. 32 Charter Oak.
" Philip, laborer, h. 95 Harper.
" Rebecca, boardinghouse, 191 Lawrence.
**WEST A. B. & CO.** carpenters and builders, 101½ Hudson. *See page* 514.
Andrew B. West.            A. M. West.
" Walter H. timekeeper at Colts, h. Burnside v.
" William, h.u. 165 State.
" William, laborer, h.u. 22 Goodman.
" Wm.B.druggist atT.Sisson729 Mn.b.90Ann.
Westbrook Geo. A. cigarmaker at 867 Main, h.u. 10 Brown.
Westcott Harriet C. wid. Edward Y. h. 195 Sig.
" Sarah, wid. George H. b.u. 271 High.
" ☞*see also Wescott.*
Wester Christ, laborer, Pope Tube Co. b. 12 South Forest.
Western Automatic Screw Co. of Hfd. 476 Capitol.
" Union Telegraph Co. 6 Central.
Westland Andrew, apprentice, b. 52 Seymour.
" Cornelia A. housekeeper, 48 Ashley.
" Delia, wid. Chester, h.u. 153 Market.
" Frank W. coachman, 138, b. 138 Wash.
" Isaac I. waiter, l.2u. 8 State.
" Richard C. carpenter, h.u. 153 Market.
" William, builder, b. 64 Capitol.
Westling Gustaf, dropforg.142 Russ,h.880 Broad.
Weston Eugene F. painter, 72 Albany, b.u. 90 Williams.
" John B. h.u. 8 Foot Guard.
Westphal Ernest, carpenter, h.2u. 44 Pleasant.
" Wm. leaf tobacco, 221 State, h.u. 1273 Main.
" William Jr. salesm. at 221 State, h.5 Barbour.
Westwood Minnie E.wid. Fred R.b.156 Franklin.
Wetherbee Frank M. shipper at 40 Governor, h. 39 Dean.
" Guy, clerk at L. L. Ensworth & Son, iron merchants, 104 Front, b. 39 Dean.
Wetherby William P. gardener at, b. 9 Fales.
Wetherell Mary A. girls supervisor, 690 Asylum.
" ☞*see also Witherell; Withrel.*
Wetmore Florille, wid. Samuel, b. 98 Capen.
Wettberg ☞*see Von Wettberg.*
Wetter Carl, clerk, 39 Church, h. 12 Talcott ct.
Wey Joseph, waiter at 98 Wells, h.u. 52 Linden.
Weyand Jacob, bootfitter, 14 Mul. h. 411 Maple.
" James C. enameler at Popes, b. 411 Maple.
" Mary J. b. 411 Maple.
Weyant Roland J. rubberworker at 690 Park, h.u. 10 Rose.
Whalen Catherine, domestic at 36 Jefferson.
" Charles.J. messenger at 98 Kil.b.69 Williams.
" Daniel, blacksmith at 1 Laurel, h. 7 Willow.
" Edward, roofer, b. 11 Sigourney pl.
" Elizabeth, wid. Michael P. h. 75 Francis.
" Frank C. clerk, 690 Park, b. 128 Madison av.
" Frank S. baggagem. N.E.R. b. 69 Williams.
" George W. painter, h. 6 West.
" James, driver at 103 Asy. h.u.r. 26 Front.

Whalen James B. clerk, h.3u. 18 Sheldon.
" James P. molder, 54 Arch, h.2u. 86 Windsor.
" John, clerk, b. 999 Main.
" John, laborer, h.u. 41 Mechanic.
" John, stationmaster, N.E.R. h. 69 Williams.
" John A. carpenter at N.Y.R. b. 70 Hung.
" John F. clerk, 33, b.3u. 18 Sheldon.
" John P. painter, b. 214 Allyn.
" John W. buffer at 62 Market,b.Glastonbury t.
" Keron, roofer r. 52 Pratt, b.3u. 18 Sheldon.
" Michael J. laborer, h.2u. 89 Main.
" Lucy, dressmaker, 50, b. 50 John.
" Nicholas, carpenter, b.2u. 50 Lawrence.
" Patrick,helper at Pope Tube Co.h.u.36 Law.
" Thomas J. carpenter, h. 24 Smith.
" William F. polisher at Popes, h.u. 250 Law.
" ☞*see also Whalon.*
Whaley Josiah, laborer, h. 16 Warren.
Whalon ☞*see Whalen.*
Whaples Anna Mrs. h. 1088 Main.
" Heywood H. student at Yale, b. 955 Asylum.
" Meigs H. pres't Ct. Trust & Safe Deposit Co. treasurer Collins Co. 785 Main; *police commissioner*, h. 955 Asylum.
Wharton William P. student Trinity college, 18 Jarvis hall, Summit.
Wheaton Alice J. Mrs.: artist, b.u. 111 Trumbull.
" Eleazur C. b. 185 Ashley.
Wheelan Kathleen, bookkeeper at 90 Albany, b. 22 Canton.
Wheeler Adaline H. wid. Mark H. h. 911 Asy.
" Albert M. conductor St.Ry. b. 57 Pratt.
" Calvin H. painter & decor. 85, h. 85 Vine.
" Charles H. student Trinity college, 35 Jarvis hall, Summit.
" Charles R. carpenter, h. 23 Florence.
" Cyrus E.trav.salesm. at Popes,b.815 Asylum.
" Edward R. clerk, P.&R. b. 25 Spring.
" Elbert L. (*American Cycle Repair Co.*) h. 37 Mulberry.
" Elizabeth, wid. Lorenzo, h. Quaker lane.
" Emily E. wid. William R. h. 64 Tremont.
" Floren A. woodcarver, 28 Mul. l. 1224 Main.
" Frank P. bricklayer, h. 20 Winter.
" Fred. A. conductor, St.Ry. h. 22 Goodman.
" George B. confectioner, h.u. 259 High.
" George L. b. 277 Main.
" George L. clerk, 267 Main, h. Wethersfield.
" George L. driver, 2 American,h.u.4 Bellevue.
" H. Frank, baggagem. N.E.R. h.u. 90 Wms.
" Henry E. carpenter, h. 277 Main.
" Henry R. laborer, h.u.r. 24 South Prospect.
" Henry S. mason, h. 887 Park.
" Hulbert, painter, h. 62 Dean.
" James K.mach. at 13 Central, h. 98 Wooster.
" Jane S. Mrs. florist, 64, h.r. 64 Dean.
" Jerome H. die sharpener at 252 Pearl, h. 53 Hungerford.
" John E. clerk at 1031 Main, h. Holyoke t.
" John P.treasurer Connecticut Trust and Safe Deposit Co. 785 Main, h. 14 Niles.
" Joseph E. bookkeeper at A. Mugford, engraver, 177 Asylum, h. 36 Lincoln.
" Judson M. brakeman P.&R. h. Pleasant.
" Leon A. clerk at 201 Asylum, b. 85 Vine.

**Want Advertisements Bring Results in THE POST.**

Wheeler Louis, laborer, b. 94 Walnut.
" Mary, wid. J. I. b. 259 High.
" Norman S. clerk, b.u. 14 Winter.
" Olin, clerk at 164 State, h. Buckland v.
" Robert F. Rev. pastor Talcott st. Congregational church, h. 47 Fairmount.
" Sophia A. wid. Chas. W. h.u. 189 Main.
" Vesta L. stenographer at Beach & Co. 209 State, b.u. 6 Belden.
" William L. painter, h.u. 7 Sigourney pl.
" William R. machinist, b. 60 Tremont.
" & Wilson sewing mach. agency,11 Goodman.
    Joseph E. Stanley, agent.
Wheelock John H. rubberworker at 690 Park, b. 236 Sigourney.
" Kate P. b. 236 Sigourney.
" Paul L. clerk at Popes, b. 236 Sigourney.
" Thomas S. at Conn. Mutual Life Ins. Co. 783 Main, h. 236 Sigourney.
" William G. traveling salesman, 15 Trumbull, h. Greenwich, R. I.
Whelan Frederick C. timekpr.b.u. 28 Madison av.
" John B. shipping clerk at 690 Park, b.u. 128 Madison av.
" Lizzie, clerk at 835 Main, b. 75 Francis.
" Mollie, clerk at 835 Main, b. 75 Francis.
" Samuel T. bkkpr. at 690 Park, h. 45 Smith.
" Sarah wid. Wm. S. h.u. 128 Madison av.
" ☞ see also Whalen.
Wheldon ☞ see Weildon; Weldon; Welton.
Whipple Frank H. (Olds & W.) h.u. 274 Laurel.
" John C. clerk, 164 State, h. 274 Laurel.
" Louis, harnessm at 8 Sig. h.u. 8 Chestnut.
" P. B. Mrs. b. 888 Asylum.
Whitaker Emma, dressmaker, 23, h. 23 N.B.
" F. P. fresco painter, l. 720 Main, rm. 10.
" George H. laborer, h.2u.r. 41 Mather.
" ☞ see also Whittaker.
White A. M. at 1 Flower, b. 284 Asylum.
" Addie C. wid. William H. h.u. 76 Retreat.
" Agnes B. wid. Frank G. b. 57 Buckingham.
" Albert P. nightwatchman at Brown, Thomson & Co. 942 Main, h. 27 Seyms.
" Alexander, cook, b. 175 Windsor.
" Almira, wid Edwin A. b.2u. 4 Martin.
" Alonzo P. at Phœnix Ins. Co. 64 Pearl, h. 148 Seymour.
" Annie E. stenog. at Popes, b. Manchester t.
" Bridget,wid.Christopher, b.u.14 Wadsworth.
" Calvin J. city expresser, 38, h. 38 Vernon.
" Catherine L. wid. John, b.3u. 284 Pearl.
" Charles E. theological student, 1507 Broad.
" Charles P. tailor, 25 Asy. h.u. 283 Market.
" Cornelia A. wid. Francis A. h. 37 Main.
" Daniel J. waiter, b. 999 Main.
" David A. machinist, b. 15 Rose.
" Dora A. dressmaker, b.u. 14 Wadsworth.
" E. Mrs. h.2u. 6 Ford.
" Edward, helper at N.Y.R. h. 15 Rose.
" Edward, mach. 1 Flower, h.2u. 42 Lawrence.
" Edward A. pressman, b.2u. 1060 Broad.
" Edward D. h.u. 23 Seymour.
" Edwin P. upholstr. 219 Asy. b. 31 Windsor.
" Elizabeth, wid. Richard, h. 31 Windsor.
" Elmer L. clerk 661 Main, b. 18 Lincoln.

White Elmer M. cashier of Hartford St.Ry. Co. 115 State, h. 21 Sherman.
" Elmira A. Mrs. b.u. 23 Martin.
" Frank, laborer at 20 South Hudson.
" Frank P. overseer at East Hartford Manufacturing Co. h. 24 Windsor av.
" Frederick C. foreman at Popes, h. E.H.t.
" Fred'k John, motorm. St.Ry. h.u. 106 Tru.
" Frederick T. painter, h. 27 Seyms.
**WHITE FRED. W.** stoves, tinware, 1124 Main, h. 10 John.    *See page 507.*
" Fred'k W. bookkeeper at L. L. Ensworth & Co. iron store,104 Front, h.u. 72 Congress.
" George, coachman at 187 High, b. Huntley.
" George, painter, h.r.u. 44½ John.
" George A. clerk at 95 Ple. b. 60 Allen pl.
" Georgie, wid. H. Tudor, h. 65 Babcock.
" Harris, irondealer, 242, h.u. 242 Front.
" Harry S. asst. auditor at Popes, h. 871 Broad.
" Harry W. bookkeeper First National Bank, 50 State, b. 37 Main.
" Henry C. artist, b. 69 Gillett.
" Herbert B. clerk at 71 Asy. h.u. 76 Retreat.
WHITE HERBERT H. *alderman 10th ward,* ass't cashier Phœnix Nat. Bank, h. 21 Girard.
" Ida E. dressmaker, h. 74 Spring.
" Isaac R. h. 39 Willard.
" Isabelle G. teacher Second North school, 249 High, b. 136 Trumbull.
" J. L. paints, oils, 185 Asylum, h. 24 Chapel.
" James, bricklayer, b. Windsor av.
" James, enameler at Popes, b.u. 38 S.Pro.
" James L. painter at 185 Asylum, h. E.H.t.
" John, b. 2 Holcomb.
" John clerk at 26 State, b.u. 69 Pleasant
" John,plumber at 599 Main,h.2u. 1060 Broad.
" John A. machinist at 54 Arch, b.26 Governor.
" John A. painter, h.u. 52 Green.
" John B. h. 47 Park.
" John F. brakeman, b. 1202 Main.
" John H. att'y, 756 Main, rm. 26, h. 69 Gillett.
" John L. toomaker at Popes, h. 38 Park.
" Joseph L. Jr. b. 24 Chapel.
" Josephine, b. 141 Washington.
" Laura A. wid. James H. h. 59 Webster.
" Leroy, clerk at 575 Main, b. 18 Lincoln.
" Lizzie F. h.u. 39 John.
" Mabel F. teacher, Ch.O. sch. b. 148 Seymour.
" Maria, wid. John, b. 752 Park.
" Marie M. teacher, 690 Asy. l. 122 Garden.
" Mary A. dressmaker, 27, b. 27 Seyms.
" Mary A. clerk at Brown, Thomson & Co. 942 Main, b. 259 Lawrence.
" Mary E. clerk at Brown, Thomson & Co. 942 Main, b. 38 Park.
" Michael Mrs. h. 9 Wilson.
" Michael J. mechanic at Popes, h. 31 Grand.
" N. G. ( White & W.) h. West Hartford t.
" Nettie Mrs. laundress, h. 489 Main.
" Patrick, laborer at 15 Albany, b.u. 22 Center.
" Patrick, laborer, h.2u. 146 Grove.
" Patrick J. mach. 110 Com. b.u. 14 Wads.
" Prescott H. city expresser, b. 38 Vernon.
" Richard, measurer, 37 Wells, b. 31 Windsor.

**The Up to Date Merchant ADVERTISES in The Post.**

White Robert G. collector 185 Asy. b. 24 Chapel.
" S W. wid. Dr. Moses, h. 223 Asy. rm. 120.
" Sarah E. Mrs. milliner, h.u. 704 Main.
" Susan, wid. John S. h.u. 41 Flower.
" Thomas, machinist, b. 15 Rose.
" Thomas, roadmaker, h.r. 18 So. Prospect.
**WHITE WESTON L.** real estate and investment broker, auctioneer, 884 Main, h. 51 Girard.　　*See page 503.*
" & Warner, publishers, 115 State.
　　Elmer M. White.　　Herbert O. Warner.
" & Whitmore, mantels, 38 Ann.
　　N. G. White.　　W. F. Whitmore.
" William, helper at 26 Mec. b. 115 Barbour.
" Wm.A.forem.Johns-Pratt Co. h.53 Sargeant.
" William E. motorman, St.Ry. h.u. 206 Fkn.
" William F. helper at 70 Huy. h. 18 John.
" William J. finisher at 556, h.2u. 289 Capitol.
" ☞ *see also Wight.*
Whitefield Washington, blacksmith, h. 38 Smith.
Whitehead Etta F. Mrs. dressm. h. 2 Martin av.
" Fred C. mach. at 1 Flower, b. 389 Capitol.
" George I. mach. at N.Y.R. h. 2 Martin av.
" Horatio, mfr. 302 Asylum, h. 50 Allen pl.
" Martha R. Mrs. attendant, 30 Washington.
" Sophia Mrs. h. 78 New Britain.
" William, h. 78 New Britain.
" William H. mach. at 1 Flower, l. 389 Cap.
" William W. policeman, h. 84 New Britain.
Whitehurst James E. clerk, h. 853 Park.
Whitelaw W. H. collector, h. 104 Capitol.
Whiteley Ellen F. wid. James, b.4u. 90 State.
" William E. at 942 Main, b.4u. 90 State.
Whiteside John, mach. 690 Park, h.3u.r.44½ John.
Whitestone Gustave, trim. 921 Mn. h.31 Bellevue.
Whiteford Ernest R. dentist, 68 Pratt,h.14 Grand.
" Wm. H. blacksm. carriagepa. h. 31 Amity.
Whiting Alfred, florist, Whiting lane, h. Farmington av. just west of Vanderbilt hill.
" Archie L. treas. of Wm. H. Post Carpet Co. 219 Asylum, h. 116 Wooster.
Whiting Charles B. president Orient Ins. Co. 5 Haynes, h. 887 Asylum.
　　　　　　　　　*See page 461.*
" Charles E. at Hartford Fire Insurance Co. 53 Trumbull, h. 184 Bellevue.
" Charles H. at 24 Mec. b. 17½ Wadsworth.
" Charles S. secy. and treas. Whitney Mfg. Works, 70 Huyshope, h. 15 Annawan.
" Ellsworth M. casehard. at Colts, h. 39 Huy.
" Elsie B. wid. Robert, h. 427 Main, rm. 15.
" Frank D. h. 54 Capen.•
" Gordon S. Mrs. h. 146 Washington.
" Henry S. mach. Popes, h. 17½ Wadsworth.
" Isaac P. painter at 234, h.u. 234 Franklin.
" Jennie A. carpetm. 17½, h. 17½ Wadsworth.
" Loren A. machinist, h. 1361 Main.
" Robert P. clerk, 618 Cap. h. 44 Hungerford.
" Walter F. mach. at 13 Central, h. 1361 Main.
" William H. C. at Phœnix Insurance Co. 64 Pearl, h. 427 Main, rm. 15.
Whitman Eden M. at Neal, Goff & Inglis Co. 980 Main, b. 22 Hopkins.
" Franklin J. laborer, b. 61 Potter.

Whitman George, at 25, b.u. 25 Fairfield.
" George. laborer, h. 61 Potter.
" James L. teamster at 234 State, h. 47 Com.
Whitmock Neils P. laborer, 54 Arch, h.29 Elliott.
Whitmore C. O. architect, 75 Pratt.
" Charles L. motorman St.Ry. h. 158 Franklin.
" Frank C. helper at 26 Potter, b.u. 25 Front.
" Franklin G. *park commissioner;* real estate, 700 Main, h. 1 Highland.
" George H. clerk at 843 Main, h. 45 Mahl.
" Geo. L. toolkpr. 476 Cap. b. 39 Lawrence.
" Harriette, wid. Orrin H. h. 1400 Main.
" Harold B. clerk at Factory Ins. Association, 95 Pearl, b. 1 Highland.
" James, laborer, h. 47 Commerce.
" John O. laborer at 618 Cap. b. 22 Babcock.
" John S. mach. at 1 Flow. h.2u. 3 Seymour.
" Louis D. carpenter at 158 Woodland, b.u. 158 Franklin.
" Maria L. h. 74 Buckingham.
" Mary A. wid. Jabez H. h. 47 Mahl.
" Ness B. tailor at 41 Asy. h. 9 Sigourney pl.
" William F. agent Walsbach Light Co. 190 Pearl and 38 Ann, h. 17 Beacon.
" ☞ *see also Whittemore.*
Whitney Alfred W. peddler extracts, h. 144 Bab.
" Amos, first vice president and superintendent Pratt & Whitney Co. 1 Flower, h. 568 Farmington.
" Charles H. screwm. 476 Cap. h. 72 Chestnut.
" Clarence E. president and manager Whitney Mfg. Co. b. 568 Farmington.
" Clifton W. at 13 Haynes, b. 144 Babcock.
" E. M. Miss, teacher, b.u. 49 Spring.
" Edward P. forem. at Colts, h. 55 Huyshope.
**WHITNEY EMORY C.** (*W. & Rothwell,*) patent attorney, 49 Pearl, h. 193 Ashley.　　*See page 502.*
" Frank E. machinist at Pratt & Whitney Co. 1 Flower, b. 57 Imlay.
" George H. h. 107 Jefferson.
" George F. foreman at Pratt & Whitney Co. 1 Flower, h. 568 Farmington.
" George Q. foreman at Pratt & Whitney Co. 1 Flower, h. 4 Sumner.
" Harry,at Ætna Life Ins.Co.650,h.u.757Main.
" Henry D. special attorney, Conn. Building and Loan Asso. 252 Asy. h. 42 Barbour.
" James A. undertakers assistant at 387 Main, h. 59 Crown.
" James F. mach. at 1 Flower, h.u. 57 Imlay.
" Leon D. printer at 25 Asy. h.u. 1303 Main.
" Mfg. Co. machine tools, etc. 70 Huyshope.
**WHITNEY & ROTHWELL,** solicitors of patents, 49 Pearl. *See p. 502.*
　　Emory C. Whitney.　　Percy Rothwell.
" Russell, toolm. at 581 Capitol, h. 730 Park.
" Walter F. mach. at 581 Cap. b. 1361 Main.
Whiton Andrew, electrical supplies, 5 Kinsley, h. 68 Bellevue.
" Clara A. kindergarten teacher at 1205 Asy.
" Frank W, architect, 78 Tru. b. 68 Bellevue.
Whittaker Frederick A. clerk P.&R. b. 25 Spring.
" Russell H. salesman, h. 28 Hopkins.

Whittelsey Archie B. salesman at 126 Church, b.u. 10 Avon.
" Charles B. at Travelers Insurance Co. 56 Prospect, h. 23 Crown.
" Charles M. h.u. 6 Church.

**WHITTELSEY D. L. & CO.** contractors and builders, 212 Asylum. *See page 513.*
D. L. Whittelsey.      Rev. E. F. Atwood.
" D. L. *(D. L. W. & Co.)* h. 94 Wooster.
" E. G. *(E. G. W. & Co.)* h. 427 Main, rm. 62.
" E. G.&Co. commis'n,butter,flour, 140 State.*
" Frank H. paper mfr. h. 286 Farmington.
" George C. h.u. 10 Avon.
" Jennie A. Mrs. b. 8 Trinity.
" Julia F. bkkpr. at 338 Main, b. 136 Retreat.
" Mahlon H. h. 74 Brook.
" Mary A. b. 36 Jefferson.
" Samuel,engraver at 618 Cap.h.u.136 Retreat.
" William F. h. 11 Avon.
" William F. Jr. at Ætna Insurance Co. 666 b. 986 Main.
" ☞*see also Whittlesey.*
Whittemore Edmund J. general agent National Life Asso. 53 Trumbull, h. 1176 Main.
" Herbert L. mach. at 70 Huy. b.u. 59 Sey.
" John A. foreman, N.Y.R. h. Springfield t.
" Wm.E.*(W.L.W.&Son,)*b.307 Wethersfield.

**WHITTEMORE W. L. & SON,** brushmakers, 176 Allyn.  *See page 483.*
William L. Whittemore.   William E. Whittemore.
" Wm L.*( W.L.W.&Son,)* h.307 Wethersfield.
" ☞*see also Whitmore.*
Whittermore Matilda, b. 74 Arch.
Whittier William, bkkpr. at Popes, h. 16 Clark.
Whittle Francis, painter, b.2u. 15 Goodman.
" Joseph, b.2u. 15 Goodman.
" Joseph F. painter at 185 Asy. h. 170 Main.
" Joseph F. Jr. helper, 135 Shel. b. 15 Good.
Whittlesey David L. carpenter, h. 94 Wooster.
" ☞*see also Whittelsey.*
Whitty Walter G. mach. at 1 Laurel, h. 267 Park.
Wiant John L. mach. at 690 Park, b. 12 Sisson.
Wibber Ave, laborer, b.2u. 55 Pleasant.
Wiberg Victor, insp. at 690 Park, b. 279 Capitol.
Wicker Conrad, baker, 305, b. 305 Lawrence.
Wickes Isaac C.carptr.PopeTubeCo.b.88 Church.
Wickham Clarence H., U. S. envelope works, 1 So.Ann, P.O. address box 645, Hartford, sec'y & treas. Hartford Manilla Co. treas. Hfd. Manchester & Rockville Tramway Co. b. Manchester t.  *See pages 479, 557.*
" Edwin H. clerk, h.r. 1225 Main.
" Horace J., U. S. envelope works, 1 So. Ann; P. O. address box 645, Hartford, vice pres't. & general sup't Htfd. Manilla Co. general manager Hartford, Manchester & Rockville Tramway Co. h. Manchester t.
" Irving,chief traindespatcher N.Y.R.h.2 East.
" Rosa, wid. Wm. H. vestmkr. b.r. 1225 Main.
" William, laborer at 889 Allyn, h. E.H.t.
Wickirzer Frederick M. butcher, h. 18 Ashley.
Wicks Louisa, wid. Peter, h. 23 Russell.
Wickstrom Henry, b. New Park.

Wickward M. H. compositor, 141 Pearl.
Widell Frank G. at N.Y.R. shops, h. 16 Squire.
Widows' Homes, 133 Market, 214 and 216 Windsor av. and 13 So. Hudson.
Wiedeman Charles F. draughtsman, b. 119 High.
Wieder Isaac, laborer at 581 Cap. b. 30 Flower.
" Jacob, *(M. W. & Sons,)* h. 34 Williams.
" M. & Sons, wholesale meats, 91 Morgan.
Moritz Wieder.   Jacob Wieder.   Milton Wieder.
" Milton, *(M. W. & Sons,)* h. 137 Bellevue.
WIEDER MORITZ, alderman 2nd ward, *(M. W. & Sons,)* h. 26 Morgan.
Wiegel Jacob, peddler, h. 64 Avon.
Wier Grace L. stenog. 197 Asy. b. 16 Beach.
" Joseph H. clerk at National Home for disabled volunteers, 783 Main, h. 193 Jef.
Wiese Max J. cutter at 28 High, b. Rocky Hill t.
Wiesner Charles, carpet layer at 921 Main, b. 162 Franklin.
" Henry W. mach. at 1 Flower, h. 1436 Broad.
Wiessman ☞*see Weisman.*
Wiggin G W. watchmaker, 2 Am. h. 926 Main.
" G. W. Mrs. throat protectors, 926, h. 926 Main, rm. 59.
Wiggins Frank, clerk, b. 5 Wolcott.
Wight Robert, carptr. at r. 334 Asy. h.84 Putnam.
Wightman Abbie P. wid. J.C.h. 18 Huntington.
" Alanson H. clerk at Hartford Fire Ins. Co. 53 Trumbull, b. 18 Huntington.
" Hubert J. clerk, b. 18 Huntington.
WIGHTMAN WALTER V. secretary New England Granite Works, 1260 Main, h. 18 Huntington.        *See page 533.*
Wilber E. F. painter at Baxter the Decorator, 231 Asylum, h. 76½ Park.
" Harry, attorney, h. Highland, south of Far.
Wilbor Anson G. inspector at Factory Ins. Association, 95 Pearl, h. Albany, N. Y.
Wilbraham Geo. tinner, 14 Hicks, h.u. 1407 Main.
Wilbur Charles D. clerk at 33 Market, b. W.t.
" Elizabeth, wid. Gilderay, b. 1112 Main.
" Eugene C. trav. salesman, h. 60 Woodland.
" George, joiner, l.2u. 19 Church.
" J. Nelson, mach. 328 Asylum, l. 1224 Main.
" Marion, h.u.r. 26 Temple.
" Martha A. wid. Curtis S. b. 60 Woodland.
" Mortimer A. agent, h.2u. 21 Windsor.
" S. E. Mrs. nurse. h.u. 71 Asylum, rm. 18.
Wilcox Albert H.porter, Adams Ex.Co.h.110 Fkn.
" Amelia G. wid. Thos. N. h. 37 Huntington.
" Arthur C. mason, b. 86 Wooster.
" Benjamin F. harnessm. 68 Mor. h. 7 Chapel.
" C. Amelia, wid Austin A. b. 69 Chestnut.
" Carlos A. watchm. at 40 Gov. h.110 Franklin.
" Catharine S. wid. Dr. Lucian S. h. 122 High.
" Charles H. bkkpr. at 111 Sheldon, b. W.t.
" Clara, b. 58 Church.
" Clarence M. watchmaker at 4, b. 80 State.
" David A. fireman at 40 Gov. h. 28 Benton.
" David & Co. hatters, 50 Asylum, Charles H. Martin, manager.
" Ebenezer C. h. 86 Wooster.
" Edmund M. stenog. P.&R.h. Wethersfield t.
" Florence, cook at 1150, b. 1150 Main.
" Frank D. plumber at 164 State, b. 110 Pratt.

Wilcox Fred. B. printer at Times, 716, h. 1295 Mn.
" Fred. M. at Ætna Life Ins. Co. 650, b. 1255 Mn.
" Frederick S. tinner at 164 State, h. 1074 Mn.
" George E. machinist at 80 Huyshope, b. 108 Franklin.
" George K. reporter at Hartford Daily Times, 716 Main, h. East Hartford. t.
" Harry E. mach. at 1 Laurel, b. 102 Kenyon.
" Herbert R. pressm. 154 Pearl, h. Rocky Hill t.
" Howard N. salesm. 273 Asy. h. u. 51 Sumner.
" Ida N. music teacher, b. 347 Windsor av.
" Imri M. at Ætna Life Insurance Co. 650, Main, h. 347 Windsor av.
" Lina D. teacher West Middle school, 927 Asylum, b. Middletown t.
" M. Clark, butcher, 123 Anu, h. 2u. 119 Albany.
" Margaret, wid. Henry L. h. 2u. 488 Main.
" Maria R. h. 41 Sumner.
" Marianna, wid. Augustine, h. 253 Capen.
" Martha A. Mrs. h. u. 5 Center.
" May, clerk, b. 86 Wooster.
" Robert N. toolm. at 476 Cap. b. 100 Laurel.
" Sherrill E. forem. 164 State, h. u. 33 Canton.
" Walter G. rubberw. 690 Park, b. 218 N. P.
" Warren W. clerk, b. 86 Wooster.
WILCOX WILBUR A. (*Rowley & W.*) builders, b. 253 Capen.          *See page 562.*
" ☞ *see also Willcox.*
Wilde Marcus, japanner, b. 18 Central.
" Wm. H. clerk at 590 Park, h. u. 49 Webster.
Wilder Frank E. toolmaker at Popes h. 2u. 56 Putnam.
" George H. head entry clerk at Popes, b. 24 Hopkins.
" Nahum C. superintendent Spring Grove Cemetery, h. 196 Windsor av.
Wildes Frederick J. salesman 66 Market, b. 57 Farmington.
Wildman Mary F. manicure and chiropodist, 212, h. 212 Asylum, rm. 2.
Wile Benjamin F. lineman at W. U. Telegraph Co. 6 Central, h. 739 Asylum.
Wilen Fred, shoemaker, b. u. 125 Ward.
" Gustav F. shoe repairer at Brown, Thomson & Co. 942 Main, b. 125 Ward.
Wilensky Charles, salesman, h. 104 Windsor.
" Morris, tailor at 892 Main, h. 182 Front.
Wiley Clarence H. at 59½ Tru. b. 122 Collins.
" Clarence W. mach. b. 27 Elmer.
" George A. toolmaker at 1 Flower, b. u. 110 Hungerford.
" Herbert A. ins. clk. at 197 Asy. b. u. Ashley.
" James Allen, (*W. H. W. & Son,*) h. 176 Collins.

**WILEY LOUIS G.** job printer, 174 Pearl, h. u. 11 Belden.  *See page 477.*
" Louis N. dentist, 884 Main, h. 230 Ashley.
**WILEY L. A. & SON,** art store, manufacturers picture frames, 251 Pearl.
*See page 546.*
" Lyman A. (*L. A. W. & Son,*) h. 27 Elmer.
" M. G. wid. Wm. H. h. 122 Collins.
" Oscar, driver 48 Ann, h. West Hartford t.
" Robert E. printer 174 Pearl, b. u. 11 Belden.
" Roy H. (*L. A. W. & Son,*) 251 Pearl, b. 27 Elmer.
" W. H. & Son, overgaiter mfrs. r. 59½ Trumbull.
Mrs. M. G. Wiley.          James Allen Wiley.
" ☞ *see also Willey; Wyllie.*
Wilhelm Charles, mach. at 142 Russ, h. u. 280 Park.
Wilhelmy Geo. F. shoemaker, 22, b. u. 24 Church.
" Mina, assistant at 171 Putnam.
Wilhemy Marie M. clerk at 142 Asy. b. 13 Belden.
Wilke A. cabinetm. 69 Front, h. Springfield t.
Wilkes Nathan, peddler, h. 2u. 3 Pleasant ct.
" Thomas, filer at 581 Cap. h. Bloomfield t.
" Thos. Jr. filer at 581 Cap. b. Bloomfield t.
Wilkie Alexander, carpenter at 155 Charter Oak, h. 11 Russell.
" Ida, dressmaker, b. 11 Russell.
Wilkinson Clara B. music teacher, 96, h. 3u. 96 Walnut.
" Joseph E. carpenter, 109 Windsor av. b. 65 Hawthorn.
" Martha J. nurse, b. 14 Church, rm. 5.
" William H. h. 65 Hawthorn.
" William H. Jr. modelmaker at Popes, h. 108 Laurel.
Willard Abbie, wid. Chas. E. b. 1210 Main.
" C. L. Mrs. b. 119 Capitol.
" Dennis, teamster, h. 3 John.
" Elizabeth, h. 13 Clinton.
" Eugene W. mach. at 133 Shel. h. 2u. 7 S. Pro.
" Frances G. wid. W. F. h. 13 Clinton.
" Leone, fruits, etc. 59 Spruce, b. 28 Flower.
" Lizzie H. stenographer, 49 Pearl, h. Weth. t.
" Palmer S. traveling salesman at 399 Allyn.
" Ruth A. wid. W. H. seamstress, h. u. 71 Asy.
" Samuel P. agent State Board of Education, room 42 State Capitol, b. Colchester t.
" Will L. clerk at 76 Trumbull, h. Weth. t.
" William A. assistant treasurer Mechanics Savings Bank, 815 Main, h. 13 Clinton.
" William B. h. 12 Willard.
Willcox Reginald N. student at Trinity college, 25 Jarvis hall, Summit.
" Washington F. railroad commissioner at State capitol, room 41-43, h. Chester t.
Willday Frank, repairer at Popes, h. u. 55 Kibbe.
Willehan John, engineer, h. u. 107 Wooster.
Willerup E. cabinetmaker, 9, h. 9 Winship.
Willes Ida, b. 67 Windsor av.
" Jabez H. art store, 1013 Main, h. 9 Avon.
" ☞ *see also Wills.*
Willet Joseph S. carptr. at 1 Laurel, h. 306 Park.
" Samuel, painter, b. 306 Park.
Willette John, mason, h. 5 New Park.
Willey Guy L. foreman. 581 Capitol, h. 57 Hung.
" ☞ *see also Wiley; Wyllie.*

## ALFRED WILLIAMS & SON,

Furriers to the People.

**SEAL JACKETS AND SACQUES.**

Full line of capes, muffs, boas and trimmings, robes, rugs and all kinds of fancy furs.

**99 PRATT ST.** *Old Nos. 41 to 45.*

**WM. ROGERS MFC. CO.** 66 Market.          *See outside back cover.*

Williams A. E. burnisher at 62 Mar. h. Meriden t.
" A. N. special agent at Ætna Insurance Co. 666 Main, b. 53 Trumbull.
" Aaron W. C. treasurer and gen'l manager, Capewell Horse Nail Co. 40 Governor, h. 27 Charter Oak pl.          *See page 524.*
" Albert F. h. 26 Sanford.
" Alfred, drug clerk at 254, b. 230 Asy. rm. 7.
WILLIAMS Alfred & Son, furriers, 99 Pratt.
          *See page 379.*
    Estate of Alfred Williams. Alfred C. J. Williams.
" Alfred C. J. *(Alfred Williams & Son)* furrier, 99 Pratt, h. 79 Edwards.
" Alfred P. laborer at 690 Park, b. u. 26 Grand.
" Alice E. clerk at 44 Ann, b. 18 Russell.
" Alice Mrs. washer, b. 118 Albany.
" Alonzo, laborer, h. r. 213 Pearl.
" Andrew J. policeman, h. u. 167 Babcock.
" Arthur, h. u. 69 Chestnut.
" Anna Francis Mrs. h. r. 48 Elm.
" Anna L. wid. Samuel W. h. u. 80 Hopkins.
" Annie M. wid. Joseph, h. 2u. 37 Mulberry.
" Arthur E. packer at 57 Alb. h. u. 43 Chestnut.
" Asenath, wid. Francis, b. 11 Rowe.
" August, baggagemaster str. Middletown, h. Essex t.
" C. D. machinist, 13 Central.
" C. Louise, teacher drawing, High school, b. 3u. 370 Asylum, rm. 16.
" Carleton, motorman St. Ry. b. u. 230 Weth.
" & Carleton Co. wholesale druggists, 206 State.
" Catherine, wid. William J. h. u. r. 139 Martin.
" Charles F. cook, 2 Holcomb.
" Charles H. Rev. h. 650 Main, rm. 18.
" Charles H. janitor, h. 90 Fairmount.
" Charles Henry, carpenter at 158 Woodland, h. 1 Warren.
" Charles M. h. Hamilton heights.
" Charles M. Jr. draughtsman at 142 Russ, b. Vanderbilt hill.
" Charles R. letter carrier, h. 8 Marsh.
" Chas. S. pres't Williams & Carleton Co. h. 92 Farmington.
" Cilanda A. laundress, h. 8 Green.
" Clara L. teacher West Middle school, b. 370 Asylum.
" Clarence B. toolm. 30 Cush. h. 19 Riverside.
" Clark H. cigarm. at 1115 Main, h. 1 Warren.

## E. H. WILLIAMS,

### MANUFACTURING

### CONFECTIONER.

#### SPECIALTIES IN

# FINE GOODS.

## 366 ASYLUM STREET.

Williams Cyrus C. at Hartford Fire Insurance Co. 53 Trumbull, h. 216 Sargeant.
" David E. clerk, b. Hamilton heights.
" David J. laborer, b. u. 740 Main.
" Dora Mrs. wid. John, at 84 Pratt, h. E. H. t.
" E. silverplater, l. 1032 Main.
" Ebenezer B. printer at Case, Lockwood & Brainard Co. 141 Pearl, h. 23 Riverside.
" Edward, goldbeater 41 Tru. b. 193 Weth.
" Edward C. salesman at 38 Ann, b. 56 Capitol.
" Edw. D. cigar mfr. r. 1263 Main, h. 48 Green.
" Edward F. printer at R. S. Peck & Co. 26 High, h. Windsor t.
" Edward J. brakeman, b. 26 Sanford.
" Edwin H. foreman at Colts, b. 119 Jefferson.
" Edwin L. mach. at 30 Cush. h. 85 Sargeant.
" Edwin R. nickelplater at 135 Sheldon, b. 50 John.
" Elind W. paperhanger, h. 42½ Windsor.
" Elisabeth J. h. 10 Wyllys.
" Eliza, wid. George, h. 25 Pawtucket.
" Elizabeth, nurse, l. 981 Main, rm. 27.
" Ella M. teacher, b. 10 Suffield.
" Emma, wid. David, h. 22 Walnut.
" Emma L. teacher 2d North school, 249 High, h. 68 Pratt.
" Ethel L. stenog. at 20 Sargeant, b. 10 Suffield.
" Eugene B. supt. Hartford & N. Y. Transportation Co. 285 State, b. 88 Capitol.
WILLIAMS Eugene H. mfr. confectionery, 366 Asylum, h. u. 183 Retreat. *See page 379.*
" Eugene L. traveling salesman at Andrews & Peck, 88 Market, h. 95 Laurel.
" Everett S. mach. at 54 Arch, h. South Weth. t.
" Everett S. mach. at 40 Governor, h. E. H. t.
" F. A. motorman St. Ry. 115 State.
" Fannie S. housekeeper, b. u. 13 Fairmount.
" Francis E. clerk at 117 Asy. h. u. 397 Capitol.
" Francis J. clerk at 272 Asylum, b. 281 Main.
" Frank, furrier at 99, b. 114 Pratt.
**WILLIAMS FRANK B.** attorney at law, 847 Main, rm. 8, h. 195 Sigourney.
          *See page 496.*
" Frank R. molder, 690 Park, h. 247 Franklin.
" Fred, clerk, b. 2u. 37 Mulberry.
" Fred, nickleplater at Popes, b. 25 Pawtucket.
" Fred H. filer at Colts, h. 14 Westland.
" Frederick, b. 145 High.
" G. F. Mrs. h. u. 230 Asylum.
" G. Grant, barber, 209 Pearl, h. 2u. 29 Wolcott.

**If you have anything to Sell, Advertise it in The Post.**

Williams George, b. 25 Pawtucket.
" George A. clerk at 64 Asylum, b. 37 Mulberry.
WILLIAMS GEORGE C. F. Dr., sec'y and asst. treas. Capewell Horse Nail Co. 40 Gov. h. 17 Atwood.  *See page 524.*
" George G. h. 28 Prospect.
" George H. finisher at Seidler & May, furniture store, 306 Pearl, h. Windsor t.
" George H. Jr. mach. at 1 Flow. b. 234 Putnam.
" George S. clerk at 372 Asy. h. 151 Albany.
" II. DeWitt Rev. pastor, Glenwood church, h. 87 Laurel.
" H. Edgar, timekpr. at 1 Flow. h. 95 Laurel.
" Harry B. clerk at Conn. General Life Ins. Co. 49 Pearl, h. Windsor t.
" Harry F. organist Christ church, b. 986 Main.
**WILLIAMS HARRY R.** patent expert, 756 Main, h. 24 Marshall.
*See outside back cover.*
" Helen J. stenographer at 20 Sargeant, b. 151 Collins.
" Heman C. pilot str. Hartford, 285 State, h. Haddam t.
" Henry, carptr. at r. 8 Ashley, h. 2u. 17 Seyms.
" Henry E. druggist, 839, h. 899 Park.
" James, cigarmaker, 104 Asylum, h. E.H.t.
" James A. quartermaster str. Middletown, 285 State, h. Essex t.
" James A. salesman 42 Un.pl. h. 10 Atwood.
" James A. teamster at 154 Charter Oak, h. r. 41 Mather.
" Jas. E. foreman, 54 Windsor av. h. 26 Chapel.
" James F. clerk at Brown, Thomson & Co. 942 Main, h. 15 Fairmount.
" James H. repairer Popes, h. 12 Ellsworth.
" James J. laborer, h.u.r. 176 Front.
" Job, principal, 690, b. 690 Asylum.
" John, ostler, h. 2 Elm pl.
" John, teamster at 82 Francis, b. Ford.
" John A. horseshoer, h. 2 Elm pl.
" John F. coachman, 888 Asy. h. 100 Walnut.
" John H. cabinetm. 69 Front, b. 37 Mulberry.
" John H. furniture repairer, 133, h.u. 133 Mn.
" John H. music teacher, 17, b. 2u. 17 Seyms.
WILLIAMS JOHN K. *alderman 5th ward*, apothecary, 973 Main, h. 370 Asylum, Batterson block, rm. 54.
" John W. gardener, h. 11 Curcombe.
" Kate B. clerk at 835 Main, l.u. 80 Pearl.
" King H. waiter at 152 Asy. h. 3 Wolcott.
" Laura C. h. 1492 Broad.
" Lewis E. conductor St.Ry. h. 10 Elliott ct.
" Lewis J. molder at 225 Shel. b. 10 Suffield.
" Lewis W. cook, h.u. 15 Gold.
" Lizzie C. clerk at 45 Asylum, h. 10 Wyllys.
" Louis J. molder, b. 10 Suffield.
" Lucy H. teacher 690 Asylum, b. 1492 Broad.
" Mabel, clerk at Brown, Thomson & Co. 942 Main, b. 2u. 20 Seyms.
" Margaretta, wid. Ralph, h. 10 Suffield.
" Mary, wid. John. h. 174½ Front.
" Mary A. wid. Alfred, h.u. 156 Washington.
" Mary E. wid. Elizur W. h. 650 Main, rm. 33.
" Mary E. wid. Ezra H. h. 88 Capitol.

Williams Mary R. artist, h. 1492 Broad.
" Minerva A. dressmaker, 26, b. 26 Sanford.
" Morris, cigarmaker, h. 2u. 20 Seyms.
" Nancy, wid. William, h. 36 Wooster.
" Nellie, wid. Joseph, h.u. 18 Russell.
" Olive E. operator, 3 Central, b. 215 Garden.
" Peter, coachman, h.u. 5 Riverside pl.
" Peter, laborer, h. 1220 Asylum.
" Philip, baker at 57 Albany, h. 55 Fairmount.
" Philip K. b. 92 Farmington.
" Rachel Mrs. h.u. 35 Spruce.
" Rosa, clerk at 70 Huy. b. 25 Pawtucket.
" Rosamond M. elocutionist, 847 Main, rm. 7, b. 25 Foot Guard.
" Ruby M. teach. W. Mid. school, b. 26 Chapel.
" Samuel H. supt. Adams Ex. Co. stable, h. 15 Foot Guard.
" Samuel P. asst. treas. W. & Carleton Co. 206 State, h. 110 Kenyon.
" Seymour E. toolmaker at Colts, b.u. 119 Jef.
" Thomas, filer at Popes, h. 177 Zion.
" Thomas, mach. at 690 Park, h. 177 Zion.
" Thomas, painter, b. 145 High.
" Thos. E. stereotyper at Post, b. 145 High.
" Thos. H. timekeeper N.Y.R. h. 21 Riverside.
" Typewriter Co. 77 Pratt, M.J.Lehwald,mgr.
" Walter, teamster Robt. Price & Son, h. Ford.
" William, b. 373 Capitol.
" William, carpetfitter, b. 150 Albany.
" William A. laborer, h.r. 139 Martin.
" William C. conductor St.Ry. h. 73 Congress.
" William D. clerk at 78 Asy. h. 44 Ashley.
" Wm. F. foreman 40 High, h.u. 36 Wooster.
" William H. driver, Adams Ex. b. 31½ Russell.
" William P. steward, 690, h. 690 Asylum.
" William S. at 149 State, h. Manchester t.
" William S. stevedore, commission merchant, *port warden*, 285 State, h.u. 17 Russ.
" Wm. W. painter at 20 Central, b. 12½ Windsor.
Williamson Clifford B. joiner, b. 181 Bellevue.
" Herbert C. foreman at Colts, b. 181 Bellevue.
" John, blacksmith at 54 Arch, b. 80 State.
" Leroy A. forem. at 581 Cap. b. 181 Bellevue.
" Peter L. patternm. at Popes, b. 123 Oak.
" Randolph W. carptr. 556 Mn. h. 11 Woodbine.
" Thomas J. peddler, h. 181 Bellevue.
" Wm. H. toolm. 476 Capitol, h.u. 13 Simon.
Williard Samuel, laborer, b. 2u. 1 Riverside pl.
**WILLIMANTIC LINEN CO.** factory 34 Morgan, office 391 Allyn, c. High
*See page 544.*
Willing Mark, cigarm. at 867 Main, b. 163 Front.
Willinsky Charles, salesman, b. 104 Windsor.
Willis Albert H. ( *W. & Wilson*, ) h. Boston, Mass.
" Caroline M. wid. Charles O. h. 47 Main.
" Chas. H. carptr. at 141 Tru. h. 36 Seymour.
" Clarissa T. b. 36 Jefferson.
" George S. helper, b. 112 Albany.
" Samuel, carpenter, N.Y.R. h.u. 265 Asylum.
" Sarah, Mrs. h. 13 So. Hudson, room 6.
" & Wilson, clothiers, 115–119 Asylum.
Albert H. Willis.    George W. Wilson.
" William B. machinist, h. 1107 Main.
" William T. clerk at 729 Main, b. 73 Babcock.
" Wylie, coachman, l. 11 Myrtle.

Williston Charles E. clerk 921Mn. h.u. 874Broad.
" Rhoda, wid. Josiah F. b. 24 East.
Wills Frederick C. diesinker 142 Russ, b. 73 Bab.
" Thomas H. carptr. N.Y.R. h. 73 Babcock.
" ☞see also Willes.
Willson Everett C. clerk at Hartford Times, 716 Main, h. 95 Wethersfield.
" Jane D. dressmaker, 25, b. 25 Madison.
" Leslie H. manager at R. N. FitzGerald, 44 Market, h.u. 15 East.
" Susan C. wid. Henry, h.u. 95 Wethersfield.
" Vesta H. stenog. 904 Main, rm.88, b.34 Mahl.
" William C. engineer,N.Y.R. h. 129 Sargeant.
" ☞see also Wilson.
Wilmarth Clara, at 336 Asy. b. 38 Woodbine.
" Edward, harnessm. at 8 Sig. b. 38 Woodbine.
" Gardner Mrs. h. 38 Woodbine.
Wilsey Erminie, rubberw. 690 Park, b. 30 Smith.
" John N. chief clerk U. S. stamped envelope works, 1 So. Ann, h.u. 257 Windsor av.
Wilson Abraham, mech. at 690, h. 868 Park.
" Albert E. mach. at 1 Flower, b.Manchester t.
" Albert E. printer at 581 Cap. h. Bloomfield.
" Alexander H. b. 386 Windsor.
" Alice M. nurse, 151, b. 151 Retreat.
" Ann, wid. George, b.u. 86 Wooster.
" Anne Burr, teach. Ars'l sch. b.18 Windsor av.
" Arthur A. actuary insurance department, rm. 20, State Capitol, h. 31 Russ.
WILSON ARTHUR M. vice pres't and treas. E. S. Kibbe Co. 149 State, h. Wilson station.
  See page 587.
" B. E. Mrs. h. 151 Retreat.
" B. VanLew, asst. phys. director, 315 Pearl, b. 58 Buckingham.
" Barbara, h. 147 State.
" Benj. A. screwm. at 476 Cap. h. 51 Laurel.
" Bruce C. at 556 Capitol, b. 6 So. Forest.
" Charles E. at Ætna Life Ins. Co. 650 Main, b. 21 Seyms.
" Charles E. clerk at Popes, b. 251 Capitol.
" Chas. E. poolroom, 26 Ford, b.r. 156Mather.
" Chas. E. toolm. at Colts, h. 24 Woodbridge.
" Charles S. b. 565 Park.
" Cora, h. 933 Main, rm. 25.
" David A. clerk at Brown, Thomson & Co. 942 Main, b. 151 Retreat.
" Edward, mach. at 133 Sheldon, h. 53 Elliott.
" Edward D. waiter, h. 235 Bellevue.
" Edward E. at Ætna Life Ins. Co. 650 Main, h. 21 Seyms.
" Elisha, clerk at 131 Main, h. E.H.t.
" Elizabeth N. wid. William H. b. 1506 Broad.
" Florence A. clerk at Brown, Thomson & Co. 942 Main, b. 151 Retreat.
" Foster, broomm. 336, b. 334 Wethersfield.
" Frank, teamster, h.u. 61 Elm.
" Frank B. sec'y Jewell Pin Co. 31 Hicks, h.u. 132 Jefferson.
" George, h.u. 79 Bellevue.
" George B. jobber, h.u. 42 Hicks.
" George C toolm. Colts, b. 26 Woodbridge.
" George E. nurse, b. 1261 Main
" George H. carpenter, h.u. 86 Wooster.

Wilson George W. (Willis & W.) h. 2 Florence.
" George W. porter, b. 156 Mather.
" Henry Mrs. h. 2 Sumner.
" J. Frank, clerk at 885 Main, h.2u. 208 Park.
" James, h. 34 Williams.
" James, shipcarptr. 285 State, h. 54 Wdbg.
" James A. painter at Baxter the Decorator, 231 Asylum, h. 41 Lincoln.
" James H. laborer at 70 Com. b.u. 5 Wolcott.
" James Jr. gardener, b. New Park.
" James L. teamster, 70 Com. h.u. 5 Wolcott.
" James P. repairer 40 Gov. h.u.r. 27 John.
" Jane Mrs. b. 2 Holcomb.
" Jane Mrs. h.r. 114 Albany.
" Jason, mach. at 1 Flow. h.r. 13 Huntington.
" John, carpenter, h. Park c. Oakwood, W.H.t.
" John, decorator at Baxter the Decorator, 231 Asylum, b. 34 Williams.
" John, operator at 40 Gov. h.u. 81 Seymour.
" John C. factorymgr. 690 Park, b. Far. n. Pro.
" John C. farmer, h. 656 Park.
" John C. rubberw. 690 Park, h. 633 Pro. av.
" John E. cigarm. at 867 Main, h.u. 18 Alden.
" John H. painter, b. 151 Retreat.
" John H. rubberworker at 690, h. 868 Park.
" John L. deputy sheriff, 85 Tru. h. Suffield t.
" Joseph, machinist at 1 Flower, l. 28 Spring.
" Jos. teamster at 93 Ch.O. b. 94 New Britain.
" Joseph A. machinist at 690, b. Park, W.H.t.
" Joseph F. planer 335 Shel. h. 386 Windsor av.
" L. May, music teacher, 83, b.u. 83 Seymour.
" Leland P. clerk at Conn. Fire Insurance Co. 51 Prospect, h. Wilson station.
" Lizzie A. b. 26 Woodbridge.
" Mary A. Mrs. cashier at 119 Pearl, h. G.t.
" Martha H. clerk, b.u. 71 Williams.
" Martin F. b.u. 1199 Main.
" Mary Ann Mrs. h. 76 Ferry.
" Mary L. dressmaker, b.u. 1199 Main.
" Mary L. wid. Peter B. h. 121 Madison av.
" Nellie, domestic, 20 South Hudson.
" Nicholas E. clerk, b. 151 Retreat.
" Patrick, saloon, 255 State, h.u. 1199 Main.
" Phœbe C. wid. Charles E. b. 26 Woodbridge.
" Richard F. mech. at Popes, h. 39 Lawrence.
" Robert J. salesman, l. 1224 Main.
" Robert J. steamfitter at 690, b. 565 Park.
" Samuel, boilermaker at H. B. Beach & Son, 185 Grove, h.u. 4 Union.
" Sarah, wid. James, h. New Park.
" Sarah T. wid. Cornelius, h.u. 21 Seyms.
" Severin, bookbdr. at 141 Pearl, h.u. 13 Talcott.
" Thomas, cordmaker at Jewell Belting Co. 15 Trumbull, h. 3 Pliny's ct.
" Thomas, laborer, h. 92 Walnut.
" Thomas, lineman, b.u. 59 Market.
" Thomas F. clerk at Popes, h.u. 76 Franklin.
" Thomas J. screwm.476 Cap.h.u. 1086 Broad.
" Thomas K. molder, 1 Flow. b. 370 Asy. rm. 6.
" Thomas M. h. 370 Asylum, rm. 36.
" Virgil, clerk, h.u. 6 Squire.
" William, laborer, h.u. 94 Walnut.
" William, laborer, h. 31 Mechanic.
" William, lineman, h.u. 59 Market.
" William, poolroom, 26 Ford, b.r. 156Mather.

**THE POST DELIVERED AT YOUR HOME DAILY, PER MONTH, FIFTY CENTS.**

Wilson William, porter str. Hartford, 285 State.
" William C. engineer N.Y.R. h.127Sargeant.
" William F. enameler at Popes, b. 13 Law.
" Wm. G. mach. at Colts, h.u. 83 Seymour.
" William G. porter at T. Sisson & Co. 729 Main, b. 156 Mather.
" William H. trimmer at 618 Cap. h. B.t.
" William J. at Travelers' Ins. Co. 56 Prospect, h. Suffield t.
" William J. telegraph oper. b.u. 1199 Main.
" William W. clerk at 197, b. 370 Asylum.
" ☞ see also Willson.
Wilton Samuel, bricklayer, l.u. 12 Church.
Wiltsie Irving L. assistant treasurer, 732 Main, h. So. Highland.
Wilund Charles F. h.4u. 66 Hicks.
Winchester Chas. R. clerk 466 Mn.h.2u. 96 Park.
Wind Hans, b. 273 Capen.
" Holger, screwm. at 476 Cap. h. 50 Willow.
" Lillian M. nurse 54, l.u. 54 Church.
" Thomas J. beltm. at 15 Tru. h. 310 Capen.
**WINDSOR RED STONE CO.**
M. J. O'Connor, president. See p. 508.
" The, 986 Main.
Winek Samuel, carpenter, h.2u. 62 Pleasant.
Winer Jacob, tailor, 892 Main, b. 305 Market.
Winestein Isaac, laborer, h.2u. 30 Kilbourn.
" Israel B. tailor, h. 3 North.
" Morris, tailor, h.2u. 34 Avon.
Wing Belle Mrs. nurse at 102 Pearl.
" Charlie, laundry, 92½, h. 92½ Trumbull.
" Chung, laundry, 41 Hawthorn.
" Mary J. Mrs. h. 1008 Park c. Prospect av.
" Oliver F. clerk at Mechanics' Savings Bank, 815 Main, h.u. 164 Seymour.
" Sing, laundry, 21 Park.
" Tung, laundry, 58½ Front.
" Yee, laundry, 487 Main.
Winkel Henry, baker, h. 179 Albany.
" Henry F. farmer, b. 82 Vine.
" John, driver, 59, h.u. 59 Sheldon.
" John P. clerk at 78 Asylum, h. 82 Vine.
Winkleman B. M. teacher at E. M. Huntsinger, 30 Asylum, b. 234 High.
" Wm. A. repairer at Popes, h. 623 Capitol.
Winn E. L. decorator at Baxter the Decorator, 231 Asylum, b. 80 Church.
" Mary Mrs. h. 364 Main.
" Peter, laborer, h.u. 18 Wolcott.
Winnerberg John, coppers.141 Com. h. Temple.
Winnewski Adam, cementw. h.2u. 43 Bellevue.
Winnie Wm. teamster at 2 Chapel, h. 37 Hudson.
Winott May, clerk at 1407 Main.
Winship Chas. B. carptr. b. 478 Wethersfield.
" Ellen M. dressmaker, 11, b. 11 Wethersfield.
" Henry, h. 11 Wethersfield.
" Henry C. cabinetmaker at 556, b. 345 Main.
" Mary E. wid. Chauncey H. h. 391 Weth.
" Wm. L. supt. at Mrs. Colts, 30, h. 373 Weth.
Winslow Emma E. prin. prim. dept. West Middle school, 927 Asylum, b. 171 High.
" Everett, teamster, h.r. 34 So. Prospect.
" Fred. G. at Ætna Life Ins. Co. 650 Main, b. 51 Grove.

Winslow Gideon D. treas. Hartford Dredging Co. 721 Main, rm. 30, h. 51 Grove.
" Herbert J. tel.oper. 10 Central,l.62 Edwards.
" Miranda, wid. Daniel, b. 74 Brook.
" Nelson, teamster at r. 1263 Main, b. 74 Brook.
Winter Charles J. h. 120 Retreat.
" Charles O. at Ætna Life Insurance Co. 650 Main, h. 34 Congress.
" Jacob A. clerk at Brown, Thomson & Co. 942 Main, h. 2 Goodman.
" Neils, peddler, b. 987 Main.
" Peter, laborer, b. 2 Goodman.
" Rose A. clerk at Brown, Thomson & Co. 942 Main, b.u. 117 Benton.
" Susan, wid. Zina, h.2u. 33 Windsor.
" Thomas J., Earle House, 368 Allyn,74 High.
Winters Jennie, assistant, 171 Putnam.
" Joseph, joiner, b. 75 Windsor.
" Thomas, instructor,11 Grove, b. 75 Windsor.
Winther Nicholas, molder 690 Park, b.533 Broad.
Winzig Joseph, machinist at Pratt & Whitney Co. 1 Flower, h. Elmwood v.
Wippit Louis, harnessm. at 8 Sig. b. 8 Chestnut.
Wirth Theodore, sup't of city parks, h. 501 Park.
Wisdom Louis A. helper at 37 Wells, l.24 Church.
Wise Daniel, b. 255 Asylum.
" Henry J. clerk at 133 State, h.u. 66 Flower.
" Isidore (W., Smith & Co.) h. 11 Mahl.
" John, carptr. at 155 Charter Oak, h.19 John.
" Michael J. clerk at quartermaster general office, State capitol, rm. 56, l. 278 Main.
" Moses, clerk, 364 Asylum, b.u. 13 Belden.
" Norton, mach. at 388 Cap. h. 102 Windsor.
" Robert E.pressfdr.141 Pearl, h.2u.147 State.
" Samuel C. nightwatchm. h. 373 Asy. rm. 33.
" Smith & Co. drygoods, 921 Main.
　　I. Wise. Gottfried Olschefskie, Jr., S. Youngman
　　　　Robert Smith.　　　Solomon Wohl.
" William J. mach. at Colts, h. 73 Huyshope.
Wiseman C. deckhand, scow Newton, 285 State.
" John C. mach. at Hfd. Cycle Co. h. 433 Cap.
" ☞ see also Weisman.
Wishart William, foreman at 286 Sheldon, b.u. 35 Buckingham.
Wisner Christian, driver at 351, b. 353 Asylum.
" Fred. K. driver at 48 Ann, h. W.H.t.
Wissel Konrad, cooper at 245 Winsor, b. 36 Sanford.
" Konrad Jr. wirew. 247 Asy. b. 36 Sanford.
" Margaret Mrs. grocery, 36, h. 36 Sanford.
Wissker Fred, clerk, 245 Windsor, h.73 Bellevue.
Witham Aurilla R. proofreader Hartford Times, 716 Main, b. 79 Seymour.
" Harriet E. clerk at Brown, Thomson & Co. 942 Main, b. 79 Seymour.
" Nelson J.printer at 141 Pearl, h.79 Seymour.
Witherell Geo. E. mech. engineer, 476 Capitol, h.u. 3 Linden.
" Georgia M. teacher Northeast school, b. 3 Linden.
" ☞ see also Wetherell; Withrel.
Withers John T. nurseryman, h. 126 Westland.
Withrel Edwin, salesman at Sage, Allen & Co. 898 Main, h.2u. 1 Wooster.
" ☞ see also Wetherell; Witherell.

Witkin Lena Mrs. groceries, 110, h. 110 Barbour.
" Moris, carpenter, b. 110 Barbour.
Witte Albert, clerk at 842 Asylum, b. High.
" Charles J. engineer at Wm. Rogers Mfg. Co. 66 Market, h. 85 Brown.
" Henrietta, wid. Emil, b. 71 Bellevue.
" Herman C. machinist, b. 77 Hungerford.
" Julia wid. Charles, h.u. 219 Main.
" Robert C. cutlery, etc. r. 215, h.u. 219 Main.
Witter William H. clerk at Popes, h. 16 Clark.
Wittig Abbie, wid. J. R. h. 22 Babcock.
" Charles R. carpenter, b. 22 Babcock.
" Louis H. polisher, 581 Cap. h.2u. 134 Bab.
" Mather Mrs. photo artist, 14, h. 14 Goodman.
Wittmaack Niels P. laborer, h.2u. 29 Elliott.
Wittman Frank, painter, b. 6 Elliott pl.
" Henry, machinist, b. 6 Elliot pl.
" John, tailor, h. 6 Elliott pl.
" John J. upholstr. at 104 Asy. h. 6 Elliott pl.
" William H. painter, b. 6 Elliott pl.
Wittmann Chas. J. clerk, 904 Mn. h.102 Windsor.
" Sophie, wid. Frank, tailoress, h. 6 Queen.
Wittstein William, barber at 187, b. 187 Front.
Wodal John, laborer at Pope Tube Co. b.40 Park.
" Michael A. helper at 142 Russ, b. 40 Park.
Woerner Louis E. asst. forem. at 1 Flow. h. E.H.t.
" ☞ see also Warner.
Woglom Howard C. asst. foreman at Popes, b.u. 109 Babcock.
Wohl Solomon ( Wise, Smith & Co. )h.u. 20 Seyms.
Wolcott Almira, wid. Wm. Henry, b. 17 Lafayette.
**WOLCOTT & DARBY,** mechanical engirs. surveyors, 49 Pearl. See p. 493.
Henry A. Wolcott.      John Darby.
" Emma, stenographer, adjt. gen. office, rm. 19, State capitol, b.u. 97 Washington.
" Frank, carpenter, b.u. 29½ Lewis.
" Frank, clerk at 921, l. 750 Main, room 20.
" Grace, teacher Law. st. school, b. 97 Wash.
Wolcott Henry A. ( W. & Darby, ) h. 22 Highland.      See page 493.
" Julia M. clerk at Brown, Thomson & Co. 942 Main, b. East Hartford t.
" Julia M. forewmn. of bindery, Case, Lockwood & Brainard Co. 141 Pearl, h. 17 Lafayette.
" Mary E. nurse, 20 South Hudson.
" Mary E. wid. Samuel, h.u. 97 Washington.
" William A. ticket agt. at P.&R. l. 14 Spring.
Wolden Timothy, chipper, h. 9 Curcombe.
Wolf Charles, baker, h. 156 Brown.
" Charles, butcher at 295 Asy. b. 120 Babcock.
" Charles, machinist at 26 Laurel, h. Weth. t.
" Charles, shuttlemkr. at 34 Mor. h.u.1413 Mn.
" Chas. A. pressman, 252 Pearl, h. 92 Retreat.
" Charles F. mach. at 1 Flow. h. 168 Putnam.
" Chas. R. mach. at 1 Flower, h. 114 Lawrence.
" Frederick J. mach. at 1 Flow. h. 1088 Broad.
" Harry, peddler, h.u. 66 Avon.
" Harry D. b.u. 284 Pearl.
" Herman, groceries, 92, h. 92 Windsor.
" Jacob F. mach. at 1 Flow. h. 111 Lawrence.
" Karl J. machinist at 1 Flower, h.u. 2 Francis.
" Max, clerk at 908 Main, h. 29 Morris.
" Robert, mach. at 70 Huyshope, b.36 Temple.
" Susan T. wid. William, h.u. 13 Grand.

Wolfe Fred A. beltist at Jewell Belting Co. 15 Trumbull, h. 85 Portland.
" Kate F. stenographer at 68 Pratt, rm. 11, b. Windsor t.
Wolff Arthur J. physician, 1, h. 1 Spring.
" Samuel, helper at 1 Flower, h. 279 Market.
" Walter A. mach.hand, at Colts, h.u. 109 Law.
" William, bkkpr. at 921 Main, h. 23 Pleasant.
" ☞ see also De Wolf.
Wolfinger John S. fireman, h. 260 New Park.
Wollerton S. Harvey, compositor at Hartford Times, 716 Main, h. 62 Capen.
Wollmann Carrie, wid. F. William, h.3u. Kil. ct.
" Emil K. E. upholstr. 1052 Mn. b.3u. Kil. ct.
Wolsendon Ella, wid. Luke B. h. 31 John.
" Florence M. operator at 6 Central, b.31 John.
" Mary E. bkkpr. at 701 Main, b. 31 John.
Wolsieffer Herman J. printer at 1 Flow. b.29 Ward.
Wolters Henry J. brewer at N.E. brew. h.22 Mahl.
Woltersdorf Albert, mineral waters, b.u. 16 Chas.
" August, bottler, 16, b.u. 16 Charles.
" Eva, wid. August, h. 16 Charles.
" William, clerk at 278 Asylum, b. 16 Charles.
Wolven John W. officer superior court, 85 Trumbull, h. 37 Mahl,
Woman's Aid Society, 1 Pavilion.
" Christian Association, 58, Industrial Department, 54 Church.
" Exchange, 73 Pearl, Isabel Lyon, supt.
" Shelter, Mattie J. Halstead, matron, 76 Temple.
Wombacher Adam, laborer, h. 5 Kilbourn et.
Wong C. H. laundry, 556 Asylum.
" Charlie, laundry, 76 Albany.
" Edward, laundry, 5 Heath, h. 47½ Morgan.
" Fred, laundry, 34 Grand.
Wood Alfred B. b. 68 Farmington.
" Alfred P. stew'd. at Hfd. Club, h. 7½ Grove.
" Arthur O. mach. at 581 Cap. b.2u. 32 Wells.
" Bert L. painter at 185 Asy. h.u. 84 Albany.
" Charles E. bottler, b. 16 Warren.
" Chas. H. clerk, Pope Tube Co. h. 191 Sisson.
" Ethel, b. 675 Asylum.
" Frances H. wid. William J. h. 675 Asylum.
" Francis C. carpenter, h. 243 Jefferson.
" Frank, h. 1 John.
" Frank L. mach. at 30 Cush. b. 43 Sigourney.
" Fred C. hosedriver No. 7, 480 Windsor av. h. 7 Sanford.
" George E. ostler, 14 Huntington, b.5 Sumner.
" H. Russell, bookkeeper at 185 Pearl, b. 53 Allen pl.
" Harmon & Co. real estate, 721 Main, rm. 19.
C. E. Wood, N.Y.; W. E. Harmon, C. B. Harmon.
" Harry G. clerk at 98 Kil. b. Wethersfield t.
" Harry J. salesm. at 252 Pearl, h. 43 Willard.
" Hubert K. h. 124 Garden.
" Inspector, E. D. Roberts, City hall, 800 Mn.
" James W. machinist at I. B. Davis & Son, 40 Cushman, h. E.H.t.
" Jesse, painter, l. 200 Allyn.
**WOOD JOHN A.** livery and boarding stable, 19, h. 15 Mather. See page 551.
" John F. blacksmith, h. 40 Glendale.
" John J. traveling salesman, h. 10 Canton.
" Julia A. wid. Charles E. h. 186 Barbour.

**As A NEWSPAPER, THE POST LEADS.**

Wood Julia P. wid. J. E. h. 43 Willard.
" Leslie C. at 281 Asylum, b. 42 Church.
" Lucy T. Mrs. b. 104 Clark.
" Marguerite G. R. Mrs. teacher, b. 104 Clark.
" Mary, wid. William, h. 63 Hungerford.
" Milton L. machinist at Colts, b. 14 Westland.
" Oliver W. janitor at Halls of Records, 114 Pearl, b. 38 Lewis.
" Prudence Mrs. dressm. 111, h. 111 Windsor.
" Sarah, laundress, b.u. 659 Main.
" Thomas H. clerk at 98 Kil. h. 10 Russell.
" William, engineer at 926, h.2u. 1343 Main.
" William E. assember at Colts, h. E.H.t.
" Wm. H. elevatorer, 650 Mn. h.u.r. 88½ Fmt.
" Wm. O. engir. at 133 Shel. h.2u. 32 Wells.
" ☞ see also Woods.
Woodard Arthur J. clerk at Brown, Thomson & Co. 942 Main, b. 59 Capitol.

**WOODARD HERBERT M.** real estate broker and expert appraiser, office 92 Pearl, h. 63 Church.

Woodbridge H. C. Mrs. nurse, b. 74 Arch.
" John W. with Travelers Ins. Co. 56 Prospect, h. Windsor t.
" Louise E. nurse, h. 124 Windsor.
Woodbury Alfred D. salesman at 45 Asylum, h.u. 43 Huntington.
" Francis H. letter carrier, b.2u.18 Windsor av.
" Larkin, laborer at 30, b. 30 Washington.
Woodcock Adella M. teacher at West Middle school, h. 39 Willard.
Wooden Fred. fireman, P.&R. b.u. 140 Mather.
Woodford A. E. law student, 49 Pearl, b. Unionville t.
" Ada M. b. 2 Sumner.
" D. R. coal dealer, 15 Pearl, b. 57 Farmington.
" Ernest G. clerk at 884 Main, b. W.H.t.
" L. J. Mrs. boardinghouse, 56 Winthrop.
" Lucius H. h. 38 Church.
" M. C. Mrs. b. 8 Avon.
Woodhouse Edwd. R. salesm. at 219 Asy. h. Weth.t.
Wooding Mary E. teacher at 2d North school, 249 High, b. 18 Windsor av.
Woodmancy Chas. S. mach. at 1 Flow.h. 15 Imlay.
Woodruff Asahel H. carpenter at 581 Capitol, b. 255 Putnam.
" Belle D. wid. James E. b. 84 Ann.
" Frank D. agent for pies, b. 561 Garden.
" H. A. wid. Elias N. b. 11 Florence.
" Orrin D. h. 84 Ann.
" William N. contractor 1 Flower, h. 1544 Broad.
" William N. toolmaker at Popes, b. 129 Sig.
Woods Albert F. pianos, 227 Asy. h. 135 Ashley.
" Arthur G. clerk at Brown, Thomson & Co. 942 Main, b. 161 Maple.
" Charles J. mech. at Popes, b. 65 Glendale.
" Dennis, blacksm. at 8 Front, h. Burnside v.
" Emma, wid. Alexander G. h. 246 Bellevue.
" Enoch S. sculptor, h. 828 Broad.
" George H. real est. 754 Main, h. 19 Grand.
" Henrietta E. teach. Parkv. school. b. 19 Grand.
" Henry, laborer at Colts, h.u. 15 Curcombe.
" Hugh, ostler, b.u. 10 Queen.
" & Hurley, printers, 9 Grove.*

**WOODS JAMES,** manager A. W. Scoville Wood Working Co. Vredendale e. Taylor, h. 55 Charter Oak.      *See p. 516.*
" James, painter, 110, h.u. 110 Ward.
" James J. clerk, 867, h. 1305 Main.
" James R.O. carptr. 30 Cush. h.u. 65 Glendale.
" John, bartender, b. 110 Trumbull.
" John C. boxmaker, b.u. 65 Glendale.
" John C. salesman at 227, b. 223 Asylum.
" John H. mach. at 28 High, b. Burnside v.
" Lizzie V. dressmaker, h.u. 54 Governor.
" Margaret, h. 8 Squire.
" Mary C. h.u. 54 Governor.
" Michael J. printer, 9 Grove, b. 54 Governor.
" Patrick, collarmaker at 8 Sig. h.u. 10 Queen.
" W. fireman tug Ward, 285 State.
" William, laborer on city parks, h. 514 Broad.
" ☞ see also Wood.

**WOODSIDE SEMINARY** for girls, Miss Sara J. Smith, 1204 Asylum.
      See page 710.
Woodstock Chas. F. molder 690 Park, b. 232 Putnam
Woodward Benjamin P. b. 46 Hudson.
**WOODWARD BENJAMIN S.** *( W. & Rogers,)* 133-135 Shel. h. 17 Florence. *See page 526.*
" Burt J. distributor at Evening Post, 23 Asylum, b. 46 Hudson.
" Carrie M. b. 809 Asylum.
" Charles G. b. 742 Asylum.
" Chas. H. patternm. at 33 Wells, h. 72 Allen pl.
" Chas. S. steward almshouse, b. 2 Holcomb.
" Clinton S. bkkpr. 133 Shel b. 17 Florence.
" Frances, wid. Nathaniel, b. 14 Huntley pl.
" Fred. E. carpenter, b. 46 Hudson.
" Fred W. clerk at 338 Asylum, b. 33 Mahl.
" H. J. printer at 23 Asylum, b. 46 Hudson.
" Hattie R. teacher at 2d North school, 249 High, b. 40 Pliny.
" Jennie M. wid. Wm. boardingh. 809 Asylum.
" Joseph, rubberwkr. 690, b. 771 Park.
" Joseph G. stockbroker, 39 Pearl, h. 85 Elm.
" Joseph Hooker, student, b. 85 Elm.
" Julia A. b. 17 Florence.
" Leon A. clerk at Popes, b. 56 Buckingham.
" Newell S. teamster at 149 State, h. 33 Mahl.
" P. Henry, secretary Hartford Board of Trade, 49 Pearl, h. 742 Asylum.
" Percy E. wid. J. Everett, h. 46 Hudson.
" Richard W. chemist at 83 Woodbine h. 2 Park ter.

**WOODWARD & ROGERS,** machinists, 133-135 Sheldon.   *See page 526.*
Benjamin S. Woodward.    Wm. W. Rogers.
" Rolland E. bookeeper at 86 Morgan, h. Springfield, Mass.
" Susan E. dressmaker, b. 17 Florence.
" Wilder L. conductor at St.Ry. h. 55 Lincoln.
" William N. bunker engine 5, b.u. 129 Sig.
" William S. printer at 49 Pearl, b. 46 Hudson.
Woodworth Charles R. clerk at 341 Main, h.2u. 83 Seymeur.
" Edwd. C. driver, Eng. Co. No. 5, h.u. 129 Sig.
" Elizabeth M. teacher at Lawrence street school, b. 129 Sigourney.

Woodworth Emma, forewoman at 219 Asylum, h.2u. 6 Trumbull.
" Fannie A. wid. Arthur C. hairdresser, h. 1341 Main.
" Flavel W. machinist at Pratt & Whitney Co. 1 Flower, h. Wilson station.
" Harry R. operator at 40 Gov. h.2u. 9 S.Pro.
" Henry S. laborer, 252 Pearl, b. 9 S.Pro.
" Henry S. sawyer, at 155 Ch.O. b.2u. 9 S.Pro.
" Jas. Henry, porter, Adams Ex. h.u. 23 N.B.
" Jessie M. nurse, b.u. 17 Chapel.
" Polly A. wid. Lyman, b. 139 Ashley.
" Walter G. wirewkr. 618 Cap. b. 1341 Main.
Wooley Horace G. driver, h. 227 Capen.
" Robert H. silverworker, b. 279 Asylum.
Woolley Adelbert P. woodwkr. 366, b. 372 Main.
" Arthur G. president and treas. L. T. Frisbie Co. 79 Talcott, h. 800 Asylum.
" Chas. P. trav. salesman, b. 146 Washington.
" Frederick P. manager at 366 Main, b. 5 N.B.
" George H. (G. W. W. & Son) h. 763 Asy.
" Geo. W. (G.W.W. & Son) h. 88 Buckingham.
" George W. & Son, undertakers, 556 Main. George W. Woolley.    George H. Woolley.
" Hardware Co. hardware, etc. 44 Asylum.
" James N. carpenter, h.2u. 19 Church.
" James W. conductor St.Ry. h. 57 Ward.
" Joseph C. sec'y and treas. Woolley Hardware Co. 44 Asylum, h. 111 Oak.
" Joseph M. mason, b. 21 John.
" Kate A. musicteacher, 63, h. 63 Huntington.
" Leonard D. b. 372 Main.
" Wesley, carpenter, b.2u. 19 Church.
" William F. fruits, 34 Church, b. 265 Asylum.
" William P. livery stable, 366, h. 372 Main.
" William S. builder, 63, h. 63 Huntington.
Woolner Wm. C. draughtsman, b. 74 Grove.
Woolsey Wm. A. clairvoyant, b. 30 Charlotte.
Wooster ☞ see Worcester.
Woottan Edward, clerk, 12 Central.
Wootton Fred W. civil engineer, b. 40 Pliney.
" George Mrs. h. 74 Grove.
Wopschal Charles, plumber at 548 Asylum, b.u.r. 2 Pleasant ct.
" Julius, tailor, h.u.r. 2 Pleasant ct.
" Julius E. tailor, h.u. 15 Windsor.
" Rudolph, tailor, b.u.r. 2 Pleasant ct.
" William, tailor, b.u.r. 2 Pleasant ct.
Worcester ☞ see also Wooster.
Worden Frank H. conductor St.Ry. h. 14 Bond.
" ☞ see also Warden.
Work Almira, wid. Thomas, h.u. 209 Jefferson.
" Asa B. bootcutter, h.u. 68 Chestnut.
" Frederick S. coal, 746 Mn. h. 235 Sigourney.
" John, conductor St.Ry. b. 80 State.
" Minnie E. b.u. 209 Jefferson.
" Norman P. educational sec'y at Y.M.C.A. 323 Pearl, h.u. 209 Jefferson.
Wormeck Charles, laborer, b.u. 24 Smith.
Worron Lewis C. mach. 490 Cap. b. 275 Asylum.
Worshovisky Joseph, baker, 204, h. 204 Front.
Worth Fannie, b. 15 Capitol.
" ☞ see also Wirth.
Worthington A. D. (A. D. W. & Co.) h.63 Willard.
" A. D. & Co. book publishers, 438 Asylum.*

Worthington Charles A. bookkeeper at 438 Asylum, h.u. 243 Sigourney.
" Edward A. clerk at 122, b. 126 Capen.
" Elizabeth M. teacher at Second North school, 249 High, b. 12 Florence.
" Frederick L. opera. 247 Pearl, b.63 Willard.
" Harry, apprentice at Colts, b. 86 Whitmore.
" Henry R. borer at Colts, h. 86 Whitmore.
" Howard H. clerk at Factory Ins. Association, 95 Pearl, b. 63 Willard.
" Ida H. b. 86 Whitmore.
" John D. h. 10 Girard.
" Mary A. wid. James, h. 12 Florence.
Worton Elizabeth, wid Samuel, h.u. 1172 Main.
Wraight Walter T. mach. 1 Flower, b. 211 Barb.
" ☞ see also Wright.
Wray John C. salesman at L. T. Fenn's furniture store, 613 Main, h.u. 53 Franklin.
" ☞ see also Ray.
Wrench George, carpenter, b. 80 State.
Wright Andrew J. condtr. St.Ry. h.u. 21 Canton.
" Arita, b.2u. 37 Liberty.
" Arthur J. molder at 1 Flow. h.u. 213 Law.
" Asahel J. clerk at State Board of Education, room 42 State capitol, h. 485 Farmington.
" Benjamin, compositor at 25 Asy. h. 76 Park.
" Bertha, stenographer at Hartford Life Ins. Co. b. 60 Maple.
" Bridget, wid. Charles, h.u. 147 Zion.
" Carl H. repairer at Popes, l. 196 Russ.
" Charles A. b. 341 Laurel.
" Charles E. foreman 197 Main, h. 36 Wolcott.
" Charles E. gearcutter, 1 Flow. b. 38 Wolcott.
" Charles J. ostler at r. 50 State, h.u. 9 Kinsley.
" Charles W. lather, b.u. 147 Zion.
" Clarissa A. wid. John B. b. 36 Jefferson.
" Daniel M. sec'y at 135 Shel. h. 55 Maple.
" Dora E. at 141 Pearl, b. 145 Collins.
" Dudley E. bricklayer, h. 63 Park.

**WRIGHT & DUNHAM, dentists, 911 Main, rm 1.**
Joel F. Wright.    Frank W. Dunham.
" Dwight H. mach. at Colts, b. Glastonbury t.
" Edward A. clerk at Hartford Life Insurance Co. 252 Asylum, h. 92 Ashley.
" Elina, wid. George F. artist and teacher of languages, 55, h. 55 Maple.
" Eliza Mrs. laundress, b. 53 Mather.
" Elizabeth, clerk at Hartford Life Ins. Co. 252 Asylum, b. 124 Wethersfield.
" Elizabeth C. teacher, b. 55 Maple.
" Ellen M. wid. George A. h. 9 Sherman.
" Ellsworth R. blacksmith at Ed. Balf's, h.u.r. 22½ Alden.
" F. H. conductor St.Ry. 115 State, b. E.H.t.
" F. May Mrs. b. 93 Russ.
" Frank, h.u. 8 Center.
" Frank H. helper at 1 Laurel, h. E.H.t.
" Frank O. mach. 9 Sigourney, b. 1470 Broad.
" Frederick B. clerk at Factory Ins. Association, 95 Pearl, b. 9 Sherman.
" George, painter, b. 31 Chapel.
" Geo. A. mach. at 13 Cen. b.2u. 18½ Church.
" George C. ostler, b. 9 Kinsley.

Wright George E. h. 1388 Main.
" Geo. W. foreman at Wm. Rogers Mfg Co. 66 Market, h. Glastonbury t.
" Henry E. h. 29 Townley.
" Hannah, wid. H. L. b.u. 35 Benton.
" Harriet L. wid. J. D. massage, b.u. 213 Law.
**WRIGHT HARRY B.** dentist, 51 Pratt, b. 21 Canton.
" James, carpenter, h. 35 Buckingham.
" James, carpenter, h. 6 Pleasant ct.
" James F. compositor at Case, Lockwood & Brainard Co. 141 Pearl, b. 27 Smith.
WRIGHT JOEL F. ( *W. & Dunham,* ) h. 13 Niles.
" John, clerk at Hartford Life Ins. Co. 252 Asylum, b. 124 Wethersfield.
" John E. machinist, h.u. 109 Babcock.
" Julia A. wid. William, h.u. 103 Pratt.
" Leverett, condtr. St.Ry. h.2u. 18½ Church.
" Marcus A. mach. at 581 Cap. b. 55 Maple.
" Martha, wid. Robert, h. 124 Wethersfield.
" Mary A. Mrs. cook, h.u. 105 Front.
" Mary C. teacher, b. 55 Maple.
" Mary E. clerk, b.u. 103 Pratt.
" Mary J. nurse, b. 14 Church, rm. 5.
" Minnie J. b.u. 60 Maple.
" Ralph B. stock clerk, Popes, h. 24 Babcock.
" Ralph B. Mrs. nurse, h. 7 Affleck.
" Samuel, cordwainer, 95, h. 95 Windsor.
" Thomas, engineer, h.u. 31 Union.
" Thos. machinist at 1 Flower, h. Unionville t.
" Thomas G. inspector, b.u. 31 Union.
" Thomas G. Rev. h.u. 60 Maple.
" Wm. L. machinist at 1 Flow. h. 140 Retreat.
Wrisley Chas. B. boxm. 42 Un.pl. h. 74 Spring.
" Francis, foreman, 285 State, h. Glastonbury t.
" W. H. collector steamer Hartford, h. G.t.
Wrulich Simon, filer, h.r. 44 Wells.
Wunder Bertha, dressmaker, b.u. 152 Seymour.
" Emil L. barber 94 Pearl, h. 37 So. Hudson.
" Karl A. stenographer, b.u. 37 So. Hudson.
" Lawrence, cigarm. 867 Main, h. 177 Weth.
Wurth Geo. machinist, 1 Flower, b. 179 Babcock.
Wurtz Alfred C. clerk at 273 Asy. b. 59 Capitol.
Wuzo Joseph, laborer, h.2u. 102 Windsor.
Wyand James, carpenter, h. 1430 Broad.
Wyatt William, carpenter, b. 64 Capitol.
Wybell J. Walter, woodworker at 556 Main, h.u. 25 Mulberry.
**WYCKOFF, SEAMANS & BEN-EDICT,** Remington Standard Type writer, Phœnix Life Ins. Building, 49 Pearl, rm. 19.
" Walter D. clerk at 83 Asylum, h. 6 Seyms.

Wyler Louis E. master mech. N.Y.R. h. 79 Clark.
" Louis E. Jr. fireman N.Y.R. b. 79 Clark.
Wylie James, at 62 Market, b. 41 Harbison.
Wyllie Edward, carpenter, h. 1522 Broad.
" Edward C. mason, b. 1522 Broad.
" Fred. W. carpenter, b. 1522 Broad.
" James, toolmaker at Popes, h.u. 383 Park.
" Miss, nurse, b. 14 Church, rm. 5.
Wylund Chas. foreman 247 Pearl, h. 66 Hicks.
Wyman Alonzo J. h. 24 Morris.
" Simon, b. 2 Holcomb.
" William E. finisher, 225 Shel. h.u. 90 State.
Wynkoop Augustus T. student at Trinity college, 33 Jarvis hall, Summit.
Wynn Joseph, helper at 54 Arch, b.2u. 18 Tru.
Wyrfel Annie, at 83 Woodbine, b. 66 Babcock.
" Christie, at 15 Trumbull, h.u. 66 Babcock.
" Nicholas, pressm. 252 Pearl, b. 66 Babcock.
" Samuel, at 98 Asylum, b. 66 Babcock.
Wythe D. Frank, compositor at Hartford Post, 23 Asylum, b. 964 Broad.
" Frances Mme. dressmaker, h. 964 Broad.

XELTA ☞ *See Selta.*
Xwirz Fred E. helper at 581 Cap. b. 86 Windsor.

YACKAVON Frank, laborer, h.u. 22 Kilbourn.
" James, h.u. 22 Kilbourn.
" Joseph, grocery, b.u. 22 Kilbourn.
" Michael, peddler, h.3u. 1 Charles.
" Peter, carpenter, h. 17 Kilbourn.
Yale Charles F. printer at Hartford Times, 716 Main, h. East Hartford t.
" Charles M. stenographer, 466 Asy. b. E.H.t.
" Frances E. girls' matron, 171 Putnam.
" John D. h. 248 Laurel.
Yannelli Bernardino, carpenter, h.u. 15 Charles.
Yanner John, brewer, h. 56 Bellevue.
Yanz George T. polisher at 581 Cap. h. 90 Heath.
Yarnall Benjamin, lab. 70 Com. b.u. 45 Albany.
Yarrow Philip W. theolog. student, 1507 Broad.
Yates Alva W. butter and eggs, h. 550 Asylum.
" Chas. E. saddler at 8 Sig. h. 218 New Park.
" E. P. & Co. hay, grain, straw, 1411 Main.
      Erton P. Yates.          William A. Benton.
" Erton P. ( *E. P. Y. & Co.* ) h. 30 Vine.
" Wells, carpenter, h.3u. 703 Main, rm. 13.
Yauch Charles, clerk, 267 Main, b. 46 Annawan.
Yeadi Vito Nicolo, laborer, h.3u. 2 Charles.
Yeager Charles, upholsterer at L. T. Fenn, 613 Main, h. Newington t.
Yellen Nathan, tailor, 283 Asy. h. 136 Grove.
Yellop James, laborer, h.u. 14 Arch.
Yeomans Albert F. baggagemaster N.Y.R. h. 8 Walnut.
" Edward M. attorney, 756 Mn. h. Andover t.
" Henry E. livery stables, 51, h. 51 Farmington.
" Raymond S. student, Trinity college, 43 Jarvis hall, Summit.
Yerardi Frank, laborer, h. 17 Morgan.
Yergason Edgar S. decorator, 391 Aly. h. 143 Sig.
Yerrington Henry C. mach. N.Y.R. h. 1463 Broad.
" Jane, wid. Charles, h. 1463 Broad.
Yockisch Charles, cabinetmaker, h.u.r. 165 Front.
Yoreo Paul, fruiterer, 353, h. 253 Main.

Yorgensen Charles R. machinist at 133 Sheldon, b. 10 Cottage.
" Daniel S. cabinetm. 633 Main, h. 10 Cottage.
" Paul L. L. machinist at 133 Sheldon, b. 10 Cottage.
York Etta, at 83 Woodbine, b. 91 Laurel.
" John, fireman, 70 Commerce, h.u 45 Albany.
Yost John, carpenter, b. 999 Main.
Youell Louis, helper at N.Y.R. h. 166 Ward.
" Thomas E. fireman, h.u. 99 Arch.
Young A. R. Mrs. nurse, h.u. 76 Ann.
" C. Howard, prof. of language, b. 230 Asylum.
" Charles C. operator 40 Gov. h.2u. 63 Dean.
" Charles F. mach. 388 Cap. h. 252 Putnam.
" Charles L. civil engir. b.u. 52 Wadsworth.
" Chas. L. Jr. draughtsm. 800 Main, b. Weth. t.
" Colburn L. motorman St.Ry. b. 67 Congress.
" Cora B. cashier 843 Main, b. Middletown t.
" E. M. & Co. teas and coffee, 782 Park.
   Elsie M. Young.    Harry A. Treadwell.
" Edward S. registrar of electors, 114 Pearl, h. 54 Washington.
" Edwin C. inspector at 581 Cap. h. 155 Law.
" Elizabeth Mrs. h. 74 Williams.
" Elsie M. (E. M. Y. & Co.) h. Windsor t.
" Ernest E. mech. 335 Sheldon, h.u. 14 Union.
" Ferdinand, h. 102 Prospect av.
" Frank R. clerk at 782 Park, b. Windsor t.
" Frank S. policeman, b. 1080 Main.
" George, b. 79 Clark.
" George, diesinker Popes, h. 370 Asy. rm. 41.
" George, jobber, b. 19 Sanford.
" George A. clerk, 908 Main, h. Rockville t.
" Harry H. operator at 40 Gov. b. 12 Sisson.
" Henry, painter, h. 32 Kinsley.
" Henry C. accountant, b. 52 Park.
" Herschel C. molder 1 Flower, h. 12 Sisson.
" J. Albert, carpenter, b.u. 887 Park.
" James, carpenter, l. 90 Pearl.
" James, florist, 30 Whitney, h. 10 Cone.
" John, brakeman, b.2u. 71 Albany.
" John, laborer at stonepits, h. New Britain av.
" John B. cigarmaker, h. 155 Lawrence.
" John B. Jr. painter, h.u. 33 Hungerford.
" John E. blacksmith, 1 Flower, h. 175 Russ.
" John W. printer, b. 9 Avon.
" Joseph, carpenter, h. 16 Union.
" Lillian I. stenographer, 223 Asy. b. 462 Far.
" Mamie A. clerk, b.2u. 71 Albany.
" Mary, wid. James J. h.2u. 71 Albany.
" Mary J. wid. Arthur P. h. 120 Huntington.
" Mary J. wid. Lewis J. h.u. 27 Lewis.
YOUNG MEN'S CHRISTIAN ASSOCIATION, 315, 323 Pearl, c. Jewell.  *See pp. 704, 705.*
" Men's Total Abstinence Society, 14 State.
" Nellie J. clerk, b.2u. 71 Albany.
" R. D. Mrs. h. 32 John.
" Tamar, wid. Walter H. h. 45 Wolcott.
" Warren, painter, h. 137 Babcock.
" William, florist, Elmwood, h. Lubeck.
" Wm. E. mail. clerk post office, h. 80 Brook.
" William F. bookkeeper at Hartford Cycle Co. 581 Capitol, h. 123 Hungerford.
" Women's Boarding Home, Mrs. Harriet A. Platt, matron, 58 Church.

**YOUNGBLOOD WILLIAM S.** dentist, 68, h. 68 Pratt, room 17.
Younger Thomas W. painter, b.u. 24 S.Pro.
Youngman L. & Co. gents' furnishings, 364 Asy.*
" Louis (L. Youngman & Co.) b.u. 17 Mahl.
" Solomon, (Wise, Smith & Co.) h.u. 17 Mahl.
Youngmann William, cook at 430 Asylum, h.2u. 56 Village.
Youngs Emma, wid. Edwin T. h. 41 Niles.
" Eugene R. at Conn. Mutual Life Ins. Co. 783 Main, b. 41 Niles.
" Susan E. wid. J. R. h. 41 Niles.
Youngson James, carpenter at r. 334 Asylum, h. 90 Pearl.
YUEN, SING & Co. teas, silk, etc. 118 State. *See page 387.*
Yungk Edward, molder, h. New Park, n. Prospect av.
" John, foreman at Pope Tube Co. grocery, 171, h. 171 Wethersfield.
Yuon Jow, laundry, 24 Trumbull.

ZABACK Frank, belter at Popes, h.2u. 34 Flower.
Zabel Herman, bartender at 27, b. 27 Mulberry.
Zacher Carrie M. stenographer, b. 15 Ashley.
" Edmund L. clerk at Farmers & Mechanics Nat. Bank 106 State, b. 15 Ashley.
" L. H. lithographer, h. 15 Ashley.
" Mary B. wid. Louis, h. 303 Market.
Zachs Annie, b.2u. 304 Market.
Zackrison M. motorman St.Ry. b.u. 289 Asylum.
Zalanka Frank, blacksm. at 308 Allyn, h. 29 Vine.
Zalor Jacob, h. 304 Market.
Zalenca Frank, blacksmith, h.u. 91 Windsor.
Zanccgmino Canio, laborer, h. 7 Charles.
" Donato, laborer, b.3u. 5 Charles.
Zandegiocomo Daniel, laborer, h.u. 82 Morgan.
Zander Otto, driver, h. 7 Warren.
Zangenberg Henry, painter, h.u.r. 44½ John.
Zantow Wm. F. casehardener 26, h.u. 82 Laurel.
Zaritsky Solomon, cutter, h.u.r. 174 Front.
Zawodski Anthony, laborer, 690, h. 15 Park.
" Michael, rubberworker, 690, b. 15 Park.
Zeiser Leo, b. 19 Crown.
Zemke Fred. molder, h.u. 24 Smith.
Zepp Frederick, cook, h. 2 Wooster.
Zerser William, operator at 388 Cap. b. 19 Crown.
Zettergreu Augustaf G. machinist at 476 Capitol, b.u. 58 Woodbine.
Zibbdeo Joseph, laborer, b.u. 67 Morgan.

Zibbeda John, laborer, h. 190 Front.
Zich Fred. C. A. machinist 1 Flower, h. 847 Park.
Ziegler John C. mechanic, h.u.r. 60 Vanblock.
" Reinhold, bartender at 245 Windsor, b.2u. 98 Albany.
" Walter J. mach. at 1 Flower, b. Elmwood.
Ziesing Charles Fred. nickleplater at Popes, h. 113 Windsor av.
" Fred. C. mach. at 1 Flow. b. 113 Windsor av.
Ziff Joel, shoemaker at 86 State, h. 70 Village.
" Morris, clerk at 198 State, b. 70 Village.
" Myers, peddler, h.u. 30 Kilbourn.
Ziglatzki Albert, baker 30 Wash. h.u. 120 Retreat
" Henry, clerk at 843 Main, b.u. 120 Retreat.
" Paul J. salesman, 843 Mn. b.u. 120 Retreat.
Zillhart Agnes E. b.3u. 1 Kilbourn ct.
" Albert, clerk at 618 Capitol, b. 12 Village.
" Charles, painter 618 Cap. h.3u. 1 Kilbourn ct.
Ziuman Meyer, shoem. at 524 Asy. b. 80 Morgan.
Zimmer Benedict J. stonemason, b.u. 71 Temple
" W. C. baker at 69 Morgan, b. 71 Temple.
Zimmerman Charles, sweeper at 1 Flower, h. New Britain t.
" Chas. H. waiter at 47 Prospect, l. 703 Main.
" Eugene, bottler, h.2u.r. 124 Market.
" Harry J. cigarm. at 104 Asy. b. 212 Fkn.
" Henrietta H. Mrs. attendant at 30 Wash.
" Ike, barber, 1 Spruce, h. 201 Front.
" Jacob, screwmaker, 476, b. 381 Capitol.
" Joseph E. machinist, h. 78 Martin.
" Louis, shoemaker, 112 Albany, b. 66 Village.
**ZIMMERMAN PHILIP,** baker, 55, h. 57 Judson.　　*See page 482.*
" Sam, cutter, h.u. 3 North.
" Solomon, shoem. 1167 Main, h.u. 80 Morgan.

Zinn George, carpenter, b. 131 Madison av.
" Jacob F. forem. 476 Cap. h. 131 Madison av.
Zink Joseph, baker, b. 5 Pleasant.
Zion Hill Cemetery, c. Ward and Zion.
" Isaac, cigarmaker, h. Market, c. Marsh.
Zipp Charles A. collector at 315, h.u. 298 Park.
Zisk Joseph, at 420, b. 420 New Britain.
Ziskey Harris, driver at 314 Asylum.
Zitari Gaetano, laborer, 20 Charles.
Zito Dominick, bootblack, 34 Mul. h. 58 Pleasant.
Zoels Gustave, machinist at Pratt & Whitney Co. 1 Flower, b. 835 Park.
" John, painter, 25, h. 25 Mulberry.
Zonit Joseph, laborer, h.u. 95 Sheldon.
Zorich Lorenzo, laborer, h.u. 41 Mechanic.
Zozolo Frank, laborer, h.r. 20 Charles.
Zuchtmann Friedrich, teacher of music at Washington st. school, h. Springfield t.
Zundel Conrad, baker at 78 Morgan.
Zunner Bernhardt, brewer at Columbia Brewing Co. 245 Windsor, h. 5 Nelson.
**ZUNNER JOHN,** treasurer and manager Columbia Brewing Co. 245 Windsor, h. 73 Bellevue.　　*See page 417.*
Zurhorst Alfred H. packer at Linus T. Fenn, 613 Main, h. 52 Windsor.
" Alfred J. engraver at 177 Asy. b. 52 Win.
" Louise K. cashier at 372 Asy. b. 52 Windsor.
Zuselman Aron, peddler, h.u. 207 Front.
Zychowski Andrew, blacksmith, 295 Albany, h.2u. 34 South Prospect.
Zweygartt Casper, brewer, 52 Bellevue. h. Lifkey.
" H. J. Mrs. h. 105 Ann.
Zwirz Ferdinand, mason, h. 86 Windsor.
Zwyko John, chipper at 556 Cap. b. 92 Francis.

**You'll Get ALL THE NEWS, if you READ THE POST.**

### PUBLIC BATHING HOUSE.

The first free public bathing house was opened July 20, 1872; the second was built and opened for use July 22, 1884. The present house, to replace the 1884 structure which floated off to the sound in this spring freshet, was designed and its construction supervised by Captain John K. Williams, Alderman from the 5th Ward, and Chairman of the "Bathing House Committee." It was built by S. Gildersleeve & Sons, shipbuilders, Portland, Conn., in the most substantial manner and upon entirely different principle from the others. It is supported or floated by three pontoons or floats on a side, each 20 feet long, 7 wide and 4 in depth; and these are surrounded by 12x12 timbers, and in every way protected from any possible injury even if the house sank. These floats are detachable at any time and are independent from the others for any repairs by simply opening the sea valve in the bottom and partially filling with water so as to sink the pontoon away from the load. This house contains 36 dressing-rooms and 50 hooks, together with benches for the clothes of smaller children not using the rooms; an office with closets for valuables; one tank, 50 feet by 5 feet, with water depth of 2½ for young children, and one tank 56 by 20 feet, with water depth of 4 feet. Hours for men and boys, 7 to 10 A. M.; 1 to 4 and 7 to 9 P. M.; Sundays, 6 to 10 A. M.: For women and girls, 10.30 A. M. to 12.30 P. M.; 4.20 to 6.30 P. M.; week days only. Size of structure, 60x40 feet. Cost, $3,500. Opened July 4, 1896. Attendance 1896, 41,000; 1897, 31,000. Alderman John K. Williams, chairman; Councilmen John D. Lapaugh, A. L. Newton.

### VOTES IN HARTFORD FOR GOVERNOR, 1873-'96.

| Year. | Dem. | Rep. | Proh. | Greenb. | Lab. | Scat. | Total. |
|---|---|---|---|---|---|---|---|
| 1873 | 3,612 | 3,147 | 23 | ... | ... | ... | 4,782 |
| 1874 | 4,087 | 2,880 | 124 | ... | ... | ... | 7,091 |
| 1875 | 4,488 | 3,226 | 56 | ... | ... | ... | 7,765 |
| 1876 | 3,986 | 3,260 | 19 | 167 | ... | 2 | 7,394 |
| 1876* | 5,021 | 4,033 | 4 | 78 | ... | 1 | 9,137 |
| 1878 | 3,792 | 3,167 | 24 | 541 | ... | ... | 7,524 |
| 1880 | 4,707 | 4,527 | 5 | 85 | ... | ... | 9,324 |
| 1882 | 4,684 | 3,831 | 15 | 112 | ... | ... | 8,642 |
| 1884 | 5,346 | 4,528 | 61 | 111 | ... | ... | 10,061 |
| 1886 | 4,764 | 3,843 | 124 | ... | 141 | ... | 8,872 |
| 1888 | 5,537 | 5,595 | 138 | ... | 26 | ... | 11,296 |
| 1890 | 5,209 | 4,484 | 152 | ... | 27 | 3 | 9,875 |
| 1892 | 6,376 | 5,567 | 185 | ... | 62 | 48 | 12,190 |
| 1894 | 5,748 | 5,881 | 90 | ... | 108 | 39 | 11,866 |
| 1896 | 4,184 | 9,016 | 78 | ... | ... | ... | 14,221 |

* Time of election changed from April to November.

### HARTFORD GRAND LIST.

| | | | | |
|---|---|---|---|---|
| Grand List of Hartford for Oct. | | | 1886, | $46,437,816 |
| " | " | " | 1887, | 48,345,381 |
| " | " | " | 1888, | 48,541,890 |
| " | " | " | 1889, | 47,360,439 |
| " | " | " | 1890, | 48,429,308 |
| " | " | " | 1891, | 47,912,501 |
| " | " | " | 1892, | 48,890,080 |
| " | " | " | 1893, | 49,566,010 |
| " | " | " | 1894, | 49,294,922 |
| " | " | " | 1895, | 53,311,681 |
| " | " | " | 1896, | 54,348,859 |
| " | " | " | 1897, | 60,059,133 |

# National Banks of Connecticut.

Report of the condition of the National Banks of Connecticut, for the years 1890, 1891, 1892, 1893, 1894, 1895, 1896, 1897, 1898.

## RESOURCES.

| | 84; May 17,'90. | 84; May 4,'91. | 84; May 17,'92. | 84; May 4,'93. | 84; May 4,'94. | 83; May 7,'95. | 82; May 7,'96. | 82; May 14,'97. | 80; May 5,'98. |
|---|---|---|---|---|---|---|---|---|---|
| No. Banks, date, report. | | | | | | | | | |
| Loans and Discounts. | $48,089,644.29 | $47,456,832.17 | $49,318,094.70 | $50,666,926.18 | $46,026,287.16 | $46,333,763.97 | $44,922,623.31 | $44,969,400.68 | $44,489,963.94 |
| Overdrafts. | 170,187.58 | 148,968.09 | 137,981.16 | 114,480.91 | 176,186.83 | 177,287.90 | 146,921.28 | 140,280.34 | 124,384.88 |
| U.S. Bonds for Circulation. | 6,470,600.00 | 6,142,600.00 | 6,186,000.00 | 6,335,000.00 | 8,150,600.00 | 7,296,600.00 | 8,919,600.00 | 8,108,600.00 | 8,249,660.00 |
| U.S. Bonds for Deposits. | 1,607,000.00 | 1,026,000.00 | | 250,000.00 | 250,000.00 | 250,000.00 | 250,000.00 | 250,000.00 | 250,000.00 |
| U.S. Bonds on hand. | 100,200.00 | 60,200.00 | 60,200.00 | | 185,000.00 | 176,000.00 | 171,500.00 | 171,500.00 | 310,600.00 |
| Other Stocks, Bonds, etc., | 4,127,691.71 | 4,095,906.02 | 4,658,184.38 | 6,072,510.90 | 6,925,998.70 | 7,837,313.06 | 7,187,906.72 | 7,679,375.99 | 7,883,217.71 |
| Due from Reserve Agents. | 5,641,580.88 | 6,039,879.43 | 6,975,645.06 | 6,072,118.00 | 7,402,409.49 | 6,049,829.79 | 6,137,844.75 | 8,140,241.29 | 7,744,011.00 |
| Due from National Banks. | 1,987,737.80 | 1,667,133.03 | 1,366,503.84 | 2,083,384.70 | 1,872,638.31 | 2,169,168.33 | 2,346,793.89 | 3,023,251.30 | 1,929,437.97 |
| Due from State Banks, etc. | 270,186.51 | 178,384.43 | 600,746.71 | 839,059.01 | | 1,837,364.45 | 265,566.65 | 397,303.64 | 401,078.69 |
| Real Estate, Furniture, etc. | 1,519,929.64 | 1,663,790.04 | 661,155.87 | 1,833,487.81 | 1,670,653.46 | 2,055,064.82 | 2,073,259.60 | 2,169,617.66 | 2,169,617.66 |
| Real Est. & Mortgee owned. | 166,767.99 | 200,396.91 | 177,884.69 | 197,308.48 | 181,305.16 | 149,515.64 | | 304,637.43 | 298,300.23 |
| Current Expense paid. | 288,586.78 | 242,621.92 | 265,073.90 | 268,301.86 | 479,397.66 | 436,182.81 | 644,183.25 | 530,891.26 | 488,082.00 |
| Premiums paid. | 381,511.57 | 490,467.72 | 466,563.79 | 446,517.44 | 295,409.76 | 356,960.95 | 315,647.16 | 392,108.44 | 340,509.23 |
| Checks and Cash Items. | 418,184.32 | 408,446.36 | 321,399.90 | 301,808.94 | 206,672.36 | 231,968.01 | 192,407.19 | 209,707.00 | 280,964.38 |
| Exchange for Clearing. | 370,710.17 | 361,478.80 | 801,667.88 | 300,016.04 | 211,478.35 | 632,387.00 | 668,691.00 | 598,981.00 | 718,964.00 |
| Bills of National Banks. | 477,066.00 | 446,392.00 | 612,486.00 | 638,433.00 | 624,905.00 | | 28,694.68 | 28,694.68 | 23,793.87 |
| Fractional Currency. | 91,215.80 | 20,201.98 | 35,421.40 | 25,240.00 | 35,722.80 | 34,553.99 | | | |
| Specie. | 1,995,245.99 | 3,985,605.96 | 4,771,269.19 | 2,905,280.31 | 2,949,421.59 | 2,910,287.11 | 3,116,819.00 | 3,249,287.83 | |
| Legal Tender Notes. | 381,089.00 | 770,087.00 | 761,766.00 | 984,111.00 | 944,446.00 | 888,578.00 | 986,982.00 | 885,212.00 | 918,777.00 |
| Five per ct. Redemptions. | 343,093.60 | 328,112.60 | 275,960.00 | 278,080.00 | 841,417.60 | 804,975.00 | 401,877.60 | 396,772.60 | 363,113.50 |
| Due from U.S. Treasury. | 19,170.00 | 31,986.00 | 30,900.00 | 36,460.00 | 36,185.00 | 23,310.40 | 36,125.00 | 56,110.00 | 31,060.00 |
| **Total,** | **$73,968,908.46** | **$73,898,082.60** | **$78,082,787.87** | **$78,223,448.14** | **$77,486,521.98** | **$77,948,381.60** | **$78,351,077.69** | **$83,259,796.63** | **$80,165,371.50** |

## LIABILITIES.

| | 84; May 17,'90. | 84; May 4,'91. | 84; May 17,'92. | 84; May 4,'93. | 84; May 4,'94. | 83; May 7,'95. | 82; May 7,'96. | 82; May 14,'97. | 80; May 5,'98. |
|---|---|---|---|---|---|---|---|---|---|
| Capital Stock paid in. | $22,874,870.00 | $22,774,870.00 | $23,024,870.00 | $22,999,370.00 | $22,991,070.00 | $22,391,070.00 | $22,391,070.00 | $22,391,070.00 | $21,281,070.00 |
| Surplus Fund. | 7,214,612.46 | 7,602,556.77 | 7,616,946.47 | 7,768,288.74 | 7,705,288.38 | 7,689,866.94 | 7,791,000.00 | 7,890,806.36 | 7,888,460.00 |
| Other Undivided Profits. | 2,481,886.16 | 2,775,581.11 | 3,094,866.18 | 3,110,889.14 | 2,716,573.08 | 2,686,662.07 | 2,782,014.46 | 2,761,848.07 | 2,778,688.00 |
| Nat. Bk. Notes outstanding. | 4,878,679.00 | 4,578,465.00 | 5,490,785.00 | 5,925,980.00 | 7,196,966.00 | 6,432,469.00 | 7,940,085.00 | 7,960,414.60 | 7,367,819.60 |
| State Bank Notes outsr'd'g. | 4,817.00 | 4,817.00 | 4,817.00 | 4,817.00 | 4,817.00 | 4,817.00 | 4,817.00 | 4,817.00 | 4,317.00 |
| Dividends unpaid. | 48,748.17 | 516,832.56 | 38,886.41 | 41,299.00 | 80,160.40 | 81,795.88 | 20,022.48 | 83,494.76 | 39,068.43 |
| Individual Deposits. | 30,961,215.96 | 30,310,548.07 | 29,715,577.87 | 29,284,901.96 | 24,073,589.49 | 24,072,888.49 | 24,878,888.35 | 24,987,069.99 | 29,926,788.25 |
| U.S. Deposits. | 1,508,997.70 | 1,086,373.58 | 189,408.51 | 190,480.36 | 224,583.45 | 236,306.55 | 282,994.65 | 313,758.18 | 324,489.38 |
| Deposits of U.S. Dis.Officers. | 16,796.79 | 27,300.00 | 6,774.61 | 6,668.84 | 11,613.74 | 10,542.82 | 8,194.92 | 16,057.69 | 11,661.36 |
| Due to other Nat. Banks. | 3,830,222.14 | 1,767,961.60 | 2,478,797.88 | 3,149,990.35 | 6,697,485.36 | 3,354,029.28 | 3,892,440.97 | 4,770,720.34 | 1,848,502.70 |
| Due to State Banks, etc. | 662,740.39 | 611,237.60 | 580,394.72 | 651,616.02 | 656,474.22 | 669,209.16 | 718,432.71 | 1,242,071.04 | 861,577.02 |
| Notes, etc. Re-discounted. | 69,471.90 | 91,898.33 | 17,574.90 | 48,108.88 | 30,608.80 | 9,900.00 | 17,880.00 | 14,000.00 | 25,000.00 |
| Bills Payable. | 180,000.00 | 25,000.00 | 86,975.59 | 361,100.00 | 61,898.94 | 144,287.07 | 164,000.00 | 20,000.00 | 396,000.00 |
| Liabilities other thanabove | | | | 99,411.42 | 8,952.88 | 10,957.99 | 10,118.86 | 16,308.88 | 8,588.87 |
| **Total,** | **$73,966,908.46** | **$73,898,085.65** | **$78,082,787.87** | **$78,252,448.14** | **$77,486,521.98** | **$77,948,381.60** | **$78,351,077.69** | **$83,259,796.63** | **$80,165,371.50** |

Of the millions of dollars settled between Hartford banks and their customers, not $100,000 of currency or gold was used. A recent report of the U.S. Comptroller of the currency shows that 96.18 per cent of the cash transactions of all the banks in the United States are performed with checks, drafts and other credit taken.

# Elevations at Hartford,

Above mean low water mark at Saybrook; prepared for GEER'S HARTFORD CITY DIRECTORY.

| | | FEET. |
|---|---|---|
| Albany, corner | Bloomfield, | 112 |
| | Bluehills, | 64.3 |
| | East, | 57.2 |
| | Garden, | 51 |
| | Prospect, | 148 |
| | Vine, | 58.6 |
| | Williams, | 58 |
| | Woodland, | 64 3 |
| Ann, | Asylum, | 39.5 |
| | Main, | 62.5 |
| Asylum, | Atwood, | 68 |
| | Farmington, | 80 |
| | Garden, | 58.4 |
| | Girard, | 83 |
| | High, | 85.5 |
| | Main, | 65.7 |
| | Prospect, | 149 |
| | Spring, | 59.5 |
| | Spruce, | 41 |
| | Sumner, | 83.6 |
| | Trumbull, | 56 |
| | Willard, | 71.5 |
| | Woodland, | 69 |
| Barbour, | Capen, | 89 |
| | Frankfort, | 76.7 |
| | Tower, | 76 |
| | Westland, | 83 |
| Bluehills, | Albany, | 64.3 |
| | Holcomb, | 143 |
| | Tower, | 147 |
| Broad, | Capitol, | 49.5 |
| | New Britain, | 115 |
| | Vernon, | 90.5 |
| Brook, | Fairmount, | 47 |
| | Liberty, | 46 |
| | Mather, | 58 |
| Capen, | Barbour, | 89 |
| | Clark, | 94.5 |
| | Garden, | 78.4 |
| Capitol building, | | 85 |
| Capitol, | Broad, | 49.5 |
| | Main, | 51.2 |
| | Putnam, | 48 |
| | Trinity, | 74 |
| | Washington, | 81 |
| | Willow, | 56.8 |
| | Woodbine, | 54 |
| Charter Oak av.. | Ch. Oak pl. | 52 |
| | Governor, | 32 |
| | Main, | 55.5 |
| | Union, | 20 |
| | Vandyke, | 32.5 |
| | Woodbridge, | 24.5 |
| Colt's dyke, | | 32.5 |
| Collins, | Garden, | 78.1 |
| Fairfield, | Maple, | 153 |
| | New Britain, | 155 |
| | White, | 159 |
| Farmington, | Asylum, | 80 |
| | Flower, | 82 |
| | Girard, | 74 |
| | Laurel, | 68 |
| | Prospect, | 100.5 |
| | Sigourney, | 75.5 |
| | Smith, | 76.5 |
| | Woodland, | 57 |

| | | FEET. |
|---|---|---|
| Franklin, corner | Annawan, | 51 |
| | Benton, | 48 |
| | Maple, | 55 |
| | Preston, | 42 |
| | South, | 43 |
| Front, | Arch, | 27.4 |
| | Grove, | 29.2 |
| | Morgan, | 27 |
| | North, | 24.5 |
| | Pleasant, | 26.3 |
| | Potter, | 27 |
| | State, | 34 |
| | Temple, | 29 |
| Garden street reservoir, | | 128 |
| Garden, | Albany, | 51 |
| | Asylum, | 58.4 |
| | Capen, | 78.4 |
| | Collins, | 73.1 |
| | Sargeant, | 51.5 |
| | Westland, | 72.4 |
| Girard, | Asylum, | 83 |
| | Farmington, | 74 |
| Governor, | Ch. Oak av. | 32 |
| | Sheldon, | 34.8 |
| | Wyllys, | 41.4 |
| Harper, | Love lane, | 83 |
| High, | Asylum, | 85.5 |
| | Main, | 62.5 |
| Holcomb, | Bluehills, | 141 |
| | Vine, | 90 |
| Kinsley, | Market, | 49 |
| Main, | Asylum, | 65.7 |
| | Capen, | 78 |
| | Capitol, | 51.2 |
| | Ch. Oak av. | 55.5 |
| | Church, | 72.5 |
| | Fishfry, | 28.7 |
| | Morgan, | 68.5 |
| | Pearl, | 59.2 |
| | Seyms, | 78 |
| | Sheldon, | 44.5 |
| | State, | 64 |
| | Trumbull, | 75 |
| | at Tunnel, | 62.5 |
| | Westland, | 49.5 |
| | Windsor, | 65 |
| | Wyllys, | 67.7 |
| Maple, | Benton, | 82.5 |
| | Fairfield, | 153 |
| | Franklin, | 55 |
| | Retreat, | 59 |
| | South, | 99 |
| | Webster, | 85 |
| | Whitmore, | 86 |
| Market, | Kinsley, | 49 |
| | Marsh, | 26 |
| | Morgan, | 85.5 |
| | State, | 49.5 |
| Martin, | Westland, | 78.4 |
| Morgan, | Front, | 27 |
| | Main, | 68.5 |
| New Britain, | Broad, | 115 |
| | Fairfield, | 155 |
| | Summit, | 137 |
| | Washington, | 105.8 |

| | | FEET. |
|---|---|---|
| Niles, corner | Laurel, | 66.3 |
| | Sigourney, | 72 |
| | Woodland, | 73 |
| Park, | Broad, | 67.5 |
| | Laurel, | 55 |
| | Prospect av. | 74 |
| | Putnam, | 88.7 |
| | Sisson, | 67 |
| | Washington, | 83 |
| | Zion, | 93 5 |
| Pavilion, | Bellevue, | 70 |
| | Wooster, | 84 |
| Prospect st | Central row, | 54 |
| Prospect av. | Albany, | 148 |
| | Asylum, | 149 |
| | Farmington, | 100.5 |
| Seyms, | Center, | 72 |
| | Main, | 78 |
| Sheldon, | Governor, | 34.8 |
| | Main, | 44.5 |
| State, | American, | 49.5 |
| | Commerce, | 22.5 |
| | Front, | 34 |
| | Main, | 64 |
| | Market, | 49.5 |
| Summit, | New Britain, | 137 |
| | Vernon, | 149.2 |
| Vernon, | Broad, | 90.5 |
| | Summit, | 149.2 |
| | Washington, | 107 |
| Vine, | Albany, | 58.6 |
| | Holcomb, | 90 |
| Washington, | Buckingham, | 86.5 |
| | Capitol, | 81 |
| | Jefferson, | 88 |
| | New Britain, | 105.8 |
| | Park, | 83 |
| | Retreat, | 107 |
| | Webster, | 105.8 |
| Wethersfield, | Benton, | 57.8 |
| | Bond, | 60.5 |
| | Brown, | 52 |
| | at the Folly, | 40 |
| | Preston, | 56 |
| | South, | 52 |
| | Warwarme, | 57 |
| | Wyllys, | 67.7 |
| Westland, | Barbour, | 83 |
| | Clark, | 86 |
| | Garden, | 72.4 |
| Windsor, | Avon, | 25.5 |
| | Canton, | 35 |
| | Main, | 66 |
| | Pleasant, | 32.6 |
| | Suffield, | 30.6 |
| Woodland, | Albany, | 64.3 |
| | Asylum, | 69 |
| | Farmington, | 57 |
| | Niles, | 73 |
| Wyllys, | Ch. Oak pl. | 61 |
| | Governor, | 41 4 |
| | Vanblock, | 21.3 |
| | Vandyke, | 32.5 |
| Zion, | Flatbush, | 120 |
| | Park, | 93 5 |
| | Ward, | 100.7 |

The low water mark at Hartford is 1.84 feet above mean low water at Saybrook bar, or Long Island Sound, sixty miles south of this city.

## HACKMEN AND PUBLIC CARRIAGES.

For distances to any part of Hartford see the half mile circles on our map, in this Directory, having the Union Railroad Station, 466 Asylum st. for the center.

THE HACK STANDS are "west of the west entrance on the north side of the City Hall square, and on the west side of the City Hall square, the north side of the South Park (so called), and in front of the house of Engine Company No. 2;" and east side of Union place, between Allyn and Church streets; and their prices or rates of fare shall be as is in the amended Dec. 27, 1888, city ordinances, as follows:—

LEGAL PASSENGER FARES.

One or two persons to or from any place within the following limits, viz.: beginning at the Connecticut river and running thence westerly on a line with the north line of Pavilion street to the west line of Garden street; thence southerly down Garden street to the north line of Collins street; thence westerly along Collins street to the west line of Sigourney street; thence southerly down Sigourney street to Summit street; thence through Summit street to the south line of Jefferson street; thence easterly through Jefferson and Wyllys streets to the Connecticut river, and including both sides of all of said streets, 50 cents. One passenger to or from any place within said limits, to or from any other place beyond said limits, and within the city, 50 cents. For each extra person carried from any point to any point, within the city, 25 cents. Passengers in any carriage may have carried, without extra charge, their ordinary baggage, not exceeding one trunk or ordinary small baggage, or one hundred pounds of general baggage. For each extra trunk or equivalent baggage, 25 cents. Children under four years of age, in company with an adult, free; and between the ages of four and twelve years, half price. Fare between 12 o'clock at night and 6 o'clock in the morning, double the above rates. Public carriage, first hour, $1.50. Public sleigh, first hour, $2.00. Public carriage or sleigh, each succeeding hour or fraction, $1.00. Weddings and parties, $3.00. Funerals, $2.50. Any person who shall violate any of the provisions of this ordinance or any amendment, shall be deemed guilty of a misdemeanor, and may be prosecuted before the police court of the city, and subjected to a fine of not less than *two* or more than *twenty dollars* for each offence.

Licenses are required in all cases and prices are established on a printed card which every driver must give to each passenger. Passengers can secure a carriage to a remote part of the city, as it is provided in this revision that there shall be an accommodation, or the carriage will not be allowed to remain on a public stand either at the cars or boat. The police can enforce the ordinance.

Hackmen and Expressmen when soliciting custom are required to have No. of their vehicles on their caps.

## EXPRESS WAGONS.

Regulations are provided for the baggage express wagons, the rates for carrying being as follows:—

LEGAL RATES FOR BAGGAGE.

For one trunk, valise, carpetbag, bandbox, hat box, bundle, or other similar package, carried to or from any railroad or steamboat station, to or from any place within the following limits, viz.: beginning at the Connecticut river and running thence westerly on a line with the north line of Pavilion street, to the west line of Vine street; thence southerly along the west line of Vine street and in a line in continuation thereof to the line of the Philadelphia, Reading and New England R. R. Co.; thence along the line of said railroad company to the west line of Sigourney street; thence southerly through Sigourney street and in a line in continuation thereof to Summit street; thence easterly in a straight line to the south side of Jefferson street; thence through Jefferson and Wyllys streets, and including both sides of all of said streets, to the Connecticut river, and thence along the west bank of said river to the place of beginning, 25 cents. For each extra trunk or similar package, carried with another trunk or similar package at the same time and between the same points, 15 cents. For each extra valise, carpetbag, bandbox, hat box, bundle, or other similar parcel carried with other baggage between the same points, 5 cents. To or from any railroad or steamboat station to or from any point *without* said limits, and within the limits of the city: 15 cents additional. Each extra valise, or package, not exceeding two, at the same time and between the same point five cents additional. Fines not less than five dollars nor over fifteen, also revocation of the license or a criminal prosecution.

## ELECTRIC LIGHT, GAS AND LAMPS.

Nov. 6th, 1821, lighting the street of this city was first began at the public expense, by a by-law.

Electric lights made its first show as a commercial article in 1876, and were first used in this city for lighting of stores, streets, etc., April 7, 1883. They had been on exhibition in our streets occasionally two years previously, and December 22, 1881, were first used, experimentally, a few evenings in several stores on Main st. In May, 1884, street lights were established. June 28, 1890, the city began to light entirely by electric lights, being the first in New England to use them exclusively.

1898, there are 674½ electric lights in the streets of this city. Cost during the year:

| | | |
|---|---|---|
| 1879... $30,697.93 | 1886... $40,699.06 | 1893... $42,197.86 |
| 1880... 31,508.74 | 1887... 40,584.81 | 1894... 39,644.17 |
| 1881... 35,080.42 | 1888... 38,993.48 | 1895... 46,281.71 |
| 1882... 46,647.51 | 1889... 38,824.37 | 1896... 49,676.52 |
| 1883... 48,699.06 | 1890... 41,644.38 | 1897... 51,668.49 |
| 1884... 43,039.12 | 1891... 44,607.02 | |
| 1885... 43,170.74 | 1892... 46,616.99 | |

## REMOVING GARBAGE.

The law of May 16, 1887, relating to garbage (except ashes) was superseded in 1894 by contract with Edward Balf.

## ASHES

Will be removed, free of expense, for the citizens of Hartford by Edward Balf under contract with city.

## FIRE DEPARTMENT WORKING EXPENSES.

Of the last full year of the Volunteer Fire Department, ending April, 1864, were $22,450.37; April, 1867, the Paid Fire Department expenses were $18,000. The working expenses since then have been:

| | | |
|---|---|---|
| 1868... $22,431.71 | 1878... $48,106.20 | 1888... $61,474.72 |
| 1869... 23,292.27 | 1879... 48,273.57 | 1889... 71,887.88 |
| 1870... 25,942.90 | 1880... 47,439.84 | 1890... 62,934.83 |
| 1871... 30,805.28 | 1881... 58,352.51 | 1891... 60,998.14 |
| 1872... 33,920.85 | 1882... 58,144.10 | 1892... 85,498.56 |
| 1873... 42,099.08 | 1883... 65,807.85 | 1893... 68,862.02 |
| 1874... 45,833.60 | 1884... 62,762.30 | 1894... 67,485.81 |
| 1875... 64,299.61 | 1885... 62,473.70 | 1895... 82,450.08 |
| 1876... 52,720.85 | 1886... 64,854.83 | 1896... 100,195.79 |
| 1877... 45,671.45 | 1887... 59,946.19 | 1897... 98,872.80 |

## MILD WINTERS.

1774-5; 1782-3; 1806-7; 1828-9; 1831-2; 1841-2; 1847-8; 1877-8; 1879-80.

## UNITED STATES STAMPED ENVELOPE AGENCY

CORNER JEWELL AND SOUTH ANN STREETS.

CHAS. A. FIELD, *Agent* of the P. O. department, in charge; John N. Wilsey, *Chief Clerk.*

# Divorces

*To residents of Hartford, May 21, '97, to June 10, '98.*

Alderman Lucy C. from Allen C., adultery.
Allen Nathan H. from Elizabeth M., desertion.
Alling Alma L. from Benjamin B., desertion.
Anderson Jeff H. from Selma, desertion.
Barrows Arthur C. from Alice, adultery.
Billotte Isabelle C. from Peter, intolerable cruelty.
Blume Emma M. from Henry L., desertion.
Bogue John C. from Harriet M., desertion.
Borgman Elizabeth L. from Jos., intolerable cruelty.
Brewer Emily from George, intemperance.
Briggs Helen W. from Arthur L., desertion.
Broderick John H. from Margaret, desertion.
Broderick Thomas from Addie, desertion.
Bronson Clara L. from Robert T., adultery.
Brusie Lillian A. from Charles F., intemperance.
Burns Mary A. from Richard, desertion.
Buttles Anise A. from Wallace L., adultery.
Champlin Jennie B. from William C., desertion.
Chapman Adelbert from Elsie, adultery.
Clark Frederick P. from Alice, desertion.
Clark Sallie E. from James, intemperance.
Clarke James M. from Myrtle V., desertion.
Clen Charles E. from Nellie F., adultery.
Colburn Susie A. from Herbert L., desertion.
Cook Ida M. from Joseph E., desertion.
Cook Mary from Charles J., intemperance.
Crary David from Etta J., adultery.
Decker Margaret J. from Theodore, intol. cruelty.
Deloury Ella J. from John, adultery.
Eustice Clara L. from Francis L., intemperance.
Fager Louise G. from Karl G., intemperance.
Fitzgerald Martin from Julia, adultery.
Fletcher Elizabeth A. from William A., desertion.
Goulet William from Parmilee, adultery.
Green William A. from Annie, desertion.
Hall Lillian A. from Charles C., desertion.
Hanson John N. from Clara, desertion.
Herbert Maurice from Catharine, intemperance.
House Mary A. from Charles D., intemperance.
Hubbard Louisa D. from Wilbur E., desertion.
Ingraham Margaret S. from Charles F., desertion.
Keith Flora A. from Wilford A., intemperance.
Kenyon Annie A. from John M., adultery.
Lee Mary Jane from Frank, desertion.
Levy Elizabeth from Wolf, desertion.
Lipp Jacob from Clara C., intemperance.
Lynch Frances B. from John F., intemperance.
Morris Julia S. from Augustus H., bigamy.
Nordstrom Peter A. from Emily P., desertion.
North Mary G. from Harry J., desertion.
Norton George B. from Lizzie, adultery.
O'Brien Mary from Timothy, intemperance.
Olmsted Amy W. from Fred L., desertion.
Patti Veronika from Joseph, desertion.
Perry Florence P. from Arthur C., adultery.
Powell Lizzie M. from Benjamin, desertion.
Price Henry E. from Lydia A., adultery.
Ritchie Jordon W. from Kate, intemperance.
Schaefer Roxanna from George C., desertion.
Segur Frank P. from Harriet M., desertion.
Semple Lilla B. from William A., desertion.
Seymour Julius L. from Carrie M., desertion.
Sisson Dwight E. from Mary L., desertion.
Sperry E. Knight from Clara M., desertion.
Stackpole Charles O. from Emma L., desertion.
Stuart Millie from Max, intemperance.
Sweeney Delia from Edward, desertion.
Sweet Elizabeth T. from William A., intemperance.
Taylor C. Nellie from George W., adultery.
Tibbals Anna B. from Addison E., desertion.
Tifft Ada L. from William B., adultery.
Tillottson Kate E. from Fred A., intemperance.
Towne Elizabeth from Joseph M., intolerable cruelty.
Tuller Harriet A. from Wilson F., desertion.

Washburn Anna from Thomas B., intemperance.
Weyant Louise K. from John R., intolerable cruelty.
Wheeler Albert M. from Grace E., intemperance.
Wheeler Sarah E. from Norman S., intemperance.
Whitman Nettie F. from Elmore, intemperance.
Wilson Eva L. from Peter H., adultery.
Wilson William from Jane, desertion.

## BUSINESS FAILURES IN THE UNITED STATES.

There were 1,095,541 business houses or firms in the United States, on the first Jan. 1898—and the failures the past twenty-four years, as reported by the Bradstreet Commercial Agency, is as follows:—

| Year. | Number. | Total Liabilities. | Av'ge Liab. |
|---|---|---|---|
| 1874, | 5,830 | $155,239,000 | $26,628 |
| 1875, | 7,740 | 201,060,853 | 25,977 |
| 1876, | 9,092 | 191,117,786 | 21,030 |
| 1877, | 8,872 | 190,669,936 | 21,490 |
| 1878, | 10,478 | 234,366,132 | 22,367 |
| 1879, | 6,658 | 98,149,053 | 14,741 |
| 1880, | 4,735 | 65,752,000 | 13,896 |
| 1881, | 5,582 | 81,155,932 | 14,529 |
| 1882, | 6,738 | 101,547,564 | 10,070 |
| 1883, | 9,184 | 172,874,172 | 15,921 |
| 1884, | 10,968 | 226,343,427 | 20,302 |
| 1885, | 10,637 | 124,220,321 | 11,678 |
| 1886, | 9,834 | 114,644,119 | 11,658 |
| 1887, | 9,634 | 167,560,944 | 17,392 |
| 1888, | 10,679 | 123,829,973 | 11,595 |
| 1889, | 11,719 | 140,359,490 | 11,906 |
| 1890, | 10,668 | 175,082,886 | 16,119 |
| 1891, | 12,394 | 193,173,000 | 15,586 |
| 1892, | 10,270 | 108,595,248 | 10,574 |
| 1893, | 15,508 | 382,155,676 | 24,645 |
| 1894, | 12,724 | 151,548,520 | 11,910 |
| 1895, | 12,958 | 153,727,682 | 13,249 |
| 1896, | 15,112 | 247,062,343 | 16,347 |
| 1897, | 13,099 | 156,166,273 | 11,922 |

## BUSINESS FAILURES IN CONNECTICUT.

AS REPORTED BY THE BRADSTREET MERCANTILE AGENCY, P. P. BENNETT, AGENT.

| | | |
|---|---|---|
| 1874, | 151 failures; | liabilities, $1,286,000 |
| 1875, | 191 failures; | liabilities, 2,851,926 |
| 1876, | 197 failures; | liabilities, 4,136,548 |
| 1877, | 314 failures; | liabilities, 5,821,649 |
| 1878, | 281 failures; | liabilities, 4,680,586 |
| 1879, | 158 failures; | liabilities, 2,474,844 |
| 1880, | 173 failures; | liabilities, 1,672,817 |
| 1881, | 180 failures; | liabilities, 836,788 |
| 1882, | 88 failures; | liabilities, 808,962 |
| 1883, | 119 failures; | liabilities, 744,242 |
| 1884, | 169 failures; | liabilities, 1,464,296 |
| 1885, | 176 failures; | liabilities, 1,714,486 |
| 1886, | 132 failures; | liabilities, 1,906,684 |
| 1887, | 117 failures; | liabilities, 3,500,484 |
| 1888, | 187 failures; | liabilities, 1,265,103 |
| 1889, | 171 failures; | liabilities, 2,012,000 |
| 1890, | 178 failures; | liabilities, 2,018,000 |
| 1891, | 249 failures; | liabilities, 3,889,000 |
| 1892, | 211 failures; | liabilities, 1,182,543 |
| 1893, | 298 failures; | liabilities, 2,756,700 |
| 1894, | 243 failures; | liabilities, 2,098,000 |
| 1895, | 225 failures; | liabilities, 2,425,750 |
| 1896, | 280 failures; | liabilities, 2,189,450 |
| 1897, | 330 failures; | liabilities, 2,491,600 |

## NORTHAM MEMORIAL CHAPEL.

Entrance to Cedar Hill Cemetery on Maple av. near its junction with Fairfield av. Consecrated Nov. 12, 1883. It is a cemetery chapel, as a house for performing the last services to the dead, on entering the cemetery. It is of the English gothic style—cruciform in plan, steep roofs of gray rock faced Westerly granite, relieved by lighter granite dressings.

# Hartford Volunteers for Spanish War, 1898;

## ARMY AND NAVY.

Abram Robert.
Ackerman Sidney W.
Ahern Edward F.
Aninger Benjamin C.
Aninger Frank B.
Appleton Frederick L.
Arnold Alfred C.
Ashwell Robert R.

Bailey Herbert G.
Bailey James C.
Baldwin Henry F.
Barber Arthur W.
Barlow John A.
Barrows Charles D.
Bassett Merton W.
Barton Seymour B.
Baxter George S.
Beebe Robert L.
Beers Robert C.
Belisle Tancrede.
Bennett Thomas A.
Bernard Isadore.
Berry Howard.
Bigelow Henry W.
Billings Fred H.
Bissell Herbert G.
Blake Charles L.
Blake Frank.
Blake John T.
Blakeslee Fred G.
Blicher August W.
Boniface John D.
Borland Henry L.
Bosworth Fred. E.
Bowen Edward.
Brandt Frederick.
Breman William J. J.
Brennan Michael.
Brigham William E.
Brimble Ernest W.
Bronson Arthur H.
Brown William H.
Brust Frank.
Bryant Harry E.
Buckley Jeremiah.
Burby John A.
Burdett Charles L.
Burke John F.
Burke Patrick J.
Burns William H.
Burrell Francis C.
Bush Simon J.

Cadwell Frank J.
Callaghan Patrick.
Camp George.
Camp Henry P.
Campbell William A.
Canales Fred.
Cannon Archie L.
Carlson Otto.
Carroll Charles A.
Carroll Frank G.
Carter Horace A.
Case Archibald L.
Case Robert A.

Case William O.
Chapin Robert D.
Chapman Morton L.
Chase Nelson L.
Claffey Frank.
Clark Frank E.
Clark William M.
Clarkin Peter A.
Cleary Thomas.
Cloman James H.
Coffey James F.
Coggeshall Murry H.
Colby George E.
Cole Henry J.
Collins Frank W.
Converse Lawrence A.
Corrigon John F.
Cosgrove Edward J.
Cosgrove Patrick J.
Covey George W.
Cowles Royal M.
Coyle Frank P.
Coyle Thomas J.
Crane Frank.
Cranick Charles A.
Crilly Thomas L.
Cuff Edward C.
Cunningham Thomas H.
Cuntz Herman F.
Cutting Arthur S.

D'Arche Raoul.
Dahill John F.
Daley John J.
Davis Charles E.
DeLamater Richard W.
Denison Frank E.
Denison Frederick R.
Dimock Stanley K.
Dolbeare William B.
Doolittle Lewis J.
Donahue Thomas J. Jr.
Doran Edward J.
Dougherty John J.
Douthwaite Harry W.
Doyle William A.
Dresser Wilfred H.
Driesnack Albert M.
Drury Henry W.
Duffy James A.
Duffy Joseph P.
Duffy Michael J.
Duffy Thomas F.
Dunn Daniel J.
Dwyer George K.

Ellison James.
Embler Ralph H.
Eno John E.
Ensling Phillip Jr.

Fairfield Philip E.
Falknor Clark T.
Fargo Theodore C.
Farrell Patrick A.
Ferguson Owen J.
Field Francis E.
Finney Charles H.

Finigan Patrick.
Fisher Alfred M.
Fisher Irving L.
Fletcher Emerson C.
Flint Fred C.
Flood Edward N.
Fogarty Cornelius J.
Foley Daniel.
Foley Maurice C.
Foley Thomas W.
Forrest George C.
Foster George.
Fox Martin J.
Franke Paul.
Frederickson Nick.
Freund Simon.
Fritzson Charles W.
Fuller Frank E.
Fulton Albert C.
Furlong Thomas V.

Gabrielle Burton L.
Gaffey William F.
Gallivan Murty J.
Gallup Christopher M.
Gates Benjamin.
Geary Patrick J.
Geer William A.
Gibbons Thomas F.
Giddings Howard A.
Gillett Frank W.
Gillette Henry C.
Golden Peter J.
Gooding Earl W.
Gorman John J.
Goulet William.
Grady James J.
Green Harry D.
Green Samuel W.
Griswold Richard S.
Grop Frank.
Grusner Theodore.
Guckin Thomas.

Hadsell G. Arthur.
Hall George R.
Hall Henry H.
Hansen Hans.
Hansen Steve.
Hanson Harry J.
Harkins Fred B.
Harper Joseph P.
Hastings Walter S.
Hatton William H.
Hawkins Wallace V.
Hawley James J.
Hayden Edgar G.
Hays Robert L.
Healey Joseph F.
Hebron Robert F.
Hedberg Charles V.
Hefferman Charles C.
Hefferman James.
Henderson James D.
Henson Stephen F.
Herron Robert.
Herter Louis A.
Hindley George A.

Hines James J.
Hines Thomas J.
Hoban John J.
Hogan Thomas F.
Holan William F.
Holcombe George A.
Holmes Richard J.
Holt Henry T.
Holt Rodney A.
Hollingsworth Harry E.
Hollis Eben C.
Horton Thomas.
Howard James L. Jr.
Humphrey Robert M.
Huntington Charles A.
Huntington Henry L.
Huntington Samuel G.
Hurd William M.
Hurley William.
Hutchins Nelson.

Iffland Alexander.

Jackson Edward Q.
Johnson Francis M.
Johnson Frank E.
Johnson William C.
Jones Frank M.
Judson Edward W.

Kalber Conrad C.
Keena Michael.
Kelleher William.
Kelly James.
Kelsey Henry H.
Kennedy James.
Kennedy Patrick D.
Kenyon Lorenzo W.
Kerrigan John J.
Kershaw William.
Keyes Frank R.
Kilmartin Edward J.
Kirkley Robert.
Knox John B. Jr.
Kollenz Christian.
Kostenbeader Fred.
Kowalcky Frank E.
Krull George R.

Lacey Herbert V.
Lamb Edwin E.
Landrigan John F.
Lane Albert E.
Lane Robert.
Larsen Christie.
Lee Frank H.
Lehnemann John W.
Leonard Martin C.
Leslie Howard.
Leslie William H.
Lewis Fred H.
Lewis George.
Libutzke John G.
Liebert George S.
Lincoln Robert M.
Little Harry R.
Lohs Fred W.
Long Michael C.
Lotze Frederick.
Loveland Edward E.
Low William B. Jr.
Low William W.
Lowenhaupt Ralph.
Lutz Frank G.
Lyons Philip.

Mack Herbert D.
Madsen Elith N. C.
Madsen Lorens J.

Mahoney William E.
Mahoney William H.
Malm O. William.
Mantei Otto.
Marion Otis D.
Marsh Frank T.
Marshall Andrew B.
Martin Fred M.
Martin George R.
Marvel Eugene T.
Mayer Joseph.
Maynard Anson H.
McAdams Thomas J.
McAuliffe James.
McCarthy Dennis F.
McCarthy John.
McCarthy Thomas.
McCarthy Thomas A.
McCrea Mark C.
McCreary Ralph W.
McCook John B.
McCook George S.
McCollum Oleon.
McCue Thomas J.
McDonough James P.
McGrath Michael E.
McGregor John B.
McKee Robert A.
McKenney Benjamin C.
McKone John J.
McMahon Henry P.
McMahon John J.
McManus Ward.
McPherson John.
McVane John J.
Meara James.
Merenholtz Fred T.
Merrill Charles O.
Middlebrook Louis F.
Miller Eugene D.
Miller Guy P.
Miller Hugh I.
Miller Richard.
Mills John H.
Missel Jacob J.
Missel William E.
Moran John F.
Mooney James P.
Mooney Matthew.
Morgan James H.
Morgan Victor F.
Morley Reuben H.
Morris Shiras.
Moseley Edward E.
Moses Linwood K.
Mottram Alfred.
Mountain John A.
Muhleib William H.
Mullaney John J.
Mullen Thomas F. Jr.
Munro Kenneth McK.
Munsell William F.
Murphy Edward T.
Murphy Thomas E.
Myers Clinton H.

Neddo Joseph R.
Newberry Henry G.
Newman James F.
Newton Charles W.
Neilson Carl.
Nielson Henry.
Noble Edward J.
Noonan Edward C.
Nord Charles.
Norris Louis A.
Northam Edward T.
Northam Robert C.
Nunan Edward P.

Nutter Harrie Y.

O'Brien Daniel J.
O'Brien Joseph F.
Obryon Thompkins H.
Olschefakie Charles.
O'Neil John J.
O'Toole Richard.
Oviatt Edward M.
Owen Ernest L.
Owen Hans C.

Parker Arthur V.
Parker Felton.
Parker Howard.
Pasco Arthur J.
Pattison George E.
Payne Frederick E.
Payne Herbert R.
Pearson Adolf.
Pearson William T.
Peterson Alfred K.
Peterson Andrew.
Pettys George J.
Pickard Ward W.
Piddock John E.
Pierce Charles W.
Pierce Ralph B.
Pierson Wilbur B.
Pimm Alfred B.
Pinchon Lauriston F. L.
Potter James H.
Prescott Albert N.

Quinn Edward W.

Rathbun Edward H.
Reese William E.
Reeve William R.
Reidel Rudolph C.
Rich Alfred T.
Richard Don C.
Richardson Ralph R.
Riley Charles S.
Riordon Michael F.
Ripley Herbert J.
Robertson William B. L.
Robins George D.
Roemer George A.
Rohrmayer George M.
Root Herbert E.
Root Lyman.
Rosengreu John.
Rosheck Joseph.
Ross Fred H.
Ross Herbert A.
Roulston Archibald J.
Roulston Archibald W.
Rowland Guy F.
Ryan James B.
Ryberd Gottfried.

Sanderson Edward F.
Sanford Harrison.
Saunders Charles C.
Saunders Henry H.
Scanlan Thomas J.
Schiesell Max.
Schiverdtfeger Otto W.
Schuler Louis A.
Schults Carl H.
Schulze Edward.
Schwerdtferger Henry.
Scoville Albert W. Jr.
Scoville Lester H.
Scrivener William H.
Seaver Frederic A.
Seidler Frederick A.
Seinsoth Frank A.

Selleck Edwin H.
Seymour Edward S.
Seymour Freeman P.
Shannon Owen.
Shapiro Samuel.
Sharper Ernest A.
Shea Frank E.
Shea Maurice B.
Sheedy Thomas F.
Shepard Forrest
Shields Howard L.
Silvernail Louis.
Simmons William Cayton.
Smith Edmund S.
Smith Frank H.
Smith George H.
Smith James.
Sobieralski John A.
Sparks William A.
Stedman John E.
Steele Clinton L.
Steele Henry W.
Stephan Maurice.
Stevens John B.
Storrs Herbert E.
Sullivan Eugene J.

Tabor Mallory W.
Talcott Morton C.
Talcott William H.
Thayer George B.
Thomas John U. B.
Thomas Noel D.
Thompson Walter.
Tinkham Charles A.
Tinkham George H.
Tregoning William C.
Tripp Harold W.
Twardoks John F.
Twichell David C.

Upler Jonathan K.

Valentine Nathaniel G.
VanBuren Henry S.
Vibert Robert N.
Vinton Louis E.
Vinton William O.

Wadsworth George H.
Wainwright Jonathan M.
Walsh Daniel.
Walsh John J.
Walsh Thomas H.
Ward Edward M.
Waterman Edward H.
Watson William T.
Webster Roy C.
Welch William J.
Welles Ralph C.
Wells Richard B.
Westcott Alexander.
Whalen Cyrus E.
Wheelock Paul L.
White John F.
White Patrick J.
Wightman Alanson H.
Wiley Herbert H.
Wiley Royal H.
Wilcox George E.
Wilcox Harry E.
Wilcox Robert.
Williams Frank J.
Williams Frederick E.
Williams George.
Williams John H.
Wilson Louis B.
Wilton Charles H.
Wittig Charles H.

Wittig Louis H.
Wolcott Charles B.
Wolf Charles F.
Wood Arthur.
Woods James C.
Woodworth Walter G.
Wucherer Julius.

Zwitz William.

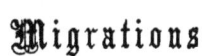

# Migrations

*From Hartford, for one year to
July, 1898, were 1,804.*

Abbey Grove H., Wilsons Station.
Abbott George E., Bristol.
Abbott James, Portland.
Abbott William John, New Britain.
Ackerson John W., Unionville.
Adams C. G., Boston, Mass.
Adams Charles G., Cromwell.
Adams Lewis D., Simsbury.
Ahern Mary Mrs., Glastonbury.
Albee W. J., Springfield, Mass.
Alexander Reuben, New London.
Allen Bernard, Windsor.
Allen Eli H., Springfield, Mass.
Allen Fletcher T., Chicopee Falls.
Allen Henry T., Farmington.
Allen Henry W., Pittsfield, Mass.
Allen Richard F., Manchester.
Alling George B., East Hartford.
Alling James, East Hartford.
Allyn Noyes B., Gales Ferry.
Anderson Charles, Wethersfield.
Anderson Edward, So. Manchester.
Anderson George H., Canada.
Andrews Charles, New Haven.
Andrews Elizabeth P., New York.
Angel D., Worcester, Mass.
Anglem John, West Hartford.
Antone Charles, New York.
Apgar William F., Wilsons Station.
Appold William F., Boston, Mass.
Armes Frederick, West Hartford.
Arnold Frank W., East Hartford.
Arnold May, Bridgeport.
Arnold O. Y., Mechanicville, N. Y.
Arnold William, New York.
Arrowsmith W. W., Thompsonville.
Arthur Catherine D., Cleveland, O.
Atkinson John H., Holyoke, Mass.
Attleton Nancy Mrs., Arizona.
Atwell Harry E., Middletown.
Atwood Eugene E., Wethersfield.
Atworth Theo. W., Brooklyn, N. Y.
Austin Delia A., Avon.
Austin Lucius C., Rocky Hill.
Austin Wm. M., Washington, D. C.
Avery George O., So. Manchester.

Babcock Carl, East Hartford.
Bacon Charles R., New York.
Badger John P. Jr., New York.
Bailey Harry E., Newington.
Bailey Henry L., Newington.
Bailey W. H., Brooklyn, N. Y.
Bain Mary Mrs., Bolton.
Baisvert Louis, Meriden.
Baker Samuel, New Britain.
Balch Fred'k A., Detroit, Mich.
Balcom William H., West Hartford.

Rainman George H., Boston, Mass.
Bancroft Isaac C., Talcottville.
Barber Norman, East Hartford.
Barlow Richard A., Providence, R. I.
Barnes Jos. B., Springfield, Mass.
Barney William R., Cincinnati, O.
Barrett Joseph L., Bridgeport.
Barrett Michael, Bridgeport.
Barrett Thomas, South Norwalk.
Barrett Walter E., Putnam.
Bartholms George, Bridgeport.
Bartholomew Harry J., Ohio.
Bartlett Catherine H., Springfield.
Barton E. E., East Hartford.
Bass Nellie A., Andover.
Bassin Augusta Mrs., Waterbury.
Bassin John, Waterbury.
Bean Leon H., Springfield; Mass.
Beardsley Edward J., Philadelphia.
Beardsley Edwin W., New Britain.
Beatty H. L., New York.
Beaumont George F., Colchester.
Beckley Frank E., Meriden.
Beckley Jacob, Glastonbury.
Beebe A. G. Mrs., Staten Island.
Beecroft E. C., Pelham Manor, N. Y.
Beers Maria L., Rockville.
Beij Karl J., Sweden.
Belanger Ernest L., East Hartford.
Belden C. H., Seneca Falls, N. Y.
Belfi Anthony, New York state.
Belknap Ernest, Rockville.
Bemont Ed., Rocky Hill.
Bender Ewald, Wethersfield.
Benedict Fred S., Waterbury.
Bennett Austin N. Jr., New Britain.
Bennett Frederick E., East Hartford.
Bennett Joseph W., New Britain.
Benson John A., Warehouse Point.
Bernard William, East Hartford.
Berry James, East Hartford.
Berry John, East Hartford.
Best George L., Boston, Mass.
Bettes Ruth E. Mrs., Oak Hill.
Bibbins Edwin S., Guilford.
Bill Alvin H., Manchester.
Bill & Co., South Manchester.
Bill G. Ezra, Colchester.
Billings Peter, Waterbury.
Birdsall Harriet A. Mrs., New York.
Bishop D. C., Lakeville.
Bissell Annie W. Mrs., Cleveland, O.
Bjorklund Carl, Sweden.
Blake Charles A., Windsor.
Blake G. Irving, New York.
Blamberg John, East Hartford.
Blumgren John, Portland.
Boardman Ralph H., New Britain.
Bodge Cordelia Mrs., Plantsville.
Bogin Abe, East Hartford.
Bohus Frank H., Rockville.
Boland John F. Rev., Waterbury.
Booton Frank, Elmwood.
Borg Albert, Collinsville.
Borthwick William, Barry, Ill.
Boss Charles, Clifton Springs.
Bosworth Joseph M., East Hartford.
Bowe Ellsworth, Wethersfield.
Bowe Eugene L., North Manchester.
Bowes Pollard, Boston, Mass.
Boyd David, Maine.
Boynton Fred. O., Manchester.
Bradden Philip J., New Britain.
Brainard Fred'k L., So.Glastonbury.
Brainerd Jennie F., Cobalt.
Bramley William G., Elmwood.
Brand Charles A., Oberlin, O.
Bratton David B., New Britain.
Brett Patrick, Windsor Locks.

Brewer Lewis, Boston, Mass.
Brickley Genevieve V., W.Hartford.
Brickley George, West Hartford.
Brightman Max, Boston, Mass.
Broadwell C. M.D., Forestville.
Broderick James, Rocky Hill.
Broderick John, Windsor Locks.
Broderick Patrick, Rocky Hill.
Bromley Daniel T., Scotland, Conn.
Bronson Willis W., Bridgeport.
Brooks Edward J., Lynn, Mass.
Brooks Samuel A., Colchester.
Brown Emily A., New York.
Brown Julius, Brooklyn, N. Y.
Brown Michael, Portland.
Brown Wm. C., Springfield, Mass.
Brown William W., New York.
Brunette Frank Jr., Wallingford.
Buck Frank E., Fall River, Mass.
Buck Frederick Earle, Winsted.
Buck Silas, Wethersfield.
Buckland Charles, Boston, Mass.
Buckland Clarence E., E. Hartford.
Bucklee Alfred, Klondike.
Bull Edward Jr., New London.
Bull Mary E., Boston, Mass.
Bullard A. L. Mrs., Brooklyn, N. Y.
Bullard Arthur H., Brooklyn, N. Y.
Bunker Amos, Gilead.
Buoncore Guidon, Philadelphia, Pa.
Burch C. S., New York.
Burke Anna L., Massachusetts.
Burkette James, England.
Burkette Jeremiah, Pittsfield, Mass.
Burkhardt Wallace, Canaan.
Burnham Harry M., New York.
Burnham Jennie L, Burnside.
Burnham Julia, West Hartford.
Burnham Myron J., West Hartford.
Burns Thomas, England.
Burr Emma M. Mrs., Wethersfield.
Burr Martin J., Cheshire.
Burton George W., Beacon Falls.
Buscall D. T., Springfield, Mass.
Buss Cearles H., Clinton Springs.
Byxbee John C., Meriden.

Cadman Robert C., So. Manchester.
Cadwell Edward T., West Hartford.
Cady Corancy, East Hartford.
Cady Edward, Collinsville.
Cakerson Fred, West Hartford.
Callahan David F., New Britain.
Callahan Ed., New York.
Callahan Edward, Salem, Mass.
Callat Ernest, New York.
Callender W. R., Providence, R.I.
Cameron John, Holyoke, Mass.
Camp William O., East Hartford.
Canfield George S., Wethersfield.
Capen Edward W., Boston, Mass.
Capron Eugene, New York.
Capron Margaret, New York.
Carl William H., East Hartford.
Carley George, West Hartford.
Carlson John, Sweden.
Carlson Pete. Middletown.
Carney Frank, East Hartford.
Carney Patrick, Worcester.
Caroll Patrick, New York.
Carpenter Fred H., Lowell, Mass.
Carpenter George S., Bridgeport.
Carr B. J., Chicago.
Carr C. F., Worcester, Mass.
Carter Geo. Wm. Rev., West Haven.
Carter Julian S., Baltimore, Md.
Carutners William. Norwich.
Cartwright M. R., Ridgeway, Pa.
Case A. Curtis, Bloomfield.

Case George, Wethersfield.
Casey Benjamin, Middletown.
Casey Myron, South Manchester.
Cavanaugh David, Charter Oak Pk.
Cavenaugh Michael J., Burnside.
Cawn C. Frank, Brockton, Mass.
Chaffee E. W., Newington.
Chamberlin Albert H., Wilsons Sta.
Chamberlin G. M., Gt. Barrington.
Champlin J. M., Wethersfield.
Chaney Cora I., New York.
Chapin Chas. A., Springfield, Mass.
Chapin Fred'k N., Springfield, Mass.
Chapin Martha B., Springfield, Mass.
Chapman Annie B., Harvard Col.
Chapman Frank H., Philadelphia.
Chapman Henry A., Rocky Hill.
Charest Alphonse, Springfield, Mass.
Chalton John B., Springfield, Mass.
Charter Geo. D. Mrs., Minneapolis.
Chase March F., Mineral Point, Wis.
Chelliz Margaret, Vermont.
Chiarizio Donato, Manchester.
Chido Benezario, Windsor.
Christian Robert, England.
Christoff Fred C., New Haven.
Clapp Burt S., Wethersfield.
Clapp Richard S., Wethersfield.
Clark C., New York.
Clark Charles, East Hartford.
Clark Michael, Burnside.
Clark Samuel J., East Hartford.
Clark Sherman, Windsor.
Clay Albert A., East Hartford.
Clemons F. A., New York city.
Cloonan John-Joseph, Stafford.
Clough Emeline E. Mrs., Unionville.
Coates Edward W., New Britain.
Coates Jas. P., North Adams, Mass.
Coats Wm. E., Springfield, Mass.
Cobine Walter L., East Hartford.
Cochran John L., Windsor.
Cody Alfred J., New York.
Coe George H., Schenectady, N. Y.
Coer William H., Waterbury.
Cogswell George E., Jamaica, N. Y.
Cohn Abram, Waterbury.
Colt Charles K., Brooklyn, N. Y.
Colburn Susan Mrs., Boston, Mass.
Cole Wm. J., Poughkeepsie, N. Y.
Collins John, Glastonbury.
Commeant Antoine, Klondike.
Condon James, New York.
Cone George, Lyme.
Cone Gertrude J., West Hartford.
Conn. Indemnity Co., Waterbury.
Connell Lizzie, Wethersfield.
Connell Michael, Newington.
Conners Charles R., Waterbury.
Connor Joseph J., Stafford Springs.
Connor Thomas C. Jr., Waterbury.
Connor Thomas E., Manchester.
Conovey Maila R., Bridgeport.
Cooledge Nellie J., East Hartford.
Cooley James D., Westfield. Mass.
Coolidge Lawrence E., E. Hartford.
Coop David W., Newington.
Cooper Edwin, Wethersfield.
Coppinger John, East Hartford.
Cormier Josephine, Wallingford.
Cornell Oliver D., Europe.
Corrigan John, Ireland.
Cook Aaron Jr., Manchester.
Cook Antoinette Mrs., California.
Cook Fred E., Higgannm.
Cook Philip, Kansas City.
Cooke Frank W., Windsor.
Cosker John J., New Jersey.
Coslo John, New York.

Cotter Ellen Mrs., Bridgeport.
Coughlin Nellie M., Stamford.
Courtney Owen, So. Manchester.
Couture Wm. G., Providence, R.I.
Couture Edward, Canada.
Cowen John, Birmingham, England.
Cowen William, England.
Cowles Eliza, Plainville.
Cowles Fred M., Wallingford.
Cowles William H., East Hartford.
Crane Edward A., Bridgeport.
Crane George, East Hartford.
Crane John, East Hartford.
Crego Charles D., Windsor.
Critchell Wm. M., East Hartford.
Croft John, Wethersfield.
Crosby Allyn, Wethersfield.
Crossett Caria, East Hartford.
Crossman Francis, New Haven.
Crowe Michael, Unionville.
Crowell Myron D., Brooklyn, N. Y.
Cummings M. L., Bridgeport.
Cunliffe James T., Klondike.
Curran James P., Saybrook.
Curran Thomas J., Saybrook.
Curry Thomas Albert, Chester, Pa.
Cutler Forrest R., New London.
Cycle Tool Mfg. Co., Springfield.

Daley Bernard J., Rockville.
Danforth W. F., Springfield, Mass.
Daniels Edward R., Glastonbury.
Danher Walton S., Boston, Mass.
Darby Joseph, Hoosac Falls.
Darling Frank H., Bloomfield.
Davenport John S. 3d, New York.
Davis Charles S., Arlington, N. J.
Davis Harry, New York city.
Davis Perry, Middletown.
Day John C., New York city.
Dearborn Samuel S., Bridgeport.
DeForest Mrs., Middletown.
Deloury E. J. Mrs., Oswego, N. Y.
Deloury John, New Orleans, La.
Delvin P., New York.
Deming Vernon H., Rootstown, O.
Desjardins Bertha, Salem, Mass.
Deuse John, Waterbury.
Devlin Patrick, New York.
Diggle Charles W., Plainville.
Dimes Joseph F., Burnside.
Dodd Alfred W., New York.
Dodd Charles B., New York.
Donahue Daniel E., Brooklyn, N.Y.
Dong Wong, Meriden.
Donohue William, New York.
Dooley Edward J., Bridgeport.
Dooling Andrew A., Denver, Col.
Douglass James C., Windsor Locks.
Dow David, Norwich.
Dow Everett E., New York.
Dow James M., Elgin, Ill.
Dowd Timothy P., Windsor Locks.
Dowden F. H., Springfield, Mass.
Dowed George J., Burnside.
Dowen Ralph, Burnside.
Drake Fred, West Hartford.
Dubois Joseph, West Hartford.
Dubord Edward M., Canada.
Duclos Charles H., New York.
Dunbar Eugene A., East Hartford.
Duncan George, Springfield, Mass.
Dunnell Charles E., Unionville.
Dunning Wyatt, New York.
Durgan J. E., Thompsonville.
Dutton Winifred Mrs., New Haven.
Dwight Jane Mrs., New Haven.

Eagan Margaret Mrs., Farmington.

Easton Sidney, New Britain.
Eaves Fred. W., Boston, Mass.
Eberle Munroe M., New York.
Eckholm Otto, Sweden.
Edmond Arthur, Mansfield.
Ehret John, Stamford.
Eklund August, Sweden.
Elcock Alfred, New Haven.
Elert John, Wethersfield.
Ellsworth David J., Windsor.
Ellsworth Janette, East Windsor.
Elmer Harmon S., Naubuc.
Elmer Harmon S. Mrs., Naubuc.
Elwin Kate Mrs., Wethersfield.
Emery Abel, Warehouse Point.
Emmett Arthur, New Britain.
Engstrom Oscar, New York.
Erickson John, New York.
Evans Franklin P., Glastonbury.
Evans William A.,East Windsor Hill.
Ewen Laura, New London.

Fahy Michael J., New York.
Farmer Fred, Canada.
Farnham Andrew E., So. Windsor.
Fay Adelia C., Rochester, N. Y.
Fay Harry E., South Manchester.
Featherstone Cath., East Hartford.
Fengeralo Domencio, New York.
Fenner Joseph, New York.
Fenner Ruth T., Massachusetts.
Ferguson John L., Manchester.
Fieber Minor M., Middletown.
Field Arthur, Albany, N. Y.
Fields George, New York.
Fischer Kittie, Windsor Locks.
Fisher Richard A., East Hartford.
Fiske George W., Holliston, Mass.
Fiske Louis S., San Diego, Cal.
Fitts Horace G., Elliott, Maine.
Fitzgerald Mary G., Meriden.
Fitzgerald Thomas, West Hartford.
Fitzpatrick Patrick, New York.
Flaherty D. J., Thompsonville.
Flanagan William J., New London.
Flanigan Timothy B., Wethersfield.
Flannery Edward A. Rev., Stamford.
Flavin T., New York.
Fleming James, Springfield.
Fletcher Dolphin S., Wash., D. C.
Fletcher Thomas, Chicago, Ill.
Fletcher W. C., Bridgeport.
Fogarty John, New York.
Foran Nellie, East Hartford.
Foricke Everett H., East Hartford.
Foss W. J., Roxbury, Mass.
Foster Edwin B., South Coventry.
Foster Harry Phelps, New York.
Foster Howard B.,Wilmington, Del.
Fox Burdette M., East Hartford.
Fox Robert, Manchester.
Francis Fannie, Wethersfield.
Fratter August, Bloomfield.
Freer Susan M., West Hartford.
French Albert E., Quincy, Mass.
French Edwin C., Wilmington, Del.
Frieberg Edward, New Britain.
Frost E. C. Mrs., West Hartford.
Fuhrmann Richard, New York.
Fuller Albert, Philadelphia, Penn.
Fuller Catherine M. Mrs.,Fall River.
Fuller Edgar, Providence, R. I.
Fuller Samuel R., Buffalo, N. Y.
Fuller William, East Hartford.
Furbwash George, New York.

Gaard George, Providence, R. I.
Gabin Robert C., Meriden.
Gager Louise A., Glastonbury.

Galacar Chas. E., Springfield, Mass.
Galacar Fred'k E.,Springfield,Mass.
Gallagher Thomas, Providence, R. I.
Gallup Albert, Scotland.
Gardner Sophia L. Mrs., Addison.
Garrison Albert, Windsor.
Garrity Thomas W., East Hartford.
Gaskins Cæsar, Maple Cypress, N.C.
Gates D. W., Lyme.
Gatewood S., New York.
Gathers Arthur, New York.
Gatling Richard J. Dr., New York.
Gaudet Dennis, West Virginia.
Gaudet Frederick, Winsted.
Gaudet Levi, East Hartford.
Gauggel Otto H., New Haven.
Gay Herbert, Farmington.
Getz Sigmond, Glastonbury.
Gevek George, Montreal, Canada.
Gibson Howard J. Wethersfield.
Giddings David, Suffield.
Giebelhausen Ludw'k E.,Weth'field.
Gilbert Albert W., New York.
Gilbert George L., East Hartford.
Giller George L., New York.
Gilnite William H., Hockanum.
Gilnite William H. Jr., Hockanum.
Gladwin Robert H., Brooklyn.
Glancy P. J., Port Norfolk, Va.
Gleason Thomas W., Buffalo, N. Y.
Glenn John, N. Y.
Goddard Frank Archie, Win. Locks.
Goldberg Jacob, New London.
Goldman Barney, Philadelphia, Pa.
Goldthwaite Arch., Galveston, Tex.
Gonyai William, Buffalo, N. Y.
Goodwin Harley E., Bloomfield.
Goodwin Mary Mrs., West Hartford.
Goodwin Scott G., New Hartford.
Goodwin Wilbur, New York.
Gordon John R., New York.
Gordon William J., Burnside.
Gorman Betsey Mrs., California.
Gorman E. P., Springfield.
Gorman Frank, East Hartford.
Goulet Louis, Providence, R. I.
Gowdy George W., East Hartford.
Graham David, West Hartford.
Graham William S., Waterbury.
Grant George E., Springfield, Mass.
Graves Dudley C., Burlington, Vt.
Grayson Samuel, England.
Greaves William H., Cromwell.
Green John, Warehouse Point.
Green Rose Mrs., South Manchester.
Green Wm. A., N. Indianapolis, Ind.
Greenberg Samuel,Springfi'ld,Mass.
Greenblatt Meyer, New London.
Griffin Edward A., South Windsor.
Griffin John, Windsor.
Griffin William, New York.
Griggs Hattie A., Thomaston.
Griggs Maitland F., New York.
Grinnell Henry,Westport Har.Mass.
Griswold Alfred H., New Britain.
Griswold M. R. Mrs., West Hartford.
Grogan Michael, Wethersfield.
Grogan W., Wethersfield.
Gross Frank, Austria.
Grough John, Colorado.
Grover William, Norwich.
Grundler Henry, East Hartford.
Guider Daniel, Colchester.
Guilfoil William F., Bloomfield.
Gundacker Henry J., New York.

Hagan John, Chicago, Ill.
Haggerty Charles, New York.
Haggerty Frank, East Hartford.

Haggerty Mary, East Hartford.
Haglin John G. Glastonbury.
Hagman Gustav A. Jr., Europe.
Hague William T., Klondike.
Hale Edward W. Wethersfield.
Hale Frank L. Manchester.
Hale Laura J. Mrs., Gt. Barrington.
Hale William H., Middletown.
Haley James, Windsor Locks.
Halfpenny James, Boston, Mass.
Hall Nicholas, Boston, Mass.
Hallas Benjamin G., Thompsonville.
Hamaker Harry, Jamaica Plains.
Hamel Frank, Vermont.
Hamilton Harry, New York.
Hamilton John, Windsor.
Hammond George K., East Hartford.
Hancock Horace O., Virginia.
Hand P., New York.
Hannifin John F., Springfield, Mass.
Hanmer Edward S., Wethersfield.
Hanson Charles, New York.
Hanson Nelson, New York.
Hanson Paul, Middletown.
Harmon Edward L., Plainville.
Harris Chauncey K.,Wethersfield.
Harris Myron, West Hartford.
Hart Myron A., Springfield, Mass.
Hart Patrick, New Britain.
Hfd. Fertilizer Mfg. Co., Rocky Hill.
Hartzell Carl, New York.
Haskins Herman H., West.
Haskins Washington C., West.
Hastings Homer, Meriden.
Hastings Panet M., Cincinnati, O.
Hatch Frank P., New York state.
Hatch Otis M., Bloomfield.
Hathaway E. T. May, Boston, Mass.
Hatton Maria, England.
Hauver Perley J., Boston, Mass.
Haviland Amanda H., Danbury.
Hawksford William, East Hartford.
Hawley John Amon, Farmington.
Hayden Henry R. Jr., East Hartford.
Hayes Carrie L., East Hartford.
Hayes Edwin J., Wilson Station.
Hayes Gordon W., Windsor.
Hayes William J., Windsor.
Hayward Harry W.,Presque Isle,Me.
Hayward Walter D., Brooklyn, N.Y.
Hazard Flora, Brooklyn, N. Y.
Hazard Mary A., Warehouse Point.
Hazel Dora A., Holyoke, Mass.
Healy J. D., Meriden.
Healy John F., Windsor.
Healy William, East Hartford.
Heavey Katie A., Norwich.
Heghinian Sam'l, Marash, Turkey.
Helm Mary W. Mrs., Simsbury.
Hendy John B., East Hartford.
Henry Edward, Ireland.
Henry Lewis, Canterbury, Vt.
Henry Michael, Springfield, Mass.
Herman Alex., Naubuc.
Hermann Christian, New Britain.
Hershnow J. B., New Britain.
Hersom Arthur F., Boston, Mass.
Hewitt Frank G., Waterbury.
Heymann Henry B., Boston, Mass.
Hickmott George H., Boston, Mass.
Hicks J. H., Northampton, Mass.
Higbee Ira M., Watsontown, Pa.
Higgins Mary, New Haven.
Hill George A., Manchester.
Hill H. Clinton, Buffalo, N. Y.
Hill & King, Buffalo, N. Y.
Hills Marie L., East Hartford.
Holley Charles H., Waterbury.
Hollis Clara W., Mt. Vernon, N. Y.

Hollister Edward B., Windsor.
Hollister Sherman E., Bloomfield.
Holmes E. M., Fitchburg, Mass.
Holmes Howard A., East Hartford.
Holmes Mary E. Mrs., East Hartford.
Holmgren Gust. A., Burnside.
Holton Eugene P., West Winsted.
Homey Fred, Klondike.
Hood James, West Hartford.
Hopkins George W., Willimantic.
Horan Kittie, Manchester.
Horngeen Gus, Burnside.
Horsman Richard, Ireland.
Horton Amenus, Michigan.
Howard Alfred E., Buffalo, N. Y.
Howard Charles, Washington, D. C.
Howe Lottie, Washington, D. C.
Howell Sheridan, New York.
Hoyer Fred F., New York.
Hoyt Walter, Farmington.
Hruby & Heintzes, Manchester.
Hubbard Charles E., Cincinnati, O.
Hubbard George R., Bridgeport.
Huff August, New Jersey.
Hull William, Norwich.
Humphrey Louise J. Mrs., N.Haven.
Humphreys F. E., Kansas.
Humstone Edward M., Phila., Pa.
Hunter Frank H., Portland. Oregon.
Huntley Charles H., East Hartford.
Huntley Grace L., New Britain.
Huntley Helen B., New Britain.
Hunter Mitchell A., New Britain.
Husband John, East Hartford.
Hutchinson Annab.M.Mrs., Paris,Fr.
Hutchinson Verna,Newtonv'le,Mass.
Hutt Charles F., Glastonbury.
Hutton Isaac, Springfield, Mass.
Hyde Carrie A. Mrs., St. Paul, Minn.

Ingraham Edwin, New York.
Ingraham George A., Enfield.
Iverson Charles, Bridgeport.
Iverson John, Bridgeport.
Ives Harry G., Southington.

Jacobs Moses, Brooklyn, N. Y.
Jacobs William, Windsor.
Jackson Fannie E. Mrs., N. Britain.
Jacquart Michael, New York.
Jacques William P., South Killingly.
James Charles, New York.
James Henry, Derby.
Jepson John, Denmark.
Jerusalemsky M., East Hartford.
Jessen Henry A., East Hartford.
Johns A. M. Mrs., Windsor.
Johnson Bert, Clayton, Mass.
Johnson Chris, East Hartford.
Johnson Emil, Klondike.
Johnson Eugene A., Waterbury.
Johnson Eric E., Seattle.
Johnson Harry, New York.
Johnson John J., East Hartford.
Johnson Leopold, Klondike.
Johnson Rob't B., Beachmont, Mass.
Johnson Walter, New York.
Johnston John, Philadelphia, Pa.
Jonas John A., New York.
Jones Edward, Portland.
Jones Edwin C., Poughkeepsie, N.Y.
Jones George A., Wethersfield.
Jones James W., New Britain.
Jones John T., Avon.
Jones L. Mrs., Worcester, Mass.
Jones William Horace, New Britain.
Joyce Joseph F., Italy.
Judd Martin, Ireland.
Judson Arthur S., Brockton, Mass.

Kahn Leopold, New York.
Kamm Archie, Glastonbury.
Kampfmann Jacob. Spring'd,Mass.
Katzensohn M., New York.
Kearns Daniel,Willimantic.
Keating Peter, Meriden.
Keeler Charles W., Windsor.
Keeler J., New York.
Keeling William, England.
Keith Flora Mrs., Canterbury, N. H.
Kelley Fannie, Boston, Mass.
Kelley John H. Wethersfield.
Kelley Lucy L., Meriden.
Kellogg Kenneth E., New York.
Kelly William, Waterbury.
Kennedy John A., Springfield, Mass.
Kennedy John C., Boston, Mass.
Kenney John, Waterbury.
Kenson George F., Enfield.
Keough James, Bloomfield.
Kern Samuel L., New York.
Kernan John, East Hartford.
Kessler Joseph, Boston, Mass.
Kiersted Charles, West Hartford.
Kilbourne A. E., East Hartford.
Kilburn William B., Washington.
Kilby Mary A., Berlin.
Killen Ernest L., Indianapolis, Ind.
Killian John J., East Hartford.
Kilmartin James, New London.
Kimball M. A. Mrs., New Haven.
Kimball Martin, East Hartford.
King Emeline S.Mrs.,Franklin,Mass
King J. Walter, East Hartford.
King William, East Hartford.
King Victor J., New York.
Kinghorn John, East Hartford.
Kingsley John M., Newington.
Knee Lewis, Windsor Locks.
Knight Charles W., New Haven.
Knight Robert, Virginia.
Knott Ruby A., West Hartford.
Knott William W., West Hartford.
Knox Charles D., Springfield, Mass.
Knox William H. H., Boston, Mass.
Kohn Leopold, New York.
Krohn Gustav, New York.
Kurz George, Unionville.

Ladd M. D., Los Angeles, Cal.
Ladd Merton D., Plainfield, Vt.
Laidler Stephen W. Rev., Brooklyn.
Lane Egbert, Thompsonville.
Langford Arichib. M., Bayonne,N.J.
LaRocque Henrietta Mrs., Canada.
Larson Andrew, Portland.
Lasso Louis, Italy.
Lathrop P. C. Mrs., Boston, Mass.
Latham Maud E., Windsor Locks.
Lauritz Lauritzen, Denmark.
Leach Willis E., West Willington.
Leas John H., Wethersfield.
Lecomp Benjamin H., Montreal.
Lecour Joseph H. Jr., Brooklyn,N.Y.
Lee Warren W., Klondike.
Leppens F. C. B., Hayden Station.
LeRoy Charles H., Putnam.
Lester Julius M., East Hartford.
Lester William H., Wethersfield.
Levy Ike, New York.
Levy Isaac H., West Haven.
Levy Leon, New York.
Lewis Edward C., Waterbury.
Lewis Lorena, Hartford, Vt.
Lincoln Carter, South Manchester.
Lincoln Walter, South Manchester.
Lindell Charles, Waterbury.
Lindo Charles. New York.
Linton James H., Burnside.

Linton Samuel, A., West Hartford.
Lisle Frank D. Rochester, N. Y.
Lockwood George F., New Britain.
Lonsdale John, Springfield, Mass.
Lord E. Elmer, West Hartford.
Lord James W., Ballston Lake, N.Y.
Lorenz Herman, Holyoke, Mass.
Lucas Henry, Newington.
Luchine Cæsar, Boston.
Ludington Myron, Rockville.
Luntz A. Saul, East Hampton.
Lyman Mary Mrs., Wethersfield.
Lynch Dennis J., New York.
Lynch John, Farmington.
Lynch John T. Rev., Wethersfield.
Lynge Carl Hugo, Bridgeport.

Mack James A., Ohio.
Madden Patrick J., Ireland.
Madden Thomas J., New Haven.
Maher John E., Windsor Locks.
Maher William F.,Washington,D.C.
Maine Ferdinand W., East Hartford.
Malone Martin J., New Haven.
Manchock Michael, Glastonbury.
Mann Samuel, New Haven.
Manner George, Burnside.
Mannix Martin S., New York.
Marceau Arthur, Wallingford.
Marion Nelson, East Hartford.
Marion Otis D., East Hartford.
Marsh Edward, New Britain.
Marshall Edwin D., East Hartford.
Marshall Sarah C. Mrs., E. Hartford.
Martin Warren C., Boston, Mass.
Martson Edward Robert, Norfolk.
Mason Mary E. Mrs., New York.
May Frank D., East Hartford.
May Frank D. Jr., East Hartford.
May Harry A., Middletown.
Mayer Frederick W., New York.
Mayer Maurice A., New York.
McCabe James, Burnside.
McCabe P. James, Burnside.
McCarthy John J., Glastonbury.
McCarthy Patrick, New York.
McCarthy William J., Winsted.
McChesney James, New York city.
McClellan Frank, East Hartford.
McCormick Joseph, West Hartford.
McCue Charles T., Springfield, Mass.
McCutcheon Charles, East Hartford.
McCutcheon Geo.Kennebunkp't,Me
McDonnell Thomas F., Norfolk.
McDougall W. L., Meriden.
McEvitt William, Manchester.
McFarlan John H., Wethersfield.
McGrath John J., Waterbury.
McGregor John, New Britain.
McGurk Wm. J. Rev., Manchester.
McKenna Bernard, Rockville.
McKenzie William, Unionville.
McKeoun Edgar W., Brooklyn, N.Y.
McNamara Nora, Manchester.
McTernan James, Brooklyn, N.Y.
Mechtold Roland H., New York.
Meier Phillip, Middletown.
Mercer Frank B., West Hartford.
Mercer Fred, Canada.
Mercer John, New Haven.
Merringer William, Thomsonville.
Messenger Edwin E., Bloomfield.
Metro Clifford, Berlin.
Meyer Frederick, East Hartford.
Miller Albert A., Holyoke, Mass.
Miller Alfred W., New Britain.
Miller Gustav E., Manchester.
Miller William, Springfield, Mass.
Milliken Charles O., Auburn, N. Y.

Mills Charles S., Westville, Mass.
Minigero Angelo, East Hartford.
Minton M. M., New York.
Minton T. M., New York.
Mitchell James, Trabo, Wyoming.
Mohr Henry, Burnside.
Molenat Julius, North Manchester.
Monk Ed. E., Baltimore, Md.
Moon George C., New York.
Mooney Annie J., Meriden.
Moore Edward E., Providence, R. I.
Moore Eugene E., East Hartford.
Moore Fred T., East Hartford.
Moore Jairus A., Deep River.
Moore Lucius H., Springfield.
Morgan Sherman F., Elmwood.
Morhardt Frank W., Springfield.
Mork George, East Hartford.
Morley E. F., Glastonbury.
Moroney Thomas, Manchester.
Morse Levi G., Newark, N. J.
Morse Selden S., Suffield.
Moses Mary H. Mrs., Concord, N. H.
Mosher Fannie Mrs., West Hartford.
Mott Dexter R., Boston, Mass.
Moulton Alfred W., West Hartford.
Moulton Annie J., Wethersfield
Moulton Joel C., Wethersfield.
Moyer P. J. A., New Haven.
Moynihan Cornelius, Manchester.
Mueller J. H., Rockville.
Muldoon Peter J., East Hartford.
Mullen John, New York.
Mumford Harry S., East Hartford.
Mumford Rolland K., East Hartford.
Murburg S. Emil, Bridgeport.
Murdock William B., Taunton, Mass.
Murlless H. Walter, Guilford.
Murnane Patrick F., New Britain.
Murphy John B., New York.
Murphy John B., Elmwood.
Murphy John R., East Hartford.
Murray Daniel W., Meriden.
Murray John W., Philadelphia, Pa.
Myers Albert E., California.
Myers Frederic, Middletown.
Myers Henry, Florida.
Myers Sarah T. Mrs., Florida.
Myers William F., Corry, Pa.
Myers William H. Florida.

Namar Donald, Scranton, Pa.
Nason Andrew C., Bluehills.
Nathlis Harry, Burnside.
Nauman Bruno, Klondike.
Neal Alonzo L., Meriden.
Needham Frank R., Washington, D.C.
Neher Louis, Windsor.
Nelson Christian, Parkville.
Netter Gabriel, Baltimore, Md.
Neuhans Edward G., Windsor.
Neumann Edward, New York.
Newcomb A. H., Middletown.
Newmann Henry, Springfield, Mass.
Newton Isaac R., Soldiers' Home.
Nichols Frederick A., Wethersfield.
Nichols George W., Wethersfield.
Nicholson May, East Hartford.
Nixon Charles, Port Norfolk, Va.
Nock August, East Hartford.
Nodine Isaac P., East Hartford.
Noonan John F., East Hartford.
Norman A. P., Springfield.

O'Brien Edward J., Wethersfield.
O'Brien James F., Chicopee, Mass.
O'Brien Mary Mrs., Waterbury.
O'Brien Michael C., New Britain.
O'Brien Thomas, East Hartford.

O'Brien William P., Chicago, Ill.
O'Connen Michael, Northampton.
Odber William B., Boston, Mass.
O'Donnell John, Tennessee.
O'Donnell John, Tennessee.
O'Donnell William, New Britain.
Oldershaw William H., New Britain.
Oliver William E., East Hartford.
Olund John U., New Britain.
O'Meara John, Bridgeport.
Orcutt H. M., Cambridge, N. Y.
O'Rourke Mary Mrs., Hayden Sta'n.
Osborn Joseph E., Warehouse Point.
Osborn Newton, Newington.
Osborne Frank H., Hayden Station.
Osgood Charles, Brooklyn, N. Y.
O'Shaughnessy Patrick, New York.
Outerson Joseph, Windsor Locks.
Owen Hans C., Middletown.

Pagelau Rudolph, Wethersfield.
Pagram Pahl A., Springfield, Mass.
Parlee Ernest S., New Brunswick.
Parker Florence E., Springfield.
Parker L. J., Brooklyn, N. Y.
Parker Theodore H., Unionville.
Parrott Sarah Mrs., Norfolk.
Pattison Arthur E., Brooklyn, N.Y.
Pearson Henry, England.
Pease Belle, New Hampshire.
Peline Michael, Unionville.
Penfield Frank H., Boston, Mass.
Perkins Frederick, Griswoldville.
Perkins George J., Quebec, Canada.
Perkins Julian L., Wethersfield.
Perret George J., Danbury.
Perry Florence Peltier Mrs., N. Y.
Perry Orville Y., East Hartford.
Person Peter, Windsor.
Petersen Peter, Denmark.
Petsch Lotta Mrs., Brooklyn, N. Y.
Phillips Hubert, New York.
Phillips Lillian, Syracuse, N. Y.
Phillips Nathaniel, Boston, Mass.
Pierson Edward, West Hartford.
Pingree Arthur H., Boston, Mass.
Pinto John, Italy.
Pitkin Joseph F., Newtonville, Mass.
Pond Charles F., Brooklyn, N. Y.
Porch George W., England.
Porter John, Manchester.
Posser Frederick, New York.
Poulter Henry, Glastonbury.
Pratt Alex. Jr., New Britain.
Pratt George C., Denver, Colorado.
Prentiss Wm. C., So. Hadley, Mass.
Preston Charles W., New York.
Prince William O., Unionville.
Proffett Charles, Enfield.
Pulsifer Harry B., New Haven.
Pulsifer Herbert B., Boston, Mass.
Putnam Israel C., East Hartford.

Quick Henry J., Chicago, Ill.
Quilligan Mollie T., East Hartford.

Rabs John Michael, Europe.
Rabs Theresa M., Europe.
Rady David W., Springfield, Mass.
Randall Eugene E., Brooklyn, N.Y.
Randall Mary D. Mrs., Westogue.
Rankin James, Waterbury.
Rau George, Burnside.
Raymond James H., Elmwood.
Reaney George H., Easton, Pa.
Redfield Charles P., Vernon.
Reed Charles O., Scotland.
Reeve Philip H., East Hartford.
Rehse Frank A., Torrington.
Reilly John A., Meriden.

Reineking F. C. M., Germany.
Reineking George, Germany.
Remsen Henry R., Babylon, N. Y.
Reynolds Andrew, New York.
Reynolds Lloyd G., Erie, Pa.
Rhine John V., Windsor Locks.
Rice Herbert H., Providence, R. I.
Rice Richard W., E. Windsor Hill.
Richardson Clarence S., Ellington.
Richardson Louis G., New York.
Richardson Orono M., Ellington.
Riley William, Bridgeport.
Ripley Jay F., New York.
Roane Thomas M., West Hartford.
Roarke Mary Mrs., Ireland.
Roberts George, Newfane, Vt.
Roberts James H. Rev., China.
Roberts Jennie, New York.
Roberts Joseph F., Philadelphia, Pa.
Roberts Morris F., Newfield.
Roberts William J., New Jersey.
Robertson Henry G., East Hartford.
Robinson Frank, West Hartford.
Rodgers Hart J., Windsor.
Rodgers Stanley E., Windsor.
Rogers George I., Milford.
Rogers John, Springfield, Mass.
Rogers William M., California.
Rohan Martin, Holyoke, Mass.
Rohrs Henry, Worcester, Mass.
Roland Clarence A., Pennsylvania.
Root George N., East Hartford.
Root Patrick Kennedy, Waterbury.
Rose John W., South Windham.
Rosenthal Emil, East Hartford.
Rowe Jennie C., Wethersfield.
Ruben Ellis, Boston, Mass.
Rudinsky Abram, New York.
Rudinsky & Katzensohn, New York.
Ruff John, Hockanum.
Russell Charles, East Hartford.
Russell William E., Wethersfield.
Ryan Cornelius, West Hartford.

Sadler Ernest, Windsor Locks.
Samuels Nathan, Windsor.
Sanderson Lydia E., Cleveland, O.
Sanford Edward D., New York.
Sanford H. B., New York.
Sankey Henry, Manchester.
Santhouse Robert, Meriden.
Sardowski Carl, Wethersfield.
Saul C. Frederick, Thomaston.
Scanlon John, Saybrook.
Schauffler Henry P., Cleveland, O.
Scheer John, New York.
Scheidler Charles, Germany.
Scheidler Edward, Germany.
Scheller Paul, Germany.
Schleicher Valentine, New Britain.
Schmidt John C., Germany.
Schneider Minnie, Rocky Hill.
Schneider Theresa Mrs., N. Haven.
Schufft Herman, Burnside.
Schulte Edward D. N., New York.
Schulte Herman V. W., New York.
Schultz Louis V., New Britain.
Schur Fritz, New Britain.
Scribner George G., Boston, Mass.
Seegers Dora, Holyoke, Mass.
Seymour Edw., Bedford, Canada.
Seymour Jno. Mrs., Hopkint'n, Mass.
Shanahan Daniel, Norwich.
Shannahan Matthew, Waterbury.
Shaughnessy Annie T., New Haven.
Shaw Joseph, East Hartford.
Shea James F., Burnside.
Sheldon Arthur T., California.
Sheldon Ellsworth A., New Britain

Shellrain Carl, West Hartford.
Shepard George Mrs., East Hartford.
Shepard Wallace E., Colchester.
Sherman James T.,Springfield,Mass.
Sherman Silas, Niantic.
Sherriff Herbert T., Detroit, Mich.
Shippee Cullen M., Liberty Hill.
Shippee Edward M., Liberty Hill.
Shubert Ernest L., Bristol.
Siezer Joseph, West Hartford.
Sigmund Anna, East Hartford.
Silverman David, New York.
Silverman Thomas, England.
Simington George J., East Hartford.
Simmons Edward, Jersey City, N. J.
Simons George, Pine Meadow.
Simpson Albert, East Hartford.
Singer Charles, Meriden.
Shatts Albert W., Wethersfield.
Skinner Charles F., So. Manchester.
Skinner Cyrus C., New York.
Slade William, New York.
Slater John, New York.
Slipp Fred C., Waterbury.
Sloan Charles, Ansonia.
Small Thomas, Ireland.
Smead George, East Hartford.
Smedberg John, West Hartford.
Smith Abraham, Manchester.
Smith Allie M., East Hartford.
Smith Arth'rW.,Spring Rapids,Minn
Smith C. W., East Hartford.
Smith Caroline F. Mrs.,Wash., D. C.
Smith Edward C., Saybrook.
Smith Fred H., Rochester, N. Y.
Smith Fred J., Bluehills.
Smith Frederick, Bloomfield.
Smith George R., Canada.
Smith H. Howard, Syracuse, N. Y.
Smith Henry M., Newtown.
Smith J. W., New York.
Smith James A., Haverhill, Mass.
Smith James J. Rev., Norwich.
Smith Joseph J., East Hartford.
Smith Nellie A., Washington.
Smith Nemiah, East Hartford.
Smith Otis E., Cincinnati, O.
Smith Peter S., East Hartford.
Smith Walter S., Wethersfield.
Smith William F., Rhinecliff, N. Y.
Smithe Percival S.,Germantown,Pa.
Smithson Nettie B., Thompsonville.
Snow Max, Boston.
Snow Samuel F., Burnside.
Solomon John, New York.
Sorenson Samuel, East Hartford.
Souer Andrew, Meriden.
Sowers David W., Stamford.
Spalding James A. Jr., Colorado.
Sparks William A., Waterville, Me.
Spear Minnie, Manchester.
Spedding William, Wethersfield.
Spencer Daniel Mrs., Troy, N. Y.
Sperry B. Wells, Soldiers' Home.
Squire Norman H., West.
Stacey Willard E., Cincinnati.
Stack J. B., Washington.
Staples Joseph C., Philadelphia, Pa.
Staples Susan A. Mrs., Phila., Pa.
Starkweather Henry, Pawtucket.
Stevens Alfred H., Derby.
Stevens Alice A., Windsor, Vt.
Stevens J. Eugene, East Hartford.
Stevens William H., East Hartford.
Steves William, Simsbury.
Stewart Amanda Mrs., Farmington.
Stewart Charles A., New Jersey.
Stewart Mitchell, Windsor.
Stillman Charles, Sweden.

Stimpson George A., New Orleans.
Stock James, New Hampshire.
Stoddard Edw'd S., Plymouth,Conn.
Stone Alexander, New York.
Stone Josephine L. Mrs.,Middlefield.
Stone Wilbur M., Brooklyn.
Storrs William E., East Hartford.
Stoney Emma Mrs., Brooklyn.
Strong George, Hayden Station.
Strong Irving E., Philadelphia, Pa.
Stueck George H., New Haven.
Stumpf William E., Burnside.
Stumph Richard, New Britain.
Sullivan Daniel J., Manchester.
Sutcliff Edwin R., New Haven.
Sutton McWalter B., New Rochelle.
Svenson John, Chicago, Ill.
Swindell George, New York.
Sylverstein Henry C., Norwich.

Taft Charles C., East Hartford.
Taylor Charles A., Meriden.
Taylor Charles W., Waterbury.
Taylor Dana, East Hartford.
Taylor Edward, Gildersleeve.
Taylor George W., Bloomfield.
Taylor J. M., Springfield, Mass.
Taylor Lincoln, New Britain.
Tennant Chester W., Klondike.
Teper Sam, Russia.
Thayer Fred G., East Hartford.
Thayer Louis E., New London.
Theoudx Henry J., Springfield.
Thomas Samuel O., Thornton Park.
Thompson Arthur R., Klondike.
Thompson Edwin J., Boston, Mass.
Thompson Edwin S., Boston, Mass.
Thompson Frank E., Cincinnati, O.
Thompson Harry A., West Hartford.
Thompson Mrs., New York.
Thompson Watson E., New York.
Thomson John, Palmer, Mass.
Thrall Charles D., New Haven.
Thrall Egbert J., New Haven.
Thrall Luther J., Poultney, Vt.
Throughgood C., New York
Tibbals William J., Windsor.
Tilton Frederick W., New York.
Tiney Alfred T., Waterbury.
Tolles Fred H., Windsor.
Tolles Samuel J., Meriden.
Towers Leslie W., Windsor.
Townsend S. M., Canada.
Tracy C. H. Mrs., Norwich.
Tracy Charles, Putnam.
Tracy John, Providence, R. I.
Tracy John F., Providence, R. I.
Tracy Richard B., Norwich.
Travers Edw. S., Middletown.
Treat William E., Meriden.
Tregastic Hubert A.,Thompsonville.
Trudeau Adelard P.,Windsor Locks.
Turner Charles J., Philadelphia, Pa.
Turner John, Waterbury.
Turner Joseph L., Derby.
Turtloot William, East Hartford.
Tyler George E. Rev., Bristol.
Tyler John F., South Glastonbury.

Ulrich George P., New Haven.
Underwood George, Barry, Ill.
Usinskie John F., Nanticoke, Pa.

Valentine Robert F., Waterbury.
Valleau Andrew J., East Hartford.
Vallentine Arthur A., Klondike.
Vehring H. M., West Hartford.
Verder Daniel H., Rutland, Vt.
Vieberg Victor, New Britain.

Waghorn Thomas E., Elmwood.
Wagner Margaret Mrs., Holyoke.
Wald H., New York city.
Waldo Emma L., France.
Waldo Ida A., East Hartford.
Wales Linus B., Plainville.
Walker John, West Hartford.
Walker William T., Canton, Mass.
Wallace W. B., New Britain.
Walsh John, New Britain.
Walsh John G., New York.
Walsh Thomas, Springfield.
Ward Delia B. Mrs., Middletown.
Ward Frank J., Middletown.
Ward Jennie C., Wethersfield.
Warner Harriet F., Wethersfield.
Warner Marietta E. Mrs., Tolland.
Washington James N., New York.
Waterman Chas. F., Cottage Grove.
Waterman E. F., Middletown.
Way Robert F., West Hartford.
Weaver Electa L. Mrs.,Willimantic.
Webb Helen, Jersey City, N. J.
Webb William H., Windsor.
Weed E. W., Boston, Mass.
Weed Truman Rev.,Three Mile Bay.
Weeks Asa T., Springfield, Mass.
Weeks May F. Mrs., Bridgeport.
Weissel Julius, West Hartford.
Welbraham F. M., Windsor.
Weldon Watson, Springfield, Mass.
Wells Clarence S., Middletown.
Welsh John Jr., Berlin.
Wentworth F. A., Hopevale.
West Albon, Rockville.
Weston Charles, Wethersfield.
Weyant John R., New York.
Wheeler Amos B., Manchester.
Wheeler Fred, New York.
Wheeler Harry, Lynn, Mass.
White Robert, New York.
White William, Schnectady, N. Y.
White William A., New Britain.
White William C., Utica, N. Y.
Whitmore Nancy Mrs., Rocky Hill.
Whitney Edward B., New Britain.
Whittermore John A., Springfield.
Wiant Clark, Pennsylvania.
Wierzdrolski Joseph, New York.
Wigg Alfred, New York.
Wilcox Charles W., New York.
Wilcox Chester Eng., Cottage Grove.
Wilcox Frank H., Brooklyn, N. Y.
Wildman Walter B., Wallingford.
Wilkinson Frank, South Windsor.
Wilkinson L. J., Springfield, Mass.
Williams Benjamin, Columbus, O.
Williams George, Danbury.
Williams Herbert, New Haven.
Williams M. Jr., West Hartford.
Wilson George, New York.
Wilson Richard, Charter Oak Park.
Winter Eugenie, East Hartford.
Wolgast Henry F., New York.
Wood Percival M., Huntington,N.Y.
WoodbridgeCharles S.,Wethersfield
Woodle Allan S. Jr., Altoona, Pa.
Worth Albert, New Britain.
Wren E. Y., North Adams, Mass.
Wright C. L., Waterbury.
Wright Charles A., Boston, Mass.
Wufling Henry, New York.

Young Jennie E., Windsor Locks.
Young John J., Windsor Locks.
Ziegle Carl G., Detroit, Mich.
Ziegle George, New York.
Zimmerman Edward M., Rockville.
Zwicker Fred Mrs., New York.

# Deaths

In Hartford, Year ending May 31, 1898.

*The months June (6), July (7) August (8), September (9), October (10), November (11), December (12), are in the year 1897, and the months of January (1), February (2), March (3), April (4), May (5), are in the year 1898. Figures in first column represent the month, those in second column the day of month, and those after name the age. If the age is not given they are under one year of age.*

6- 1-Abbe Lydia, 67.
7- 5-Ackerman Lizzie.
3-30-Adams John W. 65.
3-13-Adams Sarah H. 81.
10-21-Ahern Armanda, 66.
7- 7-Ahern David, 32.
4-14-Allen Ann E. 78.
5-17-Allen Edward, 68.
10-21-Allen Harriet L. 47.
10-25-Allen Harry, 5.
10- 1-Allen Joshua W. 33.
1-12-Allen Mary.
12-28-Allen William, 34.
11-18-Allge Sophia L. 66. .
12-21-Anderson Alexander, 22.
5- 9-Anderson Alma B. 31.
7-24-Anderson Axel, 25.
5- 9-Anderson Elsie E.
11-20-Anderson Ernest.
5-25-Anderson Helen.
7-23-Anderson Joseph.
8-30-Anderson Minnie H. 30.
10-20-Anderson Peter, 50.
1-27-Andrews Hudson, 69.
2-21-Ash Frank M. 20.
3-10-Ash Luke 70.
11-16-Atwater Otis E. 46.

1- 1-Babcock George H.
10-16-Babcock Nathan L. 86.
1-11-Backus Harriet, 61.
6-12-Bacon Elizabeth C. 78.
1- 5-Bailey Martha, 69.
10- 9-Bailey Pluto.
10-28-Baker Aloney, 69.
1-21-Balf George, 26.
9-10-Barbour Florence J.
2-11-Barbour Verue E. 30.
5- 1-Baribeault Katie, 1.
8-23-Barlow Edgar James.
12-14-Barnard William E. 55.
10-26-Barnes Abbie, 60.
1- 1-Barrett Margaret M.
8-23-Barry Hazel.
2- 9-Basey Sidney S. 50.
12- 8-Becker Mamie, 6.
4-23-Beerman Abe 1.
2-15-Belcourt Nora.
11- 1-Bell Henry.
3-11-Bell Sarah M. 73.
7- 5-Bentley Antone, 64.
7- 7-Bernard Oscar, 46.
1-12-Berry James, 65.
4-25-Berry Michael F.
10-15-Bidwell Alfred, 79.

4-29-Bigelow Mary, 83.
7-11-Birden Francis A. 43.
5-22-Birge Charles N. 57.
2-10-Birmingham Catherine, 39.
2-15-Birmingham John, 31.
1-12-Birmingham Thomas F. 40.
6- 6-Bissell Josephine, 59.
9 -29-Bjerman Hans, 61.
6-18-Black Cynthia A. 80.
1- 2-Blackstone Lucy L. 70.
10-25-Blake Lydia A. 65.
1-16-Blake Margaret, 62.
5-23-Blake Mary E. 28.
3-11-Blanchard Abigail, 70.
4-30-Blaney Roger W.
11-30-Blaud Patrick, 35.
6-18-Blazier Teresa.
8-30-Blinn Frederick, 20.
8- 3-Bliss Edward A. 68.
7-23-Blodgett Francis C. 83.
7-21-Bolles Francis.
6-28-Bonayna Celia.
6-15-Bonnell George, 48.
11-29-Bourn Benjamin A. 70.
7-26-Bovino Joseph, 37.
11- 4-Boyd Frank W. 23.
8-18-Boyden Helen, 50.
5- 6-Bracken Francis A. 12.
8-15-Brady Mary A. 60.
8-17-Brainard Elliot W. 65.
2-23-Braineny Katie.
9- 4-Brandenburg Ernestina, 63.
6-24-Brassill Martin, 42.
2- 1-Braun Laura Kayes, 29.
2- 7-Breetman Lena.
5-10-Brewer Fanny E. 88.
8- 3-Briggs Eugene, 48.
10-12-Brigham Charles A. G. 73.
5-10-Brimble Minnie, 21.
7-25-Brink August A. 56.
8-23-Brisbois John.
8-19-Brissnin Albert.
12- 2-Brodener Mary Ann Louise.
1- 8-Broderick John H. 65.
5- 2-Bronson Alice E. 50.
12-25-Broughton Bessie, 24.
11-24-Brown Cora M. 23.
6-19-Brown Cyntha A. 81.
6- 3-Brown George E. 59.
6-23-Brown Martha W. 71.
10-21-Brown Mattie, 20.
6-12-Brown Thomas, 76.
7-22-Brown William, 34.
10-17-Brown William H. 22.
5-23-Brownlee Thomas D. 3.
11- 6-Bruce Cora B. A. 27.
2- 5-Bruton Mary, 31.
10-20-Buckley Lewis W. 2.
2-10-Budd James, 50.
3- 3-Bugbee Alanson, 93.
10-15-Bullard Charles Henry, 77.
11-22-Bumstead Harriett A. 69.
9-26-Burgess Henry, 40.
8- 6-Burk Joseph J. 68.
9- 2-Burke Annie F. 9.
1-26-Burke Catherine, 65.
10- 6-Burke Edward M. 17.
10- 2-Burke James Thomas.
12-23-Burke Erne E. 29.
5-24-Burleson Rowena, 89.
1-29-Burnett Thomas H. 45.
3-24-Burns John.
9- 9-Burns Mary.
1-10-Burr John B. 62.
8-24-Burr Owen, 52.
12- 5-Bushnell William F. 4.
7-20-Buss Percis H. 78.
10-29-Butler Kate, 60.
6-29-Butler Keron, 26.

5- 5-Butler Thomas, 55.
6- 1-Buttero Peter A.
5-22-Cadwell Charles S. 69.
7-11-Cadwell Lizzie, 43.
12-27-Cahill William J. 21.
11- 5-Caldwell Florence C. 2.
9-17-Calio Ann.
10- 4-Callahan James, 1.
5- 5-Callazo Lolita L. 7.
7-10-Camp Phillip L. 67.
3-11-Canning Thomas, 67.
1-18-Capetto Michael, 19.
4-10-Carey Ann A. 59.
3-29-Carey Bessie, 3.
4- 5-Carey Francis, 5.
8-16-Carey John, 6.
8-30-Carl James F. 31.
11-30-Carlin Ann, 51.
9-24-Carlo James.
7- 5-Carlson Andrew, 28.
4-13-Carlson Sophia, 47.
7-16-Carmichael Jennie P. 30.
2-11-Carmody Edward J.
11-27-Carney Ann, 62.
3-16-Carney John P. 28.
2-20-Carniski John.
5-27-Carrier Ellen J. 61.
6-16-Carroll Ellen D. 66.
11-16-Cartarina Ida.
4-15-Carter Paul.
8-14-Cartwell James, 65.
9-18-Case Horace, 69.
9- 9-Cashen Annie, 32.
4-30-Cassidy Mary E. 1.
4-23-Cassionne Toney, 19.
9-12-Castonguye Mary J.
7-25-Cavanaugh William, 88.
10-22-Chaffee O. William, 72.
11-30-Chamberlain Mary, 86.
1-24-Chamberlain Samuel S. 36.
11-12-Champion Helen A.
5-19-Chapman Robert B. 48.
8-16-Chapin Henry, 54.
12- 9-Chase Calista, 71.
12-25-Chase Estella A. 46.
2- 3-Cheney Thomas S. 30.
7-21-Chikie John.
3-17-Chippato Mary G. 1.
5-14-Christiansen Harry, 3.
4-15-Christensen Niels, 39.
8-23-Chussee Francois, 45.
10- 2-Cirigliano Antonio, 9.
1-30-Claffey Matilda, 36.
4-29-Clarey William 1.
11-23-Clark George R.
11-16-Clark James, 45.
11-26-Clark Martha, 15.
3-22-Clark Philip, 39.
5- 6-Clark Susan B. 74.
12-18-Clark Susan S. 75.
10-10-Clarkin Sister Mary A. 25.
11-25-Clary James F. 28.
9-21-Cleary Lillie M.
12-29-Clement Henry, 67.
5-12-Cloyes Charles E. 23.
1-14-Clynch William, 25.
4-22-Coburn Merrena.
11-17-Cohen Charles.
4- 7-Cohen David, 1.
11- 7-Cohen Sarah M. 59.
1- 4-Coleman Daniel, 65.
1- 4-Collazo Nichols, 5.
5-19-Collins Daisey.
1-23-Collins James.
7-26-Cologiorauni Catherine, 25.
12-21-Colton Horatio, 74.
6- 6-Colton Lester H. 61.
8-20-Conklin Annie, 35.
11-16-Conlan Francis B.

8-12-Connell William J. 29.
9-28-Conner Edward, 23.
5-28-Conner Stephen, 25.
8-18-Connerton Thomas.
1-24-Conniff Thomas J. 38.
7-14-Connor Elizabeth, 12.
-22-Connor O. Mary.
6- 8-Conrey Milfred, 65.
9-30-Conroy Harry E. 1.
9-22-Conroy Frank H. 1.
6- 5-Conway Maggie, 29.
6-23-Conway Martin, 58.
3-14-Cook Catherine.
9-20-Cook Hezekiah S. 75.
8- 6-Cooke Edward Ludlow, 57.
10-25-Cooper Annie.
5-17-Cooper Carlyle, 1.
9-16-Copeland Alice E. 28.
1-25-Corcoran Daniel, 38.
12- 7-Corr Austin B. 67.
5-16-Cosgrove Winnefred, 80.
8-20-Costello Irene.
10-10-Coughlin John.
7-17-Courtney Owen P. 1.
8- 7-Courttey May, 1.
10-13-Cragg Lydia A. 73.
2- 1-Crigliano Sarceno, 50.
7-28-Crimmins Marion E.
8- 8-Cronan William J.
6-17-Crondahl Herman, 45.
6-13-Crossfield Samuel.
11- 8-Crummey Mary, 44.
11-10-Cuddigan Maurice, 65.
8-21-Cudworth Leroy J. 3.
4-16-Cudworth T. Judson B.
4-28-Cunningham Eliza, 70.
6- 3-Cunningham William.
4-17-Curry Jean L. 1.
11-26-Curry Mary, 57.
7- 2-Curtin Patrick, 55.
6-14-Curtis Ellen M. 48.
10- 7-Curtis Maria A. 31.
2-14-Curtis Barbara M.

1-30-Dacey Patrick, 64.
8-14-Dahlquist Regina, 18.
8-20-Dailey Catherine, 50.
9-15-Dailey James, 48.
5-25-Daily Patrick, 31.
12-29-Dalton James, 48.
4- 9-Daly Alice, 5.
7- 1-Daly Francis E.
12-16-Daly Gertrude.
4-22-Daly Helen, 3.
4- 8-Daly Margaret, 32.
8- 6-Damery Raymond G.
4- 4-Damon Almada E. 55.
3-20-Dane Mary, 20.
8-31-Daniels Frederick H.
3-11-Davis Ellen M. 47.
5-26-Davis Jennie E. 40.
8-23-Davis Joseph S. 50.
10-27-Dean Rosie, 1.
1- 1-DeAunato B.
4-11-Deberdeue Juenne D.
6-25-Deegan Martin, 67.
3-22-Deegar Bessie.
2- 7-Delehanty John J. 62.
5-11-Dellafera Chester.
6-27-Demarto Mary.
9- 9-Deming Elizabeth, 50.
3-20-Dempsey Benjamin, 37.
7- 7-Dempsey Patrick, 70.
4- 1-Denslow Dayton N.
8- 8-Deream Margaret E.
7-29-Desmond Edward, 50.
8-12-DeSopo Joseph, 54.
4-12-Dibble Betsey, 76.
10-13-Diefendorf Lyman S. 67.

10-28-Dillon Margaret, 25.
12-19-Dolan Annie M. 18.
8- 9-Dolgandi A. M. J. 7.
1-25-Donahue John J. 38.
7-26-Doocey Charles A.
6-23-Doody Margaret, 57.
2-20-Doolan Catherine, 67.
5- 8-Doolittle Minnie E. 36.
1- 8-Dorcy James, 26.
5- 3-Doris Georgie, 48.
9-24-Doty Mary Elizabeth, 70.
11-12-Dougherty Philip, 90.
4- 1-Dow Riou D. 58.
4-18-Dowden Beulah D.
6-12-Dower William.
9-19-Dowling Mary, 55.
6-15-Downs James, 80.
8- 6-Downs Mary, 58.
12- 4-Downs Michael, 60.
11-13-Doyle Edward, 54.
4-23-Doyle Ellen, 1.
2-26-Doyle John, 26.
10-16-Doyle Maude, 8.
9-28-Doyle Nellie, 2.
2-13-Drake Sidney, 86.
4- 1-Driscoll Patrick, 26.
8-12-Drolker Tuedre, 36.
12-10-Dubiel Andro.
10-26-Duffy Henry, 38.
11- 2-Dungan William, 61.
3-11-Dunn Frank.
9- 4-Dunn James.
12-24-Dunn James.
12- 8-Dunn John, 19.
1-29-Dunn Sarah.
6-17-Duprea Theodore E. 37.
8-10-Duroshe William, 30.
11- 3-Dutton Ida, 39.
10-17-Dwyer Annie M.
1-28-Dwyer Bridget, 28.
10-27-Dwyer Catherine.
3-20-Dwyer John, 58.
1-22-Dwyer William.
8-11-Earle Cornelius, 38.
8- 2-Earley John, 58.
7-27-Eaton Roselle.
11- 8-Eberle Jacob, 66.
8-20-Eddy Maria W. 82.
12-16-Edwards Charles F. 18.
4-25-Egan Martin, 13.
3-18-Egan Mary, 50.
4-27-Eggleston ——.
11- 1-Elcha Annie Bell, 9.
7-21-Ellsworth Ellen T. 60.
2-10-Emmett Robert, 47.
12-11-Emmett William, 37.
7- 4-Endress Charles D. 37.
5- 7-English Edward J. 6.
7-16-Erickson Huda, 31.
11-29-Essymont Alexander, 32.
7- 1-Eustice Annie, 67.

4- 6-Fagan Peter, 84.
8- 9-Fahey James J.
8-10-Fallon Joseph, 1.
6- 6-Farquhar John, 40.
1-25-Farrington May, 1.
11-26-Fassetta Dennis H. 36.
8- 4-Faust Annie M. 24.
8-21-Faust Idabelle.
1- 4-Featherstone Mary A. 25.
10-30-Feeney Josephine, 32.
7-10-Feeney Nellie, 17.
1-18-Feigher Ann, 58.
12-24-Felhage Withemia H. 66.
8-11-Feuklistern Barnet, 40.
1-28-Fields George H. 57.
10-15-Fien Lena, 7.
10- 8-Filiter Martin, 52.

4-22-Finn Annie, 3.
8- 2-Finnegan John, 65.
8-14-Fischer Lillian.
11-17-Fish Minnie L. R.
2-27-Fisk Harold.
7- 5-Fiske Louis S. 26.
4- 6-Fitts Joseph P. 80.
8- 8-Fitzgerald Catherine, 75.
9-29-Fitzgerald Thomas G. 25.
2-16-Fitzmorris Mary, 80.
4-16-Fitzpatrick Michael, 61.
12- 2-Flad Charles F. 35.
2- 8-Flagg Abigail W. 70.
7-11-Flint Alvin S. 64.
2- 2-Flynn Catherine C.
11- 9-Flynn Margaret.
1- 8-Flynn Mary, 47.
1-19-Foley Elizabeth H. 25.
1-21-Foote Catherine S. 86.
7-30-Ford Catherine, 60.
1-15-Fortinato Carmino.
6- 2-Forst Henry.
7-24-Fowler George W. 52.
8-17-Fox Eugene, 30.
1-14-Fox Martin E. 61.
10-23-Fox Nellie, 17.
8-14-Freeman Ella G.
9-16-Freeman Eva R. 40.
5- 7-Friedman George, 3.
3- 2-Friend Henry, 60.
9- 5-Fuller Elthade G. 86.
11-17-Fuller James, 72.
11-12-Fullerton Alexander, 75.
11-26-Furey Wilbert H.
7-22-Furgeson —— 67.

5-13-Gaeovone John, 4.
2-28-Gaffey Keron, 61.
5-21-Gaggin Willie, 10.
9-28-Gallagher Charles E. 52.
4-25-Galvin Frank J. 21.
10-31-Ganyon John, 72.
11-25-Ganz Frank, 4.
3-23-Gardiner William G.
2-16-Gardner Catherine, 60.
4-17-Gardner Isabella, 20.
3- 9-Garland Alfred J. 22.
6-13-Garrity Michael, 55.
10- 6-Garrity James, 67.
1-17-Garrity Peter, 32.
5- 4-Garvan Elizabeth Frances,24.
1- 6-Gaughan Francis.
1-29-Gebo Harry, 8.
10-20-Geer Eliza Evans, 39.
5- 1-Geidel ——.
1-28-George Rocco, 4.
9-11-Georgia Annia.
9-15-Georgia Vincens, 2.
9-11-Gevard Dominick.
7-24-Gibbons William A. 17.
11- 4-Gillett Jerome, 76.
10- 4-Gilligan Mary.
8-15-Gilman Ike.
8-25-Glazier Saphronia M. 83.
3-19-Gleason James F. 22.
9-25-Goba Peter, 20.
9-12-Gogozoreski Francis, 1.
2-17-Golden ——.
12-20-Goldenblum Reuben, 71.
11-12-Goldstein Shone W.
7- 3-Gompf Ella M. 44.
1-20-Goodman Sarah L. 71.
3-23-Goodwin Charles S. 79.
6-24-Goodwin Mary A. 79.
12-18-Googan Stephen J. 24.
5-26-Gordon Harry W. 22.
2-18-Gorman Ellen, 55.
8-17-Gorman William, 45.
11-10-Goss Annie.

5— 1-Gotthold Ester G. 69.
8–21-Gowdy Emma R. 48.
10–22-Grady Sarah, 55.
8— 8-Graff William, 39.
3–20-Green Arthur O. 19.
4— 8-Green Ora, 22.
10–12-Greenland Katherine.
5–22-Greenleaf Lucy Ann, 66.
9–28-Gray George, 56.
4–21-Greley Annie, 3.
8–14-Griffin Charles D. 57.
4–11-Griffin Mary, 69.
2–24-Griffin Pauline E.
8— 9-Griswold Edwin D. 84.
10— 6-Griswold Francis B. 81
3–28-Griswold Lillian A. 39.
1–24-Griswold Mary E. 70.
2–28-Grociunger Elizabeth.
2— 4-Guilfoil Patrick, 61.
10–81-Guinan John, 70.
4–28-Gunning Charles.
2— 5-Gunning William, 59.

4— 4-Hack Arthur, 40.
5–20-Haffey Bridget, 70.
11–80-Haffke Frederick, 89.
12–21-Hagelin Frank, 22.
9–26-Hale Amelia, 38.
5— 8-Hall Electa Fisk, 63.
6–28-Hall Milton R.
2–14-Hallahan John, 55.
11–25-Halloran Michael, 45.
4–14-Hamilton Bessie A. 1.
1— 7-Hamilton Elizabeth A. 25.
2–19-Hammond Helen F.
6— 9-Hanger William, 67.
12.21-Hanlon Margaret, 16.
6–30-Hanlon Mary, 12.
5–20-Hanophy Charles, 2.
9–17-Hansen Iver V. 42.
3–81-Hansen Martha L.
2–15-Hansen Minnie J.
7–20-Hansen Peter H.
10–11-Harding Joseph A. 40.
2–24-Harney Alice, 85.
1–16-Harrigan David, 62.
8–14-Harris Samuel, 58.
7— 6-Harris Samuel H. 83.
5— 2-Harris William, 13.
4–21-Harrison William H.
12–21-Hass Anna, 60.
1–25-Hatheway Hazel M. 4.
10–24-Haub Hedrig, 40.
4— 5-Hawley Margaret M. 40.
5— 4-Hayes Richards, 66.
9— 8-Hayes Thomas, 30.
4–18-Healy John P. 42.
2–12-Healy Mary E. 38.
4–24-Hearnes Frank P. 2.
4–28-Henderson Sarah A. 25.
7— 9-Hendrickson Eddie P.
9— 1-Hennessy Margaret, 19.
6–11-Henson George F. 6.
5— 5-Henson Thomas, 27.
4— 9-Herb William H. 57.
11–12-Herbert ——.
10–14-Hess ——.
8–80-Hevrin Margaret C. 22.
4–29-Hewitt George F.
8— 5-Heywood George M. 85.
8— 4-Hickey Patrick, 32.
4–29-Hickmott Julia A. 73.
7–10-Hiespe Ida F. E. 5.
7— 4-Higgins Mary, 63.
8–80-Hill William, 62.
1–81-Hills Florinda A. 85.
8— 8-Hills Jane E. 69.
10— 6-Hines Annie, 17.
4–28-Hines Thomas, 50.

8–14-Kilbourn Joseph K. 73.
12–17-Kilbourn Viola.
9–19-Killian James.
8–20-Killin Mary, 85.
7–21-Kiltz Willie.
11–80-Kilniakie John, 26.
4–17-King George, 4.
2–16-Kingsley Betsey W. 84.
11–28-Kingsley Lucina D. 73.
5–19-Kinnure Thomas, 34.
6–16-Kirby John J.
8— 2-Kilne Anton, 40.
4— 7-Knightly James.
6–15-Korpusky Alexander.
11–28-Koch ——.
4–20-Krah Christina, 76.
1–19-Kumler Luno.
9–11-Kunze Frederick H. 71.

8–17-Lacara Peter, 38.
5— 8-Lacasse Ernest, 9.
18–16-Ladella Christina.
0–25-Ladragen Michael, 26.
9— 6-Laird William, 78.
8— 8-Lang Herbert M. 26.
7–19-Laporte ——.
8–21-La Pruce John, 81.
14–20-Larmeer ——.
1–19-Larsen Louise.
17–17-Laschever David.
0–19-Lathrop Grace E. 25.
7— 7-Lauranti Joseph.
16–19-Lavary Osker.
8–30-Lawler John, 69.
8–11-Lawrence James, 44.
11–11-Lawton Wells, 67.
0— 2-Leahy John, 88.
4–16-Leahy Katie.
8–19-Lee Marie Gertrude, 35.
8— 5-Leggett William H. 51.
9— 4-Lehan Mary, 46.
6–12-Lehner Frank W. 27.
6–17-Lehr Raymond S.
4— 6-Lennox Alexander, 71.
8–25-Leroy Mary A.
6–29-Lester Porter E. 70.
6–17-Leuca Thomas, 1.
4— 7-Lincoln Brooks M. 45.
7–26-Lindstrom Jennie, 3.
7–11-Lipie Joseph H. 22.
8–20-Lobdell Edwin R. 56.
8— 2-Logan Gladias.
2–28-Logan Henry.
7–30-Looney Daniel, 48.
5–21-Loprete Lucia, 4.
8–27-Lord Arthur F. 64.
12–28-Lord Henry S. 58.
4–23-Lord Jane R. 79.
7–11-Lougent ——.
5— 2-Lowrey Sarah, 81.
12— 8-Loyden Urania J.
1— 5-Lucas Charles E. 75.
5–22-Lucas Frank, 61.
9–80-Lundstrom John, 30.
8–12-Lurain Thomas, 40.
8— 2-Lutz Dorothy, 62.
4— 1-Lycett Susan, 78.
6–14-Lynch John.
1— 2-Lynch Welter, 75.

10–28-Mack Carrie E. 26.
2— 8-Maddox John E. 1.
4–15-Maher Margaret, 40.
8–15-Maher Nellie B. 21.
5— 8-Mahoney David, 22.
11–15-Mahoney Mary, 70.
12— 8-Main Charles E. 42.
11— 4-Main Jennie, 9.
10–22-Malloy Bridget, 68.

5–18-Hiscock Edward, 25.
11— 1-Hoben Mary I. 38.
9–12-Hogan John Edward, 46.
7— 6-Hogman Magnus, 28.
5–19-Holden Anna Bell, 42.
6— 1-Holehouse John, 68.
10–17-Holmquist Edward, 37.
7–18-Hollister Martin T. 49.
11— 6-Hooker Helen Frances, 61.
7— 8-Hotchkiss Ashbel C. 83.
10–15-House Philo B. 72.
10–21-Howard Mary, 41.
11— 4-Howorth William, 55.
1–16-Hubbard Fidelia C. 90.
2–27-Hubbard George H. 50.
7— 5-Hubbard George R. 53.
12–19-Hubbard Maria R. 80.
5— 4-Hubbard Reuben L. 64.
5–10-Hunn George A. 76
2–12-Hunter Joseph, 83.
8— 8-Huntington Andrew J. 64.
8–28-Hussey Eliza F. 78.
12–28-Hutchins Ezra, 76.
10–18-Hutter Samuel, 58.
8–12-Hutton James, 15.
9–24-Hydoush ——.
6— 7-Hyland Joseph.
12— 2-Hyland Thomas, 1.
6— 4-Ingraham Henry D. 77.

1— 8-Jacklyn William, 80.
8— 8-Jackson Andrew D.
8–29-Jackson George J. 36.
1–29-Jackson Susan, 17.
2–28-Jahn Loren.
4–14-Jaywith Emma.
8–22-Jessen Edward J. 2.
1— 7-Jewett Sarah J. 68.
4–27-Johnsen Larence, 83.
7–28-Johnson ——.
2–11-Johnson Chandler, 79.
11— 2-Johnson Charles H. 34.
2— 9-Johnson Charles P.
4— 8-Johnson Levi B. 45.
7— 4-Johnson Louisa H. 39.
11–11-Johnson Viola.
8–19-Johnson William G. 60.
5–16-Jonasson Manfred T. 28.
12–24-Jones Ella, 39.
10–24-Jones Marietta, 66.
1–20-Jorgensen Annie.

9–15-Kampfanam ——.
4–19-Kane Mary A.
12— 5-Kapp Mary M. 3.
10–28-Katz Beckie, 1.
5–21-Knutzki Louis, 55.
11–26-Keane Catherine E. 22.
5–11-Keane Patrick T. 21.
12— 5-Keating Maggie, 85.
7— 9-Keeling Emma, 76.
6— 4-Keenehan John, 58.
6— 2-Keeney Harriet J. 60.
8–25-Keeney Lee S. 83.
4–18-Kehoe John.
5–21-Keighley Nancy, 80.
5— 5-Keleher Catherine, 65.
9— 5-Kelley Rose, 72.
10–10-Kellogg Charles F. 80.
12— 5-Kelly Teresa, 15.
8–22-Kennedy Mary, 85.
12— 8-Kennedy Thomas, 70.
1–19-Kenneely William F. 21.
8— 6-Kenney Martin, 61.
2–26-Kenyon H. 1.
8–11-Keough Sarah, 60.
8–18-Kerwin Pearl, 30.
8–80-Ketz Bessie.
8–81 Kilbourn Abbie M. 69.

| | | |
|---|---|---|
| 9-12-Malone William H. 36. | 11-11-Mooney James, 78. | 11-15-Patton Alice I. |
| 10-17-Maloney Charles H. 29. | 4-30-Mooney Thomas, 40. | 12-26-Patz Ferdinand, 56. |
| 10-24-Maloy John, 71. | 1-24-Moore Mary J. 57. | 4-15-Payne Emily J. N. 24. |
| 8- 9-Manion Frank, 12. | 10- 9-Moore Patrick, 25. | 7- 8-Pelton John T. 73. |
| 7-14-Manion James. | 8-29-Moore William, 50. | 12-30-Percy Martha N. 37. |
| 10- 1-Manion Willie. | 1-27-Moran John F. 24. | 3-18-Percy Mary M. 28. |
| 8- 2-Manion William H. 43. | 8- 7-Moran Kitty A. 27. | 1-10-Perrien Baghdasar, 28. |
| 11-29-Manka Frederick, 21. | 1-15-Moran Patrick, 46. | 7-10-Pete Frankie, 2. |
| 9-10-Manley Johanna A. 1. | 8- 6-Morgan Adam, 81. | 12- 8-Peters August, 59. |
| 8-15-Manley John E. 1. | 8- 1-Morgan Joseph M. 84. | 3-22-Peters Mary A. 50. |
| 8-24-Manning William, 24. | 12-10-Morgan Mary. | 11- 5-Peterson August', 32. |
| 2-26-Maradei Freduci, 52. | 4-16-Moriarty John. | 6-26-Peterson L. 69. |
| 4-23-Marcai Maria. | 1-31-Morris James L. 39. | 11-25-Petigall Mary. |
| 6-16-Marison ——. | 4-25-Morse Everett L. 46. | 12-13-Pettibone Frederick L. 12. |
| 1-28-Marks Walter H. 40. | 4-17-Morse Lodice, 85. | 8-17-Pfeiffer Edward, 65. |
| 1-12-Marsh Affa B. 85. | 7- 6-Mulcahy Bridget, 51. | 2- 4-Phelps Clarinda, 94. |
| 7-27-Martin Bridget, 50. | 7- 6-Mulcahy George L. | 1-16-Pierson Denison, 62. |
| 8-16-Martin John, 65. | 11-21-Mulcahy Willie, 2. | 11-29-Pillett Charles N. 41. |
| 5-22-Martin John, 4. | 1- 6-Mulhall Julia, 55. | 12- 5-Pillion Willie, 5. |
| 4- 2-Martin John. | 3-18-Munster Charles F. 46. | 4-17-Pinney George H. 57. |
| 11-25-Martin Prudence B. 77. | 11- 4-Murdane Rose. | 12-12-Pitkin Emily F. 70. |
| 12-29-Martin Russell. | 5- 7-Murphy Daniel, 39. | 1- 2-Polette Thelisphore, 26. |
| 4-17-Massier Felix. | 6-27-Murphy Jeremiah, 87. | 1-16-Polk Mary A. 86. |
| 1-26-Mayer David, 68. | 2-26-Murphy John, 62. | 6-10-Porter Leander, 60. |
| 5-16-McAleer Patrick J. 24. | 2-12-Murphy John, 75. | 4-17-Porter Mary L. 92. |
| 9- 7-McCabe James, 30. | 9-11-Murphy J. Maria. | 6-11-Post Caroline C. 19. |
| 5-23-McCabe Sister Mary F. 20. | 8-27-Murphy Kate, 70. | 11-18-Post Julius P. 83. |
| 5-11-McCafferty Jeannette, 40. | 4- 7-Murphy Katherine, 1. | 7-17-Poupe Alfred. 53. |
| 10-16-McCann Michael, 67. | 8- 3-Murray Anuie, 3. | 4-15-Pratt Ogden E. 88. |
| 9- 3-McCarthy Catherine, 38. | 10-15-Murray Charles, 67. | 6-28-Premo Francis L. |
| 1- 5-McCarthy Dennis J. 43. | 4-22-Murray John E. 21. | 4-23-Preston John B. |
| 5- 4-McCarthy Jeremiah, 34. | 11-20-Myers Annie J. 28. | 6-21-Pritchard George. |
| 12-15-McCarthy John, 12. | 7-29-Myers Esther, 81. | 3-18-Puffer Charles F. 59. |
| 8-17-McCormack Richard, 32. | | 5- 8-Puglisk Leonascho. |
| 12- 1-McCready Frank, 33. | 11- 3-Nason Almond F. 55. | 10- 2-Putnam Carrie B. |
| 6-20-McCue ——. | 4-17-Neale Lucinda, 89. | 6-28-Purcell Martin, 39. |
| 10- 4-McCue Patrick F. 25. | 1-26-Nearing Henry T. 72. | 11- 5-Purdy James F. |
| 3-20-McDonald James P. | 11-14-Neff Mary, 89. | |
| 4-27-McDonald Mary, 70. | 8-23-Nevers Melissa, 85. | 8-29-Quilty William, 44. |
| 7- 1-McElroy George, 57. | 2-15-Newman Abagail, 78. | 7-19-Quish George. |
| 7-16-McGann Mary, 36. | 10-18-Nicola Maria. | |
| 9-23-McGee Alice, 18. | 7-17-Noonan Agnes, 18. | 4-26-Rabinowitz Channa. |
| 4- 2-McGill Hugh, 42. | 5-21-Noonan Edward, 19. | 2- 2-Raimondi Tony. |
| 8-18-McGill Rose, 84. | 9-29-Nordstrom Ruth C. J. | 3-23-Ramsdell Oliver W. 4. |
| 2-25-McGinn John, 36. | 8-23-North Wallace H. 32. | 6- 8-Randall William E. 89. |
| 8-13-McGovern Charles S. 38. | 11- 3-Norton Howard A. 22. | 9- 2-Rasmussen Nelson P. 46. |
| 8-13-McGowne John, 56. | 1-15-Nyrol Andrew, 50. | 6-10-Rathburn Lucy A. 75. |
| 4- 8-McGuire John, 21. | | 4-13-Rau Frederick, 1. |
| 2- 3-McIntyre Hugh, 66. | 10-16-Ober Margaret E. 52. | 5-21-Rau George, 6. |
| 2-13-McIntyre Margaret, 47. | 6- 4-O'Brien Alice A. | 10-16-Raymond Henry S. 84. |
| 3-15-McKay Daniel. | 8-18-O'Brien Margaret. | 8- 1-Read Spencer, 81. |
| 5-29-McKee Nancy, 81. | 1-10-O'Brien Nomie, 1. | 6-17-Reardon Ellen, 8. |
| 12-27-McKenna Mary A. 46. | 7-28-O'Brien Willie. | 4-18-Reardon George A. 26. |
| 1- 6-McLaughlin Mary, 46. | 12-12-O'Connor Elizabeth. | 9- 8-Reardon Mary E. |
| 11- 6-McLean Lillian F. 10. | 5-17-O'Connor William L. | 5-27-Reardon Sarah, 48. |
| 4-20-McLean William A. 3. | 12-25-O'Donnell James P. 25. | 9-11-Redding Philip D. |
| 8-11-McManus James, 56. | 3-24-O'Hare James. 66. | 8-22-Redway George M. 65. |
| 1-29-McManus William, 60. | 8-28-O'Keefe Hannah. | 2- 1-Reed Martin, 68. |
| 12-10-McNamara Martin, 58. | 3- 5-O'Laughlin ——. | 10- 1-Regan Edwin J. 2. |
| 2-26-McTernan Robert, 1. | 6-16-Oliver John. | 12-11-Rete John. |
| 4-26-McVean William, 84. | 8-26-O'Mara John. | 5-25-Reynolds Charlotte C. 65. |
| 4-30-Meader Samuel K. 88. | 9- 4-O'Neil Margaret, 30. | 18-22-Reynolds Thomas, 58. |
| 10- 7-Meanly William, 65. | 7-29-O'Neil Mary, 80. | 1-24-Richards Winifred D. 6. |
| 6-14-Merrill Oliver C. 58. | 12-22-Oppelt Annie C. 28. | 4- 1-Richardson Willie E. 42. |
| 2- 5-Michaels Joseph. | 9- 8-O'Reilly Ann, 88. | 4-19-Riche Florence M. |
| 6-16-Milde Charles, 49. | 3-18-Orisne Maria R. 1. | 1- 2-Richmond Augusta R. 57. |
| 2- 4-Miller Charles G. 71. | 7-29-Osburne Catherine, 65. | 9-26-Rider Emily F. 71. |
| 11- 7-Miller Ernest, 21. | 2-16-Ostman Carl I. 28. | 3-24-Riley Flavia G. |
| 12-28-Miller Esther R. 1. | 9-21-Overlando Christen. | 2-15-Riley John, 39. |
| 10-11-Miller James C. 76. | | 5-11-Riordon Eddie. |
| 4-24-Miller Jennie, 81. | 1-10-Page Lewis B. 88. | 3-21-Risby Arthur, 1. |
| 3-19-Miller Margaret, 67. | 6-22-Page Nancy, 49. | 3-17-Robbins Benjamin G. 81. |
| 11-28-Miller Martha. | 10-24-Palassi Frank, 5. | 5-22-Roberts William W. 84. |
| 2- 8-Mitchill Margaret, 65. | 4-21-Palmer Mary A. 39. | 8-29-Robinson Harriet E. 34. |
| 8-14-Mitchill Robert. | 11-21-Parker James H. 52. | 9- 3-Roune Fannie. |
| 1-28-Mitchill William F. 63. | 11- 9-Parks Elnia D. 89. | 4-24-Rouvier Harriet, 73. |
| 2- 2-Montgomery Margaret. | 3-11-Parsons John C. 65. | 7-12-Roux Arthur. |
| 6-30-Moodig Milcher, 17. | 10-23-Patterson Mary C. A. 68. | 8-15-Roberts Roxana S. 43. |
| 5- 7-Mooney Mary, 65. | 5-31-Patterson Robert, 48. | 2-24-Roberts William S. 79. |

9–30–Robins Albert.
9–17–Rochette Mary Anna, 51.
8–25–Roedel ——.
1–12–Roehrer Catherine, 46.
10–31–Rogers Alice M. 34.
6–21–Rogers William, 68.
7– 5–Rohwei Raymond V.
6– 4–Rood Ella D. 37.
7– 1–Rooney Katie. 8.
10– 9–Rosa Axel E.
10– 6–Rubright E. M. 6.
8– 1–Rudolph Julius, 60.
2–12–Russell John, 45.
12–10–Russell Mary T. 42.
8–21–Ryan George W. 24.
10–14–Ryan John, 48.
7–25–Ryder John.
3–17–Rymarozyk John.

8– 1–St. John Frank H. 1.
12–25–Saganio Francis, 56.
2–16–Sage Olive, 79.
1–12–Salad Julius, 37.
5–81–Sall George, 1.
11–16–Samson Annie T. 3.
7– 8–Samuels Louis L. 41.
12–30–Samuelson John A. 33.
5– 9–Sanso Anna B.
5– 8–Sanzo M. Carmina.
1–22–Sayers Garrett, 44.
10–17–Scanlon Delia A. 19.
3–11–Sceery Francis.
10–11–Schall Annie J. D. 35.
10–11–Schall August.
9– 6–Schenwasky Mary.
12–24–Scherman Amelia.
3–27–Schleicher Mabel E.
2–20–Schnieder Minnie B. 8.
11–22–Schudlick William, 42.
6–23–Schuh Frederick, 67.
12– 9–Schulze George, 75.
1–18–Schroeder Frederick C.
9–19–Schwartz Helena, 11.
7–29–Schwete Helena, 11.
11–23–Scully Thomas, 1.
8–21–Searey E. G. 54.
12–11–Seltzer Annie, 19.
8– 4–Seraphin Oliver.
3– 8–Sessions George, 19.
12–22–Seymour Ada H. 29.
12–24–Seymour Arthur, 50.
9–26–Seymour Henry P. 32.
5– 7–Seymour Nellie, 78.
10–25–Seymour Sarah B. 71.
5– 1–Shano Robert, 58.
8– 5–Sharp ——.
10– 8–Shaughnessy Michael W. 40.
11–29–Shaughnessy Peter, 65.
10–20–Shea Cornelius, 8.
9–17–Shea Daniel Jr., 13.
11– 6–Shea Hannah, 65.
2– 7–Shea Rose.
2–19–Shea Thomas F. 1.
8– 1–Sheedy Frank.
8– 2–Sheehan Johanna, 37.
5– 8–Sheehan Margaret, 70.
6–28–Sheehan Michael J. 1.
1– 8–Shepard Pastoria E. 51.
4– 4–Shepperd Harriet L. 75.
10–18–Sheridan Catherine, 54.
7– 6–Sheridan James.
12–31–Shew Jacob W. 78.
7–12–Shnoo George.
8–19–Siebert Adolph, 13.
7–22–Sigall ——.
7– 6–Sigfried Bertha.
12–14–Sillence Cora E. 4.
12–15–Silvester Emerico.
4–14–Simmons Ichabod Rev. 66.

10–19–Thompson Edith C.
8–12–Thompson Mary A. 87.
6–23–Thompson Sarah M. 87.
3– 8–Thompson Violet.
6– 9–Thrall William, 83.
2–25–Thurman Laura, 24.
12–18–Todd Evalyn, 20.
8–29–Toles Kate, 62.
6–24–Tomlins Fannie, 45.
8–25–Tontaine Charles, 17.
3–21–Townsend Gertrude.
6– 3–Tracy Edward, 5.
4–18–Tracy Thomas, 62.
7–22–Trainor Thomas, 38.
8– 3–Trerice Robert P. 49.
8–19–Trostel Carrie, 53.
8– 5–Trumbull J. H. 76.
3– 3–Tryon Henry R. 79.
7–22–Tryon William J. 15.
5–26–Tuller Jane E. 74.
8–22–Tuller Sarah E. 88.
5– 9–Turner Mary, 22.
11–24–Tyske Wadersle.
11–24–Tyske William.

3–22–Underwood Sanford G. 80.

5–14–Valhall Frank.
7– 9–Vallario Angelina, 1.
4– 5–Varoll Willie.
7–17–Ventento Frank.
5– 8–Vesey Nellie, 17.
12– 3–Vesland Anna E. 54.
6–30–Vingno Annie.
11–25–Vossler Marx C. 16.

3–20–Walker Elsie, 2.
9–22–Wallace William D. 5.
9– 5–Walsh Nora M.
9–23–Ward Kate, 31.
10– 7–Ward Lizzie, 30.
7– 7–Warnecke Mary, 36.
2–11–Warner Charles S. 58.
12– 7–Warner Nellie M. 32.
3– 7–Warriner Charles J. 24.
3–28–Washburn George P.
3–11–Washburn Hiram F. 55.
10– 4–Wasileuski Lepold, 44.
9–26–Waterman Edgar, 75.
10– 8–Waterman Edith M.
3–22–Waterman Howard, 1.
2–19–Waters Abigal L. 72.
9–10–Waters Chancy, 74.
2–23–Watrous Mattie E. 40.
8–11–Watson Edward J. 28.
2–28–Watson Julia, 88.
10–15–Webb Maria L. 55.
5–11–Wedberg Johanna C. 20.
5–11–Weed Mary Ann, 76.
9– 5–Weedeir Walter W. 21.
4– 4–Weidell Signie.
1–18–Weidell Tekla L. 38.
8–14–Weidlich Welhelmine, 62.
1–20–Weir Walter, 65.
12–28–Welch John.
1–24–Welch Joseph, 18.
8– 4–Welch Mary, 21.
4–24–Wells Edward W. 78.
7–31–Wenis Mary.
5–26–Wenk Margaret B. 60.
11–15–West Berzella, 84.
1– 8–West Evlyn A. 1.
12–12–West Mary.
12–12–Westcott Edward G. 75.
9–22–Wetherill Gertrude L. 16.
4–29–Wey Joseph.
12–30–Wheeler Addison, 71.
6–30–Wheeler Gertrude F. 28.
12–27–White Arthur D.

10– 2–Simons Annie, 48.
9–28–Simons Jacob, 64.
11– 7–Simons William, 79.
5–27–Simpkins ——.
4–20–Sinnott William, 56.
4– 4–Sisson Mary N. 73.
5–10–Skeaba Ottam.
10– 1–Sladitch Jacob, 65.
9– 8–Slattery Clarence.
11– 5–Smith Annie, 28.
4–18–Smith Annie, 7.
2–18–Smith Edith I.
4–20–Smith Elizabeth A. 23.
3– 5–Smith Ellen, 7.
8– 2–Smith Ernest, 61.
5–11–Smith George B.
7–31–Smith Helen A. 27.
1– 5–Smith John I. 76.
2– 7–Smith Joseph B.
6–20–Smith Jossie L. 33.
8– 1–Smith Mary A. 20.
6–23–Smith Nellie, 86.
12– 3–Smith Sarah, 48.
8–19–Soboleffsky Annie D.
10–17–Somers Mary, 55.
3–15–Southergill Charles J. 26.
2–25–Spencer Alice F. 26.
9– 9–Squires Luman A. 91.
12–18–Stamp Henry, 67.
5–14–Stanton Bessie.
4–22–Stark ——.
8–18–Starkey Robert M.
1–29–Stearns Hulda, 77.
11– 2–Stearns Julia M. 70.
4–16–Stedman Mildred M. 2.
11–17–Stelmetz Annie L. 50.
6–30–Stewart Margaret S. 73.
8–26–Sticklor Ise, 1.
7– 8–Stockofski Annie.
1–14–Stokes Josephine D. 57.
9–17–Stoll John, 65.
4–27–Stone Grace H. 1.
7–31–Stone Henry.
7– 8–Stoty Jacob, 25.
6– 5–Stowe Bridget 41.
7– 9–Stowe Jeremiah, 75.
11–18–Stratton Lily L. 24.
3–12–Strauss Nathan.
9–23–Strong Maria, 77.
11–29–Strumer Bertha, 1.
12– 6–Studley Frederick T. 46.
8–10–Suess Charles, 54.
8–21–Sullivan Ellen, 35.
9– 6–Sullivan Francis, 5.
7–25–Sullivan Mary.
12–24–Sullivan Nora, 51.
12–17–Sullivan Patrick, 48.
4– 5–Sullivan Patrick, 60.
2–18–Sullivan Philip.
10– 6–Sullivan Teresa.
10–12–Sullivan Timothy J. 22.
12–28–Sumner William, 71.
10–22–Sutherland Electa T. 56.
7–30–Svenson Charles R.
8–19–Sweeney Irene.
11–25–Sweet Laura A. 87.
4–29–Sweet William, 55.
7–14–Sydenham Mary L. 1.
5–26–Sykes Caroline S. 86.

10–30–Taylor Diana M. 67.
5–11–Taylor Hattie, 88.
1–22–Taylor James, 27.
2–11–Taylor Sidney R. 71.
6–13–Taylor William, 22.
6– 4–Thayer Cora M. 35.
1–17–Thomas Charles A. 41.
4– 5–Thomas Edith May.
5–28–Thompson ——.

10-30- White John, 80.
5-25-White Mary Jane 56.
9-30-White Michael, 55.
7-12-White Peter F.
12- 4-Whitehead Alfred, 25.
8- 3-Whitman Harriett N. 75.
9- 8-Willard Francis S.
12- 6-Williams Clifford.
8- 6-Williams Horace, 63.
12-10-Williams John F. 28.
10-18-Williams Lucy H. 27.
2-15-Williams Mary E. 64.
4- 2-Williams Wightman, 95.
5- 6-Wills Lavinia, 75.
10- 5-Wilson Frederick, 23.
2-10-Wilson Willie.
10-27-Wilson William H. 44.
12-28-Wind ——. 
12-28-Wind ——.
12-26-Winship Chauncey H. 86.
11-19-Wittig John F. 26.
12-28-Wolf Matilda, 34.
4-10-Woodbeck Harriett, 70.
1- 1-Woodhouse Jane E. 75.
4- 4-Woods Beatrice M.
3-21-Woods Phœbe, 51.
9-25-Wootton George L. 21.
12-22-Wren John, 27.
11- 8-Wright Francis K.
2- 5-Wright Mary E. 70.
1-15-Wulle Christian C. 8.

8-25-Young Alice G. 3.
12- 4-Young Mary E. 5.
7- 6-Young Olinie M. 2.
4-20-Young Walter A. 55.

6-29-Zillhart Louisa, 35.
1- 8-Zitkins Peter, 28.
3-12-Zodkus Auduheim, 36.
2-23-Zuhurst Catherine, 51.
8-27-Zygment John.

# Marriages
## IN HARTFORD, DURING 1897.

*The first figures in the line indicate the month in the year 1897, and the second figures the date of the month of marriage; first name is of the Groom, the second of the Bride.*

12-27-Abram Pat'k J.- Doyle Marg't.
5- 8-Ackerman MC-Nordstrom AC
7- 1-Adams Henry-Mullen Katie.
11-18-Albin Jas.-Monahan Delia.
6-16-Allen R. J.-Allen Charlotte M.
2-24-Allen H. R.-Williams Cath.
2-10-Ames B.T.-Thibault Am'da E
12- 4-Anderson A.-Peterson A. B.
9-25-Anderson C. H.-Danielson W.
7- 3-Anderson C. J.-Neilson Ella.
5-22-Anderson J.-Anderson Aug'a
5-16-Anderson J. A.-Johnson A. E.
11- 1-Anderson J. E.-Johnson H. E.
5-13-Anderson M. P.-Kundsen A.
11-24-Andretta A.-Pallotti Felici.
4-20-Andrews H.M-Woodward E.R
5-19-Angus D.-Newton Grace S.
1- 9-Appleby G. A.-Barrows G.

7-26-Armstrong A.-Parker Clara.
10-13-Ashwell C. E.-Martin Sadie L.
8- 1-Augell Jos.-Jambor Mary.
7-12-Aurnhammer C.F.-Kress H.F.
2- 5-Ayers W. H.-Miller Adesta F.

2- 1-Badger Degar-Hook C. Belle.
1- 6-Barbeau L.-Brousseau Marie.
11-10-Barone G. A.-Dunn Katie E.
5- 5-Barrows F. W.-Flanagan M. J.
2- 2-Barry David-Martin Susie G.
11-22-Barry John J.-Cashen Nellie E.
4-28-Barry Michael-Moore Mary.
4-27-Bartlett A. M.-Perry Kate B.
5-12-Beaumier Jos.-Robus Bertha.
12-27-Beck T.C.-Coomes Rebecca M.
10-26-Bedford Wm.-Thomas Sara J.
4-20-Begg Wm. R.-Spencer Louise.
9-16-Benton Geo.-Jones Lizzie.
9-30-Bergquist D.-Carlson Anna L.
3-28-Berry T. A-Breen Josephine L.
12-25-Bill A. C.-Fowler Fannie S.
5-20-Birney R.-Johnson Grace E.
5-24-Bishop K. F.-Sweet Jennie.
9-12-Blair R. C.-Durie Bessie C.
8-17-Blish F. T.-Hollister Edna M.
10- 6-Bloom S.-Cooper Ida.
9-18-Bondy B.-Nussbaum Julia.
2-12-Bowers P. P.-Henry Matilda.
6-30-Boyce J. Y.-Paterson Maggie.
6-15-Bracken Frank-Andrus Ellen.
3-26-Brainerd H.F.-Wilson Hattie F
2-25-Branagan T.J.-Reagan Eliz'bh.
1-20-Brehm Jas. S.-Reidmann ——
2-20-Broineng A.-Crupp Augusta.
6- 2-Brennan J.P.-Crowley Ellen C
12-31-Brennan T.J.-Leeney Mary J.
9-22-Bride Thos. H -Keefe Fannie.
6-10-Brink R. A.-Terhune Mary A.
6- 3-Britton W. A.-Percy Minnie L
12- 8-Bronson R.T-English Marg't C.
11- 1-Brooks J.T.-Dibble Edna B.
3- 2-Brown G.H.-Goulet Georgiana.
3-24-Brown J.H.T.-Henderson E. B.
6-30-Brown L. D.-Burns Ada E.
9-21-Brown Wm.-Woods Delia.
11- 4-Brunett W.-Whelen Elizabeth
5- 9-Brure E.-Ceriglians Angiolni
11-21-Bupo L.-Zaccamine Jennie.
1-18-Burcrynski J-Maziasz Antonia
4-28-Burke Thos.-McWalter Mary.
10-20-Burns William-Wall Nellie.
4-10-Burrows F. O.-Pease Lizzie M
3- 8-Butler D. B.-Jackson Mary.
6- 9-Buttles G. H.-Hammersley A.

9-25-Calkins Wm. L.-Prior Susie.
4-28-Callahan C.-Keilly Mary.
7- 1-Callender F. E.-Rosein M. A.
10-25-Campbell N.-McCarthy Sara.
4-21-Carey Thos. E.-Hile Kittie.
6-19-Carlson Olof-Erikson Anna.
6-16-Carney D. P.-O'Brien M. M.
1- 1-Carnick F.J.-Schwab Emma.
3- 6-Case Frank D.-Case Edna M.
10- 5-Case Herb't S.-Atwood Lulu.
6-17-Casey Thos.-Higgins Mary.
5-12-Cassels B. J.-Dooley Annie T.
6- 2-Catlin C. F.-Bidwell Annie B.
12-17-Ceiderfeld J. V.-Schulte M.
11-10-Cella Jos.-McLaughlin Nellie.
10-26-Chamberlin S.S.-Fox Louise T
11-17-Cheney F.L.-McLean Jennie M
4-22-Childs C. R.-Smith Grace D.
8-15-Chludick J.-Klimesak Mary.
11- 4-Christensen C. P.-Clausen A.
12- 3-Christensen C.-Terkelsen S.
10-21-Christiansen J.-Beck Gert'de.
6-30-Christensen J. C.-Hansen H.

11- 4-Christensen P.C.-Andersen C-
12- 6-Claffey F.-Dupree Hattie E.
6-19-Clancy Michael-Fagan Nellie.
3-17-Clapp B. S.-Harland Clara M.
11- 1-Clark Alvin J.-Prilly Katie.
11- 4-Clark F. P.-Harvey Rose A.
10-23-Clark Geo.-Leary Helen C.
8-15-Clark Ira A.-Quinn Delia.
1-28-Clarkin Wm.-Doocy Fanny J.
9-22-Cleary S.-Otis Katherine.
5-23-Cleggett C.F.-Sherman Cora E
8- 6-Codey G. W.-Heffern Nora L.
6- 7-Coffee Patrick-Dix Margaret.
9-27-Coffey P. G.-Murray Sarah J
9-22-Collard L. W -Sands Esther J.
8- 2-Collins C.-Higley Bessie.
9- 6-Collins J. B.-Goodwin Katie.
9- 1-Collins J. H.-Hogan Ellen M.
4-14-Colpitts A.B.-Cooley Jessie M
4-28-Conners Patrick-Riley Mary.
3-28-Cook A. N.-Belden Alice D.
12-22-Cook E.-Stockham Mary N.
12- 1-Coombs C.-Brown Millie.
10-25-Copinos J.-Myzga Karolme.
6-29-Coranfeld H.-Silversmith M.
4-28-Corrigan J. A.-Barry Nellie J.
9-21-Cotter Edw'd J.-Doty Rosie.
2-10-Cowles Samuel-Fuld Emma.
12-31-Cox H.A.-O'Brien Josephine T
10-26-Coyle Jas. J.-Dacey Helen F.
1- 6-Crawford Jas.-Becton Annie.
10-19-Crowell E.S.-Fuller Catherine
11-18-Crussberg G. A.-Johnson S. C.
1- 7-Cullen T. A.-Morse Jane E.
2- 3-Currie G. W.-Dagle Minnie I.
6-23-Curtin F. H.-McCartney M.F.
8- 9-Czaruieck K.-Cwitka Jozefa.

6-21-Daley Alfred L.-Welch Helen.
5-11-Daley M.F.-Kennedy Nellie R
9-15-Daly Thos.-Powers Margaret.
3- 1-Dalut Botris-Detz Annie.
1-19-Dandurand R.-Carter Martha
5- 5-Daniels F.A.-Bishop Adelia D
11-27-Danielson C.G.-Johnson E.A.
1-24-Davies Emanuel-Ball Yetta.
6-29-Davis Edw'd-Wissell Teressa.
2-22-Dean Geo. J.-Noonan Anna E.
2-15-Deegan Jas.-Moran Sarah.
2-18-Delaney J.-McCarthy Bridget
5-12-Delap Edw'd-Nichols Bridget.
5- 5-Dennehy W.-Mulvihill Annie
5-18-Densmore H.A.-Allen Jennie A
6-21-Depatie L.-Lavoie Marie E.
10- 6-Desmarais H.-Allen Lizzie.
8-31-Dewitt E. A.-Havens Nellie.
12-27-Dickenson W. A.-Neilson P.
5-29-Dillon J. E.-Sullivan Mary A.
7-14-Dillon J. E.-Sullivan Nora M.
4-25-Dixon B. C.-Banite Lenora.
6- 8-Donaghue J.-O'Keefe Maggie
7- 2-Donaghue Thos.-Nestor Katie
7- 7-Donovan J. J.-Connolly B.
4-28-Donovan T.-Haggerty Mary.
12- 7-Dore Jos. A.-Clark Sarah E.
9-15-Dormitzer S.-Morris Hannah
5- 5-Drechsler W.-Parker Louise H
10-18-Dube A.-LeCleaire Clara.
10-21-Ducey J. J.-Garriety M. A.
4-26-Ducey W. J.-Kelly Delia.
10-25-Duffy John P.-Lagan Sarah J.
9-22-Duffy P. F.-Mulcahey Kitty.
4-28-Dully Jos. F-Havens Delia A.
1- 4-Dundon John-Trainor Annie.
1-13-Dunlap H. H.-Weeks Bessie C
11-18-Dunlop J.-Parlee Amanda.
1-12-Dunn James-Glynn Delia.
5-12-Dunne John J.-Shea Julia.
6-28-Dutton L.-Loveland Alice M.

| | | |
|---|---|---|
| 2- 6-Dwyer A. E.-Moran Isabella. | 5-16-Gustafson E. W.-BrownM. E. | 11-24-Jordan J.Jr.-Hutchinson S.J. |
| 10- 4-Dwyer John J.-Kelly Annie. | | 12-18-Joseph John-Mellor Agnes. |
| 4-27-Dwyer R. O.-O'Brien Bridget | 2-22-Hackett T. J.-Green Susie E. | 11-16-Joyce William-Eagan Lena. |
| | 4-28-Haffner R.-Quinn Nellie J. | |
| 10-27-Eagan O. Jr.-DonnellyMarg't | 11-15-Haglund G.-Resare Albertine. | 5-19-Katz L.-Rosenbloom Lottie. |
| 2- 9-Eagan Wm.-Ronan Mary. | 12-24-Hakins R.M.-TalbotMary O. | 6- 9-Katz Lewis-Katz Ida. |
| 6- 1-Eaves F. W.-Morley Kate L. | 3-29-Hale F. W.-Dixon Bertha E. | 11-25-Katzenstein M.-Lyon Sophia. |
| 10- 4-Ebert G. F-Burns Elizabeth J | 5-18-Hall Andrew-Diggs Ada. | 6- 9-Keeney C.H.-Strong MinnieE |
| 8- 9-Eccles P. J.-McCann Mary. | 6- 6-Hall H. M.-Woodward MaryE. | 5- 6-Keily James-King Lizzie. |
| 2- 8-Egan E. J.-Roberts Catherine | 5- 5-Hallberg B.-WidellEllenM.T. | 6-30-Kellen C. J.-Axelson HildaT. |
| 11-24-Eisle Louis F.-Fox Caroline E. | 3-18-Hallman Jacob-WattonLizzie | 11-23-Kelley E. W.-Hale Harriett E |
| 6- 9-Ellis Geo.W.-Corson Annie F. | 9-27-Hamel P. F.-Gratton Anna M. | 6-80-Kelley J.D.-Connor Sabina A |
| 4-21-Elmer E. O.-Rowley Carrie L. | 6-12-Hamilton F.-Bowman Ellen. | 6- 1-Kelley J. H.-Tenney Alice E. |
| 5-17-Emond Joseph-Drolet Mary. | 6-12-HamiltonJ.H.-Peterson Cath. | 2-30-Kelley J. M.-Donohue MaryE |
| 6-30-Enauder C.O.-Hanson Matilda | 6- 9-HamiltonM.C.-BurnhamM.A. | 4-21-Kelley T. J.-Selden Julia G. |
| 2-27-Erickson E.-Freidenfelt T. | 10-26-Hamilton W. T.-Hall Etta M. | 10- 6-Kelly Jas.-Allen Elizabeth. |
| 6-11-Evans Hugh-Colburn Mary. | 2-17-Hansel C. R.-Hastings H. D. | 2-20-Kelly Paul-Johnson Rose. |
| | 3-12-Hansen Ernest-Toft Anna. | 11-10-KennedyH.M-Broderick L.M |
| 6-30-Fanelli L.-Cardone Delna. | 4- 2-Hansen Paul-Leide Karoline. | 9- 8-KennedyT.J.-DannaherB.M. |
| 6-16-Farley G. P.-Ingalls Grace. | 6-23-Harder L. D.-Holmes Lora E. | 10- 4-Kenyon F. H.-Maslen C. L. |
| 1- 7-Felder Chas.-Nitsch Annie. | 8-31-Harriman E.A.-Ray Bertha C. | 12-24-Kenyon M. G.-Phelps Alice F. |
| 3-18-Felix Frank-Pesci Mary. | 7-27-Harrington J.-Martin May. | 8-16-Kiffe John R -Wescott Bessie |
| 6-17-FieldW.E-Williams Charlotte | 10- 7-Haskell W. R.-Cook Kittie S. | 12-29-Killiard T.-Curtin Agnes B. |
| 6-30-Fischer G. B.-Frosin Annie M. | 10-29-Hayden J. D.-Dubuschere E. | 8- 4-Killin J. A.-SullivanDelia A. |
| 9-25-Fish A. W.-Johnson Effie M. | 2- 2-Hayes J.-Gorman Antonella. | 1-26-Kilmurra y W.-Flannery Kate |
| 12-14-Fisk Wm. L.-Hall Amelia. | 7-28-Heath William-Jones Millie. | 11-25-King M.-Carrahle Mary B. |
| 6-23-Fitzpatrick F.J.-Winters A.J. | 6-16-Hebb D. B.-Norcross Edna M. | 2-17-King Wm. H.-Locker Mary. |
| 7-10-FitzpatrickJ.-MorganBridget | 1-14-Helder Max-Brewer Nellie L. | 4-29-Kingsley R. C.-FarnhamM.B. |
| 7- 5-Fitzpatrick P.-Poland Cath. | 1-11-Hellberg G.F.-WarnerMary T | 6-15-Klein Jacob-Miles Rose. |
| 6-10-Flint E. R.-Brown Harriet D. | 1-21-HensonF.-ThompsonGraceL. | 5-15-Knuschke C.D.-Myers Carrie |
| 11-10-FlintW.E.-TaylorFlorenceM. | 6-16-Herman A. A.-Barwold Sadie | 4-24-Koch A.-Polovitz Juliana. |
| 5- 1-PlipowskiK.-RadwillsEliz'bh | 12-18-Higgins C. J.-Donovan Nora. | 10-27-Krauth A. G.-Brown Mary I. |
| 11-10-Flynn C. P.-Kelley Cath. C. | 2-24-Hill C. C.-Turner Fannie G. | 9-22-Kuerett T. M.-Rotchford A. |
| 12-22-Fogg E. H.-Wilcox Mary E. | 6-16-Hill F. A.-Marenholtz Josie J. | 12-23-Kuhm E.-McGintyBridget D. |
| 12-23-Ford T. E.-Minnehan Nellie. | 9- 4-Hill Percival H.-Lewis Ella F. | 11-17-Kummell H. J.-Scott F. A. |
| 1- 6-Forgie J. R.-SpenceMargaret. | 10-27-Hills A. K.-Collins Jennie E. | |
| 7- 1-Forster John B.-Taft Mary R. | 6- 8-Hills A. M.-Pierson Hettie A. | 10-26-Lahey L. S.-Connor Mary C. |
| 7-81-Fowler H.-Farquhor Hannah. | 6-16-Hills E. S.-GubitzCaroline M. | 11-25-Laing John-Tisdall Lizzie. |
| 6-28-Franklin G. A.-Anderson M. | 6-80-Hills Frank F-Little Lida M. | 2-25-Lamphone G.-Drago Annie. |
| 10-16-Franks J. B.-Gunshannon A. | 1- 7-Hirsh Jacob-Lorsch Mary A. | 9-80-Langdon J. F.-Riley Emma S |
| 12-16-Fraser William-Burns Mary. | 7-14-Hitchcock W. E.-Allen Ida M. | 8-26-Laranche E.-Powers MinnieJ. |
| 2-27-Frendberg A.-Peterson Aug. | 7- 2-Hoffman H. E.-BeebeAnna E. | 12- 8-Lardau Emil-Brown Emily. |
| 8-25-Furlong Wm.-Shea Maggie. | 6-10-Hogle H.H.-Forsyth Addie C. | 1-20-Larock J.-McCollough Mary |
| 10-12-Fusler W. H.-Kemp Annie M. | 2-24-HolcombE.L.-McAviny Helen | 12- 4-Larson J.-NoeringSelma C.T. |
| | 5- 6-Hollfelder J.-Welke Edith M. | 10-27-Larson P. N.-Larson H. E. |
| 2-10-Gaffey J.J.-KeenanCatherine | 11-17-Hollis F. G.-Bates Edith M. | 2-24-LaurentA.-GervaisJoseph'ne |
| 6-12-Gaffney P. F.-McLagan A. D. | 1- 9-HolmK.J-NeilsonElizabeth F | 1- 6-Layland E. W.-VogelAnna J. |
| 6-39-Gallagher J. J.-Ganley Kate. | 2- 8-Holt Frank C.-Connell Lizzie. | 4-10-Leclerc M.-Freeman Mary. |
| 2-22-Gammon P. F.-Marra Minnie | 10-20-Hooper C. E.-Phelan Anna N. | 5-22-Lee H. A. H.-Redell Marie. |
| 8- 9-Garrity T.F.-Cummings A.M. | 11-28-Horgan John-O'Keefe Ellen. | 11-25-Lewis H. G.-Donovan C. V. |
| 11-25-Gasner A.-Killpatrick Annie. | 5-11-Horsman R.-Walsh Mary A. | 1- 4-Lewis L. B.-Brewster H. A. |
| 4-19-Geiger B.-Knauss Marie. | 1- 7-Horton A. G.-Stace Emma J. | 9- 8-Lewis Thomas-Hatch Clara. |
| 4-12-German Isaac-Towler Ida B. | 4- 7-Horwltz C.-Gerstein Minnie. | 11-24-Lincoln R. M.-Smith Julia A. |
| 7-24-Gibbs J. W.-Seaton Mary E. | 5- 1-Houghland A.P.-Gustofson E. | 4- 8-Lindgren P. O.-Beckman M.J |
| 12-11-Gibstein Sam'l-Falk Rebecca. | 6-30-Huling Chas. S.-Dart Addie A. | 10-24-Linser F.-McGuire Mary. |
| 6- 2-Gilligan Thos.-Branick Mary. | 5-12-Hunt James-Scanlon Mary. | 6-28-Linsley H. G.-Stannard E. |
| 9-27-Giorgio A.-Pietro Anna T. | 2-28-Hurley C.-Winkler Amelia. | 9- 4-LittleR.S.-Haythorn Edith M. |
| 5- 2-GiosciaM.-DeAmatoCarmela. | 1-16-Husted N. N.-Olesen Julie. | 8-22-Little Robert-Sibley Annie. |
| 8-30-Giovenal G.-Botasso Paulina. | 5-19-Hyde F. W.-Miller A. L. | 11-18-Lockwood L.V.-Bunnell A.G. |
| 6- 9-Giodell L. M.-McCarthy A.M | 2-28-Hyland T.-Murphy Nellie J. | 4-19-Longdon A.C.-Cooper Effie L. |
| 6-16-GlueckBernhare-HahmMary. | | 6-16-Loomis A. C.-Markham A. L. |
| 8- 2-Goldenthal B.-Kantrovitz A. | 6- 9-Ierardi N.-DeCorleto MarieG. | 11-17-Loomis F.W.-Clapp Louise C. |
| 8-81-Goldstein G.-Blumenthal R. | 8-16-Ingraham W. A.-Clegg M. A. | 10-11-Loomis R. W.-Fuller Anna D. |
| 10-12-Goodrich D. T.-Smith Etta J. | 11- 8-Ives Ralph B.-King Edith M. | 1-28-Lord A. E.-Warner MildredE. |
| 1- 6-Gordon J. E.-Thompson F.E. | | 2-17-Loughlin J. J.-Joyce Bridget. |
| 4-18-Gough A. C.-Rodda Emma. | 8- 4-Jackson Chas.-Carlson Annie. | 6- 1-Lufkin DavidT.-Lufkin A.A. |
| 9-15-Gourlie W. P.-Henry H. E. | 10-14-Jackson J. D.-Cameron J. | 6-80-Lull L.-Harrison Carrie. |
| 9- 1-Grady John-McCann Maggie. | 2-20-Jacobson A.-Sanelen Selma. | 8- 2-Lux Carl E.-Clark Alice D. |
| 6-16-Grady J. J.-Munsell Grace M. | 11- 1-Janke Julian-Nass Annie. | 9- 4-Lux Geo. L.-Rowe Nellie N. |
| 9-15-Graham C. J.-Ahearn Gert'de. | 11-27-James A.-Osmond Lillie R. | 6-16-Lyons Michael-Belden Mary. |
| 2- 8-Graham Geo.-Cooney Mary. | 9-15-Johnson A. W.-Manion Clara. | 11-25-Lyons Thos. J.-Long Bridget. |
| 6- 9-Green J. S.-Taylor Maria F. | 7-22-Johnson C.A.-KelleherKittie. | 7-14-Lynch D. J.-Coughlin E. R. |
| 1-16-Griffin Geo. F-Nihill Mary. | 11-24-Johnson E.E.-Fielding MaryE | 8-27-Lynch Jos.-Sullivan Mary. |
| 6-26-Griggs J. B.-Bolter Mary E. | 6-29-Johnson G. L.-Coan Delia A. | |
| 10-12-Griswold J. P.-Brown Mary J. | 3- 5-Johnson H. W.-Thayer M. L. | 2- 1-MacDonald W. B.-Nielson K. |
| 6- 1-Griswold G. T.-East A. M. | 12-16-Johnson J.A.-Peterson Clara. | 10-27-Madden F. O'Connor Annie. |
| 10- 5-GuertinN.P.-BelangerMaryL | 3-5-Johnson Jas G.-Hafey ―― | 6- 9-MadiganM.-Donovan Elizb'h. |
| 7-20-Guilfoil W. J.-KelleyMaryE. | 12- 8-Johnson L. S.-Holcombe C. F. | 8-28-Madsen C.-Carlson Kirstine. |
| 2-24-Guinan M. J.-Fitzpatrick A. | 7- 8-Jones Wm. A.-Carter Mary. | |

12- 1-Main Louis S.-Butler May E.
4-29-Malone Jas. F.-Green Bridget
10-80-Marrain E.A.-Parker AliceM.
4- 5-Marston R. E.-Root Emily.
6-16-Martin J. F.-McKeough J. J.
5-19-Martin Leon E.-Minse Nellie.
7-30-MartinsonC.-Johanson Hilma
6- 9-Marvel L.M.-DuCharmie M.E
10- 9-Marvin C. H.-Litchfield L. L.
6-16-Mason A. J.-Bartlett M. M.
12-22-Matthews A. V.-French M. E.
7-18-Maurice J. H.-Torrey L. G.
11- 8-McAdams F.A.-Buckley M.E.
10-14-McCarthyC.J.-CondronNellie
1-12-McCarthy Wm.-King Marg't.
5-26-McCatee Chas.-Rohn Mary.
6- 4-McClarren M.-Sweeney B.
2-24-McClean Jos. -Watson Anna.
6-30-McClunie G.G.-CallenderA.S.
6- 9-McDermott J.F.-Connell C.J.
1-27-McDonald JW-BatchellerME
4-21-McHenry T.-Jackson Hattie.
10-27-McIntyre E. T.-Cassells M. E.
9-16-McKay John-Whaska Mary.
4-20-McKee P. F.-Tracy Lillie.
10-27-McMonegle D.-Pokrain V.
6- 1-Meehan John-Dolan Annie.
8-18-Meehan P.J.-Doheny Bridget
8-14-Menges Wm.-Rosen Annie.
6-22-Mere Frank-Donahue Mamie
4-12-MerrittG.S.-KibbeFlorenceA.
6-12-Messinger E.E.-PeckAnnieL.
12-27-Micheloritz W.-Katz Rosa.
7-22-Milikowski A.J.-Dorsey M.E.
5- 2-Miller A. W.-Kastner Louise.
12- 2-Miller W.E.-JohnsonAnnieC.
4-28-Miner E. M.-Abell Rose I.
2-24-Missett Jas. E.-Cotter Cath.
9-28-Mitchill Lee-Harris Pattie.
8-23-Moffitt P.-Sullivan Nellie.
6-16-Mooney N.-Cronin Julia.
1-18-Moore W. H.-McMaster M.J.
1-11-Moran J. P.-Smith Kittie A.
6-24-Morana Henry-Speigel Etta.
2-10-Morris James J.-Daly Rose.
8- 8-Moser Julius-Taksir Marie.
6-26-Moynihan F.-Beiswanger M.
10-18-Mucke E. E.-Rosenberg A.
11-17-Mullady P.-Duham Cath.
10-18-Mulrane T.-Grennan Ellen.
8- 4-Munro Jas.-Harvey Mary A.
2-10-Murphy Patrick-Grady Nora.
9-20-Murphy S. A.-Walsh Mary F.
9-30-MurphyW.H.-O'ConnorK.A.
12-21-MurrayP.J-O'Connell Annie.
8-31-MurrayW.H.-Vessells Bessie.
6-30-Murtagh M. M.-HansonKate.

8- 8-NashG.-BuckleyElizabeth A.
4-24-Naumann R.-Miller Annie.
8-24-Neal C. W.-Roloff Lillian B.
12-29-Nelson E.-Stromquist E. L. B.
6-28-Nichols E. B.-Carleton M. L.
6-30-Nichols G. W.-StoneJennie A
10-26-Nichols W. C.-Speath E. M.
10- 6-Nordlund E.-Johanson M, G.
3-17-Nordstrom P.-Pierson Emma.
10-80-Nugent Dan'l-Walters Nellie.
7- 8-Nyman N.-Swenson HilmaE.

11-20-O'Brien Daniel-Curtin Lizzie
3-17-O'Connor J. W.-Hadley J. E.
8-18-O'Connor T.-BrennanJuliaT.
2-27-O'Donnell W.J.-Reiley Annie.
10- 6-Ogden F.S.-Hancock Gert'de
2-24-O'Hern P.-Featherstone K.
12-31-Ohliger A.-Schmidt Annie.
11- 8-O'Keefe M.-Mulcahy MaryL.
12-81 OlderAbraham-LavineBessie

10- 5-O'Leary D.-Brennan Ellen.
9- 6-O'Neil J. F.-Bailey Stella G.
7-31-O'Neil W. H.-Keegan C. T.
6-16-O'NeillA.F.-McLaughlinE.M
6- 9-O'Neill T.-Devine Elizabeth.
3-10-Oppelt W.-Wilkinson Sarah.
7-21-Owen J.-Rowley Jennie P.

4-21-Paine O. T.-Hart Sarah M.
7-12-Palmer E.-Stace Mary E.
8-27-Parchall J.F.-Beakerr Mary.
10-14-Parmelee C. C.-Turner M. A.
8-22-Pasco W. E.-Leicock B. E.
10- 4-Pease O. L.-Gibbs Maude E.
10-12-Pease Wm. H.-Wright V. E.
12-28-Percy C. D.-Robinson E. J.
10- 5-Peterson A.-Svendsen Else.
4-29-Peterson J. E -Erikson J. J.
4-17-Peterson O. L.-Svenson E. G.
9-25-Peterson P. C.-Hehbe Eva M.
1-28-Phelps F. S.-Bradley L. A.
1-23-Phillips C. A.-Robinson F. A.
1- 6-PikeSherman-Bogart Jennie.
9-30-Pitkin C. A.Jr.-Fox Lidia A.
5-28-Potholu C. P.-Peterson C.M.
5-16-Prairie C. A.-Millet Exina.
1-19-Prass Fred-Miller Elizabeth.
5-18-Pratt A.B-HempreeBertha E.
8-16-Press Harvy-Kramer Harvy.
11-10-Purdue A. J.-Hopkins A. B.
4- 9-Putney L. G.-Buckland Julia

12-25-Radway C.-McCulley H.
12- 2-Ragan T.-McGovern Cath.
8- 4-Ramsdell C. A.-Tucker A.B.
6-22-RandallB W-MillerAugustaA
11-24-Ray Chas. R -Noyes Lena M.
3-28-Read G. H.-Gallagher Annie.
10- 6-Reardon C. J.-Flynn Ellen T.
10-14-Reiche H. C. Jr.-Grauer A.
4-27-Reilly John-Donovan Kate.
8-16-Reinhart M.-Abraham Lena.
2-11-ReynoldsA.-FentonJennieM.
12-29-RichardsD.T.-KeneosonA.R.
11-25-Richards L.W-KelleyEliz'bth
6-23-Riggs T. D.-Lanman Laura T.
4-28-Riley C. F.-Hines Mary L.
9-28-Riley W. J.-Gallagher Julia.
5-16-Rioux Olivier-LaRose Julia.
2-25-RobertsG.L-DrewGertrudeE.
6-15-RobinsD.-JacobsonHenrietta
11-17-Rock J. J.-CrowleyMargaret.
8-25-Ronan Thos.-Bannon Mary J.
8-22-Root E. B.-Carroll Clara M.
8-23-Root L. S.-Bulkeley Bertha L.
11-23-Rousseau A.-Croistiere M.
5- 8-Rouzina Jos.-Maffia Carmila.
10-14-Rowley W. H.-Thurston S. K
2-16-Rubright B. A.-Bridle Sadie.
11-13-Rudis Wm.-Zukanski Agnes.
7-17-Rudkins C.-Maleuski Annie.
3-30-Ruoff.John-LudwigCatherine.
6-28-Russell L. H.-Harris Lilla M.
1-10-Russo Tony-Domato Rosie.
3-16-Ryan Jas. F.-Kuss Agnes.
4-28-Ryan M. W.-Loughlin Marg't

9-22-Sargent F. A.-Roberts A. M.
11- 3-Sawyer E. M.-Kimball W. L.
10-25-Sayers T.-Landers Josephine
8- 6-Scanlon J.-Sinhee Johanna.
4-28-Scanlon J. W.-Cotter Sara A.
11-17-Scannell T.-Bermingham E.
10- 2-Schofield H. B.-Huntley G.
3-18-Schmid John-GompperC. L.
12-18-Schmidt M.-Schwirz Martha.
4-29-Schmitter F. K.-Knauth M.

1-20-Schuler L. A.-Mitchill J. J.
2- 8-Schuman W. H.-Little M. E.
10-28-Schwarting H.-Kantzki L.
6-28-Scott L.-Fuller Florence.
7-28-Seders R. S.-Grannis Edith.
1-26-Segur N.-Simpson Mary E.
11-12-SeinsothF.A.-GreenLouiseD.
4-21-Shaffer C. O.-Shipman E. H.
6-28-Shea John-Joyce Julia L.
5-15-Sheehan Thos.-Noone Delia.
9-18-Shepard H.H.-Patten Alice R.
10-27-Shields D. P.-Kenny Julia A.
6-14-Silver Wolf-Mazier Jennie.
3-28-Simon G. A.-Selde Esther.
2-10-Simonson A. H.-Miller B. C.
6- 2-Simpkins W. F.-Mertens J.
10-18-SimpsonJ.M.-Jones AbbieM.
10-20-Skelly J. F.-Spollen Mary J.
1-19-Skelley M.-Reilly Annie Y.
10-18-Sloan Michael-King Mary.
10-28-Smith F. J.-Maher Anastasia.
6- 9-Smith F. M.-Abernethy S. E.
2-18-Smith G.C.-O'Connell Maggie
1-21-Smith J.C.-Thompson Grace.
6-28-Smith J.M-Watson IsabellaC.
10- 6-Smith S. R.-Willis Hattie E.
1-28-Solomon J.-Berkovitch M. E.
6-30-Somerville W.J.-Dudley M.J.
2-10-Soper A. A.-Rivers Mary J.
10-10-Sorcio P.-Ferrada Rafhal.
11- 7-Sorehr H. V.-Leining E. L.
11-14-Stager F.-Bongrauz Mary.
6-19-Starkey F.D.-KelseyEmma L.
1- 2-Starr Edward-Quinn Kittie.
11-24-Starr J. C.-Schonhaar A. M.
11-16-States F. O.-Russell Mary E.
7- 8-Staufenbil R.-Pond Cora S.
6-28-Steele G.W.-Thirkeld MaryE.
10-11-Stevens Wm.-Court Mary E.
7-21-Still Wm.C.-Moran Margaret.
9- 8-Stone C. E.-Tavenia Selma.
10-25-Storm E. C.-Merrifield Mary.
10-30-StrausHerman-KahlAugusta
2-16-Sturtevant E.W.-GreeneH.L.
6-23-Sullivan D.-Cronin Catherine
3- 2-Sullivan H.-Kenney Mary.
6- 1-Sullivan T.-Crane Elizabeth.
8-14-Swanson A.-Johnson Emma.

3- 2-Tait HarveyJ.-Hare Blanche.
2- 6-Talcott G. J.-Clapp Grace P.
2-Tatro F.J.-Bidgood Ida May.
12- 9-Taylor A.-Battle Nanie H.
7-14-Taylor Frank-Camp Hattie.
9-28-Taylor J. E.-Rodgers Elsie M.
1-18-Taylor R. T.-Lewis Mary E.
9- 8-Teeney M. A.-Thornton M.A.
9- 5-Tony Nysot-Romato Mary.
10- 5-Thacker W.R.-Murdock C.L.
7- 5-Thompson I.J.-WebbGrace L.
9-21-ThompsonL.W.-HoskinsH.F.
11-24-Tiagwad C.-FrederiksenA.M.
10-15-Tonng Geo.-Jordan Julia A.
5- 5-Tooley Chas.M.-RabsAnnaA.
9-14-Tracey James-Green Esther.
12-15-Traute A.H.-Woerner Emily.
8-18-Trelor W. J.-Potter Grace.
5-18-Trolin C. L.-Ledin Jennie A.
4-29-Tully P. J.-TierneyMargaret
7-5-Turner Jos.-O'Neil Maggie.
5-24-Twaddle James-Robb Jessie.
2-17-Twaddle Wm.-Odette Mary.
1-16-Tygeson J.-Johnson Matilda.

11-25-Urichio G.-Marzanio Rosina.

5- 5-Valentine E.-Wurther Anna.
2-11-Valentine G.L.-Wheeler H.H.

9- 4-Vester Thos.-Swenson Olga.
4-31-Vincent H. M.-Debler Mary.
6-24-Vincent Jas.-Snow Lizzie G.
6-27-Vincenzo S.-Salvato Francis.
10-20-Vining E. W.-Crocker May L.

1-20-Waldron Thos.-Naster Bridget
9- 8-Wall J. E.-Turnstall Louise.
3-24-Walsh R. M.-Barnard Eva.
5-20-Walsh S.-Dalton Bridget.
7-21-Ward Jas. A.-Rice Edith W.
9-29-Warren Wm.-Brown Earsular.
12-28-Washburn A. L.-Hollister N.B
3-10-Waters Geo.-Strickland I. L.
6- 2-Watrous F.C.-Fargo Lillian C.
3-24-Watson Jas.-Wright Robina.
9-15-Webster D.-Dicks Annie M.
12- 1-Wedberg F.E.-Osterlund A.M.
2-23-Weed E.S.-McKnight Emma
4- 8-Weider J.-Gutman Leola.
5- 6-Weir Warren M.-Smith Ettie.
9-22-Welch G. H.-Marble Sarah M.
10-26-Welch P.-Halloran Catherine.
1-21-Weller Fred-Herold Selma.
2-24-Wells L. E.-Lyman Lena L.
6-12-Wesnstein M.-Lachner Ann.
10-28-West H. J.-Whitney Grace M.
1-27-Weyant R. J.-Bonel Effie.
10-18-Wheeler C. E.-McIntyre M.
8-30-White Ralph-Pillon Annie.
3- 2-Whitman Geo.-Lee Mary A.
4- 8-Whitman J. L.-Whitman N.
4-14-Whittemore E. J.-Still Annie E.
6-13-Wiggins Geo. E.-Keith F. E.
1-28-Wilcox D. A.-Hurlburt C. A.
3- 9-Wilensky C.-Applebaum Ette.
10-29-Williams G. W.-Smith Maria.
12- 8-Williams Jas. Gardner Sarah.
11- 2-Williams Wm. H.-Page Ida F.
5-25-Willson E. C.-Francis B. E.
6-11-Wind H.G.-Nielsen Dorthea M.
11-24-Wood Bert L.-Hyland Rose.
12-20-Wooley A.E.-Greany Marion A.
11-24-Wright F. O.-Taylor Alice F.
1-25-Wright L. F.-Holmes Mary J.
3-15-Wyckoff C. S.-Day Harriet B.

4-29-Yocovone J.-Perigal Isabella.
9-28-Young E. C.-Downs Lulu.
5-11-Young J.C-Shelton Frances E.

4-21-Zantow W. F.-McGrath A. E.
6-22-Zoels Gustav-Berger Lizzie.

---

## Births

## IN HARTFORD, DURING 1897.

*The first figures in each line indicate the month in the year 1897, and the second figures the date of the month of birth; d for daughter, s for son; the first name is of the husband, the second of the wife.*

4- 4-d-Abesantra Luke-Maggie.
11-20-s-Abramorwitz M. -Sophia.
2- 4-s-Abske Louis-Merkine.
8-d-20-Aconco Peter-Quassn M.
1- 9-d-Addison Alfred-Mary R.
2- 8-s-Adkins Frank H.-Ella H.

7-d- 9-Adodo Jehn-Jerka U.
9- 9-d-Aeno Mori-Mary.
9-24-d-Ahern Michael-Kittie.
10-20-s-Ahern Michael F.-Mary A.
3-21-s-Ahern Morris-Annie.
6-12-d-Ahern William-Nellie.
12-23-d-Alban Abraham-Betoey
10-23-d-Alexander Loui-Fannie.
2-19-d-Allarde Jeffred R.-Louisa.
3-26-d-Allen Bernard-Charlotte.
2-26-s-Allen Elmer A.-Mabel V.
5-20-s-Allen Oscar-Margaret.
7-26-d-Allen William-Mary.
1-26-d-Allesandre Joseph-Annie.
1-16-s-Allis Ferdinand-Anna.
8- 3-s-Allison F. A.-Margaret J.
8-11-s-Alphonse F. C.-Melina.
5-17-s-Alston John-Jennie.
1-11-s-Ambrowzo Alphonse-Mary
8-16-s-Anderson Alml E.-M. L.
7-21-d-Anderson Aug. W.-Ella A.
7-19-d-Anderson C. M.-Christlin.
8-29-d-Anderson James W.-A.
12-28-s-Anderson J. D.-Jennie.
12- 7-s-Anderson Marten-Julia.
11-14-s-Anderson Oscar-Olida.
1-16-d-Anderson Paul-Johanna.
8-10-s-Anderson Peter-
9-28-s-Anderson Peter-Agnes.
1-24-s-Anderson Peter-Anna
12-17-s-Anderson Thos.-Christine.
12-29-d-Argard Charles-Kate.
1-12-s-Angelo James-Christina.
8-3-d-Arnold Walter-Helena.
4-26-d-Aroin Bernard-Bertha.
6- 5-s-Aroson Herman-Fueda.
8- 8-s-Arthur Geo. T.-Anna L.
8- 3-d-Asgard Charles-H. A.
10- 9-s-Ashmore Andrew-Ellen.
8-11-d-Askeland John-Augustus.
6-27-d-Austin Edwin L-Jennie A.

12-31-s-Babcock E. J.-Margaret
10-d-20-Babom Henry-Jerusha
8-12-s-Back Meyer-Rosie.
12-17-s-Baker Robert-Celia.
10-19-s-Balance Joseph-Emma.
8-23-s-Baldwin C. R.-Alice A.
2-19-d-Balfour James-Grace.
4-29-s-Balinson Rudolph-Mariah
9-'5-d-Ball Julius-Hattie.
7-15-d-Ballahfsky Halle-Minnie.
12-25-d-Bane Thomas J.-Susie E.
2-15-s-Bannon John-Bridget.
9-26-d-Barber Andrew-Lucy B.
5-24-d-Barbour Wilbur-Florence.
11- 8-s-Bardwell Arthur-Hattie S.
8-24-d-Barey Thomas-Mary.
7-16-s-Barggoman John-Mary.
2-20-s-Barlow Chas. H.-Ida May.
10-11-s-Barnesky Edward-Maudy.
11- 2-d-Barrett George-Annie.
6-30-s-Barrows E. R.-Annie L.
8-17-s-Barrows F. W.-Margaret.
8- 1-d Barry John-Winifred.
4-26-d-Bartha Charles-Lizzie. }
4-26-d-Bartha Charles-Lizzie. }
10-11-d-Bartlett John L.-Annie G.
10-21-d-Bartlett William-Grace.
7- 4-s-Bartner Samuel-Fannie.
7- 5-s-Bashman Ike-Ida.
5-24-d-Baxon Henry-Ida.
5-19-d-Batchelder J.W.-Margaret
2-28-s-Batty William H.-Mary.
5-19-s-Baudren Henry-Elizabeth
4- 3-d-Baus Julia-Eniske.
11- 7-d-Bayne John-Mary.
9-d- 8-Beam Jacob-Susan W.

1-11-d-Bean Leon H-Lula E.
2-27-s-Beardslee C. S.-Emma G.
2-28-s-Beaudry Ray F.-Alice.
8-14-d-Beck Abraham-Anna.
2-12-s-Beck Jacob-Minnie.
4-14-d-Becker C. W.-Fanny R.
7- 2-s-Becker Benjamin-Rachel.
11- 8-d-Beebe Edward-Aeline.
11- 6-d-Behrman J. D.-Tilda.
4-17-d-Bekowitch Abe-Annie.
12-28-s-Belanger Joseph-Agnes.
6-19-d-Belcher Jonathan W.-Ella.
2- 6-Belden Chas. H.-Hattie E.
9- 5-d-Belisky -Sophia.
6- 6-d-Bennett Michael-Margaret
8-29-s-Benson Edward-Mary A.
1- 3-d-Benson Joseph-Annie.
6-20-d-Benson Lin-Annie.
10-27-s-Berg George-Theresa.
12-22-s-Berge Chas. N.-Martha. }
12-22-s-Berge Chas. N.-Martha. }
6-30-s-Bering Peter-Fanny.
11- 6-d-Berman Abe-Sarah.
9-11-s-Bernard Napoleon-Fanny.
11- 6-d-Berregan Keron-Mary.
11- 6-s-Berry Barney-Ethe.
12-21-s-Berry George-Grace.
1- 7-d-Berry William-Nora.
10-27-s-Bidwell F. W.-Elizabeth.
6-16-d-Bill Albert C-Bessie.
9-18-d-Bill Fred R.-Minnie J.
7-18-s-Bird Charles-Laura.
9-14-s-Bishop F. L.-Florence L.
12-23-s-Bissell Henry-Martha J.
1-16-s-Blair Frank-Mary Belle.
5-26-s-Blair James-Isabella C.
5-26-s-Blair N-
7-17-s-Blake John F.-Gertrude.
4-18-d-Blazer Frank-Mary.
12-1-d-Blazer Juon-Mary.
7- 8-s-Blivins William-Caroline.
8-22-d-Blonlguist Martin-H-
9-30-Blumenthal Max-
8-21-s-Bogardees A. N.-Elizabeth
5-17-s-Bogeir Bernard-Jetti.
4- 5-d-Bohman Alfred-Ida.
9-25-s-Boisrert-Felix-Marie.
8-16-s-Boissein John-Harriet.
12-24-s-Bonee Dominoc-Angela.
2- 1-s-Bonifacio L.-Philomena.
7-30-s-Bonner William-Mary.
11- 8-d-Booth Edwin-Lousi C.
10-27-d-Bordenstein H.-Katie L.
9-24-s-Borgenholtz John-T-
8-25-s-Boss Walter-Julia.
10-31-s-Bourselski Frank E.-Olin.
4-18-d-Bowe Albert H.-Tillie.
7-21-d-Bowers Frank-Emma E.
1-10-d-Boyce George J.-Margaret
4-10-s-Boyce Robt. H.-Elizabeth.
2- 4-s-Bradley Josiah-Hanna.
8-30-s-Brado Johano-Margaret.
3-12-s-Brady John-Lizzie.
12-15-s-Brainard Fred'k J.-Sarah.
6-17-d-Brandt Edward-Matilda.
2-17-s-Brassell Edward-Anna.
11-27-s-Brazell William-Bridget.
11- 2-d-Breen John H.-Delia.
11- 2-d-Brennig Anton-Augusta.
2-17-s-Brenser C. F.-Josie.
8-21-d-Bresson Joseph-Vitaline.
5-19-s-Brett John H.-Betty.
8- 4-s-Brewer Chas. H.-Minnie.
2-d-Brewer Michael-Mary.
5-19-d-Brewster John-Bridget.
4-22-s-Briggs C. O.-Gertrude. }
4-22-d-Briggs C. O.-Gertrude. }
12-12-s-Brink Frederick-Maggie.

1-18-s-Brink Fritz-Maggie.
5- 2-s-Britt S.-Caroline.
4-17-s-Brizina Tonil-Maria.
2-10-s-Broadhurst Leon P.-Alice.
5-17-s-Broccosin Joseph-Mary.
11-22-d-Brodecina H. H.-Evelina.
6-18-s-Broden Archie J.- ————
11- 7-d-Broderick Dennis-Mary. }
11- 7-d-Broderick Dennis-Mary. }
5-10-s-Broderick T. A.-Elizabeth
10-25-d-Brodrib John-Alice M.
2-15-s-Brody Israel-Jennie.
9-24-s-Brott George-Carrie M.
3-17-s-Bro't James O.-Mattie.
4-29-s-Broughel John J.- ————
6-13-s-Brown Andrew-Maria.
1- 5-d-Brown Chas. M.-Hattie.
4-16-s-Brown Edw. V.-Cora E. }
4-16-d-Brown Edw. V.-Cora E. {
10-23-d-Brown Harry-Flora.
7-16-d-Brown William-Edith.
6-30-s-Bruce Benjamin- ————
11-22-s-Bruce Geo. P.-Daisy May.
9-26-s-Bruce William H.-Cora B.
1-17-s-Bublitz John-Anna.
10-33-d-Buckley D. P.-Annie B.
7-23-d-Buckley Edw. L.-Agnes.
12- 1-s-Buckley James W.-Ellen.
7-29-s-Buckley Lawrence.-Alice.
12- 4-d-Buckley Wm. J.-Kittie.
1-15-d-Budd James-Rebecca.
8-20-d-Budge Edw. C.-Annie B.
1- 2-s-Bugron John-Isabella.
7- 3-s-Bulkeley John C.-Mabel L.
5-29-s-Burgey Fred W.-Jennie.
2- 7-d-Burk J. J.-Elizabeth M.
1- 3-s-Burke James L -Catherine
5-14-d-Burns Bernard-Julia.
12-26-s-Burns Daniel-Mary.
9- 8-d-Burns Edward-Annie.
10-19-s-Burns Edward-Margaret.
8- 7-s-Burns James-Mary.
3-21-d-Burns James-Mary A.
9-d-27-Burns Zalmon-Xena J.
6-23-d-Burton Geo. W.-Jennie.
7- 6-s-Butler George-Hattie.
8-26-d-Byxbie Edward-Effie.

4- 2-s-Cahill Daniel-Kate.
12-20-d-Cahill John-Catherine.
8-14-d-Cahill M.-Margaret.
5-11-d-Cahill Patrick-Celia.
1-18-s-Cahill William-Evelyn.
8-28-d-Cahill William-Mary.
12-18-s-Cairnes Edw. T-Elizabeth.
7- 8-d-Calder John-Elizabeth.
2-18-d-Callaghan J. J. O.-Julia.
8-20-d-Callahan Thomas-Mary.
7-31-d-Calloni John- ————
8-21-s-Cameron Robt.-Margaret.
1-27-s-Campagna John- ————
11-28-d-Campbell Geo. A.-Clara L.
4-25-d-Campble John-Bridget.
2-19-s-Cannon Edward-Mary.
7-29-d-Cannon Thomas-Mary.
5-81-s-Carbo John-Rosii.
10-14-s-Carey Daniel J.-Annie.
8- 6-s-Carey David-Mary.
1-12-d-Carey John-Mary.
12-23-s-Carey Thos. E.-Catherine.
12- 4-s-Carich Tony-Lena.
10-24-d-Carleton John W.- ————
7- 9-s-Carlson August-Amanda.
10-26-s-Carlson Emil-Matilda C.
3- 2-s-Carmel Frank-Delia.
4-16-s-Carmine Della.
10-21-s-Carney Peter-Minnie.
3-16-d-Carricia — -Christina.
2-11-s-Carro'l Deg'an-Hanna.

12-11-d-Carroll John L.-Maggie.
7-24-s-Casey N.-Alice.
6-13-s-Cassale Carmeni-Anna.
9-11-d-Cassidy Edward-Bridget.
11-18-s-Carter James-Ethel M.
5-11-s-Carua John-Mary.
5-16-s-Cavensela Sigmond-Alice.
8- 9-d-Cersosimo F.-Minnie A.
2-27-d-Cersosimo Joseph-Annie.
4-25-d-Cersosimo T.-Philomena.
11- 9-d-Champion C.-Charlotte.
6-18-d-Chapman M. J.-Elizabeth.
8- 6-s-Chaputre B.-Frances.
2- 2-s-Charbouneau O P.-Annie.
12-26-s-Charnagelin Geo.-Annie.
4-27-s-Chase F. H- ————
6-15-s-Chase Oak A.-Annie.
1- 9-s-Chausse Michael-AnnieM.
11- 6-d-Chesler Benjamin-Fanny.
12-11-d-Childs John-Mary.
7-22-s-Chraigia John M.-C——
7- 1-s-Christensen C.-Bertha.
12- 8-d-Christensen Iver-Alma.
10- 7-d-Christensen N.-Annie.
2- 9-d-Christensen Neil-Katrina.
5-31-d-Christensen Peter-Mary.
11- 2-d-Christie Fred'k-Lizzie. }
11- 2-d-Christie Fred'k-Lizzie. }
7-20-d-Chump Peter-Catherine.
12-12-d-Church Edgar E.-Clara.
7-15-d-Church William-Mary.
6-26-s-Claffey George R.-Kitty.
12- 7-s-Chaffey Keron-Lizzie.
10-17-s-Clark Charles H.-Mary.
1-31-s-Clark Chester J.-Lottie.
6-16-s-Clark Henry-Annie.
9-18-s-Clark Henry-Annie.
1- 7-d-Clark John S.-Florence A.
10- 1-s-Clark Roscoe N.-Florence.
11- 4-d-Clarke Wm. F.-Helen E.
5-26-d-Clary John-Lillian.
3-10-d-Clegg Frank-Elizabeth.
8- 3-d-Clemansky Antonio-Mary
2- 2-d-Cleveland Orange-Rebeca
4- 5-s-Clifford Frank-Nellie.
8-24-d-Clough Geo. H.-Margaret.
9-25-d-Clough John R.-Dora.
6-19-d-Cody John-Kate.
7-10-d-Coer William H.-L. J.
6-10-s-Cohen Gustaf-Minnie.
4-13-d-Cohen Jacob-Annie.
11-12-s-Cohn Jacob-Lena.
11-21-d-Coleman James J.-Madge.
1-17-s-Coleman John-Emma.
3- 1-d-Coleman Michael-Nellie J.
9- 8-d-Coleman T. P.-Mabel L.
5- 8-s-Collins C. W.-Besse.
1- 2-d-Collins William J.-Ellen.
7- 8-s-Colton Edward M.-Minnie.
6-16-d-Cook Curtis C.-Georgia L.
1-14-d-Cook Joseph L.-Grace E.
7-31-d-Cook Patrick-Mary.
1- 9-s-Cook Robert J.-Annie.
8- 1-s-Conlon James-Mary.
2-14-s-Connant Patrick-Marg't.
2-11-s-Connelly Wm. L -Mary T.
11-12-s-Conners Hugh-Nellie.
11-30-d-Conners John-Nellie.
7- 6-d-Conners John R.-J. M.
5- 9-d-Conners Thomas-Bridget.
8-22-d-Connerton Pat'k-Bridget.
3-28-d-Connor Thomas-Elizabeth
6-23-d-Connors ——Alice.
11-11-d-Connors Thomas-Sarah.
6-25-s-ConnoverHerb't J.-Alice B
10-30-s-Conran James-Mary K.
2-23-d-Copeland Chas. H.-Minnie.
5- 7-s-Corcoran Michael-Jennie.

11-80-d-Costello Dominick-Mary.
12-16-d-Costello John-Mary.
11- 2-s-Costello Martin J.-Mary
1-30-s-Cotter Jerry-Mary.
10-10-s-Coughlin J. J.-Minnie.
4-11-s-Coughlin Patrick-Julia.
10-13-d-Coughlin Patrick-Marg't.
5- 2-s-Court John-Mary.
9- 4-s-Cowles Edwin T.-Ella C.
4-27-d-CowlesFred'k M-Charity S
6-25-s-Cowles James-Margaret.
6- 8-d-Cowles Samuel-Emma.
8- 4-s-Cowles Wm. H.-Alice L
12-d-25-Cramps Nat-Nancy Y.
10- 6-d-Crane Eugene-Mary.
8-27-d-Crane Martin-Hattie.
10-27-s-Crapulli Leo-Ausams.
3-11-s-Craven Martin-Annie.
6-21-d-Crimmons John-Mary.
1-10-d-Cristoff Fred-Emily.
12-26-s-Cuddegan Wm.-Cath. H.
2-10-d-Cunninghm Thos.-Mary.
8-15-d-Cunningham Tim'y-Mary.
9-18-d-Cunningham W-Claudine.
5-31-s-CunninghamWm.H-Susan
8-23-d-Curley David-Lizzie.
1-30-d-CurryHowardW-BerthaM.
1-16-d-Curtis Henry T.-Rose M.
1- 1-d-Curtis John W. ————
7- 4-d-Cusick Edward-Margaret.
8-25-d-Cusick William-Sarah.

7-22-d-Dabette — -Nellie.
12-30-d-Daffie Raphael-Sarafonia.
7-28-d-Dailey Matthew-Nellie.
5-30-d-Dailey William C.-Minnie.
8- 8-s-Daley George-Mary.
2-14-d-Daley James-Mary.
7-24-d-Daley Thomas- ————
5-14-s-Daly Jaines-Nellie.
6- 9-d-Daly James R.-Kate.
3-18-s-Daly Lawrence-Mary.
2- 2-d-Daly Thomas-Margaret.
6-14-s-Damery Wm. H.-Elizabeth
9-21-s-Daniel Lorenzo-Mabel.
11-28-d-Daniels Leonard C.-Grace.
12- 5-d-Danielson Gustav-Ellen.
8-d- 9-Dany Ambrose-Anna J.
6- 8-s-Darby James-Margaret.
1-14-s-Darno Lorenzo-Mamie.
5-29-s-Davidson John F.-Mary E.
1-14-d-Davies James- ————
8-22-s-Davis Arthur-C.
2-26-d-Davis Edger-Rose E.
11- 2-d-Davis Fred'k W.-Mary E.
8-15-s-Davis Reuben- ————
12-26-d-Davis W.-Mabel.
12- 4-s-Day George H.-Katherine.
10-16-s-Day Noah D.-Fannie I.
4- 6-s-Deago Nucenzio-Johanno.
10-16-d-Deaurieg Wm.Francis-Ella
10- 7-d-Deegan James-Sarah.
6-19-s-Deegan James F.-Annie.
4- 2-s-DeForen Geo. H. MinnieE.
12-31-s-D'Esopo Dominici-Teresa.
6-22-d-D'Esopo Leo-Rosie.
3-22-s-Delaney Wm. L.-Florence
10-18-d-DeLauriel Victor-Thresa.
5-81-s-Dellafera Michael-Mary.
7- 4-s-DeLoury John-Kate.
10-11- -Delliber Charles R.-M.
4-22-d-Deluhery John-A.
4- 9-d-Deming W. W.-Mary.
9- 6-s-Denslow Edward-Julia.
4- 9-d-Denui John-Minnie.
4- 2-d-Deonne Frank-Adelade.
7-29-d-Depres Rocco-Maria.
12- 3-d-Deranney Thomas-Martha
2- 2-d-Dereau Clandino A.-Carrie

7-16-d-Derito Joseph-Almena.
3-17-d-Deromac Leonard-Carmel.
2- 4-s-Deroron John-Annie.
10- 5-d-Descharme Michael-Irene.
2-17-s-Desfard George-Mary.
12-18-s-Desopo Michael-William.
3- 7-d-Dettenbom L. F.-Annetta.
12- 1-s-Deubil Joseph-Kate.
10-20-d-Dicks George B.-Edna H.
8-16-d-Dicks George B.-Edna L.
9-10-s-Dickerman Chas. W-Alice.
9-15-d-Didricksen Severin K-Ida.
7-18-s-Dietrich Carl J.-Lillian.
1- 3-s-Dignam Thomas-Lucy.
1-31-s-Dillon Chas. J.-Hannah M.
6- 9-s-Dillon Jas. Edward-Mary.
10-38-s-Dillon John-Catherine.
10-29-s-Dillstein Isaac-Sarah.
5-20-s-Dingwell ArthurE.-Bertha
8-25-s-Dissell Joseph O.-Annie.
8-26-s-Dixon Wm. H.-Florence.
3-11-s-Dobunier Mike-Louisa.
1-15-d-Dolan ——-Maggie.
4-18-d-Dolan Frank-A. F.
5- 3-d-Donaghue Michael-Rose.
9-19-d-Donaghue Wm.-Mary H.
2-14-s-Donahue John-Mary. }
2-14-s-Donahue John-Mary. }
12-19-s-Donato Tonisa-Carmel.
7-10-s-Donlon Thomas-Bridget.
10-29-d-Dooley Daniel-Bridget.
11- 1-s-Dooley Wm. J.-Sadie.
5-12-s-Dorsey Edward J.-Kate.
6- 8-s-Doucey John-Nellie.
1-17-d-Dowder John-Lavinia.
7-12-s-Dower Jas. P.-Ellen.
9-19-d-Dower Wm.M-Elizabeth T.
7-25-s-Down Eugene C.-Adelin.
3-30-d-Doyle Albert-Mary.
3- 1-d-Doyle John-Maggie.
12-12-s-Drake Frank-Mary.
2-17-d-Droboski Joseph-Ellen.
1-19-d-Drolet Frederick-Florence.
5-26-d-Dudley Wm. A.-Annie.
6- 5-s-Duer Lewis- ——
7-12-s-Dumas Wm. H.-Lizzie.
8-21-d-Dungan Francis-Mary A.
2-21-s-Dunn George-Libby.
9- 3-s-Dunn James-Bridget.
8- 2-s-Dunn Jerry J.-Grace.
7-13-d-Dunn Joseph-Mary.
12-24-s-Dunn Lawrence-Ann.
4-12-s-Dunn Stephen-Julia.
5-31-s-Dunn Thomas-Delia.
6-30-d-Dwight Henry C. Jr-Edith
6-17——Dworski William-Dora.
10-16-d-Dwyer R -Catherine.
8- 7-s-Dwyer Thomas-Lizzie.

6-17-s-Eakson Oland-Agnes E.
5-29-d-Eames Harold-Clara.
1-16-s-Earl Richard P.-Lilla.
1- 3-s-Easterby Alfred J.-Eliz'bth
10- 4-d-Easterby Chas.-May E.
4- 9-s-Eaton John William-Anna
10- 1-d-Eccles Patrick-Mary.
5- 1-d-Echols Frank G.-Emma A.
8-28-d-Edlure Peter-Caroline.
9-17-s-Edwards Alex J.-Lizzie A.
5- 1-s-Egan Daniel-Katie.
6-11-s-Egan Keron-Ellen.
8-20-d-Egan William F.-Mary.
4- 5-d-Ehlers Hans-Mary.
3-31-d-Elche William J.- ——
4-19-d-Eichler J. T.-C.
7-17-s-Ellis John-Emma.
10-11-s-Ellison Geo. F.-Alice R.
7-26-s-Ellovitch Elias-Lizzie.
7-26-s-Elmer Herbert T.-Maretta

7-10-s-Elorich Louis-Jennie.
4-15-d-Elwin William-Luella. •
8- 2-d-Emerick George-Carrie L.
12-10-d-Emory Joseph-Gertrude.
4-29-s-Epstein Jacob-Annie.
10-19-d-Epstein Max-Sophia.
9-10-s-Eruno David-Teresa C.
12-28-s-Erickson Edward- ——
8- 3-d-Ericson Emil-Amnda.
1-13-s-Erving Rollin-Clara A.
9-26-s-Eschols Herman-Catherine
8-14-s-Espen Leonard-Kate.
9-19-d-Etherington J. T.-Ella.
9-23-s-Ethier Joseph-Georgianna
12-25-s-Evans Isaiah F.-Marguret.
10- 9-s-Evans Wm. W.-Margaret.

6- 1-s-Fagan John-Mary E.
5- 3-d-Fagan L.-Catherine.
7-14-s-Fagerholm Karl-S.
4-19-s-Fahey James-Margaret.
4- 9-s-Falvey Jeremiah-Mary.
7-28-s-Fanning Wm. E.-Ada M.
7- 2-d-Farley Patrick-Mary.
9- 2-s-Farnsworth Wm.E.-MaryL
2- 5-s-Farrell James-Elizabeth.
12- 7-d-Farrell Patrick-Margaret.
8-16-d-Farrell Wm. J.-Mary.
6-30-d-Feeley Matthew-Minnie.
11-26-d-Feidman Simon-Rosa.
8-20-s-Feil Louis-Coralena.
11- 4-s-Feinblum Meyer-Cicill.
11- 5-s-Fellessey John-Mary.
3- 6-s-Fenn Jerry-Emily.
13- 7-s-Fenn Louis-Lena.
12- 5-s-Fenn P. S.-Sarah E.
10-27-d-Fennell Michael-Margaret.
2- 8-d-Fennessey John-Mary.
9-80-d-Fennicers John J.-Mary.
1-17-d-Fenoglio Alex. A.-Adel M.
6-26-s-Fenton James-Nellie.
6-19-d-Fenton Michael-Bridget.
4-28-d-Ferguson Alvin S.-MaryA.
11- 9-s-Fern John-Kate.
1-20-s-FethergillEdw'dW-AliceR
11-30-s-Feui James-Fannie.
8-16-s-FickthorneChas.E.-Emma
4-26-d-Filan Thomas-Mary.
4-27-d-Filander Roceo-Maggie.
10-18-d-Finck George-Mary.
5-23-s-Fine Philip-Fannie.
7-31-d-Finerty Edward-Annie.
7-17-d-Finlay Patrick J.-Mary E.
5-20-s-Finley Michael-Nellie.
5- 2-d-Finley William F.-Sarah.
2-30-d-Firber Morris-Rebecca.
11- 8-d-Fish Arthur W.-Effie M.
9-28-d-Fisher Andrew-Augusta.
4-21-s-Fisher Warren R.-Lillie M.
12-10-d-Fitch Charles G.-Hattie.
12- 7-d-Fitzpatrick Jos.-Bridget.
9-13-s-Fitzpatrick Mich'l-Minnie.
7-27-s-Fitzsimmons Chas.-Julia.
4-17-s-Flanagan James-Margaret
12-5-d-Flanagan John-Julia.
10-21-d-Flanagin Patrick-Kate.
5- 3-d-Flanagan Thos. F.-Mary.
12- 5-d-Flanigan Jas.-Margaret.
8-16-s-Flannery Peter-Kate.
9-80-d-Flannigan Thos.-Angelina.
9-23-s-Flint Michael-Mary E.
10- 4-d-Flynn James-Catherine.
1-d-Flynn John C.-Annie M.
11- 7-d-Flynn Thomas-Ann.
12-25-d-Flynn William-Catherine.
8-29-d-Ford Michael-Mary C.
1-11-s-Ford W. Harry-Maria.
6-23-s-Forristall——-Lucretia.
1-17-s-Forshaw Rob't H.-Elizab'h

2-21-s-Forst Charles-Elizabeth.
5-31-s-Forster Charles-Katie.
11- 6-d-Foster Charles A.-Emma.
8-22-d-Foster HowardB.-Marg'tL
11-25-s-Fowler George-Ada W.
7-30-s-Fox Eugene-Catherine.
8- 7-s-Fox Martin-Annie.
3-21-s-Fox Patrick J.-Bridget.
4-19-s-Fox Samuel P.-Maggie.
9-20-s-Franco Joseph-Mary.
2-21-d-Franzen Frank J.-Anna E.
6-18-s-Fraudbury Aug.-Augusta.
7-12-s-Fraudella Christ-Annie.
4-26-d-Freberg Emel-Christina.
6-25-d-Freedman Harris-Eva.
11-26-d-Freeman Samuel-Olga.
8-13-s-Fresher Samuel-Nora.
12-20-s-Frildich Henry- Anita.
9-18-d-Fritz John L.-Hannah.
10-31-s-Frobel Albert D.-Annie.
3-17-d-Froch Bernard-Pascer.
11- 1-d-Fudol George-Rose.
4- 1-d-Fulberg Bernard-Rose.
2-15-d-Furey Frank-Mary J.
7- 1-s-Furey Wm. Edward-C.C.
5- 8-d-Furlong John-Annie.

9-25-s-Gabelina Morris-Jennie.
8-17-d-Gable Bess-Annie F.
7-13 d-Gabriel Oscar A.-Mary E.
8- 6-s-Gaffey Patrick-Margaret.
10- 3-d-Gaffey Peter J.-Anna E.
1-12-s-Gaffney Jas. A.-Annie M.
2- 4-d-Gaggins James-Hannah.
9- 8-s-Gaghan John-Kate.
3-12-d-Gallagher Barnard-E.
8- 7-d-Gallichio Nicolo-Adelina.
7-17-d-Gallio Joseph- ——
8-19-s-Garalone John-Martha.
6-51-s-Garneau Xavier-Mary.
3-10-s-Garotry John-Lena.
2-28-s-Garvey Jos.P.-Gertrude L.
5-23-d-Gaskins George-Etta.
7-25-s-Gaudet Timothy- ——
3-20-d-Gauggle Otto-Emma.
11-24-d-Gaughan Frank-Bessie.
2- 6-s-Gelman Jacob-Beckie.
6-21-d-George Rocco-Mary.
8- 9-d-Geraldhardt Ludwig-Maria
8- 6-d-Getchel Frank H.-Lucella.
6-27-s-Gett George-Jennie.
4- 2-d-Gettersloh Fred-Ellen.
12-10-d-Gibson James H.-Nellie.
12-29-s-Gifford James-Louise.
9-80-d-Gillen Robert-Julia.
8- 9-d-Giller George L.-Annie.
10- 4-d-Gilligan James-Annie.
7-26-s-Gilliland John T.-Nellie J
4-21-s-Gilliland Wm. M.-Nellie.
2- 9-s-Gilmore ——
3-18-s-Gilmore John-Emma.
5- 9-d-Gilmore John-Jennie.
10-22-s-Gilmore John-Kate.
11-11-s-Gladden Chas.-Maybell A.
7-12-d-Gladden Louis-Annie A.
3-21-d-Ginuz Morris-Fannie.
6-18-d-Glover Benj.-Margaret.
8- 7-d-Glynn John-Mary.
2-19-d-Goedon Morris-Mark.
5- 5-s-Goetz Frederick-LouiseM.
8-17-s-Gofeind David-Annie.
6-12-d-Goldberg Maitoch-Rachel.
6-15-s-Goldberg Millz-Anna.
11- 6-s-Goldberg Nathan-Becky.
6-25-d-Goldman Louis-Rachel.
1-29-d-Goldstein David-Sarah.
7-16-s-Goldstein Henry-Nettie.
9-21-d-Goldstein Simon- ——
8-20-d-Goodacre Frank-Agnes.

3-17-s-GoodmanAbraham-Sophie
8-31-s-Goodman Adolph-Mary.
12-19-s-Goodrich Charles-Bertha.
8- 9-s-Goodrich James-Etta H.
2- 9-d-Goodwin C. E.-Margaret.
3-26-d-Goodwin Geo. H.-Ethel M.
1- 3-s-Gordon James-Mary.
9-15-s-Gordon Loui-Anna.
7- 4-s-Gorerman Herman-Beka.
11-29-s-Gorman Patrick-Bridget.
9-28-d-Gouche Charles-Mary.
7-14-d-Govan William G.-Clara.
11-38-s-Grady Dennis-Hannah.
9-30-s-Graff Richard-Clara L.
12-15-s-Gray Charles A.-Emily J.
2- 7-s-Green David J.-Mary.
2-27-d-Green John-Mary.
3- 1-d-Greenberg Jacob-Minnie.
3- 4-d-Greenberg William-Clara.
10-23-s-Greenland Geo. W.-Bessie.
4-13-s-Gregory Napaloen-Agnes.
10-19-d-Gridley John P.-Carrie.
7- 4-s-Griffin Emanual-Mary A.
6-14-s-Griffin George-Mary.
8-13-s-Griffin John-Agnes.
7- 8-d-Griffin William L.-Pauline
4-33-s-Grifford Chas. R.-Margaret
8-16-d-Groesbeck Fred'k-MinnieL
3-16-d-Grogan Patrick-Kate.
9- 8-d-Gross Adolph-Hanna.
4-14-d-Gross Isador-Rosy. }
4-14-Gross Isador-Rosy. }
2-15-s-Grossman Morris-Mache.
2-10-s-Grsh J. N.-Carrie.
9- 3-s-Gsoell ——
7- 9-d-Guethlein G. T.-Barbura.
5-12-d-Guethlein L. F.-Catherine.
5-31-d-Guilmantin John-Mary.
7-17-d-Guisberg Solomon-Bessie.
7-31-d-Gunkel John-Pauline.
3- 3-s-Gunning Thos. J.-Sarah.
4-25-d-Gunshannon Jno.-Maggie.
5- 9-s-Gunshannon Thos.-Mary.
11-15-d-Gustafson Chas. A.-Annie.
12- 4-d-Gutherz Mark-Fannie.

8-31-s-Haas Felix S.-Carrie.
3-17-s-Haff August-Henrotta.
1-13-d-Haggerty Joseph-Annie.
10-12-s-Haley James-Katie.
11-22-d-Hall Charles R.-Louisa.
5- 6-s-Hall James E.-Effie.
5-12-s-Hall Louis H.-Sarah G.
9- 9-d-Halliday Thos. S.-Estelle.
7-21-s-Hallisey Patrick-Mary.
11-16-s-Halmer Frank-Annie.
11-29-s-Hamilton Edward-Sarah.
9- 4-d-Hammond—— -Aron.
10- 1-s-Hammond F.H.L.-Bertha.
7- 8-s-Hancock Walter-Jessie.
6-19-s-Hansen Carl-Fannie.
2- 6-d-Hansen Charles-Hellen.
11-22-s-Hansen Christian A.-Mary.
5-14-s-Hansen Easmess-Juga M.
10-25-s-Hansen Ernest-Anna.
8-18-d-Hansen Hubert-Margaret.
5-23-s-Hansen Martin-Mary.
4- 4-d-Hansen Peter-Catherine.
8- 3-s-Hansen Wm. M.-Charlott.
11-15-d-Hapgood Edw. T.-Mary E.
3-14-s-Harbison John P.-Vida.
9- 4-s-Harding Caleb-Emma D.
5-29-d-Harrington J. B.-Susan E.
10- 9-d-Harris M.-Alma.
12-20-d-Harris Walter-Ellen C.
12-13-d-Harris Walter-Ellen E.
2- 2-s-Hart Edward-Mary E.
10-22-d-Hart N. L.-Jessie G.
7-30-s-Hart William-Elizabeth.

2-10-s-Hartnet John-Nora.
1-29-d-Hartung William-Kate L.
3-28-d-Hastings Frank-Alice.
7- 6-s-Hatch C. E.-Elizabeth A.
10-20-s-Hatch Charles L.-Lottie. }
10-20-d-Hatch Charles L.-Lottie. }
5-24-s-Hatch Ernest G.-Jennie.
4-10-d-Hatch Henry-Margaret.
8-23-s-Hatheway Edw.F.-Eunice.
1-28-d-Haueston James-Johanna.
12-31-s-Hauger Wm. J.-Elizabeth.
8-30-s-Hausman William-Louisa.
1-31-s-Hausolt Louis-Clara.
2-13-d-Havens Edw. F.-Mary A.
6-12-s-Havens James-Mary.
4-17-d-Haverbeck I-rael-Mamie.
8- 6-s-Hawley Louis F.-Lucia.
10- 8-s-Hayes Henry-Rosa.
11- 7-d-Hayes Jeremiah-Nellie.
9-29-s-Hayes Thomas- ——
1- 8-d-Hazel William H.-Agnes.
12- 2-d-Heacox Chas. E.-Idella M.
2-21-s-Healy Dennis-Kate.
1-24-d-Heffernon James-Bridget.
4-25-—Heins Frank W.-Louise.
·1-26-d-Henderson G. A.-Ophelia.
8-29-d-Henrochon John-Lizzie.
8-20-s-Henry Charles-Lulu.
11- 5-s-Herrup Samuel E.-Esther.
6-12-s-Hervin Jus. F.-Margerite.
2- 2-d-Herzberg Hertz-Annie.
12- 9-d-Herzog John-Annie.
11-27-d-Hess Abraham-Jennie.
10-14-s-Hess Charles T.-Emma.
9-29-d-Hess Conrad- ——
2-23-d-Hewett Geo. F.-Nettie E.
4-16-d-Hickey Michael-Bridget.
8- 1-s-Hicks Edward-Clara.
9-20-s-Hiedersham M.F.-AnnieF.
5- 1-s-Higher Oscar-Lottie.
2- 4-s-Highland Edward-Annie.
5-26-d-Hill George-Margaret.
12-29-s-Hill Henry J.-Grace E.
12-27-s-Hill James A.-Mary.
5-18-d-Hillard John-Margaret.
2-20-s-Hilliard Michael-Bridget.
9-25-d-Hills Charles-Agnes.
5-20-d-Hills Frank J.-Florence M.
1-19-s-Himmel Heiman-Ida.
7-12-s-Hoban Edward-Annie.
1-28-d-Hoban James-Mary.
10-12-d-Hodge Frank C.-Bessie.
2- 2-s-Hofer John-Franzisker.
5-24-d-Hoffer Theo-Mary A.
1- 8-d-Hoffman Louis-Rachel.
12-30-d-Hoffman Max-Beckey.
4-30-s-Hogan Martin-Mary.
9-14-s-Hogan Michael-Mary.
11-20-d-Holsten Leonard-Elizabeth
4- 2-s-Holtz William-Minnie.
2- 1-s-Honce Johnson-Emily.
8-16-s-Honiss Wm. H.-Catherine.
6-25-s-Horan John-Maria.
11- 8-s-Horan Michnei-Margaret.
8- 6-s-Horton ——
5- 3-s-Hoskins Earnest-Francis.
6-28-d-Howard William-Mary.
9-17-d-Howland Edw. D.-Annie.
12-27-—Hubbard Edward-Susin.
12-d-Hubbard Geo. R.-Mary L.
9- 9-d-Hubert Samuel-M.
7-12-s-Huble Paul-Lena.
2-23-s-Hughes J. C.-Evangelina.
9-28-d-Hughes Thomas-Lizzie.
9-28-d-Hunter Edward J.-Janet.
4- 8-s-Huntington R. D.-Judith.
8-30-d-Hurd Herbert L.-Eva.
8-10-d-Hussey Edward-Annie.

9-13-s-Hutchinson E. G.-Susan.
7-22-s-Hutchinson R.-Margaret.
7-23-s-Hutchinson R.-Margaret.
2-17-s-Hyerpe Emil-Mathilde E.
11-19-s-Hynes James-Jennie.
7-31-s-Hyser John-Josephine.

9-24-d-Ibbot Charles-Kate.
9- 8-d-Ingram Walter-Ella M.
12-29-d-Iuskep Frederick-Beatrice.

2- 6-d-Jacaromni A.-Terminie.
9- 2-d-Jacklyn Wm. H.-Sarah L.
7-22-s-Jackson Allen-Virginia.
8- 1-s-Jackson James-Gertrude.
4-24-d-Jackson N. S.-Catherine S.
1-16-s-Jackson Peter-Annie.
2-26-s-Jacobs Herbert-Rosa.
8-25-s-Jacobs Mathew-Kate.
9-12-s-Jacobson Alex-Selma.
7-31-s-Jacobson Andrew-Nellie.
11-18-d-Jncorro Anzelo-Augie.
4-24-s-Jaffar Abe-Annie.
6- 2-d-Jal James-J——
11- 2-d-James Alfred-Mary.
9- 4-d-Jansan John-Mary.
8-27-s-Jennings Robert-Etta M.
10- 6-d-Jennings W. R.-Margaret.
6- 2-d-Jensen James P.- ——
9- 6-s-Jode Leonard-Agie.
7-23-s-Johansen Mads-Sophia.
3-19-s-John Henry-Mary.
4- 8-s-Johnson August-Helen.
11- 6-s-Johnson Carl A.-Amandi.
11- 6-s-Johnson Chas. A.-Katie K.
7-30-d-Johnson Chas. J.-Annie.
9-25-d-Johnson Christian- ——
9-10-d-Johnson Fred-Catherine.
2- 8-d-Johnson John-Annie.
8- 4-s-Johnson John-Charlotte.
2- 8-d-Johnson John-Selma.
4-21-s-Johnson John A.-Amanda.
8-30-s-Johnson John A.-Jacobin.
7- 9-s-Johnson Louis-Mary.
10-17-d-Johnson P. A.-Amanda C.
8- 9-s-Johnson Peter-Marie.
10-24-d-Johnson Reynald-Francis.
2-18-s-Johnson Stewart-Bridget.
2- 1-d-Johnson William-Edna.
9-24-s-Jones Benjamin-Kate.
8-25-s-Jones Edward-Mary.
1-30-d-Jones Moses-Isabella.
10-15-d-Jones W N.-Josephine.
8-31-s-Jones Wm. Francis.-Mary.
11- 1-d-Jones Workman-Carrie.
7-28-d-Joseph Samuel- ——
8- 1-d-Judatz Osualth-Anna.
8-21-s-Juella Valentine-Rosie.

12- 8-d-Knices Leon-Anna.
10-29-s-Kamerer Fred'k-Mary J.
10- 9-d-Kameukos Simon-Sarah.
1- 3-s-Kammvitz August-Annie.
8-28-s-Kane Joseph-Sarah T.
7-20-d-Kane Mathew-Mary.
4- 8-d-Kapp Martin-Kate.
11-21-d-Karitz Daniel-Willimar.
7-29-d-Kashman Simon-Rosie.
2- 6-d-Kask Axle-Augusta.
4-15-s-Katten Abraham-Jenne.
12- 1-d-Katz Esau-Nellie.
11- 7-s-Katz Jacob-Rachel.
1-21-d-Katz Joseph-Louise.
1- 9-d-Katz Max-Millie.
2- 8-d-Katz Max-Rachel.
4-23-d-Katz Nathan-Fannie.
4-14-s-Katz Nathan-Fannie.
1-20-d-Katz Samuel-Edith.
11-17-s-Katz Samuel-Rachel.

9- 9-s-Katzman Samuel-Bella.
12-21-d-Kaufman Philip-Lena.
9-15-s-Kaupfman Adam-Mary.
2- 6-s-Keane Samuel L.-Annie C.
7- 5-s-Keating Maurice- ——
1- 1-d-Keefe Christopher-Annie.
8- 7-d-Keefe James-Kate.
9-19-d-Keefe Michael W.-Mary.
1- 3-s-Keefe Patrick-Bridget.
11-26-s-Keefe Thomas-Margaret.
11-30-d-Keelmer Fred'k-Matilda.
6- 4-s-Keen Charles B.-Annie.
3- 8-d-Keenan John-Bridget.
11-13-d-Keenan John-Bridget.
12-25-d-Kehoe Chas. F.-Catherine.
8-15-s-Kehoe Patrick-Mary.
9-11-d-Keilg Michael J.-Ellen.
8-19-d-Keller Henry-Amelia.
6-14-s-Kelley Daniel-Lizzie.
12- 6-s-Kelley John- ——
9-23-s-Kellson Peter-Mary E.
4-23-s-Kelly James B.-Dealia.
11-22-d-Kelly James M.-Mary.
4-26-d-Kelly Patrick J.-Catherine.
7-19-s-Kelly Samuel-Lizzie.
9-27-d-Kelly William-Bridget.
2- 8-d-Kemler Jacob-Lena.
8- 2-d-Kennedy James-Mary.
9-20-s-Kennedy John-Lizzie.
12- 1-s-Kenyon James H.-Maria.
10-15-d-Keough Thomas-Joseph.
4-24-s-Kerr William-Ellen. }
4-24-s-Kerr William-Ellen. }
3-28-s-Kersche Richard-Annie.
10- 8-d-Keumani Frank-Katherine
4-13-d-Kilbourn Charles-Jennie.
10-17-s-Kilfoil John-Margaret.
5-24-s-Kilfoil Thomas-Annie.
1-28-s-Killian Terrence-Bridget.
8-18-s-Kilmartin Joseph-Annie.
4-20-s-Kimmer A. W.-Charlotte.
9-18-s-King Frank E.-Lottie R.
12-20-s-King George S.-Sadie.
7-15-s-King Herbert S.-Ada J.
2-18-s-King James-Mary.
2-24-s-King Peter A.-Marion.
9-10-s-Kinghorn Harry-Kate.
6-30-d-Kinghorn Jas. R.-Bridget.
5-31-d-Kingsbury Frank P.-Edith.
11- 5-s-Kinsella Rich'd-Catherine
6-15-——Kirby Cornelius-Kate.
8-28-s-Kirney Thomas-Marey.
2- 6-s-Kissler David-Becky.
10- 1-s-Kline Adolph-Lena.
2-28-s-Klingelsmith Z. M.-May E.
1-21-d-Klinger Charles-Nellie.
11- 9-d-Koch Antone-Julia.
10-26-d-Kofsky Bernard-Katie.
5-17-s-Kotosky Wladyrian-Maria
6- 5-d-Kowslaki John-Antonine.
4-11-s-Krauss Louis-Lena.
10-10-s-Kress Reinhart-Anna.
4-20-d-Kreuter Louis J.-Ida.
12-16-d-Kromer John-Mary.
8-25-d-Kuebler Geo. F.-Annie S.
10- 6-s-Kulu Henry J.- ——
10-24-d-Kulu Jacob-Mary.
2- 3s-d-Kumuski Charles-Marie.
1-15-s-Kuris Morris-Bessie.

7-17-s-Labadie Aural-Mary. }
7-17-s-Labadie Aural-Mary. }
7- 9-d-Labneck Domonick- ——
8- 4-s-Lache Frank-Isabella.
1- 7-s-Lackard Joseph-Mary L.
1-29-d-LambRichard F.-Virginia.
10-15-s-Lane Patrick-Kate.
12-29-d-Lankton Geo. H.-Viola M.
9- 8-s-Lano P. S.-Jennie.

2-15-d-Lapointe J. H.-Milina.
6-25-s-Lappen Israel-Dora.
7-18-d-Larkin Michael-Maggie.
11- 5-d-Larsen Peter-Christena.
11-14-d-Larson Andrew G.-Annie.
8-27-s-Larson Michael-Anna.
7-19-d-Later Morris-Pauline.
4-12-d-Laudry Joseph P.-Eva.
12-25-d-Laughlin John-Bridget.
10- 9-s-Lauritzen L. C.-Dortha.
8-10-s-Lavaidson Lavsido- ——
1-19-s-Lavane Tony-Laura.
3-20-s-LavenderMichael-Augusta
11-24-d-Lavenson Hyman-Sarah.
1- 1-d-Lavery John-Mary.
9-14-s-Lavery John-Mary.
3- 5-d-Laville George-Jennie.
5-11-s-Lawler Andrew-Margaret.
1-30-s-Lawler Michael J.-Jennie.
6-14-d-Lawlor Raymond-Alice.
5-12-d-Lawson John-Jane.
5-19-d-Lawton Franklin L.-Lucy.
11-29-s-Leaug Hugh-Nora.
10- 4-d-Lee George-Mirtel.
6- 8-d-Lee Thomas-Mary J.
5-25-s-Leeuer John J.- ——
11- 1-d-Lefkowitz Mano-Mary.
6-22-d-Lego Dominick-Anna.
2-24-d-Leitz John E.-Francis.
7- 6-s-Lemanto Joseph-Mary.
1- 5-d-Lenderman Sam-Sprincy.
1-10-s-Lennihan Thomas-Mary.
11- 8-s-Lennon James F.-Mary E.
8- 8-d-Lennon Mathew-Bridget.
10- 4-s-Leo Frank-Mary.
2-25-d-Leon John J.-Mary.
2-12-s-Leonard Charles R.-Mary.
7-14-d-Leporte Mitchill-Mary.
6- 1-d-LeRoy D.-Mary.
5-10-s-Leroy Dominic-Thressa.
9-22-s-Lesondray Frank-Vets.
1-12-s-Lessor Arthur-Enterdeur.
10-25-d-Leuneder Charles-Nancy.
2- 8-s-Leventhal Simon-Bessie.
6- 5-d-Levi Leo-Minnie.
1-26-d-Levin Samuel-Jennie.
6-25-s-Levinson A.-Pauline.
10-23-d-Levy Louis-Pauline.
4-13-s-Levy Morris-Anna.
3- 5-s-Levy Morris-Nettie.
8-21-d-Lewis Charles-Sadie.
3-80-s-Lewis Frank-Catherine.
12-16-s-Lewis Robert H.-Lillian.
8-23-s-Leyman James C.-Jennie.
3-13-s-Lilia Julius-Anna M.
8-18-d-Lindsley Samuel-Kitty.
1-21-s-Lippert Charles-Dagmar.
5-14-d-Littlefield A. B.-Laura A.
2-17-s-Livingston Geo. E.-Mary.
10-29-d-Long George S.-Josephine.
6-26-d-Longdon Arthur C.-Effie L.
3-13-s-Loomis Charles-Jennie J.
11- 2-d-Lopenansky Morris-Ida.
4-18-s-Lopez Harvey-Elizabeth.
12-23-s-Losker Martin-Julia.
1-23-d-Losty James-Susan.
4- 9-s-Lotker Carl-Lena.
6-21-s-Louis John-Minnie.
9- 3-d-Lourin William- ——
11-26-s-Low Robert-Elizabeth.
9-24-s-Lowe William B.-Mary.
11-27-d-Loydon F. R.-Mary L.
8- 3-d-Luca John-Mary.
6- 2-s-Luce Joseph-Caroline.
9- 3-d-Lucy James A.-Mary.
8-12-s-Ludington Myron E.-Eva.
11-30-s-Ludwig Fred F.-Mary H.
9-28-d-Ludwig Solomon-Rachel.
8-11-s-Luetzenkirchen-Elizabeth.

7-11-d-Lugane Andrew-Mary.
5- 8-s-Luidholm August-Mary.
10-80-s-Luke John A.-Mabel S.
4- 8-d-Lutton Joseph-Rosanna.
11-25-d-Lutz Reinhold-Phillipena.
10-80-d-Lyhhe J. Peter-Maria.
2- 5-s-Lyman Henry-Annie.
8- 4-s-Lyman Richard P.-Bertha.
11-22-d-Lynch Declan J.-Nellie.
2-25-s-Lynch Michael W.-Delia.
3- 6-d-Lyon Gilbert-Harriet.
5- 1-s-Lyon John J.-Mary A.
12-27-s-Lyons James-Margaret.
8-20-d-Lyons Michael-Kate.
8-12-s-Lyons Thomas-Nora. }
8-12-d-Lyons Thomas-Nora. }
9-15-d-Lyons William-Catherine.

9- 8-d-Mack Crohan-Mary.
2- 3-s-Mack John-Gladys.
11-14-s-Maddox Frank H.-Jane F.
7-25-s-Madir John-Mary.
9-26-d-Madress Joseph-Rosie.
11-15-s-Maercklein H. L.-Effie.
11-25-s-Magazuier Joseph-Fanny.
6-29-s-Magrade Frederick-Rosa.
8- 8-s-Malcolm Thomas-Annie.
3-20-d-Malley Patrick-Bridget.
1-31-d-Malley Thomas-Annie.
8-27-s-Malley William-Susan.
10-29-d-Malone Philip-Mary.
1- 1-d-Maloy John-Annie.
6- 5-d-Maloy John-Josephine.
1-25-d-Maloy William-Annie.
8-11-d-Malthrof Jas. E.-Jennie S.
10-12-s-Manion Patrick J.-Mary.
8-19-s-Manion Richard J.-Mary.
11-26-d-Mannion William-Bridget.
6-13-d-Mansfield John-Katie.
8-13-s-Marcone Peter- ——
4- 1-d-Marcus Anton-Katherine.
6-14-d-Marisen Fred'k-Josephine.
10-27-s-Marks Rudolph-Ida.
1-21-s-Marquette J. L.-Harriet L.
1-27-d-Marsh Joseph-Rosie.
1-20-s-Marsh William-Mary.
3-17-s-Marshall Joseph-Minnie.
8-22-d-Martin C. A.-Nellie.
7-11-d-Martin Charles-Minnie.
4-14-s-Martin John G.-Mary T.
12- 2-s-Martin Russell-Martha.
2- 5-s-Marvel Walter S.-Annie J.
8-16-d-Marvel Winship W.-Effie.
1-20-d-Mather Arthur-Fannie B.
7-25-s-Mather Frank J.-Ida M.
6-28-s-Mathers John T.-Emma.
8- 2-d-Mathewson Duncan-Jessie
4-28-d-Mathieu Archibald-Elvnia
11-21-s-Mathieu Julius-Caroline.
2-25-s-Mauseault Stephen-L——
11- 4-d-McCaffery Edward-Ida.
8-25-s-McCall Patrick- ——
7- 2-d-McCarthy Dennis-Marg't.
7-29-s-McCarthy Dennis-Marg't.
1-19-s-McCarthy Jeremiah- ——
6-13-d-McCarthy Patrick J.-Jane.
3-22-s-McCarthy T. F.-Lena. }
3-22-d-McCarthy T. F.-Lena. }
12- 3-d-McCollun John-Rhoda.
7- 7-s-McCormick Wm.-Kittie.
8-18-d-McCourt James-Margaret.
9- 6-d-McCrone Richard-Annie.
6-20-s-McCue Martin-Kate.
5- 1-s-McDonald J.-Margaret.
8-31-d-McDonough Patrick-Kate.
8-19-d-McFetridge Robert-Emma.
11-14-d-McFetridge Thomas-Sarah.
8-28-s-McGalloy Martin-Mary.
7-11-d-McGann Thomas-Mary.

9-28-d-McGeary Alex.-Elizabeth.
10-12-d-McGlory Henry-Mary.
5-22-McGovern Chas.-Mary C.
2- 1-s-McGrath Michael-Mary.
8- 4-s-McGrath Timothy-Mary.
10- 5-s-McGuire John-Ellen.
2-19-d-McHenry Geo. W.-Emma.
6-13-s-McIntosh George-Clara.
6-19-s-McIntyre Hugh A.-Elsa.
2-14-s-McIver H.-Christine.
10-18-d-McKenna Lewis-Maria.
8-27-s-McKenzy John-Kate.
6-11-s-McKerney P.-Josephine.
10- 9-s-McKnight Jas. B.-Elmore.
2- 2-s-McLaughlin Arthur-Ellen.
5-23-s-McLaughlin D.-Catherine.
6-10-d-McLeod Arthur-Katherine.
7-29-d-McLeod Donald-Delia.
3-26-d-McMonagle Edward-Nora.
8-27-d-McQuillan John J.-Maggie.
4-14-d-Meaher Joseph-Margurite.
11-16-s-Meloney Thomas-Rose.
9- 4-d-Meniman Philip-Emma.
1-17-s-Merritt Chas. B.-Margaret.
9-15-s-Merwith ——Sarah.
9-19-d-Meyer Joseph-Rose.
11-26-d-Meyers George-Mary.
11-30-s-Mi hael Isaac E.-Sophia.
9-29-d-Mich el Jacob-Jennie.
10-25-s-Michelli Augustine- ——
5-19-s-Michelson Peter-H. M.
10-10-d-Middlebrook L. F.-Mary.
11-25-s-Miland Candalorn-Rosie.
6-17-d-Miles Oscar-Jane G.
3-31-d-Mill Ernest-Marion.
12- 3-d-Miller Chandler E.-Anna.
8- 7-d-Miller Fred'k-Catherine.
11-28-d-Miller George-Martha.
5- 4-d-Miller Oscar-Nellie.
1-17-d-Miltimore R. C.-Martha.
10- 3-d-Minuerly Ferris-D——
12-13-d-Miro Dominici- ——
1- 2-s-Missa Ignalaus-Annie.
2-19-d-Mitchill George-Grace.
12-28-s-Mitchill Victor E.-Bessie.
2- 9-d-Molgnard Peter-Christine.
12-14-d-Molnar Lucis-Ross.
3-16-s-Monda Franz-Franciska.
4- 7-s-Monguli Angel-Lena.
9-12-s-Moore Robert-Minnie.
7-11-d-Moran Albert-Mary.
8-11-d-Moran Daniel-Annie.
3-17-d-Moran Frank-Hannah.
4-27-d-Moran James F.-Mary.
8-10-d-Moran James T.-Lizzie E.
6- 1-d-Moran John-Kate.
2-15-s-Moran Michael C.-Mary.
12- 2-s-Morgan John- ——
8-29-s-Moriarty Thomas-Mary.
8-23-s-Morkardt Frank-Margaret.
4-18-d-Morris Eugene-Maggie.
10-30-Morris Henry-Emma.
11- 3-d-Morris James-Julia.
11- 8-s-Morris James-Rose.
6- 6-d-Morris Joseph-Agnes.
11-23-d-Mosier Julius-Mary.
8- 4-d-Moskovitz Charles- ——
5-27-s-Moskowitz Samuel-Bessie.
8-30-d-Mulcahey Arthur W.-L. M.
4-22-s-Muldoon Pat'k J.-Mary A.
5-23-s-Mullalley Wm. J.-Marg't.
2- 2-s-Muller John-Emma.
5- 3-d-Muller Martin-Helen A.
10-24-d-Muller Samuel-Sarah.
1-28-d-Mundine Charlie-Marie.
10-11-s-Murphy Arthur P.- ——
10-24-d-Murphy Daniel-Mary.
8-22-d-Murphy Edw'd J.-Kate A.
12-18-d-Murphy John-Etta.

11-28-d-Murphy John-Thresa.
5-23-s-Murphy John P.-Annie.
2-16-s-Murphy Joseph-Abbe.
6-15-s-Murphy Joseph-Abbe.
3-27-d-Murphy Michael-Mary.
2-12-d-Murphy Park-Bridget.
1u- 2-s-Murphy Patrick-Bessie.
6-26-d-Murphy Patrick-Bessie.
12-27-s-Murphy Steven A.-Mary.
11- 6-d-Murphy William-Bridget.
8- 7-d-Murphy Willim-Nora.
9-26-s-Murray Bartholmew-Cath.
5- 6-s-Murray Jas. T.-Minnie.
8-18-d-Murray John-Kate.
10-25-d-Murray Oscar-Martinoniss
1- 9-s-Murray Patrick-Mary J.
9- 9-d-Murk Herman G.-Annie.
1- 4-d-Musey James-Mary.
6-12-s-Mussgung Martin-M.
1- 4-d-Myers George P.-Bertha.

1-25-d-Nagle Thomas-Annie.
3-29-d-Nalley James-Annie E.
11-19-d-Neal Christoph'r F.-Fissi.
11-28-d-Needham Wm. F.-Ada.
1-12-s-Neilson John A.-Augusta.
10- 5-d-Neircot Benjamin-Jennie.
7- 8-s-Nelson Albert-Christian.
6-18-s-Nelson Charles-Christian.
10- 2-s-NelsonEdw'dG.-Augusta E
5-11-d-Nelson John-Gertrude.
5-20-d-Nelson John V.-Nora.
6-12-d-Nelson Joseph V.-Mary E.
5-14-s-Nomser Louis-Minnie.
4-29-s-Nerille James-Bessie.
7-18-s-Nesbitt William-Sarah E.
9-15-d-Nevins Michael-Margaret.
6-12-s-Nostrand Wm. C.-Julia.
4-21-d-Newell George E.-Emelia.
10-28-d-Newman Solomon-Sarah.
11- 5-d-Newton Allin-Emily K.
6-24-d-Nezzo Tony-Rosie.
9- 4-d-Nichols H. F.-Katherine.
12-10-s-Nicholas Berri-Mary.
5- 9-s-Nicholos Collotti-Angelo.
7- 9-d-Nichols Arthur C.-Lizzie.
7-14-d-Nielson James-Mary.
3-31-s-Nielson Jeff-Christine.
11-25-s-Noble Richard H.-Grace B.
12- 6-d-Noble Wm. B.-Nettie B.
4-11-d-Nolan John-Mary.
4-11-d-Nolan Mary.
8-20-s-Noll Jacob- ——
8-28-s-Norige Edward-Annie.
1-25-s-Norris Michael-Delia.
11-13-s-Northam Robt. C.-Elsie E.
8-30-d-Northstrom Peter-Emma.

9-21-s-Oakes Thomas E.-Helen.
5- 5-d-Obert Joseph-Lena.
11-25-s-o. Brien Daniel-Norah.
4-17-d-O'Brien Edward-Margaret.
5- 5-d-O'Brien James-Annie.
11- 9-d-O'Brien John-Mary.
4-30-d-O'Brien John F.-Maude E.
4-19-s-O'Brien John H.-Maggie.
7-22-d-O'Brien Morris-Annie.
8- 5-s-O'Brien Thomas-Mary.
3-31-d-O'Brien T. J.-Margaret.
10- 8-s-O'Donnell Owen-Elizabeth
5- 5-d-O'Donnell Thos. F.-Nellie.
7-21-s-O'Keefe John-Mary L.
5-18-d-O'Keefe Patrick-Margaret.
1-28-s-O'Laughlin John-Catherine
2-17-s-O'Laughlin John J.-Ellen.
8-12-s-O'Laughlin Wm.-Maggie.
2-17-d-O'Leary Timothy-Annie.
2-24-d-Olin John-Anna.
6-26-s-Olliger Ernest-Mary.

7-17-Olschleger Joseph-Paulina.
8- 8-s-O'Mara James-Margaret.
10-12-d-O'Neal Timothy-Kate.
11- 8-s-O'Neal T. J.-Kate.
6-16-d-O'Neil Patrick-Nellie.
5- 5-d-O'Neil Thomas-Nellie.
3- 6-d-Oppelt Michael-Anne K.
1-13-d-Upper Frederick-Lena.
3-19-s-O'Reustein Mendel-Spuize
1-30-d-O'Rourke Frank-Mary.
1-30-d-Orzino Danato-Rosie.
9- 7-d-Osborn Wm. E -Sarah A.
10- 1-s-O'Shea Gerald-Lizzie.
9-25-s-Osher Joseph-Mary E.
2-15-d-Ostlund Ovel R.-Lena.
11-27-s-Ottowitz Peter-Maria.
8- 9-d-Ouellette John-Julia.
1-15-d-Ough John-Charlotte.
8-16-s-Owen John--Addie E.

10- 6-s-Page Irving W.-Alice R.
7- 3-s-Page Ralph E.-May.
11- 4-s-Paiso Willinm-Louise.
7-26-d-Palisetta John-Rosie.
1-10-s-Pallotta Domenico-Maria.
12-28-s-PalmerNicholasL.-Addie W
9- 7-d-Palotta Rosco-Anna M.
7-19-s-Parel Harris-Ida.
10-28-s-Parker Fred'k-Elizabeth.
12-10-d-Parker Fred J.-Lizzie.
6-28-d-Parker John D.-Carol ma.
8-12-s-Parker John D.-Edith T.
4-14-d-Parker Percy P.-Emma.
6-22-d-Parlee Edw'd D.-Henretta.
7- 1-s-Parsons Alonzo H.-Abbie.
12-14-s-Parsons Robert E.-Mary A.
7-14-d-Pasquale Bennett-Lucy.
6-10-d-Patrice Tony-Antonia.
4-17-d-Patrigo Tony-Maria.
12-30-d-Pauell Martin-Elizabeth.
6-24-d-Pearson John L.-Hulda.
4-18-d-Pease Charles E.-Julia T.
2-23-s-Peaune Michael-Conshet.
5-13-d-Pellingill Fred-Hannah.
3-12-s-Peltier Fred'k D.-Jane M.
2-28-s-PenfieldRaym'dW-Eliz'bh
9- 5-d-Peoples Eldridge-Mary.
2-29-d-Perkins Tim'y-Mollie A.
11-17-s-Perlitz Henry-Augusta.
12-23-d-Perlmortter Jacob-Mary.
3-14-s-Perry Alfred T.-Anna.
3-10-s-Perry Melledge-Loretta.
10-11-s-Peters Chas. H.-Marg't E.
6-19-s-Peters Joseph H.-Sarah J.
2- 8-s-Peterson Edward-Thora.
11- 9-s-Peterson John-Lizzie.
8-30-Peterson Peter L.-Mary.
11-16-s-Phelan Daniel-Margaret.
7- 2-d-Phelps Wilbur-Christine.
1-22-s-Phillips Chas. G.-Eva M.
8- 3-s-Phillips Nathan-Etta.
2-19-d-Phillips Thomas-Cora.
9- 1-s-Picard Charles-Mary.
5- 8-s-Pierce Austin D.-Maud M.
10-18-s-Pierce Charles-Grace.
1-19-s-Pierce Clinton-Delia.
4-15-d-Pierce H. W.-Florence M.
2-26-d-Pillion John-Mary.
12-18-s-Pillon Thos. J.-Mary E.
1- 1-d-Pindar Alfred-Gertrude.
5——d-Plaisikouski Aug.-Serena.
10- 8-s-Plat Charles-Lena.
2-20-s-Poder Frank-Rosie.
6-14-s-Poindexter Leroy.- ——
12-21-d-Pollack Irar- ——
2- 3-d-Pomery Everett C.-Edith.
11- 6-d-Porter William-Hattie.
5-17-s-Posener Isaac-Tillie.
11-28-d-Poste Lawrence-Christina.

8–19–d–Power Declan–Kate.
9– 7–d–Powers Wm. Arthur–Lena.
12– 9–d–Powetza John–Mary.
8– 5–d–Pracety Walter S.–Harriet.
11–27–s–Pratt Lawrence M.–Louisa.
1–30–d–Prentiss C. C.–Hattie.
7–16–d–Preston Fred'k–Elizabeth.
7–15–d–Price Harry–Mary.
5– 6–d–Price Jacob–Jennie.
11–23–s–Price Louis S.–Friede.
7–24–s–Priesner Julius–Mary.
2– 1–d–Proller Morris–Annie.
10– 7–s–Provost Napolian L.–Rose.
5– 6–d–Pruno David–Emma.
5–19–s–Prutting Arthur–Minnie.
2–24–s–Pulaski Michael– ——
5– 6–s–Purtell Thomas M.–Nora.
9–28–d–Pu nam Wm. H.–Carrie.
12–25–s–Pyott Geo. D.–Elizabeth.

11–26–d–Quail Michael–Hannah.
3–12–d–Quinn William–Rose.
4–11–d–Quiris John–Catherine.
12– 5–s–Quish Hanford–Mary.

12–21–d–Rabuiowitz Isidore–Sadie,
5–19–d–Radigan Michael–Annie.
9–18–s–Ragna Sahvatore–Mary.
11– 8–s–Rahowsky Jacob–Hattie.
1–29–d–Rand Henry E.–Elizabeth.
9– 5–d–Rannigan James–Josie.
10– 6–d–Raplad Aron–Jennie.
11–18–s–Raymond Frank–Rosie.
10– 5–s–Raynois James–Mary.
7–29–s–Reardon John J.–Mary E.
6– 4–s–Reardon Patrick–Maggie.
1– 8–d–Reardon Pat'k E.–Marg't.
3–28–s–Reardon T. F.–Lizzie.
4–16–d–Reardon Timothy–Mary.
2– 1–s–Redfield Edw'dD.–Marietta
2– 4–s–Redlund Adolph W.–Ida.
3–80–s–Reheseir Simon–Sarah.
5– 6–d–Reiser Martin–Rosie.
11–17–s–Rengstrom Joseph–Emilie.
7– 2–s–RennackerChas. H.–Minnie
8–23–s–Ressadier Louis–Rosie.
4– 6–d–Reudlinger Conrad–Rosina.
5–26–s–Reynolds James–Ellen.
12–35–s–Reynolds James–Mary A.
10–12–s–Rheaune Edward–Laura.
6–13–d–Rice Ole T.–Mary.
6–19–d–Richard Ge rgo–Mary.
12– 3–s–Ridda Miller–Mary.
10–21–s–Riley C. F.–Mary.
8–28–s–Riordan Patrick–Annie.
12– 7–d–Rioux Horace L.– ——
4–16–s–Rioux Ledger–Eugene.
9– 5–s–Roach Frank–Mary.
12–16–d–Roach Thomas–Kate.
1– 2–s–Roach Thomas H.–Maggie.
9–26–d–Roatman Samuel–Annie.
9–23–s–Robbins D. W.–Henrietta.
1–27–s–Robbins Edward–Rose.
1–15–s–Robbins James–Lizzie.
5– 5–d–Robbins John–Mary.
2–24–s–Roberts Charles T.–Agnes.
1–16–d–Roberts Enoch C.–Kate.
1– 3–s–Robertson Robert–Annie.
4–17–s–Robinson Charles–E. H. J.
9– 9–s–Robinson James–Julia.
9–14–s–Robinson John E.–Lydia J.
6– 6–s–Robinson Lucius F.–Elnor.
12–30–s–Rochett Patrick–Margaret.
7–28–d–Rockenfeller M. W.–C.C.E.
8–25–s–Roedel Ernest B.–Amelia.
12–22–s–Roemer Geo. A.–Mary E.
10– 1–s–Rogers James H.–Alice.
10–26–d–Rogers William H.–Etta.
8– 4–s–Roivett Peter–Elizabeth.

4– 8–d–Romano George–Theresia.
11–14–s–Romato John–Philomena.
2– 1–s–Rome Louis–Hannah.
2–24–d–Rood Alfred H.–Crucia.
8– 3–d–Rooney Frank–Nellie.
4–21–s–Rooney Hugh–Hannah.
2–26–s–Root F. H.–Jennie.
7– 9–s–Rosana Nicola–Margaret.
8– 7–s–Rosenbaum Sam'l–Esther.
6– 2–d–Rosenbaum Solomon–Yetta
11–26–d–Rosenbaum William–Lena.
4–10–d–Rosenblatt Israel–Dora.
1– 4–s–Rosenfeldt Isaac–Sarah.
9–12–d–Rosenwall F.–Christina.
5– 7–d–Ross Jackson–Mary.
7– 3–s–Roszelle Edw. M.–Isabella.
2–15–d–Roulston Robert G.–Annie.
11–23–s–Rousa Mike–Rosalie.
3– 1–d–Rouselle John– ——
3–21–s–Rouske Michael–Mary.
5–15–s–Rowe Benj.–Francis M.
7– 4–d–Roys L. C.–Liddie D.
12–15–s–Rozen Max–Mary.
12–10–d–Rubenbauner Martin–C.
10– 1–s–Ruddell R. V.–Mary L.
6– 8–d–Rudolf Philip–Margaretha.
3–19–s–Ruoff Charles–K.
7–19–s–Russell Frank H.–Mary F.
8–22–s–Russell Jos. J.–Margaret C.
7– 9–d–Russell Raymond–Edith.
11–18–d–Russell Thos. J.–Mary E. }
11–18–s–Russell Thos. J.–Mary E. }
2–24–d–Russell Wm. A.–Clara M.
8–16–s–Ryan James–Mary.
1–23–s–Ryder Thomas–Ellen.

7–15–d–Sado Tony– ——
7–12–d–Sudusky Harris–Lizzie.
2–27–d–Sagarins Roceo–Rosie.
4–12–s–St. John Raymond–Delia.
6– 1–d–Sall John A.–Anna E.
5– 8–d–Salvatore Safferan–Annie.
8– 4–d–Samblanaio Frank–Louisa.
1–10–d–Sanboon Charles H.–Mary.
4–10–s–Sanford Charles–Mary.
7– 4–d–SargentFrank D.–Fannie E.
6– 6–s–Saul Fred C.–Mary.
11– 9–s–Saun Edward E.–Nell.
8–12–s–Saunders Alfred E.–Lizzie.
7–31–d–Saunders Frank–Hudu.
7–16–s–Saunders Wm. R–M. M.
10–23–d–Sauski Thomas–Carrie.
7–26–d–Sauso Lawrence–Angelo.
12– 7–d–Savage John–Katherine.
5–27–s–Sawyer DeF. A.–Carrie M.
2–14–d–Scanlon Michael–Bridget.
11–20–s–Scannell Thomas–Eva.
5–17–d–Sceery Thomas–Kate.
8– 2–d–Schenkel August–Hattie.
12–24–d–Scherm Frank–Ernestein.
11– 6–d–Scherman Isaac–Minnie.
7– 8–d–Schief John–Ida.
2–28– –Schienauski Valentine–F.
2– 7–d–Schiessel Peter–Maggie.
9–18–s–Schiftgiesser Emil–Anna.
2– 2–d–Schinder Morris–Annie.
3–20–d–Schleicher Wm.–Rebecca.
5–24–d–Schlitz John–Minnie.
2– 4–s–Schmidt Martin V.–Mary.
3–28–s–Schnee Max–Dorothy.
8– 2–d–Schrepfer Michael–Annie.
9–15–s–Schroeder Chas.H.–Bertha.
1– 7–s–Schuckerow Jas. F.–Eliza.
12– 4–s–Schulz Wm.–Helena C.
6– 5–d–Schwartz Geo. B.–Pauline.
2–27–s–Scott Dennis–Alice.
2–25–d–Scott John–Sarah.
1– 4–s–Scott Patrick–Helen.
12–11–d–Scott Thomas–Maria.

11–10–d–Scott Thomas–Mary.
7–12–d–Scoville Oscar–Elizabeth.
7–24–s–Sculley Thomas–Mary.
4–18–d–Sedlesky Barney–Mary.
12– 9–s–Segel Heinrich–Rosie.
6–21–s–Segal Israel–Fannie.
10–24–s–Seide Henry W.–Ida.
8–21–d–SeinsothJol.nJ.–Elizab'h L.
12–22–s–Sellen Geo. C.–Marie.
6–17–d–Semindenger Theo.–Annie.
10–17–s–Senatre James–Maria.
4– 6–s–Setterl erg Edw'd–Hilda.
11–21–s–Seusico Carl F.–Carmel.
12–81–d–ShafferChas.O.–Eliz'bhH }
12–81–d–ShafferChas.O.–Eliz'bhH }
7– 6–s–Shak Tony–Mary.
11–27–s–Shanalian Peter J.–Bridget.
2– 8–d–Shappin Abraham–Annie.
8– 5– –Sharp Harvey–Annie.
10–16–d–Shaumen Thomas–Annie.
6–22–d–Shaw William E.–Mabel.
6–10–d–Shay Daniel–Lizzie.
1–14–s–Shea Cornielus–Kate.
7–11–d–Shea Daniel– ——
6– 9–d–Shea F. E.–Mary.
7–25–s–Shea John–Annie.
3–13–s–Shea John–Mary.
2–16–d–Shea John–Mary.
6–18–s–Shea John B.–Ellen.
10– 7–d–Shea Michael–Julia.
8– 2–d–Shea Patrick– ——
4– 2–s–Sheedy Mathew–Rose.
2–11–s–Sheedy Wm.–Catherine A.
8–24–d–Shepard George–Margaret.
1– 2–s–Shield Richard M.–Mary J.
2– 4–s–Shipman Lewis J.–Nettie.
12– 4–d–Shirley Chas. H.–Emma.
9–29–d–Shoesfer Andrew–Helen.
7– 7–s–Shuckerow James J.–Eliza.
9– 5–s–Shuethiers John F.– ——
5–21–s–Shulausky Henry–Jennie.
8–23–s–Silberman ——Celia.
5–28–d–Silberman Harris–Beckie.
11–14–s–Silk Patrick J.–Delia.
8–19– –Sillman Jakie–Beckey.
11–18–s–Silversmith Nathan–Ida.
9–17–s–Silvester Michael–Amelia.
7–12–s–Simkins Frank R.–Annie.
12–16–s–Simpson Irvin A–Elizabeth
7–29–s–Simpson James F.–Ros.
5–18–s–Skaw Peter L.–Annie C.
7– 9–s–Skinner Geo. L.–Annie L.
12–18–d–Slade Parish–Katherine.
8–31–d–Slattery John–Mary.
6–17–s–Slattery John A.–Mary. }
6–17–s–Slattery John A.–Mary. }
9– 2–s–Slichoski Martin–Redfia.
12–12–d–Slocum Chas. H.–Hester.
12–12–d–Small Char'es G.–Mary.
11–28–d–Smallyon Edw. J.–Etta A.
10–30–d–Smart John–Seline.
7–12–s–Smith C. H.–Matilda.
12–25–d–Smith Chas. E.–Christena.
9–13–s–Smith Christin–Bertha.
9– 8–d–Smith Fred'k H.–Minnie.
8–20–d–Smith George–Annie.
11–28–s–Smith John C.–Grace.
10–18–d–Smith Louis–Minnie.
10–18–s–Smith Nelson–Anna.
9– 4–d–Smith Silas N.–Bertina.
5–28–s–Smith Walter H.–Lillian S.
12– 1–d–Smith William–Mary.
12– 1–d–Snell Carl E.–Helma.
9– 9–d–Snow Charles L.–Julia.
5– 5– –Snyder Henry–Minnie.
10– 6–d–Sobolofsky F.– ——
12–10–s–Solomon Israel–Sarah.
4– 9–d–Solomon Jos. H.–Esther M.

11- 3-d-Solomon William-Katie.
4-27-d-Souther Henry-Elizabeth.
5- 4-s-Southurland A. G.-Alice.
8-14-s-Soutner Joseph- ——
4-17-s-Spencer Truman- ——
10-10-s-Spiegel David-Hattie.
10-19-s-Spielrogol John-Bertha.
12-16-d-Spoorer Mathias- ——
9-18-s-Spring Theo. L.-Lottie.
11-29-d-Spurr George W.-Alice M.
11-19-d-Stack Loren-Krestine.
9-15-s-S'annard Mason S.-Mary L.
8-14-s-Starkey John J.-Nora A.
11-17-s-S'arkweather C. M.-Lucy.
8-22-d-Starola Guiseppe- ——
9-27-s-Starr Jerome-Catherine.
3- 4-d-Steaberuz George-Maggie.
6- 4-d-Steane Isaac J.-Lybulla.
10- 2-s-Stedman Harry B.-Marg't E
10-14-s-Steeres W. H.-Cyenthia.
6- 7-d-Steidel Henry-Wilhelm.
6- 8-s-Stein Joseph-Sarah.
12-15-d-Steinmetz Wm. P.-Rosa.
10- 5-d-Stengelin Andrew-Joseph'e
3-25-s-Steres Wm. H.-Catherine.
7-28-d-Stermer John- Annie.
3-19-s-Stern Isaac-Mary.
1-23-d-Steven William F.-Agnes.
7-24-s-Stevens Joseph-Lottie.
9- 6-d-Stewart Frank O.- ——
1- 9-d-S'ewart John D.-Eliza.
12-13-s-Stickler C. M.-Ethel.
6-80-s-Stiles Frank B.-Charlotte.
10- 1-d-Stocker Thos.-Caroline.
3-16-d-Stone Frank E.-Marcia.
11-24-s-Stone Thomas-Elizabeth.
12-21-d-Storlor N.-Clara
12-21-d-Stoughton D. G.-Mary.
12-13-d-Stewart Charles-Phœbe.
2- 7-d-Strahan John-Lillian M.
1- 3-s-Street John-Lilly.
12-10-s-Sturtevant Ernst W.-H. L.
12-22-d-Sucher Mich-Margaret.
9-20-d-Suguduska John-Helena.
9-23-d-Sullivan Christher-Annie.
6-24-d-Sullivan Daniel-Hannah.
3- 6-d-Sullivan Dan'el-Mary.
4-15-s-Sullivan Dan'l F.-Eliza'bh.
5- 9-d-Sullivan Dennis-Margaret.
7- 1-s-Sullivan Dennis-Nellie.
5-10-d-Sullivan Ignatius A.-Sarah
12-29-d-Sullivan Jeremiah-Norah.
11-21-d-Sullivan John-Mary.
2- 1-d-Sullivan Joseph P.-Mary.
5- 1-d-Sullivan Patrick-Mary.
5-24-d-Sullivan Patrick-Mary.
10-14-s-Sunderland Peter-Mary A.
12-11-d-Supzauski Meyer-Mary.
6-30-s-Surgason Edw'd-Margaret.
6- 4-d-Suvenson Gus. L.-Matilda.
7- 6-s-Swanson —— -Matilda.
7-26-d-Swift Joseph-Rose L.
11-12-s-Sylvester Anari-Annie.
12-14-d-Sylvester George-Adelaine

8- 3-d-Taillefer Leon-Adelia.
8- 6-s-Talcott Wm. H.-Edith E.
10-23-d-Talui Nathan-Becky.
11-15-d-Taylor Fred'k E.-Emma.
5-15-d-Taylor Geo. W.-Lizzie L.
3- 6-d-Taylor Herman-Esther.
6-19-s-Taylor Samuel-Myran.
10-20-s-Taylor Solon T.-Bessina.
10-12-d-Taylor William F.-Helen.
11- 8-d-Tedford Joseph-Emma.
11-30-d-Tellassie Augeto-J.
1-10-d-Teuine Roco-C.
8- 6-s-Thalheimer A. L.-Julia.
3-23-s-Thayer Edward E.-Esther.

6-24-d-Thomas David-Millie.
9-13-s-Thomas Milton-Sarah H.
9-23-d-Thompson Edw'd M-Minnie
4-27-d-Thompson Michael-Mary.
6- 2-s-Thornton John-A.
5-25-d-Thoyet Wilbur-Cora M.
11- 2-s-Tilliman Charles-Ida.
11-19-d-Tiliman Louis-Ida.
10-29-d-Tischenbach Nicolas-Lizzie
11- 8-d-Tolles Chas. L.-Annie L.
12- 6-s-Toner John F.-Elizabeth.
4-16-d-Toohey Thomas-Mary.
2-22-d-Tooker Wm. L.-Margaret.
10- 8-s-Toomey John-Agnes.
4-25-s-Torp Christian-Kissten.
12-26-s-Toutant Eugene- ——
5-28-s-Towler John-Mary A.
7- 5-s-Tracey Willis S.-Ellen J.
7-23-s-Tracy Garrett-Mary L.
5-26-s-Tracy Louis A.-Mary A.
9-17-d-Tracy Thomas-Mary.
6- 1-d-Tremonta Joseph-Mary.
8- 7-d-Triebert Henry-Mary.
6-21-d-Tripp Richard E-Elizabeth
10-23-d-Trobeck Enock-Alice.
8-27-s-Trolui Charles-Johanna.
4-21-d-Trowbridge Isra-Mary.
12- 1-s-Trumbull C. P.-Annie.
6-80-d-Truth Francis-L. L.
7-14-s-Tucker Frederick A.-Lula.
3-22-d-Tucks S.-Fannie.
7-17-s-Tully Owen-Mary.
7- 1-d-Tuminons Philip-Bridget.
6- 3-s-Tunick Samuel-Yetti.
2- 1-s-Tunillo Michael-Mellie.
1-11-s-Turnbull J. A.-Frances H.
1-25-d-Turner Guy-Jean A.
10-27-s-Tyler George C.-Lula.
11-10-s-Tyska Martin-Louise. }
11-10-s-Tyska Martin-Louise. }

12-24-d-Urbandke Wm.-Bertha.
7-27-d-Uricchio D.-Philomena.
1-17-d-Uricchio Joseph-Milla.

7- 2-d-Valente Joseph-Carolina.
4-30-d-Valentine Geo. L.-Helen H.
10-13-s-Valentine N. G.-Carrie.
2-17-d-Vedal John-Christina.
7- 8-s-Vedner Solomon-Marie.
9- 3-s-Veranie Luke-Catherine.
10-24-d-Vilette Edward-Annie.
1-15-s-Vilhage Frank R.-Margaret
10-20-d-Vizner Marcel F.-Nellie.
12-17-d-Vonna Peter-Matilda.

4-17-s-Wade Arthur C.-Margaret.
10-25-d-Wade Benjamin-May.
8-19-d-Wakefield W. L.-Alice G.
7-16-d-Waldron James-Louisa A.
8-14-s-Walker Frederick-Hattie.
5-24-s-Walker John-Magaret.
10- 9-d-Walker Wilbur C.-Mary A.
3-21-s-Wall Charles-Annie.
7-28-d-Wall Garrer-Delia E.
6-27-s-Wallace E. S. J.-Nellie.
8- 9-d-Walsh John-Hanora.
5- 4-s-Warhoe Lowny-Mary.
9- 4-s-Warner George L.-Flora E.
3- 1-d-Warring Robert H.-Annie.
3- 2-d-Waten David-Mary.
3-18-s-Watrous Charles D.- ——
6-25-d-Watrous E. R.-Larella.
1- 9-s-Watrous Thomas-Marilla.
2-23-s-Watson Francis P.-Mary.
8-17-d-Watson James- ——
4-14-d-Webster Benj. F.-Amelia.
2- 8-s-Webster Chas. S.-Isabella.
8-14-d-Weeks C. A.-Mary D.

10-14-d-Weidel Frank-Tichla.
12-18-d-Weider Frank E.-Alrena.
7-30-s-Weinstein Israel-Clara.
9-20-s-Weinstein Samuel-Dora.
7- 8-d-Weir Charles-Alice.
8-27-d-Weirup Suvard-Anna.
1-16-d-Weiser Meyer-Sara.
10-15-d-Weitmaun Auschel-Sara.
3-25-d-Weitzel Conrad-Rosia.
4-12-d-Well Otto-Bridget.
3- 9-s-Weller Robert- ——
6-15-s-Wells M. O.-Mary.
10-30-d-Weltman Chas. J.-Carrie.
1-29-s-Welch Edward-Ellen M.
9-20-s-Welch James-Kate.
10-25-s-Welch John-Rose.
8-16-d-Welch Joseph-Annie.
9-14-s-Welch Michael-Mary.
12-28-s-Welch Thomas-Annie.
5-23-s-Wentworth Lucius M.-Etta
7-11-s-Werner Solomon-Mary.
12-11-d-West A. E.-Mary A.
9-28-s-Weston Peter-Florence K.
7- 4-d-Wetherill Herb't M.-Jessie.
4- 5-d-Weuis Thomas-Annie.
7-22-s-Weuzloff Wm. P.-Julia.
1-30-d-Whaley Josiah-Mary A. J.
1-30-s-Whalon Patrick-Bridget.
7-18-s-Wheelock John-F. W.
12-27-s-White Alexander-Minnie.
9- 7-d-White Harry-Ada.
3- 5-s-Whitford E. R.-Addie.
6-13-s-Whitford W. H.-Emma B.
3- 5-d-Whiting Chas. E.-Julia E.
8-17-d-WhitingEllsw'th M.-Selena
3-25-s-Whitmore Geo. H.-Susie R.
1- 2-d-Whittelsey F. H.-Laura V.
8- 3-s-Wilcox David- ——
12-18-d-Wilensky Charles-Etta. }
12-18-d-Wilensky Charles-Etta. }
11-21-d-Willerup Eric C.-Thea.
12-14-s-Wileuski Joseph-Pauline.
3-23-d-Williams And'w J.-Selma.
2-11-d-Williams Edward L.-Mary
2- 9-d-Williamson Frank R-Lettie.
2-20-s-Williamson P.-Annie.
8- 4-d-Williams Thos. H.-Lizzie E
11- 6-d-Wilson Benj. A.-Mary.
6-21-s-Wilson F. Potter-Joseph'e.
8-13-s-Wilson George-Annie.
1- 3-d-Wilson John-Mary.
7- -d-Wilson Richard-Mary D.
2- 2- -Wilson Thomas-Mary.
12- 8-d-Wilson William H.-Ida L.
12-28-s-WindHolgerG-Dorothy M }
12-28-d-WindHolgerG-Dorothy M }
7-28-s-Winnie Wm. M.-Carrie A.
9- 1-d-Wise Robert F.-Catherine.
5- 4-s-Wolf Charles- ——
5- 4-s-Wood William H.-Georg'a.
9- 8-s-Woodmancy Chas. S.-Clara
2- 6-s-Woods James-Maggie.
9- 4-d-Woods John F.-Lillinn.
1- 8-s-Wooley Fred'k-Isabella C.
3- 2-d-Wright Benjamin-Alice E.

10-13-d-Yarrick Julius-Annie.
1-17-s-Yellot James-Anna.
6- 9-s-Yelsorsky Steven-Kallas.
8-19-d-Yorune Meclea A. D.- ——
9- 7-d-Young James-Mary.
12- 9-s-Young John-Bertha.

2-22-s-Zabuck Frank-Pauline.
2- 9-s-Zillhart Albert-Louisa.
10- 8-s-Zimmerman Harry J.-Ella.
3-28-s-Zimmerman Louis-Ida.
10- 7-d-Zimmerman Philip-Minnie
11-11-s-Zimmerman Sim'l-Fannie

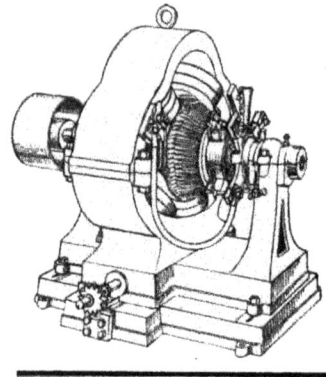 

# FRANCIS R. COOLEY,

## BANKER.

### Bonds, Local Securities, Investment Stocks,

#### Letters of Credit, Foreign Exchange.

**49 PEARL ST.,**                **Hartford, Conn.**

---

G. N. MERRILL,                E. O. HATHAWAY.                F. P. COBB.
Mem. Am. Soc. C. E.

## GEO. N. MERRILL & CO.,

### Civil and Consulting Engineers,

75 PRATT ST., Room 36,      Stearns Building,      **HARTFORD, CONN.**

Surveys, Plans, Estimates, and Specifications made for

**Steam and Street Railroads, Water Works, Bridges, Sewerage, Highways and Subdivision of Estates.**

## SPECIAL ATTENTION GIVEN TO CONSTRUCTION.

#### WORK SUPERINTENDED.

---

FRANK E. HUBBARD.          GEORGE MORTSON.

# HUBBARD & MORTSON,

## Automatic
## Time Switch Clock.

Special Attention given to Horologi
Astronomical and Electrical Work.

**42 UNION PLACE, Opp. Depot, Hartford,**

# 7 and 8 Per Cent. INTEREST

## NET TO THE INVESTOR.

### Choice Applications in

# FARM MORTGAGES

## DAILY RECEIVED BY US.

Do not speculate in uncertain securities, but seek safe investments. First Mortgages on Productive Land in the rapidly developing States of the West and South, when carefully selected by experienced men, will not fail in SECURITY and PROFIT.

We call your attention to the experience of our firm, and its methods of selecting and earning for these mortgages, and invite the examination of their record at our office.

JAMES H. TALLMAN, Att'y at Law.
JAMES B. MOORE.

## GEO. W. MOORE & CO.

### 759 MAIN STREET, Cor. Pearl St., Hartford, Conn.

---

# THIS IS THE KIND I BUILD.

But if you prefer a different style of architecture, let me get it up for you. I can please you, let your wants be what they may.

**See My Plans.**
**See My Houses.**
**See My People.**
(Those for whom I have built.)
**See My References.**

# E.F.EDE,

### 3 MORRIS ST.,
### HARTFORD, CONN.

---

# Ætna National Bank.

[Incorporated as a State Bank, Sept. 1857.  Reorganized as a National Bank, Jan. 1865.]

## 644 MAIN STREET,

Ætna Life Insurance Building, · · · · · · · HARTFORD, CONN.

### Capital, $525,000.   Surplus and Undivided Profits, $400,000.

**A. G. LOOMIS, President.     ALFRED SPENCER, Jr., Cashier.**

DIRECTORS.

Hon. LEVERETT BRAINARD, Ex-Mayor of City; Pres't of the Case, Lockwood & Brainard Co.
A. R. HILLYER, Ex-President.
Hon. MORGAN G. BULKELEY, Ex-Governor of Connecticut; President Ætna Life Insurance Co.
A. G. LOOMIS, President.     JAMES R. CONE, Capitalist.

### Discount Days, Mondays, Wednesdays, and Fridays, at 12 M.

**DIVIDENDS JANUARY AND JULY.**

Hours, 10 A. M. to 3 P. M.; Saturday, 12 M.          Annual Meeting, Second Thursday in January.

# American National Bank.

Organized as a State Bank, 1852.  Reorganized as National Bank, 1865.

## 803 MAIN STREET, Hartford, Conn.

### Capital, $600,000.   Surplus, $253,000.

*ROWLAND SWIFT, President.     JOSEPH H. KING, Cashier.*

DIRECTORS.

SILAS W. ROBBINS, Wethersfield, Conn.
WILLIAM H. BULKELEY, Capitalist; Ex-Lieutenant Governor of Connecticut.
ROWLAND SWIFT, President.
HENRY C. DWIGHT, firm of Dwight, Skinner & Co.
SAMUEL TAYLOR, firm of E. Taylor & Sons.
LYMAN B. JEWELL, Vice President Jewell Belting Co.
GEORGE ROBERTS, President and Treasurer Hartford Carpet Co.
CHARLES H. NORTHAM, firm of Smith, Northam & Co.
JOHN M. HOLCOMBE, Vice President Phœnix Mutual Life Ins. Co.
GEORGE L. CHASE, President Hartford Fire Ins. Co.
GEORGE H. DAY, Vice President Pope Mfg Co.

### Discount Days, Mondays, Wednesdays, and Fridays, at 12 M.

**DIVIDENDS JANUARY AND JULY.**

10 A. M. to 3 P. M.; Saturday, 12 M.          Annual Meeting, Second Thursday in January.

# CHARTER OAK NATIONAL BANK,

## 124 ASYLUM STREET.

### DEPOSITORY OF THE UNITED STATES.

State Bank, October, 1853.     National Bank, June 25, 1864.

### CAPITAL, $500,000.00     SURPLUS, $128,435.00

Charter Extended June 25, 1884, to June 15, 1904.

### J. P. TAYLOR, President.     M. A. ANDREWS, Cashier.

#### DIRECTORS.

JAMES NICHOLS, President National Fire Insurance Company.
LUCIUS A. BARBOUR, President Willimantic Linen Co.
JONATHAN F. MORRIS, formerly President of this Bank.
SILAS CHAPMAN, JR., Insurance.
E. C. FRISBIE, firm of Talcott, Frisbie & Co.
J. P. TAYLOR, President of this Bank.
ALBERT P. DAY, Superintendent Pope Manufacturing Co.
CHARLES C. COOK, Contractor and Builder.
JOHN O. ENDERS.

**Discount Days, Mondays, Wednesdays, and Fridays, at 11.30 A. M.**

### SAFE DEPOSIT DEPARTMENT.

A new vault has been constructed, combining the latest inventions of modern skill and science. Secure your papers and valuables against **Fire, Burglary, and Mob Violence.**

**Safe Deposit Boxes to Rent from $5.00 Upwards.**

Hours, 9 A. M. to 4 P. M.          Annual Meeting Second Tuesday in January.

---

# City Bank of Hartford,

## 783 MAIN STREET.

Incorporated in 1851.          Capital, $440,000.00.          Surplus, $160,000.00.

### CHARLES T. WELLES, President.

### CHAS. B. WHITING, Vice President.          EDWARD D. REDFIELD, Cashier.

#### DIRECTORS.

CHARLES A. JEWELL, Treasurer Jewell Belting Co.
RUSSELL M. BURDICK, firm of C. S. Brewer & Co.
WILLIAM B. CLARK, President Ætna Insurance Co.
CHAS. B. WHITING, President Orient Insurance Co.
MARO S. CHAPMAN, Sup't U. S. Envelope Works.
THEODORE M. LINCOLN, Sec'y and Treas. The Lincoln Co.
EDWARD D. ROBBINS, Attorney at Law.
GEORGE POPE, President Hartford Cycle Co.
ELIZUR S. GOODRICH, President Hartford Street Railway Co.
CHARLES T. WELLES, President.
GEORGE ELLIS, Secretary Travelers Insurance Co.
EDWARD W. HOOKER, Treas. Perkins Electric Switch

**Discount Days, Mondays, Wednesdays, and Fridays, at 12**

**Hours, 10 A. M. to 3 P. M.          Annual Meeting, First Tuesday in A**

It transacts a general Banking Business, and is authorized to act as **Trustee**, whether of ........ or of Corporations.     It also acts, whether by individual or court appointment, as Executor or Admini Guardian, or in any fiduciary capacity whatever. It is also

**A LEGAL DEPOSITORY OF TRUST FUNDS.**

# Connecticut River Banking Company,

**761 Main Street,**    Southwest corner of Pearl,    **Hartford, Conn.**

**Capital, $150,000.    Incorporated, May 1825.    Surplus, $80,000.**

SAMUEL E. ELMORE, President.          H. W. ERVING, Cashier.

HERMAN J. MAERCKLEIN, Assistant Cashier.

### DIRECTORS.

SAMUEL E. ELMORE, President.

HERBERT R. COFFIN, firm of C. H. Dexter & Sons.

J. M. ALLEN, Pres't Hfd. Steam Boiler Inspection and Ins. Co.

MILES W. GRAVES, Treasurer State Savings Bank.

STANLEY B. BOSWORTH, Manufacturer.

LOUIS R. CHENEY.

ARTHUR F. EGGLESTON, Attorney at Law.

WILLIAM H. WATROUS, Treasurer Wm. Rogers Mfg. Co.

E. O. WEEKS, Vice President Ætna Insurance Co.

## DISCOUNT DAYS, TUESDAYS AND FRIDAYS.

**Dividends, January and July.**

Hours, 10 A. M. to 3 P. M.; Saturday, 12 M.      Annual Meeting, First Tuesday in January.

---

# Farmers & Mechanics National Bank,

Organized as a State Bank in 1833.    Reorganized as a National Bank in 1865.

## 106 STATE STREET, HARTFORD, CONN.

**CAPITAL, $500,000.00.**      **SURPLUS AND UNDIVIDED PROFITS, $150,000.00.**

**JOHN G. ROOT, President.**      **WM. W. SMITH, Cashier.**

**CHARLES F. SEDGWICK, Assistant Cashier.**

### DIRECTORS.

FRANKLIN CLARK, Retired Merchant.

JOHN H. WHITE, Ex-Judge of Probate Court, Attorney at Law.

JOHN G. ROOT, Ex-Mayor City of Hartford.

WM. O. CARPENTER, Real Estate.

C. WILLIAMS, Treasurer Capewell Horse Nail Co.

HENRY H. GOODWIN, firm of Tucker & Goodwin.

A. O. CROSBY, Treas. Crosby Mfg. Co., East Glastonbury, Conn.

ATWOOD COLLINS, President Security Company.

## Discount Days, Tuesdays and Fridays, at 12 M.

**Dividends, January and July.**

rs, 10 A. M. to 3 P. M.; Saturday 12 M.      Annual Meeting, Second Tuesday in January.

# The First National Bank of Hartford,

**807 MAIN STREET, during the construction of their New Building at**

## No. 50 STATE STREET, HARTFORD, CONN.

Organized as a State Bank in 1857.          Reorganized as a National Bank, February, 1864.

**Capital, $650,000.     Surplus and Undivided Profits, $190,000.**

J. H. KNIGHT, Pres't.          C. D. RILEY, Cashier.          WARD W. JACOBS, Vice Pres't.

### DIRECTORS.

THOMAS SISSON, of T. Sisson & Co., Wholesale Druggists.
WARD W. JACOBS, Treasurer Mechanics Savings Bank
LESTER L. ENSWORTH, of L. L. Ensworth & Son, Iron Merchants.
E. C. HILLIARD, Manufacturer, Manchester, Conn.
J. H. KNIGHT, President of this Bank.
RAPHAEL BALLERSTEIN, of R. B. & Co., Importers of Millinery.
LUCIUS F. ROBINSON, of Robinson & Robinson, Attorneys at Law.
ASA S. COOK, Manufacturer of Machinery.
FRANCIS A. PRATT, Consulting Engineer, The Pratt & Whitney Co.
EDWIN S. BARTLETT, Real Estate.
RIENZI B. PARKER, President Hartford Life Insurance Co.

*Discount Days, Mondays, Wednesdays, and Fridays, at 11.30 A. M.*

**Dividends, January and July.**

Hours, 10 A. M. to 3 P. M.; Saturday 12 M.          Annual Meeting, Second Tuesday in January.

# Hartford National Bank.

**LATE HARTFORD BANK, INCORPORATED IN 1792.**

## 58 STATE STREET, HARTFORD, CONN.

*CAPITAL, $1,200,000.          SURPLUS, $700,000.*

**JAMES BOLTER, President.**          **W. S. BRIDGMAN, Cashier.**
**W. S. ANDREWS, Assistant Cashier.**

### DIRECTORS.

JAMES BOLTER, President.
HENRY C. JUDD, firm of H. C. Judd & Root.
PLINY JEWELL, President The Jewell Belting Co.
RALPH H. ENSIGN, firm of Ensign, Bickford & Co., Simsbury, Conn.
D. W. C. SKILTON, President Phœnix Insurance Co.
GEORGE A. FAIRFIELD, President Hartford Machine Screw Co.
JOHN H. HALL, Vice President Colt's Patent Fire Arms Mfg. Co.
CHARLES E. CHASE, Assistant Secretary Hartford Fire Ins.
PHILIP CORBIN, President P. & F. Corbin, New Britain, 
GEORGE A. GAY, of Brown, Thomson & Co.
JAMES G. BATTERSON, President Travelers I

*Discount Days, Mondays, Wednesdays, and Fridays, at 12 M.*

**DIVIDENDS, JUNE AND DECEMBER.**

Hours 10 A. M. to 3 P. M.; Saturday, 12 M.          Annual Meeting, Second Tuesday in

# National Exchange Bank,

## 76 STATE ST., HARTFORD, CONN.

Organized as a State Bank in 1884.     Reorganized as a National Bank in 1864.

### CAPITAL, $500,000.00.     SURPLUS, $200,000,00.

JOHN R. REDFIELD, President.     F. B. COOLEY, Vice President.     ELIJAH C. JOHNSON, Cashier.

### ⤙DIRECTORS.⤚

Hon. FRANCIS B. COOLEY.
JOHN C. DAY, Attorney.
AUSTIN C. DUNHAM, firm of Austin Dunham & Sons.
WILLIAM E. SUGDEN, of The Charles R. Hart Co.
MARTIN BENNETT, Manager Scottish Union and National Insurance Company of Edinburgh,
and the Lion Insurance Company of London.
DANIEL R. HOWE, Treasurer Hartford Street Railway Co.
J. R. REDFIELD, President.
N. B. ALLYN, formerly of Allyn & Blanchard Co.
JOHN D. BROWNE, President Connecticut Fire Insurance Co.
JULIUS GAY, Treasurer Farmington Savings Bank.
EDWARD A. FULLER, firm of E. A. & W. F. Fuller.
SYLVESTER C. DUNHAM, of The Travelers Ins. Co.

### Discount Days, Mondays, Wednesdays, and Fridays, at 12 M.

#### DIVIDENDS, JANUARY AND JULY.

Hours, 10 A. M. to 3 P. M.; Saturday, 12 M.     Annual meeting, second Tuesday in January.

# Phœnix National Bank

## 803 Main Street, Hartford, Conn.

Incorporated as a State Bank in 1814.     Reorganized as a National Bank, December, 1864.

### CAPITAL, $1,000,000.     SURPLUS, $500,000.

HENRY A. REDFIELD, President.     FREDERIC L. BUNCE, Cashier.
HERBERT H. WHITE, Assistant Cashier.

### DIRECTORS.

JAMES L. HOWARD, President of James L. Howard & Co., manufacturers car goods.
CHARLES M. BEACH, firm of Beach & Co.
JONATHAN B. BUNCE, President Phœnix Mutual Life Insurance Co.
JAMES M. THOMSON, firm of Brown, Thomson & Co.
HENRY A. REDFIELD, President.
SAMUEL G. DUNHAM, firm of Austin Dunham & Sons.
DANIEL SHIPMAN, Judge United States Circuit Court.
JACOB L. GREENE, President Connecticut Mutual Life Insurance Co.
WM. C. SKINNER, of Dwight, Skinner & Co.
ELLIS G. RICHARDS, Vice Pres't and Sec'y National Fire Ins. Co.

### Discount Days, Mondays, Wednesdays, and Fridays, at 12 M.

#### DIVIDENDS, JANUARY AND JULY.

Hours, 10 A. M. to 3 P. M.; Saturday, 12 M.     Annual Meeting, Second Tuesday in January.

# STATE BANK,

## INCORPORATED IN 1849.

### 795 MAIN STREET, HARTFORD, CONN.

Capital, $400,000.00          Surplus and Undivided Profits, $130,000.00

**GEORGE F. HILLS, President.**          **GEORGE H. BURT, Cashier.**

### DIRECTORS.

GEORGE F. HILLS, President of this Bank.
ERASTUS GAY, Farmington.
A. E. HART, Treasurer Society for Savings.
CLARENCE B. INGRAHAM, firm of Ingraham, Swift & Co.
E. G. WHITTELSEY, of E. G. Whittelsey & Co., Commission.
C. H. LAWRENCE, Secretary Phœnix Mutual Life Insurance Co.
GEORGE E. TAINTOR, with J. J. & F. Goodwin.
PATRICK GARVIN, Paper and Paper Stock.
JOHN R. BUCK, ex-member of Congress.

### Authorized to Act as Executor, Administrator, Treasurer, and every Fiduciary Capacity.

**Safe Deposit Boxes to Rent from $5.00 Upward.**

Hours, 9 A. M. to 4 P. M.          Annual Meeting, First Tuesday in October.

---

# United States Bank,

## CHARTERED 1872.

### 872 Main Street, corner Kinsley Street, Hartford, Conn.

Capital, $100,000.      Surplus and Undivided Profits, $282,000.

**HENRY L. BUNCE, President.**          **WM. H. BULKELEY, Vice President.**
**FREDERICK G. SEXTON, Cashier.**

### DIRECTORS.

MORGAN G. BULKELEY, Ex-Governor of Connecticut, President Ætna Life Ins. Co.
WILLIAM H. BULKELEY, Ex-Lieut. Governor of Connecticut.
SAMUEL G. DUNHAM, Treasurer Dunham Hosiery Co.
JOHN R. HILLS, Contractor and
ATWOOD COLLINS, President The Security Co.
LEVERETT BRAINARD, President Case, Lockwood & Braina-
JOHN O. ENDERS, Capitalist.
HENRY L. BUNCE, Pr

## DISCOUNT DAY, TUESDAY, 12 M.

Hours 10 A. M. to 3 P. M.          Annual Meeting, First Tuesda-

# Connecticut Trust and Safe Deposit Co.

### Incorporated, July 19, 1871.

## 777 and 785 MAIN ST., Corner Pearl St., HARTFORD, CONN.

### Cash Capital Paid in, $300,000. Surplus and Undivided Profits, $247,000.

### Banking Business.

Conducts a General Banking Business. Accounts opened and Deposits received subject to check at sight. Accounts solicited. Also

### Safe Deposit Vault,

The most capacious and impregnable in the city. 1000 Safe Boxes for rent from $10 to $100 per annum, according to size.

### Trust Department.

Is authorized by its charter to act as Trustee for Individuals and Corporations, Executor or Administrator of Estates, Guardians of Minors, etc.

**M. H. WHAPLES, Pres't. JACOB L. GREENE, Vice Pres't. JOHN H. WHEELER, Treas.**

**HENRY S. ROBINSON, Sec'y. H. P. REDFIELD, Ass't Treas.**

#### TRUSTEES.

| | | | |
|---|---|---|---|
| HENRY C. ROBINSON, | JACOB L. GREENE, | GEORGE ROBERTS, | DANIEL R. HOWE, |
| GEORGE L. CHASE, | HENRY CORNING, | JOHN M. TAYLOR, | MEIGS H. WHAPLES. |
| CHARLES H. SMITH, | JAMES J. GOODWIN, | JONATHAN B. BUNCE. | |

Annual Meeting, Second Wednesday in January. Dividends, January and July.

# HARTFORD TRUST COMPANY

## 764 Main St., cor. Central Row, Hartford, Conn.

### CAPITAL STOCK, $300,000.00. SURPLUS AND UNDIVIDED PROFITS, $175,000.00.

### Transacts a General Banking Business. Discounts Daily.

#### OFFICERS.

**RALPH W. CUTLER, President. CHAS. M. JOSLYN, Vice President. FRANK C. SUMNER, Sec'y and Treas.**

#### TRUSTEES.

RODNEY DENNIS, Pres't Conn. Humane Society.
J. C. WEBSTER, Vice Pres't Ætna Life Ins. Co.
CHARLES M. JOSLYN, Hungerford, Hyde, Joslyn & Gilman, Attorneys.
THEODORE LYMAN, Attorney at Law.
RALPH W. CUTLER, President of this Company.

PLINY JEWELL, Pres't Jewell Belting Co.
HENRY ROBERTS, Pres't H'f'd Woven Wire Mattr's Co.
CHARLES E. BILLINGS, Pres't Billings & Spencer Co.
Dr. HENRY P. STEARNS, Sup't Retreat for the Insane.
M. BRADFORD SCOTT, Hartford Fire Ins. Co.

**TRUST DEPARTMENT.**—This Company is authorized to act as Executor, Administrator, Guardian, Trustee. (Circular on Application.)

**SAFE DEPOSIT DEPARTMENT.**—We beg to call your attention to our Fire and Burglar SAFE DEPOSIT VAULT. It cannot be assailed by fire, being entirely outside the building, and under the very granite double sidewalk. Private boxes, strong in themselves, are protected by massive steel safes of the most improved construction, and these can only be reached through two sets of heavy vault doors, guarded by a Yale Time Lock. There are **seventy-six distinct plates of welded steel and iron** between the outside of the vault and the **inner** boxes. Trusty night watchmen pass entirely around the vault at stated intervals, and register their visits on a Watchman's Time Clock. We regard the vault as **ABSOLUTELY SAFE** and offer it with confidence, that it is the **strongest in New England.** Boxes, under the entire control of the renter, are $10, $15, $20 per annum.—a small sum for the **perfect security** we offer

**SILVER VAULT.**—We have also constructed a vault for storage of Family Silver, Laces, Jewels, etc., which has been built to supply an increasing demand for a place where heirlooms and other articles cherished for association, may be stored in safety. We cordially invite your inspection. FRED P. HOLT, *Superintendent.*

**Annual Meeting in January. Organized, October, 1868. Dividends, January and July.**

# The Fidelity Company,

### 49 PEARL STREET, HARTFORD, CONN.

#### Capital Stock, $50,000.

**JOHN M. HOLCOMBE, President.      CHARLES P. COOLEY, Treas.**

**LOOMIS A. NEWTON, Secretary.**

#### TRUSTEES.

This Company assumes the care of Property of all kinds, including the collection of Rents
and general management of Real Estate.
Acts as Trustee, Guardian, Conservator, Administrator, Executor, Agent and Attorney-in-fact
Is a lawful Depository of Trust Funds.
Undertakes the Presentation and Collection of Claims.
Receives money in Trust and on Deposit.
Places Insurance in strong and reliable companies.

### ANNUAL MEETING, SECOND TUESDAY IN APRIL.

# SECURITY COMPANY

*INCORPORATED 1875.*

### 62 PEARL STREET, HARTFORD, CONN.

## CAPITAL, $200,000.      RESERVE FUND, $100,000.

### ATWOOD COLLINS, Pres't.

**HENRY E. TAINTOR, Vice Pres't.          CHAS. EDW. PRIOR, Treas.**

#### TRUSTEES.

Acts as Executor, Administrator, Guardian, Conservator, and Trustee, and transacts
fiduciary business of every description.

Pays interest on moneys deposited for long periods, and loans money on approved collateral
security.

### Annual Meeting, Second Wednesday in January.

# DIME SAVINGS BANK

## OF HARTFORD,

In State Bank Building, 791 MAIN STREET, Hartford, Conn.

### DIMES SAVED INCREASE TO DOLLARS.

ALFRED E. BURR, President.　　　　　JOHN W. WELCH, Secretary.
　　P. H. WOODWARD, Vice President.　　　THOMAS M. SMITH, Treasurer.

### DIRECTORS.

ALFRED E. BURR, firm of Burr Brothers.
JAMES BOLTER, Pres't Hartford National Bank.
JOHN R. REDFIELD, Pres't National Exchange Bank.
C. C. KIMBALL, firm of Kimball & McCray.
S. G. DUNHAM, Treasurer Dunham Hosiery Company.
THOMAS SISSON, firm of T. Sisson & Co.
P. H. WOODWARD, Sec'y Hartford Board of Trade.
C. R. WHITING, Pres't Orient Insurance Company.
JOHN H. HALL, Vice President Colt's Patent Fire Arms Manufacturing Company.
HENRY L. BUNCE, President United States Bank.
WM. WALDO HYDE, Gross, Hyde & Shipman, Att'ys
GEORGE H. DAY, Vice Pres't Pope Manufacturing Co

JOHN W. WELCH, Secretary of this Bank.
C. S. DAVIDSON, Supt. N. Y., N. H. & H. R. R. Co.
D. A. ROOD, Proprietor United States Hotel.
SILAS GOODELL, Contractor.
R. H. ENSIGN, of Toy, Bickford & Co., Simsbury.
E. O. GOODWIN, Merchant, East Hartford.
R. P. CHAPMAN, Pres't Hartford B'ld'g & Loan Ass'n.
JOHN FAIRMAN, Merchant.
THOMAS M. SMITH, Treasurer.
EDWARD B. HATCH, President Johns-Pratt Co.
JOHN O. ENDERS, Capitalist.
E. C. HILLIARD, Manufacturer.
N. W. HAYDEN, Insurance.

AUDITORS—WM. L. SQUIRE, Treas. N. Y., N. H. & H. R. R.; JOHN K. WILLIAMS, Druggist,

Deposits draw interest from the first of each month, free from all taxes.

*Incorporated, May, 1870. Annual Meeting in July.*

**DEPOSITS AND SURPLUS, MAY 1, 1898, $1,070,000.00.**

**Call and get one of our New Auxiliary Banks. They will encourage and help you to save money.**

Banking Hours, 9 a. m. to 4 p. m.　　Dividends, April and October.

---

# Mechanics Savings Bank,

## 815 MAIN ST., 2d Door South of Asylum St.,

### HARTFORD, CONN.

++++++++++

## DEPOSITS AND SURPLUS, May 1, 1898, $4,419,436.57.

++++++++++

### INCORPORATED, JUNE, 1861.

HENRY C. DWIGHT, Pres't.　WARD W. JACOBS, Sec'y and Treas.　WM. A. WILLARD, Asst. Treas.

### DIRECTORS.

.EL PHILLIPS, Retired.
VARD W. PARSONS, Real Estate.
RD W. JACOBS, Treasurer.
R HARBISON, Retired.
RLES L. LINCOLN, of Lincoln & Co.
. A. FAIRFIELD, Pres't Hartford Mach. Screw Co.
N G. ROOT, Pres't Farm. & Mech National Bank.
HOLCOMBE, V. Pres't Phœnix Mut. Life Ins. Co.
RY C. DWIGHT, of Dwight, Skinner & Co.
TRICK R. FOSTER, of Foster & Co.

EDWARD M. BUNCE, Sec'y Conn. Mutual Life Ins. Co.
WM. B. CLARK, Pres't Ætna Insurance Co.
JAMES B. MOORE, of George W. Moore & Co.
JAMES H. KNIGHT, Pres't First Nat. Bank, Hartford.
LESTER L. ENSWORTH, Iron Merchant.
FRANK C. SUMNER, Treasurer Hartford Trust Co.
GEORGE POPE, President Hartford Cycle Co.
EDWIN P. TAYLOR, of E. Taylor & Sons.
JAMES U. TAINTOR, Secretary Orient Insurance Co.
WILLIAM H. KING, Secretary Ætna Insurance Co.

**Dividend Days, January 1st and July 1st.**　　**Interest Commences 1st of Every Month.**

Hours of Business, 9 A. M. to 4 P. M.　　Annual Meeting in July.

# State Savings Bank

## 39 PEARL STREET, HARTFORD.

INCORPORATED, JUNE, 1858.

## DEPOSITS AND SURPLUS, MAY 1, 1898, $4,100,000.

SAMUEL TAYLOR, President.  CHARLES E. BILLINGS, Vice President.

MILES W. GRAVES, Secretary and Treasurer.

### TRUSTEES.

MILES W. GRAVES, Secretary and Treasurer.
D. W. C SKILTON, Pres't Phœnix Insurance Co.
SAMUEL TAYLOR, firm of E. Taylor & Sons.
HENRY E. TAINTOR, Attorney at Law.
GEO. E. HATCH, Hatch & North Coal Co.
CHAS. E. BILLINGS, Pres't Billings & Spencer Co.

HENRY ROBERTS, Pres't Hfd. Woven Wire Mat Co
SAMUEL M. BRONSON, Treas. National Machine Co.
STANLEY B. BOSWORTH, Manufacturer of Pott'y
FREDERICK W. DAVIS, with J. J. & P. Goodwin.
JOHN P. WHEELER, Tr. Conn. Trust & Safe Deposit Co.
EGBERT O. WEEKS, Vice Pres't Ætna Ins. Co.

**Annual Meeting, Third Wednesday in July.**

Deposits commence drawing interest on the first day of the month after they are made.
Banking hours 9 A. M. to 4 P. M.

**DIVIDENDS, FEBRUARY AND AUGUST.**

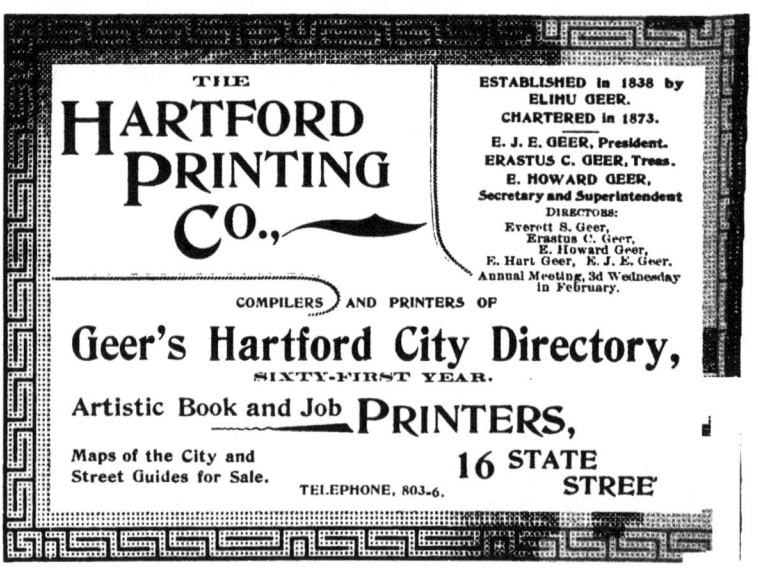

THE

# HARTFORD PRINTING Co.,

ESTABLISHED in 1838 by
ELIHU GEER.
CHARTERED in 1873.

E. J. E. GEER, President.
ERASTUS C. GEER, Treas.
E. HOWARD GEER,
Secretary and Superintendent

DIRECTORS:
Everett S. Geer,
Erastus C. Geer,
E. Howard Geer,
E. Hart Geer,  E. J. E. Geer.
Annual Meeting, 3d Wednesday
in February.

COMPILERS AND PRINTERS OF

## Geer's Hartford City Directory,

SIXTY-FIRST YEAR.

Artistic Book and Job **PRINTERS,**

Maps of the City and
Street Guides for Sale.    **16 STATE STREE'**

TELEPHONE, 803-6.

# THE. ÆTNA

*Is the Leading American Insurance Company.*

**Incorporated 1819.**

Organized upon a National basis, with Agencies in the principal Cities and Towns in the Union. Applications for Insurance against loss or damage by **FIRE** or the Perils of **INLAND**

**Charter Perpetual.**

**NAVIGATION,** made to any duly authorized Agent, promptly attended to.

Rates as liberal as is consistent with solvency and fair profit. Losses equitably adjusted and promptly paid.

## OFFICE: No. 666 MAIN ST., HARTFORD, CONN.

### OFFICERS.

### WILLIAM B. CLARK, President.

E. O. WEEKS, Vice President.　　　　WM. H. KING, Secretary.

A. C. ADAMS, HENRY E. REES, Assistant Secretaries.

### DIRECTORS.

DRAYTON HILLYER, firm of Dwight, Skinner & Co.
FRANCIS B. COOLEY, late President National Exchange Bank.
NATHANIEL SHIPMAN, Judge United States Circuit Court.
AUSTIN C. DUNHAM, firm of Austin Dunham & Sons.
MORGAN G. BULKELEY, Pres't Ætna Life Ins. Co.
J. PIERPONT MORGAN, firm of J. P. Morgan & Co.
ATWOOD COLLINS, President Security Company.
WILLIAM B. CLARK, Director of City Bank of Hartford.
FRANCIS GOODWIN, Capitalist.
CHARLES E. GROSS, firm of Gross, Hyde & Shipman.
JAMES H. KNIGHT, President First National Bank.
GEO. H. DAY, Vice President Pope Mfg Co.
E. O. WEEKS, Director Conn. River Banking Co.

Annual Election Third Thursday in January.

### SPECIAL AGENTS.

F. W. JENNESS, C. H. HOLLISTER, W. A. WARBURTON, J. B. HUGHES, O. H. KING, H. L. HISCOCK, C. J. IRVIN, H. O. KLINE, H. B. SMITH, ALFRED ROWELL, ALEXANDER BAYNE, PRIOLEAU ELLIS, A. N. WILLIAMS, A. W. SELKIRK, J. T. THOMAS, JAMES S. MIDDLETON.

*BRANCH OFFICE--413 Vine Street, Cincinnati, Ohio.*
Keeler & Gallagher, General Agents.

*NORTHWESTERN BRANCH--Omaha, Neb.*
W. H. Wyman, General Agent.　W. P. Harford, Assistant General Agent

### INLAND DEPARTMENT.

*EASTERN OFFICE--52 William Street, New York.*
Scott, Alexander & Talbot, Agents.

*WESTERN OFFICE--179 LaSalle Street, Chicago.*　J. S. GADSDEN, Superintendent.

*PACIFIC BRANCH*—Boardman & Spencer, Gen

**L. A. DICKINSON & CO.,** 664 Main St., Local Agents for Hartford and Vicinity

# SEVENTY-NINTH ANNUAL STATEMENT

## JANUARY 1, 1898.

OF THE

# ÆTNA Insurance Company,

## HARTFORD, CONN.

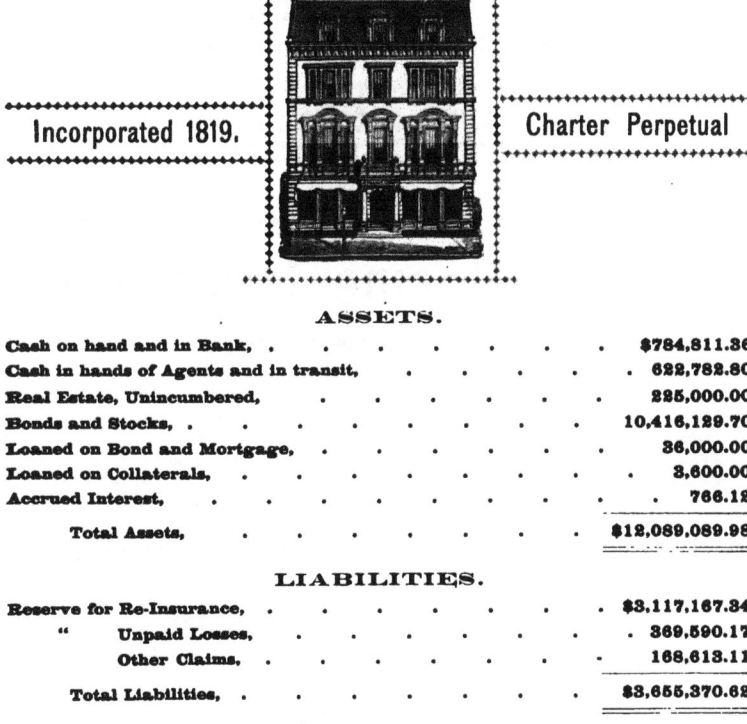

**Incorporated 1819.**            **Charter Perpetual**

### ASSETS.

| | |
|---|---:|
| Cash on hand and in Bank, | $784,811.36 |
| Cash in hands of Agents and in transit, | 622,782.80 |
| Real Estate, Unincumbered, | 225,000.00 |
| Bonds and Stocks, | 10,416,129.70 |
| Loaned on Bond and Mortgage, | 36,000.00 |
| Loaned on Collaterals, | 3,600.00 |
| Accrued Interest, | 766.12 |
| **Total Assets,** | **$12,089,089.98** |

### LIABILITIES.

| | |
|---|---:|
| Reserve for Re-Insurance, | $3,117,167.34 |
| "        Unpaid Losses, | 369,590.17 |
| Other Claims, | 168,613.11 |
| **Total Liabilities,** | **$3,655,370.62** |

] Surplus, $4,433,719.36.   Surplus as to Policy-Holders, $8,433,719.36.

## Losses Paid in 79 Years, $81,125,621.50.

## THE PIONEER COMPANY OF AMERICA.

# ❧ The ❧
# Hartford Steam Boiler Inspection and Insurance Company,

## 650 MAIN ST., HARTFORD CONN.

J. M. ALLEN, President.
WM. B. FRANKLIN, Vice President.
FRANCIS B. ALLEN, 2d Vice President.

J. B. PIERCE, Secretary and Treasurer.
L. B. BRAINARD, Assistant Treasurer.
L. F. MIDDLEBROOK, Ass't Secretary.

## ABSTRACT OF STATEMENT,
### January 1, 1898.

#### ASSETS.

| | |
|---|---:|
| Cash in Office and Bank, | $69,431.76 |
| Premiums in course of collection (net), | 238,158.42 |
| Loaned on Bond and Mortgage, first liens, | 335,775.00 |
| Bonds and Stocks, market value, | 1,503,841.50 |
| Real Estate, | 55,655.39 |
| Interest accrued, | 34,776.74 |
| Total Assets, | $2,237,638.81 |

#### LIABILITIES.

| | | |
|---|---:|---:|
| Premium Reserve, | | $1,275,786.77 |
| Losses in process of adjustment, | | 14,692.38 |
| Capital Stock, | $500,000.00 | |
| Net Surplus, | 447,159.66 | |
| Surplus as regards Policy-holders, | $947,159.66 | $947,159.66 |
| Total Liabilities, including Capital and Surplus, | | $2,237,638.81 |

#### INSPECTIONS.

All Boilers under the care of this Company are carefully inspected annually, internally and externally, by competent, practical men, and frequent visits of inspection are made beside. Steam Gauges are tested, safety valves properly adjusted and weighted. Boiler Connections carefully examined, and information given relative to setting and management—all with a view to economy in use of fuel, and safety to fire and property. Thorough inspection is the foundation of this business, and the best safeguard against accidents occurring in the use of steam boilers; nevertheless, circumstances arise beyond the control of the steam user independent of any inspection, however thorough, which would result in disaster, involving not only destruction of property, but loss of life and personal injury. It is therefore well to consider these points when affecting Insurance.

The work of the Company thus far has brought to light many and dangerous defects; and we risk nothing in saying that disastrous explosions have been prevented. Where boilers are left unexamined for months and years together, incrustation, internal and external corrosion, burned plates and blisters, shorten their working age and render them positively dangerous. The usual mode of inspection, applying the hydraulic test, take no cognizance of these defects, and does but little towards insuring safety.

HOME OFFICE OF
CONNECTICUT MUTUAL LIFE INSURANCE COMPANY, No. 783 MAIN STREET,
HARTFORD, CONNECTICUT.

(See opposite page.)

# "The Strongest Financial Institution in New England."

# The Connecticut Mutual
## Life insurance Co.
### 1846-1898.

THE CONNECTICUT MUTUAL TAKES FOR ITS SINGLE AIM THE ONE PECULIAR SERVICE WHICH LIFE INSURANCE ALONE CAN RENDER, AND WHICH NO OTHER INSTITUTION CAN RIVAL: THE PERFECT PROTECTION OF DEPENDENT FAMILIES, AT THE LOWEST POSSIBLE COST —THE CHEAPEST, SIMPLEST, MOST THOROUGH FAMILY PROTECTION. BY DINT OF INCESSANT CARE AND ECONOMY AT EVERY POINT, IT HAS SUCCEEDED AND DOES SUCCEED IN THIS PURPOSE AS NONE OTHER HAS DONE OR IS DOING. IT SECURES THE BEST AND HIGHEST OBTAINABLE RESULTS FROM THE PRUDENT AND UNSELFISH POLICY-HOLDER'S POINT OF VIEW; AND TO MAKE SURE OF AND TO MAINTAIN THESE, IT STEADILY FOREGOES THOSE THINGS FOR WHICH OTHERS STRIVE AT SUCH FEARFUL COST, TO WIT: RAPID GROWTH AND ENORMOUS SIZE: THINGS VERY IMPRESSIVE, EVEN STARTLING TO THE GENERAL EYE, BUT WHICH DO NOT BENEFIT THE POLICY-HOLDER IN THE SLIGHTEST, AND WHICH CAN BE HAD ONLY AT AN ENORMOUS COST WHICH HE MUST PAY.

## OFFICERS.

JACOB L. GREENE, President.  
JOHN M. TAYLOR, Vice President.  
EDWARD M. BUNCE, Secretary.  
JOHN D. PARKER, Ass't Secretary.  
DANIEL H. WELLS, Actuary.  
CHAS. HILDERBRAND, Ass't Actuary  
WILLIAM H. DEMING, Ass't Secretary.  
GEORGE R. SHEPHERD, M. D., Medical Director.  
EDWARD K. ROOT, M. D., Ass't Medical Director.  
CHARLES D. ALTON, M. D., Medical Referee.  
ELISHA RISLEY, Superintendent of Agencies.

## DIRECTORS.

| | | |
|---|---|---|
| HENRY C. ROBINSON, | WILLIAM B. FRANKLIN, | JOHN M. TAYLOR, |
| THOMAS SISSON, | EDWARD M. BUNCE, | CHARLES HOPKINS CLARK, |
| JACOB L. GREENE, | JAMES J. GOODWIN, | WILLIAM C. SKINNER, |
| FRANK W. CHENEY, | CHARLES M. BEACH, | CHARLES E. CHASE. |

ALFRED T. RICHARDS, General Agent, Room 16, Company's Building.  
JAMES H. JARMAN, Special Agent, Home Office.

HOME OFFICE OF
THE PHOENIX MUTUAL LIFE INSURANCE COMPANY.
49 PEARL STREET, HARTFORD, CONN.

(See opposite page.)

**1851.**           FORTY-SEVENTH ANNUAL STATEMENT           **1898.**

OF THE

# PHŒNIX MUTUAL LIFE

## INSURANCE COMPANY,

### OF HARTFORD, CONN.

### January 1, 1898.

## ASSETS.

| | |
|---|---|
| Loans on First Mortgages of Real Estate, | $5,463,730.12 |
| Premium Notes and Loans on Policies in force, | 727,159.38 |
| Loans on Collateral, | 6,600.00 |
| Cost Value of Real Estate owned by the Company | 1,151,828.59 |
| City and Municipal and Railroad Bonds and Stocks, | 2,685,536.43 |
| Bank Stocks, | 188,376.00 |
| Cash in Office, | 157.03 |
| Cash Deposited in Banks, | 459,526.16 |
| **Add:** | **$10,682,913.71** |
| Market Value of Stocks and Bonds over cost, $ 51,759.73 | |
| Interest accrued and due, 147,181.41 | |
| Net Deferred and Outstanding Premiums, 172,818.49 | $371,759.63 |
| **Gross Assets January 1, 1898,** - - - - - | **$11,054,673.34** |

## LIABILITIES.

| | | |
|---|---|---|
| Reserve on Policies in force at 4 per cent. interest, | $10,183,846.00 | |
| Claims by death outstanding and notified, | 37,774.00 | |
| Premiums paid in Advance, | 11,244.00 | |
| Special Reserves, | 197,934.00 | $10,430,798.00 |
| **Surplus at 4 per cent.,** - - - - - - - - - | | **$623,875.34** |

| | 1895. | 1896. | 1897. |
|---|---|---|---|
| Policies issued, | 6,161 | 5,193 | 6,110 |
| Insurance written, | $11,170,117 | $9,186,356 | $11,007,200 |
| New Premiums received, | 307,719 | 268,651 | 315,307 |
| Total Premiums received, | 1,330,804 | 1,430,228 | 1,589,531 |
| Policies in force, | 24,999 | 25,981 | 28,269 |
| Insurance in force, | 40,460,331 | 42,216,841 | 46,021,069 |

*This Company has paid since organization for DEATH LOSSES, MATURED ENDOWMENTS, DIVIDENDS TO POLICY-HOLDERS and SURRENDERED POLICIES, more than* **37,000,000.00.**

### BOARD OF DIRECTORS.

JONATHAN B. BUNCE, President Phœnix Mutual Life Insurance Company.
JAMES NICHOLS, President National Fire Ins. Co.
NATHANIEL SHIPMAN, Judge U. S. Circuit Court.
JOHN M. HOLCOMBE, Vice President Phœnix Mutual Life Insurance Company.
ISAAC W. BROOKS, Treas. Torrington Savings Bank.
FRANCIS B. COOLEY, Vice President National Exchange Bank.
GEORGE H. DAY, Vice President Pope Mfg. Co.
SILAS W. ROBBINS, Director American Nat'l Bank.

CHARLES H. LAWRENCE, Secretary Phœnix Mutual Life Insurance Company
CHAS. E. GROSS, of Gross, Hyde & Shipman, Attorneys at Law.
JOHN H. HALL, Vice President of Colt's Patent Fire Arms Manufacturing Company.
JOHN D. BROWNE, President Conn. Fire Ins. Co.
EDWARD D. ROBBINS, formerly of Hamersley & Robbins, Attorneys at Law.
DAVID S. PLUME, Treasurer Plume & Atwood Company, Waterbury.

Annual Meeting, last Tuesday in February.

### OFFICERS.

**JONATHAN B. BUNCE, President.**

CHARLES H. LAWRENCE, Secretary.
WILLIAM A. MOORE, Assistant Secretary.
WM. D. MORGAN, M. D., Medical Director.

JOHN W. HOLCOMBE, Vice President.
ARCHIBALD A. WELCH, Actuary.
GEO. S. MILLER, Superintendent of Agencies.

# ..THE..

# Hartford Life Insurance Co.,

### HARTFORD, CONN.

*Organized, 1867.*

## R. B. PARKER, President.

**DIRECTORS.**
Hon. DWIGHT LOOMIS,
R. B. PARKER,
E. C. HILLIARD,
JAS. H. KNIGHT,
JOHN D. PARKER,
F. S. SNOW,
N. M. LEARNED.

E. C. HILLIARD,
1st Vice President.

J. D. PARKER,
2d Vice President.

CHAS. H. BACALL,
Secretary.

F. S. SNOW,
Medical Director.

### HOME OFFICE.

This Company issues the best all-round up-to-date policy contracts upon the most desirable plans, and most liberal in terms. January 1, 1894, the capital and surplus of the Hartford Life was $294,265. The capital and surplus January 1, 1898, was $570,797; showing a gain for the period of $276,532.

| | |
|---|---:|
| **INSURANCE IN FORCE,** | $90,520,000 |
| **PAID BENEFICIARIES,** | 14,225,000 |
| **MEMBERS' SAFETY FUNDS,** | 1,192,191 |
| **PAID DIVIDENDS TO POLICY HOLDERS,** | 800,000 |
| **SECURITIES DEPOSITED WITH CONN. STATE TREAS.,** | 100,000 |

## HOME OFFICE,

# 252 ASYLUM ST., - Hartford, Conn.

### S. F. BRONSON, General Agent for Connecticut.

**HOME OFFICE,**

# No. 53 TRUMBULL ST., - Hartford, Conn.

## STEPHEN BALL, President.

L. L. ENSWORTH and CHAS. B. ANDRUS, Vice Presidents.

FREDERIC H. CALKINS, Secretary.

E. E. SMITH, Treasurer.

F. E. BUTLER, Manager Claim Department.

F. H. PELTIER, M. D., Assistant Medical Director.

CHAS. E. PERKINS and SIDNEY E. CLARKE, Counsel.

O. H. BLANCHARD, Manager New England Division of Agents.

### BOARD OF DIRECTORS.

CHAS. E. PERKINS, Attorney, and President Hartford Bar.
O. H. BLANCHARD, Manager New England Division of Agents, Hartford.
L. L. ENSWORTH, Iron Merchant and Bank Director, Hartford.
JAMES AHERN, President Plumbers' Association of Conn., Hartford.
SIDNEY E. CLARKE, Attorney, Hartford.
R. BALLERSTEIN, Merchant and Bank Director, Hartford.
EBEN E. SMITH, Treasurer, Hartford.
H. B. PHILBRICK, Contractor, Hartford.
CHAS. B. ANDRUS, Contractor, Hartford.
SELAH A. HULL, of S. A. Hull & Co., Investment Broker and Director
Meriden Savings Bank, Meriden, Conn.
FREDERIC H. CALKINS, Secretary, Hartford.
STEPHEN BALL, President, Hartford.

### JANUARY 1, 1898.

## ASSETS, - - - - - $330,346.55
## INSURANCE IN FORCE, $25,028,221.00

# THE

# TRAVELERS,

of
Hartford,
Conn.

### JAMES G. BATTERSON,
**President.**

## Largest Accident Company in the World,

## and a Leading Life Company.

### ISSUES ACCIDENT POLICIES

*Covering Accidents of Travel, Sport, or Business, at Home and Abroad,*

Yearly, or premium paid up in Ten Years with return of all premiums paid, and running till 70. Death only, or Death and Weekly Indemnity. No medical examination required. Not forfeited by change of occupation, but paid *pro rata*. No extra charge for foreign travel or residence.

### All Forms of LIABILITY INSURANCE, Covering

The liability of Manufacturers and other Employers to strangers who may be injured upon their premises. The liability of Contractors to Employees and to strangers for injuries sustained upon buildings or other works under contract. The contingent liability of Owners having buildings or other works under contract. The liability of owners of buildings for accidents, (including Elevator). The liability of Owners of Horses and Vehicles for driving accidents.

### LIFE and ENDOWMENT POLICIES.

All Forms, Low Rates, and Non-Forfeitable. *Its Increasing Life Plan* affording options of conversion into temporary or life annuities, with liberal surrender values, is offered by no other Company.

| Assets, | Liabilities, | Surplus, |
|---|---|---|
| $22,868,994.16 | $19,146,359.04 | $3,722,635.12 |

#### Returned to Policy Holders since 1864,

#### $34,360,626

GEORGE ELLIS, Secretary.            JOHN E. MORRIS, Ass't Secretary.

# CONNECTICUT
# FIRE INSURANCE CO.

## of Hartford, Conn.

### Office, No. 51 PROSPECT STREET, Cor. of GROVE ST.

INCORPORATED JUNE, 1850.

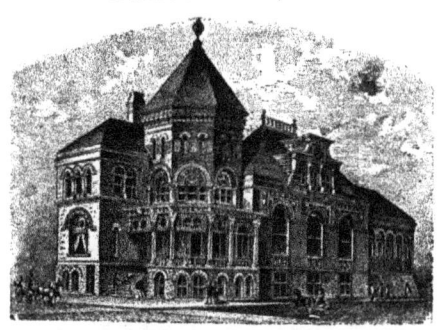

CONNECTICUT FIRE INSURANCE CO'S BUILDING.

### Forty-Eighth Annual Statement, Jan. 1, 1898.

| | |
|---|---:|
| *Cash Capital,* . . . . . . . . . . | *$1,000,000.00* |
| *Cash Assets, January 1, 1898,* . . . . . . . . | *3,559,327.18* |
| *Net Surplus to Policy-Holders,* . . . . . . . | *1,984,017.65* |

#### OFFICERS.

**JOHN D. BROWNE, President.**

**CHARLES R. BURT, Secretary.**          **L. W. CLARKE, Ass't Secretary.**

#### DIRECTORS.

HENRY C. ROBINSON, Attorney at Law, Director N. Y., N. H. & H. R. R.
A. E. BURR, Editor Hartford Daily Times.
JOHN R. REDFIELD, President National Exchange Bank.
RODNEY DENNIS, President Connecticut Humane Society.
FRANKLIN G. WHITMORE, Real Estate.
T. W. RUSSELL, President Connecticut General Life Insurance Co.
J. D. BROWNE, President.
D. R. HOWE, Treasurer Hartford Street Railway Company.
H. P. STEARNS, Superintendent and Physician, Retreat for Insane.
J. M. HOLCOMBE, Vice President Phœnix Mutual Life Insurance Co.

*Western Department—*P. D. McGREGOR, Asst. Manager, Rookery Building, Chicago, Ill.
*Pacific Department—*BENJ. J. SMITH, Manager, San Francisco, Cal.

### W. E. BAKER & SON, Local Agents, Gas Co's Building.

# THE HARTFORD
# Fire Insurance Company,

### OF HARTFORD, CONN.

————53 TRUMBULL STREET.————

Devoted exclusively to Insurance against Loss or Damage by Fire.  All classes
of Fire Risks accepted at rates graded to hazard Involved.

**Incorporated May, 1810.**

Charter Perpetual.

**GEO. L. OHASE,**
President.

**P. O. ROYOE,**
Secretary.

**T. TURNBULL,**
Ass't Sec'y.

**OHAS. E. OHASE,**
Ass't Sec'y.

*Annual Meeting,*
*January 8.*

**DIRECTORS.**

Geo. L. Ohase,
Jon'n B. Bunce,
Jas. J. Goodwin.
Jacob L. Greene,
Theodore Lyman,
George Roberts,
John O. Day,
Wm. O. Skinner,
M. H. Whaples.

Has a Capital of One and One-quarter Million Dollars.

Has Total Assets of Over Ten Million Eight Hundred and Nineteen Thousand Dollars.

Has a Net Surplus of Over Four Million Two Hundred and Forty-Nine Thousand Dollars.

Has Paid Over Fifty-Six Million Dollars in Losses.

### SILAS CHAPMAN, Jr., Resident Agent,
#### 51 TRUMBULL STREET.

**Offices and Apartments To Let**
**In the Hartford Fire Insurance Company's Building,**
**Apply to M. O. Wells, Agent, 9 Central Row.**

CHARTERED, MAY, 1869.    ORGANIZED, NOV. 27, 1871.

# NATIONAL
# FIRE INSURANCE COMPANY,

### OF HARTFORD, CONN.

## No. 95 PEARL STREET.

### *Statement, January 1, 1898.*

CAPITAL STOCK, All Cash,................................................. $1,000,000.00
FUNDS RESERVED TO MEET ALL LIABILITIES:
    Re-Insurance Reserve, Legal Standard,............................. 1,734,945.34
    Unsettled Losses and Other Claims,................................. 317,654.02
Net Surplus over Capital and Liabilities,................................. 1,380,419.50
TOTAL ASSETS, January 1, 1898,........................................ $4,433,018.86

### JAMES NICHOLS, President,

#### E. G. RICHARDS, Vice President and Secretary.

#### B. R. STILLMAN, Assistant Secretary.

##### *DIRECTORS.*

JAMES NICHOLS, President.
HOMER BLANCHARD, formerly Pres't Broad BrookCo.
JAMES BOLTER, President Hartford National Bank.
WILLIAM B. FRANKLIN, formerly Vice President Colt's Patent Fire-Arms Manufacturing Co.
FRANK W. CHENEY, Treasurer Cheney Brothers, Silk Manufacturers, etc., etc.
JOHN R. BUCK, Attorney at Law, Ex-Congressman.

JONATHAN F. MORRIS, formerly President Charter Oak National Bank.
JOHN L. HOUSTON, President Hartford Carpet Co.
HENRY C. JUDD, firm of H. C. Judd & Root.
FRANCIS T. MAXWELL, Treasurer Hockanum Co., Rockville.
ELLIS G. RICHARDS, Secretary.
BYRON A. SIMMONS, Capitalist.

*Annual Meeting, the Last Thursday in January.*

DIVIDENDS JANUARY AND JULY.

*WESTERN DEPARTMENT, Office, 174 LaSalle Street, Chicago.*
    FRED S. JAMES, GENERAL AGENT; GEORGE W. BLOSSOM, Ass't General Agent.
    CHARLES RICHARDSON, 2d Assistant General Agent.

*PACIFIC DEPARTMENT, Office, 409 California Street, San Francisco.*
    GEORGE D. DORNIN, MANAGER; GEORGE W. DORNIN, Assistant Manager.

# W. T. PRICE & CO., Local Agents, 95 PEARL ST., Hartford.

## TIME TRIED AND FIRE TESTED.

# The Phœnix Insurance Company,

## 64 PEARL STREET, Hartford, Conn.

**Chartered, June, 1854.**       **Annual Meeting in January.**

### Cash Capital,

## $2,000,000

### Loses Paid,

*♪ OVER ♪*

## $41,385,760.27

### CONDITION JANUARY 1, 1898.

#### ASSETS.

| | |
|---|---:|
| Cash on Hand, in Bank, and with Agents, | $747,147.73 |
| State Stocks and Bonds, | 29,250.00 |
| Hartford Bank Stocks, | 569,280.00 |
| Miscellaneous Bank Stocks | 359,907.00 |
| Corporation and Railroad Stocks and Bonds, | 2,774,416.00 |
| County, City, and Water Bonds, | 344,270.00 |
| Real Estate, | 527,696.67 |
| Loans on Collateral, | 20,200.00 |
| Real Estate Loans, | 132,340.70 |
| Accumulated Interest and Rent, | 33,871.40 |
| TOTAL CASH ASSETS, | **$5,538,379.50** |

#### LIABILITIES.

| | |
|---|---:|
| Cash Capital, | $2,000,000.00 |
| Reserve for Outstanding Losses, | 375,470.73 |
| Reserve for Re-Insurance, | 2,139,993.40 |
| NET SURPLUS, | 1,022,915.37 |
| TOTAL ASSETS, | **$5,538,379.50** |

### Surplus to Policy-holders,    $3,022,915.37

**D. W. C. SKILTON, President.**

J. H. MITCHELL, Vice Pres't.      EDWARD MILLIGAN, Sec'y.      JOHN B. KNOX, Ass't Sec'y.

H. M. MAGILL, General Agent Western Department, Cincinnati, Ohio.
THEO. F. SPEAR, Assistant General Agent Western Department, Cincinnati, Ohio.
HERBERT FOLGER, General Agent Pacific Department, San Francisco, Cal.
DIXWELL HEWITT, Assistant General Agent.
J. W. TATLEY, Manager Canadian Department, Montreal, Canada.

#### DIRECTORS.

CHARLES M. BEACH,    HENRY A. REDFIELD,    HENRY C. DWIGHT,    CHAS. H. NORTHAM,
MILO HUNT,    HENRY K. MORGAN,    WARD W. JACOBS,    JOHN H. HALL,
PLINY JEWELL,    CHARLES H. SMITH,    D. W. C. SKILTON,    GEORGE RIPLEY,
     LYMAN B. JEWELL,    J. H. MITCHELL,      Boston.

### EDWARD W. BEARDSLEY, Local Agent, Hartford and Vicinity.

#### Office, 64 PEARL STREET.

# Orient ✳ Insurance ✳ Company,

## 5 HAYNES ST., Cor. PEARL, HARTFORD, CONN.

Incorporated, June 28, 1867.

Began Business, January, 1872.

Annual Meeting, Second Wednesday in February. Dividends, January and July.

### Statement of Condition, January 1, 1898.

| | |
|---|---:|
| CAPITAL STOCK, PAID UP IN CASH, | $500,000.00 |
| NET SURPLUS OVER ALL LIABILITIES, | 735,278.41 |
| RESERVE FOR RE-INSURANCE, | 959,900.72 |
| OUTSTANDING LOSSES AND ALL OTHER LIABILITIES, | 151,505.36 |
| **Total Cash Assets,** | **$2,346,684.49** |
| **Surplus, as Regards Policy-holders,** | **$1,235,278.41** |

### SCHEDULE OF ASSETS.

| | |
|---|---:|
| Bank Stocks, | $333,090.00 |
| Railroad Stocks, | 473,115.00 |
| Railroad Bonds, | 466,722.00 |
| State, County, City, and Town Bonds, | 432,161.63 |
| Cash in Bank and in Agents Hands, | 295,306.39 |
| Real Estate, | 58,959.43 |
| Interest Accrued, and Rents, | 18,229.38 |
| Loans on Mortgages, first lien, | 267,350.66 |
| Loans Secured by Stocks and Bonds, | 1,750.00 |
| **Total Assets,** | **$2,346,684.49** |

### Losses Paid Since Organization to Date, $11,224,028.47.

**CHARLES B. WHITING, President.**

JAMES U. TAINTOR, Secretary.      HOWARD W. COOK, Ass't Secretary.

### DIRECTORS.

DANIEL PHILLIPS, ex-Pres't Mechanics Savings B'k.
LEVERETT BRAINARD, President of the Case, Lockwood & Brainard Co.
WILLIAM H. BULKELEY, Ex-Lieut. Gov. of Conn.
JOHN R. HILLS, Mason and Builder.
JOHN G. ROOT, President Farmers and Mechanics National Bank.
ARTHUR W. ALLEN, Merchant, Chicago, Ill.
CHAS. B. WHITING, Vice Pres't City Bank of Hartford

J. M. ALLEN, President Hartford Steam Boiler Inspection and Insurance Company.
P. HENRY WOODWARD, Sec'y H'f'd Board of Trade.
B. W. FRENCH, General Agent, Chicago, Ill.
GEORGE POPE, President Hartford Cycle Company.
M. S. CHAPMAN, Vice Pres't Plimpton Mfg. Co.
JAMES U. TAINTOR, Secretary.
WM. WALDO HYDE, Attorney at Law, Gross, Hyde & Shipman.

*Western Department*—B. W. FRENCH, General Agent, CHICAGO, ILL.

*Pacific Department*—W. J. CALLINGHAM, SAN FRANCISCO, CAL.

*Southwestern Department*—TREZEVANT & COCHRANE, DALLAS, TEXAS.

## SILAS CHAPMAN, JR., Local Agent, 51 Trumbull Street.

## CITY JURORS

Chosen by Court of Common Council, April 25, 1898, for the year ending April 1, 1899.

| | |
|---|---|
| Allen John | Kinsella R. J. |
| Anderson Montague | Kinyon F. S. |
| Baker William E. | Kohn Henry |
| Bartlett Alonzo | Lamb John W. |
| Bidwell Samuel W. | Lawler Edward |
| Blake Thomas J. | Lepard Frederick P. |
| Boardman Thos. J. | Long John C. |
| Bosworth S. B. | Lull Lysander |
| Bourn William | Madigan Charles R. |
| Bragaw Isaac | Mahl George |
| Brainerd Amaziah | Marcy Frederick A. |
| Bremer B. Z. | McDonnell John B. |
| Burnham Edgar F. | McKee Geo. C. |
| Butler Patrick F. | Messenger J. T. |
| Cadden Abraham | Moody Geo. F. |
| Cambridge Ichabod L. | Morse J. H. |
| Camp Howard A. | Mulcahy Edward J. |
| Case Horace J. | Norris Michael H. |
| Child A. Kennedy | Noyes Geo. N. |
| Collins Samuel | Oakey P. Davis |
| Cook James S. | Oakley Ernest F. |
| Cowles Samuel W. | O'Donnell Frank |
| Cummings Francis A. | Otis John Henry |
| Cummings Leonard G. | Packard Caleb L. |
| Davenport Joseph | Peek DeWitt J. |
| Dillon James D. | Persse T. B. |
| Donaghue William | Post Charles A. |
| Ehret John | Prentice Charles H. |
| Farrell Robert J. | Pye Thomas F. |
| Freeman S. G. | Russell Henry B. |
| Garvie John B. | Sage Edwin J. |
| Gaffey P. J. | Schall Ernst |
| Gilman Julius S. | Schmidt Emil |
| Govan James | Schwab Joseph |
| Halliday W. H. | Shelton Edward |
| Hayden George A. | Smith Willis E. |
| Haspey William | Sperry Henry T. |
| Hatch George E. | Stewart Chas. W. |
| Herrick Lewis B. | Talcott William H. |
| Heublein Louis F. | Thrall Edward B. |
| Hill Eben B. | Tillinghast A. H. |
| Hinckley Nelson G. | Tuller George W. |
| Hogan Matthew | Tuttle Charles L. |
| Hudson Wm. M. | Welton Henry A. |
| Hurd Charles F. | West Frederick A. |
| Judd Edward H. | Winship William L. |
| Keane H. P. | Wood H. R. |
| Kennedy Henry | Woods George H |
| King Charles | |

## UNITED STATES INTERNAL REVENUE.

*Post Office Building*, 65 *State street.*

Thos. A. Lake, Rockville, *Collector.* Geo. R. Case, *Chief Deputy Collector.* Theo. M. Byxbee, Hartford; J. J. Kennedy, New Haven; Chas. W. Murphy, Providence, *Stamp Deputies.* H. J. Hirsch, New London; G. M. Phelps, Bloomfield; Herman Hoffman, Waterbury; J. V. Squier, Hartford; J. Flahavan, New Haven; E. N. Sloan, Bridgeport; J. J. Gilmartin, T. F. Cavanaugh, Providence; *Division Deputies.* R. A. Rathbun, Providence; Joseph Mairson, E. T. Case, Hartford; Thomas F. Clarke, Providence, *Office Department.* Thomas Langdon, Bridgeport; J. R. Daly, Hartford; C. H. Owen, Providence; E. A. Jonchinson. New Haven, George C. McKee, *Gaugers.* Fred M. Godard, Melrose; W. H. Coggswell, Warehouse Point, *Store-keepers and Gaugers.* Bernard C. Lynch, Warehouse Point; M. F. Delaney, Melrose; J. A. Linsley, New Haven, *Storekeepers.* T. F. Daily, *Storekeeper and Gauger* special bonded warehouse, Wallingford.

## BUSINESS PANICS AND DEPRESSIONS,

1825; 1836-39; 1847; 1857; 1866; 1873; 1883-4; 1886; 1893-8, over silver, lack of confidence, war with Spain.

## COLD WEATHER.

1641—50 days crossing Conn. river on ice.
1664—Large comet seen in New England.
1669—In February, deep snow storms.
1691—Terrible snow storms.
1717—Snow 11 feet deep; one storm commenced 17th lasting until 24th.
1740—Sleighing Nov. 13 to April 20.
1761—Very cold; deep snows.
1773—Very severe winter.
1774—Largest snow storm known.
1780—May 19, the dark day in Northern states; winter very severe; the sound frozen over.
1784, 1785, 1788, 1792, 1796 and 1799, severe winters.
1791—One snow storm of four days; snow 6 feet deep.
1798—Feb. 4, 34° below zero.
1800—Snow 3 feet deep, three months.
1808—May 8, snow fell over a foot in depth—freezing for two nights.
1807—Cold so intense Feb. 7, that forest trees cracked like reports from guns firing.
1816—Jan. 16-17, snow four feet deep; cold summer; frost every month in the year.
1818—May 17, snow lasted five days.
1821—Intense cold so long and continuous that Long Island sound was frozen over.
1823—Nov. 6, first snow; sleighing for 151 days.
1827—Oct. 17, snow fell fifteen inches deep, and in all New England; a few miles above Hartford it did not go off until spring opened. Thousands of bushels of potatoes remained undug until spring, when they were found in good condition.
1835—Cold winter of this century; February, from 1° to 28° below zero, with deep snows.
1837—Was noted for deep snows.
1841—Oct. 3, snow fell one foot deep.
1855—Below zero 47 times, and crossing the ice on Conn. river, to near the sound, was continuous until the the 1st day of April, 1856, inclusive, and the next day steamboats steamed up to Hartford.
1857—Jan. 22-24, for 42 consecutive hours it was 18° to 30° below zero.
1859—Jan. 9-12, from 2° to 27° below zero. July 4 mercury was 86°, and a slight frost in several towns.
1861—Jan. 13 and Feb. 8, 18° below zero.
1866—Jan. 8, 18° below zero.
1871—Feb. 6, 12° below zero.
1873—Jan. 30, 32° below zero; 36 zero mornings this winter, and 102 days sleighing.
1874—April 25, 28-30, snow storms.
1875—Jan. 10, 10° below zero.
1878—Jan. 9, 18° below zero. May 11, snow in several states; frost in Conn. for three successive nights.
1879—Jan. 10, 10° below zero.
1880—35 snow storms and 43½ inches snow fell. Several times below zero.
1881—Jan. 1—12° below zero.
1882—Jan. 24, 16° below zero. Feb. 4th, a severe snow storm that drifted so as to universally stop all traveling—many churches were not opened for service.
1883—Dec. 22, 18° below zero.
May 29, 30, 1884, there were severe frosts throughout all New England and western states. Ice formed from ¼ to 1 inch in thickness, killing early beans, potatoes, corn, etc. Thermometer 24° in this city. A snow storm in Litchfield county. The frosts extended southerly to Virginia. It was a huge polar wave that made a "Black Friday" for the farmers.
June 15, 1884, another severe frost, killing all tender vegetables, throughout the most of New England and the West. Aug. 25, another frost; but September following was intensely hot.
1885—Last of January and month of February, intensely cold weather, from zero to 20° below.
1886—January 10-13, 10 to 20° below zero.

# THE

# Hartford Courant.

### Established: WEEKLY, 1764; DAILY, 1836.

*The Oldest Newspaper in America.*   *A Representative Journal of New England.*

## PUBLISHED BY

# The Hartford Courant Co.

### DIRECTORS.

*JOSEPH R. HAWLEY.*
*CHARLES DUDLEY WARNER, President.*
*CHARLES HOPKINS CLARK, Vice President.*
*ARTHUR L. GOODRICH, Treasurer.*
*FRANK S. CAREY, Secretary.*

## COURANT BUILDING, 66 STATE STREET, Hartford, Conn.

# The Daily Courant

Is the leading Republican paper in Connecticut; fourteen and sixteen pages, and has all the news of the day, and has *no superior* as an Advertising Medium.   No effort or expense is spared to maintain its position at the head of the newspaper press of the state.

# The Connecticut Courant,

Published Semi-weekly (Monday and Thursday evenings), for $1.00 a year, is carefully made up of the most valuable matter appearing in the Daily. Its circulation extends to all parts of the Country, making it one of *the best* Advertising Mediums in New England.

### SUBSCRIPTIONS:

**Daily, $8.00.**   **Semi-Weekly, $1.00.**   **Postage Paid.**

Specimen Papers sent on application.

# The Globe.

## ISSUED EVERY SUNDAY MORNING.

**Complete City News and Telegraph Reports to the Hour of Going to Press.**

# LEADING
# SUNDAY Newspaper in Connecticut.

*Only Homeprint Sunday Newspaper in America's Wealthiest City of its Population.*

**FILLS THE FIELD Vacated by the Dailies on the Best Reading Day of the Week.**

## ITS ADVERTISERS PROSPER.

# 'HE GLOBE PUBLISHING COMPANY,

**No. 25 Asylum Street, Hartford, Conn.**

_____THE_____

# HARTFORD JOURNAL,

### 284 Asylum Street,   -   Hartford, Conn.

ESTABLISHED, 1867. . . . .
AS A SUNDAY PAPER, 1874.

## LARGE CIRCULATION IN HARTFORD AND VICINITY.

### Special Editions for Country Towns.

VALUABLE . . .

ADVERTISING .

MEDIUM. . . . .

**JOSEPH H. BARNUM,**

**Editor and Proprietor,**

_____THE_____

# CONNECTICUT FARMER .

### ESTABLISHED IN 1879.

### *284 Asylum St., Foster Block, Hartford, Conn.*

**The only Agricultural Paper published in Southern
New England, and is THE BEST Advertising Medium
in Connecticut to reach the people outside the large
cities. Terms, $1.00 per Year. Always in Advance.**

—→ *ADVERTISING RATES.* ←—

| | | |
|---|---|---|
| One Inch, one week, . . . . | $1.00 | Three months, . . . . . ‸0 |
| Each consecutive continuance, . . | .75 | One year, . . . . . 0 |

## The Farmer Publishing and Printing C

### PUBLISHERS.

NOAH CRESSY, M. D., V. S. Ph. D.,        LOUIS A. CRESSY,
       President and Editor.             Secretary and T

# The Catholic Transcript

PUBLISHED BY

THE CONNECTICUT CATHOLIC PUBLISHING CO.,

## No. 704 Main St., - Hartford, Conn.

This paper is published in the interest of the Catholics of the Diocese of Hartford. It is an eight-page, fifty-six column sheet, 33¼ x 44 inches, and circulates throughout the State. Being the only journal of its kind published in the State of Connecticut, it finds its way into the homes of thousands of Catholic families in this Diocese, making it

## THE BEST MEDIUM for Advertisers.

## CIRCULATION, 4500.

The Rates of Advertising are Reasonable, and will be furnished on application.

ᴜrms of Subscription, $1.50 Per Annum, in Advance.

➤POSTAGE FREE.↩

# The Weekly

*Established*
*1881.*

# Examiner.

## ROBERT PYNE, Editor.

## AN INDEPENDENT JOURNAL

Devoted to the Discussion of Questions relating to the
Social and Material Advancement
of the People.

# The Examiner

### IS PUBLISHED EVERY SATURDAY AT

## No. 45 Brown Street, { OFF WETHERSFIELD AVENUE, } Hartford, Conn.

It is designed to speak THE TRUTH regardless of conse-
quences; and its pages are open to all having
the welfare of Humanity at heart.

### TO LOCAL ADVERTISERS

THE EXAMINER offers SPECIAL INDUCEMENTS. Its large number of shareholders are
pledged to a reciprocation of advertising patronage bestowed; besides many friends to
principles not otherwise interested, giving preference in their purchases to those adv     ig
in its columns.   Rates given on application.

### TERMS, IN ADVANCE:

One Year, $1.00.        Six Months, 50 cents.        Sample Copies     ¼

# Farmington Valley
## Herald and Journal,

### NORTH & LATE, Publishers.

JOHN A. NORTH,                                                  J. C. LATE,
Editor, Collinsville, Conn.                          Business Manager, West Hartford, Conn.

### HERALD AND JOURNAL Circulation, 3,000.

*Subscription Price, $1.00 per Annum.*      *Advertising Rates on Application.*

It is a fact that the country towns in Hartford County, lying west of the Connecticut, are the wealthiest in the state. Advertisers who wish to reach the people living in these towns, should advertise in the FARMINGTON VALLEY HERALD AND JOURNAL, the most wide-awake country weekly paper in the state. It reaches more people of wealth, and has more readers in that locality than any other paper. The towns this paper represents, and it is practically alone in the field, have a population, according to the last census, of over 26,000. Do you wish to reach them? If so, advertise in the FARMINGTON VALLEY HERALD AND JOURNAL.

### NORTH & LATE, Publishers,
**336 Asylum Street,** . . . . . . **Hartford, Conn.**

ESTABLISHED 1883.

# HARTFORDER HEROLD

## ( GERMAN.)

## PAUL F. PFEIFFER, PUBLISHER.

31 MULBERRY STREET,        -        HARTFORD, CONN.

### ISSUED EVERY SATURDAY.

THIS IS THE ONLY GERMAN PAPER IN THIS PART OF THE S™
As an ADVERTISING MEDIUM among a large and well-to-do
class of people IT HAS NO EQUAL.

### CIRCULATION 2500

*'For Sale' and*
*'To Rent' Cards*
*in Stock*
*and For Sale.*

*LAW BLANKS*
*For Sale.*

**WE SOLICIT YOUR PATRONAGE.**

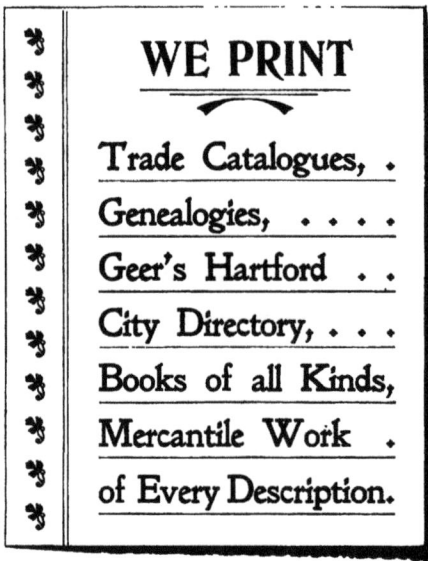

# WE PRINT

Trade Catalogues, .

Genealogies, . . . .

Geer's Hartford . .

City Directory, . . .

Books of all Kinds,

Mercantile Work .

of Every Description.

**WE WILL CALL ON YOU OR SHOULD BE PLEASED
TO HAVE YOU CALL ON US.**

E. J. E. GEER, PRESIDENT.
ERASTUS C. GEER, TREASURER.
E. HOWARD GEER, SEC'Y AND SUPT.

*Our Office is 16 STATE STREET.*
*Our Telephone No. is 803-6.*

# The Hartford
# Printing
# Co. *(Elihu Geer's Soi*

Hartford, Coi

# The Case, Lockwood & Brainard Co.

**L. BRAINARD, President.**　　　　**J. H. TURNER, Treasurer.**
**MARCUS A. CASEY, Vice President.**　　**JOHN REARDEN, Secretary.**

## DIRECTORS.

A. E. Burr,　　L. Brainard,　　J. G. Batterson,　　W. H. Lockwood,　　J. M. Allen.

Annual Meeting, Third Tuesday in February.

# Printers, Bookbinders,

### and Manufacturers of

Flat Opening Blank Books,　　　　The "American" Diary,
and "Peerless" Daily Calendar.

### MISCELLANEOUS FINE LEATHER WORK.

'.E FACILITIES TO EXECUTE ORDERS PROMPTLY.

## PEARL AND TRUMBULL STREETS,

### HARTFORD, CONN.

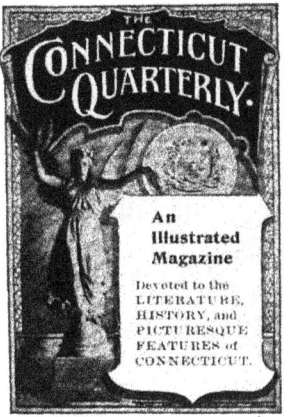

# THE HARTFORD MANILLA CO.,

Office, No. 1 South Ann St.,      Woodland Mills,

TELEPHONE, 722.                TELEPHONE, 226.2,

HARTFORD, CONN.      BURNSIDE, CONN

MANUFACTURERS OF FIRST-CLASS

# Envelope Manillas
# and Box Paper.

CAPACITY SEVEN TONS PER DAY.

WICKHAM, President.          L. B. PLIMPTON, Vice President.

C. H. WICKHAM, Secretary and Treasurer.

DIRECTORS.

| | |
|---|---|
| CHAPMAN, Sup't U. S. Stamped Env. Works. | H. J. WICKHAM, at U. S. Stamped Envelope Works. |
| PLIMPTON, Pres't Plimpton Manufacturing Co. | DANIEL MORRELL, Sec'y Hartford Mach. Screw Co. |
| IA MORGAN, Pres't Morgan Envelope Co. | JONATHAN F. MORRIS, ex-Pres't CharterOak Nat. Bk |

C. H. WICKHAM.

CHARTERED, 1881.          CAPITAL, $100,000.

Address all communications to P. O. Box 645, Hartford, Conn.

# HUBERT FISCHER BREWERY

## *Extra Bottling Lager for Hotels and Family Use a Specialty.*

### 315 PARK, Cor. LAWRENCE STREET, HARTFORD, CONN.

HUBERT FISCHER, Pres't.          CAMILLO L. FISCHER, Vice Pres't and Treas.          C. E. JOHNSON, Sec'y.

---

## Leonard Morse,

### Attorney and Counselor at Law,

Trust Company Building,

Judge City Court.                                      Hartford, Conn.

---

# The HARTFORD COAL COMPANY,

## WHOLESALE AND RETAIL DEALERS IN

ANTHRACITE COAL BITUMINOUS

## OLD COMPANY'S LEHIGH A SPECIALTY.

### No. 754 MAIN ST., and Nos. 100 to 108 COMMERCE ST., HARTFORD, CONN.

*CHAS. R. BELDEN, Pres't and Treas.*
*JOHN R. HILLS, Sec'y.*
*FREDERICK S. BELDEN, Ass't Sec'y.*

DIRECTORS: John R. Hills,      Chas. R. Belden,      Frederick S. Belden.

# EARL HATHEWAY,

# Contractor and Builder.

### ESTIMATES GIVEN ON ALL CLASSES OF WORK.

## Shop and Residence, - 29 IMLAY STREET, - Hartford, Conn.

**Special Attention given to WOOD WORK, JOBBING,
and Superintendance of Work for Owners and Architects.**

Telegraphic Code for Foreign Countries.

Kime's International Law Directory.

## Lewis E. Stanton,

### Attorney and Counselor at Law,

### 16 State Street,

Established 1860.
Geer's Directory Building.

Hartford, Conn.

# ROBERT PORTEUS,

# Contractor and Builder,

### ESTIMATES FURNISHED
### ON ALL CLASSES OF WORK.

## Office and Shop, 13 Forest St., Hartford, Conn.

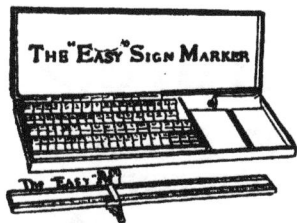

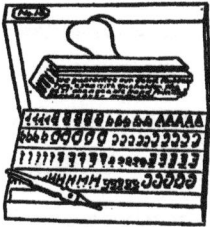

For making Display Signs of all kinds. The most complete Price Marker in the market. Very large variety of Sizes.

CATALOGUES SENT ON REQUEST.

Telephone your orders when more convenient.

Rubber Type in Sets. Over 100 different styles.

## AT THE TOP.

That is my position in the stamp business, AT THE TOP. A position gained by some fifteen years steady and intelligent effort to produce good work and to satisfy customers. My Rubber Stamp work is admitted to be of the very highest quality. Assortment of type for styles of letters is large and well selected, and is used exclusively for Stamp Work. My mail trade extends all over the United States and Canada. There is no reason why anyone in this vicinity should give his trade to traveling agents, or send his orders away, when one of the best equipped stamp works in New England is here to serve him, with best work at right prices, and everything guaranteed. I carry a full supply of all the goods generally handled by a first-class stamp house, some of which will be found mentioned here.

Steel Stamps for mechanics and manufacturers.

Rubber Hand Stamps.
Check Punches.
Brass Wheel Dating Stamps.
Pads and Inks.
Brass Checks.

Numbering Machines.
Stencils to order, and in Sets.
Branding Irons.
Stencil Brushes and Blacking.
Nickel Badges.

# GEO. W. BURCH,
## The Stamp Maker,
### 91 ASYLUM ST.

Buck's Patent Flexible Stamp. Best Stamp on Earth.

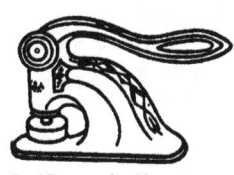

Seal Presses, for Notaries Societies and Corporations. All Guaranteed.

Self-Inkers in all sizes.

Expert Dating Stamp.

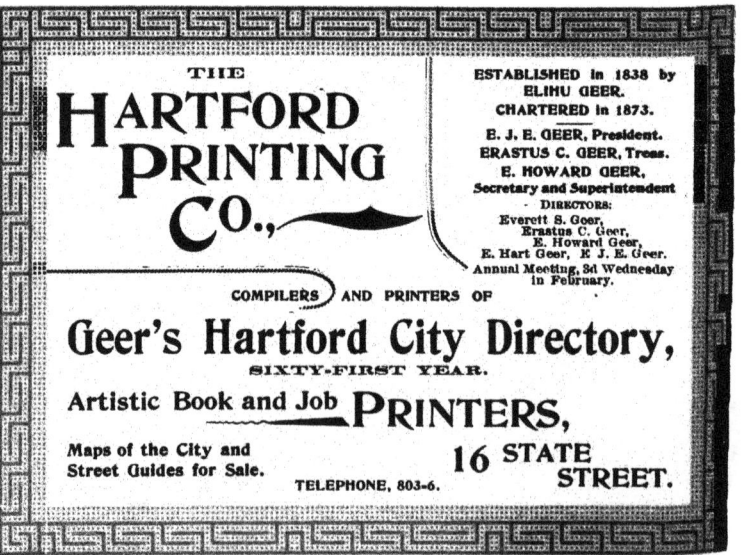

# BROWN, THOMSON & Co.,

GEORGE A. GAY.
HARRY B. STRONG.

Cheney Block,

Hartford, Conn.

920, 930, 932, 934, 936, 938, 940 and 942 MAIN STREET.

16, 18, 20 and 22 TEMPLE STREET.

*Wholesale and Retail Dealers in Domestic and Foreign*

# DRY GOODS.

SPECIAL ATTENTION IS GIVEN TO OUR STOCK OF

## Linens, Towelings, Muslins and Cottons,

While our other Departments, embracing

Silks, Dress Goods, Flannels, Skirts, Laces, Ribbons, Trimmings, Gloves, Hosiery, Notions, Handkerchiefs, Underclothing, Druggist Sundries, Boys' Clothing, Ladies' and Children's Boots and Shoes, Shawls, Cloaks, Millinery, Carpets, Books, Furniture, House Furnishing Goods, and Bicycles, Will be found replete with the LATEST NOVELTIES.

++++++++++++++++++

*LADIES' RESTAURANT, WAITING AND TOILET ROOMS.*

# FENN,
## The Furniture Man,

Manufacturer of and Dealer in

# FURNITURE OF ALL KINDS,

### AGENCY FOR THE

## CELEBRATED Household Stoves and Ranges.

# LINUS T. FENN,
## No. 613 Main Street,

Opposite Atheneum.                    HARTFORD, CONN.

# REYNOLDS & CO.,

Every description of electrical work carefully executed. The installation of electric lights, bells, annunciators, burglar alarms, gas lighting apparatus, ventilating fans, watchmen's time registers, and all electric work appertaining to private residences, stores, hotels, churches, manufacturing plants, and public buildings. We make it a special point to employ only competent and experienced workmen, and will guarantee all work to be entirely satisfactory.

Motors, dynamos, electrical supplies, and specialties in great variety always in stock.

## *Electrical Engineers* and *Contractors.*

Wiring for Incandescent Electric Lighting.

ESTIMATES FURNISHED.

### No. 85 PRATT STREET, Hartford, Conn.

Local and Long Distance Telephone Connection.

---

# ROBERT BRAND,

## *Practical* Cabinet Maker.

**Dealer in**
### Antique Furniture.

Removed from 5 GROVE ST. to 5½ MORRIS ST.

**FURNITURE REPAIRED, UPHOLSTERED AND REPAIRED AT REASONABLE RATES. FURNITURE PACKING.**

### No. 5½ MORRIS STREET, Hartford, Conn.

---

ESTABLISHED 1840.

# F. W. WHITE,

Dealer in

## Stoves, Funiture, and Ranges.

A large variety of

Stove Repairs, Roofing, and particular attention paid to JOBBING.

TIN, COPPER, and SHEET IRON WARE Manufactured to Order.

### 1124 MAIN ST., Old Number, 538, HARTFORD, CONN.

Persons wanting STOVES, or any article in our line, will find it to their advantage to CALL AT 1124 MAIN ST., BEFORE PURCHASING ELSEWHERE.

# H. H. PECK,
# Dealer in LUMBER.

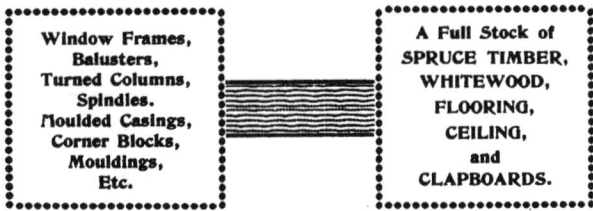

| Window Frames, Balusters, Turned Columns, Spindles. Moulded Casings, Corner Blocks, Mouldings, Etc. | A Full Stock of SPRUCE TIMBER, WHITEWOOD, FLOORING, CEILING, and CLAPBOARDS. |

## MILL WORK DONE at SHORT NOTICE.

TELEPHONE, 1048-3,

## Office and Yard, Rear 32 CHURCH ST., HARTFORD, CONN.

# ANDREWS & PECK,
Manufacturers, Wholesale and Retail Dealers in

# DOORS, WINDOWS AND BLINDS.

AND IN EVERY WAY SUPERIOR TO SCOTCH, CEMENT, OR GLAZED PIPE

IMPORTED and AMERICAN Window Glass and Putty.

THIS PIPE IS IMPERMEABLE, STRONGER,

Zimmerman's Patent

*Blind or Shutter Adjuster.*

NEW ENGLAND AGENTS FOR

Vitrified, Salt-Glazed Sewer Pipe.

*All Sizes and Connections constantly on hand.*

FOR SEWERS, HOUSE CONNECTIONS ETC.

Plate and Ornamental Glass.

SPECIAL ATTENTION GIVEN TO PUBLISHING

## No. 88 MARKET STREET, Hartford, Conn.

Local Mills, Junction Charter Oak & Vredendale Aves.    Lumber at Wholesale.

FLUE LINING AND WALL COPING.

# E. TAYLOR & SONS,

### Dealers in all kinds of

## Lumber, Timber, Shingles, and Lath,

### At Steam Planing Mill, 335 SHELDON ST., Colt's Dyke, Hartford, Conn.

*ALWAYS ON HAND:—Pine, Spruce, Hemlock, Flooring, Ceiling, Mouldings, Whitewood,
Maple, Mahogany, Oak, Black Walnut, Ash, Butternut, Quartered Oak.*

### SOUTHERN PINE A SPECIALTY.

---

*JAMES H. GROZIER, 50 Warrenton Ave.*          *ROBERT MOORE, 203 Franklin Ave.*

# GROZIER & MOORE,

## Builders & Mason Contractors.

*Estimates cheerfully furnished on Buildings and all kinds of Mason Work,
large or small.    JOBBING promptly attended to.*

### Office and Yard, VREDENDALE AVE., Cor. Taylor St.

### HARTFORD, CONN.

---

# D. W. HOLLIS,    Successor to KNIGHT & HOLLIS.

## Contracting Builder.

*Estimates Cheerfully Furnished.
All Work Strictly First Class.
Contracts Fulfilled Promptly.*

**Contracts taken for all kinds
of work, large or small.**

## No. 62 LAUREL STREET,
Hartford, Conn.

---

## Hartford Maps and Street Guides,

### PUBLISHED BY ELIHU GEER'S SONS, 16 STATE STREET.

### PRICE TWENTY-FIVE CENTS.

# A. W. SCOVILLE,

**Architect,**
**Contractor,**
**and Builder,**

Office, **700 MAIN STREET,**
Old Number, 236,
HARTFORD, CONN.

---

D. L. WHITTLESEY.          E. F. ATWOOD.

# D. L. Whittlesey & Co.,

## CONTRACTORS
## AND BUILDERS,

OFFICE, ROOM 5,
212 ASYLUM STREET,

SHOP,
590 GARDEN STREET,

HARTFORD, CONN.

---

# THOMPSON BROTHERS,

**Masons, Builders**
**and Contractors,**

SPECIAL ATTENTION
GIVEN TO JOBBING.

**19 ROWE AVENUE, Hartford, Conn.**

---

# MALLERY TABOR,

Personal Attention
Given to Repair Jobs.

# CARPENTER
# AND BUILDER.

REAR 281 ALLYN STREET, Hartford, Conn.

# W. T. ARNOLD,
## CONTRACTOR AND BUILDER,

Residence, 47 So. Hudson St.,
Office, 82 Pearl St., Hartford, Conn.

## BUILDING IN ALL ITS BRANCHES,

Including Decorative Work, Stained Glass, and Interior Finish.
Skilled Workmen promptly furnished for Repairs and Alterations.

**Preliminary Sketches, Full Working Plans, Specifications and Estimates Furnished.**

---

ANDREW B. WEST.                                          A. M. WEST.

# A. B. WEST & CO.,
# ×Builders.

## Contractors for all Classes of Buildings.

With good facilities, small expenses, and close application to business, we can do work
at prices that ought to insure a fair share of public patronage.

**OFFICE OPEN EVENINGS.**

Office and Shop, 101½ HUDSON ST., Hartford, Conn.

---

D. W. HOLLIS.                    Telephone, 628-6                    E. C. HOLLIS.

# D. W. HOLLIS & SON,
# Contracting Builders.

Contractors for all kinds of Works, Business Blocks, Churches,
Dwellings, etc. Estimates cheerfully furnished. Prompt
attention given to all transactions. Cabinet Work of all kinds, Store Fronts, Counters, Cases, Mantels, Panel Work, Turning, Variety Work of all kinds. All
work strictly first class, at prices most reasonable.

Office, 212 ASYLUM ST.,    Factory, 26 POTTER ST.,    Hartford

# EDMUND BROWNE,

## CONTRACTOR AND BUILDER.

Contracts of all kinds taken, both large and small.
Jobbing will receive prompt attention.

Shop, 1419 MAIN ST., (Old Number, 719.)    Residence, 13 FLORENCE ST.,

HARTFORD, CONN.

---

S. D. STODDARD.                Telephone, 401-5.                W. E. CAULKINS.

## STODDARD & CAULKINS,

# Contractors and Builders.

Cabinet Work, Interior Finish, and General Jobbing,
Turning, Sawing and all kinds of Machine Work.
PLANS and SPECIFICATIONS FURNISHED.

Junc. CHARTER OAK & VREDENDALE AVES., Hartford, Conn.

---

## GEO. E. DENISON,

# GENERAL CONTRACTOR.

ESTIMATES given on all classes of Work.
PLANS and SPECIFICATIONS furnished.

Office, 190 PEARL STREET,   Hartford, Conn.
Shop, 207 LAUREL STREET,                        Telephone.

---

F. L. BONFOEY, 17 Avon Street.
B. C. BONFOEY, 25 Spring Street.

## BONFOEY BROTHERS,

# Contractors and Builders.

Special attention given to

JOBBING.

109 WINDSOR AVE.

HARTFORD, CONN.

# ISAAC A. ALLEN, JR.,

### Successor to F. S. NEWMAN,

## ARCHITECT AND DESIGNER. EXPERT ON CONSTRUCTION.

904 MAIN STREET, Cor. Temple Street,

Old Number, 372.

BALLERSTEIN Building, Rooms 87, 89, and 91. Hartford, Conn.

✺ ✺ ✺ Plans of all kinds furnished for Schools, Dwellings, Mills, Blocks, etc. ✺ ✺ ✺

# H. B. PHILBRICK,

# Building Contractor.

### Estimates made on all classes of building.

Office and Residence; 111 Edwards St., Hartford, Conn.

### TELEPHONE CONNECTION, 813-2.

ALEX. ANGUS, 27 Warner Street.     E. L. CHESEBRO, 51 Seymour Street.

# ANGUS & CHESEBRO,

# Building Contractors.

### Agents for GRANVILLE MOSAIC WOOD FLOORS.

### ⤛ JOBBING PROMPTLY ATTENDED TO. ⤜

27 WARNER STREET, Hartford, Conn.

# F. W. BARKER & CO.,

# Doors, Windows and Blinds,

Window Frames, Weights and Cord.    Posts, Rails, Brackets and Balustrades.

All Kinds of Mill Work and Interior Finish.

Leaded Art Glass. ✺ ✺ ✺ ✺ Plate and Window Glass. ✺ ✺ ✺

No. 86 MORGAN STREET, Hartford, Conn.

# D. J. DONAHUE,
# BRICK MANUFACTURER,
### BUILDING, SEWER, PAVING, PLAIN, AND
### SPECIAL ANGLE BRICK.

YARD, 685 WINDSOR AVENUE.
RESIDENCE, 171 BARBOUR STREET.     HARTFORD, CONN.

---

# GEO. F. GRENIER,
## Practical Painter, Grainer & Decorator,
PAPER-HANGING, KALSOMINING, GLAZING, SIGN-WRITING,
WOOD-FINISHING, ENAMELING, AND POLISHING, ETC.

☞ JOBBING ATTENDED TO AT REASONABLE PRICES.
RESIDENCE AND SHOP, 19 EAST STREET,
HARTFORD, CONN.

---

# EDWARD O'NEIL,

## JOINER AND BUILDER.
*JOBBING PROMPTLY
ATTENDED TO.*
*Contracts Taken. Estimates Given.*

SHOP and RESIDENCE, 68 HUDSON ST.,
HARTFORD, CONN.

---

# T. F. McGRATH & CO.,
# Contractors and Builders.
## JOBBING WILL RECEIVE PROMPT ATTENTION.
No. 820 PARK STREET, HARTFORD, CONN.

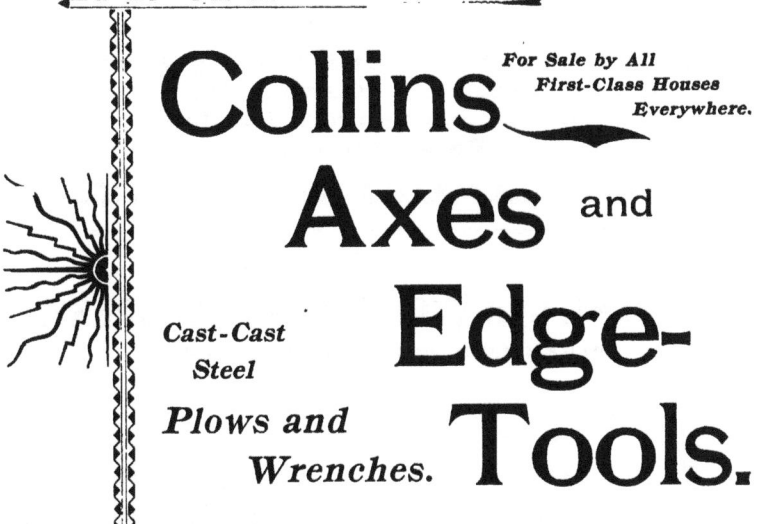

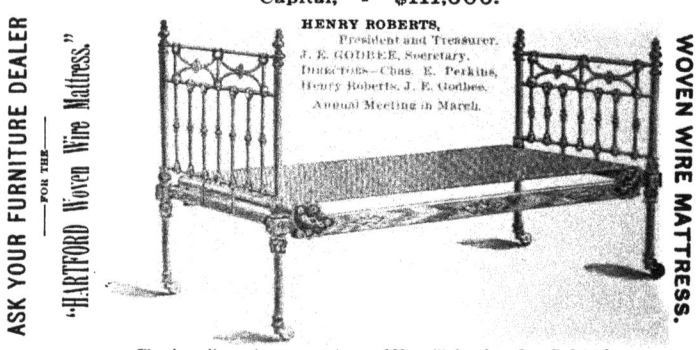

# The Pratt & Whitney Co.

## 1 Flower Street, - Hartford, Conn.,

### MANUFACTURES

Planers, Shapers, Drilling Machines, Speed, Cutting-Off and Engine Lathes, Monitor Lathes, Turret-Head Screw and Chucking Machines, Milling, Profiling, Tapping, Cutter and Taper Reamer Grinding Machines, Boring Mills, Bolt Cutters, Die Sinkers. Metal Band Sawing Machines, Two Spindle Centering Machines, Flour Mill Roll-Grooving Machines, Drop Hammers, Punching Presses, United States Standard Thread, Ring, Plug and Caliper Size Gauges, Hand, Machine Nut, Machine Screw, Pipe, Staybolt, and Pulley Taps, Die-Stocks and Dies, Milling Cutters in great variety, solid and with inserted teeth.

Cutters for Teeth of Gear Wheels, Combination Lathe Chucks, Straight and Taper, Solid and Shell Reamers.

## Brass Finishing Machines,

## Automatic

## Weighing Machines,

MILLING CUTTER.

## Special Machinery.

## Also Machinery and Tools for Bicycle Manufacture.

Factories Equipped with Complete Plants of Machines, Fixtures, Small Tools and Gauges for the Manufacture of Guns, Sewing Machines, and Similar Articles Requiring Interchangeability of Parts.

## IRON CASTINGS MADE TO ORDER.

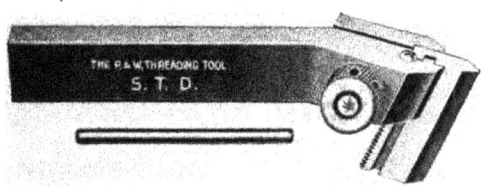

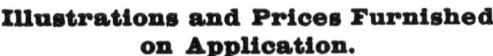

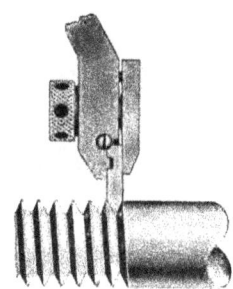

### Illustrations and Prices Furnished
### on Application.

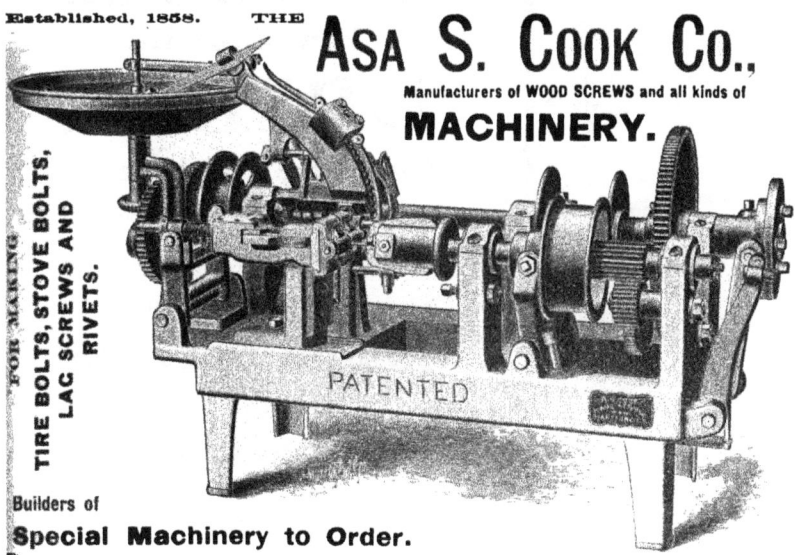

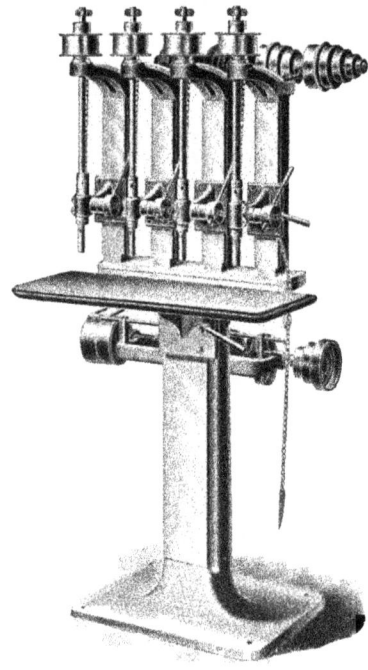

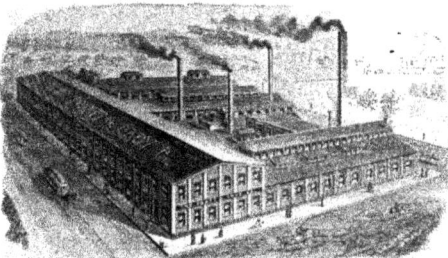

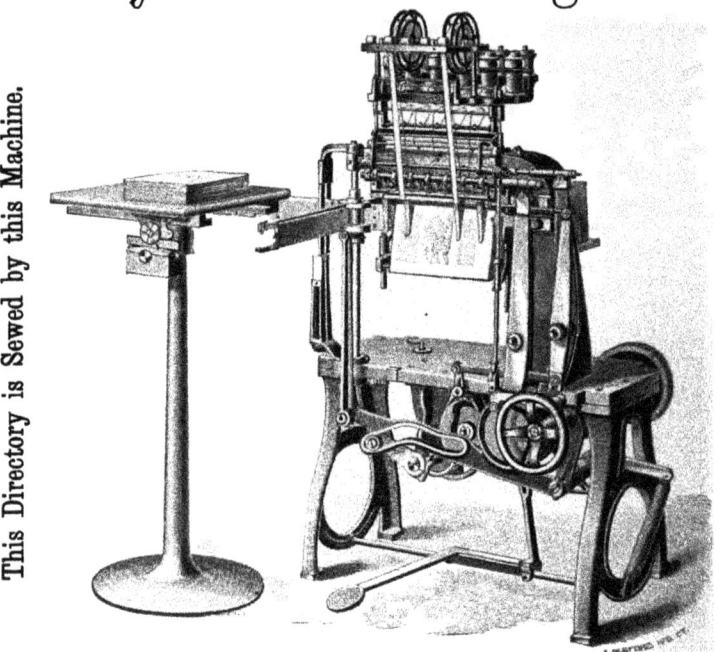

Established, 1848.　　Chartered, 1880.　　Organized, April 16, 1883.　　Capital, $800,000.

PLINY JEWELL, President.　LYMAN B. JEWELL, Vice President.
CHAS. A. JEWELL, Treas.　CHAS. E. NEWTON, Secretary.

DIRECTORS.—Pliny Jewell, Lyman B. Jewell, Chas. A. Jewell, Charles E. Newton, Edward H. Bingham.

# THE JEWELL BELTING CO.,

### MANUFACTURERS OF

# Leather Belting, Lace Leather,

## METALLIC TIPPED

# BELT LACINGS,

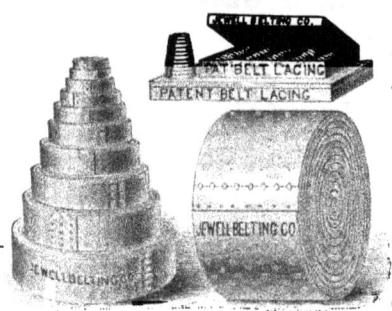

### AND DEALERS IN

# HIDES AND LEATHER,

## Walrus and Buff Leather

———Always on Hand.

## POLISHING BELTS

of All Kinds Made to Order.

Office and Manufactory,

# 15 TRUMBULL, JEWELL, and HICKS STREETS, Hartford, Conn.

# The Billings & Spencer Co.,

## 216 LAWRENCE ST., HARTFORD, CONN., U. S. A.

### Manufacturers of Drop Forgings of Iron, Steel, and Copper; FIRST-CLASS MACHINISTS' TOOLS.

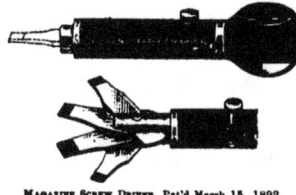

MAGAZINE SCREW DRIVER, Pat'd March 15, 1892.

### Commutator Segments
#### For Railway Motors and Dynamos.

Made of a single piece of unalloyed Copper, having a homogeneous molecular structure throughout, of the greatest density, with an increased efficiency.

Ball Pene Machinists' Hammers, drop-forged from best Tool Steel; Horseshoe Turning Hammers; Billings' Wire Cutters.

## Overhead Trolley Equipment, Colophite Insulation.

The great advantage of this material is that all the parts that are subject to strain are made from material that has a tensile strength of 80,000 pounds per square inch, and an electrical potential and resistance of 337,000 megohms.

Send
for
Illustrated
Catalogue.

Selling
Agents for
THE C. E.
BILLINGS
MFG. CO.

### Drop-Forged Pole and Rein Snaps
#### For Fire Department Service and All Classes of Heavy Work.

**Billings'** Patent Double Acting Ratchet Drills for Morse Taper and Square Shank Drills; original Packer Ratchet Drills for both Morse Taper and Square Shank Drills; Billings' Patent Cutting-off Tool; Lineman's Hand Vises; Forged Steel Snap Gauge Blanks, from $1\frac{1}{4}$ to $2\frac{1}{8}$ inches.

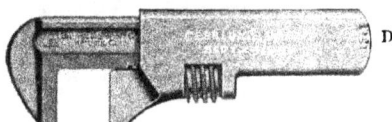

Drop Hammers, Trimming Presses and Forges.
Drop-Forged Eye-Bolts, from $\frac{3}{8}$ to 2 inches diameter; Combination Pliers.
Drop-Forged Machine and Engineer's Wrenches in 120 different styles.

# DROP FORGINGS OF EVERY DESCRIPTION,

### For Pistols, Sewing Machines, Locomotives, Stationary Engines, and Machinery Generally.

## FREE DIRECTORY LIBRARY,

—— AT ——

## ELIHU GEER'S SONS,
## PRINTERS,

### 16 STATE STREET, - HARTFORD, CONN.

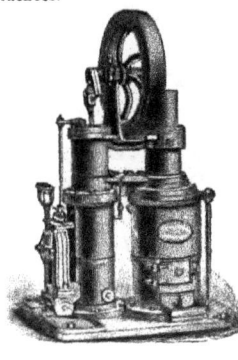

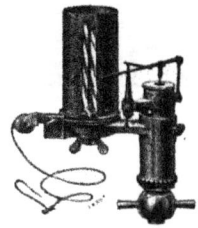
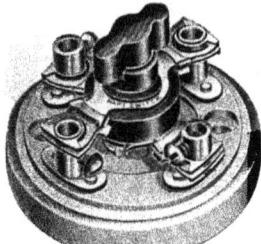

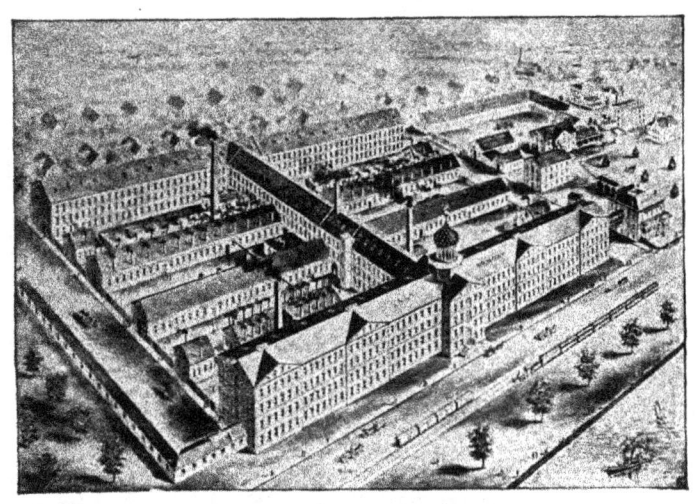

R. W. H. JARVIS, President.                          F. E. BELDEN, Secretary.
JOHN H. HALL, Vice President and Treasurer.          L. C. GROVER, Superintendent.

# COLT'S
# Patent Fire-Arms Mfg. Co.,

**17 VANDYKE AVE., Hartford, Conn.**

Manufacturers of

## REVOLVERS, RIFLES & SHOT GUNS.

## Colt Automatic Machine Gun.
## Colt Armory Printing Presses.
## Gatling Guns.

# Colt Revolvers,

Adopted by the U. S. ARMY AND NAVY,      STATE NATIONAL GUARDS,
New York City and other POLICE DEPARTMENTS.

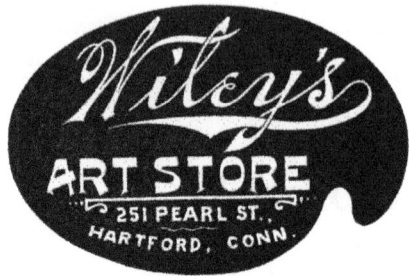
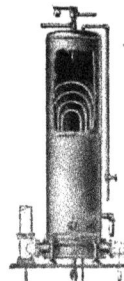

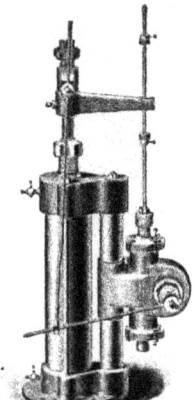

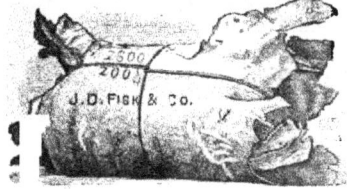

# Hartford and New York Boats.

Formerly Connecticut River Steamboat Company, and now owned by the

## HARTFORD AND NEW YORK TRANSPORTATION COMPANY.

### OFFICE AND WHARF,

Hartford Office, 285 STATE STREET,
Foot of the Street.

New York Office, PECK SLIP,
Pier 24, East River.

*Two New Steel Twin-Screw Boats.*

## Middletown, Leaves Hartford TUESDAY, THURSDAY AND SATURDAY AT 5 P. M. Until OCTOBER 15th.

Captain, R. H. Hills.          Steward, G. H. Jones.

## Hartford, Leaves Hartford MONDAY, WEDNESDAY, AND FRIDAY.

Captain, Fred H. Beebe.          Steward, J. W. Smith.

**Leave New York each Alternate Day,** from Pier 24, East River, at 5 P. M. until October 15.
From October 15 to close of navigation, leave Hartford at 4 P. M.; New York at 5 P. M.

### PASSENGER FARES.

| | |
|---|---|
| One way, with berth,............$1.50 | Deck Fare,............................$1.15 |
| Round trip, good for season,............ 2.50 | State Room, one way,.................... 1.00 |
| Round trip, good for six days,.......... 2.25 | Children from 6 to 12 yrs. of age, Half Price. |

E. GOODRICH, Pres't.    EDGAR L. SMITH, Sec'y and Ass't Treas.    C. C. GOODRICH, Gen'l Manager.
E. B. WILLIAMS, Superintendent.
GEO. C. HILLS, General Freight and Passenger Agent, Pier 24, East River, N. Y.
W. B. SMITH, New York Agent, Pier 24, East River, N. Y.

E. **GOODRICH, Local Agent,  -  No. 285 STATE STREET, Hartford, Conn.**

For Distances of and Between all Landings, see Index to Contents

# Distances to all Towns in Connecticut from Hartford,

By RAILROAD and TOWN ROAD, also, year Towns were Organized.    CITIES AND BOROUGHS.

* City Charters in these Towns—18 Cities in State.    † Borough Charters in these Towns—22 Boroughs in State.
F Fairfield County; H Hartford; L Litchfield; M Middlesex; NH New Haven; NL New London; T Tolland; W Windham.

*Copyrighted for "GEER'S HARTFORD CITY DIRECTORY"*

| Towns | County | Town Road | Rail road | Organized | Towns | County | Town Road | Rail road | Organized | Towns | County | Town Road | Rail road | Organized |
|---|---|---|---|---|---|---|---|---|---|---|---|---|---|---|
| Andover, | T | 18 | 23 | 1848 | Griswold, † | N L | 53 | 53 | 1815 | Portland, | M | 17 | 18 | 1841 |
| Ansonia*, | NH | 45 | 48 | 1889 | Groton, | N L | 50 | 65 | 1705 | Preston, | N L | 45 | 55 | 1687 |
| Ashford, | W | 31 | 46 | 1710 | Guilford, † | NH | 36 | 52 | 1639 | Prospect, | NH | 30 | 29 | 1827 |
| Avon, | H | 12 | 20 | 1880 | HADDAM, | M | 25 | 27 | 1662 | Putnam, | W | 45 | 56 | 1855 |
| Barkhamsted, | L | 24 | 34 | 1746 | Hamden, | NH | 38 | 34 | 1786 | Redding, | F | 65 | 67 | 1767 |
| Beacon Falls, | NH | 43 | 41 | 1871 | Hampton, | W | 38 | 44 | 1786 | Ridgefield, † | F | 75 | 84 | 1708 |
| Berlin, | H | 13 | 13 | 1785 | HARTFORD, * | H | — | — | 1686 | Rocky Hill, | H | 7 | 8 | 1843 |
| Bethany, | NH | 36 | 45 | 1832 | Hartland, | H | 26 | 39 | 1753 | Roxbury, | L | 43 | 92 | 1801 |
| Bethel, † | F | 58 | 89 | 1855 | Harwinton, | L | 23 | 53 | 1731 | Salem, | N L | 34 | 53 | 1819 |
| Bethlehem, | L | 36 | 45 | 1787 | Hebron, † | T | 22 | 39 | 1704 | Salisbury, | L | 54 | 62 | 1738 |
| Bloomfield, | H | 7 | 6 | 1835 | Huntington, † | F | 52 | 62 | 1789 | Saybrook, | M | 38 | 36 | 1635 |
| Bolton, | T | 14 | 20 | 1716 | Kent, | L | 49 | 80 | 1738 | Scotland, | W | 34 | 40 | 1867 |
| Bozrah, † | N L | 34 | 50 | 1786 | Killingly, † | W | 47 | 64 | 1700 | Seymour, | NH | 44 | 44 | 1850 |
| Branford, † | NH | 40 | 45 | 1644 | Killingworth, | M | 37 | 43 | 1668 | Sharon, | L | 51 | 71 | 1739 |
| BRIDGEPORT, * | F | 52 | 53 | 1821 | Lebanon, | N L | 30 | 42 | 1700 | Sherman, | F | 60 | 98 | 1802 |
| Bridgewater, | L | 45 | 96 | 1856 | Ledyard, | N L | 50 | 88 | 1836 | Simsbury, | H | 13 | 15 | 1670 |
| Bristol, † | H | 17 | 18 | 1785 | Lisbon, | N L | 42 | 50 | 1786 | Somers, | T | 24 | 24 | 1706 |
| Brookfield, | F | 60 | 82 | 1788 | LITCHFIELD, † | L | 30 | 55 | 1788 | Southbury, | NH | 43 | 55 | 1673 |
| BROOKLYN, | W | 44 | 66 | 1786 | Lyme, | N L | 40 | 48 | 1664 | Southington, † | H | 19 | 20 | 1779 |
| Burlington, | H | 18 | 23 | 1806 | Madison, | NH | 36 | 56 | 1826 | South Windsor, | H | 8 | 8 | 1845 |
| Canaan, | L | 43 | 61 | 1789 | Manchester, | H | 9 | 8 | 1823 | Sprague, | N L | 38 | 42 | 1862 |
| Canterbury, | W | 40 | 50 | 1703 | Mansfield, | T | 27 | 36 | 1703 | STAFFORD, † | T | 23 | 33 | 1718 |
| Canton, | H | 17 | 22 | 1806 | Marlborough, | H | 16 | 30 | 1803 | Stamford, * | F | 77 | 78 | 1641 |
| Chaplin, | W | 33 | 44 | 1822 | Meriden, * | NH | 17 | 18 | 1806 | Sterling, | W | 49 | 61 | 1794 |
| Chatham,.., | M | 22 | 25 | 1767 | Middlebury, | NH | 36 | 38 | 1807 | Stonington, † | N L | 57 | 75 | 1649 |
| Cheshire, | NH | 26 | 21 | 1728 | Middlefield, | M | 26 | 21 | 1866 | Stratford, | F | 49 | 50 | |
| Chester, | M | 32 | 34 | 1836 | MIDDLETOWN, * | M | 15 | 15 | 1650 | Suffield, | H | 18 | 17 | |
| Clinton, | M | 38 | 51 | 1838 | Milford, | NH | 45 | 46 | 1639 | Thomaston, | L | 28 | 27 | |
| Colchester, † | N L | 25 | 40 | 1701 | Monroe, | F | 52 | 67 | 1823 | Thompson, | W | 43 | 61 | |
| Colebrook, | L | 31 | 40 | 1765 | Montville, | N L | 37 | 55 | 1786 | TOLLAND, * | T | 19 | 22 | |
| Columbia, | T | 23 | 28 | 1800 | Morris, | L | 34 | 62 | 1859 | Torrington, † | L | 28 | 46 | |
| Cornwall, | L | 39 | 71 | 1740 | Naugatuck, * | NH | 36 | 37 | 1844 | Trumbull, | F | 56 | 57 | |
| Coventry, | T | 21 | 28 | 1709 | New Britain, * | H | 10 | 9 | 1850 | Union, | T | 33 | 60 | |
| Cromwell, | M | 13 | 13 | 1851 | New Canaan, † | F | 78 | 86 | 1801 | VERNON, * | T | 13 | 17 | |
| DANBURY, * | F | 61 | 92 | 1684 | New Fairfield, | F | 65 | 97 | 1707 | Voluntown, | N L | 59 | 60 | |
| Derby, * | NH | 45 | 43 | 1654 | New Hartford, | L | 22 | 29 | 1738 | Wallingford, † | NH | 23 | 24 | 1 |
| Darien, | F | 73 | 74 | 1820 | NEW HAVEN, * | NH | 35 | 36 | 1637 | Warren, | L | 44 | 76 | 1 |
| Durham, | M | 21 | 24 | 1698 | Newington, | H | 5 | 5 | 1871 | Washington, | L | 44 | 58 | |
| Eastford, | W | 34 | 50 | 1847 | NEW LONDON, * | N L | 45 | 61 | 1646 | WATERBURY, * | NH | 30 | 32 | 1677 |
| East Granby, | H | 16 | 20 | 1858 | New Milford, | L | 48 | 90 | 1707 | Waterford, | N L | 48 | 58 | 1801 |
| East Haddam, | M | 33 | 33 | 1784 | Newtown, † | F | 50 | 74 | 1708 | Watertown, | L | 30 | 39 | 17 |
| East Hartford, | H | 4 | 2 | 1784 | Norfolk, | L | 36 | 45 | 1744 | Westbrook, | M | 49 | 48 | 1840 |
| East Haven, | NH | 40 | 45 | 1785 | North Branford, | NH | 35 | 45 | 1831 | West Hartford, | H | 4 | 4 | 1854 |
| East Lyme, | N L | 44 | 56 | 1839 | North Canaan, | L | 44 | 55 | 1858 | Weston, | F | 67 | 63 | 1787 |
| Easton, | F | 63 | 63 | 1845 | North Haven, † | NH | 28 | 29 | 1786 | Westport, | F | 64 | 65 | 1835 |
| East Windsor, | H | 11 | 14 | 1680 | North Stonington, | N L | 55 | 80 | 1808 | Wethersfield, | H | 4 | 4 | 1634 |
| Ellington, | T | 15 | 20 | 1786 | Norwalk, * | F | 67 | 70 | 1651 | Willington, | T | 25 | 48 | 1719 |
| Enfield, | H | 17 | 18 | 1681 | NORWICH, * | N L | 38 | 50 | 1660 | Wilton, | F | 73 | 75 | 1802 |
| Essex, | M | 37 | 39 | 1854 | Old Lyme, | N L | 45 | 55 | 1855 | Winchester, | L | 30 | 35 | 1756 |
| Fairfield, | F | 67 | 58 | 1639 | Old Saybrook, | M | 49 | 43 | 1852 | WINDHAM, * | W | 30 | 35 | 1692 |
| Farmington, | H | 10 | 19 | 1640 | Orange, † | NH | 41 | 42 | 1822 | Windsor, | H | 8 | 8 | 1633 |
| Franklin, | N L | 36 | 42 | 1786 | Oxford, | NH | 42 | 48 | 1798 | Windsor Locks, | H | 12 | 12 | 1854 |
| Glastonbury, † | H | 9 | 12 | 1690 | Plainfield, | W | 45 | 50 | 1699 | Wolcott, | NH | 26 | 37 | 1796 |
| Goshen, | L | 32 | 52 | 1738 | Plainville, | H | 16 | 14 | 1869 | Woodbridge, | NH | 38 | 40 | 1784 |
| Granby, | H | 18 | 18 | 1786 | Plymouth, | L | 23 | 26 | 1795 | Woodbury, | L | 37 | 45 | 1673 |
| Greenwich, † | F | 83 | 84 | 1640 | Pomfret, | W | 40 | 50 | 1686 | Woodstock, | W | 47 | | 1686 |

| Cities, | In Town of | Cities, | In Town of | Boroughs, | In Town of | Borough |
|---|---|---|---|---|---|---|
| Ansonia | Ansonia | Norwalk | Norwalk | Bethel | Bethel | New Ca... |
| Bridgeport | Bridgeport | Norwich | Norwich | Branford | Branford | Newtown |
| Danbury | Danbury | Putnam | Putnam | Bristol | Bristol | Ridgefield,.... Ri. |
| Derby | Derby | Rockville | Vernon | Colchester | Colchester | Shelton.... Hun. |
| Hartford | Hartford | South Norwalk | Norwalk | Danielson | Killingly | Southington.... Sout. |
| Meriden | Meriden | Stamford | Stamford | Fair Haven, E. | New Haven | Stafford Spring... |
| Middletown | Middletown | Waterbury | Waterbury | Greenwich | Greenwich | Stonington.... Sto |
| New Britain | New Britain | Willimantic | Windham | Guilford | Guilford | Torrington .... Torr. |
| New Haven | New Naven | | | Jewett City | Griswold | Wallingford |
| New London | New London | | | Litchfield | Litchfield | West Haven |
| | | | | Naugatuck | Naugatuck | Winsted.. |

# LAUREL PARK,

## MANCHESTER, CONN.

## Nicest Grove in Connecticut.

### OPEN DURING THE SUMMER SEASON.

DANCING Wednesdays and Saturdays, "BEEMAN & HATCH" Orchestra.
FROM 3 TO 6 P. M.

Sacred Concert by HATCH'S MILITARY BAND Every Pleasant Sunday During June, July, Aug. and Sept.

## BOATING FOR ALL.

F . SWINGS AND ELECTRIC MERRY-GO-ROUND IN THE STATE, FOR CHILDREN.

Manchester and Rockville Cars from City Hall, Hartford.

Managed by the Hartford, Manchester & Rockville Tramway Co.

| | |
|---|---|
| 3 10 S. CHAPMAN, President. | RICHARD O CHENEY, Vice President. |
| J ' HAYNES, Sec'y and Supt. | C. H WICKHAM, Treasurer. |

H. J. WICKHAM, General Manager.

A RESS ALL COMMUNICATIONS TO P. O. DRAWER B, SOUTH MANCHESTER, CONN.

# Railroad Distances and Fares from Hartford, July, 1898.

## NEW YORK, NEW HAVEN AND HARTFORD RAILROAD,

### TO NEW YORK.

Passengers paying on trains, 5 cts. extra

| Hartford to | Miles. | Fares. |
|---|---|---|
| Newington........ | 5 | .10 |
| Berlin............ | 10⅝ | .25 |
| Meriden.......... | 18 | .40 |
| Yalesville ........ | 20½ | .45 |
| Wallingford ...... | 24 | .50 |
| North Haven.. ... | 29½ | .60 |
| New Haven.. .... | 36 | .75 |
| West Haven....... | 38 | .80 |
| Milford........... | 45 | .95 |
| Naugatuck Junc... | 48 | 1.00 |
| Stratford ....... | 50 | 1.05 |
| Bridgeport........ | 54 | 1.10 |
| Fairfield......... | 58 | 1.20 |
| Southport........ | 60 | 1.25 |
| Green's Farms.... | 61 | 1.30 |
| Westport......... | 64 | 1.35 |
| South Norwalk... | 67 | 1.40 |
| Rowayton......... | 70 | 1.40 |
| Darien........... | 71 | 1.45 |
| Noroton ......... | 73 | 1.50 |
| Stamford......... | 75 | 1.55 |
| Riverside......... | 79 | 1.65 |
| Coscob........... | 80 | 1.65 |
| Greenwich....... | 81 | 1.65 |
| 9 Stations in N. Y.. | | |
| New York,........ | 110 | 2.25 |

### TO SPRINGFIELD AND BOSTON.

| Hartford to | Miles. | Fares. |
|---|---|---|
| Windsor.......... | 7 | .15 |
| Haydens.......... | 9½ | .20 |
| Windsor Locks.... | 13 | .25 |
| Warehouse Point... | 13½ | .30 |
| Thompsonville ... | 18¾ | .35 |
| Long Meadow..... | 22 | .45 |
| Pecowsic......... | 24 | .50 |
| Springfield....... | 26 | .50 |
| Palmer........... | 41 | .86 |
| West Brookfield... | 55 | 1.18 |
| Worcester ....... | 82 | 1.75 |
| South Framingham. | 108 | 2.25 |
| Boston........... | 124 | 2.75 |

### VALLEY DIVISION TO SAYBROOK.

Formerly the Hartford & Connecticut Valley R. R.

| Hartford to | Miles. | Fares. |
|---|---|---|
| State st. Station ... | 1½ | .10 |
| Wethersfield...... | 4 | .10 |
| South Wethersfield. | 5½ | .15 |
| Rocky Hill........ | 7½ | .20 |
| North Cromwell.. | 11½ | .30 |
| Cromwell......... | 12½ | .35 |
| Middletown....... | 15 | .40 |
| Maromas......... | 20 | .55 |
| Higganum........ | 23½ | .60 |
| Haddam.......... | 26 | .65 |
| Arnolds.......... | 27 | .70 |
| Goodspeeds....... | 29½ | .75 |
| Hadlyme......... | 32½ | .80 |
| Chester.......... | 33½ | .80 |
| Deep River....... | 34 | .85 |
| Essex............ | 38 | .90 |
| Saybrook Junction. | 42 | 1.00 |
| Saybrook Point.... | 44 | 1.00 |
| Fenwick ......... | 45 | 1.00 |

## NEW YORK AND NEW ENGLAND RAILROAD,

### TO BOSTON.

10 cts. disc't on Tickets purchased at Ticket Offices.

| Hartford to | Miles. | Fares. |
|---|---|---|
| East Hartford ..... | 2.7 | .17 |
| Burnside . ........ | 4.1 | .21 |
| Buckland.......... | 7.5 | .29 |
| Manchester....... | 8.7 | .32 |
| So. Manchester.... | 11 | .35 |
| Talcottville........ | 11.3 | .39 |
| Vernon........... | 12.3 | .41 |
| Rockville......... | 16.2 | .52 |
| Bolton........... | 16.6 | .52 |
| Andover.......... | 22.5 | .66 |
| Hop River........ | 26.3 | .76 |
| Willimantic....... | 31.5 | .89 |
| North Windham... | 35.8 | 1.00 |
| Chaplin.......... | 39.9 | 1.10 |
| Hampton......... | 43.3 | 1.19 |
| Elliott........... | 47.2 | 1.28 |
| Abington......... | 49 | 1.33 |
| Pomfret.......... | 51.8 | 1.38 |
| Putnam.......... | 56.1 | 1.50 |
| Worcester*........ | | 1.75 |
| Thompson........ | 60.2 | 1.61 |
| East Thompson.... | 64.6 | 1.72 |
| Boston........... | 117.3 | 2.85 |

### TO PROVIDENCE.

Same Stations & Miles as above from

| Hartford to | Miles. | Fares. |
|---|---|---|
| Willimantic....... | 31.5 | ·89 |
| New London*...... | | 1.50 |
| South Windham... | 34.9 | .98 |
| Scotland.......... | 38.5 | 1.07 |
| Baltic............ | 41.9 | 1.15 |
| Versailles ........ | 44.7 | 1.22 |
| Jewett City....... | 47.4 | 1.29 |
| Canterbury....... | 50.2 | 1.36 |
| Plainfield......... | 54.5 | 1.47 |
| Moosup.......... | 57.7 | 1.55 |
| Sterling.......... | 61.1 | 1.63 |
| Oneco........... | 62.9 | 1.68 |
| Greene........... | 65.9 | 1.75 |
| Summit.......... | 68.4 | 1.81 |
| Coventry......... | 71.9 | 1.90 |
| Washington....... | 75.6 | 1.99 |
| Anthony ......... | 76.6 | 2.02 |
| Quidnick......... | 77 | 2.08 |
| Centreville....... | 77.9 | 2.05 |
| Riverpoint........ | 79.2 | 2.08 |
| Natick........... | 81 | 2.13 |
| Pontiac.......... | 81.6 | 2.14 |
| Oak Lawn........ | 82.8 | 2.17 |
| Cranston ........ | 86 | 2.25 |
| Providence........ | 90 | 2.85 |

### TO SPRINGFIELD.

| Hartford to | Miles. | Fares. |
|---|---|---|
| East Hartford ..... | 2.7 | .17 |
| Burnhams........ | 4.7 | .22 |
| South Windsor.... | 6.2 | .26 |
| East Windsor Hill.. | 8.8 | .32 |
| Osborn........... | 12.9 | .43 |
| Broad Brook ..... | 14.6 | .47 |
| Melrose.......... | 16.3 | .51 |
| Hazardville—Scitico | 19.6 | .59 |
| Shaker Station.... | 21.6 | * .50 |
| East Longmeadow. | 25.1 | * .50 |
| Water Shops...... | 28.4 | * .50 |
| Armory Station.... | 29.3 | * .50 |
| Springfield........ | 31.9 | * .50 |

*Limited tickets, no discount.

## To ROCKVILLE, Branch via Melrose

| | Miles. | Fares. |
|---|---|---|
| Ellington,........ | 19.8 | .60 |
| Windermere,...... | 21.7 | .64 |
| West Street,...... | 23.6 | .65 |
| Rockville,........ | 24.8 | .69 |

### TO HUDSON RIVER.

| Hartford to | Miles. | Fares. |
|---|---|---|
| Parkville......... | 1.6 | .15 |
| Charter Oak Park.. | 3 | .20 |
| Elmwood......... | 3.7 | .20 |
| Claytons.......... | 6.6 | .27 |
| Pratts........... | 7.5 | .29 |
| New Britain...... | 9.1 | .33 |
| Plainville......... | 13.7 | .45 |
| Forestville........ | 15.5 | .49 |
| Bristol........... | 17.9 | .55 |
| Terryville........ | 22.2 | .66 |
| Tolles ........... | 24.9 | .73 |
| Hancock.......... | 26.1 | .76 |
| Wheatons......... | 27.1 | .78 |
| Greystone........ | 27.8 | .80 |
| Waterville........ | 29.9 | .85 |
| Waterbury........ | 32.4 | .91 |
| Union City,....... | 35.7 | 1.00 |
| Towantic......... | 40.6 | 1.12 |
| Southford......... | 43.9 | 1.20 |
| Pomperaug Valley. | 46.9 | 1.28 |
| Sandy Hook...... | 51.4 | 1.39 |
| Newtown ........ | 54.1 | 1.46 |
| Hawleyville....... | 56.6 | 1.52 |
| Danbury.......... | 63 | 1.68 |
| Mill Plain........ | 67.6 | 1.79 |
| Brewsters........ | 73.1 | 1.93 |
| New York........ | | |
| Poughkeepsie*..... | | 1.75 |
| Fishkill Landing ... | 133 | 2.66 |
| Newburg.......... | 110.5 | 2.94 |

## PHILA., READING & N. E. R. R.

### TO RHINEBECK, POUGHKEEPSIE, AND CAMPBELL HALL.

| Hartford to | Miles. | Fares. |
|---|---|---|
| Cottage Grove..... | 4 | .10 |
| Bloomfield........ | 6 | .15 |
| N. Bloomfield...... | 10 | .25 |
| Tariffville ........ | 12 | .32 |
| Hoskins .......... | 14 | .40 |
| Simsbury......... | 15 | .45 |
| Stratton Brook.... | 18 | .50 |
| Canton .......... | 22 | .65 |
| Collinsville....... | 24 | .65 |
| Cherry Brook .... | 25 | .70 |
| Pine Meadow..... | 28 | .80 |
| New Hartford..... | 29 | .80 |
| East Winsted..... | 35 | 1.00 |
| Naugatuck Station. | 36 | 1.00 |
| West Winsted..... | 36 | 1.00 |
| Colebrook........ | 39 | 1.15 |
| Grants........... | 41 | 1.25 |
| Norfolk.......... | 46 | 1.35 |
| West Norfolk..... | 48 | 1.45 |
| East Canaan..... | 52 | 1.55 |
| Canaan.......... | 55 | 1.65 |
| Twin Lakes...... | | |
| Chapinville....... | | |
| Salisbury......... | | |
| Lakeville......... | | |
| Ore Hill.......... | | |
| State Line........ | 66 | |
| Millerton......... | 69 | |
| Boston Corners ... | 75 | |
| Poughkeepsie ..... | 113 | |
| Rhinecliff........ | | |
| Campbell Hall.... | | |

For distance to every Town in Connecticut from Hartford, see page 556.

---

Telephone Connection.        Special Rates to Stores.

## J. M. HERR,
### Hartford, East Hartford and Burnside Express.

Orders left at the following stores promptly attended to:
Wm. E. Truesdell & Co., 566 Burnside Av.
C. A. Rapelye, 853 Main St., Hartford.
Wm. B. Noble, 732 Main St., East Hartford,
Premium Stamp Co., 78 Pearl St., Hartford.
Leave Burnside, daily, for Hartford, 7 A. M.; East Hartford, 7.30 A. M.; and Hartford for Burnside, 5 P. M.

## LEE'S BRISTOL EXPRESS,
### L. L. NEARING, Proprietor.

Orders left with Bill Brothers, 46 Ann street, will receive prompt attention.
Leave Bristol, daily, at 7.40 A. M., arriving in Hartford at 9 A. M., returning, leaves Hartford at 12 noon.
Charges Reasonable.

## MAHER'S
## SOUTH MANCHESTER EXPRESS,
### JERRY MAHER, Proprietor.

Leaves Hartford, Daily except Sundays, from Tuttle & Maher's, 2 American Row, 3 P. M.  Arrives 10.30 A. M.
Leaves South Manchester at 9 A. M.  Arrives at 6 P. M.

## Wethersfield Accommodation
## EXPRESS,
### CHARLES WESTON, Proprietor.

Leaves Wethersfield at 7.30 A. M.
Leaves Hartford at 5 P. M.  Orders will receive prompt attention if left at either of the following places:
755 Main St.,    131 Main St.,    171 Wethersfield Ave.

## HALL'S
## Rocky Hill Express,
### N. J. HALL, Proprietor.
### STATE STREET.

Leav{    1 Post Office at 8 A. M.
         artford from 64 State St. at 4 P. M.
         hone at Clapp & Treat's.

## GL    URY EXPRESS,
### DGE, Proprietor.

Leav    ... rear 50 State St., United States
        s, at 2 P. M.

A

## EAST HARTFORD EXPRESS,
### FRED J. BUSIERE, Proprietor,
#### 26 WOODBRIDGE STREET.

Leaves East Hartford at 8.30 A. M., and 2 P. M.
Returning, leaves Hartford at 11 A. M. and 5 P. M.
Orders will receive prompt attention if left either at my house, Stoughton & Pelton's, or W. B. Noble's, East Hartford; and at Kashman's, 12 State. St.; McClunie's, 805 Main St., Hartford.
An extra team is kept at the house in East Hartford for special calls.
Also Agent for H. E. Patten Dye and Carpet Cleaning Works.
Telephone connection at Noble's and McClunie's.

## WINDSOR EXPRESS,
### GEO. M. WEBB, Manager.

Orders left at New York & Boston Despatch 236 Asylum St., or St. John's Stables, rear 995 Main St,
Leaves Windsor at 9.30 A. M., arriving in Hartford at 12 M.  Leaves St. John's stables at 3 P. M.

## GLASTONBURY EXPRESS,
### D. W. MAY, Proprietor

*Office, St. John's Stables, 995 Main St., and 64 State St., Hartford.*

Leaves Glastonbury 7 A. M.  Arrives at Hartford 10 A. M.
Leaves Hartford at 2 P. M. from 64 State st. where all freight and express may be left.

## Wethersfield Express,
### JAMES CRILLY, Proprietor.

Leaves T. Sisson & Co's, 729 Main st., at 1 P. M., arriving at 11 A. M.
Leaves Wethersfield at 9 A. M.

## SMITH'S
## Manchester & Hartford
## EXPRESS

Leaves Hartford, rear 50 State st., at 1 P. M.  Arrives in Hartford at 11 A. M.
Leaves Manchester at 8 A. M.  Arrives in Manchester at 6 P. M.
### THOMAS J. SMITH, Proprietor.

XPRESS CO., SEE PAGE 553.

# R. A. GREENSTEIN,

## Fashionable ∻ Ladies' ∻ Tailoring.

Tailor Made Suits and Dresses.
Bicycle Suits and Riding Habits Made to Order.
Perfect Fit and Style Guaranteed.
We solicit the Elite trade, and our workmanship is the best.
Re-fitting and Altering at Reasonable Rates.

ROOM 4, 903 MAIN ST., Columbia Building, - - HARTFORD, CONN.

---

## H. MAERCKLEIN,

### Upholsterer and Decorator, Patentee and Manufacturer of "SIMPLICITY."

AS A BED.

AS A SOFA.

SOFA AND LOUNGE BED.

Furniture Repairing a Specialty.

The best in the Market. Upholstered Furniture made to order. Carpets made and fitted. Old carpets made over or refitted. Carpet and Shade Work.

104 ASYLUM ST.,        Hartford, Conn.

---

Lowest Possible Prices.                              Satisfaction Guaranteed.

# N. NISSEN & CO.,

# Job and Card Printers,

1362 BROAD ST.,    - -    HARTFORD, CONN.

Printing in English, Danish, German, and Sweedish Languages.

---

JOHN H. ROWLEY, 188 Capen St.                    WILBUR A. WILCOX, 253 Capen St.

# Rowley & Wilcox,

# CARPENTERS AND BUILDE   S.

## ✄ Painters and Decorators. ✄

JOBBING A SPECIALTY.        All Work Personally Supervised        ed.

Office and Shop, 39 ANN ST., Hartford, Conn.

# United States:

### CAPITALS, AREA, POPULATION AND VOTES FOR PRESIDENT.

These 1896 Census returns and areas in square miles are from the July, 1890, and final revision.

| STATES. | CAPITALS. | Square Miles. | Population 1880. | Population 1890. | Rep. McKinley. | Dem. Bryan. | N. Dem. Palmer. | Pro. Levering. | Electoral Vote. R. | Electoral Vote. D. |
|---|---|---|---|---|---|---|---|---|---|---|
| Alabama | Montgomery | 51,540 | 1,262,505 | 1,513,017 | 54,787 | 130,807 | 6,462 | 2,147 | .. | 11 |
| Arkansas | Little Rock | 53,045 | 802,525 | 1,128,179 | 37,512 | 110,103 | ...... | 889 | .. | 8 |
| California | Sacramento | 155,980 | 864,694 | 1,208,130 | 146,170 | 148,373 | 1,780 | 2,573 | 8 | 1 |
| Colorado | Denver | 103,645 | 194,327 | 412,198 | 26,271 | 161,153 | 1 | 1,717 | .. | 4 |
| Connecticut | Hartford | 4,845 | 622,700 | 746,258 | 110,285 | 56,740 | 4,334 | 1,808 | 6 | .. |
| Delaware | Dover | 1,960 | 146,608 | 168,493 | 16,804 | 13,424 | 877 | 355 | 3 | .. |
| Florida | Tallahassee | 54,240 | 269,493 | 391,422 | 11,288 | 32,736 | 654 | 1,778 | .. | 4 |
| Georgia | Atlanta | 58,980 | 1,542,180 | 1,837,353 | 60,091 | 94,232 | 2,708 | 5,613 | .. | 13 |
| Idaho | Boise City | 84,290 | 32,610 | 84,385 | 6,324 | 23,192 | .... | 179 | .. | 3 |
| Illinois | Springfield | 56,000 | 3,077,871 | 3,826,351 | 607,186 | 464,632 | 6,390 | 9,796 | 24 | .. |
| Indiana | Indianapolis | 35,910 | 1,978,301 | 2,192,404 | 323,754 | 305,573 | 2,145 | 3,056 | 15 | .. |
| Iowa | Des Moines | 55,475 | 1,624,615 | 1,911,896 | 289,293 | 223,741 | 7,516 | 3,192 | 13 | .. |
| Kansas | Topeka | 81,700 | 996,096 | 1,427,096 | 159,541 | 171,810 | 1,209 | 1,921 | .. | 10 |
| Kentucky | Frankfort | 40,000 | 1,648,690 | 1,858,635 | 218,171 | 217,890 | 5,114 | 4,781 | 12 | 1 |
| Louisiana | Baton Rogue | 45,420 | 939,946 | 1,118,587 | 22,037 | 77,175 | 1,884 | ...... | .. | 8 |
| Maine | Augusta | 29,895 | 648,936 | 661,086 | 80,465 | 34,688 | 1,870 | 1,570 | 6 | .. |
| Maryland | Annapolis | 9,860 | 934,943 | 1,042,390 | 136,959 | 104,735 | 2,507 | 5,918 | 8 | .. |
| Massachusetts | Boston | 8,040 | 1,783,085 | 2,238,943 | 278,976 | 105,711 | 11,749 | 2,998 | 15 | .. |
| Michigan | Lansing | 57,430 | 1,636,937 | 2,093,889 | 293,582 | 286,714 | 6,879 | 5,025 | 14 | .. |
| Minnesota | St. Paul | 79,205 | 780,773 | 1,301,826 | 193,501 | 189,626 | 3,202 | 4,343 | 9 | .. |
| Mississippi | Jackson | 46,340 | 1,131,597 | 1,289,600 | 5,180 | 63,859 | 1,071 | 485 | .. | 9 |
| Missouri | Jefferson City | 68,735 | 2,168,380 | 2,679,184 | 304,940 | 363,667 | 2,355 | 2,169 | .. | 17 |
| Montana | Helena | 145,310 | 39,159 | 132,159 | 10,494 | 42,537 | ...... | 186 | .. | 3 |
| Nebraska | Lincoln | 76,840 | 452,402 | 1,058,910 | 102,304 | 115,880 | 2,885 | 1,193 | .. | 8 |
| Nevada | Carson City | 109,740 | 62,266 | 45,761 | 1,988 | 8,377 | ...... | ..... | .. | 3 |
| New Hampshire | Concord | 9,005 | 346,991 | 376,530 | 57,444 | 21,650 | 3,520 | 779 | 4 | .. |
| New Jersey | Trenton | 7,455 | 1,131,116 | 1,444,933 | 221,367 | 133,675 | 6,373 | 5,614 | 10 | .. |
| New York | Albany | 47,620 | 5,082,871 | 5,997,853 | 819,838 | 551,369 | 18,950 | 16,052 | 36 | .. |
| North Carolina | Raleigh | 48,580 | 1,399,750 | 1,617,947 | 155,222 | 174,488 | 578 | 675 | .. | 11 |
| North Dakota | Bismarck | 70,195 | ...... | 182,719 | 26,335 | 20,686 | ...... | 358 | 3 | .. |
| Ohio | Columbus | 40,760 | 3,198,062 | 3,672,316 | 525,991 | 477,494 | 1,857 | 5,068 | 23 | .. |
| Oregon | Salem | 94,560 | 174,768 | 313,767 | 48,779 | 46,662 | 977 | 919 | 4 | .. |
| Pennsylvania | Harrisburg | 44,985 | 4,282,891 | 5,258,014 | 728,300 | 433,228 | 11,000 | 19,274 | 32 | .. |
| Rhode Island | Newp.&Prov. | 1,085 | 276,531 | 345,506 | 37,437 | 14,459 | 1,166 | 1,160 | 4 | .. |
| South Carolina | Columbia | 30,170 | 995,577 | 1,151,149 | 9,281 | 58,798 | 828 | ...... | .. | 9 |
| South Dakota | Pierre | 76,850 | ...... | 328,808 | 41,042 | 41,225 | ...... | 685 | .. | 4 |
| Tennessee | Nashville | 41,750 | 1,542,359 | 1,767,518 | 148,773 | 166,268 | 1,951 | 3,098 | .. | 12 |
| Texas | Austin | 262,290 | 1,591,749 | 2,235,523 | 167,520 | 370,434 | 5,046 | 1,786 | .. | 15 |
| Utah | Salt Lake C'y | 82,190 | 143,963 | 207,905 | 13,484 | 64,517 | 21 | ...... | .. | 3 |
| Vermont | Montpelier | 9,135 | 332,286 | 332,422 | 51,127 | 10,637 | 1,331 | 733 | 4 | .. |
| Virginia | Richmond | 40,125 | 1,512,565 | 1,655,980 | 135,868 | 154,709 | 2,129 | 2,350 | .. | 12 |
| Washington | Olympia | 24,645 | 618,457 | 762,794 | 39,153 | 51,646 | 1,668 | 968 | .. | 4 |
| West Virginia | Charleston | 66,880 | 75,116 | 349,390 | 104,414 | 92,927 | 677 | 1,203 | 6 | .. |
| Wisconsin | Madison | 54,450 | 1,315,497 | 1,686,880 | 268,135 | 165,523 | 4,584 | 7,509 | 12 | .. |
| Wyoming | Cheyenne | 97,575 | 20,789 | 60,057 | 10,072 | 10,655 | ...... | 186 | .. | 3 |
| Population | of 45 States, | ...... | ...... | 62,116,811 | 7,104,779 | 6,502,925 | 133,148 | 132,007 | 271 | 176 |

| Territories. | Capitals. | Square Miles. | Population 1880. | Population 1890. |
|---|---|---|---|---|
| Alaska, | Sitka, | 531,409 | 33,426 | 30,329 |
| Arizona, | Phœnix, | 112,920 | 40,440 | 59,620 |
| District Columbia, | Washington, | 60 | 177,624 | 230,392 |
| Indian, etc. | Talequa, | 31,000 | ...... | 179,321 |
| New Mexico, | Santa Fe, | 122,460 | 119,565 | 153,593 |
| Oklahoma, | Guthrie, | 39,030 | 38,830 | †61,834 |
| Population, 6 Territories, | | | | 561,768 |
| Total, States and Territories, | | 3,540,439 | 50,189,209 | 62,678,579 |

r-five thousand, six hundred Square Miles of Water Surface. Alaska not included.

Republican Party; D, Democratic Party.

udes 5,338 in Greer County (in Indian Territory), claimed by Texas.

# ARBA LANKTON,
## Practical Helminthologist.

Manufacturer of and Dealer in

### ARBA LANKTON'S
# Tape Worm Expeller,

### PRICE, $5.00.

Tape Worms of the following sizes have been successfully removed: One of 14 feet, consisting of 225 joints, from a man in Manchester; one of 21 feet and 4 inches, from a girl seven years old, in Hartford; one of 12 feet, consisting of 590 joints, from a young woman in Hartford; one of 44 feet, consisting of 1,650 joints, from a man in Jewett City. I have also in bottles at my house some thirty specimens of Tape Worms removed with this medicine.

#### THREE OF MANY TESTIMONIALS.

*Arba Lankton.*—Dear Sir: This is to certify that I have used your Tape Worm Expeller, and it had the desired effect in three and one-half hours' time after using. I have tried various other remedies without effect. It measured about thirty feet. I cheerfully recommend it as being perfectly harmless and causing no sickness.

J. LINKINS,
Harness maker at Smith & Bourn's.
Hartford, Conn., Dec. 3, 1889.

This is to certify that I have used Arba Lankton's Tape Worm Expeller, by which my little child, 3½ years old, passed a tape worm eighteen feet long, containing 675 joints. I recommend it as a safe and sure cure to all afflicted in a similar manner. Yours respectfully.
MRS. MARKS, 356 Main Street.
Hartford, Conn., Sept. 1889.

*Dr. Arba Lankton*, Hartford, Conn.—Dear Sir: I had been in poor health for more than ten years. I heard of Dr. Lankton's Tape Worm Expeller; I sent to him for it. I took it as he ordered; the worm was entirely removed in six hours; it had 500 joints. This was in October, 1883. Now I am quite strong and can do all my own work. I can heartily recommend this Tape Worm Expeller, believing it to be a simple yet sure remedy.
Very gratefully yours.
Granby, Conn., Jan. 20, 1886. Mrs. M. W. CLARK.

# CORN SALVE,

An Infallible Remedy for Hard and Soft Corns, Bunions, or Calloused Soreness of the Toes and Feet, and for Ingrowing Nails.

| ARBA LANKTON'S | ARBA LANKTON'S |
|---|---|
| ### PILE OINTMENT | ### WORM SYRUP, |

ARBA LANKTON'S **PILE OINTMENT**

Should be used in all cases of Painful Itching, Blind, Bleeding and Ulcerated Piles.

Price, - 50 Cents a Box.

ARBA LANKTON'S **WORM SYRUP,**

A safe and certain preparation for the Removal of Worms.

A Sure Cure for Dyspepsia, Sour Stomach, Want of Appetite, and Diseases of Debility. For Children or Adults in all cases of Worms known as Lumbrici or Long Round Worms, and Ascarides, or small thread or Pin Worms.

Price, 25 Cents a Bottle. Large Bottles, 50 Cents.

### ARBA LANKTON'S
# Compound for Pain

For relieving Rheumatism, Neuralgia and Headache; for Coughs, Colds, Bronchitis, Sore Throat; for Cholera, Cholera Morbus, Colic, Diarrhea, Pain or Cramp of the Stomach and Bowels; for Sprains, Bruises, Burns, Pain in the Back, Limbs, Feet, Corns, Chilblains, Bites, or Piles. *25 Cents a Bottle.*

Address *ARBA LANKTON, Practical Helminthologist,*
2 MARSH COURT, Hartford.

☞ All my medicines can be sent, securely packed, by express to any part of the United States or Canada. For sale at wholesale by T. SISSON & CO., 729 Main Street, Hartford, Conn., and by all Druggists.

# CHARLES K. SWENSON,

Choice Carnations. # FLORIST.

### Roses and Violets. Floral Designs a Specialty.

## BIRDS AND CAGES.

Greenhouses
ON NEW PARK AVENUE.
Telephone Connection.

210 Asylum St.,
HARTFORD, CONN.

# THE JOURNAL OF INEBRIETY

### WAS ESTABLISHED IN 1876,

As the Organ of the American Association for the Study and Cure of Inebriety.

It has been published from the beginning by the Case, Lockwood & Brainard Company, and
also edited by Dr. T. D. Crothers from the commencement.

### IT IS A HUNDRED PAGE QUARTERLY,

Devoted exclusively to the scientific study of the inebriate and the alcoholic problem. It is the
only journal published, especially confined to the medical side of the subject.

## Grand List of State by Counties.

| | Hartford County. | New Haven County. | New London County. | Fairfield County | Windham County. | Litchfield County. | Middlesex County. | Tolland County. | Total. |
|---|---|---|---|---|---|---|---|---|---|
| 1879 | $81,992,176 | $88,188,994 | $38,915,476 | $60,893,019 | $17,106,115 | $25,320,007 | $16,340,821 | $8,317,077 | $327,082,685 |
| 1880 | 83,582,044 | 89,513,761 | 39,456,270 | 51,357,423 | 17,363,554 | 25,720,672 | 16,782,571 | 8,394,561 | 332,170,856 |
| 1881 | 87,084,778 | 87,273,557 | 39,772,794 | 52,701,297 | 17,653,364 | 26,154,758 | 19,361,613 | 8,411,915 | 338,413,076 |
| 1882 | 87,229,238 | 90,127,888 | 39,446,763 | 53,508,928 | 17,629,958 | 26,479,259 | 19,384,657 | 8,436,375 | 342,242,566 |
| 1883 | 87,335,513 | 92,815,588 | 39,227,512 | 57,280,854 | 17,752,753 | 26,272,021 | 19,639,486 | 8,451,152 | 348,774,879 |
| 1884 | 86,221,817 | 94,305,094 | 39,182,839 | 58,592,556 | 17,537,540 | 26,142,044 | 19,519,190 | 8,476,259 | 349,977,339 |
| 1885 | 87,069,872 | 94,032,137 | 39,035,235 | 58,491,849 | 17,335,108 | 26,006,202 | 18,945,403 | 8,261,791 | 349,177,597 |
| 1886 | 87,585,276 | 94,236,915 | 39,057,701 | 59,010,690 | 16,962,346 | 25,743,048 | 18,985,382 | 8,299,022 | 389,475,856 |
| 1887 | 88,771,185 | 94,846,235 | 39,339,079 | 58,801,499 | 16,870,363 | 25,918,045 | 18,914,105 | 8,340,465 | 352,795,926 |
| 1888 | 88,976,969 | 96,243,614 | 38,855,667 | 60,677,697 | 16,909,977 | 25,685,957 | 18,995,741 | 8,211,893 | 354,557,515 |
| 1889 | 87,715,289 | 97,121,067 | 36,764,096 | 66,404,900 | 18,405,806 | 24,929,690 | 19,152,049 | 8,421,009 | 358,913,804 |
| 1890 | 90,811,864 | 99,122,806 | 36,872,011 | 68,699,857 | 18,058,566 | 26,686,667 | 19,414,581 | 8,484,950 | 368,150,802 |
| 1891 | 92,133,946 | 99,866,080 | 37,347,897 | 70,607,918 | 18,005,013 | 27,137,069 | 18,609,877 | 8,537,642 | 372,245,442 |
| 1892 | 95,980,761 | 103,480,761 | 87,332,817 | 72,036,919 | 18,086,985 | 27,084,780 | 18,680,247 | 8,579,049 | 381,261,607 |
| 1893 | 96,716,342 | 106,429,424 | 37,965,234 | 101,715,966 | 17,993,764 | 28,081,896 | 18,901,751 | 8,518,875 | 416,323,257 |
| 1894 | 96,575,791 | 109,955,702 | 38,013,511 | 98,416,178 | 17,643,022 | 26,363,652 | 18,840,832 | 8,450,268 | 414,258,956 |
| 1895 | 100,252,839 | 118,462,571 | 38,163,889 | 113,675,978 | 17,872,358 | 28,534,267 | 18,718,888 | 8,641,145 | 444,321,927 |
| 1896 | 123,392,307 | 153,529,035 | 43,127,595 | 125,870,009 | 20,316,702 | 31,381,647 | 19,394,488 | 12,609,382 | 529,621,165 |
| 1897 | 124,768,443 | 154,043,938 | 43,309,415 | 127,539,620 | 19,585,278 | 31,916,588 | 19,441,059 | 13,560,016 | 534,465,257 |

## JOB PRINTING ~~~FOR~~~ Business Men

### RECEIVES OUR PARTICULAR ATTENTION.

## THE HARTFORD PRINTING CO.,

CHU GEER'S SONS. 16 STATE STREET.

# Parks.

*For Commissioners, see page 677.*

### BUSHNELL PARK.

Was laid out in 1853, and voted for in 1854, contains 48½ acres with the 15 acres purchased of Trinity College in 1872, and is bounded north by Asylum st., east and west by Park river, south by Elm st. and Capitol av. Total cost of land and construction, not including the annual care thereof, $1,082,400.

There are over 150 distinct varieties of trees, and over 500 specimens, all labeled with their botanical and common names, besides hundreds of shrubs, flowers, etc. Also, concrete and other walks in all directions, and roads for vehicles.

There are four and a half miles of walks in this Park. The Common Council of this city at a regular meeting held Feb. 14th, 1876, only three days previous to the decease (which occurred on Feb. 17), of the late Rev. HORACE BUSHNELL, D.D., unanimously passed, and on the same evening, officially sent to him sundry resolutions concerning this park laid out by the city in 1854 which owes its origin and successful execution in a large degree to his foresight, to his able and earnest advocacy, and to his influence, freely and with generous persistence exerted in public, in private and through the press, and in recognition of his invaluable services thereon, they *Resolved*, That the public park now commonly called "The Park," be and hereby is named "BUSHNELL PARK."

June 17th, 1874, a Bronze Statue 8 feet in height, of Gen. ISRAEL PUTNAM, weighing 1,200 lbs. was erected on this Park which with the pedestal of Quincy granite cost $14,000—presented by the late J. P. Allyn.

July 22, 1875, a Bronze Statue of Dr. HORACE WELLS, the discoverer of Anæsthesia, in September, 1844, was erected on this Park at a cost of $10,000—one half paid by this State and the other half by the city of Hartford.

### BUCKINGHAM PARK.

Buckingham, north side, between Main and Whitman sts., laid out and fenced in 1890.

### CITY HALL SQUARE

So called since 1879; is by arrangement with City Hall Committee cared for by the Park Commissioners.

### FRANKLIN AVENUE PARK.

Junction of Franklin and Maple avs., laid out in 1876.

### KENEY PARK.

The gift of Henry Keney. RRev. Francis Goodwin, Judge J. H. White, Mr. Henry H. Goodwin, Mr. Geo. E. Taintor, Trustees. Olmsted Brothers, Brookline, Mass., Landscape Architects. Mr. G. A. Parker, 12 Blue Hills avenue, Superintendent. Thh purchase of land commenced early in 1896, and was completed in 1897. 663.4 acres of land was purchased in thirty-five different lots. Keney Park is bordered by Windsor avenue on the east, by Blue Hills avenue and Park river on the west, and on the northwest by Holcomb street. Its north boundary line is the north line of the city. Tower avenue, Vine street and Love lane pass through it, and Barbour street, Waverly avenue, Harper street and Woodland street extension connect with it. With the exception of the Metropolitan Reservations near Boston, Keney Park is the largest park in New England, and with the other parks of Hartford, will make this city second only to Boston in the park work of New England. It is a driving or country park, which requires minimum cost of maintenance.

### LAUREL PARK.　*See page 557.*

### POND PARK.

The gift of Charles M. Pond, comprising about 90 acres of land in the western part of the city, on Prospect and Asylum avenues, with $200,000 for the development of the same.

### POPE PARK.

The gift of Colonel Albert A. Pope, comprising over 78 acres of land in the southwestern section of the city, on Capitol avenue, Laurel and Park streets for use by the citizens as a public park for all time without restriction. Conditioned that the city procure 18 acres adjoining this, from the Watkinson Farm School, and 6 acres from the Hartford Orphan Asylum.

### RIVER FRONT PARK.

Purchased by the commissioners, in the eastern section of the city, on the river front, between the East Hartford bridge and the New England Railroad bridge.

### SIGOURNEY SQUARE PARK,

Between Ashley, Sigourney Sargeant and May streets, laid out by the town in 1890, improvment began 1896.

### SOUTH PARK.

Junction of Main, Park, Jefferson and Wyllys streets, Wethersfield and Franklin avs. Mar. 26, 1816, the town voted a fence for this Park, then called South Green.

### TUNNEL PARK.

Junction of Main st. and Albany av., improved as a park in 1891 by an agreement with the N.Y.N.H.&H. R.R. and the N.Y.&N.E.R.R.

### VILLAGE STREET PARK.

At the divergence of Windsor street from Village st.

### WASHINGTON STREET PARK.

At the junction of Washington, Buckingham and Lafayette streets. Laid out in 1881.

### WINDSOR STREET PARK.

At a special city meeting held in October, 1875, the Court of Common Council were authorized to lay out at public expense, a park between Avon, Front, North and Windsor streets,—not begun, July, 1896.

---

# Streets.

*For Commissioners, see page 677.*

In 1826 the Street Commissioner's salary was raised from $52.00 per year, or $1 per week, to $75 per year. Now it is $2,400 and an Assistant paid by city.

There are 132 miles of stone sidewalks, besides many miles of plank walks, in this city.

Union place was paved with granite blocks in 1894 at $3.50 per square yard. Pearl street with block asphalt at $3.00 per square yard in 1894-5. State street and Central Row was paved with block asphalt in 1895-6. Main and Athenæum streets were paved with sheet asphalt in 1896-7.

There are nearly 110 miles of streets in this city under 348 different names, over 58 miles of which are macadamized. The expenses of the street department were:

| | | | |
|---|---|---|---|
| 1872.. | $187,100.88 | 1881.. | $64,239.28 |
| 1873.. | 173,595.86 | 1882.. | 72,948.43 |
| 1874.. | 190,700.46 | 1883.. | 71,959.26 |
| 1875.. | 131,188.17 | 1884.. | 76,967.80 |
| 1876.. | 101,182.63 | 1885.. | 83,121.56 |
| 1877.. | 68,908.50 | 1886.. | 92,451.56 |
| 1878.. | 53,242.01 | 1887.. | 109,385.69 |
| 1879.. | 48,715.97 | 1888.. | 99,717.41 |
| 1880.. | 62,252.67 | 1889.. | 118,251.54 |
| | | 1890.. | $142,065.73 |
| | | 1891.. | 140,487.70 |
| | | 1892.. | 112,944.61 |
| | | 1893.. | 118,~~~~ |
| | | 1894.. | 127, |
| | | 1895.. | 149, |
| | | 1896.. | 157, |
| | | 1897 | ~~~ |

---

WINTER EVENING PUBLIC SCHO

ASYLUM STREET EVENING SCHOOL—162 As
MORGAN STREET EVENING SCHOOL—52 I'

# Bridges.

## ALBANY AVENUE BRIDGE.
Built in 1850, cost $1,800.

## ASYLUM AVENUE BRIDGE.
Built in 1860, cost $1,924.05.

## ASYLUM ST. R. R. AND CHURCH ST. BRIDGES,
Including the approaches of both to the Union Station, completed in 1890, costing $395,049.84, of which amount the City of Hartford has paid $197,-524.92, being one-half of the cost. June 9, 1891, there commenced a hearing before the Railroad Commissioners for an adjustment, whereby the city should not pay more than thirty per cent, and June 2, 1892, they rendered their decision that the city pay one-half.

## ASYLUM STREET (PARK) BRIDGE.
Asylum street to west drive on Park; erected 1858, of wood, cost $2,500. Repaired in 1893 at a cost of $2,000.

## BROAD STREET BRIDGE,
Over railroad tracks, of the Truesdell pattern, erected of iron in 1867, cost $52,111.79—Railroad Companies paying $7,550 thereof.

## CAPITOL AVENUE BRIDGE,
Across Park river, connecting Capitol av., with Sigourney street, 1872, cost $30,163.71. Re-built in 1895 at a cost of $10,000.

## COMMERCE STREET BRIDGE,
A swing or draw-bridge, costing $14,000, built in the fall of 1859. Town paid $8,750. This has been superseded by a new iron swing bridge which was finished in 1887, and cost $9,100.

## CONNECTICUT RIVER BRIDGE.
Built in 1809, was an open bridge, carried away by a freshet March 2, 1818, (as was also the bridge at Springfield, 26 miles north of this city) and rebuilt Dec. 1818. It was 1060 feet in length. and cost with the raising of the causeway over East Hartford meadows, in 1859, the sum of $135,000, divided into 600 shares. This was re-built after the Legislature had abolished the ferry between the two towns, that had been running from 1681, first from foot of Kilbourn st. then changed to Ferry street. In 1836 the ferry was re-established, and boat propelled by two horses, one on each side of the boat. In 1841 this right was rescinded by the legislature. The next year it was restored. The case then went through all the courts, and was decided that the restoration was in violation of the 1818 contract, by which the bridge was re-built. The travel of the bridge by actual count was over 1,000 vehicles and over 1,600 footmen, daily. The 1887 legislature voted to make this a free bridge. June 11, 1888, Edward W. Seymour, Fred. J. Kingsbury and Thomas Sanford, the commission appointed by the 1887 legislature to assess the damages, gave their decision which amounted to $210,000. The legislature of 1889 voted to pay $84,000 and the towns of Hartford, East Hartford, Glastonbury, Manchester and South Windsor the balance, $126,000 which was paid, making it a free bridge September 1 889. May 17, 1890, the Hartford Bridge Co. voted a al dividend of $25 per share; making a total of 1 50 per share paid to its stockholders. The bridge approaches were taken by the State of Connecticut under Public Act CCXXXIX, session of 1893. 1 le legislature of May 24, 1895, repealed the act of 1 and in June, 1895, passed an act creating a "dge District," comprising the original five towns, Hartford, East Hartford, Glastonbury, Manchester ad South Windsor, thus placing the rebuilding, and maintainance of the bridge and causeway on t 'ld five towns. For commissioners, see page 658.

The old bridge was totally destroyed by fire at 7.15 P. M. on Friday, May 17, 1895. A temporary bridge on spiling was built by the Berlin Bridge Co. and opened for travel Saturday afternoon, June 8, 1895; the west end was carried away by freshet, Dec. 28, 1895, at 1.10 A. M.; the remaining portion, except a short length on the East Hartford side was swept away by freshet, March 1, 1896, and the steam ferryboats "Schuykill" and "Nellie" for foot passengers, the "F. C. Fowler" and "Cora" for teams, were run for public travel, comfort and convenience between the two towns. A new temporary iron bridge, to cost over $30,000, was commenced by the Berlin Iron Bridge Co., May 4, 1896, and opened for travel June 12, 1896.

## EDWARDS STREET BRIDGE,
Built by Railroad Co.

## FARMINGTON AVENUE BRIDGE
Was built in 1871, of stone, across North branch Park river, cost $27,901.54.

## FLATBUSH AVENUE BRIDGE,
Built in 1862, cost $1,974.

## FLOWER STREET FOOT BRIDGE,
Connecting said street with Lawrence st., cost $464.50; finished December 21, 1878. This bridge was rebuilt of stone and brick, with a 77 feet arch span, 46 feet wide, 11 feet high, with height of 16 feet above average low water, with stone abutments, brick arch and parapets, two sidewalks, each 6 feet wide with a roadway 30 feet wide, costing $19,557.24, including curbs and sidewalks, and opened for travel July 1, 1885.

## FORD STREET BRIDGE
Cost about $15,000, and was built in the year 1850; is 35 feet wide, 174 feet long, of five free stone arches,—the north and south of fifteen feet span each—the other three of 18 feet each; width of arches 26 feet; width of piers 5½ feet; height from top of center arch to top of sides, 7 feet. In 1885 the sidewalks on this bridge were extended over the sides on stone brackets, and road bed widened at an expense of $11,287.64.

## FRONT STREET BRIDGE
Cost $10,000, and was built in the year 1853; is 44 feet wide, 148 feet long,—of three free stone arches—two of 34 feet span, and one of 35 feet—all semi-circular, and divided or supported by two piers, each six feet wide.

## HAMILTON STREET BRIDGE
Was erected in 1872, at a cost of $800.

## LAUREL STREET (RAILROAD) BRIDGE,
Over the railroad tracks at Laurel street crossing, was erected in 1875, at an expense of $17,357.21—of which the city paid $9,215.13—the Railroad Companies the balance.

## LAUREL STREET (RIVER) BRIDGE,
Over the Park river was built in 1894, at a cost of $23,000, in place of the wooden pile bridge which was constructed by citizens, and finished July, 1872, at a cost of $1,500.

## MAIN STREET STONE BRIDGE
Is of a single arch, on rock foundation, and is one hundred feet wide, seven feet in thickness at the base, and three feet two inches at the center — the chord span of it is 104 feet, and it is 30 feet 9 inches from the bed of river to top of arch. Cost $31,526.20 It was planned by the late Bishop Potter, who in 1830 was a professor in Trinity—then called Washington college. The first stone for the foundation of this bridge was laid June 18, 1833, and key-stone of arch inserted Nov.

21st of same year. This bridge was completed in the fall of 1833—less than one year from the time it was begun, by Elias Rathbun, the contractor, whose indefatigable labors thereon brought on a paralyzed side, including arm and leg. The bridges of wood on high trestle work that preceded this one, had rows of stores on either side on Main st. over the river, and was called market bridge. The generally expressed opinion of that day, after over half a century's use of this bridge is as true in 1896 as it was in 1833, on the unanimous town vote of its acceptance, that this bridge "combines strength with elegance of architecture, and is honorable to the town." The largest stone arch in this state.

## MULBERRY STREET FOOT BRIDGE,

Built of wood at the time of laying out of Bushnell Park, and rests on the abutments of the old Railroad bridge which was built about 1839.

## NEWFIELD AVENUE BRIDGE

Was erected in 1873, at a cost of $730.

## PARK STREET BRIDGE,

Built in the year 1858, cost $1,977.40.

## TRUMBULL STREET FOOT BRIDGE,

Erected of iron in 1864, cost $4,000, and is 75 feet long, 10 feet wide and 18 feet from bottom of river, of one span, and bears ten tons in the center.

## WATER STREET BRIDGE.

An arched stone bridge, at junction of Front, was built in 1857, costing $3,140.

## WOODLAND STREET BRIDGE

Was built by the Railroad Co.

## PRESIDENTS OF THE UNITED STATES.

| NAMES. | INAUGURATED. | BORN. | DIED. |
|---|---|---|---|
| 1. George Washington, of Va. | Apr.30, 1789 | 1732 | 1799 |
| 2. John Adams, of Mass. | Mar. 4, 1797 | 1735 | 1826 |
| 3. Thomas Jefferson, of Va. | Mar. 4, 1801 | 1748 | 1826 |
| 4. James Madison, of Va. | Mar. 4, 1809 | 1751 | 1886 |
| 5. James Monroe, of Va. | Mar. 4, 1817 | 1758 | 1831 |
| 6. J. Quincy Adams, of Mass. | Mar. 4, 1825 | 1767 | 1848 |
| 7. Andrew Jackson, of Tenn. | Mar. 4, 1829 | 1767 | 1845 |
| 8. Martin Van Buren, of N. Y. | Mar. 4, 1837 | 1782 | 1862 |
| 9. Wm. Henry Harrison, of O. | Mar. 4, 1841 | 1773 | 1841 |
| 10. John Tyler, of Va. Vice P. suc. | P.Harrison | 1790 | 1862 |
| 11. James K. Polk, of Tenn.* | Mar. 4, 1845 | 1795 | 1849 |
| 12. Zachary Taylor, of La. | Mar. 4, 1849 | 1784 | 1850 |
| 13. Millard Fillmore, N.Y. Vice P. suc. | Taylor | 1800 | 1874 |
| 14. Franklin Pierce, of N. H. | Mar. 4, 1853 | 1804 | 1869 |
| 15 James Buchanan, of Pa. | Mar. 4, 1857 | 1791 | 1868 |
| 16. Abraham Lincoln, of Ill.† | Mar. 4, 1861 | 1809 | 1865 |
| 17. Andrew Johnson, Vice P. suc. | A. Lincoln | 1808 | 1875 |
| 18. Ulysses S. Grant, of Ill. | Mar. 4, 1869 | 1822 | 1885 |
| 19. Rutherford B. Hayes, of O. | Mar. 4, 1877 | 1822 | 1893 |
| 20. James A. Garfield, of O.‡ | Mar. 4, 1881 | 1831 | 1881 |
| 21. Chester A. Arthur, of N. Y. | Sep. 20, 1881 | 1830 | 1886 |
| 22. Grover Cleveland, of N. Y. | Mar. 4, 1885 | 1837 | |
| 23. Benjamin Harrison, of Ind. | Mar. 4, 1889 | 1833 | |
| 24. Grover Cleveland, of N. Y. | Mar. 4, 1893 | 1837 | |
| 25. William McKinley, of Ohio | Mar. 4, 1897 | 1843 | |

* President Polk's term expired on Saturday, March 3, 1849, at 12 o'clock midnight. The next day, the 4th, occurring on Sunday, General Taylor, the then President elect, was not inaugurated until Monday, the 5th, at 12 M. Therefore, David R. Atchinson of Missouri, the then President elect of the U. S. Senate (the Vice President, W. R. King, having deceased), was nominally President for one day, but did not take the oath of office.

† Assassinated in a Washington Theater and died April 14, 1865, about 8 P. M.

‡ Assassinated in Railroad Station, Washington, 10 A. M. July 2d, 1881, died 10:30 P. M. Sept. 19, 1881.

## POLITICAL ORGANIZATIONS.

DEMOCRATIC TOWN COMMITTEE.— James Campbel Chairman; John F. Spellacy, 1st ward; John H. Pitts 2d; Walter J. Mather, 3d; John J. Hickey 4th; Micham O'Brien, 5th; James T. Farrell, 6th; Thos. F. Meagher, 7th; J. Dunn, 8th; James J. Coyle, 9th; Daniel J. O'Brien, 10th.

REPUBLICAN TOWN AND CITY COMMITTEE.—Frank H. Parker, Chairman; G. D. Winslow, 1st ward; Wm. A. Baedor, 2d; Samuel McFadyen, 3d; Horace M. Andrews, 4th; Robert A. Griffing, 5th; Samuel N. Benedict, 6th; Robert D. Bone, 7th; F. E. Simonds, 8th; Lyman Root, 9th; Andrew F. Gates, 10th.

PROHIBITION TOWN COMMITTEE.—L. W. Bartlett, Chairman; Myrton Smith, Sec'y; Henry Cowlishaw, Treas.; Geo. S. Swaine, Charles F. Agard, John P. Harding, Marion F. Levee, E. D. Matthews, C. W. Whiting, Marion Pulver.

REPUBLICAN STATE CENTRAL COMMITTEE.—O. R. Fyler, Torrington, Chairman; Samuel A. Eddy, Canaan, Secretary. Wm. B. Dwight, Hartford; Perry S. Bryant, East Hartford; George P. McLean, Simsbury; Robert A. Potter, Bristol; Chas. E. Turner, Waterbury; Leverett M. Hubbard, Wallingford; Frederick L. Gaylord, Ansonia; James A. Howarth, New Haven; Frederick Farnsworth, New London; Wm. H. Palmer, Jr., Norwich; Geo. O. Jackson, Colchester; Whitman S. Mead, Greenwich; Edmund E. Crowe, Norwalk; Allan W. Paige, Bridgeport; Samuel S. Ambler, Bethel; George A. Hammond, Putnam; Charles N. Daniels, Willimantic; O. R. Fyler, Torrington; A. T. Bowaba, Canaan; N. L. Webster, Thomaston; W. C. Reynolds, East Haddam; W. E. McDonald, Cromwell; Thomas A. Lake, Rockville; Harry S. Abel, Stafford Springs.

PROHIBITION STATE COMMITTEE.—Henry B. Brown, East Hampton, Chairman; L. W. Bartlett, Hartford, Treas.; W. D. Martin, Rockville; C. P. Hodgson, Stafford Springs; E. L. G. Hokenthal, So. Manchester; John B. Smith, Berlin; F. C. Bradley, North Haven; F. S. Clark, New Haven; B. J. Gardner, Stonington; Stephen Crane, Norwich; W. F. Peebles, Stamford; A. N. Sherwood, So. Norwalk; O. G. Beard, Shelton; Allen B. Lincoln, Willimantic; C.H.Cabler,Thomaston; E. C. Barton, East Hampton; C. D. Rice, Middletown.

DEMOCRATIC NATIONAL COMMITTEE.—James K. Jones, Washington, Ark., Chairman; C. A. Walsh, Ottumwa, Iowa, Sec'y; Alexander Troupe, New Haven, Conn., and one from each State.

REPUBLICAN NATIONAL COMMITTEE.—Mark Hanna, Cleveland, Ohio, Chairman; Chas. Dick, Chicago, Ill., Wm. Osborne, N. Y., Sec'ys; C. N. Bliss, N. Y., Treas; Samuel Fessenden, Stamford, Conn., and one from each State.

PROHIBITION NATIONAL COMMITTEE.—Sam'l Dickie, Albion, Mich., Chairman; William T. Wardwell, 33 Broadway, New York, Sec'y; Samuel D. Hastings, Green Bay, Wis., Treas.; F. C. Bradley, North Haven, J. N. Stanley, Highland Park, Conn., and two from each State.

## NET TONNAGE OF DOCUMENTED VESSELS.

*Belonging to District of Hartford, July*

| Year. | No. | Tons. | Year. | No. | Tons. | Year. | No. |
|---|---|---|---|---|---|---|---|
| 1797 | — | 4,509 | 1880 | — | 15,790 | 1890 | 914 |
| 1800 | — | 2,070 | 1882 | 116 | 16,840 | 1891 | 117 |
| 1810 | — | 5,368 | 1883 | 117 | 15,850 | 1892 | 8 125 |
| 1820 | — | 10,172 | 1884 | 120 | 15,970 | 1893 | 319 |
| 1830 | — | 11,859 | 1885 | 101 | 14,422 | 1894 | 394 |
| 1840 | — | 12,193 | 1886 | 100 | 12,267 | 1895 | 143 |
| 1850 | — | 11,861 | 1887 | 89 | 10,860 | 1896 | 95 148 |
| 1860 | — | 16,815 | 1888 | 86 | 10,320 | 1897 | 341 |
| 1870 | — | 17,128 | 1889 | 83 | 9,805 | | |

# Tucker & Goodwin,

WILLIAM TUCKER.
HENRY H. GOODWIN.

Successors to KENEY, ROBERTS & CO.

## Wholesale Grocers and Flour Merchants,

R. R. Warehouse and Office,
8, 10, and 12 HURLBURT STREET, } *Hartford, Conn.*
Just South of Union Station.

*AGENTS FOR THE*

### WASHBURN-CROSBY CO'S GOLD MEDAL FLOUR,

The best flour in the world,
Try it once and you will always use it.

*We make a Specialty of*

*Teas, Coffees and Spices.*

---

# INGRAHAM, SWIFT & CO.

# Swift's Dressed Beef, Mutton, Veal,

 PROVISIONS AND POULTRY,
BUTTER, CHEESE AND EGGS.
SWIFT'S WASHING POWDER.

## 126 Church Street,      Hartford, Conn.

---

# The L. T. FRISBIE CO.,

DEALERS IN

# Hides, Calf Skins, Wool Skins,

TALLOW, SOAP STOCK, AND SALT.

# Soap Manufacturers.

# 71 TALCOTT STREET, Hartford, Conn.

CHARLES H. NORTHAM.                                    E. V. MITCHELL.

**Established 1860.**

# SMITH, NORTHAM & CO.,

Office, No. 129 STATE STREET, Hartford, Conn.

**Warehouse and Mills,    -    165 WINDSOR STREET,**

At Junction of the N. Y., N. H. & H. R. R. and the N. E. R. R.

**CAPACITY:**

Mills: 7,500 bushels corn daily.                    Elevator: 200,000 bushels grain.

Warehouses: 600 cars flour, feed, etc.

☞ Our conveniences for handling flour, grain, and feed, and grinding meal, are superior to any in New England.

**SPECIALTIES:** *GRAIN by the Carload delivered at any station in New England. A large amount of Corn, Oats, and Mill Feed constantly in transit.*

*MILLERS' AGENTS FOR* "PILLSBURY'S BEST," "SURPRISE," "H. C. COLE'S FFFG," "ALLEN'S PATENT," "GOLDEN SHEAF," and other choice brands of FAMILY and BAKERS' FLOUR.

*BALED HAY AND STRAW, by the carload, on commission.*

*PEAT MOSS, FOR STABLE BEDDING, a superior substitute for straw.   Send for Circul*

1☞ Special attention to supplying private stables with the best of hay, or ALL KINDS OF FEED.

*CREAM AND CHICAGO GLUTEN MEAL, the best thing in the world for Milch Cows.*

# ELIHU GEER'S SONS'

# BUSINESS DIRECTORY

## OF THE

# CITY OF HARTFORD,

## JULY, 1898.

Names in Capitals are Firms that Advertise in this Book; for pages of such, see Advertisers' Index, Pages 9 and 12.

## ACADEMIES.
*See Schools; Bands of Music.*

## ACCIDENT INSURANCE.
ÆTNA LIFE INS. CO. *See page 449.*
TRAVELERS INSURANCE CO. *See page 456.*

## ACCOUNT BOOKS.
CASE, LOCKWOOD & BRAINARD CO. 141 Pl. *See page 475.*

## ACCOUNTANT.
*See also Expert Accountant.*
Knapp Frederic, 14 Columbia.
STEWART GORDON W., P. O. address, Portland, Conn.

## ACIDS.
*See Apothecaries.*
SISSIONS T. & CO. 729 Main. *See page 560.*

## ADMINISTRATORS.
CONN. TRUST & SAFE DEPOSIT CO. 777 Main. *See page 487.*
SECURITY CO. 62 Pearl. *See page 488.*
THE FIDELITY CO. 49 Pearl *See page 488.*

## ADVERTISEMENT WRITER
O'Keef M. 908 Main.

## ADVERTISING AGENCY.
DILLINGHAM E. B. 709 Main. *See page 122.*
Parsons Albert R. 71 Asylum.

## AGENCIES IN THIS CITY.
*Particulars on advertising*   PAGES.

| | PAGES. |
|---|---|
| Allens Patent Flour | 590 |
| Am. Security Co. of N. Y. | 444 |
| American Traveler Bicycles | 484 |
| Belle of Nelson Whiskey | 589 |
| Berryman Heaters | 546 |
| Billings C. E., Mfg. Co. | 521 |
| Bonds of Suretyship | 444 |
| British Alizarine Co. | 591 |
| Brookway Carriages | 550 |
| Brooke, Simpson & Spiller, Lon. | 591 |
| Buckeye Engine | 539 |
| Bucklow & Co. | 591 |
| Butterfly Flour | 589 |
| Ceresota Flour | 589 |
| Clipper Bicycles | 837 |
| Coles H. C. FFFG Flour | 590 |
| Collins Co's Axes | 521 |
| Columbia Bicycle | 485 |
| Commercial Union Assurance Co. London | 444 |
| Conway, Mass. Co-operative Creamery | 586 |
| Crockers Best Flour | 589 |
| "Crown Jewells" Cigars | 111 |
| Dayton Bicycles | 484 |
| Delaware Ins. Co. | 444 |
| Depository United States | 432 |
| Dodge Patent Wood Split Pulleys | 592 |
| Farwell Cherry Bounce | 589 |
| Fidelity & Deposit Co. | 108 |
| Franklin Ins. Co., Phila. | 444 |
| German-American Ins.Co. N.Y. | 108 |
| Golden Grain Flour | 586 |
| Golden Sheaf | 590 |
| Granville Mosaic Wood Floors | 519 |
| Greylock Cheese | 587 |
| Hartford Bicycle | 485 |
| Hartford Engine | 539 |
| Hartford Extension Ladder | 60 |
| Hartford Hot Water Heater | 180 |

| | PAGE. |
|---|---|
| Helmet Brand | 587 |
| Hermitage Rye Whisky | 589 |
| Homeopathic Medicines | 801 |
| Hot Water Heaters | 524 |
| Household Stoves and Ranges | 501 |
| Imperial Insurance Co. London | 444 |
| India Pale Ale | 589 |
| India Wharf Ale | 589 |
| Indiana Limestone | 508 |
| Insurance Co. of N. A. | 444 |
| Jessop William & Sons Steel | 592 |
| London Art Union | 418 |
| Manchester Fire Assurance Co. Manchester, England | 444 |
| Marine Ins. Co. of London | 444 |
| Mass. Mu. Life I. Co. of Sprfi'd. | 64 |
| Melrose Cocktails | 589 |
| Mercer & Gold, Boilers | 542 |
| Merchants Insurance Co. Newark, N. J. | 444 |
| Merchants and Manufacturers Fire Ins. of Baltimore City | 427 |
| Mutual Benefit Life Ins. Co. of Newark, N. J. | 174 |
| Mutual Life Ins. Co. of N. Y. | 108 |
| Nagle Engines and Boilers | 587 |
| National Fire Insurance Co. | 459 |
| New Home Sewing Machine | 149 |
| Northern Ins. Co. London | 444 |
| Old Crow, whisky | 589 |
| Onogagu Electrical Apparatus | 420 |
| Palatine Insurance Co. Manchester, Eng. | 444 |
| Pennsylvania Fire Ins. Co. | 445 |
| Pepper James E. whiskey | 589 |
| Phenix Ins. Co., New York | 444 |
| Philadelphia India Pale Ale | 589 |
| Philadelphia Underwriters | 444 |
| Pickering Governor | 587 |
| Pillsbury Best Flour | 590 |
| Plate Glass Insurance | 444 |
| Pleasant Valley Twins Cheese | 587 |
| Potter's Pat. Belt Hooks | 548 |

PAGE.

Queen Insurance Co.New York 444
Racycle Bicycle.............. 484
Rider & Ericsson, Hot-Air
 Pumping Engines.......... 224
Robert Smith's India Pale Ale. 589
Royal Fire Insurance Co...... 445
Scandinavia Belting.......... 591
Singer, Nimick & Co's Steel... 592
Societe Chimique Des Wines
 Du Rhone, Lyons.......... 591
Standard Arkron Salt Glazed
 Pipe........ .............. 508
State Mutual Ins. Co......... 445
Surprise Flour............... 590
Tarbell Factory Cheese....... 587
Transatlantic Fire Insurance
 Co. Hamburg, Germany.... 444
Tribune Bicycles............. 295
Union Assurance Society of
 London............... ...... 444
Victoria Fire Insurance Co.
 New York................. 444
Vitrified Salt Glazed Sewer
 Pipe,..................... 509
Washburn, Crosby & Co. Flour 585
White Sponge Flour.......... 586
Winchester Hot Water Heating 542
Windsor Creamery Butter..... 586
Windsor Folding Bed......... 500
Zimmerman's Patent Shutter
 Adjuster ................. 509

### AGENTS.
*See also Real Estate.*

Adams C. F. & Co. 261 Asylum.
Associated Press, 7 Central.
Atwood E. F. 212 Asylum.
Barnard William C. 52 Liberty.
BARTLETT F. W. & F. E. 212
 Asylum. *See page 420.*
Bennett P. P., Bradstreet, 49 Pearl.
BLANCHARD, G. G. 40 Vine. *See
 page 61.*
Bodge Geo. R. 81 Asylum.
Brainard Fred J. 20 Lincoln.
Brett M. A. 190 Pearl.
Conroy John F. 548 Main.
Down E. C. 847 Main.
Driscoll James C. 42 High.
DWIGHT SLATE MACHINE CO.
 18 Central. *See page 525.*
Forbes W. L. 942 Mn. *See page 499.*
Frisbie Thomas S. 221 Garden.
GRIFFITH WILLIAM RICHARD,
 66 State. *See page 427.*
Henney Charles M. 18 State.
Hodge George W. 904 Main.
Internat'l Correspondence Schools,
 Scranton, Pa. 75 Pratt.
Jacobs Ward W. & Co. 815 Main.
Kilbourn J. F. 118 Asylum.
Martin Horatio, 721 Main.
Middlesex Banking Co. 49 Pearl.
Morse Albert B. 200 Allyn.
National Cash Register Co. 118 Asy.
N. Y. Leather Co. 21½ Mulberry.
New England Trading Coupon Co.
 77 Pratt.
O'Brien Patrick, 58 Fairmount.
Palmer H. 231 State.
Park Bros. & Co. 18 Central.
Parsons Adv. Agency, 71 Asylum.
Payson H. N. 532 Garden.
Premier Mfg. Co. 487 Main.
Rourke John, 389 Main.
Schmidt Emil, 8 Bond.
Standard Account Co. of N. Y. 75
 Pratt.

---

Stacy Ina B. (corsets) 58 Church.
St. Clair Hector B. 1½ East.
Schierholz Emil C. 182 Market.
Storrs F. H. & Co. 42 Church.
Syndicate Premium Co. 78 Pearl.
Tifft A. L. 115 Oak.
Whitmore William F. 190 Pearl.

### AGENTS WANTED.
AMERICAN PUBLISHING CO.
 . 424 Asylum.    *See page 473.*

### AGRICULTUBAL TOOLS.
### M'F'R.
*See also Hardware.*
COLLINS CO.        *See page 521.*

### ALE BREWERS.
COLUMBIA BREWING CO, 245
 Windsor.       *See page 417.*
NEW ENGLAND BREWING CO.
 217 Windsor.  *See page 504.*

### ALIZARINES.
BEACH & CO. 209 State. *See p. 591.*

### AMUSEMENTS.
Capitol City Chute Co.Wethersfield.

### ANILINE DYES.
BEACH & CO. 209 State.   *See
 page 591.*

### ANTI-FRICTION METALS.
BLAKE T. J. & SON, 141 Commerce.   *See page 489.*

### ANTIQUES.
Brooks A. E. 911 Main.
Russell John S. 1140 Main.

### ANTIQUE FURNITURE.
FENN L. T. 613 Main. *See p. 501.*
NEAL, GOFF & INGLIS CO. 980
 Main.   *See page 498.*

### ANVILS.
ENSWORTH L. L. & SON, 104
 Front. *See page 592.*

### APOTHECARIES.
*See also Drug Stores, Medicines.*
GOODRICH S. & CO. 1208 Main.
 *See page 164.*
GOODWIN L. H. 852 Main.  *See
 page 165.*
Hartford Drug Co. 852 Main.
NEWTON PHILO W. 142 Asylum.
 *See page 35.*
RAPELYE CHARLES A. 876
 Asylum and 853 Main. *See p. 301.*
Risley Leon S. 386 Capitol.
SEINSOTH JOHN J. 12 Maple.
 *See page 324.*
SISSON T. & CO. 729 Main. *See
 page 560.*
Talcott, Frisbie & Co. 273-277 Asy.

### BOXES.
HARTFORD BOX CO. *See p. 532.*

### APPRAISERS.
*See Real Estate.*
CONN. BUILDING AND LOAN
 ASSO. 252 Asylum. *See p. 480.*
GRIFFITH WM. RICHARD, 66
 State. *See page 427.*

---

LINCOLN FRED. M. 911 Main.
 *See page 427.*
MULHALL JAMES, 29 Pearl. *See
 page 367.*
SHELTON E. 66 State. *See p. 425.*
STEINMETZ WILLIAM P. 29
 Pearl. *See page 342.*
WHITE W. L. 384 Main.  *P. 502.*

### ARCHITECTS.
*See also Draughtsmen.*
ALLEN ISAAC A. Jr. 904 Main.
 *See page 519.*
ARNOLD WALTER T. 82 Pearl.
 *See page 514.*
BARNES PHILIP, 416 Franklin av.
 *See page 481.*
Bayley & Goodrich, 700 Main.
Becker Willis E. 756 Main.
Brocklesby William C. 756 Main.
Buckland G. W. Mrs. 926 Main.
BUTTS & CROSBY, 49 Pearl. *See
 page 427.*
Chesebro J. L. 757 Main.
Comstock Frederick R. 252 Asylum.
Curtis & Johnson, 926 Main.
Dwyer John J. 78 Trumbull.
Gerstel Max, 576 Main.
Gilbert George H. 67 Willard.
Hapgood & Hapgood, 141 Tru.
Jackson Edward, 847 Main.
Keller George, 756 Main.
McCarthy John J. 793 Main.
McCLUNIE J. ALEX. 177 Asylum.
 *See page 249.*
O'Donohue Michael, 93 Hawthorn.
Perkins Martin, 887 Park.
Relyea W. H. 260 Wethersfield.
 *See page 304.*
Rogers George B. 49 Pearl.
SCOVILLE A. W. 700 Main.
 *See page 513.*
SCOVILLE WILLIAM H. 729 Main.
 *See page 515.*
Storrs Henry W. 50 State.
Whitmore C. O. 75 Pratt.

*Architectural Ornament.*
SANFORD CO., 438 Asylum.  *See
 page 448.*

*Architectural Sculptor.*
ENTRESS ALBERT, 598 Main.
 *See page 511.*

### ARMORIES.
*See Military Companies, page 680.*
First Regiment, 51 Elm.
GOVERNOR'S FOOT GUARD
 HALL, 159 High. *See page 496.*
Governor's Horse Guard, 460 Main.
Putnam Phalanx, Haynes c. Pearl.

### ART MATERIALS.
PEPION JOHN & CO. 25 Church.
 *See page 289.*

### ART STORES, Etc.
*See also Pictures and Frames.*
Athen. Gallery Paintings, 624 Main.
ECKHARDT J. H. CO. 687-695
 Main. *See page 413.*
Goodrich W. Wells, 86 Pratt.
Historical Society, 624 Main.
VORCE A. D. CO. 752 Main. *See
 page 413.*
WILEY LYMAN A. & SON, 251
 Pearl. *See page 546.*
Willes Jabez H. 1013 Main.

## ARTESIAN WELLS.
See Wells.

GRANT C. L. 22 Belden. See page 535.
KING H. B. 38 Williams. See page 484.

## ARTIFICIAL TEETH.
See also Dentists.

CHAPMAN L. G. 86 Pratt. See outside front cover.

## ARTIST PENMAN.
Winter Charles O. 650 Main.

## ARTISTIC MEMORIALS.
THE NEW ENGLAND GRANITE WORKS,1260 Main. See page 533.

## ARTISTS.
Art Society of Hartford, 624 Main.
Bundy Harriet M. 904 Main.
Butler Jeannette E. 29 John.
Carney W. C. 904 Main, rm. 106.
Chaese Nora, 753 Main.
Dantrich Fred. L. 57 Park.
Dickenson H. Wallace, 847 Main.
Duffy Catherine E. 747 Main
Dunham Isabella B. 8 Spring.
Durand Fannie B. Miss, 943 Main.
Fenety Andrew C. 904 Main, rm. 105
Finesilver Nathan, 277 Market.
Flagg C. Noel, 904 Main.
Goodrich W. Wells, 86 Pratt.
Hall Charles H. 45 Pratt.
Hastings Mary A. 35 Spring.
Herbert Art Co. 726 Main.
Herrmann Charles L. 111 Trumbull.
Holtz Abraham, 61 Pleasant.
Loomis Charles R. 15 Vernon.
MacGowan James P. 365 Main.
Majestic Portrait Studio, 721 Main.
Pitblado Colin S. 156 Sargeant.
Sanford Walter, 438 Asylum.
Smith J. M. Mrs 370 Asylum.
Snow Ellen, 99 Washington.
Steele T. Sedgwick, 904 Main.
Tiffany Miss M. A 757 Asylum.
Webster Mrs. E. S. 210 Windsor av.
Wentworth D. F. 904 Main, rm. 101.
Wheaton Alice J. Mrs. u. 111 Tru.
White Henry C. 69 Gillett.
Williams C. Louise, 370 Asylum.
Williams Mary R. 1492 Broad.
Wittig Mather Mrs. 14 Goodman.
Wright George F. Mrs. 55 Maple.

## ARTISTS' MATERIALS.
BONNER–PRESTON CO. 843 Main. See page 425.
ECKHARDT J. H. CO. 687 Main. See page 418.
WALKER ROBERT, 14 Church. See page 866.
WILEY LYMAN A. & SON, 251 Pearl. See page 546.

## ASBESTOS, M'F'R.
JOHNS–PRATT CO. See page 540

## ASBESTOS PACKING MFG.
JOHNS–PRATT CO. 555 Capitol. See page 540.

## ASSESSORS.
114 Pearl. See page 668.

## ASYLUMS.
See Hospitals; Orphan Asylums.

## ATHLETIC FOOT WEAR.
WEBB E. M. 546 Asy. See page 796.

## ATTORNEYS AT LAW.
Adams Sherman W. 700 Main.
ALCORN HUGH M. 57 Pratt. See page 485.
ANDREWS JAMES P. 926 Main, reporter Supreme C't, State Cap'l.
Austin Leverett N. 847 Main.
Barbour Joseph L. 50 State.
Barbour Sylvester, 756 Main.
BENNETT & BROTT, 847 Main. See page 483.
BENNETT EDWARD B. 847 Main. See page 483.
BILL ALBERT C. See page 482.
BILL & TUTTLE, 847 Main. See page 482.
BRAINARD AUSTIN. See p. 494.
BRISCOE CHARLES H. 926 Main, Cheney Building. See page 484.
Brooklesby John Henry, 756 Main.
Brooks C. M. 71 Asylum.
BROTT GEO. OLNEY, 847 Main. See page 488.
Broughel Andrew J. Jr. 739 Main.
BRYANT PERCY S. 57 Pratt. See page 485.
BUCK & EGGLESTON, 926 Main. See page 481.
BUCK JOHN H. 926 Main. See page 481.
Burke Harry M. 756 Main.
Bullard Herbert S. 2 Central.
Burdett Charles L. 68 Pratt.
Calhoun David S. 877 Main.
Calhoun J. Gilbert, 877 Main.
Case Uriah, 798 Main.
CASE WILLIAM C. 57 Pratt. See page 485.
CASE WILLIAM S. 57 Pratt. See page 485.
Chambers Frederick, 68 Pratt.
Clarke Charles H. 8 Asylum.
Clarke Sidney E. 884 Main.
Cleaveland F. E. 66 State.
Collins L. J. 847 Main.
Conant George A. 85 Trumbull.
Coogan James T. 2d, 877 Main.
Coogan John W. 877 Main.
Cook Albert S. 90 Gillette.
Cornwall Horace, 68 Pratt.
Day Edward M. 847 Main.
Dickenson Robert C. 847 Main.
Dunham S. C. 56 Prospect.
Dyer John J. 68 Pratt.
Eaton William W. 86 Church.
Eberle Frederick. 811 Main.
Eberle Fred G. 811 Main.
Eddy Willard, 756 Main.
EGGLESTON ARTHUR F. 926 Main. See page 481.
Elmore Samuel D. 98 Farmington.
Ellsworth Ernst B. 877 Main.
Fellowes Charles E. 85 Trumbull.
Fenn J. Lincoln, 85 Trumbull.
Fowler George B. 926 Main.
Freeman Harrison B. Jr. 750 Main.
Garvan Edward J. 877 Main.
Gates Andrew F. 11 Central.
GILMAN GEORGE H. See page 488.
Goslee Henry S. 877 Main.
Grant Ralph M. 847 Main.

GROSS CHAS. E. See page 486.
GROSS, HYDE, & SHIPMAN, 2 Central. See page 486.
Hall Mary, 98 Pratt.
Hamersley William, Judge Supreme Court, 789 Main.
Hamlin John, 721 Main.
Healy Frank E. 750 Main.
Henney William F. 11 Central.
HOLCOMB & PIERCE, 68 Pratt. See page 487.
HOLCOMB M. H. See page 487.
Holden Benedict M. 11 Central.
Hooker John, 16 Marshall.
HUNGERFORD F. L. See p. 488.
HUNGERFORD WM. C. See page 488.
Huntington Henry A. 2 Central.
HYDE E. HENRY, Jr. See p. 488.
HUNGERFORD, HYDE, JOSLYN & GILMAN, 49 Pearl. See p. 488
HYDE WM. W. See page 486.
JOSLYN CHAS. M. See page 488.
Kellogg George A. 789 Main.
Kennedy Henry, 798 Main.
Kennedy Thomas K. 10 Wyllys.
Knight Franklin H. 11 Central.
Leete Wm. H. 926 Main.
Levy Josiah W. 9 Asylum.
Loomis Dwight, referee Superior Court, 789 Main.
Lounsbury Cooke, 75 Pratt.
Lyman Theodore, 847 Main.
MALTBIE T. M. 8 Asylum. See page 489.
Markham Daniel A. 877 Main.
Marvin E. E. clerk U. S. Courts, 65 State.
Marvin L. P. Waldo, 2 Central.
McConville Wm. J. 847 Main.
McLEAN GEO. P. See page 494.
McMANUS THOMAS, 847 Main. See page 490.
Mildeberger Henry D. 798 Main.
MILLS HIRAM R. 847 Main. See page 491.
MORSE LEONARD, 2 Central. See page 492.
Newberry Leslie W. 877 Main.
O'Flaherty Hugh, 798 Main.
PARKER FRANCIS H. 863 Main. See page 493.
Parsons Francis, 877 Main.
Perkins & Perkins, 14 State.
Prentice Samuel O. 85 Trumbull.
PIERCE N. E. See page 487.
Quinn James J. 847 Main.
RICHARDS FRANCIS H. 803 Mn. See outside front cover.
Robbins Edward D. 739 Main.
Robinson Henry S. 785 Main.
Robinson & Robinson, 11 Central.
Rose Herbert A. 847 Main.
Safford Charles A. 750 Main.
Scott Fred A. 750 Main.
SHIPMAN ARTHUR L. See p. 486.
Shipman Nathaniel, Judge U. S. Court, 65 State.
Sill George G. 863 Main.
SIMONDS W. EDGAR, 2 Central. See outside back cover.
Smith Herbert Knox, 847 Main.
SPERRY LEWIS. See page 494.
SPERRY, McLEAN & BRAINARD. 650 Main. See page 494.
STANTON LEWIS E. 16 State. See page 495.
Steele & Steele, 863 Main.
Stoeckel Robbins B. 847 Main.

Stoughton John A. 863 Main.
Sumner George G. 739 Main.
Taintor Henry E. 847 Main.
Tilton George E. 9 Asylum.
Toohey John A. 49 Pearl.
TUTTLE JOSEPH P. *See p.* 482.
Vail Thomas G. 863 Main.
Walker Albert H. 133 Hawthorn.
Waterous Thos. C. 49 Pearl.
Welles Roger, 847 Main.
White John H. 756 Main.
WILLIAMS FRANK B. 847 Main.
*See page* 496.
Yeomans Edward M. 756 Main.

### ATTORNEYS' COPYING.

COOK L. H. Mrs. 80 State. *See page* 710.

### AUCTION and COMMISSION

*See also Real Estate and Loans.*
Hannum F. N. 208 Asylum.
Johnson Horace, 170 Commerce.
LINCOLN FRED. M. 911 Main. *See page* 427.
Kendrick H. H. 370 Asylum.
SHELTON E. 66 State, rm. 6. *See page* 426.
WHITE W. L. 884 Main. *See page* 508.

### AUTHORS.

Clemens Samuel L. 351 Farmington
VanZile Edward S. 19 Columbia.

### Automatic Gear Cutters.

SIGOURNEY TOOL CO. 9 Sigourney. *See page* 537.

### Automatic Time Switch Clock

HUBBARD & MORTSON, 42 Union. *See page* 428.

### AWNINGS.

*See Tents and Awnings.*
ROBERTS S. F. 124 State. *See page* 502.

### AXES, KNIVES, PLOWS.

COLLINS CO. *See page* 521.

### AXLES, SPRINGS, HUBS.

BLODGETT & CLAPP CO. 51 Market. *See page* 541.
ENSWORTH L. L. & SON, 104 Front. *See page* 592.

### BABY CARRIAGES.

*See also Trunks, etc.*
FENN LINUS T. 618 Main. *See page* 501.
FULLER C. C. & CO. 16 Ford. *See page* 500.
NEAL, GOFF & INGLIS CO., 980 Main. *See page* 498.

### BAKERS.

*See also Confectioners.*
BACKES F. W. 167 Asylum. *See page* 45.
BOSTON BAKERY. *See page* 482.
Bridgman George J. 27 Sherman.
Brucker Charles F. 548 Main.
Chaney Etta M. Mrs. 44 Pratt.
Deming Charles A. 1218 Main.
Dobmeier Michael, 70 Morgan.

Eschholz Herman, 238 New Park.
Feil Louis, 115 Windsor.
Flint Benjamin F. 150 Capen.
Forst Charles, 484 Main.
Fritz August, 121 Front.
Goldstein Fannie Mrs. 216 Front.
Goldstein Samuel, 46 North.
Graff Joseph, 255 Park.
Graul August E. 292 Park.
Hillard Maria, 44 Park.
Huntington Bert D. 185 Albany.
Journeymen's International Union Bakery, 78 Morgan.
Kessler John, 305 Lawrence.
Lamb Edwin J. 132 Trumbull.
Lincks John F. 156 Front.
Magazina Joseph A. 46 North.
MUZZEY MARY R. MRS. 14½ Church. *See page* 561.
Nelson Gustaf, 106 Jefferson.
Pearson August, 84 Spring.
Pelton Charles N. 41 Laurel.
Preisaner Bros. 59 Sheldon.
Ricco Tony, 178 Front.
Sanders J. C. Mrs. 94 Hudson.
SCHREPFER MICHAEL, 368 Asylum. *See page* 321.
Schuman Bros. 69 Morgan.
Schuman Edward, 466 Windsor.
Sickles Charles H. 385 Main.
STUECK J. WILLIAM, Jr. 1036 Main. *See page* 348.
Thorstenson John, 12 Queen.
Utzig Henry, 56 Front.
VIENNA BAKERY. *See page* 45.
Vitt Max, 151 Maple.
Warren Sidney, 84 Albany.
Weltner Adam, 68 Windsor.
Werschafskie Joseph, 204 Front.
ZIMMERMAN PHILIP, 55 Judson. *See page* 482.

### PEELMAKER.

Sullivan Cornelius B. 60 Loomis.

### BANDS OF MUSIC.

*See also Music Teachers ; Schools.*
Allen Drum Corps, 253 State.
BEEMAN & HATCH ORCHESTRA 18 Windsor av.
Colts Armory Band, 51 Elm.
Cook's Orchestra, 92 State.
D'Esopo Brothers, 1179 Main.
First Reg't Drum Corps, 51 Elm.
HATCH'S MILITARY BAND, 18 Windsor av.
Leroy Bros., 1363 Main.
Popes Military Band, 104 Asylum.
Severn's Orchestra, 167 Asylum.

### BANK LOOK REPAIRING.

HALLIDAY W. H. 181 Front. *See page* 506.

### BANKERS.

*See also Brokers.*
ABBOTT JOHN C. 49 Pearl. *See page* 430.
COOLEY FRANCIS R. 49 Pearl. *See page* 428.

### BANKS.

ÆTNA NATIONAL, 644 Main. *See page* 431.
AMERICAN NATIONAL, 803 Main. *See page* 431.
CHARTER OAK NATIONAL, 124 Asylum. *See page* 432.
CITY BANK OF HARTFORD, 783 Main. *See page* 432.

CONN. RIVER BANKING CO. 761 Main. *See page* 433.
FARMERS & MECHANICS NATIONAL, 106 State. *See p.* 433.
FIRST NATIONAL, 50 State. *See page* 434.
HARTFORD NATIONAL, 58 State *See page* 434.
Mercantile National, office 53 Tru.
NATIONAL EXCHANGE, 76 State.
*See page* 435.
PHŒNIX NATIONAL, 803 Main. *See page* 435.
STATE, 795 Main. *See page* 436.
UNITED STATES, 872 Main. *See page* 436.
UNITED STATES DEPOSITARY, 124 Asylum. *See page* 422.

#### SAVINGS BANKS.

CONN BUILDING AND LOAN ASSO. 252 Asylum. *See p.* 430.
DIME SAVINGS, 791 Main. *See page* 439.
MECHANICS SAVINGS, 815 Main. *See page* 439.
Society for Savings, 31 Pratt.
STATE SAVINGS, 39 Pearl. *See page* 440.

#### TRUST COMPANIES.

CONN. TRUST & SAFE DEPOSIT CO. 777 Main. *See page* 427.
HARTFORD TRUST CO. 764 Main. *See page* 427.
Loan and Guarantee Co. of Conn. 49 Pearl.
SECURITY COMPANY, 62 Pearl. *See page* 438.
THE FIDELITY COMPANY, 49 Pearl. *See page* 438.

### BANK STAMPS.

BURCH GEORGE W. 91 Asylum. *See page* 457.

### BANNERS.

FORBES EDWARD P. 3 Asylum *See page* 148.
McCLUNIE J. ALEXANDER, 177 Asylum. *See page* 242.

### BARBER SUPPLIES.

COWLISHAW HENRY, 162 Pearl. *See page* 535.

### BARBERS.

Abrouza Alphonso, 20 Kilbourn.
Ambro Michael, 144 Front.
Antz Henry, 27 Pearl.
Arcari Bros., 456 Main.
Baldassario Gabriel G. 18 Kilbourn.
Ball Julius, 1069 Main.
Ball Samuel L. 46 Church.
Bechstedt Charles O. 258 Lawrence.
Berenson Brothers, 296 Asylum.
Brink Otto, 92 Flower.
Brit John M. 34 Temple.
Brunnotte William, 58 Front.
Bureau Alphonse T. 932 Main.
Buthario George, 3 Asylum.
Callandrillo John, 15 Charles.
Carroll Stephen A. 46 Asylum.
Cirigliano Joseph, 1237 Main.
Cohn Frank, 296 Front.
Collins Ira, 985 Main.
Cropulli Raphael, 9 Mar. 120 Front.
Crosby Frederick A. 391 Park.
Davis & Beattie, 36½ Church.

Davis Ernest, 39 Windsor av.
Demuro Giovanni, 83 Windsor.
Diano Leonordo, 253 State.
Eisenberg Henry A. 356 Park.
Fisher Gilbert, 85 Front.
Flentye Fred H. 34 Temple.
Fletcher & Rosenthal, 703 Main.
Giannettino Bros. 3 State.
Gipstein Harry G. 615 Capitol.
Gipstein Samuel, 98 Francis.
Goldstein Max, 281 Main.
Goulet Edmund, 34 Mulberry.
Grapalli Raphael, 120 Front.
Greenberg Meyer, 175 State.
Grosch Edward H. 789 Main.
Guerriero Luca, 75 Morgan.
Harris Jacob, 22 Sheldon.
Herrup Sam, 484 Asylum.
Healy & Ledoux, 46 Asylum.
Henning William L. 77 Trumbull.
Herrup & Raphael, 278 Asylum.
Kane Joseph L. 66 Sheldon.
Katz Joseph R. 9 Morgan.
Katzman Samuel, 178 State.
Kinlser David, 42 Pleasant.
Lacava & Domenier, 16 Morgan.
Lavelli Joseph A. 22 State.
Levautow Samuel, 51 Windsor.
Leduc G. M. 91 Windsor.
Lanctan William A. 275 High.
Laprete Pasquale, 47 Albany.
Loprete Rodolf, 9½ Wells.
Lowry Daniel, 37 Albany.
Manns George W. 933 Main.
March John G. 9 Asylum.
Marenholtz Otto, 415 Main.
Marte Paul H. 362 Asylum.
McAuley George A. 647 Main.
McCarthy John J. 347 Allyn.
McGee John, 3 Asylum.
Mercantande F. P. 884 Trumbull.
Muller Ernest, 523 Main.
Missell J. W. 1151 Main.
Muzio & Bertucci, 222 Asylum.
Notine John, 108 Main.
Notine Joseph, 454 Asylum.
Obert & Puglisi, 124 Asylum.
O'Keefe Daniel, 55 High.
Pillion John H. 76 Pleasant.
Plant Solomon, 5 Central.
Proffitt James H. 86 Benton.
Raphael Isaac, 32 Sheldon.
Riley Wm. J. 281 Park.
Rollo Louis M. 1159 Main.
Rosenburg Benjamin, 187 Front.
Rosenblatt & Shevitz, 327 Capitol.
Saraceno Battista, 1151 Main.
Scharff Louis, 46 Temple.
Seide David, 706 Main.
Seide Morris M. 57 Maple.
Senger Martin, 272 Park.
Shield Bros. 334 Pearl.
Sloan Neil P. 80 State.
Smith Fred'k J. 42 Union pl.
Smith Joseph P. 86 Trumbull.
Stern & Weidl, 6 Charter Oak.
Ullrich Louis, 5 Vandyke.
Uricchio Joseph, 219 Sheldon.
Valiquette Cyrille, 887 Park.
Vallenta Joseph, 46 Temple.
Viggiano Antonio, 877 Capitol.
Viggiano James, 14½ New Britain.
Warren Sidney, 84 Albany.
Williams G. Grant, 209 Pearl.
Wunder Emil L. 94 Pearl.

### BARREL Mfrs.
Butler Thomas, 30 Ferry.

### BASKETS.
Gillette C. O. 25 Warren.

### BATHING HOUSE.
River Front Park.    See contents.

### BATHS.
*See also Barbers.*
Caporale Rocco, 18 State.
ELECTRO AND VAPOR, Merriam,
A. E. Colt Mrs. 926 Main, rm. 51.
    See page 257.
Henning Wm. L. 77 Trumbull
JONES GEORGE E., Turkish, etc.
609 Main.    See page 421.
Sodasky Joseph, 79 Morgan.
Y.M.C.A. 323 Pearl.
    See pages 704, 705.

### BEDDING.
Farber M. 8 Walnut.
FLINT GEO. W. & CO. 61 Asylum.
    See page 147.

### BEEF AND PROVISIONS.
WHOLESALE.
*See also Markets.*
Armour & Co. 508 Asylum.
CHAMBERLIN S. D. & SONS,
179 State.    See page 89.
INGRAHAM, SWIFT & CO. 126
Church.    See page 585.
Hartford Beef Co. 54 Huntley.
HARTFORD PROVISION CO.
Valley st.    See page 586.
HURLBURT E. E. Valley st.    See
page 199.
Wieder M. & Sons, 91 Morgan.

### BEER.
*See Root Beer; Brewers.*

### BELL HANGERS.
*See also Cutlers; Electric.*
Clark William M. 22 Church.
HALLIDAY W. H. 131 Front.    See
page 506.

### BELT HOOK Mfrs.
JEWELL BELT HOOK CO. 15
Trumbull    See page 548.
JEWELL BELTING CO. 15 Trum-
bull.    See page 530.

### BELT MAKERS & LACINGS.
*See also Leather Belting.*
JEWELL BELTING CO. 15 Trum-
bull.    See page 530.

### BELT PUMPS.
LEE H. K. 223 State.    See p. 589.

### BERRYMAN HEATERS.
DAVIS I. B. & SON, 40 Cushman.
See page 546.

### BICYCLE FORGINGS.
BILLINGS & SPENCER CO. 142
Russ.    See page 581.

### BICYCLE Mfrs.
HARTFORD CYCLE CO., 581
Capitol.    See page 796.
POPE MANUFACTURING CO.
436 Capitol.    See page 796.

### BICYCLE SHOEMAKER.
WEBB E. M. 546 Asylum. See page
795.

### BICYCLE SUNDRIES.
Smith & Whitney, 13 Haynes.
Stanley F. G. & Co. 11 Goodman.

### BICYCLE WRENCHES.
BILLINGS & SPENCER CO. 142
Russ.    See page 581.

### BICYCLE DEALERS.
*See also Hardware; Sporting Goods.*
Alexander & Elmer, 744 Main.
ANDRUSS & HERMANN, 300
Asylum.    See page 484.
ANDRUS & NAEDELE CO.
272 Asylum.    See page 485.
BROWN, THOMSON & CO., 942
Main.    See page 499.
Brunner & Co. 198 Pearl.
Pomeroy Albert H. 98 Asylum.
Olmsted G. N. 186 Pearl.
Smith & Whitney, 13 Haynes.

### BICYCLES REPAIRED.
American Cycle Repair Co. 540 Mn.
ANDRUS & HERMANN, 300 Asy-
lum.    See page 484.
ANDRUS & NAEDELE CO. 272
Asylum.    See page 485.
Barnett John F. 322 Pearl.
Beam Alfred C. 431 Main.
Bellew F. F. 532 Asylum.
Kibbe Wm. E. 1100 Main.
Leitz John E. 328 Asylum.
Meloney Wm. H. Jr. 317 State.
Smith Alexander, 10 Mulberry.

### BILL POSTER.
Hartford Bill Posting Co. 159 High.

### BILLIARD TABLE MAKER.
Reiche C. E. r. 599 Main.

### BILLIARD SALOONS.
*See also Saloons.*
Hewins Matt H. 734 Main.
Lord F. J. 32 Asylum.

### BIRDS AND CAGES.
SWENSON CHARLES K. 210 Asylum.    See page 565.

### BISCUIT Mfrs.
*See Bakers.*
National Biscuit Co. 59 Albany.

### BITTERS.
*See also Medicines.*
Hopkins A. S. r. 138 Windsor av.
Quinn Mary, r. 570 Main.

### BLACKSMITH SUPPLIES.
BLODGETT & CLAPP COM-
PANY, 51 Market    See page 541
CAPEWELL HORSE NAIL CO
40 Governor.    See page 524.
ENSWORTH L. L. & SON, 104
Front.    See page 592.

### BLACKSMITH
### POWER SHEARS.
PRATT & WHITNEY CO. 1 Flower
See page 523.

## BLACKSMITHS, HORSESHOERS, Etc.

*See also Carriages and Wagons.*

Alexander Joel S. 54 Commerce.
Aronson Charlie, 207 Front.
Burnham O. H. 866 Allyn.
Calhoun J. J. 843 Park.
DECKER J. A. 201 Smith. *page* 548.
Evarts Frank L. 16 Hicks.
Filian Joseph T. r. 580 Windsor av.
Flynn Michael A. 92 Albany.
Gearin Michael J. 20 Morgan.
Glater Morris, r. 46 North.
Grandohl John A. 10 Charter Oak.
Haley Jeremiah, 84 Elm.
Hart P. H. 14 Huntington.
Horenson C. H. 207 Front.
Hughes Peter, 59 New Britain.
Keefe James, 7 Spruce.
Kinghorn Harry H. 10 Charles.
Kowalshy Godfrey, r. 1068 Main.
Lamb James, 10 Ferry.
Locke Thomas F. 29 Wells.
Mannix James, 22 Wells.
Mansuy & Smith, 17 Elm.
McDermott John T. 18 Front.
McGinn Hugh M. 41 Annawan.
McGurk B. L. 852 Albany.
Moore Martin J. 276 Allyn.
Nelson John N. 697 Windsor av.
North End Carriage Co. r. 84 Capen.
Pearl Samuel, 481 Windsor av.
Price Robt. T. & Son, 90 Francis.
Pullar James & Co. 5 Mechanic.
Ryan Michael J., Donald.
SCHIRM FRANK F. 28-30 Sheldon.
*See page* 551.
Single A. R. & Co. 295 Sheldon.
Sugrue Michael, Albany cor. Bio.
Wadsworth F. E. r. 44½ John.
Webster Charles E. 84 Elm.
Whitefield Washington, 88 Smith.
Zychowski Andrew, 295 Albany.

## BLANK BOOKS.

*See also Bookbinders.*

CASE, LOCKWOOD & BRAIN-ARD CO. 141 Pl.    *See page* 475.
GEER'S ELIHU SONS, 16 State.
*See page* 474.
TALCOTT WM. H. 856 Main.
*See page* 478.

## BLANKET MACHINE Mfr.

MERROW MACHINE CO. 26 Laurel.    *See page* 535.

## BLEACHERS.

*See also Dyers.*

## BLIND ADJUSTERS.

ANDREWS & PECK, 88 Market.
*See page* 509.

## BLINDS, SASH & DOORS.

*See Doors, Sash and Blinds.*

## BOARD OF TRADE.

Hartford Board of Trade, 49 Pearl.

## BOARDING HOUSES.

*See also Restaurants; Hotels; Lodging Rooms.*

Abel Orpha Mrs. 1153 Main.
Adams Elizabeth Mrs. 1080 Main.
Allen Emily J. Mrs. 518 Main.
Allen S. H. 999 Main.

Barrett Elizabeth J. 452 Main.
Burns James Mrs. 61 Ann.
Buzzell F. E. Mrs. 11 Goodman.
Campbell A. C. Mrs. 97 Trumbull.
Carlidge William Mrs. 21 Central.
Carron Salome Mrs. 197 State.
Church Lewis Mrs. 19 Central.
Clark Thomas J. Mrs. 1202 Main.
Coclough Kate, 198 Allen.
Collins Alice Mrs. 1173 Main.
Corrigan Ester J. 265 Main.
Clodgo Jennie Mrs. 234 Allyn.
Colonial The, 981 Main.
COMMERCIAL HOUSE, G. F. Johnson. prop. 165 Asylum. *See page* 100.
Crystal House, 249 Asylum.
Cummings Mrs. C. D. 581 Main.
Cummings Mary, 16 Trumbull.
Cunningham Maria J. Mrs. 1183 Mn.
Davis Ferdinand J. 82 Church.
DULEY J. E. Mrs. 119 High.
*See page* 561.
Elliott Matilda Mrs. 1096 Main.
Ellsworth W. J. Mrs. 19 Spring.
Elmwood House, 145 High.
Empire House, 58 Trumbull.
Estlow Elizabeth Mrs. 542 Main.
Evers M. E. Mrs. 28 Spring.
Fenwick House, 90 Pearl.
Fischer Fannie Mrs. 845 Main.
Florence House, 114 State.
Gates F. E. Mrs. 48 Asylum.
German Republic House, 163 Front.
Glynn Elizabeth, 10 Arch.
Goodale House, 114 State.
Gould Elizabeth E. Mrs. 1140 Main.
Hepburn George H. 225 High.
Hickey Catharine Mrs. 40 So. Pro.
Hills F. R. Mrs. 98 Trumbull.
Hines Mary, 192 Sheldon.
Hoban Edward Mrs. 23 Spring.
HOTEL PROSPECT, 119 High.
*See page* 561.
JOHNSON G. F. 165 Asylum. *See page* 100.
Lawrence The, 231 Lawrence.
Livingston Wm. F. Mrs. 41 Wdbg.
Lucas Amelia Mrs. 401 Capitol.
Martin Mary V. 1086 Main.
McCabe Ellen F. 227 High.
McCarty Mary, 18 Central.
McGrath Rose E. 5 Chapel.
Meafoy Ellen F. Mrs. 1255 Main.
Merrick J. T. Mrs. 27 Spring.
Merriman G. A. Mrs. 25 Spring.
Metropolitan Hotel, 255 Asylum.
Miner John F. 842 Main.
Miner O. H. 149 High.
Mooney John Mrs. u. 1421 Broad.
Moran Mary, 1172 Main.
Moriarty Mary, 1163 Main.
Moyer Oliver J. Mrs. 64 Capitol.
MUZZEY M. R. Mrs. 14½ Church.
*See page* 561.
Nason Cora B. Mrs. 1104 Main.
Neary Annie E. 88 Charter Oak.
Nelson Frank Mrs. 1094 Main.
Nihill Mary Mrs. 69 Governor.
Nihill Nora, 147 Sheldon.
O'Connell Maurice Mrs. 76 Bellevue.
Olsen Ada, 80 Front.
OWEN JOSEPHINE M. Mrs. 57 Church; after Oct. 1, 164 High.
Park View House, 8 Lewis.
Paquette Melvina, 192 State.
Pitkin Mary F. 157 Capitol.
Porter Ella C. Mrs. 8 Village.
Puffer E. J. Mrs. 1210 Main.

Rahba Sophia Mrs. 42 Morgan.
Rood H. T. Mrs. 147 Babcock.
Russell Charles Mrs. 76 Hopkins.
Sargent Mary E. Mrs. 84 Flower.
SIGOURNEY HOUSE, 1150 Main.
*See page* 561.
Smith Alice W. 1209 Main.
Smith Mary J. Mrs. 1228 Main.
Smith Matilda Mrs. 1096 Main.
Southergill Margaret, 1223 Main.
Stoll Lisetta, Mrs. 1213 Main.
Sullivan John, 4 Huntley.
Sunny Side House, 80 Church.
Thomas Abbie S. Mrs. 52 Laurel.
Wallace Jane E. 79 Front.
Webster Wm. H. 98 Babcock.
Windsor The, 986 Main.
Woodford L. J. Mrs. 56 Winthrop.
Woodward Jennie M. Mrs. 809 Asy.
Young Women's Boarding H. 48 Ch.

## BOARDING STABLES.

*See also Livery Stables.*

## BOILER FEED Mfrs.

PRATT & CADY, 556 Capitol.
*See page* 527.

## BOILER INSURANCE.

HARTFORD STEAM BOILER IN-SPECTION & INSURANCE CO. 650 Main. *See pages* 446, 447.

## BOILER MAKERS.

*See Machinists.*

Amerman Peter & Son. 109 Commerce.
BEACH H. B. & SON, 135 Grove.
*See page* 538.
DAVIS J. B. & SON, 40 Cushman.
*See page* 546.
Pitkin Bros. & Co. 152 State.
STRONG IRA J. 267 Asylum. *See page* 534.

## BOLOGNA.

*See Markets; German Delicacies.*

Maurer Theo. r. 490 Windsor av.

## BOLTS, NUTS.

BLODGETT & CLAPP CO. *See page* 541.
CLAPP JOHN B. & SON, 61 Market. *See page* 529.
ENSWORTH L. L. & SON, 104 Front. *See page* 592.

## BOND DEALERS.

COOLEY FRANCIS R. 49 Pearl.
*See page* 428.
DENISON CHARLES, 756 Main.
*See page* 428.

## BONDED WAREHOUSES.

84 Trumbull.

## BOOKBINDERS.

AMERICAN PUB. CO. 424 Asylum. *See page* 478.
CASE, LOCKWOOD & BRAIN-ARD CO. 141 Pl.    *See page* 475.
TALCOTT WM. H. 856 Main. *See page* 478.

## BOOKBINDERS' THREAD.

SMYTH MFG. CO.    *See page* 532.

## BOOKBINDERS' MACHINERY.
SMYTH MFG. CO. 648 Main. *See page 528.*

## BOOKBINDERS' SEWING MACHINE.
SMYTH MFG. CO. 648 Main. *See page 528.*

## BOOKKEEPER.
STEWART GORDON W., P.O. Address, Portland, Conn.

## BOOK PUBLISHERS.
AMERICAN PUBLISHING COMPANY, 424 Asy. *See page 478.*
Arms Publishing Co. 336 Asylum.
Barnard Henry, 118 Main.
BELKNAP & WARFIELD, 77 Asylum. *See page 421.*
Burr Index Co. 336 Asylum.
Burr J. B. & Co. 236 Asylum.
CASE, LOCKWOOD & BRAINARD CO. 141 Pl. *See page 475.*
Case O. D. & Co. 302 Asylum.
CONN. QUARTERLY, 66 State. *See page 477.*
FLETCHER N. P. & CO. *Page 146.*
Gillum F. G. 6 Charter Oak pl.
HARTFORD PRINTING CO. *p. 474.*
MERRIAM G. & C. Co., Springfield, Mass. *See page 497.*
Scranton S. S. & Co. 281 Asylum.
Webster's Dictionary, G. & C. Merriam Co. *See page 497.*
Worthington A. D. & Co. 488 Asy.

## BOOK STORES, NEWS, Etc.
Anderson, Larson & Co. 322 Asy.
Barlow Joseph R. 366 Asylum.
BELKNAP & WARFIELD, 77 Asylum. *See page 421.*
BROWN, THOMSON & CO. 942 Main. *See page 499.*
Chapin Lyman A. 865 Main. (N. Y. Sunday papers.)
Conroy John, 648 Main.
Cook D. P. 92 State.
Dickerson Mrs. J. L. 56 Trumbull.
FISCHER GUSTAVE, 259 Asylum. *See page 142.*
Hotel and R R. News Co. Union Depot, 456 Asylum.
Kelleher P. J. 534 Asylum.
Molin Carl P. 205 Park.
N. Y. & Eastern News Co. Union depot, 456 Asylum.
Pfeiffer George, 81 Mulberry.
Regan Bridget Mrs. 298 Main.
Sill E. M. Mrs. 89 Trumbull.
Sill L. B. 1187 Main.
Smith & McDonough, 801 Main.

### OLD BOOKS RE-BOUND.
CASE, LOCKWOOD & BRAINARD CO. 141 Pl. *See page 475.*
HARTFORD PRINTING CO. 16 State. *See page 474.*

## BOOT and SHOE MAKERS.
Ahern Morris, 176 Windsor av.
Ahern Thomas P. 91 Windsor.
Albro James W. 18 New Britain.
Alexander Louis, 251 Park.
Anderson Alfred, 59 Farmington.
Barchfeld B. 4 Kinsley.
Barrila Rocco. 3 Charles.
Bertelsen Hans, 15 Morgan.
Brodman H. 187 State.
Canterwit Harris, 51 Albany.
Carroll Patrick, 7 Huntley.
Childs John E. M. 69 Asylum.
Cigal Moses, 86 Windsor.
Cohen Morris, 115 Front.
Costello James V. 21 Main.
Cross Frederick O. 1263 Main.
Cross George, 328 Pearl.
Dalesso Tony, 355 Park.
Debler F. Joseph, 755 Main.
Devito Joseph, 42 Pratt.
DOW PETER, JR. 278 Asylum. *See page 551.*
Dowd John, 89 Clark.
Duchesne F. 27 Lewis.
Eakins James, 1086 Broad.
Epstein Louis, 199 Front.
Elf Max, 205 Front.
Engel William, 10 State.
Forastiere Antonio, 57 Woodbridge.
Ford William, 78 Clark.
Fox George H. 8 Spruce.
Friedman Max, 189 Trumbull.
Friedman & Kaplan, 65 Morgan.
Fungaroli Gelsemino, 114 Laurel.
Goldfer Harris, 244 Front.
Goldman Lewis, 145 Front.
Goldstein Simon, 359 Asylum.
Grandahl John A. 10 Charter Oak.
Hanlon Jeremiah, 79 Front.
Hartman Adam, 27 Lafayette.
Healy Thomas, 8 Potter.
Herbst W. Edward, 71 Asylum.
Hoff Isaac, 146 State.
Hogan Michael, 41 Woodbine.
Horowitz Samuel, 40 State.
Johnson Charles S. 59 Farmington.
Kay William W. 78 Windsor.
Kershaw Thomas, 42 Bonner.
Kirch Jacob, 81 Flower.
Krause Philip H. 14 Mulberry.
Leahy Patrick, 26 Howard.
Lechner Nicholas, 55 Laurel.
Levin George, 147 Front.
Levin Max, 11 Park.
Levy Louis, 1192 Main.
Lutz Frederick, 187 Market.
Lyons Frank, 22 Union pl.
Madsen Mathias C. 89 Ann.
Mahon Patrick, 18 Grace.
Maloy Thomas F. 270½ Park.
Manock Edmund, 1109 Main.
Marconvitz Samuel, 59 Maple.
Markowitz Heyman, 287 Main.
Marks Matthew, 1 Martin.
Mathiew Archibald, 784 Park.
Mattia G. 24 Albany.
Michaelson Harris, 52 Sheldon.
Miller Moritz, 19 Church.
Mittau F. 172 Pearl.
Meshorsky Meyer, 1857 Main.
Morgan Patrick J. 25 Albany.
Murray Michael. 30 Park.
Noll Harris, 116 State.
Noll Jacob, 173 State..
Oppelt Michael, 224 New Park.
Palmberg Justice, 169 Main.
Patronsky Isaac, 34 North.
Pearl Harris, 30 Mulberry.
Perham Melvin A. 65 Albany.
Pownall Thomas B. 68 Albany.
Priove Joseph, 994 Main.
Puglise Peter, 40 Church.
Siegle Morris, 32 Portland.
Sirrigalli Frank, 73 Morgan.
Silverman K. 169 State.
Smith Philip J. 582 Asylum.
Smytheman George T. 92 Trumbull.
Sturm I. 154 Front.
Strum Simon, 14 Sheldon.
Viola Frank, 260 New Park.
Walter August, 888 Park.
WEBB ELDORUS M. 546 Asylum. *See page 795.*
Wehner George, 28 Trumbull.
Weins Thomas, 62 Francis.
Weinstein Hyman, 206 Front.
Wilhelmy George F. 22 Church.
Ziff Joel, 86 Albany.
Zimmerman Louis 2d, 112 Albany.
Zimmerman Solomon, 1165½ Main.
Zimmon Michael, 524 Asylum.

### SUPPLIES.
DOW PETER, Jr. 278 Asylum. *See page 551.*

## BOOTS AND SHOES.
*See also Overgaiter Mfr.*

### WHOLESALE AND MFRS.
DOW PETER, Jr. *See page 551.*
Marcy Brothers & Co. 14 Ford.

### RETAIL.
Aishberg Edwin, 913 Main.
Avery Charles, 160 Asylum.
BROWN, THOMSON & CO. 942 Main. *See page 499.*
Cygolf Shoe, 218 Asylum.
Douglass W. L. Co. 192 Asylum.
Eckstein Louis, 199 Front.
Gavin James J. 83 Trumbull.
Goodell George M. 1081 Main.
Goodwin C. B. & Co. 163 Asylum.
Goodwin C. L. & G. R. 755 Main.
Henry Albert W. mgr. 1028 Main.
King Horace H. 1078 Main.
Larned & Hatch, 945 Main.
Lawrence James, 531 Main.
Lawrence William J. 1105 Main.
Mittau Frederick, 172 Pearl.
Noll Bros. 485 Main.
Samuels J & Co. 882 Main.
Schmeltz & Hammer, 1005 Main.
Simmons Wm. G. & Co. 901 Main.
Standard Boot & Shoe Co. 589 Main.
Strong David E. 928 Main.
WEBB E. M. 546 Asylum. *See page 795.*

## BOSTON BROWN BREAD.
ZIMMERMAN PHILIP, 55 Judson. *See page 482.*

## BOTTLERS.
*See also Saloons; Brewers.*
Ayers Charles J. 25 Union.
Bacon Marcus M. r. 13 Morris.
Brady Brothers, 1 Brady pl.
COLUMBIA BREWING CO. 245 Windsor. *See page 417.*
Davenport & Co. 89 Front.
GROSS HERMAN. 198 Front. *See page 171.*
Heublein G. F. & Bro. 74 Trumbull.
Preston James, r. 141 Front.
ROPKINS & CO. 282 Sheldon. *See page 491.*
Rubenbauer Martin, 7 Affleck.
Woltersdorf Albert, 16 Charles.

## BOTTLES—OLD.
Gross Edward, 63 Ferry.

### BOWLING ALLEYS.
Hartford Bowling Co. 645 Main.
Y.M.C.A. 328 Pearl.

### BOX MAKERS.
*See also Paper Boxes.*
Bonsilate Box Co. 24 Mechanic.
CALLAGHAN C. J. 44 Union pl.
          *See page 82.*
HARTFORD BOX CO. r. 223
State.          *See page 532.*
Hill & Robinson, r. 133 Sheldon.
Rockwell J. W. 65 Front.

### BOYS' CLOTHING.
*See also Children's Wear; Merchant Tailors.*
BROWN, THOMSON & CO. 942
Main. *See page 499.*

### BRASS FOUNDERS.
*See also Metals.*
Birkery Mfg. Co. 65 Suffield.
BLAKE T. J. & SON, 141, 143
Commerce. *See page 489.*
Donovan James G. 38 Ferry.
Eastern Brass Works, r. 223 State.
HOWARD JAS. L. & CO. 440 Asy-
lum. *See page 527.*
Phoenix Brass Foundry Co. r. 223
State.
PRATT & CADY CO. 556 Cap-
itol. *See page 527.*

### BRASS WIRE SCRATCH
BRUSH Mfrs.
WHITTEMORE W. L. & SON, 176
Allyn.          *See page 488.*

### BREWERS.
COLUMBIA BREWING CO. 245
Windsor.          *See page 417.*
NEW ENGLAND BREWING CO.
217 Windsor. *See page 504.*
ROPKINS & CO. 242 Sheldon.
*See page 491.*
THE HUBERT FISCHER BREW-
ERY, 315 Park. *See page 492.*

### BRICKS, DRAIN PIPE,
TILE, Etc.
BELDEN SETH & SON, 69 Com-
merce. *See page 508.*
BISSELL HIRAM, 43 Wadsworth.
*See page 516.*
Capitol Brick Co. 268 Prospect av.
CURTIS D. J. & SON, 787 Wind-
sor av.          *See page 517.*
Dennis Thomas, Prospect av.
DONAHUE DANIEL, Jr. r. 685
Windsor av.          *See page 520.*
Dorr Cephas, New Park.
Dusette & Wrisley, Frankfort.
Kane Michael, 170 New Park.
Mills & Son, Tower av.

### BROKERS.
*See Bankers, Real Estate and Loans.*
ABBOT JOHN C. 49 Pearl. *See
page 480.*
Barnes R. T. H. 650 Main.
Benedict Samuel N. 75 Pratt.
Broker's Board, 808 Main.
Bunce B. F. 7 Central.
Catlin Abijah, 210 Pearl (cotton).

---

DENISON CHARLES, 756 Main.
*See page 426.*
Hobby James & Co. 75 Pratt.
Holmes & Co. 10 Central.
Hough N. P. 10 Central.
Johnston E. P. 721 Main.
MARQUARDT H. C. 904 Main. *See
page 243.*
Matson William L. 55 Trumbull.
Maxfield Bros. 722 Main.
Pike L. E Co. 904 Main.
Skinner Henry H. 803 Main.
Smith Charles H. 49 Pearl.
Spencer Donald R. 373 Asylum.
Stoughton George H. 7 Central.
Woodward Joseph G. 39 Pearl.

### BROOM & BRUSH MAKERS
Conn. Institute and Indust. School
for the Blind, 336 Wethersfield.
WHITTEMORE WM. L. & SON,
176 Allyn.          *See page 488.*

### BUILDERS
AND CONTRACTORS.
*See also Carpenters; Masons.*
ANGUS & CHESEBRO, 27 Warner.
*See page 519.*
BARNES PHILIP, 416 Franklin av.
*See page 481.*
BONFOEY BRO. 109 Windsor av.
*See page 518.*
BISSELL HIRAM, 43 Wadsworth.
*See page 516.*
BRAY WILLIAM J. 85 Imlay.
*See page 512.*
BROWNE EDMUND, r. 1419 Main.
*See page 518.*
CONN. BUILDING & LOAN AS-
SOCIATION, 252 Asylum. *See
page 480.*
COOK CHARLES C. 141 Trum-
bull. *See page 419.*
DART EDMUND, 14 Hicks. *See
page 552.*
DWYER JOHN W. 386 Park. *See
page 132.*
EDE E. F. 8 Morris. *See page 429.*
Gerety & Sullivan, 703 Main.
GROZIER & MOORE, Vredendale,
c. Taylor. *See page 510.*
HATHEWAY EARL, 29 Imlay.
*See page 495.*
HILLS & FOX, 22 John. *See
page 515.*
HOLLIS D.W. & SON, 212 Asylum.
*See page 514.*
McGRATH T. F. & CO. 820 Park.
*See page 520.*
Morris William S. 624 Broad.
New England Construction Co. 720
Main.
O'NEIL EDWARD, 68 Hudson.
*See page 520.*
O'Neil William T. 172 Farmington.
Parker G. S. r. 190 Asylum.
PHILBRICK H. B. 111 Edwards.
*See page 519.*
PORTEUS ROBERT, r. 18 Forest.
*See page 495.*
Potter Maurice H. 38 Lewis.
PURVES & MALCOLM, r. 334.
Asylum. *See page 422.*
Relyea W. H. 260 Wethersfield.
Roemer George A. r. 190 Asylum.
ROWLEY FRANK H. r. 190 Asy-
lum. *See page 441.*

---

ROWLEY & WILCOX, 29 Ann
*See page 562.*
SCOVILLE A. W. 700 Main. *See
page 512.*
SCOVILLE WILLIAM H. Office
720 Main. *See page 515.*
SIMMS W. J. 54 Pratt. *See p. 517.*
STODDARD & CAULKINS, junc.
Charter Oak and Vredendale av.
*See page 518.*
SVENSON CHAS. 64 Woodbine.
*See page 482.*
TAYLOR GEORGE M. 1274 Main.
*See page 353.*
THE NEW ENGLAND GRANITE
WORKS, 1260 Mn. *See page 533.*
THOMSON BROS. 19 Rowe. *See
page 513.*
TRYON EDWARD S. 23 Temple.
*See page 360.*
WEST A. B. & CO. 101½ Hudson.
*See page 514.*
WHITTLESEY D. L. & CO. 212
Asylum. *See page 513.*
WINDSOR RED STONE CO. 1543
Broad. *See page 508.*

### BUILDERS, IRON WORKS.
LINCOLN & CO. *See page 522.*

### MOULDINGS.
THE HARTFORD MOULDING
WORKS, 26 Potter. *See page 517.*

### BUILDERS' MATERIALS.
Gillespie & Co. 219 State.

### BUILDING AND LOANS.
CONN. BUILDING & LOAN AS-
SOCIATION, 252 Asylum. *See
page 430.*
Co-operative Savings Society of
Conn. 782 Main.
HARTFORD BUILDING & LOAN
ASSOCIATION, 370 Asylum.
*See page 424.*

### BUILDING DESIGNING.
NEW ENGLAND GRANITE
WORKS, 1260 Main. *See page 533.*

### BUILDING MOVERS.
Brazel Matthew, 220 Ashley.
Malone James T. 12 Center.

### BUNTING.
ROBERTS S. F. 124 State. *See
page 502.*

### BURGLAR ALARMS.
AHERN JAMES, 280 Asylum.
*See page 505.*
HALLIDAY W. H. 131 Front. *See
page 506.*
RICE & BALDWIN, 214 Pearl.
*See page 554.*

### BUILDINGS.
*See Public Buildings.*

### BURIAL CASKETS.
*See Undertakers.*

### BUSHELERS.
*See Tailors.*

## BURNING BRANDS.
ÆTNA STAMP WORKS, 25 Asylum. *See page 429.*
BURCH GEORGE W. 91 Asylum. *See page 497.*
PARKER T.M. 71 Asy. *See page 534.*

## BUSINESS COLLEGES.
*See Schools; Type Writers.*
HARTFORD BUSINESS COLLEGE, 370 Asylum. *See page 711.*
HONEY FREDERICK R. 904 Main. *See page 422.*
HUNTSINGER E. M. 30 Asylum. *See outside back cover.*

## BUTCHERS.
*See Beef; Markets.*

## BUTTER.
BLANCHARD G. G. 40 Vine. *See page 61.*
DAY C.W. 53 High. *See page 586.*

## BUTTER and CHEESE.
*See Commission Merchants, Produce.*
Hartzler George C. 75 Park.
Kingsley & Smith, 571 Main.
Leroy Bros. 1359 Main.
NEWTON, ROBERTSON & CO. 342 Asylum. *See page 586.*
POTTER & PAYNE, 405 Allyn. *See page 586.*
Russell Chas. H. 711 and 909 Main.
Tracy H. C. 940 Park.
Whittlesey E. G. & Co. 140 State.

## CABINET MAKERS.
*See also Furniture; Patterns.*
BELLER BERNHARD, 43 Linden. *See page 511.*
BRAND ROBERT, 5½ Morris. *See page 507.*
Dresser Charles H. 225 Sheldon.
ENTRESS ALBERT, r. 597 Main. *See page 511.*
Mannix & Ritchie, 133 Sheldon.
Schwarzer Albert, 32 Wells.
TOPPING JAMES R. 734 Main. *See page 541.*
Willerup E. 9 Winship.

## CAFE.
*See Restaurant; Saloon.*

## CALCIUM LIGHTS.
Lincoln Fred M. 911 Main.
U. S. PHOTO CHEM. MFG. CO. 29 Pearl. *See page 419.*

## CALIPER Mfrs.
BILLINGS & SPENCER CO. 142 Russ. *See page 531.*

## CAMPAIGN BANNERS.
FORBES EDWARD P. 3 Asylum. *See page 148.*

## CANDY MAKER.
*See Confectionery.*
WILLIAMS E. H. 366 Asylum. *See page 379.*
SCHROEDER F. *See page 322.*

## CANDLE Mfr.
FRISBIE L. T. CO. 79 Talcott. *See page 585.*

## CANNED GOODS.
FITZGERALD RANSOM H. 44–46 Market. *See page 144.*
KIBBE E. S. CO. 149 State. *See page 587.*

## CANOPY FOR WEDDINGS.
ROBERTS S. F. 124 State. *See page 502.*

## CANVAS CEILINGS.
BAXTER WM. H. 231 Asylum. *See page 52.*
LANGE & FLAD, 13 Central. *See page 512.*

## CAR GOODS.
HOWARD JAMES L. & CO. 488 Asylum. *See page 527.*

## CAR SEATS.
HARTFORD WOVEN WIRE MATTRESS CO. 618 Capitol. *See page 522.*

## CARMEN.
*See also Expresses; Livery Stables.*
BALF EDWARD CO. 2 Chapel. *See page 426.*
Bolf Wm. M. 51 Martin.
BILL BROS. 46 Ann. *See page 550.*
Chamberlin N. H. 27 Hudson.
Deming Roswell M. 478 Wethersfield.
DOWNING & PERKINS, 128 Commerce. *See page 552.*
Edwards Alonzo, 75 Hudson.
Farrell James, 67 Main.
George Henry, 4 Central.
HEBARD & CO. 213 State. *See page 552.*
LeGeyt James, George cor. Preston.
Nugent Michael, 31 Mather.
Palmer H. W. & Co. 250 State.
Sherman & Pigott, 284 State.
SPENCER GEORGE F. & CO. 71 Asylum. *See page 550.*
Sullivan Dennis, 354 Broad.
Tuttle & Mather, 2 American.

## CARPENTERS, BUILDERS.
*See also Stair Builders.*
ANGUS & CHESEBRO, 27 Warner. *See page 519.*
ARNOLD W. T. 82 Pearl. *See page 514.*
Bailey Wm. E. 78 Chestnut.
Barlow James W. r. 22 Grand.
Barnes L. Algernon, 30 Oxford.
Barnes Loren W. 50 Oxford.
Barnes Philip S. 416 Franklin.
Barrett Bros. 10 Trumbull.
Benner A. J. 99 Babcock.
Bentley W. F. 219 Ashley.
Bernard Oscar, Gilman, c. George.
Best James J. 24 New Britain.
Bliss Watson H. & Sons, 158 Woodland. Office 17 Lewis.
Bone William, 48 Bond.
BONFOEY BROS. 109 Windsor av. *See page 518.*
Brady Edward, 72 Ward.
Bragg George S. 22 Canton.
BRAY W.J. 35 Imlay. *See page 512.*
Brooks Philip A. 496 Broad.
BROWNE EDMUND, r. 1419 Main. *See page 518.*

Burdette E. J. 50 Heath.
Burr Jason F. 13 Goodman.
Cairns James R. 41 Seyms.
Cairns Robert, 80 Clark.
Calder Geo. 288 Sigourney.
Camp Samuel J. 110 Capitol.
Caya Bernard, Prospect av. c. Caya.
Clark George B. 199 Barbour.
Columbus Joseph L. 27 Judson.
COOK CHARLES C. 141 Trumbull. *See page 419.*
Crane Patrick W. 52 John.
Dart Edmund, 14 Hicks.
Day P. R. & Sons, 1196 Main.
DENISON GEORGE E. 190 Pearl. *See page 518.*
D'Esopo Brothers, 1179 Main.
Donovan Anthony, r. 116 Market.
Downs Albert C. 257 Capen.
DWYER J. W. r. 386 Park. *See page 182.*
Eagan Frank, 47 Linden.
Ede Edgar F. 24 Preston.
Ford J. M. r. 1231 Main.
Fox George J. 64 New Britain.
Furrey L. M. 1185 Main.
Garvie John B. 754 Main.
Gerety George, 247 Wethersfield.
Gilbert John W. 15 Capitol.
Goldenberg Israel, 24 Kennedy.
Gradisky L. W. H. 30½ Ann.
GROZIER & MOORE, Vredendale, cor. Taylor. *See page 510.*
Gustafson Elen W. 49 Webster.
Hamilton Thomas, Warrington av.
Hardendorf Horatio, 102 Hudson.
HATHEWAY EARLE, 29 Imlay. *See page 495.*
HOLLIS D. W. & SON, 212 Asylum. *See page 514.*
Hollister George, 234 Wethersfield.
Hopkins Leroy, 26 Mahl.
Jameson William J. 908 Park.
Jordan James, 20 Canton.
Joubert Moses, 750 Main.
Keep William E. 97 Webster.
Kent Brothers, 3 Barnard.
Kinberg & Gilmour, 23 Squire.
Lapaugh J. D. r. 46 John.
Larendeau Mederick, 255 Asylum.
Leische Frank, 217 Franklin.
Loomis Charles, r. 128 Jefferson.
Low William B. 37 Hamilton.
Mahl Hermann, 12 Pavilion.
McCoy William, 55 Lincoln.
McKenna John, 11 Bellevue.
McKone Bros. 145 Sheldon.
McKone Patrick, r. 131 Oak.
McKone Robert A. 131 Oak.
Moon Frank D. 78 Bond.
Morris Alfred J. 52 Washington.
Mulcahy John J. 11 Kennedy.
Newton Roswell W. 29 Pearl.
Newton Theo. & Sons, 77 Pearl.
Nolan J. F. r. 988 Main.
Norton Malcolm A. 32 Highland.
O'Brien William, 136 Retreat.
O'Connor Michael, Lubeck.
O'Neil Edward, 68 Hudson.
Parlee Murray, 57 Elliott.
Pellett A. D. 190 Smith.
Perry Peter A. 159 Russ.
PHILBRICK HALSEY B. 111 Edwards. *See page 519.*
PORTEUS ROBERT, r. 13 Forest. *See page 495.*
Priessner Emanuel, 206 Franklin.
Provost Napoleon L. 142 Brown.

PURVES & MALCOLM, r. 334
Asylum.  *See page 422.*
Rice Henry W. 1 Rice.
Rioux H. L., Prospect av. n. Park.
Rosen Brothers, 296 Market.
Root Fred H. 166 Clark.
ROWLEY & WILCOX, 39 Ann.
*See page 562.*
SCOVILLE ALBERT W. office 700
Main.  *See page 513.*
SCOVILLE WM. H. office, 720 Main.
*See page 515.*
Sinnott Brothers, 26 Harbison.
Sinnot Patrick C. r. 597 Main.
Slattery Austin P. 25 Harbison.
Smith Franklin, 8 Ashley.
Snow & Maloney, 27 Spring.
Squires W. L. 149 Clark.
STODDARD & CAULKINS, cor.
Charter Oak & Vredendale.  *See
page 518.*
SVENSON CHARLES, 54 Wood-
bine.  *See page 482.*
TABOR MALLERY, r. 281 Allyn.
*See page 513.*
TAYLOR GEORGE M. 1274 Main.
*See page 353.*
Taylor John E. 347 Wethersfield.
Taylor Peter, Bartholomew.
TEYON EDWARD S. 26 Temple.
*See page 360.*
Tyler Samuel, r. 55 Park.
WEST A. B. & Co. 101½ Hudson.
*See page 514.*
Woolley William S. 68 Huntington.

## Carpets Relaid, Sewed.
Fisher Charles F. 22 Preston.
MAERCKLEIN H. 104 Asylum.  *See
page 562.*

### CARPET CLEANERS.
PATTEN HENRY E. 87 Wells.  *See
page 591.*
Standard Rug and Carpet Renovating Co. r. 13–15 Wells.

### CARPET STORES and WALL
PAPER.
*See also Wall Paper.*
BRAINERD HARVEY B.    84
Pratt.  *See page 503.*
BROWN, THOMSON & CO. 942
Main.  *See page 499.*
FLINT GEORGE W. & CO. 61
Asylum.  *See page 147.*
HART CHARLES R. CO. 896 Main.
*See page 179.*
NEAL, GOFF & INGLIS CO. 980,
Main.  *See page 498.*
Post William H. Carpet Co. 219
Asylum.

### CARPET SWEEPERS.
HART CHARLES R. CO.    896
Main.  *See page 179.*

### CARRIAGE HARDWARE.
ENSWORTH L. L. & SON, 104
Front.  *See page 592.*

### CARRIAGE MAKERS
SUPPLIES.
BLODGETT & CLAPP CO. 51
Market.  *See page 541.*
ENSWORTH L. L. & SON, 104
Front.  *See page 592.*

### CARRIAGE PAINTERS.
*See also Carriages.*
Adams & Atkins, 10 Charles.
Johnson J. Edmund, 580 Windsor av.
NORTH END CARRIAGE CO.
r. 34 Capen.  *See page 277.*

### CARRIAGE REPAIRS.
Calback Robert, 5 Mechanic.
Gridley John L. r. 35 Front.
Keeney Charles R., 123 Church.
McGurk B. L. 352 Albany.
NORTH END CARRIAGE CO.
r. 34 Capen.  *See page 277.*
SCHIRM FRANK F. 28 and 30
Sheldon.  *See page 551.*

### CARRIAGE TRIMMINGS.
ENSWORTH L. L. & SON, 104
Front.  *See page 592.*

### CARRIAGES and WAGONS.
*See also Blacksmiths; Wheelwright.*
BROCKWAY & TUTTLE, 19–21
Mather.  *See page 550.*
Bushnell Russell H. r. 792 Windsor
av.
Capitol City Carriage Co. 291 Allyn.
Gregg Geo. W. & Co. 2 Union pl.
Hart Henry H. 41 Albany.
HARTFORD CARRIAGE CO. 300
Allyn.  *See page 549.*
Katzman David, 36 Ferry.
Mansuy & Smith, 17 Elm.
McGurk Bernard L. 352 Albany.
Moody William A. 87 New Britain.
Moseley G. W. & Son, 393 Allyn.
Murray Bros. 25 Wells.
Phoenix Carriage Works, 597 Main.
Pullar James & Co. 5 Mechanic.
Saunders James H. r. 16 New Britain.
SCHIRM FRANK F. 28 and 30
Sheldon.  *See page 551.*
Tuttle N. J. 19 Mather.
Warren F. M. 393 Allyn.
Webster Alvier D. 308 Allyn.
Webster & Lotze, r. 597 Main.
Whitford William H. 31 Amity.

### CARRIAGES MANUFAC-
TURED.
McGurk B. L. 352 Albany.

### CASH REGISTERS.
National Cash Register Co. 118
Asylum.

### CATERERS.
*See also Bakers.*
BESSE P. & J. 701 Main.  *See p. 57.*

### CATTLE DEALERS.
*See also Markets.*
Capen James R. 57 Barbour.

### CEILING CUT-OUTS.
PERKINS ELECTRIC SWITCH
MFG. CO. 83 Woodbine.  *See
page 536.*

### CEMETERIES.
*See page 735.*
*See also Marble Works.*

### CEMETERY WORK.
*See also Marble Works.*
BELDEN SETH & SON, 69 Com-
merce.  *See page 508.*

### CHAIR Mfrs.
BISHOP E. C. & CO. 34 Capen.
*See page 60.*

### CHAIR SETTINGS.
Hartford Chair Co. 42 Seyms.
MARTIN J. HENRY, 42 Seyms.
*See page 244.*

### RESEATING.
MARTIN J. HENRY, 42 Seyms.
*See page 244.*

### Chandeliers Replated.
HOWARD JAMES L. & CO. 440
Asylum.  *See page 527.*

### CHARITIES.
*See also Hospitals; Orphan Asylums.*
Charity Commissioners' office, 222
Pearl.
Charity Organization Society, 57
Trumbull.
City Missionary Society, 224 Pearl.
City Store, 184 Pearl.
Conn. Children's Aid Society, 222
Asylum.
Hartford Dispensary, 2 Talcott.
HARTFORD HOSPITAL. 20 South
Hudson.  *See pages 700, 701.*
OLD PEOPLE'S HOME. 36 Jeffer-
son.  *See pages 702, 703.*
Open Hearth, 185 Front.
RETREAT FOR INSANE, 30
Washington.  *See pages 696, 699.*
St. Francis Hospital, 110 Woodland.
St. Mary's Home for the Aged, Alb.
Sheldon St. Mission and Coffee
House, 100 Sheldon.
Shelter for Women, 76 Temple.
Stillman Wm. H. supt. 222 Pearl.
Union for Home Work, 239 Market.
United Worker's Club, 700 Main.
Widows Home, 133 Market, 214 and
216 Windsor av. 18 So. Hudson.
Woman's Exchange, 73 Pearl.
Womens Aid Society, 1 Pavilion.
Y. M. C. A. 323 Pearl.  *See pages
704, 705.*

### CHECK PUNCHES.
BURCH GEORGE W. 91 Asylum.
*See page 497.*

### CHEMICALS.
BEACH & CO. 209 State.  *See
page 591.*
SISSON T. & CO. 729 Main.  *See
page 560.*
U. S. PHOTO CHEM. MFG. CO.
29 Pearl.  *See page 419.*

### CHICAGO DRESSED BEEF.
*See Beef Wholesale.*

### CHILDREN'S WEAR.
*See also Boys' Clothing.*
Hodge A. B. & Co. 64 Pratt.
Rennacker & Co. 141 Asylum.

### CHINA.
CASE C. H. & CO. 851 Main.  *See
outside front cover.*

### CHINESE GOODS.
YUEN, SING & CO. 118 State.
*See page 387.*

## CHIROPODISTS.
*See Physicians.*
BENEDICT CARRIE M. H. 721 Main. *See page 55.*

## CHUCK Mfr.
PRATT & WHITNEY CO. 1 Flower. *See page 528.*

## CHURCH ARCHITECT.
O'Donohue Michael, 98 Hawthorn.

## CHURCHES.
*See list of Clergymen, page 603.*
*For full information regarding Pastors, Officers, etc., see pages 683-697.*

### ADVENT.
Life & Advent Meetings, 370 Asylum.
Second Advent, Foot Guard pl. *See page 697.*
Seventh Day Adventist Society, 724 Main. *See page 697.*

### BAPTIST.
Asylum Avenue, 866 Asylum. *See page 688.*
First, 1014 Main. *See page 687.*
Memorial, Washington c. Jefferson. *See page 688.*
Olivet Baptist Church, Parkville. *See page 696.*
Shiloh Baptist, 127 Mather. *See page 697.*
South, 455 Main. *See page 687.*
Suffield Street Chapel, 10 Suffield. *See page 687.*
Swedish. *See page 696.*
Union, 85 Wooster. *See page 688.*

### CATHOLIC APOSTOLIC.
1520 Broad. *See page 690.*

### CHAPELS.
Allyn Memorial Chapel, Spring Grove Cemetery. *See page 692.*
Bethel Mission Church, 1216 Main. *See page 690.*
Elizabeth, 26 Washington. *See page 690.*
New Britain Av. Sunday School, No. 1 New Britain. *See page 696.*
Northam Memorial, Cedar Hill Cemetery. *See page 892.*
Warburton Chapel, 61 Temple. *See page 692.*

### CONGREGATIONAL.
Asylum Hill, 814 Asylum. *See page 685.*
Center, 675 Main. *See page 683.*
Fourth, 1091 Main. *See page 684.*
Glenwood, 87 Laurel. *See page 684.*
Morgan St. Mission Sch. 52 Morgan.
Park, 390 Asylum. *See page 685.*
Pearl St. 40 Pearl. *See page 684.*
South, 307 Main. *See page 685.*
Talcott St. 30 Tal. *See page 686.*
Wethersfield Avenue, 250 Wethersfield. *See page 684.*
Windsor Avenue, 302 Windsor av. *See page 686.*
Zion (Swedish) 87 Russ, c. Hungerford. *See page 696.*

### DANISH LUTHERAN.
Our Saviour's Danish Evangelical Lutheran Church, Russ, c. Babcock. *See page 697.*

Swedish Evangelical Lutheran Emanuel, Russ, corner Babcock. *See page 692.*

### EPISCOPAL.
Christ, 955 Main. *See page 689.*
Good Shepherd, Colt's Meadows, Wyllys. *See page 690.*
Grace, Parkville. *See page 695.*
St. James, 145 Park c. Washington. *See page 689.*
St. John's, 580 Main. *See page 689.*
St. Thomas, 245 Windsor av. *See page 690.*
Trinity, 128 Sig. *See page 690.*
Trinity Col. Chapel. *See page 697.*

### GERMAN LUTHERAN OF THE REFORMATION.
125 Market street. *See page 688.*

### HEBREW.
Association Adas Israel, 11 Pratt. *See page 694.*
Association Brothers Children of Israel, r. 194 Front. *See page 696.*
Congregation Beth Israel, 21-23 Charter Oak. *See page 686.*

### METHODIST EPISCOPAL.
African Zion, 269 Pearl. *Page 691.*
First, 205 Asylum. *See page 691.*
First Swedish, 302 Asylum. *See page 696.*
First German, 99 Jefferson. *See page 692.*
Harbison Av. Chapel. *See page 695.*
North, 313 Windsor av. *See page 691.*
South Park, 75 Mn. *See page 695.*

### NEW JERUSALEM.
Conn. Association of New Jerusalem Church. *See page 692.*

### PRESBYTERIAN.
First, 186 Capitol. *See page 695.*

### ROMAN CATHOLIC.
Church of Sacred Heart, 33 Windsor. *See page 696.*
Immaculate Conception, 260 Park.
Italian, 125 Market. *See page 84.*
Our Lady of Sorrows, Parkville. *See page 694.*
St. Ann's, 362 Park. *See page 690.*
St. Joseph's Cathedral, 150 Farmington. *See page 694.*
St. Lawrence, Wilson cor. Laurel. *See page 698.*
St. Patrick's, 88 Ch. *See page 693.*
St. Peter's, 170 Mn. *See page 693.*
St. Stephanus, Winthrop, cor. Ely. *See page 694.*

### SWEDISH.
*See Baptist ; Congregational.*

### UNITARIAN.
First, 62 Pratt. *See page 692.*

### UNIVERSALIST.
Church Redeemer, 686 Main. *See page 695.*

## CHURCH WORK.
STRICKLAND & SHEA, 20 Potter. *See page 516.*

## CIGAR BOX Mfrs.
*See Box Makers.*
CRYGIER F. H. 248 Asylum. *See page 111.*
Hill & Robinson, 138 Sheldon.

## CIGAR MANUFACTURERS.
CRYGIER F. H. 248 Asylum. *See page 111.*
Hartford Cigar Co. 54 Pratt.
Krug, Powers & Co. 741 Main.
Leschke & Pletcher, 1087 Main.
Lynch John F. r. 192 Asylum.
Lyon Cigar Co. 48 Wells.
Oehlhof C. 30 Park.
SALOMON & DeLEEUW, 7 Asy.
Schott James S. 6 State.
Soby Charles, 867 Main.

## CIGARS.
*See Tobacco and Cigars.*

## CITY DIRECTORY.
THE HARTFORD PRINTING CO.
*See page 474.*

## CITY EXPRESS.
*See Expresses.*

## CITY WEIGHERS.
*See page 676.*

## CIVIL ENGINEERS.
Allen Julian S. 859 Prospect av.
Ayers Henry W. 66 State.
Boland Fred'k A. 64 Vernon.
Bunce Charles H. 800 Main.
BURT LUTHER W. 89 Pearl. *See page 421.*
Drake Timothy, 1415 Main.
Graves & Robinson, 650 Main.
HOFFMAN JOHN R. 721 Main. *See page 441.*
Loomis Frank W. 114 Pearl.
Loomis Hiram G. 114 Pearl.
McKenzie Theodore H. 75 Pratt.
MERRILL GEORGE N. & CO. 75 Pratt. *See page 428.*
PHELPS J. WESSON, 13 Belden, *See page 508.*
Starkweather Nathan, 948 Asylum.
Vorce C. B. 904 Main.
WOLCOTT & DARBY, 49 Pearl. *See page 493.*

## CLERGYMEN.
*See Churches, pages 683 to 697.*
Allen Samuel H. 859 Prospect av.
Andrews Samuel J. 956 Asylum.
Atwood Eugene F. 590 Garden.
Beardslee Clark S. 1507 Broad.
Beckwith Isbon T. 14 Seabury hall, Summit.
Bell George H. S. 183 Capen.
Bingham J. Foote, 484 Farmington.
Bjorkman L. W. A. 87 Russ.
Blake Edwin A. 98 Edwards.
Bradin James W. 6 Park ter.
Breckenridge W. W. 61 Oak.
Brewster Chauncey B. 98 Woodland.
Bristol Cornelius G. 92 Wethersfield
Broderick Bonaventure, 352 Collins.
Broderick Edward J. 158 Main.
Broderick Thomas W. 158 Main.
Broman Frank E. 1152 Broad.
Bruckner Karl P. 64 Babcock.
Carr William M. 25 Sisson.
Clark George H. 125 Washington.

Connell James B. 39 Sisson.
Cooper J. Sulla, 17 South Ann.
Culver A. J. 433 Windsor av.
Curtis Lucius Q. 52 Imlay.
Dahme Hubert, 1861 Main.
Davenport John S. 1057 Asylum.
Dixon Frank, 28 Capitol.
Donovan James P. 140 Farmington.
Downey John J. 82 Church.
Duggan Thomas S. 140 Farmington.
Dustin George, 171 Putnam.
Ek Nils, West Hartford.
Elkin Meyer, 14 Florence.
Faucon James P. 427 Main, rm. 40.
Ferguson Henry, 123 Vernon.
Fitzgerald Robert F. 352 Collins.
Forbes Samuel B. 206 Wethersfield.
Fox John, 35 So. Prospect.
Frazen S. C. 187 Russ.
Gilbert William H. 714 Asylum.
Gillette Arthur L. 1 Wethersfield.
Gillette Henry J. 17 Suffield.
Gleason Dennis, 82 Church.
Goodwin Francis, 108 Woodland.
Griffin Duane N. 411 Wethersfield.
Guy Albert, 90 Edwards.
Hammond E. Payson, 25 Atwood.
Hart Samuel,22 Jarvis hall,Summit.
Hartranft Chester D. 82 Gillett.
Hausser G. F. 99 Jefferson.
Hicks Lewis W. 1 Farmington.
Hine Sylvester,25 Huntington.
Hoskins Francis D. b. 34 Ch.O. pl.
Huntington John T. 17 Clinton.
Jacobus Melancthon W.14 Marshall.
Jaeger J. H. W. 28 Julius.
Kelsey Henry H. 108 Ann.
Kena Thomas J. 18 South Laurel.
Kennedy Wm. P. 82 Church.
Kimball John C. 926 Main, rm. 23.
Kramm Joseph, 58 Morgan.
Laden Thomas J. 158 Main.
Lally Francis J. 158 Main.
Lamson Chas. M. 142 Washington.
Learned Newton M. 176 Sigourney.
Lemke Paul, 62 Babcock.
Loftus J. J. 82 Church.
Love William D. L. Jr. 354 Laurel.
Luther Flavel S. 1 Columbia.
MacDonald Duncan B. 315 Asylum.
MacNaught George K. 7 Sisson.
Mayo March C. 13 Vernon.
McClean P. H. 140 Farmington.
McCook John J. 396 Main.
McGuinness J. L. 140 Farmington.
McGurk William J.140 Farmington.
Mead Charles M. 152 Asylum.
Merriam Alex R. 314 Collins.
Miel Ernest DeF. 120 Sigourney.
Miles Harry R. 294 Windsor av.
Mitchell Edwin Knox, 57 Gillette.
Moore Wm. H. 15 Columbia.
Mulcahy John A. 82 Church.
Mulville Frank, 352 Collins.
Norris Kingsley F. 16 Belden.
Parker E. P. 47 Buckingham.
Paton Lewis B. 50 Forest.
Pattison Harold, 31 Winthrop.
Pearl Samuel T. 41 Sumner.
Pearl William M. 41 Sumner.
Perkins Fred. W. 34 Collins.
Perry Alfred T. 731 Asylum.
Piddock Charles A. 185 Sigourney.
Pynchon Thomas R. 15 Seabury,
  Summit.
Ranny Wm. W. 811 Asylum.
Richard William A. 187 Jefferson.
Robbins Silas W. 5 Preston.
Rogers J. A. R. Windsor t.

Roy Paul E. 364 Park.
Ryan John F. 82 Church.
Saltonstall Lindall W. 16 Winthrop.
Sanborne George E. 51 Russ.
Shanley Walter J. 140 Farmington.
Smith Geo. Williamson, 115 Vernon.
Stearns C. C. 126 Garden.
Stiles Samuel M. 141 Washington.
Stone George M. 22 Townley.
Suchawolsky Louis, 265 Market.
Synnott John, 352 Collins.
Thompson H. M. 17 Vernon.
Tierney Michael, 140 Farmington.
Twichell Joseph H. 125 Woodland.
Tyler George W. 14 Martin.
Waite Joseph, 109 Kenyon.
Walker George Leon, 46 Prospect.
Warner George R. 50 Capen.
Wheeler Robert F. 47 Fairmount.
Williams Charles H. 650 Main.
Williams H. DeWitt, 87 Laurel.
Wright Thomas G. 60 Maple.

### CLOAKS and SUITS.
*See also Dry Goods.*

BROWN, THOMSON & CO. 942
  Main. *See page* 499.
Cooper James, 904 Main.
Geary Thomas J. & Co. 845 Main.
Pratt C. W. 937 Main.
SAGE, ALLEN & CO. 896 Main.
  *See page* 317.

### CLOCK REPAIRERS.
*See Jewelers.*

### CLOTHES CLEANERS.
*See Dye Works; Merchant Tailors.*
Arons Sam, 296 Pearl.
PATTEN H.E. 37 Wells. *Page* 591.

### CLOTHING.
*See also Merchant Tailors.*

Ackerman Samuel, 149 Front.
BROCKWAY U. H. & Co. 132 State.
  *See page* 71.
Cohn Isaac, 110 State.
Daniel H. & D. 75 Trumbull.
Foster A. L. & Co. 45 Asylum.
Freeman-Tibbals Co. 34 Asylum.
Geeley Henry, 27 Asylum.
Gemmill, Burnham & Co. 66 Asy.
Gilman Michael, 160 Front.
Hartford One Price Clothing Co.
  116 Asylum.
Hollander's A. Sons, 82-88 Asylum.
Koffman M. 324 Asylum.
Lewis Henry & Co. 174 State.
Mulcahy E. J. 33-41 Asylum.
Nussman Joe, 157 Front.
People's Credit Clothing Co. 933
  Main.
Proller Morris, 134 Front.
RENNACKER & CO. 141 Asylum.
  *See page* 305.
Rhein Rubien, 68 Talcott.
Sedelsky Barrett, 86 Sheldon.
Silverstein Samuel, 198 State.
Union Clothing Co. 100 Asylum.
Willis & Wilson, 109 Asylum.

#### RESTORER.
PATTEN H. E. 37 Wells.  *See*
  *page* 591.

#### SECOND HAND.
Alexander Moses, 144 Front.
Getz Jacob, 122 State.
Helene Manuel, 91 Front.
Rohowsky Maurice, 86 Front.

### CLUBS.
*See Index to Contents for full information of each.*

Camera Club, 53 Pratt.
Cathedral Lyceum, 221 Lawrence
City Club of Hartford, 904 Main.
Colonial Club, 17 Prospect.
Conn. Congregational Club, 225 Pl.
Fencers' Club, 51 Elm.
Franklin Rifle Club, 274 Main.
Gentlemen's Driving Club,7 Central.
Germania Cycle Club, 730 Main.
Good Will Club, 98 Pratt.
H. C. Robinson Troop, 809 Main.
Hartford Club, 33 Prospect.
Hartford Prohibition Club, 91 Asy.
Hartford Turnhalle, 8 Morgan.
Hartford Wheel Club, 704 Main.
Hercules Athletic Asso. 29 Pearl.
Hibernian Rifle, 104 Asylum.
Hubbard Escort, 7 Central Row.
Jefferson Social Club, 265 Park.
Kokomo Social Club, 245 Main.
McKinley Club. 92 Pearl.
Musicians Social Club, 405 Main.
Prospect Casino, 649 Farmington.
Republican Club, 676 Main.
United Workers Club, 700 Main.
Veteran Volunteer Fireman's Asso.
  27 Arch.
Woman's Exchange, 73 Pearl.
Young Italian American Association, 64 Morgan.
Young Men's Christian Association,
  323 Pearl. *See pages* 680-681.
Young Men's Hebrew Association,
  603 Main.

### COACH SCREWS.
CLAPP JOHN B. & SON, 61 Market. *See page* 529.

### COAL.
BURGESS HENRY C. 15 Albany.
  *See page* 493.
Farr George, 15 Kinsley.
FRAYER & FOSTER, 446 Asylum.
  *See page* 490.
HARTFORD COAL CO. 754 Main;
  100 Commerce.   *See page* 491.
HATCH & NORTH COAL CO. 861
  Main and 56 Com. *See page* 491.
MASON W. C. & CO. 746 Main, 169
  Front, 178 Com. *See page* 417.
McClory Henry S. 146 Trumbull.
Mitchell Charles E. 1554 Broad.
NEW ENGLAND COAL CO. 722
  Main. *See page* 273.
Newton Geo. W. & Son, 107 Grove.
Price Robert & Son, 82 Francis.
Shackley Frank W., Park, W.Hd.
Slocum F. R. 340 Pearl.
Slonim Bernard, 238 Front.
Taft Joel C. 29 Albany.
Tyler Edwin S. 746 Main.
Woodford D. R. 15 Pearl.

#### WHOLESALE.
MASON W. C. & CO. 746 Main.
  *See page* 417.

### COCK Mfrs.
PRATT & CADY CO. 554 Capitol.
  *See page* 527.

## COFFEE ROASTERS.
KIBBE E. S. CO. 149 State. *See page 587.*
LINCOLN, SEYMS & CO. 34 Market. *See page 588.*

## COFFEE & SPICES.
*See Tea, etc.*
LINCOLN, SEYMS & CO. whl. 34 Market. *See page 588.*

## COLLECTORS.
*See also Mercantile Agencies; Attorneys at Law.*
ADAMS EXPRESS COMPANY, 805 Main. *See page 552.*
Emery & Co. 721 Main.
MULHALL JAMES, 29 Pearl. *See page 267.*
Rhodes Chauncey A. 82 Pearl.
WARD WILLIAM, 868 Main. *See page 368.*

## COLLEGES.
*See also Schools.*
HARTFORD BUSINESS COLLEGE, 370 Asylum. *See p. 711.*
HARTFORD THEOLOGICAL SEMINARY, 1507 Broad. *See pages 708, 709.*
TRINITY COLLEGE, Summit. Office of Treasurer 89 Pearl. *See pages 706, 707.*
OLMSTEAD ELLA M. 756 Main. *See page 710.*

## Commercial Agencies.
Bradstreet Co. 49 Pearl.
Dun R. G. & Co. 223 Asylum.

## COMMERCIAL PAPER.
*See also Bankers; Brokers.*
Stedman & Redfield, 5 Central Row.

## COMMISSION MERCHANT.
*See also Flour; Produce; Butter; Cheese; Fruit, Wholesale.*
BREWER C. S. & CO. 238 Asylum. *See page 69.*
Dunham Austin & Sons, 66 State.
FITZGERALD RANSOM N. 44–46 Market. *See page 144.*
Fowler & Huntting, 47 Ann.
Haskell Charles B. 145 State.
Judd H. C. & Root, 389 Allyn.
POTTER & PAYNE, 405–407 Allyn. *See page 586.*
Slate D. N. & Co. 40 Ann.
SMITH NORTHAM & CO. 129 State. *See page 590.*
Whittelsey E. G. & Co. 140 State.

## Commission Stock Brokers.
DENNISON CHARLES, 750 Main. *See page 426.*

## COMMISSIONER of DEEDS.
*See Attorney at Law.*
PARKER FRANCIS H. *See page 493.*

## Commissioners Sup. Court.
*See page 669.*

## COMMUTATOR BARS.
BILLINGS & SPENCER CO. 142 Russ. *See page 531.*

## COMPOSITION RELIEF ORNAMENTS.
SANFORD CO. 488 Asylum. *See page 448.*

## CONDUCTOR Mfrs.
BISHOP E. C. & CO. 84 Capen. *See page 60.*

## CONFECTIONERY.
*See also Bakers.*
BACKES F. W. 169 Asylum. *See page 45.*
Bartha Frank J. 150 Russ.
BESSE P. & J 701 Main. *Page 57.*
Booth & Condos, 224 Asylum.
Cohn Rosie, 55 Morgan.
Curley John, 575 Main.
Elsner Morritz, 129 Front.
Goldberg Nathan, 22 Howard.
Hetzel George J. Mrs. 149 Market.
Hoadley E. J., 19 Foot Guard pl.
Kilby Arthur E. 39 Sargeant.
Oiley George, 174 Windsor av.
Quinlan Patrick H. 263 High.
Raphael Aaron, 183 Front.
Sansone Salvadore, 851 Park.
Schlemmer Oscar P. 44 Ann.
SCHROEDER Fred G. 941 Main. *See page 322.*
Silver Brothers, 1174 Main.
Stoughton D. G. 219 State.
Vining A. C. 570 Main.
Weiss Joseph, 59 Morgan.
Werder Fritz, 607, 815 Main.
Wheeler George B. 259 High.
WILLIAMS EUGENE H. 366 Asylum. *See page 379.*

## CONSULTING ENGINEERS.
BUTTS & CROSBY, 49 Pearl. *See page 427.*
MERRILL GEO. N. & CO. 75 Pratt. *See page 428.*

## CONSTABLES.
*See page 668.*

## CONTRACTORS.
*See also Carpenters.*
ANGUS & CHESEBRO, 27 Warner. *See page 519.*
Aspromonte L. 81 Windsor.
BALF EDWARD CO. 2 Chapel. *See page 426.*
Belden Eugene S. 217 Laurel.
BISSEL HIRAM, 43 Wadsworth. *See page 516.*
BONFOEY BROS. 109 Windsor. *See page 513.*
COOK CHARLES C. 141 Trumbull. *See page 419.*
DWYER JOHN W. 386 Park. *See page 182.*
Ferranto Joseph M. 17 Charles.
GROZIER & MOORE, Vredendale, cor. Taylor. *See page 510.*
Harrison P. H. & Sons, 343 Main.
HATHEWAY EARL, 29 Imlay. *See page 495.*
HOLLIS D. W. & SON, 212 Asylum. *See page 514.*
Keenen D. F. 721 Main.
Lapaugh J. D. 46 John.
McGRATH T. F. & CO. 820 Park. *See page 520.*
O'Loughlin James, 25 Central.

O'NEIL EDWARD, 68 Hudson. *See page 520.*
PORTEUS ROBERT, r. 12 Forest. *See page 495.*
PURVES & MALCOLM, r. 334 Asylum. *See page 422.*
ROWLEY & WILCOX, 39 Ann. *See page 562.*
SCOVILLE A. W. 700 Main. *See page 518.*
SHERMAN M. W. & SON. *See page 551.*
Sharp Harry, 153 Clark.
SIMMS W. J. 54 Pratt. *See p. 517.*
Stafford Thomas 65 New Britain.
SVENSON CHARLES, 54 Woodbridge. *See page 482.*
THOMPSON BROS. 19 Rowe av. *See page 513.*
TRYON EDWARD S. 28 Temple. *See page 360.*
WHITTLESEY D. L. 212 Asylum. *See page 513.*
WINDSOR RED STONE CO. 1542 Broad. *See page 508.*

## COOPERS.
Butler Thomas, 30 Ferry.
Wissel Konrad, 38 Sanford.

## COPPER.
KATZ JACOB, 7 North. *See p. 502.*

## COPPER NEEDLE BRUSH MANUF'R'S·
WHITTEMORE W. L. & SON, 176–178 Allyn. *See page 483.*

## COPPERPLATE PRINTERS.
*See also Engravers; Printers.*
PERKINS JAMES A. & CO. 863 Main. *See page 290.*

## COPPERSMITHS.
*See also Brass Founders.*
BLAKE T. J. & SON, 141–143 Commerce. *See page 489.*

## COPYING OFFICE.
Brooks E. E. Mrs. 801 Main.
COOK L. H. Mrs. 80 State. *See page 710.*
Smith Mary L. Mrs. 2 Central.

## COPYING PADS.
TUCKER'S E. SONS. *See page 481.*

## COPYISTS.
*See Type Writer.*
COOK L. H. Mrs. 80 State. *See page 710.*
OLMSTEAD COMMERCIAL COLLEGE, 756 Main. *See page 710.*

## CORDAGE.
FRANCIS & CO. 859 Main. *See page 546.*

## CORK DEALER.
GROSS HERMAN. *See page 171.*

## CORN SALVE.
LANKTON ARBA, 2 Marsh. *See page 564.*

## CORONERS.

*County Coroners see page 666.*
Fuller Horace S. 95 Trumbull.
Taintor Henry E. 847 Main.

## CORSETS.

Corpe Laura A. Mrs. 81 Church.
Leek A. M. Mrs. 290 Main.
Stacy I. B. Miss 58 Church.

## CORPORATIONS.

*For full particulars, see Index to Contents and Advertisers' Index.*
A. D. Vorce Co. 752 Main.
Acme Machine Screw Co. Vredendale.
Ætna Indemnity Co. 650 Main.
Ætna Machine Co. 75 Commerce.
American Emigrant Co. 25 Forest.
American Publishing Co. 424 Asy.
American School for Deaf, 690 Asy.
American Specialty Co.135 Sheldon
Art Society of Hartford, 624 Main.
Balf Edward Co. 2 Chapel.
Beach Mfg. Co. 211 State.
Beacon Falls Mill & Power Co. 211 State.
Berryman Mfg. Co. 40 Cushman.
Billings C. E. Mfg. Co. 142 Russ.
Billings & Spencer Co. 142 Russ.
Billings Sidewalk and Masons' Sup-Co. 154 Charter Oak.
Birkery Mfg. Co. 65 Suffield.
Blodgett & Clapp Co. 51 Market.
Board of Trade, 49 Pearl.
Boardman Wm. & Sons Co. 304 Asy.
Bonner, Preston Co. 843 Main.
Bonsilate Box Co. 24 Mechanic.
Broad Brook Co. 211 State.
Burr Index Co. 386 Asylum.
Calhoun Printing Co. 29 Union pl.
Capewell Horse Nail Co. 40 Gov.
Capitol City Chute Co.Wethersfield.
Capitol City Lumber Co. 25 Front.
Case, Lockwood & Brainard Co. 141 Pearl.
Charitable Soc. in Hartford, 57 Tru.
Cheney Bros. Silk Manufacturers, 84 Morgan.
Citizens Grocery and Provision Co. 285 Main.
City Missionary Society, 284 Pearl.
Collins Co. 785 Main.
Colts Patent Fire Arms Mfg. Co. Vandyke av.
Columbia Brewing Co. 245 Windsor.
Conn. Building and Loan Association, 252 Asylum.
Conn. Catholic Publishing Co. 704 Main.
Conn. Historical Society, 624 Main.
Conn. River Co. 761 Main.
Cook Asa S. Co. Colt's West Armory
Cook C. P. H. Co. 721 Main.
Curtis-Hull Mfg. Co. 904 Main.
Cushman Chuck Co. 30 Cushman.
Dart Marking Machine Co.235 State.
Directors of the Missionary Society of Conn. 426 Asylum.
Dunham Hosiery Co. 66 State.
Dwight Slate Machine Co. 13 Cen.
Eckhardt J. H. Co. 695 Main.
Eddy Electric Mfg. Co. Windsor t.
Evening Post Association, 23 Asy.
Examiner Publishing Co. 45 Brown.
Farmer Printing & Publishing Co. 284 Asylum.
Farmington RiverPower Co. 50 Sta.

Farnham Type Setter Mfg. Co. 281 Asylum.
Fowler & Miller Co. r. 857 Main.
Francis Gowdy Distilling Co. Melrose t.
Fraternity of I. K. A. of Trinity College, 70 Vernon.
Freeman, Tibbals Co. 34 Asylum.
Gatling Gun Co. Colt's Armory.
Gray Telephone Pay Station, r. 64 Asylum.
Guilfoil Grocery Co. 493 Asylum.
Hart Charles R. Co. 902 Main.
Hart & Hageman, Mfg. Co. 26 High.
Hartford Beef Co. Huntley av.
Hartford Bowling Co. 645 Main.
Hartford Building & Loan Asso. 870 Asylum.
Hartford Carpet Co. 10 Market.
Hartford Chemical Co. 285 State.
Hartford City Gas Light Co. 700 Mn.
Hartford Club, 33 Prospect.
Hartford Coal Co. 754 Main.
Hartford & Conn. V. R. Co. 450 Asy.
Hartford & Conn. Western R.R. Co. 59 Spruce.
Hartford Courant Co. 66 State.
Hartford Cycle Co. 581 Capitol.
Hartford Diamond Polish Co. 118 Asylum.
Hartford Dispensary, 2 Talcott.
Hartford Dredging Co. 721 Main.
Hartford Elec. Light Co. 266 Pearl.
Hartford Heating Co. 267 Asylum.
Hartford Hospital, 20 So. Hudson.
Hartford Ice Co. 4 Central.
Hartford Lumber Co. Lumber st.
Hartford Mach. Screw Co. 476 Cap.
Hartford Manilla Co. 1 So. Ann.
Hartford and New York Transportation Co. 285 State.
Hartford Orphan Asylum, 171 Put.
Hartford Paper Co. 141 Pearl.
Hartford Printing Co. 16 State.
Hartford Provision Co. Valley st.
Hartford Public Library Assoc. 5 Athenæum.
Hartford Real Estate Improvement Co. 436 Capitol.
Hartford Rubber Works Co. 690 Park.
Hartford Telegram Co. 12 Central.
Htfd. Theolog. Seminary,1507 Broad.
Hartford Typewriter Co. 476 Cap.
Hartford Street Ry. Co. 115 State.
Hartford Street Sprinkling & Supply Co. 868 Main.
Hartford Woven Wire Mattress Co. 618 Capitol.
Hatch & North Coal Co. 801 Main.
Health Underwear Co. 66 State.
Heublein Hotel Co. 98 Wells.
Hitchcock & Curtiss Knitting Co. 1189 Broad.
Horne Vacuum Co. 55 Trumbull.
Howard James L. & Co. 488 Asy.
Insurance Journal Co. 53 Trumbull.
Jacobs, Avery & Northam Co. 875 Main.
Jewell Belting Co. 15 Trumbull.
Jewell Pad Co. 49 Hicks.
Jewell Pin Co. 31 Hicks.
Johns–Pratt Co. 555 Capitol.
Kellogg & Bulkeley Co. 175 Pearl.
Kibbe E. S. Co. 149–155 State.
League Cycle Co. 11 Central.
Lincoln Co. 54 Arch.
Lovell & Tracy Oil Co. 218 State.
Mellen & Hewes Co. 725 Main.

Merchants National Trading Ass. 66 State.
Mt. St. Joseph's Convent Corp. of Hartford, 150 Farmington.
National Machine Co. 111–123 Shel.
National Trotting Asso. 650 Main.
Neal, Goff & Inglis Co. 980 Main.
New England Coal Co. 722 Main.
New England Granite Works, 1268 Main.
New York & New England R.R. Co. 478 Asylum.
New York, New Haven & Hartford R.R. Co. 450 Asylum.
Old People's Home, 36 Jefferson.
Overman Wheel Co. 847 Main.
Palace Amusement Co. 933 Main.
Perkins Electric Switch Mfg. Co. 83 Woodbine.
Plimpton Mfg. Co. 254 Pearl.
Pope Mfg. Co. 436 Capitol.
Post Wm. H. Carpet Co. 219 Asy.
Pratt & Cady, 556 Capitol.
Pratt & Whitney, 1 Flower.
Retreat for Insane, 30 Washington.
Rhodes L. E. Co. 28 High.
Rogers Cutlery Co. 66 Market.
Rogers Wm. Mfg. Co. 66-72 Market.
Sanford Co. 438 Asylum.
Sigourney Tool Co. 9 Sigourney.
Schall Ernst Co. 5 Asylum.
Shedd J. N. Co. 109 Asylum.
Smith, Northam & Co. 129 State.
Smyth Mfg. Co. 648 Main.
Southern New England Paving Co., 141 Trumbull.
Spencer Motor Co. 216 State.
Spring Brook Ice Co. 4 Central.
Sterling Washing Compound Co. 284 Asylum.
Syracuse Coal and Salt Co.682 Main.
Taft Co. Lumber st.
Trinity College, office 39 Pearl.
Trustees Good Will Club, 98 Pratt.
Tru. of the Widows' Home,133 Mar.
Tucker Stop Motion Co. 124 Collins.
Tunxis Worsted Co. 66 State.
Union for Home Work, 239 Market.
Union Grove Co. Wethersfield av.
United Workers Club, 700 Main.
Wadsworth Athenæum, 634 Main.
Walnut Lodge Hospital Co. 56 Fairfield av.
War Photo. Ex. Co. 137 Kenyon.
Warner & Willard Co. 108 Asylum.
Watkinson Juvenile Asylum and Farm School, Albany cor. Bloomfield avenues.
Watkinson Library, 5 Athenæum.
Way Hardware Co. 866 Main.
Western Automatic Machine Screw Co. of Hartford, 476 Capitol.
Whitney Mfg. Co. 70 Huyshope.
Widows' Society. *See page 728.*
Williams & Carleton Co. 206 State.
Willimantic Linen Co. 389 Allyn.
Woman's Aid Society, 1 Pavilion.
Woman's Christian Association of Hartford. 58 Church.
Woman's Cong. Home Miss. Union of Conn. *See page 729.*
Woman's Shelter, 76 Temple.
Young Men's Chris.Asso.,315 Pearl.

## COTTON BROKER.

Catlin A. Jr. 210 Pearl.

## COTTON THREAD.
WILLIMANTIC LINEN CO. 289 Allyn. *See page 544.*

## COTTON & WOOL WASTE.
*See also Wool.*
HOWARD JAS. L. & CO. 438. Asylum. *See page 527.*

## COUGH CHERRIES Mfr.
Stoughton D. G. 219 State.

## COUGH DROPS.
Colton S. B. & Son, 90 Bluehills.
WILLIAMS E. H. 366 Asylum. *See page 379.*

## COUNSELLORS.
*See Attorneys.*

## COUNTY JAIL.
*See page 667.*

## COUNTY OFFICERS.
*See page 668.*
CLERKS OF COURT. *See page 649.*

## Coverings for Boilers, Etc.
Remington E. A. 249 Pearl.
Rogers William H. 259 Asylum.

## CRACKER Mfr.
National Biscuit Co. 59 Albany.
U. S. Biscuit Co. 409 Allyn.

## CREAMERY.
DAY C. W. 53 High. *See p. 586.*
NEWTON, ROBERTSON & CO. 342 Asylum. *See page 486.*

## CROCHET MACHINE MFR.
MERROW MACHINE CO. 26-28 Laurel. *See page 535.*

## CROCKERY.
*See also Pottery.*
BROWN, THOMSON & CO. 942 Main. *See page 499.*
Fineberg Louis, 201½ Front.
Jacobs, Avery & Northam Co. 875 Main.
Mellen & Hewes Co. 725 Main.

## CURBING.
*See Sidewalk Layers.*

## CURTAINS.
BRAINERD H. B. 84 Pratt. *See page 503.*

## CURTAINS HUNG.
*See Carpet Stores.*
BRAINERD H. B. 84 Pratt. *See page 503.*
MAERCKLEIN H. 104 Asylum. *See page 562.*

## CURTAINS (SILK) MFRS.
CHENEY BROS. 34 Morgan, *See page 545 and inside front cover.*

## CUT GLASS.
CASE C. H. & CO. 851 Main. *See outside front cover.*
HANSEL, SLOAN & CO. 886 Main. *See page 176.*

## CUT OUTS.
HART & HEGEMAN MFG. CO 26 High. *See page 539.*

## CUTLERS.
*See also Bell Hangers, Hardware.*
COWLISHAW HENRY, 162 Pearl. *See page 535.*
HALLIDAY W. H. 181 Front. *p 506.*
ROGERS CUTLERY COMPANY, 66 Market. *See page 471.*
Stengelin Fred C. 5 Grove.
Witte Robert C. r. 215 Main.

## CUTTER GRINDERS.
WOODWARD & ROGERS, 133-135 Sheldon. *See page 526.*

## CUTTING BLOCKS.
LITTLE H. B. & CO. 33 Wells. *See page 232.*

## CYLINDER BORING,
*without removing from bed.*
LEE R. K. 223 State. *See page 539.*

## DEAD ANIMALS.
*See Undertakers.*

## DANCING.
*See also Music Teachers; Schools.*
Beers Edith D. 64 Allen pl.
Church William, 104 Clark.
Goldstein B. J. 759 Main.
MARSH HENRY T. 1084 Main. *See page 496.*
Prutting George Jr. 53 Trumbull.
Reilly Julie Smith, 234 Pearl.
Reilly P. Harvard, 6 Haynes.

## Decorative Ornaments.
SANFORD CO. 438 Asylum. *See page 448.*

## DECORATORS.
*See Florists; Carpets; Painters.*
BAXTER W. G. 231 Asylum. *See page 52.*
BECK CURT E. 262 Allyn. *See page 506.*
BLAKE WALTER P. 219 Pearl. *See page 61.*
BONNER-PRESTON CO. 843 Main. *See page 425.*
BRAINERD H. B. 84 Pratt. *See page 503.*
COOK CHAS. C. 141 Trumbull. *See page 419.*
DARBY THEODORE T. 37 Martin. *See page 529.*
HART CHAS. R. CO. 596 Main. *See page 179.*
McCLUNIE J. A. 177 Asylum. *See page 249.*
NEAL, GOFF & INGLIS CO. 980 Main. *See page 498.*
PEPION J. & CO. 25 Ch. *See p. 289.*
Rogers George B. 49 Pearl.
ROWLEY & WILCOX, 39 Ann. *See page 562.*
SANFORD CO. 438 Asylum. *See page 448.*
Warburton G. B. 999 Main.
Yergason Edgar S. 389 Allyn.

## DENTISTS.
ASSOCIATE DENTISTS, 943 Main. *See page 423.*
Barrett Charles E. 753 Main.
Barrett George F. 926 Main.
Boston Dental Asso. 759 Main.
Bryant Charles K. 926 Main.
Bullock Henry C. 868 Main.
CAHILL W. H. 75 Pratt. *See page 423.*
Carr Ellen R. 68 Pratt, rm. 44.
CHAPMAN LESLIE G. 86 Pratt *See front cover outside.*
Crane S. L. G. 8 State.
Damon William A. 103 Pratt.
Doebler John F. 903 Main.
Duval Arthur E. 9 Asylum.
Eberle Edward, 68 Pratt. *See page 133.*
Erichson & McLean, 3 Asylum.
Fisk Henry J. 53 Trumbull.
Fisk Louis H. 53 Trumbull.
Goodwin Nelson J. 753 Main.
Griswold Gilbert M. 904 Main.
Griswold Monroe, 51 Pratt.
Harper J. Warren, 50 State.
Henry George H. 943 Main.
Keeler Ralph H. 903 Main.
KIMBERLY THOMAS A. 86 Pratt. *See outside back cover.*
KUMPITSCH P. F. 75 Pratt. *See outside back cover.*
Lane Davis E. 17 Pratt.
LAW & PRENTISS, 926 Main *See page 427.*
Little Samuel A. 904 Main.
Mallery J. Hammond, 981 Main.
McMANUS JAMES & SONS, 80 Pratt. *See page 428.*
Mix Frederick E. 904 Main.
Parmele George L. 65 Pratt.
Pillion Henry J. 903 Main.
Pomeroy W. H. 721 Main, rm. 2.
Prentiss Charles C. 926 Main.
Riggs Chas. H. 68 Pratt, rm. 34.
Starr Thomas K. 926 Main.
Taylor L. C. 68 Pratt.
Welles John M. 793 Main.
Whitford Ernest R. 68 Pratt.
Wiley Louis N. 884 Main.
Wright H. B. 51 Pratt.
Wright & Dunham, 911 Main.
Youngblood William S. 68 Pratt.

## DENTISTS SUPPLIES.
Messinger W. C. 96 Trumbull.

## DESIGNERS.
BUTTS & CROSBY, 49 Pearl. *See page 427.*
Reuss Hugo, 30 Asylum.
RICHARDS F. H. 803 Main. *See outside front cover.*
Rogers George B. 49 Pearl.
Scheck Theo. G. 118 Main.
Sherman E. A. 756 Main.
WOLCOTT & DARBY, 49 Pearl. *See page 493.*

## DESKS.
NEW ENGLAND TYPEWRITER EXCHANGE, 847 Mn. *See p. 422.*

## DEVELOPING.
U. S. PHOTO. CHEMICAL MFG. CO. 29 Pearl. *See page 419.*

### DIAMOND COMPOSITION.
Altemus W. F. & Co. 9 Asylum.

### DIAMONDS and SETTERS.
See also Jewelers, etc.
CASE C. H. & CO. 851 Main. See outside front cover.
HANSEL, SLOAN & CO. 886 Main. See pages 176 and 333.
KOHN HENRY & SONS, 890 Main. See page 797.
Pease Allison L. 756 Main.

### DIARIES.
CASE, LOCKWOOD & BRAINARD CO. 141 Pearl. See p. 475

### DICTIONARIES.
MERRIAM G. & C. CO. See p. 797.
WEBSTER'S. See page 797.

### DIE SINKERS.
JOHNS-PRATT CO. 555 Capitol. See page 540.

### DIES.
See also Machinists.
BILLINGS & SPENCER CO. 142 Russ. See page 531.
BURCH GEORGE W. 91 Asylum. See page 497.
Ideal Machine Works, 328 Asylum.
PARKER T. M. 71 Asy. page 584.
PRATT & WHITNEY CO. page 523.

### DINING ROOMS.
See Restaurants.

### DIRECTORY.
TROW'S DIRECTORY PRINTING & BOOKBINDING CO. 21-27 University pl. See page 33.

### DISPENSARIES.
See Hospitals.

### DOCKS.
See Wharfs.

### DOG KENNELS.
Hartford Kennel Club. See p. 723.
Pitkin Howard S., E.H.t.
Smith James H. 25 Fairfield av.

### DOOR PLATES.
ÆTNA STAMP WORKS, 25 Asylum. See page 497.
BURCH GEORGE W. 91 Asylum. See page 497.
Cross L. D. 103 Ann.

### DOORS, SASH & BLINDS.
See Sash, Blinds and Doors.
ANDREWS & PECK, 88 Market. See page 509.
BARKER FRANK W. & CO. 86 Morgan. See page 519.
FRENCH HARRY A. 554 Main. See page 512.
Joslyn Clarence R. 23 Wells.
NIMS, WHITNEY & CO. 1170 Mn. See page 511.
SCOVILLE A. W. 700 Main. See page 513.

### DOOR SCREENS.
AMIDON F. S. rear 60 Temple. See page 40.

### DRAIN PIPE & TILE.
See Bricks, etc.
BELDEN SETH & SON, 69 Commerce. See page 508.

### DRAPERIES,
BRAINERD H. B. 84 Pratt. See page 508.

### DRAPERIES (SILK) MFRS.
CHENEY BROS. 84 Morgan. See page 545 and inside front cover.

### DRAUGHTSMEN.
See Architects.

### DREDGING.
Hartford Dredging Co. 721 Main.

### DRESSED BEEF.
See Beef, wholesale.
Armour & Co. 501 Asylum.

### DRESS GOODS.
CHENEY BROS. 84 Morgan. See page 545 and inside front cover.

### DRESSMAKERS.
See also Seamstresses.
Aab Kate Mrs. 15 Imlay.
Ahern Kate, 144 Capitol.
Alderman A. C. Mrs. 14 Ch. rm. 12.
Alexander Emma J. 51 Windsor.
Alling Alma Mrs. 721 Main.
Anderson Carrie, 17 So. Ann.
Apgar Maud, 45 Vine.
Bacon Elizabeth D. Mrs. 106 Capen.
Baker Frank P. Mrs. 37 Barbour.
Baker Hattie Mrs. 1836 Main.
Baldwin Ada L. Mrs. 1281 Main.
Barnes Fannie C. 67 Willard.
Barnum Belle M. 25½ Florence.
Bascomb C. H. Mrs. 2 Wadsworth.
Baytopp Mary Mrs. 37 Maple.
Beers George M. Mrs. 64 Allen pl.
Bell Azilda, 46 Canton.
Benson Jennie C. 10 Village.
Billings Sarah F. 79 Willow.
Blumenthal Mollie, 72 Hungerford.
Bogue Harriet Mrs. 375 Main.
Boyle Mary, 21 Sumner.
Boyle W. B. Mrs. 389 Allyn.
Boynton Susan E. 265 Asylum.
Brace Eveline Mrs. 277 Main.
Brant N. M. Mrs. 37 Amity.
Brennan Lizzie, 903 Main.
Bridgman Luella, 171 Collins.
Brierton Margaret, 103 Mather.
Brierton Mary, 103 Mather.
Britt Lena H. 9 Asylum.
Brodersen Nessine, 222 Park.
Brooks Louise M. Mrs. 42 Village.
Brown Frances P. 13 Goodman.
Brown Nellie A. 574 Windsor av.
Brusie Lillian A. Mrs. 61 Hudson.
Bryant Frances A. Mrs. 4 Marsh.
Buckley Anna L. 12 Liberty.
Buckley Mary G. 25 Seyms.
Burke Margaret, 85 Governor.
Burke Mary E. 29 Bellevue.
Burnham Annie M. 107 Jefferson.
Burnham Sarah F. Miss, 15 Sherman.

Burns Phœbe Mrs. 54 Sumner.
Burr Clara S. Mrs. 155 Franklin.
Cadwell Hattie J. Mrs. 1158 Main.
Cady Mary A. 2u. 15 Goodwin.
Cambridge Annie B. 67 Green.
Cambridge Eva L. 67 Green.
Cameron Catherine, 76 Albany.
Carberry Mary A. 53 Wadsworth.
Carey Lillian, 9 Blumenthal.
Carrier Margaret, 96 Hudson.
Carroll Agnes A. 199 Sheldon.
Carroll Mary A. 6 Pavilion.
Carney Margaret, 24 Canton.
Carter Eliza L. Mrs. 188 Laurel.
Claffey Kate Mrs. 151 Main.
Clark Emma H. Mrs. 1208 Main.
Clark May E. 199 Barbour.
Clements W. H. Mrs. 68 Heath.
Coleman Annie E. 15 Belden.
Collaze Lilla S. 67 Green.
Collins Adella E. 71 Asylum.
Conway Mary A. 517 Main.
Cook Caroline A. Mrs. 406 Weth.
Cooper L. M. Mrs. 58 Grove.
Cordier Kate, 22 Chestnut.
Costello Sadie E. 1293 Main.
Costello Sarah E. 14 Pratt.
Crane Iphigenia E. Mrs. 7 Belden.
Critchley Agnes, 16 Spring.
Cross Maria D. Mrs. 10 Martin.
Cummings Margaret E. 128 Ann.
Daley Nellie, 48 Windsor.
Damon Fannie E. 54 Maple.
Dare E. C. Mrs. 71 Asylum.
Davis Georgene A. 192 High.
Day Elizabeth Mrs. u. 9 Park.
Delahanty Lottie E. 118 Mather.
Derrick John A. Mrs. 73 Congress.
Desmond Nora J. 354 Park.
Deutsch D. Mrs. 54 Village.
Dow Alice J. Mrs. 899 Wethersfield.
Dowling Elizabeth M. 1315 Main.
Doyle Nora, 943 Main.
Dubes Mary, 721 Main.
Duff Mary J. 53 Church.
Duffy Mary, 30 Temple.
Dunn Bridget, 136 Maple.
Eberle Susan, 152 Wethersfield.
Egan Alice, 122 Heath.
Egan Maria J. 700 Main.
Emmett Sarah, 59 New Britain.
Farrell Mary, 73 Huyshope.
Fay Nellie F. 49 Sigourney.
Feeney Mary E. 76 Walnut.
Ferrall Mary, 225 Barbour.
Filley Sophia, 32 Canton.
Fish Ella E. 13 East.
Fiske Carrie Mrs. 284 Asylum.
Flynn Margaret, 391 Allyn.
Flynn Mary G. 148 Washington.
Foley Elizabeth, 15 Goodman.
Foley Kittie, 22 Affleck.
Forshaw Harry Mrs. 140 New Park.
Forsyth Clara J. Mrs. 14 Ch. rm. 9.
Fox H° P. Mrs. 868 Main.
French Mabel P. 54 Sanford.
Fuller Josephine L. 36 Russ.
Fullerton Jennie, 5 Sigourney pl.
Ganley Margaret, 9 So. Prospect.
Gardner C. C. Mrs. 1201 Main.
Gardner Elizabeth B. 650 Main.
Gavin Mary A. 38 Spring.
Gavin Misses, 19 Alden.
Geddes Annie, 227 Sigourney.
Gillespie Lucia C. 49 Governor.
Gloster Mary, u. 51 Portland.
Godman Mary, u. 101 Main.
Goff Angie D. Mrs. 884 Main.
Goulet Georgina M. 721 Main.

Graml Annie Mrs. 143 Front.
Grannis Susan H. Mrs. 926 Main.
Grassier Helen M. 168 Franklin.
GREENSTEIN R. A. 903 Main, room 4. *See page 562.*
Gregg A. L. Mrs. 165 Capen.
Guinan Anna C. 23 Beach.
Guinan Elizabeth, 22 Beach.
Gunning Sarah A. 9 Zion.
Hackett Minnie A. 88 Charter Oak.
Hallinan Katherine, 29 Beach.
Handel Rose L. 721 Main.
Hanley Nora A. 53 Grove.
Hart Lizzie I. Mrs. 51½ Wooster.
Hatch Misses, 11 Goodwin.
Hatheway Sara, 29 Imlay.
Heath C. J. Mrs. 926 Main.
Hedican Misses, 903 Main.
Heinze Meta A. 1143 Broad.
Hitchcock Carrie M. Mrs. 650 Main.
Hodge A. B. & Co. 84 Pratt.
Hoffman Mary J. Mrs. 88 Whitmore.
Hogan Margaret A. 17 Morris.
Holden Mary, 56 Albany.
Holley Hattie M. Mrs. 152 Allyn.
Horey Margaret, 67 Franklin.
Hotchkiss Lizzie, 46 John.
Howe Joseph Mrs. 926 Main.
Hughes Rose, Mrs. 110 Trumbull.
Hunt C. M. Miss, 187 Trumbull.
Hyland Mary A. 54 Pratt.
James Flora, u. 27 Avon.
Johnson Amanda, 48 New Britain.
Johnson Emily P. 171 Seymour.
Johnson Helma, 193 Russ.
Jordan Kate A. 20 Canton.
Joyner E. P. Mrs. 864 Broad.
Keefe Misses, 926 Main.
Keenan Mary C. 80 Trumbull.
Kelly John D. Mrs. 183 Babcock.
Kennedy Julia A. Mrs. 721 Main.
Kennedy Nellie B. Mrs. 56 Asylum.
Kenneth Annette, 75 Niles.
Kerwin Kate, 161 Zion.
Kessler Ida, 42 North.
Kidney M. Mrs. u. 32 Park.
Kilbourn Fannie A. Mrs. 83 Windsor
Kimberly Carrie A. 38 Ashley.
King Mary Mrs. 721 Main.
Knowlton Blanche, 48 Hopkins.
Knudsen Katrina, r. 36 Temple.
Kumpitsch Mary, 6 Kilbourn ct.
Lagan Mary W. 57 Annawan.
Landrigan Kate M. Mrs. 72 Law.
LaRocque Mary Mrs. 18 Kennedy.
Larson Ida, 173 Babcock.
Lathrop Ella S. 20 Union.
Laylor Mary E. Mrs. 120 Wooster.
Lenihan Catherine, 50 Francis.
Leonard Estelle Mrs. 53 Maple.
Leven Jacob, 164 Front.
Lewis Mary Mrs. 489 Main.
Logan Matilda & Theresa, 229 Pearl.
Longworth Mary, 29 North.
Loomis Carrie M. Mrs. 721 Main.
Loper Mary Mrs. 168 Windsor av.
Lyman Mary J. 214 Jefferson.
Lynch Ada, 75 Pratt.
Mahoney Ellen J. 10 Atlantic.
Mallon Jennie, 10 Chapel.
Mandrus Delia, 182 Market.
Mangan Mary, 102 Hungerford.
Manogue Kate, 108 Windsor.
Marceau Corrinne, 767 Park.
Marceau R. Mrs. 767 Park.
Marlow Agnes, 19 Wadsworth.
Marlow Mary M. 19 Affleck.
Maroney Lizzie I. 6 Village.
Maroney Mary, 6 Village.

Marsh Ellen Mrs. 1034 Main.
Marshall Julia, 37 Brook.
Marshall Sarah A. 50 Cedar.
Mathies Nettie Mrs. 566 Main.
McCarty Elizabeth A. 214 Bellevue.
McClunie Annie, 464 Farmington.
McCormick L. J. Mrs. r. 59 Albany.
McDonnell Elizabeth, 65 Flower.
McFarlan Bert, u. 89 Main.
McGrath Nora A. 43 Madison av.
McKenzie Jessie, 294 Maple.
McKeon Mary L. 789 Main.
McKeown Annie, 205 Woodland.
McKinnon James Mrs. 50 Albany.
McLaughlin Kate, 1232 Main.
McLean Annie Mrs. 117 Jefferson.
McNerny Margaret E. 721 Main.
McNulty Sarah, 1416 Broad.
Miller Emory H. Mrs. 18 Benton.
Mills Hattie V. 370 Asylum, rm. 7.
Milton Carrie A. 211 Barbour.
Miskill Minnie, 721 Main.
Mooers M. E. Mrs. 49 Park.
Moore Emma N. 635 Main.
Mulcahy Johanna, 114 Hungerford.
Mullen Mary E. 21 Grace.
Mullen N. A. 68 Pratt, room 26.
Murphy Cath. A. J. 83 Avon.
Murphy John Mrs. 20 Walnut.
Myers Hattie W. Mrs. 312 Asylum.
Nelson Cora A. Mrs. 241 Bellevue.
Nolan Jennie C. 27 Beach.
Noonan Alice F. 18 Beach.
Noonan Mary, 18 Beach.
Northrup Geo. Mrs. 150 Franklin.
O'Callaghan Julia, 1081 Main.
O'Callaghan Nana, 1081 Main.
O'Day Minnie, 48 John.
Officer John W. Mrs. 149 Weth.
O'Neil Mary E. 904 Main.
O'Neill Annie, 64 Ashley.
Parnell Nora, 2u. 1828 Broad.
Patten Bessie, 206 Asylum.
Peck Mary A. W. Mrs. 1 Goodman.
Peckham Mary J. Mrs. 64 Williams.
Phelps Mary J. 289 Allyn.
Porter Gertrude L. 13 Ellsworth.
Potter L. T. Mrs. 1208 Main.
Pratt George W. Mrs. 1199 Main.
Price Dora, 868 Park.
Quirk Kate, 1 Imlay.
Reardon Abbie J. 115 Collins.
Renshaw Mary, 203 High.
Ressler Ida, 42 North.
Riordon Mary E. 71 Sigourney.
Roach Mary J. 51 Spring.
Robinson H.M. J. Mrs. 312 Asylum.
Rockwell E. H. Mrs. 44 Hopkins.
Roessler Marie, 127 Albany.
Rogers Ellen M. Mrs. 943 Main.
Rogers Laura A. Mrs. 546 Main.
Rooney Kate, 1071 Main.
Root E. Buell Mrs. 124 Ann.
Root Louise Mrs. 166 Windsor.
Root Winifred, 39 Elm.
Sammis Lydia N., New Park.
Sansabrino Rosie, 12 Kilbourn.
Schaffer Pauline, 277 Market.
Scollon Mary, 110 Windsor.
Seery Mary, 60 Fairmount.
Senior Susan A. Mrs. 51 Pratt.
Seymour Myra A. 81 Wadsworth.
Shaw Nellie D. Mrs. 177 Asylum.
Sheedy Cassie, 1232 Main.
Sheridan Annie F. 8 Wellington.
Sherlock Mattie L. 987 Main.
Sjogren Amanda, 14 Affleck.
Smith Alvina M. 3 Pleasant.
Smith Mary E. 39 Congress.

Smith S. C. Mrs. 69 Laurel.
Soloman M. Mrs. r. 22 Trumbull.
Sparks Ella Mrs. 16 Buckingham.
Spear John M. Mrs. 14 Benton.
Sperry Susan M. Mrs. 877 Main.
Stewart Jennie L. 200 Wethersfield.
St. John Daness Mrs. 42½ Windsor.
Stone Anna M. 11 Squire.
Storrs Ella Mrs. r. 875 Main.
Stowe Henry Mrs. 1112 Main.
Sutherland Margaret Mrs. 22 Elm.
Talcott W. L. Mrs. 1059 Main.
Tansley M. A. 75 Pratt.
Thibeault Lucy, 545 Main.
Toohey Thomas J. Mrs. 45 Park.
Towne Elizabeth Mrs. 4 Village
Towne Hattie A. 43 Seyms.
Treat Emeline Mrs. 110 High.
Varney Jennie S. Mrs. 270 Main.
Vibbert L. M. Mrs. 71 Asylum.
Vossler Adella E. 160 Allyn.
Warren Jessie C. Mrs. 363 Main.
West Harriet Mrs. 7 Pleasant.
Welch & Farrell, 1295 Main.
Welch Margaret, 13 Belden.
Welsh Mary A. 80 Walnut.
Wells N. G. Mrs. 68 Pratt.
Werner Nellie L. 847 Main.
Whalen Lucy, 50 John.
Whitaker Emma, 23 New Britain.
White Ida E. 74 Spring.
White Mary A. 27 Seyms.
Whitehead Etta F. Mrs. 2 Martin.
Whitehurst L. M. Mrs. 858 Park.
Wilkie Ida, 11 Russell.
Williams Menervia A. 26 Sanford.
Wilson Jane D. 322 Wethersfield.
Wilson Mary L. 1199 Main.
Winship Ellen M. 11 Wethersfield.
Wood Prudence Mrs. 111 Windsor.
Woods Lizzie V. 54 Governor.
Woodward Susan E. 17 Florence.
Wythe Frances Mrs. 964 Broad.

## DRILLING MACHINES.

DWIGHT SLATE MACHINE CO. 13 Central. *See page 526.*
PRATT & WHITNEY CO. 1 Flower. *See page 523.*
SIGOURNEY TOOL CO. 9 Sigourney. *See page 527.*
WOODWARD & ROGERS, 133–135 Sheldon. *See page 526.*

## DRILL MACHINES.

SLATE DWIGHT & CO. 13 Central. *See page 525.*

## DRILLS.

BILLINGS & SPENCER CO. 142 Russ. *See page 531.*

## DRIVEN WELLS.

GRANT C. L. 22 Belden. *See page 535.*

## DRIVING PARKS.
*See Trotting Parks.*

## Drop Forging Furnaces.

BILLINGS & SPENCER CO. 142 Russ. *See page 531.*

## DROP FORGINGS.

BILLINGS & SPENCER CO. 142 Russ. *See page 531.*

## DROP HAMMERS.

BILLINGS & SPENCER CO. 142 Russ. *See page* 531.
PRATT & WHITNEY CO. 1 Flower. *See page* 528.

## DRUGGISTS BOX Mfrs.

HARTFORD BOX CO. 223 State. *See page* 532.

## DRUGGISTS SUNDRIES.

BROWN, THOMSON & CO. 942 Main. *See page* 499.
McGee Mfg. Co. 78 Park.

## DRUG STORES.

*See Apothecaries.*

Bell Charles H. 639 Main.
Coleman William H. 1391 Main.
Crary Edwin, 206 Park.
Daley Joseph T. 200 Franklin.
Drobegg Charles, 60 Village.
Edwards Fred. B. 55 Farmington.
GOODRICH S. & CO. 1203 Main. *See page* 164.
GOODWIN L. H. 852 Main. *See page* 165.
Graves Frank E. 115 Main.
Greenbaum Moses, 90 Albany.
Griswold Charles R. 1129 Main.
Hannon Charles P. 110 Trumbull.
Hawley V. E. Co. 254 Asylum.
Hubbard Charles L. 407 Main.
Kennelly & Co. 329 Main.
Lester Wm. W. 367 Capitol.
Loeffler George J. 705 Main.
Marwick A. Jr. 877 Asylum.
McCorkle Geo. A. 1189 Main.
Modern Pharmacy, 299 Main.
Morgan Nath'l K. 320 Windsor av.
NEWTON PHILO W. 142 Asylum. *See page* 35.
Noble Drug Co. 153 Wethersfield.
O'Flaherty M. 391 Main.
Packard C. F. 12 New Britain.
Parkville Pharmacy, Park corner New Park.
Pierce Austin D. 379 Windsor av.
RAPELYE CHARLES A. 376 Asylum & 853 Main. *See page* 301.
Risley Leon S. 385 Capitol.
Sawtelle Alfred W. 808 Main.
Service John W. 243 Park.
SEINSOTH JOHN J., South End Drug Store, 12 Maple & 5 Congress. *See page* 324.
Shannon T. R. & Co. 143 Trumbull.
Sissa A. P. 56 Windsor.
Stoughton D. G. & Co. 204 State and Park c. New Park.
Townsend Heber, 9 New Britain.
Tracy D. Wallace, 515 Main.
Trinity Pharmacy, 169 Zion.
Umberfield Burton L. 619 Capitol.
Veterinary Drug Store, 214 Pearl.
Williams H. E. 839 Park.
Williams John K. 973 Main.

## DRUM CORPS.

*See Bands of Music.*

## DRY DOCKS.

HARTFORD & N. Y. TRANSPORTATION CO. "Dutch Point," office 285 State. *See page* 554.

## DRY GOODS.

*See also Carpets; Milliners, etc.*

WHOLESALE.

BROWN, THOMSON & CO. 942 Main. *See page* 499.
Goldschmidt H. & Co. 52 Ann.

RETAIL.

*See also Yankee Notions.*

Alexander Moses, 144 Front.
Atkins Samuel, 128 Maple.
BROWN, THOMSON & CO. 942 Main. *See page* 499.
Cohen Gustav, 115 Front.
Fox G. & Co. 956 Main.
Furmansky Abe, 142 Front.
Goldberg Minnie, 881 Park.
Greenberg Kune, 84 Morgan.
Griswold John H. 347 Main.
Hills C. S. & Co. 885 Main.
Horwitz Charles, 174½ Front.
Israeli E. 232 Front.
Keller Bros. 579 Main.
Kofsky Bernhard, 300 Park.
Libman Lewis, 208 Front.
Malley Abram, 87½ Windsor.
Malley Simon, 142 Front.
McFarland Elizabeth, 761 Park.
Pintus Sarab, 64 Morgan.
Proller Moriss, 111 Front.
Resnick Philip, 207 Front.
Richmond Jacob, 172 Front.
Rome & Ganz, 202 Front.
Sack Harris, 70 Morgan.
SAGE, ALLEN & CO. 896 Main. *See page* 317.
Sawyer George O. 885 Main.
Simon, Ragovin & Co. 78 Pratt.
Stein Moriss, 140 Front.
Teisler H. A. & Co. 54 Pleasant.
Wise, Smith & Co. 921 Main.

## DYERS.

*See also Clothes Cleaners.*

Arons Sam, 296 Pearl.
Mosesson S. 148 Front.
New England Fancy D. Wks. 94 Tru.
PATTEN H. E. 37 Wells. *See page* 591.
Perrault Louis, 36 Pratt.
Rohrmayer George, 11 Wells & 88 Trumbull.

## DYE STUFFS.

BEACH & CO. 209 State. *See page* 591.

## DYE WOODS.

BEACH & CO. 209 State. *See page* 591.

## DYNAMO ELECTRIC MACHINE Mfrs.

*See also Electric.*

EDDY ELECTRIC MFG. CO. *See page* 536.

## EARTHENWARE.

*See Crockery.*

## EDGE TOOL Mfrs.

COLLINS CO. *See page* 521.

## EGG FOOD.

Sturtevant F. C. 216 State.

## EGGS.

BLANCHARD G. G. 40 Vine. *See page* 61.

## EGGS FOR HATCHING.

ELM POULTRY YARD. *See pages* 185–170.

## ELASTIC STOCKINGS.

GOODRICH S. C. & CO. 1203 Main. *See page* 164.
RAPELYE CHARLES A. 376 Asylum & 853 Main. *See page* 301.

## ELECTRIC BELL HANGERS.

AHERN JAMES, 280 Asylum. *See page* 505.
HALLIDAY W. H. 131 Front. *See page* 506.
REYNOLDS & CO. 85 Pratt. *See page* 507.
TRUMBULL BROS. 190 Pearl. *See page* 420.

## ELECTRIC BURGLAR ALARMS.

HALLIDAY W. H. 131 Front. *See page* 506.

## ELECTRIC DROP FORGINGS.

BILLINGS & SPENCER CO. 142 Russ. *See page* 531.

## ELECTRIC FANS.

RICE & BALDWIN, 214 Pearl. *See page* 554.

## ELECTRIC GAS LIGHTING.

HALLIDAY W. H. 131 Front. *See page* 506.
STARBUCK R. M. & SON, 249 Pearl. *See page* 425.
TRUMBULL BROS. 190 Pearl. *See page* 420.

## ELECTRIC LAMPS.

PERKINS ELECTRIC SWITCH MFG. CO. *See page* 536.

## ELECTRIC LIGHTING.

TRUMBULL BROS. 190 Pearl. *See page* 420.

## ELECTRIC LIGHTS.

HALLIDAY W. H. 131 Front. *See page* 506.
Hartford Light and Power Co. 266 Pearl.
HARTFORD ELECTRIC LIGHT CO. 266 Pearl. *See page* 542.
HART & HEGEMAN MFG. CO. 26 High. *See page* 539.
Knox Charles N. 210 Pearl.
REYNOLDS & CO. 85 Pratt. *See page* 507.
STARBUCK R. M. & SON, 249 Pearl. *See page* 425.

## ELECTRIC MASSAGE.

Ponsaing John, 1524 Broad.

## ELECTRIC MFR'S.

EDDY ELECTRIC MFG. CO. *See page* 536.

## ELECTRIC MOTORS.
EDDY ELECTRIC MFG. CO. See page 586.
LEE H. K. 223 State. See p. 539.
TRUMBULL BROS. 190 Pearl. See page 420.

## Electric Power Furnished.
HARTFORD ELECTRIC LIGHT CO. 266 Pearl. See page 542.

## ELECTRIC PROTECTION.
Fielding W. C. 847 Main.
Holmes Electric Protection Co. 903 Main.

## ELECTRIC SCHOOL.
Y. M. C. A. 823 Pearl. See page 704–705.

## ELECTRIC SWITCHES.
PERKINS ELECTRIC SWITCH MFG. CO. 83 Woodbine. See page 586.

## ELECTRICAL ENGINEERS.
See Electricians.
WOLCOTT & DARBY, 49 Pearl. See page 493.

## Electrical Instrument Mfg.
HART & HEGEMAN MFG. CO. 26 High. See page 589.
SIGOURNEY TOOL CO. 9 Sigourney. See page 537.

## ELECTRICAL INSULATION Mfr.
BILLINGS & SPENCER CO. 142 Russ. See page 531.
JOHNS–PRATT CO. 555 Capitol. See page 540.

## Electrical Maintenance.
TRUMBULL BROS. 190 Pearl. See page 420.

## Electrical St. R. R. Supplies.
BILLINGS & SPENCER CO. 142 Russ. See page 531.
JOHNS–PRATT CO. 555 Capitol. See page 540.

## ELECTRICAL SUPPLIES.
AHERN JAMES, 280 Asylum. See page 505.
Berkshire Electrical Co. 284 Asy.
BILLINGS & SPENCER CO. 142 Russ. See page 531.
EDDY ELECTRIC MFG. CO. See page 586.
FRANCIS & CO. 859 Main. See page 546.
Gibbs Electric Co. 302 Asylum.
HART & HEGEMAN MFG. CO. 26 High. See page 589.
LEE H. K. 223 State. See page 539.
OAKES THOMAS & SON, 11 Haynes. See page 278.
REYNOLDS & CO. 85 Pratt. See page 507.
SIGOURNEY TOOL CO. See page 537.
TRUMBULL BROS. 190 Pearl. See page 420.
Whiton Andrew, 5 Kinsley.

## ELECTRICAL WIRING CONTRACTORS.
OAKES THOMAS & SON, 11 Haynes. See page 278.

## ELECTRICAL WORK.
HUBBARD & MORTSON, 42 Union pl. See page 428.

## ELECTRICIANS and ENGINEERS.
Carroll Samuel J. 596 Main.
Campbell Terence J. 20 Park.
Clark W. M. 22 Church.
Dustin Charles E. 11 Central.
Furlong L. F. 287 Asylum.
Knox Charles N. 210 Pearl.
Hurley & Staudinger, 223 State.
Mather Richard H. 1169 Windsor av.
OAKES THOS. & SON, 11 Haynes. See page 278.
REYNOLDS & CO. 85 Pratt. See page 507.
RICE & BALDWIN, 214 Pearl. See page 554.
STARBUCK R. M. & SON, 249 Pearl. See page 425.
Stirling Clarence C. 66 State.
TRUMBULL BROS. 190 Pearl. See page 420.
WOLCOTT & DARBY, 49 Pearl. See page 493.

## ELECTRO BATHS.
MERRIAM A. E. COLT MRS. 926 Main. See page 257.

## ELECTRO-PLATER.
Alexander John, r. 39 Trumbull.
Hotchkiss Eugene E. 182 Allyn.

## ELECTRO PLATING MACHINE Mfrs.
EDDY ELECTRIC MFG. CO. Windsor t. See page 586.

## ELECTRO-THERAPEUTICS.
TAYLOR NELLIE L. Mrs. 24 Hopkins. See page 353.
Benedict Carrie M. H. 721 Main.

## ELECTROTYPERS.
AMERICAN PUBLISHING CO. 424 Asylum. See page 473.
Lockwood William H. 41 Trumbull.
MUGFORD A. 177 Asylum. See page 476.

## ELEVATOR MOTORS.
EDDY ELECTRIC MFG. CO. Windsor t. See page 586.

## ELEVATORS.
IN THE FOLLOWING BUILDINGS:
See also Public Halls, etc.
Ætna Ins. Co. 666 Main.
Ætna Life Insurance Co. 650 Main.
Allyn House, 152 Asylum.
Ballerstein building, 904 Main.
Batterson building, 870 Asylum.
Belmont The, 14 Church.
Capitol, on Bushnell Park.
Cheney building, 926 Main.
Conn. M. L. I. Co. building, 783 Mn.
County building, 85 Trumbull.
Courant building, 66 State.
First National Bank, 50 State.
Fox building, 956 Main.
Goodwin building, 17 Haynes.
Hartford Hotel, 865 Allyn.
Hartford Fire Ins. Co. 58 Trumbull.
Hartford Life Ins. Co. 252 Asylum.
Hfd. Trust Co. building, 764 Main.
Heublein Hotel, 98 Wells.
Hills building, 88 Asylum.
Hotel Capitol, 389 Main.
Linden, 427 Main.
Munsill Mary J. 2 Wethersfield.
Neal, Goff & Inglis Co. 980 Main.
Phœnix Fire Ins. Co. 64 Pearl.
Phœnix Mutual Life Ins. Co. 49 Pl.
Phœnix Nat Bank building, 808 Mn.
Plimpton Mfg. Co. 252 Pearl.
Post Office, 65 State.
Robbins Bros. 633 Main.
Sage–Allen, 900 Main.
Sawyer G. O. & Co. 885 Main.
Seidler & May, 318 Pearl.
Tucker E. Sons, 100 Trumbull.
Unity building, 68 Pratt.
Waverly building, 721 Main.
Way Hardware Co. 866 Main.
Wise, Smith & Co. 921 Main.
Y. M. C. A. building, Pearl c. Jewell.

## EMBALMERS.
See also Undertakers.
FOSTER & FURREY, 1166 Main. See page 150.
HILLS & MARCHANT, 58 Ann. See page 189.
McCARTHY & AHERN, 194 Pearl. See page 248.

## EMBROIDERY and STAM'G·
See also Paper Patterns.
Herbert Art Co. 726 Main.
Homan N. L. Miss, 82 Trumbull.
Hudson Hattie B. Mrs. 119 Allyn.
Hunt James Mrs. 89 Pratt.

## EMIGRANT AGENTS.
See Tickets.
Conroy John F. 548 Main.

## EMORY STROPS.
HURD OLIVER. See page 586.

## EMPLOYMENT.
Buckley B. A. Miss, 119 Trumbull.
Dibble Emma E. Mrs. 54 Pratt.
Dodge Employment Agency, 98½ Trumbull.
Fox Alice S. 119 Trumbull.
Hetzel Geo. J. Mrs. 149 Market.
Martel Ann Mrs. 596 Main.
Registry for Nurses, 67 Farmington.
Webster B. F. Jr. 154 Allyn.

## ENAMELING OVENS.
CULLEN M. 44 Ann. See page 506.

## ENGINES.
STRONG IRA J. 267 Asylum. See page 524.

## ENGINE BUILDERS.
LEE H. K. 223 State. See p. 539.
STRONG IRA J. 267 Asylum. See page 524.

## ENGINE MFRS.
*See Steam Engines.*

## ENGINE REPAIRERS.
*See Machinists; Steam Engines.*
LEE H. K. 223 State. *See p.* 539.
STRONG IRA J. 267 Asylum. *See page 524.*

## ENGINEERS.
*See also Machinists; Mechanical Engineers.*
BUTTS & CROSBY, 49 Pearl. *See page 427.*
LEE H. K. 223 State. *See page* 539.
Perkins T. C. & Co. 14 State.
PICKERING W. H. & CO. 110 Commerce. *See page* 537.
RICHARDS F. H. 803 Main. *See outside front cover.*
Stibbs George H. 50 Church.
STRONG IRA J. 267 Asylum. *See page 524.*

## ENGINEERS' SUPPLIES.
ANDREWS & CREEDON, 446 Asylum. *See page 542.*
KNOX FRANK J. 2 So. Ann. *See page 220.*
PICKERING W. H. & CO. 110 Commerce. *See page* 537.

## ENGRAVERS.
Clark Alfred C. 871 Main.
Gelbart Theo. F. 427 Main.
Hampshire Parker, 847 Main.
HARTFORD ENGRAVING CO. 66 State. *See page* 477.
Leigh Enoch, 32 Ward.
MUGFORD A. 177 Asylum. *See page* 476.
PECK R. S. & CO. 26 High. *See page* 473.
PERKINS JAMES A. & CO. 863 Main. *See page 290.*
Reuss Hugo, 30 Asylum.
Weller Robert Jr. 180 Asylum.

## ENVELOPE Mfrs.
Plimpton Mfg. Co. 252 Pearl.

## ENVELOPE MOISTENER.
Dawson Joseph, 704 Main.

## ENVELOPE PAPER Mfrs.
HARTFORD MANILLA CO. 1 So. Ann. *See page 479.*

## ETCHINGS.
ECKHARDT J. H. CO. 687 Main. *See page 418.*
VORCE A. D. CO. 752 Main. *See page 418.*

## EXECUTORS.
*See Administrators.*

## EXHAUST HEADS.
LEE H. K. r. 223 State. *See p.* 539.

## EXPERT BOOK-KEEPER.
Knapp Frederic, 14 Columbia.
STEWART GORDON W., P. O. address, Portland, Conn.

## EXPERT IN PATENTS.
RICHARDS F. H. 803 Main. *See outside front cover.*

## EXPRESSES.
*Out of Town Stages and Expresses, see page 559.*
ADAMS EXPRESS CO. 805 Main and Union Depot. *See page 552.*
Bristol Express, 46 Ann. *See p.* 559.
Burnside Express. *See page 559.*
East Hartford Ex. *See page 559.*
Glastonbury Expresses. *See p.* 559.
Manchester Express. *See p.* 559.
New England Despatch Co. (Bill Brothers). *See page 550.*
N. Y. & Boston Despatch Express Co. 236 Asylum.
Rocky Hill Express. *See p.* 559.
South Manchester Ex. *See p.* 559.
Wethersfield Accommodation Express. *See page 559.*
Wethersfield Ex. *See page 559.*
Windsor Express. *See page 559.*

### CITY.
*See also Carmen.*
Banning William A. 188 Barbour.
Barnard E. R. agent, 35 Woodbridge.
BILL BROS. 46 Ann. *See page* 550.
Carlin Joseph. 42 Hudson.
Carr Peter, 42 New Britain.
Clough Bros. 11 Morris.
Cornwell Albert E. 335 Sheldon.
Deming Frederick A. 20 Morgan.
Deming Roswell M. 478 Wethersfield.
Dickinson Calvin P. 46 Pratt.
Doody Thomas, 57 Hudson.
DOWNING & PERKINS, 128 Commerce. *See page 552.*
Eagan James T. 48 Wilson.
Egan John, 25 Greenwood.
Eakins John, 15 Hawthorn.
Finnerty Peter, 873 Broad.
Gaffey Peter J. Union Depot.
Gaines David L. 16 Alden.
George Henry, 4 Central.
George William H. 20 Chapel.
Gunshanan James, 19 Affleck.
Kallenbach John M. 42 Madison.
Losty Patrick, 115 Zion.
Martin David, 20 Affleck.
McKone Peter, 152 Zion.
McLean Dwight, 186 Albany.
Merchants Package Delivery, 44 Asylum.
O'Brien Dennis, 141 Barbour.
O'Brien Thomas, 66 Windsor.
Pendergast Dennis, 20 Cedar.
PEOPLE'S EXPRESS CO. 42 Union. *See page 559.*
Porter A. Leonard, 115 Barbour.
Powers George, 53 Windsor.
Rau Edward F. 7 Central.
Roberts John W. 930 Park.
Ryan Edward, 413 Broad.
Smith John M. 1029 Main.
Sullivan Jeremiah, 470 Broad.
Stafford John, 71 New Britain.
Steer Trayton, 84 Fairmount.
Waterman Jas. H. 1281 Main.
White C. J. 88 Vernon.

## EXTRACTS.
BEACH & CO. 209-211 State. *See page 591.*
Morse Charles S. 529 Broad.
SISSON T. & CO. 729 Main. *See page 560.*

## FANCY DRY GOODS.
*See Dry Goods—Retail.*

## FARM LOANS.
*See Western Farm Loans.*

## FAST FREIGHT.
BILL BROS. 46 Ann. *See page* 550.
Penn. R. R. Freight Office, 18 State.

## FEATHER BEDS CLEANED.
PATTEN H. E. 37 Wells. *See page 591.*

## FEATHER DUSTER Mfrs.
WHITTEMORE W. L. & SON. 176-178 Allyn. *See page 482.*

## FEED WATER HEATERS.
DAVIS I. B. & SON, 40 Cushman. *See page 546.*
LEE H. K. 223 State. *See page* 539.

## FENCE MFR.
Day P. R. & Son, 1196 Main.
LINCOLN & CO. 54 Arch. *See page 522.*

## FERTILIZERS.
Bowler Fertilizer Co. 218 State.
Ellsworth Frederick, 44 Market.
Stafford H. H. 242 State.

## FINANCIAL AGENT.
Chapman & Mucklow, 370 Asylum.

## FIRE ARMS Mfrs.
COLT'S PATENT FIRE-ARMS MF'G. CO. 17 Vand. *See page* 542.
Gatling Gun Co. 17 Vredendale.

## FIRE BRICKS.
BLODGETT & CLAPP CO. 51 Market. *See page 541.*
ENSWORTH L. L. & SON, 104 Front. *See page 592.*

## FIRE ENGINES.
*See page 677.*

## FIRE ESCAPES.
BUELLESBACH W. 75 Commerce. *See page 478.*

## FIRE HOSE MFR.
JEWELL BELTING COMPANY, 15 Trumbull. *See page* 539.

## FIRE HYDRANT Mfg.
PRATT & CADY, 556 Capitol. *See page 527.*

## FIREPLACES.
*See Mantels.*

## FIREWORKS.
Ætna Pyrotechnic Co. 377 Asylum.
BREWER C. S. & CO. 240 Asylum. *See page 62.*

## FISHING TACKLE.
*See also Sporting Goods.*
ANDRUS & HERMANN, 300 Asylum. *See page 464.*
ANDRUS & NÆDELE CO. 272 Asylum. *See page 485.*

## FISH MARKETS.
*See also Markets.*
WHOLESALE.
CHAMBERLIN S. D. & SONS, 179 State. *See page 89.*
FITZGERALD RANSOM N. 44–46 Market. *See page 144.*
RETAIL.
Abbe L. G. 188 State.
CITIZENS MEAT & FISH, JOHN FLYNN, 493 Main. *See page 587.*
- Clark & Crane, 323 Asylum.
Harding & Holbrook, 1165 Main.
HONISS T. A. 30 State. *See p. 589.*
Jones Wayland H. 419 Garden.
Michael Solomon, 205 Front.
Moore & Holbrook, 275 Main.
NEWTON & BURNET,319 Asylum. *See page 487.*
Thresher Arthur, 494 Wethersfield.

## FLAGGING.
*See Stone Yards.*

## FLAG Mfrs.
CHENEY BROS. ( ☞ silk )84 Mor. *See page 545 & inside front cover.*
FORBES EDWARD F. 3 Asylum. *See page 148.*
HARTFORD DECORATING CO. 177 Asylum. *See page 249.*

## FLAGS.
McCLUNIE J. ALEX. 177 Asylum. *See page 249.*
ROBERTS S. F. 124 State. *See page 502.*

## FLORISTS, NURSERYMEN.
*See Seed Stores; Landscape Gardeners.*
Bassinger Paul A. 126 Albany.
Brooks David W. 53 Farmington and 5 Fairfield.
BROWN, THOMSON & CO. 942 Main. *See page 499.*
Coombs John,702 Main & 118 Benton
Harper John M. 2 Windsor av.
Marchant Robert, 13 Huntington.
McClunie George G. 805 Main.
McRonald Thomas, 66 Mahl.
Munsell Charles C. 37 Trumbull.
Newton J. G. D. 810 Park.
Osborn Geo. S. 248 Sargeant.
RICHARDSON F. W. 680 Main. East Hartford. *See page 731.*
Scheld Theodore, Caya av.
Spear David A. 242 Asylum.
SWENSON CHARLES K. 210 Asylum. *See page 565.*
Wheeler Jane Mrs. r. 64 Dean
Whiting Alfred, Whiting st. W.H. t.
Young James, 80 Whitney.
PRIVATE GARDENERS.
Delbar Stephen, for Gov. Bulkeley, 136 Washington.
Drake John, for Mrs. Colt, 30 Weth.
Goodwin George A. for Alfred Whiting, W.H.t.
May Wm. B. for J. J. Goodwin, 83 Woodland.
O'Neil John, for Mark Twain, 351 Farmington.
Patchet Robert, for Rev. F. Goodwin, 185 Woodland.
Relihan Michael J. for Miss Collins, 1064 Asylum.
Smith James,for Miss Ellen M.Case, 305 Farmington.

## FLOUR, GRAIN, FEED.
*See also Grist Mills.*
Daniels Mill Co. 40 Elm.
PEASE CHARLES A. 462 and 1123 Main. *See page 586.*
POTTER & PAYNE, 405–407 Alyn. *See page 586.*
SMITH, NORTHAM & CO. 129 State. *See page 590.*
TUCKER & GOODWIN, 8 and 12 Hurlburt. *See page 585.*
Yates E. P. & Co. 1411 Main.

## FLOWER SEEDS.
*See Seed Stores.*

## FLUE LININGS.
ANDREWS & PECK. *See p. 509.*

## FLY ROD MAKERS.
ANDRUS & HERMANN, 300 Asylum. *See page 484.*
ANDRUS & NÆDELE CO. 272 Asylum. *See page 485.*

## FOLDING BEDS.
FULLER C. C. & CO. *See p. 500.*

## FORGINGS & CASTINGS.
COLLINS CO. *See page 521.*

## FORGING SCHOOL.
Y.M.C.A. 323 Pearl. *See pages 704–705.*

## FORWARDERS.
*See Expresses.*

## FOUNDRY.
Laragy Patrick, 114 Grove.
Phœnix Brass FoundryCo.223State.

## FRAME MAKER.
*See also Pictures, Frames, etc.*
Wentworth George B. 730 Main.

## FRESCO PAINTERS.
*See House Painters.*
BONNER, PRESTON & CO., 843 Main. *See page 425.*
Crosscup & Gaudett, 75 Pratt.
DARBY THEODORE T. 37 Martin. *See page 529.*
Grierson P. C. 41 Laurel.
Kassenbrook Theodore, 262 Allyn.
LANGE & FLAD, 13 Central. *See page 512.*
Pietsch & Hinkley, 1148 Main.
VanHoudt Louis, 9 John.

## FRUIT.
WHOLESALE.
*See Commission Merchants.*
Berry P. & Sons, 4 American.
BREWER C. S. & Co. 240 Asylum. *See page 69.*
Chesky H. & Co. 1076 Main.
Marks Brothers, 39 Church.
Slate D. N. & Co. 12 Ann.
RETAIL.
Albert Louis, 213 Front.
Alfarno Tony, 31 Laurel.
Angelo Dan. 365 Capitol.
Atro James D. 1007 Main.
Bennedetto George, 64 Morgan.
Bertly George, 261 Main.
Blazier J. F. & Co. 413 Main.

Bonee Joseph, 1043 Main.
Bonee Michael, 2 Ford.
Bonee Peter, 488 Asylum.
Boniface James, 47½ Francis.
Calano Joe, 25 Flower.
Calanos J. 216 Allyn.
Campagna John, 519 Main.
Carmine Delia, 83 Windsor.
Cersosimo Joseph &Co. 553 Asylum.
Champmadi Tony, 225 Park.
Colano Joseph, 15 Central.
Dabato Carmine, 491 Main.
Daleno G. A. 262 New Park.
DeNezzo Frank, 82 Morgan.
D'Esopo Domonic, 1175 Main.
D'Esopo D. & M. 269 Asylum.
D'Esopo James, 197 State.
Ferguson Albin S. 53 Albany.
George A. 1197 Main.
Gilstein Jacob, 215 Front.
Harris Max, 80 Morris.
HILLS & CO. 872–874 Asylum. *See page 485.*
Huberman Moriss, 198 Front.
Lamenza Tony, 48 Union pl.
Lavria Donato, 1055 Main.
LeRoy Bros. 1363 Main.
Manecy Frank, 335 Asy.& 336 Pearl.
Manelli Dominick, 36 State.
Monacella Angelina Mrs.79 Windsor
Motto Nicola, 8 Maple.
Muscarie Thomas, 18 Church.
NEWTON, ROBERTSON & CO. 342 Asylum. *See page 486.*
Potenza James, 85 Albany.
Preston James, 141 Front.
Rago Frank, 22 Union pl.
Rates Michael, 81 Albany.
Rates Thomas & Co. 90½ Albany.
Rizy Joseph A. 41 Laurel.
Rizzo Leon, 59 Spruce.
Robertson Lafayette J. 990 Main.
Rosenbaum Jake, 55 Windsor.
Rosita Salvador, 295 Park.
Sardella Leberato, 173 Main.
Senato Samuel, 85 Sigourney.
Shetchman Louis,81 Windsor.
Soby James, 195 State.
Spugnardo Liborio, 10½ Village.
Tremont Antonio, 81 Pearl.
Ursone Donato, 130½ Trumbull.
Viola Tony, 950 Broad.
Wechsler Sam, 51 Morgan.
Woolley William F. 34 Church.
Yoreo Paul, 353 Main.

## FUNERAL DIRECTORS.
FOSTER & FURREY, 1166 Main. *See page 150.*
HILLS & MARCHANT, 58 Ann. *See page 189.*
McCARTY & AHERN, 149 Pearl. *See page 248.*

## FURNACES.
*See Agents; Stoves, etc.*
Allen Ripley D. 8 Grove.
BLISS EDWARD, 1263 Main. *See page 494.*

## FURNACES REPAIRED.
BLISS EDWARD, 1263 Main. *See page 494.*

## FURNISHED ROOMS.
Cunningham Michael, 114 State.
MARTIN MARY V. 180 Ann.

## FURNITURE.
### See Mantels.
Abels George F. 1180 Main.
BECK CURT E. 262 Allyn. See page 505.
BRAND ROBERT, 5½ Morris. See page 507.
BROWN, THOMSON & CO. 942 Main. See page 499.
Bruce, Filley & Co. 103 Asylum.
Capitol City Furniture House, 78 Sheldon.
FENN LINUS T. 613 Main. See page 501.
FLINT GEO. W. & CO. 61 Asylum. See page 147.
FULLER C. C. & CO. 16 Ford. See page 500.
Kellogg Julius A. Boston Furniture House, 149 Asylum.
MÆRCKLEIN H. 104 Asylum. See page 562.
Meyer Henry, r. 585 Main.
NEAL, GOFF & INGLIS CO. 980 Main. See page 498.
NEW ENGLAND TYPE WRITER EXCHANGE, (typewriters) 847 Main. See page 422.
Robbins Bros. 633 Main.
Sceery Thomas, 10 Church.
SEIDLER & MAY, 306 to 318 Pearl. See page 500.
Smith Brothers, 1079 Main.
Spieske Henry, 1052 Main.

### MANUFACTURERS.
BISHOP E. C. & CO. 34 Capen. See page 60.

### POLISH.
Hartford Diamond Polish Co. 118 Asylum.
SMITH H. M. & CO. 301 Allyn. See page 419.

### REPAIRERS.
BECK CURT E. 262 Allyn. See page 505.
BRAND ROBERT, 5½ Morris. See page 507.
MARTIN J. H. 42 Seyms. See p. 244.
O'Brien Thomas J. 12 Elm.
Phipps Edward D. r. 1419 Main.
Schwarzer A. 38 Wells.
Stevens Daniel H. 81 Bentley.
TOPPING JAS. R. 784 Main. See page 541.
Williams John H. 133 Main.

### SECOND HAND.
Berkovitch Abraham, 64 Morgan.
Churchill George G. 643 Main.
Goodman Don Alonzo A., estate of 1090 Main.
Lux Peter & Son, 593 Main.
Porass Reuben, 298 Market.

## FURNITURE PACKING.
BRAND ROBERT, 5½ Morris. See page 507.

## FURS; FURRIERS.
### See also Hats, Caps, Etc.
Bassevitch & Glotzer, 1235 Main.
Burton Sperry Mrs. 68 Pratt.
Geary Thomas J. & Co. 845 Main.
Kenyon R. P. Co. 91 Pratt.
LOTKER KARL, 189 Main. See page 420.
Plasikowski A. 47 Pratt.

STILLMAN & CO. 59 Pratt. See outside front cover.
WILLIAMS ALFRED & SON, 99 Pratt. See page 379.

## Galvanised Iron CORNICES.
CULLEN C. A. 44 Ann. See p. 489.
STELLING FRED W. 93 Franklin. See page 487.

## GAME.
### See Market.
STEVENS NEWELL H. 329 Asylum. See page 845.

## GARBAGE CONTRACTOR.
BALF EDWARD CO. 2 Chapel. See page 426.

## GARDENERS.
### See Florists; Landscape Gardeners. Market Gardeners.

## GARDEN SEEDS.
### See Seed Stores.

## GAS ENGINES.
GRANT C. L. 22 Belden. See page 535.
HANNUM T. W. JR. 700 Main. See page 503.
NATIONAL MACHINE CO. 133 Sheldon. See page 540.

## GAS FITTERS.
Burns John J. 14 Trumbull.
MURRAY WM. A. 450 Main. See page 270.
STARBUCK R. M. & SON, 249 Pearl. See page 425.

## GAS FITTERS' TOOLS.
KNOX F. J. 2 So. Ann. See p. 220.
LANGDON THOMAS H. 228 Pearl. See page 224.

## GAS FIXTURES.
### See also Stoves and Tin Ware.
AHEARN JAMES, 280 Asylum. See page 505.
CONRAN FRANK E. 237 Asylum. See page 103.
CRAIG JOHN S. 59 Farmington. See page 109.
HOGAN W. B. & BRO. 81 Trumbull. See page 192.
LANGDON THOMAS H. 228 Pearl. See page 224.

### RE-FINISHED.
HOWARD JAMES L. & CO. 438 Asylum. See page 527.

## GASOLINE.
SISSON T. & CO. 729 Main. See page 560.

## GASOLINE ENGINES.
GRANT C. L. 22 Belden. See page 535.

## GAUGE Mfrs.
BILLINGS & SPENCER CO. 142 Russ. See page 581.
PRATT & WHITNEY CO. 1 Flower. See page 528.

## GEAR CUTTERS.
SIGOURNEY TOOL CO. 9 Sigourney. See page 527.

## GENERAL JOBBERS.
### See Whitewashers.
Phipps Edward D. r. 1419 Main.

## GENTS FURNISHINGS.
### See Men's, etc.
BROWN, THOMPSON & CO. See page 499.

## GERMAN DELICACIES.
### See Bologna.
Blumenthal Benjamin, 229 Market.
Conti Angelo & Co. 161 Front.

## GERMAN MASSAGE.
STUTZ EUGENE, 9 Asylum, rms. 3 and 4. See page 422.

## GERMAN TARTS.
STUECK J.W. JR. 1036 Main. See page 348.

## GILDERS.
### See Picture Frames; Art Galleries.

## GLASS.
### See House Painters.
ANDREWS & PECK, 88 Market. See page 509.
NIMS, WHITNEY & CO. 1170 Main. See page 511.
Peck Edward A. 88 Market.

## GLASSWARE.
### See Crockery.

## GOLD BEATERS.
Ashmead J. H. & Son, 41 Trumbull
Bladon Geo. L. 41 Trumbull.
Ney John M. & Co. 265 Asylum.
Swift M. & Sons, 100 Love Lane.

## GOLD MINES.
Seward Gold Mining Co. 49 Pearl.

## GRADING, &c.
### See Contractors.
Blanchfield John, 49 Sanford.

## GRAIN.
PEASE CHAS. A. 464 & 1122 Main. See page 589.
Phillips John R. 86 Hartford av. East Hartford t.
SMITH, NORTHAM & CO. 129 State. See page 590.

## GRAIN ELEVATORS.
SMITH, NORTHAM & CO. See page 590.

## GRAMOPHONE.
Gramophone The Hartford, 118 Asy.

## GRANITE WORKS.
THE NEW ENGLAND GRANITE WORKS, 1260 Main. See p. 555.

## GRASS SEEDS.
### See Seed Stores.

## GRATES.

Stoughton & Taylor, 38 Ann.

## GRAVESTONES,

*See Marble Yards.*

BREEN PATRICK J. 1070 Main
*See outside front cover.*
Slocumb F. R. 1 Ford & 40 Albany.
THE NEW ENGLAND GRANITE
WORKS. *See page 533.*

## GRINDING MACHINES.

DWIGHT SLATE MACHINE CO.
13 Central. *See page 525.*

## GRINDING MACHINE for TOOLS.

DWIGHT SLATE MACHINE CO.
13 Central. *See page 525.*

## GRINDSTONES.

FRANCIS & CO. 859 Main. *See page 546.*
Tuttle & Sons, 1072 Main.

## GRIST MILLS.

*See also Flour and Feed.*
Daniels' Mill Co. 40 Elm.
SMITH, NORTHAM & CO. 165
Windsor. *See page 590.*

## GROCERS, Wholesale.

Boardman Wm. & Sons Co. 304 Asy.
FITZGERALD RANSOM N. 44–46
Market. *See page 144.*
Foster & Co. 72 Front.
KIBBE E. S. CO. 149 State. *See page 587.*
LANE JOSEPH G. 224 State. *See page 589.*
LINCOLN, SEYMS & CO. 34 Market. *See page 588.*
Moseley G. W. & Son, 401 Allyn. *See page 586.*
POTTER & PAYNE, 406 Allyn. *See page 586.*
TUCKER & GOODWIN, 8 and 12
Hurlburt. *See page 585.*

RETAIL.

Adelsohn Sam, 70 Windsor.
Alderman James S. 472 Windsor av.
Alfier Vittorio, 174 Front.
Allen Brothers, 466 Main.
Andrews Geo. C. & Son, 20 N.B.
Ardinolfi Antonio, 176 Front.
Ashberg Harry, 84 North.
Avery George, 614 Capitol.
Barrows Charles L. Park c. Sisson.
Barrows & Thalheimer, 1111 Main.
Bashner Louis, 40 Commerce.
Bennes Abraham, 19 Hawthorn.
Bernard Luke, 121 Windsor av.
Berry Patrick E. 74 Franklin.
Blanchard George G. 170 Capen.
Bleik Isaac, 75½ Pleasant.
Block Himan, 72 Temple.
Blumenthal Benjamin, 229 Market.
Blumenthal Sarah, 80 Morgan.
Bonee Joseph, 81 Morgan.
Boston Branch, 745–751 Main.
Bowdoin & Son, 48 Clark.
Brandriss M. M. 34 Front.
Breen P. J. 75 Windsor.
Britt John, 102 Mather.
Burns Dominick, 304–310 Park.
Burns James, 184 Windsor.
Cady & Lombard, 69 Albany.

Callahan Mary Mrs. 36 North.
Callere Joseph, 264 Front.
Cannon & Flanagan, 230–236 Park.
Cardamon Peter, 5 Charles.
Carter David, 8 Church.
Case H. J. & Co. 983 Main.
Chase Oak A. 88 Walnut.
Cherniavsky Samuel, 42 North.
Cirelli Antonio, 26 Kilbourn.
Cirgiliano Vito, 40 Village.
Cit. Grocery & Provision Co. 267 Main.
Cohn Henry, 29 Mulberry.
Cohn Rosie, 55 Morgan.
Cole Henry, 2 Talcott.
Coledezky Ozias, 68 Morgan.
Conti Angelo, 161 Front.
Conway Charles, 293 Lawrence.
Co-operative Provision Co. 149 Bab.
Crawford Charles, 75 Charter Oak.
Crawford Co. 1248 Main.
Curtin Mary, 10 Ellery.
Dalton John, 77 Sheldon.
Davidson David, agent, 281 Park.
Davis Bros. 1451 Broad.
Davis J. W. 88 Grand.
DeBone Gustave, 38 Canton.
Delap Edward, 30 Trumbull.
D'Elia Carmine, 88 Windsor.
DeNezzo Frank, 82 Morgan.
DePalma Vincenzo, 280 Front.
DeWolfe Ephraim, 344 Windsor av.
Dianza Teresa, 92 Francis.
Dillon J. D. 244 Pearl.
Divinsky Josie, 192 Front.
Donahue Peter, 309 Park.
Dow & Hatch. 2 Church.
Downey James, 38 New Britain.
Dwyer John E. 146 Ward.
Easterby Alfred J. 26 Commerce.
Eff Louis, 203 Front.
Elsner Morritz, 129 Front.
Eustace William, 119 Pearl.
Falk Tillie Mrs. 176 Sheldon.
Farmington Av. Grocery, 67 Far.
Feeley Matthew J. 26 Front.
Ferranto Joseph, 17 Charles.
Fitzsimmons James, 126 Martin.
Flanagan J. J. 97 Windsor.
Flannery Anna Mrs. 189 Zion.
Fleming Thomas G. 428 Main.
Fling Ferdinando, 180 Front.
Frad N. 194 Front.
French Grenville W. Franklin, c.
Annawan.
Frost Henry D. 1195 Main.
Furlong & Howard, 160 Windsor av.
Gardner Mary A. 15 Ellery.
Gelman Davis, 82 Avon.
Giese Charles H. 51 Ferry.
Glynn John F. 144 Maple.
Goldberg Kolman, 24 North.
Goldstein Gus. 237 Park.
Goodman Dora, 85 Front.
Goodrich D. T. 43 Windsor.
Gordon Morris, 73 Windsor.
Gowdy Lorin B. 1 Whitmore.
Graham Jason, 125 Albany.
Griswold Hosmer, 547 Main.
Gross Isadore, 209 Front.
Guilfoil Grocery Co. 198 Asylum.
Haggarty Joseph, 75 Front.
Hart L. C. 63 Albany.
Hartford Grocery Co. 369 Capitol.
Hastings Arthur B. 80 Grand.
Heffernan Patrick Mrs. 66 Front.
HILLS & CO. 372–374 Asylum.
*See page 485.*
Hills H. E. & Son, 1143 Main.
Hirschfield Annie Mrs. 56 Market.

Hyman Morris, 246 Front.
Jonas Henry, 50 Temple.
Kahn Henry, 105 Mather.
Kane James, 258 Front.
Katz Nathan, 215 Front.
Kennedy Philip S. 1046 Main.
Kingsley & Co. 436 Asylum.
Klein Jacob, 270 Market.
Koenig C. A. A. 42 Temple.
Kramer Sarah, 6 Kibbe.
Kuhn Rosie Mrs. 25 North.
Kutscher Ferdinand, 75 Temple.
Landerman S. 18 Cedar.
Landurand Joseph, Prospect av.
Lane Thomas Mrs. 33½ Morris.
Lane Willis A. 37 Church.
Larson Frank, 22 Park.
Laviere George, 10 North.
Lavin Hyman, 160 Front.
Leichner B. 80 Talcott.
Loeb Helena Mrs. 54½ Wooster.
Lopianski Benjamin, 20 Russell.
Lopianski Morris, 19 Morgan.
Losty Mary Mrs. 115 Zion.
Loughman Patrick F. Mrs. 40 Flow.
Lotz Otto H. 3 Clark.
Lovell Charles D. 50 Front.
Macini & Silvestri, 88 North.
Magines Joseph, 19 Mechanic.
Mahon Maria Mrs. 47 Sheldon.
Mahon W. J. A. 105 Windsor.
Malley Joel, 137 Front.
Marcus Solomon, 72 Park.
Mays John E. 122 Capen.
McGinn Charles Mrs. 29 Liberty.
McLaughlin John J. 141 Zion.
McLean Geo. C. 16 Maple.
Meheran James, 45 Lafayette.
Menaservitz Fannie, 204 Front.
Miltimore Rufus C. 151 Weth.
Moody John, 120 Albany.
Moran Michael, 46 Sheldon.
Morrissey James F. 84 Albany.
Moshinsky Nathan, 54 Avon.
Murphy Ann Mrs. 143 Zion.
Murray John, 3 Wawarme.
Natile G. 136 Front.
NEWTON, ROBERTSON & CO.
338–342 Asylum. *See page 486.*
Nirenstein E. 76 Sheldon.
Northwood Geo. & Son, 36 Walnut.
O'Brien Bridget, 106 Huyshope.
O'Hara James, 71 Potter.
O'Keefe Margaret Mrs. 105 Zion.
Oppelt Barthel, 284 New Park.
Opperman Henry, Crown c. Julius.
Palmer Edgar M. 120 Albany.
Pilgard John A. 1030 Main.
Post Charles A. 1409 Main.
Rabinovitz E. 89 Portland.
Raphael Aaron, 184 Front.
Rapport George L. 86 Retreat.
Rates Frank & Co. 348 Park.
Rezzo James, 100 Park.
Rosenblatt Moses, 44 Village.
Rosenfeldt Libbie, 196 Front.
Ross A. E. 55 Vernon.
Russell Charles H. 711, 909 Main.
Sagarino Dominick, 15 Mechanic.
Satter Jacob, 234 Front.
Seltzer Nathan, 24 Lawrence.
Senk William, 8 Capen.
Sessarsky Nathan, 30 North.
Sizkind Barney Mrs. 79 Governor.
Sloan Michael, 44 Benton.
Soboleosky Samuel, 106 Windsor.
Spiegelman Max, 106 Ward.
Strong Charles H. 131 Main.
Suchadolski John, 64 Sheldon.

Sullivan Bridget Mrs. 78 Avon.
Taub Johanna, 52 Pleasant.
Tillinghast A. H. 341 Main.
Tolhurst W. J. 55 Maple.
Tracy H. C. 814 Park & 95 Main.
Tremont Bros. 53 New Britain.
Tucker Charles W. New Park.
Vail James, 87 Windsor.
Vile William, 280 Front.
Vogel Solomon, 361 Main.
Walz Jacob, 54 Temple.
Warren F. M. 899 Allyn.
Warren Michael J. 222 Sheldon.
Weinstein Max, 80 Talcott.
Wissell Margaret Mrs. 36 Sanford.
Witkin Lena Mrs. 110 Barbour.
Wolf Herman, 92 Windsor.
Yackavon Joseph, 22 Kilbourn.
Yungk John, 171 Wethersfield.

### GROVES.
Kenyon's Grove, Albany av.
LAUREL PARK. See page 557.
Werder's Park. 444 Wethersfield.

### GUN POWDER.
ANDRUS & NÆDELE CO. 272
Asylum. See page 485.

### GUARANTEE CO.
COWLES E. S. 25 Pearl.  p. 108.
KIMBALL & McCRAY, 658 Main.
See page 444.

### GUNN FOLDING BED.
FULLER C. C. & CO. 16 Ford. See
page 500.

### GUNS and RIFLES.
ANDRUS & NÆDLE CO. 372
Asylum. See page 485.

### GUNSMITHS.
*See also Firearms; Hardware.*
ANDRUS & NÆDELE, 272 Asy-
lum. See page 485.

### GUTTERS.
CULLEN C. A. 44 Ann.  See p. 489.
STELLING FRED W. 93 Franklin.
See page 487.

### GYMNASIUMS.
Hartford Turnehalle Co. 10 Mor.
Young Men's Christian Associa-
tion. See pages 704–705.

### HACKS, Etc.
*See Livery Stables.*

### HAIR WORK and Manicure.
*See Barbers.*
Bascom Mary M. 68 Pratt.
Brasgrove A. G. 25 Central.
Fry M. A. Mrs. 942 Main.
Gelston M. Olive, 26 Chapel.
Helene Madame, 228 Asylum.
Hempsted Adelaide R. 881 Main.
Mason E. J. Mrs. 240 Sigourney.
McQuillan Alice T. 17 Pratt.
Mill Misses, 903 Main.
Powers Mary J. 721 Main.
Seymour Edith C. 68 Pratt.
Welldon Thomas C. 871 Main.

### HALF TONES.
HARTFORD ENGRAVING CO.
66 State.  See page 477.
U. S. PHOTO. CHEMICAL MFG.
Co. 29 Pearl.  See page 419.

### HALLS.
*See Public Halls, Etc.*

### HAMMER Mfr.
BILLINGS & SPENCER CO. 142
Russ.  See page 531.

### HAND STAMPS.
*See Stamps, etc.*
BURCH GEORGE W. 91 Asylum.
See page 497.

### HARD OIL POLISH.
SMITH H. M. & CO. 301 Allyn.
See page 419.

### HARD WOOD WORK.
FRENCH H. A. 554 Main.  See
page 512.
SCOVILLE A. W. WOODWORK-
ING CO. Vredendale av. c. Tay-
lor.  See page 516.

### HARDWARE AND AGRICULTURAL TOOLS.
Cadwell & Jones, 1084 Main.
Clapp & Treat, 64 State.
Cohen Myers, 180 Front.
Cone J. H. & W. E. 87 Asylum.
FRANCIS & CO. 859 Main.  See
page 546.
Levitt Louis, 176 Front.
Olds & Whipple, 164–168 State.
Thrall Edward B. 62 Church.
Tracy & Robinson, 78 Asylum.
Way Hardware Co. 866 Main.
Wooley Hardware Co. 44 Asylum.

### HARNESS SUPPLIES.
ENSWORTH L. L. & SON, 104
Front.  See page 591.

### HARNESS and SADDLES.
*See also Carriages.*
Broduer Peter, 784 Park.
Brown William, 1148 Main.
Corning H. F. & Co. 83 Asylum.
HARTFORD CARRIAGE CO. 300
Allyn.  See page 549.
Herbert Nathan, 186 Front.
Hunter Harness Co. 162 Asylum.
JEWELL PAD CO. 15 Trumbull.
See page 584.
Marchant George, 425 Main.
MELONEY WILLIAM H. Capitol
City Oil Co. 195 State.  See p. 541.
Ryan Patrick J. 1222 Main.
Smith Alexander, 523 Main.
SMITH, BOURN & CO. 334 Asy-
lum and 8 Sig.  See page 547.
Stalker Mfg. Co. 452 Asylum.
Warren F. M. 893 Allyn.
Webster William S. 996 Main.
Wilcox B. F. 68 Morgan.

### HATS, CAPS and FURS.
*See also Furs: Men's Furnishings.*
Burke Hannah M. Mrs. 419 Main.
Danbury Hat Co. 214 Asylum.
Dix & Co. 551 Main
Hartford Hat Mfg. & Repair Co. 71
Asylum.
Holman & Meister, 76 Asylum.
Horsfall & Rothschild, 97 Asylum.
Kenyon R. P. Co. 91 Pratt.
STILLMAN & CO. 59 Pratt.  See
*outside front cover.*

Shedd J. N. Co. 109 Asylum.
Wilcox David & Co. 50 Asylum.
WILLIAMS ALFRED & 945
(fur).  See page 171.

### HAY and STRAW.
*See also Flour, Grain, Fed.*
Cummings & Garvin, 37 Spruce.
Goldberg Kalman, 67 Morgan.
PEASE CHARLES A. 464 & 122
Main.  See page 582.
Phillips John R. 36 Hartford rd.
East Hartford t.
Price Robert & Son, 84 Francis.
SMITH, NORTHAM & CO. 120
State.  See page 590.
Yates Erton P. 1411 Main.

### HEALTH UNDERWEAR.
DUNHAM HOSIERY CO. 66 State.
See page 547.

### HEATING ENGINEER.
HARTFORD HEATING CO. 90
Asylum.  See page 180.

### Heating and Ventilating.
*See Steam Heating; Hot Water.*

### HELMINTHOLOGIST.
LANKTON ARBA, 2 Marsh.  See
page 564.

### HIDES, TALLOW, & SKINS.
FRISBIE L. T. CO. 79 Talcott.
See page 585.
JEWELL BELTING COMPANY,
15 Trumbull.  See page 129.
Sage E. W. & Co. 64 Albany.

### HOLLOW WARE Mfr.
WM. ROGERS MFG. CO. 66 Market.
*See outside back cover & page 471.*

### HORIZONTAL TUBULAR BOILERS.
BEACH H. B. & SON, 125 Grove.
See page 538.

### HORSE DEALERS.
*See Sale Stables, Livery Stables.*

### HORSE FOOD.
Schmidt Emil, 8 Bond.

### HORSE GOODS.
*See Harness and Saddles.*
Capitol City Carriage Co. 203 Allyn.
Corning H. F. & Co. 83 Asylum.
HARTFORD CARRIAGE CO. 300
Allyn.  See page 549.
Stalker Mfg Co. 452 Asylum.
MELONEY WILLIAM H. Capitol
City Oil Co. 195 State.  See p. 541.

### HORSE GOODS MACHINE Mfr.
MERROW MACHINE CO. 26
Laurel.  See page 535.

### HORSE RADISH.
Birden J S. & Co. 84 Vine.

### HORSE-SHOE CALKS.
ROWE A. H. & CO. 5 Rowe.  See
page 529.

## HORSE SHOE NAIL Mfr.
CAPEWELL HORSE NAIL CO.
40 Governor. *See page 524.*

## HORSE SHOERS.
*See Blacksmiths.*
NORTH END CARRIAGE CO.
r. 34 Capen. *See page 277.*

## HOSPITALS.
*See Orphan Asylums; Insane Retreat.*
Hartford Dispensary, 2 Talcott.
HARTFORD HOSPITAL, 20 So.
Hudson. *See pages 700, 701.*
Industrial Home for the Blind, 335
Wethersfield.
Nursery & Kindergarten for Blind
Children, 1205 Asylum.
OLD PEOPLE'S HOME, 86 Jefferson. *See pages 702, 703.*
St. Francis Hospital, 110 Woodland,
c. Collins.
St. Mary's Home for Aged, Albany
av. W.H.t.
WALNUT LODGE, 56 Fairfield.
*See page 712.*

## Hotel Copper Utensils.
BLAKE T. J. & SON, 141-143 Commerce. *See page 489.*

## HOTELS.
*See Restaurants; Boardinghouses.*
Adams Hotel, 370 Albany.
Allyn House, 152 Asylum.
American Hotel, 103 State.
Arlington House, 999 Main.
Brainard Hotel, 119 Capitol.
Brower House, 25 Central.
City Hotel, 651 Main.
Colonial The, 981 Main.
Columbia House, 26-28 Market.
COMMERCIAL HOUSE, 165 Asylum. *See page 100.*
Earle House, 74 High.
Fairview House, 87 High.
Farmington Avenue Hotel, 57 Far.
Quincy House, 1233 Main.
Heins Bros. 430 Asylum.
Hotel Capitol, 389 Main.
Hotel Hartford, 343 Allyn.
Hotel Heublein, 98 Wells.
HOTEL PROSPECT, 119 High.
*See page 561.*
LONG BROS. 80 State. *See page 232.*
Madison House, 110 Pratt.
Merrill L. D. 54 Prospect.
New Dom, 109 Trumbull.
SIGOURNEY HOUSE, 1150 Main.
*See page 561.*
United States Hotel, 26 State.
Wadsworth Daniel D. 401 Albany.

## HOT WATER HEATING.
AHERN JAMES, 280 Asylum.
*See page 505.*
ANDREWS & CREEDON, 446
Asylum. *See page 542.*
HARTFORD HEATING CO. 267
Asylum. *See page 180.*
King A. G. & Co. 440 Asylum.
LANGDON, THOMAS H. 228
Pearl. *See page 224.*

## HOUSE DECORATORS.
*See Decorators.*

## HOUSE FURNISHING.
*See Carpet Stores; Stoves, etc.*

## HOUSE PAINTERS.
*See Decorators, Signpainters.*
Abild Ludig C. 93 Whitmore.
Beckwith Albert F. 39 Ann.
BLAKE WALTER P. 219 Pearl.
*See page 61.*
BONNER-PRESTON CO. 843 Main.
*See page 425.*
Bradley Henry E. 1106 Main.
Bragg Fred S. r. 190 Asylum.
Brimble Joseph, 130 Ward.
Brookbanks Henry & Son, 463
Broad.
Buckley Bros. & Co. 10 Ford.
Butts James M. 245 Park.
Camp Charles W. 1120 Main.
Condron Patrick, 63 Ward.
Crosscup & Gaudette, 75 Pratt.
DARBY THEODORE T. 37 Martin.
*See page 529.*
Delahanty John J. Jr. 12 Warner.
Daly & Eardley, r. 1331 Broad.
Fagerhorn Carl, 277 Main.
French Charles S. 1092 Main.
French & Hurlock, 1153 Main.
Gillespie & Co. 219 State.
Girard Edmund, 229 Pearl.
GRENNIER G. F. 19 East. *See page 520.*
Griffing C. P. 1166 Main.
Harding Thomas H. 1212 Main.
Hargey John M. 24 Charlotte.
Hart Henry C. 56 Hudson.
Hitchcock Hiram, 12 Sisson.
Horan James, 4 Waverley.
Hussey Samuel J. & Co. 20 Central.
Hutchins Llewellyn A. 2 Webb.
Ingraham Wm. Thos. 34 Lawrence.
Jacobson & Hamarstrom, 14 Hung.
Johnson J. Edmund, 580 Windsor av.
Kassenbrook Theodore, 262 Allyn.
Kibbe & Penfield, r. 1231 Main.
Lang F. C. 212 Asylum.
LANGE & FLAD 13 Central. *See page 512.*
Lynch R. 111 Front.
Mallender John G. 185 Asylum.
Marsh Thomas & Co., 1076 Main.
Martin & Kelley, 265 Asylum.
Moran Thomas J. 14 Charter Oak.
Morse Fred, 32 Lawrence.
Nibbe & Penfield, r. 1231 Main.
Parkes Alfred, 19 Bond.
Peak Daniel, 192 Vernon.
PEPION JOHN & CO. 25 Church.
*See page 289.*
Pietsch & Hinkley, 1146 Main.
Richmond Frank L. r. 28 Temple.
ROWLEY & WILCOX, 39 Ann.
*See page 562.*
Scheck Theo. G. 113 Main.
Stowe Henry E. 1112 Main.
Tufts Charles H., Cava.
WALKER ROBERT & CO. 12
Church. *See page 366.*
Warburton G. B. 999 Main.
Wells Jordan C. 60 Benton.
Wheeler Calvin H. 85 Vine.
White Joseph L. & Co. 185 Asylum.
Whiting Isaac P. 234 Franklin.
Woods James, 110 Ward.
Zoells John, 25 Mulberry.

## ICE CREAM FREEZERS.
*See Stoves; Hardware.*

## HOUSE RENTING.
WARD WILLIAM, 863 Main. *See page 368.*

## HUBS AND SPOKES.
BLODGETT & CLAPP CO. *See page 541.*
ENSWORTH L. L. & SON, 104
Front. *See page 592.*

## Hydraulic Air Compressors.
RHODES L. E. CO. 28 High. *See page 548.*

## Hydraulic Engineers.
BUTTS & CROSBY, 49 Pearl. *See page 427.*

## HYDRAULIC PRESS MFR.
NATIONAL MACHINE CO. 138
Sheldon. *See page 540.*

## ICE CREAM.
*See also Confectionery.*
BACKES F. W. 169 Asylum. *See page 45.*
BESSE P. & J. 701 Main. *See page 57.*
SCHROEDER F. 941 Main. *See page 323.*
STUECK J. W. Jr. 1036 Main. *See page 348.*

## ICE DEALERS.
Consumers Ice Co. 80 State.
Drivers Ice Co. 342 Wethersfield.
Hartford Ice Co. 4 Central.
Main Lewis S. 391 Main.
Spring Brook Ice Co. 4 Central.
Trout Brook Ice & Feed Co. 48 Ann.

## ICE PLANTS.
FISCHER HUBERT BREWERY,
315 Park. *See page 492.*

## INDEMNITY BONDS.
KIMBALL & McCRAY, 658 Main.
*See page 444.*

## ILLUSTRATIONS.
MUGFORD A. 177 Asylum. *See page 476.*

## IMPORTERS.
BALLERSTEIN R. & CO. 908
Main. *See page 421.*
BEACH & CO. 209 State. *See page 591.*
BONNER-PRESTON CO. 843 Main.
*See page 425.*
BROWN, THOMSON & CO. 942
Main. *See page 499.*
CHENEY BROS. 34 Morgan. *See inside front cover and page 545.*
COLT PATENT FIREARMS MFG.
CO., Vandyke. *See page 543.*
Craig J. E. & Co. 239 State.
Donaghue P. 133 State.
Donchian S. B. 75 Pearl.
Dunham A. & Sons, 66 State.
DWIGHT, SKINNER & CO. 207
Allyn. *See page 488.*
ECKHARDT J. H. CO. 687 Main.
*See page 418.*
Fox G. & Co. 956 Main.
Hartford Carpet Co. 10 Market.

Hartford Woven Wire Mattress Co. 618 Capitol.
Henning Otto, 31 Temple.
Heines Bros. 480 Asylum.
Heublein G. F. & Bro. 74 Trumbull.
Hirth Joseph, 279 Main.
Horsfall & Rothschild, 93 Asylum.
HOWARD J. L. & CO. 440 Asylum. *See page 527.*
JEWELL BELTING CO. 15 Trumbull. *See page 530.*
KOHN HENRY & SONS, 890 Main. *See page 797.*
Krug, Powers & Co. 741 Main.
LANE J. G. 224 State. *See p. 589.*
Lathrop W. H. 314 Asylum.
LINCOLN, SEYMS & CO. 34 Market. *See page 588.*
Melrose & Keane, 33 Main.
Peck Edward A. 88 Market.
POPE MFG. CO. *See page 796.*
PRATT & CADY CO. *See p. 527.*
ROGERS WM. MFG. CO. 66 Market. *See outside back cover and page 471.*
SAGE, ALLEN & CO. 896 Main. *See page 817.*
Soby Charles, 667 Main.
TUCKER'S E. SONS, *See p. 481.*
VORCE A. D. CO. 752 Main. *See page 418.*
Westphal William, 221 State.
YUEN, SING & CO. 118 State. *See page 887.*

## Incandescent Arc Lamps.
PERKINS ELECTRIC SWITCH MFG. CO. 88 Woodbine. *See page 536.*

## INCANDESCENT LAMPS.
Hubbard & Monson, 858 Asylum.
PERKINS ELECTRIC SWITCH MFG. CO. 88 Woodbine. *See page 536.*

## INDEX Mfg.
Burr Index Co. 386 Asylum.

## INFANTS' OUTFITS.
*See also Children's Wear.*

## INK EXTRACTS.
Bairstow Ink Co. 281 Allyn.
BARBER INK EXTRACT CO. 5 Haynes. *See page 488.*
FLETCHER N. P. & CO. 31 Niles. *See page 146.*

## INNS.
Wadsworth Inn, 401 Albany.

## INSANE RETREAT.
*See also Charities.*
RETREAT FOR THE INSANE, 30 Wash. *See pages 698, 699.*

## INSTALLMENT GOODS.
Adams Charles F. & Co. 261 Asy.
Gately & Brennan, 118 Asylum.

## INSTITUTE.
HARTFORD BUSINESS COLLEGE, 370 Asylum. *See p. 711.*

## INSULATING MATERIAL.
BILLINGS & SPENCER CO. 142 Russ. *See page 531.*

## INSURANCE COMPANIES.
Foreign companies having agencies, see "Agent," page 593.

### ACCIDENT.
ÆTNA LIFE INSURANCE CO. 650 Main. *See page 449.*
TRAVELERS INSURANCE CO. 56 Prospect. *See page 456.*

### EXPLOSION.
HARTFORD STEAM BOILER INSPECTION & INS. CO. 650 Main. *See pages 446, 447.*

### FIRE.
ÆTNA INSURANCE CO. 666 Main. *See pages 442, 448.*
CONNECTICUT FIRE INS. CO. 51 Prospect. *See page 457.*
Factory Insurance Asso. 96 Pearl
HARTFORD COUNTY MUTUAL FIRE INS. CO. 798 Main. *See page 445.*
HARTFORD FIRE INSURANCE CO. 58 Trumbull. *See pages 458.*
NATIONAL FIRE INS. CO. 95 Pearl. *See page 459.*
ORIENT INSURANCE CO. 5 Haynes. *See page 461.*
PHŒNIX INSURANCE CO. 64 Pearl. *See page 460.*
Scottish Union & National Insurance Co. 197 Asylum.
STATE MUTUAL FIRE, 750 Main. *See page 445.*

### INDEMNITY.
Ætna Indemnity Co. 650 Main.

### LIFE.
ÆTNA LIFE INSURANCE CO. 650 Main. *See page 449.*
CONNECTICUT GENERAL LIFE INS. CO. 49 Pearl. *See p. 448.*
CONNECTICUT MUTUAL LIFE INS. CO. 788 Main. *Pages 450, 451.*
HARTFORD LIFE INS. CO. 252 Asylum. *See page 454.*
NATIONAL LIFE ASSOCIAT'N, 58 Trumbull. *See page 455.*
PHŒNIX MUTUAL LIFE INS. CO. 49 Pearl. *See pages 452, 453.*
TRAVELERS INSURANCE CO. 56 Prospect. *See page 456.*

### FOREIGN COMPANIES.
Conn. Indemnity Association, 252 Asylum.
Fidelity and Casualty Co. 49 Pearl.
German-American, 25 Pearl.
John Hancock, 750 Main.
MASSACHUSETTS MUTUAL LIFE INS. CO. 847 Main. *See page 64.*
Metropolitan Life Ins. Co. of New York, 721 Main.
Mutual Life Insurance Co. of New York, 50 State.
New York Life Ins. Co. 847 Main.
Northwestern Mutual Life Ins. Co. 721 Main.
Prudential Ins. Co. 811 Main.
Royal Insurance Co. 720 Main.

## INSURANCE AGENTS.
### FIRE.
Arnold Charles E. 97 Asylum.
Baker W. E. & Son, 700 Main.
BEARDSLEY EDWARD W. 64 Pearl. *See page 460.*

Belden Oscar C. 721 Main.
Bennett Martin, 197 Asylum.
Chapman & Mucklow, 870 Asylum.
Chapman Silas, Jr. 51 Trumbull.
CONKLIN H. W. & CO. 9 Central. *See page 101.*
COWLES E. S. 25 Pearl. *See p. 108.*
CROSS & MORLEY, 750 Main. *See page 445.*
DICKINSON L. A. & CO. 564 Main. *See page 444.*
DILLINGHAM E. B. 709 Main. *See page 122.*
Eldridge & Co. 2 State.
Fisher George B. 197 Asylum.
Gillett Albert B. 744 Main.
Gorton Philip G. 654 Main.
GREENE JACOB H. 721 Main. *See page 425.*
Hough Niles P. 10 Central.
Johnstone Charles, 9 Asylum.
KIMBALL & McCRAY, 658 Main. *See page 444.*
MARQUARDT H. C. 904 Main. *See page 248.*
PRICE W. T. & CO. 96 Pearl. *See page 445.*
Rogers William H. 259 Asylum.
Schwab Joseph, 51 Trumbull.
Small Henry T. 252 Asylum.
Street F. F. 118 Asylum.
TULLER GEO. W. 847 Main. *See page 860.*
WAKEFIELD WALTER L. 720 Main. *See page 445.*
Webster & Baker, 721 Main.

### LIFE.
Betancourt P. B. 92 Pearl.
Birney Reginald, 29 Pearl.
BOND ALBERT H. 847 Main. Mass. Mutual Life Ins. Co. *See page 64.*
Bronson Sanford F. 252 Asylum.
Buckland C. Edward, 721 Main.
Burnham Frank G. 29 Pearl.
Carroll Joseph R. 904 Main.
COWLES EDWIN S. 25 Pearl. *See page 108.*
Everett Martin R. 811 Main.
Green Alfred W. 82 Pearl.
GRISWOLD FREDERICK A. 721 Main. *See page 170.*
HALL JAMES P. 29 Pearl. *See page 174.*
Harbison Alexander, 2 Central.
Harrington Henry E. 50 State.
Hart Ferdinand A. 650 Main.
Hutchins J. Herbert, 721 Main.
JARMAN JAMES H. 783 Main. *See page 203.*
Kellogg E. N. 873 Asylum.
Knox Robert C. 721 Main.
Lamb John W. 49 Pearl.
Learned Newton M. 252 Asylum.
Murray Richard, 756 Main.
Norris Richard D. 82 Canton.
Peek DeWitt J. 118 Asylum.
Pike L. E. 904 Main.
Pitkin Albert H. 783 Main.
Pittman Edward H. 239 Jefferson.
RATHBUN FRED. D. 118 Asylum. *See page 302.*
Rathbun Julius G. 80 Pearl.
RICHARDS ALFRED T. 783 Main. *See page 306.*
Risley Elisha, 783 Main.
ROGERS F. WILLSON, 847 Main. *See page 311.*
Segur F. P. 999 Main.

Seide Henry W. 904 Main.
Shepard Charles E. 654 Main.
SMITH JAMES E. & SON, 49 Pearl.
See page 336.
STAPLES GEORGE W. 847 Main.
See page 342.
Street F. F. 118 Asylum.
Thompson Frank A. 49 Pearl.
Todd M. A. 756 Main.
Trante & Loeser, 704 Main.
Tyler Heman A. 756 Main.

INSURANCE COMMISS'R.
Frederick A. Betts, State Capitol.

## INTELLIGENCE OFFICES.
See Employment.

## INTERIOR DECORATIONS.
BONNER-PRESTON CO. 848 Main.
See page 425.
SCOVILLE A. W. 700 Main. See page 513.

## INTERIOR FINISH Mfr.
SCOVILLE A. W. 700 Main. See page 513.

## INVENTORS.
DES JARDINS BENJAMIN M. 904 Main. See page 490.
RICHARDS F. H. 808 Main. See outside front cover.
Wiggin M. E. Mrs. 926 Main.

## INVESTMENTS.
See Brokers; Real Estate and Loans.
ABBOT JOHN C. 49 Pearl. See page 430.
Boynton E. B. 904 Main.
CONN. BUILDING & LOAN ASSO. 252 Asy. See page 430.
COOLEY FRANCIS R. 49 Pearl. See page 428.
DENISON CHARLES, 750 Main. See page 426.
Dustin Charles E. 11 Central.
Gladwin R. S. 49 Pearl.
LOAN & GUARANTEE CO. OF CONN. 49 Pearl. See page 441.
Pike L. E. & Co. 904 Main.
Townsend S. P. 49 Pearl.
WHITE W. L. 884 Main. See page 503.

## IRON CORNICES.
CULLEN C. A. 44 Ann. See page 489.
STELLING F. W. 93 Franklin. See page 487.

## IRON AND BRASS BEDSTEADS.
HARTFORD WOVEN WIRE MATTRESS CO. 618 Cap. See p. 522.

## IRON FOUNDERS.
Donovan J. G. 38 Ferry.
Laragy Patrick, 114 Grove.
LINCOLN & CO. 54 Arch. See page 522.
PRATT & CADY CO. 556 Capitol. See page 527.
PRATT & WHITNEY CO. 1 Flower. See page 523.

## IRON WORKS.
See Machinists; Scrap Iron.

## IRON PIPE & FITTINGS.
ANDREWS & CREEDON, 446 Asylum. See page 542.
KNOX FRANK J. 2 So. Ann. See page 220.

## IRON RAILING.
BUELLESBACH WILLIAM, 75 Commerce. See page 478.
LINCOLN & CO. 54 Arch. See page 522.

## IRON SIDINGS.
CULLEN C. A. 44 Ann. See p. 489.

## IRON and STEEL.
BLODGETT & CLAPP CO. 51 Market. See page 541.
CLAPP JOHN B. & SON, 61 Market. See page 529.
ENSWORTH L. L. & SON, 104 Front. See page 592.
Park Brothers & Co. 18 Central.
FORGINGS AND CASTINGS.
COLLINS CO. See page 521.

## Isolated Lighting Plants.
LEE H. K. 228 State. Page 589

## JAPANESE GOODS.
Japan Product Co. 367 Main.

## JAPANESE OVENS.
CULLEN M. 44 Ann. See page 506.

## JEWELERS and WATCHMAKERS.
See Diamonds and Setters.
Alexander George W. 125 Maple.
Blinn D. H. & Co. 175 Asylum.
Brown Edward J. 162 Asylum.
CASE C. H. & CO. 851 Main. See front cover outside.
Coggswell Henry J. 84 Trumbull.
Cohn Elias, 104 Trumbull.
Deming Henry A. 87 Pratt.
Fromberg Thomas, 992 Main.
Gallevsky Harry, 2 State.
Garfinkel Morris, 996 Main.
Garfinkel William, 154 Front.
Grace Jewelry Co. 40 Asylum.
Gundlach E. & Co. 20 State.
HANSEL, SLOAN & CO. 886 Main. See pages 176 and 333.
Harris Henry, 82 Asylum.
Houston George H. 82 Temple.
KOHN HENRY & SONS, 890 Main. See page 797.
LaPointe S. S. 883 Park.
Leonard Augustus T. 1212 Main.
Leventhal Frank, 15 Florence.
Levy H. P. 862 Main.
Mittau Adolph, 551 Main.
Neal Charles W. 847 Main.
Rist Owen D. 847 Main.
Roberts Walter W. 847 Main.
Schall Ernst Co. 5 Asylum.
Schirmaier Frederick, 847 Main.
Schmidt & Fox, 19 Pearl.
Smith Charles F. 865 Main.
STEVEN WILLIAM T. 4 State. See page 344.
Teske Charles, 214 Asylum.
Tobias Theodore, 399 Franklin.
BOXES.
HARTFORD BOX CO. 228 State. See page 532.

REPAIRERS.
Ball George W. 25 Asylum.
Beeman Wm. M. 272 Asylum.
Callery William C. 847 Main.
CASE C. H. & CO. 851 Main. See front cover outside.
Jackson J. L. 1076 Main.
Wiggin G. W. 2 American.

## JEWELRY Mfr.
Blair & Coxeter, 911 Main.

## JOBBING.
McGRATH T. F. & CO. 820 Park. See page 520.

## JOBBERS.
See Whitewashers.

## JOINERS.
See Carpenters and Builders.

## JOINERS and BUILDERS.
See Carpenters and Masons.

## JUNK SHOPS.
Bares Nathan, 80 Front.
KATZ JACOB, 7 North. See page 502.
Lacava Rocco. 27 Charles.
Loveland A. C. & Co. 65 Pleasant.
Pierce William H. 83 Ferry.
White Harris, 242 Front.

## JURORS.
See page 462.

## JUSTICES OF PEACE.
See page 669.
McMANUS THOMAS, 847 Main. See page 490.

## KEROSENE OIL.
See Grocers; Oils.
SISSON T. & CO. 729 Main. See page 560.

## KEY RINGS.
BILLINGS & SPENCER CO. 142 Russ. See page 531.

## KID GLOVES.
See Dry Goods.

## KID GLOVES CLEANED.
PATTEN H. E. 87 Wells. See page 591.

## KINDLING WOOD.
Coleman John, 938 Park.
Gydsen Hans, 25 Belmont.
HARTFORD COAL CO. 754 Main. See page 492.
Hartford Wood Yard Co. 116 Charter Oak.
HATCH & NORTH COAL CO. 801 Main. See page 419.
Johnson Jacob, 30 Union.
MASON W. C. & CO. 746 Main and 169 Front. See page 419.
Mullarky Charles. 135 CharterOak.
RICKER ALFRED T. 26 Potter. See page 517.
Scott Dennis, r. 72 Pleasant.

## KITCHEN FURNITURE.
See also Stoves, Etc.

## Knit Goods Machine Mfr.
MERROW MACHINE CO. 26 Laurel. *See page 535.*

## KNIT GOODS Mfrs.
*See also Textile Mfrs.*
Health Underwear, 66 State.
DUNHAM HOSIERY CO. 66 State. *See page 547.*
Park Knitting Works, 336 Asylum.
Whitehead Horatio, 302 Asylum.

## LACES.
NEAL, GOFF & INGLIS CO. 980 Main. *See page 498.*

## LACE CLEANER.
*See Real Lace.*

## LACE LEATHER Mfr.
JEWELL BELTING CO. 15 Trumbull. *See page 530.*

## LADDER Mfr.
BISHOP E. C. & CO. r. 34 Capen. *See page 60.*

## Ladies' Furnishing Goods.
*See also Dry Goods, Children's Wear*
BROWN, THOMSON & CO. 942 Main. *See page 499.*
Corpe L. A. Mrs. corsets, 31 Church.
Pratt Charles W. 937 Main.
SAGE ALLEN & CO. 896 Main. *See page 317.*

## LADIES' RESTAURANT.
BROWN, THOMSON & CO. 942 Main. *See page 499.*
SCHROEDER F. 941 Main. *See page 322.*

## LADIES' TAILOR.
GREENSTEIN R. A. 903 Main, room 4. *See page 562.*

## LADIES' WRAPPERS.
Levey Samuel, 228 Front.

## LAGER BEER.
*See Brewers.*
COLUMBIA BREWING CO. 245 Windsor. *See page 417.*
FISCHER HUBERT BREWERY, 315 Park. *See page 492.*
NEW ENGLAND BREWING CO. 217 Windsor. *See page 504.*

## LAGER CASES.
GROSS HERMAN, 198 Front. *See page 171.*

## LAMP Mfrs.
HOWARD JAMES L. & CO. 488 Asylum. *See page 527.*

## LAMP SOCKETS.
PERKINS ELECTRIC SWITCH MFG. CO. 88 Woodbine. *p. 586.*

## LANDSCAPE GARDENING.
*See also Florists.*
BURT L. W. 39 Pearl. *See p. 421*
Church Albert, 108 Prospect av.
McCLUNIE J. ALEXANDER, 177 Asylum. *See page 249.*
McClunie T. 464 Farmington.
PHELPS J. WESSON, 13 Belden. *See page 508.*

## LANTERN SLIDES.
U. S. PHOTO. CHEMICAL MFG. CO. 29 Pearl. *See page 419.*

## LATHE DOGS.
BILLINGS & SPENCER CO. 142 Russ. *See page 581.*

## LAUNDRIES and WASHERWOMEN.
Adams Jane A. Mrs. 51 Mather.
American St'm Laundry, 788 Park.
Branch Maria Mrs. u. 659 Main.
Broomhall Louisa Mrs. 545 Main.
Buck Elizabeth, r. 14 Martin.
Buckley Fannie Mrs. 100 Walnut
Charlie Bros. 14 New Britain.
Chong Fang, 100½ Trumbull.
Chong Sung, 229 Park.
Chung Charles, 114 Laurel.
Chung George, 96 Flower.
Chung Lee, 98 Park.
Chung W. 954 Broad.
Clements W. H. 788 Park.
Conway Maria, 49 Mather.
Crane Sarah Mrs. u. 36 Flower.
Dean Charles M. 379 Main.
Empire Steam Laundry, 34 Pratt.
Fellerter Ann Mrs. 2u. 80 Windsor.
Foo Wong, 17 Church.
Gaudet Patrick Mrs. 403 Franklin.
Gee Ying 130 Windsor.
Goss Jennie Mrs. 175 Windsor.
Griffin Chat. A. 863 Main.
Gun Chung, 769 Park.
Hartford Apron and Toilet Supply Co. 49 Market.
Hartford Laundry, 403 Franklin.
Hayden John M. 851 Asylum.
Henn Christina Mrs. 9 Kinsley.
Hing Charles W. 258 Allyn.
Hing Wing, 299 Windsor av.
Hong Fred W. 851 Main.
Hop Gwong, 76½ Temple.
Johnson Mary Mrs. 108 Huyshope.
Kane Barbara Mrs. 139 Martin.
Kee Sing, 297 Lawrence.
Layton Emma H. 8 Gold.
Lee Charlie, 99 Main.
Lee Quong, 182 Front.
Lee Sam, 59 Maple.
Lee Sing, 92 Sheldon.
Lee Sing, 175 State.
Lee Wing, 1108 Main.
Ling Hong, 780 Park.
Long Wah, 287 Asylum.
Looney Sisters, 85 Church.
Loong Ching, 108 State.
Lung Lee Sam, 90 Albany.
Lung Sam, 861 Asylum.
Lung Wong, 11 Morgan.
Mack Sarah Mrs. 86 Pratt.
Martel Louis J. 568 Main.
Mow Charlie, 135½ Lawrence.
Mow Quong, 54 Sheldon.
Murphy Johannah Mrs. 9 Sig.pl.
Murphy Hannah Mrs. r. 106 Win.
New England Steam Laundry, w. Hawthorn.
New Method Laundry, 438 Asylum.
New York Laundry, 35 Church.
No-Pareil Laundry Co. r. 366 Windsor av.
Palace Laundry, 4 Lewis.
Paul Desdemons, 25 Wolcott.
Perkins Alice, 489 Main.
Pierce Mary F. Mrs. 1130 Main.
Pierce Roxanna Mrs. 18 Fairmount.
Powers Adelia, 74 Sanford.
Randall Harriett, 139 Capen.
Randall Susan Mrs. 2u. 51 Sanford.
St. John Adele Mrs. 42½ Windsor.
Sand Lan, 486 Asylum.
Sheriden Ellen Mrs. u. 51 Mechanic.
Sing Charlie, 24 Mulberry.
Sing Charlie, 1360 Broad.
Sing Charlie Wong, 116 Albany.
Sing Frank, 1225 Main.
Sing Lung, 57 Windsor.
Sing Quong, 18 Morgan.
Sing Tam, 1100 Main.
Sing Tong, 294 Asylum.
Sing Wah, 294 Main.
Sing Wing, 117 Windsor av.
Sing Wing, 105 State.
Sing Wong T. 62 Trumbull.
Sing Yee, 273 Lawrence.
Song Charlie, 102 Trumbull.
Smith Lottie A. 10 Green.
Sturtzel Sarah Mrs. u. 41 Canton.
Vew Shin, 157 Maple.
Wah Charlie A. 454 Main.
Wah Chung, 954 Broad.
Wah Sam, 278 Pearl.
Wah Sing, 1075 Broad.
Wah Yet, 211 Lawrence.
War Charlie, 47 Morgan.
Wells Anna Mrs. 14 Warren.
White Nettie Mrs. 489 Main.
Williams Alanda A. 8 Green.
Wing Charlie, 92½ Trumbull.
Wing Chung, 41 Hawthorn.
Wing Sing, 21 Park.
Wing Tung, 58½ Front.
Wing Yee, 487 Main.
Wong Charlie, 76 Albany.
Wong C. H. 556 Asylum.
Wong Edward D. 5 Heath.
Wong Fred. 34 Grand.
Wood Sarah L. u. 659 Main.
Wright Eliza Mrs. 53 Mather.
Yee C. W. 188 Asylum.
Yuon Jow, 24 Trumbull.

## LAUNDRY MACHINES Mfr.
LINCOLN & CO. 54 Arch. *See page 521.*

## LAWN MOWERS.
*See Hardware.*

## Lawn Mowers SHARPENED.
CLARK E. W. 31 Wells. *See p. 536.*
COWLISHAW HENRY, 162 Pearl. *See page 535.*
Leitz John E. 328 Asylum.

## 'LAWN SETTEE Mfr.
BISHOP E. C. 34 Capen. *See p. 60.*

## LAWYERS.
*See Attorneys at Law.*

## LEADED ART GLASS.
BARKER F. W. & CO. 86 Morgan. *See page 512.*

## LEATHER BELTING MFRS.
JEWELL BELTING CO. 15 Trumbull. *See page 530.*
KNOX FRANK J. 2 So. Ann. *See page 220.*

## LEGGINS Mfr.
Wiley W. H. & Son, 59½ Trumbull.

## LEATHER and FINDINGS.
ARMS POCKETBOOK CO. 396 Asylum. *See page 504.*
Brewster A. L. 186 Pearl.
Cohn R. & Co. 1234 Main.
DOW PETER JR. 278 Asylum. *See page 561.*
JEWELL BELTING COMPANY, 15 Trumbull. *See page 530.*
New York Leather Co. 21½ Mulberry

## LEDGER PAPER Mfr.
EAST HARTFORD MANUF. CO. *See page 480.*

## LIBRARIES.
*See also list of: Index to Contents*
Circulating Library, 89 Trumbull.
Girls' Reading Room, 243 Market.
Good Will Club Library, 96 Pratt.
Hartford Medical, 33 Prospect.
Hartford Public Libr'y,5Athenæum.
Historical Library, 624 Main.
Law Library Association, 85 Tru.
Medical Jou. & Lib. Ass'n,2 Talcott
State Library in Capitol.
United Workers Club, 700 Main.
Watkinson Library, 624 Main.
Women's Christian, 58 Church.

## LIFE INSURANCE.
*See Insurance Agents.*

## LIGHTING.
HARTFORD ELECTRIC LIGHT CO. 266 Pearl. *See page 542.*

## LIME and CEMENT.
*See also Stone Yards.*
BELDEN SETH & SON, 69 Commerce. *See page 508.*
Coburn Charles, 154 State.

## LINEN DRAPERS.
*See Gent's Furnishing; Shirts.*

## LINEN PAPER Mfr.
EAST HARTFORD MANUF. CO. *See page 480.*

## LININGS.
*See also Trimmings.*
Fish H. 48 Pratt.

## LIQUORS.
*See also Saloons; Bottlers.*
Craig J. E. & Co. 239 State.
Dolan Frank, 39 Kinsley.
Donaghue Patrick, 133 State.
Donaghue William, 28–80 Union pl.
FISHEL & LEVY, 189 State. *See page 144.*
Heublein G. F. & Bro. 74 Tru.
HILLS & CO. 372–374 Asylum. *See page 485.*
Killin James & Sons, 74 Morgan.
LANE JOSEPH G. 224 State. *See page 539.*
Lathrop W. H. 314 Asylum.
Smith M. B. 288 Asylum.

## LITHOGRAPHERS.
*See also Printers.*
Dodd Wm. H. & Co. 42 Union pl.
Kellogg & Bulkeley Co. 175 Pearl

## LOAN BROKERS.
*See Real Estate and Loans.*

## LODGING HOUSES.
*See Boarding Houses.*

## LIVERY STABLES,
*See also Carmen and Expresses.*
BOARDING AND SALES.
Baker Frank A. 16 Squire.
Barrows F. P. 291 Allyn.
Bedford William R. 16½ Babcock.
Black Madison J. 560 Main.
Blumenthal Isaac R. 20 Morgan.
Boardman Chauncey B. 356 Main.
Clark & Phelps, 995 Main.
Cotter William, 19 Buckingham.
Cronin Timothy, 12 Wells.
CUMMINGS F. B. 820 Asylum. *See page 112.*
Dorsey James T. 10 Commerce.
Garrity Michael, 1231 Main.
Hicks Bros. rear 173 State.
Honce Alfred E. 82 Hudson.
Kenyon Edwin F. 287 Albany.
Landon Frank H. 212 Park.
LEWIS HENRY B. 22 Trinity. *See page 231.*
McNamara Thomas, 678 Main.
Niles Daniel B. r. 1177 Main.
Nott Charles D. r. 1128 Main.
Otis J. Henry, r. 1214 Main.
Pibbles John, r. 1063 Main.
RAYMOND & SLOAN, 19 Mather. *See page 549.*
Reilly James H. r. 173 State.
Reilly Philip, 19 Gold.
Strant C. H. & Co. r. 50 State.
Terrett John, r. 106 Hopkins.
Tewksbury Wilbur, 87 High.
Trumbull Joseph H. 833 Park.
WOOD JOHN A. 19 Mather. *See page 551.*
Wooley William P. 366 Main.
Yeomans Henry E. 51 Farmington.

## LOANS.
*See also Banks and Brokers.*
Capitol Loan Office, 32 Asylum.
CONN. BUILDING AND LOAN ASSO. 252 Asv. *See page 480.*
GRIFFITH WILLIAM RICHARD, 66 State. *See page 427.*
HARTFORD BUILDING & LOAN ASSOCIATION, 370 Asylum. *See page 424.*
SHELTON E. 66 State, rm. 6. *See page 426.*

## LOUNGE BOTTOMS.
HARTFORD WOVEN WIRE M. CO. 618 Capitol. *See page 522.*

## LOCKSMITHS.
*See Cutlers.*
Clark W. M. 22 Church.
COWLISHAW HENRY, 152 Pearl. *See page 585.*
Epstein A. 201 Front.
HALLIDAY WILBUR H. 131 Frpnt *See page 506.*

## LUMBER.
*See Sawmills.*
ANDREWS & PECK, 88 Market. *See page 509.*
Bidwell S. W. 72 Buckingham.
Capitol City Lumber Co. 25 Front.

Conn. River Lumber Co. 756 Main.
HARTFORD LUMBER CO. r. 17 Albany. *See page 515.*
Hill Marshall L. 57 Albany.
Hubbard Charles E. 69 Bluehills.
Peck Austin L. Lumber Co. 88 Mar
PECK HARRY H. r. 32 Church. *See page 509.*
Taft Co. r. 15 Albany.
TAYLOR E. & SONS,335 Sheldon. *See page 510.*

### KILN DRIED.
HARTFORD MOULDING WORKS 26 Potter. *See page 517.*

## MACHINERY.
RHODES L. E. CO. 28 High. *See page 548.*
RICHARDS F. H. 808 Main. *See outside front cover.*
STRONG IRA J. 267 Asylum. *See page 524.*
Trio Tool & Mach. Co. 858 Asylum.

## MACHINERY AGENTS.
STRONG IRA J. 267 Asylum. *See page 524.*

## MACHINERY DEALERS.
DWIGHT SLATE MACHINE CO. 13 Central. *See page 525.*

## MACHINERY OIL.
SISSON T. & CO. 729 Main. *See page 560.*

## MACHINISTS.
ÆTNA MACHINE CO. 77 Commerce. *See page 532.*
BILLINGS & SPENCER CO. 142 Russ. *See page 531.*
CLARK EDRED W. 31 Wells. *See page 526.*
COLTS PATENT FIRE ARMS MANUFACTURING CO. 17 Vandyke. *See page 548.*
COOK ASA S. CO. 80 Huyshope. *See page 525.*
DWIGHT SLATE MACHINE CO. 13 Central. *See page 525.*
Hurley Bros. r. 228 State.
Hurley & Standinger, r. 228 State.
Ideal Machine Co. 328 Asylum.
JOHNS-PRATT CO. 555 Capitol. *See page 540.*
Judd E. H. & Son, 24 Mechanic.
LEE H. K. 228 State. *See page 589.*
LINCOLN & CO. 54 Arch. p. 532.
MERROW MACHINE CO. 26 Laurel. *See page 535.*
NATIONAL MACHINE CO. 183 Sheldon. *See page 540.*
PICKERING W. H. & CO. 110 Commerce. *See page 537.*
PRATT & WHITNEY CO. 1 Flower. *See page 528.*
RHODES L. E. CO. 28 High. *See page 548.*
Robbins Eliphalet D. 54 Pratt.
SIGOURNEY TOOL CO. 9 Sigourney. *See page 537.*
WOODWARD & ROGERS, 183 Sheldon. *See page 526.*

## MAGICIAN.
Jewett Fred. D. r. 240 Windsor av.

## MACHINISTS' SUPPLIES.

BILLINGS & SPENCER CO. 142 Russ.        *See page 581.*
DWIGHT SLATE MACHINE CO. 13 Central.        *See page 525.*
FRANCIS & CO. 859 Main. *See page 546.*

## MACHINISTS' TOOLS Mfrs.

BILLINGS & SPENCER CO. 142 Russ.        *See page 581.*
DWIGHT SLATE MACHINE CO. 13 Central.        *See page 525.*
LINCOLN & CO. 54 Arch. *See page 522.*
PRATT & WHITNEY CO. 1 Flower.        *See page 523.*

## MAGAZINES.

CONN. QUARTERLY, 66 State.        *See page 477.*

## MANICURE.

*See Chiropodist, Hair Work, Etc.*
Bascom Mary M. 68 Pratt.
BENEDICT CARRIE M. H. 721 Main.        *See page 55.*

## MANILLA PAPER Mfrs.

HARTFORD MANILLA CO. 1 So. Ann.        *See page 479.*

## MANTELS.

*See Wood Turners; Marble Works.*
Dunn P. H. 218 Pearl.
SCOVILLE A. W. 700 Main. *See page 513.*
SCOVILLE A. W. WOODWORKING CO. Vredendale, c. Taylor.        *See page 516.*
Smith & Hutton, 1446 Broad.
White & Whitmore, 38 Ann.

## Manual Training School.

Y. M. C. A.        *See pages 704-705.*

## MANUFACTURERS.

*See also Corporations; Machinists.*
Acme Machine Screw Co. Vre'dale.
Ætna Machine Co. 75 Commerce.
Allen Shade Holder Co. 284 Asylum.
American Specialty Co. 185 Shel.
ARMS POCKET BOOK CO. 336 Asylum.        *See page 504.*
BEACH H. B. & SON, 185 Grove.        *See page 538.*
Beach Manufacturing Co. 211 State
Beacon Falls Mill & Power Co. 209 State.
BILLINGS & SPENCER CO. 142 Russ.        *See page 531.*
Birkery Mfg. Co. 65 Suffield.
Bonsilate Box Co. 24 Mechanic.
Broad Brook Co. 211 State.
CALLAGHAN C. J. 44 Union pl.        *See page 88.*
CAPEWELL HORSE NAIL CO. 40 Governor.        *See page 524.*
CASE, LOCKWOOD & BRAINARD CO. 141 Pearl. *See page 475.*
CHENEY BROS. silk mfrs. 84 Morgan. *See inside front cover and page 545.*
COLLINS & CO.        *See page 521.*
Collum Manufact'g Co. 9 Asylum.
COLT'S PAT. FIRE-ARMS MFG. CO. 17 Vandyke. *See page 543.*

Comfort Powder Co. 61 Albany.
COOK A. S. Co. 80 Huyshope. *See page 525.*
Curtis-Hull Mfg. Co. 42 Union pl.
Cushman Chuck Co. 30 Cushman.
Dart Marking Mach. Co. 285 State.
DAVIS I. B. & SON, 40 Cushman.        *See page 546.*
Dunham Hosiery Co. 66 State.
Eagle Eyelet Works, 24 Mechanic.
Eastern Brass Works, 228 State.
EDDY ELECTRIC MFG. CO. *See page 586.*
Eldredge Co. 110 Commerce.
Farber Morris, r. 8 Walnut.
FRISBIE L.T.CO. 79 Talcott. *See page 586.*
Gatling Gun Co. 17 Vredendale.
Gibbs Electric Mfg. Co. 302 Asy.
Gold Star Overall Co. 26 High.
Gray's Tel. Station Co. r. 64 Asy.
Green & Bauer, 33 Wells.
HART & HEGEMAN MFG. CO. 26 High.        *See page 539.*
Hartford Boltless and Noiseless Thill Coupling Co. 173 Asylum.
HARTFORD BOX CO. 223 State.        *See page 582.*
Hartford Carpet Co. 10 Market.
Hartford Chemical Co. 235 State.
HARTFORD CYCLE CO. 581 Capitol.        *See page 796.*
HARTFORD HEATING CO. 267 Asylum.        *See page 180.*
Hartford Machine Scr. Co. 476 Cap.
HARTFORD MANILLA CO. *See page 479.*
HARTFORD MOULDING WORKS, 26 Potter.        *See page 517.*
HARTFORD PAPER COMPANY. 141 Pearl.        *See page 480.*
HARTFORD PRINTING COMPANY (ELIHU GEER'S SONS), 16 State.        *See page 474.*
HARTFORD RUBBER WORKS, 690 Park.        *See page 796.*
Hartford Typewriter Co. 476 Cap.
HARTFORD WOVEN WIRE MATTRESS CO. 613 Capitol.        *See page 523.*
Health Underwear Co. 66 State.
Hitchcock & Curtiss Knitting Co. 1189 Broad.
Hogan Mfg. Co. r. 56 Grove.
Holly Steam Eng. Co. 28 High.
HOWARD JAMES L. & CO. 440 Asylum.        *See page 527.*
HURD OLIVER.        *See page 586.*
JEWELL BELT HOOK CO. *See page 548.*
JEWELL BELTING CO. 15 Trumbull.        *See page 530.*
JEWELL PAD CO. 49 Hicks. *See page 534.*
JEWELL PIN CO. 31 Hicks. *See page 534.*
JOHNS-PRATT CO. 555 Capitol.        *See page 540.*
LEE H. K. 223 State. *See page 539.*
LINCOLN CO. 54 Arch. *See p. 522.*
LINCOLN, SEYMS & CO. 84 Market. *See page 588.*
Mansuy & Smith, 17 Elm.
Manufacturers Governors Co. 228 Asylum.
McClary John, 69 Front.
MERROW MACHINE CO. 28 Laurel.        *See page 535.*
Morgan Wm. D. & Co. 9 Columbia.

NATIONAL MACHINE CO. 133 Sheldon.        *See page 540.*
Nonotuck Silk Co. 133 Sheldon
PERKINS ELECTRIC SWITCH MFG CO. 83 Woodbine. *See p. 536.*
PICKERING W. H. & CO. 119 Commerce.        *See page 537.*
Pomroy George W. 279 High.
POPE MFG. Co. 436 Capitol. *See page 796.*
POPE MFG. CO. Motor Carriage Dept. 1 Laurel. *See page 796.*
POPE TUBE CO. Hamilton. *See page 796.*
PRATT & CADY CO. 556 Capitol.        *See page 527.*
PRATT & WHITNEY CO. 1 Flower.        *See page 522.*
Premier Mfg. Co. 437 Main.
Quint Alanson D. 80 Huyshope.
RHODES L. E. CO. THE 28 High. *See page 548.*
ROGERS CUTLERY COMPANY.        *See page 471.*
ROGERS WM. MFG. CO. 66, 68 Market. *See outside back cover and page 471.*
ROWE A. H. & CO. 5 Rowe av.        *See page 522.*
SANFORD CO. 438 Asylum. *See page 448.*
SCOVILLE A. W. 700 Main. *See page 513.*
SCOVILLE A. W. WOODWORKING CO. THE, Vredendale av. c. Taylor.        *See page 516.*
Side Weight Horse Shoe Co. 9 Cen.
SIGOURNEY TOOL COMPANY. 9 Sigourney.        *See page 527.*
SLATE DWIGHT MACHINE CO. 13 Central.        *See page 525.*
SMITH, BOURN & CO. 334 Asy. 8 Sigourney.        *See page 547.*
SMITH H. M. CO. 279 High. *See page 419.*
SMYTH MFG. CO. 648 Main. *See page 528.*
STELLING FRED. W. 93 and 95 Franklin. *See page 487.*
STEVEN W. T. 4 State. *See p. 344.*
Stoughton D. G. 219 State.
Tifft A. L. Mrs. 115 Oak.
Tunxis Worsted Co. 66 State.
Tyler Manufacturing Co. 754 Main.
U. S. PHOTO-CHEMICAL CO. 29 Pearl.        *See page 419.*
Veeder Mfg. Co. 20 Sargeant.
Whitney Mfg. Co. 80 Huyshope.
WHITTEMORE W. L. & SON. 176-178 Allyn.        *See page 462.*
WILLIMANTIC LINEN COMPANY, 389 Allyn. *See page 544.*
WOODWARD & ROGERS, 133-135 Sheldon.        *See page 536.*

## Manufacturers' SUPPLIES.

FRANCIS & CO. 859 Main. *See page 546.*
KNOX F. J. 2 So. Ann. *See p. 220.*

## MAP COLORER.

Herzer Charles, 40 Wolcott.

## MAP PUBLISHERS.

Elihu Geer's Sons, 16 State. *See page 474.*

## MARBLE WORKS.
*See also Stone Yards; Sculptors.*
BREEN PATRICK J. 1070 Main.
*See outside front cover.*
Burnham C. D. & H. D. 54 Win. av.
MASLEN STEPHEN, 40 High. *See outside back cover.*
NEW ENGLAND GRANITE WORKS,1260 Main. *See page 533.*

## MARINE ENGINES.
COLTS PATENT FIRE-ARMS MFG. CO. *See page 543.*
LEE H. K. 228 State. *See page 539.*
PICKERING W. H. & CO. 100 Commerce. *See page 587.*

## MARKET GARDENERS.
*See also Markets.*
Colton Frank B. 90 Bluehills.
Forster Ludwig, 375 New Britain.
Gladding Timothy, 23 Harrison.
Newton Frank E. 810 Park.

## MARKETS.
*See also Grocers, Provisions, Bologna.*
Antupitzky Sam. 186 Front.
Bach Abram, 206 Front.
Bacharach Henry, 13 Park.
Bacon Franklin N. 490 Main.
Bansemer Gottleib, 34 Front.
Barrows Charles A. 42 Pleasant.
Barrows & Thalheimer, 1111 Main.
Barry John J. 128 New Britain.
Bartlett John, 552 Asylum.
Breen Patrick J. 156 Windsor.
Burns William J. 544 Asylum.
Cady & Lombard, 69–75 Albany.
Carter David, 8 Church.
Caswell Charles S. 295 Asylum.
Chandler Arthur W. 58 Sheldon.
CITIZEN'S MEAT & FISH MARKET, 587 Main. *See page 587.*
City Market, 1065 Main.
Co-operative Provision Co. 149 Bab.
Crane Charles E. r. 175 Ashley.
Crowell J. W. 455 Garden.
Curtis Alfred C. 16 Queen.
Davis Bros. 1451 Broad.
Davis J. W. 88 Grand.
Day Charles E. 158 Capen.
Dodge & Brewer, 340 Main.
Dutton Daniel, 1150 Broad.
Elmer & McClellan, 108 Trumbull.
Ensworth & Parsons, 77 Front.
FAIR HAVEN OYSTER DEPOT, 30 State. *See page 589.*
FLYNN JOHN, 493 Main. *See page 587.*
Franklin Market, 516 Main.
Furlong & Howard,160 Windsor av.
Foley John J. 1065 Main.
Goldberg David, 26 North.
Goldstein Henry, 218 Sheldon.
Graves Elmer C. 11 Elmer.
Hall Joel E. 38 Capen.
Hansling Philip, 73 Williams.
Harrington Daniel J. 302 Main.
Hart L. C. & Co. 68 Albany.
Hermann Wenzel, 162 Front.
Hewitt Henry H. 1157 Main.
HILLS & CO. 372–374 Asylum. *See page 485.*
INGRAHAM, SWIFT & CO. 126 Church. *See page 555;*
Itzak W. 80 Potter.
Kashman Jacob, 162 Clark.
Kashman Joseph, 26 Mulberry.

Kashman Simon, 46 Sumner.
Katz Louis, 205 Front.
Katz M. H. 51 Morgan.
Katzenstein Bros. 132 Windsor, 201 Front.
Keegan Michael A. 283 Park.
Kellogg George F. 125 Ann.
Later Morris, 196 Front.
Lawler John A. 271 New Britain.
Longworth John C. 250 New Britain.
Mahon Wm. J. A. 105 Windsor.
Marcus Solomon, 72 Park.
McGurk Bernard, 1149 Main.
McLean George C. 16 Maple.
Montgomery Hugh G. 373 Main.
Moore & Holbrook, 275 Main.
Morse Matthew O. 179 Asylum.
Murphy John F. 29 Hawthorn.
Newman Solomon, 40 North.
NEWTON & BURNET, 319 Asylum. *See page 487.*
Nussbaum K. 533 Main.
Palmer Clarence L. & Co. 115 Pearl.
Palmer Edgar M. 180 Albany.
Patterson George, 1397 Main.
Peckham Bros. 8 Ford and 331 Cap.
Pilgard John A. 1050 Main.
Preston Thos. P. M. 308 Asylum and 48 Front.
Public Market Co. 653 Main.
Ruderman Jacob, 56 Pleasant.
Samuels Isaac F. 42 Wooster.
Shippe C. N. 116 Albany.
Slonne Henry A. 82 Walnut.
Smith George F. 2 Washington.
Squires Alvin & Son, 33, 43 Market.
Stedman John A. 25 Greenwood.
STEVENS NEWELL H. 329 Asylum. *See page 345.*
Stokes Frederick, 371 Asylum.
Sullivan Patrick J. 188 Front.
Thomas Albert L. 1417 Main.
Tolhurst W. J. corner Maple and Retreat.
Wade & Sampson, 201 State.
Walter Wm. 19 Elmer.
Wehrly Herman, 52 Temple.

## Marking Metal Surfaces.
THE DWIGHT SLATE MACHINE CO. 13 Central. *See page 525.*

## MASONS and BUILDERS.
Ahearn Daniel, 38 Crown.
Andrus Chas. B. 11 Seyms.
Angus William, 110 Oak.
BISSELL HIRAM, 43 Wadsworth. *See page 516.*
BRABAZON ANDREW, Garden and Liberty. *See page 511.*
Bridgman Federal B. 45 Sumner.
Brown Joseph Henry, 51 N. Britain.
Budde A. W. 107 Hungerford.
Chapin A. D. 74 Seymour.
COOK CHAS. C. 141 Trumbull. *See page 419.*
CURTIS D. J. & SON, 787 Windsor av. *See page 517.*
Deming Edwin N. 39 Seyms.
Donnelly Francis, 66 Green.
Farmilo Henry, 91 Buckingham.
Flannery James, 62 Governor.
Flynn John M. 856 Broad.
Flynn Martin, 721 Main.
Flynn Thomas 148 Washington.
Harrison John, 156 Franklin.
Hills John R. 754 Main.
HILLS & FOX, 22 John. *See p. 515.*

Hills Nelson P. 64 Clark.
HOLLIS D. W. & SON, 212 Asylum. *See page 514.*
GROZIER & MOORE, Vredendale, cor. Taylor. *See page 510.*
Mahl Benj. F. 1152 Main.
Newton Thomas S. 116 Clark.
O'Neil Michael, 172 Farmington.
Ryder Thomas F. 9 Arch.
Sheedy Michael, 75 Franklin.
Simpson Charles W. 68 Wooster.
Sullivan Michael, 373 Broad.
Thayer F. J. 39 Linden
Thompson Bros. 19 Rowe.
Westland William, 64 Capitol.
Zwirz Ferdinand, 92 Windsor.

## MASSAGE.
BENEDICT CARRIE M. H. 721 Main. *See page 56.*
Ponsaing John, 1524 Broad.
Ponsaing Matilda Mrs. 1524 Broad.
STUTZ EUGENE, 9 Asylum. *See page 422.*

## MATCHING and PLANING.
HARTFORD MOULDING WORKS 26 Potter. *See page 517.*

## MATTRESS Mfrs.
HARTFORD WOVEN WIRE MATTRESS COMPANY, 618 Capitol. *See page 522.*
FARBER M. 8 Walnut. *See p. 189.*

## MEAT MARKET.
*See Markets.*

## Mechanical Drawing School.
HONEY FREDERIC R. 904 Main, room 111. *See page 422.*
Y. M. C. A. *See pages 704–705.*

## MECHANICAL ENGINEER.
Boland Frederic A. 64 Vernon.
Caswell Frederick K. 238 Laurel.
Clausen Ed. E. 904 Main.
DES JARDINS BENJAMIN M. 904 Main. *See page 490.*
HONEY FREDERIC R. 904 Main. *See page 422.*
Honiss William H. 370 Asylum.
LEE H. K. 228 State. *See page 539.*
Lorenz Wm. A. 370 Asylum.
Merritt Joseph, 581 Capitol.
NATIONAL MACHINE CO. 133 Sheldon. *See page 540.*
RICHARDS FRANCIS H. 808 Main. *See outside front cover.*
SVENSON CHARLES, 58 Woodbine. *See page 482.*
Thalheimer A. L. 2 Central
WHITNEY & ROTHWELL, 49 Pearl. *See page 502.*
WOLCOTT & DARBY, 49 Pearl. *See page 498.*

## MEDICAL SOCIETIES.
*See page 784.*

## MEDICINES.
*See also Apothecaries.*
Bloomingdale James, 377 Main.
Dickinson George K. 25 Evergreen.
Hopkins Alexander S. r. 138 Windsor av.
LANKTON ABBA. *See page 564.*

PEASE HENRY A. 58 Wooster.
See page 287.
SEINSOTH JOHN J. 12 Maple. See page 824.
Street F. F. 270 Laurel.
Watrous J. Hubbard 71 Asylum.
Williams & Carleton Co. 206 State.

## MEERSCHAUM PIPES.
Solomon & DeLeeuw, 7 Asylum.
See page 818.

## MEMORANDUM BOOK Mfr.
ARMS POCKET BOOK CO. 336 Asylum.    See page 504.

## MEN'S FURNISHINGS.
See Clothing; Merchant Tailors.
Ballerstein Benjamin, 858 Main.
BROCKWAY U. H. & CO. 132 State.
See page 71.
BROWN, THOMSON & CO. 942 Main. See page 499.
Burke John E. 419 Main.
Chamberlin & Shaughnessey, 65 Asylum.
Greenwald William, 486 Main.
Horsfall & Rothschild, 97 Asylum.
Kashman Isaac, 12 State.
Koffman Mitchell, 324 Asylum.
Model Tailoring Co. 222 Pearl.
Moran John F. 869 Main.
Rennacker & Co. 141 Asylum.
Salad Witte, 325 Capitol.
Shedd J. N. Co. 109 Asylum.
Walder Bros. 120 State.
Youngman L. & Co. 364 Asylum.

## MERCANTILE AGENCY.
Bradstreet Co. 49 Pearl.
Dun R. G. & Co. 228 Asylum.
National Mercantile Co. 66 State.

## MERCHANT TAILORS.
See Clothing; Seamstresses; Clothes Cleaned.
AKENLIND JOHN A. 205 Park.
See page 424.
Alexander Edward W. 856 Main.
Bartlett George D. 25 Asylum.
Billings P. Harry, 11 Asylum.
Booth Albert F. 55 Pratt.
BROCKWAY U. H. & CO. 132 State.
See page 71.
Cahill E. P. 105 Pratt.
Clarke & Duffey, 73 Asylum.
Coughlin D. J. & Co. 180 Asylum.
Cusick F. H. 740 Main.
Foster & Morrill, 719 Main.
Gemmill, Burnham & Co.66Asylum.
Greibel Wm. H. 56 Pearl.
Hansel Charles & Son, 69 Pearl.
Hartford Tailoring Establishment, 881 Main.
Haub & Son, 721 Main.
Hitchcock H. P. 10 State.
Hollander's A. Sons, 82 Asylum.
Levy Morris H. 46 Asylum.
Lewis Henry & Co. 174 State.
Low David, 60 Asylum.
Maginn William F. 908 Main.
Nicoll, the tailor, 52 Asylum.
Reid James W. 1212 Main.
Rennacker & Co. 141 Asylum.
Rines James A. 80 Asylum.
Ryan Patrick D. 76 Asylum.
Saunders P. H. B. & Son, 730 Main.
Simon, Ragovan & Co. 73 Pratt.

South Sidney F. 77 Pearl.
Tilton Abner F. 697 Main.
Warner & Willard Co. 110 Asylum.

## MESSENGER COMPANIES.
American District Telegraph and Messenger Co. 6 Central.
Hartford Messenger Co. 8 Central.
Postal Telegraph Cable Co. 8 Central, 1 Flower, 42 Union place.

## METALS.
KATZ J. 7 North.    See page 502.

## METAL CAR TRIMMINGS.
HOWARD JAS. L. & CO 438 Asylum.    See page 527.

## METAL CEILINGS.
BAXTER WM. H. 281 Asylum.
See page 52.
LANGE & FLAD, 18 Central. See page 512.
NEAL, GOFF & INGLIS CO. 980 Main. See page 498.

## METAL SKY-LIGHTS.
CULLEN C. A. 44 Ann. See p. 489.
STELLING FREDERIC W. 98 Franklin. See page 487.

## METALLIC SHINGLES.
CULLEN C. A. 44 Ann. See page 489.

## METALS.
See Junks.
BLODGETT & CLAPP CO. 51 Market.    See page 541.
FRANCIS & CO. 859 Main. See page 546.
GROSS HERMAN, 198 Front. See page 171.

## MILITARY ARMORIES.
See Armories.

## MILKMEN.
Of the 190 milkmen, who July 12, 1898, are supplying Hartford residents with milk, only the following licensed 50 are residents of Hartford:
Akerberg C., Fishfry.
Antrim Elmer, 1016 Windsor av.
Anderson Christian J. 1 Flatbush.
Barber Henry G. 375 New Britain.
Barnard George H., Bloomfield av.
Beerwort W. G. 286 New Britain.
Bissell William P. 10 Holcomb.
Conrey William, Bloomfield av.
Cowles Truman, 21 South.
Crockford E. M. & Co. 301 N.B.
Curry James A. 39 Vine.
Daly T. M. 86 Woodbridge.
Dart J. & Son, 286 New Britain.
Denslow Edward D. 915 Windsor av.
Denslow P. & W. 1180 Windsor av.
Dower J. P. 50 New Park.
Epstein Herman, 79 Avon.
Febre H. 1087 Windsor av.
Gates Thomas, 868 Windsor.
Hubbard Joseph T. 116 Bluehills.
Hynes Martin, 80 Fairfield.
Hynes William F. 40 Fairfield.
Katz E. 82 Pleasant.
Kenyon Elijah A. 105 Bluehills.

King M. 145 Flatbush.
Lally T. W. 74 Vanblock.
Lynch A. E. 7 Washington.
Lane Charles M. 40 Clark.
Mather Arthur, 926 Windsor av.
Mather Frank H. 926 Windsor av.
Mather Oliver T. 1040 Windsor av.
Mertzking Manuel, 145 Flatbush.
Moylan D. 44 Glendale.
Peterson A. 36 Village.
Petersen N. C. 125 Bluehills.
Rosen Charles, 296 Market.
Selden Edward M. 54 Eaton.
Seymour Freeman, Estate,10 Fair.
Seymour J. L. 15 Fairfield.
Seymour Lemuel W. 347 New Brit.
Seymour S. F. 420 New Britain.
Smith C. P. 25 Fairfield.
Smith G. F. 2 Washington.
Smith James H. 25 Fairfield.
Sope Oscar, 21 Windsor.
Southergill Geo. 1017 Windsor av.
Tuttle Charles L. 47 Bluehills.
Utley C. H. 71 Bluehills.
Utley Herbert S. 55 Bluehills.
West I. H. 100 Hudson.

## MILL SUPPLIES.
See Manufacturers' Supplies.
KNOX FRANK J. 2 So. Ann. See page 220.

## MILLINERS.
BALLERSTEIN R. & CO. 908 Main.    See page 421.
Beattie Robert Mrs. 37½ Church.
Brown & St. John, 65 Pratt.
BROWN, THOMSON & CO. 942 Main. See page 499.
Caswell Lizzie S. Mrs. 75 Pratt.
Cody Helen, 16 Jefferson.
Douthwaite Fannie M. 904 Main.
Dowling Jennie J. 721 Main.
Duffy C. T. Miss 19 Pratt.
Evans & Hanmer, 75 Pratt.
Ferrall Frances, 903 Main.
Franks Adella, 36 Pratt.
Granniss Cora L. 926 Main.
Harris Harriet, 86 Laurel.
Hunt E. S. Miss 137 Trumbull.
Pierce & Roulston, 926 Main.
Pierson M. S. Miss, 70 Pratt.
Rogers Ellen M. 943 Main.
Saunders Kate C. 721 Main.
Turner Annie F. 904 Main.

## MILLINERY GOODS.
Wholesale.
BALLERSTEIN R. & CO. 908 Main.    See page 421.
BROWN, THOMSON & CO. 942 Main.    See page 499.
Lewis George S. 145 Asylum.

## MILLING CUTTER Mfr.
PRATT & WHITNEY CO.1 Flower.
See page 523.

## MILLING MACHINE Mfr.
COOK ASA S. CO. 80 Huyshope.
See page 525.
DWIGHT SLATE MACHINE CO. 18 Central.    See page 525.
PRATT & WHITNEY CO.1 Flower.
See page 523.

## MINERAL WATER Mfr.
See Bottlers.

## MIRRORS.

ECKHARDT J. H. CO. 687 Main.
*See page 418.*
VORCE A. D. CO. 752 Main.   *See page 418.*

## MODEL-MAKERS.
*See Patterns and Models.*

## MONUMENTS.
*See also Marble Works.*

BREEN PATRICK J. 1070 Main.
*See outside front cover.*
MASLEN STEPHEN, 40 High.
*See outside back cover.*
NEW ENGLAND GRANITE
WORKS, 1260 Main. *See p. 533.*
Slocum F. R. 1 Ford and 40 Albany.

## MOTORS.
*See Electrical.*

EDDY ELECTRIC MFG. CO.
Windsor t.   *See page 536.*

## MOTOR SWITCH Mfr.

PERKINS ELECTRIC SWITCH
MFG. CO. 83 Wbn. *See page 536.*

## MOULDED MICA MFR.

JOHNS-PRATT CO. 555 Capitol.
*See page 540.*

## MOULDINGS.

HARTF'D MOULDING WORKS,
26 Potter.   *See page 517.*
TAYLOR E. & SONS, 335 Sheldon.   *See page 510.*

## MOULDS

FOR RUBBER MANUFACT'RS.
CLARK EDRED W. 31 Wells. *See
page 526.*

## Mowing Machine Repairers.

CLARK EDRED W. 31 Wells. *See
page 526.*
HALLIDAY W. H. 131 Front. *See
page 506.*

## MUSIC STORES and INSTRUMENTS.
*See also Music Teachers.*

Barker L. & Co. 155 Asylum.
Cook D. P. 92 State.
Farris John, 173 Asylum.
FERNSIDE G. W.   *See page 770.*
Gallup & Metzger, 201 Asylum.
Gramophone, 118 Asylum.
Hartford Graphophone Co. 80 Tru.
Sedgwick & Casey, 227 Asylum.
Wander William & Son, 241 Asy.
Woods A. F. 227 Asylum.

PIANO TUNERS.
Barker William E. 58 Asylum.
Bissell Samuel T. 851 Main.
Child Edgar A. 201 Asylum.
Fray Louis C. 801 Main.
Goodrich Samuel R. 153 Asylum.
Hollings John F. 28 Mulberry.
Moeller August, 92 Pearl.
Pratt Ambrose E. 241 Asylum.
Raymond John W. 82 New Britain.
Sadd Fred T. 80 Trumbull.
Schmidt Louis C. 35 Chapel.

## NEWS OFFICES.
*See also Books, News, Etc.*

## MUSIC TEACHERS.
*See also Bands of Music, Schools.*

Allen Nathan H. 926 Main.
Allen Olive M. 284 Sigourney.
Ames May D. Mrs 131 Trumbull.
Bacon F. J. 223 Asylum.
Barker William E. 119 Albany.
Barrington Alfred, 904 Main.
Bartschmid Alois, 55 Russ.
Beard Amanda F. Mrs. 61 Elm.
Beeman Mary L. 18 Windsor av.
Bissell Lillian L. 44 Spring.
Bissell Samuel T. 851 Main.
Bloomingdale Martha, 719 Asylum.
Bradley Ruth A. 926 Main.
Bronson Nettie L. Mrs. 18 Wind. av.
Bryan Agnes C. 389 Main.
Burnham Ida J. 337 Windsor av.
Cambridge Eb. S. Mrs. 67 Green.
Camp John S. 391 Allyn.
Carr Mary L. 33 Mather.
Casey Eugene R. 25 Beach.
Chapman May E. 29 Girard.
Churchill William T. 16 Wellington.
Conway K. R. 2 Orchard.
Cook Edith L. 173 High.
Crocker Charles D. 36 Mahl.
Cummings Hattie L. 66 Allen pl.
Dailey Warren C. 153 Capen.
Dietrich M. Mary Mrs. 3 Asylum.
Downs Elizabeth, 12 Wooster.
Eaton Harriet I. 26 Wethersfield.
Eitel Emil, 558 Main.
Elmore Charles M. 5 Center.
Emerson Irving, 63 Girard.
Fagan Mary E. 64 Hungerford.
Flynn Mary E. & Margaret F. 119
Hungerford.
Gebhardi Gustav, 46 New Britain.
Hardy Herbert C. 700 Main.
Harvey L. W. 171 High.
Harrington Edith M. 24 Hopkins.
Hart Mary Mrs. 166 Russ.
Hascall H. E. Miss 650 Main.
Hastings Emma B. 1185 Broad.
Hatch Charles P. 18 Windsor av.
Hawkins Walter E. 27 Pliny.
Johnson Harriett H. 23 Wadsworth.
Karr Mary L. 2 Atwood.
Kilbourn Ella C. Mrs. 34 Annawan.
King L. Elizabeth, 20 Beach.
Koenig Oscar, 71 Church.
Landfear Louise B. 102 Wooster.
Leavenworth A.J.Mrs. 56 Winthrop.
Lord S. Clarke, 111 Elm.
Marsh Mary I. 106 Clark.
Marshall George, 1205 Asylum.
Marwick Virginia P. Mrs. 97 Far.
Merz Mamie C. 35 Park.
Moran David S. 16 Ely.
Murphy Malvina E. 19 Russell.
Newton Clinton H. 926 Main.
Newton Clinton H. Mrs. 926 Main.
Pearson George W. 25 Bellevue.
Peiler Ernst, 721 Main.
Perrin H. Foot, 125 Huntington.
Perrin P. Mrs. 125 Huntington.
Perry Mary A. 61 Russ.
Phelps Richard O. 18 Suffield.
Phoenix Walter, 177 Babcock.
Pitblado Harriet C. 156 Sargeant.
Prutting George S. 241 Pearl.
Raymond Carrie, 82 New Britain.
Roulston Martha L. Mrs. 255 Main.
St. John Carrie L. 835 Asylum.
Schirm Rose, Maple, corner King.
Schulz Carl, 202 Capen.
Severn Edmund, 45 Farmington.

Shirrell Ida V. 7 Belden.
Slesinger Lotta L. 57 Oak.
Sturmdorf Leonice C. M. 98 Sarg't.
Smith Lottie Korn, 25 Niles.
Spieske Bertha, 77 Edwards.
Spieske Emma, 77 Edwards.
Spieske Louisa, 77 Edwards.
Stancheski Eva H. 561 Garden.
Starbuck Bessie, 43 Niles.
Starbuck Mary, 43 Niles.
Steele George W. 8 Spring.
Walz Jacob, 103 Pratt.
Warner Grace M. 30 Sumner.
Warner Minnie C. 60 Capen.
Webster Cora M. 29 Vine.
Weidlich August, 40 Lewis.
Wilcox Ida N. 347 Windsor av.
Williams John H. 17 Seyms.
Wilson L. May, 88 Seymour.

## NAILS.

BLODGETT, CLAPP & CO. 47-55
Market.   *See page 541.*
CAPEWELL HORSE NAIL CO.
40 Governor.   *See page 524.*
CLAPP JOHN B. & SON, 61 Mar-
ket.   *See page 529.*
ENSWORTH L. L. & SON, 104
Front.   *See page 592.*
FRANCIS & CO. 859 Main. *See
page 546.*

## NEWSPAPERS, Etc.
*See also Printers, Book Publishers
Magazines.*

Ætna The, quarterly, 650 Main.
Am. Journal of Education, 118 Mn.
Bulletin, Hfd. Lib. Ass'n, quarterly,
624 Main.
CATHOLIC TRANSCRIPT, 704
Main. *See page 467.*
Chronicle, monthly, by High School.
CHURCH REVIEW, monthly, 8
State. *See page 472.*
CITY DIRECTORY, 16 State. *See
preface.*
CONNECTICUT COURANT,
Weekly, 66 State. *See page 463.*
CONNECTICUT FARMER, 284
Asylum.   *See page 466.*
CONNECTICUT POST, Weekly,
28 Asylum.
Cyclopædia of Insurance, 53 Tru.
Farmers & Mechanics Journal, 45
Brown.
FARMINGTON VALLEY HER-
ALD & JOURNAL, 836 Asylum.
*See page 470.*
Fraternal News, monthly, 2 State.
GLOBE (Sunday) 30 Asylum. *See
page 465.*
HARTFORD DAILY COURANT,
66 State. *See page 463.*
HARTFORD DAILY TIMES, 716
Main.
HARTFORD JOURNAL, Sun-
day, 284 Asylum. *See page 466.*
HARTFORD POST, Daily, 28
Asylum.
Hartford Seminary Record, bi-
monthly, 1507 Broad.
HARTFORD TELEGRAM, Daily,
12 Central. *See page 464.*
HARTFORD WEEKLY TIMES,
716 Main.
HARTFORDER HEROLD, 31 Mul-
berry.   *See page 470.*
Insurance Journal Co. 53 Trumbull.

Journal of Inebriety, quarterly, Dr.
T. D. Crothers, editor, 56 Fairfield.
RELIGIOUS HERALD, 336 Asylum.                    *See page 469.*
Safety Fund Advocate, by Hartford
Life Ins. Co. 252 Asylum.
Travelers' Record, monthly, 56 Pro.
Trinity Tablet, by Trinity students.
WEEKLY EXAMINER, 45 Brown.
*See page 468.*
Weekly Underwriter, 53 Trumbull.

### AGENTS.

Chapin Lyman A. 865 Main.
Dickerson Josephine L. Mrs. 56
Trumbull.
Sill Emile M. Mrs. 89 Trumbull.
FISCHER GUSTAVE, 259 Asylum.
*See page 148.*

### NICKELPLATERS.
*See also Silversmiths.*

HOWARD JAMES L. & CO. 488
Asylum.          *See page 527.*
Tuttle Plating Co. 41 Trumbull.

### NIGHT LUNCH.
Card Herbert C. 87 Seyms.

### NOTARIES PUBLIC.
*See page 668.*
GRIFFITH WM. RICHARD, 66
State.            *See page 427.*
McMANUS THOMAS, 847 Main.
*See page 490.*
STEINMETZ WILLIAM P. 80
Pearl.            *See page 848.*
WHITE W. L. 884 Main. *See p. 508.*

### NOTARY SEALS.
PARKER T. M. 71 Asylum. *See
page 534.*

### NOTE BROKERS.
*See also Bankers.*
Stedman & Redfield, 5 Central.

### NUMBERING MACHINES.
BURCH GEORGE W. 91 Asylum.
*See page 497.*

### NURSERY.
Children of laboring women, 248
Market.

### NURSERYMEN.
*See also Florists.*
Hartford Nursery, 75 New Britain.
Hunt W. W. & Co. 24 State.
Stanley Peter, 7 Lenox.
WALLACE W. E. Farmington, bet.
Whiting&Quakerlanes.*See p.867.*

### NURSES.
Abbe E. M. Miss, 48 Church.
Adams Sarah Mrs. 22 Winthrop.
Albro Mrs. 33 Wooster.
Allen Libbie M. 96 Church.
Andrews Oregon F. Mrs. 124 N. B.
Avery Julia M. Mrs. 14 Church.
Bachmeyer Annie Mrs. 175 Maple.
Bailey Bessie M. 13 Avon.
Barrett Grace L. 236 Asylum.
Bassett Mary E. Mrs. 56 Albany.
Bates Helen A. Mrs. 82 Maple.
Beadle E. Elizabeth, 205 Ashley.
Beck Lottie E. 75 Allen place.
Beers Eliza, 11 Elmer.
Belyea Annie Mrs. 61 Spring.
Bingham Frances A. 14 Spring.

Bodwell E. A. Mrs. 127 Oak.
Bolton L. Mrs. 13 South Hudson.
Brazos Annie E. 54 Church.
Bridgeman Delia L. 171 Collins.
Brooks M. S. Mrs. 71 Asylum.
Brown Margaret Mrs. 290 Market.
Brown Mary E. 30 Wethersfield.
Brown Mary M. 73 Buckingham.
Brown Josie M. 230 Asylum.
Bryson Jane A. 14 Church, rm. 4.
Burpee Caroline L. 230 Windsor av.
Carman Florence E.14 Church,rm.4.
Chapin M. A. Miss, 122 High.
Chapman Mary, 12 Squire.
Cheney Minnie P. 5 Main.
Clarke Elma A. 28 Hopkins.
Clarkin C. M. Mrs. 147 Sheldon.
Coburn Julia Miss, 122 High.
Colby Mary Mrs. 100 Madison av.
Cooley Sarah Mrs. 216 Windsor av.
Cornelius Alice L. 98½ Ann.
Crocker Hattie C. 95 Jefferson.
Dalton Ada, 14 Church, rm. 10.
Davenport Jane C. Mrs. 449 Broad.
Davis A. P. Mrs. 14 Church, rm. 1.
Delaney Catharine Mrs. 56 Hicks.
Denison Learned B. 26 Huntington.
Dennison Jessie K. 427 Main.
Donahue E. T. 14 Church, rm. 1.
Drummond Alice G. 9 Park.
Duff Maggie M. 703 Asylum.
Duhr Pauline, 217 Ashley.
Elder Elizabeth H. 14 Church,rm. 3.
Farnsworth Mary, 54 Church.
Ferguson Julia E. 257 New Park.
Field Alice B. 97 Trumbull.
Field Jennie R. 108 Ann.
Fish Helen M. Mrs. 13 East.
Garrity Margaret, 28 Madison.
Giesler Mary Mrs. 52 Temple.
Goodrich J. B. Mrs. 16 Belden.
Gourley Jessie R. Mrs. 32 Park.
Graham Mabel A. 29 Allen pl.
Greeno Margaret, Barnard st.
Hardiman W. B. 48 Church.
Hendrick Harriet, 14 Church, rm. 3.
Hicks Minnie, 97 Webster.
Hills Anna M. 370 Asylum, rm. 28.
Hobson Mary C. 221 Capen.
Hough F. Marie, 49 Governor.
Hubbell Elizabeth, 650 Main, rm. 58.
Hunter W. B. Miss, 48 Church.
Jacobs Jacob Mrs. 45 Morgan.
Jenison Mary E. 9 Chapel.
John M. C. 427 Main.
Johnson Alma, 193 Russ.
Johnson Helen, 193 Russ.
Jones Marion E. 87 Laurel.
Jons Mary F. 14 Church, rm. 4.
Kenyon Francis, 19 Wadsworth.
Kirkpatrick Elizabeth Mrs.33 Julius.
Knapp Jessie E. 427 Main.
Laidlow Hannah, 2 Marsh.
Layton O. J. Mrs. 144 Capen.
Lewis Daisy, 48 Church.
Lloyd Addie J. 200 Allyn.
Loomis H. Mrs. 39 Wadsworth.
Lorber Harriet A. 14 Church, rm. 10.
Marchant Caroline Mrs. 189 Ashley.
Marsh Mary L. 14 Church, room 3.
Masterton Elizabeth, 52 Seymour.
Mather Lephe L. Mrs. 13 S.Hudson.
McGarry M. 48 Church.
Meafoy Florence, 1255 Main.
Mittag Francis A. Mrs. 144 Albany.
Morehouse E. K. Mrs. 14 Church.
Morgan Annie, 1304 Main.
Morrell M. A. Mrs. 926 Main.
Munson A.G. Miss,14 Church,rm.10.

Murray May Mrs. 926 Main.
Nuttell Mattie F. 427 Main.
Nutting Mary H. 14 Spring.
Packer Emily J. 22 Winthrop.
Page Jeanette A. 223 Garden.
Palmer Emily, 70 Wooster.
Peck Lois S. 94 Church.
Petersen Kathrine, 884 Main.
Pilgard Katherine D. 14 Ch. rm. 4.
Profitt Mary Mrs. 36 Benton.
Rattray Cecelia A. 64 Russ.
Reed L. M. Mrs. 981 Main.
Riley Mary E. 205 Ashley.
Roche Bridget, 20 Sheldon.
Rust Eliza T. 13 So. Hudson.
Schlatter Lottie Mrs. 488 Main.
Schulz C. F. Mrs. 33 Elliott.
Senior Bridget, 1445 Broad.
Seymour C. M. Mrs. 38 Woodbridge.
Sharpe Howard J. 1220 Asylum.
Sheldon Sarah M. 14 Church, rm. 4.
Simpson Eliza, 279 Asylum.
Skinner Harriet Mrs. 41 Vine.
Skinner Sarah E. 545 Main.
Smith E. J. Mrs. 71 Asylum, rm. 21.
Smith Mary J. Mrs. 48 Grand.
Smith Alice M. 14 Church, rm. 10.
Snow A. G. 58 Church.
Soper Helen G. 14 Church, room 2.
Stowe Etta W. Mrs. 14 Church,rm. 4.
Straw Henrietta, 97 Webster.
Sweeney Della Mrs. 20 Marshall.
Tattam Louisa A. 457 Windsor av.
Terrell Emma J. 14 Church.
Walsh Elizabeth, 1255 Main.
Ware M. F. Mrs. 721 Main.
Waters Emma Mrs. 14 Grand.
Watson Sarah Mrs. 13 King.
Wilbur S. E. Mrs. 71 Asylum.
Wilkinson Martha J. 14 Ch. rm. 12.
Williams Elizabeth, 981 Main.
Wilson George E. 1261 Main.
Wind Lillie, 54 Church.
Wing Belle Mrs. 102 Pearl.
Woodworth Jessie M. 1201 Main.
Wright Ralph B. Mrs. 7 Affleck.
Young A. R. Mrs. 76 Ann.

### OCEAN STEAMERS.
*See Tickets.*

### OFFICE FIXTURES.
*See Scroll Sawyers.*

### OILS.
*See Apothecaries; House Painters.*
CAPITOL CITY OIL CO. 196
State.            *See page 541.*
Gardner Samuel A. 1100 Main.
Lovell & Tracy Co. 218 State.
Osborn George, 278 Market.
Ozon Wallace, 52 Smith.
SISSON T. & CO. 729 Main. *See
page 560.*
Standard Oil Co. 370 Front.
Sweet Charles F. 174 Pearl.

### OIL CLOTHS.
NEAL, GOFF & INGLIS CO. 980
Main.           *See page 494.*

### OIL PAINTINGS.
*See Art Stores.*

### OIL POLISH.
SMITH H. M. & Co. 301 Allyn.
*See page 419.*

### OIL STOVES.
*See also Stoves and Tin Ware.*

## OMNIBUSES.
See Expresses page 559.

## OPERA GLASSES.
STEVEN W. T. 4 State. See page 344.

## OPERA HOUSES.
See Theatres.

## ORCHESTRA.
See also Bands of Music.
Beeman & Hatch, 18 Windsor av.

## OPTICIANS.
Harvey & Lewis, 865 Main.
Sparks Frederic, 82 Pearl.
STEVEN W. T. 4 State. See page 344.
Taylor Frederick N. 162 Asylum.
Wells & Devine, 904 Main.

## ORGANS.
See Music Stores.

## ORGAN MOTORS.
RHODES L. E. CO. 28 High. See page 548.

## ORGAN TEACHERS.
See Music Teachers.

## Ornamental Iron Work.
BUELLESBACH W. 75 Commerce See page 478.

## ORIENTAL RUGS.
See Carpet Store.
Donchian S. B. 75 Pearl.
NEAL, GOFF & INGLIS CO. 980 Main. See page 498.

## ORPHAN ASYLUMS.
See also Charities.
Hartford Orphan Asylum, 171 Put.
St. Catharine C. O. A. for girls, 89 Ch.
St. James C. O. A. for boys, 98 Ch.

## OVENS.
CULLEN M. 44 Ann. See page 506.

## Overhead Trolley Equipment.
BILLINGS & SPENCER CO. 142 Russ. See page 531.

## OYSTERS.
See also Markets.
FLYNN JOHN, 498 Main. See page 587.
HONISS T. A. 30 State. See page 589.
NEWTON & BURNET, 319 Asylum. See page 487.

## PACKAGE EXPRESS.
See Express.

## PACKING.
See Rubber Packing.

## PACKING BOXES.
See Box Makers.

## PAINTERS.
See House Painters.

## PAINTERS' SUPPLIES.
BONNER-PRESTON CO. 843 Main. See page 425.

## PAPER HANGINGS.
See Wall Paper; Carpet Stores.

## PAINTINGS, ENGRAVINGS.
CLEANED and RESTORED.
ECKHARDT J. H. CO. 687 Main. See page 418.
VORCE A. D. CO. 752 Main. See page 418.

## PAINTS, OILS and GLASS.
See also House Painters.
ANDREWS & PECK, 88 Market. See page 509.
BONNER-PRESTON CO. 843 Main See page 425.
ENSWORTH L. L. & SON, 104 Front. See page 592.
NIMS, WHITNEY & CO. 1170 Main. See page 511.
PEPION J. & CO. 25 Church. See page 289.
SISSON T. & CO. 729 Main. See page 560.
WALKER ROBERT, 12 Church. See page 366.

## PAPER BOX MACHINERY.
TUCKER'S E. SONS, 100 Trumbull. See page 481.

## PAPER BOXES.
CALLAGHAN C. J. 42 Union pl. See page 83.
HARTFORD BOX CO. 223 State. See page 532.
Nichols Paper Box Co. 356 Asylum

## PAPER DEALERS.
See also Paper Mfrs. Paper Stock.
CASE, LOCKWOOD & BRAINARD CO. 141 Pearl. See p. 475.
EAST SIDE PAPER CO. 59 Morgan. See page 472.
GARVAN PATRICK, 205 State. See page 472.
Keep C. D. 49 Pearl.
Kemler Michael, 53 Morgan.
TUCKER'S E. SONS, 100 Trumbull. See page 481.

## PAPER HANGINGS.
PEPION JOHN & CO. 25 Church. See page 289.

## PAPER PATTERNS.
See Embroidery.

## PAPER MILLS.
EAST HARTFORD MFG. CO. mill in Burnside. See page 480.
HARTFORD MANILA CO. 1 So. Ann. See page 479.
HARTFORD PAPER COMPANY, 141 Pearl. See page 480.

## PAPER RULERS.
See also Book-Binders.
CASE, LOCKWOOD & BRAINARD CO. 141 Pearl. See page 475.
McNIE MALCOLM, 336 Asylum. See page 504.
TALCOTT WM. H. 856 Main. See page 478.

## PARASOLS.
See Umbrellas.

## PAPER STOCK.
See Paper Dealers.
CASE, LOCKWOOD & BRAINARD CO. 141 Pearl. See page 475.
GARVAN P. 207 State, See p. 472.
HARTFORD PAPER CO. 141 Pearl. See page 480.
Kelly Patrick J., Dutch point.
Levin Max, 41 North.
Pierce William H. 33 Ferry.

## PARKS.
See Trotting Parks; Public Halls, etc.

## PARQUET FLOORINGS.
BAXTER WM. H. 231 Asylum. See page 52.

## PASTEURIZED CREAM.
Bryant & Co. 5 Lenox.

## Pastors, Priests, Rectors.
See Clergymen, and page 683.

## PASTRY OVENS.
CULLEN M. 44 Ann. See page 506.

## PATENT EXPERTS.
WILLIAMS HARRY R. 756 Main. See outside back cover.

## PATENT MEDICINES.
See Medicines.

## PATENT RIGHTS.
See Attorneys at Law.
DESJARDINS BENJAMIN M. 904 Main. See page 490.
RICHARDS F. H. 803 Main. See outside front cover.
SIMONDS WM. E 2 Central. See outside back cover.
WHITNEY & ROTHWELL, 49 Pearl. See page 502.
WILLIAMS HARRY R. 756 Main. See outside back cover.

## PATTERNS.
See Paper Patterns; Stamping.

## PATTERNS & MODELS.
See also Metals.
DWIGHT SLATE MACHINE CO. 15 Central. See page 525.
LITTLE H. B. & CO. 33 Wells. See page 232.
NATIONAL MACHINE CO. 188 Sheldon. See page 540.
TOPPING JAMES R. 784 Main. See page 541.

## PAVING.
Hartford Paving & Construction Co. 868 Main.
Southern New England Paving Co. 141 Trumbull.

## PAWNBROKERS.
Capitol Loan Co. 82 Asylum.
Knoek Leviat S. 188 State.
SHARPE FRANK N. 71 Asylum.

## PEANUTS, Etc.
See Fruit, retail.

## PEAT MOSS.
SMITH, NORTHAM & CO. See page 590.

## PEDDLERS.
Osborn George, 278 Market.
Oxon Wallace, 52 Smith.
Solomon William, 369 Park.
Sprague Elwin L. 46 Bond.

## PEEL MAKER.
Sullivan C. B. 60 Loomis.

## PETROLEUM ENGINE Mfr,
NATIONAL MACHINE COM-
PANY, 133 Sheldon. See p. 540.

## PHOTOGRAPHIC GOODS.
BONNER-PRESTON CO. 848 Main.
See page 425.
U. S. PHOTO CHEM. MFG. CO. 29
Pearl. See page 419.

## PHOTO ENGRAVING.
HARTFORD ENGRAVING CO.
66 State. See page 477.
MUGFORD A. 177 Asylum. See
page 476.
U. S. PHOTO CHEMICAL M'FG.
CO. 29 Pearl. See page 419.

## PHOTO TYPING.
MUGFORD A. 177 Asylum. See
page 476.

## PHOTOGRAPHERS.
Brewer Fred R. 903 Main.
Bundy Horace L. 904 Main.
CARBON PHOTO STUDIO, 92
Pratt. See outside front cover.
DeLamater & Son, 902 Main.
Harney Wm. J. 759 Main.
Johnson Frank M. 1089 Main.
Johnstone C. A. 45 Pratt.
Kellogg Edwin P. 789 Main.
King Herbert, 49 Park.
Lay Horace E. 212 Asylum.
Lloyd Wm. B. Mrs. 11 Pratt.
Nyser John C. F. 2 Ford.
Olsen Johann, 89 Pratt.
Orgill Studio, 753 Main.
Stuart Charles T. 747 Main.
U. S. PHOTO CHEMICAL M'FG.
CO. 29 Pearl. See page 419.
Warren Photograph Co. 75 Pratt.

## PHYSICIANS.
* Regular Allopathic.
† Homoeopathic.
Officers see page 734.
See also Nurses.

Abrams A. E.* 78 High.
Hours—9 to 10 A. M., 2 to 4 P. M.
daily.
Sundays, no office hours.
Mondays, Wednesdays, and Satur-
days, 7 to 8 P. M.
Office Telephone 601-2.
House Telephone 973.
Albu Max,* 703 Main.
Hours—2 to 3.30 P.M., 6 to 7.30
P.M.
Alling Buel B. 56 Fairfield.
Alton C. D.* 86 Farmington.
Andre G. A.* 303 Park.
Hours—8 to 10 A.M., 1 to 3 and 7
to 9 P.M.
Telephone 429-3.
Andross George, (Botanic) 724 Main.

Angell Augustus,† 904 Main.
Hours—9 A.M. to 1 P.M., 2 to 5 P.M.
Tuesday and Saturday, 7 to 8 P.M.
Arms P. H. C.* 94 Walnut.
Hours—8 to 10 A.M., 1 to 3 and 6
to 8 P.M.
Telephone 236-12.
Axtelle J. Frank * 685 Main.
Bacon William T.* 11 Pratt.
Bailey George C.* 85 Church.
Bailey Michael A.* 65 Church.
Barrows B. S.* 78 High.
Beach Charles C.* 58 Trumbull.
Hours—2 to 5 P.M.
Sundays, 4 to 5 P.M.
Telephone 549.
Beardsley Benjamin F. 90 Edwards.
Bell Geo. N.* 44 High.
Bickford Henry, (Eclectic) 98 Ann.
Hours—8 to 9 A.M., 1 to 2 and 7
to 8 P.M.
Telephone 849-2.
Booth James W.* 293 Main.
Botsford Charles P.* 1898 Main.
Boucher John B.* 306 Main.
Hours—8 to 9 A.M., 1 to 3.30 and
7 to 9 P.M.
Telephone 1014-12.
Brewer Clarissa A. Mrs.† 120 Trum-
bull.
Hours—8 to 10 A.M., 2 to 4 and 7
to 8 P.M.
Brigham L. Louise,† 52 Church.
Hours—9 to 10 A.M., 2 to 4 and
6.30 to 7.30 P.M.
Sundays, 2 to 2 P.M.
Telephone 908.
Bunce Philip D.* 50 Pratt.
Hours—9 to 10 A. M., 2 to 4, and 7
to 8 P.M.　Sundays, 3 to 4 P.M.
Telephone connection.
Cahill Joseph H.* 51 Church.
Campbell James,* 2 Congress.
Carlon Philip P.* 284 Main.
Case Erastus E.† After Sept. 1,
office 902 Main.
Hours—10.30 to 12 A.M., 2 to 4 P.M.
Thursday, 10.30 to 12 A.M. only.
Sundays, 12 to 1 P.M. only.
109 Ann, Evenings, 7 to 8, except-
ing Thursday and Sunday.
Telephone at office & residence.
Chester Weston,* 110 High.
Hours—8 to 9 A.M., 2 to 4 and 7
to 8 P.M.
Sundays, 12 to 1 P.M.
Cochran L. B.* 48 Farmington.
Cole F. Hills,† 926 Main.
Hours—9 to 12 A.M., 1 to 5 P.M.
Telephone, 1012-6.
Cole Harlan P.† 926 Main.
Hours—11 to 12 A.M., 3 to 4 P.M.
Telephone, 1012-6.
Cook Ansel G.* 164 High.
Craig W. G. 11 Pratt.
Crary David, Jr.* 1074 Main.
Hours—8 to 9 A.M., 1.30 to 4 and
7 to 9 P.M.
Crossfield Fred S.* 75 Pratt.
Hours—9 A.M. to 4 P.M.
Crothers T. D.* 56 Fairfield av.
See page 712.
Davis G. Pierrepont,* 56 Prospect.
Davison Luther A.* 11 Pratt.
DeBonis Dominick,* 24 Morgan.
Dickerman W. E.* 51 Pratt.
Hours—8 to 10 A.M., 2 to 4 and 7
to 8 P.M.
Telephone 967.

Douglass E. K.* 36½ Church.
Dowling John F.* 1315 Main.
Hours—Until 9 A. M., 2 to 4 and
7 to 9 P.M.
Telephone 716.
Down Edwin A. 2 State.
Eaton W. Bradford,* 2 Garden.
Edgar Alexander F.* 219 Park.
Elmer Edward O. 813 Park.
Farrar I. 152 Asylum.
Every 3d Friday and Saturday of
each month.
Hours—Fridays, 1 to 10 P.M.
Saturdays, 8 to 11 A.M.
Felty J. Wellington,* 340 Wind-
sor av.
Froelich Charles E.* 108 Pratt.
Fuller Horace S.* 95 Trumbull.
Gill M. H. 151 Windsor av.
Gladwin Ellen Hammond,*765 Asy.
Hours—8.30 to 9.30 A.M., 2 to 4 P.M.
Telephone 308.
Grana Giovanni, 70 Morgan.
Griggs John B.* 1067 Asylum.
Griswold R. S.* 44 Church.
Hours—Until 10 A.M.
1.30 to 3.30 and 7 to 8
P.M.
Sundays, 2 to 4 P.M.
Telephone.
Hall Joseph B.* 57 Pratt.
Hours—9 to 10 A.M., 2 to 4 and 7
to 8 P.M.
Telephone.
Hayes Arthur D.* 18 Spring.
Hooker Edward B.† 721 Main.
Hours—10.30 to 12 A.M., except
Saturdays, 2 to 3.30 P.M.
Saturdays, 10 A.M. to 1 P.M.
Sundays, 12 to 1 P.M.
Evenings at Residence, 70 Farm-
ington av.
Telephone residence 723.
Howard John,* 119 Trumbull.
Howe Harmon G.* 137 High.
Hours—8 to 9 A.M., 3 to 4 and 7
to 8 P.M.
Sunday, 3 to 4 P.M.
Telephone 529.
Hudson Wm. M.* 105 Elm.
Hann Paul R. 47 John.
Husinsky M. J.* 1042 Main.
Ingalls P. H.* 112 High.
Hours—11.30 A.M. to 3 P.M.
Telephone 842.
Isham Oliver K.* 211 High.
Hours—11.45 A.M. to 3 P.M., 7 to
8 P.M.
Telephone 1110.
Jarvis Geo. Cyprian,* 98 High.
Hours—2 to 5 P.M.
Telephone 333.
Johnson M. M.* 92 Pearl.
Hours—9 to 10 A.M., 2 to 3.30, and
7 to 8 P.M.
Telephone office 573.
Sanitarium 201-6.
Jones Chas. E.† 116 Ann.
Hours—9 to 10 A.M., 3 to 4 and 7
to 8 P.M.
Wednesdays, 9 to 10 A.M. only.
Sundays, 3 to 4 P.M. only.
Telephone 965.
Judd Etta M. Mrs. 141 Ashley.
Kane Thomas F.* 517 Main.
Kean L. J. D. Mrs.* 67 Pearl.
Kellogg Arthur B. 53 Trumbull.

Kellogg Edward W.† 53 Trumbull, rm. 209.
  Hours—9 to 10 A.M., 2.30 to 4 P.M.
    At office daily, except Thursday and Sunday P.M.
    Telephone residence 859.
    Telephone office 137-2.
Kilbourn Joseph A.* 771 Park.
King E. C.† 21 Capitol.
  Hours—8 to 10 A.M., 2 to 4 and 7 to 8 P.M.
  Sundays, 2 to 8 P.M.
    Telephone 548.
Knight William W.* 96 Trumbull.
Law Homer L.* 100 Washington.
Lawton Franklin L.* 18 Congress.
Lewis John B.* 56 Prospect.
Look Frank B.* 104 Church.
Lynch William J.* 272 Park.
  Hours—Until 9 A.M., 1 to 2.30 P. M. and 7 to 8.80 P.M.
    Telephone office 429-6.
Mahon William J. 985 Main.
Mayer Nathan,* 742 Main.
McCook John B.* 390 Main.
McKnight E. J.* 110 High.
  Hours—8 to 9 A.M., 2 to 4 and 7 to 8 P.M.
  Sundays, 2 to 8 P.M.
    Telephone office 608-2.
    Telephone residence 608-3.
Miller George R.* 182 High.
Morgan Ely,* 721 Main.
Morgan William D.* 700 Main.
Morris Charles E.* 721 Main.
Morse Fred J.* 55 Church.
Naylor James H.* 153 Main.
O'Flaherty John,* 406 Main.
O'Leary James F.* 4 Village.
Olmsted Charles E. 868 Main.
Peltier Frank H.* 926 Main.
  Hours—11 A.M. to 1 P.M., 7 to 8 P.M.
    Telephone 214-2.
Peltier P. D.† 926 Main.
  Hours—8.30 to 10 A.M., 3 to 5 and 7 to 8 P.M.
  Thursdays, 8.30 to 10 A.M. only.
  Sundays, 5 to 7 P.M. only.
    Office Telephone 214-2.
    Residence Telephone 585.
Porter Wm. Jr.* 391 Allyn.
Reinert Emil G.* 553 Main.
Richardson Leonard E.† 99 Park.
Root Edward K.* 700 Main.
Root E. A. Mrs. (eclectic) 1201 Main.
Root Joseph E.* 67 Pearl.
  Hours—10.30 A.M. to 12 M., 3.30 to 5.30 and 7.30 to 9 P.M.
  Sundays, 12 M. to 2 P.M.
    Telephone 728.
Rose John Henry,* 11 Pratt.
Russegue H. Elmore,† 95 Farmington
  Hours—8 to 9 A.M, 2 to 8.30 and 7 to 7.45 P.M.
  Sundays, 8 to 4 P.M. only.
    Telephone 1187.
Russell G. W.* 207 Farmington.
St. John Samuel B.* 68 Pratt.
Scott John R. 71 Asylum.
Segur Gideon C.* 67 Farmington.
Shannon J. B. 119 Capitol.
Shepherd George R.* 82 Farmington.
Simpson Fred T.* 122 High.
Sleeper George E.* 1395 Main.
Smith Howard F.* 609 Main.
  Hours—9 to 10 A.M., 2 to 4 and 7 to 8 P.M.
  Sundays, 8 to 4 P.M.
    Telephone, office and residence.

Smith Oliver C.* 44 High.
  Hours—9 to 10 A. M., 2 to 3.30, and 7 to 8 P.M.
    Office Telephone 288-2.
    Residence Telephone 1016-4.
Standish J. Herbert,* 878 Windsor av.
Starr Pierre S.† 811 Main.
  Hours—8 to 9.30 A.M., 2 to 3.30 and 7.30 to 8.80 P.M.
    House Telephone 1027-3.
Stearns Henry P.* 190 Retreat.
Stern Charles S.* 75 Pratt.
  Hours—10 A.M., to 8 P.M., and 6.80 to 7.30 P.M.
  Sundays 9 to 10 A. M.
    Telephone 121-13.
Stocker Frank H.† 40 Allen pl.
  Hours—8.30 to 9.30 A.M., 2 to 3 and 7 to 8 P.M.
  No. 116 Ann, 10 to 11 A.M.
  Sundays, 2 to 8 P.M.
    Telephone connection.
Storrs Melancthon,* 91 Ann.
Sullivan Daniel F.* 64 Church.
Sweet Henry T. 1205 Main.
Taft C. E.* 98 High.
Waite F. L.* 68 Pratt.
Waldron Wm. F.* 708 Main.
  Hours—7 to 9 A. M., 2 to 4 and 7 to 9 P. M.
    Telephone 410-5.
Ward J. W.* 487 Capitol.
Waters J. B.* 108 Trumbull.
  Hours—8 to 10 A.M., 1 to 8 and 7 to 9 P.M.
    Telephone 950.
Weir Janet M.* 88 West.
Welch Geo. K.* 108 Pratt.
Wolff A. J.* 1 Spring.

BOTANIC;
MERRIAM A. E. COLT Mrs. 926 Main. *See page 257.*

CHIROPODIST.
Bascom Mary M. 68 Pratt.
Benedict Carrie M. H. 721 Main.
Gelston M. Olive, 26 Chapel.
Hathaway Charles H. 926 Main.
Hathaway Louis C. 926 Main.
LANKTON ARBA, 2 Marsh. *See page 564.*
Mason Ella Mrs. 240 Sigourney.
Murphy Mary A. 942 Main.
Scofield Viola M. Mrs. 255 Main.
Seliger Wendel, 15 Waverly.
Varney William S. 270 Main.
Wildman Mary F. 212 Asylum.

CHRISTIAN SCIENTISTS.
*See also Metaphysicians.*
Bartlett John O. 53 Trumbull.
Graves Mary J. Mrs. 98 Russ.
Mather Lizzie D. Mrs. 1040 Windsor av.

CLAIRVOYANT.
Bascom Caroline L. Mrs. 68 Pratt.
Clark Mme M. E. 1273 Main.
Dowd Nora J. Mrs. 89 Clark.
Fuller Cynthia B. Mrs. 96 Webster.
Greenleaf M. A. Mrs. 350 Main.
Hatch E. J. Mrs. 280 Putnam.
MERRIAM A. E. COLT Mrs. 926 Main. *See page 257.*
Pierce A E. Mrs. 1118 Main.
Sweet S. A. Mrs. r. 878 Main.
Thrall Flavia A. Mrs. 1295 Main.
Tinkham Emily A. r. 878 Main.
Tracy Gertie Daniels, 19 Chapel.

ECLECTIC.
Mead James A. 80 Pearl.
MERRIAM A. E. COLT Mrs. 926 Main.
Rowe C. O. 926 Main.
Woolsey William A. 80 Charlotte.

HELMINTHOLOGIST.
LANKTON ARBA, 2 Marsh. *See page 564.*

MAGNETIC, MASSAGE AND RUBBING.
Backus Jason, 1110 Main.
Benedict Carrie M. H. Mrs. 721 Main.
Clark M. E. Mme. 1273 Main.
House C. A. Mrs. 258 Wethersfield.
JONES GEO. E. 609 Main.
  8 A.M. to 9 P.M. *See page 421.*
MERRIAM A. E. COLT Mrs. 926 Main. *See page 257.*
Moore M. J. Mrs. 1147 Main.
Osborne Adelaide E. 167 High.
PEASE HENRY A. 38 Wooster. *See page 287.*
STUTZ EUGENE, 9 Asylum, rm. 3. *See page 423.*
TAYLOR NELLIE L. Mrs. u. 24 Hopkins. *See page 853.*
Tracher Michael L. 789 Main.
Wright Harriet L. Mrs. 213 Law.

METAPHYSICIAN.
Barrows Julia R. Mrs. 127 Trumbull.
Browne Sarah E. Mrs. 870 Asylum.
Davis Minnie G. 192 High.
Skinner Jennie S. 127 Trumbull.

PILE OINTMENT.
LANKTON ARBA, 2 Marsh. *See page 564.*

MIDWIFE.
Giesler Mary Mrs. 52 Temple.
Jacobs Anna M. Mrs. 45 Morgan.
Lehmann Pauline Mrs. 189 Front.
Oakley M. Jane Mrs. 255 Putnam.
Perlitz Madeline, 150 Front.
Williams Anna M. 87 Mulberry.

## PHYSICIANS SUPPLIES.
ALLYN HOUSE DRUG STORE, 142 Asylum. *See page 35.*
GOODRICH STEPHEN & CO. 1203 Main. *See page 164.*

## PIANOS RE-BUILT.
BATTALIA LEO H. 943 Main.

## PIANO TUNERS.
*See also Music Stores.*

## PIANOS and ORGANS.
*See Music.*
BATTALIA LEO H. 943 Main.
GALLUP & METZGER, 201 Asylum. *See page 258.*

## PICKLE Mfr.
Birden J. S. & Co. 84 Vine.

## PICTURES and FRAMES.
*See Art Galleries ; Photographers.*
Deutsch Morris, 1198 Main.
ECKHARDT J. H. CO. 687 Main. *See page 418.*
VORCE A. D. CO. 752 Main. *See page 418.*
Wentworth George B. 780 Main.

WILEY LYMAN A. 251 Pearl.
    See page 546.
Willes J. H. 1018 Main.
    MOULDING MFR.
HARTF'D MOULDING WORKS,
26 Potter.    See page 517.

## PIN Mfr.
JEWELL PIN COMPANY, 81
Hicks.    See page 584.

## PIPE WRENCHES.
BILLINGS & SPENCER CO. 142
Russ.    See page 531.

## PLANING MILLS.
    See Saw Mills.
HFD. MOULDING WORKS, 26
Potter.    See page 517.

## PLATE GLASS.
BARKER F. W. & CO. 86 Morgan.
    See page 519.

## PLATE GLASS INS.
DICKINSON L. A. & CO. 664 Main.
    See page 444.

## PLASTERITE.
SANFORD CO. THE, 488 Asylum.
    See page 448.

## PLATE PRINTING.
    See Engravers; Printers.
PERKINS JAMES A. & CO. 863
Main.    See page 290.
Barnes George H. 704 Main.

## PLOW Mfr.
COLLINS CO.    See page 521.

## PLUMBERS.
    See also Steam Fitters.
AHERN JAMES, 280 Asylum. See
    page 505.
Birch Richard, 26 Church.
BULL N. B. & SON, 599-601 Main.
    See page 76.
Burns John J. 14 Trumbull.
Buths Karl A. 36 Temple.
Clapp Fred C. 24 Church.
CONRAN FRANK E. 287 Asylum.
    See page 108.
Cope Bros. 94 State.
Couch George M. 1072 Main.
CRAIG J. S. 59 Farmington. See
    page 109.
Davies & Sawyer, 53 Farmington.
Dowling Thomas L. 446 Asylum.
Duffy James F. 433 Main.
Ellison James, 46 Smith.
Garvie Robert, 12 Mulberry.
Harris James M. 302 Pearl.
Hogan Malachi, 760 Main.
HOGAN WM. B. & BROTHER, 81
Trumbull.    See page 192.
Hopper & Sweeney, 1092 Main.
Langdon & Dailey, 1280 Main.
LANGDON THOMAS H. 228 Pearl.
    See page 224.
Lawler Edward, 550 Main.
Lawler John J. 548 Asylum.
Leitch Henry, 291 Asylum.
Mahl George & Son, 1152 Main.
Mahl Edward, 1204 Main.
Melicovsky J. 207 Front.
McCarty Timothy M. 288 Main.

McGrath Edward A. 842 Park.
Murray Charles, 425 Main.
Murray John F. 186 Maple.
MURRAY WILLIAM A. 450 Main.
    See page 270.
OAKES THOMAS & SON, 11
Haynes.    See page 278.
Pepion Charles, 120 Market.
Sinnot T. J. 248 Park.
Smith John, 18 Ford.
Smith Louis, 72 Morgan.
Snow Charles L. 1076 Main.
STARBUCK R. M. & SON, 249
Pearl.    See page 425.
Trant Thomas, 889½ Main.

### SUPPLIES.
Hogan Mfg. Co. 74 Grove.
Jones Owen H. 279 High.
KNOX FRANK J. 2 So. Ann. See
    page 220.
MURRAY WILLIAM A. 450 Main.
    See page 270.

## PLUSH MFRS.
CHENEY BROS. 34 Morgan. See
    inside front cover and page 545.

## POCKET BOOK Mfr.
ARMS POCKET BOOK CO. 886
Asylum.    See page 504.

## Pole and Rein-Snap Hook.
BILLINGS & SPENCER CO. 142
Russ.    See page 531.

## POET.
Van Zile Edward S. 19 Columbia.

## POOL ROOMS.
    See also Saloons.
Dalessio Toney, 637½ Main.
Griffith Charles, 285 Asylum.
Keene Patrick F. 19 Park.
Mosco Salvator, 180 Front.
Older Abraham, 211 Front.
Russ Andrew J. 26 Church.
Taylor Charles E. 6 Ford.
Y. M. C. A. 828 Pearl. See pages
    704-705.

## POOL TABLES.
Reiche C. E. r. 599 Main.

## POP CORN.
LANKTON ARBA, 2 Marsh. See
    page 564.

## PORTER.
COLUMBIA BREWING CO. 245
Windsor.    See page 417.

## PORTIERES.
NEAL, GOFF & INGLIS CO. 980
Main.    See page 498.

## PORTRAITS.
    See also Photographers.
PORTRAIT ENGRAVING.
MUGFORD A. 177 Asylum. See
    page 476.

## POST OFFICES.
65 State.    See page 755.
Parkville P.O. 761 Park.

## POTATO CHIPS.
Plummer Chas. B. 388 Wethersfield.

## POTTERY.
    See also Crockery.
Bosworth Stanley B. 33 Front.
PURINGTON C. O. 77 New
Britain.    See page 182.

## POWDER.
    See Gun Powder.

## POULTRY.
    See Game.
ELM POULTRY YARD, 30 Sumner.    See pages 135 and 170.
STEVENS NEWELL H. 229 Asylum.    See page 345.
TAYLOR GEORGE M. 1274 Main.
    See page 353.

## PRECIOUS STONES.
    See also Diamonds.
CASE C. H. & CO. 851 Main.
    See outside front cover.
HANSEL, SLOAN & CO. 886 Main.
    See page 176.

## PRESS CLIPPINGS.
Fernald R. P. 212 Asylum.

## Pressed Paper Hangings.
BRAINERD H. B. 84 Pratt. See
    page 503.

## PRINTERS.
See also Newspapers; Lithographers;
    Copper Plate Printers.
AMERICAN PUBLISHING CO. 434
Asylum.    See page 472.
Baedor Wm. A. & Co. 90 Asylum.
Barnard William H. 154 Pearl.
BURCH & TARBOX, 91 Asylum.
    See page 497.
Calhoun Printing Co. 29 Union pl.
CASE, LOCKWOOD & BRAINARD CO. 141 Pearl. See page 475.
CLARK & SMITH, 49 Pearl. See
    page 95.
Comstock John P. 25 Asylum.
Daniels Newell P. 25 Asylum.
Daniels Henry C. 284 Asylum.
Deming Printing Co. 2 State.
ELIHU GEER'S SONS, 16 State.
    See page 474.
Finlay Bros. 25 Asylum.
Fowler & Miller Co. r. 857 Main.
Funck C. H. 258 Lawrence.
GAINES CHARLES M. 66 State.
    See page 478.
Hartford Advertising Co. 7 Central.
HARTFORD PRINTING CO. 16
State.    See page 474.
Johnson George F. 724 Main.
Meyer & Noll, 302 Asylum.
MOSELEY DAVID S. 336 Asylum.
    See page 477.
NISSEN N. & CO. 1362 Broad.
    See page 562.
Pease L. & Co. 18 Haynes.
PECK R. S. & CO. 26 High. See
    page 473.
Pfeiffer Paul F. 81 Mulberry.
Pfund William A. 62 Morgan.
Plimpton Mfg. Co. 252 Pearl.
Pyne Robert, 45 Brown.
Roeske & Fernald, 708 Main.
Turner Robert E. 3 Spruce.
Union Printing Co., W. A. Baedor
    & Co. 90 Asylum.
WILEY LOUIS G. 174 Pearl. See
    page 477.
Woods & Hurley, 9 Grove.

## PRINTERS' MATERIALS.

PHELPS, DALTON & CO. Dickinson Foundry, Boston. See p. 471.

## PRINTERS' ROLLERS.

ÆTNA STAMP WORKS, 25 Asylum.          See page 429.

## PRINTING PRESS Mfr.

COLTS PAT. FIRE ARMS MFG. CO. 17 Vandyke.   See page 543.
NATIONAL MACHINE CO. 183 Sheldon.          See page 540.

## PRINTERS OF SILKS.

CHENEY BROS. 34 Morgan. See page 545 and inside front cover.

## PRIVATE SCHOOLS.

See also Schools, Business Colleges.
WOODSIDE SEMINARY. See page 710.

## PRODUCE.

FITZGERALD RANSOM N. 44–46 Market.      See page 144.
CHAMBERLIN S. D. & SONS, 179 State. See page 89.
Haskell Chas. B. 145 State.
Noble C. S. 9 Morgan.
Weiner Bros. 54 Morgan.

## PUBLIC CHARITIES.

See Charities.

## PUBLIC SCHOOLS.

See Schools, and page 715.

## PROVISIONS.

BREWER C. S. & CO., 240 Asylum. See page 69.
INGRAHAM, SWIFT & Co. 126 Church. See page 585.
CHAMBERLIN S. D. & SONS, 179 State. See page 89.
Handy H. L. 81 Church.
HARTFORD PROVISION CO. Valley st. See page 586.
HURLBURT E. E. Valley st. See page 199.
KIBBE E. S. CO. 149 State. See page 587.
POTTER & PAYNE, 405–407 Allyn. See page 586.

## PUBLIC HALLS, PUBLIC BUILDINGS, Etc.

See Trotting Parks; Clubs, Armories.

PUBLIC HALLS.

Alliance Hall, r. 26 Chapel.
Alumni Hall, Trinity College.
Arba Lankton Total Abstinence, 143 Commerce.
Auditorium, 180 Asylum.
Bliss Hall, 11 Pratt.
Bliss New Hall, 881 Main.
Bolden Hall, 26 Elm.
Centennial Hall, 6 Hungerford.
Central Hall, 11 Central.
City Hall, 800 Main.
City Mission Hall, 234 Pearl.
Columbian Hall, 903 Main.
Conrads Hall, 52 Market.
Elk Hall, 7 Central.
FOOT GUARD ARMORY HALL, 159 High.      See page 496.
Fraternity Hall, 323 Pearl.
Germania Hall, 1056 Main.

Glenwood Hall, 614 Capitol.
Good Templars Hall, 881 Main.
Good Will Hall, 93 Pratt.
Grand Army Hall, 926 Main.
Harbison Hall, 458 Main.
Hartford Turnehalle Co. 10 Morgan.
Hibernian Hall, 5 American.
Hibernian Rifle Club Hall, 104 Asy.
Hosmer Hall (Hartford Theol. Seminary), 1507 Broad.
Jarvis Hall, Trinity College.
Jewell Hall, 323 Pearl.
Kastner Hall, 52 Market.
Keney Hall, 98 Pratt.
Knights of Labor Hall, 11 Central.
Mænnerchor Hall, 5 American.
Masonic Hall, 51 Ann, c. Allyn.
Memorial Hall, (Eldridge) Congregational, 426 Asylum.
Odd Fellows Hall, 976 Main.
Olsen Hall, 19 Mulberry.
Opera House, 933 Main.
Parkville Hall, 718 Park.
Parsons Theatre, 66 Prospect.
Putnam Phalanx Hall, 6 Haynes.
Pythian Hall, 757 Main.
Sangerbund Hall, 11 Central.
Spiritual Hall, 81 Asylum.
Stangler Hall, New Park, c. Ham.
St. Augustine Hall, 726 Main.
St. James Hall, 300 Allyn.
St. Johns Hall, 458 Main.
Temple of Honor Hall, 302 Asylum.
Turnerbund Hall, 1056 Main.
Unity Hall, 62 Pratt.
Weller Hall, 52 Market.
Wright Hall, 234 Pearl.

BUILDINGS.

Acme, 37½ Church.
Ætna Life Ins. Co.'s Bldg, 650 Main.
American School for Deaf, 690 Asy.
Ballerstein Building, 904 Main.
Batterson Block, 870 Asylum.
Belmont, 14 Church.
Boardman Building, 302 Asylum.
Bonded Warehouse, 74 Trumbull.
Brown, Thomson & Co's Building, 926 Main.
Buckingham Block, 261 to 285 Main.
Bushnell Flats, 34 West.
Cadden The, 1042–1044 Main.
Capitol, on Bushnell Park.
Cheney Building, 926 Main.
City Mission Building, 234 Pearl.
Collins Building, 81 Asylum.
Columbia Building, 903 Main.
Cone Building, 87 Asylum.
Conn. Mutual Life Ins. Bldg. 783 Mn.
Cooks Building, 86 Pratt.
County Building, 85 Trumbull and 86 Allyn.
County Jail, 42 Seyms.
Courant Building, 62–68 State.
Ely Block, 645 Main.
Exchange Block, Main, c. State.
Fire Bell, 48 Pearl.
First National Bank, 50 State.
Florence The, 14–16 Florence.
Foster Block, 284 Asylum.
Fox Building, 958 Main.
Geer's Directory Building, 16 State.
Goodwin Block, 323 Asylum, elevator entrance, 17 Haynes.
Halls of Record, 114 Pearl, c. Tru.
Hartford Fire Ins. Co. Bldg. 53 Tru.
Hartford Hospital, 20 South Hudson.
Hartford Theological Seminary, 1507 Broad.

Hartford Lib. Assoc'n, 5 Athenæum.
Hartford Trust Co. Block 750 Main
   2 Cen. elevator entrn. 756 Main.
Hills Block, 847 Main.
Home for the Aged, 36 Jefferson.
Howard Building, 440–448 Asylum.
Hunt Memorial Bldg. 38 Prospect.
Hurlbut Block, 873 Asylum.
Imperial Building, 545 Main.
Industrial Building, 581 Capitol.
Judd & Root Building, 389 Allyn.
Loomis Block, 46–54 Ann.
Marble Block, 9–15 Central.
McGoodin Block, 346 Windsor av.
Metropolitan Block, 980–986 Main.
Miller Building, 943 Main.
Morgue, 38 Kinsley.
Northam Towers, Trinity College.
Parsons Building, 875–885 Main.
Phœnix Bank Building, 803 Main.
Phœnix Ins. Co. bldg. 54–66 Pearl.
Phœnix Mutual Life Ins. Co. 49 Pearl.
Pierson Building, 16–22 State.
Police Office and Station, 38 Kinsley.
Post Office, cor. State, American and Central.
Putnam Building, 706 Main.
Retreat for the Insane, 80 Wash.
Roof Garden, 80 State.
Roxbury, 1308–1305 Main.
Saengerbund Hall, 8 Morgan.
Sage-Allen Building, 900 Main.
Sceery's Block, 46 Wells.
Seabury Hall, Trinity College.
Silsby Block, 152 Allyn.
State Arsenal, 264 Windsor av.
Stearn Building, 75 Pratt.
St. Clair, 7–9 Canton.
The Linden, 427 Main.
Times Building, 716 to 724 Main.
Town House, 2 Holcomb.
Trinity College, Summit one mile south of the Capitol.
Union for Home Work Building, 239 Market.
Unity Building, 68 Pratt.
Wadsworth Athenæum, 624 Main, opposite Mulberry.
Warburton Building, 230 Asylum.
Watkinson Library, 624 Main.
Waverly Block, 721 Main.
Wellington Building, 488 Main.
Winthrop, 1293–1295 Main.
Woods Building, 784 Main.
Young Men's Christian Association, 315, 323 Pearl.

PARKS.

See also page 567.

Hartford Baseball Park, Weth.
LAUREL PARK, Manchester t. See page 557.
Werders Park, Wethersfield.

## PUBLISHERS.

See also Book Publishers; Printers.

HARTFORD POCKET GUIDE, 252 Asylum.      See page 505.
HARTFORD WEEKLY GUIDE, 252 Asylum.
Monk George D. 7 Central.
White & Warner, 115 State.

## PUMPING ENGINES.

GRANT C. L. 22 Belden. See page 535.
LANGDON THOMAS H. 228 Pearl See page 224.

### PULLEY Mfr.
LEE H. K. 223 State. *See page 539.*
LINCOLN & CO. 54 Arch. *See page 522.*
PICKERING W. H. & CO. 110 Commerce. *See page 537.*
PRATT & WHITNEY CO.1 Flower. *See page 523.*

### PUMPS.
ANDREWS & CREEDON, 446 Asylum. *See page 542.*
DAVIS L B. & SON, 40 Cushman. *See page 546.*
GRANT C. L. 22 Belden. *See page 535.*

### PUNCHES.
Hill Warren Co. The, 174 Pearl.

### QUARRIES.
WINDSOR RED STONE CO. *See page 508.*

### RAGS.
*See also Junk Shops.*
GARVAN P. 205 State. *See p. 472.*
Stone Jesse E. 44 Woodbridge.

### RAILROAD COMMISS'RS.
Room 42 in Capitol.
*See page 663.*

### RAILROAD LAMP Mfr.
HOWARD JAMES L. & CO. 438 Asylum. *See page 527.*

### RAILROAD TICKETS.
*See Tickets.*

### RAILWAY SUPPLIES.
HOWARD JAMES L. & CO. 438 Asylum. *See page 527.*

### RAILROAD OFFICES.
H. & C. W. R. R. 59 Spruce.
Hartford & Conn. Valley R.R. 450 Asylum.
Hartford Street Railway, 115 State.
New York & New England R. R. 460 Asylum.
New York, New Haven & Hartford R. R. 450 Asylum.
Philadelphia, Reading & New England R. R. 59 Spruce.

### RAILROAD PASSENGER STATIONS.
Hartford & Conn. Valley R. R. Stations, 466 Asylum, and 265 State,
Hartford & Conn. Western R. R. Station, 59 Spruce.
New York & New England R. R. Station, 466 Asylum.
New York, New Haven & Hartford R. R. Station, 466 Asylum.
Philadelphia, Reading & N.E.R.R. office 59 Spruce.

### R. R. FREIGHT DEPOTS.
New York & New England R. R. 95 Pleasant.
New York, New Haven & Hartford R. R. 98 Kilbourn.
Philadelphia, Reading & N.E.R.R. freight depot, 69 Spruce.

### RANGES.
*See also Stoves.*
BLISS EDWARD, 1263 Main. *See page 494.*
FENN L. T. 613 Main. *See p. 501.*
FLINT GEO. W. & CO. 61 Asylum. *See page 147.*

### RATCHET DRILLS.
BILLINGS & SPENCER CO. 142 Russ. *See page 531.*
PRATT & WHITNEY CO. 1 Flower. *See page 523.*

### RAZOR GRINDER.
*See Cutlers, etc.*

### RAZOR MFR.
COWLISHAW HENRY, 162 Pearl. *See page 535.*

### RAZOR STRAPS.
HURD OLIVER. *See page 586.*

### READING ROOMS.
*See Libraries.*
Christian Science, 252 Asylum.
Christian Science, 53 Trumbull.
H'tf'd Public Library, 5 Athenæum.
Temperance Reading room, 102 Sheldon
Yoke Fellows Band, Fourth Church, 1091 Main.
YOUNG MEN'S CHRISTIAN ASSOCIATION. *See pages 704–705.*

### READY MADE CLOTHING.
*See Clothing.*

### REAL ESTATE and LOANS.
*See also Auction and Commission, Brokers.*
Barber George W. r. 843 Park.
BARTLETT F. W. & F. E. 212 Asylum. *See page 420.*
Beator Howard G. 82 Pearl.
Bissell Thomas H. 95 Ann.
BOYNTON E. B. 904 Main. *See page 66.*
BRAY W. J. 85 Imlay. *See p. 512.*
Bullard, Johnson & Shipman, 175 Asylum.
Butler & Helion, 756 Main.
Chapman & Muchlow, 870 Asylum.
Coleman John J. 545 Main.
Collateral Loan Co. 71 Asylum.
CONKLIN H. W. 9 Central. *See page 101.*
CONN. BUILDING & LOAN ASSO. 252 Asy. *See page 480.*
Cowles S. W. 295 Windsor av.
Cumnings L. G. 100 Edwards.
Curtis John F. 792 Main.
Delliber Charles H. 218 Park.
DILLINGHAM E. B. 709 Main. *See page 122.*
Donovan Patrick B. 92 Pearl.
Doty Samuel C. 757 Main.
Edwards Charles W. B. 68 Albany.
Eldridge James W. 2 State.
FIDELITY CO. 49 Pearl. *p. 488.*
Flint Harold F. C. 252 Asylum.
Forrest Geo. C. 847 Asylum.
Glazier A. Judson, 8 State.
Gleszer & Seltzer, 2 State.
Goodwin J. J. & F. 783 Main, rm. 7.
GREENE JACOB H. 721 Main. *See page 425.*

Gridley Henry R. 18 State.
GRIFFITH WM. RICHARD, 66 State. *See page 427.*
Hamilton Joseph D. 2 State.
Hart E. G. 18 State.
Hartford Building & Loan Association, 870 Asylum.
Hartford Real Estate & Investment Co. 118 Asylum.
Healey Thomas L. 756 Main.
Huntington Chas.G.23 Wethersfield.
Hub Loan Co. 180 Asylum.
Hurd Charles F. 80 Pearl.
International Loan Office, 2 State.
Kempner Nathan & Son, 57 Morgan.
Kennedy Henry, 793 Main.
Lamb Lorenzo. 541 Main.
LINCOLN FREDERICK M. 911 Main. *See page 427.*
Loan & Guarantee Co. 49 Pearl.
MARQUARDT H. C. 904 Main. *See page 243.*
Marrett Thomas A. 58 Trumbull.
Mayer & Bartholomew, 7 Central.
Merril Arthur H. 373 Asylum.
MOORE GEO W. & CO. 759 Main. *See page 429.*
MULHALL JAMES, 29 Pearl. *See page 267.*
New England Loan and Trust Co. 757 Main.
Parsons Edward W. 9 Central.
Pierson Frederick A. 721 Main.
Pitkin Ralph, 575 Farmington.
Plato B. H. 71 Asylum.
Prentice Charles H. 847 Main.
Price Louis S. 225 Market.
Price Robert C. 722 Main.
Rhodes William H. 49 Pearl.
Roberts Charles F. 190 Pearl.
Rosenfeld & Eosenblatt, 15 Morgan.
Rundbaken John, 2 State.
SECURITY CO. 62 Pearl. *See page 488.*
Sheldon E. A., Whiting.
SHELTON EDWARD, 66 State. rm. 6. *See page 426.*
Stearns Charles S. 75 Pratt.
Steinmetz Bros. 32 Asylum.
STEINMETZ WILLIAM P. 80 Pearl. *See page 343.*
Taintor George E. 223 Asylum.
Traute & Loeser, 704 Main.
TULLER GEO. W. 847 Main. *See page 360.*
WAKEFIELD AGENCY, 720 Main. *See page 424.*
Walder Aaron, 10 Morris.
WARD WILLIAM, 862 Main. *See page 368.*
Waterous Richard G. 2 Asylum.
West End Land Co. 703 Main.
WHITE WESTON L. 884 Main. *See page 508.*
Whitmore Franklin G. 700 Main.
Wood, Harmon & Co. 721 Main.
Woods George H. 754 Main.
Woodard Herbert M. 92 Pearl.

### REAMING MACHINE Mfr.
PRATT & WHITNEY CO. 1 Flower. *See page 523.*

### REAL LACES CLEANED.
Eaton Henry J. Mrs. 92 Pearl.

### RED SAND STONE.
WINDSOR RED STONE CO. *See page 508.*

## REFRIGERATING ROOMS.
FISCHER HUBERT BREWERY, 315 Park. *See page 492.*

## REFRIGERATORS.
*See also Stoves and Tinware.*

## REGISTRARS of ELECTORS
Cotter William, 114 Pearl.
Young E. S. 114 Pearl.

## RELIEF WORK.
NEAL, GOFF & INGLIS OO. 980 Main. *See page 498.*
SANFORD CO. THE, 488 Asylum. *See page 443.*

## RENTING.
GRIFFITH WM. RICHARD, 66 State. *See page 427.*
Woodard Herbert M. 92 Pearl.

## RENTS COLLECTED.
BARTLETT F. W. & F. E. 212 Asylum. *See page 420.*
CONKLIN H. W. 9 Central. *See page 101.*
SHELTON E. 66 State, room 6. *See page 426.*

## REPAIRER.
Robbins E. D. 54 Pratt.

## RE-SEATING CHAIRS.
MARTIN J. HENRY, 42 Seyms. *See page 244.*

## RESTAURANTS.
*See also Hotels; Boardinghouses.*
Abroza Charles, 189 Front.
Anderson Augusta, 301 Lawrence.
Anderson Charles J. 618 Capitol.
Needham, 1049 Main.
BACKES F. W. 169 Asylum. *See page 45.*
Bagot John R. (oysters), 107 State.
Ball Harry, 8 Central.
Banks J. H. 244 State.
Barnard W. Mrs. 12 Ford.
Bates George D. 196 Asylum.
BESSE P. & J. 701 Main. *See page 57.*
BROWN, THOMSON & CO. 942 Main. *See page 499.*
Bushnell Park Restaurant, 323 Pl.
Callender Bros. 296 Asylum.
Capitol Av. House 276 Lawrence.
Central Row Restaurant, 8 Central.
Cross W. P. H. 257 State.
Crocker E. A. 18 Central.
Daigneau Eli, 276 Lawrence.
Davenport Joseph C. 7 American.
DeFea Raphael, 260 Front.
DeFelice Alonzo, 52 Front.
DeJorio Frank, 74 Talcott.
Dillon R. J., R.R. depot, 466-478 Asy
Farr Frank, 148 Front.
Fenwick David, 111 Pearl.
Goebel Fred Jr. & Co. 358 Asylum.
Guethlein Leo F. 33 Pearl.
Habenstein E. 53 Ann.
Hamel George, 19 Goodman.
Hammond C. L. 326 Asylum.
Heins Brothers, 430 Asylum.
Herrman W. D. & Co. 106 Asylum.
HONISS T. A. ( *Oysters* ) 30 State. *See page 589.*
Koch August, 29 Central.

Lawlor B. S. manager, 375 Asylum.
LONG BROS. 78-82 Sta. *See p. 233.*
LOW DO YON, 182 State. *See page 512.*
Mascovitz Solomon, 201 Front.
McClean Joseph, 10 Gold.
Merrill L. D. 54 Prospect.
MIRROR PALACE DINING ROOMS, 78 State. *See p. 233.*
MUZZEY MARY R. Mrs. 14½ Church. *See page 561.*
Neill Henry W. 3 American.
Park View Hotel, 430 Asylum.
Payton Frank P. 330 Pearl.
Praedella Joseph, 90 Front.
Roesner August, 1098 Main.
Russell Joseph D. 246 State.
SCHROEDER F. 941 Main. *See page 322.*
Strempfer John, 60 Front.
Strong Henry N. 189 Asylum.

## RETREAT FOR INSANE.
*See also Hospitals; Orphan Asylum.*
CONNECTICUT RETREAT FOR INSANE, 30 Washington. *See pages 698, 699.*

## RIDING STABLES.
*See Livery Stables.*

## RIFLE RANGES.
Companies of 1st Reg't, So. Meadow.
Franklin, So. Meadow.
German. 300 Wethersfield.

## ROMAN BATHS.
JONES GEORGE E. 609 Main. *See page 421.*

## ROOFERS and SLATERS.
*See also Tinners.*
Blevins David, 383 Park.
Capitol City Roofing-Co. 110 Pratt.
Clark Merlin F. 19 Center.
Clark Samuel P. 114 Mather.
Clarke E. W. & Son, r. 32 Village.
Dunlap George G. 4 American.
Ford J. P. 373 Asylum.
Gans Louis A. 199 Front.
Lyman Eleazer H. 18 Elmer.
Sherman Seth E. 238 Martin.
WHITE F. W. 1124 Main. *See page 507.*

## ROOM MOULDING.
BAXTER WM. H. 231 Asylum. *See page 52.*

## ROOMS TO RENT.
Freeman Mary E. 1136 Main.
Krog Hans P. 24 Gold.
Robinson Fannie, 1264 Main.
Tillotson Florence, 1221 Main.
Tillotson Katherine E. Mrs. 1082 Main.
Wall Josephine Mrs. 1122 Main.

## ROSES.
WALLACE W. E. Farmington av. between Whiting and Quaker lane. *See page 367.*

## RUBBER BELTING, PACKING and HOSE.
JOHNS-PRATT, 555 Capitol. *See page 540.*

## RUBBER CLOTHING, Etc.
Bidwell John C. & Co. 237 Asylum.
DOW PETER Jr. 278 Asylum. *See page 561.*
Pitkin & Harlow, 28 Asylum.
McGee Mfg. Co. r. 78 Park.

## RUBBER MOULD Mfr.
CLARK EDRED W. 31 Wells. *See page 526.*

## RUBBER STAMPS.
*See Stamps and Stencils.*
ÆTNA STAMP WORKS, 25 Asylum. *See page 429.*
BURCH GEORGE W. 91 Asylum. *See page 497.*
PARKER T. M. 71 Asylum. *See page 534.*

## RUGS.
*See Carpet Stores.*
Donchian S. C. 75 Pearl.
LOTKER KARL, 189 Main. *See page 420.*
NEAL, GOFF & INGLIS CO. 980 Main. *See page 498.*

## Rug and Carpet Cleaning.
Standard Rug and Carpet Renovating Co. r. 13-15 Wells.

## RUSSIAN BATHS.
*See also Baths.*
JONES GEORGE E 609 Main. *See page 421.*

## SADDLE Mfrs.
*See Harness, Etc.*
SMITH, BOURN & CO. 334 Asylum. *See page 547.*

## SAFE DEPOSIT VAULTS.
*See Banks and Trust Co's.*

## SAFES.
Ashmead James H. & Son, 41 Tru.
BILL BROS. 46 Ann. *See p. 550.*

## SAFE and LOCK REPAIRING.
HALLIDAY W. H. 131 Front. *See page 506.*

## SAFE MOVERS.
BILL BROS. 46 Ann. *See page 550.*
HEBARD & CO. 213 State. *See page 552.*

## SAILS.
ROBERTS S. F. 124 State. *See page 502.*

## SALE STABLES.
*See Livery Stable.*
Blumenthal Isaac R. 20 Morgan.
Frink George H. 140 Trumbull.
Gaines Fred. S. 522 Windsor av.
Kenyon Edward F. 287 Albany.
Price Robert T. & Son, 82 Francis.
RAYMOND & SLOAN, 19 Mather. *See page 549.*

## SALOONS.
*See also Brewers; Bottlers; Liquors.*
Ahern William T. 49 Sheldon.
Allyn House Cafe, 148 Asylum.
Arnold & Phelan, 1242 Main.

Banning John, 17 Mulberry.
Barrows John, 1 Morgan.
Barry Albert, 1181 Main.
Barry Thomas, 217 Front.
Becher Frank, 841 Main.
Bergen Keron, 84 Walnut.
Berry & Cosgrove, 997 Main.
Bondy Sigmund, 42 Asylum.
Buckley & O'Laughlin, 22 Central.
Burns George H. 136 Windsor.
Burns John J. 288 Zion.
Butler James E. 35 Mulberry.
Camp G. W. 161 State.
City Hotel, 651 Main.
Claffey John R. 223 Main.
Clancy Timothy A. 1167 Main.
Clark John J. 245 State.
Clifford Michael P. 117 Windsor.
Colbert Daniel, 130 Front.
Colburn Chas. M. 370 Albany.
Coleman Cornelius F. 107 Main.
Conners William, 14 Albany.
Conrad Philip, 50 Market.
Coppelli Michael, 146 Front.
Copperberg Julius Jr. 107 Asylum.
Costello William, 86 Albany.
Curtin John D. 526 Main.
Day Frederick E. 336 Main.
Dolin J. F. 1061 Main.
Donaghue Edward, 352 Asylum.
Donaghue William, 28 Union pl.
Donahue Thomas, 268 Park.
Donaghue William & Co. 1047 Main.
Dougherty Philip, 44 Spruce.
Doyle Patrick, 28 Spruce.
Driscoll David C. 22 Albany.
Dwyer John J. 30 Albany.
Emmonds Joseph, 88 Front.
Ernst Henry, 27 Mulberry.
Fagan Martin, 1076 Broad.
Farrell John A. 340 Park.
Farrell John H. 532 Main.
Farrell Morris, 20 Ford.
Farrell & Co. 208 State.
Feeley Matthew J. 24 Front.
Fenton James M. 34 South Prospect.
FISCHER HUBERT, 315 Park and
  158 Front.          See page 492.
Flaherty Daniel J. 17 Central.
Foley Daniel, 6 Franklin.
Foley William A. 98 State.
Fox Martin, 214 Sheldon.
Fox Michael J. 57 Market.
Franzen Frederick W. 359 Main.
Gaffey John F. 116 State.
Gallagher Thomas F. 75 Windsor.
Giovanni Motta, 79 Windsor.
Goggins J. S. & Co. 71 Windsor.
Goodacre William H. 788 Main.
Gorman J. O. 287 Allyn.
Gothers John J. 65 Sheldon.
Govan James, 119 Front.
Grady John C. 147 Windsor.
Graf Adolph, 36 Temple.
Greenberg Leon, 72 Trumbull.
Griffin John, 82 So. Prospect.
Guethlein Leo F. 33 Pearl.
Hackett Thomas J. 269 Main.
Hale Edwin C. 30 Church.
Hardie Thomas C. 287 Park.·
Hartnett & Bartley, 1061 Main.
Hawksworth Henry, 111 Main.
Heingartner Sutter, 39 Mulberry.
Heins Bros. 430 Asy. & 26 Union pl.
Heneghan William, 141 Windsor.
Henning Otto, 31 Temple.
Heublein Edmund, 605 Main.
Heublein G. F. & Bro. 931 Main.
Hewins Matt H. 734 Main.

Hirth Joseph, 279 Main.
Hudner William F. 61 Front.
Huebler Alfred, 287 Asylum.
Hunter & Clark, 123 Pearl.
Hurter Rudolph, 84 Front.
Hynes Matthew, 134 State.
Janson Henry, 1056 Main.
Johnson Andrew, 282 Park.
Johnson Andrew, 44 Temple.
Johnson Charles E. 183 Front.
Kehoe & Geary, 167 State.
Kelley James M. 15 Spruce.
Kiely Michael J. 1119 Main.
Killian Terrence, 77 Sheldon.
Kilmartin & O'Brien, 88 Sheldon.
King M. H. 2 Lawrence.
Kooh August, 29 Central.
Kroher John, 66 Temple.
Krumgold Henry, 60 Pleasant.
Lacy Thomas, 529 Main.
Lathrop Walter H. 314 Asylum.
Lawler James F. 202 State.
Lennehan Michael G. 125 Pearl.
Leroy D. & N. N. 212 Front.
Loeser F. C. & A. W. 289 Park.
LONG BROS. 78 State.  See p. 233.
Long John C. 583 Main.
Longworth Joseph, 27 North
Lundy Edward M. 46 Windsor.
Madden Michael, 36 Park.
Lawler, John J. 637 Main
Mainello Felix, 222 Front.
Manion Wm. F. 55 Potter.
McCarty John, 53 Windsor.
McDermott James J. 25 Temple.
McGrath William, 29 Sheldon.
McIntyre Edward F. 109 State.
McKee William J. 220 Front.
McKeough Martin, 110 Albany.
McKernan Edward F. 532 Main.
Meehan Patrick J. 1177 Main.
Melrose & Keane, 330 Main.
Michael Solomon, 182 Front.
Melekoske Andrew, 125 Front.
Miller Willis E. 200 Asylum.
MIRROR PALACE DINING
  ROOMS.  See page 283.
Mohon Thomas, 61 Elm.
Monahan Thomas, 70 Front.
Morrissey John J. 122 Albany.
Motta Giovanni, 79 Windsor.
Murphy Robert, 212 State.
Nolan John F. (manager), 365 Asy.
O'Brien & Connell, 194 State.
O'Brien W. W. 178 Asylum.
O'Connell William M. 69 Pleasant.
Olson & Jacobson, 80 Front.
Pagram John, 68 Hicks.
Pannone Peter, 190 Front.
Pattison Joseph, 1211 Main.
Pearson Henry, 172 Sheldon.
Plikunas Justin, 92 Front.
Ragan Peter, 48 Temple.
Reiche Herman C. 357 Asylum.
Rice H. W. 257 Asylum.
River House, 76 Ferry.
Rogers Barnett, 165 Front.
Russell Frank H. 109 Front.
Russell Joseph D. 246 State.
St. Germain Remi, 85 Front.
Saunders Frank J. 302 Park.
Schott Carl, 6 State.
Sexton James J. 116 Front.
Shea Michael J. 53½ Windsor.
Sheehan C. J. 657 Main.
Sichler George E. 44 Union pl.
Silk Patrick J. 25 Spruce.
Smith Frank P. 62 Front.
Smith P. B. & Co. 989 Main.

Spollen Patrick, 186 Sheldon.
Spring Henry, 187 State.
Steinbruck & Kuehn, 70 Temple.
Steiner & Stern, 29 Temple.
Stephen Charles C. 197 Front.
Strempfer John, 60 Front.
Stickney Charles L. 1219 Main.
Sullivan Timothy, 18 Market.
Trout Frank, 21 Kilbourn.
Turner William J. 46 Union pl.
Ullrich Ferd. 17 Sanford.
United States Hotel, 26 State.
Vail James, 87 Windsor.
Vaillant Henry L. 36 Wells.
Wall Garrett, 184 State.
Warren & Kenney, 3 Front.
Weidlich Herman, 5 American.
Weinman Philip, 132 Market.
Weisman John, 76 Front.
Welch James, 16 Sheldon.
Wilson Patrick, 255 State.
Winter Thomas J. 368 Allyn.

### SALT; and SALT FISH.

Betts Edward H. 216 State.
CHAMBERLIN S. D. & SONS, 179
  State.  See page 89.
FITZGERALD RANSOM N. 44-46
  Market.  See page 144.
FRISBIE L. T. CO. 79 Talcott.  See
  page 586.
KISBE E. S' CO. 149 State.  See
  page 587.
POTTER & PAYNE, 405-407 Allyn.
  See page 586.

### SAND.

SHERMAN M. W. & SON, Donald.
  See page 551.

### SANITARIUMS.

  See Hospitals.
WALNUT LODGE, 56 Fairfield. See
  page 712.

### SANITARY PLUMBING.

  See Plumbers.
AHERN JAMES, 280 Asylum.  See
  page 605.
CRAIG J. S. 59 Farmington.  See
  page 109.
OAKS THOS. & SON, 11 Haynes.
  See page 278.

### SASH AND BLINDS.

  See also Doors, Etc.

### SAVINGS.

  See Banks.
CONN. BUILDING & LOAN AS-
  SOCIATION, 252 Asylum.  See
  page 480.
HARTFORD BUILDING & LOAN
  ASSOCIATION, 270 Asylum.
  See page 445.
WAKEFIELD W. L. 720 Main.  See
  page 424.

### SAW FILER.

COWLISHAW H. 162 Pearl.  See
  page 535.
HALLIDAY W. H. 131 Front.  See
  page 506.

### SAW MILL MFG.

LEE H. K. 223 State.  See p. 539.

## SAW MILLS and PLANING.

FRENCH H. A. 554 Main. *See page 512.*
HARTFORD MOULDING W'KS. Alfred T. Ricker, 26 Potter. *See page 517.*
Otis & Burr, 169 Front.
SCOVILLE A. W. WOODWORK-ING CO. Charter Oak, junction Vredendale. *See page 516.*
TAYLOR E. & SONS, 335 Sheldon. *See page 509.*

## SCALLOP MACHINE MFR.

MERROW MACHINE CO. 28 Laurel. *See page 585.*

## SCHOOL FURNITURE.

Case O. D. & Co. 302 Asylum.

## SCHOOLS.

*For full information, see pages 715 to 717. See Business Colleges, Seminaries, Dancing Schools, Music Teachers, and Writing Teachers.*
Academy Imma. Concep. 89 Church.
Academy of Mt. St. Joseph, 150 Farmington.
Academy of Sacred Heart, 158 Main.
American Asylum, Deaf, 690 Asy.
Arsenal (Dist. 5), 264 Windsor av.
Bachimont Stephane 721 Main.
Barbour Lucy A. 44 Beacon.
Bartlett Margaret, 31 Farmington.
Brandt E. M. Miss, 25 Sherman.
Brown (1), 160-170 Market.
Burbank Julia B. 714 Asylum.
Catholic Free School, 71 Ann.
Catholic Orphan Asylum, for boys, 91 Church.
Catholic Orphan Asylum, for girls, 89 Church.
Catholic Parish School, 353 Capitol.
CHANDLER SHORTHAND SCHOOL, 252 Asy. *See p. 710.*
Charter Oak Av. (2), 91 Charter Oak.
Connecticut Institute & Industrial School for the Blind, 334 Wethersfield, 1205 Asylum.
Hannum T. W. 302 Asylum.
HARTFORD BUSINESS COL-LEGE, 370 Asylum. *See p. 711.*
Hartford Grammar, 89 Hopkins.
Hartford Orphan Asylum, 171 Putnam.
Hartford Public High, 89 Hopkins.
HONEY FREDERIC R. 904 Main, room 99. *See page 422.*
HUNTSINGER E. M. 30 Asylum. *See outside back cover.*
Lawrence Street (2), 85 Lawrence.
MORSE E H. 370 Asylum. *See page 711.*
Northeast (8), Westland.
Northwest (9), Albany.
OLMSTEAD COMMERCIAL COL-LEGE, 756 Main. *See page 710.*
Parkville (2), New Park.
Second North (3), 249 High.
Seybold Mmd. 926 Main.
Smith Elizabeth G. 650 Main.
SMITH SARA J. 1204 Asylum. *See page 710.*
Sperry Mary B. 323 Pearl.
Southwest (7), White.
St.Anne's Convent,246 Farmington.
St. Augustine School, 152 Far.
St. Catherine's Orphan Asylum, 93 Church.

St. James Orphan Asy. 93 Church.
St. Patrick's Free School, 71 Ann.
St. Patrick's Orphan Asylum, 93 Ch.
St. Peter's Parochial, rear 170 Main.
St. Thomas Seminary, 352 Collins.
Steele George W. 8 Spring.
Steele Mary K. 8 Spring.
Thrall Ida R. 63 Church.
TRAINING SCHOOL NURSES, 20 So. Hudson. *See pages 700-701.*
Wadsworth St. (2), 86 Wadsworth.
Washington (6), 1 Washington.
Watkinson Juvenile Farm School, Albany, c. Bloomfield.
West Middle (4), 927 Asylum.
Wethersfield Avenue (2), 175 Weth.
Wilson Street (6), Wilson.
WOODSIDE YOUNG LADIES SEM. 1204 Asy. *See page 710.*
Y. M. C. A., 328 Pearl. *See pages 704-705.*

## SCRAP IRON and METALS.

*See Junk Shops.*
KATZ JACOB, 7 North. *See p. 502.*

## SCREEN DRESSING.

AMIDON F. S. r. 60 Temple. *See page 40.*

## SCREENS.

AMIDON F. S. r. 60 Temple. *See page 40.*

## SCREW Mfr.

Atlantic Screw Works, 70 Huyshope.
Spencer Automatic S. Co. 133 Shel.

## SCREW PLATES and DIES.

BILLINGS & SPENCER CO. 142 Russ. *See page 531.*

## SCROLL SAW GOODS.

Pomeroy A. H. 98 Asylum.

## SCROLL SAWYERS.

*See also Wood Turners.*
STRICKLAND & SHEA, 20 Potter. *See page 516.*

## SCULPTORS.

*See also Marble Works, Stone Yards.*
Conrads Carl H. 1260 Main.
ENTRESS ALBERT, r. 597 Main. *See page 511.*

## Sealer Weights, Measures.

Roberts E. D. 800 Main, City Hall.

## SEAL PRESSES.

*See also Stamps.*
ÆTNA STAMP WORKS, 25 Asylum. *See page 429.*
BURCH GEORGE W. 91 Asylum. *See page 497.*
PARKER T. M. 71 Asylum. *See page 584.*

## SEAL SACQUE Mfr.

*See also Hats, Caps, etc.*
STILLMAN & CO. 59 Pratt. *See outside back cover.*
WILLIAMS ALFRED & SON, 99 Pratt. *See page 379.*

## SEAMSTRESSES.

*See also Dressmakers; Tailors.*
Andrews Margaret, 877 Main.
Barber Jane, u. 42 Village.

Beach Sarah, 877 Main.
Birmingham Mary, 271 Jefferson.
Cambridge Carrie S. 67 Green.
Christensen Christain, 41 Asylum.
Condron Mary L. u. 133 Market.
Degnan Annie L. u. 50 Retreat.
Foley Elizabeth, 15 Goodman pl.
Foley Hannah, 68 Church.
Gaffey Mary A. 121 Maple.
Goodwin Grace, u. 23 Canton.
House Mary Mrs. 289 Asylum.
Jackson Sarah J. 877 Main.
Kelsey Sarah J. 16 Spring.
McClellan Ann Mrs. u. 133 Market.
Merz Grace M. 35 Park.
Peck Mary A. 1 Goodman.
Primus T. R. Miss, 20 Wadsworth.
Ragne Salvator, 41 Asylum.
Roberta Eliza J. Mrs. 18½ Church.
Root Martha C. 111¾ Ann.
Scarritt Jennie, 120 Jefferson.
Sullivan Catherine, 20 Spring.
Whiting Jennie A. 17¾ Wadsworth.
Wickham Rosa Mrs. u.r. 1225 Main.
Willard Ruth A. Mrs. u.71 Asylum.
Wittman Sophia, 6 Queen.

## SEED STORES.

*See also Florists, Hardware.*
Cadwell & Jones, 1082 Main.
CHAMBERLIN S. D. & SONS, 179 State. *See page 87.*

## SELECT SCHOOL.

*See Schools.*

## SELF-TIMING SPEED IN-DICATOR Mfrs.

EDDY ELECTRIC MFG. CO. Windsor t. *See page 536.*

## SEMINARIES.

*See Schools.*
HARTFORD THEOLOGICAL SEMINARY, 1507 Broad. *See pages 708-709.*
LaSalette Seminary, New Park av.
WOODSIDE SEMINARY, 1204 Asylum. *See page 710.*

## SENSITIVE DRILLS.

*See Drilling Machines.*
DWIGHT SLATE MACHINE CO. 13 Central. *See page 525.*

## SETTEE Mfr.

BISHOP E. C. & CO. 34 Capen. *See page 60.*
HARTFORD WOVEN WIRE M. CO. 618 Capitol. *See page 522.*

## SEWER BRICK.

DONAHUE D. J. r. 685 Windsor av. *See page 520.*

## SEWER PIPE.

*See also Bricks; Tiles.*
ANDREWS & PECK, 88 Market. *See page 509.*

## SEWING MACHINE SHUT TLE Mfr.

BILLINGS & SPENCER CO. 142 Russ. *See page 531.*

## SEXTONS.

*See Churches, page 683.*

## SEWING MACHINE Mfrs.
SMYTH MFG. CO. 648 Main. *See page 528.*

### AGENCIES.
Domestic Sewing Machine, 726 Mn.
NEW HOME, 920 Main. *See p. 149.*
Singer's, J. W. Osborn, 9 Haynes.
Wheeler & Wilson, 80 Trumbull.

## Sewing Machine THREAD.
WILLIMANTIC LINEN CO. 389 Allyn. *See page 544.*

## SHAD.
*See also Markets.*
FITZGERALD RANSOM N. 44-46 Market. *See page 144.*

## SHADE TREES.
BIDWELL M. A. 24 Vine. *See page 59.*

## SHAFTING.
STRONG IRA J. 267 Asylum. *See page 524.*

## SHAFTING HANGERS.
LEE H. K. 223 State. *See p. 539.*
LINCOLN & CO. 54 Arch. *See page 522.*
PICKERING W. H. & CO. 110 Commerce. *See page 537.*

## SHELL FISH.
*See Fish Markets.*

## SHEET METAL WORK.
STELLING F. W. 93 Franklin. *See page 487.*

## SHEET MUSIC.
*See Music, etc.*

## SHERIFF and DEPUTIES.
*See page 667.*
Smith E. J. 85 Trumbull.

## SHIP BUILDING, & RE-PAIRING.
HARTFORD & N. Y. TRANS. CO. 285 State. *See page 554.*

## SHIRT & COLLAR Mfrs.
*See also Men's Furnishings.*
Griffin C. A. 863 Main.
Moyer Wm. N. 545 Main.
Tulin Isaac, 285 Market.
Springer E. O. 28 High.

## SHOEMAKERS.
*See Boot and Shoemakers.*

## SHOE UPPERS
*See also Leather.*
DOW PETER, JR. *See page 551.*

## SHORTHAND SCHOOLS.
HUNTSINGER E. M. 30 Asylum. *See outside back cover.*
MORSE E. H. 870 Asy. *See p. 711.*
OLMSTEAD COMMERCIAL COLLEGE, 756 Main. *See p. 710.*

## SHOW CARD ENGRAVING.
MUGFORD A. 177 Asylum. *See page 476.*

## SIDEWALKS AND LAYERS.
*See also Stone Yards.*
BELDEN SETH & SON, 69 Commerce. *See page 508.*
Clarke E. W. & Son, r. 82 Village.
Hartford Pavement and Construction Co. 868 Main.
McLaughlin John, 22 Squire.
Owen Thomas, r. 38 Annawan.
Southern New England Paving Co. 141 Trumbull.
Watson Alex, 82 Lincoln.

## SIGN PAINTERS.
*See also House Painters.*
Atcheson Albert C. 12 Smith.
Bradley W. G. (X.L.C.R.) 8 Kinsley.
Cohn Brothers, 1174 Main.
Crane Charlie L. 1274 Main.
Ellsworth Henry S. 1243 Main.
FORBES E. P. 3 Asylum. *See page 148.*
Lynch Richard D. 111 Front.
Major & Dundon, 104 Asylum.
PEPION JOHN & CO. 26 Church *See page 289.*
Preston & Kenyon, 185 Pearl.
Tibbals William A. 68½ Market.

## SILK Mfrs.
CHENEY BROTHERS, 34 Morgan. *See inside front cover and p. 645.*

## SILVERSMITHS and PLATERS.
*See also Jewelers.*
Alexander John, 89 Trumbull.
Barbour Silver Co. 62 Market.
Hartford Plating Co. 249 Pearl.
Hartford Silver Ware Co. 249 Pearl.
HOWARD JAMES L. & CO. 488 Asylum. *See page 527.*
Pitkin H. E. 36 Capen.
THE ROGERS CUTLERY CO. 66 Market. *See page 471.*
THE WILLIAM ROGERS MFG. CO. 66 Market. *See outside back cover.*

### SILVERWARE.
CASE C. H. & CO. *See outside of front cover.*

## SINGING TEACHERS.
*See Music Teachers; Schools.*
Emerson Irving, 63 Girard.

## SKY-LIGHTS.
CULLEN C. A. 44 Ann. *See p. 489.*
STELLING F. W. 93 Franklin. *See page 487.*

## SLATERS.
*See Roofers.*

## SLEIGHS.
HARTFORD CARRIAGE CO. 800 Allyn. *See page 549.*

## SMALL TOOLS.
*See Machinist.*
JOHNS-PRATT CO. 555 Capitol. *See page 540.*

## SNOW SHOVEL Mfr.
BISHOP E. C. 34 Capen. *See 60 p.*

## SOAP Mfrs.
FRISBIE L. T. & SON, 79 Talcott. *See page 536.*
Hartford Chemical Co. 225 State.

### SHAVING SOAP.
COWLISHAW HENRY, 160 Pearl. *See page 536.*

## SODA WATER.
*See Bottlers.*
WILLIAMS E. H. 366 Asylum. *See page 379.*

## SOFA BED Mfrs.
MAERCKLEIN HERMAN, 104 Asylum. *See page 562.*
SEIDLER & MAY, 306 to 318 Pearl. *See page 500.*

## SOLICITORS OF PATENTS.
*See Patent Rights.*
RICHARDS F. H. 803 Main. *See outside front cover.*
WHITNEY & ROTHWELL, 49 Pearl. *See page 502.*

## SPEAKING TUBES.
RICE & BALDWIN, 214 Pearl. *See page 554.*

## SPECIAL ANGLE BRICK.
DONAHUE D. J. r. 685 Windsor av. *See page 530.*

## SPECIAL MACHINERY.
*See also Machinists.*
ÆTNA MACHINE CO. 77 Commerce. *See page 532.*
CLARK EDRED W. 31 Wells. *See page 526.*
COOK ASA S. CO. Colt's West Armory, 80 Huy. *See page 525.*
DWIGHT SLATE MACHINE CO. 13 Central. *See page 525.*
LEE H. K. 223 State. *See p. 539.*
LINCOLN & CO. 54 Arch. *See page 522.*
MERROW MACHINE CO. 28 Laurel. *See page 535.*
NATIONAL MACHINE CO. 123 Sheldon. *See page 540.*
POPE MFG. CO. 436 Capitol. *See page 796.*
PRATT & WHITNEY CO. 1 Flower. *See page 523.*
SIGOURNEY TOOL CO. 9 Sigourney. *See page 537.*
WOODWARD & ROGERS, 125-135 Sheldon. *See page 526.*

## SPECTACLES.
*See Opticians.*

## SPEED INDICATOR Mfr.
EDDY ELECTRIC MFG. CO *See page 536.*

## SPICE MILLS.
*See Tea, Coffee, etc.*
KIBBE E. S. CO. 149 State. *See page 587.*
LINCOLN, SEYMS & CO. 34 Market. *See page 588.*

## SPOOL COTTON.
WILLIMANTIC LINEN CO. 389 Allyn. *See page 544.*

## SPORTING GOODS.
*See also Hardware, Yankee Notions.*
ANDRUS & HERMANN, 800 Asylum. *See page 484.*
ANDRUS & NÆDELE COMPANY. 272 Asylum. *See page 485.*

## SPORTING SHOES.
WEBB E. M. 546 Asylum. *See page 795.*

## SPRING BEDS.
*See Mattresses.*

## STABLES.
*See also Livery Stables.*

## STAIR BUILDERS.
*See Carpenters.*
Ericsen & Harman, 133 Sheldon.
SCOVILLE A. W. WOODWORKING CO. THE Vredendale c. Taylor. *See page 516.*
Turner John, 24 Potter.

## STALL GUARDS.
HARTFORD WOVEN WIRE MATTRESS CO. 618 Capitol. *See page 522.*

## STAMPING.
*See Embroidery; Paper Patterns.*

## STAMPS and STENCILS.
*See Rubber Stamps.*
ÆTNA STAMP WORKS, 25 Asylum. *See page 429.*
Baldwin Charles O. 8 State.
PARKER T. M. 71 Asylum. *See page 534.*

## STATIC ELECTRICIAN.
Cornish James P. 926 Main.

## STATIONERS.
*See Book Stores; Paper Dealers.*

## STATUARY.
*See Marble Works.*
NEW ENGLAND GRANITE WORKS, 1260 Mn. *See page 533.*

## STEAMBOATS.
*See Transportation.*
HFD. & N. Y. TRANS. CO. 285 State. *See page 554.*

## STEAM BOILER INS.
HARTFORD S. B. INSPECTION & I. CO. 650 Main. *See pages 446-447.*

## Steam Boiler Inspector.
*See page 663 for Deputies.*

## STEAM BOILERS.
*See Boiler Maker.*
Pitkin Bros. Co. 152 State.
STRONG IRA J. 267 Asylum. *See page 524.*

## STEAM ENGINE CONDENSER.
LEE H. K. 223 State. *See p. 539.*

## STEAM ENGINEERS.
HARTFORD HEATING CO. 267 Asylum. *See page 180.*

## STEAM ENGINE Mfrs.
*See also Gas Engines; Boilermakers; Machinists.*
COLT'S PATENT FIRE ARMS MFG. CO. 17 Van Dyke av. *See page 548.*
HARTFORD HEATING CO. 267 Asylum. *See page 180.*
LEE H. K. 223 State. *See p. 539.*

## STEAMER TICKETS.
*See Tickets.*

## STEAM FITTINGS & PIPES.
AHERN JAMES, 280 Asylum. *See page 505.*
ANDREWS & CREEDON, 446 Asylum. *See page 542.*
KNOX FRANK J. 2 So. Ann. *See page 220.*
LANGDON THOMAS H.,228 Pearl. *See page 224.*
Murray James T. 253 Asylum.
Starr John C. 16 Kinsley.

## STEAM HEATING.
*See also Plumbers; Stoves, etc.*
AHERN JAMES, 280 Asylum. *See page 505.*
ANDREWS & CREEDON, 446 Asylum. *See page 542.*
DAVIS I. B. & SON, 40 Cushman. *See page 546.*
HARTFORD HEATING CO. 267 Asylum. *See page 180.*
Harris James, 302 Pearl.
King A. G. & Co. 440 Asylum.
Stibbs Geo. H. 50 Church.

## STEAM PUMPS.
LEE H K. 223 State. *See p. 539.*

## STEAM SAW & PLANING.
*See Saw Mills.*

## STEAM TUGS.
HARTFORD & N. Y. TRANS. CO. 285 State. *See page 554.*

## STEEL.
*See Iron and Steel.*
CLAPP JOHN B. & SON, 61 Market. *See page 529.*

## STEEL PLATE PRINTER.
*See Plate Printers.*

## STEEL STAMPS.
*See Stamps.*
BURCH GEORGE W. 91 Asylum. *See page 497.*

## STEEL WIRE BRUSH Mfrs.
WHITTEMORE W. L. & SON, 176-178 Allyn. *See page 488.*

## STENCILS.
*See Stamps.*
BURCH GEORGE W. 91 Asylum. *See page 497.*

## STENOGRAPHERS.
*See Type Writer agents.*
Bacon Alice C. 106 Capen.
Bacon Alta M. 120 Maple.
Ballou Lydia W. 252 Asylum.
Barnard Grace M. 58 Church.
Bell Lillian G. 273 Asylum.

Billsborrow F. H. 666 Main.
Bingham Grace J. 486 Capitol.
Bond Marion W. 847 Main.
Brooks, Emma E. 801 Main.
Brown Christine W. 389 Allyn.
Case Raymond W. 15 Atwood.
Coffrin Erma P. 58 Pratt.
COOK LOUISE H. Mrs. 80 State. *See page 710.*
Denney Pearl A. 555 Capitol.
DOWN E. C. 847 Main. *See p. 422.*
Earl Katherine M. 21 Girard.
Ellis Kate F. 11 Central.
Evans Emma M. 2 State.
Fowler Emma G. 808 Main.
Fuller Fred E. 2 Central.
Galvin May F. 126 Church.
George Isabelle L. 29 Pearl.
Gompf Willard C. 51 Prospect.
Graham Winfield C. 904 Main.
Grayson Marion C. 51 Prospect.
Guiney Catherine L. 756 Main.
Hills Leonie May, 58 Trumbull.
Hugentobler Georgie L. 904 Main.
Jenkins A. B. 68 Pratt.
Lally Mary J. 51 Capen.
Lozell Walter J. 56 Prospect.
Malone Emma J. 56 Prospect.
McCreary H. S. 650 Main.
McDonnell Mary E. 65 Flower.
McGurk Minnie F. 200 Ashley.
Mix Gertrude, 700 Main.
Monagan Kittie I. 34 Market.
Morrison L. W. 926 Main.
Moyer Mahlon H. 904 Main.
NEW ENGLAND TYPE WRITER EXCHANGE, 847 Main. *See page 422.*
O'Flaherty Grace, 40 Buckingham.
OLMSTEAD COMMERCIAL COLLEGE, 756 Main. *See p. 710.*
Perkins Clara, 31 Ashley.
Pitkin Susie H. 95 Pearl.
Platt Ada L. 53 Trumbull.
Platt Edith J. 5 Haynes.
Ryan Katie, 6 Atlantic.
Sayles Mina R. 94 Capitol.
Scanlon Mary E. 25 Alden.
Shaw May E. 15 Trumbull.
Skinner Bessie M. 43 Elm.
Smith Grace M. 75 Pratt.
Smith Pauline, 25 Elm.
Stiles S. M. 141 Washington.
Storrs Rose W. 122 Clark.
Wheeler Vesta L. Miss, 6 Belden.
Willson Vesta H. 904 Main.
Wolcott Emma, 97 Washington.
Warren Mabel B. 66 Charter Oak.
Wood Leslie C. 281 Asylum.
Young Lillian, 462 Farmington.

## STEP LADDERS.
*See Ladder Mfr.*

## STEREOTYPING.
ÆTNA STAMP WORKS, 25 Asylum. *See page 429.*

## STEVEDORES.
Williams W. S. 285 State.

## STOCK BROKERS.
*See Brokers.*
COOLEY F. R. 49 Pearl. *See page 428.*
DENISON CHARLES, 754 Main. *See page 426.*

### STOCK FARM.
Bingham Herbert C. 856 Pro. av.
Dart J. & Son, 286 New Britain.
ELM POULTRY YARD. *See page 185-170.*

### STONE CUTTERS.
*See Stone Yards.*

### STONE CUTTERS' TOOLS.
SCHIRM FRANK F. 28-30 Sheldon
*See page 551.*

### STONE MASON.
GROZIER & MOORE, 889 Sheldon.
*See page 510.*

### STONE AND SAND.
BALF EDWARD CO. 2 Chapel.
*See page 426.*

### STONE YARDS.
*See also Marble Works; Side Walk Layers.*
BELDEN S. & SON. *See page 508.*
Billings Sidewalk & Masons Supply Co. 154 Charter Oak.
BRABAZON ANDREW, Garden, cor. Liberty. *See page 511.*
Collins Samuel & Co. 283 Sheldon.
Kelly Bros. 93 Charter Oak.
O'Brien & Flannery, r. 6½ Ellery.
SHERMAN M. W. & SON, Donald. *See page 551.*
WINDSOR RED STONE Co. 1542 Broad. *See page 508.*

### STORAGE.
BARTLETT F. W. & F. E. 212 Asylum. *See page 420.*
BILL BROTHERS, 46 Ann. *See page 550.*
Johnson Horace, 170 Commerce.
PEOPLES EXPRESS CO. 42 Union pl. *See page 559.*
Public Warehouse, 288 State
Smith J. Charles, r. 86 Buckingham.
Stoughton D. G. 204 State.

### STORE FIXTURES.
*See Scroll Sawyers.*

### STOVE REPAIRS.
Thrall Edward B. 63 Church.
WHITE F. W. 1124 Main. *See p. 507.*

### STOVES and TIN WARE.
BLISS EDWARD, 1268 Main. *See page 494.*
BULL, N. B. & SON, 599-601 Main. *See page 76.*
Daly Lawrence, 860 Main.
FENN L. T. 205 Main. *See p. 501.*
FLINT GEO. W. & CO. 61 Asylum. *See page 147.*
Friedman Elias, 210½ Front.
FULLER C. C. & CO. 16 Ford. *See page 500.*
Lappin D. 166 Front.
Leitch Henry, 291 Asylum.
Lyon Jacob & Son, 128 State.
McManus John C. 346 Main.
Meisterling Charles, 60 Temple.
Olds & Whipple, 164-168 State.
Webster Edward, 580 Asylum.
Weigelt Wm. P. 16 Mulberry.
WHITE FRED W. 1124 Main. *See page 507.*
Wilbraham George, 14 Hicks.

### STRAIGHT WAY VALVES.
*See Valve Manufacturers.*

### STRAW.
*See Flour, Feed, &c.*
SMITH, NORTHAM & CO. 129 State. *See page 590.*

### STREET BANNERS.
FORBES E. P. 8 Asylum. *See page 148.*

### STREET RAILWAYS.
HARTFORD, ROCKVILLE & MANCHESTER TRAMWAY CO. *See page 557.*
Hartford Street Ry. Co. 115 State.

### STREET SPRINKLERS.
Hartford Street Sprinkling and Supply Co. 868 Main.

### STRUCTURAL IRONWORK.
BUELLESBACH W. 75 Commerce. *See page 478.*

### SURETY BONDS.
COWLES E. S. 25 Pearl. *See p. 108.*

### SURFACE GRINDING.
WOODWARD & RODGERS, 188-185 Sheldon. *See page 526.*

### SURGICAL INSTRUMENTS.
GOODRICH STEPHEN & CO. 1208 Main. *See page 164.*
NEWTON PHILO W. 142 Asylum. *See page 85.*

### SURVEYORS.
*See Civil Engineers.*
WOLCOTT & DARBY, 49 Pearl. *See page 498.*

### SUNDAY PAPERS.
*See Books, News.*

### SWIMMING BATHS.
Y. M. C. A. 328 Pearl. *See pages 704-705.*

### SWITCH Mfrs.
HART & HEGEMAN MFG. CO. 26 High. *See page 589.*
PERKINS ELECTRIC SWITCH MFG. CO. 83 Woodbine. *See p. 586.*

### TAGS.
TUCKER'S E. SONS, 100 Trumbull. *See page 481.*

### TAILORS.
*See Merchant Tailors.*
Adams Edward T. 25 Asylum.
Ackerman Samuel, 149 Front.
Akerlind John A. 205 Park.
Aldrich S. P. 40 Asylum.
Alexander Benjamin, 168 Front.
Barnett Simon, 1196 Main.
Bercovitz Jacob, 299 Market.
Bibbins Frances, 28 Julius.
Braun William, u. 248 Main.
Brown Frances A. u. 21 Albany.
Buch George, 10 Charter Oak av.
Byrne John, 6 State.
Chesba B., 29 Church.
Cohen & Silberman, 64 Trumbull.
Cohn Gustave, 154 Front.
Cohn Myer, 85 Sheldon.
Davis Harris, 94½ Trumbull.

Dudrowicz John, 28 Sheldon.
Eichelman Isaac, 214 Front.
Eiswirth John, 100 Seymour.
Epsar Frank, r. 1128 Main.
Epstein Sam, 114 Trumbull.
Forlen John, 85 Asylum.
Fox Joseph, 878 Park.
Frank August F. 86 Trumbull.
Friedman Himan, 77 Windsor.
Gelman Michael, 160 Front.
Goodman Abraham, 19 Church.
Green Carl A. 57 Pratt.
Greenstein Ross A. 903 Main.
Gruber Jacob, 298 Park.
Gruninger Fred, 14 Goodman.
Guerra Sulvon, 65 Pleasant.
Haaser Joseph, 19 Goodwin.
Hedlund Levin, 81 Putnam.
Helene Mannel, 91 Front.
Hendrickson Peter, 45 Ann.
Hoffman David, 104 Trumbull.
Hoffman L. 24 Morgan.
House Eugene G. 289 Asylum.
Hull Philetta H. 20 Lewis.
Hurst Stephen, 21 New Britain.
Johnson Gustavus, 98 Pratt.
Kalkhof Bros. 2 Kilbourn ct.
Kasanof Reuben, 822 Park.
Kelley Jeremiah, 14 Ellery.
Kessler Abraham B. 730 Main.
Krohn Gustave E. 23 Squire.
Leschever L. 29 Church.
Laschever Nathan, 1259 Main.
Levin Samuel, 526 Asylum.
Lewis Isaac, 80 State.
Lohs Frederic A. 88 Pearl.
Lutz Reinhold, 720 Main.
Maginn William F. 903 Main.
Maher Patrick J. 219 Pearl.
McGovern T. J. 76 Asylum.
Meranski David, 15 Morgan.
Merz Frederick, 85 Park.
Miller Max, 544 Main.
Missal Isaac S. 2 State.
Missell Charles, 30½ Temple.
Model Tailoring Co. 222 Pearl.
Murphy Daniel, 59 Pleasant.
Nieretz August, 77 Temple.
Norrgard A. Arnold, 812 Asylum.
Petit Joseph, 868 Main.
Pfeil John, 81 Asylum.
Reid James W. 1212 Main.
Resnik Philip, 88 Windsor.
Reuber Henry, 8 State.
Riedmann Matthias, 5 Orchard.
Rodowsky M. 88 Front.
Roeder Frederick, 186 State.
Rosenberg David, 17 Albany.
Rudy Isaac, 82 Front.
Rutt Morris, 50 Sheldon.
Saled David, 171 Main.
Schaffman Bennett, 206 Front.
Scheer Eugene, 85 Church.
Schwalb Max, 118 Asylum.
Sillman Ike, 582 Asylum.
Sizkind Barney, 79 Governor.
Slabossewski Hilari A. 552 Main.
Solar Peter, 117 Market.
Spollen Patrick, 186 Sheldon.
Stasne Frank, 730 Main.
Stinson R. W. 71 Asylum.
Stone Henry, 1069 Broad.
Taylor Philip, 20 Church.
Thompson Robert, 18 Park.
Weis Emil, 58 Temple.
Werner W. F. 29 Pearl.
White Charles P. 25 Asylum.
Wopschal Julius, u.r. 2 Pleasant ct.
Yellen Nathan, 288 Asylum.

## TANNERY.

JEWELL BELTING CO. 15 Trumbull. *See page 530.*

## TAP and DIE Mfrs.

BILLINGS & SPENCER CO. 142 Russ. *See page 531.*
PRATT & WHITNEY CO. 1 Flower. *See page 523.*

## TAPE WORM EXPELLER.

LANKTON ARBA, 2 Marsh. *See page 564.*

## TAPPING MACHINE Mfr.

WOODWARD & ROGERS, 133–135 Sheldon. *See page 526.*

## TAXIDERMIST.

Ullrich Ferdinand, 5 Vandyke.
Aldrich Pertia W. Franklin pl.

## TEA, COFFEE, and SPICES.

*See also Grocers.*

WHOLESALE.

Boardman Wm. Sons Co. 304 Asy.
KIBBE E. S. CO. 149 State. *See page 587.*
TUCKER & GOODWIN, 8 and 12 Hurlburt. *See page 585.*
LINCOLN, SEYMS & CO. 34 Market. *See page 588.*
POTTER & PAYNE, 405–407 Allyn. *See page 586.*
Quinn Patrick H. 997 Main.

RETAIL.

Buckley & Reardon, 28 Wells.
Capitol Tea & Coffee Co. 1200 Main.
Centennial American Tea Co. 575 Mn.
Frost John A. 42 Beach.
Grand Union Tea Co. 715 Main.
Great Atlantic & Pacific Tea Co. 979 Main.
HILLS & CO. 372 Asylum. *p. 485.*
McGuire John H. 16 Church.
NEWTON, ROBERTSON & CO. 338, 342 Asylum. *See page 486.*
New York Tea Store, 1046 Main.
Sing Frank, 1225 Main.
Union Pacific Tea Co. 174 Asylum.
Young E. M. & Co. 782 Park.
YUEN, SING & CO. 118 State. *See page 589.*

## TEACHERS.

*See also Music; Dancing; Artists.*

Brandt Elizabeth M. 25 Sherman.
Flynn Jane, 148 Washington.
Francolini Domenico, 17 Morgan.
Martin Edwina, 97 Washington.
Pearl Arthur, 24 Julius.
Stevens Clara, 107 Washington.
Vogel Annie E. 719 Asylum.
Wolcott Grace, 97 Washington.

## TELEGRAPH COMPANIES.

American District Tel. & Mes. Co., 6 Central.
Commercial Cable Co.—Mackey-Bennett—8 Central.
Fire Alarm Tel. 43 Pearl.
Postal Telegraph Cable Co. 8 Central, branch 42 Union pl. 1 Flower.
Western Union. 6 Central, branches Union R.R. Station, 152 Asylum, 1 Flower, 98 Wells and 54 High.

## TELEGRAPHY.

MORSE E. H. 370 Asylum. *See page 711.*
OLMSTEAD COMMERCIAL COLLEGE, 756 Main. *See page 710.*

## TELESCOPE MAKER.

Hale John, 18 Clark.

## TENEMENTS TO RENT.

BARTLETT F. W. & F. E. 212 Asylum. *See page 420.*
STEINMETZ WM. P. 50 Pearl. *See page 343.*

## TENTS AND AWNINGS.

Daggett W. H. H. 71 Asylum.
ROBERTS S. F. 124 State. *p. 502.*
Simons & Fox, 7 Haynes.

## TEXTILE Mfrs.

Beach Mfg. Co. 211 State.
DUNHAM HOSIERY CO. 66 State. *See page 547.*
Hartford Carpet Co. 10 Market.
Health Underwear, 66 State.

## THEATRE.

*See also Public Halls, Etc.*

Auditorium, 180 Asylum.
FOOT GUARD HALL, 159 High. *See page 496.*
Hartford Opera House, 233 Main.
Parsons, 66 Prospect.

## THEOLOGICAL SEMINARY.

*See Schools.*

HARTFORD THEOLOGICAL SEMINARY, 1507 Broad. *See pages 708–709.*

## THREAD Mfr.

WILLIMANTIC LINEN CO. 389 Allyn. *See page 544.*

## TICKETS.

*Ocean Steamers and Railroads.*

Conroy John F. 548 Main.
Gridley H. R. 18 State.
Hartford and New York boats, 285 State.
Jacobs Ward W. & Co. 815 Main.

## TILE.

*See Bricks; Drain Tile, Etc.*

Atwood Faience Co. Faience st.
Winslow Nelson, r. 1263 Main.

## TIME CLOCKS.

HUBBARD & MORTSON, 42 Union pl. *See page 318.*

## TIME REGISTERS,

RICE & BALDWIN, 214 Pearl. *See page 554.*

## TINNERS.

*See also Stoves; Roofers; Slaters.*

Behner F. Edward, 1115 Main.
BLISS EDWARD, 1263 Main. *See page 494.*
Brown W. B. r. 464 Windsor.
Clapp Joseph B. 26 Kinsley.
Couch George M. 1072 Main.
CULLEN C. A. 44 Ann. *See page 489.*

Dalton M. H. 446 Asylum.
Egan Keron Jr. 48 Wilson.
Francis Daniel W. 848 Park.
Friedman Elias, 210½ Front.
Goldenthal Moses, 1192 Main.
Greene Daniel E. 4 Ford.
Henry James J. 1162 Main.
Jones Joseph, 26 Hicks.
Meisterling Charles, 60 Temple.
Rowland A. B. 342 Pearl.
STELLING FRED. W. 98 Franklin. *See page 487.*
WHITE F. W. 1124 Main. *See page 507.*
Wilbraham George, 14 Hicks.

## TIN TYPES.

*See Photographers.*

## TOBACCO and CIGARS.

*See Tobacco—Leaf; Saloons; Grocers.*

WHOLESALE.

KIBBE E. .S. CO. 149 State. *See page 587.*
LINCOLN, SEYMS & CO. 34 Market. *See page 588.*
POTTER & PAYNE, 405–407 Allyn. *See page 586.*

RETAIL.

Bee Cigar Co. 220 State.
Bodenstein Herman, 29 Brook.
Chlopkowiak L. 58 Temple.
Cion Isaac, 51 Morgan.
Crane S. D. 213 Pearl.
CRYGIER FRANK H. 248 Asylum. *See page 111.*
D'Esopo R. A. & Co. 88 State.
Gilbert Wm. J. 159 Asylum.
Gleason Edward N. 222 Asylum.
Green Joseph, 355 Main.
Grundshaw Edward J. 52 Pratt.
Goodacre Bros. r. 788 Main.
Hartford Cigar Co. 54 Pratt.
Herting Theodore M. r. 173 State.
Horenstein Bros. 1118 Main.
Katz Max, 1874 Broad.
Krauthoff Charles, 155 Market.
Krug & Powers, 741 Main.
Kuenhold Frederick W. 68 Temple.
Leschke & Pletcher, 1037 Main.
Lutwack William, 191 Front.
Lyons Cigar Co. The, 40 Mulberry.
Malone John J. r. 597 Main.
McManus Bros. 183 Main.
Murphy William J. 217 Main.
Nathan & Cole Cigar Mfg. 88 State.
Oehlholf Christian, 30 Park.
Pfund Wm. 62 Morgan.
Rice Abraham, 92 New Britain.
Rockenfeller Philip, 600 Garden.
Rosenthal Charles, 591 Main.
Russ Andrew J. 28 Church.
SALOMON & DeLEEUW, 7 Asylum. *See page 318.*
Schott James S. 6 State.
Soby Charles, 867 Main.
Stodel Charles J. 36 Temple.
Stoehr Henry W. r. 75 Bluehills.
Suisman Max, 206 Front.
Valiquette Alfred, r. 90 Heath.
Wadsworth Alfred J. 1115 Main.
Wakefield Atwood, 259 Asylum.
Weeks George H. 1015 Main.
Williams Edward D. r. 1263 Main.

## TOILET GOODS.

*See Apothecaries.*

Hartford Apron & Toilet Supply Co. 49 Market.

## TOBACCO—LEAF.
See also Tobacco and Cigars.
Bissell James M. 220 State.
Brace John M. G. 214 State.
Clark, Diamond & Clark, 225 State.
Cohn A. & Co. 281 State.
Dibble Hinman A. 85 Capen.
Dickinson & Miller, 215 State.
Fuller E. A. & W. F. 280 State.
Gershel L. & Bro. 284 State.
Haas L. B. 150 State.
Huntting Wm. L. & Co. 214 State.
Miller Jonas, 210 State.
Way Henry R. & Co. 219 State.
Watrous John H. 280 State.
Westphal William, 221 State.

## TOOL GRINDING MACHINE Mfr.
SLATE DWIGHT MACHINE CO.
18 Central. See page 525.

## TOOL Mfrs.
See Machinists.

## TOWING.
See Steam Tugs.

## TOYS.
See Yankee Notions.

## TRADING COUPONS.
MERCHANTS' NATIONAL
TRADING ASSOCIATION, 66
State. See outside back cover.

## TRANSPORTATION.
See also Railroad; Steamboat and Express Companies.

## Transportation INSURANCE.
KIMBALL & McCRAY, 658 Main.
See page 444.

## TREES.
See Nurserymen.
BIDWELL M. A. 24 Vine. See page 59.

## TRICYCLE Mfr.
POPE MFG. CO. 486 Capitol. See page 796.

## TRIMMING PRESSES.
BILLINGS & SPENCER CO. 142
Russ. See page 531.

## TRIMMINGS.
See also Linings.
Samilson & Shulman, 108½ Trum.

## TROTTING PARKS.
See Public Halls.
Charter Oak Park, New Park av.
Gentlemen's Driving Club Park, Albany av.

## TRUCKING.
BALF EDWARD CO. 2 Chapel. See page 426.
Bolf William M. 51 Martin.
McCarty Cornelius, 33 Hudson.
SHERMAN M. W. & SON. See page 551.

## TRUNK Mfrs.
Fuller Geo. W. 182 Asylum.

## TRUSSES.
See also Apothecaries.
ALLYN HOUSE DRUG STORE,
142 Asylum. See page 85.
Babcock A. H. Mrs. 265 Asylum.
Flint Ruptnre Cure, 252 Asylum.
GOODRICH S. & CO. 1208 Main. See page 164.

## TRUST COMPANIES.
See Banks.

## TUGS.
HARTFORD & N. Y. TRANS. CO.
285 State. See page 554.

## TURKISH BATHS.
JONES GEORGE E. 609 Main. See page 421.

## TWINE.
TUCKER'S E. SONS, 100 Trumbull. See page 481.

## TYPE FOUNDERS.
PHELPS, DALTON & CO., Boston, Mass. See page 471.

## TYPE WRITER AGENTS.
See also Stenographers.
COOK LOUISE H. Mrs. 80 State. See page 710.
Lehwald M. J. 77 Pratt.
NEW ENGLAND TYPEWRITER
EXCHANGE, 847 Main. P. 422.
Remington Typewriter, 49 Pearl.
Stafford N. E. 7 Central.
Underwood Mr. 42 Church.
Williams Typewriter Co. 77 Pratt.
Wyckoff, Seamans & Benedict, 49 Pearl.

## TYPEWRITERS.
HUNTSINGER E. M. 80 Asylum. See outside back cover.
MORSE E. H. 870 Asylum. See page 711.
OLMSTEAD COMMERCIAL
COLLEGE, 756 Mn. See p. 710.

## TYPE WRITER SUPPLIES.
See Type Writer Agents.
COOK LOUISE H. Mrs. 80 State. See page 710.
NEW ENGLAND TYPEWRITER
EXCHANGE, 847 Main. See p. 422.
OLMSTEAD COMMERCIAL
COLLEGE, 756 Mn. See p. 710.
Wyckoff, Seamans & Benedict, 49 Pearl.

## UMBRELLA MFG.
Feingold George, 13 Morgan.

## UNDERTAKERS.
See also Embalmers.
FOSTER & FURREY, 1166 Main. See page 150.
Hfd. Undertaking Co. 106 Trumbull.
HILLS & MARCHANT, 58 Ann. See page 189.
Kenny & Dillon, 30 Wells.

McCARTHY & AHERN, 194 Pearl. See page 248.
McIntyre & Clarkin, 12½ Church.
Miller & Burnham, 180 Allyn.
Morgan & Pratt, 387 Main.
Scott & Smith, 26 Church.
Woolley G. W. & Son, 556 Main.

## UNDERWEAR Mfrs.
See also Textile Mfrs.; Knit Goods.
DUNHAM HOSIERY CO. 66 State. See page 547.
Heath Underwear Co. 66 State.

## U. S. DEPOSITARY.
CHARTER OAK NAT'L BANK
124 Asylum. See page 482.

## U. S. OFFICERS of all kinds
See Index to Contents.

## UPHOLSTERER Mfr. SILK.
CHENEY BROS. 84 Morgan. See page 545 and inside front cover.

## UPHOLSTERERS.
See also Furniture.
BECK CURT E. 262 Allyn. See page 505.
Bleehdorn William, 2 Trumbull.
BRAND ROBERT, 6½ Morris. See page 507.
Elkin Bros. r. 1068 Main.
Farber Morris, 8 Walnut.
MAERCKLEIN H. H. 104 Asylum. See page 562.
Missell Wm. E. 988 Main.
Sommerman August A. 219 Pearl.

## VALVE Mfrs.
PRATT & CADY CO. 556 Capitol. See page 527.

## VAPOR BATHS.
See also Baths.
JONES GEO. E. 609 Main. See page 421.
MERRIAM A. E. COLT MRS. 926 Main. See page 257.

## VAPOR LAUNCHES.
HANNUM T. W. Jr. 700 Main. See page 503.

## VARNISHES & COLORS.
ENSWORTH L. L. & SON, 104 Front. See page 592.

## VEGETABLE MARKETS.
See also Markets; Market Gardeners.

## VELVET Mfrs.
CHENEY BROS. See page 545 and inside front cover.

## VENTILATING.
King A. G. & Co. 440 Asylum.

## VERANDAS.
SCOVILLE A. W. WOODWORKING CO. THE, Vredendale av. c. Taylor. See page 516.

## VETERINARY SURGEONS.
*See also Physicians.*

### VETERINARY.
Black Madison J. 560 Main.
Burton J. S. 2 American.
Dudley Joseph L. 560 Main.
Gale A. S. 20 Morgan.
Gardner Julian E. r. 50 State.
Hertel Albert G. r. 871 Main.
Ingram Frank A. 17 Foot Guard.
Lee Thomas J. r. 1068 Main.
LYMAN RICHARD P. r. 995 Main, St. Johns Stables. *See page 237.*
Stroud Thompson C. 356 Main.

### DOG DISEASES.
Brown William, 114 Albany.

## VINEGAR Mfr.
Seymour John, 16 Park.

## VIOLIN REPAIRER.
Cook D. P. 92 State.
FERNSIDE G. W. *See page 777.*

## VIOLIN TEACHERS.
*See Music Teachers.*

## VULCABESTON Mfr.
JOHNS–PRATT CO., 555 Capitol.
*See page 540.*

## WALL COPING.
ANDREWS & PECK, 88 Market.
*See page 509.*

## WALL PAPER.
*See also Carpet Stores.*
BAXTER WILLIAM G. 231 Asylum. *See page 52.*
BONNER PRESTON CO. 843 Main. *See page 425.*
BRAINERD HARVEY B. 84 Pratt. *See page 503.*
Drew Fannie L. 564 Main.
HART CHAS. R. CO. 896 Main. *See page 179.*
NEAL, GOFF & INGLIS CO. 980 Main. *See page 498.*
PEPION JOHN & CO. 25 Church. *See page 289.*
WALKER ROBERT & CO. 14 Church. *See page 366.*

## WAREHOUSE.
*See Storage.*

## WASHERWOMEN.
*See Laundries.*

## WASTE, COTTON & WOOL.
HOWARD JAMES L. & CO. 488 Asylum. *See page 527.*

## WASTE PAPER.
Pierce William H. 38 Ferry.

## WATCHES and JEWELRY.
*See Jewelers.*
CASE C. H. & CO. 851 Main. *See outside front cover.*
Clarke Eugene A. 208 Asylum.
KOHN HENRY & SONS, 890 Main. *See page 797.*

## WATCHMAKERS.
*See Jewelers.*
Ball George W. 25 Asylum.
Beeman William M. 272 Asylum.
Brown Edward J. 162 Asylum.
Luftig L. 29 Church.
Teske Charles, 214 Asylum.
STEVEN W. T. 4 State. *See p. 844.*
Vogel William, 191 Front.

## WATER ARTESIAN.
GRANT C. L. 22 Belden. *See page 535.*
KING H. B. 38 Williams. *See page 484.*

## WATER FRONT BOILERS.
BEACH H. B. & SON, 135 Grove.
*See page 538.*

## WATER GATE Mfrs.
PRATT & CADY CO. 556 Capitol.
*See page 527.*

## WATER HEATERS.
ANDREWS & CREEDON, 446 Asylum. *See page 542.*
DAVIS I. B. & SON, 40 Cushman. *See page 546.*
HARTFORD HEATING CO. 267 Asylum. *See page 180.*

## WATER MOTORS.
RHODES L. E. CO. 28 High. *See page 548.*

## WATER WHEEL Mfr.
Cushman Dwight, r. 29 Church.
LEE H. K. 228 State. *See p. 539.*

## WEIGHING MACHINE Mfr.
PRATT & WHITNEY CO. 1 Flower. *See page 528.*

## WELL DIGGER.
GRANT CHARLES L. 22 Belden.
*See page 535.*
KING H. B. 38 Williams. *See page 484.*

## WESTERN LOANS.
*See also Brokers; Real Estate.*
MOORE GEORGE W. & CO. 759 Main. *See page 429.*

## WHITEWASHERS.
*See General Jobbers.*

## WHARVES.
W. S. Williams, Dock Agent for—
Dutch Point, east of bridge to foot of Potter, H. & N. Y. Trans. Co.
Foot of Potter st. by H. C. Gas L. Co.
" " Ferry, Mrs. M. W. Chapin.
" " Grove, Beach & Co. 400 feet south of.
" Keeney, P. Smith & H. Beach.
Foot of Grove, State to Ferry st., H. & N. Y. Transport'n Co.
" " Kilb. J. J. Poole & Co.
" " Kilb., N. Y., N. H. & H. R. Co.
Park River west of Railroad bridge.

## WHEELWRIGHT.
*See also Carriages.*

## WHEELS, SHAFTS, SPOKES
BLODGETT & CLAPP CO. 51 Market. *See page 541.*
ENSWORTH L. L. & SON, 104 Front. *See page 592.*

## WIND MILLS.
GRANT C. L. 22 Belden. *See p. 535.*

## WINDOWS and FIXTURES.
*See also Doors; Sash and Blinds.*
ANDREWS & PECK, 88 Market. *See page 509.*
NIMS, WHITNEY & CO. 1170 Main. *See page 511.*

## WINDOW GLASS.
*See Paints, Oils and Glass.*

## WINDOW SCREENS.
CROSTHWAITE F. H. 247 Asylum. *See page 488.*

## WINDOW SHADES.
*See also Wall Papers.*
BONNER, PRESTON CO. 843 Main. *See page 425.*
BRAINERD H. B. 84 Pratt. *See page 503.*
NEAL, GOFF & INGLIS CO. 980 Main. *See page 498.*

## WINDSOR FOLDING BED.
FULLER C. C. & CO. 16 Ford
*See page 500.*

## WINES.
SISSON T. & CO. (Communion). *See page 560.*

## WINE STORE.
*See also Saloons.*

## WIRE BRUSHES.
WHITTEMORE W. L. & SON, 176–178 Allyn. *See page 488.*

## WIRE FENCING.
CROSTHWAITE F. H. 247 Asylum. *See page 488.*

## WIRE MATTRESS Mfrs.
HARTF'D WOVEN WIRE MATTRESS CO. 618 Cap. *See page 522.*

## WIRE WINDOW GUARDS.
AMIDON F. S. r. 60 Temple. *See page 40.*
HARTFORD WOVEN WIRE MATTRESS CO. 618 Capitol.
*See page 522.*

## WIRE WORKS and SCREEN.
AMIDON FREDERICK S. r. 60 Temple. *See page 40.*
HARTFORD WIRE WORKS, 247 Asylum. *See page 488.*

## WIRE WORKS of all KINDS
CROSTHWAITE F. H. 247 Asylum. *See page 488.*

## WOMAN'S EXCHANGE.
*See Charities.*

### WOOD CARVING.
Entress A. 597 Main.
Wheeler F. A. 28 Mulberry.

### WOOD ENGRAVERS.
*See also Engravers.*
MUGFORD A. 177 Asylum. *See page 476.*
PECK R. S. & CO. 26 High. *See page 478.*

### WOOD—HARD FINISH.
*See also Wood Turners.*
FRENCH H. A. 554 Main. *See page 512.*
SCOVILLE A. W. 700 Main. *See page 513.*

### WOOD MANTELS.
SCOVILLE A. W. 700 Main. *See page 513.*
STRICKLAND & SHEA, 20 Potter. *See page 516.*

### WOOD YARD.
*See Kindling Wood.*

### WOOD SCREW Mfrs.
COOK ASA S. CO. 80 Huyshope. *See page 525.*

### WOODEN EAVE TROUGHS.
BISHOP E. C. & CO. 34 Capen. *See page 60.*

### WOOD TURNERS.
*See also Scroll Sawing.*
Dresser Charles H. 225 Sheldon.
LITTLE H. B. & CO. 33 Wells. *See page 232.*
McClary John Co. 69 Front.
RICKER A. T. 26 Potter. *See page 517.*

SCOVILLE A. W. 700 Main. *See page 513.*
STRICKLAND & SHEA, 20 Potter. *See page 516.*
Taft Co. Lumber st.

### WOOL and COTTON.
Broad Brook Co. 211 State.
Catlin Abijah, Jr. 210 Pearl.
Dunham Austin & Sons, 66 State.
DWIGHT, SKINNER & CO. 207 Allyn. *See page 488.*
Judd H. C. & Root, 389 Allyn.
Kellogg N. O. 378 Asylum.

### WOOLEN UNDERCLOTHES.
DUNHAM HOSIERY CO. 66 State. *See page 547.*

### WOOLENS.
Pember M. W. Sons, 292 Asylum.
Tolles E. & Co. 49 Ann.

### WORM SYRUP.
LANKTON ARBA, 2 Marsh. *See page 564.*

### WRENCH Mfr.
BILLINGS & SPENCER CO. 142 Russ. *See page 581.*

### WRITING SCHOOL.
*See also Type Writers.*
Y. M. C. A. 323 Pl. *See pp. 704–705.*

### WRITING INKS.
BARBER INK EXTRACT CO. 5 Haynes. *See page 488.*
FLETCHER N. P. & CO. *See page 146.*

### WRITING PAPER Mfrs.
EAST HARTFORD MFG. CO. *See page 480.*

### WRITING TEACHERS.
*See also Schools.*
Bender E. E. 502 Windsor av.
Martin David T. 847 Main.
Pearl Arthur, 24 Julius.
Smith Lyman D. 83 Madison.
Titcomb John W. 24 Charter Oak.

### WROUGHT IRON.
BUELLESBACH W. 75 Commerce. *See page 478.*

### YEAST.
Fleischmann Com. Yeast, 42 High.
Graves G. A. Mrs. 22 Barbour.
Vienna Pressed Yeast Co. 281 Allyn.

### YANKEE NOTIONS.
*See also Dry Goods.*
RETAIL.
Anderson Wm. J. 1399 Main.
Birmingham Mary, 74 Ward.
Charlton E. P. & Co. 929 Main.
Churchill George G. 643 Main.
Conniff Mary Mrs. 64 Front.
Cook D. P. 92 State.
Dworski L. 372 Park.
McFarland Elizabeth, 761 Park.
McTigue Catherine, 69 Potter.
Oppelt Michael, 224 New Park.
Prindle George E. Mrs. 31 Elm.
Pulver Marvin, 820 Park.
Rositer S. 371 Park.
Samilson & Shulman, 106½ Tru.
Schwartz Joseph, 20 Talcott.
Sill L. B. 1187 Main.
Street Edwin R. 225 Sheldon.

### YOUNG MEN'S CHRISTIAN ASSOCIATION.
Rooms 323 Pearl, cor. Jewell. *See pages 704–705.*

## Business of Hartford Clearing House.

FIFTEEN Banks and Trust Companies settle their daily balances in this city, alternating monthly, at the banks.

| | 1891. | 1892. | 1893. | 1894. | 1895. | 1896. | 1897. |
|---|---|---|---|---|---|---|---|
| June...... | $8,375,571.40 | $8,975,652.41 | $9,814,766.66 | $7,988,807.17 | $9,040,318.07 | 10,809,575.51 | 10,358,922.02 |
| July...... | 11,220,561.18 | 10,961,785.34 | 11,035,363.30 | 10,179,713.96 | 12,269,952.87 | 12,215,152.35 | 11,599,213.43 |
| August ... | 6,766,978.87 | 7,782,401.82 | 6,894,158.54 | 7,216,806.41 | 8,420,590.84 | 8,026,070.67 | 8,500,499.39 |
| September | 7,570,611.45 | 7,976,780.98 | 7,145,094.12 | 7,457,757.44 | 8,541,075.27 | 8,404,557.43 | 9,810,841.06 |
| October... | 9,810,105.56 | 9,667,288.34 | 9,150,785.45 | 9,721,601.11 | 12,207,407.98 | 9,676,587.57 | 11,055,555.36 |
| November. | 7,522,750.21 | 9,086,001.29 | 8,126,961.95 | 8,181,788.79 | 9,950,911.86 | 7,986,777.94 | 9,514,146.73 |
| December. | 9,475,361.51 | 10,141,919.38 | 8,010,704.14 | 9,464,364.89 | 10,648,999.46 | 9,459,614.66 | 10,757,264.45 |
| | 1892. | 1893. | 1894. | 1895. | 1896. | 1897. | 1898. |
| January .. | 11,608,042.84 | 15,045,050.89 | 10,572,982.86 | 11,605,462.09 | 12,473,011.93 | 12,637,385.53 | 13,447,395.89 |
| February.. | 8,811,680.33 | 8,643,243.00 | 7,042,472.52 | 7,981,212.73 | 9,909,143.48 | 9,339,158.13 | 8,981,983.07 |
| March .... | 8,890,288.04 | 10,527,500.66 | 8,240,168.48 | 8,750,344.01 | 10,009,477.48 | 10,317,972.50 | 10,316,782.39 |
| April ..... | 9,216,388.64 | 10,342,470.86 | 8,356,297.10 | 9,346,835.25 | 10,988,649.93 | 10,151,471.92 | 10,345,655.99 |
| May...... | 9,765,403.75 | 9,658,779.11 | 7,915,756.92 | 9,926,881.28 | 9,103,629.89 | 9,900,252.19 | 9,366,655.83 |
| Totals..... | 109,688,943.78 | 118,758,878.02 | 101,808,461.49 | 107,816,574.52 | 123,566,316.80 | 118,424,571.40 | 124,055,626.13 |

# Governments of the World;

Collated from authentic sources, for GEER'S HARTFORD CITY DIRECTORY, No. 61, July, 1898.

| COUNTRY. | CAPITAL. | NAME OF RULER. | TITLE. | TERM BEGAN. | POPULATION. | AREA SQ. M. |
|---|---|---|---|---|---|---|
| Abyssinia,...... | Massowah.... | Menelik II,.... | King............ | March 12, 1889 | 3,500,000 | 150,000 |
| Afghanistan,... | Cabul,........ | Abdur Rahman Khan,. | Amir........... | July 12, 1880 | 4,000,000 | 300,000 |
| Annam,......... | Hue,......... | Thanh Thai,...... | King........... | Jan. 31, 1889 | 6,000,000 | 81,042 |
| Argentine Repb. | Buenos Ayres. | Senor Uriburu,.... | President....... | Jan. 22, 1895 | 3,954,911 | 1,778,195 |
| Austria-Hung'y, | Vienna,...... | Franz Josef I,.... | Emperor....... | Dec. 2, 1848 | 41,358,886 | 240,942 |
| Baluchistan,... | Khelat,....... | Mir Mahmud Khan,.. | Chief.......... | Aug. 1893 | 500,000 | 130,000 |
| Belgium,...... | Brussels,..... | Leopold II,...... | King........... | Dec. 10, 1865 | 6,495,886 | 11,373 |
| Bolivia,....... | La Paz,...... | Sev'o Fernandes Alonso | President....... | Aug. 15, 1896 | 2,019,549 | 567,360 |
| Borneo,........ | Zwolle,...... | A. van der Wyck,.. | Governor Gen'l. | July 15, 1893 | 1,163,820 | 212,937 |
| Brazil, Un. St. of | Rio de Janeiro, | Dr. De Campos-Salles, | President....... | March, 1898 | 14,332,530 | 3,209,878 |
| British Empire, | London,...... | Victoria,........ | Queen.......... | June 20, 1837 | 381,037,374 | 11,335,806 |
| Bulgaria,...... | Sofia,........ | Ferdinand of Saxe Cob'g | Prince......... | Aug. 14, 1887 | 3,309,816 | 24,360 |
| Canada,........ | Ottawa,...... | Earl of Aberdeen,. | Governor Gen'l. | Sept. 1893 | 4,833,239 | 3,315,647 |
| Chili,.......... | Santiago,..... | Senor Errazuris,.. | President....... | June 25, 1896 | 2,712,145 | 293,970 |
| China,......... | Peking,...... | Tsait'ien,........ | Emperor....... | Jan. 21, 1875 | 402,680,000 | 4,218,401 |
| Columbia, U.S. of | Bogota,...... | M. A. Caro,...... | President....... | Sept. 1896 | 3,878,600 | 504,773 |
| Congo, Free Sta. | Boma,........ | Leopold II,...... | Sovereign....... | Aug. 2, 1889 | 30,000,000 | 900,000 |
| Corea,......... | Seoul,........ | Li-Heui,......... | King........... | Jan. 1864 | 10,519,000 | 82,000 |
| Costa Rica,.... | San Jose,..... | Rafael Yglesias,.. | President....... | Nov. 1897 | 243,205 | 23,000 |
| Dahomey,...... | Abomey,...... | Guthili,......... | King........... | Jan. 1894 | 150,000 | 14,000 |
| Denmark,...... | Copenhagen,.. | Christian IX,..... | King........... | Nov. 15, 1803 | 2,185,335 | 15,289 |
| Ecuador,....... | Quito,........ | General Alfaro,... | President....... | July 1, 1894 | 1,271,861 | 120,000 |
| Egypt,......... | Cairo,........ | Abbas Hilmi,..... | Khedive........ | Jan. 7, 1892 | 9,734,405 | 400,000 |
| France,........ | Paris,........ | M. Felix Faure,.. | President....... | Jan. 17, 1895 | 38,517,975 | 204,092 |
| Germany,...... | Berlin,....... | Wilhelm II,...... | Emperor....... | June 15, 1888 | 52,279,915 | 208,830 |
| Prussia,....... | Berlin,....... | Wilhelm II,...... | King........... | June 15, 1848 | 31,855,123 | 134,603 |
| Bavaria,....... | Munich,...... | Otto,........... | King........... | June 13, 1886 | 5,818,544 | 29,286 |
| Saxony,........ | Dresden,..... | Albert,.......... | King........... | Oct. 29, 1873 | 3,787,688 | 5,787 |
| Wurtemberg,... | Stuttgart,.... | Wilhelm II,...... | King........... | Oct. 6, 1891 | 2,081,151 | 7,533 |
| Baden,......... | Karlsruhe,.... | Friedrich I,...... | Grand Duke.... | Sept. 5, 1856 | 1,725,464 | 5,822 |
| Hesse,......... | Darmstadt,... | Ernst Ludwig,.... | Grand Duke.... | March 13, 1892 | 1,039,020 | 2,966 |
| Lippe,......... | Detmold,..... | Alexander,....... | Prince,........ | March 20, 1895 | 134,854 | 469 |
| Anhalt,........ | Dessau,...... | Friedrich,....... | Duke........... | May 22, 1871 | 293,298 | 906 |
| Brunswick,.... | Brunswick,... | Prince Albrecht,.. | Regent......... | Oct. 21, 1885 | 434,213 | 1,424 |
| Mechb'g-Schw. | Schwerin,.... | Friedrich Frans IV,. | Grand Duke.... | April 10, 1897 | 596,436 | 5,135 |
| " Strelz | Neu Strelitz,. | Friedrich Wilhelm I,. | Grand Duke.... | Sept. 6, 1860 | 101,540 | 1,131 |
| Oldenburg,.... | Oldenburg,... | Peter, I,......... | Grand Duke.... | Feb. 27, 1853 | 373,739 | 2,479 |
| Saxe-Altenb'rg | Altenburg,.... | Ernst,.......... | Duke........... | Aug. 3, 1853 | 180,313 | 511 |
| " Cob.& Go. | Gotha,....... | Alfred,.......... | Duke........... | Aug. 22, 1893 | 216,603 | 755 |
| " Mein'gen | Meiningen,.... | Georg II,........ | Duke........... | Sept. 20, 1866 | 234,005 | 953 |
| " Weimar, | Weimar,...... | Carl Alexander,... | Grand Duke.... | July 8, 1853 | 339,217 | 1,388 |
| Waldeck,...... | Arolsen,...... | Friedrich,....... | Prince.......... | May 12, 1893 | 57,766 | 433 |
| Greenland,..... | Godthaab,.... | Christian IX, Denmark | King........... | Nov. 15, 1863 | 10,516 | 46,740 |
| Greece,........ | Athens,...... | Georgios I,...... | King........... | Nov. 2, 1863 | 2,433,806 | 25,014 |
| Guatemala,.... | Guatemala,... | Senor Cabrera,... | President....... | August, 1897 | 1,364,678 | 63,400 |
| Hawaii,*...... | Honolulu,.... | Sandford B. Dole,. | President....... | July 4, 1894 | 109,020 | 6,640 |
| Hayti,......... | Port au Prince, | Gen T. Simon Sam,. | President....... | April 1, 1896 | 572,000 | 10,204 |
| Honduras,..... | Tegucigalpa,.. | Policarpo Bonilla,. | President....... | Jan. 1, 1895 | 400,000 | 43,000 |
| Iceland,....... | Rejkjavik,.... | Christian IX, Denmark | King........... | Nov. 15, 1863 | 70,927 | 39,756 |
| India (British), | ............ | Victoria,........ | Empress........ | Jan. 1, 1877 | 287,123,350 | 1,500,160 |
| Italy,......... | Rome,....... | Umberto, I,..... | King........... | Jan. 9, 1878 | 28,953,480 | 114,410 |
| Japan,......... | Tokio,........ | Mutsu Hito,..... | Emperor....... | Feb. 13, 1867 | 42,270,620 | 147,655 |
| Khiva,......... | Khiva,........ | Seyd M. Rahim Khan,. | Sovereign...... | 1865 | 700,000 | 22,320 |
| Liberia,....... | Monrovia,.... | W. D. Coleman,... | President....... | Nov. 13, 1896 | 1,068,000 | 14,360 |
| Luxemburg,.... | Luxemburg,.. | Adolf,.......... | Grand Duke.... | Nov. 23, 1890 | 217,583 | 998 |
| Madagascar,... | Tananarivo,.. | M. Felix Faure,.. | President....... | Feb. 27, 1897 | 3,500,000 | 228,500 |
| Monaco,....... | Condamine,.. | Albert,......... | Prince.......... | Sept. 10, 1889 | 13,304 | 8 |
| Mexico,........ | Mexico,...... | Gen. D. Porfirio Diaz, | President....... | Dec. 1, 1896 | 12,578,861 | 767,005 |
| Montenegro,... | Cettinje,..... | Nicholas, I,...... | Prince......... | Aug. 14, 1860 | 228,000 | 3,630 |
| Morocco,....... | Fez,......... | Mulai-Abd-el-Aziz,. | Sultan......... | June 7, 1894 | 9,400,000 | 219,000 |
| Nepal,......... | Katmandu,... | S. B. Shamsher Jang. | Sovereign...... | May 17, 1881 | 2,000,000 | 54,000 |
| Netherlands,... | Hague,....... | WilhelminaHelenaP.M. | Queen.......... | Nov. 23, 1890 | 4,928,658 | 12,648 |
| Nicaragua,..... | Managua,.... | Gen. Santos Zelaya,. | President....... | Oct. 1, 1894 | 360,000 | 49,200 |
| Oman,......... | Muscat,...... | Seyyid Feysal'b. Turki, | Sultan......... | June 4, 1888 | 1,500,000 | 82,000 |
| Orange, Free St. | Bloemfontein, | M. Th. Steyn,.... | President....... | Feb. 21, 1896 | 207,503 | 48,326 |
| Paraguay,...... | Asuncion,..... | General Egusquiza,. | President....... | Nov. 25, 1894 | 329,645 | 98,000 |
| Persia,......... | Teheran,..... | Muzaffer-ed-Din.. | Shah.......... | May 1, 1896 | 9,000,000 | 628,000 |
| Peru,.......... | Lima,........ | Nicolas de Piecola,. | President....... | Aug. 12, 1895 | 2,621,844 | 463,747 |
| Portugal,...... | Lisbon,....... | Carlos I,........ | King........... | Oct. 19, 1889 | 5,049,729 | 36,038 |
| Roumania,..... | Bucharest,.... | Carol I,......... | King........... | March 20, 1881 | 5,800,000 | 48,307 |
| Russian Empire, | St. Petersburg | Nicholas II,...... | Emperor....... | Nov. 1, 1894 | 129,200,000 | 8,644,100 |
| Salvador,...... | San Salvador,. | General R. A. Gutierrez | President....... | March 3, 1895 | 651,130 | 7,225 |
| Samoa,........ | Apia,......... | Malietoa Lauppea,. | King........... | Nov. 9, 1889 | 34,000 | 1,701 |
| Santo Domingo, | Santo Domingo | Gen. Ulisses Henreaux, | President....... | Sept. 1, 1897 | 610,000 | 18,045 |
| Sarawak,...... | Kuching,..... | Sir Ch. Johnson Brooke, | Rajah......... | June 11, 1868 | 300,000 | 50,000 |
| Servia,........ | Belgrade,..... | Alexander I,..... | King........... | April 13, 1893 | 2,314,153 | 19,050 |
| Siam,.......... | Bangkok,..... | Chulalongkorn I,.. | King........... | Oct. 1, 1868 | 8,000,000 | 300,000 |
| Spain,......... | Madrid,...... | Alfonso XIII. (a minor) | King........... | May 17, 1886 | 17,565,632 | 197,670 |
| Sweden-Norway | Stockholm,.... | Oscar II,........ | King........... | Sept. 18, 1872 | 6,920,177 | 297,321 |
| Switzerland,... | Berne,........ | Eugene Ruffy,.... | President....... | Jan. 1, 1898 | 2,917,754 | 15,976 |
| Tonga,......... | Nukualofa,.... | George II,....... | King........... | 1893 | 17,500 | 374 |
| Transvaal, S.A.R | Pretoria,...... | S. J. Paul Kruger,. | President....... | Feb. 1898 | 867,897 | 119,139 |
| Tripoli,........ | Tripoli,....... | Abdul Hamid II,.. | Sultan......... | Aug. 31, 1876 | 800,000 | 398,900 |
| Tunis,......... | Tunis,........ | Sidi Ali,........ | Bey........... | Oct. 28, 1882 | 1,700,000 | 51,000 |
| Turkey,........ | Constantino'le, | Abdul Hamid II,.. | Sultan......... | Aug. 31, 1876 | 38,790,736 | 1,576,677 |
| United Sts. of A. | Washington,.. | William McKinley,. | President....... | March 4, 1897 | 74,500,000 | 3,602,990 |
| Uruguay,...... | Montevideo,.. | Juan L. Cuestas,.. | President....... | March 1, 1898 | 843,408 | 72,110 |
| Venezuela,..... | Caracas,...... | General Andrade,.. | President....... | 1897 | 2,323,527 | 593,943 |
| Zanzibar,...... | Mombasa,..... | Mahomed-bin Said,. | Sultan......... | Aug. 27, 1896 | 150,000 | 625 |

* Annexed by United States July, 1898.

## GREAT BRITAIN COLONIES.

| | SQ. M. | POPULATION. |
|---|---|---|
| *Africa:*—Ascension | | |
| Islands,..... | 38 | 200 |
| Cape Colony,..221,310 | | 1,527,224 |
| Gambia,....... | 2,700 | 50,000 |
| Gold Coast,.... | 15,000 | 1,473,882 |
| Lagos ......... | 1,500 | 100,000 |
| Mauritius,.... | 1,063 | 892,500 |
| Natal........ | 21,150 | 543,913 |
| St. Helena,... | 47 | 4,116 |
| Sierra Leone,.. | 15,000 | 300,000 |
| *America:*—Baha- | | |
| mas,........ | 5,450 | 47,565 |
| Barbadoes,.... | 166 | 189,000 |
| Bermuda,..... | 40 | 16,000 |
| Brit. Honduras, | 7,562 | 28,000 |
| Brit. Guiana,..109,000 | | 285,315 |
| Canada,.......563,700 | | |
| British Colum.382,300 | | |
| Manitoba,.... | 64,066 | |
| N. Brunswick. | 28,100 | 3,315,647 |
| Nova Scotia.. | 20,550 | |
| Prince Ed. Isl.. | 2,000 | |
| Western Ter. 2,254,931 | | |
| Faulkland Isl's, | 7,500 | 1,992 |
| Jamaica,...... | 4,424 | 694,865 |
| Newfoundland, | 42,200 | 202,040 |
| Trinidad and | | |
| Tobago..... | 1,868 | 268,367 |
| Grenada, .... | 133 | 60,367 |
| St. Vincent,.. | 132 | 41,054 |
| St. Lucia,... | 233 | 46,671 |
| Leeward Isl's, | 701 | 127,728 |
| *Asia:*—Aden,So- | | |
| mali Coast & | | |
| Socotra,.... | 69,457 | 94,910 |
| Ceylon,...... | 25,365 | 3,008,289 |
| Cyprus,...... | 3,584 | 187,000 |
| Hong Kong,... | 30½ | 221,441 |
| India,including | | |
| Burma,..1,800,258 | | 287,223,431 |
| Labuan,...... | 31 | 5,853 |
| British North | | |
| Borneo.... | 31,000 | ·150,000 |
| Straits Settle- | | |
| ments, etc.. | 2,500 | 935,726 |
| *Australia:*—Fiji. | 8,045 | 120,500 |
| New So. Wales | | |
| and Norfolk | | |
| Islands,....310,710 | | 1,312,190 |
| New Guinea,.. | 88,460 | 350,000 |
| New Zealand..104,471 | | 703,360 |
| Queensland,..668,497 | | 460,550 |
| So. Australia, | 903,690 | 320,481 |
| Tasmania,.... | 26,385 | 146,667 |
| Victoria,..... | 87,884 | 1,177,304 |
| W. Australia,..975,920 | | 49,782 |
| *Europe:*—Gibral- | | |
| tar,........ | 2 | 26,658 |
| Malta, etc..... | 117 | 176,231 |
| | | |
| Total..... 8,779,150 | | 306,386,614 |

## NETHERLANDS—COLONIES.

| | SQ. M. | POPULATION. |
|---|---|---|
| *East Indies:*—Ce- | | |
| lebes,Sumatra, | | |
| Java, Borneo, | | |
| New Guinea, | | |
| Muluccas, etc..736,400 | | 34,090,000 |
| *West Indies:*—Cu- | | |
| racao and five | | |
| Islands,..... | 403 | 43,744 |
| Surinam,..... | 46,060 | 68,000 |
| | | |
| Total,.......782,863 | | 34,201,744 |

## GERMANY—STATES.

| | SQ. M. | POPULATION. |
|---|---|---|
| Anhalt,........ | 906 | 293,298 |
| Alsace-Lorraine, | 5,601 | 1,640,986 |
| Baden,........ | 5,822 | 1,725,464 |
| Bavaria,....... | 29,286 | 5,818,544 |
| Bremen,....... | 99 | 196,404 |
| Brunswick,.... | 1,424 | 434,213 |
| Hamburg,..... | 158 | 681,632 |
| Hesse,........ | 2,966 | 1,039,020 |
| Lippe,........ | 469 | 134,854 |
| Lubeck,....... | 115 | 88,324 |
| Meck'g-Schwerin | 5,135 | 596,436 |
| Meck'g-Strelitz,.. | 1,131 | 101,540 |
| Oldenburg,..... | 2,479 | 373,739 |
| Prussia,.......184,603 | | 31,855,123 |
| Reuss-Greiz,.... | 122 | 67,468 |
| Reuss-Schleiz,.. | 319 | 132,130 |
| Saxony,....... | 5,787 | 3,787,688 |
| Saxe-Altenburg, | 511 | 180,313 |
| Saxe-Cob'g-Goth. | 755 | 216,603 |
| Saxe-Meiningen, | 953 | 234,005 |
| Saxe-Weimar,.. | 1,388 | 339,217 |
| Schaumb'g-Lippe | 181 | 41,224 |
| Schz. Rudolstadt, | 363 | 88,685 |
| Schz.Sondershau | 333 | 75,074 |
| Waldeck,....... | 433 | 57,766 |
| Wurttemberg,..: | 7,553 | 2,081,151 |
| | | |
| Total,.......209,544 | | 52,278,901 |

## MEXICO—STATES.

| | SQ. M. | POPULATION. |
|---|---|---|
| Aguascalientes,. | 2,950 | 106,645 |
| Campeche,..... | 18,087 | 88,121 |
| Chiapas,....... | 27,222 | 315,190 |
| Chihuahua.... | 87,802 | 266,831 |
| Coahuila,...... | 63,569 | 235,638 |
| Colima,....... | 2,272 | 55,677 |
| Durango,...... | 38,009 | 294,366 |
| Federal District. | 463 | 484,608 |
| Guanajuato,.... | 11,370 | 1,047,288 |
| Guerrero,..... | 24,996 | 417,621 |
| Hidalgo,....... | 8,917 | 548,089 |
| Jalisco,....... | 31,846 | 1,107,863 |
| Lower California | 58,328 | 42,245 |
| Mexico,....... | 9,247 | 837,368 |
| Michoacan,..... | 22,874 | 889,795 |
| Morelos,...... | 2,773 | 159,800 |
| Nuevo-Leon,... | 23,592 | 809,262 |
| Oaxaca,....... | 85,382 | 882,529 |
| Puebla,....... | 12,204 | 979,723 |
| Queretaro,.... | 3,556 | 227,233 |
| San Luis Potosi,. | 25,316 | 570,814 |
| Sinaloa, .... | 33,671 | 258,845 |
| Sonora,....... | 76,900 | 191,281 |
| Tabasco,...... | 10,072 | 134,794 |
| Tamaulipas,... | 32,128 | 208,102 |
| Tepic (Ter.).... | 11,275 | 148,776 |
| Tlaxcala,...... | 1,595 | 166,803 |
| Vera Cruz,.... | 29,201 | 855,975 |
| Yucatan,...... | 35,203 | 298,089 |
| Zacatecas,..... | 24,757 | 452,720 |
| | | |
| Total,........767,005 | | 12,578,861 |

## DENMARK—COLONIES.

| | SQ. M. | POPULATION. |
|---|---|---|
| Greenland,...... | 46,740 | 10,516 |
| Iceland,........ | 39,756 | 70,927 |
| West Indies,.... | 118 | 32,786 |
| | | |
| Total,........ | 86,614. | 114,229 |

## FRANCE—COLONIES.

| | SQ. M. | POPULATION. |
|---|---|---|
| *Asia:* — French | | |
| India, Cochin- | | |
| China,........ | 23,000 | 2,034,452 |
| *Africa:* — Algeria, | | |
| Senegal, Rivie- | | |
| res,duSud,French | | |
| Soudan,Niger,Ga- | | |
| bun, Guinea Coast, | | |
| Congo Eegan, Re- | | |
| union, Mayotte, | | |
| Nosi-Be, Ste. Ma- | | |
| rie, Obock,....336,196 | | 12,062,545 |
| *America:* — Gui- | | |
| ana,or Cayenne, | | |
| Guadeloupe de- | | |
| pendencies, Mar- | | |
| tinique,St.Pierre, | | |
| Miquelon, .... | 1,162 | 385,563 |
| *Oceania:* — New | | |
| Caledonia, Mar- | | |
| quesas Islands, | | |
| Tahiti & Moorea, | | |
| Tubuai Raiva- | | |
| vae, Tuamotu, | | |
| Gambier, Wallis | | |
| Islands,....... | 9,135 | 78,280 |
| *Protected Coun-* | | |
| *tries*—Tunis, | | |
| Madagascar, | | |
| Annam,Cambo- | | |
| dia,Comoro, Isl. | | |
| Sahara Reg'n,2,090,210 | | 15,053,000 |
| | | |
| Total...... 3,009,703 | | 29,614,241 |

## SPAIN—COLONIES.

| | SQ. M. | POPULATION. |
|---|---|---|
| *America:*—Cuba,41,655 | | 1,631,687 |
| Porto Rico,.... | 3,670 | 806,704 |
| *Asia:*—Philippine | | |
| Islands,.....114,326 | | 7,000,000 |
| Caroline Is- | | |
| land & Palaos, | 560 | 36,000 |
| Sulu Islands,.. | 950 | 75,000 |
| Marianne Is- | | |
| lands,....... | 420 | 10,172 |
| *Africa:*—Ferdinan- | | |
| do Po,Annabon, | | |
| Corsico, Elobey, | | |
| San Juan,.... | 850 | 30,000 |
| Rio de Oro and | | |
| Adrar,.......243,000 | | 100,000 |
| Ifni (near Cape | | |
| Nun).......... | 27 | 6,000 |
| | | |
| Total,........ 405,458 | | 9,695,567 |

## PORTUGAL—COLONIES.

| | SQ. M. | POPULATION. |
|---|---|---|
| *Africa:* — Cape | | |
| Verde Islands, | 1,480 | 114,120 |
| Guinea,...... | 4,440 | 820,000 |
| Prince's & St. | | |
| Thomas Is'lds, | 360 | 24,660 |
| Angola, Am- | | |
| briz, Mossam- | | |
| edes, Benguela | | |
| and Congo,....484,800 | | 4,119,000 |
| East Africa...301,000 | | 3,120,000 |
| *Asia:*—Goa,.... | 1,290 | 494,836 |
| Damao, Diu,etc. | 168 | 77,454 |
| Indian Archi- | | |
| pelago,...... | 7,458 | 300,000 |
| China,Macao, etc. | 4 | 78,627 |
| | | |
| Total,........ 801,000 | | 9,148,767 |

# State & Territorial Governments; United States of America.

Copyrighted for GEER'S HARTFORD CITY DIRECTORY, No. 61, July, 1898.

District of Columbia was ceded March 30, 1791, to the U. S. by Virginia and Maryland; governed by Congress.
* Original 13 States. ‡ Democratic. † Republican. || Silver Party. ¶ Populist. § Legislature, biennially.

| 45 States, 4 Ter's. | When Formed or Admitted | GOVERNORS | Yrs. | Terms Expire | Legislature begins | Time of next Election in each State. |
|---|---|---|---|---|---|---|
| Alabama, ‡.... | Dec. 14, 1819 | Joseph F. Johnston | 2 | Dec. 1898 | Nov.§ 1898 | 1st Monday,..............Aug. 1898 |
| Alaska Ter'y, ‡. | July 27, 1868 | .............. | 4 | Sept. 1897 | .... | .... |
| Arizona Ter'y,‡. | Feb. 24, 1863 | Benj. J. Franklin.. | 4 | April,1900 | Jan.§ 1899 | Tuesday after 1st Monday, Nov. 1899 |
| Arkansas,‡.... | June 15, 1836 | Daniel W. Jones... | 2 | Jan. 1899 | Jan.§ 1899 | 1st Monday, September,.......1898 |
| California,‡.... | Sept. 9, 1850 | James H. Budd.... | 4 | Jan. 1899 | Jan.§ 1899 | Tuesday after 1st Monday, Nov. 1898 |
| Colorado,‡..... | Aug. 1, 1876 | Alva Adams...... | 2 | Jan. 1899 | Jan.§ 1899 | 2d Tuesday,............Nov. 1898 |
| Connecticut,*†. | Jan. 9, 1788 | Lorrin A. Cooke... | 2 | Jan. 1899 | Jan.§ 1899 | Tuesday after 1st Monday, Nov. 1898 |
| Delaware,*†... | Dec. 7, 1787 | Ebe W. Tunnell... | 4 | Jan. 1901 | Jan.§ 1899 | Tuesday after 1st Monday Nov. 1898 |
| Florida,‡...... | March 3, 1845 | Wm. D. Bloxham.. | 4 | Jan. 1901 | Apr.§ 1899 | 1st Tuesday............Nov. 1900 |
| Georgia,*‡... | Jan. 2, 1788 | Wm. Y. Atkinson.. | 2 | Oct. 1898 | Oct. 1898 | 1st Wednesday,..........Oct. 1898 |
| Idaho, ‡........ | March 3, 1868 | Frank Steunenberg | 2 | Jan. 1899 | Jan.§ 1899 | Tuesday after 1st Monday, Nov. 1899 |
| Illinois,†...... | Dec. 3, 1818 | John R. Tanner... | 4 | Jan. 1901 | Jan.§ 1899 | Tuesday after 1st Monday, Nov. 1898 |
| Indiana,†...... | Dec. 11, 1816 | James A. Mount... | 4 | Jan. 1901 | Jan.§ 1899 | Tuesday after 1st Monday, Nov. 1898 |
| Iowa,†........ | March 3, 1845 | Leslie M. Shaw,... | 2 | Jan. 1900 | Jan.§ 1900 | 1st Saturday,............Nov. 1898 |
| Kansas,¶...... | Jan. 29, 1861 | John W. Leedy... | 2 | Jan. 1899 | Jan.§ 1899 | Tuesday after 1st Monday, Nov. 1898 |
| Kentucky,-†.... | June 1, 1792 | Wm. O. Bradley.. | 4 | Jan. 1900 | Jan. 1900 | Tuesday after 1st Monday, Nov. 1900 |
| Louisiana,‡.... | April 30, 1812 | Murphy J. Foster.. | 4 | May, 1900 | May§ 1898 | Tuesday after 3d Monday, April, 1900 |
| Maine,†....... | Mar. 15, 1820 | Llewellyn Powers. | 2 | Jan. 1899 | Jan.§ 1899 | 2d Monday,............Sept. 1898 |
| Maryland,*†.. | April 28, 1788 | Lloyd Lowndes.... | 4 | Jan. 1900 | Jan.§ 1900 | 1st Monday,............Nov. 1899 |
| Massachus'tts*† | Feb. 6, 1788 | Roger Wolcott.... | 1 | Jan. 1899 | Jan.§ 1899 | Tuesday after 1st Monday, Nov. 1898 |
| Michigan,†.... | Jan. 26, 1837 | Hazen S. Pingree.. | 2 | Jan. 1899 | Jan.§ 1899 | 1st Monday............Nov. 1898 |
| Minnesota,†... | May 11, 1858 | David M. Clough.. | 2 | Jan. 1899 | Jan.§ 1899 | Tuesday after 1st Monday, Nov. 1898 |
| Mississippi,‡.. | Dec. 10, 1817 | A. J. McLaurin... | 4 | Jan. 1901 | Jan. 1901 | 1st Saturday............Nov. 1900 |
| Missouri,‡..... | Aug. 10, 1821 | Lon V. Stephens.. | 4 | Jan. 1900 | Jan.§ 1899 | Tuesday after 1st Monday, Nov. 1898 |
| Montana,¶..... | Nov. 8, 1889 | Robert B. Smith.. | 4 | Jan. 1901 | Jan.§ 1899 | Tuesday after 1st Monday, Nov. 1898 |
| Nebraska,¶.... | March 1, 1867 | Silas A. Holcomb,. | 2 | Jan. 1899 | Jan.§ 1899 | Tuesday after 1st Monday, Nov. 1898 |
| Nevada,||...... | Oct. 31, 1864 | Reinhold Sadler... | 4 | Jan. 1899 | Jan.§ 1899 | Tuesday after 1st Monday, Nov. 1899 |
| N. Hampshire,*† | June 21, 1788 | Geo. A. Ramsdell.. | 2 | Jan. 1899 | Jan.§ 1899 | 1st Monday,............Nov. 1898 |
| New Jersey,*†. | Dec. 18, 1787 | FosterM. Voorhees, | 3 | Jan. 1899 | Jan.§ 1899 | Tuesday after 1st Monday, Nov. 1898 |
| N.Mexico Ter'y† | Sept. 9, 1850 | Mignel Otero,..... | 4 | June,1901 | Jan.§ 1899 | Tuesday after 1st Monday, Nov. 1898 |
| New York,*†.. | July 26, 1788 | Frank S. Black... | 2 | Jan. 1899 | Jan.§ 1899 | Tuesday after 1st Monday, Nov. 1898 |
| No. Carolina,*†. | Nov. 21, 1789 | Daniel L. Russell.. | 4 | Jan. 1901 | Jan.§ 1899 | Tuesday after 1st Monday, Nov. 1900 |
| North Dakota†.. | Nov. 2, 1889 | Frank A. Briggs.. | 2 | Jan. 1899 | Jan.§ 1899 | Tuesday after 1st Monday, Nov. 1898 |
| Ohio,†......... | Nov. 29, 1802 | Asa S. Bushnell... | 2 | Jan. 1900 | Jan. 1900 | Tuesday after 1st Monday, Nov. 1899 |
| Oklahoma Ter.‡ | May 2, 1890 | Cassius M. Barnes,. | 4 | May, 1901 | Jan.§ 1899 | 1st Friday............June 1898 |
| Oregon,†...... | Feb. 14, 1859 | William P. Lord... | 4 | Jan. 1899 | Jan.§ 1899 | 1st Monday,............Nov. 1898 |
| Pennsylvania,*† | Dec. 12, 1787 | Daniel H. Hastings. | 4 | Jan. 1899 | Jan.§ 1899 | Tuesday after 1st Monday, Nov. 1898 |
| Rhode Island,*‡ | May 29, 1790 | Elisha Dyer.... | 1 | May, 1899 | May, 1899 | 1st Wednesday,.........April,1899 |
| So. Carolina,*‡ | May 23, 1788 | William H. Ellerbe. | 2 | Jan. 1899 | Jan. 1899 | Tuesday after 1st Monday, Nov. 1898 |
| South Dakota,||. | Nov. 3, 1889 | Andrew E. Lee.... | 2 | Jan. 1899 | Jan.§ 1899 | Tuesday after 1st Monday, Nov. 1898 |
| Tennessee,‡.... | June 1, 1796 | Robert L. Taylor .. | 2 | Jan. 1899 | Jan.§ 1899 | Tuesday after 1st Monday, Nov. 1898 |
| Texas,‡........ | Dec. 29, 1845 | Chas. A. Culberson. | 2 | Jan. 1899 | Jan.§ 1899 | Tuesday after 1st Monday, Nov. 1898 |
| Utah, †........ | Sept. 9, 1850 | Heber M. Wells... | 4 | Jan. 1901 | Jan. 1899 | 1st Saturday............Nov. 1898 |
| Vermont, †..... | March 4, 1791 | Josiah Grout..... | 2 | Oct. 1898 | Oct.§ 1898 | 1st Tuesday,............Sept. 1898 |
| Virginia,*‡... | June 26, 1788 | J. Hoge Tyler,..... | 4 | Jan. 1902 | Dec.§ 1899 | Tuesday after 1st Monday, Nov. 1898 |
| Washington,¶... | Nov. 11, 1889 | John R. Rogers,... | 4 | Jan. 1901 | Jan.§ 1899 | Tuesday after 1st Monday, Nov. 1900 |
| West Virginia,† | June 19, 1863 | Geo. W. Atkinson.. | 4 | Mar. 1901 | Jan.§ 1899 | Tuesday after 1st Monday, Nov. 1901 |
| Wisconsin,†.... | May 29, 1848 | Edward Scofield... | 2 | Jan. 1899 | Jan.§ 1899 | Tuesday after 1st Monday, Nov. 1898 |
| Wyoming, †..... | July 25, 1868 | WilliamA.Richards. | 4 | Jan. 1899 | Jan.§ 1899 | 1st Monday,............Nov. 1898 |

# United States of America.

## UNITED STATES EXECUTIVE OFFICERS, JULY, 1898.

WILLIAM McKINLEY, of the State of Ohio, PRESIDENT,...............................Salary, $50,000
GARRET A. HOBART, of the State of New Jersey, VICE PRESIDENT,....................   "    8,000

### CABINET OFFICERS:

WILLIAM R. DAY, of the State of Ohio, SECRETARY OF STATE............................Salary, $8,000
LYMAN J. GAGE, of the State of Illinois, SECRETARY OF THE TREASURY,.................   "    8,000
RUSSELL A. ALGER, of the State of Michigan, SECRETARY OF WAR,......................   "    8,000
JOHN D. LONG, of the State of Massachusetts, SECRETARY OF THE NAVY,................   "    8,000
CORNELIUS N. BLISS, of the State of New York, SECRETARY OF THE INTERIOR,.........   "    8,000
CHARLES EMORY SMITH, of the State of Pennsylvania, POSTMASTER GENERAL,...........   "    8,000
JOHN W. GRIGGS, of the State of New Jersey, ATTORNEY GENERAL,.....................   "    8,000
JAMES WILSON, of the State of Iowa, SECRETARY OF AGRICULTURE,.....................   "    8,000

## FIFTY-FIFTH
# United States Congress.

A new Congress begins on the 4th of March, each alternate year—the odd-number year. By Act of Congress, the election of Congressmen throughout the country (except Oregon, which is first Monday in June, even years), takes place on Tuesday after the 1st Monday in November, every even year. The regular sessions of Congress begin annually on the 1st Monday of December. The pay of a member of Congress, whether Senator or Representative is $5,000 per year with mileage at the rate of 20 cents per mile. Republicans unmarked; * Democrats; † Independents; ‖ People's Party; ¶ Silver Party; § Populist. Senatorial terms expire March 3d of years as indicated.

### SENATE.

GARRET A. HOBART, New Jersey, *President.*

| Term Exp | Senators. | Home Post Office. |
|---|---|---|
| | **ALABAMA.** | |
| 1901. | John T. Morgan,* | Selma. |
| 1903. | Edmund W. Pettus* | Selma. |
| | **ARKANSAS.** | |
| 1901. | James H. Berry,* | Bentonville. |
| 1903. | James K. Jones,* | Washington. |
| | **CALIFORNIA.** | |
| 1899 | Stephen M. White,* | Los Angeles. |
| 1903. | George Clement Perkins, | Oakland. |
| | **COLORADO.** | |
| 1901. | Edward O. Wolcott, | Denver. |
| 1903. | Henry M. Teller, | Central City. |
| | **CONNECTICUT.** | |
| 1899. | Joseph R. Hawley, | Hartford. |
| 1903. | Orville H. Platt, | Meriden. |
| | **DELAWARE.** | |
| 1899. | George Gray,* | Wilmington. |
| 1901. | Richard R. Kenney* | Dover. |
| | **FLORIDA.** | |
| 1899. | Samuel Pasco,* | Monticello. |
| 1903. | Stephen R. Mallory,* | Pensacola. |
| | **GEORGIA.** | |
| 1901. | Augustus O. Bacon,* | Macon. |
| 1903. | Alexander S. Clay,* | Marietta. |
| | **IDAHO.** | |
| 1901. | George L. Shoup, | Boise. |
| 1903. | Henry Heitfeld,§ | Lewiston. |
| | **ILLINOIS.** | |
| 1901. | Shelby M. Cullom, | Springfield. |
| 1903. | William E. Mason, | Chicago. |
| | **INDIANA.** | |
| 1899. | David Turpie*, | Indianapolis. |
| 1903. | Charles W. Fairbanks, | Indianapolis. |
| | **IOWA.** | |
| 1901. | John H. Gear, | Burlington. |
| 1903. | William B. Allison, | Dubuque. |
| | **KANSAS.** | |
| 1901. | Lucien Baker, | Leavenworth. |
| 1903. | William A. Harris,§ | Linwood. |
| | **KENTUCKY.** | |
| 1901. | William Lindsay,* | Frankfort. |
| 1903. | William J. Deboe, | Marion. |
| | **LOUISIANA.** | |
| 1901. | Donelson Caffery,* | Franklin. |
| 1903. | Samuel D. McEnery,* | New Orleans. |
| | **MAINE.** | |
| 1899. | Eugene Hale, | Ellsworth. |
| 1901. | William P. Frye, | Lewiston. |
| | **MARYLAND.** | |
| 1899. | Arthur P. Gorman,* | Laurel. |
| 1903. | George L. Wellington | Cumberland. |
| | **MASSACHUSETTS.** | |
| 1899. | Henry Cabot Lodge, | Nahant. |
| 1901. | George F. Hoar, | Worcester. |
| | **MICHIGAN.** | |
| 1899. | Julius C. Burrows, | Kalamazoo. |
| 1901. | James McMillan. | Detroit. |
| | **MINNESOTA.** | |
| 1899. | Cushman K. Davis, | St. Paul. |
| 1901. | Knute Nelson, | Alexandria. |
| | **MISSISSIPPI.** | |
| 1899. | Hernando De S. Money,* | Carrolliton. |
| 1901. | Edward C. Walthall,* | Grenada. |
| | **MISSOURI.** | |
| 1899. | Francis M. Cockrell,* | Warrensburg. |
| 1903. | George G. Vest,* | Kansas City. |
| | **MONTANA.** | |
| 1899. | Lee Mantle, | Butte. |
| 1901. | Thomas H. Carter, | Helena. |
| | **NEBRASKA.** | |
| 1899. | William V. Allen,§ | Madison. |
| 1901. | John M. Thurston, | Omaha. |
| | **NEVADA.** | |
| 1899. | William M. Stewart, | Carson City. |
| 1903. | John P. Jones, | Gold Hill. |
| | **NEW HAMPSHIRE.** | |
| 1901. | Wm. E. Chandler, | Concord. |
| 1903. | Jacob H. Gallinger, | Concord. |
| | **NEW JERSEY.** | |
| 1899 | James Smith, Jr.,* | Newark. |
| 1901. | William J. Sewell, | Camden. |
| | **NEW YORK.** | |
| 1899. | Edward Murphy, Jr.,* | Troy. |
| 1903. | Thomas C. Platt, | Owego. |
| | **NORTH CAROLINA.** | |
| 1901. | Marion Butler,§ | Elliot. |
| 1903. | Jeter C. Pritchard, | Marshall. |
| | **NORTH DAKOTA.** | |
| 1899. | William N. Roach,* | Larimore. |
| 1903. | Henry C. Hansbrough, | Devils' Lake. |
| | **OHIO.** | |
| 1898. | Marcus A. Hanna, | Cleveland. |
| 1903. | Joseph B. Foraker, | Cincinnati. |
| | **OREGON.** | |
| 1901. | George W. McBride, | St. Helens. |
| | **PENNSYLVANIA.** | |
| 1899. | Matthew S. Quay, | Beaver. |
| 1903. | Boies Penrose. | Philadelphia. |
| | **RHODE ISLAND.** | |
| 1899. | Nelson W. Aldrich, | Providence. |
| 1901. | George P. Wetmore, | Newport. |
| | **SOUTH CAROLINA.** | |
| 1901. | B. R. Tillman,* | Trenton. |
| 1903. | John L. McLaurin,* | Marlboro Co. |
| | **SOUTH DAKOTA.** | |
| 1901. | Richard F. Pettigrew, | Sioux Falls. |
| 1903. | James H. Kyle,† | Aberdeen. |
| | **TENNESSEE.** | |
| 1899. | William B. Bate,* | Nashville. |
| 1901. | Thomas B. Turley, | Memphis. |
| | **TEXAS.** | |
| 1899. | Roger Q. Mills,* | Corsicana. |
| 1901. | Horace Chilton,* | Tyler. |
| | **UTAH.** | |
| 1899. | Frank J. Cannon, | Ogden. |
| 1903. | Joseph L. Rawlins,* | Salt Lake City. |
| | **VERMONT.** | |
| 1899. | Redfield Proctor, | Proctor. |
| 1903. | Justin S. Morrill, | Strafford. |
| | **VIRGINIA.** | |
| 1899. | John W. Daniel,* | Lynchburg. |
| 1901. | Thomas S. Martin,* | Scottsville. |
| | **WASHINGTON.** | |
| 1899. | John L. Wilson, | Spokane. |
| 1903. | George Turner,‖ | Spokane. |

**WEST VIRGINIA.**

1899. Charles J. Faulkner,*.....Martinsburg.
1901. Stephen B. Elkins,........Elkins.

**WISCONSIN.**

1899. John L. Mitchell,*.........Milwaukee.
1903. John C. Spooner,...........Madison.

**WYOMING.**

1899. Clarence D. Clark,.........Evanston.
1901. Francis E. Warren,.........Cheyenne.

## HOUSE OF REPRESENTATIVES.

District. **ALABAMA.**

1. George W. Taylor.*  6. John H. Bankhead.* ·
2. Jesse F. Stallings.*  7. Milford W. Howard.§
3. Henry D. Clayton.*  8. Joseph Wheeler.*
4. William F. Aldrich.*  9. Oscar W. Underwood.*
5. Willis Brewer.*

**ARKANSAS.**

1. PhilipD.McCulloch,Jr*  4. William L. Terry.*
2. John S. Little.*  5. Hugh A. Dinsmore.*
3. Thomas C. McRae.*  6. Stephen Brundidge,Jr.*

**CALIFORNIA.**

1. John A. Barham.  5. Eugene F. Loud.
2. Marion DeVries.*  6. Charles A. Barlow. ‖
3. Samuel G. Hilborn.  7. Curtis H. Castle.§
4. James G. Maguire.*

**COLORADO.**

1. John F. Shafroth.  2. John C. Bell.*

**CONNECTICUT.**

1. E. Stevens Henry.  3. Charles A. Russell.
2. Nehemiah D. Sperry.  4. Ebenezer J. Hill.

**DELAWARE.**

Levin I. Handy,* at large.

**FLORIDA.**

1. S. M. Sparkman.*  2. Robert W. Davis.*

**GEORGIA.**

1. Rufus E. Lester.*  7. John W. Maddox.*
2. James M. Griggs.*  8. William M. Howard.*
3. Elijah B. Lewis.*  9. Farish C. Tate.*
4. Wm. C. Adamson.*  10. William H. Fleming.*
5. L. F. Livingston.*  11. William G. Brantley.*
6. Charles L. Bartlett.*

**IDAHO.**

James Gunn,§ at large.

**ILLINOIS.**

1. James R. Mann.  12. Joseph G. Cannon.
2. William Lorimer.  13. Vespasian Warner.
3. Hugh R. Belknap.  14. Joseph V. Graff.
4. Daniel W. Mills.  15. Benjamin F. Marsh.
5. George E. White.  16. Wm. H. Hinrichsen.*
6. Henry S. Boutell.  17. James A. Connolly.
7. George E. Foss.  18. Thomas M. Jett.*
8. Albert J. Hopkins.  19. Andrew J. Hunter.*
9. Robert R. Hitt.  20. James R. Campbell.*
10. George W. Prince.  21. Jehu Baker.‡
11. Walter Reeves.  22. George W. Smith.

**INDIANA.**

1. James A. Hemenway.  8. Charles L. Henry.
2. Robert W. Miers.*  9. Charles B. Landis.
3. William T. Zenor.*  10. Edgar D. Crumpacker.
4. Francis M. Griffith.*  11. George W. Steele.
5. George W. Faris.  12. James M. Robinson.
6. Henry U. Johnson.  13. Lemuel W. Royse.
7. Jesse Overstreet.

**IOWA.**

1. Samuel M. Clark.  7. John A. T. Hull.
2. George M. Curtis.  8. William P. Hepburn.
3. David B. Henderson.  9. A. L. Hager.
4. Thomas Updegraff.  10. Jonathan P. Dolliver.
5. Robert G. Cousins.  11. George D. Perkins.
6. John F. Lacey.

**LOUISIANA.**

1. Adolph Meyer.*  4. Henry W. Ogden.*
2. Robert C. Davey.*  5. Samuel T Baird.*
3. Robert F. Broussard.*  6. Samuel M. Robertson.*

**KANSAS.**

1. Case Broderick.  Jeremiah D. Botkin,§ at large.
2. Mason S. Peters.*  5. William D. Vincent.§
3. Edwin R. Ridgely.*  6. N. B. McCormick.§
4. Charles Curtis.  7. Jerry Simpson.*

**KENTUCKY.**

1. Charles K. Wheeler.*  7. Evan E. Settle.*
2. John D. Clardy.*  8. George M. Davison.
3. John S. Rhea.*  9. Samuel J. Pugh.
4. David H. Smith.*  10. T. Y. Fitzpatrick.*
5. Walter Evans.  11. David G. Colson.
6. Albert S. Berry.*

**MAINE.**

1. Thomas B. Reed.  3. Edwin C. Burleigh.
2. Nelson Dingley, Jr.  4. Charles A. Boutelle.

**MARYLAND.**

1. Isaac A. Barber.  4. William W. McIntire.
2. William B. Baker.  5. Sydney E. Mudd.
3. William S. Booze.  6. John McDonald.

**MASSACHUSETTS.**

1. Geo. P. Lawrence.  8. Samuel W. McCall.
2. Frederick H. Gillett.  9. John F. Fitzgerald.*
3. Joseph H. Walker.  10. Samuel J. Barrows.
4. Geo. W. Weymouth.  11. Charles F. Sprague.
5. William S. Knox.  12. William C. Lovering.
6. William H. Moody.  13. John Simpkins
7. William E. Barrett.

**MICHIGAN.**

1. John B. Corliss.  7. Horace G. Snover.
2. George Spalding.  8. Ferdinand Brucker.*
3. Albert M. Todd.*  9. Roswell P. Bishop.
4. Edw'd L. R. Hamilton.  10. Rousseau O. Crump.
5. William A. Smith.  11. William S. Mesick.
6. Samuel W. Smith.  12. Carlos D. Shelden.

**MINNESOTA.**

1. James A. Tawney.  5. Loren Fletcher.
2. James T. McCleary.  6. Page Morris.
3. Joel P. Heatwole.  7. Frank M. Eddy.
4. Frederick C. Stevens.

**MISSISSIPPI.**

1. John M. Allen.*  5. John S. Williams.*
2. Will V. A. Sullivan.*  6. William F. Love.*
3. Thomas C. Catchings.*  7. Patrick Henry.*
4. Andrew F. Fox.*

**MISSOURI.**

1. James T. Lloyd.*  9. Champ Clark.*
2. Robert N. Bodine.*  10. Richard Bartholdt.
3. AlexanderM.Dockery.*  11. Charles F. Joy.
4. Charles F. Cochrane.*  12. Charles E. Pearce.
5. William S. Cowherd.*  13. Edward Robb.*
6. David A. DeArmond.*  14. Willard D. Vandiver.*
7. James Cooney.*  15. Mæcenas E. Benton.*
8. Richard P. Bland.*

**MONTANA.**

Charles S. Hartman, at large.

**NEBRASKA.**

1. Jesse B. Strode.  4. William L. Stark.*
2. David H. Mercer.  5. R. D. Southerland.*
3. Samuel Maxwell.*  6. William L. Greene.§

**NEVADA.**

Francis G. Newlands, at large. ¶

**NEW HAMPSHIRE.**

1. Cyrus A. Sulloway.  2. Frank G. Clark.

**NEW JERSEY.**

1. Henry C. Loudenslager.  5. James F. Stewart.
2. John J. Gardner.  6. Richard W. Parker.
3. Benjamin F. Howell.  7. Thomas McEwan, Jr.
4. Mahlon Pitney.  8. Charles N. Fowler.

**NORTH CAROLINA.**

1. Harry Skinner.‡  6. Charles H. Martin.§
2. George H. White.  7. A. C. Shuford.§
3. John E. Fowler.§  8. Romulus Z. Linney.
4. W. F. Strowd.§  9. Richmond Pearson.*
5. William W. Kitchin.*

**NEW YORK.**

1. Joseph McC. Belford.
2. Denis M. Hurley.
3. Edmund H. Driggs.*
4. Israel F. Fischer.
5. Charles G. Bennett.
6. James R. Howe.
7. John H. G. Vehslage.*
8. John M. Mitchell.
9. Thomas J. Bradley.*
10. Amos J. Cummings.*
11. William Sulzer.*
12. George B. McClellan.*
13. Richard C. Shannon.
14. Lemuel E. Quigg.
15. Philip B. Low.
16. William L. Ward.
17. Benj. B. O'Dell, Jr.
18. John H. Ketcham.
19. Aaron V. S. Cochrane.
20. George N. Southwick.
21. David F. Wilbur.
22. Lucius N. Littauer.
23. Wallace T. Foote, Jr.
24. Charles A. Chickering.
25. James S. Sherman.
26. George W. Ray.
27. James J. Belden.
28. Sereno E. Payne.
29. Charles W. Gillet.
30. James W. Wadsworth.
31. Henry C. Brewster.
32. Roland B. Mahany.
33. DeAlva S. Alexander.
34. Warren B. Hooker.

**NORTH DAKOTA.**

Martin N. Johnson, at large.

**OHIO.**

1. William B. Shattuc.
2. Jacob H. Bromwell.
3. John L. Brenner.*
4. George A. Marshall.*
5. David Meekison.*
6. Seth W. Brown.
7. Walter L. Weaver.
8. Archibald Lybrand.
9. James H. Southard.
10. Lucien J. Fenton.
11. Charles H. Grosvenor.
12. John J. Lentz.*
13. James A. Norton.*
14. Winfield S. Kerr.
15. Henry C. VanVoorhis.
16. Lorenzo Danford.
17. John A. McDowell.
18. Robert W. Tayler.
19. Stephen A. Northway.
20. Clifton B. Beach.
21. Theodore E. Burton.

**OREGON.**

1. Thomas H. Tongue.
2. William R. Ellis.

**PENNSYLVANIA.**

Galusha A. Grow; S. A. Davenport, at large.

1. Henry H. Bingham.
2. Robert Adams, Jr.
3. William McAleer.*
4. James R. Young.
5. Alfred C. Harmer.
6. Thomas S. Butler.
7. Irving P. Wanger.
8. Wm. S. Kirkpatrick.
9. Daniel Ermentrout.*
10. Marriott Brosius.
11. William Connell.
12. Morgan B. Williams.
13. Charles N. Brumm.
14. Marlin E. Olmsted.
15. James H. Codding.
16. Horace B. Packer.
17. Monroe H. Kulp.
18. Thaddeus M. Mahon.
19. George J. Benner.*
20. Josiah D. Hicks.
21. Edward E. Robbins.
22. John Dalzell.
23. William A. Stone.
24. Ernest F. Acheson.
25. Joseph B. Showalter.
26. John C. Sturtevant.
27. Charles W. Stone.
28. William C. Arnold.

**RHODE ISLAND.**

1. Melville Bull.
2. Adin B. Capron.

**SOUTH CAROLINA.**

1. William Elliott.*
2. W. Jasper Talbert.*
3. Asbury C. Latimer.*
4. Stanyarne Wilson.*
5. Thomas J. Strait.*
6. James Norton.*
7. J. William Stokes.*

**SOUTH DAKOTA.**

Freeman Knowles§; John E. Kelley,‖ at large.

**TENNESSEE.**

1. Walter P. Brownlow.
2. Henry R. Gibson.
3. John A. Moon.*
4. Benton McMillin.*
5. James D. Richardson.*
6. John W. Gaines.*
7. Nicholas N. Cox.*
8. Thetus W. Sims.*
9. Rice A. Pierce.*
10. E. W. Carmack.*

**TEXAS.**

1. Thomas H. Ball.*
2. Sam B. Cooper.*
3. R. C. DeGraffenried.*
4. John W. Cranford.*
5. Joseph W. Bailey.*
6. Robert E. Burke.*
7. Robert L. Henry.*
8. Sam'l W. T. Lanham.*
9. Joseph D. Sayers.*
10. R. B. Hawley.
11. Rudolph Kleberg.*
12. James L. Slayden.*
13. John H. Stephens.*

**UTAH.**

William H. King,* at large.

**VERMONT.**

1. H. Henry Powers.
2. William W. Grout.

**VIRGINIA.**

1. William A. Jones.*
2. William A. Young.*
3. John Lamb.*
4. Sydney P. Epes.*
5. Claude A. Swanson.*
6. Peter J. Otey.*
7. James Hay.*
8. John F. Rixey.*
9. James A. Walker.
10. Jacob Yost.

**WASHINGTON.**

James H. Lewis,* William C. Jones, at large.

**WEST VIRGINIA.**

1. Blackburn B. Dovener.
2. Alston G. Dayton.
3. Charles P. Dorr.
4. Warren Miller.

**WISCONSIN.**

1. Henry A. Cooper.
2. Edward Sauerhering.
3. Joseph W. Babcock.
4. Theobold Otjen.
5. Samuel S. Barney.
6. James H. Davidson.
7. Michael Griffin.
8. Edward S. Minor.
9. Alexander Stewart.
10. John J. Jenkins.

**WYOMING.**

John E. Osborne, at large.

*TERRITORIAL DELEGATES.*

**ARIZONA.**

Marcus A. Smith,* Tucson.

**NEW MEXICO.**

H. B. Fergusson,* Albuquerque.

**OKLAHOMA.**

James Y. Callahan.§

SENATE.—48 Republicans; 33 Democrats; 3 Populists; 2 Independent; 1 Peoples. Total, 90.
HOUSE.—215 Republican; 123 Democrats; 12 Populists; 1 Independent; 2 Peoples. Total, 354.

# Courts.

**SUPREME COURT OF THE UNITED STATES.**

Annual sessions commence on the 2d Monday in Oct.

CHIEF JUSTICE, Salary, $10,500.

|  | BORN. | APPOINTED. |
|---|---|---|
| Melville W. Fuller, Ill., | 1833, | by Cleveland, in 1888. |

ASSOCIATE JUSTICES, Salary of each, $10,000.

|  | BORN. | APPOINTED. |
|---|---|---|
| John M. Harlan, Ky., | 1833, | by Hayes, in 1877. |
| Horace Gray, Mass., | 1828, | by Arthur, in 1881. |
| David J. Brewer, Kan., | 1837, | by Harrison, in 1889. |
| Henry B. Brown, Mich., | 1836, | by Harrison, in 1890. |
| George Shiras, Jr., Pa., | 1832, | by Harrison, in 1892. |
| Edward D. White, La., | 1845, | by Cleveland, in 1894. |
| Rufus W. Peckham, N.Y., | 1838, | by Cleveland, in 1896. |
| Joseph McKenna, Cal., | 1843, | by McKinley, in 1896. |

**CIRCUIT COURT OF APPEALS.**

The Supreme Court Justice for each Circuit and the Circuit Judges, constitute the new Circuit Court of Appeals in each Circuit, with limited appellate jurisdiction in relief of Supreme Court of the U. S.  Salary $6,000.

| | Appointed in |
|---|---|
| Don A. Pardee, La., | 1881. |
| William J. Wallace, N. Y., | " 1882. |
| LeBarron B. Colt, R. I., | " 1884. |
| E. Henry Lacombe, N. Y., | " 1888. |
| Henry C. Cadwell, Ark., | " 1890. |
| Marcus W. Acheson, Pa., | " 1891. |
| William L. Putnam, Me., | " 1892. |
| Nathaniel Shipman, Conn., | " 1892. |
| George M. Dallas, Pa., | " 1892. |
| Nathan Goff, West Va., | " 1892. |
| Andrew P. McCormick, Texas, | " 1892. |
| William H. Taft, Ohio, | " 1892. |
| William A. Woods, Ind., | " 1892. |

Walter H. Sanborn, Minn.,........Appointed in 1892.
William B. Gilbert, Oregon,...... " 1892.
Charles H. Simonton, S. C.,....... " 1893.
Horace H. Lurton, Tenn.,........ " 1893.
James G. Jenkins, Wis.,.......... " 1893.
John W. Showalter,.............. " 1895.
Amos M. Thayer,................ " 1895.
Erskine M. Ross,................ " 1895.

## U. S. CIRCUIT & DISTRICT COURTS IN CONN.
### 65 State street, in Post Office building.

*Circuit.*—Hartford, 2d Tuesday in October; New Haven, 4th Tuesday in April. *District.*—Hartford, 4th Tuesday in May and 1st Tuesday in December; New Haven, 4th Tuesday in February and August.

*Circuit Judges, (2d J. Dist.)*—Wm. J. Wallace, Syracuse, N. Y., E. Henry Lacombe, N. Y. City, Nathaniel Shipman, Hartford, Conn., Salary $6,000.

*District Judge*—Wm. K. Townsend, N. H. Sal. $5,000.

*Circuit & District Clerk*—E. E. Marvin, 65 State st., Hartford; *deputy*, Richard F. Carroll.

*District Attorney*—Charles W. Comstock, Montville.

*Marshal*—Richard C. Morris, New London.

*Deputy Marshals* — Daniel Lake, New London; James T. Farrell, Hartford; Stephen B. Hayes, Bridgeport.

*Extradition Commissioner*—E. E. Marvin.

*Commissioner of U. S. Circuit Court in Hartford*—E. E. Marvin.

## SUPREME COURT OF ERRORS, CONNECTICUT.

*Chief Justice*—CHARLES B. ANDREWS, Litchfield, May 27, 1905. Salary, $4,500.

### ASSOCIATE JUDGES.

DAVID TORRANCE, Birmingham, till Feb. 9, 1906.
AUGUSTUS H. FENN, Winchester, till 1901.
SIMEON E. BALDWIN, New Haven, till 1901.
WILLIAM HAMERSLEY, Hartford, till Jan. 1902.
Salaries of each of the above $4,000, and $500 for expenses, per annum..

*Reporter*—J. P. ANDREWS, Hartford; Salary, $3,000.

*State Referee*—DWIGHT LOOMIS, Hartford. Salary, $2,000.

The *State Referee* was created by special act of the Legislature in June, 1889, whereby any case pending in the Superior Court can be referred to either State Referee by consent of the parties, for trial of law and fact.

*First Judicial District*—HARTFORD, TOLLAND, MIDDLESEX, LITCHFIELD and WINDHAM COUNTIES, at Hartford, on the first Tuesdays of Oct., Jan., Mar. and May.

*Second Judicial District*—NEW LONDON CO., at Norwich, last Tuesday of May and third Tuesday of Oct.

*Third Judicial District*—NEW HAVEN and FAIRFIELD Co., at New Haven, 3d Tues. Jan. and 1st Tues. in June. At Bridgeport, 3d Tues. in April, and 4th Tues. in Nov.

Passes on QUESTIONS of LAW only, with a full bench of judges; (a full bench may be waived, however, by consent of counsel,) hears appeals from the city courts, courts of common pleas, and the superior court.

## SUPERIOR COURT OF CONNECTICUT, Created in 1798.—JUDGES.

FREDERIC B. HALL, Bridgeport, till April 1, 1905.
SAMUEL O. PRENTICE, Hartford, till July 1, 1905.
JOHN M. THAYER, Norwich, till July, 1905.
SILAS A. ROBINSON, Middletown, till Feb. 11, 1905.
GEORGE W. WHEELER, Bridgeport, till 1901.
RALPH WHEELER, New London, till 1901.
MILTON A. SHUMWAY, Killingly. Jan. 14, 1902.
WILLIAM T. ELMER, Middletown, till 1903.
Salary of Superior Judges, $4,000, and $500 expenses.
State Judges elected for eight years by the Legislature.

### HARTFORD COUNTY.

ARTHUR F. EGGLESTON, States Att'y; Salary, $2,500.
G. A. CONANT, Clerk. | J. LINCOLN FENN, Ass't Clerk.
J. W. Wolven, Messenger.

## ALLOTMENT OF JUDGES, AND COURT TERMS;
### FOR THE YEAR, BEGINNING JULY 1st, 1898.

### HARTFORD COUNTY.

PRENTICE, J.—Oct. 7, '89, and assignment. Short Cal.
PRENTICE, J.—2d Tuesday in Oct. '98. Oct. Term.
THAYER, J.—Dec. 30, '98, and ass'nm't. Short Cal.
THAYER, J.—1st Tuesday in Jan. 1899. Jan. Session.
G. W. WHEELER, J.—Mar. 31, 1899, and as'm't. Short Cal.
G. W. WHEELER, J.—1st Tuesday in April, 1899. Session.
PRENTICE, J.—2d Tuesday in Sept. 1898. Criminal.
SHUMWAY, J.—1st Tuesday in Dec. 1898. "
ROBINSON, J.—1st Tuesday in March, 1899. "
RORABACK, J.—1st Tuesday in June, 1899. "

### NEW HAVEN COUNTY.

RORABACK, J.—Sept. 23, '98, and ass'nm't. Short Cal.
RORABACK, J.—4th Tuesday in Sept. '98. Sept. Term.
SHUMWAY, J.—Dec. 30, '98, and ass'nm't. Short Cal.
SHUMWAY, J.—1st Tuesday in Jan. '99. Session.
PRENTICE, J.—Jan. 6, 1899, and ass'nm't. Short Cal.
PRENTICE, J.—2d Tuesday in Jan. 1899. Spec. Ses.
ROBINSON, J.—Mar. 31, 1899, and ass'nm't. Short Cal.
ROBINSON, J.—1st Tuesday in April, 1899. Session.
RORABACK, J.—1st Tuesday in July, 1898. Criminal.
THAYER, J.—1st Tuesday in Oct. 1898. "
WHEELER, J.—1st Tuesday in Jan. 1899. "
SHUMWAY, J.—1st Tuesday in April, 1899. "

### WATERBURY TERMS.

SHUMWAY, J.—Oct. 14, 1898, and ass'nm't. Short Cal.
SHUMWAY, J.—3d Tuesday in Oct. '98. Oct. Term.
RORABACK, J.—Feb. 17, '99, and assignm't. Short Cal.
RORABACK, J.—3d Tuesday in Feb. '99. Feb. Term.
THAYER, J.—June 16, 1899, and ass'nm't. Short Cal.
THAYER, J.—3d Tues. in June, '99. June Term.
RORABACK, J.—Apr. 28,'99, civil & ass'mt. Short Cal.
RORABACK, J.—1st Tuesday in May, '99. May Term.

### NEW LONDON COUNTY.

#### NEW LONDON TERMS.

ROBINSON, J.—Sept. 16, 1898, and ass'nm't. Sh. Cal.
ROBINSON, J.—3d Tuesday in Sept. 1898. Sept. Term.
ROBINSON, J.—Feb. 10, '99, and ass'nm't. Short Cal.
ROBINSON, J.—2d Tues. in Feb. '99. Civ. & Crim. Term.
ROBINSON, J.—1st Tuesday in Sept. 1898. Criminal.

#### NORWICH TERMS.

G. W. WHEELER, J.—Oct. 28, '98, and ass'nm't. S. Cal.
THAYER, J.—1st Tuesday in Nov. '98. Nov. Session.
ELMER. J.—May 19, 1899, and assignment. Short Cal.
ELMER. J.—4th Tuesday in May, 1899. May Session.
RORABACK, J.—1st Tuesday in Jan. 1899. Criminal.
ELMER, J.—1st Tuesday in May, 1899. "

### FAIRFIELD COUNTY.

#### DANBURY TERMS.

ELMER, J.—Sept. 16, 1898, and assignment. Sh. Cal.
ELMER. J.—3d Tuesday in Sept. 1898. Sept. Term.
ROBINSON, J.—Jan. 13, 1899, and ass'nm't. Short Cal.
ROBINSON, J.—3d Tuesday in Jan. 1899. Jan. Session.
ELMER, J.—3d Tuesday in Oct. 1898. Criminal.
THAYER, J.—2d Tuesday in May, 1899. "

#### BRIDGEPORT TERMS.

G. W. WHEELER, J.—Oct. 7, '98, and ass'nm't. Sh. Cal.
G. W. WHEELER, J.—2d Tuesday in Oct. 1898. Session.
ELMER, J.—Dec. 30, 1898, and assignment. Sh. Cal.
ELMER, J.—1st Tuesday in Jan. 1899. Jan. Ses.
R. WHEELER, J.—Mar. 31, '99, and ass'nm't. Short Cal.
R. WHEELER, J.—1st Tues. in April, 1899. Apr. Session.
THAYER, J.—2d Tuesday in Sept. '98. Criminal.
G. W. WHEELER, J.—3d Tuesday in Feb. 1899. "

## WINDHAM COUNTY.
### PUTNAM TERMS.
R. WHEELER, J.—Sept. 2, '98, and ass'nm't. Sh. Cal.
R. WHEELER, J.—1st Tuesday in Sept. 1898, Civil and Criminal Term.
R. WHEELER, J.—March 3, '98, and ass'm'nt. Sh. Cal.
R. WHEELER, J.—1st Tuesday in March, 1899. Civil and Criminal Term.

### WINDHAM TERMS.
ROBINSON, J.—Oct. 14, 1898, and assignment. Sh. Cal.
ROBINSON, J.—3d Tues. in Oct. '98. Civ. & Crim. Term.
SHUMWAY, J.—April 28, '99, and assignm't. Short Cal.
SHUMWAY, J.—1st Tues. in May, '99. Civ. & Crim. Term.

## LITCHFIELD COUNTY.
R. WHEELER, J.—Sept. 30, '98, and assignment. Sh. Cal.
R. WHEELER, J.—1st Tues. in Oct. '98. Civ. & Crim. Term.
RORABACK, J.— { March 31, 1899, and assignment. New Milford. Short Cal.
RORABACK, J.— { 1st Tuesday in April, 1899, Civil and Criminal Term.
SHUMWAY, J.— { June 2, 1899, and assignment. Winchester. Short Calendar.
SHUMWAY, J.— { 1st Tuesday in June, 1899, Winchester, Civil & Criminal Term.

## MIDDLESEX COUNTY.
### MIDDLETOWN TERMS.
SHUMWAY, J.—Sept. 23, '98, and assnm't. Short Cal.
SHUMWAY, J.—4th Tues. in Sept. '98. Civ. & Crim. Term.
ROBINSON, J.—Nov. 4, 1898, and ass'nm't. Short Cal.
ROBINSON, J.—2d Tuesday in Nov. 1898. Session.
G. W. WHEELER, J.—Jan. 20, '99, and assnm't. Short Cal.
G. W. WHEELER, J.—4th Tues. in Jan. '99. Jan. Session.
PRENTICE, J.—April 7, '99, and ass'nm't. Short Cal.
PRENTICE, J.—2d Tuesday in April, 1899. Apr. Session.
ELMER, J.—1st Tuesday in Dec. 1898. Criminal.
THAYER, J.—1st Tuesday in April, 1899. "

## TOLLAND COUNTY.
R. WHEELER, J.—Sept. 2, '98, and ass'ment. Short Cal.
G. W. WHEELER, J.—1st Tu. in Sept. '98. Civ. & Cr. Term.
R. WHEELER, J.—Dec. 2, '98, and assignment. Sh. Cal.
R. WHEELER, J.—1st Tues. in Dec. '98. Civ. & Cr. Term.
ELMER, J.—April 7, 1899, and assignment. Short Cal.
ELMER, J.—2d Tues. in April, '99. Civil & Crim. Term.
PRENTICE, J.—June 2, 1899, and assignment. Sh. Cal.
PRENTICE, J.—1st Tues. in June, '99. Civ. & Crim. Term.

## COURT OF COMMON PLEAS.
Meets in County house, 127 Allyn and 85 Trumbull sts., 1st Mondays in Sept., Nov., Jan., March and May.
WILLIAM S. CASE, Judge, till July 1, 1901.
EPAPHRODITUS PECK, Associate Judge till April, 1901.
CHARLES E. FELLOWES, Clerk.
EDWIN J. HALE, Messenger.
Created in 1869 for civil cases, where values do not exceed $500; amended so as to have concurrent jurisdiction with the superior court in amounts from $500 to $1,000.
There is a court of common pleas in counties of Hartford, New Haven, Fairfield, New London and Litchfield.

## CITY COURT OF HARTFORD.
Regular sessions every Monday, Tuesday, Wednesday and Saturday of the first week of each term, and every Monday and Saturday of the remaining weeks. All other sessions on days specially designated by the court.
LEONARD MORSE, Recorder.
EDWARD J. GARVAN, Clerk.
WILLIAM J. McCONVILLE, City Attorney.
JOSEPH DAWSON, City Marshal.
CHARLES E. OLMSTED, Messenger.

Was established in 1784 to try civil cases arising within the city limits, whenever one or both parties reside therein, and jurisdiction is unlimited as to amounts.

## POLICE COURT.
Daily at 9 A. M. in Police Court Room, 44 Kinsley st.
ALBERT C. BILL, Judge, till April, 1899.
ARTHUR PERKINS, Assistant Judge.
J. GILBERT CALHOUN, Prosecuting Attorney.
HARRISON B. FREEMAN, Jr. Special Pros. Attorney.
ROBERT C. DICKENSON, Clerk.
Bennett H. Pepper, Messenger. Salary, $400.
Was established in 1852; jurisdiction in criminal cases, and final jurisdiction in all offenses where the penalty does not exceed a fine of $200, or six months' imprisonment, or both; all other hearings are simply preliminary. Appeals are taken only to the superior court. Previously these cases were tried before the Justice of Peace.

### JUDGES OF THE POLICE COURT OF HARTFORD.
| | |
|---|---|
| 1852–1854 | Eliphalet A. Bulkeley. |
| 1855–1857 | Goodwin Collier. |
| 1858 | George S. Gilman. |
| 1859 | Goodwin Collier. |
| 1860 | George S. Gilman. |
| 1861 | Elisha Johnson. |
| 1862 | George S. Gilman. |
| 1863 | Elisha Johnson. |
| 1864–1865 | George S. Gilman. |
| 1866 | Samuel F. Jones. |
| 1867–1870 | Monroe E. Merrill. |
| 1871–1873 | Harrison B. Freeman. |
| 1874–1876 | Monroe E. Merrill. |
| 1877–1882 | Arthur F. Eggleston. |
| 1883–1888 | William F. Henney. |
| 1889–1892 | William J. McConville. |
| 1893–1894 | Sylvester Barbour. |
| 1895– | Albert C. Bill. |

## PROBATE COURT.
(District includes Towns of Hartford, Bloomfield, Glastonbury, Newington, Rocky Hill, West Hartford, Wethersfield and Windsor Locks.)
Regular sessions, daily, except holidays, at 114 Pearl street, Halls of Record, from 9 A. M. to 5 P. M.
HARRISON B. FREEMAN, Judge.
FRANK M. MATHER, Clerk.

## GRAND LIST OF HARTFORD, OCT. 1ST, 1897.
| | |
|---|---|
| 10 per cent for making lists | $ 291,978 |
| 7,481 Dwelling Houses | 27,452,670 |
| 666 Acres of Land | 1,419,471 |
| 962 Stores, Manufactories and Mills | 12,919,550 |
| 2,164 Horses | 134,690 |
| 278 Neat Cattle | 6,790 |
| Carriages | 129,345 |
| Time Pieces, Jewelry, etc. | 27,570 |
| Musical Instruments | 35,495 |
| Furniture and Libraries | 149,161 |
| Bank Stock | 1,304,924 |
| Insurance Stock | 10,101,915 |
| State, Canal and all other Stocks | 25,972 |
| Railroad, City, and other Corporation Bonds | 34,500 |
| Amount employed in Merchandise & Trade | 2,322,985 |
| Investments in Mechanical and Mnf'g op'ns. | 2,562,429 |
| " in Vessels, Steamboats and Com. | 107,800 |
| Money at Interest | 77,162 |
| " on hand or on deposit | 276,797 |
| Taxable property not specified | 63,844 |
| | $60,350,873 |
| Less Soldiers exemption etc. | 291,760 |
| As returned to State Comptroller | $60,059,123 |

*Motto:*—HE WHO TRANSPLANTED, STILL SUSTAINS.

# State of Connecticut.

Description of Capitol, see pages 658–655.

The LEGISLATURE meets biennially at Hartford, on Wednesday after 1st Monday in January (odd years).

Next State election will be for Members of Congress, State Officers, Senators, Representatives and Justices of th~ Peace, for two years, on the Tuesday after the 1st Monday in November, 1898.

For TOWN OFFICERS, annually, on the 1st Monday in October, excepting Hartford, Bridgeport and New Haven.

## Connecticut State Officers, 1898.

| OFFICERS IN CAPITOL. | SALARY. |
|---|---|
| LORRIN A. COOKE, Winsted, *Governor*, | $4,000 |
| JAMES D. DEWELL, New Haven, *Lieut. Gov.* | 500 |
| GEORGE HAVEN, Adjutant General, | 1,200 |
| WM. E. F. LANDERS, Assistant Adjutant General, | 1,800 |
| THERON C. SWAN, Hartford, Clerk. | |
| WALTER PEARCE, Hartford, Clerk. | |
| LORENZO D. CONVERSE, New London, Clerk. | |
| LOUIS N. VANKUREN, Quartermaster General, | 1,200 |
| HENRY C. MORGAN, Assistant Q. M. General. | |
| MICHAEL J. WISE, Clerk. | |
| GEORGE E. KEENEY, Somers, Paymaster General, | 600 |
| ALBERT P. DAY, Hartford, Commissary General. | |
| ALBERT W. PHILLIPS, Surgeon General. | |
| JOHN F. CARPENTER, Putnam, Judge Advocate Gen'l. | |

JAS. B. HOUSTON, Thompsonville,
CLAYTON H. CASE, Hartford, } Aids-de-Camp to
CHAS. W. PICKETT, New Haven, } Governor.
WILLIAM B. McCRAY, Hartford, }

| | |
|---|---|
| JOHN H. BUCK, Executive Secretary, | 1,200 |
| FRANK D. ROOD, Hartford, Executive Clerk, | 1,800 |
| CHARLES PHELPS, Rockville, *Secretary*, | 1,500 |
| ROBINSON S. HINMAN, Chief Clerk. | |
| RICHARD J. DWYER, Hartford, Clerk. | |
| ALBERT R. PARSONS, Hartford, Clerk. | |
| CHAS. W. GROSVENOR, Pomfret, *Treasurer*, | 1,500 |
| B. FRANK MARSH, Chief Clerk. | |
| ROBERT J. MATHEWSON, Pomfret, Clerk. | |
| CHARLES F. SUMNER, Jr., Clerk. | |
| BENJ. P. MEAD, New Canaan, *Comptroller*, | 1,500 |
| F. CLARENCE BISSELL, Willimantic, Chief Clerk. | |
| JOHN H. WADHAMS, Clerk. | |
| HERBERT E. BENTON, *School Fund Commis'er*, | 2,000 |
| CARNOT O. SPENCER, Hartford, Chief Clerk. | |
| WILLIAM H. POND, Hartford, Clerk. | |
| FREDERICK A. BETTS, *Insurance Commissioner*, | 8,500 |
| ARTHUR A. WILSON, Hartford, Actuary. | |
| THERON UPSON, Hartford, Chief Clerk. | |
| FREDERICK W. SKIFF, West Haven, Clerk. | |
| GEORGE D. BLAKESLEY, Hartford, Clerk. | |
| HARLEY M. BLAKESLEY, Hartford, Clerk. | |
| SAMUEL B. HORNE, Winsted, *Labor Commis'er*, | 8,000 |
| WILLIAM W. IVES, Norwich, Clerk. | |
| CHARLES J. HOADLY, Hartford, *Librarian*, | 1,800 |

For State Institutions, Officers, etc., see page 658.

## ROLL OF THE SENATE

All Republicans.
* Resigned November, 1897.  † Resigned March, 1898.
Lieut. Gov. JAMES D. DEWELL, New Haven, *President.*
Hon. WM. H. MARIGOLD, Bridgeport, *Pres't pro tem.*
SAMUEL A. EDDY, North Canaan, *Clerk.*

| Dist. | | |
|---|---|---|
| 1, | Hon. | LINUS B. PLIMPTON, Hartford. |
| 2, | " | ELIZUR S. GOODRICH, Wethersfield. |
| 3, | " | GEORGE F. KENDALL, Suffield. |
| 4, | " | ERASTUS GAY, Farmington. |
| 5, | " | EDWARD D. STEELE, Waterbury. |
| 6, | " | JOHN W. MIX, Wallingford. |
| 7, | " | DWIGHT W. TUTTLE, East Haven. |
| 8, | " | WILLIAM S. BEECHER, New Haven. |
| 9, | " | BENJAMIN H. LEE, New London. |
| 10, | " | LUCIUS BROWN, Norwich. |
| 11, | " | JOHN N. LEWIS, Voluntown. |
| 12, | " | GEORGE E. LOUNSBURY, Ridgefield. |
| 13, | " | EDWIN O. KEELER, Norwalk. |
| 14, | " | *WILLIAM H. MARIGOLD, Bridgeport. |
| 15, | " | JOHN N. WOODRUFF, Sherman. |
| 16, | " | MONROE F. LATHAM, Eastford. |
| 17, | " | GEORGE M. HARRINGTON, Windham. |
| 18, | " | SAMUAL A. HERMAN, Winsted. |
| 19, | " | DONALD T. WARNER, Salisbury. |
| 20, | " | BURTON H. MATTOON, Watertown. |
| 21, | " | ALFRED M. WRIGHT, Essex. |
| 22, | " | CHARLES G. R. VINAL, Middletown. |
| 23, | " | †THOMAS A. LAKE, Rockville. |
| 24, | " | J. CARL CONVERSE, Stafford. |

## ROLL OF HOUSE OF REPRESENTATIVES,

Republican, except * Democrats ; † Nat'l Democrats ; ‡ Dead; || Resigned.

JOSEPH L. BARBOUR, Hartford, *Speaker.*

### HARTFORD COUNTY.

| | |
|---|---|
| Avon | Robert J. Holmes. |
| Berlin | *Daniel E. Bradley. |
| Bloomfield | George F. Humphrey. |
| Bristol | George H. Hall, Adrian J. Muzzy. |
| Burlington | Samuel G. Winchester. |
| Canton | Walter L. Wilder. |
| East Granby | George L. Viets. |
| East Hartford | Norman S. Brewer, A. W. Wickham. |
| East Windsor | Louis F. Helm, Sylves'r D. Rockwell. |
| Enfield | Hugh Young, Jr., Thompson S. Grant. |
| Farmington | A. N. Wadsworth, ‡Samuel Frisbie. |
| Glastonbury | P. Henry Goodrich, Chas. O. Tryon. |
| Granby | Hector Case, Marcus A. Griffin. |
| Hartford | Joseph L. Barbour, Rob't A. Griffing. |
| Hartland | Bryant J. Marks, Edgar B. Case. |
| Manchester | Francis H. Whiton, W. R. Tinker. |
| Marlborough | Charles E. Carter. |
| New Britain | Chas. J. Parker, Morris C. Webster. |
| Newington | †John H. Fish. |
| Plainville | Burwell Carter. |
| Rocky Hill | Luther B. Williams. |
| Simsbury | Alex. T. Pattison, Chauncey H. Eno. |
| Southington | Sherman F. Guernsey, Wm. L. Ames. |
| South Windsor | Norman F. Stoughton. |
| Suffield | Horace K. Ford, Edwin J. Sheldon. |
| West Hartford | William H. Mansfield. |
| Wethersfield | Robert S. Griswold, Frank J. Welles. |
| Windsor | James J. Merwin, Eli S. Hough. |
| Windsor Locks | Alfred W. Converse. |

### NEW HAVEN COUNTY.

| | |
|---|---|
| Ansonia | Reuben H. Tucker, Franklin Burton. |
| Beacon Falls | *Daniel J. Carrington. |
| Bethany | Dwight L. Humiston. |
| Branford | *Charles S. Bradley. |
| Cheshire | Fred'k Doolittle, Herbert J. Morse. |
| Derby | Edwin Hallock, *Albert K. Kennedy. |
| East Haven | Francis F. Andrews. |
| Guilford | Herbert E. Parmelee, †Wm. P. Hill. |
| Hamden | John O. Shares. |
| Madison | Edwin W. Munger |
| Meriden | Wm. G. Gallager, George W. Couch. |

Middlebury ....G. Fred. Abbott.
Milford.........Dumond P. Merwin, Theo. Thompson.
Naugatuck.....James Hughes, *William J. Neary.
New Haven....T. Atwater Barnes, Fred'k L. Averill.
North Branford. Ralph Beers.
North Haven...Anson B. Clinton.
Orange.........Charles E. Graham.
Oxford.........Samuel W. Buckingham.
Prospect........Stephen A. Talmadge.
Seymour.......Theodore B. Beach.
Southbury......Curtiss H. Smith.
Wallingford....W. J. Leavenworth, Sam. Hodgkinson.
Waterbury.....George H. Cowell, Warren L. Hall.
Wolcott........Albert N. Lane.
Woodbridge ....Henry E. Baldwin.

**NEW LONDON COUNTY.**

Bozrah.........F. Judson Miner.
Colchester ....Edward M. Day, William Daudey.
East Lyme.....*Arthur B. Calkins.
Franklin.......James H. Hyde.
Griswold.......*Ira F. Lewis.
Groton.........Robert P. Wilder, Donald Gunn.
Lebanon.......George A. Mills, George A. Fuller.
Ledyard.......Nathan S. Gallup.
Lisbon.........*Charles B. Bromley.
Lyme.........James L. Lord, E. Hart Geer.
Montville .....George N. Wood.
New London....Robert Coit, *Cyrus G. Beckwith.
No. Stonington..Amasa M. Main, Samuel Thompson.
Norwich.......John H. Barnes, Currie Gilmour.
Old Lyme......*John H. Noble.
Preston ........Chas. F. Boswell, Chas. B. Chapman.
Salem.........Albert Morgan.
Sprague ......Ebenezer Allen.
Stonington.....James Pendleton, Elias Williams.
Voluntown.....*Charles E. Main.
Waterford......*John L. Payne.

**FAIRFIELD COUNTY.**

Bethel .........William S. Wortman.
Bridgeport.....Matthew H. Rogers, Geo. E. Somers.
Brookfield .....*James Lee.
Danbury.......Charles S. Peck, Frank L. Butler.
Darien.........*George Gregory.
Easton.........Ellis F. Wheeler.
Fairfield.......H. N. Wakeman, Sherwood Banks.
Greenwich .....Seaman Mead, John F. Close.
Huntington ....Sturges Whitlock.
Monroe........David A. Nichols.
New Canaan...Russell L. Hall.
New Fairfield...*Daniel A. Murphy.
Newtown.....*Martin F. Houlihan, *Aaron Sanford.
Norwalk.......J. Belden Hurlbutt, Russell Frost.
Redding.......Henry S. Osborn, Nathan Perry.
Ridgefield.....Louis L. Valden, Hiram J. Kellogg.
Sherman.......George A. Barnes.
Stamford.......Michael Kenealy, Charles E. Rowley.
Stratford.......J. Henry Blakeman.
Trumbull ......Arthur E. Plumb.
Weston ........Iverson C. Fanton.
Westport......Joseph G. Hyatt.
Wilton.........Frederick D. Benedict.

**WINDHAM COUNTY.**

Ashford........E. Lincoln White, H. R. Woodward.
Brooklyn ......John G. Potter.
Canterbury ....*Charles S. Hyde, *Oliver S. Francis.
Chaplin.......Theron L. Neff.
Eastford.......Leander H. Snow.
Hampton ......Addison J. Greenslit.
Killingly.......James M. Paine, John A. Paine.
Plainfield......Charles E. Barber, Walter Kingsley.
Pomfret .......I. W. Trowbridge, ‡Reuben G. Weeks.
Putnam.......Wm. R. Barber, Charles H. Brown.
Scotland ......William M. Burnham.
Sterling........*Orren W. Bates.
Thompson .....Geo. T. Bixby, ‖Cornelius V. Chapin.
Windham......Huber Clark, ‡John Brown.
Woodstock .....Geo. M. Sampson, Francis B. Chaffee.

**LITCHFIELD COUNTY.**

Barkhamsted...Hubert B. Case, Baker Cleveland.
Bethlehem .....*William Griswold.
Bridgewater....‡Reuben M. Warner.
Canaan.......Edwin W. Spurr.
Colebrook......Samuel A. Cooper, Wm. H. Baldart.
Cornwall.......Chas. W. Everett, *Rob't N. Cochrane.
Goshen.........Frank W. Griswold, Lorrain Apley.
Harwinton .....Patrick Hogan, Jr., D. B. Mansfield.
Kent ..........Thomas D. Barclay.
Litchfield......Geo. W. Mason, *Edw'd E. Champlin.
Morris ........‡Samuel J. Bissell.
New Hartford...Henry C. Messenger, C. F. Loomis.
New Milford....Turney Soule, George H. Jackson.
Norfolk ........Leopold J. Curtiss, ‡Fred M. Darrow.
North Canaan..Alberto T. Rorsback.
Plymouth......Richard Baldwin.
Roxbury .......Edward W. Seeley.
Salisbury ......James M. Selleck, ‖Hubert Williams.
Sharon .........Simeon B. Jewett, *M. F. Whitney.
Thomaston.....Byron W. Pease.
Torrington.....Ed. H. Hotchkiss, Willard V. Barber.
Warren ........Robert H. Perkins.
Washington.....Henry Upson, *Charles P. Lyman.
Watertown.....Edson B. Lockwood.
Winchester.....Lester C. Strong, S. Landon Alvord.
Woodbury......Asahel W. Mitchell, G. H. Drakeley.

**MIDDLESEX COUNTY.**

Chatham.......Henry T. Sellew, C. F. Shepard, Jr.
Chester........James Smith Deuse.
Clinton........Henry C. Hull.
Cromwell......Charles B. Frisbie.
Durham ........John H. Ball, *Henry I. Page.
East Haddam...Frank C. Fowler, Charles H. Rich.
Essex..........John I. Hutchinson.
Haddam .......Roland R. Tyler, Henry E. May.
Killingworth ...Edward P. Nichols, Nathan H. Evarts.
Middlefield.....Otis A. Smith.
Middletown....D. Luther Briggs, Dale D. Butler.
Old Saybrook...Joseph L. Hayden.
Portland.......George G. McLeau.
Saybrook......Milon Pratt, Louis D. Pratt.
Westbrook.....William I. Lewis.

**TOLLAND COUNTY.**

Andover.......Albert H. Lyman.
Bolton.........‡Charles G. Tryon.
Columbia....  *Warren A. Collins.
Coventry.......Charles E. Hunt, George Keeney.
Ellington......Charles A. Thompson.
Hebron........Horace F. Porter, Charles D. Way.
Mansfield......Charles T. Crane, Martin W. Atwood.
Somers ........Amos Pease, Charles H. Ricketts.
Stafford........John M. Leach, Adorno S. Eaton.
Tolland........Edwin S. Agard, *John S. Usher.
Union .........Harry E. Back, Henry F. Corbin.
Vernon........Edwin L. Heath, George Arnold, Jr.
Willington.....William H. Hall, Frederick C. Junl.

---

POLITICAL RECAPITULATION; 1897.

Senate: Republicans, 24. House: Republicans, 218, Democrats, 29, National Democrats, 5. Total, 252.

Republican majority in Senate, 24; Republican in House, 184; on joint ballot, 208.

There are 101 Farmers, 84 Merchants, 19 Manufacturers, 15 Attorneys, the balance are from one to six each in other vocations.

Of the 24 Senators, 19 were born in Connecticut; of the Representatives, 214 were born in this state.

---

AUDITORS PUBLIC ACCOUNTS.

F. B. Noyes, Stonington, July 1, 1899; D. Ward Northrop, Middletown, July 1, 1899.

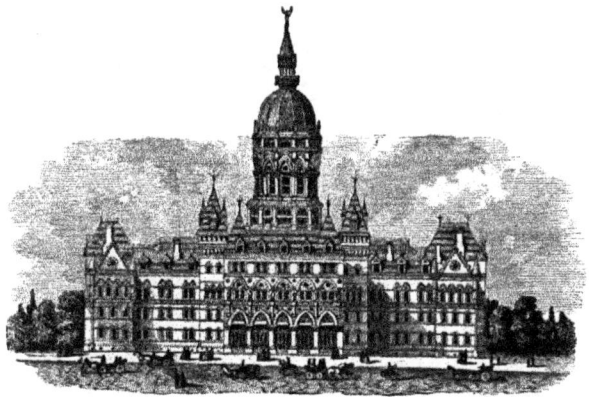

# State Capitol in the City of Hartford;

*Approached from Asylum, Ford, Pearl, Trumbull, Jewell, Mulberry, Wells, Elm, West, Clinton, Trinity, Washington, Lafayette, and Hungerford streets, and Capitol avenue.*

CHARLES H. BUTLER, *Sup't*, room 13, salary, $1,600     BENJ. C. McKENNEY, *Ass't Sup't*, room 13, salary, $1,400

DOME open at 10 and 11.30 A. M.; 2 and 3.30 P. M.     ELEVATORING, 4 stories, from 7 A. M. till 6 P. M.

## OCCUPANCY AND LOCATION OF THE ROOMS.

*See page 617 for the State Officers occupying these rooms.*

All even numbered rooms are on the north side of the building—all the odd numbered on the south side The rooms on the east end are numbered 1 to 19 on the first floor; 21 to 30 on the second floor; 41 to 50 on the third floor; 61 to 70 on the fourth floor. On the west end are Nos. 11 to 19 on first floor; 81 to 39 on second floor; 51 to 61 on third floor; 72 to 80 on fourth floor.

Adjutant General, room 19, 1st floor.
Agricultural Committee, room 50, 8d floor.
Ante room, House, room 33, 2d floor.
Appropriations Committee, room 26, 2d floor.
Attorney's retiring room, 60, 8d floor.
Bank Commissioners, room 55, 8d floor.
Bank Committee, room 55, 8d floor.
Battle Flags of Connecticut, in west corridor.
Cities and Boroughs Committee, room 60, 8d floor.
Claims Committee, room 5, 1st floor.
Comptroller of Public Accounts, r'ms 2 & 4, 1st floor.
Connecticut Prison Association, room 45, 8d floor.
Constitutional Amendments, room 72, 4th floor.
Dairy Commissioners, room 54, third floor.
Education Committee, room 42, 3d floor.
Executive Secretary, room 35, 2d floor.
Engrossed Bills, room 36, 2d floor.
Finance Committee, room 54, 8d floor.
Fisheries Committee, room 25, 2d floor.
Forfeited Rights, room 75, 4th floor.
Governor's room, 39, 2d floor.
Grand Army of the Republic, room 70, 4th floor.
Hall of Representatives, south side on 2d floor.
Highway Commission, rooms 25 and 27, 2d floor.
House coat rooms, 30 and 32, 2d floor.
House Members retiring rooms, 27 and 33, 2d floor.
Humane Institutions Committee, room 47, 8d floor.
Incorporations Committee, room 27, 2d floor.
Inspector of Factories, room 26, 2d floor.
Insurance Commissioner, rooms 14, 16, 18, 20, 1st floor.
Insurance Committee, room 14, 1st floor.
Janitor's room, 11, 1st floor.

Judges retiring room, 59, 8d floor.
Judiciary Committee in Supreme Court room.
Labor Statistics, room 48, 8d floor.
Ladies' reception room, 58, 8d floor.
Lieutenant Governor's room, 21, 2d floor.
Manufactures, room 76, 4th floor.
Military Affairs Committee, room 15, 1st floor.
New Towns and Probate Districts, room 79, 4th floor.
Paymaster General, room 19, 1st floor.
Pharmacy Commission, room 72, 4th floor.
Quartermaster General, rooms 56, 58, 8d floor.
Railroad Commission, room 48, 8d floor.
Railroad Committee, room 41, 8d floor.
Restaurant, room 8, 1st floor.
Roads and Bridges, room 78, 4th floor.
School Fund Commissioner, rooms 5 and 7, 1st floor
School Fund Committee, room 7, 1st floor.
Secretary of State, rooms 38 and 40, 2d floor.
Senate Chamber, east end, 2d floor.
Senate Clerk's and Coat room, 24, 2d floor.
Senator's retiring room, 22, 2d floor.
Speaker's room, 23, 2d floor.
State Board of Charities, room 80, 4th floor.
State Board of Education, room 42, 3d floor.
State Board of Health, room 47, 8d floor.
State Library, north room, 8d floor.
State Prison Committee, room 45, 8d floor.
Superintendent's room, 13, 1st floor.
Stuart's painting of Washington, Senate Chamber.
Supreme Court, west end, 8d floor.
Supreme Court Clerk's room, 57, 8d floor.
Supreme Court Reporter's room, 57, 8d floor.
Temperance Committee, room 80, 4th floor.
Treasurer of State, rooms 1 and 3, 1st floor.
United States Standard Scales, Weights and Measures for this State, room 76, 4th floor.
Washrooms, 28 and 34, 2d floor.
Water Closets, 12, 1st floor; 28 and 34, 2d floor; 49 8d floor.

THE CONNECTICUT CAPITOL COMMISSIONERS advertised for plans for a Capitol edifice in 1871. Among the several plans which were first submitted, was one modeled from the Bradford Town Hall, in England. The present edifice is *not* modeled therefrom, but was planned solely in reference to the site on which it stands, and to the wants of the State.

The main idea of the architect was to follow the order of the 13th Century Gothic, though the strict rules of this order were materially modified at every step in the construction of the building. It is not even Victoria Gothic, but a modernized and Americanized improvement upon all the various changes that have been made in many centuries upon the order of Gothic architecture. The ground was first broken therefor in the spring of 1872. But before the foundation was completed, so much public dissatisfaction was exhibited, with the plan first adopted, and the universal desire expressed for a fire proof building, that the first commission resigned, and a new one appointed, that went forward, in the year 1874, to erect the present edifice on an improved plan.

### GENERAL DESCRIPTION.

The portion of Bushnell Park allotted to the State Capitol, is bounded, north by a roadway, east by Trinity street, south by Capitol avenue, and west by Broad street and the Park river; without any fences.

The edifice on Bushnell Park, in the City of Hartford, of the modern secular Gothic in style, is unrivaled in location. The general ground plan of building is that of a parallelogram. It has four fronts, nearly corresponding with the four cardinal points of the compass. Its extreme length is 295 feet 8 inches ; depth of center part 189 feet 4 inches; depth of wings, 111 feet 8 inches; depth of intermediate parts, 102 feet 8 inches; height from ground line to top of crowning figure 256 feet 6 inches; level of building ground line is 84.7 feet above mean low water at Saybrook. Material, white marble. The frame work of slated roof is iron. The building is fire proof—probably the only fire proof Capitol in this world. There are over 500 windows, 200 doors, and over two acres of flooring to be swept and kept clean. The Commissioners spent about $400,000 annually, during its erection, of the $2,000,000 that was appropriated for this fire proof structure; and upon completion of their labors they reported to the State about $13,000 unexpended of the amount the State had appropriated. Competent critics from other states pronounce it as "unique and unrivaled among structures of this kind in America."

The Connecticut Legislature met in the new Capitol March 26, 1878, and its annual sessions on Wednesday, Jan. 8, 1879. The State Offices were moved therein, Oct. 26, 1878. Since January, 1888, the Legislature has met here biennially.

When a State flag is raised over the west wing of the Capitol the Governor is in his office; and when over the east wing the Senate is in session; and when over the south wing the House of Representatives is in session—aside from public occasions.

| | |
|---|---|
| Completed in January, 1880, costing.... | $2,534,024.46 |
| Land, 14 acres paid by City, April 15, 1872, | 600,000.00 |
| Half acre of ground paid for by State,' 82, | 7,200.00 |
| Furniture, carpets, gas fixtures, etc.,..... | 98,740.00 |
| Five grading appropriations,............ | 70,594.80 |
| Compensation of Capitol Commissioners, | 15,000.00 |
| Paid for a defaulting contractor in 1881, | 5,041.87 |
| "         "         "         1882, | 5,000.00 |
| Commission for grading around Capitol. | 1,500.00 |
| Completing four unfinished rooms, Jan. '85, | 5,000.00 |
| Drinking fountain in Capitol, Jan. 1885, | 450.00 |

| | |
|---|---|
| Total cost of land, building, furniture, etc., | $3,342.550.73 |
| Of above, Hartford donated land, $600,000 | |
| "         "         " cash, 500,000 | |

Hartford pays two-fifths of taxes,
which adds as paid by Hartford, 860,000, 1,960,000.00

Leaving, as paid by rest of State, about $1,382,550.73

Four steam boilers of fifty horse power each are set in a vault outside of the building, and are working satisfactorily in every respect. Much attention has been given to properly warming and ventilating this spacious building, and from results already attained, efforts in this respect are entirely successful. Thirty miles in length of steam, water and gas pipes were laid as the building progressed.

The statues of Roger Sherman[*], Thomas Hooker[†], Jonathan Trumbull[‡] and John Davenport[‖], cut in fine statuary marble, seven feet in height, also medallions of Noah Webster[§] and Horace Bushnell[7] are placed on each side of the center tympanum over the east entrance, upon which a correct representation of the historical Charter Oak Tree is cut. Places have been left for many marble statues, busts, and historical designs upon the tympana.

In the Agricultural room, No. 50, third floor, is a rare exhibit of Connecticut productions.

On the second floor near Representatives hall is that celebrated Vienna premium fountain, presented this State, on a marble base.

### ARRANGEMENT OF ROOMS.

As the interior of the rooms of the building have been arranged by the Commissioners, the rooms of the State Officers are on the first floor, the Executive and Legislative rooms on the second or main floor, the Legislative Committee rooms on the third and fourth floors, above the Senate and House floors. Except the floors of the Legislative halls and offices, which are of hard pine, the only woods used in the building for finishing, fittings and furniture, are oak, black walnut and ash. There is no veneer or varnish used in the entire building. The woods are left in their natural state, except that the pores are filled with some preparation and rubbed down with hard oil finish, thus giving a smooth surface without a shining polish.

In the corridor is the celebrated HISTORICAL WHEEL, battle scarred, etc. Also in the office of the Adjutant General is a portrait of Gen. NATHANIEL LYON, who was born at Ashford, July 14, 1819; graduated at West Point; entered U. S. Army as Lieutenant, July, 1841; was in the Florida Indian war; also in the Mexican war; was in command of U. S. Arsenal at St. Louis at breaking out of the rebellion in 1861; and was killed while leading his command at the battle of Wilson Creek Mission, Aug. 10, 1861; and his remains were interred at Eastford, Conn., Sept. 5, 1861.

### THE SENATE CHAMBER

Has a floor 50 by 40 feet with a height from floor to ceiling of 37 feet. Three windows on the east front of the building admit herein direct light, and the central panel in the ceiling is also a skylight. The desks are placed in three lines of eight each, one facing the President's desk and the others on the sides at right angles; on the east or fourth side there are six desks for Reporters, corresponding with Senators' desks, leaving a large rectangular area in the center and ample passage ways around the outside. Rows of desks do not meet at the corners, leaving passage ways toward the several angles of the room. The

[*]ROGER SHERMAN, born in Newtown, Mass., 1721; a shoemaker; lawyer; representative of Milford and New Haven in Conn. Colonial Assembly; statesman; judge of the Superior Court of Connecticut; treasurer of Yale College; member of Convention that framed United States Constitution, 1795; in United States Senate 19 years, and died July 23, 1793.

[†]THOMAS HOOKER, born in England, 1586, came to Hartford in 1636, and was pastor here until his death in 1647.

[‡]JONATHAN TRUMBULL, born in Lebanon, Conn., June 10, 1710, graduated at Harvard, 1727; elected to the Assembly 1733; its speaker 1739; judge of courts; lieut. governor 1766; then ex officio chief justice and court; governor 1769, and until resigning, 1783; died at Lebanon, Aug. 17, 1785. Washington called him "Brother Jonathan."

[‖]JOHN DAVENPORT, born in England, 1597, went to New Haven, 1638; died in Boston, 1670.

[§]NOAH WEBSTER, born in Hartford, Conn., in 1758; author of Webster's Spelling Book and Webster's Unabridged Dictionary; died in New Haven, Conn., in 1843.

[7]HORACE BUSHNELL, born in Litchfield, Conn., April 14, 1802, graduated at Yale, 1827; called at North Congregational Church of Hartford, Feb. 1833; ordained May 22, 1833; settled only over this church, resigned in April, 1859, on account of ill health; died at Hartford, Feb. 17, 1876.

entire chamber is finished in oak. The carpet has a small pattern agreeable to the eye and in harmony with the walls. The gas fixtures, also, for these halls and the Supreme Court room, which are all of similar pattern, and are of plain, solid finished brass, with no imitations. These fixtures are typical of everything throughout the entire building—being solid, substantial, honest and durable. The desks and chairs of the Senate are oak. The top levels or backs of the desks have a covered recess for the reception of pens, ink and pencils, and under the desks—which is also a receptacle for papers, documents, etc. The chairs have cane seats and backs covered with crimson leather, the back upholstering bearing in emboss work the State coat of arms. The chairs move on hard rubber casters, which are noiseless.

In the Senate Chamber is the celebrated ORIGINAL FULL LENGTH PORTRAIT OF WASHINGTON, taken from life by STUART, for which this State in 1800 paid less than the sum of $800—now it has a priceless value. And a copy of the same, by another artist, is in the Aldermen's chamber in the City Hall. Also, the Lieutenant Governor's Chair, carved from Charter Oak wood, is in the Senate Chamber.

The Colonial Legislature of Connecticut was without a Senate for the first sixty years after its settlement. From the union of the colonies of New Haven and Connecticut under the new charter in 1662 to 1701, all the sessions of the General Court or Legislature, were held in Hartford; but at the latter date, it was enacted that the October session should be held in New Haven, and this prevailed till the Constitution of 1818 was adopted, when annual sessions were held the even years, as 1820, at New Haven, and the odd years, as 1819, at Hartford. This remained till the amendment to our State Constitution was adopted in 1873, to take effect on and after first Wednesday in May, 1875, restoring Hartford as the sole capital. So it seems to be no new thing to have one capital, and that, Hartford. And on and after January, 1877, it met here annually, on the Wednesday after the first Monday in January. Since January, 1888, the Legislature has met here biennially.

### THE REPRESENTATIVES' HALL

Is on the central projecting building of the south front, and supported on an arcade of polished granite columns with carved marble caps, and is lighted by windows on the east, south and west. It has a floor area 84 by 56 feet, and a height of 48 feet. The gallery for spectators being on the north side, on which side is the Speaker's desk. The length of the Representatives hall is from east to west, and the floor is a series of platforms four feet six inches wide, with risers, or steps, of seven inches. On these the members' desks and seats, in amphitheatrical form, are arranged with radial aisles, having the space around the Speaker's desk for the center. There is a central aisle, and two running to the corners of the desk with a shorter aisle in the center of each section of seats, the largest groups or sections having seven seats, and there being only two of this number. By this arrangement no member in reaching his seat is obliged to pass by more than two of his fellow members. In this hall the woodwork and furniture are of black walnut, similar to those in the Senate chamber, except that they are upholstered in maroon leather. The gallery has seats for about 250 persons.

### THE GOVERNOR'S ROOMS.

The Governor's rooms consist of a private office, audience room and private secretary's room, finished in oak and furnished with adjoining safety vault. In the southwest corner of the second floor, lighted by windows on the south and west.

In the Governor's room is the portrait of Major Gen. ISRAEL PUTNAM, commander at "Battle of Bunker Hill," June 17, 1776; born at Salem, Mass., Jan. 7, 1718; died at Brooklyn, Conn., May 19, 1790.

### LIEUTENANT GOVERNOR'S ROOMS.

The corner rooms south of the Senate chamber at the east end of the building are for the Lieutenant Governor and Speaker of the House. They are connected by a doorway In these rooms are portraits of several Lieutenant Governors and ex-Speakers of the House.

### THE COMMITTEE ROOMS,

Twenty-three in all, are on the second, third and fourth floors, in close vicinity to the halls of the assembly, and are amply sufficient in number for all the business of a session. In all there are eighty rooms for the use of State officers, committees, and the convenience of them and members of the legislature.

### STATE DEPARTMENT ROOMS.

On the first floor are rooms for the Treasurer, Comptroller, School Fund Commissioner, Insurance Commissioner, Adjutant General, Paymaster General; on second floor, the Secretary of State; on third floor, the Quartermaster General and Labor Commissioner.

### THE SUPREME COURT ROOM

Is on the third floor in the west portion of the building, and is lighted by six windows on the west side, arranged in two rows. It is 50 by 31 feet on the floor, and has a height of 35 feet from floor to ceiling. It is finished in ash.

### THE STATE LIBRARY ROOM

Is on this floor, and has a superficial area of 85 by 55 feet with a height same as the supreme court room— 35 feet. It is situated on the west center; its north windows overlook the northern entrance.

In the State Library are the portraits of all the Governors of the State of Connecticut, up to 1898 inclusive, excepting those of John Haynes, Edward Hopkins, Thomas Wyllys, Thomas Welles, John Webster, William Leet, Robert Treat, Joseph Talcott, Jonathan Law, Roger Wolcott, Thomas Fitch, William Pitkin, Matthew Griswold, Roger Griswold, also the old original State Charter.

### A CLOCK

Is located in room No. 71, on the fourth floor, with 17 dials, connected by the electric system in the several rooms.

### ELEVATOR AND FLOORS.

A steam elevator, six by eight feet, is located near the center of the building. The floors throughout the Capitol are built with brick arches turned against iron beams. In the construction of the roof, iron has been extensively used, so that the building is considered thoroughly fire proof.

### THE CAPITOL DOME

Has an area of 4,100 square feet, requiring 87,500 leaves of gold 3⅜ inches square, 23 karats fine. The gilding and dome were finished October 11, 1879. It is reached by 275 steps from the first floor, or by 212 steps from the elevator's landing. The view therefrom extends nearly fifty miles in all directions, embracing the rivers, the cities, numerous villages, etc.

The central and commanding feature of the building is the dome, which is richly adorned with arcades, columns, galleries, etc. Is is constructed of marble like the rest of the building. The dome, in plan, is a duodecagon (twelve sided), and on each terminal, at angles, is placed a female figure, representing Force, Art, Law, Commerce, Science, Agriculture, (two each); one-half size models are standing at entrance of House gallery, third floor. The large figure representing the Genius of Connecticut surmounts the cupola, and holds two wreaths, one of immortelles and one of laurel, and on its head a crown of oak leaves; the model stands on the first floor in the north wing.

### THE FINISH.

The wood finish presents a pleasing variety of oak, ash and black walnut, the details being in conformity with the general work. Substantial vaults with iron and steel doors, and also combination locks, and all the most approved guards for safety are provided for the Treasurer, School Fund Commissioner, and other officers.

## 1890, 1880, 1870, 1850 and 1830

# Census of Connecticut Towns;

*Compiled from U. S. Census Returns*

**FOR GEER'S HARTFORD CITY DIRECTORY.**

For Census of 1810, see page 500 of 1890 Directory.

**HARTFORD COUNTY.**

Organized in 1666. 738 square miles. 4 Senators and 45 Representatives.

| Towns. | 1890. | 1880. | 1870. | 1850. | 1830. |
|---|---|---|---|---|---|
| Avon,....... | 1,182 | 1,057 | 987 | 995 | 1,025 |
| Berlin,........ | 2,600 | 2,385 | 2,436 | 1,869 | 3,087 |
| Bloomfield,... | 1,308 | 1,346 | 1,473 | 1,412 | .... |
| Bristol,....... | 7,382 | 5,347 | 3,788 | 2,884 | 1,707 |
| Burlington,... | 1,302 | 1,224 | 1,319 | 1,161 | 1,801 |
| Canton,...... | 2,500 | 2,301 | 2,639 | 1,986 | 1,487 |
| East Granby,.. | 661 | 754 | 858 | .... | .... |
| East Hartford,. | 4,455 | 3,500 | 3,007 | 2,497 | 2,287 |
| East Windsor, | 2,890 | 3,019 | 2,882 | 2,633 | 3,536 |
| Enfield,....... | 7,199 | 6,755 | 6,322 | 4,460 | 2,129 |
| Farmington,... | 3,179 | 3,017 | 2,616 | 2,630 | 1,901 |
| Glastonbury,.. | 3,457 | 3,580 | 3,580 | 3,390 | 2,980 |
| Granby,...... | 1,251 | 1,340 | 1,517 | 2,498 | 2,788 |
| Hartford,..... | 53,230 | 42,551 | 37,743 | 13,555 | 9,789 |
| Hartland,..... | 565 | 643 | 789 | 848 | 1,221 |
| Manchester,.. | 8,222 | 6,462 | 4,223 | 2,546 | 1,576 |
| Marlborough,.. | 582 | 391 | 476 | 832 | 704 |
| New Britain,,. | 19,007 | 13,979 | 9,480 | 3,029 | .... |
| Newington,*.. | 953 | 984 | 778 | .... | .... |
| Plainville,.... | 1,992 | 1,930 | 1,483 | .... | .... |
| Rocky Hill,... | 1,069 | 1,108 | 971 | 1,042 | .... |
| Simsbury,..... | 1,874 | 1,830 | 2,051 | 2,737 | 2,221 |
| Southington,.. | 5,501 | 5,411 | 4,314 | 2,135 | 1,844 |
| South Windsor, | 1,736 | 1,902 | 1,688 | 1,838 | .... |
| Suffield,...... | 3,169 | 3,225 | 3,277 | 2,962 | 2,690 |
| West Hartford,. | 1,930 | 1,828 | 1,582 | 4,411 | .... |
| Wethersfield,.. | 2,271 | 2,173 | 1,915 | 2,523 | 3,853 |
| Windsor,..... | 2,954 | 3,058 | 2,783 | 3,294 | 2,220 |
| Windsor Locks, | 2,758 | 2,332 | 2,154 | .... | .... |
| Total,.. | 147,180 | 125,382 | 109,007 | 69,967 | 51,141 |

*Set off from Wethersfield in 1870.

**NEW HAVEN COUNTY.**

Organized in 1666. 619 square miles. 4 Senators and 36 Representatives.

| Towns. | 1890. | 1880. | 1870. | 1850. | 1830. |
|---|---|---|---|---|---|
| Ansonia,...... | 10,342 | .... | .... | .... | .... |
| Beacon Falls,*. | 505 | 879 | .... | .... | .... |
| Bethany,...... | 550 | 637 | 1,185 | 914 | .... |
| Branford,..... | 4,460 | 3,047 | 2,488 | 1,423 | 2,332 |
| Cheshire,..... | 1,929 | 2,284 | 2,344 | 1,626 | 1,780 |
| Derby,........ | 5,969 | 11,650 | 8,020 | 3,824 | 2,253 |
| East Haven,... | 955 | 3,057 | 2,714 | 1,670 | 1,229 |
| Guilford,...... | 2,780 | 2,782 | 2,576 | 2,653 | 2,344 |
| Hamden,...... | 3,882 | 3,408 | 3,028 | 2,164 | 1,666 |
| Madison,...... | 1,429 | 1,672 | 1,814 | 1,837 | 1,809 |
| Meriden,...... | 25,423 | 18,340 | 10,495 | 3,559 | 1,708 |
| Middlebury,... | 566 | 687 | 696 | 763 | 816 |
| Milford,....... | 3,811 | 3,347 | 3,405 | 2,465 | 2,256 |
| Naugatuck,... | 6,218 | 4,274 | 2,880 | 1,720 | .... |
| New Haven,... | 86,045 | 62,882 | 50,840 | 20,345 | 10,678 |
| North Branford, | 825 | 1,025 | 1,085 | 998 | .... |
| North Haven,. | 1,862 | 1,768 | 1,771 | 1,325 | 1,264 |
| Orange,....... | 4,587 | 3,341 | 2,634 | 1,476 | 1,341 |
| Oxford,....... | 902 | 1,130 | 1,338 | 1,564 | 1,768 |
| Prospect,..... | 445 | 492 | 551 | 666 | 651 |
| Seymour,..... | 3,300 | 2,318 | 2,122 | 1,677 | .... |
| Southbury,.... | 1,089 | 1,740 | 1,318 | 1,484 | 1,557 |
| Wallingford,.. | 6,584 | 4,686 | 3,676 | 2,595 | 2,418 |
| Waterbury,... | 33,202 | 20,270 | 13,106 | 5,187 | 3,070 |
| Wolcott,...... | 522 | 493 | 491 | 608 | 848 |
| Woodbridge,.. | 926 | 829 | 880 | 912 | 2,052 |
| Total,....... | 209,058 | 156,523 | 121,257 | 65,588 | 43,848 |

*Set off from Bethany, Naugatuck, Oxford and Seymour in 1871.

**LITCHFIELD COUNTY.**

Organized in 1751. 948 square miles. 3 Senators and 41 Representatives.

| Towns. | 1890. | 1880. | 1870. | 1850. | 1830. |
|---|---|---|---|---|---|
| Barkhamsted,. | 1,180 | 1,297 | 1,439 | 1,524 | 1,715 |
| Bethlehem,... | 548 | 655 | 750 | 815 | 906 |
| Bridgewater,.. | 617 | 708 | 877 | .... | .... |
| Canaan,....... | 970 | 1,157 | 1,257 | 2,627 | 2,361 |
| Colebrook,.... | 1,098 | 1,148 | 1,141 | 1,317 | 1,332 |
| Cornwall,..... | 1,288 | 1,583 | 1,772 | 2,041 | 1,714 |
| Goshen,...... | 972 | 1,098 | 1,223 | 1,457 | 1,734 |
| Harwinton,... | 943 | 1,016 | 1,044 | 1,175 | 1,516 |
| Kent,......... | 1,333 | 1,522 | 1,744 | 1,848 | 2,001 |
| Litchfield,.... | 3,304 | 3,410 | 3,113 | 3,953 | 4,456 |
| Morris,........ | 584 | 637 | 701 | .... | .... |
| New Hartford, | 3,160 | 3,302 | 3,078 | 2,643 | 1,766 |
| New Milford,.. | 3,917 | 3,907 | 3,586 | 4,058 | 3,979 |
| Norfolk,...... | 1,546 | 1,418 | 1,541 | 1,643 | 1,485 |
| North Canaan, | 1,683 | 1,537 | 1,695 | .... | .... |
| Plymouth,.... | 2,147 | 2,350 | 4,149 | 2,568 | 2,064 |
| Roxbury,..... | 936 | 950 | 919 | 1,114 | 1,122 |
| Salisbury,..... | 3,420 | 3,715 | 3,303 | 3,103 | 2,550 |
| Sharon,....... | 2,149 | 2,580 | 2,441 | 2,507 | 2,615 |
| Thomaston,*.. | 3,278 | 3,225 | .... | .... | .... |
| Torrington,... | 6,048 | 3,327 | 2,893 | 1,916 | 1,651 |
| Warren,....... | 477 | 639 | 673 | 830 | 986 |
| Washington,.. | 1,633 | 1,590 | 1,563 | 1,802 | 1,621 |
| Watertown,... | 2,328 | 1,597 | 1,598 | 1,583 | 1,500 |
| Winchester,.. | 5,183 | 5,142 | 4,096 | 2,179 | 1,766 |
| Woodbury,.... | 1,815 | 2,149 | 1,931 | 2,150 | 2,045 |
| Total,..... | 53,542 | 52,044 | 48,727 | 45,253 | 42,856 |

*Set off from Plymouth in 1875.

**WINDHAM COUNTY.**

Organized in 1726. 520 square miles. 2 Senators and 24 Representatives.

| Towns. | 1890. | 1880. | 1870. | 1850. | 1830. |
|---|---|---|---|---|---|
| Ashford,...... | 778 | 1,041 | 1,241 | 1,295 | 2,661 |
| Brooklyn,..... | 2,626 | 2,308 | 2,354 | 1,514 | 1,415 |
| Canterbury,... | 947 | 1,272 | 1,543 | 1,669 | 1,880 |
| Chaplin,...... | 542 | 627 | 704 | 796 | 867 |
| Eastford,..... | 561 | 855 | 984 | 1,127 | .... |
| Hampton,..... | 632 | 827 | 891 | 946 | 1,101 |
| Killingly,..... | 7,027 | 6,921 | 5,712 | 4,543 | 3,257 |
| Plainfield,.... | 4,582 | 4,021 | 4,521 | 2,732 | 2,289 |
| Pomfret,...... | 1,471 | 1,470 | 1,488 | 1,848 | 1,975 |
| Putnam,...... | 6,512 | 5,827 | 4,192 | .... | .... |
| Scotland,..... | 506 | 590 | 648 | .... | .... |
| Sterling,...... | 1,051 | 957 | 1,022 | 1,025 | 1,240 |
| Thompson,... | 5,580 | 5,051 | 3,804 | 4,638 | 3,380 |
| Voluntown,*.. | .... | 1,186 | 1,062 | 1,064 | 1,204 |
| Windham,..... | 10,032 | 8,264 | 5,412 | 4,508 | 2,812 |
| Woodstock,... | 2,809 | 2,639 | 2,965 | 3,381 | 2,917 |
| Total,...... | 45,158 | 43,856 | 38,518 | 31,081 | 27,077 |

*Transferred to New London County in 1881.

**TOLLAND COUNTY.**

Organized in 1786. 403 square miles. 2 Senators and 22 Representatives.

| Towns. | 1890. | 1880. | 1870. | 1850. | 1830. |
|---|---|---|---|---|---|
| Andover,...... | 401 | 428 | 461 | 500 | .... |
| Bolton,....... | 452 | 512 | 576 | 600 | 744 |
| Columbia,*... | 740 | 757 | 891 | 876 | 962 |
| Coventry,..... | 1,875 | 2,043 | 2,057 | 1,984 | 2,119 |
| Ellington,..... | 1,539 | 1,569 | 1,452 | 1,399 | 1,455 |
| Hebron,....... | 1,089 | 1,243 | 1,279 | 1,345 | 1,937 |
| Mansfield,*... | 1,911 | 2,154 | 2,401 | 2,517 | 2,661 |
| Somers,....... | 1,407 | 1,242 | 1,247 | 1,508 | 1,429 |
| Stafford,...... | 4,535 | 4,455 | 3,405 | 2,940 | 2,515 |
| Tolland,...... | 1,037 | 1,169 | 1,216 | 1,406 | 1,698 |
| Union,........ | 431 | 539 | 627 | 738 | 711 |
| Vernon,....... | 8,808 | 6,915 | 5,446 | 2,900 | 1,164 |
| Willington,... | 906 | 1,086 | 942 | 1,388 | 1,205 |
| Total,....... | 25,081 | 24,112 | 22,000 | 20,091 | 18,700 |

*Transferred from Windham County.

**FAIRFIELD COUNTY.**
Org. 1666. 540 sq. m. 4 Senators, 32 Representatives.

| Towns. | 1890. | 1880. | 1870. | 1850. | 1830. |
|---|---|---|---|---|---|
| Bethel, | 3,401 | 2,727 | 2,811 | .... | .... |
| Bridgeport,† | 48,866 | 29,148 | 19,835 | 7,560 | 2,800 |
| Brookfield, | 989 | 1,152 | 1,198 | 1,859 | 1,255 |
| Danbury, | 19,473 | 11,666 | 8,753 | 5,964 | 4,311 |
| Darien, | 2,276 | 1,949 | 1,808 | 1,454 | 1,212 |
| Easton, | 1,001 | 1,145 | 1,288 | 1,482 | .... |
| Fairfield,* | 3,868 | 3,748 | 5,645 | 3,614 | 4,226 |
| Greenwich, | 10,131 | 7,892 | 7,644 | 5,086 | 3,801 |
| Huntington, | 4,006 | 2,499 | 1,527 | 1,301 | 1,371 |
| Monroe, | 994 | 1,157 | 1,226 | 1,442 | 1,522 |
| New Canaan, | 2,701 | 2,673 | 2,497 | 2,600 | 1,830 |
| New Fairfield, | 670 | 791 | 870 | 927 | 989 |
| Newton, | 3,539 | 4,013 | 3,681 | 3,338 | 3,096 |
| Norwalk, | 17,747 | 13,956 | 12,119 | 4,651 | 3,792 |
| Redding, | 1,546 | 1,540 | 1,524 | 1,754 | 1,686 |
| Ridgefield, | 2,235 | 2,028 | 1,919 | 2,287 | 2,305 |
| Sherman, | 668 | 828 | 846 | 984 | 947 |
| Stamford | 15,700 | 11,297 | 9,714 | 5,000 | 3,707 |
| Stratford, | 2,608 | 4,251 | 3,032 | 2,040 | 1,814 |
| Trumbull, | 1,453 | 1,323 | 1,335 | 1,309 | 1,242 |
| Weston, | 772 | 918 | 1,054 | 1,056 | 2,997 |
| Westport | 3,715 | 8,447 | 8,361 | 2,651 | .... |
| Wilton, | 1,722 | 1,864 | 1,994 | 2,066 | 2,097 |
| Total, | 150,081 | 112,042 | 95,276 | 59,775 | 46,950 |

*In July, 1870, part annexed to Bridgeport.
†West Stratford annexed in 1890 Census.

**NEW LONDON COUNTY.**
Org. 1666. 687 sq. m. 3 Senators, 30 Representatives.

| Towns. | 1890. | 1880. | 1870. | 1850. | 1830. |
|---|---|---|---|---|---|
| Bozrah, | 1,005 | 1,155 | 984 | 867 | 1,079 |
| Colchester, | 2,988 | 2,974 | 3,383 | 2,468 | 2,073 |
| East Lyme, | 2,048 | 1,731 | 1,506 | 1,382 | .... |
| Franklin, | 585 | 686 | 731 | 895 | 1,194 |
| Griswold, | 3,113 | 2,746 | 2,575 | 2,065 | 2,212 |
| Groton, | 5,539 | 5,128 | 5,124 | 3,748 | 4,805 |
| Lebanon,* | 1,670 | 1,845 | 2,211 | 1,901 | 2,555 |
| Ledyard, | 1,188 | 1,373 | 1,392 | 1,558 | .... |
| Lisbon, | 548 | 630 | 502 | 938 | 1,166 |
| Lyme, | 977 | 1,025 | 1,181 | 2,668 | 4,092 |
| Montville, | 2,344 | 2,664 | 2,495 | 1,848 | 1,972 |
| New London, | 13,757 | 10,537 | 9,576 | 8,991 | 4,356 |
| No.Stonington, | 1,463 | 1,769 | 1,759 | 1,936 | 2,840 |
| Norwich, | 23,048 | 21,143 | 16,653 | 10,265 | 5,179 |
| Old Lyme, | 1,319 | 1,387 | 1,362 | .... | .... |
| Preston, | 2,555 | 2,523 | 2,161 | 1,842 | 1,935 |
| Salem, | 481 | 574 | 717 | 764 | 959 |
| Sprague, | 1,106 | 3,207 | 3,463 | .... | .... |
| Stonington, | 7,184 | 7,355 | 6,313 | 5,431 | 3,401 |
| Voluntown,† | 1,060 | .... | .... | .... | .... |
| Waterford, | 2,661 | 2,701 | 2,482 | 2,259 | 2,477 |
| Total, | 76,634 | 73,152 | 66,570 | 51,821 | 42,295 |

*Transferred from Windham County. †Do. in 1881.

**MIDDLESEX COUNTY.**
Org. 1785. 390 sq. m. 2 Senators, 22 Representatives.

| Towns. | 1890. | 1880. | 1870. | 1850. | 1830. |
|---|---|---|---|---|---|
| Chatham, | 1,949 | 1,967 | 2,771 | 1,525 | 3,646 |
| Chester, | 1,301 | 1,177 | 1,094 | 992 | .... |
| Clinton, | 1,384 | 1,402 | 1,404 | 1,344 | .... |
| Cromwell, | 1,987 | 1,640 | 1,856 | .... | .... |
| Durham, | 856 | 990 | 1,086 | 1,026 | 1,116 |
| East Haddam, | 2,599 | 3,032 | 2,951 | 2,610 | 2,664 |
| Essex, | 2,085 | 1,855 | 1,669 | 950 | .... |
| Haddam, | 2,095 | 2,419 | 2,071 | 2,279 | 3,025 |
| Killingworth, | 582 | 748 | 856 | 1,107 | 2,484 |
| Middlefield, | 1,002 | 928 | 1,053 | .... | .... |
| Middletown, | 15,205 | 11,732 | 11,126 | 8,441 | 6,892 |
| Old Saybrook, | 1,484 | 1,302 | 1,215 | .... | .... |
| Portland, | 4,687 | 4,157 | 4,698 | 2,886 | .... |
| Saybrook, | 1,484 | 1,362 | 1,267 | 2,904 | 5,018 |
| Westbrook, | 874 | 878 | 987 | 1,202 | .... |
| Total, | 39,524 | 35,589 | 36,099 | 27,216 | 24,845 |

## RECAPITULATION.

| Counties. | 1890. | 1880. | 1870. | 1850. | 1830. |
|---|---|---|---|---|---|
| Hartford, | 147,180 | 125,382 | 109,007 | 69,967 | 51,141 |
| New Haven, | 209,058 | 156,523 | 121,257 | 88,556 | 43,848 |
| Litchfield, | 53,542 | 52,044 | 48,727 | 55,285 | 42,855 |
| Windham, | 45,158 | 43,856 | 38,518 | 31,081 | 27,077 |
| Tolland, | 25,081 | 24,112 | 22,000 | 20,091 | 18,700 |
| Fairfield, | 150,081 | 112,042 | 95,276 | 59,775 | 46,950 |
| New London, | 76,684 | 73,152 | 66,570 | 51,821 | 42,295 |
| Middlesex, | 39,524 | 35,589 | 36,099 | 27,216 | 24,845 |
| Total, | 746,258 | 622,700 | 537,454 | 370,792 | 297,711 |

## SENATORIAL DISTRICTS.

District in bold type; p. population, 1890; v. votes,1896. No. of Towns in, at the end of each District.

HARTFORD COUNTY.—**1st Dist.**—Hartford; 1. P. 53,230. v. 14,160. **2d Dist.**—Berlin, East Hartford, Glastonbury, Manchester, Marlborough, Newington, Rocky Hill, Southington, South Windsor, Wethersfield, 10. P. 30,846. v. 6,964. **3d Dist.**—Bloomfield, Canton, East Windsor, East Granby, Enfield, Granby,Hartland, Simsbury, Suffield, Windsor, Windsor Locks; 11. P. 27,129. v. 6,105. **4th Dist.**—Avon, Bristol, Burlington, Farmington, New Britain, Plainville, West Hartford; 7. P. 35,975. v. 8,913.

NEW HAVEN COUNTY.—**5th Dist.**—Beacon Falls, Bethany, Middlebury, Naugatuck, Oxford, Prospect, Southbury, Waterbury, Wolcott; 9. P. 48,999. v. 11,120. **6th Dist.**—Cheshire, Guilford, Madison, Meriden, North Branford, Wallingford; 6. P. 38,970. v. 9,151. **7th Dist.**—Ansonia, Branford, Derby, East Haven, Hamden, Milford, North Haven, Orange, Seymour, Woodbridge; 10. P. 29,702. v. 9,410. **8th Dist.**—New Haven; 1. P. 86,045. v. 22,355.

NEW LONDON COUNTY.—**9th Dist.**—Groton, New London, North Stonington, Stonington; 4. P. 27,043. v. 6,088. **10th Dist.**—Ledyard, Norwich, Preston; 3. P. 26,786. v. 5,737. **11th Dist.**—Bozrah, Colchester, East Lyme, Franklin, Griswold, Lebanon, Lisbon, Lyme, Montville, Old Lyme, Salem, Sprague, Voluntown, Waterford; 14. P. 21,905. v. 4,248.

FAIRFIELD COUNTY.—**12th Dist.**—Darien, Greenwich, New Canaan, Ridgefield, Stamford, Wilton; 6. P. 34,765. v. 7,806. **13th Dist.**—Fairfield, Norwalk, Stratford, Trumbull, Westport, Weston, 6. P. 30,163. v. 6,895. **14th Dist.**—Bridgeport; 1. P. 48,866. v. 12,248. **15th Dist.**—Bethel, Brookfield, Danbury, Easton, Huntington, Monroe, New Fairfield, Newton, Redding, Sherman; 10. P. 36,287. v. 8,699.

WINDHAM COUNTY.—**16th Dist.**—Ashford, Eastford, Killingly, Putnam, Thompson, Woodstock; 6. P. 22,767. v. 3,575. **17th Dist.**—Brooklyn, Canterbury, Chaplin, Hampton, Plainfield, Pomfret, Scotland, Sterling, Windham; 9. P. 22,391. v. 4,085.

LITCHFIELD COUNTY.—**18th Dist.**—Barkhamsted, Colebrook, Goshen, Harwinton, New Hartford, Norfolk, Torrington, Winchester; 8. P. 21,080. v. 5,070. **19th Dist.**—Bridgewater, Canaan, Cornwall, Kent, New Milford, North Canaan, Roxbury, Salisbury, Sharon; 9. P. 16,358. v. 3,386. **20th Dist.**—Bethlehem, Litchfield, Morris, Plymouth, Thomaston, Warren, Washington, Watertown, Woodbury; 9. P. 16,130. v. 3,535.

MIDDLESEX COUNTY.—**21st Dist.**—Chatham, Chester, Clinton, Durham, East Haddam, Essex, Haddam, Killingworth, Old Saybrook, Saybrook, Westbrook; 10. P. 16,643. v. 3,868. **22d Dist.**—Cromwell, Middlefield, Middletown, Portland; 4. P. 22,881. v. 4,113.

TOLLAND COUNTY.—**23d Dist.**—Andover, Bolton, Columbia, Coventry, Hebron, Vernon; 6. P. 13,115, v. 2,556. **24th Dist.**—Ellington, Mansfield, Somers, Stafford, Tolland, Union, Willington; 7. P. 11,966. v. 2,877.

## LEGISLATIVE SESSIONS.

Commencement and ending of the sessions of the General Assembly of the State of Connecticut, from 1850.

| YEAR. | COM. | END. | YEAR. | COM. | END. |
|---|---|---|---|---|---|
| 1850 | May 1 | June 22. | 1872 | May 1 | Aug. 2. |
| 1851 | May 7 | July 2. | 1873 | May 7 | July 12. |
| 1852 | May 5 | June 29. | 1874 | May 6 | July 25. |
| 1853 | May 4 | July 1. | 1875 | May 5 | July 22. |
| 1854 | May 3 | July 1. | 1876 | May 3 | June 28. |
| 1855 | May 2 | June 30. | 1877 | Jan. 3 | Mar. 23. |
| 1856 | May 1 | June 29. | 1878 | Jan. 9 | Mar. 28. |
| 1857 | May 6 | June 27. | 1879 | Jan. 8 | Mar. 28. |
| 1858 | May 5 | June 17. | 1880 | Jan. 7 | Mar. 25. |
| 1859 | May 4 | June 24. | 1881 | Jan. 5 | April 14. |
| 1860 | May 2 | June 23. | 1882 | Jan. 4 | April 26. |
| 1861 | May 1 | July 3. | 1883 | Jan. 3 | May 3. |
| 1862 | May 7 | July 3. | 1884 | Jan 9 | April 4. |
| 1863 | May 6 | July 11. | 1885 | Jan. 7 | April 23. |
| 1864 | May 4 | July 9. | 1886 | Jan. 6 | April 14. |
| 1865 | May 3 | July 29. | 1887 | Jan. 5 | May 19. |
| 1866 | May 2 | June 30. | 1889 | Jan. 8 | June 22. |
| 1867 | May 1 | July 27. | 1891 | Jan. 7 | Jan. 3, '93. |
| 1868 | May 2 | Aug. 1. | 1893 | Jan. 4, June 30, '93. | |
| 1869 | May 3 | July 10. | 1895 | Jan. 9, July 9, '95. | |
| 1870 | May 4 | July 22. | 1897 | Jan. 6, June 12, '97. | |
| 1871 | May 3 | July 28. | | | |

## BANK COMMISSIONERS.
Sidney W. Crofut, Killingly, July, 1899; Charles H. Noble, New Milford, July, 1901.

## BOARD OF EDUCATION OF THE BLIND.
Gov. Lorrin A. Cooke, ex officio; Charles B. Andrews, Litchfield; Frank E. Cleaveland, Sec'y, room 47 State Capitol, Hartford; Emily W. Foster, Ass't Sec'y, Hartford.

## BOARD OF PARDONS.
Gov. Lorrin A. Cooke, Winsted; Charles B. Andrews, Litchfield; Ernest Cady, Hartford, June, 1901; Francis Bacon, M. D., New Haven, June, 1901; Morris W. Seymour, Bridgeport, June, 1899; Edward Harland, Norwich, June, 1899. Salary $5 per day each, and expenses, while actually thus employed. George P. McLean, Simsbury, Clerk, salary $200 per annum. Created April, 1883. Organized Nov. 20, 1883. This board has jurisdiction for "granting commutation of punishment, conditional or absolute, from the State Prison." Board meets at Capitol in June and December. A unanimous vote, by this board, for liberating from State Prison, is required.

## BAPTIST SOCIAL UNION OF CONN.
Carnot O. Spencer, Hartford, Pres't; Edward Miller, Meriden; H. A. Hull, Stonington, Vice Presidents; Frederick W. Payne, Hartford, Sec'y & Treas.; Organized 1871. Annual election in October.

## BRIDGE COMMISSIONERS.
Hartford.—Morgan G. Bulkeley, Meigs H. Whaples, John G. Root, John H. Hall, Hartford; Charles W. Roberts, East Hartford; James W. Cheney, Manchester; Alembert O. Crosby, Glastonbury; Lewis Sperry, South Windsor.

Middletown and Portland.—E. B. Strong, Middletown; E. I. Bell, Portland.

Rope Ferry Bridge.—J. L. Payne, Waterford; Frederick A. Beckwith, East Lyme.

Thompsonville and Suffield.—George T. Matthewson, Thompsonville; Herbert L. Viets, Suffield.

Windsor Locks and Warehouse Point.—F. J. Barnes, East Windsor; Arthur F. Saxton, Windsor Locks.

## COMMISSIONER ON DOMESTIC ANIMALS.
William B. Sprague, Andover, July 1, 1899.

## COMMISSIONERS OF THE ISRAEL PUTNAM MEMORIAL CAMP GROUND, REDDING, CONN.
George G. Durant, Bethel; Henry S. Osborn, Redding; Morris W. Seymour, Bridgeport; W. S. Wortman, Bethel; John H. Ferris, Norwalk; John N. Woodruff, Sherman; William W. Lee, Meriden.

## COMMISSION OF SCULPTURE.
C. Dudley Warner, Chairman, Hartford, July 1, 1899; Henry W. Farnam, New Haven, Sec'y, July, 1903; Francis Goodwin, Hartford, July 1, 1903; A. E. Burr, July, 1899; Kirk H. Leavens, Norwich, July, 1901; J. Q. A. Stone, Killingly, July, 1901.

## COM. ON BUILDING & LOAN ASSOCIATIONS.
Edwin L. Scofield, Stamford, July 1, 1899.

## COMMISSION ON UNIFORM STATE LAWS.
Lyman D. Brewster, Danbury; Earliss P. Arvine, New Haven, E. Henry Hyde, Jr., Hartford.

## CONN. AGRICULTURAL EXPERIMENT STATION.
Lorrin A. Cooke, West Winsted, President ex officio of Board of Control; T. S. Gold, West Cornwall, July, 1898, Vice President; William H. Brewer, New Haven, July, 1898, Sec. and Treas.; S. W. Johnson, New Haven, Director; E. H. Jenkins, Vice Director; Edwin Hoyt, New Canaan, 1899; W. O. Atwater, Middletown, July, 1900; James H. Webb, Hamden, July, 1899, S. M. Wells, Wethersfield, 1900. Board of Control; A. L. Winton, Jr., T. B. Osborne, A. W. Ogden, G. F. Campbell, W. L. Mitchell, Chemists; W. G. Sturgis, Mycologist; W. E. Britton, Horticulturist; C. S. Green, Clerk; J. B. Olcott, Grass Gardener; Charles J. Rice, Janitor.

## CONNECTICUT AND RHODE ISLAND CHIEFS OF POLICE UNION.
George F. Bill, Hartford, Pres't; Joseph R. Johnson, New Britain, Vice Pres't; William Hillhouse, Willimantic, Sec'y; Geo. R. Bevans, Danbury, Treas. Meets annually third Tuesday in May.

## CONN. ASSOCIATION OF CLASSICAL AND HIGH SCHOOL TEACHERS.
Edward G. Coy, Lakeville, Pres't; Isaac M. Agard, Rockville, Vice Pres't; Miss Clara Pease, Hartford, Treas.; Miss M. A. Howe, Farmington, Sec'y. Organized 1892. Annual meeting last Saturday in Feb.

## CONN. ASS'N OF FARMERS AND SPORTSMEN FOR THE PROTECTION OF GAME AND FISH.
Abbott C. Collins, Hartford, Pres't; Geo. P. McLean, Hartford, Sec'y; Geo. P. McLean, J. C. Chamberlin, John R. Pitt, Francis B. Skinner, F. W. Whitlock, Samuel A. Eddy, Geo. A. Reed, Z. R. Robbins, Directors; A. C. Collins, C. H. Smith, Jr., A. E. Hart, Geo. P. McLean, Executive Committee. Meets upon call of President. Annual meeting in September.

## CONNECTICUT ASS'N OF MASTER PLUMBERS.
J. S. Craig, Hartford, Pres't; F. J. Reynolds, Ansonia, William H. Hazel, New Haven, Vice Pres'ts; James Donovan, Middletown, Treas.; G. S. Bull, Hartford, Rec. and Cor. Sec'y; E. A. Creevey, Bridgeport, Fin. Sec'y. Organized October 14, 1891.

## CHURCH CLUB OF THE DIOCESE OF CONN.
W. W. Skiddy, Stamford, President; P. C. Royce, Hartford, B. R. English, New Haven, Vice Presidents; Chas F. Chase, New Britain, Sec'y; Burton Mansfield, New Haven, Treas.; N. Albert Hooker, New Britain, John H. Sage, Portland, Samuel Taylor, Hartford, John A. Buckingham, Waterbury, Geo. M. Curtis, Meriden, Executive Committee. Organized October 19, 1892. Meets 4th Tuesday in January, May, October and November. Annual election in January.

## CONN. ASS'N UNION EX-PRISONERS OF WAR.

Lester D. Phelps, Rockville, *President;* Ebenezer Bishop, North Woodstock, E. Dart, South Manchester, *Vice Presidents;* George Q. Whitney, 4 Sumner street, Hartford, *Secretary;* L. J. Filley, Bloomfield, *Treas.;* E. F. Atwood, Hartford, *Chaplain.*

## CONN. BAPTIST BIBLE SCHOOL UNION.

Rev. J. R. Stubbert, New London, *Pres't;* C. L. Rhodes, Stamford, C. H. Brown, Ashford, H. A. Hull, Stonington, R. O. Sherwood, Fairfield, R. Maplesden, Middletown, *Vice Pres'ts;* C. A. Piddock, Hartford, *Treas.;* Rev. B. H. Hatfield, Danielson, *Secretary.* Annual meeting at Crescent Beach in July or August.

## CONN. BEE KEEPERS ASSOCIATION.

Geo. H. Yale, Wallingford, *Pres't;* C. H. Chittenden, Killingworth, Miss H. L. Johnson, Middle Haddam, *Vice Pres'ts;* Porter L. Wood, Waterbury, *Treas.;* Mrs. W. E. Riley, Waterbury, *Sec'y.* Organized May 13, 1891. Meets at State Capitol in May and Nov.

## CONNECTICUT BIBLE SOCIETY.

Rev. Joseph Anderson, Waterbury, *Pres't;* Rev. James W. Bradin, Hartford, Rev. L. D. Warner, Naugatuck; Francis Wayland, New Haven, Rev. 1. Simmons, Hartford, *Vice Pres'ts;* Rev. Wm. H. Gilbert, Hartford, *Sec'y;* Chandler E. Miller, Hartford, *Treas.;* Rodney Dennis, Hartford, *Auditor;* Rev. W. H. Gilbert, Hartford, *Superintendent of Distribution, etc.* Rev. Jos. Anderson, Waterbury, Rev. Jas. W. Bradin, Hartford, David N. Camp, New Britain, Rodney Dennis, Hartford, Rev. A. C. Eggleston, Simsbury, F. D. Glazier, South Glastonbury, Rev. David E. Jones, Broad Brook, Rev. W. H. Kelsey, John W. Lamb, Rev. C. M. Lamson, Rev. Wm. H. Moore, Hartford, A. R. Pierce, Suffield, Wm. H. Talcott, Williston Walker, Hartford, James B. Williams, Glastonbury, *Executive Committee.* Rev. Jas. W. Bradin, David N. Camp, Rodney Dennis, F. D. Glazier, John W. Lamb, Rev. W. H. Moore, A. R. Pierce, Williston Walker, J. B. Williams, *Finance Committee.* Organized 1809. Incorporated, 1816. Rechartered, 1879. Amended, and authorized to do evangelistic work, 1884. Auxiliary of the American Bible Society. Annual election, 1st Tuesday in May.

This Society, with one exception, is the oldest Bible Society in America, and was organized but seven years later than the British and Foreign Bible Society.

The Depositories are in charge of the Y. M. C. A., 323 Pearl street, Hartford; The Treat & Shepard Company, 849 Chapel street, New Haven; T. I. Gwillim, Bristol.

## CONNECTICUT BOARD OF CIVIL ENGINEERS.

William O. Seymour, Ridgefield; T. H. McKenzie, Southington; Nelson J. Welton, Waterbury; H. G. Scofield, Bridgeport; Charles E. Chandler, Norwich.

## CONN. CHILDREN'S AID SOCIETY.

John T. Huntington, Hartford, *Pres't;* George L. Chase, Hartford, E. Stevens Henry, Rockville, Rev. Samuel B. Forbes, Hartford, *Vice Pres'ts;* Charles E. Curtis, New Haven, *Treas.;* Mrs. Virginia T. Smith, Hartford, *Sec'y;* Josephine M. Griswold, *Ass't Treas. and Agent,* office of society, 10 Goodwin building, Hartford Organized in 1892.

## CONN. CIVIL ENGINEERS, AND SURVEYORS, ASSOCIATION.

R. A. Cairns, Waterbury, *Pres't;* L. W. Burt, Edwin D. Graves, Hartford, George K. Crandall, New London, *Sec'y and Treas.;* Wm. G. Smith, R. A. Cairns, W. B. Palmer, C. H. Bunce, L. W. Burt *Executive Committee.* Organized Jan. 15, 1884.

## CONN. COMMERCIAL TRAVELERS ASSO'N.

John E. McPartland, New Haven, *Pres't;* F. P. Chapman, Hartford, C. M. Bradstreet, Bridgeport, *Vice Pres'ts.* L. H. Bates, New Haven, *Secretary and Treas;* W. H. Hardy, L. M. Dyer, F. H. Crygier, E. C. Bogart, E. H. Beers, A. N. Trott, *Executive Committee.* Organized August 30, 1878. Annual meeting in January.

## CONN. COMMISSIONERS OF PHARMACY.

Richard F. Kimball, Hartford, June 1, 1898, *Pres't;* Henry M. Bishop, New Haven, June 1, 1899, *Sec'y;* Frederick S. Stevens, Bridgeport, June, 1900, *Treas.*

## CONN. CREAMERY ASSOCIATION.

E. A. Russell, Suffield, *Pres't;* Hiram Carter, Plainville, *Vice Pres't;* Frank Avery, Wapping, *Sec'y and Treas.;* H. P. Deming, Robertsville; R. F. Case, Canton Centre; B. E. Phelps, Windsor; E. D. Hammond, Cromwell; John Thompson, Ellington; Francis Deming, Berlin; C. B. Little, Somers; John Brown, Merrow, *Directors.* Organized Jan. 1890. Meets upon call of Secretary. Annual meeting in January.

## CONNECTICUT DAIRYMEN'S ASSOCIATION.

A. R. Wadsworth, Farmington, *Pres't;* Wm. B. Sprague, Andover, *V. Pres't;* W. I. Bartholomew, Putnam, *Treasurer;* F. H. Stadtmuller, Elmwood, *Secretary;* J. S. Kirkham, Newington; George E. Manchester, West Winsted; Wm. O. Seymour, Ridgefield; Richard Davis, Middletown; John B. Noble, East Windsor; Richard B. Eno, Westogue; J. G. Schwink, Jr., Meriden; Harry T. Miner, Vernon, *Directors.* Organized, 1882. Incorporated 1889. Meets in January.

## CONNECTICUT DENTAL COMMISSIONERS.

Charles P. Graham, Middletown, *Pres't,* July, 1899; Geo. L. Parmele, Hartford, *Recorder,* July, 1899; William J. Ryder, Danbury, July, 1899; Richard W. Browne, New London, July, 1899; Charles B. Baker, New Haven, July, 1899.

## CONNECTICUT FARMERS' ALLIANCE.

Charles L. Tuttle, Hartford, *Pres't;* S. C. Colt, Farmington, *Vice Pres't;* James H. Smith, Hartford, *Sec'y;* J. Cleveland Capen, Bloomfield, *Treas.* Organized Jan 9, 1897.

## CONNECTICUT HORTICULTURAL SOCIETY.

George S. Osborn, *Pres't;* T. J. McRonald, J. T. Withers, Robert Veitch, Robert Coit, T. S. Gold, L. P. Chamberlain, S. Hoyt, D. A. Lyman, A. N. Pierson, *V. Pres'ts;* C. M. Rodgers, *Sec'y;* J. B. Bruce, *Treas.* Incorporated May, 1889.

## CONNECTICUT HOSPITAL FOR THE INSANE,

IN MIDDLETOWN.

His excellency the Governor : W. B. Foster, Vernon, July, 1901; W. D. Morgan, Hartford, July, 1901; Costello Lippitt, Norwich, July, 1901; Hart D. Munson, New Haven, July, 1899; James G. Gregory, Norwalk, July, 1899; Wm. Bissell, Salisbury, July, 1899; Henry Woodward, Middletown, July, 1899; E. Irving Bell, Portland, July, 1899; E. K. Hubbard, Middletown, July, 1901; Frank B. Weeks, Middletown, July, 1901; Samuel Russell, Middletown, July, 1899; Timothy E. Hopkins, Killingly, July, 1901, *Board of Trustees.* M. B. Copeland, Middletown, *Treasurer;* Henry S. Noble, M.D., *Acting Superintendent;* William E. Fisher, M.D., Charles E. Stanley, M.D., James M. Keniston, M.D., A. B. Coleburn, M. D., J. W. Duke, M. D., R. E. Savage, M.D., *Ass't Physicians;* Thomas M. Durfee, *Clerk;* Mrs. Margaret Dutton, *Matron;* P. W. Sanderson, *Farmer.* Number of patients, July 1, 1897, 858 males and 951 females; total, 1,809.

Visitors are not admitted on Sunday. On any other day of the week, patients may be seen by their friends, unless in the opinion of the physicians the visit is liable to injure the patient. The general public are permitted to inspect the Hospital, between the hours of 10 and 12 M., and between 2 and 5 P. M. on Mondays, Wednesdays and Fridays. Express packages may be addressed to any patient, "In care of the Hospital for the Insane." Letters relating to the patients or the affairs of the Hospital, should be addressed to the Superintendent.

### CONN. HOTEL ASSOCIATION.

Tracy B. Warren, Bridgeport, *President;* A. A. Pocock, Hartford, *V. Pres't;* John J. Dahill, Hartford, *Sec'y;* W. P. Merritt, Bridgeport, *Treas.* Organized Dec. 1892.

### CONNECTICUT HUMANE SOCIETY.

Rodney Dennis, Hartford, *Pres't;* Chandler E. Miller, Hartford, *Sec'y;* Ralph W. Cutler, Hartford, *Treas.;* G. Pierrepont Davis, Hartford, *Ass't Sec'y;* Dwight W. Thrall, Hartford, *Gen'l Agent;* Wallace S. Moyle, New Haven; C. H. Sawyer, Meriden; Lyman S. Burr, New Britain; Robert S. Alexander, Danbury; Samuel B. Harvey, Willimantic; Andrew J. Ewen, Derby; Jas. Huntington, Woodbury; L. J. Nickerson, West Cornwall; Edgar M. Warner, Putnam; John M. Sweeney, Naugatuck; Clayton B. Smith, New London; Harold R. Durant, Waterbury; Elbert O. Hull, Monroe; Edward M. Lockwood, Norwalk; Richard T. Higgins, Winsted; Homer S. Cummings, Stamford; John A. Stoughton, Hartford, *Prosecuting Officers;* Dr. J. E. Gardner, *Veterinary Surgeon.* Chartered March, 1881. Annual meeting in January.

### CONNECTICUT INDIAN ASSOCIATION.

Mrs. Sara T. Kinney, 1162 Chapel street, New Haven, *President;* Miss Sarah Porter, Mrs. G. Williamson Smith, Miss Katharine Hunt, Mrs. Homer Curtiss, Sr., Mrs. Edward Sterling, Miss M. E. Ives, Mrs. F. E. Castle, Mrs. J. N. Harris, Miss Sarah A. Stoddard, Mrs. Geo. W. Lane, Mrs. Stephen Walkley, Mrs. John H. Whittemore, Mrs. Allan McLean, Mrs. C. J. Camp, Mrs. M. S. Foster, *Vice Presidents;* Miss Sara B. Huntington, 886 Collins street, Hartford, *Treas.;* Mrs. Sara A. Booth, 61 Dwight street, New Haven, *General Secretary;* Mrs. George Williamson Smith, Hartford, *Chairman Executive Committee;* Mrs. Kate Foote Coe, Meriden, *Chairman Missionary Committee;* Mrs. Sara T. Kinney, New Haven, *Chairman Home Building Committee;* Mrs. C. F. Chapin, Waterbury, *Chairman Educational Committee;* Miss Mary K. Talcott, Hartford, *Chairman Leaflet Committee;* Miss Mary Hall, Hartford, *Chairman Petitions Committee;* Mrs. John D. Tucker, Hartford, *Chairman Distribution Committee;* Miss Katharine Burbank, Hartford, *Chairman Press Committee;* Hon. Joseph R. Hawley, Hartford; Right Rev. John Williams, Bishop of Connecticut, Middletown; Hon. Francis Wayland, Hon. Henry B. Harrison, Mr. S. A. Galpin, New Haven; Mr. Moses Pierce, Norwich; Rev. Joseph Anderson, D. D., Waterbury; Hon. Jas. L. Howard, Rev. George Williamson Smith, S. T. D., Gen. William B. Franklin, Col. Jacob L. Greene, Rev. Joseph H. Twichell, Col. Charles M. Joslyn, Mr. James P. Andrews, Hartford; Rev. R. P. H. Vail, D. D., Rev. Samuel Scoville, Stamford, *Advisory Committee;* Charles T. Welles, City Bank, Hartford, *Auditor.* Organized November, 1881. Annual meeting in November.

### CONN. INDUSTRIAL SCHOOL FOR GIRLS,
#### IN MIDDLETOWN.

Henry D. Smith, Plantsville, *President;* Clarence E. Bacon, Middletown, *Sec'y and Treasurer;* Rodney Dennis, Hartford, Edward Payne, John M. Van Vleck, Clarence E. Bacon, Samuel Russell, Middletown, Lorrin A. Cooke, Barkhamsted, Stephen O. Bowen, Eastford, Morris W. Seymour, Bridgeport, H. D. Smith, Plantsville, Eugene V. Raynolds, New Haven, William H. Burrows, Calvin L. Harwood, Norwich, *Directors.* The Governor, Lieutenant Governor and Secretary, *Directors ex-officio.* W. G. Fairbank, *Sup't;* Margaret E. Fairbank, *Ass't Sup't.* Incorporated 1868.

### CONN. JERSEY CATTLE BREEDERS ASSO'N.

Samuel C. Colt, Elmwood, *Pres't;* M. W. Terrell, Middlefield, *V. Pres't;* Robert A. Potter, Bristol, *Sec'y;* Benj. W. Collins, Meriden, *Tr.;* S. C. Colt, Elmwood, James I. Inglis, Middlefield, D. D. Bishop, Cheshire, Charles L. Tuttle, Hartford, George A. Bowen, Woodstock, Frederic Bronson, Southport, R. B. Eno, Simsbury, W. E. Hotchkiss, Burlington, *Directors.* Organized Feb. 2, 1888.

### CONN. POMOLOGICAL SOCIETY.

J. H. Hale, South Glastonbury, *Pres't;* J. H. Merriman, New Britain, *V. Pres't;* R. A. Moore, Kensington, *Treas.;* H. C. C. Miles, Milford, *Sec'y.* Organized Dec. 15, 1891. Annual election in February.

### CONNECTICUT PRESS ASSOCIATION

Robert J. Vance, New Britain, *Pres't;* John A. J. Orr, Bridgeport, *V. Pres't;* A. W. Green, Hartford *Secretary and Treasurer;* Arthur B. Underwood, Bridgeport; Herbert W. Baker, Meriden; John Rodemeyer, Jr., New Haven, William R. Sill, Hartford: Harry M. Loomis, Waterbury, *Executive Committee;* N. G. Osborn, New Haven; A. N. Hall, Meriden; J. J. Redmond, Wallingford, *Trustees of the Stevenson Fund.* Organized April 11, 1879, as the Connecticut Reporters' Association. Re-organized July 4, 1887. Annual meeting for the election of officers in the spring.

### CONNECTICUT PRISON ASSOCIATION.

Francis Wayland, New Haven, *Pres't;* Carnot O. Spencer, Hartford, *Treas.;* John C. Taylor, *Sec. and Agent,* room 45 in State Capitol; Francis Wayland, Edward Harland, Henry W. Farnam, Frank Miller, Carnot O. Spencer, H. M. Thompson, John C. Taylor, S. O. Preston, W. H. Pond, G. P. Chandler, Wm. C. Jillson, Alfred R. Goodrich, Thos. R. Pynchon, Wm. G. Fairbanks, *Executive Committee.* Organized Jan. 21, 1876. Incorporated, March, 1879. Annual meeting in January.

### CONNECTICUT PROBATE ASSEMBLY.

Martin H. Smith, Suffield, *Pres't;* Wm. D. Holman, West Willington, John D. Carpenter, Putnam, *Vice Pres'ts;* Joseph B. Banning, Deep River, *Secretary and Treas.* Two regular meetings each year, on second Wednesdays of May and November. Annual meeting second Wednesday in February at Capitol in Hartford. May and November meetings held at such places as the Assembly directs.

### CONN. PUBLIC LIBRARY COMMITTEE.

Charles D. Hine, New Britain, *Chairman;* Caroline M. Hewins, Hartford, *Sec'y;* Storrs O. Seymour, Litchfield; Nathan L. Bishop, Norwich; Charles E. Graves, New Haven. Appointed annually by the State Board of Education.

### CONNECTICUT SCHOOL FOR IMBECILES,
#### LAKEVILLE, CONN.

George B. Burrall, *Pres't;* G. W. Russell, Henry Gay, J. C. Goddard, *V. Pres'ts;* the above officers and W. W. Knight, T. L. Norton, E. W. Spurr, M. B. Richardson, G. H. Knight, George P. McLean, with the Governor, *Directors;* T. L. Norton, *Treas.;* G. H. Knight, *Sec'y and Supt.*

### CONN. SHEEP BREEDERS' ASSOCIATION.

R. S. Hinman, Hartford, *Pres't;* Julius W. Yale, F. W. Chambers, *Vice Pres'ts;* B. C. Patterson, Torrington, *Treas.;* John H. Wadhams, Goshen, *Sec'y.* Meets upon call by President. Annual meeting in December.

### CONN. SOCIETY FOR UNIVERSITY EXTENSION.

Chester D. Hartranft, *President,* office 1567 Broad street, Hartford.

## CONNECTICUT SOCIETY SONS OF THE AMERICAN REVOLUTION.

Jonathan Trumbull, Norwich, *Pres't*; E. S. Greeley, New Haven, *Vice Pres't*; Louis R. Cheney, Hartford, *Sec'y*; John C. Hollister, New Haven, *Treas.*; Joseph G. Woodward, Hartford, *Historian*; H. L. Hotchkiss, New Haven, *Registrar*; E. S. Lines, New Haven, *Chaplain.* Organized April 2, 1889. Incorporated December, 18, 1893.

## CONNECTICUT SOLDIERS HOSPITAL BOARD,

AND MANAGERS FITCH'S HOME FOR SOLDIERS AT NOROTON HEIGHTS, CONN.

Gov. Lorrin A. Cooke; Adjutant Gen. Geo. Havens; Surg. Gen. Albert W. Phillips, *ex-officio*; Gen. L. A. Dickinson, Hartford, March 29, 1900; Judge Alfred B. Beers, Bridgeport, March 29, 1900; Col. William E. Morgan, New Haven, *Sec'y,* January 1, 1900; Gen. L. A. Dickinson, Hartford, *Treasurer*; Capt. Alfred B. Beers, Bridgeport, *Chairman Ex. Com.* Officers of the Home and Hospital.—James N. Coe, *Sup't*; Franklin Dart, *Q. M.*; W. G. Brownson, *Surgeon*; C. S. Page, *Assistant Surgeon.* All applications for admission to the Home, to be sent to Capt. A. B. Beers, Bridgeport. Authorized to provide for the maintenance of honorably discharged soldiers, sailors or marines, who have become disabled, in the hospitals at Hartford, New Haven, Bridgeport, Hospital for Insane, Middletown, and at the Soldiers' Home at Noroton, Conn., the expense to be defrayed by the state.

## CONN. STATE AGRICULTURAL SOCIETY.

George A. Hobson, Wallingford, *Pres't*; James A. Bill, Lyme; Samuel C. Colt, Farmington; John W. Bacon, Danbury, *Vice Pres'ts*; Eugene A. Hall, Meriden, *Treasurer*; B. W. Collins, Meriden, *Cor. Sec'y*; T. S. Gold, West Cornwall, *Rec. Sec'y.* Annual meeting second Wednesday in January at Meriden.

## CONNECTICUT STATE BAR ASSOCIATION.

Charles E. Perkins, *Pres't*; Simeon E. Baldwin, Henry C Robinson, *Vice Pres'ts*; Charles M. Joslyn, *Sec'y*; Edward D. Robbins, *Treas.*; Lyman D. Brewster, Wm. T. Elmer,Wm. K. Townsend, Solomon Lucas,Chas. E. Searles, *Executive Committee.* Annual meeting second Wednesday after the meeting of the General Assembly.

## CONN. STATE BOARD OF AGRICULTURE.

Hartford County, Edmund Halladay, Suffield; New Haven County, Fred. Doolittle, Cheshire; New London County, E. J. Miner, Bozrah; Fairfield County, Seaman Mead, Greenwich; Windham County, M. F. Latham, Eastford; Litchfield County, E. G. Seeley, Roxbury; Middlesex County, G. G. McLean, Portland; Tolland County, C. A. Thompson, Ellington; T. S. Gold, *Sec'y,* West Cornwall. Organized 1866. Re-organized 1871. Annual meeting third Wednesday in January.

## CONN. STATE BOARD OF CHARITIES.

Heman C. Whittlesey, *Pres't,* Middletown; July 1, 1899; Charles P. Kellogg, *Sec'y,* Waterbury; Edwin A. Down, Hartford, July 1, 1901; Miss Rebekah G. Bacon, New Haven, July 1, 1901; Miss Mary Hall, Hartford, July 1, 1901; George F. Spencer, Deep River, July 1, 1899. Regular meetings of the Board are held on the first Wednesday of each month in room 80, State Capitol.

## CONN. STATE FIREMEN'S ASSOCIATION.

Howard L. Stanton, Norwich, *President*; Fred. S. Young, Willimantic; Charles H. O'Neil, New Haven; George S. Pitt, Middletown; Frank J. Riley, Derby; Wm. M. Gibb, Hartford; John W. Hefferon, Rockville, Thomas F. Burns, Winsted, William Dyson, Norwich, Morris Meyers, Danbury, *Vice Pres'ts*; Samuel C. Snagg, Waterbury, *Treas.*; John S. Jones, Westport, *Sec'y.* Annual election in August. Chartered, March, 1885. Capital, $10,000.

## CONNECTICUT STATE BOARD OF TRADE.

James D. Dewell, New Haven, *Pres't*; William H. Mathews, Ansonia, and 17 associate, *Vice Pres'ts*; T. Attwater Barnes, Box 224, New Haven, *Sec'y and Treas.* Organized April 16, 1890. Annual meeting in October.

## CONNECTICUT STATE GRANGE—PATRONS OF HUSBANDRY.

Stephen O. Bowen, Eastford, *Master*; Mrs. Estella H. Barnes, Southington, *Lecturer*; G. C. Beckwith, Nepaug, *Overseer*; Henry E. Loomis, Glastonbury, *Sec'y*; Norman S. Platt, Cheshire, *Treas.*; Rev. D. B. Hubbard, Little River, *Chaplain*; B. C. Patterson, Torrington, J. H. Hale, South Glastonbury, Orson S. Wood, Ellington, *Executive Committee.* Annual meeting second Tuesday in January.

## CONN. STATE POULTRY SOCIETY.

John E. Bruce, Hartford, *Pres't*; Fred. W. Morgan, Windsor, C. P. Jordan, New Haven, George B. Fisher, Hartford, C. A. Thompson, Melrose, Fred. Sterling, Bridgeport, E. F. Badmington, Rockville, W. H. Hamilton, Danielsonville, George E. Taft, Unionville, C. P. Nettleton, Derby, *Vice Pres'ts*; B. S. Woodward, Hartford, *Treas. and Sec'y*; S. E. Clark, Hartford, *Attorney.* Organized, 1870. Re-organized,1891. Meets at 103 Asylum street. Annual election, 2d Tuesday in February.

## CONNECTICUT STATE PRISON.

IN WETHERSFIELD.

Electric Cars pass the City Hall, Hartford, every 16 minutes from 6.23 A. M. Fare 5 cents each way. The Prison is open to visitors on Wednesday of each week; they must have a permit from the Warden or one of the Directors; no charge for admission.

Prisoners can write one letter a month, and receive all letters sent them if containing nothing conflicting with the rules; prisoners are allowed one visit each month on Friday.

James W. Cheney, South Manchester, *President*; Thomas D. Wells, Waterbury, *Sec'y*; Frank C. Sumner, Hartford; Willie O. Burr, Hartford; Wilson C. Reynolds, East Haddam; Frederick M. Salmon, Westport; Edward C. Frisbie, Hartford, *Directors.* Jabez L. Woodbridge, *Warden*; George E. Baisden, *Deputy Warden*; Albert Perkins, *Ass't Deputy Warden*; H. Kirk Woodbridge, *Clerk*; Walter N. Thayer, M. D., *Physician*; Mrs. E. M. Cusick, *Matron.*

This institution was begun in 1826, and on the night of Sept. 28th, 1827, the prisoners were removed from Newgate at Simsbury, which place the State Prison had been since 1790. Grated doors to the cells were first used in 1853, in room of the doors of plank covered inside with sheet iron, with a small orifice near the upper part. The long established uniform of the inmates is now changed from the striped black and gray to a deep plain gray color. There are 400 cells in new, 50 in old block.

## CONNECTICUT STATE SCHOOL FOR BOYS,

IN MERIDEN.

J. S. Lathrop, Norwich, *Pres't*; George Richardson, Bridgeport; John W. Coe, Meriden; W. S. Beecher, New Haven; George P. Crane, Woodbury; Joseph Hutchins, Columbia; George O. Balch, Ashford; John C. Byxbee, Nathan L. Bradley, Meriden; Frederick DePeyster, Portland; Eugene Hall, Meriden, *Trustees.* Frank Perine, *Acting Sup't.*

The whole cost of farm of 195 acres and buildings $218,000. The first boy was received March 1st, 1854. The whole number received to Sept. 30, 1896, has been 5,815. The number of boys in the school Sept. 30, 1896, was 469. Boys between seven and sixteen are received for truancy and crime. Boy boarders are also received from parents and guardians, at $3.00 per week.

## CONNECTICUT STATE SPIRITUALIST ASSOCIATION.
A. A. Gustin, Meriden, *Pres't;* Mrs. J. A. Chapman, Norwich, *Vice Pres't;* Mrs. J. B. Dillon, 943 Main street, Hartford, *Sec'y and Treas.*

## CONN. STATE TEACHERS' ASSOCIATION.
Edwin H. Forbes, Torrington, *Pres't;* S. P. Willard, Colchester, *Cor. Sec'y;* J. F. Williams, Bristol, *Rec. Sec'y;* G. B. Hurd, New Haven, *Treas.;* C. N. Kendall, New Haven; J. A. Graves, Hartford; J. B. Stanton, Norwich; E. C. Andrews, Willimantic; I. M. Agard, Stafford Springs; F. A. Curtis, Saybrook; L. E. Funnill, Fairfield; E. G. Coy, Lakeville, *Vice Pres'ts.* Annual meeting in October.

## CONN. STREET RAILWAY ASSOCIATION.
H. Holten Wood, Derby, *Pres't;* Henry S. Parmelee, New Haven, *V. Pres't;* E. S. Goodrich, Hartford, *Treas.;* E. S. Breed, New Britain, *Sec'y;* A. M. Young, Waterbury, G. A. W. Dodge, New Haven, Israel A. Kelsey, New Haven, *Executive Committee.* Annual meeting in May.

## CONN. SUNDAY SCHOOL ASSOCIATION.
*Organized,* 1857. *Incorporated,* 1893.
Cullen B. Foote, New Haven, *Pres't;* Geo. S. Deming, New Haven, *Field Sec'y;* Mrs. Ada B. Falley, New Haven, *Cor. Sec'y;* John D. Converse, Putnam, *Treas.;* C. H. Platt, New Haven, *Auditor;* Miss Lucy G. Stock, New Haven, *Primary Sup't.* The above officers and 24 Executive Committee constitute the State Central Committee.

## CONNECTICUT TYPOTHETÆ.
C. S. Morehouse, New Haven, *Pres't;* Leverett Brainard, Hartford; W. H. Marigold, Bridgeport; E. E. Smith, Meriden, *V. Pres'ts;* George M. Adkins, New Haven, *Sec'y;* O. A. Dorman, New Haven, *Treas.;* W. H. Lee, Rial S. Peck, F. S. Buckingham, George H. Tuttle, J. D. Jackson, *Executive Committee.* Annual meeting in February.

## CONN. WOMAN SUFFRAGE ASSOCIATION.
Mrs. Isabella Beecher Hooker, Hartford, *Pres't;* Mrs. L. D. Bacon, Hartford, *Vice Pres't at Large;* Mrs. Jane F. Kooms, Mansfield; Mrs. Ella G. Brooks, Southington; Mrs. Emma Hurd Chaffee, Moodus; Mrs. Annie C. Fenner, New London; Mrs. Ella S. Bennett, Willimantic; Mrs. Abby B. Sheldon, New Haven; Mrs. Mary C. Hickox, Litchfield County, *V. Pres'ts;* Miss F. Ellen Burr, 102 Windsor av., Hartford, *Sec'y;* Mrs. Ella B. Kendrick, Hartford, *Cor. Sec'y;* Mrs. Mary J. Rogers, Meriden, *Treas.;* Mrs. E. J. Warren, Collinsville, *Auditor.*

## COUNTY COMMISSIONERS.
Terms expire July 1, of year mentioned.
*Hartford Co.*—Robert A. Potter, Bristol, 1899; Edward W. Dewey, Granby, 1901.

*New Haven Co.*—Jacob D. Walter, Cheshire, 1899; Albert B. Dunham, Seymour, 1899; Hart D. Munson, 1901.

*New London Co.*—John T. Batty, Groton, 1899; Richard W. Chadwick, Old Lyme, 1899; Gilbert L. Hewitt, Norwich, 1901.

*Fairfield Co.*—Henry Lee, Bridgeport, 1899; James E. Miller, Redding, 1899; Whitman S. Mead, Greenwich, 1901.

*Windham Co.*—Edwin H. Hall, Windham, 1899; Edwin L. Palmer, Killingly, 1899; E. Herbert Corttis, 1901.

*Litchfield Co.*—Newell L. Webster, Thomaston, 1899; Sylvester N. Pettibone, New Hartford, 1899; George W. Hall, Canaan, 1901.

*Middlesex Co.*—John J. Hubbard, Middletown, 1899; William H. Scoville, East Haddam, 1899; George A. Olcott, Clinton, 1901.

*Tolland Co.*—Milo P. J. Walker, Stafford Springs, 1899; John H. Buell, Hebron, 1899; John Thompson, Ellington, 1901.

## DAIRY COMMISSIONER.
John B. Noble, East Windsor, May 1, 1900; Robert O. Eaton, North Haven, *Deputy.*

## FERRY AND CANAL COMMISSIONERS.
*East Haddam and Tylerville.*—Roland R. Tyler, Haddam; Wilbur S. Comstock, East Haddam.

*Hadlyme and Chester*—William F. Comstock, Hadlyme; F. S. Smith, Chester.

*Middle Haddam and Maromas.*—William F. Simpson, Chatham; John J. Cone, Middletown.

*New London and Groton.*—Henry G. Keeney, New London; Frank W. Allen, Groton.

*Saybrook and Lyme Ferry.*—Richard W. Chadwick, Old Lyme; John H. Tileston, Old Saybrook.

## FISH AND GAME COMMISSIONERS.
George H. Knight, Lakeville, *Pres't;* A. C. Collins, Hartford, *Secretary;* James A. Bill, Lyme, *Treasurer,* May, 1899.

## FUNERAL DIRECTORS ASSO'N OF CONN.
Wm. T. Marchant, Hartford, *Pres't;* C. E. Lewis, Birmingham, *Vice Pres't;* Edward C. Root, Thomaston, *Cor. Sec'y;* C. A. Cadwell, Southington, *Rec. Sec'y;* H. W. Crawford, New Haven, *Treasurer* Organized May, 1889.

## GENERAL CONFERENCE OF THE CONGREGATIONAL CHURCHES OF CONNECTICUT.
Geo. F. Tinker, New London, *Moderator;* Rev. E. K. Holden, Bridgeport, *Scribe;* Rev. Charles F. Clarke, Whitneyville, Rev. J. R. Danforth, West Mystic, *Ass't Scribes;* Rev. W. H. Moore, Hartford, *Registrar;* Ward W. Jacobs, Hartford, *Treas.;* Charles E. Thompson, Hartford, *Auditor.* Annual meeting in November.

## GIDEON WELLES NAVAL VETERAN ASSOCIATION OF CONN.
Henry F. McCullum, New Haven, *Captain;* Henry Jaquet, New Haven, *Commander;* Charles H. Thompson, Meriden, *Lieut. Commander;* Joline J. Butler, West Haven, *Lieut.*

## HARBOR COMMISSIONERS.
Wm. S. Williams, Hartford, Dec. 22, 1898; Wm. E. Morgan, Sept. 26, 1900; Frank W. Bradley, *Deputy,* New Haven; Aurelius J. Meeker, July 9, 1898; Hezekiah S. Bartlett, July 9, 1898; William H. Allen, *Deputy,* New London; John McNeil, Bridgeport Aug. 29, 1900; Roger Kennedy, Middletown, July 9, 1898; Daniel P. Weeks, July 9, 1898, Five Mile River; Merritt W. Merwin, July 9, 1898, Milford; James Pendleton, Oct. 14, 1899; M. W. Chamberlin, *Deputy,* Stonington; George W. Brush, Dec. 27, 1900, Greenwich.

## HARRISON VETERANS OF 1840 ASSOCIATION.
R. J. Gatling, Hartford, *Pres't;* H. A. Stillman, Hartford; James B. Williams, Glastonbury, *Vice Pres'ts;* Nathan Starkweather, Hartford, *Sec'y and Treas.* Organized Sept. 13, 1888. Annual meeting first Thursday in October.

## HIGHWAY COMMISSIONER.
James R. MacDonald, New Haven, July, 1901; Geo. I. Allen, *Clerk,* rooms 25 and 27, State Capitol.

## INSPECTOR GENERAL OF GAS METERS AND ILLUMINATING GAS.
William G. Mixter, New Haven.

## INSPECTORS OF FACTORIES.

George L. McLean, Ellington, July 1, 1899; W. W. Kirk, New Canaan; Preston B. Sibley, Danielson, *Special Agents.*

## INSPECTORS OF STEAM BOILERS.

George E. Cooley, Hartford, for the 1*st Congressional District,* Sept. 4, 1898; Fred'k H. Laforge, Waterbury, *2d Congressional District,* Sept. 30, 1900; Jeremiah Sullivan, Norwich *3d Congressional District,* March 8, 1899; Daniel Olihan, Bridgeport, *4th Congressional District,* March 8, 1899.

## NEW ENGLAND RIFLE ASSOCIATION.

H. M. Pope, Hartford, *Pres't;* C. H. Merriman, Meriden, *Vice Pres't;* W. B. Hall, New Britain, *Sec'y;* J. C. Weisman, Hartford, *Treas.*

## NEW ENGLAND TOBACCO GROWERS ASSO'N.

H. S. Frye, Poquonock, *Pres't;* Thaddeus Graves, Hatfield, Mass., *Vice Pres't;* Samuel C. Hardin, Glastonbury, *Sec'y and Treas.* Organized December 22, 1882. Meets annually in Hartford in January.

## NEW ENGLAND TYPOGRAPHICAL UNION AND ALLIED TRADES.

John Moffitt, Fall River, Mass., *Pres't;* Charles Ashton, Boston, Mass.; Thomas F. Hannan, Salem, Edward Phelan, Boston, Mass., *V. Pres'ts;* John F. Duggan, Worcester, *Sec'y and Treas.*

## PENSION EXAMINING SURGEONS.

Doctors P. D. Peltier, *Pres't;* Nathan Mayer, *Sec'y;* E. H. Griswold, *Treas.,* as the Board of Examining Surgeons in this city, for the U. S. Pension office. Meet every Wednesday, 10 A. M. at 742 Main street.

## RAILROADS IN CONNECTICUT.

Wm. O. Seymour, Ridgefield, July, 1899; Orsamus R. Fyler, Torrington, July, 1901; Washington F. Wilcox, Chester, July, 1901, *Commissioners;* Henry F. Billings, *Clerk.* Room 43, State Capitol, Hartford.

There are 18 railroad corporations in the State, owning 1,784.72 miles of single track in this State.

Capital stock issued, $100,893,050.88. The funded debt is reported at $43,480,000 00.

Total gross earnings, $36,353,269.83, of which $18,-376,363.86 was from passengers, and $17,596,267.50 from freight. Gross earnings per mile of road operated $15,-713.96. Net earnings have been $11,217,511.28. Operating expenses, $25,136,737.70. Amount paid for taxes, $1,996,938.28. Dividends paid, $4,756,328.00.

Number of passengers carried, 49,783,689; tons of freight carried, 14,815,851. Total miles run were 25,-502 060, of which 12,724,761 were by passenger trains, and 6,970,893 by freight trains.

There are 384 stations in the state, with an average distance of 2.63 miles between each. Number of highway grade crossings in the state, 1,015. The total number of locomotives is 975; number of cars, 18,986. The number of employees, including officers, in operating the roads is 25,877; compensation for same, $16,079,950.74.

During the past year, 28 passengers were injured, 1 of these fatally; of employees 220 were injured, 27 fatally; trespassers, 156, of which 89 were fatal.

## SENATE CLUB, 1889-90.

E. S. Cleveland, Hartford, *Pres't;* John M. Hall, New Haven, *V. Pres't;* Geo. N. Morse, Meriden, *Sec'y;* Philip Corbin, New Britain, *Treas.;* Jas. Graham, Isaac N. Bartram, Lucius H. Fuller, Raymond H. Parish, *Executive Committee.*

## SHELL FISH COMMISSIONERS.

Christian Swartz, Norwalk, July 1, 1901; George C. Waldo, Bridgeport, July, 1899; Geo. W. Hallock, Danbury, July, 1899. McC. Mathewson, New Haven, *Clerk.*

## SHERIFFS:

For term ending June 1, 1899.

*Hartford Co.,* ....Edwin J. Smith, Hartford, r.
*New Haven Co.,* ...Charles R. Spigel, New Haven, r.
*New London Co.,* .George O. Jackson, New London, r.
*Fairfield Co.,* ......Sidney E. Hawley, Bridgeport, r.
*Litchfield Co.,* .....Edward A. Nellis, Winchester, r.
*Windham Co.,* .....Charles B. Pomeroy, Willimantic, r.
*Middlesex Co.,* ....Thomas S. Brown, E. Hampton, r.
*Tolland Co.,* .......Amasa P. Dickinson, Rockville r.

## STATE BOARD OF EDUCATION.

Gov. Lorrin A. Cooke, West Winsted, *Pres't;* Lieut. Gov. James D. Dewell, New Haven, *ex officio;* Edward D. Robbins, Wethersfield, July 1, 1899; Anthony Ames, Danielson, July 1, 1900; George M. Carrington, West Winsted, July 1, 1901; William G. Sumner' New Haven, July 1, 1902; Charles D. Hine, New Britain, *Secretary;* Giles Potter, New Haven, *Agent;* A. J. Wright, Hartford, *Clerk.* Rooms 42 and 44, State Capitol. The first appropriation for a Normal School was $5,000 in 1839.

## STATE BOARD OF MEDIATION AND ARBITRATION.

George A. Parsons, Hartford, July 1, 1899; Gilbert L. Smith, Sharon, April 20, 1899; Franklin T. Ives, Meriden, April 20, 1899.

## STATE CHEMISTS.

Robert B. Riggs, Hartford, Dec. 16, 1899; Herbert E. Smith, New Haven, November 20, 1899; Sylvester P. Wheeler, Bridgeport, June 21, 1899; R. B. West, Guilford, Jan. 18, 1900; Henry Souther, Hartford, Jan. 10, 1900.

## STATE LIBRARY COMMITTEE.

The Governor, the Secretary, and William Hamersley, Hartford, *Committee.* Charles J. Hoadly, *Librarian;* Chas. W. Butler, *Assistant.* In Capitol, 3d floor, north room.

## STATE NORMAL TRAINING SCHOOL,

### NEW BRITAIN.

*Incorporated,* 1849. *Opened, May,* 1850.
*First Graduates,* 1851.

*Board of Education.*—Gov. Lorrin A. Cooke, West Winsted; Lieut. Gov. James D. Dewell, New Haven; Geo. M. Carrington, West Winsted, 1901; William G Sumner, New Haven, 1902; Edward D. Robbins, Wethersfield, 1899; Anthony Ames, Danielson, 1900; Charles D. Hine, *Sec'y,* New Britain. A. J. Wright, Hartford, *Clerk;* Giles Potter, New Haven, *Agent.*

Marcus White, *Principal,* with the following *Assistants:* Ralph G. Hibbard, M. Gertrude Fenn, Jane Darlington, Elizabeth L. Allyn, Emily J. Parker, Helen J. Bunce, Gertrude L. Rhoades, Mary G. Peabody, Jessie E. Guernsey, Bertha M. McConkey, Georgianna Minor, Minnie L. Clark, Margaret S. Hubbell, Mary A. Spear, Emily B. Scarborough, Caroline T. Robbins, Frederick A. Verplanck, Clara M. Washburn, Anna L. Parker, Maud L. Gridley, Marie Curtis, Mary E. Goodrich, Estelle M. Hart, Florence M. Prince, Mary E. Wardwell, Estelle I. Pierpont, Hannah M. Gartland, Anna A. Bubser, Ada M. Harding, Annie T. Banister, Alice O'Grady, Charles H. Morrill, Grace E. Mowry, Sarah T. Palmer, Belle W. Hanna.

Examinations are only in Spelling, English Grammar, Arithmetic, Geography, and United States History. Examinations for entrance are held in different parts of the State in the months of July and August, and at the school building August 25 and September 5, 1898. Number enrolled in 1897-98, 200; graduated, 70. The Fall and Winter term of 1898 begins Tuesday, September 6.

**STATE NORMAL TRAINING SCHOOL,**
WILLIMANTIC.

*Incorporated* 1889. *Opened Sept.* 3, 1889.
The Board of Education is the same as the New Britain school.
George P. Phenix, *Principal*, with the following *Assistants:* Jennie E. Chapin, Grace L. Bell, Emelene A. Dunn, Mary G. Henderson, Mabel I. Jenkins, Caroline E. Meacham, Harriette Wilson, Sarah J. Walter, Mary E. Davison, Julia W. Swift, Eliza Graeme Graves, Jennie E. Dennehy, Lucy Chandler, Frederick W. Staebner, Helen E. Bennett, Fannie A. Bishop, Edwin C. Andrews, Edith W. Griffith Margaret A. Egan.
Fall and Winter term begins Tuesday, Sept. 6, 1898.

**STATE NORMAL TRAINING SCHOOL,**
NEW HAVEN.

*Incorporated* 1893. *Opened Sept.* 11, 1893.
For Trustees and Board of Control, see Table of Contents, for State Board of Education.
Arthur B. Morrill, *Principal*, with the following *Assistants:* Ella M. Broderick, Ellen A. Kenny, Anna S. Hart, Lillian E. Bradley, Lottie M. Hall, Herbert N. Loomis, S. Lillian Brooks, Martha A. Quinlan, Georgiana Norman, Mary A. Maltby, Lottie J. Thompson, Helen M. Thomas, Nora A. Sweeney, Helen A. Austin, Edna C. Lines, Anna L. Wilson, Edward B. Birge, Sara H. Fahey, Julia H. Doyle, Annie E. McNulty, Josephine M. Sheldrick Dr. E. H. Arnold, Louise Schmahl, Mary A. McFarland, Eleanor T. Quinlan.

**STORRS AGRICULTURAL COLLEGE AND EXPERIMENT STATION.**
MANSFIELD, CONN. P. O. ADDRESS, STORRS, CONN.

*Board of Trustees:* Gov. Lorrin A. Cooke, West Winsted, *Pres't, ex officio;* Monroe F. Latham, Phœnixville, *Vice Pres't;* T. S. Gold, West Cornwall, *Sec'y;* Charles A. Thompson, Melrose, *Treas.;* S. W. Johnson, New Haven, *Chemist;* W. C. Sturgis, New Haven, *Botanist;* N. S. Platt, Cheshire, *Pomologist.* Edmund Halladay, Suffield, Hartford Co.; Frederick Doolittle, Cheshire, New Haven Co.; E. Judson Miner, Bozrah, New London Co.; Seaman Mead, Greenwich, Fairfield Co.; Monroe F. Latham, Phœnixville, Windham Co.; Edwin G. Seeley, Roxbury, Litchfield Co.; George G McLean, Portland, Middlesex Co.; Charles A. Thompson, Melrose, Tolland Co., *Members appointed by the General Assembly. Officers College:* B. F. Koons, PH. D. M. A., *Principal;* L. P. Chamberlain, *Farm Sup't.;* A. B. Peebles, B. S., *Prof. of Chemistry and Physics;* C. S. Phelps, B.S., *Prof. of Agriculture;* Nelson S. Mayo, *Prof. of Veterinary Science;* A. G. Gulley, *Prof. of Horticulture;* Lucretia J. Barber, H. S. Patterson, Lulie G. Lincoln, W. L. Chamberlain, C. L. Beach, Rufus W. Stimson, Henry A. Ballou, *Instructors;* Capt. C. H. Murray, *Prof. of Military Science and Tactics;* C. A. Wheeler, *Mathematics;* Maud Knapp, *Domestic Science;* Lucy E. Saxton, *Matron.* Four years course in agriculture and sciences related thereto. Tuition, free. Board at cost. Fall term begins September 9, 1898. All communications should be addressed to the Storrs Agricultural College, Storrs, Conn. The Station is located at Mansfield (P. O. Storrs,) as a department of the Storrs Agricultural College. The chemical and other more abstract research is carried out at Wesleyan University, Middletown.

**TEMPORARY HOMES FOR DEPENDENT AND NEGLECTED CHILDREN.**

Between 2 and 18 years of age. The Board of Managers are the County Commissioners for each in said county.
*Hartford County*—In Warehouse Point, East Windsor. Henry M. Adams, *Sup't;* Mrs. H. M. Adams, *Matron.*

*New Haven Co.*—In New Haven, cor. Shelton and Dixwell. Willard Matthews, *Sup't.*
*New London Co.*—In Preston, near railroad station. Miss Jessie Gibson, *Matron.*
*Fairfield Co.*—In Norwalk, Miss Martha A. Boughton, *Matron.*
*Windham Co.*—In Putnam, three miles from station. J. D. Converse, *Sup't.*
*Litchfield Co.*—In West Winsted, near station. Dwight S. Case, *Sup't.*
*Tolland Co.*—In Vernon Center. E. S. Talbot, *Sup't.*
*Middlesex Co.*—In Haddam, southwest from station. John H. Odber, *Sup't.*

**GOVERNORS OF CONNECTICUT.**

| | |
|---|---|
| 1639–1655...John Haynes and Edward Hopkins, Hartford, chosen Gov. alternate years except | |
| 1642–1648...George Wyllys | Hartford. |
| 1655–1656...Thomas Wells | Hartford. |
| 1656–1657...John Webster | Hartford. |
| 1657–1658...John Winthrop | New London. |
| 1658–1659...Thomas Wells | Hartford. |
| 1659–1676...John Winthrop | New London. |
| 1676–1680...William Leete | Guilford. |
| 1680–1687...Robert Treat | Milford. |
| 1687–1689...Sir Edmund Andros | Boston, Mass. |
| 1689–1696...Robert Treat | Milford. |
| 1696–1707...Fitz John Winthrop | New London. |
| 1707–1724...Gurdon Saltonstall | New London. |
| 1724–1741...Joseph Talcott | Hartford. |
| 1741–1751...Jonathan Law | Milford. |
| 1751–1754...Roger Wolcott | Windsor. |
| 1754–1766...Thomas Fitch | Norwalk. |
| 1766–1769...William Pitkin | Hartford. |
| 1769–1784...Jonathan Trumbull | Lebanon. |
| 1784–1786...Matthew Griswold | Lyme. |
| 1786–1796...Samuel Huntington | Norwich. |
| 1796–1798...Oliver Wolcott | Litchfield. |
| 1798–1809...Jonathan Trumbull | Lebanon. |
| 1809–1811...John Treadwell | Farmington. |
| 1811–1813...Roger Griswold | Lyme. |
| 1813–1818...John Cotton Smith | Sharon. |
| 1818–1827...Oliver Wolcott | Litchfield. |
| 1827–1831...Gideon Tomlinson | Fairfield. |
| 1831–1833...John S. Peters | Hebron. |
| 1833–1834...Henry W. Edwards | New Haven. |
| 1834–1835...Samuel A. Foote | Cheshire. |
| 1835–1838...Henry W. Edwards | New Haven. |
| 1838–1842...William W. Ellsworth | Hartford. |
| 1842–1844...Chauncey F. Cleveland | Hampton. |
| 1844–1846...Roger S. Baldwin | New Haven. |
| 1846–1847...Isaac Toucey | Hartford. |
| 1847–1849...Clark Bissell | Norwalk. |
| 1849–1850...Joseph Trumbull | Hartford. |
| 1850–1853...Thomas H. Seymour | Hartford. |
| 1853–1854...Charles H. Pond, (acting) | Milford. |
| 1854–1855...Henry Dutton | New Haven. |
| 1855–1857...William T. Minor | Stamford. |
| 1857–1858...Alexander H. Holley | Salisbury. |
| 1858–1866...William A. Buckingham | Norwich. |
| 1866–1867...Joseph R. Hawley | Hartford. |
| 1867–1869...James E. English | New Haven. |
| 1869–1870...Marshall Jewell | Hartford. |
| 1870–1871...James E. English | New Haven. |
| 1871–1873...Marshall Jewell | Hartford. |
| 1873–1876*...Charles R. Ingersoll | New Haven. |
| 1877–1879...Richard D. Hubbard | Hartford. |
| 1879–1881...Charles B. Andrews | Litchfield. |
| 1881–1883...Hobart B. Bigelow | New Haven. |
| 1883–1885...Thomas M. Waller | New London. |
| 1985–1887...Henry B. Harrison | New Haven. |
| 1887–1889...Phineas C. Lounsbury | Ridgefield. |
| 1889–1893...Morgan G. Bulkeley | Hartford. |
| 1893–1895...Luzon B. Morris | New Haven. |
| 1895–1897...O. Vincent Coffin | Middletown. |
| 1897—...Lorren A. Cooke | Winsted. |

* Terms expiration changed from May to January.

# State Board of Health.

Wm. H. Brewer, New Haven, *Pres't*, 1908; Charles A. Lindsley, 15 Elm st., New Haven, *Sec'y and Treas.;* Grove H. Wilson, Meriden, 1901; Ralph S. Goodwin, Thomaston, 1908; Nathaniel E. Wordin, Bridgeport, 1899; George P. Ingersoll, New Haven, 1899; Grove H. Wilson, Meriden, 1901; Theodore H. McKenzie, Southington, 1901; Room 47, third floor, State Capitol. Chartered, 1877. The following Cities and Towns (Boroughs marked with a *) in this state have regularly organized Boards of Health; the name after the town is the health officer.

## HARTFORD COUNTY.

Avon............J. L. North.
Berlin..........R. E. Ensign.
Bloomfield.....O. K. Isham.
Bristol*........H. D. Brennan.
Burlington....John Luby.
Canton........W. H. Crowley.
East Granby..W. C. Foster.
East Hartford..E. H. Griswold.
East Windsor..H. O. Allen.
Enfield........Geo. T. Finch.
Farmington....S. J. Edgerton.
Glastonbury....C. G. Rankin.
Granby.........A. J. Weed.
Hartford.......Dan'l A. Markham.
Hartland......Clifford Cowdry.
Manchester....M. S. Bradley.
Marlborough...W. W. Hall.
New Britain...W. P. Bunnell.
Newington....John S. Kirkham.
Plainville....J. N. Bull.
Rocky Hill....F. L. Burr.
Simsbury......C. M. Wooster.
Southington*..Jas. H. Osborne.
South Windsor. H. A. Deane.
Suffield........J. K. Mason.
West Hartford..F.H. Staudtmueller
Wethersfield...E. G. Fox.
Windsor.......Newton S. Bell.
Windsor Locks. J. A. Coogan.

## NEW HAVEN COUNTY.

Ansonia.......L. E. Cooper.
Beacon Falls..Edward Gruber.
Bethany.......S. G. Davidson.
Branford*.....W. H. Zink.
Cheshire......M. N. Chamberlin.
Derby.........L. D. LaBonte.
East Haven...C. W. Holbrook.
Guilford*.....R. B. West.
Hamden.......G. H. Joslin.
Madison.......A. D. Ayres.
Meriden.......E. A. Wilson.
Middlebury....A. L. Schuyler.
Milford.......E. B. Heady.
Naugatuck....W. P. Smith.
New Haven....F. W. Wright.
North Branford. C. W. Gaylord.
North Haven...R. B. Goodyear.
Orange........J. F. Barnett.
Oxford........L. Barnes.
Prospect......J. R. Platt.
Seymour.......F. A. Benedict.
Southbury....J. M. Shepherd.
Wallingford*..W. P. Wilson.
Waterbury....B. A. O'Hara.
Wolcott.......J. H. Garrigus.
Woodbridge...J. W. Barker.

## LITCHFIELD COUNTY.

Barkhamsted...H. D. Moore.
Bethlehem.....L. P. Judd.
Bridgewater....L. J. Pons.

Canaan........F. S. Skiff.
Colebrook......H. L. Culver.
Cornwall......G. H. Beers.
Goshen........Joseph H. North.
Harwinton....C. L. Blake.
Kent..........J. F. Gibbs.
Litchfield*....C. I. Page.
Morris........S. E. Stockman.
New Hartford..Jerry Burwell.
New Milford..J. C. Barker.
Norfolk.......J. C. Kendall.
North Canaan..C. W. Camp.
Plymouth......M. P. Robinson.
Roxbury......L. J. Pons.
Salisbury.....W. B. Bissell.
Sharon........B. P. Knight.
Thomaston....T. St. John.
Torrington*...Elias Pratt.
Warren........Wm. Forestelle.
Washington...Robert Marcy.
Watertown....W. S. Munger.
Winchester*..G. G. Howd.
Woodbury....E. L. Smith.

## FAIRFIELD COUNTY.

Bethel*.......A. E. Barber.
Bridgeport....E. A. McClelland.
Brookfield....A. W. Griswold.
Danbury......G. E. Lemmer.
Darien .......George H. Noxon.
Easton........B. W. White.
Fairfield......W. H. Donaldson.
Greenwich*...L. P. Jones.
Huntington...W. S. Randall.
Monroe.......J. G. Stevens.
New Canaan..C. B. Keeler.
New Fairfield...W. S. Watson.
Newtown*....E. M. Smith.
Norwalk......W. J. Tracey.
Redding......E. H. Smith.
Ridgefield*...W. E. Weed.
Sherman......J. N. Woodruff.
South Norwalk. W. J. Tracey.
Stamford......F. J. Rogers.
Stratford......G. F. Lewis.
Trumbull......E. S. Fairchild.
Weston........F. Gorham.
Westport......L. T. Day.
Wilton........A. B. Gorham.

## MIDDLESEX COUNTY.

Chatham......E. S. Parmelee.
Chester.......S. W. Turner.
Clinton.......H. S. Reynolds.
Cromwell.....C. E. Bush.
Durham.......E. A. Markham.
East Haddam..M. W. Plumstead.
Essex.........C. H. Hubbard.
Haddam......E. D. Gilbert.
Killingworth..E. P. Nichols.
Middlefield...J. E. Bailey.
Middletown...F. E. Coudert.
Old Saybrook..J. H. Granniss.

Portland......F. E. Potter.
Saybrook......E. Bidwell.
Westbrook....T. B. Bloomfield.

## NEW LONDON COUNTY.

Bozrah........N. Johnson.
Colchester*...M. W. Robinson.
East Lyme....F. H. Dart.
Franklin......E. L. Danielson.
Griswold......Geo. H. Jennings.
Groton........John Gray.
Lebanon......E. L. Danielson.
Ledyard......Edwin W. Case.
Lisbon........Henry Lyon.
Lyme.........J. G. Ely.
Montville.....W. M. Burchard.
New London..M. J. Roche.
Norwich......E. H. Linnell.
No. Stonington E. H. Knowles.
Old Lyme.....W. H. H. Wallace.
Preston.......O. F. Harris.
Salem........C. F. Congdon.
Sprague......T. I Stanton.
Stonington*...O. M. Barber.
Voluntown....W. R. Davis.
Waterford.....G. M. Minor.

## TOLLAND COUNTY.

Andover......P. H. Edwards.
Bolton........C. F. Sumner.
Columbia.....W. H. Yeomans.
Coventry.....W. L. Higgins.
Ellington.....E. T. Davis.
Hebron.......C. H. Pendleton.
Mansfield ...E. G. Sumner.
Rockville......T. F. Rockwell.
Somers.......A. L. Hurd.
Stafford......F. L. Smith.
Stafford Springs. H. H. Smith.
Tolland.......E. S. Agard.
Union.........E. W. Upham.
Vernon.......A. R. Goodrich.
Willington....C. C. Essex.

## WINDHAM COUNTY.

Ashford.......F. B. Converse.
Brooklyn.....A. H. Tanner.
Canterbury...J. O. Smith.
Chaplin......F. C. Lummis.
Danielson*...W. H. Judson.
Eastford......E. K. Robbins.
Hampton.....Horace Jackson.
Killingly......A. E. Darling.
Plainfield.....W. W. Adams.
Pomfret.......C. O. Thompson.
Putnam.......J. J. Russell.
Scotland......A. M. Clark.
Sterling.......O. W. Bates.
Thompson....L. Holbrook.
Willimantic...William A. King.
Windham.....F. E. Wilcox.
Woodstock....Joseph Spalding.

# County Coroners and Medical Examiners.

THE law of June 1, 1883, provides for the appointment of County Coroners for three years, and each Coroner to have appointment of a Deputy, and a Medical Examiner, for each town. SECTION 4.—"When any person shall come to a sudden, violent, or untimely death, and when any person shall be found dead, the manner of whose death is not known, any one who shall become aware of such death shall forthwith report the same to the Medical Examiner for the Town in which the body lies," etc. If the Medical Examiner is satisfied that the death was not caused by the criminal act, omission or carelessness of another, he reports the case to the Coroner for record; but if, in the opinion of the Medical Examiner, such death was caused by the criminal act, omission or carelessness of another, or is attended with suspicious circumstances, he immediately notifies the Coroner who proceeds forthwith to take charge of the body and make all necessary inquiry concerning the cause and manner of death.

## HARTFORD COUNTY;
H. E. TAINTOR, *Hartford*, CORONER.
J. G. Calhoun, *Hartford*, DEP. COR.

MEDICAL EXAMINERS,
*Avon*, John L. North.
*Berlin*, R. E. Ensign.
*Bristol*, George S. Hull.
*Burlington & Canton*, G.F. Lewis.
*East Granby*, C. M. Wooster.
*East Hartford*, Edward H. Griswold.
*East Windsor*, H. A. Deane.
*Enfield*, Edward F. Parsons.
*Farmington*, S. J. Edgerton.
*Glastonbury*, H. C. Bunce.
*Granby & Hartland*, A. J. Weed.
*Hartford*, H. S. Fuller.
*Manchester*, J. N. Parker.
*Marlborough*, H. C. Bunce.
*New Britain*, B. N. Comings.
*Newington*, W. W. Knight.
*Plainville*, T. G. Wright.
*Rocky Hill*, Rufus W. Griswold.
*Simsbury*, C. M. Wooster.
*Southington*, W. G. Steadman.
*South Windsor*, H. A. Deane.
*Suffield*, J. K. Mason.
*West Hartford*, W. W. Knight.
*Wethersfield*, Abner S. Warner.
*Windsor*, N. S. Bell.
*Windsor Locks*, S. R. Burnap.

## NEW HAVEN COUNTY;
CORONER,
ELI MIX, *New Haven*.
MEDICAL EXAMINERS,
*Ansonia*, Wm. H. Conklin.
*Beacon Falls*, Edwin H. Johnson.
*Bethany*, John W. Barker.
*Branford*, C. W. Gaylord.
*Cheshire*, E. T. Cornwall.
*Derby*, George L. Beardsley.
*East Haven*, Gustavus Eliot.
*Guilford*, Redfield B. West.
*Hamden*, George H. Joslyn.
*Madison*, Daniel M. Webb.
*Meriden*, G. H. Wilson.
*Middlebury*, Aug. A. Crane.
*Milford*, E. B. Heady.
*Naugatuck*, Franklin B. Tuttle.
*New Haven*, Moses C. White.
*North Branford*, C. W. Gaylord.
*North Haven*, Robert B. Goodyear.
*Orange*, John F. Barnett.
*Oxford*, Lewis Barnes.
*Prospect*, F. G. Graves.
*Seymour*, Elias W. Davis.
*Southbury*, John M. Shepherd.
*Wallingford*, Jas. D. McGaughey.
*Waterbury*, Thomas L. Axtelle.
*Wolcott*, Thomas L. Axtelle.
*Woodbridge*, J. W. Barker.

## NEW LONDON COUNTY;
F.H. BROWN, *Norwich*, CORONER.
*Bozrah*, Nathan Johnson.
*Colchester*, Myron W. Robinson.

MEDICAL EXAMINERS,
*East Lyme*, F. H. Dart.
*Franklin*, T. I. Stanton, *Baltic*.
*Griswold*, George H. Jennings.
*Groton*, James L. Weaver.
*Lebanon*, Edward L. Danielson.
*Ledyard*, N. B. Lewis.
*Lisbon*, Sanford H. Holmes.
*Lyme*, Joseph G. Ely.
*Montville*, Wm. M. Burchard.
*New London*, Chas. B. Graves.
*No. Stonington*, Edwin H. Knowles.
*Norwich*, Lewis S. Paddock.
*Old Lyme*, George W. Harris.
*Preston*, Geo. R. Harris, *Norwich*.
*Salem*, Charles F. Congdon.
*Sprague*, T. I. Stanton.
*Stonington*, George D. Stanton.
*Voluntown*, Sanford H. Holmes.
*Waterford*, G. Maynard Minor.

## FAIRFIELD COUNTY;
CORONER,
CHARLES A. DOTEN, *Bridgeport*.
MEDICAL EXAMINERS,
*Bethel*, Alvin E. Barber.
*Bridgeport*, Frederick B. Downs.
*Brookfield*, Junius F. Smith.
*Danbury*, W. C. Wile.
*Darien*, George H. Noxon.
*Easton*, M. V. B. Dunham.
*Fairfield*, Wm. H. Donaldson.
*Greenwich*, L. P. Jones.
*Huntington*, G. A. Shelton.
*Monroe*, J. G. Stevens.
*New Canaan*, Charles B. Keeler.
*New Fairfield*, E. A. Stratton.
*Newtown*, E. M. Smith.
*Norwalk*, Wm. C. Burke, Jr.
*Redding*, Ernest H. Smith.
*Ridgefield*, Russell W. Lowe.
*Sherman*, John N. Woodruff.
*Stamford*, Charles E. Rowell.
*Stratford*, William B. Cogswell.
*Trumbull*, C. C, Godfrey.
*Weston*, Frank Gorham.
*Westport*, Frederick Powers.
*Wilton*, Andrew B. Gorham.

## LITCHFIELD COUNTY;
CORONER,
RICHARD T. HIGGINS, *Winsted*.
MEDICAL EXAMINERS,
*Barkhamsted*, Howard D. Moore.
*Bethlehem*, H. S. Karrman, *Woodb'y*.
*Bridgewater*, George F. Staub.
*Canaan*, Francis S. Skiff.
*Colebrook*, Wm. S. Hulbert, *Winsted*.
*Goshen*, Joseph Howard North.
*Harwinton*, Thacher S. Hanchett.
*Kent*, Walter M. Barnum.
*Litchfield*, C. I. Page.
*Morris*, C. I. Page, *Litchfield*.
*New Hartford*, Jerry Burwell.
*New Milford*, Frederick E. King.
*Norfolk*, L. L. Hamant.
*North Canaan*, Charles W. Camp.
*Plymouth*, Wm. W. Wellington.

*Roxbury*, L. J. Pons.
*Salisbury*, Wm. B. Bissell, *Lakeville*.
*Sharon*, William W. Knight.
*Thomaston*, George D. Ferguson.
*Torrington*, Thacher S. Hanchett.
*Warren*, R. A. Marcy.
*Washington*, Orlando Brown.
*Watertown*, Walter S. Munger.
*Winchester*, William S. Hulbert.
*Woodbury*, Henry S. Karrman.

## WINDHAM COUNTY;
A. G. BILL, *Danielson*, CORONER.
DEPUTY CORONER,
J. F. Carpenter, *Putnam*.
MEDICAL EXAMINERS,
*Ashford*, Elisha K. Robbins.
*Brooklyn*, Alfred H. Tanner.
*Canterbury*, W. W. Adams, *Moosup*.
*Chaplin*, Charles N. Knight.
*Eastford*, Elisha K. Robbins.
*Hampton*, Lewis W. Spencer.
*Killingly*, Renzi Robinson.
*Plainfield*, W. W. Adams, *Moosup*.
*Pomfret*, S. B. Overlock.
*Putnam*, John B. Kent.
*Scotland*, Robert C. White.
*Sterling*, W. W. Adams, *Moosup*.
*Thompson*, Lowell Holbrook.
*Windham*, Robert C. White.
*Woodstock*, J. D. Spaulding.

## TOLLAND COUNTY;
CHAS. PHELPS, *Rockville*, CORONER.
MEDICAL EXAMINERS,
*Andover*, William L. Higgins.
*Bolton*, Charles F. Sumner.
*Columbia*, Cyrus H. Pendleton.
*Coventry*, William L. Higgins.
*Ellington*, Edward T. Davis.
*Hebron*, Cyrus H. Pendleton.
*Mansfield*, Edwin G. Sumner.
*Somers*, William B. Woods.
*Stafford*, D. B. Newton.
*Tolland*, Willard N. Simmons.
*Union*, C. L. Ormsbee.
*Vernon*, Thomas F. Rockwell.
*Willington*, Frederick E. Johnson.

## MIDDLESEX COUNTY;
S. B. DAVIS, *Middlet'n*, CORONER.
MEDICAL EXAMINERS,
*Chester*, Sylvester W. Turner.
*Chatham*, G.N. Lawson, *M. Haddam*.
*Clinton*, Herbert S. Reynolds.
*Cromwell*, Charles E. Bush.
*Durham*, Earl Mathewson.
*Essex*, Charles H. Hubbard.
*East Haddam*, Matt. W. Plumstead.
*Haddam*, Miner C. Hazen.
*Killingworth*, H. S. Reynolds.
*Middlefield*, J.E.Loveland, *Middlt'n*.
*Middletown*, J. F. Calef.
*Old Saybrook*, John H. Grannis.
*Portland*, C. A. Sears.
*Saybrook*, H. T. French, *Deep River*.
*Westbrook*, Thomas B. Bloomfield.

# Hartford County.

Incorporated 1666, originally comprised entire County of Tolland, most of Middlesex and Windham Counties, and part of Litchfield and New London Counties.

Hartford County Court house building, corner of Trumbull and Allyn streets, completed, Jan. 5, 1886, is in general design fire proof, of the modern French school; is 80 feet on Trumbull street and 141 feet on Allyn street, three stories, with a basement. The material is Philadelphia pressed brick, with Portland stone trimmings. The main entrance is at 85 Trumbull st., and another corridor entrance at 127 Allyn st.

## COUNTY COMMISSIONERS.

Edward W. Dewey, Granby, July, 1901; Robert A. Potter, Bristol, July, 1899. Marcus H. Holcomb, Southington, *County Treasurer;* Chas. D. Barnes, Southington, James Roach, New Britain, *County Auditors;* Andrew F. Gates, Hartford, Lyman S. Burr, New Britain, Epaphroditus Peck, Bristol, Chas. R. Hathaway, South Manchester, *Prosecuting Agents;* ArthurF. Eggleston, Hartford, *State Attorney;* John H. Buck, Hartford, *Ass't State Attorney;* Geo. A. Conant, Hartford, *Clerk of Courts;* J. Lincoln Fenn, Hartford, *Assistant Clerk.* Meet Tuesdays, Wednesdays, Thursdays and Fridays, from 9 A. M., till 3 P. M., in County building, 85 Trumbull st.

## SHERIFF AND DEPUTIES.

*Sheriff,* Edwin J. Smith. *Deputies,* Richard B. Hetherton, Thomas B. Chapman, George Senk, W C. Fielding, Hartford; F. H. Dibble, East Granby; Chas. Heath, East Windsor; John M. Foote, Jr., West Hartford; Albert L. Morse, Bristol; Frank Stark, Canton; George L. Wilson, Enfield; Jas. L. Sheffield; Glastonbury; Geo. H. Hall, Manchester; Leroy M. Cowles, New Britain; John W. Phelps, Simsbury; Thos. F. Egan, Southington; John L. Wilson, Suffield; Wm. H. Gibney, Berlin; Edson A. Welch, Windsor; Gustavus Cowles, Farmington. For Sheriffs of each county, see page 663.

## COUNTY JAIL.

THE FIRST JAIL in Hartford was erected in rear of a building on the northwest corner of State and Market streets. In 1793 the first Hartford County Jail was erected on the southwest corner of Pearl and Trumbull streets, and removed June, 1837, from thence to 107 Pearl st., from thence to 42 Seyms st., July 11, 1874, ground for which building was broken, April 17, 1878.

There are 315 cells for the accommodation of prisoners. The number of commitments for the year ending June 30, 1897, was 2,470—remaining in Jail, 310; of whom 2,193 were males and 277 females; 799 natives of Conn.; other states, 603; foreigners, 1,068; habitually intemperate, 83; moderate drinkers, 2,378; strictly temperate, 9; burglary, 53; drunkenness, 902; breach of the peace, 228; assault, 183; adultery, 10. Daily average, 295.9.

Edwin J. Smith, *Jailor;* Robert W. Kellogg, Michael D. Conners, Oliver Cleveland, *Deputy Jailors;* Joseph Tatem, *Turnkey;* Wm. F. Clarke, *Night Deputy;* Wm. F. Smith, *Hospital Steward;* Chas. F. Campbell, *Engineer;* Gertrude C. Smith, *Matron.*

## COUNTY POST SURGEONS.

H. Walter Murliess, Levi B. Cochran, Hartford; George Clary, New Britain; Edward P. Woodward, Bristol; Edward F. Parsons, Enfield; E. H. Griswold, East Hartford; James H. Osborn, Southington; Henry C. Bunce, Glastonbury; George F. Lewis, Canton; Charles M. Wooster, Tariffville; Charles Carrington, Farmington; S. R. Burnap, Windsor Locks; Julian N. Parker, Manchester; Edward G. Fox, Wethersfield; Alfred J. Wood, Granby.

## RECEIPTS AND EXPENSES OF HARTFORD CO.

MARCUS H. HOLCOMB, *Treasurer.*

*For year ending June 30, 1897.*

RECEIPTS.

| | |
|---|---|
| From state, for board of prisoners,.......... | $35,336.10 |
| " City of Hartford, for board of prisoners, | 425.11 |
| " United States on civil process,........ | 71.44 |
| " earnings of prisoners................ | 1,700.00 |
| " sales at jail,....................... | 108.14 |
| " temporary loans,.................... | 73,000.00 |
| " licenses, 5 per cent,................ | 8,463.40 |
| " license transfers,................... | 210.00 |
| " state for county home,.............. | 11,089.68 |
| " interest on deposits,................ | 629.56 |
| Glastonbury,............................. | 18.14 |
| East Windsor school money,.............. | 276.75 |
| Coal,.................................... | 129.66 |
| Balance on hand June 30, 1896,........... | 814.72 |
| Total,...........................| $152,696.64 |
| Key fees,................................ | 1,198.50 |

AMOUNT DUE TO THE COUNTY.

| | |
|---|---|
| From state, for board of prisoners,....... | $3,828.53 |
| " United States, for board of prisoners, | 88.54 |
| " Civil process,...................... | 1.92 |
| Total,........................... | $3,918.99 |

EXPENDITURES.

| | |
|---|---|
| Paid at jail for provisions,.................. | $11,625.67 |
| Clothing,............................... | 1,984.28 |
| Bedding,................................ | 768.98 |
| Fuel,................................... | 3,054.54 |
| Light,.................................. | 464.08 |
| Medicines,.............................. | 448.76 |
| Medical attendance,..................... | 167.00 |
| Salary of jailor,........................ | 1,000.00 |
| " assistants,........................ | 6,202.88 |
| " chaplain,......................... | 200.00 |
| Building and repairs,.................... | 1,698.85 |
| Furniture,.............................. | 491.50 |
| Board of sick prisoners,................. | 26.00 |
| Water and ice,.......................... | 824 00 |
| Telephone,.............................. | 97.87 |
| Addition to jail,........................ | 44,000.00 |
| Transportation,......................... | 76.17 |
| Stationery and stamps,.................. | 62.18 |
| Supplies,............................... | 2,578.92 |
| Advertising for jail report,............. | 88 00 |
| Insurance,.............................. | 260.00 |
| Court house for repairs,................. | 590.21 |
| Bar library,............................ | 800.00 |
| Telephone,.............................. | 211.85 |
| Gas,.................................... | 129.97 |
| Janitor and assistants,.................. | 2,031.00 |
| Furnishings,............................ | 149.00 |
| Water and ice,.......................... | 150.78 |
| Coal,................................... | 309.27 |
| Insurance,.............................. | 100.00 |
| County home, building and repairs,...... | 5,681.82 |
| " expenses,................ | 12,158.44 |
| " school furniture,........ | 249.80 |
| Salary of county commissioners,......... | 4,785.34 |
| " treasurer,.............. | 800.00 |
| " auditors,............... | 20.00 |
| Stationary, blanks and stamps,......... | 327.01 |
| Legal expenses,......................... | 165.00 |
| License blanks,......................... | 104.00 |
| Loans paid,............................. | 5,000.00 |
| Interest on loans,....................... | 6,796.43 |
| Towns for highway,..................... | 20,646.36 |
| Violation of liquor law,................. | 22.20 |
| Balance in hands of county treasurer,.... | 7,198.40 |
| " managers of county home, | 268.25 |
| Total,...........................| $12,696.64 |

INDEBTEDNESS OF THE COUNTY.

Accepted orders on the county treasurer,..$166,000.00

**HARTFORD COUNTY BAR ASSOCIATION.**
Charles E. Perkins, *Pres't;* Henry C. Robinson, *Vice Pres't;* Wm. F. Henney, *Clerk.* Organized March 20, 1795. Regular meetings at Superior Court room on Friday before the civil terms, and on each Friday during the term, at 2 P. M. Annual election in March.

**COUNTY HEALTH OFFICERS.**
*Hartford County*—Daniel A. Markham, Hartford.
*New Haven County*—C. E. Hoadley, New Haven.
*New London County*—Charles F. Thayer, Norwich.
*Fairfield County*—Geo. E. Hill, Bridgeport.
*Windham County*—Wm. A. King, Willimantic.
*Litchfield County*—Frank W. Etheridge, Thomaston.
*Middlesex County*— Wesley U. Pearne, Middletown.
*Tolland County*—Myron P. Yeomans, Andover.

# Town of Hartford.

**HARTFORD TOWN OFFICERS, JULY, 1898.**
Offices, 114 Pearl street.

☞ Annual Town Election, 1st Monday in April.
See also City Officers.

The Act of Consolidation has transferred to City Commissions all but the following Town Officers.

*Town Clerk.*—Henry F. Smith.

*Assistant Town Clerk.*—Wilbur T. Halliday.

*Selectmen.*—August W. Budde, Hart Talcott, Halsey B. Philbrick, Frederick A. Marcy, Frederick P. Lepard.

*Assessors.*—Elected for three years from June 1, 1898, Robert D. Bone, Samuel N. Benedict, James T. Farrell. *Clerk,* Charles E. Giddings.

*Constables.*—Thomas B. Chapman, Willis A. Pierce, Charles W. Cole, Charles B. Greene, Richard B. Hetherton, Seymour P. Agnew, Charles Taussig.

*Grand Jurors.*—Austin Brainard, Lucius F. Robinson, John W. Coogan, Timothy E. Steele, James J. Quinn, Edward L. Steele.

*Registrars of Electors.*—Wm. Cotter, Jr., Edward S. Young.

*Janitor Halls of Record.*—Oliver W. Wood.

**TOWN SINKING FUND.**
In Account with HARTFORD TRUST Co., Agent; R. W. CUTLER, President.
*For fiscal year ending April 1, 1898.*
The Fund is invested as follows:

| | | |
|---|---|---:|
| 7 Town of Hartford 4½ per cent. Bonds,.. | | $7,000.00 |
| 31 " " 3 " | | 31,000.00 |
| 2 " " 5 " Notes,.. | | 40,000.00 |
| Cash on hand.......................... | | 4,428.17 |
| | | $42,428.17 |

HARTFORD TRUST CO., Treasurer.

**TOWN DEPOSIT FUND.**
Amount of Fund April 1, 1898, was $23,481.43; invested in Town's Note, dated October 1, 1888, at 6 per cent. Proceeds from same the past year was $1,408.88, which amount was paid for the benefit of the public schools.        C. C. STRONG, *Treasurer.*

**POPULATION OF HARTFORD.**

| | | | | |
|---|---|---:|---|---:|
| 1756 Census, | ....... | 3,027 | 1820 Census,....... | 6,909 |
| 1761 " | ..... | 3,988 | 1830 " ....... | 9,789 |
| 1774 " | ....... | 5,081 | 1840 " ....... | 12,793 |
| 1782 " | ....... | 5,495 | 1850 " ....... | 17,966 |
| 1790 " | ...... | 4,090 | 1860 " ....... | 29,152 |
| 1800 " | ....... | 5,347 | 1870 " ....... | 37,743 |
| 1810 " | ....... | 6,003 | 1880 " ....... | 42,551 |

1890 Census, 53,230.

1898 population, see Preface of this book, page 7.

Adams Sherman W.
Alderman Allen C.
Allen Charles Dexter,
Andetta Antonio,
Andrews James P.
Andrews W. S.
Atwood Eugene F.
Augur William C.

Babcock H. E.
Bailey Herbert G.
Baker George W.
Barbour Joseph L.
Barbour Sylvester.
Barker Wm. L. B.
Bartholomew D. W.
Bates Ezra F.
Beadle H. Leonard,
Belden Frank E.
Bennett Edward B.
Bestor Howard G.
Bidwell. Frank W.
Bill Albert C.
Bissell Henry.
Boland Fred. A.
Bone Robert D.
Brainard Austin
Brewer Geo. A.
Bridgman Myron H.
Brocklesby Arthur K.
Brocklesby John H.
Bronson Samuel M.
Brott George Olney.
Broughel Andrew J. Jr.
Brower Edwin.
Bruce Willard H.
Bryant P. S.
Buck John H.
Budge Edward C.
Bulkeley John C.
Bullard Herbert S.
Burdett Charles L.
Burdick Francis L.
Burnham Charles R.
Burnham E. D.
Burt George H.
Butler Patrick F.
Buths Joseph.

Calhoun J. Gilbert,
Carroll John A.
Carroll Richard F.
Carter Charles P.
Caswell Thomas M.
Chapman Silas, Jr.
Chapman R. P.
Chase J. Seymour,
Cheney Howard.
Clark Mahlon N.
Clarke Charles H.
Clarke Sidney E.
Collins Atwood.
Comstock Royal D.
Conklin Mahlton W.
Conklin Harry S.
Conklin J. H.
Conklin Wm. P.
Coogan James F. 2d.
Coogan John W.
Cook Albert S.
Cook Edward B.
Cooley Francis R.
Corkins Willington M.
Cornwell Silas H.
Cottrell Harry L.
Cowles Edwin S.
Cunts Herman F.

Darcy Patrick J.
Dart Frederick W.
Davidson Charles S.
Davis Frederick W.
Day Albert P.
Day Edward M.
Dennis James W.
Dickinson L. A.
Dickenson Robert C.
Dillingham Edmund B.
Dixon Wm. J.
Dodd Charles A.
Dole Fred J.
Donovan P. B.
Doty S. C.
Dunham Sylvester C.
Dwyer John J.
Dwyer Robert W.
Dwyer William S.

Eberle Frederick.
Eberle Frederick G.
Eddy Willard.
Ellis George
Ellsworth Ernest B.
Elmore Samuel E.

Faxon Walter C.
Fenn John Roberts,
Fenn J. Lincoln.
Fitts Henry E.
Flagg Charles E.
Flint Harold F. C.
Ford Nelson G.
Fowler Clarkson N.
Freeman Harrison B. Jr.
Fuller Frederick E.
Fuller Henry W.

Galotti Nicola.
Garvin Edward J.
Gates Andrew F.
Gillett Albert B.
Gilman George H.
Gladwin Sidney M.
Glazier A. Judson,
Glazier D. J.
Glazier Robert C.
Graham Winfield C.
Graves Miles W.
Green Alfred W.
Green Sarah E.
Greene Jacob H.
Griffing Robert A.
Griffith John E.
Griffith Wm. Richard.
Grosbeck Frederick O.
Gross Chas. E.

Hall Mary.
Halliday Wilbur T.
Hamilton Joseph D.
Hannum Geo. A.
Hansling Philip, Jr.
Harrington Henry E.
Hart Edward G.
Havens Irving W.
Hawley John G.
Henney William F.
Hickmot Wm. J.
Hillyer Appleton R.
Hoadley E. J.
Hoadley Francis A.
Hoadly Charles J.
Hodge Geo. W.
Hoffman C. F. Paul,
Hollister Martin T.

Holt Fred P.
Honiss Wm. H.
Hotchkiss Laura A.
Hotchkiss Samuel M.
Howard Arthur E.
Howard Frank E.
Howe Albert S.
Hubbard Frederick H.
Hungerford William C.
Huntington Henry A.
Huntington Robert W. Jr.
Hyde E. Henry.
Hyde William Waldo.

Jackson Rufus H.
Jacobs Ward W.
Jenkins Arthur B.
Johnson Charles E.
Johnson Elijah C.
Joslyn Charles M.

Kellogg George A.
Kellogg W. H.
Kempner Isadore,
Kilbourn John F.
King H. S.
Knight Chas. W.
Knight Franklin H.
Knoek L. S.
Knox Harry R.

Laraja G. Battiste,
Larkum Horace H.
Lawrence Charles H.
Learned Newton M.
Leroy Daniel.
Levy Josiah W.
Lincoln Frederick M.
Lincoln George F.
Linke William L.
Lipsey Robert G.
Long Henry C.
Loomis A. G.
Loomis A. H.
Lounsbury Cooke.
Loveland G. C.
Lunny Robert.

Marcy Merrick A.
Markam Daniel A.
Marvin Edwin E.
Marvin L. P. W.
Matson William L.
McConville William J.
McCorkell Alex. K.
McGovern Patrick.
McKenney Benjamin C.
McManus Thomas.
Merritt George P.
Mildeberger Henry D.
Milliken John B.
Mills Hiram A.
Miner Samuel A.
Morgan William.
Morse Leonard.
Morley F. A.
Morton George E.
Myers Charles E.
Maercklein Herman J.
Mairson Joseph.

Newberry Leslie W.
Newton Allen H.
Newton George B.
Newton Loomis A.
Nichols George.
Noonan J. T.

Oakey P. Davis,

Parker Chas. E.
Parker Felton.
Parker Francis H.
Parsons Francis,
Pearce Walter.
Pearson Edward J.
Peck Edward B.
Peck Nathan F.
Perkins Arthur.
Petherbridge Emelyn.
Phillips J. Henry.
Pierce Wm. J.
Plimpton Frederick
Powell James B.
Powell Ward C.
Pratt Walter W.
Price George T.
Price William T.
Prior Charles E.

Quinn James J.

Rathbun Fred D.
Redfield Hosmer P.
Reynolds George A.
Rhone Chas. W.
Richards Alfred T.
Richards Francis H.
Riley Charles D.
Risley Albert E
Roberts Hosmer C.
Robinson Henry C.
Robinson Henry S.
Robinson John T.
Robinson Lucius F.
Rood David A.
Rosenthal Charles.
Rowley William H.

Safford Charles A.
Satriano S.
Sawtelle Alfred W.
Schriftgiesser Emil.
Schwab Joseph.
Scott M. B.
Sedgwick Charles F.
Sexton Frederick G.
Seymour Fred B.
Shaffer Charles O.
Shannon Thos. A.
Shelton Charles E.
Shelton Edward.
Shepard Charles E.
Shipman James.
Sill George G.
Skinner Charles W.
Small Frederick F.
Smith Andrew T.
Smith Chas. H.
Smith Eben E.
Smith Edgar L.
Smith Frank B.
Smith Henry F.
Smith Herbert Knox.
Smith James A.
Smith Mary L. Mrs.
Smith Thomas M.
Smith Wm. W.
Spencer Alfred, Jr.
Spencer Carnot O.
Stagg Charles E.
Stanton Lewis E.
Staples Geo. W.
Steele Edward L.
Stevens Robert D.
Steinmetz Wm. P.
Stillman William W.
Stocker E. H.
Stone Frank E.

Stoughton John A.
Street Frederick F.
Sumner George G.
Swan Charlotte E.
Swan Theron C.

Taintor George E.
Taintor Henry E.
Tallman James H.
Thacher John H.
Thompson Charles E.
Thompson Frank A.
Thompson H. J.
Thompson Isabelle.
Tilton Geo. E.
Todd Milo A.
Toohey John A.
Traute Alfred H.
Trumbull Joseph P.
Trux Melville E.
Tucker Edwin H.
Tucker William.
Turner J. H.
Tuttle Joseph P.
Tyler Heman A.
Ulrich George.
Vail Thomas G.

Very William.
Wakefield W. L.
Walker Albert H.
Ward William.
Waterous Thos. C.
Webster Charles M.
Welles Charles T.
Welles Roger.
White Herbert H.
White Weston L.
Whitmore Franklin G.
Whitney Henry D.
Wilder Nahum C.
Willard William A.
Williams A. N.
Williams Frank B.
Williams Harry R.
Williams William S.
Willson Leslie H.
Wing Oliver F.
Wolven John W.
Woodard Herbert M.
Woods George H.
Wright A. J.

Young Edward S.
Young William F.

---

## JUSTICES OF THE PEACE FOR HARTFORD.

Election biennially at the same time as for State officers.

Adams Sherman W.
Alderman Allen C.
Barbour Joseph L.
Barbour Sylvester.
Bill Albert C.
Brainard Austin.
Brott George O.
Broughel Andrew J. Jr.
Bullard Herbert S.
Calhoun J. Gilbert.
Carroll John A.
Case Uriah.
Clarke Charles H.
Coogan John W.
Dwyer John J.
Eberle Frederick.
Eberle Frederick G.
Eggleston Arthur F.
Fellowes Charles E.
Freeman Harrison B. Jr.
Henney William F.
Higgins John E.

Kennedy Thomas K.
Lyman Theodore.
McConville William J.
McManus Thomas.
Mildeberger Henry D.
Morse Leonard.
Murphy Dennis J.
Perkins Charles E.
Quinn James J.
Robinson Lucius F.
Safford Charles A.
Shipman Arthur L.
Sill George G.
Stanton Lewis E.
Steele Edward L.
Steele Timothy E.
Stillman William W.
Taintor Henry E.
Toohey John A.
Tuttle Joseph P.
Watrous Thomas C.
Williams Frank B.

---

## COMMISSIONERS OF SUPERIOR COURT; HARTFORD COUNTY.

Brooks Calvin M.*
Brott George O.
Brown Arthur T.
Buck John H.
Buck John R.
Bullard Herbert S.
Chambers Francis.
Clarke Sidney E.
Day Edward M.
Dickinson Robert C.
Dwyer John J.
Ellsworth Ernest B.
Freeman Harrison B. Jr.
Garvan Edward J.
Gates Andrew F.
Gibson George P.
Gilman Geo. H.
Goslee Henry S.
Healy Frank E.*
Healy John P.*

Holden Benedict M.*
Hooker John.
Hungerford William C.*
Hyde E. Henry, Jr.
Hyde Wm. Waldo.
Joslyn Chas. M.
Levy Josiah W.
Markham Daniel A.
Marvin L. P. Waldo.
McLean Geo. P.*
Mills Hiram R.*
O'Flaherty Hugh.
Parker Francis H.
Perkins Arthur.
Robinson John T.
Steele Edward L.
Tilton George E.
Toohey John A.
Vail Thomas G.
White John A.

* Not residents of Hartford.

---

## GAME AND FISH WARDEN.

A. C. Collins, Hartford, Conn.

# Boundaries.

## City of Hartford.

ON THE NORTH. In 1830 the Selectmen of Hartford and Windsor towns, assisted by Chauncey Barnard, Surveyor, followed a former survey made in the year 1808, and erected monuments as follows: commencing at an ancient and well-known monument, being a pile of stones on the East side of the highway leading from Hartford to Windsor, and running as the Needle now stands, N. 41 degs. E. 2360 links to a hickory tree—thence North 50 d. E. 575 l. to a ditch—thence N. 88 d. E. 560 l. to a ditch—thence S. 87½ d. E. 860 l. to a stone monument near the house of widow Hezekiah Marsh—thence S. 82½ d. E. 1409 l. to a maple tree which is marked—thence 1819 l. to the west bank of the Connecticut river. Commencing back at the aforesaid pile of stones near the highway, and running N. 88 d. W. 1013 l. to an old ditch; thence 1010 l. to a ditch—thence 996 l. to a ditch—thence 1034 l. to a ditch—thence 1000 l. to a ditch—thence 1015 l. to a ditch—thence 2018 l. to a ditch—thence 2038 l. to a ditch—thence 1006 l. to a ditch—thence 895 l. to an ancient and well-known monument, being a large pile of stones in Brick-kiln swamp—thence N. 11½ d. W. 1000 l. to a ditch—thence 1000 l. to a ditch—thence 1000 l. to a ditch—thence 1075 l. to a hickory tree and a large pile of stones on land of Thos. Moore—thence N. 86 d. W. 1200 l. to a stone monument on the east side of the highway, near the house of Thos. Moore, thence 1878 l. to a ditch—thence 900 l. to a ditch—thence 1990 links to a large pile of stones on Nath'l Terry's farm, being an ancient and well-known monument; thence 1775 l. to a ditch—thence 2000 l. to a ditch; thence 1044 l. to a ditch; thence 1017 l. to a ditch; thence 1590 l. to the east bank of Wood's river; thence 406 l. to a pile of stones; thence 775 l. to the middle of the new road (so called) leading from Hartford to Wintonbury meeting house.

ON THE EAST. By the east bank of Connecticut river.

ON THE SOUTH. In April, 1817, the following division line was run between the towns of Hartford and Wethersfield, under G. Gillett, Surveyor General, assisted by John Hempsted, Jonathan Wells and Elijah Keach, of Wethersfield, and monuments properly placed; beginning at the northeast corner of Wethersfield on a line between the towns of Wethersfield and East Hartford, near a place called pewter pot brook S. 87° west at a stone monument—thence across Connecticut river, 28 chains 67 links, thence to a stone monument in the middle of Standish's Island 22 chains 61 links—thence to a stone east of Standish's creek 2 chains 60 links—thence to a stone on the west side of Standish's creek to the stone N. F. distant from the stone N. F. 16 chains 97 links, thence 8 chains 56 links to the fence on the east side of the main road leading from Wethersfield to Hartford, near the north side of the Folly bridge—thence 1 chain 64 links to the stone monument on the west side of said road, marked H. & W. near the northwest corner of said bridge—thence 9 chains 28 links to a heap of stones in the fence running east and west—thence 80 rods to a stone monument in the fence—thence 80 rods to an elm tree marked—thence 89 rods to a stone monument—thence 80 rods to a heap of stones in the fence—thence 28 rods to the east side of the Rocky Hill road to a stone monument—thence till it strikes the line between Hartford and West Hartford, as established in 1854.

ON THE WEST. From Farmington avenue on the west line of Prospect avenue north to Albany avenue, and from thence on the same line prolonged to town of Bloomfield; the line from Farmington avenue, south commencing at the northwest corner of Farmington avenue at the present boundary stone, it shall cross Prospect hill road, to the northeast corner of said road and Farmington avenue, from thence running south on the east line of said Prospect hill road to Park street road, thence in a direct line across Park street road on Prospect avenue (formerly McKegg road); and thence south on the east line of Prospect avenue (formerly McKegg road) and the east line of New Park avenue (formerly Baker road), until it strikes the present boundary line; thence south on the present boundary line between Hartford and West Hartford, as set off in 1854.

## City of Hartford.

By Legislative Act, approved April, 1881:—"The territorial limits of the body politic and corporate existing under the name of the City of Hartford shall hereafter consist of all the land and territory situate within the present limits of the Town of Hartford, so that hereafter the limits of said city and town shall be the same."

The new Charter, uniting City and Town under one set of officers, passed by the Legislature, July 9, 1895, took effect June, 1896.

## City Wards,

*As enacted by the Legislature, July, 1895, Re-districting the City and Town of Hartford into ten wards.*

### FIRST.

Beginning at a point on Main street, opposite the center of Charter Oak street, thence running easterly through the center of Charter Oak street to the Connecticut river, thence northerly along the west bank of the Connecticut river to a point opposite the center of Talcott street, thence westerly through the center of Talcott street to the center of Main street, thence southerly through the center of Main street to place of beginning.

### SECOND.

Beginning at a point in the center of Main street opposite Talcott street, thence running easterly through the center of Talcott street to the Connecticut river, thence northerly by the Connecticut river to the city line, thence westerly by the northern boundary line of the city to a point where the New York, New Haven and Hartford railroad crosses, thence southerly along the center of the track of the New York, New Haven and Hartford railroad to the center of Canton street, thence westerly through the center of Canton street to the center of Main street, thence southerly through the center of Main street to the place of beginning.

### THIRD.

Beginning at a point on Main street opposite Canton street, thence running easterly through the center of Canton street to the center of the track of the New York, New Haven and Hartford railroad, thence northerly along the center of the track of the New York, New Haven and Hartford railroad to the northern boundary line of the city, thence westerly by the northern boundary line of the city to a point opposite the center of Vine street, thence southerly in a straight line coincident with Vine street produced to the center of Vine street, thence southerly through the center of Vine street to the center of Albany avenue, thence easterly through the center of Albany avenue to the center of Belden street, thence easterly through the center of Belden street to the center of Main street, thence northerly to the place of beginning.

### FOURTH.

Beginning at a point on Little river, opposite the center of Union place, thence running northerly through the center of Union place to the center of

Church street, thence easterly through the center of Church street to the center of High street, thence northerly through the center of High street to the center of Main street, thence northerly through the center of Main street to the center of Belden street, thence westerly through the center of Belden street to the center of Albany avenue, thence westerly through the center of Albany avenue to the center of Vine street, thence northerly through the center of Vine street to Holcomb street, thence northerly in a straight line coincident with Vine street produced, to the northern boundary line of the city, thence westerly on the northern boundary line of the city to the western boundary line of the city, thence southerly on the western boundary line of the city to the center of Asylum avenue, thence easterly through the center of Asylum avenue to the center of Woodland street, thence northerly through the center of Woodland street to the center of Collins street, thence easterly through the center of Collins street to the center of Garden street, thence southerly through the center of Garden street to the center of Asylum street, thence easterly through the center of Asylum street to the center of Union place, thence southerly in a straight line to the place of beginning.

#### FIFTH.

Beginning at a point on Main street, opposite Mulberry street, thence running westerly through the center of Mulberry street to the center of Little river, thence westerly by the Little river to a point opposite the center of Union place, thence northerly through the center of Union place to the center of Church street, thence easterly through the center of Church street to the center of High street, thence northerly through the center of High street to the center of Main street, thence southerly through the center of Main street to the place of beginning.

#### SIXTH.

Beginning at a point on Main street, opposite Mulberry street, thence westerly through the center of Mulberry street to the center of Little river, thence westerly by the center of Little river to a point opposite the center of Hungerford street, thence southerly through the center of Hungerford street to the center of Park street, thence easterly through the center of Park street, to the center of Main street, thence northerly through the center of Main street to the place of beginning.

#### SEVENTH.

Beginning at a point on Main street, opposite the center of Charter Oak street, thence easterly through the center of Charter Oak street to the Connecticut river, thence southerly by the Connecticut river to the southern boundary line of the city, thence westerly by the southern boundary line of the city to the center of Maple avenue, thence northerly through the center of Maple avenue to the center of Webster street, thence northerly through the center of Webster street to the center of Washington street, thence northerly through the center of Washington street to the center of Park street, thence easterly through the center of Park street to the center of Main street, thence northerly through the center of Main street to the place of beginning.

#### EIGHTH.

Beginning at a point on Park street, opposite the center of Washington street, thence southerly through the center of Washington street to the center of Webster street, thence southerly through the center of Webster street to the center of Maple avenue, thence southerly through the center of Maple avenue to the southern boundary line of the city, thence westerly by the southern boundary line of the city to the western boundary line of the city, thence northerly by the western boundary line of the city to a point where the New York, New Haven and Hartford railroad crosses,

thence northerly along the center of the track of the New York, New Haven and Hartford railroad to the center of Park street, thence easterly through the center of Park street to the place of beginning.

#### NINTH.

Beginning at a point on Little river, opposite the center of Union place, thence running northerly to the center of Asylum street, thence westerly through the center of Asylum street to the center of Garden street, thence northerly through the center of Garden street to the center of Collins street, thence westerly through the center of Collins street to the center of Sigourney street, thence southerly through the center of Sigourney street to the Little river, thence southerly in a straight line coincident with Sigourney street produced, to the center of Park street, thence easterly through the center of Park street to the center of Hungerford street, thence northerly through the center of Hungerford street to the Little river, thence easterly along the center of Little river to the place of beginning.

#### TENTH.

Beginning at a point on Sigourney street, opposite the center of Collins street, thence running westerly through the center of Collins street to the center of Woodland street, thence southerly through the center of Woodland street to the center of Asylum street, thence westerly through the center of Asylum avenue to the western boundary line of the city, thence southerly along the western boundary line of the city to a point where the New York, New Haven and Hartford railroad crosses, thence northerly through the center of the New York, New Haven and Hartford railroad track to the center of Park street, thence easterly through the center of Park street to a point opposite the center of Sigourney street, thence northerly in a straight line coincident with Sigourney street produced, to the center of Sigourney street, thence northerly through the center of Sigourney street to the place of beginning.

## School Districts.

ARSENAL DISTRICT, (No. 5). On the South, beginning at a point on west bank of Connecticut river due east of the center of the eastern termination of Avon street, thence running westerly to and through the center of said Avon street to Windsor avenue, thence southerly through the center of Windsor avenue to Belden street, thence westerly through the center of Belden street and diagonally across Albany avenue to Edwards street, thence southerly through the center of Edwards street to Walnut street, thence westerly through the center of Walnut street to brick-kiln brook; thence on the West, northerly by the course of said brook crossing the north line of Walnut street between Nos. 78 and 80, Liberty street at No. 28, Albany avenue at No. 145, to a point about 150 feet south of the south line of Capen street; thence on the North, easterly in a direct line, crossing Windsor avenue in division line between Hubbell's and Hawley's and at the north line of Suffield street and diagonally across said Suffield street, passing near or just south of No. 92 Bellevue street to the Connecticut river; thence on the East, southerly by said river to the place of beginning.

FIRST DISTRICT, (No. 1)—CENTER DISTRICT, BROWN SCHOOL. On the North and on the West by the south line of the Second North District to a point where the Brick-kiln brook crosses No. 442 Asylum street, then southerly by said brook to Park river; thence on the South, easterly by Park river to the Connecticut river; thence on the East, northerly by Connecticut river to the place of beginning.

NORTH EAST DISTRICT, (No. 8). On the North by the town of Windsor; on the East by the Connecticut river; on the South by the north line of the Arsenal District; on the West by Brick-kiln brook, crossing Capen street at No. 255.

NORTH WEST DISTRICT, (No. 9). On the West, beginning at a granite stone marked "W. M. District" and "N. W. District," 1,034 feet northerly on the intersection of the north line of Asylum street with the east line of Prospect avenue, thence following the northerly boundary line between the town of Hartford and the town of West Hartford to the intersection of that line with the boundary line of the town of Bloomfield; on the North, by the boundary line between the town of Hartford and the town of Bloomfield; on the East, by the boundary line of the town of Bloomfield and the Brick-kiln brook to Love lane; thence following the Brick-kiln brook to the center of Walnut street and about 35 feet south of said center of Walnut street; thence on the South, due west on north line of West Middle District to the center of the north branch of the Park river; thence on the West, northerly, by said river, to a granite stone marked "W. M. District" and "N. W. District"; thence westerly in a straight line along the boundary line of the West Middle District to the point of beginning.

SECOND NORTH DISTRICT, (No. 3), sometimes called NORTH MIDDLE DISTRICT. On the North, by the south line of Arsenal District to the center of Albany avenue and Edwards street; thence on the West, southerly through the center of Edwards street to Brick-kiln brook, thence southerly by said Brick-kiln brook to the center of and crossing at No. 442 Asylum street; thence on the South, easterly through the center of Asylum street to its intersection with Ann street, thence north through the center of Ann street to the center of Church street, thence easterly through the center of Church street to the center of Trumbull street, thence northerly through the center of Trumbull street to the center of Main street, thence southerly through the center of Main street to its intersection with Village street, thence northeasterly through the center of Village street to the center of Pleasant street, thence easterly through the center of Pleasant street to Front street, thence east to a point on the Connecticut river; thence on the East, northerly by said river to the place of beginning.

SOUTH DISTRICT, (No. 2). On the North, beginning at a point 380 feet south of the southeast corner of Warrenton street and Prospect avenue, (the western boundary of the town of Hartford); thence easterly crossing Sisson avenue at the culvert, and following the course of that stream to the north branch of Park river; thence southerly by said branch of Park river, thence easterly by said Park river to the west bank of the Connecticut river; thence on the East by the west bank of the Connecticut river to the southern boundary of the town of Hartford; thence on the South, westerly by Wethersfield town line to a point in the center of Franklin avenue; thence running northerly in the center of said avenue to a point 200 feet south of the south line of South street; thence running westerly parallel to said south line of South street, 200 feet distant therefrom to a point 200 feet west of the west line of George street produced; thence running northerly parallel to said west line of George street, 200 feet distant therefrom to a point 200 feet south of the south line of Preston street; thence running westerly parallel to said south line of Preston street, 200 feet therefrom to a point 200 feet west of the west line of Webster street produced; thence running northerly in a straight line to the east line of Maple avenue to a point where said east line of Maple avenue is intersected by the south line of the Washington School District; thence running easterly in said south line of the Washington School District to a point 200 feet east of Franklin avenue, and some 475 feet south of the south line of Bond street; thence north in a line parallel with the east line of Franklin avenue, and 200 feet distant therefrom at all points, to a point in the

center of Wawarme avenue produced; thence westerly in the center line of said Wawarme avenue produced to No. 337 Maple avenue; thence in a straight line to the center of Seymour street in the north line of Retreat avenue; thence northerly in the center of and to No. 85 Seymour street at a point in the center of Madison street produced, crossing Washington street; thence westerly in the center of Madison street, and in the center of said street produced, in a straight line to a pile of stone some 400 feet north of Hamilton avenue in the south branch of Park river; thence southerly by said south branch to its intersection with the westerly boundary of the town; thence on the West, northerly by said western boundary, New Park avenue and Prospect avenue, to the place of beginning.

SOUTH WEST DISTRICT, (No. 7). On the North by the south branch of Park river and south line of the Washington District; on the East by the South District; on the South by the town of Wethersfield; on the West by the town of West Hartford.

WASHINGTON DISTRICT, (No. 6). On the South, beginning at a point in the center of the south branch of the Park river and Flatbush avenue and running easterly through the center of Flatbush avenue to a point nearly 200 feet east of the western line of Zion street, intersecting a line produced from the center of Fairfield avenue, thence southerly by said line and through the center of Fairfield avenue to a point intersecting E. W. Moseley's north division line, thence northeasterly in the direction of said Moseley's line to a point 200 feet east of Franklin avenue in the division line between this and the South District and some 475 feet south of the south line of Bond street; thence on the East, on the North and on the West to the place of beginning by the line of the South District.

WEST MIDDLE DISTRICT, (No. 4). On the East, beginning at the center of Park river at the mouth of the Brick-kiln brook and running thence crossing Asylum street at No. 442 northwesterly by said brook to the center of Edwards street, thence northerly through the center of Edwards street to the center of Walnut street; thence on the North, westerly through the center of Walnut street to the center of Brick-kiln brook between Nos. 78 and 80 Walnut street, thence southerly by said brook about 35 feet to the culvert intersecting a line from the southeast corner of said culvert that is a due east and west line which passes exactly over the northeast corner stone of an "old well" near the south wall of the present Alms house, and through the north part of the house No. 336 Collins street, diagonally across said Collins street and 26 feet from the southeast corner of Collins street with its intersection with Woodland street, crossing Woodland street and passing 32 feet south of the southeast corner of the present residence of Rev. Francis Goodwin, 103 Woodland street, to its intersection with the center of Asylum avenue, thence northerly, following the north branch of the Park river to a mere stone situated on the north bank of said north branch of Park river, said mere stone being marked "W. M. District" and "N. W. District"; thence easterly in a straight line to a mere stone on the west side of Scarborough street, situated 1,308 4.10 feet from the intersection of the north line of Asylum avenue with the west line of Scarborough street; thence continuing in a straight line to a mere stone situated on the east side of Prospect avenue at a point 1,034 feet northerly from the intersection of the north line of Asylum avenue with the east line of Prospect avenue; thence on the West, southerly, by said west boundary of the town (Prospect avenue) to a point 380 feet south of the southeast corner of Warrenton street with its intersection with Prospect avenue; thence on the South, easterly, crossing the culvert at Sisson avenue and the course of that stream to the north branch of Park river; thence southerly by said north branch of Park river and easterly by said Park river to the place of beginning.

**CITY HALL, 800 MAIN STREET.**

ERECTED and used as a STATE HOUSE from May, 1796, till it was transferred by the State of Connecticut to the CITY OF HARTFORD, March 13, 1879, and formally dedicated as the City Hall, October 22, 1879.

*Motto:*—"AFTER THE CLOUDS, THE SUN."

CITY SEAL.—The Eagle, emblem of the United States; the Grapevine, from the seal of the State of Connecticut; the Hart, a favorite and abundant animal here in 1636 — and little river ford — for HARTFORD.

## City Officers.

ANNUAL ELECTION FIRST MONDAY IN APRIL.
The City of Hartford is divided into ten Wards. Polls open from 6 A. M. till 5 P. M. The Mayor, Clerk, Treasurer, Collector, Auditor, and Marshal, elected for two years, even number of year. One Alderman elected annually to each ward for two years; all other city officers are chosen or appointed annually, except members of the several commissions.

| | | |
|---|---|---|
| Hon. MILES B. PRESTON, Mayor; | salary | $3,000 |
| HENRY F. SMITH, City Clerk; | " | 2,000 |
| CHARLES C. STRONG, Treasurer; | " | 3,600 |
| RANSOM N. FITZGERALD, Collector; | " | 3,600 |
| CHARLES H. ROBINS, Auditor; | " | 2,100 |
| JOSEPH DAWSON, City Marshal; | " | 500 |
| JOS. B. HALL, Registrar of Vital Statistics, | " | 1,650 |

REGULAR MEETINGS OF THE COUNCIL, 2d and 4th MONDAY EVENINGS, MONTHLY, IN CITY HALL.

**FIRST WARD.**
Alderman.........John J. Dunn,* 219 Sheldon.
  "         John F. Conniff, 63 Ward.
Councilman......William J. Kelleher, 29 Windsor.
  "         Ferdinand Richter, 75 Temple.
  "         Henry Goldstein, 29 Woodbridge.
  "         Albert S. Chamberlin, 16 Prospect.

**SECOND WARD.**
Alderman.........Moritz Wieder,* 26 Morgan.
  "         William H. Killin, 72 Morgan.
Councilman......Patrick H. Daley, 11 Pleasant.
  "         Sidney L. Bacharach, 9 Canton.
  "         William A. Sullivan, 120 Windsor.
  "         John F. Schuman, 69 Morgan.

**THIRD WARD.**
Alderman.........Henry F. Hart,* 104 Capen.
  "         Charles E Shelton, 310 Windsor av.
Councilman......Edward L. Steele, 27 Clark.
  "         George L. Vannais, 42 Mahl.
  "         George M. Deming, 145 Barbour.
  "         Freeman W. Barrows, 123 Bellevue.

**FOURTH WARD.**
Alderman.........Frederick A. West,* 238 Sigourney.
  "         Horace M. Andrews, 80 Williams.
Councilman......Willard D. Hastings, 11 Atlantic.
  "         Edward B. Boynton, 26 Williams.
  "         Dwight Chapman, 131 Sargeant.
  "         Charles G. Stone, 240 Ashley.

**FIFTH WARD.**
Alderman.........William Bailey, Jr.,* 703 Main.
  "         John K. Williams, 370 Asylum.
Councilman......George F. Kellogg, 1337 Main.
  "         Thomas W. Morgan, 92 Pearl.
  "         Franklin A. Morley, 223 Asylum.
  "         Charles W. Fenn, 175 Pearl.

**SIXTH WARD.**
Alderman.........Ralph Burnham,* 49 Oak.
  "         Henry Roberts, 59 Lafayette.
Councilman......Frederick P. Chapman, 58 Russ.
  "         James Eadie, 158 Washington.
  "         John D. Lapaugh, 68 Park.
  "         Robert C. Lawson, 72 Hungerford.

**SEVENTH WARD.**
Alderman.........Edward Mahl,* 24 Annawan.
  "         William H. Scoville, 7 Alden.
Councilman......Ellery D. Burnham, 269 Wethersfield.
  "         Jordan C. Wells, 60 Benton.
  "         Sanford A. Gabrielle, 60 Dean.
  "         Arthur E. Hobson, 21 Wethersfield.

**EIGHTH WARD.**
Alderman.........Philip Hansling, Jr.,* 385 Park.
  "         George O. Brott, 117 Washington.
Councilman......Peter Taylor, Bartholomew.
  "         Frederick W. Prince, 66 Vernon.
  "         Adolphus J. Orgill, 33 New Britain.
  "         Andrew L. Newton, 15 Hamilton.

**NINTH WARD.**
Alderman.........Howard H. Keep,* 202 Sigourney.
  "         Jos. M. Birmingham, 256 Putnam.
Councilman......Edward Schulze, 1256 Broad.
  "         Chas. F. Gladding, 36 Huntington.
  "         Emil Hjerpe, 1151 Broad.
  "         Forrest Shepherd, 667 Asylum.

**TENTH WARD.**
Alderman.........Thomas Smart,* 8 Sisson.
  "         Herbert H. White, 21 Girard.
Councilman......William A. Countryman, 204 Sisson.
  "         Louis R. Cheney, 40 Woodland.
  "         George E. Smart, 192 Laurel.
  "         Egbert O. Weeks, 580 Farmington.

\* Two years to serve.

**BOARD OF ALDERMEN.**

Hon. MILES B. PRESTON, Mayor, Presiding Officer.
HORACE M. ANDREWS, Acting President.
HENRY F. SMITH. Clerk.
JAMES S. SECOR, Messenger.

**BOARD OF COUNCILMEN.**

WILLIAM A. COUNTRYMAN, President.
GEORGE L. VANNAIS, Vice President.
HENRY C. SHEFFIELD, Clerk.
FRED F. PAYNE, Messenger.

**JOINT STANDING COMMITTEES.**

*Amusements*—Alderman, George O. Brott; Councilmen, George F. Kellogg, William A. Sullivan.

*Auditing*—City Auditor, Alderman, William Bailey, Jr.; Councilman, Edward B. Boynton.

*Cemeteries*—Alderman, Philip Hansling, Jr.; Councilmen, Robert C. Lawson, William J. Kelleher.

*City Buildings*—Alderman, Charles E. Shelton; Councilmen, Peter Taylor, Patrick H. Daley.

*Claims*—Alderman, Frederick A. West; Councilmen, Franklin A. Morley, Edward L. Steele, Sidney L. Bacharach.

*Education*—Alderman, Ralph Burnham; Councilmen, Charles G. Stone, Charles F. Gladding.

*Fire*—Alderman, Henry F. Hart; Councilmen, Dwight Chapman, Frederick P. Chapman.

*Manufactures*—Alderman, Joseph M. Birmingham; Councilmen, Arthur E. Hobson, Edward Schulze.

*Municipal Lighting*—Alderman, William H. Scoville; Councilmen, Ellery D. Burnham, James Eadie.

*Nominating*—Alderman, Horace M. Andrews; Councilmen, Willard D. Hastings, Thomas W. Morgan, Albert S. Chamberlin.

*Ordinances*—The Mayor; City Attorney; Alderman, Herbert H. White; Councilmen, Forest Shepherd, Henry Goldstein.

*Printing*—Alderman, Edward Mahl; Councilmen, Charles W. Fenn, John F. Schuman.

*Public Bath*—Alderman, John K. Williams; Councilmen, John D. Lapaugh, Andrew L. Newton.

*Railroads*—Alderman, Thomas Smart; Councilmen, Freeman W. Barrows, Egbert O. Weeks.

*Water Works*—Alderman, Howard H. Keep; Councilmen, Jordan C. Wells, George M. Deming.

*Ways and Means*—Alderman, Henry Roberts; Councilmen, Louis R. Cheney, Sanford A. Gabrielle, Ferdinand Richter.

**APPOINTED OFFICERS.**

*Alms House*—W. W. Stillman, *Sup't*; Charles S. Woodward, *Steward*; Thomas B. Ackerly, *Physician*; Mrs. L. A. Cornwall, *Matron*; Mrs. L. A. Rowley, *Ass't Matron*; George Cavens, *Orderly*; John H. Gildav, *Engineer*; James Devine, *Hospital Steward*; Hugh F. McGinley, *Watchman*.

*Charity Commissioners*—See page 677.

*City Attorney*—William J. McConville.

*City Auditor*—Charles H. Robins.

*Abatement of Taxes*—Francis Coles, Amos Reynolds, John H. McCann.

*Assessors*—Robert D. Bone, Samuel N. Benedict, James T. Farrell.

*Board of Relief*—Franklin P. Carter, Robert A. Griffing, John P. Collins; Charles E. Giddings, Clerk.

*Building Inspector*—James M. Dow.

*City Recorder*—Leonard Morse.

*City Store Keeper*—Michael H. Gunshanan.

*City Surveyor*—Charles H. Bunce.

*Port Warden*—William S. Williams.

*Prosecuting Attorney*—J. Gilbert Calhoun.

*Special Prosecuting Attorney*—Harrison B. Freeman, Jr.

*Rate Maker*—Robert D. Bone.

*Registrars of Elections*—114 Pearl.—William Cotter, E. S. Young.

*Sealer of Weights and Measures and Inspector of Fire Wood and Milk.*—Edmund D. Roberts.

*Street Superintendent*—Charles W. Sprague. Salary $2,000; Horse hire, $400; *Foreman*, William McEvoy.

*Superintendent Stone Pits*—John Gunning.

*Janitor City Hall*—Peter Conner.

*Janitor Halls of Record*—Oliver W. Wood.

## City Treasurer's Report.

CHARLES C. STRONG, Treasurer, in account with the CITY OF HARTFORD, for year ending March 31, 1896.

**RECEIPTS.**

| | |
|---|---:|
| Balance from old account, | $ 14,589.24 |
| Taxes, | 852,637.76 |
| County Commissioner, | 89,462.45 |
| Hartford Street R. R. Co. tax, | 8,130.51 |
| National Bank tax, | 5,566.36 |
| Street department, | 1,171.33 |
| Fire " | 847.10 |
| Police " | 395 15 |
| Health " | 836.50 |
| City court, | 6.00 |
| Police court, | 6,754.64 |
| Farragut Day Committee, | 500.00 |
| Legal Claims, | 8,000.00 |
| Committee on Public Buildings, | 1,004.38 |
| " Amusements, | 880.43 |
| Town Clerk, | 2,715.13 |
| Milk Inspector, | 49.25 |
| Charity Department, | 3,444.51 |
| Committee on Cemeteries, | 1,676.89 |
| School Appropriation, | 81,070.25 |
| State Evening School Appropriation, | 863.37 |
| Town Deposit Fund, | 1,408.58 |
| Sewers, | 18,974.88 |
| Sidewalks, | 136.06 |
| Street improvements, | 1,269.71 |
| State Street Pavement, | 275.86 |
| Main " " | 33,943.61 |
| Asylum " " | 10,066.29 |
| Church " " | 2,805.53 |
| Trinity " " | 1,752.46 |
| Intercepting Sewer, | 3,399 68 |
| Refunding Town Bonds, | 270,000.00 |
| Committee on Sale of Old Town Farm, | 19,439.41 |
| State Pension for Children of Deceased Soldiers, | 278.50 |
| Police Department Bonds, | 75,000.00 |
| Paving Bonds, | 100,000.00 |
| High School and Bridge Bonds, | 200,000.00 |
| Temporary loans, | 60,896.98 |
| | $1,867,658.14 |

**DISBURSEMENTS.**

| | |
|---|---:|
| Street department, | $215,222.54 |
| Public Lamps " | 52,183.28 |
| Fire " | 107.313.65 |
| Police " | 102,227.17 |
| Health " | 9,055.62 |
| Sewer ventilation, | 125.00 |
| City Court, | 2,724.83 |
| Police Court, | 6,325.71 |
| Public Library, | 9,000.00 |
| Park, | 27,626.00 |
| Water, | 13,969.20 |
| Common Council, | 8,404.00 |

| | |
|---|---|
| Legal and Claims.............. ........... | $16,187.58 |
| Public Buildings,....................... | 8,063.40 |
| Election,............................ | 10,452.60 |
| Advertising,............................ | 1,213.66 |
| Mayor,............................. | 3,365.05 |
| Collector,............................ | 9,798.82 |
| Treasurer,......................... | 5,652.88 |
| Auditor,............................ | 3,443.70 |
| Marshal,............................ | 526.25 |
| Town Clerk,........................ | 5,506.58 |
| Building Inspector,................. | 2,523.34 |
| Sealer of Weights and Measures,....... | 1,270.36 |
| Assessors,........................... | 11,435.80 |
| Charity,............................ | 89,968.62 |
| Cemetery,........................... | 3,928.19 |
| Military Commutation tax,........... | 14,778.60 |
| Police Reserve Fund, ............... | 4,473.12 |
| Fireman's Relief Fund,............... | 48.22 |
| School Visitors,...................... | 15,898.97 |
| School, ............................ | 87,743.77 |
| High School, ........................ | 42,500.00 |
| Liquor prosecution,.................. | 732.42 |
| Bath House,......................... | 1,207.38 |
| Miscellaneous,...................... | 1,440.82 |
| Interest,............................ | 92,926.32 |
| Permanent improvement debt, ........ | 44,623.34 |
| Town floating debt,............... | 29,000.00 |
| Sewers,............................ | 40,013.48 |
| Sidewalks, ......................... | 1,010.87 |
| Street improvements,................ | 7,318.10 |
| Street liens,......................... | 54.00 |
| Main Street Pavement,............... | 66,713.23 |
| Asylum " " ............... | 15,099.59 |
| Church " " ............... | 3,628.03 |
| Trinity " " ............... | 13,597.50 |
| Capitol Bonds,...................... | 7,000.00 |
| Intercepting sewer,................. | 67,937.47 |
| Expense Issuing Bonds,.............. | 1,417.75 |
| Park Street Bridge,................. | 271.59 |
| Broad " " ............... | 7,366.00 |
| Asylum Av. " ............... | 10,000.00 |
| " " " Approach,......... | 2,634.00 |
| High School addition,................ | 105,500.00 |
| Children of Deceased Soldiers,....... | 278.50 |
| Re-assessment Committee,........... | 928.35 |
| Manual Training School,.............. | 35,000.00 |
| Police Building,.................... | 29,250.00 |
| Pope Park,......................... | 3,580.00 |
| New Ten-Twenty-five Bonds,......... | 270,000.00 |
| | $1,768,059.95 |
| Balance to new account, March 31, '98,.. | 99,598.19 |
| | $1,867,658.14 |

### WATER DEPARTMENT.
#### RECEIPTS.

| | |
|---|---|
| Balance from old account,............. .. | $2,205.00 |
| Board Water Commissioners, interest due on bonds and notes,.................. | 43,862.47 |
| To call and redeem Water Bonds, ...... | 45,000.00 |
| | $91,067.47 |

#### DISBURSEMENTS.

| | |
|---|---|
| Interest on bonds,................... | 43,442.47 |
| Called and redeemed Water Bonds,.... | 45,000.00 |
| Balance to new account, ............. | 2,625.00 |
| | $91,067.47 |

### PARK DEPARTMENT.
#### TAX FUND RECEIPTS.

| | |
|---|---|
| Balance from old account, April 1, 1897,.. | 4,672.45 |
| Appropriation from city......... ... | 27,626.00 |
| Special tax collected on list of 1894,.... | 88.78 |
| Elizabeth Park Fund,................. | 10,585.28 |
| Bond Fund,......................... | 2,716.97 |
| | $45,689.48 |

#### TAX FUND DISBURSEMENTS.

| | |
|---|---|
| Orders drawn by Board of Park Commissioners for current expense,......... | 20,711.59 |
| Adv. Elizabeth Park Fund,............ | 10,585.28 |
| Bond Fund,......................... | 2,716.97 |
| Balance to new account, March 31, 1898.. | 11,675.64 |
| | $45,689.48 |

#### BOND FUND RECEIPTS.

| | |
|---|---|
| Balance from old account, April 1, 1897,. | 61,636.51 |
| Sale of $150,000 Park Improvement Bonds at 106.5-29,..................... | 159,723.50 |
| Interest on Deposit,.................. | 1,119.00 |

#### BOND FUND DISBURSEMENTS.

| | |
|---|---|
| Land purchase,...................... | 21,905.25 |
| Expense account,................... | 23,424.47 |
| | $45,329.72 |
| Balance to new account, March 31, 1898,. | 177,219.84 |
| Total,............... ................. | $222,549.56 |

#### ELIZABETH PARK FUND RECEIPTS.

| | |
|---|---|
| Hartford Trust Co. (Trustee of C. M. Pond Estate),..................... | $6,671.00 |
| Sale of stock,......................... | 10,779.22 |
| Dividends,.................... .... | 2,586.48 |
| | $20,036.70 |

#### DISBURSEMENTS.

| | |
|---|---|
| For Greenhouses,..................... | $17,895.15 |
| Balance to new account,............. | 2,141.55 |
| | $20,036.70 |

### NILES CHARITY FUND.

This fund consists of $40,000, invested in local bank stocks. The income, $2,649.00, is paid to the Hartford Charitable and Hartford Widows' Societies.

### RESERVE FUND OF THE POLICE DEPARTMENT.
#### RECEIPTS.

| | |
|---|---|
| Balance April 1, 1897,.............. | $7,447.61 |
| Interest on deposits,................ | 202.67 |
| County Commissioners, 5 per cent. of the licenses,........................... | 4,473.12 |
| | $12,123.40 |

#### DISBURSEMENTS.

| | |
|---|---|
| Paid members of Veteran Reserve,...... | $3,066.64 |
| Balance to new account,............. | 9,056.76 |
| | $12,123.40 |

### CITY DEBT, April 1, 1898.

| | |
|---|---|
| Water bonds, 4 to 6 per cent.,........... | $925,000.00 |
| Consolidated bonds, 1909, 3 per cent ,.... | 750,000.00 |
| Funding bonds, 1918, 4 per cent.,....... | 290,000.00 |
| Public Imp. bonds, 1922, 3½ per cent.,.... | 250,000.00 |
| Re funding Capitol bonds, 1922, 3½ p. c.,.. | 800,000.00 |
| Re-funding Town bonds, 1922, 3½ per cent. | 270,000.00 |
| Police Dept. bonds, 1923, 3½ per cent.,... | 75,000.00 |
| Park Imp. bonds, 1926, 3½ per cent.,..... | 800,000.00 |
| Paving bonds, 1938, 3½ per cent.,........ | 100,000.00 |
| School and Bridge bonds, 1938, 3½ p. c.,.. | 700,000.00 |
| Bonded debt,........................ | $3,960,000.00 |
| Demand note, Town Deposit Fund, 6 p. c., | 23,481.00 |
| Demand Notes, Permanent Improvement debt, 4 per cent...................... | 90,474.00 |
| Demand Notes, Town Floating debt, 4½ and 5 per cent.,.................... | 7,500.00 |
| Total debt,........................ | $4,081,455.00 |
| Less Sinking Funds,................. | 313,732.00 |
| | $3,767,723.00 |
| Less Water debt....................... | 925,000.00 |
| Net debt,........................ | $2,842,723.00 |

## Hartford Police.

### OFFICE, 38 KINSLEY ST.

*Chief of Police, from 7 A. M. till 6 P. M.*

GEORGE F. BILL, *Chief;* salary, $2,000 per annum.

| | | |
|---|---|---|
| CORNELIUS RYAN, *Captain;* | 1,500 | " |
| WILLIAM F. GUNN, *Lieutenant;* | 1,200 | " |
| JAMES P. CARTER, *Sergeant;* | 1,080 | " |
| LYMAN SMITH, " | 1,080 | " |
| B. L. UMBERFIELD, " | 1,080 | " |
| W. W. SMITH, " | 1,080 | " |
| JOHN F. BUTLER, *Acting Serg't;* | 1,000 | " |

Patrolmen $1,000 each: and sixty supernumeraries at $2.73 per day when called into active service. Following are regular policemen:

| | | | | | |
|---|---|---|---|---|---|
| Beecher Edward...No. | 34 | Liebut M. O......No. | 75 |
| Brazel Thad. W... " | 56 | Lloyd Charles H... " | 14 |
| Brown Wm. G..... " | 52 | Losty Ed. T....... " | 68 |
| Burns John J...... " | 54 | McCue Thomas,... " | 15 |
| Case Albert M.... " | 21 | Mahoney Patrick.. " | 11 |
| Costello E. H...... " | 67 | Maloy Keron....... " | 13 |
| Creedon John..... " | 33 | Marshall Wm. H.. " | 57 |
| Dietrich Theodore. " | 41 | McDermott John F. " | 45 |
| Dillon Edward F.. " | 47 | McLeod Arthur... " | 50 |
| Doran Patrick.... " | 69 | Maloney James.... " | 4 |
| Dunn James D.... " | 46 | Mantle Charles... " | 44 |
| English Edward ... " | 77 | Morgan' James.... " | 66 |
| Fagan Mathew.... " | 9 | Noonan James F.. " | 36 |
| Fagan J. T.:..... " | 58 | O'Brien J. E...... " | 72 |
| Farrell Ed. J...... " | 71 | O'Malley John..... " | 19 |
| Farrell Garrett J.. " | 40 | O'Neil Barth'lmw. " | 8 |
| Finley Patrick J.. " | 22 | O'Sullivan John.. " | 39 |
| Flannery John.... " | 49 | Palmer John E.... " | 24 |
| Florence William.. " | 64 | Peck G. Herbert.. " | 53 |
| Flynn James D.... " | 74 | Pillion T. J....... " | 73 |
| Flynn John P..... " | 61 | Quinn Felix....... " | 25 |
| Gaffey Michael.... " | 16 | Ramsden Chas. L.. " | 28 |
| Gavin Michael.... " | 5 | Riley S. J........ " | 62 |
| Geary Frank P.... " | 43 | Russell Charles E.. " | 35 |
| Goodwill Justin... " | 10 | Santorra Frank... " | 42 |
| Grady Mark...... " | 31 | Schiller Charles A.. " | 17 |
| Gunning Thos. J.. " | 65 | Schulze Benj. G.... " | 37 |
| Harris William H.. " | 6 | Sheehan John..... " | 60 |
| Harvey George P.. " | 12 | Steele William C.. " | 8 |
| Havens James F.. " | 55 | Strickland Geo. E.. " | 1 |
| Heise Frank A.... " | 59 | Sullivan John F... " | 26 |
| Heise George C... " | 30 | Sullivan Peter A... " | 29 |
| Hennessey Jas. F. " | 51 | Tinker Herbert E.. " | 7 |
| Hogaboom Homer A" | 48 | Tobin William F... " | 18 |
| Johnson Edwin.... " | | Tucker Wm. E.... " | 2 |
| Lally James F..... " | 23 | Weltner Wm...... " | 63 |
| Langrish Edward J. " | 27 | Whitehead W. W.. " | 32 |

T. J. Elwood, Michael Finley, F. S. Young, D. T. Molloy, S. W. Edwards, W. F. Redmond, J. J. Powers, A. J. Williams, Frank Trask, W. M. Dower, *Special Policemen.*

Edward O'Brien, day driver; Edward Hayes, night driver of patrol wagon.

Louisa D. Hubbard, Matron; W. B. Clark, Electrician.

The force consists of one chief, one captain, one lieutenant, four sergeants, 85 regular policemen and 100 supernumeraries. For the year ending April 1, 1898, the police made 6,367 arrests—of whom 2,006 were tried by police court; 2,609 were drunkards: 260 assaults; 248 thefts; 40 burglaries, etc.; breach of peace, 317; vagrants, 588.

The police force of Hartford was organized and uniformed July, 1860. A night watch had been previously maintained since March, 1815.

### THE POLICE TELEGRAPH.

Was adopted in 1885, at an expense of $45,000, was finished Feb. 4, 1886, and has 22 stations, viz:

No. 12, Morgan and Front streets.
" 13, Main and Morgan streets.
" 14, Windsor and Avon streets.
" 15, Main and Pavilion streets.
" 16, Judson and Barbour streets.
" 21, Union Depot, Asylum street.
" 22, Main and Ann streets.
" 23, Albany avenue and East street.
" 24, Albany and Bluehills avenues.
" 25, Asylum and Woodland streets.
" 26, Sigourney and Collins streets.
" 27, Farmington avenue and Laurel street.
" 31, State and Front streets.
" 32, Sheldon and Front streets.
" 33, Commerce and Potter streets.
" 34, Main and Arch streets.
" 35, Charter Oak avenue and Union street.
" 41, Pearl street, Hook and Ladder House.
" 42, Park and Broad streets.
" 43, Zion street and Glendale avenue.
" 44, Broad and Howard streets.
" 45, Sisson avenue and Park street.
" 46, Park and Laurel streets.
" 51, Wethersfield avenue and Bond street.
" 52, Main and Congress streets.
" 53, Washington and Vernon streets.
" 54, Lafayette and Russ streets.
" 56, Maple avenue and Webster street.
" 61, Pearl street, Selectmen's office.
" 62, Trumbull street, near County building.
" 63, House of Comfort, Bushnell park.
" 72, Farmington avenue and Smith streets.

Five new boxes have been added, viz: cor. Maple av. and Webster st.; house of comfort on Bushnell Park; Laurel st. and Farmington av.; Smith st. and Farmington av.; Trumbull st. near County building.

Keys to these boxes are with the police and reputable citizens. One key fits all the locks of the outer doors. Citizens wanting police assistance must insert the key into the key hole in the center of box marked "Citizens' Key."

### CITY WEIGHERS.

| | |
|---|---|
| Ball John E. | Kellogg Robert W. |
| Bartlett Frank E. | Kilmurry William. |
| Barrows C. L. | Marvel Sylvester. |
| Belden C. R. | McCormick Michael. |
| Boyd James. | McEntee John. |
| Brewer Alfred R. | Newton Charles W. |
| Burgess Henry C. | Newton George W. |
| Burke Fred E. | North A. W. |
| Campbell John. | Perkins D. C. |
| Carpenter Wm. O. | Phelps C. R. |
| Chamberlin G. B. | Price Geo. T. |
| Chapin A. D. | Ray Frank E. |
| Charter George H. | Roberts E. D. |
| Collins Samuel. | Ryan Edward W. |
| Cooksley C. E. | Sage Edwin A. |
| Courtice Charles. | Sage Edwin W. |
| Day A. P. | Sage F. L. |
| Deming Edward. | Sage George W. |
| Elmer H. T. | Sage Harry D. |
| Farnham E. B. | Shackley F. W. |
| Foster W. H. | Skirrow R. W. |
| French G. W. | Slocumb W. R. |
| Fury M. C. | Smith Frank G. |
| Goodrich E. S. | Spencer Charles E. |
| Gunning John. | Swords Joseph F. |
| Hafey Michael J. | Strong C. H. |
| Hayward A. J. | Taft J. C. |
| Hubbell Gershom W. B. | Taft W. E. |
| Hunt W. C. | Thatcher Herbert E. |
| Jones Edwin A. | Wells Richard B. |
| Kellogg Frank S. | Woolley Arthur G |
| Work F. S. | |

# Commissioners.

*Charity Commissioners.*—E. Henry Hyde, Jr., Pres't, 1901; Thomas J. Blake, 1899; Frank S. Kellogg, 1899; Joseph F. Swords, 1898; Clarkson N. Fowler, 1900; Louis B. Haas, 1900; Wm. W. Stillman, Supt.; H. G. Bailey, Clerk; T. B. Ackerly, Physician. Office, 2 Holcomb street.

*Fire Commissioners.*—Chas. E. Billings, 1901, Pres't; George Ulrich, 1898; Daniel Readett, 1900; Ransom N. Fitzgerald, 1899; Ralph W. Cutler, 1899; John D. Bonner, 1900; George A. Reynolds, Clerk. Regular meetings, 1st and 3d Tuesday evenings each month. Office, 43 Pearl street.

*Health Commissioners.*—Mayor Miles B. Preston; Dr. Jas. Campbell, Pres't, 1900; Frank C. Sumner, 1900; John M. Holcombe, 1901; Thomas F. Kane, 1899; Samuel G. Dunham, 1899; Edward R. Doyle, 1901; Joseph B. Hall, Clerk; Harry L. Cottrell, Ass't Clerk; Patrick J. Darcy, Inspector; Dr. E. K. Root, Medical Inspector; Dr. Arthur J. Wolff, Bacteriologist. Office, 800 Main street.

*Park Commissioners.*—Patrick Garvan, Pres't, 1905; Lucius F. Robinson, Vice Pres't, 1902; Franklin G. Whitmore, Sec'y; W. DeLoss Love, 1899; Gurdon W. Russell, 1907; Geo. A. Fairfield; Willis I. Twichell, 1901; Charles E. Gross, 1903; George H. Day, 1904; Chas. Dudley Warner, 1906; Francis Goodwin, 1906. Office, 700 Main street.

*Police Commissioners.* — Mayor Miles B. Preston. President *ex officio*; Phineas H. Ingalls, 1898; Thos. A. Smith, 1898; William B. Davidson, 1899; Henry Osborn, 1900; Charles H. Lawrence, 1900; Meigs H. Whaples, 1899; Geo. N. Holcomb, Sec'y. Office 800 Main st.

*Street Commissioners.*—Charles H. Northam, Pres't; 1899; Joseph Buths, 1899; Edward J. Mulcahy, 1898; George Pope, 1900; Wm. Waldo Hyde, 1900; John R. Hills, 1901, Salary of Board $2,000, to be divided between the members. George Nevers, Clerk; Charles W. Sprague, Supt. Office, 800 Main street.

*Water Commissioners.*—John S. Hunter, President, 1900; Edward S. Cleveland, 1901; John M. Fairfield, 1901; Ernest Cady, 1900; Jeffrey O. Phelps, Jr., 1899; Ulysses H. Brockway, 1899; J. Seymour Chase, Sec'y. Meets 2d Tuesday in each month. Office, 800 Main st.

# Fire Department.

**43 Pearl st. For Commissioners, see page 677.**

An ordinance was passed by the City Council, Oct. 10, 1864, creating a paid Fire Department, and on the 24th of the same month the first Board of Fire Commissioners was elected. This new department took possession of fire apparatus, December 1st, 1864.

The Department consists of one Chief Engineer; salary $2,500; three assistant Engineers, $850; eight steam fire engines, two spare hose carriages, four wagons, one chemical engine, two hook and ladder trucks, and forty-two horses. The propeller companies having 14 men each, the horse engine companies 13 men each, officers included; the hook and ladder trucks a foreman and 20 men. At the present time there are 16,000 feet of serviceable Hose in the Department.

Superintendent of Telegraph system, salary, $1,700; Assistant Superintendent, $1,000; Engineer's, $1,000; Assistant Engineer's, Engine Driver's, Truck Driver's and Steamers' Tillermen, $900; Permanent Substitute, $1,000; Hose Driver's and Truck Tillerman, $850; Firemen—bunker, $225; lodge in the houses of the Company to which they respectively belong; Foremen $300; other call men of the Department, $200 each annually; Linemen, $800; Bunkers, $225.

*Telegraphic Fire Alarm,* costing $11,000, and bell tower over 70 feet in height, and new fire bell of 8,175 lbs. weight, erected in 1881 at an expense of $807.52 to replace the one that became cracked, which weighed 9,000 lbs. that was erected in 1867 at an expense of $9,091, with 29 miles of wire, 51 signal boxes, 17 gongs. Telephonic communication between the nine stations. In May, 1897, there were 50 miles of wire and 96 call boxes.

*Chief Engineer,* Henry J. Eaton. No. 43 Pearl st.

*Assistant Engineers*—Louis Krug, Edwin H. Williams, Hamlet P. Barber.

*Superintendent Fire Alarm,* George W. Hamilton.

*Assistant Superintendent,* Walter B. Clark.

*Linemen,* David DeMar; *Permanent Substitute,* John C. Moran.

*Engine Company No. 1.*—197 Main street.—Charles E. Wright, Foreman; William J. Smith, Engineer; Thos. A. O'Brien, Engine Driver; Herbert C. Edwards, Hose Driver; William R. Hays, Fireman.

*Engine Company No. 2.*—5 Pleasant st.—Fred. C. Krug, Foreman; George W. Kingsley, Engineer; Chas. W. Griffith, Engine Driver; David F. McSweegan, Hose Driver; Wm. C. Case, Fireman.

*Engine Company No. 3.*—124 Front st.—Charles Tarbox, Foreman; John R. Davis, Engineer; John J. McIntyre, Ass't Engineer; James Magonigal, Tillerman; Benjamin D. Bailey, Hose Driver.

*Engine Company No. 4.*—60 Ann street.—George Fatlow, Foreman; Edward Sommerman, Engineer; Charles F. Grundt, Ass't Engineer; Warren A. Bingham, Tillerman; Ernest M. Quigley, Hose Driver.

*Engine Company No. 5.*—129 Sigourney st.—Robert Marchant, Foreman; Aug. P. Lyons, Engineer; Ed. C. Woodworth, Engine Driver; George L. Stiles, Hose Driver; William N. Woodruff, Fireman.

*Engine Company No. 6.*—98 Huyshope av.—John A. Staib, Foreman; Albert B. Camp, Engineer; John Glynn, Engine Driver; John F. Dungan, Hose Driver; Herbert Bagshaw, Fireman.

*Engine Company No. 7.*—480 Windsor av.—William Senk, Foreman; Augustus Loomis, Engineer; John J. Broughel, Engine Driver; Fred C. Wood, Hose Driver; Joseph W. McClellan, Fireman.

*Engine Company No. 8.*—341 Park street.—James S. Secor, Foreman; Willis P. Barker, Engineer; Robert Magonigal, Engine Driver; Anthony F. Bolan, Hose Driver; Solomon Birmingham, Fireman.

*Hook and Ladder Company No. 1.*—275 Pearl st.—Samuel C. Cooper, Foreman; John E. Carey, Driver; Wm. J. Annis, Ass't Driver; John E. Street, Tillerman.

*Hook and Ladder Company No. 2.*—275 Pearl st.—Peter F. O'Brien, Driver; John O'Meara, Tillerman.

*Chemical Engine Company No. 1.*—43 Pearl st.—John F. Dungan, Acting Foreman and Pipeman; Thomas J. Kellhan, Driver; John G. Barnard, Assistant Driver; Dennis J. Sullivan, Pipeman.

## FIRE ALARM TELEGRAPH

Was erected and first used in this city January, 1868. Railroad time is given daily at noon and 9 P. M. by one stroke on the fire alarm bell.

Two strokes for *Fire is Out.*

Ten strokes for *General Alarm.*

Twelve strokes twice for *Military Alarm.*

Number and Location of Fire Alarm Boxes and engines which respond to first alarm; Chemical Engine to all alarms in the center of the city; and one of the Hook and Ladder Co's to all alarms.

| BOX | LOCATION. | ENGINES. |
|---|---|---|
| 12—Asylum st. cor. Union pl. | | 2-3-4-5 |
| 122—Myrtle st. cor. Edwards st. | | 4-5 |
| 123—159 High st., Foot Guard Armory,. | | 2-3-4 |
| 124—247 Pearl st. | | 1-2-3-4 |
| 13—Asylum st. cor. Farmington av. | | 2-4-5 |
| 14—Walnut st. opp. Chestnut st. | | 2-4-5 |
| 141—Lumber st. | | 2-3-4-7 |
| 142—Albany av. cor. East st. | | 2-4 |
| 143—42 Seyms st., Hartford Co. Jail, | | 2-4-7 |
| 15—1 Flower st., Pratt & Whitney Co. | | 4-5-8 |
| 16—275 Pearl st., Hook & Ladder Co. | | 1-2-3-4 |
| 17—60 Ann st., Engine 4's house, | | 1-2-3-4 |
| 18—r. 481 Asylum st., N. Y., N. H. & H. R. | | 1-4-5-8 |
| 19—Trumbull st. cor. Chapel st. | | 2-3-4 |
| 21—Asylum st. cor. Trumbull st. | | 1-2-3-4-6 |
| 213—Church st. cor. Trumbull st. | | 1-2-3-4 |
| 23—Main st. cor. Pearl st. | | 1-2-3-4-6 |
| 231—Main st. cor. Asylum st. | | 1-2-3-4-6 |
| 24—Market st. near State st. | | 1-2-3-4-6 |
| 25—124 Front st., Engine 3's house, | | 1-2-3-4-6 |
| 251—Kilbourn st. cor. Commerce st. | | 2-3-4-6 |
| 26—Grove st. cor. Commerce st. | | 1-3-4-6 |
| 27—Main st. cor. Pratt st. | | 1-2-3-4-6 |
| 28—Main st. cor. Morgan st. | | 1-2-3-4 |
| 29—Morgan st. cor. Front sts. | | 2-3-4 |
| 31—Arch st. cor. Front st. | | 1-3-4-6 |
| 312—Charter Oak av. cor. Governor st. | | 1-3-6 |
| 313—40 Governor st. | | 1-3-4-6 |
| 314—Sheldon st. cor. Taylor st. | | 1-3-4-6 |
| 315—Governor st. cor Sheldon st. | | 1-3-4-6 |
| 32—Main st. cor. Gold st. | | 1-2-3-4-6 |
| 34—15 Trumbull st. cor. Hicks st. | | 1-2-3-4-6 |
| 35—Main st. cor. Elm st. | | 1-2-3-4-6 |
| 36—Capitol av. cor. West st. | | 1-2-3-4-6 |
| 37—Colt's Armory, | | 1-3-4-6 |
| 38—Main st. cor. Buckingham st. | | 1-3-4-6 |
| 39—98 Huyshope av. Engine 6's house,.. | | 1-3-6 |
| 41—436 Capitol av. front Pope's Factory, | | 1-4-5-8 |
| 412—Russ st. cor Lawrence st. | | 1-5-8 |
| 42—Park st. cor. Washington st. | | 1-4-8 |
| 421—Buckingham st. cor. Cedar st. | | 1-4-8 |
| 423—Jefferson st. cor. Washington st. | | 1-4-8 |
| 43—Russ st. cor. Oak st. | | 1-8 |
| 45—Summit st. cor. New Britain av. | | 1-8 |
| 451—White st. cor. Fairfield av | | 1-8 |
| 46—Zion st. opp. Vernon st. | | 1-8 |
| 461—Hamilton st. cor. Wellington st. | | 5-8 |
| 47—Park st. cor. Lawrence st. | | 1-8 |
| 471—341 Park st. Engine 8's house | | 1-8 |
| 48—Broad st. cor. Vernon st. | | 1-6-8 |
| 5—197 Main st., Engine 1's house, | | 1-4-6-8 |
| 51—Congress st. cor. Maple av. | | 1-6-8 |
| 512—Franklin av. cor. Pawtucket st. | | 1-6 |
| 513—Morris st. cor. Franklin av. | | 1-6 |
| 514—20 Hudson st., Hartford Hospital,.. | | 1-6-8 |
| 52—109 Wethersfield av. | | 1-6 |
| 521—Wethersfield av. cor. Preston st. | | 1-6 |
| 522—Wethersfield av. opp. Union Grove, | | 1-6 |
| 53—Washington st. cor. Retreat av. | | 1-6-8 |
| 54—Wethersfield av. opp. Alden st. | | 1-6 |

| BOX. | LOCATION. | ENGINES. |
|---|---|---|
| 56—New Britain av. cor. Washington st. | | 1-8 |
| 561—Bond st. cor. Maple av. | | 1-8 |
| 57—80 Washington st. Retreat for Insane, | | 1-4-8 |
| 6—Asylum st. opp. Sumner st. | | 4-5 |
| 61—Asylum st. cor. Smith st. | | 4-5 |
| 62—129 Sigourney st., Engine 5's house,. | | 4-5 |
| 621—150 Farmington av., Cathedral,... | | 4-5-8 |
| 63—Farmington av. cor. Gillett st. | | 4-5 |
| 64—Park st. cor. Sisson av. | | 1-8 |
| 641—Smith st. cor. Davenport st. | | 5-8 |
| 642—Park st. cor. Heath st. | | 1-8 |
| 65—Capitol av. cor. Laurel st. | | 1-5-8 |
| 651—581 Capitol av. | | 1-5-8 |
| 652—Park and Laurel sts., (Pope's),... | | 1-5-8 |
| 67—Sigourney st. cor. Cushman st. | | 1-5-8 |
| 7—Albany av. cor. Williams st. | | 2-4 |
| 71—Woodland st. cor. Collins st. | | 4-5 |
| 712—Collins st. west of Sigourney st. | | 4-5 |
| 713—Ashley st. cor. Huntington st. | | 4-5 |
| 72—Holcombe and Vine sts., Alms-house, | | 2-7 |
| 73—Garden st. cor. Collins st. | | 4-5 |
| 74—Albany av. cor. Bluehills av. | | 2-4 |
| 75—23 Vine st., opp. T. J. Blake's, | | 2-7 |
| 8—Main st. cor. Canton st. | | 2-7 |
| 81—Main st. cor. Capen st. | | 2-7 |
| 812—Main st. cor. Mahl av | | 2-4-7 |
| 82—Clark st. cor. Westland st. | | 2-7 |
| 821—Charlotte st. cor. Barbour st. | | 2-7 |
| 83—Main st. cor. Frankfort st. | | 2-7 |
| 831—480 Windsor av. Engine 7's house, | | 2-7 |
| 84—Capen st. cor. Garden st. | | 2-7 |
| 9—Main st. cor. High st. | | 2-4-7 |
| 91—5 Pleasant st., Engine 2's house,... | | 2-3-4-7 |
| 92—Windsor st. cor. Pleasant st. | | 3-4-7 |
| 93—165 Windsor st. | | 2-4-7 |

### FIRES IN THIS CITY

*From April 1, 1897, to April 1, 1898.*
*Amount of Losses not estimated by the Department this year.*

| 1897. | LOCATION. | OCCUPANT OR OWNER. |
|---|---|---|
| April 14, | Vine, | S. C. Arnold. |
| " 25, | Preston, | M. Harris. |
| " 26, | Dutch Point, | Conn. River Lumber Co. |
| May 2, | 48 Vernon, | Hartford Street R'y Co. |
| " 5, | 320 Asylum. | |
| " 27, | 133 Maple, | C. Silberman. |
| " 30, | 1090 Main, | Frank H. Mather. |
| June 1, | Asylum & Ford, | A. M. Hurlburt Est. |
| " 15, | rear 470 Bond, | J. Sullivan, |
| " 18, | Main and Grove, | Hartford Times. |
| " 27, | 324 Asylum. | |
| " 28, | Woodland, | B. R. Allen Est. |
| July 5, | 31 Pearl. | |
| " 5, | r. No. 6 Eng. House, | Est. Samuel Colt. |
| " 7, | 48 Park. | |
| " 27, | 12 Wells, | Barrett Bros. |
| Aug. 19, | P. R. & N. E. R. R. | P. R. & N. E. R. R. |
| " 21, | Sheldon & Governor. | |
| " 24, | 11 Charter Oak, | Mrs. Thos. G. Welles. |
| " 29, | 159 Main, | Dix & Co. |
| " 29, | 90 Front, | A. Augusta. |
| " 30, | 17 Charles, | Jos. Ferranti. |
| " 31, | 218 Sheldon, | Mrs. Clarissa Holcomb. |
| Sept. 5, | 88 Woodbine, | Perkins Electric Switch Co. |
| " 18, | Sanford. | |
| Oct. 8, | Park and Putnam, | W. Solomon. |

**1897.**   **LOCATION.**   **OCCUPANT OR OWNER.**

Oct.  4, 63 Pleasant.
"   4, 83 Washington,  S. Maslen.
"   5, Woodland.  W. H. Bliss Sons.
"  19, Glendale,  P. Horan.
"  19, Maple and Fairfield, J. Perango.
"  22, 206 Front,  Hartford Pants Co.
"  22, Maple & Fairf'd, Ernest Hannon and others.
"  23, 219 Sheldon.
"  26, 615 Main,  D. H. Murphy.
"  29, 115 Windsor st.  International Bakery.
"  30, American row.
Nov. 19, 84 Morgan,  K. Greenberg.
"  25, Pleasant.
"  26, 41 Winthrop,  M. J. Goodale.
"  30, 79 Governor.
Dec.  2, Potter and Ellery.
"   2, 1074 Broad.
"   3, 245 Pearl.
"  22, rear 212 Oak,  A. Dallas.
"  25, Brown,  W. H. Relyea.
"  26, So. Ann and Hicks, F. J. Knox.
"  28, Winthrop opposite Ely.
**1898.**
Jan.  3, American row,  P. Berry Sons.
"   3, 1 Cushman,  Pratt & Cady Co.
"   5, 52 Chestnut,  Mrs. W. H. Coughlin.
"  13, 510 Main,  Frank Nelson.
"  15, 90 Main,  Mr. Fagan.
"  16, 52 Bellevue,  I. & J. Silver.
"  18, 191 Front,  W. Lutwack.
"  21, 436 Asylum,  Kingsley Co.
"  25, 19 Kilbourn.
"  30, 97 Windsor st.  J. J. Flanigan.
Feb. 20, rear 577 Main.
"  26, Main and Pratt,  Sage, Allen & Co.
Mar.  7, 120 Albany.
"   7, 484 Main,  Germania Hall.
"  10, So. side Capen.
"  14, Ellery.
"  15, Park r. Heath.
"  26, 204 High,  Mrs. John Sullivan.

## MAYORS OF THE CITY OF HARTFORD.

Until 1825, the Mayor held his office during the pleasure of General Assembly; since elected for two years.

THOMAS SEYMOUR,*  June 18, 1784—May 28, 1812
CHAUNCEY GOODRICH, June  8, 1812—Sept.  9, 1815
JONATHAN BRACE,  Sept.  8, 1815—Nov. 22, 1824
NATHANIEL TERRY,  Nov. 22, 1824—Mar. 28, 1831
THOMAS S. WILLIAMS,  Mar. 28, 1831—April 27, 1835
HENRY L. ELLSWORTH,† April 27, 1835—June 15, 1835
JARED GRISWOLD,‡  June 15, 1835—Nov. 22, 1835
HENRY HUDSON,  April 18, 1836—April 20, 1840
THOMAS K. BRACE,†  April 20, 1840—April 17, 1843
AMOS M. COLLINS,  April 17, 1843—April 21, 1847
PHILIP RIPLEY,  April 19, 1847—April 21, 1851
EBENEZER FLOWER,  April 18, 1851—April 18, 1853
WM. J. HAMERSLEY,  April 18, 1853—April 17, 1854
HENRY C. DEMING,  April 17, 1854—April 12, 1858
TIMOTHY M. ALLYN,  Apr l 12, 1858—April  8, 1860
HENRY C. DEMING,†  April  9, 1860—Jan. 27, 1862
CHARLES BENTON,§  Feb. 10, 1862—April 14, 1862
WM. J. HAMERSLEY,  April 14, 1862—April 11, 1864
ALLYN S. STILLMAN,  April 11, 1864—April  9, 1866
CHARLES R. CHAPMAN, April  9, 1866—April  1, 1872
HENRY C. ROBINSON,  April  1, 1872—April  6, 1874
JOSEPH H. SPRAGUE,  April  6, 1874—April  1, 1878
GEORGE G. SUMNER,  April  1, 1878—April  5, 1880
MORGAN G. BULKELEY, April  5, 1880—April  2, 1888
JOHN G. ROOT,  April  2, 1888—April  7, 1890
HENRY C. DWIGHT,  April  7, 1890—April  4, 1892
WM. WALDO HYDE,  April  4, 1892—April  2, 1894
LEVERETT BRAINARD,  April  2, 1894—April  7, 1896
MILES B. PRESTON,  April  7, 1896—

*Resigned to the General Assembly. †Resigned. ‡Died in office. §Elected by Court of Common Council.

## Hartford Water Works.

OFFICE 800 MAIN STREET.

John S. Hunter, President and Sup't; J. Seymour Chase, Secretary; W. E. Johnson, Engineer in Charge at Reservoirs; William Russell, Bookkeeper; Fred. D. Berry, Assistant Bookkeeper; Albert A. Fox, Inspector; Dudley W. Havens, Assistant Inspector; Bartholomew Dwyer, Foreman Main Pipe Dep't; Thomas Carmody, Foreman of Service Pipe Dep't; Lawrence Lowe, Foreman of Repairs and Pumping Station.

For Commissioners, see page 677.

Bills due May 1 and Nov. 1—5 per cent. added ten days after due—1 per cent. on 1st day of each month after.

Surveys for these works were commenced Oct. 1853; ground broke June, 1854 and first pumping of water, Oct. 23, 1855. The engines and pumps were used in supplying water to the Garden Street Reservoir from the Connecticut river up to Jan. 2, 1867, at 2 P. M., at which time water from West Hartford was substituted.

Pumps were started Oct. 3, 1891, 2.30 P.M., and run till Dec. 8th; they were also run Dec. 22d to the 30th inst., to supply a large part of the city, owing to the failure in the supply of the reservoirs. Its hourly capacity is 154,000 gallons for delivering at reservoir, which is at an elevation of 125 feet above the river, and 1½ miles distant from it. The load upon the engine at low water, and with a full Reservoir, is 11,934 pounds.

The pier in the river, to protect the receiving pipe, is where at low water, there is 12 feet in depth, the water running into a well 140 feet from the river.

The ORIGINAL GARDEN STREET RESERVOIR, 97-175 Garden street, is connected by 6,879 feet of 16 inch iron pipe, with Pumps on Water st.; holds 8,600,000 gallons.

The head is as follows:—

| | Garden st. Reservoir. | West H'fd Reservoir. |
|---|---|---|
| Main street near Trumbull street, | 52 feet. | 187 feet. |
| "   " the Tunnel, | 67 " | 202 " |
| "   " Temple street, | 57 " | 192 " |
| " in front of City Hall, | 66 " | 201 " |
| " on Stone Bridge, | 83 " | 218 " |
| " by South Church, | 73 " | 208 " |
| At Charter Oak place, highest point, | 51 " | 186 " |
| Highest point on Capitol grounds, | 40 " | 175 " |
| Washington st. at Buckingham st., | 43 " | 178 " |
| "   " Park street, | 44 " | 179 " |
| Spring street, corner Myrtle street, | 52 " | 187 " |
| Windsor avenue, at Arsenal Gate, | 44 " | 179 " |
| Front street, at State street, | 98 " | 233 " |
| "   " Morgan street, | 101 " | 236 " |
| Pleasant street, at Winthrop st., | 68 " | 208 " |
| "   " Windsor street, | 96 " | 231 " |

THE WEST HARTFORD RESERVOIR was completed and water furnished the city therefrom at 2 o'clock P. M., January 2d, 1867, at which time the pumps ceased working, and have been used since only occasionally.

The receipts from Water Rents collected for the year ending March 1, 1898, amounted to $238,576.22; from sale of pipe, etc., $5,117.11; cash on hand, March 1, 1898, $14,435.38; total receipts, $258,128.71. Disbursements as follows: Construction, $66,705.80; repairs, $16,507.60; current expenses, $39,083.74; interest on water bonds, $43,862.47; redemption of water bonds, $45,000.00; cash on hand, $46,969.60; total disbursements, $258,128.71.

Total consumption of water for the year ending March 1, 1869, when it was all measured at the pumping works, was 700,000,000 gallons. Under the direct distribution from the West Hartford reservoir during 1876 was 1,808,500,000 gallons, equal to 4,954,795 gallons per day. During the drought of 1879 the average daily supply from Sept. 22, 1879, to Jan. 23, 1880, pumped from the river, for use in the eastern part of the city, was 3,298,315 gallons, which shows an average daily supply to the city of 6,000,000 gallons; in 1897 the average daily supply was 10,000,000 gallons.

Reservoir No. 1 is five miles from City Hall, and at high water flows 82 acres. Its capacity of 84 feet in depth is 145,985,543 United States gallons. The altitude of the reservoir at top water above low water of Connecticut River is 260 feet, and gives a head at the City Hall of 185 feet over the old works.

Reservoir No. 2 is 1¼ miles beyond Reservoir No. 1, covering a water surface of 49 acres with 41 feet depth and capacity of 283,694,375 gallons. Forty acres of land was purchased in 1890 for additional water shed.

Reservoir No. 3, is located about one mile northwesterly from Reservoir No. 1, and was completed October 30, 1875, with a capacity, when filled to depth of 36 feet, of 145,595,829 gallons, covering 25 42-100 acres at top water line. Total cost $59,117.78.

Reservoir No. 4, located in towns of New Britain and Farmington. It is 8½ miles from the city by the south road. The reservoir overflows 160 of the 188 acres. The land cost $9,764.90; construction, $84,124.86. Its capacity of 20 feet in depth is 601,358,592 gallons.

Reservoir No. 5, on Mine Brook, about half a mile from No. 1, with a capacity 20 feet in depth of 94,132,-000 gallons; constructed in 1884, at an expense of $18,549 and paid from receipts of water rents.

Reservoir No. 6 is located about 2 miles north of the first water shed, and covers about 109 acres, with a capacity 27 feet in depth of 765,115,175 gallons; it was completed Oct. 1, 1895, and cost $594,731.06.

Making a total supply of over 2,000,000,000 gallons in the six reservoirs.

Mountain Stream Canal has been thoroughly excavated, bringing a supply of water from three rivulets into Reservoir No. 2, constructed in 1888.

Brandy Brook Canal, 1½ miles long, 16 feet deep, 12 feet wide at bottom, connecting Brandy Brook with Reservoir No. 4, constructed in 1883.

Total amount of cast iron pipe now in use is 112 miles and 260 feet.

There are 8,672 service pipes now in use.

769 Public hydrants and 497 water meters are in use

The total construction outlay since this water system has been introduced, has been $2,734,869.82; bonded debt is $970,000.00.

From the commencement of these works in March, 1898, the amount received for water rents has been $3,565,558.80. Paid for repairs and current expenses, $1,175,125.58; paid interest, $1,845,875.02.

### UNITED STATES CUSTOM HOUSE.
#### DISTRICT OF HARTFORD.

JOHN H. BROCKLESBY, Collector, No. 65 State st., Hartford. ARTHUR E. HOWARD, Special Deputy Collector and Inspector; Philip G. Gorton, Deputy Collector and Inspector; Robert D. Stevens, Deputy Collector and Inspector; Thomas W. Gunshanan, Deputy Collector and Inspector; Wilbur H. Blake, Sidney W. Andrews, Storekeepers. Offices in Federal Building, 65 State st.

Hartford as the port of entry. The district of Hartford comprises the waters and shores of the towns of Lyme, Saybrook, Clinton, Westbrook, Old Saybrook, Chester, Essex, Haddam, East Haddam, Middletown, Cromwell, Chatham, Portland, Wethersfield, Rocky Hill, Glastonbury, Hartford, East Hartford, Windsor, Windsor Locks, East Windsor, South Windsor, Suffield and Enfield, in Connecticut, and Springfield in Massachusetts, in which Hartford shall be the port of entry; and Saybrook, Clinton, Westbrook, Old Saybrook, Essex, Haddam, East Haddam, Chester, Portland, Cromwell, Rocky Hill, Middletown, Chatham, Wethersfield, Glastonbury, East Hartford and Enfield, Connecticut, and Springfield, Mass., ports of delivery.

## Military Companies;
#### BRIGADE OFFICERS, C. N. G.

Governor and Staff, see State Officers.

Russell Frost, South Norwalk, Brigadier General; Francis G. Beach, New Haven, Ass't Adj. General; John H. Wade, Norwalk, Inspector; W. H. Marigold, Bridgeport, Quartermaster; James K. Crofut, Simsbury, Commissary; Henry S. Terrell, Winsted, Inspector of Small Arms, etc.; Tracy Waller, New London, Judge Advocate; Wilbur S. Watson, Danbury, Medical Director; Howard A. Giddings, Hartford, Signal Officer; Robert G. Mitchell, Norwalk; Lucius H. Fuller, Putnam, Aide-de-Camp.

THE CONNECTICUT NATIONAL GUARD is composed of Battery A, Four Regiments and 1st Separate Company (colored) Infantry, Signal Corps, Machine Gun Battery, and Naval Battalion, numbering 2,791 enlisted officers and men.

#### LOCATED IN THE CITY OF HARTFORD.

[The following returns of the various companies of the 1st Regiment were made before they were called into the regular U. S. Service May 4, 1898.]

All Hartford Companies of 1st Regiment C. N. G., meet at their Armory, 51 Elm st., which was dedicated with appropriate military ceremonies, March 16, 1880. The organization of the 1st Regiment dates June, 1672.

The First Regiment was composed of ten Companies, Band, and a Hospital Corps. Five companies were in Hartford; three in New Britain; one in South Manchester; one in Rockville. Regimental headquarters, Hartford.

#### FIELD, STAFF AND NON-COMMISSIONED OFFICERS, FIRST REGIMENT.

Charles L. Burdett, Hartford, Colonel; Henry S. Redfield, Hartford, Lieut. Colonel; John Hickey, South Manchester, Edward Schulze, Hartford, Majors; Jonathan M. Wainwright, Hartford, Adj.; Patrick J. Cosgrove, Frank E. Johnson, Hartford, Battalion Adjts.; Arthur H. Bronson, Hartford, Quartermaster; Raymond G. Keeney, Somersville, Paymaster; Thomas F. Rockwell, Rockville, Surgeon; H. Walter Murliss, Hartford, J. B. McCook, Hartford, Ass't Surgeons; Henry H. Kelsey, Hartford, Chaplain; Edward E. Mosely, Sergeant Major; John D. Milne, Rockville; Thomas J. Hines, Hartford, Battalion Sergeant Majors; William S. Inglis, Hartford, Quartermaster Serg't; Albert C. Bill, Hartford, Com. Serg't; Charles L. Hubbard, Hospital Steward; William C. Steele, Drum Major, Hartford; William H. Scheu, Chief Trumpeter, New Britain; Frank H. Bilson, Rockville; Horace X. Saunders, New Britain, Color Sergeants; Alfred B. Pimm, Hartford, Corporal and Orderly.

### FIRST SECTION, BRIGADE SIGNAL CORPS.

Philip E. Fairfield, Lieut. and Pres't; Robert A. Wadsworth, 1st Serg't; Irving L. Wittsie, Serg't; Arthur P. Towne, Charles H. Whitney, Corporals; Charles H. Whitney, Treas.; Philip E. Fairfield, Chas. P. Carter, Arthur P. Towne, Ex. Com. Organized Sept. 1, 1889. Drills Tuesday evenings, November to May, at 51 Elm st. Annual meeting in April.

### HARTFORD GERMANIA GUARD.
#### COMPANY A, 1st REGT. CONN. NATIONAL GUARD

James C. Bailey, Capt.; Edward E. Lamb, 1st Lieut.; Charles F. Wolf, 2d Lieut.; Frank J. Williams, 1st Serg't; Otto Mantel, Q. M.; Joseph R. Neddo, George A. Roemer, Daniel D. Lane, Wm. H. Leslie, Sergeants; William H. Leslie, Rec. Sec'y; James C. Bailey, Treas.; George E. Berry, F. Sec'y; Charles F. Wolf, Charles S. Riley, Otto Mantel, Executive Committee. Drills Thursday evenings at 51 Elm st. Business meeting, first Thursday of each month. Organized January 23, 1872. 68 men.

## HILLYER GUARD.

**COMPANY B, 1st REGT. CONN. NATIONAL GUARD.**
John F. Moran, Capt.; Frank E. Shea, 1st Lieut.; Patrick A. Farrell, 2d Lieut.; J. W. Kennedy, 1st Sergt.; Henry Brooks, Q. M. Sergt.; T. J. Leahy, E. F. Ahern, D. F. Keleher, W. T. Slater, Sergts.; J. J. McMahon, J. A. Barlow, J. F. Dahill, M. W. Malumphy, G. Covey, W. Smith, Corporals; J. F. Moran, Treas.; J. J. McMahon, Rec. Sec'y; John J. Nagle, F. Sec'y; P. A. Farrell, John A. Barlow, Thos. J. Skelley, Executive Committee; Patrick A. Farrell, Historian. Drills Tuesday evenings at 51 Elm st. Regular meeting, 2d Tuesday in each month. Annual meeting 2d Tuesday in January. Organized September, 1862. Reorganized September, 1865. 68 men.

## HARTFORD CITY GUARD.

**COMPANY F, 1ST REGT. CONN. NATIONAL GUARD.**
Charles W. Newton, Capt.; George W. Ripley, 1st Lient.; Frank H. Smith, 2d Lieut.; M. H. Whittlesev, 1st Serg't.; A. D. Pierce, Q. M. Sergeant; W. H. Bruce, W. H. Talcott, Jns. W. Dennis, H. H. Dunlap, Sergeants; A. M. Bond, C. E. Whiting, J. P. Tuttle, H. F. Billings, W. C. Simmons, G. S. Douthwaite, E. S. Mugford, H. G. Bailey, Corporals; Foster E. Harvey, Treas.; Frank M. Jones, Sec'y; W. H. Talcott, Collector; Charles W. Newton, M. H. Whittelsey, J. P. Tuttle, Executive Committee. Annual meeting, 2d Monday in January. Regular meeting, 2d Monday of each month. Drills Monday evenings at 51 Elm st. Organized Jan. 8, 1861. 68 men.

## HARTFORD LIGHT GUARD.

**COMPANY H, 1ST REGT. CONN. NATIONAL GUARD**
William E. Mahoney, Capt.; Wm. A. Sparks, 1st Lieut.; James Smith, 2d Lieut.; Fred F. Connolly, Q. M. Sergeant; P. Jarvis White, John F. Landrigan, Thomas J. Coyle, Maurice F. Foley, John J. Grady, Serg'ts; William F. Duffy, David J. Garrity, P. Callaghan, F. J. Mather, Joseph Healy, William Clarke, John Stevens, John F. White, Corporals; Joseph P. Healey, Fin. Sec'y; F. P. Horan, Rec. Sec'y; John F. Landrigan, Treas.; E. J. Crowley, W. H. Mahoney, J. J. Grogan, Executive Committee. Drills Friday evenings at 51 Elm st. Annual meeting, 2d Friday in Jan. Regular meeting, 2d Friday in each month. Organized 1835. Re-organized October 22, 1872. 68 men.

## COMPANY K.

**1ST REGT. CONN. NATIONAL GUARD.**
Henry H. Saunders, Capt.; E. H. Waterman, 1st Lieut; Nathaniel G. Valentine, 2d Lieut.; Reginald Birney, 1st Serg't; Benjamin N. Bull, Q. M. and Com. Serg't; S. G. Huntington, W. C. Prescott, R. W. DeLamater, G. S. Batterson, Serg'ts; H. L. Huntington, H. T. Holt, H. S. King, A. A. Hunt, J. D. Boniface, R. L. Beebe, Charles S. Stern, C. A. Carroll, Corporals; Robert L. Beebe, Fin. Sec'y; W. C. Prescott, Treas.; F. D. Rood, Rec. Sec'y. Monthly meetings 1st Wednesday evening. Annual meeting 1st Wednesday in Dec. Drills Wednesday evening at 51 Elm st. Organized Feb. 10, 1879. 62 members.

## FIRST SECTION MACHINE GUN BATTERY,
**CONN. NATIONAL GUARD.**
John D. Bonner, 1st Lieut.; Frank A. Keen, John A. Wood, Serg'ts; Osmyn P. Clarke, Henry R. Haynes, Corporals; Emil D'Arche, Secretary, 46 Canton st.; Henry R. Haynes, Treasurer. Organized July 1, 1886. Drills Thursday evenings at 51 Elm street. Monthly meetings last Thursday of each month. Annual meeting last Thursday in January.

## SECOND DIVISION NAVAL BATTALION, C. N. G.
Felton Parker, Lieut. Comd'g; Hermann F. Cuntz, Lieut. (Jr. Gr.); Louis F. Middlebrook, Lyman Root, Ensigns; Daniel S. Morrell, Edward H. Crowell, Bontswain's Mates; Robert C. Northam, F. G. Blakeslee,

Gunner's Mates; Philip D. Burnham, Walter L. Meek, James H. Morgan, Samuel H. Havens, Coxswains; Alanson H. Wightman, Fred E. Bosworth, Quartermasters; Herbert G. Bissell, Bugler; R. D. Chapin, Custodian; Harry Y. Nutter, Treas.; Richard B. Wells, Fin. Sec'y; Hugh I. Miller, Rec. Sec'y. Organized, May 12, 1896. Drills Wednesday evenings 7 P. M. Civil meetings 2d Wednesday of each month at 51 Elm street. 85 men.

## FIRST CO. GOVERNOR'S FOOT GUARD.
E. Henry Hyde, Jr., Major-commandant; Robert R. Pease, Captain and 1st Lieut.; Fred R. Bill 2d Lieut.; George Hays, 3d Lieut.; Wm. E. A. Bulkeley, 4th Lieut. and Adj.; Fred J. Dole, Ensign; C. C. Strong, Treas. and Paymaster; M. M. Johnson, Surg.; A. G. Cook, Ass't Surg.; Rev. J. W. Bradin, Chaplain; G. H. Folts, Engineer; L. R. Cheney, Inspector; Austin Brainard, Judge Advocate; Wm. B. Davidson, Qr. Master; Henry Bryant, Commissary; G. A. Cornell, Sergt. Major; Edson Session, Q. M. Sergeant; W. H. Foster, Com. Sergt.; E. J. Andrews, Asst. Com. Sergt.; T. R. Shannon, Hospital Steward; T. H. Goodrich, Signal Sergt.; T. Hooker, Ord. Sergt.; Albert F. Wood, Ass't Ord. Sergt.; A. H. Brooks, J. E. Tennyson, Color Sergeants; E. E. Johnson, T. J. Lewis, Color Corporals; Geo. E. Cox, A. E. Snow, Harry Prutting, Wm. H. Wilson, W. L. Fenn, William Melrose, H. S. Ellsworth, T. W. Laiman, Sergeants; J. C. Pratt, E. W. Alexander, A. H. Speath, Hugo E. Patz, C. E. Stedman, J. C. Gorton, F. H. Forbes, R. D. Condray, Corporals; J. C. Pratt, G. J. A. Neadele, Auditors; Warren T. Bartlett, Rec. Sec'y; Thos. F. Pye, Jr., Clerk; H. S. Ellsworth, Collector; Armory, 159 High street, cor. Foot Guard place. Chartered Oct. 19, 1771. Annual meeting in April. Drills Monday evenings. 112 men.

## FIRST CO.—GOVERNOR'S HORSE GUARD.
Gilbert P. Hurd, Maj. Com.; Charles B. Rhodes, Capt. and 1st Lieut.; William H. Shannon, 2d Lieut.; Alfred T. Rich, Cornet; Joseph A. Prisk, Q. M.; John B. Clapp, Capt. and Adj't; Joseph E. Root, Surgeon; Dominick DeBonis, Ass't Surgeon; Clarence W. Allen, Commissary; Henry D. Middleberger, Inspector; Jas. R. Goodrich, Paymaster; Jared B. Standish, Engineer; Joel C. Taft, Ass't Q. M.; Henry Lewis, Herbert W. Wells, Chas. H. Dillings, Fred R. Cunliffe, Lieuts.; C. M. D. Brondwell, Serg't Major; Richard P. Lyman, Hospital Steward; Fred A. Hill, Harry Treadwell, Q. Sergts.; Wm. Church, Com. Sergt.; Horace L. Center, Vet. Sergt.; William A. Griffith, Alden J. Allen, D J. Mullane, Geo. I. Whitehead, Charles C. Hutchings. J. H. Trumbull, Geo. A. Wilczarlk, Sergts.; John F. Butler, Herbert S. Fowler, Color Sergts.; E. C. Lindsley, William F. Simon, Fred W. Bowe, R. W. Cunliffe, Harry Young, C. A. Vining, W. G. Smith, Wm. A. Hinds, Corporals; Daniel J. Mullane, Secretary; Henry Lewis, Treas. Armory, 450 Main st. Chartered May 8, 1778. About 100 men. Drills Monday evenings. Annual meeting third week in January.

## PUTNAM PHALANX.
J. N. Shedd, Major; Henry F. Smith, Adjutant; H. B. Philbrick, Chief of Staff; B. W. Edwards, Secretary, P. O. Box, 828; Wm. S. Dwyer, Treasurer; Sidney E. Clarke, Historian and Judge Advocate; W. H. Barnard, Quartermaster; Alexander Harbison, Inspector; E. M. Huntsinger, Paymaster; P. D. Peltier, Surgeon; Francis P. Bacheler, Chaplain; F. H. Richards, Engineer; A. E. Brooks, Commissary; Miles B. Preston, Ass't Inspector; Luther A. Davison, Ass't Surgeon; Cyrus G. Beckwith, Assistant Paymaster; William J. McConville, Ass't Engineer; Arthur M. Wilson, Ass't Quartermaster; W. H. Lathrop, Ass't Commissary; Frank H. Johnston, Sergeant Major; William C. Steele, Drum Major; George E. Strickland, James O. Griswold, Standard Bearers; DeForest Sellew, William C. Smith, Color Guards; J. N. Shedd, C. B. Andrus, Geo.

W. Scailes, F. H. Richards, H. B. Philbrick, Henry Bickford, Executive Committee. Active members, 219; veterans, 9; associate members, 22; life members, 48; musicians, 14—total, 307.
*First Company*—Charles B. Andrus, Captain.
*Second Company*—George W. Scailes, Captain.
*Veteran Corps*—L. W. Bartlett, Captain.
Organized Aug. 26, 1858. Incorporated Mar. 9, 1877. Independent military organization consisting of two active companies and a veteran corps. Annual meeting, February 22. Regular meeting, 1st Wednesday in each month. Armory, 6 Haynes st. cor. Pearl st.

### VETERAN ASSOC'N, HARTFORD CITY GUARD.
John B. Clapp, Pres't; James R. Stevens, Vice Pres't; Henry P. Hitchcock, Sec'y; Ward W. Jacobs, Treas.; James P. Taylor, James W. Cheney, J. D. Parsons, Ex. Com.; Charles T. Wells, Historian. Annual meeting 2d Wednesday in Jan. Organized in 1866.

### FIRST CO. GOV. FOOT GUARD VET'N CORPS.
J. H. White, Pres't; R. D. Burdick, Wm. B. Clark, Vice Pres'ts; Geo. P. Merritt, Sec'y; H. J. Case, Fin. Sec'y; A. C. J. Williams, Treas. and Major; C. E. Shelton, Captain and 1st Lieut.; F. H. Dean, Thomas Oakes, Geo. S. Penfield, Lieuts.; George P. Merritt, Ensign; J. H. White, R. D. Burdick, Wm. B. Clark, A. C. J. Williams, Fred A. West, Edward Mahl, Ex. Com.; Chas. E. Gilbert, Historian; William S. Dwyer, Ass't Historian. Organized March, 1870. Annual meeting 1st Tuesday in October. Quarterly meetings 1st Tuesday in January, April and July.

### VETERAN CITY GUARD BATTALION.
Edwin Strong, Major; Edward Reisel, Adjutant; Howard N. Hinckley, Quartermaster; H. C. Dwight, Judge Advocate; Geo. L. Parmelee, Surgeon; P. W. Newton, Hospital Steward; Fred C. Burnham, Sergt. Major; L. P. Broadhurst, Sec'y and Treas.; Edwin Strong, Curtis P. Gladding, A. Harbison, A. W. Green, L. P. Broadhurst, Edward Reisel, Chas. T. Wells, Executive Committee.
*Company A*—Norman L. Hope, Captain.
*Company B*—Frank B. Wilson, Captain.
Incorporated April, 1885. Organized in 1877. Members, 174. Annual meeting 2d Wednesday in March.

### COMPANY K. VETERAN CORPS.
Charles S. Robbins, Capt.; John D. Candee, 1st Lieut.; Henry S. Redfield, 2d Lieut.; Charles H. Slocum, 1st Serg't; George N. Holcomb, 2d Serg't; Howard H. Keep, Sec'y; Hubert W. Chapman, Treas.; Wm. B. Dwight, Historian; Silas H. Cornwall, Chas. H. Slocum, Frank E. Johnson, Executive Committee. Organized March 2, 1887. 130 members. Annual meeting 1st Tuesday in February.

### HILLYER GUARD VETERAN ASSOCIATION.
———— President; Edward J. Claffey, Vice Pres't; Dennis J. Murphy, Sec'y; August J. Meyer, Treas.; James Cunningham, Michael J. Hafev, Patrick J. Cosgrove, Thos. F. Flannigan, William E. Hogan, Thos. J. Ward, Executive Committee; Chas. J. Dillon, Collector. Organized Nov. 1882. Meets 2d Thursday evening quarterly. Annual meeting in June.

### HORSE GUARD VETERAN ASSOCIATION.
C. B. Boardman, Pres't; C. L. Perrington, Sec'y and Treas.; John Spencer, Collector.

### LIGHT GUARD VETERANS.
W. M. Clark, Pres't; E. C. Stone, Vice Pres't; J. E. Ball, Sec'y; G. W. Lynch, Treas.; C. H. Patterson, W. J. Collins, J. J. Grady, Ex. Com. Organized 1835. Reorganized 1872. Meets 2d and 4th Thursday at Armory, 51 Elm street.

## Credit Table
### FOR THE USE OF MERCHANTS.

| Date. | Four Months. | Six Months. | Eight Months. |
|---|---|---|---|
| JANUARY. | MAY. | JULY. | SEPT. |
| FEB. | JUNE. | AUGUST. | OCT. |
| MARCH. | JULY. | SEPT. | NOV. |
| APRIL. | AUGUST. | OCT. | DEC. |
| MAY. | SEPT. | NOV. | JANUARY. |
| JUNE. | OCT. | DEC. | FEB. |
| JULY. | NOV. | JANUARY. | MARCH. |
| AUGUST. | DEC. | FEB. | APRIL. |
| SEPT. | JANUARY. | MARCH. | MAY. |
| OCT. | FEB. | APRIL. | JUNE. |
| NOV. | MARCH. | MAY. | JULY. |
| DEC. | APRIL. | JUNE. | AUGUST. |

### SAVINGS BANKS IN CONNECTICUT.
As reported Oct. 1, 1897, by the Bank Commissioners to the Legislature of Connecticut, there were 89 Savings Banks, holding $165,969,797.95 of deposits, and with total assets of $166,175,213.67, being an increase over last year in deposits of $8,284,253.09. Whole number of depositors are 366,661, a net increase of 10,216 over 1896. Loans on real estate, $62,606,501.07. Loans on stock, bonds, and personal security, $11,085,082.87.

### STATE BANKS OF DISCOUNT IN CONN.
Commissioners report Oct. 1, 1897, eight banks with the following summary of their condition on that date:

| | |
|---|---|
| Loans and Discounts, | $5,475,472.62 |
| Overdrafts, | 28,695.03 |
| Due from Banks and Bankers, | 1,335,945.10 |
| Stocks, Bonds, and Mortgages, | 1,661,458.76 |
| Current Expenses, | 10,695.91 |
| Specie and Currency, | 499,228.62 |
| Real Estate, | 200,279.00 |
| Checks and Cash Items, | 180,864.32 |
| Other Assets, | 42,493.06 |
| Total Assets, | $9,435,142.35 |
| Capital Stock, | $2,240,000.00 |
| Deposits, | 5,692,908.72 |
| Due to Banks and Bankers, | 604,618.09 |
| Surplus, | 480,000.00 |
| Dividends Unpaid, | 6,612.00 |
| Undivided Profits, | 402,749.66 |
| Other Liabilities, | 8,253.87 |
| Total Liabilities, | $9,435,142.35 |

### TRUST CO'S DOING BANKING BUSINESS.
There are twelve Trust Companies in this state, and their assets and liabilities on the 1st day of Oct. 1897, were as follows:

| | |
|---|---|
| Loans and Discounts, | $3,940,936.18 |
| Stocks, Bonds and Mortgages, | 2,416,415.85 |
| Due from Banks and Bankers, | 1,058,118.81 |
| Overdrafts, | 11,502.97 |
| Specie and Currency, | 848,734.12 |
| Checks and Cash Items, | 93,765.28 |
| Current Expenses, | 26,305.90 |
| Real Estate, Furniture and Fixtures, | 401,472.55 |
| Checks and Cash Items, | 93,765.28 |
| Other Assets, | 10,149.53 |
| Total Assets, | $8,307,407.49 |
| Capital Stock, | $1,245,000.00 |
| Due to Banks and Bankers, | 89,719.71 |
| Surplus, | 395,965.13 |
| Undivided Profits, | 357,320.43 |
| Dividends Unpaid, | 1,194.72 |
| Deposits, | 6,091,166.72 |
| Other Liabilities, | 97,140.75 |
| Total Liabilities, | $8,307,407.49 |

# Churches in the City of Hartford.

FIRST CHURCH OF CHRIST IN HARTFORD.

SECOND CHURCH OF CHRIST.

## FIRST CHURCH OF CHRIST;
(CENTER CONGREGATIONAL.) 675 MAIN ST.

The first organization was at Cambridge, Mass., in 1632; removed to Hartford with Rev. Thomas Hooker as Pastor and Rev. Samuel Stone as Teacher, in June, 1636.

The present edifice was erected in 1807; it is 114 feet in length by 79 in width. There are 150 slips on the lower floor, and 56 in the gallery, which will seat about 1200 persons. Spire is 185 feet in height. The conference room was occupied in 1832. In 1822 this church had the first organ in this city. Services 10.45 A. M.

Rev. CHARLES M. LAMSON, D. D., Pastor; Rev. GEORGE LEON WALKER, D. D., Pastor Emeritus; Daniel H. Wells, Melancthon Storrs, Williston Walker, Solon P. Davis, Rowland Swift, Daniel R. Howe, Deacons; Charles T. Wells, Clerk and Registrar; Chas. T. Welles, Treas.; Rowland Swift, Auditor. 648 members. Annual meeting in Feb.

*Sabbath School.*—Rev. Arthur L. Gillett, Sup't; Mrs. A. H. Pitkin, Elliot F. Talmadge, Ass'ts; Mrs. C. A. Jewell, Sup't Primary Dept.; Miss Clara Wells, Miss Mary C. O. Pierson, Ass'ts; William T. Pitkin, Sec'y; Knighton Smith, Treas.; Thos. W. Hooker, Librarian; Teachers, 25; Scholars, 200; School, 12.15 P. M.; 375 volumes in Library; 2,843 volumes in Teachers' Library. Annual meeting in Jan.

*Society.*—Charles P. Cooley, Charles A. Jewell, Henry Roberts, Committee; Rowland Swift, Treas.; John D. Parker, Clerk; D. H. Wells, Herbert Knox Smith, Auditors. Annual meeting in January. N. H. Allen, Organist; W. B. Edwards, Sexton.

## SECOND CHURCH OF CHRIST;
(SOUTH CONGREGATIONAL,)

307 MAIN ST. *Organized Feb. 22, 1670.*

*This third edifice was dedicated April 11, 1827.*

The building is 96 feet in length by 63 feet in breadth, with a portico in front 42 by 12 feet, and a chapel in the rear 36 by 80 feet. The porch is 60 by 16 feet. The audience room is 60 by 77 feet, with galleries. Estimated to seat 1,100 persons.

Rev. EDWIN P. PARKER, D.D., Pastor; Geo. H. Woods, Henry E. Harrington, G. F. Hills, Joseph A. Graves, Hosmer Griswold, John L. Dalgleish, Deacons; H. E. Harrington, Treas.; Olin H. Clark, Clerk. Number of communicants, 640. Annual meeting in January.

*Sabbath School.*—I. F. Robinson, Sup't; Olin H. Clark, Alice H. Goodwin, Ass'ts; Mrs. E. P. Parker, Sup't Primary Dep't; Merrick W. Chapin, Sec'y; A. H. Loomis, Treas.; N. G. Valentine, Librarian; E. J. Noble, R. D. Chapin, Assistants; Mrs. Bidwell, Librarian Primary Dep't. About 1000 volumes in Library; Teachers, 35; Scholars, 260; School, 12.15 P. M. Annual election in January.

*Society.*—H. C. Robinson, C. H. Northam, H. E. Harrington, W. E. Baker, J. H. Knight, Committee; J. E. Morris, Clerk; E. F. Harrington, Treas.; A. G. Loomis, J. W. Titcomb, Auditors. Annual meeting, 2d week in March. J. M. Gallup, Organist; John Hassett, Sexton.

FOURTH CONGREGATIONAL CHURCH.

PEARL STREET CONGREGATIONAL CHURCH.

**FOURTH CONGREGATIONAL CHURCH,** 1091 MAIN ST. *Organized Jan. 10, 1832. This second edifice was dedicated April 3, 1850.* Service 10.45 A. M.; Evangelistic service, 7.30 P. M.; also, Thursday evening meeting. Rev. H. H. KELSEY, Pastor; Rev. KINGSLEY F. NORRIS, Assistant Pastor; T. W. Hannum, J. B. Pierce, J. N. Bardin, F. W. Hawley, F. H. Basson, B. D. Field, S. B. Mallett, H. J. Gillett, Deacons; Mrs. John G. Parsons, Mrs. E. G. Lasbury, Mrs. J. M. Owen, Mrs. Franklin Smith, Mrs. J. S. Kepler, Mrs. J. L. Benham, Mrs. E. F. Kenyon, Mrs. E. R. Clarke, Deaconesses; J. N. Bardin, Clerk; C. E. Miller, Treas.; Michael Burnham, Musical Director; Rev. H. H. Kelsey, Registrar. No. of members, 902. Annual meeting in Jan.

*Evangelistic Fund.*—J. B. Pierce, Treas.; the Pastor and Deacons, Official Board.

*Sunday School.*—Rev. K. F. Norris, Superintendent; Mrs. H. G. Howe, Carrie L. St. John, Mrs. Wilcox, Associates; Horace Howe, Sec'y; E. S. Cook, Treas.; Frank H. Adkins, Librarian; Robert Gardner, W. W. Brouson, W. Weller, Assistant Librarians; 700 vols. in Library; Teachers, 50; Scholars, 706; School, 12.15 P.M. Annual election in Jan.

*Society.*—Joseph B. Pierce, E. E. Case, C. E. Miller, F. H. Bosson, M. J. Mack, Committee; F. A. Searle, Treas.; Mrs. A. N. Daniels, Ass't Treas.; S. B. Mallett, Clerk; Hyman F. Smith, Auditor. Annual meeting in March. Mrs. N. S. Bronson, Organist; J. T. Lyman, Sexton.

**PEARL STREET CONGREGATIONAL CHURCH, 40 PEARL STREET.** *Edifice dedicated Dec. 1852.* This building including the spire 212 feet in height with its apex, is built entirely of Portland stone. The corner stone was laid August 2, 1851. Services 10.45 A.M. Rev. WILLIAM D'L. LOVE, JR., Pastor; Stephen C. Brownell, Nathaniel Shipman, Wm. P. Williams, Chas. R. Burt, Horace E. Mather, Deacons; Francis N. Allen, Clerk; George E. Sanborne, Treas. Number of members, 422. Annual meeting second Thursday in January.

*Sabbath School.*—David Calhoun, Sup't; A. L. Shipman, Miss Anna H. Andrews, Mrs. F. N. Allen, Ass'ts; Mrs. L. W. Ripley, Sup't Chinese Department; Mrs. W. P. Williams, Sup't Home Dep't; Edward R. Cook, Sec'y and Treas.; Fred. G. Winslow, Librarian; 1000 volumes in Library; Teachers' Library, 600 volumes; Officers and Teachers, 34; Scholars, 270; School, 12.10 P.M. Annual meeting 2d Thursday in January.

*Society.*—Wm. P. Williams, Charles R. Burt, Lyman B. Brainard, Committee; Henry H. Goodwin, Treas.; A. A. Welch, Clerk; H. P. Hitchcock, U. H. Brockway, Auditors. Annual meeting 2d week in Jan. Benjamin W. Loveland, Organist and Musical Director. Ephraim Cook, Sexton.

**WETHERSFIELD AV. CONGREGATIONAL CHURCH, 250 WETHERSFIELD AV.** *Church organized May 28, 1873.* Rev. SAMUEL B. FORBES, Pastor; J. Wilson Shew, Austin Smith, William Porter, Lucius W. Burt, Deacons; George K. Marvin, Treas.; Robert C. Dickenson, Clerk; J. Wilson Shew, Alex. Angus, George K. Marvin, Financial Committee; Robert D. Bone, Luther W. Burt, Auditors. Church members, 122. Annual meeting first week in January.

*Sabbath School.*—Albert H. Brooks, Sup't; E. N. Tarbell, Matilda Burchfield, Ass't Sup'ts.; Richard H. Noble, Clerk and Treas.; William A. Shew, Robert C. Dickenson, Librarians; Teachers, 15; Scholars, 200; volumes in Library, 680; School, 12 M. Annual meeting, first week in January.

## PARK CONGREGATIONAL CHURCH,
### (FORMERLY THE NORTH CHURCH,)
**390 ASYLUM ST.** *Organized Sept. 23, 1824.*
*This 2d edifice was dedicated March 29, 1867.*

This building has sittings for about 1000 persons, with gallery for organ and choir, costing with land $150,000. Dimensions inside are 115 feet long and 66 wide, height of nave 60 feet, chapel with other rooms in rear and connection therewith is 82 by 40 feet with 500 sittings. This edifice is of the early English ornamented style with true Gothic windows and doors, walls of brown Portland stone in blocks rough hewn. All of the ornamental portions are of the yellow Dorchester or commonly called Nova Scotia stone. Services at 10.45 A. M., and 7.45 P. M. 800 members.

Rev. W. W. RANNEY, Pastor; Thomas W. Russell, A. L. Hunt, A. E. Abrams, F. T. Simpson, Deacons; Willis E. Smith, Treas.; H. R. Hovey, Clerk. Annual meeting in Jan.

*Sabbath School.*—Walter R. Blackman, Sup't; Joseph H. King, Assistant Sup't; Mrs. T. W. Russell, Sup't Infant Department; Mary L. Plimpton, Ass't; Charles R. Childs, Sec'y and Treas.; E. M. Stone, Librarian; 600 volumes in Library; Teachers, 15; Scholars, 118; School 12.15 P. M. Annual meeting, Jan. 6.

*Society.*—F. L. Howard, C. C. Kimball, Wm. Tucker, Ellis G. Richards, J. H. King, Com.; George H. Burt, Treasurer; Allen H. Newton, Clerk. Annual meeting 3d Wednesday in January. J. S. Camp, Organist; Fred. Richards, Sexton.

ASYLUM HILL CONGREGATIONAL CHURCH.

## ASYLUM HILL CONG. CHURCH,
### 814 ASYLUM STREET.

*Society organized June 25, 1864. Church organized March 23, 1865. Edifice dedicated June 15, 1866. Incorporated March 21, 1895.*

It is built of Portland stone; corner stone was laid May 5, 1865; the length of church and chapel is 184 feet; audience room of the church is 68 by 112 feet; 182 pews for 1,050 sittings. The chapel is 42 by 65 feet; seats 250. The spire is of stone, 230 feet in height. Services 10.45 A. M. Young People's meeting 6.30 P.M., and service of praise first Sunday of the month at 7.30 P.M.

Rev. JOSEPH H. TWICHELL, Pastor; Samuel A. Bacon, Atwood Collins, Chas. E. Thompson, Alfred T. Richards, Abel S. Clark, Waldo S. Pratt, Deacons; C. E. Thompson, Treas.; Harry S. Conklin, Clerk. 787 communicants. Annual meeting third Thursday in January.

*Sabbath School*—Rev. J. H. Twichell, Sup't; Waldo S. Pratt, Mrs. F. P. Bartlett, Miss Susan T. Clark, Ass'ts; Calvin J. Burnell, Sup't Home Dep't; S. A. Bacon, Sec'y; Fred'k H. Forbes, Treas.; Paul E. Stevens, Librarinn; Miss Harmony Twichell, Historian. Library, 609 vols. Officers and Teachers, 57; Scholars, 399; Mrs. Lester H. Goodwin, Sup't Primary Dep't; School 2.30 P. M. Annual meeting in January.

*Society.*—Chas. E. Chase, F. B. Allen, Samuel O. Prentice, James R. Stevens, James E. Tucker, Committee; H. P. Redfield, Treas.; F. E. Bliss, Clerk. Annual meeting during week following 1st Sunday in March. S. Clarke Lord, Organist; Wm. Livingston, Sexton.

PARK CONGREGATIONAL CHURCH.

## WINDSOR AV. CONGREGATIONAL CH.

302 WINDSOR AV. *Organized, March 23, 1876.*

Rev. HARRY R. MILES, Pastor; F. A. Brackett, Chas. King, S. N. Benedict, Hart Talcott, Deacons; Laura C. Camp, Agnes J. McCoy, Helena R. Rossiter, L. D. Hutchinson, Deaconesses; Walter G. Camp, Clerk; Henry H. Pease, Treas.; the Deacons with Walter G. Camp and A. R. Hillyer, Standing Committee. Annual election 2d Wednesday evening in Jan. Services 10.45 A. M.; 7.30 P. M. 353 members.

*Sabbath School.*—F. A. Brackett, Sup't; F. M. Dawson, Miss A. B. Cairnes, Assistants; Miss Etta Belden, Sec'y; C. A. Pease, Treas.; A. H. Pease, Librarian; W. J. Gardner, Assistant Librarian; 671 volumes in Library; Miss A. L. Olmsted, Sup't of Infant Dep't; Mrs. C. H. Brigham, Sec'y and Treas. Infant Dep't; Scholars, Senior Dep't, 197; Junior, 130; School, 12 M. Annual election 2d Wednesday evening in Jan.

---

## PAVILION CONGREGATIONAL SOCIETY
### TO WINDSOR AV. CONGREGATIONAL CHURCH.

*Organized December 10, 1870.*

*Committee.*—Hart Talcott, F. A. Brackett, Isaac Bragaw, Edward Deming, H. A. Dibble; P. P. Bennett, Clerk; H. A. Dibble, Treas.; S. N. Benedict, N. C. Wilder, Auditors; Clement H. Bingham, Collector. Annual meeting first Monday in May.

---

## TALCOTT STREET CONGREGATIONAL CHURCH, 30 TALCOTT STREET.

*Organized Aug. 28, 1833.*

The Rev. Dr. J. Hawes, pastor of the First Church, and the Pastor of the Second Church officiated on the occasion. Services 10.45 A.M. and 7.45 P.M. Social meetings, Thursdays at 8 P.M.

Rev. ROBERT F. WHEELER, Pastor; A. I. Plato, T. A. Lane, George W. Lane, Deacons; Mrs. C. C. Peterson, Mrs. M. F. Stevens, Deaconesses; Albert Peterson, Clerk; A. I. Plato, Treas.; Theodore A. Lane, B. F. Peterson, Albert Peterson, Mrs. S. J. Jackson, Mrs. R. P. Thomas, Committee. Annual meeting 2d Tuesday in January.

*Sabbath School.*—Rev. R. F. Wheeler, Sup't; Alfred Plato, Mrs. R. P. Thomas, Ass'ts; Miss May A. Green, Sec. and Tr.; Library, 350 vols.; Teachers, 8; Scholars, 98; School, 12.10 P M.

*Society.*—F. O. Cross, Chairman; A. I. Plato, George W. Lane, Theodore A. Lane, B. F. Peterson, Com.; Albert Peterson, Clerk; A. I. Plato, Treas. Annual meeting 1st Monday in January.

---

## CONGREGATION BETH ISRAEL,

21 CHARTER OAK AVENUE. *Organized, 1847.*

The synagogue was erected in 1876, is 100 feet long, by 50 feet wide, and an elevation of 60 feet from basement to roof, of Gothic style, and will seat 600 persons. The building and land cost $65,000. Dedicated May 26, 1876.

Rev. M. ELKIN, Rabbi; M. Wieder, Pres't; Ludwig Hellman, Vice Pres't; Chas. Rosenthal Sec'y; Leopold DeLeeuw, Tr.; Isadore Wise, R. Ballerstein, W. B. Rothschild, F. C. Opper, with the above officers, Trustees; L. Goldschmidt, Collector. Annual meeting 1st week in January. Richard O. Phelps, Organist; Simon Borochelsky, Sexton. Services, Fridays at 7.30 P. M.; Saturdays, 10 A. M.

FIRST BAPTIST CHURCH.

SOUTH BAPTIST CHURCH.

## FIRST BAPTIST CHURCH,
### 1014 MAIN STREET.

Organized March 23, 1790; in 1798 erected building on the cor. of Market and Temple sts., which they occupied until 1831, when they erected a house of worship, now 940 Main st. Their present and third structure of Portland sandstone, was dedicated April 23d, 1856. Seats for 1,100. 619 members. Preaching at 10.45 A. M. Sunday School 12.15 P. M.; Young Peoples' Meeting 6.30 P. M.

Rev. HAROLD PATTISON, Pastor; James L. Howard, Luther C. Glazier, Rush P. Chapman, Carnot O. Spencer, J. G. Burnet, Deacons; C. P. Gladding, Clerk; Luther C. Glazier, Treasurer. Annual meeting in January.

*Sunday School.* — Edward B. Boynton, Superintendent; Dwight Chapman, C. S. Shumway, Miss Harriet I. Eaton, Assistants; Carrie L. McClure, Mrs. Isaac Glazier, Sup'ts Primary Dep't; Mrs. Homer Belfield, Sup't Kindergarten Dep't; Mrs. E. B. Bennett, Sup't Home Dep't; W. D. Johnson, Sec'y and Tr.; E. B. Bliss, Hattie G. Morse, Ass't Sec'ys; F. A. West, George N. Clark, J. G. Burnet, A. D. Mitchell, Mrs. A. D. Mitchell, Librarians; Geo. Davis, Collector; 1,427 volumes in Library; Officers, 18; Teachers, 33; Home Dep't Visitors, 12; Scholars, 512; Home Dep't Members, 117; total membership, 692; School, 12.15 P. M. Annual election last Sunday in Dec.

*Society.* — Rush P. Chapman, Fred A. West, Silas Chapman, Jr., W. D. Johnson, C. S. Shumway, Wm. A. Erving, Committee; Carnot O. Spencer, Treas; Dwight Chapman, Auditor; Silas Chapman, Jr., Clerk. Annual meeting, January. H. L. Bolles, Organist.

## SOUTH BAPTIST CHURCH,
### 455 MAIN STREET.

Organized Oct. 21, 1834. Dedicated April 23, 1854. 585 members. Preaching at 10.45 A. M. and 7.30 P. M.; Young Peoples' meeting Sunday evening at 6.15 P. M.; Prayer meeting in Chapel, Thursdays, 7.45 P. M.

Rev. FRANK DIXON, Pastor; H. M. Jacobs, F. A. Carey, E. B. Squires, J. A. Conklin, Stephen Maslen, H. L. Strong, F. A. Butler, James Eadie, Deacons; O. H. Ham, Clerk.

*Sunday School.* — Rev. Frank Dixon, Sup't; Geo. M. Smith, Sec'y; H. W. White, Treas.; Frank Tolhurst, Ass't Treas.; L. B. Seymour, Librarian; F. H. Butler, John G. Hawley, Ass't Librarians; Mrs. Allen W. Brown, Sup't Infant Dep't; 1,200 vols. in Library; Officers, 11; Teachers, 28; Scholars, 350; School 12.15 P. M. Annual election in October.

*Society.* — W. C. Augur, W. J. Tolhurst, W. H. Rhodes, Com.; Nelson G. Ford, Clerk; H. M. Jacobs, Treas; W. H. Whitelaw, Ass't Treas. Annual meeting in Jan. C. Walter Gaylord, Organist; George McCann, Sexton.

---

## SUFFIELD STREET BAPTIST CHAPEL,
### 10 SUFFIELD STREET.
Dedicated June 11, 1871.

*Officers.* — Silas Chapman, Jr., H. M. Twiss, Albert Guy, Wm. Clay, Committee.

*Sabbath School.* — H. M. Twiss, Superintendent; L. A. Wiley, Mrs. A. C. Thompson, Assistants; Charles Parkhurst, Sec'y; Clark Williams, Ass't; Silas Chapman, Jr., Treas.; A. L. Brewster, Librarian; R. Dale Smith, Ass't. 500 volumes in Library; Scholars, 143; School, 2.30 P. M.

ASYLUM AVENUE BAPTIST CHURCH.

MEMORIAL BAPTIST CHURCH.

**ASYLUM AVENUE BAPTIST CHURCH,**

**866 ASYLUM ST.**     *Organized Nov. 2, 1872.*

GEORGE M. STONE, D.D., Pastor: Edward V. Preston, D. N. Slate, J. L. Denison. Deacons; Wilbur M. Stone, Clerk; J. A. Williams, Treasurer.

*Sabbath School.*—C. E. Prior, Superintendent; A. Spencer, Jr., Assistant; Mrs. D. G. Smythe, Sup't Prim. Dep't; L. E. Hatheway. Sec'y and Treas.; C. E. Prior, Jr., Librarian; Lawrence Howard, Ass't Librarian; 600 vols. in Library; 150 Teachers and Scholars. Annual meeting 1st Sunday in January.

*Society.*—Daniel N. Slate, W. B. Case, A. Spencer, Jr., Committee; F. A. Thompson, Clerk; E. V. Preston, Treas.; H. H. White, Auditor. Annual meeting second Monday evening in March., Mrs. Colin Pitblado, Organist.

---

**MEMORIAL BAPTIST CHURCH,**

**WASHINGTON, CORNER JEFFERSON STREET.**

*Org. July 10, 1884. Incor. Nov. 19, 1889.*

Rev. H. M. THOMPSON, Pastor; John W. Lamb, Chairman; E. M. Hurlbut, Fred. R. Simonds, Geo. E. Moses, H. H. Dickinson, Deacons; A. O. Dole, Clerk, 15 Seymour st.; F. M. Hale, Treas.; F. L. Barton, H. H. Dickinson, Wm. O. Shelley, Trustees; Wm. A. Hurd, Auditor. Preaching at 10.45 A.M. and 7.30 P.M. Prayer meetings Thursdays at 7.45 P.M. and Young People's meeting, Sundays 6.15 P.M.

*Sunday School.*—Henry H. Dickinson, Sup't: George R. Reed, Ass't Sup't; Mrs. Emily A. Baldwin, Sup't Primary Dep't; C. W. Evans. Sec'y; Howard D. Burnham, Ass't Sec'y; F. L. Barton, Treas.; Geo. T. Fowler, Librarian; F. L. Purinton, Assistant Librarian. Officers and Teachers, 29; Scholars, 372; School, 12.15 P.M. 375 volumes in Library.

---

**UNION BAPTIST CHURCH, 35 WOOSTER ST.**

Rev. J. W. ANDERSON, Pastor: R. M. Richie, J. O. Taylor, Mark Collins, Geo. W. Litchfield, John Epps, James Allen, Lawrence Washington, Deacons; C. W. Custis, Treas.; H. S. Johnson, Sec'y; Chas. Nelson, Thomas Cole, Moses Braxton, Trustees. Services, 11 A.M. at 7.30 Friday evenings.

*Sunday School.*—John O. Taylor, Superintendent; Booker Jones, Tr.; Miss Ella Litchfield, Secretary; Teachers, 6; Scholars, 55; School, 12.30 M. Annual meeting in June.

---

**GERMAN LUTHERAN CHURCH OF THE REFORMATION, 125 MARKET ST.**

Organized June 6, 1880; corner stone laid July 25, 1854; completed Apr. 1855; Seats free.

Rev. J. H. W. JAEGER, Pastor: Wm. Braun, Pres't; Karl Fritsche, Sec'y; Richard Gabitz, Treas.; Fred'k Eberle, Augustus W. Budde, William Westphal, F. W. Heublein, Richard Gubitz, Edward Schumann, Society Committee. Gustav Gebhardi, Organist. Service at 10.30 A.M. in German. Annual meeting 1st Tuesday in June.

*Sunday School.*—Frederick Eberle, Sup't; Anna Jaeger, Ass't Sup't; Chas. Fritsche, Sec'y; Officers and Teachers, 10; Scholars, 125; School, 9 A.M. in church.

## CHRIST CHURCH.—EPISCOPAL,

955 MAIN ST.          *First Organization*, 1762.

This second edifice of Christ Church was begun in 1827. The corner stone was laid May 13, 1828, and consecrated Dec. 23, 1829. The Church is built of freestone and is 121½ feet long and 76 feet wide. It was the first specimen of Gothic church architecture in this country. The first edifice was wood on opposite corner to present, began in 1762, finished in 1786, and moved to Talcott st. in 1829. The chancel, new chapel and parish building on Church st., were opened Dec. 23, 1879. Services Sundays, 8; 10.45 A. M.; 7.30 P. M.; week days, 12 M. Sunday School at 12.30 P.M. 883 communicants.

Rev. LINDALL W. SALTONSTALL, Rector; Rev. JAMES P. FAUCON, Ass't; George Ellis, John F. Tracy, Wardens; S. B. Curtis, Wm; H. Dodd, Edwin S. Bartlett, H. H. Hollister, J. D. Tucker, T. Belknap Beach, Charles C. Beach, G. W. Russell, Geo. Beach, James J. Goodwin, Vestrymen; H. H. Hollister, Clerk; Sidney B. Curtis, Treas.; T. B. Beach, J. D. Tucker, Auditors. Annual meeting, Easter Monday. H. F. Williams, Organist and Choirmaster; R. W. Hyde, Sexton.

*Sunday School.*—The Rector, Sup't; Rev. J. P. Faucon, Ass't Sup't; F. A. B. Wenk, Treas.; Carl S. Jasper, Sec'y; A. F. Donley, W. A. Pocock, Librarians. 543 volumes in Library; Teachers, 24; Scholars, 267; School, 12.30 P.M. during Winter, and 9.30 A. M. in Summer.

---

## ST. JOHN'S CHURCH.—EPISCOPAL,

580 MAIN ST.          *Organized March* 18, 1841.

The corner stone was laid July 14, 1841, and consecrated April 20, 1842. Sittings free. Services at 10.45 A. M., and 7.30 P. M.

Rev. JAMES W. BRADIN, Rector; George W. Woolley, Edwin P. Taylor, Wardens; J. T. Pratt, Frederick S. Crossfield, Wm. C. Pease, William O. Taylor, A. H. Pense, T. B. Persse, Peter Lux, E. B. Johnson, H. R. Hayden, Austin Brainard, Henry L. Bunce, J. L. English, Vestrymen; R. A. Wadsworth, Clerk and Auditor; Charles A. Pease, Treasurer; E. N. Emmons, Choirmaster. S. B. Harrison, Sexton. 375 communicants. Annual meeting, 1st Monday in May.

*Sunday School.*—Rev. Jas. W. Bradin, Sup't; Chas. A. Pease, Sec'y and Treas: A. H. Watkinson. Librarian; 425 vols. in Library; Teachers, 20; Scholars, 125; School, in Summer, 9.45 A. M.; other times at 2.45 P. M.

---

## ST. JAMES CHURCH.—EPISCOPAL,

145 PARK ST., COR. WASHINGTON.

Edifice dedicated Nov. 18, 1868. Services 10.45 A. M. and 7.30 P. M. Seats free.

Rev. JOHN T. HUNTINGTON. Rector; Theo. Herzer, Wm. T. Smith, Wardens; Wm. Hawkins, Frank Goodman, Aven Allen, A. L. Mitchell, J. H. Spencer, Wm. Monks, L. P. Edgerton, J. A. Owen, Ray Goodman, F. A. Taylor, W. H. C. Pynchon, James Goodacre, Harry White, E. Lorenzen, Vestrymen; C. Ray Goodman, Clerk; W. H. C. Pynchon, Treas. O. P. Colloque, Organist. Annual meeting, Easter Monday.

*Sunday School.*—Rev. John T. Huntington, Superintendent and Treasurer; John Owen, Sec'y; Charles Zipp, Librarian; Miss C. E. Huntington, Organist; Teachers, 25; Scholars, 200; 800 vols.; School, 12.15 P. M.

**TRINITY CHURCH.—EPISCOPAL.—128 SIGOURNEY ST.** *Organized Sept.* 12, 1859.

The corner stone of the first edifice was laid Thursday, Oct. 27, 1860; and the church was consecrated in May, 1861. It was enlarged and improved in 1875. The last service was held in it Jan. 24, 1892, after which it was torn down to make way for a new church which is being built on the same site. This edifice will be 144 feet in length by 62½ feet wide, with a square tower 152 feet high. In connection with this there has been already built as a Memorial and gift to the parish a Chapel and Parish house, which are used for services until the new edifice is finished. Annual meeting, Easter Monday. Seats free. Services 10.45 A. M. and 7.30 P. M. Communicants, 360.

Rev. ERNEST DEF. MIEL, Rector; Jacob L. Greene, George E. Hatch, Wardens; L. Walter Clarke, G. Pierrepont Davis, John S. Gray, C. B. Ingraham, C. H. Lawrence, Frederick P. Lepard, P. C. Royce, Vestrymen; G. Pierrepont Davis, Treas.; Frank E. Johnson, Clerk.

*Sunday School.*—Rev. Ernest DeF. Miel, Sup't; Fred. B. Wright, Treas.; Richard Goodman, Librarian; 300 volumes in Library; Teachers, 20; Scholars, 196; School. 2.45 P. M.

CHURCH OF THE GOOD SHEPHERD.

MEMORIAL CHURCH OF ST. THOMAS.

**CATHOLIC APOSTOLIC CHURCH.** 1520 BROAD ST. *Organized October, 1868.*

Rev. S. J. ANDREWS, Elder in charge; Rev. S. H. Allen, Rev. J. A. R. Rogers, John Ponsaing, S. T. Pearl, Pastors; L. R. Cheney, W. M. Brigham, G. D. Pyott, C. T. Mitchell, Deacons. Sunday services: Holy Eucharist, 10 A. M., evening prayer 5 o'clock.

**CHURCH OF THE GOOD SHEPHERD.**—EPISCOPAL, WYLLYS ST. *Organized,* 1866.

Edifice is situated on the corner of Wyllys st. and Hendricxsen avenue. It was erected by Mrs. Samuel Colt as a memorial to her deceased husband and children, and was consecrated Jan. 28, 1869. It is built in the Gothic style, of Portland hewn stone finished with Ohio white stone. Sittings free. 250 Communicants. Services 10.45 A. M. and 5.00 P. M.

Rev. CORNELIUS G. BRISTOL. Rector; John H. Hall, William H. Gilbert, Wardens, Wm. B. Franklin, George H. Day. Ralph Burnham, H. A. Kippen, Philomen W. Robbins, Samuel Taylor, Joseph M. Birmingham, Horace S. Seymour, E. H. Cowell, Vestrymen; Horace S. Seymour, Clerk; Ward C. Powell, Treas.; A. M. Hollingshead, Organist. Annual meeting first Monday in May.

*Sunday School.*—Rev. C. G. Bristol, Sup't; Frederick W. Addis, Sec'y and Treas.; Alfred Barker, Librarian; Teachers, 12; Scholars, 180; 600 vols. in Library; School, 9.30 A. M.

**MEMORIAL CHURCH OF ST. THOMAS.**—EPISCOPAL, 245 WINDSOR AV.

Organized July, 1870; corner stone laid Sept. 27, 1871; dedicated Dec. 21, 1872. Services 10.45 A.M. and 7.30 P.M.

Rev. GEORGE R. WARNER, Rector; L. A. Dickinson, E. H. Crosby, Wardens; E. H. Judd, Wm. F. Whittelsey, J. Henry Martin, Edward Shelton, Geo. F. Douthwaite, Robert H. Burton, A. D. Pierce, Edward Reisel, Vestrymen; Austin D. Pierce, Treasurer; Henry W. Richards, Clerk; Walter E. Hawkins, Organist; Alonzo M. Seymour, Sexton. Annual meeting first Monday in May.

*Sunday School.*—Robert H. Burton, Sup't; Edwin S. Mugford, Sec'y and Treas.; H. W. Richards, R. H. Burton, Jr., Librarians; School at 12.15 P. M.; Teachers, 18; Scholars, 175.

**ELIZABETH CHAPEL, 26 WASHINGTON ST.**

This memorial Chapel, erected on the Retreat for the Insane grounds, is for the use of the inmates of said institution, for religious worship, and was dedicated Dec. 24, 1875. Its cost was $14,000, including organ, etc.

**ST. ANN'S CHURCH—FRENCH CATHOLIC,** 362 PARK STREET. *Organized, Jan.* 6, 1889.

Rev. P. E. ROY, Pastor. Mass every Sunday, at 8.30 and 10.30 A. M.; Vespers at 4.00 P. M. Holy days at 5 and 9 A. M. About 1,100 members. Sunday School, 3.00 P. M. Teachers, 2; scholars, 69. H. I. Linesque, L. Beaune, Trustees.

**FIRST METHODIST EPISCOPAL CHURCH.**

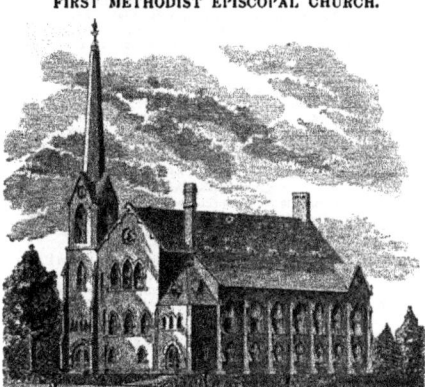

**NORTH METHODIST EPISCOPAL CHURCH.**

**AFRICAN METHODIST EPISCOPAL ZION'S CHURCH.**

### FIRST METHODIST EPISCOPAL
#### CHURCH, 305 ASYLUM ST.

Organized in 1820; present edifice dedicated April 4, 1860, and will seat 1000 people. Seats free. 512 members.

Rev. SAMUEL L. BEILER, Pastor; Geo. W. Newton, Pres't and Treas.; Richard P. Martin, Sec'y; I. H. Coe, Clerk; W. H. Newell, I. M. Wilcox, P. H. Reeve, B. F. Beardsley, Charles E. Parker, Chas. W. Hills, Trustees. Annual meeting 1st Monday in Sept.

*Stewards.*—Miles B. Preston, C. F. Remsen, T. F. Hill, George W. Post, W. H. Hipple, W. R. Sage, G. F. Warfield, W. H. Wilde, Elmer H. Fogg, E. W. Gustafson, Charles H. Ewing, E. C. Linn.

*Sabbath School.*—W. H. Newell, Sup't; Imri M. Wilcox, I. H. Coe, Mrs. W. H. Hipple, Ass'ts; T. F. Hill, Sec'y; A. M. Waldron, Ass't Sec'y; C. E. Parker, Treas.; W. R. Sage, Librarian; Theo. I. Coe, C. E. Parker, C. E. Cooper, Assistant Librarians. 700 vols. in Library; Teachers, 46; Scholars, 370; School, 12.15 P. M. Annual meeting, 1st week in Jan.

### NORTH METHODIST EPISCOPAL
#### CHURCH, 313 WINDSOR AV.

This church erected and dedicated a chapel, April 9, 1871. The corner stone for this edifice was laid July 11, 1873, and dedicated Oct. 1874. Gothic style, of brick, fire stone trimmings; length 96 feet, width 60 feet; seats 500 persons.

Rev. DUANE N. GRIFFIN, Pastor; Robert Cairnes, H. D. Burnham, H. A. Camp, Clerk, Geo. N. Seidler, J. E. Marsh, Charles May, E. S. Gardner, Wm. H. Watrous, Julius Weed, Trustees. Annual election, 3d Monday, Sept.

*Stewards.*—Julius Weed, John M. Parker, Howard A. Camp, James S. Birden, S. H. Wollerton, Ira J. Strong, Frank A. Davoll, E. L. Furrey, J. Harry Goodrich, Samuel H. Havens, Louis H. Scranton, Frank H. Waterhouse.

*Sabbath School.*— Howard A. Camp, Sup't; S. H. Wollerton, Fannie S. Williams, Ass'ts; Frank H. Waterhouse, Sec'y; J. Harry Goodrich, Treas.; Ira J. Strong, Librarian; Charles B. Krug, J. C. Waterhouse, Harry Brewer, Assistants; 350 vols. in Library; Officers and Teachers, 34; Scholars, 316; School, 12.15 P M. Annual meeting, 3d Monday in December.

### AFRICAN M. E. ZIONS CHURCH,
#### 269 PEARL ST. *Established,* 1836.

Their edifice, with a lecture room, was erected in 1857. It is 34 by 60 feet; contains 56 slips and seats 445; cost $6,000. Members, 130. Services, 11 A. M., and 7.45 P. M.

Rev. J. STELLA COOPER, Pastor; Vincent E. Davis, Pres't; W. S. James, Treas.; Henry Green, Sec'y; Morris Mitchell, Vincent E. Davis, Sanford Harrison, Wm. James, Walter Young, Virgil Wilson, Henry Green, W. S. James, Charles Percy, Trustees.

*Sunday School.*—Morris Mitchell, Sup't; Wm. D. Battle, Sec'y, J. S. Taylor. Treas.; Prim Batson, Librarian; 275 volumes in Library; Teachers, 10; Scholars, 125; School 1.30 P. M. Annual meeting in Jan.

## SO. PARK METHODIST EPISCOPAL CHURCH,
75 MAIN ST.  *Organized* 1869.  *Dedicated Jan.* 1869.

The corner stone of this church edifice of Gothic style was laid September 1, 1874. It is of brick with brown stone trimmings and about 700 sittings Edifice dedicated April 2, 1875. Seats free. A chapel in the rear was dedicated Feb. 23, 1886.

Rev. WM. A. RICHARD, Pastor; S. M. Stiles, Pres't; E. K. Ives, Sec'y; D. E. Lyman, Treas.; S. M. Stiles, D. A. Spear. C. W. Clark, R. R. Latimer, D. E. Lyman, W. G. Simmons, Louis E. Parkhurst, I. Cross, Jr., H. Cowishaw, Trustees; George S. Bull, C. B. Averill, R. H. Southergill, H. D. Clemens, D. E. Lyman, H. Cowlishaw, W. H. Pomeroy, C. E. McCausland, W. G. Wilson, M. H. Moyer, E. K. Ives, Stewards. 385 members. Mrs. C. N. Green, Organist; John Williams, Sexton.

*Sunday School.*—Harry E. Parkhurst, Sup't; W. H. Pomeroy, Miss L. May Wilson, Ass'ts; Clayton P. Chamberlin, Sec'y; G. W. Sanford, Ass't Sec'y; E. K. Ives, Treas.; H. W. Conklin, G. A. Embury, Librarians; 1,022 vols. in Library; Mrs. Geo. A. Embury, Sup't Inf. Dep't; Gertrude L. Boutelle, Sup't Int. Dep't; Officers and Teachers, 40; Scholars, 450; School, 12.15 P.M Annual election, 2d Monday in December.

## FIRST GERMAN M. E. CHURCH.—99 JEFFERSON ST.
*Organized November* 13, 1885.

Rev. GUSTAV F. HAUSSER, Jr., Pastor and President; Joseph Gallon, Secretary; G. Mannz, Treasurer; G. Mannz, Charles Bickel, A. Goetz, Joseph Gallon, G. F. Hausser, Jr., Trustees; Joseph Gallon, G. Mannz, Charles Bickel, G. Loescher, Christ Gammerdinger, Anton Loescher, A. Goetz, Stewards. Services at 10.45 A. M., and 7.45 P. M., Sundays; also on Thursday evening. Annual election first Thursday in September. Frank Loescher, Sexton.

*Sabbath School.*—Charles Bickel, Sup't; G. Mannz, Ass't; H. Loescher, Sec'y; Frank Loescher, Treas.; Aug. Bickel, Librarian; Teachers, 8; Scholars, 60; School, 9.30 A. M. 200 volumes in Library.

## CONN. ASS'N OF NEW JERUSALEM CHURCH.
*Incorporated March* 11, 1879.

Henry G. Thompson, Milford, Pres't; A. Marwick, Jr., Hartford, Rec. Sec'y; Mrs. G. O. Sawyer, 4 Townley street, Hartford, Cor. Sec'y and Librarian; George W. Bancroft, Hockanum, Treas. Meets quarterly, at Hartford and New Haven. Annual meeting at Hartford in February.

## UNITY CHURCH.—62 PRATT ST.
FIRST UNITARIAN CONGREGATIONAL SOCIETY.
*Organized July* 27, 1844.  *Reorganized April* 12, 1879.

This edifice was dedicated April 3, 1881.

Rev. JOSEPH WAITE, Pastor; Horace Cornwall, President; Gilbert Lincoln, Vice President; E. M. Cutting, Clerk; Joseph Dawson, Treasurer; William Francis, William E. Dickinson, Josiah Q. Baker, Ex. Com.; E. A. Perry, Charles H. Field, Auditors. Annual meeting first Monday in April. Services at 10.45 A.M. Church year from September to 2d Sunday in July inclusive.

*Sunday School.*—Mrs. Lizzie C. Baker, Sup't; Mrs. Helen M. Root, Ass't Sup't; E. M. Cutting, Sec'y; Wm. F. Young, Treas.; L. A. Cressy, Librarian; W. F. Friebe, Ass't Librarian; Officers and Teachers, 12. Scholars, 80. 625 vols. in Library. School, 12.15 P. M. Annual meeting last Tuesday in May.

## WARBURTON CHAPEL.—61 TEMPLE ST.
*Chapel dedicated June* 18, 1866.

Religious services Sunday afternoons in English.

*Trustees.*—F. B. Cooley, D. R. Howe, J. B. Pierce, Henry Roberts, Solon P. Davis, J. C. Hills. Annual meeting in Dec. Henry Sorensen, Sexton.

*Sunday School.*—O. A. Phelps, Sup't; Solon P. Davis, Ass't; Miss Margaret B. Lee, Sup't Primary Dep't; Mrs. O. A. Phelps, Ass't Primary Dep't; Mrs. S. P. Davis, Sup't Home Dep't; Ferdinand Richter, Sec'y; J. C. Hills, Treas. and Librarian; Newman Hungerford, Ass't; Teachers, 33; Scholars, 181; Home Dep't, 50; Library, 500 vols. School at 2 P.M.

## SWEDISH EVANGELICAL LUTHERAN EMANUEL CHURCH.—COR. BABCOCK AND RUSS STS.
Rev. S. C. FRANZEN, Pastor; August Hanson, C. J Anderson, Gus. Hellstgom, Deacons; David Stromberg, Neils Nelson, P. Alfred Johnson, J. M. Johnson, C. O. Anderson, John Nelson, Trustees; John Anderson. Sec'y; C. O. Anderson, Treas. Services Sundays, 10.30 A.M., 7.45 P.M.; Thursdays, 7.45 P.M. Organized Nov. 12, 1889. Annual meeting 1st Monday in Jan.

*Sunday School.*—Gustave Nelson, Sup't: meets at 12 noon. *Young People's Society Fortuna.*—Meets 1st and 3d Tuesday evenings monthly. *Ladies' Aid and Missionary Society.*—Meets last Thursday in each month.

## ALLYN MEMORIAL CHAPEL.
Entrance of Spring Grove Cemetery, 301 Windsor avenue, finished Jan. 1, 1883; cost $40,000; paid for by the late T. M. Allyn. First funeral services held therein, March 12, 1884.

ST. PATRICK'S CHURCH.

ST. PETER'S CHURCH.

## ST. PATRICK'S CHURCH.—ROMAN CATHOLIC.—83 CHURCH ST.

This Church was first formed in June, 1823, in Talcott street, and was destroyed by fire May 11, 1853. Their recent edifice was dedicated Dec. 14, 1851, and was destroyed by fire Jan. 24, 1875. Their present edifice was dedicated Nov. 26, 1876; consecrated Oct. 4, 1884. The length from the outside of tower to outside of chancel, is 166½ feet, and the breadth is 78 feet; the height of tower and spire from ground is 216 feet; and cost $175,000. Seats for 2000 persons; 240 pews on main floor and 96 in galleries. About 5,000 members.

Very Rev. JOHN A. MULCAHY, Vicar-General, Pastor; Rev. J. J. Downey, Rev. John Loftus, Rev. John F. Ryan, Rev. Wm. P. Kennedy, Assistants; Rev. D. L. Gleason, D. D., Pastor for the Italians; David S. Moran, Organist; F. X. Fury, Sexton. Mass at 7; two at 9 and 10.30 A. M.; Vespers, 4 P. M.

*Sunday School*—Very Rev. John A. Mulcahy, Sup't; and in charge of the Sisters of Mercy, 18 Assistants; Teachers, 19; Scholars, 1050; School, 9 A. M.

## ST. PATRICK'S PAROCHIAL SCHOOL, 71 ANN STREET.

Opened September, 1897; has twenty rooms including two kindergarten rooms. Taught by the Sisters of Mercy; Very Rev. John A. Mulcahy, Pastor; No. of children, 1035.

## ST. PETER'S CHURCH—ROMAN CATHOLIC.—170 MAIN ST.

The building at this location, first occupied as a School House, then by Protestant Methodist Episcopal, and afterward rented as a Free Mission Chapel, was, September, 1859, purchased for Roman Catholic purposes, and an addition attached. It was dedicated by Bishop McFARLAND, on Sunday, December 4, 1859. In April, 1865, a freestone structure was commenced, which is 75 feet broad and 164 feet long, and it is one of the largest church edifices in the State. Its entire cost, when completed, will be over $200,000. There are church sittings in the basement, which at present are used for Sunday school and church society purposes. About 4500 members.

Rev. T. W. BRODERICK, Pastor; Rev. F. J. Lally, Rev. E. J. Broderick, Rev. T. J. Laden, Ass'ts; E. V. Caulfield, Organist. 1st Mass in church at 7 A. M.; 2d Mass at 9 A. M.; Special Mass for Children at 9.00 A. M. in basement Chapel; High Mass at 10.30 A. M.; Vespers, 3 P. M.

*Sunday School.*—Rev. Sister M. Antonia, Sup't; Teachers, 35; Scholars, 1262; School, 10 to 11 A. M. Sunday School in basement.

CONVENT OF OUR LADY OF THE SACRED HEART.—188 Main st. Rev. Sister M. Antonia, Superioress, and 16 Sisters.

## ST. PETER'S PAROCHIAL SCHOOL, NEAR 170 MAIN STREET.

Under charge of Sisters of Mercy; No. in male dep't, 446; in female dep't, 448.

## ST. LAWRENCE CHURCH—ROMAN CATHOLIC,
WILSON STREET, COR. LAUREL.

Cornerstone laid Sept. 3, 1876. Rev. THOS. J. KENA, Pastor. Mass every Sunday, 8.30 and 10.30 A. M.; Holy days at 5.30 and 8 A. M. Vespers 3.30 P. M. About 900 members. Sunday School at 3 P. M.; Miss Alice Guinan, Sup't; Teachers, 24; Scholars, 160.

## ST. JOSEPHS CATHEDRAL.—ROMAN CATHOLIC,
### 150 FARMINGTON AV.

Corner stone was laid April 29, 1877; consecrated May 8, 1892. Material used is Portland brown stone. Gothic architect, 264 ft. long, 178 ft. wide, 93 ft. high. Rt. Rev. MICHAEL TIERNEY. D.D., Bishop of Hartford; Rev. W. J. SHANLEY, Rector; Rev. JAMES P. DONOVAN, D.D., Chancellor and Sec'y; Rev. THOS. S. DUGGAN, Rev. P. H. McCLEAN, Rev. J. L. McGUINNESS. Masses 7.00; 9.00; 10.30 A.M.; Vespers 4 P.M.; School 9 A.M.; Scholars, 815.

MT. ST. JOSEPH'S CONVENT. 160 Farmington av.; building dedicated Nov. 27, 1873; it is of brick, four stories high with basement and cellar.

----

## ST. STEPHÆN'S BEN. SOCIETY (ST. STEPHANUS KRANKEN UNTERSTUTZUNGS VEREIN).—
### GERMAN ROMAN CATHOLIC.
*Organized, March 10, 1889.*

Frank Herding, Pres't; Albert Frobel, Vice Pres't; Charles J. Wittmann, Cor. Sec'y; Fred Becker, Fin. Sec'y; Paul M. Beck, Treas.; Joseph Schmidt, John Graf, John Schuessler, Trustees. Meets first Sunday monthly, at 4 P.M. Edifice corner Winthrop and Ely streets; dedicated April 9, 1893.

----

## OUR LADY OF SORROWS CHURCH,
### ROMAN CATHOLIC.                    PARKVILLE.

The corner stone was laid May 30, 1887. Church dedicated Sept. 18, 1887. Masses Sundays at 8 and 10.30 A.M., Vespers at 4 P.M. Sunday School at 2.30 P.M., in charge of Our Lady of LaSalette Missionaries.

## HARTFORD SOCIAL SETTLEMENT,
### 6 NORTH STREET.    *Organized March 1, 1896.*

Miss May G. Jones, Pres't; Mrs. Charles A. Jewell, Vice Pres't; Mrs. Frank I. Prentice, Treas.; Miss Irmagarde Rossiter, Sec'y.

*Board Managers.*—Mrs. Charles E. Dustin, Miss Harriet Gillette, Mrs. F. H. Hastings, Miss C. M. Hewins, Miss Catharine Howard, Mrs. Charles A. Jewell, Miss May G. Jones, Mrs. Charles Lamson, Prof. Alexander Merriam, Mr. Edward M. Ney, Miss F. Z. Niles, Mrs. L. B. Paton, Mrs. Arthur Perkins, Mrs. T. I. Prentice, Miss I. Rossiter, Miss Alice Stillman, Miss Margaret Warner, Mr. P. W. Yarrow, Miss Faith Collins.

*Advisory Board.*—George Pope, Clarence B. Ingraham, George R. Shepherd, Geo. H. Day, W. F. Gordy, F. S. Luther, Charles E. Dustin, John M. Holcombe, P. Henry Woodward, Rodney Dennis, Ralph W. Cutler, James P. Andrews, Lewis F. Reid, Chester D. Hartranft, E. K. Mitchell, James B. Cone, Atwood Collins, Frank H. Hastings, Lewis B. Paton, Henry Ferguson, Frank I. Prentice. Annual meeting, first Wednesday in March.

----

## ASSOCIATION ADAS ISRAEL.
### *Organized 1862.*

Meets 11 Pratt st. Saturdays and holidays, mornings and evenings. Nathan Kempner, Pres't; L. Price, Vice Pres't; Joel Samuels, Treasurer; Louis S. Price, Secretary; H. Jonas, P. Resnick, M. Dorenbaum, Trustees; M. Levy, S. Silverstein, I. Holstein, Ex. Committee; L. S. Price, J. Salad, M. Dorenbaum, A. Raphael, S. Silverstein, Burial Ground Committee. Annual election first Sunday in October.

CHURCH OF THE REDEEMER.

## CHURCH OF THE REDEEMER.—
UNIVERSALIST, 686 MAIN ST.

*Organized June 18, 1827.*

This edifice is 58 feet in width by 116 feet in length, with a tower at southwest corner 104 feet in height. There are 172 pews on the floor and 86 in the galleries. Dedicated in the fall of 1860 Services 10.45 A. M.

Rev. FREDERIC W. PERKINS, Pastor; Abner Church, L. L. Ensworth, Francis H. Richards, George H. Hebard, Deacons; Charles G. Lincoln, Clerk.

*Sabbath School.*—George H. Hebard, Sup't; F. S. Carey, Mrs. G. F. Whitney, Mrs. L. L. Ensworth, Ass'ts; Miss Emma Fowler, Sec'y; Frank Mellen, Ass't Sec'y; Arthur L. Brown, Treas.; L. Ellis, C. S. Woodward, Librarians; Library 900 vols.; Teachers, 21; Scholars, 250; School, 12.10 P. M. Annual election, Dec.

*Society.*—C. N. Fowler, R. W. Farmer, F. H. Richards, E. S. Belden, Joseph Buths, Com.; C. G. Lincoln, Clerk; W. I. Wakefield, Treas. Annual meeting, last Monday in March. Wm. T. Plimpton, Org.; A. Sommermann, Sexton.

## GRACE CHAPEL.—EPISCOPAL.
NEW PARK AVENUE.

*Edifice Consecrated November 11, 1868.*

GEO. K. MACNAUGHT, Minister in charge; Christopher Johnson, Herman Luchrig, Prudential Committee; Hiram W. Elmer, Sec'y; Christopher S. Johnstone, Treas. The meetings of the Prudential Committee are opened to all members of the chapel. Services Sundays, 10.45 A. M. and 7 P. M., Fridays, 7.45 P. M.

*Sunday School.*— George K. MacNaught, Sup't; James Monks, Sec'y. Meets at 2.30 P. M.; Teachers, 14; Scholars, 150; 250 vols. in Library; 300 vols. in Guild Library.

## HARBISON AVENUE CHAPEL,
WEST END OF HARBISON AV.

*Dedicated June 11, 1875.* School 4.15 P.M.

## FIRST PRESBYTERIAN CHURCH,
136 CAPITOL AVE., COR. CLINTON STREET.

*Organized November 4, 1851.*

This second edifice was dedicated May 17th, 1870. The Church is built of Connecticut granite, with trimmings of Portland and Ohio stone. The tower and spire to rise 135 feet. The whole building is 123 by 57 feet. The audience room of the Church is 86 by 50 feet. Services at 10.45 A. M. and 7 30 P. M.; Young People's meeting at 6.30 P. M. 303 members.

Rev. W. W. BRECKENRIDGE, Pastor; Alexander Watson, John Johnston, Robert J. Carey, John Gray, Ruling Elders.

*Society.*—Samuel Collins, Henry Ford, John Johnston, Wm. B. Low, James Pullar, Chas. Pullar, John J. Laing, Trustees; Fred. D. Berry, Clerk; John Johnston, Treas.; Charles G. Small, Ass't Treas. Annual meeting 3d Tuesday in March.

*Sabbath School.*—Rev. W. W. Breckenridge, Sup't; John Gray, Ass't Sup't; Miss L. J. Harrison, Sec'y; James Johnson, Ass't Sec'y; S. H. Berry, Tr.; J. A. M. Bell, Librarian; Fred. Lycett, Ass't Librarian; 600 vols. in Library; Teachers, 22; Scholars, 179; School, 12.15 P.M.

FIRST PRESBYTERIAN CHURCH.

**SWEDISH ZION CONGREGATIONAL CHURCH,**
87 RUSS STREET CORNER HUNGERFORD STREET.
*Organized October 25, 1889.*

Rev. L. W. A. BJORKMAN, Pastor; John Nilson, C.
J. Carlson, John Johnson, L. R. Larson, J. A. Magnuson,
I. Ringstrom, Deacons; Mathilda J. Engstrom, J. Ma-
thilda Svenson, Hulda Lindgren, Ebba Nilson, Ida
Thompson, Emma L. Johnson, Deaconesses; F. E.
Wedberg, Binzen Johnson, F. W. Larson, Amandus
Carlson, John A. Sandberg, John Olsen, Trustees; A.
Gust. Anderson, Clerk; F. E. Wedberg, Treas.; Wall
Seaholm, A. W. Gidart, Auditors; L. Gustaf Svenson,
Organist; I. Ringstrom, Sexton.

Services, Sunday 10.30 A.M. and 7.30 P.M.; Wednesdays and Fridays, 7.30 P.M. Members, 173.

*Sunday School.*—Rev. L. W. A. Bjorkman, Sup't;
Wall Seaholm, Ass't; P. N. Nyman, Sec'y; Gust. A.
Edstrom, Treas.; Bergen Johnson, Auditor; Anna S.
Soderstrom, Organist. Teachers, 7; Scholars, 92;
School, 12 noon. Annual meeting 1st Sunday in Jan.

**SWEDISH BAPTIST CHURCH.**
*Organized Oct 27, 1888.*

Rev. NILS EK, W. Hartford, Pastor; J. Erickson, G.
A. Johnson, Deacons; A. G. Zettergren, Treas.; Fred
Wilen, August Johnson, Committee. Services in the
South Baptist Church Chapel, Sundays at 10.45 A.M.
and 7.45 P.M.; Wednesdays, 7.45 P.M. Communion,
first Sunday monthly. Annual meeting in Jan.

Young People's Society meet Sundays at 6 P.M., at
234 Pearl st.; O. Johnson, Pres't; A. G. Zettergren,
Secretary.

**SWEDISH EMANUEL M. E. CHURCH,**
302 ASYLUM ST.          *Organized Sept. 21, 1895.*

Rev. FRANK E. BROMAN, Pastor; Emil Hjerpe, Sec'y
and Treas.; A. P. Nelson, Emil Friberg, P. A. Edlund,
Charles Ackerman, Gustaf Engstrand, Trustees. Ser-
vices Sunday at 10.45 A.M. and 7.45 P.M.; Tuesdays
Classmeetings at 7.45 P.M. Epworth League meet on
Sundays at 6.45 P.M.

*Sunday School.*—Alex R. Nylin, Sup't; meets at 12
noon.

**CHURCH OF SACRED HEART,** 33 WINDSOR ST.
ITALIAN ROMAN CATHOLIC.

Rev. D. L. GLEESON, D.D., Pastor. Number of communicants in Hartford 1,500.

**ASSO'N BROTHERS, CHILDREN OF ISRAEL,**
REAR 194 FRONT STREET.

Rev. JOSEPH KRAMM, Rabbi; Rev. Barnet Feinstein.
Ass't Rabbi; N. Kempner, Pres't; L. Katz, Vice Pres't;
Israel Brody, Sec'y; Abraham Hess, F. Sec'y; I. Rosen-
feld, L. Sablidowsky, H. Sidowsky, Trustees; S. Fine,
Sexton. Organized October, 1884. Meet Saturdays
at 10 A.M. Annual meeting in October.

**BROTHERHOOD OF ANDREW AND PHILIP,**
FOURTH CONGREGATIONAL CHURCH.
*Organized July, 1891.*

Rev. H. H. Kelsey, Pres't; Frank M. Johnson, Treas.;
Robert E. Lee, Cor. Sec'y. Meets at call of the President.

**GLENWOOD CONGREGATIONAL CHURCH,**
87 LAUREL STREET.          *Organized July 17, 1894.*

A Chapel which seats 225, was built in 1896, costing
$3,500. Services at 10.45 A.M.

Rev. H. DeWITT WILLIAMS, Pastor; H. M. Smith,
R. T. Huntington, A. A. Lewis, Deacons; S. P. Phipps,
Clerk; R. W. Williamson, Treas.; J. B. Sexton, Pres't;
S. P. Phipps, Clerk, C. W. Crane, S. E. Doane, E J.
Horner, R. W. Williamson, S. L. Gibbs, F. A. Seaver,
George H. Williams, Trustees. 57 members. Annual
meeting 1st Thursday after 1st Sunday in January.

*Sabbath School.*—F. Haskell Smith, Sup't; Albert A.
Lewis, Ass't; Fred A. Seaver, Treas.; Miss Maud B.
Wills, Sec'y; James Grierson, Librarian. 125 mem-
bers. 300 volumes in Library.

**HARTFORD BAPTIST UNION.**

Curnot O. Spencer, President; Frederick W. Payne,
Vice President; H. H. Dickinson, Secretary; John
Gemmill, Treas. Election 3d Wednesday in April.

**HARTFORD PRAYING BAND.**
*Organized Jan. 31, 1896.*

Charles W. Hills, Pres't; James Nichols, V. Pres't;
Rev. N. M. Learned, Leader; James P. Mumford, Rec
Sec'y; H. Cowlishaw, Treas.; Charles F. Agard, Chor
ister; Thomas F. Hill, Ass't Chorister; Alice Agard
Organist. Meets at 305 Asylum st., Room 2, 2d Fri-
day evening, monthly. Annual election 1st Friday in
January. 15 members.

**HARTFORD CHRISTIAN ENDEAVOR UNION.**
*Organized Oct. 19, 1887.*

Nelson B. Bassett, Pres't; Harry E. Parkhurst, Sec'y
and Treas.; H. DeWitt Williams, Ira Strong, Jr., N.
B. Bassett, Harry E. Parkhurst, Leila M. Smart, Mar-
ion Engelke, H. DeWitt Williams, Ira J. Strong, Annie
R. McDonnell, Mary E. Coleman, William A. Willard,
Executive Committee. Meets in Feb., April, June,
October and Dec. Annual meeting in October.

**NEW BRITAIN AVENUE SUNDAY SCHOOL,**
1 NEW BRITAIN AV.          *Organized June, 1878.*

C. F. Agard, Sup't; H. S. House, Mrs. Henry House,
Ass't Sup't; Richard L. Joslyn, Treas.; Miss M. B.
Watrous, Sec'y; R. W. Walkey, Librarian; Richard L.
Joslyn, Ass't Librarian; Miss I. L. Mill, Choirister,
H. K. Gage, Sup't Mission Work; Miss E. J. Whitta-
ker, Chairman Mission Committee; Miss L L. Mill.
Chairman Local Committee. Meets 3 P.M. Sundays.
Annual election in January.

**OLIVET BAPTIST CHURCH,** PARKVILLE.
*Chapel built in 1888. Enlarged and renovated in 1896.*
*Church organized March 26, 1896.*

Rev. JAS. B. CONNELL, Pastor; Wm. G. Reid, Wm.
C. Lee, Deacons; G. B. Turner, Clerk; J. G. D. Newton, Treas.; Nellie M. Barrows, Ass't Tr. 48 members.

*Sunday School.*—G. B. Turner, Sup't; Wm. G. Reid.
Ass't; Fred Gould, Sec'y; Caira C. Crossett, Treas.;
S. Hastings, Librarian; 15 Teachers; 112 Scholars;
600 vols. in Library. Meets in Parkville Baptist Chapel
at 12.15 P.M. Preaching at 10.45 A.M. and 7 P.M. Sundays. Organized in 1874. Annual meeting in March.

## OUR SAVIOUR'S DANISH EVANGELICAL LUTHERAN CHURCH, RUSS, COR. BABCOCK ST.

Org. *May*, 1883. *Dedicated May* 31, 1891.
Rev. K. P. BRUCKNER, Pastor; N. Due, President; R. Bahnson, Secretary; S. Hansen, Treas. and Trustee; L. Esbensen, Cashier; P. C. Toft, Andrew Martensen, B. Holst, C. Christensen, P. Christensen, Directors. Services on Sunday, 10.30 A.M. and 7.30 P.M.; Thursday, 8 P.M. Annual meeting 2d Sunday in July.

## SECOND ADVENT CHURCH,

FOOT GUARD PLACE. Org. 1859. *Reorganized*, 1879. This edifice is built of wood 35x60 feet, and was dedicated May 27, 1838. Pastorship vacant; Lucian Tiffany, Miles Clark, S. B. Colton, M. G. Dunham, H. E. Kinsman, Deacons; Mrs. M. G. Dunham, Mrs. P. A. Pierson, Mrs. H. E. Kinsman, Mrs. Emily Roland, Mrs. Matilda Dart, Mrs. H. M. Goodell, Deaconesses; M. G Dunham, H. M. Andrews, A. P. Sloan, H. E. Kinsman, M. E. Lord, Committee; William J. Pierce, Treas. and Clerk. Service at 10.45 A.M., and 7.30 P.M. Sunday School at 12 M. Annual meeting last week in March.

## SHILOH BAPTIST CHURCH, 127 MATHER ST.

*Organized Jan.* 9, 1890.
Rev. GEORGE W. TYLER, Pastor; J. H. Ellis, E. R. Jones, Jackson Lewis, J. S. Taylor, Deacons; David Robb, Treas.; John S. Taylor, L. S. Johnson, Clerks. Services at 10.45 A.M. and 7.30 P.M. *Sunday School.*— E. R. Jones, Sup't; Sad Jones, 81 Green street, Clerk; Mrs. M. Shaw, Treas. Meet at 12.15 P.M. Annual meeting in March.

## SEVENTH DAY ADVENTIST SOCIETY.

*Organized July* 8, 1893.
Elder D. B. PARMELEE, Pastor; Timothy B. Stewart, Deacon and Treas.; O. M. Hatch, Clerk; D. B. Parmelee, John Drake, Timothy B. Stewart, O. M. Hatch, Church Committee. 23 members. Services in Hall, 724 Main st., Saturdays at 3 P.M. Annual meeting in January. *Sabbath School*—O. M. Hatch, Sup't; W. R. Andrews, Ass't Sup't; Mrs. Jennie Hatch, Sec'y and Treas.; Mrs. L. S. Stevens, Ass't. Teachers, 5; Scholars, 30; School on Saturdays at 2 P.M. Election in June.

## SOCIETY OF CHRISTIAN ENDEAVOR

OF WINDSOR AVENUE CONGREGATIONAL CHURCH.
*Organized December*, 1886.
Charlotte S. Hull, Pres't; Raymond E. Stronach, Vice Pres't; Mabel Stronach, Sec'y; Allen C. Bragaw, Treas.; Mrs. C. H. Brigham, Cor. Sec'y. Meets Monday evenings in chapel.

## SOCIETY OF CHRISTIAN ENDEAVOR

OF THE PEARL STREET CONGREGATIONAL CHURCH.
*Organized Nov.* 29, 1886.
William A. Willard, Pres't; Wm. G. Baxter, Vice Pres't; Miss Grace D. Thayer, Sec'y; Miss M. Louise Allen, Cor. Sec'y; Wm. B. Bassett, Treas. Meets at Pearl street church every Sunday evening at 6.30.

## SOCIETY OF CHRISTIAN ENDEAVOR

OF SOUTH PARK METHODIST EPISCOPAL CHURCH.
*Organized May* 21, 1889.
Fulton Q. Lawson, Pres't; R. E. McCausland, Vice Pres't; Ida J. Wells, Rec. Sec'y; H. E. Parkhurst, Cor. Sec'y; Richard G. Cook, Treas. Meets Sunday at 6.15 P.M. Business meeting 1st Friday following 1st Sunday.

## SOCIETY OF CHRISTIAN ENDEAVOR

OF SWEDISH ZION CONGREGATIONAL CHURCH.
John Olson, President; Alex Peterson, Vice Pres't; Gust A. Edstrom, Sec'y; Arthur A. Engstrom, Treas. Members 62. Meet Sundays at 6 P.M. from October to May, and Mondays at 7 P.M. from May to October. Annual meeting 1st Monday in Jan.

## YOUNG PEOPLE'S SOCIETY

OF THE WARBURTON CHAPEL. *Organized*, 1897.
Oscar A. Phelps, Pres't; Mary L. Hastings, Sec'y; Mrs. J. C. Hills, Treas. Mrs. O. A. Phelps, Chairman Social Committee. Mrs. N. Hungerford, Chairman Missionary Committee. Mrs. J. C. Hills, Chairman Prayer Meeting Committee.

## IN HIS NAME,

CIRCLE OF KING'S DAUGHTERS.
Emma E. Campbell, 165 Collins st., Leader; Mrs. C. F. Gordon, Vice Leader; Carrie F. Hamilton. Rec. Sec'y; Edith M. Harrington, 24 Hopkins st., Cor. Sec'y; Lena A. Burwell, Treas.

## SOCIETY OF CHRISTIAN ENDEAVOR

OF THE ASYLUM AVENUE BAPTIST CHURCH.
Charles E. Prior, Pres't; Howard H. Burdick, Vice Pres't; Carrie F. Hamilton, Sec'y; Emma E. Campbell, Cor. Sec'y; Lena A. Burwell, Treas.

## TRINITY COLLEGE CHAPEL.

The President is Chaplain.—Daily Prayers, 8.30 A.M. Sundays: Holy Communion, at 7.45 A.M.; Morning Prayer and Sermon, 9.15 A.M.; Evening Prayer, 5 P.M. Special services in Lent.

## YOUNG PEOPLE'S ASSOCIATION

OF FIRST PRESBYTERIAN CHURCH.
*Organized June*, 1878.
John Gray, Pres't; Hugh Purdy, Jr., Vice Pres't; Miss Isabel Eadie, Sec'y; J. Harry Ford, Treas.; Mrs. N. F. Tilton, Stewardess. Meets last Tuesday evening of each month. Annual meeting last Tuesday, Sept.

## YOUNG PEOPLE'S ASSOCIATION

OF FIRST BAPTIST CHURCH.
*Organized December*, 1877.
Francis H. Spencer, Pres't; Wm. H. Sloane, Ida F. Nichols, Vice Pres'ts; Fred. S. Chapman, Sec'y; Annie B. Brown, Ass't Sec'y; Guy E. Beardsley, Treas.; Bert W. Chapman, E. B. Bliss, Auditors. Annual meeting 2d Tuesday in March.

## YOUNG PEOPLE'S GUILD

OF CHURCH OF THE REDEEMER.—UNIVERSALIST.
*Organized November*, 1888.
Frank G. Mellen, President; Ernest C. Day, Vice Pres't; Garrett Brown, Rec. Sec'y; Lottie Champlin, Cor. Sec'y; Clinton S. Woodward, Treas.; Arthur L. Brown, Historian. Meets Sunday evenings at 6.15. Semi-annual election of officers, first Wednesdays in Oct. and March.

## YOUNG PEOPLE'S SOCIETY

OF THE CENTER CHURCH.
Lucius H. Holt, Pres't; Elliott F. Talmadge, Sec'y; Carl W. Davis, Treas. Formed February, 1897 from the Society of Christian Endeavor organized 1885 and reorganized 1895. Meets Sundays at 6.45 P.M. in chapel.

## YOUNG MEN'S UNION

OF THE SOUTH CONGREGATIONAL CHURCH.
*Organized Nov.* 1889.
A. H. Loomis, Pres't; Geo. B. Thayer, Merrick W. Chapin, V. Pres'ts; Philip D. Burnham, Sec'y; Henry S. Robinson, Treas; the above officers, Lucius F. Robinson, C. Howard Gillette, Edwin T. Northam, L. P. White and Philip Montgomery, Executive Committee. Meets in the chapel on Thursday evenings. Annual election in October.

## YOUNG PEOPLE'S SOCIETY "ENIGHET"

OF FIRST SWEDISH METHODIST EPISCOPAL CHURCH.
*Organized March* 1, 1897.
Aug. P. Syreen, Pres't; Emil Hedlund, C. Winell, Oscar Hjerpe, Vice Presidents; Oscar Larson, Sec'y; Emma Nelson, Treas. Meetings Sundays at 6.45 P.M. and 1st Thursday each month at 7.45 P.M. Business meetings 1st Saturday each month at 7.45 P.M.

RETREAT FOR THE INSANE.

# The Retreat for the Insane

## No. 30 WASHINGTON STREET.

WAS Incorporated in 1822, and was opened for the reception of patients April 1, 1824. There were at that time but three or four like Institutions in the country, and the necessity of this one had been strongly urged. The funds for its establishment came mostly from individuals of benevolent character, who were kindly disposed, and who saw how great the need was. As its reputation increased under the judicious administration of Dr. Todd, it became necessary to furnish further accommodations. These have been increased until now there are various apartments for one hundred and sixty patients. A handsome double cottage costing $18,000 is one of the improvements for the year; a $5,900 cottage adjoins it. Also two new cottages have been erected which are not only of great utility, but add materially to the already attractive surroundings.

There are but few institutions better equipped than this, and the Directors have determined to offer to the friends of these unfortunate people all the comforts, conveniences and means of restoration to health that it is possible to furnish. The prices of board necessarily vary with the accommodations offered; but all have the same medical skill and kind attention.

The Retreat is but filling a demand for an institution of its character. It might with as much propriety be said that all hotels should be of a third or fourth rate class, as that all asylums for the care and treatment of the Insane should be alike. The well furnished rooms, the increased number of attendants, the best medical skill,—everything which money can afford to the sane, and which is frequently demanded by the Insane,—is here offered.

It ought to be remembered that neither the directors nor any others engaged with them in this charitable work receive any compensation whatever, excepting that the Treasurer is paid two hundred dollars per annum for his care of the accounts, and that the Medical Visitors receive ten dollars each, as part payment of their traveling expense. This is all the compensation paid to any one, excepting to the immediate personal officers and servants. The Retreat has but a comparatively small amount of permanent invested funds, and so necessarily derives its support from the board of patients. The great improvements which have been made have been chiefly from this source. The small endowments we have enable us to help some of the poor Insane, whose education and former circumstances in life render this a fitting place for their abode. With increased endowments we should be enabled to do much more.

Religious services have been conducted as usual during the past year by our chaplain, and there has been about the same number of patients as usual, in which the form of disease was such as to admit of attendance on the daily exercises.

The usual entertainments conducted in the amusement hall have again this year been supplemented by a daily practice of light gymnastics, conducted by Dr. Down. The readings, which have not usually exceeded an hour in length, have been anticipated with interest by all concerned, as affording a change to the current of thought and usual games and occupations of the halls.

A training school for attendants has been conducted by recitations and examinations in such elementary branches as have been deemed best.

The grounds are open to visitors on the afternoon of each day, excepting Sunday, and visitors may be admitted by card from either of the Managers, Rodney Dennis, Jonathan B. Bunce or William B. Clark.

There have been twenty-nine recoveries during the year, amounting to thirty-three per cent. of the admissions. There have been fifteen deaths, amounting to six per cent. on total number present. Total number in Retreat April 1, 1897, 164; 78 females, 76 males.

No patient is admitted for a shorter term than three months; and payment for *that term only* is to be made *in advance to the Steward or Treasurer.*

Letters relating to quarterly bills and clothing should be addressed to Henry J. Thompson, the Steward. Clothing and packages sent for the use of the inmates should be sent to the care of the Steward.

All letters in relation to the situation and health of the patients, etc., will, of course, be addressed to Dr. Henry P. Stearns, the Superintendent.

Application for the admission of patients must be made to Superintendent, Dr. H. P. Stearns, at Retreat, *previous to the patient's being brought to the Retreat,* in all cases. A brief statement of the case should accompany the application.

The meetings of the Board of MEDICAL VISITORS are held during the year at the regular quarterly periods, and frequent occasional tours of inspection are also made by members of the Board. Patients are afforded frequent opportunities of talking with members of the Board, and of making such statements as they please regarding their own condition, their treatment and their own surrounding. It is believed that no reasonable ground for serious dissatisfaction has been found during the year, and the general morale of the patients is remarkably good. Changes are continually making in the direction of increasing the beauty, cheerfulness, and homelikeness of their abode; if any expenditures of thought or money will help to solve the important problem of employment for the Insane, it will, in the opinion of the Medical Visitors, be well bestowed as a sanitary means.

MEDICAL VISITORS.—Gurdon W. Russell, M.D.; Harmon G. Howe, M. D.; Francis Bacon, M. D.: Geo. L. Porter, M.D.: George R. Shepherd, M.D.; L. B. Almy, M.D.

VISITING COMMITTEE OF LADIES.—Mrs. F. B. Cooley, Mrs. Thomas Sisson, Mrs. J. H. Sprague, Mrs. James B. Cone. Mrs.T. O. Enders, Mrs. J. M. Holcomb, Mrs. G. G. Williams.

Visitations are made often by four Directors, with a change every month of these visitors.

THE PRESIDENT AND DIRECTORS OF THE RETREAT FOR THE INSANE.—80 *Washington.*
GURDON W. RUSSELL, *President.*
NATH'L SHIPMAN,*V.Pres't.* | THOMAS SISSON, *Treas.*
JAMES B. CONE, *Sec'y.* | ROWLAND SWIFT, *Aud'r.*
*Directors.*—James L. Howard, Jona. B. Bunce, Francis B. Cooley, Chas. M. Beach, Nath'l Shipman, T. Sisson, Gen. Joseph R. Hawley, Rodney Dennis, Rev. Francis Goodwin, John C. Day, Rowland Swift, James B. Cone, Henry P. Stearns, Col. Frank W. Cheney, Wm. B. Clark, J. M. Allen, D. R. Howe, J. D. Browne, Dr. G. Pierrepont Davis, P. H. Woodward.
*Managers.*—Rodney Dennis; Jonathan B. Bunce, Pres. Phœnix Mutual Life Ins. Co.; Wm. B. Clark, Pres. Ætna Ins. Co.
HENRY P. STEARNS, M.D., *Superintendent & Physician.*
JAMES R. BOLTON, M.D., *Assistant Physician.*
EDWARD ATKINSON, 2d *Assistant Physician.*
HENRY J. THOMPSON, *Steward.*
Mrs. C. J. MERRIMAN, *Clerk.*
Rev. J. W. BRADIN, *Chaplain.*
Miss H. E. BACON, *Matron.*
ANDREW J. SIZER, *Supervisor.*
EVA F. KILBY, *Supervisor.*

CHARTERED IN 1854. HARTFORD HOSPITAL. 20 So. HUDSON STREET.

# Hartford Hospital;

Dedicated May 19, 1859. Cost of building and grounds, $244,803; all of which was donated by individuals except $50,000 from this state. A "Contagious Ward" department, now completed at a cost of $25,000, containing 19 beds, has been opened for contagious diseases.

## OFFICERS OF THE HARTFORD HOSPITAL.

GURDON W. RUSSELL, M. D., *President.*
JONATHAN B. BUNCE, Esq., *Vice President.* WARD W. JACOBS, *Secretary and Treasurer.*
*Executive Committee.*—Henry K. Morgan, Harmon G. Howe, M. D., Thomas Sisson.
*Finance Committee.*—Jonathan B. Bunce, Henry A. Redfield, Henry C. Dwight.
*Auditors.*—Jonathan B. Bunce, Henry A. Redfield.
*Directors.*—Gurdon W. Russell, M.D., Jonathan B. Bunce, Henry C. Robinson, Henry K. Morgan, Thomas Sisson, Harmon G Howe, M. D., Henry A. Redfield, Melancthon Storrs, M. D., Henry C. Dwight, James J. Goodwin, G. Pierrepont Davis, M. D., Atwood Collins, Miles B. Preston, *ex-officio.*
*Medical and Surgical Staff.*—Gurdon W. Russell, M. D., *Chairman;* P. H. Ingalls, M. D., *Secretary.*
*Consulting Physicians and Surgeons.*—Gurdon W. Russell, M.D., George R. Shepherd, M.D., William Porter, M.D.
*Visiting Physicians and Surgeons*—George C. Jarvis, M. D., G. Pierrepont Davis, M. D., Harmon G. Howe, M.D., Melancthon Storrs, M.D., Horace S. Fuller, M.D., William W. Knight, M.D., Edward K. Root, M.D., Charles C. Beach, M.D.
*Assistant Surgeons*—Ansel G. Cook, M. D., James Campbell, M. D.
*Ophthalmic and Aural Surgeons.*—Wm. T. Bacon, M.D., Sam'l B. St. John, M.D. *Gynecologist.*—P. H. Ingalls, M.D.
*Pathologist and Bacteriologist.*—Philip S. Bunce, M. D. *Orthopedic Surgeon.*—Everett J. McKnight, M. D.
*Lady Sup't Training School.*—Miss Elisabeth M. Friend. *Superintendent.*—Benjamin S. Gilbert.
*Apothecary.*—Henry W. Fuller. Annual meeting second Wednesday in December.

The growth of the Hospital from the first opening of the present building in 1860, will be better realized by comparing the number of beds available at that and the present time. In 1860 the number of beds was 48—40 in the wards, and 8 private rooms. The present capacity is 200 beds—145 in the five wards, 22 private rooms, 21 beds in children's ward, and 12 in the lying-in department. So rapidly has the demand for hospital care increased that, at some periods of the year, present accommodations are barely sufficient.

The number of patients remaining at date of last report was 161; admitted during the year, 1,558; the daily average was 144; the largest number for one day was 166; the smallest number for one day was 113.

The deaths numbered 187. Of these 16 were the result of accidents, and lived but a short time after admission; 26 were received as hopeless cases, and 31 were due to consumption. The appropriation from the State, of $5,000, has partially supported 1,121 patients, at the rate of 99½c. per week for each patient. The average cost per week for each patient was $8.26. Patients have been received from 76 different towns in the State.

The pavilion for contagious diseases built within the amount subscribed by citizens, namely, $25,000, and is 109 by 48 feet, has 7 rooms and 19 beds for patients.

THE TRAINING SCHOOL FOR NURSES, under the direction of Miss Elizabeth M. Friend has been ably conducted. The graduates of the year, 13 in number, under examination, proved themselves fully competent, and we can confidently recommend them to whoever may need intelligent and efficient service.

The graduates of previous years who have remained in the city and vicinity have been in demand, and are fully appreciated by those persons who have had occasion to employ them.

The Executive Committee direct the internal management, including the grounds and buildings, both of the Hospital and Home.

The visiting physicians and surgeons take charge of the medical and surgical departments, and arrange their time for visiting the Hospital. Acute cases are visited every day, and chronic cases as often as necessity requires.

All moneys for board of patients at the Hospital and inmates of the home must be paid to the Superintendent.

Patients to the Hospital may be admitted by either member of the Executive Committee, subject to the approval of said Committee at their regular Hospital meeting.

Inmates of the home must be admitted and discharged by a unanimous vote of said Committee present at said meeting.

Neither the Medical Staff nor Executive Committee shall receive from the Hospital or Home compensation in any form for duties performed in their behalf.

The regular visits of the visiting physicians and surgeons are made daily between the hours of 8 A. M. and 1 P. M.

Extra visits shall be made whenever the necessity of the case demands.

They shall report to the Superintendent patients who are in a proper condition to be discharged from the Hospital.

No operation shall be performed without the consent of the patient; but if consent cannot be obtained after all the surgeons in consultation have decided that the patient's safety demands it, the visiting surgeon shall advise the discharge of the patient from the Hospital.

The resident physician and surgeon shall visit the patients in their respective wards every morning and evening, and be prepared to report their condition to the visiting physicians and surgeons.

No ardent spirits or other stimulating drinks shall be brought into the Hospital by the patients or their friends; neither shall patients be furnished fruit or any article of food, without the knowledge or permission of the Superintendent.

All patients are admitted by permit from one of the Executive Committee or Superintendent, who arranges the price per week, according to the circumstances of the case and accommodations required.

OLD PEOPLE'S HOME.

CHARTERED IN 1873.

96 JEFFERSON STREET.

# Old People's Home.

## Executive Officers of the Old People's Home.

### Executive Committee,

HENRY K. MORGAN,  HARMON G. HOWE, M. D.,  THOMAS SISSON.

Physician, JOSEPH B. HALL, M. D.

BENJAMIN S. GILBERT, *Superintendent.*

Mrs. E. J. FOX, Matron.  CARRIE M. FOX, Assistant Matron.

THIS department of the Hospital was opened for the reception of inmates December 1, 1884.

The present number of permanent inmates is 57; boarders, 6; —total, 63.

*There is a class of aged and infirm persons who cannot find homes* with their relatives or friends, either through inability in adapting themselves to new surroundings, or whose habits and disposition render them disagreeable and uncomfortable to their friends or relatives, who may be willing, or are morally bound, to afford them a home in their old age. These should not be considered objects of public charity. While it might be proper to admit them as boarders, their friends should be chargeable for their full support. The Home should not assume any responsibility for their future, unless a sum, the interest of which would be sufficient for this purpose, should be paid into the treasury of the Hospital, and become a part of the permanent fund.

*Another class of applicants includes those aged and homeless persons* who are in possession of some small amount of money, but insufficient for their comfortable support, and if their years are prolonged, the dreary prospect of the almshouse is before them. These ought to be received as permanent inmates, provided the conditions of admission are satisfied; and as the admission fee will only cover the expense of support for a year or two, any property they may possess over and above this amount should be paid over to the Treasurer of the Hospital, to indemnify the institution in some slight degree for the responsibility assumed.

*Still another class* comprises those aged, infirm and homeless ones who are destitute of friends and means of support. This class is a large one, and appeals strongly to our sympathy.

*The liberality of our citizens toward the Hospital encourages us* in the firm belief that, when the needs of the "Old People's Home" are fully appreciated and the vast amount of good to be accomplished by its agency is understood, it will not suffer for lack of funds, and that in the near future, the terms of admission may be made more liberal. It has been a source of regret to those in its management that for want of money they have been obliged to refuse admission to many worthy aged and infirm persons, who have been looking forward to this Home for shelter in their declining years.

*This department has some unique features,* differing in many respects from institutions of similar purpose in our country. Many of the Homes for the aged and infirm are established and maintained by religious denominations for the care of those members of their own churches in need. Others are limited to residence in the city or town where they are located. Others, still, are established for the benefit of a particular race. Few receive both sexes.

In some respects the Old People's Home is a novel experiment, restricted neither by religious tenets, residents in the city, sex or race.

The building has proved to be admirably fitted in every respect for the purpose designed, furnishing a pleasant and comfortable home for the aged and infirm. It offers shelter, wholesome food, warmth, and medical service (a not inconsiderable item with the aged). Its doors are open and cannot be closed upon those of its inmates who desire to withdraw at any time.

Persons desiring temporary accommodation, in the Home will be charged such a sum as the Executive Committee may find necessary to cover the expenses of board, etc.

*Applicants for admission* to the Old People's Home must be citizens of Hartford County, persons of good character, not under 60 years of age, and in reduced circumstances.

Applications for admission must be made to the Executive Committee, and a full statement of circumstances of applicant must be given.

*The friends of inmates* and the public generally may visit the Home on Thursday, between the hours of 10 and 12 o'clock A. M., and from 2 to 4 o'clock P. M. At other times visitors will be admitted only by permission of the Superintendent or Matron.

No physician except those connected with the Hospital will be allowed to attend the inmates, except by permission of the Chairman or some member of the Executive Committee.

No spirituous liquors shall be brought into the Home, nor shall any be used by any inmate unless the same be prescribed by the attending physician, and placed in charge of and administered by the Matron.

Two trained nurses are in attendance continuously upon the feeble and sick.

# Young Men's Christian Association of Hartford.

## 315 to 323 PEARL STREET, Corner of JEWELL and FORD STREETS.

Open from 9 A. M. to 10 P. M..          ▪ ▪ ▪                    SUNDAYS, 1 to 6 P. M.

President, CHARLES A. JEWELL.          Treasurer, CHARLES T. WELLES.
General Secretary, GEORGE M. HERSEY.
Treasurer Board of Trustees, APPLETON R. HILLYER.

**Organized in 1878.**          ▪ ▪ ▪          **Incorporated in 1884.**

First rooms were located southwest corner Grove and Prospect streets, and were opened April 29, 1878. Later the house on the opposite corner, (southeast) was occupied by the Association. In January, 1887, the Association removed to the Foster Building, corner of Asylum and Ann streets, occupying a large portion of the second floor, and introducing a *Physical Department.* On November 8, 1893, the new and commodious building now occupied was opened to the public, with appropriate exercises. This building is the center of the youthful advocates of a large and interested membership, numbering May 1, 1331.

The Association is organized into departments, such as *Business,. Educational, Information and Relief, Junior, Physical, Social, Religious,* and *Workingmen's Exchange.* Under these different departments, the needs of a varied and very large class of young men are met. All creeds and races are welcome to join, the one requirement being: self-respect and regard for the rights of others. The fees charged for the many privileges offered being placed at a moderate figure, and adjusted by departments, so that a member is not obliged to pay for features in which he is not particularly interested.

The *Educational Department* is worthy of the remaining space on this page. It was endowed with fifty thousand dollars ($50,000) by Mr. A. R. HILLYER and Miss CLARA E. HILLYER, as a memorial to their deceased father, General CHARLES T. HILLYER. It is known as

## HILLYER INSTITUTE.

*Industrial, Commercial,* and other branches are taught. Some twenty teachers are employed, giving instruction in the following: Architectural, Freehand, and Mechanical Drawing, Woodwork, Forging, Plumbing, Electricity, Physics, Chemistry. Arithmetic, English Grammar and Composition, Spelling, Bookkeeping. Penmanship, Shorthand, Algebra, and Geometry. If the class is large, it is subdivided, and has more than one teacher

The instruction is given in the evening, in order to reach those who are employed in the day time. There are two terms of twenty lessons each. The fall term will open about October 10, 1898. Last winter the total enrollment in all classes was 433.

Applications for membership in any department of the Association, should be made at the Business Office at the building.

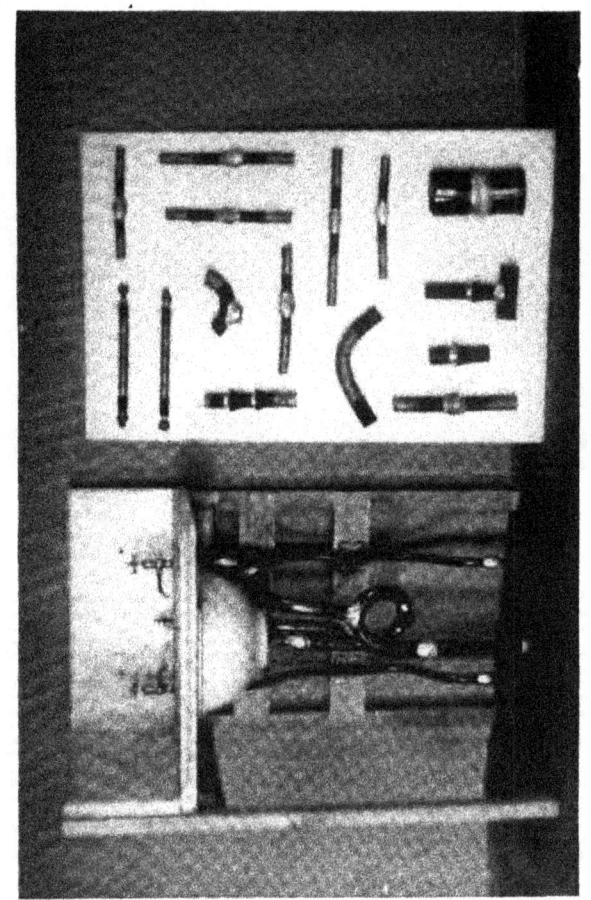

WORK OF PLUMBING CLASS PUPILS, HILLYER INSTITUTE.

See opposite page.

# Trinity College,

## SUMMIT STREET, HARTFORD, CONN.

The Charter of Washington College was granted by the General Assembly in 1823; and, in consequence of the generous gifts of the citizens of Hartford to the new institution, it was located by the Trustees in that city. The Rt. Rev. T. C. Brownell, D.D., LL.D., Bishop of Connecticut, was chosen president; and in 1824, two buildings afterwards known as Seabury Hall, and Jarvis Hall, were erected on an ample site of fourteen acres, now the Capitol grounds, but then described as about three-quarters of a mile from the city. Academic work was begun, in buildings temporarily engaged for that purpose, on the 23d day of September, 1824. The beginning of a good library was soon made, and in a few years the collection of books, with those belonging to the Rev. Prof. Jarvis, was said to be the most select in the country and only less in number than that in the library of one other college. There was soon, also, a valuable cabinet. Two things proposed in the scheme of instruction were novel in their character: the arrangement for practical work in the scientific department, and the admission of partial students to pursue select courses of study. In 1845 the name of the College on the petition of the Alumni and the Corporation, was changed to Trinity College; in the same year a third Building, Brownell Hall, was erected. In 1871 it was proposed to the College authorities that they should sell the campus to the city to be used as the site of the new State Capitol. The sale was effected, the College reserving the use of the grounds and part of the building till 1877. A new site of some eighty acres on high land south of the western part of the city, was purchased, and ground was broken in 1875 for buildings in accordance with very elaborate plans which had been secured. Two blocks of buildings, in accordance with modifications of those plans, were ready for occupancy in 1878; and in 1882 the west side of the great quadrangle, 600 feet in length, was completed by the erection of the central towers, the gift of Col. Charles H. Northam. Seabury Hall contains the Chapel, the Library, the Cabinet, the Dining Hall, and Lecture Rooms, besides a few suites of apartments; Jarvis Hall and Northam Towers are arranged for students' rooms. The St. John Observatory was built on the south campus in 1883, and the President's house on the North campus in 1885. The new gymnasium and Alumni Hall was completed in 1887, and the Jarvis Laboratories, providing for the Departments of Chemistry and Physics, for which a large gift was made by the late Geo. A. Jarvis, was occupied in 1888. Within a few years liberal additions, from gifts and legacies, have been made to the funds of the College by Stephen M. Buckingham, Mrs. Frances J. Holland, (daughter of Bishop Brownell), Henry Keney, Mrs. Walter Keney, Judge D. W. Pardee, George A. Jarvis, Henry E. Russell, and others.

The College offers four courses of instruction, viz:

1, a Course in Arts; 2, a Course in Letters and Science; 3, a Course in Science; 4, a Course in Letters.

These courses extend over four years, with the exception of the Course in Science, which begins with the Sophomore year.

Students completing the Course in Arts receive the degree of Bachelor of Arts ; those completing the Course in Letters and Science, or the Course in Science, receive the degree of Bachelor of Science; and those completing the Course in Letters receive the degree of Bachelor of Letters. The Statutes provide that students who do not propose to attend the whole course of instruction may be permitted,under the name of Students in Special Courses, to recite with regular classes in such studies as, upon examination, they shall be found qualified to pursue.

The requirements for admission to the Course in Arts are as follows:

*Greek:*—Grammar; Anabasis, four books; Iliad three books; Prose Composition; History.

*Latin:*—Grammar; Cæsar, four books; Æneid, six books; Cicero, five orations; Extempore Translation from prose and verse; Prose Composition; History and Geography.

*Mathematics:*—Arithmetic; Algebra, through Quadratics, together with Proportion, Progressions, and the Binominal Theorem: Plane Geometry.

*English:*—Grammar: Composition on a subject from assigned works in English Literature.

Candidates for admission to other courses substitute elementary French or German for the requirements in Greek; those for the Course in Letters and Science also omit the requirement in extempore Latin translation; and Candidates for admission to the Course in Science are also examined in six books of Cæsar with Latin Grammar and Composition, in Algebra as far as the Theory of Equations, in the whole of Geometry, in Plane Trigonometry, in Trench's *Study of Words,* and in the History of the United States.

In addition to the Religious Studies (to which one hour a week is assigned throughout each course) each student is required to take at least fifteen hours a week. The Sophomores are allowed a choice of four out of seven studies, with certain restrictions, besides a course in English ; and four-fifths of the work of the last two years is in elective studies, in which over sixty courses are offered. The Freshmen and the Sophomores have regular work in the gymnasium, under the charge of an instructor.

Two Examinations for admission are held at the College in each year; the first at the end of June, in Commencement Week, and the second in September, immediately before the beginning of Christmas Term (in 1898, September 20, 21, and 22).

The academic year is equally divided into two terms. The year begins with examinations for Admission about the 15th of September, and extends to Commencement, which falls on the last Thursday in June (in 1898, June 30th). There is a recess of two or three weeks at Christmas, and another of ten days in the spring.

Honors are conferred in fifteen studies or groups of studies. The honor grade is obtained by students having, in both term-mark and examination-mark in any study, an average of nine on a scale of ten.

Three appointments to speak at Commencement are based on the aggregate standing at the end of Christmas term in Senior year; and three other speakers are ordinarily selected from the remaining members of the class after competition.

The Library, which is open every week day, contains about 38,000 volumes, exclusive of many duplicates and unbound pamphlets. The Burgess, Elton, Sheffield, Peters, Athenæum, Alumni, and Northam Library Funds amount to about $40,000.

The Cabinet, open every week day, contains valuable collections in Natural History, Geology and Mineralogy, including a complete suite of Ward's casts, a large collection of skeletons, specimens of rocks, photographic views, etc.

The Observatory has been recently provided with a new telescope of excellent make.

The Treasurer's bills including tuition, room rent, heat and incidentals, vary from $242.50 to $177.50, according to the location of rooms. The amount of these bills is considerably reduced to holders of scholarships. For holders of those scholarships which remit the entire charges for tuition and room rent, the Treasurer's bills are reduced to $42.50; and the necessary expenses of such students, including board and other personal items, will not exceed $250 or $300 a year. Application for any scholarship should be made in writing to the President by the parent or guardian, at or before the beginning of the term in which the student intends to enter.

Most of the rooms in the College buildings are so arranged as to provide that two students rooming together have a common study and separate bedrooms. All the rooms are heated by steam, and ventilation is secured by open fire-places. Water is carried into each section.

Prizes are awarded each year for excellence in special work, as tested by written theses or examinations; for some of which special endowments have been provided ; and also for excellence in composition and declamation. To these prizes have been added recently the three Holland Prize Scholarships, each having the annual value of about $600, and the Russell Fellowship. There is also a prize offered to students for Hartford for the best examinations for admission.

The number of the Alumni of the College is 1200, of whom about 745 survive.

The faculty is at present constituted as follows:

The Rev. GEORGE WILLIAMSON SMITH,D.D.,LL.D.

PRESIDENT; *and Hobart Professor of Metaphysics.*

The Rev. THOMAS R. PYNCHON, D.D., LL.D.,
*Brownell Professor of Moral Philosophy.*

The Rev. SAMUEL HART, D.D.,
*Professor of the Latin Language and Literature.*

The Rev. IBSON T. BECKWITH, PH. D.,
*Professor of the Greek Language and Literature.*

The Rev. FLAVEL S. LUTHER, M.A.,
*Seabury Professor of Mathematics and Astronomy,
and Secretary.*

The Rev. HENRY FERGUSON, M.A.,
*Northam Professor of History and Political Science.*

CHARLES FREDERICK JOHNSON, M.A.,
*Professor of English Literature.*

The Rev. JOHN J. McCOOK, M.A.,
*Professor of Modern Languages.*

WM. LISPENARD ROBB, PH. D,,
*Professor of Physics.*

ROBERT BAIRD RIGGS, PH. D.,
*Scovill Professor of Chemistry and Natural Science.*

W. R. MARTIN, LL.B, PH. D.,
*Professor of Oriental and Modern Languages.*

There are also instructors in Natural Science, Drawing, Elocution, History, English, Physics, and Physical Culture, and Lecturers on Law, Anatomy, Hygiene, and English and Italian Literature.

Copies of Examination papers and of Catalogues, and information of every kind touching the Courses of Instructions, Scholarships, etc., can be obtained from the President, or from the Secretary of the Faculty.

*For Societies, see page 726.*

CASE MEMORIAL LIBRARY.     THE HARTFORD THEOLOGICAL SEMINARY.     HOSMER HALL.

# The Hartford Theological Seminary;

Formerly known as "THE THEOLOGICAL INSTITUTE OF CONNECTICUT."

**Sixty-fifth Year, 1898-99.**

This Seminary is managed by Trustees elected by THE PASTORAL UNION OF CONNECTICUT, a large and increasing association of Congregational ministers.

THE PASTORAL UNION was formed in 1833; and the charter of the Seminary was secured in 1834. The first building was erected at East Windsor Hill, in 1834, where the Seminary remained for over 30 years. In October, 1865, it was removed to 33 Prospect street, Hartford. The corner-stone of its present commodious building, HOSMER HALL, 1507 Broad street, was laid May 8, 1879. This building was the gift of the late James B. Hosmer. It is of brick and stone, three stories and French roof, 160 feet front, with two wings over 100 feet deep. It contains a chapel, music-room, reading-room, several lecture-rooms, office, about sixty students' rooms, dining-room, kitchen and laundry, with every appliance for comfort and efficiency. A fully equipped GYMNASIUM, 32 by 60 feet, is placed somewhat in the rear.

The LIBRARY contains over 67,000 books and 35,000 pamphlets, the larger part of which was secured through the liberality of the late NEWTON CASE. It includes many rare and valuable books, and is especially rich in biblical texts, bibliography, Arabic literature, Reformation history, Lutherana and Hymnology. It is open to students and the public generally for consultation and the drawing of books from 7.30 A.M. to 9.30 P.M., Sundays excepted. The CASE MEMORIAL LIBRARY is a large, fully-equipped, fire-proof building, ample for the needs of the Library for many years to come.

The READING ROOM is supplied with nearly 500 periodicals, including several daily papers, the various religious weeklies, and the leading American and European reviews.

The MUSEUM contains the large collection of curiosities from missionary lands, gathered by the American Board, together with many acquired by the Seminary, forming an unusually rich and instructive exhibit.

The calendar provides but a single session, beginning the last Wednesday in Septmeber and closing the last Thursday in May, with recesses at Thanksgiving, Christmas, and Easter.

## PRESIDENT OF THE SEMINARY.

Rev. CHESTER D. HARTRANFT, D. D.

## BOARD OF TRUSTEES.

*President*, REV. EDWIN B. WEBB, D.D.
*Secretary*, REV. GEORGE W. WINCH.
*Treasurer*, JOHN ALLEN.
*Auditor*, DAVID W. WILLIAMS.

*For Three Years.*—Rev. James L. Barton, D.D., Elbridge Torrey, Boston, Mass.; Rev. Michael Burnham, D.D., St. Louis, Mo.; Rev. Lewis W. Hicks, Rev. Henry H. Kelsey, Jeremiah M. Allen, John Allen, George R. Shepherd, M.D., Hartford, Conn.; Rev. Anthony R. Macoubrey, D.D., White Plains, N. Y.; Rev. George W. Winch, Holyoke, Mass.; Francis A. Palmer, New York City.

*For Two Years.*—Rev. Chester D. Hartranft, D.D., Hartford, Conn.; Rev. Franklin S. Hatch, Monson, Mass.; Rev. Lewellyn Pratt, D.D., Norwich, Conn.; Rev. Charles M. Southgate, Auburndale, Mass.; Rev. Augustus C. Thompson, D.D., William F. Day, Boston, Mass.; Rev. Edwin B. Webb, D.D., Wellesley, Mass.; Thomas Duncan, Poquonock, Conn.; William Ives Washburn, New York City; David W. Williams, Glastonbury, Conn.

*For One Year.*—Rev. Asher Anderson, Meriden, Conn.; Rev. Luther H. Cone, Springfield, Mass.; Rev. Frederick W. Greene, Middletown, Conn.; Rev. John E. Tuttle, D.D., Worcester, Mass.; George E. Barstow, Providence, R. I.; His Excellency Lorrin A. Cooke, Riverton, Conn.; Rodney Dennis, Jonathan F. Morris, Rowland Swift, Hartford; Silas H. Paine, New York.

*Executive Committee.*—Rodney Dennis, *Chairman;* John Allen, J. M. Allen, J. F. Morris, C. D. Hartranft, Rowland Swift, L. W. Hicks.

## FACULTY.

CHESTER DAVID HARTRANFT, D.D., *President.* Riley Professor of Christian Theology, and Instructor in Encyclopædia and Methodology.

WALDO SELDEN PRATT, A.M., MUS.D., Professor of Ecclesiastical Music and Hymnology.

MELANCTHON WILLIAMS JACOBUS, D.D., Hosmer Professor of New Testament Exegesis.

WILLISTON WALKER, PH.D., D.D., Waldo Professor of Germanic and Western Church History.

EDWIN KNOX MITCHELL, D.D., Professor of Græco-Roman and Eastern Church History.

CLARK SMITH BEARDSLEE, A.M., Professor of Biblical Dogmatics and Ethics.

ALEXANDER ROSS MERRIAM, A.B., Samuel Hawes Professor of Practical Theology and Christian Sociology.

ARTHUR LINCOLN GILLETT, A.M., Professor of Apologetics.

ALFRED TYLER PERRY, A.M., Professor of Bibliology, Instructor in Church Polity, and Librarian.

LEWIS BAYLES PATON, PH.D., Associate Professor of Old Testament Exegesis and Criticism, Instructor in Assyrian and Cognate Languages, and Registrar.

DUNCAN BLACK MACDONALD, B.D., Associate Professor of Semitic Languages.

EDWARD EVERETT NOURSE, A.M., Instructor in Biblical Theology and in New Testament Canonicity and Textual Criticism.

CECIL HARPER, A.M., Boston, Mass., Instructor in Oratory.

AUGUSTUS C. THOMPSON, D.D., Boston,Mass., Lecturer on Foreign Missions.

AUSTIN B. BASSETT, B.D., Ware, Mass., Lecturer on Experiential Theology.

M. WOOLSEY STRYKER, D.D., LL.D., Clinton, N. Y.; ST. CLAIR MCKELWAY, LL. D., Brooklyn, N.Y.; MARCELLUS BOWEN, Constantinople; CHARLES E. GORMAN, D.D., Amherst, Mass., Carew Lecturers, 1897-'98.

WILLIAM CUSHMAN HAWKS, Tutor in Aramaic and Assistant Librarian.

OTTO SCHLUTTER, Tutor in the German Language and Literature.

Letters of inquiry should be addressed to Professor Mitchell.

# ONLY ONE BUSINESS COLLEGE

## IN HARTFORD

Trains its Students for Business by

# Actual
### Business
#### Practice.

*THAT ONE IS*

# Morse's

370
ASYLUM ST. *Hartford Business College* Corner of HIGH ST.

# "Walnut Lodge Hospital,"
## HARTFORD, CONN.

### A Private Asylum for the Special Treatment of ALCOHOL AND OPIUM INEBRIATES.

This Institution is founded on the modern view that inebriety is a Disease and Curable. Each Case is made the subject of special study and special medical treatment, suited to meet the exact requirements of the case.

This is accomplished by Turkish, Russian and Saline Baths, with Electricity, Massage, and various other appliances which Art, Science, and Experience have proved to be valuable.

Each one is under the direct personal care of the Physician and attendant; and experience shows that a large proportion of these cases are restored by the application of exact means and remedies.

Application for Admission, Terms and Letters of Inquiry, should be addressed,

## T. D. CROTHERS, M.D.,
### Fairfield Ave., Hartford, Conn.

HARTFORD PUBLIC HIGH SCHOOL, 39 HOPKINS STREET.

# Public Schools.

*Schools are Graded except Southwest.*
*Annual meeting in June.*

Admission to the lowest grade of primary department in each public district school shall be on the first Tuesday of each term, and the first Mondays of October, February, and June, and at such other times as the acting school visitor, for cause, shall order.

For Boundaries of School Districts, see page 671.

*High School hours,* 9 A. M. *to* 1.85 P. M.

*All other Schools,* 9 A. M. *to* 12 M. *and* 2 *to* 4 P. M.

## BOARD OF SCHOOL VISITORS.

Herbert S. Bullard, 1901: Thomas S. Weaver, 1901; Howard G. Bestor, 1901; Henry S. Bryant, 1899; Joseph P. Tuttle, 1899; Jas. H. Jarman, 1899; Welthea T. Day, 1900; Leonard A. Dickinson, 1900; Thomas F. Kane, 1900. James H. Jarman, *Pres't;* Joseph P. Tuttle, *Sec'y;* Herbert S. Bullard, *Sup't of Public Schools.*

## HARTFORD PUBLIC HIGH SCHOOL.—89 *Hopkins.*

*Expenses past year,* $52,593.22.

THE FIRST HIGH SCHOOL BUILDING was erected in 1847, at the corner of Asylum and Ann streets. It was a plain three story brick structure, about 70 feet long by 40 feet wide, with desks for about 300 pupils.

In 1869 a SECOND BUILDING was erected upon the present High School lot on Hopkins st., with desks for 380 pupils; it was enlarged in 1877, the addition contained four school rooms, recitation and dressing rooms, etc., giving 200 additional desks for pupils. This building, with all its contents, was destroyed by fire on Jan. 24, 1882. Only four recitations were lost before the school was in its temporary rooms, 870 and 878 Asylum street.

The THIRD BUILDING was occupied January 3, 1884. The building is in the secular gothic style, and is fire proof; the basement walls are of rock faced brown stone; the outer walls above the basement are of Philadelphia pressed brick, with the dressings of the doors and windows of brown stone. All the floors are laid upon brick arches supported by iron beams; the stairs are of stone supported by brick arches. The building is 236 feet long. In 1897 an extensive addition, built in harmony with the south portion, of 190 feet in length was made, the whole making a building of 426 feet in length, with an average of 50 feet in width; two stories high with an attic and basement. It is finished in the very best manner with all the modern appliances for heating, ventilating, laboratories, gymnasium, etc. In the rear of this extension is a manual training building, two stories and basement, 132 feet long and 64 feet wide. Number of pupils enrolled for the year 1897, 735; graduated, 299.

*High School Committee.*—Chas. E. Thompson, *Chairman;* Joseph Schwab, *Treasurer;* Francis R. Cooley, *Sec'y;* Archibald A. Welch, *Auditor;* Edward J. Mulcahy.

*Teachers.*—Edward H. Smiley, *Principal;* Frederick S. Morrison, Frank P. Moulton, R. Eston Phyfe, David G. Smyth, Homer W. Brainard, Otto B. Schlutter, Clement C. Hyde, Franklin H. Taylor, Burleigh S. Annis, Alfred M. Hitchcock, Charles B. Howe, Katherine Burbank, Mary B. Mather, Clara A. Pease, Lucy O. Mather, Anna H. Andrews, Mary L. Hastings, Frank J. Preston, Jennie A. Pratt, Agnes W. Garvan, Mary R. Beach, Marie de la Niepce, May B. Bald, Elizabeth W. Stone, Idelle B. Watson, Caroline A. Jacobs, Alice L. Cole, Margaret T. Hedden, Anna .C Walter, Elma A. Nichols, C. Louise Williams, Sophia D. Tracy, Annie L. Holcomb, Ralph G. Hibbard, Irving Emerson. A Library of 4,650 vols. Patrick McCarthy, Janitor.

## COST OF BUILDINGS, ETC.

First one, cor. Asy. and Ann, Dec. 1847, cost $15,000.00
Second, on Hopkins st., Dec., 1869,.... " 160,000.00
Addition to second one in 1877,........ " 24,000.00
New 1884 edifice, apparatus, library,.. " 285.000.00
Additional land in 1893 for............... 50,000.00
In 1897 for extension to building, etc.,..... 176,000.00
Total,.................................$710,000.00

## HARTFORD GRAMMAR SCHOOL.—89 *Hopkins st.*

A classical school was founded in Hartford in 1638, which was partly supported by the town and partly by tuition fees. It received its first bequests in 1655, 1659, 1664 and 1680. The town for more than a century managed this school, when they petitioned in 1798 for an act of incorporation, and it was thus continued until 1847, when it was merged with the Classical Department of the Hartford Public High School. Previous to this merging, the school was held in a two story brick building on the southwest part of Linden place. It is *free* to residents of Hartford. The number of scholars is limited to 35.

Amount of funds Sept. 1, 1895.............$50,000.00
Income for the last year.................... 2,684.00
Expenditure for the last year.............. 2,240.00

The Conn. Trust and Safe Deposit Co., *Treasurer.*

*Trustees.*—Nathaniel Shipman, *Chairman;* Francis Parsons, *Clerk;* Jonathan B. Bunce, Austin C. Dunham, Francis Goodwin, Edw'd B. Hooker, Henry C. Robinson. Frank P. Moulton, Hartford Grammar School, Teacher.

### District No. 1.—Expenses past year, $38,248.69.

FIRST OR CENTER DISTRICT—BROWN SCHOOL.

*Nos.* 160—170 *Market street.*

This building is four stories high, 140 by 70 feet, contains in upper story an assembly hall 70 by 84 feet; 22 school rooms 28 by 32 feet; accommodates 1,200 pupils; cost with land, $185,000. Occupied, Nov. 1868.

*Committee.*—Geo. C. Bailey, Leviat Knoek, Edwin Strong; *Treasurer,* Hartford Trust Co.; *Clerk,* Ferdinan Richter; *Coll.,* Ransom N. FitzGerald; *Auditors,* G. D. Winslow, A. D. Hunt; *Rate Maker,* G. B. Preston. Tax, 2 mills.

*Teachers.*—Charles L. Ames, *Principal;* Henry C. Mayer, *Asst. Principal; Grammar Department*—Alida B. Clark, Hannah F. Bailey, Calista A. Dean, Agnes G. Shipman; *Intermediate Department*—Josephine F. St. John, Lucy M. Parker, Ella A. Fuller, Minnie A. Bailey; *German Department*—Josephine Schwab, Annie L. Guilfoil, Mary S. Waterman, Kate S. Murphy, Mary A. Dooley, Ida M. Ellis, M. Alice Shipman, Mary E. Muller; *Primary Department*—Harriet F. Barrows, Hattie E. Pease, M.Matilda Kane, Minna Hellmann, Francesca A. Henke, May E. Robbins, Rose A. Maloy, Florence M. Spencer, Winifred A. Ryan, Julia C. Spellacy, Mary C. Ryan; J. A. Martin, *Penmanship;* S. P. Davis, *Drawing;* Irving Emerson, *Vocal Music;* Rose Guttmann, *Drawing.*

KINDERGARTEN SCHOOL.—34 *Talcott st.*— This was the first public Kindergarten School building erected in this State, is two stories high, 78 by 52 feet, with six school rooms, cloak rooms, teacher's room, matron's room, bath room, and main exercising hall 50 by 40 feet. The building is heated by steam and ventilated with chimneys in each school room, fitted for grate fires; has folding chairs and tables to accommodate 150 pupils, fitted with black-boards and sand boxes. Cost with furnishings $16,000. Occupied May 13, 1889. *Teachers.*—Kate W. Hutchinson, Letty H. Learned, Margaret B. Lee, Evelyn E. Atwood, Winnibelle M. Clark, Edith L. Bunnell, Mary Bissell; Mary E. Fuller, *Matron.*

ANNEX.—Market corner of Morgan streets—with land costing $125,000; built in 1897; accommodates 600; has 12 rooms besides a hall and manual training and cooking departments.

*District No. 2.*—Expenses past year, $76,161.12.

## SOUTH SCHOOL DISTRICT.

*Committee.*—Rodney Dennis, Henry C. Dwight, Leverett Brainard; *Treas.*, Charles T. Welles; *Clerk*, Ralph W. Cutler; *Auditors*, James S. Belden, J. H. Knight; *Collector*, Ransom N. FitzGerald; *Rate Maker*, Robert D. Bone.

SOUTH SCHOOL (formerly called Wadsworth st. School), 36 *Wadsworth and 87 Hudson sts.* The present building is of stone and brick, fire proof, three stories high above the basement, and contains 24 school rooms on first and second floors, with accommodations for 1200 pupils. Hall in third story seats 1200. Building is 255 feet long by 86 feet wide, fronts both on Wadsworth and Hudson sts. Cost, with land and furniture, $200,000. First occupied, Jan. 1887. Tax 2½ mills.

*Teachers.*—Joseph A. Graves, *Principal; Grammar Department.*—Mary M. Harris, Victoria B. Jamieson, Mary I. Patterson, Mary L. Linehan, Mary I. Paige, Sarah A. Stevens, Ella A. Parish, Carrie L. Gridley, Bertha H. Griswold. *Intermediate Dep't*—Mary E. Barber, Bertha Taylor, Mary J. Kane, M. Elizabeth Tate, Anna M. Trumbull, Delia A. Bidwell, Julia A. Stevens, Mary G. Foster. *Primary Department*—Mary A. Maloy, Charlotte G. Case, Mary M. Bristol, Minnie B. Chamberlain, Charlotte A. Butler, Anna B. Geer, Alice N. Fowler, Katharine L. Newton. *Kindergarten Dep't*—Charlotte L. McMurray, Jennie P. Forbes, Amalie B. Henke, Effie M. Hollingworth, Annie J. Ahern, Jane B. Bailey. Lyman D. Smith, Writing; Agnes C. Bryan, Music; Katharine F. Smith, Gymnastics; Jessie M. Newell, Drawing; Ann Kennedy, Assistant. 500 vols. in Library.

CHARTER OAK AVENUE SCHOOL, 91 *Charter Oak av.*—Building erected in 1871, four stories, of brick 56 by 94 feet; ten recitation rooms, seats for 540 pupils; cost $50,000. *Teachers.*—Marion G. Chapman, *Principal; Grammar Dep't*—Helen McClunie, *Intermediate Dep't*—Mary Marchant, Christine F. Glen, Mary A. Riley; *Primary Dep't*—Nellie B. Washburn, Margaret Helion. *Kindergarten Dep't*—Mabel White, Suzanne C. Thompson. 200 vols. in Library.

LAWRENCE STREET SCHOOL, 85 *Lawrence street.*—Built in 1878 of brick; two stories; 54 by 92 feet, eight recitation rooms, and seats 432 pupils; cost $33,000. *Teachers*—Clara A. Stevens, *Principal; Grammar Dep't*—Eliza S. Geer; *Intermediate Dep't*—Edwina B. Martin, Lillian A. Andrews, Margaretta J. McGowan, Marion G. Smith, Mary E. McLean; *Primary Department*—Mary E. Tuite, Grace Wolcott, Elizabeth L. Woodworth, May E. Rigby, Nellie B. Hogan; *Kindergarten Department*—Eva L. Marshall, Mabel Weeks, Mabel E. Giddings, Sarah Sprague, Rose Galbraith.

PARKVILLE SCHOOL, *New Park avenue.*—Built of brick in 1873; two stories; cost $27,000. Addition completed in 1885 at an additional cost of $10,000; seats 432 pupils. Second addition completed in 1896, cost $20,000. *Teachers.*—Franc E. Potter, *Principal.* A. Marie Hansen, Assistant; *Grammar Dep't*—Katharine A. Callahan, Janet E. Gray. *Intermediate Dep't*—Kate E. Guilfoil, Hilma C. Fernquist, Mary Noonan, Cora J. Seaver. *Primary Dep't*—Josephine Barchfeld, Nora E. McEvoy, Jessie D. Griswold, Hattie L. Seymour. *Kindergarten Dep't*—Kate P. Safford, Lillie M. Nangle, Henrietta E. Woods, Jennie B. Elmer. 100 vols. in Library.

WETHERSFIELD AVENUE SCHOOL, 291 *Wethersfield av.*—School building is 26 by 75 feet; two stories with two school rooms with coat rooms adjoining; high basement with two large play rooms; seats for 108 pupils; built of brick and stone; first occupied, Oct. 1, 1883; cost $8,000. *Teachers.*—Anna C. Day, Lillian M. Cody, Helen Barchfield, Jennie P. Forbes, Alice M. Farnham.

*District No. 3.*—Expenses past year, $22,282.33.

## SECOND NORTH SCHOOL DISTRICT.—249 *High st.*

The original building 48 by 57 feet was first occupied in 1854; subsequently an annex building of 47 by 57 feet was built thereto in 1864; both of brick; three stories high; twelve rooms—one to accommodate 115 pupils the others 46 each—total 621; cost $24,500. This building was torn down and a new building erected in 1891 with 15 rooms to accommodate 700 pupils, and was occupied January, 1892, with additional land and furnishing; cost, $140,000.

*Committee.*—Frank S. Kellogg, Herman Goldschmidt, U. H. Brockway; *Treas.*, Security Co.; *Clerk*, George O'Neil; *Auditors*, E. S. Sykes, John K. Williams; *Collector*, Ransom N. FitzGerald; *Rate Maker*, Eugene G. Billings; Tax, 3½ mills.

*Teachers.*—Wilbur F. Gordy, *Principal; Grammar Department*—Annie I. House, Elizabeth M. Worthington, Cornelia A. Watrous; *Intermediate Department*—Hattie R. Woodward, Mary E. Guinan, Winifred K. Kenney, Mary E. Wooding; *Primary Department*—Clara A. Pausch, Susan P. Clapp, Harriet M. Olmsted, Sarah A. Backus, Emma L. Williams, Helen C. Foley, Isabelle G. White, Mary A. Ensign, Kate B. Owen. *Kindergarten*—Susan E. Towne, Mary P. Gillette, Mary Clissold Knapp, Bessie M. McManus, Francella Goodenough, Irving Emerson. Music: Solon P. Davis, Drawing; John W. Titcomb, Writing; Bertha H. Klinger, Science. 1,000 volumes in Library.

*District No. 4.*—Expenses past year, $31,788.06.

## WEST MIDDLE SCHOOL DISTRICT.—927 *Asylum st.*—This building of brick, three stories with sixteen rooms, and accommodations for fifty pupils to each room—800—is 89 by 148 feet in size; first occupied in 1873; building and land cost $154,165. $15,000 was appropriated June 28, 1886, for additions to building. A building for Kindergarten and Primary, opened Dec. 1894.

*Committee.*—James H. Tallman, A. E. Hart, L.L. Ensworth; *Treas.*, J. P. Taylor; *Auditors*, S. E. Elmore, C. H. Field; *Clerk*, Charles E. Chase; *Collector*, Nelson G. Hinckley; *Rate Maker*, H. H. Keep. Tax, 1¾ mills.

*Teachers.*—Esther C. Perry, *Principal; Grammar Department*—Mary C. Cone, Carolyn A. Goodwin, Kate L. Smith, Rosilla R. Newton, Adalaide M. Westcott. *Intermediate Dep't*—Ruby M. Williams, Nellie C. Skilton, Carrie E. Hollister, Bessie A. Brown, Clara M. Klinger. *Primary Dep't*—Emma E. Winslow, Mabel E. Stone, Lillian B. Conant, Mabel F. Terry, Mary E. Ball, Lina D. Wilcox, Ruth S. Crampton, Carolyn Nichols, Helen B. Rathburn. *Kindergarten Department*—Adella M. Woodcock, Lillian M. Reis, Anna W. Bullard, Julia G. Simonds, Edith E. Richards. John W. Titcomb, Writing; Irving Emerson, Music; Clara L. Williams, Drawing; Bertha H. Klinger, Science. Capt. C. H. Slocum, Military Instructor.

*District No. 5.*—Expenses past year, $20,160.63.

## ARSENAL SCHOOL DISTRICT.—180 *Windsor st.*

This building is three stories high, with annex, and cost, with land, $30,000. In 1886, an additional building of two stories, 98 by 56 feet, was erected, at an expense of $16,500 as was voted in district meeting, May 26, 1886, under direction of a building committee. Additional land, costing $15,000, was purchased in 1892, and a Kindergarten building erected at a cost of $11,272, and occupied in May, 1893.

*Committee.*—Howard A. Camp, Edmund Browne, C. P. Gladding; *Treas.*, Geo. H. Burt; *Clerk*, Clarence L. Beardsley; *Auditors*, H. B. Philbrick, Betsey M. Parsons; *Collector*, R. N. FitzGerald; *Rate Maker*, Thomas Boyd.

*Teachers.*—Willis I. Twitchell, *Principal;* Mrs. Grace H. Phelps, *Assistant; Grammar Department*—Belle C. Davis, Maud E. Davis; *Intermediate Department*—Mary E. Bentley, Emily F. Pausch, Alice M. Baker, Jennie D. Strong, Edwina M. Pratt, Gertrude E. Dickenson; *Primary Department*—Martha A. Patterson, Carrie S.

Allen, A. Mabel Parkhurst, Etta M. Dow, Elizabeth V. Adams, Mary A. Long, Mabel E. Lester; *Kindergarten*—Anne Burr Wilson, Leila H. Blakeslee, M. Grace Brown, H. Viola Glazier; Irving Emerson, Music; Solon P. Davis, Drawing; John A. Martin, Penmanship. 500 vols. in Library. Tax 4 mills.

*District No. 6.*—Expenses the past year, $11,268.71.

WASHINGTON DISTRICT SCHOOL.—1 *Washington st.*—This building of brick is two stories high; four school rooms; accommodates 200 pupils; cost $25,000. *Committee.*—Isaac J. Steane, Joseph Buths, William Sinnot, Jr.; *Clerk*, Charles Dexter Allen, *Treas.*, W. L. Wakefield; *Collector*, Ransom N. FitzGerald; *Auditors*, Charles F. Watrous, C. O. Purinton; *Rate Maker*, R. D. Bone.

*Teachers.*—Elizabeth J. Cairns, *Principal*; *Grammar Department*—Isabella M. Mulligan, N. Florence Bullock; *Intermediate Department*—A. Elizabeth Heppe, Isabelle Eggleston, Coval E. Tracy; *Primary Dep't*—Mary E. J. Patterson, Ida G. Holcomb, Mary E. Fisk; *Kindergarten Dep't*—Marion Van Vleet, Myra G. Hills; Alice L. Moore; Frederick Zuchtmann, Music; S. P. Davis, Drawing; W. K. Cook, Penmanship. Tax 5 mills.

WILSON STREET BRANCH.— *Wilson st.* This building of wood is two stories high; three school rooms; seats for 180 pupils; cost $5,000. *Teachers*, Nellie T. Mulhall, Elizabeth E. Sinnot, Jane C. Flynn, Mary M. Bennett.

*District No. 7.*—Expenses the past year, $698.62.

SOUTHWEST SCHOOL DISTRICT.— *White street.* Built in 1844, of wood; one story; 25 by 45 feet; seats for 50 pupils; cost $3,500. *Committee.*—Fred. Tucker; *Treas.*, John L. Seymour; Clarise Raymond, *Principal.*

*District No. 8.*—Expenses the past year, $11,289.87.

NORTHEAST SCHOOL DISTRICT.— *Westland st.* *Committee.*—George R. Warner, Marshall L. Hill, George Stronach; *Clerk*, James D. Bacon; *Treas.*, Security Company; *Auditors*, Ludwig Heimann, C. S. Hutchinson; *Collector*, R. N. FitzGerald; *Rate Maker*, R. D. Bone. Tax 7 mills.

*Teachers.*—F. A. Brackett, *Principal*; *Assistant in Grammar Dep't*—Rose A. Hopkins, Annie M. Cairns; *Intermediate Dep't*—Mary E. Coleman, Hattie A. Miller, Lillie L. Huntington; *Primary Dep't*—Annie R. McDonnell, Minnie F. Eaves, Elsie A. Rood, Grace E. Bradley, Ella A. Washburn; *Kindergarten Dep't*—Georgia M. Moseley, Grace C. Spencer, Sadie L. Hawkins, Alice M. Deming, Georgia M. Witherell, W. K. Cook, Writing; Leila M. Smart, Music; S. P. Davis, Rose Guttman, Drawing. 150 vols. in Library. Rufus C. Banning, Janitor.

*District No. 9.*—Expenses the past year, $8,350.53.

NORTHWEST DISTRICT SCHOOL.— *Albany avenue.* Building of brick; two stories; two rooms, accommodates 100 pupils; first occupied in 1870. An addition, costing $15,000, built in 1891, making six rooms and accommodating 250 pupils. Tax 4 mills.

*Committee*, Chas. G. Stone, Joseph H. Twichell, R. L. Russell; *Treas.* Security Co.; *Clerk*, James Shipman; *Auditors*, Mrs. Ariadne K. Smith, George Calder; *Rate Maker*, Thomas Boyd; *Collector*, Ransom N. FitzGerald.

*Teachers.*—J. Isabella Price, *Principal*; *Grammar Dep't*—L. Eudora Price, Minnie Stern. *Intermediate Dep't*—Lucy E. Cobey, Alice E. Gladding. *Primary Dep't*—Minnie J. Gilbert, Emma M. Jarman. *Kindergarten Dep't*—Alice S. Hawkins. Minnie Stern, Science; Wm. K. Cook, Writing; William D. Monnier, Singing.

VACATIONS—Two weeks in April; one commencing with the close of the usual school exercises on the last Friday afternoon in June, and ending on Tuesday preceding the second Wednesday in September following, and one commencing with the day before Christmas, and closing the day after New Year's. Holidays are Fast day, Thanksgiving day with the day following, Washington's Birthday, Decoration day, Commencement day at Trinity College (High School only), and every Saturday.

## SCHOOL FUND.

FOR SUPPORT OF HARTFORD SCHOOL CHILDREN. As annually returned, by law, with the rate per child and amounts received from the State School Fund, during the years that this Directory has been published. This State, since July 29, 1873, has allowed $1.50 from the State Treasury to the Towns, towards the education of each child enumerated between the ages of 4 and 16 years, in addition to the dividends from the School Fund of the State.

| Year. | No. of Children. | Am't from School Fund. | Rate per Sch'r. | Year. | No. of Children. | Am't from School Fund. | Rate per Sch'r. |
|---|---|---|---|---|---|---|---|
| 1838– | 2,555 | $3,076.00 | $1.20 | 1868– | 7,475 | $8,222.50 | $1.10 |
| 1839– | 2,609 | 3,219.80 | 1.25 | 1869– | 7,846 | 7,846.00 | 1.00 |
| 1840– | 2,711 | 3,375.35 | 1.25 | 1870– | 7,834 | 7,834.00 | 1.00 |
| 1842– | 2,787 | 3,694.95 | 1.35 | 1871– | 8,258 | 8,258.00 | 1.00 |
| 1842– | 2,731 | 3,823.40 | 1.40 | 1872– | 9,124 | 9,124.00 | 1.00 |
| 1843– | 2,709 | 3,792.60 | 1.40 | 1873– | 9 188 | 9,138.00 | 1.00 |
| 1844– | 2,824 | 3,953.60 | 1.40 | 1874– | 9,684 | 9,684.00 | 1.00 |
| 1845– | 2,924 | 4,093.60 | 1.40 | 1875– | 9,332 | 10,265.20 | 1.10 |
| 1846– | 2,921 | 4,089.40 | 1.40 | 1876– | 9,598 | 9,598.00 | 1.00 |
| 1847– | 2,888 | 4,087.60 | 1.45 | 1877– | 9,621 | 9,621.00 | 1.00 |
| 1848– | 2,969 | 4,305.05 | 1.45 | 1878– | 9,661 | 9,661.00 | 1.00 |
| 1849– | 3,117 | 4,675.50 | 1.50 | 1879– | 9,525 | 8,572.50 | .90 |
| 1850– | 3,358 | 5,037.00 | 1.50 | 1880– | 9,652 | 7,721.60 | .80 |
| 1851– | 3,396 | 4,754.40 | 1.40 | 1881– | 9,590 | 6,713.00 | .70 |
| 1852– | 3,648 | 5,107.20 | 1.40 | 1882– | 9,660 | 7,245.00 | .75 |
| 1853– | 3,738 | 5,046.80 | 1.35 | 1883– | 9,816 | 7,362.00 | .75 |
| 1854– | 4,118 | 5,765.20 | 1.40 | 1884– | 10,098 | 7,574.20 | .75 |
| 1855– | 4,390 | 5,487.50 | 1.25 | 1885– | 9,775 | 7,820.00 | .80 |
| 1856– | 4,601 | 5,982.30 | 1.30 | 1886– | 9,909 | 7,927.00 | .80 |
| 1857– | 4,892 | 6,848.80 | 1.40 | 1887– | 9,991 | 7,493.25 | .75 |
| 1858– | 4,937 | 6,911.80 | 1.40 | 1888– | 9,605 | 7,203.75 | .75 |
| 1859– | 5,269 | 6,849.70 | 1.30 | 1889– | 9,984 | 7,488.00 | .75 |
| 1860– | 5,442 | 6,803.75 | 1.25 | 1890– | 10,376 | 7,782.00 | .75 |
| 1861– | 5,897 | 6,781.55 | 1.15 | 1891– | 10,474 | 7,855.50 | .75 |
| 1862– | 6,375 | 7,650.00 | 1.20 | 1892– | 10,789 | 8,064.25 | .75 |
| 1863– | 6,464 | 7,756.80 | 1.20 | 1893– | 11,021 | 8,265.75 | .75 |
| 1864– | 6,819 | 8,160.80 | 1.20 | 1894– | 11,262 | 8,446.50 | .75 |
| 1865– | 6,965 | 8,009.75 | 1.15 | 1895– | 12,059 | 9,044.25 | .75 |
| 1866– | 7,294 | 8,023.40 | 1.10 | 1896– | 12,175 | 9,181.25 | .75 |
| 1867– | 7,855 | 8,090.50 | 1.10 | | | | |

## ENUMERATION OF SCHOOL CHILDREN.

| Districts. | Oct.'93. | Oct.'94. | Oct.'95. | Oct.'96 | Oct.'97. |
|---|---|---|---|---|---|
| First, | 2,352 | 2,313 | 2,430 | 2,458 | 2,470 |
| South, | 3,758 | 3,880 | 4,292 | 4,659 | 4,997 |
| Second North, | 1,407 | 1,548 | 1,536 | 1,582 | 1,669 |
| West Middle, | 1,118 | 1,201 | 1,220 | 1,293 | 1,380 |
| Arsenal, | 1,007 | 981 | 1,072 | 1,154 | 1,278 |
| Washington, | 509 | 487 | 655 | 730 | 867 |
| Southwest, | 58 | 48 | 45 | 58 | 76 |
| Northeast, | 546 | 573 | 600 | 636 | 660 |
| Northwest, | 239 | 248 | 268 | 355 | 412 |
| Total, | 11,021 | 11,262 | 12,159 | 12,875 | 13,809 |

There are 20 Schools and School Houses in Hartford; 182 School Rooms; 261 Teachers, with 10,445 Registered Scholars. In the High School there has been a regular increase of scholars from 180 in 1865 to 826 in 1897. The total cost for schools during the past year was $278,806.05. Teachers' wages paid the past year, $176,412.98.

# Societies.

## AGENTS—SUNDRY BENEVOLENT SOCIETIES.

*American Board of Commissioners for Foreign Missions.*—Ward W. Jacobs, 815 Main st., *Receiver for Hartford County.*

*Hartford Baptist Association, Ministers' and Widows' Fund.*—Henry W. Erving, *Treasurer*, 761 Main st.

## ALLEN DRUM BAND.

C. W. Myers, *Pres't and Major;* T. L. Sheiber, *Vice Pres't;* H. J. Gubitz, *R. Sec'y;* A. Waltersdorf, *F. Sec'y and Treas.* Organized June 21, 1880. Meets Thursday evenings at 258 State street.

## ALUMNI ASSOCIATION OF THE HARTFORD PUBLIC HIGH SCHOOL.

Edward H. Smiley, *Pres't ex-officio;* A. A. Welch, Lucy O. Mather, *Vice Pres'ts;* F. S. Morrison, *Sec'y;* Atwood Collins, *Treas.* Incorporated April, 1889. Annual meeting, 3d Monday in March.

## AMATEUR BOWLING LEAGUE OF CONN.

Charles O. Winter, *Pres't;* D. L. Macomber, *Vice Pres't;* D. S. Hawkins, *Sec'y;* W. W. Pratt, *Treas.* Organized in January, 1894. Annual meeting first Wednesday in October. Headquarters 66 Temple st.

## AMERICAN EMIGRANT COMPANY.

G. H. Warner, *Pres't;* G. H. Warner, Charles E. Dustin, Wm. H. Gillette, Chas. E. Gross, *Directors.* Chartered 1863. Annual meeting in Dec. Office 25 Forest st.

## AMERICAN SCHOOL AT HARTFORD FOR THE DEAF.

(Formerly American Asylum for the Deaf and Dumb.)

*690 Asylum. Chartered, 1816. Dedicated, 1821.*

Francis B. Cooley, *Pres't;* Nathaniel Shipman, Jonathan B. Bunce, Rowland Swift, John C. Day, William M. Hudson, F. W. Cheney, S. W. Kellogg, *Vice Pres'ts;* D. R. Howe, *Treas.;* Archibald A. Welch, *Sec'y;* D. R. Howe, L. A. Barbour, Atwood Collins, W. L. Matson, J. B. Cone, C. H. Clark, Archibald A. Welch, W. Waldo Hyde, H. K. Smith, E. B. Bennett, *Directors.*

Job Williams, *Principal;* Gilbert O. Fay, A. S. Clark, George F. Stone, John E. Crane, Mary A. Mann, Caroline C. Sweet, Jane B. Kellogg, Lucy H. Williams, Mollie J. Noyes, Sarah T. Sprague, Grace W. Robinson, *Instructors;* Mary Allen, Adelia C. Fay, Elizabeth Fay, Mary L. Geer, *Teachers of Articulation;* Solon P. Davis, *Drawing;* W. P. Williams, *Steward;* F. T. Simpson, *Attending Physician.* Chartered 1816. Dedicated 1821. Annual meeting Saturday after 2d Thursday in May. 690 Asylum street.

## ANCIENT ORDER OF HIBERNIANS.

*Chartered 1875.*

Company B, Hibernian Rifles. H. J. McInnis, 109 Windsor street, *Capt. and Treas.;* Wm. E. Hogan, J. F. Flanigan, *Lieuts.;* James King, J. F. Sayer, M. King, J. K. Sullivan, J. Moynahan, *Serg'ts;* M. Kelley, Q. M. Serg't; P. Rearder, P. Lynch, Simon King, John Desmond, J. T. O'Brien, J. Curtin, *Corporals.* Organized April 1, 1886. Meets Friday evenings at 104 Asylum street.

2d Division, re-organized 1885. E. J. Claffey, *Pres't;* D. J. Sullivan, *Vice Pres't;* Wm. H. Killian, *Tr.;* J. O'Callaghan, *Fin. Sec'y;* Edward Keating, 1 Orchard st., *Rec. Sec'y.* Meets at 92 Asylum st. 2d Sunday of each month.

3d Division, organized November, 1871. Meets at 4 American row 3d Sunday of each month. P. J. Silk, *Pres't;* Martin Dwyer, *Vice Pres't;* Patrick Nolan, *Treas.;* Wm. J. Keleher, *Fin. Sec'y;* John J. McNamara, *Rec. Sec'y,* 184 State st.

4th Division, organized Feb. 26, 1888. Meets at 6 American row 4th Sunday of each month. John J. Hickey, *Pres't;* John J. Mulcahy, *Vice Pres't;* Thos. J. Ward, *Fin. Sec'y;* John P. Carmody, *Rec. Sec'y;* James Harris, *Treas.*

5th Division meets at 6 American row 4th Thursday evenings. William J. Buckley, *Pres't;* Charles L. Dillon, *Vice Pres't;* Charles P. Hannon, *Treas.;* Edward D. O'Brien, *Rec. Sec'y;* P. J. Reardon, *F. Sec'y.*

## ARARAT LODGE, No. 13,

INDEPENDENT ORDER OF B'NAI BRITH.

A. Heutter, *Pres't;* Jacob Wieder, *Vice Pres't;* Milton Wieder, *Cashier;* Chas. Rosenthal, *R. and F. Sec'y,* 158 Asylum st.; Joseph Kashmann, Nathan Kempner, Abe Cadden, *Trustees.* Organized 1853. Meets 1st, 3d, 5th Sunday evenings at 739 Main st. Annual election 1st Sunday in Jan.

## ART SOCIETY OF HARTFORD.

Mrs. F. G. Whitmore, *Pres't;* Miss S. R. Dunham, Mrs. E. H. Perkins, *Vice Pres'ts;* Mrs. Jas. B. Cone. *Treas.;* Mrs. William E. Collins, *Ass't Treas.;* Mrs. T. W. Russell, *Rec. Sec'y;* Mrs. W. Walker, *Cor. Sec'y;* Mrs. Charlotte M. Ely, Mrs. John C. Day, Mrs. George Kellar, Miss Mary F. Collins, Miss Alice Taintor, *Honorary Managers;* Mrs. W. H. Palmer, Miss Frances A. Beach, Mrs. C. C. Beach, Miss Emily Cheney, Mrs. A. K. Bunce, Miss Mary Talcott, Miss C. Louise Williams, Miss Emily Barnard, Mrs. A. A. Welch, Mrs. F. W. Cheney, Mrs. J. L. English, Mrs. Charles D. Warner, Mrs. George G. Williams, Miss Sarah Day, Miss Eliza Robinson, Miss Sarah Goodwin, Mrs. Henry Ferguson, Mrs. George Keller, Mrs. George H. Warner, Miss Alice Taintor, *Managers.* Organized June, 1877. Incorporated March, 1886. Studio in the Atheneum building, 624 Main st. Annual meeting 2d Thursday in Jan.

## BACHELORS.

Hermann F. Cuntz, Felton Parker, R. H. C. Keltan, Mark W. Reeves, J. J. Hawley. 2 Columbia st.

## BAPTIST YOUNG PEOPLE'S UNION OF CONN.

Rev. F. E. Robbins, Norwalk. *Pres't;* R. Maplesden, C. W. Martin, Noank, *Vice Pres'ts;* James L. Chase, Norwich, *Tr.;* H. A. Edgcomb, Box 131, Groton, *Sec'y.*

## B. H. WEBB COUNCIL, No. 702,

ROYAL ARCANUM.

George L. Vannais, *R.;* Edward B. Boynton, *V. R.;* Geo. K. Wilcox, P. O. Box 993, *Sec'y;* Thos. M. Smith, *Treas.;* Elisha Ryder, R. P. Martin, W. H. Nugent, *Trustees.* Meets at 976 Main st. 1st and 3d Wednesday evenings of each month. Instituted Aug. 22, 1882. Annual election 1st Wednesday in Dec.

## BOARD TRUSTEES YOUNG MEN'S CHRISTIAN ASSOCIATION.

Charles A. Jewell, *Chairman;* Appleton R. Hillyer, *Sec'y and Treas.;* James G. Batterson, Daniel E. Howe, G. Pierpont Davis, John F. Tracy, W. H. Talcott, Arthur L. Shipman. This Board has the care of property interests of the Association.

BOARD OF TRADE OF THE CITY OF HARTFORD.
Charles E. Gross, *Pres't;* C. C. Kimball, Pliny Jewell, *Vice Pres'ts;* P. H. Woodward, *Sec'y;* Chas. P. Cooley, *Treas.;* J. M. Allen, C. C. Kimball, Geo. A. Fairfield, Judson H. Root, John F. Morris, Charles E. Billings, M. H. Whaples, John G. Root, Charles B. Whiting, Clarence B. Ingraham, Ernest Cady, H. C. Dwight, Morgan G. Bulkeley, F. A. Pratt, Charles M. Beach, A. E. Burr, George H. Day, Charles E. Gross, Asa S. Cook, A. B. Gillett, S. M. Bronson, Leverett Brainard, Charles H. Clark, Albert A. Pope, James M. Thomson, *Directors;* F. R. Cooley, *Chairman Membership Committee;* John M. Holcombe, *Chairman Reception Committee;* Chas. B. Whiting, *Chairman Finance Committee;* Geo. H. Day, *Chairman House Committee;* J. F. Swords, *Chairman Transportation Committee;* James Nichols, *Chairman Railway Proxies;* Francis Goodwin, *Chairman Public Affairs Committee.* Organized July, 1888. Annual meeting 2d Tuesday in Jan. Rooms 49 Pearl st.

BRANCH No. 86, NATIONAL ASSOCIATION OF LETTER CARRIERS.
William H. Shaffer, *Pres't;* H. E. Beebe, *V. Pres't;* James J. Preston, *Cor. Sec'y;* J. B. Gossman, *Fin. Sec'y;* Francis H. Woodbury, *Treas.* Organized Dec. 20, 1890. Meets second Tuesday of each month.

BRICKLAYERS' AND PLASTERERS' UNION, No. 1, OF CONNECTICUT.
William J. Sheedy, *Pres't;* T. J. Sullivan, *V. Pres't;* J. F. Conniff, *Treas.;* Frank McLaughlin, *C. Sec'y;* George W. Butler, *Fin. Sec'y;* John Spellacy, Thomas Flynn, Michael Roach, *Trustees.* Meets 1st and 3d Fridays at No. 92 Asylum st. Annual meeting first Friday in April.

BROKERS' BOARD.
J. G. Woodward, *Pres't;* F. R. Cooley, *Treas.;* F. Reichter, *Sec'y.* Meets Thursdays at 11.30 A. M. at 808 Main street.

BROWN, THOMSON & CO'S EMPLOYEES' MUTUAL AID ASSOCIATION.
*Organized June,* 1893.
H. M. Twiss, *Pres't;* G. W. Valentine, Miss M. Buckley, *Vice Pres'ts;* Hector Johnstone, *Treas.;* J. A. Thomson, *Financial Sec'y.* Meets in June and Dec.

BUCKINGHAM ASSEMBLY, No. 213,
ROYAL SOCIETY GOOD FELLOWS.
D. S. Moseley, *R.;* Charles S. Potter, *Sec'y;* Adelbert J. Cooper, *F. Sec'y;* William F. Harrison, *Treas.;* Charles E. Crane, H. C. Daniels, Edw. S. Gardiner, *Trustees.* Meets 1st and 3d Thursday evenings monthly at 11 Pratt st. Annual election in Dec.

BUSHNELL COUNCIL, No. 213,
ORDER OF UNITED FRIENDS.
F. W. Colby, *C. C.;* Geo. D. Stebbins, *V. C.;* W. G Wilson, *R. and F. Sec'y;* G. M. Beers, *Treas.* Instituted April 10, 1886. Meets at 881 Main st. 2d and 4th Wednesday evenings of each month. Annual meeting in January.

CAPITOL CITY BOWLING CLUB.
D. L. Macomber, *President;* J. F. Galvin, *Captain;* F. H. Mayberry, *Sec'y.* Organized March 28, 1888. Meets Thursday evenings at 66 Temple st. Elections April and October.

CAPITOL CITY LODGE, No. 119,
L. O. B. A.
Max Sueaman, *Pres't;* Wolf Furspan, *Treas.;* Nathan Wilkes, *Sec'y;* David Goldenthal, Mayer Beck, *Trustees.* Organized Aug. 19, 1894. Meets 2d and 4th Sunday at 10 A. M. monthly at 798 Main street. Semi-annual elections June and Dec.

CARPENTERS' & JOINERS' UNION, No. 43.
George Gregory, *Pres't;* John Calder, *Vice Pres't;* Alex Forbes, *R. Sec'y;* Alex Mackay, *F. Sec'y;* Jas. R. Cairns, *Treas.;* F. C. Walz, *Business Agent,* 1332 Broad street; Warren H. Higley, William A. Nielson, *Trustees.* Organized October 22, 1882. Meets on Tuesday evenings at 11 Central row. Semi-annual election in June and December.

CASE, LOCKWOOD & BRAINARD MUTUAL BENEFIT ASSOCIATION.
Leverett Brainard, *Honorary President;* Theodore Herzer, *President;* Miss Margaret Kane, *Vice Pres't;* E. H. Rathbun, *Rec. Sec'y;* Walter H. Price, *Fin. Sec'y;* Anson P. Filer, *Treas.*
*Trustees*—Marcus A. Casey, J. H. Turner, Bernard Allen. Organized Dec. 2, 1893. Meets quarterly upon call. Annual election of officers in December.

CATHEDRAL LYCEUM.
Joseph M. McNamara, *Pres't;* John J. Foley, *Vice Pres't;* William J. White, 289 Capitol avenue, *Rec. Sec'y;* Mark Bain, *Fin. Sec'y;* Peter I. McCabe, *Treas.* Meets 221 Lawrence st.

CATHOLIC CLUB OF HARTFORD.
James Ahern, *Pres't;* James J. Quinn, *V. Pres't;* Charles J. Reardon, *Treas.;* Thomas J. Hagerty, *Fin. Sec'y;* Robert H. Fox, *Rec. Sec'y;* Frank H. Fallon, T. F. Kane, J. T. Lynch, R. J. Dwyer, J. O'Flaherty, E. Lancaster, George C. Bailey, D. J. Shea, Patrick Garvan, Patrick J. Heffernan, Andrew J. Broughel, Frank A. Hagarty, M. A. Bailey, E. W. Wall, Charles E. Barrett, *Directors.* Organized Dec. 28, 1893. Meets first Tuesday evenings, monthly, at 11 Grove street. Annual election second Tuesday in January.

CATHOLIC LADIES' BENEVOLENT ASSOC'N.
Annie M. Fox, *Pres't;* Mrs. J. C. Ryan, *Vice Pres't;* Mrs. Edward Donaghue, *Fin. Sec'y;* Miss Mary Guinan, *Rec. Sec'y;* Mrs. P. D. Ryan, *Treas.* Organized Jan. 1884. Annual election in Jan. Office 3 Pratt st. Meets third Wednesday evening, monthly.

CENTRAL LABOR UNION.
William Crawley, *Pres't;* Geo. E. Bradford, *Treas.;* D. A. Fitzpatrick, *Rec. Sec'y;* R. J. Anderson, *Fin. Sec'y.* Meets 1st and 3d Wednesday evenings at Central Labor Union hall, 11 Central row.

CHARITABLE SOCIETY IN HARTFORD.
Rodney Dennis, *Pres't;* C. T. Welles, *Sec'y and Tr.;* W. A. Willard, *Auditor;* E. B. Farnham, A. H. Tillinghast, Ralph Foster, G. P. Chandler, H. J. Case, *Almoners.* Formed Nov. 28, 1792. Chartered May, 1809. Annual meeting 2d Tuesday in Oct.

CHARITY ORGANIZATION SOCIETY.
David I. Green, *Sup't;* Helena R. Rossiter, *Assis't Sup't,* 57 Trumbull street; Jacob L. Greene, *Pres't;* P. C. Royce, *Vice Pres't;* Atwood Collins, *Secretary;* Rodney Dennis, *Treasurer;* Francis Goodwin, Jacob L. Greene, P. C. Royce, Charles A. Jewell, Mrs. A. R. Hillyer, Jonathan B. Bunce, Rodney Dennis, J. D. Browne, Atwood Collins, Nathaniel Shipman, Mrs. Robert E. Day, P. H. Woodward, John J. McCook, Leverett Brainard, L. B. Haas, A. R. Merriam, Miss Ellen W. Gray, Mrs. Chas. R. Burt, Mary Hall, Mrs. Wm. A. Ayres, Mrs. Isaac Cross, Samuel N. Benedict, C. M. Lamson, J. A. Mulcahy, Mrs. E. L. Sluyter, Ernest DeF. Miel, Edwin K. Mitchell, G. P. Davis, Miles B. Preston, E. Henry Hyde, F. W. Perkins, Wilbur F. Gordy, Oscar A. Phelps, Mrs. B. M. Parsons, *Directors.* Organized Nov. 30, 1890. Meets second Thursday, monthly, at 57 Trumbull st. Annual meeting first Wednesday in Nov.

## CHARTER OAK QUARTETTE.
Norris B. Bull, A. H. Dole, H. Seaman, F. W. White. Organized 1885. Meets as may be called.

## CHURCH HOME.
John Williams, *Pres't;* L. W. Saltonstall, *V. Pres't;* H. Lilienthal, *Sec'y;* George E. Hatch, *Treas;* Mrs. G. W. Russell, Mrs. H. Kennedy, Miss Alice Bolter, Mrs. J. W. Gray, Mrs. G. L. Bulkley, Mrs. G. A. Wright, Mrs. J. E. Ball, Mrs. C. Ehbitts, Mrs. T. G. Talcott, Mrs. H. R. Hayden, Mrs. H. B. McKinney, Mrs. J. E. Russell, Mrs. H. S. Seymour, Mrs. T. J. Boardman, Mrs. H. W. Richards, Mrs. A. Mugford, Mrs. H. C. Hawley, *Managers.* Dr. G. W. Russell, Henry K. Morgan, L. A. Dickinson, G. H. Day, *Advisory Board.* G. W. Russell, G. E. Hatch, Charles A. Pease, *Trustees.* Mrs. M. F. Weeks, *Matron,* 76 Bellevue st. Chartered 1876. Annual meeting Wednesday following 2d Sunday after Easter.

## CHURCH SCHOLARSHIP SOCIETY.
Rt. Rev. John Williams, Middletown, *Pres't;* Rev. C. G. Bristol, Hartford, *Sec'y and Treas.* T. R. Pynchon, *Chairman,* F. Goodwin, J. W. Bradin, J. H. Barbour, F. W. Harriman, James Stoddard, S. Taylor, A. C. Goodman, F. J. Kingsbury, G. W. Russell, C. G. Bristol, Benj. Page, O. H. Raftery, *Board of Education.* Incorporated 1874. Annual meeting 2d Tuesday in June, where convened by Bishop.

## CIGAR MAKERS' UNION, No. 42.
J. J. Doyle, *Pres't;* Thomas W. Mathers, *V. Pres't;* Geo. F. Scheflin, P. O. Box 970, *Cor. and Rec. Sec'y;* W. J. Dolan, *F. Sec'y.* Meets at 11 Central row, first Thursday in each month. Executive board meets Mondays at 5.15 P.M. Organized Dec. 1880. Officers elected in Jan. and July.

## CITY CLUB OF HARTFORD.
Wm. Waldo Hyde, *Pres't;* James P. Andrews, Geo. H. Day, *Vice Pres'ts;* Archibald A. Welch, *Sec'y;* George C. F. Williams, *Treas.;* James P. Andrews, Wm. Waldo Hyde, George C. F. Williams, Ernest Cady, George H. Day, A. A. Welch, J. G. Calhoun, Charles E. Gross, Arthur L. Shipman, *Directors.* Organized March 3, 1894. Annual election in April. Meets at 904 Main st.

## CITY MISSIONARY SOCIETY.
S. N. Benedict, *Pres't;* C. H. Prentice, *Vice Pres't;* Olin H. Clark, *Sec'y;* George F. Hills, *Treas.;* A. L. Hunt, D. R. Howe, *Auditors;* H. J. Gillette, *Missionary.* Chartered in 1859. Their building at 234 Pearl street was dedicated March 25, 1891. This Society employs a city missionary with the united efforts of the Congregational churches of this city. Annual meeting in October.

## CIVIC CLUB.
Mrs. Appleton R. Hillyer, *Pres't;* Miss Annie Eliot Trumbull, Mrs. T. Belknap Beach, *Vice Pres'ts;* Miss Lucy A. Perkins, *Rec. Sec'y;* A. Holly Rudd, 282 Sigourney street *Cor. Sec'y;* Mrs. J. Humphrey Greene, *Treas.* The above officers and Mrs. Jonathan B. Bunce, Mrs. George C. Perkins, Mrs. C. D. Alton, Mrs. Wm. A. Ayers, F. Louise Bushnell, Mrs. John C. Day, Mrs. Henry Ferguson, Caroline Hewins, *Directors.* Organized January 10, 1895. Meets 1st Friday in each month. Annual election in January.

## CLAN GORDON, No. 19,
### ORDER OF SCOTTISH CLANS.
John Gray, *Chief;* John MacCallum, *Sec'y;* Hector Johnstone, 35 Canton st., *Fin. Sec'y;* George H. Brown, *Treas.;* Andrew Pullar, G. B. Riddell, Peter Dow, *Trustees.* Organized March 31, 1886. Meets at 11 Pratt st. 1st and 3d Monday evenings each month. Annual election in December.

## CLEYAKA CLUB.
Arthur P. Towne, *Pres't;* Irving Dimock, *Vice Pres't;* Merrick W. Chapin, *Treas.;* John K. Groesbeck, *R. Sec'y.* The above officers and William Penrose, Martin Stokes, Howard Buck, Milan Harlan, *Directors.* Organized March 1, 1898. Meets second Thursday, monthly, at 902 Main street. Annual meeting in April.

## COLONIAL CLUB.
Francis R. Cooley, *Pres't;* Henry Ferguson, *Vice Pres't;* Henry S. Robinson, *Sec'y;* Wm. P. Conklin, *Treas.;* A. A. Welch, P. H. Ingalls, R. W. Huntington, Jr., Louis R. Cheney, Edward M. Bunce, G. C. F. Williams, *Directors;* R. W. Huntington, Jr., Louis R. Cheney, A. A. Welch, *House Com.* Meets at club rooms, Prospect st., first Tuesday, monthly. Annual meeting first Tuesday in February.

## COLT BICYCLE CLUB.
L. C. Grover, *Pres't;* E. H. Williams, *V. Pres't;* F. W. Weatherhead, *Sec'y;* C. B. Mellen, *Treas.;* A. L. Allen, *F. Sec'y;* H. S. Roberts, E. P. Whitney, H. G. Lord, A. L. Ulrich, F. N. Tilton, L. C. Grover, G. C. Green, A. L. Allen, C. B. Mellen, F. W. Weatherhead, C. C. Bulkeley, J. J. Peard, F. B. Griswold, E. H. Williams, C. N. Goodrich, *Board of Managers;* J. N. Fletcher, C. N. Goodrich, L. B. Bushnell, J. A. Staib. G. C. Green, *House Committee.* Organized Feb. 17, 1890. Annual meeting 2d Monday in February.

## COLT BOWLING CLUB.
L. C. Grover, *President;* T. H. Cook, *Sec'y;* A. L. Allen, *Treas.;* L. C. Glover, E. P. Whitney, *Capts.* Meeting every Wednesday evening at the Hartford Alleys.

## COLT HAMMERLESS GUN CLUB.
J. A. Pitkin, *President;* Fred Bishop, *Vice Pres't;* M. F. Cook, *Sec'y and Treas.;* M. F. Cook, J. A. Pitkin, L. C. Grover, Fred Bishop, *Ex. Com.* Organized August 13, 1884. Annual meeting in August. Club house south of Colt's armory.

## COLT MUTUAL BENEFIT ASSOCIATION.
James J. Peard, *Pres't;* E. H. Williams, *Vice Pres't;* C. C. Bulkley, *Sec'y;* J. H. Hall, *Treas.* Membership comprises 450 employees of the Colt Patent Fire Arms Manufacturing Co. Annual meeting first Monday in June.

## COLT'S FIRST REGIMENT BAND.
James R. Daly, *President;* George F. Johnson, *Sec'y and Treas.* Office 720 Main street.

## CONNECTICUT BRANCH OF THE WOMAN'S AUXILIARY TO THE BOARD OF MISSIONS,
### OF THE PROTESTANT EPISCOPAL CHURCH.
Mrs. Samuel Colt, Hartford, *Pres't;* Mrs. Harriette F. Giraud, Middletown, *Vice Pres't;* Miss C. L. Thomas, North Washington st., Norwich, *Treas.;* Miss Edith Beach, care Beach & Co., 211 State st., Hartford, *Cor. Sec'y;* Mrs. T. Belknap Beach, 99 Elm st., *Ass't Sec'y;* Miss Sara B. Huntington, 336 Collins st., Hartford, *R. Sec'y.* Miss Mary E. Beach, Lock Drawer 13, Hartford, *Sec'y and Ass't Treas.* of the Junior Auxiliary Publishing Company. Annual meeting in autumn, as may be called.
*Managers for the Hartford Archdeaconry.*—Miss S. E. Davis, 95 Trumbull st., Hartford; Mrs. Stephen Terry, 771 Asylum st., Hartford; Miss Mary E. Holkins Warehouse Point.

## CONNECTICUT LADIES' COMMISSION ON SUNDAY SCHOOL BOOKS.
### UNDER CARE OF CONN. CONGREGATIONAL CLUB.
Mrs. D. E. Bartlett, *Pres't;* Miss Charlotte A. Jewell, *Treas.;* Miss Susan T. Clark, *Sec'y.* Organized June, 1881. Meets at 420 Asylum st. Annual election in March.

### CONNECTICUT CONGREGATIONAL CLUB.

Chas. E. Gross, Hartford, *Pres't;* Jos. H. Twichell, C. D. Hartranft, Charles A. Jewell, Hartford, F. R. Waite, Talcottville, H. R. Coffin, Windsor Locks, Wm. Maxwell, Jas. Nichols, John B. Talcott, *Vice Pres'ts;* S. H. Williams, Glastonbury, *Sec'y;* Daniel H. Wells, Hartford, *Treas.* Organized May 14, 1877. Meets 3d Tuesday in March, May, Sept. and Dec. at Jewell hall. Annual meeting third Tuesday in March.

### CONN. HISTORICAL SOCIETY.

Charles J. Hoadly, *Pres't;* Samuel Hart, James J. Goodwin, Hartford; James Terry, New Haven; R. A. Wheeler, Stonington; Morris W. Seymour, Bridgeport; Theodore S. Gold, Cornwall; Frank F. Starr, Middletown; Miss Ellen D. Larned, Thompson, *Vice Pres'ts;* Albert C. Bates, *Rec. Sec'y and Librarian;* W. DeLoss Love, *Cor. Sec'y;* Jonathan F. Morris, *Treas.* Chartered in 1825. The Library is at 624 Main street; open 9.30 A. M. to 12.30 P. M., 1.30 to 5 P. M., and contains over 22,000 volumes. Annual election 4th Tuesday in May. Meets 1st Tuesday evening in each month, from October to May.

### CONN. LIFE UNDERWRITERS' ASSOCIATION.

Benedict F. Ess, New Haven, *Pres't;* Eli D. Weeks, Litchfield; Rodney Kellogg, Hartford, *Vice Pres'ts;* F. A. Thompson, Hartford, *Sec'y;* Jos. Schwab, Hartford, *Treas.;* J. G. Rathbun, A. T. Richards, A. H. Bond, Alexander Harbison, Hartford, L. H. Lyon, Bridgeport, *Executive Committee.* Organized Oct. 27, 1891. Annual meeting 2d Tuesday in February.

### CONVERSATION CLUB.

Mrs. John R. Buck, *Pres't;* Mrs. Martha I. Cone, *Sec'y.* Organized 1888. Meets Mondays, at 10:30 A.M. November to May, at members' houses.

### DEVOTION, No. 145,

L. O. L.

James H. Jones, *W. M.;* Thomas McFetridge, *Sec'y.* Meets first and third Friday evenings at 302 Asylum st. Annual election first Friday in March.

### DIRECTORS OF THE MISSIONARY SOCIETY OF CONNECTICUT.

Ward W. Jacobs, *Treas.;* W. H. Moore, *Sec'y;* Rev. C. M. Lamson, Nathaniel Shipman, David N. Camp, Joel S. Ives, George W. Banks, Watson L. Phillips, E. P. Parker, S. H. Fellows, Azel W. Hazen, Jos. Anderson, J. W. Backus, E. W. Marsh, H. L. Reade, W. H. Catlin, J. L. R. Wyckoff, Rev. D. C. Eggleston, Rev. J. H. Twichell, Rev. David E. Jones, H. G. Talcott, W. F. Stevens, *Directors;* D. N. Camp, George M. Carrington, W. H. Catlin, *Auditors.* Annual meeting in February in Memorial hall, 426 Asylum street. These Directors have five Trusts:—Western Work; Everest Fund; Memorial Hall Estate; State Work; and Special Trusts Organized 1798, chartered October, 1802, and took the above title by legislative enactment March 12, 1880.

### DRIVERS' PROTECTIVE AND BENEVOLENT UNION, No. 6229, OF HARTFORD.

Robert L. Myers, *Pres't;* Henry Phelan, *V. Pres't;* Charles W. Hunt, *Treasurer;* Benj. P. Woodward, 46 Hudson st., *Cor. Sec'y;* Wm. Haupt, *Fin. Sec'y;* D. Pendergast, Clinton Myers, T. F. Knightley, *Trustees.* Organized Jan. 1, 1895. Meets 1st and third Friday evenings at 11 Central row.

### EMERALD BENEVOLENT SOCIETY.

T. W. Gunshanon, *Pres't;* J. R. Bowen, *Vice Pres't;* D. J. Stafford, *Secretary;* John H. McCann, *Fin. Sec'y;* Patrick McCarthy, *Treas.* Annual meeting in January. Monthly meetings first Thursday at 52 Market.

### EQUAL RIGHTS CLUB.

Mrs. Emily P. Collins, *Hon. Pres't;* Mrs. E. O. Kimball, *Pres't;* Elizabeth D. Bacon, Mrs. J. G. Parsons, *Vice Pres'ts;* F. Ellen Burr, *Sec'y;* C. H. Young, *Foreign Cor. Sec'y;* Mrs. A. S. Cressy, *Treasurer.* Meets every other Wednesday evening at Unity Church parlors. Organized March, 1885. Annual election in January.

### FACTORY INSURANCE ASSOCIATION.

Geo. P. Sheldon, Brooklyn, N.Y., *Pres't;* J. H. Mitchell, Hartford, *Vice Pres't and Treas.;* E. O. Weeks, Hartford, *Secretary;* E. G. Richards, J. H. Mitchell, H. W. Eaton, J. R. Mullikin, A. G. McIlwaine, John H. Washburn, J. H. Brewster, J. A. McDonald, *Executive Committee.* Annual meeting third Thursday in April. Began business 1890. Office 95 Pearl st. Chas. G. Smith, *Manager.*

### FATHER MATTHEW CADET DRUM CORPS.

D. P. Broderick, *Pres't;* J. J. Derley, 992 Main st. *Treas.;* John Butler, *Sec'y.* 100 Asylum st.

### FIREMEN'S BENEVOLENT SOCIETY OF THE CITY OF HARTFORD.

N. G. Hinckley, *Pres't;* Louis Krug, *Vice Pres't;* D. W. Havens, *Sec'y;* C. C. Strong, *Treas.;* S. P. Agnew, *Collector;* T. J. Blake, F. P. Lepard, *Auditors.* Louis Krug, *Chairman;* George Keasley, Engine No. 1; C. C. Champlin, No. 2; Chas. Tarbox, No. 3; G. B. Hale, No. 4; W. E. Tucker, No. 5; J. J. McIntyre, No. 6; J. J. Kemmerer, No. 7; J. C. Secor, No. 8; S. C. Cooper, Hook & Ladder Co., *Board of Trustees of Firemen's Benevolent Society.* John C. McManus, Alfred Milton, *Trustees for the Old Veteran Department.* Annual meeting 1st Monday in June. 232 members. Organized June, 1836. Incorporated May, 1839.

### FRANKLIN RIFLE CLUB.

W. W. Tucker, *Pres't;* D. S. Seymour, *Vice Pres't;* H. M. Jacobs, *Treas.;* Otto Klett, *Sec'y;* T. W. Fahy, *Instructor;* E. J. Hale, *Collector;* William E. Smith, *Steward.* Organized 1867. Annual meeting 1st Friday, in Jan. Monthly meetings on 1st Fridays. Club room, 750 Main. Range, 450 Wethersfield avenue. Shootings, 1st Saturday afternoon each month.

### FRIDAY NIGHT BOWLING CLUB.

George N. Holcomb, *Pres't;* William B. Davidson, *V. Pres't;* Charles S. Robbins, *Sec'y and Treas.* Organized April, 1891. Meets Friday evenings at 66 Temple street.

### FRIENDLY VISITORS CLUB.

Miss Laura H. Sluyter, *President;* Miss Mary Robinson, *Vice Pres't;* Miss Lillian C. Cone, *Sec'y and Treas.* Miss Laura Sluyter, Miss Mabel Johnson, Miss Lillian Cone, Miss Louise Bunce, Miss Mary S. Robinson, *Executive Committee.* Organized October, 1880. Meets at Union for Home Work building, 239 Market street, October to May, on Tuesdays.

### GENERAL ASSOCIATION OF CONN.

Rev. J. G. Davenport, Waterbury, *Moderator;* Rev. G. H. Cummings, Thompson, *Scribe;* Rev. W. H. Moore, Hartford, *Sec'y and Treas.* The one hundred and eighty-eighth annual meeting was held in 1897.

### GENTLEMEN'S DRIVING CLUB.

R. N. FitzGerald, *Pres't;* M. J. Black, *Vice Pres't;* C. W. B. Edwards, Hartford, *Sec'y;* Monroe Griswold, *Treas.;* Charles Crawford, I. R. Blumenthal, J. H. Otis, W. C. Wade, Hartford; J. L. Jencks, East Hartford; C. S. Capen, Bloomfield, *Directors.* Room 10, Cheney building, 926 Main street.

### GERMAN AID SOCIETY.
SECTIONS OF 50.

*First Section*—William Braun, *Pres't;* Emil Rueger, *Vice President;* William Vater, *Secretary;* Theodore Kassenbrook, *Treas.;* Henry F. Smith, Emil Leschke, *Trustees.* Organized Feb. 10, 1875. Meets 2d Thursday evenings monthly, at 52 Market st.

*Second Section*—Carl Wagner, *President;* Theodore Scheck, *V. Pres't;* August Rudolph, *Rec. Sec'y;* Emil Eitel, *Fin. Sec'y;* H. Antz, *Treas.* Meets at Weller's Hall, first Friday evening, monthly.

### GERMANIA BOWLING CLUB.
Herman Eschholz, *Pres't;* M. Schrepfer, *V. Pres't;* A. W. Loeser, *Sec. and Treas.;* H. Wehrly, *Captain.* Organized Nov. 1890. Meets Tuesday afternoon at 66 Temple street. Election in January.

### GERMANIA CYCLE CLUB.
George Kiefar, *Pres't;* Richard Naumann, *Vice Pres't;* Gustav Holland, *Rec. Sec'y;* Wm. Muehlelr, *Fin. Sec'y;* Charles Wormeck, *Treas.;* John Libutzky, *Capt.* Organized Oct. 2, 1894. Meet at 730 Main st.

### GERMANIA LODGE, No. 388,
D. O. H.

C. F. Schulz, *O. B.;* C. R. Wolf, *Sec'y;* C. A. A. Koenig, *Treas.* Instituted April 3, 1874. Elections 2d Tuesday in January and July. Meets 2d and 4th Tuesday evenings at 793 Main st.

### GERMAN RIFLE CLUB OF HARTFORD.
Cuno Helfricht, *President;* L. B. Moller, *Vice President;* Henry Janson, *Treasurer;* Alb. Ziglatzki, *Sec'y;* T. Buettner, *Collector.* Organized in May, 1865, Annual meeting in April. Headquarters, 1056 Main st. Shoots each alternate Monday in Union Grove.

### GOOD WILL CLUB—98 PRATT ST.
Miss Mary Hall, *Pres't and Treas.;* Mrs. Daniel R. Howe, *Sec'y;* Mrs. Edward Curtis, *Auditor.* Annual election in May.

### HARTFORD ARCHÆOLOGICAL SOCIETY.
Geo. R. Shepherd, *Pres't;* Charles C. Stearns, *Vice Pres't;* Julia B. Burbank, *Sec'y;* Edward B. Bennett, *Treas.* The above officers and Prof. W. S. Pratt, L. F. Reed, S. S. Sterns, D. R. Howe, *Executive Committee.* Organized in 1887. Meets Saturday evenings in January, February and March. Annual election, April.

### HARTFORD ARCHDEACONRY.
Rev. Arthur H. Wright, Warehouse Point, *Archdeacon;* Charles H. Lawrence, Hartford, *Treas.;* Rev. H. Lilienthal, Wethersfield, *Sec'y.* Organized in 1877 by the Protestant Episcopal Church in the diocese of Connecticut. Annual election in June.

### HARTFORD BAR LIBRARY ASSOCIATION.
Lewis E. Stanton, *Pres't;* Charles J. Hoadly, John R. Buck, *Vice Pres'ts;* Hiram R. Mills, *Sec'y and Treas.;* Charles E. Perkins, Charles H. Briscoe, Chas. E. Gross, *Library Committee;* J. W. Wolven, *Librarian.* Chartered March, 1880. Organized April 10, 1880. Rooms in Court House. 1,000 vols. in Library. Annual meeting, March.

### HARTFORD BOARD OF FIRE UNDERWRITERS.
Charles E. Chase, *Pres't;* Charles M. Webster, *Vice Pres't;* L. A. Dickinson, *Sec'y and Surveyor;* C. M. Goddard, *Treas.;* John B. Knox, Frederick Samson, Charles B. Whiting, E. G. Richards, William F. Rice, *Rate Committee;* Wm. B. McCrary, Joseph Buths, Isaac Cross, Jr., W. L. Wakefield, E. S. Cowles, *Executive Committee.* Annual meeting second Tuesday in January. Meets second Tuesday each month at office of National Fire Insurance Company.

### HARTFORD BOWLING CLUB.
Fred. J. Dole, *Pres't;* W. F. Williams, *Cap't;* E. W. Alexander, *Sec. and Treas.* Organized June 8, 1892. Meets Wednesday evenings at 66 Temple street. Elections in June and December.

### HARTFORD BRANCH AMERICAN TRACT SO'Y.
Nathaniel Shipman, *Pres't;* J. M. Allen, *Vice Pres't, Treasurer and Trustees;* J. B. Pierce, *Sec'y;* Francis B. Cooley, Edward W. Parsons, Wm. H. Post, H. C. Robinson, Charles A. Jewell, Rodney Dennis, A. L. Hunt, *Directors.* Annual meeting in January.

### HARTFORD BRANCH OF SOCIETY FOR INSTRUCTION IN FIRST AID TO THE INJURED.
Mrs. Watson Webb, *Pres't;* Annie E. Trumbull, Mrs. James B. Cone, *Vice Pres'ts;* Mrs. G. Williamson Smith, *Treas.;* Mrs. Seth Talcott, *Sec'y;* Mrs. Henry P. Stearns, Mrs. Henry T. Sperry, Mrs. Geo. Watson Beach, Mrs. J. C. Kinney, Mrs. G. C. Jarvis, Mrs. W. T. Bacon, Helen Rathbun, Mrs. F. W. Davis, Miss Maida Sisson, Miss Lizzie Robinson, Mrs. Storrs O. Seymour, Mrs. Geo. Roberts, Jr., Mary C. Spencer, *Executive Committee.*
*Medical Directors*—Dr. William Porter, Jr., Dr. Oliver C. Smith. Organized 1884. Meets at 49 Pearl st. 1st Wednesday, monthly. Annual meeting 1st Wednesday in May.

### HARTFORD BRANCH OF THE CONN. CHILDREN'S AID SOCIETY.
Mrs. Virginia T. Smith, *Pres't;* Mrs. Isabella B. Hooker, Mrs. B. M. Parsons, Mrs. H. N. Simmons, *Vice Pres'ts;* Mrs. C. H. Boardman, *Treas.;* Josephine M. Griswold, *Rec. Sec'y;* Mrs. S. L. G. Crane, *Cor. Sec'y;* Mrs. Geo. H. Warner, Mrs. J. M. Allen, Miss Lucy A. Brainard, Mrs. M. Parsons, Mrs. Richard Seymour, *Executive Committee.* Organized March 8, 1888, as Hartford City Mission Association. Name changed in 1892 to the Children's Aid Society. Office, 223 Asylum street, room 10.

### HARTFORD BRANCH OF THE WOMAN'S NATIONAL ALLIANCE.
Mrs. S. L. G. Crane, *Pres't;* Mrs. Joseph Waite, Mrs. W. E. Dickinson, *Vice Pres'ts;* Mrs. J. Q. Baker, *Sec'y and Treas.;* Mrs. W. E. Dickinson, *Cor. Sec'y.* Organized April 16, 1883. Meets in Unity Church parlors 1st and 3d Thursday, at 3 P. M. Annual election in April.

### HARTFORD CANOE CLUB.
Geo. L. Parmele, *Pres't;* Daniel S. Morrell, *Commodore;* A. H. Wightman, *Treas.;* Francis H. Hills, *Sec'y;* L. S. Hickmott, *Ass't Sec'y;* officers above, and W. B. Davidson, *Executive Committee.* Organized April, 1880. Chartered 1884. Annual meeting 3d Tuesday in January. Club house, East Hartford.

### HARTFORD CLEARING HOUSE ASSOCIATION.
James Bolter, *Pres't;* Geo. H. Burt, *Sec'y and Treas.* John R. Redfield, John G. Root, *Clearing House Com.* It is composed of the fourteen city Banks and Trust Companies, who settle at 10 A. M. their daily balances, at the clearing house, in the Phœnix National Bank building. Annual election in Feb.

### HARTFORD CLUB.
Joseph R. Hawley, *Pres't;* George Pope, D. W. C. Skilton, *Vice Pres'ts;* Chas. E. Chase, *Sec'y;* R. G. Watrous, Jr., *Treas.;* W. R. Davidson, Ernest Cady, Henry Osborn, W. E. A. Bulkeley, James Campbell, Lyman B. Jewell, George Ellis, *Managers;* J. C. Sterling, James P. Taylor, *Auditors.* Organized Nov. 1873. Chartered July, 1874. Annual meeting, 3d Monday in October. 88 Prospect st.

### HARTFORD COMEDY CO.
H. I. Horton, *Pres't;* H. H. Larkum, *Treas. and Stage Manager.* Org. Feb. 1892. Meets on call of Pres't.

## HARTFORD CONFERENCE CONG. CHURCHES.
Rev. W. W. Ranney, *Moderator;* Rev. Richard Wright, *Treas. and Registrar.* Organized Feb. 21, 1871. Meets spring and fall. Annual election, in the fall.

## HARTFORD CONCLAVE, No. 259.
IMPROVED ORDER HEPTASOPHS.
William F. Finlay, *Archon;* A. D. McKinnon, *Sec'y;* Geo. R. Bodge, *Financier;* William A. Willard, *Treas.;* Grenville W. French, William H. Pond, Clarkson N. Fowler, *Trustees.* Organized March 21, 1893. Meets 1st and 3d Tuesdays at 881 Main st. Annual meeting 3d Tuesday in Dec.

## HARTFORDER TURNERBUND.
Wilmar Schlag, *Pres't;* Adam Lepper, *Vice Pres't;* Karl Sterner, *Cor. Sec'y;* R. C. Stadermann, *Rec. Sec'y;* Henry Spieske, *Treas.;* Wm. C. Winkelman, *Ins.;* H. Spieske, John Yungk, Jacob Walz, A. Trante, Sr., *Trustees.* Organized May 19, 1878. Incorporated April, 1885. Capital $10,000. Meet at 8 Morgan st., monthly, 2d Monday evening. Election in Jan. and July. 200 members.

## HARTFORD FOX CLUB.
Cleveland Capen, *Pres't;* Joseph G. Lane, *Treasurer and Secretary;* George L. Deming, *Master of Hounds.* Annual meeting 1st Monday in January at 224 State. Result of 1896-8 winter field days, 21 skins.

## HARTFORD GOLF CLUB.
S. O. Prentice, *Pres't;* F. R. Cooley, *Captain;* Arthur P. Day, *Sec'y;* J. J. Nairn, *Treas.;* L. R. Cheney, J. C. Stirling, J. M. Taylor, R. W. Cutler, C. P. Howard, *Directors.* Organized June 3, 1896.

## HARTFORD INDIAN ASSOCIATION.
Mrs. G. Williamson Smith, *Pres't;* Mrs. A. E. Hull, Mrs. Jacob Knous, *Vice Presidents;* Mrs. Henry E. Taintor, *R. Sec'y;* Mrs. Frederick Jones, *C. Sec'y;* Mrs. Seth Talcott, *Treas.* Organized April 26, 1887. Meets last Tuesday in Jan., April and Oct. in Center church parlors at 11 A. M. Annual meeting in Oct.

## HARTFORD KENNEL CLUB.
William L. Matson, *Pres't;* Archibald A. Welch, *Vice Pres't;* Abbott C. Collins, *Sec'y;* John D. Parker, *Treas.* Incorporated, 1886. Annual meeting, first Wednesday after the first day in January in each year.

## HARTFORD LAWN CLUB.
Francis R. Cooley, *Pres't;* James A. Turnbull, *Vice Pres't;* Jas. Terry, *Sec'y;* Loomis A. Newton, *Treas.* Annual election 2d Tuesday in April.

## HARTFORD LODGE, No. 19,
BENEVOLENT AND PROTECTIVE ORDER OF ELKS.
Robert D. Bone, *E. R.;* Thos. A. Shannon, P. O. Box 557, *Sec'y;* Albert F. Woods, *Treas.;* S. D. Chamberlin, M. F. Cook, E. M. Graves, James Campbell, P. McGovern, *Trustees.* Organized Feb. 11, 1883. Incorporated 1893. Meets at 7 Central row on Friday evenings. Annual election last Friday in March.

## HARTFORD LODGE, No. 108,
INDEPENDENT ORDER OF SONS OF BENJAMIN.
Henry Jonas, *Pres't;* Morris Dorenbaum, *Vice Pres't;* Julius Herzfeld, *Rec. Sec'y;* Israel Brody, *Fin. Sec'y;* Sol. Silverstein, *Treas.;* Joel Samuels, Louis S. Price, Nathan Kempner, *Trustees.* Meet at 11 Pratt st. 2d and 4th Sunday in each month at 2.30 P. M. Organized March 13, 1887. Elections semi-annually, June and December.

## HARTFORD LODGE, No. 120,
ORDER OF FRATERNAL GUARDIANS.
In the hands of Assignee. E. Howard Geer, R. S.

## HARTFORD MÆNNERCHOR.
Frank Schirm, *Pres't;* Albert Baumgarten, *Vice Pres't;* Henry Schwerdtfeger, 27 Mulberry st., *Sec'y;* Christian Woerner, *Fin. Sec'y;* Nicholas Kohlus, *Treas.;* Frank Schirm, Edward Santer, Herman Werhly, *Trustees.* Organized, Sept. 11, 1884. Incorporated May 5, 1898. Monthly meetings first Friday evening at Turnerbund Hall, 1056 Main st.

## HARTFORD MALE CHORUS.
Ludlow Barker, *Leader.* Organized 1877. 155 Asy.

## HARTFORD McALL AUXILIARY.
Mrs. A. H. Pitkin, *Pres't;* Miss Annie E. Olmsted, Mrs. R. C. Mayer, Miss M. C. Holaday, *Vice Pres'ts;* Miss Harriet Rowell, *Treas.;* Miss Mary B. Lewis, *Sec'y;* A. A. Welch, *Auditor,* and Board of thirty-two Managers. Organized April, 1887. Meets first Monday of each month. Annual election 1st Monday in May.

## HARTFORD OPERA COMPANY.
Irving Emerson, *Director and Manager.* Organized Dec. 17, 1881. Meets as notified at Unity hall.

## HARTFORD ORPHAN ASYLUM.
Mrs. Charles F. Howard, *Pres't;* Mrs. A. P. Hyde, Mrs. F. B. Cooley, Mrs. F. Goodwin, Mrs. L. Brainard, *Vice Pres'ts;* D. R. Howe, *Treas.;* Mrs. W. W. Hyde, *Ass't Treas.;* Mrs. E. B. Bennett, *Cor. Sec'y;* Mrs. C. F. Sedgwick, *Rec. Sec'y;* Mrs. John Allen, Mrs. Lucius A. Barbour, Mrs. George M. Bartholomew, Mrs. Edward B. Bennett, Mrs. James Bolter, Mrs. Leverett Brainard, Mrs John R. Buck, Miss E. Blythe, Mrs. G. R. Shepherd, Mrs. J. S. Camp, Mrs. W. C. Skinner, Mrs. Francis B. Cooley, Mrs. J. S. Curtis, Mrs. F. R. Foster, Mrs. James J. Goodwin, Mrs. Frances Goodwin, Mrs. Charles E. Gross, Mrs. D. R. Howe, Mrs. A. P. Hyde, Mrs. Havemeyer, Mrs. Charles F. Howard, Charlotte A. Jewell, Mrs. J. F. Judd, Mrs. George W. Moore, Mrs. George R. Shepherd, Mrs. G. E. Taintor, Mrs. H. E. Taintor, Mrs. J. J. Nairn, Mrs. George W. Beach, Mrs. W. W. Hyde, Mrs. Charles F. Sedgwick, Mrs. J. A. Smith, Mrs. Wilder Smith, Mrs. W. H. Palmer, Antoinette R. Phelps, Mrs. DeWitt, Miss Ellen Case, Miss Clara E. Hillyer, Mrs. J. W. Bradin, Mrs. William E. Collins, Mrs. Harlan P. Kline, *Managers;* Miss Elizabeth Blythe, 799 Asylum st.; Mrs. George W. Beach, 54 Main st., *Admission Committee.* Rev. George Dustin, *Sup't;* Mrs. George Dustin, *Matron.* Chartered June 22, 1865. Annual meeting first Monday in June. Managers' meeting 1st Mon. each month. 171 Putnam st.

## HARTFORD PUBLIC LIBRARY.
Chartered 1878 as Hartford Library Association, successors of the Hartford Young Men's Institute that was chartered in 1887. Said Young Men's Institute purchased the books of the Hartford Library that was chartered in 1799. Present name taken and opened to the public as a free Library Sept. 15, 1892. Samuel O. Prentice, *Pres't;* W. I. Twitchell, *Vice Pres't;* Charles H. Clark, *Treas.;* Robert A. Griffing, *Sec'y;* Samuel B. St. John, W. F. Gordy, Lucius F. Robinson, S. O. Prentice, Francis Goodwin, Charles M. Joslyn, Edward D. Robbins, W. W. Hyde, Willis I. Twitchell, Robert A. Griffing, Charles Hopkins Clark, Chas. P. Howard, *Directors;* Caroline M. Hewins, *Librarian;* Alice T. Cummings, Alice M. Crocker, Mary G. Huntington, Jane E. Hastie, Florence H. Kellogg, Mary I. Bartlett, Alice P. Tallman, Grace A. Child, Annie Fischer, Herbert P. Stedman, *Assistants;* Karl P. Morba, Alfred Zurhorst, William L. Carter, John Walmsley, *Extra Assistants.* Library, 624 Main st., open from 9 A. M. to 8 P. M.; Reading room from 8 A. M. to 10 P. M. Annual election 1st Tuesday in June. Volumes in Library, 57,500; Periodicals, 175.

## HARTFORD RETAIL GROCERS' ASSOCIATION.
John A. Conklin, *Pres't;* Chas. H. Strong, *Treas.* Organized, April, 1891. Meets upon call of President.

### HARTFORD, No. 5,
**NATIONAL ASSOCIATION OF STATIONARY ENGINEERS.**
E. J. Markel, *Pres't;* Louis M. Marvel, P. O. box 751, *Sec'y;* Geo. Miller, *Treas.;* Thomas Wright, Patrick J. Barrett, M. O'Brien, *Trustees.* Meets at 720 Main st., room 15, on Monday evenings. Instituted April 16, 1885. Annual election last Monday in Dec.

### HARTFORD ROWING AND ATHLETIC CLUB.
John C. Long, *Pres't;* Wm. L. Crowley, *Vice Pres't;* J. M. McCunn, *Rec. Sec'y;* D. J. Murphy, *Fin. Sec'y;* L. S. Knoek, *Treas.;* Edward J. Ryan, *Capt.;* Henry Beaune, *Lieut.* Organized in Nov. 1889, as Hartford Rowing Club, and present name, April 6, 1893. Annual meeting first Tuesday in April. Boat house on east side Conn. river, south of bridge. Meets 1st Sunday in each month.

### HARTFORD SÆNGERBUND.
Henry Antz, *Pres't;* Henry Preissner, *Vice Pres't;* Emil Rueger, *Rec. Sec'y;* H. Seegers, *Cor. Sec'y;* W. Meyer, *Fin. Sec'y;* F. D. Mann, *Treas.;* Ernest Schall, H. Meyer, *Trustees.* Organized Jan. 28, 1858. Incorporated 1893. Meetings 1st Monday evening each month at Sængerbund hall, 11 Central row. Elections January and July.

### HARTFORD SCHUETZEN VEREIN.
Cuno Helfrich, *Pres't;* L. B. Moller, *Vice Pres't;* Henry Jansen, *Treas.;* Alb. Ziglatzki *Sec'y;* T. Buettner, *Collector.* Organized in May, 1865. Annual meeting in April. Headquarters 1056 Main st. Shoots each alternate Monday in Union Grove.

### HARTFORD SCIENTIFIC SOCIETY.
George L. Parmele, *Pres't;* W. H. C. Pynchon, *Vice Pres't;* W. E. Treat, *Sec'y;* Oliver H. Ham, *Treas.* Organized, December 18, 1885. Chartered April, 1886. Reorganized June, 1894. Room 65 Pratt st.

### HARTFORD THEOSOPHICAL SOCIETY.
Louisa D. Kean, *Pres't;* W. H. Witham, *Vice Pres't;* Frances Ellen Burr, *Sec'y and Treas.* Meets Thursday in Unity parlors. Annual meeting first Thursday in January.

### HARTFORD TURNHALLE COMPANY.
William Westphal, *Pres't;* Joseph Schwab, *Vice Pres't;* A. Traute, *Sec'y;* Joseph Hirth, *Treas.;* William Westphal, Joseph Hirth, T. Kassenbrook, Joseph Schwab, O. E. Froehlich, H. Spieske, A. Traute, Hubert Fischer, Wilmar Schlag, *Directors;* H. Spieske, *Hall Agent.* Organized May 2, 1888. Capital, $20,000. Annual election 2d Tuesday in May.

### HARTFORD TYPOGRAPHICAL UNION, No. 127.
Thomas Crosby, *Pres't;* T. H. Dignam, *Vice Pres't;* A. F. Miles, *Treas.;* Daniel A. Fitzpatrick, *Rec. Sec'y;* S. T. Pfund, *Fin. Sec'y.* Re-organized Dec. 3, 1883. Meets at 11 Central row, Central Labor Union hall, 2d Wednesday of each month, at 8 P. M. Annual election last Wednesday in July.

### HARTFORD WHEEL CLUB.
A. H. Schumaker, *Pres't;* F. R. Loyden, *V. Pres't;* H. C. Bill, *R. Sec'y;* W. A. Damon, *F. Sec'y;* W. A. Shew, *Treas.;* A. B. Smith, *Capt.;* R. E. Prendergast, *1st Lieut.;* R. B. Tracy, *2d Lieut.;* A. E. Sisson, *Color Bearer;* H. G. Bailey, *Bugler.* Organized Nov. 2, 1885. Incorporated, April 19, 1887. Meets at 704 Main st. 2d Tuesday evening, monthly. Annual meeting 2d Tuesday, November.

### HARTFORD WOMAN'S BAPTIST FOREIGN MISSIONARY CONFERENCE.
Mrs. G. M. Stone, *Pres't;* Mrs. I. F. Stidham, Mrs. H. F. Thompson, Mrs. Frank Dixon, *Vice Pres'ts;* Mrs. H. L. Strong, 19 Vernon street, *Cor. Sec'y;* Mrs. J. M. Lester, *Rec. Sec'y;* Miss Frances Z. Niles, *Treas.* Annual meeting, Dec. Semi-annual meeting, June.

### HARTFORD YACHT CLUB.
H. L. Maercklein, *Commodore;* E. N. Way, *Vice Commodore;* E. L. Miller, Middletown, *Rear Commodore;* C. J. Doolittle, Windsor, *Fleet Cap't.;* F. H. Varney, 270 Main st. *Sec'y;* C. H. Way, *Treas.;* C. H. Northam, Ernest N. Way, W. W. Frayer, C. M. Spencer, John McFadyen, Walter Pearce, *Trustees.* Organized May 3, 1895. Annual election in February. Club house, foot of Grove st.

### H. C. ROBINSON TROOP.
James P. Andrews, *Pres't;* H. A. Tyler, *V. Pres't;* Robert D. Bone, *Sec'y;* Geo. H. Woolley, *Treas.;* H. C. Robinson, *H. Commander;* S. E. Chamberlain, *Major;* J. N. Wilsey, H. A. Tyler, *Captains;* C. H. Case, G. H. Woolley, R. P. Kenyon, O. H. Blanchard, *Lieutenants;* James R. Goodrich, *Ensign.* Organized Feb. 14, 1889. 676 Main street.

### HEARTHSTONE CLUB.
Mrs. S. L. G. Crane, *Pres't;* Mrs. T. E. Steele, *Vice Pres't;* Mrs. F. A. Brackett, *Sec'y;* Mrs. Linus Dickenson, *Cor. Sec'y;* Mrs. L. S. Lee, *Treas.;* Mrs. S. B. Forbes, Mrs. E. J. E. Geer, Mrs. C. P. Gladding, *Directors.* Organized Jan. 1895. Meets 1st and 3d Monday evening Oct. to May. Annual meeting in April.

### HEBREW BENEVOLENT ASSOCIATION.
M. Wieder, *Pres't;* A. Walder, *V. Pres't;* Joel Samuels, *Treas.;* Louis S. Price, *Secretary;* H. Bacharach, N. Kempner, I. F. Samuels, and above officers, *Board of Directors.* Reorganized 1866. Meets Thursdays at 4 P. M. at 91 Morgan st. Annual meeting in January.

### HELPING HAND AUXILIARY SOCIETY VETERAN VOLUNTEER FIREMEN'S ASSOCIATION.
Mrs. Ada Belcher, *President;* Mrs. Charles Stickney, *Vice President;* Mrs. Margaret Cooper, *Treas.;* Mrs. Carrie Graham, *Rec. Sec'y;* Mrs. Jennie Fox, *Fin. Sec'y.* Organized Jan. 17, 1895. Meets Friday evening at 27 Arch street. Annual meeting in January.

### HOSMER HALL CHORAL UNION.
Joseph A. Graves, *Pres't;* F. H. Forbes, *Registrar of Rheinberger Club;* J. W. Titcomb, *Sec'y;* W. S. Brown, *Librarian;* J. M. Gallup, C. L. Ames, J. W. Titcomb, J. A. Graves, R. P. Paine, *Business Committee;* C. D. Hartranft, H. H. Kelsey, Gail B. Munsill, E. K. Mitchell, A. T. Perry, E. B. Hooker, J. M. Gallup, Jos. A. Graves, J. W. Titcomb, Arthur E. Hobson, C. L. Ames, *Directors;* R. P. Paine, *Conductor.* Organized 1880. Annual meeting in May. The Chorus of over 200 voices rehearses every Friday evening; from October 1 to May 1, at Hosmer Hall, 1507 Broad street. Several concerts are given during the year, and a May Festival at the close of the season.

### HUBBARD ESCORT.
Leopold DeLeeuw, *President;* Edwin Brower, Wm. G. Boardman, *Vice Pres'ts;* Joseph Buths, *Sec'y and Treas.;* H. C. Daniels, *Serg't at Arms;* Thomas P. M. Preston, *Historian.* The above officers and E. P. Forbes and R. P. Curtis, *Ex. Com.* Organized Sept. 1880. Annual meeting in March. Meets quarterly.

### ISAAC LEESER LODGE, No. 142,
**KESHER SHEL BARZEL.**
S. Marcus, *Pres't;* Isidor Kempner, *Vice Pres't;* Charles Taussig, *Treas.;* Julius Herzfeld, *Rec. and Fin. Sec'y;* Joel Samuels, Abraham Cadden, Nathan Kempner, *Trustees.* Organized April 4, 1875. Meets at 11 Pratt st., first Sunday, monthly, 2.30 P. M. Annual meeting in Jan.

## ITALIAN SOCIETY, UMBERTO FIRST.

Vincent Bertucci, *Pres't;* Joseph Prior, *Vice Pres't;* Joseph Uricchio, 219 Sheldon st., *Secretary;* Michael Forastiri, *Vice Sec'y;* John Motto, *Treasurer;* Antoni Arcari, John Nicolina, Nicola Delena, *Ex. Committee.* Meets at 11 Central row, second Sunday monthly.

## JUDITH LODGE, No. 33,

**INDEPENDENT ORDER OF THE FREE SONS OF ISRAEL.**

Henry W. Seide, *Pres't;* Joseph W. Levy, *Vice Pres't;* Charles Rosenthal, *Rec. Sec'y;* Gustav Simon, *Fin. Sec'y;* Victor Minke, *Cashier;* Ludwig Hellman, William Bacharach, Nathan Kempner, *Trustees.* Organized March 25, 1870. Meets at Bliss hall, 2d and 4th Sundays, monthly. Semi-annual meeting 4th Sunday in June and December.

## KNIGHTS OF SHERWOOD FOREST.

Joseph R. Neddo, *Com.;* John F. Kilmartin, *Adj.;* Nicholas D. Baldwin, *Sergt. Maj. and Sec'y.* Organized Oct. 1896. Meets 1st and 3d Wednesday evenings at 104 Asylum st.

## LADIES' BENEVOLENT SOCIETY OF CHRIST CHURCH.

Mrs. H. H. Hollister, *President;* Mrs. J. F. Tracy, Mrs. Grace Robinson, *Vice Pres'ts;* Miss Mary N. Davis, *Treasurer;* Mrs. A. R. Barrows, *Ass't Treas.;* Mrs. John D. Tucker, *Sec'y;* Mrs. H. E. Kellogg, *Rec. Sec'y.* Organized 1829. Annual meeting in October. Meets bi-weekly, Fall, Winter and Spring.

## LADIES' MUTUAL BENEVOLENT SOCIETY.

Miss Margaret Welch, *Pres't;* Miss Mary Felleter, *Vice Pres't;* Miss Alice Campbell, 651 Main st., *Rec. Sec'y;* Mamie Morgan, Allie Brenan, *Fin. Sec'ys;* Miss Sadie Ledwith, *Treas.* Organized August 1887. Meets 1st and 3d Tuesday evenings.

## LARRABEE FUND ASSOCIATION.

Mrs. Jacob Knous, *Pres't;* Ellen W. Gray, 198 Farmington av., *Sec'y and Treas.;* Miss A. S. McManus, Mrs. J. G. Parsons, Mrs. Chas. R. Burt, Mrs. E. B. Bennett, Mrs. L. H. Brainard, Miss Sarah Fisher, Mrs. Howard A. Camp, Miss Susan T. Clark, Mrs. A. L. Hunt, *Executive Committee.* Annual meeting in Oct. Organized Dec. 1864. Meet at 426 Asylum st. Trust Fund, $23,242.02. Annual income to be appropriated to the relief of the lame, maimed and deformed females of Town of Hartford. C. C. Strong, *Treas.;* Mayor and Aldermen of City and Selectmen of Hartford, *Trustees.*

## LES CHATS NOIRE.

Membership limited to thirteen men, who meet fortnightly for the study of modern literature. E. B. Field, 83 Niles st., *Sec'y.* Organized May, 1895. Rooms, rear 243 Laurel st.

## L. L. T. SOCIETY OF PHILOSOPHY OF HEALING.

E. A. Sheldon, *Pres't;* Mrs. E. W. Fuller, *Vice Pres't;* Miss H. M. Lyman, *Sec'y;* Mrs. E. M. Sill, *Treas.*

## MASTER PLUMBERS.

J. J. Lawler, *Pres't;* G. S. Bull, *Vice Pres't;* T. Edward Oakes, *Rec. Sec'y;* T. H. Langdon, *Fin. Sec'y;* B. J. Lyon, *Cor. Sec'y;* Edward Lawler, *Treas.*

## McKINLEY CLUB OF HARTFORD.

Alex Harbison, *Pres't;* I. Wise, W. A. Countryman, C. E. Shelton, R. S. Hinman, W. H. Watrous, *V. Pres'ts;* W. H. Nugent, *Treas.;* W. F. Taylor, *Sec'y;* B. C. McKinney, *Fin. Sec'y.* Organized Nov. 23, 1893. Regular meeting 1st Tuesday of each month at 92 Pearl street. Annual meeting 1st Tuesday in June.

## MERCHANTS' EXCHANGE.

Joseph F. Swords, *Pres't;* Ezra F. Bates, *Vice Pres't;* P. H. Woodward, *Sec'y;* H. H. Goodwin, *Ass't Sec'y;* Charles A. Pease, *Treas.;* William Tucker, R. N. Fitzgerald, Charles G. Lincoln, Geo. P Chandler, Arthur M. Wilson, *Directors. Committees:* Arthur M. Wilson, C. S. Hutchinson, R. N. FitzGerald, H. H. Goodwin, C. B. Ingraham, *Transportation;* C. A. Pease, E. F. Bates, H. F. Boardman, *Printing;* E. C. Frisbie, H. Goldschmidt, D. N. Hewes, *Arbitration.* Edwin W. Sage, S. B. Bosworth, *Auditors.* Regular meeting 4th Monday evening, monthly, 89 Pearl street.

## METHODIST UNION.

Geo. W. Newton, *Pres't;* E. Ryder, Geo. F. Warfield, N. J. Witham, L. E. Parkhurst, R. S. Eldridge, E. S. Gardner, H. A. Camp, Julius Weed, James Adair, John R. Holehouse, Martin Pulver, *Vice Pres'ts;* Ira J. Strong, *Sec'y;* Jordon C. Wells, *Treas.* Organized May, 1892.

## MISSIONARY DAUGHTERS OF DYSON.

Miss Desdemona Paul, *Pres't;* Mrs. J. A. Curtis, *V. Pres't;* Mrs. Fannie E. Randall, 48 Wolcott st., *Sec'y and Treas.;* Mrs. Elizabeth Christian, Mrs. Augusta Commeraw, Mrs. Ruby A. Mitchell, Mrs. Rebecca Strong, Mrs. Bell, *Matrons.* J. S. Cooper, *Chaplain.* Organized May, 15, 1870. Meets 1st Thursday of each month, 284 Pearl st.

## MT. HOLYOKE COLLEGE ALUMNI ASSOC'N.

Mrs. George L. Clark, Farmington, *Pres't;* Mrs. A T. Richards, Hartford, Mrs. C. D. Talcott, Talcottville, Miss Charlotte A. Jewell, Mrs. Emily O. Kimball, Hartford, Mrs. Lydia S. Woodworth, Berlin, Mrs. Julia M. Carrington, Winsted, Miss Jessie Usher, Higganum, Mrs. Solomon Richards, Unionville, Miss Julia I. Williams, Windsor, *Vice Pres'ts;* Mrs. Sidney W. Clark, Hartford, *Secretary;* Miss Lucy Day, Hartford, *Treas.;* President, Secretary, Treasurer, and Miss Charlotte A. Jewell, Mrs. N. F. Allen, Mrs. C. D. Talcott, Mrs. A. T. Richards, Miss Lucy Way, *Advisory Board.* Organized April 17, 1886. Semi-annual meetings in May and October.

## MT. HOPE TABERNACLE, No. 408.

**DAUGHTERS OF MOUNT TABOR.**

Mrs. Fannie E. Randall, *C. P.;* Mrs. Emeline Smith, *V. P.;* Miss Desdamona F. Paul, *C. Recorder;* Mrs. Ella Daniels, *C. Treas.* Meets 2d and 4th Friday evenings at 302 Asylum st.

## MUSURGIA CLUB.

N. H. Allen, *Pres't;* Mrs. V. P. Marwick, F. L. Burdick, *V. Pres'ts;* C. S. Shumway, *Sec'y.* Organized October 1890. Meets Mondays at 926 Main st. Annual meeting in April.

## MUTUAL AID SOCIETY OF JEWELL MFG. CO.

W. C. Colton, *Pres't;* George Stronach, *Vice Pres't;* E. A. Shaw, *Sec'y;* L. D. Hubbard, *Treas.;* W. C. Colton, S. H. Townsend, George Stronach, G. H. Fulton, *Executive Committee.*

## NUT-MEG CLUB.

Edward G. Graves, *Pres't;* John J. Starkey, Jr., *Vice Pres't;* Ralph H. Foster, *Sec'y and Treas.* Organized October, 1892. Meets first Tuesday evening, monthly, at rear 49 Wooster street. Elections, January and July.

## PIONEER LODGE, No. 315,

**KNIGHTS OF HONOR.**

J. H. Coe, *D.;* Edward R. Faxon, *Reporter;* F. P. Carter, *Treas.;* C. E. Cooksley, 71 Asylum st., *F. Rep.;* J. N. Shedd, Geo. M. Johnson, C. H. Clark, *Trustees.* Instituted June 26, 1876. Meets 2d and 4th Monday evenings in each month at 815 Pearl st. Annual election 2d Monday evening in December.

## POLICE MUTUAL AID ASSOCIATION.

George F. Bill, *Pres't*; John J. Golden, *V. Pres't*; Cornelius Ryan, *Treas.*; Herbert E. 'Linker, *Sec'y*; Lyman Smith, Thomas McCue, Walter Smith, Edward F. O'Brien, George P. Harvey, John Creedon, James F. Lally, Wm. Weltner, Chas. L. Ramsden, *Trustees*. Benefits paid since organization, $5,400. Members, 192. Organized, April 1, 1880. Annual meeting 1st Thursday in April. Rooms, Police Office.

## POPE'S MILITARY BAND.

George L. Bladon, *Pres't*; George Rudolph, *Vice Pres't*; N. A. Sperry, *Sec'y and Treas*. Annual meeting in January. 104 Asylum street.

## PRATT & WHITNEY FELLOWSHIP CLUB.

F. A. Pratt, *Pres't*; Philip Bardons, *V. Pres't*; Fred. A. West, *Treas.*; Frank Harrington, *Secretary*. Organized Dec. 1894. Annual election 1st Monday in Oct.

## PRESS CLUB OF HARTFORD.

Charles E. Clay, *President*; Fred E. Perine, *Treas.*; A. H. Loomis, *C. Sec'y*; Alphonse Dumont, *R. Sec'y*; W. A. Countryman, *Historian*; W. D. Freer, *Sergeant-at-Arms*. Organized Jan. 23, 1892. Meets monthly. Annual meeting in January.

## PRIVATE COACHMEN'S BENEVOLENT ASSOC'N.

T. P. Quirk, *Pres't*; James Clark, *Vice Pres't*; Wm. Feeley, 77 Wethersfield av., *R. and C. Sec'y*; Wm. R. Jones, *F. Sec'y*; Patrick Golden, *Treas.*; James Clark, Louis Thompson, P. Scanlon, A. S. Tillotson, J. McCarty, *Directors*. Chartered in April, 1884. Annual meeting 2d Tuesday in January. Meets monthly, 2d Tuesday evening at 92 Asylum st.

## REBEKAH LODGE, No. 17,

O. K. S. D.

Henry Jonas, *Pres't*; Mrs. L. Levy, *Vice Pres't*; Mrs. B. R. Blumenthal, *Rec. and Fin. Sec'y*; Mrs. Nonie Minke, *Treas.*; Mrs. J. Lyon, Mrs. L. Greenberg, Miss Bertha Tannebaum, *Trustees*. Organized April 15, 1888. Meets 3d Sunday each month at 881 Main st.

## REPUBLICAN CLUB OF HARTFORD.

Henry C. Dwight, *Pres't*; James L. Howard, William B. Clark, *Vice Pres'ts*; John T. Robinson, *Sec'y*; Joseph L. Blanchard, *Treas.*; Wm. H. Whitelaw, *Collector*; Gail B. Munsill, Albert P. Day, Henry P. Hitchcock, George E. Taintor, Wm. M. Hudson, Frank S. Kellogg, *Executive Committee*; H. P. Hitchcock, Wm. M. Hudson, F. S. Kellogg, *House Committee*. Organized 1894. Annual meeting 1st Monday in March. Members 325. Meets at 676 Main street.

## RETREAT FOR THE INSANE.—80 *Washington.*

*See pages 798, 799.*

## ROSE OF ENGLAND LODGE, No. 4,

DAUGHTERS OF ST. GEORGE.

Mrs. Alice Whitehead, *Pres't*; Mrs. E. Dawe, *Vice Pres't*; Mrs. Sophia Whitehead, 78 New Britain av., *Rec. Sec'y*; Mrs. L. Garner, *Fin. Sec'y*; Mrs. M. E. Oakes, *Treas.*; M. Ives, L. Hooper, E. Thompson, *Trustees*. Organized April 28, 1887. Meets 2d and 4th Friday evenings, monthly, at 724 Main street. Elections June and December.

## SACKMAIER BOWLING CLUB.

James Johnston, *President*; James C. Bailey, *Vice Pres't*; Carl Schott, *Treas.*; Chas. O. Winter, *Sec'y*. Organized Oct. 23, 1882. Meets Monday evenings at 66 Temple street. Annual, third Monday in October.

## SOCIALOGICAL CLUB.

Chester D. Hartranft, *Pres't*; Alex R. Merriam, *Vice Pres't*; Miss May Jones, *Treas*. General meeting the 2d Wednesday evening monthly at Hosmer Hall.

## SHELTER FOR WOMAN.

Mrs. John M. Taylor, *Chairman and Sec'y*; Mrs. J. G. Calhoun, *Treas.*; Mrs. Stephen Terry, Mrs. James J. Goodwin, Mrs. E. B. Turner, Annie E. Cooke, Mrs. A. L. Goodrich, Augusta H. Williams, Mrs. J. G. Calhoun, Mrs. Pierre S. Starr, Mrs. Chas. M. Lamson, *Committee*. Jacob L. Greene, Ernest DeF. Miel, B. N. B. Miller, *Advisory Board*. Organized Oct. 1891. 76 Temple st.

## SOCIETY FOR INCREASE OF THE MINISTRY OF THE PROTESTANT EPISCOPAL CHURCH.

Rt. Rev. John Williams, Middletown, Conn., *Pres't*; Rev. T. R. Pyncheon, *Rec. Sec'y*; Rev. F. D. Hoskins, *Cor. Sec'y*; James Bolter, *Treas.*; Rev. S. O. Seymour, *Chairman Ex. Com*. Annual election 2d Tuesday, Sept. Organized 1857. Incorporated 1859. 37 Spring st.

## SONQUASSEN TRIBE, No. 2,

IMPROVED ORDER OF RED MEN.

Herman Seegers, *S.*; John F. Lehr, *C. of R.*; Thos. A. Kimberly, *C. of W.*; William H. Pond, *K. of W.*; W. H. Goodell, *Trustee*. Instituted January 21, 1857. Meets every Friday evening at 908 Main st. Elections last Friday in June and December.

## ST. JOHN'S SICK AND BURIAL SOCIETY.

James Connelly, *Pres't*; Lawrence Low, *Vice Pres't*: Daniel A. Hern, *Treas.*; P. D. Ryan, *Sec'y*. Chartered July 18, 1848. Meets 3d Sunday, quarterly, at 92 Asylum st. Annual election in Jan.

## ST. PATRICK'S BENEVOLENT SOCIETY.

Wm. Dungan, *Pres't*; Joseph Dillon, *Vice Pres't*: Edward T. Lyons, *Treas.*; James Watson, *F. Sec'y*: John Tagerty, *R. Sec'y*. Chartered 1842. Meetings first Sunday, monthly, at 104 Asylum street. Annual meeting 1st Sunday in January.

## SWEDISH SICK HELP SOCIETY.

SWEDISH ZION CONGREGATIONAL CHURCH.

J. Gust. Johnson, *Pres't*; E. Gust. Anderson, *Vice Pres't*; Arthur A. Engstrom, *Sec'y*; Oscar E. Carlson, *Tr*. Meets 3d Friday monthly in church. 40 members.

## SWISS SOCIETY OF HARTFORD.

Robert Brandenberger, *Pres't*; Carl Welter. *Vice Pres't*; Rudolph Spring, *Rec. Sec'y*; N. Ruedlinger. *Fin. Sec'y*; Rudolph Hurter, *Treas*. Organized May 24, 1896. Meets at Weller's Hall every second and fourth Wednesday.

## THEOLOGICAL INSTITUTE OF CONNECTICUT.

*Now Hartford Theological Seminary.*
*For full particulars see pages 708, 709.*

## THOMAS HOOKER ASSOCIATION.

John Hooker, *Pres't*; Mrs. Isabella Beecher Hooker, Edward B. Hooker, Miss Mary K. Talcott, Frank F. Starr, Joseph G. Woodward, Charles E. Mitchel, Henry G. Newton, Mrs. Seth Talcott, Mrs. Emily C. Curtis. Mrs. Samuel Hotchkiss, Edward Hooker, James B. Olcott, Clara L. Bowman, Charles S. Smith, William A. Hooker, Mrs. John C. Day, Mrs. Cordelia N. Barnes. Mrs. Martha W. Hooker, *Vice Pres'ts*; Mrs. Cornelia Hooker Chapin, 8 Wadsworth street, *Sec'y and Treas*. The foregoing officers *Prudential Committee*. Organized May 13, 1889. Meets in May or June, yearly.

## TRINITY COLLEGE SOCIETIES.

MISSIONARY SOCIETY.

*Founded*, 1832.

J. M. Nicholls, *President*; E. G. Littell, *Sec'y*; R. N. Willcox, *Treas.*; Rev. Profs. Pynchon and Hart, *Chaplains*. Meets Monday evenings in the Latin room.

CONNECTICUT BETA OF PHI BETA KAPPA.

*Founded*, 1845.

Professor Pynchon, *Pres't*; Professor Hart, *Sec'y*. Six undergraduate members in class of 1898.

LOCAL FRATERNITY OF I. K. A.
*Founded, 1829.*
Hon. John T. Wait, LL. D., *President of Corporation.* Meets at Hall on Vernon st. Ten resident members.

FRATERNITY OF DELTA PSI, EPSILON CHAPTER.
*Founded, 1850.*
Chapter House, corner of Summit street and Allen place. Thirteen resident members.

FRATERNITY OF ALPHA DELTA PHI, PHI KAPPA CHAPTER.
Founded as Phi Kappa Society, 1835; Chapter chartered, 1878. Chapter House, 122 Vernon st. Seventeen resident members.

FRATERNITY OF DELTA KAPPA EPSILON, ALPHA CHI CHAPTER.
*Chapter chartered,* 1879.
Sixteen resident members.

FRATERNITY OF PSI UPSILON, BETA BETA CHAPTER.
Founded as Beta Beta Society, 1842; Chapter chartered, 1880. Chapter House, corner of Washington and and Park streets. Nineteen resident members.

FRATERNITY OF SIGMA ALPHA EPSILON, CONNECTICUT ALPHA CHAPTER.
*Chapter chartered,* 1892.
Five resident members.

FRATERNITY OF PHI GAMMA DELTA, TAU ALPHA CHAPTER.
*Chapter chartered,* 1893.
Two resident members.

FRATERNITY OF ALPHA CHI RHO.
*Organized,* 1895.
Twenty-five resident members.

TRUMBULL COUNCIL, No. 21,
NATIONAL PROVIDENT UNION.
Sylvester Marvel, *Pres't;* George R. Bodge, *Vice Pres't;* Edwin Brower, *Sec'y and Treas.;* C. N. Fowler, F. H. Parker, W. H. Pond, *Trustees.* Meets at 881 Main street, 1st and 3d Wednesday evenings monthly. Instituted May 7, 1885. Annual meeting 1st Wednesday in Dec.

TRUSTEES OF DONATIONS AND BEQUESTS FOR CHURCH PURPOSES.
Rt. Rev. John Williams, Middletown, *Pres't;* Elijah C. Johnson, Hartford, *Sec'y and Treas.* Chartered in 1863.

TRUSTEES OF NATIONAL COUNCIL OF CONGREGATIONAL CHURCHES.
W. H. Moore, S. B. Forbes and others, *Corporators.* Chartered in April, 1885. Capital $80,000. Annual meeting in September.

TRUSTEES OF THE FUND FOR MINISTERS.
Same officers as "Directors of the Missionary Society of Connecticut." Incorporated 1868.

TRUSTEES OF THE GOOD WILL CLUB.
A. E. Burr, *Pres't;* Francis Goodwin, *Vice Pres't;* Charles H. Clark, *Treas.;* Harry S. Conklin, *Sec'y;* Mary Hall, *Manager;* A. E. Burr, Francis Goodwin, Chas. H. Clark, Atwood Collins, W. W. Hyde, S. G. Dunham, D. R. Howe, Edward Curtis, Samuel Hart, Alex. R. Merriam, Harry S. Conklin, Francis Parsons, *Trustees.* Incorporated Jan. 28, 1888. Building dedicated Feb. 22, 1889. Special Charter April, 1889. Keeney hall, 40 Pratt st.; Good Will hall, side entrance. Annual meeting 2d Monday in May.

TRUSTEES OF THE WIDOWS HOME.
Rev. J. W. Bradin, *Pres't;* R. A. Wadsworth, *Sec'y and Agent;* Security Co., *Treas.;* E. P. Taylor, *Auditor.* Incorporated 1860. Authorized capital, $25,000. Annual meeting, Easter Tuesday. Homes at 133 Market st. and 13 South Hudson st. This corporation consists of the Rectors and Wardens of Christ, St. John's and Trinity Churches in Hartford.

TUESDAY NIGHT BOWLING CLUB.
R. W. Dwyer, *Pres't;* E. S. Crowell, *Sec'y;* S. S. Chamberlin, *Captain.* Meets at 66 Temple st.

TWENTIETH CENTURY CLUB.
Wilbur F. Gordy, *Pres't;* George Pope, *Vice Pres't;* Robert H. Schutz, *Sec'y;* Edward D. Redfield, *Treas.* Henry Ferguson, Charles C. Stearns, Henry S. Robinson, S. O. Prentice, E. DeF. Miel, W. H. St. John, *Executive Committee.* Organized March 31, 1892. Annual meeting in April.

UNION FOR HOME WORK.
Mrs. Samuel Colt, *Pres't;* Mrs. N. Shipman, Mrs. G. W. Russell, *Vice Pres'ts;* Mrs. M. G. Bulkeley, *Treas.;* Mrs. J. R. Buck, *Sec'y;* Mrs. L. R. Cheney, *C Sec'y;* Mrs. Samuel Colt, Mrs. Nathaniel Shipman, Mrs. John R. Buck, Mrs. G. W. Russell, Mrs. W. H. Palmer, Mrs. J. B. Bunce, Mrs. M. G. Bulkeley, Mrs. J. S. Jarvis, Mrs. O. H. Whitmore, Mrs. H. C. Robinson, Mrs. G. C. Perkins, Mrs. F. W. Russell, Mrs. L. R. Cheney, Miss Margaret Blythe, *Executive Committee;* Mrs. Frank L. Howard, Mrs. Chas. E. Gross, Mrs. Wm. H. Bulkeley, Mrs. John Hall, Miss Lydia Brooks, Mrs. James McManus, Miss C. A. Jillson, Mrs. Geo. H. Day, Mrs. J. S. Camp, Mrs. P. H. Ingalls, *Finance Committee.* Mrs. E. L. Sluyter, *Superintendent,* 239 Market st., office hours 8 A.M. to 12 M.; Mrs. N. Shipman, Miss Margaret Blythe, *Day Nursery.* Chartered July, 1872. Annual meeting, first Tuesday in January.

UNITED ASSOCIATION JOURNEYMEN PLUMBERS.—LOCAL UNION, 76.
Daniel J. Farrell, *Pres't;* James Murphy, *V. Pres't;* John White, *Treas.;* P. J. McLoughlin, *Rec. Sec'y;* A. J. McNab, *Fin. Sec'y;* Thomas Keefe, John J. Dunn, James Mahoney, *Trustees.* Organized Sept. 22, 1892. Meets 2d and 4th Wednesday at 92 Asylum st.

UNITED WORKERS CLUB.
Miss Hattie G. Pratt, *Pres't;* Alfreda Dickinson, Mrs. John J. Coughlin, Frances McCook, *Vice Pres'ts;* Mabel C. Washburn, *Sec'y;* Grace Turnbull, *Treas.;* M. Sullivan, *Ass't Treas.;* Lillie O. Mullane, *Lib.;* Herbert H. White, *Aud.;* Marie E. Johnson, *Chairman Educational Committee;* Kittie Connor, *Chairman Membership Committee;* Caroline Hansell, *Chairman Social Committee;* Emily M. Morgan, *Chairman Vacation Committee.* Organized March 13, 1888. Incorporated April, 1888, as United Workers and Woman's Exchange. Incorporated under present name, April, 1893. 700 Main street.

UNIVERSALIST SABBATH SCHOOL TEACHERS' ASSOCIATION.
C. G. Lincoln, *President;* Miss Kate F. Ellis, *Vice Pres't;* Miss Emma Fowler, *Sec'y;* Frank G. Mellen, *Ass't Sec'y;* Arthur L. Brown, *Treas.* Organized April, 1864. Annual meeting 2d Friday in Dec. Meets on call.

U. S. CIVIL SERVICE EXAMINING BOARD.
Fred C. Jackson, *Chairman;* Julian H. Gates, *Secretary;* Frederick W. Kreimendahl, Daniel S. McGrath. Examinations 1st Tuesday in February, 65 State street.

VETERAN VOLUNTEER FIREMEN'S ASS'N.
Edwin O. Goodwin, *President;* Alfred Milton, *Vice Pres't;* Edward H. Fox, *Sec'y;* Charles A. Barrows, *Treas.;* Charles Milton, *Collector;* H. S. Brown, H. A. King, S. L. Barker, *Auditors;* Alexander Harbison, E. H. Judd, E. O. Goodwin, J. C. McManus, Chas. A. Barrows, *Trustees.* Organized, Nov. 25, 1889. Meets 1st Monday evening, monthly, at 27 Arch street. Annual meeting first Monday in January.

## WADSWORTH ATHENEUM,

624 Main st., is a granite building of 100 ft. in length and 80 ft. in depth in center wings, and 70 ft. in depth in outside wings. It is of the castelated structure, with central towers 70 feet in height and corner buttresses 56 ft. in height, with an extensive brick addition on the east of Tudor architecture, which is used, on the first floor, for the Library of the HARTFORD LIBRARY ASSOCIATION; and, on the second floor, for the WATKINSON LIBRARY with the library of the HISTORICAL SOCIETY adjoining. The first floor of the main building on the North is used for the PUBLIC READING room and TRUSTEES room. The whole South division of the main building is occupied by the CONNECTICUT HISTORICAL SOCIETY. The Central and Northern portions of the main building on the 2d floor are occupied as a PUBLIC ART GALLERY and for the ART SCHOOL. The building was erected by voluntary contributions of citizens, with the land and fence, cost over $200.000. Commenced April, 1842, and completed in July, 1844, and the additions in January, 1893. Francis Goodwin, Pres't; Nathaniel Shipman, James G. Batterson, Vice Pres'ts; James B. Cone, Sec'y; J. F. Morris, Treas.; Charles E. Gross, Auditor; Charles J. Hoadly, Jonathan F. Morris, Henry C. Robinson, John C. Day, James B. Cone, Charles Hopkins Clark, Charles E. Gross, Theodore Lyman, Jacob L. Greene, James J. Goodwin, and ex officio, the Mayor of the City of Hartford, Trustees; Frank B. Gay, Sup't of Building; Francis Goodwin, Charles E. Gross, Theodore Lyman, James B. Cone, House Committee; Francis Goodwin, J. F. Morris, Jacob L. Greene, Finance Committee. Annual meeting in June.

## WALNUT LODGE HOSPITAL COMPANY.

T. D. Crothers, Pres't; B. B. Alling, Treas; S. B. Crothers, Sec'y. Chartered April 21, 1886. A private asylum for the special medical care and treatment of INEBRIATES and OPIUM CASES. Special facilities provided for each one. Address, T. D. Crothers, M. D. Superintendent, Fairfield av., Hartford, Conn.

See page 712.

## WASHINGTON FIRE ENGINE CO. No. 1.

Charles A. Barrows, Foreman; James McCabe, Edward J. Lamb, Assistants; George Jones, Sec'y; James Mulhall, Treasurer; Edward Downs, Steward. Organized June 26, 1891.

## WATKINSON JUVENILE ASYLUM AND FARM SCHOOL.

Francis Goodwin, Pres't; D. H. Wells, Sec'y; Daniel R. Howe, Treas.; Henry Barnard, F. W. Cheney, N. Shipman, G. Pierrepont Davis, A. C. Dunham, Francis Goodwin, D.R. Howe, Jacob L. Greene, Chas. M. Beach, Philander C. Royce, Charles Hopkins Clark, Daniel H. Wells, Geo. E. Taintor, Lucius F. Robinson. C. B. Brewster, Trustees; Edwin B. Smead, Principal; Selden W. Hayes, Assistant; Honora C. Whiting, School Teacher; Miss Florence Girdwood, Matron. Chartered May, 1862. School opened June 1, 1881. Annual meeting 2d Tuesday in February. Lands and Funds, about $245,000. New buildings on "Handicroft Farm," Albany and Bloomfield avenues.

## WATKINSON LIBRARY.

Nathaniel Shipman, Pres't; Roland Swift, Treas.; James B. Cone, Sec'y; Henry Barnard, Rowland Swift, Nathaniel Shipman, Francis Goodwin, Austin C. Dunham, Chas. Hopkins Clark, Theo. Lyman, J. B. Cone, J. L. Greene, Lucius F. Robinson, James J. Goodwin, Charles Dudley Warner, Governor of Connecticut, President of the Connecticut Historical Society, President of the Wadsworth Atheneum, President of the Hartford Library Association, President of Trinity College, and Mayor of the City, Trustees; Frank B. Gay, Librarian. Chartered 1858. Rooms, 624 Main street, open from 9.30 A. M. to 5.30 P. M. and free to every one. Library 46,526 vols. Annual election 2d Tuesday, Dec.

## WAWAUME COUNCIL, No. 1, DAUGHTERS OF POCAHONTAS.

Mrs. Lilla L. Lloyd, Pocahontas; Mrs. Emma Nicholson, Prophetess; Mrs. Hattie Deming, Wenonah; Wm. F. Booth, Powhatan; Mrs. Floribelle A. Kummell, 139 Retreat ave., K. of R.; Mrs. Josephine Barchfeld, K. of W. Instituted June 29, 1888. Meets at Grand Army Hall, 926 Main st., on 1st and 3d Monday evenings, monthly. Semi-annual meetings January and July.

## WIDOWS' SOCIETY.

Mrs. Robert E. Day, Pres't; Mrs. Charles R. Burt, Treas.; Mrs. Charles A. Jewell, Sec'y; Miss Mary Bigelow, Mrs. Robert E. Day, Mrs. Harmon G. Howe, Mrs. Albert L. Hunt, Almoners. Organized 1825. Incorporated 1847. Annual meeting in September. Miss Sarah E. Davis, Mrs. Arthur F. Eggleston, Mrs. C. A. Jewell, Mrs. Thos. Sisson, Niles Fund Almoners.

## WOMEN'S ADVISORY COMMITTEE OF HARTFORD THEOLOGICAL SEMINARY.

Miss M. F. Collins, Pres't; Mrs. M. D. Thompson, Treas.; Miss Clara E. Hillyer, Ass't Treas.; Mrs. F. B. Cooley, Secretary; Miss F. L. Bushnell, Mrs. L. M. Barbour, Mrs. R. E. Day, Mrs. F. D. Glazier, Mrs. C. M. Lamson, Mrs. G. W. Smith, Mrs. George G. Williams.

## WOMAN'S AID SOCIETY.

Mrs. E. B. Turner, Pres't; Mrs. F. Goodwin, Mrs. A. R. Hillyer, Mrs. H. F. Taintor, Vice Pres'ts; Mrs. T. W. Russell, Treas.; Mrs. J. R. Buck, Ass't Treas.; Mrs. Stephen Terry, Rec. Sec'y; Mrs. J. G. Calhoun, Cor. Sec'y. Organized Feb. 1878. Chartered 1881. Home, 1 Pavilion st. Annual meeting in Jan.

## WOMAN'S AUXILIARY YOUNG MEN'S CHRISTIAN ASSOCIATION.

Mrs. E. H. Smiley, Sec'y; Mrs. O. B. Colton, Treas.; Chairman, Mrs. W. P. Williams; Social, Mrs. J. H. Cone; House, Mrs. Charles A. Jewell; Devotional, Mrs. S. M. Stiles; Supplies for Sick, Mrs. H. E. Hollister; Membership, Mrs. Elihu Geer; Finance, Mrs. S. L. Barbour; Press and Printing, Mrs. G. P. Merritt; Junior Work, Mrs. Lee Jackson; Vice Chairman, Mrs. T. E. Steele. Annual meeting third Thursday in May.

## WOMAN'S BOARD OF MISSIONS.

Mrs. Charles A. Jewell, President; Mrs. J. W. Backus, Mrs. E. W. Hooker, Mrs. J. M. Talcott, Mrs. C. D. Talcott, Mrs. C. D. Davison, Miss Mary D. Eastman, Mrs. Chas. M. Lamson, Mrs. H. A. Castle, Mrs. George Kellogg, Miss Clara E. Hillyer, Mrs. H. R. Haisington, Miss Clara Lee Bowman, Vice Pres'ts; Mrs. M. Bradford Scott, Treas.; Mrs. W. P. Williams, Rec. Sec'y; Mrs. Charles R. Burt, Home Sec'y; Mrs. Louise S. Baker, Ass't Sec'y; Miss Clara E. Wells, Sec'y Junior Work; Miss Lizzie J. Holcomb, Ass't Sec'y Junior Work; Charles T. Welles, Auditor. Hartford Branch organized October, 1874. Meetings fourth Tuesdays of each month at chapel of Center Church, at 3 P. M. Executive meetings second Tuesday of each month at 10.30 A. M. at Memorial hall. Annual meeting 3d Wednesday in October. Auxiliary societies exist in the several Congregational Churches in Hartford and Tolland Counties.

## WOMEN'S CHRISTIAN ASSOC'N OF HARTFORD.

Mrs. Geo. Kellogg, Pres't; Mrs. F. B. Cooley, Mrs. Thos. Sisson, Mrs. P. Jewell, Vice Pres'ts; Mrs. E. P. Curtis, Cor. Sec'y; Mrs. Robert E. Day, Rec. Sec'y; Miss C. A. Jewell, Treas.; John Allen, Auditor; Mrs. George Kellogg, Mrs. Francis B. Cooley, Mrs. Thomas Sisson, Mrs. R. E. Hooker, Mrs. John Allen, Mrs. Pliny Jewell, Mrs. Stephen Terry, Mrs. Chas. H. Boardman, Mrs. Seth Talcott, Mrs. S. C. Preston, Mrs. L. A. Barbour, Mrs. G. M. Stone, Mrs. W. N. Pelton, Mrs. P. C. Royce, Mrs. M. M. Johnson, Mrs. John H. White, Mrs.

D. H. Wells, Mrs. William J. Tuller, Mrs. R. E. Day, Mrs. Edward A. Smith, Mrs. John S. Camp, Miss Charlotte A. Jewell, Mrs. E. W. Hooker, Mrs. Arthur L. Gillett, Mrs. Charles R. Hansel, Mrs. Everett P. Curtis, Mrs. Williston Walker, Miss Elizabeth C. Blythe, Mrs. M. W. Jacobus, Miss Charlotte Huntington, Mrs. J. J. Nairn, Mrs. Francis R. Cooley, *Directresses.* Organized June 6, 1867. Incorporated 1869. Annual meeting in Oct. *Young Women's Boarding Home,* 58 Church st., Mrs. Harriet A. Platt, *Matron. Industrial Department,* 54 Church st., Miss E. C. Maxwell, *Sup't.*

## WOMAN'S CHRISTIAN TEMPERANCE UNION.

Mrs. C. B. Forbes, *Pres't;* Mrs. J. H. Spencer, Mrs. C. R. Parsons, *V. Pres'ts;* Mrs. A. S. Cressy, *Treas.;* Mrs. A. D. Cross, *Rec. Sec'y;* Mrs. William H. Parker, 151 Capitol av., *Cor. Sec'y.*

*Superintendents*—Mrs. H. S. Whiting, *Flower Mission;* Mrs. J. H. Spencer, *Press Work;* Mrs. J. B. Rogers, *Union Signal;* Miss Elizabeth Taylor, *Literature;* Mrs. B. M. Parsons, *Franchise;* Miss Lucy A. Brainard, *Scientific;* Mrs. C. R. Parsons, *Evangelistic;* Mrs. L. M. Parker, *Colored Work;* Mrs. A. D. Cross, *Narcotics;* Mrs. A. S. Cressy, *Juvenile.* Organized December, 1881. Meets 1st and 3d Tuesdays at 3 P. M., in room 5, 302 Asylum st. Annual election in October.

## WOMANS CONGREGATIONAL HOME MISSIONARY UNION OF CONNECTICUT.

Miss Ellen R. Camp, 9 Camp street, New Britain, *Pres't;* Mrs. F. B. Cooley, Mrs. Geo. L. Walker, Mrs. Henry Gay, Mrs. S. M. Hotchkiss, Mrs. E. Hubbard, *Vice Pres'ts;* Mrs. Ward W. Jacobs, Hartford, *Treas.;* Mrs. C. T. Millard, Hartford, *Gen. Sec'y;* Mrs. George Follett, *Fin. Sec'y;* Mrs. A. H. Pitkin, Hartford, *Rec. Sec'y;* Mrs. O. Vincent Coffin, Mrs. Francis Williams, Mrs. E. Ackley, Mrs. Luman Cowles, Miss Alice H. Goodwin, Mrs. Nathan Merwin, Mrs. J. A. Kippen, Miss Mathewson, Mrs. D. F. Gulliver, Mrs. John Hopson, Mrs. E. E. Hubbell, Mrs. H. P. Hitchcock, Mrs. C. W. Shelton, Mrs. Washington Choate, Miss E. Danielson, Mrs. E. P. Parker, Mrs. Philo Bevin, Mrs. W. R. Carr, Mrs. E. C. Smith, Mrs. W. R. Burnham, *Executive Committee;* Mrs. George W. Moore, Mrs. Francis B. Cooley, Mrs. Henry Gay, *Finance Committee;* Cornwall T. Millard, *Auditor.* Organized Jan. 14, 1885. Incorporated 1886. Meets 2d Monday of each month at Memorial hall. Annual election in May.

## WOMAN'S EXCHANGE.

Mrs. F. H. Adriance, *Pres't;* Mrs. T. B. Beach, Mrs. L. R. Cheney, Mrs. M. G. Bulkeley, *Vice Pres'ts;* Emma Foster, *Rec. Sec'y;* Mrs. T. B. Chapman, *Cor. Sec'y;* Miss P. H. Ingalls, *Treas.;* Mrs. Leverett Brainard, Mrs. Morgan G. Bulkeley, Mrs. Edwin Strong, Mrs. M. Bradford Scott, Mrs. A. R. Hillyer, Mrs. A. G. Loomis, Mrs. F. A. Hart, Miss Hattie G. Pratt, Mrs. P. H. Ingalls, Mrs. Louis R. Cheney, Mrs. John J. Nairn, Miss Helen Whiting, Mrs. F. H. Adriance, Mrs. H. S. Redfield, Mrs. R. N. Seyms, Mrs. T. Belknap Beach, Miss Josephine E. Barnard, Mrs. J. H. Greene, Miss Mary S. Robinson, Miss Laura W. Taft, Mrs. T. B. Chapman, Mrs. F. C. Billings, Mrs. G. C. F. Williams, Miss Sarabelle Goodwin, Miss Mary Johnson, Miss Emma Foster, *Board of Managers.* Organized April, 1893. 73 Pearl st.

## WORKMEN'S SICK AND DEATH BENEFIT FUND OF THE U. S.

BRANCH NO. 52.

F. Fellermann, *Chairman;* O. Gernreich, *V. Chairman;* Wm. Wentze, *Treas.;* Theo. Hinz, *Rec. Sec'y;* R. L. Sander, 186 Putnam st., *Fin. and Cor. Sec'y.* Organized Oct. 24, 1891. Meets last Tuesday evening, monthly, at 50 Market street. Annual meeting in January.

## YALE ALUMNI ASSOCIATION OF HARTFORD.

Harrison B. Freeman, *Pres't;* Wm. Waldo Hyde, *Vice Pres't;* Chas. P. Cooley, *Sec'y and Treas.;* L. F. Robinson, Andrew F. Gates, W. H. St. John, J. B. Hall, E. H. Cady, E. B. Ellsworth, Ward Cheney, *Executive Committee.* Orgnized April 8, 1885. Annual meeting in December.

## YOUNG GERMAN AMERICAN ASSOCIATION

George Speath, *Pres't;* L. Cley, *V. Pres't;* F. Fisher, *R. Sec'y;* O. Lotze, *F. Sec'y;* William Noll, *Treas.;* C. F. Koenig, *C Sec'y;* Wm. Noll, H. Bordenstein, F. F. Heussler, *Trustees.* Officers chosen quarterly. Org. Feb. 25, 1878. Meets Sundays, 4 P. M., 793 Main st.

## YOUNG MEN'S CHRISTIAN ASSOCIATION.

Charles A. Jewell, *Pres't;* Rodney Dennis, H. H. Goodwin, Herbert K. Smith, L. F. Robinson, *Vice Pres'ts;* Charles T. Wells, *Treas.;* G. M. Hersey, *Gen. Sec'y;* Charles A. Pease, *Rec. Sec'y;* A. L. Hunt, *Auditor;* J. Allen Wiley, C. D. Alton, John Gemmill, Gail B. Munsill, Atwood Collins, John S. Camp, S. P. Davis, J. H. Jarman, Wm. H. Talcott, Wilbur M. Stone, Herbert Knox Smith, Henry E. Rees, *Directors.* Organized Feb. 7, 1878. Chartered April, 1884. Annual meeting in May. Rooms open week days from 9 A. M. till 10 P. M.; on Sundays from 1 till 6 P. M. Song service for men, on Sundays, 3.30 P. M. The average age of members is 22½ years. Total membership Jan. 1, 1898, 1,369. There are 112 different occupations represented in the enrollment. Young men of all creeds, no creeds may join. The control of property interests and the voting privilege are limited to the members of Protestant Evangelical Churches. Educational classes are maintained evenings during the fall and winter months. There was an enrollment of over 437 students season of 1897-8. The Educational Department known as the Hillyer Institute has an endowment of $50,000. A Workingman's Exchange is maintained as one of the many departments of the Association. Recreation rooms furnished with pool tables, and other games are provided. The workingmen of the city assemble in large numbers at these rooms where social privileges are enjoyed free from the demoralizing influences of the saloon. All workingmen 18 years or over may join this department as well as that of the main association. The new building, cor. Jewell, Ford and Pearl streets, was opened November 8, 1893. It is a superior building in all respects. *See pages 704, 705.*

## Masonic.

There are 16,813 members in Connecticut; 802,282 in the United States.

## GRAND COMMANDERY OF CONNECTICUT.

KNIGHTS TEMPLAR.

Wm. E. Withey, New London, G. C.; Wm. E. Risley, Waterbury, D. G. C.; E. S. Davis, Middletown, G. G.; A. S. Comstock, Norwich, G. C. G.; Frank Street, Norwalk, G. S. W.; Alfred E. Fuller, Danbury, G. J. W.; Wm. R. Higby, Bridgeport, G. T.; Eli C. Birdsey, Meriden, G. Rec.; Edward E. Fuller, Willimantic, G. P.; J. W. Knowlton, Bridgeport, G. S. B.; Frank E. Stoddard, New Haven, G. W.; N. F. Allen, Hartford, G. S.

## GRAND CHAPTER OF CONNECTICUT.

ROYAL ARCH MASONS.

I. T. Stidham, New Britain, G. H. P.; Welsey N. Pearne, Middletown, G.K.; John L. Hill, Norwich, G.S.; Isaiah Baker, Jr., Hartford, G. T.; James McCormick, Hartford, G.S.; James Callan, Waterbury, G.C.of H.; E. J. Beardsley, Derby, G. R. A. C.; Edgar T. Main, Hartford, G. T. Election in May.

### GRAND COUNCIL OF CONNECTICUT.
#### ROYAL AND SELECT MASTERS.
R. H. Tucker, Ansonia, M. P. G. M.; Edgar W. Latham, Suffield, D. P. G. M.; Stephen J. Lyon, Collinsville, T. I. G. M.; Henry O. Canfield, Bridgeport, G. P. C. of W.; Isaiah Baker, Jr., Hartford, G. T.; James McCormack, Hartford, G. R.; Albert S. Comstock, Norwich, G. C. of G.; J. S. Stokes, Meriden, G. C.; Edgar T. Maine, Hartford, G. S. Election in May.

### GRAND LODGE OF CONNECTICUT.
Frank W. Havens, Hartford, G. M.; Geo. C. McNall, Greenwich, D. G. M.; John O. Rowland, Fair Haven, G. S. W.; Fred. S. Stevens, G. J. W.; Miles W. Graves, Hartford, G. Tr.; John H. Barlow, Hartford, G. Sec'y; Nelson G. Hinckley, Edmund Tweedy, W. R. Higby, *Trustees.* Organized June 6, 1788.

### WASHINGTON COMMANDERY, No. 1,
#### KNIGHTS TEMPLAR.
Philo W. Newton, E. C.; George N. Delap Gen.; John B. Clapp, C. Gen.; Frederick W. Payne, Prelate; M. W. Graves, Treas.; Richard P. Martin, Rec.; James W. Matthews, S. W.; W. G. Simmons, J. W.; Curtis P. Gladding, Warden; E. T. Maine, Tyler; Charles E. Billings, John G. Root, Charles S. Davidson, Trustees. H. B. Philbrick, Trustee Masonic Hall Association. Organized July, 1796. Stated conclaves 1st and 3d Tuesday evenings in each month, except July and August, at Masonic Temple. Annual conclave 1st Tuesday evening in January.

### PYTHAGORAS CHAPTER, No. 17. R. A. M.
Geo. N. Delap, H. P.; Geo. O. Brott, E. K.; Geo. A. Loomis, E. S.; Miles W. Graves, Treas.; Wm. J. Morrow, Sec'y; Wm. W. Frayer, C. of H.; Herbert F. Seymour, P. S.; Geo. P. Merritt, R. A. C.; John G. Root, S. B. Bosworth, Frank J. Knox, Trustees; James M. Dow, Trustee Masonic Hall Association. Instituted Oct. 2, 1817. Stated meetings, every Friday evening at Masonic Temple. Annual convocation 1st Friday in January.

### WOLCOTT COUNCIL, No. 1, R. & S. M.
Chas. A. Jones, T. I. M.; Albert A. Fox, R. I. D. M.; Alfred C. J. Williams, I. P. C. of W; Miles W. Graves, Treasurer; William J. Morrow, Rec.; Thomas W. Morgan, C. of G.; William H. Babcock, Cond.; E. T. Main, Sentinel; Miles W. Graves, Trustee Masonic Hall Association. Instituted Feb. 17, 1818. Stated assemblies 1st Thursday evening in each month, at Masonic Temple. Annual in January.

### ST. JOHN'S LODGE, No. 4, A. F. & A. M.
Theodore H. Goodrich, W. M.; A. C. J. Williams, S. W.; A. F. Booth, J. W.; Lester H. Goodwin, Treas.; B. F. Wile, Sec'y; Chas. H. Riggs, S. D.; Edward Eberle, J. D.; Henry S. Strong, S. S.; George R. Miller, J. S.; C. G. Bristol, Chaplain; Frank J. Knox, Marshal; S. T. Bissell, Organist; Edward T. Main, Tyler; Nelson G. Hinckley, H. B. Philbrick, Edward Mahl, Trustees; Edward Mahl, Trustee Masonic Hall Association. Stated communications Wednesday evenings at Masonic Temple. Annual communications last Wednesday in December.

### SPHINX TEMPLE, A. A. O. N. M. S.
Rial S. Peck, Ill. Potentate; Jas. H. Jarman, C. R.; W. G. Simmons, A. R.; Albert A. Fox, H. P. & P.; John McClary, O. G.; Alfred Spencer, J. W.; Charles E. Shelton, Recorder; S. B. Bosworth, 1st C. M.; Dr. Joseph E. Root, 2d C. M.; Frank D. May, Director; J. N. Shedd, Marshal; Fred Stokes, Capt. of G.; George H. Foster, O. Guard. Instituted April 27, 1896. Meets 2d Thursday evenings at Masonic Temple.

### HARTFORD LODGE, No. 88, A. F. & A. M.
Edward S. Tryon, W. M.; L. Howard Tracy, S. W.; A. W. Comstock, J. W.; Miles W. Graves, Treas.; Benjamin W. Edwards, Sec'y; Henry A. Fox, S. D.; Irving W. Havens, J. D.; H. Lillenthal, Chaplain; W. C. Steele, Marshal; S. T. Bissell, Organist; Addison P. Carter, S. S.; Harry F. Kohn, J. S.; Edward T. Main, Tyler; D. Wallace Tracy, Jas. M. Dow, Robert Moore, Trustees. George W. Scailes, Trustee Masonic Hall Association. Stated meetings every Monday evening, from first Monday in September to last Monday in June, at Masonic Temple. Annual election 2d Monday, Dec.

### LAFAYETTE LODGE, No. 100, A. F. & A. M.
John M. Parker, Jr., W. M.; Geo. A. Loomis, S. W.; Augustus Loomis, J. W.; Frederick J. Bacon, S. D.; Geo. A. Chandler, J. D.; Henry E. Fitts, S. S.; James W. Ward, J. S.; George P. Chandler Marshal; Joseph Buths, Treasurer; Isaiah Baker, Jr., Secretary; Irving Emerson, Organist; Edward T. Main, Tyler; Stephen Ball, Isaiah Baker, Jr., Thomas Boyd, Trustees; Jos. E. Marvel, Masonic Board of Relief; Wm. G. Simmons, Trustee Masonic Hall Association. Stated meetings 2d and 4th Tuesday evenings, except in July and August, at Masonic Temple. Annual election 2d Tuesday, Dec.

### CHARTER OAK LODGE OF PERFEC'ON A. A. S. R.
Norman F. Allen, T. P. G. M.; Silas Chapman, Jr., H. of T. D. G. M.; Jas. H. Jarman, V. S. G. W.; Samuel M. Bronson, G. O.; Lester L. Ensworth, G. Treas; Isaiah Baker, Jr., G. S. Sec'y; Jas. W. Boardman, G. M. of C.; David J. Jordan, G. C. of G.; Stanley R. Bosworth, G. H.; Edward T. Main, G. Tyler. Rial S. Peck, Trustee Masonic Hall Association. Stated communication 2d Tuesday, monthly, at Masonic Temple. Instituted July 27, 1864.

### HARTFORD COUNCIL PRINCES OF JERUSALEM.
Charles E. Billings, M. E. S. P. G. M.; W. Waldo Goodell, G. H. P. D. G. M.; Silas Chapman, Jr., M. E. S. G. W.; Frank W. Havens, M. E. J. G. W.; Edward Mahl, M. E. G. O.; L. L. Ensworth, V. G. Treas; Isaiah Baker, Jr., V. G. Sec'y; James W. Boardman, V. G. M. of C.; Stanley Bosworth, V. G. A.; James H. Jarman, V. G. M. of E.; Edward T. Main, V. G. T. Charles E. Billings, Trustee Masonic Hall Association. Stated assembly, 3d Thursday, monthly, at Masonic Temple.

### CYRUS GOODELL CHAPTER OF ROSE CROIX.
Frank W. Havens, M. W. and P. M.; Stanley R. Bosworth, M. E. and P. K. S. W.; Rial S. Peck, M. E. P. K. J. W.; Normand F. Allen, M. E. and P. K. G. O.; L. L. Ensworth, R. and P. K. Treas.; Isaiah Baker, Jr., R. and P. K. Sec'y; Silas Chapman, Jr., R. and P. K. H.; James W. Boardman, R. and P. K. M. of C.; H. B. Philbrick, R. and P. K. C. G.; Edward T. Main, R. and P. K. T. Isaiah Baker, Jr., Trustee Masonic Hall Association. Stated meeting 4th Thursday evening of each month and St. John's day, at Masonic Temple. Annual meeting in Dec.

### MASONIC HALL ASSOCIATION.
C. E. Billings, Pres't; Halsey B. Philbrick, V. Pres't; Isaiah Baker, Jr., Sec'y; M. W. Graves, Treas.; C. E. Billings, Halsey B. Philbrick, Isaiah Baker, Jr., Executive Committee. Isaiah Baker, Jr., Geo. W. Scailes, Wm. G. Simmons, Miles W. Graves, H. B. Philbrick, C. E. Billings, Rial S. Peck, J. M. Dow, Edward Mahl, Directors. Chartered April, 1886. Annual meeting 3d Monday in January at Masonic Temple.

### MASONIC BOARD OF RELIEF.
J. Seymour Chase, Pres't; Joseph E. Marvel, Vice Pres't; Geo. W. Tuller, Treas. and Sec'y. The first three officers of each Lodge in this city are also as *officio* members. Organized 1883. Meets quarterly at Masonic Hall. Annual election in December.

## HARTFORD MASONIC CLUB.

Frank W. Havens, Pres't; H. B. Philbrick, Charles E. Billings, V. Pres'ts: Isaiah Baker, Jr., Treas.; the above officers and John H. Barlow, Normand F. Allen, John A. Crilly, Luke Horsfall, George P. Chandler, Irving Emerson, Stanley B. Bosworth, Directors: Geo. P. Merritt, Sec'y *pro tem.* and Collector. Organized March 5, 1896. Annual meeting in March. Club Rooms in Masonic Temple.

## MASONIC MUTUAL BENEFIT ASSOCIATION OF CONNECTICUT.

S. M. Bronson, Pres't; C. E. Billings Vice Pres't ; Silas Chapman, Jr., Treasurer; Frank W. Havens, Secretary; Joseph Schwab, Henry Ensign, Ernest Cady, Trustees; W. W. Goodell, J. E. Marvel, Robert Moore, Auditors, and a Board of 26 Directors, including the above officers. Regular meetings of Directors are held on 4th Thursday evenings of March, June, September, and December. Annual meeting 4th Thursday in-March.

## EXCELSIOR LODGE No. 3, F. & A. M.

C. H. Babcock, W. M.; J. S. Taylor, S. W.; J. C. Lee, J. W.; R. E. Snyder, 56 Grand street, Sec'y; T. H. Rose, Treas; G. B. Wilson, Tyler. Meets 2d and 4th Monday evenings at 302 Asylum st. Annual meeting in June.

## IVANHOE CHAPTER, No. 10, EASTERN STAR.

Mrs. Abbie S. Foster, W. M.; Wm. E Foster, W. P.; Mrs. Kate L. Merriman, A. M.; Mrs. Mary J. Silloway, Sec'y; Mrs. M. E. Dow, Treas.; Mrs. Mary F. Richards, C.; Mrs. Ida J. Fahrenbach, A. C.; Mrs. Rachel Case, W.; Mrs. Ida H. Fiske, C.; R. G. Merriman, Sentinel; Mrs. Jennie E. Perry, A.; Mrs. Hannah H. Francis, R.; Mrs. Mary A. White, E.; Mrs. Mary E. Lyon, M.; Mrs. M. Jennie Eastman, E.; Mrs. Ella Readette, Pianist. James M. Dow, Lucius Chapman, Trustees. Meets 2d and 4th Tuesday evenings, monthly, in Masonic Temple. Annual communication first meeting in Dec.

# Odd Fellows.

There are 15,817 members in Connecticut; 804,557 in the United States.

## GRAND LODGE OF CONNECTICUT.

Zebulon R. Robbins, Norwich, G. M.; Horace H. Jackson, Bridgeport, D. G. M.; Selah G. Blakeman, G. W.; Frederick R. Botsford, New Haven, G. Sec'y; William H. Marigold, G. Treas.

## MIDIAN ENCAMPMENT, No. 7.

Loren Davis, C. P.; Eugene Webster, H. P.; Wm. T. Hayden, Box 813, Scribe; S. B. Mallett, Tr.; Grant U. Kierstead, S. W.; David A. Wilcox, J. W. Instituted Dec. 24, 1844. Reinstituted February 17, 1873. Meets 1st and 3d Monday evenings, at Odd Fellow's hall, 972 Main st.

## CHARTER OAK LODGE, No. 2.

Wm. H. Williamson, N. G.; Fred. Parker, V. G.; Wm. Hooper, Rec. Sec'y ; R. E. Nichols, Perm. Sec'y; Isaac H. Coe, Treasurer; Nelson G. Ford, Frank H. Crygier, Frederick A. West, Trustees. Instituted April 21, 1840. Reinstituted March 6, 1872. Meets Friday evenings at Odd Fellow's hall, 972 Main street.

## SUMMIT LODGE, No. 45.

H. D. Middleberger, N. G.; George P. Sturtevant, V. G.; Charles B. Greene, P. O. Box 146, Rec. Sec'y; A. S. Bishop, Perm. Sec'y ; Charles A. Bowles, Treas.; J. O. Gorman, J. H. Mallery, C. A. Q. Norton, Trustees. Instituted March 29, 1898. Meets at G. A. R. hall, 926 Main st., Thursday evenings. Elections, June and Dec.

## HARTFORD LODGE, No. 82.

Wm. J. Murray, N. G.; W. J. Lozell, V. G.; E. W. Alexander, Perm. Sec'y; George A. McCorkle, Treas.; Clarkson N. Fowler, Elwin L. Sprague, Trustees. Meets Tuesday evenings at Odd Fellow's hall, 972 Main st.

## CONNECTICUT LODGE, No. 93.

G. Herbert Peck, N. G.; James G. Bacon, V. G.; Frank C. Goodrich, 126 Retreat av., Rec. Sec'y; H. H. Larkum, Perm. Sec'y; Francis Coles, Treas.; Ralph Burnham, George D. Schaubel, Eugene F. Weston, Trustees. Instituted April 27, 1874. Meets Thursday evenings at Odd Fellow's hall, 972 Main st. Semi-annual meetings in June and Dec.

## BEETHOVEN LODGE, No. 98.

Geo. Fisher, N. G.; R. Vranz, V. G.; Ernest Roedel, R. Sec'y; Albert Zillhart, Perm. Sec'y; Henry Janson, Treas.; Joseph Hirth, T. Kassenbrook, L. Hellman, Trustees. Instituted April 27, 1876. Meets Wednesday evenings at 793 Main st. Semi-annual elections January and June.

## TYCHO BRAHE LODGE, No. 13.

Hans Micklesen, N. G.; Michael Larsen, V. G.; Robert Ellegard, Rec. Sec'y; Henry Jessen, Perm. Sec'y; Hans N. Hansen, Treasurer. Instituted Oct. 31, 1888. Meets Tuesday evenings at 793 Main st. Elections semi-annually, June and December.

## JOHN ERICSSON LODGE, No. 67.

Gustaf Anderson, N. G.; Peter Larson, V. G.; Alfred Carlson, Treas.; Charles A. Orlander, Rec. Sec'y; Gabriel Crusberg, Perm. Sec'y; Chas. J. Anderson, Chas. A. Anderson, John Bjorklund, Trustees. Organized April 18, 1893. Meets Friday evenings at 747 Main st. Elections June and December.

## CHARTER OAK SICK AND BENEFIT ASSOC'N OF CHARTER OAK LODGE, NO. 2.

Thomas S. Birch, Pres't; George I. Bodge, V. Pres't; Wm. T. Hayden, Sec'y; Fred A. West, Treas. Organized Nov. 10, 1887. Meets at Odd Fellow's hall, 1st Fridays. Annual meeting in Nov.

## MUTUAL AID ASSOCIATION OF CONNECTICUT LODGE, No. 93.

Geo. D. Schaubel, Pres't; John E. Palmer, V. Pres't; Frank C. Goodrich, Sec'y; James G. Bacon, Treas. Annual election second Monday in April. Quarterly meetings second Monday in Jan., April, July and Oct. Organized April 30, 1888. Incorporated July 11, 1888. Meets at 972 Main street.

## MINERVA LODGE, No. 2, DAUGHTERS OF REBEKAH.

Mrs. Bertha Hogaboom, N. G.; Mrs. Caroline Eberwein, V. G.; Mrs. Alwine Wehner, 28 Trumbull street, Sec'y; Miss Louisa Ziglatzky, Treas. Instituted March 16, 1892. Meets 2d and 4th Monday evenings at 757 Main street. Annual meeting in January.

## MIRIAM LODGE. No. 18, DAUGHTERS OF REBEKAH.

Mrs. Blanch Phelps, N. G.; Mrs. Lena Reuger, V. G.; Mrs. L. A. Gladwin, Broad corner Lincoln street, R. S.; Mrs. Eliza Ellsworth, 1243 Main street, F. S.; Mrs. Etta Birch, 173 Ashley street, Treas.; Mrs. Henry Avery, Mrs. Georgie McKeoun, Mrs. W. W. Tucker, Trustees. Meets at Odd Fellow's hall, 972 Main st., 2d and 4th Wednesday evenings. Annual meeting in December.

## CELESTIAL LODGE, No. 2,093, GRAND UNITED ORDER OF ODD FELLOWS.

John F. Jones, N. G.; Morris Mitchell, V. G.; Patrick H. Mills, P. O. Box 503, P. S.; Thos. H. Rose, Treas.; Charles W. Custis, John H. Jones, John F. Jones, Finance Com. Meets 1st and 3d Tuesdays, monthly, at 26 Kinsley street. Organized May 4, 1880.

## Knights of Pythias.

There are 6,033 members in Connecticut; 469,291 in the United States.

### GRAND LODGE OF CONNECTICUT.

F. W. Chesson, Waterbury, G.C.; J. S. Stokes, Meriden, G. V. C.; F. E. Cutler, Bridgeport, G. P.; H. O. Case, Hartford, G. K. of R. and S.; W. N. Potter, Willimantic, G. M. E.; Edward Schulze, Hartford, G. M. A.; D. W. Benjamin, Jr., Norwich, G. I. G.; Wm. Reid, East Hartford, G. O. G. Annual meeting Oct. 18, 1898, at Norwich.

### CRESCENT LODGE, No. 7.

W. B. Deming, C. C.; W. S. Leek, V. C.; Ervin L. Furrey, 1166 Main st., K. of R. and S.; E. J. Hale, M. of F.; H. C. Burgess, M. of E.; G. M. Deming, F. E. Day, Frank Bryden, Trustees. Established April 19, 1869. Meets Monday evenings at 7 Central row.

### WASHINGTON LODGE, No. 15.

H. G. Bestor, C. C.; A. L. Whiting, V. C.; Charles H. Phelps, 45 Ann st., K. of R. and S.; H. J. Case, M. of E.; F. A. E. Mason, M. of F.; A. L. Whiting, David Seide, H. G. Bestor, Trustees. Instituted May 12, 1870. Meets Wednesday evenings at 901 Main street.

### HERMANN LODGE, No. 16.

Louis Dettenborn, C. C.; J. E. Palmer, V.C.; Chas. F. Miller, K. of R. and S.; Theo. G. Scheck, M. of F.; Frank Schirm, M. of E.; Wm. Weigelt, John Palmer, H. A. Slaboszewski, Trustees. Instituted May 18, 1870. Meets 1st and 3d Thursday evenings, monthly, at 798 Main st.

### LINCOLN LODGE, No. 55.

F. S. Stearns, P. O. Box 716, K. of R. and S. Organized Nov. 23, 1894. Meets Friday evenings at Fraternity Hall, Y. M. C. A. building. Semi-annual election last Friday in June and Dec.

### SUMNER COMPANY, No. 1, UNIFORM RANK.

William Haspey, Capt.; E. L. Furrey, 1st Lieut.; G. W. Lynch, 2d Lieut.; George M. Deming, Recorder; George M. Couch, Treas.; O. W. Chaffee, Jr., Guard; G. H. Langdon, Sentinel; Robert Hunter, D. B. Russell, Wm. Haspey, Geo. M. Deming, George W. Lynch, Ex. Committee. Instituted Nov. 29, 1886. Meets at 456 Main street, 1st and 3d Tuesday evenings monthly. Annual meeting 2d Friday in Feb.

### ENDOWMENT RANK, SECTION 186.

F. D. Parker, Pres't; H. C. Burgess, Vice Pres't; Ervin L. Furrey, Sec'y and Treas.; J. F. Axtelle, Med. Examiner. Annual meeting in Dec. subject to call.

### HARTFORD PYTHIAN BUILDING ASSOCIATION.

George E. Wright, Pres't; George M. Deming, H. C. Burgess, Vice Pres'ts; Archie L. Whiting, Sec'y; Edward Schulze, Treas.; Henry F. Smith, H. J. Case, Frank F. Heussler, Trustees; David Seide, William Haspey, Jas. A. Robertson, Committee on Credentials.

## Fraternal Order of Connecticut.

### GRAND COUNCIL OF CONNECTICUT.

Arthur Hirsch, Hartford, G.C.; I. P. Turney, Bridgeport, G. V. C.; Wm. T. Hartwell, Bridgeport, G. R.; H. O. Case, Hartford, G. T.; Jacob May, Bridgeport, G. M. E.; John H. Stevenson, Parkville, G. C.; Samuel F. Powell, Bridgeport, G. G.; Robert E. Pyne, Hartford, G. S. G.; Geo. P. Harvey, Hartford, G. J. G.; E. R. Faxon, Amanda M. Dane, Hattie L. Graham, G. Trustees. Instituted March 18, 1892. Incorporated May 2, 1895. Annual meeting 3d Tuesday in May.

### HARTFORD COUNCIL No. 2.

Charles A. Allen, C. C.; William H. Carter, V. C.; E. Howard Geer, Sec'y; Royal S. Hoxie, F.; George H. Lycett, Treas.; George P. Harvey, Henry C. Burgess, Edward R. Faxon, Trustees. Instituted May 5, 1892. Meets at 881 Main st., 2d and 4th Thursday evenings, monthly. Elections, June and December.

### FRATERNAL RELIEF ASSOCIATION.

#### HARTFORD COUNCIL.

E. R. Faxon, Pres't; George P. Harvey, Vice Pres't; Charles A. Allen, Sec'y; George H. Lycett, Treas. Organized Feb. 27, 1896. Annual election in May.

### LAFAYETTE COUNCIL, No. 4.

John J. Lawler, C. C.; Herbert Johnson, V. C.; Pauline R. Simendinger, Sec'y; H. C. Stevenson. F.; J. H. Stevenson, T.; Richard Record, Annie Stevenson, Theo. Simendinger, Trustees. Instituted Dec. 16, 1893. Meet in Parkville hall, 1st and 3d Wednesday evenings. Annual meeting in January.

### LAFAYETTE RELIEF ASSOCIATION.

#### LAFAYETTE COUNCIL.

E. C. Blushdorn, Pres't; Theo. Simendinger, Vice Pres't; H. E. Miller, Secretary; M. Murray, Treasurer. Organized October 2, 1895. Annual meeting third Wednesday evening in January.

## United American Mechanics.

### STATE COUNCIL OF CONNECTICUT.

A. L. Thompson, New Britain, S. C.; A. T. Boon, S. V. C.; Charles H. Adams, 4 Grove st., South Norwalk, S. C. Sec'y; E. F. Atwood, Hartford, S. C. Treas. Instituted May 19, 1873.

### CHARTER OAK COUNCIL. No. 3.

Albert Chaney, C.; M. J. Burnham, V. C.; T. H. Cook, Box 571, Rec. Sec'y; E. D. Clark, Fin. Sec'y; C. B. Mellen, Treas.; Charles E. Crane, Wm. K. Ford, H. P. Fox, Trustees. Instituted June 15, 1886. Elections, January and July. Meets every Tuesday evening at Grand Army Hall, 926 Main street.

### CUSTER COUNCIL, No. 85.

J. F. Baker, Councilor; F. W. White, V. C.; H. R. Hovey, Treas.; A. S. Bishop, Rec. Sec'y, P. O. Box 562; A. H. Nearing, F.S.; Hart Talcott, T. B. Chapman, F. W. White, Trustees. Organized July 24, 1893. Meets Friday evening at 926 Main street. Elections in January and July.

### CHARTER OAK COMMANDERY, No. 26,

#### LOYAL LEGION, U. R. OF THE O. U. A. M.

C. F. Crane, Capt.; A. H. Seymour, 1st Lieut.; T. J. McCabe, 2d Lieut.; Albert Chaney, M. F. Pellet, G. H. Andrews, H. A. Clough, Serg'ts; Albert Chaney, Treas.; M. E. Horton, 447 Capitol ave., Rec. and Fin. Sec'y; A. H. Seymour, M. M. Smith, George D. Scott, Trustees. Organized March 2d, 1891. Meets every Monday evening at 603 Main street.

### BUCKINGHAM COUNCIL, No. 4,

#### JUNIOR ORDER UNITED AMERICAN MECHANICS.

F. S. Stratton, C.; E. E. Eno, V. C.; Geo. D. Scott, 884 Main street, R. Sec'y; F. M. Wetherbee, F. Sec'y; LeRoy F. Johnson, Treas.; E. E. Eno, W. C. Nichols, F. R. Dickerson, Trustees. Organized Oct. 4, 1894. Meets Saturday at 971 Main st.

# Grand Army of the Republic.

There are 5,773 members in Connecticut; 319,456 in the United States.

## DEPARTMENT OF CONNECTICUT.

W. E. Simonds, Hartford, C.; Thomas Bourdren, Bridgeport, S. V. C.; W. H. Loomis, Rockville, J. V. C.; Charles Rawling, New Haven, M. D.; Rev. Henry Upson, New Milford, Chaplain; John H. Thacher, Hartford, A. A. G.; Wm. E. Morgan, New Haven, A. Q. M. G.; C. C. Kinne, Meriden, I.; Robert Pyne, Hartford, J. A.; Edward C. Buck, Winsted, C. M. O.; Edson S. Bishop, Norwich, C. of S.

## NATHANIEL LYON POST, No. 2.

John W. Drew, C.; George Jones, S. V. C.; E. D. Ames, J. V. C.; John R. Sloan, Adj.; Hobart W. Deming, Q. M.; Charles Jackson, Chaplain; Hiram Edward, Surg.; P. J. Callahan, O. D.; Joseph Horey, O. G.; Robert Pyne, S. M.; A. M. Cadwell, Q. M. S. Meets 1st, 3d and 5th Tuesday evenings, 724 Main st.

## ROBERT O. TYLER POST, No. 50.

John N. Wilsey, C.; Henry E. Taintor, S. V. C.; C. A. Q. Norton, J. V. C.; E. Howard Geer, Adj.; John A. Dresser, Q. M.; Dr. L. D. McLean, Surg.; John W. Longdon, Chaplain; Benj. W. Kenyon, O. D.; Charles C. Munsell, O. G.; Charles H. Case, S. M.; W. L. Earl, Q. M. S.; Henry C. Storrs, George Hetzel, C. B. Leonard, C. S.; E. V. Preston, John G. Root, L. A. Dickinson, Trustees Relief Fund. Organized July 29, 1879. Chartered April, 1885. Meets every Wednesday evening, excepting July and August, in G. A. R. hall, 926 Main st.

## WOMAN'S RELIEF CORPS, No. 2,

AUXILIARY TO NATHANIEL LYON POST, NO. 2.

Mrs. Laura A. Sanders, Pres't; Mrs. Alice C. Whitehead, S. V. P.; Mrs. Kate A. Martin, J. V. P.; Miss Carrie M. Roberts, 30 West st., Secretary; Miss Alice A. Slater, 42 Ward st., Treas.; Mrs. Sarah D. Coombs, Chaplain; Mrs. Nellie F. Neville, Cond.; Mrs. Hattie R. Hale, Guard. Organized 1882. Meets at 724 Main st., 2d and 4th Tuesday evenings, monthly. Annual meeting in Dec.

## WOMAN'S RELIEF CORPS, No. 6.

AUXILIARY TO ROBERT O. TYLER POST, NO. 50.

Mrs. Alice L. Gregg, President; Mrs. Rachel Case, S. V. P.; Mrs. Mary F. Richards, J. V. P.; Mrs. Mary E. Manderville, 27 Martin st., Sec'y; Mrs. Emma A. Coomes, Treas.; Mrs. Alta Star Cressy, Chaplain; Mrs. Sarah Pidge, Cond.; Mrs. Maria Smith, Guard. Organized April 28, 1884. Meets 2d and 4th Saturday evenings at 926 Main st. Election last meeting in Dec.

## GRIFFIN A. STEDMAN CAMP, No. 6,

SONS OF VETERANS.

Arthur T. Bogue, Capt.; G. Lester Wheeler, 1st Lieut; Wm. E. Caulkins, 2d Lieut; C. C. Saunders, Chaplain; A. O. Warner, 1st Sergt.; C. H. Burlingham, Q.-M. Serg.; Charles E. Boswell, H. E. Gage, R. D. Landon, Wm. Murdock, Jr., Levi B. Benson, Sergeants; Samuel C. Cooper, Jr., R. H. Noble, Chas. E. Boswell, Jr., Corporals. Organized April 21, 1887. Meets at 926 Main st. 2d and 4th Monday evenings. Annual election in December.

# Knights of the Maccabees of the World.

## HARTFORD TENT, No. 1,

Thomas W. Gunshanan, C.; Fred. H. Butts, L. C.; John F. Johnson, R. K.; Joseph A. Swift, F. K. Organized April 27, 1881. Annual election first regular review in Dec. Meets at 7 Central row 2d and 4th Wednesday evenings, monthly.

## MIZPAH TENT, No. 11.

M. B. Trant, C.; W. J. Doyle, L. C.; Thos. J. Sceery, F. K.; Edward L. Buggee, R. K.; Charles Miller, Christopher McKone, A. H. Tyler, Trustees. Organized Sept. 15, 1894. Meets 1st and 3d Tuesday evenings monthly at 7 Central row. Annual election 1st Tuesday in Dec.

## EMILY E. MORGAN HIVE,

LADIES OF THE MACCABEES.

Mary Mahan, Com.; Julia McCarthy, Lieut. Com.; Mary Bolan, 39 Harbison av., Rec. Keeper; Katie J. Ryan, 30 Florence st., Finance Keeper.

## HARRIET BEECHER STOWE HIVE, No. 1,

LADIES OF THE MACCABEES.

Miss Mary Felletter, Com.; Miss Lizzie Hines, Lieut. Com.; Annie Nolan, Rec. Keeper; Mrs. Susan H. M. Graff, Fin. Keeper. Organized July 20, 1893. Meets 1st and 3d Wednesday evenings at 51 Ann st. Election in December.

# Ancient Order of United Workmen.

## NATHAN HALE LODGE No. 39.

Clarendon C. Bulkeley, M. W.; Fred N. Miller, F.; Dennis Kearns, Recorder; Wm. S. Dwyer, Receiver; Edwin J. Hale, Financier; G. W. French, William Westland, J. Frank Axtelle, Trustees. Organized Jan. 28, 1889. Meets 2d and 4th Thursday evenings at Columbia Hall, 903 Main st. Annual meeting in Jan.

## PARKVILLE LODGE, No. 66.

Clarence W. Hart, M. W.; Henry C. Tracy, Foreman; William M. Buckmayer, Receiver; J. W. Roberts, F.; Henry S. Baker, 11 Greenwood st., Recorder; Henry C. Tracy, Alex R. Trimble, A. Grecy, Trustees. Organized Nov. 11, 1893. Meets 2d and 4th Friday evenings, monthly, at Parkville Hall. Annual election in January.

## WADSWORTH LODGE, No. 60.

B. C. Seymour, M. W.; J. McDonald, F.; John E. Ball, Receiver; R. E. Nichols, Recorder; W. D. Hastings, R. H. Lewis, F. H. Seymour, Trustees. Organized March 5, 1893. Meets 2d and 4th Tuesday evenings at 828 Pearl street. Annual election in Dec.

# Ancient Order of Foresters of America.

## COURT BUCKINGHAM, No. 25.

John F. Kilmartin, Chief Ranger; Mathew Montgomery, Treas.; E. J. Sheehan, F. Sec'y; N. D. Baldwin, Rec. Sec'y; M. H. Kelly, James Struthers, P. D. Kennedy, Trustees. Organized March 18, 1886. Meets 1st and 3d Wednesday evenings at 6 American row.

## COURT ERICSSON, No. 48.

Frank E. Shea, C. R.; Herbert Foley, Treas.; Eugene D. Fox, Fin. Sec'y; John J. Gaffey, Rec. Sec'y; John L. Cahill, James Williams, James B. Duffy, Trustees. Organized April 29, 1889. Meets 2d and 4th Monday evenings at 972 Main street.

## COURT SAMUEL COLT, No. 93.

James L. Roper, C. R.; Arthur M. Dignam, Treas.; D. A. Fitzpatrick, Sec'y; P. J. Timmons, P. J. Reardon, John McMahon, Trustees. Organized Oct. 15, 1896. Meets at 7 Central row. Semi-annual elections in Jan. and July.

## COURT CAPITOL CITY, No. 7,899.

T. Stanners, C. R.; R. E. Turner, Treas; A. J. Easterby, F. Sec'y; H. G. Morris, 224 Park st., Rec. Sec'y. Meets 2d and 4th Thursday evenings at 11 Pratt st.

COURT ABRAHAM LINCOLN, No. 121.
J. B. Schwartz, C. R.; Louis Leviton, Treas.; B.
Meyers, Fin. Sec'y; I. Noll, Rec. Sec'y; S. Tuck, A.
Kessler, Trustees. Organized Feb. 22, 1898. Meets
2d and 4th Thursday evenings at 798 Main street.

## Knights of Columbus.

GREEN CROSS COUNCIL, No. 11,
James J. Coleman, G. K.; Philip A. Ledwith Rec.
Sec'y; John A. Carroll, F. Sec'y; P. D. Ryan, Treas.;
Wm. Murray, P. J. McLaughlin, Wm. D. Casker, M. H.
Gunshanan, Trustees. Annual election in December.
Meets 1st and 3d Monday evenings of each month, at
908 Main street.

CHARTER OAK COUNCIL, No. 19,
John Mulhall, G. K.; H. J. Golden, R. Sec'y; James
P. Tobin, F. Sec'y; E. J. Mulcahy, Treas.; Thomas P.
M. Preston, William J. Sullivan, James Williams,
Patrick F. Brassill, Michael Clarkin, Trustees. Organ-
ized, March, 1885. Meets at 709 Main street 2d and
4th Tuesday evenings in each month. Annual meet-
ing in January.

HARTFORD COUNCIL, No. 161.
D. F. Shea, G. K.; E. L. Scott, Treas.; J. F. Callahan, F. Sec'y; J. E. Kelly, Rec. Sec'y; J. J. Ryan, J.
J. Helion, P. J. Green, J. J. Hutchinson, L. J. Godbout, Trustees. Organized March 22, 1896. Meets
1st and 3d Thursday evening at 908 Main st. Annual
election in January.

JEWEL COUNCIL, No. 51.
T. J. Burke, G. K.; T. J. Ward, 9 Center st., R. Sec'y;
William J. Dooley, F, Sec'y; Patrick Golden, Treas.;
C. A. Cullen, W. J. Conlin, R. J. Casey, J. B. McCabe,
T. P. Quirk, Trustees. Meets 2d and 4th Monday
evenings, monthly, at 908 Main st. Annual meeting
in December.

## Temperance.

ARBA LANKTON TOTAL ABSTINENCE AND
ANTI-TOBACCO SOCIETY.
Arba Lankton, Pres't and Treas. This Society
holds meetings at the Tabernacle, 124 Commerce st.,
from Oct. 1, to May 1, and at Valley Railroad depot
from May 1 to October 1, every Sunday, at 5 P. M.
Organized September 29, 1876.

CATHOLIC TOTAL ABSTINENCE UNION OF
CONNECTICUT.
Rev. John T. Winters, South Norwalk, Pres't; John
J. McDonald, Waterbury; Mrs. Harriet Granger, Meri-
den, Vice Pres'ts; John Kelly, New Britain, Sec'y;
Charles Fitzgerald, Middletown, Treas.; Thomas F.
Fitzgerald, Winsted, State Editor; Rt. Rev. Michael
Tierney, D. D., Hartford, Chaplain. 86 Societies in the
State—14 Ladies; 55 Adults; 17 Cadets. 6,280 Mem-
bers. Organized August 15, 1870.

CONNECTICUT TEMPERANCE UNION.
Thomas L. Norton, Lakeville, Pres't; M. W. Terrill,
Middletown, J. B. Williams, Glastonbury, J. M. Talcott, Ellington, S. L. Blake, New London, H. A. Davenport, Bridgeport, K. T. Sheldon, Winsted, A. G. Bill,
Danielson, C. B. Foote, New Haven, Vice Pres'ts; W.
A. Willard, Hartford, Treas.; Rev. J. H. James, Rockville, Sec'y. Organized 1865. Incorporated 1893. Hartford office, 426 Asylum street.

GOOD TEMPLARS.
HARTFORD LODGE, NO. 214.
Organized June 22, 1852. Meets 881 at Main street,
Friday evening.

HAWLEY DIV. No. 82, SONS OF TEMPERANCE.
W. A. Baedor, W. P.; H. W. F. Cheney, Rec. Sec'y;
Annie R. Reimann, F. Scribe; H. H. Quintard, Treas.
Organized Feb. 3, 1888. Meets Tuesday evenings at
Y. M. C. A. building. Annual meeting in October.

TEMPLES OF HONOR AND TEMPERANCE.
PERSEVERANCE TEMPLE, No. 3. J. A. Decker, W.
C. T.; R. E. Sage, W. R.; J. S. Baisden, W. F. R.; C. E.
Boswell, W. Treas. Instituted Feb. 18, 1869. Meets
at 302 Asylum st. on Tuesday evenings.
FIDELITY COUNCIL, No. 2. F. H. Sage, Jr., C. of C.;
R. E. Sage, R. of C.; J. A. Decker, Treas. Meets Satur-
day evenings at 302 Asylum st.
CHARITY SOCIAL, No. 20. Luella F. Billings, S. P.
T.; Eugenia Sage, S. R.; Mrs. Martha S. Estes, Fin.
Sec'y, 545 Main st. Organized April 10, 1883. Meets
at 302 Asylum st. 1st Wednesday evening of month.

LEAGUE OF THE CROSS.
Thomas J. Butler, Pres't; Bernard Burns, P. B.
Donovan, Vice Pres'ts; Frank P. Garvan, Sec'y.

YOUNG MEN'S TOTAL ABSTINENCE SOCIETY.
John Hutchinson, Pres't; John L. Quinn, V. Pres't;
John Derby, Treas.; Timothy J. Ryan, Sec'y; Bernard
Fitzsimmons, Rec. Sec'y. Organized Oct. 11, 1896.
Meets 2d and 4th Thursday at 14 State st.

## Medical.

For Physicians, Dentists and Nurses, see the classified
Business Directory.

CONN. ECLECTIC MEDICAL SOCIETY.
W. L. Adams, Hazardville, Pres't; G. W. H. Wil-
liams, Grosvenordale, Vice Pres't; LeRoy A. Smith,
Higganum, Treasurer; George A. Faber, Waterbury
Secretary; George A. Faber, Waterbury, Leonard
Bailey, Middletown, Thomas S. Hodge, Torrington,
Thos. Mulligan, New Britain, J. D. S. Smith, Bridgeport,
Censors. Annual meeting 2d Tuesday in May. Semi-
annual meeting 2d Tuesday in September.

CONNECTICUT MEDICAL SOCIETY.
Henry P. Stearns, Hartford, Pres't; C. S. Rodman,
Waterbury, Vice Pres't; N. E. Wordin, Bridgeport,
Sec'y; W. W. Knight, Hartford, Treas. Organized,
1791. Annual meeting 4th Wednesday and Thursday
in May, alternately at Hartford and New Haven.

CONN. HOMEOPATHIC MEDICAL SOCIETY.
Charles Vishno, New Haven, Pres't; E. S. Smith,
Bridgeport, Vice Pres't; E. C. M. Hall, New Britain,
Sec'y; E. J. Walker, New Haven, Treas.; Theodore
St. John, Thomaston, Adelaide Lambert, New Haven.
C. N. Payne, Bridgeport, A. J. Givens, Stamford, C.
E. Stark, Norwich, Censors. Organized 1851. Incor-
porated Oct. 1864. Annual meeting in May, alternate-
ly in Hartford and New Haven.

CONN. PHARMACEUTICAL ASSOCIATION.
N. Douglas Sevin, Norwich, Pres't; John W. Lowe,
New Haven, Richard H. Kimball, Hartford, Vice
Pres'ts; John B. Ebbs, Waterbury, Treas.; Arthur
S. Clark, Waterbury, Sec'y. Organized, 1876. Incor-
porated 1889. Annual meeting in June.

CONN. STATE DENTAL ASSOCIATION.
A. J. Cutting, Southington, Pres't; H. G. Provost,
Winsted, Vice Pres't; Edw'd Eberle, Hartford, Sec'y;
Daniel A. Jones, New Haven, Treas.; J. F. Wright,
Hartford, P. A. Powers, Meriden, J. T. Barker, Wal-
lingford, Executive Committee. Organized 1864. In-
corporated 1875. Annual meeting 3d Tuesday in May.

## HARTFORD COUNTY MEDICAL ASSOCIATION.

James Campbell, Hartford, *Pres't*; Joseph A. Coogan, Windsor Locks, *Vice Pres't*; Wilton E. Dickerman, Hartford, *Sec'y*; Samuel W. Irving, Jos. B. Hall, Howard O. Allen, *Censors*. Established 1792. Annual meeting 8d Wednesday in April.

## HARTFORD DRUGGISTS' ASSOCIATION.

Fred B. Edwards, *Pres't*; John W. Service, D. W. Tracy, *Vice Pres'ts*; Chas. L. Hubbard, *Treas.*; Chas. H. Bell, *Sec'y*; Fred B. Edwards, C. H. Bell, *Censors*; A. D. Pierce, F. B. Edwards, C. P. Gladding, J. K. Williams, L. H. Goodwin, A. Marwick, Jr., J. W. Service, *Ex. Com.*; Fred H. Chapin, John K. Williams, *Entertainment Com.* Organized December, 1878. Annual meeting in January.

## DUNHAM MEDICAL CLUB OF HARTFORD.

F. Hills Cole, *Sec'y and Treas.* Meets last Saturday of each month at the houses of members, in rotation.

## HARTFORD MEDICAL SOCIETY.

**88 PROSPECT ST., HUNT MEMORIAL BUILDING.**

G. P. Davis, *Pres't*; H. S. Fuller, *Vice Pres't*; Gideon C. Segur, *Sec'y*; C. D. Alton, *Treas.*; E. K. Root, *Librarian*; E. E. Taft, P. H. Ingalls, F. T. Simpson, *Censors*; G. W. Russell, M. Storrs, Geo. R. Shepherd, *Trustees*; G. C. Segur, C. D. Alton, E. K. Root, H. L. Law, T. F. Kane, *Executive Committee*; M. Storrs, G. P. Davis, G. R. Shepherd, *Building Committee*. Organized Sept. 15, 1846. Chartered July 1, 1889. Annual meeting, first Monday in Jan. Regular meetings 1st and 3d Monday evenings of each month, except July and August.

A medical reference library open to the public, under the supervision of Dr. E. K. Root, the librarian, has been established in the Society building.

Nurses' Registry at the office of the Secretary, Dr. G. C. Segur. Only recommended nurses are placed on the list; over 100 names registered. The public can secure a nurse through the registry on payment of $1.

# Cemeteries.

## ANCIENT BURYING GROUND ASSOCIATION.

Chas. T. Welles, *Treas. and Sec'y.* Annual meeting in September. One acre.

## CEDAR HILL CEMETERY.

Jonathan B. Bunce, *Pres't*; George G. Sumner, *Vice Pres't*; Ward W. Jacobs, *Sec'y and Treas.*; George Beach, Jonathan B. Bunce, Daniel Phillips, Francis B. Cooley, Jonathan F. Morris, James G. Batterson, Rowland Swift, George A. Fairfield, Ward W. Jacobs, Austin C. Dunham, Pliny Jewell, George G. Sumner, Drayton Hillyer, James B. Moore, Edwin P. Taylor, Olapd H. Blanchard, Edward M. Gallaudet, Henry C. Dwight, William B. Clark, Atwood Collins, *Directors*; James B. Moore, Edwin P. Taylor, *Auditors.* Robert Scrivner, *Sup't.* Incorporated, 1864. First interment July 17, 1866. Annual meeting 1st Thursday in December. 268 acres, three miles south of City Hall, Maple and Fairfield avs. Office, 815 Main st.

## NORTH BURYING GROUND.

In charge of the Cemetery Committee. A new iron fence, costing $8,500, was put up in front of this Cemetery by the Town in 1868. Another fence on south side, put up July, 1884. A Chapel and office, erected at a cost of $1,495, north of main entrance, in the Spring of 1889. The first interment in these grounds was that of Mrs. Anna Olcott, who died Feb. 6, 1807, aged 71. There have been several additions made to the area of this burial place since that time. Rollin D. Lane, *Sexton.* 197 Windsor av.

## HEBREW CEMETERY.

Leopold DeLeeuw, R. Ballerstein, Joseph Kashmann, *Committee*; Rymon Bocorselski, *Sexton.* Deborah Mortuary Chapel thereon was dedicated Oct. 17, 1886. 71 Ward street, adjoining Zion Hill Cemetery.

## OLD SOUTH BURYING GROUND.

In charge of *Cemetery Committee.* Two acres. 370 Maple av., cor. Benton st.

## MOUNT ST. BENEDICT CEMETERY.

Very Rev. John A. Mulcahy, 82 Church st., *Sup't*; B. Higgins, *Sexton.* First burial, Nov. 1874. 71 acres. Bluehills avenue, about ¼ mile north of City line.

## ST. PATRICK'S AND HOLY TRINITY CEMETERY.

Very Rev. John A. Mulcahy, *Sup't*; John Broderick, *Sexton.* 12 acres. Cemetery st., west of the North Burying Ground.

## SPRING GROVE CEMETERY ASSOCIATION

Alfred E. Burr, *Pres't*; W. E. Sugden, *Vice Pres't*; John G. Root, *Treasurer and Secretary*; Alfred E. Burr, W. E. Sugden, J. G. Root, M. W. Graves, John K. Williams, Henry C. Judd, D. A. Rood, C. D. Burnham, William L. Matson, W. O. Carpenter, D. W. C. Skilton, L. A. Dickinson, Willis E. Smith, H. M. Andrews, *Directors*; M. W. Graves, Wm. L. Matson, *Auditors*; Nahum C. Wilder, *Sup't.* Present Association was organized in 1867; with recent enlargement, there are 33 acres, and more than 7,000 bodies interred therein. First burial was Mrs. Stephen Page in 1845. Annual meeting 1st Wednesday in June. 303 Windsor av.

## ZION'S HILL.

David Blevins, *Sup't and Sexton.* 23 acres. 89 Zion st., junction Ward st.

### CLOSING OF CONN. RIVER NAVIGATION.

| | | |
|---|---|---|
| 1855, Dec. 9. | 1870, Dec. 19. | 1884, Dec. 18. |
| 1856, Dec. 6. | 1871, Nov. 80. | 1885, Dec. 6. |
| 1857, Dec. 12. | 1872, Dec. 1. | 1886, Dec. 5. |
| 1858, Dec. 1. | 1873, Nov. 29. | 1887, Dec. 26. |
| 1859, Dec. 10. | 1874, Nov. 28. | 1888, Dec 15, 2d. |
| 1860, Dec. 10. | 1874, Dec. 24. | 1889, Jan.11 (90). |
| 1861, Dec. 21. | 1875, Nov. 80. | 1890, Dec. 10. |
| 1862, Dec. 6. | 1876, Dec. 1. | 1891, Jan 8 (92). |
| 1863, Dec. 9. | 1877, Jan. 1, '78. | 1892, Dec. 23. |
| 1864, Dec. 12. | 1878, Dec. 20. | 1893, Dec. 13. |
| 1865, Dec. 17. | 1879, Dec. 21. | 1894, Dec. 28. |
| 1866, Dec. 15. | 1880, Nov. 22. | 1895, Dec. 22. |
| 1867, Dec. 8. | 1881, Jan. 4 (82). | 1896, Dec. 20. |
| 1868, Dec. 11. | 1882, Dec. 4. | 1897, Dec. 24. |
| 1869, Dec. 5. | 1883, Dec. 15. | |

### OPENING OF CONN. RIVER NAVIGATION.

| | | |
|---|---|---|
| 1835, March 1. | 1857, March 18. | 1878, March 1. |
| 1886, April 1. | 1858, March 20. | 1879, March 15. |
| 1887, March 22. | 1859, March 12. | 1880, Jan. 23. |
| 1838, March 4. | 1860, March 5. | 1881, March 14. |
| 1839, Jan. 26. | 1861, Feb. 28. | 1882, March 8. |
| 1840, March 11. | 1862, March 29. | 1883, March 19. |
| 1841, Feb. 26. | 1863, March 22. | 1884, March 15. |
| 1842, Feb. 3. | 1864, March 5. | 1885, March 28. |
| 1843, April 7. | 1865, March 17. | 1886, March 16. |
| 1844, March 15. | 1866, March 14. | 1887, March 11. |
| 1845, March 2. | 1867, March 5. | 1888, March 80. |
| 1846, March 14. | 1868, March 24. | 1889, March 8. |
| 1847, March 13. | 1869, March 25. | 1890, Feb. 18. |
| 1848, March 9. | 1870, March 2. | 1891, March 1. |
| 1849, March 17. | 1871, March 10. | 1892, Feb. 24. |
| 1850, March 6. | 1872, March 81. | 1893, March 14, |
| 1851, Feb. 7. | 1873, March 30. | 1894, March 8. |
| 1852, March 15. | 1874, March 16. | 1895, March 14. |
| 1853, Feb. 25. | 1874, Dec. 5. | 1896, March 1. |
| 1854, March 12. | 1875, April 7. | 1897, March 8. |
| 1855, March 8. | 1876, March 17. | 1898, Feb. 25. |
| 1856, April 7. | 1877, March 10. | |

# Corporations.

For Banks, Fire and Life Insurance Companies, Trust and Security Companies, full particulars will be found on the advertising pages by referring to the Index of Contents, or the Business Directory under each appropriate head.

For Corporations, Societies, etc., too late to arrange alphabetically, see Index of Contents.

In order to facilitate the finding of any particular Corporation, we have arranged them in alphabetical order, and have omitted the usual prefix to each one, of the word "THE."

*Chartered* Companies are organized under *special* charters from Conn. Legislature. *Incorporated* Companies are under the Joint Stock Laws of this State.

### A. D. VORCE COMPANY.
*See page 718.*

### ACME MACHINE SCREW CO.
*Foot of Sheldon street.*
E. C. Henn, *Pres't.*  |  A. W. Henn, *Sec'y-Treas.*
R. Hakewessell, *Assistant Treasurer.*
Annual meeting second Monday in January.

### ÆTNA INDEMNITY COMPANY.
*Office 650 Main street.*
Rob't A. Griffing, *Pres't.* | Geo. L. Chase, *V. P.*
Edward S. Pegram, *Sec'y.*
*Directors.*—Morgan G. Bulkeley, James G. Batterson, George L. Chase, John C. Webster, William H. Bulkeley, Appleton R. Hillyer, John O. Enders, Wm. B. Clark, Leverett Brainard, Chas. C. Cook, Ralph W. Cutler, Austin Brainard, Robert A. Griffing, P. H. Quinn.

### ÆTNA MACHINE CO.
*Org. Feb. 17, 1891.   Capital, $15,000.   75 Commerce.*
L. F. Robinson, *Pres't.* Austin Brainard, *Sec. & Tr.*
*Directors*—Austin Brainard, Lucius F. Robinson, Andrew F. Gates.
Annual meeting third Thursday in February.

### AMERICAN PUBLISHING COMPANY.
*See page 473.*

### AMERICAN SPECIALTY MANUFACTURING CO.
*Incorporated 1894.   Capital $100,000.   135 Sheldon st.*
Geo. J. Capewell, *Pres't.*  |  C. E. Billings, *V. Pr.*
Frank B. Richmond, *Treas. and Gen. Mgr.*
*Directors,* G. J. Capewell, A. W. C. Williams, J. H. Knight, Charles R. Forrest, E. C. Lewis, Charles Flint, C. E. Billings.
Annual meeting in July.

### EDWARD BALF CO.
*Office 2 Chapel street.*        *See page 426.*

### BEACH MANUFACTURING CO.
*Org. March 12, 1888.   Capital, $50,000.   211 State st.*
George Watson Beach, *President.*
Geo. H. Day, *Vice Pres't.* | C. J. Burnell, *Treas.*
*Directors.*—Geo. Watson Beach, C. J. Burnell, Geo. H. Day.
Annual meeting 1st Monday in April.

### BEACON FALLS MILL AND POWER CO.
*Organized 1889.   Capital $58,000.   Office 211 State st.*
John S. Camp, *President.* | Chas. M. Beach, *Treas.*
T. B. Beach, *Secretary.*

### C. E. BILLINGS MANUFACTURING COMPANY.
*Org. May 28, 1884. Capital $20,000. Office 216 Lawrence.*
Factory: Dividend Station, Town of Rocky Hill.
Product handled by The Billings & Spencer Co.
Chas. E. Billings, *Pres't.* | E. H. Stocker, *Secretary.*
L. H. Holt, *Treasurer.* | Fred. C. Billings, *Sup't.*
*Directors.*—C. E. Billings, L. H. Holt, E. H. Stocker, F. C. Billings.
Annual meeting 1st Tuesday in July.

### BILLINGS & SPENCER CO., OF HARTFORD, CT.
*Organized 1869.   Chartered 1872.   Capital $200,000.*
*Office 142 Russ st. corner of Lawrence st.*
Chas. E. Billings, *Pres't and General Manager.*
E. H. Stocker, *Secretary.* | L. H. Holt, *Treasurer.*
Fred. C. Billings, *Superintendent.*
H. E. Billings, *Assistant Superintendent.*
*Directors.*—C. E. Billings, M.W. Graves, H. P. Stearns, C. M. Spencer, L. H. Holt, Silas Chapman, Jr., E. H. Stocker.
Annual meeting third Monday in February.
*See page 531.*

### BILLINGS SIDEWALK & MASONS' SUPPLY CO.
*Incorporated Jan. 17, 1898.   Capital $5,500.*
*154 Charter Oak av.*
H. E. Billings, *Pres't.*
J. D. Candee, *Treas.*  |  H. F. Billings, *Sec'y.*
*Directors.*—H. E. Billings, H. F. Billings, J. D. Candee.
Annual meeting in February.

### BIRKERY MANUFACTURING COMPANY.
*Incorporated April 4, 1892.   65 Suffield st.*
C. J. Birkery, *Pres't.* | Thos. Standish, *Tr. & Sec'y.*
*Directors.*—Ernest Cady, William J. Thompson, Cornelius J. Birkery, Thomas Standish, Harry E. Williams.
Annual meeting 1st Monday in February.

### BLODGETT & CLAPP COMPANY.
*Org. Dec. 31, 1879.  Capital $41,825.  Office 61 Market st.*
Jeffry O. Phelps, *Pres't.* | James K. Crofut, *Sec'y.*
Geo. Breed, *Vice Pres't.* | J. O. Phelps, Jr., *Treas.*
*Directors.*—R. F. Blodgett, J. O. Phelps, Jr., George Breed, J. O Phelps, James K. Crofut, S. H. Hascall.
Annual meeting third Tuesday in April.
*See page 541.*

### WM. BOARDMAN & SONS CO.
*Incorporated Jan. 13, 1897.   Office 304 Asylum st.*
T. Jefferson Boardman, *President.*
Arthur H. Bronson, *Sec'y.* | H. F. Boardman, *Treas.*
*Directors.*—T. Jefferson Boardman, Howard F. Boardman, Arthur H. Bronson.
Annual meeting second Wednesday in February.

## BONNER-PRESTON COMPANY.
*Incorp. May, 1893.　Capital, $40,000.　848 Main st.*
JOHN D. BONNER, *President.*
MILES B. PRESTON, *Secretary and Treasurer.*
*Directors.*—John D. Bonner, Miles B. Preston, Oscar
A. Ziglatzki.　Annual meeting 1st Monday in Feb.
*See page 425.*

## BONSILATE BOX CO.
*Org. Feb. 15, 1888.　Capital, $20,000.　24 Mechanic st.*
J. W. ROCKWELL, *Pres't.* | F. C. ROCKWELL, *Sec. & Tr.*
*Directors*—J. W. Rockwell, F. S. French, F. C.
Rockwell.　Annual meeting 1st Wednesday in Feb.

## BROAD BROOK COMPANY.
*Organized, 1847.　Capital, $400,000.　Office 211 State st.*
F. B. COOLEY, *Pres't.* | CHAS. M. BEACH, *Sec'y & Tr.*
*Directors.*—F. B. Cooley, George Beach, Willis L.
Ogden, Charles H. Northam, J. H. Simonds.　Annual
meeting second Wednesday in Dec.

## BURR INDEX COMPANY.
*Org. April 7, 1883.　Capital, $50,000.　Office 336 Asylum.*
L. BRAINARD, *Pres't.* | R. K. ERVING, *Sec. & Tr.*
*Directors.*—L. Brainard, J. O. Enders, J. W. Welch,
J. M. Allen, Charles King, Silas Chapman, Jr., Philo
W. Newton.　Annual meeting, 3d Tuesday in April.

## CALHOUN PRINTING COMPANY.
*Established 1852.　Org. Oct. 13, 1879.　Capital $25,000.*
*Office, 29 Union place.*
Annual meeting 2d Monday in July.

## CAPEWELL HORSE NAIL COMPANY.
*Org. Jan. 17, 1881.　Capital $400,000.　Office 40 Governor.*
E. C. LEWIS, *President.* | G.J.CAPEWELL, *V.P.& S.*
A. W. C. WILLIAMS, *Treas. and Gen. Manager.*
G. C. F. WILLIAMS, *Sec'y and Ass't Treas.*
*Directors.*—E. C. Lewis, George J. Capewell, A. W. C.
Williams, John E. Gillette, John H. White, J. M. Allen,
George C. F. Williams.　Annual meeting in January.
*See page 524.*

## CAPITOL CITY CHUTE CO.
*Organized June 10, 1897.*
R. BALLERSTEIN, *Pres't.* | CHAS. S. ROBBINS, *Sec'y*
FRANK P. FURLONG, *V.Pres.* | JOHN P. HARBISON, *Tr.*
*Directors.*—R.Ballerstein, C. A. Jewell, E. D. Graves,
F. P. Furlong, J. P. Harbison, C. S. Robbins, L. F.
Robinson, John A. Crilly, George A. Reynolds.

## CAPITOL CITY LUMBER COMPANY.
*Inc. May 31, 1893.　Capital, $10,000.　25 Front st.*
H. W. FOX, *Pres't & Tr.* | TIMOTHY J. BURKE, *Sec'y.*
*Directors.*—H. W. Fox, John Kimball, Timothy,
J. Burke.　Annual meeting first Tuesday after 2d
Monday in June.

## CASE, LOCKWOOD & BRAINARD COMPANY.
*49 Trumbull st. and 141 Pearl st.　　See page 475.*

## CHENEY BROTHERS, SILK MANUFACTURERS.
*Chartered July, 1854.*
*Mills, 34 Morgan st., Hartford: and South Manchester.*
KNIGHT D. CHENEY, *President.*
FRANK CHENEY, JR., *Vice President.*
FRANK W. CHENEY, *Treasurer-Secretary.*
*Directors.*—Frank W. Cheney, Knight D. Cheney,
James W. Cheney, John S. Cheney, Harry G. Cheney,
Frank Cheney, Jr., Richard O. Cheney.
*See inside page to cover fronting the title page
and also Colored page 545.*

## COLT'S PATENT FIRE ARMS MFG. CO.
*Vandyke avenue.　Capital $1,000,000.　Chartered 1855.*
Annual meeting first secular day of April.
*See page 543.*

## CITIZENS GROCERY AND PROVISION COMP'Y.
*Incorporated Jan. 1868.　Capital $10,000.　285 Main st.*
HENRY M. JACOBS, *Pres't.* | JOHN A. CONKLIN, S.& Ag't.
*Directors.*— F. A. Thompson, H. M. Jacobs, J. W.
Lamb, E. P. Whitney, Ed. Williams, E. W. Buck, H.
Freeman, F. Chambers, S. Goodell.　Annual meeting
in January.

## COLLINS COMPANY.
*Estab. 1826.　Chart. 1834.　Capital $1,000,000.　785 Main.*
EDWARD H. SEARS, *Pr.* | MEIGS H.WHAPLES, *Tr. & Sec.*
*Directors.*—Howard S. Collins, Drayton Hillyer,
James J. Goodwin, John R. Redfield, Charles Hopkins
Clark, Nathaniel Shipman, Edward H. Sears, Daniel R.
Howe, Henry C. Wells.
Dividends in Jan. and July.　Works in Collinsville.
*See page 521.*

## COLUMBIA BREWING COMPANY.
*Incorporated 1879.　Office 235-245 Windsor st.*
OSCAR KOENIG, *President.*
E. HEROLD, *Secretary.* | JOHN ZUNNER, *Tr. & Man.*
*Directors.*—James Melrose, William McKone, Harry
Pearson, Philip Conrad.　Annual meeting 1st Wednes-
day in April.　　　　　*See page 417.*

## CONN. CATHOLIC PUBLISHING CO.
*Established 1876.　Incorp. June, 1896.　704 Main st.*
Rt. Rev. BISHOP MICHAEL TIERNEY, *President.*
WILLIAM F. O'NEIL, *Vice President.*
THOMAS F. KANE, M.D., *Treas.*
M. J. SLATTERY, *Manager.*
*Directors.*—Rt. Rev. Michael Tierney, William F.
O'Neil, Thos. F. Kane.　　　　*See page 467.*

## CONNECTICUT RIVER COMPANY.
*Chartered 1824.　Capital $203,500.　Office 761 Main.*
H. R. COFFIN, *President.* | M. W. GRAVES, *Sec. & Tr.*
*Directors.*—Samuel H. Allen, H. R. Coffin, S. E.
Elmore, Miles W. Graves, J. R. Montgomery, Ezra B.
Bailey, H. W. Erving, Charles E. Chaffee, Arthur F.
Eggleston.　Annual election, 4th Tuesday in January.

## ASA S. COOK COMPANY.
*Incorporated Dec. 15, 1896.　Colt's West Armory.*
ASA S. COOK, *Pres't and Treas.*
JOHN F. COOK, *Secretary.* | M. F. COOK, *Ass't Treas.*
*Directors.*—Asa S. Cook, M. F. Cook, John F. Cook,
Albert S. Cook, Mrs. H. E. Robbins.　Annual meeting
1st Wednesday in February.　　　*See page 525.*

## C. P. H. COOK COMPANY.
*Incorporated March 24, 1898.　Capital $5,000.*
*Office 721 Main street.*
C. P. H. COOK, *Pres't.* | JAMES C. PRATT, *Treas.*
WM. H. MELONEY, *V. Pr.* | JAMES B. CONROY, *Sec'y.*
*Directors.*—C. P. H. Cook, W. H. Meloney, James C.
Pratt, Francis Chambers, J. Warner Rockwell.　An-
nual meeting 3d Thursday in Sept.

## CURTIS-HULL MF'G CO.
*Incorp. April 25, 1894.　Capital $250,000.　904 Main st.*
E. C. WILSON, *Pres't.* | F. H. HASTINGS, *Sec'y.*
ERNEST CADY, *V. Pres't.* | H. J. CURTIS, *Treas.*
*Directors.*—E. C. Wilson, F. H. Hastings, Ernest
Cady, H. J. Curtis, L. A. Corbin, A. E. Hull, H. J.
Wickham.　Annual meeting in April.

## CUSHMAN CHUCK COMPANY.
*Est. 1862.　Inc. Sept. 1885.　Cap. $80,000.　30 Cushman.*
A. F. CUSHMAN, *Pres't;* | E. L. CUSHMAN, *Sec. & Tr.*
*Directors.*—A. F. Cushman, E. L. Cushman, A. P.
Sloan.　Annual meeting 2d Monday in September.

### DART MARKING MACHINE COMPANY.
*Chartered June 24, 1895.*　　235 *State street.*
W. E. GOODWIN, *President.*
F. C. ROCKWELL, *V.Pres't.* | W. W. SAVAGE, *S. & Tr.*
*Directors.*—W. E. Goodwin, F. C. Rockwell, W. M. Savage, W. W. Savage, A. H. Merrill, H. F. Hatch. Annual meeting 1st Tuesday in Jan.

### DUNHAM HOSIERY COMPANY.
*Incorporated June 21, 1880.　Capital $50,000.* 66 *State.*
AUSTIN C. DUNHAM, *Pres.* | HENRY OSBORN, *Sec'y.*
S. G. DUNHAM, *Treas.* | Mills at Naugatuck.
*Directors.*—A. C. Dunham, Sam'l G. Dunham, Edw. Dunham, Henry Osborn, D. P. Mills. Annual meeting 4th Wednesday in January. *See page 547.*

### DWIGHT SLATE MACHINE COMPANY.
*See page 526.*

### J. H. ECKHARDT COMPANY.
*Incorp. Feb. 15, 1893.　Capital, $50,000.* 695 *Main st.*
Mrs. J. H. ECKHARDT, *Pr.* | C. H. MOYER, *Sec'y & Tr.*
*Directors.*—Mrs. J. H. Eckhardt, C. H. Moyer, J. C. Ripley. Annual meeting 3d Monday in February. *See page 418.*

### EDDY ELECTRIC MANUFACTURING CO.
*Incor.* 1885.　*Capital $250,000　Factory, Windsor, Conn.*
A. H. EDDY, *President.* | A. D. NEWTON, *Sec. & Tr.*
GEORGE T. BRIGGS, *Sup't* | M. E. BAIRD, *Gen. Mgr.*
*Directors.*—A. H. Eddy, Arthur D. Newton, C. E. Newton, Geo. T. Briggs, M. E. Baird. Annual meeting in February This Company's extensive works are located near the station in Windsor. *See page 536.*

### ELECTRIC GENERATOR COMPANY.
*Incorporated April, 1890.　Capital $1,000,000.*
GEORGE H. DAY, *Pres't.* | ERNEST CADY, *Treas.*
G. W. WARD, N. Y., *V.P.* | E. H. HYDE, JR., *Sec'y.*
*Directors.*—Ernest Cady, E. Henry Hyde, Jr., Geo. H. Day, George G. Ward, New York; Henry Barringer Cox, C. H. Patrick. Annual meeting in April.

### ERNST SCHALL COMPANY.
*Incorporated Apr. 1, 1892.　Capital $30,000.* 5 *Asylum.*
ERNST SCHALL, *Pres't.* | FRANK D. MANN, *Sec. & Tr.*
*Directors.*—Ernst Schall, Frank D. Mann. Annual meeting 1st Monday in January.

### EVENING POST ASSOCIATION.
*Established* 1856.　*Incorporated July, 1881.*
*Capital $75,000.*　23 *Asylum street.*
JOHN A. PORTER, *President.* | GEO. L. FIELDER, *Tr.*

### FARMER PRINTING AND PUBLISHING CO.
*Incor. July, 1894.　Capital $15,000.* 284 *Asylum st.*
Annual meeting 1st Monday in July.

### FARMINGTON RIVER POWER COMPANY.
*Org. June 3, 1890.　Capital $110,000.　Office 50 State.*
A. C. DUNHAM, *Pres't.*
E. B. BENNETT, *Treas.* | E. C. TERRY, *Sec'y.*
*Directors.*—James L. Howard, E. C. Terry, L. A. Barbour, E. B. Bennett, Henry Roberts, Atwood Collins, Rodney Dennis, A. C. Dunham. Annual meeting 3d Mon. in June.

### FARNHAM TYPE SETTER MANUF'G CO.
*Chartered April, 1875.　Capital $190,000.* 281 *Asylum.*
JAMES NICHOLS, *Pres't.* | WM. L. MATSON, *Sec. & Tr.*
*Directors.*—Henry C. Robinson, Samuel C. Elmore, Henry P. Stearns, James Nichols, J. G. Rathbun, William L. Matson. Annual meeting 3d Tuesday in May.

### FOWLER & MILLER CO.
857 *Main street.*
WM. MCKONE, *Pres't.* | FRED. P. HOLT, *Treas.*
JOHN E. COX, *Sec'y.*
*Directors.*—S. M. Bronson, Patrick Garvan, Fred P. Holt, Charles M. Joslyn, William McKone, E. P. Miller, John G. Cox.

### FREEMAN-TIBBALS COMPANY.
*Incorporated March 1, 1897.　Office* 34 *Asylum st.*
S. I. FREEMAN, *President.*
I. N. TIBBALS, *Sec'y & Mgr.* | S. G. FREEMAN, *Treas.*
*Directors.*—S. I. Freeman, S. G. Freeman, I. N. Tibbals. Annual meeting 1st Monday in February.

### L. T. FRISBIE COMPANY.
*Incorporated* 1897.　　79 *Talcott st.*
ARTHUR G. WOOLLEY, *President and Treasurer.*
EDWARD DEMING, *Secretary.*
*See page 585.*

### GATLING GUN COMPANY.
*Capital $250,000.　Office Colt's Armory.*
JOHN H. HALL, *Pres't & Tr.* | FRED'K W. PRINCE, *Sec.*
LEWIS C. GROVER, *Vice Pres't & Sup't.*
*Directors.*—John H. Hall, William Waldo Hyde, Frank E. Belden, Lewis C. Grover, James S. Bryant. Annual meeting, first Wednesday in October.

### FRANCIS GOWDY DISTILLING COMPANY.
*Incorporated* 1890.　*Capital, $50,000,　Melrose, Conn.*
EDWIN J. BLAKE, *Pres't* | E. P. ATKINSON, *Sec'y & Tr.*
*Directors.*—S. A. Ryan, G. S. Barry, Springfield, Mass., Edward P. Atkinson, Melrose; J. G. Lane, Edwin J. Blake, E W. Lindsey, W. H. Killin, Hartford. Annual meeting 2d Tuesday in January.

### GRAY TELEPHONE PAY STATION COMPANY.
*Org. Nov.* 1891.　*Capital $100,000.　Rear 64 Asylum st.*
AMOS WHITNEY, *Pres't.* | CHARLES SOBY, *Sec'y & Tr*
WM. GRAY, *General Sup't.*
*Directors.*—Amos Whitney, Francis A. Pratt, Franklin Clark, William Gray, Chas. Soby, E. W. Kellogg, H. R. Mills. Annual meeting, 1st Thursday in Nov.

### GUILFOIL GROCERY COMPANY.
*Incorporated April 1, 1897.*　193 *Asylum st.*
HYMAN F. SMITH, *President and Treasurer.*
JOSEPH P. GUILFOIL, *Sec'y, Ass't Treas & Gen. Man.*
*Directors.*—Hyman F. Smith, Joseph P. Guilfoil, Wm. E. Bradley. Annual meeting second Monday in February.

### HART & HEGEMAN MFG. CO.
*Incorporated* 1892.　*Capital $21,000.*　26 *High st.*
GERALD W. HART, *President.*
ALFRED H. PEASE, *Secretary and Treasurer.*
*Directors.*—G. W. Hart, A. H. Pease, A. L. Shipman. Annual meeting 3d Wednesday in Jan.

### CHARLES R. HART COMPANY.
*Incorporated Mar. 23, 1897.　Capital $30,000.*
898–902 *Main street.*
CHARLES R. HART, *Pres't.* | WM. E. SUGDEN, *Treas.*
G. W. CURTIS, *Vice Pres't.* | SAMUEL A. BACON, *Sec'y*
*Directors*—Charles R. Hart, Grosvenor W. Curti,
William E. Sugden, Samuel A. Bacon. Annual meeting 4th Monday in January.

### HARTFORD & CONN. WESTERN RAILROAD CO.
*Leased to the Central New England & Western Railroad Company; in 1892 to the Philadelphia, Reading and New England Railway.*
H. O. SEIXAS, *President.* | E. R. BEARDSLEY, *Sec. & Tr.*
*Directors.*—W. R. Taylor, John W. Brock, W. W. Gibbs, Charlemagne Tower, Jr., Philadelphia, Pa.; A. A. McLeod, H. O. Seixas, James Armstrong, New York; J. H. Appleton, Springfield, Mass.; C. E. Gross, Hartford; J. O. Phelps, Simsbury; Henry Gay, West Winsted; D. L. Freeman, Canaan; E. W. Spurr, Falls Village. Annual meeting 3d Tuesday in Dec. Office, Church cor. Spruce sts.

### HARTFORD & N. Y. TRANSPORTATION CO.
*See page 554.*

**HARTFORD & WEST HARTFORD HORSE R.R. CO.**
*Incorporated* 1868.     *Capital* $247,000.
DAVID HENNEY, *President.*
W. J. CARROLL, *Secretary and Treasurer.*
T. L. MCCORMICK, *Superintendent.*
*Directors.*—David Henney, W. E. Goodwin, Erastus Gay, H. B. Goodwin, J. B. Henney. Annual meeting in November.

**HARTFORD BEEF COMPANY.**
*Organized Feb.* 1889. *Capital* 10,000. *Huntley av.*
ROBT. A. PERKINS, *Pres't.* | GEO. D. ROBERTS, *Treas.*
W. P. COFFIN, *V. Pres't.* | J. E. CHAPMAN, *Sec'y.*
*Directors.*—Robert A. Perkins, Boston, W. P. Coffin, New York City, James D. Standish, Detroit, Mich.
*See index for adv.*

**HARTFORD BUILDING & LOAN ASSOCIATION.**
*Organized March* 19, 1889. *Incorporated July* 1, 1898.
*Office* 870 *Asylum st.*
R. P. CHAPMAN, *Pres't.* | GEO. STRONACH, *V. Pres't.*
ALBERT S. HOWE, *Sec'y.* | LUTHER C. GLAZIER, *Tr.*
*Directors.*—Thos. S. Birch, F. P. Carter, F. K. Rand, F. D Parker, Francis Coles, Justus P. Lewis, Joseph Buths, Henry M. Jacobs, H. B. Philbrick, W. H. Scoville, August Schmelzer. *Auditors.*—Edward R. Faxon, Carnot O. Spencer, R. S. Peck.
*See page 424.*

**HARTFORD CHEMICAL COMPANY.**
*Incorporated Jan.* 18, 1888.     285 *State street.*
F. C. ROCKWELL, *Pres't.* | W. W. SAVAGE, *Tr. & Sec.*
*Directors.*—F. C. Rockwell, W. E. Goodwin, W. W. Savage. Annual meeting 8d Tuesday in Jan.

**HARTFORD CARPET COMPANY.**
*Chartered* 1854.   *Capital* $1,500,000.   10 *Market st.*
GEO. ROBERTS, *Pr. & Tr.* | J. B. BUNCE, *V. Pres't.*
GEORGE B. NEWTON, *Secretary.*
*Directors.*—Jonathan B. Bunce, James J. Goodwin, Geo. Roberts, C. M. Beach, James B. Cone, Morgan G. Bulkeley. Annual meeting 4th Wednesday in January. Works at Thompsonville, Conn.

**HARTFORD CITY GAS LIGHT COMPANY.**
*Chartered May,* 1848. *Capital* $750,000. 700 *Main st.*
JAMES L. HOWARD, *President.*
JOHN P. HARBISON, *Treas.* | THOMAS EVANS, *Secretary.*
*Directors.*—Hugh Harbison, Francis B. Cooley, Jas. L. Howard, Henry K. Morgan, George Roberts, John P. Harbison, Atwood Collins, Nathaniel Shipman, Henry A. Redfield. *Auditors.*—James L. Howard, Atwood Collins. Annual meeting 2d Tuesday in Jan.

**HARTFORD COAL COMPANY.**
*Incorp. May* 1, 1888.   *Capital,* $10,000.   754 *Main st.*
C. R. BELDEN, *President and Treasurer.*
JOHN R. HILLS, *Sec'y.* | FRED. S. BELDEN, *A. Sec'y.*
*Directors.*—John R. Hills, Charles R. Belden, Fred'k S. Belden. Annual meeting 1st Monday in May.
*See page 499.*

**HARTFORD DIAMOND POLISH COMPANY.**
*Capital,* $2,500.   118 *Asylum st.*
W. L. B. BARKER, *Pres't and Manager.*

**HARTFORD COURANT COMPANY.**
*Established Jan.* 1764. *Organized Jan.* 1, 1891.   66 *State st.*
CHAS. DUDLEY WARNER, *President.*
CHAS. H. CLARK, *V.Pres't.* | ARTHUR L. GOODRICH, *Tr.*
FRANK S. CAREY, *Sec'y.*
*Directors.* — Joseph R. Hawley, Charles Dudley Warner, Charles Hopkins Clark, Arthur L. Goodrich, Frank S. Carey. Annual meeting in January.
*See page 468.*

**HARTFORD CYCLE COMPANY.**
*Org. Nov.* 1889. *Capital* $200,000. 581 *Capitol av.*
A. A. POPE. *President.* | GEORGE POPE, *Treasurer.*
G. H. DAY, *Vice Pres't.* | ALBERT L. POPE, *Sec'y.*
*Directors.*—A. A. Pope, G. H. Day, E. W. Pope, Harry M. Pope, George Pope. Annual meeting 1st Tuesday in February.         *See page 796.*

**HARTFORD DISPENSARY.**
*Incorporated* 1871.     2 *Talcott, cor. Main st.*
THOMAS SISSON, *Pres't* | JOSEPH E. ROOT, *Sec'y & Tr.*
*Attending Physicians and Surgeons.*—M. M. Johnson, J. E. Root, Janet M. Wier, John Howard, L. Darnstaedt Kean. *Visiting Committee.*—A. R. Hillyer, Charles M. Joslyn, James L. Howard. *Executive Committee.*—M. M. Johnson, E. H. Hyde, Thos. Sisson. Dispensary open daily from 8 to 4 P. M. Annual meeting 2d Tuesday in December.

**HARTFORD DREDGING COMPANY.**
*Incorporated* 1881. *Capital* $40,000. *Office* 721 *Main st.*
Contractors, and owners of dredges No. 2 and No. 8, and tug McDermott.
A. H. CHARLTON, *President.*
G. D. WINSLOW, *Tr. & Sec.* | C. H. LATHAM, *Sup't.*
*Directors.*—G. D. Winslow, E. G. Lasbury, James P. Amerman, A. H. Charlton, E. H. Judd, F. W. Backes, C. H. Latham, Joseph C. Davenport. Annual meeting 2d Wednesday in January.      *See page 554.*

**HARTFORD ELECTRIC LIGHT COMPANY.**
266 *Pearl street.*
*Chartered* 1881. *Organized Mar.* 1883. *Cap'l* $500.000.
A. C. DUNHAM, *President.* | D. N. BARNEY, *Treasurer.*
E. B. BENNETT, *V. Pres't.* | D. P. COLTON, *Secretary.*
R. W. ROLLINS, *Superintendent.*
*Directors.*—A. C. Dunham, William H. Bulkeley, Willie O. Burr, Henry Roberts, Atwood Collins, E. B. Bennett, Rodney Dennis, D. N. Barney, E. K. Root, W. L. Robb, Lucius F. Robinson, W. F. Henney. Annual meeting 2d Tuesday in Feb.

**HARTFORD HOLLOW WARE COMPANY.**
*Org. April* 24, 1888. *Capital,* $10,000. 17 *Florence st.*
JOHN W. COOKE, *Pres't.* | THOS. M. SMITH, *Sec'y & Tr*
J. R. R. MOORE, *General Manager.*
Annual meeting in April.

**HARTFORD HEATING CO.**
*Organized* 1896. *Capital,* $10,000. 267 *Asylum st.*
R. W. FARMER, *Pres't & Tr.* | F. J. JOHNSON, *Sec'y.*
*Directors.*—R. W. Farmer, F. J. Johnson, Burton Hills.

**HARTFORD HOSPITAL, 20 So. Hudson st.**
*See pages 700, 701.*

**HARTFORD ICE COMPANY.**
*Incorp. Dec.* 2, 1868. *Capital,* $50,000. 4 *Central row.*
F. R. FOSTER, *President.*
E. W. SAGE, *Treasurer.* | WM. W. TAINTOR, *Sec'y.*
*Directors.*—Atwood Collins, F. R. Foster, H. Bissell, G. E. Taintor, E. W. Sage. Annual meeting 2d Wednesday in March.

**HARTFORD LIGHT AND POWER COMPANY.**
*Organized Jan.* 1887. *Capital* $250,000. 266 *Pearl st.*
DAVID HENNEY, *President.*
E. G. WHITTLESEY, *V. Pres't.* | W. J. CARROLL, *Sec'y.*
J. B. HENNEY, *General Manager.*
*Directors.*—David Henney, W. F. Henney, E. G. Whittlesey, P. H. Quinn, James B. Henney, W. E. Goodwin, A. H. Pitkin. Annual meeting in January.

**HARTFORD LUMBER COMPANY.**
*Organized Aug. 22, 1889. Capital $30,000. Lumber st.*
THOMAS A. LAKE, *President.*
EVERETT J. LAKE, *Secretary and Treasurer.*
*Directors.*—T. A. Lake, Everett J. Lake, Sadie M.
Lake. Annual meeting 1st Monday in Feb.
*See page 515.*

**HARTFORD MACHINE SCREW CO.**
*Chartered June, 1876. Capital $100,000. 476 Capitol av.*
G. A. FAIRFIELD, *Pr. & Tr.* | J. K. LANMAN, *Ass't Treas.*
DANIEL MORRELL, *Sec'y.* | J. W. MORRELL, *Ass't Sec.*
*Directors.*—George A. Fairfield, Charles M. Beach,
J. K. Lanman, Daniel Morrell, J. W. Morrell, William
Stanton Andrews. Annual meeting, 1st Tuesday in
February.

**HARTFORD MANILLA COMPANY.**
1 So. Ann st. *See page 479.*

**HARTFORD PAPER COMPANY.**
141 Pearl st. *See page 480.*

**HARTFORD PRINTING COMPANY.**
16 State st. *See pages 474. 498.*

**HARTFORD PROVISION CO.**
*Incorporated Nov. 1, 1892. Capital $100,000. Valley st.*
W. W. BARTHOLOMEW, *President and Treasurer.*
W. C. BARTHOLOMEW, *Secretary.*
*Directors.*—W. W. Bartholomew, W. C. Bartholomew,
K. A. Bartholomew. Annual meeting in July.
*See page 586.*

**HARTFORD REAL ESTATE IMPROVEMENT CO.**
*Organized May, 1890. Capital $100,000.*
JAMES L. HOWARD, *Pres't.* | GEO. H. DAY, *Treasurer.*
JOSEPH L. BLANCHARD, *Secretary.*
*Directors.*—James L. Howard, Geo. H. Day, Joseph
L. Blanchard. Annual meeting 2d Thursday in June.

**HARTFORD RUBBER WORKS COMPANY.**
*Established 1881. Incorporated July, 1888.*
*Capital $200,000. Factory Parkville.*
ALBERT A. POPE, *President.*
GEO. H. DAY, *V. Pres't.* | J. D. ANDERSON, *Sec'y.*
LEWIS D. PARKER, *Treasurer and Manager.*
FRANK H. TURNER, *Superintendent.*
*Directors.*—Albert A. Pope, George H. Day, George
Pope, Albert P. Day, Albert R. Pope.
Annual meeting 3d Tuesday in July.
*See Advertisers' Index.*

**HARTFORD STREET RAILWAY COMPANY.**
*Capital $200,000. Office 115 State st.*
E. S. GOODRICH, *Pres't.* | D. R. HOWE, *Sec'y & Treas.*
SAM'L G. DUNHAM, *V.P.* | N. McD.CRAWFORD, *G.Man.*
*Directors.*—James J. Goodwin, E. S. Goodrich, Chas.
L. Lincoln, Daniel R. Howe, Atwood Collins, S. G.
Dunham, Geo. E. Taintor. Annual meeting in Jan.

**HARTFORD STREET SPRINKLING & SUPPLY
COMPANY.**
*Incorporated 1895. 863 Main st.*
FRANK D. PERRY, *President.*
WARD W. JACOBS, *Secretary and Treasurer.*
*Directors.*—Frank D. Perry, Ward W. Jacobs, Mary
C. McKennan, Helen M. Spalding, J. Spalding.

**HARTFORD THEOLOGICAL SEMINARY.**
For particulars and engraving *see pages 708, 709.*

**HARTFORD TELEGRAM COMPANY.**
*Est. Nov. 1, 1888. Capital $60,000. 12 Central row.*
EDWARD R. DOYLE, *Pres't.*
A. M. GROGAN, *Secretary and Treasurer.*
*See page 464.*

**HARTFORD TYPEWRITER COMPANY.**
*Organized 1893. Capital $100,000. 476 Capitol av.*
JOHN M. FAIRFIELD, *Pr.&Tr.* | E. J. FAIRFIELD, *Sec'y.*
*Directors.*—John M. Fairfield, A. C. Dunham, Lucius
A. Barbour, P. C. Royce, Ernest Cady. Annual meet-
ing 1st Wednesday in June.

**HARTFORD WOVEN WIRE MATTRESS CO.**
*Capital $80,000.*
Annual meeting in March. *See page 522.*

**HATCH & NORTH COAL COMPANY.**
*Incorp. April, 1893. Capital $30,000. 801 Main st.*
GEORGE E. HATCH, *Pres't.* | A. W. NORTH, *Treasurer.*
THOMAS M. CASWELL, *Secretary.*
*Directors.*—George E. Hatch, A. W. North, Thomas
M. Caswell. Annual meeting 2d Monday in April.
*See page 491.*

**HEALTH UNDERWEAR COMPANY.**
*Incorp. June 21, 1887. Capital $30,000. 66 State st.*
A. C. DUNHAM, *President.* | HENRY OSBORN, *Sec. & Tr.*
*Directors.*—A. C. Dunham, S. G. Dunham, Henry Os-
born. Annual meeting in Jan. Mills in Poquonock.

**HEUBLEIN HOTEL CO.**
*Org. 1891. Capital $150,000. Wells and Gold sts.*
G. F. HEUBLEIN, *Pres't.* | F. M. PECK, *Sec'y & Treas.*
*Directors.*—Gilbert F. Heublein, Andrew Heublein,
Frederick M. Peck. Annual meeting in March.

**HITCHCOCK & CURTISS KNITTING CO.**
*Organized Oct. 1886. Capital $18,000. 1189 Broad st.*
M. HITCHCOCK, *President.* | E.P.CURTISS, *Sec.& Treas.*
*Directors.*—M. Hitchcock, Everett P. Curtiss, Henry
L. Bunce. Annual meeting in Feb.

**HORNE VACUUM COMPANY.**
*Incorp. Nov. 26, 1887. Capital $100,000. 55 Trumbull st.*
WILLIAM L. MATSON, *President.*
*Directors.*—Norman Day, William L. Matson, O. B.
Arnold, Robert Bowman. Annual election 2d Tuesday
in January.

**JAMES L. HOWARD & CO.**
*440 Asylum st.*
*Established 1841. Chor. June, 1876. Capital $200,000.*
JAMES L. HOWARD, *Pres.* | CHAS. E. HOWARD, *Sec'y.*
GEO. E. HOWARD, *V. Pres.* | FRANK L.HOWARD, *Treas.*
*Directors.*—James L. Howard, George E. Howard,
Frank L. Howard, Charles P. Howard.
Annual meeting in February. *See page 527.*

**INSURANCE JOURNAL COMPANY.**
*Incorp. Feb. 1896. Capital $2,500. 53 Trumbull st*
F. M. Earl, *Sec'y and Treas.* Annual meeting in
February.

**JACOBS, AVERY & NORTHAM CO.**
*Organized Jan. 1898. Capital $25,000. 575 Main st.*
H. M. JACOBS, *Pres't.* | FRED'K H. AVERY, *Treas.*
HENRY W. BURRILL, *V.P.* | ROB'T C. NORTHAM, *Sec'y.*
*Directors.*—H. M. Jacobs, H. W. Burrill, Frederick
H. Avery, S. E. Jennings. Annual meeting in Feb.

**JEWELL PIN COMPANY.**
81 Hicks st. *See page 524.*

**JEWELL BELTING COMPANY, 15 Trumbull street.**
In 1848 Pliny Jewell, a practical tanner, established what is now this company and began the manufacture of leather belting. He was the third person
in the United States in this business. The belts produced are acknowledged the best, are largely exported
to Europe and other foreign countries. Now, belts su-
persede gearing for driving heavy machinery. The
factory as shown in the advertisement is five stories
44x185 feet with a three story addition. Employing
100 hands, pays monthly wages of $5000. *See page 530.*

## JOHNS-PRATT COMPANY.
*Org.* 1886.  *Capital* $150,000.  *Office* 555 *Capitol av.*
EDWARD B. HATCH, *President.*
CHAS. H. PATRICK, *V.Pres't.* | R. N. PRATT, *Treasurer.*
H. H. LUSCOMB, *Secretary and Manager.*
*Directors.*—Chas. H. Patrick, Rufus N. Pratt, E. B.
Hatch, Daniel Morrell, H. H. Luscomb, C. W. Trainer,
H. W. Johns, Jr.  Annual meeting 1st Tuesday in Feb.
*See page 540.*

## KELLOGG & BULKELEY CO.
*Organized Jan.* 31, 1871.  *Capital* $33,175.  175 *Pearl st.*
WM. H. BULKELEY, *Pr.* | WALLACE T. FENN, *S.&Tr.*
*Directors.*—W. H. Bulkeley, J. R. Hills, Charles C.
Cook, M. G. Bulkeley, W. T. Fenn.  Annual meeting
1st Wednesday in February.

## E. S. KIBBE COMPANY.
*Estab.* 1878.  *Incor. April,* 1893.  *Capital* $100,000.
149 *to* 155 *State st.*
E. C. QUIGGLE, *President.*
A. M. WILSON, *V. Pr. & Tr.* | R. D. BALDWIN, *Sec'y.*
*Directors.*—E. C. Quiggle, R. D. Baldwin, A. M. Wil-
son, W. K. Butler, F. E. Beach.  Annual meeting 1st
Saturday after 3d Monday in May.  *See page 587.*

## LEAGUE CYCLE COMPANY.
*Organized, Nov.* 1, 1892.  *Capital* $100,000.
ANDREW F. GATES, *Receiver,* 11 *Central row.*

## LINCOLN COMPANY.
*Estab.* 1834.  *Incorp.* 1898.  *Capital* $125,000.
54 *Arch st.*
CHARLES L. LINCOLN, *President.*
THEODORE M. LINCOLN, *Secretary and Treasurer.*
*Directors.*—Charles L. Lincoln, Theodore M. Lin-
coln, Charles P. Lincoln.  *See page 522.*

## LOVELL & TRACY OIL CO.
*Incor. Nov.* 22, 1897.  *Capital* $2,500.  218 *State st.*
JOHN F. TRACY, *Pres't.* | S. G. TRACY, *Secretary.*
H. N. ROBINSON, *Treasurer.*

## MELLEN & HEWES CO.
*Incorp. April* 13, 1896.  *Capital* $40,000.  725 *Main st.*
MOSES MELLEN, *President.*
FRANK G. MELLEN, *Treas.* | DWIGHT N. HEWES, *Sec'y.*
*Directors.*—Moses Mellen, Dwight N. Hewes, Levi
Drake.  Annual meeting 3d Tuesday in March.

## MERCHANTS' NATIONAL TRADING ASSOC'N.
*Organized* 1898.  66 *State st.*
WM. E. ALVORD, *Pres't.* | WM. H. WEBSTER, *V. Pr.*
DANIEL WEBSTER, *Secretary and Treasurer.*
*Directors.*—Geo. G. Sill, Alfred R. Goodrich, Wm.
H. Webster, Daniel Webster, Joel W. Martin, Wm. E.
Alvord, Howard K. Wood.

## MORTGAGE INVESTMENT CO. OF CONN.
*Office,* 265 *Main street, Hartford, Conn.*
CHAS. T. WELLES, *Pres't.* | EDW'D D. ROBBINS, *Treas.*
*Directors.*—S. W. Robbins, Thomas Sisson, Chas. T.
Welles, E. D. Robbins, Theo. Lyman, Geo. A. Kellogg.

## MT. ST. JOSEPH'S CONVENT CORPORATION OF HARTFORD.
*Organized Nov.* 6, 1876.  *Office* 150 *Farmington av.*
Rev. Mother M. FABIAN, *President.*
Mother M. CYRIL, *V. Pres.* | Mother M. AGNES, *Treas.*
Election, August, 1897, and tri-ennially thereafter.

## NATIONAL MACHINE CO.
111-133 *Sheldon street.*
*Established* 1887.  *Organized* 1891.  *Capital* $100,000.
CHAS. E. BILLINGS, *Pres't.* | S. M. BRONSON, *Sec. & Tr.*
SILAS CHAPMAN, JR., *V. Pr* | WM. F. LOOMIS, *Asst. Sec.*
*Directors.*—Chas. E. Billings, S. M. Bronson, Ernest
Cady, Silas Chapman, Jr., F. R. Cooley, Ralph Crit-
tenden, Lester L. Ensworth.  Annual meeting in Feb.
*See page 540.*

## NATIONAL TROTTING ASSOCIATION.
*Organized* 1870.  *Chartered* 1884.  650 *Main st.*
P. P. JOHNSTON, Lexington, Ky., *President.*
DAVID BONNER, New York, 1st *Vice President.*
N. T. SMITH, San Francisco, Cal., 2d *V. Pres't.*
LEWIS J. POWERS, Springfield, Mass., *Treas.*
W. H. GOCHER, Hartford, *Secretary.*
Officers elected biennially (even years) 2d Wed. Feb.

## NEAL, GOFF & INGLIS COMPANY.
*Incorp. Nov.* 1893.  *Capital* $50,000.  980 *Main st.*
WILLIAM SLOANE INGLIS, *President.*
EDW. F. GOFF, *V. Pr. & Sec.* | C. R. NEAL, *Treasurer.*
*Directors.*—W. Sloane Inglis, E. F. Goff, C. R. Neal.
Annual meeting in January.  *See page 498.*

## NEW ENGLAND COAL COMPANY.
*Organized July* 7, 1888.  *Capital authorised* $50,000.
*Capital paid in* $25,000.
*Offices* 722 *Main and* 276 *Market sts.*
JOSEPH F. SWORDS, *P. & Tr.* | EDWIN A. JONES, *Sec'y.*
*Directors.*—J. F. Swords, Edwin A. Jones, Frank
W. Shackley.  Annual meeting 2d Tuesday in April.

## NEW ENGLAND GRANITE WORKS.
*Established* 1845.  *Chartered May* 1, 1875.
*Capital* $250,000.  1260 *Main st.*
JAMES G. BATTERSON, *President and Treasurer.*
J. G. BATTERSON, Jr., *Vice President.*
W. V. WIGHTMAN, *Sec'y.* | CARL CONRADS, *Sculptor.*
JAMES GOURLAY, *General Manager,* Westerly, R. I.
Annual meeting 2d Wednesday in May.
*See page 533.*

## NEW YORK & NEW ENGLAND RAILROAD CO.
*Capital* $25,000,000.
*Hartford Office and Station, Union Depot,* 478 *Asylum st.*
C. P. CLARK, *Pres't.* | GEO. B. PHIPPEN, *Treas.*
E. D. ROBBINS, *V. Pres't.* | W. H. DUDLEY, *Auditor.*
J. W. PERKINS, *Secretary.* | F. E. DEWEY, *Gen. Sup't.*
C. PETER CLARK, *G. Mgr.* | J. W. WILLIAMS, *G. F. A.*
T. H. FENNELL, *Sup't West Division, East Hartford.*
*Directors.*—Francis L. Higginson, N. W. Rice, Charles
L. Lovering, Boston; Jesse Metcalf, Gorham P. Pom-
roy, Providence; Frederick J. Kingsbury, D. S. Plume,
Waterbury; Charles P. Clark, New Haven; Robert
Bacon, New York; J W. Doane, Chicago; E. D. Rob-
bins, Hartford, Ct.  Annual meeting in October.

## NEW YORK, NEW HAVEN AND HARTFORD RAILROAD COMPANY, 450 *Asylum st.*
*General Office in Railroad Building, New Haven.*
*Authorized Capital,* $100,000,000.  *Issued,* $37,942,000.
CHARLES P. CLARK, *President.*
JOHN M. HALL, *Vice President.*
W. L. SQUIRE, *Treasurer.* | W. D. BISHOP, Jr., *Sec'y.*
H. M KOCHERSPERGER, *Comptroller.*
C. H. PLATT, *General Superintendent.*
O. M. SHEPARD, Sup't N. Y. Div. New York.
C. S. DAVIDSON, Sup't Hartford Division, Hartford.
W. A. WATERBURY, Sup't New London Div. N. Haven.
F. C. PAYNE, Sup't Air Line Division, New Haven.
GEO W. BEACH, Sup't Naugatuck Div. Waterbury.
J. V. A. TRUMBULL, Sup't Valley Div. Hartford.
R. G. CURTIS, Sup't Northampton Division, N. Haven.
J. B. GARDINER, Sup't Providence Division.
F. G. SPENCER, Sup't Worcester Division.
*Directors.*—George MacCulloch Miller, New York ;
Arthur D. Osborne, New Haven ; William D. Bishop,
Bridgeport ; I. De Ver Warner, Bridgeport ; H. C. Rob-
inson, Hartford; Charles P. Clark, New Haven; Joseph
Park, New York; Chauncey M. Depew, New York;
Henry S. Lee, Springfield; Wm. Rockefeller, New York;
Leverett Brainard, Hartford; J. Pierpont Morgan, New
York; George J. Brush, New Haven; John M. Hall,
New Haven ; Charles F. Choate, Boston; Nathaniel
Thayer, Boston ; Royal C. Taft, Providence; Charles
F. Brooker, Torrington; Carlos French, Seymour.
Annual meeting in Oct.

OLD PEOPLE'S HOME.—*See pages* **702, 703.**

## OVERMAN WHEEL COMPANY.
*Incorp.* Feb. 1, 1882.    *Capital* $250,000.    847 *Main st.*
A. H. OVERMAN, *President.*
LUTHER WHITE, *V. Pres't.* | H. R. MILLS, *Secretary.*
*Directors.*—A. H. Overman, Rodney Dennis, Luther White, Geo. D. Seymour, Rudolph R. Reeder. Annual meeting 4th Saturday in Nov.

## PALACE AMUSEMENT CO.
*Incorporated March* 15, 1898.    *Capital* $20,000.
*Office* 983 *Main st.*
P. McGOVERN, *President.*
P. H. QUINN, *Treas.* | E. M. GRAVES, *Sec'y.*
*Directors.*—P. McGovern, P. H. Quinn, E. M. Graves, John C. Long, John A. Crilly, N. McD. Crawford, George Ulrich. Annual meeting 2d Wednesday in March.

## PERKINS ELECTRIC SWITCH M'F'G CO.
*Org.* Sept. 1890. *Capital* $125,000. 83 *Woodbine st.*
C. G. PERKINS, *Pres't.* | EDW. W. HOOKER, *S. & Tr.*
*Directors.*—C. G. Perkins, P. H. Woodward, J. M. Allen, E. C. Frisbie, R. A. Griffin, Charles B. Whiting, Edward W. Hooker. Annual meeting 2d Wednesday in Feb.          *See page* **586.**

## PHENIX BRASS FOUNDRY COMPANY.
*Organized* 1885.    *Capital* $18,000.    *Office,* 223 *State st.*
JOHN S. HUNTER, *Pres't.* | JAMES TERRY, *Treasurer.*
*Directors.*—John S. Hunter, Edward C. Terry, James Terry. Annual meeting in January.

## PHŒNIX IRON WORKS—THE LINCOLN CO.
54 *to* 70 *Arch street.*
These works were established in 1834 by Mr. Levi Lincoln. The firm is extensively known throughout the United States for their very fine and artistic architectural designs in building iron work of every description, such as fronts, columns, girders, lintels, etc., vault and jail doors, illuminated tiling, vases, fences, and in fact everything that can be cast from iron. They also manufacture machinists' tools, lathes, planers, milling machines, shafting, pulleys, hangers, etc., etc.
*See page* **522.**

## PLIMPTON MANUFACTURING COMPANY.
*Incorp.* Dec. 1872.    *Capital* $300,000.    254 *Pearl st.*
LINUS B. PLIMPTON, *President.*
MARO S. CHAPMAN, *Vice President.*
FREDERICK PLIMPTON, *Treasurer.*
JAMES M. PLIMPTON, *Secretary.*
*Directors*—Linus B. Plimpton, Maro S. Chapman, Daniel Morrell, R. O. Cheney, Frederick Plimpton, Horace J. Wickham, James M. Plimpton. Annual meeting last Tuesday in Jan.

## POPE MANUFACTURING COMPANY.
*Incorporated under the Laws of Maine.*
*Capital* $2,000,000.          436 *Capitol av.*
ALBERT A. POPE, *President.*
GEO. H. DAY, *V. President.* | ALBERT L. POPE, *Sec'y.*
GEORGE POPE, *Treasurer.*
*Directors.*—Albert A. Pope, Geo. H. Day, Edward W. Pope, George Pope, Albert L. Pope. Albert P. Day, *Superintendent.* Annual meeting 2d Wednesday in June.          *See page* **796.**

## POTTER BELT HOOK COMPANY.
*Incorp.* Oct. 1, 1891.    *Capital,* $27,000.    884 *Main st.*
JOHN A. DECKER, *President and Secretary.*
JOHN B. HOLADAY, *Treasurer.*
*Directors.*—John A. Decker, H. B. Millard, John B. Holaday.

## WILLIAM H. POST CARPET COMPANY.
*Established* 1850.  *Incorporated* 1894.  219 *Asylum st.*
WILLIAM H. POST, *Pres't.* | ARCHIE L. WHITING, *Tr.*
WILLIAM STRONG POST, *Vice President and Secretary.*
*Directors.*—Wm. H. Post, Wm. Strong Post, Archie L. Whiting. Annual meeting in Jan.

## PRATT & CADY COMPANY.
*Organized* 1878.  *Incorporated* 1882.  *Capital* $400,000.
556 *Capitol av.*
JOHN S. CAMP, *Vice Pres't and Treas.*
F. F. STREET, *Sec'y.*
Annual meeting, last Tuesday in January.
*See page* **527.**

## PRATT & WHITNEY COMPANY,
1 *Flower street.*
*Established* 1860.          *Incorporated July* 8, 1869.
*Re-organized* 1898 *with Capital of* $3,000,000.
AMOS WHITNEY, *President.*
ROWLAND SWIFT, 1st *Vice President.*
GEO. W. M. REED, 2d *Vice President.*
CHARLES C. TYLER, *Superintendent.*
FRANCIS A. PRATT, *Consulting Engineer.*
R. F. BLODGETT, *Sec'y.* | J. C. STIRLING, *Treas.*
*Directors.*—F. A. Pratt, A. Whitney, R. F. Blodgett, H. C. Robinson, R. Swift, Daniel R. Howe, W. W. Hyde, J. R. Redfield, George W. M. Reed, F. C. Sumner, Hartford; C. C. Cuyler, A. C. Vaughn, Horace J. Morse, Robert S. Walker, New York. Annual meeting in March.          *See page* **523.**

## L. E. RHODES COMPANY.
28 *High street*          *See page* **548.**

## RIPLEY BRO'S COMPANY.
*Incor.* 1890.    *Capital* $60,000.    84 *Pratt st.*
L. W. RIPLEY, *Pres't.* | WM. H. STEVENS, *V. Pres't.*
J. F. RIPLEY, *Sec'y and Treas.*
*Directors.*—L. W. Ripley, Wm. H. Stevens, J. F. Ripley, G. W. Ripley. Annual meeting in January.

## SANFORD COMPANY.
*Incorporated April,* 1896.          438 *Asylum st.*
CHAS. E. NEWTON, *Pres't* | WALTER SANFORD, *S. & Tr.*
*Directors.*—Charles E. Newton, Walter Sanford, Charles L. Tolles, Edward J. Pearson. Annual meeting 1st Tuesday in February.

## ROGERS CUTLERY COMPANY.
*Incorp.* Sept. 1, 1871.    *Capital* $25,000.    66 *Market st.*
WM. H. WATROUS, *President and Treasurer.*
GEORGE W. WATROUS, *Secretary.*
*Directors.*—Wm. H. Watrous, George W. Watrous, George Rockwell, Geo. H. Wilcox. Annual meeting 4th Tuesday in January          *See page* **471.**

## WILLIAM ROGERS MANUFACTURING CO.
*Established* 1865.    *Incorporated* 1872.
*Capital* $25,000.          66–72 *Market st.*
WILLIAM H. WATROUS, *President and Treasurer.*
GEORGE W. WATROUS, *Secretary.*
*Directors.*—William H. Watrous, George Rockwell, George H. Wilcox, Geo. W. Watrous. Annual meeting fourth Tuesday in January. *See outside back cover.*

## J. N. SHEDD CO.
*Incorporated April* 1, 1896.          109 *Asylum st.*
J. N. SHEDD, *Pr. & Tr.* | E. S. COOK, *Sec'y & & Tr.*
*Directors.*—J. N. Shedd, E. S. Cook, O. H. Blanchard. Annual meeting in January.

## SIGOURNEY TOOL COMPANY,
9 *Sigourney street.*          *See page* **537.**

## SMITH, NORTHAM & CO.
*Office,* 129 *State street; Mills* 165 *Windsor street.*
*See page 590.*

## SMYTH MANUFACTURING COMPANY.
*Organized Dec.* 8, 1879.     *Chartered April* 17, 1883.
*Capital* $300,000.     *Office* 648 *Main st.*
C. C. KIMBALL, *President.* | GEO. C. KIMBALL, *S. & Tr,*
     ROBERT H. SCHUTZ, *Ass't Sec'y.*
*Directors.*—D. M. Smyth, C. C. Kimball, Chas. H.
Smith, Chas. E. Gross, H. W. Conklin, Wm. C. Skinner, Atwood Collins. Annual meeting 1st Monday in
December.            *See page 528.*

## SOUTHERN NEW ENGLAND PAVING CO.
*Incorporated May* 16, 1895.     *Capital* $100,000.
            141 *Trumbull st.*
WILLIAM P. ENO, *Pres't.* | CHAS. C. COOK, *V. Pres't.*
    GEO. W. S. WHITNEY, *Sec'y and Treas.*
*Directors.*—William P. Eno, Wm. H. Bulkeley, Geo.
H. Day, John H. Hall, Charles C. Cook, G. W. S.
Whitney.

## SPENCER MOTOR COMPANY,
*Reorg. Feb.* 10, 1897. *Capital* $2,500. *Office,* 216 *State.*
         S. P. TURNER, *Pres't.*
E. S. KIBBE, *V. Pres't.* | WM. E. GATES, *Sec. & Tr.*
*Directors.*—S. P. Turner, E. S. Kibbe, W. E. Gates,
E. H. Betts, Ira H. Spencer. Annual meeting 2d
Wednesday in Feb.

## SPRING BROOK ICE COMPANY.
*Incorp. Jan.* 16, 1880. *Capital* $30,000. 4 *Central row.*
      LEWIS SPERRY, *President.*
  G. D. WINSLOW, *Treas.* | ALEX. ALLEN, *Sec'y.*
*Directors.*—Lewis Sperry, G. D. Winslow, Alex.
Allen, Wm. P. Bunnell.

## STERLING WASHING COMPOUND CO.
*Incorporated Sept.* 1895.      284 *Asylum st.*
CYRUS S. BESTOR, *P. & Tr.* |   C. E. ARNOLD, *Sec'y.*
*Directors.*—Charles P. Barto, C. S. Bestor, Charles
E. Arnold, J. M. Birmingham, Clinton Smith, Charles
D. Rice. Annual meeting Sept. 5.

## SYRACUSE COAL AND SALT CO.
*Incorp. Aug.* 1854. *Capital* $500,000. 683 *Main st.*
R. O. CHENEY, *President.* | P. W. ROBBINS, *Sec. & Tr.*
      L. H. BRIDGEMAN, *Gen. Manager.*
*Directors.*—Richard O. Cheney, John Blair, F. A.
Robbins, C. G. Munyan, Jonathan F. Morris, C. W.
Everest, Geo. C. Gilbert, W. W. Jacobs, L. H. Bridgeman, A. R. Hillyer, George H. Parker. Annual meeting 2d Thursday in February.

## TRINITY COLLEGE, *Chartered* 1823.
Rev. GEO. WILLIAMSON SMITH, D. D., LL. D., *Pres't.*
CHAS. E. GRAVES, *Treas.; office* 39 *Pearl street.*
  The former site was west of Trinity street and north
of Capitol avenue, now that part of Bushnell Park
known as the Capitol grounds. Three brown stone
buildings stood on the crest of the hill, facing the east.
The first class graduated was in 1827. In 1878 the
college was removed to its new site on Summit street,
where the buildings stand on west part of a campus
of seventy-eight acres. The library contains about
38,000 volumes. There is a large cabinet, a fine science
building, an astronomical observatory, and a gymnasium with public hall. The annual commencement
is held on the last Thursday in June.
*For full particulars see pages 706, 707.*

## TUCKER STOP MOTION CO.
         124 *Collins st.*
*Chartered April* 12, 1881.     *Capital,* $50,000.
F. P. CARTER, *Pres't & Tr.* | H. R. MILLS, *Secretary.*
*Directors.*—John Johnston, Hiram Carter, Curtis
Hakes, H. R. Mills, F. P. Carter. Annual meeting in
September.

## TUNXIS WORSTED COMPANY.
*Incorporated* 1880. *Capital* $162,000. *Office* 66 *State st.*
S. G. DUNHAM, *Pres't.* | A. C. DUNHAM, *Treas.*
HENRY OSBORN, *Sec'y.* | Mills at Poquonock.
*Directors.*—A. C. Dunham, S. G. Dunham, E. Dunham,
H. Osborn. Annual meeting 4th Wednesday in Jan.

## UNION GROVE COMPANY.
*Char. May* 28, 1883. *Capital* $6,000. *Wethersfield av.*
C. J. HELFRICHT, *Pres't.* | JOSEPH HIRTH, *Tr. & Ag't.*
PHILIP CONRAD, *V.Pres't.* | C. A. HELFRICHT, *S. & Sup't*
*Directors.*—Chas. J. Helfricht, Joseph Hirth, Philip
Conrad, Cuno A. Helfricht. Annual meeting 2d Tuesday in February.

## WARNER & WILLARD COMPANY.
*Incorp. Feb.* 19, 1894. *Capital* $48,400. 108 *Asylum st.*
WILLIAM BAILEY, *Sec'y.* | FRED. W. WARNER, *Treas.*
*Directors.*—Frederick W. Warner, John C. Warner,
William Bailey. Annual meeting 1st Monday in Jan.

## WAR PHOTOGRAPH AND EXHIBITION CO.
*Incorp. Dec.* 27, 1890. *Capital* $1,125. 187 *Kenyon st.*
W. H. POND, *President.* | J. C. TAYLOR, *Sec'y & Treas.*
*Directors.*—W. H. Pond, J. C. Taylor, M. S. Taylor.
Annual meeting last Monday in December.

## WAY HARDWARE COMPANY.
*Incorporated Feb.* 1, 1894. *Capital* $50,000. 366 *Main.*
SAMUEL L. WAY, *President.*
CHARLES L. WAY, *Treas.* | ISAAC BRAGAW, *Manager.*
*Directors.*—Samuel L. Way, Charles L. Way, Isaac
Bragaw. Election 1st Wednesday in February.

## WESTERN AUTOMATIC MACHINE SCREW
## COMPANY OF HARTFORD, CONN.
*Incorporated,* 1882. *Capital* $300,000. 476 *Capitol av.*
GEO. A. FAIRFIELD, *Pres't* | S. H. CURTISS, *Sec. & Tr.*
CHAS. M. BEACH, *V. Pr.* | M. H. LEVAGOOD, *C.Sec'y.*
*Directors.*—Geo. A. Fairfield, Daniel Morrell, James
U. Taintor, Leverett Brainard, Charles E. Gross, Chas.
M. Beach, Geo. H. Day, T. Belknap Beach, Joseph K.
Lanman. Works located at Elyria, Ohio. Annual
meeting 2d Thursday in August.

## THE WILLIAMS & CARLETON CO.
*Incorp. Nov.* 1893. *Capital,* $100,000. 206 *State st.*
CHAS. S. WILLIAMS, *Pres't.* | D. CARLETON, *Sec. & Tr.*
      S. P. WILLIAMS, *Ass't Treas.*
*Directors*—Chas. S. Williams, D. Carleton, M. Carleton, S. P. Williams. Annual meeting in February.

## WILLIMANTIC LINEN COMPANY.
*Office* 389 *Allyn st., Hartford. Mills, Willimantic, Conn.*
    LUCIUS A. BARBOUR, *Pres't and Treas.*
A. C. DUNHAM, *V. Pres't.* | E. H. CLARK, *Secretary.*
*Directors.*—Morgan G. Bulkeley, A. C. Dunham,
Nathaniel Shipman, Francis B. Cooley, Lucius A.
Barbour, Atwood Collins, Theodore M. Ives, of New
York, Frank W. Cheney, of South Manchester, Leverett Brainard. *For engraving of No.* 4 *mill and*
*other particulars see page 544.*

## OPEN HEARTH MISSION, 135 FRONT ST.
By the Open Hearth Association. Founded in 1888.
Incorporated 1891. Gospel services every evening.
Christian work among children and adults. Lodging
house; lunch room; reading room; wood yard; sand
yard; and childrens' outing parties.
*Trustees*—Jas. J. Goodwin, Jacob L. Greene, John
M. Taylor, O. D. Alton, John F. Tracy, E. DeF. Meil,
B. N. B. Miller, Sup't; George R. Bodge, Treas.

# Geer's Connecticut Geographical Directory:

### CITIES, TOWNS, BOROUGHS, POST OFFICES, SCHOOL DISTRICTS, VILLAGES, HAMLETS, PRECINCTS; RAILROAD, EXPRESS, TELEGRAPH AND TELEPHONE STATIONS; MOUNTAINS, ISLANDS, LAKES AND PONDS;

### IN STATE OF CONNECTICUT, WITH THE TOWNS AND COUNTIES WHERE LOCATED.

Compiled for GEER'S HARTFORD CITY DIRECTORY, and Copyrighted in 1897, by The Hartford Printing Co.

H for Hartford County; NH New Haven; NL New London; F Fairfield; T Tolland; L Litchfield; M Middlesex; W Windham County.

Cities, 18; Towns, 168; Boroughs, 22; School Districts, 1447; Villages, Hamlets, 1867; Post Offices, 482; Railroad Express Stations, 410; Telegraph, 822; Telephone, 958; Mountains, 50; Islands, 90; Lakes, 59; Ponds, 282. In the Towns marked !! the School Districts make returns as Towns or by numbers, etc.

| Stations, Villages, etc. | Town. | County. |
|---|---|---|
| Abington*§?†!.. | Pomfret. | W |
| Abington 4 cor's?! | Pomfret | W |
| Aboveall | Sherman | F |
| Abrigador! | Waterbury | NH |
| Ackley!. | East Haddam | M |
| Adams! | Easton | F |
| Addison?!† | Glastonbury | H |
| Aftondale§ | North Haven | NH |
| Allen! | Canterbury | W |
| Allenhill! | Brooklyn | W |
| Allentown! | Plymouth | L |
| Allingtown§!† | Orange | NH |
| Allynapoint* | Ledyard | NL |
| Almyville! | Plainfield | W |
| Amenia?! | Sharon | L |
| American! | Sterling | W |
| Amesville?! | Salisbury | L |
| Amity | Woodbridge | NH |
| Andover*§†‖!! | Andover | T |
| Andovercenter | Andover | T |
| Ansonia*§?†‡‖! | Ansonia | NH |
| Appequag! | Hampton | W |
| Arlington 4 cor's. | Pomfret | W |
| Armsmear?.7th Ward, Hartford | | H |
| Arnolds*§ | Haddam | M |
| Arnoldtown! | Woodstock | M |
| Arrowanna | Middletown | M |
| Arsenal?! | Hartford | H |
| Ashford§?†‖!! | Ashford | H |
| Ashhouse! | N. Stonington | NL |
| Ashwillett | East Lyme | NL |
| Aspetuck†! | Easton | F |
| Asylum! | Salisbury | L |
| Asylumhill?.10th Ward, Hartford | | H |
| Attawaugan?! | Killingly | W |
| Atwoodville?†! | Mansfield | T |
| Augerville?! | Hamden | NH |
| Averyhill! | Ledyard | NL |
| Avon*§?†‖!! | Avon | H |
| Axefactory! | Eastford | W |
| Babcockhill! | Lebanon | NL |
| Backroad! | Windham | W |
| Bagwell! | Lisbon | NL |
| Bailey! | Sterling | W |
| Baileys* | Andover | T |
| Baileys* | Middletown | M |
| Baileyville | Middlefield | M |
| Bakersville†! | New Hartford | L |
| Baldhill! | East Haddam | M |
| Baldhill! | Wilton | F |
| Baldwin! | Canterbury | W |
| Baldwin! | Plymouth | L |
| Baldwins* | Milford | NH |
| Ballahack | East Haddam | M |
| Ballouville?†! | Killingly | W |
| Baltic*†§?! | Sprague | NL |
| Bangall | Meriden | NH |
| Bank! | East Lyme | NL |
| Banks N.! & S.!. | Fairfield | F |
| Banksville! | Greenwich | F |
| Bantam*§?†! | Litchfield | L |
| Bantamfalls | Litchfield | L |
| Banuch! | Canaan | L |
| Bareplain! | No. Branford | NH |
| Barkhamstedt†‖. | Barkhamsted | L |
| Barnes! | Burlington | H |
| Barnes! | Montville | NL |
| Barnum?! | Bridgeport | F |
| Barracks | Caanan | L |
| Bartlett* | Montville | NL |
| Bashan! | East Haddam | M |
| Bashbish | Salisbury | L |
| Bayport*?! | Greenwich | F |
| Beachdale | Voluntown | NL |
| Beachhill! | Colebrook | L |
| Beachstreet! | Litchfield | L |
| Beaconfalls*§?†‖! | Beaconfalls | NH |
| Beanhill? | Norwich | NL |
| Beaverbrook?! | Danbury | F |
| Beaverhill | Windham | W |
| Beaverplain?! | Derby | NH |
| Beavermeadow! | Haddam | M |
| Beckley*†! | Berlin | H |
| Bedlam! | Chaplin | W |
| Beebehill! | Canaan | L |
| Beebehill! | Salisbury | L |
| Beecher! | Bethany | NH |
| Beldenshill! | Wilton | F |
| Bell! | Enfield | H |
| Bell! | Seymour | NH |
| Bell! | Windsor | H |
| Bendofriver! | Lisbon | NL |
| Bennett! | Cornwall | L |
| Bennettbrook! | Enfield | H |
| Bennettsbridge | Southbury | NH |
| Berkshire | Newtown | F |
| Berlin*§?†‖! | Berlin | H |
| Bethany!§?†‖! | Bethany | NH |
| Bethel*§?†‖¶ | Bethel | F |
| Bethel! | Griswold | NL |
| Bethlehem§?†‖!! | Bethlehem | L |
| Betw'ntherivers! | Old Lyme | NL |
| Bicknell! | Ashford | W |
| Bigelow! | Union | T |
| Bigelow N.! & S.!. | Hampton | W |
| Billhill?†! | Lyme | NL |
| Birdsleyplain! | Monroe | F |
| Birmingham*§?! | Derby | NH |
| Bitgood! | Voluntown | NL |
| Blackhall*†! | Old Lyme | NL |
| Blackhill! | Plainfield | W |
| Blackrock§?†! | Bridgeport | F |
| Blackrock! | Durham | M |
| Blackrook! | Killingworth | M |
| Blackstreet! | Lyme | NL |
| Bloomfield*§?†‖. | Bloomfield | H |
| Bluehill | Berlin | H |
| Bluehill | Franklin | NL |
| Bluehill?.4th Ward, Hartford. | | H |
| Bluff | Durham | M |
| Boardman! | Griswold | NL |
| Boardman† | New Milford | L |
| Bokum | Chester | M |
| Bolton*§†‖!! | Bolton | T |
| Bolton Notch! | Tolland | T |
| Boothshill! | Huntington | F |
| Bossichville | Bridgeport | F |
| Boston! | East Lyme | NL |
| Boston! | Redding | F |
| Bostonhollow | Ashford | W |
| Bostonneck*. | Suffield | H |
| Bostonstreet! | Madison | NH |
| Botsford*†§ | Newtown | F |
| Bowershill! | Orange | NH |
| Bowlane! | Middletown | M |
| Bozrah§‖! | Bozrah | NL |
| Bozrahville?†! | Bozrah | NL |
| Bradleyhill! | Tolland | T |
| Bradleyville*! | Middlebury | NH |
| Bradyville | Weston | F |
| Brainard! | Enfield | H |
| Brainerdhill! | Haddam | M |
| Branchville*?†. | Redding | F |
| Branchville§! | Ridgefield | F |
| Brandybrookcanal? | Farmington | H |
| Brandyhill! | Thompson | W |
| Branford*§?†¶ | Branford | NH |
| Branfordpoint? | Branford | NH |
| Breakneck! | Middlebury | NH |
| Brewster! | Griswold | NL |
| Brewstersneck!. | Preston | NL |
| Brickschool! | Bristol | H |
| Brickschoolhouse! | Ledyard | NL |
| Brickschoolhouse! | Lisbon | NL |
| Bricktop! | Windham | W |
| Bridge! | Preston | NL |
| Bridgeport*§?†‖ | Bridgeport | F |
| Bridgewater§?†‖! | Bridgewater | L |
| Briggs! | Voluntown | W |
| Bringay! | Seymour | NH |
| Bristol*§?†¶! | Bristol | H |
| Bristolcenter | Bristol | H |
| Broadbrook*§?†! | East Windsor | H |
| Broadbrook! | Preston | NL |
| Broadriver! | Norwalk | F |
| Broadstreet! | Norwich | NL |
| Broadstreet! | Wethersfield | H |
| Broadway! | Norwich | NL |
| Brockways§?! | Lyme | NL |
| Brookfield*§?†‖!! | Brookfield | F |
| Brookfieldcenter† | Brookfield | F |
| Brookfieldjunc.*? | Brookfield | F |
| Brooklyn§?†‖!! | Brooklyn | NH |
| Brooklyn! | Waterbury | NH |
| Brookmead | Canton | H |
| Brooksidepark* | Redding | F |
| Brooksvale† | Cheshire | NH |
| Brown! | Hartford | H |
| Brown! | Preston | NL |
| Brundage | Greenwich | F |
| Brunswick! | Scotland | W |
| Buckhollow | Portland | M |
| Buckingham§† | Glastonbury | H |
| Buckland*§?† | Manchester | H |
| Buckleys! | Fairfield | F |
| Buckscorners | Glastonbury | H |
| Buckshill! | Waterbury | NH |
| Bucktown | Portland | M |
| Buffcap! | Tolland | T |
| Bugbee! | Woodstock | W |
| Bulkeleyhill! | Colchester | NL |

* Railroad and Express Stations; § Telegraphs; ? Telephones; † Post Offices; ‡ Cities; ‖ Towns; ¶ Boroughs; ! School Districts.

| Stations, Villages, etc. | Town. | County. |
|---|---|---|
| Bullethill! | Southbury | NH |
| Bullsbridge†! | Kent | L |
| Bundyhill! | Lisbon | NL |
| Bungay! | Seymour | NH |
| Bunkerhill! | Waterbury | NH |
| Burlington*†‖!! | Burlington | H |
| Burlingtonstation | Burlington | H |
| Burnap! | Andover | T |
| Burnett! | Groton | NL |
| Burnhams*? | East Hartford | H |
| Burnside*§?†! | East Hartford | H |
| Burr! | Haddam | M |
| Burritt! | New Britain | H |
| Burritt! | Roxbury | L |
| Burrowshill! | Hebron | T |
| Burrs! | Fairfield | F |
| Burrville*§?† | Torrington | L |
| Burton! | Griswold | NL |
| Bushpoint | Groton | NL |
| Bushyhill! | Granby | H |
| Bushyhill! | Simsbury | H |
| Byram! | Greenwich | F |
| Calhounstreet! | Washington | H |
| Calkins! | Sharon | L |
| Campbell! | Voluntown | NL |
| Campbellsmills† | New London | NL |
| Camptown | Derby | NH |
| Campville*† | Harwinton | L |
| Cannan*§?†‖!! | Canaan | L |
| Canaanvalley | Canaan | L |
| Candlewoodhill! | Haddam | M |
| Cannon*§†! | Wilton | F |
| Canoebrook! | Branford | NH |
| Canterbury*†‖ | Canterbury | W |
| Canterburygreen! | Canterbury | W |
| Canton*§†‖ | Canton | H |
| Cantoncentre*† | Canton | H |
| Cantondistrict | Canton | H |
| Capitolcity*§?†‖ | Hartford | H |
| Carmelhill! | Bethlehem | L |
| Casesfarms | Simsbury | H |
| Casestreet! | Granby | H |
| Catswamp! | Woodbury | L |
| Cedarhill?..8th Ward, Hartford | | H |
| Cedarhill | Canaan | L |
| Cedarhill | Haddam | M |
| Cedarhill! | Hamden | NH |
| Cedarhill*§?.. | New Haven | NH |
| Cedarridge! | Seymour | NH |
| Cedarstreet?! | New Haven | NH |
| Cedarswamp | Canterbury | W |
| Cedarswamp! | Tolland | T |
| Center! | Stafford | T |
| Centerbeach! | Branford | NH |
| Centerville?! | New Fairfield | F |
| Central | East Granby | H |
| Centralvillage*?† | Plainfield | W |
| Centre Groton†! | Groton | NL |
| Centre! | Meriden | NH |
| Centre | Wolcott | NH |
| Centrebrook§?†‡ | Essex | NH |
| Centrehill†! | Barkhamsted | L |
| Centreville*?! | Hamden | NH |
| Centreville | Vernon | T |
| Chaffeeville§? | Mansfield | NH |
| Chalybes | Roxbury | L |
| Chandler! | Woodstock | W |
| Chapelhill! | Montville | NL |
| Chapelstreet*?! | New Haven | NH |
| Chapinville*§†! | Salisbury | L |
| Chaplin?†‖ | Chaplin | W |
| Chapmanmeadow | East Haddam | M |
| Chapmanpoint | Old Saybrook | M |
| Charter Oak City*§?† | Hartford | H |
| Char.Oak Park*? | West Hartford | H |
| Chatham*?‖ | Chatham | M |
| Checkerberry! | Sterling | W |
| Cherrybrook* | Canton | H |

| Stations, Villages, etc. | Town. | County. |
|---|---|---|
| Cherrygrove | Wallingford | NH |
| Cherrypark | Canton | H |
| Cheshire*§?†‖!! | Cheshire | NH |
| Cheshirestreet?! | Cheshire | NH |
| Chester*§?†‖ | Chester | M |
| Chester & Hadlyme Ferry* | | M&NL |
| Chesterfi'd†!Mt.Wa'd E L & Sal.NL | | |
| Chestnuthill! | Chatham | M |
| Chestnuthill*! | Colchester | NL |
| Chestnuthill†! | Columbia | T |
| Chestnuthill! | Litchfield | L |
| Chestnuthill?! | Killingly | W |
| Chestnuthill! | Killingworth | M |
| Chestnuthill! | Mansfield | T |
| Chestnuthill! | Trumbull | F |
| Chestnuthill! | Wilton | F |
| Chestnutland! | New Milford | L |
| Chestnuttreehill! | Oxford | NH |
| Chewink* | Hampton | W |
| Chickenhill! | New Milford | L |
| Christiancorner! | Brooklyn | W |
| Christianlane! | Berlin | H |
| Christianstreet! | Oxford | NH |
| Christianstreet! | Washington | L |
| Christianstreet! | Windham | W |
| Church! | Brooklyn | W |
| Churchhill! | Ledyard | NL |
| Churchhill! | Washington | L |
| Ciderbrook! | Avon | H |
| Ciderhill! | Ledyard | NL |
| Citydistrict! | Portland | M |
| Clapboardridge! | Greenwich | F |
| Clapboardhill! | Guilford | NH |
| Clapboardhill! | New Canaan | F |
| Clarkshill! | Chatham | M |
| Clarkscorner† | Windham | W |
| Clarksfalls†! | N. Stonington | NL |
| Claybanks | Wethersfield | H |
| Clayhill,? 3d Ward, Hartford | | H |
| Clayton*? | Newington | H |
| Clayville | Griswold | NL |
| Clinton*§?†‖!! | Clinton | M |
| Clintonville†! | North Haven | NH |
| Coalpithill! | Danbury | F |
| Cobalt*§?† | Chatham | M |
| Cobblehill | Norwalk | F |
| Cohanzie! | Waterford | NL |
| Colchester*§?†‖¶!! | Colchester | NL |
| Coldspring | Newtown | F |
| Colebrook*§?†‖! | Colebrook | L |
| Colebrookrivers?†! | Colebrook | L |
| Coleyville! | Westport | F |
| Collegefarms! | Warren | L |
| Collins! | Montville | NL |
| Collinsville*§?†! | Canton, Avon | H |
| Columbia†‖ | Columbia | T |
| Compo! | Westport | F |
| Compounce | Southington | H |
| Comstock! | Essex | NH |
| Comstocksbri'ge† | Col.&Chat. | NL&M |
| Conantville§? | Mansfield | W |
| Conn.river? | Old Saybrook | M |
| Cookhill.! | Wallingford | NH |
| Cooks* | Plainville | H |
| Cookshill | Windsor | H |
| Cooper* | Ridgefield | F |
| Cooper! | Woodstock | W |
| Copperhill†! | East Granby | H |
| Coreyville! | Lebanon | NL |
| Corner! | Huntington | F |
| Corner! | Meriden | NH |
| Cornfieldpoint | Old Saybrook | M |
| Cornwall§?†‖!! | Cornwall | L |
| Cornwallbridge*§?†! | Cornwall | L |
| Cornwallcentre† | Cornwall | L |
| Cornwallhollow?†! | Cornwall | L |
| Cornwallplain! | Cornwall | L |
| Corwin! | Huntington | F |

| Stations, Villages, etc. | Town. | County. |
|---|---|---|
| Cos Cob†*§?! | Greenwich | F |
| Cottagegrove* | Bloomfield | H |
| Cottonhollow | Glastonbury | H |
| Couchhill! | Redding | F |
| Cove?! | Stamford | F |
| Coventry†‖!! | Coventry | T |
| Coverahill | Killingworth | M |
| Cowhill! | Clinton | M |
| Cowsethill | Portland | M |
| Cranberry† | Norwalk | F |
| Cranberryplains.! | Norwalk | F |
| Crary! | Preston | NL |
| Creamhill! | Cornwall | L |
| Crescent† | East Lyme | NL |
| Crescentbeach*§. | East Lyme | NL |
| Cromwell*§?†!! | Cromwell | M |
| Crookedlane! | Suffield | H |
| Crosshighway! | Westport | F |
| Crownpoint | Groton | NL |
| Crowhill! | Stafford | T |
| Crystal Lake† | Ellington | T |
| Cutlersfarm! | Monroe | F |
| Daleville! | Willington | T |
| Daleyville | Ellington | T |
| Damascus! | Branford | NH |
| Damonhill! | Redding | F |
| Danbury*§?†‡ | Danbury | F |
| Danburyquarter! | Winchester | L |
| Danielsfarm! | Trumbull | F |
| ∴ Danielson*§?†¶! | Killingly | W |
| Dantown! | Stamford | F |
| Darien*§?†‖ | Darien | F |
| Darkhollow! | Salem | NL |
| Dart! | South Windsor | H |
| Davenport! | New Haven | NH |
| Davenportpoint? | Stamford | F |
| Davishollow! | Washington | L |
| Daytonville | Torrington | L |
| Dayville*§?‖! | Killingly | W |
| Deaconpoint! | Stratford | F |
| Deansville | Stamford | F |
| Deepriver*§?†! | Saybrook | M |
| Deerfield! | Fairfield | F |
| Deerhill! | Danbury | F |
| Deming! | Woodstock | W |
| Den! | Weston | F |
| Denisonhill | Voluntown | W |
| Depot! | Litchfield | L |
| Derby*§†?‡‖ | Derby | NH |
| Derbyhill | Derby | NH |
| Derbynarrows! | Derby | NH |
| Derbyneck! | Derby | NH |
| Devilsblowhole | Cromwell | M |
| Devilsden | Weston | F |
| Devilsden | Sterling | W |
| Devilshopyard | East Haddam | M |
| Diamondhill! | Redding | F |
| Dividend? | Rockyhill | H |
| Dixwell?! | New Haven | NH |
| Doaneville | Griswold | NL |
| Dobsonville | Vernon | T |
| Dodgeingtown | Newtown | F |
| Doncaster! | Bloomfield | H |
| Doublebeach? | Branford | NH |
| Downtown! | Lebanon | NL |
| Downtown! | Norwalk | F |
| Downtown! | Woodbury | L |
| Drakeville | Winchester | L |
| Drybrook | South Windsor | H |
| Dublin?! | Colchester | NL |
| Dublin | Farmington | H |
| Dublin | New Hartford | L |
| Dublin! | Waterbury | NH |
| Dunbarhill! | Hamden | NH |
| Duncan† | Haddam | M |
| Duncaster! | Bloomfield | H |
| Durant?! | Middletown | M |
| Durfeehill! | Waterford | NL |

*Railroad and Express Stations; §Telegraphs; †Telephones; †Post Offices; ‡Cities; ‖Towns; ¶Boroughs; !School Districts.

| Stations, Villages, etc. | Town | County |
|---|---|---|
| Durham§?†‖‖ | Durham | M |
| Durhamcenter§?† | Durham | M |
| Dwight! | New Haven | NH |
| Dyerhill! | Brooklyn | W |
| Eaglerock? | Thomaston | L |
| Eagleville• | Lisbon | NL |
| Eagleville•?†! | Mansfield | T |
| East Aspeteck | Washington | L |
| East Berlin•§?†! | Berlin | H |
| E. Bridgeport§?! | Bridgeport | H |
| East Bristol | Bristol | H |
| East Brooklyn?! | Brooklyn | W |
| Eastbury.....? | Glastonbury | H |
| East Canaan•§?† | North Canaan | L |
| Eastchestnuthill! | Litchfield | L |
| East Cornwall†! | Cornwall | L |
| Easterly | Stonington | NL |
| Easternpoint | Groton | NL |
| Eastfarms! | Farmington | H |
| Eastfarms! | Wallingford | NH |
| Eastfarms! | Waterbury | NH |
| Eastford?†‖! | Eastford | M |
| E. Glastonb'ry§?† | Glastonbury | H |
| East Granby†‖!! | East Granby | H |
| Eastgreatplain?! | Norwich | NL |
| East Greenwich | Greenwich | W |
| E. Haddam•§?†‖ | East Haddam | M |
| E. Haddamlanding?!E. | Haddam | M |
| E. Hampton•§?† | Chatham | M |
| E. Hartford•§?†‖ | East Hartford | H |
| E. Hfd. Meadow†.E. | Hartford | H |
| East Hartland† | Hartland | H |
| East Haven•§?†‖! | East Haven | NH |
| Easthill! | Canton | H |
| Easthill! | Eastford | W |
| Eastironworks! | Brookfield | F |
| East Kent†! | Kent | L |
| East Killingly?† | Killingly | W |
| E. Litchfield•§?† | Litch'd,Harw'n. | L |
| East Lyme•§?†‖ | East Lyme | NL |
| East Meriden§? | Meriden | NH |
| East Morris?† | Morris | L |
| Eastneck! | Waterford | NL |
| East Norwalk? | Norwalk | F |
| Easton§†‖!! | Easton | F |
| Eastoncenter! | New Fairfield | F |
| Eastplains | Hamden | NH |
| East Plymouth! | Plymouth | L |
| EastPortchester?! | Greenwich | F |
| East Putnam?! | Putnam | W |
| East River•§?†! | Madison | NH |
| Eastrock? | New Haven | NH |
| East Saugatuck! | Westport | F |
| East Sharon | Sharon | L |
| Eaststreet | Cornwall | L |
| E. Thompson•§†! | Thompson | W |
| Eastvillage | Monroe | F |
| E. Wallingford§† | Wallingford | NH |
| Eastwallop! | Enfield | H |
| East Weatogue! | Simsbury | H |
| East Willington†! | Willington | T |
| East Windsor•‖!! | East Windsor | H |
| E.Windsorhill•§†! | South Windsor | H |
| E. Woodstock?†! | Woodstock | W |
| Eaton?! | New Haven | NH |
| Edgewood | New Haven | NH |
| Edwards?! | New Haven | NH |
| Ekonk†! | Sterling & Vol. | W&NL |
| Ellington•?†‖!! | Ellington | T |
| Elliott•?† | Pomfret | W |
| Elliotville? | Killingly | W |
| Ellithorpe• | Stafford | T |
| Ellsworth†! | Sharon | L |
| Elmcity•§?† | New Haven | NH |
| Elmgrove! | Windsor | H |
| Elmstreet! | Stamford | F |
| Elmstreet! | Monroe | F |
| Elmwood! | Bethel | F |
| Elmwood | Windsor | H |
| Elmwood•?† | West Hartford | H |
| Elyslanding | Lyme | NL |
| Enfield§?†‖!‖ | Enfield | H |
| Enfieldbridge• | Enfield | H |
| Enfieldstreet! | Enfield | H |
| Englishneighborhood | Woodstock | W |
| Equivalent! | Ellington | T |
| Esquire Parker! | Salem | NL |
| Essex•§?†‖! | Essex | M |
| Essexferry | Essex to Lyme | M |
| Exeter N.!S.!E.! | Lebanon | NL |
| Fairfield•§?†‖ | Fairfield | F |
| Fairfieldwoods! | Fairfield | F |
| Fair Ground† | | NL |
| Fairground• | Danbury | F |
| Fairhaven E.•§?†¶! | New Haven | NH |
| Fairhavenhei'ts? | New Haven | NH |
| Fairstreet?! | New Haven | NH |
| Falls! | Middlefield | M |
| Falls?! | Norwich | NL |
| Fallsvillage•§?† | Canaan | L |
| Farmhill! | Middletown | M |
| Farmington•§?†‖ | Farmington | H |
| Farmingville! | Ridgefield | F |
| Farms! | Bloomfield | H |
| Farms! | Meriden | NH |
| Farms! | Stamford | F |
| Farms! | Simsbury | H |
| Faxon! | East Haven | NH |
| Fellsmere | | NH |
| Fenwick•§? | Old Saybrook | M |
| Fernside | East Haddam | M |
| Ferry! | Milford | NH |
| Ferry! | Huntington | F |
| Finchville | Norwalk | F |
| Fisherville | Thompson | W |
| Fitchshouse! | Darien | F |
| Fitchville?†! | Bozrah | NL |
| Fivemilehill! | Oxford | NH |
| Fivemilepoint | East Haven | NH |
| Fivemileriver•?! | Norwalk | F |
| Flanders | Chatham | M |
| Flanders! | East Lyme | NL |
| Flanders! | Groton | NL |
| Flanders! | Kent | L |
| Flanders! | Southington | H |
| Flanders! | Woodbury | L |
| Flatrock! | Plainfield | W |
| Flatrock! | Ridgefield | F |
| Flatswamp! | Newtown | F |
| Flaxhill | Norwalk | F |
| Florida! | Ridgefield | F |
| Fluteville•§! | Litchfield | L |
| Flyingpoint | Branford | NH |
| Foleys• | Salisbury | L |
| Footville | Morris | L |
| Forestcity! | Middletown | M |
| Forestville•§?†! | Bristol | H |
| Forge! | Colebrook | L |
| Forge! | Weston | F |
| Forthale | East Haven | NH |
| Forthill | Groton | NL |
| Forttrumbull | New London | NL |
| Foster! | Union | T |
| Fosterhill | Portland | M |
| Foundry! | Redding | F |
| Fourmileriver! | Old Lyme | NL |
| Foxon! | New Haven | NH |
| Foxtown! | East Haddam | M |
| Foxville! | Stafford | T |
| Franklin•?†‖! | Franklin | NL |
| Franklinhill! | Franklin | NL |
| Fraryville | Meriden | NH |
| French! | Huntington | F |
| Froghollow! | Ellington | T |
| Froghollow?.8th Ward, | Hartford | H |
| Frost! | Canterbury | W |
| Furnacehollow?! | Stafford | T |
| Gage! | Woodstock | W |
| Galesferry§†! | Ledyard | NL |
| Gallup! | Ledyard | NL |
| Gallup! | Voluntown | NL |
| Gardner Lake† | Salem | NL |
| Gary! | Putnam | W |
| Gate! | Bethany | NH |
| Gate! | Chatham | M |
| Gaylordsbridge | New Milford | L |
| Gaylordsville†! | New Milford | L |
| Gaystreet! | Sharon | L |
| Geer! | Ledyard | NL |
| Georgetown•§?†! | Red'g Wilt.W't'n | F |
| Germanville | Stonington | NL |
| Giantaneck | East Lyme | NL |
| Gilbert! | Brooklyn | W |
| Gilbert! | Litchfield | L |
| Gilberttown! | Easton | F |
| Gildersleeve§?†! | Portland | M |
| Gilead† | Hebron | T |
| Gilead! | Waterford | XL |
| Gileadhill | Hebron | L |
| Gladdingsville | Plainfield | W |
| Glasgo?† | Griswold | NL |
| Glassfactory?! | Willington | T |
| Glastonbury†§?‖ | Glastonbury | H |
| Glenbrook•?† | Stamford | F |
| Glengrove | Chatham | M |
| Glenville•§†! | Greenwich | F |
| Glenwood•?.10th Ward, | Hartford | H |
| Goffsbridge | Rockyhill | H |
| Goldenhill?! | Bridgeport | F |
| Goodhill! | Roxbury | L |
| Goodhill! | Weston | F |
| Goodspeeds•§ | Haddam | M |
| Goodspeedsl'g..? | East Haddam | M |
| Goodspeed station•§? | Haddam | M |
| Gooselane! | Tolland | T |
| Goshen?†‖!‖ | Goshen | L |
| Goshen•§! | Hampton | W |
| Goshen•N.!S.!E.!W.! | Lebanon | NL |
| Goshen! | Plainfield | W |
| Goshen! | Waterford | NL |
| Goslee! | Glastonbury | H |
| Grainhill | Portland | M |
| Granby•§†‖!! | Granby | H |
| Grand! | New Haven | NH |
| Granite! | Sterling | W |
| Graniteville | Norwalk | F |
| Granitville?! | Waterford | NL |
| Grantahill! | Tolland | T |
| Grantville•† | Winchester | L |
| Grasshill! | Ashford | W |
| Grasshill N!&S! | Lyme | NL |
| Grassyplain! | Bethel | F |
| Gravelhill! | Hartford | H |
| Graysplain! | Newtown | F |
| Greathill! | Cornwall | L |
| Greathill! | Seymour | NH |
| Greathollow! | New Fairfield | F |
| Greatmeadow! | New Fairfield | F |
| Greatneck | Waterford | NL |
| Greatplain! | Danbury | F |
| Green! | Barkhamsted | L |
| Green! | Glastonbury | H |
| Greene! | Ashford | W |
| Greenfieldhill§?†! | Fairfield | F |
| Greenhollow! | Plainfield | W |
| Greenmanville? | Stonington | NL |
| Greensfarms•†! | Westport | F |
| Greenharbor | New London | NL |
| Greenville•§?†! | Norwich | NL |
| Greenwich•§?†‖¶ | Greenwich | F |
| Greenwoods! | New Hartford | L |
| Gregorysorchard! | Newtown | F |
| Greystone•†! | Plymouth | L |

| Stations, Villages, etc. | Town. | County. |
|---|---|---|
| Griswold§?†|||.. | Griswold | NL |
| Griswoldville!.... | Wethersfield | H |
| Grosvenordale*†?! | Thompson | W |
| Groton*§?†§||!.. | Groton | NL |
| Grotonbank!..... | Groton | NL |
| Grotonheights ... | Groton | NL |
| Grovebeach*†... | Clinton | M |
| Grovelane!...... | Tolland! | T |
| Guilford*§?†|¶.. | Guilford | NH |
| Guilfordpoint?.. | Guilford | NH |
| Gulf........... | Milford | F |
| Gurleyville †!.. | Mansfield | T |
| Gurnseyhill!.... | Litchfield | L |
| Gurnseytown!.... | Waterford | NL |
| Gypseyville .... | Manchester | H |
| Haddam*§?†||.. | Haddam | M |
| Haddamcenter!.. | Haddam | M |
| Haddamneck†!.. | Haddam | M |
| Haddamquarter .. | Durham | M |
| Haddamroad!... | Middletown | M |
| Hadlyme*§?†!!. | Lyme,E.Had.NL. | M |
| Halfwayriver!.. | Newtown | F |
| Hall!......... | Sharon | L |
| Hall!......... | Stafford | T |
| Hallington...... | Litchfield | L |
| Hallmeadow!.... | Goshen | L |
| Hallsville...... | Willington | T |
| Hamburg!...... | Hamden | NH |
| Hamburg§?†!.. | Lyme | NL |
| Hamden*†?†||!.. | Hamden | NH |
| Hamdenplains!.. | Hamden | NH |
| Hamilton!...... | New Haven | NH |
| Hammertown.... | Salisbury | L |
| Hammonasset!.. | Madison | NH |
| Hampsted†...... | | L |
| Hampton*?†||!!. | Hampton | W |
| Hancock*.... | Plymouth | L |
| Handlin!....... | Sharon | L |
| Hanginghills... | Southington | H |
| Hanover!...... | Meriden | NH |
| Hanover!...... | Newtown | F |
| Hanover!...... | South Windsor | H |
| Hanover?†!... | Sprague | NL |
| Harbor!....... | Stonington | NL |
| Harbor!....... | Windsor | H |
| Harborview.... | Stamford | F |
| Hardhill!...... | Bethlehem | L |
| Harrison!...... | Salisbury | L |
| Harrisons*.... | Waterford | NL |
| Harrisplain!... | Litchfield | L |
| Harrisville!.... | Woodstock | W |
| Hartford*§?†§||. | Hartford | H |
| Harthollow!.... | Goshen | L |
| Hartland||†!!... | Hartland | H |
| Hartlandcenter .. | Hartland | H |
| Hartwell!...... | Sharon | L |
| Harwinton§?†§||!. | Harwinton | L |
| Haskell!....... | Preston | NL |
| Hastingshill... | Suffield | H |
| Hattertown..... | Newtown | F |
| Haughton!...... | Montville | NL |
| Hawkshill...... | Mansfield | T |
| Hawleysbridge.. | Bridgewater | L |
| Hawleyville*§?†. | Newtown | F |
| Hawthorne†...... | | F |
| Hayden!....... | Westbrook | M |
| Haydenhill!.... | Fairfield | F |
| Haydens*!..... | Windsor | H |
| Haywardville.... | East Haddam | M |
| Hazardville*§?†!. | Enfield | H |
| Hazelplains!... | Woodbury | L |
| Headofmeadow!.. | Newtown | F |
| Headquarters!.. | Litchfield | L |
| Hebron*§†||!!.. | Hebron | T |
| Hemlockville... | East Haddam | M |
| Hewitt!....... | N.Stonington. | NL |
| Higganum*§?†!E&W. | Haddam | M |
| Highhill......... | E.&S.Windsor. | H |
| Highlandpark,†700 ft. | Manchester | H |
| Highland*§.... | Middletown | M |
| Highlandterrace.. | Seymour | NH |
| Highlandterrace.. | Stafford | T |
| Highridge †!... | Stamford | F |
| Highriver...... | Columbia | T |
| Highrock*§?.. | Beacon Falls | NH |
| Highstreet!.... | Wethersfield | H |
| Hightower?.... | Warren | L |
| Highwood†........... | | NH |
| Hill!........... | East Lyme | NL |
| Hill!........... | Glastonbury | H |
| Hill!........... | Morris | L |
| Hill!........... | Naugatuck | NH |
| Hill!........... | South Windsor | H |
| Hillandplain!.. | New Milford | L |
| Hillsidepark.... | Watertown | L |
| Hillstown!†... | East Hartford | H |
| Hinckleyhill!.. | Stonington | NL |
| Hitchcocks*... | Southington | H |
| Hoadleyneck!.. | Branford | NH |
| Hoadleyville!.. | Plymouth | L |
| Hockanum§?†!.. | East Hartford | H |
| Hockanum?.... | Westport | F |
| Holcomb!...... | Burlington | H |
| Holland........ | Union | T |
| Holland!....... | Fairfield | F |
| Hollow! N & S.. | Barkhamsted | L |
| Hollow!....... | Kent | L |
| Hollow!....... | Willington | T |
| Holmes!....... | Darien | F |
| Hookertown.... | Stonington | NL |
| Hophill......... | Derby | NH |
| Hopbrook*.... | Naugatuck | NH |
| Hopevale†..... | Hebron | T |
| Hopeville!..... | Greenwich | F |
| Hopeville!..... | Griswold | NL |
| Hopeville?!.... | Waterbury | NH |
| Hopewell§..... | Thomaston | L |
| Hopewell!..... | Newtown | F |
| Hopewell†..... | Glastonbury | H |
| Hopmeadow!.. | Simsbury | H |
| Hopriver*§?†!.. | Columbia | T |
| Hopswamp!... | Middlebury | NH |
| Hopyardplain... | Branford | NH |
| Horsehill!...... | Killingly | W |
| Horsehill!...... | Westbrook | M |
| Horseneck..... | Greenwich | F |
| Hoskins*...... | Simsbury | H |
| Hotchkissville§?†! | Woodbury | L |
| Howardvalley †.. | Hampton | W |
| Hoytville...... | Stamford | F |
| Hoydens!...... | Fairfield | F |
| Hubbard!...... | Enfield | H |
| Hubbard!...... | Middletown | M |
| Huckleberryhill!. | Avon | H |
| Huckleberryhills! | Brookfield | F |
| Hull!.......... | Redding | F |
| Hull!.......... | Stafford | T |
| Hullshill!...... | Oxford | NH |
| Hullsbill....... | Southbury | NH |
| Humaston...... | Plymouth | L |
| Humphrey!.... | New Haven | NH |
| Hungary!...... | Granby | H |
| Hunt!......... | New Milford | L |
| Huntingridge!.. | Stamford | F |
| Huntington§?†||. | Huntington | F |
| Huntington!.... | Lebanon | NL |
| Huntingtoncentre§. | Derby | NH |
| Huntingtonstreet. | Harwinton | L |
| Huntingtown!.. | Newtown | F |
| Huntsville?†!... | Cannan | L |
| Hurlbutt†!..... | Wilton | F |
| Hyde!......... | Canterbury | W |
| Hyde!......... | Lisbon | NL |
| Hydeville?!.... | Stafford | T |
| Indianneck?.... | Branford | NH |
| Indiantown...... | N.Stonington. | NL |
| Industrial?!..... | Middletown | M |
| Iranistan?...... | Bridgeport | F |
| Iron Works,E!&W! | Brookfield | F |
| Isinglass!...... | Huntington | F |
| Islandbrook!... | Bridgeport | F |
| Ivesville?!..... | Hamden | NH |
| Ivoryton§?†!... | Essex | M |
| Jabbok!....... | Enfield | H |
| Jamestreet!.... | Bridgeport | F |
| Jerico!........ | Pomfret | W |
| Jerusalem!..... | New Milford | F |
| Jerusalem!..... | Windham | W |
| Jewettcity*§?†!¶ | Griswold | NL |
| Jobshill!....... | Ellington | T |
| Johnsonhollow !.. | Cornwall | L |
| Johnsonlane!... | Middletown | M |
| Johnsonville?.. | East Haddam | M |
| Jordan!....... | Waterford | NL |
| Joshuatown?!.. | Lyme | NL |
| Joyceville ..... | Salisbury | L |
| Judd!......... | Easton | F |
| Juddsbridge*†.. | Roxbury | L |
| Judea......... | Washington | L |
| Judgescave..... | New Haven | NH |
| Kasson!....... | Bethlehem | L |
| Kennedycity.... | Plainfield | W |
| Kenosia....... | Danbury | F |
| Kensington§?†!.. | Berlin | H |
| Kent*§?†||..... | Kent | L |
| Kenthollow !... | Stafford | T |
| Kentonville.... | Woodstock | W |
| Kentfurnace†... | Kent | L |
| Kentorehill.... | Kent | L |
| Kenyonville ... | Woodstock | W |
| Kettlehill....... | East Haddam | M |
| Kettletown!.... | Southbury | NH |
| Kibbe †........ | Somers | T |
| Killingly§..... | Killingly | W |
| Killinglycenter.. | Killingly | W |
| Killingworth*§||. | Killingworth | M |
| Kimball!....... | Ellington | T |
| Kimball!....... | Preston | NL |
| Kingstreet!.... | Danbury | F |
| Kingstreet..... | East Windsor | H |
| Kingstreet!.... | Enfield | H |
| Kingstreet!.... | Greenwich | F |
| Kinney?!...... | Griswold | NL |
| Kirtland!....... | Westbrook | M |
| Kissewaug!.... | Middlebury | NH |
| Kittemaug*.... | Montville | NL |
| Knifeshop..... | Thomaston | L |
| Knowlton?!.... | Ashford | W |
| Lafayette!..... | Bridgeport | F |
| Lakeville*§?†!.. | Salisbury | L |
| Lamb!......... | Ledyard | NL |
| Landsend!..... | Newtown | F |
| Lane!......... | Groton | NL |
| Lane!......... | Killingworth | M |
| Lanesville*§?†!. | New Milford | L |
| Lanternhill!.... | Ledyard | NL |
| Latham!....... | N.Stonington. | NL |
| Laurelglen†!... | N.Stonington. | NL |
| Laurelhill...... | Montville | NL |
| Laurelhill!..... | Norwich | NL |
| Laysville!...... | Old Lyme | NL |
| Leachhollow!.. | Sherman | F |
| Lebanon*§?†||!. | Lebanon | NL |
| Ledge!......... | Berlin | H |
| Ledge!......... | Killingly | W |
| Ledge!......... | Lyme | NL |
| Ledyard†||!!... | Ledyard | NL |
| Ledyardcenter!. | Ledyard | NL |
| Leesville§?!.... | East Haddam | M |
| Leete Island†... | Guilford | NH |
| Leffingtown?!.. | Bozrah | NL |
| Leffingwell†?!.. | Bozrah | NL |
| Leonardbridget*. | Lebanon | NL |
| Lester!........ | Ledyard | NL |

*Railroad and Express Stations; § Telegraphs; ! Telephones; † Post Offices; ‡ Cities; || Towns; ¶ Boroughs; ! School District.

| Stations, Villages, etc. | Town. | County. |
|---|---|---|
| Lewiswoods | New London | NL |
| Libertyhill*†! | Lebanon | NL |
| Libertystreet! | Stonington | NL |
| Limerock*§?†! | Salisbury | L |
| Limestone! | Ridgefield | F |
| Lindencroft | Bridgeport | NH |
| Linkfield! | Waterford | NL |
| Linkfield! | Watertown | L |
| Lisbon§!! | Lisbon | NL |
| Litchfield*§?†‖¶!! | Litchfield | L |
| Littleboston | Redding | F |
| Littlecity! | Haddam | H |
| Little Haddam† | East Haddam | M |
| Littleriver† | Middletown | M |
| Littlerock | Haddam | M |
| Lockwood! | New Canaan | F |
| Lockwood† | Stamford | F |
| London! | Enfield | H |
| Lonetown! | Redding | F |
| Longbrook | Stratford | F |
| Longcove! | Ledyard | NL |
| Longhill§! | East Hartford | H |
| Longhill§! | Huntington | F |
| Longhill!! | South Windsor | H |
| Longhill*†! | Trumbull | F |
| Longhill E&W?! | Middletown | M |
| Longlots!E&W | Westport | F |
| Longmeadowhill! | Brookfield | F |
| Longridge! | Danbury | F |
| Longridge†! | Stamford | F |
| Longsociety! | Preston | NL |
| Lovelystreet! | Avon | H |
| Lovett! | South Windsor | H |
| Lovett! | Sprague | NL |
| Lovettstation! | Lisbon | NL |
| Lowercity! | Canaan | L |
| Lowermerryall! | New Milford | L |
| Lowerscotland! | Scotland | W |
| Lowerwhitebills! | Huntington | F |
| Ludington! | Goshen | L |
| Lull! | Stafford | T |
| Lydalville? | Manchester | H |
| Lymanviaduct* | Colchester | NL |
| Lyme?‖ | Lyme | NL |
| Lyme*§?† | Old Lyme | NL |
| Lymeferry | Old Lyme to O.Sayb'k | M |
| Lymestreet! | Old Lyme | NL |
| Lymevillage?! | Old Lyme | NL |
| Lyndepoint | East Haven | NH |
| Lyonsplain†! | Weston | F |
| Macedonia! | Kent | L |
| Mackhill! | East Lyme | NL |
| Macksmill!! | East Lyme | NL |
| Madison*§?†‖ | Madison | NH |
| Mainstreet! | Bridgeport | F |
| Main st. branch† | Meriden | NH |
| Mallet! | Bridgewater | L |
| Mallory! | Barkhamsted | L |
| Malmanack | Waterbury | NH |
| Manchester*§?†‖!! | Manchester | H |
| Manchestergreen?† | Manchester | H |
| Mansfield*§†‖? | Mansfield | T |
| Mansfieldcenter†?! | Mansfield | T |
| Mansfieldcity! | Mansfield | T |
| Mansfielddepot*§?†! | Mansfield | T |
| Mansfield 4 Cor's! | Mansfield | T |
| Mansfieldhollow! | Mansfield | T |
| Manwaring! | Montville | NL |
| Maplegrove | Canterbury | W |
| Mapleton† | | H |
| Marbledale§?†! | Washington | L |
| Marcy! | Woodstock | W |
| Marion?†! | Southington | H |
| Marlborough†‖!! | Marlborough | H |
| Marlboroughmills† | | H |
| Maromas*§! | Middletown | M |
| Marsh! | Litchfield | L |
| Maryland! | New Milford | L |

| Stations, Villages, etc. | Town. | County. |
|---|---|---|
| Mashapaug†! | Union | T |
| Mashcutuck! | Killingly | W |
| Mashentuck! | Killingly | W |
| Masonville | Thompson | W |
| Massapeag*?† | Montville | NL |
| Matsonhill! | Glastonbury | H |
| McKinney! | Ellington | T |
| Meadow! | East Hartford | H |
| Meadowpark, 2d Ward, Hartford, | | H |
| Meadowplain! | Simsbury | H |
| Meadowwoods! | Essex | M |
| Mechanicsville | Granby | H |
| Mechanicsville*?† | Putnam | W |
| Mechanicsville! | Thompson | W |
| Meekertown! | Goshen | L |
| Meekertown! | Norfolk | L |
| Meetinghouse! | Greenwich | F |
| Melrose*§†! | East Windsor | H |
| Meriden*§?†‡‖ | Meriden | NH |
| Merrill! | New Hartford | L |
| Merrow*?†! | Mansfield | T |
| Merryall | New Milford | L |
| Merrybrook! | Danbury | F |
| Merwinspoint? | Milford | NH |
| Merwinstation! | Mansfield | T |
| Merwinsville*§ | New Milford | L |
| Meshomasick | Chatham | M |
| Mianus§?†! | Greenwich | F |
| Middle! | Naugatuck | NH |
| Middlebrook! | Wilton | F |
| Middlebury§?†‖!! | Middlebury | NH |
| Middlefield*§?†!! | Middlefield | M |
| Middlefieldcenter*§? | Middlefield | M |
| Middle5mileriver! | Norwalk | F |
| Middlegate! | Newtown | F |
| Middlehaddam§?† | Chatham | M |
| Middlehill! | Franklin | NL |
| Middleriver! | Danbury | F |
| Middletown*§?†‖‖ | Middletown | M |
| Middlet'n Junc*? | Middletown | M |
| Middlequarter! | Woodbury | L |
| Milecreek! | Old Lyme | NL |
| Milford*§?†‖!! | Milford | NH |
| Milfordpoint | Milford | NH |
| Mill! | Hartland | H |
| Mill! | Huntington | F |
| Mill! | Morris | L |
| Millbrook† | Colebrook | L |
| Milldale?†! | Southington | H |
| Millerfarm?! | Middletown | M |
| Millerhill | Chatham | M |
| Millhill? | Fairfield | F |
| Millington!! | East Haddam | M |
| Millingtongreen! | East Haddam | M |
| Millplain! | Branford | NH |
| Millplain*?†! | Danbury | F |
| Millplain ! | Fairfield | F |
| Millriver! | New Canaan | F |
| Millstone?† | Waterford | NL |
| Milltown! | N. Stonington | NL |
| Millville! | Naugatuck | NH |
| Milton?†! | Litchfield | L |
| Mine! | Bristol | H |
| Minebrook? | West Hartford | H |
| Minehill | Roxbury | L |
| Miner! | N. Stonington | NL |
| Minersgrove | East Hartford | H |
| Minortown†! | Woodbury | L |
| Mirybrook! | Danbury | F |
| Mixville?! | Cheshire | NH |
| Mohawktower | Cornwall | L |
| Mohegan*†! | Montville | NL |
| Monroe?†‖ | Monroe | F |
| Montowese*?†! | North Haven | NH |
| Montville*§?†‖!! | Montville | NL |
| Moodus§?†! | East Haddam | M |
| Moosehill! | Guilford | NH |
| Moosemeadow§† | Willington | T |

| Stations, Villages, etc. | Town. | County. |
|---|---|---|
| Moosup*§?†! | Plainfield | W |
| Morgan! | Clinton | M |
| Morgan! | Ledyard | NL |
| Morgan! | Waterford | NL |
| Morganpoint | East Haven | NH |
| Morris*§?†‖!! | Morris | L |
| Morrispoint§ | New Haven | NH |
| Mossfarm! | Cheshire | NH |
| Mountain! | Bristol | H |
| Mountain! | Canaan | L |
| Mountain! | Morris | L |
| Mountcarmel† | Hamden | NH |
| Mountcarmelcentre† | Hamden | NH |
| Mounthope† | Mansfield | T |
| Mountoemon! | Southington | H |
| Mudgetown! | Sharon | L |
| Munger! | Bethlehem | L |
| Mungerlane! | Bethlehem | L |
| Musicvale | Salem | NL |
| Mystic*§?†! | Stonington | NL |
| Mysticbridge§?! | Stonington | NL |
| Mysticriver?! | Groton | NL |
| Narrows! | Derby | NH |
| Narrows! | Easton | F |
| Natchaug! | Chaplin | W |
| Natchaug! | Windham | W |
| Naubuc§?†! | Glastonbury | H |
| Naugatuck*§?†‖¶ | Naugatuck | NH |
| Naugatuckjunc.* | Milford | NH |
| Naugatuckjunc.* | Winchester | L |
| Naunawague! | Bethlehem | L |
| Navyyard? | Groton | NL |
| Nayaug! | Glastonbury | H |
| Nayumps | Stratford | F |
| Neck! | Derby | NH |
| Neck! | Madison | NH |
| Neck?! | Old Lyme | NL |
| Neck! | Preston | NL |
| Neck! E&W | Waterford | NL |
| Nepaug† | New Hartford | L |
| New Boston! | Salem | NL |
| New Boston?†! | Thompson | W |
| N. Britain*§?†‡‖! | New Britain | H |
| N. Canaan*§?†‖¶!! | New Canaan | F |
| Newcity? | Meriden | NH |
| Newdistrict! | Avon | H |
| Newdistrict! | Simsbury | H |
| Newent! | Lisbon | NL |
| Newcomb! | Goshen | L |
| New Fairfield†‖ | New Fairfield | F |
| Newfield! | Stratford | F |
| Newfield! | Torrington | L |
| Newfield*§! | Middletown | M |
| Newgatehill | Granby | H |
| Newhallville§ | New Haven | NH |
| N. Hartford*?†‖ | New Hartford | L |
| New Hart'd Cen.? | New Hartford | L |
| New Haven*§?†‡‖! | New Haven | NH |
| Newington*§?†‖! | Newington | H |
| Newington Jun*?† | Newington | H |
| N.London*§?†‖!! | New London | NL |
| New Milford*§?†‖ | New Milford | L |
| New Preston*?†! | Washington | L |
| New Prestonhill! | Washington | L |
| New Saybrook§ | Saybrook | M |
| Newtown*§?†‖¶ | Newtown | F |
| New York! | Stratford | F |
| Niantic*§?†! | East Lyme | NL |
| Nichols?† | Fairfield | F |
| Nicholsfarm?! | Trumbull | F |
| Ninevah | Madison | NH |
| Nipsic! | Glastonbury | H |
| Nisopark | Ridgefield | F |
| Noank*§?†! | Groton | NL |
| Nod! | Avon | H |
| Nod! | Wilton | F |
| Nonewaug! | Woodbury | L |
| Norfield! | Weston | F |

| Stations, Villages, etc. | Town. | County. |
|---|---|---|
| Norfolk*§?†‖ | Norfolk | L |
| Noroton*§?†! | Darien | F |
| Norotonheights† | Darien | F |
| North Ashford†! | Ashford | W |
| Northbanks! | Fairfield | F |
| North Bayport | Greenwich | F |
| North Branford†‖!! | No. Branford | NH |
| Northbrick! | Wethersfield | H |
| North Bridgeport*? | Bridgeport | F |
| North Bigelow! | Hampton | W |
| North Canaan?‖! | North Canaan | L |
| North Canton† | Canton | H |
| Northchippenhill! | Bristol | H |
| NorthColebrook§† | Colebrook | L |
| NorthCornwall§! | Cornwall | L |
| North Coventry | Coventry | T |
| North Cromwell* | Cromwell | M |
| Northend? | Southington | H |
| Northfarms! | Litchfield | L |
| Northfarms! | Wallingford | NH |
| Northfield§?†! | Litchfield | L |
| Northford*§?†! | No. Branford | NH |
| North Franklin† | Franklin | NL |
| N. Glastonbury§! | Glastonbury | H |
| North Granby†! | Granby | H |
| North Greenwich | Greenwich | F |
| N.Grosvenordale*?†! | Thompson | W |
| North Guilford† | Guilford | H |
| No. Guilfordbluff! | Guilford | NH |
| North Hampton | Hampton | W |
| North Hartland*§ | Hartland | H |
| NorthHaven*§?†‖!! | NorthHaven | NH |
| Northhill! | North Haven | NH |
| North Kent†! | Kent | L |
| North Lyme†! | Lyme | NL |
| North Madison† | Madison | NH |
| N.Manchester*§? | Manchester | H |
| North Mianus! | Greenwich | F |
| North Norfolk! | Norfolk | L |
| Northplain† | | M |
| Northplains† | Guilford | NH |
| No. Ridgebury! | Ridgefield | F |
| North Somers§! | Somers | T |
| North Stamford†! | Stamford | F |
| North Stanwich! | Greenwich | F |
| North Sterling† | Sterling | W |
| No. Stonington†‖!! | N.Stonington | NL |
| Northstreet! | Glastonbury | H |
| Northstreet | Greenwich | F |
| Northville§? | Bristol | H |
| Northville§†! | New Milford | L |
| No. Westchester† | Colchester | NL |
| North Wilton†! | Wilton | F |
| No.Windham*§†! | Windham | W |
| Northwoodbury† | | L |
| N. Woodstock*?†! | Woodstock | W |
| Nortontown! | Madison | NH |
| Norwalk*§?†‡‖ | Norwalk | F |
| Norwich*§?†‡‖ | Norwich | NL |
| Norwichfalls! | Norwich | NL |
| Norwichtown *?†! | Norwich | NL |
| Nott! | Essex | M |
| Novascotia! | Waterford | NL |
| Nutplains N!&S! | Guilford | NH |
| Nyumphs! | Beacon Falls | NH |
| Oakdale§?† | Montville | NL |
| Oakland?! | Manchester | H |
| Oakland! | South Windsor | H |
| Oaks§?! | Windham | W |
| Oakstreet?! | New Haven | NH |
| Oakville*§?†! | Watertown | L |
| Obtuse! | Brookfield | F |
| Occum§? | Norwich | NL |
| Oldchurch! | Glastonbury | H |
| Oldchurch! | New Canaan | F |
| Oldfield? | Stonington | NL |
| Oldfurnacehol'w? | Stafford | T |
| Oldgreenwich! | Greenwich | F |
| Old Lyme*§?‖!! | Old Lyme | NL |
| Oldmystic† | ? | NL |
| Oldprison | East Granby | H |
| Oldroad! | Meriden | NH |
| OldSaybrook*§?‖!! | Old Saybrook | M |
| Oldwell§ | Norwalk | F |
| Olivet! | Bridgeport | F |
| Olmstead! | New Canaan | F |
| Olmstead! | East Haddam | M |
| Oneco*§?†! | Sterling | W |
| Orange*§?†‖!! | Orange | NH |
| Orcutts*? | Stafford | T |
| Orehill§! | Kent | L |
| Orehill*?†! | Salisbury | L |
| Oronoke! | Waterbury | NH |
| Uronoque†! | Stratford | F |
| Orton† | | L |
| Osborn* | East Windsor | H |
| Osborntown* | Naugatuck | NH |
| Osgoodhill! | New Britain | H |
| Oswegatchie | East Lyme | NL |
| Overriver! | Norwalk | F |
| Oviatt! | Goshen | L |
| Oxbridge! | Darien | F |
| Oxford§?‖ | Oxford | NH |
| Oxridge! | Darien | F |
| Oysterpoint§ | New Haven | NH |
| Oysterriver! | Old Saybrook | M |
| Pachaug?! | Griswold | NL |
| Packerville*†! | Canterbury | W |
| Packwoodville | Colchester | NL |
| Paconset?! | Portland | M |
| Paine! | Thompson | W |
| Painterhill! | Roxbury | L |
| Painters swamp | New Britain | H |
| Palestine! | Newtown | F |
| Palmer! | Preston | NL |
| Palmerhill | Greenwich | F |
| Palmerstreet! | Stonington | NL |
| Palmertown?! | Montville | NL |
| Pamecha | Middletown | M |
| Paran | Colchester | NH |
| Parkerfarm! | Wallingford | NH |
| Parkerville | Manchester | L |
| Parklane! | New Milford | L |
| Parkville*§?.9th Ward, Hartford | | H |
| Parlorrock | Trumbull | F |
| Patten! | Stafford | T |
| Pauchaug | Griswold | NL |
| Pautipaug | Sprague | NL |
| Pavedstreet! | Branford | NH |
| Pawcatuck! | Stonington | NL |
| Pawsonpark | Branford | NH |
| Paywell! | Lisbon | NL |
| Peaceable! | Bristol | H |
| Pearlville | East Windsor | H |
| Pease! | Ellington | T |
| Peck! | Canterbury | W |
| Peckhollow * | Franklin | NL |
| Pecksbridge! | Tolland | T |
| Pecksland! | Greenwich | F |
| Pegville! | Granby | H |
| Pemberville*! | Greenwich | F |
| Pembroke! | Bridgeport | F |
| Pembroke! | Danbury | F |
| Pendletonhill†! | N. Stonington | NL |
| Penfieldhill! | Portland | M |
| Pequabuck*§?† | Plymouth | L |
| Pequonnock | Bridgeport | F |
| Pequonoc! | Groton | NL |
| Peqnothill | Mystic | NL |
| Pequotmills? | Montville | NL |
| Perrin! | Woodstock | W |
| Perry! | Sharon | L |
| Perryville | Norwalk | F |
| Peterparleyville | Southbury | NH |
| Phelpshill! | Lebanon | NL |
| Phœnixville†! | Eastford | W |
| Pick! | Canterbury | W |
| Picketsridge! | Redding | F |
| Pickett! | New Milford | L |
| Piercehollow! | Southbury | NH |
| Pigville§ | 2d Ward, Hartford | H |
| Pimpewaug! | Wilton | F |
| Pinchstreet† | Scotland | W |
| Pinebridge | Beacon Falls | NH |
| Pinebrook! | Chatham | M |
| Pinebrook! | Haddam | M |
| Pinemeadow*§?†! | New Hartford | L |
| Pinemeadow! | Windsor Locks | H |
| Pineorchard§?! | Killingworth | M |
| Pineorchard*† | Branford | N.H |
| Pinesbridge! | Oxford | NH |
| Pinestreet! | Columbia | T |
| Pineswamp! | Sharon | L |
| Pineville | Killingly | W |
| Pinney! | Ellington | T |
| Pistolpointbar | Portland | M |
| Pitch! | Morris | L |
| Plain! | Canaan | L |
| Plain! | South Windsor | H |
| Plainfield*§?†‖ | Plainfield | W |
| Plainfieldjunc'n*§ | Plainfield | W |
| Plainhill! | Norwich | NL |
| Plainhill? | Woodstock | W |
| Plains! | East Haddam | M |
| Plains! | Kent | L |
| Plains! | Preston | NL |
| Plainville*§?†‖!! | Plainville | L |
| Plantsville*§?†! | Southington | H |
| Plattsville! | Easton | F |
| Plattsville! | Meriden | NH |
| Pleasantbeach | Waterford | NL |
| Pleasantvalley?†! | Barkhamsted | L |
| Pleasantvalley | Groton | NL |
| Pleasantvalley! | Lyme | NL |
| Pleasantvalley! | South Windsor | H |
| Plumhill | Derby | NH |
| Plumtrees! | Bethel | F |
| Plymouth§?†‖! | Plymouth | L |
| Plymouthhollow | Plymouth | L |
| Pocansett | Portland | M |
| Pocotopaug | Chatham | M |
| Podunk! | S. Win.&E.Hfd. | H |
| Pohtatuck! | Newtown | F |
| Polk! | Watertown | L |
| Polkville?! | Bristol | H |
| Pomfret*§?†‖!! | Pomfret | W |
| Pomfretcentre§?† | Pomfret | W |
| Pomfretlanding†! | Pomfret | W |
| Pomperaug! | Southbury | NH |
| Pomperaug* | Woodbury | L |
| Pomperaugvalley*? | Southbury | NH |
| Pompeyhollow | Ashford | W |
| Poncesstreet! | New Canaan | F |
| Pond! | Burlington | H |
| Pond! | Morris | L |
| Pond! | Thompson | W |
| Pond! | Warren | L |
| Pondhill! | Naugatuck | NH |
| Pondhill! | Plainfield | W |
| Pondhill! | Wallingford | NH |
| Pondmeadow | Killingworth | M |
| Pondmeadow! | Westbrook | M |
| Pondpoint! | Milford | M |
| Ponds! | Norfolk | L |
| Pondville | Chester | M |
| Pondville! | New Fairfield | F |
| Ponsett! | Haddam | M |
| Pontoosuc | Glastonbury | H |
| Pootatuck! | Southbury | NH |
| Poplarplain! | Westport | F |
| Poquetannoc | Ledyard | NL |
| Poquetanuck*?†! | Preston | NL |
| Poquonoc*?! | Groton | NL |
| Poquonockbridge† | Groton | NL |

* Railroad and Express Stations; § Telegraphs; † Telephones; † Post Offices; ‡ Cities; ‖ Towns; ¶ Boroughs; ! School Districts.

| Stations, Villages, etc. | Town. | County. |
|---|---|---|
| Poquonock§?†... | Windsor | H |
| Portchester*?... | Greenwich | F |
| Portersville...... | Groton | NL |
| Portipaug!....... | Sprague | NL |
| Portland*§?†||!!. | Portland | M |
| Post......... | Westbrook | M |
| Potatolane...... | East Windsor | H |
| Potopogue!..... | Sprague | NL |
| Porter!....... | South Windsor | H |
| Potter!....... | Willington | T |
| Poundhill!..... | Canterbury | W |
| Poundridge...... | Stamford | F |
| Povertystreet!.. | Waterford | NL |
| Pratts*....... | New Britain | H |
| Prattsville?!.... | Meriden | NH |
| Pressbarnbar.... | Glastonbury | H |
| Preston§?†||.... | Preston | NL |
| Prestoncity?!... | Preston | NL |
| Pricehollow!.... | Southbury | NH |
| Prospect!...... | Bridgeport | F |
| Prospect!...... | Litchfield | L |
| Prospect†||!!... | Prospect | NH |
| Prospecthill?L.. | Hfd and W Hfd | H |
| Prospecthill*.... | Litchfield | L |
| Prospecthill.... | Norwalk | F |
| Prospecthill.... | Waterford | NL |
| Providencestreet!Norwich | | NL |
| Puckshire!...... | Woodbury | L |
| Puddinghill!.... | Scotland | W |
| Puddletown...... | New Hartford | L |
| Puffingham!.... | Cornwall | L |
| Pumpkinhill!... | Ashford | T |
| Pumpkinhill.... | New Milford | L |
| Pumpkintown.... | Rockyhill | H |
| Purgatory....... | Avon | H |
| Purchase!...... | Southbury | NH |
| Put!......... | Rockyhill | H |
| Putnam*§?†‡||!.. | Putnam | W |
| Putnamheights?†! | Putnam | W |
| Putnam Memorial Park, Redding | | F |
| Putney!........ | Stratford | F |
| Putshill!...... | Greenwich | F |
| Quadic!....... | Thompson | W |
| Quailtrap!...... | Griswold | NL |
| Quakerfarms†!.. | Oxford | NH |
| Quakerhill!U&L.† | Waterford | NL |
| Quakerridge!... | Greenwich | F |
| Quakertown.... | Groton | NL |
| Quakertown.... | Ledyard | NL |
| Quarry!....... | Durham | M |
| Quarry?!...... | Portland | M |
| Quarry....... | Milford | NH |
| Quarry....... | Thomaston | L |
| Quarryville†.... | Bolton | T |
| Quarter!....... | Branford | NH |
| Quassapaug!... | Woodbury | L |
| Quasset!....... | Woodstock | W |
| Queach!....... | Branford | NH |
| Quiambog?!.... | Stonington | NL |
| Quinebaug!.... | Brooklyn | W |
| Quinebaug*†.... | Thompson | W |
| Quinnipiac*§!.. | North Haven | NH |
| Raggedhill!!.... | Pomfret | W |
| Railroad!....... | Meriden | NH |
| Rainbow§†?.... | Windsor | H |
| Randall!....... | Stonington | NL |
| Ransomhill!.... | Salem | NL |
| Rathbunhill!... | Salem | NL |
| Rawson†....... | Hampton | W |
| Ray!......... | Voluntown | NL |
| Raymond!...... | Canterbury | W |
| Raymondhill.... | Montville | NL |
| Read!......... | Lisbon | NL |
| Reading*....... | Redding | F |
| Readsfield...... | Wilton | F |
| Redcity!....... | Oxford | NH |
| Redding*?†||... | Redding | F |
| Redding Ridge†!. | Redding | F |
| Redlane!....... | East Haddam | M |
| Redoak!....... | *Orange | NH |
| Reynolds!...... | Voluntown | NL |
| Reynoldsbridge*§† | Plymouth | L |
| Rhodesville!.... | Putnam | W |
| Rider!....... | Willington | T |
| Ridge!....... | Redding | T |
| Ridgebury†!N&S. | Ridgefield | F |
| Ridgefarm..... | West Hartford | H |
| Ridgefield*§†||¶. | Ridgefield | F |
| Riggsstreet!.... | Oxford | NH |
| Rimmon!....... | Beacon Falls | NH |
| Rinebank!...... | Stamford | F |
| Ringstreet...... | Danbury | F |
| Ripton....... | Huntington | F |
| River!....... | Bridgewater | L |
| River!....... | Canton | H |
| River!....... | Colebrook | L |
| River!....... | Cornwall | L |
| River!....... | Montville | NL |
| Riverbank†!... | Stamford | F |
| Riverdale!..... | Greenwich | F |
| Riverhead*!... | East Lyme | NL |
| Riverside*§?†!. | Greenwich | F |
| Riverside?!.... | Orange | NH |
| Riverton§?†!... | Barkhamsted | L |
| Riverview!..... | Essex | M |
| Riverview§?... | New Haven | NH |
| Riversville!.... | Greenwich | F |
| Rixtown!...... | Griswold | NL |
| Road!........ | Stonington | NL |
| Roadrock...... | East Lyme | NL |
| Roaringbrook!.. | Willington | T |
| Roastmeathill... | Killingworth | M |
| Roathavenue!... | Norwich | NL |
| Robertsville§†.. | Colebrook | L |
| Rock!........ | Colebrook | L |
| Rock!........ | Kent | L |
| Rockhouse!.... | Easton | F |
| Rockhousehill!.. | Oxford | NH |
| Rockfall*§?†... | Middlefield | M |
| Rockland!..... | Madison | NH |
| Rockland...... | Durham | M |
| Rocklanding... | Haddam..:.. | M |
| Rockmeadow!.. | Union | T |
| Rocknook..... | Preston | NL |
| Rockville*§?†‡!. | Vernon | T |
| Rockwell!..... | New Britain | H |
| Rockwellhill!... | Stafford | T |
| Rockyglen*.... | Newtown | F |
| Rockyhill*§?†||!. | Rockyhill | H |
| Rockyneck..... | Greenwich | F |
| Rogers!....... | Salem | NL |
| Romford*†...... | Washington | NH |
| Rosehill!...... | Portland | M |
| Roselandpark... | Woodstock | W |
| Roseofnewengland | Norwich | NL |
| Rotonpoint*?... | Norwalk | F |
| Roundhill...... | Farmington | H |
| Roundhill*?†!.. | Greenwich | F |
| Rowayton†...... | Norwalk | F |
| Roxbury*§?||†.. | Roxbury | L |
| Roxbury?!...... | Stamford | F |
| Roxburyfalls?... | Roxbury | L |
| Roxburystation?† | Roxbury | L |
| Ryestreet!...... | E. & S. Windsor | H |
| Sabin!......... | Pomfret | W |
| Sabtown........ | Old Lyme | NL |
| Sachemshead§?†!. | Guilford | NH |
| Sachemswoods?.. | New Haven | NH |
| Saddsmills*..... | East Windsor | H |
| Salem†||!!..... | Salem | NL |
| Salisbury*§?†||!. | Salisbury | L |
| Salmonbrook!.. | Granby | H |
| Salmonriver... | East Haddam | M |
| Sampmortar... | Fairfield | F |
| Sandbank!..... | Burlington | H |
| Sandbanks..... | Portland | M |
| Sandybrook!... | Colebrook | L |
| Sandyhill!..... | Middlebury | NH |
| Sandyhook*§?†!. | Newtown | F |
| Sanford!....... | Hamden | NH |
| Sanford*§?†... | Redding | F |
| Sangwauk!..... | Stonington | NL |
| Satanskingdom... | New Hartford | L |
| Saugatuck*§?†!E!W!&S!Westp'rt | | F |
| Savinrock*§?... | Orange | NH |
| Sawmillplain!... | Waterbury | NH |
| Sawyer!....... | Putnam | W |
| Saybrook§?§||!.. | Saybrook | M |
| Saybrook*§?†!!. | Old Saybrook | M |
| Saybrookferry!L.. | Old Saybrook | M |
| Saybrookjunc'n*§ | Old Saybrook | M |
| Saybrookpt.*§?†! | Old Saybrook | M |
| Scantic§!...... | East Windsor | H |
| Schoolstreet!... | Norwich | NL |
| Scitico*§†!..... | Enfield | H |
| Scofieldtown!... | Stamford | F |
| Scotchcap...... | Montville | NL |
| Scotland!N!&S!.. | Bloomfield | H |
| Scotland!...... | Ridgefield | F |
| Scotland*?†||!.. | Scotland | W |
| Scotland*....... | Simsbury | H |
| Scotlandroad!... | Norwich | NL |
| Scottsswamp!... | Farmington | H |
| Seasidepark.... | Bridgeport | F |
| Sebetha....... | Cromwell | M |
| Secondhill!..... | New Milford | L |
| Seymour*§?†||!. | Seymour | NH |
| Shailerville†!... | Haddam | M |
| Shakerstation*§†! | Enfield | H |
| Sharon†§?||.... | Sharon | L |
| Sharonvalley§†.. | Sharon | L |
| Sharphill!...... | Ashford | W |
| Shelterockhill... | Bethel | F |
| Shelton§?†¶.... | Huntington | F |
| Shennecosset!.. | Groton | NL |
| Shepaug*...... | Southbury | NH |
| Sherman§?†||!.. | Sherman | F |
| Shetucket!..... | Sprague | NL |
| Shetucketbridge.. | Norwich | NL |
| Shewville!...... | | NL |
| Shingleohollow .. | Glastonbury | H |
| Shipman!...... | New Britain | H |
| Shippanpoint... | Stamford | F |
| Shippee!...... | Eastford | W |
| Shortbeach§?†!.. | Branford | NH |
| Shruboak!...... | Orange | NH |
| Shruboak!...... | Seymour | NH |
| Shume!....... | N. Stonington | NL |
| Siam......... | Portland | M |
| Sibley!....... | Eastford | W |
| Silltown?!...... | Old Lyme | NL |
| Silvercity?!.... | Meriden | NH |
| Silverlane†..... | East Hartford | H |
| Silvermine..... | Middletown | M |
| Silvermine!.... | New Canaan | F |
| Silvermine†.... | Norwalk | F |
| Silverstreet.... | Coventry | T |
| Simeapog...... | East Lyme | NL |
| Simonsville!.... | Waterbury | NH |
| Simsbury*§†||.. | Simsbury | H |
| Simsbury†!..... | Stamford | F |
| Skinner?!...... | New Haven | NH |
| Skinner!....... | Woodstock | W |
| Skunkamaug!.. | Tolland | T |
| Slaterville....... | Haddam | M |
| Smith!....... | Bethany | NH |
| Smith!....... | Canterbury | W |
| Smithscorner... | Franklin | NL |
| Smithscrossing*. | Middletown | M |
| Smithsridge.... | New Canaan | F |
| Snipsic?!...... | Tolland | T |
| Somers§†||!.... | Somers | T |
| Somersville§†!.. | Somers | T |

* Railroad and Express Stations; § Telegraphs; † Telephones; ‡ Post Offices; ‡ Cities; || Towns; ¶ Boroughs; ! School Districts

| Stations, Villages, etc. | Town. | County. |
|---|---|---|
| Sonetown l | Redding | F |
| Soperville | Windsor | H |
| Soundbeach*§?†!Greenwich | | F |
| Southbankl | Fairfield | F |
| South Bigelowl | Hampton | W |
| South Britain§?!†Southbury | | NH |
| Southbury*§?†‖ | Southbury | NH |
| South Canaan†l | Canaan | L |
| So. Canterbury† | Canterbury | W |
| South Cheshire? | Cheshire | NH |
| Southchestnuthill!Mansfield | | T |
| So. Chippenhill! | Bristol | H |
| So. Coventry*§?†Coventry | | T |
| Southfarms? | Middletown | M |
| Southfarms | Morris | L |
| South5mileriver!Norwalk | | F |
| Southford*§†! | Southbury | NH |
| S.Glastonbury§?†Glastonbury | | H |
| South Goshen? | Goshen | L |
| South Hampton | Hampton | W |
| South Haven§?! | New Haven | NH |
| Southhill! | Wethersfield | H |
| Southhollow! | Barkhamsted | L |
| Southhollow! | Hartland | H |
| Southhollow! | New Hartford | L |
| Southingt'n*§?†‖¶!!Southington | | H |
| Southingtoncor.? | Southington | H |
| South Kent*†! | Kent | L |
| South Killingly†!Killingly | | W |
| South Lyme*†§ | Old Lyme | NL |
| S.Manchester*§?† | Manchester | H |
| South Meriden§?†!Meriden | | NH |
| South Norfolk?†l | Norfolk | L |
| S. Norwalk*§?†!Norwalk | | F |
| Southplain! | Litchfield | L |
| Southport*§?†! | Fairfield | F |
| Southridgebury! | Ridgefield | F |
| Southriver! | Warren | L |
| South Roxbury? | Roxbury | L |
| South Saugatuck!Westport | | F |
| South Stamford! | Stamford | F |
| South Stanwick! | Greenwich | F |
| Southstreet,* | Suffield | H |
| Southvillage | Bristol | H |
| Southville†! | Bridgewater | L |
| So. Wethersfield*§† | Wethersfield | H |
| So. Willington*§†?Willington | | T |
| South Wilton*† | Wilton | F |
| So.Windham*§?†!Windham | | W |
| So.Windsor*§†‖!South Windsor | | H |
| So. Woodstock?†.Woodstock | | W |
| Sparks! | Killingly | W |
| Spencerhill | East Hartford | H |
| Spencerhill | Old Saybrook | M |
| Spithead! | Waterford | NL |
| Spoonville! | East Granby | H |
| Sprague‖! | Sprague | NL |
| Sprindlehill | Wolcott | NH |
| Springdale*†! | Stamford | F |
| Springhill†! | Mansfield | T |
| Springs! | Stafford | T |
| Springvalley | Montville | NL |
| Sprucedale | Woodstock | W |
| Spunkeyhollow! | Lyme | NL |
| Squabblehollow.North Canaan | | L |
| Squantuck | Seymour | NH |
| Square Pond | Ellington | T |
| Squashhollow | New Milford | L |
| Staddlehill N.&S.?!Middletown | | M |
| Stadleyrough | Danbury | F |
| Stafford! | Bristol | H |
| Stafford*?†‖ | Stafford | T |
| Staffordhollow? | Stafford | T |
| Staffordsprings.§?†¶!Stafford | | T |
| Staffordstreet?! | Stafford | T |
| Staffordville†?! | Stafford | T |
| Stamford*§?†‡‖!!Stamford | | F |
| Standishhill | Lebanon | NL |

| Stations, Villages, etc. | Town.County. | |
|---|---|---|
| Stanford* | Stamford | F |
| Stanleyquarter! | New Britain | H |
| Stantonl | Voluntown | NL |
| Stanwich*?†!N&SGreenwich | | F |
| Starrhill | Danbury | F |
| Starrplain! | Danbury | F |
| Stateline* | Salisbury | L |
| Stateline* | Stafford | T |
| Steeles* | Bolton | T |
| Steephollow | Greenwich | F |
| Stepney*§†! | Monroe | F |
| Stepneydepot*† | Monroe | F |
| Sterling*?† | Sterling | W |
| Sterlingcity! | Lyme | NL |
| Sterlinghill§! | Sterling | W |
| Sterlingstreet! | Bridgeport | F |
| Stevenson† | | F |
| Stillmanville | Stonington | NL |
| Stillwater? | Stamford | F |
| Stilsonhill | New Milford | L |
| Stockingscorner | Berlin | H |
| Stoddard! | Ledyard | NL |
| Stonefactory! | Sterling | W |
| Stonehill! | Griswold | NL |
| Stonehill! | Plainfield | W |
| Stonehouse! | Killingworth | M |
| Stoneyhill! | Windsor | H |
| Stonington! | Southbury | NH |
| Stonington*§?†‖¶.Stonington | | NL |
| Stoningt'njunc.*§?Stonington | | NL |
| Stonycreek*§?†!.Branford | | NH |
| Stonyhill! | Bethel | F |
| Stonyhill! | Griswold | NL |
| Storrs† | Mansfield | T |
| Straitsville! | Naugatuck | NH |
| Stratfield | Bridge. & Fairf. | F |
| Stratford*§?†‖ | Stratford | F |
| Strattonbrook* | Simsbury | H |
| Strawberryhill | Stamford | F |
| Strongtown?! | Southbury | NH |
| Stubtown! | N. Stonington.NL | |
| Suagatchie | Waterford | NL |
| Suckerbrook l | Winchester | L |
| Suffield*§?†‖!! | Suffield | H |
| Suffrage§! | Canton | H |
| Sugarhill! | Tolland | T |
| Summerhill! | Madison | NH |
| Summit* | Norfolk | L |
| Swift! | Cornwall | L |
| Taftville*§?†! | Norwich | NL |
| Talcottville*§?†!Vernon | | T |
| Talmadgehill*!New Canaan | | F |
| Tangwank! | Stonington | NL |
| Tariffville*§?†! | Simsbury | H |
| Tarsia | Chatham | M |
| Tashua! | Trumbull! | F |
| Taterhill! | East Haddam | M |
| Tatnickhill! | Brooklyn | W |
| Taunton! | Newtown | F |
| Taylortown! | Glastonbury | H |
| Tebtown | East Hartford | H |
| Terracehill | Lyme | NL |
| Terryplain! | Simsbury | H |
| Terryville*§?†!..Plymouth | | L |
| Thamesgrove* | Montville | NL |
| Thamesville*§? | Norwich | NL |
| Thomaston*§?†‖!!Thomaston | | L |
| Thompson*§?†‖!!Thompson | | W |
| Thomps'nville*§?†!Enfield | | H |
| Threadfactory!..Willington | | T |
| Ticknor! | Salisbury | L |
| Tilestonhill! | Fairfield | F |
| Tinbridge?. 8th Ward, Hartford | | H |
| Tinkerfield | Newtown | F |
| Titicus†! | Ridgefield | F |
| Titus! | Sterling | W |
| Toadrockl | East Lyme | NL |
| Tobaccostreet! | Lebanon | NL |

| Stations, Villages, etc. | Town. | County. |
|---|---|---|
| Toddyhill! | Newtown | F |
| Toilsomehill! | Fairfield | F |
| Tolland*§?†‖! | Tolland | T |
| Tollandstreet! | Tolland | T |
| Tolles* | Plymouth | L |
| Torringford§?† | Torrington | L |
| Torrington*§?†‖¶!!Torrington | | L |
| Totoket† | | NH |
| Towantic* | Oxford | NH |
| Town! | New Britain | H |
| Townhill! | East Haddam | M |
| Townhill! | New Hartford | L |
| Townhill | New London | NL |
| Townhill! | Plymouth | L |
| Townhill! | Salisbury | L |
| Townplot! | Waterbury | NH |
| Townsend! | Andover | T |
| Townstreet?! | Norwich | NL |
| Tracy† | | NH |
| Transylvania! | Woodbury | L |
| Trapfall! | Huntington | F |
| Treat! | Bridgewater | L |
| Trumbull§?‖ | Trumbull | F |
| Trumbullchurch*Trumbull | | F |
| Tryontown | Portland | M |
| Tucker! | Killingly | W |
| Turkeyhill! | East Granby | H |
| Turkeyhill! | Haddam | M |
| Turkeyhill* | Orange | NH |
| Turnerville*§† | Hebron | T |
| Turnofriver! | Stamford | F |
| Twinemill! | Glastonbury | H |
| Tyler! | Griswold | NL |
| Tylercity*?†l | Orange | NH |
| Tylermills! | Wallingford | NH |
| Tylerville*§?† | Middlebury | NH |
| Tylerville*§?†! | Haddam | M |
| Umpawaug! | Redding | F |
| Uncasville§?†! | Montville | NL |
| Union! | Bridgeport | F |
| Union! | Cheshire | NH |
| Union! | Clinton | M |
| Union! | Farmington | L |
| Union! | Goshen | L |
| Union! | Guilford | NH |
| Union! | Hampton | W |
| Union! | Killingworth | M |
| Union! | Madison | NH |
| Union! | New London | NL |
| Union! | N. Stonington.NL | |
| Union! | Orange | NH |
| Union! | Plainfield | W |
| Union! | Simsbury | H |
| Union! | Stratford | F |
| Union†‖! | Union | T |
| Unioncenter! | Naugatuck | NH |
| Unioncity*?†! | Naugatuck | NH |
| Uniondale! | Plainfield | W |
| Uniongrove | Hartford | H |
| Unionvillage | Manchester | H |
| Unionville! | Avon | H |
| Unionville! | Colchester | NL |
| Unionville! | Ledyard | NL |
| Unionville*§?† | Farmington | H |
| Unionville! | Ledyard | NL |
| Upham! | Thompson | W |
| Upperend! | Washington | L |
| Uppermerryall! | New Milford | L |
| Uppermystic! | Stonington | NL |
| Upperoank! | Groton | NL |
| Upperparish! | Weston | F |
| Uptown! | Derby | F |
| Uptown! | East Haddam | M |
| Uptown! | Lebanon | NL |
| Uptown! | Woodbury | L |
| Valley! | Barkhamsted | L |
| Valley! | Killingly | W |
| Valley! | South Windsor | H |

*Railroad and Express Stations; §Telegraphs; ?Telephones; †Post Offices; ‡Cities; ‖Towns; ¶Boroughs; !School Districts.

| Stations, Villages, etc. | Town | County |
|---|---|---|
| Valleyforge! | Weston | F |
| Val'y & NE Junc* | Hartford | H |
| Vermont! | Union | T |
| Vernon*§?†‖!! | Vernon | T |
| Vernoncenter?† | Vernon | T |
| Vernonstat.*§? | Vernon | T |
| Versailles! | South Windsor | H |
| Versailles*§?† | Sprague | NL |
| Vexation! | Wethersfield | H |
| Village! | Stafford | T |
| Village! | Voluntown | NL |
| Villagedistrict! | Wolcott | NH |
| Villagehill! | Lebanon | NL |
| Villagehill! | Willington | T |
| Vinton! | South Windsor | H |
| Vintons Mills† | South Windsor | H |
| Voluntown§?†‖!! | Voluntown | NL |
| Wadawannuc | Stonington | NL |
| Waldermere? | Bridgeport | F |
| Waldo! | Canterbury | W |
| Wadostation* | Scotland | W |
| Walkersfarm! | Monroe | F |
| Walkleyhill! | Haddam | M |
| Walle! | New Milford | L |
| Wallingford*§?†‖¶ | Wallingford | NH |
| Wallinhill!?† | Winchester | L |
| Wallup! | Enfield | H |
| Walnuthill! | East Lyme | NL |
| Walnuttreehill! | Huntington | L |
| Walnuttreehill! | New Milford | L |
| Walnuttreehill! | Newtown | F |
| Walterville! | Bridgeport | F |
| Wamphassuc | Stonington | NL |
| Wapping! | Newtown | F |
| Wapping! | Southbury | NH |
| Wapping† | South Windsor | H |
| Warehousepoint*§?†!E. | Windsor | H |
| Warner! | Windham | W |
| Warnerhill! | Roxbury | L |
| Warnertown! | Hamden | NH |
| Warren! | Killingly | W |
| Warren§?†‖!! | Warren | L |
| Warrenville†! | Ashford | W |
| Washapaug | Union | T |
| Washburn! | Stafford | T |
| Washington! | Bridgeport | F |
| Washington! | Hartford | H |
| Washington?! | New Haven | NH |
| Washington*§?†‖ | Washington | L |
| Washingtonbri'ge? | Stratford | F |
| Washingtonhill! | Barkhamsted | L |
| Washingtondepot*† | Washington | L |
| Wassuc! | Glastonbury | H |
| Waterbury*§?†‖¶ | Waterbury | NH |
| Waterford*?†‖ | Waterford | NL |
| Waterside? | Stamford | F |
| Watertown*§?†‖ | Watertown | L |
| Waterville?! | Farmington | H |
| Waterville*§?†! | Waterbury | NH |
| Waterworks§? | West Hartford | H |
| Wauregan*?†! | Plainfield | W |
| Wauwakushill! | Norwich | NL |
| Weantenuck! | New Milford | L |
| Weatogue*†! | Simsbury | H |
| Webster! | New Haven | NH |
| Weekeepeemee! | Woodbury | L |
| Weller! | Roxbury | L |
| Wequatucket | Stonington | NL |
| Wequetequock! | Stonington | NL |
| Wequonnoc! | Norwich | NL |
| West Ansonia! | Derby | NH |
| West Ashford†! | Ashford | W |
| West Avon*†! | Avon | H |
| Westbrook*§†‖!! | Westbrook | M |
| West Chelsea?! | Norwich | NL |
| West Cheshire?†! | Cheshire | NH |
| Westchester*§†! | Colchester | NL |
| West Cornwall*§?†! | Cornwall | L |
| Westcottcove | Stamford | F |
| West Cromwell* | Cromwell | M |
| Westdistrict§ | Farmington | H |
| Westend! | Milford | NH |
| Westfield*§?!1,2,3&4, | Middletown | M |
| Westford† | Ashford | W |
| West Goshen?†! | Goshen | L |
| West Granby†! | Granby | H |
| W. Hartford§?†‖!! | West Hartford | H |
| West Hartland† | Hartland | H |
| WestHaven*§?†¶ | Orange | NH |
| Westhill! | New Hartford | L |
| Westhill! | Wethersfield | H |
| Westironworks! | Brookfield | F |
| West Killingly§ | Killingly | W |
| Westlane! | Ridgefield | F |
| Westmiddle! | Hartford | H |
| Westminster*†! | Canterbury | W |
| West Morris†! | Morris | L |
| West Mystic*†! | Groton | NL |
| Westneck! | Waterford | NL |
| West Norfolk*†! | Norfolk | L |
| W. Norwalk§?†! | Norwalk | F |
| Westpeak! | Meriden | NH |
| Westport*§?†‖ | Westport | F |
| Westoverplain! | Simsbury | H |
| West Redding§?† | Redding | F |
| West Rockyhill! | Rockyhill | H |
| West Saugatuck! | Westport | F |
| W. Stratford, now | Bridgeport | F |
| Westside! | Madison | NH |
| Westside! | Woodbury | L |
| West Simsbury†! | Simsbury | H |
| West Stafford?.† | Stafford | T |
| West Stamford?! | Stamford | F |
| Weststreet* | Vernon | T |
| Weststreet! | New Canaan | L |
| West Suffield†! | Suffield | H |
| W. Thompson*†! | Thompson | W |
| West Torrington† | Torrington | L |
| Westtownstreet!? | Norwich | NL |
| Westville! | Danbury | F |
| Westville§?†! | New Haven | NH |
| West Westogue | Simsbury | H |
| West Willington?† | Willington | T |
| W. Winsted*§?†! | Winchester | L |
| Westwoods! | Hamden | NH |
| Westwoods! | Sharon | L |
| W.Woodstock?†! | Woodstock | W |
| Wethersfield*§?†‖!! | Wethersfield | H |
| Wetogue! | Salisbury | L |
| Weymouth! | Enfield | H |
| Whalebonecreek | Lyme | NL |
| Wheaton! | Pomfret | W |
| Wheatons* | Stamford | F |
| Wheeler! | N.Stonington | NL |
| Wheeler! | Stonington | NL |
| Wheelerfarm! | Milford | NH |
| Whigville?†! | Burlington | H |
| Whipstick! | Ridgefield | F |
| Whisconier! | Brookfield | F |
| Whistcorner! | Brookfield | F |
| Whistletown | East Lyme | NL |
| Whistleville | Norwalk | F |
| White! | Griswold | NL |
| Whitebeach | East Lyme | NL |
| Whitebird! | Salem | NL |
| Whitehall! | Plainfield | W |
| Whitehills!U&L. | Huntington | L |
| Whitehollow! | Sharon | L |
| Whiteoak! | New Britain | H |
| Whiteoak! | Plainville | H |
| Whiteoak! | Southbury | NH |
| Whiteoakshade! | New Canaan | F |
| Whiteplain! | Trumbull | F |
| Whiteschoolhouse! | Pomfret | W |
| Whiteschoolhouse! | Tolland | T |
| Whiting! | New Haven | NH |
| Whitingriver* | Canaan | L |
| Whitneyville§?†! | Hamden | NH |
| Whittlesey! | Salisbury | L |
| Wicketlane! | East Haddam | M |
| Wighill | Chester | M |
| Wildwood? | 8th ward, Hartford | H |
| Williams! | Glastonbury | H |
| Williams! | Stonington | KL |
| Williamsville?! | Killingly | W |
| Willimantic! | Tolland | T |
| Willimantic*§?†‡! | Windham | W |
| Willington*§?†‖! | Willington | T |
| Willisville! | Stamford | F |
| Willoughby! | Canterbury | W |
| Willowbrook | East Hartford | H |
| Willowbrook | Wethersfield | H |
| Wilsons*† | Windsor | H |
| Wilsonspoint*§?! | Norwalk | F |
| Wilsonstreet! | Easton | F |
| Wilsonville*†! | Thompson | W |
| Wilton*§†‖!! | Wilton | F |
| Wiltonstation* | Wilton | F |
| Winchester§‖!! | Winchester | L |
| Winchestercenter§†!! | Winchester | L |
| Windermere*! | Ellington | T |
| Windham?‖ | Windham | W |
| Windham!N&S. | Windham | W |
| Windsor*§?†‖! | Windsor | H |
| Windsorlocks*§?†!! | Windsorl'cks | H |
| Windsorville†! | East Windsor | H |
| Winnipauk*§?†! | Norwalk | F |
| Winsted*§?‡¶! | Winchester | L |
| Winthrop†! | Saybrook | M |
| Witter! | Brooklyn | L |
| Wolcott§†‖! | Wolcott | NH |
| Wolfhill | Southington | H |
| Wolfneck! | Stonington | NL |
| Wolfpits! | Bethel | F |
| Wolfsden | Pomfret | W |
| Woodbridge§?‖!! | Woodbridge | NH |
| Woodbury§?†§ | Woodbury | L |
| Woodchuckhill | Canterbury | W |
| Woodchuckhill | Canton | H |
| Woodcreek! | New Fairfield | F |
| Woodhill! | Woodstock | W |
| Woodland*? | East Hartford | H |
| Woodland! | Ashford | W |
| Woodlawn | Pomfret | W |
| Woodlawn | Stafford | T |
| Woodmont*§?†! | Milford | NH |
| Woodneck! | Bethlehem | L |
| Woods! | Madison | NH |
| Woodside? | 1st Ward, Hfd. | H |
| Woodstation* | Suffield | H |
| Woodstock§?†‖!! | Woodstock | W |
| Woodstockhill! | Woodstock | W |
| Woodstockval.?†! | Woodstock | W |
| Woodtick | Wolcott | NH |
| Woodtick§ | Waterbury | NH |
| Woodvalley! | Woodstock | W |
| Woodville | Somers | T |
| Woodville†! | Washington | L |
| Woodward! | Griswold | NL |
| Woolsey! | New Haven | NH |
| Wooster! | New Haven | NH |
| Works?! | Stafford | T |
| Wormwoodhill! | Mansfield | T |
| Worthington?! | Berlin | H |
| Wylie! | Voluntown | NL |
| Yaleeville*?†! | Wallingford | NH |
| Yantic*§?†! | Norwich | NL |
| Yellowschoolhouse! | Easton | F |
| Youngsville! | Barkhamsted | L |
| Zionshill? | 8th Ward, Hartford | H |
| Zionshill | Suffield | H |
| Zoar*! | Newtown | F |
| Zoarbridge | Oxford | NH |

*Railroad and Express Stations; §Telegraphs; †Telephones; ‡Post Offices; ‡Cities; !Towns; ¶Boroughs; !School District

## MOUNTAINS.

| Name. | Town. | County. |
|---|---|---|
| Archer | Lyme | NL |
| Asprooma | Ridgefield | F |
| Ayers | Franklin | NL |
| Bear, 2,354 feet | Salisbury | L |
| Beaverbog | New Fairfield | F |
| Bald, 1,750 feet | Norfolk | L |
| Bald, 1,700 feet | Stafford | T |
| Blake | Lebanon | NL |
| Bolton | Bolton | T |
| Brace, 2,300 feet | Salisbury | L |
| Bradford, 1,910 feet | Canaan | L |
| Burr | Norfolk | L |
| Bushnell | Washington | L |
| Canaan 11950 feet | North Canaan | L |
| Candlewood | Sherman | F |
| Carmel*‡?†l | Hamden | NH |
| Coltsfoot | Cornwall | L |
| Delectable | Bolton | T |
| East l | Waterbury | NH |
| Eastrock | North Haven | NH |
| French | Watertown | L |
| Fuller | Kent | L |
| General l | Kent | L |
| Haystack, 1,678 feet | Norfolk | L |
| Hope†l | Mansfield | T |
| Ivy, 1,642 feet | Goshen | L |
| Kent | Kent | L |
| Lamentation | Berlin | H |
| Lone l | New Milford | L |
| Long | Milford | NH |
| Mohawk, 1,600 feet | Cornwall | L |
| North | Brookfield | F |
| Parnassus | East Haddam | M |
| Pisgar | East Lyme | NL |
| Pleasant? | Derby | NH |
| Prospect | Litchfield | L |
| Riga*l | Salisbury | L |
| Sharon l | Sharon | L |
| Skiff l | Kent | L |
| Talcott | Avon | H |
| Toby*? | Plymouth | L |
| Tom l | Milford | NH |
| Tom l | Morris | L |
| Totoket | Guilford | NH |
| Tower? | Avon | L |
| Towndale | Cornwall | L |
| Under | Canaan | L |
| Vernon l | Southington | H |
| West l | Ridgefield | F |
| Westrock, Hamden, New Haven. | | NH |

## ISLANDS.

| | | |
|---|---|---|
| Bells island | Norwalk | F |
| Box island | Waterford | NL |
| Bradford island | Groton | NL |
| Branford 3-4 islands | Branford | NH |
| " Belden, Blackstone, Clam | Crib, | |
| " Cutintwo, Darrow, Eastcrib, | | |
| " Foot, Governor, Green, High, | | |
| " Horse, Hut, Jeffrey, Lewis, | | |
| " Mermaid, Money, Oldcow, Pot, | | |
| ' Owlsnest, Pages, Pierson, Reed, | | |
| " Pumpkin, Sedge, Spectacle, | | |
| " Sumac, Stony, Stoopingbush, | | |
| " Squaw, Taunton, Twotree, | | |
| " Westcrib, Whitetop. | | |
| Captains islands | Greenwich | F |
| Charles island | Milford | NH |
| Cockenoes island | Westport | F |
| Comstock island | Wilton | F |
| ContentmentislandDarien | | F |
| Cows island | Fairfield | F |
| Cows islands | Stamford | F |
| Crab island | Darien | F |
| Dog island | Norwalk | F |
| Duck island | Westbrook | M |

| Name. | Town. | County. |
|---|---|---|
| Elihus island | Stonington | NL |
| Eustatia island | Saybrook | M |
| Fairweatherisland | Fairfield | F |
| Faulkners island | Guilford | NH |
| Fish island | Darien | F |
| Fishing island | Stamford | F |
| Fosdick island | Guilford | NH |
| Goose island | Guilford | NH |
| Goose island | Norwalk | F |
| Goose island | Waterford | NL |
| Grass island | Norwalk | F |
| Haddam island | Haddam | M |
| Hadlyme island | Lyme | NL |
| Hammock island | Norwalk | F |
| Hay island | Norwalk | F |
| Hen and Chickens | Old Saybrook | M |
| High island | Branford | NH |
| Horse island | Guilford | NH |
| Kitts island | Westport | F |
| Leets island*‡†l | Guilford | NH |
| Lords island | East Haddam | M |
| Masons island | Stonington | NL |
| Mouse island | Middletown | M |
| Mystic island, Groton, Stonington. | | NL |
| Narrows island | Guilford | NH |
| Nells island | Stratford | F |
| Nomans island | Guilford | NH |
| Notts island | Lyme | NL |
| Pine island | Groton | NL |
| Poverty island | Old Lyme | NL |
| Ram island | Norwalk | F |
| Salt island | Westbrook | M |
| Sheffield island | Norwalk | F |
| Smiths island | Norwalk | F |
| Spite island | Norwalk | F |
| Tavern island | Norwalk | F |
| Thimble islands | Branford | NH |
| Tuxis island | Madison | NH |
| Tweed island | Greenwich | F |
| Twelvemileisland | Saybrook | M |
| Twotree island | Waterford | NL |
| Vincent island | Stamford | F |
| Waite island | Stamford | F |

## LAKES.

| | | |
|---|---|---|
| Bantam lake | Litchfield, Morris | L |
| Bashan lake | East Haddam | M |
| Billings lake | N. Stonington | NL |
| Black lake | Woodstock | W |
| Breakneck lake | Union | T |
| Bride lake | East Lyme | NL |
| Cedar lake | Chester | M |
| Collequam lake | Greenwich | F |
| Community lake | Wallingford | NH |
| Congomond lake | Suffield | H |
| Creamhill lake | Cornwall | L |
| Crystal lake | Groton | NL |
| Crystal lake | Union | T |
| Crystal | Eastford, Woodstock | W |
| Diamond lake | Glastonbury | H |
| Eastlake l | Waterford | NL |
| Fairy lake | Salem | NL |
| Fountain lake | Newtown | F |
| Gardnerslake†Salem, Boz. Mont. | | NL |
| George l | Newtown | F |
| Greenwood lake | Cornwall | L |
| Hamden lake | Hamden | NH |
| Holbrook lake | Bolton | T |
| Kanamoe lake | Waterford | NL |
| Kanoha lake | Danbury | F |
| Kenosha lake | Danbury | F |
| Konomuc lake | Montville | NL |
| Long lake | Winchester | L |
| Maltby lake | New Haven | NH |
| Mamanasco lake | Ridgfield | F |
| Mashapaug lake | Union | T |
| Millriver lake | Fairfield | F |
| Mountain lake | Salem | NL |

| Name. | Town. | County |
|---|---|---|
| North reservoir lake | Wallingfd. | NH |
| Okseboksee lake | Montville | NL |
| Pattagansettlake | East Lyme | NL |
| Pickerel lake | Colchester | NL |
| Pocotopogue lake | Chatham | M |
| Poquonoc lake | Ledyard | NL |
| Powers lake | East Lyme | NL |
| Quassepaug lake | Middlebury | NH |
| Reservoir lake | Middletown | M |
| Rimmon lake | Seymour | NH |
| Rogers lake | Old Lyme | NL |
| Saltonstall | Branford, E. Haven. | NH |
| Shaws lake | East Haddam | M |
| Shuttlemeadow lake | New Britain | H |
| Snipsic | Vernon, Ellington, Tolland. | T |
| Taunton lake | Newtown | F |
| Twin lakes* | Salisbury | L |
| Wangambaug lake* | Coventry | T |
| Wanonpakok lake | Salisbury | L |
| Waramaug.*Warren, Washington. | | L |
| Whitney lake | Hamden | NH |
| Windermere lake | Wallingford | NH |
| Wintergreen lake | Hamden | NH |
| Wocoons lake | Portland | M |
| Wononscopomac lake | Salisbury | L |
| Wyassup lake | N. Stonington. | NL |

## PONDS.

| | | |
|---|---|---|
| Alexander's pond | Killingly | W |
| Allens mills pond | Sprague | NL |
| Andrews pond | Danbury | F |
| Angers pond | Thompson | W |
| Avery pond | Preston | NL |
| Babcocks pond | Colchester | NL |
| Bacons pond | Woodbury | L |
| Baileys pond | Voluntown | NL |
| Balcolm pond | Norfolk | L |
| Baldwins pond | Plymouth | L |
| Bulls pond† | New Fairfield | F |
| Baltic pond | Sprague | NL |
| Bashan pond | East Haddam | M |
| Bates pond | Canterbury | W |
| Beach pond | Norwich | NL |
| Beach pond | Voluntown | NL |
| Beaconfalls pond | Beacon Falls | NH |
| Beardsley pond | Sharon | L |
| Bears pond | New Fairfield | F |
| Beasley pond | Salisbury | L |
| Beaver pond | Meriden | NH |
| Beaver pond | Milford | NH |
| Beaverbrook pond | Sprague | NL |
| Beckley pond | Norfolk | L |
| Beckwiths pond | Woodbury | L |
| Beeds pond | Fairfield | F |
| Benedict pond | Norfolk | L |
| Bennetts pond | Ridgefield | F |
| Big pond | Bloomfield | H |
| Big pond | Watertown | L |
| Big pond | Windsor | H |
| Bigelow pond | Hampton | W |
| Bigelow pond | Norfolk | L |
| Bigelow pond | Union | T |
| Birds pond | Lebanon | NL |
| Birnsley pond | Branford | NH |
| Black pond | Meriden | NH |
| Black pond | Middlefield | M |
| Blackhall pond | Old Lyme | NL |
| Blakeley pond | Norfolk | L |
| Blissville pond | Lisbon | NL |
| Boggs pond | Danbury | F |
| Bogmeadow pond | Sharon | L |
| Breakneck pond | Union | T |
| Briggs pond | New London | NL |
| Brookside pond | Montville | NL |
| Brown Brothers pond | Colchester | NL |
| Buddington pond | Ledyard | NL |
| Carrs pond | Salem | NL |
| Cedar pond | Lyme | NL |

*Railroad and Express Stations; ‡ Telegraphs; †Telephones; † Post Offices; ‡Cities; ‖Towns; ¶ Boroughs; l School Districts.

| Name. | Town. | County. |
|---|---|---|
| Cedar pond.....No. | Branford.NH | |
| Cedarswamp pond.Bristol........H | | |
| Chapmans pond.. East Haddam.. M | | |
| Chaubamaug pond.. Killingly.... W | | |
| Cherry pond.....Avon. ........H | | |
| Cherry pond.....Canton........H | | |
| Clayville pond...Griswold.....NL | | |
| Columbia reservoir.Columbia.... T | | |
| Compounce pond.Southington ...H | | |
| Cove pond......Stamford......F | | |
| Cranberry pond..Granby.......H | | |
| Cranberry pond..Litchfield.....L | | |
| Dairy pond.....Norwalk......F | | |
| Davis pond.. .Lisbon.....NL | | |
| Diamond pond...Glastonbury...H | | |
| Dixies pond...Fairfield......F | | |
| Dog pond........Goshen......L | | |
| Doolittle pond..Norfolk......L | | |
| Dunhams pond..Mansfield.....T | | |
| East pond.....Cornwall......L | | |
| EastKillinglypond.Killingly....W | | |
| Eastlake pond!..Waterford....NL | | |
| Empewaug pond.Redding......F | | |
| Empewaug pond.Ridgefield......F | | |
| English pond....Windsorlocks..H | | |
| Five mile pond...Wallingford..NH | | |
| Fourteen acre pond. Norwalk....F | | |
| Foxs pond......Montville....NL | | |
| Fresh pond.....Stratford......F | | |
| Frisbies pond....Wallingford..NH | | |
| Frog pond......Windham.....W | | |
| Fuller pond....Kent.........L | | |
| Fullers pond....Hampton.....W | | |
| Gales pond......Preston......NL | | |
| Giddings pond...Lisbon.......H | | |
| Gorhams pond...Darien.......F | | |
| Goshen pond.....No. Branford. NH | | |
| Greenwood pond.New Hartford..L | | |
| Great pond.....Ridgefield.....F | | |
| Great pond.....Simsbury.....H | | |
| Great pond......Windsor.....H | | |
| Greathill pond...Portland......M | | |
| Hadlyme cove...Lyme.......NL | | |
| Ramlin pond....Plainville.....H | | |
| Harts pond.....Southington...H | | |
| Hatchet pond. Union, Woodstock..W | | |
| Hatch pond....Kent.........L | | |
| Hayward Cos pond.Colchester..NL | | |
| Hazelmeadow pond.Simsbury...H | | |
| Hoadleys pond...Plymouth.....L | | |
| Hodge pond.....Voluntown...NL | | |
| Hog pond......Lyme......NL | | |
| Hog pond......Windham.....W | | |
| Holbrook pond...Windsorlocks..H | | |
| Holly pond.....Darien........F | | |
| Horse pond.....Madison.....H | | |
| Humiston pond ..Wallingford.. NH | | |
| Hurds pond.....Fairfield......F | | |
| Indian pond.....Sharon......L | | |
| Jobs pond.....Portland......M | | |
| Jordan mill pond.Waterford....NL | | |
| Kent pond......Lebanon.....NL | | |
| Kettlebrook pond.Windsorlocks ..H | | |
| Kenyons pond...Colchester...NL | | |
| Kings pond.....Thompson....W | | |
| Lake pond......Southington...H | | |
| Lakes pond!....Waterford....NL | | |
| Lanternhill. Ledyard N. Stoning.NL | | |
| Lawrence pond..Lisbon......NL | | |
| Leachs pond....Ledyard.....NL | | |
| Leonard pond...Kent........L | | |
| Lewis pond.....New London..NL | | |
| Lilly pond......Avon.......H | | |
| Lilly pond.....Glastonbury...H | | |
| Lilly pond.....Southington...H | | |
| Linsleys pond...No. Branford..NH | | |
| Little pond.....Danbury......F | | |
| Little pond.....Farmington...H | | |

| Name. | Town. | County. |
|---|---|---|
| Little pond.....Litchfield.....L | | |
| Little pond.....Ridgefield.....F | | |
| Little pond.....Simsbury.....H | | |
| Little pond.....Thompson....W | | |
| Little pond.....Winchester....L | | |
| Little pond.....Windsor.....H | | |
| Locust pond.....Beacon Falls. NH | | |
| Lockwood pond..Watertown..... L | | |
| Long pond......Old Lyme....NL | | |
| Long pond......Salisbury.....L | | |
| Long pond.N.Stonington,Leyard.NL | | |
| Long pond......Thompson....W | | |
| Longmeadow pond.. Bethlehem...L | | |
| Longmeadow. Oxford. Mid'lb'ry.NH | | |
| Longridge mills pond.Stamford... F | | |
| Loomis pond....Killingly.....W | | |
| Lost pond......Union.......T | | |
| Mamonasco pond. Ridgefield.....F | | |
| Margorie pond..Danbury......F | | |
| Marlboroughpond.Marlborough...H | | |
| Marsh pond....East Granby...H | | |
| Marshapaug pond.Goshen......L | | |
| Marshy pond...Bristol.......H | | |
| Mathews pond.. Stamford......F | | |
| Meadow pond...Killingworth...M | | |
| Messenger pond..Colebrook.....L | | |
| Middlesex Mfg pond.Middletown..M | | |
| Mill pond.....Branford....NH | | |
| Mill pond......Stamford.....F | | |
| Mill pond......Litchfield.....L | | |
| Millers pond....Waterford....NL | | |
| Millers pond....Durham......M | | |
| Millpond.......Windsorlocks ..H | | |
| Mixs pond.....Wallingford..NH | | |
| Mohawk pond...Cornwall......L | | |
| Morgan pond....Ledyard......NL | | |
| Mountain pond..Danbury......F | | |
| Mount Tom { Morris,Litchfield, } L | | |
|    pond { Washington...... } | | |
| Mud pond......Cornwall......L | | |
| Mud pond..New Milford, Kent..L | | |
| Mud pond.....Norfolk......L | | |
| Mud pond......Sharon......L | | |
| Muddy pond....Woodstock....W | | |
| Mudge pond....Salisbury......L | | |
| Neversink pond..Danbury......F | | |
| Nichols pond.....Oxford......NH | | |
| Norfolk reservoir.Norfolk......L | | |
| North pond.....Goshen.......L | | |
| North pond.. Hebron. Lebanon. NL | | |
| North pond.....Salisbury.....L | | |
| North Spectacle pond.Kent......L | | |
| Norwich pond...Lyme.......NL | | |
| Oldmarsh pond..Plymouth.....L | | |
| Old Marsh pond. Bristol.......H | | |
| Oxboro pond....Montville....NL | | |
| Pachaug pond...Griswold.....NL | | |
| Palmer pond....Middletown...M | | |
| Pamecha pond...Middletown...M | | |
| Park pond.....Winchester....L | | |
| Parkers pond....Wallingford.. NH | | |
| Patchogue pond..Westbrook.....L | | |
| Paug pond..N.Brandfd,Walngfd.NH | | |
| Peconsett pond...Portland......M | | |
| Pequot pond....Montville....NL | | |
| Pestapaugh pond. Wallingford. . NH | | |
| Phelps pond....Colebrook.....L | | |
| Phillips pond...Stamford......F | | |
| Pisteraugh { Wallingford, No. } NH | | |
|   pond, { Branf'd,Durham, } M | | |
| Posey pond.....Norfolk......L | | |
| Potters pond....Woodstock....W | | |
| Poverty pond....Redding......F | | |
| Pratling pond....Farmington....H | | |
| Preston City pond.Preston......NL | | |
| Pritchards pond..Waterbury...NH | | |
| Quadiclowerpond.Thompson....W | | |
| Quasapaug pond. Middlebury ..NH | | |

| Name. | Town. | County. |
|---|---|---|
| Beads pond.....Lisbon......NL | | |
| Reservoir ponds..Watertown....L | | |
| Reservoir pond...Windsorlocks..H | | |
| Respect pond....Brookfield....F | | |
| Rockfall pond. ...Middletown...M | | |
| Rockland pond ..Montville....NL | | |
| Rose pond......Branford....NH | | |
| Round pond.....Ridgefield.....L | | |
| Round pond.....Salisbury.....L | | |
| Round pond.....Danbury......F | | |
| Rowley pond....Winchester....L | | |
| Roxbury mills pond.Stamford....F | | |
| Russell Mfg Co. pond.Middletown.M | | |
| Russell&Erwinspond.New Britain.H | | |
| Quinebaug pond Killingly.....W | | |
| Quinnipaug pond.Guilford.....NH | | |
| Quinnipiac pond. Wallingford.. NH | | |
| Scotch pond.....Southington...H | | |
| Schofields pond..Montville....NL | | |
| Seyms pond.....Colchester...NL | | |
| Shepherds pond..New Hartford..L | | |
| Shermans pond...Colchester...NL | | |
| Sherwood pond ..Westport.....F | | |
| Simpson, Hall & M. Wallingford.NH | | |
| Spalding pond...N. Stonington.NL | | |
| Spaldings pond...Norwich.....NL | | |
| Spectacle pond..Kent........L | | |
| Sperrys pond...Bolton.......T | | |
| Spring pond....Granby.......H | | |
| Spring pond....Windsorlocks..H | | |
| Squants pond...Sherman......F | | |
| Square pond†!Ellington, Stafford T | | |
| Squntz pond....New Fairfield..F | | |
| Smith pond.....Watertown.....L | | |
| South Spectacle pond.Kent......L | | |
| Standishs pond..Colchester...NL | | |
| Starr pond.....Middletown...M | | |
| Stillwater pond..Stamford......F | | |
| Straddlehill pond.Middletown...M | | |
| Strongs pond...Colchester...NL | | |
| Stroud pond....Middletown...M | | |
| Sturges pond....Fairfield......F | | |
| Sugarhollowpond.Danbury......F | | |
| Swan pond.....Old Lyme....NL | | |
| Sympaug pond..Bethel.......F | | |
| Thomaston W. Co. pond Plymouth.L | | |
| Three corner pond.Granby.......H | | |
| Tobez pond....Norfolk......L | | |
| Towantic pond...Oxford......NH | | |
| Tower pond....Avon........H | | |
| Town pond.....Mansfield.....T | | |
| Transylvania pond. Southbury..NH | | |
| Trauts pond....New Britain..H | | |
| Troutbrook pond. Wethersfield...H | | |
| Tryons pond....Farmington....H | | |
| Tuxis pond.....Madison.....NH | | |
| Turtle pond....Southbury...NH | | |
| Tylers pond....Goshen.......L | | |
| Tylers pond....Wallingford..NH | | |
| Uncasville pond..Montville....NL | | |
| Umperwaug pond.Redding......F | | |
| Vencels pond....New Britain..H | | |
| Vincents pond...Montville....NL | | |
| Wakeley pond...Easton.......F | | |
| Waterworks pond.Stamford......F | | |
| Watrous pond...Chester......M | | |
| West pond......Guilford.....NH | | |
| Westhill pond...West Hartford.H | | |
| Westlake pond!..Waterford....NL | | |
| West Hartland pond.Hartland....H | | |
| Wheaton pond...Killingly.....W | | |
| Wilcox pond....Middletown...M | | |
| Williams pond...Lebanon.....NL | | |
| Willimantic reservoir.Bolton.....T | | |
| Wolf pond......Danbury......F | | |
| Woods pond....Portland.....M | | |
| Woodings pond..Wallingford..NH | | |
| Woodstock pond..Woodstock....W | | |

# Hartford Post Office,

**65 State street, and opposite 14 Central row.**

FRANK P. FURLONG, *Postmaster.*

HENRY E. BABCOCK, *Assistant Postmaster.*

Henry J. Hall, *Cashier and Bookkeeper.*

**CLERKS.**

*Money Order:* A. T. Bogue, Sup't, Catharine E. Costain, Carrie E. Hall.

*Stamps:* Julian H. Gates, Ernest E. C. Bassett.

*Registry:* Frank D. Munger, Sup't; Annie G. Dooley.

*General Delivery:* F. A. Smith, C. R. Harrington.

*Box Division:* Sidney O. Dickinson, Chief Clerk, R. C. Thomas, E. R. Scott, E. W. Goodale, F. A. Connolly, C. J. Steele.

*Mailing:* R. N. Watrous, foreman; Robt. H. Roulston, Wm. S. Goodrich, Wm. E. Young, Thomas Curtis, H. F. Roberts, A. E. Lennox.

*Letter Carriers:* F. C. Jackson, Sup't, P. E. Sheehan, Eugene G. Austin, O. D. Brown, J. B. Gossman, D. W. C. Graves, Charles H. Halladay, Thomas F. Hayes, Julius Herzfeld, Charles Jackson, D. S. McGrath, John O'Farrell, W. C. Elwin, A. C. Reuthe, Garrett Roach, Lloyd E. Seymour, L.W. Smith, S. E. Waters, John F. Smith,William C. Preston, Thomas F. Daly, C. J. Mulligan, Aaron D. Cook, Ambrose Mulligan, W. H. Shaffer, George F. Ebert, P. E. Kenney, L. C. Nelison, Fred. W. Seymour, Watkins W. Christian, Henry E. Beebe, Fred. Kreimendahl, C. R. Williams, G. H. Lankton, J. J. Preston, A. C. Gough, Niels Husted, Thos. Leahy. *Sub-Carriers:* A. T. Rich, Ernest S. Kepler, Francis H. Woodbury, Albert B. Hart.

*Night:* W. A. Morgan, E. R. Benedict, F. E. Collins, H. R. Taylor, Howard Crocker.

*Messengers:* W. H. Nodine, Frank Sarvan, Edward G. Kober, Philip Carlin, C. F. Meyers, E. B. Bunce, G. H. Ryder.

*Porter:* William D. Cross.

*At Station A:* M. P. Keane, Wm. Maguire, W. R. Purple; A. M. Green, *Janitor.*

There will be four deliveries and fourteen collections within the business section of the city, and three deliveries and three collections beyond, except outskirts, two deliveries and two collections; and a collection from 100 boxes after 8 P. M. The business deliveries will leave the office at 7 and 10.30 A. M., and 2 and 3.30 P.M.; and outside at 7 and 10.30 A.M. and 3.30 P.M. Letters must be deposited in the Post Office five minutes before the carriers leave.

*For Stamp Agencies see page 34.*

**STREET MAIL LETTER BOXES.**

Carriers from this office hereafter will not stop while on their routes to collect mail matter except from the street mailing boxes, from doors where they are delivering mail at the same time, and from persons on the sidewalk; and in *no case* will they receive mail matter on which the postage *has not been prepaid.* The boxes are located as follows:

Albany av.; Nos. 90, 131.
Ann; Nos. 91, 57.
Asylum; Nos.117.201,270, 370,377,378,635,784,878, 948, 1073, Union Depot, cor. Ford, cor. High, cor. Farmington.
Ashley, cor. May, cor. Garden.
Babcock, cor. Russ.
Bellevue; No. 94.
Bluchills av.; No. 71.
Broad; Nos. 840,1478,1507.
Buckingham; No. 54.
Canton; No. 32.
Capen; No. 68.
Capitol; Nos. 93, 193, 374, 475, 612.
Center; No. 16.
Charter Oak place; No. 9.
Ch. Oak; Nos. 28, 58, 154.
Church; Nos. 45, 82.
Collins; 31, 155, 189, 227, cor. Atwood, cor. Sigourney.
Congress; No. 35.
Elm; No. 71.
Fairfield av.
Farmington av.; 67, 116, 180,250,305,480,536,670.
Forest; No. 9.
Franklin av.; No. 163.
Front; Nos.25,157,181,225.
Garden; Nos. 100,174,221, 574.
Gillett; No. 70.
Grand; No. 31.
Harrison av.; No. 39.
High; Nos. 137, 211.
Hopkins; No. 39.
Hotel Hartford.
Hotel Heublein.
Huntington, cor. Ashley.
Huyshope; No. 75.
Jefferson; No. 61.
Lafayette; No. 13.
Laurel; No. 20.
Main; Nos. 54,117,310,407, 427,484,539,613,650, 709, 716,721,901,904,926,958, 973,1048,1131,1248,1389.

Maple; No. 144.
Market; No. 67.
Morris; No. 17.
N. Britain; Nos. 10, 98.
Oak, cor. Russ.
Park; Nos. 70, 113, 171, 227, 311, 371.
Pearl; Nos. 49, 129, 190, 255, 315.
Pleasant; No. 74.
Pratt; No. 68.
Prospect; No. 33.
Prospect av. cor. Fern.
Retreat av.; No. 120.
Riverside av. Laurel.
Seyms; No. 18.
Sheldon; No. 227.
Spring; No. 34.
"The Linden."
State; by City Hall; Nos. 26, 106, 204.
Townley; No. 2.
Trinity College.
Trumbull; Nos. 53, 86.
Unity Building.
Vernon; No. 102.
Vine; No. 1.
Walnut; Nos. 26, 62.
Ward; No. 44.
Washington; Nos. 40, 77.
Wells; No. 95.
Westland; No. 25.
Weth. av; Nos. 73, 145,242.
Weth. av. cor. Brown.
Windsor; Nos. 56, 117.
Windsor av.; Nos. 64, 108, 156,268,373,588,807, 912.
Woodland; No. 110.
Zion, near Hamilton.

**PARKVILLE DISTRICT.**

Amity st; 37.
Francis av.; 32.
Madison av. and Park st.
New Park av. and Grace st.
New Park av. and Kibbe st.
Post Office.
Railroad station.

**PAPER & PACKAGE BOXES.**

Union Depot.

# Hours for Closing Conn· Mails in Hartford.

Corrected to July 18, 1898.

*Money Order Post Offices. †Also International or Foreign Money Order Office.

| | A. M. | P. M. | | A. M. | P. M. | | A. M. | P. M. |
|---|---|---|---|---|---|---|---|---|
| Abington,* | 7½ | 1½ | Berlin,* | 7½, 11½ | | Bristol,*† | 5½,9½, 12 | 3, 5½ |
| Addison, | 6, 10.30 | 2½ | Bethany, | 1, 7½, 9½ | 2½, 4½, 6, 7 | Broad Brook.* | 1, 9½ | 1½, 5½ |
| Allingtown,1,5½, 7½, 9½ 11½ 2½, 4½, 6,7 | | | Bethel.*† | 1, 7½, 11½ | 6 | Brockway,* | 5½ | 5 |
| Andover.* | 4, 7½ | 4½ | Bethlehem,* | 5½, 7½ | 2½ | Brookfield,* 1, 7½, 11½ | | |
| Ansonia,*† | 1, 7½, 11½ | 2½ | Bill Hill, | 1, 5½ | 3, 9 | Brookfield Cent.*1, 7½, 11½ | | |
| Ashford, | 1, 4½ | 1½, 4½ | Black Hall,* | 1, 5½ | 1½, 3½, 9 | Brooklyn.* | 4, 7½ | 11½, 10 |
| Ashwillet, | 1, 4, 7½ | 1½, 4½ | Black Rock.*1, 7½, 11½ | | 4½, 6, 7 | Brooks Vale, 1, 7½, 11½ | | 2½ |
| Aspetuck, 1, 7½, 11½ | | 4, 6 | Bloomfield,* | 7½ | 2½ | Buckingham, | 6, 10 | 2½ |
| Atwoodville,* | 7½, 4 | 1½, 4½ | Boardman, | 1, 7½, 11½ | 8 | Buckland, | 4, 7½ | 4½ |
| Avon.* | | 3½ | Bolton,. | | 4 | Bull's Bridge, | 1, 11½ | |
| Bakersville.* | 7½ | 2½, 5½ | Bolton Notch, | | 1½ | Burlington, | | 5½ |
| Bellouville,* | 1, 4 | 1½, 9 | Botsford,* | 1, 11½ | 7 | Burnside.* | 6, 10½ | 2½, 5½ |
| Baltic,* | 4 | 1½, 9 | Bozrahville,* | 1, 4, | 1½, 10 | Burrville, | 1, 7½ | 2½, 5½ |
| Bantam,* | 1, 7½, 11½ | 2½, 6 | Branchville.* | 1, 11½ | 7 | Campbells Mills, 1, 4 | | 1½, 10 |
| Barkhamsted,* | 7½ | 2½, 5½ | Branford.*† | 1, 11½ | 8 | Campville, | 1, 7½ | 2½, 5½ |
| Beacon Falls,* | 1, 7½ | 2½, 5½ | Bridgeport,*†1,7½, 9½,11½ | | 4½, 6, 7 | Canaan,* | 7½ | 2½ |
| Beckley, | 5½, 11½ | 8½, 5½ | Bridgewater,* 1, 7½, 11½ | | | Cannon, | 1, 7½, 11½ | 6 |

| | A. M. | P. M. |
|---|---|---|
| Canterbury,* | 1, 4, 8 | 1½, 9 |
| Canton, | 7½ | 2½ |
| Canton Center,* | 7½ | 2½ |
| Central Village,* | 1, 4, 11 | 1½, 9 |
| Center Brook,* | 5½ | 1½, 8 |
| Center Groton, | 1, 5½, 8 | 1½, 9 |
| Center Hill, | 7½ | 2½ |
| Chapinville, | 7½ | 2½ |
| Chaplin,* | 4, 7½ | 1½ |
| Cheshire,* | 1, 7½, 11½ | 2½ |
| Chestnut Hill, | 5½, 11½ | 4½ |
| Chester,*† | 5½ | 1½, 8 |
| Chesterfield, | 1, 8 | 1½, 8, 9 |
| Clarks Corner, | 1, 4, 7½ | 1½ |
| Clarks Falls, | 1, 4 | 1½, 9 |
| Clinton,* | 1, 5½ | 8 |
| Clintonville,* | 5½, 11½ | 8 |
| Cobalt,* | 5½, 11½ | 4½ |
| Colchester,*† | 5½, 11½ | 4½, 7 |
| Colebrook, | 7½ | 2½ |
| Colebrook River, | 7½ | 2½ |
| Collinsville *† | 7½ | 2½, 3½, 5½ |
| Columbia,* | 4, 7½ | 1½ |
| Comstocks Bridge, | 5½ | 1½, 4½ |
| Copper Hill, | 5½ | |
| Cornwall,* | 1, 11½ | |
| Cornwall Bridge,* | 1, 11½ | |
| Cornwall Centre, | 1, 11½ | |
| Cornwall Hollow, | 1, 11½ | |
| Coscob,* | 1, 7½, 11½ | 6 |
| Coventry, | 4, 7½ | 9, 10 |
| Cranbury, | 1, 7½, 11½ | 7 |
| Crescent, | 1, 5½, 7½, 8 | 3, 3½, 9 |
| Cromwell,* | 5½ | 3½ |
| Crystal Lake, | 1, 4, 11 | 1½, 4, 9 |
| Danbury,*† | 1, 5½, 12 | 5½ |
| Danielson,*† | 1, 4, 11 | 1½, 9 |
| Darien,* | 1, 7½, 11½ | 6 |
| Deep River,* | 5½ | 1½, 3½ |
| Derby,*† | 1, 7½, 11½ | 3½, 6 |
| Duncan, | 5½ | 1½, 3½ |
| Durham,* | 1, 5½, 11½ | 3 |
| Durham Center,* | 1, 5½, 11½ | 3 |
| Engleville, | 1, 4 | 1½, 9 |
| East Berlin,* | 7½, 11½ | |
| East Canaan,* | 1, 7½ | 2½ |
| East Cornwall, | 1, 11½ | |
| Eastford,* | 1, 4 | 1½, 4½ |
| East Glastonbury,* | 6, 10½ | 2¾ |
| East Granby,* | 8½, 11 | 4 |
| East Haddam,* | 5½ | 1½, 3 |
| East Hampton,* | 5½, 11½ | 4½, 6 |
| East Hartford,* | 6, 10¼ | 2¼, 5¼ |
| E. H. Meadow,* | 6 | 2¾ |
| East Hartland, | 7½ | 2½, 3½ |
| East Haven,* | 1, 5½ | 3 |
| East Kent, | 1, 7½, 11½ | |
| East Killingly,* | 1, 4, 11 | 1½, 9 |
| East Litchfield, | 1, 7½ | 2½, 5½ |
| East Lyme,* | 1, 5½, 8 | 3, 3½, 9 |
| East Morris, | 1, 7½, 11½ | 7 |
| Easton, | 1, 7½, 11½ | 7 |
| East River,* | 1, 5½ | 3½ |
| East Thompson, | 1, 4 | 1½ |
| East Wallingford, | 5½, 11½ | 4½ |
| East Willington, | 1, 4 | 1½, 9 |
| East Windsor, | 9½ | |
| East Windsor Hill,* | 9½ | 5½ |
| East Woodstock,* | 1, 4, 7½ | 1½, 4½ |
| Ekonk, | 1, 5½, 4 | 1½ 9 |
| Ellington,* | 5½, 9½ | 1½ |
| Elliott, | 4, 7½ | 1½, |
| Ellsworth, | 1, 11½ | |
| Elmwood,* | 7, 12 | |
| Enfield,* | 1, 8½, 11 | 4 |
| Essex,* | 5½ | 1½, 3 |
| Fairfield,* | 1, 7½, 11½ | 6 |
| Fair Ground, | 1, 5½, 11 | 1, 9 |
| Fair Haven, | 1, 7½, 11½ | 2½, 5, 6 |
| Falls Village,*† | 1 11½ | |
| Farmington,* | 1, 6, | 2½, 3, 5½ |
| Fitchville,* | 1, 4 | 9 |
| Forestville,* | 5½, 12 | 5½ |
| Franklin, | 1' 4, | 1½, 4½ |
| Gales Ferry, | 1, 4, | 1½, 9 |
| Gardner Lake, | 1, 4 | 1½, 3½, 4½, 9 |
| Gard's Lake, | 1, 4, | 1½, 9 |
| Gaylordsville,* | 1, 11½ | |
| Georgetown, | 1, 7½, 11½ | 7 |
| Gildersleeve,* | 5½, 11½ | 3½, 4½ |
| Gilead, | 5½, 11½ | 4½, 6 |
| Glasgo,* | 1, 4 | 1½, 9 |
| Glastonbury,* | 6, 10½ | 2¾ |
| Glenbrook,* | 1' 7½, 11½ | 6 |
| Glenville,* | 1, 7½, 11½ | 6 |
| Goshen,* | 1, 7½ | 2½, 5½ |
| Granby,* | 5½ | 2½, 3½ |
| Grantville, | 7½ | |
| Greystone, | 1, 5½, 12 | |
| Greens Farms,* | 1, 7½, 11½ | 7 |
| Greenfield Hill,* | 1, 7½, 11½ | 7 |
| Greenville,*† | 1, 4, 8, 11 | 1½ |
| Greenwich,*† | 1, 7½, 11½ | 7 |
| Griswold,* | 1, 4, 11 | 1½, 9 |
| Grosvenordale,* | 1, 4, 11 | 1½, 9 |
| Groton,* | 1, 4, 8 | 1½, 9 |
| Grove Beach, | 1, 5½ | 3 |
| Guilford,*† | 1, 5½ | 3 |
| Gurleyville, | 1, 4, 7½ | 1½, 4½ |
| Haddam,* | 5½ | 1½, 3½ |
| Haddam Neck, | 1, 5½, 11½ | 4½ |
| Hadlyme,* | 5½ | 1½, 3½ |
| Hamburg,* | 1, 5½ | 3, 3½, 9 |
| Hamden,* | 1, 10, 11½ | 3 |
| Hampsted, | 7½ | 2½, 3½ |
| Hampton,* | 4, 7½ | 1½ |
| Hanover,* | 4, 7½ | 1½, |
| Hartland | 7½ | 2½, 5½ |
| Harwinton,* | 1, 11½, | 6 |
| Hawleyville,* | 1, 12 | 2½ |
| Hawthorne, | 1, 7½, 11½ | 6 |
| Hazardville,* | 1, 9½ | 5½ |
| Hebron,* | 1, 5½ | 4½ |
| Higganum,* | 5½ | 1½, 3½ |
| Highland Park,* | 6, 10½ | 3, 6 |
| High Ridge, | 1, 7½, 11½ | 2½, 6 |
| Highwood,* | 1, 7½, 11½ | 2½, 6 |
| Hillstown, | 6, 10½ | 3 |
| Hockanum,* | 6, 10½ | 2¾ |
| Hopevale, | 5½, 11½ | 4, 7, 9 |
| Hopewell, | 5½, 10 | 2¾ |
| Hop River, | 4, 7½ | 1½ |
| Hotchkissville,* | 5½, 12 | |
| Howard Valley, | 4, 7½ | 1½ |
| Huntsville, | 1, 11½ | |
| Huntington, | 1, 7½, 11½ | 4½, 6 |
| Hurlbutt, | 1, 7½, 11½ | 6 |
| Ivoryton,* | 5½ | 1½, 3½ |
| Jewett City,*† | 1, 4, 11 | 1½, 9 |
| Judds Bridge, | 1, 7½, 11½ | 2½ |
| Kensington,* | 1, 7½, 11½ | 3, 6 |
| Kent,* | 1, 11½ | |
| Kent Furnace, | 1, 11½ | |
| Kibbe, | 1, 8½ | 1½, 5½ |
| Killingly,* | 1, 4, 11 | 1½, 9 |
| Killingworth, | 1, 5½ | 3, 3½ |
| Lakeville,* | 7½ | 2½ |
| Lanesville, | 1, 11½ | |
| Laurel Glen, | 1, 4 | 1½, 9 |
| Lebanon,* | 1, 4, | 9 |
| Ledyard, | 1, 4, | 1½, 9 |
| Leete's Island,* | 1, 5½ | 3, 3½ |
| Leffingwell, | 1, 4, | 1½, 9 |
| Leonard Bridge, | 1, 5½, 11½ | 4½ |
| Liberty Hill, | 5½, 11½ | 4½ |
| Lime Rock,* | 1, 11½ | |
| Litchfield,*† | 1, 7½, | 2½ |
| Little Haddam, | 5½ | 1½, 3½ |
| Little River, | 5½, 11½ | 5½ |
| Lockwood, | 1, 7½, 11½ | 6 |
| Long Hill,* | 1, 11½ | 6 |
| Long Ridge,* | 1, 7½, 11½ | 6 |
| Lyme,* | 1, 5½ | 3, 3½, 9 |
| Lyons Plain, | 1, 7½, 11½ | 6 |
| Madison,* | 1, 5½ | 3, 3½ |
| Manchester,* | 6, 10¼ | 1½, 5¼ |
| Manchester Green,* | 5, | 4½ |
| Mansfield, | 1, 5½, 4, | 1½, 9 |
| Mansfield Centre,* | 1, 4 | 1½, 4½ |
| Mansfi'd Dep't, | 1, 4, 5½ | 1½, 9 |
| Mapleton, | 1, 8½, 11 | 4 |
| Marble Dale, | 1, 7½, 11½ | |
| Marion, | 1, 7½, | 1½, 3 |
| Marlborough, | 5½, 11½ | 4½, 6 |
| Marlborough Mills,* | 5½ | 4½, 6 |
| Mashapaug, | 1, 4, 11 | 1½, 4, 9 |
| Massapeag, | 1, 4, | 1½, 4½ |
| Mechanicsville, | 1, 4, 11 | 1½, 9 |
| Melrose,* | 1, 9½ | 1½, 5½ |
| Meriden,*† | 1, 7½ 11½ | 2½, 4, 6, 7 |
| Merrow, | 1, 4, | 1½, 9 |
| Mianus,* | 1, 7½, 11½ | 6 |
| Middlebury, | 5½, 7½, 12 | |
| Middlefield,* | 1, 5½ | 4½ |
| Middle Haddam,* | 1, 5½, 11½ | 4½ |
| Middletown,*† | 5½, 11½ | 3, 5 |
| Milford,*† | 1, 7½, 11½ | 3 |
| Millbrook, | 5½ | 2½ |
| Milldale,* | 1, 7½, 11½ | 3 |
| Millington,- | 5½ | 1½, 3½ |
| Millplain, | 1, 7½, 12 | 7 |
| Millstone, | 1, 5½, 7½, 8 | 3½, 9 |
| Milton, | 1 | 2½ |
| Minortown, | 1, 7½, 12 | |
| Mohegan, | 1, 5½ | 1½, 9 |
| Monroe. | 1, 11½ | 7 |
| Montowese,* | 1, 5½, 11½ | 3 |
| Montville,* | 1, 4, | 1½, 9 |
| Moodus,*† | 5½ | 1½, 3½ |
| Moose Meadow, | 1, 4 | 1½, 9 |
| Moosup,* | 1, 4, 5½ | 1½, 9 |
| Morris, | 1, 7½, 11½ | 6 |
| Mount Carmel,* | 1, 11½ | 1½, 3 |
| Mt. Carmel Centre,* | 1, 11½ | 1½, 3 |
| Mount Hope, | 1, 4 | 1½, 4½ |
| Mystic,*† | 1, 5½ | 1½, 10 |
| Naubuc, | 6, 10½ | 3¾ |
| Naugatuck,*† | 1, 7½ | 2½ |
| Nepaug, | 5½ | 2½ |
| New Britain,*† | 5½, 7½, 12 | 3½, 5½ |
| New Boston,* | 1, 8 | 1½, |
| New Canaan,* | 1, 11½ | 6 |
| New Fairfield, | 1, 12, | 6 |
| New Hartford,* | 5½ | 2½, 5½ |
| N. Haven,*† | 1, 5½, 7½, 9½, 11½, | 2½, 4, 6, 7 |
| New London,*† | 1, 5½, 8 | 1½, 3½, 4½, 10 |
| New Milford,*† | 1, 7½, 11½ | |
| New Preston,* | 1, 7½, 11½ | 2½, 6 |
| Newington,* | 7½ | 3½ |
| Newington Junc.* | 7½, 12 | 3½ |
| Newtown,* | 1, 11½ | 6 |
| Niantic,*† | 1, 5½, 7½, 8 | 3, 3½, 9 |
| Nichols, | 1, 7½, 11½ | 6 |
| Noank,*† | 1, 5½, 8 | 1½, 9 |
| Norfolk,* | 7½ | 2½ |
| Noroton, | 1, 7½, 11½ | 6 |
| Noroton Heights,* | 1, 7½, 11½ | 6 |
| North Ashford, | 1, 4 | 1½, 4½ |
| N. Branford, | 1, 7½, 11½ | 3 |
| No. Canton, | 7½ | 2½ |
| North Colebrook, | 7½ | 2½ |
| Northfield,* | 1, 7½ | 2½, 5½ |
| Northford,* | 1, 5½, 11½ | 3 |

| | A. M. | P. M. |
|---|---|---|
| North Franklin, 1, 4, 5½ | | 9 |
| North Granby, | 7½ | 2½, 3½ |
| N. Grosvenordale,*1, 4. 7½,11 | | 1½, 9 |
| North Guilford, 7½, 11½ | | 3 |
| North Haven,* 1, 7½ 11½ | | 2½ |
| No. Kent, | 1, 4 | |
| North Lyme, | 1, 1⅜ | 3, 9 |
| North Madison, | 8¼, ½ | 3 |
| North Plain, | 1, 4 | 3, 9 |
| North Stamford, 1, 7½, 11½ | | 2½ |
| North Sterling, 1, 5½, 4, 7½,11 | | 1½, 9 |
| North Stonington,* 1, 5½ | | 1½, 9 |
| Northville, 1, 7½, 11½ | | |
| North Westchester,* 1, 5½, 11½ | | 4½ |
| North Wilton, 1, 7½, 11½ | | 6 |
| North Windham,* 4, 7½ | | 1½ |
| No. Woodbury, *5½, 2 | | |
| North Woodstock,* 1, 4, 7½ | | 1½, 4½ |
| Norwalk,* 1, 7½, 11½ | | 6 |
| Norwich,*† 1, 4 | | 1½,8½,4½,9 |
| Norwich Town,* 1, 4 | | 1½, 9 |
| Oakdale, 1, 5½ | | 1½, 9 |
| Oakville,* 1, 7½ | | 2½, 5½ |
| Old Mystic * 1, 5½ | | 1½, 9 |
| Oneco,* 1, 4, 5½ | | 1½, 9 |
| Orange, 1, 7½, 11½ | | 6 |
| Ore Hill, 7½ | | 2½ |
| Oronoque, 1, 7½, 11½ | | 3, 6 |
| Orton, 1, 7½, 11½ | | 6 |
| Oxford,* 1, 7½ | | 2½ |
| Packerville, 1, 4, 5½ | | 1½, 9 |
| Pendleton Hill, 1, 5½ | | 1½, 9 |
| Pequabuck,* 5½, 12 | | 5½ |
| Phœnixville, 4, 7½ | | 1½ |
| Pine Meadow,* 6 | | 5½ |
| Pine Orchard, 1, 5½ | | 3 |
| Plainfield,* 1, 4, 5½, 7½ | | 1½, 9 |
| Plainville, 5½, 12 | | 5½ |
| Plantsville,* 1, 7½ | | 1½, 3 |
| Plattsville, 1, 7½ | | |
| Pleasant Valley, 7½ | | 2½, 5½ |
| Plymouth,* 1, 5½, 7½, | | 5½ |
| Pomfret, 1, 4, 7½ | | 1½, 4½ |
| Pomfret Center,* 4, 7½ | | 1½ |
| Pomfret Landing, 1, 4, 7½,11 | | 1½, 9 |
| Poquetanuck, 1, 4, 5½ | | 1½, 9 |
| Poquonock,* 8½, 11 | | 4 |
| Poquonock Bridge, 1, 4, 5½ 1½, 4½ | | 9 |
| Portland, *† 5½, 11½ | | 3½, 4½ |
| Preston, 1, 4, 5½ | | 1½, 9 |
| Prospect, 1, 7½, 11½ | | 3 |
| Putnam,*† 1, 4, 7½ | | 1.20, 4,9 |
| Putnam Heights, 1, 4, 7½ | | 1½, 9 |
| Quaker Hill, 1, 5½ | | 1½, 9 |
| Quaker Farms, 5½, 12 | | 5½ |
| Quarryville, 4 7½ | | 9 |
| Quinebaug,* 1, 4, 5½, 7½ | | 1½ |
| Rainbow,* 8½, 11 | | 4 |
| Rawson, 4, 7½ | | 1½ |
| Redding.* 1, 7½, 11½ | | 6 |
| Redding Ridge, 1, 7½, 11½ | | 6 |
| Reynold'sBridge,* 1, 7½ | | 2½, 5½ |
| Ridgebury, 1, 5½, 7½ 12 | | 6 |
| Ridgefield,* 1, 7½, 11½ | | 6 |
| Riverbank, 1, 7½ 11½ | | 6 |
| Riverside,* 1, 7½, 11½ | | 6 |
| Riverton,* 7½ | | 2½, 5½ |
| Robertsville, 7½ | | 2½, 5½ |
| Rockfall*, 1, 5½, 11½ | | 4½ |
| Rockville.*† 4, 9½ | | 1½, 4½ |
| Rocky Hill,* 5½ | | 3½ |
| Romford, 1, 7½, 11½ | | 6 |
| Round Hill, 1, 7½ 11½ | | 6 |
| Rowayton.*† 1, 7½, 11½ | | 6 |
| Roxbury,* 1, 7½, 11½ | | 6 |
| Roxbury Station,*1, 7½, 11½ 2½. 6 | | |
| Sachem Head, 1, 5½ | | 3 |

| | A. M. | P. M. |
|---|---|---|
| Salem, 1, 5½, | | 1½, 9 |
| Salisbury,* 7½ | | 2½ |
| Sandy Hook,*1, 7½, 12 | | |
| Sanford. 1, 7½, 11½ | | 6 |
| Saugatuck,* 1, 7½, 11½ | | 6 |
| Saybrook,* 5½, 7½ | | 3½ |
| Saybrook Point,* 5½ 7½ | | 3½ |
| Scitico, 1, 8½ | | 1½, 5½ |
| Scotland,* 1, 4 | | 1½, 4½ |
| Seymour,* 1, 7½ | | 2½ |
| Shailerville,* 5½ | | 1½, 3½ |
| Shaker Station, 1, 9½ | | 1½, 5½ |
| Sharon,* 1, 7½, 11½ | | 6 |
| Sharon Valley,* 1, 7½, 11½ | | 6 |
| Shelton, 1, 11½ | | 2½ |
| Sherman,* 1, 7½, 11½ | | |
| Shewville, 1, 5½, | | 1½, 9 |
| Short Beach,* 1, 5½, 7½ | | 3 |
| Silver Lane,* 6, 10½ | | 2½ |
| Silver Mine. 1, 7½, 11½ | | 7 |
| Simsbury,* 5½ | | 2½ |
| Somers,* 1, 8½ | | 1½, 5½ |
| Somerville,* 1, 8½ | | 1½, 5½ |
| Sound Beach,* 1.7½, 11½ | | 6 |
| South Britain,* 5½, 12 | | |
| Southbury,* 5½, 12 | | |
| South Canaan, 1, 11½ | | |
| South Canterbury, 1, 4, 5½ | | 1½, 9 |
| South Coventry,* 1, 4, 5½ | | 1½, 4, 9 |
| South Glastonbury,* 5½, 10 | | 2½, 9 |
| Southford,* 1, 7½, 12 | | 6 |
| Southington,*†1, 7½, 11½ | | 2½ |
| South Kent, 1, 7½, 11½ | | |
| South Killingly, 1, 4, 5½, 11 | | 1½, 9 |
| South Lyme, 1, 5½, 7½ | | 1½ |
| South Manchester,*† 6, 10½ | | 2½, 5½ |
| South Meriden,*1, 7½, 11½ | | 3, 4½, 6 |
| South Norfolk, 1, 5½ | | 2½ |
| South Norwalk,*† 1, 7½, 11½ | | 6 |
| Southport,* 1, 7½, 11½ | | 6 |
| Southville, 1, 7½, 11½ | | 6 |
| South Wethersfield,* 5½ | | 3½ |
| South Willington, 1, 4 | | 1½, 9 |
| South Wilton,* 1, 7½, 11½ | | 6 |
| South Windham,* 1, 4 | | 1½, 9 |
| South Windsor,* 9½ | | 5½ |
| South Woodstock,* 1, 4 | | 1½, 4½ |
| Springdale, 1, 11½ | | 7 |
| Spring Hill,* 1, 4 | | 1½, 4, 9 |
| Stafford,* 1, 4, 11 | | 1½, 4, 9 |
| Stafford Springs,*†1, 4, 11 | | 1½, 4, 9 |
| Staffordville*, 1, 4,11 | | 1½, 4, 9 |
| Stamford,*† 1, 7½, 11½ | | 2½ |
| Stanwich, 1, 7½, 11½ | | 6 |
| Stepney, 1, 12 | | 6 |
| Stepney Depot,* 1, 12 | | 6 |
| Sterling,* 1½, 5½, 8 | | 1½, 9 |
| Stevenson, 1, 7½, 11½ | | 6 |
| Stonington,*† 5½, 8 | | 1½, 9 |
| Stony Creek,* 1, 5½, 7½ | | 3, 3½ |
| Storrs, 1, 4 | | 1½, 9 |
| Stratford,* 1, 7½, 11½ | | 3, 6 |
| Suffield,* 1, 8½, 11 | | 4 |
| Taftville,* 1, 5½, 11 | | 1½, 9 |
| Talcottville,* 4, 7½ | | 4½ |
| Tariffville,* 7½ | | 2½ |
| Terryville,* 5½, 12 | | 5½ |
| Thomaston,*† 1, 7½ | | 2½, 5½ |
| Thompson,* 1, 4, 5½ | | 1½, 9 |
| Thompsonville,*†1½, 8½, 11 | | 4 |
| Titicus, 1, 7½, 11½ | | 6 |
| Tolland,* 5½, 9½ | | 4½ |
| Turringford, 7½ | | 2½ |
| Torrington,*† 1, 7½ | | 2½, 5½ |
| Totoket,* 1, 7½, 11½ | | 3 |
| Tracy,* 1, 7½, 11½ | | 3 |
| Trumbull,* 1, 12 | | 6 |

| | A. M. | P. M. |
|---|---|---|
| Turnerville,* 5½, 11½ | | 4½, 7, 9 |
| Tyler City, 1, 7½, 11½ | | 3, 6 |
| Tylerville, 5½ | | 3 |
| Uncasville,* 1, 4, 5½ | | 1½, 9 |
| Union, 1, 4, 11 | | 1½, 4, 9 |
| Union City,* 1, 7½ | | 2½, 7 |
| Unionville, 1, 6 | | 3 |
| Vernon,* 4 | | 4½ |
| Vernon Center, | | 4½ |
| Versailles, 1, 5½, | | 1½, 9 |
| Vinton Mills, | | 5½ |
| Voluntown,*† 1, 5½, | | 1½, 9 |
| Wallingford,*†1, 7½, 11½ | | 3 |
| Wapping, 5½, 5 | | 4½ |
| Warehouse Point,*1, 8½, 11 | | 4 |
| Warren, 1, 7½, 11½ | | 2½ |
| Warrenville, 1, 4, 7½ | | 1½, 9 |
| Washington,* 1, 7½, 11½ | | 6 |
| Wash'ton Dpt.*1, 7½, 11½ | | 6 |
| Waterbury.*† 5½, 12, | | 2½, 5½ |
| Waterford,* 1, 5½, 7½ | | 1½ |
| Watertown,* 5½, 7½ | | 2½ |
| Waterville,* 1, 7½ | | 2½, 5½ |
| Wauregan, 1, 4, 11 | | 1½, 9 |
| Weatogue, 4, 5½ | | 3½ |
| West Ashford, 1, 7½ | | 1½, 9 |
| West Avon, 5½ | | 3½ |
| Westbrook,* 1, 5½, 7½ | | 3, 3½ |
| West Cheshire,*1, 7½, 11½ | | 3 |
| Westchester, 1, 5½, 11½ | | 4½ |
| West Cornwall,*1, 7½, 11½ | | |
| Westford, 1, 4 | | 1½, 4½ |
| West Goshen, 1, 5½, 7½ | | 2½, 5½ |
| West Granby, 5½ | | 2½, 3½ |
| West Hartford,* 6, | | 2½, 6½ |
| W. Hartland,Mon.,Fri., 7½ | | 2½, 5½ |
| West Haven,*1, 7½, 11½ | | 3, 6 |
| Westminster, 1, 4 | | 1½, 9 |
| West Morris, 1, 7½, 11½ | | 7 |
| West Mystic, 1, 5½, | | 1½, 9 |
| West Norfolk, 1, 5½ | | 2½ |
| West Norwalk,1, 7½, 11½ | | 6 |
| Weston, 1, 7½, 11½ | | 6 |
| Westport,*1, 2½, 7½, 11½ | | 6 |
| West Redding, 1, 7½, 11½ | | 6 |
| West Simsbury, 7½ | | 2½ |
| West Stafford, 1, 4, 11½ | | 3, 4½, 6 |
| West Suffield, 1, 8½, 11 | | 4 |
| West Thompson, 1, 5½, 8 | | 1½, 9 |
| West Torrington,* 1, 7½ | | 2½, 5½ |
| Westville,* 1, 7½, 11½ | | 2, 6 |
| West Willington, 1, 4 | | 1½, 9 |
| West Winsted,*† 7 | | 2½ |
| West Woodstock, 1, 4, 7½ | | 1½, 4½ |
| Wethersfield,* 5½ | | 3½ |
| Whigville, 5½, 10, 12 | | |
| Whitneyville,1,1½, 10, 11½ | | 2, 5, 6 |
| Willimantic,*† 1, 4, 7½ | | 1½, 4½ |
| Willington, 1, 4 | | 1½, 9 |
| Wilsonville, 1, 5½, 7½, 11 | | 1½, 9 |
| Wilton,* 1, 7½, 11½ | | 6 |
| Winchester Center, 7½ | | 2 |
| Windham,* 1, 4 | | 1½, 4½ |
| Windsor,* 1, 8½, 11 | | 4 |
| Windsor Locks,*† 1, 8½, 11 | | 4 |
| Windsorville, 9½ | | |
| Winnipauk,* 1, 7½, 11½ | | 6 |
| Winsted,*† 7 | | 2½, 5½ |
| Winthrop, 5½ | | 1½, 3½ |
| Wolcott, 5½, 7½, 12 | | |
| Woodbury,* 5½, 12 | | |
| Woodmont,* 1, 7½, 11½ | | 3, 6 |
| Woodstock,* 1, 4, 7½ | | 1½, 4½ |
| Woodstock Valley, 1, 4, 7½ | | 1½, 4½ |
| Woodville, 1, 2½, 7½, 11½ | | 7 |
| Yalesville,* 1, 7½, 11½ | | 3 |
| Yantic,* 1, 4 | | 1½, 10 |

# Hartford Post Office, Mail Arrangements, July 18, 1898.

COPYRIGHTED FOR No. 61 of GEER'S HARTFORD CITY DIRECTORY.

OFFICE HOURS.—Week days, from 7.30 A.M. to 8 P.M.; Sundays, 5 to 6 P.M., Holidays, 8.30 A.M. to 1 P.M.
REGISTRY DEPARTMENT.—Open 8 A. M. to 6 P.M. except Sundays. Fee, 8 cents in addition to postage.
SPECIAL DELIVERY SERVICE.—Letters delivered by messengers, week days, from 7 A.M. to 11 P.M.; Sundays, 7 to 8 A.M. and 7.30 to 8.30 P.M. Special stamps, 10 cents.

## ARRIVAL AND DEPARTURE OF MAILS

*For hours that Mails close to every Post Office in Connecticut, see pages 755–757.*

| CLOSE. | | | | | | | LOCALITIES AND ROUTES. | OPEN. | | | | | | |
|---|---|---|---|---|---|---|---|---|---|---|---|---|---|---|
| A. M. | | | | P. M. | | | | A. M. | | | P. M. | | | |
| 1 | 8½ | ... | .... | 1¾ | ... | 6 | Albany, Saratoga and Northern New York, | 7 | 9 | ... | 1½ | ... | ... | 8 |
| 1 | 8½ | ... | 11 | 1 | 3¾ | 6, 9 | Boston, | 7 | ... | 11 | 1½ | 3½ | ... | 8 |
| 1 | 8½ | ... | 11 | 1¾ | ... | 6 | Boston & Albany Railroad, West of Springfield, | 7 | 9 | ... | ... | 3 | ... | 8 |
| 1 | 8½ | ... | .... | ... | ... | 6 | Boston, Canada East and Connecting Routes, | 7 | 9 | 11 | 1½ | 3 | ... | 8 |
| 1, 7 | 8½ | ... | .... | 1¾ | ... | 6 | Buffalo and Western New York, | 7 | 9 | ... | 1½ | 3 | ... | 8 |
| 1 | 8½ | ... | .... | 1¾ | ... | 6 | Chicago and the West, | 7 | 9 | ... | 1½ | ... | 5½ | 8 |
| ... | 7 | ... | 11 | 1¾ | ... | 6 | Connecticut River Railroad and Vermont, | ... | 9 | ... | ... | 3 | ... | 8 |
| 1 | 7½ | 8½ | 11 | 1 | 3¾ | 6, 9 | Maine, New Hampshire and Eastern Massachusetts, | 7 | ... | 11 | 1½ | 3 | ... | 8 |
| 1 | 7½ | 9½ | 11½ | 1¾ | 6 | 7, 9 | New York, | 7 | 10 | 11½ | 12½ | 3 | 5½ | 7, 8 |
| 1 | 7 | 8½ | 11 | 1¾ | 3¾ | 6 | Northampton and Holyoke, | 7 | 9 | ... | 1½ | 3 | ... | 8 |
| 1 | 7½ | ... | 11½ | 1¾ | 6 | 9 | Philadelphia and Baltimore, | 7 | 10 | ... | 12½ | 3 | 5½ | 8 |
| 4 | 5½ | 7½ | 11 | 1 | 4½ | 6, 9 | Providence, | 7 | ... | 11 | 1½ | 4 | 5½ | 9 |
| 4 | 5½ | 7½ | 11 | 1 | ... | 9 | Providence and Way Stations, | 7 | ... | 11 | 1½ | ... | 5½ | 9 |
| 1 | 8½ | 9½ | 11 | 1¾ | 3¾ 6 | 8¼ | Springfield, | 7 | 9 | ... | 1½ | 3½ | 6 | 8 |
| 1 | 7½ | ... | 11½ | 1¾ | 6 | 9 | Washington, D. C., | 7 | 10 | ... | 12½ | 3 | 5½ | 8 |
| 1 | ... | 8½ | 11 | 1¾ | 3¾ | 6 | Worcester, Palmer and Way Stations, | 7 | ... | 11 | 1½ | 3½ | ... | 8 |
| | | | | | | | *CONNECTICUT.* | | | | | | | |
| ... | 5½ | ... | 11½ | 3 | 4½ | ... | Air Line Railroad, East of New Haven, | 7 | ... | ... | 1½ | ... | 7 | ... |
| 4 | ... | ... | .... | ... | 4½ | ... | " West of Willimantic, | 7 | ... | ... | ... | ... | 5½ | ... |
| 1 | 7½ | ... | 11½ | ... | 4½ | 6, 7 | Bridgeport, | 7 | 10 | ... | 12½ | 3½ | 5½, 8 | 10½ |
| 1 | 7½ | ... | 11½ | ... | ... | 7 | Bridgeport, Norwalk and Stamford, | 7 | 10 | ... | 12½ | ... | 5½, 8 | 10½ |
| ... | 5½ | ... | .... | ... | 3½ | ... | Canal Railroad, North of Plainville, | 7 | ... | ... | 1 | 3 | 6½ | ... |
| 1 | ... | ... | 11½ | ... | 3½ | ... | " South of " | 7 | ... | ... | 1 | 3 | ... | 10½ |
| 1 | ... | 9½ | .... | ... | 5½ | ... | Connecticut Central Railroad, | 7 | 10 | ... | ... | 3 | ... | 7 |
| ... | 5½ | ... | .... | 1 | 3½ | ... | Connecticut Valley Railroad, | 7 | ... | 11 | ... | ... | ... | 7 |
| 1 | 5½ | ... | 11½ | ... | ... | 7 | Danbury, | 7 | 10 | ... | ... | 2½ | ... | ... |
| ... | 5½ | 10¼ | .... | ... | 2¼ | 5¼ | East Hartford and Burnside,* | ... | 2½ | 10¼ | ... | 2 | 6½ | 8¼ |
| ... | 5½ | ... | .... | ... | 2¾ | ... | E. H. Meadow, Hockanum, Silver Lane and Naubuc* | ... | ... | 10¼ | ... | ... | ... | 8¼ |
| ... | 5½ | ... | .... | ... | 3½ | 5½ | Farmington and Unionville* | ... | 10½ | ... | ... | ... | ... | 8¼ |
| ... | 5½ | ... | 10¼ | ... | 2¾ | ... | Glastonbury and South Glastonbury,* | ... | 11 | ... | ... | 2 | ... | 8½ |
| 1 | 7½ | ... | 11½ | ... | ... | ... | Housatonic Railroad, | 7 | ... | ... | 1 | 3 | ... | 8 |
| ... | 5½ | 10¼ | .... | ... | 2½ | 5¼ | Manchester and South Manchester,* | ... | 10¾ | ... | 2 | ... | 6½ | 8¼ |
| 1 | 7½ | ... | 11½ | 3 | 4½ | 6, 7 | Meriden, | 7 | 10 | ... | 12½ | 3½ | 5½ | 8 |
| ... | 5½ | ... | 11½ | 3½ | 5 | ... | Middletown, | 7 | 10 | 11 | 1 | 3 | 7 | 9 |
| 1 | 7½ | ... | 11½ | 2 | ... | ... | Naugatuck Railroad, | 7 | ... | ... | 1 | 3 | ... | 8 |
| 1 | ... | 7½ | .... | 2 | 5½ | ... | " North of Waterbury, | 7 | ... | 12 | ... | ... | ... | 8 |
| ... | †5½ | 7½ | 11½ | ... | 3½ | 5½ | New Britain, | 7 | 10 | ... | 12 | 2½ | †7½ | 10½ |
| 1 | 5½ | 7½ | 11½ | 3 | 4½ | 6, 7 | New Haven, | 7 | 10 | ... | 12½ | 3½ | 5½, 8 | 10½ |
| 1 | 7½ | ... | 11½ | ... | ... | 7 | New Haven and Way Stations, | 7 | 10 | ... | 12½ | 3 | 5½ | ... |
| 4 | 8 | ... | 1 | ... | 3¾ | 9 | New London Northern, North and South of Willimantic, | 7 | ... | ... | 1½ | ... | ... | 8 |
| 1 | ... | 8½ | 11 | ... | 3¾ | ... | N. Y., N. H. & H. Railroad, North of Hartford, | 7 | 9 | ... | 1½ | ... | ... | 8 |
| 1 | 7½ | ... | 11½ | ... | ... | 7 | " " between New Haven and New York, | 7 | 10 | ... | 1 | ... | 5½ | 10½ |
| ... | 5½ | ... | 11½ | ... | 5½ | ... | New York & New England Railroad, West of Hartford, | ... | 10 | ... | ... | 2½ | ... | 10½ |
| 4 | 7½ | .... | .... | 1 | 4½ | ... | " " East of " | ... | ... | 11 | 1½ | ... | ... | 9 |
| 1 | 5½ | 7½ | .... | 1 | 4½ | 9 | Norwich and New London, | 7 | ... | 11 | 1½ | ... | 5½ | 9 |
| 4 | ... | 9½ | .... | 1 | 4½ | ... | Rockville, | 7 | ... | 11 | 1½ | 3 | ... | 9 |
| ... | 5½ | 7½ | .... | ... | 3½ | 9 | Shore Line Railroad, bet. Saybrook and New London, | 7 | ... | 11 | ... | ... | 5½ | 7 |
| 1 | 5½ | 7½ | .... | 1 | 3½ | ... | " " " " New Haven, | 7 | ... | 11 | 1 | ... | 5½ | ... |
| ... | †5½ | 7½ | 11½ | 3½ | 5½ | ... | Waterbury, | 7 | 10 | ... | 12½ | 2½ | 6 | 10½ |
| ... | 5½ | ... | .... | 2½ | ... | 5½ | West Hartford,* | ... | ... | 11 | ... | ... | 5 | 8½ |
| 1 | 4 | 7½ | .... | 1 | 4½ | ... | Willimantic and Putnam, | 7 | ... | 11 | 1½ | ... | ... | 9 |
| ... | ... | 7 | .... | 2 | ... | ... | Winsted and Stations on Phila. & Reading Railroad, | ... | 9 | ... | 1 | ... | ... | 8 |
| | | | | | | | *FOREIGN.* | | | | | | | |
| 1 | 7½ | 9½ | 11½ | 1¾ | 6 | 7, 9 | By Steamers from New York, | 7 | 10 | ... | 1½ | 3½ | 5½ | 8½ |

* Electric cars. †Also on Sunday.

# War Revenue Taxes, July 1, 1898.

| | |
|---|---|
| Bank check, draft, or certificate of deposit, non-interest bearing | $0.02 |
| Beer and other fermented liquor, per bbl | 1.00 |
| Berth sold in a parlor or sleeping car | .01 |
| Bill of exchange, in land, draft or certificate or deposit, drawing interest, promissory note, U. S. money orders—Sums not exceeding $100 | .02 |
| Each additional $100 or fraction | .02 |
| Bill of exchange (foreign), letters of credit, money orders by telegraph, payable out of U. S.—Drawn singly, for $100 or less | .04 |
| Each additional $100 or fraction | .04 |
| Drawn in sets of two or more—Every bill of each set not over $100 | .02 |
| Each additional $100 or fraction | .02 |
| Bill of lading or receipt, export merchandise | .10 |
| Bill of lading, manifest, or receipt, and each duplicate thereof, express and freight | .01 |
| Bonds or certificates of stock and debt, on each $100 of face value | .05 |
| On issue of stock, original or on reorganization, each $100 face value | .05 |
| Bonds of indemnity | .50 |
| Broker's note or memorandum of sale | .10 |
| Certificates of profit and transfers thereof, each $100 or part of | .02 |
| Certificates issued by port warden or surveyor | .25 |
| Certificates required by law, not elsewhere specified | .10 |
| Charter contracts or agreements, or renewals of transfers of—Vessels not exceeding 300 tons | 3.00 |
| Vessels exceeding 300 and not ex. 600 tons | 5.00 |
| Exceeding 600 tons | 10.00 |
| Chewing gum or substitutes—Each jar, box, or other package of not more than $1 retail value | .04 |
| Each additional $1.00 or part thereof | .04 |
| Cigars weighing more than 3 pounds per 1,000 | 3.60 |
| Weighing not more than 3 pounds per 1,000 | 1.00 |
| Cigarettes weighing more than 3 pounds per 1,000 (per M.) | 3.60 |
| Weighing not more than 3 pounds per 1,000 | 1.50 |
| Conveyance deed or instrument transferred realty—Where value exceeds $100 and does not exceed $500 | .50 |
| Each additional $500 or fraction | .50 |
| Custom house entry of merchandise—Less than $100 in value | .25 |
| Exceeding $100 and not exceeding $500 | .50 |
| Exceeding $500 | 1.00 |
| Entry for withdrawal of merchandise from customs bonded warehouse | .50 |
| Fire, marine, accident, fidelity, etc., insurance policies, except purely co-operative—Each $1 of premium | ½ of 1 per cent. |
| Lease, agreement, or contract for rent—Not exceeding one year | .25 |
| Exceeding one year and not exceeding three | .50 |
| Exceeding three years | 1.00 |
| Life insurance policies, except fraternal companies and associations—each $100 or frac. part, | .08 |
| On policies issued on weekly payment plan, 40 per cent. of first weekly premium. | |
| Manifest for entry or clearance of vessel for foreign port—Where registered tonnage does not exceed 300 tons | 1.00 |
| Where registered tonnage exceeds 300 tons and does not exceed 600 tons | 3.00 |
| Where registered tonnage exceeds 600 tons | 5.00 |
| Medicinal proprietary articles and preparations, (on every packet, box, bottle, pot, phial or other inclosure)—Retail value not exceeding 5 cents | ⅛ of .01 |
| Exceeding 5c. and not exceeding 10c. | ¼ of .01 |
| Exceeding 10c. and not exceeding 15c. | ⅜ of .01 |
| Exceeding 15c. and not exceeding 25c. | ⅝ of .01 |
| Each additional 25c. of retail price or fractional part thereof | ⅝ of .01 |
| Mortgage or pledge of lands or property, real or personal, or assignment, transfer or renewal of—Exceeding $1,000 and not exceeding $1,500 | .25 |
| Each $500, or frac. part of, in excess of $1,500 | .25 |
| Passage tickets from United States to foreign ports—Not over $30 | $1.00 |
| More than $30 and not over $60 | 3.00 |
| More than $60 | 5.00 |
| Perfumery, cosmetics, and other similar articles, (on every packet, box, bottle, etc.)—Retail value not exceeding 5 cents | ⅛ of .01 |
| Exceeding 5c. and not exceeding 10c | ¼ of .01 |
| Exceeding 10c. and not exceeding 15 | ⅜ of .01 |
| Exceeding 15c. and not exceeding 25c | ⅝ of .01 |
| Each additional 25c. or fract'l part thereof. | ⅝ of .01 |
| Power of attorney, or proxy for voting at any election of officers of any incorporated company or association, except religious, charitable, or literary, or public cemeteries | .10 |
| Other | .25 |
| Protests of notes, etc | .25 |
| Sale or agreement to sell stock of any company, each $100 face value | .02 |
| Sale or agreement to sell any products or merchandise at any exchange or board of trade—Each $100 in value | .01 |
| Each additional $100 or fraction | .01 |
| Sparkling or other wines, bottled—Each bottle containing 1 pint or less | .01 |
| Each bottle containing more than 1 pint | .02 |
| Tea, per lb | .10 |
| Telegraphic dispatch | .01 |
| Telephone messages at 15 cents or over | .01 |
| Warehouse receipt | .25 |

## *EXCISE TAXES.*

| | |
|---|---|
| Estates exceeding $10,000 and not exceeding $25,000, brother or sister | 75c. on $100 |
| Decedent of brother or sister | $1.50 on 100 |
| Aunt or uncle | 3.00 on 100 |
| Great aunt or great uncle | 4.00 on 100 |
| Corporation or stranger in blood | 5.00 on 100 |
| Between $25,000 and $100,000 | Multiply by 1½ |
| Between $100,000 and $500,000 | " " 2 |
| Between $500,000 and $1,000,000 | " " 2½ |
| Over $1,000,000 | " " 3 |
| Refiners of petroleum or sugar whose gross annual receipts exceed $250,000 | ¼ of 1 p.c. |

## *SPECIAL TAXES, ANNUALLY.*

| | |
|---|---|
| Bankers—Capital, (including surplus,) not exceeding $25,000 | $50.00 |
| Each $1,000 in excess of $25,000 | 2.00 |
| Bowling alleys and billiard rooms, for each alley or table | 5.00 |
| Brokers, (except those paying tax as bankers) | 50.00 |
| Cigar manufacturers—Annual sales less than 100,000 cigars | 6.00 |
| Annual sales over 100,000 and less than 200,000 | 12.00 |
| Annual sales over 200,000 | 24.00 |
| Commercial brokers | 20.00 |
| Custom house brokers | 10.00 |
| Owners of circuses | 100.00 |
| Theaters, museums, and concert halls | 100.00 |
| Other public exhibitions or shows for money. | 10.00 |
| Leaf tobacco and manufactures—If annual sales do not exceed 50,000 pounds | 6.00 |
| If annual sales exceed 50,000 and do not exceed 100,000 pounds | 12.00 |
| If annual sales exceed 100,000 pounds | 24.00 |
| Mixed flour, manufacturers of, per year | 12.00 |
| Pawnbrokers | 20.00 |
| Tobacco and snuff, manufactured, per pound | .12 |

# Charter Oak.

**THE CHARTER OAK TREE, Nov. 7, 1853,**

In the trunk of which was concealed the Charter of Connecticut, from October 31st, 1687, to May 9th, 1689. This old Charter was won by Gov. John Winthrop, to the colonists, from Charles II., King of England, April 23, 1662. This tree stood on lot No. 29 Charter Oak av. The above engraving we had made for our use, by a Hartford artist, Nov. 7, 1853, just as it then appeared. It measured at its base thirty-three feet in circumference, and where the stump was broken off seven feet above the ground, was twenty-one feet in circumference. Twenty-seven persons have stood up in its hollow, where the charter was hid. It was blown down in a severe storm, Aug. 21, 1856. The following engraving has been made especially for this Directory, by the same artist who made the above engraving, and is from a drawing taken on the day of this sad disaster. The tree stood inside of a wooden picket fence, and a marble stone in a stone offset wall, now marks the spot where this tree stood, with the inscription, "CHARTER OAK FELL Aug. 21, 1856."

May 7, 1896, James J. Goodwin of Hartford presented to the Connecticut Society of Sons of Colonial Wars the narrow strip of land, about 100 feet long, the point of which intersects Charter Oak avenue and Charter Oak place. A suitable monument will be erected upon this plot of ground to take the place of present almost obscure mark where the old tree stood.

A special session of the GENERAL COURT held in Hartford, July, 1687, "publiquely declare and protest against the said Major Edmond Andross and these his illegal proceedings, as also against all his aiders and abettors as disturbers of the publique peace." This court also "commanded all good people, subject in this Colony of Connecticut, under our present government, utterly to refuse to attend, countenance, or obey the sayd Major Edmond Andross, or any under him, in any order, instruction or command, contrary to the laws of this colony, established under the aforesaid charter." The unsuccessful attempt to wrest this charter from this State was made by Sir Edmond Andross, Oct. 31, 1687. The General Court was assembled at the Inn, (which was then kept, under order of the General Court, on the lot where now is the Universalist church, 234 Main street,) to meet Governor Andross. When there assembled, the lights being put out, by arrangement, where Andross and the authorities had the Charter and were discussing it, Capt. Joseph Wadsworth carried it off in the dark and hid it so effectually in the hollow of the Charter Oak tree, that it could not be found. There it remained until May 9, 1689. The original Charter, engrossed on three parchment skins, is in the State Library room, framed in wood from the tree that concealed it from the minions of James II. Duplicate of this charter engrossed on two parchment skins is in the room of the Conn. Historical Society. All North American colonies or states were subjected to the kingly veto power, except Connecticut. This charter was the grain of mustard seed, planted in Hartford, April 23, 1662, that sprang up, grew, and bore fruit in the revolution, by

**CHARTER OAK TREE, August 21, 1856.**

expanding into a large and liberty-enjoying nation of towns and states; having thus been nurtured in its unexampled growth, by the terms of this charter, that gave free action to the original town system of government, in the liberty of the wilderness. The mode of government, established by this instrument, was reasserted, etc., by the adoption of our present constitution, in 1818. On the 23d day of April, 1897, this Charter was 235 years old.

Trees propagated from acorns from the Charter Oak tree are growing:—one about twenty feet in height, on Bushnell Park, in the triangular plot near the Trumbull st. bridge; one on this Park, nearly opposite 98 Elm st.; one in yard to 5 Collins st.; and one in yard 82 Ann st., and one at "Armsmere," just south of Mrs. Colt's house, 80 Wethersfield avenue.

---

# State Capitol, Hartford.

## CAPITOL COMMISSION.

THE members composing the FIRST Commission appointed May session, 1871, under whom the first steps were taken to erect a new Capitol, were Marshall Jewell, Chairman, and William D. Shipman, Hartford; William A. Buckingham, Norwich; Wm. H. Barnum, Salisbury; Wm. D. Bishop, Bridgeport. Wm. D. Bishop resigned; Wm B. Franklin was appointed Jan. 21, 1872, and Chairman, Sept. 16, 1872. Wm. A. Buckingham died Feb. 5, 1875, and Henry P. Haven of New London was appointed. Marshall Jewell resigned and Charles D. Warner, Hartford, was appointed April 14, 1873. This committee resigned in June, 1873, and the SECOND Commission appointed July, 1873, were: Alfred E. Burr and Austin Dunham of Hartford; Jeremiah Halsey, Norwich; Nathaniel Wheeler, Bridgeport; William P. Trowbridge, New Haven. Austin Dunham died March, 1877; Gardner P. Barker was appointed in August. Mr. Barber died in 1879, and Franklin Chamberlain was appointed to said vacancy, Oct. 28, 1879. *This Capitol edifice was accepted by the State Legislature, Jan. session, 1880.* R. M. Upjohn, Architect. Wm. B. Franklin, Sup't. Wm. C. Gunnell, Civil Engineer. James G. Batterson, Contractor.

This edifice has proved universally acceptable to all occupants, from year to year, and is pronounced by all visitors,—the model Capitol building of the world.

## BATTLE FLAGS OF CONNECTICUT.

In the West Vestibule are the remnants of the BATTLE FLAGS of the Connecticut Regiments which were marshalled in fine array and deposited there in handsome and substantial glass cases, under escort of the surviving members of the several Connecticut regiments, who made a grand triumphal march on Sept. 17, 1879, through the streets of this City, to their final resting place. June 18, 1884, a statue of Gov. Buckingham was placed with these battle flags.

## THE OLD TOMBSTONE OF GEN. PUTNAM.

Is in the west vestibule, which has been replaced in Brooklyn, Conn., with a monument by the State at a cost of $10,000.

# GEER'S

# EAST HARTFORD

# DIRECTORY,

# 1898.

For Index to East Hartford, see page 12.

Entered according to Act of Congress, in the year 1898, by the HARTFORD PRINTING CO., in the office of the
Librarian of Congress, Washington, D. C.

# STREETS IN EAST HARTFORD.

| Names. | District. | Beginning at. | Direction. | Ending at. |
|---|---|---|---|---|
| Ash street | Meadow | Meadow hill | South West | Connecticut River wharf. |
| Beaumont | Center | Burnside avenue | South. | |
| Belden street | Second North | Webster | East and North | Park avenue. |
| Bidwell street | Second North | Tolland street | East | Burnside avenue. |
| Bigelow | Center | 3 Burnside avenue | North | Rector street. |
| Bissell street | Center | Main | East | Elm street. |
| Blinn street | Center | 1 Main street | West and South | Pitkin street. |
| Bragg street | Center | Burnside avenue | South | Olmsted. |
| Brewer street | Hockanum, etc. | Cemetery | East | Manchester line. |
| Broad street | Hockanum | Main street | West | Naubuc avenue. |
| Brook street | North | Main street | West | Meadow Island. |
| Burnham street | Next South Windsor line | King street | East | Manchester line. |
| Burnside avenue | Center, etc. | Main street | East | Manchester line. |
| Carroll lane | Center | Main street | West | Towards River. |
| Central street | Center | Main street | East | Elm street. |
| Church street | Burnside Center | Burnside avenue | South | Paper mills. |
| Clark street | Center | Burnside avenue | North | Railroad track. |
| Colt street | Second South | Main street | West | Connecticut River. |
| Comstock place | Second North | Park avenue | N. and N. West | Main street. |
| Cottage street | Burnside South | Forbes | West | The Reservoir. |
| Cotton Road | Second South | Tolland street | North West | Main street. |
| Darlin street | Meadow | Hartford avenue | South | Pitkin street. |
| Ellington street | North | King street | North East | South Windsor line. |
| Elm street | Center | Burnside avenue | South | Central street. |
| Ensign street | Hockanum | Main | West | Connecticut River. |
| Ferry street | Meadow | Governor street | West | Connecticut River. |
| Florence | Meadow | Pitkin | South. | |
| Forbes street | Burnside, etc. | Church street | South | Glastonbury line. |
| Forest street | South Middle | Forbes street | East | Manchester line. |
| Franklin street | Second North | Park avenue | North | To a road. |
| Garvan | Center | Main street | West | Towards River. |
| Gilbert street | Meadow | Ash street | South | Through South Meadow. |
| Gilman street | North | King street | West | Gilman's meadow. |
| Goodwin street | North | Ellington street | East | Long Hill street. |
| Goodwin's lane | Center | Main street | East | Elm street. |
| Governor street | Center and Meadow | Main street | West and South | Hartford avenue. |
| Hartford avenue | Center and Meadow | Main street | West | Hartford line. |
| High street | Hockanum | Ellery Brewer's | South and East | Naubuc avenue. |
| Highland street | Center | Burnside avenue | North | Railroad track. |
| Hills street | South Middle and So. East | Forbes street | East | Manchester line. |
| Howard | Center | Orchard | North | Railroad track. |
| Hudson street | Burnside (south) | Forbes street | East | Great Hill. |
| Jencks | Meadow | Village | North | Railroad track. |
| Kennedy street | Burnside (south) | Forbes street | East and North | Silver street. |
| King street | Second North and North | Main street | N. E. and North | South Windsor line. |
| Larrabee street | Burnside | Burnside avenue | North East | Tolland street. |
| Latimer | Center | Burnside avenue | South | To a fence. |
| Lewis | Center | Bissell street | North | Wells street. |
| Lester | Meadow | Ash street | South and East | Darlin street. |
| Linden street | Second North | Main street | East | Webster street. |
| Long Hill street | Long Hill | Main street | North | South Windsor line. |
| Lynn street | Center | Hartford avenue | North. | |
| Main street | Hockanum Ctr. & 2d North | Glastonbury line | North | South Windsor line. |
| Maple street | Hockanum, etc. | Main street | East | Forbes street. |
| Meadow lane | Hockanum | High street | West | Hockanum meadow. |
| Naubuc avenue | Hockanum | Main street | South | Glastonbury line. |
| Oak street | Hillstown | Main street | South | Glastonbury line. |
| Olmsted | Center | Elm street | East | To a road. |
| Orchard street | Second North and Center | Main street | West | Prospect street. |
| Park avenue | Second North, etc | Main street | East | School street. |
| Phelps | Center | Goodwin lane | East | Elm street. |
| Pitkin street | Center and Meadow | Main street | West | Conn. River in South Meadow. |
| Pleasant street | Meadow | Hartford avenue | South | Pitkin street. |
| Porter street | Hockanum | Main st. at Broad | South and East | Main street. |
| Prospect street | Second North and Center | Main street | West and South | Hartford avenue. |
| Ranney street | Second North | Main street | East | Cotton Road. |
| Rector | Second North | Main street | East | Bigelow. |
| Reservoir street | Burnside | Forbes street | West | By Hockanum River. |
| Roberts lane | Center | Main, corner Pitkin | South West. | |
| Roberts street | Second South and Burnside | Silver street | North and East | Forbes street. |
| Saunders | Center | Main street | East and North | Central avenue. |
| School street | Burnside | Burnside avenue | North | Ellington street. |
| Sherman avenue | Center | Orchard street | South. | |
| Silver street | Second South and Burnside | Main street | East | Manchester line. |
| Spring street | Center | Olmsted | South | Hockanum. |
| Stanley street | Second North | Main street | West | Towards Prospect. |
| Thayer street | Second North | Orchard street | North | Railroad track. |
| Tolland street | Second North, etc | Burnside avenue | North East | Manchester line. |
| Village street | Meadow | Governor street | North | Through North Meadow. |
| Wadsworth street | Hockanum | Main street | West | High street. |
| Webster street | Second North | Woodbridge avenue | North | Park avenue. |
| Wells avenue | Center | Main street | East | Elm street. |
| William street | Burnside | Burnside avenue | North | Tolland street. |
| Willow street | Second South | Main street | East and North | Silver street. |
| Woodbridge street | Second North | Main street | East | Cotton Road. |
| Woodland | Second North | Burnside avenue | East | Manchester. |

# GEER'S

# East Hartford Directory,

## No. 9, July, 1898.

### EXPLANATIONS:

The letter h. signifies house; b. boards; l. lodges or rooms at; st. street; av. avenue; r. rear; u. upper tenement; pl. place; ct. court; c. corner; rd. road; t. town; v. village; n. near; e. s. east side of; w. s. west side of; s. s. south side of; n. s. north side of; B. Burnside Post Office; G. Glastonbury; H. Hockanum Post Office; S. L. Silver Lane Post Office; Brnsd. av. Burnside avenue; M. Meadow. See also Street Directory on opposite page. Even numbers are on the North and East side of all streets, except Main street, re-numbered 1898, even numbers are on West side.

## WM. K. ACKLEY,

### Agent for

## The McCormick Harvesting Machine Co.,

### And also the WIARD PLOW CO.

Also dealer in General Lines of Agricultural Implements.

## 1175 MAIN ST.,

### East Hartford, Conn.

ABBEY Franklin H. painter, h. 29 Burnside av.
Abery Harry, plumber, h. 1 Willow, H.
Ackley Elijah, *auditor*, h. 1175 Main c. Gilman.
ACKLEY WILLIAM K. agricultural implements, h. 1175 Main c. Gilman. *See page 763.*
Adams A. Mrs. h. 679 Main.
" Fred. S. (*W.H.A.& Son,*) b. 2 Burnside av.
" Harry A. machinist, h. 679 Main.
" W. H. & Son, grocers, 16 Burnside av.
  William H. Adams.    Frederick S. Adams.
" William H. (*W. H. A.& Son,*) h. 2 Brnsd. av.
Ætna Hose Co. 119 Hartford av. M.
Afostina Louis, farmer, b. Silver, w. of Forbes.
Agnew James, nightwchm. N E.R. h.16 Franklin.
" Margaret, b. 16 Franklin, B.
Ahern Thomas, papermaker, h. 87 Burnside av.
" Thomas Jr. b. 87 Burnside av.
Ahl George N. marketman, h. 61 Garvan.
" Michael, h.u. 61 Garvan.
Ahlgrimm Charles, fireman, h. Woodland, B.
Alexander George W. brakem. h. 29 Woodbridge.
Allen Charles, sealer, N.E.R. b. 4 Clark.
Alling Charles, machinist, b. 33 Pleasant, M.
" George B. poolrooms, 89, h. 85 Hfd av. M.
" George W. blacksm. at 9, h. 33 Pleasant, M.

Alms House, 62 High, H.
Alton Charles, farmer, h. 85 Silver.
Amelunxen John P. machinist, h. Florence.

**AMERICAN ENTERPRISE,** Jas. A. Martin, pub. 866 Main. *See p. 795.*
Ames Francis, b. 18 Wells.
Amidon Martha B. wid. Chas. D. h. 32 Governor.
Anderson Andrew J. at Popes, h. 100 Larrabee.
" Charles, clerk, h. 4 Ash. M.
" Charles, farmer, h.u, 1035 Main.
" Charles H. laborer, h. 120 Hartford av. M.
" Delcena E. wid. Henry, h. 7 Central.
" Emma D. b. 7 Central.
" Frank H. farmer, b. 1 King.
" George F. farmer, h. 38 Silver.
" Harry, farmer, b. 37 Naubuc av. H.
" Ira, farmer, h. 54 Naubuc, H.
" John, farmer, b. 534 Main.

**ANDREWS CHARLES,** steam heating, h. 7 Ash, M. *See page 542.*
" Herbert L. farmer, b. 54 High, H.
Andross James B. bkkpr. h. 3 Comstock pl.
ANDROSS WILLIAM F. wagons, carriages and fertilizers, h. Main, north end.
Archer Beatrice, wid. John, b. 27 Burnside av.
" James H. h. 27 Burnside av.
Arms Alvah C. mach. h. 46 Goodwin c. School.
Arnold Everett E. bookkeeper,b. 38 Hartford av.
" Frank W. machinist, b. 525 Burnside av. B.
" John F.carptr. at 1 Forbes, h.525 Brnsd av.B.
" Sarah Mrs. h. 38 Hartford av.
" Sophronia, h.u. 47 School, B.
" William E. machinist, b. 253 Main, H.
Arnurius Gustavus, farmer, h. 144 Main, H.
Arrant Joseph, farmer, h. Park, B.
Asblund William, mach.N.E.R.h.10 Comstock pl.
Atkins Annie, wid. William H. b. 121 Larrabee.
" Frances, wid. George S. b. 4 Comstock pl.
" William H. h. 121 Larrabee, B.

# WILLIAM A. BECK,

## Practical Plumber,
## Steam and Gas Fitter.
## Hot Water Heating.

Estimates on all kinds of work cheerfully
given.

Office and Shop, 46 GOVERNOR ST.

East Hartford, Conn.

Atwood Julia T. h. 749 Main c. Wells av.
Austin Thomas, finisher at 1 Forbes.
Avery Caroline wid. William H. h. Naubuc av. H.
" Frederick D. Rev. h. 13 Orchard.
" Frederick H. crockery, h. 19 Orchard.
Ayers Franklin W. truckman and general job-
ber, h.u. 620 Main.

BABCOCK Carlos A. carpenter, h. 18 Bissell.
" Caroline G. wid. Augustus W. h. 12 Village.
" Charles, b. 18 Bissell.
" George, b. 18 Bissell.
Bacheler F. P. Rev. pastor So. Cong. Church,
Hockanum, h. 4 High n. Main, H.
Bacon Frederick, butcher, h. 38 Central.
Baedor George H. clerk, h.2u. 102 Hfd. av. M.
Bailey Ada B. teacher, b. Brewer, H.
" Andrew, farmer, b. Silver, e. of Kennedy.
" Asher S. carpenter, h.u. 75 Hartford av. M.
" Frank, farmer, b. Brewer, H.
" George R. butcher, h. 12 Broad, n. Main, H.
" Harry C. b. 19 Darling, M.
" Orra B. Jr. machinist, h. Brewer, H.
Bahn Fred, blacksmith, b. 97 Pitkin, M.
Baker Ezra E. machinist, h. 2 Beaumont.
" Frederic C. pastor Burnside M. E. church,
h. 576 Burnside av. B.
Ball Arthur, farmer, b. Hudson, B.
" John, farmer, h. Hudson, B.
" John Jr. b. 110 Larrabee, B.
" Mary, b. 576 Burnside av. B.
Bancroft George W. farmer, h. Hills, Hillstown.
" James W. farmer, b. Hills, Hillstown.
Bantle Jacob, farmer, h. Forbes, n. Maple, H.
Bantly Anton, farmer, h. Maple, H.
" William, farmer, h. Forbes, c. Maple, H.
Barber Arthur E. painter, b. 16 Governor.
" Edwin C. carpenter, h. 16 Governor.
Barnes Charles, engineer, h. 20 Elm.
" Charles S. farmer, h.90 Prospect, no. of R.R.
" James, machinist, b. 32 William, B.
" Jane, wid. Franklin, h. 12 Church, B.
" Robert, papermaker, h. 32 William, B.
Barnett Daniel, farmer, h. Forbes.
Barrett Samuel A. Rev. pastor of first Congrega-
tional church, h. 654 Main.
Barrows Isaac C. boxmaker, h. 46 Central.
" John, carpenter, b. Forbes, n. Hudson.
" Walter C. brassfinisher, b. 46 Central.
Bartholomew Annie, h. 5 Belden, n. R.R. track.

Bartlett Charles, farmer, b. Willow, H.
" George, farmer, h. Forbes c. Brewer.
Bartolmes Frederick, farmer, h. Maple, H.
Barton Albert J. painter, b. 12 Gilbert, M.
" George H. painter, b. 12 Gilbert, M.
" Lewis, jantr. Hfd. Canoe clb. h. 12 Gilbert, M.
" Louis L. gas inspector, b. 12 Gilbert, M.
" Willard, painter, h. 96 Pitkin, M.
" William E. plumber, b. 12 Gilbert, M.
Bately Walter N. farmer, b. 1175 Main.
Bates Albert H. machinist, h. 17 Central.
" Geo. A. teamster, 100 Hfd. av. b. 9 Garvan.
" Herbert S. clerk, b.u. 9 Garvan.
Bauder Edward L. chief of conductors, h. 10
Garvan.
Baugh John, finisher at 1 Forbes, h. Larrabee, B.
Beach Emilius E. boilermaker, h. 123 Silver.
" Frederick W. farmer, b. 123 Silver.
" William S. Mrs. h. 84 Silver.
Beauchamp Leopold, firem. N.E.R. h.13 Highland.
" Lexie, dressmaker, b. 13 Highland.
Beaumont Alice M. b. 53 Burnside av.
" Clara W. b. 53 Burnside av.
" Electa L. h. 51 Burnside av. c. Bragg.
" Emeline R. Mrs. h. Elm, n. Burnside av.
" Henry G. h. 53 Burnside av.
" Jeanette E. h. 51 Burnside av. c. Bragg.
" John R. h. 12 Burnside av.
" William D. h. 43 Burnside av.
Beebe Stephen R. at I.D.Blinn & Son, h. Blinn st.
Beck Alice, clerk, b. 5 Pleasant.
" Clara, clerk, b. 5 Pleasant.
" Curt F. plumber, 46, h. 46 Governor.
" Frank H. Mrs. h. 94 Larrabee.
" Henry, bartender, b. 7 Pleasant.
" Henry, printer, h. 42 Ranney.
BECK WILLIAM A. plumber, 46, b. 46 Governor.
See page 764.
Beers Arthur B. condr. St.Ry. h. 21 William, B.
" George, teamster, b. 112 Hartford av. M.
Belcher Clarence, stenog. b.u. 115 Hartford av. M.
" Mary E. wid. Richard S. h.u. 115 Hfd. av. M.
Bell Eugene R. machinist, h. 96 Pitkin, M.
" Harriet, wid. Edward, h. 96 Pitkin, M.
" John H. conductor, St.Ry. l. 679 Main.
" Michael R. ins. agent, h. 12 Ranney.
Bellevue Arthur, carptr. N.E.R. h. 3 Highland.
Bennett Alvin, mechanic, h. Forbes, n. Hudson.
" Clarence, farmer, b. 56 Silver.
" Elizabeth A. h. 56 Silver.
" Fred, papermaker at 1 Forbes, h. Roberts.
" Frederick E. silverplater, h. 36 Pleasant, M.
" James C. carpenter, N.E.R. h. 8 Central.
Bennis Annie E. b. 107 Burnside av.
" Bridget, wid. Patrick, h. 107 Burnside av.
" John, at N.E.R. b. 107 Burnside av.
Benson Edward, engineer, h. 23 Olmsted.
Bentley John F. farmer, h. (304) Main.
Benton James, farmer, h. Long Hill st.
Berge Mitchel, barber, 741 Main, b. 1 Beaumont.
Bernard Ida, b. 103 Larrabee, B.
" Moses, brakeman, N.E.R. h. 518 Tolland, B.
" Peter, h. 103 Larrabee, B.
Berrington George H. patternm. h. 23 Village.
Berry James, laborer, b. 19 Belden.

## I. N. BLINN & SON,

### Contractors and Builders.

*Dealers in Wood and Lumber.*

Estimates cheerfully furnished on all kinds of work.

Shop and Office,

*Corner PITKIN AND MAIN STREETS,*

*Near Street Railway Car House,*

**EAST HARTFORD, CONN.**

Berry John, helper, N.E.R. h.u. 78 Main.
" Margaret, wid. Thomas, h. 19 Belden.
" Nelson M. at I. N. Blinn & Son, b. Blinn.
" Wolferd, driver, b. Lewis, c. Bissell.
Bevan John, boilermaker, N.E.R. h. 89 Brnsd.av.
Bevier John, clerk at 566 Brnsd. av b. School, B.
Bidgood Edward H. clerk, h.u. 1 Phelps.
Bidwell Adele E. h. 124 Burnside av.
" Andrew S. farmer, h. 23 King,n. town line.
" Chas. M. real estate, 124, h. 124 Burnside av.
" Daniel D. reporter for Hartford Times, h. (106) Main.
" Edward E. farmer, b. 536 Burnside av.
" Eliza M. wid. Samuel A. h.u. 536 Brnsd. av.
" Emma W. B. Mrs. b. 27 High.
" Frank L. painter, h. 2 Spring.
" George C. publisher and author, h. 612 Main.
" Howard E. bookkeeper, b. 30 Wells av.
" John N., Yankee doughnuts, h. Prospect.
" Lonzo E. machinist, b. 536 Burnside av. B.
" Samuel, laborer, b. 536 Burnside av. B.
" Samuel C. painter, 51, h. 51 Governor.
Bigelow Hall, 720 Main, c. Governor.
Bihl Rose, wid. Wendelin, h. 55 High, H.
" William, farmer, h. 55 High H.
Bingham Charles F. engineer N.E.R. h. 34 Wdbg.
" Hezekiah C. iceman, h.u. 2 Ash, M.
Birch Herbert R. bookkeeper, h. 8 Rector.
" Richard, plumber, h. 8 Burnside av.
Bissell Alice L. teach. Brnsd. sch. b. 20 Brnsd.av.
" George, real estate, h. 20 Burnside av.
" Jennie L. teach. Brnsd. sch. b.20Burnside av.
" Lewis, real estate, h. 745 Main, n. Bissell.
Blake Charles H. ice and coal, h. 14 Linden.
" Willard J. papermaker, b. 3 William, B.
Bligh James, h. 8 Bissell.
BLINN I. N. & SON, sawmill, Main cor. Pitkin.
See page 765.
Isaac N. Blinn. I. DeForest Blinn.
Blinn I. DeForest, (I.N.B. & Son,) h. 596 Main.
" Isaac N. (I. N. B. & Son,) h. 586 Main.
Blisque John, farmer, h. Maple, H.
BOARDMAN JOSEPH H. woodyard, 6, h. 6 Pleasant, M. See page 765.
" Nelson J. plumber. b. 6 Pleasant.
" William J. b. 6 Pleasant, M.
Bockus Wm. A. electrician St.Ry. h.38 Brnsd. av.
Bogle Richard, fireman N.E.R. b. 5 Belden.
Bogue Frank, clerk at 102, h.u. 113 Hfd. av. M.

## Joseph H. Boardman,

### Dealer in

# ICE AND WOOD,

**Also Second-Hand Doors, Windows, Lumber, and Brick.**

**Contracts made for removing trees and old buildings at short notice.**

**6 PLEASANT STREET,**

**East Hartford, Conn.**

**Telephone Connection.**

BOGUE LINCOLN H. postmaster Silver Lane P. O.; grocer and general store, h. Main, c. Silver. *See page 765.*
Bolger John J. conductor, h. 28 Olmsted.
Bosworth Joseph M. janitor, h. Saunders.
Boughton Frank J. engineer, h. 32 Hartford av.
Bowe James J. barber, (88) Main, n. railroad, h.u. (86) Main.
Bowen William, engineer N.E.R. b. 27 Linden.
Bowman Geo. A. Rev. private school, 32, h. 32 Burnside av. c. Clark.
Bowne Edgar B. painter, h. 413 Tolland, B.
Bowser Edwin, b. 318 Tolland, B.
Boyd Oliver, painter, h. 7 Saunders.
Boyes Maggie, wid. Thomas H. h. cor. Howard and Orchard.
Boyle Edward, farmer, b. 10 Phelps.
" Hugh, h. 10 Phelps.
" Kate E. compositor, b. 10 Phelps.
" Patrick, farmer, h. 10 Phelps.
" Wm. F. clerk at N.E.R. h. 8 Lynn.
Bracken Frank, mach. b. 44 Burnside av.
" Jeremiah, sectionman, h. 44 Burnside av.
Bradley Arthur J. insurance agent, h. 2 Wells.
" Carrie, box trimmer, b. 9 Comstock.
" Henry A. engineer, h. 9 Comstock.
Brady Edward, papermaker, h. 26 William, B.
Braga Geo. H. brakeman N.E.R. h. 75 Tolland.
Bragg Caroline K. wid. John, h. 7 Elm.
" Charles H. clerk, b. 3 Stanley.
" Edward, h. 3 Stanley.
" Frank C. carpenter, h. 15 Elm.

# L. H. BOGUE,

### Dealer in

# Groceries, Flour, and Feed,

**MAIN ST., Cor. SILVER ST.,**

**EAST HARTFORD, CONN.**

**The Silver Lane Post Office is in this store.**

**TELEPHONE, 313-2.**

# S. N. BRAINARD,
## Real Estate, Loan Agency,
▲ ▲ AND ▲ ▲
## General Insurance,
**Office and House,**
## No. 9 BURNSIDE AVENUE,
**EAST HARTFORD, CONN.**

Bragg Fred L. clerk, b. 7 Elm.
" J. Merrick, contractor and builder, 7, h. 7 Elm, n. Olmsted.
Brainard Geo. W. h.u. 104 Hartford av. M.
BRAINARD S. N. real estate and loan agency, 9, h. 9 Burnside av. *See page 766.*
" Wm. H. trunkmaker, h. 14 Wells av.
Brand Adam, conductor N.Y.R. h. 100 Brnsd. av.
Brasch Emilie Mrs. h. 120 Silver, e. of Willow.
Breen Thomas, fireman N.E.R. b. 22 Woodbridge.
Brennan Jas. A. engineer, h. 31 Woodbridge.
" Mary, stenographer, b. 31 Woodbridge.
" Stephen, fireman N.E.R. b. 22 Woodbridge.
Brewer Alfred R. clerk, h. 261 Main, H.
" Ashbel, farmer, h. 5 High, n. Main, H.
" Ashbel H. capt. barge, h. (147) Main, H.
" Burton G. farmer, b. Brewer, H.
" Cassius K. h. 265 Main, H.
" Clifford F. b. (320) Main, S.L.
" Edgar L. farmer, h. (184) Main, H.
BREWER EDWARD, meats, etc. 21, h. 21 Central. *See page 766.*
" Elisha Curtis, farmer, h. 145 Silver.
" Ellen, b. 27 High, H.
" Ellery L. farmer, h. 8 High, near Main, H.
" Ernest J. bookkeeper, b. (292) Main.
" Esther, wid. Franklin, h. (320) Main, H.
" Everett E. pilot str. Hartford, h. 568 Main.
" Everett P. clerk, h. (248) Main, S.L.
" Frank C. clerk, b. 301 Main.
" Harry, b. 12 High, H.
" Hoadley C. farmer, h. (259) Main, H.
" Howard E. clerk, b. 568 Main.
" Janeway E. marketman, b. 21 Central.
" Joel H. *selectman*, farmer, h. Hills, H.
" Julia A. wid. George C. h. (303) Main.
" Julia E. b. 3 High, H.
" Lena H. stenographer, b. 327 Main, S.L.
" Leslie S. b. (327) Main.
" Linwood R. bookkeeper, b. (292) Main.
" Lowell H. farmer, h. 12 High, near Main, H.
" Lowell H. Jr. b. 12 High, H.
" Millard V. farmer, b. 12 High, H.
" Monroe J. gen. store 275, h. 275 Main, H.
" Norman S. *board of relief*, h. 27 High, H.
" Philo S. farmer, h. 424 Main, S.L.
" Ralph C. collarmaker, h. 34 Pleasant, M.
" Royal H. farmer, h. Brewer, H.
" Rudolph, boathand, b. 147 Main, H.

# EDWARD BREWER,
**Dealer in**
## Meats and Vegetables
**OF ALL KINDS IN THEIR SEASONS.**
**Cart runs through East Hartford, Burnside, and So. Windsor.**
## No. 21 CENTRAL AVENUE,
**EAST HARTFORD, CONN.**

Brewer Sidney, farmer, h. Silver.
" William E. brassmolder, b. 21 Central.
" William E. framemaker, h. 44 Pleasant, M.
" William H. *board of relief*, h. (292) Main.
Briesbois Joseph, h. Jencks, M.
Brigham James, asst. secretary East Hartford Mfg. Co. h. Springfield, Mass.
" Mary E. b. Tolland, n. School.
Brink Jason, carpenter N.E.R. h. 316 Tolland.
Brinton Joseph, plumber, h. 1 Saunders.
Broderson Andrew, carpenter, h. 15 Darlin, M.
Brooks John, mason, N.E.R. h. 41 Olmsted.
Broughton Wm. engineer N.E.R. h. 29 Linden.
Brown Abbie N. Mrs. h. 561 Main.
" Charles, electrician, h. 22 Pleasant, M.
" Charles, gardener, h. 32 Prospect.
" Edwin J. conductor N.E.R. h. 102 Brnsd. av.
" Eugene W. conductor St Ry. b. 19 Elm.
" Everett H. teamster, b. 324 Tolland, B.
" Frank, engineer N.E.R. b. 98 Tolland.
" Frank A. brakeman N.E.R. h. (74) Main.
" Fred'k J. shipping clerk, h. 16 Pleasant, M.
" John A. h. Woodland, B.
" Thomas, papermaker, b. 424 Tolland, B.
" Walton H. timekeeper, h. 561 Main.
Browning Benjamin, salesman, h. 17 Church.
Bruce George B. inspector, b. 9 Village, M.
Brucher Gustave D. paperm. h. 420 Tolland.
Brusie Harry L. clerk, b. 12 Village, M.
Bruton Edward H. farmer, b. Carroll lane, n. Main.
" John F. farmer, b. Carroll lane, n. Main.
" Mary, wid. James, b. Carroll lane, n. Main.
Brutt Fred, mechanic, h. 118 Main.
Bryan Daniel L. supt. CenterCem. h. 18 Wells av.
" John E. painter, h. School, B.
Bryant Hannah W. stenog. b. 19 Burnside av.
" Percy L. student, b. 953 Main.
**BRYANT PERCY S.** attorney at law, h. 953 Main near Park. *See page 485.*
" Sarah E. wid. William, h. 19 Burnside av.
Buckland Clarence, artist, b. 51 Governor.
" Francis, h. 19 Bissell.
" George P. clerk, b. 58 Governor.
" Lee H. h. 58 Governor.
Buckley Edward, fireman N.E.R. b. 413 Tolland.
" Elizabeth Mrs. h. 12 Main, H.
Bunnell Newton D. cond. N.E.R. b. 330 Tolland.
Burden H. h. 47 School, B.
" Sarah, wid. Edward, h. 47 School, B.

Burhans H. M. salesman, h. 108 Hartford av. M.
Burk George W. trunkmaker, h.u. 28 Village, M.
Burke Herman, farmer. h. Brewer, c. Forbes, H.
" Otto, farmer, h. Hills, H.
" William, fireman, h.r. (163) Main.
Burnham Alice, bkkpr. 70, b. 70 Burnside av.
" Allison E. farmer, steam saw mills, h. Long
Hill, So. Windsor, B.
" Amy M. clerk, b. 13 Village, M.
" Archibald S. farmer, h. 129 Silver.
" Arthur C. farmer, h. 1220 Main.
" Austin, farmer, h. 21 King, c. Brook.
" Clarence P. farmer, b. 21 King, c. Brook.
" David C. papermaker, h. 87 Larrabee, B.
" Dwight L. b. Ellington c. Burnham.
" Edgar A. ins. clerk, b. Ellington, c. Burnham.
" Edwin F. wagonmaker, shop and house,
Forbes, near paper mills.
" Frank E. horseshoer, h. Forbes, n. paper mills.
" Frank J. farmer, h. Brook, c. Main.
" Geo. D. coal, wood, h. 70 Burnside av.
" Henry R. farmer. h. 8 King, opp. Gilman.
" John H. farmer, h. 1203 Main, c. Brook.
" John T. farmer, h. Ellington, c. Burnham.
" Mary S. b. 20 King.
" Millie, wid. Ransom M. h. 4 Olmsted.
" Samuel P. farmer, h. 20 King, opp. Brook.
" Sarah A. b. 20 King.
" Spencer H. carpenter, h. 10 King.
" W. S. at Colts, h. 22 Governor.
" Wilbur S. farmer, h. 20 King.
" Willie B. farmer, h. 1228 Main, c. Brook.
" Zenas A. Mrs. h. 1220 Main, c. Brook.
Burns Edward G. stonecutter, b. 22 Village, M.
" Michael J. forem. N.E.R. h. 107 Burnside av.
" Patrick, laborer, h. 22 Village, M.
" Robert. brakeman, h. Olmsted, n. Bragg, B.
Burnside Hall, Church, n. Burnside av.
" Hose House No. 3, Church, n. Burnside av.
" M. E. church, Church, n. Burnside av.
" Post Office, 566 Burnside av. B.
" School, School st. B.
Burr Eugene, farmer, h. 29 Naubuc, H.
Burridge Geo. N. engineer N.E.R. h. 945 Main.
Burt William E. brakeman N.E.R. h. 4 Elm.
Burton Clinton S. farmer, Long Hill c. Burnham.
Bush Winfield S. machinist, b. 711 Main.
Bushnell Giles R. machinist, h. 9 Ash, M.

**BUSIERE FRED. J.** prop. East Hartford Express, h. 26 Woodbridge av.
See page 559.

Butler Edwin H. collector, 100, h. 75 Hfd. av. M.
" Edwin M. h. 65 Hartford av. M.
" George, b. 65 Hartford av. M.
" Harvey T. engineer N.E.R. h. 21 Highland.
Byers James B. salesman, h. 8 Wells.

CADY Corancey, jobber, h. 110 Hartford av. M.
Callahan Andrew, carpenter, h. 23 Woodbridge.
" Eugene, at N.E.R. b. 23 Woodbridge.
" Julia Mrs. b. 23 Woodbridge.
" Morris, brakeman, N.E.R. b. 8 Tolland.
" William H. conduc. N.E.R. h.u. 2 Beaumont.
Callaher Edward, engineer, h.u. 51 Burnside.

Callander Charles E. at Colts, h. Governor, M.
" Charles E. Jr. at Colts, h. Governor, M.
" Ralph, laborer, h. Governor, M.
Calverley Charles, h. 97 Hartford av. M.
" John, carpenter, h.u. 620 Main.
Campbell Charles, gateman, b. 22 Central.
" Thomas, operator at N.E.R. b. 22 Central.
Canner Isaac C. floorwalker, b. 8 Elm.
Carberry Bessie, wid. James, b. (177) Main, H.
" James, farmer, b. (177) Main, H.
" Thomas, b. (177) Main, n. Wadsworth, H.
Carey James, engineer, h. 12 Bissell.
" Thomas, b. 12 Bissell.
" William. steamfitter, h. 14 Bissell.
Carlson August, carpenter, h. 316 Tolland.
Carmel Alexander, carptr. h.u. 19 Woodbridge.
Carney Augustus A. farmer, b. (192) Mn. c. King.
" Henry F. farmer, b. (192) Main, c. King.
" James H. clerk, b. 26 Village, M.
" John J. carpenter, h. 26 Village, M.
" John Jr. plumber, h. 26 Village, M.
" Lizzie, h. (192) Main, n. King.
" Thomas G. farmer, b. (192) Main, n. King.
" Thomas L. bicycle repairer, b. 26 Village, M.
Carroll Alice, wid. William, h. Burnham.
" Winfred, farmer, h. Burnham.
" E. P. & Co. market gardeners, 614 Main.
Edward P. Carroll. Edward J. Carroll.
" Edward J. paper dealer, h. 616 Main.
" Edward P. *(E. P. C. & Co.)* h. 614 Main.
" John, foreman N.E.R. b. 70 Park av.
" Joseph E. builder, 15, h. 15 Central.
" Joseph R. insurance agent, h. 757 Main.
" Lawrence F. at Colts, b. 616 Main.
" M. May, b. 616 Main.
" Ruth W. teacher 2d N. School, b. 616 Main.
CARSON & TAYLOR, groceries, etc. 98–102
Hartford av. M. See page 767.
" William H. *(C. & Taylor,)* 102 Hartford
av. h. 24 Darlin, M.
Carter Ellen M. wid. Newton, b. 21 Burnside av
Case Horace O. sec'y K. of P. h. 46 Hartford av.
" Jairus, car inspector N.E.R. h. 66 Tolland.
" Mabel D. stenographer, b. 46 Hartford av.
" Robert A., U. S. Army, b. 48 Hartford av.
Cassidy Margaret, wid. Joseph, b. 28 Woodbridge.
" Wm. J. paperm. h. 28 Woodbridge.
Catholic Church, Main cor. Woodbridge.
Cavanaugh John, h. 543 Burnside av. B.
" John Jr. b. 543 Burnside av. B.

Cavanaugh Michael, b. 543 Burnside av. B.
" Patrick, clerk, 25 Church, b. Brnds. av. B.
" Thomas, b. 543 Burnside av. B.
Caverly Dubois, electrician, h. 85 Larrabee.
" Henry, helper, h. Woodland, B.
" Hiram, machinist, h. 83 Larrabee, B.
Center Cemetery, 693 Main, opp. Cong. church.
" District school, 671 Main.
" Hose No. 1, Bissell.
Chaffee Cornelia, musictea. 78 Park, b.u. 6 Clark.
Chalker Allen, b. 62 High, H.
Champlin Philip, painter, h. 32 Gilbert, M.
" William H. ( W. E. T. & Co.) h. 8 Church, B.
Chandler Betsey A. Mrs. h. 22 Church, B.
Chapman Obed, h. 21 Village, M.
" William R. insur. b. 546 Main, s. of Silver.
Chickering John W. shoemaker, r. 743 Main.
Childs Henry E. physician, h. Elm, n. Bissell.
" Mary L. b. 800 Main, n. Orchard.
Christia Angelo, farmer, h. Silver, w. Forbes.
" Michael, farmer, h. Silver, w. Forbes.
Christiansen Severn, h. 27 Olmstead.
Christoffersen Rasmus, upholsterer, b. 5 Lester, M.
Clancy Edward, forem. N.E.R. h. Larrabee, B.
" Morris, blacksmith, 555, b. 561 Main.
• " Patrick, foreman N.E.R. h. 8 Franklin.
Clark Calvin, h. 650 Main.
" Duett C. h. 12 Olmsted.
" Edward, switchman N.E.R. b. 20 Tolland.
" Frederick B. h. 761 Main.
" Fred. C. farmer, h. 29 Naubuc av. c. High, H.
" George A. engineer, h. 739 Main.
" John at N.E.R. b. 20 Tolland.
" Joseph, carpenter, h. 24 Burnside av.
" Kate, wid. Edward, h. 20 Tolland.
" Lester R. h. Tolland, near Manchester, B.
Clarkson James H. decorator, h. 1 Beaumont.
Clause Matthew, farmer, h. Forbes c. Maple, H.
Clay George, twister, h. 114 Larrabee, B.
" William, carpenter, h. 110 Larrabee, B.
Clement Deloss, conductor St.Ry. h. 59 Hfd. av.
Cleveland John E. laborer, h. Colt.
Cloughsey Pat'k, lab. N.Y.R. h. Tolland, n. School.
Clune John, boardinghouse, 70 Park av.
Cobb Sirus P. laborer, h. 51 Central.
Coburn Ernest, farmer, b. (323) Main.
" Frank E. clerk, h. 39 Pleasant, M.
" Herbert E. teamster, h. 370 Main, H.
" Leonard B. farmer, b. (323) Main.
" William B. teamster, b. (323) Main.
Cole Etta E. bookkeeper, b. 2 Olmsted.
Coleman Lester H. farmer, h. (298) Main.
Collins Charles H. h. 1 Belden.
" William, foreman N.E.R. b. 98 Tolland.
Comstock Franklin G. h. 1030 Main.
" Frederick, ( W. G. & F. C.) h. 981 Main.
" Frederick H. b. 981 Main.
" Harry F. b. 183 Main.
" Memorial Chapel, Main, north of Prospect.
" Tracy S. accountant, b. 981 Main.
" Wm. G. h. (175) Main, n. of Prospect.
" Wm. G. & F. horses, etc. 1022 Main.
" William G. Jr. ( W.G. & F.C.) b. 1022 Main.
Condon Michael P. supervisor N.E.R. h. 9 Elm.
Condron Samuel, laborer, h.c. Main and Pitkin.

Conklin Cyril E. driver, h. 20 Gilbert, M.
" John J. plumber, b. 25 Church, B.
" Kate, wid. Bernard, h. 25 Church, B.
" William, plumber, b. 25 Church, B.
Conlin Mary, housekeeper, 2 Goodwin.
Connelly Jeremiah, laborer, h.105 Silver, c. Willow.
" Timothy J. laborer N.E.R. h. 10 Church, B.
Conners Christopher, farmer, b. 9 King.
" John, h. 9 King.
Constantine Henry J. N.E.R. h. 7 Comstock pl.
Conway Thomas, blacksmith, b. 20 Church.
Conwell Francis, firem. 1 Forbes. h. Burnside av.
Cook Edith L. b. 975 Main.
" Frank A. foreman, 13 Wells av.
" Mary P. Mrs. housekpr. High, n.c. Naubuc.
" Thomas, farmer, h. Silver, w. of Forbes.
Cooke John B. collector, h. 34 School, B.
Coolidge Clarence E. draughtsman, b. 2 Olmsted.
" Edwin B. salesm. h. 848 Main, n.R.R. track.
" Walter B. plumber, 848, b. 848 Main.
Cooney Michael, laborer N.E.R. b. Burnside av.
     c. Highland.
" Timothy, farmer, h. 68 Prospect, n. of R.R.
" William, papermaker, h. 34 William, B.
Cooper Charles, at Colts, h.u. 28 Village, M.
" Richard, musician, b. 50 Hartford av.
Coren Albert, laborer, h. 6 Pleasant, M.
" Richard, laborer, h. 6 Pleasant, M.
Corey Charles, architect, h.u. 586 Main.
Cornwell Francis, papermaker, h.u. 33 Burnside.
Cosgrove Margaret, h. 39 Silver.
Coster William, laborer, h. Woodland, B.
Cotton Julius H. with Brown, Thomson & Co. h.
     2 Tolland.
Covey A. D. machinist, h. 106 Pitkin, M.
" George W., U. S. Army, b. 106 Pitkin, M.
" Harry L. machinist, b. 106 Pitkin, M.
Cowles Erastus R. burnisher, h. 35 Naubuc av. H.
" Henry S. patternmaker, h. 11 Village, M.
" J. Frank, salesm. 724 Mn. h. 43 Burnside av.
" Julius T. farmer, h. 9 Woodbridge.
" Laura G. b. 2 Governor. c. Main.
" Lewis, farmer, h. 38 Goodwin.
" Lewis L. carbuilder N.Y.R. h. 3 Beaumont.
" William H. butcher, h. 16 Phelps.
Cox Edward M. salesman, Main, h. 3 Bigelow.
" Frank S. butcher, h. 1156 Main.
" Howard, h. 144 Main, H.
" Isaac P. farmer, h. (291) Main, S.L.
" William J. grist mill, 140, h. 244 Main.
Coyendall Dennis M. clerk, h.u. 22 Bissell.
Crabbe Sarah Mrs. h. 47 Central.
Cragan John, h. School, n. Goodwin, B.
" Wm. J. farmer, h. School, n. Goodwin, B.
Cramer Henry, tinner, h.u. 7 Pleasant, M.
Crane George, at St.Ry. h. 9 Garvan.
" Harry S. printer, h. 23 Darlin, M.
" Irving H. clerk 63 Woodland, b. 34 Brnsd. av.
" John, clerk, h. 48 Hartford av.
Crimmins Dennis, millhand N.E.R. b. 63 Tolland.
" John, millhand N.E.R. h. 63 Tolland.
Critchett William M. bookkeeper, h. Gilbert.
Crosson Nicholas, lab. N.E.R. h.r. 69 Burnside av.
Crowley James J. conductor, h. 15 Burnside av.
" William, laborer N.E.R. b. 4 Webster.

# GEORGE W. DARLIN,

## Livery Stable and Trucking.

REAL ESTATE AND TENEMENTS.

Dealer in COAL AND WOOD.

### 114 HARTFORD AVENUE,

Corner Village St., Near the Bridge,

Office, 102 HARTFORD AVE., East Hartford Meadow.

Cullen Patrick, laborer N.E.R. b. 70 Park av.
Cumming Charles P. farmer, h. Hills, H.
Cummings Thomas, engineer, h.u. 15 Silver.
" Waterman C. farmer, h. Hills, H.
Curtin Cornelius, N.E.R. h. 14 Ranney.
Curtis Nathan, conductor, h. 15 Wells av.
Cushman Erskine, engineer, b. 62 High, H.
" Julia Mrs. h. Colt.
" Louis, farmer, h. 122 Silver.

DAGLE Henry, screwmaker, h. 22 Linden.
Dailey Ralph J.laborer, h.Park av. n. School, B.
Daley David, joiner, b. 54 High.
" Patrick, teamster, h. 40 Governor.
" Peter, paperm. 1 Forbes, h. Burnside av.B.
" Thomas, farmer, h. Forbes, opp. Kennedy, B.
Dalton William, brakeman, N.E.R. b. 4 Clark.
Daly John, at N.E.R. h. 10 Ranney.
" John, clerk at (87) Main, b. Goodwin.
Daniels Charles H. farmer, b.118 Main,s. M.E.ch.
" Henry, farmer, h. 128 Main, s. of M. E. ch.
" Joseph R. carpenter, h.u. 21 Church.
" N. P. printer, h. 44 Hartford av.
Dannaher Michael, papermaker at 1 Forbes, h. 94 Larrabee.
" Thomas J. barbershop, 562 Burnside av. h. Burnside av. c. School, B.
Darlin G. Ellery, bkkpr. h. 112 Hartford av.
DARLIN GEO. W. postmaster, livery stable, 114, h. 112 Hartford av. M.    See page 769.
Darling James L. engineer, h. 12 Linden.
Darlin's Block, 102–112 Hartford av. c. Gov.
Dart Benjamin, h. Lewis, c. Bissell.
" Walter C. machinist, h. 22 Bissell n. Lewis.
Davis Charles M. woodmoulder, h. 21 Governor.
" Henry, farmer, b. 419 Tolland, B.
" John F. engineer, h. Prospect, no. of Hfd.av.
" Walter G. blacksmith, N.E.R. h.Park av.B.
" William R. satin finisher, h. 13 Olmsted.
Dawes William H. at Colts, h.u. 104 Hfd. av.
Dawley George, teamster at 100 Hartford av. b. 9 Village.
Dean George A. joiner, h. Roberts.
" John, painter, h. 22 School.
DeBarthe May, wid. Peter, nurse, h. 5 Elm.
Delaney David, farmer, h. School, e. Ellington, B.
" Kieran, engraver, h. 512 Burnside av.
" Michael, b. School, e. of Ellington.

# WILLIAM DUFFY,

## Horseshoeing, Blacksmithing,

and General Jobbing.

### No. 1 VILLAGE STREET,

Cor. Hartford Avenue,

EAST HARTFORD, CONN.

Deming Lucius T. clerk at Charles Merriman, insurance, 650, b. 650 Main.
Dennerlein P. & Sons, Hartford av. c. Prospect.
Denney George, fireman, N.E.R. b. 13 Linden.
" J. Thomas, engineer, h. 13 Linden.
" Pearl A. stenographer, b. 13 Linden.
Derby Cornelia, wid. William, h. 6 Clark.
Detweiler Alfred, engir. N.E.R. b. 11 Franklin.
" Samuel, brakeman, N.E.R. 11 Franklin.
Deuse Simeon, machinist, h. 250 Main.
Devitt James, farmer, b. Kennedy, B.
" John, brakeman, h. Woodland, B.
" Richard, farmer, h. Kennedy, B.
" Richard J. farmer, b. Kennedy B.
Devon Janette, wid. Benjamin, h.u. 430 Tolland.
Dickinson Mr. h.3u. 6 Pleasant, M.
" Elias H. farmer, h. 8 Olmsted.
" Herbert F. machinist, h. 30 Olmsted.
Dimes Joseph, watchman, h. 25 Linden.
Dimon Arthur L. machinist, b. 25 Burnside av.
" Hannah S. wid. John, h. 25 Burnside av.
" Lita, b. 25 Burnside av.
Dixon Frederick W. molder, h. 30 Central.
Dolan Thomas J. cond. N.E.R. h. 15 Brnsd. av.
Donahue Francis, papermaker, b. Woodland, B.
" John, papermaker, b. Woodland, B.
" Patrick, papermaker, h. 580 Tolland.
" Patrick, Jr. b. 580 Tolland.
" Patrick J. papermaker, b. Woodland, B.
" William, papermaker, h. Woodland, B.
" William J. papermaker, b. Woodland, B.
Donaldson Edward J. blacksmith at 1 Village,M.
Donovan James, laborer, h. 26 School, B.
" Jeremiah, laborer, h. 4 Webster.
" Nellie, b. 4 Webster.
Doo Charles Y. H. laundry, 4 Governor.
Dover James, fireman, N.E.R. h. 72 Brnsd. av.
Dowd Josephine, b. 345 Main.
" Louise, b. 345 Main.
Dowden Andrew, papermaker, h. Burnside, B.
Dowds Bernard, far. h. 41 Goodwin, n.R. R. track.
" Mary, b. 6 Burnside av.
" Rose A. h. 6 Burnside av.
" William J. (Foran, D. & Co.) h. 6 Brnsd. av.
Dowen James, papermaker, h. 8 William, B.
" Ralph, groceries, 14 Church, b. 8 William, B.
" Trythena, papermaker, b. 8 William, B.
Dowley George,driver,100 Hfd. av. b.9 Village, M.
Downs Byron C. carpenter, h. 73 Burnside av.
" Frank, at 63 Woodland, b. 73 Burnside av.

Dresser John A. clerk N.Y.R. h. 34 Hartford av.
Driggs Alfred W. b. 62 Hartford av.
" Frank, mechanic, b. 47 School, B.
" Waldo J. builder, 62, h. 62 Hartford av.
Driscoll Daniel, farmer, h. 1132 Main, n. Gilman.
" Dennis, h. 852 Main.
" Edward, conductor, St.Ry. b. 10 Garvan.
" F. Frank, conductor, h. 34 Woodbridge.
Drolet George, bridgebuilder, h. Jencks, M.
Drown Alvin R. train dispatcher N.E.R. b. 4 Elm.
Dudley William, painter, h. 8 Pleasant, M.
DUFFY WILLIAM, blacksmith 1, h. 3 Village, cor. Hartford av. M.   See page 769.
" William L. bookkeeper, b. 3 Village, M.
Dunbar E. R. laborer, h. Lester, M.
" Joseph, ostler, h. 39 Village.
" William J. clerk, b. 41 Village.
Dunham William T. farmer, h. 66 Main.
Dunlap Robert, driver, h. 8 Pleasant, M.
Dunray Henry, b. Naubuc, av.
Duprey Alfred, laborer, b. 30 Gilbert, M.
" Joseph, carpenter, b. 30 Gilbert, M.
" Mitchell, h. 30 Gilbert, M.
Dush Louis, farmer, h. High, n. Naubuc & Broad.
Dutton Leslie, mason, h. 1 Bigelow.
Dwight Edward F. toolmaker, h. 36 Hartford av.
Dwyer William L. engineer, h. 30 Bissell.

EAGAN Martin, farmer, h. Roberts. B.
" Thomas, farmer, h. 4 Silver, s. of P. O.
Eagar Robert, helper, 1 Forbes, b. Kennedy, B.

" Hartford P.O., Eugene H. Merriam, P. M. 720 Main.
" Hartford Street Lighting Association, Main n. Burnside av.
" Hartford Water Co. Arthur P. Moore, supt. 952 Main.
Easterby Thos. W. cigarmfr. 32, h. 32 Pleasant.
Easton Clarence D. farmer, h. Forbes, B.
" Frances, wid. of Agis, b. Forbes, B.
Eaton Louis D. meat & groceries, 153, h. 155 Mn.
Edelman William P. gunm. h. 28 School, B.
Edgar Hannah, wid. Jas. D. h. Cottage, n. bridge.

Edgar John, Sr. b. Cottage, B.
" Robert, papermaker, h. Spencer hill.
Edgerly Charles H. carpenter, h. 2 Webster.
Edwards Charles A. teamster, h. 113 Hfd. av. M.
Ehlers Ernest, milkman, b. 3 William.
Elmer Frances Mrs. h. 563 Burnside.
" Harmon S. farmer, h. 32 High, H.
" John H. farmer, h. 563 Burnside av. B.
" Lucius H. bicycles, b. 32 High.
Elmore Mary P. wid. Milton, h. 112 Silver.
Enler William, brakeman, N.E.R. b. 98 Tolland.
Ensign Alfred J. (E., R. E. & Sons,) farmer, h. 390 Main, Silver Lane.
" Annie T. wid. M. E. b. 319 Main, S.L.
" E. R. & Sons, tobacco inspectors, west side Main, near Colt street, Silver Lane.
Elisur R. Ensign.  F. Howard Ensign.  A. J. Ensign.
" Edwin L. machinist, b.u. 3 Garvan.
" Elizur R. farmer, h. (319) Main, S.L.
" F. Howard, tobacco dealer, h. 380 Main.
" Maria W. wid. Chas. A. h. 65 Naubuc av. H.
" Owen L. farmer, h. 312 Main, Silver Lane.
" Sarah, wid. George, h.u. 3 Garvan.
Episcopal Church, Main n. Burnside av.
Erving John J. farmer, h. 242 Main.
" Waldo, boxmaker, h. Woodland, B.
Evans E. S. machinist, h. 20 Pleasant, M.
Evleth Jas. W. emp. N.E.R. h. 5 Elm, n. Olmsted.
FAHEY John, papermaker, b. 3 William, B.
Fairbanks Charles P. mason, h. 1234 Main.
" Edwin S. salesman, h. 5 Village, M.
Fallon Joseph, carpenter, h. 8 Olmsted.
Falls W. H., Imperial hotel, 99 Hartford av. M.
Farnham Frank P. carpenter, h. 1056 Main.
" Sarah, h. Forbes, B.
Farrell Thomas M. firem. N.E.R. h. 1 Highland.
" Wm. H. at N.E.R. h. 318 Tolland.
Fay Edward, machinist, N.E.R. b. 70 Park.
Feeney Patrick, laborer, h. 588 Burnside av. B.
Felber Peter, electrician, h. Burnside av. c. Highland.
Ferguson Jas. lab. Woodland, b. Manchester t.
" Lawrence W. poolroom, 90; boots & shoes, 92 Main.
FERNSIDE GEORGE W. carpenter, 5 Orchard.
See page 770.
Ferry King F. carpenter, h.u. 718 Main.
Fiala Frank, farmer, h. Forbes, e. of Brewer, H.
Field Calvin S. engineer, h.u. 27 Village, M.

First Congregational church, 660 Main.
" Methodist Episcopal church, Hockanum.
Fisher Albert C. cigarmaker, b. 95 Pitkin.
" Ferdinand, machinist, N.E.R. h. 70 Park.
Fisk Wilbur N. farmer, h. 44 School, B.
Fitch Clark, b. 10 Olmsted, opp. Spring.
" Dwight H. molder, h. 51 Governor.
" E. R. Mrs. h. Forbes, B.
" Fred L. brassm. h. 10 Olmsted, opp. Spring.
FITZGERALD WM. J. painter and decorator, r.
820 Main, h. Beaumont, c. Olmsted.
*See page 770.*
Fitzpatrick Margaret, wid. Connell, h. Park,
n. School, B.
" Michael, laborer, b. Park, n. School, B.
Flaherty John, carpenter, b. 12 William, B.
" John, gardener, h. 36 Woodbridge.
Flanigan James E. printer, h. 64 Burnside av.
" Nellie M. and Kate F. b. 75 Burnside av.
" Patrick, farmer, h. 75 Burnside av.
" Wm. H. *registrar of voters*, b. 75 Brnsd. av.
Fletcher Robert R. brakeman, N.E.R. b. 15
Franklin.
Flint Sarah E. wid. John H. b. 20 Church.
Flynn Dominick, farmer, h. 63 Hartford av.
" Frank J. b. 63 Hartford av.
" Thomas, b. 63 Hartford av.
" William, laborer, b. 63 Hartford av.
Fogarty James, gardener, h. 3 Garvan.
" James F. cond. N.E.R. h. 6 Burnside av.
Folan James, at N.E.R. h. 11 Belden.
Foley Daniel, bluer, b. 30 Silver.
" Edward, laborer, b. 582 Burnside, B.
" John, machinist, h. 30 Silver.
" John J. h. 20 Woodbridge.
" Thomas F. b. 30 Silver.
" William A. h. 25 Central.
" William J. supt. East Hartford Mfg. Co. b.
41 Church, B.
Foot Henry, lather, h. 39 Silver.
Foran, Dowds & Co. grocers, (87) Main.
   John J. Foran.   William J. Dowds.
" James, machinist, N.E.R. h. 89 Park av. B.
" John, machinist, N.E.R. b. 89 Park av. B.
" John J. (*Foran, D.& Co.*) h. 18 Woodbridge.
" John P. farmer, b. 1086 Main, n. King.
" Margaret Mrs.h.1086 Mn. n.of Memo.Chapel.
" Mary, dressmaker, b. 1068 Main.
" Michael, laborer, h. 89 Park av.
" Patrick J. farmer, h. 1086 Main, n. King.
" William, blacksm. N.E.R. b. 89 Park av. B.
Forbes Albert A. farmer, h. 138 Silver.
" Fred. E. teamster, 70 Burnside av.
" Charles R. *board of relief*, h. 31 Church, B.
" Charles R. Sr. Mrs. h. 31 Church, B.
" Charles T. farmer, h. High, n. c. Naubuc, B.
" Charles W. farmer, b. 318 Main, S. L.
" E. Hart, farmer, h. Forbes, B.
" Edwin, farmer, h. 44 Goodwin, s. School.
" Elizabeth, wid. George, h. Forbes, B.
" Ellery S. farmer, h. 318 Main, S. L.
" Emma S. Miss, h. Forbes, s. of Roberts, B.
" Frank, farmer, h. Forbes, B.
" Frank E. clerk at 25 Church, h. Forbes, c.
Roberts, B.

Forbes Frank S. reporter, Hartford Courant, h.
19 Wells av.
" George L. h. Forbes, B.
" James S. h. Forbes, s. of Roberts, B.
" John W. papermaker, h. Forbes, B.
" Lawrence S. pres't and tr. East Hartford
Mfg. Co. h. 720 Main, opp. Wells av.
" Leonard H. grocery, 25 Church, b. Forbes,
s. of Roberts, B.
" Mary A. wid. Samuel, h. 138 Silver.
" Stephen P. Mrs. h. Brewer, H.
" Timothy O. h. Silver, cor. Forbes, B.
" Walter H. h. 45 Hartford av.
" William G. farmer, h. 134 Silver.
Ford John, fireman, N.E.R. h. 24 Linden.
" Thomas, plumber, b. 9 Bissell.
Forrest Patrick T. conductor, h. 2 Lynn.
Foster Charles, carptr. N.E.R. h. 31 Woodbridge.
" Estella M. h. 16 Village, M.
" Hannah, wid. Thomas, b. 31 Woodbridge.
" Mabel E. stenographer, b. 16 Village, M.
" Truman R. clerk, 16 Brnsd. av. h. Woodland.
" William A. mach. N.E.R. h. 71 Brnsd. av.
Foughey Martin, farmer, h. Goodwin, e. R.R.
Fountain Alexander G. h. 107 Pitkin, M.
Fournier Cyril, h. 19 Woodbridge.
Fowler Joel H. grocer, postmaster and h. Hills, H.
" William H. carpenter, h. 263 Main.
Fox Charles A. Mrs. h. 5 Stanley.
" Edmund A. farmer, h. 69 Naubuc av. H.
" Henry C. farmer, b. 59 Naubuc av. H.
" Hiram C. farmer, h. 36 Naubuc av. H.
" Janette, wid. Anson, h. 5 Stanley.
" Leonard, farmer, h. 59 Naubuc av. H.
" Lucy A. wid. Clement, h. 53 Naubuc av. H.
" Robert C. farmer, h. 53 Naubuc av. H.
Frank Everett, brakeman, N.E.R. h. 12 Tolland.
Franklin Elizabeth L. wid. Orrin, h. 426 Tolland, B.
" Geo. B. carpenter, h. 422 Tolland, B.
Freiheit Fred. engir. h. Burnside av. Wdld. B.
French Erwin R. toolmaker, b. 8 Olmsted.
Fresher Cicero, b. 8 Tolland.
Fricke Albert E. farmer, b. 24 Village, M.
" Charles, farmer, h. Forest, e. of Forbes, H.
" Edward F. farmer, h. Forbes, B.
" Everett H. engraver, b. 24 Village, M.
" Henry, tin peddler, 24, h. 24 Village, M.
Fricker Frank, papermaker, h. 2 Church.
Frink George, farmer, h. Woodland, B.
Frye Louis D. mach. h. Tolland, near William.
Fuller Edgar W. bkkpr. h. 28 Hartford av.
" Fred E. stenographer, h. 15 Orchard.
Furman Ezra, brakeman, N.E.R. h. 45 Central.
Furner ☞ *see Ferner.*
Futh William, painter, h. 7 Highland.

GAINES Albert, harness store, (57) Main, h. 22
Hartford av.
" Howard C. trav. salesm. h. 28 Burnside av.
" Raymond S. clerk, b. 28 Burnside av.
Gainey William, brakeman, b. 98 Tolland.
Gale L. P. foreman at 1, h. 1 Forbes.
Galuly Thomas, papermaker, h. 3 William.
Galvin Christopher, bartndr, h.u. 24 Village, M.
Gannon Edward, fireman, N.E.R. b. 20 Tolland.

Gardner Emmet, conductor, N.E.R. b. 8 Tolland.
" George, conductor, N.E.R. b. 8 Tolland.
" Samuel A. oils, h. 27 William, B.
Garrity David J. printer, h. 69 Burnside av.
" John, mechanic, b. 65 Burnside av.
" Thomas, teamster, h. 65 Burnside av.
" Thomas J. polisher, h. 65 Burnside av.
Gatling John R. farmer, h. 29 High, H.
Garvey Henry, h. 39 Olmsted.
Garvie George S. h. 39 Silver.
Gaudet Levi, carptr. St.Ry. h.u.561 Main,c.S.L.
Geer Editha L. trained nurse, h. 12 Garvan.
" Erastus C. treas. The Hartford Printing Co. 16 State st. Hartford, h. 12 Garvan.
Gehan Fred, b. 63 High, H.
" John B. carpenter, h. 63 High, H.
" Norman, b. 63 High, H.
Geiselman John Jr. farmer, h. 242 Main, S.L.
" Simeon E. farmer, h. Willow, e.s. of Main.
Gellert Anton, carpenter, h. 39 Olmsted.
George Frederick, flagman, b. 60 Burnside av.
Gerror Mary, wid. John, b. 19 Highland.
Getto Frank, farmer, h. 150 Larrabee, B.
" Fred, farmer, b. Forbes, s. Silver, B.
" John, farmer, h. Forbes, s. of Silver, B.
" John Jr. paperm. h. Forbes, s. of Silver.
Ghagan Henry, car despatcher, h. Saunders.
Gibbons Edward P. emp. N.E.R. h. 109 Brnsd.av.
Gibbs George S. agent, h. 13 Central.
" J. W. Rev. evangelist, h. 22 Burnside av.
" Marshall S. baker, 10, h. 10 Central.
Gibson George, carpenter, h. 68 Tolland.
" George, Jr. inspector,N.E.R. b. 68 Tolland.
" James, fireman, h. 526 Burnside av. B.
" John, laborer, h. 117 Larrabee, B.
Giddings Perry M. painter, h. 21 Linden.
Gilbert Frederick W. farmer, h. 19 Elm.
" Lewis S. mechanic, h. 14 William, B.
" Walter, at 63 Woodbine, b. 19 Elm.
Gilde A. H. cigarmaker, h. 5 Olmsted.
Gile Loren D. conductor, h. 4 Lynn.
Gillette Augustus, clerk, (86,) b. 844 Main.
" Laura, h. 52 High, H.
Gilman Relzaman, h. 661 Main.
Gilnite Frank, b. 1203 Main.
" William H. carpenter, h. 573 Burnside av.
Gladding Arthur A. engineer, h. 26 Wells av.
Glazier Dwight, h. (385) Main.
" Franklin P. farmer, h. 512 Burnside av. B.

Gleeson James J. Rev. pastor St. Mary's church, Main, c. Woodbridge, h. 10 Woodbridge.
Glendenning Ellen, housekeeper, 23 Burnside av.
" George E. carbuilder, h. 20 Linden.
Goble John P. fireman at 1, h. Forbes.
Goetz Sigmund, filer. h. Brewer, H.
Gonnella George, clerk, N.E.R. h. 6 Olmsted.
Goodale Benjamin F. mason, b. Governor, M.
" Frederick, laborer, h. Governor, M.
" Julius B. compositor.Rector,b.Glastonbury t.
Goodrich Charles, farmer, h. 60 School, B.
" Charles H. b. Governor, M.
" Chauncey W. farmer, h. 67 School, B.
" George F. engineer, h. 20 Church.
" Loren H. blacksmith, 67, h. 67 School, B.
" Orrin H. farmer, h. 45 High, H.
Goodwin Edward O. leaf tobacco, h. 711 Main.
" George, clerk, h. 592 Burnside av. B.
" George H. Mrs. h. 592 Burnside av. B.
" Henry L. acc't, h. 26 Church, c. Forbes, B.
" Joseph O. *town clerk*, h. 717 Main. c. Goodwin's lane.
GOODWIN SAMUEL O. flour and feed store, 701, h. 705 Main, n. of Hfd. av. *Page 772.*
Gordon Moses, teamster, h. 8 Church, B.
Goslee Anna, wid. Wm. T. h. Forbes, B.
" William T. farmer, b. Forbes, B.
Gould Andrew B.sta. agt. N.E.R. h.u.28School,B.
" Frank C. market gardener, h. 161 Silver.
" Sophronia D. wid. Edwin A.b.u.28 School,B.
Gowdy Edward, farmer, School, e. Ellington.
Grady Peter, b. 8 Tolland.
Graham Francis A. farmer, h. 185 Main.
" Jessie, b. Forbes, n. Kennedy, B.
" John R. laborer, N.E.R. b. 15 Franklin.
Grange Hall, Hills st.
Granger Cyrus, clerk, 14 Church, b. Larrabee, B.
" Horace D. butcher, h. 18½ Village, M.
GRANT HERBERT W. livery r. 743 Main, h. 11 Orchard. *See page 772.*
" John, carpenter, N.E.R. h. 26 Ranney.
Green Daniel W. carpenter, h. 26 Central.
Griffin Patrick, papermaker, h.r. 62 School, B.
Griffing Charles R. painter, h. 12 Central.
Grisel Louis, piper. N.E.R. h. 415 Tolland.
Griswold Edward H. physician, 7, h. 7 Wells av.
" Harriet Mrs. b. 745 Main.
" John B. brass molder, h. 35 Central.
" Marietta Mrs. h. 5 High, n. Main.

Griswold Walter, farmer, b. 39 Broad, c. Nau.
Grover S. Wesley, machinist, h. 171 Brnsd. av.
Gunn James H. bkkpr. h. 59 Hartford av.
Gurtin Andrew, carpenter, h. 35 Governor.

HACKETT John, machinist, b. 610 Main.
" Michael, machinist, h. 610 Main.
" William, at N.E.R. b. 70 Park av. B.
Hadley Edgar L. painter, h. 7 Highland.
Hagan James, b. High, n.c. Naubuc.
" John, b. 25 High, H.
Hagedorn A. groceries, Main, c. Linden, h. Man. t.
" Max, brassworker, h. Church, n. Brnsd. av.
Hagenow Ida, h. 525 Burnside av. B.
" Minnie, h. 525 Burnside av. B.
Hagerty Daniel, motorman, b. 9 Belden.
" Jeremiah, laborer, N.E.R. h. 9 Belden.
Haist Albert R. stenographer, h. 25 Village, M.
Hakeman Harry, ostler at 50, b. 50 Hartford av.
Hale Edwin C. farm. h. 1167 Main, n. of Gilman.
" Henry B. editor Weekly Gazette, Rector, h. 20 Wells av.
" J. Wilbur, salesman, h. 23 Wells av.
" John D. carpenter at St.Ry. h. Tolland, B.
" Stephen, brakem. N.E.R. h.u. Elm, n. Bissel.
" Truman, farmer, h. 12 Broad, H.
Haley Joseph, papermaker, b. Roberts.
Hall Albert, farmer, h. 66 Main, c. Maple.
" Carrie L. at Hartford P.O. b. 129 Main.
" J. Knox, farmer, h. 129 Main, H.
" William K. farmer, b. 129 Main, H.
Hallett John, conductor N.E.R. b. 70 Park av. B.
Hamblet Mrs. h. Tolland, n. School.
Hamilton Joseph D. real estate, h. 24 Central.
" Mary, dressmaker, b. 117 Larrabee.
Hammond Amos, b. 24 Central.
" George, clerk, b. 24 Central.
" John K. agent, h. 24 Central.
Hamson Henry, papermaker, Brnsd. av. Man. t.
Hancock Harvey G. painter, h. (219) Main.
" Howard, clerk, h.u. 266 Main, H.
Handel Christ'n, farmer, h. Forbes, s. of Maple, H.
" Edward, farmer, b. Forbes, s. Maple, H.
" Gotlieb, farmer, h. Forbes, s. of Maple, H.
Hanley L. W. at N.E.R. b. 22 Woodbridge.
Hanmer Charles C. h.u. 21 Burnside av.
" Charles F. h. 756 Main, opp. Wells av.
" Franklin H. farmer, h. 584 Burnside av. n. William, B.
Hansen John, engir. h. Brnsd. av. Woodland, B.
Harmon Ernest, teamster at I. N. Blinn & Son, h. 592 Main.
" John P. farmer, h. Naubuc av. H.
Harris John B. brakeman, h. Olmsted, n. Bragg.
Harrison Benjamin, blacksmith, h. 11 Olmsted.
" Bridget, wid. James, paperm. h. Forbes, B.
" George B. mach. h. Olmsted, opp. Bragg.
" Henry, farmer, h. Forbes, B.
" Lucinda R. Mrs. private school, 16, h. 18 Burnside av.
" Robert, b. Forbes, B.
" Samuel G. mechanic, b. 526 Burnside av.
Hart Henry T. coalyard and h. Tolland, B.
" John, farmer, Forbes, s. of Silver, B.
Hartford Canoe Club, Gilbert, M.

**HARTFORD MANILLA CO.** *See* page 479.
" Rowing & Athletic Club, Hartford av. M.
Hartley Wm. N. plumber, b. 34 Burnside.
Hartz John, farmer, h. Forbes, s. of Silver, B.
Harvey James G. farmer, b. 312 Main, S.L.
Harwood F. W. Mrs. b. 24 Wells av.
" Fred. A. ins. clerk, h. 22 Wells av.
Hastings Herbert E. patrnm. h. 40 Naubuc av. H.
Hatch Kate A. Mrs. h. 3 Beaumont.
" L. S. Mrs. h. 433 Main, S.L.
" Maria L. wid. Ephraim P. b. 22 Church.
Haughton Edward, barber at (88) Main.
" Elizabeth H. wid. Ralph W. h. 861 Main, n. Burnside av.
Haven Frank C. machinist, h. Roberts, B.
Hawkins David, bartender, h. Goodwin lane.
Hawksford William, at Colts, h. 19 Village.
Hayden Edgar G., U. S. Army, b. 702 Main.
" Henry R. ed. Weekly Underwriter, h. 702Mn.
" Henry R. Jr. architect, h. 19 Governor.
" Jessie W. librarian Raymond Lib. b. 702 Mn.
" Joseph A. student, b. 702 Main.
" Warren, editor Insurance Journal, b. 702 Mn.
" William G. engineer N.E.R. h. 5 Bragg.
Hayes Chester, paperm. 1 Forbes, h. Larrabee.
" Clarence, papermaker, b. 591 Burnside av. B.
" Edw'd D. undrtkr. (53) Main, h. 37 Olmsted.
" Eliza J. h. 3 Bragg.
" Frederick, laborer, h. Long hill, B.
" Frederick A. engineer at 1 Forbes, h. Long hill, B.
" John L. farmer, h. Long hill, B.
" Patrick D. engineer, h. 8 Ash, M.
" Waldo, farmer, h. 591 Burnside av. B.
" Wilbur, paperm. 1 Forbes, h. Spencer hill.
" William, paperm. at 1 Forbes, h. Kennedy.
Healey James, baggageman, h. Goodwin.
" John, planer, h. 18 Gilbert, M.
Heath Calvin, clerk at 101 Hartford av.
Heck Albert J. cigarmaker, b. 46 Darlin, M.
" Charles, cigarmaker, b. 46 Darlin, M.
" Joseph, cigarmfr. 135Hfd.av. h. 46 Darlin, M.
Heimer Bruno, machinist, h. 15 Garvan.
" Edward, mason, h. 15 Garvan.
" Paul, mason, b. 15 Garvan.
Helgren Louise, tchr. 2d North, b.Park av. n. Mn.
" Oliver, clerk, b. Park av. n. of Main.
" Pierre A. shoemaker, h. Park av. n. Main.
Hemming Wm.P. drugclk. 743 Mn.b.15Brnsd.av.
Hendee James, blacksmith, b. 2 Goodwin.
" Kate, dressmaker, b. 2 Goodwin.
" Tobias, Jr. b. 2 Goodwin.
Henderson Oscar, filer at Popes, h. 37Naubuc, H.
Henson James, operator, b. Gov. c. Village, M.
" Michael, plumber, h. Governor, n.Village, M.
Herr John N. express, b. 34 School.
Hickey Daniel J. engir. N.E.R. h. 66 Burnside.
" John J. farmer, h. (203) Main.
" Margaret Mrs. b. Silver, cor. Forbes, B.
" Michael, teamster, h. 575 Burnside.
" Patrick, farmer, h. Silver lane, c. Forbes, B.
Higbie Wallace, butcher, b. Forbes, B.
High School, 760 Main.
Hildreth Frank, carpenter, h.u. 16 Burnside.

## C. M. HILLS,
# TIN ROOFING

### AND JOB WORK.

## Stove and Furnace Repairs and Plumbing.

Agent for BOYNTON FURNACES.

## SHOP, REAR 696 MAIN STREET,

### EAST HARTFORD, CONN.

Hilley Andrew, laborer N.E.R. b. 70 Park av. B.
Hills Alonzo P. farmer, h. 23 Silver.
" Arthur, farmer, h. Hills, H.
" Charles, mason, h.u. 250 Main, H.
" Chelsea O. carriagemaker, h. Oak, H.
HILLS CHESTER M. tinner, r. 696, h. 696 Main.
See page 774.
" Chris. E. farmer, h. (294) Main.
" Edward F. farmer, h. Hills, H.
" Elliott, farmer, h. Oak, H.
" Everett, farmer, h. Oak, H.
" Frank F. laborer, b. 161 Silver.
" Fred. M. farmer, h. 287 Main.
" George A. farmer, b. 23 Silver.
" Herbert C. asst. supt. Hartford & N. Y.
Transportation Co. h. 293 Main.
" Howard, farmer, h. Hills, H.
" Jerome, farmer, h. Oak, H.
" John, farmer, h. Brewer, H.
" Lucius, farmer, b. 320 Main, S.L.
" Ruez H. capt. str. Middletown, h. 570 Main.
" Samuel A. farmer, h. 3 Willow.
" Sarah, wid. Francis, h. Oak, H.
" Waldo Jr. clerk, b. 7 William, B.
" Waldo M. carpenter, h. 7 William, B.
" Walter, farmer, b. Hills, H.
" Wiley, farmer, h. 266 Main.
" William H. farmer, h. Hills, H.
" William P. mason, h. 51 High, H.
Hillstown Grange hall, Hills. n. Oak.
Hilton James, carpenter, h. Prospect.
Hindle Thomas, h. 1 Church, B.
Hines Thomas, farmer, h. Prospect, n. R.R.
" Wm. J. carpenter, h. 30 Orchard, n. Pros.
Hinton Harry, painter, b. 324 Main, S.L.
" John, machinist, h. 324 Main, S. L.
Hobbs Alexander, ostler, b. 2 Bissell.
Hockanum Cemetery, 11 High, H.
" District School, 519 Main.
" M. E. Church, 308 Main.
" Post Office, (120) Main, opp. Wadsworth.
Hoffman Joseph, farmer, b. Hills, H.
Hogan Timothy, teamster, 70, b. 70 Burnside av.
Holbrook Erving P. butcher, 9, h. 2 King, n. Gil.
Holden Herbert, mach. at Naubuc, h. 250 Main, H.
Holland Harry A. machinist, h. 59 Village.
" Peter, laborer, b. 161 Silver, B.
Hollis William M. h. Saunders.
Hollister Charles T. farmer, h. 116 Silver.

Hollister Chauncey, farmer, h. 41 Naubuc av. H.
" Ellen Miss, h. 21 Church.
" Frank F. farmer, b. 308 Main.
" W. Stannard, mechanic, h.u. 28 Ranney.
" William, engineer, h. 11 Gilbert, M.
" William T. mason, h. 116 Silver.
Holmes Howard A. paperm. h. Woodland, B.
Holstein John, paper finisher, h. 6 Clark, B.
Homewood Albert, h.u. 26 Wells av.
Hooper Harry, machinist N.E.R. b. 5 Belden.
Hopewell Carl, plumber, b. 3 Lester, M.
" James, machinist, h. 3 Lester, M.
Horan Keron, fireman, h. 155 Larrabee.
Horton John W. carptr. N.E.R. h. 35 Park av.
Hotchkiss Charles W. crullers, h.u. 1 Garvan.
House Albert, farmer, b. 15 High, H.
" Elisha E. farmer, h. Maple, H.
" Eugene H. laborer, b. 16 Darlin, M.
" George M. mason, h. (291) Main.
" Herbert B. driver NY&B.D.Ex. h. 16 Darlin.
" Marshall D. carpenter, h. 8 Garvan.
Houseman Jacob, helper 1 Forbes, h. Sch. c. Brnsd.
Hovey Andrew J. carpenter, h. 11 Bragg.
Howard Arthur A. engineer N.E.R. h. 9 Linden.
" James A. farmer, h. Brewer, H.
Howard's Hall, 568 Burnside, B.
Howe Alfred C. farmer, h. 345 Main.
" William, machinist, b. 5 Belden.
Howlett Charles A. decorator, b. 15 Wells.
" H. Leroy, painter, b. 15 Wells.
" Henry G. h. 15 Wells.
Hubbard Caroline, wid. Luther, h. High, n. Broad.
" Christian, motorman St. Ry. h.u. 4 Blinn.
" Wilbur B. farmer, h. Hills, H.
Hughes Mary, dressmaker, h. Rector.
Hunn Mary, wid. John, h. 80 Larrabee, B.
Huntley Charles, teamster, h. 34½ Governor.
" Joseph W. millwright, h. Woodland, B.
Huntting Henry J. b. 812 Main.
" John, tobacco, h. Main, opp. Comstock pl.
" Lillian, music teacher, 812, b. 812 Main.
" William L. (W. L. H. & Co.) h. 812 Main.
" Wm. L. & Co. tobacco dealers, 812 Main.
William L. Huntting.
" William S. b. 812 Main.

**HURD OLIVER,** mfr. emery strop knife sharpener, 6, b. 6 Governor. See p. 586.
Hurlburt Charles E. farmer, h. Hills, H.
" Lucy M. Mrs. h. (263) Main.
Hutchings Charles C. blacksm. h. 97 Pitkin, M.
Hyde Claude, laborer, b. 244 Main, H.
" Frederick E. papermaker, h. 2 William, B.
" John, clerk, b. c. Main and Pitkin.
Hyland Matthew, blacksm. b.u. 18 Woodbridge.
" Michael, blacksm. r. (85) Main, h. Howard.
" Timothy F. carpenter, h.u. 9 Garvan.
Hymer ☞ see Heimer.
Hynes John, at N.E.R. h. 24 Ranney.

Imperial Hotel, 99 Hartford av.
Ingraham Clarence W. farmer, h. 25 High, H.
Irish Charles, cabinetmaker, h.u. 5 Central.
Isenberg Harry, capmaker, h. 22 Village, M.

JACKSON George V. emp. N.E.R. h. 34 Olmsted.

*Charles L. Jencks.*　　　　*John L. Jencks.*

## JENCKS BROS.,

### Dealers in

*PINE, SPRUCE* **Lumber,**
*and CHESTNUT*

*Also Window Frames and*
*Turned Columns, Brackets*
*and Mouldings, Banisters, etc.*

### 100 HARTFORD AVENUE,

*Cor. Governor St., Near the Bridge,*

*Telephone, 266-2.*　　*East Hartford Meadow.*

James Thomas, papermaker, h. 11 William, B.
" William, papermaker, b. 11 William, B.
Jarman Charles, h. 161 Silver.
" Emma M. teacher, b. 18 Church.
" William S. clerk, h. 18 Church.
" William S. Jr. clerk, h. 18 Church.
JENCKS BROS. lumber, 100 Hartford av. c.
　Governor, M.　　*See page 775.*
" Charles L. (*Jencks Bros.*) h. 7 Village, M.
" John L. (*Jencks Bros.*) h. (303) Main, S.L.
" Wm. H. farmer, h. 12 King, near Ellington.
Jensen Neils, stonecutter, h. 25 Darlin, M.
Jepson Christian, laborer, h.u. 23 School, B.
Jessen Ernest, carpenter N.E.R. h. 4 Blinn.
Jesson Chris. carpenter, h. Nelson, M.
" Henry A. painter, b. 2 Ash, M.
" John M. teamster, 100 Hfd. av. b. 2 Ash, M.
" Niels, painter, h. 2 Ash, M.
Johnson Christ, laborer, h. Jencks, M.
" Fred. E. clerk, b. 5 Pleasant.
" John A. hodcarrier, h. Nelson, M.
" John Oscar, paperm. h. 589 Burnside av. B.
Jones Charles Addison, carpenter, 161, h. 161
　Burnside av.
" George S. farmer, h. Naubuc av. n. Hock-
　anum schoolhouse, H.
" Hansey, wid. William, h. Naubuc.
" Isaac, paperm. 1 Forbes, h. 1 Church, B.
" James, blacksmith, h. 26 Gilbert, M.
" John P. blacksmith, h. 848 Main.
Jordan Edward, farmer, h.r. 124 Burnside.
" George S. butcher, h. Larrabee st. B.
Jordon John, teamster, b. 112 Hartford av. M.
Joseph John, at Colts, h. 27 Village, M.
Judson Albert A. salesman, h. 358 Main.
" Dwight, clerk, b. 358 Main.
" Edwin A. farmer, h. 374 Main.
" Herbert A. glazier, h. 378 Main.
" Louis T. farmer, b. 374 Main.
Juskip Fred, machinist, h.u. 24 School.

KAFINK Arthur, at Colts, h. Roberts, B.
Kahl Charles, farmer, h. Silver, w. of Forbes.
Kaiser William H. plumber, h. 16 Pleasant, M.
Kane John, laborer, h. 687 Main, n. cemetery.
" Thos. fireman N.E.R. b. 22 Woodbridge, B.
Kantz Charles, mach. Naubuc, b. 53 Main, H.
" John, farmer, h. 53 Main.
" Katie, wid. Simeon, h. 53 Main.

Kappenberg Robt. W. constable, h. Roberts, B.
Kasche Edward, farmer, h. Hills, H.
" Paul, farmer, b. Hills, H.
Kask Axel J. cabinetmaker, h. 12 Franklin, B.
Kearns James, farmer, h. School, n. Goodwin, B.
" James Jr. b. School, n. Goodwin.
" John F. printer, b. School, n. Goodwin.
" Lawrence P. ticket agent, h. Stanley.
" Michael H. printer, h. 14 Pleasant.
Keating Thomas, ostler, b. 112 Hartford av.
Keeler John, fireman N.E.R. b. 70 Park av. B.
Keeney Asahel L. farmer, h. Forbes, n. Brewer, H.
" Herbert E. farmer, h. Silver, c. of Forbes, H.
" William, brassworker, h.u. 12 Central.
Kehoe Patrick, farmer, h. Ellington, n. Goodwin.
Kellar Fred B. at N.E.R. h. (68) Main.
Kelleher Timothy, sectionhand, h. 3 Goodwin.
Keller William W. plumber, h. 22 Darlin, M.
Kelley Abner, carpenter, h. 42 Governor.
" Annie, b. 635 Main.
" Edward, mach. N.E.R. b. 24 Woodbridge.
" Francis J. machinist, b. 635 Main.
" John T. brakeman N.E.R. b. 6 Burnside av.
" Joseph J. foreman N.E.R. h. 41 Park av.
" Marcella, clerk, b. 635 Main.
" Mary, wid. John, h. 635 Main.
Kenefick Timothy, laborer, b. Kennedy, B.
Kennedy George A. farmer, b. Silver, e. of
　· Forbes, B.
" Harriet, wid. Osborn, b. Silver, c. of Kennedy.
" Herbert, farmer, h. Silver, e. of Forbes, B.
" John, farmer, h. 56 Governor.
" John E. b. 24 Woodbridge.
" Julia A. Mrs. h. 16 School, B.
" Leon, carinspector, b. 21 School.
" Samuel H. papermaker, h. 1 Church, B.
" William, foreman N.E.R. h. 24 Woodbridge.
Kenney John P. farmer, h. 21 Main, H.
Kent John, farmer, b.r. 124 Burnside.
Kepley Charles, brakeman N.E.R. h. 98 Tolland.
Kernan John, mason, h. 16 Central.
Kiernan John F. mason, h. 38 Governor.
" Kate, wid. Francis, h. 38 Governor.
" Sylvester, bricklayer, b. 38 Governor.
Kilbourne A. E. h. 1235 Main, So. Windsor line.
" Charles P. b. 350 Tolland.
" Henry P. emp. paper mill, h. 350 Tolland, B.
" Wm. H. carpenter, N.E.R. h. 26 Ranney.
Kilgariff Austin, h. 25 Woodbridge.
" Michael, section boss N.E.R. h. Park av. B.
Killian John, h. Tolland, n. School, B.
Kilner William, steamfitter, h. 584 Brnsd. av. B.
Kilty Patrick, farmer, h. 21 Goodwin.
Kimball Clarence S. carpenter, h. 318 Tolland, B.
" Daniel Martin, h. 108 Burnside.
" Tamson A. wid. E. P. h. 318 Tolland, B.
" Willis S. b. 318 Tolland, B.
King Annie K. b. 56 Governor.
" Charles H. bookkeeper, h. 115 Hfd. av. M.
" E. C. L. b. 115 Hartford av. M.
" Edward E. *selectman*, tobacco warehouse,
　Hartford av. c. Prospect, h. 56 Governor.
" Everett, machinist, b. 21 Bissell.
" Frederick, fireman, b. 60 Tolland.
" George, h. 60 Tolland.

King George Jr., U. S. Army, b. 60 Tolland.
" J. Walter, machinist, h. 642 Main.
" Hortense G. wid. Wilbur J. h. (88) Main.
" Louis H. silverplater, b. 115 Hartford av.M.
" Mowlee, laundry, 854 Main.
" Nellie, housekeeper at 24 Ranney.
" Rose S. wid. Ernest, h. 13 Burnside av.
" William, machinist, b. 60 Tolland.
Kinghorn David, blacksmith, h. 36 Governor.
" Harry H. blacksmith, h. 48 Hartford av.
" William, machinist, b. 547 Main.
Kinnane John, papermaker, h. Church, B.
" Lawrence, papermaker, b. Church, B.
Kirbell Benjamin, h. 40 Silver.
" Joseph, harnessmaker, 571 Main, h. 9 Silver.
Kirchen William, New England Wood Yard, Ranney c. Mn. h. 1 Bissell.
Kleban Edward, painter, h. 100 Tolland, B.
Klett Louis, furrier, h.u. 58 Village, M.
Klopfer Louis, brakeman N.E.R. b. 2 Webster.
Kossick Simon, cigarmaker, h. Spring.
Kostenpider John, h. Pitkin, cor. Main.
Kowalski Charles, farmer, h. (174 South) Main.
" Frederick W. farmer, h. Hills, H.
" Godfrey, blacksmith, b. (174) Main, H.
Kramer George, fireman N.E.R. h. 67 Burnside.
Krapsch Frank W. carpenter, h. Park av. B.
Kuebler John M. Jr. laborer, b. 20 Prospect.
" Robert B. printer, b. 20 Prospect.
" Teresa, wid. John M. h. 20 Prospect.
" William, cigarm. h. Orchard, cor. Prospect.
Kugler John Mrs.: h. High, H.
Kuhn Fred, stonecutter, h. 98 Pitkin, M.

LAFFARGUE Frederick, farmer, b. 12 Main, H.
La Fortune Victor E. conductor St.Ry. h. Blinn.
La Grange Grant, ins. agent, b. 2 Wells.
Lahie Louis, carpenter, h. Roberts.
Lamb George, W. carpenter, h. 34 Village, M.
Landers Morris, h.u. 67 Tolland.
" Patrick, helper N.E.R. b. 65 Tolland.
" Thomas, h. 40 Tolland.
" Thomas, b.u. 67 Tolland.
Landon Will P. clerk, N.E.R. h. 51 Burnside.
Landry William, carptr. N.E.R. b. 63 Tolland.
Lane Davis E. dentist, h. (75) Main, n. Orchard.
" Farnum H. musicteacher, b. (75) Main.
Lang John, gardener at 518 Main.
Langdon John, engineer N.E.R. b. 98 Tolland.
Larenson John, carpenter, h. Jencks, M.
Laroque Charles, laborer, b. 6 Pleasant, M.
Larson Albert, laborer at and b. Silver, n. Ken.
" August, laborer, b. Silver, c. Kennedy.
" Nels, clerk, h. 421 Tolland, n. School, B.
Lathrop Albert H. livery, 63, h. 63 Main.
" Charles W. h. 188 Burnside av. B.
Lave Charles, oiler, h. Woodland, B.
" Frank, laborer, h. Woodland, B.
" Louis, laborer at 161 Silver.
Lawler Michael, brakeman N.E.R. h. 17 Belden.
Layland William, machinist, h. 31 Pleasant, M.
Leadbitter Francis G. cigarmaker, h. Bragg.
Leary Mary, wid. John, h. 40 Ranney.
" Minnie, b. 40 Ranney.
" Timothy, driver, h.r. 16 Pleasant, M.

Leavitt Floyd, engraver, h. 58 Village, M.
LeCourt Eugene, iceman, h. Brewer.
" Leon, iceman, h. Brewer.
Leddy P. machinist, h.u. 11 Village, M.
Lee James L. machinist, h. 8 Willow.
Leonard John, farmer, Forbes, s. of Silver.
Lester Albert J. h.u. 3 Lester, M.
" Andrew M. peddler, h. Lester, M.
" Charles E. W. cutter, h. 99 Pitkin, M.
" Charles H. clerk, h. 26 Darlin, M.
" Charles R. H. plater, b. 26 Darlin, M.
" Henry, b. 9 Darlin, M.
" Henry H. silverplater, h. 27 Darlin, M.
" Howard W. clerk, b. 28 Pleasant, M.
" James G. machinist, h. 9 Darlin.
" Julius M. clerk, h. 28 Pleasant, M.
" Lawrence V. farmer, h. 60 Silver.
" Mabel E. teacher b. 60 Silver.
" Martin K. farmer, h. 99 Pitkin, M.
" Sarah E. wid. Porter, h. 101 Willow.
Levy Julius, drugstore, h. Burnside, opp. School. B.
Lewis Anna, wid. Wm. J. h. 106 Burnside av.
" John, plumber, h.u. 8 Burnside av.
" T. Jarvis, ins. clerk, h. 11 Sherman.
" William B. clerk, b. 106 Burnside av.
Liebert Arthur C. cashier Conn. Mutual Life Ins. Co. h. 949 Main, c. Park.
" Gustave Mrs. b. 949 Main, c. Park.
Lilly Hanson, brakeman N.E.R. h. 31 Wdbg.
Linberg Jacob, glazier, h. 17 Broad, H.
Line Andrew, farmer, Silver, w. of Forbes, B.
Linton Earl, machinist, b. 12 William, B.
" James, carpenter, h. 12 William, B.
Lloyd John Jr. teamster at 100 Hartford av. M.
" Thomas F. policeman, h. 35 Pleasant.
Lockman Frank, h. 16 Gilbert, M.
Lockwood Frank, farmer, h. Silver. e. Kennedy.
Long Albert A. farmer, h. Ellington, n. Goodwin.
" George H. farmer, h. School and Ellington.
" Hill District School, B.
" Thomas, laborer N.E.R. b. 67 Tolland.
Loomis Charles B. clerk at (84) Main.
" Herbert W. transfer office, N.E.R. h. 10 Wells av.
" Mary, wid. Chester M. h. 800 Main.
" Walter A. h. 26 Hartford av.
Loveland A. L. nurse, b. Governor.
" Selden, b. 1 Bigelow.
" William, laborer, h. Governor.
Lowe Frank P. machinist, h. 15 Wells.
Lowenhanft Edward, clerk, b. 30 William, B.
" John P. electrician, h. 30 William, B.
Lowry William A. drugstore, 743 Main, c. Bissell, b. 13 Burnside av.
Lucy Cornelius, laborer, b. Forbes, B.
" Mary, wid. Martin, b. Forbes, B.
Ludcig Barbara, wid Jacob, b. Park av. B.
Lull DeForest, carpenter, h. 21 Church.
Lumis George, clerk, h. 1 Clark.
Lund John, at Popes, h. 102 Larrabee, B.
Lyman Edith B. b. 13 Village, M.
" L. Warren, h. 13 Village, M.
Lyons Daniel, helper N.E.R. b. 63 Tolland.
Lysaght Mich. foreman N.E.R. h. 44 Burnside av

MAOATEE Charles, tel. operator, h.u. 4 Olmsted.
Machie Albert, farmer, h. King.
Mackey Newton, painter, h. 24 Ranney.
MacLean Charlotte E. h. 12 Wells.
" Mary E. h. 12 Wells.
Magner Patrick, laborer, h. 72 Hartford av. M.
Mahan John, caller N.E.R. h. 8 Ranney.
" Joseph, U.S. Army, b. 8 Ranney.
" Martin, farmer, h. 8 Ranney.
Mahoney William, machinist, h. 24 School.
Maine Ferdinand, helper at Popes, h. 5 Saunders.
Malloy Daniel, laborer N.E.R. h. Park av.
Manning Morris Mrs. b. 62 High, H.
Manock Edmund, shoemaker, h. 91 Burnside.
Mans George, barber, b. 37 Pleasant, M.
Marceau Napoleon, brakeman N.E.R. h.u. 34
    Woodbridge.
Marcy Ann, wid. Anson H. h. 5 Village, M.
Marion Edward T. manager, h. 6 Wells.
" Nelson, b. 6 Wells.
" Otis D., U. S. Army, b. 6 Wells.
Maroney Dennis, farmer, h. Hills, H.
Marshall E. D. h.2u. 105 Hartford av. M.
Marston David D. at Colts, h. 40 Pleasant, M.
Martin Eva M. postmistress, H.P.O. and grocery,
    So. Main, opp. Wadsworth, b. 17 Broad.
" Harvey, fireman N.E.R. b. 5 Belden.
" Henry F. printer, b. 23 Central.
" Hugh J. printer, h. 23 Central.
**MARTIN JAMES A.** publisher Ameri-
can Enterprise, 866 Main, n. R.R. depot,
    h. 866 Main.          *See page 795.*
" John A. farmer, h. 17 Broad, n. Main, H.
Matthies Louis, cigarmaker, h. 66 Naubuc av. H.
Mattisen Thomas, paperm. h. Burnside av. B.
May Frank D. traveling salesman, h. 330 Main.
Mayberry F. H. physician, h. 575 Burnside av. B.
Maynard George W. farmer, h. 19 Elm, n. Bissell.
Mayo Minnie, wid. William, h. Gilbert, M.
McAloon Mary, h. 91 Prospect.
" Patrick, farmer, h. 57 Prospect, c. Orchard.
McAuliff Cornelius, asst. yardmaster N.E.R. h.
    7 Woodbridge.
McCabe James, tinsmith, b. 10 William.
" Richard, bricklayer, b. 10 William.
" Thomas J. papermaker, h. 10 William.
McCARTHY & AHERN, undertakers. *See p. 248.*
" Edw. J. engineer, h. 45 Governor.
" Jeremiah, boilerman N.E.R. h.u. 14 Wdbg.
" Patrick, helper, h. 30 Ranney.
" William, brakeman N.E.R. b. 8 Tolland.
McCarty Daniel, at N.E.R. h. Forbes, B.
" Michael, farmer, h. Roberts, B.
" Thomas J. farmer, b. Roberts, B.
McClelland Belle, widow Thomas, h. Tolland,
    n. Larrabee, B.
" Mary, bookkeeper, b. 330 Tolland, B.
" Mary J. widow William J. h. 330 Tolland, B.
" Milton H. teamster, h. 20 Governor.
" Robert, farmer, h. Long hill st.
" Robert, papermaker, h. Woodland, B.
McClelland William, at N.E.R. h. 330 Tolland.
McCormick John H. leathercut. b. 1 Goodwin ln.
" S. B. watchmaker, r. 743, h. 743 Main.
" Wm. L. h. 1 Goodwin lane.

**S. B. McCORMICK,**
**Watchmaker and Jeweler,**
**743 MAIN STREET,**
Corner of BISSELL,          Over LOWRY'S Drug Store,
**EAST HARTFORD, CONN.**
Repairer of all kinds of Watches, Clocks, Jewelry, and
Silverware. Repairing of Fine Watches, French Clocks, Hall
Clocks, and Music Boxes a Specialty. 30 years' experience.

Drop a Postal.          Lock Box 121.

McCourt James, at N.E.R. h. 4 Webster.
" Mary, wid. Samuel, b. 4 Webster.
" Thomas, at N.E.R. b. 4 Webster.
McCown Joseph G. conductor, h. 10 Rector.
McCreery Frank, printer American Enterprise,
    b. 866 Main.
McCudden James F. bookkeeper, b. 30 Silver.
McCullough Bridget, wid. John, h. 28 Village.
" Felix, h. 34 Village, M.
" Henry, sailor, b. 32 Village.
" William E. engineer, h. Village, n. R.R.
McCune Edward, fireman, N.E.R. b. 22 Wdbg.
McCutcheon Chas. M. brakem. N.E.R. b.8 Tolland.
" Henry, b. 8 Tolland.
" Thomas, laborer, h. 8 Tolland.
McDonald Bernard, blacksmith, h. 310 Tolland, B.
" John, carpenter, h. (76) Main.
McDonough John, laborer, N.E.R. b. 14 Ranney.
McGehan Anthony, farmer, h. (269) Main, H.
McGinnis Thomas, laborer, h. 41 Governor.
McGregor James A. farmer, h. Forbes.
McGuire Michael, helper, N.E.R. b. 8 Franklin.
McIntosh Herbert, farmer, h. King.
" Nill, machinist, h.u. 14 Church, B.
McKee James F. carpenter, h. 3 King.
" John J. carpenter, b. 3 King.
" Mary, wid. William, h.u. 16 Pleasant, M.
" William J. b.u. 16 Pleasant, M.
" William J. carpenter, h. 3 King.
McKeig James, fireman, N.E.R. b. 5 Belden.
McKenzie Albert L. cond. N.E.R. h.62 Brnsd.av.B.
McKibbin James A. associate editor American
    Enterprise, b. 866 Main.
McKinney Jas. employe N.E.R. h. 20 Ranney.
McMahon Daniel, farm.h.24 Goodwin, n. Ellington.
" John, helper at 70, b. 70 Park av.
McManus F. G. clerk Woodland mills.
" Hugh, laborer, N.E.R. b. 8 Franklin, B.
McNair Christina Mrs. drssm. h. 29 Bissell, n. Lewis.
" James, clerk, h. 29 Bissell, n. Lewis.
McNeil Catherine Mrs. b. 5 Stanley.
McNerney John, car insp. N.E.R. h. 21 Wdbg.
Medway John M. engir. N.E.R. b. 12 Linden.
Mehan Edward, fireman, b. 22 Woodbridge.
Meighan Patrick J. clerk, N.E.R. b.39 Park av. B.
Meisterling Lizzie H. clerk, b. 34 School, B.
Meredith Edw. H. engineer, N.E.R. h. 31 Park,
    n. Main.
" Mary E. wid. Charles, b. 31 Park n. Main.

# Charles Merriman,

### FIRE, LIFE, AND
### ACCIDENT

# INSURANCE.

### REAL ESTATE and LOAN Agency,

### No. 650 MAIN STREET,

*Cor Garvan St.,        East Hartford, Conn.*

MERRIMAN CHARLES, *town treasurer*, insurance agent, 650, h. 650 Main. *See page 778.*
" Ella E. wid. Frank B. h. 667 Main.
" Eugene H. postmaster, h. Elm, e. of Wells.
Merritt John W. cond. N.E.R. h. 73 Brnsd. av.
Methodist Episcopal church, Main, n. Naubuc av.
Meyer Fred, painter, h. Bragg.
Mikkelsen Rasmus P. watchman, h. 13 Lester, M.
Mikleheit Fred, laborer, b. Kennedy.
Miller August, mason, h. 513 Burnside.
" Benjamin T. papermaker, h. 44 Olmsted, B.
" Don Alonzo, farmer, h. 18 Ranney.
" Francis, polisher, h.u. 18 Governor.
" George, carpenter, b. Park av. B.
" Harry L. printer, b. 11 Highland.
" Joseph, farmer, h. 32 Olmsted.
" Peter, brewer, h. Burnside av. c. Highland.
Milton John, carriage painter, 9 Pleasant, h. Hfd.
Miner Eliza M. wid. Jesse L. h. 149 Main.
" George, machinist, h. Silver, s. of Kennedy.
" Walter, clerk, h. 79 Silver.
Mitchell Frank A. engineer, h. Olmsted.
Moffat James, mechanic, b. 3 William, B.
Mohr Henry, printer, b. Tolland, B.
" Joseph, inspector, N.E.R. h. Tolland, B.
Monahan Dennis, farmer, h. 36 Goodwin.
" Dennis, Jr. farmer, h. 36 Goodwin.
Monnier W. D. music teacher, h. 29 Central.
Montgomery Hugh, h. 2 Church, c. Brnsd. av. B.
Moody Charles C. market gardener, 105, h. 105 Burnside av.
" Frank, teamster, 70, b. 70 Burnside av.
" Lillie M. b. 105 Burnside av.
" O. W. h. Tolland, n. William, B.
Moonan John, paperm. h. Cottage, n. Bridge.
Moore Arthur P. supt. E. H. water works, tax collector, constable, h. 952 Main, c. Pros.
" Clarissa, wid. Jas. A. boardinghouse, 2 Governor, c. Main.
" Edward F. machinist, b. 22 Goodwin.
" Ernest A. b. 951 Main.
" Eugene E. machinist, b. 951 Main.
" Fred T. toolmaker, b. 344 Main, S.L.
" Harvey, h. 113 Hartford av. M.
" James, farmer, b. 22 Goodwin.
" Joseph, brakeman N.E.R. h. Tol. e. Larrabee.
" Robert, employee N.E.R. h. 22 Goodwin.
" Sarah, wid. George, h. 52 High, H.
Moran James F. stairbuilder, h. Prospect.

Moran Mary C. clerk, b. 25 Governor.
" Sarah F. Mrs. h. 25 Governor.
Morgan James, engineer, h. 24 Wells.
Moriarty James, h. 943 Main.
Morrison Catherine, h. 1 Goodwin lane.
Morrissey James, b. 70 Tolland.
Morse Frank, silverturner, b. 34 Burnside av.
" James L. farmer, h. 34 Burnside av.
Mosgrove Thomas, b. Darlin, M.
Mostmean Robert, teamster, b. 112 Hfd. av. M.
Mott Orville, conductor N.E.R. h. 15 Highland.
Moulton Newton H. farmer, h. (194) Main.
Muir James A. brakeman, h. 32 Ranney.
Mulcahy Matthew, farmer, h. Hills, H.
" William, farmer, h. Hills, H.
" William Jr. farmer, b. Hills, H.
Muldoon Daniel, emp. N.E.R. h. 38 Ranney.
" Michael, b. 29 Governor.
" Patrick, tracklayer, h. 29 Governor.
" Peter, machinist, b. 29 Governor.
Mulally Peter, papermaker, h. Woodland, B.
Mulligan David, brakeman, b. 28 Ranney.
" Peter, fireman, b. 28 Ranney.
Mumford Harry S. b. 36 Governor.
" James P. bookbinder, b. 36 Governor.
" Rolland K. signpainter, b. 36 Governor.
Munsell Franklin E. motorm. St. Ry. h. 12 Lynn.
Murkett Herbert E. pastor Hockanum M. E. church, h. 49 High, H.
Murphy Cecilia, wid. Denslow, h. Brnsd. n. Sch. B.
" David, farmer, h. 162 Silver.
" Edward, laborer, h. Burnside av.
" George, papermaker, h.u. 44 School, B.
" James J. farmer, h. 162 Silver.
" Walter G. physician, 802, h. 802 Main.

WALTER G. MURPHY, Physician and Surgeon. Office 802, h. 802 Main, (old No. 81,) c. Orchard, opposite Episcopal Church.
Office Hours—7 to 8 A. M.
1 to 3 P. M.
7 to 8 P. M.
Telephone.

Murray Daniel, master mech. N.E.R. h. 1 Comstock.
" Ellen, wid. Patrick, h. 63 School, B.
" James, farmer, h. 515 Burnside av.
" James, papermaker, b. 580 Tolland.
" James, papermaker, b. Woodland, B.
" James F. farmer, b. Ellington, n.c. School.
" John, papermaker, h. 120 Larrabee, B.
" John M. machinist, b. 120 Larrabee, B.
" Martin, laborer, h. 56 Prospect, c. Orchard.
" Patrick, real estate, h. 192 Burnside. av. B.
" Thomas, farmer, h. Ellington, cor. School.
Myers Mary, housekeeper, 68 Tolland.

NAVIN Michael, cond. N.E.R. h. 17 Highland.
Neild Robert A. engir. N.E.R. h. 12 Comstock.
Nelson Beverley, h. Elm, c. Central.
" Leland E. machinist, h. 22 Burnside.
" Ludwig, carpenter, h. Park av. n. School, B.
" Peter J. polisher, h. 9 Saunders.
Nevils Dennis, laborer, N.E.R. b. 98 Tolland.
New England House, Jas. E. Spellicy, 808 Main.
" England R. R.; office at depot; shops, Pk. av.

# Samuel Newman & Co.,
## WATCHMAKERS
## AND JEWELERS,
### East Hartford Meadow, Conn.

*Watch Repairs Guaranteed
One Year.*

*Fine REPAIRING on Watches and Jewelry a
Specialty.*

Newman Fred. machinist, b. 98 Hartford av. M.
" Lucy, wid. George M. h. 98 Hartford av. M.
" Samuel, (S.N.& Co.) b. 98 Hartford av. M.
NEWMAN SAMUEL & CO. watchmakers & jewelers, 98 Hartford av. *See page 779.*
Newton Murray A. conductor St. Ry. b. 6 Lynn.
" R. S. Mrs. b. 11 Sherman av.
Nichol Leslie B. firem. N.E.R. b. 2 Beaumont.
Nicholson Emma M. wid. H.A. b. 20 Village, M.
" Frank H. turner, b. 20 Village, M.
" Robert, teamster, b. 5 Pleasant, M.
" Ruel H. mason builder, and building mover, 20, h. 20 Village, M.
Nicoll David S. emp. N.E.R. h. 37 Park av.
" John S. fireman, b. 37 Park av.
Nielson Lars E. letter carrier, h. 5 Lester, M.
Nillson Andrew, cabinetmaker, h. 375 Main.
Niver James, carpenter, N.E.R. b. 34 Olmsted.
Noathlich Charles W. farmer, h. Roberts, B.
Noble Brothers, fruit, cigars, etc., 874 Main.
T. M. Noble.   W. B. Noble.
" Charles S. clerk, b.u. 45 Hartford av.
" Henry D. baker, 1, h. 1 Garvan.
" James M. clerk, h.u. 45 Hartford.
" Thomas M. (N. Bros.) h.u. 858 Main.
" William B. druggist. (61) Main, h.15 Wells av.
Nodine Isaac P. machinist, h.u. 28 Wells.
" William H. lettercarrier, b.u. 28 Wells.
Nolan Frank, clerk, b. 15 Highland.
North District School, 7 King, c. Gilman.
" John C. farmer, h. Prospect, e. of Main.
" Mill Dist. School, 15 School, n. Burnside av. B
Northam Helen R. b. 41 Burnside.
Nuthman Edward, machinist, h. Tolland.

O'BRIEN William, carptr. b. 112 Hartford av. M.
" William, teamster, h. 74 Hartford av. M.

THOMAS S. O'CONNELL Physician and Surgeon. Office 14, h. 14 Burnside av.
Office Hours—7 to 8 A.M.
2 to 3 and 7 to 8 P.M.

O'CONNELL Thomas S. physician, 14, h. 14 Burnside av.
O'Connor John, plater, b. (12) Main, H.
Oelkuck Edward, harnessm. h.u. 20 Pleasant, M.
" Henry, stonecutter, h.u. 20 Pleasant, M.
Ogden Charles, paper finisher, h. 14 William, B.
O'Hearn Peter, brakeman, N.E.R. h.u. (68) Main.
Olcott Elmer I. farmer, h. Brewer, H.

# W. H. OLMSTED,
## Civil Engineer and General Contractor,

Will furnish Surveys, Plans, Estimates, and Blue Prints for opening new Streets, Bridges, and Highways, and for Developing Public or Private Property.

LAND DRAINAGE AND SANITARY ENGINEERING,
Dealer in VITRIFIED SEWER PIPE of all Sizes.

### No. 1032 MAIN STREET,
Near Memorial Chapel,   North of Railroad Tracks.
### EAST HARTFORD, CONN.

Olin Charles F. editor, h. Forbes, B.
Oliver Rachel Mrs. h.u. Brewer, n. Main, H.
Olmstead Caroline E. Mrs. h. 14 School, B.
Olmsted A. Edward, h. 101 Prospect.
" Aaron F. farmer, b. 1089 Main.
" Alice Mrs. h. Elm, n. Bissell.
" Amy Mrs. h. 60 Silver.
" Angeline, wid. Edward, b. 16 School, B.
" Anna M. h. 101 Prospect.
" Annie E. b. (119) Main, no. of R.R. tracks.
" Arthur G. *selectman*, h. (156) Main.
" C. Henry, civil engineer, b. 1032 Main.
" Clarence G. b. 14 School, B.
" Elihu, machinist, h. (176) Main, n. King.
" G. Frank, b. (124) Main.
" George Howell Jr. salesman, h.(124) Main.
" Harry D. insurance, h. (119) Main.
" Harry W. b. (124) Main.
" Sophronia, wid. Chase E. h. (168) Main.
" William A. teamster at 101 Hartford av. h. 6 Pleasant, M.
OLMSTED WILLIAM H. civil engir. h. 1032 Main, next to Memorial chapel. *See page 779.*
O'Neil Daniel, fireman N.E.R. h. 39 Woodbridge.
" Francis, farmer, h. Forest, e. of Forbes, H.
" John, farmer, Forest, e. Forbes, H.
" Maggie, dressmaker, b. 6 Comstock.
" Margaret, wid. Daniel, h. 6 Comstock.
Osborn Ferdinand R. paperm. b. 7 William, B.
" Samuel L. carpenter, h. Stanley.
Osterhout Andrew, brakeman, h. Woodland, B.
" Cornelius, farmer, h. Woodland, B.
" Jacob, papermaker, h. Woodland, B.
" Norman, papermaker, b. Woodland, B.
Ostrout Lewis J. emp. N.E.R. h. 144 Burnside, B.
Ott Charles, farmer, h. Forbes, s. of Silver, B.
" Charlotte, h. Hudson, B.
" Jacob, farmer, h. Forbes, s. of Silver, B.
Oullet Alphonse, carptr. N.E.R. b. 92 Larrabee.
Overton Delos, farmer, h. Willow, n. Silver.
" Frank H. farmer, h. Willow, n. Silver.
" George A. salesman, h.w.s. Mn. s. of Willow.
" William J. farmer, h. Willow, n. Silver.

PADDLEFORD Frank, brakeman N.E.R. b. 24 William, B.
Painter R. F. toolmaker, h. 3 Bragg.
Palmer John, h. 91 Burnside av.
" Mary J. wid. James L. h. 388 Main.
" Walter H. farmer, h. 388 Main.

## J. R. PHILLIPS,

**New Store!**   ::::   **New Firm!**

Wholesale and Retail Dealer in

# HAY, GRAIN, AND FEED,

At Lowest Cash Prices in Town.

## 86 HARTFORD AVENUE,

**EAST HARTFORD, CONN.**

Near Jondis Brothers' Lumber Yard.

Papanineau John, shoem. r. 860, h. 860 Main.
Paradis Fred. h. 92 Larrabee, B.
Parsons Myron P. painter, h. 420 Tolland.
" Sarah H. wid. Elias, h. 40 Nau. n. Broad, H.
Patnod Edward, sawyer, h. Blinn, n. Main.
Pearce Fred'k, clerk N.Y.R. b.Tolland, n.Sch.B.
" Jos. carriagem. h. Tolland, n. School, B.
Pease Alexis, motorman, h. 10 Lynn.
" John F. h. 74 Burnside av.
" John W. clerk, b. 74 Burnside.
" M. S. Mrs. h. 20 William, B.
" Maurice, (*Thompson&P.*) h. 20 William,B.
Pebbles Cornelia, wid. Edward, h. 16 Village, M.
" Watson, mason, h. High, H.
Peck Arthur N. transfer agent, h. 587 Brnsd. av.
Peltier Frank H. physician, h. 49 School, B.
Pelton Charles N. machinist, h.u. 19 Brnsd. av.
Peoples Drug Store, J.Levy, Brnsd,opp.School,B.
Perkins Henry, helper, Woodland, b. Man.t.
Perrune Raffael, farmer, h. Silver, w. of Forbes.
Perry Charles O. plater, h. 6 Gilbert, M.
Peters Lucinda Mrs. h. Park av. n. School, B.
Peterson Charles, carpenter, h. Bragg, c. Olm.
Pfeifer Jacob, farmer, h. Maple hear Main, H.
Phelps Alvin M. carpenter, h. 103 Hartford av.
" Katie Mrs. h. Saunders.
PHILLIPS JOHN R. hay and grain, 86 Hartford av. h. Nelson.   *See page 780.*
" Sidney, conductor St.Ry. h. 30 Tolland.
Pierce Luella Mrs. b. 4 Burnside av.
Pitkin Frank H. h. 80 Hartford av.
" Howard M. farmer, h. 2 King.
" Howard S. reporter Evening Post, h. 23 Burnside av.
" Louisa, wid. Addison M. h. 297 Main, S. L.
Place Benton E. brakeman N.E.R. b. 4 Clark.
" Edward E. yardmaster N.E.R.h. 4 Clark.
Planter George, tinsmith, b. 10 William, B.
Poland Peter, carpenter, h.3u. 6 Pleasant, M.
Porter Albert, restaurant, 53, h. 53 Park.
" Charles W. farmer, h. Porter, n. Main, H.
" Edgar, helper, N.E.R. b. 51 Park av. B.
" Frank W. farmer, h. 34 Main, H.
" Garfield C. farmer, b. Porter, n. Main.
" George H. emp. N.E.R. h. 51 Park av.
Post Office, Meadow, 102 Hartford av.
" Office, 720 Main, c. Governor.
Potter Marcus A. at N.E.R. h. 18 School.
Powers James, printer, h. 40 Goodwin.
" John, laborer, h. 40 Goodwin.

Pratt Anna, wid. George W. h. 14 Central.
" Delia, wid. Algernon, h. 15 Silver.
" Edward W. dentist, 638, h. 638 Main.
" Fannie E. Mrs. dressmaker, 13, h. 13 Bragg, n. Olmsted.
" George Edwin, carpenter, h. 157 Silver.
" George Ely, farmer, h. 564 Main, opp. Silver.
" Grace L. stenog. b. 564 Main, opp. Silver.
" Howard R. carpenter, b. 157 Silver.
" James P. farmer, b. 157 Silver.
" S. Arthur, farmer, h. 153 Silver.
" Walter W. farmer, b. 157 Silver.
" Wm. O. clerk, h. 13 Bragg, n. Olmsted.
Prentice James R. h. 723 Main.
Pritchard Charles H. painter, h. 590 Brnsd. av. B.
Probate Office, Wells hall, 771 Main.
Proctor Jas. supt. 53 Church, h. Springfield,Mass.
Prudhomme Oscar E. painter16 Wells, b.(85)Mn.
Prumbaum John, machinist, h. 20 Gilbert, M.
" Nicholas W. machinist, b. 23 Village.
" Peter, tinner, h. 27 Village, M.
Public warehouse, A. E. Kilbourn, Ranney st.
Purple Edson, carpenter, b. 85 Burnside.
Putnam Frederick S. farmer, h. (141)Mn. c. Pros.
" George K. patternmaker, b. 22 Governor.
" Giles H. inspector, h. 22 Governor.
" I. C. b. 22 Governor.

QUILLIGAN Morris, laborer, h. 15 Belden.
Quinn Alex, at 6 Governor, b. Central.
" Ellen, wid. Daniel, b. 517 Burnside av.
" John, foreman, h. 517 Burnside av.

RAFFE Gustave, mechanic, h. Main, s. Maple, H.
Ramsey Louisa A. wid. Rufus, h. (385) Main.
Rand Harry E. machinist, b. 89 Burnside.
Randall Wm. C. switchm. N.E.R. h.r.18Brnsd.av.
Ranney Burt J. clerk, b. 5 Beaumont.
" Mary J. Mrs. h. 5 Beaumont.
" Robert K. undertaker, b. 5 Beaumont.
" Walter K. clerk, h. 1031 Main.
Rasmussen Rasmus, clerk, h. 21 Darlin, M.
Rathbun Frederick H. painter, h. 15 High, H.
Rathgeb John, l. 8 Pleasant, M.
" John, grocer, h. 95 Pitkin, M.
" Henry, cigarmaker, b. 95 Pitkin, M.
Raymond Public Library and Hall, Mn.c. Central.
Reardon Hannah, wid. Wm. J. h. 33 Central, M.
" Jeremiah M. shoem. 133, h. 133 Hartford av.
" John conductor St.Ry. b. 10 Garvan.
Recor Alfred H. polisher, h. 31 Central.
Reeve Philip H. engineer, h. 22 Gilbert, M.
Reid Edward Y. h. 34 Gilbert.
" Robert K. sawyer, h. 32 Village, M.
" Thomas, constable, h. 10 Governor, M.
" William, salesman, h. 37 Village, M.
Reiff Charles, cigarmaker, h. Olmsted, n. Bragg.
Rentch Matthew, b. 62 High.
Reynolds Robert, b. Naubuc, n. Hockanum sch.
Rice Thomas, machinist, h.u. 60 Burnside av.
Rich Caroline M. Mrs. h. 13 Burnside.
Richards Alfred, machinist, h. 5 Woodbridge.
" Alfred Jr. machinist, b. 5 Woodbridge.
" William, b. 5 Woodbridge.
Richardson Frank, florist at 680, b. 680 Main.

RICHARDSON FRANK W. florist, 680, h. 680 Main. *See page 781.*
"   Lorenzo D. farmer, h. 975 Main.
Richmond Andrew, h. 131 Silver.
"   George W. h. Forbes, n. of Kennedy, B.
"   James, painter, h. 19 Darlin, M.
"   John A. engineer, h. 9 Linden.
Riggy John, potter, h.r. Park av. n. R.R. shop.
Riley Alice M. h. 20 Church.
"   Annie E. stenographer, b. 79 Burnside av.
"   Charles B. farmer, h. Forbes, B.
"   George, sawyer, b. 79 Burnside av.
"   Helen, b. 20 Church.
"   John C. boilermaker N.E.R. h. 1 Webster.
"   Joseph, brakeman N.E.R. b. 324 Tolland.
"   Matthew, h. 79 Burnside av.
"   William A. bookkeeper, b. 14 School.
Ripley George W., U. S. Army, h. Sherman av.
Risley Adella A. b. 43 High, H.
"   Cassius E. b. 68 Naubuc av. H.
"   Charles R. farmer, h. 87 Silver.
"   Charles S. motorman St.Ry. h.u. 9 Garvan.
"   Daniel S. farmer, h. 344 So. Main, S.L.
"   Delia A. wid. William H. h. 43 High, H.
"   Edward, farmer, h. 348 Main.
"   Elmer, farmer, h. 68 Naubuc av. H.
"   Frank, teamster at 70, b. 70 Burnside av.
"   Frederick S. groc. (267,) h. (267) Main.
"   Irvin L. helper at 100 Hfd.av. h. 9 Village, M.
"   J. Albert, mechanic, h. 344 Main, S.L.
"   John E. driver 101 Hfd.av. h.u. 14 Village, M.
"   Lyman, h. 12 Village, M.
"   Meltire B. laborer, h. Governor, M.
"   Olive, wid. Lucius, b. 27 Darlin, M.
"   Ralph, farmer, h. 72 Naubuc av. H.
"   Ralph M. machinist, h. 96 Silver.
"   Selden S. carpenter, h. 635 Main.
"   William E. farmer, h. Brewer, H.
Rist O. Dewitt, h. 397 Main, s. of Silver.
Ritter Harry, machinist, b. 15 Franklin.
Rival Peter, mach. at Colts, h. Forbes, s. Hills, H.
Robbins Ernest, machinist, b.u. 32 Gilbert, M.
Roberts Alonzo, farmer, h. Porter, s. of Maple.
"   Andrew, carriages, etc. 9 Pleasant, h. 18 Burnside av.
"   Arthur, mechanic, h. Porter, s. of Maple, H.
"   Augustus, farmer, h. Saunders.
"   Charles A. farmer, b. Saunders.
"   Charles S. h. 17 Burnside av.
"   Charles W. *bridge commissioner*, farmer, h. 531 Main, s. of Silver, S. L.
"   David, bicycle repairer, 40, b. 40 Brnsd. av.
"   Ella R. Mrs. h. 60 Garvan.
"   Ernest, farmer, b. Porter, s. of Maple.
"   Frances L. h. 3 Central.
"   Frank, farmer, h. 146 Silver.
"   Frank T. farmer, b. 146 Silver.
"   Fred. H. b. Porter, s. Maple, H.
"   Henry C. poultry, 20, h. 20 Silver.
"   Homer C. ins. clerk, h. 527 Main, s. Silver.
"   J. Wilbur, farmer, b. 398 Main.
"   John F. laborer, h. Saunders.
"   Joseph William, h.u. 40 Burnside av.
"   Martha, h. 3 Central.
"   Martin, farmer, h. 398 Main, s. of Silver, S.L.

F. W. RICHARDSON,

# Florist.

Cut Flowers, Bouquets, and Floral Designs of Every Description.

Greenhouse and Vegetable Plants.

GREENHOUSES,

## 680 MAIN STREET,

Corner Hartford Avenue,

EAST HARTFORD, CONN.

Roberts Mary, wid. Watson, h. 22 Central.
"   Mary E. wid. Jason, h. 20 Silver.
"   Roland J. poultry, 20, h. 20 Silver.
"   Samuel E. farmer, h. Maple, H.
"   Walter R. farmer, b. 398 Main, s. Silver, S.L.
"   William, farmer, h. 537 Main, s. of Silver.
Robertson Henry G. clerk, h. 28 Darlin.
Robinson Henry C. farmer, h. Pitkin. n.of Main.
Roche Dennis, bricklayer, h. 22 Woodbridge.
"   William, papermaker, h. Woodland, B.
Rockwell Walter, laborer, h.u. 109 Hartford av.
Rodman Daniel C. Post, No. 65, G.A.R., Wells hall, 771 Main.
"   Samuel, farmer, h. Oak, H.
Rood Ephraim, builder, h. 7 Orchard, n. Main.
Root George N. cabinetm. h. 43 Hartford av.
Rosbrook Charles A. b. 1 Olmsted.
"   William R. buffer, h. 1 Olmsted.
Rose Albert, mason, h. 586 Burnside av. B.
"   Mary, wid. Samuel, h.u. 16 Village, M.
Rosenthal Emil, grocer & confec. 33, h. 33 Brnsd.
Rosenwald E. & Bro., Goodwin lane, n. Main.
Rossler Henry, screwm. h. 33 Main.
Rowe John, machinist, h. Silver, c. Forbes.
"   Patrick, farmer, h. Oak, H.
"   Patrick, Jr. farmer, h. Hills, H.
Ruoff Edwin M. farmer, b. Hills, H.
"   Frank, farmer, h. 25 Broad, H.
"   John, farmer and keeper of Town house, h. 62 High, H.
"   John G. farmer, h. Hills, H.
Russell Claude, prin. Sec. No. sch. h. 12 Brnsd. av.
Ruther Adolph, lettercarrier, h. (22) Main, H.
Ryan Dennis, conductor, h. 19 Highland.
Ryant Elmer E. engineer N.E.R. h. 11 Highland.

ST. JOHN Josephine F. teacher, b. 31 Hartford av.
"   Kittie, milliner, b. 31 Hartford av.
"   Marshall, gunstocker, h. 31 Hartford av.
"   Philomena, clerk, b. 31 Hartford av.
St. John's Episcopal church, 799 Main.
St. Mary's Roman Catholic church, Main, c. Woodbridge.
Sadler Fred. bicycle repairer, (70,) h. (68) Main.
Saeuer Andrew, shoemaker, h. Forbes, B.
Salerno Nicodamo, fruit, etc. 94, h. 94 Hfd. av. M.
Salsmo Louis J. farmer, h. Silver, no. of Forbes.
Sanderson William H. dispatcher, h. Elm, c. Wells.
Sanford Charles B. clerk, h. 15 Garvan.

Sargent Peter, laborer, b. 38 Central.
Satterthwaite R. M. Mrs. b. 953 Main.
Sauer John, machinist, h. Forbes, B.
Saunders George E. clerk, h. 3 Saunders.
" Kate A. wid. Henry, h. 3 Saunders.
Scarborough Edwin, timekeeper, h. 4 Wells.
" Emily T. b. 4 Wells.
" Luke, farmer, h. Park av. B.
Sceery Edward J. cigarmaker, b. 20 Ranney.
" Sarah A. wid. Edwd.J. housekpr.20 Ranney.
Schleicher Ernest, sawyer, h. 52 Central.
Schmidt Alexander, carpenter, h. 70 Hfd.av. M.
" Alex. Jr. harnessm. b. 70 Hartford av. M.
Schofield Lena Mrs. h.u. 32 Gilbert, M.
School street school, School, n. Burnside av.
Schroeder HenryF.teams.70 Brnsd.av.h.Latimer.
Schufts Herman, mech. h. Burnside, c.Tolland,B.
Schug Nicholas, farmer, h. Forbes, s. of Silver, B.
Schultz August, b. Naubuc av.
Schumaker Frank, salesm. at 100 Hartford av.
Scranton Charles, farmer, b. School, c. Goodwin.
" James, farmer, h. School, c. Goodwin.
Second North District School, Main, c. Linden.
" South School, Main, s. of Silver.
Selectmen's Office, Town hall, 771 Main.
Sellew George, machinist, h. 3 Ensign.
" William, machinist, h. Stanley.
Sergeant Abbie J. wid. William M. h. 982 Main.
Seware Fred C. brakeman, N.E.R. h. 5 Clark.
Sexton Cornelia, wid. Harlin P. h. 387 Main.
" Timothy, mechanic, h. 21 Elm, n. Bissell.
Sharpe Arthur, at Colts, b. 4 Gilbert, M.
" Edward, shipping clerk, h. 4 Gilbert, M.
" Thomas D. cigarmaker, b. 4 Gilbert, M.
Shaw David, carpenter, N.E.R. h. 7 Franklin, B.
" Joseph, mason, h. 28 Gilbert.
Shea Daniel, engineer, h. 25 Burnside av.
" James F. assembler, h. 22 William, B.
Shearer William, brakeman, N.E.R. b.8 Tolland.
Sheehan H. R. painter, h.u. 20 Governor.
" John, laborer, h. 70 Tolland.
" John H. Rev. pastor St. Marys church, h.
10 Woodbridge.
Sheldon Everett E. electrician, b.38 Pleasant,M.
Shepard Almyr J. clerk, h. 574 Burnside.
Sheperd George, filer, h.r. 98 Pitkin, M.
Sherman William W. h. 98 Tolland, c. Bidwell.
Shive William, brakeman, N.E.R. b. 2 Webster.
Shley Bernard, b. 59 Hartford av.

Shook Elmer E. h. 32 Woodbridge.
" Frank, fireman, b. 17 Woodbridge.
" Ruth Mrs. h. 11 Linden.
" Theodore, h. 17 Woodbridge.
Sickles George H. tel. oper. h. 30 Hartford av.
" Peter H. silversmith, h. 10 Park av. c. Main.
Signor O. J. Jr. b. 80 Burnside av.
" Oswald J. farmer, h. 80 Burnside av.
Silver Lane Post Office, Lincoln H. Bogue Post-
master, Silver st. c. Main.
Simington George, farmer. h. Carroll lane.
Simmons Nina, teacher Hockanum school, b.
Naubuc, c. Broad.
Simon Walter, carpenter, h. 54 High.
" William, papermaker, h. Woodland.
Simons Charles, mech. b. 512 Burnside av. B.
" Peter, farmer, h. Brewer, e. of Forbes, H.
" Robert A. farmer, h. Brewer, H.
Simpson Albert, fireman, b. 6 Bissell.
" Charles E. teamster, h. Goodwin lane.
" George, drug clerk, b. Phelps.
" George S. h. 7 Stanley.
" James K. teamster, b. 31 Park av.
" Nancy, wid. George, b. 6 Bissell.
" William H. gunmaker, h. 6 Bissell.
Sinclair James K. painter, h. 38 Pleasant, M.
Sing Charlie, laundry, (52) Main.
Singer Martin, farmer, h. 126 Silver.
Sisson Alexander G. flagm. N.E.R. h. 28 Linden.
" Lester F. farmer, h. 10 Silver.
Skelley Ann, wid. Patrick, b. 316 Tolland, B.
Skinner Edward S. clerk N.E.R. h. 16 Wells.
" Hervey D. b. 2 Governor.
Slater Charles C. h. Church, n. Burnside av.
" Fred, laborer, h. 47 Central.
" Silas, farmer, h. Hills, Hillstown P.O.
Smart George W. 385 Main, s. of Silver.
" Lottie C. b. 385 Main.
" Merritt, job printing, Rector, b. 385 Main.
Smead George, h. 683 Main.
Smith Alex Jr. harnessmaker, foreman Ætna
Hose, b. 70 Hartford av. M.
" Allie M. plumber, h. 28 Wells.
" Ann, wid. Samuel, h. 61 School.
" Cecil J. engineer, b. 17 Garvan.
" Charles D. clerk, b. Forbes, s. Maple, H.
SMITH CHARLES M. assessor, coaldealer, r. 895
Main, opp. R.R. depot, h. Forbes, s. of
Maple, H.          *See page 782.*
" Charles W. engineer, h. 36 Burnside.
" Chrissie, b. 11 Central av.
" Coleman, motorman, St.Ry. b. 10 Rector.
" Eber C. carpenter, h.u. Elm, n. Bissell.
" Edgar, captain N.Y.T.Co. h. 11 Village, M.
" Edgar B. conductor, h. 9 Garvan.
" Edmund S., U.S.A. b.Forbes, s. of Maple, H.
" Ernest J. electrician, St.Ry. h. 17 Garvan.
" Francis C. farmer, h. 43 Naubuc av. H.
" Frank E. farmer, b. Forbes, s. Maple, H.
**SMITH FRANK E.** rubber stamps, h.
19 Linden.          *See page 429.*
" Frank M. clerk, L. H. Forbes, b. 3 William,B.
" Fred. M. carpenter, b. 83 Silver.
" George, emp. N.E.R. b. 11 Orchard.

Smith James H. market, 689 Main, b. 3 Rector.
" John E. clerk, b. 17 Garvan.
" Joseph J. at N.E.R. h. 33 Woodbridge.
" Josiah H. farmer, h. 81 Silver.
" Lawrence, machinist, b. School, n. R.R.
" Neils, blacksmith, h. School, n. R.R.
" Orrin E. roofer, h. 52 Hartford av.
" Patrick, laborer, h. 9 High.
" Peter, engineer, h. 536 Burnside av.
" Seymour C. engineer, h. 8 Gilbert.
" William K. h. 69 Hartford av. c. Darlin, M.
Snow Ernest W. electrician, b. 426 Tolland, B.
" George A. plumber, b. 426 Tol. c. School, B.
" Harry, laborer, b. 2 Clark.
" Hiram. shoemaker, h. Brewer, H.
" Samuel F. b. 426 Tolland, B.
" Wade, h. 2 Clark.
Sope Frank, farmer, h. Silver, w. of Forbes.
" Guisseppe, farmer, h. Silver, n. Forbes.
" Tony, farmer, b. Silver, n. Forbes.
Sopi Oscar, farmer, h. Silver, B.
Sorensen Peter, blacksmith, h. 23 School, B.
South Congregational church, High, n. Main.
Spafford Mary E. Mrs. housekpr. 12 Burnside.
Spalding Marshall T. engineer, h. 23 Linden.
Speed E. M. Miss, h. 433 Main, S.L.
Spellicy James E. prop. N. E. House, (85) Main.
Spencer Block, 887-895 Main.
" Jane A. h. Silver lane, n. Kennedy.
" Selden W. h. 859 Main.
Sprague Kate J. wid. Gilbert E. h. (15) Main.
Squires Charles B. silverplater, b. 41 Central.
" Edson E. farmer, h. Forbes, n. Brewer, H.
" Eliza A. b. 41 Central.
" George F. brassmolder, h. 43 Central.
" Lillian M. teacher Hockanum school, b. Hfd.
" Stephen S. farmer, h. Roberts, B.
" Thomas H. tinsmith, h. 41 Central.
" William, horsedealer, b. 50 Hartford av.
" William G. fireman, N.E.R. b. 37 Park.
Stager Cornelius C. clerk, 566, b.540 Brnsd. av.B.
" Edward F. *assessor*, builder, 540, h. 540
Burnside av. B.
Stahl Arthur W. dispatcher, N.E.R. h. Stanley.
Stanley Kate S. and Nellie C. b. 1005 Main.
" William P. farmer, h. 1005 Main.
Stanton George, miller, h.u. 155 Main, H.
Stapleton John, blacksmith, b. 15 Bragg.
" Patrick, blacksmith, b. 15 Bragg.
" Matthew, at N.E.R. b. 15 Bragg.
" William, machinist, b. 15 Bragg.
Stark Gertrude, teacher, b. Forbes, c. Brewer, H.
" William, farmer, h. Forbes, c. Brewer, H.
Starks Alfred E. carpenter, h. 85 Burnside. av.
" George A. blacksmith, 1057 Main, h. 4 King.
Statton Walter W.cond, N.E.R. h.24 William, B.
Stebbins Alfred F. h.u. 44 School, B.
Stedman Hosmer P. carpenter, h. 16 Ranney.
Steele Eli, teamster, b. 45 Central.
" George, carpenter, b. 45 Central.
" George S. farmer, h. Forbes, s. Silver, B.
" Howell A. farmer, h. 21 School, B.
**STEELE JOHN H.** meat market, 20, h.
20 School, B. *See page 795.*
" Joseph A. *registrar of voters*, b. 21 School.

Steele Samuel, h. 45 Central.
" William E. electrician, h. 10 Ash, M.
" William M. h. Tolland, n. School, B.
Sterner Isaac C. engineer, N.E.R. h. 9 Clark.
Stevens George, farmer, b.119 Main, c. Wads.H.
" J. Eugene, mach. at Colts, h. 58 Garvan.
" W. H. painter, h.u. 52 Hartford av.
" Willard, teamster, h. 1 Bragg.
" William I. farmer, h. 119 Main, c. Wads. H.
Stewart Alexander, mason, b. 5 Central.
" James K. farmer, b. Hills, n. Forbes, H.
" John, fireman, N.E.R. h. 29 Woodbridge.
Stickney George G. at Colts, b. 23 Governor.
" George R. at Colts, h. 23 Governor.
Stiles Austin, emp. N.E.R h. 36 Ranney.
Stillman Albert M. baker, h. Elm, n. Burnside av.
" Mark W. baker, h. Elm, n. Bissell.
Stone Charles, mechanic, h. (344) Main.
" Francis P. laborer, h. Colt.
Storrs William E. hop beer, h. 5 Central.
Stoughtner John, at N.Y.R. b. (85) Main.
Stoughton Eliza A. wid. Edwin, h. 844 Main.
" Helen Mrs. h. 17 Wells.
" John A. lawyer, h. (117) Main.
" William G. grocer 887, h. 844 Main.
Stowell Charles, papermaker, h. Roberts, B.
Strasinger William, farmer, h. 123 Silver.
Strickland Allen M. carpenter. h. 26 Pleasant, M.
" Edwin V.machinist N.E.R. h.99 Burnside av.
Strohl George, foreman N.Y.R. h.u. 38 Hfd. av.
Strong Emerson E. farmer, b. Hills, H.
Strout George E. helper at 100, b. 98 Hfd. av. M.
Stumpf Geo. H. farmer, h. 22 Church, B.
" William E. machinist, h. 47 School, B.
Sturgis Isaac M. flagman, b. 8 Tolland.
Suckau Cecilia, wid. Theodore, h. 6 Gilbert.
" Theo. screwmaker, b. 6 Gilbert.
Sullivan Charles J. papermaker, b. Forbes, B.
" Daniel J. machinist, h. 513 Burnside.
" Dennis, farmer, h. Goodwin, e. R.R.
" James, laborer, h. 66 Burnside av.
" John C. engineer, b. Elm, c. Olmsted.
" John J. conductor, b. 12 Tolland, c. Cotton
" John J. laborer, h. 15 Franklin.
" John P. painter N.E.R. b. 15 Franklin, B.
" Mary, employed papermill, h. Roberts, B.
Sundman Gustave, carpenter, h. 8 Central.
Sutherland Frank W. cond'r St.Ry. h. 679 Main.
Sutter Bros.. A. E. Kilbourn, agt. Clark, n. R.R.
Swain George E. engineer, h. 17 Linden.
Swartfiguer Sam, painter, h. 18 Village, M.
Sweeney Christopher, farmer, h. Pitkin, n. Main.
" John, farmer, b. Pitkin, n. Main
" Katie and Nellie, b. Pitkin, n. Main.
Syncox John, fireman N.E.R. b. 98 Tolland, B.

**TAFT** Albert J. clerk, b. (112) Main, c. Linden.
" Fred, laborer, h. Burnside. n. School, B.
" Harry, teamster 26 Wbdg. b. Linden, n. Mn.
" Joel C. coal, city, h. (112) Main, c. Linden.
" William E. clerk, b. (112) Main, c. Linden.
Tatro Felix J. carpenter, h. 1 Phelp.
Taylor Amelia E. wid. Azel, b. 17 Church, B.
" & Beckman, tobacco warehouse, 31 Brnsd.av.
Henry G. Taylor. Benj. F. Beckman, res. N. Y.

TAYLOR FRANK S. (*Carson & T.*) 98 Hartford av. h. Hfd. city. *See page 767.*
" Mfg. Co. 53 Church.
" Oscar L. electrician, h. 17 Church.
" Sarah, wid. Nelson, h. 29 Naubuc c. High.
Teed George, b. 22 Woodbridge.
Tefft Jennie, wid. Geo. H. b. 146 Silver.
Teller James, at N.E.R. h. 4 Clark.
Terry Loren C. clerk, 887 Main, h. 17 Orchard.
Thayer Albert, conductor, h.u. 97 Burnside av.
" Andrew L. undertaker, h. 19 Village, M.
Thomas D. Webster, butcher, h. 36 Central.
" Lavinia Mrs. h. High, n. Broad, H.
" Philip, peddler, h. 1 Church, B.
" Marshall, farmer, b. Maple, n. Main.
Thompson Fred C. (*T.& Pease,*) b. 20 William, B.
" Grace J. bookkeeper, b. 4 Burnside av.
" Juliette, wid. Newton, h. 4 Burnside av.
" Katherine P. musicteach. 4, b. 4 Burnside av.
" & Pease, photographers, 20 William, B.'
  Fred C. Thompson,     Maurice Pease.
" Thomas W. conductor N.E.R. b. 20 Tolland.
Thorpe Edward, laborer, h.r. 53½ Burnside.
Thuer Ann, wid. Alexander, h. Maple, n. Main, H.
" John, machinist, h. Maple, n. Main, H.
Tiernan Edward, brakem. N.E.R. b. 346 Tolland.
" Kate J. wid. James, h. 316 Tolland, B.
" Thomas, mechanic, b. 316 Tolland, B.
Tistone Rocco, farmer, h. Silver, w. of Forbes.
Tobin James P. auditor, b. 33 Governor.
" Nora, wid. David, h. 33 Governor.
**TOPPING JAMES R.** patternmaker, h. 1 Woodbridge. *See page 541.*
Tourtellotte William F. plumber, h. 27 Central.
Town Clerk, Jos. O. Goodwin, office, 771 Main.
" Hall, Wells hall, 771 Main.
Trask Abner, farmer, h. 63 Silver.
" William W. b. 63 Silver.
Traver Fred C. laborer, h.u. 430 Tolland, B.
Treat Clarence B. teacher, b. 299 Main, H.
" Delia, h (346) Main.
" Edwin, farmer, h. Willow, s. of Silver.
" Ellery, farmer, h. 360 Main, s. of Silver.
" Frank, b. 62 High, H.
" H. Ella, h. 33 Main, H.
" Lyman, farmer, h. 317 Main, S.L.
" Owen, h. 299 Main, S.L.
" Willard E. ornithologist, b. 334 Main, S.L.
" William H. farmer, h. Brewer, H.
Tripp George W. tinner, h. 31 Governor.

Truesdell Wm. E. & Co. grocers, 566 Burnside av.
  Wm. E. Truesdell.     Wm. H. Champlin.
" William E. (*W. E. T. & Co.*) h. 8 Church, B.
Tryon E. E. h. 22 Pleasant, M.
" Frank E. h. 16 Church, B.
" Mary A. wid. A. F. h. 16 Church, B.
" Nelson D. butcher, h. Porter, n. Main, H.
Tucker John J. brakem. N.E.R. h.u. (84) Main.
Turner Louis, farmer, b. 386 Main.
" Sarah W. wid. Ezra A. h.u. 32 Central.

ULRICH Wm. H. farmer, h. Forbes, n. Brewer, H.
" William J. farmer, h. Forbes, n. Brewer, H.
Union District School, 16 Tolland.
Upson Benjamin A. carpenter, b. 46 Olmsted.
Upton William, millwright, h. Roberts, n. Forbes, B.
" William Jr. farmer, b. Roberts, n. Forbes, B.
Ure Walter B. clerk at 102 Hartford av.

VANBENSCHOTEN John W. fireman N.E.R. h. 27 Linden.
Vandenburg Henry, engir. h.u. 21 Woodbridge.
Vanderburg Charles, cigarmanufacturer, c. Ranney and Main, h. (90) Main.
Vandusen, James R. varnisher, h.u. 18 Village, M.
VanDyne Frank W. carpenter, h. 24 Burnside.
Vansplunder Anna, wid. Dingman, b. 80 Hfd. av. M.
Vibberts Burton G. b. 183 Main, H.
" Charles F. farmer, h. 34 High.
" Charles H. farmer, h. 183 Main, H.
Vibert Chauncey, farmer, h. Brewer, H.
" Cynthia, wid. Andrew, b. Brewer, H.
" Duane, farmer, h. Brewer, H.
Vincent Ellen, wid. William, h. 18 School, B.
Vining Amanda, wid. James, h. 39 Silver.
VINTON C. C. grocer, 724 Main, grain, feed, lumber, P.O. Vinton's Mills. *See page 784.*
VINTON HENRY WILBUR, agent for C. C. Vinton, grocer, 724 Main, h. 12 Sherman.
Vogt Francis T. engineer N.E.R. h. 4 Comstock pl.
Volunteer Hose Co. No. 2, 6 Park av.

WADSWORTH Elsie, wid. Milton S. b. 39 Broad.
" Stanley, farmer, h. 39 Broad, c. Naubuc av. H.
Wagner Edward, machinist, b. 22 Woodbridge.
" Eugene, laborer, h.u. 190 Main, H.
" Eugene, machinist N.E.R. h. 11 Belden.
Wait Luzerne C. h. 574 Burnside av. B.
Waite George E. clerk, h. 3 Olmsted.
Walding William, foreman, h. 9 Wells.
Waldo Harold B. reporter, b. Naubuc av. G.
Waldron Francis R. buffer, h. 105 Pitkin, M.
Walker Elijah C. supt. h. Forbes, n. the Mills.
" Geo. K. bookkeeper, b. Forbes, near bridge.
" John H., Eagle papermills, 1 Forbes, B.
" William, carpenter, h. 419 Tolland.
" William H. papermaker, h. 18 William, B.
Wallace Bella, h. 186 Burnside av.
" Eliza Miss, h. 186 Burnside av.
Walsh John, machinist N.E.R. h. 97 Burnside av.
Warren Alice M. b. 46 Silver.
" Cyrena A. wid. Walter P. b. Tolland, B.
" Frederick R. farmer, h. 46 Silver.
" George A. farmer, h. 54 Silver.
" Leander H. farmer, b. 46 Silver.
" Louis N. farmer, h. 56 Silver.

Warriner Albert D. emp. N.E.R. h. Elm, n. Cen.
" Elizabeth H. Mrs. b. Elm, n. Central.
Waterhouse Clarence, caller N.E.R. b. 21 Belden.
" James D. fireman, h. 21 Belden.
Waterman James, finisher, b. Woodland, B.
Waterous Richard G. real estate, h. 56 Hartf'd av.
Waters George, farmer, h. Brewer, w. of Forbes, H.
Watson Charles H. motorman, h. 18 Central.
Waugh James, teamster at 100 Hartford av.
Way J. H. Mrs. h. 681 Main.
Webster Norman, b. 27 Burnside av.
Weed William T. conductor St.Ry. h. 7 Bragg.
Welch John, farmer, h. Maple, H.
" Joseph, mechanic, h. Maple, H.
" Paul, farmer, h. Maple, H.
Weldon Edward G. farmer, h. Brewer, H.
" Monroe W. farmer, h. Brewer, H.
Wells Benjamin, h. 21 Wells.
" Hall, 771 Main, n. Burnside av.
" William B. clerk at 102 Hartford av. M.
Wemett Cornelius, brakeman, h.u. 1031 Main.
West Walter H at Colts, h. 4 William, B.
" William, butcher, h. Elm. n. Bissell.
Weston Arthur F. lather, b. (291) Main, S.L.
" Clarence A. lather, b. (291) Main, S.L.
Wetherell Herbert M. upholsterer, (68) Main,
    h. 21 Bissell.
Whalen John J. farmer, h. 1149 Main.
Whaley Alfred M. builder, h. 25 Olmsted.
Whalon George, clerk, b. 164 Main.
" John D. buffer, b. (164) Main.
" John W. buffer, h. (164) Main.
Whaples Frank L. carpenter, h. 1 Spring.
" John F. (J. F. W. & Son,) h. 2 Olmsted.
" John F. & Son, buillders, 2 Olmsted.
    John F. Whaples.          Nelson P. Whaples.
" Nelson P. (J.F.W.&Son,) h.Elm,n.Olmsted.
" Mary, wid. William, b. 1 Spring.
Whitcomb Ernest C. carpenter, b. 12 Rector.
" Lewis B. sawyer, b. 12 Rector.
" Mary E. wid. John F. h. 12 Rector.
White A. B. Jr. (G. M. White & Co.) b. W.H. t.
" Charles E. meat dealer, h. 148 Main.
" Frank P. papermaker, Burnide, h. Hartford.
" Frederick C. inspector, h. 11 Darlin, M.
WHITE G. M. & Co. flour, grain, etc. 101 and          See page 785.
    107 Hartford av.          A. B. White, Jr.          Glover M. White.
" Glover M. (G. M. White & Co.) 101 and
    107 Hartford av. b. W.H.t.
" James, painter, b. 43 Governor.
" John, painter, b. 43 Governor.
" Morris, h. 1038 Main.
" Thomas C. laborer, b. 1038 Main.
Whitney Martin V. teamster, h. 187 Main.
Whiton Harriet L. wid. Porter, b. 16 School, B.
Wickham Almeron W. foreman, 598 Burnside av.
" Horace C. farmer, h. Hills, Hillstown.
" William H. clerk, b. 29 Olmsted.
" William P. farmer, h. Hills, H.
Wickward M. H. printer, h. 14 Pleasant, M.
Wiganowski Charles, bricklayer, h. 593 Tolland.
Wilcox George K. reporter Hartford Times, h.
    24 Pleasant, M.
Williams Belcher (W. Bros.) 50, b. 50 Hfd. av.

# G. M. WHITE & CO.,

Successors to G. M. WHITE,

Wholesale and Retail Dealers in

# Flour, Grain, and Feed,

## 101 HARTFORD AVENUE,

Corner Pleasant Street,          Near the Bridge,

### EAST HARTFORD, CONN.

Williams Bros. horse dealers, 50 Hartford av.
    Noah Williams.
    Richard Williams.          Belcher Williams.
" Charles H. farmer, h. Long hill, B.
" David L. farmer, h. Long hill, B.
" Dora, wid. J. A. b. 18 Ranney.
" Edward A. farmer, h. Long hill, B.
" Edward E. h. Long hill,n. Burnham road, B.
" Everett S. machinist, h. 9 Central.
" G. A. & H. B. market gardens, 534 Main.
    George A. Williams.          Horace B. Williams.
" George A. (G. A. & H. B. W.) h. 534 Main.
" Horace B. (G. A. & H. B. W.) h. 518 Main.
" James, cigarmaker, h. 3 Spring.
" John, laborer, b. 981 Main.
" Mahala, wid. Francis, h. 11 Central.
" Marietta, wid. Samuel, h. 1156 Main.
" Noah, (Williams Bros.) b. 50 Hartford av.
" Rena B. teacher Sec. So.school, b. 518 Main.
" Richard, (Williams Bros.) b. 50 Hfd. av.
" Samuel A. firem. N.E.R. h. 57 Tolland.
Wilson Elijah W. clerk, h. 16 Pleasant, M.
" Henry P. shoem. 868 Main, h. 16 Linden.
Wirtella Karl, papermaker, h. Woodland, B.
Wistoski August, helper 1 Forbes, h. Spencer hill.
Woener Christian, stonecutter, h. 41 Pleasant, M.
" Louis, machinist, b. 41 Pleasant, M.
Wolcott Francis, machinist, b. 35 Olmsted.
" Frank, laborer, h. 32 Governor.
" Julia, clerk, b. 35 Olmsted.
" Julius M. farmer, h. 35 Olmsted, n. Bragg.
Wolverton George, brakem. N.E.R. b.2 Webster.
Wood Charles H. teamster, h. 21 Tolland.
" Ida A. wid. L. S. h. 55 Park av.
" James W. machinist, h. 574 Main.
" William, at Colts, h. Saunders.
Woodbridge Alfred W. h. (108) Main, c. Wdbg.
" Mary A. h. (108) Main, c. Woodbridge.
Woodland Schoolhouse No. 8 Burnside av.
Woods Dennis, blacksmith, h. 88 School, B.
Woolridge Richard, laborer, h. 91 Larrabee, B.
Wright Frank H. at Popes, b. 125 Main.
" William A. teamster, h. (125) Main.
Wrisley Clarence E. driver, 100, h. 98 Hfd. av.
YALE Charles F. printer, h. 67 Hartford av. M.
" Charles M. stenographer, b. 67 Hfd. av. M.
" Maribel A. teacher 9th district school, Dar-
    lin, b. 67 Hartford av. M.
Yauch Charles, farmer, h. 56 Main, H.
" Frederick, farmer, b. 56 Main, H.
" William, farmer, b. 56 Main, H.
Young John, brakeman, N.E.R. b. 98 Tolland.
Yoiergeson Hans, painter, h. 13 Village.

## 𝔐arriages, 𝔅irths and 𝔇eaths in 𝔈ast 𝔥artford,

### For one year ending June 30, 1898.

The 1st column of figures indicate the month; the 2d column, the day of the month; *d* for daughter; *s* for son.

### MARRIAGES.

9- 1-Aupry A. C.-Beauchamp R.
9-29-Babcock G. C.-Cadwell S. S.
12- 6-Ballou W. H.-Smead Ella L.
6-22-Bidwell H. E.-Fox Grace E.
12- 8-Bogue J. C.-Sickles Alida A.
6-14-BrewerF.C.-VanWagnerM.E.
6- 8-Bruce G. P.-Risley Daisy M.
11- 7-Buddi M.-Slewzaroy Albenia
12- 8-Burton H. C.-Judson Eva G.
2-21-Christian M.-Clafis Beneretta
6- 7-Fagan R: C.-Williams J. M.
12-20-Foster C. T.-Bennett Matilda.
8-24-French E.R.-Dickenson G.M.
6-20-Gagnon O -Collins Agilda.
10-20-GalvinJ.C.-McCullough E.B.
11- 7-Harrington D.-Sullivan K.
8-24-Hawes A. H.-Harrison A. C.
2-21-HaydenHR.Jr.-WilliamsMA.
10- 6-Hollister F. T.-Forbes E. N.
8- 7-Johnson H. S.-Wethereli M.
12-11-Kastberg E. F.-Molin M. L.
10-20-Kelleher D. M.-Moore M. A.
11- 9-Keough W. J.-Kenney Katie.
11-10-Kersey P. F.-McAvoy M. E.
2- 5-Kiernan S. J.-Curran J. F.
8-24-Maher M. M.-Monroe A. S.
8-25-Manierre G. L.-Scanlon N.A.
6-19-McCue A. A.-Yard Mary L.
11-10-Myers C. W.-Daley Rose.
10-29-Petraitsi A.-AthucanicekiW.
10-27-Roy Jas. P.-Foley Mary A,
8- 6-Simon W. F.-Schug Lena.
11-12-Stewart J. T.-Allen Isabella.
12-29-Vibert Sid.-Gould Edith M.
1- 1-Wagner Eug.-Roach Katie.
6- 8-WhitcombW.H.-Warner J.S.
11- 8-Wiley Oscar-Scott Nellie.
7- 5-Williams C. C.-Cooper E. M.
5-23-Willerup E.-Thorstensen T.

### BIRTHS.

5-12-d-Ackley Wm. K.-Helen.
7-31-s-Agnew James-Jennie.
12-16-d-Alling Geo. B.-Gertrude.
1-30-s-Anderson Chas.-Elizabeth.
12- 2-d-Archer James H.-Amy.
4- 8-Baedor G. H.-Georgiana H.
3-30-d-Baker Ezra E.-Christine E.
8-22-d-Beck Henry F.-Annie L.
3-19-s-Beck Henry-Marie.
12-21-d-Berry Thomas-Maggie.
5-17-s-Brainard Sam'l N.-Nellie.
12- 1-d-Brand Adam-Grace.
6-18-d-Brewster George-Martha.
2- 1-s-Brewer Frank-Mary.
10-18-d-Brown James-Anna.
2-11-d-Burden Harold-Hattie L.
8-30-d-Callender C. E. F.-Mary F.
8- 1-d-Carroll Edwd. P.-Annie B.
11- 9-d-Carroll Joseph R.-Carrie.
12- 5-s-Carson Henry-Emma.
4-28-d-Clune John-Nellie.
7-30-s-Colbert Patrick-Ella.
12-29-d-Collins Charles-Annie.

5-20-s-Cook Frank-Mary P.
11-19-s-Cooley Walter C.-Ethel C.
6-25-s-Coolidge Edward C.-Eva.
6-20-d-ConnellyTim'thy-Bridget.
11- 8-d-Cooney William-Eliza.
8-31-s-Cowles Lewis L.-Hilda.
4- 5-d-Crimmins John-Susan.
9-20-d-Cushman Arthur L.-Julia.
9-22-d-Davis Walter-Emily.
5-19-d-Dawes William-Flora.
5-20-d-Delmore James-Georgie.
6-11-s-Devitt John-Maggie.
1-14-d-Detweiler Alfred-Emma.
9-25-s-Dixon Fred-Margaret.
8-16-d-Edgecomb E.-Elizabeth.
2-16-s-Eidleman Wm. P.-Tiley.
3-20-s-Enes Pierce-Mary.
7- 8-s-Evans Edwd. E.-Blanche.
11-14-s-Fallon Joseph-Ethel.
4-30-s-Fila Frank J.-Josie.
4- 7-d-Fogarty James-Mary.
10- 1-d-Folon James-Bridget.
12- 8-d-Fox Henry C.-Lillian A.
12-17-s-Frink George A.-Rose.
3-16-s-Getto Frank-Jennie.
5-22-d-Goodale Fred-Nellie.
7- 8-s-Grennan Law.-Christine.
5-28-d-Hale Henry B.-Celia M.
10-30-d-Hansen John-Johanna.
4- 8-d-Hatch William F.-Katie.
9-27-s-Haugh Christian-Mary.
8-10-s-Hertsch Benjamin-Emllie.
1-21-d-Hickey Patrick F.-Mary.
7-25-s-Hills Elliott-Gertrude.
12-23-d-Hyde Fred E.-Lucinda.
8- 1-d-Ingraham Clar. W.-Mary.
8- 9-d-Jencks Chas L.-Mamie.
8-19-s-Jessen Ernest-Elena.
9-30-s-Johnson Jno. A.-Christine.
12- 5-d-Jordan Edward-Mary.
4-26-s-Kask Axle-Augusta S.
11-21-d-Kearns Law. P.-Grace.
8 10-d-Kearns Mich'el H.-Mary J.
5- 8-s-Keeney Wm. W.-Annie.
10- 4-d-Kennedy Herbert-Ada F.
4- 4-d-Kennedy William-Mary.
2-27-d-Kiernan Sylvester-Jennie.
8- 8-s-Killen Ernest L.-Emma M.
5- 4-d-Kilty Patrick-Nellie.
5-16-d-Kilty Patrick-Nellie.
5-12-s-King Everett E.-Mary.
8-20-d-Kline Jason-Emma.
12-16-s-Koster William-Sophia.
7-10-d-Landers John-Maggie.
8-27-d-Larson Aug.-Josephine. }
8-27-d-Larson Aug.-Josephine. }
5- 2-s-Larson Niels-Meta M.
3-14-s-Lathrop Fred'k-Minnie.
5-28-s-Lorenson Simon-Hulda.
11-22-d-Loveland Arthur-Jennie.
7-10-d-Lyceth Michael-Susie.
5-10-d-McCarthy Daniel-Mary.
5- 9-d-McCourt James-Nora.
1- 7-s-Maloy Daniel-Margaret.
8-10-s-Mandeville Carle.-Annie.

9-17-d-March John-Rose.
1-31-d-Maynard George-Mary.
9-27-d-Mikolat Leo.-Catherine.
5- 5-d-Miller Angust-Mary.
12-28-d-Monahan Michael-Bridget
1-27-s-Moulton Newton H.-Clara.
5-12-d-Muir James-Florence.
10- 2-d-Murray James-Maggie.
7- 4-d-Nathlick Charles-Elvina.
3-24-s-Nelson L. E.-Jennie E.
5- 6-s-Nield Robert-Elizabeth.
12- 5-d-Noble William B.-Nettie B.
7-14-d-Norman Charles N.-Clara.
5- 5-d-O'Connell T. S.-Nellie M.
2-11-d-Oelkuck Edward-Annie.
5- 6-d-O'Hearn Peter-Catherine.
6-27-d-Olmsted Wm. A.-Grace.
12-18-d-Osterbandt And'w-Elsie.
5-25-d-Overton George A.-Ross.
4-28-d-Paine James L.-Sarah.
11- 4-s-Peterson Charles-Susan.
8-12-d-Prumbaum John-Maggie.
10- 1-s-Reardon Edward-Mary.
8-22-s-Reichart H.-Hannah E.
3-30-d-Riley Wm. A.-Carrie G.
5-21-d-Risley Charles S.-Bertha.
6- 8-d-Risley Mellire B.-Phebe J.
5- 8-Roberts John F.-Mary.
5- 7-d-Schleicher Ernest-Amelia.
5-31-d-Sellew William-Margaret.
5-26-s-Sheehan Howard-Lizzie.
5-13-s-Sheldon Everett-Florence.
5-30-d-Shook Elmer-Bulah B.
1-30-d-Smith A. C.-Cora.
11-18-d-Smith Elwood-Anna.
9-29-d-Stanton George E.-Mary.
8-30-d-Stevens Philip H.-Julia H.
12-36-d-Stevenson James-Harriet.
5-12-s-Stowell Charles P.-Kate.
12- 8-d-Sullivan John J.-Mary.
1- 1-s-Sunner F. S.-Mabelle M.
7- 9-s-Taylor Oscar L. W.-Lena.
5-14-s-Thorpe Edward-Mary.
8-13-d-Ulrich Wm. J.-Charlotte.
7-23-s-Vanderburg Henry-Nellie.
1-28-d-VanDyne Frank-Frances.
7- 9-s-Waterhouse George-Rose.
4-26-s-Weldon E. G.-Jennie H.
4-23-s-Wesley S. Wesley-Lena.
8-12-s-White James-Louise.
5-16-d-Williams Belcher-Sophia.
10-18-d-Wilson Elijah-Mary.
8- 8-Winslow Harrison-Emma.
9-21-s-Wirtella Carl-Sophia.
6-11-d-Wood Wm. E.-Jennie M.
8- 8-d-Woods Francis-Lillian.

### DEATHS.

11- 3-Ahearn John, 32.
9- 9-Anderson Thomas, 84.
6- 4-Arnold Mary A. 91.
1-10-Baldwin Merritt, 61.
8-31-Bantley Anton, 64.
1-26-Barbour Jessie, 1.
4- 1-Bartholomew Elizabeth, 78.

8- 8-Belknap Mabel May.
5-12-Bernard Freeman.
12-26-Berry Lizzie.
11- 2-Berry Thomas, 31.
6-12-Boardman William J. 12.
9-20-Boss Francis G. 4.
1- 4-Brown Willie G. 5.
5-26-Calaher Nickloe Mrs. 68.
8-23-Carlos Thomas, 82.
8- 8-Carmill Alice, 2.
6- 3-Carpenter Ira, 66.
4- 9-Carroll Margaret Ruth.
5- 5-Carson Harold G.
12-25-Cassiday Joseph, 70.
3-29-Clark Harriet T. 82.
8-30-Clarkson Helen A.
5-20-Clune Beatrice.
11-20-Cooper Robert, 33.
5-25-Daley Mary, 65.
8- 7-Dammerall Mary A. 34.
5- 4-Dimon John, 70.
9-13-Duffy Margaret, 55.
8-11-Edgecomb Stella.
7-30-Edgerly Edward T. 1.
5- 6-Elmer William H. 39.
9-23-Farrell Madelene R. 8.
2-26-Flaherty Dennis, 66.
12- 2-Folan Hanora.
5-31-Foran Nellie M. 37.
11-21-Forbes Anna B. 34.
7-21-Forbes Charlotte A. 81.
5-27-Gates Arthur.

10-20-Geer Eliza Evans, 39.
6-18-Gillis A. 35.
5-14-Helner Martha, 7.
5- 9-Hendee Tobias, 86.
2- 8-Hills James, 88.
5-28-Hurd Charles O. 33.
3-23-Inskip Frederick.
8- 8-Johnson Harry.
10-16-Jones Mary Wood, 86.
5-24-Kane Bridget, 68.
10-10-Keeney Dwight H. 79.
8-11-Kennedy Abby R. 82.
10-29-King Wilbur J. 45.
7-15-La Fortune Gertrude R. 4.
7-27-Lahaie Geo. L.
12- 8-Lave Minnie, 72.
5-15-Leary Minnie, 34.
8- 7-Lessen Homo.
8- 7-Lessen Homo Lapieus. }
10-19-Lewis Lucy A. 72.
5-27-Lorenhaupt Donald R. 3.
4- 8-McCullough Charles L. 4.
5-29-Mackey Elizabeth, 35.
8-30-Mahoney John P. 28.
2- 1-Murray Mary, 65.
12-12-Murray Thomas, 65.
4-24-Nathlick Amelia.
1-29-Olmsted Chas. E. 88.
6-27-Olmsted Stanley P. 49.
11- 4-O'Niel Alice, 2.
5-14-Paradis Albert, 1.
3-13-Pebbles Elizabeth A. 79.

5- 6-Peck Alice W. 28.
8- 2-Peck Carl H.
5- 8-Pratt Geo. W. 85.
11-20-Prumbaum Ella.
8- 8-Ranney Daisy, 21.
8-19-Ran Jacob, 72.
2-23-Richmond Hattie E. 52.
5-29-Risley Mary, 79.
5- 6-Roberts Francis A.
5-15-Roberts Levi, 82.
12-26-Ross Michael, Jr. 3.
2- 7-Sairena Carmela.
10-28-Schaefer Jacob, 20.
11-30-Sergeant William M. 87.
9- 9-Shea Bridget, 32.
9-22-Sloan Lenora F. 76.
5-10-Snyder Chas. H. 65.
2-33-Spaulding Marshall T. 42.
2-18-Stanton Florence B.
11- 6-Sullivan Cornelius, 53.
8-11-Sullivan James M.
6-16-Taylor Samuel, 70.
5-28-Thuer Alexander, 71.
7-28-Touhey Martin W. 2.
4- 5-Tryon Julia E. 60.
8- 5-Vanderburg Eva, 16.
11-15-Waite Elizabeth L. 46.
7-23-Warner Eli, 94.
5-27-Warner George N. 20.
4- 1-Weaver Harriet T. 78.
5-20-Whaples Delia, 41.
4-30-Wilson Geo. E. 59.

# Town Officers, Churches, Societies, Corporations, etc.

## Town Officers.

EAST HARTFORD TOWN OFFICERS, JULY, 1898.

*Selectmen.*—Edward E. King, Arthur G. Olmsted, Joel H. Brewer. Meet 1st Monday monthly from 1 to 5 P. M.

*Assessors.*—Charles M. Smith, Edward T. Stager, Waldo J. Driggs.

*Board of Relief.*—Norman S. Brewer, Charles R. Forbes, William H. Brewer.

*Town Clerk.*—Joseph O. Goodwin.

*Treasurer.*—Charles Merriman.

*Tax Collector.*—Arthur P. Moore.

*Auditors.*—Elijah Ackley, James P. Tobin.

*Committee on New Cemetery.*—Edward W. Pratt, Elijah C. Walker, Joel H. Fowler, Andrew S. Bidwell, Lawrence V. Lester.

*High School Committee.*—Joseph O. Goodwin, Elijah C. Walker, Horace B. Williams, William E. Truesdell, William L. Huntting.

*Registrars of Voters.*—William H. Flanigan, Joseph A. Steele.

*Alms House Superintendent.*—John Ruoff.

*Health Officer.*—E. H. Griswold.

PROBATE COURT.

Regular sessions in Wells Hall, Main street, on Mondays from 9 to 10 a. m., and on Saturdays from 4 to 5 p. m. All other days by special appointment. JOHN A. STOUGHTON, *Judge.* District includes the town of East Hartford only.

GRAND JURORS.

| James S. Forbes, | Michael H. Kearns, |
| William Hawksford, | Michael Price, |
| Truman Hale, | Charles W. Roberts. |

CONSTABLES.

| Erastus R. Cowles, | Thos. D. Reid, |
| Robert W. Kappenberg, | John Ruoff, |
| Arthur P. Moore, | Alexander Schmidt Jr. |

JUSTICES OF THE PEACE.

| Asher S. Bailey, | Edward O. Goodwin, |
| Philo S. Brewer, | Henry L. Goodwin, |
| Percy S. Bryant, | J. Knox Hall, |
| Edward P. Carroll, | Henry T. Hart, |
| W. C. Cummings, | Ralph Risley, |
| Henry Daniels, | Peter Smith, |
| | John A. Stoughton. |

SCHOOL VISITORS.

1900.

Elijah Ackley, George A. Bowman, F. Howard Ensign.

1899.

Francis P. Bachelor, Thos. S. O'Connel, Annie E. Olmsted.

1898.

Joseph O. Goodwin, Franklin H. Mayberry, Walter G. Murphy.

TOWN COURT.

*Judge.*—John A. Stoughton.

*Deputy Judge.*—George K. Wilcox.

*Prosecuting Attorney.*—Charles W. Roberts.

*Assist. Prosecuting Attorney.*—Frederick E. Forbes.

## Churches.

### FIRST CONGREGATIONAL CHURCH.
660 Main street.

Organized as the third church in Hartford about 1694. Incorporated, 1894. 818 members.

Rev. SAMUEL A. BARRETT, Pastor; Alfred E. Kilbourne, David L. Williams, George W. Smart, Wm. H. Olmsted. Deacons; George W. Smart, Clerk; Erastus C. Geer, Treas. William H. Olmsted, Chairman of Trustees. Service 10.45 a. m. and 7.00 p. m. Annual meeting 2d Wednesday in January.

Sunday School.—H. B. Williams, Supt.; Miss Annie E. Olmsted, Ass't. Supt.; Miss Katharine A. Stoughton, Supt. of Infant Dep't; Miss Hattie T. Kilbourne, Sec'y; Wilbur S. Burnham, Treas.; Chas. H. Williams, W S. Burnham, Librarians; Merritt Smart, Registrar. Teachers 36, Scholars 395. Average attendance 213. Service 12 noon.

### SOUTH CONGREGATIONAL CHURCH.
High street, near Main street.

Rev. F. P. BACHELER, Pastor; Elizur R. Ensign, Charles T. Forbes, Deacons; F. Howard Ensign, Clerk; Alfred J. Ensign, Treas. Services at 10.45 a. m. and 6.00 p. m. Organized 1870.

Sunday School—J. Knox Hall, Supt.; Rev. F. P. Bacheler, Ass't Supt.; Clifford Brewer, Clerk; F.Howard Ensign Treas.; Laura Griswold, Librarian; Teachers 13; Scholars, 85. Volumes in library 600. Service 12noon.

### FIRST METHODIST EPISCOPAL CHURCH
OF EAST HARTFORD, 308 Main street, Hockanum.

REV. HERBERT E. MURKETT, Pastor; J.P. Kenney, Recording Steward; Chauncey Hollister, Monroe J. Brewer, W. H. Waterman, J. P. Kenney, E. S. Forbes, W. H. Myers, Trustees. Organized 1846. Preaching at 10.45 a. m. and 7.30 p. m. Prayer meeting, Thursday evenings 7.30.

Sunday School.—J. P. Kenney, Supt.; E. S. Forbes, Ass't Supt.; Frank A. Graham, Librarian. Teachers 9, Scholars 80. Meets at 12 noon.

Epworth League Meetings at 6.30 Sunday evenings.

### ST. JOHN'S CHURCH—EPISCOPAL.
799 Main, near Burnside av.

Consecrated June 22, 1869. Sunday services at 10 and 10.45 A.M., 3d Sunday monthly at 10.45 A.M. Other holy days at 8 A.M.

Rev. Prof. JOHN J.McCOOK, Rector; Wm.H.Brainard, Percy S. Bryant, Wardens; A. C. Liebert, Anthony McGehan, Richard Birch, Walter G. Murphy, Alfred T. Richards, Vestrymen; Rev. J. J. McCook, Treas.; A. C. Liebert, Clerk; A. C. Liebert, Choirmaster; Arthur S. Joyner, Organist.

Sunday School—12.30 p.m. Rev.J. J. McCook,Supt.; Francis A. McCook, Librarian.

St. Agnes Guild meets on Wednesdays.

Choir rehearses Friday evenings at 7.30 o'clock.

### ST. MARY'S CHURCH.
ROMAN CATHOLIC.
Main street cor. Woodbridge street.

This Church was organized in 1873. The corner stone was laid in 1877, the edifice was finished and occupied the same summer. Seats 700, cost $15,000.

Rev. JAMES J. GLEESON, Pastor; Rev. Patrick Daley, assistant. Services Sundays, 1st Mass at 8.30 a.m., High Mass at 11 a.m.; Vespers at 3.30 p.m.

Sunday School—Wm. J. Dowds, Supt.; Lizzie Kearney, Ass't Supt.; Teachers, 18; Scholars, 250; School, 9 a.m.; Library, 150 vols.

### BURNSIDE METHODIST EPISCOPAL CHURCH.
Church street.

REV. F. C. BAKER, Pastor; J. S. Forbes, L. S. Forbes, J. H. Burnham, W. S. Jarman, F. C. Gould,

Henry Lathrop, S. A. Gardner, Trustees; L. S. Forbes, Treas. Organized, 1896. Services 11 a. m. and 7 p. m. 100 members. Frederick Hyde, Sexton.

Sunday School—12.30 p. m. James S. Forbes, Supt.

### COMSTOCK MEMORIAL CHAPEL,
Main street, north of railroad track.

## Public Schools.

DISTRICT No. 1. North, King Street—William J. McKee, Chairman of Committee ; E. Ackley, Treas.; Wilber S. Burnham, Clerk.

DISTRICT No. 2. Second North, Main c. Woodbridge—James J. Moriarity, Charles F. Brigham, Daniel D. Bidwell, Committee; Eugene Moore, Clerk; William G. Comstock, Jr., Treasurer.

DISTRICT No. 3. Center, 671 Main, opp. Hartford av—J. Wilbur Hale, E. E. King, Erastus C. Geer, Committee; Edward O. Goodwin, Treas.; Joseph O. Goodwin, Clerk ; Arthur P. Moore, Collector.

DISTRICT No. 4. Second South ( Willow Brook), east side of Main, south of Silver Lane—Frank Roberts, F. Howard Ensign, George A. Williams, Committee; Horace B. Williams, clerk.

DISTRICT No. 5. Hockanum, 519 Main street—Norman S. Brewer, John Kenney, Cassius Brewer, Committee; Charles Daniels, Treas.; Clarence Forbes, Collector.

DISTRICT No. 6. South Middle, Forbes below Brewer. Christen Handel, Chairman Committee. Charles M. Smith, clerk and treasurer ; Joseph Welch, collector.

DISTRICT No. 7. South East, Hills street—Chester Manning, Committee; Horace C. Wickham, treas.; H. B. Hubbard, clerk; Monroe Hills, collector.

DISTRICT No. 8. Burnside, 16 School street.—F. H. Mayberry, F. J. Hartz, A. W. Wickham, Committee; L. H. Forbes, Clerk; J. A. Steele, Collector; H. L. Goodwin, Treas.; S. A. Gardner, Auditor.

DISTRICT No. 9. Meadow, Darlin street, near Hartford avenue.—Charles F. Yale, Mrs. Ellen C. Lester, Charles Andrews, Committee; Geo. K. Wilcox, Clerk; Geo. W. Darlin, Treasurer; Henry E. Jessen, Collector.

DISTRICT No. 10. Long Hill, Burnside P. O.—D. L. Williams, Chairman Committee; E.A.Williams, Treas. and Clerk; C. E. Lathrop, Collector.

UNION, No. 11. Burnside av.—John H. Walsh, Will P. Landon, Henry G. Beaumont, Committee; H. C. Gaines, Clerk; Nelson A. Whaples, Treas.; George V. Lester, Collector; W. R. Rosebrook, C. Addison Jones, Auditors.

HIGH SCHOOL, 760 Main street, opposite Wells hall.—Horace B. Williams, Elijah C. Walker, W. L. Huntting, W. E. Truesdale, Joseph O. Goodwin, Committee.

Town tax rate, .015. 36 teachers, 1898-99.

Election of committees in June.

Enumeration of children in October, 1897, 1,476.

## Public Halls.

Bigelow Hall, P. O. Block, 720 Main, cor. Governor.
Burnside Hall, 568 Burnside av.
Raymond Hall, 651 Main, seats 300.
Sons of Temperance Hall, 45 Church st., Burnside Vil.
Wells Hall, 771 Main, 1st floor, seats 200.
    "    2nd floor, seats 250.    [seats 100.
    "    (Rodman Post G. A. R. Hall) 3d floor,

## Public Libraries.

### RAYMOND LIBRARY CO.

Organized 1889 in accordance with provisions of the will of the late Albert C. Raymond.

Henry R. Hayden, Prest.; Henry L. Goodwin, V. Prest.; Joseph O. Goodwin, Secy.; Lawrence S. Forbes, Treas. Directors, Henry R. Hayden, F. F. Street, E. J. Carroll, Henry L. Goodwin, Alonzo P. Hills, Davis E. Lane, Patrick Garvan, Joseph O. Goodwin. About 2,500 volumes. Building cost $9,900.00. Permanent fund $10,000.00. Library open Tuesdays, Thursdays and Saturdays from 2 to 5 and from 7 to 9 P.M. Miss Jessie Hayden, Librarian. Located in Raymond Park, 651 Main st., cor. Central av.

### EAST HARTFORD PUBLIC LIBRARY.

Organized February 10, 1896. 651 Main street. William H. Olmsted, Pres't; F. Howard Ensign, Sec'y; Aaron F. Olmsted, Treas. Directors for one year, William H. Olmsted, John W. Forbes, Walter G. Murphy; for three years, Charles F. Yale, Joel H. Brewer, Percy S. Bryant; for two years, Aaron F. Olmsted, F. Howard Ensign, J. Knox Hall.

## Corporations.

### EAST HARTFORD FIRE DISTRICT.

*Incorporated by Special Act, 1889.*

Committee—John P. Hunting, Chairman; Charles Merriman, Treas.; Almeron W. Wickham, Clerk; Jos. A. Steele, Collector.

Edward Bragg, Chief.

ÆTNA HOSE No. 4, 115 Hartford av—Alexander Smith, Jr., Foreman; Thomas D. Reid, John M. Jessen, Ass'ts.; Robert L. Nicholson, Sec'y; Henry A. Jessen, Treas.; C. S. Goodrich, Steward; Henry S. Cowles, E. Y. Reid, H. A. Yergasan, Trustees; William Dawes, Collector.

BURNSIDE HOSE No. 3, Church Street extention—James McCabe, Foreman; Edward Clancy, John Kinnane, Assistants; Frank Smith, Sec'y; Thomas Galuby, Treas.

CENTER HOSE No. 1. 6 Bissell street—Walter C. Dart, Foreman; Edward Bruton, Thomas Ahern, Assistants; Lucius T. Deming, Sec'y; Michael F. Muldoon, Fin. Sec'y; Robert B. Kuebler, Treas.; Patrick E. Muldoon, Stewart.

VOLUNTEER HOSE No. 2, 3 Park av.—John F. White, Foreman; Charles E. Simpson, Julius T. Cowles, Assistants; F. J. Bracken, Sec'y; James F. McKee, Treas.; Elmer Shook, Stewart.

EAST HARTFORD MFG. CO., paper. *See page 480.*

THE HARTFORD MANILLA CO. *See page 479.*

### THE EAST HARTFORD & GLASTONBURY HORSE RAILROAD CO.

*Incorporated 1866. Capital $100,000.*

Office, 115 State st. Hartford.

E. S. Goodrich, Hartford, Prest.; Samuel G. Dunham, Hartford, Vice Prest.; George D. Curtis, Hartford, Sec'y; Daniel R. Howe, Hartford, Treasurer; E. S. Goodrich, General Manager; Directors—P. Henry Goodrich, James J. Goodwin, Daniel R. Howe, Atwood Collins, E. S. Goodrich, Leverett Brainard, George D. Curtis, John R. Redfield, Samuel G. Dunham, Hartford. Annual meeting in January.

### EAST HARTFORD STREET LIGHTING ASSO'N.

*Organized October, 1881.*

Edward O. Goodwin, Pres't & Treas.; Lawrence S. Forbes, Secretary. Annual meeting second Monday evening in October.

### EAST HARTFORD VILLAGE IMPROVEMENT CO.

*Organized 1877. Incorporated 1879.*

Henry R. Hayden, Prest.; Henry L. Goodwin, Secy.; Joseph O. Goodwin, Treas. Executive Committee, 13 members. Annual meeting 1st Tuesday in October.

### EAST HARTFORD WATER CO.

Percy S. Bryant, President; Arthur C. Liebert, Sec'y; Charles L. Goodhue, Treas.; Arthur P. Moore, Supt. Directors, Percy S. Bryant, Arthur C. Liebert, Charles L. Goodhue, George A. Fernald, Arthur P. Moore.

## Societies.

### ORIENT LODGE No. 62, F. & A. M.

William H. Brewer, W. M.; James Harvey, S. W.; T. Jarvis Lewis, J. W.; E. E. King, Treasurer; Will P. Landon, Sec'y; E. C. Walker, S. D.; W. R. Rosbrook, J. D.; P. M. Giddings, S S.; Fred M. Hills, J. S.; E. Hart Forbes, Tyler; E. W. Pratt, Marshal; J. Knox Hall, Chaplain; J. Knox Hall, F. W. Richardson, Edward F. Stager, Trustees. Organized Sept. 2. 1822. Meets 1st and 3d Wednesday evening monthly in Masonic Hall. Annual meeting 1st Wednesday in December.

### BIGELOW CHAPTER.

ORDER OF THE EASTERN STAR.

Mrs. B. A. Chandler, W. M.; E. C. Walker, W. P.; Miss Elizabeth Shook, Sec'y; Mrs. I. I. King, Treas. Organized April 28, 1890. Meets 2d and 4th Wednesday evenings except months of July and August in Bigelow Hall.

### ANCIENT ORDER OF HIBERNIANS.

Patrick Healy, Prest.; Michael Hyland, V. Prest.; David J. Garrity, Fin. Sec'y; John F. White, Rec. Sec'y; John J. Foran, Treas. Organized May 26, 1890. Meets 3rd Monday evening monthly at Wells' Hall.

### DANIEL C. RODMAN POST No. 65,

GRAND ARMY OF THE REPUBLIC.

Josiah H. Smith, Commander; John F. Arnold, S. V. C.; Charles S. Roberts, J. V. C.; Duett C. Clark, Adjutant; Edward J. Carroll, Q.; William H. Brewer, O. D.; Arthur G. Olmsted, O. G.; Davis E. Lane, S. M.; E. B. Coolidge, S.; Frank Graham, C.; G. Harvey Hancock, Davis E. Lane, E. B. Coolidge, Trustees. Meets 2d and 4th Tuesday evenings, G. A. R. hall, Main street. Annual meeting in December.

### JOHN F. CARROLL CAMP, No. 27,

SONS OF VETERANS.

Chas. P. Stowell, Capt.; Arthur C. Robertson, First Lieut.; Frank W. Arnold, Second Lieut.; Lon. Carroll, Quartermaster Sergt.; E. P. Carroll, First Sergt.; J. R. Carroll, Chaplain. Meets in G. A. R. hall 1st and 3d Friday evenings monthly.

### WOMANS RELIEF CORPS, No. 19,

AUXILIARY TO D. C. RODMAN POST NO. 65.

Clara E. Lester, Prest.; Austina Barrows, Sr. Vice Prest.; Emma Lester, Jr. Vice Prest.; Mary E. Roberts, Sec'y; Georgia Arnold, Treas.; Sarah Bryant, Chaplain. Organized Feb. 7, 1887. Meets 1st and 3d Tuesday, monthly, in Wells Hall. Annual meeting in December.

### NUTMEG LODGE No. 55, A. O. U. W.

George Stroh, P. M. W.; John H. Walsh, M. W.; Thomas P. Hayes, F.; T. F. Hyland, O.; James W. Wickham, Recorder; Everett E. Arnold, Fin.; Wm. A. Lowry, Rec.; John Flaherty, G.; James E. Flanigan, I. W.; H. G. Hancock, O. W.; C. F. Brandon, H. Jergensen, D. J. Mullaly, Trustees. Instituted June 17, 1892. Meets 1st and 3d Wednesday evenings in Wells Hall.

**EAST HARTFORD DRAIN COMPANY.**
William H. Olmsted, Treas.; Wm. P. Stanley, Sec'y;
the above officers and Arthur P. Moore, William H.
Olmsted, Percy S. Bryant, Directors. Organized in
1878.  Annual meeting first Monday in March

**EAST HARTFORD GRANGE No. 87,**
PATRONS OF HUSBANDRY.
L. V. Lester, Master; Laura Griswold, Sec'y; Elijah
Ackley, Treasurer. Organized Jan. 28, 1886.  Meets
Friday evenings at Wells hall.  Annual meeting 3d
Friday in December.

**EAST HARTFORD COUNCIL No. 1287,**
ROYAL ARCANUM.
Frank Roberts, Regent; Everett E. Arnold, Sec'y;
H. Wilber Vinton, Treas.; Edward Risley, A. W.
Wickham, L. H. Bogue, Trustees.  Organized Feb.
3, 1890.  Meets 2d and 4th Wednesday evenings in
Wells hall.  Annual meeting in January.

**EAST HARTFORD WHEEL AND SOCIAL CLUB.**
W. B. Noble, Pres't; Lucius T. Deming, Sec'y and
Treas.; Organized June, 1884.  Re-organized Jan.
18, 1897.  Meets first Monday evening monthly in
Goodwin hall.  Annual meeting in December.

**COURT RAYMOND,**
FORESTERS OF AMERICA.
James Fogerty, C. R.; Chas. Myers, R. Sec'y; Wm.
B. Noble, Treas.: Thomas Galuly, Michael Hickey,
Wm. J. Fitzgerald, Trustees.  Meets 2d and 4th Mon-
day evenings at Wells hall.

**ST. MARY'S T. A. B. SOCIETY.**
Thomas W. Garrity, Pres't; John B. Sullivan, Rec.
Sec'y; Timothy J. Kelleher, Fin. Sec'y; Wm. J. Dowd,
Treas.; John F. Daley, John F. Graham, John W. Har-
rington, Trustees.  Meets 2d and 4th Sunday r. 895 Main.

**SCHOOL CHILDREN, OCTOBER, 1896 AND 1897.**

| | | 1896 | 1897 |
|---|---|---|---|
| North District | | 44 | 46 |
| Second North District | | 303 | 312 |
| Center | " | 347 | 348 |
| Second South | " | 91 | 90 |
| Hockanum | " | 68 | 78 |
| South Middle | " | 39 | 37 |
| South East | " | 28 | 25 |
| Burnside | " | 280 | 323 |
| Meadow | " | 185 | 199 |
| Long Hill | " | 13 | 12 |
| Total | | 1,398 | 1,476 |

**GROWTH OF EAST HARTFORD, 1881—1898.**

| Year. | Dwell-ing houses | Stores and Mfrs. | School Chil-dren. | Hors's | Neat Cattle | Total Grand List. |
|---|---|---|---|---|---|---|
| 1881 | 745 | 111 | 786 | 585 | 778 | $1,856,351 |
| 1882 | 752 | 125 | 807 | 583 | 746 | 1,813,724 |
| 1883 | 755 | 124 | 836 | 580 | 750 | 1,792,356 |
| 1884 | 758 | 125 | 823 | 540 | 613 | 1,689,756 |
| 1885 | 765 | 109 | 827 | 556 | 666 | 1,681,974 |
| 1886 | 770 | 125 | 883 | 581 | 705 | 1,798,040 |
| 1887 | 784 | 127 | 885 | 572 | 722 | 1,702,235 |
| 1888 | 825 | 112 | 886 | 571 | 709 | 1,713,547 |
| 1889 | 868 | 182 | 989 | 582 | 824 | 1,760,138 |
| 1890 | 903 | 180 | 1095 | 635 | 763 | 2,276,430 |
| 1891 | 963 | 149 | 1151 | 680 | 731 | 2,574,146 |
| 1892 | 997 | 161 | 1199 | 662 | 680 | 2,637,364 |
| 1893 | 1032 | 183 | 1199 | 696 | 583 | 2,601,845 |
| 1894 | 1080 | 182 | 1191 | 679 | 545 | 2,682,337 |
| 1895 | 1151 | 182 | 1313 | 689 | 530 | 2,731,555 |
| 1896 | 1165 | 182 | 1398 | 680 | 499 | 2,749,542 |
| 1897 | 1203 | ... | .... | 749 | 489 | 2,825,780 |

EUGENE H. MERRIMAN, P. M.—706 Main st.

| Mail leaves, | Mail arrives, |
|---|---|
| 7.05 A.M....for the East. | 7.05 A.M..from Hartford. |
| 10.25 A.M....for Hartford. | 11.05 A.M..from  " |
| 11.05 A.M....for Burnside. | 12.55 P.M..from the East. |
| 12.55 P.M....for Hartford. | 3.05 P.M..from Hartford. |
| 5.25 P.M.....for " | 6.05 P.M...from  " |
| 7.25 P.M....for " | |

Mails close fifteen minutes before leaving time.

**BURNSIDE POST OFFICE.—25 Church street.**
L. H. FORBES, P. M.

| Mail leaves. | Mail arrives. |
|---|---|
| 10.00 A.M. for Hartford. | 7.20 A.M. from Hartford. |
| 12.50 P.M. " " | 11.20 A.M. " " |
| 5.00 P.M. " " | 3.20 P.M. " " |
| 7.00 P.M. " " | 6.20 P.M. " " |
| 7.00 A.M. Boston & East. | 1.00 P.M. Boston & East. |

**HILLSTOWN POST OFFICE.**
JOEL H. FOWLER, P.M.
Mail leaves 5.15 P. M., for Hockanum.
Mail arrives 6.00 P. M., from Hockanum.

**HOCKANUM POST OFFICE.**
Main st. opposite Wadsworth st.
EVA M. MARTIN, P.M.

| Mail leaves, | Mail arrives, |
|---|---|
| 10.15 A.M. for Hartford. | 7.15 A.M. from Hartford. |
| 7.15 P.M. " | 3.45 P.M. " |
| 6.15 P.M. for Hillstown. | 6.00 P.M. from Hillstown. |

**MEADOW P. O.—102 Hartford av. corner Village st.**
GEO. W. DARLIN, P.M.; G. ELLERY DARLIN, Ass't.

| Mail leaves, | Mail arrives, |
|---|---|
| 10.35 A.M. for Hartford. | 7.00 A.M. from Hartford. |
| 7.85 P.M. " | 3.30 P.M. " |

**SILVER LANE P. O.—Main st. cor. Silver Lane.**
L. H. BOGUE, P.M.

| Mail leaves, | Mail arrives, |
|---|---|
| 10.20 A.M. for Hartford. | 7.05 A.M. from Hartford. |
| 7.20 P.M. " | 3.85 P.M. " |

**GRAND LIST OF EAST HARTFORD, OCT. 1, 1897.**

| | |
|---|---|
| 1,203 Dwelling Houses | $1,820,875 |
| 8,675 1-6 Acres of Land | 898,454 |
| 219 Mills, etc. | 263,065 |
| 649 Horses | 24,830 |
| 489 Neat Cattle | 9,110 |
| 214 Carriages,etc | 6,510 |
| Time Pieces, Jewelry, etc. | 1,215 |
| Musical Instruments | 6,060 |
| Bank, Insurance and mfg. Stocks | 214,281 |
| Stores and amount employed in Trade | 59,300 |
| Money at Interest | 20,775 |
| " on hand or on deposit | 2,900 |
| Taxable property not specified | 30,650 |
| Invested in Steamboats | 300 |
| Sheep, Swine and Poultry | 153 |
| Ten per cent. for making lists | 30,402 |
| | $2,884,182 |
| Less Soldiers exemption, etc. | 58,452 |
| As returned to State Comptroller | $2,825,730 |

# GEER'S
# East Hartford Business Directory,
## JULY, 1898.

**AGRICULT'RAL IMPLEMENTS**
*See also Farming Tools; Fertilizers.*
Ackley William K. 1175 Main.
   See page 768.
Vinton C. C. 710 Main. See p. 784.

**APOTHECARIES.**
*See Drug Stores.*

**ATTORNEYS AT LAW.**
BRYANT PERCY S. 953 Main.
   See page 485.
Stoughton John A. (117) Main.

**AUTHORS.**
*See Publishers.*

**BAKERS.**
Gibbs Marshall S. 10 Central.
Hotchkiss C. W. 1 Garvan.
Noble H. D. 1 Garvan.
Stillman M. W. Elm n. of Bissell.

**BARBERS.**
Berge Mitchel, 741 Main.
Bowe James J. 847 Main, n. R.R.
Dannaher Thos. J. 562 Burnside av.

**BICYCLE REPAIRER.**
Sadler Frederick, 771 Main.

**BLACKSMITHS AND HORSESHOERS.**
*See also Carriages.*
Burnham Frank E., Forbes.
Clancy Morris, 555 Main.
Duffy William, 1 Village. Page 769.
Goodrich Loren H. 67 School, B.
Hutchins Chas. C. 97 Pitkin.
Hyland Michael, r. 810 Main.
Kinghorn David, 86 Governor.
Roberts Andrew, 9 Pleasant.
Starks George A. 1057 Main.

**BOARDINGHOUSES.**
*See also Hotels, Restaurants.*
Clune John, 70 Park av.
King Hortense G. (88) Main.
Moore Clarissa Mrs. 2 Governor.

**BOARDING STABLES.**
*See Livery Stables.*

**BOOT AND SHOE STORE.**
*See also Grocers.*
Ferguson L. W. 843 Main.

**BUILDERS & CARPENTERS.**
Blinn I. N. & Son, Main c. Pitkin.
   See page 765.
Bragg J. Merrick, 7 Elm, n. Olmsted.
Carroll Joseph E. 15 Central.
Driggs Waldo J. 62 Hartford av.
Fairbanks Charles P. 1234 Main.
Gehan John B. 68 High.

Jones C. Addison, 161 Burnside.
Nicholson Ruel H. 20 Village.
Rood Ephraim, 7 Orchard, n. Main.
Whaples John F. & Son, 2 Olmsted.

**BUILDING MOVER.**
Nicholson Ruel H., 20 Village.

**BUTCHERS.**
*See also Meat Markets.*
Bailey Geo. R. 12 Broad, n. Main, H.
Holbrook Erving P. 9 King n. Gilman.
Steele John H. 20 School, B. See page 795.
Tryon Nelson D. Porter, n. Main.

**CARMEN.**
*See also Expresses; Truckmen.*
Burnham George D. 70 Burnside
Darlin George W. 114 Hartford av.
   See page 769.

**CARPENTERS.**
*See Builders.*

**CARRIAGES AND WAGONS.**
*See also Blacksmiths.*
Ackley Wm. K. 1175 Main. See page 768.
Andross W. F., Main st., north end.
Burnham E.F., Forbes st. near paper mills, B.
Fowler William H. 263 Main.
Milton John, 9 Pleasant.
Roberts Andrew, 9 Pleasant.

**CHURCHES AND CHAPELS.**
*See page 788.*

**CIGAR MANUFACTURERS.**
Easterbey Thomas W. 32 Pleasant.
Heck Joseph, 135 Hartford av.
Vanderburg Charles, cor. Ranney and Main.

**CIGARS AND TOBACCO.**
Carson & Taylor, 102 Hartford av.
   See page 767.
Goodwin Samuel O. 701 Main. See page 772.

**CIVIL ENGINEER.**
Olmsted Wm. H. 1082 Main next to Mem. Chapel. See page 779.

**CLERGYMEN.**
Barrett Samuel A. 654 Main.
Bacheler F. P., 4 High.
Bowman George A. 32 Burnside av.
Gibbs J. W. 22 Burnside.
Gleeson Jas. J. 10 Woodbridge.
Sheehan John H. 10 Woodbridge.
Waldron S. R. 40 Tolland.

**CLUBS.**
Art Club.
Hartford Canoe Club, Gilbert.
Hartford Rowing & Athletic Club, Hartford av.
St. Mary's Catholic Club for Boys.
Wheel and Social Club, 701 Main.

**COAL YARDS.**
Burnham Geo. D. 70 Burnside av.
Hart H. T., Tolland, B.
Smith Chas. M. r. 841 Main opposite R.R. depot. See page 782.

**CONFECTIONERS.**
*See Fruit and Confectionery.*
Rosenthal Emil, 38 Burnside av.
Slater Charles C., Church.

**CONSTABLE.**
Moore Arthur P. 951 Main, c. Pros.

**CONTRACTORS & BUILDERS.**
*See Builders.*

**DECORATOR.**
Fitzgerald W. J. r. 820 Main. See page 770.

**DENTIST.**
Pratt E. W. 685 Main.

**DRESSMAKERS.**
Flanigan Kate F. and Nellie M. 75 Burnside.
Hendee Kate, 2 Goodwin.
Hughes Mary A. 16 Rector.
McNair Christina Mrs., Bissell n. Lewis.
O'Neil Maggie, 6 Comstock.
Pratt Fannie E. Mrs. 18 Bragg n. Olmsted.

**DRUG STORES.**
Levy Julius, Burnside av. opp. Sch.
Lowry Wm. A. 743 Main c. Bissell.
Noble Wm. B. 716 Main.

**DRY GOODS.**
*See Grocers.*

**EMERY STROP MFR.**
Hurd Oliver, 6 Governor. Page 586.

**EXPRESS.**
*See also Carmen, Trucking.*
Busiere Fred'k J. 261 Woodbridge. See page 559.
Kirchen William, Main c. Bissell. See page 559.

**FARMING TOOLS.**
*See Agricultural Implement Mfr.*
Ackley William K. 1175 Main.
   See page 768.

Carson & Taylor, 100 Hartford av.
See page 767.
Vinton C. C. 710 Main. See p. 784.

**FEED STABLES.**
Grant H. W. r. 743 Main. See p. 772.

**FERTILIZERS.**
*See also Agricultural Implements.*
Andross W. F., Main, north end.
Smith C. M., Main, opp. R.R. Depot.
See page 782.

**FIRE DEPARTMENT.**
Ætna Hose Co.No.4,119 Hartford av.
Burnside Hose, No. 3, Church st. B.
Center Hose, No. 1, 6 Bissell.
Volunteer Hose No. 2, 3 Park av.

**FLORIST.**
Richardson Frank W. 680 Main.
See page 781.

**FLOUR, GRAIN & FEED.**
*See also Grocers.*
Bogue L. H., Main cor. Silver.
See page 765.
Cox W. 841 Main.
Goodwin Samuel O. 701 Main, east
side,north H'frd av. See page 772.
Phillips John R. 86 Hartford av.
See page 780.
Truesdell W. E. & Co. 566 Burn-
side av.
Vinton C. C. 71C Main. See p. 784.
White Glover M. 101 Hartford av.
See page 785.

**FRUITS.**
Carson & Taylor, 100 Hartford av.
See page 767.
Noble Bros. 874 Main.

**FRUIT AND CONFECTIONERY.**
Rosenthal Emil, 33 Burnside.
Salreno Nicadamo, 94 Hartford av.
Slater Charles C., Church.

**FURNITURE MOVER.**
Ayers Frank D. 626 Main.

**GAS FITTER.**
Beck Wm. A. 46 Governor. See
page 764.

**GENERAL JOBBING.**
Ayers Frank D. 626 Main.
Duffy William, 1 Village. See
page 769.

**GENERAL STORES.**
*See Grocers; Provisions.*

**GRIST MILLS.**
Cox William J., So. Main, H.
Vinton C. C., P.O. address Vinton's
Mills.

**GROCERS.**
Adams W. H. & Son,16 Burnside av.
Bogue Lincoln H., Main, c. Silver.
See page 765.
Brewer Monroe J. 275 Main.
Carson & Taylor, 102 Hartford av.
See page 767.
Foran, Dowds & Co. 810 Main.
Forbes Leonard H. 25 Church, B.
Fowler Joel H., Hills n. Oak, H.
Goodwin Samuel O. 701 Main, east
side,north H'f'd av. See page 772.
Hagedorn A., Main c. Linden.
Martin Eva M. So.Main, opp. Wads.
Rathgeb John, 95 Pitkin.
Risley F. S. (267) Main.

Stoughton W. G. 851 Main.
Truesdell Wm. E. & Co. 566 Brnsd.
Vinton C. C. 710 Main, cor. Gov-
ernor. See page 784.

**HACKS.**
*See Livery.*

**HALLS AND BLOCKS, ETC.**
*See Public Halls, Etc.*
See page 780.

**HAY, GRAIN, AND FEED.**
Phillips J. R. 86 Hartford av. See
page 780.

**HORSE SHOERS.**
*See Blacksmiths.*

**HARNESS STORES, ETC.**
Gaines Albert, 712 Main.
Kirbell Joseph, 571 Main.
Oelkuck Edward, 20 Pleasant.

**HORSE DEALERS.**
Williams Bros. 50 Hartford av.

**HOT WATER HEATING.**
Beck Wm. A. 46 Governor. See
page 764.

**HOTELS AND BOARDING
HOUSES.**
*See also Restaurants.*
Hotel Imperial, 99 Hartford av.
Moore Clarissa Mrs. 2 Governor.
New England House, 808 Main.

**HOUSE PAINTERS.**
*See Painters.*

**ICE.**
Blake Charles H. 14 Linden.
Boardman J. H. 6 Pleasant. See
page 765.
LeCourt Leon, (166) Main.

**ICE CREAM.**
*See Fruits and Confectioners.*

**INSURANCE AGENTS.**
Brainard S. N. 2 Burnside av. See
page 766.
Carroll Joseph R. 757 Main.
Chapman Wm. R. 546 Main.
Merriman Charles, 650 Main. See
page 778.

**JEWELERS.**
Newman Samuel, 98 Hartford av.
See page 779.
McCormick S. B. 743 Main. See
page 777.

**KINDLING WOOD.**
*See also Wood Yards.*
Boardman Joseph H. 6 Pleasant.
See page 765.

**LAUNDRIES.**
Doo Chas. Y. H. 4 Governor.
Goodwin Samuel O. agent for, 701
Main, north of Hartford av.
See page 772.
Sing Charlie, 727 Main.
Sing Young, Pleasant c. Hfd. av.

**LEAF TOBACCO.**
*See also Tobacco Warehouse.*
Ensign F. Howard, 850 Main.
Goodwin Edward O. 711 Main.

Huntting William L. 812 Main.
Kilbourne A. E. 1235 Main.
King Edward E., Hfd. av. c. Pros.

**LIBRARIES.**
Raymond Library Co. 655 Main.
East Hfd. Public Library,655 Main.

**LIVERY STABLES.**
*See also Sale Stables.*
Darlin George W. 114 Hartford av.
See page 769.
Grant Herbert W. r. 743 Main.
See page 772.
Lathrop Albert H. 718 Main.

**LOAN AGENCY.**
Merriman Charles, 650 Main. See
page 778.

**LUMBER YARDS.**
Blinn I. N. & Son, 596 Main. See
page 765.
Burnham A. E. & Co., Long Hill,B.
Jencks Bros. 100 Hartford av. See
page 775.

**MANUFACTURERS.**
*See also Paper Manufacturers.*
East Hartford Mfg Co. 49 Church.
See page 480.
Hurd Oliver, 6 Governor. Page 586.

**MARKETS.**
*See Meat Markets.*

**MARKET GARDENERS.**
Ahl George N. 81 Garvan.
Carroll Edward P. & Co. 614 Main.
Moody Charles C. 105 Burnside av.
Williams G. A. & H. B. 534 Main.

**MASONS AND BUILDERS.**
*See also Carpenters.*
Fairbanks Charles P. 1234 Main.
Kiernan John F. 38 Governor.
Nicholson Ruel H. 20 Village.
Whaley A. M. 25 Olmsted.

**MEAT MARKETS, ETC.**
*See also Butchers.*
Bailey Geo. R. 12 Broad, n. Main B.
Brewer Edward, 21 Central. See
page 766.
Steele John H. 20 School, B. See
page 795.
Tryon Nelson D., Porter, n. Main.
White Charles E. 148 Main.

**MUSIC INSTRUMENTS.**
*See also Violins.*
Fernside G. W. 5 Orchard. See
page 770.

**MUSIC TEACHERS.**
Bauder Edward L. Mrs. 10 Garvan.
Huntting Lillian, 812 Main.
Lane Farnum H. 796 Main.
Monnier W. D. 29 Central.
Olmsted Anna M. 101 Prospect.
Thompson Katherine P. 4 Burnside.

**NEWSPAPERS.**
American Enterprise, 866 Main,
near R.R. depot. See page 795.
Weekly Gazette, Rector.

**NURSE.**
DeBarthe Mary Mrs. 5 Elm.
Loveland A. L., Governor.

ORNITHOLOGIST.
Treat Willard E. 334 Main,s. Willow.

PAINTERS, PAPER HANGERS.
*See also Sign Painters.*
Bidwell Samuel C. 51 Governor.
Fitzgerald Wm. J. 820 Main.
See page 770.
Griffing C. R. Central.
Hancock Harvey G. (219) Main.
Hinton Harry, 824 Main.
Milton John, 9 Pleasant.
Parsons Myron P. 420 Tolland.
Prudhome O. E. 16 Wells av.

PAPER DEALER.
Carroll Edward J. 616 Main.

PAPER MANUFACTURERS.
*See also Manufacturers.*
EAST HARTFORD MFG. CO. 49
Church, Burnside P.O. Page 480.

HARTFORD MANILLA CO. Woodland. See page 479.
Walker John H. 1 Forbes, near Ch.

PEDDLERS.
*See Tin Peddlers.*
Lester Andrew M., Lester st.

PHYSICIANS.
Childs Henry E., Elm n. Bissell.
Griswold Edward H. 7 Wells av.
Mayberry Franklin H. 575 Burn-
side av. B.
Murphy Walter G. 802 Main.
O'Connell Thos. S. 15 Burnside av.

PLUMBERS.
Beck William A. 46 Governor.
See page 764.
Hills C. M. r. 696 Main. See p. 774.

POOL ROOMS.
*See also Saloons.*
Alling George B. 89 Hartford av.
Ferguson L. W. 845 Main.

PRINTERS.
*See also Newspapers.*
Martin James A. 886 Main.
Smart Merritt, Rector.

PROVISIONS.
*See also Grocers.*
Vinton C. C. 710 Main. See p. 784.

PUBLIC BUILDINGS.
*See also Halls.*
Darlin's block, 102-112 Hartford av.
cor. Village.
Garvan's block, 722 Main.
Grange Hall, Hillstown, Hills st.
Howard's Hall, 568 Burnside.
Raymond Public Library and Hall,
655 Main, c. Central.
Spencer's Block, 889 Main.
Wells Hall, 761 Main.

PUBLISHERS AND AUTHORS.
Bidwell Geo. C. 618 Main.
Martin James A. 866 Main. See
page 795.

RAZOR STROP MFR.
Hurd Oliver, 6 Governor. Page 586.

REAL ESTATE.
Bidwell Chas. M. 124 Burnside av.
Bissell Lewis, 745 Main, n. Bissell.
Brainard S. N. 9 Burnside. See
page 766.
Darlin Geo. W. 114 Hartford av.
See page 769.
Merriman Charles, 650 Main. See
page 778.

RESTAURANTS.
*See also Hotels.*
Porter Albert, 53 Park av.

ROOFING.
Hills C. M. 696 Main. See page 774.

SALOONS.
Alling George B. 89 Hartford av.
Falls W. H. 99 Hartford av.

SAW MILLS.
Blinn I. N. & Son, 596 Main. See
page 765.
Burnham Allison, Long Hill, So.
Windsor, B.

SCHOOLS.
*See Public Schools, page 788.*
Bowman George A. Rev. 82 Burn-
side av.
Harrison Lucinda Mrs. 16 Brnsd. av.

SCHOOL BOOKS.
Goodwin S. O. 701 Main, east side,
north Hartford av. See page 772.

SEAMSTRESS.
*See Dressmakers.*

SHOEMAKERS.
*See also Boot and Shoe Stores.*
Chickering John W. r. 748 Main.
Manock Edmund, 91 Burnside av.
Reardon Jeremiah, 188 Hartford av.
Snow Hiram, Brewer.
Wilson Henry P. 868 Main.

STAGES AND EXPRESSES.
East Hartford. See page 559.

STEAM SAW MILLS.
Blinn I. N. & Son, 596 Main. See
page 765.
Burnham Allison, Long Hill, So.
Windsor, B.

STOVE AND FURNACE
REPAIRS.
Hills C. M. 696 Main. See p. 774.

STREETS.
See page 762.

STROPS.
Hurd Oliver, 6 Governor.

SURVEYOR.
Olmsted Wm. H. 1032 Main,1st house
north of Mem. chapel. Page 779.

TAILORS.
Berman M. 708 Main.

TEAMSTERS.
*See Carmen.*

TIN PEDDLER.
Fricke Henry A. 24 Village.

TINNERS AND ROOFERS.
Hills Chester M. 696 Main.

TOBACCO.
*See Leaf Tobacco.*

TOBACCO INSPECTORS.
Ensign E. R. & Son, Main, n. Colt.

TOBACCO WAREHOUSES.
*See also Leaf Tobacco.*
Dennerlein P. & Sons, Hartford av.
Ensign F. Howard, 850 Main.
Hunting Wm. L. & Co. 812 Main.
Kilbourne A. E. 1235 Main.
Rosenwald E. & Bro., Goodwin lane.
Taylor & Beckman, 81 Burnside av.

TOWN OFFICERS.
See page 787.

TRUCKMEN.
Ayers Frank D. 620 Main.
Darlin George W. 114 Hartford av.
See page 769.
Lathrop Charles W. 188 Burnside.

UNDERTAKERS.
Hayes Edward D. 708 Main.
McCarthy & Ahern. See page 248.

UPHOLSTERER.
Wetherell Herbert M. 769 Main.

VEGETABLE PLANTS.
Richardson F. W. 680 Main cor.
Hartford av. See page 781.

VEGETABLES.
Carson & Taylor, 100 Hartford av.
See page 767.
Steele John H. 20 School, B. See
page 796.

VIOLINS REPAIRED.
Fernside G. W. 5 Orchard. See
page 770.

WAGON MFR.
*See also Carriages*
Burnham E F.Forbes,n. Papermills.

WATER WORKS.
East Hartford Water Co. 952 Main.

WATCHMAKERS.
Newman Samuel, 98 Hartford av.
See page 779.
McCormick S. B. r. 748 Main. See
page 777.

WOOD.
Blinn I. N. & Son, 596 Main. See
page 765.
Boardman Joseph H. 6 Pleasant.
See page 765.
Burnham G. D. 70 Burnside av.
Darlin G. W. 114 Hartford av. See
page 769.
Kirchen William, Ranney, c. Main.

YANKEE DOUGHNUTS.
Bidwell John N., Prospect, c. Governor.

## POPULATION OF CONNECTICUT.

| | | | |
|---|---|---|---|
| 1890, | 746,258 | 1820, | 275,148 |
| 1880, | 622,700 | 1810, | 261,942 |
| 1870, | 537,454 | 1800, | 251,002 |
| 1860, | 460,147 | 1790, | 237,946 |
| 1850, | 370,792 | 1782, | 208,850 |
| 1840, | 309,978 | 1774, | 197,865 |
| 1830, | 297,675 | 1756, | 130,611 |

## SAILING VESSELS

Have been so numerous heretofore that we refer inquirers to our annual Directories for half a century past.

*Vessels belonging in the Customs District of Hartford.*

| NAME. | CAPT. |
|---|---|
| A. G. Pease | Albee |
| A. M. Smith | Reed |
| Acme | Miller |
| Adaline | Davis |
| Addie | Lord |
| Admiral Farragut | Bacon |
| Aggie | McFadyen |
| Agnes | Watrous |
| Alga | Reid |
| Alice | Beckwith |
| Barges Nos. 1, 2, 3, 4, 5, 6, 7, 8, 9, 10, 11 of Hartford & New York Trans. Co. | |
| Blanche | Bugbee |
| Cactus | Beers |
| Chas. T. Marston | Rubright |
| Christine | Cunningham |
| City of Springfield | Beebe |
| Clifford | Davis |
| Clio | Williams |
| Coot | Spencer |
| Cora | Miner |
| Cynthia | Mead |
| Dandy | Lackmann |
| Dauntless | —— |
| David Currie | Pease |
| Dolphin | Dupree |
| E. S. Tyler, Jr. | Bowe |
| Emily A. Wright | Alger |
| Emma | Goken |
| Engineer | Bishop |
| Era | Tyler |
| F. C. Fowler | Fuller |
| Flying Dutchman | Palmer |
| Frances | Storrs |
| Frank Jones | Lucas |
| G. Stancliff | Eikrem |
| G. A. Hayden | Green |
| G. B. Newton | Thompson |
| G. E. Williams | Wentworth |
| Game Cock | Pratt |
| Gen. Sheridan | Stewart |
| Geo. E. Hatch | Wentworth |
| Geo. W. Hunt | Rankin |
| Gildersleeve | Buell |
| Gipsey | Hooker |
| Goodspeed | Clark |
| Gypsy | Alexander |
| H. N. Conklin | Deming |
| Harriet | Hollister |
| Hartford | Beebe |
| Hfd Dr'g Co. No. 2 | Butler |
| Hfd Dr'g Co. No. 3 | Reilly |
| Helen | Davis |
| Helen Augusta | Pratt |
| Helen P. | Rowland |
| Hollister | Hollister |
| Hornet | Buell |
| Huntress | Fowler |
| Idell | Davis |
| Irene | Doolittle |
| Irene | Kelsey |
| J. H. Chaffee | Buell |
| J. W. Coulston | Brewer |
| James Duffield | Jones |
| Jay K. | Dexter |
| John McDermott | Arnold |
| Josie C. Williams | Payson |
| Lady Fenwick | Bates |
| Leda | Sadler |
| Lizzie | Gildersleeve |
| Lottie | Rustemeyer |
| Lucy | Mosher |
| Lucy F. | Cunningham |
| Luther C. Ward | Gaines |
| Luzette | Spencer |
| Mabel | Sanders |
| Margaret | Hill |
| Maria | Varney |
| Marian | Oakes |
| Marion | Mahl |
| Mary | Gildersleeve |
| Mascot | Smith |
| Mattabesett | Rowland |
| Maud | Markham |
| Middletown | Hills |
| Midget | Perkins |
| Minnie | Alexander |
| Minnie May | Sweet |
| Mollie B. | Hayden |
| Mystic Shrine | Odber |
| Nauticus | Peterson |
| Nellie | Theur |
| Nomad | Hayden |
| Normandie | Horton |
| Owl | Munger |
| Priscella | Leshure |
| Prospector | Beckwith |
| R. Wrisley | Smith |
| Racer | Holmes |
| Raymond | Douglass |
| Raymond | Davis |
| Rebecca | Benson |
| Richard | Burns |
| S. B. Hubbard | Mehaffey |
| S. S. Scranton, | Bruce |
| Sarah | Gildersleeve |
| Schuylkill | Munger |
| Sensation | Myers |
| Seriatim | Tryon |
| Seventy-six | Davis |
| Sibyl | Williams |
| Sprite | Mugford |
| Sunshine | Blydenburgh |
| Surf | Bogue |
| Surprise | Stedman |
| Thistle | Raynor |
| Toxotes | O'Callaghan |
| Traveler | McMann |
| Trio | Reed |
| Uncle Joe | Stevens |
| Undine | Green |
| Viola | Mack |
| Volunteer | Rubright |
| Wawa | Smith |
| Wenonah | Webster |
| Wm. W. Wood | Collins |
| Ylo | Munger |
| Zette | Miner |
| Zuella | Souther |

## DISTANCES, CONN. RIVER, HARTFORD TO

| | MILES. |
|---|---|
| * Wethersfield | 4½ |
| * Glastonbury | 6 |
| * South Glastonbury | 10½ |
| Rocky Hill | 11 |
| * Gildersleeve's | 16 |
| Cromwell | 18 |
| * Portland | 21 |
| * Middletown | 22 |
| * Tibbals | 27 |
| * Middle Haddam | 28 |
| Higganum | 31 |
| * Rock Landing | 33 |
| Haddam | 36½ |
| East Haddam | 40 |
| * Goodspeed's | 41 |
| * Hadlyme | 44 |
| * Deep River | 46 |
| * Brockway | 49 |
| * Ely's | 51 |
| * Essex | 52 |
| * Lyme | 56 |
| * Saybrook | 58 |
| Saybrook bar or Sound | 60 |

*The New York Steamboats make these Landings.

## VITAL STATISTICS—TOWN OF HARTFORD.

| Year. | Births. | Marriages. | Deaths. | Year. | Births. | Marriages. | Deaths |
|---|---|---|---|---|---|---|---|
| 1838 | No record made until the year 1848. | 126 | No record made until the year 1848. | 1868 | 861 | 380 | 497 |
| 1839 | | 124 | | 1869 | 848 | 459 | 461 |
| 1840 | | 116 | | 1870 | 922 | 426 | 478 |
| 1841 | | 187 | | 1871 | 905 | 466 | 461 |
| 1842 | | 140 | | 1872 | 980 | 467 | 700 |
| 1843 | | 187 | | 1873 | 939 | 505 | 773 |
| 1844 | | 127 | | 1874 | 946 | 476 | 594 |
| 1845 | | 184 | | 1875 | 994 | 445 | 567 |
| 1846 | | 168 | | 1876 | 961 | 422 | 953 |
| 1847 | | 155 | | 1877 | 858 | 429 | 743 |
| 1848 | 298 | 110 | 313 | 1878 | 886 | 366 | 756 |
| 1849 | 345 | 100 | 209 | 1879 | 1190 | 375 | 713 |
| 1850 | 368 | 120 | 235 | 1880 | 1018 | 385 | 841 |
| 1851 | 467 | 78 | 225 | 1881 | 1138 | 430 | 1012 |
| 1852 | Laws changed | | | 1882 | 1162 | 481 | 1057 |
| 1853 | 616 | 202 | 258 | 1883 | 1342 | 450 | 1205 |
| 1854 | 662 | 229 | 368 | 1884 | 1236 | 440 | 989 |
| 1855 | 692 | 299 | 281 | 1885 | 1371 | 431 | 1011 |
| 1856 | 758 | 307 | 325 | 1886 | 1295 | 526 | 977 |
| 1857 | 802 | 294 | 427 | 1887 | 1331 | 494 | 1034 |
| 1858 | 878 | 323 | 395 | 1888 | 1234 | 506 | 1098 |
| 1859 | 824 | 380 | 429 | 1889 | 1250 | 438 | 1067 |
| 1860 | 878 | 302 | 427 | 1890 | 1230 | 525 | 1138 |
| 1861 | 925 | 332 | 489 | 1891 | 1344 | 603 | 1202 |
| 1862 | 912 | 358 | 574 | 1892 | 1401 | 633 | 1277 |
| 1863 | 844 | 326 | 583 | 1893 | 1549 | 571 | 1321 |
| 1864 | 773 | 367 | 525 | 1894 | 1548 | 525 | 1081 |
| 1865 | 715 | 411 | 435 | 1895 | 1620 | 654 | 1111 |
| 1866 | 708 | 425 | 598 | 1896 | 1513 | 665 | 1257 |
| 1867 | 882 | 399 | 521 | 1897 | 1814 | 678 | 1155 |

## STATE OF CONNECTICUT GRAND LIST.

| | | |
|---|---|---|
| Grand List, State of Conn. Oct. | 1886, | $339,475,856 |
| " " " " | 1887, | 352,795,925 |
| " " " " | 1888, | 354,557,515 |
| " " " " | 1889, | 358,913,906 |
| " " " " | 1890, | 368,150,802 |
| " " " " | 1891, | 372,245,442 |
| " " " " | 1892, | 381,261,607 |
| " " " " | 1893, | 416,323,257 |
| " " " " | 1894, | 414,258,956 |
| " " " " | 1895, | 444,321,927 |
| " " " " | 1896, | 529,611,165 |
| " " " " | 1897, | 534,465,257 |

## POSTAL AREAS OF ENGLAND AND U. S.

England's total postal areas is 122,000 square miles, with one penny postage on over half ounce letters; and that of the United States is over 3,500,000 square miles with two cents on half ounce letters.

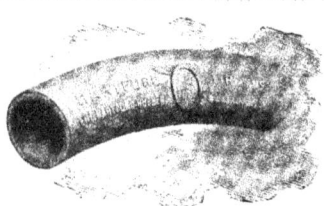
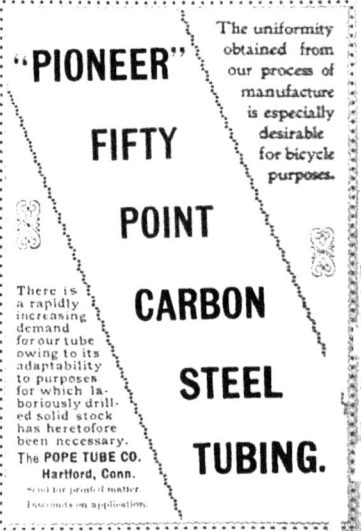

Lightning Source UK Ltd.
Milton Keynes UK
UKHW020848110119
335238UK00009B/955/P